AMERICAN AUTHORS AND BOOKS
1640 TO THE PRESENT DAY

AMERICAN AUTHORS

AND BOOKS

1640 TO THE PRESENT DAY

Third Revised Edition

W. J. Burke and Will D. Howe

revised by

IRVING WEISS and ANNE WEISS

CROWN PUBLISHERS, INC.   NEW YORK

APR 73

Cy - REF

Preface to the Third Revised Edition

The decade 1960–70 was marked by significant changes in literary theory and practice, the uses of language in print, the expressive use of print as a medium, the form and content of journalism, and the publishing of periodicals and books. The so-called alternate, or counter, culture introduced many new trends in reading, writing, publishing, and related means of conveying information in the United States. Developments in politics, religion, art, the humanities and sciences, and the fields of civil, sexual, and human rights introduced others. The editors have attempted to account for all such trends not only in the author and title entries but also in the general articles. Additions were made to many of them and the new ones have been written under such headings as *Black Humor, Hippie, Pop Writing,* and *Underground Press.*

The 1960s were particularly distinguished by a merging of elements in the usually ignored popular arts with those of traditional book culture, such as in the more relaxed acceptance of obscenity and pornography on most levels of reading, in the wide practice of experimental graphic and typographic styles, and in the serious attention paid to popular song lyrics. Indeed, the decade confirmed the original importance of this work as an encyclopedic distillation of the national culture defined by the medium of print. *American Authors and Books* thus becomes more than ever a compendium of information for everyone interested in American studies, the sociology of American literature, and the history of printed sources since colonial times.

As in the last edition, author entries have been updated and new authors and book titles added, again with the intention of representing material ranging from the fashionable, novel, and commonly known to the scholarly, esoteric, regional, or otherwise limited in readership. Nothing new was added at the cost of omitting any information previously included.

We think that this volume should be of interest to occasional or curious readers as well as to researchers, all of whom may find in its pages references to authors and books, literary works and the pen names of their authors, newspapers and magazines, publishers and printers, institutions and societies, ordinarily found only in much larger collections.

I would like to thank the reference staff of the Sojourner Truth Library of the State University College of New York at New Paltz for their help in suggesting reference materials and their readiness to trace details of all kinds.

I.W.

AMERICAN AUTHORS AND BOOKS
1640 TO THE PRESENT DAY

ABBREVIATIONS

anon., anonymous

assoc., associate

b., born

c., circa, about

comp., compiler

cop., copyrighted

d., died

dept., department

ed., edited, editor

fl., flourished

illus., illustrated

lit., literary

M.S., MSS., manuscript, manuscripts

n.d., no date

prod., produced (plays)

prof., professor

q.v., quod vide, which see

trans., translated, translator

AMERICAN
AUTHORS AND BOOKS

A

A.L.A. Bulletin. Chicago, Ill. Issued monthly by the American Library Association. Founded 1907.

AARON, DANIEL (Aug. 4, 1912–); Educator. *Men of Good Hope: A Story of American Progressives* (1951); *Writers on the Left* (1961); *Child's Play: A Creative Approach to Play-Spaces for Today's Children* (with B. P. Winawer, 1965). Editor: *The Memoirs of an American Citizen* (1963). English dept., Smith College.

ABARBANELL, JACOB RALPH (Dec. 6, 1852–Nov. 9, 1922); b. New York City. Lawyer, novelist, playwright. *A Model Pair* (1882); *Flirtation* (1884); *The Rector's Secret* (1892); *Ma* (1902); etc.

ABBATT, WILLIAM (Nov. 16, 1851–Sept. 7, 1935); b. New York City. Historian. *The Crisis of the Revolution* (1899); *Colloquial Who's Who,* 2 v. (1924). Editor and publisher, *The Magazine of History with Notes and Queries.*

ABBE, GEORGE [Bancroft] (Jan. 28, 1911–); b. Somers, Conn. Author. *Voices in the Square* (1938); *Dreamer's Clay* (1940); *Wait for These Things* (poems, 1940); *Letter Home* (poems, 1945); *Mr. Quill's Crusade* (1948); *Bird in the Mulberry; Collected Lyrics, 1937-1954* (1954); *The Incandescent Beast* (poems, 1957); *The Winter House* (1958); *Collected Poems* (1961); *The Larks* (1965); *The Non-Conformist* (1966); *The Funeral* (1967); *Yonderville* (1968); *You and Contemporary Poetry: An Aid to Appreciation* (1969). Editor: *Stephen Vincent Benét on Writing* (1964).

ABBEY, HENRY (July 11, 1842–June 7, 1911); b. Rondout (now Kingston), N.Y. Poet. *May Dreams* (1862); *Ralph, and Other Poems* (1866); *Stories in Verse* (1869); *The Poems of Henry Abbey* (1885); *Dream of Love* (1910); etc.

ABBOT, WILLIS J[ohn] (Mar. 16, 1863–May 19, 1934); b. New Haven, Conn. Editor, author. *Blue Jackets of '76* (1888); *Battle Fields and Campfires* (1890); *American Merchant Ships and Sailors* (1902); etc. Editor, *Christian Science Monitor,* 1921–34.

Abbott, A. A. Pen name of Samuel Spewack.

ABBOTT, AUSTIN (Dec. 18, 1831–Apr. 19, 1896); b. Boston, Mass. Lawyer, novelist. Pen name, used jointly with brothers, Benjamin Vaughan Abbott and Lyman Abbott, "Benauly." Co-author: *Cone Cut Corners* (1855); *Matthew Canby* (1859); etc.

ABBOTT, BENJAMIN VAUGHAN (June 4, 1830–Feb. 17, 1890; b. Boston, Mass. Lawyer, novelist. Pen name, used jointly with brothers, Austin Abbott and Lyman Abbott, "Benauly." Co-author: *Cone Cut Corners* (1855); *Matthew Canby* (1859); etc.

ABBOTT, BERENICE (July 17, 1898–); b. Springfield, O. Photographer, author. *Changing New York* (photography, 1939); *A Guide to Better Photography* (1941); *The View Camera Made Simple* (1948); *Greenwich Village, Today and Yesterday* (photography, 1950); *A Portrait of Maine* (with Chenoweth Hall, 1968); *Magnet* (with Evans G. Valens, 1964); *Motion* (1965); *Attractive Universe* (1969). Instructor, New School for Social Research, 1934–58.

ABBOTT, CHARLES C[onrad] (June 4, 1843–July 27, 1919); b. Trenton, N.J. Naturalist, author. *Naturalist's Rambles About Home* (1884); *Days Out of Doors* (1889); *Notes of the Night* (1895); etc.

ABBOTT, EDWARD (July 15, 1841–Apr. 5, 1908); b. Farmington, Me. Congregational clergyman, author. *Revolutionary Times* (1876); *The Long-Look Books,* 3v. (1877–80); etc. Editor, *The Literary World,* 1878–88, 1895–1903.

ABBOTT, ELEANOR HALLOWELL (Mrs. Fordyce Coburn) (Sept. 22, 1872–); b. Cambridge, Mass. Author. *Molly Make-Believe* (1910); *White Linen Nurse* (1913); *Little Eve Edgerton* (1914); *The Indiscreet Letter* (1915); *Old Dad* (1919); *Love and the Ladies* (1928); *Being Little in Cambridge When Everybody Else Was Big* (1936); etc.

ABBOTT, GEORGE (June 25, 1889–); b. Forestville, N.Y. Actor, playwright, producer. *The Fall Guy* (with James Gleason, prod. 1925); *Broadway* (with Philip Dunning, prod. 1926); *Love 'Em and Leave 'Em* (with John V. A. Weaver, prod. 1926); *Coquette* (with Ann Preston Bridges, prod. 1927); *Four Walls* (with Dana Burnet, prod. 1927); *Those We Love* (with S. M. Lauren, prod. 1930); *Ladies' Money* (prod. 1934); *Three Men on a Horse* (with John Cecil Holm, prod. 1935); *The Boys from Syracuse* (prod. 1938); *Where's Charley?* (prod. 1948); *The Pajama Game* (prod. 1954); *Damn Yankees* (prod. 1955); *Tenderloin* (with Jerome Weidman, prod. 1960); etc.

Abbott, Helen Raymond. See Helen Abbott Beals.

ABBOTT, JACOB (Nov. 14, 1803–Oct. 31, 1879); b. Hallowell, Me. Author. The *Rollo* series, begun in 1835; the *Lug Books;* the *Gay Family* series; the *Marco Paul* series; the *Jonas Books;* the *Franconia Stories; The Young Christian* (1832); etc. See *The Colophon,* 1939. His manuscripts are now in Hubbard Hall, Bowdoin College.

ABBOTT, JANE [Ludlow] DRAKE (July 10, 1881–); b. Buffalo, N.Y. Novelist. *Keineth* (1918); *Highacres* (1920); *Polly Put the Kettle On* (1925); *Juliet Is Twenty* (1926); *Heyday* (1929); *Fiddler's Corn* (1934); *Low Bridge* (1935); *Row of Stars* (1937); *Angels May Weep* (1938); *To Have, To Keep* (1939); *Yours for the Asking* (1943); *River's Rim* (1950); *Neighbors* (1952); *Open Way* (1955); etc.

ABBOTT, JOHN STEVENS CABOT (Sept. 18, 1805–June 17, 1877); b. Brunswick, Me. Congregational clergyman, historian. *The History of Napoleon Bonaparte* (1855); *The Em-*

pire of Austria (1859); *The Empire of Russia* (1860); *Italy* (1860); *The History of the Civil War in America,* 2v. (1860, 1866); *The History of Napoleon III* (1868); *The Romance of Spanish History* (1869); *History of Frederick the Second, Called Frederick the Great* (1871); etc.

ABBOTT, KEENE (d. July 5, 1941); b. Fremont, Neb. Drama editor, author. *A Melody in Silver* (1911); *Wine o' the Winds* (1920); *Tree of Life* (1927); etc. Drama editor, Omaha *World Herald,* 1903–35.

ABBOTT, LYMAN (Dec. 18, 1835–Oct. 22, 1922); b. Roxbury, Mass. Congregational clergyman, editor. Co-author, with brothers Austin Abbott and Benjamin Vaughan Abbott, using joint pen name, "Benauly." *Cone Cut Corners* (1855); *Matthew Canby* (1859). Author: *Life of Henry Ward Beecher* (1883); *Reminiscences* (1915); etc. Editor, "The Literary Record" of *Harper's Magazine,* assoc. editor, *The Christian Union,* 1876–81; editor, 1881–93; *The Outlook,* 1893–1922.

ABBOTT, WENONAH STEVENS (Aug. 1865–Mar. 16, 1950); b. Tionesta, Pa. Novelist. *Love's Legacy* (1892); *A Jealous Father* (1894); *From Pilgrimage to Pilgrimage* (1934); etc.

ABBOTT, WILBUR CORTEZ (Dec. 28, 1869–Feb. 3, 1947); b. Kokomo, Ind. Educator, historian, essayist. *Colonel Blood, Crown Stealer, 1618–1680* (1911); *The New Barbarians* (1925); *New York in the American Revolution* (1929); *Adventures in Reputation* (1935); etc. Editor: *The Writing and Speeches of Oliver Cromwell,* 2v. (1937–39). Prof. history, Yale University, 1908–20; Harvard University, 1920–37; etc.

ABDULLAH, ACHMED (Syyed Shaykh Achmed Abdullah Nadir Khan el-Idrissyieh el-Durani) (May 12, 1881–May 12, 1945). Novelist, playwright. *Chansons Couleur Puce* (1900); *The Red Stain* (1915); *Bucking the Tiger* (1917); *The Man on Horseback* (1919); *Night Drums* (1921); *Shackled* (1924); *Steel and Jade* (1927); *Black Tents* (1930); *The Cat Had Nine Lives* (autobiography, 1933); *Flower of the Gods* (with Fulton Oursler, 1940); *Shadow of the Master* (with same, 1940).

Abe Lincoln in Illinois. Play by Robert Sherwood (prod. 1938). Twelve episodes in the life of Lincoln before he became President of the United States.

ABEL, LIONEL (Nov. 28, 1910–) b. New York. Critic, playwright. *Metatheatre* (1963); *Moderns on Tragedy* (1967). Translator: *Some Poems of Rimbaud* (1939); Jean-Paul Sartre's *Three Plays* (1949); Ghelderode's *Escurial* (1957); Racine's *Andromaque* in *Genius of the French Theater* (1961), ed. by Albert Bermel.

Abelard-Schuman, Ltd. New York. Founded 1945. President, Lew Schwartz. Publishes trade books of all kinds, including mystery fiction and works of Jewish interest. Acquired Criterion Books (founded 1953) in 1960. Taken over by Intext Educational Publishers in 1969.

ABELL, ARUNAH SHEPHERDSON (Aug. 10, 1806–Apr. 19, 1888); b. East Providence, R.I. Journalist. One of the founders of the Philadelphia *Public Ledger,* Mar. 24, 1836; and of the *Baltimore Sun,* May 17, 1837. William M. Swain and Azariah Simmons were his co-founders in both instances. His sons succeeded him in the ownership of the Baltimore *Sun* in 1878, and in the management of the A. S. Abell Co.

ABELL, WALTER [Halsey] (Feb. 23, 1897–1956); b. Brooklyn, N.Y. Educator, author. *Eternal Springtime* (poems, 1927); *Representation and Form* (1936); *The Collective Dream in Art* (1957).

ABEND, HALLETT [Edward] (Sept. 15, 1884–Nov. 27, 1955); b. Portland, Ore. Editor, author. *Tortured China* (1930); *Can China Survive?* (1936); *Pacific Charter* (1943); *Half Slave, Half Free* (1950); etc. Chief China correspondent, *New York Times,* 1927–41.

ABERNETHY, THOMAS PERKINS (Aug. 25, 1890–); b. Collirene, Ala. Historian. *The Formative Period in Alabama* (1922); *From Frontier to Plantation in Tennessee* (1932); *Western Lands and the American Revolution* (1937); *Three Virginia Frontiers* (1940); *The Burr Conspiracy* (1954); *The South in the New Nation, 1789–1819* (1961). Chairman, Corcoran School of History, University of Virginia, 1946–1955.

Abie's Irish Rose. Comedy in three acts, by Anne Nichols (prod. 1922). Abie marries an Irish girl and a family feud is engendered. The couple are married three times, once by a Rabbi, once by a Methodist Minister, and once by a Roman Catholic Priest. The birth of twins reconciles the two warring families. The play ran for 2,532 consecutive performances, a record until Erskine Caldwell's *Tobacco Road.*

Abingdon Press. Nashville, Tenn. The present name of a merger of several Methodist book publishers. It was once a subsidiary of the Methodist Book Concern (q.v., later Methodist Publishing House) and has now replaced it. Cecil D. Jones and, later, T. E. Carpenter have been managers. Publishes religious books, juveniles, biographies.

Able McLaughlins, The. Novel by Margaret Wilson (1923. Pulitzer Prize for fiction, 1924). Pioneer life in Iowa.

About the House. Collection of poems by W. H. Auden (1965).

"*Abraham Davenport.*" Poem by John G. Whittier, in *Atlantic Monthly,* May, 1866. Based on the protest of Abraham Davenport against the adjourning of the Massachusetts legislature on the famous Dark Day, May 19, 1780, which many people thought was the end of the world.

"*Abraham Lincoln: An Horatian Ode.*" By Richard Henry Stoddard (1865).

Abraham Lincoln: The Prairie Years. By Carl Sandburg, 2v. (1926); *The War Years,* 4v. (1939). A one-volume abridgment of both appeared in 1954.

"*Abraham Lincoln Walks at Midnight.*" Poem by Vachel Lindsay (1914). The spirit of the "prairie lawyer" is represented as pacing up and down near the old court-house in Springfield.

ABRAHAMS, ROBERT DAVID (Sept. 24, 1905–); b. Philadelphia, Pa. Lawyer, author. *Come Forward* (poems, 1928); *New Tavern Tales* (1930); *The Pot-Bellied Gods* (poems, 1932); *Death After Lunch* (1941); *Death in 1-2-3* (1942); *Three Dozen* (poems, 1945); *Mr. Benjamin's Sword* (1948); *Room for a Son* (1951); *The Commodore* (1954); *The Uncommon Soldier* (1959); *Sound of Bow Bells* (1962); *Humphrey's Ride* (1964); *The Bonus of Redonda* (1969).

ABRAHAMSEN, DAVID (June 23, 1903–); b. Trondheim, Nor. Psychiatrist, psychoanalyst. *Crime and the Human Mind* (1944); *Men, Mind, and Power* (1945); *The Mind and Death of a Genius* (1946); *Who Are the Guilty?—A Study of Education and Crime* (1952); *The Road to Emotional Maturity* (1958); *The Psychology of Crime* (1960); *The Emotional Care of Your Child* (1969).

ABRAMOVITZ, MOSES (Jan. 1, 1912–); b. Brooklyn, N.Y. Economist, educator. *Price Theory for a Changing Economy* (1939); *Inventories and Business Cycles* (1950); *The Growth of Public Employment in Great Britain* (with Vera Eliasberg, 1957). Prof. economics, Stanford University, since 1948.

ABRAMS, CHARLES (Sept. 20, 1901–Feb. 22, 1970); b. Vilna, Pol. Lawyer. *Revolution in Land* (1939); *The Future of Housing* (1946); *Forbidden Neighbors* (1955); *Man's Struggle for Shelter in an Urbanizing World* (1964); *The City Is the Frontier* (1967); etc.

Abrams, Harry N., Inc. *See* Times-Mirror Co.

ABRAMS, MEYER HOWARD (July 23, 1912–); b. Long Branch, N.J. Educator, critic. *The Milk of Paradise* (1934); *The Mirror and the Lamp: Romantic Theory and the Critical Tradition* (1953); *A Glossary of Literary Terms* (1957). Editor: *The Poetry of Pope* (1954); *Literature and Belief* (1958); *The Romantic Poets: Modern Essays in Criticism* (1960); *The Norton Anthology of English Literature* (1962). Professor, English department, Cornell University, since 1945.

Absalom, Absalom! Novel by William Faulkner (1936). A reconstructed sequence of incidents in the life of Thomas Sutpen, whose ambition to found a family dynasty founders on his inability to accept other human beings for what they are. The story is told by his descendant Quentin Compson.

"Absence: A Pastoral." Poem by Jonathan Boucher (c. 1775). Perhaps the earliest poem treating of the peculiarities of the English language in America. See *Dialect Notes,* Dec., 1933.

Abstracts of English Studies. Boulder, Colorado. Monthly. Founded 1958. Publishes abstracts of articles dealing with English and American literature and language.

Accent on Youth. Comedy by Samson Raphaelson (prod. 1935). Stephen Gaye, a playwright, writes a play which causes its cast to rebel because of the implausibility of the plot. Gaye's secretary, who knows how true the plot is, marries him to prove it.

Ace Books. New York. Publishers. Founded 1952. A subsidiary of Ace Publishing Corp. Issues paperback reprints and originals.

ACHELIS, ELIZABETH (Jan. 24, 1880–); b. Brooklyn, N.Y. Calendar reformer. *The World Calendar* (1930); *The Calendar for Everybody* (1943); *Of Time and the Calendar* (1955); *The Calendar of the Modern Age* (1959); *Be Not Silent* (autobiography, 1961).

ACHESON, DEAN GOODERHAM (Apr. 11, 1893–Oct. 12, 1971); b. Middletown, Conn. Lawyer, government official. *Pattern of Responsibility* (1952); *A Democrat Looks at His Party* (1955); *A Citizen Looks at Congress* (1957); *Power and Diplomacy* (1958); *Sketches from the Life of Men I Have Known* (1961); *Morning and Noon* (1965); *Private Thoughts on Public Affairs* (1967); *Present at the Creation: My Years in the State Department* (1969). Secretary of State, 1949–53.

ACHESON, EDWARD (b. 1902). Novelist. *Red Herring* (1932); *A Grammarian's Funeral* (1935); *Gone Away!* (1935); *Murder to Hounds* (1939); etc.

Acheson, Lila Bell. See Lila Acheson Wallace.

Achievement in American Poetry, 1900–1950. By Louise Bogan (1951). One of the most authoritative works on the poetry of the period, by the poetry editor of *The New Yorker.*

ACKERMAN, CARL WILLIAM (Jan. 16, 1890–Aug. 23, 1954); b. Richmond, Ind. Educator, publicist, author. *Mexico's Dilemma* (1918); *Trailing the Bolsheviki* (1919); *Biography of George Eastman* (1930); etc. Dean, Columbia University Graduate School of Journalism, since 1931.

ACKERMAN, EDWARD AUGUSTUS (Dec. 5, 1911–); b. Post Falls, Ida. Educator. *New England's Fishing Industry* (1941); *American Resources* (with J. R. Whitaker, 1951); *Japan's Natural Resources* (1953); *Technology in American Water Development* (1959). Prof. geography, University of Chicago, since 1948.

Acme Edition. A series of cheap reprints of popular and standard authors, begun in 1879 by John B. Alden.

ACOSTA, MERCEDES DE (Mrs. Abram Poole) (Mar. 1900–); b. Paris, France. Poet, novelist, playwright. *Wind Chaff* (1918); *Moods* (poems, 1919); *Sandro Botticelli* (prod. 1923); *Until the Day Breaks* (1928); *Here Lies the Heart* (autobiography, 1960); etc.

Acres of Diamonds. Lecture by Russell Herman Conwell. It was given over 6,000 times, and the proceeds were devoted to the education of more than 10,000 young men.

Across the River and Into the Trees. Novel by Ernest Hemingway (1950).

Across the Wide Missouri. Historical work by Bernard De Voto (1947). About the Rocky Mountain fur trade.

Act One. By Moss Hart (1959). Autobiography of a playwright.

ADAIR, JAMES (c. 1709–c. 1783); b. in Co. Antrim, Ireland (?). Indian trader, author. *The History of the American Indians, Particularly Those Nations Adjoining to the Mississippi, East and West Florida, Georgia, South and North Carolina, and Virginia* (1775).

ADAMIC, LOUIS (Mar. 23, 1899–Sept. 4, 1951); b. Blato, Austria. Novelist. *Dynamite: the Story of Class Violence in America* (1931); *Laughing in the Jungle* (autobiography, 1932); *The Native's Return* (1934); *Grandsons* (1935); *Cradle of Life* (1936); *The House of Antigua: A Restoration* (1937); *My America, 1928–1938* (1938); *From Many Lands* (1940); *Two-Way Passage* (1942); *What's Your Name?* (1942); *My Native Land* (1943); *Dinner at the White House* (1946); *The Eagle and the Roots* (1952). Publisher and editor, *The Trends of the Times,* 1945–51.

ADAMS, ABIGAIL [Smith] (Nov. 11, 1744–Oct. 28, 1818); b. Weymouth, Mass. Wife of John Adams, second president of the United States. Noted letter writer. *Letters of Mrs. Adams* (1840), ed. by Charles Francis Adams.

ADAMS, ANDY (May 3, 1859–Sept. 26, 1935); b. in Whitley Co., Ind. Cowboy, miner, author. *The Log of a Cowboy* (1903); *A Texas Matchmaker* (1904); *The Outlet* (1905); *Cattle Brands* (1906); *Reed Anthony, Cowman* (1907); *Wells Brothers* (1911); *The Ranch on the Beaver* (1927).

ADAMS, BROOKS (June 24, 1848–Feb. 13, 1927); b. Quincy Mass. Historian. *The Law of Civilization and Decay* (1895); *The New Empire* (1902); *The Theory of Social Revolution* (1913); etc. See *Harvard Graduates' Magazine,* v. 35, 1927; Thorton Anderson's *Brooks Adams, Constructive Conservative* (1951); Timothy Paul Donovan's *Henry Adams and Brooks Adams* (1961); Warner Berthoff's *The Ferment of Realism: American Literature 1884–1919* (1965).

ADAMS, CEDRIC M. (May 27, 1902–Feb. 18, 1961); b. Adrian, Minn. News columnist, commentator. *The Country Plumber* (1929); *Poor Cedric's Almanac* (1952). Columnist, *Minneapolis Star and Tribune,* from 1934; commentator, C.B.S. radio and television, from 1950.

ADAMS, CHARLES FOLLEN (Apr. 21, 1842–Mar. 8, 1918); b. Dorchester, Mass. Poet. *Leedle Yawcob Strauss* (1876); *Dialect Ballads* (1888); *Yawcob Strauss, and Other Poems* (1910).

ADAMS, CHARLES FRANCIS (Aug. 18, 1807–Nov. 21, 1886); b. Boston, Mass. Diplomat. Editor: *The Works of John Adams,* 10v. (1850–56); *Memoirs of John Quincy Adams,* 12v. (1874–77).

ADAMS, CHARLES FRANCIS (May 27, 1835–Mar. 20, 1915); b. Boston, Mass. Publicist, author. *Episodes in New England History* (1883), extended to two volumes as, *Three Episodes in Massachusetts History* (1892); *Charles Francis Adams, 1835–1915* (autobiography, 1916). See *A Cycle of Adams Letters, 1861–65* (1920); Edward Kirkland's *Charles Francis Adams, Jr.* (1966).

ADAMS, CHARLES KENDALL (Jan. 24, 1835–July 26, 1902); b. Derby, Vt. Educator, historian, biographer. *Democracy and Monarchy in France* (1874); *Manual of Historical Literature* (1882); *Christopher Columbus* (1892). Editor: *Representative British Orations,* 3v. (1884). See Charles Foster Smith's *Charles Kendall Adams: A Life-Sketch* (1924).

ADAMS, EDWARD C[larkson] L[everett] (1876–); b. in Richmond Co., S.C. Author. *Congaree Sketches* (1927); *Nigger to Nigger* (1928); etc.

ADAMS, ELEANOR N., b. Lebanon, O. Educator, author. *Old English Scholarship in England* (1917). Editor: Sarah Sullivan's *The Old Flatboatman's Trail* (1955). President, Oxford College for Women, Ohio, 1918–28.

ADAMS, EPHRAIM DOUGLASS (Dec. 18, 1865–Sept. 1, 1930); b. Decorah, Ia. Educator, historian. *British Interests and Activities in Texas, 1838–1846* (1910); *The Power of Ideals in American History* (1913); *A History of the United States* (with John C. Almack, 1931); *Great Britain and the American Civil War,* 2v. (1925); etc.

ADAMS, EUSTACE L[ane] (July 12, 1891–); b. Saco, Me. Author. *Over the Polar Ice* (1928); *Racing Around the World* (1928); *Pirates of the Air* (1929); *The Mysterious Monoplane* (1930); *Wings of Adventure* (1931); *The Young Sky Riders* (1931); *Wings of the Navy* (1936); *War Wings* (1938); *Fools Rush In* (1940); *Death Charter* (1943); etc.

ADAMS, FRANK R[amsay] (July 7, 1883–Oct. 8, 1963); b. Morrison, Ill. Novelist. *Five Fridays* (1915); *Molly and I* (1915); *The Long Night* (1929); *Peter and Mrs. Pan* (1929); *Gangway* (1931); *King's Crew* (1932); *Gunsight Ranch* (1939); *Arizona Feud* (1941); *When I Come Back* (1944); etc. Author or co-author of musical comedy librettos and screenplays.

ADAMS, FRANKLIN P[ierce] (Nov. 15, 1881–Mar. 23, 1960); b. Chicago, Ill. Journalist, columnist, poet. Wrote under initials, "F. P. A." *In Other Words* (poems, 1912); *By and Large* (poems, 1914); *Weights and Measures* (poems, 1917); *Something Else Again* (poems, 1920); *The Diary of Our Own Samuel Pepys,* 2v. (1935); *The Melancholy Lute* (poems, 1936); *Nods and Becks* (1944); etc. Editor: *Innocent Merriment* (1942); *F. P. A. Book of Quotations* (1952); etc. With *Chicago Journal,* 1903–1904; *New York Evening Mail,* 1904–13; *New York Tribune,* 1914–1921; *New York World,* 1922–1931; *New York Herald Tribune,* 1931–37; *New York Post,* from 1938. Conducted daily column, *The Conning Tower,* selections from which have been published as *The Conning Tower Book* (1926); and *The Second Conning Tower Book* (1927). On radio program "Information Please." *See* Fred B. Millett's *Contemporary American Authors* (1940).

ADAMS, FREDERICK UPHAM (Dec. 10, 1859–Aug. 28, 1921); b. Boston, Mass. Inventor, novelist. *John Henry Smith* (1905); *The Bottom of the Well* (1906); *The Revolt* (1907); etc.

ADAMS, GEORGE BURTON (June 3, 1851–May 26, 1925); b. Fairfield, Vt. Educator, historian. *Civilization during the Middle Ages* (1894); *History of England* (1905); *Constitutional History of England* (1920); etc. Editor, *American Historical Review,* 1895–1913. Prof. history, Yale University, 1888–1925.

ADAMS, GEORGE MATTHEW (Aug. 23, 1878–Oct. 28, 1962); b. Saline, Mich. Columnist. *You Can* (1913); *Take It* (1917); *Up* (1920); *Just Among Friends* (1928); *Better Than Gold* (1949); *The Great Little Things* (1953); etc.

ADAMS, G[eorge] P[limpton] (1882–Apr. 20, 1961). *Idealism in the Modern Age* (1918); *Man and Metaphysics* (1948). Editor, University of California publications in philosophy, 17v., 1923–40. Philosophy dept., University of California, 1908–54.

ADAMS, HAMPTON (Mar. 2, 1897–); b. Hamilton, Ky. Disciples of Christ clergyman. *The Pastoral Ministry* (1932); *You and Your Minister* (1940); *Calling Men for the Ministry* (1945); *Ambassador in Chains* (1947); *Vocabulary of Faith* (1956); etc.

ADAMS, HANNAH (Oct. 2, 1755–Dec. 15, 1831); b. Medfield, Mass. Author. *Alphabetical Compendium of the Various Sects Which Have Appeared in the World from the Beginning of the Christian Era to the Present Day* (1784); *A Summary History of New England* (1799); *The History of the Jews,* 2v. (1812).

ADAMS, HARRIET S. b. in New Jersey. Director of Stratemeyer Literary Syndicate (*see* Edward L. Stratemeyer) after 1930. Best known for juvenile series *Dana Girls* and *Nancy Drew,* written under pen name "Carolyn Keene."

Adams, Harrison. Pen name of St. George Henry Rathbone.

ADAMS, HELEN SIMMONS (1897–). Author. Writes under pen name "Nancy Barnes." *Carlota, American Empress* (1943); *The Wonderful Year* (1946); etc.

ADAMS, HENRY AUSTIN (Sept. 20, 1861–1931); b. Santiago, Cuba. Story-writer, playwright. *Orations* (1902); *The Mortgage on the Brain* (1905); *'Ception Shoals* (prod. 1917); etc.

ADAMS, HENRY BROOKS (Feb. 15, 1838–Mar. 27, 1918); b. Boston, Mass. Historian, essayist. *Democracy* (1880); *John Randolph* (1882); *Esther* (under pen name, "Francis Snow Compton," 1884); *History of the United States,* 9v. (1889–91); *Mont-Saint-Michel and Chartres* (1904); *The Education of Henry Adams* (1918, Pulitzer prize for American biography, 1919); *A Cycle of Adams Letters, 1861–1865,* 2v. (1920); *Letters of Henry Adams, 1858–1891,* (1930); and *Letters of Henry Adams, 1892–1918* (1938), ed. by Worthington C. Ford; etc. Editor: *North American Review,* 1870–76. *See* James Truslow Adams's *Henry Adams* (1933); Ernest Samuels' *The Young Henry Adams* (1948), *Henry Adams: The Middle Years, 1877–1891* (1958), and *Henry Adams: The Major Phase* (1964).

ADAMS, J[ames] **DONALD** (Sept. 24, 1891–Aug. 22, 1968); b. New York. Editor, critic. *The Shape of Books to Come* (1944); *Literary Frontiers* (1951); *Copey of Harvard* (1960); *Speaking of Books and Life* (1965). Editor: *The Treasure Chest: An Anthology of Contemplative Prose* (1945); *The New Treasure Chest* (1953); *Triumph Over Odds* (1957); *The Magic and Mystery of Words* (1963); etc. Editor, *New York Times Book Review,* 1925–43; contributing editor, since 1943.

ADAMS, JAMES LUTHER (Nov. 12, 1901–); b. Ritzville, Wash. Theologian, author. *The Changing Reputation of Human Nature* (1943); *Taking Time Seriously* (1957). Translator: Paul Tillich's *The Protestant Era* (1948); Erich Fromm's *The Dogma of Christ* (1963). Professor of Christian Ethics, Harvard Divinity School, since 1956.

ADAMS, JAMES TRUSLOW (Oct. 18, 1878–May 18, 1949); b. Brooklyn, N.Y. Historian. *The Founding of New England* (1921, Pulitzer prize for American history, 1922); *Revolutionary New England, 1691–1776* (1923); *New England in the Republic, 1776–1850* (1926); *Provincial Society, 1690–1763* (1927); *The Adams Family* (1930); *The Epic of America* (1931); *The March of Democracy,* 2v. (1932–33); *Henry Adams* (1933); *America's Tragedy* (1935); *The Living Jefferson* (1936); *Building the British Empire* (1938); *Empire on the Seven Seas* (1940); *An American Looks at the British Empire* (1940); *The American* (1943); *Frontiers of American Culture* (1944); *Big Business in a Democracy* (1945); etc. Editor: *Dictionary of American History,* 6v. (1940); *The Atlas of American History* (1943); *Album of American History,* 5v. (1944–48); etc.

ADAMS, JOHN (Oct. 19, 1735–July 4, 1826); b. Braintree, Mass. Second president of the United States, author. *Thoughts on Government* (1776); *Discourses on Davila* (1805); etc. *See* Charles F. Adams's *Life and Work of John Adams,* 10v. (1850–56); Catherine Drinker Bowen's *John Adams and the American Revolution* (1950); *The Adams-Jefferson Letters,* ed. by Lester J. Cappon, 2v. (1959); *The Adams Papers: Diary and Autobiography of John Adams* (1961), *Family Corre-*

spondence (1963), and *The Earliest Diary of John Adams* (1966), ed. by L. H. Butterfield.

ADAMS, JOHN COLEMAN (Oct. 25, 1849–June 22, 1922); b. Malden, Mass. Clergyman, author. *Christian Types of Heroism* (1891); *Nature Studies in Berkshire* (1899); *An Honorable Youth* (1906); *Santa Claus's Baby and Other Christmas Stories* (1911); etc.

ADAMS, JOHN CRANFORD (Oct. 11, 1903–Oct. 11, 1952); b. Boston, Mass. Educator, scholar. *The Globe Playhouse: Its Design and Equipment* (1942). President, Hofstra College, New York, from 1944.

ADAMS, JOHN QUINCY (July 11, 1767–Feb. 23, 1848); b. Braintree, Mass. Sixth president of the United States, author. *Lectures on Rhetoric and Oratory*, 2v. (1810); *Poems of Religion and Society* (1848); *Diary of John Quincy Adams,* ed. by Charles F. Adams, 12v. (1874–77); *Writings of John Quincy Adams,* ed. by W. C. Ford, 7v. (1913–1917; rev. ed. 1968). See J. T. Adams's *The Adams Family* (1930); Bennett Champ Clark's *John Quincy Adams* (1932); biography by John T. Morse in *American Statesmen Series;* and George Lipsky's *John Quincy Adams* (1950).

ADAMS, JOHN TURVILL (1805–1882). Author. *Poems* (1925); *The Lost Hunter* (anon., 1856); *The Knight of the Golden Melice* (anon., 1857); republished as *The White Chief Among the Red Men* (1859).

ADAMS, JOSEPH QUINCY (Mar. 23, 1881–Nov. 11, 1946); b. Greenville, S.C. Librarian, Shakespearean scholar, author. *A Life of William Shakespeare* (1923); *A Register of Bibliographies of the English Language and Literature* (with C. S. Northup, 1925); etc. Editor: *Chief Pre-Shakespearean Dramas* (1924); *The Dramatic Records of Sir Henry Herbert* (1917); *Oenone and Paris* (1943); general editor, *A New Variorum Edition of Shakespeare;* etc. Director and editor of publications, The Folger Shakespeare Library, Washington, D.C., (1931–46).

Adams, Julia Davis. See Julia Davis.

ADAMS, KATHARINE, b. Elmira, N.Y. Novelist, poet. *Irish Day* (poems, 1916); *Light and Mist* (1918); *Mehitable* (1920); *Midsummer* (1921); *Wisp, a Girl of Dublin* (1922); *Red Caps and Lilies* (1924); *The Silver Tarn* (1924); *Midwinter* (1927); *Thistle Down* (1930); *Blackthorn* (1931); *Scarlet Sheath* (1936); etc.

ADAMS, LEONIE [Fuller] (Mrs. William E. Troy) (Dec. 9, 1899–); b. Brooklyn, N.Y. Poet. *Those Not Elect* (1925); *High Falcon, & Other Poems* (1929); *This Measure* (1933); *Poems: A Selection* (1954), (1959). Editor: *Lyrics of François Villon* (1932). Lecturer, Columbia University, since 1947.

Adams, Lucy Lockwood. See Lucy Lockwood Hazard.

ADAMS, MARY [Jane] M[athews] (Mrs. Charles Kendall Adams) (Oct. 23, 1840–Dec. 10, 1902); b. Granard, near Dublin, Ireland. Poet. *The Choir Visible* (1897); *Sonnets and Songs* (1901); *The Song at Midnight* (1903).

Adams, Moses. Pen name of George William Bagby.

ADAMS, NICHOLSON BARNEY (1895–). Educator. *The Romantic Dramas of Garcia Guttiérrez* (1932); *Brief Spanish Review Grammar* (1933); *The Heritage of Spain* (1943). Editor: *Don Juan Tenorio* (1931). Co-editor: *Spanish Folktales* (1932); *Spanish Literature, A Brief Survey* (with J. E. Keller, 1962); etc. Prof. Spanish, University of North Carolina, since 1924.

ADAMS, OSCAR FAY (1855–Apr. 30, 1919); b. Worcester, Mass. Story-writer, poet, anthologist. *A Brief Handbook of American Authors* (1884), augmented as *A Dictionary of American Authors* (1897); *Post-Laureate Idyls* (1886); *Dear Old Story-Tellers* (1889); *The Archbishop's Unguarded Moment, and Other Stories* (1899); *Sicut Patribus, and Other Verse* (1906).

ADAMS, RAMON FREDERICK (1889–). Author. *Cowboy Lingo* (1936); *Western Words* (1944); *Come an' Get It: The Story of the Old Cowboy Cook* (1952); *Six-Guns and Saddle Leather* (1954); *The Best of the American Cowboy* (1957); *A Fitting Death for Billy the Kid* (1960); *The Old-Time Cowhand* (1961); *Book of the American West* (with others, 1963); *Burrs Under the Saddle* (1964).

ADAMS, RANDOLPH GREENFIELD (Nov. 7, 1892–Jan. 4, 1951); b. Philadelphia, Pa. Librarian, historian. *Political Ideas of the American Revolution* (1922); *A Gateway to American History* (1927); *Pilgrims, Indians and Patriots* (1928); *Three Americanists* (1939). Director, William L. Clements Library of American History, University of Michigan, 1923–51.

ADAMS, ROBERT MARTIN (1915–); Educator, author. *Ikon: John Milton and the Modern Critics* (1955); *Stendhal: Notes on a Novelist* (1959); *Surface and Symbol* (1962); *Nil: Episodes in the Literary Conquest of Void during the Nineteenth Century* (1966). Prof. English, University of California at Los Angeles.

ADAMS, ROBERT McCORMICK, JR. (July 23, 1926–); b. Chicago, Ill. Anthropologist, author. *Land Behind Baghdad* (1965); *The Evolution of Urban Society: Early Mesopotamia and Prehispanic Mexico* (1966). Editor: *City Invincible: A Symposium on Urbanization and Cultural Development in the Ancient Near East* (with C. H. Kraeling, 1960). Faculty, Oriental Institute, University of Chicago, since 1955.

ADAMS, SAMUEL (Sept. 27, 1722–Oct. 2, 1803); b. Boston, Mass. Revolutionary statesman, one of the leaders in the Boston Tea Party, Dec. 16, 1773, author. *The Writings of Samuel Adams,* ed. by H. A. Cushing, 4v. (1904–08). *See* James K. Hosmer's *Samuel Adams* (1885); Stewart Beach's *Samuel Adams: The Fateful Years, 1764–1776* (1966).

ADAMS, SAMUEL HOPKINS (Jan. 26, 1871–Nov. 15, 1958); b. Dunkirk, N.Y. Author. *The Flying Death* (1902); *The Secret of Lonesome Cove* (1913); *Our Square and the People in It* (1917); *From a Bench in Our Square* (1922); *Flaming Youth* (pen name "Warner Fabian," 1923); *Revelry* (1926); *The Gorgeous Hussy* (1934); *It Happened One Night* (scenario, 1934); *Perfect Specimen* (1936); *Maiden Effort* (1937); *Incredible Era: The Life and Times of Warren Gamaliel Harding* (1939); *The Harvey Girls* (1942); *A. Woollcott, His Life and His World* (1945); *Sunrise and Sunset* (1950); *Grandfather Stories* (1955); *Chingo Smith of the Erie Canal* (1958); etc.

ADAMS, SHERMAN (Jan. 8, 1899–); b. East Dover, Vt. Government official. *Firsthand Report: The Story of the Eisenhower Administration* (1961). Governor of New Hampshire, 1949–53; assistant to the President, 1953–58.

ADAMS, WILLIAM TAYLOR (July 30, 1822–Mar. 27, 1897); b. Bellingham, Mass. Novelist. Pen names, (books for boys) "Oliver Optic," (novels) "Irving Brown," (travel books) "Clingham Hunter, M. D."; also "Old Stager." *The Boat Club* (1855); the *Great Western* series; the *Lake Shore* series; the *Army and Navy* series; the *Yacht Club* series; *Woodville* stories, the *Blue and Gray* series; etc. Editor, *Oliver Optic's Magazine for Boys and Girls,* 1867–75.

Adams Family, The. Biography by James Truslow Adams (1930).

ADAMSON, HANS CHRISTIAN. (1890–). Author. *Lands of New World Neighbors* (1941); *Eddie Rickenbacker* (1946); *Keeper of the Lights* (1955); *Admiral Thunderbolt* (1959); *Rebellion in Missouri* (1961); *Blood on the Midnight Sun* (with Per Klem, 1964); etc. With Charles Andrews Lockwood: *Hellcats of the Sea* (1955); *Through Hell and Deep Water* (1956); *Tragedy at Honda* (1960); *Battles of the Philippine Sea* (1967).

ADDAMS, CHARLES [Samuel] (Jan. 7, 1912–); b. Westfield, N.J. Cartoonist, author. *Drawn and Quartered* (1942); *Addams and Evil* (1947); *Monster Rally* (1950); *Homebodies* (1954); *Nightcrawlers* (1957); *Black Maria* (1960); *The Groaning Board* (1964); *The Charles Addams Mother Goose* (1967). Editor: *Dear Dead Days* (1959). Cartoons have appeared in *The New Yorker* since 1935.

ADDAMS, JANE (Sept. 6, 1860–May 21, 1935); b. Cedarville, Ill. Settlement worker, sociologist, author. *Democracy and Social Ethics* (1902); *Twenty Years at Hull House* (1910); etc.

Adding Machine, The. Play by Elmer Rice (prod. 1923). Satire on the "machine age."

ADDINGTON, LUTHER FOSTER (1899–). Author. *Story of Wise County, Virginia* (1956); *Little Fiddler of Laurel Grove* (1960); *Sugar in the Gourd* (1961); *Tip-off to Win* (1962).

ADDINGTON, SARAH (Mrs. Howard C. Reid) (Apr. 6, 1891–Nov. 7, 1940); b. Cincinnati, O. Author. *The Boy Who Lived in Pudding Lane* (1922); *The Pied Piper in Pudding Lane* (1923); *Pudding Lane People* (1926); *Hound of Heaven* (1935); etc.

ADDISON, DANIEL DULANY (Mar. 11, 1863–Mar. 27, 1936); b. Wheeling, W. Va. Episcopal clergyman, biographer. *Lucy Larcom: Life, Letters and Diary* (1894); *Phillips Brooks* (1894); *The Life and Times of Edward Bass, First Bishop of Massachusetts* (1897); *The Clergy in American Life and Letters* (1900); etc.

ADDISON, JAMES THAYER (Mar. 21, 1887–Feb. 13, 1953); b. Fitchburg, Mass. Episcopal clergyman, educator, author. *Chinese Ancestor Worship* (1925); *Our Expanding Church* (1930); *Parables of Our Lord* (1940); *The Christian Approach to the Moslem* (1942); *The Episcopal Church in the United States 1789–1931* (1951); etc.

ADDISON, JULIA DE WOLF (Feb. 24, 1866–); b. Boston, Mass. Artist, musician, author. *Florestane the Troubadour* (1903); *Arts and Crafts in the Middle Ages* (1908); *The Spell of England* (1912); etc. Composed music for "The Night Hath a Thousand Eyes" (1888).

Address on Thomas Jefferson and John Adams. Delivered by William Wirt in the House of Representatives in 1826. One of the classic American orations.

Address to the Roman Catholics of the United States. By Bishop John Carroll (1784). The first example of Catholic writing published in the United States.

Addresses upon the American Road. By Herbert Hoover, 3v. (1946, 1949, 1951).

ADE, GEORGE (Feb. 9, 1866–May 16, 1944); b. Kentland, Ind. Humorist, playwright. *Doc Horne* (1899); *Fables in Slang* (1900); *Breaking Into Society* (1904); *The County Chairman* (Prod. 1903); *The Sultan of Sulu* (prod. 1903); *Peggy from Paris* (prod. 1903); *The College Widow* (prod. 1904); *The Sho-Gun* (prod. 1904); *Father and the Boys* (prod. 1907); *The Fair Co-Ed* (prod. 1908); *The Old-Time Saloon* (1931); etc.

Adeler, Max. Pen name of Charles Heber Clark.

ADER, PAUL [Fassett] (Oct. 20, 1919–); b. Asheville, N.C. Author. *We Always Come Back* (pen name "James Allen," 1945); *The Leaf Against the Sky* (1947).

"Adirondacs, The." Poem by Ralph Waldo Emerson (1867).

ADLER, CYRUS (Sept. 13, 1863–Apr. 7, 1940); b. Van Buren, Ark. Educator, Semitic scholar and archeologist, editor. *Told in the Coffee House: Turkish Tales* (with Allan Ramsay, 1898); *Jacob H. Schiff: His Life and Letters,* 2v.

(1928). Editor: *Jewish Encyclopedia; American Jewish Year Book.* President of Dropsie College, Philadelphia, 1908–40; Jewish Theological Seminary, New York, 1924–40.

ADLER, ELMER (July 22, 1884–Jan. 11, 1962); b. Rochester, N.Y. Printer, publisher, editor, author. *On Books, Etc.* (1953). Editor: *Breaking Into Print* (1937). Founder, The Pynson Printers, New York, 1922; director, 1923–40. One of the founders of Random House, 1927, vice-president, 1927–32. Founder, *The Colophon;* co-editor, 1930–40; *New Colophon,* 1947; *La Casa Del Libro,* Puerto Rico, 1958. Curator in graphic arts, Princeton University, 1940–52.

ADLER, FELIX (Aug. 13, 1851–Apr. 24, 1933); b. Alzey, Germany. Lecturer, author. *Creed and Deed* (1877); *An Ethical Philosophy of Life* (1918); etc. Founder, The New York Society for Ethical Culture, 1876.

ADLER, IRVING (1913–). Author. Under pen name "Robert Irving": *Energy and Power* (1958); *Sound and Ultrasonics* (1959); *Electronics* (1961); etc. Under own name: *The Secret of Light* (1952); *Fire in Your Life* (1955); *Time in Your Life* (1955); *Tools in Your Life* (1956); *How Life Began* (1957); *Man-Made Moons* (1958); *Seeing the Earth from Space* (1959); *Light in Your Life* (1961); *Shadows* (with Ruth Adler, 1961); *Color in Your Life* (1962); *Inside the Nucleus* (1963); *Wonders of Physics* (1966); *Groups in New Mathematics* (1968); *Mathematics: Exploring the World of Numbers* (1968); etc.

ADLER, JULIUS OCHS (Dec. 3, 1892–Oct. 3, 1955); b. Chattanooga, Tenn. Editor, publisher. *History of the 77th Division* (1919); *History of the 306th Infantry* (1935). With *New York Times,* from 1914; general manager, from 1935; publisher *Chattanooga Times,* 1935.

ADLER, MORTIMER [Jerome] (Dec. 28, 1902–); b. New York. Educator, author. *Dialectic* (1927); *Art and Prudence* (1937); *St. Thomas and the Gentiles* (1938); *How to Read a Book* (1940); *A Dialectic of Morals* (1941); *How to Think About War and Peace* (1944); *The Idea of Freedom,* 2v. (1958, 1962); *The New Capitalists* (with Louis Kelso, 1961); etc. Editor: *The Negro in American History,* 3v. (with others, 1969). Associate editor, *Great Books of the Western World,* since 1945; editor, *The Great Ideas.* Prof. philosophy of law, University of Chicago, 1942–1952. Pres. and director, Institute of Philosophical Research, since 1952.

ADLER, POLLY (1900–June 9, 1962). Author. *A House Is Not a Home* (1953).

ADLER, RENATA, b. Milan, It. Book and motion-picture reviewer. *Toward a Radical Middle* (1969); *A Year in the Dark* (1969). Writer-reporter, *The New Yorker,* since 1962; film critic, *The New York Times,* 1968–69. Film Critic, *The New Yorker,* from 1970.

ADSHEAD, GLADYS LUCY (Apr. 25, 1896–); b. West Didsbury, Manchester, Eng. Author. *Brownies—Hush!* (1938); *Something Surprising* (1939); *Casco* (1943); *What Miranda Knew* (1944); *Brownies—It's Christmas!* (1955); *Brownies, Hurry!* (1959); *Smallest Brownie's Fearful Adventure* (1961); etc.

Adulateur, The. Drama by Mercy Otis Warren (1773). Political satire following the Boston Massacre.

Adventure. New York. Magazine of adventure stories. Founded, 1910. Arthur Sullivant Hoffman was editor, 1911–27.

Adventures in Contentment. Essays by "David Grayson" (Ray Stannard Baker), 9v. (1907). Also *Adventures in Understanding* (1925); and *Adventures in Solitude* (1931).

Adventures of a Young Man. Novel by John Dos Passos (1939). First of a trilogy continued in *Number One* (1943) and *The Grand Design* (1949).

Adventures of Augie March, The. Novel by Saul Bellow (1953). The adventures of a spirited and Bohemian young man from Chicago, written as a picaresque tale.

Adventures of Captain Bonneville. By Washington Irving (1837). Story of roving trappers in the West.

Adventures of Captain Simon Suggs. By Johnson J. Hooper (1846). A classic of Southern humor, written in the vernacular.

Adventures of François, The. Historical novel by S[ilas] Weir Mitchell (1898). Paris during the French Revolution.

Adventures of Huckleberry Finn, The. By Mark Twain (1885). Continuation of the experiences set forth in *The Adventures of Tom Sawyer.* The background was the author's own childhood in Hannibal, Mo., on the Mississippi. Written in the form of a juvenile adventure tale, this account of the river journey of Huck and the Negro slave Jim is a landmark in American literature, distinguished for its colloquial style and the depth of its perception into the moral conditions of mid-nineteenth-century frontier life. See Walter Blair's *Mark Twain and Huck Finn* (1960); Walter Blair and Hamlin Hill's *The Art of Huckleberry Finn* (1962); John Seelye's *The True Adventures of Huckleberry Finn* (1970).

Adventures of Three Worthies, The. Collection of stories by Clinton Ross (1891).

Adventures of Tom Sawyer, The. By Mark Twain (1876). Classic picture of life on the Mississippi, recounting the escapades of a boy who could not stay out of mischief, and who keeps his Aunt Polly in a constant state of apprehension. See *The Adventures of Huckleberry Finn.*

Advertisements for Myself. Collection of essays and stories by Norman Mailer (1959). Contains the essay *The White Negro.*

Advise and Consent. Novel by Allen Drury (1959). About the personalities and political intrigues of U.S. Senators.

Affluent Society, The. By John Kenneth Galbraith (1958). Attack on the principle that modern economic health rests on constant consumption of goods and overproduction.

Afloat and Ashore; or, The Adventures of Miles Wallingford. By James Fenimore Cooper, 2v. (1844). Mainly experiences of the author.

Afoot and Alone: A Walk From Sea to Sea, by the Southern Route. By Stephen Powers (1872). Record of a walking tour through the Southern States.

Africa Report. Washington, D.C. Monthly, Oct. through June. Founded 1956.

African Game Trails. By Theodore Roosevelt (1910). Account of his African wanderings, and his big game hunts.

"After All." Civil War poem by William Winter (1865).

"After Apple Picking." Poem by Robert Frost.

"After the Ball." Poem by Nora Perry, in the *Atlantic Monthly,* 1859. Sometimes reprinted under the title "Maud and Madge."

After the Lost Generation. By John W. Aldridge (1951). A critical study of the American writers who wrote about the two World Wars.

Aftermath. Novel by James Lane Allen (1896). Sequel to *A Kentucky Cardinal* (1894).

Agapida, Fray Antonio. Fictitious writer to whom Washington Irving originally attributed authorship of his *Conquest of Granada.*

AGAR, HERBERT [Sebastian] (Sept. 29, 1897–); b. New Rochelle, N.Y. Editor, author. *Fire and Sleet and Candlelight* (poems, with Eleanor Carroll Chilton and Willis Fisher, 1928); *Bread and Circuses* (1930); *The People's Choice* (1933, Pulitzer prize for American history, 1934); *Land of the Free* (1935); *Pursuit of Happiness* (1938); *A Time for Greatness* (1942); *A Declaration of Faith* (1952); *The Price of Power* (1957); *The Saving Remnant, An Account of Jewish Survival* (1962); *Perils of Democracy* (1965); etc. Editor, Louisville *Courier-Journal,* 1940–42. Conducted syndicated column "Time and Tide," 1935–39.

AGARD, WALTER RAYMOND (Jan. 16, 1894–); b. Rockville, Conn. Educator. *The Greek Tradition in Sculpture* (1930); *What Democracy Meant to the Greeks* (1942); *Classical Myths in Sculpture* (1951); *The Greek Mind* (1957); *The Humanities of Our Time* (with others, 1968); etc. Prof. classics, University of Wisconsin, since 1927.

"Agassiz." Long poem by James Russell Lowell (1874).

AGASSIZ, ELIZABETH [Cabot] CARY (Mrs. Louis Agassiz) (Dec. 5, 1822–June 27, 1907); b. Boston, Mass. Educator, author. *Seaside Studies in Natural History* (with stepson, Alexander Agassiz, 1865); *A Journey in Brazil* (with husband, 1868); *Louis Agassiz: His Life and Correspondence,* 2v. (1885); etc. See Lucy Allen Paton's *Elizabeth Cary Agassiz* (1919).

AGASSIZ, LOUIS [Jean Louis Rodolphe] (May 28, 1807–Dec. 14, 1873); b. Motier-en-Vully, Switzerland. Naturalist, author. *Contributions to the Natural History of the United States,* 4v. (1857–62); *Essay on Classification,* ed. by Edward Lurie (1962). See *Louis Agassiz: His Life and Correspondence,* ed. by Elizabeth Cary Agassiz, 2v. (1885); and Jules Marcou's *Life, Letters, and Works of Louis Agassiz,* 2v. (1896).

Age of Anxiety, The: A Baroque Eclogue. Dramatic poem by W. H. Auden (1946). A woman and three men, during World War II, discuss their own lives and the period they live in. The settings are a New York City bar and the apartment of one of the characters.

Age of Innocence, The. Novel by Edith Wharton (1920 Pulitzer Prize for fiction, 1921). A picture of high society in the New York of the eighteen-seventies.

Age of Jackson, The. Historical study by Arthur M. Schlesinger, Jr. (1945. Pulitzer Prize for history, 1946.)

Age of Reason, The. By Thomas Paine (1795). Had an important influence on American thought in the early nineteenth century.

Age of Roosevelt, The. Biographical and historical work by Arthur M. Schlesinger, Jr. It comprises *The Crisis of the Old Order* (1956); *The Coming of the New Deal* (1958); and *The Politics of Upheaval* (1960).

AGEE, JAMES (Nov. 27, 1909–May 16, 1955); b. Knoxville, Tenn. Author. *Permit Me Voyage* (poems, 1934); *Let Us Now Praise Famous Men* (with Walker Evans, 1941); *Religion and the Intellectuals* (with others, 1950); *The Morning Watch* (1951); *A Death in the Family* (1957); *On Film: Reviews and Comments* (1958); *On Film: Five Film Scripts* (1960).

AGER, WALDEMER [Theodor] (Mar. 23, 1869–Aug. 1, 1941); b. Fredericksstad, Nor. Editor, author. Translations of his books have been published as: *Sons of the Old Country* (1926); *I Sit Alone* (1931). Editor, *Reform* (Norse annual).

Ages, and Other Poems, The. By William Cullen Bryant (1821). This volume grew out of his Phi Beta Kappa poem delivered at Harvard, and was one of the most significant volumes of American poetry up to that time.

AGETON, ARTHUR AINSLIE (Oct. 25, 1900–); b. Fromberg, Mont. Naval officer, author. *Dead Reckoning Altitude and Azimuth Table* (1932); *Naval Officer's Guide* (1943); *Naval Leadership and the American Bluejacket* (1944); *Mary*

Jo and Little Liu (1945); *The Jungle Seas* (1954); *Admiral Ambassador to Russia* (with William H. Standley, 1955); *Manual of Celestial Navigation* (1961); etc.

AGNEW, JOHN HOLMES (May 9, 1804–Oct. 12, 1865); b. Gettysburg, Pa. Editor, publisher. Editor, *The American Eclectic,* 1842, *The Eclectic Museum,* 1843, *The Eclectic Magazine,* 1844–46; *The Knickerbocker Magazine,* 1864–65.

Agony and the Ecstasy, The. Novel by Irving Stone (1961). Based on the life of Michelangelo.

Agrarians. A group of Southern writers, including notably John Crowe Ransom, Allen Tate, Robert Penn Warren, and Donald Davidson, that argued in the 1920's and 1930's for an agrarian economy and regional ideals in the South. They were associated either as founders of or contributors to *Fugitive, The American Review,* and *Southern Review* (qq.v.). Members were also the leading exponents of the New Criticism (q.v.). Their collective manifesto, *I'll Take My Stand,* appeared in 1930.

Agricola. Pen name of William Elliott.

Aguecheek. A collection of travel sketches and essays by Charles Bullard Fairbanks (1827–1859), which had appeared originally in the Boston *Saturday Evening Gazette* under the pen name "Aguecheek," and were published anonymously in 1859. It was republished by Henry Garrity in 1912 under the title *My Unknown Chum: "Aguecheek."*

Ah, Wilderness. Comedy by Eugene O'Neill (prod. 1933). Depicts American family life about 1906. The boy Richard rebels against custom and tradition, but his father wisely lets him have his fling.

AIKEN, ALBERT W. One of the leading dime novelists. He averaged a dime novel a week for many years. *The Brigand Captain* (1871); *Abe Colt, the Crow-Killer* (1878); *Sol Ginger, the Giant Trapper* (1879); *Red Richard* (1885); *Lone Hand, the Shadow* (1889); *Dick Talbot, the Ranch King* (1892); *Fresh, the Race-Track Sport* (1894); etc. These dates are not necessarily those of first editions.

AIKEN, CONRAD [Potter] (Aug. 5, 1889–); b. Savannah, Ga. Poet, novelist, critic. *Earth Triumphant and Other Tales in Verse* (1914); *The Jig of Forslin* (poem, 1916); *Turns and Movies and Other Tales in Verse* (1916); *Nocturne of Remembered Spring and Other Poems* (1917); *The Charnel Rose,* (poems, 1918); *Scepticism, Notes on Contemporary Poetry* (1919); *The House of Dust* (poems, 1920); *Punch, the Immortal Liar* (poems, 1921); *Priapus and the Pool* (poems, 1922); *The Pilgrimage of Festus* (poems, 1923); *Senlin: a Biography, and Other Poems* (1925); *Selected Poems* (1929, Pulitzer prize for poetry, 1930); *Bring! Bring! and Other Stories* (1925); *Blue Voyage* (1927); *Costumes by Eros* (1928); *Gehenna* (1930); *The Coming Forth by Day of Osiris Jones* (poems, 1931); *Preludes for Memnon* (poems, 1931); *And in the Hanging Gardens* (poems, 1933); *Great Circle* (1933); *Landscape West of Eden* (poems, 1934); *Among the Lost People* (1934); *Time in the Rock* (poems, 1936); *A Heart for the Gods of Mexico* (1939); *Conversation* (1940); *And in the Human Heart* (poems, 1940); *Brownstone Eclogues* (1942); *The Soldier* (poem, 1944); *The Kid* (poem, 1947); *The Divine Pilgrim* (poem, 1949); *Short Stories* (1950); *Ushant* (autobiography, 1952); *Collected Poems* (1953); *A Letter from Li Po* (poems, 1956); *Mr. Arcularis* (play, 1957); *A Reviewer's ABC* (1958); *Collected Short Stories* (1960); *The Morning Song of Lord Zero* (1963); *Collected Novels* (1964); *A Seizure of Limericks* (1964); *Thee* (1967); *Collected Criticism* (1968). *See* Jay Martin's *Conrad Aiken, A Life of His Art* (1962); F. J. Hoffman's *Conrad Aiken;* Reuel Denney's *Conrad Aiken* (1964).

AIKEN, EDNAH [Robinson] (Mrs. Charles Sedgwick Aiken) (Sept. 7, 1872–); b. San Francisco, Calif. Novelist. *The River* (1914); *If Today Be Sweet* (1923); *Snow* (1930).

AIKEN, GEORGE DAVID (Aug. 20, 1892–); b. Dummerston, Vt. Governor, agriculturist, author. *Pioneering with Wild Flowers* (1933); *Pioneering with Fruits and Berries* (1936); *Speaking from Vermont* (1938). Governor of Vermont, 1937–41; U.S. Senator 1940–50, and since 1956.

AIKEN, GEORGE L. (Dec. 19, 1830–Apr. 27, 1876); b. Boston, Mass. Dime novelist, playwright. *The Household Skeleton* (1865); *Cynthia, the Pearl of the Points* (1867); *Josie; or, Was He a Woman?* (1870); *Fergus Fearnaught* (1882); etc. Dramatizer of Harriet B. Stowe's *Uncle Tom's Cabin* (prod. 1852); Ann S. Stephens's *The Old Homestead* (prod. 1856); etc.

AIKMAN, DUNCAN (1889–Dec. 14, 1955); b. Terre Haute, Ind. Author. *The Home Town Mind* (1926); *Calamity Jane and the Lady Wildcats* (1927); *All-American Front* (1940); *Turning Stream* (1948); etc. Editor: *The Taming of the Frontier* (1925).

Aikman, Henry G. Pen name of Harold Hunter Armstrong.

AINSLIE, HEW (Apr. 5, 1792–Mar. 11, 1878); b. Bargeny Mains, Ayrshire, Scotland. Poet. *Scottish Songs, Ballads and Poems* (1855).

AINSWORTH, EDWARD MADDIN (June 7, 1902–June 15, 1968); b. Waco, Tex. Journalist. *Pot Luck* (1940); *Eagles Fly West* (1946); *California Jubilee* (1948); *California* (1951); *Death Cues the Pageant* (1954); *Beckoning Desert* (1962); *Cowboy in Art* (1968); etc. State editor and columnist, *Los Angeles Times,* since 1924.

Air-Conditioned Nightmare, The. A personal critique of America, by Henry Miller (1945).

Airs from Arcady. Poems by Henry C. Bunner (1884).

AITKEN, ROBERT (1734–July 15, 1802); b. Dalkeith, Scotland. Editor, publisher, bookseller, printer, engraver. Publisher, *Aitken's General American Register* (1773); *The Pennsylvania Magazine; or, American Monthly Museum,* Jan. 1775–June, 1776. He printed the first American Bible in 1782.

AKELEY, CARL ETHAN (May 19, 1864–Nov. 17, 1926); b. in Orleans Co., N.Y. Explorer, author. *In Brightest Africa* (1923); *Lions, Gorillas and Their Neighbors* (1932); etc.

Akeley, Delia. See Delia Akeley Howe.

AKELEY, MARY L. JOBE (Mrs. Carl Akeley) (Jan. 29, 1886–July 19, 1966); b. Tappan, O. Educator, explorer, author. *Carl Akeley's Africa* (1929); *Adventures in the African Jungle* (with husband, 1930); *Lions, Gorillas and Their Neighbors* (1932); *Restless Jungle* (1936); *The Wilderness Lives Again: Carl Akeley and the Great Adventure* (1940); *Congo Eden* (1950).

Akens, Floyd. Pen name of L. Frank Baum.

AKERS, BENJAMIN PAUL (July 10, 1825–May 21, 1861); b. Saccarappa, Me. Sculptor, author. His early essays were published in the *Atlantic Monthly.* Husband of Elizabeth Chase Akers.

AKERS, ELIZABETH CHASE (Oct. 9, 1832–Aug. 7, 1911); b. Strong, Me. Poet, novelist. Pen name, "Florence Percy." *Forest Buds, from the Woods of Maine* (poems, 1856); *Poems* (1866); *The Silver Bridge, and Other Poems* (1886); *The Triangular Society* (1886); *The High Top Sweeting, and Other Poems* (1891); *The Proud Lady of Stavoren* (poem, 1897); *The Sunset Song, and Other Verses* (1902); etc. Her most famous poem is "Rock Me to Sleep, Mother" (1860).

"Akhoond of Swat, The." Humorous poem by George Thomas Lanigan (1878). Based on a headline in the *London Times,* Jan. 22, 1878.

AKINS, ZOË (Oct. 30, 1886–Oct. 29, 1958); b. Humansville, Mo. Playwright, poet. *Interpretations* (poems, 1911); *Déclassée* (prod. 1919); *Foot-Loose* (prod. 1920); *Daddy's Gone a Hunting* (prod. 1921); *The Furies* (prod. 1928); *The Greeks Had a Word For It* (prod. 1930); *The Old Maid* (dramatized from story by Edith Wharton, prod., 1935, Pulitzer prize play, 1935; *Forever Young* (1941); *Mr. January and Mrs. Ex* (1944); *Another Darling* (prod. 1950); *The Swallow's Nest* (prod. 1951).

Al Aaraaf, and Minor Poems. By Edgar Allan Poe (1829).

Alain. Pen name of Daniel Brustlein.

Alan Swallow. Denver, Colo. Founded 1940. Has used the following imprints: Alan Swallow, for fiction, poetry, biography; Swallow Paperbooks, for fiction and poetry; Sage Books, for works concerning the West. Directed by Alan Swallow until his death in 1966. Now known as the Swallow Press.

Albany Knickerbocker News. Albany, N.Y. Newspaper. Founded 1843, as the *Knickerbocker.* The *Albany Press* was founded 1877, and merged with the *Knickerbocker.* From 1899 to 1910 the name was the *Press-Knickerbocker-Express.* Publishers have included Frank E. Gannett and Gene Robb. Duane La Fleche is book critic and R. Fichenburg is editor.

Albany Times-Union, Albany, N.Y. Newspaper. Founded 1856, as the *Albany Courier,* becoming the *Albany Morning Times* in 1861, and the *Evening Times* until 1865. In 1891 John Henry Farrell and associates founded the *Times-Union* by consolidating the *Evening Union* with the *Albany Times* and *Albany Daily Sun.* M. H. Glynn sold the paper to William Randolph Hearst in 1924.

ALBEE, EDWARD [Franklin] (Mar. 18, 1928–). Playwright. *The Zoo Story; The Death of Bessie Smith; The Sandbox: Three Plays* (1960); *The American Dream* (prod. 1960); *Who's Afraid of Virginia Woolf?* (prod. 1961); *The Ballad of the Sad Cafe* (dramatized from novel by Carson McCullers, prod. 1963); *Tiny Alice* (prod. 1964); *Malcolm* (prod. 1966); *A Delicate Balance* (prod. 1966. Pulitzer Prize for drama, 1967); *Everything in the Garden* (1968); *Box;* and *Quotations from Chairman Mao* (1970). See *Edward Albee at Home and Abroad: A Bibliography, 1958–June, 1968,* ed. by R. E. Amacher and Margaret Rule (1970).

ALBEE, ERNEST (Aug. 8, 1865–May 26, 1927); b. Langdon, N.H. Educator, author. *A History of English Utilitarianism* (1902). Editor, *Philosophical Review,* 1903–8. Philosophy dept., Cornell University, 1892–1927.

ALBEE, JOHN (Apr. 3, 1833–May 24, 1915); b. Bellingham, Mass. Poet, essayist. *Literary Art* (1881); *Poems* (1883); *Prose Idyls* (1892); *Remembrances of Emerson* (1901); *Confessions of Boyhood* (1910); etc.

ALBERS, JOSEF (Mar. 19, 1888–); b. Bottrop, Germany. Painter, educator, author. *Poems and Drawings* (1958); *Interaction of Color* (1963). Professor of Art, Bauhaus, Yale University, 1950–1960.

Albion, a Journal of News, Politics, and Literature. New York. Newspaper. Founded 1822. Expired 1875. Valuable for its commercial news, especially the shipping news of New York Port.

ALBION, ROBERT GREENHALGH (Aug. 15, 1896–); b. Malden, Mass. Educator, historian. *Brief Biographies* series, 4v. (with Jennie B. Pope, 1929–31); *The Rise of New York Port* (with same, 1939); *Sea Lanes in Wartime: The American Experience, 1775–1942* (1942); *The Navy at Sea and Ashore* (with S. H. P. Read, 1947); *Seaports South of Sahara* (with Jennie B. Pope, 1959); *Forrestal and the Navy* (1962); *Naval and Maritime History* (1969); etc. Co-editor: *Philip Vickers Fithian: Journal, 1775–1776* (1934). Prof. history, Harvard University, since 1949.

Albion, The. Boston. Magazine. Founded June 22, 1822, by John S. Bartlett. Expired Dec., 1875.

Albrand, Alberta. Pen name of Heidi Huberta Loewengard.

Albrand, Martha. Pen name of Heidi Huberta Loewengard.

ALBRECHT-CARRIE, RENÉ (Jan. 20, 1904–); b. Izmir, Turkey. Educator, author. *Italy at the Paris Peace Conference* (1938); *Italy from Napoleon to Mussolini* (1950); *Diplomatic History of Europe since the Congress of Vienna* (1958); *France, Europe and the Two World Wars* (1960); *One Europe* (1965); *The Meaning of the First World War* (1965). Professor of History, School of International Affairs, Columbia University, since 1953.

ALBRIGHT, WILLIAM FOXWELL (May 24, 1891–); b. Coquimbo, Chile. Educator, orientalist. *Excavations at Gibeah of Benjamin* (1924); *The Archaeology of Palestine and the Bible* (1932); *The Excavation of Tell Beit Mirsim,* 3v. (1932–38); *Recent Discoveries in Bible Lands* (1936); *Archeology and the Religion of Israel* (1942); *Archeology and Christian Humanism* (1964); etc. Prof. Semitic languages, Johns Hopkins University, since 1929.

ALCOTT, [Amos] BRONSON (Nov. 29, 1799–Mar. 4, 1888); b. Wolcott, Conn. Educator, author. Father of Louisa May Alcott. *Orphic Sayings* (1840); *Ralph Waldo Emerson* (priv. pr. 1865, publ. 1882); *Tablets* (1868); *Concord Days* (1872); *Table Talk* (1877); *Sonnets and Canzonets* (1882). See Odell Shepard's *Pedlar's Progress: The Life of Bronson Alcott* (1937); *The Journals of Bronson Alcott,* ed. by Odell Shepard (1938); and Dorothy McCuskey's *Bronson Alcott, Teacher* (1940).

ALCOTT, LOUISA MAY (Nov. 29, 1832–Mar. 6, 1888); b. Germantown, Pa. Novelist. *Flower Fables* (1854); *Hospital Sketches* (1863); *Moods* (1864); *Little Women* (1868); *An Old Fashioned Girl* (1870); *Little Men* (1871); *Work* (1873); *Eight Cousins* (1875); *Rose in Bloom* (1876); *Silver Pitchers* (1876); *A Modern Mephistopheles* (1877); *Under the Lilacs* (1878); *Jack and Jill* (1880); *Aunt Jo's Scrap Bag,* 6v. (1872–82); *Proverb Stories* (1882); *Spinning Wheel Stories* (1884); *Lulu's Library,* 3v. (1886–89); *Jo's Boys* (1886); *A Garland for Girls* (1888). Editor, *Merry's Musuem.* See Lucile Gulliver's *Louisa May Alcott: A Bibliography* (1932); Cornelia Meigs's *The Story of the Author of Little Women: Invincible Louisa* (1933); Katharine S. Anthony's *Louisa May Alcott* (1938); Madeleine B. Stern's *Louisa May Alcott* (1950).

ALCOTT, WILLIAM A. (Aug. 6, 1798–Mar. 29, 1859); b. Wolcott, Conn. Educator, author. *Confessions of a Schoolmaster* (1839); *Lectures for the Fireside* (1851); etc. Editor, *The Juvenile Rambler; Parley's Magazine.*

ALDAN, DAISY (Sept. 16, 1923–); b. New York. Poet. *Poems* (1946); *The Masks Are Becoming Faces* (1965); *The Destruction of the Cathedrals and Other Poems* (1964); *Seven: [sic] Seven* (with Stella Sneed, 1965); *Poems of India* (1968). Translator: Mallarmé's *A Throw of the Dice Will Never Abolish Chance* (1959).

ALDANOV, M. A. [Mark Aleksandrovich Landau-Aldanov] (1888–1957); b. in Russia. *Lenin* (1922); *The Ninth Thermidor* (1926); *The Devil's Bridge* (1928); *The Key* (1931); *The Fifth Seal* (1943); *For Thee the Best* (1945); *Before the Deluge* (1947); *Tenth Symphony* (1948); *Escape* (1950); *To Live As We Wish* (1952); *Nightmare and Dawn* (1957); etc.

ALDEN, HENRY MILLS (Nov. 11, 1836–Oct. 7, 1919); b. Mt. Tabor, Vt. Editor, author. *Magazine Writing and the New Literature* (1908). Managing editor, *Harper's Weekly,* 1869; editor, *Harper's Magazine,* 1869–1919. See *Bookman,* v.50, 1919.

ALDEN, ISABELLA [Macdonald] (Nov. 3, 1841–Aug. 5, 1930); b. Rochester, N.Y. Editor, novelist. Pen name, "Pansy." *Helen Lester* (1865); and many Sunday school stories. Editor, *Pansy,* juvenile magazine, 1873–96.

ALDEN, JOHN (Aug. 30, 1869–Mar. 4, 1934); b. Hoosick Falls, N.Y. Editor, poet. Editorial writer, *Brooklyn Eagle,* 1901–34; wrote daily poem for the *Brooklyn Eagle,* signed "J.A."

ALDEN, JOHN B[erry] (Mar. 2, 1847–Dec. 4, 1924); b. in Henry Co., Ia. Editor. Publisher, *Hearth and Home,* 1874–75; began the publication in 1879 of classical and standard works, encyclopedias, etc., including the "Elzevir Library," in cheap editions.

ALDEN, JOHN RICHARD (Jan. 23, 1908–); b. Grand Rapids, Mich. Historian. *John Stuart and the Southern Colonial Frontier* (1944); *General Gage in America* (1948); *General Charles Lee* (1951); *The American Revolution, 1775–1783* (1954); *The South in the Revolution, 1763–1789* (1957); *The American Revolution: 1775–1783* (1962); *Rise of the American Republic* (1963); *A History of the American Revolution* (1969). Prof. history, Duke University, since 1955.

ALDEN, JOSEPH (Jan. 4, 1807–Aug. 30, 1885); b. Cairo, N.Y. Educator, editor, author. *Alice Gordon; or, The Uses of Orphanage* (1847); *The Young Schoolmistress* (1848); *Anecdotes of the Puritans* (1849); *Studies in Bryant* (1876); etc.

ALDEN, RAYMOND MacDONALD (Mar. 30, 1873–Sept. 27, 1924); b. New Hartford, N.Y. Educator, author. *English Verse* (1903); *Knights of the Silver Shield* (1906); *An Introduction to Poetry* (1909); *Why the Chimes Rang* (1909); *The Sonnets of Shakespeare* (1916); *Shakespeare* (1922); etc.

ALDEN, TIMOTHY (Aug. 28, 1771–July 5, 1839); b. Yarmouth, Mass. Presbyterian clergyman, educator, antiquarian, author. *A Collection of American Epitaphs and Inscriptions,* 5v. (1814); etc. President, Allegheny College, Meadville, Pa., 1816–31.

ALDEN, WILLIAM LIVINGSTON (Oct. 9, 1837–Jan. 14, 1908); b. Williamstown, Mass. Journalist, author. *Domestic Explosives, and Other Sixth Column Fancies* (1877), republished as *The Comic Liar* (1883), and as *The Coming Girl* (1884); *Shooting Stars as Observed from the "Sixth Column" of the Times* (1878); *The Canoe and the Flying Proa* (1878); *The Moral Pirates* (1881); *The Adventures of Jimmy Brown* (1885); *A New Robinson Crusoe* (1888); *Told by the Colonel* (1893); *Among the Greeks* (1896); *Drewitt's Dream* (1902); *Jimmy Brown Trying to Find Europe* (1905); etc. Wrote humorous pieces for the *New York Times* which appeared in the "sixth column" of the editorial page.

ALDERMAN, EDWIN ANDERSON (May 15, 1861–Apr. 29, 1931); b. Wilmington, N.C. Educator, orator, biographer. *J. L. M. Curry* (with Armistead C. Gordon, 1911); *Woodrow Wilson: Memorial Address* (1925); etc. Editor-in-chief (with Joel Chandler Harris): *Library of Southern Literature,* 17v. President [the first in its history], the University of Virginia, 1904–31.

Aldine Club. A club founded in 1889, at Lafayette Place, New York. Its membership was made up exclusively of publishers, authors, and journalists.

Aldington, Hilda Doolittle. See Hilda Doolittle.

ALDIS, DOROTHY [Keeley] (Mrs. Graham Aldis) (Mar. 13, 1897–June 28, 1966); b. Chicago, Ill. Novelist, poet. *Everything and Anything* (1926); *Murder in a Haystack* (1930); *Any Spring* (poems, 1933); *Time at Her Heels* (1936); *Before Things Happen* (1939); *Poor Susan* (1942); *Dark Summer* (1947); *Lucky Year* (1951); *All Together* (poems, 1952); *We're Going to Town!* (1952); *Ride the Wild Waves* (1957); *The Boy Who Cared* (1958); *Hello Day* (poems, 1959); *Quick as a Wink* (1960); *Is Anybody Hungry?* (1964); etc.

ALDIS, MARY REYNOLDS (Mrs. Arthur T. Aldis) (June 8, 1872–June 20, 1949); b. Chicago, Ill. Poet, playwright. *Plays for Small Stages* (1915); *Flashlights* (verse, 1916); *No Curtain* (1935). Founder, The Aldis Playhouse, 1910.

ALDRICH, ANNE REEVE (1866–1892); b. New York. Poet. *The Rose of Flame, and Other Poems of Love* (1889); *The Feet of Love* (1890); *Songs about Love, Life and Death* (1892); *A Village Ophelia* (1899).

ALDRICH, BESS STREETER (Mrs. Charles S. Aldrich) (Feb. 17, 1881–Aug. 3, 1954); b. Cedar Falls, Ia. Novelist. *Mother Mason* (1924); *The Rim of the Prairie* (1925); *The Cutters* (1926); *A Lantern in Her Hand* (1928); *Miss Bishop* (1933); *Song of the Years* (1939); *The Drum Goes Dead* (1941); *The Lieutenant's Lady* (1942); *Journey into Christmas* (stories, 1949); etc. *See* Blanche Colton Williams' *Bess Streeter Aldrich, Novelist* (1935).

ALDRICH, CLARE CHAPLINE THOMAS (Mrs. Chilson Darragh Aldrich); b. Richmond, Ind. Novelist, playwright. Writes under name "Darragh Aldrich." *Enchanted Hearts* (1917); *Spuds; or, Diana of Babylon, Texas* (1927); *Peter Good for Nothing* (1929); *Girls Are Like That* (1932); *The Luck of the Irish* (1934); *Red Headed School Ma'am* (1935); *Earth Never Tires* (1936); *Girl Going Nowhere* (1939); *Some Trails Never End* (1941); *Lady at Law* (1950).

Aldrich, Darragh. Pen name of Clare Chapline Thomas Aldrich.

ALDRICH, MILDRED (Nov. 16, 1853–Feb. 1928); b. Providence, R.I. Author. *A Hilltop on the Marne* (1915); *Told in a French Garden* (1916); *On the Edge of the War Zone* (1917); *Peak of the Lead* (1918); *When Johnny Comes Marching Home* (1919).

ALDRICH, RICHARD (July 31, 1863–June 2, 1937); b. Providence, R.I. Music critic, author. *Musical Discourse From the New York Times* (1928); etc. Music critic, *New York Times,* 1902–37.

ALDRICH, THOMAS BAILEY (Nov. 11, 1836–Mar. 19, 1907); b. Portsmouth, N.H. Poet, story-writer. *The Story of a Bad Boy* (1870); *Marjorie Daw* (1873); *Prudence Palfrey* (1874); *The Queen of Sheba* (1877); *The Stillwater Tragedy* (1880); *An Old Town by the Sea* (1893); *Two Bites at a Cherry* (1894); *A Sea Turn and Other Matters* (1902); *Ponkapog Papers* (1903); *Judith of Bethulia* (1904). Best known poems are "Fredericksburg," "Nocturne," and "Elmwood." Editor *Every Saturday,* 1865–72; *Atlantic Monthly,* 1881–90. *See* Ferris Greenslet's *Life of Thomas Bailey Aldrich* (1908).

ALDRIDGE, GORDON JAMES (Oct. 19, 1916–); b. Toronto, Can. Educator, author. *Social Welfare and the Aged* (1959); *Social Issues and Psychiatric Social Work Practice* (1959); *Social Welfare of the Aging* (with J. Kaplan, 1962); *Liberal Education and Social Work* (with Earl J. McGrath, 1965). Professor of Social Work, Michigan State University, since 1952.

ALDRIDGE, JOHN W[atson] (Sept. 26, 1922–); b. Sioux City, Ia. Critic, novelist. *After the Lost Generation* (1951); *In Search of Heresy: American Literature in an Age of Conformity* (1956); *Party at Cranton* (1960); *Time to Murder and Create* (1966); *In the Country of the Young* (1970); *Devil in the Fire* (1971). Editor: *Critiques and Essays on Modern Fiction, 1920–1951* (1952). Prof. literature, New York University, since 1958.

Aleichem, Sholom. Pen name of Solomon J. Rabinowitz.

ALEXANDER, ARCHIBALD (Apr. 17, 1772–Oct. 22, 1851); b. Lexington, Va. Clergyman, educator, author. *Biographical Sketches of the Founder, and Principal Alumni of the Log College* [forerunner of Princeton University] (1845); etc.

ALEXANDER, EDWARD PORTER (May 26, 1835–Apr. 28, 1910); b. Washington, Ga. Confederate artillerist, author. *Catterel Ratterel* (1888); *Military Memoirs of a Confederate* (1907).

ALEXANDER, FRANCESCA (Feb. 27, 1837–Jan. 21, 1917); b. (Esther Frances Alexander) Boston, Mass. Artist, author. Friend of John Ruskin, who gave her the name "Francesca." *The Story of Ida* (1883); *Roadside Songs of Tuscany* (1885); *Christ's Folk in the Apennines* (1888), these books edited by Ruskin; *Tuscan Songs* (1897); *The Hidden Servants, and Other Very Old Stories* (poems, 1900). *See* Constance Grosvenor's *Francesca Alexander, a Hidden Servant* (1927).

ALEXANDER, FRANZ [Gabriel] (Jan. 22, 1891–Mar. 8, 1964); b. Budapest, Hung. Psychiatrist. Author or co-author: *The Criminal, the Judge, and the Public* (1931); *Roots of Crime* (1935); *Fundamentals of Psychoanalysis* (1948); *Psychoanalysis and Psychotherapy: Developments in Theory, Technique and Training* (1956); *The Scope of Psychoanalysis: 1921–1961* (1962); *Psychoanalysis and the Human Situation* (1964).

ALEXANDER, HARTLEY BURR (Apr. 9, 1873–July 27, 1939); b. Lincoln, Nebr. Educator, editor, author. *Poetry and the Individual* (1906); *Odes on the Generation of Man* (1910); *Odes and Lyrics* (1922); *Nature and Human Nature* (1923); *Manito Masks* (1925); *Taiwa* (1934); etc.; also, in *Mythology of All Races*; vol. X, *North American* (1916); and vol. XI, *Latin American* (1920).

ALEXANDER, HOLMES MOSS (Jan. 29, 1906–); b. Parkersburg, W. Va. Author. *The American Talleyrand: the Career and Contemporaries of Martin Van Buren, Eighth President* (1935); *Aaron Burr, the Proud Pretender* (1937); *American Nabobs* (1939); *Dust in the Afternoon* (1940); *Selina* (1942); *Tomorrow's Air Age: A Report on the Foreseeable Future* (1953); *The Famous Five* (1958); *Shall Do No Murder* (1959); *West of Washington* (1962); *The Equivocal Men: Tales of the Establishment* (1964); *The Spirit of '76* (1966). Nationally syndicated political columnist since 1947.

ALEXANDER, T[ruman] **H**[udson] (Oct. 20, 1891–Sept. 1, 1941); b. Birmingham, Ala. Journalist, author. *Loot* (1932). Wrote syndicated column, "I Reckon So" from 1922.

ALGER, HORATIO, Jr. (Jan. 13, 1834–July 18, 1899); b. Revere, Mass. Author of boys' books. *Bertha's Christmas Vision* (1850); *Helen Ford* (1866); *Ragged Dick* (1868); *Luck and Pluck* (1869); *Ben, the Luggage Boy* (1870); *Tattered Tom* (1871); *From Canal Boy to President* (1881); *From Farm Boy to Senator* (1882); *Abraham Lincoln, the Backwoods Boy* (1883); *Frank Fowler, the Cash Boy* (1887); *Tom Temple's Career* (1888); etc. *See* Herbert R. Mayes's *Alger: A Biography Without a Hero* (1928). The popular Alger books pointed a moral, and their heroes triumphed over adversity.

ALGER, WILLIAM ROUNSEVILLE (Dec. 28, 1822–Feb. 7, 1905); b. Freetown, Mass. Clergyman, author. *The Poetry of the East* (1856); *The Friendships of Women* (1868); *Life of Edwin Forrest, the American Tragedian*, 2v. (1877); etc.

Algerine Captive, The. Novel by Royall Tyler, 2v. (1797). One of the first dealing with American life. Adventures of a New England boy, Updike Underhill, in Boston, Philadelphia, Virginia, London, and finally as a captive of the Algerian pirates.

Algonquin Hotel. 59 W. 44 Street, New York. Celebrated literary rendezvous. Many novels and plays have been written here and an informal club called the "Round Table" (q.v.) was formed here in 1919. *See* Frank Case's *Tales of a Wayward Inn* (1938), and his *Do not Disturb* (1940).

ALGREN, NELSON (Mar. 28, 1909–); b. Detroit, Mich. Author. *Somebody in Boots* (1935); *Never Come Morning* (1942); *The Neon Wilderness* (1947); *The Man with the Golden Arm* (1949); *Chicago: City On the Make* (1951); *A Walk on the Wild Side* (1956); *Who Lost an American?* (1963); *Notes From A Sea Diary* (1965).

Alhambra. By Washington Irving (1832). Vivid description of Spain, and the architectural splendors of the old Moorish palace, with tales and legends of the days of Boabdil.

Alias Jimmy Valentine. Detective play by Paul Armstrong (prod. 1909). Based on O. Henry's *A Retrieved Reformation*.

Alice Adams. Novel by Booth Tarkington (1921. Pulitzer Prize for fiction, 1922). Study of social deterioration, in which the plucky heroine, a small town girl, tries to keep up appearances against overwhelming odds.

Alice of Old Vincennes. Novel by Maurice Thompson (1900). Old Vincennes on the Wabash in 1778; it describes the life of the Northwest Territory during the Revolution.

ALINSKY, SAUL [David] (Jan. 30, 1909–); b. Chicago, Ill. Sociologist, author. *Reveille for Radicals* (1946); *John L. Lewis, a Biography* (1949).

Alison's House. Play by Susan Glaspell (prod. 1930). The story of an American poet, Alison Stanhope, and her sister Agatha, who preserves Alison's love poems in spite of Alison's wish to destroy them. Emily Dickinson was the model for Alison.

All Brides Are Beautiful. Novel by Thomas Bell (1936). Idyllic romance of the Bronx, in New York.

All God's Chillun Got Wings. Play by Eugene O'Neill (prod. 1924). The complex problem of a white woman married to a Negro and the tragic attempt to solve it.

"All Quiet Along the Potomac." Poem by Ethel Lynn Beers, first published in *Harper's Magazine*, Nov. 30, 1861, under the title "The Picket Guard." Signed merely "E. B.," its authorship was claimed by Lamar Fontaine, and others. *See* James Wood Davidson's *The Living Writers of the South* (1869), and Lamar Fontaine's *My Life and My Lectures* (1908).

All This, and Heaven Too. Novel by Rachel Field (1938). Henriette, having fallen in love with the father of the French children to whom she is governess, is unjustly implicated in the murder of the mother. The father dies, and Henriette, through the intervention of an American clergyman whom she afterward marries, comes to America, there to live down the notoriety caused by the trial.

All-Story. New York. Weekly. Fiction magazine. Founded 1889. Later merged with *Argosy.*

ALLAN, ELIZABETH RANDOLPH PRESTON (1848–Apr. 1933); b. Lexington, Va. Author. *The Life and Letters of Margaret Junkin Preston* (1903); *A March Past* (reminiscences, 1938), ed. by daughter, Janet Allan Bryan.

ALLEE, MARJORIE HILL (June 2, 1890–Apr. 30, 1945); b. Carthage, Ind. Novelist. *Susanna and Tristram* (1929); *Judith Lankester* (1930); *Jane's Island* (1931); *The Road to Carolina* (1932); *Ann's Surprising Summer* (1933); *The Great Tradition* (1937); *The Little American Girl* (1938); *The House* (1944); *Smoke Jumper* (1945); etc.

ALLEN, ALEXANDER VIETS GRISWOLD (May 4, 1841–July 1, 1908); b. Otis, Mass. Episcopal clergyman, educator, biographer. *Continuity of Christian Thought* (1884); *Jonathan Edwards* (1889); *Christian Institutions* (1897); *Life and Letters of Phillips Brooks*, 2v. (1900); etc.

ALLEN, ALFRED (Apr. 8, 1866–June 18, 1947); b. Alfred, N.Y. Playwright, novelist. *The Heart of Don Vega* (1888); *Chivalry* (1901); etc.

ALLEN, ARTHUR AUGUSTUS (Dec. 28, 1885–Jan. 17, 1964); b. Buffalo, N.Y. Ornithologist, author. *The Book of Bird Life* (1930); *American Bird Biographies* (1934); *Stalking Birds with Color Camera* (1951); etc.

ALLEN, BENJAMIN (Sept. 29, 1789–Jan. 13, 1829); b. Hudson, N.Y. Episcopal clergyman, poet. *Miscellaneous Poems, on Moral and Religious Subjects* (under pen name "Osander," 1811); *United We Stand: Divided We Fall* (under pen name "Juba," 1812); *Columbia's Naval Triumphs* (1813); *Urania, or The True Use of Poesy: a Poem* (1814); etc.

ALLEN, CHARLES DEXTER (1865–Sept. 10, 1926); b. Windsor Locks, Conn. Author. *American Book-Plates* (1894); *Ex-Libris Essays of a Collector* (1896); *A Talk on Book Plates* (1901); etc.

ALLEN, DEVERE (June 24, 1891–Aug. 27, 1955); b. Providence, R.I. Editor, author. *The Fight For Peace* (1930). Editor: *Pacifism in the Modern World* (1929); *Adventurous Americans* (1932). Editor, *The World Tomorrow*, 1925–33; assoc. editor, *The Nation*, 1931–32.

ALLEN, DON B. (Sept. 27, 1889–June 8, 1966); b. Kansas City, Mo. Author. Co-author (with Terry D. Allen under pen name "T. D. Allen"): *Doctor in Buckskin* (1951); *Troubled Border* (1954); *Prisoners of the Polar Ice* (1962); *Navahos Have Five Fingers* (1963); *Doctor, Lawyer, Merchant, Chief* (1965). Co-author of screenplays.

ALLEN, DON CAMERON (Dec. 5, 1903–June 9, 1966); b. St. Louis, Mo. Educator, editor, author. *The Star-Crossed Renaissance* (1941); *The Harmonious Vision: Studies in Milton's Poetry* (1954); *Image and Meaning: Metaphoric Traditions in Renaissance Poetry* (1960); *The Legend of Noah: Renaissance Rationalism in Art, Science, and Letters* (1963); *Doubt's Boundless Sea* (1964); *The Ph.D. in English and American Literature* (1968); etc. Editor: *Francis Meres's Treatise "Poetrie"* (1933); *Francis Meres's Palladis Tamia* (1938); *The Owles Almanacke* (1943); *Essayes by Sir William Cornwallis, the Younger* (1946); *A Strange Metamorphosis* (1949); etc. Prof. English, Johns Hopkins University, since 1945.

ALLEN, DONALD M. Editor. *Garcia Lorca's Selected Poems* (with Francisco Garcia Lorca, 1954); *The New American Poetry, 1945–1960* (1961); *New American Story* (with Robert Creeley, 1965).

ALLEN, EDWARD FRANK (June 9, 1885–); b. Newark, N.J. Editor, author. *Red-Letter Days of Samuel Pepys* (1910); *A Guide to the National Parks of America* (1915); *Effective English* (1939). Editor: *A Dictionary of Abbreviations* (1946); *The Complete Dream Book* (1949). Editor, *Lippincott's Magazine*, 1914–15, *McBride's Magazine*, 1915–16, *Travel*, 1910–14, 1916–17.

ALLEN, EDWARD MONINGTON (May 23, 1899–); b. Dover, N.J. Educator, author. *America's Story as Told in Postage Stamps* (1930); *The Author's Handbook* (1938).

ALLEN, EDWARD WEBER (May 12, 1885–); b. Oshkosh, Wis. Lawyer, author. *North Pacific* (1936); *The Vanishing Frenchman or the Mysterious Disappearance of Lapérouse* (1959).

Allen, Elizabeth Akers. See Elizabeth Akers.

ALLEN, ERIC WILLIAM (Apr. 4, 1879–Mar. 5, 1944); b. Appleton, Wis. Educator, author. *Printing for the Journalist* (1927). Founder, Department of Journalism, University of Oregon, 1912. Manager, University Press, University of Oregon.

ALLEN, ETHAN (Jan. 10, 1737/8–Feb. 12, 1789); b. Litchfield, Conn. Revolutionary soldier, author. *A Narrative of Colonel Ethan Allen's Captivity* (1779); *Reason the Only Oracle of Man* (1784); etc. *See* Stewart H. Holbrook's *Ethan Allen* (1940).

ALLEN, F. STURGES (Oct. 1, 1861–Aug. 8, 1920); b. Norwalk, Conn. Editor, lexicographer. Compiler: *Dictionary of Synonyms and Antonyms* (1920); etc. On editorial staff, *Webster's International Dictionary*, for many years.

ALLEN, FRANCIS HENRY (Aug. 3, 1866–Oct. 24, 1953); b. Jamaica Plain, Mass. Editor, ornithologist. Compiler: *Nature's Diary* (1897); *A Bibliography of Henry David Thoreau* (1908). Editor: *The Journal of Henry David Thoreau* 14v. (1906); *The Letters of Robert Burns*, 4v. (1927); *Men of Concord* (1936); etc. Editor, Houghton, Mifflin Co., 1894–1934.

ALLEN, FRANK WALLER (Sept. 30, 1878–); b. Milton, Ky. Disciples clergyman, novelist. *My Ships Aground* (1900); *Back to Arcady* (1905); *The Golden Road* (1910); *The Lovers of Skye* (1913); *Painted Windows* (1918); *My One Hundred Best Novels* (1919); *Wings of Beauty* (1929); etc.

ALLEN, FREDERICK LEWIS (July 5, 1890–Feb. 13, 1954); b. Boston, Mass. Editor, author. *Only Yesterday* (1931); *Metropolis* (1934); *The Lords of Creation* (1935); *Since Yesterday* (1940); *I Remember Distinctly* (with A. Rogers, 1947); *The Great Pierpont Morgan* (1949); *The Big Change* (1952); etc. Assoc. editor, *Harper's*, 1931–41; editor, 1941–54.

ALLEN, GARDNER WELD (b. Jan. 19, 1856); b. Bangor, Me. Surgeon, naval historian. *Our Navy and the Barbary Corsairs* (1905); *Our Naval War with France* (1909); *A Naval History of the American Revolution*, 2v. (1913); *Massachusetts Privateers* (1927); *Our Navy and the West Indian Pirates* (1929); *Papers of John Davis Long* (1939); etc.

ALLEN, GAY WILSON (Aug. 23, 1903–); b. Lake Junaluska, N.C. Educator, author. *American Prosody* (1935); *Walt Whitman Handbook* (1946); *The Solitary Singer: A Critical Biography of Walt Whitman* (1955); *Walt Whitman As Man, Poet and Legend* (1961); *William James: A Biography* (1967). Co-editor: *Literary Criticism: Pope to Croce* (1941); *Masters of American Literature* (1949); *Walt Whitman's Poems* (1955). Prof. English, New York University, since 1946.

ALLEN, GINA (July 4, 1918–); b. Trenton, Neb. Author. *Prairie Children* (1941); *On the Oregon Trail* (1942); *Rustics for Keeps* (1948). Coauthor, with R. V. Hunkins: *Tepee Days* (1941); *Trapper Days* (1942); *Sod-House Days* (1945); *The Forbidden Man* (1962); *Gold!* (1964).

Allen, Graham. Pen name of George Arnold.

ALLEN, HENRY. (1912–). Author. Writes under pen names "Clay Fisher" and "Will Henry." *Yellow Hair* (1953); *Yellowstone Kelly* (1957); *The Crossing* (1958); *The Seven Men at Mimbres Springs* (1958); *From Where the Sun Now Stands* (1960); *Nino* (1961); *Valley of the Bear* (1964); etc.

ALLEN, HERVEY (Dec. 8, 1889–Dec. 28, 1949); b. Pittsburgh, Pa. Author. *Wampum and Old Gold* (poems, 1921); *Carolina Chansons* (with DuBose Heyward, 1922); *Israfel, the Life and Times of Edgar Allan Poe* (1926); *New Legends* (poems, 1929); *Anthony Adverse* (1933); *Action at Aquila* (1938); *It Was Like This* (1940); *The Disinherited* (series of novels: *The Forest and the Fort*, 1943; *Bedford Village*, 1944; *Toward the Morning*, 1948). Editor, with Thomas Oliver Mabbott: *Poe's Brother: The Poems of William Henry Leonard Poe* (1926).

ALLEN, IDA [Cogswell] **BAILEY**; b. Danielson, Conn. Home economist, author. *Youth After Forty* (1950); *Solving the High Cost of Eating* (1952); *Step-by-Step Picture Cook Book* (1952); *Sandwich Book* (1957); *Cook Book for Two* (1957); *Gastronomique* (1958).

Allen, James. Pen name of Paul Ader.

ALLEN, JAMES LANE (Dec. 21, 1849–Feb. 18, 1925); b. Lexington, Ky. Novelist. *Flute and Violin, and Other Kentucky Tales and Romances* (1891); *A Kentucky Cardinal* (1895); *Aftermath* (1896); *The Choir Invisible* (1897); *The Reign of Law* (1900); *The Mettle of the Pasture* (1903); *The Bride of the Mistletoe* (1909); *A Cathedral Singer* (1916); *The Emblems of Fidelity* (1919); etc. *See* Grant C. Knight's *James Lane Allen and the Genteel Tradition* (1935).

ALLEN, JOSEPH HENRY (Aug. 21, 1820–Mar. 20, 1898); b. Northboro, Mass. Clergyman, editor. Author of Latin text books. Editor, *The Unitarian Review*, 1887–91.

ALLEN, LYMAN WHITNEY (Nov. 19, 1854–Jan. 27, 1930); b. St. Louis, Mo. Presbyterian clergyman, poet. *Abraham Lincoln: A Poem* (1896); *A Parable of the Rose, and Other Poems* (1908); *The Triumph of Love* (1910); *An Epic Trilogy*, 3v. (1929).

ALLEN, PAUL (Feb. 15, 1775–Aug. 18, 1826); b. Providence, R.I. Editor, poet. *Original Poems, Serious and Entertaining* (1801); *Noah* (poem, 1821). Editor: *History of the Expedition under the Command of Captains Lewis and Clark* (1814). Wrote for the *Portico* under the pen names of "Pasquin" and "St. Denis le Cadet."

ALLEN, PHILIP SCHUYLER (Aug. 23, 1871–Apr. 27, 1937); b. Lake Forest, Ill. Educator, author. *The Romanesque Lyrics* (1927); *Medieval Latin Lyrics* (1931). German dept., University of Chicago, 1903–37.

ALLEN, ROBERT S[haron] (July 14, 1900–); b. Latonia, Ky. Journalist. *Washington Merry-Go-Round* (with Drew Pearson, 1931); *More Washington Merry-Go-Round* (with same, 1932); *The Nine Old Men* (with same, 1936); *Lucky Forward* (1947); *The Truman Merry-Go-Round* (with W. V. Shannon, 1950). Editor: *Our Fair City* (1946); *Our Sovereign State* (1949). Writes syndicated column on national and world affairs.

ALLEN, STEVE [Stephen Valentine Patrick William] (Dec. 26, 1921–); b. New York. Television humorist, songwriter. *Fourteen for Tonight* (1955); *The Funny Men* (1956); *Wry on the Rocks* (poems, 1956); *Mark It and Strike It* (autobiography, 1960); *Not All Your Laughter, Not All Your Tears* (1962); *Letter to a Conservative* (1965); *The Ground Is Our Table* (1966).

Allen, T. D. Pen name of Don B. Allen and Terry D. Allen.

ALLEN, TERRY D. Co-author of books with Don B. Allen (q.v.) under pen name "T. D. Allen."

ALLEN, WILLIAM (Jan. 2, 1784–July 16, 1868); b. Pittsfield, Mass. Congregational clergyman, educator, lexicographer, author. *Wunnissoo; or, The Vale of Housatonnuck* (poem, 1856); *Sacred Songs* (1867); etc. Compiler: *An American Biographical and Historical Dictionary* (1809), one of the earliest undertakings of its kind. He published a 10,000 word supplement to *Webster's Dictionary*.

ALLEN, WILLIAM FRANCIS (Sept. 5, 1830–Dec. 9, 1889); b. Northboro, Mass. Educator, author. *A Short History of the Roman People* (1890). Compiler: *Slave Songs of the United States* (with Charles P. Ware and Lucy M. Garrison, 1867).

ALLEN, WILLIS BOYD (July 9, 1855–Sept. 10, 1938); b. Kittery Point, Me. Author. *Pine Cones* (1885); *Kelp: A Story of the Isles of Shoals* (1888); *Cloud and Cliff* (1889); *The Red Mountain of Alaska* (1889); *In the Morning* (poems, 1890); *The Boyhood of John Kent* (1891); *John Brownlow's Folks* (1891); *Gulf and Glacier* (1892); *Lost on Umbagog* (1894); *Great Island* (1897); *Pineboro Quartette* (1898); *Under the Pine Tree Flag* (1902); *The North Pacific* (1905); *The Violet Book* (1909); etc.

ALLEN, WOODY (Dec. 1, 1935–); b. New York. Entertainer, author. *What's New, Pussycat?* (screenplay, 1964); *Don't Drink the Water* (play, 1967); *Take the Money and Run* (screenplay, 1969); *Play It Again, Sam* (play, 1969); *Bananas* (screenplay, 1971); *Getting Even* (1971).

ALLIBONE, SAMUEL AUSTIN (Apr. 17, 1816–Sept. 2, 1889); b. Philadelphia, Pa. Lexicographer, librarian. Compiler: *A Critical Dictionary of English Literature, and British and American Authors Living and Deceased, from the Earliest Accounts to the Middle of the Nineteenth Century,* 3v. (1858–1871); *Poetical Quotations, from Chaucer to Tennyson* (1873); *Prose Quotations, from Socrates to Macaulay* (1876). Librarian, the Lenox library; prepared card catalogue written in his own hand.

ALLINSON, ANNE CROSBY EMERY (Mrs. Francis Greenleaf Allinson) (Jan. 1, 1871–Aug. 16, 1932); b. Ellsworth, Me. Educator, author. *Greek Lands and Letters* (with husband, 1909); *Roads from Rome* (1913); *Children of the Way* (1923); *Friends With Life* (1924); *Selections from the*

Distaff (1932); *Selected Essays* (1933). Columnist, "The Distaff," in *Providence* (R.I.) *Evening Bulletin.*

ALLINSON, FRANCIS GREENLEAF (Dec. 16, 1856–June 23, 1931); b. Burlington, N.J. Educator, author. *Greek Lands and Letters* (with A. C. E. Allinson, 1909); *Lucian: Satirist and Artist* (1926); etc. Classical philology dept., Brown University, 1898–1928.

ALLIS, MARGUERITE (1886–Aug. 6, 1958); b. Ludlow, Vt. Author. *Connecticut Trilogy* (1934); *English Prelude* (1936); *Connecticut River* (1939); *Not Without Peril* (1941); *The Splendor Stays* (1942); *All in Good Time* (1944); *Charity Strong* (1945); *Water over the Dam* (1947); *Law of the Land* (1948); *The Bridge* (1949); *Now We Are Free* (1952); *Brave Pursuit* (1954); *The Rising Storm* (1955); *Free Soil* (1958).

ALLIS, OSWALD THOMPSON (Sept. 9, 1880–); b. Wallingford, Pa. Theologian. *The Five Books of Moses* (1943); *Bible Numerics* (1944); *Prophecy and the Church* (1945); *Revision or New Translation?* (1948); *The Unity of Isaiah* (1950); *God Spake by Moses* (1952); etc.

ALLISON, ANNE OSTERSTROM; b. Des Moines, Ia. Public affairs specialist, author. *Road to Romance* (1950); *Romance in Rio* (1953); *Love Lies South* (1960); *Siren in White* (1964); *The Secret Wife* (1965); etc.

ALLISON, YOUNG EWING (Dec. 23, 1853–July 7, 1932); b. Henderson, Ky. Editor, author. *The Ogallallas* (opera, prod. 1893); *Insurance at Piney Woods* (1896); *The Delicious Vice,* 2 series (1907–09); *Select Works* (1935), ed. by J. Christian Bay. Best known for his poem "The Derelict."

ALLOWAY, LAWRENCE (Sept. 17, 1926–); b. London. Art critic, author. *Nine Abstract Artists* (1954); *Ettore Colla* (1960); *The Metalization of a Dream* (1963).

ALLPORT, GORDON W[illard] (Nov. 11, 1897–Oct. 9, 1967); b. Montezuma, Ind. Psychologist, educator. Author or co-author: *Studies in Expressive Movement* (1933); *Personality: A Psychological Interpretation* (1937); *The Psychology of Rumor* (1947); *The Nature of Personality* (1950); *The Nature of Prejudice* (1954); *Personality and Social Encounter* (1960); *Pattern and Growth in Personality* (1961); *Personality and Social Encounter* (1964); *Letters from Jenny* (1965). Prof. psychology, Harvard University, since 1942.

ALLSOPP, FREDERICK WILLIAM (June 25, 1868–Apr. 9, 1946); b. Wolverhampton, England. Publisher, author. *Twenty Years in a Newspaper Office* (1907); *Little Adventures in Newspaperdom* (1922); *History of the Arkansas Press for a Hundred Years and More* (1922); *Rimeries* (1926); *Albert Pike, A Biography* (1928); *Folklore of Romantic Arkansas* (1931); *The Poets and Poetry of Arkansas* (1933). With the *Arkansas Gazette* from 1884; publisher, from 1896. Founder, Allsopp & Chapple Book Store, Little Rock, Ark.

ALLSTON, WASHINGTON (Nov. 5, 1779–July 9, 1843); b. Waccamaw, S.C. Artist, poet. *The Sylphs of the Seasons, with Other Poems* (1813); *Monaldi: A Tale* (1841). See Jared B. Glass's *The Life and Letters of Washington Allston* (1892).

ALMAN, DAVID (1919–). Author. *Hour Glass* (1947); *Well of Compassion* (1948); *World Full of Strangers* (1949); *Conquest* (1963).

Almanac for Music Lovers, An. By Elizabeth C. Moore (1940). Day-by-day commemorations of important musical events and personages.

Almanacs. The first almanac printed in America was *An Almanac Calculated for New England,* by William Peirce, printed by Stephen Daye at Cambridge (1639). Benjamin Franklin's *Poor Richard's Almanac* (1732–57) was perhaps the best known. Numerous editions of *The Farmer's Almanac* have appeared since 1872, and it is still in publication. Among current almanacs of general information are *World Almanac* (1868–76; since 1886) and *Information Please Almanac* (since

1947). *See* George Lyman Kittredge's *Old Farmer and His Almanac* (1905); Charles Lemuel Nichols's *Checklist of Maine, New Hampshire and Vermont Almanacs* (1929), his *Notes on the Almanacs of Massachusetts* (1912), and his *A Collection of Photographic Reproductions of Massachusetts Almanacs, 1646–1700.*

ALMOND, LINDA STEVENS; b. Seaford, Del. Author. *Peter Rabbit* books, beginning 1921; *Buddy Bear* series; *Penny Hill* stories.

Alnwick Castle, with Other Poems. By Fitz-Greene Halleck (1827). Includes "Marco Bozzaris."

ALPERT, HOLLIS (Sept. 24, 1916–); b. Herkimer, N.Y. Author, editor. *Summer Lovers* (1958); *Some Other Time* (1960); *The Dreams and the Dreamers* (1962); *For Immediate Release* (1963); *The Barrymores* (1964). Contributing editor, *Saturday Review,* since 1959.

ALSOP, GEORGE (b. 1638); b. in England, came to America in 1658. Author. *A Character of the Province of Mary-Land* (1666); *An Orthodox Plea for the Sanctuary of God* (1669).

ALSOP, JOSEPH W[right], JR. (Oct. 11, 1910–); b. Avon, Conn. Journalist. *The 168 Days* (with Turner Catledge, 1938); *Men Around the President* (with Robert E. Kintner, 1939); *American White Paper: The Story of American Diplomacy and the Second World War* (with same, 1940); *We Accuse* (with Stewart Alsop, 1954); *The Reporter's Trade* (with same, 1958); *From the Silent Earth* (1964). Author, with Robert E. Kintner, of column "Capitol Parade," 1937–40; with Stewart Alsop, of column "Matter of Fact," 1945–58.

ALSOP, RICHARD (Jan. 23, 1761–Aug. 20, 1815); b. Middletown, Conn. Satirist, poet, one of the "Hartford Wits." *A Poem: Sacred to the Memory of George Washington* (1800); *The Echo, with Other Poems* (1807). Chief contributor to *The Echo* (1791–1805). *See* Karl P. Harrington's *Richard Alsop* (1939).

ALSOP, STEWART [Johonnot Oliver] (May 17, 1914–); b. Avon, Conn. Journalist, author. *Sub Rosa* (with Thomas Braden, 1946); *We Accuse* (with Joseph Alsop, 1954); *The Center: The Anatomy of Power in Washington* (1968); etc. Author, with Joseph Alsop, of column "Matter of Fact," 1945–58.

ALSTON, WALLACE McPHERSON (July 16, 1906–); b. Decatur, Ga. Presbyterian clergyman, author. *The Throne Among the Shadows* (1945); *Break Up the Night* (1947).

ALSTON, WILLIAM PAYNE (Nov. 29, 1921–); b. Shreveport, La. Educator, author. *Religious Belief and Philosophical Thought* (1963); *Readings in Twentieth Century Philosophy* (with G. Nakhnikian, 1963); *Philosophy of Language* (1964); etc.

ALTER, J. CECIL (Mar. 31, 1879–); b. near Rensselaer, Ind. Meteorologist, editor, historian. *James Bridger, Trapper, Frontiersman, Scout and Guide; a Historical Narrative* (1925); *Through the Heart of the Scenic West* (1927); *Utah, the Storied Domain* ... (1932), 3v. (1932); *Early Utah Journalism; a Half Century of Forensic Warfare, Waged by the West's Most Militant Press* (1938). Editor, *Utah Historical Quarterly,* since 1928.

ALTGELD, JOHN PETER (Dec. 30, 1847–Mar. 12, 1902); b. Nieder Selters, Germany. Governor, author. *Live Questions* (1890). Governor of Illinois, 1893–97. He was a member of the literary group which met with Finley Peter Dunne at McGarry's Saloon in Chicago. *See* Waldo Ralph Browne's *Altgeld of Illinois* (1924); Harry Barnard's *Eagle Forgotten* (1938); Vachel Lindsay's poem "The Eagle That Is Forgotten."

ALTROCCHI, JULIA [Cooley] (Mrs. Rudolph Altrocchi) (July 4, 1893–); b. Seymour, Conn. Poet. *The Poems of a Child* (1904); *The Dance of Youth, and Other Poems* (1917); *Snow Covered Wagons: A Pioneer Epic; the Donner Party Expedi-*

tion, 1846–1847 (poem, 1936); *The Spectacular San Franciscans* (1949); *Girl with Ocelot* (1964).

ALTSHELER, JOSEPH ALEXANDER (Apr. 29, 1862–June 5, 1919); b. Three Springs, Ky. Editor, novelist. *The Sun of Saratoga* (1897); *A Herald of the West* (1898); *The Last Rebel* (1899); *The Wilderness Road* (1901); *The Candidate* (1905); *The Forest Runners* (1908); *The Last of the Chiefs* (1909); *The Riflemen of the Ohio* (1910); The Horsemen of the Plains (1910); *The Texan Star* (1912); *The Texan Scouts* (1913); *The Guns of Bull Run* (1914); *The Star of Gettysburg* (1915); *The Rock of Chickamauga* (1915); *The Tree of Appomattox* (1916); *The Shadow of the North* (1917); *The Master of the Peaks* (1918); etc.

ALVAREZ, WALTER C[lement] (July 22, 1884–); b. San Francisco, Cal. Physiologist, physician. *Mechanics of the Digestive Tract* (1928); *The Neuroses* (1951); *Danger Signals* (1953); *Practical Leads to Puzzling Diagnoses* (1958); *Minds That Came Back* (1961); *Incurable Physician* (autobiography, 1963); *Little Strokes* (1966). Editor, *Journal of General Practice,* since 1950. Prof. medicine, Mayo Foundation, University of Minnesota, 1934–50. Author, syndicated medical column for New York *Herald Tribune,* from 1952. Tribune expired 1967.

ALVORD, CLARENCE WALWORTH (May 21, 1868–Jan. 24, 1928); b. Greenfield, Mass. Historian. Editor: *Illinois Historical Collections,* 14v.; *Centennial History of Illinois,* 5v. (1920). Founder, *The Mississippi Valley Historical Review,* 1914.

Amazing Stories. New York. Magazine featuring science fiction. Founded 1926, by Hugo Gernsback. Expired 1966.

Ambassadors, The. Novel by Henry James (1903). The story of Lambert Strether's mission to Paris to bring back Chad Newsome, who has inherited a business concern, but has no inclination to obey his mother's request that he return to Massachusetts to take charge of it.

Amber. Pen name of Martha Everts Holden.

Amber Gods, and Other Stories, The. By Harriet Prescott Spofford (1863). Among the first stories to depict New England life.

Ambitious Woman, An. Novel by Edgar Fawcett (1883). Analysis of an American woman imbued with social ambition. A revealing portrait of life in New York City.

AMBLER, CHARLES HENRY (Aug. 12, 1876–Aug. 31, 1957); b. near Mattamoras, O. Educator, historian. *Thomas Ritchie* (1913); *The Life and Diary of John Floyd* (1918); *George Washington and the West* (1936); *West Virginia: Stories and Biographies* (1937); *West Virginia, the Mountain State* (1940); *A History of Education in West Virginia from Early Colonial Times to 1949* (1951); *Sectionalism in Virginia from 1776 to 1861* (1964); etc.

AMBLER, ERIC (June 28, 1909–); b. London. Author. *The Dark Frontier* (1936); *Background to Danger* (1937); *Cause for Alarm* (1939); *A Coffin for Dimitrios* (1939); *Journey into Fear* (1940); *Intrigue* (1943); *Judgment on Deltchev* (1951); *Epitaph for a Spy* (1952); *The Schirmer Inheritance* (1953); *State of Siege* (1956); *Passage of Arms* (1960); *The Light of Day* (1962); *The Ability to Kill* (1963); *A Kind of Anger* (1964); *The Intercom Conspiracy* (1969).

Ambrose and Eleanor; or, The Disinherited Pair. Anonymous novel (1834). A story of the American Revolution.

Amee Brothers. Booksellers. Cambridge, Mass. John and Albert Amee ran a bookshop in Brattle Square, in Cambridge, Mass. The bookstore was the rendezvous of many Harvard professors and students. The bookshop was founded in 1833 by a man named Monroe.

Amelia. See Amelia B. Welby.

Amelia; or, The Faithless Briton; An Original American Novel, Founded Upon Recent Facts; to Which is Added: Amelia; or, Malevolence Defeated. Anonymous novel (1798).

Amelia; or, The Influence of Virtue. Novel by Sarah Sayward Barrell (1802).

America. New York. Roman Catholic weekly. Founded 1908, by Michael Kenny and others. Now edited by the Rev. Donald R. Campion.

"America." National hymn written by Samuel Francis Smith in 1831, and first published in Lowell Mason's *The Choir* (1832).

America in Contemporary Fiction. By Percy H. Boynton (1940). Critical study of 20th-century American novelists.

"America the Beautiful." Poem by Katharine Lee Bates in *The Congregationalist,* 1905. Usually sung to the tune "Materna" by Samuel A. Ward.

American, The. Novel by Henry James (1877). Story of Christopher Newman, cultivated American, who meets the widow Madame de Cintre in Paris and discovers many barriers to marriage.

American, The. Philadelphia. Monthly magazine. Founded 1880, by Wharton Barker. Walt Whitman was one of its leading contributors. Suspended 1891–94; expired 1900.

American Academy of Arts and Letters. New York. Founded 1904, as an outgrowth of the National Institute of Arts and Letters (founded 1898). New members are elected each May. Medals are awarded yearly and fifteen $1,500 grants are made for distinguished achievement.

American Academy of Arts and Sciences. Boston, Mass. Founded 1780. Publishes *Daedalus* (quarterly), *Modicum* (bimonthly).

American Antiquarian Society. Worcester, Mass. Founded Oct. 24, 1812, by Isaiah Thomas. Concerned exclusively with American history until 1877. Its *Proceedings* were first published in 1812 and its *Transactions* in 1820.

American Archives. Founded by Peter Force, and authorized by Act of Congress, Mar. 2, 1833. After nine volumes, 1837–53, the project was discontinued.

American Avatar. Roxbury, Mass. Monthly. Founded 1969, a merger of *Avatar, Boston Avatar,* and *New York Avatar.* Underground newspaper publication.

American Bee, The. An anthology of twenty-six tales (1797).

American Bible Society. New York. Founded 1816, by delegates from thirty-one local Bible Societies. Elias Boudinot, first president. Has published the Bible or its parts in more than a thousand languages and dialects.

American Bibliography, A Chronological Dictionary of all Books, Pamphlets and Periodical Publications Printed in the United States of America from 1639 down to 1820. Vols. 1–12 (1639–1799), by Charles Evans, were published 1903–34. Vol. 13 (1799–1800) was completed by Clifford K. Shipton in 1954. Roger Pattrell edited Volume 14 (1959) and a *Supplement* (1962). Evans changed the 1820 outer date to 1800 while completing Vols. 1–12, and the same time span obtains for all later volumes.

American Book Company. New York. Publishers. Founded 1890, when the educational departments of Harper & Brothers; A. S. Barnes & Co.; Ivison, Blakeman & Co.; D. Appleton & Co.; and Van Antwerp Bragg & Co., were amalgamated. In later years the following houses were added: Werner School Book Co., Chicago; Standard School Book Company, St. Louis; D. D. Merrill, St. Paul; Cowperthwait & Co., Philadel-phia; Taintor Brothers and Co., New York; E. H. Butler & Co., Philadelphia; Western School Book Co., Chicago; Sheldon & Co., New York; Williams and Rogers, Rochester; and the elementary list of The University Publishing Co., New York. Frederick H. Blake, Norvell B. Samuels, Craig T. Senft have been president. Bought by Litton Educational Publishing, Inc., in 1967.

American Booksellers' Guide. New York. Monthly. Founded 1869. Published by the American News Company. Succeeded in 1876 by the *American Bookseller,* semi-monthly, which expired 1893.

American Boy. Detroit, Mich. Boy Scouts monthly. Founded 1899. Elmer Presley Grierson has been publisher since 1939. Absorbed *Youth's Companion,* Oct. 1929.

American Caravan: A Yearbook of American Literature. 5v. (1927–29, 1931, 1936). Editors, Van Wyck Brooks, Alfred Kreymborg, Lewis Mumford, and Paul Rosenfeld, 1927; Alfred Kreymborg, Lewis Mumford, and Paul Rosenfeld, 1928–36.

American Catholic Quarterly Review. Philadelphia. Founded 1876. Edited by James A. Corcoran, followed by Archbishop Patrick John Ryan, 1890–1911, and others. Among its contributors were Orestes Brownson, John Boyle O'Reilly, George Parsons Lathrop, T. P. O'Connor, and John Gilmary Shea. Expired 1924.

American Catholic Who's Who, The. Detroit, Mich. Vol. 1, ed. by Georgina P. Curtis, was published at St. Louis, 1911. No more volumes were published until 1934, when it was revised at Detroit, and biennially since then.

American College Dictionary, The. Edited by Clarence L. Barnhart (1947–53). A one-volume dictionary for general use. The definitions are based on the Thorndike-Lorge Semantic Count.

American Council of Learned Societies. Washington, D.C. Founded 1919. Many scholarly works have been published under its auspices, notably the *Dictionary of American Biography* (q.v.). The constituent societies include: American Philosophical Society, 1727; American Academy of Arts and Sciences, 1780; American Antiquarian Society, 1812; American Oriental Society, 1842; American Numismatic Society, 1858; American Philological Association, 1869; Archaeological Institute of America, 1879; Society of Biblical Literature and Exegesis, 1880; Modern Language Association of America, 1883; American Historical Association, 1884; American Economic Association, 1885; American Philosophical Association, 1900; American Anthropological Association, 1902; American Political Science Association, 1903; Bibliographical Society of America, 1904; Association of American Geographers, 1904; American Sociological Society, 1905; American Society of International Law, 1906; History of Science Society, 1924; Linguistic Society of America, 1924; Mediaeval Academy of America, 1925.

American Dialect Society, The. New Haven, Conn.; Washington, D.C. Publishes *Publications of the American Dialect Society.*

American Dramatists Club. New York. Founded 1890, by Bronson Howard. The occasion was a private dinner given to the veteran playwright Charles Gaylor.

American Dream, An. Novel by Norman Mailer (1965). Written serially for *Esquire.* A fantasy novel with a "superhero," combining elements from comic-strip and movie exaggerations of plot and character with black-humor naturalism, it ranges over politics, class and race conflict, sexual aggression, and crime.

American English Grammar. By Charles C. Fries (1940). The most influential early work on the then new linguistic approach to grammar.

American Fiction. By Arthur Hobson Quinn (1936). Historical survey of American literature.

American Fiction Guild. New York. National organization of writers, with local branches in various cities. Founded 1931. Its *Bulletin* was published 1933–37.

"American Flag." Poem by Joseph Rodman Drake, in the *New York Evening Post,* May 29, 1819.

American Girl. New York. Girl Scouts monthly. Founded 1917.

American Guide Series. A series of illustrated travel guides for every state in the Union. It was sponsored and subsidized by the Federal Government and compiled by members of the Federal Writers Project. Each guide has bio-bibliographical notes on the literary men and women of the region described, with historical notes on literary landmarks, etc.

American Heritage, The Magazine of History. New York. Published six times yearly in book form. Founded 1954. Editorial directors have been Joseph J. Thorndike, Jr., and Oliver Jensen. Bought by McGraw-Hill in 1969.

American Heritage Dictionary of the English Language (1969). Edited by William Morris, with the assistance of Morton Bloomfield, Henry Lee Smith, Calvert Watkins, and other scholars. Published by American Heritage and Houghton Mifflin. A remarkable lexicographical undertaking, noted especially for its marginal illustrations, maps, and explanations of Indo-European derivations and roots.

American Hero: A Sapphic Ode, The. By Nathaniel Niles (1776). Written in celebration of the Battle of Bunker Hill. Set to music, it became very popular during the Revolution.

American Historical Association. Washington, D.C. Founded 1884, at Saratoga, N.Y. Incorporated by Act of Congress, Jan. 4, 1889, and moved to Washington, D.C. Its founders were Andrew D. White, George Bancroft, Justin Winsor, William F. Poole, Herbert B. Adams, Clarence W. Bowers, and others. It established the *American Historical Review* in 1895.

American Historical Magazine. See Americana.

American Historical Review, The. New York. Founded 1895, by the American Historical Association.

American Institute of Graphic Arts. New York. Founded Feb., 1914. In 1923 it began its selection of "The Fifty Books of the Year," now an annual exhibition, the formal opening of which is held in The New York Public Library. It conducts a Book Clinic. William B. Howland was its first president. In 1922 the Institute began its series of the *Keepsake,* a finely printed souvenir.

American Journal of Psychology. Austin, Tex.; Urbana, Ill. Founded 1887. Published at the University of Illinois.

American Journal of Sociology. Chicago, Ill. Bimonthly. Founded 1894. Published by the University of Chicago Press.

American Judaism. New York City. Quarterly. Founded 1873. Published by the Union of American Hebrew Congregations and Affiliates.

American Language, The. By H. L. Mencken (1919). A standard study of the speech of Americans. It supports the view that the English spoken in the United States is diverging from the mother tongue of England to form a new language. Supplements were published in 1945 and 1948.

American Legion Magazine. New York. Monthly. Founded 1919, at Indianapolis, Ind., as the *American Legion Weekly.* Became the *American Legion Monthly* in 1926; present name adopted 1937.

American Library Association. Chicago, Ill. Founded 1876, as a result of the Centennial Exhibition at Philadelphia. It publishes the *A.L.A. Bulletin* (monthly), *A.L.A. Booklist and Subscription Books Bulletin* (fortnightly), *Choice* (monthly), *College and Research Libraries* (bimonthly), and over 20 other serial publications. The *A.L.A. Catalog* (1893), revised in 1926, with later supplements, is an annotated basic list of books. Numerous other catalogs in special fields are issued under the A.L.A. imprint. It is affiliated with many educational projects, associations, etc.

American Literary Manuscripts: A Checklist of Holdings in Academic, Historical, and Public Libraries in the United States. Standard reference work prepared by the Committee on Manuscript Holdings of the American Literature Section of the Modern Language Association (1960). Revision being undertaken by J. A. Robbins, project chairman, for publication in 1975.

American Literature. By Carl Van Doren (1933). An introductory survey of our literature.

American Literature. By George Edward Woodberry (1903). A critical analysis.

American Literature. Durham, N.C. Quarterly. Founded 1928. A journal of literary history, criticism, and bibliography, published by the Duke University Press. Edited by Arlen Turner.

American Literature Abstracts. San Jose, Cal. Semiannual. Founded 1967. Abstracts current scholarship. Published at San Jose State College. Edited by James K. Bowen and R. Van der Beets.

American Lutheran. New York. Monthly. Founded 1918.

American Magazine, or A Monthly View of the Political State of the British Colonies, The. Philadelphia. Founded Feb. 13, 1741. Printed by Andrew Bradford and edited by John Webbe. Expired Mar., 1741. This was the first magazine published in America and appeared just three days before Benjamin Franklin's *General Magazine.* Both of these magazines were erroneously dated Jan. 1741 on the title-page.

American Magazine, The. New York. First monthly to be published in New York. Founded Dec., 1787, by Noah Webster. Barlow, Dwight, and Trumbull were among the contributors. Expired Nov. 1788.

American Magazine, The. New York. Monthly. Founded 1906 by John S. Phillips, Ida Tarbell, Lincoln Steffens, and others when they purchased *Frank Leslie's Popular Monthly* (q.v.) and changed its name to *The American Magazine.* Published by Crowell Publishing Company after July, 1916. In its earlier years, known as a Muckrackers' organ; later popular for its success stories and sentimental fiction. Discontinued 1956.

American Magazine and Historical Chronicle, The. Boston. Founded Sept. 1743. Published by Rogers and Fowle. Editor, Jeremiah Gridley. Expired Dec. 1746.

American Magazine and Monthly Chronicle for the British Colonies, The. Philadelphia. Founded Oct. 1757, by William Bradford. Editor: William Smith. The first American magazine of literary pretensions. The poets, Joseph Shippen, Francis Hopkinson, Thomas Godfrey, Jr., and James Sterling wrote for it. Expired Oct. 1758.

American Memoir. Social and literary critique by Henry Seidel Canby (1947).

American Mercury. New York. Monthly magazine. Founded Jan. 1924. H. L. Mencken and George Jean Nathan were its first editors. They had been co-editors of *The Smart Set.* Mencken was editor until 1933, Henry Hazlitt, 1933–34, Charles Angoff, 1934–35, Paul Palmer, 1935–39, Lawrence Spirak, 1939–50. Now edited by La Vonne Doden Furr. The present magazine, published in Oklahoma City, Okla., is unrelated in outlook to that founded by Mencken.

American Mind, The. By Bliss Perry (1912).

American Mirror. By Halford E. Luccock (1940). The social, ethical, and religious aspects of American literature from 1930 to 1940.

American Monthly Magazine, The. New York. Literary monthly. Founded Mar. 1833, by Henry William Herbert, better known as "Frank Forester," writer of sporting books. Charles Fenno Hoffman, Park Benjamin and Herbert were its chief editors and contributors. Expired Oct. 1838.

American Museum, The. Philadelphia. Eclectic monthly. Founded Jan. 1787, and edited by Mathew Carey. Trumbull's *M'Fingal* appeared in it. Washington, Franklin, Paine, Timothy Dwight, and Rush were among the contributors. Expired Dec., 1792.

American Notes & Queries. New York; New Haven, Conn. Literary monthly. Founded 1941, by Walter Pilkington and B. Alsterlund.

"American Patriot's Prayer, The." Attributed by some to Thomas Paine (1776).

American Peoples Encyclopedia, The. Edited by Franklin J. Meine and others, 20v. (1953). Distributed by Sears, Roebuck and Co. A popular encyclopedia written in simple language, based on *Nelson's Encyclopedia,* and with an annual year book.

American Philosophical Society. Philadelphia. Founded 1743, by Benjamin Franklin. Publishes scholarly books and gives grants for research.

American Place-Names: A Concise and Selective Dictionary for the Continental United States of America. By George R. Stewart (1970).

American Poetry: A Miscellany. Four volumes of original contributions by American poets, entitled: *A Miscellany of American Poetry, 1920; American Poetry, 1922: A Miscellany; American Poetry, 1925: A Miscellany;* and *American Poetry, 1927: A Miscellany.*

American Poetry Magazine. Milwaukee, Wis. Founded May 1919, by Clara Catherine Prince.

American Political Science Review. Washington, D.C. Quarterly. Founded 1906.

American Politician, An. By F. Marion Crawford (1884). Political novel setting forth the methods of choosing a United States Senator.

American Portraits, 1875–1900. By Gamaliel Bradford (1920). Short sketches of Mark Twain, Henry Adams, Sidney Lanier, James McNeill Whistler, James G. Blaine, Grover Cleveland, Henry James, and Joseph Jefferson.

American Prefaces. Iowa City, Ia. Quarterly literary journal. Founded 1935, as a monthly, by the University of Iowa. Became quarterly in 1941. Edited by Wilbur Schramm, Paul Engle, Jean Garrigue. Discontinued 1943.

American Quarterly. Quarterly journal of American studies. Founded 1949, at the University of Minnesota. Published since 1951 at the University of Pennsylvania.

American Review. New York. Founded 1933. Concerned with social and economic affairs as well as literature. Discontinued 1937. *See* Agrarians.

American Review, The. New York. Monthly. Founded 1895.

American Review, The. New York. Founded 1933. Edited by Seward Collins. Discontinued 1938.

American Review of History and Politics, and General Repository of Literature and State Papers, The. Philadelphia. First standard quarterly review in the United States. Founded Jan. 1811, and edited by Robert Walsh. Expired Oct. 1812.

American Scene, The. An appreciation of the United States, published in 1907 by Henry James. It describes his impressions and thoughts about American customs, attitudes, and places, and the quality of American life.

American Scholar, The. Phi Beta Kappa oration delivered by Ralph Waldo Emerson at Harvard, Aug. 31, 1837, which has been called "our intellectual Declaration of Independence."

American Scholar, The. Washington, D.C. Literary quarterly. Founded at New York City in 1932, by the United Chapters of Phi Beta Kappa.

American Society of Composers, Authors and Publishers, The. Organized 1914, by Victor Herbert and others, to protect the rights of musicians, particularly royalties and performing rights; later broadened to include all literary property and rights. Generally known as ASCAP.

American Sociological Review. Washington, D.C. Founded 1936. Published by the American Sociological Association.

American Songbag, The. Compilation of songs and ballads by Carl Sandburg (1927).

American Spectator, The. New York. Literary monthly. Founded 1932. Edited by George Jean Nathan, Theodore Dreiser, Eugene O'Neill, Ernest Boyd, and James Branch Cabell. Expired 1937.

American Speech. New York. Quarterly. Founded 1925, by Louise Pound, Kemp Malone, and Arthur G. Kennedy. First published at Baltimore, Md. Moved to New York in 1933. Monthly to Sept. 1927; bi-monthly, Oct. 1927–Aug. 1932.

"American Times, The." Poem by "Camille Querno" (the loyalist Jonathan Odell) (1779). Bitter, denunciatory poem against the American cause.

American Tract Society. New York. Founded 1825. One of the largest distributors of religious literature for many generations. Published the juvenile magazines *Child's Paper,* 1852–97; *Child at Home,* 1863–73; *Apples of Gold,* 1871.

American Tragedy, An. Novel by Theodore Dreiser, 2v. (1925). The story of Clyde Griffiths, the drowning of Sondra Finchley, his sweetheart, and the ensuing murder trial.

American Tramp and Underworld Slang. By Godfrey Irwin (1931). Dictionary of the argot of low life.

American Way of Death, The. By Jessica Mitford (1963). A critical examination of the business of undertaking in the United States and of American attitudes toward death.

American Weave. University Heights, Ohio; Cleveland, Ohio. Quarterly of verse. Founded 1935.

American Weekly, The. New York. Sunday magazine section distributed by various newspapers. Founded 1896.

American Weekly Mercury, The. Philadelphia. Founded Dec. 22, 1719, by Andrew Bradford and John Copson. First newspaper published in Pennsylvania. Expired 1723. Republished in facsimile by the Colonial Society of Pennsylvania, 1898–1907.

American West, The. Palo Alto, Cal. Quarterly. Founded 1964. Devoted to Western Americana. Editorial board has included Wallace Stegner and Roger Olmsted.

American Whig Review, The. New York. Monthly. Founded 1845. George H. Colton was its chief editor. Colton was the author of the long poem "Tecumseh." Poe was a contributor, along with Lowell, Tuckerman, Greeley, Webster and Calhoun and other notable writers. Distinguished for its mezzotint engravings of American statesmen. Expired 1852.

American Whig Society, The. Literary society at Princeton University. Founded 1769, by Hugh Henry Brackenridge, Philip Freneau, James Madison, and others. See Jacob N. Beam's *The American Whig Society* (1933).

American Zionist, The. New York. Monthly. Founded 1921. Published by Zionist Organization of America.

American-Scandinavian Review, The. New York. Monthly. Founded 1913. Hannah Astrup Larson was literary editor, 1913–21, editor from 1921.

Americana; or, A New Tale of the Genii. Anonymous play (1798). See Benjamin Franklin.

Americanisms. Words and phrases peculiar to America. See John Russell Bartlett's *Dictionary of Americanisms* (1848); Maximilian Schele de Vere's *Americanisms* (1872); R. H. Thornton's *An American Glossary,* 2v. (1912); *A Dictionary of American English,* edited by Sir William Craigie and others, 4v. (1938–43); H. L. Mencken's *The American Language* (1919 and later editions); W. J. Burke's *The Literature of Slang* (1939); Stuart Berg Flexner's *American Dialect Dictionary* (1944); Margaret M. Bryant's *Current American Usage* (1962); Mitford M. Mathews' *Americanisms: A Dictionary of Selected Americanisms on Historical Principles* (1966); Stuart Berg Flexner's and Harold Wentworth's *Dictionary of American Slang* (rev. with supplement; 1967); Sylvia Clapin's *A New Dictionary of Americanisms* (1968).

Americanization of Edward Bok, The. Autobiography of Edward W. Bok (1920).

Americans in Paris; or, A Game of Dominoes. Play by William Henry Hurlbert (prod. 1858).

America's Lost Plays. Little-known plays by popular dramatists of the 18th and 19th centuries. Collected in 20 volumes (1940–41) under the general editorial direction of Barrett H. Clark.

America's Tragedy. By James Truslow Adams (1935). History of the Civil War.

AMES, EDWARD SCRIBNER (Apr. 21, 1870–June 29, 1958); b. Eau Claire, Wis. Disciples of Christ clergyman, educator, author. *Psychology of Religious Experience* (1910); *The Higher Individualism* (1915); *The New Orthodoxy* (1918); *Religion* (1929); *Beyond Theology: Autobiography* (1959); etc. Philosophy dept., University of Chicago, 1900–35.

AMES, ELEANOR MARIA [Easterbrook] (Oct. 7, 1831–1908); b. Warren, R.I. Author. Pen name, "Eleanor Kirk." *Information for Authors* (1888); *Up Broadway, and Its Sequel: A Life Story* (1870); etc.

AMES, FISHER (Apr. 9, 1758–July 4, 1808); b. Dedham, Mass., son of Nathaniel Ames (1708–1764). Statesman, publicist, author. *Works of Fisher Ames* (1809).

AMES, LOUISE BATES (Oct. 29, 1908–); b. Portland, Me. Child psychologist. *Child Rorschach Responses* (with others, 1952); *Rorschach Responses in Old Age* (with others, 1954); *Child Behavior* (with Frances L. Ilg, 1955); *Adolescent Rorschach Responses* (with others, 1959); *The Guidance Nursery School* (with Evelyn G. Pitcher, 1964); *Is Your Child in the Wrong Grade?* (1967). Co-founder, Gesell Institute of Child Development.

AMES, MARY CLEMMER (May 6, 1839–Aug. 18, 1884); b. Utica, N. Y. Journalist, novelist, poet. *Victoire (1864); Eirene; or, A Woman's Right* (1871); *A Memorial of Alice and* Phoebe Carey (1873); *Outlines of Men, Women, and Things* (1873); *Ten Years in Washington* (1873); *His Two Wives* (1874); *Poems of Life and Nature* (1882). Her last book and reissues of her earlier books appeared under her maiden name. Wrote "A Woman's Letters from Washington" for the New York *Independent,* 1866–84; wrote daily column for the *Brooklyn Daily Union,* 1869–72.

AMES, NATHANIEL (July 22, 1708–July 11, 1764); b. Bridgewater, Mass. Physician, almanac maker. He published his first almanac in 1725, eight years before Franklin's *Poor Richard.* See *The Essays, Humor and Poems of Nathaniel Ames, Father and Son, of Dedham, Massachusetts, from Their Almanacks, 1726–1775, with Notes and Comments, by* Sam. Briggs (1891).

AMES, NATHANIEL (d. Jan. 18, 1835); b. Dedham, Mass. Mariner, author. *A Mariner's Sketches* (1830); *Nautical Reminiscences* (1832); *An Old Sailor's Yarns* (1835).

AMES, VAN METER (1898–). Author. *Aesthetics of the Novel* (1928); *Faith of the Free* (with others, 1940); *André Gide* (1947); *Zen and American Thought* (1962). Editor: E. S. Ames' *Beyond Theology* (1959).

AMHERST, J. H. (1776–Aug. 12, 1851); b. London, England. Playwright, actor. *Will Watch; or, The Black Phantom* (1825); *Ireland As It Was* (1850); *The Battle of Waterloo* (1850); etc.

AMMONS, ARCHIE RANDOLPH (Feb. 18, 1926–); b. Whiteville, N. C. Educator, poet. *Ommateum* (1955); *Expressions of Sea Level* (1964); *Corson's Inlet* (1965); *Tape for the Turn of the Year* (1965); *Northfield Poems* (1966); *Uplands* (1970). English dept., Cornell University, since 1964.

AMORY, CLEVELAND (Sept. 2, 1917–); b. Nahant, Mass. Author. *The Proper Bostonians* (1947); *Home Town* (1950); *The Last Resorts* (1952); *Who Killed Society?* (1960); *The Last Resort* (1963); *Lost, Strayed or Stolen* (1967). Editor: *Vanity Fair* (with Frederic Bradlee, 1960).

AMORY, THOMAS COFFIN (Oct. 16, 1812–Aug. 20, 1889); b. Boston, Mass. Lawyer, antiquarian, poet. *Life of James Sullivan* (1858); *Old Cambridge and New* (1871); etc. His poem *William Blaxton, Boston's First Inhabitant,* published anonymously in 1877, helped to prevent the razing of the Old South Church.

Amos, Judd. Novel by John Ames Mitchell (1895). A child rajah is smuggled from India by two Hindus and an American and is removed to a Connecticut farmhouse. He takes the name of Amos Judd and is brought up in ignorance of his royal background.

Amsterdam News. See *New York Amsterdam News.*

Analectic Magazine, The. Philadelphia. Founded 1813 by Moses Thomas. Editors, Washington Irving and Thomas Isaac Wharton. In reality this magazine was a new series of *Select Reviews,* founded 1809. Expired 1821.

Anarchiad: A New England Poem, The. By David Humphreys, Joel Barlow, John Trumbull, and Leonard Hopkins; first printed in the *New Haven Gazette and Connecticut Magazine,* Oct. 26, 1786 to Sept. 13, 1787. First published in book form in 1861.

ANASTASI, ANNE (Mrs. John Porter Foley, Jr.) (Dec. 19, 1908–); b. New York City. Psychologist. *Differential Psychology* (1949); *Human Relations and the Foreman* (with J. P. Foley, Jr., 1951); *Psychological Testing* (1954); *Fields of Applied Psychology* (1963); *Individual Differences* (1965). Prof. psychology, Fordham University, since 1951.

Anatomy of Criticism. By Northrop Frye (1957). Divides the task of literary criticism into analysis of four types, according to theories of modes, symbols, myths, and genres.

Anchor Books. New York. In 1952 Jason Epstein launched this paperback series, which fostered interest in "quality" reprints in soft-cover format. Among the early titles were Bergson's *Two Sources of Morality and Religion*, A. E. Taylor's *Socrates*, and D. H. Lawrence's *Studies in Classic American Literature. See* Doubleday and Co.

And Keep Your Powder Dry. By Margaret Mead (1942). An anthropological analysis of the American character.

ANDERSON, ADA WOODRUFF (Mrs. Oliver Phelps Anderson) (July 4, 1860–); b. San Francisco, Calif. Novelist. *The Heart of the Red Firs* (1908); *The Strain of White* (1909); *The Rim of the Desert* (1915).

ANDERSON, ALEXANDER (Apr. 21, 1775–Jan. 17, 1870); b. New York City. America's first wood engraver. Illustrated more than one hundred volumes of English classics. Made engravings for *Webster's Spelling Book*. Illustrated Bewick's *General History of Quadrupeds* (1804); and Irving and Paulding's *Salmagundi* (1814). *See* Benson Lossing's *A Memorial of Alexander Anderson* (1872); and Frederic M. Burr's *Life and Works of Alexander Anderson* (1893).

ANDERSON, BARBARA [Tunnell] (Sept. 27, 1894–); b. Mansfield, Mass. Author. *The Days Grow Cold* (1941); *Southbound* (1949); *The Tall Kentuckian* (prod. 1953).

ANDERSON, BERNHARD WORD (Sept. 15, 1916–); b. Dover, Mo. Methodist clergyman, educator. *Rediscovering the Bible* (1951); *Understanding the Old Testament* (1957); *The Old Testament and Christian Faith* (1963); *Creation versus Chaos* (1967). Prof. Biblical theology, Drew Univeristy, since 1954.

ANDERSON, BRAD[ley] JAY (May 14, 1924–); b. Jamestown, N.Y. Cartoonist, author. *Marmaduke* (1955); *More Marmaduke* (1958); *Marmaduke Rides Again* (1968); etc.

ANDERSON, CARL THOMAS (Feb. 14, 1865–Nov. 4, 1948); b. Madison, Wis. Cartoonist, author. *How to Draw Cartoons Successfully* (1935); *Henry* (1935). Creator of the cartoon "Henry" for *Saturday Evening Post.*

ANDERSON, CHARLES ROBERTS (Oct. 17, 1902–); b. Macon, Ga. Educator, author: *Melville in the South Seas* (1939); *Emily Dickinson's Poetry: Stairway of Surprise* (1960). Editor: *Journal of a Cruise in the Frigate United States, with Notes on Melville* (1937); *Centennial Edition of Sidney Lanier*, 10v. (1945); *American Literary Masters* 2v. (1965). Prof. English, Johns Hopkins University, since 1946.

ANDERSON, EUGENE N[ewton] (July 24, 1900–); b. Tehuacana, Tex. Educator. *The First Moroccan Crisis, 1904–1906* (1930); *Nationalism and the Cultural Crisis in Prussia, 1806–1815* (1939); *Social and Political Conflict in Prussia, 1858–1864* (1954); *Modern Europe in World Perspective* (1958). Editor: *Europe in the 19th Century*, 2v. (with others, 1961). Prof. history, University of California at Los Angeles, since 1955.

ANDERSON, FLORENCE MARY BENNETT (Mrs. Louis Francis Anderson) (May 20, 1883–); b. Chateaugay, N. Y. Educator, classicist, author. *An Off Islander* (1921); *The Garland of Defeat* (1927); *Spindrift* (1930); *Through the Hawse-Hole: The True Story of a Nantucket Whaling Captain* (1932); *The Black Sail* (1948); *Leaven for the Frontier* (1953); *The Shadow of the Tower* (1955); *Rebel's Daughter* (1957).

ANDERSON, FRANK MALOY (Feb. 3, 1871–); b. Omaha, Neb. Educator. *Constitutions and Documents Illustrative of the History of France, 1789–1902* (1904); *The Mystery of a Public Man* (1948); etc. Prof. history, Dartmouth College, 1914–41.

ANDERSON, FREDERICK IRVING (Nov. 14, 1877–Dec. 24, 1947); b. Aurora, Ill. Author. *The Farmer of Tomorrow* (1913); *The Adventures of the Infallible Godahl* (1914); *Electricity for the Farm* (1915); *The Book of Murder* (1930). Also

many short stories for the *Saturday Evening Post* and other magazines. Staff, New York *World*, 1898–1908.

ANDERSON, [Hobson] DEWEY (Jan. 14, 1897–); b. Grand Forks, N.D. Economist. Author or co-author: *Ballots and the Democratic Class Struggle* (1943); *Recent Occupational Trends in American Labor* (1945); *Natural Resources—Their Protection and Development* (with others, 1959); etc.

ANDERSON, ISABEL [Weld Perkins] (Mrs. Larz Anderson) (Mar. 29, 1876–Nov. 3, 1948); b. Boston, Mass. Author. *The Great Horse* (1909); *The Spell of Japan* (1914); *Presidents and Pies: Life in Washington, 1897–1919* (1920): *From Corsair to Riffian* (1927); *Circling South America* (1928); *Circling Africa* (1929); *A Yacht in Mediterranean Seas* (1930); *A Musical Extravaganza* (1932); *I Hear a Call* (poems, 1933); *Zigzagging the South Seas* (1936); *The Whole World Over* (poems, 1945); *Near and Far* (poems, 1949); etc. Editor: *General Nicholas Longworth Anderson's Letters and Journals* (1942).

ANDERSON, JACK (June 15, 1935–); b. Milwaukee, Wis. Journalist, author. *The Hurricane Lamp* (1968). News editor, *Dance Magazine.*

ANDERSON, JOHN [Hargis] (Oct. 18, 1896–July 16, 1943); b. Pensacola, Fla. Drama critic. *Box Office* (1929); *American Theatre* (1938); etc. Drama critic, *New York Evening Post*, 1924–28; *New York Journal*, since 1928.

ANDERSON, MARGARET C. Editor. *My Thirty Years' War* (1930); *Fiery Fountains* (1951). Founded *The Little Review* in Chicago in 1914, moved it to New York, finally to Paris. First chapters of *Ulysses* by James Joyce appeared in *The Little Review.*

ANDERSON, MAXWELL (Dec. 15, 1888–Feb. 28, 1959); b. Atlantic, Pa. Playwright. *What Price Glory* (with Laurence Stallings, prod. 1924); *Saturday's Children* (prod. 1927); *Elizabeth the Queen* (prod. 1930); *Both Your Houses* (prod. 1932, Pulitzer prize play, 1933); *Mary of Scotland* (prod. 1933); *Valley Forge* (prod. 1934); *Winterset* (prod. 1935); *High Tor* (prod. 1937); *The Essence of Tragedy, and Other Footnotes and Papers* (1939); *Key Largo* (prod. 1939); *The Eve of St. Mark* (prod. 1942); *Truckline Café* (prod. 1945); *Joan of Lorraine* (prod. 1946); *Off Broadway* (essays, 1947); *Anne of the Thousand Days* (prod. 1948); *Lost in the Stars* (prod. 1949); *Barefoot in Athens* (prod. 1951); *The Bad Seed* (prod. 1955); *The Golden Six* (prod. 1958); etc.

ANDERSON, MELVILLE BEST (Mar. 28, 1851–June 22, 1933); b. Kalamazoo, Mich. Educator, author. *Some Representative Poets of the Nineteenth Century* (1896); *The Happy Teacher* (poems, 1910); *The Florence of Dante Alighieri* (1929); *The Fate of Virgil as Conceived by Dante* (1931).

ANDERSON, PATRICK (1936–). Author. *The President's Men* (1968); *The Approach to Kings* (1970).

ANDERSON, PAUL RUSSELL (Sept. 27, 1907–); b. Akron, O. Educator, author. *Science in Defense of Liberal Religion; A Study of Henry More's Attempt to Link Seventeenth Century Religion with Science* (1933); *Platonism in the Midwest* (1963). President, Temple University, since 1967.

ANDERSON, POUL (1936–). Author. *Vault of the Ages* (1952); *The Broken Sword* (1954); *Star Ways* (1956); *Earthman's Burden* (with G. R. Dickson, 1957); *Enemy Stars* (1959); *High Crusade* (1960); *Three Hearts and Three Lions* (1961); *Twilight World* (1961); *After Doomsday* (1963); *Is There Life on Other Worlds?* (1963); *Flandry of Terra* (1965); *Ensign Flandry* (1966); *Brain Wave* (1969); *The Infinite Voyage: Man's Future in Space* (1969); *Seven Conquests: An Adventure in Science* (1969).

ANDERSON, RASMUS BJORN (Jan. 12, 1846–Mar. 2, 1936); b. Albion, Mich. Diplomat, educator, editor, author. *Norse Mythology* (1875); *Life Story* (1915); etc. Translator and editor: *Viking Tales* (1877); *The Younger Edda* (1880); *The Elder Eddas* (1906).

ANDERSON, ROBERT GORDON (Apr. 18, 1881–Sept. 25, 1950); b. Somerville, N.J. Author. *Leader of Men* (1920); *Seven o'Clock Stories* (1920); *Half-Past Seven Stories* (1922); *Eight O'Clock Stories* (1923); *Those Quarrelsome Bonapartes* (1927); *An American Family Abroad* (1931); *The Tavern Rogue* (1934); *Villon; a Lyric Drama of François Villon* (1937); *Biography of a Cathedral* (1944); *The City and the Cathedral* (1948); etc.

ANDERSON, ROBERT [Woodruff] (Apr. 28, 1917–); b. New York City. Playwright. *Come Marching Home* (prod. 1946); *Eden Rose* (1948); *Love Revisited* (prod. 1951); *Tea and Sympathy* (prod. 1953); *Silent Night, Lonely Night* (prod. 1959); *The Days Between* (1965); *You Know I Can't Hear You When the Water's Running* (prod. 1967).

ANDERSON, SHERWOOD (Sept. 13, 1876–March 8, 1941); b. Camden, O. Essayist, novelist. *Windy McPherson's Son* (1916); *Marching Men* (1917); *Mid-American Chants* (poems, 1918); *Winesburg, Ohio* (1919); *Poor White* (1920); *The Triumph of the Egg* (1921); *Many Marriages* (1923); *Horses and Men* (1923); *A Story Teller's Story* (autobiography, 1924); *Dark Laughter* (1925); *Sherwood Anderson's Notebook* (1926); *Tar: A Midwest Childhood* (1926); *Perhaps Women* (1931); *Beyond Desire* (1932); *Death in the Woods* (1933); *No Swank* (1934); *Puzzled America* (1935); *Kit Brandon* (1936); *Home Town* (1940); *Memoirs* (1948); etc. *See* Howard Mumford Jones's *Letters of Sherwood Anderson* (1953). *See also* Irving Howe's *Sherwood Anderson* (1951); J. Schevill's *Sherwood Anderson: Life and Works* (1951); R. Burbank's *Sherwood Anderson* (1964); David D. Anderson's *Sherwood Anderson: An Introduction and Interpretation* (1967).

ANDERSON, WILLIAM (Oct. 25, 1888–); b. Minneapolis, Minn. Educator. *A History of the Constitution of Minnesota* (1921); *American City Government* (1925); *American Government* (1938); *The National Government of the United States* (1946); *The Nation and the States* (1946); *Man's Quest for Political Knowledge* (1964). Editor: *Intergovernmental Relations* series (1950–1953). Political science department, University of Minnesota, 1916–57.

Andersonville. Novel by MacKinlay Kantor (1955). About the scandalous conditions in the Confederate prison in Sumter Co., Ga., during the Civil War.

ANDREWS, CHARLES McLEAN (Feb. 22, 1863–Sept. 9, 1943); b. Wethersfield, Conn. Educator, historian. *The River Towns of Connecticut* (1889); *The Old English Manor* (1892); *The Historical Development of Modern Europe*, 2v. (1896–98); *The Fathers of New England* (1919); *Colonial Folkways* (1919); *The Colonial Period of American History*, 4v. (1934–38, vol. I awarded Pulitzer prize for American History, 1935); etc. Editor: *Yale Historical Publications*, 50v. (1912–33); *Journal of a Lady of Quality* [Janet Schaw] (with wife, Evangeline Holcombe Walker, 1921). Farnham Professor, American History, Yale University, 1910–31.

ANDREWS, CHARLTON (Feb. 1, 1878–Aug. 13, 1939); b. Connersville, Ind. Educator, playwright. *A Parfait Gentil Knight* (1901); *The Interrupted Revels* (1910); *The Drama To-Day* (1913); *His Majesty the Fool* (prod. 1913); *The Lady of Gestures* (1927); *Get Me in the Movies* (with Philip Dunning, prod. 1927); *The Golden Age* (with Lester Lonergan, prod. 1928); *The Butterfly Murder* (1932); *The Affair of the Malacca Stick* (1936); etc.

ANDREWS, C[hristopher] C[olumbus] (Oct. 27, 1829–Sept. 21, 1922); b. Hillsboro, N.H. Lawyer, historian. *Minnesota and Dacotah: In Letters Descriptive of a Tour Through the North-West, in the Autumn of 1856* (1857); *Brazil: Its Condition and Prospects* (1887); *Recollections* (1928).

ANDREWS, ELISHA BENJAMIN (Jan. 10, 1844–Oct. 30, 1917); b. Hinsdale, N.H. Educator, historian. *The History of the Last Quarter-Century in the United States, 1870–1895* (1896), enlarged as *The United States in Our Own Time* (1903); *The Call of the Land* (1913); etc. President, Brown University, 1889–98.

ANDREWS, ELIZA FRANCES [Fanny] (b. Aug. 10, 1840); b. Washington, Ga. Botanist, novelist. Pen name, "Elzey Hay." *A Family Secret* (1876); *A Mere Adventurer* (1879); *Prince Hal* (1882); *The War-Time Journal of a Georgia Girl, 1864–1865* (1908); etc.

ANDREWS, F[rank] EMERSON (Jan. 26, 1902–); b. Lancaster, Pa. Foundation executive. *New Numbers* (1935); *The Gingerbread House* (1943); *I Find Out* (1946); *For Charlemagne* (1949); *Philanthropic Giving* (1950); *Corporation Giving* (1952); *Attitudes Toward Giving* (1953); *Grugan's God* (1955); *Philanthropic Foundations* (1956); *Upside-Down Town* (1958); *Numbers Please* (1961); *Knights and Daze* (1966). Director, Russell Sage Foundation Library Center, since 1956.

ANDREWS, JANE (1833–1887); b. in Massachusetts. Author. *The Seven Little Sisters Who Live on the Round Ball That Floats in the Air* (1861); *Ten Boys Who Lived on the Road from Long Ago to Now* (1886).

ANDREWS, JOHN WILLIAMS (Nov. 10, 1898–); b. Bryn Mawr, Pa. Lawyer, author. *History of the Founding of Wolf's Head* (1934); *Prelude to "Icaros"* (1936); *Georgia Transport* (radio verse play, 1938); *A Ballad of Channel Crossings* (1941); *First Flight* (poem, 1963); *Hill Country North: A Vermont Cycle* (1965); *The Story of Flying* (1968); *A.D. Twenty-One Hundred: A Narrative of Space* (poem) (1969). Editor, *St. Lawrence Seaway Fact Sheet*, since 1958.

ANDREWS, MARY RAYMOND SHIPMAN (1865?–Aug. 2, 1936); b. Mobile, Ala. Novelist. *The Perfect Tribute* (1906); *The Enchanted Forest* (1909); *The Lifted Bondage* (1910); *The Eternal Masculine* (1913); *The Eternal Feminine* (1916); *Yellow Butterflies* (1922); *A Lost Commander: Florence Nightingale* (1929); etc.

ANDREWS, MATTHEW PAGE (July 15, 1879–June 20, 1947); b. Shepherdstown, W. Va. Editor, author. *A History of the United States* (1913); *A Heritage of Freedom* (1918); *History of Maryland* (1929); *The Old Dominion* (1937); *Social Planning by Frontier Thinkers* (1944); *Ye Fountain Inn Diary* (1947); etc.

Andrews, Robert D. See Robert Hardy Andrews.

ANDREWS, ROBERT HARDY (Charles Robert Douglas Hardy Andrews) (Oct. 19, 1903–); b. Effingham, Kans. Author, motion picture scenarist. *The Truth About Artists* (1926); *The Truth About Pirates* (1927); *Three Girls Lost* (1929); *Windfall* (1930); *Burning Gold* (1945); *Legend of a Lady* (1949). Author of first daytime radio serial and 29 others. Scenarist, under name Robert D. Andrews, of *If I Had a Million* and more than 50 other motion pictures.

ANDREWS, ROY CHAPMAN (Jan 26, 1884–Mar. 11, 1960); b. Beloit, Wis. Zoologist, explorer, author. *Whale Hunting with Gun and Camera* (1916); *Camps and Trails in China* (with wife, 1918); *Across Mongolian Plains* (1921); *On the Trail of Ancient Man* (1926); *Ends of the Earth* (1929); *The New Conquest of Central Asia* (1932); *This Business of Exploring* (1935); *Under a Lucky Star* (1943); *Meet Your Ancestors* (1945); *An Explorer Comes Home* (1947); *Nature's Ways* (1951); *All About Dinosaurs* (1953); *Quest of the Snow Leopard* (1964). Director, American Museum of Natural History, New York (retired, 1942).

ANDREWS, WAYNE (Sept. 5, 1913–); b. Kenilworth, Ill. Author. *The Vanderbilt Legend* (1941); *Battle for Chicago* (1946); *Architecture, Ambition and Americans* (1955); *Architecture in America* (1960); *Germaine: A Portrait of Madame* *de Stael* (1963). Editor: *Best Short Stories of Edith Wharton* (1957); *Concise Dictionary of American History* (1962).

ANDREWS, WILLIAM LORING (Sept. 9, 1837–Mar. 19, 1920); b. New York City. Bibliophile, author. *Jean Grolier* (1892); *Among My Books* (1894); *The Old Booksellers of New York* (1895); *Gossip About Book Collecting,* 2v. (1900); *Bibliopegy in the United States* (1902); *New York as Washington Knew It After the Revolution* (1905); etc. Co-founder, The Grolier Club, 1884; founder, The Society of Iconophiles, 1895. *See* Addison Van Name's *Catalogue of the William Loring Andrews Collections of Early Books* (1913).

Androboros: A Bographical [*sic*] *Farce in Three Acts, viz.: The Senate, The Consistory, and the Apotheosis.* Farce by Robert Hunter and Lewis Morris (New York: William Bradford, 1714). The first drama written and printed in this country. Only two copies are known, one in the Henry E. Huntington Library, and one in the Bodleian.

Andromeda Strain, The. By Michael Crichton (1969). Science-fiction tale of extra-terrestrial invasion of microorganisms. Uses print-graphics as integral parts of the story, in the form of top-secret documents, computer print-outs, etc., to achieve realistic effects.

Andros Tracts, The. Ed. by William H. Whitmore, 3v. (1868–74). Collection of colonial papers, particularly of the Mather family, and of Sir Edmund Andros (1637–1714), colonial governor associated with the "Charter Oak" incident, the founding of William and Mary College, etc.

ANGELL, JAMES BURRILL (Jan. 7, 1829–Apr. 1, 1916); b. Scituate, Mass. Educator, editor, author. *Selected Addresses* (1912); *The Reminiscences* (1912). Editor, *The Providence Journal,* 1860–65. Co-founder, the American Historical Association, 1884; president, 1893–94. President, University of Michigan, 1871–1909.

ANGELL, JAMES ROWLAND (May 8, 1869–Mar. 3, 1949); b. Burlington, Vt. Educator, author. *Chapters from Modern Psychology* (1911); *Introduction to Psychology* (1913); *American Education* (1937); etc. President, Yale University, 1921–37.

ANGELL, JAMES WATERHOUSE (May 20, 1898–); b. Chicago, Ill. Economist. *The Theory of International Prices* (1926); *Financial Foreign Policy of the U.S.* (1933); *The Behavior of Money* (1936); *Investment and Business Cycles* (1941). Prof. economics, Columbia University, since 1931.

ANGELL, ROBERT COOLEY (Apr. 29, 1899–); b. Detroit, Mich. Sociologist. *The Campus* (1928); *The Family Encounters the Depression* (1936); *The Integration of American Society* (1941); *Free Society and Moral Crisis* (1958). Prof. sociology, University of Michigan, since 1935.

ANGELLOTTI, MARION POLK, b. San Rafael, Calif. Novelist. *The Burgundians* (1912); *The Firefly of France* (1918); *Three Black Bags* (1922); etc.

ANGELO, VALENTI (June 23, 1897–); b. Massarosa, It. Author, illustrator. *Nino* (1937); *Paradise Valley* (1940); *Look Out Yonder* (1943); *The Bells of Bleecker Street* (1949); *The Marble Fountain* (1951); *Candy Basket* (1960); *The Merry Marcos* (1963); *Tale of a Donkey* (1966). Illustrations for the Limited Editions Club, the Peter Pauper Press, etc.

"Angels of Buena Vista, The." Poem by John Greenleaf Whittier, in the *National Era,* May 20, 1847.

ANGLE, PAUL McCLELLAND (Dec. 25, 1900–); b. Mansfield, O. Librarian, author. *Mary Lincoln, Wife and Widow* (with Carl Sandburg, 1932); *Lincoln, 1854–1861* (1933); *"Here I Have Lived": a History of Lincoln's Springfield* (1935); *A Shelf of Lincoln Books* (1946); *Bloody Williamson: A Chapter in American Lawlessness* (1952); *Tragic Years, 1860–1865,* 2v. (with Earl S. Miers, 1960); *Crossroads: 1913* (1963); *Pictorial History of the Civil War Years* (1967). Edi-

tor: *The Lincoln Reader* (1947); *By These Words* (1954); *The American Reader* (1958); *Prairie State: Impressions of Illinois, 1673–1967* (with M. L. McCree, 1968). Librarian, Illinois State Historical Library, 1932–45; director, Chicago Historical Society, since 1945.

Anglomaniacs, The. Novel by Mrs. Burton Harrison (1890). Satirizes the aping of English life and manners.

ANGLUND, JOAN WALSH (Jan. 3, 1926–); b. Hinsdale, Ill. Author, illustrator. *A Friend is Someone Who Likes You* (1958); *The Brave Cowboy* (1959); *Look Out the Window* (1959); *Love Is a Special Way of Feeling* (1960); *In a Pumpkin Shell* (1960); *The Cowboy and His Friend* (1961); *Christmas Is a Time of Giving* (1961); *Nibble Nibble Mousekin* (1962); *Spring Is a New Beginning* (1963); *Cowboy's Secret Life* (1963); *A Pocketful of Proverbs* (1964); *Childhood Is a Time of Innocence* (1964); *A Book of Good Tidings* (1965); *What Color Is Love* (1966); *A Year Is Round* (1966); *A Cup of Sun* (1967).

ANGOFF, CHARLES (Apr. 22, 1902–); b. Minsk, Russia. Editor, author. *A Literary History of the American People,* v. 1–2 (1931); *Moment Musical* (prod. 1943); *Adventures in Heaven* (1945); *The Fathers of Classical Music* (1947); *In the Morning Light* (1953); *H. L. Mencken, A Portrait from Memory* (1956); *The Bitter Spring* (1961); *Summer Storm* (1963); *The Bell of Time* (1966); *Memoranda for Tomorrow* (poems) (1968); *Memory of Autumn* (1968). On editorial staff, *American Mercury,* 1925–50; managing editor, 1943–50.

Anna Christie. Play by Eugene O'Neill (prod. 1921). Drab story of river-front life, with "de old Davil" sea as a powerful force of destiny. Chris Christopherson tries to save his daughter from the curse of the sea, but fails.

"Annabel Lee." Poem by Edgar Allan Poe, in the *New York Tribune,* Oct. 9, 1849. Written in memory of his wife Virginia.

Annals of the West. By James Handasyd Perkins (1846), revised and enlarged by John Mason Peck (1850).

Anne. Novel by Constance Fenimore Woolson (1882). The love story of the orphan Anne Douglas and Ward Heathcote, setting forth the awards of staunch character and high ideals.

Annie Kilburn. Novel by William Dean Howells (1888). The heroine returns to New England village life after long residence in Rome. Foreign culture changed her outwardly, but inwardly she remained a Puritan.

Anonyms; A Dictionary of Revealed Authorship. By William Cushing (1889). *See also* his *Initials and Pseudonyms,* 2v. (1885–88).

ANSHEN, MELVIN LEON (July 2, 1912–); b. Boston, Mass. Educator. *Modern Marketing* (with C. W. Barker, 1939); *An Introduction to Business* (1942); *Private Enterprise and Public Policy* (1954). Faculty, Carnegie Institute of Technology, since 1951.

ANSLEY, CLARKE FISHER (Dec. 29, 1869–Feb. 14, 1939); b. Swedona, Ill. Editor, educator. Editor: *The Columbia Encyclopedia* (1935). Editor-in-chief, Columbia University Press, 1937–39.

ANSPACHER, LOUIS KAUFMAN (Mar. 1, 1878–May 10, 1947); b. Cincinnati, O. Playwright. *Tristan and Isolde* (drama in verse, 1904); *A Woman of Impulse* (prod. 1909); *Our Children* (prod. 1915); *The Unchastened Woman* (1915); *All the King's Horses* (prod. 1919); *The Rhapsody* (prod. 1930); *This Bewildered Age* (1935); *Slow Harvest* (poems, 1943); *Challenge of the Unknown* (1947); etc.

Anthology Society. Boston, Mass. Founded Oct. 3, 1805 for the purpose of financing and supplying literary material for the newly organized *Monthly Anthology or Magazine of Polite Literature* (1803–1811). Founded by John Sylvester, William Emerson, and John Gardiner. Among the other members were

William Tudor, Joseph S. Buckminster, Nathan Hale, William Smith Shaw, George Ticknor, Samuel C. Thatcher, John T. Kirkland, etc. The society disbanded, July, 1811. Known also as The Anthology Club, and as A Society of Gentlemen. See *Journal of the Proceedings of the Society . . . October 3, 1805, to July 2, 1811,* ed. by M. A. De Wolfe Howe (1910).

ANTHON, CHARLES (Nov. 19, 1797–July 29, 1867); b. New York. Educator, classicist, author. *Classical Dictionary* (1841); and about fifty other classical school books.

ANTHONY, ANDREW VARICK STOUT (Dec. 4, 1835–July 2, 1906); b. New York City. Wood engraver. Illustrated John W. Palmer's *Folk Songs* (1860); Whittier's *Snow Bound* (1866); Longfellow's *Skeleton in Armor* (1877).

ANTHONY, EDWARD (Aug. 4, 1895–Sept. 13, 1971); b. New York City. Author. *Merry-Go-Roundelays* (1921); *The Pussycat Princess* (1922); *The Fairies Up-to-Date* (1923); *Bring 'Em Back Alive* (with Frank Buck, 1930); *Wild Cargo* (with same, 1932); *The Big Cage* (with Clyde Beatty, 1933); *Nowhere Else in the World* (with G. B. Enders, 1935); *Every Dog Has His Say* (poems, 1947); *Oddity Land* (1957); *This Is Where I Came In* (1960); *O Rare Don Marquis* (1962); *Facing the Big Cats* (1965).

ANTHONY, HENRY BOWEN (Apr. 1, 1815–Sept. 2, 1884); b. Coventry, R.I. Statesman, editor. Editor, *The Providence Journal,* 1838–59. A portion of his library known as the "Harris Collection of American Poetry" was bequeathed to Brown University. Governor of Rhode Island, 1849–50, U.S. Senator, 1859–84.

ANTHONY, JOSEPH (Apr. 9, 1897–); b. New York City. Editor, author. *Rekindled Fires* (1918); *The Gang* (1921); *The Golden Village* (1924); *Casanova Jones* (novel in verse, 1930); *A Ship Comes In* (play, 1934). Editor, *The Golden Book* magazine, 1934; *The Invisible Curtain* (1957).

ANTHONY, KATHARINE SUSAN (Nov. 27, 1877–Nov. 20, 1965); b. Roseville, Ark. Biographer. *A Psychological Biography* (1920); *Catherine the Great* (1925); *Queen Elizabeth* (1929); *Marie Antoinette* (1933); *Louisa May Alcott* (1938); *The Lambs* (1945); *Dolly Madison* (1949); *Susan B. Anthony* (1954).

ANTHONY, PIERS [Piers A.D. Jacobs] (1934–); b. in England. Author. *Chthon* (1967); *Sos the Rope* (1968); *Omnivore* (1968).

Anthony Adverse. Novel by Hervey Allen (1933). A composite picture of the merchant adventurers who came to America from Europe in our early days of expansion, concentrated in the picturesque personality of Anthony Adverse, ardent lover, bold businessman, and reckless adventurer.

Anti-Intellectualism in American Life. By Richard Hofstadter (1963). A critique of American society and culture which uses the idea of anti-intellectualism as a device for looking at the less attractive aspects of American life.

ANTIN, MARY (Mrs. Amadeus W. Grabau) (June 1881–Apr. 15, 1949); b. Polotzk, Russia. Essayist, *From Polotzk to Boston* (1899); *The Promised Land* (1912); *They Who Knock at Our Gates* (1914).

Antioch Review. Yellow Springs, O. Quarterly of articles, stories, and verse. Founded 1941. Noted for its scholarly essays in the humanities and social sciences. Edited by faculty members of Antioch College.

Antiquamania, Edited by Kenneth L. Roberts: The Collected Papers of Professor Milton Kilgallen. Illustrated by Booth Tarkington. Published 1928. A parody of books on collecting, based on the papers of an imaginary professor.

Antiworlds. Collection of poems by Andrei Voznesensky (1966). The translations of these poems from the Russian by W. H. Auden, Richard Wilbur, Stanley J. Kunitz, William Jay

Smith, and others represents one of the most successful attempts of this kind made in recent decades.

ANTRIM, MINNA THOMAS (b. 1861); b. Philadelphia, Pa. Author. *Naked Truths and Veiled Allusions* (1901); *Wisdom of the Foolish* (1903); *Sweethearts and Beaux* (1905); etc.

Apache Gold and Yaqui Silver. By J. Frank Dobie (1939). Folk-stories of Texas and the Southwest, and an account of buried Spanish treasure.

Apartment in Athens. Novel by Glenway Wescott (1945). A Nazi officer billeted with a Greek family during the German occupation of World War II. The family decides to participate in the resistance movement.

Ape, the Idiot, and Other People, The. Tales by W. C. Morrow (1897).

APEL, WILLI (Oct. 10, 1893–); b. Konitz, Ger. Musicologist. Author: *The Notation of Polyphonic Music, 900–1600* (1942); *Harvard Dictionary of Music* (1944); *Masters of the Keyboard* (1947); *Gregorian Chant* (1958). Editor: *Historical Anthology of Music,* 2v. (1946, 1950). *Essays in Musicology* (with H. Tischler, 1968). Prof. music, Indiana University, 1950–64.

APES, WILLIAM (b. Jan. 31, 1798); b. Colrain, Mass. Pequot Indian, missionary, author. *A Son of the Forest* (autobiography, 1829); *The Experiences of Five Christian Indians; or, The Indian's Looking-Glass for the White Man* (1833); *Eulogy on King Philip* (1836).

Apostle, The. Novel by Sholem Asch (1943). Based on the life of St. Paul, this novel interprets Christianity as a clear outgrowth of Judaism.

APP, AUSTIN JOSEPH (May 24, 1902–); b. Milwaukee, Wis. Author. *History's Most Terrifying Peace* (1946); *The True Concept of Literature* (1949); *The Way to Creative Writing* (1954); *Making the Later Years Count* (1960). Co-founder, with Eugene P. Willging, *Best Sellers, 1941.*

Appeal to Reason. Girard, Kan. Socialist journal. Founded 1897, by J. A. Wayland. Taken over by E. Haldeman-Julius in 1912. Name changed to *Haldeman-Julius Weekly* in 1922, later to *The New Appeal,* and then to *The American Freeman.*

APPEL, BENJAMIN (Sept. 13, 1907–); b. New York City. Author. *Brain Guy* (1937); *The Dark Stain* (1943); *Fortress in the Rice* (1951); *We Were There at the Battle for Bataan* (1957); *The Raw Edge* (1958); *Shepherd of the Sun* (1961); *The Illustrated Book About South America* (1963); *Why the Russians Are the Way They Are* (1966); *Why the Chinese Are the Way They Are* (1968); *Age of Dictators* (1968).

APPEL, JOSEPH HERBERT (July 19, 1873–July 26, 1949); b. Lancaster, Pa. Merchant, author. *My Own Story* (1912); *Seeing America* (1916); *Living the Creative Life* (1918); *A World Cruise Log* (1926); *John Wanamaker; A Study* (1927); *Africa's White Magic* (1928); etc.

Appledore Island. Isles of Shoals. Thomas B. Laighton opened a summer hotel here in 1848. It became the haunt of James Russell Lowell, Henry David Thoreau, John Greenleaf Whittier, Childe Hassam, and others. Laighton's daughter, Celia Thaxter, has written about it in her *Among the Isles of Shoals* (1873). *See also* Willis Boyd Allen's *Kelp: A Story of the Isles of Shoals* (1888); and James R. Lowell's poems on Appledore in *The Crayon,* 1855.

APPLEGARTH, MARGARET [Tyson] (July 8, 1886–); b. New Brunswick, N.J. Novelist. *Lamp-Lighters Across the Sea* (1920); *At the Foot of the Rainbow* (1930); *Right Here, Right Now!* (1950); *Men as Trees Walking* (1952); *Moment by Moment* (1955); *Twelve Baskets Full* (1957); *Heirlooms* (1966).

APPLEGATE, FRANK GUY (Feb. 9, 1882–Feb. 13, 1932); b. Atlanta, Ill. Artist, educator, author. *Indian Stories from the Pueblos* (1929); *Native Tales of New Mexico* (1932).

APPLEGATE, JESSE (July 5, 1811–Apr. 22, 1888); b. in Kentucky. Surveyor, publicist, author. *A Day with the Cow Column in 1843* (1877); *Recollections of My Boyhood* (1914).

APPLEMAN, JOHN ALAN (May 14, 1912–); b. Webster Groves, Mo. Lawyer. Author: *Automobile Liability Insurance* (1938); *Military Tribunals and International Crimes* (1954); *Approved Appellate Briefs* (1958); *How to Increase Your Money-Making Power* (1959); etc. Editor: *Successful Jury Trials* (1952); etc.

Appleseed, Johnny. Nickname of John Chapman.

APPLETON, DANIEL (Dec. 10, 1785–Mar. 27, 1849); b. Haverhill, Mass. Founded publishing house of D. Appleton & Co., N.Y. 1825. Published first book in 1831. *See* G. M. Overton's *Portrait of a Publisher* (1925).

APPLETON, EMILY. Novelist. *Alice Mannering; or, The Nobleman's Son* (1845); *The Miser's Daughter; or, The Coined Heart* (1846).

APPLETON, THOMAS GOLD (Mar. 31, 1812–Apr. 17, 1884); b. Boston, Mass. Essayist, poet, artist. *Faded Leaves* (poems, 1872); *Fresh Leaves* (poems, 1874); *A Sheaf of Papers* (1875); *Windfalls* (1878); *Chequer-Work* (1879). *See* Susan Hale's *Life and Letters of Thomas Gold Appleton* (1885).

Appleton, Victor. Pen name of Edward L. Stratemeyer.

Appleton, Victor II. Pen name under which Tom Swift, Jr., Books have been written since 1954.

APPLETON, WILLIAM HENRY (Jan. 27, 1814–Oct. 19, 1899); b. Haverhill, Mass. Became partner in D. Appleton & Co. in 1838. Co-founder, *Popular Science Monthly,* 1872. He was largely responsible for *Appleton's Cyclopedia of Biography.*

APPLETON, WILLIAM WORTHEN (Nov. 29, 1845–Jan. 27, 1924); b. Brooklyn, N.Y. Publisher with D. Appleton & Co., and was responsible for the American editions of Carroll's *Alice's Adventures in Wonderland;* the *International Education Series* under editorship of W. T. Harris. Prominent in promoting idea of circulating libraries. *See* G. M. Overton's *Portrait of a Publisher* (1925).

Appleton-Century-Crofts. New York. Publishers. Founded 1825, by Daniel Appleton, who opened a general store which featured books, among other things. In 1831 he began to publish books as D. Appleton & Co. The first book published was *Crumbs from the Master's Table,* measuring three inches square. On Appleton's death in 1849 his four sons, headed by William H. Appleton, took over the business. The firm was noted for such reference works as *New American Cyclopedia, Appleton's Cyclopedia of American Biography,* and *Picturesque America.* Thirty-five million copies of *Webster's Blue-Back Speller* were sold from 1855 to 1890. Appleton published the first American edition of *Alice in Wonderland.* A popular series of novels was called *Appleton's Town and Country Library,* started in 1888, which reached 312 volumes. The firm issued the magazine *Appleton's Journal* (1869–81) and founded, in May, 1872, *The Popular Science Monthly,* which was taken over by McClure, Phillips & Company in 1900. In 1933 the Century Company, founded 1881, merged with D. Appleton & Co. to form the D. Appleton-Century Company; in 1948 a consolidation was effected with F. S. Crofts Co., founded 1924, to form Appleton-Century-Crofts. Allan W. Ferrin is president. The firm was bought by Meredith Publishing Co.

Appleton's Annual Cyclopaedia. New York, 1862–1903. Edited by William Jewett Tenney, 1861–84, who was followed by Rossiter Johnson. The first 15 volumes (1861–76) appeared under the name *American Annual Encyclopaedia.*

Appleton's Cyclopaedia of American Biography. Ed. by James Grant Wilson and John Fiske, 6v. (1887–89). Six supplementary volumes, by various editors, were published.

Appleton's Journal. New York. Literary magazine. Founded Apr. 3, 1869, by D. Appleton & Company. Editors, Edward Livingston Youmans, 1869–70; Robert Carter, 1870–72; Oliver Bell Bunce and Charles Henry Jones, 1872–81. Started as a scientific journal, it soon developed into a literary one. William Cullen Bryant's "Picturesque America" was an early feature, and "Table Talk" was a popular department. It began as a weekly and became a monthly in 1876. Stressing original articles by American authors at first, it became an eclectic magazine with emphasis on English, French, and German articles. Expired Dec. 1881. *See* F. L. Mott's *A History of American Magazines,* v.3 (1938).

Appointment in Samarra. Novel by John O'Hara (1934). A quick-moving narrative, realistic in every detail, about high-living members of a Pennsylvania social set.

Approach. Rosemont, Pa. Quarterly. Founded 1947. Published verse, fiction, critical articles. Suspended 1967.

"April is the cruellest month." First words of *The Waste Land* (1922) by T. S. Eliot.

APTHEKER, HERBERT (1915–); Historian. *The Negro in the Abolitionist Movement* (1941); *American Negro Slave Revolts* (1943); *Essays in the History of the American Negro* (1945); *History and Reality* (1955); *The Colonial Era* (1959); *Dare We Be Free?* (1961); *Soul of the Republic* (1964). Editor: *A Documentary History of the Negro* (1969).

APTHORP, WILLIAM FOSTER (Oct. 24, 1848–Feb. 19, 1912); b. Boston, Mass. Music and drama critic. *Musicians and Music Lovers* (1894); *By the Way* (1898); *The Opera, Past and Present* (1901); etc. Editor (with J. D. Champlin, Jr.): Scribner's *Cyclopedia of Music and Musicians,* 3v. Music editor, *Atlantic Monthly;* Boston *Transcript.*

ARBAUGH, GEORGE BARTHOLOMEW (Dec. 28, 1905–); b. Frankfort, Ind. Lutheran clergyman, educator. *Revelation in Mormonism* (1932), *Growth of a Christian* (1953); *Gods, Sex and Saints* (1957); *Kierkegaard's Authorship* (1967). Prof. philosophy and psychology, Augustana College, since 1945.

Archer, Lane. Pen name of Louise Platt Hauck.

Archibald, Mrs. George. *See* Anna Campbell Palmer.

Archy and Mehitabel. Humorous verse by Don Marquis (1927). The doings and sayings of a cockroach named Archy.

Arcturus: A Journal of Books and Opinions, The. New York. Monthly magazine. Founded Dec. 1840, by Cornelius Mathews and Evert A. Duyckinck. Hawthorne and Longfellow were contributors. Contained much literary criticism by William A. Jones. Expired May 1842.

ARDREY, ROBERT (1908–); b. Chicago, Ill. Playwright, author. *Star Spangled* (prod. 1936); *How to Get Tough About It* (prod. 1938); *Casey Jones* (prod. 1938); *Thunder Rock* (prod. 1939); *Worlds Beginning* (1944); *Jeb* (prod. 1946); *Brotherhood of Fear* (1952); *Sing Me No Lullaby* (prod. 1954); *Shadow of Heroes* (prod. 1961); *African Genesis* (1961); *Territorial Imperative* (1966).

Are You Running with Me, Jesus? A book of prayers by Malcolm Boyd (1965). The prayers are couched in the words and conveyed according to the feelings of social activists.

ARENDT, HANNAH (Oct. 14, 1906–); b. Hanover, Ger. Political scientist, philosopher. *The Origins of Totalitarianism* (1951); *The Human Condition* (1958); *Between Past and Future* (1961); *Eichmann in Jerusalem* (1963); *On Revolution* (1963), *Men in Dark Times* (1968). Prof. philosophy, Princeton University, since 1959.

ARENSBERG, CONRAD MAYNADIER (Sept. 12, 1910–); b. Pittsburgh, Pa. Anthropologist, sociologist. *Irish Country-man* (1936); *Family and Community in Ireland* (with S. T. Kimball, 1946); *Measuring Human Relations* (with Eliot D. Chapple, 1940); *Culture and Community* (with Solon T. Kimball, 1965); *Introducing Social Change* (with Arthur Niehoff, 1964). Editor: *Research in Industrial Human Relations* (with others, 1957). Prof. anthropology, Columbia University, since 1953.

ARENSBERG, WALTER CONRAD (Apr. 4, 1878–Jan. 29, 1954); b. Pittsburgh, Pa. Author. *Poems* (1914); *Idols* (1916); *The Louise and Walter Arensberg Collection,* 2v. (with wife, 1954); and many books on the Bacon-Shakespeare controversy.

AREY, HARRIET ELLEN GRANNISS (b. Apr. 14, 1819); b. Cavendish, O. Editor, poet. *Household Songs, and Other Poems* (1855). Editor, Beadle's *Youth's Casket,* and *Home Monthly,* 1856–58.

AREY, LESLIE BRAINERD (Feb. 15, 1891–); b. Camden, Me. Anatomist. *Developmental Anatomy* (1954); *Human Histology* (1957). Prof. anatomy, Northwestern University Medical School, 1919–56.

Argonaut, The. San Francisco, Cal.; Burlingame, Cal. Weekly journal. Founded Apr., 1877, by Frank M. Pixley and Fred M. Somers.

Argosy. New York. Monthly. Founded 1882, by Frank Munsey, as *Golden Argosy,* a magazine for young people. Name was changed to *The Argosy* in 1888, when it became a fiction magazine. Among its contributors were Jack London, Edgar Rice Burroughs, and O. Henry. In 1920 it became *Argosy All-Story Weekly,* after merging with *All-Story Weekly.* In 1929 it was merged with *Munsey's Magazine* as *All-Story Combined with Munsey's.* It was revitalized in 1942 as *New Argosy* but sold the same year to Popular Publications, Inc., and appeared as *Argosy,* featuring men's action stories as well as book condensations.

Ariel. Collection of poems by Sylvia Plath (1966).

Arion. Austin, Tex. Quarterly. Founded 1962. Published at the University of Texas. Concerned with classical studies. William Arrowsmith, D. S. Carne-Ross, and others helped edit the publication.

Arizona Quarterly. Tucson, Ariz. Quarterly of poetry, fiction, and articles. Founded 1945. Published at the University of Arizona. Contributors have included Wallace Stevens, Randall Jarrell, and Yvor Winters.

Arizona Republic. Phoenix, Ariz. Newspaper. Founded 1890. Now combined with the *Phoenix Gazette.* Publishes rotogravure Sunday magazine, "Arizona Days and Ways," and separate section, "Sun Living."

Ark, The. San Francisco, Calif. Founded 1947. Literary quarterly.

Arkansas Gazette, The. Little Rock, Ark. Founded at Arkansas Post, Nov. 20, 1819, by William Edward Woodruff (1795–1885). Probably the first newspaper published west of the Mississippi. Woodruff sold the paper in 1838, repurchased it in 1841. In 1846 he founded the *Arkansas Democrat* and combined it with the *Gazette* in 1860. The *Gazette* moved to Little Rock in 1821. Frederick W. Allsopp (q.v.) was with the *Gazette* from 1884 (and publisher, 1896–1946). John Netherland Heiskell became editor in 1902.

Arkansas Traveler, The. Little Rock, Ark. Comic magazine. Founded 1882, by Opie Read. He moved it to Chicago in 1888. Expired 1916.

ARLEN, MICHAEL J. (Dec. 9, 1930–); b. London, Eng. Television critic, author. *Living-Room War* (1969); *Exiles* (1970). Television critic, *The New Yorker* magazine.

ARLING, EMANIE NAHM; b. Bowling Green, Ky. Author. *Talk* (1924); *Red Damask* (1926); *The Terrible Siren—Victoria Woodhull* (1929); *The Octangle* (1930).

ARLT, GUSTAV OTTO (May 17, 1895–); b. Lock Haven, Pa. Educator. Translator; Franz Werfel's *Jacobowsky and the Colonel* (1944), *Star of the Unborn* (1946). Editor, *Modern Language Forum, 1937–42;* associate editor, *California Folklore,* since 1942. Prof. German, University of California at Los Angeles, since 1935.

Armed Services Editions. Inexpensive, lightweight paperbacks issued to members of the armed forces during World War II. Created 1943 by the Council of Books in Wartime (1942–46), which was sponsored by the Book Publishers' Bureau and various library, educational, and booksellers' organizations. The Armed Services Editions totaled 108,500,000 copies in more than 1,000 titles, ranging from classics to light fiction and mystery stories.

ARMER, LAURA [Adams] (Jan. 12, 1874–Mar. 3, 1963); b. Sacramento, Calif. Author. *Waterless Mountain* (1931); *Southwest* (1935); *The Forest Pool* (1938); etc.

ARMES, ETHEL MARIE; b. Washington, D.C. Author. *Midsummer in Whittier's Country* (1909); *Stratford Hall, the Great House of the Lees* (1936). Editor: *Nancy Shippen: Her Journal Book* (1935).

ARMITAGE, MERLE (Feb. 12, 1893–); b. Mason City, Ia. Impresario, author. *Post-Caviar: Barnstorming with Russian Grand Opera* (1939); *Accent on America* (1944); *Railroads of America* (1952); *George Gershwin* (1958); *Stella Dysart of Ambrosia Lake* (1959); *Pagans, Conquistadores, Heroes and Martyrs* (1964); *Accent on Life* (1965); *Martha Graham* (1966); *Dance Memoranda* (1969).

ARMOUR, RICHARD [Willard] (July 15, 1906–); b. San Pedro, Cal. Educator. *Yours for the Asking* (poems, 1942); *Golf Bawls* (poems, 1946); *For Partly Proud Parents* (poems, 1950); *It All Started with Columbus* (1953); *It All Started with Europa* (1955); *It All Started with Eve* (1956); *Twisted Tales from Shakespeare* (1957); *Nights with Armour* (poems, 1958); *Drug Store Days* (1959); *Classics Reclassified* (1960); *Golf Is a Four-Letter Word* (1962); *Armour's Almanac* (1962); *Through Darkest Adolescence* (1963); *Our Presidents* (1964); *Going Around in Academic Circles* (1965); *A Dozen Dinosaurs* (1968); *English Lit & Relit* (1969); *It All Started with Hippocrates* (1966); *On Your Marks* (1969). Prof. English, Scripps College and Claremont Graduate School, since 1945.

ARMS, GEORGE WARREN (Feb. 1, 1912–); b. LaGrande, Ore. Educator. *The Fields Were Green* (1953). Compiler: *A Bibliography of William Dean Howells* (with W. M. Gibson, 1948); *Poetry Explication: A Checklist* (with J. M. Kuntz, 1950). Editor: *Symposium* (with L. G. Locke, 1954); *Twelve American Writers* (with William Gibson, 1962). Editor, *The Explicator,* since 1942. Prof. English, University of New Mexico, since 1945.

ARMSTRONG, A. JOSEPH (Mar. 29, 1873–Mar. 31, 1954); b. Louisville, Ky. Educator, author: *Operatic Performances in England Before Handel* (1918); *Browning Through French Eyes* (1932). Editor: *Baylor Browning Interests,* 5 series; Vachel Lindsay's *Letters to A. Joseph Armstrong* (1940). Donor of Browning Collection to Baylor University. Head, English dept., Baylor University, 1912–52; director, Armstrong-Browning Library, since 1952.

ARMSTRONG, CHARLOTTE (May 2, 1905–July 19, 1969); b. Vulcan, Mich. Author. *Ring Around Elizabeth* (play, 1942); *Lay on Mac Duff!* (1942); *The Innocent Flower* (1945); *The Chocolate Cobweb* (1948); *The Black-Eyed Stranger* (1951); *The Better to Eat You* (1954); *Duo* (1959); *The Seventeen Widows of Sans Souci* (1959); *A Little Less Than Kind* (1963); *The Witch's House* (1963); *The Turret Room* (1965); *I See You* (1966); *Lemon in the Basket* (1967); *The Balloon Man* (1968); *Seven Seats to the Moon* (1969).

ARMSTRONG, HAMILTON FISH (Apr. 7, 1893–); b. New York City. Editor, author: *The New Balkans* (1926); *Where the East Begins* (1929); *Hitler's Reich: The First Phase* (1933); *Europe Between Wars* (1934); *We or They* (1937); *The Calculated Risk* (1947); *Tito and Goliath* (1951); *Those Days* (1963). Editor, *Foreign Affairs*, since 1928.

ARMSTRONG, HAROLD HUNTER (Apr. 9, 1884–); b. Morenci, Mich. Novelist. Pen name, "Henry G. Aikman." *The Groper* (1919); *Zell* (1921); *For Richer, For Poorer* (1922); *The Red-Blood* (1923).

ARMSTRONG, MARGARET NEILSEN (Sept. 24, 1867–July 18, 1944); b. New York. Author. *Five Generations* (1930); *Fanny Kemble: A Passionate Victorian* (1938); *Murder in Stained Glass* (1939); *Trelawney* (1940); *The Blue Santo Murder Mystery* (1941); etc.

ARMSTRONG, PAUL (Apr. 25, 1869–Aug. 30, 1915); b. Kidder, Mo. Journalist, playwright. Pen Name "Right Cross." *The Heir to the Hoorah* (1905); *Ann Lamont* (1905); *St. Ann: In a Blaze of Glory* (1906); *For a Woman* (1909); *Alias Jimmy Valentine* (1909); etc.

ARMSTRONG, ROBERT ALLEN (Sept. 23, 1860–Sept. 15, 1936); b. Frenchton, Va. (now W. Va.). Educator, author. *Life Out of Death* (1906); *The Law of Service* (1907); *Dramatic Interpretation of Shakespeare's Tragedies* (1907). Prof. English, West Virginia University, 1901–36.

ARMSTRONG, WILLIAM (1856–May 18, 1942); b. in Frederick Co., Md. Author. *Thekla: A Story of Viennese Musical Life* (1887); *An American Nobleman: A Story of the Canaan Wilderness* (1892); *The Romantic World of Music* (1922).

ARNETT, ALEX MATHEWS (Feb. 13, 1888–Aug. 7, 1945); b. Sylvania, Ga. Educator, historian. *Story of North Carolina* (1933); *The South Looks at Its Past* (with B. B. Kendrick, 1935); etc.

ARNHEIM, RUDOLF (July 5, 1904–); b. Berlin. Educator, author. *Art and Visual Perception* (1954); *Film as Art* (1957); *Picasso's Guernica* (1962); *Toward a Psychology of Art* (1966). Faculty, Sarah Lawrence College.

ARNO, PETER (Jan. 8, 1904–Feb. 22, 1968); b. (Curtis A. Peters, Jr.) New York City. Illustrator. Most of his humorous illustrations have appeared in *The New Yorker.* Among published collections of his cartoons are *Peter Arno's Circus* (1931); *Peter Arno's Favorites* (1932); *Whoops Dearie!* (1937); *Man in the Shower* (1944); *Sizzling Platter* (1949); etc.

Arnold, Birch. Pen name of Alice Elinor Bartlett.

ARNOLD, ELLIOTT (Sept. 13, 1912–); b. New York. Author. *Two Loves* (1934); *Personal Combat* (1936); *Only the Young* (1939); *Finlandia* (1941); *The Commandos* (1942); *Mediterranean Sweep* (with Richard Thruelsen, 1944); *Big Distance* (with Donald Hough, 1945); *Blood Brother* (1947); *Everybody Slept Here* (1948); *Deep in My Heart* (1949); *Walk with the Devil* (1950); *Time of the Gringo* (1953); *Broken Arrow* (1954); *White Falcon* (1955); *Flight from Ashiya* (1959); *A Night of Watching* (1967); *A Kind of Secret Weapon* (1969); *Forests of the Night* (1971).

ARNOLD, GEORGE (June 24, 1834–Nov. 9, 1865); b. New York City. Journalist, poet. Pen names, "Graham Allen," "Pierrot." *Drift: A Sea-Shore Idyl and Other Poems* (1866); *Poems Grave and Gay* (1867); *"McArone Papers"* (1860–65); *Poems* (1871). Author of the popular poem, "The Jolly Old Pedagogue." The "McArone Papers" began in *Vanity Fair,* Nov. 24, 1860, continued in the *Leader,* and concluded in the *Weekly Review,* Oct. 14, 1865.

ARNOLD, HENRY HARLEY [Hap] (June 25, 1886–Jan. 15, 1950); b. Gladwyne, Pa. Soldier, author. *Bill Bruce* series (1928); *Airmen and Aircraft* (1926). Co-author (with Ira Eaker): *This Flying Game* (1936); *Winged Warfare* (1941); *Army Flyer* (1942).

ARNOLD, JOSIAS LYNDON (1768–1796). Poet. *Poems* (1797).

ARNOLD, THURMAN WESLEY (June 2, 1891–); b. Laramie, Wyo. Lawyer, author. *The Symbols of Government* (1935); *The Folklore of Capitalism* (1937); *The Bottlenecks of Business* (1940); *Democracy and Free Enterprise* (1942); *Fair Fights and Foul—A Dissenting Lawyer's Life* (1965); etc. Prof. law, Yale University, 1931–38.

ARNOLD, WILLIAM HARRIS (Mar. 18, 1854–Jan. 2, 1923); b. Poughkeepsie, N.Y. Book collector, author. *First Report of a Book-Collector* (1897–98); *Record of American First Editions* (1901); *A Record of Books and Letters* (1901); *Ventures in Book Collecting* (1923).

ARNOW, HARRIETTE [Louisa Simpson] (July 7, 1908–); b. Wayne Co., Ky. Novelist. *Mountain Path* (1936); *Hunter's Horn* (1949); *The Dollmaker* (1954); *Seedtime on the Cumberland* (1960); *Flowering of the Cumberland* (1963). *Weedkiller's Daughter* (1970).

ARNY, CLARA MAUDE BROWN (June 19, 1888–); b. Grand Island, Neb. Home economist. Author (as Clara Maude Brown): *Evaluation and Investigation in Home Economics* (1941); *The Effectiveness of the High School Program in Home Economics* (1952); *Evaluation in Home Economics* (1953). Prof. home economics, University of Minnesota, 1938–53.

ARNY, MARY TRAVIS (Oct. 13, 1909–); b. Montclair, N.J. Educator, author. *Seasoned with Salt* (1954); *A Goodly Heritage* (1963); *A Common Sense Garden Guide* (1964); *Zoology* (1966); etc. Biology dept., Montclair State Teacher College, since 1955.

Arp, Bill. Pen name of Charles Henry Smith.

ARQUETTE, CLIFF (1906?–). Author. Writes under pen name "Charley Weaver." *Charley Weaver's Letters from Mama* (1959); *Things Are Fine in Mount Idy* (1960); etc.

ARRINGTON, ALFRED W. (Sept. 17, 1810–Dec. 31, 1867); b. Iredell Co., N.C. Lawyer, journalist, poet. Pen name, "Charles Summerfield." *The Desperadoes of the South-West* (1847), republished as, *The Lives and Adventures of the Desperadoes of the South-West* (1849), and as, *Illustrated Lives and Adventures of the Desperadoes of the New World* (1849); *The Rangers and Regulators of the Tanaba* (1856); *Poems by Alfred W. Arrington* (1869).

ARROW, KENNETH J[oseph] (Aug. 23, 1921–); b. New York. Economist. Author: *Social Choice and Individual Values* (1951); *Studies in the Mathematical Theory of Inventory and Production* (with others, 1958); *Studies in Linear and Non-Linear Programming* (1959). Prof. economics and statistics, Stanford University, since 1953.

"Arrow and the Song, The." Poem by Henry Wadsworth Longfellow (1845).

ARROWOOD, CHARLES FLINN (Nov. 9, 1887–Feb. 6, 1951); b. in Cabarrus Co., N.C. Educator, author. *Thomas Jefferson and Education in a Republic* (1930); *Development of Modern Education* (with F. Eby, 1934); *The History and Philosophy of Education* (with same, 1939); etc. Editor, translator: George Buchanan's *The Powers of the Crown in Scotland* (1949). Dept. of education, University of Texas, from 1926.

Arrowsmith. Novel by Sinclair Lewis (1925). Based on the medical profession. Arrowsmith, a dreamer, is concerned with pure science rather than making money, and his important discovery in the field of bacteriology is ironically the cause of tragedy and unhappiness.

ARROWSMITH, WILLIAM (Apr. 13, 1924–). b. Orange, N.J. Translator, editor. Translator: Petronius' *Satyricon* (1959); Aristophanes' *The Birds* (1961); Aristophanes' *The*

Clouds (1962). Editor: *Craft and Context of Translation* (with Roger Shattuck, 1961); *Five Modern Italian Novels* (1964). Editor, *Hudson Review.*

"Ars Poetica." Poem by Archibald MacLeish (1926).

"Arsenal at Springfield, The." Poem by Henry Wadsworth Longfellow, in *Graham's Magazine,* Apr., 1844.

Art of Courting, The. By Ebenezer Bradford, published anonymously (1795). Described in a series of letters.

ARTHUR, TIMOTHY SHAY (June 6, 1809–Mar. 6, 1885); b. Newburgh, N.Y. Editor, author. *Married and Single* (1843); *The Lady at Home* (1847); *Ten Nights in a Bar Room* (1854); *Madeline* (1855); *Three Years in a Man-Trap* (1872); *Cast Adrift* (1873); *Strong Drink* (1877); etc. An extensive list of these temperance novels is given in Lyle H. Wright's *American Fiction, 1774–1850* (1939). Founder, *Arthur's Home Gazette,* 1850; *Arthur's Home Magazine,* 1852; *The Children's Hour,* 1867; etc. Editor, *Baltimore Athenaeum; Baltimore Saturday Visitor.* A voluminous contributor to *Godey's Lady's Book; Graham's Magazine;* etc.

Arthur Mervyn. Novel by Charles Brockden Brown (1799). A country boy comes to Philadelphia, blunders into the secret of a murder, and is persecuted by the murderer. The yellow-fever plague in Philadelphia serves as a background.

Arts and Letters. New Orleans, La. Illustrated magazine. Founded 1887, and edited by Mary Ashley Townsend and Mary E. Moore Davis.

Arts in Society. Madison, Wis. Three times a year. Founded 1958. Published by Research Studies and Development in the Arts, University Extension, University of Wisconsin. Devoted to the advancement of education in the arts and the augmenting of the arts in society. Edited by Edward L. Kamarck.

ARTZ, FREDERICK BINKERD (Oct. 19, 1894–); b. Dayton, O. Educator, historian. *Reaction and Revolution, 1814–32* (1934); *The Intellectual History of Europe from St. Augustine to Marx: A Guide* (1941); *The Mind of the Middle Ages, 200–1500 A.D.: An Historical Survey* (1953); *France Under the Bourbon Restoration (1814–1830)* (1963); *From the Renaissance to Romanticism* (1963). Prof. history, Oberlin College, since 1934.

ARTZYBASHEFF, BORIS MICHAILOVITCH (May 25, 1899–July 16, 1965); b. Kharkov, Russia. Artist, author. *Poor Shaydullah* (1931); *Seven Simeons: a Russian Tale* (1937); *As I See* (1954); etc. Editor: *Aesop's Fables* (1933). Illustrator of books by Padraic Colum, Alfred Kreymborg, Rabindranath Tagore, Edmund Wilson; etc.

ARVIN, NEWTON (Aug. 23, 1900–Mar. 24, 1963); b. Valparaiso, Ind. Educator. *Hawthorne* (1929); *Whitman* (1938); *Herman Melville* (1950); *Longfellow: His Life and Work* (1963). Editor: *The Heart of Hawthorne's Journals* (1929); *Hawthorne's Short Stories* (1946); *The Selected Letters of Henry Adams* (1952). Prof. English, Smith College, 1940–60.

As a Man Thinks. Play by Augustus Thomas (prod. 1911). Concerns conventional morality and race prejudice.

As I Lay Dying. Novel by William Faulkner (1930). The children of Addie Bundren journey with her dead body, laid in its coffin, to bury her in her native town, Jefferson, Mississippi.

"As I Like It." Literary column conducted by William Lyon Phelps in *Scribner's Magazine,* 1922–36. Selections were reprinted in book form in three series, 1923, 1924, 1926.

ASBURY, FRANCIS (Aug. 20/21. 1745–Mar. 31, 1816); b. near Birmingham, England. Methodist bishop, author. *The Journal,* 3v. (1821). See *The Heart of Asbury's Journal,* ed. by Ezra S. Tipple (1904). *See also* William P. Strickland's *The Pioneer Bishop* (1858); Ezra S. Tipple's *Francis Asbury* (1916); Herbert Asbury's *A Methodist Saint* (1927); William Duren's *Francis Asbury* (1928).

ASBURY, HERBERT (Sept. 1, 1891–Feb. 24, 1963); b. Farmington, Mo. Journalist, author. *Up from Methodism* (1926); *A Methodist Saint* (1921); *The Gangs of New York* (1928); *Carrie Nation* (1929); *Ye Olde Fire Laddies* (1930); *The Barbary Coast* (1933); *The French Quarter* (1936); *Gem of the Prairie* (1940); *The Golden Flood* (1942); *The Great Illusion* (1950); etc.

ASCAP, *See* American Society of Composers, Authors and Publishers.

ASCH, NATHAN (July 10, 1902–Dec. 23, 1964); b. Warsaw, Poland. Author. *The Office* (1925); *Love in Chartres* (1927); *Pay Day* (1930); *The Valley* (1925); *The Road: In Search of America* (1937).

ASCH, SHALOM [Sholem] (Nov. 1, 1880–July 10, 1957); b. Kutno, Poland. Yiddish author. Translations of his books have been published as: *The God of Vengeance* (1918); *Three Cities* (1933); *Mother* (1937); *Three Novels* (1938); *The Nazarene* (1939); *The Apostle* (1943); *East River* (1946); *Mary* (1949); *Moses* (1951); *The Prophet* (1955); etc.

ASCHAM, JOHN BAYNE (Feb. 12, 1873–Nov. 14, 1957); b. Vanlue, O. Methodist clergyman, author. *Help from the Hills* (1910); *A Syrian Pilgrimage* (1914); *The Religion of Israel* (1918); *Apostles, Fathers, and Reformers* (1921); etc.

ASCOLI, MAX (June 25, 1898–); b. Ferrara, It. Editor, author. *Intelligence in Politics* (1936); *Fascism for Whom* (with Arthur Feiler, 1938); *The Power of Freedom* (1949). Editor: *The Fall of Mussolini* (1948); *The Best of the Reporter* (1960). Founder, *The Reporter,* 1949; editor, 1949–68. Grad. faculty, New School for Social Research, since 1933.

Ash, Peter. Pen name of Louise Platt Hauck.

ASHBERY, JOHN (July 28, 1927–); b. Rochester, N. Y. Poet, playwright. *The Heroes* (prod. 1953), *Some Trees* (1956); *The Compromise* (prod. 1956); *Selected Poems* (1967); *A Nest of Ninnies* (with James Schuyler, 1969).

Ashe, Penelope. See *Naked Came the Stranger.*

ASHE, SAMUEL A'COURT (Sept. 13, 1840–Aug. 31, 1938); b. Wrightsville Sound, N.C. Lawyer, historian. Editor: *Biographical History of North Carolina from Colonial Times to the Present,* 8v. (1905–1917); *History of North Carolina,* 2v. (1908–1925).

ASHEIM, LESTER EUGENE (Jan. 22, 1914–); b. Spokane, Wash. Librarian, educator. *The Library's Public* (with Bernard Berelson, 1949); *Humanities and the Library* (with others, 1957); *Librarianship in the Developing Countries* (1966). Editor: *The Core of Education for Librarianship* (1954); *The Future of the Book* (1955); *Persistent Issues in American Librarianship* (1961). Faculty, University of Chicago, since 1948.

"Ashes of Glory, The." Poem by Augustus Julian Requier. Martial lyric, in reply to "The Conquered Banner," by Abram J. Ryan.

ASHLEY, CLIFFORD WARREN (Dec. 18, 1881–Sept. 18, 1947); b. New Bedford, Mass. Marine artist, author. *The Yankee Whaler* (1926); *Whaleships of New Bedford* (1929); *The Ashley Book of Knots* (1944); etc.

ASHLEY, FREDERICK WILLIAM (Jan. 12, 1863–June 14, 1943); b. Mansfield, O. Librarian, author. *Three Eras in the Library of Congress* (1929); *In Praise of Print* (1934); *Story of the Vollbehr Collection of Incunabula* (1934); *History of the Library of Congress, 1897–1939* (1939); etc. Compiler: *Catalogue of the John Boyd Thacher Collection of Incunabula* (1915). With Library of Congress, 1900–36.

ASHMORE, HARRY S[COTT] (July 28, 1916–); b. Greenville, S.C. Editor, author. *The Negro and the Schools* (1954); *An Epitaph for Dixie* (1958); *The Other Side of Jordan* (1960); *The Man in the Middle* (1966); *Mission to Hanoi: A Chronicle of Double Dealing in High Places* (with W. C. Baggs 1968). Executive editor, *Arkansas Gazette*, since 1948 (Pulitzer prize for editorial writing, 1958).

ASHMUN, MARGARET ELIZA (d. Mar. 13, 1940); b. Rural, Wis. Author. The *Isabel Carlton* series, 5v. (1916–19); *Topless Towers* (1921); *The Lake* (1924); *Brenda Stays at Home* (1926); *David and the Bear Man* (1929); *The Singing Swan* (1931); etc.

ASHTON, DORE (May 21, 1928–); b. Newark, N.J. Art critic, educator. *Abstract Art Before Columbus* (1957); *The Unknown Shore* (1962); *Modern American Sculpture* (1966). Art critic, *The New York Times;* associate art critic, *The New York Times,* 1955–60. Head, Humanities division, School of Visual Arts, since 1965.

Asia. New York. Monthly magazine of literature and travel. Founded 1898. It was first called the *Journal of the American Asiatic Association.* Discontinued 1917.

ASIMOV, ISAAC (Jan. 2, 1920–); b. Petrovichi, U.S.S.R. Author. *Pebble in the Sky* (1950); *I, Robot* (1950); *The Stars, Like Dust* (1951); *David Starr, Space Ranger* (under pen name "Paul French," 1952); *Foundation and Empire* (1952); *Triangle* (1961); *Realm of Algebra* (1961); *Facts and Fancy* (1962); *The Genetic Code* (1963); *Adding a Dimension* (essays, 1964); *An Easy Introduction to the Slide Rule* (1965); *The Noble Gases* (1966); *The Roman Republic* (1967); *The Dark Ages* (1968); *Asimov's Guide to the Bible,* 2v. (1968–1969); *Is Anyone There?* (1968). Prof. chemistry, Boston University School of Medicine, since 1950.

Aspen. New York. Quarterly. Founded 1965. Edited and published by Phyllis Johnson. Published in container form with each contribution designed as a separate item. Interested in all aspects of cultural modernism and the "non-linear" uses of print.

Aspern Papers, The. Novel by Henry James (1888). Strife between the former mistress of the famous Jeffrey Aspern and the critic who wishes to publish the poet's letters.

Assistant, The. Novel by Bernard Malamud (1957). A guilt-ridden thief is redeemed through the humanity and love of those he has wronged.

Association of Literary Magazines of America. Organization of the literary and little magazines of America, founded in 1961 at St. Paul, Minnesota, with headquarters established in New York.

ASTOR, MARY (May 3, 1906–); b. Quincy, Ill. Actress, novelist. *My Story* (autobiography, 1959); *The Incredible Charlie Carewe* (1960); *The Image of Kate* (1962); *The O'Conner's* (1964); *A Place Called Saturday* (1969).

ASTOR, WILLIAM WALDORF ASTOR, VISCOUNT (Mar. 31, 1848–Oct. 18, 1919); b. New York City. Novelist. *Valentino* (1885); *Sforza* (1889); *Pharaoh's Daughter* (1900). In 1893 he established in London the *Pall Mall Magazine.* In 1899 he became a British subject, in 1916 was raised to the peerage.

Astor Library, The. New York. Founded by John Jacob Astor in 1849. Merged with the Lenox Library and The Tilden Trust in 1895 to form The New York Public Library (q.v.).

Astor-Honor, Inc. *See* Obolensky, Ivan, Inc.

Astoria. By Washington Irving (1836). Account of the Far West during the period of the fur trade and the rise of John Jacob Astor.

ASWELL, JAMES (Apr. 27, 1906–1955); b. Baton Rouge, La. Author. *We Know Better* (poems, 1926); *The Midsummer Fires* (1948); *There's One in Every Town* (1951); *The Birds and the Bees* (1953).

Asylum, The. Anonymous romance attributed to Isaac Mitchell (1811).

"At Melville's Tomb." Poem by Hart Crane.

Atheneum; or Spirit of the English Magazine, The. Boston. Weekly magazine. Founded 1817. Expired 1832.

Atheneum Publishers. New York. Founded 1959. The executive committee consisted of Alfred A. Knopf, Jr., Simon Michael Bessie, and Hiram Haydn. Russell and Russell is its scholarly reprint house.

Athenia of Damascus. Tragedy by Rufus Dawes (1839).

ATHERTON, GERTRUDE FRANKLIN HORN (Oct 30, 1857–June 14, 1948); b. San Francisco, Calif. Novelist. *The Doomswoman* (1893); *A Whirl Asunder* (1895); *Patience Sparhawk and Her Times* (1897); *His Fortunate Grace* (1897); *The Californians* (1898); *The Valiant Runaways* (1898); *A Daughter of the Vine* (1899); *Senator North* (1900); *The Aristocrats* (1901); *The Conqueror; Being the True and Romantic Story of Alexander Hamilton* (1902); *Rulers of Kings* (1904); *The Travelling Thirds* (1905); *Rezánov* (1906); *Ancestors* (1907); *The Gorgeous Isle* (1908); *Tower of Ivory* (1910); *Julia France and Her Times* (1912); *Perch of the Devil* (1914); *California: An Intimate History* (1914); *The Living Present* (1917); *The White Morning* (1918); *The Avalanche* (1919); *The Sisters-in-Law* (1921); *Sleeping Fires* (1922); *Black Oxen* (1923); *The Crystal Cup* (1925); *The Immortal Marriage* (1927); *The Jealous Gods* (1928); *Dido, Queen of Hearts* (1929); *The Sophisticates* (1931); *Adventures of a Novelist* (1932); *Golden Peacock* (1936); *The House of Lee* (1940); *The Horn of Life* (1942); *Golden Gate Country* (1945); *My San Francisco* (1946); etc. Editor: *A Few of Hamilton's Letters* (1903). *See* Fred B. Millett's *Contemporary American Authors* (1940).

ATHERTON, LEWIS ELDON. Author. *Pioneer Merchant in Mid-America* (1939); *The Southern Country Store, 1800–1860* (1949); *Main Street on the Middle Border* (1954); *The Cattle Kings* (1961); etc.

ATHERTON, SARAH [Henry]. Novelist. *Blow Whistles, Blow!* (1930); *Brass-Eagles* (1935); *Mark's Own* (1941).

ATKESON, MARY MEEK; b. near Buffalo, W. Va. Author. *A Study of the Local Literature of the Upper Ohio Valley, . . . 1820–1840* (1920); *A Study of the Literature of West Virginia, 1822–1922* (1922); *The Woman on the Farm* (1924); *The Shining Hours* (1927).

ATKINS, STUART [Pratt] (Mar. 8, 1914–); b. Baltimore, Md. Educator, author. *The Testament of Werther* (1949); *Goethe's Faust: A Literary Analysis* (1958). Editor: *The Age of Goethe: An Anthology of German Literature* (1969). Prof. German, Harvard University, since 1956.

ATKINSON, ELEANOR (1863–Nov. 4, 1942); b. Rensselaer, Ind. Author. *Mamzelle Fifine* (1903); *The Boyhood of Lincoln* (1908); *Lincoln's Love Story* (1909); *Greyfriars Bobby* (1912); *Johnny Appleseed* (1915); *Hearts Undaunted* (1917); *Poilu, a Dog of Roubaix* (1918); etc.

ATKINSON, GEORGE WESLEY (June 29, 1845–Apr. 14, 1925); b. in Kanawha Co., Va. (now W. Va.). Governor, historical writer. *History of Kanawha County* (1876); *Prominent Men of West Virginia* (1890). Governor, West Virginia, 1897–1901.

ATKINSON, [Justin] BROOKS (Nov. 28, 1894–); b. Melrose, Mass. Drama critic, author. *Cleo for Short* (1940); *Broadway Scrapbook* (1947); *Once Around the Sun* (1951); *Tuesdays & Fridays* (1963); *Brief Chronicles* (1966); etc. Editor: *Walden* *and Other Writings of Henry David Thoreau* (1937); *Complete Essays and Other Writings of Ralph Waldo Emerson* (1940). Drama critic, *The New York Times,* 1925–42, 1946–59; columnist, "Critic at Large," *The New York Times,* since 1960.

ATKINSON, ORIANA [Torrey McIlveen] (Mrs. Justin Brooks Atkinson). Author. *Over at Uncle Joe's* (1947); *Big Eyes* (1949); *The Twin Cousins* (1951); *The Golden Season* (1953); *Manhattan and Me* (1954); *The South and the West of It* (1956).

ATKINSON, WILMER (June 13, 1840–May 10, 1920); b. in Bucks Co., Pa. Journalist, author. *Wilmer Atkinson: An Autobiography* (1920). Founder, with Howard M. Jenkins, *The Wilmington Daily Commercial,* 1866; founder, *The Farm Journal,* Philadelphia, 1877. In 1910 he began a series of almanacs called *Poor Richard's Almanac Revived.*

Atlanta Constitution. Atlanta, Ga. Newspaper. Founded 1868. Among its early and notable editors were Cary W. Styles, Evan Park Howell and Henry W. Grady. Joel Chandler Harris was on the staff for many years. The poet, Frank Lebby Stanton, conducted his "Just from Georgia" column in the *Atlanta Constitution* for nearly forty years. Clark Howell (1863–1936) was editor, 1897–1936. In 1950 it incorporated the *Atlanta Journal.* Jack Spalding and Eugene Patterson are editors. William Westbrook is book-review editor.

Atlanta Times. Atlanta, Ga. Newspaper. Founded 1964 by James C. Davis. Expired 1965.

Atlantic Magazine, The. New York. Monthly. Founded, 1824, by Robert C. Sands, who was a member of the so-called "Knickerbocker Group," including Irving, Halleck, Bryant, and Paulding. Suspended Apr. 1825, to be replaced in June by *New York Review and Atheneum Magazine,* which expired 1826. Bryant, Henry J. Anderson and Sands were editors of the latter. *See* Frank L. Mott's *A History of American Magazines,* v. 1 (1938).

Atlantic Migration, The: 1607–1860. *A History of the Continuing Settlement of the United States.* By Marcus Lee Hansen (1940). Pulitzer prize for history, 1941.

Atlantic Monthly, The. Boston, Mass. Founded Nov., 1857, by Moses Dresser Phillips, of the publishing firm of Phillips, Sampson & Co. Editors: James Russell Lowell, 1857–61; James T. Fields, 1861–71; William Dean Howells, 1871–81; Thomas Bailey Aldrich, 1881–90; Horace E. Scudder, 1890–98; Walter Hines Page, 1898–99; Bliss Perry, 1899–1909; Ellery Sedgwick, 1909–38; Edward A. Weeks, Jr., 1938–65; Robert Manning, since 1965. Francis H. Underwood was the originator of the magazine. He was literary adviser to Phillips, Sampson & Co. Also connected with the early numbers were Longfellow, Lowell, Emerson, Cabot, Motley and Hale. Holmes was the most voluminous early contributor, continuing in it *The Autocrat of the Breakfast Table* papers started twenty-five years earlier in *The New England Magazine.* The name tentatively selected for the new magazine was *Orient,* but Holmes suggested that it be called *The Atlantic.* In 1859 the magazine was purchased by Ticknor & Fields. In 1876 Ticknor & Fields was absorbed by the Houghton, Mifflin Co. The magazine was then published by Houghton, Mifflin & Co. and by the Atlantic Monthly Co., founded by MacGregor Jenkins in 1908. Julia Ward Howe's "Battle Hymn of the Republic"; Whittier's "Barbara Frietchie"; Lowell's "Commemoration Ode"; and Hale's "The Man Without a Country" appeared in *The Atlantic,* along with *Marjorie Daw,* by Aldrich and hundreds of poems and essays which have passed into our permanent literature. *See* M. A. DeW. Howe's *The Atlantic Monthly and Its Makers* (1919); Frank L. Mott's *A History of American Magazines,* v.2 (1938).

Atlantic Souvenir. Boston. Literary annual. Founded 1826. Noted for its short stories by such writers as J. K. Paulding, William Penn Smith, Maria Sedgwick, and Lydia Maria Child. Expired 1833.

Atlas Shrugged. Novel by Ayn Rand (1957). About business leaders who relinquish their freedom of action for the security of government regulation and lose their social creativity thereby. The basic philosophical idea underlying this work is the need for ruthless selfishness in order to release creative energy.

"Attack, The." Civil War poem by Thomas Buchanan Reed (1862). Celebrating the duel between the *Merrimack* and the *Cumberland.*

ATTAWAY, WILLIAM (1912–); b. in Mississippi. Author. *Let Me Breathe Thunder* (1939); *Blood on the Forge* (1941).

ATTERIDGE, HAROLD RICHARD (July 9, 1886–Jan. 16, 1938); b. Lake Forest, Ill. Playwright. *The Honeymoon Express* (with Joseph W. Herpert, prod. 1913); *The Passing Show of 1912–1919, 1921–1923, 1925* (prod. 1912–19, 1921–23, 1925); *The Man with Three Wives* (with Agnes Bangs Morgan and Paul Potter, prod. 1913); *Sinbad* (prod. 1918); *Monte Cristo, Jr.* (prod. 1919); *The Little Blue Devil* (prod. 1919); *The Last Waltz* (prod. 1921); etc.

ATTWOOD, WILLIAM (July 14, 1919–); b. Paris. Editor, author. *The Man Who Would Grow Hair* (1949); *Still the Most Exciting Country* (1955); *The Decline of the American Male* (with G. Leonard and J. I. Moskin, 1958); *The Red and the Black* (1967).

ATWATER, RICHARD TUPPER (Dec. 29, 1892–); b. Chicago, Ill. Author. Pen name, "Riq." *Rickety Rimes of Riq* (1925); *Doris and the Trolls* (1931); *The King Sneezes* (operetta, 1933); *Mr. Popper's Penguins* (with Florence Atwater, 1938). Translator: Procopius' *Secret History* (1961).

ATWOOD, MILLARD V. (Aug. 6, 1886–Nov. 3, 1941); b. Groton, N.Y. Editor, author. *The Country Newspaper* (1923); *Some Other Power* (1937); *Sawdust in His Shoes* (1940). With *Rochester Times-Union,* from 1927.

ATWOOD, WALLACE WALTER (Oct. 1, 1872–July 24, 1949); b. Chicago, Ill. Geographer, geologist, author. *Home Life in Far Away Lands* (1928); *The Americas* (1929); *Nations Beyond the Seas* (1930); *The United States Among the Nations* (1930); *The World at Work* (1931); *The Growth of Nations* (1936); *The United States in the Western World* (1944); *The Rocky Mountains* (1945); *Our Economic World* (with Ruth E. Pitt, 1948). Founder, *Economic Geography,* 1925; editor, from 1925. President, Clark University, 1920–1945.

AUCHINCLOSS, LOUIS STANTON (Sept. 17, 1917–); b. Lawrence, N.Y. Novelist. *The Indifferent Children* (under pen name "Andrew Lee," 1947); *The Injustice Collectors* (1950); *Sybil* (1952); *A Law for the Lion* (1953); *The Romantic Egoists* (1954); *The Great World and Timothy Colt* (1956); *Venus in Sparta* (1958); *Pursuit of the Prodigal* (1959); *Reflections of a Jacobite* (essays, 1961); *Powers of Attorney* (1963); *The Rector of Justin* (1964); *Pioneers and Caretakers* (1965); *The Embezzler* (1966); *A World of Profit* (1968); *Motiveless Malignity* (1969); *Second Chance* (1970).

AUDEN, W[ystan] H[ugh] (Feb. 21, 1907–); b. York, Eng. Poet, critic. *Poems* (1930); *The Orators* (1932); *The Dance of Death* (play, 1933); *The Dog Beneath the Skin* (play, with Christopher Isherwood, 1935); *The Ascent of F6* (play, with same, 1936); *Look, Stranger* (1936); *Letters from Iceland* (with Louis MacNeice, 1937); *Spain* (1937); *On This Island* (1937); *Selected Poems* (1938); *Journey to a War* (with Christopher Isherwood, 1939); *On the Frontier* (play, with same, 1939); *Education Today—and Tomorrow* (with T. Worsley, 1939); *Some Poems* (1940); *Another Time* (1940); *The Double Man* (1941); *New Year Letter* (1941); *For the Time Being* (1944); *Collected Poetry* (1945); *The Age of Anxiety* (1947); *Collected Shorter Poems, 1930–1944* (1950); *The Enchaféd Flood* (criticism, 1950); *Nones* (1959); *The Shield of Achilles* (1955); *Homage to Clio* (1960); *The Dyer's Hand* (essays, 1962); *About the House* (1966); *City Without Walls* (1970);

A Certain World (prose, 1970); etc. Author, with Chester Kallman, of librettos, *The Rake's Progress, Elegy for Young Lovers.* Editor: *Poet's Tongue* (with John Garrett, 1925); *The Oxford Book of Light Verse* (1938); *A Selection from Tennyson's Poems* (1944); *Poets of the English Language,* 5v. (with Norman Holmes Pearson, 1950); *Van Gogh: A Self-Portrait* (1961); etc. See Richard Hoggart's *Auden* (1951); Joseph Warren Beach's *The Making of the Auden Canon* (1957); Monroe K. Spears' *Auden* (1964); Justin Replogle's *Auden's Poetry* (1969).

Audience. Cambridge, Mass. Quarterly. Founded 1954. Devoted to publishing poetry, fiction, articles, plays, drawings, etc., especially by unknown writers. Edited by Firman Houghton.

AUDUBON, JOHN JAMES (Apr. 26, 1785–Jan 27, 1851); b. Les Coyes, Santo Domingo. Ornithologist, artist, author. *Birds of America* (in parts, 1827–38); *Viviparous Quadrupeds of North America* (in parts, 1842–54); etc. See Elliot Coues's *Audubon and His Journals,* 2v. (1897); Francis Hobart Herrick's *Audubon the Naturalist* (1938); *Audubon's America,* ed. by Donald Culross Peattie (1940); Robert Penn Warren's *Audubon: A Vision* (1969).

Augsberg Publishing House. Minneapolis, Minn. Founded 1891. Devoted to works of Protestant interest. In 1960 Augsberg Publishing House, Wartburg Press, & Lutheran Publishing House merged.

Augusta Chronicle and Herald. Augusta, Ga. Newspaper. Founded 1785, as *Augusta Chronicle.* Now merged with *Augusta Herald,* founded 1890. W. S. Morris is editor and publisher. Kenneth C. Crabbe is book critic.

AULD, ALEXANDER (Apr. 15, 1816–1889?); b. near Harrisburg, Pa. Music teacher. Compiler: *The Key of the West* (1836); *The Ohio Harmonist* (1847); *The Farmer's and Mechanic's Minstrel* (1863); etc.

Aunt Abby's Neighbors. Short stories by Annie Trumbull Slosson (1902).

Aunt Fanny. Pen name of Frances Elizabeth Mease Barrow.

Aunt Hattie. Pen name of Harriette Newall Woods Baker.

Aunt Phillis's Cabin; or, Southern Life As It Is. Novel by Mary H. Eastman (1852). Written as a Southern answer to *Uncle Tom's Cabin.*

AURANDT, PAUL HARVEY (Sept. 4, 1918–); b. Tulsa, Okla. News analyst, columnist, author. Writes under pen name "Paul Harvey." *Remember These Things* (1952); *Autumn of Liberty* (1954); *The Rest of the Story* (1956). News analyst and commentator, American Broadcasting Company, since 1944; syndicated columnist, General Features Corp., since 1954.

Aurelian. Historical novel by William Ware (1849). First published as *Probus* (1838), but better known by the later title.

Aurifodina. Satire by George Washington Peck, under pen name "Cantrell A. Bigly" (1849). In the manner of *Gulliver's Travels.*

AURINGER, OBADIAH CYRUS (June 4, 1849–Oct. 2, 1937); b. Glens Falls, N.Y. Clergyman, poet. *The Voice of a Shell* (1878); *Scythe and Sword* (1887); *The Heart of the Golden Roan* (1891); *The Book of the Hills* (1896); *The Death of Maid McCrea* (1909); *The Eagle's Bride* (1911); *Quest of the Lamp* (1922); *In Praise of Books* (1930); *The Eye of the Plain* (1931); etc.

Aurora. Philadelphia, Pa. Newspaper. Founded Oct. 1, 1790, by Benjamin Franklin Bache, as the *General Advertiser.* Name changed to the *Aurora,* Nov., 1794.

Aurora Esmeralda. Pen name of Ella Sterling Mighels.

Auroras of Autumn, The. Collection of poems by Wallace Stevens (1950).

AURTHUR, ROBERT ALAN (June 10, 1922–). Author. *Glorification of Al Toolum* (1953); *The Relation of the Writer to Television* (with others, 1960).

AUSLANDER, JOSEPH (Oct. 11, 1896–June 22, 1965); b. Philadelphia, Pa. Author. *Sunrise Trumpets* (1924); *Cyclops' Eye* (1926); *The Winged Horse* (with Frank Ernest Hill, 1927); *Hell in Harness* (1930); *Letters to Women* (1930); *No Traveler Returns* (1933); *Will Shakespeare* (1934); *Prose Cavalcade* (1934); *More Than Bread* (1936); *Riders at the Gate* (1938); *The Unconquerables* (poems, 1943); *My Uncle Jan* (with wife, 1948); *Islanders* (with same, 1951). Editor: *The Winged Horse Anthology* (with Frank Ernest Hill, 1928); *Song of America* (with wife, 1934).

AUSTIN, JANE GOODWIN (Feb. 25, 1831–Mar. 30, 1894); b. Worcester, Mass. Novelist. *Fairy Dreams* (1859); *Dora Darling* (1865); *Outpost* (1867); *The Novice* (1865); *A Nameless Nobleman* (1881); *Nantucket Scraps* (1882); *Standish of Standish* (1889); *Dr. Le Baron and His Daughters* (1890); *Betty Alden* (1891); *It Never Did Run Smooth* (1892); etc.

AUSTIN, JOHN OSBORNE (Dec. 28, 1849–Oct. 27, 1918); b. Providence, R.I. Author. *More Seven Club Tales* (1900); *Philip and Philippa* (1901); *A Week's Wooing* (1902); *Impressions and Reflections of Sixty Years, 1857–1917* (1917); and genealogical works.

AUSTIN, MARY [Hunter] (Mrs. Stafford W. Austin) (Sept. 9, 1868–Aug. 14, 1934); b. Carlinville, Ill. Essayist, novelist, playwright. *The Land of Little Rain* (1903); *The Arrow Maker* (prod. 1911); *The American Rhythm* (1923); *Earth Horizon, Autobiography* (1932); etc. See T. M. Pearce's *The Beloved House* (1940).

AUSTIN, STEPHEN FULLER (Nov. 3, 1793–Dec. 27, 1836); b. in what is now Wythe Co., Va. Pioneer, founder of Texas. *The Austin Papers,* 4v. (1924–28); ed. by E. C. Barker. See Eugene Campbell Barker's *Life of Stephen F. Austin* (1925); and his *The Father of Texas* (1935). The city of Austin, Tex., is named for him. Secretary of State, Republic of Texas, 1836.

AUSTIN, WILLIAM (Mar. 2, 1778–June 27, 1841); b. Lunenburg, Mass. Lawyer, author. *Letters from London* (1804); etc. His most famous short story is "Peter Rugg, the Missing Man," *New England Galaxy,* Sept 10, 1824, Sept l, 1826, and Jan. 19, 1827, and published separately in 1910. See Walter Ainslie's *William Austin* (1925).

Author and Journalist, The. Boulder, Colo.; Wash., D.C. Monthly. Founded 1916. Magazine for the professions.

"Author to Her Book, The." Poem by Anne Bradstreet (1678).

Authors and Publishers. By G.H.P. (George Haven Putnam) and J.B.P. (John Bishop Putnam) (1883). A standard manual of suggestions for beginners in literature. It ran into many editions over a period of years.

Authors Club. New York. Founded 1882 by Brander Matthews and others, at "The Studio," 103 East 15th St., New York, the home of Richard Watson Gilder. See *Liber Scriptorum.*

Author's Guild. New York. Founded 1920.

Authors' League Bulletin. New York City. Founded 1913. Issued monthly by the Authors' League.

Authors' League of America, The. New York City. Founded 1911, by Arthur Train, Gelett Burgess, Joseph Vance and Lloyd Osbourne, for the purpose of safeguarding the rights of authors. Described at length in Arthur Train's *My Day in Court* (1939).

Autobiography of Alice B. Toklas. Book of reminiscences by Gertrude Stein (1933).

Autobiography of Benjamin Franklin, The. First published in Paris as *Memoires de la Vie Privée de Benjamin Franklin* (1791); all editions in English until 1868 were either translations from the French or partial editions from the manuscript; the first complete edition from the original manuscript was published by John Bigelow as, *The Autobiography of Benjamin Franklin* (1868). *See* Samuel A. Green's *The Story of a Famous Book: An Account of Dr. Benjamin Franklin's Autobiography* (1871).

Autocrat of the Breakfast Table, The. By Oliver Wendell Holmes (1858). A series of essays consisting of imaginary conversations around a boarding-house table, and containing many of his most famous poems such as "The Deacon's Masterpiece; or, The Wonderful One Hoss Shay"; "The Chambered Nautilus"; "The Old Man Dreams."

Avant-Garde. New York. Bimonthly. Founded 1967. Edited by Ralph Ginzburg. In form and content concerned with modernism in the arts and society.

AVARY, MYRTA LOCKETT, b. Halifax, Va. Author. *A Virginia Girl in the Civil War* (1903); *Dixie After the War* (1906); etc. Editor: *A Diary from Dixie, as written by M. B. Chesnut* (1905); *Recollections of A. H. Stephens* (1910).

Ave Maria. Notre Dame, Ind. Roman Catholic literary monthly. Founded 1865, by Father Granger, Father Sorin, and Mother Angela (1824–1887). Eleanor Cecilia Donnelly, sister of Ignatius Donnelly, was one of the editors.

Average Man, An. Novel by Robert Grant (1883). The story of two young Harvard graduates who enter law practice in New York. One takes the hard road to success, the other the easy road, and the latter oversteps the bounds of ethics and comes to disaster.

AVERILL, CHARLES E. Novelist. *The Corsair King* (1847); *The Mexican Ranchero* (1847); *The Secret Service Ship* (1848); *The Wanderers* (1848); *Kit Carson, the Prince of the Gold Hunters* (1849); *Life in California* (1849); *The Secrets of the Twin Cities* (1849); etc.

AVERILL, ESTHER [Holden]. Author. *Voyages of Jack Cartier* (1937); *Adventures of Jack Ninepins* (1944); *Jenny's First Party* (1948); *King Philip the Indian Chief* (1950); *Jenny's Birthday Book* (1954); *Jenny Goes to Sea* (1957); *Jenny's Bedside Book* (1959); *Fire Cat* (1960); *Eyes on the World* (1968); etc.

AVERILL, LAWRENCE AUGUSTUS (May 1, 1891–); b. Alna, Me. Educator, author. *Introductory Psychology* (1943); *Psychology of the Elementary School Child* (1949); *Pie for Breakfast* (with Marion P. Averill, 1953); *Psychology Applied to Nursing* (with F. C. Kempf, 1956). Prof. psychology, Worcester State Teachers College, Worcester, Mass. 1915–50.

Avery, Al. Pen name of Rutherford George Montgomery.

AVERY, BENJAMIN PARKE (Nov. 11, 1828–Nov. 8, 1875); b. New York City. Journalist, author. *California Pictures In Prose and Verse* (1878). Editor, San Francisco *Bulletin,* 1861–71; *Overland Monthly,* 1874–1875.

Avon Books. New York. Founded 1941, as a division of The Hearst Corporation. Peter M. Mayer is publisher and editor-in-chief. Issues reprints and originals in paperback editions. Its first reprint was a twenty-five cent edition of Sinclair Lewis' *Elmer Gantry.*

Avon's Harvest. Melodrama in verse by Edward Arlington Robinson (1921). A study of a fear-hunted, hate-driven man.

Awake and Sing! Play by Clifford Odets (prod. 1935).

Awkward Age, The. Novel by Henry James (1899). The intricacies of London social life as they entangle the lives of two young girls.

AXELROD, GEORGE (June 9, 1922–); b. New York. Author. *Beggar's Choice* (1947); *Small Wonder* (revue, with Max Wilk, 1948); *The Seven Year Itch* (play, 1953); *Will Success Spoil Rock Hunter?* (play, 1956); *Where Am I Now That I Need Me?* (1971); etc. Also screenplays.

Axel's Castle: A Study in the Imaginative Literature of 1870–1930. By Edmund Wilson (1931). Essays on W. B. Yeats, Paul Valery, T. S. Eliot, Marcel Proust, James Joyce, Gertrude Stein, "Axel" and Rimbaud. "Axel" was a long poem by Villiers de l'Isle-Adam.

AYDELOTTE, FRANK (Oct. 16, 1880–Dec. 17, 1956); b. Sullivan, Ind. Educator. *Elizabethan Rogues and Vagabonds* (1913); *The Oxford Stamp* (1917); *Oxford Today* (with others, 1922); *Breaking the Academic Lock Step* (1944); *The American Rhodes Scholarship* (1946). Pres., Swarthmore College, 1921–39; director, Institute for Advanced Study, Princeton, N.J. 1939–47.

Ayer, John. See Guy Carlton Lee.

AYRES, CLARENCE [Edwin] (May 6, 1891–); b. Lowell, Mass. Educator, author. *Science—the False Messiah* (1927); *Holier Than Thou* (1929); *Huxley* (1932); *The Theory of Economic Progress* (1944); *The Industrial Economy* (1952); *Toward a Reasonable Society* (1968). Prof. economics, University of Texas, since 1930.

AYRES, SAMUEL GARDINER (Apr. 25, 1865–Dec. 29, 1942); b. Peru, N.Y. Methodist clergyman, librarian, author. *Fifty Literary Evenings,* 2v. (1897–1904); *History of the English Bible* (1899); *Methodist Heroes of Other Days* (1916); *Asbury and His Helpers* (1916); etc.

Ayscough, Florence. See Florence Ayscough MacNair.

AZARIAS, BROTHER (Patrick Francis Mullany) (June 29, 1847–Aug. 20, 1893); b. in Co. Tipperary, Ireland. Educator, author. *An Essay Contributing to a Philosophy of Literature* (1874); *Development of English Literature* (1880); *Books and Reading* (1890); *Phases of Thought and Criticism* (1892); etc.

B

B. L. T. See Bert Leston Taylor

Babbitt. Novel by Sinclair Lewis (1922). Satire on small town business as represented by George F. Babbitt, town booster, uplifter, joiner, handshaker, hustler, who misses the enduring things of life through preoccupation with business, which has become a fetish and a tyrant.

BABBITT, IRVING (Aug. 2, 1865–July 15, 1933); b. Dayton, O. Educator, critic. *Literature and the American College* (1908); *The New Laokoön* (1910); *Rousseau and Romanticism* (1919); *Democracy and Leadership* (1924); *On Being Creative and Other Essays* (1932); *Spanish Character* (1940); etc. Prof. French literature, Harvard University, 1894–1933. *See* Fred B. Millett's *Contemporary American Authors* (1940).

BABCOCK, EDWINA STANTON b. Nyack, N.Y. Poet. *Greek Wayfarers, and Other Poems* (1916); *The Flying Parliament, and Other Poems* (1918); *Nantucket Windows* (1924); etc.

BABCOCK, FREDERIC (Oct. 31, 1896–); b. Ord, Neb. Author, editor, lecturer. *Blood of the Lamb* (1932); *Hang Up the Fiddle* (1954). Editor, *Magazine of Books,* since 1942.

BABCOCK, JAMES STAUNTON (Nov. 7, 1815–Apr. 13, 1847); b. South Coventry, Conn. Poet. *Visions and Voices* (1849).

BABCOCK, WINNIFRED [Eaton] (1879–); b. Nagasaki, Japan. Novelist. Pen name, "Onoto Watanna." *A Japanese Nightingale* (1901); *The Wooing of Wistaria* (1903); *The Heart of Hyacinth* (1903); *Daughters of Nijo* (1904); *The Honorable Miss Moonlight* (1912); *Me: A Book of Remembrance* (1915).

BABSON, NAOMI LANE (1895–); b. Cape Ann, Mass. Novelist. *The Yankee Bodleys* (1936); *All the Tomorrows* (1939); *Look Down From Heaven* (1942); *I Am Lidian* (1951); *Another Sky* (1956); *Young Fair Maidens* (1958).

Babylon Revisited. Short story by F. Scott Fitzgerald in his *Taps at Reveille* (1935).

"Bacchus." Poem by Ralph W. Emerson (1847).

BACH, GEORGE LELAND (Apr. 28, 1915–); b. Victor, Ia. Economist. *Economic Analysis and Public Policy* (with M. J. Bowman, 1943); *Economics* (1954); *Inflation: A Study in Economics, Ethics, and Politics* (1958). Co-author: *Management and Corporations* (1960); *Microeconomics* (1966); *Macroeconomics* (1966). Prof. economics, Carnegie Institute of Technology, since 1946.

BACH, MARCUS LOUIS (Dec. 15, 1906–); Sauk City, Wis. Educator, author. *While Mortals Sleep* (1935); *Within These Walls* (1936); *Report to Protestants* (1948); *Of Faith and Learning* (1952); *The Circle of Faith* (1956); *Adventures in Faith* (1959); *Strange Sects and Curious Cults* (1961); *The Unity Way of Life* (1963); *Let Life Be Like This!* (1964); *The Power of Perception* (1966); *The Chiropractic Story* (1968). Director and prof., School of Religion, University of Iowa, since 1942.

BACHE, BENJAMIN FRANKLIN (Aug. 12, 1769–Sept. 10, 1798); b. Philadelphia, Pa., grandson of Benjamin Franklin. Editor. Founder, the *Philadelphia General Advertiser,* 1790, which became the *Aurora* in 1794. *See* Carl Van Doren's *Benjamin Franklin* (1938).

BACHELLER, IRVING [Addison] (Sept. 26, 1859–Feb. 24, 1950); b. Pierpont, N.Y. Novelist. *Eben Holden* (1900); *D'ri and I* (1901); *Darrel of the Blessed Isles* (1903); *Silas Strong* (1906); *The Turning of Griggsby* (1913); *The Light in the Clearing* (1917); *A Man for the Ages* (1919); *In the Days of Poor Richard* (1922); *The Scudders* (1923); *Coming Up the Road: Memories of a North Country Boyhood* (1928); *The Oxen of the Sun* (1935); *From Stores of Memory* (autobiography, 1938); *The Winds of God* (1941); etc.

BACKMAN, JULES (May 3, 1910–); b. New York. Economist, educator, author. *Adventures in Price Fixing* (1936); *Surety Rate Making* (1949); *Economics of Armament Inflation* (1951); *Wage Determination* (1959); *Inflation and the Price Indexes* (1966); etc. Editor: *Price Practices and Price Policies* (1953). Editorial writer, *New York Times,* 1943–48. Prof. economics, New York University, since 1950.

BACKUS, TRUMAN JAY (Feb. 11, 1842–Mar. 25, 1908); b. Milan, N.Y. Educator, author. *The Great English Writers from Chaucer to George Eliot* (1889); *The Outlines of Literature, English and American* (1897).

Backwoodsman, The. Novel by James Kirke Paulding (1818). An idyl of the West.

BACON, ALBION FELLOWS (Apr. 8, 1865–Dec. 10, 1933); b. Evansville, Ind. Social reformer, author. *Songs Ysame* (with Annie Fellows Johnston, 1897); *Beauty for Ashes* (1914); *Consolation* (1922); *The Path to God* (1928); *The Charm String* (1929); etc.

BACON, ALICE MABEL (Feb. 6, 1858–May 1, 1918); b. New Haven, Conn. Educator, lecturer, author. *Japanese Girls and Women* (1891); *A Japanese Interior* (1893); *In the Land of the Gods; Some Stories of Japan* (1905).

BACON, DAISY SARAH, b. in Pennsylvania. Editor, author. *Love Story Writer* (1954). Editor: *Detective Story Annual; All Fiction Detective Stories* (annual); *All Fiction Stories* (annual); *Love Story Annual.* Editor, *Love Story,* since 1928; *Detective Story* and *Romantic Range,* 1940.

BACON, DELIA SALTER (Feb. 2, 1811–Sept. 2, 1859); b. Tallmadge, O., sister of Leonard Bacon. Proponent of the Baconian théory of Shakespeare's plays, author. *Tales of the Puritans* (anon., 1831); *The Bride of Fort Edward* (anon., 1839); *The Philosophy of the Plays of Shakespeare Unfolded* (1857).

BACON, EDGAR MAYHEW (June 5, 1855–Dec. 14, 1935); b. Nassau, New Providence, Bahamas. Editor, lecturer, author. *Chronicles of Tarrytown and Sleepy Hollow* (1897); *The Hudson River* (1902); *Narragansett Bay* (1904); *Henry Hudson* (1907); etc.

BACON, EDWIN MUNROE (Oct. 20, 1844–Feb. 24, 1916); b. Providence, R.I. Editor, author. *Historic Pilgrimages in New England* (1898); *Literary Pilgrimages in New England* (1902); *The Connecticut River and the Valley of the Connecticut* (1906); *Rambles Around Old Boston* (1914); *The Book of Boston, Fifty Years' Recollections* (1916); etc. Editor, *Boston Globe,* 1873–78.

BACON, FRANK (Jan. 16, 1864–Nov. 19, 1922); b. Marysville, Calif. Actor, playwright. *Lightnin'* (with Winchell Smith, prod. 1918), which ran for 153 weeks and 1291 performances; etc.

BACON, JOSEPHINE DODGE DASKAM (Feb. 17, 1876–July 29, 1961); b. Stamford, Conn. Poet, story-writer. *Smith College Stories* (1900); *Middle-Aged Love Stories* (1903); *Poems* (1903); *The Domestic Adventurers* (1907); *In the Border Country* (1909); *The Inheritance* (1912); *To-Day's Daughter* (1914); *Medusa's Head* (1926); *Counterpoint* (1927); *Luck of Lowry* (1931); *Kathy* (1933); *The Root and the Flower* (1939); *The World in His Heart* (1941); etc. Compiler: *Best Nonsense Verse* (1901).

BACON, LEONARD (Feb. 19, 1802–Dec. 24, 1881); b. New Haven, Conn., brother of Delia Bacon. Clergyman, editor, author. *Slavery Discussed in Occasional Essays* (1846); etc. Co-founder, *The New Englander,* 1843, and sometime editor; co-founder, *The Independent,* 1848; senior editor, 1848–61.

BACON, LEONARD (May 26, 1887–Jan. 1, 1954); b. Solvay, N.Y. Poet. *Ulug Beg* (1923); *Animula Vagula* (1926); *Guinea-Fowl and Other Poultry* (1927); *The Legend of the Quincibald* (1928); *Lost Buffalo, and Other Poems* (1930); *The Furioso* (1932); *Dream and Action* (1934); *The Voyage of Autoleon* (1935); *Bullinger Bound, and Other Poems* (1938); *Semi-Centennial* (autobiography, 1939); *Sunderland Capture, and other Poems* (1940); *Day of Fire* (1943); etc. Translator: Luiz de Camões, *The Lusiads.*

BACON, MARY SCHELL [Hoke] (Mrs. Charles E. Bacon) (Nov. 20, 1870–June 2, 1934); b. Atchison, Kan. Pen name, "Dolores Marbourg." Author. *I Will Ne'er Consent* (1888); *Juggernaut* (with George Cary Eggleston, 1891); *The Soul of a Woman* (1897); *The Diary of a Musician* (1904); etc. Compiler: *Songs That Every Child Should Know* (1906); etc.

BACON, PEGGY (Mrs. Alexander Brook) (May 2, 1895–); b. Ridgefield, Conn. Illustrator, author. *The Lion-Hearted Kitten* (1927); *Mercy and the Mouse* (1928); *The Ballad of Tangle Street* (1929); *Mischief in Mayfield* (1933); *Catcalls* (1935); *The Mystery of East Hatchett* (1939); *Starting from Scratch* (1945); *The Inward Eye* (1952); *The Good American Witch* (1957); etc. *See* William Murrell's *Peggy Bacon* (1922).

BADEAU, ADAM (Dec. 29, 1831–Mar. 19, 1895); b. New York City. Author. *The Vagabond* (1859); *Military History of Ulysses S. Grant,* 3v. (1868–1881); *Grant in Peace* (1887).

BAGBY, ALBERT MORRIS (Apr. 29, 1859–Feb. 26, 1941); b. Rushville, Ill. Musician, novelist. *Miss Traumerei* (1895); *Mammy Rosie* (1904). Director for many years of the "Musical Mornings" at the Waldorf Astoria in New York.

BAGBY, GEORGE WILLIAM (Aug. 13, 1828–Nov. 29, 1883); b. in Buckingham Co., Va. Editor, lecturer, author. *The Letters of Mozis Addums to Billy Ivvins* (1862); *What I Did With My Fifty Millions* (under pen name, "Moses Adams," 1874); *Meekin's Twinses, a Perduckshun of Mozis Addums* (1877); *Canal Reminiscences* (1879); *The Old Virginia Gentleman, and Other Sketches* (1910); Editor, *The Southern Literary Messenger,* 1860–1864.

BAGDIKIAN, BEN HAIG (Jan. 30, 1920–); b. Marash, Turk. Author. *In the Midst of Plenty: The Poor in America* (1964). Contributor: *The Kennedy Circle* (1961). Editor: *Man's Contracting World in an Expanding Universe* (1959).

BAGG, HELEN F., b. Chicago, Ill. Novelist, playwright. Pen name, "Jarvis Hall." *Through Mocking Bird Gap* (1921); *Across the Mesa* (1922); *Up the Rito* (1925).

BAGG, ROBERT ELY (Sept. 21, 1935–); b. Orange, N.J. Poet. *Poems, 1956-57* (1957); *Madonna of the Cello* (1961).

BAGLEY, WILLIAM C[handler] (Mar. 15, 1874–July 1, 1946); b. Detroit, Mich. Educator, author. *The Educative Process* (1908); *History of the American People* (with Charles A. Beard, 1918); *Determinism in Education* (1925); *Education and Emergent Man* (1934); *America, Yesterday and Today* (with R. F. Nichols and C. A. Beard, 1938); etc. Prof. education, Columbia University, 1917–40.

BAILEY, CAROLYN SHERWIN (Mrs. Eben Clayton Hill) (Oct. 25, 1875–Dec. 23, 1961); b. Hoosick Falls, N.Y. Author. *The Peter-Newell Mother Goose* (1905); *Songs of Happiness* (1913); *Boy Heroes in Making America* (1919); *Flint: The Story of a Trail* (1922); *Boys and Girls of Pioneer Days* (1924); *Boys and Girls of Discovery Days* (1926); *Plays for the Children's Hour* (1931); *Stories from an Indian Cave* (1935); *Country Stop* (1942); *Pioneer Art in America* (1944); *Miss Hickory* (1946); *Enchanted Village* (1950); *A Candle for Your Cake* (1952); *Finnegan II, His Nine Lives* (1953); *Little Red School House* (1957); *Flickertail* (1962); etc. Editor, *American Childhood,* 1928–34.

BAILEY, CHARLES. Novelist. *The Jilted Doctor* (1844); *The Reclaimed Student* (1844).

BAILEY, FLORENCE AUGUSTA MERRIAM (Aug. 8, 1863–deceased); b. Locust Grove, N.Y. Ornithologist, author. *Birds Through an Opera Glass* (1889); *My Summer in a Mormon Village* (1895); *A-Birding on a Bronco* (1896); *Birds of Village and Field* (1898); etc.

BAILEY, FRANCIS (c.1735–1815); b. in Lancaster Co., Pa. Printer, almanac maker. Founder, *The United States Magazine,* 1779; *The Freeman's Journal; or, North American Intelligencer,* 1781. In his almanac for 1779 appears a portrait of Washington with the caption "Des Landes Vater" giving rise to the popular "Father of His Country." Official printer to the Continental Congress.

BAILEY, GAMALIEL (Dec. 3, 1807–June 5, 1859); b. Mt. Holly, N.J. Editor. Founder of the anti-slavery journal, *The Cincinnati Philanthropist,* 1836; and *The National Era,* Washington, 1847, in which Harriet Beecher Stowe's *Uncle Tom's Cabin* first appeared.

BAILEY, [Irene] TEMPLE (d. July 6, 1953); b. Petersburg, Va. Novelist. *Judy* (1907); *Glory of Youth* (1913); *Mistress Anne* (1917); *The Trumpeter Swan* (1920); *The Gay Cockade* (1921); *Peacock Feathers* (1924); *The Blue Window* (1926); *Wallflowers* (1927); *Silver Slippers* (1928); *Burning Beauty*

(1929); *Wild Wind* (1930); *Little Girl Lost* (1932); *Enchanted Ground* (1933); *The Radiant Tree* (1934); *Fair as the Moon* (1935); *I've Been to London* (1937); *Tomorrow's Promise* (1938); *The Blue Cloak* (1941); *The Pink Camellia* (1942); *Red Fruit* (1945); etc.

BAILEY, JAMES MONTGOMERY (Sept. 25, 1841–Mar. 4, 1894); b. Albany, N.Y. Editor, humorist. Known as "The Danbury News Man." *Life in Danbury* (1873); *They All Do It* (1877); *England from a Back Window* (1878); *The Danbury Boom* (1880); etc. Editor, *The Danbury* (Conn.) *Times,* 1865–70; founder, *The Danbury News,* 1870; editor, 1870–94. First to use humor in "column" form.

Bailey, Jessie Emerson. See Jessie [Emerson] Moffat.

BAILEY, LIBERTY HYDE (Mar. 15, 1858–Dec. 25, 1954); b. South Haven, Mich. Educator, horticulturist, author. *Survival of the Unlike* (1896); *Outlook to Nature* (1915); *The Holy Earth* (1915); *Wind and Weather* (verse, 1916); etc. Editor: *Cyclopedia of American Horticulture,* 2v. (1907–1909); etc.

BAILEY, MARGARET EMERSON (1880–Oct. 29, 1949); b. Providence, R.I. Author. *Robin Hood's Barn* (1922); *The Wild Streak* (1932).

BAILEY, MARGERY (May 12, 1891–); b. Santa Cruz, Calif. Educator, editor, author. *Seven Peas in a Pod* (1919); *Little Man with One Shoe* (1921); *Whistle for Good Fortune* (1940); etc. Editor: *The Hypochondriack, Being the Seventy Essays by the Celebrated Biographer, James Boswell,* 2v. (1928); *Boswell's Column* (1951).

BAILEY, VERNON HOWE (Apr. 1, 1874–Oct. 27, 1953); b. Camden, N.J. Artist, author. *Little Known Towns of Spain* (1928); *New Trails in Old Spain* (1928); etc.

BAILY, THOMAS LLOYD (1884–1914). Novelist. *Possibilities* (1887); *Dr. Wallsten's Way* (1889); *An Entire Stranger* (1891).

BAILYN, BERNARD (Sept. 10, 1922–); b. Hartford, Conn. Educator, historian. *New England and Merchants in the Seventeenth Century* (1955); *Massachusetts Shipping, 1697–1714* (with wife, Lotte Lazarsfeld, 1959); *Education in the Forming of American Society* (1960); *The Ideological Origins of the American Revolution* (1967, Pulitzer Prize, 1968); Prof. history, Harvard University, since 1961; editor-in-chief, John Harvard Library, since 1962.

BAINBRIDGE, JOHN (Mar. 12, 1913–); b. Monticello, Minn. Author, editor. *Little Wonder; or, The Reader's Digest and How It Grew* (1946); *The Wonderful World of Toots Shor* (1951); *Biography of an Idea* (1952); *Garbo* (1955); *Like a Homesick Angel* (1964); *Another Way of Living: A Gallery of Americans Who Choose To Live in Europe* (1969). With *The New Yorker,* since 1938.

Baines-Miller, Minnie Willis. See Minnie Willis Baines Miller.

BAIRD, CHARLES WASHINGTON (Aug. 28, 1828–Feb. 10, 1887); b. Princeton, N.J., brother of Henry Martyn Baird. Presbyterian clergyman, historian. *History of the Huguenot Emigration to America,* 2v. (1885); etc.

BAIRD, HENRY CAREY (Sept. 10, 1825–Dec. 30, 1912); b. Bridesburg, Pa. Publisher, economist. Founder, Henry Carey Baird & Co., 1849; this was the first American firm to specialize in publishing technical and industrial books.

BAIRD, HENRY MARTYN (Jan 17. 1832–Nov. 11, 1906); b. Philadelphia, Pa. Presbyterian clergyman, historian. *Modern Greece* (1856); *History of the Rise of the Huguenots,* 2v. (1879); *The Huguenots and Henry of Navarre,* 2v. (1886); *The Huguenots and the Revocation of the Edict of Nantes,* 2v. (1895); etc. Prof. Greek, New York University, 1859–1906.

BAIRD, THOMAS (1923–). Author. *The Old Masters* (1963); *Sheba's Landing* (1964); *Triumphal Entry* (1964); *Nice Try* (1965); *Finding Out* (1967); *People Who Get You Down* (1970).

BAIRD, WILLIAM BRITTON (Aug. 15, 1904–); b. Grand Island, Neb. Puppeteer, author. *The Art of the Puppet* (1966).

BAITY, ELIZABETH CHESLEY (1907–). Author. *Man Is a Weaver* (1942); *Americans Before Columbus* (1951); *America Before Man* (1953); etc.

BAKELESS, JOHN [Edwin] (Dec. 30, 1894–); b. Carlisle, Pa. Editor, author. *The Economic Causes of Modern War* (1921); *The Origin of the Next War* (1926); *Magazine Making* (1931); *Christopher Marlowe: The Man in His Time* (1937); *Daniel Boone* (1939); *The Tragicall History of Christopher Marlowe*, 2v. (1942); *Fighting Frontiersman* (1948); *Eyes of Discovery* (1950); *Background to Glory: Life of George Rogers Clark* (1957); *Traitors, Turncoats and Heroes* (1959); *The Adventures of Lewis and Clark* (1962). Lit. editor, *Living Age*, 1921–23, editor, 1928–29; lit. editor, *The Literary Digest*, 1937–38; etc.

BAKER, BENJAMIN A. (Apr. 4, 1818–Sept. 6, 1890); b. New York City. Actor, playwright. *A Glance at New York* (prod. Feb. 15, 1848), rewritten as *New York As It Is* (prod. Mar. 17, 1848).

BAKER, BETTY (June 20, 1928–); b. Bloomsburg, Pa. Author. *The Sun's Promise* (1962); *Killer-or-Death* (1963); *Walk the World's Rime* (1965); *Blood of the Brave* (1966); etc.

BAKER, CARLOS [Heard] (May 5, 1909–); b. Biddeford, Me. Educator, author. *Shelley's Major Poetry* (1948); *Hemingway: The Writer as Artist* (1952); *A Friend in Power* (1958); *The Land of Rumbelow* (1963); *Ernest Hemingway: A Life Story* (1969). Editor: *The American Looks at the World* (1944); *Wordsworth's Prelude* (1948); *Shelley's Selected Poetry and Prose* (1951); *Hemingway and His Critics* (1961); etc. Faculty, Princeton University, since 1938.

BAKER, CHARLES H[enry], JR. (1895–June 17, 1968). Author. *The Gentleman's Companion,* 2v. (1939); *Blood of the Lamb* (1946); *South American Gentleman's Companion,* 2v. (1951); *The Esquire Culinary Companion* (1959).

BAKER, COLGATE (d. June 25, 1940); b. Kobe, Japan. Critic. Drama critic, *The New York Review,* 1909–1931.

BAKER, DOROTHY DODDS (Apr. 21, 1907–); b. Missoula, Mont. Novelist. *Young Man With a Horn* (1938); *Trio* (1943); *Our Gifted Son* (1948); *Cassandra at the Wedding* (1962).

BAKER, ELLIOTT. Author. (Dec. 15, 1922–) *A Fine Madness* (1964); *Penny Wars* (1968); *Pocock and Pitt* (1971).

BAKER, EMILIE [Addoms] KIP (Mrs. Franklin Thomas Baker), b. Brooklyn, N.Y. Author. *Out of the Northland* (1904); *Stories of Old Greece and Rome* (1913); *Stories of Northern Myths* (1914). Compiler: *The Children's First* [*Second,* and *Third*] *Book of Liberty,* 3v. (1915).

BAKER, ETTA IVA ANTHONY, b. Cincinnati, O. Author. *The Fairmount* series, 4v. (1909–14); *Miss Mystery* (1913); etc.

BAKER, FRANKLIN THOMAS (Sept. 12, 1864–Feb. 3, 1949); b. Hagerstown, Md. Educator, author. *The Teaching of English* (1903); *Every Day English* (with Ashley H. Thorndike, 1913); etc. Editor: *Browning's Shorter Poems* (1899); *Macaulay's Poems* (1904); etc. Prof. English, Teachers College, Columbia University, 1893–1933.

BAKER, GEORGE (May 22, 1915–); b. Lowell, Mass. Cartoonist. *The Sad Sack* (1944); *The New Sad Sack* (1946). Creator of "Sad Sack" cartoon, *Yank,* 1942.

BAKER, GEORGE BARR (Apr. 1, 1870–July 29, 1948); b. Wyandotte, Mich. Assoc. editor, *Everybody's Magazine,* 1907–10; lit. editor, *Delineator,* 1911–14.

BAKER, GEORGE MELVILLE (1832–Oct., 1890); b. in Maine. Playwright. *Sylvia's Soldier* (1866); *Amateur Dramas* (1867); *An Old Man's Prayer* (poem, 1868); *Down by the Sea* (prod. 1869); *The Last Loaf* (prod. 1871); etc. Wrote for *Oliver Optic's Magazine.*

BAKER, GEORGE PIERCE (Aug. 4, 1866–Jan. 6, 1935); b. Providence, R.I. Educator, author. *The Development of Shakespeare as a Dramatist* (1907); etc. Editor: *Plays of the 47 Workshop,* 4v. (1918–25); *Yale One-Act Plays,* v. 1 (1930); etc. Founded the "47 Workshop," a school for drama writers, at Harvard University, where he taught 1888–1933. Eugene O'Neill, Sidney Howard, George Abbott, Edward Sheldon, Philip Barry, S. N. Behrman and other noted playwrights were among his pupils. Established similar department at Yale, where he taught 1933–35.

BAKER, HARRIETTE NEWALL WOODS (1815–1893); b. Andover, Mass. Author. Pen names, "Mrs. Madeline Leslie" and "Aunt Hattie." *Cora and the Doctor* (1855); *Tim, the Scissors Grinder* (1861); *Little Miss Fret* (1869); *Rebecca the Jewess* (1879); etc. *The Twin Brothers* (anon., 1843).

BAKER, JOSEPHINE TURCK (d. May 30, 1942); b. Milwaukee, Wis. Editor, author. *The Burden of the Strong* (1915); *Madame de Stael* (drama, 1927); *Songs of Triumph* (poems, 1933); etc. Founder and editor, *Correct English* magazine.

BAKER, KARLE WILSON (Oct. 13, 1878–); b. Little Rock, Ark. Educator, story-writer, poet. *Blue Smoke* (poems, 1919); *Burning Bush* (poems, 1922); *Old Coins* (1923); *Family Style* (1937); etc.

BAKER, LOUISE [Maxwell] (May 18, 1909–); b. Upland, Cal. Novelist. *Party Line* (1945); *Out on a Limb* (1946); *Ships and Sails* (1953).

BAKER, LOUISE REGINA, b. New Windsor, Md. Author. *Cis Martin* (1900); *Rosy Posy* (1901); *The Old Monday Farm* (1905).

BAKER, NEWTON D[iehl] (Dec. 3, 1871–Dec. 5, 1937); b. Martinsburg, W. Va. Statesman, author. *Frontiers of Freedom* (1918). Editor: *The American Way* (with Carlton J. H. Hayes and Roger Williams Straus, 1936). Secretary of War, 1916–21. See C. H. Cramer's *Newton D. Baker* (1961).

BAKER, NINA [Brown] (1888–1957). Author. *Cinderella Secret* (1938); *He Wouldn't Be King* (1941); *Lenin* (1945); *Peter the Great* (1943); *Cyclone in Calico* (1952); *Henry Hudson* (1958); etc.

BAKER, RAY PALMER (Sept. 21, 1883–); b. Fonthill, Ont. Educator, author. *A Tale of Rothenburg* (1906); *Croynan Hall, the Maid of the Mask* (1909); *A History of English-Canadian Literature to the Confederation; Its Relation to the Literature of Great Britain and the United States* (1920); *A Chapter in American Education* (1924); etc. Prof. English, Rensselaer Polytechnic Institute, since 1915.

BAKER, RAY STANNARD (Apr. 17, 1870–July 12, 1946); b. Lansing, Mich. Editor, biographer, essayist. Pen name, "David Grayson." Under own name: *Woodrow Wilson and World Settlement,* 3v. (1922); *Woodrow Wilson: Life and Letters,* 8v. (1927–39, v. 7 and 8 awarded Pulitzer prize for American history, 1940); *Native American* (autobiography, 1941); *American Chronicle* (autobiography, 1945); etc. Editor: *The Public Papers of Woodrow Wilson,* 6v. (with William E. Dodd, 1925–27). Under pen name: *Adventures in Contentment* (1907); *Adventures in Friendship* (1910); *The Friendly Road* (1913); *Adventures in Understanding* (1925); *Adventures in Solitude* (1931); *Under My Elm* (1942); etc.

BAKER, RUSSELL WAYNE (Aug. 14, 1925–); b. Loudoun Cy., Va. Author. *An American in Washington* (1961); *No Cause for Panic* (1964); *All Things Considered* (1965).

BAKER, WILLIAM MUMFORD (June 27, 1825–Aug. 20, 1883); b. Washington, D.C. Presbyterian clergyman, novelist. *The Life and Labours of the Rev. Daniel Baker* (1858); *Inside: A Chronicle of Secession* (under pen name, "George F. Harrington," 1866); *Oak Mot* (1868); *The New Timothy* (1870); *Mose Evans* (1874); *Carter Quarterman* (1876); *The Virginians in Texas* (1878); *Colonel Dunwoddie, Millionaire* (1878); etc.

Baker and Scribner. Publishers. 1846. *See* Charles Scribner's Sons.

Baker Street Irregulars. New York City. Literary club. Founded 1934, by Christopher Morley, Alexander Woollcott, and Vincent Starrett. Devoted to the study of "Sherlock Holmes." See *221B: Studies of Sherlock Holmes,* ed. by Vincent Starrett (1940).

Balaam and His Master. Collection of short stories by Joel Chandler Harris (1891).

"Balaklava." Best known poem of Alexander Beaufort Meek. It is similar to Tennyson's "Charge of the Light Brigade."

Balch, Mrs. Edwin Swift. See Emily Clark.

BALCH, GLENN (Dec. 11, 1902–); b. Venus, Tex. Author. *Riders of the Rio Grande* (1937); *Indian Paint* (1942); *Indian Saddle-Up* (1953); *Spotter Horse* (1961); *Keeping Horse* (1966); *Horse of Two Colors* (1969).

Balcony Stories. Stories of Louisiana by Grace King (1892).

BALDERSTON, JOHN LLOYD (Oct. 22, 1889–Mar. 8, 1954); b. Philadelphia, Pa. Playwright. *The Genius of the Marne* (1919); *A Morality Play for the Leisured Class* (1924); *Berkeley Square* (1929); *Chicago Blueprint* (1943). Co-author (plays): *Dracula* (1927); *Frankenstein* (1931); *Red Planet* (1932); *Farewell Performance* (1936). Also screenplays.

Baldridge, Mrs. C[yrus] Le Roy. See Caroline Singer.

BALDWIN, CHARLES SEARS (Mar. 21, 1867–Oct. 23, 1935); b. New York City. Educator, author. *Essays Out of Hours* (1907); *Three Medieval Centuries of Literature in England* (1932); etc. Editor: *American Short Stories* (1904). Department of English, Columbia University.

BALDWIN, FAITH (Mrs. Hugh Cuthrell) (Oct. 1, 1893–); b. New Rochelle, N.Y. Editor, novelist, poet. *Mavis of Green Hill* (1921); *Laurel of Stony Stream* (1923); *Signposts* (poems, 1924); *Those Difficult Years* (1925); *Three Women* (1926); *Alimony* (1928); *The Incredible Year* (1929); *Office Wife* (1930); *Make Believe* (1930); *Judy* (1930); *Skyscraper* (1931); *Babs and Mary Lou* (1931); *Myra* (1932); *District Nurse* (1932); *Honour Bound* (1934); *Within a Year* (1934); *American Family* (1935); *The Puritan Strain* (1935); *Station Wagon Set* (1940); *And New Stars Burn* (1941); *Breath of Life* (1942); *Arizona Star* (1945); *They Who Love* (1948); *Lookout for Liza* (1950); *Face Toward the Spring* (1956); *Many Windows* (1958); *Testament of Trust* (autobiography, 1960); *The West Wind* (1962); *The Lonely Man* (1964); *There is a Season* (1966); *Evening Star* (1966); *The Velvet Hammer* (1969); etc.

BALDWIN, HANSON W[eightman] (Mar. 22, 1903–); b. Baltimore, Md. Military editor, author. *Men and Ships of Steel* (with W. F. Palmer, 1935); *The Caissons Roll—A Military Survey of Europe* (1938); *Admiral Death* (1939); *United We Stand* (1941); *The Price of Power* (1947); *Great Mistakes of the War* (1950); *The Great Arms Race* (1958); *World War I: An Outline History* (1962); *The New Navy* (1964); *Battles Lost and Won: Great Campaigns of World War II* (1966). Military and naval correspondent, *The New York Times,* 1937–1942; military editor, since 1942.

BALDWIN, JAMES (Dec. 15, 1841–Aug. 30, 1925); b. in Hamilton Co., Ind. Editor, author. *The Book Lover* (1884); *The Horse Fair* (1895); *The Discovery of the Old Northwest* (1901); *The Conquest of the Old Northwest* (1901); *Abraham Lincoln: A True Life* (1904); *An American Book of Golden Deeds* (1907); *The Sampo* (1912); *Fifty Famous Rides and Riders* (1915); etc. Editor: *Harper's Readers,* 5v. (1887–1890); *Harper's School Speakers,* 3v. (1891); etc.

BALDWIN, JAMES (1924–); b. New York. Novelist, essayist, playwright. *Go Tell It on the Mountain* (1953); *Notes of a Native Son* (essays, 1955); *Giovanni's Room* (1958); *Nobody Knows My Name* (essays, 1960); *Another Country* (1962); *The Fire Next Time* (essays, 1963); *Blues for Mister Charlie* (play, 1964); *Going to Meet the Man* (1966); *The Amen Corner* (play, 1968); *Tell Me How Long the Train's Been Gone* (1968); *A Rap on Race* (with Margaret Mead, 1971); etc.

BALDWIN, JAMES MARK (Jan. 12, 1861–Nov. 8, 1934); b. Columbia, S.C. Educator, psychologist, author. *Between Two Wars, 1861–1921; Being Memories, Opinions and Letters Received,* 2v. (1926); etc. Editor: *Dictionary of Philosophy and Psychology,* 2v. (1901–05). Prof. psychology, Princeton, 1893–1903; Johns Hopkins, 1903–09; etc.

BALDWIN, JOHN DENISON (Sept. 28, 1809–July 8, 1883); b. North Stonington, Conn. Editor, author. *The Story of Raymond Hill, and Other Poems* (1847); *Prehistoric Nations* (1869); *Ancient America* (1872). Editor, *The Commonwealth,* 1852–59; *The Worcester Spy,* 1859–83.

BALDWIN, JOSEPH GLOVER (Jan., 1815–Sept. 30, 1864); b. Winchester, Va. Jurist, author. *The Flush Times of Alabama and Mississippi* (1853); *Party Leaders* (1855).

BALDWIN, LELAND DEWITT (Nov. 23, 1897–); b. Fairchance, Pa. Historian, novelist. *Pittsburgh: The Story of a City* (1937); *Whiskey Rebels* (1939); *The Delectable Country* (1939); *Best Hope of Earth: A Grammar of Democracy* (1948); *The Stream of American History,* 2v. (1952); *Recent American History* (1954); *The Meaning of America* (1955); *Whiskey Rebels* (1968). Editor: *The Flavor of the Past,* 2v. (1969); *Ideas in Action,* 2v. (1969). Editor, University of Pittsburgh Press, 1936–40. Prof. history, University of Pittsburgh, since 1955.

BALDWIN, THOMAS WHITFIELD (Jan. 28, 1890–); b. in Laurens Co., S.C. Educator, author. *The Organization and Personnel of the Shakespearean Company* (1927); *William Shakespeare Adapts a Hanging* (1931); *Shakespeare's Small Latine and Lesse Greeke,* 2v. (1944); *Shakespeare's Five-Act Structure* (1947); *On the Literary Genetics of Shakespeare's Poems and Sonnets* (1950); *On the Literary Genetics of Shakespeare's Plays, 1592–1594* (1959); *On Act and Scene Division in the Shakespeare First Folio* (1965). English dept., University of Illinois, since 1925.

Baldwin's Monthly. Subsidized literary magazine distributed free by the New York clothier, Oran S. Baldwin (1864–1885). Founded in 1870. It boasted some notable contributors. It was suspended c. 1886.

BALESTIER, CHARLES WOLCOTT (Dec. 13, 1861–Dec. 6, 1891); b. Rochester, N.Y. Publisher, novelist. *A Potent Philtre* (1884); *A Fair Device* (1884); *A Victorious Defeat* (1886); *The Average Woman* (1892); *Benefits Forgot* (1894). Co-author (with his brother-in-law, Rudyard Kipling): *The Naulahka* (1892). Formed partnership with William Heinemann in London to publish the "English Library" in rivalry with the Tauchnitz editions.

BALL, FRANCIS KINGSLEY (Nov. 29, 1863–June 8, 1940); b. in Mercer Co., Pa. Editor. Author (with Albert Franklin Blaisdell): *Hero Stories from American History* (1903); *Short Stories from American History* (1904); *Heroic Deeds of American Sailors* (1915); *Pioneers of America* (1919); *Log Cabin Days* (1921); etc. Editor, Ginn & Co., 1912–1938.

BALL, JOHN DUDLEY, Jr. (July 8, 1911–); b. Schenectady, N.Y. Author. *Records for Pleasure* (1947); *Operation Springboard* (1958); *Arctic Showdown* (1966); *Dragon Hotel* (1969); etc.

"Ballad of New Orleans, The." Poem by George Henry Boker.

"Ballad of Oriskany, The." By Obadiah Cyrus Auringer. Celebrating the battle between the Americans under General Herkimer and the British aided by the Indians.

"Ballad of the Babie Bell, The." Poem by Thomas Bailey Aldrich (1856). Deals with the death of an infant. It has been reprinted many times.

"Ballad of the Goodly Fere." Poem by Ezra Pound (1909).

"Ballad of the Oysterman, The." By Oliver Wendell Holmes, in the *Amateur,* July 17, 1830.

"Ballad of the Tempest." By James T. Fields. In his *Poems* (1849). It contains the oft-quoted lines, " 'We are lost!' the Captain shouted as he staggered down the stair."

BALLAGH, JAMES CURTIS (d. Sept. 28, 1944); b. Brownsburg, Va. Educator, author. *A History of Slavery in Virginia* (1902); etc. Editor: *The Letters of Richard Henry Lee,* 2v. (1911–1914). In political science dept. University of Pennsylvania from 1913.

BALLANTINE, WILLIAM GAY (Dec. 7, 1848–Jan. 10, 1937); b. Washington D.C. Educator, author. *Inductive Logic* (1896); *The Young Man from Jerusalem* (1921); *The Logic of Science* (1933); *Peggy in the Park* (1933). President, Oberlin College, 1891–96; prof. of Bible, International Y.M.C.A. College, Springfield, Mass., 1897–1920.

Ballantine Books. New York. Founded 1952, by Ian Ballantine, who is president. Published the series *New Poems by American Authors* and *New Short Novels.* A subsidiary of INTEXT (q.v.).

BALLARD, FRED[erick] (1884–). Playwright. *Believe Me, Xantippe* (prod. 1912); *Young America* (prod. 1915); *A Rainy Day* (prod. 1923); *Ladies of the Jury* (prod. 1929); *Cousin Delafield* (play, 1936); *320 College Avenue* (play, with M. G. Eberhart, 1938); etc.

BALLARD, HARLAN HOGE (May 26, 1858–Feb. 18, 1934); b. Athens, Ohio. Librarian, author. *Adventures of a Librarian* (1929). Librarian, Berkshire Athenaeum, 1888–1934.

BALLIETT, WHITNEY (Apr. 17, 1926–); b. New York. Jazz critic. *The Sound of Surprise: 46 Pieces on Jazz* (1959); *Dinosaurs in the Morning: 41 Pieces on Jazz* (1962); *Such Sweet Thunder: 49 Pieces of Jazz* (1966); *Super-Drummer: A Profile of Buddy Rich* (1968). With *The New Yorker,* since 1951.

Balloon Hoax. Written by Edgar Allan Poe for the New York *Sun,* Apr. 13, 1844. In 1836 the *Sun* had printed the "Moon Hoax."

BALLOU, HOSEA (Apr. 30, 1771–June 7, 1852); b. Richmond, N.H. Universalist clergyman, author. *A Treatise on Atonement* (1805); etc. Founder, *The Universalist Magazine,* 1819; editor, 1819–28.

BALLOU, MATURIN MURRAY (Apr. 14, 1820–Mar. 27, 1895); b. Boston, Mass. Editor, traveler, novelist. Pen name, "Lieut. Murray." Under own name: *Due West* (1884); *Due South* (1885); *Due North* (1887); also under pen name: *Red Rupert* (1845); *The Naval Officer* (1845); *The Spanish Musketeer* (1847); etc. Founder, *Gleason's Pictorial Drawing-Room Companian* (1851), later called *Ballou's Pictorial.* Editor, the Boston *Daily Globe; The Flag of Our Union;* and the Boston *Sunday Budget.*

BALLOU, ROBERT OLESON (1892–). Editor, author. *Shinto: The Unconquered Enemy* (1945); *Shortened Arrangement of the Holy Bible* (1964); *Nature of Religion* (1968); etc. Editor: *The Bible of the World: Sacred Scriptures of the Eight Basic Religions* (1939); *The Living Bible* (1952); etc.

BALLOU, WILLIAM HOSEA (Sept. 30, 1857–Nov. 30, 1937); b. Hannibal, N.Y. Biologist, novelist. *A Ride on a Cyclone* (1889); *The Bachelor Girl* (1890); *Spectacular Romances* (1892); etc.

Ballou's Dollar Monthly Magazine. Boston. Founded, 1855, by Maturin M. Ballou. The word *Dollar* was omitted beginning with 1866. Expired, 1893.

Ballou's Pictorial. See *Gleason's Pictorial.*

BALMER, EDWIN (July 26, 1883–); b. Chicago, Ill. Editor, novelist. *Waylaid by Wireless* (1909); *A Wild Goose Chase* (1915); *The Blue Man's Eye* (with William MacHarg, 1916); *The Indian Drum* (with same, 1917); *Keeban* (1923); *Fidelia* (1924); *That Royle Girl* (1925); *Flying Death* (1927); *Five Fatal Words* (with Philip Wylie, 1932); *Dragons Drive You* (1934); *The Torn Letter* (1941); *In His Hands* (1954); *The Candle of the Wicked* (1956); *With All the World Away* (1958); etc. Editor, *Red Book Magazine,* 1927–49; assoc. pub., 1949–53.

Baltimore News-American. Baltimore, Md. Newspaper. Founded 1872, as the *Baltimore News,* and merged with the *Post* (founded 1922) in 1934. Later appropriated the *Baltimore American.* W. R. Hearst, Jr., is editor-in-chief.

Baltimore Sun. Baltimore, Md. Newspaper. Founded 1837, by Arunah S. Abell. Evening edition, called *Evening Sun,* added in 1910. Known as the "Sunpapers." Frank L. Kent and H. L. Mencken were long associated with it. See *The Sunpapers of Baltimore,* by Gerald W. Johnson and others (1937).

Baltimore Sunday American. Baltimore, Md. Newspaper. Founded 1799, by William Pechin and Alexander Martin, as *The American.* Sold to Hearst Corporation in 1923. Became Sunday paper in 1928. See *Baltimore News-American.*

BAMBERGER, BERNARD JACOB (May 30, 1904–); b. Baltimore, Md. Rabbi, theologian. *Proselytism in the Talmudic Period* (1939); *Fallen Angels* (1952); *The Bible: A Modern Jewish Approach* (1955); *The Story of Judaism* (1957).

BANCROFT, FREDERIC (Oct. 30, 1860–Feb. 22, 1945); b. Galesburg, Ill. Lecturer, historian. *The Negro in Politics* (1885); *The Life of William H. Seward,* 2v. (1900); *Calhoun and the South Carolina Nullification Movement* (1928); *Slave-Trading in the Old South* (1931). Editor: *Speeches, Correspondence and Public Papers of Carl Schurz,* 6 v. (1913).

BANCROFT, GEORGE (Oct. 3, 1800–Jan. 17. 1891); b. Worcester, Mass. Diplomat, historian. *Poems* (1823); *A History of the United States,* 10v. (1834–1874); *Literary and Historical Miscellanies* (1855). *See* M. A. DeWolfe Howe's, *The Life and Letters of George Bancroft,* 2v. (1908). His collection of books was given to The New York Public Library.

BANCROFT, HUBERT HOWE (May 5, 1832–Mar. 2, 1918); b. Granville, O. Editor, publisher, historian, essayist. *Literary Industries* (autobiography, 1890); *Retrospection, Political and Personal* (1912); *In These Latter Days* (1917). Editor: *The Native Races of the Pacific States,* 5v. (1874–75); *History of the Pacific States,* 34v. (1882–90). Founder, H. H. Bancroft & Co., publishers, San Francisco. *See* Henry L. Oak's *"Literary Industries" in a New Light* (1893).

BANDELIER, ADOLPH FRANCIS ALPHONSE (Aug. 6, 1840–Mar. 18, 1914); b. Berne, Switzerland. Archaeologist, novelist. *The Delight Makers* (1890); *The Gilded Man* (1873); etc.

BANFIELD, EDITH COLBY (1870–1903). Poet. *The Place of My Desire, and Other Poems* (1904).

BANGS, JOHN KENDRICK (May 27, 1862–Jan. 21, 1922); b. Yonkers, N.Y. Editor, lecturer, humorist. *The Lorgnette* (1886); *Roger Camerden* (1887); *New Waggings of Old Tales* (1888); *Tiddledywink Tales* (1891); *The Tiddledywink's Poetry Book* (1892); *Coffee and Repartee* (1893); *The Idiot* (1895); *A House-Boat on the Styx* (1895); *The Pursuit of the House-Boat* (1897); *Cobwebs from a Library Corner* (1899); *The Idiot at Home* (1900); *Mollie and the Unwise Man* (1902); *Mrs. Raffles* (1905); *Andiron Tales* (1906); *Songs of Cheer* (1910); *A Little Book of Christmas* (1912); *The Foothills of Parnassus* (1914); *From Pillar to Post* (1916); etc. On editorial staff, *Acta Columbiana,* 1882–83; *Life,* 1884–88; *Harper's Magazine,* 1888–99; editor, *Harper's Weekly,* 1898–1900; *New Metropolitan Magazine,* 1902–03; *Puck,* etc. See Francis Hyde Bangs's *John Kendrick Bangs, Humorist of the Nineties* (1941).

BANGS, NATHAN (May 2, 1778–May 3, 1862); b. Stratford, Conn. Methodist clergyman, editor, author. *The Reformer Reformed* (1818); *Letters to a Young Preacher* (1835); *History of the Methodist Episcopal Church,* 4v. (1838–40); etc. Editor, the *Methodist Magazine,* 1821–28; 1832–36; the *Christian Advocate,* 1828. See Abel Stevens's *Life and Times of Nathan Bangs* (1863).

Banker's Daughter, The. Play by Bronson Howard (prod. 1878).

BANKOWSKY, RICHARD (1928–). Novelist. *A Glass Rose* (1958); *After Pentecost* (1961); *On a Dark Night* (1964); *Pale Criminals* (1967).

BANKS, A[lgernon] POLAN (July 21, 1906–); b. Norfolk, Va. Novelist, film producer. *Black Ivory* (1926); *The Street of Women* (1931); *The Far Horizon* (1936); *The Man From Cook's* (1938); *There Goes Lona Henry* (1941); *Carriage Entrance* (1947); etc. Also original screenplays.

BANKS, CHARLES EDWARD (July 6, 1854–Oct. 22, 1931); b. Portland, Me. Physician, author. *The History of Martha's Vineyard,* 3v. (1911–25); *The Planters of the Commonwealth* (1930); *History of York, Maine,* 2v. (1931–35); etc.

BANKS, CHARLES EUGENE (Apr. 3, 1852–Apr. 29, 1932); b. in Clinton Co., Ia. Editor, poet, novelist, playwright. *Quiet Music* (poems, 1892); *Theodore Roosevelt* (1901); *John Dorn, Promoter* (1907); *The Swami* (prod. 1909); *Heart Beats of Hawaii* (poems, 1921); etc. *An American Woman* (prod. 1905).

BANKS, EDGAR JAMES (May 23, 1866–May 5, 1945); b. Sunderland, Mass. Archaeologist, author. *Jonah in Fact and Fancy* (1899); *Bismya or The Lost City of Adab* (1912); *The Bible and the Spade* (1913); *An Armenian Princess* (1914); *The Seven Wonders of the Ancient World* (1916).

BANKS, ELIZABETH [L.] (1870–July 18, 1938); b. Taunton, N.J. Author. *Campaigns of Curiosity* (1894); *The Autobiography of a "Newspaper Girl"* (1902); *The Mystery of Frances Farrington* (1909); *Dik: A Dog of Belgium* (1914); *Captain Jinks* (of French and Russian Descent) (1915); *The Remaking of an American* (1928); etc.

BANKS, HELEN WARD, b. Brooklyn, N.Y. Author. *The Boynton Pluck* (1904); *The House of the Lions* (1924); *The Story of Mexico* (1926); etc.

BANKS, THEODORE HOWARD (Nov. 29, 1895–); b. New York. Educator. *Wild Geese* (poems, 1921); *Milton's Imagery* (1950). Editor: *The Poetical Works of Sir John Denham* (1928). Translator: *Sir Gawain and the Green Knight* (1929); *Sophocles: Three Theban Plays* (1956). English dept., Wesleyan University, since 1928.

BANKSON, RUSSELL ARDEN (Feb. 21, 1889–); b. Mt. Hope, Wash. Journalist, novelist. *Riders of the Breaks* (1931); *Bitter Grass* (1933); *Riders of the Badlands* (1934); *Disaster Island* (1935); *The Klondike Nugget* (1935).

BANNING, KENDALL (Sept. 20, 1879–Dec. 27, 1944); b. New York City. Editor, poet. *Flotsam* (1903); *Songs of the Love Unending* (1912); *Bypaths in Arcady* (1914); *Pirates* (1916); *The Great Adventure* (1925); *West Point Today* (1937); *Annapolis Today* (1938); *Submarine! The Story of Undersea Fighters* (1942); *Our Army Today* (1943); etc.

BANNING, MARGARET CULKIN (Mar. 18, 1891–); b. Buffalo, Minn. Novelist, essayist. *This Marrying* (1920); *Half Loaves* (1921); *Spellbinders* (1922); *A Handmaid of the Lord* (1924); *Money of Her Own* (1928); *The Third Son* (1933); *The First Woman* (1934); *The Iron Will* (1935); *Enough to Live On* (1940); *Letters from England* (1942); *The Clever Sister* (1947); *Give Us Our Years* (1949); *Fallen Away* (1951); *The Dowry* (1955); *The Convert* (1957); *The Vine and the Olive* (1964); *I Took My Love to the Country* (1966); *Mesabi* (1969); etc.

BANNISTER, NATHANIEL HARRINGTON (Jan. 13, 1813–Nov. 2, 1847); b. in Delaware, or Baltimore, Md. Actor, playwright. *Gaulantus* (prod. 1837); *The Gentleman of Lyons* (prod. 1837); *Robert Emmett* (prod. 1840); *The Three Brothers* (prod. 1840); *Putnam* (prod. 1844, publ. c.1859); *Richmond Hill* (prod. 1846); *Infidelity* (prod. 1847); etc.

Bantam Books, Inc. New York City. Publishers. Founded 1946. Well known for such imprints as Bantam Classics, Bantam Modern Classics, World Drama, Critical Editions. A subsidiary of Grosset and Dunlap (q.v.).

BANVARD, JOHN (Nov. 15, 1815–May 16, 1891); b. New York City. Painter, poet, playwright. *A Description of the Mississippi River* (1849); *Amasis* (prod. 1864); *Carrinia* (prod. 1875); *The Private Life of a King* [George IV] (1875); *The Tradition of the Temple* (poem, 1883); etc.

BANVARD, JOSEPH (May 9, 1810–Sept. 28, 1887); b. New York City. Baptist clergyman, author. *Plymouth and the Pilgrims* (1851); *Novelties of the New World* (1852); *Priscilla* (1854); *Old Grips and Little Tidd* (1873); *Daniel Webster, His Life and Public Services* (1875); etc. Compiler: *The Christian Melodist* (1850); etc.

Bar Sinister, The. Story by Richard Harding Davis (1903). Kid, a white bull-terrier, tells the story of his rise to fame as a blue-ribbon winner.

BARACH, FREDERICA PISEK (Mrs. Alvan L. Barach) (Aug. 1, 1904–); b. Lake Hopatcong, N.J. Editor, author. *One Hundred Best Books* (1931); editor *Golden Book Magazine.*

Barbara. Pen name of Mabel Osgood Wright.

Barbara Frietchie. Play by Clyde Fitch (prod. 1899).

"Barbara Frietchie." Poem by John Greenleaf Whittier. In *Atlantic Monthly,* Oct. 1863.

BARBE, WAITMAN (Nov. 19, 1864–Oct. 30, 1925); b. in Monongalia Co., W. Va. Educator, poet. *Ashes and Incense* (poems, 1892); *In the Virginias: Stories and Sketches* (1896); *Famous Poems Explained* (1909); *The Study of Poetry* (1925); etc.

BARBER, BERNARD (Jan. 29, 1918–); b. Boston, Mass. Educator, author. *Science and Social Order* (1952); *Social Stratification* (1957); *Drugs and Society* (1967). Editor: *Sociology of Science* (with Walter Hirsch, 1962); *European Social Class* (with Eleanor G. Barber, 1965). Prof. sociology, Barnard College, since 1961.

BARBER, ELSIE OAKES (Sept. 6, 1914–); b. in Massachusetts. Novelist. *The Wall Between* (1946); *The Trembling Years* (1949); *Hunt for Heaven* (1950); *Jenny Angel* (1954).

BARBER, JOHN WARNER (Feb. 2, 1798–June 22, 1885); b. East Windsor, Conn. Engraver, historical and religious writer. *Connecticut Historical Collections* (1836); *The Dance of Death* (1846); *Historical, Poetical, and Pictorial American Scenes* (with Elizabeth G. Barber, 1850); *Our Whole Country,* 2v. (1861); etc.

BARBOUR, ANNA MAYNARD (d. May 10, 1914). Novelist. *Told in the Rockies* (1897); republished as *The Award of Justice* (1901); *That Mainwaring Affair* (1900); *At the Time Appointed* (1903); *Breakers Ahead* (1906); etc.

BARBOUR, RALPH HENRY (Nov. 13, 1870–Feb. 19, 1944); b. Cambridge, Mass. Novelist. *The Land of Joy* (1903); *The Lilac Girl* (1909); *The Turner Twins* (1922); *Phyllis in Bohemia* (under pen name "Richard Stillman Powell," and with Luther H. Bickford, 1897); *Hurricane Sands* (1940); *Mystery on the Bayou* (1943); etc.

BARDEEN, CHARLES WILLIAM (Aug. 28, 1847–Aug. 24, 1924); b. Groton, Mass. Educator, author. *A Dictionary of Educational Biography* (1901); *A Little Fifer's War Diary* (1910); etc.

Bare and Ye Cubb, Ye. The first English play to be performed in the American colonies. Three men were brought to trial in Accomac Court House, Va., in 1665, for having acted it, but were acquitted.

Bare Souls. By Gamaliel Bradford (1924). Studies of great writers as revealed from their intimate letters. Keats, Lamb, Edward Fitzgerald, Thomas Gray, Voltaire, and Horace Walpole, are among those analyzed.

"Barefoot Boy, The." Poem by John Greenleaf Whittier, in the *Little Pilgrim,* Jan. 1855.

Barefoot in the Park. Play by Neil Simon (prod. 1963).

BARGERON, CARLISLE (July 3, 1895–Mar. 22, 1965); b. Eatonton, Ga. Publicist, author. *Confusion on the Potomac* (1941); *Joe Martin—An American Story* (1948); etc.

BARGHOORN, FREDERICK CHARLES (July 4, 1911–); b. New York. Political scientist, historian. *The Soviet Image of the United States* (1950); *Soviet Russian Nationalism* (1956); *The Soviet Cultural Offensive* (1960); *Soviet Foreign Propaganda* (1964); etc. Prof. political science, Yale University, since 1957.

Barker, The. Play by Kenyon Nicholson (prod. 1927). Chris Miller, the Barker's son, marries a snake charmer against the wishes of his father, who influences him to leave the carnival life and become a lawyer.

BARKER, BENJAMIN. Novelist. *Ellen Grafton, the Lily of Lexington* (1845); *Zoraida; or, The Witch of Naumkeag!* (under pen name, "Egbert Augustus Cowslip, Esq.," 1845); *Francisco; or, The Pirate of the Pacific* (1845); *Clarilda; or, The Female Pickpocket* (1846); *Blackbeard; or, The Pirate of the Roanoke* (1847); *The Sea Serpent; or, The Queen of the Coral Cave* (1847); *The Land Pirate; or, The Wild Girl of the Beach* (1847); etc.

BARKER, ELSA (d. Aug. 31, 1954); b. Leicester, Vt. Novelist, poet. *The Son of Mary Bethel* (1909); *The Frozen Grail, and Other Poems* (1910); *Stories from the New Testament for Children* (1911); *The Book of Love* (poems, 1912); *Songs of a Vagrom Angel* (1916); *Fielding Sargent* (1922); *The Cobra Candlestick* (1928); *The C. I. D. of Dexter Drake* (1929); *The Redman Cave Murder* (1930); etc.

BARKER, ERIC [Wilson]. Poet. *Planetary Heart* (1942); *A Ring of Willows* (1961); etc.

BARKER, EUGENE CAMPBELL (Nov. 10, 1874–); b. Riverside, Tex. Educator, author. *Life of Stephen F. Austin* (1925); *Mexico and Texas, 1821–1835* (1928); *The Father of Texas* (1935); *Speeches, Responses, and Essays* (1954); etc.

Editor, *The Austin Papers, 1765–1836,* 4v. (1924–28). Managing editor, *The Southwestern Historical Quarterly, 1910–37.* History dept., University of Texas, since 1901.

BARKER, FORDYCE (May 2, 1818–May 30, 1891); b. Wilton, Me. Physician, playwright. *The Rise in Harlem* (1864).

BARKER, JAMES NELSON (June 17, 1784–Mar. 9, 1858); b. Philadelphia, Pa. Playwright, poet. *Tears and Smiles* (prod. 1807); *The Embargo; or, What News* (prod. 1808); *The Indian Princess; or, La Belle Sauvage* (prod. 1808); *Marmion; or, The Battle of Flodden Field* (prod. 1812); *The Armourer's Escape* (prod. 1817); *How to Try a Lover* (publ. 1817, prod. 1836); *Superstition* (prod. 1824). Among his poems are "Little Red Riding Hood," and "The Three Sisters." *See* Paul Howard Musser's *James Nelson Barker* (1929).

BARKER, REGINALD C[harles] (May 15, 1881–Oct. 20, 1937); b. Brighton, Sussex, England. Novelist. *Grizzly Gallagher* (1927); *Wild-Horse Ranch* (1927); *Gentleman Grizzly* (1928); *The Hair-Trigger Brand* (1929).

BARKER, SHIRLEY [Frances] (Apr. 4, 1911–Nov. 18, 1965); b. Farmington, N.H. Author. *The Dark Hills Under* (poems, 1933); *Peace, My Daughters* (1949); *Rivers Parting* (1950); *A Land and a People* (poems, 1952); *Fire and the Hammer* (1953); *Tomorrow the New Moon* (1955); *Liza Bowe* (1956); *Swear by Apollo* (1958); *The Last Gentleman* (1960); *Corner of the Moon* (1961); *Strange Wives* (1963); *Builders of New England* (1965); etc.

BARKSDALE, LENA. Author. *First Thanksgiving* (1942); *That Country Called Virginia* (1945); *Treasure Bag* (1947); etc.

BARLOW, JOEL (Mar. 24, 1754–Dec. 24, 1812); b. Redding, Conn. Poet. One of the "Hartford Wits." *The Prospect of Peace* (1778); *The Vision of Columbus* (1787); *Advice to the Privileged Orders,* 2v. (1792–3); *The Conspiracy of Kings* (1792); *The Hasty Pudding* (1796); *The Columbiad* (1807); and many published *Letters.* See *The Anarchiad: A New England Poem;* Theodore A. Zunder's *Early Days of Joel Barlow* (1934); James Woodress's *A Yankee's Odyssey* (1958).

Barnacle, Captain Robert. Pen name of Charles Martin Newell.

BARNARD, CHARLES (Feb. 13, 1838–Apr. 11, 1920); b. Boston, Mass. Editor, playwright, novelist. *The Tone Masters,* 3v. (1870–71); *Knights of Today* (1881); *A Dead Town* (1883); *The County Fair* (prod. 1888); *The Forest Ring* (with William C. DeMille, prod. 1901); etc. Conducted column "The World's Work" in *Scribner's Monthly,* 1875–84.

BARNARD, FREDERICK AUGUSTUS PORTER (May 5, 1809–Apr. 27, 1889); b. Sheffield, Mass. Clergyman, educator, editor. *Brevity of Life* (1859); etc. Co-editor-in-chief: *Johnson's New Universal Cyclopaedia,* 4v. (1880–81). President, University of Mississippi, 1856–61; Columbia College, 1864–89. Barnard College of Columbia University is named for him.

Barnes, A. S. & Co. New York, later Cranbury, N.J. Alfred Smith Barnes began the business in Hartford, Conn., in 1831, with D. F. Robinson. He formed a partnership with Charles Davies in 1838. In 1844 he moved the business to New York. His son, Alfred Cutler Barnes, joined the firm in 1858. In 1890 the educational department of the company merged with several other publishers to form the American Book Company. Richard Green Parker and James M. Watson were among the best known textbook writers in the early days of the firm. Henry Burr Barnes (1845–1911) joined the firm in 1866. He was the editor of the *International Review,* 1878–80. The firm is now combined with Thomas Yoseloff. Julien Yoseloff is president. It publishes a paperbound line called Perpetua Books.

BARNES, ALBERT (Dec. 1, 1798–Dec. 24, 1870); b. Rome, N.Y. Clergyman, author. *Notes, Explanatory and Practical,* uv. (1832–53); *Life at Three-Score* (1859); *Life at Three-Score and Ten* (1869); etc.

BARNES, ANNIE MARIE (1857–); b. Columbia, S.C. Author. *Children of the Kalahari* (1890); *The Ferry Maid* (1899); *Lass of Dorchester* (1904); *Lost Treasures of Umdilla* (1925); etc.

BARNES, CARMAN DEE (Nov. 20, 1912–); b. Chattanooga, Tenn. Author. *Schoolgirl* (1929); *Beau Lover* (1930); *Mother, Be Careful* (1932); *Young Woman* (1934); *Time Lay Asleep* (1946).

BARNES, CHARLOTTE MARY SANFORD (Mrs. Edmon S. Conner) (1818–Apr. 14, 1863); b. New York City. Actress, playwright. *Octavia Bragaldi; or, The Confession* (prod. 1837); *The Forest Princess; or, Two Centuries* (prod. 1848); *Plays, Prose, and Poetry* (1848); also several dramatizations and adaptations.

BARNES, CLIVE [Alexander] (May 13, 1927–); b. London. Dance and drama reviewer; author. *Ballet in Britain since the War* (1953); *Frederick Ashton and His Ballets* (1961); *Ballet Here and Now* (with others, 1961). Dance critic, *The Times*, London, 1961–65; dance and drama critic, *The New York Times*, since 1965.

BARNES, DJUNA [Chappell] (June 12, 1892–); b. Cornwall-on-Hudson, N.Y. Journalist, author. *The Book of Repulsive Women* (1915); *A Book* (1923); *Ryder* (1928); *Nightwood* (1937); *The Antiphon* (play, 1958); *The Selected Works of Djuna Barnes* (1962); *The Personal Voice* (1964); *The World of Love* (1964); etc.

BARNES, [Frank] ERIC WOLLENCOTT (May 7, 1907–Dec. 31, 1962); b. Little Rock, Ark. Educator, author. *The Lady of Fashion* (1954); *The Man Who Lived Twice* (1956); *The War Between the States* (1959).

BARNES, HARRY ELMER (June 15, 1889–Aug. 25, 1968); b. Auburn, N.Y. Educator, editor, author. *Sociology Before Comte* (1917); *History: Its Rise and Development* (1919); *The Genesis of the World War* (1926); *History and Social Intelligence* (1926); *In Quest of Truth and Justice* (1928); *The Twilight of Christianity* (1929); *Intellectual and Cultural History of the Western World* (1937); *A History of Historical Writing* (1937); *History of Western Civilization*, 2v. (1935); *Society in Transition* (1939); *Social Institutions* (1942); *Historical Sociology* (1948). Editor: *Perpetual War for Perpetual Peace* (1953); *The People vs. Caryl Chessman* (1967). On editorial staff of Scripps-Howard newspapers, 1929–40.

BARNES, JAMES (Sept. 19, 1866–Apr. 30, 1936); b. Annapolis, Md. Author of boys' books. *For King or Country* (1896); *Naval Actions of the War of 1812* (1896); *A Princetonian* (1896); *Midshipman Farragut* (1896); *A Loyal Traitor* (1897); *Commodore Bainbridge* (1897); *Yankee Ships and Yankee Sailors* (1897); *The Hero of Erie* (1898); *Ships and Sailors* (1898); *David G. Farragut* (1899); *Drake and His Yeomen* (1899); *The Great War Trek* (1901); *With the Flag in the Channel* (1902); *The Giant of Three Wars* (1903); *The Unpardonable War* (1904); *The Son of Light Horse Harry* (1904); *The Blockaders* (1905); *Outside the Law* (1906); *The Clutch of Circumstances* (1908); *Commodore Perry* (1912); *Rifle and Caravan* (1912); *Through Central Africa from Coast to Coast* (1915); *The Story of the American Navy* (1919); *From Then Till Now* (autobiography, 1934); etc.

BARNES, MARGARET AYER (Mrs. Cecil Barnes) (Apr. 8, 1886–Oct. 25, 1967); b. Chicago, Ill. Author. *Prevailing Winds* (1928); *Jenny* (with Edward Sheldon, prod. 1929); *Years of Grace* (1930, Pulitzer prize novel, 1931); *Dishonored Lady* (with Edward Sheldon, 1930); *Westward Passage* (1931); *Within This Present* (1933); *Edna, His Wife* (1935); *Wisdom's Gate* (1938).

BARNES, WALTER (July 29, 1880–Aug. 27, 1969); b. Barnesville, O. Educator, author. *New Democracy in the*

Teaching of English (1923); *The Children's Poets* (1924); *English for American High Schools* (1931); *Contemporary Children's Poetry* (1938); etc. Editor, *Types of Children's Literature* (1920); *Boys Life of Mark Twain* (1939); *Realms of Reading*, 6v. (with others, 1940); etc.

BARNES, WILLIAM ROBBINS (May 12, 1866–Feb. 5, 1945); b. Hinsdale, Ill. Publisher. In book business since 1885. President Barnes & Noble, publishers, since 1917.

Barnes & Noble, Inc. New York. Publishers and booksellers. Known as an educational book house. Founded by C. M. Barnes in Wheaton, Ill., in 1874 (moved to Chicago within a year) as a jobbing business in second-hand school books. It was called C. M. Barnes Company (incorporated 1894). In 1884 William R. Barnes, a son, entered the business. John W. Wilcox joined the firm in 1898, and in 1908 the name became Barnes-Wilcox Company. In 1917 William R. Barnes withdrew, and the name was changed to J. W. Wilcox-Follett Co. In 1883, Arthur Hinds established a similar business in New York. C. Clifford Noble joined with him to form Hinds & Noble in 1887. In 1917 Hinds withdrew and Noble joined with William R. Barnes to form in New York the firm of Barnes & Noble, Inc. In 1924 John W. Barnes, grandson of the founder, entered the firm. In 1930 G. Clifford Noble sold his interest to John W. Barnes, who died Dec. 8, 1964. Celeste F. Barnes is chairman of the board. The firm supplies schools and libraries and has a department for out-of-print books.

BARNETT, LINCOLN KINNEAR (1909–). Author. *Writing on Life* (1951); *The World We Live In* (with others, 1955); *The Wonder of Life on Earth* (with others, 1960); *The Treasure of Our Tongue* (1964); etc.

BARNHART, CLARENCE L[ewis] (Dec. 30, 1900–); b. Near Plattsburg, Mo. Lexicographer. Editor: *American College Dictionary* (1948); *Thorndike-Barnhart Comprehensive Desk Dictionary* (1951); *New Century Cyclopedia of Names* (1954); *New Century Handbook of English Literature* (with W. D. Halsey, 1956); *Thorndike-Barnhart Beginning Dictionary* (1964); etc. Founder and pres., C. L. Barnhart, Inc.

BARNOUW, ERIK (June 23, 1908–); b. The Hague, Neth. Educator, author. *Open Collars* (1928); *Handbook of Radio Production* (1949); *Mass Communication* (1956); *The Television Writer* (1962); *A History of Broadcasting in the United States*, 3v. (*A Tower in Babel*, 1966; *The Golden Web*, 1968; *The Image Empire*, 1970). Prof. dramatic arts, Columbia University, since 1964.

BARNS, FLORENCE ELBERTA; b. Chicago, Ill. Editor, lecturer. *New Voices of the Southwest* (with Hilton R. Greer, 1934); *Texas Writers of Today* (1935). Editor, the *Southwester* magazine, 1935–36.

Barnum, Frances Courtenay Baylor. See Frances Courtenay Baylor.

BARNUM, PHINEAS TAYLOR (July 5, 1810–Apr. 7, 1891); b. Bethel, Conn. Publisher, showman. Called "the great American showman." Author: *Life of P. T. Barnum, Written by Himself* (1855); *The Humbugs of the World* (1865); *Lion Jack* (1876); etc. *See* Joel Benton's *Life of Hon. Phineas T. Barnum* (1891); M. R. Werner's *Barnum* (1923); Irving Wallace's *Fabulous Showman* (1959); Constance M. Rourke's *Trumpets of Jubilee* (1963).

BARON, SALO W[ittmayer] (May 26, 1895–); b. Tarnow, Austria. Educator, author. *Azariah de Rossi's Attitude to Life* (1927); *A Social and Religious History of the Jews*, 3v. (1937; rev. ed., vols. 1–14 1952–69); *The Jewish Community*, 3v. (1942); *Modern Nationalism and Religion* (1947); *The Russian Jew Under Tsars and Soviets* (1964); *History and Jewish Historians* (1964); and other works, in German. Editor: *Jewish Studies in Memory of G. A. Kohut* (1935); *The Jews of the U.S., 1790–1840: A Documentary History*, 3v. (with Joseph L. Blau, 1963); etc. Editor, *Jewish Social Studies*, since 1939. Editor-in-chief: *A Documentary History of American*

Jews, since 1954; *World History of the Jewish People,* vols. XIV–XX, since 1957. Prof. Jewish history, literature and institutions, Columbia University, since 1939; director, Center of Israel and Jewish Studies, since 1950.

BARR, ALFRED HAMILTON, JR. (Jan. 28, 1902–); b. Detroit, Mich. Art historian. *Cubism and Abstract Art* (1936); *What Is Modern Painting?* (1943); *Picasso: Fifty Years of His Art* (1946); *Matisse: His Art and His Public* (1951); *Picasso: 75th Anniversary Exhibition* (1957); etc. Editor: *Art in America* (with Holger Cahill, 1936); etc.

BARR, AMELIA EDITH HUDDLESTON (Mar. 29, 1831–Mar. 10, 1919); b. Ulverston, Lancashire, England. Author of 80 books, novels, poetry, miscellanies. *Romance and Reality* (1876); *Jan Vedder's Wife* (1885); *The Bow of Orange Ribbon* (1886); *The Maid of Maiden Lane* (1900); *The Black Shilling* (1903); *The Strawberry Handkerchief* (1908); *The House on Cherry Street* (1909); *All the Days of My Life: An Autobiography* (1913); etc.

BARR, GEORGE (1907–). Author. *Research Ideas for Young Scientists* (1958); *Epitaph for an Enemy* (1959); *More Research Ideas for Young Scientists* (1961); *Research Adventures for Young Scientists* (1964); *Fun and Tricks for Young Scientists* (1968); *Young Scientist and the Doctor* (1969).

BARR, JENE (July 28, 1900–); b. Kobrin, Russia. Author. *Conrad the Clock* (1944); *Little Circus Dog* (1949); *Good Morning, Teacher* (1957); *Mr. Zip and the U.S. Mail* (1964); *What Can Money Do?* (1967); etc.

BARR, STRINGFELLOW (Jan. 15, 1897–); b. Suffolk, Va. Educator, author. *Mazzini: Portrait of an Exile* (1935); *Pilgrimage of Western Man* (1949); *Citizens of the World* (1952); *Copydog of India* (1955); *Purely Academic* (1958); *The Will of Zeus* (1961); *The Three Worlds of Man* (1963); *The Mask of Jove* (1966). Advisory editor, *Virginia Quarterly Review,* 1926–30, 1934–37; editor, 1930–34. President, St. John's College, Annapolis, Md., 1937–46. Prof. humanities, Newark College, Rutgers University, since 1955.

BARRELL, SARAH SAYWARD (Mrs. Richard Keating; Mrs. Abiel Wood) (Oct. 1, 1759–Jan. 6, 1855); b. York, Me. Earliest Maine novelist. Under pen name, "A Lady of Massachusetts": *Julia and the Illuminated Baron* (1800); *Dorval; or, The Speculator* (1801); *Amelia; or, The Influence of Virtue* (1802); *Ferdinand and Elmira* (1804). Under pen name, "A Lady of Maine": *Tales of the Night* (1827).

Barren Ground. Novel by Ellen Glasgow (1925). Story of Dorinda Oakley, daughter of a "poor white" farmer who successfully salvages the barren acres of the farm from the encroachments of wild nature.

BARRETT, E[dward John] BOYD (Oct. 29, 1883–); b. Dublin, Ireland. Psychologist, author. *The Jesuit Enigma* (1927); *While Peter Sleeps* (1928); *The Magnificent Illusion* (1930); *Ex-Jesuit* (autobiography, 1931); *Rome Stoops to Conquer* (1935); *The Great O'Neill* (1939); *Shepherds in the Mist* (1949); *Life Begins With Love* (1952); *Shepherd Without Sheep* (autobiography, 1956).

BARRETT, LILLIAN [Foster] (June 13, 1884–Apr. 28, 1963); b. Newport, R.I., sister of Richmond Brooks Barrett. Novelist, playwright. *The Sinister Revel* (1919); *Gibbeted Gods* (1921), dramatized as *The Dice of the Gods* (prod. 1923); *The Crowd Out Front* (1927); etc.

BARRETT, RICHMOND BROOKS (Aug. 28, 1895–); b. Newport, R.I. Author. *Rapture* (1924); *The Enemy's Gates* (1926); *Madam* (1932); *Good Old Summer Days* (1941); *Truant* (1944); etc.

BARRETT, STEPHEN MELVIL (Mar. 3, 1865–deceased); b. Nebraska City, Neb. Educator, author. *Mocco, An Indian Boy* (1912); *Hoistah, An Indian Girl* (1912); *The Pawnee* (1914); *Shinkah, the Osage* (1915); *Bob, the Pioneer* (1938);

Sociology of the American Indians (1946); etc. President, Oklahoma Military Academy, 1919–25.

Barrett, Walter. Pen name of Joseph Alfred Scoville.

BARRETT, WILLIAM (1913–). Editor, author. *Aristotle's Analysis of Movement* (1938); *Irrational Man* (1958); etc. Editor, *Partisan Review;* book-review editor, *Atlantic Monthly,* since 1961. Prof. philosophy, New York University.

BARRETT, WILLIAM EDMUND (Nov. 16, 1900–); b. New York. Author. *Woman on Horseback* (1938); *Flight from Youth* (1939); *To the Last Man* (1948); *The Left Hand of God* (1951); *Shadows of the Images* (1953); *Sudden Strangers* (1956); *The Empty Shrine* (1958); *The Edge of Things* (1960); *The Fools of Time* (1963); *The Wine and The Music* (1969).

BARRETTO, LARRY [Laurence Brevoort] (May 30, 1890–); b. Larchmont, N.Y. Novelist. *A Conqueror Passes* (1924); *To Babylon* (1925); *Walls of Glass* (1926); *Old Enchantment* (1928); *Horses in the Sky* (1929); *The Indiscreet Years* (1931); *Children of Pleasure* (1932); *Three Roads from Paradise* (1933); *Bright Mexico* (1935); *Tomorrow Will Be Different* (1936); *Hawaiian Holiday* (with Bryant Cooper, 1938); *Journey Through Time* (1940); *The Great Light* (1947).

Barriers Burned Away. Novel by Edward Payson Roe (1872). Records the struggles of Dennis Fleet against a background of snobbery. The title derives from the great Chicago fire, which is strikingly described in the book.

Barritt, Frances Fuller. See Frances Fuller Victor.

BARRON, ELWYN ALFRED (Mar. 6, 1855–Sept. 28, 1929); b. Lima, N.Y. Playwright, novelist, drama critic. *Lady Ashley* (prod. 1886); *The Viking* (1888); *Lawrence Barrett* (1889); *Manders, a Tale of Persia* (1899); *In Old New York; A Romance* (with Wilson Barrett, 1900); *Marcel Levignet* (1906); *The Ruling Power* (prod. 1904); etc. Drama critic, *Chicago Inter-Ocean.*

BARRON, MILTON LEON (Feb. 25, 1918–); b. Derby, Conn. Sociologist, educator. *People Who Intermarry* (1947); *The Juvenile in Delinquent Society* (1954); *The Aging American* (1961). Editor: *American Minority* (1957); *Minorities in a Changing World* (1967). Sociology dept., College of the City of New York, since 1954.

BARROW, FRANCES ELIZABETH MEASE (Feb. 22, 1822–1894); b. Charleston, S.C. Pen name, "Aunt Fanny." Author of children's books, which were finally reissued in several series: the *Little Pet Books,* 3v. (1860); the *Good Little Hearts* series, 4v. (1864); the *Six Mitten Books,* 6v.; etc. Her most famous story is "The Letter G" (1864).

BARROWS, JOHN HENRY (July 11, 1847–June 2, 1902); b. Medina, O. Congregational clergyman, educator, biographer. *Henry Ward Beecher* (1893).

BARROWS, MARJORIE; b. Chicago, Ill. Editor, author. *The Magic Umbrella Abroad* (1930); *Who's Who in the Zoo* (1932); *Muggins Mouse* (1932); *Ezra, the Elephant* (1934); *Johnny Giraffe* (1935); *Snuggles* (1935); *Fraidy Cat* (1941); *Scamper* (1949); *Muggins Becomes a Hero* (1968); etc. Editor: *One Hundred Best Poems for Boys and Girls* (1930); *A Book of Famous Poems for Older Boys and Girls* (1931); *Read-Aloud Poems* (1957); *The Family Reader* (1956); etc. Assoc. editor, *Child Life,* 1922–31; editor-in-chief, 1931–38; editor-in-chief, *Children's Hour,* since 1952; editor, *Treasure Trails,* 1954–56.

BARROWS, WAYNE GROVE (May 12, 1880–); b. Chicago, Ill. Novelist. *The Law of the Range* (1909); *A Child of the Plains* (1911).

BARRY, ETHELRED BREEZE (Feb. 26, 1870–); Portsmouth, N.H. Author. *Little Tong's Mission* (1899); *The Countess of the Tenements* (1900); *Little Dick's Christmas* (1903); etc.

BARRY, JOHN D[aniel] (Dec. 31, 1866–Nov. 3, 1942); b. Boston, Mass. Journalist, novelist. *The Intriguers* (1896); *Mademoiselle Blanche* (1896); *A Daughter of Thespis* (1903); *Julia Marlowe* (1907); *Intimations* (1913); *The City of Domes* (1915); *Reactions and Other Essays* (1915); etc. Essayist on *San Francisco Bulletin,* 1910–18; *San Francisco Call,* 1918–26; *San Francisco News,* from 1926.

BARRY, PHILIP (June 18, 1896–Nov. 3, 1949); b. Rochester, N.Y. Playwright. *You and I* (prod. 1923); *The Youngest* (prod. 1924); *In a Garden* (prod. 1925); *White Wings* (prod. 1926); *Paris Bound* (prod. 1927); *Holiday* (prod. 1928); *Cock Robin* (with Elmer L. Rice, prod. 1928); *Hotel Universe* (prod. 1930); *Tomorrow and Tomorrow* (prod. 1931); *The Animal Kingdom* (prod. 1932); *The Joyous Season* (prod. 1934); *Bright Star* (prod. 1935); *Here Come the Clowns* (prod. 1938); *The Philadelphia Story* (prod. 1939); *Liberty Jones* (prod. 1940); *Without Love* (prod. 1942); *Foolish Notion* (prod. 1944); *Second Threshold* (1951).

BARRY, RICHARD HAYES (Sept. 10, 1881–); b. Eau Claire, Wis. Novelist, playwright. *Sandy from the Sierras* (1904); *The Events Man* (1907); *Brenda of the Woods* (1914); *The Love Bird* (prod. 1915); *Fruit of the Desert* (1919); *The Big Gun* (1925); *Barefoot* (prod. 1925); *Blue Pete* (1933); *Father and His Town* (1941); *Mr. Rutledge of South Carolina* (1942); etc. On staff, *Pearson's Magazine,* 1910–14; *New York Times Sunday Magazine,* 1914–24; etc.

BARSOTTI, CHARLES (Jan. 4, 1850–Mar. 30, 1927); b. near Pisa, Italy. Founder, *Il Progresso* in New York, the first Italian daily in the United States. Responsible for statue of Christopher Columbus at Columbus Circle, New York City, also those of Dante, Verdi, etc.

BARTH, ALAN (Oct. 21, 1906–); b. New York. Editorial writer, author. *The Loyalty of Free Men* (1951); *Government by Investigation* (1955); *The Price of Liberty* (1961); *Heritage of Liberty* (1965). Editorial Writer, *Washington Post,* since 1943.

BARTH, JOHN [Simmons] (May 27, 1930–); b. Cambridge, Md. Novelist, educator. *The Floating Opera* (1956); *End of the Road* (1958); *The Sot-Weed Factor* (1960); *Giles Goat-Boy* (1966); *Lost in the Funhouse* (1968). English faculty, State University of New York at Buffalo, since 1965.

BARTHELME, DONALD (Apr. 7, 1931–); b. Philadelphia, Pa. Author. *Come Back, Dr. Caligari* (stories, 1964); *Snow White* (1967); *Unspeakable Practices, Unnatural Acts* (stories, 1969); *City Life* (1970). Contributor to *The New Yorker* and other magazines.

Bartleby the Scrivener. Story by Herman Melville, published anonymously in *Putnam's Magazine* (1853).

BARTLETT, ALICE ELINOR (Sept. 4, 1848–Nov. 18, 1920); b. Delavan, Wis. Author. Pen name, "Birch Arnold." *Until the Daybreak* (1877); *A News Aristocrat* (1891); *The Spirit of the Inland Seas* (1901); *Birch Leaves* (1905); etc.

BARTLETT, ALICE HUNT (Mrs. William Allen Bartlett) (July 31, 1870–Sept. 14, 1949); Bennington, Vt. Poet. *Road Royal* (poems, 1927); *Caesar—the Undefeated: A Poetic Drama* (1929); *Two Thousand Years of Virgil* (1929); *Washington Pre-Eminent* (1931); *The Freedom of the Mediterranean* (play, 1938); *Six Historic and Romantic Leaders Who Visioned World Peace* (plays, 1946); etc. Editor: *The Sea Anthology* (1924); *The Anthology of Cities* (1926); etc.

BARTLETT, ARTHUR CHARLES (May 22, 1901–July 13, 1964); b. Norway, Mo. Editor, author. *Spunk, Leader of the Dog Team* (1926); *The Sea Dog* (1927); *Gumpy, Son of Spunk* (1930); *General Jim* (1931); *Pal* (1932); *Yankee Doodle* (1935); *Find Your Own Frontier* (1940); *Baseball and Mr. Spalding* (1951). Assoc. editor, *American Magazine,* 1929–30; *Country Home,* 1930–36; managing editor, 1936–37; staff writer, *This Week,* 1939–42; contributing editor, 1943–46; assoc. editor, *Country Gentleman,* 1946–47.

BARTLETT, FREDERICK ORIN (July 2, 1876–); b. Haverhill, Mass. Novelist. Pen name, "William Carleton." Under own name: *Mistress Dorothy* (1901); *The Seventh Noon* (1910); *The Wall Street Girl* (1916); *Out of the Night* (1923); etc. Under pen name: *One Way Out* (1911); *New Lives for Old* (1913); *The Red Geranium* (1915); *Big Laurel* (1922). Wrote articles for the *Saturday Evening Post* under the name "The Old Dog," in 1925–26.

BARTLETT, JOHN (June 14, 1820–Dec. 3, 1905); b. Plymouth, Mass. Editor, publisher. Compiler: *A Collection of Familiar Quotations* (1855); *The Shakespeare Phrase Book* (1881); *A New and Complete Concordance or Verbal Index to Words, Phrases, & Passages in the Dramatic Works of Shakespeare, with A Supplementary Concordance to the Poems* (1894). The 1937 revision of *Bartlett's Familiar Quotations* was made by Christopher Morley and Louella D. Everett.

BARTLETT, JOHN RUSSELL (Oct. 23, 1805–May 28, 1886); b. Providence, R.I. Librarian, bibliographer, editor. Compiler: *Dictionary of Americanisms* (1848); *The Literature of the Rebellion* (1866). Editor: *Records of the Colony of Rhode Island and Providence Plantations,* 10v. (1856–65). Librarian, John Carter Brown Library, Providence, R.I.; He prepared a four volume catalogue of its collections, 1865–82.

BARTLETT, JOSEPH (June 10, 1762–Oct. 20, 1827); b. Plymouth, Mass. Poet, eccentric adventurer. *Aphorisms* (1810); *Physiognomy* (Phi Beta Kappa poem at Harvard, 1799, publ. 1810).

Bartlett, Nancy. Pen name of Charles Stanley Strong.

BARTLETT, ROBERT ABRAM (Aug. 15, 1875–Apr. 28, 1946); b. Brigus, Newfoundland. Explorer, author. *The Last Voyage of the Karluk* (1916); *The Log of Bob Bartlett* (1928); *Sails Over Ice* (1934).

BARTLETT, ROBERT MERRILL (Dec. 23, 1899–); b. Kingston, Ind. Clergyman, educator, author. *The Great Empire of Silence* (1929); *Builders of a New World* (1933); *They Dared to Live* (1937); *They Dare to Believe* (1952); *Fighters for Freedom* (1958); *They Stand Invincible—Men Who Are Transforming Our World* (1959); *The Huguenots and Their Cross* (1964); *Thanksgiving Day* (1965); *Pilgrim Robert Bartlett 1603–1676* (1966); etc.

Bartlett & Welford. New York booksellers. Their store was a popular literary rendezvous in the 1840's. The proprietors were John Russell Bartlett (1805–86) and Charles Welford. In 1849 Bartlett withdrew, and the firm was continued as Scribner and Welford.

BARTLEY, NALBRO [Isadorah] (Nov. 10, 1888–); b. Buffalo, N.Y. Novelist. *Paradise Auction* (1917); *Gray Angels* (1920); *Fair to Middling* (1921); *Pattycake Princess* (1925); *Morning Thunder* (1926); *Her Mother's Daughter* (1926); *The Fox Woman* (1928); *The Godfather* (1929); *The Premeditated Virgin* (1930); *Breathless* (1933).

Barton, Andrew. Pen name of Thomas Forrest.

BARTON, BRUCE (Aug. 5, 1886–July 5, 1967); b. Robbins, Tenn. Congressman, advertiser, author. *More Power to You* (1917); *It's a Good Old World* (1920); *Better Days* (1924); *The Man Nobody Knows* (1925); *The Book Nobody Knows* (1926); *What Can a Man Believe?* (1927); *On the Up and Up* (1929); *He Upset the World* (1932).

BARTON, CLARA [Harlowe] (Dec. 25, 1821–Apr. 12, 1912); b. Oxford, Mass. Philanthropist, author. *History of the Red Cross* (1882); *The Story of My Childhood* (1907); etc. She established the American Red Cross in 1881. See William E. Barton's *The Life of Clara Barton,* 2v. (1921); *Clara Barton* by Mildred Pace (1941).

BARTON, GEORGE (Jan. 22, 1866–Mar. 16, 1940); b. Philadelphia, Pa. Journalist, author. *Celebrated Spies and Famous*

Mysteries of the Great War (1919); *Columbus the Catholic* (1893); *Little Journeys Around Old Philadelphia* (1925); *Walks and Talks About Old Philadelphia* (1928); *Adventures of the World's Greatest Detectives* (1908); *Real Stories of the Secret Service* (1910); *Famous Detective Mysteries* (1926); *Great Triumphs of Crime Detection* (1937); etc. Author of the "Bell Haven" stories for boys.

BARTON, GEORGE AARON (Nov. 12, 1859–June 28, 1942); b. E. Farnham, P.Q. Canada. Educator, Orientalist. *A Year's Wandering in Bible Lands* (1904); *Ecclesiastes* (in New International Critical Commentary, 1908); *Archaeology and the Bible* (1916); *Religions of the World* (1917); *A History of the Hebrew People* (1930); *Christ and Evolution* (1934); etc. Prof. Biblical literature, Bryn Mawr College, 1891–1922.

BARTON, OLIVE ROBERTS (Mrs. James Lowrie Barton) (July 26, 1880–Aug. 14, 1957); b. Allegheny, Pa. Author. *Cloud Boat Stories* (1916); *Wonderful Land of Up* (1918); *Story Riddles in Rime and Prose* (1928); *Bramble Bush Riddles* (1930); etc.

BARTON, RALPH (Aug. 14, 1891–May 20, 1931); b. Kansas City, Mo. Illustrator, author. *Science in Rhyme Without Reason* (1924); *God's Country* (1929). Has illustrated Anita Loos's *Gentlemen Prefer Blondes,* etc.

BARTON, WILLIAM ELEAZAR (June 28, 1861–Dec. 7, 1930); b. Sublette, Ill. Congregational clergyman, author. *A Tale of the Cumberland Mountains* (1887); augmented as *Life in the Hills of Kentucky* (1889); *A Hero in Homespun* (1897); *The Prairie Schooner* (1900); *The Life of Clara Barton,* 2v. (1921); *The Life of Abraham Lincoln,* 2v. (1925); *Abraham Lincoln and Walt Whitman* (1928); *The Autobiography* (1932); etc.

BARTRAM, JOHN (Mar. 23, 1699–Sept. 22, 1777); b. Marple, Delaware Co., Pa. First native American botanist. *Observations on the Inhabitants, Climate, Soil, Rivers, Productions, Animals, and Other Matters Worthy of Note; Made by Mr. John Bartram, in His Travels from Pensilvania to Onondago, Oswego, and the Lake Ontario, in Canada* (1751). *See* Ernest Earnest's *John and William Bartram* (1940); *Memorials of John Bartram and Humphrey Marshall,* ed. by William Darlington (rev. of 1849 ed., 1967). Founded first botanical garden in America, at Kingsessing, Philadelphia, Pa.

BARTRAM, WILLIAM (Feb. 9, 1739–July 22, 1823); b. Kingsessing (now in Philadelphia, Pa.), son of John Bartram. Naturalist, traveler, author. *Travels Through North and South Carolina, Georgia, East and West Florida, the Cherokee Country, the Extensive Territories of the Muscogulges, or Creek Confederacy, and the Country of the Chactaws* (1791).

BARUCH, BERNARD M[annes] (Aug. 19, 1870–June 20, 1965). Financier, author. *Making of Economic and Reparation Sections of the Peace Treaty* (1920); *A Philosophy for Our Time* (1954); *Baruch: My Own Story* (1957); *Baruch: The Public Years* (1960).

BARUCH, DOROTHY WALTER (Aug. 5, 1899–); b. San Francisco, Cal. Psychologist, author. *Four Airplanes* (1941); *Pitter Patter* (1943); *The Glass House of Prejudice* (1946); *New Ways in Discipline* (1949); *One Little Boy* (1952); *How to Live with Your Teenager* (1953); *New Ways in Sex Education* (1959); *I Would Like to Be a Pony, and Other Wishes* (1959); *Kobo and the Wishing Pictures* (1964); etc.

BARZUN, JACQUES (Nov. 30, 1907–); b. Paris. Educator, author. *Romanticism and the Modern Ego* (1943); *The Teacher in America* (1945); *Berlioz and the Romantic Century* (1950); *God's Country and Mine* (1954); *Music in American Life* (1956); *The Modern Researcher* (with Henry F. Graff, 1957); *The House of Intellect* (1959); *Science: The Glorious Entertainment* (1964); *The American University: How It Runs, Where It Is Going* (1968); etc. Editor: *Pleasures of Music* (1951); *Selected Letters of Lord Byron* (1953); Follett's *Modern American Usage* (1966); etc. Prof. history, Columbia University, since 1945.

BASCOM, JOHN (May 1, 1827–Oct. 2, 1911); b. Genoa, N.Y. Educator, philosopher. *Aesthetics* (1862); *Philosophy of Rhetoric* (1866); *Philosophy of English Literature* (1874); *Things Learned by Living* (autobiography, 1913). President, University of Wisconsin, 1874–87.

Basic Books, Inc., Publishers. New York. Founded 1950, by Arthur J. Rosenthal, who is president and editor in chief. Irving Kristol is senior editor. Known for its books in the social sciences. Bought the Natural History Book Club and The Readers' Subscription, both in 1959. Acquired by Harper and Row, Publishers (q.v.), in 1969.

BASKERVILL, CHARLES READ (Apr. 17, 1872–July 22, 1935); b. Covington, Tenn. Educator, author. *Some Evidence for Early Romantic Plays in England* (1916); *Dramatic Aspects of Medieval Folk Festivals in England* (1920); *The Elizabethan Jig and Related Song Drama* (1929). Dept. of English, University of Chicago.

BASKETT, JAMES NEWTON (Nov. 1, 1849–June 14, 1925); b. in Nicholas Co., Ky. Naturalist, novelist. *The Story of the Birds* (1896); *At You-All's House* (1898); *As the Light Led* (1900); *Sweet-Brier and Thistledown* (1902); etc.

BASLER, ROY P[rentice] (Nov. 19, 1906–); b. St. Louis, Mo. Educator, librarian, author. *Sex, Symbolism, and Psychology in Literature* (1948); *A Short History of the American Civil War* (1967); *The Lincoln Legend: A Study in Changing Conceptions* (1969). Editor: *Abraham Lincoln: His Speeches and Writings* (1946); *The Collected Works of Abraham Lincoln,* 9v. (1953). Editor, *The Abraham Lincoln Quarterly,* 1947–1952. Staff, Library of Congress, since 1952; now director of reference department.

BASSETT, JOHN SPENCER (Sept. 10, 1867–Jan. 27, 1928); b. Tarboro, N.C. Essayist, historian, biographer. *The Life of Andrew Jackson,* 2v. (1911); *A Short History of the United States* (1913); *The Middle Group of American Historians* (1917); etc. Editor, *South Atlantic Quarterly,* 1902–05. Prof. history, Smith College, 1906–28.

BASSETT, SARA WARE (Oct. 22, 1872–); b. Newton, Mass. Novelist. *Taming of Zenas Henry* (1915); *The Wayfarers at the Angels* (1917); *The Harbor Road* (1919); *The Wall Between* (1920); *Flood Tide* (1921); *Granite and Clay* (1922); *The Green Dolphin* (1926); *Bayberry Lane* (1931); *Twin Lights* (1932); *Shifting Sands* (1933); *Turning Tide* (1934); *Hidden Shoals* (1935); *Eternal Deeps* (1936); *Shining Headlands* (1937); *New England Born* (1938); *A Son of the Sea* (1939); *Cross Currents* (1941); *Anchorage* (1943); *Silver Moon Cottage* (1945); *White Sail* (1949); *Echoes of the Tide* (1951); *Beyond the Breakers* (1952); *South Cove Summer* (1956); *The Girl in the Blue Pinafore* (1957); etc.

BASSHE, EMJO (1900–Oc. 28, 1939); b. Vilna, Rus. Playwright. *Earth* (1927); *Centuries* (1928); *Doomsday Circus* (1938); etc.

BASSO, [Joseph] HAMILTON (Sept. 5, 1904–May 13, 1964); b. New Orleans, La. Novelist, biographer. *Relics and Angels* (1929); *Beauregard, the Great Creole* (1933); *Cinnamon Seed* (1934); *In Their Own Image* (1935); *Courthouse Square* (1936); *Days Before Lent* (1939); *The World from Jackson Square* (with Etolia S. Basso, 1948); *The Green Room* (1949); *The View from Pompey's Head* (1954); *The Light Infantry Ball* (1959); *Quota of Seaweed* (1960); *A Touch of the Dragon* (1964).

Bat, The. Mystery drama by Mary Roberts Rinehart and Avery Hopwood (prod. 1920).

BATCHELDER, ROGER (June 5, 1897–Dec. 13, 1947); b. Washington, D.C. Columnist. *Camp Devens* (1917); *Camp Upton* (1918); *Camp Dix* (1918); *Camp Lee* (1918); etc. Wrote "Skylines of New York" and "Footlights of Broadway" for North American Newspaper Alliance, 1932–33.

BATCHELLER, TRYPHOSA BATES (1878–Sept. 9, 1952); b. North Brookfield, Mass. Singer, author. *Glimpses of Italian Court Life* (1906); *Italian Castles and Country Seats* (1911); *Royal Spain of To-Day* (1913); *The Soul of a Queen* (1942); *France In Sunshine and Shadow* (1944); etc.

BATE, WALTER JACKSON (May 23, 1918–); b. Mankato, Minn. Educator, author. *Negative Capability* (1939); *The Stylistic Development of Keats* (1945); *From Classic to Romantic* (1946); *Criticism: the Major Texts* (1952); *The Achievement of Samuel Johnson* (1955); *John Keats* (1963; Pulitzer Prize, 1964). Prof. English, Harvard University, since 1956.

BATEMAN, SIDNEY F[rances Cowell] (Mar. 29, 1823–Jan. 13, 1881); b. New York City. Actress, playwright. *Self* (prod. 1856); *Geraldine; or, Love's Victory* (prod. 1859); etc.

BATEN, ANDERSON MONROE (Jan. 14, 1888–May, 1943); b. Brenham, Tex. Author. *Slang from Shakespeare* (1931); *Will Rogers* (1935); *Dallas* (1936); *Language of Life* (1938).

BATES, ARLO (Dec. 6, 1850–Aug. 24, 1918); b. East Machias, Me. Educator, editor, novelist, poet. *The Pagans* (1884); *A Wheel of Fire* (1885); *Berries in the Brier* (poems, 1886); *Sonnets in Shadow* (1887); *The Philistines* (1889); *The Poet and His Self* (poems, 1891); *Talks on the Study of Literature* (1895); *Talks on Writing English,* 2v. (1896–1901); *The Puritans* (1898); *Under the Beech Tree* (poems, 1899); *Love in a Cloud* (1900); *The Diary of a Saint* (1902); etc. Editor, *Boston Sunday Courier,* 1880–93.

BATES, CHARLOTTE FISKE (Mme. Adolphe Rogé) (Nov. 30, 1838–Sept. 1, 1916); b. New York City. Poet. *Risk, and Other Poems* (1879). Editor: *The Cambridge Book of Poetry and Song* (1882). Assisted Longfellow in compiling his *Poems of Places.*

BATES, CLARA DOTY (1838–1895); b. Ann Arbor, Mich. Poet, author of juveniles. *Blind Jakey* (1868); *On the Way to Wonderland* (1884); *From Heart's Content* (poems, 1892); etc.

BATES, DAVID (1809–Jan. 25, 1870); b. Philadelphia, Pa. Poet. *The Eolian* (1849), republished as *Poems* (1853); *The Poetical Works* (1870), ed. by his son, Stockton Bates. His best known poems are "Speak Gently" and "Childhood."

BATES, ERNEST SUTHERLAND (Oct. 14, 1879–Dec. 4, 1939); b. Gambier, O. Educator, editor. *This Land of Liberty* (1930); *Mary Baker Eddy: The Truth and the Tradition* (with John Valentine Dittemore, 1932); *The Story of Congress* (1936); *The Story of the Supreme Court* (1936); *Hearst, Lord of San Simeon* (with Oliver Carlson, 1936); *American Faith* (1940); etc. Editor: *The Bible Designed to be Read as Living Literature* (1936). Lit. editor, *Dictionary of American Biography,* 1926–29. Assoc. editor, *The Modern Monthly,* 1933–36.

BATES, HARRIET LEONORA VOSE (Mrs. Arlo Bates) (1856–1886). Author. Pen name, "Eleanor Putnam." *Old Salem* (1886); *Prince Vance* (with husband, 1888); *A Woodland Wooing* (1889); etc.

BATES, HERBERT (June 29, 1868–Apr. 16, 1929); b. Hyde Park, Mass. Educator, poet. *Songs in Exile* (1896). Editor: *Modern Lyric Poetry: An Anthology* (1929).

BATES, KATHARINE LEE (Aug. 12, 1850–Mar. 28, 1929); b. Falmouth, Mass. Educator, poet. *College Beautiful, and Other Poems* (1887); *American Literature* (1898); *America the Beautiful, and Other Poems* (1911); *Fairy Gold* (poems, 1916); *America the Dream* (1930); etc.

BATES, MARGRET HOLMES (Mrs. Charles Austin Bates) (Oct. 6, 1844–deceased); b. Fremont, O. Author, *Manitou* (1881); *Shylock's Daughter* (1894); *In the First Degree* (1907); *Hildegarde, and Other Lyrics* (1911); *Browning Critiques* (1921); etc.

BATES, MARSTON (July 23, 1906–); b. Grand Rapids, Mich. Naturalist. *The Natural History of Mosquitoes* (1949); *The Nature of Natural History* (1950); *Where Winter Never Comes* (1952); *The Prevalence of People* (1955); *Coral Island* (1958); *The Forest and the Sea* (1960); *Man in Nature* (1961); *The Nature of Natural History* (1962); *Animal Worlds* (1964); *The Land and Wildlife of South America* (1964). Prof. zoology, University of Michigan, since 1952.

BATES, SYLVIA CHATFIELD; b. Springfield, Mass. Novelist. *The Geranium Lady* (1916); *Andrea Thorne* (1925); *The Long Way Home* (1937); *The Floor of Heaven* (1940); *The Weather Breeder* (1948); *Silver Yoke* (1951); etc. Editor: *Twentieth Century Short Stories* (1933).

BATES, WALTER (Mar. 14, 1760–Feb. 11, 1842); b. Darien, Conn. Loyalist, author. *The Mysterious Stranger* (1816).

BATES, WILLIAM NICKERSON (Dec. 8, 1867–June 10, 1949); b. Cambridge, Mass. Educator, archaeologist, author. *Notes on the Theseum at Athens* (1901); *Etruscan Inscriptions* (1905); *Euripides, a Student of Human Nature* (1930); *Sophocles, Poet and Dramatist* (1940); etc. Editor, *American Journal of Archaeology,* 1908–20; editor-in-chief, 1920–24. Greek dept., University of Pennsylvania, 1895–1939.

BATESON, GREGORY (May 9, 1904–); b. Grantchester, Eng. Cultural anthropologist. *Naven* (1936); *Balinese Character: A Photographic Analysis* (with Margaret Mead, 1942); *Communication: The Social Matrix of Psychiatry* (with Jurgen Ruesch, 1951). Editor: *Perceval's Narrative: A Patient's Account of His Psychosis, 1830–1832* (1961).

BATTEN, LORING WOART (Nov. 17, 1859–Jan. 1946); b. Gloucester Co., N.J. Episcopal Clergyman, educator, author. *The Hebrew Prophet* (1905); *Ezra-Nehemiah* (in International Critical Commentary, 1913); *Good and Evil* (1918); etc. Lecturer on the Old Testament, in General Theological Seminary, 1904–33.

BATTENHOUSE, HENRY MARTIN (Aug. 27, 1885–Mar. 24, 1960); b. Green Garden, Ill. Educator, Author. *The Philosophy of Friedrich Nietzsche* (1917); *New Testament History and Literature* (1937); *This Seed of Faith* (1942); *Christ in the Gospels* (1952); *English Romantic Writers* (1958); etc. Prof. English literature, Albion College, 1928–52.

"Battle Cry of Freedom, The." Poem by George Frederick Root, written to celebrate the charge of the Negro troops at Port Hudson, May 27, 1863.

"Battle Hymn, A." Civil War poem by George H. Boker (1862).

"Battle Hymn of the Republic, The." Poem by Julia Ward Howe, in the *Atlantic Monthly,* Feb. 1862. Included in her *Later Lyrics* (1866).

"Battle of Bunker's Hill, The." Poem by Hugh Henry Brackenridge (1776).

"Battle of Charleston Harbor, The." Poem by Paul Hamilton Hayne (1863).

Battle of Eutaw Springs and Evacuation of Charleston, The. Play by William Ioor (prod. 1813).

"Battle of Kings Mountain, The." Anonymous ballad of the Revolution (1781).

"Battle of Lookout Mountain, The." Poem by George Henry Boker (1864).

"Battle of Lovell's Pond, The." First poem by Henry Wadsworth Longfellow (1820). It deals with the historic Indian fight in Maine, near Fryeburg, May 8, 1725, between Captain Lovewell's Massachusetts Rangers and a band of Pequawkets under Paugus.

Battle of New Orleans, The. Play by C. E. Grice (prod. 1816).

Battle of Stillwater, The. Play by Rufus Dawes (prod. 1840).

"Battle of the Kegs, The." By Francis Hopkinson (1778). Most popular of all Revolutionary ballads, it describes the alarm of the British over some empty powder-kegs which the American patriots had set floating down the Delaware River.

Battleground, The. Novel by Ellen Glasgow (1902). Virginia during the Civil War.

BAUER, FLORENCE [Anne Marvyne] b. Elgin, Ill. Author. *Behold Your King* (1945); *Abraham, Son of Terah* (1948); *Daughter of Nazareth* (1955); *Lady Besieged* (1960); etc.

BAUER, RAYMOND AUGUSTINE (Sept. 7, 1916–); b. Chicago, Ill. Psychologist. *The New Man in Soviet Psychology* (1952); *Nine Soviet Portraits* (1955); *How the Soviet System Works* (with Alex Inkeles and Clyde Kluckhohn, 1956); *American Business and Public Policy* (with others, 1963); *Social Indicators* (with others, 1966).

BAUGH, ALBERT CROLL (Feb. 26, 1891–); b. Philadelphia, Pa. Educator, author. *A History of the English Language* (1935); *Literary History of England* (with others, 1948). Editor: *Century Types of English Literature* (with G. W. McClelland, 1925); *The Literature of America,* 2v. (with A. H. Quinn and W. D. Howe, 1929); *Essays Towards Living* (with N. E. McClure, 1929); *Chaucer's Major Poetry* (1963); etc. English dept., University of Pennsylvania, since 1912.

BAUM, L[yman] FRANK (May 15, 1856–May 6, 1919); b. Chittenango, N.Y. Playwright, novelist, author of juveniles. *Father Goose: His Book* (1899); *The Wonderful Wizard of Oz* (1900; dramatic version prod. 1901); *The Land of Oz* (1904); *The Fate of a Clown* (under pen name "Schuyler Staunton," 1905); *Ozma of Oz* (1908); *Dorothy and the Wizard in Oz* (1908); *The Road to Oz* (1909); *The Emerald City of Oz* (1910); *The Patchwork Girl of Oz* (1913); *Tik-Tok of Oz* (1914); *The Scarecrow of Oz* (1915); *Rinkitink in Oz* (1916); *The Lost Princess of Oz* (1917); *The Tin Woodman of Oz* (1918); *The Magic of Oz* (1919); *Glinda of Oz* (1920); etc.; also books for boys under pen name "Floyd Akens," and for girls under pen name "Edith Van Dyne." *See* Russell R. Mac-Fall and Frank J. Baum's *To Please a Child* (1961).

BAUM, PAULL FRANKLIN (May 13, 1886–July 15, 1964); b. Dover, Del. Educator, author. *The Principles of English Versification* (1922); *Tennyson Sixty Years After* (1948); *Chaucer: A Critical Appreciation* (1958); *Ten Studies in the Poetry of Matthew Arnold* (1958); *Chaucer's Verse* (1961). Editor: *Dante Gabriel Rossetti: An Analytical List of Manuscripts in the Duke University Library* (1931); *Dante Gabriel Rossetti: Poems, Ballads and Sonnets* (1937); *The Centennial Edition of Sidney Lanier* (1945); etc. Prof. English, Duke University, since 1923; editorial director, Duke University Press, 1926–28.

BAUM, VICKI (Mrs. Richard Lert) (Jan. 24, 1896–Aug. 29, 1960); b. Vienna, Austria, came to America 1931, naturalized 1938. Novelist. *Grand Hotel* (1931); *Martin's Summer* (1931); *Helene* (1932); *Falling Star* (1934); *Sing, Sister, Sing* (1936); *Tale of Bali* (1937); *Shanghai* (1939); *Ship and Shore* (1941); *Hotel Berlin, 1943* (1944); *Headless Angel* (1948); *The Mustard Seed* (1953); *Written on Water* (1956); *Theme for Ballet* (1958); etc.

BAUMBACH, JONATHAN (July 5, 1933–). Author. *The Landscape of Nightmare: Studies in the Contemporary American Novel* (1965); *A Man to Conjure With* (1965); *What Comes Next?* Editor: *Writers as Teachers, Teachers as Writers* (1970). Faculty, New York University, since 1964.

BAXTER, JAMES PHINNEY, III (Feb. 15, 1893–); b. Portland, Me. Educator. *The Introduction of the Ironclad Warship* (1933); *Scientists Against Time* (1946; Pulitzer Prize for history, 1947). Pres. Williams College, 1937–61.

BAXTER, LYDIA (Sept. 2, 1809–Jan. 23, 1874); b. Petersburg, N.Y. Poet, hymn writer. *Gems By the Wayside* (1855). Her best-known hymn is "The Gates Ajar."

BAXTER, SYLVESTER (Feb. 6, 1850–Jan. 28, 1927); b. West Yarmouth, Mass. Publicist, author. *The Cruise of a Land-Yacht* (1891); *Old Marblehead* (1906); *The Unseen House* (poems, 1917); etc.

BAXTER, WILLIAM (July 6, 1820–Feb. 11, 1880); b. Leeds, England. Disciples clergyman, author. *Pea Ridge and Prairie Grove; or, Scenes and Incidents of the War in Arkansas* (1864). He was the author of several popular Civil War poems which appeared in *Harper's Weekly.*

"Bay Fight, The." Poem by Henry Howard Brownell (1864). On the fight in Mobile Bay, Aug. 5, 1864, when Farragut was victorious.

Bay Psalm Book, The. First book in English printed in America (1640). Edited by Richard Mather, Thomas Welde and John Eliot. It rendered the King James version of the Bible into verse. Often revised; it reached twenty-seven editions before 1750. The New York Public Library and the Huntington Library have copies of the first edition.

BAYLISS, MARGUERITE FARLEIGH (June 27, 1895–); b. Norton, N. J. Zoologist, author. *The Matriarchy of the American Turf* (monograph, 1931); *Bolinvar* (1937; republished as *The Bolinvars,* 1944); *Earth Eagles* (1947). Editor, *Offical Horse Show Blue Book.*

BAYLOR, FRANCES COURTENAY (Mrs. George Sherman Barnum) (Jan. 20, 1848–Oct. 19, 1920); b. Fort Smith, Ark. Novelist, short story writer, poet. *On Both Sides* (1885); *Behind the Blue Ridge* (1887); *Juan and Juanita* (1888); *A Shocking Example, and Other Sketches* (1889); *Claudia Hyde* (1894); *Miss Nina Barrow* (1897); *The Ladder of Fortune* (1899); *A Georgian Bungalow* (1900).

Bayou Folk. Collection of stories by Kate Chopin (1894).

BAZELON, DAVID THOMAS (March 1923–); b. Shreveport, La. Lawyer, author. *The Paper Economy* (1963); *Power in America* (1967); *Nothing But a Fine Tooth Comb* (1969).

BEACH, JOSEPH WARREN (Jan. 14, 1880–Aug. 13, 1957); b. Gloversville, N.Y. Educator, author. *Sonnets of the Head and Heart* (1903); *The Comic Spirit in George Meredith* (1911); *Meek Americans, & Other European Trifles* (1925); *The Outlook for American Prose* (1926); *Glass Mountain* (1930); *The Twentieth Century Novel* (1932); *The Concept of Nature in Nineteenth Century English Poetry* (1936); *American Fiction, 1920–1940* (1941); *Beginning With Plato* (poems, 1944); *A Romantic View of Poetry* (1944); *An Involuntary Witness* (poems, 1950); *The Making of the Auden Canon* (1957); *Obsessive Images* (1960); etc. Prof. English, University of Minnesota, 1924–28.

BEACH, MOSES YALE (Jan. 15, 1800–July 19, 1868); b. Wallingford, Conn. Journalist. Bought the New York *Sun* in 1838, having been associated with that newspaper since 1834. His brother-in-law, Benjamin H. Day, had founded the *Sun,* Sept. 3, 1833. Beach was a founder of the Associated Press in New York in 1848. He also started several weeklies. His son, Moses Sperry Beach (1822–1892), became owner of the New York *Sun,* Apr. 6, 1852, and sold the paper to Charles A. Dana in Jan., 1868.

BEACH, REX [Ellingwood] (Sept. 1, 1887–Dec. 7, 1949); b. Atwood, Mich. Novelist. *Pardners* (1905); *The Spoilers* (1906); *The Barrier* (1907); *Big Brother* (1923); *Son of the Gods* (1929); *Personal Exposures* (autobiography, 1941); *The World in His Arms* (play, 1946); *Woman in Ambush* (1951).

BEACH, STEWART [Taft] (Dec. 17, 1899–); b. Pontiac, Mich. Editor, author. *Short Story Technique* (1929); *Lend Me Your Ears* (play, with Philip Wood, 1936); *Samuel Adams: The Fateful Years 1764–1776* (1965). Editor: *This Week's*

Stories of Mystery and Suspense (1957). Exec. editor, *This Week,* since 1947.

BEACH, WILLIAM WALDO (Aug. 2, 1916–); b. Middletown, Conn. Educator, author. *Christian Ethics* (with Richard Niebuhr, 1955); *Conscience on Campus* (1958); *The Christian Life* (1967); *Christian Community and American Society* (1969). Prof. Christian ethics, Duke University, since 1946.

Beacon Biographies. Series of American biographies in pocket-sized editions published by Small, Maynard & Co., under the general editorship of M. A. De Wolfe Howe, beginning in 1899.

Beacon Press. Boston, Mass. Publishers. Founded 1902. Publishes books on world affairs, art, literature, psychology, religion, etc. Edward Darling and, later, Gobin Stair served as director.

BEADLE, ERASTUS F[lavel] (Sept. 11, 1821–Dec. 18, 1894); b. Pierstown, N.Y. Publisher of dime novels, editor, author. *To Nebraska in '57: A Diary of Erastus F. Beadle* (1923). Founder, *The Youth's Casket,* 1852; *The Home,* 1856; Beadle's *Monthly,* 1866; *The Star-Journal,* 1870; etc. Founder, Beadle & Adams, publishers of *Beadle's Dime Novels,* etc. *See* Beadle & Adams.

BEADLE, MURIEL MCCLURE BARNETT (Sept. 14, 1915–); b. Alhambra, Cal. Civic worker, author. *These Ruins Are Inhabited* (1961); *The Language of Life* (with husband, George Wells Beadle, 1966).

Beadle & Adams. New York. Founded 1859, by Erastus F. Beadle, with Irwin P. Beadle and Robert Adams as partners. They began the publication of *Beadle's Dime Novels,* etc., with Orville J. Victor as editor. The collection of these books, made by Dr. Frank P. O'Brien, is now in The New York Public Library. In 1862, Irwin P. Beadle was bought out by the others. In 1866, Robert Adams died and was succeeded by his sons, William and David. David Adams died 1886 and Erastus F. Beadle retired 1889, leaving William Adams as the sole owner. In 1897–98, the firm, still known as Beadle & Adams was purchased by M. J. Ives and Co., who continued the name for some years further. *See* Edmund L. Pearson's *Dime Novels* (1929). In 1866, George P. Munro, an employee of Beadle & Adams, left the establishment and with Irwin P. Beadle began the publication of the *New Dime Novels,* under the firm name of Irwin P. Beadle. Erastus F. Beadle enjoined the use of the name, and thereafter Munro's name was used instead. *See* Dime Novels.

BEALE, HOWARD KENNEDY (Apr. 8, 1899–Dec. 27, 1959); b. Chicago, Ill. Educator, historian. *The Critical Year: A Study of Andrew Johnson and Reconstruction* (1930); *Are American Teachers Free?* (1936); *Educational Freedom and Democracy* (with H. B. Alberty and Boyd H. Bode, 1938); *A History of Freedom of Teaching in American Schools* (1941); *Theodore Roosevelt and the Rise of America to World Power* (1956); *The Critical Year: A Study of Andrew Johnson and Reconstruction* (1958); etc. Editor: *Charles A. Beard: An Appraisal* (1954). Prof. history, University of Wisconsin, since 1948.

BEALS, CARLETON (Nov. 13, 1893–); b. Medicine Lodge, Kan. Lecturer, author. *Mexico: An Interpretation* (1923); *Brimstone and Child* (1927); *Mexican Maze* (1931); *Fire on the Andes* (1934); *The Stones Awake* (1936); *America South* (1937); *The Writer in a Changing World* (1937); *Glass Houses* (1938); *The Coming Struggle for Latin America* (1938); *American Earth* (1939); *Rio Grande to Cape Horn* (1943); *Our Yankee Heritage: New England's Contributions to American Civilization* (1955); *John Eliot: The Man Who Loved the Indians* (1958); *House in Mexico* (1958); *Nomads and Empire Builders* (1961); *Latin America: World in Revolution* (1963); *Under the Fifth Sun* (1965); *Land of the Mayas: Past and Present* (1966); etc.

BEALS, FRANK LEE (Sept. 2, 1881–); b. Morganton, Tenn. Army officer, author. *Topographical Primer* (1914); *Look Away Dixieland* (1937); *Kit Carson* (1941); *David Crockett* (1941); *Chief Black Hawk* (1943); *Buffalo Bill* (1943); *Boswell in Chicago* (1946); *Spanish Adventure Trails* (1960); etc.

BEALS, HELEN [Raymond] ABBOTT (July 7, 1888–); b. Boston, Mass. Novelist. *The Merry Heart* (1918); *These Elder Rebels* (1935); *The River Rises* (1941).

BEALS, RALPH LEON (July 19, 1901–); b. Pasadena, Cal. Anthropologist, educator. *Archeological Studies in Northeastern Arizona* (with others, 1945); *Ethnology of the Western Mixe* (1945); *No Frontier to Learning* (with N. D. Humphrey, 1957); etc. Prof. anthropology, University of California, since 1947.

BEARD, CHARLES A[ustin] (Nov. 27, 1874–Sept. 1, 1948); b. Knightstown, Ind. Educator, historian. *The Development of Modern Europe,* 2v. (with James Harvey Robinson, 1907); *American Government and Politics* (1910); *Contemporary American History, 1877–1913* (1914); *The History of the American People* (with William C. Bagley, 1918); *History of the United States* (with wife, Mary Ritter Beard, 1921); *Cross Currents in Europe Today* (1922); *Rise of American Civilization,* 3v. (with wife, 1927; v. 3 published under the title *America in Midpassage,* 1939); *American Leviathan* (with William Beard, 1930); *The Republic* (1943); *A Basic History of the United States* (with wife, 1944); *American Foreign Policy in the Making, 1932–41* (1946); *President Roosevelt and the Coming of the War, 1941* (1947); etc. Editor: *Whither Mankind* (1928); *Toward Civilization* (1930); *America Faces the Future* (1932); etc. *See* Fred B. Millett's *Contemporary American Authors* (1940).

BEARD, DAN[iel Carter] (June 21, 1850–June 11, 1941); b. Cincinnati, O. Naturalist, artist, author. *American Boys' Handy Book* (1882); *Moonlight and Six Feet of Romance* (1892); *Outdoor Handy Book* (1900); *Boy Pioneers and Sons of Daniel Boone* (1909); *The Buckskin Book* (1911); *Shelters, Shacks and Shanties* (1914); *Signs, Signals and Symbols* (1918); *Field and Forest Handybook* (1920); *The Black Wolf Pack* (1922); *Wisdom of the Woods* (1927); etc.

BEARD, JAMES ANDREWS (1903–). Author. *Cook It Outdoors* (1941); *Paris Cuisine* (with Alexander Watt, 1952); *The Treasury of Outdoor Cooking* (1960); *The James Beard Cook Book* (1961); *Delights and Prejudices* (1964); *James Beard's Menus for Entertaining* (1965); etc.

BEARD, JAMES CARTER (June 6, 1837–Nov. 15, 1913); b. Cincinnati, O. Editor, author, illustrator. *Curious Homes and Their Tenants* (1897); *Billy Possum* (1909); etc. With D. Appleton & Co. for many years and illustrated many articles for *Harper's Magazine, St. Nicholas, Century,* etc.

BEARD, MARY RITTER (Mrs. Charles A. Beard) (Aug. 5, 1876–Aug. 14, 1958); b. Indianapolis, Ind. Author. *Rise of American Civilization,* 3v. (with husband, 1927; v. 3 published under title *America in Midpassage,* 1939); *On Understanding Women* (1931); *The American Spirit: A Study of the Idea of Civilization in the United States* (with husband, 1942); *Woman as a Force in History* (1946); etc.

BEARD, PATTEN, b. Syracuse, N.Y. Author. The *Jolly Book* series, 3v. (1914–18); *Marjory's Literary Dolls* (1916); *Twilight Tales* (1929); etc.

BEARD, WILLIAM (May 18, 1907–); b. New York. Author. *The American Leviathan: The Republic in the Machine Age* (with Charles A. Beard; 1930); *Government and Technology* (1934); *Create the Wealth* (1936); *Government and Liberty: The American System* (1947); etc. Compiler: *The Economic Basis of Politics and Related Writings of Charles A. Beard* (1957).

BEARDSLEY, MONROE CURTIS (Dec. 10, 1915–); b. Bridgeport, Conn. Educator, author. *Practical Logic* (1950);

Aesthetics from Classical Greece to the Present (1966); etc. Prof. philosophy, Swarthmore College, since 1959.

Beat Generation. Young writers, painters and hangers-on in rebellion against middle-class standards and ideals, organized commercialism, and the apathetic compromises by which people accept a world supposedly heading toward atomic war and self-destruction. This rebellion centers in a quasi-religious, sensual fulfillment of personality. The "Beats" or "Beatniks," as they are often called, lead a hobo-like existence and are addicted to Oriental philosophical ideas, particularly Zen Buddhism; jazz and poetry readings to a jazz background; drug experiences; and footloose wandering. They believe in sexual freedom and the loosening of all barriers between man and man. Their writings express a dadaistic penchant for the absurd. When they first came into prominence in the early 1950's, they were associated with San Francisco haunts. In poetry, Allen Ginsberg, Lawrence Ferlinghetti and Gregory Corso are the most notable writers; in prose, there are Jack Kerouac and John Clelland Holmes. Ginsberg's poem, "Howl," and Kerouac's novel *On the Road* are the most representative examples of Beat Generation writing. These writers recognize Henry Miller and Kenneth Patchen as their forerunners; and the works of Bernard Wolfe and Chandler Brossard are also considered to be precursors of their writing. In style, Beat Generation writing is notably loose in structure and slangy in diction. The term "beat" is variously interpreted to mean "beaten, down-and-out, but full of conviction," and "beatific," in the sense of "enthusiastically inspired." *See* Lawrence Lipton's *The Holy Barbarians* (1959); T. F. Parkinson's *A Casebook on the Beats* (1961); Emily Hahn's *Romantic Rebels* (1967).

BEATTY, ARTHUR (Mar. 6, 1869–Feb. 27, 1943); b. St. Marys, Canada. Educator, author. *William Wordsworth* (1922). Editor, *De Quincey's Opium Eater* (1900); *Romantic Poets of the Nineteenth Century* (1927); etc.

BEATTY, BESSIE (Jan. 27, 1886–Apr. 6, 1947); b. Los Angeles, Calif. Editor, author. *The Red Heart of Russia* (1918); *Jamboree* (with Jack Black, prod. 1932); etc. Editor, *McCall's Magazine,* 1918–21.

BEATTY, JEROME [GRISWOLD] (Nov. 14, 1886–May 8, 1967); b. Lawrence, Kan. Author. *Americans All Over* (1940). Writer of magazine articles and fiction, since 1928, for *American Magazine, Reader's Digest, Colliers Weekly,* etc. (also under pen names "J. B. Griswold" and "Lawrence McCann").

BEATTY, JOHN (Dec. 16, 1828–Dec. 21, 1914); b. Sandusky, O. Novelist. *The Citizen Soldier; or, Memoirs of a Volunteer* (1879); *The Bell o' Becket's Lane* (1883); *McLean, a Romance of the War* (1904); etc.

BEATTY, JOHN OWEN (Dec. 22, 1890–Sept. 9, 1961); b. Crow, W. Va. Educator, author. *John Esten Cooke, Virginian* (1922); *An Introduction to Poetry* (with Jay Broadus Hubbell, 1922); *An Introduction to Drama* (with same, 1927); *Swords in the Dawn* (1937); *Image of Life* (1940); *The Iron Curtain Over America* (1952). Editor: *Facts and Ideas* (with E. E. Leisy and M. Lamar, 1930); *Famous Editions of English Poets* (with John Wilson Bowyer, 1931); *Texas Poems* (with others, 1936); etc. English department, Southern Methodist University, 1919–57.

Beau Brummell. Play by Clyde Fitch (prod. 1890). Story of the celebrated English dandy of the Regency period.

BEAUCHAMP, WILLIAM MARTIN (Mar. 25, 1830–Dec. 13, 1925); b. Coldenham, N.Y. Episcopal clergyman, archeologist, author. Adopted by the Onondaga Indians and given the name "Wah-Kat-Yu-Ten" (Beautiful Rainbow). *Iroquois Trail* (1892); *History of the New York Iroquois* (1905); *Past and Present Syracuse and Onondaga County* (1908); *Iroquois Folk Lore* (1921); *The Life of Conrad Weiser* (1925); etc. Archeologist, New York State Museum.

Beauties of Poetry, British and American, The. Published by M. Cavey at Philadelphia, in 1791, this is the first known anthology in book form of American literature.

Beautiful and Damned, The. Novel by F. Scott Fitzgerald (1922). Satirical tale of the younger generation.

BECHDOLT, FREDERICK RITCHIE (July 27, 1874–Apr. 12, 1950); b. Mercersburg, Pa. Author. *The Hard Rock Man* (1910); *When the West Was Young* (1921); *Tales of the Old-Timers* (1922); *Mutiny* (1927); *Giants of the Old West* (1930); *Riders of the San Pedro* (1931); *Horse Thief Trail* (1932); *The Tree of Death* (1937); *Hot Gold* (1942); *Hills of Fear* (1943); *Hill Racketeers* (1948).

BECK, WARREN, b. Richmond, Ind. Educator, author. *Final Score* (1944); *Pause Under the Sky* (1947); *Into Thin Air* (1951); *Man in Motion: Faulkner's Trilogy* (1961); *The Rest Is Silence, and Other Stories* (1963); etc. Prof. English, Lawrence College, Wisconsin, since 1926.

BECKER, CARL L[otus] (Sept. 7, 1873–Apr. 10, 1945); b. Blackhawk Co., Ia. Educator, historian. *The Eve of the Revolution* (1918); *Modern History* (1931); *The Declaration of Independence* (1922); *Everyman His Own Historian* (1935); *Progress and Power* (1936); *Story of Civilization* (with Frederic Duncalf, 1938); *Modern Democracy* (1941); *New Liberties for Old* (1942); *How New Will the Better World Be?* (1943); etc. Prof. history, Cornell University, 1917–45.

BECKER, HOWARD [Paul] (Dec. 9, 1899–June 8, 1960); New York. Sociologist. *German Youth, Bound or Free* (1947); *Through Values to Social Interpretation* (1950); *Man in Reciprocity* (1956); etc. Prof. sociology, University of Wisconsin, from 1937.

BECKER, MAY LAMBERTON (May Lamberton-Becker) (Aug. 26, 1873–Apr. 27, 1958); b. New York. Editor, author. *Adventures in Reading* (1927); *Books as Windows* (1929); *Under Twenty* (1932); *First Adventures in Reading* (1936); *Choosing Books for Children* (1937); *Introducing Charles Dickens* (1940); *Presenting Miss Jane Austen* (1952); etc. Compiler: *Golden Tales* series, 7v. (Our America, Old South, New England, Prairie States, Far West, Canada, Southwest, 1929–39); *Home Book of Christmas (1941); Home Book of Laughter* (1948); etc. Editor, *St. Nicholas,* 1930–32; Reader's Guide in *New York Herald Tribune* "Books," from 1933.

BECKER, STEPHEN (Mar. 31, 1927–); b. Mt. Vernon, N.Y. Author. *The Season of the Stranger* (1951); *Juice* (1959); *Comic Art in America* (1964); *The Outcasts* (1967); etc.

Bedford Village. Novel by Hervey Allen (1944). Part of the trilogy *The City in the Dawn* (1950).

BEDFORD-JONES, H[enry James O'Brien] (Apr. 29, 1887–May 12, 1949); b. Napanee, Ont. Author. Pen name "John Wyclife." *Son of Cincinnati* (1925); *This Fiction Business* (1929); *Drums of Dambala* (1932); *The Mission and the Man* (1932); *California Trail* (1948); etc.

"Bedouin Song." Poem by Bayard Taylor (1855). It has been set to music by several composers, better known as "Bedouin Love Song."

Bedtime Story Series. By Thornton Waldo Burgess, 20v. (1913–19). The Burgess Bedtime stories appeared in the daily press of the United States and Canada.

Bee-Man of Orn, and Other Fanciful Tales, The. Nine stories by Frank R. Stockton (1887). An old bee-keeper is transformed into a baby by the power of sorcery. As the story ends he is an old man again, having duplicated his earlier life.

BEEBE, LUCIUS MORRIS (Dec. 9, 1902–Feb. 4, 1966); b. Wakefield, Mass. Journalist, author. *Fallen Stars* (1921); *Corydon and Other Poems* (1924); *François Villon: Certain Aspects* (1925); *Aspects of the Poetry of Edwin Arlington Robinson* (1928); *People on Parade* (with Jerome Zerbe, Jr.,

1934); *Boston and the Boston Legend* (1935); *High Iron; A Book of Trains* (1938); *U.S. West: The Saga of Wells Fargo* (with C. M. Clegg, 1949); *Cable Car Carnival* (with same, 1950); *The American West* (with same, 1955); *The Age of Steam* (with same, 1957); *Narrow Gauge in the Rockies* (with same, 1958); *Mansions on Rails* (1959); *San Francisco's Golden Era* (1960); *Mr. Pullman's Elegant Palace Car* (1961); *The Central Pacific and the Southern Pacific Railroads* (1963); *The Trains We Rode* 2v. (1965, 1966); etc.

BEEBE, WILLIAM (July 29, 1877–June 6, 1962); b. Brooklyn, N.Y. Biologist, naturalist, author. *Log of the Sun* (1906); *Jungle Peace* (1918); *Edge of the Jungle* (1921); *Galapagos, World's End* (1924); *Jungle Days* (1925); *Pheasant Jungles* (1927); *Beneath Tropic Seas* (1928); *Nonsuch, Land of Water* (1932); *Half Mile Down* (1934); *Zaca Venture* (1938); *Book of Bays* (1942); *Book of Naturalists* (ed., 1944); *High Jungle* (1949); *Unseen Life of New York* (1953). Curator ornithology, New York Zoological Society, from 1899.

"Beechenbrook: A Rhyme of the War." Narrative poem by Margaret Junkin Preston (1865). Her experiences during the Civil War.

BEECHER, CATHARINE E[sther] (Sept. 6, 1800–May 12, 1878); b. East Hampton, L.I., N.Y. Educator, reformer, author. *A Treatise on Domestic Economy* (1841); *The Duty of American Women to Their Country* (1845); *Educational Reminiscences and Suggestions* (1874); etc.

BEECHER, CHARLES (Oct. 7, 1815–Apr. 21, 1900); b. Litchfield, Conn. Congregational clergyman, author. *The Duty of Disobedience to Wicked Laws* (1851); *The Life of David* (1861); *Spiritual Manifestations* (1879); etc.

BEECHER, EDWARD (Aug. 27, 1803–July 28, 1895); b. East Hampton, L.I., N.Y. Congregational clergyman, editor, author. *Narrative of Riots at Alton* (1838); *The Conflict of Ages* (1853); *The Concord of Ages* (1860); etc. Co-founder, *The Congregationalist,* Boston; editor-in-chief, 1849–53.

BEECHER, HENRY WARD (June 24, 1813–Mar. 8, 1887); b. Litchfield, Conn. Congregational clergyman, author. *Seven Lectures to Young Men* (1844); *Norwood* (1867); *Evolution and Religion* (1885); etc. Editor, *The Independent,* 1861–64; *The Christian Union,* 1870–81.

BEECHER, LYMAN (Oct. 12, 1775–Jan. 10, 1863); b. New Haven, Conn., father of Charles, Edward, and Henry Ward Beecher, and of Harriet Beecher Stowe. Congregational clergyman, author. *The Remedy for Duelling* (1807); *A Plea for the West* (1832); *Beecher's Works* (1852–53); *Autobiography, Correspondence,* etc., 2v. (1864–65); etc.

BEECROFT, JOHN WILLIAM RICHARD (June 23, 1902–Sept. 21, 1966); b. Superior, Wis. Editor: *The Modern Reader* (1939); *Mr. Maugham Himself* (1954); *Kipling: A Selection of His Stories and Poems* (1956); *Plain and Fancy Cats* (1958); *Rocco Came In* (1959); *What? Another Cat!* (1960). Book club editor: Literary Guild, Doubleday Dollar Book Club, etc.

Beef Steak Club of Philadelphia. An organization of artists, writers, and wits who met at the studio of William Kneass, the engraver, in Fourth Street, near Chestnut, in the 1820's.

BEER, SAMUEL HUTCHISON (July 28, 1911–); b. Bucyrus, O. Educator, author. *The City of Reason* (1949); *Treasury Control* (1956); *Patterns of Government: The Major Political Systems of Europe* (with others, 1958); *British Politics in the Collectivist Age* (1965); etc. Prof. government, Harvard University, since 1953.

BEER, THOMAS (Nov. 22, 1889–Apr. 18, 1940); b. Council Bluffs, Ia. Author. *The Fair Rewards* (1922); *Stephen Crane* (1923); *Sandoval* (1924); *The Mauve Decade* (1926); *The Road to Heaven* (1928); *Hanna* (1929); *Mrs. Egg and Other Barbarians* (1933).

BEERS, ETHEL LYNN [Ethelinda] (Jan. 13, 1827–Oct. 11, 1879); b. Goshen, N.Y. Author. *General Frankie: A Story For Little Folks* (1863); *All Quiet Along the Potomac, and Other Poems* (1879). Her best known poem is "All Quiet Along the Potomac."

BEERS, HENRY AUGUSTIN (Jan. 2, 1847–Sept. 7, 1926); b. Buffalo, N.Y. Educator, essayist, poet. *A Century of American Literature* (1878); *Odds and Ends* (poems, 1878); *Nathaniel Parker Willis* (1885); *The Thankless Muse* (poems, 1885); *A Suburban Pastoral, and Other Tales* (1894); *Brief History of English and American Literature* (1897); *Points at Issue and Some Other Points* (1904); *A Short History of American Literature* (1906); *The Connecticut Wits and Other Essays* (1920); *Poems* (1921); *A History of English Romanticism in the Eighteenth Century* (1929); etc. Prof. English literature, Yale University, 1880–1916.

BEETS, HENRY (Jan. 5, 1869–Oct. 29, 1947); b. Koedyk, Netherlands. Christian Reformed clergyman, author. *The Christian Reformed Church in North America* (1923); *The Man of Sorrows* (1935); *Johanna of Nigeria* (1937); *Toiling and Trusting* (1940); etc.

Beggar on Horseback. Play by George S. Kaufman and Marc Connelly (prod. 1924); music by Deems Taylor. The fantastic story of Neil McRae who falls asleep and dreams he is connected with Cady's "widget" factory. His real passion is music, and he murders those who interfere with his playing. He wakes up in time to save himself. Cf. Elmer Rice's *The Adding Machine.*

Begum's Daughter, The. Novel by Edwin Lasetter Bynner (1890). The complicated love tangle between Catalina Staats, Steenie Van Cortlandt, and Hester Leisler, whose parents are involved in the political battles of Old New York under the royal governorship of Sir Edmund Andros.

BEHRMAN, S[amuel] N[athaniel] (June 9, 1893–); b. Worcester, Mass. Playwright. *The Second Man* (prod. 1927); *Serena Blandish* (prod. 1929); *Meteor* (prod. 1929); *Brief Moment* (prod. 1931); *Biography* (prod. 1932); *Rain from Heaven* (prod. 1934); *End of Summer* (prod. 1936); *Amphitryon 38* (adapted from French, prod. 1937); *Wine of Choice* (prod. 1938); *No Time for Comedy* (prod. 1939); *Jacobowsky and the Colonel* (with Franz Werfel, prod. 1944); *Dunnigan's Daughter* (prod. 1945); *Duveen* (1952); *Fanny* (with Joshua Logan, prod. 1954); *The Worcester Account* (1954); *The Cold Wind and the Warm* (prod. 1958); *Portrait of Max* (1960); *The Suspended Drawing Room* (1965); *The Burning Glass* (1968); etc.

BEILENSON, EDNA (June 16, 1909–); b. New York. Publisher, book designer. *Festive Cookery* (1950); *Recipes Mother Used to Make* (1952); and other cookbooks. Partner, Peter Pauper Press, since 1930.

Being a Boy. By Charles Dudley Warner (1865). The story of the author's own boyhood in New England.

BEISSEL, JOHANN CONRAD (Apr. 1690–July 6, 1768); b. Eberbach, Germany. Founder of the Solitary Brethren of the Community of Seventh Day Baptists (Dunkers) at Ephrata, Lancaster Co., Pa.; author of more than 1000 hymns in German. He was associated with the Ephrata Press which was noted for its fine printing in the German language.

BELASCO, DAVID (July 25, 1859–May 14, 1931); b. San Francisco, Calif. Playwright, producer, actor. *The Wife* (with Henry Churchill De Mille, prod. 1887); *Lord Chumley* (with same, prod. 1888); *Men and Women* (with same, prod. 1890); *The Heart of Maryland* (prod. 1895); *Madame Butterfly* (1895, prod. 1900); *Du Barry* (prod. 1901); *The Darling of the Gods* (with Luther Long, prod. 1902); *Sweet Kitty Bellairs* (prod. 1903); *The Music Master* (with Charles Klein, prod. 1904); *The Girl of the Golden West* (prod. 1905); *The Rose of the Rancho* (with Richard Walton Tully, prod. 1906); *The Temperamental Journey* (prod. 1913); *The Theatre Through*

Its Stage Door (1919); *The Return of Peter Grimm* (prod. 1921); *Salvage* (prod. 1925). Belasco's collection of press-books, prompt books, etc., is now in The New York Public Library.

"Beleaguered City, The." Poem by Henry Wadsworth Longfellow (1839).

BELFRAGE, CEDRIC (Nov. 8, 1904–); b. London. Editor, author. *Away from It All* (1937); *Promised Land* (1938); *South of God* (1941); *They All Hold Swords* (1941); *A Faith to Free the People* (1944); *Abide With Me* (1948); *My Master Columbus* (1961); *The Man at the Door with the Gun* (1963); etc. Editor, *The National Guardian*.

"Belfry of Bruges, The." Poem by Henry Wadsworth Longfellow (1846).

Believe Me, Xantippe. Farce by Fred Ballard (1912). In which the "criminal" reveals his identity by speaking these words.

BELITT, BEN (May 2, 1911–); b. New York. Poet. *The Five-Fold Mesh* (1938); *Four Poems by Rimbaud* (1948); *School of the Soldier* (prose, 1950); *Wilderness Stair* (1955); *The Enemy Joy* (1964); *The Selected Poems of Rafael Alberti* (1965). Editor: *Selected Poems of Pablo Neruda* (1961).

BELKIN, SAMUEL (Dec., 1911–); b. in Poland. Rabbi, educator, author. *Philo and the Oral Law* (1940); *In His Image* (1961); etc. Pres. Yeshiva University, since 1943.

BELKNAP, JEREMY (June 4, 1744–June 20, 1798); b. Boston, Mass. Clergyman, historian. *The History of New Hampshire,* 3v. (1784–1792); *The Foresters: An American Tale: Being a Sequel to the History of John Bull, the Clothier* (anon., 1792); *American Biography,* 2v. (1794–98); etc.

BELL, ARCHIE (Mar. 17, 1877–1943); b. Geneva, O. Correspondent, *Seralmo* (1901); *The Bermudian* (1908); *The Clyde Fitch I Knew* (1910); *The Spell of the Holy Land* (1915); *The Spell of Egypt* (1916); *The Spell of China* (1917); *A Trip to Lotus Land* (1917); *Sunset Canada* (1918); *The Spell of the Caribbean Islands* (1926); *The Spell of Ireland* (1928); etc.

BELL, BERNARD IDDINGS (Oct. 13, 1886–Sept. 5, 1958); b. Dayton, O. Episcopal clergyman, educator, author. *Post-Modernism, and Other Essays* (1925); *Beyond Agnosticism* (1929); *Unfashionable Convictions* (1931); *A Catholic Looks at His World* (1936); *The Priestly Way* (1938); *Religion for Living* (1939); *The Altar and the World* (1944); *God Is Not Dead* (1945); *A Man Can Live* (1947); *Crisis in Education* (1949); *Crowd Culture* (1956); etc. Warden, St. Stephen's College, 1919–33.

BELL, CHARLES H[enry] (Nov. 18, 1823–Nov. 11, 1893); b. Chester, N.H. Historian, biographer. *John Wheelwright* (1876); *The Bench and Bar of New Hampshire* (1894); etc.

BELL, DANIEL (May 10, 1919–); b. New York. Educator. *Work and Its Discontents* (1956); *The End of Ideology* (1960); *The Reforming of General Education* (1968). Editor: *Toward the Year 2000* (1968). Prof. sociology, Columbia University, since 1958.

BELL, EDWARD PRICE (Mar 1, 1869–Sept. 23, 1943); b. Parke Co., Ind. Journalist, author. *Primary Diplomacy* (1933); *Studies of Great Political Personalities* (1938); *Seventy Years Deep* (autobiography, 1940); etc.

BELL, E[ric] T[emple] (Feb. 7, 1883–Dec. 20, 1960); b. Aberdeen, Scotland. Educator, mathematician, novelist. Pen name, "John Taine." Under own name *Debunking Science* (1930); *Queen of the Sciences* (1931); *The Handmaiden of the Sciences* (1937); *Men of Mathematics* (1937); *Sixes and Sevens* (1945); *The Magic of Numbers* (1947); *Mathematics, Queen and Servant of Science* (1950); *The Last Problem* (1961). Also, under pen name: *The Purple Sapphire* (1924); *Green Fire* (1928); *Seeds of Life* (1931); *Before the Dawn* (1934); etc. Prof. mathematics, University of Washington, 1921–60.

BELL, JAMES MADISON (Apr. 3, 1826–1902); b. Gallipolis, O. Poet, lecturer. *The Poetical Works of James Madison Bell* (1901).

BELL, LILIAN [Lida] (1867–July 18, 1929); b. Chicago, Ill. Novelist. *Love Affairs of an Old Maid* (1893); *Hope Loring* (1902); *Angela's Quest* (1910); etc.

BELL, MARGARET ELIZABETH (1898–). Author. *Pirates of Icy Strait* (1943); *Enemies in Icy Strait* (1945); *Watch for a Tall White Sail* (1948); *Love Is Forever* (1954); *Touched with Fire: Alaska's George William Steller* (1960); etc.

BELL, MARVIN (Aug. 3, 1937–); b. New York. Educator, author. *Poems for Nathan and Saul* (1966); *Things We Dreamt We Died For* (1966); *A Probable Volume of Dreams* (1969). Prof. English, University of Iowa, since 1966.

BELL, PEARL DOLES, b. St. Joseph, Mo. Author. *Gloria Gray, Love Pirate* (1914); *His Harvest* (1915); *The Autocrat* (1922); *Slaves of Destiny* (1926); *The First Lady* (1932); etc.

BELL, ROBERT (c. 1732–Sept. 23, 1784); b. Glasgow, Scotland, came to America c. 1766. Publisher, bookseller, author. *Illuminations for Legislators, and for Sentimentalists* (1784); *Memorial on the Free Sale of Books* (1784). Publisher of Paine's *Common Sense* (1776). Operated a circulating library.

BELL, SOLOMON. Pen name of William Joseph Snelling.

BELL, THOMAS (1903–Jan. 17, 1961). Author. *Out of This Furnace* (1941); *There Comes a Time* (1946); *In the Midst of Life* (autobiography, 1961); etc.

Bell for Adano, A. Novel by John Hersey (1944). An American officer during World War II helps an Italian village in Sicily recover its town bell, and tries to convey his own sense of democracy to the Italians. Received the Pulitzer prize for fiction, 1945.

BELLAH, JAMES WARNER (Sept. 14, 1899–); b. New York. Novelist. *Sketch Book of a Cadet from Gascony* (1923); *These Frantic Years* (1927); *Gods of Yesterday* (1928); *Sons of Cain* (1929); *Dancing Lady* (1932); *White Piracy* (1933); *The Brass Gong Tree* (1936); *South by East a Half East* (1936); *This Is the Town* (1937); *Seven Will Die* (1938); *Irregular Gentleman* (1947); *Rear Guard and the Apache* (1951); *The Valiant Virginians* (1955); *A Thunder of Drums: The Journal of Colonel Delancey* (1967); etc.

BELLAMAN, HENRY (Apr. 28, 1882–June 16, 1945); b. Fulton, Mo. Musician, novelist, poet. *A Music Teacher's Note Book* (poems, 1920); *Cups of Illusion* (poems, 1923); *Petenera's Daughter* (1926); *The Upward Pass: Poems* (1927); *Crescendo* (1928); *The Richest Woman in Town* (1932); *The Gray Man Walks* (1936); *Kings Row* (1940); *The Floods of Spring* (1942); *Victoria Grandolet* (1944).

BELLAMY, CHARLES JOSEPH (May 7, 1852–1910); b. Chicopee Falls, Mass., brother of Edward Bellamy. Publisher, novelist. *The Breton Mills* (1879); *The Way Out* (1884); *An Experiment in Marriage* (1889); *Were They Sinners?* (1890); *Return of the Fairies* (1899); *The Wonder Children* (1906); etc. Founder, *The Springfield* (Mass.) *Daily News,* 1880; publisher, 1880–1910.

BELLAMY, EDWARD (Mar. 26, 1850–May 22, 1898); b. Chicopee Falls, Mass. Author. *The Duke of Stockbridge* (serial, 1879, publ. 1900); *Dr. Heidenhoff's Process* (1880); *Miss Ludington's Sister* (1884); *Looking Backward* (1888); *Equality* (1897); etc. Founder, *The New Nation,* Boston, 1891.

BELLAMY, ELIZABETH WHITFIELD CROOM (Apr. 17, 1837–Apr. 13, 1900); b. near Quincy, Fla. Author. Pen name "Kamba Thorpe." *Four Oaks* (1870); *The Little Joanna* (1876); *Old Man Gilbert* (1888); *Penny Lancaster* (1889).

BELLAMY, FRANCIS RUFUS (Dec. 24, 1886–Feb. 2, 1972); b. New Rochelle, N.Y. Publisher, author. *The Balance*

(1917); *A Flash of Gold* (1922); *March Winds* (1924); *Spanish Faith* (1926); *We Hold These Truths* (1942); *Blood Money* (1947); *The Strange Blooming* (1948); *Private Life of George Washington* (1951); *Atta* (1953). Editor, *Outlook,* 1927–32; *New Yorker,* 1933; *Fiction Parade,* 1935–38; pres. University Publishers, Inc., since 1958.

BELLAMY, JEANNE (Nov. 15, 1911–); b. Brooklyn, N.Y. Journalist, author. *Taming the Everglades* (1947); *Communism: What It Means to You* (1961); etc. With *Miami Herald,* since 1937.

BELLAMY, PAUL (Dec. 26, 1884–Apr. 12, 1956); b. Chicopee Falls, Mass. Editor. Managing editor, *Cleveland Plain Dealer,* 1920–33; editor, 1933–53.

Belle Lamar. Play by Dion Boucicault (prod. 1874). Civil War drama, based upon the adventures of the famous Confederate spy Belle Boyd.

Belle of New York, The. Musical comedy by "Hugh Morton" (C. M. S. McClellan) (prod. 1897); music by Gustave Kerker. The story of a young man about town who falls in love with a Salvation Army girl, Violet Gray, who tries to correct his wastrel ways.

BELLI, MELVIN [Mouron] (July 29, 1907–); b. Sonora, Cal. Lawyer, author. *Modern Trials and Modern Damages,* 6v. (1954); *The Adequate Award* (1953); *Malpractice* (1955); *Dallas Justice* (with Maurice Carroll, 1964); *The Law Revolt,* 2v. (1968); etc.

Bellman, The. Minneapolis, Minn. Weekly magazine. Founded 1906. Expired 1919. William C. Edgar was its only editor. Montrose Moses was drama critic, 1910–19.

BELLOW, FRANK H. T. (Apr. 18, 1828–June 29, 1888); b. Cawnpore, Hindustan, came to America in 1860. Illustrator, caricaturist, author. *The Art of Amusing* (1866). Caricaturist for *Yankee Notions, Nick-Nax, Vanity Fair, Texas Siftings, Harper's Weekly,* and *Scribner's Monthly.* Illustrated stories for *Harper's Magazine.*

BELLOW, SAUL (July 10, 1915–); b. Lachine, Que., Can. Author. *Dangling Man* (1944); *The Victim* (1947); *The Adventures of Augie March* (1953); *Seize the Day* (1956); *Henderson the Rain King* (1959); *Herzog* (1964); *The Last Analysis* (prod. 1964); *Mosby's Memoirs* (1968); *Mr. Sammler's Planet* (1970). Editor: *The Noble Savage,* 1960.

BELLOWS, HENRY WHITNEY (June 11, 1814–Jan. 30, 1882); b. Walpole, N.H. Clergyman, editor, author. *Public Life in Washington* (1866); *The Old World in Its New Face,* 2v. (1868–69); etc. Founder, *The Christian Inquirer,* 1846.

BELLOWS, ROGER MARION (Jan. 9, 1905–); b. Springfield, O. Psychologist. *The Historical Background of Contemporary Psychology* (with R. D. Williams, 1935); *Psychology of Personnel in Business and Industry* (1949); *Employment Psychology, the Interview* (with M. F. Estep, 1954); *Creative Leadership* (1959); *Executive Skills* (1961).

"Bells, The." Poem by Edgar Allan Poe, in *Sartain's Union Magazine,* Nov. 1849.

"Bells for John Whiteside's Daughter." Poem by John Crowe Ransom.

"Bells of Lynn, The." Poem by Henry Wadsworth Longfellow (1859).

BELO, ALFRED HORATIO (May 27, 1839–Apr. 19, 1901); b. Salem (Now Winston-Salem), N.C. Publisher, editor. Became publisher, *Galveston News,* 1865; founded *Dallas News,* 1885; president of both until 1901.

BELO, ALFRED HORATIO (Aug. 1873–Feb. 27, 1906); b. Galveston, Tex., son of Alfred Horatio Belo. Publisher, editor. President, A. H. Belo & Co., publishers of the *Galveston News* and the *Dallas News,* 1901–06.

Beloit Poetry Journal. Beloit, Wis. Quarterly of poetry. Founded 1950. Published by Beloit College until 1958, subsequently by the editors: Chad Walsh, David and Marion Stocking, and Robert Glauber. Also sponsored a radio program over WFMT, Chicago, Ill., directed by Robert Glauber. Publishes occasional chapbook issues.

BELOOF, ROBERT LAWRENCE (Dec. 30, 1923–); b. Wichita, Kan. Educator, author. *The One-Eyed Gunner* (1956); *The Performing Voice in Literature* (1966). Editor: historical anthology of American poetry, 2v. LP records (1965). Chairman, speech department, University of California at Berkeley, since 1964.

BEMELMANS, LUDWIG (Apr. 27, 1898–Oct. 1, 1962); b. Meran, Austria. Painter, illustrator, author. Author and illustrator: *Hansi* (1934); *Golden Basket* (1935); *Castle Number Nine* (1936); *Quito Express* (1937); *My War with the U.S.A.* (1937); *Life Class* (1938); *Madeline* (1939); *Hotel Splendide* (1939); *Small Beer* (1940); *The Donkey Inside* (1941); *I Love You, I Love You, I Love You* (1942); *Now I Lay Me Down to Sleep* (1943); *The Blue Danube* (1944); *Sunshine* (1951); *The Happy Place* (1951); *How to Travel Incognito* (1952); *Madeline's Rescue* (1953); *Doctor Lincoln's Dog* (1953); *Madeline and the Red Hat* (1957); *The Woman of My Life* (1957); *Welcome Home* (1960); *Italian Holiday* (1961); *On Board Noah's Ark* (1962); etc.

BEMIS, SAMUEL FLAGG (Oct. 20, 1891–); b. Worcester, Mass. Educator, historian. *Jay's Treaty* (1923); *Pinckney's Treaty* (1926, Pulitzer Prize for American history, 1927); *The Diplomacy of the American Revolution* (1935); *A Diplomatic History of the United States* (1936); *John Quincy Adams and the Foundations of American Foreign Policy* (1949; Pulitzer Prize for biography, 1950); *John Quincy Adams and the Union* (1956); *A Short History of American Foreign Policy and Diplomacy* (1959); *American Foreign Policy and the Blessings of Liberty* (1962); *The Hussey-Cumberland Mission and American Independence* (1968). Editor, *The American Secretaries of State and Their Diplomacy,* 10v. (1927–29). Prof. history, George Washington University, 1924–34; lecturer, Harvard University, 1934–45.

"Ben Bolt." Song written by Thomas Dunn English, which appeared originally in the *New Mirror,* New York, Sept. 2, 1843.

Ben Hur: A Tale of the Christ. Historical novel by Lew Wallace (1880). This popular tale is laid in Jerusalem and other parts of the Roman Empire at the beginning of the Christian era. The famous chariot race is the highlight of the story. Judah Ben Hur is sent to the galleys for injury done to Valerius Gratus, the Roman governor. His adventures, and his conversion to Christianity have appealed to generations of readers. The novel was dramatized by William Young (prod. 1899), and set the vogue for mammoth stage and motion-picture spectacles.

Benauly. Pen name used jointly by the brothers Benjamin, Austin, and Lyman Abbott.

BENCHLEY, NATHANIEL [Goddard] (Nov. 13, 1915–); b. Newton, Mass. Author. *Side Street* (1950); *The Frogs of Spring* (play, 1953); *Robert Benchley* (1955); *One to Grow On* (1958); *The Off-Islanders* (1961); *Red Fox and His Canoe* (1964); *A Firm Word or Two* (1965); *The Monument* (1966); *A Ghost Named Fred* (1968); *Welcome to Xanadu* (1968). Editor: *The Benchley Roundup* (1954).

BENCHLEY, ROBERT [Charles] (Sept. 15, 1889–Nov. 21, 1945); b. Worcester, Mass. Critic, humorist. *Of All Things* (1922); *Love Conquers All* (1923); *Pluck and Luck* (1924); *The Early Worm* (1927); *The Treasurer's Report and Other Aspects of Community Singing* (1930); *From Bad to Worse* (1934); *My Ten Years in a Quandary* (1936); *After 1903, What?* (1938); *Inside Benchley* (1942); *Benchley Beside Himself* (1943); *Benchley—Or Else* (1947); *Chips Off the Old Benchley* (1949); etc. Drama editor, *Life,* 1920–29; *The New*

Yorker, 1929–40. *See* Nathaniel Benchley's *Robert Benchley* (1955); N. W. Yates' *Robert Benchley* (1968).

BENDER, ERIC J. (Aug. 8, 1902–Sept. 14, 1966); b. Cleveland, O. Editor, author. *Tickets to Fortune* (1938); *I Never Knew That* (1938); *Red Man's Treasure* (1939). Editor-in-chief, *Saint Nicholas Magazine,* 1932–35.

BENDER, HAROLD H[erman] (Apr. 20, 1882–Aug. 16, 1951); b. Martinsburg, W. Va. Educator, philologist, author. *German Short Stories* (1920); *The Home of the Indo-Europeans* (1927); *The Selection of Undergraduates* (1926); etc. Dept. of philology, Princeton University, 1909–50.

BENDER, JAMES F[rederick] (Apr. 6, 1905–); Dayton, O. Psychologist. *The Technique of Executive Leadership* (1950); *Victory Over Fear* (1952); *Make Your Business Letters Make Friends* (1952); *How to Sell Well* (1961); *10 Biggest Mistakes Speakers Make* (1963); etc.

BENDINER, [Marvin] ROBERT (Dec. 15, 1909–). b. Pittsburgh, Pa. Editor, author. *The Riddle of the State Department* (1942); *White House Fever* (1960); *Obstacle Course on Capitol Hill* (1964); *Just Around the Corner* (1967). Managing editor, *The Nation,* 1937–44; assoc. editor, 1946–50.

BENEDICT, ELSIE LINCOLN, b. in Colorado. Lecturer, author. *Our Trip Around the World* (1925); *Famous Lovers* (1927); *The Spell of the South Seas* (1930); *Inspirational Poems* (1931); *Stimulating Stanzas* (1931); *Benedictines* (1931); *So This Is Australia* (1932); *Spain Before It Happened* (1937).

BENEDICT, FRANK LEE (July 6, 1834–1910); b. Alexander, N.Y. Novelist, poet. *The Shadow Worshiper, and Other Poems* (1857); *My Daughter Elinor* (anon., 1869); *John Worthington's Name* (1874); *Mr. Vaughan's Heir* (1875); *'Twixt Hammer and Anvil* (1876); *Madame* (1877); *The Price She Paid* (1883); etc.

BENEDICT, MURRAY REED (Jan. 23, 1892–); b. Neillsville, Wis. Economist. *Farm Policies of the United States, 1790–1950* (1953); *Can We Solve the Farm Problem?* (1955); *The Agricultural Commodity Programs* (with O. C. Stine, 1956); *Farm Surpluses: U.S. Burden or World Asset* (with E. K. Bauer, 1960).

BENEDICT, RUTH [Fulton] (June 5, 1887–Sept. 17, 1948); b. New York. Anthropologist, author. *The Concept of the Guardian Spirit in North America* (1923); *Tales of the Cochiti Indians* (1931); *Patterns of Culture* (1934); *Zuni Mythology* (1935); *Race, Science and Politics* (1940); *The Chrysanthemum and the Sword* (1946). Also poems published in magazines under pen name "Anne Singleton." Editor, *Journal of American Folklore,* 1923–39. Anthropology dept., Columbia University, 1923–48.

BENEDIKT, MICHAEL (May 26, 1935–); b. New York. Poet, critic, editor. *Changes* (1961); *8 Poems* (1966). Editor and translator: *Modern French Theatre: The Avant-Garde, Dada and Surrealism* (with G. E. Wellworth, 1964); *Post-War German Theatre* (with same, 1968). Editor: *Theatre Experiment* (1968).

BENEFIELD, [John] BARRY (1877–); b. Jefferson, Tex. Author. *The Chicken-Wagon Family* (1925); *Short Turns* (1926); *Bugles in the Night* (1927); *A Little Clown Lost* (1928); *Valiant Is the Word for Carrie* (1935); *April Was When It Began* (1939); *Eddie and the Archangel Mike* (1943).

BENÉT, LAURA, b. Fort Hamilton, New York Harbor, sister of Stephen Vincent Benét and William Rose Benét. Poet, biographer. *Fairy Bread* (poems, 1921); *Noah's Dove* (poems, 1929); *Basket for a Fair* (poems, 1934); *The Boy Shelley* (1937); *The Hidden Valley* (1938); *Enchanting Jenny Lind* (1939); *Come Slowly, Eden: A Novel about Emily Dickinson* (1942); *Is Morning Sure?* (1947); *Coleridge, Poet of Wild Enchantment* (1952); *Famous American Humorists* (1959);

In Love With Time (poems, 1959); *Famous Poets for Young People* (1964); *Horseshoe Nails* (1965); *Famous English and American Essayists* (1966); *Famous Storytellers for Young People* (1968); etc.

BENÉT, STEPHEN VINCENT (July 22, 1898–Mar. 13, 1943); b. Bethelehem, Pa. Poet, novelist. *Five Men and Pompey* (poems, 1915); *Young Adventure* (poems, 1918); *Heavens and Earth* (poems, 1920); *The Beginning of Wisdom* (1921); *Jean Huguenot* (1923); *Tiger Joy* (poems, 1925); *Spanish Bayonet* (1925); *John Brown's Body* (1928; Pulitzer Prize for poetry, 1929); *Ballads and Poems, 1915–1930* (1931); *James Shore's Daughter* (1934); *Burning City* (poems, 1936); *The Devil and Daniel Webster* (1937); *Thirteen o'Clock* (1937); *Johnny Pye and the Fool Killer* (1938); *Tales Before Midnight* (1939); *Twenty-Five Short Stories* (1943); *Western Star* (poems, 1943; Pulitzer Prize for poetry, 1944); *The Last Circle* (poems, 1946). *See* Robert Van Gelder's *Writers and Writing* (1946).

BENÉT, WILLIAM ROSE (Feb. 2, 1886–May 4, 1950); b. Fort Hamilton, New York Harbor. Poet, essayist. *Merchants from Cathay* (poems, 1913); *The Falcons of God* (poems, 1914); *The Great White Wall* (poems, 1916); *The Burglar of the Zodiac* (poems, 1918); *Moons of Grandeur* (poems, 1920); *The First Person Singular* (1922); *Wild Goslings* (1927); *Man Possessed* (poems, 1927); *Starry Harness* (poems, 1933); *Golden Fleece* (poems, 1935); *With Wings as Eagles: Air Ballads* (1940); *The Dust Which Is God* (1941; Pulitzer Prize for poetry, 1942); *Day of Deliverance* (1944); *The Stairway of Surprise* (1947). Editor: *Poems for Youth* (1935); *Fifty Poets, An American Anthology* (1933); *The Oxford Anthology of American Literature* (with Norman Holmes Pearson, 1938); *The Poetry of Freedom* (1945); *The Reader's Encyclopedia* (1948); etc. Co-founder, *Saturday Review of Literature,* 1924.

BENJAMIN, CURTIS G. (July 13, 1901–); b. Providence, Ky. Publisher. Pres., McGraw-Hill Book Co., 1946–1961. Executive Consultant since 1960.

BENJAMIN, PARK (Aug. 14, 1809–Sept. 12, 1864); b. Demerara, British Guiana, of American parentage. Editor, poet. *A Poem on the Meditation of Nature* (1832); *Poetry: A Satire* (1832); *Infatuation* (1841); etc. Founded the *Norwich Spectator* in 1829. Became editor and owner of the *New England Magazine* in 1835, which merged with the *American Monthly Magazine* the same year. He was connected with *The Evening Tattler* and *Brother Jonathan.* Founded *The Evening Signal* in 1839; and the *New World* also in 1839. The latter expired in 1845.

BENJAMIN, PARK (May 11, 1849–Aug. 21, 1922); b. New York City. Lawyer, editor, author. *Shakings: Etchings from the Naval Academy* (1867); *Wrinkles and Recipes* (1873); *The Age of Electricity* (1886); *The United States Naval Academy* (1900). Assoc. editor, *Scientific American,* 1872–78. His best known short story is "The End of New York."

BENJAMIN, SAMUEL GREENE WHEELER (Feb. 13, 1837–July 19, 1914); b. Argos, Greece, of American parentage. Artist, author. *Constantinople, Isle of Pearls, and Other Poems* (1860); *The Turk and the Greek* (1867); *Contemporary Art in Europe* (1877); *The Multitudinous Seas* (1879); *Troy* (1880); *Sea-Spray* (1887); *The Story of Persia* (1887); *The Life and Adventures of a Free Lance* (autobiography, 1914); etc.

BENNET, ROBERT AMES (Feb. 3, 1870–Mar. 11, 1954); b. Denver, Colo. Novelist. *Thyra* (1901); *Into the Primitive* (1908); *The Shogun's Daughter* (1910); *The Quarterbreed* (1915); *Bloom of Cactus* (1920); *Tyrrel of the Cow Country* (1923); *Branded* (1924); *The Tenderfoot* (1928); *The Border Wolf* (1929); *Guns on the Rio Grande* (1934); *Death Rides the Range* (1935); *Sheepman's Gold* (1939); etc.

BENNETT, CHARLES EDWIN (Apr. 6, 1858–May 2, 1921); b. Providence, R.I. Educator, classicist. His Latin grammars were widely used, and he translated Horace and

Frontinus for the Loeb Classical Library. Editor, *Cornell Studies in Classical Philology,* 1892–1921. Prof. Latin, Cornell University 1892–1921.

Bennett, Dwight. Pen name of Dwight Bennett Newton.

BENNETT, EMERSON (Mar. 6, 1822–May 11, 1905); b. Monson, Mass. Novelist. *The League of the Miami* (1845); *The Bandits of the Osage* (1847); *Mike Fink* (1848); *The Prairie Flower* (1849); *The Forest Rose* (1950); *Leni-Leoti* (1850); *The Forged Will* (1853); *The Border Rover* (1857); etc. Many of his works appeared serially in the *Saturday Evening Post* and the *New York Ledger.*

BENNETT, HORACE WILSON (Sept. 4, 1862–June 9, 1941); b. Hamburg, Mich. Realtor, author. *Bright Yellow Gold* (1935); *Silver Crown of Glory* (1936); *A Modern Prince from an Ancient House* (1936).

BENNETT, JAMES GORDON (Sept. 1, 1795–June 1, 1872); b. Keith, Scotland. Author. *The Life and Writings of James Gordon Bennett* (1844). Founder, the New York *Herald,* May 6, 1835. Before that he was associated with the *New York Courier* and the *New York Enquirer.* He was succeeded by his son, James Gordon Bennett (1841–1918), who gained fame as a journalist and yachtsman.

BENNETT, JAMES GORDON (May 10, 1841–May 14, 1918); b. New York City. Journalist, Sportsman. Editor, the *New York Herald,* 1872–1918; established its Paris edition, 1887; founder, *The Evening Telegram,* New York, 1867.

BENNETT, JAMES O'DONNELL (May 1, 1870–Feb. 27, 1940); b. Jackson, Mich. Correspondent, drama critic. *Much Loved Books* (1927). Editor: *"Private Joe" Fifer: Memories of War and Peace* (1936). Drama editor, Chicago *Record-Herald,* 1902–14.

BENNETT, JAMES W[illiam] (Oct. 15, 1891–); b. Mitchell, Ind. Novelist, poet. *Plum Blossoms and Blue Incense* (1926); *The Manchu Cloud* (1927); *The Yellow Corsair* (1927); *Brush Strokes on the Fan of a Courtesan* (poems, with Dorothy Graham, 1927); *Dragon Shadows* (1928); *Son of the Typhoon* (1928); *Chinese Blake* (1930); *Spinach Jade* (1939).

BENNETT, JOHN (May 17, 1865–Dec. 28, 1956); b. Chillicothe, O. Illustrator, author. *Master Skylark* (1897); *Barnaby Lee* (1902); *Treasure of Peyre Gaillard* (1906); *Madame Margot* (1921); *The Pigtail of Ah Lee Ben Loo* (1928); *Doctor to the Dead* (1946); etc.

BENNETT, JOHN COLEMAN (July 22, 1902–); b. Kingston, Ont., Can. Educator. *Social Salvation* (1935); *Christian Ethics and Social Policy* (1946); *Christianity and Communism* (1948); *The Christian as a Citizen* (1955); *Christians and the State* (1958); *Christianity and Communism Today* (1960); *Foreign Policy in Christian Perspective* (1966). Editor: *Christian Social Ethics in a Changing World* (1966). Prof. Christian theology and ethics, Union Theological Seminary, since 1943.

BENNETT, SANFORD FILLMORE (June 21, 1836–June 11, 1898); b. Eden, N.Y. Physician, hymn writer, novelist. *The Pioneer: An Idyll of the Middle West* (1896). Compiler (with J. P. Webster): *The Signet Ring* (1871), an anthology of hymns, 100 of which were written by him. His best known hymn is "The Sweet By and By."

BENNS, FRANK LEE (Mar. 7, 1889–); b. Barre, N.Y. Educator, Historian. *The Irish Question* (1928); *Europe Since 1914* (1930); *The World in the Crucible* (1930); *European History Since 1870* (1938); etc. History dept. Indiana University since 1920.

BENSON, ALLAN L[ouis] (Nov. 6, 1871–Aug. 19, 1940); b. Plainwell, Mich. Author. *Our Dishonest Constitution* (1914); *The New Henry Ford* (1923); *Daniel Webster* (1929); etc. Founder (with William F. Cochran), *Reconstruction Magazine,* 1918.

Benson, Carl. Pen name of Charles Astor Bristed.

BENSON, EUGENE (Nov. 1, 1839–Feb. 28, 1908); b. Hyde Park, N.Y. Editor, painter, critic. *Gaspara Stampa* (1881); *Art and Nature in Italy* (1882). He wrote for *The Galaxy, The New York Evening Post,* etc.

BENSON, OLIVER EARL (Aug. 20, 1911–); b. Guthrie, Okla. Educator. *Through the Diplomatic Looking Glass* (1939); *How Vulnerable Is Communism?* (1952); *A Single Diplomatic Game* (1963); *Oklahoma Votes 1907–62* (1964); *Oklahoma Votes for Congress* (1965); *Political Science Laboratory* (1967); etc. Prof. government, University of Oklahoma, since 1947.

BENSON, SALLY [Sara Mahala Redway Smith Benson] (Sept. 3, 1900–); b. St. Louis, Mo. Short story writer. *People Are Fascinating* (1936); *Emily* (1938); *Junior Miss* (1941); *Meet Me in St. Louis* (1942); *Women and Children First* (1943); *Seventeen* (musical comedy, 1954).

Benson, Therese. Pen name of Emilie Benson Knipe.

BENT, SILAS (May 9, 1882–July 30, 1945); b. Millersburg, Ky. Editor, author. *Ballyhoo: The Voice of the Press* (1927); *Strange Bedfellows* (1928); *Buchanan of the Press* (1932); *Justice Oliver Wendell Holmes* (1932); *Newspaper Crusaders* (1939); etc.

Bent Twig, The. Novel by Dorothy Canfield Fisher (1915). The setting is a Middle Western University campus and the author's recollections of her own experiences add realism to the plot.

BENTLEY, ERIC [Russell] (Sept. 14, 1916–); b. Bolton, Lancs., Eng. Director, critic. *A Century of Hero Worship* (1944); *The Playwright as Thinker* (1946); *Bernard Shaw* (1947); *In Search of Theatre* (1953); *The Dramatic Event* (1954); *The Life of the Drama* (1964); *The Theatre of Commitment* (1968); *What Is Theatre?* (1968); etc. Editor: *From the Modern Repertoire,* 6v. (1949–60); Pirandello's *Naked Masks* (1952); etc. Translator: *The Private Life of the Master Race* by Bertolt Brecht (1944); *Mother Courage* by Bertolt Brecht (1963); etc. Drama critic, *New Republic* (1952–56). Prof. dramatic literature, Columbia University, since 1953.

BENTLEY, WILLIAM (June 22, 1759–Dec. 29, 1819); b. Boston, Mass. Unitarian clergyman, diarist. *The Diary of William Bentley,* 4v. (1905–14). Contributor to the *Salem Register.*

BENTON, JOEL (May 29, 1832–Sept. 15, 1911); b. Amenia, N.Y. Journalist, author. *Emerson as a Poet* (1883); *Life of Hon. Phineas T. Barnum* (1891); *In the Poe Circle* (1899); *Persons and Places* (1905); *Memories of the Twilight Club* (1910).

BENTON, ROBERT [Douglas] (Sept. 29, 1932–); b. Dallas, Tex. Author, screenwriter. *The In and Out Book* (with H. Schmidt, 1960); *The Worry Book* (1961); *Little Brother No More* (1961); *Superman* (musical, with David Newman, 1966). Screenplays with David Newman for *Bonnie and Clyde* (1967) and *There Was A Crooked Man* (1969).

BENTON, THOMAS HART (Mar. 14, 1782–Apr. 10, 1858); b. Hillsborough, N.C. Statesman, orator, author. *Thirty Years' View,* 2v. (1854–56); *An Abridgement of the Debates of Congress,* 15v. (1857–61). U.S. Senator from Missouri, 1821–51.

BENTON, THOMAS HART (Apr. 15, 1889–); b. Neosho, Mo. Artist, author. *An Artist in America* (1937); *An American in Art: A Professional and Technical Autobiography* (1969).

BENTON, WALTER (1907–). Poet. *This Is My Beloved* (1943); *Never a Greater Need* (1948).

BENTON, WILLIAM (Apr. 1, 1900–); b. Minneapolis, Minn. Government official, publisher, author. *This Is the Challenge* (1958); *The Voice of Latin America* (1961); *The Teachers and the Taught in the U.S.S.R.* (1966). U.S. Senator, 1949–53. Chairman of Board, *Encyclopaedia Britannica*, since 1943.

Benziger Inc. New York. Catholic book publishers. The New York firm was founded in 1853 as Benziger Brothers, a branch of the Swiss firm, which had been founded in Einsideln, Switzerland, by Joseph Charles Benziger (1762–1841) in 1792. In 1860, J. N. Adelrich Benziger and Louis Benziger began to publish books in America. A Cincinnati branch was opened in 1860, a Chicago branch in 1887, a San Francisco branch in 1929, and a Boston branch in 1937. In 1867 the Holy See conferred on the firm the title, "Printers to the Holy Apostolic See." The firm publishes religious books, text books, travel books, etc., and in 1898 established *Benziger's Magazine*, an illustrated Catholic monthly. In 1894, Louis G. Benziger succeeded his father, Louis Benziger, and in recent years the firm has been run by Xavier N. Benziger, Bernard A. Benziger, and Alfred F. Benziger. Bernard C. Benziger is now president. In 1922 the Benziger Brothers' Bookstore was opened in Philadelphia. Now a subsidiary of Crowell Collier and Macmillan, Inc.

BERCOVICI, KONRAD (June 22, 1882–Dec. 27, 1961); b. Braila, Rumania. Author. *Dust of New York* (1918); *Ghitza, and Other Romances* (1919); *Murdo* (1921); *Costa's Daughter* (1923); *Iliana* (1924); *The Marriage Guest* (1924); *On New Shores* (1925); *Singing Winds* (1926); Volga Boatman (1926); *Story of the Gypsies* (1926); *Peasants* (1928); *Alexander* (1928); *The Crusades* (1929); *For a Song* (1931); *Against the Sky* (1932); *Main Entrance* (1932); *The Incredible Balkans* (1932); *It's the Gypsy in Me* (autobiography, 1941); *The Exodus* (1947); *Savage Prodigal* (1948); etc. Editor: *Best Short Stories of the World* (1925).

BERDAHL, CLARENCE ARTHUR (June 14, 1890–); b. Baltic, S.D. Educator, author. *War Powers of the Executive in the United States* (1921); *The Policy of the United States with Respect to the League of Nations* (1932); *Presidential Nominating Politics* (1952); etc. Prof. political science emeritus, University of Illinois, since 1961.

BERELSON, BERNARD [Reuben] (June 2, 1912–); b. Spokane, Wash. Educator. *What Reading Does to People* (with others, 1940); *The Library's Public* (with L. Asheim, 1949); *Content Analysis* (1952); *Graduate Education in the United States* (1960). Editor: *Education for Librarianship* (1949); *Family Planning and Population Programs: A Review of World Developments* (with others, 1966); etc. President of the Population Council since 1968.

BERENSON, BERNARD (June 26, 1865–Oct. 6, 1959); b. in Lithuania. Art critic, author. *The Venetian Painters of the Renaissance* (1894); *The Florentine Painters of the Renaissance* (1896); *The Central Italian Painters of the Renaissance* (1897); *North Italian Painters of the Renaissance* (1907); the four combined as, *Italian Painters of the Renaissance* (1930); *Essays In Mediaeval Art* (1930); *Aesthetics and History in the Visual Arts* (1948); *Sketch for a Self-Portrait* (1949); *Rumor and Reflection* (1952); *Caravaggio: His Incongruity and His Fame* (1954); *The Arch of Constantine, or the Decline of Form* (1954); *Piero della Francesca* (1954); *Essays in Appreciation* (1958); *The Passionate Sightseer* (1960); etc. Compiler: *Catalogue of Italian Paintings in Widener Collection; Catalogue of Italian Paintings in the Michael Friedsam Collection. See* Sylvia Sprigge's *Berenson* (1960); Umberto Morra's *Conversations with Berenson* (1965).

BERENSTAIN, JANICE (July 26, 1923–); b. Philadelphia, Pa. Cartoonist, author. Co-author with husband, Stanley Berenstain (q.v.): *Marital Blitz* (1954); *Lover Boy* (1958); *Office Lover Boy* (1962); *The Bears' Picnic* (1966); *Inside, Outside, Upside Down* (1968); etc.

BERENSTAIN, STANLEY (1923–). Author. Co-author with wife, Janice Berenstain (q.v.): *The Bike Lesson* (1964); *Flipsville, Squarlesville* (1965); *The Bear Scouts* (1967); *The Bears' Holiday* (1968); *The Bears' Vacation* (1968); etc.

BERESFORD, MARCUS (Mar. 28, 1919–); b. London. Author. Writes under pen name "Marc Brandel." *Rain Before Seven* (1945); *The Rod and the Staff* (1947); *The Barriers Between* (1949); *The Choice* (1950); *The Time of the Fire* (1954).

BERG, LOUIS (June 19, 1901–); b. London, England. Psychiatrist, author. *Prison Doctor* (1931); *Prison Nurse* (1934); *Devil's Circus* (1934); *Revelations of a Prison Doctor* (1934); *Twilight Comes Early* (1939); *Day of Miracles* (play, 1946); *Sex: Methods and Manners* (with Robert Treat, 1953); *The Velvet Underground* (with Michael Leigh, 1964); etc.

BERGAUST, ERIK (Mar. 23, 1925–); b. Baerum, Oslo, Nor. Publisher, author. *The Next Fifty Years of Flight* (1954); *Rockets and Missiles* (1957); *First Men in Space* (1960); *Skin Divers in Action* (1965); *Convertiplanes in Action* (1969); *The Russians in Space* (1969); etc. Editor and publisher of various publications concerned with air and sea exploration, since 1946.

BERGENDOFF, CONRAD JOHN IMMANUEL (Dec. 3, 1895–); b. Shickley, Neb. Lutheran clergyman, educator. *Olavus Petri* (1928); *The Secular Idea of Progress and the Christian Doctrine of Sanctification* (1933); *I Believe in the Church* (1937); *One Holy Catholic Apostolic Church* (1954); *The Church of the Lutheran Reformation* (1967); etc. President, Augustana College and Theological Seminary, 1935–48; Augustana College, since 1948.

BERGENGREN, RALPH [Wilhelm] **ALEXIS** (Mar. 2, 1871–); b. Gloucester, Mass. Essayist. *The Comforts of Home* (1918); *The Perfect Gentleman* (1919); *The Seven Ages of Man* (1921); *David the Dreamer* (1922); *Susan and the Butterbees* (1947); etc.

BERGER, JOSEF (1903–); b. Denver, Col. Author of children's books. Pen name, "Jeremiah Digges." Under own name: *Captain Bib* (1929); *Come Along* (1930); *Sleepy Steve* (1931); *Pogo* (1934); *Swordfisherman Jimi* (1939); also under pen name: *Cape Cod Pilot* (1937); *Bowleg Bill, the Seagoing Cowboy* (1938); *In Great Waters* (1941); *Operation Underground* (1947); *Discoverers of the New World* (with Lawrence C. Wroth, 1960); *Who Said It?* (1963); etc. Editor: *Diary of America* (with Dorothy Berger, 1957).

BERGER, LOWE (July 17, 1896–Oct. 8, 1959); b. West Point, Ill. Publisher. With Bobbs-Merrill Co., 1928–60; pres., 1953–59.

BERGER, MEYER (Sept. 1, 1898–Feb. 8, 1959); b. New York. Journalist, author. *The Eight Million* (1942); *Men of Maryknoll* (with James G. Keller, 1943); *Growth of an Ideal: The Story of the Manhattan Savings Bank* (1950); *The Story of the New York Times, 1851–1951* (1951); *Meyer Berger's New York* (1960). Columnist, *The New York Times*, 1953–59.

BERGER, MORROE (June 25, 1917–); b. New York. Educator, author. *Equality by Statute* (1952); *Bureaucracy and Society in Modern Egypt* (1957); *The Arab World Today* (1962). Editor and translator: *Madame de Stael on Politics* (1964). Prof. sociology, Princeton University, since 1962.

BERGER, THOMAS [Louis] (July 20, 1924–); b. Cincinnati, O. Author. *Crazy in Berlin* (1945); *Reinhart in Love* (1962); *Little Big Man* (1964); *Vital Parts* (1970).

BERGERE, THEA LINDGREN (May 28, 1933–); b. New York. Author. *From Stones to Skyscrapers* (1960); *Automobiles of Yesteryear* (1961); *The Story of St. Peter's* (1966); etc.

BERGH, HENRY (Aug. 29, 1811–Mar. 12, 1888); b. New York. Humanitarian, author. *"Married Off": A Satirical Poem* (1860); etc. Founder, The American Society for the Prevention of Cruelty to Animals, Apr. 10, 1866.

BERGIN, ALFRED (Apr. 24, 1866–Mar. 6, 1944); b. Väster Bitterna, Vastergötland, Sweden. Swedish Lutheran clergyman, historian. *The Swedish Settlements in Central Kansas* (1910); *Under Pines and Palms* (1916); *The Story of Lindsborg* (1929); etc.

BERGLER, EDMUND (1899–Feb. 6, 1962); Psychoanalyst, author. *Conflict in Marriage* (1949); *The Writer and Psychoanalysis* (1950); *Neurotic Counterfeit* (1951); *The Revolt of the Middle-Aged Man* (1954); *Laughter and the Sense of Humor* (1956); *The Psychology of Gambling* (1957); *Tensions Can Be Reduced to Nuisances* (1960); *Curable and Incurable Neurotics* (1961); etc.

Berkeley Barb, The. Berkeley, Cal. Weekly. Founded 1964. Underground newspaper. Allan Coult is editor.

Berkeley Review, The. Berkeley, Calif. Quarterly. Founded 1956. Devoted to literature and the arts.

BERKOVITS, ELIEZER (Sept. 8, 1908–); b. Oradea, Rumania. Rabbi, author. *Towards Historic Judaism* (1943); *Yesterday and Tomorrow* (1945); *A Jewish Critique of the Philosophy of Martin Buber* (1962); *Prayer* (1963); *Man and God: Studies in Biblical Theology* (1969); etc.

BERKOWITZ, DAVID SANDLER (Aug. 20, 1913–); b. Pittsburgh, Pa. Educator, author. *Inequality of Opportunity in Higher Education* (1948); *Bibliotheca Bibliographica Britannica* (1963); *Ancient Civilizations and the Founding of Libraries* (1964); *From Ptolemy to the Moon* (1965); etc. Prof. history, Brandeis University, since 1949.

BERKSON, BILL [William C.] (Aug. 30, 1939–); b. New York. Poet. *Saturday Night* (1961). Editor: *Frank O'Hara: In Memory of My Feelings* (1967). Faculty, New School, New York, since 1964.

BERKSON, SEYMOUR (Jan. 31, 1905–Jan. 4, 1959); b. Chicago, Ill. Publisher, author. *Their Majesties! A Royal Merry-Go-Round* (1938); *Rise and Fall of Mussolini* (1943); *They Were There* (1944). Publisher, New York *Journal-American,* from 1955.

BERLE, ADOLF AUGUSTUS, JR. (Jan. 29, 1895–Nov. 18, 1960); b. Boston, Mass. Lawyer. *Studies in the Law of Corporation Finance* (1928); *The Modern Corporation and Private Property* (1932); *New Directions in the New World* (1940); *Natural Selection of Political Forces* (1950); *Tides of Crisis* (1957); *The Bank That Banks Built* (1959); *Power Without Property* (1959); *The Twentieth Century Capitalist Revolution* (1960); *The American Economic Republic* (1963); etc.

BERLE, MILTON [professional name of Milton Berlinger] (July 12, 1908–); b. New York. Comedian, author. *Out of My Trunk* (1945); *Earthquake* (1959).

BERLIN, ELLIN (Jan. 29, 1895–); b. Roslyn, N.Y. Author. *Land I Have Chosen* (1944); *Lace Curtain* (1948); *Silver Platter* (1957).

BERLITZ, CHARLES FRAMBACH (Nov. 22, 1913–); b. New York. Educator. Author of language-teaching books under general titles *Berlitz Method* (since 1947); *Berlitz Self Teacher* (since 1949); and others, including phrase books and dictionaries. Vice-president, Berlitz Publications, since 1947.

BERNAYS, EDWARD L. (Nov. 22, 1891–); b. Vienna. Public relations counsel, author. *Crystallizing Public Opinion* (1923); *Propaganda* (1928); *Speak Up for Democracy* (1940); *Take Your Place at the Peace Table* (1945); *Public Relations* (1952). Editor: *Engineering of Consent* (1955).

BERNBAUM, ERNEST (Feb. 12, 1879–Mar. 8, 1958); b. Brooklyn, N.Y. Educator, Author. *The Mary Carleton Narratives, 1663–1673; a Missing Chapter in the History of the English Novel* (1914); *The Drama of Sensibility; a Sketch of the History of English Sentimental Comedy and Domestic Tragedy, 1696–1780* (1915); *The Puritan Pilgrim* (poems, 1921). Editor of many textbooks in English literature. Prof. English, University of Illinois, 1916–45.

BERNE, ERIC LENNARD (May 10, 1910–July 15, 1970); b. Montreal, Can. Psychiatrist, author. *The Mind in Action* (1947); *Transactional Analysis in Psychotherapy* (1961); *Games People Play* (1964); *The Happy Valley* (1968); *Principles of Group Treatment* (1968); etc.

BERNEY, WILLIAM [Claibourne] (1920–Nov. 23, 1961). Playwright. Co-author, with Howard Richardson: *Dark of the Moon* (prod. 1945); *Design for a Stained Glass Window* (1950); *Mountain Fire* (1953); *Protective Custody* (1956); etc.

BERNSTEIN, ALINE [Frankau] (Dec. 22, 1880–1955); b. New York. Author. *Three Blue Suits* (1935); *The Journey Down* (1938); *An Actor's Daughter* (autobiography, 1941); *Miss Condon* (1947); *Masterpieces of Women's Costume of the 18th and 19th Centuries* (1959).

BERNSTEIN, HERMAN (Sept. 21, 1876–Aug. 31, 1935); b. Neustadt-Scherwindt, Russia. Editor, diplomat, author. *The Flight of Time, and Other Poems* (1899); *In the Gates of Israel* (1902); *Contrite Hearts* (1905); *Celebrities of Our Time: Interviews* (1924). Editor, *The American Hebrew,* 1916–19.

BERNSTEIN, LEONARD (Aug. 25, 1918–); b. Lawrence, Mass. Conductor, pianist, composer, author. *The Joy of Music* (1959); etc. Musical director, New York Philharmonic, 1958–70.

BERNSTEIN, RICHARD JACOB (May 14, 1932–); b. New York. Educator, author. *John Dewey on Experience, Nature, and Freedom* (1959); *Perspectives of Peirce* (1966); *John Dewey* (1966). Prof. philosophy, Haverford College, since 1966.

BERRIAN, WILLIAM (1787–Nov. 7, 1862); b. New York City. Clergyman, author. *Travels in France and Italy* (1820); *An Historical Sketch of Trinity Church, New York* (1847); *Recollections of Departed Friends* (1850); etc.

BERRIGAN, DANIEL J. (1921–). Roman Catholic clergyman, author. *World for Wedding Ring* (1962); *Encounters: poems* (1965); *They Call Us Dead Men* (1966); *No One Walks Waters* (1966); *Consequences: Truth and . . .* (1967); *Go From Here, a Prison Journal* (1968); *Love, Love at the End* (1968); *Night Flight to Hanoi* (1968); *False Gods, Real Men* (poems) (1969); etc.

BERRIGAN, PHILIP [Francis] (Oct. 5, 1923–); b. Two Harbors, Mich. Roman Catholic clergyman, author. *No More Strangers* (1965); *Prison Journals of a Priest Revolutionary* (1970).

BERRIGAN, TED [Edmund J. M., Jr.] Poet. *A Lily for My Love* (1959); *The Sonnets* (1964); *Galileo; or Finksville* (1964); *Bean Spasms* (with R. Padgett, 1967); *Many Happy Returns* (1969).

BERRYHILL, S. NEWTON (1830–1888). Known as "The Backwoods Poet." *Backwoods Poems* (1878).

BERRYMAN, JOHN [McAlpin] (Oct. 25, 1914–Jan. 7, 1972) b. McAlester, Okla. Author, poet. *Poems* (1942); *The Dispossessed* (poems, 1948); *Stephen Crane* (1950); *Homage to Mistress Bradstreet* (poems, 1956); *77 Dream Songs* (poems, 1964); *His Toy, His Dream, His Rest* (poems, 1968); etc. Contributor to *Five American Poets* (1940); *Best American Short Stories* (1946). Pulitzer Prize for poetry, 1965; National Book Award, 1968; Bollingen Prize, 1969.

BERTHOFF, WARNER [Benent] (Jan. 22, 1925–); b. Oberlin, O. Educator, author. *American Literature: Traditions and Talents* (1960); *The Example of Melville* (1962); *The Ferment of Realism: American Literature, 1884–1919* (1965). Prof. English, Harvard University, since 1967.

BESSIE, ALVAH C[ecil] (June 4, 1904–); b. New York City. Novelist. *Dwell in the Wilderness* (1935); *Men in Battle* (1939); *Bread in the Stone* (1941); *The Un-Americans* (1957); *The Symbol* (1967). Editor: *The Heart of Spain* (1952).

BEST, HERBERT (Mar. 25, 1894–); b. Chester, Eng. Author. *Garram the Hunter* (1935); *The Twenty-Fifth Hour* (1940); *Young'un* (1944); *Border Iron* (1945); *The Long Portage* (1948); *Not Without Danger* (1951); *Columbus Canon* (1954); *Sea Warriors* (1959); *Carolina Gold* (1961); *Desmond's First Case* (1961); *Desmond the Dog Detective* (1962); *Parachute to Survival* (1964); *Desmond and the Peppermint Ghost* (1965); *Desmond and Dog Friday* (1968); etc.

Best Articles and Stories. Bloomington, Ind.; Guilford, Conn. Monthly, except in summer. Founded 1957. A reprint magazine.

Best Short Stories. Annual anthology of American short stories. Founded 1916, by Edward J. O'Brien, who edited the first 26 volumes. After his death in 1941, Martha Foley became editor.

BESTER, ALFRED (Dec. 18, 1913–); b. New York. Author. *Who He?* (1953); *The Stars My Destination* (1956); *Starburst* (1958); *The Dark Side of the Earth* (1964).

BESTON, HENRY (June 1, 1888–Apr. 15, 1968); b. Quincy, Mass. Author or editor: *Full Speed Ahead* (1919); *Firelight Fairy Book* (1919); *Starlight Wonder Book* (1923); *The Book of Gallant Vagabonds* (1925); *The Sons of Kai* (1926); *The Outermost House* (1928); *London* (1929); *Herbs and The Earth* (1935); *American Memory* (1937); *Northern Farm* (1948); *White Pine and Blue Water* (1950); etc.

Beston, Mrs. Henry. See Elizabeth Coatsworth.

BESTOR, ARTHUR [Eugene], Jr. (Sept. 20, 1908–); b. Chautauqua, N.Y. Historian, author. *Chautauqua Publications* (1934); *Backwoods Utopias* (1950); *Educational Wastelands* (1953); *The Restoration of Learning* (1955); *The Reading of Jefferson* (1963); etc. Prof. history, University of Illinois, 1951–62; University of Washington, Seattle, since 1962.

Bestsellers. Besides the *Holy Bible*, Webster's *Blue-Backed Spellers*, McGuffey's *Readers*, and perennial bestsellers of this nature, the following books had large sales: *Bay Psalm Book* (1640), *New England Primer* (1727), *Public Good*, by Thomas Paine (1780), *M'Fingal*, by John Trumbull (1782), *Charlotte Temple*, by Susanna Haswell Rowson (1791), *The Coquette*, by Hannah Foster (1797), *Life and Memorable Actions of George Washington*, by Mason Locke Weems (1800), *Letters of a British Spy*, by William Wirt (1803), *Sketch Book*, by Washington Irving (1820), *The Spy*, by James Fenimore Cooper (1821); *Two Years Before the Mast*, by Richard Henry Dana (1840), *Margaret*, by Sylvester Judd (1845), *Reveries*, by Donald Grant Mitchell (1850), *St. Leger*, by Richard B. Kimball (1850), *The Wide, Wide World*, by Susan Warner (1850), *Uncle Tom's Cabin*, by Harriet Beecher Stowe (1851), *Fern Leaves*, by Fanny Fern (1853), *The Lamplighter*, by Maria S. Cummins (1854), *Tempest and Sunshine*, by Mary Jane Holmes (1854), *Ten Nights in a Bar Room*, by Timothy Shay Arthur (1854), *Nothing to Wear*, by William Allen Butler (1857), *Beulah*, by Augusta Jane Evans (1859), *Seth Jones*, by Edward Sylvester Ellis (1860), *Malaeska*, by Ann Sophia W. Stephens (1860), *Among the Pines*, by James Roberts Gilmore (1862), *Elsie Dinsmore*, by Martha Finley (1867), *Katrina*, by Josiah Gilbert Holland (1867), *The Gates Ajar*, by Elizabeth Stuart Phelps (1868), *Little Women*, by Louisa May Alcott (1868), *The Hoosier Schoolmaster*, by Edward Eggleston (1871), *Barriers Burned Away*, by Edward Payson

Roe (1872), *Farm Ballads*, by Will Car[
Daw*, by Thomas Bailey Aldrich (187[
Tom Sawyer, by Mark Twain (1876), [
Habberton (1876), *A Fool's Errand*, by[
gee (1879), *Ben Hur*, by Lew Walla[
Peppers and How They Grew, by M[
Adventures of Huckleberry Finn, b[
Personal Memoirs, by Ulysses Simp[
1886), *Little Lord Fauntleroy*, by Fr[
(1886), *Looking Backward*, by Edw[
His Steps, by Charles Monroe Shel[
Wise Man, by Henry Van Dyke (189[
by Richard Harding Davis (1897), *J[
Leicester Ford (1899), *David Har[
Westcott (1900), *Graustark*, by Ge[
(1901), *The Crisis*, by Winston Chur[
Mary Johnston (1902), *The Virg[
(1902), *The Call of the Wild*, by J[
Little Shepherd of Kingdom Come,[
Rebecca of Sunnybrook Farm, b[
(1903), *Freckles*, by Gene Stratton[
Wolf, by Jack London (1904), *The[
Raymond Shipman Andrews (190[
Hills, by Harold Bell Wright (1907[
some Pine, by John Fox, Jr. (1909)[
Barclay (1910), *The Harvester*,[
(1911), *Laddie*, by Gene Stratton P[
Eleanor H. Porter (1913), *Penro[
(1914), *Tarzan of the Apes*, by Ed[
"Over the Top," by Arthur Guy E[
by Edward Streeter (1918), *Anne[
Montgomery (1920), *Main Street[
The Covered Wagon, by Emerson[
Edna Ferber (1924), *The Story of[
(1926), *Anthony Adverse*, by H[
With the Wind, by Margaret Mi[
Friends and Influence People,[
Northwest Passage, by Kenneth[
ling, by Marjorie Kinnan Rawli[
Bell Tolls, by Ernest Hemingw[
Book, by Mortimer Adler (1940)[
Shirer (1941), *The Moon Is Dow[
Dragon Seed, by Pearl Buck (1[
grove*, by Marion Hargrove (19[
Marquand (1943), *One World,[
Strange Fruit, by Lillian Smith[
Pyle (1944), *Forever Amber*, by[
Front, by Ernie Pyle (1945), T[
Donald (1946), *Inside U.S.A.,*[
sade in Europe, by Dwight D. [
Live, by John O'Hara (1949), [
son (1950), *From Here to Ete[
The Caine Mutiny, by Hermar[
Leon Uris (1953), *Not as a St[
(1954), *Marjorie Morningstar,*[
Last Hurrah, by Edwin O'Con[
by James Gould Cozzens (195[
O'Hara (1958), *Lolita*, by Vla[
and Consent, by Allen Drur[
Ecstasy, by Irving Stone (196[
Harper Lee (1961), *Franny[
(1962), *Ship of Fools*, by Kath[
Days in May, by Fletcher [
(1963), *A Moveable Feast*, by[
zog, by Saul Bellow (1964),[
(1965), *Valley of the Dolls,*[
Cold Blood, by Truman Capc[
Elia Kazan (1967), *Myra Bre[
Ada, by Vladimir Nabokov ([
Puzo (1969), *Human Sexua[
and V. E. Johnson (1970), L[
For current bestsellers see t[
the *New York Times Book[

Bestsellers. Scranton, Pa.[
Condenses bestsellers.

hel." Poem by A. J. H. Duganne, on the Civil War battle at name.

-IUNE, GEORGE W[ashington] (Mar. 18, 1805–Apr. ?62); b. New York City. Dutch Reformed clergyman, *Lays of Love and Faith* (1847); *Orations and Occasional urses* (1850). Editor: Walton's *The Compleat Angler,* American edition (1847); *The British Female Poets* ?.

thal. Comedy by George Henry Boker (prod. 1850). with the theme of usury.

-y and I Are Out." Poem by Will Carleton, which first ed in *Harper's Weekly,* June 17, 1871, and is included *Farm Ballads* (1873). Nannette Snow Emerson (Mrs. ? F. French) claimed the authorship of this poem in a ?titled *A Thanksgiving Story; Embodying the Ballad of v and I Are Out,"* and *Other Poems* (1873), republished v *Wife and I Quarreled; by the Author of "Betsey and Out"* (1877).

:LHEIM, BRUNO (Aug. 28, 1903–); b. Vienna. ?r. *Dynamics of Prejudice* (with Morris Janowitz, *Love is Not Enough—The Treatment of Emotionally -ed Children* (1950); *Symbolic Wounds* (1954); *Tru-m Life* (1955); *The Informed Heart* (1960); *Dialogues others* (1962); *The Empty Fortress* (1967); *The Chil-' the Dreams* (1969). Prof. educational psychology, ity of Chicago, since 1952.

Homes and Gardens. Des Moines, Ia. Founded 1922. :d by Meredith Publishing Co. Appeared originally as *Garden and Home* and name changed to *Better Homes -dens* in 1924. Devoted to practical advice and instruc-ncerning domestic life.

CRAVEN LANGSTROTH (Apr. 23, 1853–July 30, St. John, N.B. Author. *The Perfume-Holder* (poem, *ales of a Garrison Town* (with Arthur W. H. Eaton, *Garland of Sonnets* (1899); *Selected Poems* (1916); *? Captains* (poems, 1921); etc.

DORIS JUNE WAUGH (June 4, 1932–); b. States-:. Author. *The Gentle Insurrection* (1954); *Tall ? Winter* (1957); *The Astronomer and Other Stories* :c.

'en. Novel by Jane G. Austin (1891). The story of the -orn to a Pilgrim family in New England, daughter ?d Priscilla Alden, best known through Longfellow's *?e Courtship of Miles Standish."* The novel gives a the joys and hardships of the Pilgrims.

?GE, ALBERT JEREMIAH (Oct. 6, 1862–Apr. b. Highland Co., O. Statesman, biographer. *The 'in Marshall,* 4v. (1916–19, Pulitzer Prize for Ameri-aphy, 1920); *Abraham Lincoln, 1809–1858,* 4v., (1928); etc.

?Y, ROBERT (ca. 1673–1722); b. in Middlesex Co., ian of Virginia. *The History and Present State of '705).

Y-GIDDINGS, ARTHUR RAYMOND (1899–); nd. Author. *Larrish Hundred* (1942); *Broad Mar-River of Rogues* (1948); *The Rival Shores* (1956).

' Graustark. Novel by George Barr McCutcheon ?el to *Graustark.* The chief characters are Grenfall the Princess Yetive. Beverly Calhoun, invited to ?y Princess Yetive, meets with a series of adven-ding the intrigues of Prince Gabriel. Her hero and 3aldos, turns out to be Prince Dantan.

?N, HELEN SMITH (1906–). Poet. *Dr. John-fall* (1946); *Nineteen Million Elephants* (1950); *A 'ky* (1956); *When Found, Make a Verse Of* (1961); *ith's Girl: A Memoir* (1965); *A Book and a Love* 3).

BEWER, JULIUS AUGUST (Aug. 28, 1877–Aug. 31, 1953); b. Ratingen, Germany. Clergyman, author. *The Book of Jonah* (in International Critical Commentary, 1912); *The Literature of the Old Testament* (1922); etc.

Beyond Baroque. Venice, Cal. Quarterly anthology of new and emerging literary trends. Founded 1968. Edited by George Drury Smith.

Beyond the Horizon. Play by Eugene O'Neill (prod. 1920). The story of the emotional conflicts of two brothers, one a man of the soil, the other an intellectual.

Beyond the Melting Pot. Sociological study of minority groups in the United States, by Nathan Glazer and Daniel P. Moynihan (1963).

"Beyond the Potomac." Poem by Paul Hamilton Hayne (1862).

BIANCHI, MARTHA [Gilbert] Dickinson (d. Dec. 21 1943); b. Amherst, Mass. Novelist, poet. *Within the Hedg* (poems, 1899); *The Cathedral, and Other Poems* (1901); *? Modern Prometheus* (1908); *The Cuckoo's Nest* (1909); *? Cossack Lover* (1911); *The Sin of Angels* (1912); *Gabrielle, and Other Poems* (1913); *The Kiss of Apollo* (1915); *The Point of View* (1918); *The Wandering Eros* (poems, 1925); *Emily Dickinson Face to Face* (1932). Editor: *The Life and Letters of Emily Dickinson* (1924); and various collections of Emily Dickinson's poems.

BIANCO, MARGERY [Williams] (Mrs. Francesco Bianco) (July 22, 1881–1944); b. London, England. Author. *The Late Returning* (1902); *Poor Cecco* (1925); *The Adventures of Andy* (1927); *The Good Friends* (1934); *Bright Morning* (1942); *Forward Commandos* (1944); etc.

BIANCOLLI, LOUIS (April 17, 1907–); b. New York. Author. *The Book of Great Conversations* (1948); *The Analytical Concert Guide* (1951); *The Opera Reader* (1953); *Forbidden Childhood* (with Ruth Slenczynska (1954). Translator: Dante's *Divine Comedy* (1966).

Bib Ballads. By Ring Lardner (1915).

Bibelot, The. Portland, Me. Literary monthly. Published and edited by Thomas Bird Mosher. Founded, 1895; expired, 1925.

Biblical Repertory, The. Princeton, N.J. Founded Jan., 1825. Underwent many changes in title. In 1875 it was called the *Princeton Review.* Its chief subject was Presbyterian Theology, but in later years it contained many essays of high literary value. Charles Hodge (1825–1871) was a dominating force as editor. Merged with *The Political Science Quarterly* in 1888. During its last two years it was called *The New Princeton Review,* the old series having suspended in 1884.

Bibliographical Society of America, The. Worcester, Mass. Founded 1904. Its *Papers* were first published in 1906 and are issued quarterly. The Society was incorporated in 1927.

Bibliotheca Americana 1820–61. By Orville Augustus Roorbach, 4v. (1852–61). A catalogue of American publications.

Bibliotheca Sacra. St. Louis, Mo.; Dallas, Tex. Calvinist magazine published by the Andover Theological Seminary, later by the Dallas Theological Seminary. Founded Feb., 1843, by Edward Robinson, at Oberlin, O.; moved to St. Louis, 1922. Among its leading editors for many years were Edwards A. Park, Bela B. Edwards, G. Frederick Wright, and John F. Walvoord.

BICKHAM, JACK M[iles] (Sept. 2, 1930–); b. Columbus, O. Author: *Feud Fury* (1959); *Wildcat on the Loose* (1967); *The Padre Must Die* (1967); *Target: Charity Ross* (1968). Under pen name Jeff Clinton: *Fighting Buckaroo* (1960); *Range Killer* (1962).

BICKMORE, ALBERT SMITH (Mar. 1, 1839–Aug. 12, 1914); b. St. George's, Me. Educator, naturalist, traveler, author. *Travels in the East Indian Archipelago* (1868).

BICKNELL, THOMAS WILLIAMS (Sept. 6, 1834–Oct. 6, 1925); b. Barrington, R.I. Educator, historian, poet. *The History of the State of Rhode Island and Providence Plantations*, 4v. (1920); etc. Founder, *The New England Journal of Education*, 1875, which became *The Journal of Education*, 1878; editor, 1875–86; founder and editor of a number of education periodicals.

BIDDLE, A[nthony] J[oseph] DREXEL (Oct. 1, 1874–May 27, 1948); b. Philadelphia, Pa. Explorer, lecturer, author. *A Dual Role* (1894); *An Allegory and Three Essays* (1894); *The Froggy Fairy Book* (1896); *Shantytown Sketches* (1897); *The Madeira Islands*, 2v. (1900); *The Land of the Wine*, 2v. (1901); etc.

BIDDLE, FRANCIS (May 9, 1886–); b. Paris. Lawyer, government official, author. *Llanfear Pattern* (1927); *Mr. Justice Holmes* (1942); *Democratic Thinking and the War* (1944); *The World's Best Hope* (1949); *The Fear of Freedom* (1951); *A Casual Past* (autobiography, 1961); *In Brief Authority* (1962). Attorney general of the U.S., 1941–45.

BIDDLE, GEORGE (Jan. 24, 1885–Oct. 4, 1968); b. Philadelphia, Pa. Painter, illustrator, author. *Green Island* (1930); *Adolphe Borie* (1937); *Boardman Robinson* (1937); *An American Artist's Story* (1939); *Artist at War* (1944); *The Yes and No of Contemporary Art* (1957); *Indian Impressions* (1960); *Tahitian Journal* (1968); etc.

BIDDLE, HORACE P[eters] (Mar. 24, 1811–May 13, 1900); b. in Hocking Co., O. Jurist, scholar, poet. *A Few Poems* (1858); *The Musical Scale* (1860); *Poems* (1868); *My Scrap Book* (1874); *American Boyhood* (1876); *Prose Miscellany* (1881); *Last Poems* (1882).

BIDDLE, NICHOLAS (Jan. 8, 1786–Feb. 27, 1844); b. Philadelphia, Pa. Litterateur, scholar, statesman. In 1809 he became a member of the "Tuesday Club" in Philadelphia and helped Joseph Dennie run the *Port Folio*. Editor, *The Port Folio*, 1812. Author of the humorous piece "Ode to Bogle." He was a benefactor of Girard College. See *The Correspondence of Nicholas Biddle*, ed. R. C. McGrane (1919); Robert V. Remini's *Andrew Jackson and the Bank War* (1967).

BIDWELL, BARNABAS (Aug. 23, 1763–July 27, 1833); b. Tyringham, Mass. Playwright. He contributed to the writing of the Society of Brothers in Unity play at Yale College, *The Modern Mistake* (prod. 1784); and was the author of another Yale play, *The Mercenary Match* (prod. 1785).

BIDWELL, DANIEL DOANE (Aug. 7, 1865–Apr. 24, 1937); b. East Hartford, Conn. Author. *Five Years with the Congo Cannibals* (with Herbert Ward, 1890); *As Far as the East Is From the West* (1910).

BIDWELL, WALTER HILLIARD (June 21, 1798–Sept. 11, 1881); b. Farmington, Conn. Editor, *The National Preacher, and Village Pulpit*, 1841–60; *The New York Evangelist*, 1843–55; owner and editor, *The Eclectic Magazine*, 1846–81; *The American Biblical Repository*, 1846–50; became owner of *The American Theological Review*, 1860.

BIERCE, AMBROSE [Gwinett] (June 24, 1842–disappeared in 1914); b. in Meigs Co., O. Journalist; author. *The Fiend's Delight* (under pen name, "Dod Grile," 1872); *Nuggets and Dust Panned Out in California* (1872); *Cobwebs from an Empty Skull* (1874); *Tales of Soldiers and Civilians* (1891); *The Monk and the Hangman's Daughter* (1892); *Can Such Things Be?* (1893); *Devil's Dictionary* (1906); *Collected Works*, 2v. (1909–1912); etc. Wrote for the *Argonaut*, the *Overland Monthly*, the *Wasp*, and the *Examiner*. He used the pen name "Town Crier" in his newspaper column. *See* Vincent Starrett's *Bibliography of Ambrose Bierce* (1928), and his *Buried Caesars* (1923); Walter Neale's *Life of Ambrose Bierce*

(1929); Percival Pollard's *Their Day in Court* (1909); Ella Sterling Cummins's *The Story of the Files* (1893); Hartley Grattan's *Bitter Bierce* (1929); Paul Fatout's *Ambrose Bierce, the Devil's Lexicographer* (1951); Richard O'Connor's *Ambrose Bierce* (1967).

BIERSTADT, EDWARD HALE (Feb. 8, 1891–); b. New York City. Editor, author. *Punishment* (play, with Louise Burleigh, 1916); *Dunsany, the Dramatist* (1917); *Sounding Brass* (1922); *The Great Betrayal* (1924); *Enter Murderers!* (1934); *Satan Was a Man* (1935); etc. Editor, *Portmanteau Plays* (1917); *More Portmanteau Plays* (1919); *Celebrated Crimes* (1928); etc.

BIERSTEDT, ROBERT (Mar. 20, 1913–); b. Burlington, Ia. Sociologist, author. *The Social Order* (1957); *Modern Social Science* (with others, 1964); *Emile Durkheim* (1966). Editor: *The Making of Society* (1959). Prof. sociology, New York University, since 1960.

Big Bear of Arkansas, The. Humorous tale by Thomas Bangs Thorpe (1845). It originally appeared in *The Spirit of the Times*, Mar. 27, 1841. In 1845 William Trotter Porter published a book with this title, including twenty-four tales by several writers.

Big Fisherman, The. Novel by Lloyd Douglas (1948). Historical fiction about Simon, called Peter, and the girl Fara, daughter of Herod Antipas.

Big Little Books. Series of 4x5 inch books published by the Whitman Publishing Company, of Racine, Wis. Sometimes know as *Better Little Books*. Many are of the dime novel type. A complete set of these books has been deposited with Harvard University.

Big Sky, The. Novel by A. B. Guthrie (1947). Set in the early nineteenth century, it deals with a Kentucky trapper who is accepted by the Indians.

Big Table. Chicago, Ill. Quarterly of literature and the arts. Founded 1959, by Irving Rosenthal and Paul Carroll, who had resigned as editors of *Chicago Review* when the University of Chicago threatend to suppress the projected Winter, 1959, issue of *Chicago Review*. *Big Table* published translations as well as work in English. Among its authors were Gregory Corso, Allen Ginsberg, Edward Dahlberg, William Burroughs, Paul Bowles. Suspended 1961.

BIGELOW, JOHN (Nov. 25, 1817–Dec. 19, 1911); b. Malden, N.Y. Editor, biographer. *Memoir of the Life and Public Services of John Charles Fremont* (1856); *The Life of Samuel J. Tilden*, 2v. (1895); *Retrospections of an Active Life*, 5v. (1900–1913); etc. Assisted William Cullen Bryant in editing the New York *Evening Post*, 1848–61. Editor: *The Complete Works of Benjamin Franklin*, 10v. (1887–88).

BIGELOW, POULTNEY (Sept. 10, 1855–May 28, 1954); b. New York. Lawyer, historian. *The German Emperor, and His Eastern Neighbors* (1892); *The Borderland of Czar and Kaiser* (1895); *History of the German Struggle for Liberty*, 4v. (1896–1905); *Prussian Memories* (1915); *Genseric* (1918); *Seventy Summers*, 2v. (1925); *Observations* (1933); etc.

BIGGERS, EARL DERR (Aug. 26, 1884–Apr. 5, 1933); b. Warren, O. Novelist, playwright. *If You're Only Human* (prod. 1912); *Seven Keys to Baldpate* (1913); *Love Insurance* (1914); *The Agony Column* (1915); *Inside the Lines* (prod. 1915); *The House Without a Key* (1925); *Fifty Candles* (1926); *The Chinese Parrot* (1926); *Behind That Curtain* (1928); *The Black Camel* (1929); *Charlie Chan Carries On* (1930); etc.

BIGGS, JOHN, JR. (Oct. 6, 1895–); b. Wilmington, Del. Jurist, author. *Demigods* (1926); *Seven Days' Whipping* (1928); *The Guilty Mind: Psychiatry and the Law of Homicide* (1955).

BIGHAM, MADGE ALFORD (Sept. 30, 1874–); b. La Grange, Ga. Author. *Tales of Mother Goose Village* (1904); *Merry Animal Tales* (1906); *Little Folks Land* (1907); *Within the Silver Moon* (1911); *More Mother Goose Village Stories* (1922); *Tales of Peanut Town* (1931); *Sunny Elephant* (1940); etc.

BIGLOW, WILLIAM (Sept. 22, 1773–Jan. 12, 1844); b. Natick, Mass. Educator. *Education* (poem, 1799); *The Youth's Library* (1808); etc. Author of the popular song, *"The Cheerful Parson."* Editor, *The Massachusetts Magazine,* July–Dec., 1796.

Biglow Papers, The. By James Russell Lowell (1848). Political satire, in verse and prose, of the War with Mexico, written in Yankee dialect. The chief narrators are Hosea Biglow, a downeast farmer, the Reverend Homer Wilbur, a country parson and antiquarian, and Birdofredum Sawin, Biglow's rascally fellow townsman who is converted to the Southern viewpoint on slavery and writes amusing letters concerning his Southern adventures. A second series was published in 1866. The first series appeared originally in part in the *Boston Courier,* in part in the *Anti-Slavery Standard;* the second series appeared originally in the *Atlantic Monthly.*

BIGNEY, MARK FREDERICK (1817–1882). Poet. *Forest Pilgrims, and Other Poems* (1867).

BILL, ALFRED H[oyt] (May 5, 1879–); b. Rochester, N.Y. Author. *The Clutch of the Corsican* (1925); *Highroads of Peril* (1926); *Alas, Poor Yorick!* (1927); *The Red Prior's Legacy* (1929); *The Wolf in the Garden* (1931); *Astrophel; or, The Life and Death of the Renowned Sir Philip Sidney* (1937); *The Beleaguered City, Richmond, 1861–1865* (1946); *The Campaign of Princeton* (1948); *A House Called Morven* (with Walter E. Edge, 1954); *Horsemen, Blue and Gray* (with James Ralph Johnson, 1960); etc.

"Bill and Joe." Poem by Oliver Wendell Holmes, in the *Atlantic Monthly,* Sept., 1868.

Billboard. Cincinnati, O. Weekly journal of the amusement world. Combined with *Funspot* to form *Amusement Business,* 1961.

BILLINGS, HENRY (1901–). Author. *Diesel Electric 4030* (1950); *Construction Ahead* (1951); *Superliner S. S. United States* (1953); *Man Under Water* (1954); *Bridges* (1956); etc.

BILLINGS, JOHN SHAW (Apr. 12, 1838–Mar. 11, 1913); b. in Switzerland Co., Ind. Surgeon, librarian. His greatest work was the *Index Catalogue* of the Library of the Surgeon-General's Office, 16v. (1880–1895), which he compiled with the assistance of Robert Fletcher (1823–1912). He and Fletcher founded the *Index Medicus* in 1879. Director, The New York Public Library, 1895–1913. *See* Harry Miller Lydenberg's *John Shaw Billings* (1924).

Billings, Josh. Pen name of Henry Wheeler Shaw.

BILLINGS, WILLIAM (Oct. 7, 1746–Sept. 26, 1800); b. Boston, Mass. Singing master and hymn writer. *The New-England Psalm-Singer* (1770). This book was engraved by Paul Revere. *The Singing Master's Assistant* (1778); *The Suffolk Harmony* (1786); *The Continental Harmony* (1794); etc. He wrote many hymns and patriotic songs. The most popular patriotic song he wrote was "Chester," a favorite during the American Revolution. *See* John Tasker Howard's *Our American Music* (1931).

BILLINGTON, RAY ALLEN (Sept. 28, 1903–); b. Bay City, Mich. Educator. *The Protestant Crusade* (1938); *American History After 1865* (1950); *American History Before 1877* (1951); *The Far Western Frontier, 1830–1860* (1956). Editorial board, *American Heritage,* since 1958. Prof. history, Northwestern University, 1944–49. Consultant Encyclopedia Americana since 1962.

Billy, Captain. Pen name of William Hamilton Fawcett.

Billy Baxter's Letters. By William J. Kountz (1867–1899), published in 1899. Interesting for its extensive use of the slang of the period.

Billy Budd. Novelette by Herman Melville, published in 1924. A study in moral contrasts, in which the sailor Billy Budd, unjustifiably hated because of his handsomeness and innocent nature by Claggart, a ship's officer, is driven to a single act of violence. Billy kills his tormentor and is hanged by the captain, who condemns him to death even though he is convinced of Billy's essential guiltlessness.

BINGHAM, ALFRED MITCHELL (Feb. 20, 1905–); b. Cambridge, Mass. Economist, author. *Insurgent America: Revolt of the Middle Classes* (1935); *Man's Estate: Adventures in Economic Discovery* (1939); *The United States of Europe* (1940); *The Techniques of Democracy* (1942); *The Practice of Idealism* (1944); etc.

BINGHAM, CALEB (Apr. 15, 1757–Apr. 6, 1817); b. Salisbury, Conn. Pioneer writer of textbooks. *The Young Lady's Accidence; or, A Short and Easy Introduction to English Grammer* (1785), the second English grammar published in the United States, Noah Webster having published his one year earlier; *The American Preceptor* (1794); *The Child's Companion* (1792); etc.

BINGHAM, HIRAM (Oct. 30, 1789–Nov. 11, 1869); b. Bennington, Vt. Congregational clergyman, missionary to the Hawaiian Islands, author. *Residence of Twenty Years in the Sandwich Islands* (1847). Co-translator of the Bible into Hawaiian.

BINGHAM, HIRAM (Nov. 19, 1875–June 6, 1956); b. Honolulu, T.H. Educator, governor, senator, traveler, author. *Journal of an Expedition Across Venezuela and Colombia* (1909); *An Explorer in the Air Service* (1920); *Inca Land* (1922); *Machu Picchu* (1930); *Elihu Yale, the American Nabob of Queen Square* (1939); *Lost City of the Incas* (1948); etc. History dept., Yale University, 1907–24.

BINGHAM, JUNE (June 20, 1919–); b. White Plains, N.Y. Author. *The Inside Story: Psychiatry and Everyday Life* (with F. C. Redlich, 1953); *Courage to Change* (1961); *U Thant: The Search for Peace* (1966); etc.

BINGHAM, MILLICENT TODD (Mrs. Walter V. Bingham) (1880–Dec. 1, 1968); b. Washington, D.C. Geographer, author. *Life of Mary E. Stearns* (1909); *Peru, Land of Contrasts* (1914); *Ancestors' Brocades: The Literary Début of Emily Dickinson* (1945); *Emily Dickinson, a Revelation* (1954). Editor: *Bolts of Melody, New Poems of Emily Dickinson* (1945).

BINKLEY, WILLIAM CAMPBELL (Apr. 30, 1889–); b. Newbern, Tenn. Educator, historian. *The Expansionist Movement in Texas* (1925); *The Texas Revolution* (1952). Editor: *New Spain and the West* (with others, 1932); *Official Correspondence of the Texan Revolution,* 2v. (1936). Editor, *Journal of Southern History,* 1943–49; *Mississippi Valley Historical Review,* since 1953. Prof. history, Tulane University, since 1953.

BINNS, ARCHIE (July 30, 1899–); b. Port Ludlow, Wash. Novelist. *Lightship* (1934); *Backwater Voyage* (1936); *The Laurels Are Cut Down* (1937); *The Land Is Bright* (1939); *Mighty Mountain* (1940); *Northwest Gateway* (1941); *You Rolling River* (1947); *The Radio Imp* (1950); *Mrs. Fiske and the American Theatre* (1955); *The Enchanted Islands* (1956); *The Headwaters* (1957); *Northwest Gateway* (1960); *Sea Pup Again* (1965); etc.

BINNS, JOHN (Dec. 22, 1772–June 16, 1860); b. Dublin, Ireland. Journalist, author. *Binn's Justice* (1840); *Recollections of the Life of John Binns* (1854). Came from England in 1801 to Northumberland, the center of the proposed Utopia on the Susquehanna dreamed of by Coleridge and Southey, and Binns was their representative. In 1807 he established the *Democratic Press* in Philadelphia.

"Birches." Poem by Robert Frost, in his *Mountain Interval* (1916).

BIRD, FREDERIC MAYER (June 28, 1838–Apr. 2, 1908); b. Philadelphia, Pa., son of Robert Montgomery Bird. Episcopal clergyman, hymnologist, novelist, editor. *A Pessimist in Theory and Practice* (under pen name, "Robert Timsol," 1888); *An Alien From the Commonwealth* (1889). Compiler (with B. M. Schmucker): *Hymns For the Use of the Evangelical Lutheran Church* (1865). Editor, *Lippincott's Magazine*, 1893–98. His library of hymns was said to be the largest in the United States.

BIRD, ROBERT MONTGOMERY (Feb. 5, 1806–Jan. 23, 1854); b. New Castle, Del. Physician, playwright, novelist. *The Gladiator* (prod. 1831); *The Broker of Bogota* (prod. 1834); *Calavar* (1834); *The Hawks of Hawk Hollow* (1835); *Nick of the Woods; or, The Jibbenainosay: A Tale of Kentucky*, 2v. (1837), republished as, *Nick of the Woods; or, Adventures of Prairie Life* (1855); *Peter Pilgrim; or, A Rambler's Recollections*, 2v. (1838); *The Adventures of Robin Day* (1938); etc., most of them anonymous. See *The Life and Dramatic Works of Montgomery Bird*, ed. by Clement E. Foust (1919).

Bird, Zenobia. Pen name of Laura Zenobia LeFevre.

Birds' Christmas Carol, The. Story by Kate Douglas Wiggin (1887).

Birds of America, The. By John James Audubon, 4v. (1827–38). Contains 1065 colored illustrations of birds. These elephant folios, first printed in England, are unsurpassed for their detailed beauty, and have long been highly prized and highly priced by book collectors.

"Birds of Killingworth, The." Poem by Henry Wadsworth Longfellow, in the *Atlantic Monthly*, Dec., 1863.

"Birds of Passage." Poem by Henry Wadsworth Longfellow, in the *Opal*, 1847.

BIRMINGHAM, FREDERIC ALEXANDER (1911–). Editor, author. *The Writer's Craft* (1958); *The Complete Cook Book for Men* (1961); *The Ivy League Today* (1961); *The Wedding Book* (with Frances Birmingham, 1964); etc. Editor: *Esquire Drink Book* (1956); etc.

BIRMINGHAM, STEPHEN (May 28, 1930–). Author. *Young Mr. Keefe* (1958); *Barbara Greer* (1959); *The Towers of Love* (1961); *Our Crowd* (1967); *The Right People: A Portrait of the American Social Establishment* (1968); *Heart Troubles* (1968); *The Grandees* (1971); etc.

Birmingham News. Birmingham, Ala. Newspaper. Founded 1881, as *The Birmingham Age;* combined 1888 with *The Birmingham Herald;* combined 1950 with *The Birmingham Post.* John Bloomer is editor. J. R. McAdory, Jr., is book-review editor. *Birmingham Post-Herald* appears mornings, except Sunday.

BIRNBAUM, MARTIN (May 10, 1878–); b. Miscolcz, Hung. Art critic, author. *Oscar Wilde: Fragments and Memories* (1920); *John Singer Sargent: A Conversation Piece* (1941); *Vanishing Eden* (1942); *Jacovleff and Other Essays* (1946); *Angkor and the Mandarin Road* (1952); *The Last Romantic* (1961).

BIRNEY, [Herman] HOFFMAN (Apr. 1, 1891–June 2, 1958); b. Philadelphia, Pa. Novelist, historical writer. *King of the Mesa* (1927); *Vigilantes* (1929); *The Pinto Pony* (1930); *Zealots of Zion* (1931); *Two Little Navajos* (1931); *Holy Murder: The Story of Porter Rockwell* (with Charles Kelly, 1934); *Forgotten Cañon* (1934); *Grim Journey: The Story of the Adventures of the Emigrating Journey Known as the Donner*

Party (1934); *Dead Man's Trail* (1937); *Montana* (1940); *Ann Carmeny* (1941); *Brothers of Doom, the Story of the Pizarros of Peru* (1942); *A Knife Is Silent* (1947); *The Dice of God* (1956).

BIRSTEIN, ANNA (May 27, 1927–); b. New York. Author. *Star of Glass* (1950); *The Troublemaker* (1955); *The Sweet Birds of Gorham* (1966).

Birth. Novel by Zona Gale (1918). The life story of a bore.

Birthmark, The. Story by Nathaniel Hawthorne (1843). It presents the conflict between the love of science and human love.

BISHOP, CORTLANDT F[ield] (1870–Mar. 30, 1935); b. New York. Book collector, author. *History of Elections in the American Colonies* (1893). He bought control of the American Art Galleries in 1923, and of the Anderson Galleries in 1928; he resigned as president of the merged firms in 1929. His collection was sold in New York in 1938–39. See *The Cortlandt F. Bishop Library* (1938).

BISHOP, ELIZABETH (Feb. 8, 1911–); b. Worcester, Mass. Poet. *Poems, North and South* (1955; Pulitzer Prize for poetry, 1956); *Brazil* (1962); *Questions of Travel* (1965); *The Complete Poems* (1969). Translator: Helena Morley's *Diary* (1957).

BISHOP, JIM [James Alonzo] (Nov. 21, 1907–); b. Jersey City, N.J. Author. *The Glass Crutch* (1945); *The Mark Hellinger Story* (1952); *The Girl in Poison Cottage* (1953); *The Making of a Priest* (1954); *The Day Lincoln Was Shot* (1955); *The Golden Ham* (1956); *The Day Christ Died* (1957); *Go with God* (1958); *The Day Christ Was Born* (1960); *The Murder Trial of Judge Peel* (1962); *Honeymoon Diary* (1963); *A Day in the Life of President Kennedy* (1964); *Jim Bishop Reporter* (1965); *A Day in the Life of President Johnson* (1967); *The Day Kennedy Was Shot* (1968). Executive editor: *Catholic Digest.*

BISHOP, JOHN PEALE (May 21, 1892–Apr. 4, 1944); b. Charles Town, W.Va. Poet, novelist. *Green Fruit* (poems, 1917); *The Undertaker's Garland* (with Edmund Wilson, Jr., 1922); *Many Thousands Gone* (1931); *Now With His Love* (poems, 1933); *Minute Particulars* (poems, 1935); *Act of Darkness* (1935); *Selected Poems* (1941). Editor: *American Harvest: Twenty Years of Creative Writing in the United States* (with Allen Tate, 1942).

BISHOP, LEONARD (1922–). Author. *Days of My Love* (1953); *Creep into Thy Narrow Bed* (1954); *The Butchers* (1956); *The Angry Time* (1960); *Make My Bed in Hell* (1961); *Against Heaven's Hand* (1963); etc.

BISHOP, MORRIS [Gilbert] (Apr. 15, 1893–); b. Willard, N.Y. Educator, author. *A Gallery of Eccentrics* (1928); *Paramount Poems* (1929); *Love Rimes of Petrarch* (1931); *The Odyssey of Cabeza de Vaca* (1933); *Pascal: The Life of Genius* (1936); *Ronsard, Prince of Poets* (1940); *Champlain, The Life of Fortitude* (1948); *The Life and Adventures of La Rochefoucauld* (1951); *A Bowl of Bishop* (1954); *Petrarch and His World* (1963); *The Exotics* (1969); *The Horizon Book of the Middle Ages* (with Horizon Magazine Editors, 1969); etc. Editor: *Blaise Pascal, Life and Works* (1966). Translator: *Eight Plays of Molière* (1957). Romance language dept., Cornell University, since 1921.

BISHOP, NATHANIEL HOLMES (1837–1902); b. Medway, Mass. Traveler, author. *The Pampas and Andes: A Thousand Miles Walk Across South America* (1869); *Voyage of the Paper Canoe* (1878); *Four Months in a Sneak-Box* (1879).

BISHOP, WILLIAM HENRY (Jan. 7, 1847–Sept. 26, 1928); b. Hartford, Conn. Author. *Detmold* (1879); *Old Mexico and Her Lost Provinces* (1884); *The Brown Stone Boy and Other Queer People* (1902); etc.

BISHOP, WILLIAM WARNER (July 20, 1871–Feb. 19, 1955); b. Hannibal, Mo. Librarian, author. *The Backs of Books, and Other Essays in Librarianship* (1925); etc. Librarian, University of Michigan, 1915–41.

Bisland, Elizabeth. See Elizabeth Bisland Wetmore.

BISSELL, RICHARD [Pike] (June 27, 1913–); b. Dubuque, Ia. Author. *A Stretch on the River* (1950); *The Monongahela* (1952); *7½ Cents* (1953; dramatic version, *The Pajama Game*, with George Abbott, prod. 1954); *High Water* (1954); *Say, Darling* (1957); *Good Bye, Ava* (1960); *You Can Always Tell a Harvard Man* (1962); *Pursuit of a Happy Cabbage* (1964); *Still Circling Moose Jaw* (1965); *How Many Miles to Galena?* (1968); *Julia Harrington, Winnebago, Iowa* (1969).

Bitter Tea of General Yen, The. Novel by Grace Zaring Stone (1930).

"Bitter-Sweet." Narrative poem by J. G. Holland (1858). Celebrating the everyday life of a New England home.

BITTNER, HERBERT G. (d. July 11, 1960); b. Breslau, Ger. Publisher, author. *Rome* (with Edward Nash, 1950). Editor: *Kaethe Kollwitz's Drawings* (1959). Publisher, Bittner Art Monograph series.

"Bivouac of the Dead, The." Poem written by Theodore O'Hara to commemorate the reinterment at Frankfort, Ky., July 20, 1847, of the Kentuckians slain at the Battle of Buena Vista.

BIXBY, JAMES THOMPSON (July 30, 1843–Dec. 26, 1921); b. Barre, Mass. Unitarian clergyman, author. *The Crisis in Morals* (1891); *The Open Secret, a Study of Life's Deeper Forces* (1912); etc.

BIXBY, WILLIAM COURTNEY (June 15, 1920–); b. San Diego, Cal. Author. *The Impossible Journey of Sir Ernest Shackleton* (1960); *The Race to the South Pole* (1961); *The Forgotten Voyage of Charles Wilkes* (1966); *Seawatchers: Oceanographers at Work* (1967); *Of Animals and Men* (1968); etc.

Bixby's Hotel. New York. Daniel Bixby, a bookseller of Lowell, Mass., for twenty-two years, came to New York and opened a hotel at Broadway and Park Place. It became a meeting place for authors and publishers. Among those seen often at the hotel were James Fenimore Cooper, Fitz-Greene Halleck, N. P. Willis, Nathaniel Hawthorne, Oliver Wendell Holmes, Ralph Waldo Emerson, Bayard Taylor, and Alice and Phoebe Cary.

BIXLER, JULIUS SEELYE (Apr. 4, 1894–); b. New London, Conn. Educator, author. *Religion in the Philosophy of William James* (1926); *Immortality and the Present Mood* (1931); *Conversations with an Unrepentant Liberal* (1946); *A Faith That Fulfills* (1951); *Education for Adversity* (1952); etc. Bussey professor of Theology, Harvard University, 1933–42; pres. Colby College, Waterville, Me., since 1942.

BIZZELL, WILLIAM BENNETT (Oct. 14, 1876–May 13, 1944); b. Independence, Tex. Educator, author. *Rural Texas* (1923); *The Green Rising* (1927); *The Relations of Learning* (1934); etc. President, University of Oklahoma, 1925–40.

BJERREGAARD, CARL HENRY ANDREW (May 24, 1845–Jan. 28, 1922); b. Fredericia, Denmark. Librarian. *The Inner Life and the Tao-Teh-King* (1912); *The Great Mother* (1913); etc. With Astor Library, New York, 1879–95; with New York Public Library, 1895–1922.

BJÖRKMAN, EDWIN [August] (Oct. 19, 1866–Nov. 16, 1951); b. Stockholm, Sweden. Journalist, author. Translator of Scandinavian authors. *Is There Anything New Under the Sun?* (1911); *Gleams: A Fragmentary Interpretation of Man and His World* (1912); *Voices of Tomorrow* (1913); *Scandinavia and the War* (1914); *The Cry of Ukraine* (1915); *The Soul of a Child* (1922); *Gates of Life* (1923); *The Search for*

Atlantis (1927); *The Wings of Azrael* (poem, 1934); etc. Translator of works by Strindberg, Björnson, etc.

BJORN, THYRA FERRÉ (Sept. 12, 1905–); b. Malmberget, Swed. Author. *Papa's Wife* (1955); *Papa's Daughter* (1958); *Dear Papa* (1963); *This Is My Life* (1966); *Then There Grew Up a Generation* (1970); etc.

BLACK, CYRIL EDWIN (Sept. 10, 1915–); b. Bryson City, N.C. Educator, author. *Establishment of Constitutional Government in Bulgaria* (1943); *Twentieth Century Europe: A History* (with E. C. Helmreich, 1959); *The Dynamics of Modernization* (1966); *Neutralization and World Politics* (with others, 1968); etc. Editor: *Challenge in Eastern Europe* (1954); *Communism and Revolution* (with Thomas P. Thornton, 1963); etc. Prof. history, Princeton University, since 1954.

BLACK, GEORGE F[raser] (Mar. 10, 1866–1948); b. Stirling, Scotland. Librarian, bibliographer, author. *Scotland's Mark on America* (1921). Compiler: *A Gypsy Bibliography* (1909); *A List of Works Relating to Scotland* (1916); *A Calendar of Cases of Witchcraft in Scotland, 1510–1727* (1938); *Some Unpublished Scottish Witchcraft Trials* (1941); *The Surnames of Scotland* (1946); etc. Asst. curator, Museum of Antiquities, Edinburgh, Scotland; with Astor Library, New York, 1896–1911; with The New York Public Library, 1911–31.

BLACK, HUGH (Mar. 26, 1868–Apr. 6, 1953); b. Rothesay, Scotland. Presbyterian clergyman, educator, author. *The Dream of Youth* (1894); *Friendship* (1898); *Culture and Restraint* (1900); *Work* (1902); *Comfort* (1910); *The Open Door* (1914); *The Adventure of Being Man* (1929); *Christ or Caesar* (1938); etc. Prof. practical theology, Union Theological Seminary, New York, 1906–38.

BLACK, JOHN DONALD (June 6, 1883–Apr. 12, 1960); b. Jefferson Co., Wis. Economist. *Introduction to Production Economics* (1926); *Agricultural Reform in the United States* (1928); *Parity, Parity, Parity* (1942); *The Rural Economy of New England* (1950); *Introduction to Economics for Agriculture* (1953); etc. Prof. economics, Harvard University, 1927–56.

BLACK, MAX (Feb. 24, 1909–); b. Baku, Rus. Educator. *Critical Thinking* (1946); *The Nature of Mathematics* (1950); *Problems of Analysis* (1954); *A Companion to Wittgenstein's Tractatus* (1964), etc. Editor: *The Social Theories of Talcott Parsons* (1961); *The Labyrinth of Language* (1968); *The Importance of Language* (1969). Editor, *The Philosophical Review*, since 1946. Prof. philosophy, Cornell University, since 1954.

Black April. Novel by Julia Peterkin (1927). Depicts Negro life on a plantation in South Carolina. April, the foreman, dominates the lives of those under him.

Black Boy. Autobiography of Richard Wright (1945). Depicts the hardening of a Negro boy's attitude toward life as he comes to realize how hopeless his condition is because of the insidiousness of the prejudice against his race.

Black Cat. Boston, Mass. Monthly short story magazine. Founded, 1895. Expired 1908.

Black Cat, The. Tale by Edgar Allan Poe (1843).

Black Cat Club, The. By James David Corrothers (1901). A series of humorous Negro "reports" written for the *Chicago Journal.*

Black Crook, The. Play by Charles M. Barras (prod. 1867). A spectacular melodrama, the performance of which lasted five hours. Revived in Hoboken, New Jersey, in 1929 by Christopher Morley.

Black Humor. A type of writing that derives from dadaism, surrealism and existentialism, as well as slapstick in vaudeville and movies, and the rhetoric of advertising. It emphasizes human folly, logical absurdity, physical and erotic crudities, and the reduction of probability to nonsense, especially by treating tragic material in deliberately bad taste. The term came into use in the mid-1960's with reference to prose fiction, especially the work of Vladimir Nabokov, Terry Southern, Joseph Heller, Peter De Vries, Bruce Jay Friedman, J. P. Donleavy, and others. See Douglas M. Davis's *The World of Black Humor* (1967).

Black Liberator. Chicago, Ill. Monthly. Founded 1969. Published by Black Liberation Alliance, Inc. Edited by Robert L. Lucas.

Black Like Me. By John Howard Griffin (1962). The white author changed the color of his skin pigmentation and traveled through the South, deliberately putting himself in situations in which his apparent blackness could be tested.

Black Mask. New York. Monthly fiction magazine. Founded 1919.

Black Mountain Review. Black Mountain, N.C. Quarterly. Founded 1951. Literary magazine.

Black Oxen. Novel by Gertrude Atherton (1923). Story of a young New York newspaperman, Lee Clavering, who falls in love with Countess Zattiany, who has recaptured her youth and beauty by the rejuvenation of her glands. A bizarre romance develops with unhappy consequences for Clavering, and the return to Europe of the Countess.

Black Panther. Oakland, Cal. Fortnightly. Founded 1966. Organ of the Black Panther Party.

"Black Regiment, The." Civil War Poem by George Henry Boker (1863).

Black Shilling, The. Novel by Amelia E. Barr (1903).

Black World. Chicago, Ill. Monthly. Founded 1970; formerly *Negro Digest,* founded 1942. Devoted to black interests.

BLACKBURN, JOHN (Dec. 21, 1924–). Author. b. Malta Bend, Mo. *A Scent of New Mown Hay* (1958); *A Sour Apple Tree* (1959); *Dead Man Running* (1961); *Blue Octavo* (1963); *Packed for Murder* (1964); *Nothing But the Night* (1968); *Bury Him Darkly* (1969).

BLACKBURN, PAUL (Nov. 24, 1926–); b. St. Albans, Vt. Poet, translator, editor. *Proensa* (1953); *The Dissolving Fabric* (1955); *Brooklyn-Manhattan Transit* (1960); *The Nets* (1961); *Sing-Song* (1966); *16 Sloppy Haiku and a Lyric for Robert Reardon* (1966). Editor and translator: *El Cid Campeador* (1966).

BLACKBURN, WILLIAM MAXWELL (Dec. 30, 1828–Dec. 29, 1898); b. Carlisle, Ind. Presbyterian clergyman, author. *The College Days of Calvin* (1865); *Admiral Coligny, and the Rise of the Huguenots,* 2v. (1869); etc.

BLACKBURNE, MARY FRANCES (Apr. 20. 1874–); b. Manchester, N.H. Author. *Child Life in Many Lands* (with sister, Etta Austin Blaisdell McDonald, 1900); *Child Life in Literature* (with same, 1900); *Polly and Dolly* (1909); *Twilight Town* (1913); *Mother Goose Children* (1916); *Pine Tree Playmates* (with sister, 1925); etc.

Blackmar, Beatrice. See Beatrice Blackmar Gould.

BLACKMUR, R[ichard] P[almer] (Jan. 21, 1904–Feb. 2, 1965); b. Springfield, Mass. Educator, literary critic, poet. *The Double Agent* (1935); *From Jordan's Delight* (1937); *The Expense of Greatness* (1940); *The Second World* (1942); *The Good European* (1947); *Language as Gesture* (1952); *The Lion and the Honeycomb* (1955); *Form and Value in Modern Poetry* (1957); *Eleven Essays in the European Novel* (1964); etc. Prof. English, Princeton University, since 1951.

BLACKWELL, ALICE STONE (Sept. 14, 1857–Mar. 15, 1950); b. East Orange, N.J. Editor, author. *The Little Grand-*

mother of the Russian Revolution—Catherine Breshkovsky's Own Story (1917); *Lucy Stone: Pioneer of Woman's Rights* (1930); etc. Translator of poems from Spanish and other languages. Editor, *Woman's Journal,* 1883–1917.

BLACKWELL, BETSY TALBOT, b. New York. Editor. With *Charm,* 1923–31; with *Mademoiselle,* since 1935; editor in chief, 1937–71.

BLAINE, JAMES GILLESPIE (Jan. 31, 1830–Jan. 27, 1893); b. West Brownsville, Pa. Statesman, author. *Twenty Years in Congress,* 2v. (1884–86); *Political Discussions* (1887); etc. See David S. Muzzey's *James G. Blaine* (1934).

BLAIR, CLAY [Drewry], Jr. (May 1, 1925–); b. Lexington, Va. Editor, author. *The Atomic Submarine and Admiral Rickover* (1954); *Beyond Courage* (1955); *Nautilus 90 North* (with William R. Anderson, 1959); *Diving for Pleasure and Treasure* (1960); *The Board Room* (1969); etc. Executive vice-president and director, Curtis Publishing Co., since 1964.

BLAIR, JAMES (1655–Apr. 18, 1743); b. in Scotland. Anglican clergyman, author. *Present State of Virginia and the College* (with Henry Hartwell and Edward Chilton, written 1697, publ. 1727); *Our Divine Saviour's Sermon on the Mount,* 5v. (1722); etc. Commissary in Virginia for the Bishop of London. Founder, College of William and Mary, 1696. See D. E. Motley's *Life of Commissary James Blair* (1901).

BLAIR, WALTER (Apr. 21, 1900–); b. Spokane, Wash. Educator, author. *Tall Tale America* (1944); *Mark Twain and Huck Finn* (1960); *American Literature, a Brief History* (1964); etc. Editor: *Selected Shorter Writings of Mark Twain* (1962); *The Art of Huckleberry Finn* (with Hamlin Hill, 1962); etc. Prof. English, University of Chicago, since 1944.

BLAISDELL, DONALD CHRISTY (Aug. 12, 1899–); b. Chautauqua, N.Y. Political scientist. *European Financial Control in the Ottoman Empire* (1929); *Government and Agriculture* (1940); *American Democracy Under Pressure* (1957); *The Riverside Democrats* (1963); *International Organization* (1966); etc. Prof. government, College of the City of New York, since 1955.

BLAKE, EMILY CALVIN (Mrs. Walter R. Blake) (deceased); b. Manchester, England. Novelist. *Marcia of the Little Home* (1911); *Quaintness of Bobby* (1912); *The Third Wearer* (1929); etc.

BLAKE, GLADYS; b. Fayetteville, Tenn. Novelist. *The Mysterious Tutor* (1925); *Even Sara* (1930); *Belinda in Old New Orleans* (1932); *Deborah's Discovery* (1933); *Fortunate Shipwreck* (1936); *Sally Goes to Court* (1937); *Mystery for Margery* (1940); *Henrietta and the Governor* (1964); etc.

BLAKE, JAMES VILA (Jan. 21, 1842–Apr. 28, 1925); b. Brooklyn, N.Y. Unitarian clergyman, poet, essayist. *Poems* (1887); *Essays* (1887); *Sonnets* (1898); *Discoveries* (poems, 1904); *Sonnets from Marcus Aurelius* (1920); etc.

BLAKE, J[ohn] L[auris] (Dec. 21, 1788–July 6, 1857); b. Northwood, N.H. Episcopal clergyman, author. *The Parlor Book; or, Family Encyclopedia of Useful Knowledge and General Literature* (1835); *A General Biographical Dictionary* (1835); *Anecdotes of the American Indians* (1843); *A History of the American Revolution* (1844); etc.

BLAKE, LILLIE DEVEREUX (Aug. 12, 1835–Dec. 30 1913); b. Raleigh, N.C. Novelist, reformer. Pen name "Tiger Lily." *Southwold* (1859); *Rockford; or, Sunshine and Storm* (1863); *Fettered for Life; or, Lord and Master* (1874); *A Daring Experiment* (1898). Contributor to the *New York Mercury.*

BLAKE, MARY ELIZABETH McGRATH (Sept. 1, 1840–Feb. 26, 1907); b. Dungarven, Ireland. Traveler, poet. *Poems* (1882); *On the Wing* (1883); *Youth in Twelve Centuries* (1886); *The Merry Months All* (1887); *Verses Along the Way* (1890); *In the Harbour of Hope* (1907).

BLAKE, PETER JOST (Sept. 20, 1920–); b. Berlin. Architect, editor, author. *The Master Builders* (1960); *God's Own Junkyard* (1965). Editor, *Architectural Forum*, since 1964.

BLAKESLEE, GEORGE HUBBARD (Aug. 27, 1871–May 5, 1954); b. Geneseo, N.Y. Educator, author. *The Pacific Area: An International Survey* (1929); *Conflicts of Policy in the Far East* (1934); etc. Editor, *Journal of International Relations*, until 1921. Prof. history and international relations, Clark University.

Blanchan, Neltze. Pen name of Neltze de Graff Doubleday.

BLANCHARD, FREDERIC T[homas] (Sept. 24, 1878–Feb. 3, 1947); b. Harvard, Mass. Educator, author. *Fielding the Novelist* (1926); *Perspective Criticism* (1930); *The Art of the Novel* (1938); etc. Dept. of English, University of California at Los Angeles, from 1920.

Blanche of Brandywine. Novel by George Lippard (1846); dramatized by J. G. Burnett (prod. 1858).

BLANCK, JACOB [Nathaniel] (Nov. 10, 1906–); b. Boston, Mass. Bibliographer, author. *Peter Parley to Penrod: A Bibliographical Description of the Best-Loved American Juvenile Books* (1938); *Jonathan and the Rainbow* (1948); *The King and the Noble Blacksmith* (1950). Editor: *Merle Johnson's American First Editions*, 3d ed. (1936). Rare book editor, *Publishers Weekly* and *Antiquarian Bookman*, 1936–52; editor, *Bibliography of American Literature*, since 1943.

BLANDING, DON (Nov. 7, 1894–June 9, 1957); b. Kingfisher, Okla. Artist, traveler, poet. *Vagabond's House* (1928); *Songs of the Seven Senses* (1931); *Stowaways in Paradise* (1931); *The Rest of the Road* (1937); *Drifter's Gold* (1939); *Floridays* (1940); *Pilot Bails Out* (1943); *Today Is Here* (1946); *A Grand Time Living* (1950); *Hawaii Says Aloha* (1955); etc.

BLANKFORT, MICHAEL (Dec. 10, 1907–); b. New York. *I Met a Man* (1937); *The Brave and the Blind* (1940); *A Time to Live* (1943); *The Widow-Makers* (1946); *The Big Yankee* (1947); *Juggler* (1952); *Goodbye, I Guess* (1962).

BLANKNER, FREDERIKA, b. Grand Rapids, Mich. Educator, poet. *All My Youth* (poems, 1932). Editor: *The History of the Scandinavian Literature* (1938); etc. Prof. language and literature, Adelphi College, Garden City, N.Y., since 1943.

BLANSHARD, BRAND (Aug. 27, 1892–); b. Fredericksburg, O. Educator. Author or co-author: *The Nature of Thought*, 2v. (1940); *Philosophy in American Education* (1945); *Preface to Philosophy* (1946); *Reason and Goodness* (1961); etc. Prof. philosophy, Swarthmore College, 1928–45; Yale University, 1945–1961.

BLANSHARD, PAUL (Aug. 27, 1892–); b. Fredericksburg, O. Author. *An Outline of the British Labor Movement* (1923); *What's the Matter with New York* (with Norman Thomas, 1932); *Democracy and Empire in the Caribbean* (1947); *American Freedom and Catholic Power* (1949); *Communism, Democracy and Catholic Power* (1951); *The Irish and Catholic Power* (1953); *The Right to Read* (1955); *God and Man in Washington* (1960); *Where Catholic Dictators Rule* (1961); *Freedom and Catholic Power in Spain and Portugal* (1962); *Religion and the Schools* (1963); *Paul Blanshard on Vatican II* (1966); etc.

BLANTON, SMILEY (May 7, 1882–Oct. 30, 1966); b. Unionville, Tenn. Psychiatrist, author. *The Art of Real Happiness* (with Norman Vincent Peale, 1950); *Love or Perish* (1956); *Now or Never* (with Arthur Gordon, 1959); *The Healing Power of Poetry* (1960).

BLASHFIELD, EDWIN HOWLAND (Dec. 15, 1848–Oct. 12, 1936); b. New York. Artist, author. *Italian Cities*, 2v. (with wife, Evangeline Wilbour Blashfield, 1900); *Mural Painting in America* (1913); *The Works of Edwin Howland Blashfield* (1937), ed. by Royal Cortissoz.

BLASHFIELD, EVANGELINE WILBOUR (Mrs. Edwin Howland Blashfield). Author. *Italian Cities*, 2v. (with husband, 1900); *Masques of Cupid* (1901); *Portraits and Backgrounds* (1917); *Manon Philipon Roland; Early Years* (1922).

BLAU, PETER MICHAEL (Feb. 7, 1918–); b. Vienna. Educator, author. *The Dynamics of Bureaucracy* (1955); *Bureaucracy in Modern Society* (1956); *Exchange and Power in Social Life* (1964); *The American Occupational Structure* (with Otis Dudley Duncan, 1967); etc. Prof. sociology, University of Chicago, since 1963.

BLAUVELT, MARY TAYLOR (1869–); b. Clinton, N.J. Lecturer, author. *The Development of Cabinet Government in England* (1902); *In Cambridge Backs* (1911); *Solitude Letters* (1912); *Ultimate Ideals* (1917); *Oliver Cromwell: A Dictator's Tragedy* (1937).

BLAVATSKY, HELENE PETROVNA [Hahn] (July 30, 1831–May 8, 1891); b. Ekaterinoslav, Russia. Founder of the Theosophical Society, 1875; author. *The Secret Doctrine*, 2v. (1888); *The Complete Works*, 4v. (1933–36). See Geoffrey Barborka's *H. P. Blavatsky, Tibet and Tulku* (1966); *Personal Memoirs of H. P. Blavatsky*, ed. by Mary Neff (1967).

BLECHMAN, BURT (Mar. 2, 1932–). Novelist. *How Much?* (1961); *The War of Camp Omongo* (1963); *Stations* (1964); *The 'Octopus' Papers* (1965); *Maybe* (1967).

BLEDSOE, ALBERT TAYLOR (Nov. 9, 1809–Dec. 8, 1877); b. Frankfort, Ky. Confederate official, educator, editor, author. *An Essay on Liberty and Slavery* (1856); *Is Davis a Traitor?* (1866); etc. Founder, the *Southern Review*, Baltimore, 1867; editor, 1867–77.

BLEECKER, ANN ELIZA [Schuyler] (Oct., 1752–Nov. 23, 1783); b. New York. Author. *The History of Maria Kittle* (1781); *The Posthumous Works of Ann Eliza Bleecker in Prose and Verse* (1793).

BLEECKER, ANTHONY (Oct. 27, 1770–Mar. 13, 1827); b. New York. Author. *Loss of the American Brig Commerce* [based on the log of James Riley] (1817).

BLEGEN, THEODORE CHRISTIAN (July 16, 1891–July 18, 1969); b. Minneapolis, Minn. Historian. *Norwegian Migration to America 1825–60*, 2v. (1931–40); *Norwegian Emigrant Songs and Ballads* (with M. B. Ruud, 1936); *Building Minnesota* (1938); *Grass Roots History* (1947); *The Land Lies Open* (1949); *Iron Face* (with Sarah Davidson, 1950); *The Crowded Box-Room* (1951); *Lincoln's Imagery* (1954); *Minnesota History* (with T. L. Nydahl, 1960); *Lincoln and His Mailbag* (1964); *Lincoln's Secretary Goes West* (1965); *The Voyageurs and Their Songs* (1966); *The Kensington Rune Stone* (1968); etc. Prof. history, University of Minnesota, from 1937.

BLENNERHASSETT, HARMAN (Oct. 8, 1765–Feb. 2, 1831); b. in Hampshire, England. Adventurer, associate of Aaron Burr. See William H. Safford's *The Life of Harman Blennerhassett* (1850); *The Blennerhassett Papers*, ed. William H. Safford (1864); Charles F. Pidgin's *Blennerhassett; or, The Decrees of Fate* (1901); Minnie K. Lowther's *Blennerhassett Island in Romance and Tragedy* (1936); Norris F. Schneider's *Blennerhassett Island and the Burr Conspiracy* (1938).

BLESH, RUDI [Rudolph Pickett Blesh] (Jan. 21, 1899–); b. Guthrie, Okla. Author. *Shining Trumpets: A History of Jazz* (1946); *They All Played Ragtime* (with Harriet Janis, 1950); *Modern Art USA* (1956); *Collage: Personalities, Concepts, Techniques* (with Harriet Janis, 1962); *Keaton* (1966); etc.

BLETHEN, JOSEPH (Apr. 16, 1870–Oct. 7, 1937); b. Farmington, Me. Publisher, playwright. *The Peacock Plume* (1897); etc.

Blind Preacher, The. Essay in *Letters of the British Spy*, by William Wirt. Included in many school readers, it was long regarded as one of the leading American essays.

BLISH, JAMES [Benjamin] (May 23, 1921–); b. East Orange, N.J. Author. *Jack of Eagles* (1951); *The Warriors of Day* (1953); *Earthman, Come Home* (1955); *They Shall Have Stars* (1956); *The Seedling Stars* (1956); *A Triumph of Time* (1958); *A Case of Conscience* (1958); *The Frozen Year* (1958); *Galactic Cluster* (1959); *The Duplicated Man* (1959); *So Close to Home* (1961); *Titan's Daughter* (1961); *The Star Dwellers* (with R. Lowndes, 1961); *Night Shapes* (1962); *A Life for the Stars* (1962); *The Vanished Jet* (1968); *Black Easter* (1969); *We All Die Naked* (1969); etc.

BLISS, PAUL SOUTHWORTH (Apr. 1, 1889–Dec. 31, 1940); b. Rice Lake, Wis. Social worker, poet. *After Supper Poems* (1929); *Rough Edges and All* (1930); *How Pan Shaped the Leaves, and Other Poems* (1931); *The Arch of Spring* (1932); *Spin Dance, and Spring Comes to Shaw's Garden* (1934); *Cirrus from the West* (1935); *The Rye Is the Sea* (1936); *Poems of Places* (1937); *The Lord Made Kansas for Wheat* (1939); etc.

BLISS, PHILIP PAUL (July 9, 1838–Dec. 29, 1876); b. in Clearfield Co., Pa. Singing evangelist, hymn writer. The published collections of his songs are: *The Charm* (1871); *The Song Tree* (1872); *The Joy* (1873); *Gospel Songs* (1874). The last contains his best known hymn, "Hold the Fort." *See* his *Memoirs*, ed. by David W. Whittle (1877).

Blithedale Romance, The. Novel by Nathaniel Hawthorne (1852). Based on the author's experiences at Brook Farm. It recounts the story of the beautiful Zenobia whose intellect and passions are frustrated. She takes her own life. Zenobia bears some resemblance to Margaret Fuller, one of the leaders of the Transcendentalist movement.

BLITZSTEIN, MARC (Mar. 2, 1905–Jan. 22, 1964); b. Philadelphia, Pa. Composer-librettist, playwright. *The Cradle Will Rock* (opera, 1937); *No for an Answer* (opera, 1941); *The Threepenny Opera* (adaptation, 1952).

BLIVEN, BRUCE (July 27, 1889–); b. Emmetsburg, Ia. Editor, author. *The Men Who Make the Future* (1942); *Preview for Tomorrow* (1953); *The World Changers* (1965). Editor: *What the Informed Citizen Needs to Know* (with A. G. Mezerik, 1945); *Twentieth Century Unlimited* (1950). Editorial staff, *The New Republic*, 1923–55. Lecturer journalism, Stanford University, since 1956.

BLOCH, HENRY SIMON (Apr. 6, 1915–); b. Kehl, Ger. Economist. Author or co-author: *Yale Law Journal Symposium on World Organization* (1946); *Technical Aid and the Progress of Underdeveloped Countries* (1952); *Economic Problems of International Trade* (1961); etc.

BLOCH, HERBERT AARON [David] (Sept. 8, 1904–May 25, 1965); b. New York. Sociologist. *Concert of Changing Loyalties* (1934); *Disorganization: Personal and Social* (1952); *The Gang: A Study in Adolescent Behavior* (with Arthur Niederhoffer, 1958); *Man, Crime and Society* (with Gilbert Geis, 1962); *Social Science & Deviance* (with Melvin Prince, 1967). Prof. sociology and anthropology, Brooklyn College, from 1955.

BLOCH, ROBERT (1917–). Author. *Psycho* (1959); *Dead Beat* (1960); *The Firebug* (1961); *Blood Runs Cold* (1961); etc.

Bloch Publishing Co. New York. Founded in Cincinnati in 1854 by Edward Bloch and Isaac M. Wise. Charles E. Bloch (1862–1940), a son of the founder, moved the business to New York in 1901. Edward H. Bloch and, later, Charles E. Bloch served as president. Publishers of Jewish religious and literary books and magazines.

BLOCK, HERBERT LAWRENCE (Oct. 13, 1909–); b. Chicago, Ill. Cartoonist, author. Pen name "Herblock." *The Herblock Book* (1952); *Herblock's Here and Now* (1955); *Herblock's Special for Today* (1958); *Straight Herblock* (1964). Editorial cartoonist, *Washington Post*, since 1946.

Block, Rudolph Edgar. See Bruno Lessing.

Blockheads; or, The Affrighted Officers, The. Play generally attributed to Mercy Otis Warren (1776). Written in reply to General John Burgoyne's *The Blockade of Boston* (prod. 1776).

BLODGETT, HAROLD W. (Mar. 24, 1900–); b. Corning, N.Y. Educator. *Walt Whitman in England* (1934); *The Story Survey* (ed., 1939); *The Roots of National Culture* (with R. Spiller, 1949). Editor: *The Best of Whitman* (1953). Prof. English, Union College, since 1936.

BLODGETT, MABLE LOUISE FULLER (Apr. 8, 1869–June, 1959); b. Bangor, Me. Author. *The Aspen Shade* (1889); *At the Queen's Mercy* (1897); *Peas Blossom* (1917); etc.

BLODGETT, RUTH ROBINSON; b. Boston, Mass. Novelist. *Birds Got to Fly* (1929); *Wind from the Sea* (1930); *Home Is the Sailor* (1932); *Easter Holiday* (1935); *Down-East Duchess* (1939).

BLOEDE, GERTRUDE (Aug. 10, 1845–Aug. 14, 1905); b. Dresden, Germany. Poet. Pen name, "Stuart Sterne." *Poems* (1875); *Angelo: A Poem* (1878); *Giorgio and Other Poems* (1881); *Beyond the Shadow, and Other Poems* (1888); *Piero da Castiglione* (1890); *The Story of Two Lives* (1891).

BLOOD, BENJAMIN PAUL (Nov. 21, 1832–Jan. 15, 1919); b. Amsterdam, N.Y. Philosopher, mystic, poet. *The Philosophy of Justice* (1851); *The Bride of the Iconoclast* (1854); *Optimism* (1860); *The Colonnades: a Poem* (1868); *Pluriverse: An Essay on the Philosophy of Pluralism* (1920).

BLOOM, HAROLD (July 11, 1930–); b. New York. Educator, author. *Shelley's Mythmaking* (1959); *The Visionary Company* (1961); *Blake's Apocalypse* (1963); *Yeats and Romanticism* (1967). Prof. English, Yale University, since 1965.

BLOOMFIELD, LEONARD (Apr. 1, 1887–Apr. 18, 1949); b. Chicago, Ill. Educator, philologist, author. *Menomini Texts* (1928); *Sacred Stories of the Sweet Grass Cree* (1930); *Language* (1933); *Plains Cree Texts* (1934); *Linguistic Aspects of Science* (1939); etc. Prof. Germanic philology, University of Chicago, 1927–40; prof. linguistics, Yale University, 1940–49.

BLOOMGARDEN, SOLOMON (Mar. 1870–Jan. 10, 1927); b. Wertzblowo, Lithuania. Poet, essayist, translator. Pen name, "Yehoash." *The Feet of the Messenger* (1923); *The Shunnamite* (1925). Translated the Old Testament from the original into Yiddish and compiled a *Yiddish Dictionary* (1911).

BLOSSOM, SUMNER NEWTON, b. Kansas City, Mo. Editor, *The American Magazine*, 1929–56. Pres. and director, Crowell-Collier Publishing Co., 1957–61.

"Blossom Time." Lyric poem by Ina Donna Coolbrith (1848).

Bloudy Tenent, of Persecution for Cause of Conscience, The. By Roger Williams (1644). A defense of religious liberty. John Cotton replied to it by writing his *The Bloudy Tenent, Washed, and Made White* (1647). Roger Williams closed the discussion with his *The Bloody Tenent Yet More Bloody* (1652).

BLOUGH, GLENN ORLANDO (Sept. 5, 1907–); b. Edmore, Mich. Educator, author. *Monkey with a Notion* (1946); *Beno the Riverburg Mayor* (1948); *The Tree on the Road to Turntown* (1953); *Lookout for the Forest* (1955); *Who Lives in This House?* (1957); *Discovering Dinosaurs* (1960); *Bird Watchers and Bird Feeders* (1963); *Discovering Plants* (1966); *Discovering Insects* (1967); etc. Education dept., University of Maryland, since 1956.

BLOW, SUSAN ELIZABETH (June 7, 1843–Mar. 26, 1916); b. St. Louis, Mo. Pioneer in kindergarten education in the United States, author. *Symbolic Education* (1894); *Kinder-*

garten Education (1900); *Educational Issues in the Kindergarten* (1900); etc. Founder, kindergarten school in St. Louis, 1873.

Blowing Weather. Novel by John T. McIntyre (1923). Story of the port of Philadelphia in the days of the clipper ships.

Blue and Gold Stories. Popular name given to the volumes of collected poems of noted American poets, published by Ticknor and Fields. Inclusion in the series, Bliss Perry once remarked, was equivalent to being elected to the French Academy.

"Blue and the Gray, The." Poem by Francis Miles Finch, in the *Atlantic Monthly,* 1867.

Blue Book. New York. Monthly fiction magazine. Founded 1905. Donald Kennicott was editor 1929–1952. Bought by McCall Corp. in 1929 and renamed *Bluebook.* Contributors included Mary Roberts Rinehart, James Oliver Curwood, Donn Byrne, and Rider Haggard. By World War II the magazine adapted itself to men's interests, carrying more nonfiction. Suspended 1956.

Blue Guitar. Long Beach, Calif. Triannual. Founded 1952. Poetry, essays, and literary criticism constitute its chief interests. Edited by G. De Witt.

Blue Hotel, The. Short story by Stephen Crane (1931).

Blue Pencil, The. New York. A magazine for authors and editors. Founded 1934, by Thomas H. Uzzell. Discontinued 1936.

Blue Ribbon Books, Inc. A reprint publishing house, established by several New York publishers in 1930. Alfred Harcourt and Eugene Reynal were prominently connected with its management. Reynal assumed complete control of the firm in 1933. In 1939 it was absorbed by Doubleday, Doran & Co.

Blue Voyage. Novel by Conrad Aiken (1927). Written in the then novel "stream of consciousness" style.

Bluff, Harry. Pen name of Matthew Fontaine Maury.

BLUM, DANIEL C. (Oct. 1, 1900–Feb. 24, 1965) b. Chicago, Ill. Author. *Great Stars of the American Stage* (1952); *A Pictorial History of Television* (1959); *A Pictorial History of the American Theatre: 1860–1960* (1960); *100 Years of American Theatre* (1961); etc.

BLUM, JOHN MORTON (Apr. 29, 1921–); b. New York. Educator, historian. *Joe Tumulty and the Wilson Era* (1951); *The Republican Roosevelt* (1954); *Woodrow Wilson and the Politics of Morality* (1956); *From the Morganthau Diaries,* Vol. I (1959); *National Experience: A History of the U.S.* (with others, 1963); *The Promise of America* (1966), etc. Prof. history, Yale University since 1957.

BLUM, ROBERT FREDERICK (July 9, 1857–June 8, 1903); b. Cincinnati, O. Painter, illustrator. Did work for *Scribner's Monthly* and *St. Nicholas.* Illustrated Sir Edwin Arnold's "Japonica" for *Scribner's Magazine* (1890–91). He and William J. Baer moved to a studio at 90 Grove St., in New York, around 1893 and became the pioneers in the Greenwich Village migration of New York artists.

BLUMENTHAL, WALTER HART (Feb., 1883–1969); b. Clinton, Ia. Editor, collector of curiosa, including Lilliputian books, odd bindings, etc.; author. *Rachel: Tragedienne* (1905); *Pageant of Moods* (1906); *Winepress; A Vintage of Verse* (1925); *In Old America* (1931); *Women Camp Followers of the American Revolution* (1952); *Bookmen's Bedlam* (1955); *Formats and Foibles* (1956); *Bookmen's Trio* (1961); *Brides from Bridewell* (1961).

Bly, Nellie. Pen name of Elizabeth Cochrane Seaman.

BLY, ROBERT [Elwood] (Dec. 23, 1926–); b. Madison, Minn. Poet. *Silence in the Snowy Fields* (1962); *The Light Around the Body* (1967; National Book Award, 1968). Editor: *Forty Poems Touching on Recent American History* (1967). Translator: *Twenty Poems of Georg Trakl* (1961); *Forty Poems of Juan Ramon Jiménez* (1967); *Twenty Poems of Pablo Neruda* (1967); etc.

BLYTHE, LE GETTE (1900–). Author. *The Bold Galilean* (1952); *Miracle in the Hills* (with Mary T. Sloop, 1953); *James W. Davis: North Carolina Surgeon* (1957); *Call Down the Storm* (1958); *Hear Me, Pilate!* (1961); *Man on Fire* (1964); *Brothers of Vengeance* (1969); etc.

BLYTHE, SAMUEL GEORGE (May 19, 1868–Jan. 17, 1947); b. Geneseo, N.Y. Author. *We Have With Us Tonight* (1909); *The Making of a Newspaper Man* (1912); *The Price of Place* (1913); *The Fakers* (1915); *Western Warwicks* (1916); *Hunkins* (1919); *The Manikin Makers* (1921); *The Revolt of Pete Purdy* (1926); *The Bootleggers* (1928); etc. Staff writer, *Saturday Evening Post,* from 1907.

BLYTHE, STUART OAKES (Mar. 5, 1890–); b. Rochester, N.Y. Editor. Assoc. editor, *Country Gentleman,* 1919–28; *Ladies' Home Journal,* 1928–35; *California Magazine of the Pacific,* 1936–39.

BOAK, ARTHUR EDWARD ROMILLY (Apr. 29, 1888–Dec. 16, 1962); b. Halifax, N.S. Educator, historian. *A History of Rome to 565 A.D.* (1921); *The Growth of European Civilization* (with Albert Hyma and Preston Slosson, 1938); *The History of Our World* (1959); etc. Editor: *University of Michigan Historical Essays* (1937); etc. History dept., University of Michigan, 1914–58.

BOAS, FRANZ (July 9, 1858–Dec. 21, 1942); b. Minden, Westphalia. Anthropologist, author. *The Growth of Children* (1896); *The Mind of Primitive Man* (1911); *Primitive Art* (1927); *Anthropology and Modern Life* (1928); *General Anthropology* (with others, 1938); *Race, Language and Culture* (1940); *Dakota Grammar* (with Ella Deloria, 1941); etc. Dept. of anthropology, Columbia University, 1896–1938.

BOAZ, MARTHA TEAROSSE, b. Stuart, Va. Educator, author. *A Guide to General Book Publishers in the United States* (with Nancy Raisbeck, 1950); *A Qualitative Analysis of the Criticism of Best Sellers* (1955); *Reviews in Library Book Selection* (with others, 1958). Compiler: *The Quest for Truth* (1961). Dean, school of library science, University of Southern California, since 1955.

Bobbs-Merrill Co. Indianapolis, Ind. Publishers. Founded in 1838 by Samuel Merrill, who opened a book store with E. H. Hood. Merrill and Hood published vol. 5 of the *Indiana Reports* in 1851, which launched them into the publishing field. Hood dropped out, and the name was changed to Merrill, Meigs & Co., after the Civil War. In 1885 the book firm of Bowen, Stewart & Co. merged with Merrill, Meigs & Co., to form the Bowen-Merrill Co., bringing into the firm Silas T. Bowen and John J. Curtis. Charles White Merrill, grandson of the founder, joined the firm in 1882. William Conrad Bobbs had joined the firm in 1879, and became its president in 1895. Called Bobbs, Merrill Company in 1895 after the death of Silas T. Bowen, and on Apr. 7, 1903, the name was shortened to Bobbs-Merrill. It is now a subsidiary of Howard W. Sams & Co. (q.v.). The firm published *The Old Swimmin'-Hole,* the first poems of James Whitcomb Riley, as well as his other books; *When Knighthood Was in Flower* by Charles Major, which was a best seller of its era; *The Man Nobody Knows,* by Bruce Barton; and *The Joy of Cooking.*

Bobbsey Twins. Series of books for children by Laura Lee Hope.

BOBULA, IDA, b. Budapest, Hung. Educator, author. *Hungarian Women of the Eighteenth Century* (1933); *Sumerian Affiliations* (1951); *The Problem of Sumerian-Hungarian Affiliations* (1961); etc. Head, dept. of sociology and anthropology, Ricker College, since 1960.

BODE, BOYD HENRY (Oct. 4, 1873–Mar. 29, 1953); b. Ridott, Ill. Educator, author. *Fundamentals of Education* (1921); *Modern Educational Theories* (1927); *Democracy as a Way of Life* (1937); *How We Learn* (1940); *Modern Education and Human Values* (1947); etc. Prof. education, Ohio State University, 1921–44.

BODE, CARL (Mar. 14, 1911–); b. Milwaukee, Wis. Educator, author. *The Sacred Seasons* (poems, 1953); *The American Lyceum* (1956); *The Man Behind You* (poems, 1959); *The Anatomy of Popular American Culture, 1840–61*; *The Great Experiment in American Literature* (1961); etc. Editor: *The Collected Poems of Henry David Thoreau* (1943); *The Correspondence of Henry David Thoreau* (1958); *Ralph Waldo Emerson: A Profile* (1968); etc. Prof. English, University of Maryland, since 1947.

BODENHEIM, MAXWELL (May 26, 1893–Feb. 7, 1954); b. Hermanville, Mass. Poet, novelist. *Advice* (poems, 1920); *The Sardonic Arm* (poems, 1923); *Against This Age* (poems, 1925); *Replenishing Jessica* (1925); *Ninth Avenue* (1926); *Returning to Emotion* (poems, 1926); *King of Spain* (1928); *Duke Herring* (1931); *Six A.M.* (1932); *New York Madness* (1932); *Run, Sheep, Run* (1932); *Lights in the Valley* (poems, 1942); *Selected Poems* (1946); *My Life and Loves in Greenwich Village* (autobiography, 1954); etc.

BODLEY, RONALD VICTOR COURTENAY (Mar. 3, 1892–); b. Paris. Author. *The Messenger* (1946); *The Quest* (1947); *The Warrior Saint* (1953); *In Search of Serenity* (1955).

BODLEY, TEMPLE (Aug. 5, 1852–Nov. 23, 1940); b. Louisville, Ky. Author. *George Rogers Clark* (1926); *History of Kentucky Before the Louisiana Purchase* (1928); *Our First Great West* (1938).

BOECKEL, RICHARD MARTIN (Oct. 17, 1892–); b. Philadelphia, Pa. Editor. *Labor's Money* (1923); *Presidential Politics* (1928); etc. Co-founder (1923) and later editorial director, *Editorial Research Reports.*

BOGAN, LOUISE (Aug. 11, 1897–Feb. 4, 1970); b. Livermore Falls, Me. Poet. *Body of This Death* (1923); *Dark Summer* (1929); *The Sleeping Fury* (1937); *Poems and New Poems* (1941); *Achievement in American Poetry, 1900–1950* (1951); *Collected Poems, 1923–53* (1954); *Selected Criticism* (1955); *The Blue Estuaries: Poems 1923–1968* (1968). Translator: *The Journal of Jules Renard* (1964). Poetry reviewer, *The New Yorker.*

BOGARDUS, EMORY STEPHEN (Feb. 21, 1882–); b. near Belvidere, Ill. Educator, sociologist, author. *Introduction to Sociology* (1917); *Essentials of Americanization* (1919); *Contemporary Sociology* (1931); *Sociology* (1934); *The Making of Public Opinion* (1951); *The Traveler* (1956); *Social Distance* (1959); *The Explorer: Much Have I Learned* (1962); *Toward a World Community* (1964); *Thrice-Seven Wonders of the World* (1965); *The Observer* (1966); etc. Prof. sociology, University of Southern California, since 1915.

BOGART, WILLIAM HENRY (Nov. 28, 1810–1888); b. Albany, N.Y. Author. *Daniel Boone, and the Hunters of Kentucky* (1854); *Who Goes There? or, Men and Events* (under pen name, "Sentinel," 1866).

BOGGS, TOM (1905–). Author, anthologist. *Millionaire Playboy* (1933); *Arenas* (poems, 1943); *Constant Mistress* (poem, 1945). Compiler: *51 Neglected Lyrics* (1937); *Lyrics in Brief, 1900–38* (1938); *Lyric Moderns in Brief* (1940); *American Decade* (1943).

Bohemian Club of San Francisco, The. Founded 1872. It owns "Bohemian Grove," a grove of virgin redwoods, comprising 2,437 acres, near Monte Rio, Calif. This grove, open to members only, contains an outdoor theatre, in which the annual "Grove Plays" are presented during the two weeks encampment of the Club. These celebrations, known as "High Jinks," date from 1879. See *The Annals of the Bohemian Club,* ed. Robert Howe Fletcher, 3v. (1898–1900); Porter Garnett's *The Bohemian Jinks* (1908); and *The Grove Plays,* ed. by Porter Graeme, 3v. (1918).

Bohemians. Artists and writers who adopt a footloose, uninhibited, and seemingly romantic way of life in rebellion against middle-class restraints and conventions. They establish communities in the poorer quarters of large cities or in rural colonies, and they often affect a mode of dress that is distinctive. The movement dates back to Du Maurier's *Trilby* and Murger's *La Bohéme.* Such locales and gathering places as Greenwich Village, Pfaff's Cellar, The Garibaldi, Carmel, Avon, Woodstock, Russian Hill, Jersey Street, are associated with Bohemian life. See Albert Parry's *Garrets and Pretenders: A History of Bohemianism in America* (1933). Henry Clapp was called "The King of Bohemia" and Jane McElheney "The Queen of Bohemia." The most recent examples of Bohemianism include the styles of life of the Beat Generation and the hippies (qq.v.).

BOK, CURTIS (Sept. 7, 1897–May 22, 1962); b. Wyncote, Pa. Jurist, author. *The Backbone of the Herring* (1941); *I, Too, Nicodemus* (1946); *Star Wormwood* (1959); *Maria* (1962); etc.

BOK, EDWARD WILLIAM (Oct. 9, 1863–Jan. 9, 1930); b. Helder, the Netherlands. Editor, author. *The Americanization of Edward Bok* (1920, Pulitzer Prize for American biography, 1921); *Twice Thirty* (1925); *A Man from Maine* (1923); etc. Editor-in-chief, *The Ladies' Home Journal,* 1889–1919; vice-president, Curtis Publishing Co., 1891–1930.

BOKER, GEORGE HENRY (Oct. 6, 1823–Jan 2, 1890); b. Philadelphia, Pa. Poet, playwright. *Calaynos* (prod. 1849); *Anne Boleyn* (1850); *The Betrothal* (prod. 1850); *The Podesta's Daughter, and Other Poems* (1852); *Leonor de Guzman* (1853); *Francesca da Rimini* (prod. 1855); *Plays and Poems,* 2v. (1856); *The Book of the Sonnet,* 2v. (1867); *Königsmark, the Legend of the Hounds, and Others* (1869); *The Book of the Dead* (poems, 1882); *Sonnets: A Sequence on Profane Love* (1929). He contributed for many years to *Lippincott's Magazine. See* Edward Scully Bradley's *George Henry Boker* (1927).

"Bold Hawthorne; or, The Cruise of the Fair American, Commanded by Capt. Daniel Hawthorne, by the Surgeon of the Vessel." Anonymous Revolutionary ballad (1777).

BOLESLAVSKI, RICHARD (1887–Jan. 17, 1937); b. Warsaw, Poland. Producer. Author (with Helen Woodward): *Way of a Lancer* (1932); *Lances Down* (1932); *Acting: The First Six Lessons* (1933).

BOLEY, JEAN (May 25, 1914–1957); b. Bayonne, N.J. Author. *The Restless* (1946); *The Baby Lamb* (1948); *A Little More Time* (stories, 1960).

BOLLES, [Edmund] BLAIR (Feb. 26, 1911–); b. St. Louis, Mo. Author. *America's Chance of Peace* (with Duncan Aikman, 1939); *Tyrant from Illinois* (1951); *How to Get Rich in Washington* (1952); *The Big Change in Europe* (1958); *Men of Good Intentions* (1960); *Corruption in Washington* (1961); etc.

BOLLES, FRANK (Oct. 31, 1856–Jan. 10, 1894); b. Winchester, Mass. Naturalist, author. *Land of the Lingering Snow* (1891); *At the North of Bearcamp Water* (1893); *From Blomidon to Smoky, and Other Papers* (1894); *Chocorua's Tenants* (poems, 1895). Founder, *Harvard Graduates Magazine,* 1893.

Bollingen Prize in Poetry. Awarded by the Library of Yale University since 1950, and by the Library of Congress in 1949, for achievement in American poetry. The awards were in the amount of $1,000 from 1949 through 1958; $2,500 from 1959 through 1962; and $5,000 from 1964. The Library of Congress award was made to Ezra Pound. In the same year the Yale University Library awarded a prize to Wallace Stevens. Since

1950 the awards have been made to John Crowe Ransom, Marianne Moore (1951), Archibald MacLeish and William Carlos Williams (1952), W. H. Auden (1953), Léonie Adams and Louise Bogan (1954), Conrad Aiken (1955), Allen Tate (1956), E. E. Cummings (1957), Theodore Roethke (1958), Delmore Schwartz (1959), Yvor Winters (1960 and 1961), John Hall Wheelock and Richard Eberhardt (1962), Robert Frost (1963), Horace Gregory (1964 and 1965), Robert Penn Warren (1967), John Berryman and Karl Shapiro (1969). The first award for poetic translation was made to Robert Fitzgerald in 1961. In subsequent years the following poets received the award: Richmond Lattimore (1962), Walter Arndt and Richard Wilbur (1963). After 1969 the Prize was discontinued.

BOLTÉ, CHARLES GUY (Jan. 19, 1920–); b. New York. Publisher, author. *The New Veteran* (1945); *The Price of Peace: A Plan for Disarmament* (1956). Vice president, The Viking Press, 1956–61. Vice president of the Carnegie Endowment for International Peace since 1966.

BOLTON, CHARLES KNOWLES (Nov. 14, 1867–May 19, 1950); b. Cleveland, O., son of Sarah K. Bolton. Antiquarian, librarian. *On the Wooing of Martha Pitkin* (1894); *The Love Story of Ursula Wolcott* (1895); *Brookline; the History of a Favored Town* (1897); *Scotch-Irish Pioneers* (1910); *American Library History* (1911); *The Elizabeth Whitman Mystery* (1912); *The Founders*, 3v. (1919–26); *The Real Founders of New England* (1929); *Terra Nova* (1935); *Workers With Line and Color in New England, 1620–1870*, 3v. (in MS at Boston Athenaeum, 1939); *Our American Language* (1945); etc. Editor, *The Athenaeum Centenary* (1907); *Sarah K. Bolton—Pages from an Intimate Autobiography* (1923); etc. Librarian, Boston Athenaeum, 1898–1933.

BOLTON, ETHEL [Stanwood] (Mrs. Charles Knowles Bolton) (Mar. 2, 1873–Jan. 9, 1954); b. Boston, Mass. Antiquarian, author. *Farm Life a Century Ago* (1909); *Wax Portraits and Silhouettes* (1915); etc. Editor, *Topliff's Travels* (1906); etc.

BOLTON, GUY REGINALD (Nov. 23, 1884–); b. Broxbourne, Eng. Playwright. *The Drone* (with Douglas J. Wood, prod. 1911); *Have a Heart* (with P. G. Wodehouse, prod. 1917); *Adam and Eva* (with George Middleton, prod. 1919); *The Light of the World* (with same, prod. 1920); *Sally* (prod. 1920); *Sitting Pretty* (with Wodehouse, prod. 1924); *Lady Be Good* (with Fred Thompson, prod. 1924); *Oh, Kay!* (with Wodehouse, prod. 1926); *Rio Rita* (with Thompson, prod. 1927); *Girl Crazy* (with John McGowan, prod. 1930); *Anything Goes* (with Wodehouse, prod. 1934); *Three Blind Mice* (with Virginia de Lanty, Prod. 1938); *Hold On to Your Hats* (prod. 1940); *Follow the Girls* (with Eddie Davis, prod. 1944); *Humoresque* (prod. 1948); *Anastasia* (adaptation, prod. 1953); *Ankles Aweigh* (with Eddie Davis, prod. 1955); *Flowers for the Living* (with Bernard Newman, 1958); *The Olympians* (1961); *The Enchantress* (1964); etc.

BOLTON, HERBERT EUGENE (July 20, 1870–1953); b. Wilton, Wis. Historian. *The Spanish Borderlands* (1921); *Anza's California Expeditions*, 5v. (1930); *The Padre on Horseback* (1932); etc. Editor: *Spanish Exploration in the Southwest, 1542–1706* (1916); *Kino's Historical Memoir of Pimería Alta*, 2v. (1919); *Historical Memoirs of New California*, by Fray Francisco Palóu, 4v. (1926); *Fray Juan Crespi, Missionary Explorer* (1927); *Wider Horizons of American History* (1939); *Coronado* (1949); etc. Professor of history, University of California, 1911–40.

Bolton, Isabel. Pen name of Mary Britton Miller.

BOLTON, SARAH K[nowles] (Mrs. Charles E. Bolton) (Sept. 15, 1841–Feb. 21, 1916); b. Farmington, Conn. Biographer, poet. *Orlean Lamar, and Other Poems* (1864); *Famous American Authors* (1887); *From Heart and Nature* (poems, with son, Charles K. Bolton, 1887); *Famous English Authors of the Nineteenth Century* (1890); *The Inevitable and Other*

Poems (1895); *Charles E. Bolton* (1907); *Pages from an Intimate Autobiography* (1923); etc.

BOLTON, SARAH T[ittle Barrett] (Dec. 18, 1814–Aug. 4, 1893); b. Newport, Ky. Poet. *Poems* (1865); *The Life and Poems of Sarah T. Bolton* (1880); *Songs of a Lifetime* (1892); *Paddle Your Own Canoe, and Other Poems* (1897).

BOLTON, THEODORE (Jan. 12, 1889–); b. Columbia, S.C. Librarian, author. *Early American Portrait Painters in Miniature* (1921); *Early American Portrait Draughtsmen in Crayons* (1923); *American Miniatures* (with H. B. Wehle, 1927); *American Book Illustrators* (1938); *The Book Illustrations of Felix Octavius Carr Darley* (1952); *Ezra Ames of Albany* (with I. F. Cortelyou, 1954); etc. Librarian, Century Club, New York, since 1926.

BONAPARTE, ELIZABETH PATTERSON (Feb. 6, 1785–Apr. 4, 1879); b. Baltimore, Md. Wife of Jerome Napoleon Bonaparte, King of Westphalia. Her romantic life-story has been the basis of various novels, plays, and poems. *See* Eugene L. Didier's *The Life and Letters of Madame Bonaparte* (1879); Rida Johnson Young's *Glorious Betsy* (prod. 1907); Elizabeth S. McNeil's *The Purple Trail* (1930); E. M. Oddie's *The Bonapartes in the New World* (1932); etc.

Bonaventura. Novel by George W. Cable (1887). A prose pastoral of Acadian Louisiana.

BOND, ALICE DIXON, b. Spring Lake, N.J. Editor, lecturer. Literary editor, *The Boston Herald,* since 1940; weekly radio program, "The Book Page of the Air."

BOND, CARRIE JACOBS (Aug. 11, 1862–Dec. 28, 1946); b. Janesville, Wis. Song writer, poet. *The Path o' Life* (1909); *Tales of Little Cats* (1918); *Tales of Little Dogs* (1921); *The Roads of Melody* (autobiography, 1927); *The End of the Road* (1941); etc. Compiler: *Old Melodies of the South* (1918). Composer of more than 200 songs, including "A Perfect Day," "I Love You Truly," "Just a-Wearyin' for You," etc.

BOND, DOROTHY ANN b. Chicago, Ill. Cartoonist, author. *Government Gertie* (1944); *All Men Are Dogs* (1950); *With Love, Bobbi Borcherdt* (1961); *Heartwarmers* (1963); etc. Syndicated cartoonist, since 1945.

BOND, NILES WOODBRIDGE (Feb. 25, 1916–); b. Newton, Mass. Foreign service officer, poet. *Arcanum* (1965); *Elegos* (1967). U.S. Foreign Service, since 1939.

BOND, RAYMOND T. Publisher, editor. With Dodd, Mead & Co., since 1920; pres., 1957–64.

BONER, JOHN HENRY (Jan. 31, 1845–Mar. 6, 1903); b. Salem, N.C. Lexicographer, poet. *Sparrows in the Snow* (1877); *Whispering Pines* (1883); *Some New Poems* (1901); *Poems* (1903). Edited several dictionaries and cyclopedias.

BONGARTZ, ROY (Dec. 8, 1924–); b. Providence, R.I. Author. *The Applicant* (1961); *Twelve Chases on West Ninety-Ninth Street* (1965).

BONHAM, MILLEDGE LOUIS (Feb. 21, 1880–Jan. 22, 1941); b. Barnwell, S.C. Educator, author. *The British Consuls in the Confederacy* (1911); *Robert R. Livingston* (1927); etc. Head of history dept., Hamilton College, 1919–41.

BONI, ALBERT (Oct. 21, 1892–); b. New York. Publisher. Editor: *Modern Book of French Verse* (1920); *A Guide to the Literature of Photography and Related Subjects* (1943); *Photographic Literature* (with others, 1963). Founded Boni and Liveright, 1917; Albert and Charles Boni, Inc., 1923.

Boni, Albert & Charles. New York. Founded by Albert and Charles Boni in 1923, when they bought out the firm of Lieber & Lewis. Its authors included Upton Sinclair, Thornton Wilder, Will Rogers, Carl Van Doren. In 1929 the firm started fifty-cent editions, known as "Boni Paper Books," of good books in paper covers. Charles Boni later started Boni & Gaer, with Joseph Gaer, in 1946. Boni withdrew in 1948 and in 1949 the firm was changed to Gaer Associates. *See* Liveright Publishing Corporation.

BONI, MARGARET [Bradford] (1893–). Editor: *Fireside Book of Folksongs* (1947); *Fireside Book of Love Songs* (1954); *Favorite Christmas Carols* (1957); *Songs of the Gilded Age* (1960); etc.

BONNER, CHARLES (Oct. 14, 1896–Mar. 21, 1965); b. Brooklyn, N.Y. Author. *Publicity* (1926); *The Fanatics* (1932); *Legacy* (1940); *Ambition* (1946); *The Last Romantic* (1949). Motion picture and television scenarist.

BONNER [Early], MARY GRAHAM (Sept. 5, 1890–); b. Cooperstown, N.Y. Author. The *Daddy's Bedtime Stories,* 4v. (1916–17); *Madam Red Apple* (1929); *A World of Our Own* (1937); *Hidden Village Mystery* (1948); *The Winning Dive* (1950); *Wait and See* (1952); *Wonders Around the Sun* (1957); *Two-Way Pitcher* (1958); etc. Author of over 3,000 "Sundown Stories."

BONNER, PAUL HYDE (Feb. 14, 1893–Dec. 14, 1968); b. Brooklyn, N.Y. Author. *Hotel Talleyrand* (1953); *S. P. Q. R.* (1954); *The Glorious Mornings* (1954); *Excelsior* (1955); *With Both Eyes Open* (1956); *Amanda* (1957); *Aged in the Woods* (1958); *The Art of Llewellyn Jones* (1959); *Ambassador Extraordinaire* (1962).

BONNER, ROBERT (Apr. 28, 1824–July 6, 1899); b. near Londonderry, Ireland. Editor and publisher. Purchased New York *Ledger* in 1851, and introduced popular and sensational journalism to America. He paid his feature writers enormous sums judged by the standards of that era. Fanny Fern was one of his most widely read contributors, and the highest paid.

Bonner, Sherwood. See Katherine Sherwood Bonner MacDowell.

BONNEY, EDWARD (1807–1864). Author. *The Banditti of the Prairies; or, The Murderer's Doom!!—A Tale of the Mississippi* (1850).

"Bonnie Blue Flag, The." Confederate song, written by Harry Macarthy (or McCarthy), an adaptation of the tune "The Irish Jaunting Car," and first sung by his sister, Marion, at the Varieties Theatre, New Orleans, in 1861. The first line of this song is "We are a band of brothers, and native to the soil." Another version beginning "Come, brothers! Rally to the right!" was written by Annie Chambers Ketchum.

BONSAL, STEPHEN (Mar. 29, 1865–June 8, 1951); b. Baltimore, Md. Correspondent. *Morocco As It Is* (1892); *The Golden Horse Shoe* (ed., 1900); *The American Mediterranean* (1912); *Heyday in a Vanished World* (1937); *Unfinished Business: Paris-Versailles, 1919* (1944; Pulitzer Prize for history, 1945); *When the French Were Here* (1945); *Suitors and Suppliants: The Lesser Nations at Versailles* (1946); etc.

BONTEMPS, ARNA WENDELL (Oct. 13, 1902–); b. Alexandria, La. Author. *God Sends Sunday* (1931); *Popo and Fifina* (with L. Hughes, 1932); *You Can't Pet a Possum* (1934); *Black Thunder* (1936); *Drums at Dusk* (1939); *Story of the Negro* (1948); *Chariot in the Sky* (1951); *Lonesome Boy* (1955); *Frederick Douglass: Slave—Fighter—Freeman* (1959); *One Hundred Years of Negro Freedom* (1961); *Famous Negro Athletes* (1964); *Black Thunder* (1968); *Hold Fast To Dreams* (1969); etc.

Book Booster, The. By Bert Leston Taylor (1901). Satire on *The Bookman.*

Book Buyer, The. Magazine published by Charles Scribner's Sons (1867–1918). It contained many original articles by leading literary figures. Since 1918 it has been revived from time to time, but chiefly as a house organ. In 1903 it was called *The Lamp,* but returned to its original name in 1905. A new series was started in 1884 by Frank Nelson Doubleday and Edward Bok.

Book clubs. Organizations that select books, usually of recent publication, for distribution to subscribers at reduced prices. Some book clubs offer "bonuses," or free choices, after a certain number of books have been purchased within a specified period; others offer an unlimited selection of almost all types of books at a discount. Many book clubs have a distinguished board of writers and critics as judges of selections, and publish a monthly magazine containing reviews. Among the best-known clubs have been the Book Find Club, Book-of-the-Month Club, Catholic Book Club, Dollar Book Club, Junior Literary Guild, Literary Guild, Marboro Book Club, Mid-Century Book Club, Reader's Subscription, Religious Book Club.

Book Digest of Best Sellers. New York. Founded Feb., 1937.

Book in America, The. By Hellmut Lehmann-Haupt, Ruth Shepard Granniss, and Lawrence C. Wroth (1939). Historical survey of book making, book selling and book collecting in America.

Book News Monthly. Philadelphia. Published by John Wanamaker's book department (1882–1918). Talcott Williams was editor, 1889–1908.

Book Notes. New York. A literary magazine. New Series. 1898–1901.

Book Notes for the Week. Providence, R.I., 1883–1916. Founded by Sidney S. Rider.

Book of Knowledge: The Children's Enclopaedia, The. 20v. (1911), revised from time to time. Published originally as an English magazine, *The Children's Encyclopedia.* In 1965 it was superseded by the *New Book of Knowledge* (q.v.).

Book Review Digest. New York. Monthly. Founded 1905.

Book Trails. Ed. by Renee B. Stern and O. Muriel Fuller, 8v. (1928).

Book Week/ Chicago Sun-Times. Chicago, Ill. Magazine section of newspaper. Founded 1967. Published by Field Enterprises, Inc. Edited by Herman Kogan.

Book World. New York. Founded 1967 as weekly literary supplement of the *Chicago Tribune* and the *Washington Post.* Superseded *Book Week* (see *New York Herald Tribune Books*) and *Books Today,* distributed by the *Chicago Tribune.* Charles Monaghan is editor.

Booklist, The, & Subscription Books Bulletin. Chicago, Ill. Quarterly, later semimonthly. Founded 1930, by the American Library Association, as *Subscription Books Bulletin.* New subscription books are evaluated, and librarians are advised of those of doubtful authority. Edna Vanek is editor.

Bookman. New York. Published monthly. Edited by John Farrar, 1921–28; Seward Collins and Burton Rascoe, 1928–29; Seward Collins, 1930–33. Discontinued 1933, with the founding of the *American Review* by Seward Collins.

Bookman's Glossary. By John A. Holden (1925). A dictionary of terms.

Bookman's Manual: A Guide to Literature. First published 1921. The first to the sixth editions were edited by Bessie Graham. The seventh edition (1954) was edited by Hester R. Hoffman, who also edited the eighth edition as *Bessie Graham's Bookman's Manual* (1958), the ninth as *Reader's Adviser and Bookman's Manual* (1962), and the tenth as *The Reader's Adviser* (1964). The eleventh edition was prepared and edited by Winifred F. Courtney (1968).

Books, Inc. New York. Monthly. Founded 1964. Published by Jerome B. Agel, who was also editor. News of latest developments in the world of writing and publishing, with special emphasis on avant-garde ideas, "pop" culture, and original ventures in all of the mass media. Suspended 1970.

Books About Books. By Winslow L. Webber. A bio-bibliography for the use of collectors (1937).

Books Abroad. Norman, Okla. Quarterly review. Founded 1927, by the University of Oklahoma. Editors have included Roy Temple House and Ivar Ivask.

Books and Battles: American Literature, 1920–1930. By Irene Cleaton and Allen Cleaton (1937).

Books and their Makers, A.D. 476–1709. By George Haven Putnam, 2v. (1896). Historical survey of bookmaking in all its aspects prior to the enactment of modern copyright laws, written by a booklover and publisher.

Books in Print: An Index to the Publishers' Trade List Annual. Published by R. R. Bowker Co. Author and title index listing the books in print of American publishers. Published annually since 1948.

Boomerang, The. Play by Victor Mapes and Winchell Smith (prod. 1915). The story of a bachelor doctor.

Boomerang, The. Newspaper. Founded 1881, by Bill Nye at Laramie, Wyo. William Edwards Chaplin was associated with Nye, and bought a half interest in the paper after Nye left Wyoming. Chaplin founded the *Laramie Republican* in 1890.

BOONE, DANIEL (Nov. 2, 1734–Sept. 26, 1820); b. near Reading, Pa. Pioneer, Indian fighter. *The Adventures of Colonial Daniel Boon* [sic] were written by John Filson (1784). *See* John Bakeless's *Daniel Boone* (1939); Reuben G. Thwaites's *Daniel Boone* (1902); Stewart Edward White's *Daniel Boone* (1922); Dixon Wecter's *The Hero in America* (1941).

BOONE, PAT (Charles Eugene Boone) (June 1, 1934–); b. Jacksonville, Fla. Singer, actor, author. *'Twixt Twelve and Twenty* (1958); *Between You, Me and the Gatepost* (1960); *The Real Christmas* (1961); *The Care and Feeding of Parents* (1967).

BOORSTIN, DANIEL J[oseph] (Oct. 1, 1914–); b. Atlanta, Ga. Educator. *The Mysterious Science of the Law* (1941); *The Lost World of Thomas Jefferson* (1948); *The Genius of American Politics* (1953); *The Americans: The Colonial Experience* (1958); *America and the Image of Europe* (1960); *The Image: Or, What Happened to the American Dream* (1962); *The Americans: The National Experience* (1965); *The Landmark History of the American People: From Plymouth to Appomattox* (1968); *The Decline of Radicalism: Reflections of America Today* (1969). Editor: *Chicago History of American Civilization,* 20v.; etc. Prof. American history, University of Chicago, since 1956.

BOOTH, BRADFORD ALLEN (Apr. 9, 1909–); b. Pittsburgh, Pa. Educator, author. *Anthony Trollope: Aspects of His Life and Art* (1958). Editor: *A Cabinet of Gems* (1938); Galt's *Gathering of the West* (1939); Trollope's *The Tireless Traveler* (1941); *Trollope's Autobiography* (1947); *Selected Poetry and Prose of Robert Louis Stevenson* (1968); etc. Prof. English, University of California at Los Angeles, since 1954.

BOOTH, CHARLES GORDON (Feb. 12, 1896–May 22, 1949); b. Manchester, England. Novelist. *Sinister House* (1926); *Gold Bullets* (1929); *Murder at High Tide* (1930); *Seven Alibis* (1932); *The Cat and the Clock* (1935); *The General Died at Dawn* (1937); *Murder Strikes Thrice* (1946). Also a number of screenplays, including *The House on 92nd Street* (Academy Award, 1945).

BOOTH, EDWIN PRINCE (Apr. 26, 1898–); b. Pittsburgh, Pa. Methodist clergyman, educator, author. *An Eighteenth Century Newspaper* (1931); *Martin Luther—Oak of Saxony* (1933); *From Experience to Faith* (1951); *Religion Ponders Science* (1964); etc. Prof. church history, Boston University, since 1925.

BOOTH, MARY LOUISE (Apr. 19, 1831–Mar. 5, 1889); b. Yaphank, L.I., N.Y. Editor, author. *History of the City of New York* (1859). Translator of about 20 volumes from French. Editor, *Harper's Bazar,* 1867–1888.

BOOTH, PHILIP (1925–); b. in New Hampshire. Poet. *Letter from a Distant Land* (1955); *The Islanders* (1961); *Weathers and Edges* (1966).

BOOTHE, CLARE [Clare Boothe Luce] (Mrs. Henry R. Luce) (Apr. 10, 1903–); b. New York. Playwright. *Stuffed Shirts* (1931); *Abide With Me* (prod. 1935); *The Women* (prod. 1937); *Kiss the Boys Goodbye* (prod. 1938); *Margin for Error* (prod. 1939); *Europe in the Spring* (1940); *Child of the Morning* (prod. 1951). Staff, *Vanity Fair,* 1931–34. Member of Congress, 1943–47; U.S. ambassador to Italy, 1953–57.

Boots and Saddles; or, Life in Dakota with General Custer. By Elizabeth B. Custer (1885). Intimate account of the cavalry leader and his exploits, and of frontier garrison life in general.

BORDEN, LUCILLE PAPIN (Mar. 30, 1873–); b. St. Louis, Mo. Novelist, essayist. *The Gates of Olivet* (1919); *Gentleman Riches* (1925); *Silver Trumpets Calling* (1931); *White Hawthorne* (1935); *Once—in Palestine* (1938); *From the Morning Watch* (1943); *Francesca Cabrini* (1945); etc.

Border Beagles. Stories by William Gilmore Simms (1840). Picaresque border tales of Mississippi.

BORGMAN, ALBERT STEPHENS (Aug. 20, 1890–Dec. 9, 1954); b. Detroit, Mich. Educator, author. *Thomas Shadwell: His Life and Comedies* (1928); *The Life and Death of William Mountfort* (1935). English dept., New York University, from 1919.

BORING, EDWIN GARRIGUES (Oct. 23, 1886–); b. Philadelphia, Pa. Psychologist. *A History of Experimental Psychology* (1929); *The Physical Dimensions of Consciousness* (1933); *Sensation and Perception in the History of Experimental Psychology* (1942); etc. Editor (with others): *Foundations of Psychology* (1948). Editor, *Contemporary Psychology,* since 1956. Prof. psychology, Harvard University, 1928–56.

BORLAND, HAL [Glen] (May 14, 1900–); b. Sterling, Neb. Author. *Heaps of Gold* (poems, 1922); *Valor* (1934); *Wapiti Pete* (1938); *America Is Americans* (poems, 1942); *An American Year* (1946); *How to Write and Sell Non-Fiction* (1956); *This Hill, This Valley* (1957); *Seventh Winter* (1959); *Beyond Your Doorstep* (1962); *King of Squaw Mountain* (1964); *Countryman: A Summary of Belief* (1965); *Homeland : A Report from the Country* (1969); etc. Under pen name "Ward West": *Trouble Valley* (1934); *Halfway to Timberline* (1935).

BORTON, HUGH (May 14, 1903–); b. Moorestown, N.J. Educator, author. *Peasant Uprisings in Japan* (1938); *Japan's Modern Century* (1955); *Japan Between East and West* (with others, 1957); etc. Prof. Japanese, Columbia University, 1948–56; pres., Haverford College, since 1957.

BOSHER, KATE [Lee] **LANGLEY** (Feb. 1, 1865–July 27, 1932); b. Norfolk, Va. Novelist. *Mary Cary* (1910); *Miss Gibbie Gault* (1911); *People Like That* (1915); etc.

BOSLEY, HAROLD A[ugustus] (Feb. 19, 1907–); b. Burchard, Neb. Methodist clergyman, author. *The Quest for Religious Certainty* (1939); *The Philosophical Heritage of the Christian Faith* (1945); *Main Issues Confronting Christendom* (1948); *Preaching on Controversial Issues* (1953); *Sermons on Genesis* (1958); *He Spoke to Them in Parables* (1963); *The Mind of Christ* (1966); *The Deeds of Christ* (1969); etc.

Boss, The. Novel by Alfred Henry Lewis (1903). An exposé of corrupt city politics.

Boss, The. Play by Edward Brewster Sheldon (prod. 1911). The sordid story of a man and woman who are ill-mated physically and who make a travesty of marriage.

BOSSARD, JAMES HERBERT SIWARD (Sept. 29, 1888–Jan. 29, 1960); b. Danielsville, Pa. Sociologist, educator. *Ritual in Family Living* (with E. S. Boll, 1950); *Parent and Child: Studies in Family Behavior* (1953); *The Large Family System* (1956); *One Marriage, Two Faiths* (with E. S. Boll, 1957); *Why Marriages Go Wrong* (with same, 1958). Prof. sociology, University of Pennsylvania, from 1925.

Boston Advertiser. Boston, Mass. Newspaper. Founded 1813, as the *Daily Advertiser.* Essentially a mercantile paper but soon published literary contributions from Edward Everett, Jared Sparks, and William Ellery Channing. Evening edition, called *Boston Record,* established 1884. *Advertiser* was bought by W. R. Hearst in 1917 and became a tabloid in 1922; *Record* was bought by Hearst in 1920 and both merged as *Boston Record* in 1922. Name changed to *Boston Daily Record* in 1929. *Boston Advertiser* is now only a Sunday newspaper.

Boston American. Boston, Mass. Newspaper. Founded 1904. Now combined with the *Boston Record* (q.v.) as the *Boston Record American.*

Boston Athenaeum. Founded 1805, by the Anthology Society, as The Anthology Reading Room. Incorporated 1807, under present name. *See* Josiah Quincy's *The History of the Boston Athenaeum* (1851); and *The Athenaeum Centenary* (1907).

Boston Authors' Club. An organization meeting was held at the home of Julia Ward Howe in Boston in 1899. The first formal meeting was held at the Hotel Vendome in Boston, Jan., 1900.

Boston Book. Boston. A literary anthology. Four volumes were published. Editors: vol. 1 (1836), Henry T. Tuckerman; vol. 2 (1837), Benjamin B. Thatcher; vol. 3 (1841), George S. Hillard; vol. 4 (1850), anon.

Boston Chronicle. Boston, Mass. Newspaper. Founded Dec. 21, 1767, by John Fleming and John Mein. Expired June 25, 1770.

Boston Evening-Post. Boston, Mass. Newspaper. Founded 1731, by Jeremy Gridley, as the *Weekly Rehearsal.* Sold to Thomas Fleet, who changed the name to the *Evening-Post.* Expired 1735.

Boston Gazette. Boston, Mass. Founded as a weekly, Dec. 14, 1719. Expired 1798, after flourishing many decades.

Boston Globe. Boston, Mass. Newspaper. Founded 1872. Charles Henry Taylor became associated with it in 1873 and remained with it until his death in 1921. He launched the *Sunday Globe* in 1877. Succeeded by his son William O. Taylor. Thomas Winship is now editor; Herbert A. Kenny is book-review editor.

Boston Herald Traveler. Boston, Mass. Newspaper. Founded 1846, by John A. French and others. Merged in 1913 with the *Boston Traveler* (q.v.) Sunday edition, the *Boston Sunday Herald,* appeared in 1861. Among its literary editors were Sidney C. Williams, John Clair Minot and Alice Dixon Bond. Publishes a special book supplement under editorship of Albert Duhamel.

Boston Journal. Boston, Mass. Newspaper. Founded 1833, as the *Boston Mercantile Journal.* In 1845, it became the *Boston Daily Journal;* in 1872, the *Boston Evening Journal.* Consolidated with the *Boston Herald* (q.v.) in 1917.

Boston Miscellany of Literature and Fashion. Boston, Mass. Monthly. Founded 1842. Editors, Nathan Hale, Jr., 1842, and Henry T. Tuckerman, 1843. Illustrated with colored fashion plates. Absorbed *The Arcturus,* in 1842. Expired 1843.

Boston News-Letter. First regularly published newspaper in America. Founded Apr. 24, 1704, by John Campbell, and published by Bartholomew Green. Called the *Boston Weekly News-Letter and New England Chronicle* until 1763; title then changed to the *Massachusetts Gazette and Boston News-Letter.* Expired Feb. 22, 1776.

Boston Post. Boston, Mass. Newspaper. Founded 1831, as the *Daily Morning Post.* Purchased 1891 by E. A. Grozier, who developed it until his death in 1924.

Boston Public Library, The. Founded 1852. George Ticknor, Edward Everett and William W. Greenough were moving forces in its development. In 1870 it established a branch library, the first in America. Among its noted collections are the John Adams Library, the Ticknor Library of Spanish books, the Prince Library, and the Barton Shakespeare collection, the Allen A. Brown Music Library, and the Nathanial Bowditch collection. Justin Winsor, Charles C. Jewett, Herbert Putnam, and Horace G. Wadlin, have been among its prominent librarians.

Boston Quarterly Review. Boston, Mass. Founded 1838, and edited by Orestes Augustus Brownson, a political writer. His religious affiliations added to his experience, for he was successively a Presbyterian, Universalist, Unitarian, and Catholic. The *Quarterly* was his mouthpiece, and few articles not written by him ever appeared in it. In 1842, he merged the *Boston Quarterly Review* with the *Democratic Review.* In Jan. 1844, Brownson established *Brownson's Quarterly Review,* which ran until Oct. 1875.

Boston Record. Founded 1884 as the evening edition of the *Boston Daily Advertiser.* The name was changed to the *Boston Record* in 1929. It is now combined with the *Boston American* (q.v.) as the *Boston Record American,* published by the Hearst Corporation.

Boston Review. Boston, Mass. Bi-monthly Congregational review; quarterly, 1866-67. Founded 1861. It was moved to Chicago in 1870; and the equipment having been destroyed in the Chicago fire of 1871, it was merged with the *New Englander.*

Boston Transcript. Boston, Mass. Newspaper. Founded 1830, by Lynde M. Walter, who edited it until 1842. Succeeding him were Cornelia Wells Walter, Epes Sargent, Robert L. O'Brien, and Henry Turner Claus, among others. Expired 1941. *See* Joseph Edgar Chamberlin's *The Boston Transcript* (1930).

Boston Traveler. Boston, Mass. Newspaper. Founded 1823, as a weekly; daily since 1845. In 1857 Curtis Guild merged the *Boston Evening Traveler, Boston Daily Atlas, Boston Chronicle,* and *Daily Evening Telegraph* as the *Boston Morning Traveler* and the *Boston Evening Traveler.* In 1913 it merged with the *Boston Herald* (q.v.) but still appeared evenings, except Sunday. Ceased separate publication in 1967. See *Boston Herald Traveler.*

Boston Two Hundred Years Ago; or, The Romantic Story of Miss Ann Carter, (Daughter of One of the First Settlers) and the Celebrated Indian Chief, Thundersquall. Anonymous novel (1830).

Boston Weekly. Boston, Mass. Founded 1802, by Samuel Gilbert and Thomas Dean. In 1805 it was sold to Joshua Belcher and Samuel T. Armstrong, and renamed the *Boston Magazine,* and finally the *Emerald.* Expired 1808. Noted for its "Thespian Dept." which reviewed the articles of the theatre, and for its fiction.

Bostonians, The. Novel by Henry James (1886). Satire on women with a "mission," stern, striving protagonists of lost causes, exemplified by the book's chief character, Olive Chancellor.

BOSTWICK, ARTHUR ELMORE (Mar. 8, 1860–Feb. 13, 1942); b. Litchfield, Conn. Librarian, author. *The American Public Library* (1910); *The Different West* (1913); *Earmarks of Literature* (1914); *Library Essays* (1920); *A Life with Men and Books* (1939); etc. Editor, *Classics of American Librarianship,* v. 1–8 (1915–29); etc. Librarian, St. Louis Public Library, 1909–38.

BOSWELL, PEYTON (May 25, 1879–Dec. 18, 1936); b. Wolf Creek, Ill. Art critic, New York *Herald;* art reviewer, New York *American;* editor, *International Studio,* 1922–25; founder, *The Art Digest,* Nov. 1, 1926.

BOTKIN, B[enjamin] A[lbert] (Feb. 7, 1901–); b. Boston, Mass. Educator. Editor: *The Southwest Scene: An Anthology of Regional Verse* (1931); *A Treasury of American Folk-Lore* (1940); *Lay My Burden Down; A Folk History of Slavery* (1945); *A Treasury of New England Folklore* (1947); *A Treasury of Southern Folklore* (1949); *New York City Folklore* (1956); *A Treasury of American Anecdotes* (1957); *A Civil War Treasury of Tales, Legends and Folklore* (1960); *The Book of the American West* (1963). Consultant, *Random House Dictionary of the English Language,* 1966. Editor, *Folk–Say: A Regional Miscellany,* 1929–32; founder, *Space,* May, 1934; editor, 1934–35.

BOTSFORD, GEORGE WILLIS (May 9, 1862–Dec. 13, 1917); b. West Union, Ia. Educator, historian. *History of the Ancient World* (1911); *Hellenic History* (1922); and many textbooks on Greece and Rome in collaboration with wife, Lillie Shaw Botsford.

BOTSFORD, MARGARET. Novelist, poet. *Adelaide* (under pen name "A Lady of Philadelphia," 1816); *Viola; or, The Heiress of St. Valverde* (poem, under same pen name, 1820); *The Reign of Reform; or, Yankee Doodle Court* (under pen name, "A Lady," 1830).

BOTTA, ANNE C[harlotte] LYNCH (Mrs. Vincenzo Botta) (Nov. 11, 1815–Mar. 23, 1891); b. Bennington, Vt. Author. *Poems* (1849); *Hand-Book of Universal Literature* (1860). Editor: *The Rhode-Island Book: Selections in Prose and Verse from the Writings of Rhode-Island Citizens* (1841). Her home in Waverly Place, New York, was a literary salon. Poe, Bryant, Willis, Stoddard, Bayard Taylor, Margaret Fuller, and others were members of her coterie.

BOTTA, VINCENZO (Nov. 11, 1818–Oct. 5, 1894); b. Cavaller Maggiore, Italy. Educator, author. *A Discourse on the Life, Character, and Policy of Count Cavour* (1862); *Dante as Philosopher, Patriot, and Poet* (1865); *Introduction to the Study of Dante* (1887); etc.

BOTTOME, MARGARET [McDonald] (Dec. 29, 1827–Nov. 14, 1906); b. New York City. Assoc. editor of *Ladies' Home Journal* and for sixteen years conducted a department called "Mrs. Bottome's Heart to Heart Talks with the King's Daughters."

Boucher, Anthony. Pen name of William Anthony Parker White.

BOUCHER, JONATHAN (Mar. 12, 1837/8–Apr. 27, 1804); b. Blencogo, County of Cumberland, England. Loyalist, author. *A Supplement to Dr. Johnson's Dictionary of the English Language* (1807), published as *Boucher's Glossary of Archaic and Provincial Words,* 2 parts (1932–33); *Reminiscences of an American Loyalist, 1738–1789* (1925).

BOUCICAULT, DION (Dec. 26, 1820–Sept. 18, 1890); b. Dublin, Ireland. Actor, playwright. *Jessie Brown; or, The Relief of Lucknow* (prod. 1858); *The Octaroon* (prod. 1859); *Arrah-na-Pogue* (prod. 1864); *The O'Dowd* (prod. 1873); *The Shaughraun* (prod. 1874); *Belle Lamar* (prod. 1874); etc. He is the author of the words of "The Wearin' of the Green." Many of his popular plays were adaptations of foreign plays and novels. *See* Margaret G. Mayorga's *A Short History of the American Drama* (1934).

BOUDINOT, ELIAS (May 2, 1740–Oct. 24, 1821); b. Philadelphia, Pa. Philanthropist, president of the Continental Congress, author. *The Age of Revolution; or, The Age of Reason Shewn to be an Age of Infidelity* (1801); *Journal or Historical Recollections of American Events During the Revolutionary War* (1894); etc.

BOUDINOT, ELIAS (c. 1803–June 22, 1839); b. in Georgia. Cherokee Indian, editor, author. Indian Name, "Galagina." *Poor Sarah; or, The Indian Woman* (text in Cherokee, 1833). Editor, *The Cherokee Phoenix.* With Samuel Austin Worcester, he translated the New Testament into Cherokee, and compiled several Cherokee hymnals.

Bought and Paid For. Play by George Broadhurst (1911). A frank presentation of an unhappy marriage and its causes.

BOUGHTON, WILLIS (Apr. 17, 1854–June 16, 1942); b. Victor, N.Y. Educator, author. *Mythology in Art* (1890); *History of Ancient Peoples* (1896); *Ode to Learning* (1912); etc.

BOULDING, KENNETH EWART (Jan. 18, 1910–); b. Liverpool, Eng. Economist. *Economic Analysis* (1941); *Economics of Peace* (1945); *There Is a Spirit* (1945); *A Reconstruction of Economics* (1950); *The Organizational Revolution* (1953); *The Image* (1956); *Principles of Economic Policy* (1958); *Conflict and Defense* (1962); *The Meaning of the 20th Century* (1964); *The Impact of the Social Sciences* (1966); *Beyond Economics: Essays on Social Religion* (1968). Prof. economics, University of Michigan, since 1949.

BOURJAILY, MONTE FERRIS (Feb. 28, 1894–); b. Ketaily, Lebanon. Editor. Editor, United Feature Syndicate, 1929–36; editor and publisher *Midweek Pictorial, Judge,* 1936–37; president Globe Syndicate, since 1937.

BOURJAILY, VANCE NYE (Sept. 17, 1922–); b. Cleveland, O. Author. *The End of My Life* (1947); *The Hound of Earth* (1955); *The Violated* (1958); *Confessions of a Spent Youth* (1960); *The Unnatural Enemy* (1963); *The Hound of the Earth* (1964); *The Man Who Knew Kennedy* (1967).

BOURKE–WHITE, MARGARET (June 14, 1906–Aug., 1971); b. New York. Photographer, author. *Eyes on Russia* (1931); *U.S.S.R.* (1934); *North of the Danube* (with Erskine Caldwell, 1939); *Say! Is This the U.S.A.?* (with Erskine Caldwell, 1941); *Shooting the Russian War* (1942); *Dear Fatherland, Rest Quietly* (1946); *Halfway to Freedom* (1949); *Portrait of Myself* (1963); etc. Illustrator: *A Report on the American Jesuits* (1956).

BOURNE, HENRY ELDRIDGE (Apr. 13, 1862–June 19, 1946); b. Hamburg, N.Y. Educator, historian, author. *Mediaeval and Modern History* (1905); *Revolutionary Period in Europe* (1914); etc. Joint editor, *Story of America and Great Americans* (1923); etc. Prof. history, Western Reserve University, 1892–1930.

BOURNE, RANDOLPH SILLIMAN (May 30, 1886–Dec. 22, 1918); b. Bloomfield, N.J. Essayist. *Youth and Life* (1913); *The Gary Schools* (1916); *Education and Living* (1917); *Untimely Papers* (1919); *The History of a Literary Radical, and Other Essays* (1920). *See* Sherman Paul's *Randolph Bourne* (1966).

BOUTELL, CLARENCE BURLEY [Clip] (Feb. 8, 1908–); b. Washington, D.C. Editor, columnist. *The Fat Baron* (1946). Co-editor: *Speak of the Devil* (1945). Author, syndicated column, "Authors Are Like People," 1943–47.

BOUTON, ARCHIBALD LEWIS (Sept. 1, 1872–Apr. 18, 1941); b. Cortland, N. Y. Educator. Editor: *Lincoln and Douglas Debates* (1905); *Matthew Arnold: Prose and Poetry* (1927); etc. English dept., New York University, 1898–1937; head, 1914–37; dean, University College, New York University, 1914–36.

BOUTON, JOHN BELL (Mar. 15, 1830–Nov. 18, 1902); b. Concord, N.H. Editor, author. *Loved and Lost* (1857); *Round the Block: An American Novel* (1864); *Round-about to Moscow* (1887); etc. Editor of *Cleveland Plain Dealer,* beginning in 1851. An editor of *Appleton's Annual Cyclopedia* for a number of years.

BOUVET, [Marie] MARGUERITE (Feb. 14, 1865–May 27, 1915); b. New Orleans, La. Author. *Sweet William* (1890);

Little Marjorie's Love Story (1891); *A Child of Tuscany* (1895); *A Little House of Pimlico* (1897); *Tales of an Old Chateau* (1899); *Bernardo & Laurette* (1901); *Clotilde* (1908); etc.

BOWDOIN, JAMES (Aug. 7, 1726–Nov. 6, 1790); b. Boston, Mass. Statesman, poet. He wrote a poetical paraphrase of Dodsley's "Economy of Human Life" (1759), and wrote an English poem for the *Pietas et Gratulatio,* a volume of poems published by Harvard College on the accession of George III. Bowdoin College was named in his honor.

BOWDOIN, WILLIAM GOODRICH (Sept. 4, 1860–1947); b. S. Hadley Falls, Mass. Art critic. *The Rise of the Book Plate* (1901); *James MacNeill Whistler: The Man and His Work* (1901); *Jack and Jill According to the Modern School of Fiction* (1906); *The Jewelled Dagger* (1908); etc. Assoc. editor, *The Independent,* 1903–10; art critic, *New York Evening World,* 1915–24; *Newark Evening News,* 1924–27; *New York World,* 1927–31.

BOWEN, ABEL (Dec. 3, 1790–Mar. 11, 1850); b. Greenbush, N.Y. Wood engraver, publisher. Made wood engravings for Caleb H. Snow's *History of Boston* (1825), etc., and was one of the publishers of the *American Magazine of Useful and Entertaining Knowledge,* Boston, 1834.

BOWEN, CATHERINE DRINKER (Jan. 1, 1897–); b. Haverford, Pa. Author. *Beloved Friend—The Story of Tchaikowsky and Nadejda von Meck* (with Barbara von Meck, 1937); *Free Artist* (1939); *Yankee from Olympus—Justice Holmes and His Family* (1944); *John Adams and the American Revolution* (1950); *The Lion and the Throne* (1957); *Adventures of a Biographer* (1959); *Francis Bacon: Temper of a Man* (1963); *The Little Girls* (1963); *The Good Tiger* (1965); *Miracle at Philadelphia* (1966); *Eva Trout* (1968); *Biography: The Craft and the Calling* (1969); etc.

BOWEN, EDWIN WINFIELD (Oct. 20, 1866–1953); b. near Prince Frederick, Md. Educator, author. *Makers of American Literature* (1907); *Questions at Issue in Our English Speech* (1909); etc. Prof. Latin, Randolph-Macon College, 1894–1950.

BOWEN, FRANCIS (Sept. 8, 1811–Jan. 21, 1890); b. Charlestown, Mass. Educator, editor, philosopher, biographer. *History and Present Condition of Speculative Philosophy* (1842); *The Principles of Political Economy* (1856); *Modern Philosophy from Descartes to Schopenhauer and Hartmann* (1877); *Gleanings from a Literary Life, 1838–1880* (1880); etc. Editor, the *North American Review,* 1843–53.

BOWEN, HERBERT WOLCOTT (Feb. 29, 1856–May 29, 1927); b. Brooklyn, N.Y. Diplomat, poet. *Verses* (1884); *Losing Ground* (1889); *In Divers Tones* (1890); *De Genere Humano* (1893); *Recollections, Diplomatic and Undiplomatic* (1926).

BOWEN, HOWARD ROTHMANN (Oct. 27, 1908–); b. Spokane, Wash. Educator. *English Grants-in-Aid* (1939); *Toward Social Economy* (1948); *Social Responsibilities of the Businessman* (1953); *Automation and Economic Progress* (with Garth L. Magnum, 1966); etc. Pres. Grinnell College, since 1955.

BOWEN, SUE PETIGRU (1824–1875); b. in South Carolina. Novelist. *The Busy Moments of an Idle Woman* (1854); *Lily* (1855); *Sylvia's World* (1859); etc.

BOWER, B[ertha] M[uzzy] (Mrs. Bertrand W. Sinclair; Mrs. Robert Ellsworth Cowan) (Nov. 15, 1871–July 23, 1940); b. Cleveland, Minn. Novelist. *Chip of the Flying U* (1906); *The Lonesome Trail* (1909); *The Range Dwellers* (1910); *The Gringos* (1913); *Flying U Ranch* (1914); *The Phantom Herd* (1916); *Skyrider* (1918); *The Quirt* (1920); *Casey Ryan* (1921); *Black Thunder* (1925); *Dark Horse* (1931); *Laughing Water* (1932); *The Flying U Strikes* (1934); *Pirates of the Range* (1937); *The Singing Hill* (1939); etc.

BOWERMAN, GEORGE FRANKLIN (Sept. 8, 1868–Aug. 6, 1960); b. Farmington, N.Y. Librarian, author. *Censorship and the Public Library* (1931); etc. Librarian, Public Library of the District of Columbia, 1904–40.

BOWERS, CLAUDE GERNADE (Nov. 20, 1878–Jan. 21, 1958); b. in Hamilton Co., Ind. Diplomat, historian, biographer. *The Party Battles of the Jackson Period* (1922); *Jefferson and Hamilton; The Struggle for Democracy in America* (1925); *The Tragic Era; The Revolution after Lincoln* (1929); *Beveridge and the Progressive Era* (1932); *Jefferson in Power; The Death Struggle of the Federalists* (1936); *The Spanish Adventures of Washington Irving* (1940); *Thomas Jefferson,* 3v. (1945); *Pierre Vergniaud: Voice of the French Revolution* (1950); *My Mission to Spain* (1954); *Chile Through Embassy Windows* (1958); etc. Ambassador to Spain, 1933–39; to Chile, 1939–53.

BOWERS, EDGAR (Mar. 2, 1924–); b. Rome, Ga. Poet. *The Form of Loss* (1956). *The Astronomers* (1965); Faculty, University of California at Santa Barbara, since 1958.

BOWERS, FAUBION (Jan. 29, 1917–). b. Miami, Okla. Author, pianist. *Japanese Theatre* (1952); *The Dance in India* (1953); *Theatre in the East* (1956); *Broadway, U.S.S.R.* (1959); *Scriabin: A Biography of the Russian Composer 1871–1915,* 2v. (1969); etc.

BOWERS, FREDSON THAYER (Apr. 25, 1905–); b. New Haven, Conn. Educator. *Principles of Bibliographical Description* (1949); *On Editing Shakespeare and the Elizabethan Dramatists* (1955); *Textual and Literary Criticism* (1959); *Bibliography and Textual Criticism* (1964); etc. Editor: *The Dramatic Works of Thomas Dekker,* 4v. (1953–60). Prof. English, University of Virginia, since 1949.

BOWIE, WALTER RUSSELL (Oct. 8, 1882–Apr. 23, 1969); b. Richmond, Va. Clergyman, author. *The Master of the Hill* (1917); *Sunny Windows* (1921); *On Being Alive* (1931); *The Heroism of the Unheroic* (1933); *The Renewing Gospel* (1935); *Great Men of the Bible* (1937); *The Story of Jesus* (1938); *Remembering Christ* (1940); *Preaching* (1954); *The Story of the Church* (1955); *The Living Story of the New Testament* (1959); *Men of Fire* (1961); *Women of Light* (1963); *The Living Story of the Old Testament* (1964); *The Compassionate Christ* (1965); *See Yourself in the Bible* (1967); *Learning to Live* (autobiography, 1969); etc. Associate editor, *The Interpreter's Bible.*

Bowker, R. R., Company. New York. Founded 1872. Frederic G. Melcher was chairman of the board until his death in 1963. Publishes books for the book trade including bibliographies, library directories, reference works. *Publishers' Weekly, American Book Publishing Record, Literary Market Place,* etc., are among the periodicals issued by the firm. Acquired by Xerox Educational Division (q.v.) in 1968.

BOWKER, RICHARD ROGERS (Sept. 4, 1848–Nov. 12, 1933); b. Salem, Mass. Editor, publisher, author. *Copyright: Its Law and Its Literature* (1886); *The Art of Life* (1900); *Copyright: Its History and Its Law* (1912); etc. One of the original "Mugwumps." Associated with Frederick Leypoldt on the *Publishers Weekly,* and succeeded him as head of the firm. Edited *Publishers Weekly* from 1884 to 1918. Formed the R. R. Bowker Company. Helped found *The Library Journal* in 1876. The R. R. Bowker Memorial Lectures have been given at the New York Public Library since 1935.

BOWLES, CHESTER (Apr. 5, 1901–); b. Springfield, Mass. Diplomat, government official, author. *Tomorrow Without Fear* (1946); *Ambassador's Report* (1954); *The New Dimensions of Peace* (1955); *American Politics in a Revolutionary World* (1956); *Africa's Challenge to America* (1956); *Ideas, People, and Peace* (1958); *The Coming Political Breakthrough* (1959); *The Conscience of a Liberal* (1962); *The Makings of a Just Society* (1963); *And Promises to Keep* (1971).

BOWLES, ELLA SHANNON (Mrs. Archie Raimond Bowles) (Jan. 9, 1886–); b. Pittsfield, N.H. Author. *Children of the Border* (1929); *Hubert the Happy* (1930); *Let Me Show You New Hampshire* (1938); *Secrets of New England Cooking* (with Dorothy S. Towle, 1947); etc.

BOWLES, PAUL [Frederic] (Dec. 30, 1910–); b. New York. Composer, author. *The Sheltering Sky* (1949); *Little Stone* (stories, 1950); *The Delicate Prey* (1950); *Let It Come Down* (1952); *The Spider's House* (1955); *Hours After Noon* (stories, 1959); *Their Heads Are Green and Their Hands Are Blue* (1963); *Time of Friendship* (1967); *Up Above the World* (1968).

BOWLES, SAMUEL (June 8, 1797–Sept. 8, 1851); b. Hartford, Conn. Editor. Founder, *The Springfield Republican,* 1824; editor, 1824–51. *See* Richard Hooker's *Story of An Independent Newspaper* (1924).

BOWLES, SAMUEL (Feb. 9, 1826–Jan. 16, 1878); b. Springfield, Mass., son of Samuel Bowles (1797–1851). Editor, author. *Across the Continent* (1865); *The Switzerland of America* (1869); the two combined as, *Our New West* (1869). Editor, *The Springfield Republican,* 1851–78. *See* George S. Merriam's *Life and Times of Samuel Bowles,* 2v. (1885).

BOWLES, SAMUEL (Oct. 15, 1851–Mar. 14, 1915); b. Springfield, Mass., son of Samuel Bowles (1826–1878). Editor, *The Springfield Republican,* 1878–1915.

"Bowling Green, The." Column by Christopher Morley in *Saturday Review.*

BOWMAN, HEATH (Aug. 7, 1910–); b. Muncie, Ind. Author. *Mexican Odyssey* (with Sterling Dickinson, 1935); *Westward from Rio* (with same, 1936); *Death Is Incidental* (with same, 1937); *All Your Born Days* (1940); *Hoosier* (1941).

BOWMAN, ISAIAH (Dec. 26, 1878–Jan. 6, 1950); b. Waterloo, Ont. Educator, geographer, author. *South America* (1915); *The Andes of Southern Peru* (1916); *The New World* (1921); *Desert Trails of Atacama* (1923); *The Pioneer Fringe* (1931); *Design for Scholarship* (1936); etc. President, Johns Hopkins University, 1935–1950.

BOWMAN, JAMES CLOYD (Jan. 18, 1880–Sept. 27, 1961); b. Leipsic, O. Educator, author. *The Knight of the Chinese Dragon* (1913); *The Gift of White Roses* (1913); *On the Des Moines* (verse, 1921); *Contemporary American Criticism* (1926); *The Adventures of Paul Bunyan* (1927); *Pecos Bill, the Greatest Cowboy of All Time* (1937); *Mystery Mountain* (1940); etc. Editor of many texts on English and American literature. Head, English dept., Northern State Teachers College, Marquette, Mich., 1921–39.

BOWMAN, JOHN WICK (Aug. 3, 1894–); b. Brownsville, Pa. Presbyterian clergyman, author. *The Intention of Jesus* (1943); *The Religion of Maturity* (1948); *Prophetic Realism and the Gospel* (1955); *Jesus' Teaching in Its Environment* (1963). Prof. New Testament interpretation, San Francisco Theological Seminary, since 1944.

BOWNE, BORDEN PARKER (Jan. 14, 1847–Apr. 1, 1910); b. Leonardville, N.J. Educator, philosopher. *The Philosophy of Herbert Spencer* (1874); *Studies in Theism* (1879); *Principles of Ethics* (1892); etc.

"Box of Gold, The." Long poem on Indians by Lew Sarett (1922).

"Boy Brittan." Poem by Forceythe Willson (1862).

Boy Emigrants, The. By Noah Brooks (1876). Popular account of an overland journey from New England to Kansas, and thence to the Pacific coast.

Boy Meets Girl. Play by Bella and Sam Spewack (prod. 1935). A satire on the movie colony of Hollywood.

Boy Travelers Series. A group of books by Thomas Wallace Knox, who also wrote the *Young Nimrod* series.

BOYCE, BENJAMIN (Nov. 26, 1903–); b. Lansing, Mich. Educator. *Tom Brown of Facetious Memory* (1939); *The Theophrastan Character in England to 1642* (1947); *The Polemic Character, 1640–1661* (1955); *The Character Sketches in Pope's Poems* (1962); *The Benevolent Man: A Life of Ralph Allen of Bath* (1967). Editor: *The Adventures of Lindamira* (1948). Prof. English, Duke University, since 1950.

BOYCE, BURKE (June 19, 1901–); b. St. Louis, Mo. *The Perilous Night* (1942); *Miss Mallett* (1948); *Cloak of Folly* (1949); *The Man from Mount Vernon* (1961); *Morning of a Hero* (1963).

Boyce, Neith. *See* Neith Boyce Hapgood.

Boyd, Barbara. Pen name of Agnes Rush Burr.

BOYD, BELLE (May 9, 1843–June 11, 1900); b. Martinsburg, Va. (now W. Va.). Confederate spy, actress, author. *Belle Boyd in Camp and Prison* (1865). Dion Boucicault's *Belle Lamar* (prod. 1874) is said to have been based on her experiences.

BOYD, ERNEST [Augustus] (June 28, 1887–Dec. 30, 1946); b. Dublin, Ireland. Author. *Ireland's Literary Renaissance* (1916); *The Contemporary Drama of Ireland* (1917); *Appreciations and Depreciations* (1917); *Portraits, Real and Imaginary* (1924); *Studies from Ten Literatures* (1925); *H. L. Mencken* (1925); *Guy de Maupassant: A Biographical Study* (1926); *Literary Blasphemies* (1927); etc. Translator of French classics.

BOYD, JAMES (July 2, 1888–Feb. 25, 1944); b. in Dauphin Co., Pa. Novelist. *Drums* (1925); *Marching On* (1927); *Long Hunt* (1930); *Roll River* (1935); *Bitter Creek* (1939); *Eighteen Poems* (1944).

BOYD, JULIAN PARKS (Nov. 3, 1903–); b. Converse, S.C. Librarian. *Number Seven: Alexander Hamilton's Secret Attempts to Control American Foreign Policy* (1964). Editor: *Miner's Essays of Poor Robert the Scribe* (1930); *Indian Treaties Printed by Benjamin Franklin* (with Carl Van Doren, 1938); *Anglo-American Union* (1941); *Declaration of Independence* (1945); *Papers of Thomas Jefferson* (to comprise about 50v., 1950–); *Susquehanna Company Papers* Vols. 1–4 (1962); etc. Librarian, 1940–52; prof. history, Princeton University, since 1952.

BOYD, LOUISE ARNER (Sept. 16, 1887–); b. San Rafael, Calif. Explorer, author. *The Fiord Region of East Greenland* (1935); *Polish Countrysides* (1937); *The Coast of Northeast Greenland* (with others, 1948).

BOYD, MADELEINE ELISE; b. St. Cirques, France. Literary agent, translator, author. *Life Makes Advances* (1939). Founder, Madeleine Boyd Literary Agency.

BOYD, MALCOLM (June 8, 1923–); b. Buffalo, N.Y. Episcopal clergyman, author. *Crisis in Communication* (1957); *Are You Running with Me, Jesus?* (1965); *Free to Live, Free to Die* (1967); *My Fellow Americans* (1970); *Human Like Me, Jesus* (1971); etc. Editor: *On the Battle Lines* (1964); *The Underground Church* (1968).

BOYD, MAURICE (Apr. 3, 1921–); b. Guthrie, Ky. Educator, author. *Cardinal Quiroga: Inquisitor General of Spain* (1955); *Eight Tarascan Legends* (1958); *American Civilization* (1964); *William Knox and Abraham Lincoln* (1966); *Contemporary America: Issues and Problems* (1968). Prof. history, Texas Christian University, since 1964.

BOYD, THOMAS [Alexander] (July 3, 1898–Jan. 27, 1935); b. Defiance, O. Novelist, biographer. *Through the Wheat* (1923); *The Dark Cloud* (1924); *Samuel Drummond* (1925); *Shadow of the Long Knives* (1928); *Simon Girty, the White*

Savage (1928); *Mad Anthony Wayne* (1929); *Light Horse Harry Lee* (1931); *In Time of Peace* (1935); *Poor John Fitch, Inventor of the Steamboat* (1935). *See* Fred B. Millett's *Contemporary American Authors* (1940).

Boyd, Woodward. *See* Peggy Shane.

BOYESEN, HJALMAR HJORTH (Sept. 23, 1848–Oct. 4, 1895); b. Frederiksvärn, Norway. Author. *Gunnar* (1874); *Tales from Two Hemispheres* (1876); *Falconberg* (1879); *Goethe and Schiller* (1879); *Ilka on the Hill-Top, and Other Stories* (1881); *A Daughter of the Philistines* (1883); *The Story of Norway* (1886); *The Modern Vikings* (1887); *Vagabond Tales* (1889); *Boyhood in Norway* (1892); *Literary and Social Silhouettes* (1894); *Essays on Scandinavian Literature* (1895).

BOYINGTON, GREGORY ["Pappy"] (1912–). Author. *Baa, Baa, Black Sheep* (1958); *Tonga* (1960).

BOYLAN, GRACE DUFFIE (Mrs. Louis Napoleon Geldert) (1862(?)–Mar. 24, 1935); b. Kalamazoo, Mich. Author. *The Old House, and Other Poems and Sketches* (1897); *If Tam O'Shanter 'd Had a Wheel, and Other Poems and Sketches* (1898); *The Supplanter* (1913); *Conquerors* (1928); etc.

BOYLE, KAY (Feb. 19, 1903–); b. St. Paul, Minn. Author. *Short Stories* (1929); *Wedding Day, and Other Stories* (1930); *Plagued by the Nightingale* (1931); *Year Before Last* (1932); *The First Lover, and Other Stories* (1933); *Gentleman, I Address You Privately* (1933); *My Next Bride* (1934); *The White Horses of Vienna, and Other Stories* (1936); *Death of a Man* (1936); *A Glad Day* (poems, 1938); *Monday Night* (1938); *The Youngest Camel* (1939); *The Crazy Hunter* (1940); *A Frenchman Must Die* (1946); *Thirty Stories* (1946); *"1939"* (1948); *His Human Majesty* (1949); *The Seagull on the Step* (1955); *Three Short Novels* (1958); *Generation Without Farewell* (1960); *Collected Poems* (1962); *Nothing Ever Breaks Except the Heart* (1966); *Pinky the Cat* (1967); *Pinky in Persia* (1968); etc.

BOYLE, VIRGINIA FRAZER (1863–Dec. 13, 1938); b. near Chattanooga, Tenn. Author. *The Other Side* (1893); *Brokenburne* (1897); *Devil Tales* (1900); *Serena* (1905); *Love Songs and Bugle Calls* (1906).

BOYLES, C. S. (1905–). Author. Writes under pen name "Will C. Brown." *Border Jumper* (1955); *The Nameless Breed* (1960); *Think Fast, Ranger* (1961); *Caprock Rebel* (1963); etc.

Boylston, Peter. Pen name of George Ticknor Curtis.

BOYNTON, HENRY WALCOTT (Apr. 22, 1869–May 11, 1947); b. Guilford, Conn. Critic. *Washington Irving* (1901); *Bret Harte* (1903); *A Reader's History of American Literature* (with T. W. Higginson, 1903); *Journalism and Literature, and Other Essays* (1904); *The World's Leading Poets* (1911); *James Fenimore Cooper* (1931); *Annals of American Book-Selling, 1638–1850* (1932); etc. Editor of many texts in English and American literature.

BOYNTON, PERCY H[olmes] (Oct. 30, 1875–July 8, 1946); b. Newark, N.J. Educator, author. *London in English Literature* (1913); *Some Contemporary Americans* (1924); *More Contemporary Americans* (1927); *The Rediscovery of the Frontier* (1931); *The Challenge of Modern Criticism* (1931); *Literature and American Life* (1936); *The American Scene in Contemporary Fiction* (1940). Editor: *American Poetry* (1918); *Milestones in American Literature* (1923); etc. English dept. University of Chicago, 1902–1941.

Boys' Life. New Brunswick, N.J. Founded 1912. Monthly. Published by the Boy Scouts of America.

Boys of New York, The. New York. Juvenile magazine featuring dime novel fiction. Founded 1875, by Norman L. Munro. It expired in 1894. The "Old Cap Collier" stories appeared in

it. The magazine was taken over by Frank Tousey in 1878 and merged with *New York Boys' Weekly.*

Boy's Town, A. By William Dean Howells (1890). Reminiscences of the author's boyhood.

Boy's Will, A. Book of poems by Robert Frost (1913).

BOYTON, NEIL (Nov. 30, 1884–Feb. 1, 1956); b. New York. Roman Catholic clergyman, editor, author. *Cobra Island* (1922); *Whoopee!* (1923); *In God's Country* (1923); *Where Monkeys Swing* (1924); *On the Sands of Coney* (1925); *Mangled Hands: A Story of the New Even Martyrs* (1926); *Mississippi Blackrobe* (1927); *In Xavier Lands* (1930); *Killgloom Park* (1938); *That Silver Fox Patrol* (1944); *Nothing Ever Happens to Me* (1951); *Circus at Madison Square Garden* (1955); etc.

Bozart. Atlanta, Ga. Bi-monthly poetry magazine. Founded 1927, by Ernest Hartsock. Absorbed *Contemporary Verse,* Jan. 1930; and *The Oracle,* Mar., 1930. Absorbed by *Westminster,* 1935, to form *The Bozart-Westminster.*

Bozart-Westminster, The. Oglethorpe University, Ga. Quarterly. Formed 1935, by the merger of *Bozart* and the *Westminster Magazine.*

BOZMAN, JOHN LEEDS (Aug. 25, 1757–Apr. 20, 1823); b. Oxford Neck, Md. Lawyer, historian. *The History of Maryland.* Contributed prose and verse to *The Port Folio,* edited by Joseph Dennie.

Brace, Benjamin. Pen name of Ben Frederick McCutcheon.

BRACE, CHARLES LORING (June 19, 1826–Aug. 11, 1890); b. Litchfield, Conn. Philanthropist, author. *Hungary in 1851* (1852); *Home Life in Germany* (1853); *The Norse-Folk* (1857); *The New West; or, California in 1867–1868* (1869); *The Life of Charles Loring Brace, Chiefly Told in His own Letters* (1894); etc.

BRACE, DONALD CLIFFORD (Dec. 27, 1881–Sept. 20, 1955); b. West Winfield, N.Y. Publisher. With Henry Holt & Co., 1904–19; one of founders of Harcourt, Brace & Co., 1919.

BRACE, GERALD WARNER (Sept. 23, 1901–); b. Islip, N.Y. Educator, author. *The Islands* (1936); *The Wayward Pilgrims* (1938); *Light on a Mountain* (1941); *The Garretson Chronicle* (1947); *A Summer's Tale* (1949); *The Spire* (1952); *The World of Carrick's Cove* (1957); *Winter Solstice* (1960); *The Wind's Will* (1964); *Between Wind and Water* (1966); *The Stuff of Fiction* (1969); etc. Prof. English, Boston University, since 1939.

BRACE, JOHN PIERCE (Feb. 10, 1793–Oct. 18, 1872); b. Litchfield, Conn. Educator, editor, novelist. *Tales of the Devils* (1847); *The Fawn of the Pale Faces; or, Two Centuries Ago* (1853). Editor, the *Hartford Courant,* 1849–63.

Brace, Timothy. Pen name of Theodore Pratt.

Bracebridge Hall. By Washington Irving (1832). Continuation of *The Sketch Book.* Squire Bracebridge is a lineal descendant of Addison's Sir Roger de Coverley.

BRACKENRIDGE, HENRY MARIE (May 11, 1786–Jan. 18, 1871); b. Pittsburgh, Pa. Lawyer, author. *Views of Louisiana* (1814); *History of the Late War* (1816); *Voyage to South America* (1819); *Recollections of Persons and Places in the West* (1834).

BRACKENRIDGE, HUGH HENRY (1748–June 25, 1816); b. in York Co., Pa. Jurist, poet, playwright. *A Poem on the Rising Glory of America* (with Philip Freneau, anon., 1772); *The Battle of Bunkers-Hill* (1776); *The Death of General Montgomery* (1777); *Modern Chivalry,* 4v. (1792–97). *See* Charles F. Heartman's *A Bibliography of the Writings of Hugh Henry Brackenridge* (1917); and Claude Milton Newlin's *The Life and Writings of Hugh Henry Brackenridge* (1932).

BRACKETT, CHARLES (Nov. 26, 1892–Mar. 9, 1969); b. Saratoga Springs, N.Y. Motion picture producer, screenwriter, novelist. *The Counsel of the Ungodly* (1920); *Week-End* (1925); *That Last Infirmity* (1926); *American Colony* (1929); *Entirely Surrounded* (1934); etc.

BRACKETT, EDWARD AUGUSTUS (Oct. 1, 1818–Mar. 15, 1908); b. Vassalboro, Me. Sculptor, poet. *Twilight Hours; or, Leisure Moments of an Artist* (1845); *The World We Live In* (1902); *My House, Chips the Builder Threw Away* (1904).

BRADBURY, BIANCA (Dec. 4, 1908–); b. Mystic, Conn. Author. *Half the Music* (1945); *Mutt* (1956); *Sam and the Colonels* (1966); *Lots of Love, Lucinda* (1966); etc.

BRADBURY, OSGOOD. Novelist. *Louise Kempton* (1844); *The Mysteries of Boston* (1844); *The Empress of Beauty: Second Series of Mysteries of Boston* (1844); *Mettallak* (1844); *Mysteries of Lowell* (1844); *The Mysterious Mother* (1844); *Henriette* (1845); *Walton* (1845); *Alice Marvin* (1845); *The Spanish Pirate* (1845); *Emily Mansfield* (1845); *Lucelle* (1845); *Monita* (1845); *The Eastern Belle* (1845); *Julia Bicknell* (1845); *Ellen Templeton* (1846); *Agnes Belmont* (1846); *Frances Carlton* (1846); *Hutoka* (1846); *The Belle of the Bowery* (1846); *Francis Abbott* (1846); *Isabelle* (1848); *Pontiac* (1848); *Elizabeth Howard* (1848); *Pierpold, the Avenger* (1848); *Manita of the Pictured Rocks* (1848); *The Old Distiller* (1851); *Therese* (1852); etc.; most of them anonymous. *See* Lyle H. Wright's *American Fiction* (1940).

BRADBURY, RAY [Douglas] (Aug. 22, 1920–); b. Waukegan, Ill. Author. *Dark Carnival* (1947); *The Meadow* (play, 1947); *The Martian Chronicles* (1950); *The Illustrated Man* (1951); *The Golden Apples of the Sun* (1953); *Fahrenheit 451* (1953); *Switch on the Night* (1955); *The October Country* (1955); *Dandelion Wine* (1957); *A Medicine for Melancholy* (1959); *Something Wicked This Way Comes* (1962); *The Machinery of Joy* (1963); *The Martian Chronicles* (screenplay) (1964); *Tomorrow Midnight* (1966); etc.

BRADBURY, WILLIAM BATCHELDER (Oct. 6, 1816–Jan. 7, 1868); b. York, Me. Music teacher, composer, compiler. Editor: *The Young Choir* (1841); *The Psalmodist* (1844); *The Shawn* (1853); *The Jubilee* (1858); *Fresh Laurels* (1867); and other collections of songs. He composed the music for several hymns, the two best known being "Just As I Am," and "He Leadeth Me."

BRADEN, ANNE McCARTY (July 28, 1924–); b. Louisville, Ky. Journalist, author. *The Wall Between* (1958); *HUAC: Bulwark of Segregation* (1964); *Southern Freedom Movement in Perspective* (1965). Editor, *Southern Patriot*, since 1957.

BRADEN, CHARLES SAMUEL (Sept. 19, 1887–); b. Chanute, Kan. Methodist clergyman, educator. *Religious Aspects of the Conquest of Mexico* (1930); *Modern Tendencies in World Religion* (1933); *The Scriptures of Mankind* (1952); *Jesus Compared* (1957); *Christian Science Today* (1958); *Spirits in Rebellion* (1963); etc. Editor, *Varieties of American Religion* (1936); etc. Founder (1937) and editor (1937–39), *World Christianity—A Digest*. Prof. history and literature of religions, Northwestern University, 1943–54.

BRADEN, JAMES A[ndrew] (July 10, 1872–June 28, 1954); b. Greensburg, O. Author. *Far Past the Frontier* (1902); *Connecticut Boys in the Western Reserve* (1903); *Captives Three* (1904); the *Auto Boys* series, 5v. (1908–13); *The Carved Sea-Chest* (1929); *That Boy at Roaring Brook Farm* (1931); etc.

BRADFORD, ALDEN (Nov. 19, 1765–Oct. 26, 1843); b. Duxbury, Mass. Editor, author. *Memoir of the Life and Writings of Rev. Jonathan Mayhew* (1838); *Biographical Notices of Distinguished Men in New England* (1842); *History of the Federal Government for Fifty Years* (1840); *History of Massachusetts for Two Hundred Years* (1835); etc. Editor, *The Boston Gazette*.

BRADFORD, AMORY HOWE (Apr. 14, 1846–Feb. 16, 1911); b. Granby, N.Y. Congregational clergyman, editor, author. *Spirit and Life* (1888); *Old Wine, New Bottles* (1892); *Spiritual Lessons from the Brownings* (1900); *Preludes and Interludes* (1911); etc.

BRADFORD, ANDREW (1686–Nov. 24, 1742); b. London, England. Pioneer printer, publisher. Founder, *The American Weekly Mercury*, Philadelphia, Dec. 22, 1719; *The American Magazine*, Philadelphia, Feb. 13, 1741, the first magazine published in America.

BRADFORD, GAMALIEL (Oct. 9, 1863–Apr. 11, 1932); b. Boston, Mass. Biographer, essayist. *Confederate Portraits* (1914); *American Portraits, 1875–1900* (1922); *Damaged Souls* (1923); *The Soul of Samuel Pepys* (1924); *Life and I, an Autobiography of Humanity* (1928); *Daughters of Eve* (1930); *Portraits and Personalities* (1933); etc. *See* Fred B. Millett's *Contemporary American Authors* (1940).

BRADFORD, JOHN (June 6, 1749– Mar. 1830); 1839); b. in Prince William Co., Va. First printer of Kentucky. Founder, *The Kentucke Gazette*, Aug. 11, 1787. He printed *The Kentucke Almanac* (1788). *See* Willard Rouse Jillson's *The First Printing in Kentucky* (1936).

BRADFORD, JOSEPH (Oct. 24, 1843–Apr. 13, 1886); b. (William Randolph Hunter) Nashville, Tenn. Actor, playwright, journalist, poet. *New German* (with F. Stinson, 1872); *Out of Bondage* (1876); *One of the Finest* (prod. 1882); *Poems* (1886); etc.

BRADFORD, RALPH (1892–); b. Kirby, Pa. Business consultant, lecturer, author. *The Purple Robe* (1929); *The White Way* (1931); *In the Image of Man* (1932); *Brief Interludes* (1934); *Three Men of Persia* (1935); *Legend of the River People* (1937); *Along the Way* (1949); etc.

BRADFORD, ROARK (Aug. 21, 1896–Nov. 13, 1948); b. in Lauderdale Co., Tenn. Novelist. *Ol' Man Adam an' His Chillun* (1928); *This Side of Jordan* (1929); *Ol' King David and the Philistine Boys* (1930); *John Henry* (1931) dramatized (prod. 1940); *Kingdom Coming* (1933); *Let the Band Play Dixie* (1934); *The Three-Headed Angel* (1937); *The Green Roller* (1949); etc.

BRADFORD, SARAH [Elizabeth] H[opkins] (b. 1818). Author. Pen name, "Cousin Cicely." Under own name: *The History of Peter the Great* (1858); *Harriet, the Moses of Her People* (1886); also, under pen name: *Aunt Patty's Mirror* (1854); *The Old Portfolio* (1854); *Ups and Downs* (1855); etc.

BRADFORD, THOMAS (May 4, 1745–May 7, 1838); b. Philadelphia, Pa. Printer, publisher. Founder, the *Merchant's Daily Advertiser*, Philadelphia, 1797, which was called the *True American* in 1798.

BRADFORD, WILLIAM (1589/1590–May 9/19, 1657); b. Austerfield, Yorkshire, England. Governor of Plymouth Colony, author. *History of Plimmoth Plantation* (written between 1630 and 1650, but not published in full until 1856). Book I was published in 1841. *See* edition published by The Mass. Hist. Soc., 2v. (1912), with notes by Worthington C. Ford. *See also* Peter Gay's *A Loss of Mastery: Puritan Historians in Colonial America* (1966).

BRADFORD, WILLIAM (May 20, 1663–May 23, 1752); b. Barnwell, England. Pioneer printer of the English Middle Colonies. Set up a printing press in Philadelphia in 1685, and the first one in New York in 1693. Began publication of the *New York Gazette* on Nov. 8, 1725.

BRADFORD, WILLIAM (Jan. 19, 1721/22–Sept. 25, 1791); b. New York City. Printer, publisher. Known as the "Patriot printer of 1776." Published the *Weekly Advertiser; or, Pennsylvania Journal*, Dec. 2, 1742. This paper existed until Sept. 18, 1793. Established *American Magazine and Monthly Chronicle*, Oct. 1757. Opened a bookstore and print shop in Philadelphia, in 1742, called "The Sign of the Bible."

BRADLEY, E[dward] SCULLEY (Jan. 4, 1897–); b. Philadelphia, Pa. Educator, biographer. *George Henry Boker, Poet and Patriot* (1927); *Henry Charles Lea: a Biography* (1931). Editor: *The Pioneer of James Russell Lowell* (1947); *Whitman's Leaves of Grass and Selected Prose* (1949). Editor, *General Magazine and Historical Chronicle,* 1945–56. Prof. English, University of Pennsylvania, since 1940.

BRADLEY, JOHN HODGDON, Jr. (Sept. 17, 1898–Aug. 18, 1962); b. Dubuque, Ia. Geologist, author. *The Earth and Its History* (1928); *Parade of the Living* (1930); *Autobiography of the Earth* (1935); *Farewell Thou Busy World* (1935); *Patterns of Survival* (1938); *World Geography* (1945); etc.

BRADLEY, MARY E[mily Neely] (1835–1898); b. Easton, Md. Novelist, poet. Pen name. "Cousin Alice." *Douglass Farm* (1858); *Handsome Is That Handsome Does* (1869); *Hidden Sweetness* (poems, 1887); *A Wrong Confessed Is Half Redressed* (1871); etc.

BRADLEY, MARY HASTINGS (Mrs. Herbert Edwin Bradley); b. Chicago, Ill. Traveler, author. *The Favor of Kings* (1912); *On the Gorilla Trail* (1922); *Caravans and Cannibals* (1926); *Alice in Jungleland* (1927); *Trailing the Tiger* (1927); *Alice in Elephantland* (1929); *Old Chicago Stories* (1933); *Pattern of Three* (1937); *A Hanging Matter* (1938); *I Passed for White* (an account by Reba Lee, 1955); etc.

BRADLEY, MILTON (Nov. 8, 1836–May 30, 1911); b. Vienna, Me. Publisher. Published *The Paradise of Childhood* (1869), the first kindergarten manual published in America. In 1893 he published the *Kindergarten Review.* He had previously published a children's magazine, *Work and Play.*

BRADLEY, PRESTON (Aug. 18, 1888–); b. Linden, Mich. Unitarian clergyman, author. *Courage for Today* (1934); *Life and You* (1939); *My Daily Strength* (1943); *Happiness Through Creative Living* (1955); *Along the Way* (1962); etc.

BRADLEY, VAN ALLEN (Aug. 24, 1913–); b. Albertville, Ala. Editor, author. *Music for the Millions* (1957); *Gold in Your Attic* (1958); *More Gold in Your Attic* (1961). Literary editor, Chicago *Daily News,* since 1948.

BRADLEY, WARREN IVES (Mar. 20, 1847–June 15, 1868); b. Bristol, Conn. Pen name, "Glance Gaylord." Author: *The Boys at Dr. Murray's* (1866); *Culm Rock* (1867); *Jack Arcombe: The Story of a Waif* (1868); *Mr. Pendleton's Cup* (1869); etc.

BRADLEY, WILL H. (July 10, 1868–Jan. 25, 1962); b. Boston, Mass. Book designer, type designer, art director, author. *Peter Poodle* (1906); *The Wonderbox Stories* (1916); *Spoils* (1928); *Lancelot and the Ladies* (1927); *Will Bradley, His Chap Book* (1955); etc. Editor: *The American Stage of Today* (1910). Editor, *Bradley: His Book* 1896–97; *The American Chapbook,* 1904–05; art director, *Collier's Magazine,* 1907–09; *Good Housekeeping,* 1911–13; *Century Magazine,* 1914–16. Founder, The Wayside Press, Springfield, Mass., 1895.

BRADLEY, WILLIAM ASPENWALL (Feb. 8, 1878–Jan. 9, 1939); b. Hartford, Conn. Editor, author. *William Cullen Bryant* (1905); *The Garden Muse* (poems, 1916); *Garlands and Wayfarings* (1917); *Old Christmas and Other Kentucky Tales in Verse* (1917); *Singing Carr, and Other Song-Ballads of the Cumberlands* (1918); etc.

BRADSHAW, LESLIE HAVERGAL; b. Liverpool, England, came to America in 1907. Producer, author. *The Right Sort* (1912). On staff, *Everybody's Magazine,* 1910–12.

BRADSHAW, MARION JOHN (Dec. 14, 1886–); b. Salem, O. Congregational clergyman, educator, author. *Third Class World* (1938); *Philosophical Foundations of Faith* (1941); *The Maine Scene* (1947); *Free Churches and Christian Unity* (1954); *Baleful Legacy* (1955). Prof. philosophy of religion, Bangor Theological Seminary, Me., 1925–57.

BRADSHAW, WESLEY. Possibly a pen name. Novelist. *Pauline of the Potomac; or, General McClellan's Spy* (anon. 1862); *The Volunteer's Roll of Honor* (1863); *General McClellan's Promise* (1864); *Washington's Vision* (1864); *The Angel of the Battlefield* (1865); *General Sherman's Indian Spy* (1865); *Brigham Young's Daughter* (anon. 1870).

BRADSTREET, ANNE DUDLEY (c. 1612–Sept. 16, 1672); b. in England, came to Massachusetts Bay in 1630. Poet. Her poems have been published in five editions. The first was called *The Tenth Muse Lately Sprung Up In America; or, Severall Poems, Compiled with Great Variety of Wit and Learning By a Gentlewoman In Those Parts* (London, 1650); the second, *Several Poems* (Boston, 1678), reprinted as the third in 1758; the fourth, *The Works of Anne Bradstreet in Prose and Verse,* edited, with additional unpublished material, by John Harvard Ellis (Charlestown, Mass., 1867); and the fifth, *The Poems of Mrs. Anne Bradstreet* (1897), with spelling modernized and an introduction by Chas. Eliot Norton. See Josephine K. Piercy's *Anne Bradstreet* (1965); *The Works of Anne Bradstreet,* ed. by Jeannine Hensley (1967).

BRADY, CYRUS TOWNSEND (Dec. 20, 1861–Jan. 24, 1920); b. Allegheny, Pa. Episcopal clergyman, novelist. *For Love of Country* (1898); *Stephen Decatur* (1900); *Border Fights and Fighters* (1902); *The Southerners* (1903); *Indian Fights and Fighters* (1904); *My Lady's Slipper* (1905); *As the Sparks Fly Upward* (1911); *Bob Dashaway, Privateersman* (1911); *Britton of the Seventh* (1914); etc.

BRADY, MARIEL; b. Stamford, Conn. Author. *Genevieve Gertrude* (1928); *Us Ladies* (1934).

BRADY, MATHEW B. (c. 1823–Jan. 15, 1896); b. Townsend, N.Y. Pioneer photographer. Took photographs of the men and battles of the Civil War, published as *Brady's National Photographic Collection of War Views and Portraits of Representative Men* (1870), a valuable source for numerous other books. Photographs of Abraham Lincoln are among the best. See James D. Horan's *Mathew Brady: Historian with a Camera (1957).*

BRAGDON, CLAUDE FAYETTE (Aug. 1, 1866–Sept. 17, 1946); b. Oberlin, O. Architect, poet. *The Golden Person in the Heart* (poems, 1898); *Architecture and Democracy* (1918); *Old Lamps for New* (1925); *The New Image* (1928); *Merely Players* (1929); *The Eternal Poles* (1930); *Delphic Woman* (1936); *More Loves Than One* (autobiography, 1938); *The Arch Lectures* (1942); *Yoga for You* (1943); etc.

Brahmin. Term used to designate the exclusive intellectual aristocrat, chiefly the cultured Bostonians. A literary cliché which is used both in a deferential or derogatory sense, depending on the individual writer and subject.

BRAINARD, DAVID LEGGE (Dec. 21, 1856–Mar. 22, 1946); b. Norway, N.Y. Army officer, arctic explorer, author. *Outpost of the Lost* (1929); *Six Came Back* (1940); both ed. by Bessie R. James.

BRAINARD, J[ohn] G[ardiner] C[alkins] (Oct. 21, 1796–Sept. 26, 1828); b. New London, Conn. Poet. *Letters Found in the Ruins of Fort Braddock* (anon., 1824), republished as *Fort Braddock Letters* (1827); *Occasional Pieces of Poetry* (1825); *Fugitive Tales* (1830); *The Literary Remains* (1832), ed. John Greenleaf Whittier; *The Poems* (1842), ed. Royal Robbins. Editor, *The Connecticut Mirror,* 1822–27.

BRAINERD, DAVID (Apr. 20, 1718–Oct. 9, 1747); b. Haddam, Conn. Presbyterian missionary to the Indians. His diary was published as *Mirabilia Dei,* in 1746, and as *Divine Grace Displayed* in the same year. In 1749 Jonathan Edwards printed additional portions of the diary, and in 1768 John Wesley published an abridgment. In 1822, Sereno E. Dwight published the diary in full, as did J. M. Sherwood in 1884.

BRAINERD, ELEANOR HOYT (1868–Mar. 18, 1942); b. Iowa City, Ia. Author. *Bettina* (1907); *How Could You, Jean?*

(1917); *In Vanity Fair* (1906); *The Misdemeanors of Nancy* (1902); *Our Little Old Lady* (1919); etc.

BRAINERD, ERASTUS (Feb. 25, 1855–Dec. 25, 1922); b. Middletown, Conn. Editor. From 1874 to 1878 he prepared five art books for James R. Osgood & Co., Boston. Editor, *The Daily News,* Philadelphia; *The Press* and the *Press Times* in Seattle; the *Seattle Post-Intelligencer;* the *San Francisco Call,* etc.

Brainerd, Norman. Pen name of Samual Richard Fuller, Jr.

BRAITHWAITE, WILLIAM STANLEY BEAUMONT (Dec. 6, 1878–June 8, 1962); b. Boston, Mass. Poet, essayist, anthologist. *Lyrics of Life and Love* (poems, 1904); *The House of Falling Leaves* (poems, 1908); *The Story of the Great War* (1919); *Our Essayists and Critics of Today* (1920); *Sandy Star* (poems, 1926); *The Story of the Years Between, 1918–39* (1940); *Poems, New and Selected* (1940); *Poems* (1948); *Bewitched Parsonage: The Story of the Brontës* (1950); etc. Editor: *Anthology of Magazine Verse,* 17v. (1913–29); *Anthology of Massachusetts Poets* (1931); *Anthology of Verse by Catholic Sisters* (1931); *Anthology of Magazine Verse for 1958* (1959); etc.

BRAKHAGE, STAN (Jan. 14, 1933–); b. Kansas City, Mo. Film-maker, author. *Metaphors on Vision* (1963); *The Moving Picture Giving and Taking Book* (1966). Conceived and produced "underground" films after 1953, including *Interim* (1953); *Desistfilm* (1954); *Reflections on Black* (1955); *Daybreak and Whiteye* (1957); *Cat's Cradle* (1959); *Blue Moses* (1962); *Dog Star Man, Parts I–IV* (1961–64); *Two Creeley McClure* (1966); *23rd Psalm Branch* (1967); etc.

BRALEY, BERTON (Jan. 29, 1882–Jan. 23, 1966); b. Madison, Wis. Poet. *Sonnets of a Freshman* (1904); *Songs of the Workaday World* (1915); *A Banjo at Armageddon* (1917); *In Camp and Trench* (1918); *Buddy Ballads* (1919); *Hurdy-Gurdy on Olympus* (1927); *Pegasus Pulls a Hack* (1934); *Morgan Sails the Caribbean* (1934); *Quaker Fortress* (1939); *Stand Fast for Freedom* (with Lowell Thomas, 1940); etc.

BRANCH, ANNA HEMPSTEAD (Mar. 18, 1875–Sept. 8, 1937); b. New London, Conn. Poet. *The Heart of the Road and Other Poems* (1901); *The Shoes that Danced, and Other Poems* (1905); *Rose of the Wind, and Other Poems* (1910); *Sonnets from a Lock Box, and Other Poems* (1929); *Last Poems* (1944).

BRANCH, E[dward] DOUGLAS (July 7, 1905–); b. Houston, Tex. Educator, historian. *The Cowboy and His Interpreters* (1926); *The Hunting of the Buffalo* (1929); *Westward: the History of the American Frontier* (1930); *The Sentimental Years, 1836–1860* (1934); *Travelways of Western Pennsylvania* (1938). Managing editor, *Frontier and Midland,* 1933–35; assoc. editor, since 1935.

BRANCH, HOUSTON (Mar. 5, 1905–Jan. 23, 1966); b. St. Paul, Minn. Publicist, author. *Dona Maria* (prod. 1922); *River Lady* (with Frank Waters, 1942); *Diamond Head* (with Frank Waters, 1948). Motion picture scenarist from 1926. Founder and director, American Library Foundation.

Brand, Max. Pen name of Frederick Faust.

BRAND, MILLEN (Jan. 19, 1906–); b. Jersey City, N.J. Novelist, poet. *The Outward Room* (1937); *The Heroes* (1939); *Albert Sears* (1947); *Some Love, Some Hunger* (1955); *Dry Summer in Provence* (poems, 1966); *Savage Sleep* (1968); *Fields of Peace* (1970); etc. Co-author (with Frank Partos) of screenplay *The Snake Pit,* (Screen Writers Guild Award, 1948). With Crown Publishers since 1952; senior editor since 1962.

BRAND, OSCAR (Feb. 7, 1920–); b. Winnipeg, Manitoba, Can. Folksinger, author. *Singing Holidays* (1957); *Bawdy Songs* (1960); *Folksongs for Fun* (1961); *Ballad Mongers* (1963).

BRANDE, DOROTHEA THOMPSON (Mrs. Seward Collins) (Jan. 12, 1893–Dec. 17, 1948); b. Chicago, Ill. Editor, author. *Most Beautiful Lady* (1935); *Wake Up and Live* (1936); *Letters to Philippa* (1937); *My Invincible Aunt* (1938). Assoc. editor, *The Bookman,* 1927–32; *American Review,* 1933–34; on editorial staff, from 1934.

"Branded Hand, The." Poem by John Greenleaf Whittier (1845). Story of Jonathan Walker, who was tried as a slave stealer in Pensacola, Florida, around 1840. "SS" was branded on his right hand ("Slave Stealer"). Walker related the story in his *Trial and Imprisonment of Jonathan Walker.*

BRANDEIS, MADELEINE [Frank] (Dec. 18, 1897–1937); b. San Francisco, Calif. Author. *The Little Indian Weaver* (1928); *The Little Dutch Tulip Girl* (1929); *The Little Mexican Donkey Boy* (1931); *Little Tom of England* (1935); *Adventure in Hollywood* (1937); *Little Eric of Sweden* (1938); etc.

Brandel, Marc. Pen name of Marcus Beresford.

BRANDT, JOSEPH AUGUST (July 26, 1899–); b. Seymour, Ind. Educator, publisher, editor, author. *Toward the New Spain* (1933). President, Henry Holt and Co., 1945–48. Prof. journalism, University of California at Los Angeles, 1949–55.

BRANDT, RICHARD BOOKER (Oct. 17, 1910–); b. Wilmington, O. Educator. *The Philosophy of Schleiermacher* (1941); *Hopi Ethics: A Theoretical Analysis* (1954); *Ethical Theory* (1959); *Value and Obligation* (1961). Prof. philosophy, Swarthmore College, since 1952.

BRANN, WILLIAM COWPER (Jan. 4, 1855–Apr. 2, 1898); b. in Coles Co., Ill. Editor. Founder, *Brann's Iconoclast,* 1891; editor, 1891, 1895–98. His writings have been collected and edited by J. D. Shaw, as: *Brann, the Iconoclast: A Collection of the Writings,* 2v. (1911); and *The Complete Works,* 12v. (1919).

BRANNON, PETER ALEXANDER (Aug. 30, 1882–Jan. 5, 1967); b. Seale, Ala. Curator, author. *By-Paths in Alabama* (1929); *Little Journeys in Alabama* (1930); *Turning the Pages* (1932); *Lillies, Lions and Bagpipes* (1934); *Corn-Bread, Creoles and Cajans* (1938); etc. Curator, Alabama Department Archives and History, 1910–41; archivist, 1941–55; director, from 1955.

Brann's Iconoclast. Waco, Tex. Monthly magazine. Founded at Austin, Tex., 1891, by William Cowper Brann; suspended that year; revived at Waco, 1895, by Brann and published until his death in 1898.

BRANT, IRVING [Newton] (Jan. 17, 1885–); b. Walker, Ia. Editor, author. *Dollars and Cents* (1933); *Storm Over the Constitution* (1937); *Life of James Madison,* 6v. (1941–61); *Road to Peace and Freedom* (1943); *The New Poland* (1946); *Friendly Cove* (1963).

BRASOL, BORIS [Leo] (Mar. 31, 1885–); b. in Province of Poltava, Russia. Lawyer, lecturer, author. *Critical Essays* (1910); *Socialism vs. Civilization* (1920); *The World at the Cross Roads* (1921); *The Elements of Crime* (1927); *Poushkin, the Shakespeare of Russia* (1931); *The Mighty Three, Poushkin, Gogol, Dostoievsky* (1934); *The Russian Wonderland* (1936); *Oscar Wilde, the Man, the Artist, the Martyr* (1938); etc.

Brass Monkey, A. Play by Charles H. Hoyt (prod. 1888). The story of a man who takes charge of a business he knows nothing about and makes a mess of it.

BRAUER, JERALD CARL (Sept. 16, 1921–); b. Fond du Lac, Wis. Educator, author. *Protestantism in America* (1953); *Basic Question for the Christian Scholar* (1954); *The Lutheran Reformation* (with J. Pelikan, 1955); *The Future of Religions* (1966). Editor: *Essays in Divinity,* 8v. (1967).

BRAUN, KURT (Sept. 13, 1899–); b. Berlin. Economist. *Union Management Co-operation* (1947); *The Right to Organize and Its Limits* (1950); *Labor Disputes and Their Settlement* (1955); *Labor in Colombia* (1962).

BRAUTIGAN, RICHARD. Author. *A Confederate General from Big Sur* (1965); *In Watermelon Sugar* (1969); *The Pill Versus the Springhill Mine Disaster* (1969); *Trout Fishing in America* (1969); *Rommel Drives Deep into Egypt* (1970); *Please Plant This Book; All Watched Over by Machines of Loving Grace; The Abortion* (1971).

Brave Bulls, The. Novel by Tom Lea (1949). Bullfighters in Mexico who conquer fear at decisive moments.

Brave Men. Collection of news reports from the Front during World War II, by Ernie Pyle (1944). Noted for their understated sympathy with the basic human concerns of American soldiers, particularly enlisted men, during the moral and psychological stress of combat.

BRAWLEY, BENJAMIN [Griffith] (Apr. 22, 1882–Feb. 1, 1939); b. Columbia, S.C. Clergyman, author. *A Short History of the American Negro* (1913); *The Negro in Literature and Art in the United States* (1918); *A Short History of the English Drama* (1921); *A Social History of the American Negro* (1921); *Doctor Dillard of the Jeanes Fund* (1930); *History of the English Hymn* (1932); *Paul Laurence Dunbar* (1936); *Negro Builders and Heroes* (1937); *The Negro Genius* (1937); etc. Editor: *Early Negro American Writers* (1935); etc.

BRAY, FRANK CHAPIN (May 7, 1866–Mar. 24, 1949); b. Salineville, O. Editor, author. *The World of Myths, A Dictionary of Universal Mythology* (1935); *Headlines in American History* (1937); *New Internationale—A Better World* (1945). Editor, "Topics of the Day" department in *Literary Digest,* 1894–99; editor *The Chatauquan,* 1899–1914; assoc. editor, *Current Opinion,* 1914–16; editorial staff, *Literary Digest,* 1920–33; etc.

BRAY, THOMAS (1656–Feb. 15, 1729/30); b. Marton, Shropshire, England. Anglican clergyman. Commissary in Maryland for the Bishop of London. Founder of many college and circulating libraries in the American colonies; including those at Annapolis, 1696; New York, 1698; and Charleston, 1700. Founder, the Society for Promoting Christian Knowledge, 1699; co-founder, the Society for the Propagation of the Gospel in Foreign Parts, 1701.

Braziller, George, Inc. New York. Founded 1954, by George Braziller, who is president. Publishes philosophy, science, art, history, architecture, and fiction.

Bread and Cheese Club, The. Founded, 1824, by James Fenimore Cooper at the City Hotel, in New York. Composed of a number of his contemporaries: Kent, Verplanck, Jarvis, Durant, DeKay, Wiley, Morse, Halleck, and Bryant.

Bread Crust Papers. Written by George Lippard for the *Spirit of the Times,* Philadelphia, in 1842. Henry B. Hirst was satirized as "Henry Bread Crust," and Thomas Dunn English as "Thomas Done Brown," a designation later revived by Poe.

Bread Line, The. By Albert Bigelow Paine (1900). Based on the famous bread line at Tenth Street and Broadway in New York City. Four men meet to lay plans for a magazine. The venture fails and the bankrupt men meet again later, at the bread line.

Bread-Winners, The. Novel by John Hay, which appeared first in the *Century Magazine,* 1883–84, and then in book form (1884), both times anonymously. Hay's name appeared on the title-page in the 1915 edition.

Breaking Into Print (1937). Stories by twenty authors telling how they started their writing careers. Reprinted from articles which appeared in the *Colophon,* 1930–37, with notes by Elmer Adler.

BREASTED, JAMES HENRY (Aug. 27, 1865–Dec. 2, 1935); b. Rockford, Ill. Educator, historian, Egyptologist. *A History of Egypt* (1905); *Ancient Records of Egypt,* 5v. (1906); *Development of Religion and Thought in Ancient Egypt* (1912); *Outlines of European History* (with J. H. Robinson, 1914); *Ancient Times* (1916); *History of Europe: Ancient and Medieval* (with J. H. Robinson, 1920); *The Dawn of Conscience* (1933); etc. University of Chicago, 1894–1935.

BREBNER, JOHN BARTLET (May 12, 1895–Nov. 10, 1957); b. Toronto, Ont. Educator, historian. *New England's Outpost-Acadia before the Conquest of Canada* (1927); *The Explorers of North America, 1492–1806* (1933); *The Neutral Yankees of Nova Scotia* (1937); *The Making of Modern Britain: A Short History* (with Allan Nevins, 1943); *North Atlantic Triangle—the Interplay of Canada, the U.S., and Great Britain* (1945); etc. Editor: *Classics of the Western World* (1927); etc. History dept., Columbia University, since 1925.

BRECHT, ARNOLD (Jan. 26, 1884–); b. Lübeck, Ger. Educator. *Prelude to Science* (1944); *Federalism and Regionalism in Germany* (1945); *The Political Philosophy of Arnold Brecht* (1954); *Political Theory* (1959). Graduate faculty, New School for Social Research, 1933–54.

Breck, Vivian. Pen name of Vivian Gurney Breckenfeld.

BRECKENFELD, VIVIAN GURNEY. Author. Writes under pen name "Vivian Breck." *High Trail* (1948); *Maggie* (1954); *White Water* (1958); *Kona Summer* (1961); etc.

Bred in the Bone. Story by Thomas Nelson Page (1905).

Bred in the Bone. Story by Elsie Singmaster (1925).

BRÉGY, KATHERINE MARIE CORNELIA; b. Philadelphia, Pa. (d. Jan., 1967). Lecturer, poet. *The Poets' Chantry* (1912); *The Little Crusaders* (1919); *Poets and Pilgrims* (1925); *Bridges* (poems, 1930); *From Dante to Jeanne d'Arc* (1933); *Ladders and Bridges* (poems, 1936).

Breitmann, Hans. Pen name of Charles Godfrey Leland.

BREMSER, RAY (Feb. 22, 1934–   ); b. Jersey City, N.J. Poet. *Poems of Madness* (1965); *Angel* (1967).

BRENNAN, FREDERICK HAZLITT (Sept. 23, 1901–June 30, 1962); b. St. Louis, Mo. Author. *God Got One Vote* (1927); *Pie in the Sky* (1931); *We Sail To-Morrow* (1934); *"Battleship Gertie"* (1935); *Stick-in-the-Mud* (1936); *Just Before the Battle* (1939); *The Wookey* (play, 1941); *Memo to a Firing Squad* (1943); *The Irish Lullaby* (1950); *One of Our H-Bombs Is Missing* (1955).

BRENT, HENRY JOHNSON (1811–Aug. 3, 1880); b. Washington, D.C. Journalist. Co-founder, *The Knickerbocker Magazine,* 1833. Editor, *The National Magazine and Republican Review,* 1839. Wrote for Porter's *Spirit of the Times* under the pen name "Stirrup."

Brent, Loring. Pen name of George Frank Worts.

BRENTANO, ARTHUR (Apr. 20, 1858–Jan. 28, 1944); b. Hoboken, N.J. Bookseller. Entered firm of Brentano's, in New York, in 1873; president, from 1915.

BRENTANO, LOWELL (Apr. 18, 1895–July 8, 1950); b. New York City. Editor, novelist, playwright. *The Melody Lingers On* (1934); *The Story Blows Over* (1934); *By That Sin Fell the Angels* (1937); *Bride of a Thousand Cedars* (with Bruce Lancaster, 1939). Co-author: *The Spider* (prod. 1927); *Zeppelin* (prod. 1929); *Family Affairs* (prod. 1929); *Great Lady* (prod. 1938); etc. Co-editor: *The Book of the Navy* (1944); *Invitation to Travel Series* (1945–48). With Brentano's Inc., 1918–33, as editor and vice-president.

Brentano's. New York. Bookstore founded by August Brentano. Brentano's Literary Emporium was started in the 1870's; in 1873 Arthur Brentano joined the firm. In 1882 August

Brentano, Jr., became president; in 1915, Arthur Brentano. Lowell Brentano was with the firm, 1918–33, first as editor, then as vice-president. The bookstore was incorporated in 1899 and published books from 1897 to 1933. Brentano's has always carried a large stock of books in foreign languages.

BRESLIN, HOWARD (1912–). Novelist. *Tamarack Tree* (1947); *The Silver Oar* (1954); *Shad Run* (1955); *Autumn Comes Early* (1956); *The Gallow Glass* (1958); *A Hundred Hills* (1960); *Concert Grand* (1963); etc.

BRESLIN, JIMMY (Oct. 17, 1930–); b. Jamaica, N.Y. Journalist, author. *Can't Anyone Here Play This Game?* (1963); *The World of Jimmy Breslin* (1967); *The Gang That Couldn't Shoot Straight* (1970).

BRETT, BRUCE Y[eomans] (Apr. 20, 1922–); b. Brooklyn, N.Y. Publisher. With The Macmillan Co., 1949–61; pres., 1958–61.

BRETT, GEORGE PLATT (1858–Sept. 19, 1936); b. London. With The Macmillan Co., 1879–1936; president of the firm for many years.

BRETT, GEORGE PLATT, JR. (Dec. 9, 1893–); b. Darien, Conn. Publisher. With The Macmillan Co., New York, 1913–61; president, 1931–58; chairman of board, 1958–61.

BRETT, WILLIAM HOWARD (July 1, 1846–Aug. 24, 1918); b. Braceville, O. Librarian. Compiled the *Cumulative Index,* which later became the *Reader's Guide to Periodical Literature.* Librarian, Cleveland Public Library, 1884–1918.

BRETT-SMITH, JOHN RALPH BRETT (Aug. 23, 1917–); b. Oxford, Eng. Publisher. With Oxford University Press, London, since 1946; with New York division, since 1955; pres., since 1958.

BREUER, BESSIE (Oct. 19, 1893–); b. Cleveland, O. Author. *Memory of Love* (1935); *The Daughter* (1938); *Bracelet of Wavia Lea, and Other Short Stories* (1947); *The Actress* (1957); *Take Care of My Roses* (1961).

BREWER, GIL. Author. *Angry Dream* (1957); *Red Scarf* (1958); *Little Tramp* (1960); *Appointment in Hell* (1961).

BREWER, LUTHER ALBERTUS (Dec. 17, 1858–May 6, 1933); b. Welsh Run, Pa. Publisher, book collector, author. *Some Lamb and Browning Letters to Leigh Hunt* (1924); *Wanderings in London* (1925); *Marginalia* (1926); *The Joys and Sorrows of a Book Collector* (1928); *Leigh Hunt and Charles Dickens* (1930); *Leaves from a Leigh Hunt Note-Book* (1932); *My Leigh Hunt Library,* 2v. (1932–38). His large collection of Leigh Hunt was bequeathed to the University of Iowa.

BREWER, NICHOLAS RICHARD (June 11, 1857–Feb. 15, 1949); b. High Forest, Minn. Artist, author. *Trails of a Paintbrush* (autobiography, 1938).

Brewsie and Willie. By Gertrude Stein (1946). An account of her meetings with American soldiers during World War II.

BREWSTER, DOROTHY (1883–); b. St. Louis, Mo. Educator, author. *Aaron Hill: Poet, Dramatist, Projector* (1913); *Dead Reckonings in Fiction* (with Angus Burrell, 1924); *Adventure or Experience* (with same, 1930); *Modern Fiction* (with same, 1934); *Modern World Fiction* (with same, 1951); *East-West Passage* (1954); *Virginia Woolf's London* (1960). Editor: *A Book of Modern Short Stories* (1928); *A Book of Contemporary Short Stories* (1937).

Brewster, Eliot. Pen name of James Noble Gifford.

BREWSTER, EUGENE VALENTINE (Sept. 7, 1871–Jan. 1, 1939); b. Bay Shore, L.I., N.Y. Editor, author. *The Art of Judging a Play* (1933); *The Devil is Dead* (1937); etc. Editor, *The Caldron,* 1894–1913, *Motion Picture Magazine,* 1911–26.

BREWSTER, OSMYN (Aug. 2, 1797–July 15, 1889); b. Worthington, Mass. Printer, publisher. Worked for Samuel Armstrong in Boston, and became a partner in publishing firm of S. T. Armstrong, Crocker and Brewster. This firm later became Crocker and Brewster, and were the publishers of the "Rollo Books," by J. S. C. Abbott. The firm merged with Houghton & Company in 1876.

BREWSTER, WILLIAM TENNEY (Aug. 15, 1869–Mar., 1961); b. Lawrence, Mass. Educator, editor, author. *English Composition and Style* (1912); *Writing English Prose* (1913). Editor: *Specimens of Narration* (1895); *Modern English Prose* (1904); *Specimens of Modern English Literary Criticism* (1907); etc. English dept., Columbia University, from 1900, provost of Barnard College, 1910–23. American editor, *University Home Library Series.*

Briarcliff Quarterly. Briarcliff Junior College, New York. Originally the *Maryland Quarterly* (q.v.). Edited by Norman MacLeod and others. Published such writers as Parker Tyler, Leane Zugsmith, W. C. Williams, Jean Garrigue, May Sarton. Discontinued 1948.

Brick. Pen name of Marcus Mills Pomeroy.

BRICK, JOHN. Novelist. *The Raid* (1951); *The Rifleman* (1953); *The King's Rangers* (1954); *Jubilee* (1956); *Panther Mountain* (1958); *Yankees on the Run* (1961); *Tomahawk Trail* (1962); *Captives of the Senecas* (1964); *They Fought for New York* (1965); *On the Old Frontier* (1967); etc.

BRICKELL, HENRY HERSCHEL (Sept. 13, 1889–May 29, 1952); b. Senatobia, Miss. Editor, critic. Editor: *O. Henry Memorial Award Prize Stories* (1941–46); *Prize Stories: The O. Henry Awards* (1947–51); *Writers on Writing* (1949). With the New York *Evening Post,* 1932–38, literary editor, 1934–38. Editor, Henry Holt & Co., 1928–33.

Bricks Without Straw. Novel by Albion W. Tourgée (1880).

BRIDENBAUGH, CARL (Aug. 10, 1903–); b. Philadelphia, Pa. Historian, educator. *Cities in the Wilderness* (1938); *Rebels and Gentlemen* (with Jessica Bridenbaugh, 1942); *Peter Harrison* (1949); *Seat of Empire* (1950); *Myths and Realities* (1952); *Cities in Revolt* (1955); *Mitre and Sceptre* (1962); *Vexed and Troubled Englishmen 1590–1642* (1968). Prof. history, University of California, since 1950.

BRIDGE, JAMES HOWARD (May 8, 1856–May 28, 1939); b. Manchester, England. Author. *A Fortnight in Heaven* (1886); *Millionnaires and Grub Street* (autobiography, 1931). Co-editor: *The Second Book of the Authors Club: Liber Scriptorum* (1921).

"Bridge, The." Long poem by Hart Crane (1930).

"Bridge, The." Poem by Henry Wadsworth Longfellow (1846).

Bridge of San Luis Rey, The. Novel by Thornton Wilder (1927). Based on the falling of an Inca bridge in Peru in 1714. Brother Juniper, who saw the accident, wonders why the five victims of the accident happened to be on the bridge at that particular moment. He reconstructs their lives for the benefit of the reader.

BRIDGES, HORACE JAMES (Aug. 31, 1880–Oct. 27, 1955); b. London. Lecturer, author. *Criticisms of Life* (1915); *Our Fellow Shakespeare* (1916); *On Becoming an American* (1919); *As I Was Saying* (1923); *The Emerging Faith* (1937); *Humanity on Trial* (1941); etc. Editor: *Erasmus in Praise of Folly* (1924).

Bridges, Madeline. Pen name of Mary Ainge De Vere.

BRIDGES, ROBERT (July 13, 1858–Sept. 2, 1941); b. Shippensburg, Pa. Editor, poet. Pen name, "Droch." *Overheard in Arcady* (1894); *Suppressed Chapters* (1895); *Bramble Brae* (poems, 1902). Asst. editor, *Scribner's Magazine,* 1887–1914; editor, 1914–30; lit. adviser, Charles Scribner's Sons, 1930–39.

BRIDGES, WILLIAM [Andrew] (Jan. 27, 1901–); b. Franklin, Ind. Editor, author: *True Zoo Stories* (1948); *Zoo Babies* (1953); *Zoo Pets* (1955); *Zoo Doctor* (1957); *Zoo Celebrities* (1959); *Walt Disney's Animal Adventures in the Lands of Ice and Snow* (1963); *A Zoo Man's Notebook* (with Lee S. Crandall, 1966); *The Bronx Zoo Book of Wild Animals* (1968). Editor and curator of publications, New York Zoological Park, since 1935.

BRIDGMAN, HELEN BARTLETT (Mrs. Herbert L. Bridgman) (1855–Oct. 17, 1935); b. Milwaukee, Wis. Author. *Gems* (1915); *Within My Horizon* (1920); *The Last Passion* (1925); etc.

BRIDGMAN, PERCY WILLIAMS (Apr. 21, 1882–Aug. 20, 1961); b. Cambridge, Mass. Physicist, author. *The Logic of Modern Physics* (1927); *The Nature of Physical Theory* (1936); *The Intelligent Individual and Society* (1938); *Reflections of a Physicist* (1950); *The Way Things Are* (1959); *Studies In Large Plastic Flow and Fracture* (1964); etc. Prof. physics, Harvard University, from 1919.

Brien, Raley. Pen name of Johnston McCulley.

BRIER, ROYCE (Apr. 18, 1894–); b. River Falls, Wis. Journalist, author. *Crusade* (1931); *Reach for the Moon* (1934); *Boy in Blue* (1937); *Last Boat from Beyrouth* (1943); *Western World* (1946). With San Francisco *Chronicle,* since 1926; news columnist, since 1937.

"Brierwood Pipe, The." Civil War poem by Charles Dawson Shanly.

"Brigade Must Not Know, Sir, The." Anonymous Civil War poem on the death of Stonewall Jackson.

BRIGANCE, W[illiam] **NORWOOD** (Nov. 17, 1896–Jan. 30, 1960); b. Olive Branch, Miss. Educator. *The Spoken Word* (1927); *Speech Composition* (1937); *Speech: Techniques and Disciplines in a Free Society* (1952); *New American Speech* (with W. G. Hedde, 1957). Prof. speech, Wabash College, 1922–36, and from 1938.

BRIGGS, CHARLES AUGUSTUS (Jan. 15, 1841–June 8, 1913); b. New York City. Episcopal clergyman, educator, author. *Critical and Exegetical Commentary on the Book of Psalms,* 2v. (1906–07); *American Presbyterianism* (1885); *History of the Study of Theology,* 2v. (1916); etc.

BRIGGS, CHARLES FREDERICK (Dec. 30, 1804–June 20, 1877); b. Nantucket, Mass. Editor, author. Pen name "Harry Franco." *The Adventures of Harry Franco: A Tale of the Great Panic* (1839); *The Haunted Merchant* (1843); *Working a Passage* (1844); *The Trippings of Tom Pepper* (1847); etc. Editor: *Bankrupt Stories* (1843). Founder, *The Broadway Journal,* 1845; editor, 1845–46; *Holden's Dollar Magazine,* c. 1850; *Putnam's Monthly Magazine,* 1853–57, 1868–69.

BRIGGS, LE BARON RUSSELL (Dec. 11, 1855–Apr. 24, 1934); b. Salem, Mass. Educator, author. *Routine and Ideals* (1904); *Girls and Education* (1911); *Riddles in Rhyme* (1927); etc. English dept., Harvard University, 1885–1925. President, Radcliffe College, 1903–23.

BRIGGS, L[loyd] **VERNON** (Aug. 13, 1863–Feb. 28, 1941); b. Boston, Mass. Psychiatrist, author. *Around Cape Horn to Honolulu in the Bark "Amy Turner"* (1926); *Experiences of a Medical Student in Honolulu* (1926); *California and the West, 1881, and Later* (1931); *Arizona and Mexico* (1932); *Capital Punishment Not a Deterrent* (1940); etc.

BRIGGS, MITCHELL PIRIE (Feb. 23, 1892–); b. Le Mars, Ia. Educator, author. *George D. Herron and the European Settlement* (1932); *If You Please!* (with Betty Allen, 1942); *Mind Your Manners* (1956); *Central Eastern Europe* (with others, 1946). Prof. history, Fresno State College, California, 1930–54.

BRIGGS, WILLIAM HARLOWE (July 22, 1876–July 31, 1952); b. Kalamazoo, Mich. Editor, playwright. *Behold Thy Wife* (prod. 1915); *Dakota in the Morning* (1942); etc. With Harper & Brothers, New York, from 1908.

BRIGHAM, CLARENCE SAUNDERS (Aug. 5, 1877–Aug. 13, 1963); b. Providence, R.I. Librarian, historian. *Memorial of Amos Perry* (1900); *History of Rhode Island* (1902); *Bibliography of Rhode Island History* (1902); *The Narragansett Indians* (1905); *Bibliography of American Newspapers,* in *Proceedings* of the American Antiquarian Society, 1913–28; *History and Bibliography of American Newspapers,* 2 v. (1947); *Journals and Journeymen* (1950); *Paul Revere's Engravings* (1954); etc. Librarian, Rhode Island Historical Society, 1900–08; American Antiquarian Society, 1908–30; director, from 1930.

BRIGHAM, GERTRUDE RICHARDSON; b. Lexington, Mass. Writer, lecturer, traveler. Pen name, "Viktor Flambeau." *The Study and Enjoyment of Pictures* (1917); *Red Letter Days in Europe* (under pen name, 1925). Art editor, *Washington Herald,* 1921–26; etc.

BRIGHT, JAMES WILSON (Oct. 2, 1852–Nov. 29, 1926); b. Aaronsburg, Pa. Educator, philologist. *West-Saxon Psalms* (1907); *Elements of English Versification* (1910); etc. Editor, *Hesperia.* Also editor of *Modern Language Notes,* 1916–25. Most of his library was sold to Goucher College.

BRIGHT, JOHN (Sept. 25, 1908–); b. Chattanooga, Tenn. Presbyterian clergyman, educator. *The Kingdom of God* (1953); *Early Israel in Recent History Writing: A Study in Method* (1956); *History of Israel* (1959); *Jeremiah* (1965); *The Authority of the Old Testament* (1967). Prof. Hebrew and Old Testament, Union Theological Seminary, since 1940.

BRIGHT, ROBERT (Aug. 5, 1902–); b. Sandwich, Mass. Author. *The Travels of Ching* (1943); *The Life and Death of Little Jo* (1944); *Georgie* (1944); *The Intruders* (1946); *The Olivers* (1947); *Me and the Bears* (1951); *The Spirit of the Chase* (1956); *Georgie's Halloween* (1958); *My Red Umbrella* (1959); *My Hopping Bunny* (1960); *Georgie and the Robbers* (1964); *Georgie and the Magician* (1966); *Gregory: The Noisiest & Strongest Boy in Grangers Grove* (1969); etc.

Bright Eyes. See Suzette La Flesche.

BRIGHTMAN, EDGAR SHEFFIELD (Sept. 20, 1884–Feb. 25, 1953); b. Holbrook, Mass. Educator, philosopher, author. *An Introduction to Philosophy* (1925); *Religious Values* (1925); *A Philosophy of Ideals* (1928); *The Finding of God* (1931); *Moral Laws* (1933); *The Future of Christianity* (1937); *A Philosophy of Religion* (1940); *Nature and Values* (1945); *Person and Reality* (1958); etc. Prof. philosophy, Boston University, from 1919.

BRILL, ABRAHAM ARDEN (Oct. 12, 1874–Mar. 2, 1948); b. in Austria. Physician, author. *Psychoanalysis* (1921); *Freud's Contribution to Psychiatry* (1944); *Lectures on Psychoanalytic Psychiatry* (1946); etc. Translator of various psychological works by Jung and Freud, etc.

BRILL, ETHEL C[laire] (1877–); b. in Minnesota. Author. *Boy Scout Crusoes* (under pen name, "Edwin C. Burritt," 1916); *The Boy Who Went to the East, and Other Indian Fairy Tales* (1917); *When Lighthouses Are Dark* (1921); *The Secret Cache* (1926); *White Brother* (1932); *Madeleine Takes Command* (1946); *Copper Country Adventure* (1949); etc.

Brimming Cup, The. Novel by Dorothy Canfield Fisher (1919). Laid in Vermont, the story centers around the development of Marise Crittenden's mature passion in a community in which passion is kept in check. She is faced with the choice of losing her husband or her new-found lover. A sequel to *Rough Hewn.*

BRINE, MARY D[ow]; b. New York. Poet, author of children's books. *Madge, the Violet Girl, and Other Poems*

(1881), containing her most famous poem, "Somebody's Mother"; *Hither and Thither* (1884); *Grandma's Memories* (1888); etc.

BRINIG, MYRON (Dec. 22, 1900–); b. Minneapolis, Minn. Author. *Singermann* (1929); *Wide Open Town* (1929); *This Man Is My Brother* (1932); *Sons of Singermann* (1934); *The Sisters* (1937); *May Flavin* (1938); *Anne Minton's Life* (1939); *You and I* (1945); *No Marriage in Paradise* (1949); *Street of the Three Friends* (1953); *The Looking-Glass Heart* (1958); etc.

BRININSTOOL, EARL ALONZO (Oct. 11, 1870–July 28, 1957); b. Warsaw, N. Y. Author. *Sonnets of a Telephone Girl* (1902); *Trail Dust of a Maverick* (poems, 1904); *The Bozeman Trail*, 2v. (with Grace R. Hebard, 1923); *A Trooper with Custer* (1925); *Capture and Death of Chief Crazy Horse* (1929); *Capt. Benteen's Story of the Custer Fight* (1933); *Little Feller* (1935); *Troopers with Custer* (1952); etc. Wrote daily column for the *Los Angeles Express*, 1905–14.

BRINK, CAROL RYRIE (Dec. 28, 1895–); b. Moscow, Idaho. Author. *Anything Can Happen on the River* (1934); *Caddie Woodlawn* (1935); *Mademoiselle Misfortune* (1936); *Baby Island* (1937); *All Over Town* (1939); *Harps in the Wind* (1947); *Stopover* (1951); *The Highly Trained Dogs of Prof. Petit* (1953); *The Headland* (1955); *The Pink Motel* (1959); *Snow In the River* (1964); *Andy Buckram's Tin Men* (1966); *All Over Town* (1968); *Two Are Better Than One* (1968); etc.

BRINKLEY, WILLIAM (Sept. 10, 1917–). Author. *Quicksand* (1948); *The Deliverance of Sister Cecilia* (1954); *Don't Go Near the Water* (1956); *The Fun House* (1961); *The Two Susans* (1962); *The Ninety and Nine* (1966); etc.

BRINLEY, KATHRINE GORDON SANGER (Mrs. Daniel Putnam Brinley) (d. Jan. 7, 1966); b. Brooklyn, N.Y. Author. *Away to the Gaspe* (1935); *Away to Cape Breton* (1936); *Away to Quebec* (1937); *Away to the Canadian Rockies* (1938); etc.

BRINNIN, JOHN MALCOLM (1916–); b. Halifax, N.S. Educator, poet. *The Garden Is Political* (1942); *The Lincoln Lyrics* (1942); *No Arch, No Triumph* (1945); *The Sorrows of Cold Stone* (1951); *Dylan Thomas in America* (1955); *The Third Rose: Gertrude Stein and Her World* (1959); *Arthur, The Dolphin Who Didn't See Venice* (1961); *William Carlos Williams* (1963); etc. Editor: *Modern Poetry* (with K. Friar, 1951); *Casebook on Dylan Thomas* (1961); *Modern Poets: An American-British Anthology* (with Bill Read, 1963); etc. English dept, University of Connecticut.

BRINTON, CHRISTIAN (Sept. 17, 1870–July 14, 1942); b. West Chester, Pa. Art critic. *Modern Artists* (1908); *Masterpieces of American Painting* (1910); *The Face of Soviet Art* (1934); etc. Compiler numerous catalogues of art exhibitions.

BRINTON, [Clarence] CRANE (Feb. 2, 1898–Sept. 7, 1968); b. Winsted, Conn. Educator, historian. *The Jacobins; an Essay in the New History* (1930); *English Political Thought in the Nineteenth Century* (1933); *A Decade of Revolution, 1789–1799* (1934); *The Anatomy of Revolution* (1938); *The Lives of Talleyrand* (1936); *The United States and Britain* (1945); *From Many, One* (1948); *Ideas and Men* (1950); *A History of Civilization* (with others, 1955); *History of Western Morals* (1959). Editor: *The Fate of Man* (1961). Prof. history, Harvard University, from 1942.

BRINTON, DANIEL GARRISON (May 13, 1837–July 31, 1899); b. Thornbury, Pa. Ethnologist, author. *The Myths of the New World* (1868); *American Hero Myths* (1882); *Aboriginal American Authors and Their Productions* (1883); *The Lenápé and Their Legends* (1885); etc.

BRISBANE, ALBERT (Aug. 22, 1809–May, 1890); b. Batavia, N.Y. Social reformer, American advocate and publicist for Fourierism. *The Social Destiny of Mankind* (1840);

Association (1843); *Ralphton; or, The Young Carolinian of 1776* (1848). Editor, *The Phalanx*, 1843–45. See Redelia Brisbane's *Albert Brisbane: A Mental Biography* (1893).

BRISBANE, ARTHUR (Dec. 12, 1864–Dec. 25, 1936); b. Buffalo, N.Y. Journalist. *Editorials from the Hearst Newspapers* (1906); *Mary Baker G. Eddy* (1908); *Today and the Future Day* (1925); etc. Managing editor, New York *World*, 1890–97; editor, New York *Evening Journal*, 1897–1921; later editor, New York *Daily Mirror*. Wrote columns "Today" and "This Week."

Briscoe, Margaret Sutton. See Margaret Sutton Briscoe Hopkins.

BRISTED, CHARLES ASTOR (Oct. 6, 1820–Jan. 14, 1874); b. New York City. Scholar, sports-writer, author. *The Upper Ten Thousand* (1852); *Five Years in an English University*, 2v. (1850); *Pieces of a Broken-Down Critic* (1858); *Anacreontics* (poems, 1872); etc. Wrote sports articles for the *Spirit of the Times* under the pen name of "Carl Benson."

BRISTED, JOHN (Oct. 17, 1778–Feb. 23, 1855); b. Sherborne, Dorsetshire, England. Episcopal clergyman, author, editor. *The Adviser*, 4v. (1802); *Edward and Anna* (1806); etc. Editor, *The Monthly Register*, Charleston, S.C., 1807.

BRISTOW, GWEN (Sept. 16, 1903–); b. Marion, S.C. Author. *Deep Summer* (1937); *The Handsome Road* (1938); *This Side of Glory* (1940); *Tomorrow Is Forever* (1943); *Jubilee Trail* (1950); *Celia Garth* (1959); *Calico Palace* (1970). With Bruce Manning: *Invisible Host* (1930); *Gutenberg Murders* (1931); *Two and Two Make Twenty-two* (1932).

"British Prison Ship, The." Narrative poem by Philip Freneau (1781). Account of the author's capture while in the ship *Aurora*, off Cape Henlopen, and of his experiences on the British prison ship *Scorpion* and hospital ship *Hunter*.

BRITT, ALBERT (Nov. 26, 1874–); b. Utah, Ill. Lecturer, educator, author. *The Wind's Will* (1912); *The Boys Own Book of Frontiersmen* (1924); *The Great Biographers* (1936); *Great Indian Chiefs* (1938); *Only the Brave Are Free* (with Donald R. Richberg, 1958); *The Hungry War* (1961); *Toward the Western Ocean* (1962); *An America That Was* (1964); etc. Editor, *Public Opinion*, 1901–06; *Railroad Man's Magazine*, 1906–09; *Outing*, 1909–23; editorial staff, Frank A. Munsey Co.; president, Knox College, 1925–36.

BRITT, GEORGE [William Hughes] (Oct. 5, 1895–); b. Millersburg, Ky. Journalist, author. *Christians Only* (with Heywood Broun, 1931); *Forty Years—Forty Millions: The Career of Frank A. Munsey* (1935); *The Fifth Column Is Here* (1940); etc. On staff, *New York World Telegram*.

Britt, Sappho Henderson. Pen name of Josiah Pitts Woolfolk.

BROADHURST, GEORGE HOWELLS (1866–Jan. 4, 1937); b. in England. Journalist, playwright. *The House That Jack Built* (prod. 1900); *The Crown Prince* (prod. 1902); *A Fool and His Money* (prod. 1903); *The Duke of Duluth* (prod. 1905); *The Man of the Hour* (prod. 1906); *The Coward* (prod. 1906); *The Mills of the Gods* (prod. 1907); *Bought and Paid For* (prod. 1911); etc.

Broadway. Comedy by Philip Dunning and George Abbott (prod. 1926). Depicts theatrical and night club life on Broadway, with a glimpse of bootleggers and their ways.

Broadway Jones. Play by George M. Cohan (prod. 1912).

Broadway Journal, The. New York. Weekly. Founded Jan. 4, 1845, by Charles F. Briggs, author of *Harry Franco: A Tale of the Great Panic*. Edgar Allan Poe was its greatest editor. Briggs had edited the first issues. Some of Poe's contributions were signed "Littleton Barry." The magazine was illustrated with woodcuts. Expired Jan. 3, 1846.

Broadway Magazine. New York. Founded 1898. It became *Hampton's Broadway Magazine,* in 1909. Suspended in 1912, after several further changes of title. Theodore Dreiser was editor in 1906.

BROCH, HERMANN (Nov. 1, 1886–May 30, 1951); b. Vienna. Author. Works translated into English: *The Sleepwalkers* (1932); *The Unknown Quantity* (1935); *The Death of Virgil* (1945).

BROCK, ROBERT ALONZO (Mar. 9, 1839–July 12, 1914); b. Richmond, Va. Historian. Editor, *Southern Historical Society Papers,* 1887–1914.

BROCKETT, LINUS PIERPONT (Oct. 15, 1820–Jan. 13, 1893); b. Canton, Conn. Physician, historian. *The Life and Times of Abraham Lincoln* (1865); *Our Great Captains* (1865); *The Camp, the Battlefield, and the Hospital* (1866); etc.

BROCKWAY, GEORGE POND (Oct. 11, 1915–); b. Portland, Me. Publisher. With McGraw-Hill Book Co., 1937–42; with W. W. Norton & Co. since 1942; pres., since 1958.

BRODHEAD, EVA WILDER McGLASSON (1870–1915). Novelist. *One of the Visconti* (1890); *Diana's Livery* (1891); *On Earthly Paradise* (1892); etc.

BRODHEAD, JOHN ROMEYN (Jan. 2, 1814–May 6, 1873); b. Philadelphia, Pa. Historian. *History of the State of New York,* 2v. (1863–1871), a projected third volume was never published.

BRODIE, BERNARD (1910–). Author. *Sea Power in the Machine Age* (1941); *Layman's Guide to Naval Strategy* (1942); *Strategy in the Missile Age* (1959); etc.

BRODKEY, HAROLD. Author. *First Love and Other Sorrows* (1958).

Brokaw, Clare Boothe. See Clare Boothe.

Broker of Bogata, The. Play by Robert Montgomery Bird, written for Edwin Forrest (prod. 1834).

BROKMEYER, HENRY C. (Aug. 12, 1828–July 26, 1906); b. Minden, Prussia. Philosopher, author. *A Foggy Night at Newport* (poetic drama, 1860); *A Mechanic's Diary* (1910). He made the first English translation of Hegel's *Larger Logic.* Founder, with William Torrey Harris, of the St. Louis Philosophical Society, Jan., 1866.

Brom. Pen name of Isaac Hill Bromley.

BROMBERG, WALTER (Dec. 16, 1900–); b. New York. Psychiatrist, author. *The Mind of Man—The Story of Man's Conquest of Mental Illness* (1937); *Mind Explorers* (with J. K. Winkler, 1939); *Crime and the Mind* (1948); *Man Above Humanity* (1954); *Mold of Murder* (1961); *Crime and the Mind* (1965); *How to Keep Out of Jail* (with Francis R. Bellamy, 1966).

BROMBERT, VICTOR HENRI (Nov. 11, 1923–); b. Berlin. Educator, author. *The Criticism of T. S. Eliot* (1949); *Stendhal et la voice oblique* (1954); *The Intellectual Hero* (1961); *The Novels of Flaubert* (1966); *Stendahl: Fiction and the Themes of Freedom* (1968). Editor: *Stendhal: A Collection of His Critical Essays* (1962); etc. Prof. Romance languages, Yale University, since 1961.

BROMFIELD, LOUIS [Brucker] (Dec. 27, 1896–Mar. 18, 1956); b. Mansfield, O. Novelist. *The Green Bay Tree* (1924); *Possession* (1925); *Early Autumn* (1926), Pulitzer Prize novel, 1927; *A Good Woman* (1927); *The Strange Case of Miss Annie Spragg* (1928); *Twenty-four Hours* (1930); *A Modern Hero* (1932); *The Farm* (1933); *The Man Who Had Everything* (1935); *It Had to Happen* (1936); *The Rains Came* (1937); *Night in Bombay* (1940); *Pleasant Valley* (1945); *Malabar Farm* (1948); *The Wild Country* (1948); *From My Experience* (1955); etc.

BROMLEY, ISAAC HILL (Mar. 6, 1833–Aug. 11, 1898); b. Norwich, Conn. Journalist. Pen name, "Brown." Founded Norwich *Bulletin* in 1858. Editor, Hartford *Evening Post,* 1868–72. With New York *Herald Tribune,* 1873–82, 1891–98.

BRONOWSKI, JACOB (Jan. 18, 1908–); b. Poland. Mathematician, author. *The Poet's Defense* (1939); *William Blake, A Man without a Mask* (1944); *The Common Sense of Science* (1951); *The Face of Violence* (1954); *Insight* (1964); *The Abacus and the Rose* (1965); *The Identity of Man* (1965); etc.

BRONSON, BERTRAND HARRIS (June 22, 1902–); Lawrenceville, N.J. Educator. *Joseph Ritson, Scholar-at-Arms* (1938); *Johnson Agonistes and Other Essays* (1946); *In Search of Chaucer* (1960); *Facets of the Enlightenment: Studies in English Literature and Its Contexts* (1968); etc. Editor: *That Immortal Garland* (1941); *Samuel Johnson: Selected Prose and Poetry* (1952); *The Traditional Tunes of the Child Ballads,* 3v. (1959, 1962, 1966). Prof. English, University of California, Berkeley, since 1945.

BRONSON, FRANCIS WOOLSEY (Feb. 6, 1901–Sept. 8, 1966); b. Minneapolis, Minn. Author. *Spring Running* (1926); *The Old Nick* (1928); *An American Hero* (1933); *Nice People Don't Kill* (1940); *The Uncas Island Murders* (1942); *The Bulldog Has the Key* (1949).

BRONSON, WALTER COCHRANE (Aug. 17, 1862–June 2, 1928); b. Roxbury, Mass. Educator, editor, author. *A Short History of American Literature* (1900). Editor: *English Essays* (1905); *English Poems,* 4v. (1907–10); *American Poems, 1625–1892* (1912); *American Prose* (1916); etc.

BRONSON, WILFRID SWANCOURT (1894–). Author. *Children of the Lea* (1940); *Horns and Antlers* (1942); *Hooker's Holiday* (1944); *Pinto's Journey* (1948); *Cats* (1950); *Freedom and Plenty* (1953); *Goats* (1959); *Beetles* (1963); etc.

Brook, Mrs. Alexander. See Peggy Bacon.

Brook Farm. Transcendentalist colony founded at West Roxbury, Mass., Apr. 1, 1841, by George Ripley, Theodore Parker, William Ellery Channing, Nathaniel Hawthorne, J. S. Dwight, Margaret Fuller, and others. Its official name was "The Brook Farm Institute of Agriculture and Education." Its purpose was "plain living and high thinking." Becoming associated with Fourierism in 1845, it collapsed in 1846. Its journal was *The Harbinger.* See J. T. Codman's *Brook Farm, History and Personal Memoirs* (1894), and Lindsay Swift's *Brook Farm, Its Members, Scholars, and Visitors* (1900).

BROOKE, [Charles Frederick] TUCKER (June 4, 1883–June 22, 1946); b. Morgantown, W.Va. Educator, author. *The Shakespeare Apocrypha* (1908); *The Works of Christopher Marlowe* (1910); *The Tudor Drama* (1911); *Shakespeare's Sonnets* (1936); etc. General editor, *The Yale Shakespeare.* English dept., Yale University, 1909–1946.

Brooklyn Eagle. Brooklyn, N.Y. Newspaper. Founded 1841, by Henry Cruse Murphy. Walt Whitman was editor from 1846 to 1848. St. Clair McKelway was another notable editor. John Aden was editorial writer, 1901–34; H. V. Kaltenborn was on the staff, 1910–30. Published by Frank D. Schroth at the time it was suspended in 1955.

BROOKS, AMY (Mrs. W. Rexter Loomis) (d. 1931); b. Boston, Mass. Illustrator, author. The *Randy* series, beginning 1900; the *Dorothy Dainty* series, beginning 1902; the *Prue* series, beginning 1908; the *Princess Polly* series, beginning 1910; and the *Rosalie Dare* series, beginning 1924; also: *At the Sign of the Three Birches* (1916); etc.

BROOKS, CHARLES STEPHEN (June 25, 1878–June 29, 1934); b. Cleveland, O. Author. *Journeys to Bagdad* (1915); *There's Pippins and Cheese to Come* (1917); *Chimney-Pot Papers* (1919); *Hints to Pilgrims* (1921); *Frightful Plays!* (1922); *Roads to the North* (1928); *Prologue* (autobiography, 1931); *English Spring* (1932); *An Italian Winter* (1933); etc.

BROOKS, CHARLES TIMOTHY (June 20, 1813–June 14, 1883); b. Salem, Mass. Unitarian clergyman, poet, translator. *German Lyric Poetry* (1842); *Aquidneck* (1848); *Songs of Field and Flood* (1854); *Poems, Original and Translated* (1885); etc. Translated various works of Schiller, Jean Paul Richter, Auerbach, Goethe, etc.

BROOKS, CHARLES WALKER (1912–); b. Richmond, Va. Poet. *Rhymes of a Southerner* (1936).

BROOKS, CLEANTH (Oct. 16, 1906–); b. Murray, Ky. Educator, author. *The Relation of the Alabama-Georgia Dialect to the Provincial Dialects of Great Britain* (1935); *Modern Poetry and the Tradition* (1939); *The Well-Wrought Urn* (1947); *Modern Rhetoric* (with R. P. Warren, 1950); *Literary Criticism: A Short History* (with W. K. Wimsatt, Jr., 1957); *The Hidden God* (1963); *Modern Poetry and the Tradition* (1963); *William Faulkner: The Yoknapatawpha Country* (1963); *The Writer and His Community* (1969); etc. Editor: *Understanding Poetry* (with Robert Penn Warren, 1938); etc. General editor: *The Percy Letters,* with David N. Smith, 6v. of projected 10v. 1944–61. Managing editor, with Robert Penn Warren, *The Southern Review,* 1935–41; editor, with same, 1941–42. Prof. English, Yale University, since 1947.

BROOKS, ELBRIDGE STREETER (Apr. 14, 1846–Jan. 7, 1902); b. Lowell, Mass. Editor, author. *Story of the American Indian* (1887); *Century Book for Young Americans* (1894); *Century Book of Famous Americans* (1896); *True Story of the United States* (1897); etc. Editor, *Wide Awake,* 1891–93. Served on editorial staff of *St. Nicholas, Publishers' Weekly,* etc., was with the publishing firms of D. Appleton; E. Steiger; D. Lothrop, etc.

BROOKS, EUGENE CLYDE (Dec. 3, 1871–Oct. 18, 1947); b. Greene Co., N.C. Educator, author. *The Story of Cotton and the Development of the Cotton States* (1911); *Education for Democracy* (1919); *Stories of South America* (1922); etc. Editor: *North Carolina Poems* (1912). President, North Carolina State College, 1923–34.

BROOKS, FRED EMERSON (Dec. 5, 1850–June 1, 1923); b. Waverly, N.Y. Poet. *Battle Ballads* (1886); *Old Lace, and Other Poems* (1894); *Pickett's Charge, and Other Poems* (1903); *The Gravedigger* (1916); etc.

BROOKS, GWENDOLYN (June 7, 1917–); b. Topeka Kan. Author. *A Street in Bronzeville* (poems, 1945) *Annie Allen* (1949; Pulitzer Prize for poetry, 1950); *Maude Martha* (1953); *Bronzeville Boys and Girls* (poems, 1956); *The Bean Eaters* (poems, 1960); *In the Mecca* (1968).

BROOKS, JAMES (Nov. 10, 1810–Apr. 30, 1873); b. Portland, Me. Editor. Founder, *The New York Evening Express,* June 20, 1836. He was assisted in its editorial management by his brother, Erastus Brooks (1815–1886).

BROOKS, JAMES G[ordon] (Sept. 3, 1801–Feb. 20, 1841); b. Red Hook (or Claverack), N.Y. Editor, poet. He collected his magazine verses and those of his wife, Mary Elizabeth Aiken Brooks, and published them as *The Rivals of Este, and Other Poems* (1829). The second part of this book, which contains his own poems, has a separate title page, *Poems* (1829), and may be found separately. He was on the editorial staff of the New York *Minerva, Morning Courier, New York Daily Sentinel, Albany Advertiser,* etc.

BROOKS, JOHN [Nixon] (Dec. 5, 1920–); b. New York. Author. *The Big Wheel* (1949); *The Man Who Broke Things* (1958); *The Fate of the Edsel* (1963); *The Great Leap* (1966); *Business Adventures* (1968); *Once in Golconda: The True Drama of Wall Street 1920–1938* (1969); etc. Editor: *The One and the Many* (1962).

Brooks, Jonathan. Pen name of John Calvin Mellett.

BROOKS, MARIA GOWEN (c. 1794–Nov. 11, 1845); b. Bedford, Me. Poet, novelist. Pen name "Maria del Occidente." *Judith, Esther, and Other Poems* (anon., 1820); *Zophiël* (poem, 1833); *Idomen; or, The Vale of Yunuri* (1843).

Brooks, Mary E[lizabeth Aiken] (Mrs. James G. Brooks). *See* James G. Brooks.

BROOKS, NOAH (Oct. 24, 1830–Aug. 16, 1903); b. Castine, Me. Editor, author. *The Boy Emigrants* (1876); *Abraham Lincoln* (1888); *The Boy Settlers* (1891); *Tales of the Maine Coast* (1894); *First Across the Continent* (1901); etc. While managing editor of the *Alta California,* San Francisco, he had as typesetter young Henry George, who later wrote *Progress and Poverty.* On editorial staff, *New York Tribune* and *New York Times.*

BROOKS, PHILLIPS (Dec. 13, 1835–Jan. 23, 1893); b. Boston, Mass. Episcopal bishop, author. *Yale Lectures on Preaching* (1877); *Essays and Addresses* (1892); etc. *See* Alexander V. G. Allen's *Life and Letters of Phillips Brooks,* 2v. (1900).

BROOKS, RICHARD (May 18, 1912–); b. Philadelphia, Pa. Author, film-maker. *The Brick Foxhole* (1945); *The Boiling Point* (1948); *Producer* (1951). Also screenplays.

BROOKS, ROBERT CLARKSON (Feb. 7, 1874–Feb. 2, 1941); b. Piqua, O. Educator, economist, author. *Corruption in American Politics and Life* (1913); *Political Parties and Electoral Problems* (1923); *Deliver Us from Dictators!* (1935); etc. Department of Political Science, Swarthmore College, since 1912.

BROOKS, SARAH WARNER (d. 1906). Poet, story writer. *The Legend of St. Christopher, and Other Poems* (1859); *Blanche; or, The Legend of the Angel Tower* (poem, 1861); *Even-Songs, and Other Poems* (1868); *My Fire Opal, and Other Tales* (1896); *Poverty Knob* (poems, 1900); *The Search of Ceres, and Other Poems* (1900); *Alamo Ranch: A Story of New Mexico* (1903).

BROOKS, VAN WYCK (Feb. 16, 1886–May 2, 1963); b. Plainfield, N.J. Critic, essayist. *The Wine of the Puritans* (1908); *John Addington Symonds* (1914); *America's Coming-of-Age* (1914); *The World of H. G. Wells* (1915); *Letters and Leadership* (1918); *The Ordeal of Mark Twain* (1920); *The Pilgrimage of Henry James* (1925); *Emerson and Others* (1927); *The Life of Emerson* (1932); *Sketches in Criticism* (1932); *Three Essays on America* (1934); *The Flowering of New England, 1815–1865* (1936); *New England: Indian Summer, 1865–1915* (1940); *On Literature Today* (1941); *Opinions of Oliver Allston* (1941); *The World of Washington Irving* (1944); *The Times of Melville and Whitman* (1947); *Malady of the Ideal* (1947); *A Chilmark Miscellany* (1948); *The Confident Years, 1885–1915* (1952); *The Writer in America* (1953); *Scenes and Portraits* (1954); *John Sloan: A Painter's Life* (1955); *Helen Keller, Sketch for a Portrait* (1956); *Days of the Phoenix* (1957); *From a Writer's Notebook* (1958); *The Dream of Arcadia* (1958); *Howells: His Life and World* (1959); *From the Shadow of the Mountain* (1961). Translator, works by Romain Rolland, Paul Gauguin, Georges Duhamel, and others.

BROOKS, WALTER ROLLIN (Jan. 9, 1886–Aug. 17, 1958); b. Rome, N.Y. Editor, author. *To and Again* (1927); *Freddy the Detective* (1930); *New York: An Intimate Guide* (1931); *Ernestine Takes Over* (1935); *The Story of Freginald* (1936); *Wiggins For President* (1939); *Freddy and the Ignormus* (1941); *Freddy and the Popinjay* (1945); *Jenny and the King of Smithia* (1947); *Freddy Rides Again* (1951); *Collected Poems of Freddy the Pig* (1953); *Freddy and the Dragon* (1958); etc.

BROOKS, WINFIELD SEARS (Mar. 6, 1902–); b. Somerville, Mass. Editor. *The Shining Tides* (1952); With Boston *American,* since 1920; managing editor, since 1940.

BROOM, LEONARD (Nov, 8, 1911–); b. Boston, Mass. Educator, author. *Removal and Return* (with Ruth Riemer, 1949); *Cherokee Dance and Drama* (with Frank G. Speck); *Sociology* (with Philip Selznick, 1955); *The Managed Casualty* (with John Kitsuse, 1956); *Transformation of the Negro American* (with N. D. Glenn, 1968). Prof. sociology, University of California at Los Angeles, 1953–57; University of Texas, since 1959.

Broom: An International Magazine of the Arts Rome, Berlin, New York. Monthly. Founded 1921. Edited by Harold A. Loeb, Alfred Kreymborg, Slater Brown, Matthew Josephson, Malcolm Cowley. Discontinued 1924.

"Broomstick Train, The." Poem by Oliver Wendell Holmes (1890).

BROSS, WILLIAM (Nov. 4, 1813–Jan. 27, 1890); b. Montague, N.J. Editor, author. *History of Chicago* (1876); *Legend of the Delaware* (1887). Founder (with John L. Scripps), the Chicago *Democratic Press,* 1852, forerunner of the Chicago *Tribune.* Established by will the Bross Foundation at Lake Forest College, 1890. Under this foundation, the college has created the Bross Library, the Bross Lectureship, and the Bross Prize.

BROSSARD, CHANDLER (1922–). Author. *Who Walk in Darkness* (1952); *The Bold Saboteurs* (1953); *The Scene Before You: A New Approach to American Culture* (1955); *The Double View* (1960); *The Girls in Rome* (1961); *The Spanish Scene* (1968); etc.

Brother Antoninus. See William Everson.

Brother Jonathan. New York. Weekly. Founded 1839, by Park Benjamin and R. W. Griswold. Noted for its serial fiction. Walt Whitman wrote poems for it. Expired 1843.

Brother Jonathan. Novel by John Neal (1825).

Brother Rat. Play by John Monks, Jr., and Fred F. Finklehoffe (prod. 1936). Based on life at the Virginia Military Institute.

Brother to Dragons. Verse narrative by Robert Penn Warren (1953). About Thomas Jefferson.

BROTHERHEAD, WILLIAM. Philadelphia bookseller, editor, author. *Forty Years Among the Old Booksellers of Philadelphia* (1891). Compiler: *The Book of the Signers: Containing Facsimile Letters of the Signers of the Declaration of Independence* (1861). Founder, *American Notes and Queries,* 1857. Established business as W. Brotherhead, 1849; suspended 1878–79; discontinued c. 1894.

BROTHERTON, ALICE WILLIAMS (d. Feb. 9, 1930); b. Cambridge, Ind. Poet, story-writer. *Beyond the Veil* (1886); *The Sailing of King Olaf, and Other Poems* (1887); *What the Wind Told the Tree-Tops* (1888).

BROUGHAM, JOHN (May 9, 1810–June 7, 1880); b. Dublin, Ireland. Actor, playwright. *Romance and Reality* (prod. 1848); *Po-ca-hon-tas; or, The Gentle Savage* (prod. 1855); *Dred; or, The Dismal Swamp* (prod. 1856); *Brougham's Dramatic Works,* v. I (1856); *Humorous Stories* (engraved title page, *The Bunsby Papers,* 1859); *Playing with Fire* (prod. 1860); *The Dramatic Review for 1868* (prod. 1869); etc., very few of which were ever published. Editor, *The Lantern,* New York, 1852. See *Life, Stories and Poems of John Brougham,* ed. William Winter (1881).

BROUGHTON, JAMES [Richard] (1913–); b. Modesto, Cal. Poet. *The Playground* (1949); *Musical Chairs* (1950); *The Right Playmate* (1952); *An Almanac for Amorists* (1955); *True and False Unicorn* (1957); *Tidings, Poems at the Land's Edge* (1965); *Look In, Look Out* (1968); *High Kukus* (1968),

BROUGHTON, LESLIE HATHAN (Oct. 3, 1877–1952); b. Delhi, N.Y. Educator, editor. Editor: *A Concordance to the Poems of John Keats* (with Dane Lewis Baldwin, and others, 1917); *A Concordance to the Poems of Robert Browning,* 2v. (with Benjamin F. Stelter, 1924–25); *Wordsworth & Reed: The Poet's Correspondence with His American Editor, 1836–1850* (1933); *Some Letters of the Wordsworth Family* (1942); *Robert Browning: A Bibliography* (with others, 1953); etc.

BROUN, HEYWOOD [Campbell] (Dec. 7, 1888–Dec. 18, 1939); b. Brooklyn, N.Y. Journalist, critic. *Seeing Things at Night* (1921); *Pieces of Hate* (1922); *The Boy Grew Older* (1922); *The Sun Field* (1923); *Gandle Follows His Nose* (1926); *Anthony Comstock, Roundsman of the Lord* (with Margaret Leech, 1927); *It Seems to Me, 1925–35* (1935); etc. Columnist, *New York Tribune,* 1913–21; *New York World,* 1921–28; Scripps-Howard Newspapers, 1928–39; *New York Post,* 1939. See Fred B. Millett's *Contemporary American Authors* (1940); and Dale Kramer's *Heywood Broun* (1949).

BROWER, BROCK (1931–). Poet. *Debris* (1967); *Other Loyalties* (1968); *Inchworm War and the Butterfly Peace* (1970).

BROWER, J[acob] V[radenberg] (Jan. 21, 1844–June 1, 1905); b. York, Mich. Explorer, archeologist, author. *The Mississippi River and Its Source* (1893); *The Missouri River and Its Utmost Source* (1896); *Quivira* (1898); *Harahey* (1899); *Kathio* (1901); *Kansas* (1903); *Minnesota* (1903); *Mandan* (1904); etc.

BROWN, [A.] CURTIS (Oct. 30, 1866–Sept. 23, 1945); b. Lisle, N.Y. Publishers' agent, author. *Contacts* (reminiscences, 1935). London representative, American Newspapers, 1898–1916. Founder, Curtis Brown, Ltd., London and New York, 1899, a literary agency.

BROWN, ABBIE FARWELL (d. Mar. 5, 1927); b. Boston, Mass. Author. *The Book of Saints and Friendly Beasts* (1900); *A Pocketful of Posies* (poems, 1902); *Heart of New England* (poems, 1920); *The Boyhood of Edward MacDowell* (1924); *The Silver Star* (poems, 1926); etc.

BROWN, ALEXANDER (Sept. 5, 1843–Aug. 25, 1906); b. Glenmore, Va. Historian. *New Views of Early Virginia History, 1606–1619* (1886); *The Genesis of the United States,* 2v. (1890); *The First Republic in America* (1898); *English Politics in Early Virginia* (1901); etc.

BROWN, ALICE (Dec. 5, 1857–June 21, 1948); b. Hampton Falls, N.H. Novelist. *Fools of Nature* (1887); *Meadow-Grass* (1895); *By Oak and Thorn* (1896); *The Road to Castaly* (poems, 1896); *The Day of His Youth* (1897); *Mercy Warren* (1898); *Tiverton Tales* (1899); *Margaret Warrener* (1901); *The Mannerings* (1903); *The County Road* (1906); *The Story of Thyrza* (1909); *Country Neighbors* (1910); *John Winterbourne's Family* (1910); *The One-Footed Fairy and Other Stories* (1911); *Robin Hood's Barn* (1913); *Children of Earth* (1915); *Bromley Neighborhood* (1917); *Homespun and Gold* (1920); *The Wind Between the Worlds* (1920); *One Act Plays* (1921); *Louise Imogen Guiney* (1921); *Old Crow* (1922); *Ellen Prior* (poem, 1923); *The Willoughbys* (1935); etc.

BROWN, ARTHUR CHARLES LEWIS (Aug. 18, 1869–June 28, 1946); b. Avon, N.Y. Educator, author. *Iwain: A Study in the Origins of Arthurian Romance* (1903); *The Origin of the Grail Legend* (1943). Editor, *Macbeth* (in the Tudor Shakespeare, 1911); etc. Prof. English, Northwestern University, 1906–39.

BROWN, ARTHUR JUDSON (Dec. 3, 1856–Jan. 11, 1963); b. Holliston, Mass. Presbyterian clergyman, traveler, author. *The New Era in the Philippines* (1903); *New Forces in Old China* (1904); *The Foreign Missionary* (1907); *The Mastery of the Far East* (1919); *Japan in the World of To-Day* (1928); *Memoirs of a Centenarian* (1957); etc.

BROWN, BOB [Robert Carlton] (June 14, 1886–); b. Chicago, Ill. Author. *What Happened to Mary* (1913); *1450–1950* (1929); *Let There Be Beer!* (1932); *Can We Co-operate?* (1940); *The Complete Book of Cheese* (1955); etc.

BROWN, BOLTON COIT (Nov. 27, 1865–Sept. 15, 1936); b. Dresden, N.Y. Artist, author. *The Painter's Palette* (1915); *Lithography* (1923); *Lithography for Artists* (1930). One of the founders of the Woodstock Art Colony, Woodstock, N.Y. He assisted George Bellows.

BROWN, CARLETON (July 15, 1869–June 25, 1941); b. Oberlin, O. Educator, philologist. Editor: *Religious Lyrics of the XIVth Century* (1924); *English Lyrics of the XIIIth Century* (1932); *Religious Lyrics of the XVth Century* (1939); etc. Prof. English, New York University, 1927–39.

Brown, Caroline. Pen name of Caroline Virginia Krout.

BROWN, CHARLES BROCKDEN (Jan. 17, 1771–Feb. 22, 1810); b. Philadelphia, Pa. Editor, novelist. *Alcuin: A Dialogue* (1798); *Wieland; or, The Transformation* (1798); *Arthur Mervyn; or, Memoirs of the Year 1793,* 2v. (1799–1800); *Ormond; or, The Secret Witness* (1799); *Edgar Huntley; or, Memoirs of a Sleep-Walker,* 3v. (1799); *Clara Howard: In a Series of Letters* (1801), republished as *Philip Stanley; or, The Enthusiasm of Love* (1807); *Jane Talbot* (1801); *The Novels,* 7v. (1827). Editor, *The Monthly Magazine, and American Review,* 1799–1800; *The American Review, and Literary Journal,* with others, 1801–02; *The Literary Magazine, and American Register,* 1803–07. See William Dunlap's *The Life of Charles Brockden Brown,* 2v. (1815); Martin S. Vilas's *Charles Brockden Brown; A Study of Early American Fiction* (1904); and David Lee Clark's *Charles Brockden Brown: A Critical Biography* (1923); Marisi Bulgheroni's *La Tentazione della chimera: Charles Brockden Brown e le origini del romanzo Americano* (1965).

BROWN, CHARLES REYNOLDS (Oct. 1, 1862–Nov. 28, 1950); b. Bethany, W.Va. Congregational clergyman, educator, author. *The Main Points* (1899); *The Modern Man's Religion* (1911); *Yale Talks* (1919); *The Art of Preaching* (1922); *These Twelve* (1926); *The Making of a Minister* (1927); *My Own Yesterdays* (1931); *They Were Giants* (1934); *Being Made Over* (1939); *Dreams Come True* (1944); etc. Dean, Divinity School, Yale University, 1911–28.

Brown, Clara Maude. See Clara Maude Brown Arny.

BROWN, CLAUDE (Feb. 23, 1937–); b. New York. Author. *Manchild in the Promised Land* (1965).

BROWN, DAVID PAUL (Sept. 28, 1795–July 11, 1872); b. Philadelphia, Pa. Orator, playwright. *Sertorius; or, The Roman Patriot* (drama in verse, 1830); *The Prophet of St. Paul's* (1830); *The Forum,* 2v. (autobiography, 1856); etc.

Brown, Demetra Vaka Kenneth. See Demetra Vaka.

BROWN, EDNA ADELAIDE (Mar. 7, 1875–June 23, 1944); b. Providence, R.I. Librarian, author. *Uncle David's Boys* (1913); *The Spanish Chest* (1917); *Journey's End* (1921); *Polly's Shop* (1931); *How Many Miles to Babylon?* (1941); etc.

BROWN, ELINOR LUELLA BAADE (Jan. 1, 1915–); b. Bennett, Neb. Author. *Fall Festival Book* (1953); *Bulletin Board Bullets* (1957); *Nebraska Travel-Rama* (1964); *Architectural Wonder of the World* (1965); etc.

BROWN, ELMER ELLSWORTH (Aug. 28, 1861–Nov. 3, 1934); b. Kiantone, N.Y. Educator, author. *The Origin of American State Universities* (1905); *Government by Influence, and Other Addresses* (1909); *Victory, and Other Verse* (1923); etc. Chancellor, New York University, 1911–33.

BROWN, EMMA ELIZABETH (Oct. 18, 1847–deceased); b. Concord, N.H. Author. *A Hundred Years Ago* (poems, 1876); *The Child Toilers of Boston Streets* (1879); *Life of*

Oliver Wendell Holmes (1884); *Life of James Russell Lowell* (1888); etc.

BROWN, [Ernest] FRANCIS (Dec. 31, 1903–); b. Amherst, Mass. Editor, author. *Joseph Hamley, Colonial Radical* (1931); *Edmund Niles Huyck: The Story of a Liberal* (1936); *The War in Maps* (1942); *Raymond of the Times* (1951). Editor: *Highlights of Modern Literature* (1954); *Page 2: The Best of Speaking of Books from the New York Times Book Review* (1969). Editor, New York Times Book Review, 1949–70.

BROWN, ESTELLE AUBREY (1877–Jan. 23, 1958); b. Constable, N.Y. Author. *A Woman of Character* (1924); *With Trailing Banners* (1930); *Around Two Worlds* (1938); *Stubborn Fool* (1952).

BROWN, FRANK CHOUTEAU (Jan. 1876–Nov. 18, 1947); b. Minneapolis, Minn, Architect, designer, author. *Book Plate Designs* (1905); *New England Colonial Houses* (1915); etc. Editor, *Architectural Review,* 1907–19; designer of many book plates, book covers, stage settings, etc.

BROWN, FREDRIC (Oct. 29, 1906–); b. Cincinnati, O. Novelist. *The Fabulous Clipjoint* (1947); *The Dead Ringer* (1948); *The Bloody Moonlight* (1949); *Death Has Many Doors* (1951); *We All Killed Grandma* (1952); *His Name Was Death* (1954); *Martians, Go Home* (1955); *The Lenient Beast* (1956); *One for the Road* (1958); *The Late Lamented* (1959); *The Murderers* (1961); *The Five-Day Nightmare* (1962); *Mrs. Murphy's Underpants* (1963); *The Shaggy Dog, and Other Murders* (1963); *Daymares* (1968); etc.

BROWN, GEORGE ROTHWELL (d. July 29, 1960) Correspondent, author. *Señora Slim's Señorita* (1902); *The Whispering Cupid* (1909); *The Tribulations of Trinity Tim* (1911); *The Other Girl* (1913); *This Is the Life* (1916); *Beyond the Sunset* (1919); *Washington, A Not Too Serious History* (1930); *The Speaker of the House* (1932). Editor: *Reminiscences of Senator William M. Stewart of Nevada* (1908). Political columnist, Hearst newspapers, from 1929.

BROWN, GOOLD (Mar. 7, 1791–Mar. 31, 1857); b. Providence, R.I. Grammarian. *Institutes of English Grammar* (1823); *First Lines of English Grammar* (1823); *Grammar of English Grammars* (1851).

BROWN, GWETHALYN GRAHAM ERICHSEN (d. Nov. 21, 1965) Novelist. Wrote under pen name "Gwethalyn Graham." *Earth and High Heaven* (1944); *Swiss Sonata* (1948).

BROWN, HARRISON SCOTT (Sept. 26, 1917–); b. Sheridan, Wyo. Chemist, educator, author. *Must Destruction Be Our Destiny?* (1946); *The Challenge of Man's Future* (1954); *The Next Hundred Years* (1957); *The Cassiopeia Affair* (1968). Prof. geochemistry, California Institute of Technology, since 1951.

BROWN, HARRY [Peter M'Nab] (Apr. 30, 1917–); b. Portland, Me. Author. *The End of a Decade* (poems, 1941); *The Poem of Bunker Hill* (1941); *The Violent* (1943); *A Walk in the Sun* (1944); *Artie Greengroin, Pfc.* (1945); *A Sound of Hunting* (play, 1946); *The Beast in His Hunger* (poems, 1949); *The Stars in Their Courses* (1960); *A Quiet Place to Work* (1968).

BROWN, HELEN DAWES (May 15, 1857–Sept. 5, 1941); b. Concord, Mass. Author. *Two College Girls* (1886); *The Petrie Estate* (1893); *Little Miss Phoebe Gay* (1895); *Her Sixteenth Year* (1901); *A Book of Little Boys* (1904); *Mr. Tuckerman's Nieces* (1907); *Orphans* (1911); *How Phoebe Found Herself* (1912); *Talks to Freshman Girls* (1914); *Little Jean* (1918); *Snapshots of Nancy and Brothers* (1939); etc.

BROWN, HELEN GURLEY (Feb. 18, 1922–); b. Green Forest, Ark. Editor, author. *Sex and the Single Girl* (1962); *Sex and the Office* (1965); *Outrageous Opinions* (1966); *Sex and the New Single Girl* (1970). Editor-in-chief, *Cosmopolitan,* since 1965.

BROWN, HENRY COLLINS (July 17, 1863–July 13, 1961); b. Glasgow, Scotland. Author. *Fifth Avenue Old and New, 1824–1924* (1924); *The Elegant Eighties* (1926); *The Golden Nineties* (1927); *The Story of Old New York* (1934); *Brown Stone Fronts and Saratoga Trunks* (1935); *A Mind Mislaid* (1937); *The Lordly Hudson* (1937); *Lincoln in New York* (1938) etc. Compiler: *Valentine's Manual* (1916–28).

BROWN, H[oward] CLARK (Jan. 27, 1898–); b. Charles City, Ia. Author. Pen name, "Donald Thistle." *Songs of the Iowa Prairie* (1921); *Appleseed Johnny* (poetic drama, 1927); *From My Medicine Sac* (1939); etc.

BROWN, H[ubert] RAP [Geroid] (1943–). Black leader, author. *Die, Nigger, Die!* (1969).

Brown, Irving. Pen name of William Taylor Adams.

BROWN, IRVING H[enry] (Oct. 29, 1888–Dec. 28, 1940); b. Madison, Wis. Educator, author. *Nights and Days on the Gypsy Trail* (1922); *Leconte de Lisle* (1924); *Gypsy Fires in America* (1924); *Deep Song* (1929); *Romany Road* (1932).

BROWN, JAMES (May 19, 1800–Mar. 10, 1855); b. Acton, Mass. Publisher, bookseller. With Hilliard, Gray & Co., Boston, 1818–1837; with Charles C. Little & Co., Boston, later Little, Brown & Co., 1837–1855.

BROWN, JOE DAVID (May 12, 1915–); b. Birmingham, Ala. Author. *Stars in My Crown* (1947); *The Freeholder* (1949); *Kings Go Forth* (1956); *India* (1963); *Sex in The 60's: A Candid Look at The Age of Mini-Morals* (with *Time* editors, 1968).

BROWN, JOHN MASON (July 3, 1900–Mar. 16, 1969); b. Louisville, Ky. Drama critic. *The Modern Theatre in Revolt* (1929); *Upstage; The American Theatre in Performance* (1930); *Letters from Greenroom Ghosts* (1934); *The Art of Playgoing* (1936); *Two on the Aisle* (1938); *Broadway in Review* (1940); *To All Hands* (1943); *Seeing Things* (1946); *Morning Faces* (1949); *Through These Men* (1956); *Dramatis Personae* (1963); etc. Drama editor, *Theatre Arts Monthly,* 1924–28; drama critic, *New York Post,* 1929–41; *Saturday Review,* 1944–53.

BROWN, KENNETH (Mar. 9, 1868–); b. Chicago, Ill. Author. *Eastover Court House* (with Henry Burnham Boone, 1901); *The Redfields Succession* (with same, 1903); *Sirocco* (1906); *The First Secretary* (with wife, Demetra Vaka, 1907); *The Duke's Price* (with wife, 1910); *In the Shadow of Islam* (with wife, 1911); *Two Boys in a Gyrocar* (1911); *In Pawn to a Throne* (with wife, 1919); *Putter Perkins* (1923); *The Medchester Club* (1938); etc.

BROWN, MRS. KENNETH. *See* Demetra Vaka.

BROWN, KENNETH H. (Mar. 9, 1936–); b. Brooklyn, N.Y. Playwright. *The Brig* (1965;) *The Narrows* (1970).

BROWN, KENNETH IRVING (Apr. 27, 1896–); b. Brooklyn, N.Y. Foundation director, author. *Campus Decade* (1940); *Not Minds Alone* (1954). Executive director, The Danforth Foundation, since 1950.

BROWN, L[awrence] GUY (Mar. 31, 1895–); b. Macomb, Ill. Educator. *Immigration: Culture Conflicts and Social Adjustment* (1933); *Social Psychology: The Natural History of Human Nature* (1934); *Social Pathology: Personal and Social Disorganization* (1942). Prof. sociology, University of Rhode Island, since 1946.

BROWN, LEE D[olph] (July 25, 1890–); b. Freedom, Md. Author. *The Yankee in the British Zone* (with Ewen Cameron MacVeagh, 1920); *Perkins Predicament* (1923); *Destiny Is a Woman* (1938).

Brown, Mahlon A. Pen name of William Henry Peck.

BROWN, MARCIA [Joan] (July 13, 1918–); b. Rochester, N.Y. Artist, author. Author and illustrator: *The Little Carousel* (1946); *Stone Soup* (1947); *Skipper John's Cook* (1951); *Once a Mouse* (1961); *Backbone of the King* (1966); *The Neighbors* (1967); *How Hippo!* (1969); etc.

Brown, Nancy. Pen name of Annie Louise Leslie.

BROWN, NORMAN O[liver] (Sept. 25, 1913–); b. El Oro, Mex. Educator. *Hermes the Thief* (1947); *Life Against Death* (1959). *Love's Body* (1966). Classics faculty, Wesleyan University, since 1946.

BROWN, PHOEBE HINSDALE (May 1, 1783–Aug. 10, 1861); b. Canaan, N.Y. Author, hymn writer. *The Tree and Its Fruits; or, Narratives from Real Life* (1836). Her best known hymn is "I love to steal a while away."

BROWN, ROBERT (Oct. 12, 1921–); b. Belfast, Me. Author. *Jeep Trails to Colorado Ghost Towns* (1963); *An Empire of Silver* (1965); *Ghost Towns of the Colorado Rockies* (1968). Teacher of western history in Colorado.

BROWN, ROBERT McAFEE (May 28, 1920–). Author. *P. T. Forsyth: Prophet for Today* (1952); *The Significance of the Church* (1956); *An American Dialogue* (with Gustave Weigel, 1960); *The Spirit of Protestantism* (1961); *The Collected Writings of St. Hereticus* (1964); *Observer in Rome* (1964); *Vietnam: Crises of Conscience* (with others, 1967); *The Ecumenical Revolution* (1969).

BROWN, ROBERT RAYMOND (June 16, 1910–); b. Garden City, Kan. Roman Catholic clergyman, author. *Miracle of the Cross* (1954); *Friendly Enemies* (1955); *Bigger than Little Rock* (1958); *Alive Again* (1964).

BROWN, ROLLO WALTER (Mar. 15, 1880–Oct. 13, 1956); b. Crooksville, O. Author. *The Creative Spirit: An Inquiry into American Life* (1925); *Dean Briggs* (1926); *Lonely Americans* (1929); *The Firemakers* (1931); *Toward Romance* (1932); *The Hillikin* (1935); *Next Door to a Poet* (1937); *I Travel By Train* (1939); *There Must Be a New Song* (1942); *Dr. Howe and the Forsyth Infirmary* (1952); *The Hills Are Strong* (autobiography, 1953); etc.

BROWN, ROSE [Johnston] (1883–1952). Author. *Two Children of Brazil* (1940); *American Emperor* (1945); *Bicycle in the Sky* (1953); etc.

BROWN, SLATER (1896–); b. Webster, Mass. Author. *Burning Wheel* (1942); *The Talking Skyscraper* (1945); *World of the Wind* (1961); *World of the Desert* (1963); etc.

BROWN, SOLYMAN (Nov. 17, 1790–Feb. 13, 1876); b. Litchfield, Conn. Swedenborgian clergyman, dentist, educator, poet. *An Essay on American Poetry* (poem, 1818); *The Birth of Washington* (poem, 1822); *Dentologia* (poem, 1833); etc.

BROWN, STERLING ALLEN (May 1, 1901–). b. Washington, D.C. Educator, author. *Southern Road* (poems, 1932); *Negro Poetry and Drama* (1937); *The Negro in American Fiction* (1937); *What the Negro Wants* (1948). Editor: *Negro Caravan* (with others, 1941). Prof. English, Howard University, since 1929.

BROWN, STUART GERRY (Apr. 3, 1912–); b. Buffalo, N.Y. Educator, editor. *The First Republicans* (1954); *Conscience in Politics: Adlai E. Stevenson in the 1950's* (1961); *Jefferson* (1963); *Adlai E. Stevenson* (1965); *American Presidency: Leadership, Partisanship and Popularity* (1966); *Government in the United States* (1967); etc. Editor: *Social Philosophy of Josiah Royce* (1950); *Religious Philosophy of Josiah Royce* (1952); *The Autobiography of James Monroe* (1959); etc. Prof. citizenship and American culture, Syracuse University, 1947–58; prof. American civilization, 1958–65; prof. American studies, University of Hawaii, since 1965.

BROWN, SYDNEY MacGILLVARY (Aug. 10, 1895–Apr. 6, 1952); b. Marblehead, Mass. Educator, historian. *Medieval Europe* (1932); *England* (with E. Wingfield Stratford, 1938); *The Royal Pedant* (1939).

BROWN, THERON (Apr. 29, 1832–Feb. 14, 1914); b. Willimantic, Conn. Baptist clergyman, editor, author. Pen name, "Park Ludlow." The *Red Shanty Boys* series (1871–78); *The Blount Family* (1873); *Walter Neil's Example* (1876); *Stories for Sunday* (1880); *Life Songs* (poems, 1894); *Nameless Women of the Bible* (1904); *The Story of the Hymns and Tunes* (with Hezekiah Butterworth, 1907); *Under the Mulberry Trees* (1909); *The Birds of God* (1912). Asst. editor, the *Youth's Companion,* 1870–1914.

BROWN, T[homas] ALLSTON (1836–Apr. 2, 1918). Author. *History of the American Stage* (1870); *The Showman's Guide* (1874); *A History of the New York Stage,* 3v. (1903). Editor, *The New York Clipper.*

BROWN, WENZELL (1912–). Author. *Hong Kong Aftermath* (1943); *Dynamite on Our Doorstep* (1945); *Angry Men —Laughing Men* (1947); *Dark Drums* (1950); *Monkey on My Back* (1953); *How To Tell Fortunes With Cards* (1963); *Lonely Hearts Killers* (1965); etc.

Brown, Will C. Pen name of C. S. Boyles.

BROWN, WILLIAM ADAMS (Dec. 29, 1865–Dec. 15, 1943); b. New York. Presbyterian clergyman, educator, author. *Musical Instruments and Their Homes* (1888); *The Essence of Christianity* (1902); *Life of Morris K. Jesup* (1910); *The Church in America* (1922); *The Creative Experience* (1923); *The Quiet Hour* (1926); *Beliefs That Matter* (1928); *Pathways to Certainty* (1930); *Finding God in a New World* (1935); *A Teacher and His Times* (autobiography, 1940); *A Creed for Free Men* (1941); *The New Order in the Church* (1943); etc. Faculty, Union Theological Seminary, 1892–1936.

BROWN, WILLIAM GARROTT (Apr. 24, 1868–Oct. 19, 1913); b. Marion, Ala. Historian, biographer. *Andrew Jackson* (1900); *The Lower South in American History* (1902); *Stephen Arnold Douglas* (1902); *The Foe of Compromise, and Other Essays* (1903); etc.

BROWN, WILLIAM HILL (1766–1793). Poet, novelist. *Ira and Isabella; or, The Natural Children* (1807). Supposed author of *The Power of Sympathy* (1789) (q.v.).

BROWN, W[illiam] NORMAN (June 24, 1892–); b. Baltimore, Md. Educator, Indologist, author. *The Pancatantra in Modern Indian Folklore* (1919); *The Story of Kalaka* (1933); *Manuscript Illustrations of the Uttaradhyayana Sutra* (1941); *The United States and India and Pakistan* (1953); *The Saundaryalahari* (ed., tr., 1958); etc. Editor: *India, Pakistan, Ceylon* (also part author, 1951). Editor, *Journal of American Oriental Society 1926–41.* Curator, Indian Art, Philadelphia Museum of Art, 1931–54.

BROWN, WILLIAM PERRY (1847–Sept. 4, 1923); b. in Indian Ty. Author. Pen name, "Capt. William B. Perry." Under own name: *A Sea Island Romance* (1888); *Roraima* (1896); *Sea Island Boys* (1903); *Nick Carter's Persistence* (1911); etc.; also, under pen name: *Our Sammies in the Trenches* (1918); *Our Jackies with the Fleet* (1918); *Our Pilots in the Air* (1918).

BROWN, WILLIAM WELLS (c. 1816–Nov. 6, 1884); b. Lexington, Ky. Reformer, historian. *Narrative of William W. Brown, a Fugitive Slave* (1847); *Illustrated Edition of the Life and Escape of Wm. Wells Brown from American Slavery* (1851); *Three Years in Europe* (1852); *Clotel; or, The President's Daughter* (1853); *The Black Man, His Antecedents, His Genius, and His Achievements* (1863); *The Negro in the American Rebellion* (1867).

BROWN, ZENITH J[ones] (Mrs. Ford K. Brown) (1898–); b. Smith River, Calif. Novelist. Pen names, "David Frome,"

and "Leslie Ford." *The Hammersmith Murders* (1930); *The Man from Scotland Yard* (1933); *The Town Cried Murder* (1939); *Old Lover's Ghost* (1940); *The Murder of the Fifth Columnist* (1941); *Siren in the Night* (1942); *All for Love of a Lady* (1943); *Date with Death* (1949); *Bahamas Murder Case* (1952); *Invitation to Murder* (1954); *The Girl from the Mimosa Club* (1957); *Trial by Ambush* (1962); etc.

Brown of Harvard. Play by Rida Johnson Young (prod. 1906). Made into a novel by Miss Young and Gilbert P. Coleman (1907).

"Brown of Osawatomie." Poem by John Greenlead Whittier, in *The Independent,* New York, Dec. 22, 1859.

BROWNE, ANITA, b. New York. Editor, publisher, poet. Compiler: *A Mosaic of Muses* (1930); *Homespun; An Anthology of Poetry* (1936); *The One Hundred Best Books by American Women During the Past Hundred Years, 1833–1933* (1933); *The Year's at the Spring* (1940); etc.

BROWNE, BENJAMIN FREDERICK (July 14, 1793–Nov. 23, 1873); b. Salem, Mass. Druggist, author. *The Yarn of a Yankee Privateer* (1926), first published in 1846 in *The U. S. Magazine and Democratic Review,* as *Papers of an Old Dartmoor Prisoner, Edited by Nathaniel Hawthorne.* Authorship not solved until after its republication in book form in 1926.

BROWNE, CHARLES FARRAR (Apr. 26, 1834–Mar. 6, 1867); b. Waterford, Me. Humorist. Pen name "Artemus Ward." *Artemus Ward: His Book* (1862); *Artemus Ward: His Travels* (1865); *The Complete Works of Charles F. Browne* (1871); etc. See Don Carlos Seitz's *Artemus Ward* (1919).

Browne, Dunn. Pen name of Samuel Wheelock Fiske.

BROWNE, FRANCIS FISHER (Dec. 1, 1843–May 11, 1913); b. South Halifax, Vt. Editor, anthologist. *The Every-Day Life of Abraham Lincoln* (1886). Compiler: *Golden Poems, by British and American Authors* (1881); *The Golden Treasury of Poetry and Prose* (1883); *Bugle-Echoes: A Collection of Poems of the Civil War, Northern and Southern* (1886). Editor, *The Lakeside Monthly,* 1869–74; founder, *The Dial,* 1880; editor, 1880–1913.

BROWNE, GEORGE WALDO (Oct. 8, 1851–Aug. 13, 1930); b. Deerfield, N.H. Lecturer, novelist, author of boys' books, historian, editor. Pen name "Victor St. Clair." Under name G. Waldo Brown: *A Daughter of Maryland* (1895); *The Woodranger* (1899); *The Paradox of the Pacific: The Hawaiian Islands* (1900); *Indian Nights* (1927); *Real Legends of New England* (1930); etc. Under name George Waldo Brown, dime novels: *The Tiger of Taos* (1876); *Dandy Rock, the Man from Texas* (1879); *The Esquimaux' Queen* (1884). etc. Under pen name: *The Boy Conjurer* (1894); *For Home and Honor* (1902); *With Axe and Flintlock* (1907); etc. Editor, *American Young Folks.*

BROWNE, IRVING (Sept. 14, 1835–Feb. 6, 1899); b. Marshall, N.Y. Editor, lawyer, author. *Our Best Society* (1876); *Iconoclasm and Whitewash* (1885); *In the Track of the Bookworm* (1897); *The House of the Heart* (poems, 1897); *Ballads of a Bookworm* (1899); etc.

BROWNE, J[ohn] ROSS (Feb. 11, 1821–Dec. 8, 1875); b. Dublin, Ireland. California pioneer, journalist, traveler, author. *Confessions of a Quack* (1841); *Etchings of a Whaling Cruise* (1846); *Yusef; or, The Journey of the Frangi* (1853); *Crusoe's Island* (1864); *An American Family in Germany* (1866); *The Land of Thor* (1867); *Adventures in the Apache Country* (1869); etc.

BROWNE, JUNIUS HENRI (Oct. 14, 1833–Apr. 2, 1902); b. Seneca Falls, N.Y. Journalist, author. *Four Years in Secessia* (1865); *The Great Metropolis: A Mirror of New York* (1869); *Sights and Sensations in Europe* (1871); etc. Civil War correspondent for the *New York Tribune.*

BROWNE, LEWIS (June 24, 1897–Jan. 3, 1949); b. London, England. Author. *Stranger Than Fiction* (1925); *This Believing World* (1926); *That Man Heine* (with Elsa Weihl, 1927); *Why Are the Jews Like That?* (1929); *Since Calvary* (1931); *Blessed Spinoza* (1932); *How Odd of God* (1934); *All Things are Possible* (1935); *Oh, Say, Can You See!* (1937); *The Wisdom of Israel* (1945); *The World's Great Scriptures* (1946); etc.

BROWNE, LEWIS ALLEN (Jan. 18, 1876–May 24, 1937); b. North Sandwich, N.H. Editor, author. *Airship Almanac* (1909); *Around the Clock with the Rounder* (1910); *Indian Fairy Tales* (1912); *Prudence Wentworth* (1914); *Please Get Married* (with James Cullen, prod. 1919); *Just Playing Around* (1930); etc. City editor, *The Boston Journal*, 1901–12; assoc. editor, *The New York Sunday American*, 1912–14; editor, Wildman Magazine Service, 1914–19; assoc. editor, *The Forum*, 1918–19.

BROWNE, MAURICE (Feb. 12, 1881–Jan. 21, 1954); b. Reading, England. Theatrical director, playwright. *Epithalamion* (1900); *Zetétés, and Other Poems* (1905); *Job* (drama in verse, 1906); *Songs of Exile* (1907); *The Nature and Function of Poetry* (1908); *Recollections of Rupert Brooke* (1927); *Wings Over Europe* (with Robert Nichols, 1929); *Too Late To Lament* (autobiography, 1956); etc. Co-founder, Chicago Little Theatre, 1912.

BROWNE, PORTER EMERSON (June 22, 1879–Sept. 20, 1934); b. Beverly, Mass. Playwright, novelist. *A Fool There Was* (prod. 1909); *The Spendthrift* (prod. 1910); *Someone and Somebody* (1917); *The Bad Man* (prod. 1920); etc.

BROWNE, RILMA MARION; b. Manchester, N.H., daughter of George Waldo Browne, Educator, author. Pen name, "Stanley Castle." *Indian Story Hour* (1920); *The Story of New Hampshire* (with father, 1925); *The Story of the Old Bay State* (with father, 1929); etc.

BROWNE, WALDO RALPH (Feb. 2, 1876–Jan. 1954); b. St. Joseph, Mich. Editor, author. *Altgeld of Illinois* (1924); etc. Compiler: *Right Reading* (1905); *Joys of the Road* (1911); *Books and the Quiet Life* (1914); *Barnum's Own Story* (1927). With the *Dial*, 1900–16, editor, 1912–16; lit. editor, *The Nation*, 1919.

BROWNE, WILLIAM HAND (Dec. 3, 1828–Dec. 13, 1912); b. Baltimore, Md. Educator, historian, editor. *Maryland: The History of a Palatinate* (1884); *George Calvert and Cecilus Calbert, Barons Baltimore* (1890); *Life of Alexander H. Stephens* (with Richard M. Johnston, 1878). Editor: *Selections from the Early Scottish Poets* (1896); *The Archives of Maryland*, v. 1–5 (1883–87). Editor, *Southern Magazine*, 1870–75; *Maryland Historical Magazine*, 1906–10. Librarian, Johns Hopkins University, 1879–81.

BROWNELL, AMANDA BENJAMIN HALL. *See* Amanda Benjamin Hall.

BROWNELL, BAKER (Dec. 12, 1887–Apr. 5, 1965); b. St. Charles, Ill. Educator, author. *The New Universe* (1926); *Earth Is Enough* (1933); *Architecture and Modern Life* (with Frank Lloyd Wright, 1937); *Art is Action* (1939); *The Philosopher in Chaos* (1941); *The Human Community* (1950); *The College and the Community* (1951); etc. Editor: *Man and His World*, 12 v. (1929); etc. Prof. philosophy, Northwestern University, 1923–53.

BROWNELL, GERTRUDE HALL (Mrs. William Crary Brownell) (Sept. 8, 1863–); b. Boston, Mass. Poet novelist. Writes under maiden name. *Far from Today* (1892); *Age of Fairygold* (poems, 1899); *The Wagnerian Romances* (1925); *William Crary Brownell* (1933); etc.

BROWNELL, HENRY HOWARD (Feb. 6, 1820–Oct. 31, 1872); b. Providence, R. I. Poet. *Poems* (1847); *Lyrics of a Day; or, Newspaper-Poetry* (anon., 1864), which contains the well-known "River Light." *War Lyrics and Other Poems* (1866); etc.

BROWNELL, MRS. JOHN ANGELL. *See* Amanda Benjamin Hall.

BROWNELL, WILLIAM CRARY (Aug. 30, 1851–July 22, 1928); b. New York City. Critic. *French Traits* (1889); *French Art* (1892); *Victorian Prose Masters* (1901); *American Prose Masters* (1909); *Criticism* (1914); *Standards* (1917); *The Genius of Style* (1924). On staff of *New York World, The Nation*, in 1888 joined the editorial staff of Charles Scribner's Sons, remained with the firm until his death. *See* Gertrude Hall Brownell's *William Crary Brownell: An Anthology of His Writings Together with Biographical Notes and Impressions of His Later Years.*

BROWNING, NORMA LEE (Nov. 24, 1914–); b. Spickard, Mo. Journalist, author. *City Girl in the Country* (1955); *Joe Maddy of Interlochen* (1963); *The Other Side of the Mind* (with W. Clement Stone, 1965); *The Psychic World of Peter Hurkos* (1970); etc. Reporter-feature writer, *Chicago Tribune*, since 1944.

BROWNING, WEBSTER E. (Apr. 14, 1869–Apr. 16, 1942); b. Sweet Springs, Mo. Presbyterian clergyman, author. *The Republic of Ecuador* (1920); *Roman Christianity in Latin America* (1924); *New Days in Latin America* (1925); *The River Plate Republics* (1928); etc.

BROWNLOW, LOUIS (Aug. 29, 1879–Sept. 28, 1963); b. Buffalo, Mo. Journalist, public administrator, author. *The President and the Presidency* (1949); *Passion for Politics* (autobiography, 1955); *A Passion for Anonymity* (autobiography, 1958); *Anatomy of the Anecdote* (1960).

BROWNSON, CARLETON LEWIS (Jan. 19, 1866–Sept. 28, 1948); b. New Canann, Conn. Educator, author. *A Shorter History of Greece* (1896); *Plato's Studies and Criticisms of the Poets* (1920). Editor: *Xenophon's Historical Works*, 3v. (1917–23); etc. Classics dept., College of the City of New York, 1897–1936.

BROWNSON, ORESTES AUGUSTUS (Sept. 16, 1803–Apr. 17, 1876); b. Stockbridge, Vt. Editor, novelist. *Charles Elwood; or, The Infidel Converted* (1840); *The Spirit-Rapper: An Autobiography* (1854); *The Convert; or, Leaves from My Experience* (1857); *The American Republic* (1866). Editor, *The Boston Quarterly Review*, 1838–42; *The United States Magazine and Democratic Review*, 1842–44; *Brownson's Quarterly Review*, 1844–64; 1873–75. *See* Americo D. Lapati's *Orestes A. Brownson* (1965).

Brownson's Quarterly Review. Boston, Mass. Theological journal founded by Orestes Brownson, Jan., 1844. Last issue, October, 1875. *See Boston Quarterly Review.*

BRUBACHER, JOHN SELLERS (Oct. 18, 1898–); b. Easthampton, Mass. Educator. *Modern Philosophies of Education* (1939); *History of the Problems of Education* (1947); *Higher Education in Transition* (with Willis Rudy, 1958). Editor: *Henry Barnard on Education* (1931); *The Public School and Spiritual Values* (1944); *Eclectic Philosophy of Education* (1951). Prof. education, Yale University, since 1946.

BRUBAKER, HOWARD (June 26, 1882–Feb. 2, 1957); b. Warsaw, Ind. Editor, author. *Ranny* (1917); *White House Blues* (1932). Assoc. editor, *Success Magazine*, 1907–11; managing editor, 1922–23; asst. editor, *Collier's Weekly*, 1914–19; contrib. editor, *The Liberator*, 1918–24; secretary, Writers' Publishing Co., from 1923.

Bruce, Arthur Loring. Pen name of Frank Crowninshield.

BRUCE, H[enry] ADDINGTON [Bayley] (June 27, 1874–); b. Toronto, Ont. Author. *The Riddle of Personality* (1908); *Historic Ghosts and Ghost Hunters* (1908); *The Romance of American Expansion* (1909); *Daniel Boone and the Wilderness Road* (1910); *Woman in the Making of America* (1912); *Adventurings in the Psychical* (1914); *Self-Development* (1921); *Your Growing Child* (1927); etc.

BRUCE, LENNY [Leonard A. Schneider] (1926–Aug. 3, 1966); b. Mineola, L.I., N.Y. Nightclub comedian, monologist. *Stamp Help Out!* (1964); *How to Talk Dirty and Influence People: An Autobiography* (1965); *The Essential Lenny Bruce,* ed. by John Cohen (1967).

BRUCE, PHILIP ALEXANDER (Mar. 7, 1856–Aug. 16, 1933); b. Staunton Hill, Charlotte Co., Va. Historian, poet. *The Rise of the New South* (1905); *Robert E. Lee* (1907); *Social Life of Virginia in the Seventeenth Century* (1907); *Institutional History of Virginia in the Seventeenth Century,* 2v. (1910); *Pocahontas, and Other Sonnets* (1912); *History of the University of Virginia, 1819–1919,* 5v. (1920–22); *History of Virginia: Volume I, Colonial Period, 1607–1763* (1924); *The Virginia Plutarch,* 2v. (1929); etc.

BRUCE, WALLACE (Nov. 10, 1844–Jan. 2, 1914); b. Hillsdale, N.Y. Poet, *The Hudson* (1881); *From the Hudson to the Yosemite* (1884); *The Yosemite* (1886); *Old Homestead Poems* (1888); *Wayside Poems* (1895); *In Clover and Heather* (1896); *Scottish Poems* (1907); *Wanderers* (1907). Under the pen name "Thursty McQuill," he wrote various guide-books on the Hudson and Connecticut rivers.

BRUCE, W[illiam] CABELL (Mar. 12, 1860–May 9, 1946); b. Staunton Hill, Charlotte Co., Va. Senator, biographer. *Benjamin Franklin, Self-Revealed,* 2v. (1917, Pulitzer Prize for American biography, 1918); *John Randolph of Roanoke, 1773–1833,* 2v. (1922); *Recollections* (1931); *Imaginary Conversations with Franklin* (1933); *The Inn of Existence* (1941); etc.

Bruce Publishing Company, The. Milwaukee, Wis. Founded in 1891 by William George Bruce. William C. Bruce was chairman of the board. Publishes books of Catholic interest and on philosophy and religion. John N. Higgins is general manager. An affiliate of Crowell Collier and Macmillan, Inc.

BRUCHÉ, COUNTESS CHARLES P. de. *See* Winifred Sackville Stoner, Jr.

BRUCKER, HERBERT (Oct. 4, 1898–); b. Passaic, N.J. Editor, educator, author. *The Changing American Newspaper* (1937); *Freedom of Information* (1949); *Eyewitness to History* (1962). On staff, *World's Work,* 1926–27; *Review of Reviews,* 1927–32; with School of Journalism, Columbia University, 1932–44; editor, *Hartford Courant,* since 1947.

BRUDNO, EZRA S[elig] (May 28, 1878–); b. in Lithuania. Author. *The Fugitive* (1904); *The Little Conscript* (1905); *The Tether* (1908); *One of Us* (1912); *The Jugglers* (1920); *Sublime Jester* (1924); *Ghosts of Yesterday* (1935); *A Guide for the Misguided* (1951); etc.

BRUESTLE, BEAUMONT (Dec. 23, 1905–); b. Philadelphia, Pa. Educator, author. *Storm Signals* (poems, 1931); *Things of Earth* (1935); *The Wonderful Tang* (play, 1952); *Know-It-All* (musical comedy, 1965); *Don't Gild Lily* (1968); etc. Editor, *Players Magazine,* since 1959. Chairman, dept. speech and English, University of Tulsa, since 1953.

BRUFF, NANCY (1915–); b. Fairfield, Conn. Poet, novelist. *The Manatee* (1945); *My Talon in Your Heart* (poems, 1946); *Cider from Eden* (1947); *The Beloved Woman* (1949); *Country Club* (1969).

BRUMM, JOHN LEWIS (Aug. 13, 1878–Aug. 16, 1958); b. Flint, Mich. Journalist, educator, playwright. *Why Print That?* (1935); etc. Dept. journalism, University of Michigan, 1924–48.

BRUNCKEN, HERBERT (1896–). Poet. *Hall Bedroom* (1936); *Last Parade* (1938); *The Long Night* (1939). Editor: *Subject Index to Poetry* (1940); *Hue and Cry* (1941); *A Noise in Time* (1949).

BRUNER, JEROME S[eymour] (Oct. 1, 1915–); b. New York. Psychologist, author. *Mandate from the People* (1941); *Opinions and Personality* (with Smith and White, 1956); *A Study of Thinking,* (with Goodnow and Austin, 1956); *The Process of Education* (1960); *On Knowing: Essays for the Left Hand* (1962); *Toward a Theory of Instruction* (1966); *Studies in Cognitive Growth* (1966); *Processes of Cognitive Growth: Infancy* (1968). Prof. psychology, Harvard University, since 1952.

BRUNINI, JOHN GILLAND (Oct. 1, 1899–); b. Vicksburg, Miss. Poet, editor. *The Mysteries of the Rosary* (poems, 1932); *Days of a Hireling* (1951). Editor or co-editor: *Return to Poetry* (1947); *Stories of Our Century by Catholic Authors* (1949); *Sealed Unto the Day* (1955); *Invitation to the City* (1960). On staff, *The Commonweal,* 1928–31; contrib. editor, since 1938. Editor, *Spirit: A Magazine of Verse,* since 1931.

BRUNO, GUIDO (Oct. 15, 1884–); b. Bohemia. Editor, author. *Adventures in American Bookshops* (1922). Editor, *Greenwich Village; Bruno Chap-Books; Bruno's Weekly,* etc.

Bruno Chap-Books. New York City. Founded 1915. Editor, Guido Bruno. Expired 1916.

BRUSH, CHRISTINE CHAPLIN (1842–Feb. 3, 1892); b. Bangor, Me. Artist, novelist. *The Colonel's Opera Cloak* (1879); etc.

BRUSH, KATHARINE (Katharine Ingham Brush) (Aug. 15, 1903–June 10, 1952); b. Middletown, Conn. Novelist. *Glitter* (1926); *Little Sins* (1927); *Night Club* (1929); *Young Man of Manhattan* (1930); *Red-Headed Woman* (1931); *Other Women* (1932); *Don't Ever Leave Me* (1935); *This Is On Me* (autobiography, 1940); *Out of My Mind* (1943); *This Man and This Woman* (1944).

BRUSTEIN, ROBERT [Sanford] (April 21, 1927–); b. New York. Educator, author. *The Theater of Revolt* (1964); *Seasons of Discontent: Dramatic Opinions, 1959–1965* (1965). Editor: *The Poems and The Plays and Prose of Strindberg* (1964); *The Third Theatre* (1969). Dramatic critic, *New Republic,* since 1959. Dean, Yale School of Drama, since 1966.

BRUSTLEIN, DANIEL (Sept. 11, 1904–); b. in France. Cartoonist, illustrator, author. *The Elephant and the Flea* (1956); *Magic Stones* (1957); *Alain's Steeplechase* (1957); *One Two Three Going to Sea* (1964); etc. Illustrator of books.

Brutus; or, The Fall of Tarquin. Historical drama, in verse, by John Howard Payne (prod. 1818).

BRUUN, GEOFFREY (Oct. 20, 1898–); b. in Canada. Historian. *Saint-Just: Apostle of Terror* (1932); *Europe and the French Imperium* (1938); *Clemenceau* (1943); *Revolution and Reaction, 1848–52* (1958); *Nineteenth Century European Civilization* (1960); etc.

BRYAN, C[ourtlandt] D[ixon] B[arnes] (Apr. 22, 1936–); b. New York. Novelist. *P. S. Wilkinson* (1964); *Great Dethriffe* (1970). Editor, *Monocle* magazine, since 1961.

BRYAN, GEORGE SANDS (Sept. 6, 1879–Dec. 2, 1943); b. Matteawan, N.Y. Editor, poet, biographer. *Sam Houston* (1917); *Yankee Notions* (poems, 1922); *The Ghost in the Attic, and Other Verses* (1926); *Edison: The Man and His Work* (1926); *The Great American Myth* (1940); *Mystery Ship* (1942); *The Spy in America* (1943). Compiler: *Poems of Country Life: A Modern Anthology* (1912).

BRYAN, JOHN STEWART (Oct. 23, 1871–Oct. 16, 1944); b. in Henrico Co., Va. Educator, editor, publisher. Succeeded his father, Joseph Bryan, as publisher of the *Richmond Times-Dispatch.* Publisher, *The News-Leader,* Richmond, Va., (from) 1940. President, College of William and Mary, 1934–42.

BRYAN, JOSEPH, III (Apr. 30, 1904–); b. Richmond, Va. Author. *Mission Beyond Darkness* (with Philip Reed, 1945); *Admiral Halsey's Story* (with Admiral Halsey, 1947); *Aircraft Carrier* (1954); *The World's Greatest Showman* (1956); *The*

Sword over the Mantel (1960). Assoc. editor, *Saturday Evening Post,* 1937–40.

BRYAN, MARY EDWARDS (May 17, 1842–June 15, 1913); b. Tallahassee, Fla. Editor, novelist, poet. *Manch* (1880); *Wild Work* (1881); *Kildee* (1886); *The Bayou Bride* (1886); etc. Editor: *Munroe's Star Recitations* (1887). Assoc. editor, *The Sunny South,* 1874–84.

BRYAN, WILLIAM JENNINGS (Mar. 19, 1860–July 26, 1925); b. Salem, Ill. Political leader, orator. *The Memoirs of William Jennings Bryan* (1925); *Speeches of William Jennings Bryan,* 2v. (1909). Founder, *The Commoner,* 1901. His best known oration is his "Cross of Gold" speech made at the Democratic National Convention in 1896, at Chicago. *See* Paxton P. Hibben's *The Peerless Leader* (1929).

BRYAN, WILLIAM LOWE (Nov. 11, 1860–Nov. 21, 1955); b. Bloomington, Ind. Educator, author. *The Spirit of Indiana* (1917); *Paradise* (1927); *The President's Column* (1934); *Farewell* (1938); *Wars of Families of Minds* (1940); *Last Words* (1951); etc. President, Indiana University, 1902–37.

BRYANT, ARTHUR HERBERT (1917–); b. Alexandria, Va. Novelist. *Double Image* (1947); *The Valley of St. Ives* (1949).

BRYANT, EDWIN (1805–1869); b. in Massachusetts. Author. *What I Saw in California in 1846–1847* (1848), an important source book for Western Americana, reprinted as *Rocky Mountain Adventures* (1885).

BRYANT, MARGARET M. (Dec. 3, 1900–); b. Trenton, S.C. Educator. *English in the Law Courts* (1930); *Proverbs and How to Collect Them* (1945); *Modern English and Its Heritage* (1948); *Current American Usage: How Americans Say It and Write It* (1962). English dept., Brooklyn College, since 1930.

BRYANT, SAMUEL WOOD, JR. (Jan. 9, 1908–); b. Annapolis, Md. Editor, author. *The Sea and the States: A Maritime History of the American People* (1947). With "March of Time," 1935–51; assoc. editor *Fortune,* since 1951.

BRYANT, SARA CONE (Jan. 4, 1873–); b. Melrose, Mass. Author. *Stories to Tell to Children* (1907); *Stories to Tell the Littlest Ones* (1916); *Gordon and His Friends* (1925); *Gordon in the Great Woods* (1928); *The Burning Rice Fields* (1963); etc.

BRYANT, WILLIAM CULLEN (Nov. 3, 1794–June 12, 1878); b. Cummington, Mass. Editor, poet. *The Embargo* (1808); *Poems* (1821); augmented (1832); *The Fountain, and Other Poems* (1842); *The White-Footed Doe, and Other Poems* (1844); *The Poetical Works* (1844); *Letters of a Traveller* (1850); *Poetical Works* (1879); *Poetical Works and Complete Prose Writings,* ed. Parke Godwin, 2v. (1883). Bryant joined the staff of New York *Evening Post,* June, 1826, and was editor, 1830–78. *See* Parke Godwin's *A Biography of William Cullen Bryant,* 2v. (1883); Allan Nevins's *The Evening Post* (1922); Richard Henry Stoddard's poem, "The Dead Master"; Curtiss S. Johnson's *Politics and a Belly-Full: Journalistic Career of William Cullen Bryant* (1962); Albert F. McLean's *William Cullen Bryant* (1964).

BRYCE, LLOYD STEPHENS (Sept. 20, 1851–Apr. 2, 1917); b. Flushing, L.I., N.Y. Diplomat, editor, novelist. *Paradise* (1887); *The Romance of an Alter Ego* (1889); *Friends in Exile* (1893); *Lady Blanche's Salon* (1899). Editor, *The North American Review,* 1889–96.

BRYSON, CHARLES LEE (Mar. 10, 1868–Apr. 18, 1949); b. in Dade Co., Mo. Editor, author. *Tan and Teckle* (1908); *Woodsy Neighbors of Tan and Teckle* (1911); *The Witch's Lane* (1918); *Chicago and Its Makers* (with Paul Thomas Gilbert, 1929); *Double Trouble* (1944); etc.

BRYSON, LYMAN [Lloyd] (July 12, 1888–Nov. 24, 1959); b. Valentine, Neb. Educator, author. *Smoky Roses* (poems, 1916); *Adult Education* (1936); *Which Way America?* (1939); *The Next America* (1952); *The Drive Toward Reason* (1954). Editor: *Aspects of Human Equality* (1957); *Outline of Man's Knowledge of the Modern World* (1960). Director, Columbia Broadcasting System program, "Invitation to Learning." Prof. education, Teachers College, Columbia University, 1935–53.

BRZEZINSKI, ZBIGNIEW (Mar. 28, 1928–); b. Warsaw, Pol. Government official, author. *The Permanent Purge–Politics in Soviet Totalitarianism* (1956); *The Soviet Bloc—Unity and Conflict* (1960); *Ideology and Power in Soviet Politics* (1962); *Alternative to Partition* (1965); *Between Two Ages: America's Role in the Technetronic Age* (1970). Prof. government, Columbia University, since 1962. Consultant, U.S. Dept. of State, since 1962.

BUCHANAN, JAMES (Apr. 23, 1791–June 1, 1868); b. near Mercersburg, Pa. Fifteenth president of the United States, author. *Mr. Buchanan's Administration on the Eve of the Rebellion* (1866); *The Works of Jas. Buchanan,* ed. by John Bassett Moore, 12v. (1908–11). *See* George T. Curtis's *Life of Jas. Buchanan* (1883); Philip G. Auchampaugh's *James Buchanan and His Cabinet on the Eve of Secession* (1926).

BUCHANAN, SCOTT (Mar. 17, 1895–Mar. 22, 1968); b. Sprague, Wash. Educator, author. *Possibility* (1926); *Poetry and Mathematics* (1929); *Symbolic Distance* (1931); *The Doctrine of Signatures* (1937); *Essay in Politics* (1953); *Poetry and Mathematics* (1962). Dean, St. John's College, Maryland, 1937–47.

BUCHANAN, THOMPSON (June 21, 1877–Oct. 15, 1937); b. New York. Journalist, playwright, novelist. *Judith Triumphant* (1905); *A Woman's Way* (prod. 1909); *The Cub* (prod. 1910); *The Bridal Path* (prod. 1913); etc.

BUCHHOLZ, HEINRICH EWALD (Jan. 19, 1879–July 25, 1955); b. Baltimore, Md. Author. *The Civil War* (1905); *Reconstruction* (1906); *The Crown of the Chesapeake* (1907); *Governors of Maryland* (1908); *U.S.: A Second Study in Democracy* (1926); etc.

BUCHLER, JUSTUS (Mar. 27, 1914–); b. New York. Editor, author. *Charles Peirce's Empiricism* (1939); *Outline-Introduction to Philosophy* (with John H. Randall, Jr., 1941); *The Concept of Method* (1961); *Metaphysics of Natural Complexes* (1966). Editor or co-editor: *Obiter Scripta by George Santayana* (1936); *Philosophy of Peirce* (1940).

BUCHMAN, FRANK N[athan] D[aniel] (June 4, 1878–Aug. 7, 1961); b. Pennsburg, Pa. Reformer. *Remaking the World* (1949). Founder, "Moral Re-Armament," June, 1938, in London.

BUCHWALD, ART [hur] (Oct. 20, 1925–); b. Mt. Vernon, N.Y. Journalist, author. *Paris* (1954); *I Choose Caviar* (1957); *A Gift from the Boys* (novel, 1958); *More Caviar* (1959); *How Much Is That in Dollars?* (1961); *I Chose Capitol Punishment* (1963); *And Then I Told the President* (1965); *Son of the Great Society* (1966); *Have I Ever Lied to You* (1968); *The Establishment Is Alive and Well in Washington* (1969); etc.

BUCK, CHARLES NEVILLE (Apr. 15, 1879–); b. Woodford Co., Ky. Novelist. *The Key to Yesterday* (1910); *The Call of the Cumberlands* (1913); *The Code of the Mountains* (1915); *Destiny* (1916); *A Pagan of the Hills* (1919); *The Roof Tree* (1921); *The Rogue's Badge* (1924); *Flight to the Hills* (1926); *Hazard of the Hills* (1932); *Mountain Justice* (1935); etc.

BUCK, FRANK (Mar. 17, 1882–Mar. 25, 1950); b. Gainesville, Tex. Wild animal collector, motion picture producer, author. *Bring 'Em Back Alive* (with Edward Anthony, 1931); *Wild Cargo* (with same, 1932); *Fang and Claw* (with Ferrin Fraser, 1935); *Tim Thompson in the Jungles* (with same, 1935); *On Jungle Trails* (with same, 1937); *Animals Are Like That* (with Carol Weld, 1939); *All in a Lifetime* (with Ferrin Fraser, 1941).

BUCK, GENE [Eugene Edward] (Aug. 8, 1885–Feb. 24, 1957); b. Detroit, Mich. Producer, song writer. Librettist for Ziegfeld Follies, and collaborator with Ring Lardner, Augustus Thomas, Jerome Kern, and others. His best-known songs are: "Hello Frisco," "'Neath the South Sea Moon," "No Foolin'," "Garden of My Dreams," "Tulip Time," and "Maybe."

BUCK, PAUL H[erman] (Aug. 25, 1899–); b. Columbus, O. Educator, historian. *The Road to Reunion, 1865–1900* (1937, Pulitzer Prize for American history, 1938); *Nature and Needs of Higher Education* (1953). Co-author: *General Education in a Free Society* (1945). Editor: *The Social Sciences at Harvard, 1860–1920* (1965). Prof. history, Harvard University, since 1942.

BUCK, PEARL S[ydenstricker] (Mrs. Richard John Walsh) (June 26, 1892–); b. Hillsboro, W. Va. Novelist. *East Wind: West Wind* (1930); *The Young Revolutionists* (1931); *The Good Earth* (1931, Pulitzer Prize for literature, 1932); *Sons* (1932); *The First Wife, and Other Stories* (1933); *The Mother* (1934); *A House Divided* (1935); *The Exile* (1936); *Stories for Little Children* (1940); *Dragon Seed* (1942); *The Promise* (1943); *Portrait of a Marriage* (1945); *Pavilion of Women* (1946); *Kinfolk* (1949); *God's Men* (1951); *The Hidden Flower* (1952); *Come, My Beloved* (1953); *My Several Worlds* (1954); *Imperial Woman* (1956); *Letter from Peking* (1957); *Command the Morning* (1959); *Fourteen Stories* (1961); *A Bridge for Passing* (1962); *The Living Reed* (1963); *Welcome Child* (1963); *The Joy of Children* (1964); *The Big Fight* (1965); *The Time Is Noon* (1967); *The New Year* (1968); *The Good Deed* (1969); etc. Nobel Prize for literature, 1938. *See* Cornelia Spencer's *The Exile's Daughter: A Biography of Pearl Buck* (1944).

BUCK, PHILO MELVIN, JR. (Feb. 18, 1877–Dec. 9, 1950); b. Morristown, N.J. Educator, author. *Social Forces in Modern Literature* (1913); *Literary Criticism* (1930); *The Golden Thread* (1931); *The World's Great Age* (1936); etc. Editor: *An Anthology of World Literature* (1934, revised 1940), and other texts. Chairman, dept. of comparative literature, University of Wisconsin, 1926–1947.

BUCK, SOLON JUSTUS (Aug. 16, 1884–May 25, 1962); b. Berlin, Wis. Archivist, historian. *The Granger Movement* (1913); *Stories of Early Minnesota* (with wife, Elizabeth H. Buck, 1925); *Planting of Civilization in Western Pennsylvania* (with wife, 1939); etc. Editor: *William Watts Folwell* (1933); etc. Superintendent, Minnesota Historical Society, 1914–31; director of publications, The National Archives, 1935–41; archivist of the United States, 1941–48; with Library of Congress, from 1948.

Buck Fanshawe's Funeral. Story by Mark Twain, which appears in his *Roughing It* (1872). Told in the slang of the Western mining camps.

BUCKHAM, JOHN WRIGHT (Nov. 5, 1864–Mar. 30, 1945); b. Burlington, Vt. Congregational clergyman, author. *Personality and the Christian Ideal* (1909); *John Knox McLean* (1914); *Mysticism and Modern Life* (1915); *Progressive Religious Thought in America* (1919); *Religion as Experience* (1922); *Christianity and Personality* (1935); *The Inner World* (1941); etc.

BUCKINGHAM, JOSEPH TINKER (Dec. 21, 1779–Apr. 11, 1861); b. Windham, Conn. Editor, author. *Specimens of Newspaper Literature, with Personal Memoirs, Anecdotes and Reminiscences,* 2v. (1850); *Personal Memoirs and Recollections of Editorial Life,* 2v. (1852). Founder, the *Polyanthos,* 1805; editor, 1805–07, 1812–14; *New England Galaxy,* 1817–28; the *Boston Courier,* 1824–48; founder, the *New England Magazine,* 1831; editor, 1831–34. It was in the *Courier,* during Buckingham's editorship, that Lowell published the first series of the "Biglow Papers."

BUCKLEY, JAMES MONROE (Dec. 16, 1836–Feb. 8, 1920); b. Rahway, N.J. Methodist clergyman, editor, author. *Travels in Three Continents* (1895); *A History of Methodism in the United States,* 2v. (1897). Editor, *The Christian Advocate,* New York, 1880–1912.

BUCKLEY, JEROME HAMILTON (Aug. 30, 1917–); b. Toronto, Ont. Educator. *William Ernest Henley* (1945); *The Victorian Temper* (1951); *Tennyson: The Growth of a Poet* (1960); *The Triumph of Time* (1966); *The Pre-Raphaelites* (1968). Editor: *Poems of Tennyson* (1958). Co-editor: *Poetry of the Victorian Period* (1955). English dept. Columbia University, since 1954.

BUCKLEY, WILLIAM F[rank] (1925–); b. New York. Editor, author. *God and Man at Yale* (1951); *Up from Liberalism* (1959); *McCarthy and His Enemies* (with L. B. Bozell, 1961); *The Committee and Its Critics* (with others, 1962); *Rumbles Left and Right* (1963); *The Unmaking of a Mayor* (1966); *The Jeweler's Eye* (1968). Editor: *Did You Ever See a Dream Walking: American Conservative Thought in the Twentieth Century* (1970). Editor, *National Review*. See *Odyssey of a Friend: Whittaker Chambers' Letters to William F. Buckley, Jr., 1954–1961* (1970).

Buckmaster, Henrietta. Pen name of Henrietta Henkle.

BUCKMINSTER, JOSEPH STEVENS (May 26, 1784–June 9, 1812); b. Portsmouth, N.H. Unitarian clergyman. Member of the "Anthology Club," Boston. Co-founder, the Boston Athenaeum, 1807.

Bucknell Review. Lewisburg, Pa. Quarterly of letters, arts, and sciences. Founded 1940. Edited at Bucknell University.

BUDENZ, LOUIS FRANCIS (July 17, 1891–); b. Indianapolis, Ind. Journalist, author. *This Is My Story* (1947); *Men Without Faces* (1950); *The Cry Is Peace* (1952); *The Techniques of Communism* (1954); *The Bolshevik Invasion of the West* (1965). Pres. and managing editor, *The Daily Worker,* 1940–45. Prof. economics, Fordham University, since 1946.

BUECHNER, [Carl] FREDERICK (July 12, 1926–); b. New York. Presbyterian clergyman, novelist. *A Long Day's Dying* (1950); *The Season's Difference* (1952); *The Return of Ansel Gibbs* (1958); *The Final Beast,* (1965); *The Magnificent Defeat* (1966); *The Hungering Dark* (1969). Chairman, dept. of religion, Phillips Exeter Academy, since 1958.

BUEL, CLARENCE CLOUGH (July 20, 1850–May 22, 1933); b. Laona, N.Y. Editor. Editor: *Battles and Leaders of the Civil War,* 4v. (1887–88). Asst. editor, *The Century Magazine,* 1881–1910; assoc. editor, 1910–13; advisory editor, 1913–14.

BUEL, JAMES WILLIAM (Oct. 22, 1849–Nov. 16, 1920). b. Golconda, Ill. Traveler, author. *Legends of the Ozarks* (1877); *Heroes of the Plains* (1881); *America's Wonderlands* (1893); etc.

BUELL, RAYMOND LESLIE (July 13, 1896–Feb. 20, 1946); b. Chicago, Ill. Publicist, author. *International Relations* (1925); *The Native Problem in Africa,* 2v. (1928); *Poland* (1939); *Isolated America* (1940); etc. Editor and co-author: *New Governments in Europe* (1934); *Democratic Governments in Europe* (1935); *Liberia: A Century of Survival* (1945).

BUFF, MARY MARSH (Apr. 10, 1890–); b. Cincinnati, O. Artist, author. *Dancing Cloud* (1937); *Dash and Dart* (with Conrad Buff, 1942); *The Big Tree* (with same, 1946); *The Apple and the Arrow* (1951); *Magic Maize* (with same, 1953); *Hurry, Skurry and Flurry* (with same, 1954); *Hah-Nee* (1956); *Elf Owl* (with same, 1958); *Trix and Vix* (with same, 1960); *The Colorado: River of Mystery* (1968); etc.

"Buffalo Bill's." Poem by E. E. Cummings in *Poems 1923–1954.*

Buffalo Courier-Express. Buffalo, N.Y. Newspaper. The *Western Star,* forerunner of the *Courier,* was founded in 1834 by James Faxon. The *Courier* was founded in 1842. The *Buffalo Express* was founded in 1846 by A. M. Clapp. The two papers were consolidated in 1926. Cy King is editor and Ed Toronto is book-review editor. Mark Twain, James M. Matthews, J. N. Larned, David Gray, Marion DeForest, Samuel G. Blythe, David Lawrence, and Frank M. O'Brien were at one time or another associated with the *Buffalo Express.*

Buffalo Days. By H. W. Wheeler (1925). An account of the Wild West.

Buffalo Evening News. Buffalo, N.Y. Newspaper. Founded Oct. 11, 1880 by Edward H. Butler. In 1873 Butler had founded the *Buffalo Sunday News,* which was the forerunner of the *Evening News.* He was succeeded by his son, Edward H. Butler. Paul E. Neville is executive editor; George H. Esselburne is book critic.

Buffalo Jones' Forty Years of Adventure. Edited by Henry Inman (1899). The life of Charles J. Jones, famous character of the Southwest.

BUFFUM, EDWARD GOULD (ca. 1820–Oct. 24, 1867); b. in Rhode Island. Journalist, California pioneer, author. *Six Months in the Gold Mines* (1850); *Sights and Sensations in France, Germany, and Switzerland* (1869).

BUFFUM, GEORGE TOWER (Mar. 16, 1846–Mar. 9, 1926); b. Winchester, N.H. Merchant, author. *Smith of Bear City, and Other Frontier Sketches* (1906); *On Two Frontiers* (1918).

Bugle Echoes: A Collection of Poems of The Civil War, Northern and Southern. Compiled by Francis F. Browne (1886).

BÜHLER, CURT FERDINAND (July 11, 1905–); b. New York. Historian, librarian. *The Sources of the Court of Sapience* (1932); *The Dicts and Sayings of the Philosophers* (ed., 1941); *Fifteenth Century Books and the Twentieth Century* (1952); *The University and the Press in Fifteenth Century Bologna* (1959); *The Fifteenth Century Book: The Scribes, The Printers, The Decorators* (1960); *The History of Tom Thumbe* (1964); etc. Assoc. with Pierpont Morgan Library, since 1934; keeper of printed books, since 1948.

"Building of the Ship, The." Poem by Henry Wadsworth Longfellow (1849). An appeal to the abolitionists to place the importance of the preservation of the Union above the slavery question.

BUKOWSKI, CHARLES (Aug. 16, 1920–); b. Andernach, Ger. Poet. *Flower, Fist and Bestial Wail* (1959); *Longshot Poems for Broke Players* (1961); *Run With the Haunted* (1962); *It Catches My Heart in Its Hands* (1963); *Cold Dogs in the Courtyard* (1965); *Crucifix in a Deathhand* (1965); *Confessions of a Man Insane Enough to Live With Beasts* (1966); *At Terror Street and Agony Way* (1968); etc.

BULEY, R[oscoe] CARLYLE (July 8, 1893–Apr. 25, 1968); b. Georgetown, Ind. Educator, historian. *The Political Balance in the Old Northwest* (1926); *The Old Northwest—Pioneer Period, 1815–1840,* 2v. (1950; Pulitzer Prize for history, 1951); *The American Life Convention—A Study in the History of Life Insurance,* 2 v. (1953); *The Equitable Life Assurance Society of the United States, 1859–1959* (1959). History Dept., Indiana University, since 1925.

BULFINCH, STEPHEN GREENLEAF (June 18, 1809–Oct. 12, 1870); b. Boston, Mass. Unitarian clergyman, poet, hymn writer. *Poems* (1834); *Lays of the Gospel* (1845); *Honor; or, The Slave Dealer's Daughter* (1864); etc.

BULFINCH, THOMAS (July 15, 1796–May 27, 1867); b. Newton, Mass. Author. *The Age of Fable* (1855); *The Age of Chivalry* (1858); *Legends of Charlemagne* (1863); *Poetry of the Age of Fable* (1863); etc.

BULLARD, F. LAURISTON (May 13, 1866–Aug. 1952); b. Wauseon, O. Editor, author. *Historic Summer Haunts* (1912); *Famous War Correspondents* (1914); *Tad and His Father* (1915); *A Few Appropriate Remarks—the Gettysburg Address* (1944). Editor: *The Diary of a Public Man* (1945); *Abraham Lincoln and the Widow Bixby* (1946). With *Boston Herald* from 1915; chief editorial writer 1919–43.

Bulwark, The. Novel by Theodore Dreiser posthumously published in 1946. The hero, of Quaker origin, finds his children attracted more and more to uncertain modern goals which are devoid of spiritual value. He eventually becomes even more confirmed in his faith in man's oneness with God, as if to compensate for his children's waywardness.

BUNCE, OLIVER BELL (Feb. 8, 1828–May 15, 1890); b. New York City. Publisher, editor, playwright, anthologist. *The Romance of the Revolution* (1853); *Love in '76* (prod. 1857); *Bensley* (1863); *Bachelor Bluff* (1881); *The Adventures of Timias Terrystone* (1885); *The Story of Happinolando, and Other Legends* (1889). Literary editor for D. Appleton & Co., for many years. Editor, *Appleton's Journal.* He did most of the literary work on *Picturesque America* (1872–74).

Bundling: Its Origins, Progress and Decline in America. By Henry Reed Stiles (1869). History of a quaint custom.

BUNDY, JONAS MILLS (Apr. 17, 1835–Sept. 8, 1891); b. Colebrook, N.H. Editor, drama critic, journalist. Editor, *New York Evening Mail,* and its successor, The New York *Mail and Express.* Dramatic critic of the New York *Evening Post* under William Cullen Bryant.

BUNGAY, GEORGE WASHINGTON (July 22, 1818–July 10, 1892); b. Walsingham, England, came to America 1827. Journalist, poet. *Crayon Sketches and Off-Hand Takings* (1852). His best known poem is "The Creed of the Bells." With the *New York Tribune.*

BUNKER, JOHN [Joseph Leo] (Apr. 11, 1884–); b. Cincinnati, O. Lecturer, poet, anthologist. *The Nativity* (poem, 1912); *Shining Fields and Dark Towers* (1919); *Revolt* (poem, 1940). Compiler: *Dreams and Images* (1919); *The Catholic Anthology* (1927); *Modern Catholic Verse* (1926); *Modern Catholic Prose* (1927).

Bunker Hill; or, The Death of General Warren. Play by John Daly Burk (prod. 1797).

BUNNER, H[enry] C[uyler] (Aug. 3, 1855–May 11, 1896); b. Oswego, N.Y. Poet, editor, short story writer. *Airs from Arcady and Elsewhere* (1884); *The Midge* (1886); *Short Sixes* (1891); *Rowen* (1892); *More Short Sixes* (1894); *Zadoc Pine* (1891); *Jersey Street and Jersey Lane* (1896); *Love in Old Clothes, and Other Stories* (1896). Editor, *Puck,* 1878–96.

Buntline, Ned. Pen name of Edward Zane Carroll Judson.

BURACK, ABRAHAM SOLOMAN (1908–). Editor: *Writing Detective and Mystery Fiction* (1945); *The Craft of Novel Writing* (1948); *Television Plays for Writers* (1957); *Writing and Selling Fillers and Humor* (1959); *A Treasury of Holiday Plays for Teenagers* (1963); etc. Editor, *The Writer's Handbook* annual, since 1936; *The Writer.*

BURCHARD, JOHN ELY (Dec. 8, 1898–); b. Marshall, Minn. Educator. *Fundamental Principles of ARP* (1943); *The Evolving House,* 3v. (with others, 1933–36); *Combat Scientists* (1947); *QED: A History of M.I.T. During World War II* (1948); *The Architecture of America* (with Albert Bush-Brown, 1961); *The Historian and the City* (1963); *The Voice of the Phoenix* (1966); *The Metropolitan Enigma* (1967); etc. Dean, school of humanities and social studies, Massachusetts Institute of Technology, since 1948.

BURDETT, CHARLES (b. 1815); b. New York. Journalist, novelist. *The Elliott Family* (1845); *The Convict's Child* (1846); *The Gambler* (1848); *The Second Marriage* (1856); *Blonde and Brunett* (anon. 1858); *Kit Carson* (1860), republished as *Life of Kit Carson* (1862); *Margaret Moncrieffe: The First Love of Aaron Burr* (1860), republished as *The Beautiful Spy* (1865), and as *The Amours of Aaron Burr* (1890); etc.

BURDETTE, ROBERT JONES (July 30, 1844–Nov. 19, 1914); b. Greensboro, Pa. Humorist, author. *The Rise and Fall of the Moustache, and Other "Hawkeyetems"* (1877); *Hawk-Eyes* (1879); *William Penn, 1644–1718* (1882); *Schooners That Pass in the Dark* (1894); *Chimes From a Jester's Bells* (1897); *The Silver Trumpets* (poems, 1911); *Old Time and Young Tom* (1912); etc. Columnist for *The Burlington* (Iowa) *Hawkeye.*

BURDICK, EUGENE [Leonard] (Jan. 1, 1918–Aug. 26, 1965); b. Sheldon, Ia. Educator, author. *The Ninth Wave* (1956); *The Ugly American* (with W. Lederer, 1958); *American Voting Behavior* (with Arthur J. Brodbeck, 1959); *The Blue of Capricorn* (1961); *Fail-Safe* (with Harvey Wheeler, 1962); *Sarkham* (with William J. Lederer, 1965); *Nina's Book* (1965). Prof. political theory, University of California at Berkeley, from 1950.

BURGAN, JOHN D. (Mar. 25, 1913–Apr. 6, 1951); b. Vintondale, Pa. Novelist. *Even My Own Brother* (1942); *Two Per Cent Fear* (1947); *The Long Discovery* (1950); *Martin Butterfield* (1950).

BURGESS, [Frank] GELETT (Jan. 30, 1866–Sept. 18, 1951); b. Boston, Mass. Humorist, author. *Vivette* (1897); *Goops and How to Be Them* (1900); *Are You a Bromide?* (1906); *The Goop Directory* (1913); *The Maxims of Noah* (1913); *The Goop Encyclopedia* (1916); *Why Men Hate Women* (1927); *Too Good Looking* (1936); *New Goops* (1940); *Ladies in Boxes* (1942); etc. Creator of such words as "bromide," "goop," and "blurb." Wrote the celebrated "Purple Cow" quatrain for the *Lark* (q.v.). He edited the *Lark*, 1895–97.

BURGESS, GEORGE (Oct. 31, 1809–Apr. 3, 1866); b. Providence, R.I. Episcopal bishop, hymn writer. *Poems* (1868). His best known hymns are "Lord, in Thy Name we spread the sail" called the "Sailor's Hymn" and "The harvest dawn is near." *See* Alexander Burgess's *Memoir of the Life of George Burgess* (1860).

BURGESS, PERRY (Oct. 12, 1886–Sept. 15, 1962); b. Joplin, Mo. Administrator, lecturer, author. *Who Walk Alone* (1940); *Born of Those Years* (autobiography, 1951).

BURGESS, THORNTON W[aldo] (Jan. 14, 1874–June 7, 1965); b. Sandwich, Mass. Author. *Old Mother West Wind* series, 8v. (1910–18); the *Bedtime Story* series, 20v. (1913–19); *Green Meadow* series, 4v. (1918–20); *Green Forest* series, 4v. (1921–23); *Tales from the Story Teller's House* (1937); *While the Storylog burns* (1938); *The Dear Old Briar Patch* (1947); *Along Laughing Brook* (1949); *At Paddy the Beaver's Pond* (1950); *Aunt Sally's Friends in Fur* (1955); *Read Aloud Peter Rabbit Stories* (1958); *Bedtime Stories* (1959); *Now I Remember* (Autobiography, 1960); and numerous Boy Scout books. Editorial Staff, Phelps Publishing Co., and Orange Judd Co., 1895–1911. Assoc. editor, *Good Housekeeping*, 1904–11.

BURK, JOHN DALY (c. 1775–Apr. 11, 1808); b. in Ireland. Editor, playwright. *Bunker Hill; or, The Death of General Warren* (prod. 1797); *Female Patriotism; or, The Death of Joan d'Arc* (prod. 1798); etc. Founder, *The Polar Star and Boston Daily Advertiser*, Oct. 6, 1796.

BURKAM, ELZEY GALLATIN (Dec. 7, 1872–Mar. 13, 1940); b. Lawrenceburg, Ind. Editor and publisher, Dayton *Journal* and Dayton *Herald*, (1910–35). President, Burkham-Herrick Publishing Co.

Burke, Fielding. Pen name of Olive Tilford Dargan.

BURKE, FRED GEORGE (Jan. 1, 1926–); b. Collins, N.Y. Educator, author. *Africa's Quest for Order* (1964); *Local Government and Politics in Uganda* (1965); *The Transforma-*

tion of East Africa* (1966); etc. Prof. political science and director, Africal Studies Program, Syracuse University, since 1960.

BURKE, KENNETH [Duva] (May 5, 1897–); b. Pittsburgh, Pa. Music critic, author. *The White Oxen, and Other Stories* (1924); *Counter-Statement* (1931); *Towards a Better Life* (1932); *Permanence and Change: An Anatomy of Purpose* (1935); *Attitudes Toward History*, 2v. (1937); *The Philosophy of Literary Form—Studies in Symbolic Action* (1941); *A Grammar of Motives* (1945); *A Rhetoric of Motives* (1950); *A Book of Moments: Poems, 1915–54* (1955); *The Rhetoric of Religion* (1961); *Perspectives by Incongruity* (1964); *Language as Symbolic Action* (1966); *Collected Poems, 1915–1967* (1968); *The Complete White Oxen* (1968). Music critic, *The Dial*, 1927–28; *The Nation*, 1934–36.

BURKHART, ROY ABRAM (Aug. 28, 1895–Dec. 9, 1962); b. Newville, Pa. Congregational clergyman, author. *From Friendship to Marriage* (1927); *Understanding Youth* (1938); *Youth and the Way of Jesus* (1939); *The Church and the Returning Soldier* (1945); *The Secret of Life* (1950); *The Freedom to Become Yourself* (1956); *The Person You Can Be* (1962).

BURLEIGH, GEORGE SHEPARD (Mar. 26, 1821–July 20, 1903); b. Plainfield, Conn. Reformer, poet. *The Maniac and Other Poems* (1849); *Signal Fires on the Trail of the Pathfinder* (1856); etc.

BURLEIGH, WILLIAM HENRY (Feb. 2, 1812–Mar. 18, 1871); b. Woodstock Conn. Editor, reformer, poet. *Poems* (1841); *The Rum Fiend, and Other Poems* (1871). Editor of several temperance magazines.

BURLIN, NATALIE CURTIS (Apr. 26, 1875–Oct. 23, 1921); b. New York City. Collector of Indian folk-songs and Negro music. Editor: *The Indians' Book* (1907); *Hampton Series Negro Folk-Songs*, 4v. (1918–19); *Songs and Tales from the Dark Continent* (1920); etc.

BURLINGAME, EDWARD LIVERMORE (May 30, 1848–Nov. 15, 1922); Boston, Mass. Editor, critic. Editor: *Stories by American Authors*, 10v. (1884–85). Editor, *Scribner's Magazine*, 1886–1914.

BURLINGAME, [William] ROGER (May 7, 1889–Mar. 19, 1967); b. New York City, son of Edward Livermore Burlingame. Author. *You Too* (1924); *Susan Shane* (1926); *High Thursday* (1928); *The Heir* (1930); *Peace Veterans* (1932); *Cartwheels* (1934); *Three Bags Full* (1936); *March of the Iron Men* (1938); *Engines of Democracy* (1940); *Whittling Boy* (biog. of Eli Whitney, 1941); *Of Making Many Books* (1946); *Inventors Behind the Inventor* (1947); *General Billy Mitchell* (1952); *Henry Ford* (1955); *The American Conscience* (1957); *Don't Let Them Scare You: The Life and Times of Elmer Davis* (1961); *Out of Silence into Sound* (1964). With Charles Scribner's Sons, 1914–26.

BURMAN, BEN LUCIEN (Dec. 12, 1895–); b. Covington, Ky. Author. *Mississippi* (1929); *Steamboat 'Round the Bend* (1933); *Blow for a Landing* (1938); *Big River to Cross* (1940); *Everywhere I Roam* (1949); *Seven Stars for Catfish Bend* (1956); *The Street of the Laughing Camel* (1959); *The Owl Hoots Twice at Catfish Bend* (1961); *It's a Big Continent* (1962); *The Generals Wear Cork Hats* (1963); *Blow a Wild Bugle for Catfish Bend* (1967).

BURNET, DANA (July 3, 1888–Oct. 22, 1962); b. Cincinnati, O. Playwright, novelist, poet. *Poems* (1915); *The Shining Adventure* (1916); *It Is a Strange House* (publ. 1925, prod. 1933); *Four Walls* (with George Abbott, prod. 1927); *The Boundary Line* (prod. 1930); *Bad Manners* (with William B. Jutte, prod. 1933); etc.

BURNETT, FRANCES ELIZA HODGSON (Nov. 24, 1849–Oct. 29, 1924); b. Cheetham Hill, England. Novelist. *That Lass o' Lowrie's* (1877); *Surly Tim* (1877); *Haworth's*

(1879); *Louisiana* (1880); *A Fair Barbarian* (1881); *Through One Administration* (1883); *Little Lord Fauntleroy* (1886); *Editha's Burglar* (1888); *Sara Crewe* (1888); *The Pretty Sister of Jose* (1889); *Little Saint Elizabeth* (1890); *Giovanni and the Other* (1892); *The One I Knew the Best of All* (1893); *A Lady of Quality* (1896); *His Grace of Osmondo* (1897); *The Dawn of a To-Morrow* (1906); *The Shuttle* (1907); *The Secret Garden* (1911); *T. Tembarom* (1913); *The Head of the House of Coombe* (1922); *Rovin* (1922). See Vivian Burnett's *The Romantick Lady* (1927).

BURNETT, HALLIE [Southgate]; b. St. Louis, Mo. Editor, author. *A Woman in Possession* (1951); *The Brain Pickers* (1957); *Watch on the Wall* (1965); *The Boarders in the Rue Madam* (1966); etc. Editor: *The Fiction of the Forties* (with Whit Burnett, 1949); *Best College Writing* (1962); *The Stone Soldier* (1964); *Story Jubilee* (1965); etc.

BURNETT, R[aymond] WILL (Sept. 9, 1912–); b. Runnels, Ia. Educator, author. *Teaching Science in the Elementary School* (1953); *Teaching Science in the Secondary School* (1957). Co-author: *Photography* (1956); *Zoology* (1958); *Life: Its Forms and Changes* (1968); *Matter: Its Forms and Changes* (1968); *Energy: Its Forms and Changes* (1968); etc. Prof. science education, University of Illinois, 1947–58; American University, Beirut, Lebanon, 1958–60.

BURNETT, VERNE EDWIN (Feb. 17, 1896–); b. St. Johns, Mich. Public relations counsel, author. *You and Your Public* (1943); *Solving Public Relations Problems* (1952).

BURNETT, WHIT (Aug. 14, 1899–); b. Salt Lake City, Utah. Editor, author. *The Maker of Signs* (1934); *The Literary Life and the Hell with It* (1939); *Immortal Bachelor: The Love Story of Robert Burns* (with John Pen, 1942). Editor: *A Story Anthology, 1931–1933* (with Martha Foley, 1933); *This Is My Best* (1942); *Time to Be Young* (1945); *The World's Best* (1950); *This Is My Best Humor* (1955); *This Is My Philosophy* (1957); *The Spirit of Man* (1958); *First of the Famous* (1962); *Prize College Stories* (1963); *The Stone Soldier* (1964); *That's What Happened to Me.* (1969); *This is My Best* (1970). Co-founder (with Martha Foley), *Story Magazine*, Vienna, 1931, brought to U.S., 1933; co-editor, 1931–41; editor, with Hallie Burnett, 1942–65; on editorial board since 1966.

BURNETT, W[illiam] R[iley] (Nov. 25, 1899–); b. Springfield, O. Novelist. *Little Caesar* (1929); *Iron Man* (1930); *Dark Hazard* (1933); *Goodbye to the Past* (1934); *The Goodhues of Sinking Creek* (1934); *The Dark Command* (1938); *High Sierra* (1940); *Nobody Lives Forever* (1944); *Tomorrow's Another Day* (1945); *The Asphalt Jungle* (1949); *Adobe Walls* (1953); *Captain Lightfoot* (1954); *Pale Moon* (1956); *Bitter Ground* (1958); *Mi Amigo* (1959); *The Goldseekers* (1962); *The Roar of the Crowd* (1964); *Coal Man* (1968).

BURNHAM, CLARA LOUISE [Root] (May 26, 1854–June 20, 1927); b. Newton, Mass. Novelist, poet. *No Gentlemen* (1881); *A Sane Lunatic* (1882); *Dr. Latimer* (1893); *Sweet Clover* (1894); *The Inner Flame* (1912); etc. She wrote poetry for *Wide Awake, St. Nicholas,* etc.

BURNHAM, FREDERICK RUSSELL (May 11, 1861–Sept. 1, 1947); b. Tivoli, Minn. Explorer, author. *Scouting on Two Continents* (1926).

BURNHAM, JAMES (Nov. 22, 1905–); b. Chicago, Ill. Author. *Introduction to Philosophical Analysis* (with Philip E. Wheelwright, 1931); *The Managerial Revolution* (1941); *The Machiavellians* (1943); *The Struggle for the World* (1947); *The Coming Defeat of Communism* (1950); *Containment or Liberation?* (1953); *The Web of Subversion* (1954); *Congress and the American Tradition* (1959); *Suicide of the West* (1964); *The War We Are In* (1967). Editorial board, *National Review,* since 1955. Prof. philosophy, New York University, 1929–53.

BURNHAM, JOHN BIRD (Mar. 16, 1869–Sept. 24, 1939); b. New Castle, Del. Conservationist, explorer, author. *The Rim of Mystery: A Hunter's Wanderings in Unknown Siberia* (1929).

BURNHAM, SMITH (Aug. 20, 1866–Dec. 14, 1947); b. Charleston, Mich. Educator, historian. *A Short History of Pennsylvania* (1912); *The Making of Our Country* (1920), republished as *The Story of Our Country* (1931); *Hero Tales from History* (1922); *The Growth of Our Country* (with F. H. Jack, (1933); etc.

BURNS, ARTHUR F. (Apr. 27, 1904–); b. Stanislau, Aus. Educator, economist. *Production Trends in the United States Since 1870* (1934); *Measuring Business Cycles* (with W. C. Mitchell, 1946); *Full Employment Guideposts and Economic Stability* (with P.A. Samuelson, 1967); *The Defense Sector and the American Economy* (with Jacob Javits and Charles Hitch, 1968); *The Business Cycle in a Changing World* (1969); etc. Prof. economics, Columbia University, since 1944.

BURNS, EDWARD McNALL (Feb. 18, 1897–); b. Burgettstown, Pa. Educator, author. *James Madison, Philosopher of the Constitution* (1938); *Western Civilization, Their History and Their Culture,* 2v. (1941); *David Starr Jordan: Prophet of Freedom* (1953); *The American Idea of Mission* (1957); *Ideas in Conflict* (1960); *The Counter Reformation* (1964); etc. Prof. history, Rutgers University, 1947–51; prof. political science, since 1951.

BURNS, JABEZ (1805–1876). Clergyman, author. *Five Hundred Sketches and Skeletons of Sermons Suited for All Occasions* (1853); etc.

BURNS, JAMES MACGREGOR (Aug. 3, 1918–); b. Melrose, Mass. Political scientist, educator. *Congress on Trial* (1949); *Government by the People* (with Jack W. Peltason, 1952); *Roosevelt: The Lion and the Fox* (1956); *John Kennedy: A Political Profile* (1960); *The Deadlock of Democracy* (1963); *Presidential Government: The Crucible of Leadership* (1966); *Roosevelt: A Soldier of Freedom* (1970); etc. Prof. political science, Williams College, since 1953.

BURNS, JOHN HORNE (Oct. 7, 1916–Aug. 10, 1953); b. Andover, Mass. Novelist. *The Gallery* (1947); *Lucifer With a Book* (1949); *A Cry of Children* (1952).

BURNS, VINCENT GODFREY (Oct. 17, 1893–); b. Brooklyn, N.Y. Congregational clergyman, author. *I Am a Fugitive from a Georgia Chain Gang* (with brother, Robert Elliott Burns, 1932); *I'm in Love With Life* (poems, 1933); *Female Convict* (1934); *Out of These Chains* (1942); *Redwood and Other Poems* (1952); *America, I Love You* (poems, 1957); *Poetry for Young Americans* (1962); *Maryland's Revolutionary Hero, Story of Col. Tench Tilghman* (1963); *Memories and Melodies of Maryland* (1964); *The Man Who Broke a Thousand Chains* (1968); etc. Editor: *The Red Harvest* (poems, 1930).

BURNS, WALTER NOBLE (Oct. 24, 1872–Apr. 15, 1932); b. Lebanon, Ky. Editor, author. *A Year with a Whaler* (1913); *The Saga of Billy the Kid* (1926); *Tombstone* (1927); *The One-Way Ride* (1931); *The Robin Hood of El Dorado* (1932).

BURNSHAW, STANLEY (June 20, 1906–) b. New York. Publisher, author. *The Wheel Age* (1928); *André Spire and His Poetry* (1933); *The Iron Land* (1936); *The Bridge* (play, 1945); *Early and Late Testament* (1949); *Caged in an Animal's Mind* (1963); *The Modern Hebrew Poem Itself* (1965); etc. Editor: *The Poem Itself* (with others, 1960). Pres. Dryden Press, 1939–58; vice-pres., Holt, Rinehart, and Winston, Inc., 1958–65.

"Burnt Norton." Poem by T. S. Eliot published as part of *Four Quartets* (1943).

BURR, AARON (Feb. 6, 1756–Sept. 14, 1836); b. Newark, N.J. Revolutionary soldier, vice-president of the United

States, lawyer, author. *Memoirs*, ed. by Matthew L. Davis, 2v. (1836–37); *The Private Journal*, ed. by same, 2v. (1838). See Johnston D. Kerkhoff's *Aaron Burr* (1931); Samuel H. Wandell's *Aaron Burr in Literature* (1936); Holmes M. Alexander's *Aaron Burr, the Proud Pretender* (1937). See also *Correspondence of Aaron Burr and His Daughter Theodosia*, ed. by Mark Van Doren (1929); Charles Burdette's *Margaret Moncrieffe: The First Love of Aaron Burr* (1860); V. B. Reed's and J. D. Williams' *Case of Aaron Burr* (1960); Donald B. Chidsey's *Great Conspiracy* (1967).

BURR, AGNES RUSH, b. Mt. Holly, N. J. Journalist, author. *Russell H. Conwell* (1905); *Alaska, Our Beautiful Northland of Opportunity* (1919); *India, The Land That Lures* (1929); *Neighbour India* (1929). Contributed to newspapers and syndicates under pen name, "Barbara Boyd."

BURR, ALFRED EDMUND (Mar. 27, 1815–Jan 8, 1900); b. Hartford, Conn. Editor. Co-editor, *The Hartford Weekly Times*, 1839–40; founder, *The Hartford Daily Times*, 1841; editor and publisher, 1841–1900.

BURR, AMELIA JOSEPHINE (1878–); b. New York City. Poet, novelist. *The Roadside Fire* (poems, 1912); *In Deep Places* (poems, 1914); *The Silver Trumpet* (poems, 1918); *The Three Fires* (1922); *Selected Lyrics* (1922); etc.

BURR, ANNA ROBESON (May 26, 1873–Sept. 10, 1941); b. Philadelphia, Pa. Novelist, biographer. *The Autobiography: a Critical and Comparative Study* (1909); *The House on Charles Street* (1921); *The Great House in the Park* (1924); *Palludia* (1928); *Weir Mitchell* (1929); *Wind in the East* (1933); *Golden Quicksand* (1936); etc.

BURR, C[harles] CHAUNCEY (1817–1883). Editor, author. *Lectures of Lola Montez* (1858). Founder, *The Old Guard*, 1862; editor, 1862–69. Also founder of *The Nineteenth Century*, Philadelphia, printed by George B. Zieber & Co.

BURR, GEORGE LINCOLN (Jan. 30, 1857–June 27, 1938); b. Oramel, N.Y. Educator, librarian, historian. *Narratives of the Witchcraft Cases, 1648–1706* (1911); etc. With Cornell University Library, 1878–1939; in charge of The President White Library there, 1891–1938.

Burr, Jane. Pen name of Rose Guggenheim Winslow.

BURRELL, [John] ANGUS (Apr. 9, 1890–June 1, 1957); b. Marysville, Mont. Educator, author. *History of Adult Education in Columbia University* (1954). Co-author (with Dorothy Brewster): *Dead Reckoning in Fiction* (1924); *Adventure or Experience* (1930); *Modern Fiction* (1934). Editor (with Bennett Cerf): *Anthology of Famous American Stories* (1953).

BURRITT, ELIHU (Dec. 8, 1810–Mar. 6, 1879); b. New Britain, Conn. Blacksmith, reformer, known as "The Learned Blacksmith," author. *Sparks from the Anvil* (1846); *Thoughts of Things at Home and Abroad* (1854); *Lectures and Speeches* (1866). See Merle Curti's *The Learned Blacksmith: The Letters and Journals of Elihu Burritt* (1937).

BURROUGHS, EDGAR RICE (Sept. 1, 1875–Mar. 19, 1950); b. Chicago, Ill. Novelist. Creator of the character "Tarzan." *Tarzan of the Apes* (1914); *A Princess of Mars* (1917); *The Land That Time Forgot* (1924); etc. The "Tarzan" and "Mars" books include many volumes. See Henry H. Heins's *A Golden Anniversary Bibliography of Edgar Rice Burroughs* (1964); Richard A. Lupoff's *Edgar Rice Burroughs, Master of Adventure* (1965).

Burroughs, Ellen. Pen name of Sophie Jewett.

BURROUGHS, JOHN (Apr. 3, 1837–Mar. 29, 1921); b. Roxbury, N.Y. Naturalist, author. *Notes on Whitman as Poet and Person* (1867); *Wake-Robin* (1871); *Birds and Poets* (1877); *Locusts and Wild Honey* (1879); *Fresh Fields* (1885); *Far and Near* (1904); *The Writings of John Burroughs*, 17v. (1904–1914); *Leaf and Tendril* (1908); *Time and Change* (1912); *The Summit of the Years* (1914); *The Breath of Life* (1915); *My*

Boyhood (1922); etc. One of his best known poems, "Waiting," was first published in *The Knickerbocker Magazine*, Mar., 1863. See Clara Barrus's *The Life and Letters of John Burroughs*, 2v. (1925); Elizabeth B. Kelly's *John Burroughs* (1959).

BURROUGHS, WILLIAM SEWARD (Feb. 5, 1914–); b. St. Louis, Mo. Author. *Junkie: Confessions of an Unredeemed Drug Addict* (1953); *Naked Lunch* (1959); *The Exterminator* (1960); *Minutes to Go* (1961); *The Soft Machine* (1961); *The Ticket that Exploded* (1962); *Dead Fingers Talk* (1963); *Nova Express* (1964); *So Who Owns Death TV?* (1967).

BURROWS, ABE (Dec. 18, 1910–); b. New York. Playwright, director. Author or co-author: *Guys and Dolls* (prod. 1950); *Three Wishes for Jamie* (prod. 1952); *Can-Can* (prod. 1953); *Abe Burrows' Song Book* (1955); *Say Darling* (prod. 1958); *How to Succeed in Business Without Really Trying* (1961); *Cactus Flower* (1968).

BURROWS, MILLAR (Oct. 26, 1889–); b. Cincinnati, O. Presbyterian clergyman, educator. *Outline of Biblical Theology* (1946). *Palestine Is Our Business* (1949); *The Dead Sea Scrolls* (1955); *More Light on the Dead Sea Scrolls* (1958); etc. Editor: *The Dead Sea Scrolls of St. Mark's Monastery*. Prof. Biblical theology, Yale University Divinity School, 1934–58.

Burt, A. L., Co. New York City. Publishers. Founded 1883, by Albert L. Burt. He died in 1913, and was succeeded by his son, Harry P. Burt (1873–1941). The latter retired in 1937, selling the business to Blue Ribbon Books, Inc. From 1902 the firm specialized in fiction reprints. Their largest series was Burt's Home Library, which included over four hundred titles. The business was sold to Garden City Books, and Burt's Home Library was purchased by Random House.

BURT, KATHERIN NEWLIN (Mrs. Struthers Burt) (Sept. 6, 1882–); b. Fishkill-on-Hudson, N.Y. Novelist. *The Branding Iron* (1919); *Hidden Creed* (1920); *The Red Lady* (1920); *Snow Blind* (1921); *"Q"* (1922); *Guest* (1925); *Cock's Feather* (1928); *A Man's Own Country* (1931); *The Tall Taddler* (1932); *Beggars All* (1933); *This Woman and This Man* (1934); *Rapture Beyond* (1935); *The Monkey's Tail* (under pen name, "Rebecca Scarlett," 1936); *When Beggars Choose* (1937); *If I Love I Must* (1939); *Fatal Gift* (1941); *Captain Millett's Island* (1944); *The Lady in the Tower* (1946); *Close Pursuit* (1947); *Still Water* (1948); *Strong Citadel* (1949); etc.

BURT, MARY ELIZABETH (June 11, 1850–Oct 17, 1918); b. Lake Geneva, Wis. Educator, author. *Browning's Women* (1887); *Literary Landmarks* (1890); *The World's Literature* (1890); etc. Co-editor: *Poems Every Child Should Know* (1904); *Prose Every Child Should Know* (1907); etc.

BURT, [Maxwell] STRUTHERS (Oct. 18, 1882–Aug. 29, 1954); b. Baltimore, Md. Novelist, poet. *In the High Hills* (poems, 1914); *John O'May and Other Stories* (1918); *Songs and Portraits* (poems, 1920); *Chance Encounters* (1921); *The Interpreter's House* (1924); *The Diary of A Dude Wrangler* (autobiography, 1924); *When I Grew Up to Middle Age* (poems, 1925); *The Delectable Mountains* (1927); *They Could Not Sleep* (1928); *The Other Side* (1928); *Festival* (1931); *Entertaining the Islanders* (1933); *Escape from America* (1936); *Powder River* (1938); *Along These Streets* (1941); *War Songs* (1942); *Philadelphia: Holy Experiment* (1945).

BURTIS, THOMSON (Oct. 2, 1896–); b. Brooklyn, N.Y. Novelist, playwright. *Russ Farrell, Airman* (1925); *Border Patrolman* (1927); *Sisters of the Chorus* (with Martin Mooney, prod. 1929); *Winged War* (1929); *Four Aces* (1932); etc.

BURTON, CHARLES PIERCE (Mar. 7, 1862–Mar. 31, 1947); b. Anderson, Ind. Author. The *Bob's Hill* series, 7v. (1905–22); etc.

BURTON, FREDERICK RUSSELL (Feb. 23, 1861–Sept. 30, 1909); b. Jonesville, Mich. Composer, author. *Shifting Sands* (1898); *The Song and the Singer* (1902); *Songs of the Ojibway Indians* (1903); *Strongheart* (1908); etc. Was on staff of *Boston Post, Boston Globe,* New York *Sun,* etc.

BURTON, JOE WRIGHT (Sept. 7 1907–); b. Miles, Tex. Clergyman, editor. *Missionary Illustrations* (1938); *Epochs of Home Missions* (1945); *Prince of the Pulpit* (1946); *Tomorrow You Marry* (1950); *Family Life—A Bible View* (1964); *Light from Above* (1968); etc. Editor, *Southern Baptist Family Life,* since 1954.

BURTON, MARION LE ROY (Aug. 30, 1874–Feb. 18, 1925); b. Brooklyn, Ia. Educator, author. *The Secret of Achievement* (1913); *Our Intellectual Attitude in an Age of Criticism* (1913); *First Things* (1915); etc.

BURTON, RICHARD [Eugene] (Mar. 14, 1861–Apr. 8, 1940); b. Hartford, Conn. Poet, critic. *Dumb in June* (poems, 1895); *Memorial Day and Other Poems* (1897); *Literary Likings* (1898); *Lyrics of Brotherhood* (1899); *Ballad of the Unsuccessful* (1900); *John Greenleaf Whittier* (1900); *Forces in Fiction and Other Essays* (1902); *Message and Melody; A Book of Verse* (1903); *Literary Leaders of America* (1903); *Three of a Kind* (1908); *From the Book of Life* (poems, 1909); *Masters of the English Novel* (1909); *The New American Drama* (1913); *Little Essays in Literature and Life* (1914); *Bernard Shaw; The Man and the Mask* (1916); *Poems of Earth's Meaning* (1917); *Charles Dickens* (1919); *The Carpenter Lad and Other Poems* (1930); *The Collected Poems* (1931); *Masters of the English Novel* (1932); *Higher Than Hills* (1937); etc. Editor: *Living Literature Series; Warner Library; The Contemporary Drama Series.*

Burton, Thomas. Pen name of Stephen Longstreet.

BURTON, VIRGINIA LEE (1909–Oct. 15, 1968); b. Newton Centre, Mass. *Mike Mulligan and His Steam Shovel* (1939); *Calico, the Wonder Horse* (1941); *The Little House* (1942); *Life Story* (1962); etc.

BURTON, WARREN (Nov. 23, 1800–June 6, 1866); b. Wilton, N.H. Unitarian clergyman, lecturer, author. *The District School As It Was* (1833); *The Scenery-Shower* (1844); etc.

BURTON, WILLIAM EVANS (Sept. 24, 1804–Feb. 10, 1860); b. London, England. Actor, editor, author. *Ellen Wareham* (1833); *Waggeries and Vagaries* (1848). Editor: *Burton's Comic Songster* (1837); *The Cyclopeadia of Wit and Humor,* 2v. (1857). Founder, *The Gentleman's Magazine,* (1837); editor, 1837–40; *The Literary Souvenir,* 1838–40.

Burton's Gentleman's Magazine. Philadelphia. Illustrated monthly. Founded July, 1837, and edited by William E. Burton. It was called *The Gentleman's Magazine* until 1839. Edgar Allan Poe was an editor, 1839–40, and was succeeded by George R. Graham. At the close of 1840 Graham bought the magazine and merged it with *The Casket,* and called the new magazine *Graham's. See* Mott's *A History of American Magazines,* v. 1 (1938).

BURTT, EDWIN ARTHUR (Oct. 11, 1892–); b. Groton, Mass. Educator, author. *Principles and Problems of Right Thinking* (1928); *Religion in an Age of Science* (1929); *Types of Religious Philosophy* (1939); *Man Seeks the Divine* (1957); etc. Editor: *The English Philosophers from Bacon to Mill* (1939). Prof. philosophy, Cornell University, 1932–41.

Burwell Papers, The. Papers of Nathaniel Burwell of Virginia, written c. 1676. Attributed to John Colton. Published in *Massachusetts Historical Society Collections* in 1814 and in 1866.

BUSCH, Bonnie [Melbourne] (Jan. 21, 1884–); b. Washington, D.C. Author. *Morality Court* (1920); *Out of the Middle West* (1922); *Eager Vines* (1925); *Progressive Marriage* (1925); *Where the Wind Listeth* (1929); *Waiting* (1934); *Society Be Damned* (1953); etc.

BUSCH, FRANCIS XAVIER (May 9, 1879–); b. Detroit, Mich. Lawyer. *In and Out of Court* (1942); *Law and Tactics in Jury Trials* (1949); *Guilty or Not Guilty* (1952); *Prisoners at the Bar* (1952); *They Escaped the Hangman* (1953); *Enemies of the State* (1954); *Casebook of the Curious and the True* (1957); *Trial Procedure Materials* (1961).

BUSCH, NIVEN (Apr. 26, 1903–); b. New York. Author. *Twenty-One Americans* (1930); *The Carrington Incident* (1941); *Duel in the Sun* (1944); *They Dream of Home* (1944); *Day of the Conquerors* (1946); *The Furies* (1948); *The Hate Merchant* (1953); *The Actor* (1955); *California Street* (1959); *The San Franciscans* (1962); *The Gentleman from California* (1965); and many motion-picture scenarios.

BUSCH, NOEL FAIRCHILD (Dec. 27, 1906–); b. New York. Editor, author. *My Unconsidered Judgement* (1944); *What Manner of Man? A Biography of Franklin Delano Roosevelt* (1944); *Lost Continent* (1945); *Fallen Sun, a Report on Japan* (1948); *Adlai E. Stevenson of Illinois* (1952); *Thailand: An Introduction to Modern Siam* (1959); *Two Minutes to Noon* (1962); *T. R.: The Story of Theodore Roosevelt* (1963); *The Emperor's Sword: Japan Vs. Russia* (1969); etc. Assoc. editor, *Time* 1927–38; senior editor, *Life,* 1938–42.

BUSH, [John Nash] DOUGLAS (Mar. 21, 1896–); b. Morrisburg, Ont. Educator, author. *Mythology and the Renaissance Tradition in English Poetry* (1932); *Mythology and the Romantic Tradition in English Poetry* (1937); *Paradise Lost in Our Time* (1945); *English Literature in the Earlier Seventeenth Century* (1945); *Science and English Poetry* (1950); *English Poetry, the Main Currents from Chaucer to the Present* (1952). Editor: *Complete Poetical Works of John Milton* (1965). English dept., Harvard University, since 1928.

BUSH, VANNEVAR (Mar. 11, 1890–); b. Everett, Mass. Administrator, electrical engineer, author. *Principles of Electrical Engineering* (with W. H. Timbie, 1922); *Operational Circuit Analysis* (1929); *Endless Horizons* (1946); *Modern Arms and Free Men* (1949); *Science in Progress* (with others, 1957); *Science Is Not Enough* (1967).

BUSH, WENDELL T. (Sept. 25, 1866–Feb. 10, 1941); b. Ridgeway, Mich. Educator, author. Founder, with Frederick J. E. Woodbridge and Sterling T. Lamprecht, of the *Journal of Philosophy* in 1923. Dept. of philosophy, Columbia University, 1905–38.

BUSHBY, D[on] MAITLAND (Nov. 7, 1900–); b. Pueblo, Col. Poet. *Mesquite Smoke* (1926); *History of Arizona* (1930); *Tusayan* (1931); *Arizona in Literature* (1933); *Essays on the Southwest* (1935); *Stories of the West* (1936); *April Will Return* (1937); *Western Characters* (1937); *Southwestern Poetry* (1940); etc. Editor: *The Golden Stallion Anthology of Southwestern Poetry* (1930). Editor, *The Tom-Tom* magazine, since 1930.

BUSHNELL, HORACE (Apr. 1, 1802–Feb. 17, 1876); b. Bantam, Conn. Congregational clergyman, essayist. *The Age of Homespun* (1851); *Work and Play; or, Literary Varieties* (1864); *Moral Uses of Dark Things* (1868); etc.

Business Week. New York. Weekly magazine. Founded 1929. Published by McGraw-Hill, Inc. Kenneth Kramer is editor-in-chief. News of and developments in business and finance.

BUSONI, RAFAELLO (1900–); b. Berlin. Illustrator, author. *Mexico and the Inca Lands* (1942); *Stanley's Africa* (1944); *The Man Who Was Don Quixote* (1958); *The Red and the Black* (1964); etc.

Busted Bibliophile and His Books, A. By George Henry Sargent (1928).

Busybody, The. Series of essays by Benjamin Franklin and Joseph Breitnal appearing in the Philadelphia *Mercury,* 1729.

BUTCHER, FANNY (Mrs. Richard Drummond Bokum) (Feb. 13, 1888–); b. Fredonia, Kan. Literary critic. With *Chicago Tribune* since 1912. Pioneer in the "Little Theatre" movement. Founder, "Fanny Butcher Books," a bookstore in Chicago.

BUTLER, CHARLES EDWARD (July 9, 1909–); b. Denver, Colo. Librarian, author. *Cut Is the Branch* (poems, 1945); *Follow Me Ever* (1950).

BUTLER, ELLIS PARKER (Dec. 5, 1869–Sept. 13, 1937); b. Muscatine, Ia. Humorist, author. *Pigs Is Pigs* (1906); *The Incubator Baby* (1906); *Mike Flannery* (1909); *Water Goats* (1910); etc.

BUTLER, HOWARD CROSBY (Mar. 7, 1872–Aug. 15, 1922); b. Croton Falls, N.Y. Archaeologist, author. *The Story of Athens* (1902); *Architecture and Other Arts* (1903); *Sardis* (1922); etc.

BUTLER, NICHOLAS MURRAY (Apr. 2, 1862–Dec. 7, 1947); b. Elizabeth, N.J. Educator, publicist, author. *The Meaning of Education* (1898); *True and False Democracy* (1907); *The American as He Is* (1908); *The International Mind* (1912); *A World In Ferment* (1917); *Is America Worth Savings?* (1920); *Scholarship and Service* (1921); *Building the American Nation* (1923); *The Faith of a Liberal* (1924); *The Path to Peace* (1930); *Looking Forward* (1932); *Between Two Worlds* (1934); *The Family of Nations* (1938); *Across the Busy Years,* 2v. (autobiography, 1939–1940); *Why War?* (1940); *Liberty, Equality, Fraternity* (1942); *The World Today* (1946). With Columbia University from 1885, president from 1902.

BUTLER, PIERCE (Jan 18, 1873–Jan. 16, 1955); b. New Orleans, La. Educator, author. *Life of Judah P. Benjamin* (1906); *Women of Medieval France* (1907); *Analytical Questions on Shakespeare's Plays* (1936); *The Unhurried Years* (1948); *Laurel Hill and Later* (1954). Compiler: *Materials for the Life of Shakespeare* (1930); etc.

BUTLER, PIERCE (Dec. 19, 1886–Mar. 28, 1953); b. Clarendon Hills, Ill. Librarian, bibliographer. *Check List of Fifteenth Century Books* (1933); *The Will of Nichols Jensen* (1928); *Introduction to Library Science* (1933); *The Origin of Printing in Europe* (1940); *The Reference Function of the Library* (1943); etc.

BUTLER, WILLIAM ALLEN (Feb. 20, 1825–Sept. 9, 1902); b. Albany, N.Y. Lawyer, biographer, novelist, poet. *Nothing to Wear* (poems, 1857); *Two Millions* (poems, 1858); *Martin Van Buren* (1862); *Dobbs, His Ferry* (poems, 1875); *Mrs Limber's Raffle* (1876); *Evert Augustus Duyckinck* (1879); *Samuel J. Tilden* (1886); *Domesticus* (1886); etc. See *Colophon,* 1936.

BUTLER, WILLIAM MILL (June 21, 1857–May 13, 1946); b. Rochester, N.Y. Editor, author. *Pantaletta* (1882); *Democracy and Other Poems* (1920); *Rough-Riding on Olympus* (1937); *Tabloid History of Greatest Rochester* (1942); *The Amazon Minstrels, a Satire* (1943); etc.

BUTTERFIELD, LYMAN HENRY (Aug. 8, 1909–); b. Lyndonville, N.Y. Historian. *John Witherspoon Comes to America* (1953). Editor: *Anticipation* (1941); *Letters of Benjamin Rush* (1951); *Papers of Thomas Jefferson,* 5v. (with others, 1950–52); John Adams's *Diary and Autobiography* (with others, 1961); etc.

BUTTERFIELD, ROGER PLACE (1907–). Author. *Al Schmid, Marine* (1944); *The American Past* (1947); *FDR* (1963); etc. Editor: *The Saturday Evening Post Treasury* (with others, 1954).

Butterfield 8. Novel by John O'Hara (1935). New York night life in its range from escapism to criminality, centering on a celebrated murder.

BUTTERS, DOROTHY GILMAN (June 25, 1923–); b. New Brunswick, N.J. Author. *Enchanted Caravan* (1949); *Ragamuffin Alley* (1952); *Four-Party Line (1954); Masquerade* (1961); *The Unexpected Mrs. Pollifax* (1966); etc.

BUTTERWORTH, HEZEKIAH (Dec. 22, 1839–Sept. 5, 1905); b. Warren, R.I. Author of travel stories for children called *Zigzag Journeys,* 17v. (1880–95); also, *The Story of the Hymns* (1875); *The Great Composers* (1884); *Brother Jonathan* (1903). Editor, *Youth's Companion,* 1870–94.

BUTTRICK, GEORGE ARTHUR (Mar. 23, 1892–); b. Seaham Harbour, Northumberland, England. Presbyterian clergyman, author. *The Parables of Jesus* (1928); *Jesus Came Preaching* (1931); *The Christian Fact and Modern Doubt* (1934); *So We Believe, So We Pray* (1951); *Faith and Education* (1952); *Sermons Preached in a University Church* (1959); *Christ and History* (1963); *God, Pain and Evil* (1966); *The Beatitudes* (1968); etc. Preacher to the university and prof. Christian morals, Harvard University, since 1955.

BUTTS, ROBERT FREEMAN (May 14, 1910–); b. Springfield, Ill. Educator, author. *The College Charts Its Course* (1939); *A Cultural History of Education* (1947); *The American Tradition in Religion and Education* (1950); *American Education in International Development* (1963); etc. Prof. education, Teachers College, Columbia University, since 1947.

By Love Possessed. Novel by James Gould Cozzens (1957). Portrays an American community, secure on the surface but ridden by corruption. The action occurs in two days' time and is presented in flashback through the viewpoint of a middle-aged lawyer.

By the Christmas Fire. Essays by Samuel McCord Crothers (1908).

BYARS, WILLIAM VINCENT (June 21, 1857–June 21, 1938); b. Covington, Tenn. Journalist, poet. *Marginalia* (collected poems, 1933); etc. Editor: *B. and M. Gratz, Merchants in Philadelphia* (1916); *Orators and Oratory of Texas* (1923); etc. See *Who's Who in America,* v. 19, 1936–37.

BYE, GEORGE T. (Oct. 21, 1887–); b. Kansas City, Mo. Literary agent. Founder, George T. Bye & Company, New York, Jan. 1, 1927. Founder, Putnam Syndicate and George Palmer Putnam, Inc., July 23, 1923.

BYERS, SAMUEL HAWKINS MARSHALL (July 23, 1838–May 24, 1933); b. Pulaski, Pa. Consul, historical writer, poet. *The Happy Isles, and Other Poems* (1884); *Iowa in War Times* (1888); *Twenty Years in Europe* (1900); *Poems . . . Selected* (1914). His best known poem is "Sherman's March to the Sea."

BYLES, MATHER (Mar. 15, 1706/7–July 5, 1788); b. Boston, Mass. Congregational clergyman, poet, wit. Known as "Punning Byles." *Poems on Several Occasions* (1744); *The Conflagration* (1755); etc. He contributed to *The New England Weekly Journal,* etc. See Joseph Green; and *Poems by Several Hands.* See also Harriet E. Tuell's *Rev. Mather Byles, Parson and Punster,* in *The Magazine of History with Notes and Queries,* Dec., 1907; and Arthur W. H. Eaton's *The Famous Mather Byles* (1914).

BYNNER, EDWIN LASSETTER (1842–Sept. 4, 1893); b. Brooklyn, N.Y. Novelist. *Nimport* (1877); *Damen's Ghost* (1881); *Agnes Surriage* (1886); *Penelope's Suitors* (1887); *The Begum's Daughter* (1890); etc.

BYNNER, WITTER (Aug. 10, 1881–June 2, 1968); b. Brooklyn, N.Y. Poet, playwright. *An Ode to Harvard, and Other Poems* (1907); *The New World* (1915); *Grenstone Poems* (1917); *The Beloved Stranger* (1919); *A Canticle of Pan, and Other Poems* (1920); *A Book of Plays* (1922); *Caravan* (1925); *Cake* (1926); *The Persistence of Poetry* (1929); *Indian Earth* (1929); *Eden Tree* (1931); *Spectra* (with Arthur D.

Ficke, under pen names "Emanuel Morgan," and "Anne Knish," 1916); *Guest Book* (1935); *Selected Poems* (1936); *Against the Cold* (1940); *Take Away the Darkness* (1947); *Journey with Genius: Recollections and Reflections Concerning the D. H. Lawrences* (1951); *A Book of Lyrics* (1955). Translator: *The Way of Life According to Laotzu* (1944); *Iphigenia in Tauris* (1956). Editor; *Sonnets of Frederick Goddard Tuckerman* (1931).

BYRD, RICHARD EVELYN (Oct. 25, 1888–Mar. 11, 1957); b. Winchester, Va. Explorer, naval officer, author. *Skyward* (1928); *Little America* (1930); *Discovery* (1935); *Exploring With Byrd* (1937); *Alone* (1938).

BYRD, WILLIAM (Mar. 28, 1674–Aug. 26, 1744); b. Virginia. Planter, colonial official, author. *History of the Dividing Line Between Virginia and North Carolina* (1728–29); *A Journey to the Land of Eden* (1732); *Progress to the Mines* (1736); all published as *The Westover Manuscripts* (1841). See *The Writings of Colonel Byrd*, ed. by John S. Bassett (1901); *William Byrd's Histories of the Dividing Line Betwixt Virginia and North Carolina*, ed. by W. K. Boyd (1929); Louis B. Wright's *The First Gentlemen of Virginia* (1940).

BYRNE, DONN (Brian Oswald Donn-Byrne) (Nov. 20, 1889–June 18, 1928); b. New York. Novelist, short-story writer. *Stories Without Woman* (1915); *The Stranger's Banquet* (1919); *Messer Marco Polo* (1921); *The Wind Bloweth* (1920); *Blind Raftery* (1924); *Hangman's House* (1926); *Crusade* (1928); *Ireland: The Rock Whence I Was Hewn* (1929); *The Field of Honor* (1929); *Poems* (1934); etc.

BYRNES, JAMES FRANCIS (1879–); b. in South Carolina. Government official, author. *Speaking Frankly* (1947); *All in One Lifetime* (1958). Secretary of State, 1945–47; governor of South Carolina, 1951–55.

C

Cabbages and Kings. Stories by "O. Henry" (William Sidney Porter) (1905).

CABELL, JAMES BRANCH (Apr. 14, 1879–May 5, 1958); b. Richmond, Va. Novelist, essayist, poet. *The Eagle's Shadow* (1904); *The Line of Love* (1905); *Gallantry* (1907); *The Cords of Vanity* (1909); *Chivalry* (1909); *The Rivet in Grandfather's Neck* (1915); *The Certain Hour* (1916); *The Cream of the Jest* (1917); *Beyond Life* (1919); *Jurgen* (1919); *Domnei* (1920); *Figures of Earth* (1921); *The Lineage of Lichfield* (1922); *The High Place* (1923); *Straws and Prayer-Books* (1924); *The Silver Stallion* (1926); *The Music from Behind the Moon* (1926); *Something About Eve* (1927); *Townsend of Lichfield* (1930); *Some of Us* (1930); *These Restless Heads* (1932); *Smirt* (1934); *Smith* (1935); *Smire* (1937); *The King Was in His Counting House* (1938); *Hamlet Had an Uncle* (1940); *The First Gentleman of America* (1942); *The St. Johns* (with A. J. Hanna, 1943); *There Were Two Pirates* (1946); *Let Me Lie* (1947); *Witch-Woman* (1948); *The Devil's Own Dear Son* (1949); *Quiet Please* (1952); *As I Remember It* (1955). *The Works of James Branch Cabell* (Storisende edition), 18v. (1927–30) contain all the novels dealing with Dom Manuel and his descendants. *Preface to the Past* (1936) contains the new prefaces to the collected novels and indicates their proper chronological order. After *These Restless Heads*, Cabell dropped the "James" from his name, for he had finished his cycle of books recording the history of Dom Manuel with which his own personality had been associated. Editor, the *American Spectator*, 1932–35. See Padraic Colum and Margaret Freeman's *Between Friends: Letters of James Branch Cabell* (1962); Desmond Tarrant's *James Branch Cabell: The Dream and the Reality* (1967).

CABELL, NATHANIEL FRANCIS (July 23, 1807–Sept. 1, 1891); b. in Nelson Co., Va. Author. *The Progress of Literature . . . Viewed from a Religious Standpoint* (1868). Editor, the "Lee Papers" in *Southern Literary Messenger*, 1858–60, etc. See Alexander Brown's *The Cabells and Their Kin* (1895).

CABLE, GEORGE WASHINGTON (Oct. 12, 1844–Jan. 31, 1925); b. New Orleans, La. Novelist. *Old Creole Days* (1879); *The Grandissimes* (1880); *The Creoles of Louisiana* (1884); *Dr. Sevier* (1885); *The Silent South* (1885); *Bonaventure* (1888); *Strange True Stories of Louisiana* (1889); *John March, Southerner* (1894); *Strong Hearts* (1899); *Cavalier* (1899); *Bylow Hill* (1902); *Kincaids Battery Gideon's Band* (1914); *The Flower of the Chapdelaines* (1918); *Lovers of Louisiana* (1918); etc. See Arlin Turner's *George Washington Cable* (1957); Louis D. Rubin's *George W. Cable: Life and Times of a Southern Heretic* (1969).

CABOT, JOHN M[oors] (Dec. 11, 1901–); b. Cambridge, Mass. Diplomat, author. *The Racial Conflict in Transylvania* (1926); *Toward Our Common American Destiny* (1955). Appointed U.S. career minister, 1948.

CABOT, RICHARD CLARKE (May 21, 1868–May 8, 1939); b. Brookline, Mass. Physician, educator, author. *What Men Live By* (1914); *Adventures on the Borderlands of Ethics* (1926); *The Meaning of Right and Wrong* (1933); *Honesty* (1938); etc.

CADBURY, HENRY JOEL (Dec. 1, 1883–); b. Philadelphia, Pa. Educator, author. *National Ideals in the Old Testament* (1920); *Style and Literary Method of Luke*, 2v. (1919–20); *The Making of Luke-Acts* (1927); *George Fox's Book of Miracles* (ed., 1949); *The book of Acts in History* (1955); etc.

CADMAN, S[amuel] PARKES (Dec. 18, 1864–July 12, 1936); b. Wellington, Shropshire, England. Congregational clergyman, author. *Charles Darwin and Other English Thinkers* (1911); *The Lure of London* (1925); *Adventure for Happiness* (1935); etc.

CADY, DANIEL L[eavens] (Mar. 10, 1861–Apr. 1, 1934); b. West Windsor, Vt. Lawyer, poet. *Stray Breaths of North East Song* (1905); *Rhymes of Vermont Rural Life*, 4v. (1919–34); *The Hill of Bennington: A Battle Poem* (1927); etc.

CADY, EDWIN HARRISON (Nov. 9, 1917–); b. Old Tappan, N.J. Educator, author. *The Gentleman in America* (1949); *The Road to Realism: The Early Years, 1837–1885, of William Dean Howells* (1956); *The Realist at War: The Mature Years, 1885–1920, of William Dean Howells* (1958); *Stephen Crane* (1962). Editor: *The War of the Critics Over William Dean Howells* (1962); *A Selected Edition of William Dean Howells* (1966). English dept., Syracuse University, 1946–59; prof., Indiana University, since 1959.

CADY, HOWARD STEVENSON (July 28, 1914–); b. Middlebury, Vt. Editor-in-chief, Little Brown and Co., 1952–54; Henry Holt and Co., 1954–57; G. P. Putnam's Sons, 1957–1962; Holt, Rinehart and Winston, Inc., 1962–64; Exec. editor, David McKay, Inc., 1964–68; senior editor, William Morrow and Co., Inc., since 1968.

CADY, JOHN F. (July 14, 1901–); b. Boonville, Ind. Educator. *The Roots of French Imperialism in Eastern Asia* (1954); *A History of Modern Burma* (1958); *Southeast Asia: Its Historical Development* (1964); *Thailand, Burma, Cambodia, Laos* (1966). Prof. history, Ohio University, since 1949.

Caesar's Column. Novel by Ignatius Donnelly (1890). A prophecy of the disintegration of civilization as a result of class warfare.

CAFFIN, CHARLES H[enry] (June 4, 1854–Jan. 14, 1918); b. Sittingbourne, England. Art critic, author. *Story of American Painting* (1907); *Art for Life's Sake* (1913); etc. Art critic: *Harper's Weekly, Evening Post, Sun, International Studio, New York American.*

CAGE, JOHN (Sept. 5, 1912–); b. Los Angeles, Cal. Musician, author. *Virgil Thomson: His Life and Music* (with Kathleen Hoover, 1959); *Silence* (1961); *A Year from Monday* (1967); *Notations* (with Alison Knowles, 1969).

Cagiati, Mrs. Gaetano. See Marie Van Vorst.

CAHAN, ABRAHAM (July 7, 1860–Aug. 31, 1951); b. Vilna, Russia. Editor, author. *Yekl, A Tale of the New York Ghetto* (1896); *The Imported Bridegroom and Other Stories* (1898); *The Rise of David Levinsky* (1917); *Bletter von Mein Leben* (autobiography in Yiddish). Editor in chief, *Jewish Daily Forward.*

CAHILL, HOLGER (Jan. 13, 1893–July 8, 1960); b. St. Paul, Minn. Art director, author. *Profane Earth* (1927); *George O. "Pop" Hart* (1928); *A Yankee Adventurer* (1930); *Max Weber* (1930); *American Folk Art* (1932); *American Sources of Modern Art* (1933); *Art in America: A Complete Survey* (1935); *Look South to the Polar Star* (1947); *Shadow of My Hand* (1956); etc.

CAHN, EDMOND [Nathaniel] (Jan. 17, 1906–Aug. 9, 1964); b. New Orleans, La. Educator. *The Sense of Injustice* (1949); *The Moral Decision* (1955); *The Predicament of Democratic Man* (1961). Editor: *The Great Rights* (1963); *The Edmond Cahn Reader* (1966). Prof. law, New York University, 1948–64.

CAIDIN, MARTIN (1927–). Author. *Rockets Beyond Earth* (1952); *The Air Force* (1957); *Countdown for Tomorrow* (1958); *Spaceport U.S.A.* (1959); *The Astronauts* (1960); *Thunderbirds!* (1961); *By Apollo to the Moon* (1963); *Everything But the Flak* (1964); *Four Came Back* (1968); *Anytime, Anywhere* (1969); etc.

CAILLIET, EMILE (Dec. 17, 1894–); b. Dampierre, Fr. Educator, author. *The Life of the Mind* (1942); *Pascal: Genius in the Light of Scripture* (1945); *The Christian Approach to Culture* (1953); *The Dawn of Personality* (1955); *The Recovery of Purpose* (1959); *Young Life* (1964); *Journey into Light* (1968); etc. Prof. Christian philosophy, Princeton Theological Seminary, since 1947.

CAIN, JAMES M[allahan] (July 1, 1892–); b. Annapolis, Md. Journalist, author. *Our Government* (1930); *The Postman Always Rings Twice* (1934); *Double Indemnity* (1936); *Serenade* (1937); *Mildred Pierce* (1941); *Love's Lovely Counterfeit* (1942); *Three of a Kind* (*Sinful Woman, Double Indemnity, The Embezzler*) (1943); *Past All Dishonor* (1946); *The Butterfly* (1947); *The Moth* (1948); *Galatea* (1953); *Mignon* (1962); *The Magician's Wife* (1965).

Caine Mutiny, The. Novel by Herman Wouk (1951). About sailors in conflict with each other aboard a minesweeper during World War II. Adapted by the author as the play *The Caine Mutiny Court-Martial* (1954).

CAIRNS, HUNTINGTON (Sept. 1, 1904–); b. Baltimore, Md. Lawyer, author. Author or editor: *Law and the Social Sciences* (1935); *The Theory of Legal Science* (1941); *Invitation to Learning* (with Mark Van Doren and Allen Tate, 1941); *Masterpieces of Painting from the National Gallery of Art* (with John Walker, 1944); *The Limits of Art* (1948); *Legal Philosophy from Plato to Hegel* (1949); *Lectures in Criticism* (1961); *Treasures from the National Gallery of Art* (with John Walker, 1962). Editor: *H. L. Mencken: The American Scene* (1965).

CAIRNS, WILLIAM B. (June 4, 1867–Aug. 2, 1932); b. Ellsworth, Wis. Educator, author. *A History of American Literature* (1912); *British Criticisms of American Writers,* 2v. (1918–22); etc. Editor: *Selections from Early American Writers, 1607–1800* (1909).

Caius Marius. Tragedy by Richard Penn Smith (1831).

Calamus. Letters by Walt Whitman (1897). Written 1868–80, to his friend Peter Doyle. Published after his death, by Richard M. Bucke.

"Calamus." Poem by Walt Whitman (1860). Presentation of the poet's views concerning man's attachment to man.

Calavar. Novel by Robert Montgomery Bird (1834). A romance of Mexico.

Calaynos. The first play written by George Henry Boker (publ. 1848, prod. London, 1849, prod. Philadelphia, 1851). Based on the antipathy of the Spanish for the Moors.

Caldecott Medal. Annual award given to an outstanding book for children, named in honor of Randolph Caldecott, English artist. The medal bears a picture of John Gilpin, done after Caldecott's representation.

CALDER, [Peter] RITCHIE (1906–). Author. *Carry On, London* (1941); *Men Against the Desert* (1952); *Science in Our Lives* (1955); *Men Against the Frozen North* (1957); *Medicine and Man* (1958); *The Inheritors* (1961); *Living With the Atom* (1962); *Two-Way Passage* (1964); *The Evolution of the Machine* (1968).

CALDWELL, ERSKINE [Preston] (Dec. 17, 1903–); b. White Oak, Ga. Novelist. *The Bastard* (1930); *Poor Fool* (1930); *American Earth* (1931); *Tobacco Road* (1932); *God's Little Acre* (1933); *We Are the Living* (1933); *Journeyman* (1935); *Kneel to the Rising Sun, and Other Stories* (1935); *Some American People* (1935); *The Sacrilege of Alan Kent* (1936); *You Have Seen Their Faces* (with Margaret Bourke-White, 1937); *North of the Danube* (with Margaret Bourke-White, 1939); *Trouble in July* (1940); *Georgia Boy* (1943); *Tragic Ground* (1944); *A House in the Uplands* (1946); *The Sure Hand of God* (1947); *Call It Experience* (1951); *The Courting of Susie Brown* (1952); *The Complete Stories of Erskine Caldwell* (1953); *Love and Money* (1954); *Gretta* (1955); *Gulf Coast Stories* (1956); *Certain Women* (1957); *Molly Cottontail* (1958); *Claudelle Inglish* (1959); *Jenny by Nature* (1961); *Close to Home* (1962); *The Last Night of Summer* (1963); *Around About America* (1964); *In Search of Bisco* (1965); *The Deer at Our House* (1966); *Miss Mamie Aimee* (1967); *Summertime Island* (1968).

CALDWELL, HOWARD WALTER (Aug. 26, 1858–Mar. 2, 1927); b. Bryan, O. Educator, historian. *History of the United States, 1815–1861* (1896); *Henry Clay, the Great Compromiser* (1899); etc.

CALDWELL, [Janet] TAYLOR (Mrs. J. Marcus Reback) (Sept. 7, 1900–); b. near Manchester, England. Novelist. *Dynasty of Death* (1938); *The Eagles Gather* (1940); *The Earth Is the Lord's* (1941); *Melissa* (1948); *Let Love Come Last* (1949); *The Balance Wheel* (1951); *The Devil's Advocate* (1952); *Never Victorious, Never Defeated* (1956); *The Sound of Thunder* (1957); *Dear and Glorious Physician* (1959); *A Prologue to Love* (1961); *Grandmother and the Priests* (1963); *A Pillar of Iron* (1965); *No One Hears But Him* (1966); *Dialogues with the Devil* (1967); *Testimony of Two Men* (1968); *The Late Clara Beame* (1969); *Great Lion of God* (1970); etc.

CALDWELL, WALLACE EVERETT (Apr. 26, 1890–); b. Brooklyn, N.Y. Educator, author. *Hellenic Conceptions of Peace* (1919); *The Ancient World* (1937); *World History* (with E. H. Merrill, 1949). Editor: *Readings in Ancient History* (with W. C. McDermott, 1951). Prof. ancient history, University of North Carolina, since 1928.

Caleb West, Master Diver. Novel by F. Hopkinson Smith (1898). Romance of the building of the Race Rock lighthouse.

CALEF, ROBERT (1648–Apr. 13, 1719); b. Boston, Mass. Merchant, writer on witchcraft. *More Wonders of the Invisible World* (1700), a reply to Cotton Mather's *Wonders of the Invisible World* (1693).

CALHOUN, JOHN CALDWELL (Mar. 18, 1782–Mar. 31, 1850); b. "Calhoun Settlement," South Carolina. Statesman, orator, author. *The Works,* ed. R. K. Crallé, 6v. (1851–55). His "South Carolina Exposition" (1828) embodied the doctrine of nullification. See William M. Meigs' *Life of John C. Calhoun,* 2v. (1917); Margaret L. Coit's *John C. Calhoun: American Portrait* (1950).

CALHOUN, PHILO CLARKE (Aug. 28, 1889–Dec. 19, 1964); b. Bridgeport, Conn. Lawyer, author. *Dickens' "Christmas Carol" after a Hundred Years* (with H. J. Heaney, 1945); *Who Dealt This Mess?* (with H. T. Webster, 1948); *Life With Rover* (with same, 1949); etc. Editor: *The Best of H. T. Webster* (1953).

CALHOUN, ROBERT LOWRY (Dec. 30, 1896–); b. St. Cloud, Minn. Educator, author. *God and the Common Life* (1935); *The Nature of Religious Experience* (1937); *The Meaning of the Humanities* (1938); *Work and Vocation* (1954); etc.

Californian, The. Monterey, Cal. Newspaper. Founded 1846. Moved to San Francisco in 1847 and expired in 1848, when the editors joined the Gold Rush.

Californian, The. See *The Overland Monthly.*

CALISHER, HORTENSE (Dec. 20, 1911–); b. New York. Author. *In the Absence of Angels* (1951); *False Entry* (1961); *Tale for the Mirror* (1962); *Textures of Life* (1963); *Extreme Magic* (1964); *Journal from Ellipsia* (1965); *The Railway Police and the Last Trolley Ride* (1966); *The New Yorkers* (1969).

CALKINS, EARNEST ELMO (Mar. 25, 1868–Oct. 4, 1964); b. Geneseo, Ill. Advertising man, author. *Care and Feeding of Hobby Horses* (1934); *They Broke the Prairie* (1937); *And Hearing Not—Annals of an Adman* (1946).

CALKINS, FRANKLIN WELLES (June 7, 1857–Dec. 20, 1928); b. in Iowa Co., Wis. Explorer, author. *Tales of the West,* 3v. (1893); *Two Wilderness Voyages* (1902); *Betty Canteen* (1924); etc. Contributed Western fiction to *Youth's Companion* for forty years.

Call It Sleep. Novel by Henry Roth (1934). One of the earliest major novels to concern itself with the American-Jewish experience of modern life. Relatively unknown for more than two decades, it was reprinted in the 1960's and received new critical appraisal.

"Call of the Bugles, The." Poem by Richard Hovey (1898).

Call of the Wild, The. Novel by Jack London (1903). Story of a dog in the Klondike named Buck, formerly a house dog, but under primitive circumstances he reverts to his wild instincts and joins a pack of wolves.

Call to Greatness. A work of personal political philosophy, by Adlai Stevenson (1954).

CALLAHAN, NORTH (Aug. 7, 1908–); b. Sweetwater, Tenn. Educator, author. *The Armed Forces as a Career* (1947); *Smoky Mountain Country* (1952); *Henry Knox: General Washington's General* (1958); *Daniel Morgan* (1961); *Royal Raiders: The Tories of the American Revolution* (1963). Syndicated columnist, "So This Is New York," 1943–68. History dept., New York University, since 1957.

CALLENDER, HAROLD (Sept. 29, 1892–Oct. 8, 1959); b. Kansas City, Kan. Journalist, author. *A Preface to Peace* (1944); etc. Correspondent, *The New York Times,* from 1926.

CALLENDER, JOHN (1706–Jan. 26, 1748); b. Boston, Mass. Baptist clergyman, historian. *An Historical Discourse in the Civil and Religious Affairs of the Colony of Rhode Island* (1739), the only history of that state for more than a century.

Calumet "K." Novel by Samuel Merwin and H. K. Webster (1901). The boss who does things, takes long shots, and makes good.

CALVERT, GEORGE HENRY (June 2, 1803–May 24, 1889); b. near Bladensburg, Md. Poet, essayist, novelist, playwright. *A Volume from the Life of Herbert Barclay* (anon., 1833); *Cabiro: A Poem* (1840); *Scenes and Thoughts on Europe,* 2v. (1845–52); *Poems* (1847); *Comedies* (1852); *The Gentleman* (1863); *First Years in Europe* (1866); *Goethe: His Life and Works* (1872); *Wordsworth* (1878); *Life, Death, and Other Poems* (1882); *Threescore, and Other Poems* (1883); etc.

CALVERTON, V[ictor] F[rancis] (June 25, 1900–Nov. 20, 1940); b. (George Goetz) Baltimore, Md. Novelist, critic, lecturer. *The Newer Spirit* (1925); *Sex Expression in Literature* (1926); *Three Strange Lovers* (stories, 1929); *The New Ground of Criticism* (1930); *American Literature at the Crossroads* (1931); *The Liberation of American Literature* (1931); *The Passing of the Gods* (1934); *The Man Inside* (1935); *The Awakening of America,* v. i (1939); *Where Angels Dared to Tread* (1941). Editor, *Anthology of American Negro Literature* (1929). Founder, *The Modern Quarterly,* 1923; editor, 1923–40.

Calvin, Mrs. Frederick. See Kate L. McLaurin.

Cambridge Dante Society. Cambridge, Mass. Founded 1881. It grew out of the informal meetings of the Dante Club at the home of Henry Wadsworth Longfellow. Its first three presidents were Longfellow, James Russell Lowell, and Charles Eliot Norton. It developed the Dante collection of Harvard University.

Cambridge History of American Literature, The. Edited by William Peterfield Trent, John Erskine, Stuart P. Sherman, Carl Van Doren, 4v. (1917–21). Historical survey of American literature, each major section of the work being written by an authority and accompanied by bibliographies. The 1933 edition appeared in three volumes.

CAMERON, D[onald] EWEN (Dec. 24, 1901–1967); b. Bridge of Allan, Scot. Psychiatrist, author. *Objective and Experimental Psychiatry* (1935); *Remembering* (1947); *Life Is for Living* (1948); *General Psychotherapy: Dynamics and Procedures* (1950); *Psychotherapy in Action* (1968).

CAMERON, GEORGE G[lenn] (July 30, 1905–); b. Washington, Pa. Educator. *History of Early Iran* (1936). Editor, posthumous works of Edward Chiera: *They Wrote on Clay* (1938). Prof. Near Eastern cultures, University of Michigan, since 1948.

CAMMANN, SCHUYLER VAN RENSSELAER (Feb. 2, 1912–); b. New York. Educator, author. *Land of the Camel* (1951); *Trade Through the Himalayas* (1951); *China's Dragon Robes* (1952); *Substance and Symbol in Chinese Toggles* (1962); etc. Faculty, University of Pennsylvania, since 1948.

CAMP, CHARLES WADSWORTH (Oct. 18, 1879–Oct. 31, 1936); b. Philadelphia, Pa. Novelist, playwright. *Sinister Island* (1915); *The House of Fear* (1916); *The Hidden Road* (1922); *Evil Tongues* (prod. 1915); etc.

CAMP, WALTER CHAUNCEY (Apr. 7, 1859–Mar. 14, 1925); b. New Britain, Conn. Athletic director, sports writer. *The Substitute* (1908); *Jack Hall at Yale* (1909); etc. See Harford Powel's *Walter Camp, the Father of American Football* (1926).

"Camp Ballad." By Francis Hopkinson (1777). A poem which did much for the American cause.

CAMPBELL, ALEXANDER (Sept. 12, 1788–Mar. 4, 1866); b. in Co. Antrim, Ireland, came to the United States in 1809. Co-founder of the Disciples of Christ, editor, author. *The Christian System* (1839); etc. Founder, the *Christian Baptist,*

1823; the *Millennial Harbinger,* 1830. Founder, Bethany College, 1840; president, 1840–66. *See* Robert Richardson's *Memoirs of Alexander Campbell* (1870).

CAMPBELL, BARTLEY (Aug. 12, 1843–July 30, 1888); b. Pittsburgh, Pa. Editor, playwright. *Through Fire* (prod. 1871); *Peril, or Love at Long Branch* (prod. 1872); *The Virginian* (prod. 1873); *How Women Love* (prod. 1877); *The Gulley Slave* (prod. 1879); *My Partner* (prod. 1879); etc. Founder, *Pittsburgh Evening Mail,* 1868; and *The Southern Monthly Magazine,* New Orleans, 1869.

CAMPBELL, CHARLES (May 1, 1807–July 11, 1876); b. Petersburg, Va. Educator, historian, editor, antiquarian. *Introduction to the History of the Colony and Ancient Dominion of Virginia* (1847), enlarged as *History of the Colony and Ancient Dominion of Virginia* (1860). Editor: *The Bland Papers,* 2v. (1840–43).

CAMPBELL, HELEN STUART (July 4, 1839–deceased); b. Lockport, N.Y. Author. The *Ainslie* series, 4v. (1864–77); *Six Sinners* (1877); *His Grandmothers* (1878); *Ann Bradstreet and Her Time* (1891); *Ballantyne* (1901); etc.

CAMPBELL, JOHN (Oct. 22, 1810–Apr. 29, 1874); b. Points Pass, Armagh, Ireland. Publisher and bookseller, author. *Campbell's Democratic Song and Recitation Book* (1842); *A Theory of Equality* (1848); *Negro-Mania* (1851); *Unionists vs. Traitors* (1861). Came to America in 1843 and in 1850 established in Philadelphia the bookselling and publishing business of John Campbell. He was succeeded by his son William J. Campbell (1850–1931). The firm name was changed to John Campbell & Son in 1871 and to William J. Campbell in 1879.

CAMPBELL, JOHN WOOD (1910–). Editor, author. *The Black Star Passes* (1930); *Islands of Space* (1956); *Invaders from the Infinite* (1961). Editor: *Astounding Stories* (1937); *Collected Editorials from Analog* (1966).

CAMPBELL, JOSEPH (Mar. 26, 1904–); b. New York. Educator, author. *Grimm's Fairy Tales: Folkloristic Commentary* (1944); *A Skeleton Key to Finnegan's Wake* (with Henry Morton Robinson, 1944); *The Hero with a Thousand Faces* (1949); *The Masks of God,* 2v. (1959, 1962); Editor: Heinrich Zimmer's *The King and the Corpse* (1948), *Philosophies of India* (1951), *The Art of Indian Asia,* 2v. (1955); *Papers from the Eranos Yearbooks,* 4v. (1954–60).

CAMPBELL, KILLIS (June 11, 1872–Aug. 8, 1937); b. Enfield, Va. Educator, author. *The Mind of Poe and Other Studies* (1933); etc. Editor: *The Poems of Edgar Allan Poe* (1917); *Poe's Short Stories* (1927); etc.

CAMPBELL, LILY BESS (June 20, 1883–Feb. 18, 1967); b. Ada, O. Educator, author. *These Are My Jewels* (1929); *Shakespeare's Tragic Heroes* (1930); *Shakespeare's "Histories"* (1947); *Divine Poetry and Drama in Sixteenth Century England* (1959); etc. Editor: *Mirror for Magistrates* (1938); *Parts Added to the Mirror for Magistrates* (1946); *Divine Poetry and Drama in 16th Century England* (1959).

CAMPBELL, OSCAR JAMES (Aug. 16, 1879–June 1, 1970); b. Cleveland, O. Educator, translator. *Comedies of Holberg* (translator, with Frederic Schenk, 1914); *A Book of Narratives* (with R. A. Rice, 1917); *The Teaching of English in American Colleges and Universities* (1934); *Comicall Satyre and Shakespeare's Troilus and Cressida* (1938); *Shakespeare's Satire* (1943); *The Sonnets, Songs and Poems of Shakespeare* (1965); etc. Prof. English, Columbia University, from 1936.

CAMPBELL, RUTH RAMSDELL (Mrs. James Francis Campbell) (Feb. 11, 1888–); b. Manistee, Mich. Author. *The All Alone House* (1923); *The Cat Whose Whiskers Slipped* (1925); *The Turtle Whose Snap Unfastened* (1927); etc.

CAMPBELL, SAMUEL ARTHUR (Aug. 1, 1895–Apr. 16, 1962); b. Watseka, Ill. Author. *How's Inky* (1943); *Too Much Salt and Pepper* (1944); *On Wings of Cheer* (1948); *Loony Coon* (1954); *Sweet Sue's Adventures* (1959); *Calamity Jane, Wise Old Raccoon* (1962).

Campbell, Scott. Pen name of Frederick William Davis.

CAMPBELL, WALTER STANLEY (Aug. 15, 1887–Dec., 1957); b. Severy, Kan. Educator, author. Pen name, "Stanley Vestal." Under own name: *New Sources of Indian History* (1934); *Professional Writing* (1938); *Writing Magazine Fiction* (1940); *Writing Non-fiction* (1944); *The Book Lover's Southwest* (1955); and under pen name: *Fandango: Ballads of the Old West* (1927); *Kit Carson* (1928); *Sitting Bull* (1932); *Warpath* (1934); *Mountain Men* (1937); *Revolt on the Border* (1938); *The Old Santa Fe Trail* (1939); *King of the Fur Traders* (1940); *Short Grass Country* (1941); *Bigfoot Wallace* (1942); *The Missouri* (1945); *Jim Bridger* (1946); *Warpath and Council Fire* (1948); *Queen of Cow Towns: Dodge City* (1952); *Joe Meek* (1952). Faculty, University of Oklahoma, from 1915–57.

CAMPBELL, WILLIAM EDWARD MARCH (Sept. 18, 1893–1954); b. Mobile, Ala. Novelist. Wrote under the name, "William March." *Company K* (1933); *Come In at The Door* (1934); *The Little Wife and Other Stories* (1935); *The Tallons* (1936); *Some Like Them Short* (1939); *Trial Balance* (1945); *The Bad Seed* (1954); etc.

CAMPBELL, WILLIAM J[ames] (Mar. 25, 1850–Sept. 9, 1931); b. Philadelphia, Pa. Bookseller, publisher. Compiler: *The Collection of Franklin Imprints in the Museum of the Curtis Publishing Company. With a Short-Title Check List of all the Books, Pamphlets, Broadsides, &c. known to have been published by Benjamin Franklin* (1918). Joined the book firm of his father, John Campbell (q.v.), Apr. 3, 1871, and the name of the firm was changed to John Campbell & Son, and in 1879 changed to William J. Campbell. William J. Campbell retired Mar. 25, 1930, and his son, John J. Campbell (b. Aug. 18, 1883), who had entered the firm in Sept., 1903, became sole proprietor. The firm dealt in rare books, prints, and autographs, and published a number of books and pamphlets. William J. Campbell was a collector of American first editions, Jeffersoniana, and the lithographic portraits of Albert Newsam.

CANADAY, JOHN E. (Feb. 1, 1907–); b. Ft. Scott, Kan. Art critic, author. *The Metropolitan Seminars in Art* (portfolios), *Mainstreams of Modern Art* (1959); *Embattled Critic* (1962); also mystery novels under pen name "Matthew Head." Art critic, *The New York Times,* since 1959.

CANBY, HENRY SEIDEL (Sept. 6, 1878–Apr. 5, 1961); b. Wilmington, Del. Educator, editor, author. *The Short Story* (1902); *Saturday Papers* (with others, 1921); *Definitions* (1922); *Classic Americans* (1931); *Designed for Reading* (with others, 1934); *The Age of Confidence* (1934) and *Alma Mater* (1936) [both included in his autobiography, *American Memoir* (1947)]; *Seven Years' Harvest* (1936); *Thoreau* (1939); *Walt Whitman: An American* (1943); *Family History* (1945); *Turn West, Turn East: Mark Twain and Henry James* (1951); etc. Editor: *The Works of Henry D. Thoreau* (1937). Co-founder, *Saturday Review of Literature,* 1924; editor, 1924–36; chairman of editorial board, 1936–58. Chairman, board of judges, Book-of-the-Month Club, 1926–58. Lecturer with professorial rank, Yale University, 1922–41.

Candid Examination of the Mutual Claims of Great Britain, and the Colonies, A. By Joseph Galloway (1731–1803), published in 1775.

Candle-Lightin' Time. Poems by Paul Laurence Dunbar (1901).

Candy. Novel by Terry Southern and Mason Hoffenberg (1958). The sexual adventures of a candid (Candide-like) young girl. Became a bestseller after the relaxation of obscenity standards in books and periodicals during the 1960's.

CANE, MELVILLE HENRY (Apr. 15, 1879–); b. Plattsburg, N.Y. Lawyer, poet. *January Garden* (1926); *Behind Dark Spaces* (1930); *A Wider Arc* (1947); *Making a Poem* (1953); *And Pastures New* (1956); *Bullet Hunting and Other New Poems* (1960); *To Build A Fire* (1964).

CANFIELD, CASS (Apr. 1897–); b. New York. Publisher, editor. *The Publishing Experience* (1969); *Up and Down and Around: A Publisher Recollects the Time of His Life* (1971). With Harper and Bros., 1927–62; pres., 1931–45; chairman of the board, 1945–55; chairman of exec. committee and editorial board, 1955–62; chairman of exec. committee and editorial board, Harper and Row, 1962–67; now senior editor, Harper and Row.

Canfield, Dorothy. See Dorothy Canfield Fisher.

CANFIELD, LEON H[ardy] (Oct. 3, 1886–); b. Binghamton, N.Y. Historian, author. *The Early Persecution of the Christians* (1913); *The United States in the Making* (with others, 1937); *The Making of Modern America* (1950); *The Presidency of Woodrow Wilson* (1966). Prof. history, Fairleigh Dickinson, since 1950.

CANFIELD, WILLIAM WALKER (July 6, 1857–Aug. 28, 1937); b. Ellicottville, N.Y. Author. *The Spotter* (1908); *Along the Way* (1909); *The White Seneca* (1911); *The Sign Above the Door* (1912); etc. Compiler: *The Legends of the Iroquois* (1902).

CANHAM, ERWIN DAIN (Feb. 13, 1904–); b. Auburn, Me. Editor, radio and television commentator, author. *Awakening: The World at Mid-Century* (with others, 1951); *New Frontiers for Freedom* (1954); *Commitment to Freedom* (1958); *The Christian Science Way of Life* (1962). Editor, *Christian Science Monitor,* since 1945.

CANNING, JOSIAH DEAN (1816–1892). Poet. Pen name, "Peasant Bard." *Poems* (1838); *The Harp and Plow* (1852); *The Shad-Fishers* (1854).

CANNON, CHARLES JAMES (Nov. 4, 1800–Nov. 9, 1860); b. New York. Poet, novelist, playwright. *Facts, Feelings and Fancies* (1835); *The Poet's Quest, and Other Poems* (1841); *The Crowning Hour, and Other Poems* (1843); *Mora Carmody* (anon., 1844); *Scenes and Characters from the Comedy of Life* (anon., 1847); *The Oath of Office* (prod. 1850); *Poems, Dramatic and Miscellaneous* (1851); *Ravellings from the Web of Life* (under pen name, "Grandfather Greenway," 1855); *Dramas* (1857); etc.

CANNON, CORNELIA JAMES (Mrs. Walter Bradford Cannon) (Nov. 17, 1876–); b. St. Paul, Minn. Author. *The Pueblo Boy* (1926); *Red Dust* (1928); *The Pueblo Girl* (1929); *Heirs* (1930); *Lazaro in the Pueblos* (1931); *The Fight for the Pueblo* (1934).

CANNON, FANNY [Venable] (1876–); b. New York City. Playwright, critic. *The Mark of the Beast* (with George Earle, prod. 1915); *Rehearsal for Safety* (1939); *Playing Fair* (1940); etc.

CANNON, LeGRAND, Jr. (Dec. 1, 1899–); b. New Haven, Conn. Author. *A Mighty Fortress* (1937); *The Kents* (1938); *Look to the Mountain* (1942); *Come Home at Even* (1951).

CANNON, WILLIAM RAGSDALE (Apr. 5, 1916–); b. Chattanooga, Tenn. Educator, author. *A Faith for These Times* (1944); *The Christian Church* (1945); *The Theology of John Wesley* (1946); *The Redeemer* (1951); *History of Christianity in the Middle Ages* (1960); *Journeys After St. Paul* (1963); etc. Dean, Candler School of Theology, Emory University, since 1953.

Canoe and the Saddle, The. By Theodore Winthrop (1863). Describes his journey across the Cascade Mountains in the Northwest.

CANONGE, LOUIS PLACIDE (June 29, 1822–Jan. 22, 1893); b. New Orleans, La. Journalist, playwright. *Gaston de St. Elmo* (1850); *Le Comte de Carmagnole* (1856); etc.

CANTACUZENE, PRINCESS (Julia Dent Grant) (June 7, 1876–deceased); b. The White House, Washington, D.C. Author. *Revolutionary Days* (1919); *Russian People* (1920); *My Life Here and There* (1921).

CANTARELLA, MICHELE FRANCESCO (June 13, 1899–); b. Giarre, It. Educator. *The Italian Heritage* (1959). Editor: *Military Dictionary: English-Italian, Italian-English* (1943). Prof. Italian, Smith College, since 1950.

Canterbury Pilgrims, The. Play by Percy Mackaye (prod. 1903).

Canticle for Liebowitz, A. By W. M. Miller, Jr. (1960). Novel about the survival of mankind after a nuclear war, cast as an allegorical fantasy.

Cantos. Long poem by Ezra Pound. Published to date in the following volumes: *A Draft of XVI Cantos* (1925); *A Draft of the Cantos 17–27* (1928); *A Draft of XXX Cantos* (1930); *A Draft of Cantos XXXI–XLI* (1935); *The Fifth Decade of Cantos* (1937); *Cantos LII–LXXI* (1940); *The Pisan Cantos* (1948); *Section: Rock Drill, 85–95 de los cantares* (1955); *Thrones: 96–109 de los cantares* (1959). This poem in progress, written in "free" verse, presents the human comedy in several dimensions and many voices. It has been Pound's major poetic effort since its inception.

CANTRIL, [Albert] HADLEY (June 16, 1906–); b. Hyrum, Utah. Psychologist, author. *Psychology of Radio* (with Gordon Allport, 1935); *The Invasion from Mars* (with others, 1941); *Gauging Public Opinion* (with others, 1944); *Understanding Man's Social Behavior* (1948); *Tensions That Cause Wars* (ed., 1950); *The Politics of Despair* (1958); *Human Nature and Political Systems* (1961); etc. Editor: *Public Opinion, 1935–46* (1951).

CANTWELL, ROBERT [Emmett] (Jan. 31, 1908–); b. Little Falls (now Vader), Wash. Novelist. *Laugh and Lie Down* (1931); *The Land of Plenty* (1934); *Nathaniel Hawthorne: The American Years* (1948); *Famous American Men of Letters* (1956); *Alexander Wilson, Naturalist and Pioneer* (1961). Editor, *Newsweek,* 1949–54. Senior editor, *Sports Illustrated,* since 1961.

CANZONERI, ROBERT (Nov. 21, 1925–); b. San Marcos, Tex. Educator, author. *"I Do So Politely": A Voice from the South* (1965); *Men with Little Hammers* (1969). Co-editor, *Per Se.* Faculty, Ohio State University, since 1966.

Cape and Smith. Publishers. The firm was founded in New York in 1929 by Jonathan Cape, an English publisher, and Harrison Smith. Dissolved in 1932.

CAPEN, OLIVER BRONSON (June 28, 1878–May 2, 1953); b. Binghamton, N.Y. Publisher. *Country Homes of Famous Americans* (1904). With Doubleday, Page & Co., 1903–07; Crowell Publishing Co., from 1924; McCall Co., from 1917, director from 1927.

CAPLAN, HARRY (Jan. 7, 1896–); b. Hoag's Corners, N.Y. Educator. Author and editor: *Gianfresco Pico della Mirandola, On the Imagination* (1930); *Mediaeval Artes Praedicandi* (1934); *Mediaeval Artes Praedicandi—A Supplementary Hand-List* (1936). Translator: Cicero's *Rhetorica ad Herrenium* (1954); *Pulpit Eloquence—English* (with H. H. King, 1955); *Pulpit Eloquence—German* (with same, 1956). Prof. classics, Cornell University, 1930–67.

CAPLES, JOHN (May 1, 1900–); b. New York. Advertising executive, author. *Tested Advertising Methods* (1932); *Advertising for Immediate Sales* (1936); *Advertising Ideas* (1938); *Making Ads Pay* (1957).

CAPLOW, THEODORE (May 1, 1920–); b. New York. Educator, author. *Sociology of Work* (1954); *The Academic Marketplace* (1957); *Principles of Organization* (1964); *Two Against One* (1968). Prof. sociology, Columbia University, since 1961.

Caponsacchi. Play by Arthur Goodrich and Rose A. Palmer (prod. 1926). Based on Browning's *The Ring and the Book.* The leading role was created by Walter Hampden.

CAPOTE, TRUMAN (Sept. 30, 1924–); b. New Orleans, La. Author. *Other Voices, Other Rooms* (1948); *Tree of Night* (stories, 1949); *Local Color* (1950); *The Grass Harp* (1951); *The Muses Are Heard* (1956); *Breakfast at Tiffany's* (1958); *Selected Writings* (1963); *In Cold Blood* (1965); *A Christmas Memory* (1966); *House of Flowers* with Harold Arlen, 1968; *A Thanksgiving Visitor* (1968).

CAPOUYA, EMILE. Editor, author. *From Rebellion to Responsibility* (1965). Executive director, Funk and Wagnalls.

CAPP, AL (Sept. 28, 1909–); b. New Haven, Conn. Cartoonist. *Fearless Fosdick* (1956); *Return of the Shmoo* (1959); *From Dogpatch to Slobbovia* (1964); etc. Originator of comic strip "Li'l Abner" for United Features Syndicate, 1934.

CAPPER, ARTHUR (July 14, 1865–Dec. 19, 1951); b. Garnett, Kan. U.S. Senator, publisher. Publisher, *Kansas City Kansan, Capper's Weekly, Capper's Farmer, Missouri Ruralist, Ohio Farmer, Topeka Daily Capital,* etc.

CAPPON, ALEXANDER P[atterson] (May 11, 1900–); b. Milwaukee, Wis. Educator. Editor-in-chief, *Kansas City Review,* 1938–42, since 1953; book reviewer, *Kansas City Star,* Prof. English, University of Kansas City, 1945–63; prof. English Literature, University of Missouri, since 1964.

CAPPON, LESTER JESSE (Sept. 18, 1900–); b. Milwaukee, Wis. Historian. *Bibliography of Virginia History since 1865* (1930); *Virginia Newspapers, 1821–1935, A Bibliography* (1936); *Virginia Gazette Index, 1736–80* (1950). Editor: *The Adams-Jefferson Letters* (1959).

CAPPS, EDWARD (Dec. 21, 1866–Aug. 21, 1950); b. Jacksonville, Ill. Educator, classicist. *From Homer to Theocritus* (1901); and other classical studies. Prof. classics, Princeton University, 1907–36.

"Captain Carpenter." Poem by John Crowe Ransom (1924).

Captain Courtesy. Novel by Edward Childs Carpenter (1906).

Captain Craig. Poems by Edwin Arlington Robinson (1902). Reprinted with revisions and additions in 1915.

Captain Jinks, Hero. By Ernest Crosby (1902).

Captain Jinks of the Horse Marines. Play by Clyde Fitch (prod. 1901).

"Captain Jinks of the Horse Marines." Street song, authorship uncertain. Sometimes attributed to William Horace Lingard, and to T. Maclagan.

CARAS, ROGER A[ndrew] (May 24, 1928–); b. Metheun, Mass. Motion picture company executive, author. *Antarctica: Land of Frozen Time* (1962); *Dangerous to Man* (1964); *Wings of Gold* (1965); *The Custer Wolf* (1966); *A Book of Mammals* (1966); *Sarang* (1968); *Monarch of Deadman Bay* (1969); *Panther!* (1969); *Death as a Way of Life* (1970). Vice-pres., Polaris Productions, since 1965.

Caravan. Lamoni, Ia. Bimonthly. Founded 1956. Published poetry only. Ceased publication 1968.

Carder, Leigh. Pen name of Eugene Cunningham.

Cardinal's Snuff-Box, The. Novel by Henry Harland (1900).

CARDOZO, BENJAMIN NATHAN (May 24, 1870–July 9, 1938); b. New York City. Jurist, author. *The Nature of the Judicial Process* (1921); *The Growth of the Law* (1924); *Law and Literature, and Other Essays* (1931); *Law Is Justice: Notable Opinions* (1938); Associate Justice, U.S. Supreme Court, 1932–38.

CARDWELL, GUY ADAMS (Nov. 14, 1905–); b. Savannah, Ga. Educator. *Twins of Genius* (1953); Editor: *The Uncollected Poems of Henry Timrod* (1942); *Readings from the Americas* (1947); *Discussions of Mark Twain* (1963); *John March, Southerner* (1969); etc. Prof. English, Washington University, St. Louis, 1949–68.

Career of Puffer Hopkins, The. Political satire by Cornelius Mathews (1841).

CARENS, THOMAS HENRY (June 19, 1893–June 29, 1960); b. Arlington, Mass. *Duty and Michael Collins* (play, 1936); *John Boyle O'Reilly, American* (1944).

CAREW, HAROLD D[avid] (Mar. 10, 1890–June 25, 1943); b. North Attleboro, Mass. Journalist, poet. *Shots from the Notebook of a Gunner* (1919); *History of Pasadena and the San Gabriel Valley, California,* 3v. (1930); *Gypsy Caravan* (poems, 1931). Literary editor, *Pasadena Star-News,* from 1923.

CAREY, HENRY CHARLES (Dec. 15, 1793–Oct. 13, 1879); b. Philadelphia, Pa., son of Mathew Carey. Publisher, economist, author. *Principles of Political Economy,* 3v. (1837–40); *Principles of Social Science,* 3v. (1858–9); etc. Head of the publishing firm of Carey, Lea & Carey.

CAREY, JANE PERRY CLARK, b. Washington, D.C. Political scientist. *Deportation of Aliens from the United States to Europe* (1931); *The Rise of a New Federalism* (1938); *The Uprooted People of Europe and European Recovery* (1948); *Italy: Change and Progress* (1963); *The Web of Modern Greek Politics* (1968).

CAREY, MATHEW (Jan. 28, 1760–Sept. 16, 1839); b. Dublin, Ireland. Publisher, economist, author. *Miscellaneous Trifles in Prose* (1796); *Autobiographical Sketches* (1829); *Miscellaneous Essays* (1830); etc. Founder, the *Pennsylvania Herald,* 1785; co-founder, *The Columbian Magazine,* 1787; *The American Museum,* 1787; editor, 1787–1792. Founder of the publishing house of Carey & Lea in 1785. *See* E. L. Bradsher's *Mathew Carey* (1912).

Carey and Hart. Philadelphia. Publishers. In 1829 Abraham Hart (1810–1885) and Edward L. Carey (d. 1845) founded the firm of E. L. Carey and A. Hart. Carey was the son of Mathew Carey (1760–1839), who had founded the parent organization in 1785. He was a brother of Henry C. Carey (1793–1879) of the publishing house of Carey & Lea. Carey and Hart made their success with the *Life of David Crockett, Major Jones' Courtship,* and *Tom Owen the Bee Hunter.* They also published a literary annual *The Gift,* and Griswold's *Poets and Poetry of America,* and Macaulay's *Essays.* The firm dissolved in 1849.

CARGILL, OSCAR (Mar. 19, 1898–); b. Livermore Falls, Me. Educator, editor, author. Author or editor: *Drama and Liturgy* (1930); *Intellectual America* (1941); *Thoreau's Selected Writings on Nature and Liberty* (1952); The Wolfe-Watt *Correspondence* (with T. C. Pollock, 1953); *The Novels of Henry James* (1961); *O'Neill and His Plays* (with others, 1963); *Toward a Pluralistic Criticism* (1965). Prof. English, New York University, since 1945.

Cargoe, Richard. Pen name of Robert Payne.

CARHART, ARTHUR H[awthorne] (Sept. 18, 1892–); b. Mapleton, Ia. Conservationist, novelist. *The Last Stand of the Pack* (with Stanley P. Young, 1929); *Colorado* (1932); *Drum Up the Dawn* (1937); *Bronc Twister* (1937); *Fresh Water Fishing* (1949); *Fishing Is Fun, Fishing in the West* (1950);

Water—or Your Life (1951); *Son of the Forest* (1952); *Timber in Your Life* (1955); *The National Forests* (1959).

CARITAT, HOCQUET (fl. 1797-1807); b. New York. Printer, bookseller, publisher. Ran a circulating library as early as 1797, which he purchased from John Fellows. Friend of Charles Brockden Brown, and published his *Wieland* in 1798. See *Colophon*, pt. 18, 1934.

Carle, Richard. Stage and pen name of Charles Nichols Carleton.

Carleton. Pen name of Charles Carleton Coffin.

Carleton, G. W. & Co. New York. Publishers. Founded, 1857, by George Washington Carleton, as Rudd & Carleton, with Edward P. Rudd (d. 1861) and then changed to G. W. Carleton & Co. Some of Carleton's greatest publishing accomplishments were in the field of humor, among his authors being "Josh Billings," "Artemus Ward," "Doesticks," "Private Miles O'Reilly," "Orpheus C. Kerr," and others. He had Victor Hugo's *Les Miserables* translated and sold thousands of copies. He also published "St. Elmo" and other works by Augusta J. Evans and William Allen Butler's *Nothing to Wear*. In 1866 he was joined by George W. Dillingham, who succeeded him.

CARLETON, HENRY GUY (June 21, 1856–Dec. 10, 1910); b. Fort Union, N. Mex. Playwright, author. *Memnon* (1881); *A Gilded Fool* (prod. 1892); *The Butterflies* (prod. 1893); etc.

CARLETON, WILL (Oct. 21, 1845–Dec. 18, 1912); b. Hudson, Mich. Poet. *Poems* (1871); *Farm Ballads* (1873); *Farm Legends* (1875); *Farm Festivals* (1881); *City Ballads* (1885); *City Legends* (1889); *City Festivals* (1892); *Song of Two Centuries* (1902). His best known poems are "Betsey and I Are Out," "Over the Hill to the Poor House," and "Gone with a Handsomer Man." Founder, *Every Where* magazine, 1894.

Carleton, William. Pen name of Frederick Orin Bartlett.

Carleton Miscellany, The. Carleton College, Northfield, Minn., Quarterly. Founded 1960. Literary magazine, edited by Reed Whittemore and others. Recent editors have included Erling Larsen and Wayne Carver.

Carlin, Francis. See James Francis Carlin MacDonnell.

CARLISLE, HELEN GRACE (June 19, 1898–); b. New York. Novelist. *See How They Run* (1929); *Mothers Cry* (1930); *Together Again* (1930); *We Begin* (1932); *The Wife* (1934); *The Merry, Merry Maidens* (1937); *The Tiger Sniffs the Rose* (1958); etc. *See* Fred B. Millett's *Contemporary American Authors* (1940).

CARLSON, EDGAR MAGNUS (July 12, 1908–); b. Amery, Wis. Lutheran clergyman, educator. *The Reinterpretation of Luther* (1948); *The Church and the Public Conscience* (1956); *Classic Christian Faith* (1959). Pres., Gustavus Adolphus College, 1944–68.

CARLSON, E[rnest] LESLIE (Oct. 14, 1893–); b. Chicago, Ill. Baptist clergyman, educator. *Elementary Hebrew* (1945); *Confirming the Scripture* (1941). Co-author: *A Study of the Prophet Micah* (1950); etc. Prof. Old Testament and Hebrew, Southwestern Baptist Theological Seminary, since 1921.

Carlson, John Roy. Pen name of Avedis Arthur Derounian.

CARLSON, LELAND HENRY (Mar. 25, 1908–); b. Rockford, Ill. Educator. *A History of North Park College* (1941); *An Alaskan Gold Mine* (1951); etc. Editor: *The Writings of Robert Harrison and Robert Browne* (with Albert Peel, 1953); *The Writings of Henry Barrow and John Greenwood, 1587–1590* (1959). Pres., Rockford College, since 1954.

CARLSON, NATALIE SAVAGE (Oct. 3, 1906–); b. Winchester, Va. Author. *The Talking Cat and Other Stories of French Canada* (1952); *Alphonse, That Bearded One* (1954);

Wings Against the Wind (1955); *Sashes Red and Blue* (1956); *The Happy Orpheline* (1957); *The Family Under the Bridge* (1958); *Carnival in Paris* (1962); *Jean-Claude's Island* (1963); *The Letter on the Tree* (1964); *The Empty Schoolhouse* (1965); *Sailor's Choice* (1966); *Chalou* (1967); *Ann Aurelia* (1968); *Befana's Gift* (1969).

Carlton, Robert. Pen name of Baynard Rush Hall.

CARLTON, WILLIAM NEWNHAM CHATTIN (June 29, 1873–Feb. 3, 1943); b. Gillingham, Kent, England. Librarian, author. *Pauline, Favorite Sister of Napoleon* (1930). Editor: *Poems and Letters of Lord Byron* (1912). Librarian, Newberry Library, Chicago, 1909–19; Williams College Library, 1922–38.

CARMAN, HARRY JAMES (Jan. 22, 1884–Dec. 26, 1964); b. Greenfield, N.Y. Educator, historian. *An Introduction to Contemporary Civilization in the West* (with others, 1919); *Social and Economic History of the United States,* 2v. (1930–32); *Jesse Buel, Agricultural Reformer* (1946); *A History of the American People,* 2v. (with Harold Syrett, 1952); *Guide to the Principle Sources for American Civilization, 1800–1900, in the City of New York* (with Arthur Thompson, 1960); *Lincoln and the Patronage* (with R. H. Luthin, 1964); etc. History dept., Columbia University, since 1921; prof., since 1931.

"Carmen Bellicosum." Poem by Guy Humphreys McMaster, in the *Knickerbocker Magazine,* 1849, under the pen name "John MacGrom."

"Carmen Triumphale." Poem by Henry Timrod (1863). Celebrating the relief of Charleston from siege by the Union fleet.

CARMER, CARL LAMSON (Oct. 16, 1893–); b. Cortland, N.Y. Author. *Frenchtown* (poems, 1928); *Deep South* (poems, 1930); *Stars Fell on Alabama* (1934); *Listen for a Lonesome Drum* (1936); *The Hurricane's Children* (1937); *The Hudson* (1939); *Genesee Fever* (1941); *Dark Trees to the Wind* (1949); *Windfall Fiddle* (1950); *The Susquehanna* (1955); *The Screaming Ghost* (1956); *Pets at the White House* (1959); *My Kind of Country* (1966); *Wildcat Furs to China* (1969); etc. Editor: *Some University of Alabama Poets,* 4v. (1924–27); *Rivers of America Series; Harper Series of Regional Histories; Calvalcade of America* (1957); *Cavalcade of Young Americans* (1958); *The Tavern Lamps Are Burning* (1964).

CARMICHAEL, STOKELY (1941–   ); b. New York . Civil rights leader. *Black Power: The Politics of Liberation in America* (with C. V. Hamilton, 1967).

CARNAP, RUDOLF (May 18, 1891–Sept. 14, 1970); b. Wuppertal, Ger. Educator, author. *The Unity of Science* (1934); *Philosophy and Logical Syntax* (1935); *Logical Syntax of Language* (1937); *Foundations of Logic and Mathematics* (1939); *Introduction to Semantics* (1942); *Formalization of Logic* (1943); *Meaning and Necessity* (1947); *Logical Foundations of Probability* (1950); *The Continuum of Inductive Methods* (1952); *Introduction to Symbolic Logic and Its Applications* (1958); *Logic and Language* (1963); *Philosophical Foundations of Physics* (1966); *The Logical Structure of the World* (1967); and other works not translated into English. Prof. philosophy, University of Chicago, 1936–52; University of California, Los Angeles, from 1954.

CARNEGIE, ANDREW (Nov. 25, 1835–Aug. 11, 1919); b. Dunfermline, Scotland. Manufacturer, philanthropist, author. *Triumphant Democracy* (1886); *The Gospel of Wealth, and Other Timely Essays* (1900); *Autobiography* (1920); *The Empire of Business* (1933). Donor of many public libraries. *See* Theodore W. Koch's *A Book of Carnegie Libraries* (1917); Joseph Frazier Wall's *Andrew Carnegie* (1970).

CARNELL, EDWARD JOHN (June 28, 1919–Apr. 25, 1967); b. Antigo, Wis. Educator, author. *An Introduction to Christian Apologetics* (1948); *Television: Servant or Master?*

(1950); *A Philosophy of the Christian Religion* (1952); *Christian Commitment* (1957); etc. Prof. theology, Fuller Theological Seminary, California, since 1948; pres. 1954–67.

Carol, Bill. J. Pen name of William Cecil Knott, Jr.

"Carolina." Poem by Henry Timrod, written early in the Civil War.

Carolina Israelite, The. Charlotte, N.C. Bimonthly. Founded 1941, by Harry Golden, who is editor and publisher. A magazine of general opinion. Merged with *The Nation* in 1968, in which Harry Golden wrote a column.

Carolina Playmakers, The. A drama workshop founded 1918, at the University of North Carolina, by Professor Frederick H. Koch. Thomas Wolfe and Paul Green were among those who wrote plays for the workshop. See *Coming of Age of the Carolina Playmakers: The Carolina Play-Book. Commemorative Issue*, June, 1940.

Carolina Quarterly. Chapel Hill, N.C. Founded 1844. Devoted to poetry, fiction, and literary criticism.

CARPENTER, DON. Author. *Hard Rain Falling* (1966); *Blade of Light* (1967); *The Murder of the Frogs and Other Stories* (1969).

CARPENTER, EDMUND JANES (Oct. 16, 1845–Feb. 21, 1924); b. North Attleboro, Mass. Journalist, author. *A Woman of Shawmut* (1891); *Hellenic Tales* (1906); also published as, *Long Ago in Greece* (1906); *Roger Williams* (1909); *The Mayflower Pilgrims* (1917); etc. Literary editor, *Boston Daily Advertiser*, 1884–96.

CARPENTER, EDWARD CHILDS (Dec. 13, 1872–Oct. 7, 1950); b. Philadelphia, Pa. Playwright, novelist. *The Chasm* (1903); *Captain Courtesy* (1906); *Remembrance* (prod. 1906); *The Code of Victor Jallot* (1907); *The Challenge* (prod. 1911); *The Easy Mark* (1912); *The Cinderella Man* (prod. 1916); *The Pipes of Pan* (prod. 1917); *Pot-Luck* (prod. 1921); *The Bachelor Father* (prod. 1928); *Whistling in the Dark* (with Laurence Gross, 1932); *Melody* (1933); *Order Please* (prod. 1934); etc.

CARPENTER, FRANCES (Mrs. William Chapin Huntington) (Apr. 30, 1890–); b. Washington, D.C. Author. *Ourselves and Our City* (1928); *Tales of a Basque Grandmother* (1930); *Our Little Friends* series, 5v. (1931–1937); *Tales of a Russian Grandmother* (1933); *Tales of a Chinese Grandmother* (1938); *Tales of a Swiss Grandmother* (1940); *Our South American Neighbors* (1942); *Canada and Her Northern Neighbors* (1946); *Wonder Tales of Horses and Heroes* (1952); *Pocahontas and Her World* (1957); *Wondertales of Seas and Ships* (1959); *African Wonder Tales* (1963); *The Mouse Palace* (1964); *The Story of East Africa* (1967); *The Story of Korea* (1968); *South American Wonder Tales* (1969).

CARPENTER, FRANK GEORGE (May 8, 1855–June 18, 1924); b. Mansfield, O. Journalist, traveler, author of many travel *Readers* for boys and girls; and *World Travels*, 20v. (1920).

CARPENTER, GEORGE RICE (Oct. 25, 1863–Apr. 8, 1909); b. Eskimo River Mission Station, Labrador. Educator, author. *Henry Wadsworth Longfellow* (1901); *John Greenleaf Whittier* (1903); *Walt Whitman* (1909); etc.

CARPENTER, MARGARET HALEY b. Frederick Hall, Va. Author. *Sara Teasdale* (1960). Editor: *Poems by Marion Cummings* (1957); *Anthology of Magazine Verse* (with William Stanley Braithwaite, 1958, 1959).

CARPENTER, RHYS (Aug. 5, 1889–); b. Cotuit, Mass. Archeologist, author. *The Tragedy of Etarre* (drama in verse, 1912); *The Sun-Thief, and Other Poems* (1914); *The Plainsman, and Other Poems* (1920); *The Land Beyond Mexico* (1921); *The Esthetic Basis of Greek Art* (1921); *The Humanistic Value of Archaeology* (1933); *The Defenses of Acrocorinth*

(1935); *Folk Tale, Fiction and Saga in the Homeric Epics* (1946); *Greek Sculpture* (1960); *Greek Art* (1963); etc. Director, American School for Classical Studies at Athens, 1927–32, 1946–48.

CARPENTER, STEPHEN CULLEN (d. 1820); b. in Ireland. Editor. Editor: *Memoirs of Hon. Thomas Jefferson*, 2v. (1809). Co-founder, *The Monthly Register, Magazine, and Review, of the United States*, Charleston, S.C., 1805; editor, *Mirror of Taste and Dramatic Censor*, Philadelphia, 1810–11.

CARPENTER, WILLIAM HENRY (1813–1899). Novelist, historian. *Claiborne the Rebel* (1845); *Ruth Emsley, the Betrothed Maiden* (1850); *The Regicide's Daughter* (1851).

Carpet-Bag, The. Boston. Humorous weekly. Founded 1851. Penhallow Shillaber was an editor, and Charles F. Browne ("Artemus Ward") was a typesetter. Browne managed to get some of his own humor into the magazine under the name of "Lieut. Chubb." Sixteen-year-old Sam Clemens ("Mark Twain") appeared in the May 1, 1852, issue. Expired 1853.

CARR, ALBERT H. Z. (Jan. 15, 1902–); b. Chicago, Ill. Government official, author. *Juggernaut: The Path of Dictatorship* (1939); *Men of Power* (1940); *America's Last Chance* (1940); *Napoleon Speaks* (1941); *Truman, Stalin and Peace* (1950); *How to Attract Good Luck* (1952); *The World and William Walker* (1963); *A Matter of Life and Death* (1966); *Business as a Game* (1968).

Carr, Mrs. Donald. See Blanche Shoemaker Wagstaff.

CARR, JOHN DICKSON (1906–); b. Uniontown, Pa. Pen names "Carr Dickson" and "Carter Dickson." *It Walks by Night* (1930); *The Lost Gallows* (1931); *The Mad Hatter Mystery* (1933); *Hag's Nook* (1933); *The Eight of Swords* (1934); *The Three Coffins* (1935); *The Peacock Feather Murders* (1937); *The Murder of Sir Edmund Godfrey* (1937); *The Judas Window* (1938); *The Reader Is Warned* (1939); *The Gilded Man* (1942); *He Who Whispers* (1946); *The Sleeping Sphinx* (1947); *The Skeleton in the Clock* (1948); *The Life of Sir Arthur Conan Doyle* (1949); *The Bride of Newgate* (1950); *Night at the Mocking Widow* (1950); *Devil in Velvet* (1951); *Behind the Crimson Blind* (1952); *The Nine Wrong Answers* (1952); *Cavalier's Cup* (1953); *The Third Bullet* (1954); *Captain Cut-Throat* (1955); *Dead Man's Knock* (1958); *In Spite of Thunder* (1960); *The Witch of the Low Tide* (1961); *The Murder of Sir Edmond Godfrey* (1962); *Most Secret* (1964); *Blind Barber* (1967); *Castle Skull* (1968); *Papa Là-bas* (1968); etc.

CARR, ROBERT KENNETH (Feb. 15, 1908–); b. Cleveland, O. Educator. *The Supreme Court and Judicial Review* (1942); *Federal Protection of Civil Rights* (1947); *American Democracy in Theory and Practice* (with others, 1951); *The House Committee on Un-American Activities, 1945–1950* (1952). Prof. law and political science, Dartmouth College, 1948–59. Pres. Oberlin College since 1960.

CARR, ROBERT SPENCER (Mar. 26, 1909–); Washington, D.C. Author. *Rampant Age* (1928); *The Bells of St. Ivan's* (1944); *The Room Beyond* (1948); *Beyond Infinity* (1951).

CARR, WILLIAM GEORGE (June 1, 1901–); b. Northampton, Eng. Educator, author. *Education for World Citizenship* (1928); *School Finance* (1933); *One World in the Making* (1946); etc.

CARRA, EMMA. Real name unknown. Novelist. *A Tale of the West* (1846); *Estelle; or, The Castle of M'Anvah* (1848); *The Hermit of the Hudson* (1848); *Viroque; or, The Flower of the Ottawas* (1848); *Ednah; or, An Antique Tale* (1858). This last was copyrighted by Avis S. Spenser, who may, therefore, have been "Emma Carra."

Carrier's Addresses. Broadsides containing verses, etc., serving as New Year's greetings, formerly presented by newsboys to their customers. The New York Public Library contains an extensive collection of them. See Frank H. Severance's *Carrier's Addresses,* in *Publications* of the Buffalo Historical Society, 1921.

CARRINGTON, FitzROY (Nov. 6, 1869–Dec. 31, 1954); b. Surbiton, Surrey, Eng. Curator, author. *Engravers and Etchers* (1917); *Prints and Their Makers* (1916); etc. Editor, *The Print Collectors' Quarterly.* Curator, Department of Prints, Museum of Fine Arts, Boston.

CARRINGTON, HENRY BEEBEE (Mar. 2, 1824–Oct. 26, 1912); b. Wallingford, Conn. Army officer, lawyer, author. *American Classics* (1849); *Battles of the American Revolution* (1876); etc.

CARRINGTON, HEREWARD [Hubert Lavington] (Oct. 17, 1880–); b. Jersey, Channel Islands. Author. *True Ghost Stories* (1915); *Loaves and Fishes* (1935); *The Psychic World* (1937); *Telepathy and Clairvoyance* (1938); *The Invisible World* (1946); *The Phenomena of Astral Projection* (with S. J. Muldoon, 1951); *Fasting for Life and Health* (1952); etc. Editor, Street & Smith's novels, 1906–1907.

CARROLL, ALEXANDER MITCHELL (June 2, 1870–Mar. 3, 1925); b. Wake Forest, N.C. Educator, philologist, author. *Great Women* (1907); *Women of Early Christianity* (with Alfred Brittain, 1907).

Carroll, Consolata. Pen name of Sister Mary Consolata.

CARROLL, EARL (Sept. 16, 1893–June 17, 1948; b. Pittsburgh, Pa. Theatrical producer, song writer, motion picture producer. Collaborator in writing over 400 songs, author of book, lyrics and music of the first two Earl Carroll Vanities, producer of 49 stage shows.

CARROLL, GLADYS [Winifred] Hasty (June 26, 1904–); b. Rochester, N.H. Author. *Cockatoo* (1929); *Land Spell* (1930); *As the Earth Turns* (1933); *A Few Foolish Ones* (1935); *Neighbor to the Sky* (1937); *Dunnybrook* (1943); *While the Angels Sing* (1947); *West of the Hill* (1949); *Christmas without Johnny* (1950); *One White Star* (1954); *Sing Out the Glory* (1957); *Come with Me Home* (1960); *To Remember Forever* (1963); *The Road Grows Strange* (1965); *The Light He Kindled* (1967); *Christmas Through the Years* (1968).

CARROLL, GORDON (Apr. 29, 1903–); b. Baltimore, Md. Editor or author: *Reader's Digest Books* (1940); *History in the Writing* (1945); *Flak Bait* (1945); *Money, Men and Machines* (1953); J. T. Trowbridge's *The Desolate South* (1956); etc. Editor, *Coronet,* 1945–48; publisher, 1952–55.

CARROLL, HOWARD (Sept. 17, 1854–Dec. 30, 1916); b. Albany, N.Y. Author. *A Mississippi Incident* (1877); *The American Countess* (prod. 1884); *Twelve Americans* (1883).

CARROLL, JOHN (Jan. 8, 1735–Dec. 3, 1815); b. Upper Marlboro, Md. Roman Catholic archbishop, author. *Address to the Roman Catholics of the United States* (1784); etc. See Daniel Brent's *Biographical Sketch of the Most Rev. John Carroll, First Archbishop of Baltimore* (1843); John G. Shea's *Life and Times of the Most Rev. John Carroll,* vol. 2 of his *History of the Catholic Church in the United States* (1888); Peter K. Guilday's *The Life and Times of John Carroll* (1922).

CARROLL, [John] WALLACE (Dec. 15, 1906–); b. Milwaukee, Wis. Journalist. *We're in This with Russia* (1942); *Persuade or Perish* (1948). Washington news editor, *The New York Times,* since 1955.

CARROLL, LOREN (Mar. 5, 1904–); b. Scanlon, Minn. Foreign service officer, editor. *Wild Onion* (1930); *Conversation Please* (1939). Chief, Paris Bureau, *Newsweek,* 1945–51; U.S. consul general, Quebec, 1956–60. Editor, *Foreign Service Journal,* since 1964.

CARROLL, RAYMOND G.; b. Buffalo, N.Y. Newspaper correspondent. Paris correspondent of *Philadelphia Public Ledger; New York Evening Post,* 1917–34; etc. Writer of stories for *Saturday Evening Post,* 1934–37.

CARRUTH, HAYDEN (Oct. 31, 1862–Jan. 3, 1932); b. near Lake City, Minn. Editor, author. *The Adventures of Jones* (1895); *The Voyage of the Rattletrap* (1897); *Mr. Milo Bush and Other Worthies* (1899); *Track's End* (1911). Editor, "Editor's Drawer" department, *Harper's Magazine,* 1900–02; on staff of *Woman's Home Companion,* 1905–32.

CARRUTH, HAYDEN (Aug. 3, 1921–); b. Waterbury, Conn. Poet. *The Crow and the Heart* (1959); *Journey to a Known Place* (1961); *Norfolk Poems* (1962); *Appendix A* (1963); *North Winter* (1964); *After the Stranger* (1965); *Nothing for Tigers* (1965); *Contra Mortem* (1967).

CARRUTH, WILLIAM HERBERT (Apr. 5, 1859–Dec. 15, 1924); b. Osawatomie, Kan. Educator, author. *Letters to American Boys* (1907); *Each in His Own Tongue, and Other Poems* (1909); *Verse Writing* (1917). Editor: *Kansas in Literature,* 2v. (1900).

Carruthers, William Alexander. See William Alexander Caruthers.

CARRYL, CHARLES E[dward] (Dec. 30, 1841–1920); b. New York. Broker, author. *Davy and the Goblin* (1885); *The Admiral's Caravan* (1892); *The River Syndicate, and Other Stories* (1899).

CARRYL, GUY WETMORE (Mar. 4, 1873–Apr. 1, 1904); b. New York. Novelist, poet, humorist. *Fables for the Frivolous* (1898); *Mother Goose for Grown-Ups* (1900); *Grimm Tales Made Gay* (1902); *Zut, and Other Parisians* (1903); *The Lieutenant-Governor* (1903); *The Garden of Years, and Other Poems* (1904); *The Transgression of Andrew Vane* (1904).

CARSON, GERALD. Author. *The Old Country Store* (1954); *Cornflake Crusade* (1957); *The Roguish World of Dr. Brinkley* (1960); *One for a Man, Two for a Horse* (1961); *Social History of Bourbon* (1963); etc.

CARSON, RACHEL [Louise] (May 27, 1907–Apr. 14, 1964); b. Springdale, Pa. Scientist, author. *Under the Sea Wind* (1941); *The Sea Around Us* (1951); *The Edge of the Sea* (1955); *Silent Spring* (1962).

CARSON, ROBERT (Oct. 6, 1909–); b. Clayton, Wash. Author. *The Revels Are Ended* (1936); *Stranger in Our Midst* (1947); *Magic Lantern* (1952); *Quality of Mercy* (1954); *Love Affair* (1958); *An End to Comedy* (1963); *The Outsiders* (1966); *The December Syndrome* (1969).

CARTER, CLARENCE EDWIN (Feb. 6, 1881–Sept. 11, 1961); b. Jacksonville, Ill. Educator, historian. Editor, *Correspondence of General Gage,* 2v. (1931–33); *Northwest Territory* 2v. (1935). Editor: *Territorial Papers,* National Archives.

CARTER, GWENDOLEN MARGARET (1906–). Educator, author. *South Africa* (1954); *The Politics of Inequality: South Africa since 1948* (1958); *The Fifth French Republic* (1959); *Government and Politics in the Twentieth Century* (1961); *The Government of the Soviet Union* (1964); *South Africa's Transkei: The Politics of Domestic Colonialism* (with others, 1967); *The Government of France* (1968). Editor: *Five African States* (with others, 1963); Prof. government, Smith College.

Carter, Henry. See Frank Leslie.

CARTER, HODDING (Feb. 3, 1907–); b. Hammond, La. Journalist, author. *Lower Mississippi* (1942); *Winds of Fear* (1944); *Flood Crest* (1947); *Southern Legacy* (1950); *Gulf Coast Country* (with A. Ragusin, 1951); *Where Main Street Meets the River* (1953); *Robert E. Lee and the Road of Honor* (1955); *Angry Scar: The Story of Reconstruction* (1958); *The South Strikes Back* (1959); *First Person Rural* (1963); *The Ballad of Catfoot Grimes* (1964); *So the Heffners Left Maccomb* (1965); *The Commandos of World War II* (1966); *The*

Past as Prelude: New Orleans 1718–1968 (with others, 1968). Editor, publisher, *Delta Star* (later *Delta Democrat-Times*), since 1936 (Pulitzer Prize for editorial writing, 1946).

CARTER, JAMES (Oct. 1, 1853–Apr. 9, 1944); b. New York. Presbyterian clergyman, author. *Songs of Work and Worship* (1899); *John Huss* (1915); *A Century of Service* (1924); etc.

CARTER, JESSIE BENEDICT (June 16, 1872–July 21, 1917); b. New York City. Educator, classicist. *The Religion of Numa* (1906); *The Religious Life of Ancient Rome* (1911).

CARTER, JOHN (July 21, 1745–Aug. 19, 1814); b. Philadelphia, Pa. Printer, editor, *The Providence Gazette,* 1768–1814.

CARTER, JOHN FRANKLIN, JR. (Jay Franklin) (Apr. 27, 1897–Nov. 28, 1967); b. Fall River, Mass. Commentator, author. Pen name, "Jay Franklin." *Conquest* (1928); *Murder in the Embassy* (1930); *Scandal in the Chancery* (1931); *Death in the Senate* (1933); *Rectory Family* (1937); *La Guardia* (1937); *Catoctin Conversation* (1947); *Republicans on the Potomac* (1953); *Power and Persuasion* (1960); etc.

CARTER, JOHN MACK (Feb. 28, 1928–); b. Murray, Ky. Editor. Managing editor, *Household,* 1953–57; editor, 1957–58; executive editor, *Together,* 1958–59; editor, *American Home,* 1959–61.

CARTER, JOHN STEWART (Mar. 26, 1912–); b. Chicago, Ill. Educator, poet. *Full Fathom Five* (1965); *The De Paolis Papers*; *Poems: an Handful with Quietness* (1966). Prof. English, Chicago Teachers College, since 1940.

Carter, Nicholas. Pen name of Frederick Van Rensselaer Dey.

Carter, Nicholas. Pen name of Frederick William Davis.

CARTER, RICHARD (Jan. 24, 1918–); b. New York. Author. *The Man Who Rocked the Boat* (1956); *The Doctor Business* (1958); *Breakthrough: The Saga of Jonas Salk* (1966); *Ainslie's Jockey Book* (1967); *Ainslie's Complete Guide to Thoroughbred Racing* (1968); etc.

CARTER, ROBERT (Nov. 2, 1807–Dec. 28, 1889); b. Earlston, Scotland. Publisher. He opened a bookstore in New York, 1834, later became publisher.

CARTER, ROBERT (Feb. 5, 1819–Feb. 15, 1879); b. Albany, N.Y. Editor, encyclopedist, author. *A Summer Cruise on the Coast of New England* (1864). Editor: *The American Cyclopedia* (1859–63). Co-editor, *The Pioneer,* 1843; editor, *The Boston Telegraph,* 1855; *Appleton's Journal,* 1870–73.

CARTER, RUSSELL GORDON (Jan. 1, 1892–May 7, 1957); b. Trenton, N.J. Author. The *Bob Hanson* series, 4v. (1921–1923); the *Patriot Lad* series, 12v. (1923–36); *Teen-Age Historical Stories* (1948); *Teen-Age Animal Stories* (1949); *Mr. Whatley Enjoys Himself* (1954); etc.

CARTWRIGHT, PETER (Sept. 1, 1785–Sept. 25, 1872); b. in Amherst Co., Va. Methodist clergyman, author. *The Autobiography of Peter Cartwright, the Backwoods Preacher* (1857). *See* Helen H. Grant's *Peter Cartwright, Pioneer* (1931).

CARTWRIGHT, WILLIAM H[olman] (Sept. 12, 1915–); b. Pine Island, Minn. Educator, author. *The Military District of Washington during the War Years* (1946); *The Teaching of History in the United States* (with Arthur C. Bining, 1950); *The Story of Our Heritage* (with Oscar O. Winther, 1962); *Teaching Social Studies in Elementary Schools* (with E. B. Wesely, 1968). Prof. education, Duke University, since 1951.

CARUS, PAUL (July 18, 1852–Feb. 11, 1919); b. Ilsenburg, Ger. Philosopher, editor, author. *Fundamental Problems* (1889); *The Gospel of Buddha* (1895); *Buddhism and Its Christian Critics* (1897); *Kant and Spencer: A Study of the Fallacies of Agnosticism* (1899); *Whence and Whither* (1900); *The Soul of Man* (1900); *The Surd of Metaphysics* (1903);

Friedrich Schiller (1905); *Amitabha: A Story of Buddhist Theology* (1906); *Our Children* (1906); *Chinese Thought* (1907); *Foundations of Mathematics* (1908); *God: An Enquiry and a Solution* (1908); *The Pleroma* (1909); *Philosophy as a Science* (1909); *Truth on Trial* (1911); *The Canon of Reason and Virtue* (1913); *Nietzsche and Other Exponents of Individualism* (1914); *Goethe: With Special Consideration of His Philosophy* (1915); *The Venus of Milo* (1916); etc. Editor, *The Open Court,* 1887–1919; *The Monist.* Founder and editor, Open Court Publishing Co.

CARUTHERS, WILLIAM ALEXANDER (ca. 1800–Aug. 29, 1846); b. in Virginia. Novelist. *The Kentuckians in New York,* 2v. (1834); *The Cavaliers of Virginia,* 2v. (1834–35); *The Knights of the Horse-Shoe* (1845). All anonymous.

CARVER, GEORGE (Dec. 19, 1888–Oct. 29, 1949); b. Cincinnati, O. Educator, author. *The Catholic Tradition in English Literature* (1926); *Points of Style* (1928); *Essays and Essayists* (1929).

Carver, John. Pen name of Richard Gardner.

CARVER, JONATHAN (Apr. 13, 1710–Jan. 31, 1780); b. New York. Traveler, author. *Travels Through the Interior Parts of North America in the Years 1766, 1767, and 1768* (1778).

CARVER, THOMAS NIXON (Mar. 25, 1865–Mar. 7, 1961); b. Kirkville, Ia. Educator, author. *The Distribution of Wealth* (1904); *Principles of Rural Economics* (1911); *Essays in Social Justice* (1915); *War Thrift* (1919); *Principles of National Economy* (1921); *The Essential Factors of Social Evolution* (1935); *Recollections of an Unplanned Life* (1949); etc. Weekly articles, *Los Angeles Times,* from 1954. Prof. economics, Harvard University, 1902–32.

CARY, ALICE (Apr. 26, 1820–Feb. 12, 1871); b. Cincinnati, O. Poet. *Poems of Alice and Phoebe Cary* (1849); *Clovernook,* 2 ser. (1852–53); *Hager, a Story of Today* (1852); *Lyra, and Other Poems* (1852); *Married, not Mated* (1856); *Pictures of Country Life* (1859); *Ballads, Lyrics, and Hymns* (1866); *Snow-Berries* (1867); *A Lover's Diary* (poem, 1868); *The Last Poems of Alice and Phoebe Cary* (1873); *Early and Late Poems of Alice and Phoebe Cary* (1887); *The Poems of Alice and Phoebe Cary,* ed. Katharine Lee Bates (1903).

CARY, EDWARD (June 5, 1840–May 23, 1917); b. Albany, N.Y. Journalist, author. *Life of George William Curtis* (1894). On Staff of *New York Times,* 1871–1917.

CARY, ELISABETH LUTHER (Mar. 18, 1867–July 13, 1936); b. Brooklyn, N.Y. Art critic, translator, author. *Alfred Tennyson* (1898); *Ralph Waldo Emerson* (1904); *The Novels of Henry James* (1905); *Artists Past and Present* (1908); etc. Art editor, *New York Times,* 1908–36.

CARY, LUCIAN (Jan. 1, 1886–); b. Hamlin, Kans. Novelist. *The Duke Steps Out* (1928); *One Lovely Moron* (1930); *The Duke Comes Back* (1933); *Second Meeting* (1938); *Guns and Shooting* (1954); *The New Lucien Cary on Guns* (1958); *The Colt Gun Book* (1961); etc.

CARY, PHOEBE (Sept. 4, 1824–July 31, 1871); b. Cincinnati, O. Poet. *Poems of Alice and Phoebe Cary* (1849); *Poems and Parodies* (1854); *Poems of Faith, Hope, and Love* (1868); *The Last Poems of Alice and Phoebe Cary* (1873); *Early and Late Poems of Alice and Phoebe Cary* (1887); *The Poems of Alice and Phoebe Cary* (1903).

Casca. Pen name of Albert Pike.

CASE, FRANCES POWELL; b. Newburgh, N.Y. Novelist. Pen name, "Frances Powell." *The By-Ways of Braithe* (1904); *The House on the Hudson* (1905); *Old Mr. Davenant's Money* (1908); etc.

CASE, JOSEPHINE [Young] (Feb. 16, 1907–); b. Lexington, Mass. Author. *At Midnight on the 31st of March* (1938);

Written in the Sand (1945); *Freedom's Farm* (1946); *Communicating Effectively through Speech* (1964); *This Very Tree* (1969); etc.

CASE, LELAND DAVIDSON (May 8, 1900–); b. Wesley, Ia. Editor, publisher, author. *Editing the Day's News* (with George C. Bastian, 1932); *Around the Copydesk* (with others, 1933). Editor of series: *A World to Live In* (1942); *Peace Is a Process* (1944); *Peace Requires Action* (1946); also, *New Hampshire to Minnesota* (with Edith Grannis, 1962); *Reader's Choice Treasury* (1964). Editor, *Rotarian*, 1930–52; founder and editor, *Together* 1956–63.

CASE, ROBERT ORMOND (Oct. 8, 1895–); b. Dallas, Tex. Author. *Just Buckaroos* (1926); *A Pair o' Mavericks* (1931); *Dynamite Smith, Cowboy* (1931); *Big Timber* (1937); *Golden Portage* (1940); *The Empire Builders* (with Victoria Chase, 1947); *We Called It Culture* (1947); *Buccaneer of the Barrens* (1951); *Cold Gold* (1956); etc.

CASE, SHIRLEY JACKSON (Sept. 28, 1872–Dec. 5, 1947); b. Hatfield Point, N.B. Educator, author. *The Historicity of Jesus* (1912); *Jesus Through the Centuries* (1931); *Makers of Christianity* (1934); *Christianity in a Changing World* (1941); *The Christian Philosophy of History* (1943); *The Origins of Christian Supernaturalism* (1946). Faculty, Bates College, 1906–38.

CASEY, KATHLEEN ASTON, b. Barrow in Furness, Eng. Editor. With *Vogue*, 1943–53; *Glamour*, 1943–50; editor-in-chief, 1953–67.

CASEY, RALPH DROZ (May 8, 1890–Dec. 4, 1962); b. Aspen, Colo. Journalist, editor, author. *Principles of Publicity* (with Glenn C. Quiett, 1926); etc. Editor: *Interpretations of Journalism* (with Frank Luther Mott, 1937); *The Press In Perspective* (1963). Editor, *Journalism Quarterly*, 1935–45.

CASEY, ROBERT JOSEPH (Mar. 14, 1890–Dec. 4, 1962); b. Beresford S.Dak. Journalist, author. *The Land of Haunted Castles* (1921); *Four Faces of Siva* (1929); *The Secret of 37 Hardy Street* (1929); *The Vest Pocket Anthology* (1929); *Cambodian Quest* (1931); *Easter Island* (1931); *The Third Owl* (1935); *I Can't Forget* (1941); *Torpedo Junction* (1942); *Such Interesting People* (1943); *More Interesting People* (1947); *The Texas Border* (1950); *Give the Man Room* (with Mary Broglum, 1952); etc.

"Casey at the Bat." Poem by Ernest Thayer (1888). A poem about a renowned baseball player who "strikes out" in the "pinch." It was popularized in recitation by De Wolf Hopper. Thayer (Aug. 14, 1863–Aug. 21, 1940) was a newspaper man and wrote the poem for the San Francisco *Examiner*. At one time Thayer was editor of the *Harvard Lampoon*.

CASH, WILBUR JOSEPH (May 2, 1901–1941); b. Gaffney, S.C. Author, editor. *The Mind of the South* (1941). Associate editor, *Charlotte News*, 1937–41. See J. L. Morrison's *W. J. Cash: Southern Prophet* (1967).

Cask of Amontillado, The. Tale by Edgar Allan Poe (1846).

Casket, Flowers of Literature, Wit and Sentiment, The. Philadelphia. Founded Jan., 1826, by Samuel C. Atkinson and Charles Alexander. Also known as *Atkinson's Casket*. George R. Graham bought the *Casket* in 1839, and later issued it under the title of *Graham's Magazine*. Both before and after Graham's connection with it the magazine had various long titles, but it is popularly known as *Graham's Magazine*. It was a noted fashion journal, rivaling *Godey's*. Cooper, Poe, Lowell, Holmes, Paulding, Longfellow, Bryant, Dana, Willis, Thomas Buchanan Read, Mrs. Sigourney, Charles Fenno Hoffman, Henry William Herbert ("Frank Forester") and others were contributors. Poe's *Murders in the Rue Morgue* appeared in Apr., 1841, "To Helen," in Sept., 1841, and "The Masque of the Red Death," in May, 1842. Charles Godfrey Leland, one of the later editors, wrote his "Hans Breitmann" series for *Graham's* in 1856 and they made him famous. Other

prominent editors were Graham, Charles J. Peterson, Rufus W. Griswold, Bayard Taylor, Mrs. Ann S. Stephens, and Mrs. Emma C. Embury. It expired Dec., 1858. See F. L. Mott's *A History of American Magazines*, v. I (1938).

CASPARY, VERA (1904–); b. Chicago, Ill. Novelist. *The White Girl* (1929); *Ladies and Gents* (1929); *Music in the Street* (1930); *Thicker than Water* (1932); *Laura* (1943); *Bedelia* (1945); *Stranger than Truth* (1946); *The Weeping and the Laughter* (1950); *Thelma* (1952); *Husband* (1958); *Bachelor in Paradise* (1961); *A Chosen Sparrow* (1964).

Caspipine, T. Pen name of Jacob Duché.

CASS, LEWIS (Oct. 9, 1782–June 17, 1866); b. Exeter, N.H. Statesman, Diplomat, soldier, author. *France: Its King, Court, and Government* (anon., 1840); *Inquiries Respecting the History, Traditions, Languages, Manners, Customs, &c. of the Indians* (1823).

Cass Timberlane. Novel by Sinclair Lewis (1945). A Minnesota judge, respected for his character, marries a girl much younger than he. The novel also deals with the relations of several husbands and wives among the principal characters' friends.

"Cassandra Southwick." Poem by John Greenleaf Whittier (1843).

CASSELS, SAMUEL JONES (1806–1853). Poet. *Providence and Other Poems* (1838); *America Discovered* (1850).

CASSIDY, CLAUDIA, b. Shawneetown, Ill. Music and drama critic. With Chicago *Journal of Commerce*, 1925–41; Chicago *Sun*, 1941–42; Chicago *Tribune*, 1942–66. Critic-at-Large since 1966.

CASSIDY, FRANCIS PATRICK (Aug. 3, 1895–); b. Danbury, Conn. Roman catholic clergyman, educator. *Catholic College Foundations in the United States* (1924); *Molders of the Medieval Mind* (1944); *History of Education* (with Patrick J. McCormick, 1946). Member of faculty, Catholic University of America, since 1924.

CASSIDY, HENRY CLARENCE (May 12, 1910–); b. Boston, Mass. Commentator. *Moscow Dateline* (1943). With Associated Press, 1933–45; National Broadcasting Co., 1946–58.

CASSIDY, MORLEY FRANKLIN (Oct. 23, 1900–); b. Shelby, Ia. Journalist, author. *Spellbinder* (play, with Phyllis H. Cassidy, 1935); etc. With the *Philadelphia Bulletin*, since 1939.

CASSILL, R[onald] V[erlin] (May 17, 1919–); b. Cedar Falls, Ia. Author. *Eagle on the Coin* (1950); *Clem Anderson* (1961); *Pretty Leslie* (1963); *The President* (1964); *The Father* (1965); *The Happy Marriage* (1966); *In An Iron Time* (1969); *Doctor Cobb's Game* (1970); etc. Also books under pen name "Owen Aherne."

Cassique of Kiawah, The. Novel by William Gilmore Simms (1859). A romance of 17th-century Carolina.

Cast, The. New York. Weekly theatrical magazine. Founded 1899.

Caste. Novel by "Sydney A. Story" (Mary Hayden Green Pike) (1856). Deals with the problem of a marriage engagement between a quadroon girl and a white man.

Caste and Class in a Southern Town. By John Dollard (1937). Results of a sociological analysis of "Southerntown," a typical town in the South, concentrating on the status of Negroes and their relations with whites.

CASTEEL, JOHN LAURENCE (Dec. 17, 1903–); b. Randolph, Neb. Congregational clergyman, educator. *Rediscovering Prayer* (1955); etc. Co-author: *Spiritual Renewal Through Personal Groups* (1957); *Promise of Prayer* (1957). Prof. pastoral theology, Union Theological Seminary, 1956–64.

CASTELL, ALBUREY (Jan. 20, 1904–); b. Toronto, Can. Philosopher, educator. *An Introduction to Modern Philosophy* (1943); *Science as a Goad to Philosophy* (1953); *An Elementary Ethics* (1954); etc. Editor: *Selections from T. H. Huxley* (1948). Prof. philosophy, University of Oregon, 1949–64; philosophy dept., College of Wooster, since 1964.

Casting Away of Mrs. Lecks and Mrs. Aleshine, The. Novel by Frank R. Stockton (1886). Two New England widows on their way to Japan are cast off on a Pacific island with a Mr. Craig. The consequences are amusingly described.

CASTLE, MARIAN JOHNSON [Marian Castle] (Nov. 5, 1898–); b. Kendall, Ill. Author. *Deborah* (1946); *The Golden Fury* (1949); *Roxana* (1955); *Silver Answer* (1960).

Castle, Stanley. Pen name of Rilma Marion Browne.

Castle Keep. Novel by William Eastlake (1965). The plight of American soldiers in the Ardennes during World War II at the time of the great German offensive there in 1944.

Castle Nowhere. Stories by Constance Fenimore Woolson (1875). Dealing with the French inhabitants of the Lake Superior area.

CASTLEMAN, VIRGINIA CARTER (Aug. 26, 1864–deceased); b. Gaston, N.C. Author. *A Child of the Covenant* (1893); *Roger of Fairfield* (1906); *Pocohontas: A Dramatic Poem; and Miscellaneous Poems* (1907); *Betweenwhiles* (1919).

Castlemon, Harry. Pen name of Charles Austin Fosdick.

Casuals of the Sea. By William McFee (1916). Story of sea adventure, and the picturesque life along the river fronts.

Cat and the Canary, The. Novelette by Margaret Cameron (1907).

Cat and the Canary, The. Play by John Willard (prod. 1922).

Cat on a Hot Tin Roof. Play by Tennessee Williams (prod. 1955).

Catalogue of Books Published in America, A. Published by John West (Boston, 1797).

"Catawba Wine." Poem by Henry Wadsworth Longfellow (1854).

Catch-22. Novel by Joseph Heller (1963). Black-humor story about the air force in World War II. Its wild improbabilities are recounted in such a way as to match the actualities of war despite apparent exaggeration.

Catcher in the Rye, The. Novel by J. D. Salinger (1951). Adventures of adolescent Holden Caulfield, who runs away from school and speculates on his own apartness from others in an adult world that lacks resilience.

CATCHINGS, WADDILL (Sept. 6, 1879–Dec. 1967); b. Sewanee, Tenn. Fund executive. Co-author: *Money* (1923); *Profits* (1925); *Business without a Buyer* (1927); *Money, Men, and Machines* (1953).

CATE, JAMES LEA (Nov. 16, 1899–); b. Little Rock, Ark. Educator. Co-editor: *Medieval and Historical Essays in Honor of James Westphal Thompson* (1938); *The Army Air Forces in World War II,* 7v. (1948–58). Prof. medieval history, University of Chicago, since 1948.

CATE, WIRT ARMISTEAD (Nov. 16, 1900–); b. Hopkinsville, Ky. Author. *Lucius Q. C. Lamar, Secession and Reunion* (1935); etc. Editor: *Two Soldiers, The Campaign Diaries of Thomas J. Key, C.S.A., and Robert J. Campbell, U. S. A.* (1938).

CATER, DOUGLASS (Aug. 24, 1923–); b. Montgomery, Ala. Editor, author. *Ethics in a Business Society* (with Mar-

quis Childs, 1953); *The Fourth Branch of Government* (1959); *Power in Washington* (1964); *The Irrelevant Man* (1970). Editor for *Reporter* magazine, 1950–64.

CATHCART, NOBLE AYDELOTTE (May 14, 1898–); b. Montgomery, Ala. Publisher. With *Saturday Review of Literature* from 1924, publisher of same, 1926–39. President, Saturday Review Co., 1933–39.

"Cathedral, The." Poem by James Russell Lowell (1869). First called *A Day at Chartres.*

CATHER, WILLA [Sibert] (Dec. 7, 1873–Apr. 24, 1947); b. near Winchester, Va. Novelist, poet. *April Twilights* (poems, 1903), augmented as *April Twilights, and Other Poems* (1923); *The Troll Garden* (1905); *Alexander's Bridge* (1912); *O Pioneers!* (1913); *The Song of the Lark* (1915); *My Antonia* (1918); *Youth and the Bright Medusa* (1920); *One of Ours* (1922; Pulitzer Prize novel, 1923); *A Lost Lady* (1923); *The Professor's House* (1925); *My Mortal Enemy* (1926); *Death Comes for the Archbishop* (1927); *Shadows on the Rock* (1931); *Obscure Destinies* (1932); *Lucy Gayheart* (1935); *Not Under Forty* (1936); *Sapphira and the Slave Girl* (1940); *The Old Beauty and Others* (1948); *Willa Cather on Writing* (1949); etc. See Mildred R. Bennett's *The World of Willa Cather* (1951); E. K. Brown's *Willa Cather: A Critical Biography* (1953); James Schroeter's *Willa Cather and Her Critics* (1967).

CATHERWOOD, MARY HARTWELL (Dec. 16, 1847–Dec. 26, 1902); b. Luray, O. Novelist. *A Woman in Armor* (1875); *The Romance of Dollard* (1889); *The Story of Tonty* (1890); *Old Kaskaskia* (1893); *The Chase of Saint-Castin, and Other Stories of the French in the New World* (1894); *The Days of Jeanne d'Arc* (1897); *Spanish Peggy* (1899); *Mackinac and Lake Stories (1899); Lazarre* (1901); etc.

Catholic Advocate. Weekly. Founded 1836 at Bardstown, Ky. Later moved to Louisville.

Catholic Digest. St. Paul, Minn. Monthly. Founded 1936. Reprint magazine, not restricted to material appearing only in Catholic publications.

Catholic Encyclopedia. Ed. by Charles G. Herbermann, Edward A. Pace, and others, 17v. (1907–27). The revised edition appeared in 1934. See *New Catholic Encyclopedia.*

Catholic Heroes and Heroines of America, The. By John O'Kane Murray (1880) *See also* his *Catholic Pioneers of America* (1883).

Catholic Historical Review. Washington, D.C. Quarterly. Founded, 1915, by Peter Guilday, who became its first editor.

Catholic Poetry Society of America, The. New York. Founded 1931, by the editors of *America, The Catholic World,* and *The Commonweal.* Its membership is open to poets of all faiths. The Society publishes a bi-monthly *Bulletin,* and *Spirit,* a bi-monthly magazine of poetry devoted exclusively to poetry submitted by members of the Society.

Catholic World, The. New York. Monthly magazine. Founded 1865, by the Paulist Fathers and the Catholic Publication Society. Its editors have included Isaac T. Hecker, A. F. Hewit, Alexander P. Doyle, John J. Burke, and John B. Sheerin, present editor. Its most prolific early contributor was Orestes A. Brownson. It published the first work of Agnes Repplier and Louise Imogen Guiney. Alice Meynell, Joyce Kilmer, Aubrey De Vere, G. K. Chesterton, and Hilaire Belloc contributed articles and poems.

Catholic Writers Guild of America. New York. Founded 1919.

CATLEDGE, TURNER (Mar. 17, 1901–); b. Ackerman, Miss. Journalist, author. *The 168 Days* (with Joseph W. Alsop, Jr., 1937), *My Life and the Times* (autobiography, 1971). Managing editor, *The New York Times,* 1951–64; exec. editor, 1964–68; Vice-pres., 1968–70; on board of directors, since 1970.

CATLIN, GEORGE (July 26, 1796–Dec. 23, 1872); b. Wilkes-Barre, Pa. Artist, author. *Letters and Notes on the Manners, Customs, and Conditions of the North American Indians,* 2v. (1841); *Catlin's North American Indian Portfolio* (1845); *Life among the Indians* (1867); *Last Rambles amongst the Indians of the Rocky Mountains and the Andes* (1867). Famous for his paintings and drawings of Indian life.

Cat's Cradle. Science-fiction satire by Kurt Vonnegut, Jr. (1963).

CATTELL, JACQUES (June 2, 1904–Dec. 18, 1960); b. Garrison, N.Y. Editor, lecturer, publisher. Editor, *American Men of Science,* from 1927; *Science,* 1944–46; *Leaders in Education,* from 1938; *American Naturalist,* 1938–46, publisher, since 1946; editor, *Biographical Directory of American Scholars,* from 1941; pres., The Science Press, 1948–56; Jacques Cattell Press, 1940–56; science editor, Pergamon Press, from 1957.

CATTELL, J[ames] McKEEN (May 25, 1860–Jan. 20, 1949); b. Easton, Pa. Editor, educator, psychologist. Editor, the *Psychological Review,* 1894–1904; *Science,* since 1894; *the Scientific Monthly* (formerly *Popular Science Monthly*), since 1900; *American Men of Science,* since 1906; the *American Naturalist,* since 1907; *School and Society,* 1915–39; *Leaders in Education,* since 1932. President, Science Press Printing Co., 1928–37. Prof. psychology, Columbia University, 1891–1917.

CATTELL, RAYMOND B. (1905–); b. Staffordshire, Eng. Psychologist, educator, author. *Personality, a Systematic Study* (1950); *Factor Analysis* (1952); *The Meaning and Measurement of Neuroticism and Anxiety* (1961); *Objective Personality Tests* (1967); etc. Research prof. psychology, University of Illinois, since 1945.

CATTON, BRUCE (Oct. 9, 1899–); b. Petoskey, Mich. Editor, author. *The War Lords of Washington* (1948); *Mr. Lincoln's Army* (1951); *Glory Road* (1952); *A Stillness at Appomatox* (1953; Pulitzer Prize for history, 1954); *U.S. Grant and the American Military Tradition* (1954); *Banners at Shenandoah* (1955); *This Hallowed Ground* (1956); *America Goes to War* (1958); *The American Heritage Picture History of the Civil War* (1961); *The Coming Fury, volume I of the Centennial History of the Civil War* (1961); *Terrible Swift Sword* (1962); *The Battle of Gettysburg* (1963); *Grant Takes Command* (1969). Editor, *American Heritage Magazine,* 1954–59; senior editor since 1959.

CAUDILL, HARRY MONROE (May 3, 1922–); b. Whitesburg, Ky. Lawyer, author. *Night Comes to the Cumberlands* (1963); *Poverty and Affluence* (1966); *Dark Hills to Westward* (1969).

CAUDILL, REBECCA (Feb. 2, 1899–); b. Poor Fork, Ky. Author. *Barry and Daughter* (1943); *Happy Little Family* (1947); *Tree of Freedom* (1949); *House of the Fifers* (1954); *Higgins and the Great Big Scare* (1960); *The Far-Off Land* (1964); *My Appalachia* (1966); *Come Along* (1969); etc.

CAUGHEY, JOHN WALTON (July 3, 1902–); b. Wichita, Kan. Historian. *History of the Pacific Coast* (1933); *McGillivray of the Creeks* (1938); *California* (1940); *Hubert Howe Bancroft* (1946); *Gold Is the Cornerstone* (1948); *In Clear and Present Danger* (1958); *Their Majesties the Mob* (1960); *The American West: Frontier and Region* (1969). Editor: *The Emigrant's Guide to California* (1932); *The Los Angeles Star* (1947); *Robert Owen, Social Idealist* (1949); *Six Months in the Gold Mines* (1958); *California Heritage: An Anthology of History and Literature* (with LaRee Caughey, 1962); *California's Own History* (1963); *School Segregation on Our Doorstep* (with LaRee Caughey, 1966).

Causes of World War III, The. By C. Wright Mills (1958). Strongly argumentative discussion of the nature of political irresponsibility and its probable consequences.

Caustic, Christopher. Pen name of Thomas Green Fessenden.

Cavalier. New York. Monthly. Founded 1952, by Fawcett Publications, Inc. General magazine for men.

Cavalier, The. Novel by George W. Cable (1901). Story of Richard Thorndyke Smith's adventures in the Confederate army during the stirring days of the Civil War.

Cavaliers of Virginia, The. Novel by William Alexander Caruthers, 2v. (1834–35). Describing "Natty Bacon," brave, swaggering and successful, who in the end leads Virginia Fairfax to the altar.

CAVALLO, DIANA (Nov. 3, 1931–); b. Philadelphia, Pa. Educator, author. *A Bridge of Leaves* (1961); *Certain Fathoms in the Earth* (1964); *New York, Its Co-Existing Past and Present* (1969). Lecturer in literature, Queens College, since 1966.

"Cavender's House." Narrative poem by Edwin Arlington Robinson (1929).

Cavendish, Pauline Bradford Mackie. See Pauline Bradford Mackie.

CAVERT, SAMUEL McCREA (Sept. 9, 1888–); b. Charlton, N.Y. Presbyterian clergyman, author. *Securing Christian Leaders for Tomorrow* (1926); *The Adventure of the Church* (1927); *The Church Through Half a Century* (with Henry P. Van Dusen, 1936); *The Church Faces the World* (1939); *On the Road to Christian Unity* (1961); *American Churches in the Ecumenical Movement 1900–68* (1968).

"Cawdor." Long title poem by Robinson Jeffers in his *Cawdor, and Other Poems* (1928).

CAWEIN, MADISON [Julius] (Mar. 23, 1865–Dec. 8, 1914); b. Louisville, Ky. Poet. *Blooms of the Berry* (1887); *The Triumph of Music and Other Lyrics* (1888); *Kentucky Poems* (1902); *The Poems,* 5v. (1907); *The Giant and the Star* (1909); etc.

Caxton Printers, Ltd. Caldwell, Ida. Founded, 1904, by James H. Gipson. Incorporated 1907. It entered the publishing field in 1925 with Luken's *Idaho Citizen,* a textbook. It is devoted to the publication in particular of Americana, and books on economics, public affairs, and statecraft. James H. Gipson, Jr. is president. The firm is interested in fine printing and the development of the graphic arts in the West. *See* Vardis Fisher's *The Caxton Printers in Idaho* (1940).

CAYTON, HORACE ROSCOE (Apr. 12, 1903–); b. Seattle, Wash. Sociologist. *Black Workers and the New Unions* (with G. S. Mitchell, 1939); *Black Metropolis* (with St. Clair Drake, 1945); *Long Old Road* (1965).

Cecil Dreeme. Novel by Theodore Winthrop (1862). Cecil Dreeme is an artist living in Washington Square, New York. The main action is inner and spiritual rather than physical, and Byng and Densdeth are used as symbols of the conflicting forces at work in man.

CEDER, GEORGIANA DORCAS b. Chicago, Ill. Author. *Ya-Ya, a Brownie Story* (1947); *Ethan the Shepherd Boy* (1948); *Winter Without Salt* (1962); *Reluctant Jane* (1966); etc.

Celebrated Jumping Frog of Calaveras County, The. Humorous story by Mark Twain, in the *Saturday Press,* Nov. 18, 1865. This started Mark Twain on his literary career, bringing him national notice. *See* Oscar Lewis's *The Origin of the Celebrated Frog of Calaveras County* (1931).

Celebrity, The. Novel by Winston Churchill (1898). A stinging satire on a well-known magazine writer of the period.

Celestial Railroad, The. Short story by Nathaniel Hawthorne (1843). A modern treatment of Bunyan's *Pilgrim's Progress.*

Censorship. Among the books banned in America have been *Jurgen,* by James Branch Cabell; *Leaves of Grass,* by Walt Whitman; *Oil,* by Upton Sinclair, *Elmer Gantry,* by Sinclair Lewis; *An American Tragedy,* by Theodore Dreiser; *Three Weeks,* by Eleanor Glyn; *Ulysses,* by James Joyce; *Bad Girl,* by Viña Delmar; *Married Love,* by Marie Stopes; *Sex Side of Life,* by Mary Ware Dennett; *Casanova's Homecoming,* by Arthur Schnitzler; *Lady Chatterley's Lover,* by D. H. Lawrence; *Tropic of Cancer* and *Tropic of Capricorn,* by Henry Miller; *Memoirs of Hecate County,* by Edmund Wilson; *Lolita,* by Vladimir Nabokov; *The Naked Lunch,* by William Burroughs. The Watch and Ward Society of Boston, and the Society for the Suppression of Vice in New York, the latter under the direction of Anthony Comstock, and, after his death, John S. Sumner, were the most vigilant of all the censoring organizations. Since the late 1950's and early 1960's, especially as a result of Grove Press v. Christenberry, involving *Lady Chatterley's Lover,* and of subsequent court decisions, censorship of supposedly obscene or pornographic works has notably relaxed. All the works mentioned above as banned have been published and sold with decreasing interference from legal authorities during the 1960's. Many other works, including those with graphic and photographic reproductions, have emerged from obscurity to be made public for the first time. In the late 1960's almost complete freedom from prosecution on the grounds of obscenity obtained for all kinds of printed material. The same freedom has been accorded motion pictures and plays. For a study of censorship of books in America, *see* Morris L. Ernst's and William Seagle's *To the Pure, a Study of Obscenity and the Censor* (1928); Anne Lyon Haight's *Banned Books* (1935); Morris L. Ernst's and Alexander Lindley's *The Censor Marches On* (1940); Redmond A. Burke's *What Is the Index?* (1952); Robert Bingham Downs's *The First Freedom: Liberty and Justice in the World of Books and Reading* (1960); and David Goldsmith Loth's *The Erotic in Literature* (1961); John McCormick's and Mairi MacInnes's *Versions of Censorship* (1962); Morris L. Ernst's *Censorship: The Search for the Obscene* (1964); Richard H. Kuh's *Foolish Figleaves?* (1967); Paul S. Boyer's *Purity in Print: The Vice-Society Movement and Book Censorship in America* (1968); Harry M. Clor's *Obscenity and Public Morality* (1969).

Centennial Hymn. By John Greenleaf Whittier, in *Atlantic Monthly,* June, 1876. Two lines were written by Bayard Taylor (17–18).

Center Magazine, The. Santa Barbara, Cal. Bimonthly. Founded 1967. Published by The Center for the Study of Democratic Institutions. Edited by John Cogley. Devoted to the study of history and the future.

Centinel of the North-Western Territory, The. Cincinnati, O. Newspaper. Founded 1793. Probably the first newspaper in Ohio. Name later changed to *Freeman's Journal.* Moved to Chillicothe in 1800; merged with the *Scioto Gazette* (founded 1800).

Century Association, The. (Century Club) New York. Founded 1846. Incorporated 1857. The incorporators were Gulian Crommelin Verplanck, William Cullen Bryant, Asher B. Durand, John Frederick Kensett, Charles M. Leupp, William H. Appleton, William Kemble. The presidents have included Gulian C. Verplanck, George Bancroft, William Cullen Bryant, John Bigelow, Elihu Root, and Charles A. Platt. The Association is composed of "authors, artists, and amateurs of letters and the fine arts" and was originally limited to 100 resident members. The first club house was at 945 Broadway. From 1857 to 1891 it was at No. 109 (old No. 42) East 50 Street. In 1891 it moved to its present quarters, 7 West 43 Street. It is popularly known as the Century Club.

Century Company, The. New York. Publishers. Founded 1881. This company was closely connected with Scribner's, for in 1870 Roswell Smith and Josiah Gilbert Holland founded *Scribner's Monthly,* published by an organization set up by Charles Scribner's Sons, publishers. Holland became editor, assisted by Richard Watson Gilder. A few books were published by this Scribner subsidiary, and in 1881 a new company was organized, called The Century Company, the Scribner interests were purchased and the magazine changed to *The Century Illustrated Monthly Magazine.* This magazine flourished under Gilder, and was printed by Theodore De Vinne. Its illustrations, under the guidance of its art director, Alexander W. Drake, set new standards of excellence. Most of the celebrated literary men and women of America were contributors over a period of years. The firm also published *St. Nicholas Magazine.* One of the major works published by the Century Company was *The Century Dictionary and Cyclopedia.* In 1933 the Century Company was merged with D. Appleton & Co., to form The Appleton-Century Co. Among the popular books published by The Century Company were: *Mrs. Wiggs of the Cabbage Patch,* by Alice Hegan Rice; *Messer Marco Polo,* by Donn Byrne; *Daddy Long-Legs,* by Jean Webster; and *Abraham Lincoln,* by Nicolay and Hay. The four presidents of The Century Company were Roswell Smith, 1881–92, Frank H. Scott, 1892–1912, W. W. Ellsworth, 1912–14, and W. Morgan Shuster, 1914–33, who became president of the D. Appleton-Century Company at the time of the merger. See *The House of Appleton-Century,* a brochure, published by the firm in 1936.

Century Magazine. See the Century Company.

Century of Dishonor, A. Novel by Helen Hunt Jackson (1881). An indictment of the United States government for its treatment of the Indians.

Ceram, C. W. Pen name of Kurt W. Marek.

CERAVOLO, JOSEPH (1934–). Author. *Fits of Dawn* (1965); *Wild Flowers Out of Gas* (1967); *Spring in the World of Poor Mutts* (1968).

CERF, BENNETT ALFRED (May 25, 1898–Aug. 27, 1971); b. New York. Publisher, editor, author. Author or editor: *Bedside Book of Famous American Stories* (1936); *Bedside Book of Famous British Stories* (with H. C. Moriarty 1940); *Try and Stop Me* (1944); *Laughing Stock* (1945); *Anything for a Laugh* (1946); *Good for a Laugh* (1952); *Life of the Party* (1956); *Reading for Pleasure* (1957); *The Laugh's on Me* (1959); *Out on a Limerick* (1960); *More Riddles* (1961); *Book of Animal Riddles* (1964); *Laugh Day* (1965); *Treasury of Atrocious Puns* (1968); *Sound of Laughter* (1970). Vice-pres., Boni & Liveright, 1923–25; founded Modern Library, in 1925; founder and pres., Random House, 1927–65; chairman of the board, from 1965; director, Bantam Books, 1945–67.

CERF, JAY HENRY (May 17, 1923–); b. Chicago, Ill. Association executive, political scientist, author. *The Intellectual Bases of Nazism* (1951); *History of the Free University* (1954). Editor: *Strategy for the 1960's* (1961); *The Alliance for Progress—a Hemispheric Response to a Global Threat* (1965).

Certain Rich Man, A. Novel by William Allen White (1909). The composite story of life in Sycamore Ridge, a small town in Kansas, during the period 1857–1903, showing the corrupting influence on character of quickly acquired wealth when the moral fibre of the recipient is weak.

Chad Hanna. Novel by Walter D. Edmonds (1940). Chad Hanna joins a small circus in upper New York State and becomes involved in many adventures, crowned by a romance which rises above the environment in which he finds himself.

Chadwick, CHARLES (Nov. 19, 1874–Sept. 28, 1953); b. Brooklyn, N.Y. Novelist. *The Cactus* (1925); *The Moving House of Foscaldo* (1926).

CHADWICK, HENRY (Oct. 5, 1824–Apr. 20, 1908); b. Exeter, England. Sportsman. One of America's earliest sports writers. Was on staff of the New York *Clipper* for thirty-one years. His annual baseball handbook was first issued in 1869 and became Spalding's *Official Baseball Guide,* which he edited 1881–1908.

CHADWICK, JOHN WHITE (Oct. 19, 1840–Dec. 11, 1904); b. Marblehead, Mass. Clergyman, poet, biographer. *A Book of Poems* (1876); *A Legend of Good Poets* (1883); *The Two Voices* (poems, 1886); *William Ellery Channing* (1903); *Later Poems* (1905); *Cap'n Chadwick, Marblehead Skipper and Shoemaker* (1906); etc.

CHAFEE, ZECHARIAH (Dec. 7, 1885–Feb. 8, 1957); b. Providence, R.I. Legal writer, educator. *Freedom of Speech* (1920); *The Inquiring Mind* (1928); *The Constitutional Convention That Never Met* (1938, 1939); *Government and Mass Communications* (1947); *The Blessings of Liberty* (1956); etc.

CHAFFEE, ALLEN; b. Corning, Ia., as Antoinette Gurney, name was legally changed in 1919. Author. *Twinkly Eyes, the Little Black Bear* (1919); *Penn, the Penguin* (1921); *Adventures on the High Trail* (1923); *Sitka, the Snow Baby* (1925); *Tony and the Big Top* (1925); *Wanda, the Wild Pony* (1933); *Tawny Goes Hunting* (1937); etc.

CHAILLÉ-LONG, CHARLES (July 2, 1842–Mar. 24, 1917); b. Princess Anne, Md. Soldier, diplomat, author. *Central Africa: Naked Truths of Naked People* (1876); *The Three Prophets* (1884); *My Life in Four Continents,* 2v. (1912); etc.

Challenge. Boston, Mass. Quarterly. Founded 1934. Little magazine of Negro intellectuals. Edited by Dorothy West. Published Arna Bontemps, Langston Hughes, Frank Yerby. Reorganized in 1937 as *New Challenge* (q.v.).

CHALMERS, ALLAN KNIGHT (June 30, 1897–); b. Cleveland, O. Educator, author. *The Commonplace Prodigal* (1934); *High Wind at Noon* (1948); *They Shall Be Free* (1951); *That Revolutionary—Christ* (1957). Prof. preaching and applied Christianity, Boston University, since 1948.

CHALMERS, STEPHEN (Feb. 29, 1880–Dec. 14, 1935); b. Dunoon, Scotland. Novelist, poet. *The Vanishing Smuggler* (1909); *The Beloved Physician: Edward Livingston Trudeau* (1916); *The Penny Piper of Saranac: An Episode in Stevenson's Life* (1916); *The Gilding-Star, and Other Poems* (1916); *Enchanted Cigarettes; or, Stevenson Stories That Might Have Been* (1917); etc.

CHAMALES, THOMAS [Tom] T. (1924–Mar. 28, 1960); Author. *Never So Few* (1957); *Go Naked in the World* (1959).

CHAMBERLAIN, ALEXANDER FRANCIS (Jan. 12, 1865–Apr. 8, 1914); b. Kenninghall, England. Anthropologist, educator, poet. *Child and Childhood in Folk Thought* (1896); *Poems* (1904); etc. Editor, *The Journal of American Folk-Lore,* 1901–07.

CHAMBERLAIN, ALLEN (May 2, 1867–deceased); b. Boston, Mass. Author. *Vacation Tramps in New England Highlands* (1919); *Beacon Hill* (1925); *The Annals of the Grand Monadnock* (1936); *Pigeon Cove—Its Early Settlers and Their Farms* (1940); etc.

CHAMBERLAIN, ARTHUR HENRY (Oct. 3, 1872–Oct. 30, 1942); b. Oak Lawn, Ill. Educator, author. *Europe* (1912); *Asia* (1913); *South America* (1913); *Africa* (1914); *Ideals and Democracy* (1913); etc. Publisher, *Overland Monthly,* and *Out West Magazine.*

CHAMBERLAIN, GEORGE AGNEW (Mar. 15, 1879–March 4, 1966); b. São Paulo, Brazil. Novelist. *Home* (1914); *Through Stained Glass* (1915); *Pigs to Market* (1920); *Taxi* (1920); *Man Alone* (1926); *River to the Sea* (1930); *Two On Safari* (1934); *In Defense of Mrs. Maxon* (1938); *Scudda-hoo! Scudda-hay!* (1946); *Lord Buff and the Silver Star* (1955); etc.

CHAMBERLAIN, JOHN [Rensselaer] (Oct. 28, 1903–); b. New Haven, Conn. Editor, critic. *Farewell to Reform* (1932); *After the Genteel Tradition* (1937); *Books That Changed Our Minds* (1939); *Farewell to Reform* (1932); *MacArthur: 1941–1951* (with Charles Willoughby, 1954); *The Enterprising Americans* (1963). Book editor, *Harper's Magazine,* 1939–47; editor, *Life,* 1945–50; staff writer, *Wall Street Journal,* since 1955. Now daily columnist, King Features Syndicate.

CHAMBERLAIN, LAWRENCE H[enry] (Mar. 15, 1906–); b. Challis, Ida. Educator, author. *President, Congress, and Legislation* (1946); *American Foreign Policy* (with R. C. Snyder, 1948); *Loyalty and Legislative Action* (1951). Dean, Columbia College, 1950–58.

CHAMBERLAIN, NARCISSE (June 17, 1924–); b. Paris. Author. Co-author with mother, Mrs. Samuel Vance Chamberlain: *The Chamberlain Calendar of French Cooking* (1957–63); *The Chamberlain Calendar of American Cooking* (1958–61); *The Chamberlain Sampler of American Cooking* (1961); *The Chamberlain Calendar of French Menus* (1965–68); etc.

CHAMBERLAIN, NEIL [Cornelius] WOLVERTON (May 18, 1915–); b. Charlotte, N.C. Educator, author. *Collective Bargaining Procedures* (1944); *The Union Challenge to Management Control* (1948); *Management in Motion* (1950); *Collective Bargaining* (1951); *Social Responsibility and Strikes* (1953); *The Impact of Strikes* (with J. M. Schilling, 1954); *A General Theory of Economic Process* (1955); *Labor* (1958); *The West in a World Without War* (1963); *Private and Public Planning* (1965); *Enterprise and Environment* (1968). Prof. economics, Columbia University, since 1954.

CHAMBERLAIN, SAMUEL (Oct. 28, 1895–); b. Cresco, Ia. Etcher, author. *Cape-Cod in the Sun* (1937); *Open House in New England* (1937); *Longfellow's Wayside Inn* (1938); *Historic Boston* (1938); *Historic Salem* (1938); *Gloucester and Cape Ann* (1938); *Lexington and Concord* (1939); *Nantucket* (1939); *Old Marblehead* (1940); *Ever New England* (1944); *Behold Williamsburg* (1947); *The Yale Scene* (1950); *Bouquet de France* (1952); *The Berkshires* (1956); *Rockefeller Center* (1961); *British Bouquet* (1963); *Etched in Sunlight* (1968); etc.

CHAMBERLIN, EDWARD HASTINGS (May 18, 1899–); b. La Conner, Wash. Educator, author. *Theory of Monopolistic Competition* (1933); *Towards a More General Theory of Value* (1957); *The Economic Analysis of Labor Union Power* (1958). Editor: *Monopoly and Competition and Their Regulation* (1954). Editor, *Quarterly Journal of Economics,* 1948–58. Prof. economics, Harvard University, since 1937.

CHAMBERLIN, FREDERICK [Carleton] (May 21, 1870–Sept. 20, 1942); b. Abington, Mass. Historical writer. *In the Shoe String Country* (1906); *Around the World in Ninety Days* (1906); *The Private Character of Queen Elizabeth* (1921); *The Private Character of Henry the Eighth* (1931); *The Great Leycester* (1938); *Elizabeth and Leycester* (1939); etc.

CHAMBERLIN, HENRY HARMON (Aug. 6, 1873–July 10, 1951); b. Worcester, Mass. Poet. *The Age of Ivory* (1904); *Poems* (1911); *The Master Knot* (1923); *Sir Aldengar* (1927); *Horace Talks* (trans. of Horace's *Satires,* 1940).

CHAMBERLIN, JOSEPH EDGAR (Aug. 6, 1861–July 6, 1935); b. Newbury, Vt. Editor, author. *The Listener in the Country* (1896); *The Listener in the Town* (1896); *John Brown* (1899); *The Ifs of History* (1907); *The Boston Transcript: A History of Its First Hundred Years* (1930).

CHAMBERLIN, THOMAS CHROWDER (Sept. 25, 1843–Nov. 15, 1928); b. Mattoon, Ill. Educator, geologist, author. *The Origin of the Earth* (1916); *The Two Solar Families* (1928); etc. Founder, the *Journal of Geology,* 1893. President, University of Wisconsin, 1887–92; prof. geology, University of Chicago, 1892–1919.

CHAMBERLIN, WILLIAM H[enry] (Feb. 17, 1897–Sept. 12, 1969); b. Brooklyn, N.Y. Author. *Soviet Russia* (1930); *The Soviet Planned Economic Order* (1931); *Russia's Iron Age* (1934); *The Russian Revolution, 1917–21* (1935); *Collectivism—A False Utopia* (1937); *Canada Today and Tomorrow* (1942); *The European Cockpit* (1947); *America's Second Crusade* (1950); *Beyond Containment* (1953); *The Evolution of a Conservative* (1959); *America's Second Crusade* (1962); *The German Phoenix* (1963). With *Christian Science Monitor*, 1922–40.

CHAMBERS, DAVID LAURANCE (Jan. 12, 1879–Jan. 12, 1963); b. Washington, D.C. Publisher, author. *Indiana: A Hoosier History* (1933). With Bobbs-Merrill Co., Indianapolis, Ind., 1903–58; president, 1935–53; chairman of board, 1953–58.

CHAMBERS, JAMES FLOYD, JR. (May 13, 1913–); b. Houston, Tex. Journalist, author. Ghost writer for several sports celebrities such as Byron Nelson, Doak Walker. With *Dallas Dispatch-Journal*, 1934–41; director, *Dallas Times Herald*, since 1952.

CHAMBERS, JULIUS (Nov. 21, 1850–Feb. 12, 1920); b. Bellefontaine, O. Journalist, author. *A Mad World and Its Inhabitants* (1876); *The Destiny of Doris* (1901); *The Mississippi River and Its Wonderful Valley* (1910); *The Book of New York: Forty Years' Recollections of the American Metropolis* (1912); *News Hunting on Three Continents* (1921). Conducted column in the *Brooklyn Eagle*, called "Walks and Talks," 1904–20.

CHAMBERS, MERRITT MADISON (Jan. 26, 1899–); b. Knox Co., O. Political scientist. *Youth-Serving Organizations* (1937); *Colleges and the Courts, 1946–50* (1952); *Financing Higher Education* (1963); *The Colleges and the Courts since 1950* (1964); *Freedom and Repression in Higher Education* (1965); *Bibliography of Higher Education* (1966); *The Colleges and the Courts, 1962–1966* (1967); *Higher Education: Who Pays? Who Gains?* (1968); etc. Editor: *Charters of Philanthropies* (1948); etc.

CHAMBERS, ROBERT W[illiam] (May 26, 1865–Dec. 16, 1933); b. Brooklyn, N.Y. Novelist. *In the Quarter* (anon., 1894); *The Red Republic* (1895); *The King in Yellow* (1895); *Lorraine* (1898); *Ashes of Empire* (1898); *Cardigan* (1901); *The Fighting Chance* (1906); *The Younger Set* (1907); *The Firing Line* (1908); *Ailsa Page* (1910); *The Common Law* (1912); *The Hidden Children* (1914); The Crimson Tide (1919); *The Slayer of Souls* (1920); *The Little Red Foot* (1921); *The Rogue's Moon* (1928); *The Rake and the Hussy* (1930); *Beating Wings* (1930); *The Painted Minx* (1930); *Whistling Cat* (1932); *Love and the Lieutenant* (1935); etc.

CHAMBERS, WHITTAKER (1901–July 9, 1961). Editor. *Witness* (autobiography, 1952). Translator: Felix Salten's *Bambi, Fifteen Rabbits;* Anna E. Weirauch's *Scorpion.* Editorial staff, *Time* magazine. See *Odyssey of a Friend: Whittaker Chambers' Letters to William F. Buckley, Jr., 1954–1961* (1970).

CHAMBRUN, CLARA [Eleanor] LONGWORTH, COMTESSE DE (Oct. 18, 1873–1954); b. Cincinnati, O. Author. *The Sonnets of William Shakespeare* (1913); *The Making of Nicholas Longworth* (autobiography, 1936); *Shakespeare Rediscovered* (1938); *Cincinnati: Story of the Queen City* (1939); *The Shadows Lengthen, The Story of My Life* (1949); *Shakespeare: A Portrait Restored* (1957); etc.

Champions of Freedom, The. Novel by Samuel Woodworth (1816). A tale of the War of 1812.

CHAMPLIN, EDWIN ROSS (May 14, 1854–Sept. 8, 1928); b. E. Westerly, R.I. Editor, poet. Pen name, "Clarence Fairchild." *Heart's Own* (1886); *Lovers' Lyrics and Other Songs* (1888); *On the White Birch Road* (1891); *At the Sign of the Song* (1907).

CHAMPLIN, JOHN DENISON (Jan. 29, 1834–Jan. 8, 1915); b. Stonington, Conn. Editor, cyclopedist, author. *Chronicle of the Coach* (1886). Compiled many cyclopedias for young folks, such as *Young Folks Cyclopedia of Persons and Places* (1887); etc. Editor: *Cyclopedia of Painters and Paintings,* 4v. (1886–87); *Cyclopedia of Music and Musicians,* 3v. (1888–90). On the staff of the *Standard Dictionary,* 1892–94.

CHAMPNEY, ELIZABETH WILLIAMS (Mrs. James Wells Champney) (Feb. 6, 1850–Oct. 13, 1922); b. Springfield, O. Novelist, traveler. Wrote also as Lizzie W. Champney, the *Witch Winnie* series, 9v. (1889-98); *Bourbon Lilies* (1883); *In the Sky-Garden* (1876); *Rosemary and Rue* (1881); *Romance of the Feudal Château* (1900); *Romance of the Renaissance Château* (1901); etc.

CHAMPNEY, JAMES WELLS (July 16, 1843–May 1, 1903); b. Boston, Mass. Painter, illustrator. He made more than five hundred sketches for the articles entitled the "Great South" written by Edward King for *Scribner's Monthly* in 1873. He also made a sketching tour of South America for Scribner's in 1878, illustrating articles by Herbert Smith.

CHAN, SHAU WING (Apr. 4, 1907–); b. Canton, China. Educator. *Chinese Reader for Beginners* (1942); *Concise English-Chinese Dictionary* (1946); *Elementary Chinese* (1951). Prof. Chinese, Stanford University, since 1950.

CHAN, WING-TSIT (Aug. 18, 1901–); b. Kwangtung, China. Educator. *Religious Trends in Modern China* (1953); *An Outline and Annotated Bibliography of Chinese Philosophy* (1959); *Reflections on Things at Hand* (1967); etc. Editor: *The Essentials of Buddhist Philosophy* (1941); *Great Asian Religions: An Anthology* (with others, 1969). Compiler and translator: *A Source Book in Chinese Philosophy* (1963). Prof. Chinese culture and philosophy, Dartmouth College, since 1942.

CHANCE, JULIE GRINNELL (Mrs. S. Van Rensselaer Cruger; Mrs. Wade Chance) (deceased); b. Paris, of American parentage. Novelist, poet. Pen name, "Julien Gordon." *A Diplomat's Diary* (1890); *A Puritan Pagan* (1891); *His Letters* (1892); *Marionettes* (1892); *A Wedding and Other Stories* (1896); *Poems* (1905); etc.

Chance Acquaintance, A. Novel by William Dean Howells (1873). The love story of Kitty Ellison, small town girl, and Miles Arbution, a snobbish Bostonian, who meet on a St. Lawrence steamer.

CHANDLER, CAROLINE A. (Dec. 7, 1906–); b. Ford City, Pa. Physician, author. *Susie Stuart, M.D.* (1941); *Dr. Kay Winthrop, Intern* (1947); *Famous Men of Medicine* (1950); *Famous Modern Men of Medicine* (1965); *Early Child Care: The New Perspectives* (with others, 1968). Co-author: *Your Child from One to Six* (1945).

CHANDLER, ELIZABETH MARGARET (Dec. 24, 1807–Nov. 22, 1834); b. Centre, Del. Poet, essayist. *Essays, Philanthropic and Moral* (1836); *The Poetical Works of Elizabeth Margaret Chandler* (1836). Her best known poem is "The Slave Ship."

CHANDLER, FRANK WADLEIGH (June 16, 1873–June 13, 1947); b. Brooklyn, N.Y. Educator, author. *The Literature of Roguery,* 2v. (1907); *Aspects of Modern Drama* (1914); *The Contemporary Drama of France* (1920); *Modern Continental Playwrights* (1931); etc. Editor: *Twentieth Century Plays* (with Richard Albert Cordell, 1934). Prof. English, University of Cincinnati, 1910–43.

CHANDLER, JOSEPH RIPLEY (Aug. 25, 1792–July 10, 1880); b. Kingston, Mass. Editor, author. *The Beverley Family* (1875). Editor, *The Gazette of the United States,* Philadelphia, Pa., 1826–47. Co-editor, *Graham's Magazine,* 1843–49.

CHANDLER, RAYMOND [Thornton] (July 23, 1888–Mar. 26, 1959); b. Chicago. Ill. Author. *The Big Sleep* (1939); *Farwell, My Lovely* (1940); *The High Window* (1942); *The Lady in the Lake* (1943); *Red Wind* (1946); *Spanish Blood* (1946); *The Little Sister* (1949); *The Simple Art of Murder* (1950); *The Long Goodbye* (1954); *Playback* (1958). See Dorothy Gardiner's and Katherine Sorley Walker's *Raymond Chandler Speaking* (1962).

CHANG, HSIN-HAI (June 24, 1900–); b. Shanghai, China. Educator, author. *Letters from a Chinese Diplomat* (1941); *The Fabulous Concubine* (1956); *Within the Four Seas* (1958); *America and China: a New Approach to Asia* (1966). Prof. English literature and Asian culture, Fairleigh Dickinson University, since 1956.

Changing Times, the Kiplinger Magazine. Washington, D.C. Monthly. Founded 1947. Edited by R. W. Harvey.

CHANLER, MRS. WINTHROP (Margaret Chanler) (Aug. 6, 1862–Dec. 18, 1952); b. Rome, Italy. Author. *Roman Spring* (1934); *Autumn in the Valley* (1936).

CHANNING, EDWARD (June 15, 1856–Jan. 7, 1931); b. Dorchester, Mass. Educator, historian. *Town and Country Government in the English Colonies of North America* (1884); *History of the United States,* 6. (1905–25, v. 6 awarded Pulitzer Prize for American history, 1926); etc.

CHANNING, EDWARD TYRRELL (Dec. 12, 1790–Feb. 8, 1856); b. Newport, R.I. Educator, editor, author. *Lectures Read to the Seniors in Harvard College* (1856). Editor, *North American Review,* 1818–19.

CHANNING, GRACE ELLERY (Mrs. Charles Walter Stetson) (Dec. 27, 1862–Apr. 3, 1937); b. Providence, R.I. Author. *The Sister of a Saint, and Other Stories* (1895); *Sea Drift* (poems, 1899); *The Fortune of a Day* (1900).

CHANNING, WILLIAM ELLERY (Apr. 7, 1780–Oct. 2, 1842); b. Newport, R.I. Unitarian clergyman, author. *The Importance and Means of a National Literature* (1830); *Discourses, Reviews, and Miscellanies* (1830); *Slavery* (1835); *The Works,* 6v. (1841–43); *The Perfect Life* (1873). See William Henry Channing's *Memoir of William Ellery Channing,* 3v. (1848).

CHANNING, WILLIAM ELLERY (Nov. 29, 1818–Dec. 23, 1901); b. Boston, Mass. Poet. *Poems,* 2 series (1843–47); *The Woodman, and Other Poems* (1849); *Near Home: a Poem* (1858); *The Wanderer* (1871) *Thoreau, The Poet Naturalist* (1873); *John Brown and the Heroes of Harper's Ferry: A Poem* (1886); *Poems of Sixty-Five Years* (1902).

CHANNING, WILLIAM HENRY (May 25, 1810–Dec. 23, 1884); b. Boston, Mass. Unitarian clergyman, abolitionist, author. *The Life of William Ellery Channing,* 3v. (1848); *Leaves of Spring Gathered in Autumn* (poems, 1883); etc.

CHANSLOR, ROY (Aug. 25, 1899–); b. Liberty, Mo. Author. *Lowdown* (1931); *Hazard* (1947); *The Naked I* (1953); *The Ballad of Cat Ballou* (1956).

CHANSLOR, TORREY [Hood] (Mrs. Roy Chanslor). Artist, author. *Our First Murder* (1940); *Artie and the Princess* (1945); *The Three Little Chipmunks* (1947); *Saturday Night Is My Delight* (1952); etc.

CHAO, YUEN REN (Nov. 3, 1892–); b. Tientsin, China. Educator. *New Book of Rhymes* (1923); *Studies in the Modern Wu Dialects* (1928); *Phonetics of Yao Folksongs* (1929); *Cantonese Primer* (1947); *Mandarin Primer* (1948); *How to Cook and Eat in Chinese* (1963); *Language and Symbolic Systems* (1968); *Readings in Sayable Chinese* (1969). Prof. Oriental languages and linguistics, University of California, Berkeley, since 1947.

Chap-Book, The. Chicago, Ill. Semi-monthly. Founded 1893, at Cambridge, Mass., by Herbert Stuart Stone and Ingalls

Kimball; moved to Chicago, 1894. Specialized in typographical effects. Merged with *The Dial,* in 1898.

CHAPEL, CHARLES EDWARD (May 26, 1904–); b. Manchester, Ia. Aeronautical ordnance engineer, author. *Forensic Ballistics* (1933); *Gun Collecting* (1939); *The Gun Collector's Handbook of Values* (1940); *The Boy's Book of Rifles* (1948); *Simplified Pistol and Revolver Shooting* (1950); *The Complete Guide to Gunsmithing* (1963); *U.S. Martial and Semi-Martial Single Shot Pistols* (1962); etc.

CHAPIN, AARON LUCIUS (Feb. 6, 1817–July 22, 1892); b. Hartford, Conn. Congregational clergyman, author. *First Principles of Political Economy* (1879); Editor, *Congregational Review* (1870–71); assoc. editor, *New Englander* (1872–73); assoc. editor, *Johnson's Cyclopedia* (1875–78).

CHAPIN, ANNA ALICE (Dec. 16, 1880–Feb. 26, 1920); b. New York City. Musician, author. *Masters of Music* (1901); *Discords* (1905); *The Heart of Music* (1906); *The Eagle's Mate* (1914); *Greenwich Village* (1917); *Mountain Madness* (1917); *Jane* (1920); etc.

CHAPIN, CHARLES E. (1858–Dec. 13, 1930). Editor, author. *Charles Chapin's Story Written in Sing Sing Prison* (1920); *The Constance Letters of Charles Chapin,* ed. by Eleanor Early and Constance (1931); *The Uncensored Letters of Charles Chapin,* ed. by Viola Irene (1931). City editor, The New York *World* for 27 years.

CHAPIN, EDWIN HUBBELL (Dec. 29, 1814–Dec. 26, 1880); b. Union Village, Washington Co., N.Y. Universalist clergyman, author. *Discourses on Various Subjects* (1841); *Moral Aspects of City Life* (1853); etc.

CHAPIN, HOWARD MILLAR (May 11, 1887–Sept. 18, 1940); b. Providence, R.I. Librarian, historian. *Bermuda Privateers,* 2v. (1923–25); *Documentary History of Rhode Island,* 2v. (1916–20); etc. Librarian of the Rhode Island Historical Society, 1912–40.

CHAPLIN, ADA C. (Jan. 25, 1842–Dec. 9, 1883); b. Falmouth, Mass. Author of numerous Sunday School books, including such titles as: *Little Nobody, Eight Years Old, Little Watchman, Charity Hurlburt,* etc.

CHAPLIN, JANE D[unbar] (Mrs. Jeremiah Chaplin) (Feb. 11, 1819–Apr. 17, 1884); b. in Scotland. Novelist, biographer. *Gems of the Bog* (1869); *Out of the Wilderness* (1870); *Life of Charles Sumner* (with husband, 1874); etc.

CHAPLIN, JEREMIAH (1813–Mar. 5, 1886; b. Danvers, Mass. Clergyman, biographer. *Life of Henry Dunster* (1872); *Life of Charles Sumner* (with wife, Jane D. Chaplin, 1874); *The Life of Benjamin Franklin* (1876); etc.

CHAPMAN, ARTHUR (June 25, 1873–Dec. 4, 1935); b. Rockford, Ill. Journalist, historical writer, poet. *Out Where the West Begins, and Other Western Verses* (1917); *Cactus Center* (poems, 1921); *The Story of Colorado* (1924); *The Pony Express* (1932); etc.

CHAPMAN, CHARLES EDWARD (June 3, 1880–Nov. 18, 1941); b. Franklin, N.H. Educator, author. *The Founding of Spanish California* (1916); *A Californian in South America* (1917); *A History of California: The Spanish Period* (1921); *Colonial Hispanic America* (1933); *Republican Hispanic America* (1937); etc. Dept. of History, University of California, from 1914.

CHAPMAN, EDWARD MORTIMER (Sept. 27, 1862– deceased); b. Old Saybrook, Conn. Congregational clergyman, author. *English Literature in Account with Religion* (1910); *Compassions of the Way* (1918); *New England Village Life* (1937); etc.

CHAPMAN, FRANK MICHLER (June 12, 1864–Nov. 15, 1945); b. Englewood, N.J. Ornithologist, author. *Camps and Cruises of an Ornithologist* (1908); *My Tropical Air Castle*

(1929); *Autobiography of a Bird-Lover* (1933); *Life in an Air Castle* (1938); and many scientific works on birds. Editor and founder of *Bird-Lore*. Curator ornithology, American Museum of Natural History, from 1908.

CHAPMAN, JOHN ("Johnny Appleseed") (c. 1775–1847); b. Boston or Springfield, Mass. Frontier character in Ohio who devoted his life to the planting of apple seed wherever he happened to wander. His legendary life has inspired numerous literary works. See Denton J. Snider's *Johnny Appleseed's Rhymes* (1894); Nell Hillis's *The Quest of John Chapman* (1904); Eleanor Atkinson's *Johnny Appleseed: The Romance of a Sower* (1915); Vachel Lindsay's "In Praise of Johnny Appleseed" (1921); Henry Bailey Stevens's *Johnny Appleseed and Paul Bunyan* (1930).

CHAPMAN, JOHN [Arthur] (June 25, 1900–Jan. 19, 1972); b. Denver, Colo. Journalist. *Tell It to Sweeney* (1961). Editor: *Best Plays, Yearbook of Drama,* 1947–53; *The Theatre,* 1953–56; *Broadway's Best,* 1957–58. With *The News,* New York, since 1920; dramatic editor, from 1929; columnist, "Mainly About Manhattan," 1931–40; drama critic since 1943.

CHAPMAN, JOHN JAY (1862–Nov. 4, 1933); b. New York. Critic, poet. *Emerson, and Other Essays* (1898); *Causes and Consequences* (1898); *Memories and Milestones* (1915); *Songs and Poems* (1919); *A Glance toward Shakespeare* (1922); etc. See Richard B. Hovey's *John Jay Chapman* (1959).

CHAPMAN, JOHN STANTON HIGHAM (May 21, 1891–); b. London, England. Novelist. Co-author (with wife, Mary Hamilton Illsley Chapman, using together the pen name "Maristan Chapman"): *Happy Mountain* (1928); *Homeplace* (1929); *Weather Tree* (1932); *Wild Cat Ridge* (1932); *Timber Trail* (1933); *Eagle's Cliff* (1934); *Rogues on Red Hill* (1937); *Gulf Coast Treasure* (1941); *Mystery of Burro Bray Canyon* (1958); *Doubloons* (1960); etc. With same, under pen name "Jane Selkirk": *Blue Smoke Mystery* (1946); *Treasure Box Mystery* (1951); etc.

CHAPMAN, KENNETH MILTON (July 13, 1875–); b. Ligonier, Ind. Artist, author. *Pueblo Indian Pottery,* 2v. (1933, 1936); *The Pottery of Santo Domingo Pueblo* (1936). Editor and translator: *Nazarus* (1964).

CHAPMAN, LUCIE [Wilson] (Mrs. Wendell Chapman) (Dec. 5, 1895); b. Pasadena, Calif. Naturalist. Co-author (with husband): *The Little Wolf* (1936); *Beaver Pioneers* (1937); *Wilderness Wanderers* (1937).

Chapman, Maristan. Pen name used jointly by John Stanton Higham Chapman and Mary Hamilton Illsley Chapman.

CHAPMAN, MARY HAMILTON ILLSLEY (Mrs. John Stanton Higham Chapman) (Sept. 10, 1895–); b. Chattanooga, Tenn. Co-author (with husband, q.v., using together the pen name "Maristan Chapman").

CHAPMAN, WENDELL (Jan. 13, 1895–); b. Formosa, Kan. Naturalist, Co-author (with wife, Lucie Chapman): *The Little Wolf* (1936); *Beaver Pioneers* (1937); *Wilderness Wanderers* (1937).

CHAPPELL, CLOVIS GILLHAM (Jan. 8, 1882–); b. Flatwood, Tenn. Methodist clergyman, author. *The Village Tragedy* (1921); *Home Folks* (1926); *Familiar Failures* (1927); *The Sermon on the Mount* (1930); *The Road to Certainty* (1940); *If I Were Young* (1945); *Anointed to Preach* (1951); *Meet These Men* (1956); *Cross Before Calvary* (1960); *Values That Last* (1964); etc.

CHAPPELL, FRED (May 28, 1936–); b. Canton, N.C. Author. *It is Time, Lord* (1963); *The Inkling* (1965); *Dagon* (1968). English dept., University of North Carolina.

CHAPPELL, GEORGE SHEPARD (Jan. 2, 1878–Nov., 1946); b. New London, Conn. Architect, author. Pen name, "Walter E. Traprock." Under own name: *Rollo in Society*

(1921); *Through the Alimentary Canal with Gun and Camera* (1930); *The Saloon in the Home* (with Ridgely Hunt, 1930); *The Gardener's Friend and Other Pests* (with same, 1931); *Animals Arise!!!* (1935); etc.; also, under pen name: *The Cruise of the Kawa* (1921); *My Northern Exposure* (1922); *Sarah of the Sahara* (1923); *Dr. Traprock's Memory Book* (1931).

CHAPPLE, JOE [Joseph] MITCHELL (July 18, 1867–Apr. 17, 1950); b. La Porte City, Ia. Editor, anthologist, novelist, biographer. *The Minor Chord* (1895); *Mark Hanna* (1903); *Heart Chord* (1915); etc. Compiler: *Heart Throbs,* 2v. (1905–11); etc. Editor, *The National Magazine,* 1900–33; founder, *Joe Mitchell Chapple's Reader's Rapid Review;* editor, 1931–34.

Character and Opinion in the United States. Collection of essays by George Santayana (1920). Discusses American philosophic thought as part of the nature of the American mind, with its practical and moralistic tendencies.

Charcoal Sketches; or, Scenes in a Metropolis. By Joseph Clay Neal (1838). Humorous sketches of fops, wastrels, and idlers in a large city, with sidelights on metropolitan manners and customs. A second series was published in 1848.

"Charge by the Ford, The." Poem by Thomas Dunn English. Deals with the later events of McClellan's first campaign in the Civil War.

CHARLES, FRANCIS (Apr. 10, 1872–); b. San Francisco, Calif. Novelist. *Siftings from Poverty Flat* (1889); *In the Country God Forgot* (1902); *The Siege of Youth* (1903); *The Awakening of the Duchess* (1903); *Pardner of Blossom Range* (1906).

Charles, Joan. Pen name of Charlotte Underwood.

Charles the Second; or, The Merry Monarch. Play by John Howard Payne and Washington Irving (prod. 1824).

CHARLESS, JOSEPH (July 16, 1772–July 28, 1834); b. Westmeath, Ireland. Printer, publisher. Founder, the *Missouri Gazette,* St. Louis, July 12, 1808. See Douglas C. McMurtrie's *The Early Career of Joseph Charless, the First Printer in Missouri* (1932).

"Charleston." Poem by Henry Timrod (1863).

Charleston Library Society, The. Founded 1748, at Charleston, S. C. Incorporated in 1755. Acquired the John M'Kenzie collection in 1771. Partly destroyed during the American Revolution, it was reorganized anew in 1790.

CHARLESWORTH, JAMES CLYDE (May 21, 1900–); b. near Greensburg, Pa. Educator. *Governmental Administration* (1951). Editor. *Bureaucracy and Democratic Government* (1954); *The Future of the Western Alliance* (1957); *Asia and Future World Leadership* (1958); *Resolving the Russian-American Deadlock* (1959); *Leisure in America: Blessing or Curse?* (1964); *Contemporary Political Analysis* (1966); *The Changing American People: Are We Deteriorating or Improving* (1968). Prof. political science, University of Pennsylvania, since 1945.

Charlotte News. Charlotte, N.C. Newspaper. Founded 1888. Perry Morgan is editor.

Charlotte Observer. Charlotte, N.C. Newspaper. Founded 1886. C. A. McKnight is editor. Harriet Doar is book-review editor.

Charlotte Temple: A Tale of Truth. Novel by Susanna Haswell Rowson (1794). First published as *Charlotte: A Tale of Truth* (London, 1791). Story of the elopement of a young English girl, and her trip to America. Montrevale, an army officer, deserts her and her baby daughter, and at the end Charlotte dies of want. This book was the first best selling novel in America. Over two hundred editions have appeared.

See R. W. G. Vail's *Susanna Haswell Rowson: The Author of Charlotte Temple* (1933).

Charlotte's Web. Story for children by E. B. White (1952).

CHARLTON, ROBERT MILLEDGE (Jan. 19, 1807–Jan. 18, 1854); b. Savannah, Ga. Jurist, poet. *Poems* (with brother, Thomas J. Charlton, 1839). Frequent contributor to *The Knickerbocker Magazine.*

Charm. New York. Monthly. Published by Street and Smith Publications. Magazine of general interest to college girls. Incorporated into *Glamour* in 1959.

CHARNLEY, MITCHELL VAUGHN (Apr. 9, 1898–); b. Goshen, Ind. Journalist, editor, educator, author. *The Boys' Life of the Wright Brothers* (1928); *The Boys' Life of Herbert Hoover* (1931); *Jean Lafitte, Gentleman Smuggler* (1934); *Magazine Editing and Writing* (with Blair Converse, 1938); *News by Radio* (1948); *Reporting* (1959). Managing editor, *Journalism Quarterly*, 1935–45. Prof., University of Minnesota, since 1940.

CHARTERIS, LESLIE (May 12, 1907–); b. Leslie Charles Bowyer Yin, Singapore. Author. *Meet the Tiger* (1928); *Enter the Saint* (1930); *The Saint vs. Scotland Yard* (1932); *The Brighter Buccaneer* (1933); *The Saint in New York* (1935); *The Ace of Knaves* (1937); *The Happy Highwayman* (1939); *The Saint Goes West* (1942); *The Saint Sees It Through* (1946); *The Saint in Europe* (1953); *The Saint to the Rescue* (1956); *Thanks to the Saint* (1959); *The Saint in the Sun* (1963); *Vendetta for the Saint* (1964); *The Saint Returns* (1968); *The Saint Abroad* (1969); etc. Editor, *The Saint Detective Magazine*, since 1953.

CHARYN, JEROME (May 13, 1937–); b. New York. Author. *Once Upon a Droshky* (1964); *On the Darkening Green* (1965); *Going to Jerusalem* (1967); *The Man Who Grew Younger* (1967); *American Scrapbook* (1969). Faculty, City College of New York, since 1968.

CHASE, ARTHUR MINTURN (June 3, 1873–Sept. 7, 1947); b. New York. Publisher, author. *The Party at the Penthouse* (1932); *Danger in the Dark* (1933); *Murder of a Missing Man* (1934); *Twenty Minutes to Kill* (1936); *No Outlet* (1940); *Peril at the Spy Nest* (1943). With Dodd, Mead & Co., 1898–1947.

CHASE, BORDEN b. Brooklyn, N.Y. Author, motion picture scenarist. *East River* (1935); *Sandhog* (1938); *Blazing Guns on the Chisholm Trail* (1948).

CHASE, BURR LINDEN (June 11, 1891–); b. Niagara Falls, N.Y. Publisher. With Silver Burdett Co., since 1920; pres., since 1942; director, Franklin Publications, since 1956.

CHASE, DANIEL (Jan. 31, 1890–); b. Newark, N. J. Author. *Flood tide* (1918); *The Middle Passage* (1923); *Hardy Rye* (1926); *Pines of Jaalam* (1929).

CHASE, ILKA, b. New York. Actress, author. *Past Imperfect* (1942); *In Bed We Cry* (1943); *I Love Miss Tilli Bean* (1946); *Free Admission* (1948); *New York 22* (1951); *The Island Players* (1956); *The Carthaginian Rose* (1961); *Elephants Arrive at Half-Past Five* (1963); *Straight from the Laundry* (1967); *The Varied Airs of Spring* (1969).

CHASE, JESSIE ANDERSON (May 6, 1865–); b. Cincinnati, O. Author. *Three Freshmen* (1898); *Mayken* (1902); *A Daughter of the Revolution* (1910); *Chan's Wife* (1919); *Paul Revere, Junior* (1932); etc.

CHASE, JOSEPH CUMMINGS (1878–Jan. 15, 1965); b. Kents Hill, Me. Artist, author. *Soldiers All* (1919); *The Romance of an Art Career* (1928); *My Friends Look Good to Me* (1933); *My Friends Look Better Than Ever* (1950); *Face Value* (1962); etc.

CHASE, LEWIS [Nathaniel] (June 27, 1873–Sept. 23, 1937); b. Sidney, Me. Educator, author. *Bernard Shaw in France* (1910); *Poe and His Poetry* (1913); etc. Co-editor (with S. Foster Damon) of the Brown University project for the publication of the life and works of Thomas Holley Chivers.

CHASE, MARY COYLE (Feb. 25, 1907–); b. Denver, Col. Playwright. *Now You've Done It* (prod. 1937); *Too Much Business* (prod. 1938); *Harvey* (prod. 1944; Pulitzer Prize for drama, 1945); *Mrs. McThing* (prod. 1952); *Bernardine* (prod. 1952); *Loretta Mason Potts* (prod. 1958); *Midgie Purvis* (1961); *The Wicked Pigeon Ladies in The Garden* (1968).

CHASE, MARY ELLEN (Feb. 24, 1887–); b. Blue Hill, Me. Educator, author. *His Birthday* (1915); *Uplands* (1927); *Thomas Hardy from Serial to Novel* (1927); *The Golden Asse, and Other Essays* (1929); *A Goodly Heritage* (autobiography, 1932); *Mary Peters* (1934); *Silas Crockett* (1935); *Dawn in Lyonesse* (1938); *A Goodly Fellowship* (1939); *Windswept* (1941); *The Bible and the Common Reader* (1944); *Jonathan Fisher: Maine Parson* (1948); *The Plum Tree* (1949); *The White Gate* (1954); *Life and Language in the Old Testament* (1955); *The Edge of Darkness* (1957); *Sailing in the Seven Seas* (1958); *Fishing Fleets of New England* (1961); *The Psalms and the Common Reader* (1961); *Victoria: A Pig in a Pram* (1963); *Dolly Moses* (1964); *A Journey to Boston* (1965); etc. Prof. English literature, Smith College, 1929–55.

CHASE, MARY M. (Aug. 12, 1822–Nov. 3, 1852); b. Chatham, N.Y. Poet. *Mary M. Chase and Her Writings* (1855).

CHASE, RICHARD (1904–). *The Jack Tales* (1943); *Jack and the Three Sillies* (1950); *The Honeymoon, and a Religious Man* (1955); etc. Editor: *Grandfather Tales* (1948).

CHASE, RICHARD VOLNEY (Oct. 12, 1914–Aug. 28, 1962); b. Lakeport, N.H. Educator, author. *Quest for Myth* (1949); *Herman Melville: A Critical Study* (1949); *Emily Dickinson* (1951); *Walt Whitman Reconsidered* (1955); *The American Novel and Its Tradition* (1957); etc. English dept., Columbia University, from 1949.

CHASE, SALMON PORTLAND (Jan. 13, 1808–May 7, 1873); b. Cornish, N.H. Statesman, Secretary of Treasury under Lincoln; Chief Justice of the Supreme Court. His diaries and letters were edited by Robert B. Warden, 1874.

CHASE, STUART (Mar. 9, 1888–); b. Somersworth, N.H. Economist, author. *The Tragedy of Waste* (1925); *Men and Machines* (1929); *Mexico* (with Marian Tyler, 1931); *A New Deal* (1932); *Rich Land, Poor Land* (1936); *The Tyranny of Words* (1938); *The New Western Front* (1939); *Idle Money, Idle Men* (1941); *The Road We Are Traveling* (1942); *Democracy Under Pressure* (1945); *The Proper Study of Mankind* (1948); *Roads to Agreement* (with Marian Tyler, 1951); *Power of Words* (1954); *Guides to Straight Thinking* (1956); *Some Things Worth Knowing* (1958); *Live and Let Live* (1959); *American Credos* (1962); *Money to Grow On* (1964); *The Most Probable* (1968); *Danger—Man Talking* (1969).

CHASIN, HELEN. Poet. *Peace Feelers* (poems, with others, 1968).

CHASINS, ABRAM (Aug. 17, 1903–); b. New York. Pianist, composer, author. *Speaking of Pianists* (1957); *The Van Cliburn Legend* (1959); *The Appreciation of Music* (1966).

CHASTAIN, MADYE LEE (Dec. 15, 1908–); b. Texarkana, Tex. Author and illustrator: *Roxana Pretends* (1945); *Loblolly Farm* (1950); *Jerusha's Ghost* (1958); *Plippen's Palace* (1961); *Magic Island* (1964); etc.

CHATFIELD-TAYLOR, HOBART C[hatfield] (Mar. 24, 1865–Jan. 16, 1945); b. Chicago, Ill. Biographer. *With Edge-Tools* (1891); *An American Peeress* (1893); *The Land of the Castanet* (1896); *The Vice of Fools* (1898); *Molière, a Biography* (1906); *Goldoni, a Biography* (1913); *Tawny Spain* (1927); *Charmed Circles* (1935); etc.

Chatterbox, Charles. Pen name of William Bigelow.

CHATTERTON, RUTH (Dec. 24, 1893–Nov. 24, 1961); b. New York. Actress, novelist. *Homeward Borne* (1950); *The Betrayers* (1953); *Pride of the Peacock* (1954); *Southern Wild* (1958).

Chautauqua. Originally a Sunday School organization, founded at Chautauqua, N.Y., Aug., 1874. Annual assemblies were held here and the visitors were given a course of instruction. In 1878 the Literary and Scientific Circle was organized and more and more stress was laid on cultural improvement. Many local assemblies sprang up, and the "tent" Chautauqua, featuring prominent lectures, plays, and music, became popular all over the United States, beginning about 1900. William Jennings Bryan was one of the favorite Chatauqua orators. Arthur E. Bestor was president from 1915 until his death in 1944; he was succeeded by Ralph McCallister.

Chautauquan, The. Chautauqua, N.Y. Monthly magazine. Founded 1880, at Meadville, Pa.; moved to Cleveland, O., 1899; then to Springfield, O., 1903; and finally to Chautauqua, N.Y., 1899. Editors: Theodore L. Flood, 1880–99; Frank Chapin Bray, 1899–1914. This magazine grew out of the cultural movement of The Chautauqua Literary and Scientific Circle, which held an annual summer assembly at Chautauqua, N.Y. Expired 1914.

CHAYEFSKY, PADDY (Jan. 29, 1923–); b. New York. Playwright, screen writer. *Television Plays by Paddy Chayefsky* (1955); *Middle of the Night* (prod. 1956); *The Tenth Man* (prod. 1959); *Gideon* (prod. 1961); *The Passion of Josef D.* (1964); *The Latent Heterosexual* (1968); etc.

Cheetah. New York. Founded 1967. An attempt to develop mass readership for the concerns of the underground youth culture: rock music, psychedelic drugs, social consciousness, eclecticism in fashion and appearance. Suspended 1968.

CHEEVER, EZEKIEL (Jan. 25, 1614/5–Aug. 21, 1708); b. London, England. Educator, author. *A Short Introduction to the Latin Tongue* (1709). This book, better known as *The Accidence,* was called "the wonder of the age."

CHEEVER, HARRIET ANNA: b. Boston, Mass. Author. *Little Miss Boston* (1890); *The Fairies of Fern Dingle* (1906); *A Little American Girl in India* (1900); *Flat Street* (1905); etc.

CHEEVER, HENRY P. Novelist. *The Rival Brothers; or, The Corsair and Privateer* (1845); *The Witch of the Wave; or, The Corsair's Captive* (1847).

CHEEVER, HENRY THEODORE (Feb. 6, 1814–Feb. 13, 1897); b. Hallowell, Me. Theologian, editor, author. *The Whale and His Captors* (1849); *Life in the Sandwich Islands* (1851); *The Island World of the Pacific* (1851). Edited and wrote memoir for Walter Colton's *The Sea and the Sailor . . . and Other Literary Remains* (1851). Editor, New York *Evangelist,* 1849–52.

CHEEVER, JOHN (May 27, 1912–); b. Quincy, Mass. Author. *The Way Some People Live* (1943); *The Enormous Radio* (1953); *The Wapshot Chronicle* (1957); *Some People, Places, and Things That Will Not Appear in My Next Novel* (1961); *The Wapshot Scandal* (1964); *Bullet Park* (1969).

CHELEY, FRANK HOWBERT (Feb. 10, 1889–Dec. 18, 1941); b. Colorado Springs, Colo. Director boys' work, author. *Buffalo Roost* (1909); *Told By the Campfire* (1911); *Boy Riders of the Rockies* (1928); *By Emberglow* (1937); etc.

Chelsea. New York. Founded 1958 as *Chelsea Review.* Edited since 1966 by Sonia Raiziss and Alfredo de Palchi. Devotes issues to special concerns, such as technology, translations of American writers into other languages, and English translations from unfamiliar languages.

CHENEY, EDNAH DOW LITTLEHALE (June 27, 1824–Nov. 19, 1904); b. Boston, Mass. Reformer, author. *Patience* (1870); *Sally Williams, the Mountain Girl* (1873); *Child of the Tide* (1875); *Life of Susan Dimock* (1875); *Nora's Return* (1890); *Stories of the Olden Time* (1890); *Reminiscences* (1902); etc. Editor: *Louisa May Alcott, Her Life, Letters, and Journals* (1889).

CHENEY, HARRIET VAUGHAN FOSTER (b. Sept. 9, 1796); b. in Massachusetts, daughter of Hannah Webster Foster. Novelist. *The Sunday School; or, Village Sketches* (with sister, Eliza Lanesford Foster Cushing, 18–?); *A Peep at the Pilgrims in Sixteen Hundred Thirty-Six* (anon., 1824); *The Rivals of Acadia* (anon., 1827).

CHENEY, JOHN VANCE (Dec. 29, 1848–May 1, 1922); b. Groveland, N.Y. Librarian, poet, essayist. *Thistle-Drift* (poems, 1887); *Wood Blooms* (poems, 1888); *The Golden Guess* (1892); *That Dome in Air* (1895); *Queen Helen, and Other Poems* (1895); *Out of the Silence* (poems, 1897); *Lyrics* (1901); *Poems* (1905); etc.

CHENEY, SHELDON [Warren] (June 29, 1886–); b. Berkeley, Calif. Art and theatre critic. *The New Movement in the Theatre* (1914); *Modern Art and the Theatre* (1921); *A Primer of Modern Art* (1923); *The Art Theatre* (1925); *Stage Decoration* (1927); *The Theatre: 3000 Years of Drama, Acting, and Stagecraft* (1929); *The New World Architecture* (1931); *Expressionism in Art* (1934); *A World History of Art* (1937); *The Story of Modern Art* (1941); *Men Who Have Walked with God* (1945); *Sculpture of the World* (1968); etc. Founder, *Theatre Arts Magazine,* 1916; editor, 1916–21.

CHENNAULT, ANNA CHAN (June 23, 1923–); b. Peking, China. Journalist, author. *Thousand Springs* (1962); *Chennault and the Flying Tigers* (1963); etc. Also author of books in Chinese, since 1948. U.S. correspondent, *Hsin Sheng Daily News,* Washington, since 1958.

CHENNAULT, CLAIRE LEE (Sept. 6, 1890–July 27, 1958); b. Commerce, Tex. Air Force officer. *Way of a Fighter: Memoirs* (1949).

Cher, Marie. Pen name of Marie Scherr.

CHERBONNIER, EDMOND LA BEAUME (1918–). Educator, author. *Hardness of Heart* (1955). Prof. religion, Trinity College, Hartford, Conn., since 1957.

CHERNE, LEO M. (Sept. 8, 1912–); b. New York. Economist, author. *Adjusting Your Business to War* (1939); *M-Day and What It Means to You* (1940); *The Rest of Your Life* (1944).

Cherokee Advocate. Tahlequah, Okla. Founded 1844. Published in Cherokee and English. Expired 1907.

Cherokee Messenger. Newspaper. First paper in Oklahoma; founded 1844, as a Baptist missionary organ, and published in Indian dialect, near the present Westville, Okla. Expired 1846.

Cherokee Phoenix. New Echota, Ga. Weekly newspaper printed in Cherokee. Founded 1828, by the National Council for Indian Education and by George Guess (or Gist), also known as "Sequoyah," an Indian who had invented a Cherokee syllabary. Elias Boudinot, or "Galagina" (his Indian name), was editor. Expired 1835.

CHERRIE, GEORGE KRUCK (Aug. 22, 1865–Jan. 20, 1948); b. Knoxville, Ia. Naturalist, author. *Dark Trails: Adventures of a Naturalist* (1930).

CHERRINGTON, BEN MARK (Nov. 1, 1885–); Educator. *The British Labor Movement* (1921); *Methods of Education in International Attitudes* (1933). Co-author: *Ten Studies in the Sermon on the Mount* (1925). Prof. international relations, University of Denver, since 1926.

CHESEBROUGH, CAROLINE (Mar. 30, 1825–Feb. 16, 1873); b. Canandaigua, N.Y. Novelist. Wrote as Caroline Chesebro'. Author: *Dream-Land by Daylight* (1852); *Isa, a Pilgrimage* (1852); *Peter Carradine* (1863); *Amy Carr; or, The Fortune Teller* (1864); *The Foe in the Household* (1871); etc.

CHESNUTT, CHARLES WADDELL (June 20, 1858–Nov. 15, 1932); b. Cleveland, O. Author. *The Conjure Woman* (1899); *Frederick Douglass* (1899); *The Wife of His Youth and Other Stories of the Color Line* (1899); *The House Behind the Cedars* (1901); *The Marrow of Tradition* (1901); *The Colonel's Dream* (1905); etc. *See* Helen M. Chesnutt's *Charles Waddell Chesnutt: Pioneer of the Color Line* (1952).

CHESSMAN, CARYL [Whittier] (May 27, 1921–May 2, 1960); b. St. Joseph, Mich. Author. *Cell 2455, Death Row* (1954); *Trial by Ordeal* (1955); *The Face of Justice* (1957). A convicted criminal awaiting execution, Chessman argued his case and attracted public attention with his books, all written in prison, which made his case an international *cause célèbre*.

CHESTER, GEORGE RANDOLPH (1869–Feb. 26, 1924); b. in Ohio. Author. *Get-Rich-Quick Wallingford* (1908); *The Cash Intrigue* (1909); *The Art of Short Story Writing* (1910); *The Early Bird* (1910); *Wallingford in His Prime* (1913); etc. Co-author (with Lillian Chester): *Cordelia Blossom* (1914); etc.

CHEVALIER, ELIZABETH PICKETT (Mar. 25, 1896–); b. Chicago, Ill. Author, *Official History of the American Red Cross Nursing Service* (1921); *The American Red Cross* (1922); *Redskin* (1928); *Drivin' Woman* (1942); etc.

CHEVALIER, HAAKON M[aurice] (Sept. 10, 1902–); b. Lakewood, N. J. Educator, author. *The Iron Temper: Anatole France and His Time* (1932); *Days of Wrath* (1936); *For Us the Living* (1949); *The Man Who Would Be God* (1959). Translator: works of André Malraux, Louis Aragon, André Maurois, Salvador Dali, Yaacov Agam. Prof. French, University of California, 1929–46.

CHEVIGNY, HECTOR (June 28, 1904–Apr. 20, 1965); b. Missoula, Mont. Author. *Lost Empire* (1937); *Lord of Alaska* (1942); *Woman of the Rock* (1949); *Russian America* (1965); etc.

CHEW, BEVERLY (Mar. 5, 1850–May 21, 1924); b. Geneva, N.Y. Bibliophile, author. *Essay and Verses About Books* (1926). His best known poem is "Old Books Are Best." His library was purchased Oct., 1912, by Henry E. Huntington, and is now in the Huntington Library at San Marino, Calif. He was the third president of the Grolier Club, and compiled many of its catalogues.

CHEW, SAMUEL CLAGGETT (Aug. 31, 1888–d.1960); b. Baltimore, Md. Educator, author. *Thomas Hardy, Poet and Novelist* (1921); *Byron in England: His Fame and After-Fame* (1924); *Swinburne* (1929); *The Crescent and the Rose: Islam and England During the Renaissance* (1937); *The Virtues Reconciled: An Iconographical Study* (1947); *Fruit Among The Leaves* (1950); *The Dramas of Lord Byron* (1964). Co-author: *A Literary History of England* (1948); *The Chief Romantic Poets* (1950). Editor: *Byron* (1936); *Tennyson* (1941). Professor, English literature, Bryn Mawr College, 1920–54.

CHEYNEY, EDWARD GHEEN (Nov. 24, 1878–deceased); b. Washington, D.C. Forester, author. The *Scott Burton* series, 6v. (1917–26); *Matu, the Iroquois* (1928); *Sylvics* (1929); *This Is Our Land* (with T. Schantz-Hansen, 1940); *American Silvics and Sillviculture* (1942); etc.

Chicago. Chicago, Ill. Founded 1954. A local magazine concerned with the life and activities of the city of Chicago. Suspended 1956.

Chicago Examiner. See *Chicago's American.*

Chicago Herald. See *Chicago's American.*

Chicago News. Chicago, Ill. Newspaper. Founded 1876, as *Chicago Daily News,* by Melville Stone and Victor Fremont Lawson. Charles Henry Dennis was editor 1925–34 and Paul Scott Mowrer succeeded him. Thomas H. Collins is present executive editor. Van Allen Bradley writes "Bradley on Books" and "Gold in Your Attic." Sold to Field Enterprises in 1959.

Chicago Record. See *Chicago's American.*

Chicago Review. Chicago, Ill. Quarterly. Founded 1946. Published at the University of Chicago. Periodical of general literary and artistic interest. Has published Kenneth Patchen, Karl Shapiro, H. H. Watts, Margaret Webster. The *Review's Anthology of Concretism* was the earliest collection of concrete writing to be published in the United States. See *Big Table.*

Chicago Sun-Times. Chicago, Ill. Newspaper. *Chicago Sun* was founded 1941, by Marshall Field III, and combined with *Chicago Times* (q.v.) in 1948. James F. Hoge is editor. Richard Takeuchi edits the Sunday magazine section, *Midwest Magazine.* Since 1967 *Book Week* has been appearing under the editorship of Herman Kogan, with Ralph Mills as poetry editor, and Alan Pryce-Jones as New York columnist.

Chicago Times. Chicago, Ill. Founded 1854. Bought by Wilbur F. Storey in 1861. See *Chicago's American.*

Chicago Times. Chicago, Ill. Newspaper. Founded 1929, by Samuel Emory Thompson. Purchased by Marshall Field III in 1947 and combined in 1948 with the *Chicago Sun,* as *Chicago Sun-Times* (q.v.).

Chicago Tribune. Chicago, Ill. Newspaper. Founded 1847, by K. C. Forrest, James J. Kelly, and John E. Wheeler. In 1852 it absorbed the *Gem of the Prairie* (1844–52); absorbed *Free West* in 1855; joined with the *Daily Democratic Press* in 1858, and after 1860 was known as the *Chicago Daily Tribune.* Connected with it were Joseph Medill, John L. Scripps, Charles Ray and Horace White. Subsequently published by Robert Rutherford McCormick. Bought *Chicago American* in 1956. See *Chicago's American.* Publishes special book supplement, *Book World* (q.v.), formerly *Magazine of Books,* edited by Robert Cromie. Fanny Butcher is literary editor, and regular book columnists include Harry Hansen and Vincent Starrett.

Chicago's American. Chicago, Ill. Newspaper. *Chicago Times,* founded 1854; *Chicago Herald,* founded 1881; merged 1895, as *Chicago Times-Herald. Chicago Record,* founded 1881; merged 1901, with *Times-Herald,* as *Chicago Record-Herald. Chicago Examiner,* founded 1900; merged 1918, with *Record-Herald,* as Chicago *Herald and Examiner.* Now merged with the *Chicago American,* founded 1900. In 1956 the *Chicago American* was bought by the *Chicago Tribune* but continued to publish under the name *Chicago's American* until 1969, when in a new format it appeared as *Chicago Today.*

CHIDESTER, ANN (1919–); b. Stillwater, Minn. Novelist. *Young Pandora* (1942); *No Longer Fugitive* (1943); *The Long Year* (1946); *Mama Maria's* (1947); *Moon Gap* (1950); *The Lost and the Found* (1963); etc.

CHIDSEY, DONALD BARR (May 14, 1902–); b. Elizabeth, N.J. Author. *Bonnie Prince Charlie* (1928); *Marlborough: The Portrait of a Conquerer* (1929); *Pistols in the Morning* (1930); *Sir Walter Raleigh* (1931); *Weeping Is for Women* (1936); *John the Great: The Times and Life of John L. Sullivan* (1942); *Panama Passage* (1946); *Stronghold* (1948); *Captain Adam* (1953); *Lord of the Isles* (1954); *Elizabeth I* (1955); *Bright Sword* (1957); *July 4, 1776* (1958); *Valley Forge* (1959); *Reluctant Cavalier* (1960); *The Battle of New*

Orleans (1961); *Victory at Yorktown* (1962); *The Birth of the Constitution* (1964); *The French and Indian War* (1969); *The Spanish-American War* (1971); *The Wars in Barbary* (1971).

CHILD, FRANCIS JAMES (Feb. 1, 1825–Sept. 11, 1896); b. Boston, Mass. Educator, philologist. Editor, *The Poetical Works of Edmund Spenser*, 5v. (1855); *English and Scottish Ballads*, 8v. (1857–58); *English and Scottish Popular Ballads*, 10v. (1882–98). Prof. of English, Harvard University, 1876–96. *See* W. D. Howells's *Literary Friends and Acquaintances* (1900); Henry James's *Notes of a Son and Brother* (1914); *Letters of James Russell Lowell* (1894).

CHILD, FRANK SAMUEL (Mar. 20, 1854–May 4, 1922); b. Exeter, N.Y. Clergyman, author. *The Colonial Parson of New England* (1896); *A Colonial Witch* (1897); *A Puritan Wooing* (1898); etc.

CHILD, JULIA [McWilliams] (Aug. 15, 1912–); b. Pasadena, Cal. Television performer, author. *Mastering the Art of French Cooking* (with Simone Beck and Louisette Bertholle, Vol. 1, 1961; Vol. 2, 1970); *The French Cookbook* (1968). Television Program "The French Chef," since 1962.

CHILD, LYDIA MARIA FRANCIS (Feb. 11, 1802–Oct. 20, 1880); b. Medford, Mass. Editor, abolitionist, novelist. *Hobomok* (anon., 1824); *The Rebels; or, Boston Before the Revolution* (1825); *The Frugal Housewife* (1829); *The First Settlers of New England* (1829); *The Coronal* (1832); *An Appeal in Favor of That Class of Americans Called Africans* (1833); *Philothea* (1836); *Letters from New York*, 2 series (1843–45); *Fact and Fiction* (1846); *A Romance of the Republic* (1867); etc. Founder, *Juvenile Miscellany*, 1826; editor, 1826–34.

CHILD, RICHARD WASHBURN (Aug. 5, 1881–Jan. 31, 1935); b. Worcester, Mass. Diplomat, novelist. *Jim Hands* (1910); *The Vanishing Men* (1919); *A Diplomat Looks at Europe* (1925); etc.

Child of the Century, A. Autobiography of Ben Hecht (1954).

CHILDERS, JAMES SAXON (Apr. 19, 1899–July 17, 1965); b. Birmingham, Ala. Educator, author. *The Uneducated Poets* (1925); *Laure and Straw* (1927); *The Bookshop Mystery* (1929); *Through Oriental Gates* (1930); *A Novel About a White Man and a Black Man: In the Deep South* (1936); *Tomorrow We Reap* (with J. H. Street, 1949); *Nation on the Flying Trapeze* (1960); etc. Editor, Atlanta *Journal*, 1953–1957. Prof. English, Birmingham Southern College, 1925–42.

Childhood and Society. By Erik Erikson (1950). Major reconsideration of the psychological development of children from a revised Freudian viewpoint that stresses the social context of a child's growth.

Children of the Night, The. Poems by Edwin Arlington Robinson (1897).

Children's Digest. New York. Monthly. Published by Parents' Magazine Enterprises. Founded 1950. Stories, articles, puzzles, and other entertainments for children aged seven through twelve.

"Children's Hour, The." Poem by Henry Wadsworth Longfellow (1860).

Children's Hour, The. Play by Lillian Hellman (prod. 1934). Suspicions of lesbianism in a boarding school.

Children's Hour, The. Philadelphia. Monthly. Founded 1867. Merged with *St. Nicholas*, July 1874.

Children's Magazine, The. Hartford, Conn. Monthly. Founded 1789. Only three numbers were published.

Children's Play Mate Magazine. Cleveland, O. Monthly. Founded 1910.

CHILDS, ELEANOR STUART (June 24, 1876–deceased); b. Orange, N.J. Novelist. Wrote under name "Eleanor Stuart."

Stonepastures (1895); *Averages* (1899); *The Postscript* (1908); *The Romance of Ali* (1913).

CHILDS, GEORGE WILLIAM (May 12, 1829–Feb, 3, 1894); b. Baltimore, Md. Publisher, author. *Recollections by George W. Childs* (1890); *Recollections of General Grant* (1885). Childs joined the publishing firm of R. E. Peterson, in Philadelphia, in 1849. In 1853 the firm published Allibone's *Critical Dictionary of English Literature*. In 1854 the firm name was changed to Childs & Peterson, and the great success of the new firm was Elisha Kane's *Arctic Explorations* (1856). Firm dissolved in 1860. Childs then joined the firm of J. B. Lippincott & Company. In 1863 he founded the *American Publishers' Circular and Literary Gazette*. In 1864 he bought the Philadelphia *Public Ledger*, with Anthony J. and Francis A. Drexel and made it a great newspaper.

CHILDS, JAMES BENNETT (June 2, 1896–); b. Van Buren, Mo. Librarian, author. *Sixteenth Century Books* (1925); *Memorias of Republics of Central America and Antilles* (1932); *German Federal Republic Official Publications* (1958); *German Democratic Republic Official Publications* (1959). Editor, publications Bibliographical Society of America, 1926–36. With Library of Congress, 1925–30, since 1934.

CHILDS, JAMES RIVES (Feb. 6, 1893–); b. Lynchburg, Va. Foreign service officer, author. *American Foreign Service* (1948); *Casanoviana* (1956); *Casanova: A Biography* (1961); *Collector's Quest* (1968); *Foreign Service Farewell* (1969).

CHILDS, JOHN LAWRENCE (Jan. 11, 1899–); b. Eau Claire, Wis. Educator, author. *Education and the Philosophy of Experimentalism* (1931); *The Educational Frontier* (with others, 1933); *America, Russia, and the Communist Party* (with George Counts, 1943); *Education and Morals* (1950); *American Pragmatism and Education* (1956). Prof. philosophy of education, Teachers College, Columbia University, 1928–54.

CHILDS, MARQUIS WILLIAM (Mar. 17, 1903–); b. Clinton, Ia. Journalist, author. *Sweden—the Middle Way* (1936); *They Hate Roosevelt* (1936); *Washington Calling* (1937); *This Is Democracy* (1938); *This Is Your War* (1942); *The Cabin* (1944); *The Farmer Takes a Hand* (1952); *The Ragged Edge* (1955); *Eisenhower, Captive Hero* (1958); *The Peacemakers* (1961); *A Taint of Innocence* (1967). With St. Louis *Post Dispatch*, 1926–44; Syndicated columnist, since 1944.

CHILDS, RICHARD S[pencer] (May 24, 1882–); b. Manchester, Conn. Association executive, publicist. *Short Ballot Principles* (1911); *Civic Victories* (1952); *First Fifty Years of the Council* (1965).

Chilmark Press. New York. Publishers. Founded 1961. Publishes poetry, fiction, and general nonfiction.

CHILTON, ELEANOR CARROLL (Mrs. Herbert Agar) (Sept. 11, 1898–Feb. 8, 1949); b. Charleston, W.Va. Novelist, poet. *Shadows Waiting* (1927); *Fire and Sleet and Candlelight* (poems, with Herbert Agar and Willis Fisher, 1928); *The Garment of Praise* (with Herbert Agar, 1929); *Follow the Furies* (1935).

Chilton Book Co. Philadelphia, Pa. Publishers. Publishes technical and professional texts in addition to general nonfiction.

Chimera: A Rough Beast. New York. Quarterly. Founded 1942. Edited by Benjamin Ford, William Arrowsmith, and others. Literary magazine. Discontinued 1948.

Chimney Pot Papers. Essays by Charles S. Brooks (1919).

China: A Memory of Last Island. By Lafcadio Hearn (1889). A tale of the terrible tidal wave that swept Last Island.

CHINARD, GILBERT (Oct. 17, 1881–); b. Châtellerault, France. Educator, author. *The Literary Bible of Thomas Jefferson* (1928); *Jefferson, the Apostle of Americanism* (1928);

etc. Editor: *The Commonplace Book of Thomas Jefferson* (1926); *Honest John Adams* (1933); *When Lafayette Came to America* (1948); etc. Author of many books in French. French dept., Princeton University, 1937–50.

"Chinese Nightingale, The." Poem by Vachel Lindsay (1917).

Ching, Ching, Chinaman. Short story by Wilbur Daniel Steele (1917).

Chinnubbie Harjo. Pen name of Alexander Lawrence Posey.

CHIPMAN, DANIEL (Oct. 22, 1765–Apr. 23, 1850); b. Salisbury, Conn. Lawyer, biographer. *The Life of Hon. Nathaniel Chipman* (1846); *The Life of Colonel Seth Warner* (1848); *A Memoir of Thomas Chittenden* (1849).

CHIPMAN, WILLIAM PENDLETON (May 11, 1854–Feb. 28, 1937); b. Old Mystic, Conn. Author. *Roy Gilbert's Search* (1889); *A Yankee Lad's Pluck* (1900); *The Young Pickets* (1910); etc.

Chippendales, The. Novel by Robert Grant. (1909).

CHISHOLM, SHIRLEY [Anita St. Hill]. Educator, Congresswoman. *Unbought and Unbossed* (1970). Educational consultant, Division of Day Care, Bureau of Child Welfare, since 1964; member New York State Assembly, 1964–68; Congresswoman, since 1969.

CHITTENDEN, HIRAM MARTIN (Oct. 25, 1858–Oct. 9, 1917); b. Yorkshire, N.Y. Army officer, author. *The American Fur Trade of the Far West,* 3v. (1901); *History of Early Steamboat Navigation on the Missouri River,* 2v. (1903); etc.

CHITTENDEN, WILLIAM LAWRENCE (Mar. 23, 1862–Sept. 24, 1934); b. Montclair, N.J. Rancher, poet. *Ranch Verses* (1893); *Bermuda Verses* (1909).

CHITWOOD, OLIVER PERRY (Nov. 28, 1874–); b. in Franklin Co., Va. Educator, author. *Justice in Colonial Virginia* (1905); *A History of Colonial America* (1931); *John Tyler, Champion of the Old South* (1939); *Richard Henry Lee: Statesman of the Revolution* (1960). Prof. history, University of West Virginia, 1907–46.

CHIVERS, THOMAS HOLLEY (Oct. 18, 1809–Dec. 18, 1858); b. Washington, Ga. Poet, playwright. *The Path of Sorrow; or, The Lament of Youth* (1832); *Nacoochee; or, The Beautiful Star, with Other Poems* (1837); *The Lost Pleiad, and Other Poems* (1845); *Eonchs of Ruby, a Gift of Love* (1850); *Virginalia; or, Songs of My Summer Nights* (1853); *The Sons of Usna: A Tragi-Apotheosis* (1858); etc. See S. Foster Damon's *Thomas Holley Chivers* (1930).

CHOATE, JOSEPH HODGES (Jan. 24, 1832–May 14, 1917); b. Salem, Mass. Lawyer, diplomat, author. *American Addresses* (1911); *The Boyhood and Youth of Joseph Hodges Choate* (1917); *Arguments and Addresses* (1926).

CHOATE, RUFUS (Oct. 1, 1799–July 13, 1859); b. Hog Island, Essex, Mass. Lawyer, statesman, author. *Works of Rufus Choate With a Memoir of His Life,* ed. by Samuel Gilman Brown, 2v. (1862); *Addresses and Orations of Rufus Choate* (1878).

CHODOROV, EDWARD (Apr. 17, 1904–); b. New York. Playwright. *Wonder Boy* (with Arthur Barton, 1931); *Cue for Passion* (with H. S. Kraft, 1940); *Those Endearing Young Charms* (1943); *Decision* (1944); *Common Ground* (1947); *Oh Men! Oh Women!* (1953); etc.

CHODOROV, JEROME (Aug. 10, 1911–); b. New York. Playwright, director. Co-author, with Joseph Fields: *My Sister Eileen* (prod. 1940); *Junior Miss* (prod. 1941); *Wonderful Town* (prod. 1952); *Anniversary Waltz* (prod. 1954); *The Ponder Heart* (prod. 1957); etc. Author: *Three Bags Full* (1966); *Dumas and Son* (1967); etc.

Choir Invisible, The. Novel by James Lane Allan (1897). Story of pioneer life in Kentucky.

CHOMSKY, [Avram] **NOAM** (Dec. 7, 1928–); b. Philadelphia, Pa. Educator, author. *Syntactic Structures* (1957); *Current Issues in Linguistic Theory* (1964); *Aspects of the Theory of Syntax* (1965); *Cartesian Linguistics* (1966); *Topics in the Theory of Generative Grammar* (1966); *American Power and the New Mandarins* (1969); *At War with Asia* (1970). Faculty, Massachusetts Institute of Technology, since 1955. See John Lyons' *Noam Chomsky* (1970).

CHOPIN, KATE O'FLAHERTY (Feb. 8, 1851–Aug. 22, 1904); b. St. Louis, Mo. Short-story writer. *At Fault* (1890); *Bayou Folk* (1894); *A Night in Acadie* (1897); *The Awakening* (1899). "Désirée's Baby" is her best known story.

Chosen, The. Novel by Chaim Potok (1967). Two teenage Jewish boys living in the Williamsburg section of Brooklyn grow up during the 1940's and face the problems of their minority status in America.

CHOUINARD, CARROLL (Dec. 19, 1907–); b. Eau Claire, Wis. Editor. Managing editor, *American People's Encyclopedia,* 1955–56; executive editor, 1956–58; editor-in-chief, since 1959.

CHRISMAN, ARTHUR BOWIE (July 16, 1889–1953); b. White Post, Va. Author. *Shen of the Sea* (1925); *The Wind That Wouldn't Blow* (1927); *Treasures Long Hidden* (1941).

CHRISMAN, LEWIS HERBERT (Aug. 21, 1883–Aug. 15, 1966); b. in Chester Co., Pa. Educator, author. *John Ruskin, Preacher; and Other Essays* (1921); *The English of the Pulpit* (1926); *Ten Minute Sermons* (1935). Prof. English, West Virginia Wesleyan, 1919–56.

CHRIST-JANER, ALBERT WILLIAM (June 13, 1910–); b. Appleton, Minn. Artist, educator. *George Caleb Bingham of Missouri* (1940); *Boardman Robinson* (1945); *Eliel Saarinen* (1948); *Modern Church Architecture* (1962). Prof. art, Pennsylvania State University, 1956–58; dean, School of Arts, Pratt Institute, since 1958.

CHRISTENSEN, ASHER NORMAN (July 11, 1903–Jan. 19, 1961); b. Little Falls, Minn. Educator. Editor: *The People, Politics, and the Politician* (with E. M. Kirkpatrick, 1941); *The Evolution of Latin American Government* (1951). Editor, *Handbook of Latin American Studies,* from 1945. Prof. political science, University of Minnesota, since 1948.

CHRISTENSEN, ERWIN OTTOMAR (June 23, 1890–); b. St. Louis, Mo. Art curator, author. *Popular Art in the U.S.* (1948); *The Index of American Design* (1950); *Early American Wood Carving* (1952); *Primitive Art* (1955); *A History of Western Art* (1959); *American Crafts and Folk Arts* (1964).

Christian Advocate, The. Park Ridge, Ill. Methodist weekly. Founded Sept. 9, 1826. It absorbed the *Missionary Journal* of Charleston, S.C., in 1827, to become *The Christian Advocate and Journal.* Since 1870 called *The Christian Advocate.* Barker Badger was its first editor. Other editors were Nathan Bangs, Thomas E. Bond, George Peck, Abel Stevens, Daniel Curry, J. M. Buckley, Edward Thomson, etc. The *Christian Advocate,* Nashville, Tenn., was founded in 1832; the *Pittsburgh Christian Advocate* in 1833; *The Western Christian Advocate* in 1834; the *Northern Christian Advocate* in 1844; the *Northwestern Christian Advocate* in 1852; the *Central Christian Advocate* in 1856; the *California Christian Advocate* in 1852; the *Pacific Christian Advocate* in 1856; and the *Southwestern Christian Advocate* in 1876. See W. F. Whitlock's *The Story of the Book Concerns* (1903).

Christian Century, The. Chicago, Ill. Weekly. Founded 1884.

Christian Examiner. Boston, Mass. Founded Jan., 1824. Bimonthly. Unitarian magazine. It grew out of the *Christian Disciple,* founded in 1813 by Channing, Lowell, Tuckerman and Francis Parkman, and edited by Noah Worcester and

Henry Ware, Jr. Among the editors of the *Christian Examiner* were John G. Palfrey, Francis Jenks, William Ware, George Putnam, E. E. Hale, and Henry W. Bellows. The "Examiner Club" was formed in 1839 to improve the book reviewing in the magazine. It expired in Nov., 1869, when it merged with *Old and New.*

Christian Herald. New York. Founded 1878. It began as a New York edition of the London journal of the same name. T. DeWitt Talmage and Louis Klopsch were associated with its early success, and it is still current. Daniel A. Poling was editor for many years until succeeded by Ford Stewart in 1966.

Christian Literature. New York. A periodical. Founded 1889. Expired 1897.

Christian Observer. Louisville, Ky. Weekly. Founded 1813. Harry Pollard Converse, managing editor since 1907. The Converse family has managed the paper since 1827.

Christian Science Monitor. Boston, Mass. Newspaper. Founded 1908. Willis J. Abbot was editor, 1921–34. James Roscoe Drummond was with paper after 1924 and its executive editor after 1934. A feature of the *Monitor* is its exclusion of all crime news and sensationalism. Erwin D. Canham is now editor. Melvin Maddocks edits the special book supplement.

Christianity and Crisis. New York. Biweekly. Founded 1940. A Christian journal of opinion. John C. Bennett is chairman of the editorial board.

CHRISTMAN, W[illiam] W[eaver] (May 20, 1865–Feb. 26, 1937); b. Delanson, N.Y. Farmer, poet. *Songs of the Helderhills* (1926); *Songs of the Western Gateway* (1930); *Wild Pasture Pine* (1934); *The Untillable Hills* (1937).

Christmas Wreck, and Other Stories, The. Nine tales by Frank R. Stockton (1887). In the title story old Silas recounts the wreck of the "Mary Auguster" on Christmas Day and the fine Christmas dinner salvaged from the floating wreckage.

"Christmas-Night in the Quarters." Poem by Irwin Russell, in *Scribner's Monthly*, Jan., 1878. One of the first examples of Negro dialect in verse. *See* Maurice Garland Fulton's *Christmas Night in the Quarters and Other Poems by Irwin Russell* (1918).

Christopher Publishing House. Boston Mass.; North Quincy, Mass. Publishers. Founded 1910. Publishes both fiction and non-fiction, including many books of poems.

CHRISTOWE, STOYAN (Sept. 1, 1898–); b. in Macedonia. Author. *Heroes and Assassins* (1935); *Mara* (1937); *This Is My Country* (1938); *The Lion of Yanina* (1941); *My American Pilgrimage* (1947).

CHRISTY, DAVID (b. 1802); b. Cincinnati, O.(?). Geologist, anti-slavery writer. *Cotton Is King; or, The Culture of Cotton, and Its Relation to Agriculture, Manufactures and Commerce; to the Free Colored People; and to Those Who Hold That Slavery Is Itself Sinful* (1855).

CHRISTY, HOWARD CHANDLER (Jan. 10, 1873–Mar. 4, 1952); b. in Morgan Co., O. Illustrator. His illustrations have appeared in *Scribner's, Harper's, Collier's Weekly, Cosmopolitan*, etc. He has also illustrated many books by James Whitcomb Riley and others. Among the collections of his drawings are: *Drawings* (1905); *The American Girl* (1906); and *The Christy Book of Drawings* (1908).

Chronicles of America Series, The. A history of America, dealing with the nation in its various lines of development. Ed. by Allen Johnson, 50v. (1918–24).

Chrysalis. Boston, Mass., Hartford, Conn. Quarterly of the arts, including dance, drama, painting, music, and poetry. Founded 1948. Edited by Lily and Baird Hastings.

CHUBB, THOMAS CALDECUT (Nov. 1, 1899–); b. East Orange, N.J. Poet, Biographer. *The White God, and Other Poems* (1920); *Kyrdoon* (poems, 1921); *The Life of Giovanni Boccaccio* (1930); *Ships and Lovers* (poems, 1933); *Cliff Pace, and Other Poems* (1936); *Aretino, Scourge of Princes* (1940); *My Daughter's World* (1941); *A Time to Speak* (poems, 1943); *If There Were No Losses* (1957); *The Byzantines* (1959); *The Northmen* (1964); *Dante and His World* (1967); *The Venetians* (1968).

Chubbuck, Emily. *See* Emily Judson.

CHUJOY, ANATOLE (Apr. 4, 1894–); b. Riga, Latvia. Editor, author. *Ballet* (1936); *Symphonic Ballet* (1937); *The Dance Encyclopedia* (ed., 1949); *New York City Ballet* (1953). Translator and editor: *Fundamentals of the Classic Dance* (1946). Editor and publisher, *Dance News*, since 1942.

CHURCH, ALONZO (June 14, 1903–); b. Washington, D.C. Educator. *Introduction to Mathematical Logic, Vol. I* (1956). Editor, *Journal of Symbolic Logic*, since 1936. Prof. mathematics, Princeton University; 1929–67; prof. mathematics and philosophy, University of California at Los Angeles, since 1967.

CHURCH, BENJAMIN (Aug. 24, 1734–lost at sea in 1776); b. Newport, R.I. Physician, poet. *Liberty and Property Vindicated, and the St—pm–n Burnt* (1765); *The Times* (poem, 1765); *The Choice: A Poem After the Manner of Pomfret* (1802).

CHURCH, FRANCIS PHARCELLUS (Feb. 22, 1839–1906); b. Rochester, N.Y. Editor. Author of the frequently reprinted editorial, "Is There a Santa Claus?" which appeared first in the New York *Sun*, Sept. 21, 1897. Founder (with brother, William Conant Church), *The Army and Navy Journal*, 1863; founder (with same), *The Galaxy*, 1866, editor (with same), 1866–78.

CHURCH, SAMUEL HARDEN (Jan. 24, 1858–Oct. 11, 1943); b. in Caldwell Co., Mo. Educator, author. *Oliver Cromwell* (1894); *John Marmaduke* (1897); *Beowulf* (poem, 1901); *Penruddock of the White Lambs* (1902); *Flames of Faith* (1914); *The Liberal Party in America* (1931); etc. President, Carnegie Institute, Pittsburgh.

CHURCH, WILLIAM CONANT (Aug. 11, 1836–May 23, 1917); b. Rochester, N.Y. Editor, biographer. *Life of John Ericsson*, 2v. (1890); *Ulysses S. Grant* (1897); etc. Founder (with brother, Francis Pharcellus Church), *The Army and Navy Journal*, 1863; editor, 1868–1917; founder (with brother), *The Galaxy*, 1866, editor (with same), 1866–78.

CHURCHILL, ALLEN (1911–). Author. *The Incredible Ivar Kreuger* (1957); *Park Row* (1958); *The Improper Bohemians* (1959); *They Never Came Back* (1960); *The Year the World Went Mad* (1960); etc.

CHURCHILL, WILLIAM (Oct. 5, 1859–June 9, 1920); b. Brooklyn, N.Y. Philologist, author. *A Princess of Fiji* (1892); *Polynesian Wanderings* (1910); *Beach-la-Mar* (1911); etc.

CHURCHILL, WINSTON (Nov. 10, 1871–Mar. 12, 1947); b. St. Louis, Mo. Novelist. Author. *The Celebrity* (1898); *Richard Carvel* (1899); *The Crisis* (1901); *The Crossing* (1904); *Coniston* (1906); *Mr. Crewe's Career* (1908); *A Modern Chronicle* (1910); *The Inside of the Cup* (1913); *A Far Country* (1915); *The Dwelling Place of Light* (1917); *A Traveller in War-Time* (1917); *Dr. Jonathan* (play, 1919); *The Uncharted Way: The Psychology of Gospel Doctrine* (1940); etc. *See* Fred B. Millett's *Contemporary American Authors* (1940).

CHURCHMAN, C[harles] WEST (Aug. 29, 1913–); b. Philadelphia, Pa. Educator. Author or editor: *Elements of Logic and Formal Science* (1940); *Theory of Experimental Inference* (1948); *Methods of Inquiry* (with R. L. Ackoff, 1950); *Introduction to Operations Research* (1957); *Measurement: Theo-*

ries and Definitions (with Philburn Ratoosh, 1959); *Prediction and Optimal Decision* (1961). *Systems Approach* (1968). Editor, *Philosophy of Science*, since 1948; *Management Science*, since 1954. Prof. business administration, University of California, since 1958.

CHURCHWARD, JAMES (1852–Jan. 4, 1936); b. in England. Author. *The Lost Continent of Mu* (1926); *The Children of Mu* (1931); *The Sacred Symbols of Mu* (1933); *Cosmic Forces As They Were Taught on Mu* (1934).

CHUTE, B[eatrice] J[oy] (Jan. 3, 1913–); b. Minneapolis, Minn. Author. *Blocking Back* (1938); *Camp Hero* (1942); *The Fields Are White* (1950); *The End of Loving* (1953); *Greenwillow* (1956); *The Blue Cup and Other Stories* (1957); *The Moon and the Thorn* (1961); *Shift to the Right* (1963); *One Touch of Nature* (1965); etc.

CHUTE, MARCHETTE [Gaylord] (Aug. 16, 1909–); b. Wayzata, Minn. Author. *Rhymes About Ourselves* (1932); *The Search for God* (1941); *Rhymes About the Country* (1941); *The Innocent Wayfaring* (1943); *Geoffrey Chaucer of England* (1946); *Rhymes About the City* (1946); *The End of the Search* (1947); *Shakespeare of London* (1949); *An Introduction to Shakespeare* (1951); *Ben Jonson of Westminster* (1953); *The Wonderful Winter* (1954); *Stories from Shakespeare* (1956); *Around and About* (1957); *Two Gentle Men: George Herbert and Robert Herrick* (1959); *Jesus of Israel* (1961); *The First Liberty: A History of the Right to Vote in America 1619–1850* (1969).

CIARDI, JOHN (June 24, 1916–); b. Boston, Mass. Educator, poet. *Homeward to America* (1940); *Other Skies* (1947); *Live Another Day* (1949); *From Time to Time* (1951); *As If: Poems New and Selected* (1955); *I Marry You* (1958); *I Met a Man* (1961); *In the Stoneworks* (1961); *Dialogue with an Audience* (1963); *Person to Person* (1964); *An Alphabestiary* (1966); etc. Translator: Dante's *Inferno* (1954); *Purgatorio* (1961). Poetry editor, *Saturday Review*, since 1956. Prof. English, Rutgers University, 1956–61.

Cimarron. Novel by Edna Ferber (1930). Story of Oklahoma in 1889, when the settlers engaged in the famous "land-rush."

Cincinnati Enquirer. Cincinnati, Ohio. Newspaper. Founded 1841, succeeding *The Advertiser and Journal,* founded 1818. Editor is Brady Black. Owen Findsen edits book reviews.

Cincinnati Gazette. Cincinnati, Ohio Newspaper. Weekly edition founded 1804; expired 1913. Daily edition founded 1827. The poet William Davis Gallagher was on the staff 1840–50. Edward Deering Mansfield was editor 1857–80. Merged with *Cincinnati Commercial* 1883, as *Cincinnati Commercial Gazette;* name changed to *Commercial Tribune,* 1896; merged with *Cincinnati Enquirer* (q.v.), 1930.

Cincinnati Post and Times-Star. Cincinnati, Ohio. Newspaper. Founded 1881, as the *Penny Paper.* Name changed 1883 to the *Penny Post,* later *Evening Post,* and later *Cincinnati Post.* Combined with *Cincinnati Times-Star* (q.v.) in 1957. Dick Thornburg is editor and book-review editor.

Cincinnati Times-Star, The. Cincinnati, Ohio. Newspaper. Founded 1840, as *Cincinnati Times,* and merged with *Cincinnati Star* (founded 1872) in 1880. Consolidated with *Cincinnati Post* in 1957, as *Cincinnati Post and Times-Star* (q.v.).

Circular Staircase, The. Detective story by Mary Roberts Rinehart (1908).

Circus in the Attic. Stories by Robert Penn Warren (1948).

Circus of Dr. Lao, The. Satirical fantasy by Charles G. Finney (1935).

CIST, CHARLES (Aug. 15, 1738–Dec. 1, 1805); b. St. Petersburg, Russia. Publisher. He published Thomas Paine's *The American Crisis* (1776); and other works. In 1784 he published The *American Herald* and in 1786 The *Columbian Magazine.*

CIST, CHARLES (Apr. 24, 1793–Sept. 5, 1868); b. (Thiel) St. Petersburg, Russia. Printer, publisher, author. *Cincinnati in 1841* (1841), augmented in 1851 and again in 1859. Compiler: *The Cincinnati Miscellany,* 2v. (1845–1846).

CIST, HENRY M[artyn] (Feb. 20, 1839–Dec. 17, 1902); b. Cincinnati, O. Soldier, military historian. *The Army of the Cumberland* (1882).

Citadel Press, Inc. New York. Founded 1939. Publishes general fiction and nonfiction.

Citizen, The. New York weekly. Founded 1864. Editors, Robert B. Roosevelt and Charles C. Halpine. After the latter's death, Roosevelt bought the *Round Table* and merged the two in 1869 as *The New York Citizen and Round Table.*

Citizen, The. Philadelphia. Monthly magazine. Founded 1839. Expired 1841.

Citizen Tom Paine. Historical novel by Howard Fast (1943).

City, The. Play by Clyde Fitch (prod. 1909). The influence of a large city on a man's soul; the thesis being that a city either makes a man or crushes him.

City and the Pillar, The. Novel by Gore Vidal (1948). Story about the trials in the life of a homosexual.

City in the Dawn. Trilogy by Hervey Allen (1950) comprising *The Forest and the Fort* (1943), *Bedford Village* (1944), and *Toward the Morning* (1948). The hero was brought up by Indians and becomes a renowned frontier fighter. The scene is Pennsylvania in the 18th century.

"City in the Sea, The." Poem by Edgar Allan Poe (1831).

City Life. By Donald Barthelme (1970). Combination of collage graphics and witty, surrealistic fantasies written in an apparently rational style.

City Lights Books, Inc. San Francisco, Cal. Publishers. Founded 1953. Lawrence Ferlinghetti is editor. Publishes radical and experimental poetry and prose, especially of Beat Generation (q.v.) writers.

City of Night. Novel by John Rechy about homosexual adventures and love (1963).

Civil Disobedience. Essay by Henry David Thoreau. See *Resistance to Civil Government.*

CLAD, NOEL (1924?–May, 1962). Novelist. *Savage* (1958); *Love and Money* (1959); *Until the Real Thing Comes Along* (1961); etc.

CLAFLIN, MARY B[uchlin] (1825–1896); b. in Massachusetts. Author. *Brampton Sketches* (1890); *Real Happenings* (1890); *Personal Recollections of John G. Whittier* (1893); *Under the Old Elms* (1895).

CLAGETT, JOHN. (b. 1916–); Author. *Cradle of the Sun* (1952) *Buckskin Cavalier* (1954); *The Slot* (1958); *The Island of Dragons* (1967); *Surprise Attack (1968); These Hallowed Grounds* (1969); etc.

CLAGETT, MARSHALL (Jan. 23, 1916–); b. Washington, D.C. Historian, educator. *Giovanni Marliani and Late Medieval Physics* (1941); *The Medieval Science of Weights* (ed. and trans. with Ernest Moody, 1952); *Greek Science in Antiquity* (1956); *The Science of Mechanics in the Middle Ages* (1959); *Archimedes in the Middle Ages* (1964); etc. Prof. history of science, University of Wisconsin, since 1954.

CLAIBORNE, CRAIG (Sept. 4, 1920–); b. Sunflower, Miss. Journalist. *The New York Times Cook Book* (1961); *Craig Claiborne's Kitchen Primer* (1969); *Cooking with Herbs and Spices* (1970). Food editor, *The New York Times,* 1957–71.

CLAIBORNE, JOHN FRANCIS HAMTRAMCK (Apr. 24, 1807–May 17, 1884); b. Natchez, Miss. Editor, historian. *Life and Correspondence of John A. Quitman,* 2v. (1860); *Life and Times of Gen. Sam Dale* (1860); *Mississippi as a Province, Territory and State* (1880).

CLAIBORNE, NATHANIEL HERBERT (Nov. 14, 1777–Aug. 15, 1859); b. in Sussex Co., Va. Congressman, author. *Notes on the War in the South* (1819).

Claire Ambler. Novel by Booth Tarkington (1928). The story of a beautiful girl who imagines that she is much more intellectual than she really is.

Clansman, The. Play by Thomas Dixon (prod. 1905). A drama of Reconstruction in the South, based on his novels *The Leopard's Spots* and *The Clansman.* It was the inspiration for the moving picture *The Birth of a Nation* (prod. 1915).

Clapp, Eva Katherine. See Eva Katherine Clapp Gibson.

CLAPP, FREDERICK MORTIMER (July 26, 1879–); b. New York City. Art curator, poet. *On the Overland, and Other Poems* (1916); *New York, and Other Verses* (1918); *Joshua Trees* (1922); *New Poems* (1936); *Said Before Sunset* (1938); *The Seeming Real* (1947); etc. Director, Frick Collection, New York, 1936–51.

CLAPP, HENRY (Nov. 11, 1814–Apr., 1875); b. on Nantucket Isl., Mass. Editor, poet. Known as "The King of Bohemia." *The Pioneer; or, Leaves from an Editor's Portfolio* (1846); *Husband vs. Wife* (verse, 1858). Founder (with Edward Howland), *The Saturday Press,* 1858.

CLAPP, HENRY AUSTIN (July 17, 1841–1904); b. Dorchester, Mass. Drama critic. *Reminiscences of a Dramatic Critic* (1902).

CLAPP, MARGARET ANTOINETTE (Apr. 11, 1910–); b. East Orange, N.J. Educator, author. *Forgotten First Citizen: John Bigelow* (1947; Pulitzer Prize for biography, 1948); *The Modern University* (ed., 1950); etc. Former president, Wellesley College.

CLAPP, WILLIAM WARLAND (Apr. 11, 1826–Dec. 8, 1891); b. Boston, Mass. Editor, playwright. *A Record of the Boston Stage* (1853); *Joseph Dennie* (1880); etc. Editor, *The Boston Journal,* 1865–91.

CLAPPE, LOUISE AMELIA KNAPP SMITH (1819–Feb. 9, 1906); b. Elizabeth, N.J. Author. Pen name "Dame Shirley." *The Shirley Letters from California Mines in 1851–52,* ed. Thomas C. Russell (1922).

CLAPPER, RAYMOND (May 30, 1892–Feb. 1944); b. in Linn Co., Kan. Newspaper correspondent. *Racketeering in Washington* (1933); *Watching the World* (ed. by Olive Clapper, 1944). Political columnist for the Scripps-Howard newspapers, from 1936.

Clara Howard: In a Series of Letters. Novel by Charles Brockden Brown (1801), republished as *Philip Stanley; or, The Enthusiasm of Love* (1807).

Clare, Ada. Pen and stage name of Jane McElheney.

CLARE, ISRAEL SMITH (Nov. 24, 1847–Mar. 1, 1924); b. in Lancaster Co., Pa. Historian. *Library of Universal History,* 8v. (1897); etc.

"Clarel." Poem by Herman Melville (1876).

Clarence. Play by Booth Tarkington (prod. 1919).

Clari. Opera by John Howard Payne (prod. 1823), in which the song "Home Sweet Home" was first sung.

CLARK, ALEXANDER (Mar. 10, 1834–July 6, 1879); b. in Jefferson Co., O. Methodist clergyman, editor, poet. *The Old Log School House* (1859); *Rambles in Europe* (1877); etc. Editor, *The Methodist Recorder,* 1870–79.

CLARK, ALLEN CULLING (Feb. 23, 1858–May 16, 1943); b. Philadelphia, Pa. Author. *William Duane* (1905); *Life and Letters of Dolly Madison* (1914); *Abraham Lincoln in the National Capital* (1925); *The Trollops* (1935); *Commodores James Barron, Stephen Decatur* (1939); etc.

CLARK, ANN NOLAN (1898–); b. Las Vegas, N.M. Author. *In My Mother's House* (1941); *Little Navajo Bluebird* (1943); *Magic Money* (1950); *Looking-for-Something* (1952); *Secret of the Andes* (1952); *Blue Canyon House* (poem, 1954); *Santos for Pasqualita* (1959); *World Song* (1960); *Father Kino, Priest to the Pimas* (1963); *Medicine Man's Daughter* (1963); *Arizona for Young People* (1968); *Sandy Trails* (1969); etc.

CLARK, ANNIE M[aria] L[awrence] (Sept. 21, 1835–Apr., 1920); b. Still River, Mass. Author, *Olive Loring's Mission* (1871); *The Alcotts in Harvard* (1902); *Poems* (1905); etc.

CLARK, ARTHUR HAMILTON (Dec. 27, 1841–July 5, 1922); b. Boston, Mass. Mariner, historian. *The History of Yachting, 1600–1815* (1904); *The Clipper Ship Era: Epitome of Famous American and British Clipper Ships,...1843–1869* (1910).

CLARK, ARTHUR HENRY (Dec. 20, 1868–May 15, 1951); b. London, Eng. Publisher, author. *Style and General Format for Publications* (1910); *Bibliography of the Publications of the Rowfant Club* (1925); etc. Founder, The Arthur H. Clark Co., publishing firm, Cleveland, O., 1902.

CLARK, BARRETT H[arper] (Aug. 26, 1890–Aug. 5, 1953); b. Toronto, Ont. Editor, author. *The Continental Drama of Today* (1914); *Contemporary French Dramatists* (1915); *British and American Drama of Today* (1915); *How to Produce Amateur Plays* (1917); *A Study of the Modern Drama* (1925); *Eugene O'Neill* (1926); *Oedipus or Pollyanna* (1927); *Speak the Speech* (1930); *An Hour of American Drama* (1930); *Intimate Portraits* (1951); etc. Editor: *World's Best Plays,* 58v. (1915–26); *Great Short Stories of the World* (1925); *Great Short Novels of the World* (1927); *Great Short Biographies of the World* (1928); *World Drama* (1932); *Favorite American Plays of the Nineteenth Century* (1943); *Nine Modern American Plays* (with W. H. Davenport, 1951); etc. Editor, Samuel French Co., New York, 1918–36. Dramatic editor, *Drama Magazine.*

CLARK, BENNETT CHAMP (Jan. 8, 1890–July 13, 1954); b. Bowling Green, Mo. Senator, author. *John Quincy Adams, Old Man Eloquent* (1932). Joint author, *Social Studies* (1934).

CLARK, [Charles] BADGER (Jan 1, 1883–Sept. 26, 1957); b. Albia, Ia. Poet. *Sun and Saddle Leather* (1915); *Grass Grown Trails* (1917); *Sun and Saddle Leather including "Grass Grown Trails" and New Poems* (1920); *Spike* (1923); *Sky Lines and Wood Smoke* (1935).

CLARK, CHARLES D[unning] (d. 1892). Dime novelist. Pen name "W. J. Hamilton." *The Shawnees' Foe* (1866); *Mohawk Nat* (1868); *Mountain Gid, the Free Ranger* (1870); *The Flying Scout* (1874); *Ben Bird, the Cave King* (1884); *Captain Paul, the Kentucky Moonshiner* (1880); etc. The dates are not necessarily those of first editions.

CLARK, CHARLES HEBER (July 11, 1847–Aug. 10, 1915); b. Berlin, Md. Journalist, author. Pen name "Max Adeler." *Out of the Hurly Burly* (1874); *Random Shots* (1879); *Captain Bluitt* (1901); *The Quakeress* (1905); etc.

CLARK, CHARLES UPSON (Jan. 14, 1875–Sept. 29, 1960); b. Springfield, Mass. Educator, author. *Greater Roumania* (1922); *Bessarabia, Russia and Roumania on the Black Sea* (1927); *United Roumania* (1932); etc. Compiler; *Voyageurs, Robes Noires, et Coureurs de Bois: Stories from the French Exploration of North America* (1934); *Racial Aspects of Roumania's Case* (1941); etc. Prof. languages, College of the City of New York, 1932–40.

CLARK, CHARLOTTE MOON. Author. Pen name "Charles M. Clay." *How She Came Into Her Kingdom* (1878); republished as *A Daughter of the Gods* (1884); *Baby Rue* (1881); *The Modern Hagar* (1882).

CLARK, DONALD LEMEN (June 30, 1888–June 27, 1966); b. South Bend, Ind. Educator, author. *Rhetoric and Poetry in the Renaissance* (1922); *Thinking, Speaking, and Writing* (with others, 1927); *Your English Problems* (with M. Esterbrook, 1935); *John Milton at St. Paul's School* (1948); *Rhetoric in Greco-Roman Education* (1957). Editor, *Columbia Poetry* (annual), 1931–40; Prof. rhetoric, Columbia University, 1947–57.

CLARK, DOROTHY PARK (1899–). Novelist. *Poison Speaks Softly* (1947); etc. Co-author with Isabella McLennan McMeekin, using together the pen name "Clark McMeekin": *Show Me a Land* (1940); *Reckon with the River* (1941); *Old Kentucky Country* (1957); *The Fairbrothers* (1961); etc.

CLARK, ELEANOR (Mrs. Robert Penn Warren) (1913–); b. in California. Author. *The Bitter Box* (1946); *Rome and a Villa* (1952); *Song of Roland* (1960); *The Oysters of Locmariaquer* (1964); *Baldur's Gate* (1970).

CLARK, ELLERY HARDING (Mar. 13, 1874–July 27, 1949); b. West Roxbury, Mass. Lawyer, author. *Dick Randall, the Young Athlete* (1910); *Reminiscences of an Athlete* (1911); *Daughters of Eve* (1924); *Carib Gold* (1925); *The Lost Galleon* (1927); etc.

CLARK, ELMER TALMAGE (Sept. 9, 1886–Aug. 29, 1966); b. Randolph Co., Ark. Educator, author, *The New Evangelism* (1915); *The Negro and His Religion* (1924); *The Small Sects in America* (1937); *The Chiangs of China* (1943); *The Warm Heart of Wesley* (1950); *Album of Methodist History* (1952); etc. Compiler, *Year Book of Methodist Missions*, annually since 1927. Editor, *World Outlook*, 1938–52.

CLARK, EMILY (Mrs. Edwin Swift Balch) (1893–July 2, 1953); b. in Virginia. Educator, author. *Stuffed Peacocks* (1927); *Innocence Abroad* (1931). Founder, *The Reviewer*, Richmond, Va., 1921; co-editor, 1921–25.

CLARK, FELICIA BUTTZ (Mrs. Nathaniel Walling Clark) (July 8, 1862–deceased); b. New York City. Novelist. *The Cripple of Nuremberg* (1900); *The Sword of Garibaldi* (1905); *Laughing Water* (1915); etc.

CLARK, GEORGE HUNT (1809–Aug. 20, 1881); b. Northampton, Mass. Poet. *Now and Then* (1855); *The News* (1856); *Undertow of a Trade-Wind Surf* (1860).

CLARK, GEORGE WHITEFIELD (Feb. 15, 1831–Nov. 10, 1911); b. South Orange, N.J. Clergyman, author. *Clark's People's Commentary*, 9v. (1910), in which were collected earlier commentaries on the several parts of the New Testament; *Struggles and Triumphs of a Long Life* (autobiography, 1914). Editor: *The Harp of Freedom* (hymnal, 1856).

CLARK, HARRY HAYDEN (July 8, 1901–June 6, 1971); b. New Milford, Conn. Educator. Editor, *Poems of Freneau* (1929); *Whittier on Writers* (with E. H. Cady, 1950); *Transitions in American Literary History* (1954); general editor, American Writers Series, American Literature Series. English dept., University of Wisconsin, since 1928; prof. from 1936.

CLARK, IMOGEN (d. Jan. 2, 1936); b. New York City. Author. *The Victory of Ezry Gardner* (1896); *Will Shakespeare's Little Lad* (1897); *God's Puppets* (1901); *Old Days and Old Ways* (1928); etc.

CLARK, JOHN BATES (Jan. 26, 1847–Mar. 21, 1938); b. Providence, R.I. Educator, economist, author. *The Philosophy of Wealth* (1885); *The Distribution of Wealth* (1899); etc.

CLARK, JONAS (Dec. 14, 1703–Nov. 15, 1805); b. Newton, Mass. Congregational clergyman, patriot. As pastor of the First Congregational Church at Lexington, he was an eye witness of the battle in 1775, and described it in a published sermon, *The Fate of Blood-Thirsty Oppressors* (1776), which has an appendix, *Opening of the War of the Revolution*.

CLARK, KATE UPSON (Mrs. Edwin Perkins Clark) (Feb. 22, 1851–Feb. 17, 1935); b. Camden, Ala. Author. *White Butterflies, and Other Stories* (1900); *Up the Witch Brook Road* (1902); *The Dole Twins* (1906); etc.

CLARK, KENNETH BANCROFT (July 24, 1914–); b. Panama Canal Zone. Educator. *Desegregation: An Appraisal of the Evidence* (1953); *Prejudice and Your Child* (1955); *The Negro Protest* (1963); *Dark Ghetto* (1965). Prof. psychology, College of the City of New York, since 1959.

CLARK, LEWIS GAYLORD (Oct. 5, 1808–Nov. 3, 1873); b. Otisco, N.Y., twin brother of Willis Gaylord Clark. Editor, poet. *Knick-Knacks from an Editor's Table* (1852). Editor: *The Literary Remains of the Late Willis Gaylord Clark* (1844); *The Lover's Gift; and Friendship's Token* (poems, 1848). Co-publisher, *The Knickerbocker* magazine, 1834–39; editor, 1834–60, 1863.

CLARK, MARGUERITE SHERIDAN, b. Madison, Wis. Editor, author. *Medicine on the March* (1949); *After the Doctor Leaves* (1954); *Medicine Today, a Decade of Progress* (1960); *Why So Tired?* (1962). Science editor, *Newsweek*, since 1941.

CLARK, MARK WAYNE (May 1, 1896–); b. Madison Barracks, N.Y. Educator, retired army officer. *Calculated Risk* (1950); *From the Danube to the Yalu* (1954). Pres., Citadel Military College of South Carolina, 1954–56.

CLARK, RAMSEY (Dec. 18, 1927–); b. Dallas, Tex. Government official. *Crime in America: Observations on Its Nature, Causes, Prevention, and Control* (1970). With U.S. Department of Justice, 1961–68; Attorney General, 1967–68.

CLARK, SYDNEY AYLMER (Aug. 18, 1890–); b. Auburndale, Mass. Author. *Old Glamors of New Austria* (1930); *Cathedral France* (1931); *France on Fifty Dollars* (1933); also, "Fifty Dollar" series on *Germany* (1933); *Italy* (1933); *Switzerland* (1934); *Spain* (1934); *England* (1934); *Scotland* (1935); *Belgium* (1935); *Sweden* (1936); *Norway* (1936); *Holland* (1936); *Denmark* (1937); *Finland* (1938); *Ireland* (1939); *Hawaii With Sydney A. Clark* (1938); *Today in Cathedral France* (1948); *All the Best in Hawaii* (1949); *All the Best in Switzerland* (1951); *All the Best in Europe* (1955); *All the Best in Germany and Austria* (1957); *All the Best in Japan* (1958); *All the Best in the South Pacific* (1962); *All the Best in Central America* (1964); *All the Best in the Caribbean* (1969); etc.

CLARK, THOMAS CURTIS (Jan. 8, 1877–Dec. 7, 1954); b. Vincennes, Ind. Poet. *Poems and Songs* (1909); *Abraham Lincoln: Thirty Poems* (1934); *Fifty Lincoln Poems* (1943); *God's Dreams and Other Poems* (1944). Compiler: *Quotable Poems*, 2v. (with E. A. Gillespie, 1928–31); *Poems for Special Days and Occasions* (1930); *Golden Book of Religious Verse* (1937); *One Thousand Quotable Poems* (1937); *Christ in Poetry. An Anthology* (with Hazel D. Clark, 1951); *The Golden Book of Immortality* (1954). Editorial staff, *The Christian Century*, Chicago, 1912–40; editor, *20th Century Quarterly*, since 1919.

CLARK, THOMAS DIONYSIUS (July 14, 1903–); b. Louisville, Miss. Educator, historian. *A History of Kentucky* (1937); *The Rampaging Frontier* (1939); *Pills, Petticoats and Plows* (1944); *The Southern Country Editor* (1948); *The Bluegrass Cavalcade* (1956); *The Emerging South* (1961); *Three Paths to the Modern South* (1965). History dept., University of Kentucky, since 1931.

CLARK, TOM (1941–); b. Chicago, Ill. Poet. *Airplanes* (1966); *The SandBurg* (1966); *The Emperor of the Animals* (1967); *Stones* (1969).

CLARK, WALTER VAN TILBURG (Aug. 3, 1909–Nov. 10, 1971); b. East Orland, Me. Novelist. *Ten Women in Gales's House, and Shorter Poems* (1932); *The Ox-Bow Incident* (1940); *The City of the Trembling Leaves* (1945); *The Track of the Cat* (1949); *The Watchful Gods and Other Stories* (1950).

CLARK, WILLIAM SMITH, II (Sept. 13, 1900–); b. Baltimore, Md. Educator. *Chief Patterns of World Drama* (1946); *The Early Irish Stage: The Beginnings to 1720* (1955); *The Irish Stage in Country Towns* (1965). Editor: *Dramatic Works of Roger Boyle, Earl of Orrery,* 2v. (1937). Prof. English, Cincinnati University, since 1940.

CLARK, WILLIS GAYLORD (Oct. 5, 1808–June 12, 1841); b. Otisco, N.Y., twin brother of Lewis Gaylord Clark. Editor, publisher, poet. *The Poetical Writings of Willis Gaylord Clark* (1847); *The Literary Remains of the Late Willis Gaylord Clark* (1844). His best known poems are "The Spirit of Life," "The Past and Present." Assoc. editor, *The Knickerbocker* magazine, 1834–41.

Clarke, Covington. Pen name of Clarke Venable.

CLARKE, DONALD HENDERSON (Aug. 24, 1887–Mar. 29, 1958); b. South Hadley, Mass. Novelist. *Louis Beretti: The Story of a Gunman* (1929); *Lady Ann* (1934); *Regards to Broadway* (1935); *Alabam'* (1935); *Millie's Daughter* (1939); *Murderer's Holiday* (1940); *A Lady Named Lou* (1941); *Joe and Jenny* (1949); *Man of the World* (1951). Editor: *The Autobiography of Frank Tarbeaux as Told to Donald Henderson Clarke* (1930).

CLARKE, FRANCES ELIZABETH; b. Albion, N.Y. Author. *Our Animal Books,* 7v. (1938); *Of Cats and Men* (1957). Compiler: *Valiant Dogs* (1926); *Poetry's Plea For Animals* (1927); *Cats and Cats* (1937); *Gallant Horses* (1938); *Wild Animals* (1939); *Great Wings and Small* (1940).

CLARKE, HELEN ARCHIBALD (Nov. 13, 1860–Feb. 8, 1926); b. Philadelphia, Pa. Musician, editor, author. *Browning's Italy* (1907); *Browning's England* (1908); *Longfellow's Country* (1909); *Hawthorne's Country* (1910); *Ancient Myths in Modern Poets* (1910); *The Poets' New England* (1911); *Browning and His Century* (1912); etc. Co-founder (with Charlotte Endymion Porter), *Poet Lore,* 1888: co-editor, 1888–1926.

CLARKE, JAMES FREEMAN (Apr. 4, 1810–June 8, 1888); b. Hanover, N.H. Unitarian clergyman, editor, author. *Ten Great Religions,* 2 parts (1871, 1883); *Memorial and Biographical Sketches* (1878); *Self-Culture* (1880); etc. Editor, the *Western Messenger,* Louisville, Ky., 1836–39. See *James Freeman Clarke: Autobiography, Diary and Correspondence,* ed. Edward Everett Hale (1891).

CLARKE, JOHN HENRIK (Jan. 1, 1915–); b. Union Springs, Ala. Educator, editor, author. *Rebellion in Rhyme* (1948); *The Lives of Great African Chiefs* (1958); *Malcom X: The Man and His Times* (1969). Editor: *Harlem: A Community in Transition* (1964); *Harlem, U.S.A.* (1965); *American Negro Short Stories* (1966); *William Styron's Nat Turner: Ten Black Writers Respond* (1968); *Black Titan: W. E. B. DuBois* (with others, 1970). Contributor, *Freedomways,* since 1962.

CLARKE, JOSEPH IGNATIUS CONSTANTINE (July 31, 1846–Feb. 27, 1925); b. Knightstown, Ireland. Journalist, playwright, poet. *Heartease* (with Charles Klein, 1896); *The Fighting Race, and Other Poems and Ballads* (1911); *Japan at First Hand* (1918); *My Life and Memories* (1925); etc. On staff *New York Herald,* 1870–83, 1903–06. Editor, *Criterion,* 1898–1900.

CLARKE, MARY BAYARD DEVEREUX (May 13, 1827–Mar. 30, 1886); b. Raleigh, N.C. Editor, poet. *Mosses from a Rolling Stone* (1866); *Clytie and Zenobia* (1871); *Poems* (1905). Editor: *Wood Notes; or, Carolina Carols* (under pen name, "Tenella," 1854); *Southern Field and Fireside* (1865).

CLARKE, McDONALD (June 18, 1798–Mar. 5, 1842); b. Bath, Me. Poet. *Poems of McDonald Clarke* (1836). Known as "The Mad Poet," he belonged to the "Bohemian" circle in New York and lived in poverty. He died in the asylum on Blackwell's Island, New York.

CLARKE, REBECCA SOPHIA (Feb. 22, 1833–Aug. 16, 1906); b. Norridgewock, Me. Author. Pen name "Sophie May." The *Little Prudy* stories, 6v. (1863–65); the *Dotty Dimple* stories, 6v. (1867–69); the *Little Prudy's Flyaway* series, 6v. (1870–73); the *Quinnebasset* series, 6v. (1871–91); the *Flaxie Frizzle* stories, 6v. (1876–84); the *Little Prudy's Children* series, 6v. (1894–1901); etc.

CLARKE, SARAH J. (b. Sept. 12, 1840); b. Norridgewood, Me. Author. The *Little Miss Weezy* series, 3v. (1886–90); *The Merry Five* (1897); the *Boy Donald* series, 3v. (1900–02); etc.

CLARKE, WILLIAM FAYAL (Mar. 12, 1855–May 12, 1935); b. near Richmond, Va. Editor. On editorial staff, *St. Nicholas* magazine, 1873–1927; asst. editor, 1878–1893; assoc. editor, 1893–1905; editor-in-chief, 1905–27.

Clark's Field. Novel by Robert Herrick (1914). Ardelle Clark, an orphan, has dreams of wealth which are always on the verge of realization.

CLARKSON, JESSE DUNSMORE (1897–). Educator, author. *Labour and Nationalism in Ireland* (1925); *War as a Social Institution* (1941); *A History of Russia* (1961); etc. Prof. history, Brooklyn College.

Classical Journal. Cedar Rapids, Ia.; Athens; O. Monthly. Founded 1905.

CLAUDY, CARL HARRY (Jan. 13, 1879–); b. Washington, D.C. Author. The *Tell Me Why* stories, 4v. (1912–16); *Partners of the Forest Trail* (1915); *The Girl Reporter* (1930); *Land of No Shadow* (1933); *Blue Grotto Terror* (1934); etc. Also books on Freemasonry.

CLAUSON, J[ames] EARL (Aug. 13, 1873–June 24, 1937); b. Troy, N.Y. Editor, author. *Cranston: A Historical Sketch* (1904). Compiler: *The Dog's Book of Verse* (1916). Sunday editor, *Providence Journal,* 1905–10; editorial staff, Frank A. Munsey Co. magazines, 1910–11; asst. mag. editor, *New York World,* 1921–31.

Clavers, Mrs. Mary. Pen name Caroline Matilda Stansbury Kirkland.

CLAWSON, MARION (Aug. 10, 1905–); b. Elko, Nev. Government administrator, economist. Author or co-author: *Western Range Livestock Industry* (1950); *Uncle Sam's Acres* (1951); *The Federal Lands: Their Use and Management* (1957); *Land for the Future* (1960); *Man and Land in the United States* (1964); *Economics of Outdoor Recreation* (1966); etc.

CLAY, ALBERT T[obias] (Dec. 4, 1866–Sept. 14, 1925); b. Hanover, Pa. Educator, orientalist, author. *Amurru, the Home of the Northern Semites* (1909); *The Empire of the Amorites* (1919); *The Origin of Biblical Traditions* (1923); etc.

Clay, Bertha M. Pen name of an English author, Charlotte Mary Brame, which was used in the United States as a "stock name" by various publishers.

Clay, Charles M. Pen name of Charlotte Moon Clark.

CLAY, HENRY (Apr. 12, 1777–June 29, 1852); b. in Hanover Co., Va. Statesman, orator. Known as "The Mill-Boy of the Slashes." See *The Life, Correspondence, and Speeches of Henry Clay,* ed. by Calvin Colton, 6v. (1857), which includes volumes published earlier under individual titles. Congressman, 1811–21, 1823–25; U.S. Senator, 1806–07, 1809–10, 1831–42, 1849–52; Secretary of State, 1825–29. *See also* Epes Sargent's *The Life and Public Service of Henry Clay* (1842);

George D. Prentice's *Biography of Henry Clay* (1931); Carl Schurz's *Henry Clay*, 2v. (1887); Bernard Mayo's *Henry Clay* (1937); Glyndon G. Van Deusen's *Henry Clay* (1937); George R. Poage's *Henry Clay and the Whig Party* (1965).

CLAY, JOHN CECIL (Apr. 2, 1875–May 24, 1930); b. Ronceverte, W.Va. Illustrator, author. *In Love's Garden* (1904); *The Portfolio of Authors* (1906); *The Lover's Mother Goose* (1905). Illustrated stories for *Saturday Evening Post* and Many other magazines.

CLAYTON, CHARLES CURTIS (June 3, 1902–); b. Cambridge, Neb. Journalist. *Newspaper Reporting Today* (1947); *Fifty Years of Freedom* (1959). With St. Louis *Globe Democrat*, 1925–55.

CLEARY, BEVERLY [Atlee] b. McMinnville, Ore. Author. *Henry Huggins* (1950); *Fifteen* (1956); *The Luckiest Girl* (1958); *Jean and Johnny* (1959); *The Mouse and the Motorcycle* (1965); *Mitch and Amy* (1967); etc.

CLEAVER, ELDRIDGE (1935–); b. Wabbaseka, Ark. Black leader, author. *Soul on Ice* (1968); *Post-Prison Writings and Speeches* (1969). Contributor, *Ramparts*, since 1966; Black Panther Party leader in exile.

CLEETON, GLEN URIEL (July 2, 1895–); b. Green City, Mo. Educator. *Executive Ability: Its Discovery and Development* (1946); *Making Work Human* (1949); etc. Dean, Division of Humanistic and Social Studies, Carnegie Institute of Technology, since 1944.

CLEGG, CHARLES MYRON, JR. (June 29, 1916–); b. Youngstown, O. Historian. Co-author, with Lucius Beebe: *U.S. West, the Saga of Wells Fargo* (1949); *Legends of the Comstock Lode* (1950); *Cable Car Carnival* (1951); *Steam Cars to the Comstock* (1957); *Narrow Gauge in the Rockies* (1958); *San Francisco's Golden Era* (1960); *When Beauty Rode the Rails* (1962); etc. Editor: *The Lucius Beebe Reader* (with Duncan Emrich, 1967).

CLEGHORN, SARAH N[orcliffe] (Feb. 4, 1876–April 4, 1959); b. Norfolk, Va. Poet. *A Turnpike Lady* (1907); *The Spinster* (1916); *Portraits and Protests* (1917); *Threescore* (autobiography, 1936); *The Seamless Robe* (1945); *Poems of Peace and Freedom* (1945); etc.

CLELAND, MABEL ROSS (Mrs. Kenneth De Witt Widdemer); b. New York. Author. *Dawn Is Silver* (1939); *Washington Irving, Boy of Old New York* (1946); *Harriet Beecher Stowe, Connecticut Girl* (1949); *Souvenir* (poems, 1956); *James Monroe, Good Neighbor Boy* (1959); *Harriet Beecher Stowe* (1962); etc.

CLELAND, ROBERT GLASS (Feb. 19, 1885–Sept. 3, 1957); b. Shelbyville, Ky. Educator, author. *A History of California: The American Period* (1922), to complement Charles E. Chapman's *A History of California: The Spanish Period* (1921); *Pathfinders* (1929); *The Place Called Sespe* (1940); *The Cattle on a Thousand Hills* (1941); *From Wilderness to Empire* (1944); *California Pageant* (1946); *California In Our Time* (1947); *This Reckless Breed of Men* (1950). Editor, *Mexican Year Book*, 1922–24. With Occidental College, 1912–43.

CLEMENS, JEREMIAH (Dec. 28, 1814–May 21, 1865); b. Huntsville, Ala. Soldier, novelist. *Bernard Lile* (1856); *Mustang Gray* (1858); *The Rivals: A Tale of the Times of Aaron Burr and Alexander Hamilton* (1860); *Tobias Wilson: a Tale of the Great Rebellion* (1865).

CLEMENS, SAMUEL LANGHORNE (Nov. 30, 1835–Apr. 21, 1910); b. Florida, Mo. Humorist. Pen name "Mark Twain." *The Celebrated Jumping Frog of Calaveras County, and Other Sketches* (1867); *The Innocents Abroad* (1869); *Roughing It* (1872); *The Gilded Age* (1873); *The Adventures of Tom Sawyer* (1876); *A Tramp Abroad* (1880); *The Prince and the Pauper* (1882); *Life on the Mississippi* (1883); *Adven-*tures of Huckleberry Finn* (1885); *A Connecticut Yankee in King Arthur's Court* (1889); *The American Claimant* (1892); *The 1,000,000 Bank-Note, and Other New Stories* (1893); *Tom Sawyer Abroad* (1894); *The Tragedy of Pudd'nhead Wilson* (1894); *Personal Recollections of Joan of Arc* (1896); *The Man That Corrupted Hadleyburg, and Other Stories and Essays* (1900); *Extract from Captain Stormfield's Visit to Heaven* (1909); *Mark Twain's Autobiography*, 2v. (1924); *The Writings of Mark Twain*, ed. by Albert Bigelow Paine, 37v. (1922–25). In progress are *The Collected Writings*, ed. by John Gerber, and a collection, *The Mark Twain Papers. See* Albert Bigelow Paine's *Mark Twain*, 3v. (1912); William Dean Howells's *My Mark Twain* (1910); Van Wyck Brooks's *The Ordeal of Mark Twain* (1920); Bernard De Voto's *Mark Twain in Eruption* (1940); *The Autobiography of Mark Twain*, ed. by Charles Neider (1959); Justin Kaplan's *Mr. Clemens and Mark Twain* (1966); Maxwell Geismar's *Mark Twain: An American Prophet* (1970).

Clement, Clara Erskine. See Clara Erskine Clement Waters.

Clement, Hal. Pen name of Harry C. Stubbs.

CLEMENTS, COLIN [Campbell] (Feb. 25, 1894–Jan. 29, 1948); b. Omaha, Neb. Playwright. *The Touchstone and Other Plays* (1919); *Plays for a Folding Theatre* (1923); *Plays for Pagans* (1924); *This Awful Age* (with wife, Florence Ryerson, 1930); *Mild Oats* (with same, 1930); *Shadows* (with same, 1934); *Through the Night* (with same, 1940); *Winnie Weeks* (1940); *Glamour Preferred* (1941); *Ever Since Eve* (1941); *Harriet* (with same, 1943); *Spring Green* (1944); *Oh! Susanna* (1947); *Strange Bedfellows* (with same, 1948).

Clements, Mrs. Colin [Campbell]. See Florence Ryerson.

Clemmer, Mary. See Mary Clemmer Ames.

CLENDENING, LOGAN (May 25, 1884–Jan. 31, 1945); b. Kansas City, Mo. Physician, author. *The Human Body* (1927); *Behind the Doctor* (1933); *Source Book of Medical History* (ed., 1942); etc.

CLEVELAND, AARON (Feb, 3, 1744–Sept. 21, 1815); b. Haddam, Conn. Congregational clergyman, poet. *The Philosopher and the Boy* (poem, 1763); *Slavery Considered* (1775).

CLEVELAND, CHARLES D[exter] (Dec. 3, 1802–Aug. 18, 1869); b. Salem, Mass. Author. *A Compendium of English Literature* (1849); *English Literature of the Nineteenth Century* (1851); *A Compendium of American Literature* (1858); etc.

CLEVELAND, GROVER (Mar. 18, 1837–June 24, 1908); b. Caldwell, N.J. 22nd and 24th president of the United States, author. *The Writings and Speeches of Grover Cleveland* (1892); *Letters of Grover Cleveland, 1850–1908* (1933). *See* Robert McElroy's *Grover Cleveland: The Man and the Statesman*, 2v. (1923); Allan Nevins's *Grover Cleveland: A Study in Courage* (1932).

CLEVELAND, HORACE WILLIAM SHALER (Dec. 16, 1814–Dec. 5, 1900); b. Lancaster, Mass. Landscape architect, author. *Voyages of a Merchant Navigator of the Days That Are Past, Compiled From the Journals and Letters of the Late Richard J. Cleveland* (1886); *Social Life and Literature Fifty Years Ago* (anon., 1888); etc.

Cleveland Herald. See Cleveland Press and News.

Cleveland News. See Cleveland Press and News.

Cleveland Plain Dealer. Cleveland, O. Newspaper. Founded 1841, as *Cleveland Advertiser*. Name changed in 1842. Artemus Ward worked as a reporter on it in 1858. Thomas Vail is editor. Alvin Beam is book-review editor.

Cleveland Press. Cleveland, O. Newspaper. Founded 1878, by Edward Wylie Scripps as *The Penny Press. See Cleveland Press and News.*

Cleveland Press. Cleveland, O. Newspaper. Founded 1868, as the *Evening News.* In 1885 it absorbed the *Cleveland Herald* to form the *Cleveland News and Herald.* Original name was resumed about 1905. Merged with *Cleveland Press* in 1960 as *Cleveland Press,* later *Cleveland Press and News,* now *Cleveland Press* again. Publishes a special book supplement. Louis Seltzer, editor of the *Press* since 1928, was succeeded after his death in 1966 by Thomas L. Boardman.

CLEWS, HENRY (Aug. 14, 1834–Jan. 31, 1923); b. in Staffordshire, England. Banker, financial writer. *Twenty-Eight Years in Wall Street* (1885); *Fifty Years in Wall Street* (1908); *Financial, Economic and Miscellaneous Speeches and Essays* (1910).

Cliff-Dwellers, The. Novel by Henry B. Fuller (1893). This story of down-town life in Chicago, showing effects of business greed upon the lives of men and women, first appeared serially in *Harper's Weekly,* 1893.

CLIFFORD, JAMES L[owry] (Feb. 24, 1901–); b. Evansville, Ind. Educator. *Hester Lynch Piozzi* (1941); *Young Sam Johnson* (1955). Editor: *Dr. Campbell's Diary* (1947); *Johnsonian Studies, 1887–1950; a Survey and Bibliography* (1951); *Eighteenth Century English Literature: Modern Essays in Criticism* (1959); *Biography as an Art* (1962); Smollett's *Peregrine Pickle* (1964); *Man Versus Society in Eighteenth-Century Britain* (1968). Prof. English, Columbia University, since 1946.

CLIFT, DENISON HALLEY (May 2, 1885–); b. San Francisco, Calif. Novelist, playwright. *The Woman Disputed* (prod. 1926); *Guns of Galt* (1927); *Scotland Yard* (prod. 1929); *Man About Town* (1932); *A Spy in the Room* (1944); *The White Terror of the Atlantic* (1954); etc.

CLIFTON, WILLIAM (1772–Dec., 1799); b. Philadelphia, Pa. Poet. *Poems, Chiefly Occasional* (1800); etc.

CLINCH, CHARLES POWELL (Oct. 20, 1797–Dec. 16, 1880); b. New York. Drama critic, playwright. *The Expelled Collegians* (prod. 1822); *The First of May in New York* (prod. 1830).

CLINCHY, EVERETT ROSS (Dec. 16, 1896–); b. New York. Author. *All in the Name of God* (1934); *The World We Want to Live in* (1942); *A Handbook on Human Relations* (1949); etc.

CLINCHY, RUSSELL JAMES (Dec. 26, 1893–); b. New York. Presbyterian clergyman, author. *A Reasonable Faith* (1936); *Human Rights and the United Nations* (1952).

CLINTON, DE WITT (Mar. 2, 1769–Feb. 11, 1828); b. Little Britain, N.Y. Governor, philanthropist, author. *The Life and Writings of De Witt Clinton,* ed. by William W. Campbell (1849); *A Memoir on the Antiquities of the Western Parts of the State of New York* (1818); *Letter on the Natural History and Internal Resources of the State of New York* (1822); etc. Governor of New York, 1817–22, 1825–28. *See* David Hosack's *Memoir of De Witt Clinton* (1829); James Renwick's *Life of De Witt Clinton* (1840); Howard L. McBain's *De Witt Clinton and the Origin of the Spoils System in New York* (1907).

Clinton, Jeff. Pen name of Jack Miles Bickham.

Clinton Bradshaw; or, The Adventures of a Lawyer. Novel by Frederick William Thomas, 2v. (1835). In the manner of Bulwer-Lytton.

Cliosophic Society, The. Literary society at Princeton University. Founded 1770, by William Paterson, Oliver Ellsworth, Luther Martin, Tapping Reeve, Robert Ogden, and others. *See* Charles Richard Williams's *The Cliosophic Society* (1916).

CLOETE, STUART (July 23, 1897–); b. Paris. Author. *Turning Wheels* (1937); *Watch for the Dawn* (1939); *Yesterday Is Dead* (1940); *The Hill of Doves* (1941); *Congo Song* (1943);

Curve and the Tusk (1952); *The African Giant* (1955); *Mamba* (1956); *The Mask* (1957); *Gazella* (1958); *The Soldier's Peaches and Other African Stories* (1959); *Fiercest Heart* (1960); *West With the Sun* (1962); *The Looking Glass* (1963); *Rags of Glory* (1963); *South Africa, Land and People* (1968); etc.

Close, Upton. Pen name of Josef Washington Hall.

CLOUD, ARTHUR DAVID (May 4, 1884–Sept. 2, 1966); b. Carroll, Ia. Publisher, author. *Pensions in Modern Industry* (1930); *The Song of the Hammer and Nail* (1940). Under pen name "George Reeder": *Lewd Moon: A Narrative in Rhythm* (1947). Founder and publisher, *Industrial Medicine,* since 1932.

CLOUD, VIRGINIA WOODWARD (deceased); b. Baltimore, Md. Poet. *Down Durley Lane, and Other Ballads* (1898); *A Reed by the River* (1902); *Candlelight* (1924).

CLOUGH, SHEPARD BANCROFT (Dec. 6, 1901–); b. Bloomington, Ind. Historian. *A Century of American Life Insurance* (1946); *Rise and Fall of Civilization* (1951); *Economic History of Western Civilization* (1959); *Basic Values of Western Civilization* (1960); *The Economic History of Modern Italy* (1964); etc. Prof. history, Columbia University, since 1937.

CLOVER, SAMUEL TRAVERS (Aug. 13, 1859–May 28, 1934); b. London, England. Journalist, author. *Paul Travers' Adventures* (1897); *Glimpses Across the Sea* (1900); *On Special Assignment* (1903); *A Pioneer Heritage* (1932); *King Hal's Fifth Wife* (1933); etc.

Clovernook Children. By Alice Cary (1855). Book for young readers. Distinct from her prose works *Clovernook,* 2v. (1852–53).

CLURMAN, HAROLD [Edgar] (Sept. 18, 1901–); b. New York. Stage director, author. *The Fervent Years: The Story of the Group Theatre* (1945); *Lies Like Truth* (1958). Drama critic, *The Nation,* since 1953.

CLUTE, WILLARD NELSON (Feb. 26, 1869–Mar. 7, 1950); b. Painted Post, N.Y. Educator, botanist, author: *Botanical Essays* (1929); *Swamp and Dune* (1931); *Off the Record* (1935); *Our Ferns, Their Haunts, Habits, and Folklore* (1938); etc.

Clyde, Kit. Pen name of Luis Philip Senarens.

CLYDE, PAUL HIBBERT (Oct. 27, 1896–); b. Victoria, B.C. Historian. *The Far East: A History of the Impact of the West on Eastern Asia* (1948); etc. Editor: *United States Policy Toward China* (1940). Prof. history, Duke University, since 1941.

CLYMER, R[euben] SWINBURNE (Nov. 25, 1878–); b. Quakertown, Pa. Physician, author. *Initiates and the People,* 5v. (1928); *Natura Physician* (1933); *Interpretation of St. Matthew,* 2v. (1945); *Divine Law* (1949); *Prenatal Culture* (1950); *The Mysteries of Osiris* (1951); *Interpretation of St. John* (1953); *Philosophic Initiation* (1955); *The Age of Treason* (1957); *The Science of Spiritual Alchemy* (1959); *Nature's Healing Agents* (1963).

Coastlines. Literary Magazine. Hollywood, Cal. Triannual. Founded 1955. Devoted to poetry, fiction, articles, reviews. Edited by Gene Frumkin.

COATES, FLORENCE EARLE (July 1, 1850–Apr. 6, 1927); b. Philadelphia Pa. Poet. *Poems* (1898); *Mine and Thine* (1904); *Lyrics of Life* (1909); *The Unconquered Air, and Other Poems* (1912); *Poems,* 2v. (1916).

COATES, GRACE STONE (May 20, 1881–); b. Ruby, Kan. Poet. *Black Cherries* (1931); *Mead and Mangel-Wurzel* (poems, 1932); *Portulacas in the Wheat* (poems, 1933).

COATES, HENRY TROTH (Sept. 29, 1843–Jan. 22, 1910); b. Philadelphia, Pa. Publisher. Editor: *Fireside Encyclopedia of Poetry* (1878); *Children's Book of Poetry* (1879). Joined Davis, Porter & Co., 1868, to form Davis, Porter & Coates; later Porter & Coates; and finally Henry T. Coates & Co.

COATES, ROBERT M[yron] (Apr. 6, 1897–); b. New Haven, Conn. Author. *The Eater of Darkness* (1929); *The Outlaw Years* (1930); *Yesterday's Burdens* (1933); *All the Year Round* (1943); *The Bitter Season* (1946); *Wisteria Cottage* (1948); *The Farther Shore* (1955); *The Hour After Westerly* (1957); *View From Here* (1960); *Beyond the Alps* (1961); *South of Rome* (1965); etc.

COATSWORTH, ELIZABETH (Mrs. Henry Beston) (May 31, 1893–); b. Buffalo, N.Y. Poet, author of children's books. *Fox Footprints* (poems, 1923); *Atlas and Beyond* (poems, 1924); *Compass Rose* (poems, 1929); *The Cat Who Went to Heaven* (1930); *The Cat and the Captain* (1930); *The Golden Horseshoe* (1936); *Here I Stay* (1938); *The Littlest House* (1940); *A Toast to the King* (1940); *Maine Ways* (1947); *The Creaking Stair* (poems, 1949); *The Enchanted* (1951); *Horses, Dogs and Cats* (1957); *The White Room* (1958); *The Cave* (1958); *The Noble Doll* (1961); *Desert Dan* (1960); *Ronnie and the Chief's Son* (1962); *The Princess and the Lion* (1963); *Jon the Unlucky* (1964); *The Place* (1966); *George and Red* (1969); etc.

COBB, BERTHA B[rowning] (Mrs. Ernest Cobb) (Oct. 23, 1867–1951); b. Waltham, Mass. Author (with husband): the *Metcalf Readers,* 3 series (1909); *Who Knows?* (1924); *Dan's Boy* (1925); *André* (1930); *Robin* (1933); *Adam Lee* (1938); *The Mind's Eye* (with M. W. Cobb, 1941); *American Eagle* (with others, 1944); *Clematis* (1955); etc.

COBB, ERNEST (Dec. 3, 1877–Nov. 18, 1964); b. Newton Upper Falls, Mass. Author (with wife, Bertha Browning Cobb): the *Metcalf Readers,* 3 series (1909); *Who Knows?* (1924); *Dan's Boy* (1925); *André* (1930); *Robin* (1933); *Adam Lee* (1938); *Clematis* (1955); etc.

COBB, FRANK IRVING (Aug. 6, 1869–Dec. 21, 1923); b. Shawnee Co., Kan. Editor. Editor, New York *World,* 1904–23. *See* J. L. Heaton's *Cobb of the World* (1924).

COBB, HUMPHREY (1899–Apr. 25, 1944); b. Florence, It. Author. *Paths of Glory* (1935).

COBB, IRVIN S[hrewsbury] (June 23, 1876–Mar. 10, 1944); b. Paducah, Ky. Humorist, storywriter, playwright. *Back Home* (1912); *Paths of Glory* (1915); *Old Judge Priest* (1915); *The Life of the Party* (1919); *A Plea for Old Cap Collier* (1921); *J. Poindexter, Colored* (1922); *Snake Doctor, and Other Stories* (1923); *Ladies and Gentlemen* (1927); *Judge Priest Turns Detective* (1936); *Azam* (1937); *Exit Laughing* (1941); *Roll Call* (1942); *Curtain Call* (1944); etc.

Cobb, John. Pen name of John C. Cooper, III.

COBB, JOSEPH BECKHAM (Apr. 11, 1819–Sept. 15, 1858); b. Lexington, Ga. Author. *The Creole* (1850); *Mississippi Scenes* (1851); *Leisure Labors* (1858).

COBB, STANWOOD (Nov. 6, 1881–); b. Newton, Mass. Educator, author. *The Real Turk* (1914); *The Essential Mysticism* (1918); *Simla: A Tale of Love* (poem, 1919); *The Wisdom of Wu Ming Fu* (1931); *Patterns in Jade of Wu Ming Fu* (1935); *Symbols of America* (verse, 1946); *What Is God?* (verse, 1955); *Islamic Contributions to Civilization* (1963); etc.

COBB, SYLVANUS (June 5, 1821–July 20, 1887); b. Waterville, Me. Story-writer. Pen names, "Austin C. Burdick" and "Walter B. Dunlap." *The Golden Eagle* (1850); *The Privateer of the Delaware* (1855); *The Patriot Cruiser* (1863); *The Smuggler of St. Malo* (1877); *Orion the Gold Beater* (1888); etc. He contributed many novelettes and short stories to the *New York Ledger. See* Ella W. Cobb's *A Memoir of Sylvanus Cobb, Jr.* (1891).

COBLENTZ, EDMOND DAVID (Sept. 30, 1882–Apr. 16, 1959); b. San Francisco, Calif. Editor. With *San Francisco Examiner,* 1907–13, 1919–27; editor, *New York American,* 1927–37; Sunday editor, *New York Journal and American,* from 1937.

COBLENTZ, STANTON A[rthur] (Aug. 24, 1896–); b. San Francisco, Calif. Critic, poet. *The Thinker, and Other Poems* (1922); *The Decline of Man* (1925); *The Lone Adventurer* (1927); *The Literary Revolution* (1927); *Shadows on a Wall* (1930); *The Enduring Flame* (1932); *Songs of the Redwoods* (1933); *The Pageant of Man* (1936); *Villains and Vigilantes* (1936); *Songs by the Wayside* (1938); *An Editor Looks at Poetry* (1947); *Garnered Sheaves* (1949); *Time's Travelers* (1952); *Under the Triple Suns* (1954); *Villians and Vigilantes* (1957); *The Long Road to Humanity* (1958); *The Swallowing Wilderness: The Life of A Frontiersman: James Ohio Pattie* (1961); *Lord of Tanerica* (1966); *The Poetry Circus* (1967); *The Pageant of the New World* (1968). Editor, *Wings; A Quarterly of Verse,* since 1933.

COBLENTZ, WILLIAM WEBER (Nov. 20, 1873–Sept. 15, 1962); b. North Lima, O. Physicist, author. *From the Life of a Researcher* (1951); *Man's Place in a Superphysical World* (1954).

COBURN, JOHN BOWEN (Sept. 27, 1914–); b. Danbury, Conn. Episcopal clergyman. *Prayer and Personal Religion* (1957); *Minister: Man-in-the-Middle* (1963); *Anne and the Sand Dobbies* (1964).

Coburn, Mrs. Fordyce. *See* Eleanor Hallowell Abbott.

Cobwebs from an Empty Skull. Collection of stories by Ambrose Bierce (1874).

COCHRAN, HAMILTON (Sept. 9, 1898–); b. Philadelphia, Pa. Author. *Rogue's Holiday* (1947); *Blockade Runners of the Confederacy* (1958); *Dram Tree* (1961); *Noted American Duels and Hostile Encounters* (1963); *Freebooters of the Red Sea* (1965).

COCHRAN, JACQUELINE (Mrs. Floyd B. Odlum), b. Pensacola, Fla. Aviator. *The Stars at Noon* (autobiography, 1954).

COCHRAN, JEAN CARTER (Nov. 24, 1876–); b. Mendham, N.J. Author. *The Rainbow in the Rain* (1912); *Foreign Magic* (1919); *The Bells of the Blue Pagoda* (1922); *Church Street* (1922); *World-wide Church* (1944); etc.

COCHRAN, THOMAS CHILDS (Apr. 29, 1902–); b. Brooklyn, N.Y. Educator, author. *Railroad Leaders, 1845–1890* (1953); *The Social Sciences in Historical Studies* (with others, 1954); *The American Business System* (1957); *The Puerto Rican Businessman* (1959); *A Basic History of American Business* (1959); *The Inner Revolution* (1965); *The Great Depression of World War II* (1968). Editor, *Journal of Economic History,* 1945–55. Prof. history, University of Pennsylvania, since 1950.

COCHRANE, WILLARD WESLEY (May 15, 1914–); b. Fresno, Cal. Economist. Author: *Economics of American Agriculture* (with W. W. Wilcox, 1951); *Economics of Consumption* (with Carolyn Bell, 1956); *Farm Prices—Myth and Reality* (1958); *The City Man's Guide to the Farm Problem* (1965); *The World Food Problem* (1969).

COCKE, ZITELLA (1831?–1929); b. in Perry Co., Ala. Poet. *A Doric Reed* (1895); *Cherokee Run, and Other Southern Poems* (1905); etc.

COCKRELL, MARIAN (Mar. 15, 1909–); b. Birmingham, Ala. Novelist. *Yesterday's Madness* (1943); *Lillian Harley* (1943); *Shadow Castle* (1945); *Something Between* (1946).

Cocktail Party, The. Verse play by T. S. Eliot (1950). Modern urbane English people suffering from the neuroses and frustrations of the age. A doctor serves as a mystical psychiatrist to help solve their problems.

CODER, SAMUEL MAXWELL (Mar. 25, 1902–); b. Straight, Pa. Presbyterian clergyman, educator. *Dobbie, Defender of Malta* (1946); etc. Editor in chief, Moody Press, 1946; dean of education, Moody Bible Institute, since 1947.

CODMAN, JOHN (Oct. 16, 1814–Apr. 6, 1900); b. Dorchester, Mass. Sea captain, author. *Sailors' Life and Sailors' Yarns* (under pen name, "Captain Ringbolt," 1847); *Ten Months in Brazil* (1867); *Winter Sketches From the Saddle* (1888); etc.

CODY, SHERWIN [Alpheus] (1868–Apr. 4, 1959); b. Cody's Mill, Mich. Author. *The Art of Short Story Writing* (1894); *How to Write Fiction* (1895); *In the Heart of the Hills* (1896); *How to Read and What to Read* (1905); *Poe—Man, Poet, and Creative Thinker* (1924); *The New Art of Writing and Speaking the English Language*, 6v. (1933); *Pocket Cyclopedia of Good English* (1940); *Coaching Children in English* (1944); *Greatest Stories, and How they Were Written* (ed., 1950).

CODY, WILLIAM FREDERICK (Feb. 26, 1846–Jan. 10, 1917); b. in Scott Co., Ia. Scout, showman, author. "Buffalo Bill." *The Adventures of Buffalo Bill* (1904); *Buffalo Bill's Own Story* (with last chapter by W. L. Visscher, 1917); *An Autobiography of Buffalo Bill* (1920); etc. The name "Buffalo Bill" was coined by Edward Zane Carroll Judson, who wrote dime novels and a play, *The Scouts of the Plains* (1872), based on Cody's exploits. Later Prentiss Ingraham became Cody's official biographer and publicist. "Buffalo Bill" became a favorite character in juvenile fiction and his exploits were followed by boy readers all over the world. See Courtney R. Cooper and Mrs. W. F. Cody's *Memories of Buffalo Bill* (1919); Richard J. Walsh's *The Making of Buffalo Bill* (1928); Edwin Sabin's *Buffalo Bill* (1914); Dixon Wecter's *The Hero in America* (1941).

COE, CHARLES FRANCIS (Nov. 25, 1890–Dec. 28, 1956); b. Buffalo, N.Y. Author. *Me . . . Gangster* (1927); *The River Pirate* (1927); *Swag* (1928); *Hooch* (1928); *The Law and the Profits* (1941); *Never a Dull Moment* (1944); *Pressure* (1951); *Ashes* (1952); etc.

COE, RICHARD LIVINGSTON (Nov. 8, 1916–); b. New York. Drama and film critic. Drama editor and film critic, Washington *Post,* since 1946.

Coeur d'Alene. Novel by Mary Hallock Foote (1894). Story of the Western mining camps.

COFFEY, EDWARD HOPE, JR. (July 14, 1896–Feb. 23, 1958); b. New Brighton, S.I., N.Y. Author. Wrote under name, "Edward Hope." *Manhattan Cocktail* (1929); *She Loves Me Not* (1933); *Spanish Omelet* (1937); etc.

COFFIN, CHARLES CARLETON (July 26, 1823–Mar. 2, 1896); b. Boscawen, N.Y. Correspondent, author. *My Days and Nights on the Battlefield* (1864); augmented (1887); *Four Years of Fighting* (1866); *The Boys of '76* (1876); *Abraham Lincoln* (1893); etc. Noted Civil War correspondent for the *Boston Journal,* under the pen name, "Carleton."

COFFIN, HENRY SLOANE (Jan. 5, 1877–Nov. 25, 1954); b. New York. Presbyterian clergyman, author. *The Creed of Jesus* (1907); *University Sermons* (1914); *The Meaning of the Cross* (1931); *God's Turn* (1934); *Religion Yesterday and Today* (1940); *The Public Worship of God* (1946); *God Confronts Man in History* (1947); *Joy in Believing* (1956); etc. President, Union Theological Seminary, 1926–45.

COFFIN, ROBERT BARRY (July 21, 1826–June 10, 1886); b. Hudson, N.Y. Journalist, author. Pen name, "Barry Gray." *My Married Life at Hillside* (1865); *Cakes and Ale at Woodbine* (1868); *Castles in the Air, and Other Phantasies* (1883); etc.

COFFIN, ROBERT P[eter] TRISTRAM (Mar. 18, 1892–Jan. 20, 1955); b. Brunswick, Me. Educator, biographer, essayist, poet. *Christchurch* (poems, 1924); *Book of Crowns and Cottages* (1925); *Golden Falcon* (poems, 1929); *Land, Storm*

Center of Stuart England (1930); *Portrait of an American* (1931); *The Duke of Buckingham* (1931); *Lost Paradise* (autobiography, 1934); *Red Sky in the Morning* (1935); *Strange Holiness* (1935, Pulitzer Prize for poetry, 1936); *John Dawn* (1936); *Kennebec, Cradle of Americans* (1937); *Saltwater Farm* (poems, 1937); *Maine Ballads* (1938); *New Poetry of New England: Frost and Robinson* (1938); *Collected Poems* (1939); *Captain Abby and Captain John* (1939); *Thomas-Thomas-Ancil-Thomas* (1941); *There Will Be Bread and Love* (1942); *Book of Uncles* (1942); *Primer for America* (1942); *Poems for a Son with Wings* (1945); *People Behave Like Ballads* (1946); *Yankee Coast* (1947); *Coast Calendar* (1949); *One-Horse Farm* (1949); *Maine Doings* (1950); *Apples by Ocean* (1950); etc.

COFFIN, ROBERT STEVENSON (July 14, 1797–May 7, 1827); b. Brunswick, Me., Poet. Pen name, "The Boston Bard." *The Life of the Boston Bard, Written by Himself* (1825); *Oriental Harp: Poems of the Boston Bard* (1826).

COFFIN, TRISTRAM (July 25, 1912–); b. Hood River. Ore. Author. *Missouri Compromise* (1947); *Your Washington* (1954); *The Sex Kick* (1966); *Senator Fulbright* (1966); etc.

COFFIN, TRISTRAM POTTER (Feb. 13, 1922–); b. San Marino, Cal. Educator, author. *British Traditional Ballad in North America* (1950); *An Analytical Index to the Journal of American Folklore* (1958); *Ancient Ballads, Traditionally Sung in New England*, Vol. I (with others, 1960). Editor: *Indian Tales of North America* (1961); *Folklore in America* (with Hennig Cohen, 1966); etc. Prof. English and folklore, University of Pennsylvania, since 1964.

COFFMAN, GEORGE RALEIGH (Oct. 22, 1880–Jan. 25, 1958); b. Ancona, Ill. Educator, author. *A New Theory Concerning the Origin of the Miracle Play* (1914). Editor: *A Book of Modern Plays* (1925); *Five Significant English Plays* (1930). English dept. University of North Carolina, 1930–51.

COFFMAN, LOTUS DELTA (Jan. 7, 1875–Sept. 22, 1938); b. Salem, Ind. Educator, author. *The State University: Its Work and Problems* (1934); etc. President, University of Minnesota, 1920–38.

COFFMAN, RAMON [Peyton] (July 24, 1896–); b. Indianapolis, Ind. Author. *The Age of Discovery* (1927); *Founding the Republic* (1931); *Uncle Ray's Story of the United States* (1934); *Famous Kings and Queens* (1947); etc. Founder *Uncle Ray's Magazine,* 1946; editor and publisher, 1946–55. Writer of daily syndicated feature called "Uncle Ray's Corner."

COGGESHALL, GEORGE (Nov. 2, 1784–Aug. 6, 1861); b. Milford, Conn. Sea captain, author. *Voyages to Various Parts of the World*, 2 series (1851–52); *History of the American Privateers and Letters-of-Marque* (1856); etc.

COGGESHALL, WILLIAM TURNER (Sept. 6, 1824–Aug. 2, 1867); b. Lewistown, Pa. Editor, diplomat, author. *Easy Warren and His Contemporaries* (1854); *Oakshaw; or, The Victims of Avarice* (1855); *The Protective Policy in Literature* (1859); *Stories of Frontier Adventure in the South and West* (1863); etc. Editor: *The Poets and Poetry of the West* (1860); See William H. Venable's *Beginnings of Literary Culture in the Ohio Valley* (1891).

COGSWELL, JOSEPH GREEN (Sept. 27, 1786–Nov. 26, 1871); b. Ipswich, Mass. Educator, librarian. Compiler: *Alphabetical Index of the Astor Library*, 5v. (1857–66). Editor, *New York Review,* 1839–42. Superintendent, the Astor Library, 1848–61. Founder (with George Bancroft), Round Hill School for boys, Northampton, Mass. See *Life of Joseph Green Cogswell as Sketched in His Letters,* ed; by Anna Eliot Ticknor (1874); Orie William Long's *Literary Pioneers* (1935); *See also* H. M. Lydenberg's *History of The New York Public Library* (1923).

COHAN, GEORGE M[ichael] (July 4, 1878–Nov. 5, 1942); b. Providence, R.I. Comedian, playwright. *Little Johnny*

Jones (prod. 1904); *The Yankee Prince* (prod. 1908); *The American Idea* (prod. 1908); *The Man Who Owns Broadway* (prod. 1908); *Forty-Five Minutes from Broadway* (prod. 1912); *Broadway Jones* (prod. 1912); *Madeleine and the Movies* (prod. 1922); *Little Nelly Kelly* (prod. 1922); *The Rise of Rosie O'Reilly* (prod. 1923); *The Song and Dance Man* (prod. 1923); *American Born* (prod. 1925); *Twenty Years on Broadway and the Years It Took to Get There* (1925); *The Baby Cyclone* (prod. 1927); *Merry Malones* (prod. 1927); *Gambling* (prod. 1929); *Pigeons and People* (prod. 1933); *Fulton of Oak Falls* (prod. 1937); etc.

COHANE, TIM (Feb. 7, 1912–   ); b. New Haven, Conn. Editor, author. *Gridiron Grenadiers, The Story of West Point Football* (1948); *The Yale Football Story* (1951); *Bypaths to Glory* (1963); *You'll Have to Pay the Price* (with Earl H. Blaik, 1960). Sports editor, *Look*, 1944–66; editor *Sunrise*, since 1966.

COHEN, ALFRED J. (May 14, 1861–May 21, 1928); b. Birmingham, England. Drama critic, novelist. Pen name, "Alan Dale." *Familiar Chats with the Queens of the Stage* (1890); *His Own Image* (1899); *A Girl Who Wrote* (1902); *The Madonna of the Future* (1918); etc. Drama critic, New York *Evening World*, 1887–95; New York *Journal*, 1895–1913; New York *American*, 1913–21.

COHEN, BERNARD CECIL (Feb. 22, 1926–); b. Northampton, Mass. Political scientist, author. *The Political Process and Foreign Policy* (1957); *The Press and Foreign Policy* (1963). Editor: *Foreign Policy in American Government* (1965). Prof. political science, University of Wisconsin, since 1963.

COHEN, HELEN LOUISE (Mrs. Willian Roswell Stockwell) Mar. 17, 1882–); b. New York. Educator, author. *The Ballade* (1915); *American English*, 4v. (with others, 1939); *Milestones of the Drama* (1940); etc. Editor: *One-Act Plays by Modern Authors* (1921); *Longer Plays by Modern Authors* (1922); etc.

COHEN, HENNIG (Aug. 1919–   ); b. Darlington, S.C. Educator, author. *The South Carolina Gazette* (1953). Editor: *The Battle Pieces of Herman Melville* (1963); *Humor of the Old Southwest* (1964); *Selected Poems of Herman Melville* (with William Dillingham, 1964); *Folklore in America* (with Tristram P. Coffin, 1966). Prof. English, University of Pennsylvania, since 1965.

COHEN, I. BERNARD (Mar. 1, 1914–); b. Far Rockaway, N.Y. Educator, author. *Benjamin Franklin's Experiments* (1941); *Science, Servant of Man* (1948); *Some Early Tools of American Science* (1950); *Benjamin Franklin: His Contribution to the American Tradition* (1953); *Issac Newton's Papers on Natural Philosophy* (ed., 1957); *Birth of a New Physics* (1960); etc. Editor: *Science before Darwin* (with Howard M. Jones, 1963). Editor, *Isis*, 1953–58. Prof. history of science, Harvard University, since 1959.

COHEN, JULIUS (Oct. 27, 1910–); b. New York. Educator. *Materials and Problems on Legislation* (1949); *Parental Authority: The Community and the Law* (with others, 1958); *The Law School of Tomorrow* (1968). Prof. law, University of Nebraska, 1946–57; Rutgers Law School, since 1957.

COHEN, LESTER (Aug. 17, 1901–July 17, 1963); b. Chicago, Ill. Author. *Sweepings* (1926); *The Great Bear* (1927); *Oscar Wilde* (play, 1928); *Two Worlds* (1936); *Billy Mitchell* (with Emile Gauvreau, 1942); *Coming Home* (1945); *Mom and Pop* (1963); *The New York Graphic* (1964). Motion picture scenarist: *Of Human Bondage*, etc.

COHEN, MORRIS RAPHAEL (July 25, 1880–Jan. 29, 1947); b. Minsk, Rus. Educator, philosopher. *Reason and Nature* (1931); *Law and Social Order* (1933); *Preface to Logic* (1944); *Faith of a Liberal* (1945); *A Dreamer's Journey* (autobiography, 1949); etc. Co-author, *Cambridge History of American Literature*, Vol. 33 (1922); etc. Prof. philosophy,

College of the City of New York, 1912–38, University of Chicago, from 1938.

COHEN, OCTAVUS ROY (June 26, 1891–Jan. 6, 1959); b. Charleston, S. C. Story-writer. *Polished Ebony* (1919); *Highly Colored* (1921); *Assorted Chocolates* (1922); *Epic Peters* (1930); *Carbon Copies* (1933); *East of Broadway* (1938); *Florian Slappey* (1938); *Romance in Crimson* (1940); *Sound of Revelry* (1943); *Danger in Paradise* (1945); *My Love Wears Black* (1948); *Borrasca* (1950); *Love Can Be Dangerous* (1955); etc.

COHEN, SEYMOUR JAY (Jan. 30, 1922–   ); b. New York. Rabbi, author. *Judaism and the Worlds of Business and Labor* (1961); *Negro-Jewish Dialogue* (1963); *Religious Freedom and the Constitution* (1963).

COHN, DAVID LEWIS (1896–Sept. 12, 1960). Author. *The Good Old Days* (1940); *New Orleans and Its Living Past* (1941); *Love in America* (1943); *Where I was Born and Raised* (1948); *The Life and Times of King Cotton* (1956); *The Fabulous Democrats* (1956).

COHON, SAMUEL SOLOMON (Mar. 22, 1888–Aug. 22, 1959); b. Lohi, Rus. Educator, author. *Christianity and Judaism Compare Notes* (with H. F. Rail, 1927); *What We Jews Believe* (1931); *Authority in Judaism* (1936); *Judaism—A Way of Life* (1948); etc. Prof. Jewish theology, Hebrew Union College, 1923–56.

COIT, DOROTHY (Sept. 25, 1889–); b. Salem, Mass. Drama coach, playwright. *The Ivory Throne of Persia* (1929); *Kai Khosru and Other Plays for Children* (1934).

COIT, MARGARET LOUISE, b. Norwich, Conn. Author. *John C. Calhoun: American Portrait* (1950; Pulitzer Prize for biography, 1951); *Mr. Baruch* (1957); *The Fight For Union* (1961); *The Sweep Westward* (1963); *Andrew Jackson* (1965); *Massachusetts* (1968).

Cokesbury Press. *See* Methodist Book Concern.

COLBRON, GRACE ISABEL (d. Sept. 8, 1948); b. New York City. Author. *The Love That Blinds* (with Clayton Hamilton, 1906); *The Man With the Black Cord* (with Augusta Groner, 1911); *The Lady in Blue* (with same, 1922); etc. Translator of many works by Scandinavian and German authors.

COLBY, ANITA (Aug. 5, 1914–); b. Washington, D.C. Editor, author. *Anita Colby's Beauty Book* (1952). Pres. and editor, Women's News Service, 1956–61.

COLBY, ELBRIDGE (Oct. 4, 1891–); b. New York. Army officer, educator, author. *The Echo Device in Literature* (1920); *English Catholic Poets* (1936); and books on military science. Editor, *The Life of Thomas Holcroft, Written by Himself*, 2v. (1925).

COLBY, FRANK MOORE (Feb. 10, 1865–Mar. 3, 1925); b. Washington, D.C. Encyclopedist, author. *Imaginary Obligations* (1904); *Constrained Attitudes* (1910); *The Margin of Hesitation* (1921). Editor: *The International Year Book*, 5v. (1899–1903); *The New International Encyclopedia*, 1900–1925; *Nelson's Encyclopedia*, 12v. (1906–07); etc.

COLBY, MERLE ESTES (Dec. 3, 1902–); b. Lodi, Wis. Author. *All Ye People* (1931); *New Road* (1933); *Brown Rifle* (1934); *A Guide to Alaska* (1939); *Alaska: A Profile, with Pictures* (1940); *The Big Secret* (1949); etc. From 1937, successively editor, Massachusetts Writers' Project, Federal Writers' Project, and in other federal departments.

COLBY, NATHALIE SEDGWICK (Feb. 4, 1875–June 10, 1942); b. New York. Novelist. *Green Forest* (1927); *Black Stream* (1927); *A Man Can Build a House* (1928); *For Life* (1936); *Glass Houses* (1937); *An American Life* (1937); *Remembering* (autobiography, 1938).

COLCORD, LINCOLN [Ross] (Aug. 14, 1883–Nov. 16, 1947); b. at sea, off Cape Horn. Novelist, poet. *The Drifting Diamond* (1912); *The Game of Life and Death* (1914); *Vision of War* (poem, 1915); *An Instrument of the Gods* (1922); *Sailing Days on the Penobscot* (with George Wasson, 1932). Assoc. editor, *The Nation,* 1919–20.

COLDEN, CADWALLADER (Feb. 7, 1688–Sept. 28, 1776); b. in Ireland, of Scots parentage. Historian, pamphleteer. *The History of the Five Indian Nations Depending on the Province of New York in America* (1727). See *The Life and Papers of Cadwallader Colden,* 9v. (1918–1937).

COLE, CHARLES WOOLSEY (Feb. 8, 1906–); b. Montclair, N.J. Educator. *French Mercantilist Doctrines Before Colbert* (1931); *Colbert and a Century of French Mercantilism,* 2v. (1939); *Economic History of Europe* (with S. B. Clough, 1941); *French Mercantilism, 1683–1700* (1943); *History of Europe* (with others, 1949). Pres., Amherst College, 1946–60.

COLE, CYRENUS (Jan. 13, 1863–Nov. 14, 1939); b. Pella, Ia. Editor, author. *Anna Marcella's Book of Verses* (1912); *I Remember, I Remember: A Book of Recollections* (1936); *I Am a Man: The Indian Black Hawk* (1938); etc.

COLE, FAY-COOPER (Aug. 8, 1881–Sept. 3, 1961); b. Plainwell, Mich. Anthropologist, author. *The Long Road* (1933); *The Story of Man* (with wife, Mabel Cook Cole, 1937); *Kincaid—A Prehistoric Illinois Metropolis* (1951); *The Bukidnon* (1955); etc.

COLE, LOIS DWIGHT (Mrs. Turney Allan Taylor), b. New York. Editor, author. Writes under pen names "Allan Dwight," "Nancy Dudley," "Anne Lattin," "Lynn Avery." *Spaniard's Mark* (1932); *Drums in the Forest* (1936); *Kentucky Cargo* (1938); *Linda Goes to the Hospital* (1954); *The Silver Dagger* (1959); *Cappy and the River* (1960); etc.

COLE, MABEL COOK (Mrs. Fay-Cooper Cole); b. Plano, Ill. Author. *Philippine Folk Tales* (1916); *Savage Gentlemen* (1929); *The Story of Man* (with husband, 1937).

COLE, THOMAS (Feb. 1, 1801–Feb. 11, 1848); b. England. Painter, poet. See *Life and Works of Thomas Cole,* ed. by Louis L. Noble (1856).

COLE, WILLIAM EARLE (July 28, 1904–); b. Crandull, Tenn. Educator, author. *Teaching of Biology* (1934); *Recent Trends in Rural Planning* (1937); *Tennessee: A Political Study* (with William H. Combs, 1940); *A Sociology in Educational Practice* (with Clyde B. Moore, 1952); *Urban Society* (1958); *Introductory Sociology* (1962); *High School Sociology: A Study in Social and Human Relations* (1963); *Social Problems: A Sociological Interpretation* (1965); *Social Foundations of Education* (1968); etc. Prof. sociology, University of Tennessee, since 1936.

COLEAN, MILES LANIER (Aug. 4, 1898–); b. Peoria, Ill. Consulting economist. *American Housing: Problems and Prospects* (1944); *Impact of Government on Real Estate Finance in the United States* (1950); *Renewing Our Cities* (1953); *Mortgage Companies* (1962); etc.

COLEGROVE, KENNETH WALLACE (Oct. 8, 1886–); b. Waukon, Ia. Educator. *The American Senate and World Peace* (1944); *Democracy versus Communism* (1957); *The Menace of Communism* (1962). Prof. political science, Northwestern University, 1926–52; Long Island University, since 1959. Assoc. editor, *Modern Age,* since 1959.

COLEMAN, CHRISTOPHER BUSH (Apr. 24, 1875–June 25, 1944); b. Springfield, Ill. Librarian, historian. *Constantine the Great* (1914); *Indiana* (1929); *The United States at War* (1943); etc. Director, Indiana Historical Collections, from 1924; director, Indiana State Library, 1936–42.

COLEMAN, EDWARD DAVIDSON (Aug. 15, 1891–Sept. 3, 1939); b. Suwalki, Lithuania. Librarian, bibliographer. *The Bible in English Drama* (1931); *Plays of Jewish Interest on the American Stage* (1934); *The Jew in English Drama* (1939); etc. Librarian, American Jewish Historical Society, 1931–39.

COLEMAN, JOHN WINSTON, JR. (Nov. 5, 1898–); b. Lexington, Ky. Tobacco planter, author. *Masonry in the Blue Grass* (1933); *Stage-Coach Days in the Blue Grass* (1935); *Lexington During the Civil War* (1938); *Slavery Times in Kentucky* (1940); *Famous Kentucky Duels* (1953); *The Springs of Kentucky* (1955); *Historic Kentucky* (1967); etc.

COLEMAN, LAURENCE VAIL (Sept. 19, 1893–); b. Brooklyn, N.Y. Educator. *Manual for Small Museums* (1927); *Museums in South America* (1929); *Historic House Museums* (1933); *The Museums in America,* 3v. (1939); *College and University Museums* (1942); *Company Museums* (1943); *Museum Buildings,* Vol. I (1950). Director, American Association of Museums, 1927–59.

COLEMAN, LONNIE [William Laurence] (Aug. 2, 1920–); b. Bartow, Ga. Author. *Hellcat Hattie and Kingdom Come* (prod. 1942); *Escape the Thunder* (1944); *The Animals in the Zoo* (1950); *Clara* (1952); *Southern Lady* (1958); *Sam* (1959); *The Golden Vanity* (1962); *King* (1967).

COLEMAN, ROY V. (July 21, 1885–); b. Oneida, Kan. Editor, author. *Roger Ludlow in Chancery* (1934); *The Old Patent of Connecticut* (1936); *The First Frontier* (1948); *Liberty and Property* (1951); etc. Managing editor: *Dictionary of American History,* 6v. (1940). With Charles Scribner's Sons, from 1911.

COLEMAN, WILLIAM (Feb. 14, 1766–July 14, 1829); b. Boston, Mass. Federalist journalist, author. *A Collection of the Facts and Documents, Relative to the Death of Major-General Alexander Hamilton* (1804). Editor and proprietor, New York *Evening Post,* 1801–29.

COLES, ABRAHAM (Dec. 26, 1813–May 3, 1891); b. Scotch Plains, N.J. Physician, poet. *Old Gems in New Settings* (1866); *The Evangel in Verse* (1874); *The Light of the World* (1884); etc.

COLES, ROBERT (Oct. 12, 1929–   ); b. Boston, Mass. Research psychiatrist, author. *Children of Crisis* (1967); *Dead End School* (1968); *The Grass Pipe* (1969); *Erik H. Erikson: The Growth of His Work* (1970).

Collected Sonnets. By Edna St. Vincent Millay (1941).

Collections, Historical and Miscellaneous, and Monthly Literary Journal. Concord, N.H. Founded 1822, by John Farmer and Jacob Bailey Moore, as bi-monthly, *Collections, Topographical, Historical, and Biographical, Relating Principally to New Hampshire.* Name changed 1823. Expired 1824.

Collector, The. New York. Magazine. Founded 1887. Edited by Walter R. Benjamin and Mary A. Benjamin. Devoted chiefly to autograph collecting and historical material.

College English. Champaign, Ill. Monthly, October through May. Founded 1939. Published by the National Council of Teachers of English.

College Humor. New York. Monthly. Founded 1920. At first made up chiefly of jokes and short stories reprinted from college humorous magazines; but later containing much original fiction portraying college life.

College Names: Their Origin and Significance. By Albert Keiser (1940).

COLLENS, THOMAS WHARTON (June 23, 1812–Nov. 3, 1879); b. New Orleans, La. Jurist, sociologist, poet, playwright. *The Martyr Patriots; or, Louisiana in 1769* (drama in verse, prod. 1836); *Humanics* (1860); *The Eden of Labor; or, The Christian Utopia* (1876).

COLLIER, JOHN (May 4, 1884–d.); b. Atlanta, Ga. Commissioner Indian Affairs, poet. *The Indwelling Splendor*

(1911); *Harp of the Human* (1913); *Shadows Which Haunt the Sun-Rain* (1917); *Indians of the Americas* (1947); *Patterns and Ceremonials of the Indian of the Southwest* (1949); *Understanding Minority Groups* (with others, 1956); *From Every Zenith* (1963); etc. Editor, *American Indian Life*, 1926–33.

COLLIER, PETER FENELON (Dec. 12, 1849–Apr. 24, 1909); b. Myshall, Co. Carlow, Ireland. Publisher. Established firm around 1877, and published the works of Dickens and Shakespeare. He also published a number of encyclopedias. In 1888 he founded the magazine *Once a Week* which in 1896 became *Collier's Weekly*. A son, Robert Joseph Collier (June 17, 1876–Nov. 9, 1918) became the head of the magazine and its editor following the death of the founder in 1909.

COLLIER, PRICE (May 25, 1860–Nov. 3, 1913); b. Davenport, Ia. Unitarian clergyman, critic. *Mr. Picket Pin and His Friends* (1894); *America and the Americans from a French Point of View* (anon., 1897); *England and the English from an American Point of View* (1909); *The West on the East from an American Point of View* (1911); *Germany and the Germans from an American Point of View* (1913); etc.

COLLIER, THOMAS STEPHENS (1842–1893); b. New York City. Soldier, poet. *Song Spray* (1889).

Collier's. New York. Founded 1888, by Peter Fenelon Collier, as *Once a Week*. Name changed to *Collier's Weekly*, 1896, and later to *Collier's*. Early editors included Norman Hapgood, Mark Sullivan, and F. P. Dunne. After World War I it became less active as an organ of influential opinion and featured mostly fiction, topical popular articles, and cartoons. Before it suspended publication in 1957, it had attained a circulation of 2,500,000.

Collier's Encyclopedia. Edited by William T. Couch, 20v. (1953). Published by P. F. Collier & Son. A comprehensive encyclopedia in easily readable format, originally copyrighted 1949–50. Bibliographies are arranged by subject in Vol. XX. A yearbook is annually issued.

COLLINGS, KENNETH BROWN (Sept. 22, 1898–); b. Lincoln, Neb. Author. *With Allenby in the Holy Land* (with L. J. Thomas, 1938); *Just for the Hell of It* (1938); *These Things I Saw* (1939).

COLLINS, CHARLES WALLACE (Apr. 4, 1879–); b. Gallion, Ala. Lawyer, author. *Whither Solid South?* (1948); *The Race Integration Cases* (1954).

COLLINS, CHARLES WILLIAM (Nov. 19, 1880–Mar. 3, 1964); b. Madison, Ind. Drama critic. *Great Love Stories of the Theatre* (1911); *The Sins of St. Anthony: Tales of the Theatre* (1925); *The Dark Island* (with Gene Markey, 1928). Dramatic critic *Chicago Tribune*, 1930–38; editor, "A Line o' Type or Two" column in the *Chicago Tribune*, 1938–51.

COLLINS, CLELLA REEVES (May 23, 1893–); b. Omaha, Neb. Author. *Woman's Handbook of Financial Facts* (1928); *Women and Their Money* (1929); *Army Woman's Handbook* (1942); *Navy Woman's Handbook* (1943); *When Your Son Goes to War* (1943); etc.

COLLINS, FRANCIS ARNOLD (June 6, 1873–1957); b. Newark, N.J. Author. *The Air Man, His Conquests in Peace and War* (1917); *Naval Heroes of Today* (1918); *Sentinels Along Our Coast* (1922); *Mountain Climbing* (1923); etc.

COLLINS, FREDERICK LEWIS (Mar. 23, 1883–July 25, 1950); b. Lawrence, Mass. Author. *This King Business* (1923); *Our American Kings* (1924); *The Christman Trail* (1928); *Glamorous Sinners* (1932); *The F.B.I. in Peace and War* (1943); *Homicide Squad* (1944); *Money Town* (1946); and various *Travelcharts and Travel Chats*. Editor, *Woman's Home Companion*, 1906–10; *McClure's Magazine*, 1913–20.

COLLINS, HENRY B[ascom] (Apr. 9, 1899–); b. Geneva, Ala. Anthropologist. *Prehistoric Art of the Alaskan Eskimo* (1929); *The Aleutian Islands, Their People and Natural History* (with others, 1946). Editor: *Science in Alaska* (1952).

COLLINS, HERMAN L[eroy] (1865–Oct. 7, 1940); b. Hepburn, Pa. Journalist. Under the pen name "Girard" he conducted a column in the Philadelphia *Public Ledger,* the Philadelphia *Evening Telegraph,* and the Philadelphia *Inquirer* for many years, beginning in 1913.

COLLINS, JAMES DANIEL (July 12, 1917–); b. Holyoke, Mass. Educator, author. *The Existentialists* (1952); *The Mind of Kierkegaard* (1953); *The Lure of Wisdom* (1962); *The Emergence of Philosophy of Religion* (1967). Prof. philosophy, St. Louis University, since 1956.

COLLINS, JOSEPH (Sept. 22, 1866–); b. Brookfield, Conn. Physician, essayist. *The Doctor Looks at Literature* (1923); *Taking the Literary Pulse* (1924); *The Doctor Looks at Biography* (1925); *The Doctor Looks at Love and Life* (1942); etc.

COLLINS, LARRY (Sept. 14, 1929–); b. Hartford, Conn. Journalist, author. *Is Paris Burning?* (with Dominique La Pierre, 1965); *I'll Dress You in Mourning* (1967). Chief Paris Bureau, *Newsweek,* 1961–64.

Collins, Mrs. Seward. See Dorothea Brande.

COLLINS, VARNUM LANSING (Dec. 1, 1870–Oct. 9, 1936); b. in Hong Kong. Educator, librarian, author. *Princeton* (1912); *President Witherspoon,* 2v. (1925); etc. Reference librarian, Princeton University, 1896–1906; with Dept. Romance Languages, 1906–36.

COLLISON, WILSON (Nov. 5, 1893–May 24, 1941); b. Gloucester, O. Author. *Up in Mabel's Room* (with Otto Harbach, prod. 1919); *The Vagabond* (prod. 1923); *The Murder in the Brownstone House* (1929); *Diary of Death* (1930); *Shy Cinderella* (1932); *Congo Landing* (1934); *Begins with Murder* (1936); etc.

COLLYER, ROBERT (Dec. 8, 1823–Nov. 30, 1912); b. Keighley, England. Unitarian clergyman, poet, lecturer. *A Man in Earnest: Life of A. H. Conant* (1875); *Ilkley, Ancient and Modern* (1885); *Three Bits of Rhyme* (1900), which includes his well-known ballad "Under the Snow"; etc.

COLM, GERHARD (June 30, 1897–); b. Hanover, Ger. Economist. Author or co-author: *Economic Consequences of Recent American Tax Policy* (with Fritz Lehmann, 1938); *Who Pays the Taxes?* (1940); *The American Economy in 1960* (1952); *Essays in Public Finance and Fiscal Policy* (1955); *The Economy of the American People* (with others, 1958).

Colonel Carter of Cartersville. Novel by F. Hopkinson Smith (1891). A picture of the Old South as illustrated in the lives of a Virginia gentleman of the old school and his loyal Negro servant, Chad.

Colonel's Daughter, The. Novel by Charles King (1883). A story of army life in the West.

Colonial Mind, The. By Vernon Louis Parrington (1927). An analysis of the intellectual currents which shaped the character of American thought and institutions from the early days to the emergence of Jeffersonian democracy.

Colophon, The. New York. Planned by Elmer Adler in 1928, organized in 1929, and the first issue printed in 1930 by the Pynson Printers. Elmer Adler, Frederick B. Adams, Alfred Stanford, and John T. Winterich were editors. Fine printing and bibliography were featured. Rockwell Kent, T. M. Cleland, and others, designed the covers and embellishments. Ceased 1940. See *New Colophon.*

Colorado Quarterly. Boulder, Colo. Founded 1952. Publishes stories and poetry, scholarly articles, and humorous essays. Edited at the University of Colorado since 1953.

Colorado Review. Fort Collins, Colo. Quarterly of literature. Founded 1956 and discontinued 1960.

COLSON, ELIZABETH FLORENCE (June 15, 1917–); b. Hewitt, Minn. Anthropologist, author. *The Makah* (1953); *Marriage and the Family among the Plateau Tonga* (1958); *The Plateau Tonga* (1962); etc. Anthropology dept., University of California at Berkeley, since 1964.

COLTON, ARTHUR [Willis] (May 22, 1868–Dec. 28, 1943); b. Washington, Conn. Novelist, poet. *The Debatable Land* (1901); *The Delectable Mountains* (1901); *Port Argent* (1904); *The Cruise of the Violetta* (1906); *Harps Hung Up in Babylon* (poems, 1907).

COLTON, CALVIN (Sept. 14, 1789–Mar. 13, 1857); b. Longmeadow, Mass. Episcopal clergyman, journalist, educator, pamphleteer, biographer and editor of Henry Clay. *Tour of the American Lakes,* 2v. (1833); *Four Years in Great Britain* (1836); *The Junius Tracts* (1864); *The Life and Times of Henry Clay,* 2v. (1846); *The Last Seven Years of the Life of Henry Clay* (1856); etc. Editor: *The Private Correspondence of Henry Clay* (1855); *The Speeches of Henry Clay,* 2v. (1857). The Clay biographies and editions were republished as, *The Life, Correspondence, and Speeches of Henry Clay,* 6v. (1857). He also wrote many political pamphlets under the pen name "Junius." Prof. political economy, Trinity College, Hartford, Conn., 1852–57.

COLTON, GEORGE H[ooker] (Oct. 27, 1818–Dec. 1, 1847); b. Westford, N.Y. Editor, poet. *Tecumseh; or, The West Thirty Years Since* (poem, 1842). Founder, *The American Review,* 1844; editor, 1844–47. *See* E. A. Poe's *The Literati* (1850).

COLTON, WALTER (May 9, 1797–Jan. 22, 1851); b. in Rutland Co., Vt. Naval chaplain, journalist, author. *Ship and Shore* (1835); *A Visit to Constantinople and Athens* (1836); *Deck and Port; or, Incidents of a Cruise in the United States Frigate Congress to California* (1850); *Three Years in California, 1846–1849* (1850); *The Sea and the Sailor* (1851); etc. Co-founder (with Robert Semple), *The Californian,* the first newspaper in California, 1846.

COLUM, MARY M[aguire] (Mrs. Padraic Colum) (1887?–Oct. 22, 1957); b. Sligo, Ire. Critic. *From These Roots* (1937); *Life and the Dream* (1947); *Our Friend James Joyce* (with husband, 1958). Lit. critic, *Forum,* 1934–40; also many other periodicals.

COLUM, PADRAIC (Dec. 8, 1881–Jan. 11, 1972); b. Longford, Ireland. Editor, poet, playwright. *Wild Earth* (poems, 1907); *My Irish Year* (1912); *The King of Ireland's Son* (1916); *The Boy Who Knew What the Birds Said* (1918); *The Golden Fleece* (1921); *The Road Round Ireland* (1926); *The Fountain of Youth* (1927); *Poems* (1932); *The Legend of Saint Columba* (1935); *The Story of Lowry Maen* (poem, 1937); *Where the Winds Never Blew and the Cocks Never Crew* (1940); *The Frenzied Prince* (1943); *The Flying Swans* (1957); *Ourselves Alone! The Story of Arthur Griffith and the Origins of the Irish Free State* (1958); *Our Friend James Joyce* (with wife, Mary Colum, 1958). Editor: *Anthology of Irish Verse* (1922); *A Treasury of Irish Folklore* (1954); *Roofs of Gold* (1964); etc.

"Columbia, the Gem of the Ocean." Patriotic song. Originally written in 1842, as *Britannia, the Pride of the Ocean,* by Stephen Joseph Meany, with music by Thomas F. Williams. In 1876, Thomas à Becket set forth a claim that he had written and composed it for David T. Shaw in 1843. It is probable that Shaw gave a copy of the English song to Becket, who adapted it to American use.

Columbia Dictionary of Modern European Literature. Edited by Horatio Elwin Smith (1947). Articles by over two hundred specialists on major figures in modern literature.

Columbia Encyclopedia. Edited by William Bridgewater, lv. (1950). Published by Columbia University Press. A widely used thumb-indexed encyclopedia without illustrations. It is entirely devoted to facts, without opinions. Supplements are issued regularly.

Columbia Forum. New York. Quarterly. Founded 1957. Published by Columbia University Press. Contributors are former students, faculty members, or associates of the University. Sent out free to alumni and faculty. For financial reasons planned to discontinue publication in 1971.

Columbia Journalism Review. New York. Quarterly. Founded 1962. Published by Columbia University graduate School of Journalism.

Columbia Lippincott Gazeteer of the World. Edited by Leon E. Seltzer (1952). An entirely new compilation, the work of many scholars.

Columbia University Press. New York. Founded 1893. *The Columbia Encyclopedia* is one of its major achievements. Frank D. Fackenthal was chairman of the board; later Charles G. Proffitt became chairman and president.

"Columbiad, The." Narrative poem by Joel Barlow (1807). Part of it had appeared as "The Vision of Columbus" in 1787.

Columbian Centinel. Boston, Mass. Newspaper. Founded 1784. Known for its maritime news. Expired 1840.

Columbian Lady's and Gentleman's Magazine, The. New York. Monthly. Founded 1844, and published by Israel Post. John Inman, the editor, secured the literary lights of the day for his contributors. The magazine was illustrated with engravings and colored fashion plates. Expired 1849.

Columbian Magazine, or Monthly Miscellany, The. Philadelphia. Founded Sept. 1786, and edited by Mathew Carey, John Trenchard, T. Seddon, William Spotswood, and Charles Cist. Illustrated with fine copperplates by Trenchard. Francis Hopkinson and Alexander James Dallas were later editors. Charles Brockden Brown wrote for it his series of essays called the "Rhapsodist." In 1790 it was merged with the projected *Philadelphia Magazine and Universal Asylum,* and the name *Universal Asylum and Columbian Magazine* was adopted. Expired 1792.

Columbus Citizen-Journal. Columbus, O. Newspaper. Founded 1899, as *Columbus Citizen.* Charles Egger is editor. Jack Keller is book-review editor.

Columbus Dispatch. Columbus, O. Newspaper. Founded 1871. Osman C. Hooper was literary editor 1893–1917. Ernest Cady is present literary editor.

Column, The. New York literary club. Founded 1825.

COLVER, ALICE [Mary] ROSS (Mrs. Frederic B. Colver) (Aug. 28, 1892–); b. Plainfield, N.J. Author. The *Babs* series, 4v. (1917–20); the *Jeanne* series, 4v. (1920–24); *The Red-headed Goddess* (1929); *One Year of Love* (1937); *Kingsridge* (1949); *The Measure of the Years* (1954); *There Is a Season* (1957); *Where Goes the Heart* (1958); *Susan, Hospital Aide* (1964).

COLVER, ANNE (1908–). Author. *Theodosia, Daughter of Aaron Burr* (1941); *Mr. Lincoln's Wife* (1943); *Shamrock Cargo* (1952); *Yankee Doodle Painter* (1955); *Lucky Four* (1960); *Florence Nightingale, War Nurse* (1961); *Thomas Jefferson: Author of Independence* (1963); etc.

COLWELL, ERNEST CADMAN (Jan. 19, 1901–); b. Hallstead, Pa. Educator, author. *The Greek of the Fourth Gospel* (1931); *John Defends the Gospel* (1936); *The Study of the Bible* (1937); *An Approach to the Teaching of Jesus* (1947); *What Is the Best New Testament?* (1952); *The Gospel of the Spirit* (with E. L. Titus, 1953); *Jesus and the Gospel* (1963); *Reader-Grammar for New Testament Greek* (1965). Pres., Southern California School of Theology, since 1957.

Comanche, El. Pen name of W. S. Phillips.

COMDEN, BETTY (May 3, 1919); b. Brooklyn, N. Y. Playwright. Co-author with Adolph Green (q.v.) of musical comedy books and lyrics.

Come Back, Little Sheba. Play by William Inge (prod. 1950). A once-alcoholic chiropractor reverts to drink and tries to murder his wife. They are saved from disaster and try to reshape their lives meaningfully.

"Come Rally Round the Flag, My Boys." Song by B. D. Taylor. Music by William Clifton (1863).

COMFORT, WILL LEVINGTON (Jan. 17, 1878–Nov. 2, 1932); b. Kalamazoo, Mich. Editor, novelist. *Routledge Rides Alone* (1910); *Midstream: A Chronicle at Half-Way* (autobiography, 1914); *Son of Power* (1920); *Samadhi* (1927); etc. Editor, *The Glass Hive,* 1930–32.

COMFORT, WILLIAM WISTAR (May 27, 1874–Dec. 24, 1955); b. Germantown, Pa. Educator, author. *Just Among Friends* (1941); *Stephen Grellet: A Biography* (1942); *William Penn: A Tercentenary Estimate* (1944); *Quakers in the Modern World* (1949). Pres., Haverford College, 1917–40.

Comfort Me with Apples. Novel by Peter De Vries (1956). Replete with puns and explosively humorous incidents, this comic novel combines a kind of Gallic raciness with description of small-town American eccentricities.

Comic World, The. New York. Magazine. Formed 1876, by a merger of *Yankee Notions* (1852–75); *Nick Nax for All Creation* (1856–75); and *Merryman's Monthly* (1868–75). Expired 1879.

COMMAGER, HENRY STEELE (Oct. 25, 1902–); b. Pittsburgh, Pa. Educator, historian. *The Growth of the American Republic,* 2v. (with Samuel Eliot Morison, 1930); *Theodore Parker* (1936); *The Heritage of America* (with Allan Nevins, 1939); *America: The Story of a Free People* (with same, 1942); *The American Mind* (1951); *Living Ideas in America* (1952); *Freedom, Loyalty, Dissent* (1954); *The Great Declaration* (1958); *The Spirit of Seventy-Six,* 2v. (with R. B. Morris, 1958); *The Great Constitution* (1961); *Crusaders for Freedom* (1962); etc. Editor: *Documents of American History* (1934, 1940, 1950); *Tocqueville's Democracy in America* (1946); *A Saint Nicholas Anthology* (1948); *The Second Saint Nicholas Anthology* (1950); *Atlas of the Civil War* (1958); *Lester Frank Ward and the Welfare State* (1965); etc. Prof. history, Columbia University, 1939–56; Amherst College, since 1956.

"Commemoration Ode." Poem by James Russell Lowell (1865) on Abraham Lincoln.

"Commencement Poem." By Edward Rowland Sill. Delivered as a class poem at Yale 1861.

Commentary. New York. Monthly. Founded 1945. Published by the American Jewish Committee. Editor Elliot E. Cohen, 1945–1960; Norman Podhoretz, since 1960. Widely read by intellectuals and civic leaders of all faiths for its articles of opinion and analysis on cultural, social, literary, and political subjects. See *The Commentary Reader,* ed. by Norman Podhoretz (1966).

Commings, Robert. Pen name of Richard Gardner.

COMMINS, SAXE (1892?–1958). Editor. Editor or co-editor: Washington Irving's *Selected Writings* (1945); R. L. Stevenson's *Selected Writings* (1947); *The World's Great Thinkers,* 4v. (1947); etc. Editor, Random House.

Common Ground. Founded 1940. Published by the Common Council for American Unity. It expired in 1949.

Common Lot, The. Novel by Robert Herrick (1904). An architect sacrifices his professional integrity.

Common Sense. Political pamphlet by Tom Paine (1775). In demonstrating the economic basis for national policies, it had a profound influence on advancing the cause of the American Revolution.

Common Sense. Founded 1932 by Selden Rodman and Alfred M. Bingham. Devoted to liberal opinion on political, economic, and social affairs. Notable contributors were John Dos Passos, John Dewey, and Archibald MacLeish. Sold to *American Mercury* in 1946.

COMMONER, BARRY (May 28, 1917–   ); b. Brooklyn, N.Y. Educator, author. *Science and Survival* (1966). Chairman, botany dept., Washington University, St. Louis, since 1965.

Commoner, The. Lincoln, Neb. Weekly review. Founded 1901, by William Jennings Bryan. Expired 1923.

Commonweal. New York. Weekly review of Catholic opinion. Founded 1924, by Michael Williams, who became its editor. Its contributors include both Catholic writers and those of other faiths.

COMPTON, ARTHUR H[olly] (Sept. 10, 1892–Mar. 15, 1962); b. Wooster, O. Educator, physicist, author. *The Freedom of Man* (1935); *The Human Meaning of Science* (1940); *Atomic Quest* (1956); etc. Co-author: *On Going to College* (1940). Nobel Prize for physics, 1927. Prof. physics, University of Chicago, 1923–45; chancellor, Washington University, 1945–53.

Compton, Francis Snow. Pen name used by Henry Adams for his novel *Esther.*

COMPTON, KARL TAYLOR (Sept. 14, 1887–June 22, 1954); b. Wooster, O. Educator, physicist. President, Massachusetts Institute of Technology, 1930–48.

Compton's Pictured Encyclopedia. Edited by Charles A. Ford and others, 15v. (1953). An encyclopedia for children, originally issued in ten volumes in 1922. Encyclopedia Britannica, Inc., purchased it from F. E. Compton, Inc., in 1961.

"Comrades." Ode by Richard Hovey (1893), read at convention of Psi Upsilon fraternity.

COMSTOCK, ANTHONY (Mar. 7, 1844–Sept. 21, 1915); b. New Canaan, Conn. Reformer, author. *Frauds Exposed* (1880); *Traps for the Young* (1883); etc. As secretary of the New York Society for the Suppression of Vice, he imposed a rigid censorship on books and plays and prosecuted their authors. *See* Heywood Broun and Margaret Leech's *Anthony Comstock, Roundsman of the Lord* (1927).

COMSTOCK, HARRIET T[heresa] (1860–); b. Nichols, N.Y. Novelist. *Molly, the Drummer Boy* (1900); *The Queen's Hostage* (1907); *The Place Beyond the Winds* (1914); *The Shield of Silence* (1921); *Penelope's Web* (1928); *The Mark of Cain* (1935); *Long Way Back* (1941); *Terry* (1943); etc.

COMSTOCK, SARAH (d. Jan. 20, 1960); b. Athens, Pa. Novelist. *The Soddy* (1912); *Old Roads from the Heart of New York* (1915); *The Valley of Vision* (1919); *The Daughter of Helen Kent* (1921); *The Moon Is Made of Green Cheese* (1929); etc.

CONANT, CHARLES ARTHUR (July 2, 1861–July 5, 1915); Winchester, Mass. Journalist, economist, author. *The United States in the Orient* (1900); *Alexander Hamilton* (1901); etc.

CONANT, ISABEL [la Howe] FISKE (1874–); b. Wellesley, Mass. Poet. *A Field of Folk* (1903); *Songs Before Birth* (1912); *Sonnets and Lyrics* (1915); *Frontier* (1924); *Dream Again* (1929); *These Coloured Balls* (1931); *Aisle-Seat* (1937).

CONANT, JAMES BRYANT (Mar. 26, 1893–); b. Dorchester, Mass. Educator, chemist, author. *Our Fighting Faith* (1942); *On Understanding Science* (1947); *Education in a Divided World* (1948); *Science and Common Sense* (1951); *Modern Science and Modern Man* (1952); *Education and Liberty* (1953); *The Citadel of Learning* (1956); *Germany and Freedom* (1958); *The Child, the Parent, and the State* (1959); *Slums and Suburbs* (1961); *The Education of American Teachers* (1963); *Two Modes of Thought* (1964); *Shaping Educational Policy* (1964); *The Comprehensive High School* (1967); and books on chemistry. Pres. Harvard University, 1933–53; U.S. high commissioner, West Germany, 1953–55; ambassador, 1955–57.

CONANT, THOMAS JEFFERSON (Dec. 13, 1802–Apr. 30, 1891); b. Brandon, Mass. Educator, philologist. Translator of the Bible for the American Bible Union, and author of *The Laws of Translation.*

"Concord Hymn." Poem by Ralph Waldo Emerson (1837).

Concord School of Philosophy, The. Concord, Mass. Founded 1879, by Bronson Alcott. It became the center for the propagation of the transcendentalist philosophy as expounded by Emerson and others. See *Dial,* Brook Farm.

Concrete poetry. Poetry in which the graphic appearance or speech sounds of the linguistic signs assume the esthetic purpose of the poem. That is, the poem's intelligibility relies on its visual appearance or phonetic notation rather than on its paraphrasable content. The term was first used in the early 1950's for the work of certain Brazilian poets. Concrete verse began to appear in American periodicals and books in the mid-1960's in the work of Richard Kostelanetz, Aram Saroyan, Dick Higgins, Jonathan Williams, and Mary Ellen Solt. *See* Emmett Williams' *Concrete Poetry* (1969) and Jean-François Bory's *Once Again* (1970).

Condition of Man. By Lewis Mumford (1944). Third volume in the series begun by *Technics and Civilization* (1934) and continued in *Culture of Cities* (1938). Argues for a reinvigorated humanism in modern life.

CONDLIFFE, JOHN B[ell] (Dec. 23, 1891–); b. Melbourne, Australia. Educator. *The Commerce of Nations* (1950); *The Welfare State in New Zealand* (1959); *The Development of Australia* (1964); etc. Prof. economics, University of California, Berkeley, 1940–58.

CONDON, RICHARD. Novelist. *The Oldest Confession* (1958); *The Manchurian Candidate* (1959); *A Talent for Loving* (1961); *Some Angry Angel* (1961); *An Infinity of Mirrors* (1964); *And God Will Do* (1966); *The Ecstasy Business* (1967); *Mile High* (1969).

CONE, HELEN GRAY (Mar. 8, 1859–Jan. 31, 1934); b. New York City. Educator, poet. *Oberon and Puck: Verses Grave and Gay* (1885); *The Ride of the Lady, and Other Poems* (1891); *A Chant of Love for England, and Other Poems* (1915); *The Coat Without a Seam, and Other Poems* (1919); *Harvest Home* (1930); etc.

"Confederate Flag, The." Poem by Henry Lynden Flash.

Confederate Girl's Diary, A. By Sarah Morgan Dawson (Mrs. Francis Warrington Dawson), ed. by her son, Warrington Dawson (1913).

Confessions of Nat Turner, The. Historical novel by William Styron (1967). About the Negro leader of the Southampton Insurrection of 1831. *See* John Clarke's *William Styron's Nat Turner: Ten Writers Respond* (1968).

Confidence-Man, The. Unfinished novel by Herman Melville (1857). This was the last of the novels published during Melville's life.

Confidential Clerk, The. Play by T. S. Eliot (prod. 1953). Verse drama about a British financier who yearns to have a son. The theme is the impossibility of satisfying fully one's aspirations and the need to find contentment in one's limitations.

"Conflagration, The." Poem by Mather Byles (1755). Description of the Last Judgment.

CONFREY, [Joseph] BURTON (Feb. 1, 1898–); b. La Salle, Ill. Educator, author. *Catholic Action* (1935); *Moral Mission of Literature* (1939); *Method in Literature* (1939); etc.

CONGDON, CHARLES TABER (Apr. 7, 1821–Jan. 18, 1891); b. New Bedford, Mass. Editor, poet. *Flowers Plucked by a Traveller on the Journey of Life* (1840); *Tribune Essays* (1869); *Reminiscences of a Journalist* (1880); etc. Associated with Horace Greeley on the *New York Tribune,* 1857–82.

CONGDON, KIRBY (Nov. 13, 1924–   ); b. West Chester, Pa. *Iron Ark* (1962); *A Century of Progress* (1963); *Juggernaut* (1966); etc. Editor: *Magazine* (1964); *Magazine 2* (1965); *Magazine 3* (1966).

CONGER, GEORGE PERRIGO (May 18, 1884–Aug. 14, 1960); b. Genoa, N.Y. Educator, author. *A Course in Philosophy* (1924); *New Views of Evolution* (1929); *A World of Epitomizations* (1931); *The Horizons of Thought* (1933); *Ideologies of Religion* (1942); *Synoptic Naturalism* (1960); etc. Philosophy dept., University of Minnesota, since 1920.

Congo, and Other Poems, The. By Vachel Lindsay (1914).

"Congress, The." Anonymous loyalist poem of the American Revolution (1776).

Congressional Record. A report of the speeches in the Congress of the United States, created by an act of Congress in 1873. Its forerunner was the *Congressional Globe,* a report of congressional debates, 1833–73, the compilation of John Cook Rives and his son, Franklin Rives.

Coniston. Novel by Winston Churchill (1906). The dramatic story of rugged Jethro Bass, political boss of a small Vermont town. His thirst for political power wrecks his own love affair and changes the lives of several other characters.

CONKLE, ELLSWORTH PROUTY (1899–); b. Peru, Neb. Educator, playwright. *Crick Bottom Plays* (1928); *Loolie and Other Short Plays* (1935); *200 Were Chosen* (prod. 1936); *In the Shadow of a Rock* (1937); *Prologue to Glory* (prod. 1938); etc.

CONKLIN, EDMUND S[mith] (Apr. 19, 1884–Oct. 6, 1942); b. New Britain, Conn. Educator, psychologist, author. *Principles of Abnormal Psychology* (1927); *The Psychology of Religious Adjustment* (1929); *Principles of Adolescent Psychology* (1935); *Introductory Psychology for Students of Education* (with F. S. Freeman, 1939); etc. Prof. psychology, Indiana University, from 1934.

CONKLIN, GROFF (1904–); Author. *How to Run a Rental Library* (1934); *All About Subways* (1938). Editor: *The Best of Science Fiction* (1946); *The Treasury of Science Fiction* (1948); *The Big Book of Science Fiction* (1950); *Science-Fiction Adventures in Dimension* (1953); *Science-Fiction Adventures in Mutation* (1956); *Great Science Fiction about Doctors* (with N. D. Fabricant, 1963); etc.

CONKLIN, JENNIE M[aria] DRINKWATER (Mrs. Nathaniel Conklin) (Apr. 12, 1841–Apr. 28, 1900); b. Yarmouth, Me. Originator of the Shut-in Society, author. *Tessa Wadsworth's Discipline* (1879); *Electa* (1881); *Bek's First Corner* (1883); *The Fairfax Girls* (1886); *Marigold* (1889); etc.

CONKLING, GRACE [Walcott] HAZARD (Mrs. Roscoe Platt Conkling) (Feb. 7, 1878–Nov. 15, 1958); b. New York. Poet. *Afternoons of April* (1915); *Wilderness Songs* (1920); *Ship's Log and Other Poems* (1924); *Flying Fish: A Book of Songs and Sonnets* (1926); *Witch, and Other Poems* (1929).

CONKLING, HILDA (Oct. 8, 1910–); b. Catskill-on-Hudson, N.Y., daughter of Grace Hazard Conkling. Poet. *Poems by a Little Girl* (1920); *Shoes of the Wind* (1922); etc.

CONKLING, WALLACE EDMONDS, (Oct. 25, 1896–); b. Beacon, N.Y. Protestant Episcopal bishop, author. *True Values* (1931); *Darkness and Light* (1931); *The Queen Mother* (1932); *Priesthood in Action* (1945); *Worship and Life* (1948).

CONLEY, PHILIP MALLORY (Nov. 30, 1887–); b. Charleston, W.Va. Publisher, author. *West Virginia Yesterday and Today* (1931); *Beacon Lights of West Virginia History* (1939); *Mountain Murder* (1939); *Everyday Philosophy* (1944); *America's Debt to Greece* (1957); *The Greatest Century in History* (1958); *History of the West Virginia Coal Industry* (1960). Pres., West Virginia Publishing Co.; Charleston Printing Co.

CONNALLY, TOM [Thomas Terry] (Aug. 19, 1877–Oct. 1963); b. McLennan, Co., Tex. Senator, 1929–53. *My Name Is Tom Connally* (1954).

"Connecticut." Poem by Fitz-Greene Halleck, in *The Poetical Works* (1847). Contains the well known lines quoted from General Stark: "For we must beat them, boys, ere set of sun, Or Mary Stark's a widow."

Connecticut Courant. Hartford, Conn. Newspaper. Founded 1764, by Thomas Green (1735–1812). Changed name later to *Hartford Courant* (q.v.).

Connecticut Gazette. See *New London Summary.*

Connecticut Quarterly. Hartford, Conn. Quarterly magazine. Founded Jan., 1895. Later called the *Connecticut Magazine.*

Connecticut Wits. See Hartford Wits.

Connecticut Yankee in King Arthur's Court, A. A story by Mark Twain (1889). A Yankee from Hartford is hit on the head and, when he regains consciousness, he finds himself in the Court of King Arthur. His modern ideas bring him into strange and humorous conflicts with Arthurian mentality and customs.

CONNELL, EVAN S[helby], Jr. (Aug. 17, 1924–); b. Kansas City, Mo. Author. *The Anatomy Lesson and Other Stories* (1957); *Mrs. Bridge* (1959); *The Patriot* (1960); *Notes from a Bottle Found on a Beach at Carmel* (1963); *At the Crossroads* (1965); *The Diary of a Rapist* (1966); *Mr. Bridge* (1969). Editor, *Contact,* 1959–65.

CONNELL, FRANCIS J. (Jan. 31, 1888–May 12, 1967); b. Boston, Mass. Roman Catholic clergyman. *Morals in Politics and Professions* (1946); *Outlines of Moral Theology* (1953); *Father Connell Answers Moral Questions* (1959); *Spiritual and Pastoral Conferences to Priests* (1962).

CONNELL, RICHARD [Edward] (Oct. 17, 1893–Nov. 22, 1949); b. Poughkeepsie, N.Y. Author. *The Sin of Monsieur Pettipon* (1922); *Apes and Angels* (1924); *Ironies* (1930); *Playboy* (1936); *What Ho!* (1937).

CONNELLY, CELIA LOGAN (1837–Jan. 18, 1904); b. in Pennsylvania. Journalist, novelist, playwright. *The Elopement* (under pen name, "L. Fairfax," 1863); *Her Strange Fate* (1888); *An American Marriage* (prod. 1886?); etc.

CONNELLY, EMMA MARY; b. near Louisville, Ky. Author. *Tilting at Windmills* (1888); *The Story of Kentucky* (1890).

CONNELLY, MARC[us Cook] (Dec. 13, 1890–); b. McKeesport, Pa. Playwright. *The Amber Empress* (prod. 1916); *Dulcy* (with George S. Kaufman, prod. 1921); *To the Ladies!* (with same, prod. 1922); *Be Yourself* (with same, prod. 1924); *The Wisdom Tooth* (prod. 1926); *The Green Pastures* (publ. 1929, prod. 1930, Pulitzer Prize play, 1930); *The Farmer Takes a Wife* (with Frank B. Elser, 1934); *Everywhere I Roam*

(with Arnold Sundgaard, 1938); *The Flowers of Virtue* (1942); *A Story for Strangers* (1948); *A Souvenir from Qam* (1965); etc. See Fred B. Millett's *Contemporary American Authors* (1940).

CONNELY, WILLARD (July 1, 1888–Mar. 27, 1967); b. Atlantic City, N.J. Educator, author. *Brawney Wycherley* (1930); *Sir Richard Steele* (1934); *The True Chesterfield* (1939); *Beau Nash* (1955); *Adventures in Biography* (1956); *Laurence Stern as Yorick* (1958); *Louis Sullivan as Yorick* (1958); *Louis Sullivan as He Lived* (1960); etc. Assistant editor, *Harper's Weekly,* 1913–14; assoc. editor, *McClure's Magazine,* 1913–15. Director, American University Union, London, from 1930.

CONNER, SABRA (Apr. 9, 1884–); b. Normal, Ill. Author. *The Quest of the Sea Otter* (1927); *Sweet Water Trail* (1928); *Captain Red Leggs* (1930); *Fighting Starrs of Oregon* (1932).

CONNERS, BARRY (1882–1933). Playwright. *The Mad Honeymoon* (prod. 1923); *So This Is Politics* (prod. 1924); *Hell's Bells* (prod. 1925); *"The Patsy"* (prod. 1926); etc.

CONNERY, ROBERT HOWE (Oct. 1, 1907–); b. St. Paul, Minn. Educator, author. *The Navy and Industrial Mobilization in World War II* (1951); *Forrestal and the Navy* (1957); *The Federal Government and Metropolitan Areas* (with Richard M. Leach, 1960); *The Politics of Mental Health* (with others, 1968).

CONNOLLY, FRANCIS X[avier] (June 24, 1909–Nov. 17, 1965); b. New York. Educator, author. *Give Beauty Back* (1950); *A Rhetoric Case Book* (1953); *St. Philip of the Joyous Heart* (1957); *Is a Christian Theory of Literature Possible?* (1962); etc. Editor: *The Types of Literature* (1955); *Man and His Measure* (1964); etc. Prof. English, Fordham University, from 1951.

CONNOLLY, JAMES B[rendan Bennet] (1868–Jan. 20, 1957); b. S. Boston, Mass. Author. *Out of Gloucester* (1902); *Deep Sea's Toll* (1905); *Open Water* (1910); *The Trawler* (1914); *Head Winds* (1916); *Tide Rips* (1922); *Book of the Gloucester Fishermen* (1927); *Coaster Captain* (1927); *Gloucestermen* (1930); *Navy Men* (1939); *Canton Captain* (1942); *Sea-Borne: Thirty Years Avoyaging* (1944); etc.

CONNOLLY, TERENCE LEO (Sept. 26, 1888–Mar. 24, 1961); b. North Attleboro, Mass. Librarian. *Francis Thompson: In His Paths* (1944). Editor: *The Man Has Wings* (1957). Prof. English, Boston College, 1926–46; director of library, 1946–58.

CONOT, ROBERT E. Author. *Ministers of Vengeance* (1964); *Rivers of Blood, Years of Darkness* (1968).

"Conquered Banner, The." Civil War poem by Abram J. Ryan (1865).

Conqueror: Being the True and Romantic Story of Alexander Hamilton, The. Novel by Gertrude Atherton (1902).

"Conqueror Worm, The." Poem by Edgar Allan Poe (1843).

"Conquest of Canaan, The." Narrative poem by Timothy Dwight (written in 1771–74, publ. 1785). An allegory, representing American heroes under the guise of Hebrew chieftains, attacking the city of Ai.

Conquest of Canaan, The. Novel by Booth Tarkington (1905). Joe Louden, a bad boy in a small Indiana town, runs away and becomes a successful lawyer. He later returns but his past has not been forgotten. Eventually he wins the respect of his townsmen, and the girl he loves.

"Conquistador." Long poem by Archibald Macleish (1932). A saga founded on Diaz's *True History of the Conquest of New Spain.*

CONRAD, BARNABY, Jr. (Mar. 27, 1922–); b. San Francisco, Cal. Artist, author. *The Innocent Villa* (1948); *Matador* (1952); *La Fiesta Brava* (1953); *Gates of Fear* (1957); *The Death of Manolete* (1958); *Encyclopedia of Bullfighting* (1961); *Famous Last Words* (ed., 1961); *Dangerfield* (1961); *How to Fight a Bull* (1968); *Fun While It Lasted* (1969).

CONRAD, ROBERT TAYLOR (June 10, 1810–June 27, 1858); b. Philadelphia, Pa. Journalist, jurist, playwright, poet. *Conrad, King of Naples* (prod. 1832); *Aylmere* (prod. 1835), rewritten as *Alymere; or, The Kentish Rebellion* (1841); and finally renamed *Jack Cade* (1852); *Aylmere; or, The Bondman of Kent, and Other Poems* (1852); *Devotional Poems* (1862); *The Heretic* (prod. 1863).

CONROY, FRANK (Jan. 15, 1936–); b. New York. Author. *Stop-Time* (1967).

CONROY, JACK (Dec. 5, 1899–); b. Moberly, Mo. Editor, author. *Mark Twain: A Study* (1931); *The Disinherited* (1933); *A World to Win* (1935); *The Fast Sooner Hound* (with Arna Bontemps, 1942); *They Seek a City* (with Arna Bontemps, 1945); *Slappy Hooper* (1946); *Midland Humor* (1947); etc. Associate editor, *The New Standard Encyclopedia,* since 1947.

Conservative Principles in Our Literature. Address by William R. Williams at Hamilton Literary and Theological Institute (now Colgate University) in 1844.

CONSIDINE, BOB (Robert Bernard) (Nov. 4, 1906–); b. Washington, D.C. Journalist, author. *MacArthur the Magnificent* (1942); *Thirty Seconds over Tokyo* (with Ted. W. Lawson, 1943); *Where's Sammy?* (with Sammy Schulman, 1943); *General Wainwright's Story* (with Jonathan M. Wainwright, 1946); *The Babe Ruth Story* (with Babe Ruth, 1948); *Innocents at Home* (1950); *Panama Canal* (1951); *Man Against Fire* (1955); *Ripley: The Modern Marco Polo* (1961); etc. Syndicated columnist, since 1937.

CONSOLATA, SISTER MARY (1892–); b. Rome, N.Y. Author, under the pen name "Consolata Carroll." *Pray Love, Remember* (1947); *I Hear in My Heart* (1949). Member of the Roman Catholic Order of the Sisters of Mercy.

Conspiracy of Pontiac, The. By Francis Parkman, 2v. (1851). Classic study of the period of American history dominated by the struggle between England and France for the control of the Great Lakes territory.

Constance Trescot. Novel by S. Weir Mitchell (1905). Constance Hood marries George Trescot, an officer in the Union army, and goes to live in the South. After winning a lawsuit, Trescot is killed by the opposing attorney. Constance harasses her husband's murderer until he finally takes his own life.

Constant Nymph, The. Novel by Margaret Kennedy (1924). Set in the Austrian Tyrol, it depicts the helter-skelter lives of the Sanger family, known as the "Sanger Circus."

Constantia. Pen name of Judith Sargent Stevens Murray.

Consumer Reports. Mount Vernon, N.Y. Monthly. Founded 1936. Published by Consumers Union of the United States with an annual buying guide. Edited by Donal Dinwiddie.

Contact. New York. Founded 1921 and edited by William Carlos Williams and Robert McAlmon until 1923. In 1933 reorganized as *Contact: An American Quarterly* and edited by William Carlos Williams. Discontinued 1933.

Contact: the San Francisco Journal of New Writing, Art, and Ideas. Sausalito, Cal. Quarterly. Founded 1958, incorporating *Western Review.* Suspended 1965.

"Contemplations." Poem by Anne Bradstreet (1678).

Contempo. Chapel Hill, N.C. Book reviewing magazine issued every three weeks. Founded 1931. Discontinued 1934.

Contemporary American Authors: A Handbook of Modern Literature. By Fred B. Millett (1940). Bio-bibliography of 219 contemporary American authors, with critical introduction and classified selective lists of books.

Contemporary American Literature. By John M. Manly and Edith M. Rickert (1922). Revised by Fred B. Millett (1929).

"Contentment." Poem by Oliver Wendell Holmes (1858).

Contrast, The. Play by Royall Tyler (prod. 1787, publ. 1790). The first comedy of American manners. It contrasts the culture of the Old World with the New. It creates the role of Jonathan, the first in a long line of stage Yankees in the American drama.

CONVERSE, FLORENCE (Apr. 30, 1871–); b. New Orleans, La. Editor, novelist, poet. *Diana Victrix* (1897); *Long Will* (1903); *The Children of Light* (1912); *Into the Void* (1926); *Sphinx* (1931); *Collected Poems* (1937); *Wellesley College: A Chronicle of the Years, 1875–1938* (1939); etc. On editorial staff, *Atlantic Monthly,* 1908–31.

Conway, Faulkner. Pen name of Frank J. Price.

CONWAY, J[ohn] GREGORY (Dec. 27, 1909–); b. Billings, Mont. Lecturer, educator, author. *Flowers East-West* (with E. W. Hiatt, 1938); *Flowers: Their Arrangement* (1940); *Conway's Treasury of Flowers* (1953); *Encyclopedia of Flower Arrangements* (1957).

CONWAY, KATHERINE ELEANOR (1853–Jan 2, 1927); b. Rochester, N.Y. Editor, poet. *On the Sunrise Slope* (1881); *A Dream of Lilies* (1893); *A Lady and Her Letters* (1895); *Making Friends and Keeping Them* (1895); etc.

CONWAY, MONCURE DANIEL (Mar. 17, 1832–Nov. 15, 1907); b. Falmouth, Va. Clergyman, editor, author. *The Wandering Jew* (1881); *Thomas Carlyle* (1881); *Demonology and Devil Lore,* 2v. (1879); *Life of Nathaniel Hawthorne* (1890); *The Life of Thomas Paine,* 2v. (1892); *Barons of the Potomack and the Rappahannock* (1892); *Autobiography, Memories and Experiences,* 2v. (1904); etc. Editor, *The Dial,* 1860.

CONWELL, RUSSELL HERMAN (Feb. 15, 1843–Dec. 6, 1925); b. South Worthington, Me. Baptist clergyman, lecturer, author. *Lessons in Travel* (1870); *History of the Great Fire in Boston* (1873); *Why Lincoln Laughed* (1922); etc. His most famous lecture was "Acres of Diamonds" (q.v.). *See* Agnes Rush Burr's *Russell H. Conwell* (1905).

CONYNGHAM, DAVID POWER (1840–1883); b. in Ireland. Editor, novelist. *Sherman's March Through the South* (1865); *Sarsfield* (1871); *Rose Parnell* (1883); etc. Editor, *The New York Tattler.*

COOK, ALBERT STANBURROUGH (Mar. 6, 1853–Sept. 1, 1927); b. Montville, N.J. Educator, philologist, author. *The Bible and English Prose Style* (1892); *The Art of Poetry* (1892); *The Artistic Ordering of Life* (1898); *The Higher Study of English* (1906). Editor, *Yale Studies in English.* Prof. English, Yale University, 1889–1921.

COOK, CLARENCE [Chatham] (Sept. 8, 1828–June 2, 1900); b. Dorchester, Mass. Art critic, journalist. *The House Beautiful* (1878); *Art and Artists of Our Time,* 3v. (1888); *Poems* (1902); etc. Art critic, *New York Tribune,* 1863–69. Editor, *The Studio,* 1884–92.

COOK, DAVID J. (Aug. 12, 1840–Apr. 29, 1907); b. in Laporte Co., Ind. Author. *Hands Up; or, Thirty-five Years of Detective Life in the Mountains and on the Plains* (1897). *See* William Ross Collier and Edwin Victor Westrate's *Dave Cook of the Rockies* (1936).

COOK, EBENEZER (c. 1672–1732); b. London, England (?). Author. *The Sot-Weed Factor; or, A Voyage to Maryland* (1708); *Sotweed-Redivivus* (1730); *The Maryland Muse* (1731); etc. See Lawrence C. Wroth's *The Maryland Muse by Ebenezer Cooke,* in Proceedings, American Antiquarian Society, Oct. 1934.

COOK, FANNIE (d. Aug. 25, 1949); b. St. Charles, Mo. Novelist. *The Hill Grows Steeper* (1938); *Boot-Heel Doctor* (1941); *Mrs. Palmer's Honey* (1946); *Storm Against the Wall* (1948); *The Long Bridge* (1949).

COOK, FRED J[ames] (Mar. 8, 1911–   ); b. Point Pleasant, N.J. Journalist, author. *The Unfinished Story of Alger Hiss* (1958); *The Warfare State* (1962); *The FBI Nobody Knows* (1964); *The Corrupted Land* (1966); *The Plot Against the Patient* (1967); *What So Proudly We Hailed* (1968).

COOK, GEORGE CRAM (Oct. 7, 1873–Jan. 14, 1924); b. Davenport, Ia. Playwright, novelist. *In Hampton Roads* (1899); *Roderick Taliaferro* (1903); *Suppressed Desires* (with Susan Glaspell, prod. 1915); *The Athenian Women* (1917); *Ticklish Time* (prod. 1919); *The Spring* (prod. 1921); *Greek Coins* (poems, 1925). Co-founder, Provincetown Players, 1915; director, 1915–24. See Susan Glaspell's *The Road to the Temple* (1926).

COOK, GLADYS EMERSON (1899–); b. Haverhill, Mass. Artist, author. *Zoo Animals* (1943); *Portfolio of Purebred Dogs* (1947); *Circus Clowns on Parade* (1956). Also many cat and dog books.

COOK, JAMES HENRY (Aug. 26, 1858–Jan. 26, 1942); b. Kalamazoo, Mich. Naturalist, scout with Texas Rangers, author. *Fifty Years on the Old Frontier* (1923).

COOK, JOSEPH[us] (Jan. 26, 1838–June 24, 1901); b. Ticonderoga, N.Y. Lecturer, author. *Biology* (1877); *Labor* (1880); *Socialism* (1880); etc. Founder, *Our Day* magazine, 1888; editor, 1888–Apr., 1895.

COOK, ROY BIRD (Apr. 1, 1886–Nov. 23, 1961); b. Weston, W.Va. Pharmacist, antiquarian, collector, author. *Washington's Western Lands* (1926); *Annals of Fort Lee* (1931); *Lewis County Journalists and Journalism* (1936); *Annals of Pharmacy in West Virginia* (1946); etc. Editor, *West Virginia History,* 1939–41. Collector of Civil War documents.

COOK, WILL[iam Everett] (1921–). Author. Writes under pen names "Wade Everett" and "James Keene." *Sabrina Kane, a Novel of Frontier Illinois* (1956); *Elizabeth, by Name* (1958); *Iron Man, Iron Horse* (1960); *The Breakthrough* (1963); etc.

COOK, WILLIAM WALLACE (Apr. 11, 1867–July 20, 1933); b. Marshall, Mich. Editor, author. *His Friend the Enemy* (1903); *A Quarter to Four* (1909); *The Fiction Factory* (under the pen name, "John Milton Edwards," 1912). With Street & Smith, publishers.

COOKE, [Alfred] ALISTAIR (Nov. 20, 1908–); b. Manchester, Eng. Journalist, author. *Douglas Fairbanks* (1940); *Generation on Trial: U.S.A. vs. Alger Hiss* (1950); *One Man's America* (1952); *Christmas Eve* (1952); *Talk about America* (1968); etc.

Cooke, Ebenezer. See Ebenezer Cook.

COOKE, GEORGE WILLIS (Apr. 23, 1848–Apr. 30, 1923); b. Comstock, Mich. Unitarian clergyman, author. *Ralph Waldo Emerson* (1881); *Poets and Problems* (1886); *A Guide-Book to the Poetic and Dramatic Works of Robert Browning* (1891); *George Eliot* (1895); *John Sullivan Dwight* (1898); *An Historical and Biographical Introduction Accompanying the Dial,* 2v. (1902); etc. Editor, *The Poets of Transcendentalism: An Anthology* (1903).

COOKE, GRACE MacGOWAN (Sept. 11, 1863–deceased); b. Grand Rapids, O. Author. *Mistress Joy* (with Annie Booth McKinney, 1901); *A Gourd Fiddle* (1904); *The Power and the Glory* (1910); *Wild Apples* (with Alice MacGowan, 1918); etc.

COOKE, JACOB ERNEST (Sept. 23, 1924–   ); b. Aulander, N.C. Educator, author. *Frederick Bancroft* (1956); *The March of Democracy,* Vols. 6 and 7 (1965). Editor: *The Federalist* (1961); *Reports of Alexander Hamilton* (1964); *The Challenge of History* (1965). Prof. history, Carnegie Institute of Technology, 1961–62; Lafayette College, since 1962.

COOKE, JAMES FRANCIS (Nov. 14, 1875–); b. Bay City, Mich. Historian of music. *Standard History of Music* (1909); *Music Masters Old and New* (1921); *Great Men and Famous Musicians* (1925); *Street of the Little Candles* (1937); *How to Memorize Music* (1947); *The Fabulous Dr. Franklin* (1956); *Memoirs—Friends Everywhere* (1958); etc.

COOKE, JOHN ESTEN (Nov. 3, 1830—Sept. 27, 1886); b. Winchester, Va. Historian, biographer, novelist. *Leather Stocking and Silk* (1854); *The Virginia Comedians,* 2v. (1854); *Henry St. John, Gentleman* (1859); *The Heir of Gaymount* (1870); *Stories of the Old Dominion* (1879); *Virginia: A History of the People* (1883); *My Lady Pokahontas* (1885); etc. See Oscar Wegelin's *A Bibliography of the Separate Writings of John Esten Cooke* (1925).

COOKE, LESLIE EDWARD (May 22, 1908–Feb. 1967); b. Brighton, Eng. Congregational clergyman, author. *Upon This Rock* (1937); *Token of Our Inheritance* (1943); *Faith Stakes a Claim* (1949); *Above Every Name* (1962); etc.

COOKE, MORRIS LLEWELLYN (May 11, 1872–Mar. 5, 1960); b. Carlisle, Pa. Consulting engineer in management, author. *Academic and Industrial Efficiency* (1910); *Snapping Cords* (1915); *Our Cities Awake* (1918); *Organized Labor and Production* (with Philip Murray, 1940); *Brazil on the March* (1944).

COOKE, PHILIP PENDLETON (Oct. 26, 1816–Jan. 20, 1850); b. Martinsburg, Va. Poet, story-writer. *Froissart Ballads, and Other Poems* (1847). His best known poem, "Florence Vane," was first published in Burton's *Gentleman's Magazine,* Mar., 1840. His only novel, *The Chevalier Merlin,* was appearing in the *Southern Literary Messenger* at the time of his death, and remained unfinished.

COOKE, PHILIP ST. GEORGE (June 13, 1809–Mar. 20, 1895); b. Leesburg, Va. Soldier, military writer. *Scenes and Adventures in the Army* (autobiography, 1857); *The Conquest of New Mexico and California* (1878).

COOKE, ROSE TERRY (Feb. 17, 1827–July 18, 1892); b. Hartford, Conn. Story-writer, poet. *Poems* (1860); *Happy Dodd* (1878); *Somebody's Neighbors* (1881); *Root-Bound, and Other Sketches* (1885); *The Sphinx's Children, and Other Peoples* (1886); *Steadfast: The Story of a Saint and a Sinner* (1889); *Huckleberries Gathered from New England Hills* (1891).

"Cool Tombs." Poem by Carl Sandburg (1918).

COOLBRITH, INA DONNA (Josephine Donna Smith) (1842–1928); b. near Springfield, Ill. Librarian, poet. *A Perfect Day, and Other Poems* (1881); *The Singer of the Sea* (1894); *Songs from the Golden Gate* (1895); *Wings of Sunset* (1929). Associated with Bret Harte on the *Overland Monthly.* Poet laureate of California, 1915.

COOLIDGE, ARCHIBALD CARY (Mar. 6, 1866–Jan. 14, 1928); b. Boston, Mass. Editor, historian. *The United States As a World Power* (1908); *The Origins of the Triple Alliance* (1917); *Ten Years of War and Peace* (1927). Co-editor, *Foreign Affairs,* 1922–28. History dept., Harvard University, 1893–1928; librarian, 1911–1928.

COOLIDGE, CALVIN (July 4, 1872–Jan. 5, 1933); b. Plymouth, Vt. 30th president of the United States, author. *Have Faith in Massachusetts!* (1919); *The Price of Freedom: Speeches and Addresses* (1924); *Foundations of the Republic: Speeches and Addresses* (1926); *The Autobiography of Calvin Coolidge* (1929); *The Talkative President*, ed. by H. H. Quint and R. H. Ferrell (1964); *Foundations of the Republic: Speeches and Addresses* (1968). See Claude M. Fuess's *Calvin Coolidge* (1940); William Allen White's *Calvin Coolidge* (1925); Gamaliel Bradford's *The Quick and the Dead* (1931).

COOLIDGE, DANE (Mar. 24, 1873–Aug. 8, 1940); b. Natick, Mass. Novelist, naturalist. *Hidden Water* (1910); *The Land of Broken Promises* (1913); *Silver and Gold* (1918); *The Navajo Indians* (with wife, Mary R. Coolidge, 1930); *Fighting Men of the West* (1932); *Death Valley Prospectors* (1937); *Texas Cowboys* (1937); *Arizona Cowboys* (1938); *Old California Cowboys* (1939); etc.

COOLIDGE, JOHN GARDNER (July 4, 1863–Feb. 28, 1935); b. Boston, Mass. Diplomat, author. *Random Letters from Many Countries* (1924); *A War Diary in Paris, 1914–17* (1931).

COOLIDGE, MARY [Elizabeth Burroughs] ROBERTS (Oct. 28, 1860–Apr. 13, 1945); b. Kingsbury, Ind. Author. *The Rain Makers* (1929); *The Navajo Indians* (with Dane Coolidge, 1930); *The Last of the Seris* (with same, 1939); etc.

Coolidge, Susan. Pen name of Sarah Chauncy Woolsey.

COOMBE, THOMAS (Oct. 21, 1747–Aug. 15, 1822); b. Philadelphia, Pa. Anglican clergyman, loyalist, poet. *The Peasant of Auburn; or, The Emmigrant* (1783); etc.

COOMBS, ANNIE SHELDON (1858–1890); b. Albany, N.Y. Novelist. *As Common Mortals* (1886); *A Game of Chance* (1887); *The Garden of Armida* (1889).

COON, CARLETON STEVENS (June 23, 1904–); b. Wakefield, Mass. Anthropologist, author. *Tribes of Rif* (1931); *Flesh of the Wild Ox* (1932); *The Riffian* (1934); *Measuring Ethiopia* (1935); *Races of Europe* (1939); *The Mountains of Giants* (1951); *Cave Explorations in Iran* (1951); *The Story of Man* (1954); *The Seven Caves* (1957); *The Origin of Races* (1962); *The Living Races of Man* (1965); *Yengema Cave Report* (with others, 1968).

COON, HORACE C. (1897–Dec. 10, 1961). Author. *Money to Burn* (1938); *American Tel and Tel* (1939); *Columbia: Colossus on the Hudson* (1947); *Triumph of the Eggheads* (1955).

COONEY, BARBARA (Aug. 6, 1917–); b. Brooklyn, N.Y. Illustrator, author. *Kellyhorns* (1942); *The Little Juggler* (1961); *Cock Robin* (1965); *Christmas* (1967); *Little Prayer* (1967); *Garland of Games* (1969).

COOPER, CLAYTON SEDGWICK (May 24, 1869–Oct. 12, 1936); b. Henderson, N.Y. Baptist clergyman, lecturer, author. *American Ideals* (1915); *The Brazilians and Their Country* (1917); *Understanding South America* (1918); etc.

COOPER, COURTNEY RYLEY (Oct. 31, 1886–Sept. 29, 1940); b. Kansas City, Mo. Journalist, showman, author. *Memories of Buffalo Bill* (with Mrs. W. F. Cody, 1919); *Under the Big Top* (1923); *The Last Frontier* (1923); *Annie Oakley* (1927); *Challenge of the Bush* (1929); *Trigger Finger* (1930); *Ghost Country* (1930); *Circus Day* (1931); *Old Mom* (1934); *Here's to Crime!* (1937); *The Pioneers* (1937); *Action in Diamonds* (1942); etc.

COOPER, ELIZABETH (Mrs. Clayton Sedgwick Cooper) (May 10, 1877–); b. Homer, Ia. Author. *The Market for Souls* (1910); *Drusilla with a Million* (1916); *The Heart of O Sona San* (1917); *My Lady of the Indian Purdah* (1927); etc.

COOPER, FREDERICK TABER (May 27, 1864–May 19, 1937); b. New York. Educator, Editor, author. *History of the Nineteenth Century in Caricature* (with Arthur Bartlett Maurice, 1904); *Some American Story Tellers* (1911); *Some English Story Tellers* (1912); *Thomas A. Edison* (1914); etc. Editor, *The Forum*, 1907–09.

COOPER, JAMES FENIMORE (Sept. 15, 1789–Sept. 14, 1851); b. Burlington, N.J. Novelist. *Precaution* (1820); *The Spy* (1821); *The Pioneers* (1823); *The Pilot* (1823); *Lionel Lincoln* (1825); *The Last of the Mohicans* (1826); *The Prairie* (1827); *The Red Rover* (1828); *The Water-Witch* (1831); *The Pathfinder* (1840); *The Deerslayer* (1841); *Wyandotte* (1843); *Ned Myers* (1843); *The Chainbearer* (1845); *Collected Works*, 32v. (1859–61), illustrated by F. O. C. Darley; *Collected Works*, 32v. (1876–84); *Correspondence of James Fenimore Cooper*, 2v. (1922); etc. See Robert E. Spiller and Philip C. Blackburn's *A Descriptive bibliography of the Writings of James Fenimore Cooper* (1934); T. R. Lounsbury's *James Fenimore Cooper* (1882); Henry W. Boynton's *James Fenimore Cooper* (1931); Donald A. Range's *James Fenimore Cooper* (1962); Warren S. Walker's *Leather-Stocking and the Critics* (1965); George Dekker's: *James Fenimore Cooper: The American Scott* (1967).

COOPER, JOHN COBB, III (Sept. 14, 1921–); b. Atlantic City, N.J. Novelist. Writes under pen name "John Cobb." *The Gesture* (1948).

COOPER, KENT (Mar. 22, 1880–Jan. 31, 1965); b. Columbus, Ind. Journalist, author. *Barriers Down* (1942); *About the Girl* (prod. 1943); *Anna Zenger, Mother of Freedom* (1946); *The Right to Know* (1956); *Kent Cooper and the Associated Press* (1959). With Associated Press since 1910; exec. director from 1943.

COOPER, LANE (Dec. 14, 1875–Nov. 27, 1959); b. New Brunswick, N.J. Educator, author. *Theories of Style* (1907); *A Manual of American Literature* (1909); *A Concordance to the Poems of William Wordsworth* (1911); *Methods and Aims in the Study of Literature* (1915); *A Concordance to the Works of Horace* (1916); *The Greek Genius and Its Influence* (1917); *Two Views of Education* (1922); *The Poetics of Aristotle* (1923); *Aristotelian Papers* (1939); etc. In English dept., Cornell University, from 1902.

COOPER, LOUISE FIELD (Mar. 8, 1905–); b. Hartford, Conn. Novelist. *The Lighted Box* (1942); *The Deer on the Stairs* (1943); *Love and Admiration* (stories, 1944); *Summer Stranger* (1947); *The Boys from Sharon* (1950); *The Cheerful Captive* (1954); *The Windfall Child* (1963); *Widows and Admirals* (1964); *A Week at the Most* (1967).

COOPER, MERIAN C. (Oct. 24, 1893–); b. Jacksonville, Fla. Explorer, moving picture producer, author. *The Sea Gypsy* (with Edward A. Salisbury, 1924); *Grass* (1925).

COOPER, PETER (Feb. 12, 1791–Apr. 4, 1883); b. New York. Manufacturer, inventor, philanthropist, author. *The Political and Financial Opinions ... With an Autobiography* (1877). Founder, Cooper Union, New York City, 1859.

COOPER, RUSSELL MORGAN (Dec. 6, 1907–); b. Newton, Ia. Educator. *American Consultation in World Affairs* (1934); *Better Colleges—Better Teachers* (1944). Dean, liberal arts, University of South Florida, since 1959.

COOPER, SUSAN FENIMORE (Apr. 17, 1813–Dec. 31, 1894); b. Cooperstown, N.Y., daughter of James Fenimore Cooper. Author. *Rural Hours* (1850); *Rhyme and Reason of Country Life* (1854); *Rural Rambles* (1854); *Elinor Wyllys* (under pen name, "Amabel Penfeather," 1845).

COOVER, ROBERT. (Feb. 4, 1932–). Author. *The Origin of the Brunists* (1966); *The Universal Baseball Association* (1968); *Pricksongs and Descants* (1969).

COPELAND, BENJAMIN (June 14, 1855–Dec. 1, 1940); b. Clarendon, N.Y. Methodist clergyman, poet, hymn writer. Writer of commemorative and occasional poems for newspapers and magazines. His additional stanza to "America" in 1935 attracted much attention.

COPELAND, CHARLES TOWNSEND (Apr. 27, 1860–July 24, 1952); b. Calais, Me. Educator, author. *Life of Edwin Booth* (1901). Editor: *The Copeland Reader* (1926); *Anthology of Translations* (1934); etc. In English dept., Harvard University, 1893–1928.

Copeland and Day. Publishing firm founded in Boston in 1895 by Herbert Copeland and Frederick Holland Day.

COPLAND, AARON (Nov. 14, 1900–); b. Brooklyn, N.Y. Composer, author. *What to Listen for in Music* (1939); *Our New Music* (1941); *Music and Imagination* (1952); *Copland on Music* (1960); *Connotations for Orchestra* (1962); *Music for a Great City* (1964); *Emblems for a Band* (1965).

COPPEE, HENRY (Oct. 13, 1821–Mar. 21, 1895); b. Savannah, Ga. Educator, critic. *A Gallery of Distinguished English and American Female Poets* (1860); *A Gallery of Famous English and American Poets* (1873); *English Literature Considered as an Interpreter of History* (1873); *History of the Conquest of Spain by the Arab Moors* (1881); etc. Editor: *The Classic and the Beautiful from the Literature of Three Thousand Years,* 6v. (1891–1892). First president of Lehigh University.

COPPOCK, JOSEPH DAVID (Feb. 10, 1909–); b. Peru, Ind. Economist. *Government Agencies of Consumer Installment Credit* (1940); *The Food Stamp Plan* (1947); *Economics of the Business Firm* (1959); *International Economic Instability* (1962); *Foreign Trade of the Middle East* (1966).

COPWAY, GEORGE (1818–c. 1863); b. in Ontario, Canada. Ojibway chief, missionary, author. Indian name, "Kah-Ge-Ga-Gah-Bowh." *The Life, History, and Travels of Kah-Ge-Ga-Gah-Bowh* (1847); *The Traditional History and Characteristic Sketches of the Ojibway Nation* (1850); *The Ojibway Conquest* (1850); etc.

Copy-Cat, and Other Stories. By Mary F. Wilkins Freeman (1914).

Coquette. Play by George Abbott and Ann Preston Bridges (prod. 1927). Coquette loves Michael Jeffrey, against the wishes of her father, who shoots Michael during a quarrel. The father pleads not guilty on the grounds of protecting the good name of his daughter. Being with child, Coquette kills herself to save her father.

Coquette; or, The History of Eliza Wharton, The. Novel by Hannah Webster Foster (1797), published anonymously. Based on the love affairs of Elizabeth Whitman, Pierpont Edwards, and Joseph Buckminster, of Hartford, Conn. This novel of seduction ran into many editions.

CORBETT, ELIZABETH [Frances] (Sept. 30, 1887–); b. Aurora, Ill. Novelist, biographer, essayist. *Cecily and the Wide World* (1916); *Puritan and Pagan* (1920); *Walt: The Good Grey Poet Speaks for Himself* (1928); *If It Takes All Summer: the Life Story of Ulysses S. Grant* (1930); *The Young Mrs. Meigs* (1931); *The Graper Girls* (1931), and other books on the Grapers; *Mr. & Mrs. Meigs* (1940); *Immortal Helen* (1948); *The Duke's Daughter* (1950); *Our Mrs. Meigs* (1954); *Family Portrait* (1955); *The Head of Apollo* (1956); *Professor Preston at Home* (1957); *The President's Wife* (1958); *Hidden Island* (1961); *The Distant Princess* (1963); *Anniversary* (1964); *Continuing City* (1965); *Old Callahan Place* (1966); *Harry Martin's Wife* (1967); *Ladies' Day* (1968); etc.

Corbin, Alice. See Alice Corbin Henderson.

CORBIN, JOHN (May 2, 1870–Aug. 30, 1959); b. Chicago, Ill. Drama critic. *An American at Oxford* (1902); *A New Portrait of Shakespeare* (1903); *The First Loves of Perilla* (1903); *The Edge* (1915); *The Unknown Washington* (1930); *Two Frontiers of Freedom* (1940); etc.

CORBY, WILLIAM (Oct. 2, 1833–Dec. 28, 1897). Roman Catholic priest, educator, author. *Memoirs of Chaplain Life* (1894). President of Notre Dame University, 1866–72, 1877–81.

CORCOS, LUCILLE (Sept. 21, 1908–); b. New York. Artist, author. *Joel Gets a Haircut* (1952); *Joel Spends His Money* (1954); *Joel Gets a Dog* (1958). Illustrator: *Grimm's Fairy Tales* (1962).

COREY, LEWIS (Oct. 13, 1894–Sept. 16, 1953); b. Louis C. Fraina, in Italy. Economist. *The House of Morgan: A Social Biography of the Masters of Money* (1930); *The Decline of American Capitalism* (1934); *The Crisis of the Middle Class* (1935); *The Unfinished Task* (1942); *Meat and Man* (1950); etc.

COREY, PAUL [Frederick] (July 8, 1903–); b. Shelby Co., Ia. Author. *Three Miles Square* (1939); *The Road Returns* (1940); *County Seat* (1941); *The Red Tractor* (1944); *Buy an Acre* (1944); *Acres of Antaeus* (1946); *Build a Home* (1946); *Five Acre Hill* (1946); *Milk Flood* (1956); *Holiday Homes* (1967); *The Planet of the Blind* (1968).

Corita, Mary. See Corita Kent.

CORLE, EDWIN (May 7, 1906–June 11, 1956); b. Wildwood, N.J. Author. *Mojave* (Short stories, 1934); *People on the Earth* (1937); *Burro Alley* (1938); *Desert Country* (1941); *Three Ways to Mecca* (1947); *The Royal Highway* (1949); *The Gila: River of the Southwest* (1951); *Billy the Kid* (1953); etc.

CORLEY, DONALD; b. Corrington, Ga. Artist, author. *The House of Lost Identity* (1927); *The Fifth Son of the Shoemaker* (1929); *The Haunted Jester* (1931).

CORLISS, ALLENE [Soule] (Mrs. Bruce R. Corliss) (Oct. 31, 1898–); b. Cambridge, Vt. Novelist. *Marry for Love* (1931); *That Girl from New York* (1932); *Smoke in Her Eyes* (1935); *It's You I Want* (1936); *Love I Dare Not* (1937); *Walk with Me Tomorrow* (1940); *Borrowed Husband* (1943); etc.

Corliss, Mrs. Charles Albert. See Anne Parrish.

"Corn Song." Poem by John Greenleaf Whittier (1847).

Corneau, Octavia Roberts. See Octavia Roberts.

Cornell University Press. Ithaca, N.Y. Founded 1869. Scholarly publications. A division, Comstock Publishing Associates, publishes books on nature study and biology.

Cornhuskers, The. Poems by Carl Sandburg (1918).

Corno Emplumado, El. Mexico City, Mex. Founded 1962. Triannual. Literary magazine publishing texts in English and Spanish. Edited by Sergio Mondragon and Margaret Randall. Also known as *The Plumed Horn.*

Cornplanter, Jesse J. See Namée Henricks.

CORNWALLIS, KINAHAN (Dec. 24, 1839–Aug. 15, 1917); b. London, England. Lawyer, editor, novelist, poet, traveler, historian. *Howard Plunkett* (1857); *An Australian Poem* (1857); *The New El Dorado; or, British Columbia* (1858); *My Life and Adventures* (1860); *The Conquest of Mexico and Peru* (poem, 1893); etc. Editor, *Knickerbocker Magazine,* 1862–63; *Albion;* etc.

CORNWELL, HENRY SYLVESTER (Apr. 13, 1831–June 8, 1886); b. Charlestown, N.H. Physician, poet. *The Land of Dreams, and Other Poems* (1878). *See* Ellen M. Frisbie's *Henry Sylvester Cornwell, Poet of Fancy* (1906). His poem, "Eulalie," was set to music by Stephen C. Foster.

CORNYN, JOHN HUBERT (July 6, 1875–deceased); b. Wingham, Ont. Journalist, author. *Mexican Fairy Tales* (1908); *Old Maya* (1909); *Around the Wigwam Fire* (1920); *When the Camp Fire Burns* (1921); etc. Translator, *The Song of Quetzalcoatl* (1930); etc.

Coronado's Children. Novel by J. Frank Dobie (1931). Folk story of Texas and the Southwest, centering about buried Spanish treasure.

Coronet. New York. Monthly, Founded 1936. Published by Esquire, Inc. until its expiration in 1961. Noted for its family-type articles on a variety of subjects and its photographic features, it achieved a readership of more than 3,000,000. In 1963, it resumed publication. Now published by Coronet Communications, Inc.

CORRINGTON, JOHN WILLIAM (Oct. 28, 1932–); b. Memphis, Tenn. Author. *Where We Are* (poems, 1962); *The Anatomy of Love* (poems, 1964); *And Wait for the Night* (1964); *Lines to the South* (poems, 1965); *The Upper Hand* (1967); *The Bombardier* (1970). Editor: *Southern Writing in the Sixties* (1966).

CORRINGTON, JULIAN DANA (Dec. 22, 1891–); b. Hot Springs, Ark. Biologist, author. *Adventures with the Microscope* (1934); *Working with the Microscope* (1941); *Exploring with Your Microscope* (1957). Prof. zoology, University of Miami, since 1947.

CORROTHERS, JAMES DAVID (July 2, 1869–Feb. 12, 1917); b. Calvin, Mich. Author. *The Black Cat Club: Negro Humor and Folk Lore* (1902); *In Spite of the Handicap* (autobiography, 1916).

CORSER, HARRY PROSPER (Apr. 13, 1864–Feb. 2, 1936); b. Portageville, N.Y. Presbyterian clergyman, author. *The Totem Lore of Alaska* (1910); *Mere Man, and Richard Kempner's Xmas* (1919); *Duel of Hamilton and Burr* (1932); etc.

CORSO, GREGORY [Nunzio] (Mar. 26, 1930–); b. New York. Poet. *The Vestal Lady on Brattle* (1955); *Gasoline* (1958); *Bomb* (1958); *The Happy Birthday of Death* (1960); *The American Express* (novel, 1961); *Long Live Man* (1962); *Selected Poems* (1962). English faculty, State University College at Buffalo, New York.

CORSON, HIRAM (Nov. 6, 1828–June 15, 1911); b. Philadelphia, Pa. Educator, author. *An Introduction to the Study of Shakespeare* (1890); *An Introduction to the Study of Browning's Poetry* (1891); *Aims of Literary Study* (1895); etc.

CORT, DAVID (July 5, 1904–   ); b. Reading, Pa. Author. *Once More Ye Laurels* (1928); *Give Us Heroes* (1932); *The Great Union* (1945); *The Big Picture* (1953); *The Minstrel Boy* (1961); *The Glossy Rats* (1967); etc.

CORTAMBERT, LOUIS RICHARD (1808–Mar. 28, 1881); b. Paris, France. French-American historian, biographer, editor. *Voyage aux Pays des Osages* (1847); *L'Histoire de la Guerre Civile Américaine,* 2v. (1867); *Le Général Grant: Esquisse Biographique* (1868); etc. Editor, *La Revue de l'Ouest* (St. Louis), 1855–58; *Le Messager Franco-Américain* (New York), 1864–81.

CORTISSOZ, ELLEN MACKAY HUTCHINSON (Mrs. Royal Cortissoz) (d. Aug. 13, 1933); b. Caledonia, N.Y. Editor, poet. *Songs and Lyrics* (1881). Editor (with Edmund Clarence Stedman): *The Library of American Literature,* 11v. (1888–90). Art editor, *New York Tribune.*

CORTISSOZ, ROYAL (Feb. 10, 1869–Oct. 17, 1948); b. Brooklyn, N.Y. Journalist, lecturer, art critic. *Art and Common Sense* (1913); *The Life of Whitelaw Reid,* 2v. (1921); *American Artists* (1923); *Personalities in Art* (1925); *The Painter's Craft* (1930). Art editor, *New York Herald Tribune,* from 1891.

CORWIN, EDWARD SAMUEL (Jan. 19, 1878–Apr., 1963); b. near Plymouth, Mich. Educator, author. *John Marshall and the Constitution* (1919); *The Constitution and What It Means Today* (1920); *The Democratic Dogma and Other Essays* (1930); *The Twilight of the Supreme Court* (1934); *Total War and the Constitution* (1947); *Liberty Against Government* (1948); *A Constitution of Powers in a Secular State* (1951); etc. Prof. jurisprudence, etc., Princeton University, 1905–46.

CORWIN, NORMAN LEWIS (May 3, 1910–); b. Boston, Mass. Radio dramatist. *They Fly Through the Air with the Greatest of Ease* (1939); *Thirteen by Corwin* (1942); *On a Note of Triumph* (1945); *Untitled and Other Radio Dramas* (1947); *The Plot to Overthrow Christmas* (1952); *Dog in the Sky* (1953); *Overkill and Megalove* (1963); etc.

CORY, CHARLES BARNEY (Jan 31, 1857–July 29, 1921); b. Boston, Mass. Ornithologist, author. *Southern Rambles* (1881); *Beautiful and Curious Birds of the World* (1880–83). Curator of ornithology, Field Museum, Chicago.

CORY, DAVID (Oct. 26, 1872–July 4, 1966); b. Oyster Bay, L.I., N.Y. Author. *Puss in Boots, Jr.,* 10v. (1917–22); *Little Indian Books,* 10v. (1922–38); etc. Daily syndicated "Little Jack Rabbit Story" for newspapers.

CORYELL, JOHN RUSSELL (1852?–July 15, 1924). Dime novelist. Pen names, "Nick Carter," "Nicholas Carter," "Milton Quarterly," "Harry Dubois Milman," "Lucy May Russell," "Julia Edwards," "Lillian R. Drayton," "Geraldine Fleming," "Bertha M. Clay," "Barbara Howard," "Margaret Grant," "Tyman Currio." Some of these pen names were used by others. *The American Marquis* (1889); *The Old Detective's Pupil* (1889); *A Wall Street Haul* (1889); *Fighting Against Millions* (1892); *Among the Nihilists* (1898); *Nick Carter's Clever Protégé* (1899); *Nick Carter Down East* (1900); *Tommy's Money* (1911); *Wife or Stenographer—Which?* (1923); etc. The dates are not necessarily those of first editions. See Russell H. Coryell's *The Birth of Nick Carter,* in *The Bookman,* July, 1929.

COSER, LEWIS ALFRED (Nov. 27, 1913–   ); b. Berlin. Educator, author. *The Functions of Social Conflict* (1956); *Sociological Theory* (with B. Rosenberg, 1964); *Men of Ideas* (1965); *Political Sociology* (1967); etc. Prof. sociology, Brandeis University, since 1960.

Cosmopolitan. New York. Monthly. Founded 1886, by Joseph N. Hallock, at Rochester, N.Y., as *The Cosmopolitan.* Later moved to New York City. In 1889 it was purchased by John Brisben Walker (1847–1931), who made it a leading fiction magazine. He sold it to William Randolph Hearst in 1905. Merged with *Hearst's International* (1925) to form *Hearst's International Combined with Cosmopolitan,* which has retained the volume numbering of *The Cosmopolitan.* Helen Gurley Brown has been editor since 1965.

COSS, CLAY (Apr. 4, 1910–); b. Wichita, Kan. Editor. Co-author, with Walter E. Myer: *The Promise of Tomorrow* (1938); *Education for Democratic Survival* (1942); *America's Greatest Challenge* (1952).

COSTAIN, THOMAS B[ertram] (May 8, 1885–Oct. 8, 1965); b. Brantford, Ont. Editor, author. *For My Great Folly* (1942); *Ride With Me* (1944); *The Black Rose* (1945); *The Moneyman* (1947); *High Towers* (1949); *Son of a Hundred Kings* (1950); *The Silver Chalice* (1952); *The Tontine* (1955); *Below the Salt* (1957); *The Three Edwards* (1958); *The Darkness and the Dawn* (1959); *The Last Plataganets* (1961); *The Last Love* (1963); etc. Editor: *Read with Me* (1965). Editor, *MacLean's Magazine* 1910–20; assoc. editor, *Saturday Evening Post,* 1920–34.

COSTIGAN, JAMES (Mar. 31, 1926–); b. Belvedere Gardens, Cal. Playwright. *Two Plays* (1959); *Little Moon of Alban* (prod. 1960); *The Beast in Me* (prod. 1962); *Baby Want a Kiss* (1964). Television Plays: *Time for the Piper* (1952); *Rain No More* (1953); *A Wind from the South* (1955); *Little Moon of Alban* (1958); etc. Television adaptations: *Cradle Song* (1956); *Wuthering Heights* (1958); *The Turn of the Screw* (1959); etc.

COTLER, GORDON, b. New York. Author. Writes under pen name "Alex Gordon." *The Bottletop Affair* (1959); *The Cipher* (1961); *Mission in Black* (1967).

COTLOW, LEWIS N[ATHANIEL] (Feb. 5, 1898–); b. Brooklyn, N.Y. Explorer, author. *Passport to Adventure* (1942); *Amazon Head-hunters* (1953); *Zanzabuku* (1953); *In Search of the Primitive* (1966); *The Twilight of Primitive Man* (1969).

COTT, TED (Jan. 1, 1917–); b. Poughkeepsie, N.Y. Radio and television executive, author. *Victor Book of Musical Fun* (1945); *How to Audition for Radio* (1946); *Isn't It a Crime?* (with others, 1947). Editor: *A Treasury of the Spoken Word* (1949).

Cottage Hearth, The. Boston. Monthly family magazine. Founded 1874, by D. L. Milliken. Edward Everett Hale, Lucy Larcom, Susan Warner, and other well-known writers were frequent contributors. Expired 1894.

COTTER, JOSEPH SEAMON (b. Feb. 2, 1861–deceased); b. in Nelson Co., Ky. Educator, novelist, poet. *A Rhyming* (1895); *Links of Friendship* (poems, 1898); *Caleb, the Degenerate* (1903); *A White Song and a Black One* (1909); *Negro Tales* (1912); *Collected Poems* (1938); *Sequel to the "Pied Piper of Hamelin," and Other Poems* (1939); etc. Founder, Paul Dunbar School, 1893; Samuel Coleridge-Taylor School, 1911, Louisville, Ky.

COTTON, JAMES HARRY (June 9, 1898–); b. Stephen, Minn. Educator. *The Christian Experience of Life* (1933); *Christian Knowledge of God* (1951); *Royce on the Human Self* (1954). Prof. philosophy, Wabash College, 1947–61; 1964–69. Prof. divinity, Harvard University, 1961–64.

COTTON, JOHN (Dec. 4, 1584–Dec. 23, 1652); b. Derby, England. Congregational clergyman, author. *The Keyes of the Kingdom of Heaven* (1644); *The Way of the Churches of Christ in New England* (1645); *Milk for Babes* (1646); *The Bloudy Tenent, Washed, and Made White* (1647); *The Way of Congregational Churches Cleared* (1648); etc.

"Cotton Boll, The." Poem by Henry Timrod (1862). One of the first Southern poems of local color.

Cotton Kingdom, The. By Frederick Law Olmsted, 2v. (1861). One of the major studies of life in the South just before the outbreak of the Civil War. Olmsted wrote the work in the form of letters sent to the *New York Times,* 1856–60.

COTTRELL, LEONARD S[later], JR. (Dec. 12, 1899–); b. Hampton Roads, Va. Social psychologist. Co-author: *American Opinion on World Affairs in the Atomic Age* (1948); *Identity and Interpersonal Competence* (1955); *Behavioral Science and Civil Defense* (with G. W. Baker, 1962); *Juvenile Delinquency: Its Prevention and Control* (with Stanton Wheeler, 1966); etc. Editor, *Sociometry,* since 1956.

COTTRELL, WILLIAM FREDERICK (Aug. 19, 1903–); b. Idaho Falls, Ida. Educator. *The Railroader* (1940); *Energy and Society* (1955). Prof. sociology and government, Miami University, Ohio, since 1930.

COUCH, WILLIAM TERRY (Dec. 4, 1901–); b. Pamplin, Va. Publisher. Editor and contributor: *Culture in the South* (1934); *These Are Our Lives* (1939). Director, University of Chicago Press, 1945–50; editor-in-chief, *Collier's Encyclopedia,* 1952–59.

COUES, ELLIOTT (Sept. 9, 1842–Dec. 25, 1890); b. Portsmouth, N.H. Ornithologist, editor, author. *Key to North American Birds* (1872); *Birds of the Northwest* (1874); *Birds of the Colorado Valley* (1878); etc. Editor of various histories and journals of early expeditions in the West (Lewis & Clark, Pike, Fowler, and others), 15 volumes in all (1893–1900). Contrib. editor, the *Century Dictionary,* 1884–91. Cofounder, the American Ornithologists' Union, 1883.

COUGHLAN, [John] ROBERT (July 17, 1914–); b. Kokomo, Ind. Journalist, author. *The Wine of Genius* (1951); *The Private World of William Faulkner* (1954); *Tropical Africa* (1962); *The World of Michelangelo* (1966); *The Great Palace* (1967). With *Fortune,* 1937–43; *Life,* 1943.

COULETTE, HENRI ANTHONY (Nov. 11, 1927–); b. Los Angeles, Cal. Educator, author. *The War of the Secret Agents* (1966). Editor: *Character and Crisis* (with Philip Levine, 1966). Prof. English, California State College, Los Angeles.

COULTER, ELLIS MERTON (July 20, 1890–); b. Hickory, Catawba Co., N.C. Historian. *History of Kentucky,* 2v. (1922); *The Civil War and Readjustment in Kentucky* (1926); *College Life in the Old South* (1928); *A Short History of Georgia* (1933); *William G. Brownlow—The Fighting Parson of the Southern Highlands* (1936); *The South During Reconstruction, 1865–1877* (1947); *Wormsloe* (1955); *Lost Generation* (1956); *Joseph Vance Bevan* (1964); *Old Petersburg and the Broad River Valley: Their Rise and Decline* (1965). Managing editor, *Georgia Historical Quarterly.* History dept., University of Georgia, since 1919–58.

COULTER, JOHN WESLEY (May 8, 1893–); b. Pettigo, Ireland. Educator. *Land Utilization in the Hawaiian Islands* (1933); *A Gazetteer of the Territory of Hawaii* (1935); *Fiji: Little India of the Pacific* (1942); *The Pacific Dependencies of the United States* (1957). Prof. geography, University of Cincinnati, 1946–49; since 1951.

Counting-Out Rhymes of Children, The. By Henry Carrington Bolton (1888).

Country Doctor, The. Story by Sarah Orne Jewett (1884).

Country Gentleman, The. Philadelphia, Pa. Monthly magazine. Founded 1853, by Luther Tucker at Albany, N.Y., as the weekly edition of the Albany *Cultivator.* Gilbert Milligan Tucker, a son, was editor, 1897–1911. Contained a "Leisure Hour Column" of selected poetry. Purchased in 1911 by the Curtis Publishing Co. of Philadelphia, and its editors were selected from the staff of *The Ladies' Home Journal,* another Curtis publication. Became a monthly in 1925, and fiction by Zane Grey, Joseph C. Lincoln, Ben Ames Williams, Corra Harris, and Courtney Riley Cooper, became an added feature. Name changed to *Better Farming* in 1955 and later that year sold to *Farm Journal.*

"Country Lover, The." Humorous poem by Thomas Green Fessenden, which appeared about 1795.

Country of the Pointed Firs, The. Novel by Sarah Orne Jewett (1896). A story of the Maine seacoast, with the quiet heroine, Mrs. Todd, maker of herb medicines, moving in and out of the idyl with provincial charm and reflecting the homely life of a small community at peace with nature.

Country People. Novel by Ruth Suckow (1924). A realistic story of farm life in the Middle West.

COUNTS, GEORGE SYLVESTER (Dec. 9, 1889–); b. Baldwin City, Kan. Author. *The Selective Character of American Secondary Education* (1922); *The American Road to Culture* (1930); *The Soviet Challenge to America* (1931); *The Prospects of American Democracy* (1938); *The Education of Free Men* (1941); *Education and American Civilization* (1952). Co-author: *The Country of the Blind—The Soviet System of Mind Control* (1949); *The Challenge of Soviet Education* (1957); *Education and the Foundations of Human Freedom* (1963).

County Chairman, The. Play by George Ade (prod. 1903).

Couples. Novel by John Updike (1968). Concerns the sexual adventures of educated suburban couples.

Courageous Companions. Novel by Charles J. Finger (1929). Story of an English boy who sailed with Magellan on his voyage around the world.

COURNOS, JOHN (Mar. 6, 1881–); b. Kiev, Rus. Author. *The Mask* (1919); *The Wall* (1921); *Babel* (1922); *The New Candide* (1924); *Miranda Masters* (1926); *O'Flaherty the Great* (1927); *A Modern Plutarch* (1928); *The Devil Is an English Gentleman* (1932); *Autobiography* (1935); *A Boy*

Named John (1941); *With Hey, Ho and The Man with the Spats* (1963); etc. Also children's books in collaboration with Helen Cournos ("Sybil Norton"). Editor of anthologies and translator of works from Russian.

COURSEY, O[scar] W[illiam] (Apr. 10, 1873–deceased); b. Forreston, Ill. Author. *History and Geography of the Philippine Islands* (1903), republished as, *The Philippines and the Filipinos* (1914); *Who's Who in South Dakota,* 5v. (1913–25); *The Woman with a Stone Heart* (1914); *Shorts* (1925); *Beautiful Black Hills* (1926); *Dakota Literature* (1928); *Pioneering in Dakota* (1937); etc. Editor: *Literature of South Dakota* (1916); etc.

Court House Square. Novel by Hamilton Basso (1936). A portrayal of South Carolina through the discovery by David Barondess of the spirit of his native town.

"Court of Fancy." Poem by Thomas Godfrey (1762).

"Courtship of Miles Standish, The." Poem by Henry Wadsworth Longfellow (1858). A record of the Pilgrim's first memorable romance, containing Priscilla's often quoted remark to John Alden "Why don't you speak for yourself, John?"

Cousin Alice. Pen name of Alice Bradley Neal Haven.

Cousin Cicely. Pen name of Sarah H. Bradford.

COUSINS, MARGARET (Jan. 26, 1905–); b. Munday, Tex. Editor, author. *Uncle Edgar and the Reluctant Saint* (1948); *Ben Franklin of Old Philadelphia* (1952); *Christmas Gift* (1952); *We Were There at the Battle of the Alamo* (1958); *Thomas Alva Edison* (1965). Co-author, with Margaret Truman: *Souvenir* (1956). Editor: *Love and Marriage* (1961). Managing editor, *McCall's,* 1958–61.

COUSINS, NORMAN (June 24, 1912–); b. Union Hill, N.J. Editor, author. *Good Inheritance: The Democratic Chance* (1942); *Modern Man Is Obsolete* (1945); *Talks with Nehru* (1951); *Who Speaks for Man?* (1953); *In God We Trust: The Religious Beliefs of the Founding Fathers* (1958); *In Place of Folly* (1961). Editor, *Saturday Review,* 1942–1971.

Coventry, John. Pen name of John Williamson Palmer.

COVER, JOHN HIGSON (Oct. 29, 1891–); b. Johnstown, Pa. Economist, statistician. *Business and Personal Failure and Readjustment* (1933); *Retail Price Behavior* (1935); *Asia Is Our Business* (1955); *Economic Procedural and Policy Papers for Barbados* (1965); etc.

Covey, Mrs. Arthur S. See Lois Lenski.

Covici-Friede. New York. Publishers. Founded 1928. Ceased 1938; most of its titles were later acquired by Crown Publishers, Inc. Before coming to New York, Pascal Covici had founded his own publishing house in Chicago.

COWAN, FRANK (Dec. 11, 1844–1905); b. Greensburg, Pa. Traveler, author. *The Three-Fold Love* (1866); *Southwestern Pennsylvania in Song and Story* (1878); *An American Story-Book* (1881); *The Poetical Works* (1892); etc.

COWAN, JOHN FRANKLIN (b. Apr. 5, 1854–); b. Griffinshire, N.Y. Methodist clergyman, author. *The Jo-Boat Boys* (1891); *Colorado River Boy Boatman* (1932); *Capturing a King's Calabash* (1934); etc.

COWAN, ROBERT ERNEST (July 2, 1862–1942); b. Toronto, Ont. Librarian, bookseller, author. *The Forgotten Characters of Old San Francisco* (1937). Compiler, *Bibliography of the History of California and the Pacific West* (1914); *The Bibliography of the Spanish Press in California* (1919); *Bibliography of California, 1510–1930* (with Robert R. Cowan, 1933); etc. Librarian, William Andrews Clark, Jr., Library, Los Angeles, 1919–33; bookseller, San Francisco, 1895–1920.

COWARD, THOMAS RIDGWAY (Aug. 5, 1896–Jan. 11, 1957); b. New York. Publisher. With Yale University Press, 1920–22; Bobbs-Merrill Co., 1922–27; founder and president of publishing firm of Coward-McCann, Inc. 1928. Former director, G. P. Putnam's Sons.

Coward-McCann. New York. Publishers. Founded in 1923 by Thomas R. Coward and James McCann. Name changed 1971, to Coward, McConn & Geoghegan. President and editor-in-chief is John J. Geoghegan.

"Cowboy's Dream, The." Cowboy song beginning with the line "Last Night as I Lay on the Prairie." Attributed to Charley Hart, circa 1873, but the authorship is not definitely established.

COWIE, ALEXANDER (Mar. 8, 1896–); b. St. Paul, Minn. Educator. *John Trumbull: Connecticut Wit* (1936); *The Yemassee* (1937); *The Rise of the American Novel* (1948); *American Writers Today* (1956). Prof. English, Wesleyan University, since 1949.

COWLES, FLEUR FENTON, b. New York. Editor, author. *Bloody Precedent* (1952); *The Case of Salvador Dali* (1959); *The Hidden World of Hadhramautt* (1963); *Tiger Flower* (1968). Editor, *Flair,* 1950–51.

COWLES, GARDNER (Feb. 28, 1861–Feb. 28, 1946); b. Oskaloosa, Ia. Publisher. Pres. The Register and Tribune Co., Des Moines, Ia, publishers of the Des Moines *Register* and *Tribune.*

COWLES, GARDNER (Jan. 31, 1903–); b. Algona, Ia. Publisher. With Des Moines *Register* and *Tribune,* since 1925; pres., since 1943; now chairman of the board, Cowles Communications, Inc.

COWLES, JOHN (Dec. 14, 1898–); b. Algona, Ia. Newspaper publisher. *Report on Asia* (1956). With Associated Press, 1929–43; board chairman, 1934–43; pres. Minneapolis *Star & Tribune,* 1935–68; board chairman, since 1968; board chairman, Des Moines *Register and Tribune.* Founder in 1932 of a perambulating library supplying books to prisons, which he called "Parnassus on Wheels."

COWLEY, CHARLES (Jan. 9, 1832–Feb. 6, 1908); b. Eastington, England. Lawyer, author. *Famous Divorces of All Ages* (1878); *Leaves from a Lawyer's Life Afloat and Ashore* (1879); etc.

COWLEY, MALCOLM (Aug. 24, 1898–); b. near Belsano, Pa. Editor, poet, translator. *Blue Juniata* (poems, 1929); *Exile's Return* (1934); *Books That Changed Our Minds* (with Bernard Smith, 1939); *The Dry Season* (1941); *The Literary Situation* (1954). Editor: *After the Genteel Tradition: American Writers Since 1910* (1937); *Writers at Work* (1958); *Fitzgerald and the Jazz Age* (with Robert Cowley, 1966); etc. Lit. editor, *The New Republic,* 1929–44.

COX, HARVEY [Gallagher] (May 19, 1929–); b. Phoenixville, Pa. Educator, author. *The Secular City* (1965); *God's Revolution and Man's Responsibility* (1965); *A Feast of Fools* (1969). Associate prof., church and society, Harvard University, since 1965.

COX, HENRY HAMILTON (c. 1769–c. 1821); b. in Ireland. Farmer, poet. *Metrical Sketches, By a Citizen of the World* (1817). Original of "Henry Donnelly" in Bayard Taylor's *The Strange Friend.*

COX, JOHN HARRINGTON (May 27, 1863–d. 1945); b. in Illinois. Educator, author. *Knighthood in Germ and Flower* (1910); *A Chevalier of Old France* (1911); *Folk Tales of East and West* (1912); etc. Editor: *Folk Songs of the South* (1925); *Traditional Ballads* (1939); *Folk-Songs from West Virginia* (1939); etc. English Dept., University of West Virginia, 1902–34.

COX, KENYON (Oct. 27, 1856–Mar. 17, 1919); b. Warren, O. Painter, art critic. *Old Masters and New* (1905); *Painters and Sculptors* (1907); *The Classic Point of View* (1911); *Artist and Public, and Other Essays* (1914); *Winslow Homer* (1914); *Concerning Painting* (1917); etc.

COX, PALMER (Apr. 28, 1840–July 24, 1924); b. Granby, P. Q. Artist, author. Creator of the "Brownies." *Squibs of California* (1875); *The Brownies: Their Book* (1887); and twelve other Brownie books for children. The "Brownies" first appeared in *St. Nicholas* magazine.

COX, SAMUEL SULLIVAN (Sept. 23, 1824–Sept. 10, 1889); b. Zanesville, O. Journalist, historical writer. Known as "Sunset Cox." *A Buckeye Abroad* (1852); *Diversions of a Diplomat in Turkey* (1887); *Arctic Sunbeams* (1882); *Orient Sunbeams* (1882); etc.

COXE, ARTHUR CLEVELAND (May 10, 1818–July 20, 1896); b. Mendham, N.J. Bishop, poet, hymnographer. *Christian Ballads* (1840); *Hallowe'en, a Romaunt; with Other Lays Meditative and Devotional* (1845); *Saul: A Mystery* (1845); *Impressions of England* (1851); etc. See G. Sherman Burrows's *Bishop Arthur Cleveland Coxe—Author,* in *The Historical Magazine of the Protestant Episcopal Church,* March, 1939.

COXE, GEORGE HARMON (Apr. 23, 1901–); b. Olean, N.Y. Author. *Four Frightened Women* (1938); *The Glass Triangle* (1940); *Charred Witness* (1942); *The Groom Lay Dead* (1944); *Dangerous Legacy* (1946); *Fashioned for Murder* (1947); *The Hollow Needle* (1948); *Inland Passage* (1949); *The Frightened Fiancée* (1950); *The Man Who Died Twice* (1951); *Never Bet Your Life* (1952); *Focus on Murder* (1954); *The Big Gamble* (1958); *Triple Exposure* (1959); *Moment of Violence* (1961); *Mission of Fear* (1962); *The Hidden Key* (1963); *Deadly Image* (1964); *An Easy Way to Go* (1969); *Double Identity* (1970).

COXE, LOUIS OSBORNE (Apr. 15, 1918–). b. Manchester, N.H. Poet. *Sea Farings and Other Poems* (1947); *Billy Budd* (stage adaptation, with R. H. Chapman, 1951); *Second Man and Other Poems* (1955); *The Wilderness* (1958); *The Middle Passage* (1960); *The Last Hero* (1965); *Edwin Arlington Robinson: The Life of Poetry* (1969).

COYKENDALL, FREDERICK (Nov. 23, 1872–Nov. 19, 1954); b. Kingston, N.Y. Book-collector and publisher. Author: *A Note on the Monk* (1935). Compiler: *Arthur Rackham: A List of Books Illustrated by Him* (1922). Managing director, later pres., Columbia University Press.

COZZENS, FREDERICK S[wartwout] (Mar. 11, 1818–Dec. 23, 1869); b. New York City. Merchant, essayist, poet. *Yankee Doodle* (1847); *Prismatics* (under pen name, "Richard Haywarde," 1853); *The Sparrowgrass Papers* (1856); *Acadia; or, A Month with the Blue Noses* (1859); *Sayings of Dr. Bushwhacker and Other Learned Men* (1867). Editor, *The Wine Press,* 1854–61.

COZZENS, JAMES GOULD (Aug. 19, 1903–); b. Chicago, Ill. Novelist. *Confusion* (1924); *Michael Scarlett* (1925); *Cock Pit* (1928); *The Son of Perdition* (1929); *S.S. San Pedro* (1931); *The Last Adam* (1933); *Castaway* (1934); *Men and Brethren* (1936); *Ask Me Tomorrow* (1940); *The Just and the Unjust* (1942); *Guard of Honor* (1948); *By Love Possessed* (1957); *Children and Others* (1964); *Morning Noon and Night* (1968); *Ask Me Tomorrow* (1969).

COZZENS, SAMUEL WOODWORTH (Apr. 14, 1834–Nov. 4, 1878); b. Marblehead, Mass. Jurist, author. *The Marvelous Country; or, Three Years in Arizona and New Mexico* (1874); *Nobody's Husband* (1878); also the *Young Trail Hunters* series; etc.

CRABB, ALFRED LELAND (Jan. 22, 1884–); b. near Bowling Green, Ky. Educator, editor, author. *Dinner at Belmont* (1942); *Supper at the Maxwell House* (1943); *Breakfast at the Hermitage* (1945); *Lodging at the Saint Cloud* (1946); *Home to the Hermitage* (1948); *A Mockingbird Sang at Chickamauga* (1949); *Reunion at Chattanooga* (1950); *Home to Kentucky* (1953); *Peace at Bowling Green* (1955); *Journey to Nashville* (1957); *Nashville: Personality of a City* (1960). Editor, *Peabody Journal of Education,* since 1932. Prof., Peabody College, since 1927.

Craddock, Charles Egbert. Pen name of Mary Noailles Murfree.

CRAF, JOHN RILEY (Aug. 4, 1911–); b. New York. Educator. *Introduction to Business Principles and Practices* (1949); *Economic Development of the United States* (1952); *Junior Boards of Executives* (1958). Dean, school of business, University of Louisville, 1953–64.

CRAFT, ROBERT (Oct. 20, 1923–   ); b. Kingston, N. Y. Musician, author. Co-author: *Conversations with Stravinsky* Vols. 1–4 (with Igor Stravinsky, 1959–63); *Retrospectives and Conclusions* (with Igor Stravinsky, 1969).

CRAFTON, ALLEN (Oct. 3, 1890–July 22, 1966); b. Quincy, Ill. Educator, author. *The Stranger Star* (with Jessica Crafton, 1920); *Self-Expression through the Spoken Word* (1926); *Process of Play Production* (1927); *The Complete Acted Play* (1943); *Free State Fortress* (1954).

CRAFTS, WILLIAM (Jan. 24, 1787–Sept. 23, 1826); b. Charleston, S.C. Lawyer, poet. *The Raciad, and Other Occasional Poems* (1810); *The Sea Serpent; or, Gloucester Hoax* (1819); *Sullivan's Island, The Raciad, and Other Poems* (1820); *A Selection in Prose and Poetry from the Miscellaneous Writings* (1828).

CRAIG, HARDIN (June 29, 1875–Oct. 13, 1968); b. Owensboro, Ky. Educator, author. *The Enchanted Glass: The Elizabethan Mind in Literature* (1936); *Types of English Fiction* (1940); *Literary Study and the Scholarly Profession* (1944). Editor: *Shakespeare: A Historical and Critical Study* (1931); *An Interpretation of Shakespeare* (1948); *The Complete Works of Shakespeare* (1951); *English Religious Drama of the Middle Ages* (1955); *A New Look at Shakespeare's Quarto* (1961); etc. Editor, *Philological Quarterly,* 1922–28. Prof. English, University of Missouri, from 1949.

CRAIG, SAMUEL G. (June 1, 1874–Oct. 7, 1960); b. in DeKalb Co., Ill. Editor, author. *Jesus as He Was and Is* (1914); *Christianity Rightly So Called* (1946); *Jesus of Yesterday and Today* (1956). Editor, *Christianity Today,* 1930–44.

CRAIGIE, PEARL MARY TERESA RICHARDS (Nov. 3, 1867–Aug. 13, 1906): b. Chelsea, Mass. Novelist, playwright. Pen name, "John Oliver Hobbes." *Some Emotions and A Moral* (1891); *Journey's End in Lovers' Meeting* (prod. 1894); *The Ambassador* (prod. 1898); *A Repentance* (prod. 1899); *Robert Orange* (1900); etc. See *The Life of John Oliver Hobbes,* ed. by her father, John Morgan Richards (1911).

Craig's Wife. Play by George Kelly (prod. 1925). Story of a fussy wife whose passion for neatness and order breaks up her home and drives away her husband.

CRAM, RALPH ADAMS (Dec. 16, 1863–Sept. 22, 1942); b. Hampton Falls, N.H. Architect, author. *The Gothic Quest* (1907); *Excalibur* (1908); *The Ministry of Art* (1914); *The Great Thousand Years* (1918); *Walled Towns* (1919); *The Catholic Church and Art* (1929); *Convictions and Controversies* (1935); *My Life in Architecture* (1936); *The End of Democracy* (1937); etc.

CRAMPTON, CHARLES GREGORY (Mar. 22, 1911–); b. Kankakee, Ill. Educator, author. *Outline History of the Glen Canyon Region 1776–1922* (1959); *Standing Up Country, The Canyon Lands of Utah and Arizona* (1964); etc. Editor: *The Mariposa Indian War* (1957); etc. Prof. history, University of Utah, since 1945.

CRANCH, CHRISTOPHER PEARSE (Mar. 8, 1813–Jan. 20, 1892); b. Alexandria, Va. Unitarian clergyman, artist, critic, poet. *Poems* (1844); *The Last of the Huggermuggers* (1856); *Kobboltozo* (1856); *The Bird and the Bell, with Other Poems* (1875); *Ariel and Caliban, with Other Poems* (1887); *Personal Recollections of Robert Browning* (1891); etc.

CRANDALL, BRUCE VERNE (Oct. 16, 1873–Nov. 19, 1945); b. Hillsdale, Mich. Editor, author. *Autocrat at the Lunch Table* (1915); *After Forty Years* (1925); *Railroading on the Rails and Off* (1927); *Reveries of an Editor* (1932); *Is This the Armageddon?* (1942); etc. Editor of several railway journals.

CRANDALL, CHARLES HENRY (June 19, 1858–Mar. 23, 1923); b. Greenwich, N.Y. Poet. *The Season* (1883); *Wayside Music* (1893); *The Chords of Life* (1898); *Songs from Sky Meadows* (1909); etc.

CRANE, ANNE MONCURE (Mrs. Augustus Seemüller) (Jan. 7, 1839–Dec. 10, 1872); b. Baltimore, Md. Novelist. *Emily Chester* (anon., 1864); *Opportunity* (1867); *Reginald Archer* (1871).

CRANE, CLARKSON (Sept. 20, 1894–); b. Chicago, Ill. Novelist. *The Western Shore* (1925); *Mother and Son* (1946); *Naomi Martin* (1947).

CRANE, ELEANOR MAUD. Author of plays for young people. *"Just For Fun"* (1899); *Next Door* (1906); *A Little Savage* (1907); *The Rainbow Kimona* (1908); *Ye Quilting Party of Long Ago* (1935).

CRANE, ELIZABETH G[reen]. Playwright, poet. *Berquin* (1897); *Sylvia* (poems, 1900); *The Imperial Republic* (drama in verse, 1902); *The Necken* (drama in verse, 1913); *Are You Men?* (1923).

CRANE, FRANCES [Kirkwood]. Author. *The Turquoise Shop* (1941); *The Applegreen Cat* (1943); *The Cinnamon Murder* (1946); *Black Cypress* (1948); *The Flying Red Horse* (1949); *The Daffodil Blonde* (1950); *Murder in Blue Street* (1951); *The Coral Princess Murders* (1954); *The Buttercup Case* (1959); *Death-Wish Green* (1960); *Body Beneath a Mandarin Tree* (1965); *A Very Quiet Murder* (1966); *Worse than Crime* (1968); etc.

CRANE, FRANK (May 12, 1861–Nov. 5, 1928); b. Urbana, Ill. Methodist and Congregational clergyman, journalist, author. *Vision* (poems, 1906); *Adventures in Common Sense* (1916); *Four Minute Essays*, 10v. (1919); *The Crane Classics*, 10v. (1920).

CRANE, GEORGE WASHINGTON, III (Apr. 28, 1901–); b. Chicago, Ill. Psychologist, author. *Radio Talks*, Vol. I (1948); *Psychology Applied* (1948); *How to Cash-in on Your Worries* (1956). Syndicated column, "The Worry Clinic" (also called "Case Records of a Psychologist").

CRANE, HART (July 21, 1899–Apr. 26, 1932); b. Garretsville, O. Poet. *White Buildings* (1926); *The Bridge* (1930); *The Collected Poems of Hart Crane* (1933); *The Letters of Hart Crane* (1952), ed. by Brom Weber. *See* Philip Horton's *Hart Crane: The Life of an American Poet* (1937); Fred B. Millett's *Contemporary American Authors* (1940); Brom Weber's *Hart Crane* (1948); H. D. Howe's *Hart Crane: A Bibliography* (1955); Samuel Hazo's *Hart Crane: An Introduction and Interpretation* (1963); Monroe K. Spears's *Hart Crane* (1965); R.W.B. Lewis's *The Poetry of Hart Crane* (1967); John Unterecker's *Voyager: A Life of Hart Crane* (1969).

CRANE, LEO (Feb. 27, 1881–); b. Baltimore, Md. Indian agent, author. *Indians of the Enchanted Desert* (1925); *Desert Drums* (1928).

CRANE, NATHALIA [Clara Ruth Abarbanel] (Aug. 11, 1913–); b. New York City. Poet, novelist. *The Janitor's Boy, and Other Poems* (1924); *The Sunken Garden* (1926); *Swear by the Night, and Other Poems* (1936); *Death of Poetry* (1941); etc.

CRANE, RONALD SALMON (Jan. 5, 1886–Aug. 27, 1967); b. Tecumseh, Mich. Educator, author. *The Languages of Criticism and the Structure of Poetry* (1953). Editor or co-editor: *The English Familiar Essay* (1916); *New Essays by Oliver Goldsmith* (1927); *Critics and Criticism, Ancient and Modern* (1952). Prof. English, Northwestern University 1925–50.

CRANE, STEPHEN (Nov. 1, 1871–June 5, 1900); b. Newark, N.J. Novelist. *Maggie* (1893); *The Black Riders, and Other Lines* (1895); *The Red Badge of Courage* (1895); *Great Battles of the World* (1901); *Men, Women and Boats* (1921); *The Collected Poems of Stephen Crane* (1930); *Twenty Stories by Stephen Crane*, edited by Carl Van Doren (1940); *Stephen Crane: An Omnibus*, ed. by R. W. Stallman (1952); *Stephen Crane: Uncollected Writings*, ed. by Olov W. Fryckstedt (1963); *Complete Short Stories and Sketches*, ed. by Thomas Gullason (1963). *See* Vincent Starrett's *Stephen Crane: A Bibliography* (1923); Thomas Beer's *Stephen Crane* (1923); John Berryman's *Stephen Crane* (1951); E. H. Cady's *Stephen Crane* (1962); Eric Solomon's *Stephen Crane in England* (1965); R. W. Stallman's *Stephen Crane* (1968).

CRANE, VERNER WINSLOW (Aug. 28, 1889–); b. Tecumseh, Mich. Educator, historian. *The Southern Frontier, 1670–1732* (1928); *Benjamin Franklin, Englishman and American* (1936); *Benjamin Franklin and a Rising People* (1954). Editor: *Benjamin Franklin's Letters to the Press 1758–1775* (1950). Prof. history, University of Michigan, since 1930.

CRANSTON, CLAUDIA (Nov. 10, 1886–June 24, 1947); b. Denton, Tex. Author. *The Murder on Fifth Avenue* (1934); *Murder Maritime* (1935); *Sky Gypsy* (1936); *I've Been Around* (1937); etc.

CHAPSEY, ADELAIDE (Sept. 9, 1878–Oct. 8, 1914); b. New York. Poet. *Verse* (1915); *A Study in English Metrics* (1918). Inventor of the cinquaine, a verse pattern. *See* Carl Sandburg's poem "Adelaide Crapsey" (1918) and Louis Untermeyer's *Modern American Poetry Since 1900* (1923).

CRAPSEY, ALGERNON SIDNEY (June 28, 1847–Dec. 31, 1927); b. Fairmount, O. Episcopal clergyman, author. *Religion and Politics* (1905); *The Rise of the Working Class* (1914); *The Last of the Heretics* (autobiography, 1924). Father of Adelaide Crapsey.

CRAVEN, AVERY ODELLE (Aug. 12, 1886–); b. in Randolph Co., N.C. Educator, historian. *Edwin Ruffin, Southerner* (1931); *To Markie* (1933); *The Repressible Conflict* (1939); *The United States: Experiment in Democracy* (1947); *The Rise of Southern Nationalism* (1953); *Civil War in the Making, 1815–1860* (1959); *An Historian and the Civil War* (1964); *Ending of the Civil War* (1968). History dept., University of Chicago, since 1928.

CRAVEN, BRAXTON (Aug. 22, 1822–Nov. 7, 1882); b. in Randolph Co., N.C. Educator, editor, author. *The Theory of Common Schools* (1850). Founder and editor, *The Southern Index*, 1850, which became *Evergreen*. First president, Trinity College (now Duke University), 1838–82.

CRAVEN, FRANK (d. Sept. 1, 1945); b. Boston, Mass. Actor, playwright. *Too Many Cooks* (prod. 1914); *The First Year* (prod. 1920); *Spite Corner* (prod. 1922); *Up She Goes* (prod. 1923); *"That's Gratitude!"* (prod. 1930); etc.

CRAVEN, THOMAS (Jan. 6, 1889–d.1969); b. Salina, Kan. Author, anthologist. *Men of Art* (1931); *Modern Art* (1934). Editor: *A Treasury of Art Masterpieces* (1939); *A Treasury of American Prints* (1939); *The Story of Painting* (1943); *Rainbow Book of Art* (1956).

CRAVEN, WESLEY FRANK (May 19, 1905–); b. Conway, N.C. Educator, author. *Dissolution of the Virginia Company* (1932); *Introduction to the History of Bermuda* (1938); *The Southern Colonies in the Seventeenth Century* (1949); *The Legend of the Founding Fathers* (1956); *New Jersey and the English Colonization of North America* (1964). Co-editor:

The Army Air Forces in World War II, Vols. I-VII (1948–58); *The Colonies in Transition 1660–1713* (1968). Prof. history, Princeton University, since 1950.

Crawdaddy. New York. Monthly. Founded 1966. Edited by Paul Williams; later by Chester Anderson. Known as "The Magazine of Rock 'n' Roll." *See* Paul Williams' *Outlaw Blues* (1969).

CRAWFORD, FRANCIS MARION (Aug. 2, 1854–Apr. 9, 1909); b. Bagni di Lucca, Italy. Historian, novelist. *Mr. Isaacs* (1882); *Doctor Claudius* (1883); *An American Politician* (1884); *Zoroaster* (1885); *Saracinesca* (1887); *Sant' Ilario* (1889); *Don Orsino* (1892); *Katharine Lauderdale,* 2v. (1894); *Corleone* (1897); *Via Crucis* (1898); *Ave Roma Immortalis* (1898); *Francesca da Rimini* (prod. 1902); *Arethusa* (1907); *Stradella* (1909); *The White Sister* (prod. 1909); *Collected Works,* 30v. (1919); etc. *See* M. H. Elliott's *My Cousin: F. Marion Crawford* (1934).

CRAWFORD, JACK [John Wallace] (Mar. 4, 1847–Feb. 28, 1917); b. in Co. Donegal, Ireland. Poet. *The Poet Scout* (1879); *Camp Fire Sparks* (1893); *Lariattes* (1904); *The Broncho Book* (1908).

CRAWFORD, JACK RANDALL (Apr. 1, 1878–d. 1968); b. Washington, D.C. Educator, playwright. *Lovely Peggy* (1910); *Robin of Sherwood* (1911); *I Walked in Arden* (1923); *What to Read in English Literature* (1928); *The Philosopher's Murder Case* (1931). Co-editor (with Tucker Brooke): *The Tragedy of Hamlet* (1947).

CRAWFORD, JAMES PYLE WICKERSHAM (Feb. 19, 1882–Sept. 22, 1939); b. Lancaster, Pa. Educator, editor, author. *Life and Works of Suarez de Figueroa* (1907); *Spanish Drama before Lope de Vega* (1923); *Spanish Pastoral Drama* (1915); etc. Editor, *Modern Language Notes,* 1920–24; *Hispanic Review,* from 1933. Romance Languages dept., University of Pennsylvania, from 1906.

CRAWFORD, KENNETH GALE (May 27, 1902–); b. Sparta, Wis. Journalist. *The Pressure Boys* (1939); *Report on North Africa* (1943). With *Newsweek,* since 1943; now senior editor.

CRAWFORD, MARY CAROLINE (May 5, 1874–Nov. 15, 1932); b. Boston, Mass. Antiquarian, author. *The Romance of Old New England Churches* (1904); *St. Botolph's Town* (1908); *Goethe and His Woman Friends* (1911); *The Romance of the American Theatre* (1913); *Social Life in Old New England* (1914); *In the Days of the Pilgrim Fathers* (1920); etc.

CRAWFORD, NELSON ANTRIM (May 4, 1888–June 30, 1963); b. Miller, S.D. Editor, author. *The Carrying of the Ghost* (poems, 1923); *A Man of Learning* (1928); *Unhappy Wind* (1930); *We Liberals* (1936); Editor: *Weavers With Words* (1921); *Today's Poetry* (1923); *Notable Short Stories* (1946); *Cats in Prose and Verse* (1947). Editor, *Household Magazine,* 1928–51; editor and publisher, *Author and Journalist,* 1951–59.

CRAWFORD, ROBERT PLATT (Dec. 7, 1893–); b. Council Bluffs, Ia. Educator, author. *These Fifty Years* (1925); *The Magazine Article* (1931); *Think for Yourself* (1937); *How to Get Ideas* (1948); *The Techniques of Creative Thinking* (1955); *Direct Creativity with Attribute Listing* (1964). Prof. journalism, University of Nebraska, 1926–59.

CRAWSHAW, WILLIAM HENRY (Nov. 6, 1861–July 2, 1940); b. Newburgh, N.Y. Educator, author. *The Interpretation of Literature* (1896); *Literary Interpretation of Life* (1900); *The Making of English Literature* (1907); *My Colgate Years* (1937). English dept., Colgate University, 1887–1930.

Crayon, Geoffrey. Pen name of Washington Irving.

Crayon, The. New York. Monthly. Founded 1855, as a weekly; became monthly in 1856. An art periodical of distinc-

tion which published poetry, including poems by Bryant and Lowell. Expired 1861.

Crayon Sketches. Humorous essays by William Cox (d. 1851), which appeared in *The New York Mirror.* They were published in 1833.

Cream of the Jest, The. Novel by James Branch Cabell (1917). Felix Kennaston's quest for the ideal lover. An ironic fantasy.

CREAMER, DAVID (Nov. 20, 1812–Apr. 8, 1887); b. Baltimore, Md. Hymnologist. Compiler: *Methodist Hymnology* (1848); etc.

CREAN, ROBERT. Playwright. *A Time to Laugh* (1962); *My Father and My Mother* (1968).

"Creed." Best known poem of Mary Ashley Townsend, in the New Orleans *Picayune,* Nov. 1, 1868.

CREEKMORE, HUBERT (1907–May 23, 1966); b. Water Valley, Miss. Author. *Personal Sun* (1940); *The Stone Ants* (1943); *The Long Reprieve* (1946); *The Fingers of Night* (1946); *Formula* (1947); *The Welcome* (1948); *No Harm to Lovers* (1950); *The Chain in the Heart* (1953); etc.

CREEL, GEORGE (Dec. 1, 1876–Oct. 3, 1953); b. in Lafayette Co., Mo. Author. *Uncle Henry* (anon., 1923); *The People Next Door* (1926); *Sons of the Eagle* (1927); *Sam Houston, Colossus in Buckskin* (1928); *Tom Paine—Liberty Bell* (1931); *War Criminals* (1944); *Rebel at Large* (1947); *Russia's Race for Asia* (1949); etc.

CREELEY, ROBERT [White] (May 21, 1926–); b. Arlington, Mass. Author. *Le Fou* (1952); *The Immoral Proposition* (1953); *The Kind of Act of* (1953); *The Gold Diggers* (1954); *A Form of Women* (1959); *For Love: Poems, 1950–60* (1962); *The Island* (1963); *Poems, 1950–65* (1966); *Words* (1967); etc.

CREELMAN, JAMES (Nov. 12, 1859–Feb. 12, 1915); b. Montreal, P.Q. Editor, war correspondent, novelist, biographer. *On the Great Highway* (1901); *Eagle Blood* (1902); etc. Assoc. editor, *Pearson's Magazine,* 1906–10; *New York Evening Mail,* 1912–15.

CREIGHTON, JAMES EDWIN (Apr. 8, 1861–Oct. 8, 1924); b. Pictou, N.S. Editor, author. *Studies in Speculative Philosophy* (1925); etc. Editor, *Philosophical Review,* 1892–1924. Philosophy dept. Cornell University, 1889–1924, dean graduate school, 1914–24.

CREIGHTON, THOMAS H[awk] (May 19, 1904–); b. Philadelphia, Pa. Architect, editor. *Planning to Build* (1945); *Homes* (1947); *Building for Modern Man* (ed., 1949); *The American House Today* (with Katherine Morrow Ford, 1952); *Designs for Living* (with same, 1955); *Comtemporary Houses* (1961); *American Architecture* (1964); etc. Editor, *Progressive Architecture,* since 1946.

CREMIN, LAWRENCE ARTHUR (Oct. 31, 1925–); b. New York. Educator, author. *The American Common School* (1951); *A History of American Education in American Culture* (with R. Freeman Butts, 1953); *A History of Teachers College, Columbia University* (with others, 1954); *The Transformation of the School* (1961); *The Genius of American Education* (1965); etc. Prof. education, Teachers College, Columbia University, since 1961.

Cresset, The. Valparaiso, Ind. Monthly except summer. Founded 1937. Devoted to literature and the arts within the area of Lutheranism.

CRESSEY, GEORGE BABCOCK (Dec. 15, 1896–Oct. 21, 1963); b. Tiffin, O. Geographer, geologist, author. *Asia's Lands and Peoples* (1944); *How Strong is Russia?* (1954); *China, Land of the 500 Million* (1955); *Crossroads* (1960). Prof. geography and geology, Syracuse University, from 1931.

CRESSON, MARGARET FRENCH, b. Concord, Mass. Sculptor. *Journey into Fame: The Life of Daniel Chester French* (1947).

Cressy. Story by Bret Harte (1889).

CRÈVECOEUR, MICHEL-GUILLAUME-ST. JEAN DE (Jan. 31, 1735–Nov. 12, 1813); b. Caen, France. Essayist. *Letter from an American Farmer* (under pen name, "J. Hector St. John," 1782); *Voyage dans la Haute Pennsylvanie et dans l'État de New-York, par un Membre Adoptif de la Nation Onéida,* 3v. (1801); *Sketches of Eighteenth Century America* (1925). See *The Colophon,* Sept. 15, 1934; Percy G. Adams' edition of *Crèvecoeur's 18th-Century Travels in Pennsylvania and New York* (1962).

CREW, FLEMING. Co-author with Alice Crew Gall: *Wagtail* (1932); *Ringtail* (1933); *Flat Tail* (1935); *Little Black Ant* (1936); *Bushytail* (1941); *Winter Flight* (1949); etc.

CREW, HELEN [Cecilia] **COALE** (Dec. 8, 1866–); b. Baltimore, Md. Novelist, poet. *Aegean Echoes, and Other Poems* (1911); *Saturday's Children* (1927); *The Trojan Boy* (1928); *Under Two Eagles* (1929); *The Lost King* (1929); *Laughing Lad* (1931); *The Shawl with the Silver Bells* (1932); *Peter Swiss* (1934); *Day Before Yesterday* (1935); *The Runaway Cousins* (1936); etc.

CREWS, FREDERICK C. (1933–   ); b. Philadelphia, Pa. Author. *The Tragedy of Manners* (1957); *E. M. Forster: The Perils of Humanism* (1962); *The Pooh Perplex* (1963); *The Sins of the Fathers: Hawthorne's Psychological Themes* (1966); *The Patch Commission* (1968); etc.

CRICHTON, KYLE SAMUEL (Nov. 5, 1896–Nov. 25, 1960); b. Peale, Pa. Editor, author. Pen name, "Robert Forsythe." Under own name: *Law and Order, Ltd.: The Rousing Life of Elfego Baca of New Mexico* (1928); *The Proud People* (1944); *The Marx Brothers* (1950); *Total Recoil* (1960); etc. Under pen name: *Redder than the Rose* (1935); *Reading from Left to Right* (1938); *My Partner-in-Law, The Life of George Morton Levy* (with Martin W. Littleton, 1957). On staff *Scribner's Magazine, Collier's,* etc.

CRICHTON, MICHAEL (Oct. 23, 1942–   ); b. Chicago, Ill. Author. *A Case of Need: A Novel by Jeffrey Hudson* (1968); *The Venom Business: A Novel by John Lange* (1969); *The Andromeda Strain* (1969); *Five Patients: The Hospital Explained* (1970).

Crime Club. Name given to a special department devoted to detective fiction established by Doubleday, Doran to promote the sales of selected titles chosen by a committee. The Dollar Mystery Club was also formed by the same publishers as an adjunct to their Star Dollar Books, reprints of books which formerly sold at higher prices. Now an imprint of Doubleday and Co., Inc.(q.v.), under the editorship of Lawrence P. Ashmead.

"Crisis, The." Poem by John Greenleaf Whittier (1848).

Crisis, The. Novel by Winston Churchill (1901). The story has for its background the incidents of the Civil War.

Crisis in the Classroom. By Charles E. Silberman (1970). Indictment of formal public schooling in America.

CRISSEY, FORREST (June 1, 1864–Nov. 5, 1943); b. Stockton, N.Y. Journalist. *The Country Boy* (1897); *In Thompson's Woods* (1901); *Biography of Alexander Legge* (1936); *Montgomery Ward* (1939); etc. Associated with *Saturday Evening Post,* from 1900.

CRIST, JUDITH [Klein] (May 22, 1922–); b. New York. Motion picture reviewer. *The Private Eye, The Cowboy and the Very Naked Girl* (1968). Film reviewer, *TV Guide,* since 1965; *New York* magazine, since 1968. Faculty, Columbia University School of Journalism, since 1966.

CRISWELL, W[allie] **A.** (Dec. 19, 1909–); b. Eldorado, Okla. Baptist clergyman, author. *The Gospel According to Moses* (1950); *These Issues We Must Face* (1953); *Did Man Just Happen?* (1957); *Expository Sermons on Revelation* (1961–66); *The Holy Spirit in Today's World* (1966); *In Defense of the Faith* (1967); etc.

Critic, The. New York. Literary magazine. Founded 1881, by Jeanette and Joseph B. Gilder. Editors: Jeannette Gilder, 1881–1906 (with Joseph B. Gilder, 1881–1901). Walt Whitman, Joel Chandler Harris, Emma Lazarus, James Lane Allen, Julia Ward Howe, Charles DeKay, Thomas Bailey Aldrich, Richard Watson Gilder, N. S. Shafer, and Edith M. Thomas were among the better-known contributors. Book notes and reviews were featured. It started as a bi-weekly, changed to a weekly in 1883, and became a monthly when it was purchased by Putnam's in 1898. Illustrated after 1898. Merged with *Putnam's Monthly,* 1906. Previously it had absorbed *Good Literature,* 1884; and *The Literary World,* 1905. See Frank L. Mott's *A History of American Magazines,* v. 3 (1938).

"Critical Fable, A." Poem satirizing contemporary poets, by Amy Lowell (1922). It is patterned after James Russell Lowell's "Fable for Critics."

Critical History of Children's Literature. By Cornelia Meigs and others (1953). Covers the period from earliest times to 1950.

CRITTENDEN, CHRISTOPHER (Dec. 1, 1902–); b. Wake Forest, N.C. Historian. *North Carolina Newspapers before 1790* (1928); *The Commerce of North Carolina 1763–1789* (1936). Editor: *Historical Societies in the United States and Canada: A Handbook* (1944). Co-editor: *The Historical Records of North Carolina,* 3v. (1938–39). Editor: *North Carolina Historical Review,* since 1935. Director, North Carolina State Dept. of Archives and History 1935–68; asst. director since 1968. History dept., University of North Carolina, 1926–35.

Croaker Papers, The. By Fitz Greene Halleck and Joseph Rodman Drake. A series of satirical poems on local celebrities, which appeared in the New York *Evening Post,* Mar. 10–July 24, 1819, under the joint pen name, "Croaker & Co." Drake was "Croaker" and Halleck was "Croaker, Jr." The series was published by The Bradford Club as *The Croakers* (1860).

Crocker, Bosworth. See Mary Arnold Crocker.

CROCKER, LIONEL GEORGE (Jan. 17, 1897–). b. Ann Arbor, Mich. Educator, author. *Argumentation and Debate* (1944); *Oral Reading* (with L. M. Eich, 1947); *Effective Speaking* (1948); *Business and Professional Speech* (1951); *An Analysis of Lincoln and Douglas as Speakers and Debaters* (1968); etc.

CROCKER, MARY ARNOLD BOSWORTH (d. Apr. 8, 1946); b. London, England. Playwright. Wrote under the name of Bosworth Crocker. *The Last Straw* (prod. 1917); *Heritage* (prod. 1925); *Iseult of the White Hands* (poetic drama, 1927); *The Tragic Three* (1931); *Child of the Waters* (1935); *Coquine* (1937); etc.

CROCKER, URIEL (Sept. 13, 1796–July 19, 1887); b. Marblehead, Mass. Publisher, author. *Autobiography* (1869); *Memorial of Uriel Crocker* (reminiscences, 1891). The publishing house and bookstore of Crocker and Brewster at 50 Cornhill, Boston, was a favorite spot of Boston literary men, and the partnership lasted for more than 75 years.

CROCKETT, ALBERT STEVENS (June 19, 1873–); b. Solomon's, Md. Author. *Revelations of Louise* (1920); *Ditties from a Ditty Bag* (1922); *When James Gordon Bennett Was Caliph of Bagdad* (1926); *Peacocks on Parade* (1931); *Old Waldorf Bar Days* (1931); etc. With *New York Sun, New York Times,* and other newspapers.

CROCKETT, DAVY [DAVID] (Aug. 17, 1786–Mar. 6, 1836); b. near Rogersville, Tenn. Frontiersman. Killed at the Alamo. Supposed author of *A Narrative of the Life of David Crockett, of the State of Tennessee* (1934). See Frank H. Murdoch's *Davy Crockett* (prod. 1872); Constance Rourke's *Davy Crockett* (1934); Dixon Wecter's *The Hero in America* (1941); K. L. Steckmesser's *The Western Hero in History and Legend* (1965).

CROCKETT, INGRAM (Feb. 10, 1856–deceased); b. Henderson, Ky. Author. *Beneath Blue Skies and Gray* (poems, 1900); *A Year Book of Kentucky Woods and Fields* (1901); *The Magic of the Woods, and Other Poems* (1908).

CROFFUT, WILLIAM AUGUST (Jan. 29, 1835–Aug. 31, 1915); b. Redding, Conn. Journalist, poet. *Bourbon Ballads* (1880); *The Prophecy, and Other Poems* (1893); *An American Procession, 1855–1914; A Personal Chronicle of Famous Men* (1931); etc. Editor: *Fifty Years in Camp and Field; Diary of Major General Ethan Allen Hitchcock* (1909).

CROFTS, FREDERICK SHARER (Jan. 10, 1883–Sept. 16, 1951); b. Hudson, N.Y. Publisher. With the Century Co., 1905–18; with Harper & Brothers, 1919–24; founder, F. S. Crofts & Co., Oct., 1924.

CROLY, DAVID GOODMAN (Nov. 3, 1829–Apr. 29, 1889); b. Cloghnakilty, Co. Cork, Ireland. Journalist, sociologist, author. *Miscegenation* (1864); *Seymour and Blair* (1868); *Primer of Positivism* (1871); *Truth* (1872); *Glimpses of the Future* (1888); etc. Editor, New York *Daily Graphic*, 1873–78. Founder, *The Modern Thinker*, 1873.

CROLY, HERBERT (Jan. 23, 1869–May 17, 1930); b. New York City. Editor, author. *The Promise of American Life* (1909); *Marcus Alonzo Hanna: His Life and Work* (1912); *Progressive Democracy* (1914); *Willard Straight* (1924). Editor, *The New Republic*, 1914–30.

CROLY, JANE CUNNINGHAM (Dec. 19, 1829–Dec. 23, 1901); b. Market Harborough, England. Editor, perhaps the first American newspaper woman, author. *For Better or Worse* (1875); etc. Asst. editor, *The Mirror of Fashion*, under pen name "Jennie June," 1860–65; and *Demorest's Monthly Magazine*, under same pen name, 1865–87. Founder, Sorosis, most famous of early women's clubs, 1868; Women's Press Club, New York, 1889.

CROMIE, ROBERT [Allen] (Feb. 28, 1909–); b. Detroit, Mich. Author. *The Great Chicago Fire* (1958); *Golf for Boys and Girls* (1965); etc. Television program, "Book Beat."

CROMWELL, GLADYS [Louise Husted] (Nov. 28, 1885–Jan. 24, 1919); b. Brooklyn, N.Y. Poet. *The Gates of Utterance, and Other Poems* (1915); *Poems* (1919).

CRONAU, RUDOLF (Jan. 21, 1855–Oct. 27, 1939); b. Solingen, Germany. Traveler, lecturer, author. *From Wonderland to Wonderland*, 2v. (1886); *Travels in the Lands of the Sioux* (1886); *In the Wild West—Trips of an Artist* (1890); *Three Centuries of German Life in America* (1909); *German Achievements in America* (1916); *In the Realm of Clouds and Gods* (1919); etc.

CRONYN, GEORGE WILLIAM (July 12, 1888–); b. Anderson, Ind. Novelist, playwright, poet. *Poems* (1914); *The Greaser* (prod. 1914); *49* (1925); *Fortune and Men's Eyes* (1935); *Mermaid Tavern: Kit Marlowe's Story* (1937); *Caesar Stagg* (1941); *Primer on Communism* (1957); etc. Editor: *The Path on the Rainbow: An Anthology of Songs and Chants from the Indians of North America* (1918).

CROSBY, ERNEST [Howard] (Nov. 4, 1856–Jan. 3, 1907); b. New York. Social reformer, poet. *Plain Talk in Psalm & Parable* (poems, 1899); *Edward Carpenter, Poet and Prophet* (1901); *Captain Jinks, Hero* (1902); *Swords and Plowshares* (poems, 1902); *Broad-Cast* (poems, 1905); *The Soul of the World, and Other Poems* (1908); etc.

CROSBY, EVERETT UBERTO (Apr. 2, 1871–June 4, 1960); b. Worcester, Mass. Author. *Handbook of Fire Protection* (1896); *Ninety-Five Per Cent Perfect* (1937); *Spoon Primer* (1941); *Nantucket in Print* (1946); etc. Editor. *Eastman Johnson* (1944).

CROSBY, FANNY [Frances Jane] (Mar. 24, 1820–Feb. 12, 1915); b. Southeast, N.Y. Poet, hymn writer. *The Blind Girl and Other Poems* (1944); *Monterey, and Other Poems* (1851); *A Wreath of Columbia's Flowers* (1858); *Bells at Evening, and Other Verses* (1897); *Fanny Crosby's Life-Story by Herself* (1903). Her best known hymn is "Safe in the arms of Jesus." See John Hawthorn's *Fanny Crosby, the Sightless Songstress, Author of 8000 Hymns* (1931).

CROSBY, HARRY [Henry Grew] (1897?–Dec. 10, 1929); b. Boston, Mass. (?). Poet. *Shadow of the Sun* (1922); *Sonnets for Caresse* (1926); *Chariot of the Sun* (1927); *Transit of Venus* (1928); *Torch Bearer* (1929); *Aphrodite in Flight* (1929); etc.

CROSBY, JOHN CAMPBELL (May 18, 1912–); b. Milwaukee, Wis. Columnist. *Out of the Blue* (1952); *With Love and Loathing* (1963). Syndicated columnist, *New York Herald Tribune*, 1946–65; columnist. *The Observer*, London, since 1965.

CROSBY, PERCY LEO (Dec. 8, 1891–). b. Brooklyn, N.Y. Artist, author. Creator of character "Skippy." *Skippy* (1925); *Skippy: A Novel* (1929); *A Cartoonist's Philosophy* (1931); *Skippy Rambles* (1932); *Always Belittlin'* (1933).

CROSS, ARTHUR LYON (Nov. 14, 1873–1940); b. Portland, Me. Educator, author. *The Anglican Episcopate and the American Colonies* (1902); *A History of England and Greater Britian* (1914). Editor, *Selected Documents From the Shelburne Papers* (1928); etc. Professor, English history, University of Michigan, 1899–1940.

CROSS, FRANK MOORE, JR. (July 13, 1921–); b. Ross, Cal. Educator. *Early Hebrew Orthography* (with David N. Freedman, 1952); *The Ancient Library of Qumran* (1958). Co-editor: *The Biblical Archeologist*, since 1952. Prof. Hebrew, Harvard Divinity School, since 1958.

Cross, James. Pen name of Hugh Jones Parry.

CROSS, MILTON [John] (1897–). Radio announcer, editor. Editor: *Complete Stories of the Great Operas* (1947); *Encyclopedia of the Great Composers and Their Music*, 2v. (with David Ewen, 1953); *New Complete Stories of the Great Operas* (1955); etc.

CROSS, TOM PEETE (Dec. 8, 1879–); b. Farmer's Delight Plantation, Nansemond Co., Va. Educator, author. *A List of Books and Articles, Chiefly Bibliographical, Designed to Serve as an Introduction to the Bibliography and Methods of English Literary History* (1916); *Motif-Index of Early Irish Literature* (1952); etc. Editor: *Good Reading for High Schools*, 5 v. (with others, 1930–31); *Ancient Irish Tales* (with C. H. Slover, 1936); *Milton's Minor Poems* (1936); etc. English dept., University of Chicago, since 1913.

CROSS, WILBUR LUCIUS (Apr. 10, 1862–Oct. 5, 1948); b. Mansfield, Conn. Educator, governor, author. *The Development of the English Novel* (1899); *The Life and Times of Laurence Sterne* (1909); *The History of Henry Fielding* (1918); *An Outline of Biography* (1924); *Modern English Novel* (1929); *Four Contemporary Novelists* (1930). Editor: *The Yale Shakespeare*; etc. Editor, *The Yale Review*, 1911–39. In English dept., Yale University, 1894–1930. Governor of Connecticut, 1931–39.

Crossing, The. Novel by Winston Churchill (1904). David Ritchie, frontiersman of Kentucky, moves to the Northwest Territory and suffers the hardships of pioneer life.

"Crossing Brooklyn Ferry." Poem by Walt Whitman (1856).

CROSWELL, WILLIAM (Nov. 7, 1804–nov. 9, 1851); b. Hudson, N.Y. Episcopal clergyman, poet, hymn writer. *Poems, Sacred and Secular* (1860).

CROTHERS, RACHEL (Dec. 12, 1878–July 5, 1958); b. Bloomington, Ill. Playwright, actress. *The Three of Us* (prod. 1906); *A Man's World* (prod. 1910); *The Herfords* (prod. Boston, 1912), also called *He and She* (prod. New York, 1920); *39 East* (prod. 1919); *Nice People* (prod. 1921); *Expressing Willie* (prod. 1924); *Let Us Be Gay* (prod. 1929); *As Husbands Go* (prod. 1931); *When Ladies Meet* (prod. 1932); *Susan and God* (prod. 1937); etc.

CROTHERS, SAMUEL McCHORD (June 7, 1857–Nov. 9, 1927); b. Oswego, Ill. Unitarian clergyman, essayist. *The Gentle Reader* (1903); *The Pardoner's Wallet* (1905); *Among Friends, and Other Essays* (1910); *Ralph Waldo Emerson: How to Know Him* (1921); etc.

CROUSE, RUSSEL (Feb. 20, 1893–Apr. 3, 1966); b. Findlay, O. Author. *Mr. Currier and Mr. Ives* (1930); *It Seems Like Yesterday* (1931); *Murder Won't Out* (1932); *The American Keepsake* (1932); *Peter Stuyvesant* (with wife, Anna E. Crouse, 1954); *Alexander Hamilton and Aaron Burr* (with same, 1958); also author or co-author of librettos for many musical comedies. Co-adapter, with Howard Lindsay, of the play *Life With Father,* by Clarence Day (prod. 1939); and co-author with same of *Strip for Action* (prod. 1942); *State of the Union* (prod. 1945, Pulitzer Prize for drama, 1946); *Life with Mother* (prod. 1948); *Call Me Madam* (prod. 1950); *Happy Hunting* (prod. 1956); *The Sound of Music* (prod. 1959); etc.

CROW, [Herbert] CARL (Sept. 26, 1883–June, 1945); b. Highland, Mo. Publicist, author. *Master Kung: The Story of Confucius* (1937); *Four Hundred Million Customers* (1937); *My Friends, the Chinese* (1938); *He Opened the Door of China: Townsend Harris and the Story of His Amazing Adventures* (1939); *Foreign Devils in the Flowery Kingdom* (1940); *Meet the South Americans* (1941); *Japan's Dream of World Empire* (1942); *The Great American Customer* (1943); *China Takes Her Place* (1944); *The City of Flint Grows Up* (1945); etc. Publicist in Shanghai, China, 1911–37.

CROW, JOHN ARMSTRONG (Dec. 18, 1906–); b. Wilmington, N.C. Educator, author. *Spanish American Life* (1941); *Epic of Latin America* (1946); *California as a Place to Live* (1953); *Mexico Today* (1957); *Spain: The Root and the Flower* (1963); *Italy: a Journey Through Time* (1965); etc. Spanish dept., University of California at Los Angeles, since 1937.

CROW, LESTER DONALD (Mar. 31, 1897–); b. Beach City, O. Educator. Co-author with wife, Alice Crow: *Mental Hygiene in School and Home Life* (1942); *Learning to Live with Others* (1944); *Our Teen-Age Boys and Girls* (1945); *Educational Psychology* (1948); *Eighteen to Eighty* (1949); *High School Education* (1951); *Understanding Our Behavior* (1956); *Outline of General Psychology* (1958); *Human Relations in Practical Nursing* (1963); *The Student Teacher in the Secondary School* (1964); etc. Prof. education, Brooklyn College, since 1956.

CROWDER, WILLIAM (1882–). Naturalist, author. *Dwellers of the Sea and Shore* (1923); *A Naturalist at the Seashore* (1928); *Between the Tides* (1931).

CROWE, PHILIP KINGSLAND (Jan. 7, 1908–); b. New York. Diplomat, author. *Sport Is Where You Find It* (1953); *Diversions of a Diplomat in Ceylon* (1957); *Sporting Journeys* (1966); *The Empty Ark* (1967). U.S. Ambassador to Ceylon, 1953–56; Union of South Africa, 1959.

CROWELL, GRACE NOLL (Mrs. Norman H. Crowell) (Oct. 31, 1877–Mar. 31, 1969); b. Inland, Ia. Poet. *White Fire* (1925); *Silver in the Sun* (1928); *Flame in the Wind* (1930); *Songs for Courage* (1935); *Light of the Years* (1936); *This Golden Summit* (1937); *Songs of Hope* (1938); *A Child*

Kneels to Pray (1950); *Come See A Man* (1956); *Proofs of His Presence* (1958); *God's Masterpieces* (1963). See Beatrice Plumb's *Grace Noll Crowell: The Poet and the Woman* (1938).

CROWELL, MERLE (Dec. 28, 1888–Aug. 14, 1956); b. North Newport, Me. Editor, publicist. With New York *Sun,* 1911–15; on staff *American Magazine,* 1915–29; editor, 1923–29; senior editor, *The Reader's Digest,* from 1944.

CROWELL, THOMAS IRVING, JR. (May 5, 1894–July 21, 1960); b. Newton Center, Mass. Business executive, publisher. Chairman board of directors, Thomas Y. Crowell Co., 1942–60.

CROWELL, THOMAS Y. (May 29, 1836–July 29, 1915); b. West Dennis, Mass. Publisher. Founded Thomas Y. Crowell Company in New York in 1876; headed firm, 1876–1915.

Crowell Collier and Macmillan, Inc. New York. Publishers. Its publications include *Collier's Encyclopedia, Harvard Classics,* Berlitz Publications, and various kinds of school materials. With the acquisition of The Macmillan Co., the firm's name was changed from Crowell-Collier Publishing Co. to Crowell Collier and Macmillan. It includes The Free Press of Glencoe, Ill., The Bruce Publishing Co., and Brentano's Inc. In 1968 it acquired *This Week* magazine, and in 1969 G. Schirmer, Inc., the music publishers, Benziger Brothers, the book publishers; and Stechert-Hafner, the booksellers and importers.

Crowell Company, Thomas Y. Publishers. Founded 1876, by Thomas Y. Crowell. Crowell may have been the first company to use cloth commercially for binding books. Reprinted the *British Poets* in the firm's *Red Line Poets,* publishing thousands of editions of Burns, Byron, Tennyson and Browning. After 1885 was among the first to issue translations of such Russian authors as Tolstoy and Gogol. Published reference works such as Roget's Thesaurus. The "success" books of Orison Sweet Marden were notably popular. Thomas Y. Crowell headed the firm until 1915; he was succeeded by his sons J. Ogden Crowell and T. Irving Crowell, who was president from 1915 to 1937. His son Robert L. Crowell succeeded him in 1937 and is now president and chairman of the board. Now a subsidiary of Dun and Bradstreet, Inc.

Crown Publishers, Inc. New York. Publishers. Founded 1936, by Nat Wartels, president, and the late Robert Simon, secretary-treasurer. Lothrop, Lee and Shepard, publishers of children's books, was added in 1943 and sold to Scott, Foresman in 1966. The company also acquired Howell, Soskin & Co.; Covici, Friede, Inc.; Long & Smith; Allen, Towne & Heath; Lear Publishers; etc. In addition to its regular trade list, it publishes the Living Language, Living Shakespeare, and Living Literature book-and-record series; reprints under the imprint of Bonanza Books and Bonanza Paperbacks; popular fiction under the Lenox Hill imprint; etc.

CROWNE, JOHN (1640–Apr., 1712); b. in Shropshire, England. "The first Harvard playwright," a student at Harvard, 1659–60. *Juliana* (prod. 1671); *Calisto* (prod. 1674); *The Country Wit* (prod. 1675–76); *The Destruction of Jerusalem* (prod. 1677); *Sir Courtly Nice* (prod. 1685); etc. See *The Dramatic Works of John Crowne,* 4v. (1873–74), ed. by James Maidment and William H. Logan. See also Arthur F. White's *John Crowne: His Life and Dramatic Works* (1922); and George P. Winship's *The First Harvard Playwright: A Bibliography* (1922).

CROWNFIELD, GERTRUDE (Oct. 26, 1867–June 2, 1945); b. Baltimore, Md. Novelist. *Princess White Flame* (1920); *Alison Blair* (1927); *Mistress Margaret* (1933); *Cristina of Old New York* (1939); *Lone Star Rising* (1940); *Proud Lady* (1942); etc.

CROWNINSHIELD, FRANK [Francis Welch] (June 24, 1872–Dec. 28, 1947); b. Paris. Editor, author. Pen name, "Arthur Loring Bruce." *Manners for the Metropolis* (1908); *The*

Bridge-Fiend (1909). Publisher, *The Bookman,* 1895–1900; *Metropolitan Magazine,* 1900–02. Art editor, *Century Magazine,* 1910–13; editor, *Vanity Fair,* 1914–35; editorial adviser, *Vogue,* from 1935.

CROWNINSHIELD, FREDERIC (Nov. 27, 1845–Sept. 13, 1918); b. Boston, Mass. Painter, poet. *Pictoris Carmina* (1900); *A Painter's Moods* (1902); *Tales in Metre, and Other Poems* (1903); *Under the Laurel* (1907); *Villa Mirifiore* (1912).

CROWNINSHIELD, MRS. SCHUYLER (Mary Bradford C.) (1854–Oct. 14, 1913); b. in Maine. Novelist. *All Among the Lighthouses* (1886); *The Ignoramuses* (1887); *Latitude 19°* (1898); *Where the Trade-Wind Blows* (1899); *The Archbishop and the Lady* (1900); *Valencia's Garden* (1901); etc.

CROWTHER, BOSLEY (July 13, 1905–); b. Lutherville, Md. Journalist. *The Lion's Share* (1957); *Hollywood Rajah: The Life and Times of Louis B. Mayer* (1960); *The Great Films* (1967). With *The New York Times,* since 1928; film critic and editor, 1940–68.

CROWTHER, SAMUEL (June, 1880–Oct. 27, 1947); b. Philadelphia, Pa. Author, farmer. *Common Sense and Labor* (1929); *John H. Patterson* (1923); *The Romance and Rise of the American Tropics* (1929); *Time to Inquire* (1942); etc.

CROY, HOMER (Mar. 11, 1883–May 24, 1965); b. near Maryville, Mo. Novelist. *Boone Stop* (1918); *West of the Water Tower* (1923); *They Had to See Paris* (1926); *Coney Island* (1929); *Sixteen Hands* (1938); *Jesse James Was My Neighbor* (1949); *Wheels West* (1955); *Last of the Great Outlaws: The Story of Cole Younger* (1956); *The Lady from Colorado* (1957); *Trigger Marshall* (1958).

Crucial Instances. Short stories by Edith Wharton (1901).

Crucible, The. Play by Arthur Miller (prod. 1953). Based on the Salem witch trials.

Cruger, Julie Grinnell. See Julie Grinnell Chance.

CRUGER, MARY (May 9, 1834–1908); b. Oscawana, N.Y. Novelist. *Hyperaesthesia* (1886); *A Den of Thieves* (1886); *The Vanderbeyde Manor-House* (1887); *How She Did It* (1888); *Brotherhood* (1891).

"Cruise of the Monitor, The." Civil War poem by George H. Boker (1862). Inspired by the fight with the *Merrimack.*

Cruise of the Snark, The. By Jack London (1911). Account of a voyage in the Pacific.

CRUM, BARTLEY CAVANAUGH (Nov. 28, 1900–Dec. 9, 1959); b. Sacramento, Cal. Lawyer. *Behind the Silken Curtain* (1947).

Crumbling Idols. By Hamlin Garland (1894). Essays on the arts.

CRUMMELL, ALEXANDER (Mar., 1819–Sept. 10, 1898); b. New York. Clergyman, scholar, author. *The Future of Africa* (1862); *Africa and America* (1891). His best known sermon was "The Greatness of Christ."

CRUMP, [James] IRVING (Dec. 7, 1887–); b. Saugerties, N.Y. Editor, author. The *Boys' Book* series, 12v. (1919–34); *Creole Wench* (1933); *Og of the Cave People* (1936); *Out of the Woods* (1940); *Our U.S. Marines* (1943); *Oil Hunters* (1947); *Our Army Engineers* (1953); *Our State Police* (1955); *Our Merchant Marine Academy* (1958). Editor: anthologies of stories reprinted from *Boys' Life.* Editor, *Boys' Life,* 1918–23; and since 1935.

Crusade in Europe. By Dwight D. Eisenhower (1948). The full, informed explanation of Eisenhower's activities, trials, and great decisions during World War II.

CRUSE, HAROLD. Author. *The Crisis of the Negro Intellectual* (1967); *Rebellion or Revolution* (1968).

CRUSE, HELOISE [Bowles] b. Fort Worth, Tex. Journalist, author. *Heloise Housekeeping Hints* (1963); *Heloise Kitchen Hints* (1964); *Heloise All Around the House* (1965). Columnist, *Hints from Heloise,* King Features Syndicate, since 1962.

CRUSO, THALASSA (1908–). Naturalist, television performer. *Making Things Grow* (1969). Regular program, NET.

CUBBERLEY, ELLWOOD PATTERSON (June 6, 1868–1941); b. Andrews, Ind. Educator, author. *Changing Conceptions of Education* (1909); *Rural Life and Education* (1913); *Public Education in the United States* (1919); *A History of Education* (1921); etc. Editor, *Riverside Textbooks in Education;* etc. With Stanford University from 1898, dean, School of Education, 1917–33.

CUBER, JOHN F[rank] (Aug. 31, 1911–); b. Chicago, Ill. Sociologist. *Sociology: A Synopsis of Principles* (1947); *Problems of American Society* (with R. A. Harper, 1948); *Marriage Counseling Practice* (1948); *Social Stratification in the United States* (with William Kenkel, 1954); *The Significant Americans* (1965).

Cudjo's Cave. Antislavery novel by John T. Trowbridge (1863). The locale is Tennessee, and the time is the Civil War. Cudjo is a dwarflike runaway slave, and has as his physical opposite the bold Pomp, also a slave. Their cave is a hangout for abolitionist sympathizers.

Cue. New York. Weekly. Founded 1932. A guide to the art and amusement world's current affairs in New York, with emphasis on the theatre.

CULBERTSON, ELY (July 22, 1891–Dec. 27, 1955); b. Poyana de Verrilao, Rum. Bridge expert, author. *Red Russia Against the World* (1932); *Contract Bridge Complete* (1936); *The Strange Lives of One Man* (autobiography, 1940); *The World Federation Plan* (1942); *Total Peace* (1943); *Must We Fight Russia?* (1946); etc.

CULLEN, COUNTEE (May 30, 1903–Jan. 9, 1946); b. New York. Poet. *Color* (1925); *The Ballad of the Brown Girl* (1927); *Copper Sun* (1927); *The Black Christ & Other Poems* (1929); *One Way to Heaven* (1931); *The Medea and Some Poems* (1935); *The Lost Zoo* (1940); *My Lives and How I Lost Them* (1942); *St. Louis Woman* (musical comedy with Arna Bontemps, prod. 1946); *On These I Stand* (poems, 1947). Editor: *Caroling Dusk, an Anthology of Verse by Negro Poets* (1927).

"Culprit Fay, The." Poem by Joseph Rodman Drake. A fanciful poem of fairy-lore, with the Hudson River region as a background, written in 1819, and published, together with his other poems, by his daughter, Janet Halleck DeKay, as *The Culprit Fay, and Other Poems* (1835).

Culture in the South. Ed. by William Terry Couch (1934). Symposium by thirty-one authors.

CUMING, FORTESCUE (Feb. 26, 1762–1828); b. Strafane, Ireland. Traveler, author. *Sketches of a Tour to the Western Country* (1810).

CUMMINGS, E[dward] E[stlin] (Oct. 14, 1894–July 3, 1962); b. Cambridge, Mass. Painter, author. *The Enormous Room* (1922); *Tulips and Chimneys* (poems, 1923); *XLI Poems* (1925); *&* (poems, 1925); *Is 5* (poems, 1926); *Him* (1927); *Christmas Tree* (poems, 1928); *By E. E. Cummings* (1930); *C I O P W* (1931); *Eimi* (1933); *No Thanks* (poems, 1935); *1/20, Poems* (1937); *Collected Poems* (1938); *One Times One* (poems, 1944); *Santa Claus* (1946); *Xaipe* (poems, 1950); *Poems, 1923–1954* (1954); *A Miscellany* (1958); *95 poems* (1958); *100 Selected Poems* (1959); *50 Poems* (1960); *73 Poems* (1963). *See* George Firmage's *E. E. Cummings: A Bibli-*

ography (1964); Charles Norman's *The Magic Maker: E. E. Cummings* (rev. ed., 1965); Robert Wegner's *The Poetry and Prose of E. E. Cummings* (1965).

CUMMINGS, PARKE (Oct. 8, 1902–); b. West Medford, Mass. Author. *The Whimsey Report* (1948); *The Dictionary of Baseball* (1950); *I'm Telling You Kids for the Last Time* (1951); *American Tennis* (1957); *The Fly in the Martini* (1961). Editor: *The Dictionary of Sports* (1949).

CUMMINS, MARIA SUSANNA (Apr. 9, 1827–Oct. 1, 1866); b. Salem, Mass. Novelist. *The Lamplighter* (1854); *Mabel Vaughan* (1857); *El Fureidis* (1860); *Haunted Hearts* (1864). *See* James A. Maitland.

Cumulative Book Index, The. Edited by Nina R. Thompson. Published by H. W. Wilson Co. since 1898. Since 1928 it has contained an author, title, and subject index to current books in English. Published monthly with semi-annual and larger cumulations.

CUNINGGIM, [Augustus] MERRIMON (May 12, 1911–); b. Nashville, Tenn. Educator. *The College Seeks Religion* (1947); *Freedom's Holy Light* (1955). Editor: *Christianity and Communism* (1958). Dean, Perkins School of Theology, Southern Methodist University, since 1951.

CUNLIFFE, J[ohn] W[illiam] (Jan 20, 1865–Mar. 18, 1946); b. Bolton, Lancashire, England. Educator, author. *A Canadian Soldier* (1917); *English Literature During the Last Half Century* (1919); *Modern English Playwrights* (1927); *English Literature in the Twentieth Century* (1933); *Leaders of the Victorian Revolution* (1934). Editor of many series of *Century Readings* and texts on English literature; *Poems of the Great War* (1916); joint editor, revised edition of *Warner Library*, 1917–18. School of Journalism, Columbia University, 1912–20, director, 1920–31.

CUNLIFFE, MARCUS. Author. *George Washington: Man and Monument* (1958); *The Nation Takes Shape, 1789–1837* (1960). Editor: *The Life of Washington* by M. L. Weems (1962).

CUNNINGHAM, ALBERT BENJAMIN (June 22, 1888–Sept. 24, 1962); b. Linden, W.Va. Educator, author. *The Manse at Barren Rocks* (1918); *The Chronicle of an Old Town* (1919); *The Singing Mountains* (1919); *Old Black Bass* (1922); *Animal Tales of the Rockies* (1925); *After the Storm* (1949); *Murder Without Weapons* (1949); *Hunter Is the Hunted* (1950); *One Big Family* (1950); *Skeleton in the Closet* (1951); *Who Killed Pretty Becky Low?* (1951); *Strange Return* (1952); etc. Under pen name "Garth Hale": *Substance of a Dream* (1951); *That Love Hath an End* (1951); *Legacy for Our Sons* (1952); etc. Under pen name "Estil Dale": *The Last Survivor* (1952); etc.

CUNNINGHAM, CORNELIUS CARMAN (Nov. 9, 1890–Sept. 15, 1958); b. Weehawken, N. J. Educator, author. *Literature as a Fine Art* (1941); *Making Words Win for You* (1953).

CUNNINGHAM, EUGENE (Nov. 29, 1896–Oct. 18, 1957); b. Helena, Ark. Author. Pen name, "Leigh Carder." *Gypsying Through Central America* (1922); *Trail to Apacaz* (1924); *Riders of the Night* (1932); *Trail of the Macaw* (1935); *Quick Triggers* (1935); *Spiderweb Trail* (1940); *Gunfighters All* (1941); *Buscadero Trail* (1951); *Gunsight Chance* (1951); *Riding Gun* (1951); also, under pen name: *Outlaw Justice* (1935); etc.

CUNNINGHAM, GUSTAVUS WATTS (Nov. 14, 1881–); b. Laurens, S.C. Educator. *A Study in the Philosophy of Bergson* (1916); *Problems of Philosophy* (1924); *The Idealistic Argument in Recent British and American Philosophy* (1933); etc. Co-editor, *The Philosophical Review*, since 1930. Prof. philosophy, Cornell University, since 1927.

CUNNINGHAM, HOLLY ESTIL (Jan. 13, 1883–Jan. 23, 1952); b. Jackson Co., W.Va. Educator, philosopher, author.

Types of Logical Theory (1918); *An Introduction to Philosophy* (1920); *New Concepts in Education* (1935); *Modern Science and Ancient Morality* (1947); etc. Dept. of philosophy, University of West Virginia, 1923–29.

CUNNINGHAM, J[ames] V[incent] (Aug. 23, 1911–); b. Cumberland, Md. Educator, literary critic, poet. *Helmsman* (poems, 1941); *The Judge Is Fury* (poems, 1947); *Woe or Wonder: The Emotional Effect of Shakespearean Tragedy* (1951); *The Journal of John Cardan* (1964); *The Renaissance in England* (1967); etc. Prof. English, Brandeis University, since 1953.

CUNNINGHAM, JULIA WOOLFOLK (Oct. 4, 1916–); b. Spokane, Wash. Author. *The Vision of Francois the Fox* (1960); *Dear Rat* (1961); *Macaroon* (1962); *Candle Tales* (1964); *Drop Dead* (1965); *Violet* (1966); *Onion Journey* (1967).

CUNNINGHAM, WILLIAM (May 13, 1901–Feb. 21, 1967); b. Okeene, Okla. Journalist, author. *Green Corn Rebellion* (1935); *Pretty Boy* (1936); *Daniel Boone* (1952); *Danny* (with Sarah Cunningham, 1953).

CUPPY, WILL[iam Jacob] (Aug. 23, 1884–Sept. 19, 1949); b. Auburn, Ind. Author. *How to be a Hermit* (1929); *How to Tell Your Friends from the Apes* (1931); *How to Become Extinct* (1941); *The Great Bustard* (1944); *Murder Without Tears* (1946); *The Decline and Fall of Everybody* (1948). Wrote weekly column in New York *Herald Tribune Books*, on current detective stories.

"Curfew." Poem by Henry Wadsworth Longfellow (1845).

"Curfew Must Not Ring To-Night." Poem by Rosa Hartwick Thorpe. Written in April, 1867, first published in the *Detroit Commercial Advertiser*, 1870.

CURIE, EVE (Dec. 6, 1904–); b. Paris. Lecturer, author. *Madame Curie* (1937); *Journey Among Warriors* (1943).

Curious Questions in History, Literature, Art, and Social Life. By Sarah H. Killikelly, 3v. (1886–1900).

Curlytops. A series of books for children by Howard R. Garis.

CURME, GEORGE OLIVER (Jan. 14, 1860–Apr. 29, 1948); b. Richmond, Ind. Educator, philologist, author. *A Grammar of the German Language* (1905); *College English Grammar* (1925); *English Syntax* (1931); *Principles and Practice of English Grammar* (1946); etc. Prof. Germanic philology, Northwestern University, 1896–1933.

CURRAN, DALE (Mar. 26, 1898–); b. Poplar, Mont. Novelist. *A House on a Street* (1934); *Piano in the Band* (1940); *Dupree Blues* (1948). Co-founder (with Art Hodes), *Jazz Record*, 1943; editor, 1943–47.

CURRAN, EDWIN (1892–). Poet. *First Poems* (1917); *The Second Poems* (1919); *Poems* (1919); *New Poems* (1921); *The Lions* (1922).

CURRAN, GEORGE EDWIN. Poet. *The Last Judgment* (1924); *The Poems*, 2v. (1928).

CURRENT, RICHARD N[elson] (Oct. 5, 1912–); b. Colorado City, Colo. Historian, author. *Old Thad Stevens* (1942); *Pine Logs and Politics* (1950); *Secretary Stimson* (1954); *The Typewriter and the Men Who Made It* (1954); *Daniel Webster and the Rise of National Conservatism* (1955); *Lincoln the President: Last Full Measure* (with J. G. Randall, 1955); *Mr. Lincoln* (ed., 1957); *The Lincoln Nobody Knows* (1958); *Lincoln and the First Shot* (1963); etc. Prof. history, Women's College of the University of North Carolina, since 1955.

Current, The. Chicago. Weekly. Founded 1883, by Edgar L. Wakeman. Outstanding for its brilliant group of contributors. Expired 1888.

Current Biography. Edited by Charles Moritz. Biographical articles about figures in the news. Issued monthly, except August, and in annual volumes.

Current Events. Columbus, O. Founded 1902. Educational magazine.

Current History. New York. Founded Dec., 1914, by the *New York Times.* Originally called *New York Times Current History.* Merged with *Forum and Century,* July, 1940.

Current History. Philadelphia, Pa. Monthly. Founded 1914.

Current Literature. See *Current Opinion.*

Current Opinion. New York. Monthly. Founded 1888, as *Current Literature.* It absorbed *Current History* in 1903, and adopted the name *Current Opinion* in 1913. E. J. Wheeler was editor, 1905–25; and Alexander Harvey, assoc. editor, 1905–22. Expired 1925.

CURRIER, CHARLES WARREN (Mar. 22, 1857–Sept. 23, 1918); b. St. Thomas, Virgin Islands. Roman Catholic bishop, historical writer, novelist. *The Rose of Alhambra; or, The Conquest of Granada* (1897); *Dimitrios and Irene; or, The Conquest of Constantinople* (1904); *Lands of the Southern Cross* (1911); etc.

CURRIER, THOMAS FRANKLIN (Feb. 26, 1873–Sept. 14, 1946); b. Roxbury, Mass. Librarian, author. *Selective Cataloging* (1928); *Elizabeth Lloyd and the Whittiers* (1939); etc. Compiler, *A Bibliography of John Greenleaf Whittier* (1937); etc. With Harvard College Library, from 1894.

Currier & Ives. New York. Lithographers. Founded by Nathaniel Currier (Mar. 27, 1813–Nov. 20, 1888) in 1835. Currier had worked for William S. & John Pendleton, Boston, and for Pendleton, Kearney & Childs, Philadelphia, before setting up his own printing establishment. In 1850 he took as partner, James Merritt Ives (Mar. 5, 1824–Jan. 3, 1895). Beginning in 1857, all lithographs issued by them bore the imprint, Currier & Ives. Currier was succeeded by his son William S., in 1880; and Ives was succeeded by his son Chauncey in 1895, who bought out Currier in 1902. The firm was sold to Daniel W. Logan in 1907 and expired. Their old prints have become collector's items. *See* Russel Crouse *Mr. Currier and Mr. Ives* (1930), and Harry T. Peters's *Currier and Ives,* 2v. (1929–31).

CURRY, CHARLES MADISON (May 16, 1869–Mar. 14, 1944); b. Whiteland, Ind. Editor, *Literary Readings* (1903); *Children's Literature* (with E. E. Clippinger, 1921); etc. Editor, Rand, McNally & Co., 1926–28; American Book Co., from 1928.

CURRY, J[abez] L[amar] M[onroe] (June 5, 1825–Feb. 12, 1903); b. in Lincoln Co., Ga. Statesman, educator, historian. *William Ewart Gladstone* (1891); *Civil History of the Government of the Confederate States* (1901).

CURRY, OTWAY (Mar. 26, 1804–Feb. 17, 1855); b. Greenfield, O. Editor, poet. *Love of the Past* (poem, 1888). Editor (with William D. Gallagher), *The Hesperian,* 1838.

CURTI, MERLE [Eugene] (Sept. 15, 1897–); b. Papillion, Neb. Educator, author. *Social Ideas of American Educators* (1934); *The Learned Blacksmith: The Letters and Journals of Elihu Burritt* (1937); *Austria and the U.S., 1848–1852* (1947); *Growth of American Thought* (1943; Pulitzer Prize for history, 1944); *Introduction to America* (1944); *Probing Our Past* (1955); *The American Paradox* (1956); *The Making of an American Community* (with others, 1959); *American Philanthropy Abroad* (1963); *Rise of the American Nation* (1966); *Human Nature in American Historical Thought* (1969); etc. Prof. history, Teachers College, Columbia University, 1937–42; University of Wisconsin, since 1942.

CURTIN, D[aniel] THOMAS (Jan. 17, 1886–Jan. 2, 1963); b. Jamaica Plain, Mass. Lecturer, author. *The Land of Deepening Shadow,* 2v. (1917); *The Edge of the Quicksands* (1918);

The Tyranny of Power (1923); *Criminal Justice, Deaf, Dumb, Blind* (1937); *Men, Oil and War* (1947). Author of numerous radio dramas.

CURTIN, JEREMIAH (Sept. 6, 1840–Dec. 14, 1906); b. Greenfield, Wis. Linguist, comparative mythologist. *Creation Myths of Primitive America* (1898); *Seneca Indian Myths* (1923); and other collections of myths of many peoples.

CURTIS, ALICE TURNER; b. Sullivan, Me. Author. The *Grandpa's Little Girl* series, 4v. (1907–10); the *Little Maid* series, 4v. (1926–36); the *Frontier Girl* series, 4v. (1929–37); etc.

CURTIS, CHARLES PELHAM (May 8, 1891–Dec. 24, 1959); b. Boston, Mass. Lawyer, author. *Hunting in Africa, East and West* (with Richard C. Curtis, 1925); *Introduction to Pareto* (with George C. Homans, 1934); *The Practical Cogitator* (with Ferris Greenslet, 1945); *Lions Under the Throne* (1947); *It's Your Law* (1954); *The Modern Prudent Investor* (1955); *The Oppenheimer Case* (1955); *A Commonplace Book* (1957); *Law as Large as Life* (1959).

CURTIS, CYRUS HERMANN KOTZSCHMAR (June 18, 1850–June 7, 1933); b. Portland, Me. Publisher. Founder, *The People's Ledger,* 1872; *Ladies Home Journal,* 1883; *Evening Public Ledger,* Philadelphia, 1914. Purchased *Saturday Evening Post* in 1897, *Country Gentleman* in 1911, and the *Public Ledger,* Philadelphia, in 1913. Founder, Curtis Publishing Company, Philadelphia, July 1, 1890. *See* Edward Bok's *A Man From Maine* (1923).

CURTIS, EDWARD S. (Feb. 19, 1868–d. 1952); b. Madison, Wis. Photographer, author. *The North American Indian,* 20v. (1907–30); etc.

CURTIS, GEORGE TICKNOR (Nov. 28, 1812–Mar. 28, 1894); b. Watertown, Mass. Constitutional lawyer, author. *History of the Origin, Formation and Adoption of the Constitution of the United States,* 2v. (1854–58); *Life of Daniel Webster,* 2v. (1870); *Life of James Buchanan,* 2v. (1883); *John Charaxes: A Tale of the Civil War* (pen name "Peter Boylston," 1889); etc.

CURTIS, GEORGE WILLIAM (Feb. 24, 1824–Aug. 31, 1892) b. Providence, R.I. Editor, orator, author. *Nile Notes of a.Howadji* (1851); *The Howadji in Syria* (1852); *The Potiphar Papers* (1853); *Prue and I* (1856); *Works,* 5v. (1856); *From the Easy Chair,* 3v. (1892–94); *Literary and Social Essays* (1895); and other books. Assoc. editor, *Putnam's Magazine,* 1853–1857; editor, "Editor's Easy Chair," in *Harper's Magazine,* 1852–92; editor, "Manners Upon the Road," in *Harper's Bazar,* where he used pen name "An Old Bachelor."

CURTIS, NEWTON MALLORY. Novelist. *The Bride of the Northern Wilds* (1843); *The Ranger of Ravenstream* (1847); *The Prairie Guide* (1847); *The Foundling of the Mohawk* (1848); *The Marksmen of Monmouth* (1848); *The Vidette* (1848); etc.

CURTIS, PAUL ALLAN, Jr. (Mar. 28, 1889–d. 1943); b. New York. Writer on guns and shooting. *Outdoorsman's Handbook* (1920); *American Game Shooting* (1927); *Upland Game Bird Shooting in America* (1930); *The Book of Guns and Gunning* (1934); *The Highlander* (1937); *Sportsmen All* (1938); etc. Editor, *Game,* 1934–35; *National Sportsman,* 1937–38.

CURTIS, WILLIAM ELEROY (Nov. 5, 1850–Oct. 5, 1911); b. Akron, O. Journalist, traveler, author. *A Summer Scamper Along the Old Santa Fe Trail* (1883); *The Capitals of Spanish America* (1888); *The Yankees of the East,* 2v. (1896); *Between the Andes and the Ocean* (1901); etc. Travel correspondent, *Chicago Record.*

CURTISS, PHILIP [Everett] (Apr. 19, 1885–May 23, 1964); b. Hartford, Conn. Novelist. *The Ladder* (1915); *Between Two Worlds* (1916); *Crater's Gold* (1919); *Wanted—A Fool*

(1920); *Mummers in Mufti* (1922); *The Gay Conspirators* (1924); *The Honorable Charlie* (1930); *An Outline of Government in Connecticut* (with James Daugherty, 1944).

CURTISS, URSULA [Reilly]. Author. *Voice Out of Darkness* (1948); *Noonday Evil* (1951); *Widow's Web* (1956); *The Stairway* (1957); *So Dies the Dreamer* (1960); *Hours to Kill* (1961); *The Forbidden Garden* (1962); *The Wasp* (1963); *Out of the Dark* (1964); etc.

CURWOOD, JAMES OLIVER (June 12, 1878–Aug. 13, 1927); b. Owosso, Mich. Novelist. *The Courage of Captain Plum* (1908); *The Gold Hunters* (1909); *The River's End* (1919); *The Valley of Silent Men* (1920); *The Flaming Forest* (1921); *The Alaskan* (1923); *The Glory of Living: The Autobiography of an Adventurous Boy* (1928); *Son of the Forest: An Autobiography* (1930).

CUSHING, CALEB (Jan. 17, 1800–Jan. 2, 1879); b. Salisbury, Mass. Statesman, scholar, author. *Review Historical and Political of the Late Revolution in France* (1853); *Reminiscences of Spain* (1833); etc. He was satirized by Lowell in the *Biglow Papers.*

Cushing, Charles Cyprian Strong. See Tom Cushing.

CUSHING, CHARLES PHELPS (Oct. 21, 1884–June 24, 1960) b. Mendota, Ill. Writer. *If You Don't Write Fiction* (1920). Managing editor, *The Stars and Stripes,* A.E.F. newspaper in France, 1918.

CUSHING, ELIZA LANESFORD FOSTER (Mrs. Frederick Cushing) (b. Oct. 19, 1794); b. in Massachusetts, daughter of Hannah Webster Foster. Novelist. *The Sunday School; or, Village Sketches* (with sister, Harriet Vaughan Foster Cheney, 18–?); *Saratoga: A Tale of the Revolution* (anon., 1824); *Yorktown: An Historical Romance* (anon., 1826); *Esther: A Sacred Drama* (1840).

CUSHING, FRANK HAMILTON (July 22, 1857–Apr. 10, 1900); b. North East, Pa. Anthropologist, ethnologist, author. *Zuñi Folk Tales* (1901); etc.

CUSHING, HARVEY [Williams] (Apr. 8, 1869–Oct. 8, 1939); b. Cleveland, O. Surgeon, biographer, essayist. *The Life of Sir William Osler* (1925, Pulitzer Prize for American biography, 1926); *Consecratio Medici, and Other Essays* (1928); etc.

CUSHING, TOM [Charles Cyprian Strong] (Oct. 27, 1874–Mar. 6, 1941); b. New Haven, Conn. Playwright. *Thank You* (with Winchell Smith, prod. 1921); *The Devil in the Cheese* (prod. 1925); also co-author of adaptations, such as *Sari* (prod. 1914); *Blood and Sand* (prod. 1921); and *Laugh, Clown, Laugh* (prod. 1923).

CUSHMAN, CLARISSA WHITE FAIRCHILD (Jan. 13, 1889–); b. Oberlin, O. Editor, author, *The New Poor* (1927); *But For Her Garden* (1935); *The Bright Hill* (1936); *This Side of Regret* (1937); *The Other Brother* (1939); *I Wanted to Murder* (1940); *Young Widow* (1942); *Fatal Step* (1953); etc.

CUSHMAN, RALPH SPAULDING (Nov. 12, 1879–Aug. 10, 1960); b. Poultney, Vt. Methodist bishop, author. *Studies in Stewardship* (1917); *Hill Top Verses* (1927); *Spiritual Hilltops* (1931); *I Have a Stewardship* (1939); *Will a Man Rob God?* (1942); *The Message of Stewardship* (1946); *The Prayers of Jesus, Meditations and Verse* (1955).

CUSTER, ELIZABETH BACON (Mrs. George Armstrong Custer) (Apr. 8, 1842–Apr. 4, 1933); b. Monroe, Mich. Author. *Boots and Saddles; or, Life in Dakota with General Custer* (1885); *Tenting on the Plains* (1887); *Following the Guidon* (1890); *The Boy General* (a condensation of the other three books, 1901). Her husband, who was massacred with all his troops in North Dakota, June 25, 1876, had written several sketches on frontier life for *The Galaxy.* These were published in 1874 as *My Life On the Plains. See* Earl A. Brininstool's *A Trooper with Custer* (1925).

CUSTIS, GEORGE WASHINGTON PARKE (Apr. 30, 1781–Oct. 10, 1857); b. "Mount Vernon," Va. Playwright. *The Indian Prophecy* (prod. 1827); *Pocahontas; or, The Settlers of Virginia* (prod. 1830); etc.; also *Recollections and Private Memoirs of Washington* (1859). The *Memoirs* had been published in the *United States Gazette* and the *National Intelligencer,* beginning in 1826.

CUTHBERT, CLIFTON (Apr. 4, 1907–); Novelist. *Joy Street* (1931); *Without Rain* (1933); *Art Colony* (1933); *Second Sight* (1934); *Another Such Victory* (1937); *The Robbed Heart* (1945).

Cuthrell, Faith Baldwin. See Faith Baldwin.

CUTLER, CARL C. (1878–). Author. *Greyhounds of the Sea* (1930); *Five Hundred Sailing Records of American Built Ships* (1952); *Queen of the Western Ocean* (1961).

CUTLER, ELBRIDGE JEFFERSON (Dec. 28, 1831–Dec. 27, 1870); b. Holliston, Mass. Educator, poet. *Poems* (1859); *War Poems* (1867); *Stella* (1868).

CUTLER, LIZZIE PETIT (1831–Jan. 16, 1902); b. Milton, Va. Novelist. *Light and Darkness: A Story of Fashionable Life* (1855); *Household Mysteries: A Romance of Southern Life* (1856); *The Stars of the Crowd; or, Men and Women of the Day* (1858).

CUTLER, ROBERT (June 12, 1895–); b. Brookline, Mass. Lawyer, author. *Louisburg Square* (1917); *The Speckled Bird* (1923); *No Time for Rest: Boston and Washington, Things Remembered* (1966).

CUTTEN, GEORGE BARTON (Apr. 11, 1874–Nov. 2, 1962); b. Amherst, N.S. Educator, Author. *Mind: Its Origin and Goal* (1925); *The Threat of Leisure* (1926); *Speaking With Tongues* (1927); *Instincts and Religion* (1940); *Should Prohibition Return* (1944); *Silversmiths of Virginia* (1952); etc. President, Colgate University, from 1922.

CUTTER, BLOODGOOD HAVILAND (Aug. 5, 1817–Sept. 26, 1906); b. Little Neck, L.I., N.Y. Poet. *The Long Island Farmer's Poems* (1886). He is associated with Mark Twain's trip to Europe, recorded in *Innocents Abroad.*

CUTTER, CHARLES AMMI (Mar. 14, 1837–Sept. 6, 1903); b. Boston, Mass. Librarian of Boston Athenaeum, 1868–93. Edited *Catalogue of the Library of the Boston Athenaeum, 1807–1871,* 5v. (1874–82); *Rules for a Printed Dictionary Catalogue* (1875); *Expansive Classification,* in parts (1891–1904). Co-founder, *The Library Journal,* 1876; editor, 1881–93.

Cutter, Elizabeth Reeve. See Mrs. Dwight Whitney Morrow.

CUTTER, GEORGE WASHINGTON (1801–Dec. 25, 1865); b. in Quebec, Canada. Poet. *Buena Vista, and Other Poems* (1848); *Poems and Fugitive Pieces* (1857); *Poems, National and Patriotic* (1857).

CUTTING, [Charles] SUYDAM (Jan. 17, 1889–); b. New York. Naturalist, author. *The Fire Ox, and Other Years* (1940). Field explorer for American Museum of Natural History, New York; Field Museum, Chicago; etc.

CUTTING, ELISABETH BROWN (d. Aug. 13, 1946); b. Brooklyn. N.Y. Editor, author. *Jefferson Davis* (1930). Editorial staff, *Harper's Bazar,* 1907–10; assoc. editor, *North American Review,* 1910–21; managing editor, 1921–27.

CUTTING, MARY STEWART (June 27, 1851–Aug. 10, 1924); b. New York. Novelist. *Little Stories of Married Life* (1902); *Heart of Lynn* (1904); *Little Stories of Courtship* (1905); *Just for Two* (1909); *Refractory Husbands* (1913); *Some of Us Are Married* (1920); etc.

CUYLER, THEODORE L[edyard] (Jan. 10, 1822–Feb. 26, 1909); b. Aurora, N.Y. Presbyterian clergyman, author. *From the Nile to Norway and Homeward* (1882); *Recollections of a Long Life* (1902); etc.

Cycle of Manhattan, A. By Thyra Samter Winslow (1923). A story of the rise of a family in New York City.

Cymon. Pen name of Frederick T. Somerby.

Cytherea. Novel by Joseph Hergesheimer (1922). Two middle-aged lovers run away to Havana in an attempt to recapture the passions of youth.

D

Da Ponte. See Ponte.

DABNEY, RICHARD (1787-Nov. 24, 1825); b. in Louisa Co., Va. Poet. *Poems, Original and Translated* (1812); *The Olive Branch; or, Faults on Both Sides, Federal and Democratic* (1814).

DABNEY, RICHARD HEATH (Mar. 29, 1860–May 16, 1947); b. Memphis, Tenn. Educator, historian, author. *The Causes of the French Revolution* (1888); *John Randolph* (1898). University of Virginia, 1889–1938.

DABNEY, ROBERT LEWIS (Mar. 5, 1820–Jan. 3, 1898); b. in Louisa Co., Va. Clergyman, educator, author. *Life and Campaigns of Lieut.-Gen. Thomas J. Jackson (Stonewall Jackson)* (1866); *A Defense of Virginia and the South* (1867); etc.

DABNEY, VIRGINIUS (Feb. 15, 1835–June 2, 1894); b. "Elmington," Gloucester Co., Va. Educator, editor, author. *The Story of Don Miff* (1886); *Gold That Did Not Glitter* (1889).

DABNEY, VIRGINIUS (Feb. 8, 1901–); b. University, Va. Editor, author. *Liberalism in the South* (1932); *Below the Potomac* (1942); *Dry Messiah: The Life of Bishop Cannon* (1949). Editor, *Richmond Times-Dispatch,* since 1936.

DABOLL, NATHAN (Apr. 24, 1750–Mar. 9, 1818); b. Groton, Conn. Educator, almanac maker. He issued *The Connecticut Almanack* (1773); *The New England Almanack* (1775); from 1776–92, the latter was issued under pen name, "Edmund Freebetter"; in 1793, Daboll resumed the use of his own name. After his death, the almanac was continued by his descendants.

Daddy-Long-Legs. By Jean Webster (1912). Story of a girl, from orphanage to college, who is befriended by the trustee "Daddy-Long-Legs."

Daedalus. Published by Wesleyan University Press, Middletown, Conn.; edited at Harvard University, Cambridge, Mass. Quarterly. Founded 1955, by the American Academy of Arts and Sciences. Each issue is devoted to a symposium topic discussed by scholars in fields related to that topic. Some of these have been Arms Control, The Russian Intelligentsia, Mass Culture and Mass Media, Symbolism in Religion and Literature, and have appeared separately in book form.

DAFFAN, KATIE; b. in Texas. Author. *Woman in History* (1908); *My Father as I Remember Him* (1908); *The Woman on Pine Spring Road* (1910); *As Thinketh a Woman* (poem, 1911); *Texas Hero Stories* (1912); *Texas Heroes* (1924). Lit. editor, *Houston Chronicle,* 1921–28.

D'AGOSTINO, GUIDO (1910–); b. New York. Novelist. *Olives on the Apple Tree* (1940); *Hills Beyond Manhattan* (1941); *My Enemy the World* (1947); *The Barking of a Lonely Fox* (1952); *Heart Is the Teacher* (with Leonard Covello, 1958).

DAHL, FRANCIS W[ellington] (Oct. 21, 1907–); b. Wollaston, Mass. Cartoonist, author. *Left-Handed Compliments* (1941); *Dahl's Cartoons* (1943); *What? More Dahl!* (1944); *Dahl's Boston* (1946); *Brave New World* (with Charles W. Morton, 1947); *Birds, Beasts and Bostonians* (1954). Cartoonist, Boston *Herald,* since 1930.

DAHL, ROBERT ALAN (Dec. 17, 1915–); b. Inwood, Ia. Educator, author. *Congress and Foreign Policy* (1950); *Politics, Economics, and Welfare* (with C. E. Lindblom, 1953); *A Preface to Democratic Theory* (1956); Editor: *Political Oppositions in Western Democracies* (1966). *Who Governs?* (1961); *Modern Political Analysis* (1963). Prof. political science, Yale University, since 1955.

DAHLBERG, EDWARD (July 22, 1900–); b. Boston, Mass. Author. *Bottom Dogs* (1930); *From Flushing to Calvary* (1932); *Kentucky Blue Grass* (1932); *Those Who Perish* (1934); *Do These Bones Live* (1941); *Sing O Barren* (1947); *Flea of Sodom* (1950); *The Sorrows of Priapus* (1957); *Truth Is More Sacred* (with H. E. Read, 1961); *Because I Was Flesh* (autobiography, 1964); *Cipango's Hinder Door* (1965); *The Carnal Myth* (1968); etc.

DAHLGREN, [Sarah] MADELEINE VINTON (Mrs. John Adolphus Dahlgren) (July 13, 1825–May 28, 1898); b. Gallipolis, O. Novelist, essayist. *Idealities* (1859); *Memoirs of Ulric Dahlgren* (1872); *South Sea Sketches* (1881); *South-Mountain Magic* (1882); *Memoir of John A. Dahlgren* (1882); *A Washington Winter* (1883); *The Lost Name* (1886); *Lights and Shadows of a Life* (1887); *Divorced* (1887); *Chim: His Washington Winter* (1892); *The Secret Directory* (1896); *The Woodley Lane Ghost, and Other Stories* (1899); etc.

"Daisy Bell." Song by an English song writer, Harry Dacre, written in New York in 1893, containing the refrain "A bicycle built for two."

Daisy Miller. Novelette by Henry James (1878). The travels of an American family in Europe. A satire on American social standards and the indifference of Americans toward European customs. Daisy, the audacious and innocent type of American girl, is unjustly compromised in her friendship with a young Italian. She dies of malaria, imprudently caught during a visit with him to the Colosseum one night. She remains in his and the readers's mind as the attractive example of American freshness toward new experiences.

Dakota Playmakers, The. A drama workshop at the University of North Dakota. Founded 1910, by Professor Frederick H. Koch. In 1918, he established a similar workshop, The Carolina Playmakers (q.v.), at the University of North Carolina.

Dale, Alan. Pen name of Alfred J. Cohen.

Dale, Estil. Pen name of Albert Benjamin Cunningham.

DALEY, ARTHUR [John] (July 31, 1904–); b. New York. Sports writer, author. *Times at Bat* (1950); *Sports of the Times* (1959); *Knute Rockne* (1961); *Pro Football's Hall of Fame* (1963); *Story of the Olympic Games* (with John Kieran, 1965). Columnist, "Sports of the Times," *The New York Times,* since 1952.

DALGLIESH, ALICE (Oct. 7, 1893–); b. Trinidad, B.W.I. Editor, author of children's books. *First Experiences with Literature* (1932); *The Smiths and Rusty* (1936); *Wings for the Smiths* (1937); *America Begins* (1938); *America Builds Homes* (1938); *The Young Aunts* (1939); *Wooden Shoes in America* (1940); *A Book for Jennifer* (1940); *St. George and the Dragon* (1941); *The Davenports Are at Dinner* (1948); *Adam and the Golden Cock* (1959); *The Silver Pencil* (1962); *Little Wooden Farmer* (1969); etc. Former editor of children's books, Charles Scribner's Sons.

DALI, SALVADOR (May 11, 1904–); b. Figueras, Sp. Artist. *Secret Life of Salvador Dali* (1942); *Dali's Mustache: A Pho-*

tographic Interview (with Philippe Halsman, 1954); *On Modern Art* (1957); etc.

DALL, CAROLINE [Wells] HEALEY (June 22, 1822–Dec. 17, 1912); b. Boston, Mass. Woman suffragist, author. *Historical Pictures Retouched* (1860); *Patty Gray's Journey to the Cotton Islands,* 3v. (1869–70); *My First Holiday; or, Letters Home from Colorado, Utah, and California* (1881); *What We Really Know About Shakespeare* (1886); *Barbara Frietchie* (1892); *Alongside* (autobiography, 1900); etc. *See* W. Goodsell's *Pioneers of Women's Education in the United States* (1931).

DALLAM, JAMES WILMER (1818–1847). Novelist. *The Lone Star* (1845); *The Deaf Spy* (1848).

Dallas News. Dallas, Tex. Newspaper. Founded 1885 as *Dallas Morning News,* by A. H. Belo. Allen Maxwell is Sunday book editor.

Dallas Times-Herald. Dallas, Tex. Newspaper. The *Herald* was founded in 1873, the *Times* in 1876; merged in 1888. Felix McKnight is editor; Olin Chism is book-review editor.

DALLIN, DAVID JULIEVICH (May 24, 1889–Feb. 21, 1962); b. D. S. Levin, Rogachow, Rus. Author. *Soviet Russia's Foreign Policy, 1939–42* (1942); *Soviet Russia and the Far East* (1948); *The Rise of Russia in Asia* (1949); *The New Soviet Empire* (1951); *Soviet Espionage* (1955); *The Changing World Of Soviet Russia* (1956); *Soviet Foreign Policy after Stalin* (1961); etc. Contributor and columnist, *The New Leader,* after 1940.

DALLMANN, [Charles Frederick] **WILLIAM** (Dec. 22, 1862–Feb. 2, 1952); b. in Germany. Lutheran clergyman, editor, author. *Portraits of Jesus* (1909); *Life of Luther* (1917); *Great Religious Americans* (1921); *Paul* (1929); *Peter* (1930); *John* (1931); *What Is Lutheranism?* (1938); *My Life* (1945); *Martin Luther* (rev., 1951); etc.

DALRYMPLE, LEONA (Mrs. C. Acton Wilson) (1884–). Author of children's books. *In the Heart of the Christmas Pines* (1913); *Diane of the Green Van* (1914); *Uncle Noah's Christmas Inspiration* (1914); *The Lovable Meddler* (1915); *Kenny* (1917); etc.

DALTON, TEST [Wane] (Sept. 13, 1875–Dec. 10, 1945); b. Chicago, Ill. Playwright, novelist. *The Role of the Unconquered* (1902); *Navarre* (1913); *Little Theatre Plays* (1917); *Uncle John* (1920); *The Mantle of Lincoln* (1921); *The Blue Orchid* (1925); *T. N. T.* (1930); *High Tide* (1940); etc.

DALY, AUGUSTIN (July 20, 1838–June 7, 1899); b. Plymouth, N.C. Producer, playwright. *Under the Gaslight* (prod. 1867); *A Flash of Lightning* (prod. 1868); *The Red Scarf* (prod. 1869); *Horizon* (prod. 1871); *Divorce* (prod. 1871); *Pique* (prod. 1875); *The Dark City* (prod. 1877); etc. Adapted and produced many French and German plays, and produced several plays of Shakespeare. *See* Joseph F. Daly's *The Life of Augustin Daly* (1917).

DALY, CARROLL JOHN (Sept. 14, 1889–Jan. 16, 1958). b. Yonkers, N.Y. Novelist. *White Circle* (1926); *Snarl of the Beast* (1927); *Tag Murders* (1930); *Murder from the East* (1935); *Emperor of Evil* (1937); *Better Corpses* (1940); *Murder After Midnight* (1948); *Cousin Oliver* (1952); *Murder for a Stuffed Shirt* (1954); etc.

DALY, CHARLES PATRICK (Oct. 31, 1816–Sept. 19, 1899); b. New York. Jurist, author. *Gulian C. Verplanck* (1870); *The Settlement of the Jews in North America* (1893); *Birthday Verses* (1897); *First Theatre in America* (1896); etc.

DALY, ELIZABETH (Oct. 15, 1878–Sept. 2, 1967); b. New York. Author *Deadly Nightshade* (1940); *The House Without a Door* (1942); *Evidence of Things Seen* (1943); *The Book of the Dead* (1944); *Night Walk* (1947); *Death and Letters* (1950); *Elizabeth Daly Mystery Omnibus* (1960); etc.

DALY, MAUREEN (Mar. 15, 1921–); b. in County Tyrone, Northern Ireland. Author. *Seventeenth Summer* (1942); *Smarter and Smoother* (1944); *Perfect Hostess* (1950); *Twelve Around the World* (1957); *Patrick Visits the Farm* (1959); *Sixteen* (stories, 1961); *Patrick Visits the Zoo* (1963); *The Ginger Horse* (1964); etc. Editor: *My Favorite Stories* (1948); *My Favorite Suspense Stories* (1968); etc. Newspaper columnist, "On the Solid Side."

DALY, T[homas] A[ugustine] (May 28, 1871–Oct. 4, 1948); b. Philadelphia, Pa. Poet. *Canzoni* (1906); *Carmina* (1909); *Madrigal* (1912); *McAroni Ballads* (1919); *The Wissahickon* (1922); *McAroni Medleys* (1932); *Late Lark Singing* (1946). Columnist, *Philadelphia Evening Bulletin,* from 1929; compiler *A Little Book of American Humorous Verse* (1926).

DALZIEL, JOHN SANDERSON (Dec. 24, 1839–Aug. 19, 1937); b. Edinburgh, Scotland. Illustrator. Came to America in 1869. Friend and schoolmate of Charles Dickens, whose works he illustrated. Also made drawings for *Punch.* Illustrated the fairy tales of Hans Andersen.

Damaged Souls. Biographical essays by Gamaliel Bradford (1922). A psycho-biographical study of Benedict Arnold, Thomas Paine, Aaron Burr, John Randolph of Roanoke, John Brown, Phineas Taylor Barnum, and Benjamin Franklin Butler.

Damascus Road. New York. Irregular periodical. Founded 1964 by a poetry workshop at Muhlenberg College, Allentown, Pa., under Charles Hanna and W. L. Kinter. Devoted to new talent.

Damnation of Theron Ware, The. Novel by Harold Frederic (1896). Story of a Methodist minister in a small New York town, who fails spiritually because his idealism is so shallow that it cannot sustain him.

Damned Thing, The. Short story by Ambrose Bierce, in his *In the Midst of Life* (1898).

DAMON, LINDSAY FOSTER (Nov. 8, 1871–May 6, 1940); b. Brookline, Mass. Educator, editor. The *Lake English Classic;* etc. Supervising editor, Scott Foresman & Co.

DAMON, S[amuel] FOSTER (Feb. 22, 1893–Dec. 26, 1971); b. Newton, Mass. Educator, poet. *William Blake: His Philosophy and Symbols* (1924); *Astrolabe, Infinitudes and Hypocrisies* (poems, 1927); *Tilted Moons* (poems, 1929); *Thomas Holley Chivers* (1930); *Amy Lowell: A Chronicle* (1935); *History of Square Dancing* (1952); *Punch and Judy* (play, 1957); *Blake Dictionary: The Ideas and Symbols of William Blake* (1965); etc. Editor: *Series of American Songs* (1936). Compiler: *Eight Harvard Poets* (with others, 1917); *Eight More Harvard Poets* (with Robert Hillyer, 1923); *Blake's Grave: A Prophetic Book* (1963). Curator, Harris Collection of American Poetry, at Brown University, since 1929.

DANA, CHARLES A[nderson] (Aug. 8, 1819–Oct. 17, 1897); b. Hinsdale, N.H. Editor, author. *Recollections of the Civil War* (1898). Editor; *The Household Book of Poetry* (1857); *The New American Cyclopedia* (with George Ripley, 1863). Became owner of the New York *Sun,* in 1868, becoming its editor on Jan. 25, 1868. *See* Candace Stone's *Dana and the Sun* (1938); and Charles J. Rosebault's *When Dana Was the Sun* (1931). *See also* Frank M. O'Brien's *The Story of the Sun* (1918).

DANA, HARVEY EUGENE (June 21, 1888–May 17, 1945); b. near Vicksburg, Miss. Baptist clergyman, educator, author. *New Testament Criticism* (1924); *Christ's Ecclesia* (1926); *Jewish Christianity* (1937); *The Ephesian Tradition* (1940); *The Heavenly Guest* (1943); etc. President, Kansas City (Kan.) Baptist Theological Seminary, from 1938.

DANA, JOHN COTTON (Aug. 19, 1856–July 21, 1929); Woodstock, Vt. Librarian, author. *Libraries: Addresses and Essays* (1916); etc. Librarian, Newark Free Public Library, 1902–29. *See* Frank Kingdon's *John Cotton Dana* (1940).

DANA, JULIAN. Formerly Morgan Mercer. Author. *Sutter of California* (1934); *The Man Who Built San Francisco: A Study of Ralston's Journey with Banners* (1936); *Lost Springtime* (1938); *The Sacramento, River of Gold* (1939); etc.

DANA, MARVIN (Mar. 2, 1867–deceased); b. Cornwall, Vt. Editor, novelist, poet. *Mater Christi, and Other Poems* (1890); *The Woman of Orchids* (1901); *A Puritan Witch* (1903); *Within the Law* (1913); *The Lake Mystery* (1923); etc.

Dana, Mary Stanley Bunce Palmer. See Mary Stanley Bunce Palmer Dana Shindler.

DANA, RICHARD HENRY (Nov. 15, 1787–Feb. 2, 1879); b. Cambridge, Mass. Editor, poet, essayist. *Poems* (1827); *Poems and Prose Writings* (1833); *The Buccaneer, and Other Poems* (1844). Founder, *The Idle Man,* 1821; editor, 1821–22. He joined the Anthology Club in Boston in 1814 and helped found the *North American Review* in 1815.

DANA, RICHARD HENRY (Aug. 1, 1815–Jan. 6, 1882); b. Cambridge, Mass. Traveler, author. *Two Years Before the Mast* (1840); *The Seaman's Friend* (1841); *To Cuba and Back* (1859). *See* Charles Francis Adams's *Richard Henry Dana* (1890).

Dancin' Party at Harrison's Cove, The. Story by Mary Noailles Murfree in the *Atlantic Monthly,* May, 1878. It created a vogue for Southern local color stories.

DANDRIDGE, DANSKE [Bedinger] (Nov. 19, 1858–deceased); b. Copenhagen, Denmark. Author. *Joy, and Other Poems* (1888); *George Michael Bedinger: A Kentucky Pioneer* (1909); *American Prisoners of the Revolution* (1911).

DANGERFIELD, GEORGE (Oct. 28, 1904–); b. Newbury, Eng. Author. *Bengal Mutiny* (1933); *The Strange Death of Liberal England* (1935); *Victoria's Heir* (1941); *The Era of Good Feelings* (1952; Pulitzer Prize for history, 1953); *The Awakening of American Nationalism, 1815–1828* (1965). Editor: *History of the United States during the Administrations of Jefferson and Madison* (1963).

DANIEL, HAWTHORNE (Jan. 20, 1890–); b. Norfolk, Neb. Editor, author. *In the Favor of the King* (1922); *Ships of the Seven Seas* (1925); *The Clipper Ship* (1928); *Peggy of Old Annapolis* (1930); *Head Wind* (1936); *For Want of a Nail (The Influence of Logistics on War)* (1948); *Judge Medina: A Biography* (1952); *The Inexhaustible Sea* (with Frances Minot, 1954); *The Ordeal of the Captive Nations* (1958); *Ferdinand Magellan* (1964); etc. Editor: *A Different Kind of War,* by Milton E. Miles. Editor, *Natural History Magazine,* 1927–35; managing editor, *The Commentator,* 1936–39.

DANIELS, JONATHAN [Worth] (Apr. 26, 1902–); b. Raleigh, N.C. Journalist, author. *Clash of Angels* (1930); *A Southerner Discovers the South* (1938); *A Southerner Discovers New England* (1940); *Tar Heels: A Portrait of North Carolina* (1941); *Frontier on the Potomac* (1946); *The Man of Independence* (1950); *The End of Innocence* (1954); *The Forest Is the Future* (1957); *Prince of Carpetbaggers (1958); Thomas Wolfe: October Recollections* (1961); *The Devil's Backbone: The Story of the Natchez Trace* (1962); *They Will Be Heard* (1965); *The Time between the Wars* (1966); *Washington Quadrille: The Dance beside the Documents* (1968); etc. With *Raleigh News and Observer,* since 1923; editor, since 1933.

DANIELS, JOSEPHUS (May 18, 1862–Jan. 15, 1948); b. Washington, N.C. Editor, diplomat, author. *The Navy and the Nation* (1919); *The Life of Woodrow Wilson* (1924); *Tar Heel Editor* (autobiography, 1939); *Editor in Politics* (1941); *The Wilson Era,* 2v. (1944–46); *Shirt Sleeve Diplomat* (1947); etc. Editor, the Raleigh *State Chronicle,* 1885–94; the Raleigh *News and Observer,* 1894–1933. Secretary of the Navy, 1913–21; ambassador to Mexico, 1933–42. See J. L. Morrison's *Josephus Daniels: The Small Democrat* (1966).

DANIELSON, RICHARD ELY (Nov. 7, 1885–May 23, 1957); b. Brooklyn, Conn. Editor, author. *Martha Doyle and Other Sporting Memories* (1938). Editor, *Boston Independent,* 1924–28; *The Sportsman,* 1927–37; president, Atlantic Monthly Publishing Co., and assoc. editor, *The Atlantic Monthly,* 1940.

DANNAY, FREDERIC. Mystery novel and story writer. Co-author with Manfred Bennington Lee, using together the pen names, "Ellery Queen" and "Barnaby Ross": *The Roman Hat Mystery* (1929); *The French Powder Mystery* (1930); *The Dutch Shoe Mystery* (1931); *The Greek Coffin Mystery* (1932); *The Egyptian Cross Mystery* (1932); *The Tragedy of X* (1932); *The Tragedy of Y* (1932); *The Tragedy of Z* (1933); *The American Gun Mystery* (1933); *Drury Lane's Last Case* (1933); *The Siamese Twin Mystery* (1933); *The Chinese Orange Mystery* (1934); *The Adventures of Ellery Queen* (1934); *The Spanish Cape Mystery* (1935); *Halfway House* (1936); *The Door Between* (1937); *The Devil to Pay* (1938); *Dragon's Teeth* (1939); *New Adventures of Ellery Queen* (1940); *The Detective Short Story: A Bibliography* (1942); *There Was an Old Woman* (1943); *The Misadventures of Sherlock Holmes* (1944); *The Murderer Is a Fox* (1945); *To the Queen's Taste* (1946); *Cat of Many Tales* (1949); *The Literature of Crime* (1950); *The Scarlet Letters* (1953); *Queen's Bureau of Investigation* (1955); *In the Queen's Parlor* (1957); *The Finishing Stroke* (1958); *XYZ Murders* (1961); *Quintessence of Queen* (1962); *To Be Read Before Midnight* (1962); *Mystery Mix* (1964); *Queen's Full* (1965); *Fourth Side of the Triangle* (1965); *Face to Face* (1967); *Q.E.D.: Queen's Experiments in Detection* (1968); *Cop Out* (1969); etc. co-editor: *Ellery Queen's Crime Carousel* (1966); etc. Co-editor, with Manfred B. Lee, of *Ellery Queen's Mystery Magazine,* 1941–71; now sole editor.

DANTON, GEORGE HENRY (May 31, 1890–); b. New York City. Educator, author. *Germany Ten Years After* (1928); *The Culture Contacts of the United States and China, 1784–1844* (1931); *The Chinese People* (1938). Co-Editor: *Four German Stories* (1947). German dept., Union College, since 1935.

DARBY, ADA CLAIRE (Dec. 31, 1883–Dec. 23, 1953); b. St. Joseph, Mo. Editor, author. *Pinafores and Pantalettes* (1927); *Sometimes Jenny Wren* (1931); *Peace-Pipes at Portage* (1938); *"Show Me," Missouri* (1938); *Jump Lively, Jeff* (1942); *Island Girl* (1951); etc. Lit. editor, *St. Joseph* (Mo.) *News Press,* 1916–24.

DARBY, WILLIAM (Aug. 14, 1775–Oct. 9, 1854); b. Lancaster Co., Pa. Geographer, author. *A Geographical Description of the State of Louisiana* (1816); *The Emigrant's Guide to the Western and Southwestern States and Territories* (1818); *Memoir on the Geography and Natural and Civil History of Florida* (1821); *View of the United States* (1828); etc.

DAREFF, HAL (May 8, 1920–); b. Brooklyn, N.Y. Editor, author. *The First Microscope* (1962); *Man in Orbit* (1962); *Jacqueline Kennedy: A Portrait in Courage* (1965); *The Story of Vietnam* (1966); etc. Editor-in-chief, juvenile and young adult books, Grosset and Dunlap, since 1967.

DARGAN, EDWIN PRESTON (Sept. 7, 1879–Dec. 13, 1940); b. Barboursville, Va. Educator, author. *Hylas, and Other Poems* (1910); *A History of French Literature* (with Albert Nitze, 1922); *Honoré de Balzac* (1932); *Anatole France* (1937); etc. Professor of French, University of Chicago, 1918–40.

DARGAN, OLIVE TILFORD (Mrs. Pegram Dargan) (b. 1869–Jan. 22, 1968); b. in Kentucky. Playwright, poet. Pen name, "Fielding Burke." *Semiramis, and Other Plays* (1904); *The Mortal Gods, and Other Dramas* (1912); *The Cycle's Rim* (poems, 1916); *Lute and Furrow* (poems, 1922); *Highland Annals* (1925); *Call Home the Heart* (1932); *A Stone Came Rolling* (1935); *From My Highest Hill* (stories, 1941); *Sons of the Stranger* (1947); *Spotted Hawk* (1958); etc.

Daring, Hope. Pen name of Anna Johnson.

Daring Young Man on the Flying Trapeze, The. Collection of stories by William Saroyan (1934).

"Darius Green and His Flying-Machine." Poem by John Townsend Trowbridge. First appeared in *Our Young Folks,* March, 1867. Included in his *The Vagabond, and Other Poems* (1869).

Dark City, The. Short story by Conrad Aiken (1925).

Dark Laughter. Novel by Sherwood Anderson (1925). John Stockton, Chicago newspaper reporter, suddenly leaves his wife, and voyages down the Illinois River in a small boat, trying to figure it all out as the "dark laughter" of the Negroes along the river beats in his ears.

DARLEY, FELIX OCTAVIUS CARR (June 23, 1822–Mar. 27, 1888); b. Philadelphia, Pa. Illustrator, author. *Sketches Abroad with Pen and Pencil* (1869); *Pen and Pencil Sketches in Europe* (1890). Most famous illustrations were for Judd's *Margaret,* Irving's *Rip Van Winkle,* and the 500 or more designs for Cooper's novels, and an equal number for B. J. Lossing's *History of the United States.*

DARLING, EDWARD (June 19, 1907–); b. Roxbury, Mass. Editor, author. *Three Oldtimers* (1936); *How We Fought for Our Schools* (1954); *Old Quotes at Home* (1966); *The Prevalence of Nonsense* (with Ashley Montagu, 1967); *Freedom and Responsibility* (1969).

DARLING, FLORA ADAMS (July 25, 1840–Jan. 6, 1910); b. Lancaster, N.H. Author. *Mrs. Darling's Letters; or, Memories of the War* (1883); *A Winning, Wayward Woman* (1889); etc. Founder, The Daughters of the American Revolution, Oct. 11, 1890; United States Daughters of the War of 1812, Jan. 8, 1892.

DARLING, JAY NORWOOD (Oct. 21, 1876–Feb. 12, 1962); b. Norwood, Mich. Cartoonist, leader in wild life conservation, author. Pen name, "J. N. Ding." *The Education of Alonzo Applegate* (1912); *A Cartoonist's Travelogue* (1931); *Ding Goes to Russia* (1932); *The Cruise of the Bouncing Betsy* (1937); etc.

DARLING, LOIS [MacIntyre] (Aug. 15, 1917–); b. New York. Illustrator-author, with husband, Louis Darling, Jr.: *Before and After Dinosaurs* (1959); *Sixty Million Years of Horses* (1960); *The Science of Life* (1961); *Bird* (1962); *Coral Reefs* (1963); *The Sea Serpents Around Us* (1965); *A Place in the Sun* (1968); etc.

DARLING, LOUIS JR. (Apr. 26, 1916–); b. Stamford, Conn. Illustrator-author: *Greenhead* (1954); *Seals and Walruses* (1955); *The Gull's Way* (1965); etc. Also collaborated with wife, Lois Darling (q.v.), on numerous books.

DARLING, MARY GREENLEAF (b. Oct. 28, 1848); b. Boston, Mass. Author. *Battles at Home* (1871); *Gladys: A Romance* (1887); *A Girl of this Century* (1902); etc.

"Darling Nelly Gray." Song by Benjamin Russell Hanby (1856).

Darling of the Gods, The. Play by David Belasco and John Luther Long (prod. 1902). A story of Japan, written in the manner of *Madame Butterfly,* which the same authors had successfully produced in 1900.

DARRELL, ROBERT DONALDSON (Dec. 13, 1903–); b. Newton, Mass. Author. *Good Listening* (1953); etc. Editor: *Gramophone Shop Encyclopedia of Recorded Music* (1936); *Schirmer's Guide to Books on Music and Musicians* (1951); *Tapes in Review* (1963).

DARROW, CLARENCE [Seward] (Apr. 18, 1857–Mar. 13, 1938); b. Kinsman, O. Lawyer, author. *A Persian Pearl, and Other Essays* (1899); *Farmington* (1904); *The Story of My Life* (1932); etc. See Charles Yale Harrison's *Clarence Darrow* (1931).

DARROW, WHITNEY (May 16, 1881–Aug. 27, 1970); b. Geneva, N.Y. Publisher, author. *A Child's Guide to Freud* (1963). A founder of the Princeton University Press, 1905, and manager, 1905–17. With Charles Scribner's Sons, publishers, New York, from 1917. President, University Club, 1941.

DARROW, WHITNEY, JR. (Aug. 22, 1909–); b. Princeton, N.J. Cartoonist. *You're Sitting on My Eyelashes* (1943); *Please Pass the Hostess* (1949); *Stop, Miss!* (1957); *Animal Etiquette* (1969); etc. Illustrator: *Unidentified Flying Elephant,* by Robert Kraus (1968).

DASH, THOMAS R[obert] (Sept. 3, 1897–); b. in Russia. Drama critic, *Women's Wear Daily* and *Daily News Record,* 1947–61.

DASHIELL, ALFRED SHEPPARD (Apr. 29, 1901–Oct. 3, 1970); b. Snow Hill, Md. Editor, author. *Editor's Choice* (with H. S. Canby, 1934); *A Study of the Short Story* (1935); etc. Assoc. editor, *Scribner's Magazine,* 1923–30, managing editor, 1930–36; assoc. editor, *The Reader's Digest,* 1936–40; managing editor, from 1940.

Daskam, Josephine Dodge. See Josephine Dodge Daskam Bacon.

DAUGHERTY, CARROLL ROOP (Dec. 3, 1900–); b. Annville, Pa. Economist, labor arbitrator. *Labor Problems in American Industry,* (1933); *Economic Principles and Problems* (1936); *Labor Problems of American Society* (with J. B. Parrish, 1952); *Conflict and Cooperation* (1968); etc.

DAUGHERTY, JAMES HENRY (June 1, 1889–); b. Asheville, N.C. Artists, author. *Their Weight in Wildcats* (1936); *Andy and the Lion* (1938); *Daniel Boone* (1939); *Poor Richard* (1941); *Wild Wild West* (1948); *Landing of the Pilgrims* (1950); *Of Courage Undaunted* (1951); *Trappers and Traders of the Far West* (1952); *Magna Charta* (1956); *Picnic* (1958); *William Blake* (1960). Editor: *Walt Whitman's America* (1964). Among his illustrations are those for *John Brown's Body,* by Stephen Vincent Benét; Washington Irving's *Knickerbocker History of New York; Uncle Tom's Cabin; Daniel Boone,* by Stewart Edward White; *Abe Lincoln Grows Up,* by Carl Sandburg; etc.

Daughter. Short story by Erskine Caldwell (1935).

Daughters of Eve. By a Lady (1826). Now identified as the work of Sarah Pogson Smith.

D'AULAIRE, EDGAR PARIN (1898–). Co-author with Ingri d'Aulaire: *Children of the Northlights* (1935); *Abraham Lincoln* (1937); *Don't Count Your Chicks* (1943); *Foxie* (1949); *Benjamin Franklin* (1950); *Buffalo Bill* (1952); *Animals Everywhere* (1954); *Magic Meadow* (1958); *Book of Greek Myths* (1962); *Norse Gods and Giants* (1967); etc.

D'AULAIRE, INGRI [Mortenson] (Mrs. Edgar Parin d'Aulaire). Co-author, with Edgar Parin d'Aulaire (q.v.), of children's books.

DAULTON, AGNES [Warner] McCLELLAND (Apr. 29, 1867–June 5, 1944); b. New Philadelphia, O. Author. *Wings and Strings* (1903); *From Sioux to Susan* (1909); *The Marooning of Peggy* (1915); *Green Gate* (1926); etc.

DAVENPORT, EUGENE (June 20, 1856–Mar. 31, 1941); b. Woodland, Mich. Educator, agriculturist, author. *Domesticated Animals and Plants* (1910); *Vacation on the Trail* (1923); *The Farm* (1927); etc. Prof. thremmatology, University of Illinois, 1896–1922.

DAVENPORT, GWEN (Oct. 3, 1910–); b. Colon, Canal Zone. Author. *A Stranger and Afraid* (1943); *Return Engagement* (1945); *Belvedere* (1947); *Family Fortunes* (1949); *The Bachelor's Baby* (1957); *Great Loves in Legend and Life* (1964); etc.

DAVENPORT, HOMER C[alvin] (Mar. 8, 1867–May 2, 1912); b. Silverton, Ore. Cartoonist, author. *The Bell of Silverton* (1899); *Other Stories of Oregon* (1900); *My Quest of the Arab Horse* (1909); *The Country Boy: The Story of His Own Early Life* (autobiography, 1910).

DAVENPORT, MARCIA (Mrs. Russell Davenport) (June 9, 1903–); b. New York City. Music critic, novelist. *Mozart* (1932); *Of Lena Geyer* (1936); *The Valley of Decision* (1942); *East Side, West Side* (1947); *My Brother's Keeper* (1954); *Garibaldi* (1957); *The Constant Image* (1960).

DAVENPORT, RUSSELL [Wheeler] (July 12, 1899–Apr. 19, 1954); b. South Bethlehem, Pa. Editor, author. *Through Traffic* (1929); *My Country* (poem, 1944); *The Dignity of Man* (1955). Co-editor: *U.S.A.: The Permanent Revolution* (1951). Editorial staff, *Fortune,* 1930–37; managing editor, 1937–40; chairman, board of editors, from 1940.

Davenport Group. Group of writers from Davenport, Iowa. It included Susan Glaspell, George Cram Cook, Floyd Dell, Harry Hansen, and Arthur Davison Ficke. Cook and Dell helped establish the Provincetown Players. *See* Alice French's *Stories of a Western Town* (1883) and Phil Stong's *Hawkeyes* (1940); *American Guide Series, Iowa* (1938).

DAVID, EVAN JOHN (1881–). Author. *Aircraft: Its Development in War and Peace* (1919); *Our Coast Guard* (1937); *As Runs the Glass* (1943); etc. Editor: *Great Moments of Adventure* (1930).

DAVID, HENRY (Dec. 5, 1907–); b. New York. Educator, labor specialist. *History of the Haymarket Affair* (1936); *Manpower Policies for a Democratic Society* (1965); etc. Editor: *The Economic History of the United States* series, since 1945. Prof. history, New School for Social Research, since 1959; president, 1961–63.

DAVID, MAURICE R[ea] (Jan. 22, 1893–); b. Toronto, Ont. Educator, sociologist, author. *A Constructive Immigration Policy* (1923); *The Evolution of War* (1929); *Problems of City Life* (1932); *World Immigration* (1936); etc. Dept. sociology, Yale University, since 1921.

David Harum. Novel by Edward N. Westcott (1899). The scene is "Homeville" in New York, and the central character is the shrewd, gruff, and homely country banker David Harum, whose passion is horse trading. His witty sayings are often quoted. Beneath his bluff exterior were many splendid traits.

David Swan. Fantasy by Nathaniel Hawthorne (1837).

DAVIDSON, BASIL (Nov. 9, 1914–). Author. *Report on Southern Africa* (1952); *The African Awakening* (1955); *The Rapids* (1957); *The Lost Cities of Africa* (1959); *Ode to a Young Love* (1959); *Black Mother* (1961); *Tira Mhurain, Outer Hebrides* (1962); *The African Past: Chronicles from Antiquity to Modern Times* (1964); *Africa: A History of a Continent* (1966); *African Kingdoms* (1966); *Growth of African Civilization: A History of West Africa 1000–1800,* ed. by F. K. Buah and J. F. Ajayi (1969); *The African Genius* (1970).

DAVIDSON, CHALMERS GASTON (June 6, 1907–); b. Chester, S.C. Educator, author. *Major John Davidson of Rural Hill* (1943); *Cloud over Catawba* (1949); *Friend of the People* (1950); *Piedmont Partisan* (1951); etc. Prof. history, Davidson College, North Carolina, since 1936.

DAVIDSON, DAVID [Albert] (May 11, 1908–); b. New York. Novelist. *The Steeper Cliff* (1947); *The Hour of Truth* (1949); *In Another Country* (1950). Also radio and television plays.

DAVIDSON, DONALD [Grady] (Aug. 18, 1893–Apr. 26, 1968); b. Campbellsville, Tenn. Educator, poet, essayist. *An Outland Piper* (poems, 1924); *The Tall Men* (poems, 1927); *Lee in the Mountains, and Other Poems* (1938); *The Attack on Leviathan* (1938); *The Tennessee,* 2v. (1946, 1948);

Twenty Lessons in Reading and Writing Prose (1955); *Still Rebels, Still Yankees, and other Essays* (1957); *Southern Writers in the Modern World* (1958); *The Long Street* (1961); etc. Editor: *British Poetry of the Eighteen-Nineties* (1937); *American Composition and Rhetoric* (1939). Literary editor, *Nashville Tennessean,* 1924–30. Prof. English, Vanderbilt University, from 1937. *See* T. D. Young's *Donald Davidson, An Essay and a Bibliography* (1965).

DAVIDSON, EDITH BOWKER; b. Gloucester, Mass. Author. *The Bunnikias Bunnies in Camp* (1909); *Nibbles Poppelty Poppett* (1911); etc.

DAVIDSON, GUSTAV (Dec. 25, 1895–Feb. 6, 1971); b. Warsaw. Publisher, author. *First Editions in American Juvenalia and Problems in Their Identification* (1940); *Mortal Hunger* (poems, 1943); *Thirst of the Antelope* (poems, 1945); *Moment of Visitation* (poems, 1950); *Ambushed by Angels, and other Poems* (1965); *A Dictionary of Angels* (1967); etc. Editor: *In Fealty to Apollo: A History of the Poetry Society of America, 1910–1950* (1950). Founder, Fine Editions Press, 1940; director, from 1940; founder, *Poetry Chap-Book,* 1942; publisher, 1942–53.

DAVIDSON, [Harry] CARTER (Sept. 23, 1905–Oct. 20, 1965); b. Louisville, Ky. Educator, author. *Poetry, Its Appreciation and Enjoyment* (with Louis Untermeyer, 1934); *Colleges for Freedom* (with Donald J. Cowling, 1947). President, Knox College, 1936–46; pres., Union College, from 1946.

DAVIDSON, ISRAEL (May 27, 1870–June 27, 1939); b. (Movshovitz) Yanova, Russia. Educator, Hebraist, author. *Parody in Jewish Literature* (1907); *Thesaurus of Mediaeval Hebrew Poetry,* 4v. (1924–33); etc.

DAVIDSON, JAMES WOOD (Mar. 9, 1829–June 15, 1905); b. in Newberry Co., S.C. Journalist, author. *The Living Writers of the South* (1869); *The Poetry of the Future* (1888); etc.

DAVIDSON, LUCRETIA MARIA (Sept. 27, 1808–Aug. 27, 1825); b. Plattsburg, N.Y., daughter of Margaret Miller Davidson. Poet. *Amir Khan, and Other Poems,* ed. by Samuel F. B. Morse (1829), augmented as *Poetical Remains,* ed. by Catharine Maria Sedgwick (1841), and again as *Poems,* ed. by Matthias Oliver Davidson (1871).

DAVIDSON, MARGARET MILLER (June 27, 1787–June 27, 1844). Poet *Slections from the Writings,* ed. by Catharine M. Sedgwick (1843). *See* Lucretia Maria Davidson *and* Margaret Miller Davidson (1823–1838).

DAVIDSON, MARGARET MILLER (Mar. 26, 1823–Nov. 25, 1838); b. Plattsburgh, N.Y., sister of Lucretia Maria Davidson. Poet. *Biography and Poetical Remains,* ed. by Washington Irving (1841).

DAVIDSON, MARSHALL B[owman] (Apr. 6, 1907–); b. New York. Editor, author. *Life in America,* 2v. (1951). With American Heritage Editors: *History of Colonial Antiques* (1967); *History of American Antiques, 1784–1860* (1968); *History of Antiques of the U.S.A., 1865–1917* (1969). Editor, publications of the Metropolitan Museum of Art, 1947–61. Senior editor, *Horizon* magazine, since 1966.

DAVIDSON, THOMAS (Oct. 25, 1840–Sept. 14, 1900); b. Aberdeenshire, Scot. Wandering scholar, philosopher, author. *Aristotle and Ancient Educational Ideals* (1892); *A History of Education* (1900); etc.

DAVIE, MAURICE R[ea] (Jan. 22, 1893–Nov., 1964); b. Toronto, Can. Sociologist. *A Constructive Immigration Policy* (1923); *The Evolution of War* (1929); *Problems of City Life* (1932); *World Immigration* (1936); *Refugees in America* (with others, 1947); etc. Co-editor: *Selected Essays of William Graham Sumner* (1924); *Social Aspects of Mental Hygiene* (1925); *Essays of William Graham Sumner,* 2v. (1934); etc. Prof. sociology, Yale University, 1932–61.

DAVIES, JOSEPH E[dward] (Nov. 29, 1876–May 9, 1958); b. Watertown, Wis. Lawyer, diplomat. *Mission to Moscow* (1942). U.S. ambassador to U.S.S.R., 1936–38; Belgium, 1938–39; etc.

DAVIES, MARY CAROLYN; b. Sprague, Wash. Poet. *The Drums in Our Street* (1918); *Youth Riding* (1919); *Marriage Songs* (1923); *Penny Show* (1927); etc. Adopted by Blackfeet Indians and given name of "Pautuxie."

DAVIES, VALENTINE (Aug. 25, 1905–July 24, 1961); b. New York. Playwright, novelist. *Three Times the Hour* (prod. 1930); *Blow Ye Winds* (prod. 1937); *Miracle on 34th Street* (1947); *It Happens Every Spring* (1949). Also screenplays.

DAVIESS, MARIA THOMPSON (Nov. 25, 1872–Sept. 3, 1924); Harrodsburg, Ky. Painter, author. *Miss Selina Lee and the Soapbox Babies* (1909); *The Melting of Molly* (1912); *Phyllis* (1914); *The Matrix* (1920); *Seven Times Seven: An Autobiography* (1924); etc.

DAVIS, ARTHUR KYLE, Jr. (Sept. 20, 1897–); b. Petersburg, Va. Educator, folklorist, editor. *Traditional Ballads of Virginia* (1929); *Folksongs of Virginia* (1949); *More Traditional Ballads of Virginia* (1960); *Matthew Arnold's Letters* (1968). English dept., University of Virginia, since 1923.

DAVIS, BERNARD GEORGE (Dec. 11, 1906–); b. Pittsburgh, Pa. Publisher. Director, Ziff-Davis Publishing Co., 1936–46; pres., 1946–57; Davis Publications, since 1957.

DAVIS, BURKE (July 24, 1913–); b. Durham, N.C. Author. *Whisper My Name* (1949); *The Ragged Ones* (1951); *Yorktown* (1952); *They Called Him Stonewall* (1954); *Gray Fox: Robert E. Lee and the Civil War* (1956); *Jeb Stuart* (1957); *To Appomatox* (1959); *Our Incredible Civil War* (1960); *America's First Army* (1962); *The Summer Land* (1965); *The Billy Mitchell Affair* (1967); *Get Yamamoto* (1969).

DAVIS, CHARLES AUGUSTUS (1795–Jan. 27, 1867); b. New York City. Merchant, author. Pen name, "J. Downing." *Letters of J. Downing, Major, Downingville Militia* (1834), reprinted under several variant titles.

DAVIS, CLYDE BRION (May 22, 1894–July 19, 1962); b. Unadilla, Neb. Journalist, novelist. *The Anointed* (1937); *The Great American Novel* (1938); *Northend Wildcats* (1938); *Nebraska Coast* (1939); *The Arkansas* (1940); *Sullivan* (1942); *Follow the Leader* (1942); *The Rebellion of Leo McGuire* (1944); *The Stars Incline* (1946); *Temper the Wind* (1948); *Thudbury* (1952); *Something for Nothing* (1956); *Unholy Uproar* (1957); *Shadow of a Tiger* (1963); etc. With *Denver Post, Buffalo Times,* and other newspapers, 1919–41.

DAVIS, DAVID BRION (Feb. 16, 1927–   ); b. Denver, Colo. Educator, author. *Homicide in American Fiction, 1790–1860: A Study in Social Values* (1957); *The Problem of Slavery in Western Culture* (1966, Pulitzer Prize, 1967). Prof. history, Cornell University, since 1963.

DAVIS, DOROTHY SALISBURY (Apr. 26, 1916–); b. Chicago, Ill. Author. *A Gentle Murderer* (1951); *A Town of Masks* (1952); *Men of No Property* (1956); *Death of an Old Sinner* (1957); *A Gentleman Called* (1958); *The Evening of the Good Samaritan* (1961); *Black Sheep, White Lamb* (1963); *The Pale Betrayer* (1965); *Enemy and Brother* (1967); *God Speed the Night* (with Jerome Ross, 1968); *Where the Dark Streets Go* (1969); etc.

DAVIS, ELMER [Holmes] (Jan. 13, 1890–May 18, 1958); b. Aurora, Ind. Commentator, author. *The Princess Cecilia* (1915); *History of the New York Times, 1851–1921* (1921); *Times Have Changed* (1923); *I'll Show You the Town* (1924); *The Keys of the City* (1925); *Friends of Mr. Sweeney* (1925); *Strange Women* (1927); *Show Window* (1927); *Giant Killer* (1928); *Morals for Moderns* (1930); *White Pants Willie* (1932); *Bare Living* (with Guy Holt, 1933); *Love among the Ruins* (1935); *Not to Mention the War* (1940); *But We Were*

Born Free (1954); *Two Minutes till Midnight* (1955). With *New York Times,* 1914–24; radio commentator, 1939–42; 1945–56.

DAVIS, FRANK MARSHALL (1905–). Poet. *Black Man's Verse* (1935); *I Am the American Negro* (1937); *Through Sepia Eyes* (1938); etc.

DAVIS, FREDERICK CLYDE (June 2, 1902–); b. St. Joseph, Mo. Author. Pen name, "Stephen Ransome." *Making Your Camera Pay* (1922); *Coffins for Three* (1938); *The Deadly Miss Ashley* (1950); *Tread Lightly, Angel* (1952); *The Shroud off Her Back* (1953); *Another Morgue Heard From* (1954); *So Deadly My Love* (1957); *Warning Bell* (1960); *Meet in Darkness* (1964); etc.

DAVIS, FREDERICK WILLIAM (1858–1933). Dime novelist. Pen names, "Nicholas Carter" and "Scott Campbell." Under pen name "Nicholas Carter": *Nick Carter's Clever Ruse* (1900); *A Victim of Circumstances* (1900); etc. Under pen name "Scott Campbell": *Union Down* (1893); *The Lion of the Law* (1900); *The Links in the Chain* (1901); *The Doctor's Secret* (1901); *Below the Dead-Line* (1906); etc. The dates are not necessarily those of first editions.

DAVIS, GWEN (May 11, 1936–   ); b. Pittsburgh, Pa. Author. *Naked in Babylon* (1960); *Someone's in the Kitchen with Dinah* (1961); *The Pretenders* (1968); *Touching* (1971).

DAVIS, HAROLD E[ugene] (Dec. 3, 1902–); b. Girard, O. Historian, educator. *Makers of Democracy in Latin America* (1945); *Latin American Leaders* (1949); *The Americas in History* (1953); *Government and Politics in Latin America* (ed., 1958); *The Study of Philosophy in the U.S.* (1964); *History of Latin America* (1968); etc. Prof. history, American University, since 1957.

DAVIS, H[arold] L[enoir] (Oct. 18, 1896–Oct. 31, 1960); b. Yoncalla, Ore. Author. *Honey in the Horn* (1935, Pulitzer prize novel, 1936); *Proud Riders* (poems, 1942); *Harp of a Thousand Strings* (1947); *Beulah Land* (1949); *Winds of Morning* (1952); *Team Bells Woke Me, and Other Stories* (1953); *The Distant Music* (1957); *Kettle of Fire* (1959).

DAVIS, HASSOLDT (1907–Sept. 10, 1959). Author. *Land of the Eye* (1940); *Half Past When* (1944); *The Jungle and the Damned* (1952); *Bonjour, Hangover* (1958); etc.

DAVIS, HERBERT JOHN (May 24, 1893–Mar. 28, 1967); b. Buckby, Northants., Eng. Educator, author. *Swift's View of Poetry* (1931); *The Satire of Jonathan Swift* (1947); etc. Editor: *The Drapier's Letters by Jonathan Swift* (1935); *The Prose Works of Jonathan Swift,* vols. 1–13 (1939–59); Joseph Moxon's *Mechanick Exercises on the Whole Art of Printing* (1958); *Elizabethan and Jacobean Studies* (with H. L. Gardner, 1959); etc. President, Smith College, 1940–49.

DAVIS, J. FRANK [James Francis] (Dec. 20, 1870–); b. New Bedford, Mass. Novelist, playwright. *Almanzar* (1918); *The Chinese Label* (1920); *Almanzar Evarts Hero* (1925); *The Ladder* (prod. 1926); *Gold in the Hills* (prod. 1931); *The Road to San Jacinto* (1936); etc.

DAVIS, JEFFERSON (June 3, 1808–Dec. 6, 1889); b. in Christian Co., Ky. President of the Confederate States, author. *The Rise and Fall of the Confederate Government,* 2v. (1881); *A Short History of the Confederate States of America* (1890). See Varina Howell Davis's *Jefferson Davis,* 2v. (1890); William E. Dodd's *Jefferson Davis* (1907); *Jefferson Davis, Constitutionalist: His Letters, Papers, and Speeches,* ed. by Dunlap Rowland, 10v. (1923); and Hudson Strode's *Jefferson Davis,* 4v. (1966).

DAVIS, JEROME (Dec. 2, 1891–); b. Kyoto, Japan. Sociologist. *Behind Soviet Power* (1946); *Character Assassination* (1950); *Peace, War and You* (1952); *Religion in Action* (1956); *On the Brink* (1959); *Citizens of One World* (1961);

World Leaders I Have Known (1963); *Adventuring for Peace and Justice* (1967); *Peace of World War III* (1969); etc. Editor: *Disarmament: A World View* (1964); etc.

DAVIS, JESSICA; b. Cartersville, Ga. Former editor-in-chief, *Vogue*.

DAVIS, JOHN (Aug. 6, 1774–Apr. 24, 1854); b. Salisbury, England. Traveler, bookseller, author. *The Farmer of New Jersey* (1800); *The Wanderings of William* (1801); *Travels of Four Years and a Half in the United States of America* (1803); *Captain Smith and the Princess Pocahontas* (1805); *Walter Kennedy: An American Tale* (1805); *The First Settlers of Virginia* (1805); *The Post-Captain; or, The Wooden Walls Well Manned* (1808); *The American Mariners* (poem, 1822); etc. See Thelma Louise Kellogg's *The Life and Works of John Davis* (1924).

DAVIS, JULIA (Julia Davis Adams) (July 23, 1900–); b. in West Virginia. Novelist. *Vaino, a Boy of New Finland* (1929); *Mountains Are Free* (1930); *Stonewall* (1931); *Remember and Forget* (1932); *No Other White Men* (1937); *Peter Hale* (1939); *The Shenandoah* (1945); *Eagle on the Sun* (1956); *Legacy of Love* (1961); etc.

DAVIS, KENNETH S[ydney] (Sept. 29, 1912–); b. Salina, Kan. Author. *In the Forests of the Night* (1942); *Soldier of Democracy* (1945); *The Years of the Pilgrimage* (1948); *Morning in Kansas* (1952); *Prophet in His Own Country: The Triumphs and Defeats of Adlai E. Stevenson* (1957); *Hero: Charles A. Lindbergh and the American Dream* (1959); *Water* (with J. A. Day, 1961); *The Experience of War: The United States in World War Two* (1965); *Cautionary Scientists* (1966); etc. Editor: *The Paradox of Poverty in America* (1969).

DAVIS, LAVINIA R[iker] (Dec. 7, 1909–Aug. 14, 1961); b. New York City. Novelist, author. *The Keys to the City* (1936); *Skyscraper Mystery* (1937); *Adventures in Steel* (1938); *Round Robin* (1943); *A Threat of Dragons* (1948); *Janey's Fortune* (1957); *Island City* (1961).

DAVIS, L[emuel] CLARKE (Sept. 25, 1835–1904); b. Sandusky, O. Editor, author. *A Stranded Ship* (1869). Assoc. editor, *Philadelphia Ledger*, 1889–1893; editor, 1893–1904.

DAVIS, MARY EVELYN MOORE (Mrs. Thomas Edward Davis) (Apr. 12, 1852–Jan. 1, 1909); b. Talladega, Ala. Novelist, poet. Best known as "Mollie E. Moore Davis." *Minding the Gap, and Other Poems* (1867); *Poems* (1869); *In War Time, at La Rose Blanche* (1888); *An Elephant's Track, and Other Stories* (1897); *Under Six Flags: The Story of Texas* (1897); *Jaconetta* (1901); *The Little Chevalier* (1903); *Selected Poems* (1927); etc. Her husband became editor of the New Orleans *Daily Picayune* in 1879. Her home on Royal Street became a great southern literary salon; among its members were Lafcadio Hearn, Grace King, George W. Cable, Eugene Field, and Cecilia Viets Dakin Jamison.

DAVIS, MARY GOULD (Feb. 13, 1882–Apr. 15, 1956); b. Bangor, Me. Author. *The Girls' Book of Verse* (1922); *The Truce of the Wolf* (1931); *The Handsome Donkey* (1933); *With Cap and Bells* (1937); *Sandy's Kingdom* (1940); *Wakaina and the Clayman* (with E. B. Kalibala, 1946); *Randolph Caldecott: An Appreciation* (1946). Editor of children's books, *Saturday Review of Literature*.

DAVIS, MARY LEE, b. Westfield, N. J. Author. *Uncle Sam's Attic: The Intimate Story of Alaska* (1930); *Alaska, The Great Bear's Cub* (1930); *We Are Alaskans* (1931); *Sourdough Gold* (1933).

DAVIS, MAXINE (Mrs. James Marshall McHugh); b. Terre Haute, Ind. Author. *The Lost Generation* (1936); They Shall Not Want (1937); *Women's Medical Problems* (1945); *Through the Stratosphere* (1946); *Facts About the Menopause* (1951); *Sex and the Adolescent* (1958); *Sexual Responsibility in Marriage* (1963); *Hope for the Childless Couple* (1965); etc.

DAVIS, NOAH KNOWLES (May 15, 1830–May 3, 1910); b. Philadelphia, Pa. Educator, philosopher, author. *The Theory of Thought* (1880); *Elements of Ethics* (1900); etc. Prof. of philosophy, University of Virginia, 1873–1906; president, Bethel College, Russellville, Ky., 1868–73.

DAVIS, NORAH (Oct. 20, 1878–deceased); b. Huntsville, Ala. Author. *The Northerner* (1905); *The World's Warrant* (1907); *Wallace Rhodes* (1909).

DAVIS, OSSIE (Dec. 18, 1917–   ); b. Cogdell, Ga. Actor, playwright, film director. *Alice in Wonder* (1953); *Purlie Victorious* (1961); *Curtain Call, Mr. Aldridge, Sir* (1963).

DAVIS, OWEN (Jan. 29, 1874–Oct. 13, 1956); b. Portland, Me. Playwright. *The Detour* (Prod. 1921); *Icebound* (prod. 1922, Pulitzer Prize play, 1923); *The Nervous Wreck* (prod. 1923); *Lazybones* (prod. 1924); *Easy Come, Easy Go* (prod. 1925); *Beware of Widows* (prod. 1925); *The Man Who Forgot* (with S. N. Behrman, 1926); *The Harbor Light* (1932); *Jezebel* (1933); *Virginia* (with Laurence Stallings, 1937); *No Way Out* (1944); etc.

DAVIS, REBECCA [Blaine] HARDING (Mrs. L. Clarke Davis) (June 24, 1831–Sept. 29, 1910); b. Washington, Pa. Novelist. *Margaret Howth* (1862); *Dallas Galbraith* (1868); *John Andross* (1874); *Kent Hampden* (1892); *Silhouettes of American Life* (1892); *Frances Waldeaux* (1897); etc.

DAVIS, RICHARD BEALE (June 3, 1907–   ); b. Accomack, Va. Educator, author. *Francis Walker Gilmer: Life and Learning in Jefferson's Virginia* (1939); *George Sandys, Poet-Adventurer* (1955); *William Fitzhugh and His Chesapeake World: 1676–1701* (1963); *Intellectual Life in Jefferson's Virginia, 1790–1830* (1964). Editor: *Correspondence of Thomas Jefferson and Francis Walker Gilmer* (1952); *Chivers' Life of Poe* (1952); *The Colonial Virginia Satirists* (1967); *Collected Poems of Samuel Davies 1723–1761* (1968); etc. Prof. English, University of Tennessee, since 1947.

DAVIS, RICHARD HARDING (Apr. 18, 1864–Apr. 11, 1916); b. Philadelphia, Pa., son of Rebecca Harding Davis. Journalist, correspondent, author. *Gallegher, and Other Stories* (1891); *Van Bibber and Others* (1892); *Soldiers of Fortune* (1897); *The Lion and the Unicorn* (1899); *Ranson's Folly* (1902); *Captain Macklin* (1902); *The Bar Sinister* (1903); *Vera, the Medium* (1908); *Notes of a War Correspondent* (1910); etc. Correspondent, New York *Sun* and *Harper's Weekly*. Many of his articles appeared originally in *Scribner's Magazine*. See Henry Cole Quinby's *Richard Harding Davis: A Bibliography* (1924); Fairfax Downey's *Richard Harding Davis: His Day* (1933);

DAVIS, ROBERT (July 29, 1881–1949); b. Beverly, Mass. Author. *Diary with Denekine* (1919); *Poem of an Old French Farm* (1931); *The Wit of Northern Vermont* (1937); *A Vermonter in Spain* (1938); *Padre Porko* (1939); *That Girl of Pierre's* (1948); etc.

DAVIS, ROBERT H[obart] (Mar. 23, 1869–Oct. 11, 1942); b. Brownsville, Neb. Editor, playwright. Wrote also under name, "Bob Davis." *Over My Left Shoulder* (1926); *Bob Davis Recalls* (1927); *Bob Davis Abroad* (1929); *The Caliph of Bagdad* (with Arthur Bartlett Maurice, 1931); *Islands Far and Near* (1933); *Bob Davis at Large* (1934); *Tree Toad: The Autobiography of a Small Boy* (1935); *"The More I Admire Dogs"* (1936); *People Everywhere* (1936); *Oriental Odyssey* (1937); *Let's Go with Bob Davis* (1940); etc. The "Bob Davis" books are compilations from his column in the New York *Sun*.

DAVIS, THURSTON N. (Oct. 12, 1913–); b. Philadelphia, Pa. Roman Catholic clergyman, editor. Editor: *A John La Farge Reader*, 1956; *Between Two Cities* (1962). With *America*, from 1953; editor-in-chief 1955–68; With *The Catholic Mind*, 1955–68. On board of directors, Georgetown University, since 1966.

DAVIS, VARINA ANNE JEFFERSON (June 27, 1864–Sept. 18, 1898); b. Richmond, Va., daughter of Jefferson and Varina Howell Davis. Known as "Winnie Davis, the Daughter of the Confederacy." Author. *An Irish Knight of the Nineteenth Century: Sketch of the Life of Robert Emmet* (1888); *The Veiled Doctor* (1895); *A Romance of Summer Seas* (1898).

DAVIS, VARINA HOWELL (Mrs. Jefferson Davis) (May 7, 1826–Oct. 16, 1906); b. Natchez, Miss. Author. *Jefferson Davis, Ex-President of the Confederate States of America*, 2v. (1890). See Evon Rowland's *Varina Howell*, 2v. (1927–31).

DAVIS, WILLIAM HEATH (1822–1909). Author. *Sixty Years in California* (1889); *Seventy-Five Years in California* (1929).

DAVIS, WILLIAM STEARNS (Apr. 30, 1877–Feb. 15, 1930); b. Amherst, Mass. Educator, historian, novelist. *A Friend of Caesar* (1900); *A Victor of Salamis* (1907); *A Day in Old Athens* (1914); *A History of France* (1919); *Life on a Mediaeval Barony* (1923); *The Beauty of the Purple* (1924); *Gilman of Redford* (1927); *Life in Elizabethan Days* (1930); etc.

DAVIS, WILLIAM THOMAS (Mar. 3, 1822–Dec. 3, 1907); b. Plymouth, Mass. Lawyer, historian. *Ancient Landmarks of Plymouth* (1883); *History of the Town of Plymouth* (1885); *Plymouth: Memories of an Octogenarian* (1906); and other books on Plymouth. Editor: *Bradford's History of Plymouth Plantation, 1606–1646* (1908).

DAVIS, WILLIAM WATTS HART (July 27, 1820–1910); b. in Bucks Co., Pa. Journalist, author. *El Gringo; or, New Mexico and Her People* (1857); etc.

Davis, Winnie. See Varina Anne Jefferson Davis.

DAVISON, ARCHIBALD T[hompson] (Oct. 11, 1883–Feb. 6, 1961); b. Boston, Mass. Music teacher, musicologist. *Protestant Church Music in America* (1934); *Choral Conducting* (1940); *Historical Anthology of Music*, 2v. (with Willi Apel, 1949, 1950); *Church Music: Illusion and Reality* (1952). Prof. music, Harvard University, 1940–1954.

DAVISON, EDWARD [Lewis] (July 28, 1898–Feb. 8, 1970); b. Glasgow, Scotland. Educator, poet. *Poems* (1920); *Poems by Four Authors* (with others, 1923); *Harvest of Youth* (1925); *Some Modern Poets, & Other Poems* (1927); *The Heart's Unreason* (1931); *The Ninth Witch, and Other Critical Essays* (1932); *Nine Poems* (1937); *Collected Poems* (1940). Editor: *Cambridge Poets, 1914–1920* (1920). Prof. English and director, School of General Studies, Hunter College, from 1953.

DAVISON, FRANK CYRIL (Feb. 3, 1893–); b. Hantsport, N.S. Pen name, "Pierre Coalfleet." Author. *Sidonie* (1921); *Solo* (1923); *Hare and Tortoise* (1925); *Meanwhile* (1927); *Family Hold Back* (prod. 1936); *Women of Property* (prod. 1937).

DAVISON, PETER HUBERT (June 27, 1928–); b. New York. Editor, poet. *The Breaking of the Day* (1964); *The City and the Island* (1966); *Pretending to Be Asleep* (1969). Director, Atlantic Monthly Press, since 1964.

Davy and the Goblin. Fanciful dream story by Charles Edward Carryl (1885).

Davy Crockett, a play by Frank Murdock (prod. New York, March 9, 1874).

DAWES, ANNE LAURENS (May 14, 1851–Sept. 25, 1938); b. North Adams, Mass. Author. *Charles Sumner* (1892); etc.

DAWES, CHARLES GATES (Aug. 27, 1865–Apr. 23, 1951); b. Marietta, O. Statesman, diplomat, author. *Essays and Speeches* (1915); *A Journal of the Great War* (1921); *Notes As Vice-President* (1935); *Journal As Ambassador to Great Britain* (1939); *A Journal of the McKinley Years* (1950); etc. Vice-president of the United States, 1925–29. Awarded (with Sir Austen Chamberlain) Nobel Peace Prize for 1925.

DAWES, RUFUS (Jan. 26, 1803–Nov. 30, 1859); b. Boston, Mass. Poet. *The Valley of the Nashaway, and Other Poems* (1830); *Geraldine; Athenia of Damascus; and Miscellaneous Poems* (1839); *Nix's Mate* (anon., 1839); *Story* (1840); *The Battle of Stillwater; or, The Maniac* (prod. 1840).

DAWSON, CONINGSBY [William] (Feb. 26, 1883–); b. High Wycombe, Bucks, Eng., son of William James Dawson. Novelist, poet. *The Worker and Other Poems* (1906); *The House of the Weeping Woman* (1908); *Murder Point* (1910); *The Road to Avalon* (1911); *The Garden Without Walls* (1913); *Florence on a Certain Night, and Other Poems* (1914); *Carry On* (1917); *The Test of Scarlet* (1919); *It Might Have Happened to You* (1921); *The Kingdom Round the Corner* (1921); *The Vanishing Point* (1922); *The Coast of Folly* (1924); *Old Youth* (1925); *Pilgrim of the Impossible* (1928); *The Unknown Soldier* (1929); *Fugitives from Passion* (1929); *A Path to Paradise* (1932); *The Moon Through Glass* (1934); *Inspiration Valley* (1936); *Tell Us of the Night* (with J. B. Browne, 1941); etc.

DAWSON, HENRY BARTON (June 8, 1821–May 23, 1889); b. Gosberton, Lincolnshire, England. Editor, historian. *Battles of the United States, by Sea and Land*, 2v. (1858); *New York City During the American Revolution* (1861); *Westchester County, New York, During the American Revolution* (1886); etc.

DAWSON, ROBERT [Merril] (Nov. 10, 1941–); b. Wells, Minn. Poet. *Six Mile Corner* (1966); *Sculpture* (1966); *Starting with Sculpture* (1968).

DAWSON, WARRINGTON (Sept. 27, 1878–); b. Charleston, S.C. Novelist. *The Scar* (1906); *The Scourge* (1908); *The Gift of Paul Clermont* (1921); *The Sin* (1923); *Adventures in the Night* (1924); *The Green Moustache* (1925); *The Crimson Pall* (1927); *Paul Clermont's Story and My Own* (1928).

DAWSON, WILLIAM JAMES (Nov. 21, 1854–Aug. 23, 1928); b. Towchester, Northampton, England. Methodist clergyman, author. *A Vision of Souls* (poems, 1884); *The Makers of Modern Prose* (1899); *The Makers of English Poetry* (1902); *The Makers of English Fiction* (1905); *The Book of Courage* (1911); *America, and Other Poems* (1914); *Robert Shenstone* (1917); *The Barrowdale Tragedy* (1920); *The Autobiography of a Mind* (1925); etc.

DAY, A[rthur] GROVE (Apr. 29, 1904–); b. Philadelphia, Pa. Educator, author. *Bluejacket* (with F. J. Buenzle, 1936); *Coronado's Quest* (1940); *The Sky Clears: Poetry of the American Indian* (1951); *James A. Michener* (1964); *Louis Becke* (1966); *Explorers of the Pacific* (1967); *Adventures of the Pacific* (1969); etc. Editor: *Despatches from Mexico by Fernando Cortes* (1935); *The Spell of the Pacific: An Anthology of its Literature* (with Carl Stroven, 1949); *Mark Twain's Letters from Hawaii* (1966); *The Spanish in Sydney, 1793* (with Virginia M. Day, 1967); etc. Prof. English, University of Hawaii, since 1944.

DAY, BENJAMIN HENRY (1810–Dec. 21, 1889). Printer, publisher. Printed first issue of New York *Sun*, Sept. 3, 1833. Started the *True Sun* in 1840, and founded *Brother Jonathan*, a monthly magazine, July, 1839, and the *New World*, a fiction magazine, June 6, 1840. His son, Benjamin Day, invented the Benday process used in photo-engraving.

DAY, CHON (1907–). Cartoonist. *I Could Be Dreaming* (1945); *What Price Dory?* (1955); *Brother Sebastian* (1957); *Brother Sebastian Carries On* (1959); *Brother Sebastian at Large* (1961).

DAY, CLARENCE [Shepard] (Nov. 18, 1874–Dec. 28, 1935); b. New York City. Author (and illustrator). *This Simian World* (1920); *The Crow's Nest* (1921); *Thoughts Without*

Words (1928); *God and My Father* (1932); *Life with Father* (1935); *Scenes from the Mesozoic and Other Drawings* (verse, 1935); *Life with Mother* (1937); *Father and I* (1940); etc.

DAY, CYRUS LAWRENCE (Dec. 2, 1900–July 5, 1968); b. New York. Critic, author. *Sailor's Knots* (1935); *The Art of Knotting and Splicing* (1947). Editor: *Songs of Dryden* (1932); *Songs of Thomas D'Urfey* (1933). Prof. English, University of Delaware, from 1946.

DAY, DAVID. Soldier, Indian agent, editor. Founder, the *Solid Muldoon,* newspaper, in Ouray, Colo., in 1879. In 1892 he moved the newspaper to Durango, Colo., and the following year changed its name to the *Durango Democrat.* Dave Day's humorous articles were often quoted in Eastern newspapers. *See* Percy Fritz's *Colorado* (1941).

DAY, FRANK PARKER (May 9, 1881–1950); b. Shubenacadie, N.S. Educator, author. *River of Strangers* (1926); *The Autobiography of a Fisherman* (1927); *Rockbound* (1928); *John Paul's Rock* (1930). President, Union College, 1929–33.

DAY, GEORGE PARMLY (Sept. 4, 1876–Oct. 24, 1959); b. New York City. Brother to Clarence Day and grandson of Benjamin H. Day, founder of the New York *Sun.* Founder, Yale University Press, 1908; president and treasurer, from 1908.

DAY, HENRY NOBLE (Aug. 4, 1808–Jan. 12, 1890); b. New Preston, Conn. Congregational clergyman, educator, author. *The Art of Rhetoric* (1850); *An Introduction to the Study of English Literature* (1869); *The Science of Aesthetics* (1872); and other books on philosophy. President, Ohio Female College, 1858–64.

DAY, HOLMAN [Francis] (Nov. 6, 1865–Feb. 19, 1935); b. Vassalboro, Me. Poet, novelist, playwright. *Up in Maine* (poems, 1900); *Pine Tree Ballads* (1902); *Kin o'Ktaadn* (poems, 1904); *Squire Phin* (1905), dramatized as *The Circus Man* (prod. 1909); *King Spruce* (1908); *The Ramrodders* (1910); *The Skippers and the Skipped* (1911); *The Red Lane* (1912); *Along Came Ruth* (prod. 1914); *The Landloper* (1915); *Blow the Man Down* (1916); *Where Your Treasure Is* (1917); *Kavanagh's Clare* (1917); *The Rider of the King Log* (1919); *All-Wool Morrison* (1920); *When Egypt Went Broke* (1921); *Joan of Arc of the North Woods* (1922); *Leadbetter's Luck* (1923); *The Loving Are the Daring* (1923); *Clothes Make the Pirate* (1925); *John Lang* (1926); *When the Fight Begins* (1924); *The Ship of Joy* (1931); etc.

Day, John Co., The. New York. Publishing House. Founded in 1926 by Richard Walsh, Guy Holt, Cleland Austin and Trell Yocum. Richard Walsh, Jr., is president. Now a subsidiary of INTEXT (q.v.).

DAY, LILLIAN (1893–); b. New York City. Author. *Paganini of Genoa* (1929); *Kiss and Tell* (1931); *Our Wife* (with Lyon Mearson, 1932); *Murder in Time* (with Norbert Lederer, 1935); *Death Comes on Friday* (with same, 1937).

DAY, RICHARD EDWIN (Apr. 27, 1852–Dec. 14, 1936); b. Granby, N.Y. Poet. *Lines in the Sand* (1878); *Thor: A Drama* (1880); *Lyrics and Satires* (1883); *Poems* (1888); *New Poems* (1909); *Dante: A Sonnet Sequence, and Other Poems* (1924); etc.

DAY, SARAH J. (Nov. 5, 1860–May 11, 1940); b. Cincinnati, O. Poet. *Mayflowers to Mistletoe* (1900); *Fresh Fields and Legends Old and New* (1909); *Wayfares and Wings* (1924); etc.

DAY, STEPHEN (c. 1594–1668); b. in England. First printer in British America. Printed the *Freeman's Oath* (1639); the *Bay Psalm Book* (1640); etc. *See* Sidney Arthur Kimber's *The Story of an Old Press: An Account of the Hand Press Known as the Stephen Daye Press* (1937); and *The Colophon,* 1938.

DAY, THOMAS FLEMING (Mar. 27, 1861–Aug. 19, 1927); b. in Somersetshire, England. Poet. *Songs of Sea and Sail* (1898); *Bristol Jack and Other Poems* (1922); *The Voyage of Detroit* (1929).

"Day is Done, The." Poem by H. W. Longfellow (1844) containing the oft-quoted lines,
"And the night shall be filled with music,
And the cares, that infest the day,
Shall fold their tents, like the Arabs,
And as silently steal away."

Day of Doom, The. By Michael Wigglesworth (1662). Long narrative poem setting forth the damnation of sinners in terms calculated to frighten them into repentance, with no promise of salvation.

Day of Faith, The. By Arthur Somers Roche (1921). On this day every person in the world was in sympathy with one another. It marked the beginning of the millennium.

Dayton Journal Herald. Dayton, O. Newspaper. *Dayton Journal,* founded 1823 as the *Miami Republican and Dayton Advertiser.* Name *Dayton Journal* adopted in 1857, after several intervening changes. Bought by James M. Cox in 1948 and merged with the *Dayton Herald.* Charles Alexander is editor; Richard Schwarze is book-review editor.

Dayton News. Dayton, O. Newspaper. Founded 1887 as *The Dayton Evening Monitor;* called *Dayton Daily News* after 1889. Bought by James M. Cox in 1898. Now known as *Dayton News.*

DAZEY, CHARLES TURNER (Aug. 13, 1855–Feb. 9, 1938); b. Lima, Ill. Playwright. *In Old Kentucky* (prod. 1893); *The War of Wealth* (prod. 1896); *Home Folks* (prod. 1904); *The Suburban* (prod. 1903); *The American Lord* (with George Broadhurst, prod. 1905); *The Stranger* (prod. 1911); *A Night Out* (with May Robson, prod. 1911); etc.

DE ANGELI, MARGUERITE [Lofft] (Mar. 14, 1889–); b. Lapeer, Mich. Author and illustrator of children's books. *Copper-toed Boots* (1938); *Bright April* (1946); *Jared's Island* (1947); *The Door in the Wall* (1949); *Just Like David* (1951); *Marguerite De Angeli's Book of Nursery and Mother Goose Rhymes* (1954); *Black Fox of Lorne* (1956); *Book of Favorite Hymns* (1963); *The Goose Girl* (1964); *Turkey for Christmas* (1965); etc. Editor and illustrator: *The Old Testament* (1960).

DE BECK, WILLIAM (Apr. 16, 1890–Nov. 11, 1942); b. Chicago, Ill. Cartoonist. Creator of the cartoons "Barney Google," "Spark Plug," "Married Life," "Bunky," "Snuffy Smith," "Feather Merchants," U.S. Army "Yard Bird," etc. With William Randolph Hearst Publications, from 1918.

DE BLOIS, AUSTEN KENNEDY (Dec. 17, 1866–Aug.10, 1945); b. Wolfville, N.S. Baptist clergyman, educator, editor, author. *Life of John Mason Peck* (1917); *John Bunyan, the Man* (1928); *Fighters for Freedom* (1929); *The Making of Ministers* (1936); *Christian Religious Education* (1939); etc. Editor, *The Christian Review,* from 1931. President, Eastern Baptist Theological Seminary, 1926–36.

De Bow's Review. New Orleans, La. Monthly magazine. Founded 1846 by James Dunwoody Brownson De Bow (July 10, 1820–Feb. 27, 1867). Originally called *The Commercial Review of the South and West.* Strictly a commercial and agricultural journal, it gave but small space to literature until 1850. History received more attention, for De Bow was one of the founders of the Louisiana Historical Society. Expired 1880. *See* Willis Duke Weatherford's *James Dunwoody Brownson De Bow* (1935).

DE CAPITE, MICHAEL (Apr. 13, 1915–); b. Cleveland, O. Novelist. *Maria* (1943); *No Bright Banner* (1944); *The Bennett Place* (1948).

DE CAPITE, RAYMOND (1926?–). Author. *The Coming of Fabrizze* (1960); *A Lost King* (1961).

DE CASSERES, BENJAMIN (1873–Dec. 6, 1945); b. Philadelphia, Pa. Author. *The Shadow-Eater* (poems, 1915); *Chameleon: Being the Book of My Selves* (1922); *Mirrors of New York* (1925); *James Gibbons Huneker* (1925); *Forty Immortals* (1925); *Anathema!* (1928); *Mencken and Shaw* (1930); *The Love Letters of a Living Poet* (1931); *Spinoza* (1932); *Works*, 3v. (1936–38); *The Muse of Lies* (1936); *Don Marquis* (1938); etc. Columnist and editorial writer, the Hearst newspapers.

DE CONDE, ALEXANDER (Nov. 13, 1920–); b. Utica, N.Y. Historian. *The Quasi-War: The Politics and the Undeclared War with France, 1797–1801* (1966); *Herbert Hoover's Latin-American Policy* (1951); *Entangling Alliance, Politics and Diplomacy under George Washington* (1958); *The American Secretary of State: An Interpretation* (1963); etc. Editor: *Patterns in American History* (1969). Prof. history, University of California at Santa Barbara, since 1961.

DE COSTA, BENJAMIN FRANKLIN (July 10, 1831–Nov. 4, 1904); b. Charlestown, Mass. Clergyman, historian. *Lake George: Its Scenes and Characteristics* (1868); *Sketches of the Coast of Maine and Isles of Shoals* (1869); *The Atlantic Coast Guide* (1873); etc. Editor, the *Magazine of American History,* 1882–83.

DE FONTAINE, FELIX GREGORY (1834–Dec. 11, 1896); b. Boston, Mass. Journalist, historian. *Marginalia; or, Gleanings from an Army Note-Book* (under pen name, "Personne," 1964); *Birds of a Feather Flock Together* (1878); etc. Compiler: *Cyclopedia of the Best Thoughts of Charles Dickens* (1873), republished as *The Fireside Dickens* (1883).

DE FORD, MIRIAM ALLEN (Mrs. Maynard Shipley) (Aug. 21, 1888–); b. Philadelphia, Pa. Author. *Love Children* (1921); *Children of Sun* (poems, 1939); *They Were San Franciscans* (biography, 1941); *Shaken with the Wind* (1942); *Uphill All the Way: Maynard Shipley* (biography, 1956); *The Overbury Affair* (1960); *Penultimates* (1962); etc. Compiler: *Who Was When? A Dictionary of Contemporaries* (1940).

DE FOREST, HENRY PELOUZE (Dec. 29, 1864–June 13, 1948); b. Fulton, N.Y. Physician, librarian, author. *One Thousand Miles Afoot* (1895); etc. Librarian, Cornell Club of New York, from 1924.

DE FOREST, JOHN WILLIAM (May 31, 1826–July 17, 1906); b. Humphreysville, Conn. Novelist, poet. *History of the Indians of Connecticut* (1851); *Witching Times* (1856); *European Acquaintance* (1858); *Seacliff* (1859); *Miss Ravenel's Conversion from Secession to Loyalty* (1867); *Overland* (1871); *Kate Beaumont* (1872); *The Wetherel Affair* (1873); *Playing the Mischief* (1875); *Honest John Vane* (1875); *The Bloody Chasm* (1881); *A Lover's Revolt* (1898); *The Downing Legends: Stories in Rhyme* (1901); *Poems* (1902).

DE GRAMONT, SANCHE (Mar. 30, 1932–); b. Geneva, Switz. Journalist, author. *The Secret War* (1962); *Epitaph for Kings* (1968); *The French: Portrait of a People* (1969). Editor and translator: *Memoirs of Duc de Saint-Simon* (1962).

DE GRAZIA, ALFRED (Dec. 29, 1919–); b. Chicago, Ill. Educator, author. *Public and Republic* (1949); *The Western Public* (1954); *Apportionment and Representative Government* (1963); *The Velikovsky Affair* (1966); *Passage of the Year* (poems, 1967). Founder and editor, *American Behavioral Scientist,* 1957–66.

DE GRAZIA, SEBASTIAN (Aug. 11, 1917–); b. Chicago, Ill. Educator, author. *The Political Community* (1948); *Of Time, Work and Leisure* (1962); *Errors of Psychotherapy* (1963). Prof. politics, Rutgers University, since 1961.

DE HARTOG, JAN (Apr. 22, 1914–); b. Haarlem, Neth. Playwright, novelist. *Skipper Next to God* (play, 1946); *This Time Tomorrow* (play, 1947); *The Fourposter* (play, 1948); *The Lost Sea* (1951); *The Distant Shore* (1952); *The Little Ark* (1953); *A Sailor's Life* (1956); *The Spiral Road* (1957);

The Inspector (1960); *Waters of the New World* (1961); *The Artist* (1963); *The Hospital* (1964); *The Captain* (1966); *The Children* (1969).

DE JONG, DAVID CORNEL (1905–Sept. 5, 1967); b. Blija, Neth. Novelist. *Old Haven* (1938); *Light Sons and Dark* (1940); *Somewhat Angels* (1945); *The Desperate Children* (1949); *Two Sofas in the Parlor* (1952); *Seven Sayings of Mr. Jefferson* (juvenile, 1957); *The Unfairness of Easter* (stories, 1959); *Around the Dom* (1964); etc.

DE KAY, CHARLES (July 25, 1848–May 28, 1935); b. Washington, D.C. Critic, poet. *The Bohemians* (1878); *Hesperus, and Other Poems* (1880); *The Vision of Esther* (1880); *The Vision of Nimrod* (1881); *The Love Poems of Louis Barnaval* (1883); *Bird Gods* (1898).

DE KAY, JOHN WESLEY (July 20, 1872–Oct. 4, 1938); b. near New Hampton, Ia. Industrialist, writer. *Longings* (1908); *The Weaver* (drama, 1908); rewritten as a play, *Judas* (prod. 1910), and again as a tragedy, *The Maid of Bethany* (1929); *The Weaver and the Way of Life* (1909); *Brown Leaves* (1911).

DE KOVEN, ANNA FARWELL (Mrs. Reginald de Koven) (Nov. 19, 1862–Jan. 12, 1953); b. Chicago, Ill. Author. *The Life and Letters of John Paul Jones*, 2v. (1913); *A Musician and His Wife* (1926); *Horace Walpole and Madame du Deffand* (1929); etc.

DE KOVEN, REGINALD (Apr. 3, 1861–Jan. 16, 1920); b. Middletown, Conn. Composer, music critic. Music critic for *Harper's Weekly, New York World,* etc. Composer of operas, "The Begum," "Robin Hood," "The Highwayman," "The Golden Butterfly," etc., and many songs, including "Oh, Promise Me."

DE KROYFT, [Susan] HELEN ALDRICH (Oct. 29, 1818–Oct. 25, 1915); b. Rochester, N.Y. Blind author and lecturer. *A Place in Thy Memory* (1850); *Little Jakey* (1871); etc.

DE KRUIF, PAUL (Mar. 2, 1890–Feb. 28, 1971); b. Zeeland, Mich. Bacteriologist, author. *Our Medicine Men* (1922); *Microbe Hunters* (1926); *Hunger Fighters* (1928); *Seven Iron Men* (1929); *Men Against Death* (1932); *Yellow Jack, a History* (with Sidney Howard, 1934); *Why Keep Them Alive?* (with Rhea [Barbarin] de Kruif, 1936); *The Fight for Life* (1938); *Health Is Wealth* (1940); *Kaiser Wakes the Doctors* (1943); *The Male Hormone* (1945); *Life Among the Doctors* (with R. B. De Kruif, 1949); *A Man Against Insanity* (1957); *The Sweeping Wind: A Memoir* (1962).

DE LA TORRE, LILLIAN (Mar. 15, 1902–); b. New York. Author. *Elizabeth Is Missing* (1945); *Dr. Samuel Johnson, Detector* (1946); *Villainy Detected* (1947); *The 60 Minute Chef* (with C. Truax, 1947); *Goodbye, Miss Lizzie Borden* (1948); *The Heir of Douglas* (1952); *The White Rose of Stuart* (1954); *Actress: The Story of Sarah Siddons* (1957); etc.

DE LA VERGNE, GEORGE H[arrison] (1868–). Author. *Hawaiian Sketches* (1898); *The Pines, and Other Poems* (1902); *At the Foot of the Rockies* (1902); *The Wilderness* (poem, 1921).

DE LEEUW, ADÈLE [Louise] (Aug., 1899–); b. Hamilton, O. Author. *Berries of the Bittersweet* (poems, 1924); *The Flavor of Holland* (1928); *Island Adventure* (1934); *Clay Fingers* (1948); *The Story of Amelia Earhart* (1955); *Donny* (1957); *Indonesian Legends and Folk Tales* (1961); *Legends and Folk Tales of Holland* (1963); *Sir Walter Raleigh* (1964); *Behold This Dream* (1968); etc. Co-author: *Caboose Club* (1957); *Apron Strings* (1959); *Where Valor Lies* (1959); *The Salty Skinners* (with Cateau De Leeuw, 1964); etc.

DE LEEUW, HENDRIK (July 18, 1896–); b. Amsterdam, Neth. Author. *Crossroads of the Java Sea* (1931); *Cities of Sin* (1933); *Java Jungle Tales* (1934); *Sinful Cities of the Western World* (1934); *Crossroads of the Caribbean Sea* (1935); *Cross-*

roads of the Buccaneers (1937); *Crossroads of the Zuider Zee* (1938); *Flower of Joy* (1939); *Peewee the Mousedeer* (1943); *Fallen Angels* (1954); *Crossroads of the Mediterranean* (1954); *The Underworld Story* (1955); *From Flying Horse to Man in the Moon* (1963); etc.

DE LEON, THOMAS COOPER (May 21, 1839–Mar. 19, 1914); b. Columbia, S.C. Editor, historian, novelist, humorist. *Four Years in Rebel Capitals* (1890); *John Holden, Unionist* (1893); *Crag Nest* (1898); *Confederate Memories* (1899); *History of Creole Carnivals* (1899). Compiler: *South Songs: From the Lays of Later Days* (1866).

DE LONG, EMMA WOLTAN (Mar. 11, 1851–Nov. 24, 1940); b. New York City. Author. *Explorer's Wife* (1938). Editor: *The Voyage of the Jeannette* (1883), the memoirs of her husband, George Washington De Long.

DE LONG, GEORGE WASHINGTON (Aug. 22, 1844–Oct. 30, 1881); b. New York City. Arctic explorer. His journals were edited by his widow under the title *The Voyage of the Jeannette* (1883). *See* John Wilson Danenhower's *Lieutenant Danenhower's Narrative of the Jeannette* (1882); Emma W. De Long's *Explorer's Wife* (1938).

DE LONG, RUSSELL VICTOR (Aug. 24, 1901–); b. Dover, N.H. Educator, author. *We Can If We Will* (1947); *The High Cost of Low Living* (1949); *Clouds and Rainbows* (1950); *Facts We Hate to Face* (1952); *A Temple or a Tavern* (1969); etc. Pres., Pasadena College, California, since 1957.

DE MILLE, AGNES, b. New York. Dancer, Choreographer, author. *Dance to the Piper* (1952); *And Promenade Home* (1958); *Lizzie Borden: A Dance of Death* (1968); etc.

DE MILLE, CECIL B[lount] (Aug. 12, 1881–Jan. 21, 1959); b. Ashfield, Mass., son of Henry Churchill De Mille. Playwright, film director. Author (with William Churchill De Mille): *The Genius,* (prod. 1904); *The Royal Mounted* (prod. 1908).

DE MILLE, HENRY CHURCHILL (Sept. 17, 1853–Feb. 10, 1893); b. Washington, N.C. Playwright. *John Delmer's Daughters on Duty* (prod. 1883); *The Wife* (with David Belasco, prod. 1887); *Lord Chumley* (with same, prod. 1888); *The Charity Ball* (with same, prod. 1889); *Men and Women* (with same, prod. 1890); etc.

DE MILLE, WILLIAM CHURCHILL (July 25, 1878–Mar. 5, 1955); b. Washington, N.C., son of Henry Churchill De Mille. Playwright. *The Genius* (with Cecil Blount De Mille, prod. 1904); *Strongheart* (prod. 1905); *The Warrens of Virginia* (prod. 1907); *Classmates* (with Margaret Turnbull, prod. 1907); *The Royal Mounted* (with Cecil Blount De Mille, prod. 1908); *The Woman* (prod. 1911); *Hollywood Saga* (1939); etc.

DE MOTT, BENJAMIN [Haile] (June 2, 1924–); b. Rockville Centre, N.Y. Educator, author. *The Body's Cage* (1959); *Hells and Benefits* (1962); *You Don't Say* (1966); *A Married Man* (1968); *Supergrow* (1969); etc. Prof. English, Amherst College, since 1951.

DE PEREDA, PRUDENCIO (Feb. 18, 1912–); b. Brooklyn, N.Y. Author. *All the Girls We Loved* (1948); *Fiesta* (1953); *Windmills in Brooklyn* (1960). Translator: Alberto Gerchunoff's *Jewish Gauchos of the Pampas* (1955).

DE PEYSTER, JOHN WATTS (Mar. 9, 1821–May 4, 1907); b. New York City. Soldier, military writer, playwright. *The Decisive Conflicts of the Late Civil War,* 2v. (1867–68); *Bothwell* (drama, 1884); etc. *See* Frank Allaben's *John Watts de Peyster,* 2v. (1908).

DE REGNIERS, BEATRICE SCHENK (Aug. 16, 1914–); b. Lafayette, Ind. Editor, author. *The Giant Story* (1953); *What Can You Do with a Shoe?* (1955); *The Snow Party* (1959); *The Little Book* (1961); *David and Goliath* (1965); *Penny* (1966); *The Day Everybody Cried* (1967); etc. Editor, Scholastic Book Services, since 1961.

DE RENNE, WYMBERLY JONES (1853–1916). Book collector. His collection was housed in a separate building on his estate near Savannah, Georgia, and its curator was the noted bibliophile Leonard L. Mackall, who died in 1937. A three-volume catalogue of the collection was privately printed in 1931. Confederate imprints and books relating to Georgia formed the bulk of the collection.

DE SANTILLANA, GIORGIO D[iaz] (May 30, 1902–); b. Rome. Historian of science. *A Historian of Science* (1933); *Aspects of Scientific Rationalism in the Nineteenth Century* (1941); Galileo's *Dialogue on the Great World Systems* (ed., 1953); *The Crime of Galileo* (1955); *The Origins of Scientific Thought* (1961). Prof. history and philosophy of science, Massachusetts Institute of Technology, since 1954.

DE SEVERSKEY, ALEXANDER PROCOFIEFF (June 7, 1894–); b. Tiflis, Rus. Aeronautical consultant, author. *Victory Through Air Power* (1942); *Air Power: Key to Survival* (1950); *America: Too Young to Die!* (1960).

DE TOLEDANO, RALPH (Aug. 17, 1916–); b. Tangier. Editor, author. *Seeds of Treason* (with Victor Lasky, 1950); *Spies, Dupes and Diplomats* (1952); *Nixon* (1956); *Lament for a Generation* (1960); *The Greatest Plot in History* (1963); *The Goldwater Story* (1964); *R.F.K.: The Man Who Would Be President* (1967); *America I Love You* (1968); *Man Alone: Richard M. Nixon* (1969); etc. Assoc. editor, *Newsweek,* since 1950.

DE TOLNAY, CHARLES ERICH (May 27, 1899–); b. Budapest. Art historian. *The Youth of Michelangelo* (1943); *The Sistine Ceiling* (1945); *The Medici Chapel* (1948); *The Drawings of Pieter Brueghel the Elder* (1952); *The Tomb of Julius II* (1954); *The Art and Thought of Michelangelo* (1964); *Hieronymus Bosch* (1966).

DE VANE, WILLIAM CLYDE (June 17, 1898–Aug. 17, 1965); b. Savannah, Ga. Educator, author. *Browning's Parleyings: The Autobiography of a Mind* (1927); *Charlotte Bronte's Legends of Angria* (with Fanny Ratchford, 1933); *Browning's Shorter Poems* (1934); *A Browning Handbook* (1935); *Tennyson* (1940); *New Letters of Robert Browning* (ed., with K. L. Knickerbocker, 1950).

DE VERE, MARY AINGE; b. Brooklyn, N.Y. Poet. Pen name "Madeline Bridges." *Love Songs, and Other Poems* (1870); *Poems* (1890); *The Wind Swept Wheat: Poems* (1904); *The Open Book, Humorous Verse* (1915).

De Vere, Maximilian Schele. See Schele de Vere, Maximilian.

DE VINNE, THEODORE LOW (Dec. 25, 1828–Feb. 16, 1914); b. Stamford, Conn. Master printer, author. *The Invention of Printing* (1876); and other books on history of printing. Founder of De Vinne Press. His firm printed *St. Nicholas; The Century;* many of the early books of Grolier Club; and *Century Dictionary.* He was one of the founders and the sixth president of Grolier Club.

DE VOTO, BERNARD [Augustine] (Jan. 11, 1897–Nov. 13, 1955); b. Ogden, Utah. Editor, novelist. *The Crooked Mile* (1924); *The Chariot of Fire* (1926); *The House of Sun-Goes-Down* (1928); *Mark Twain's America* (1932); *We Accept with Pleasure* (1934); *Forays and Rebuttals* (1936); *Minority Report* (1940); *Mark Twain at Work* (1942); *The Year of Decision: 1846* (1943); *The Literary Fallacy* (1944); *Mountain Time* (1947); *Across the Wide Missouri* (1947; Pulitzer prize for history, 1948); *The World of Fiction* (1950); *The Hour* (1951); *The Course of Empire* (1952); *The Easy Chair* (1955); etc. Editor, "The Easy Chair" in *Harper's Magazine,* from 1935.

DE VRIES, PETER (Feb. 27, 1910–); b. Chicago, Ill. Author. *But Who Wakes the Bugler?* (1940); *The Handsome Heart* (1943); *Angels Can't Do Better* (1944); *No But I Saw the Movie* (1952); *The Tunnel of Love* (1954); *Comfort Me with Apples* (1956); *The Mackerel Plaza* (1958); *The Tents of*

Wickedness (1959); *Through the Fields of Clover* (1961); *The Blood of the Lamb* (1962); *Reuben, Reuben* (1964); *Let Me Count the Ways* (1965); *The Vale of Laughter* (1967); *The Cat's Pajamas and Witch's Milk* (1968).

"Deacon's Masterpiece; or, The Wonderful 'One-Hoss Shay,' The." Poem by Oliver Wendell Holmes (1858). This poem allegorically portrays the collapse of a system of thought in New England.

Dead End. Play by Sidney Kingsley (prod. 1935). Story of a gang of boys brought up in an environment of crime. The scene is New York City in a section where slum and penthouse accentuate the social problem by their very proximity.

DEAL, BABS H. (Mrs. Borden Deal). Author. *Acres of Afternoon* (1959); *It's Always Three O'Clock* (1961); *Night Story* (1962); *The Grail* (1963); *The Walls Came Tumbling Down* (1968).

DEAL, BORDEN (1922–); Novelist. *Walk Through the Valley* (1956); *Dunbar's Cove* (1957); *The Insolent Breed* (1959); *The Dragon's Wine* (1960); *The Tempter* (1961); *The Spangled Road* (1962); *The Loser* (1964); *A Long Way to Go* (1965); *The Least One* (1967); *Advocate* (1968).

DEALEY, GEORGE BANNERMAN (Sept. 18, 1859–Feb. 26, 1946); b. Manchester, England. Publisher. With *Galveston News* and *Dallas News,* from 1874. President, A. H. Belo Corporation, publishers of the *Dallas News,* 1926–40; succeeded by his son, Edward Musgrove Dealey, who joined the *Dallas News* staff in 1915.

DEAN, ABNER (Mar. 18, 1910–); b. New York. Artist, cartoonist. *It's a Long Way to Heaven* (1945); *What Am I Doing Here?* (1947); *And on the Eighth Day* (1949); *Come As You Are* (1952); *Not Far from the Jungle* (1956); *Naked People* (1963).

DEAN, GRAHAM M. (Aug. 10, 1904–); b. Lake View, Ia. Publisher, author. *Jim of the Press* (1938); *Riders of the Gabilans* (1944); *Dusty of the Double Seven* (1948); *Deadline for Jim* (1961); etc. Publisher, *Ashland Daily Tidings,* Oregon, since 1951; *Siskiyou Daily News,* California, since 1951.

Dean, Mrs. Sidney Wallace. See Marguerite Mooers Marshall.

DEAN, VERA MICHELES (Mar. 29, 1903–); b. Petrograd, Rus. Editor, author. *Europe in Retreat* (1939); *Four Cornerstones of Peace* (1946); *Russia: Menace or Promise?* (1947); *The United States and Russia* (1947); *Europe and the United States* (1950); *Main Trends in Postwar American Foreign Policy* (1951); *Foreign Policy Without Fear* (1953); *New Patterns of Democracy in India* (1959); *Builders of Emerging Nations* (with H. D. Harootunian, 1961); *The U.S. and the New Nations* (1964); *The U.N. Today* (1965); etc. Editor: *West and Non-West* (with H. D. Harootunian, 1963). Research director, Foreign Policy Association, since 1938.

DEANE, CHARLES (Nov. 10, 1813–Nov. 13, 1889); b. Biddeford, Me. Merchant, historical writer. Eleven volumes of the *Proceedings* of the Massachusetts Historical Society were issued under his supervision. His meticulous scholarship set the standard for the editing of documents. Edited Wood's *New England Prospect* for the Prince Society (1865).

DEANE, SHIRLEY. Author. *Rocks and Olives* (1954); *Tomorrow Is Mañana* (1957); *The Road to Andorra* (1961); *Expectant Mariner* (1963); *In a Corsican Village* (1966); *Vendetta: A Story of the Corsican Mountains* (1967); *Corpses in Corsica* (1969).

DEARBORN, NED HARLAND (June 2, 1893–Aug. 1, 1962); b. Conneautville, Pa. Educator, author. *Introduction to Teaching* (1925); *The Oswego Movement in American Education* (1925); *Once in a Lifetime* (1935); etc. Dean of general education division, New York University, 1934–42.

Dearborn Independent. Dearborn, Mich. Weekly magazine. Founded, 1919. Expired, 1927.

DEASY, MARY MARGUERITE MARGARET (May 20, 1914–); b. Cincinnati, O. Author. *The Hour of Spring* (1948); *Cannon Hill* (1949); *Ella Gunning* (1950); *Devil's Bridge* (1952); *The Corioli Affair* (1954); *The Boy Who Made Good* (1955); *O'Shaughnessy's Day* (1957); *The Celebration* (1963); etc.

Death at an Early Age. By Jonathan Kozol (1967). An account of the dehumanizing effects of public school education on children.

Death Comes to the Archbishop. Novel by Willa Cather (1927). Story of two missionary priests in the southwest, Archbishop Latour and Father Vaillant. It is half idyl and half history, based chiefly on the life of Archbishop John Baptist Lamy (1814–1888).

Death in the Afternoon. By Ernest Hemingway. A detailed account of bullfighting in modern Spain (1932).

Death in the Family, A. Novel by James Agee (1957). Powerfully sensitive evocation of the spirit of American small-town life in the early twentieth century as compounded of tragedy and events of small moment.

Death of a Salesmen. Play by Arthur Miller (prod. 1949). Salesman and family-man Willy Loman, who believes in salesmanship, comes to grief because he cannot reconcile the two contradictory ideas of his job: practical shrewdness and being liked. The play is presented as a tragedy, that of an unexceptional person whose very commonness at least contains the substratum of man's will in its conflict with fate.

Death of General Montgomery, in Storming the City of Quebec, The. Tragedy by Hugh Henry Brackenridge, published anonymously (1777).

"Death of Stonewall Jackson, The." Poem by Henry Lynden Flash.

"Death of the Flowers, The." Poem by William Cullen Bryant (1825).

"Death of the Hired Man, The." Poem by Robert Frost, in his *North of Boston* (1915).

Death of the President, The. By William Manchester (1967). Controversial account of President John F. Kennedy's assassination and the events that followed.

"Decanter of Madeira." Poem by Silas Weir Mitchell (1886). A humorous greeting to George Bancroft.

DECKER, CLARENCE RAYMOND (Dec. 19, 1904–); b. Sioux City, Ia. Educator, author. Author or co-author: *Wives of the Prophets* (1935); *England* (1936); *The Victorian Conscience* (1952); *A Place of Light* (1954); etc. Editor: *Richard Le Gallienne: A Centenary Memoir* (1966). Founder, *University Review,* 1934; editor, 1934–38; editor, *Literary Review,* since 1957. Pres., University of Kansas City, 1938–53; vice-pres., Fairleigh Dickinson University, since 1956.

DECKER, MALCOLM. Author. Writes under pen name "Peter Decker." *Benedict Arnold, Son of the Havens* (1932); *The Rebel and the Turncoat* (1949); *Beyond a Big Mountain* (1959); etc.

Declaration of Independence. On July 2, 1776, the Continental Congress formally declared the independence of the American Colonies from Great Britain. On July 4, the document known as the "Declaration of Independence," drawn up by Thomas Jefferson, and slightly modified by other members of a special committee, was ratified. On Aug. 2, this document was signed by the members of the Congress present on that day, and later by the others.

Déclassée. Play by Zöe Akins (prod. 1919). The story of an honest woman who exposes a dishonest lover, and meets death by accident in a New York street.

DEDMON, EMMETT (Apr. 16, 1918–); b. Auburn, Neb. Editor, author, *Duty to Live* (1946); *Fabulous Chicago* (1953); *Great Enterprises* (1957). Managing editor, Chicago *Sun-Times,* since 1958.

Dee, Sylvia. Pen name of Josephine Moore Proffitt.

Deephaven. Novel by Sarah Orne Jewett (1877). A story of a decaying harbor town. The town of Deephaven was in reality South Berwick, Me.

DEERING, NATHANIEL (June 25, 1791–Mar. 25, 1881); b. Portland, Me. Editor, playwright. *Carabasset* (publ. 1830); *The World in a Nutshell* (1833); *The Harp* (1837); *The Clairvoyants* (prod. 1844); *Bozzaris* (1851). *See* Leola Bowie Chaplin's *The Life and Works of Nathaniel Deering, 1791–1881* (1934).

Deering at Princeton. By Latta Griswold (1913). A book for boys.

Deerslayer, The. Novel by James Fenimore Cooper (1841). One of the "Leather Stocking Tales." The story of Natty Bumppo, or Deerslayer, young hunter among the Delawares, a tribe engaged in warfare against the Hurons in New York. Judith Hutter falls in love with Deerslayer, who does not return her affections.

DEFERRARI, ROY JOSEPH (June 1, 1890–); b. Stoneham, Mass. Educator, classicist, author. *The Atticism of Lucan* (1916); *Vital Problems of Catholic Education in America* (1940); *College Organization and Administration* (1947); *Minor Works of St. Augustine* (1953); etc. Editor: *Catholic University Patristic Studies,* 65v. (1922–31); etc. Compiler: *A Concordance of Lucan* (1920); *A Concordance of Ovid* (1939); *Complete Index of Summa Theologica of St. Thomas* (1956). Catholic University of America, Washington, D.C., since 1918; secretary-general, since 1938.

DEISS, [Joseph] **JAY.** Author. *A Washington Story* (1950); *The Blue Chips* (novel, 1957); *The Great Infidel* (1963); *Captains of Fortune* (1966); *Herculaneum* (1966); *The Roman Years of Margaret Fuller* (1969).

DEJEANS, ELIZABETH; b. New Philadelphia, O. Novelist. *The Winning Chance* (1909); *The House of Thane* (1913); *The Tiger's Coat* (1917); *The Winning Game* (1925); etc.

Del Occidente, Maria. Pen name of Maria Gowen Brooks, first applied to her as a nickname by Southey.

DEL REY, LESTER (1915–   ). Author. *Day of the Giants* (originally, *When the World Tottered,* 1950); *Step to the Stars* (1954); *Outpost of Jupiter* (1963); *The Mysterious Sky* (1964); *Siege Perilous* (1966); *Prisoners of Space* (1967); etc.

DELAND, MARGARET[ta Wade Campbell] (Feb. 23, 1857–Jan. 13, 1945); b. Allegheny, Pa. Novelist. *The Old Garden and Other Verse* (1886); *John Ward, Preacher* (1888); *Florida Days* (1889); *Sidney* (1890); *The Story of a Child* (1892); *Philip and His Wife* (1894); *The Wisdom of Fools* (1897); *Old Chester Tales* (1899); *Dr. Lavendar's People* (1903); *The Common Way* (1904); *The Awakening of Helena Richie* (1906); *The Iron Woman* (1911); *Partners* (1913); *The Hands of Esau* (1914); *Around Old Chester* (1915); *The Rising Tide* (1916); *The Vehement Flame* (1922); *New Friends in Old Chester* (1924); *The Kays* (1926); *Captain Archer's Daughter* (1932); *If This Be I As I Suppose It Be* (autobiography, 1935); *Old Chester Days* (1937); *Golden Yesterdays* (autobiography, 1941); etc.

DELANEY, SAMUEL R. Author. *The Jewels of Aptir* (1968); *Empire Star; Babel 17;* etc.

DELANO, ALONZO (July 2, 1806–Sept. 8, 1874); b. Aurora, N.Y. California pioneer, correspondent. Pen name, "The Old Block." *Pen-Knife Sketches; or, Chips Off the Old Block* (1853); *Life on the Plains and Among the Diggings* (1854); *Old Block's Sketch-Book; or, Tales of California Life* (1856). See *Alonzo Delano's Pen-Knife Sketches* (reprinted 1934).

DELANO, AMASSA (Feb. 21, 1763–Apr. 21, 1823); b. Duxbury, Mass. Ship-captain, author. *A Narrative of Voyages and Travels, in the Northern and Southern Hemispheres, Comprising Three Voyages Round the World* (1817). Original of Melville's "Benito Cereno" in his *The Piazza Tales* (1856).

DELANO, EDITH BARNARD, d. Sept. 8, 1946; b. Washington, D.C. Author. *Zebedee V* (1912); *To-Morrow Morning* (1917); *The Way of All Earth* (1925).

DELAPLAINE, JOSEPH (1777–1824). Editor, publisher, author. *Delaplaine's Repository,* 2v. (1815–16). Publisher, *Emporium of Arts and Sciences,* 1812–14.

Delaplaine's Repository of the Lives and Portraits of Distinguished American Characters, 2v. (1815). Contains stipple engravings of Washington, Hamilton, Jefferson, etc. Bass Otis was one of the engravers.

Delilah. Novel by Marcus Goodrich (1941). A sea story.

Delineator, The. New York. Monthly magazine for women. Founded 1873, by Ebenezer Butterick, a tailor, of Fitchburg, Mass., who had patented a tissue-paper dress pattern and began to design fashion plates. He organized a publishing company and in 1867 bought out the *Ladies' Quarterly Report of Broadway Fashions* and merged it the next year with the *Metropolitan,* another fashion magazine. In 1872 he bought out *The Delineator.* Editors: Robert S. O'Loughlin, 1873–84; H. F. Montgomery, 1885–94; Charles Dwyer, 1895–1906; Ralph Tilton, 1906; Theodore Dreiser, 1907–10; George Barr Baker, 1911–14; Mrs. Honoré Willsie Morrow, 1914–20; Mrs. William Brown Meloney, 1920–26; Loren Palmer, 1926; Oscar Graeve, 1927–37. The first fiction did not appear in the magazine until 1896, a story by Francis Lynde. Absorbed by *The Pictorial Review* in May 1937. See Frank L. Mott's *A History of American Magazines,* v. 3 (1938).

Deliverance, The. Novel by Ellen Glasgow (1904). A romance of the Virginia tobacco fields; its main figure is Christopher Blake.

DELL, FLOYD (June 1887–July 23, 1969); b. Barry, Ill. Novelist. *Moon-Calf* (1920); *The Briary-Bush* (1921); *Janet March* (1923); *Looking at Life* (1924); *Love in Greenwich Village* (1926); *Upton Sinclair* (1927); *Little Accident* (with Thomas Mitchell, prod. 1928); *Souvenir* (1929); *Love in the Machine Age* (1930); *Diana Stair* (1932); *Homecoming: An Autobiography* (1933); *The Golden Spike* (1934); etc.

Dell Publishing Co. New York. Publishes Dell Books, reprints and originals; Laurel Editions, reprints and originals; Delta Books; Yearling Books; etc. Delacorte Press, hard-cover books, is a division of the company. Also publishes such magazines as *Hollywood Romances, Ingenue, Inside Detective, Modern Screen, Screen Stories,* and *Dell Comics.* Acquired Dial Press in 1963 and Noble and Noble, Publishers, Inc., in 1965.

Della Cruscanism. An affected and sentimental style of poetry which had a vogue in Boston around 1790. Sarah Wentworth Morton ("Philenia") and Robert Treat Paine, Jr. ("Menander") were its chief exponents. Robert Merry, an Englishman, signed his poems "Della Crusca." They were popular in England, and were immediately imitated in America. Royall Tyler's satire helped kill the fad. *The Florence Miscellany* (1785) had its influence on the movement.

DELLENBAUGH, Frederick Samuel (Sept. 13, 1853–Jan. 29, 1935); b. McConnellsville, O. Artist, explorer, author. *The North Americans of Yesterday* (1901); *The Romance of the*

Colorado River (1902); *Breaking the Wilderness* (1905); *A Canyon Voyage: The Narrative of the Second Powell Expedition* (1908); *Frémont and '49* (1914); *George Armstrong Custer* (1917).

DELLINGER, DAVE. Pacifist, author. *Triple Revolution* (with others, 1964); *What Is Cuba Really Like?* (1964); *In the Teeth of War* (with others, 1966); *Revolutionary Nonviolence* (1969).

DELMAR, VIÑA (Jan. 29, 1903–); b. New York. Novelist. *Bad Girl* (1928); *Loose Ladies* (1929); *Kept Woman* (1929); *Women Live Too Long* (1932); *Marriage Racket* (1933); *The Rich, Full Life* (play, 1946); *About Mrs. Leslie* (1950); *The Marcabboth Women* (1951); *The Laughing Stranger* (1953); *Beloved* (1956); *Breeze from Camelot* (1959); *Big Family* (1961); *Enchanted* (1965); *Grandmere* (1967); etc.

DELORIA, VINE, Jr. Author. *We Talk, You Listen; New Tribes, New Turf* (1970); *Custer Died for Your Sins* (1970).

Delphian Club. Baltimore, Md. Literary club. Founded Aug. 31, 1816, by William Sinclair, John D. Reade, Tobias Watkins, James H. McCulloh, John Pierpont, Horace H. Hayden, and John Neal. Henry M. Brackenridge, Francis Scott Key, William Wirt, John Howard Payne, Rembrandt Peale, and John P. Kennedy were among the members. Expired 1818. *See* John E. Uhler's *The Delphian Club*, in the *Maryland Historical Magazine*, Dec., 1925; John Neal's *Wandering Recollections* (1869).

Delta Wedding. Novel by Eudora Welty (1946). Preparations for a wedding on a Mississippi plantation, seen through the intense thoughts of a sensitive nine-year-old girl.

Deluge, The. Novel by David Graham Phillips (1905). The story of Matthew Blacklock, who lifts himself to a high place in the financial world centering around Wall Street, and who survives all the battles his enemies wage to dethrone him.

DELVING, MICHAEL. Author. *Smiling, the Boy Fell Dead* (1966); *The Devil Finds Work* (1969).

DEMARIS, OVID (Ovide E. Desmaris) (Sept. 6, 1919–); b. Biddeford, Me. Author. *Ride the Gold Mare* (1957); *The Hoods Take Over* (1957); *The Lusting Drive* (1958); *The Slasher* (1959); *The Long Night* (1959); *The Extorters* (1960); *The Enforcer* (1960); *Lucky Luciano* (1960); *The Gold-Plated Sewer* (1960); *Candyleg* (1961); *The Lindbergh Kidnaping Case* (1961); *Dillinger Story* (1961); *The Parasites* (1962); etc.

DEMBO, LAWRENCE SANFORD (Dec. 3, 1929–); b. Troy, N.Y. Educator, author. *Hart Crane's Sanskrit Charge: A Study of the Bridge* (1960); *The Confucian Odes of Ezra Pound* (1963); *Conceptions of Reality in Modern American Poetry* (1966). Editor, Wisconsin Studies in Contemporary Literature, since 1966. Prof. English, University of Wisconsin, since 1965.

DEMERS, ALBERT FOX (June 28, 1863–Jan. 23, 1943); b. Troy, N.Y. Editor, author. *Like and Unlike* (1888); *A Colonial MacGregor* (1893); *The Finest Lass* (1897); etc. Assoc. editor, *Troy Record*, from 1906.

DEMING, P[hilander] (Feb. 6, 1829–Feb. 9, 1915); b. Carlisle, N.Y. Lawyer, author. *Adirondack Stories* (1880); *Tompkins and Other Folks* (1885); *The Story of a Pathfinder* (1907).

DEMING, THERESE O. (Mrs. Edwin Willard Deming); (d. July 14, 1945); b. in Bavaria, of American parentage. Traveler, author. *Indian Child Life* (1899); *Red Folk and Wild Folk* (1902); *American Animal Life* (1916); *Little Eagle* (1931); *Pueblo Indian Children* (1935); *Indians of the Wigwam* (1939); etc.

Democracy. Novel by Henry Adams (1881). Sidelights on the political scene in America and its attendant evils as viewed by a society woman.

Democracy and Education. Essays by John Dewey (1916). An inquiry into the nature of education and democracy, and a clear statement of the author's philosophy of pragmatism.

Democratic Review, The. New York. Literary monthly. Founded 1837, by John L. O'Sullivan and Samuel Daly Langtree, at Washington, D.C., as *The United States Magazine and Democratic Review*. Numerous changes in title followed, beginning in 1852. In 1841 it was moved to New York. Its literary influence was great, and the foremost authors of the time contributed to it. Its illustrations were noteworthy including many engraved portraits. Expired 1859.

Democratic Vistas. Essay by Walt Whitman (1871). A statement of his democratic credo, based upon two earlier essays, *Democracy* and *Personalism*, which had appeared in the *Galaxy*, Dec., 1867, and May, 1868.

Demorest's Monthly Magazine. New York City. Magazine for women. Founded 1865, by W. Jennings Demorest, as *Demorest's Illustrated Monthly* and Mme. Demorest's *Mirror of Fashion*, replacing the quarterly fashion magazine, *The Mirror of Fashion* (founded 1860). In 1866 the name was changed to *Demorest's Monthly Magazine*, and in 1889 to *Demorest's Family Magazine*. Although devoted to women's fashions, it published many articles by Thomas Hardy, Louisa M. Alcott, Julia Ward Howe, Thomas Wentworth Higginson, Robert Louis Stevenson, and Amelia E. Barr. W. Jennings Demorest, its founder, was an ardent prohibitionist, and many temperance articles were featured. His wife, Ellen Louise Demorest, who had edited *The Mirror of Fashion*, played a prominent part in the publication of the magazine. Jane Cunningham Croly, who had been asst. editor of *The Mirror*, under the pen name "Jennie June," continued in that capacity with *Demorest's* until 1887. *Demorest's* expired 1899. *See* F. L. Mott's *History of American Magazines*.

DENBEAUX, FRED (May 8, 1914–   ); b. St. Louis, Mo. Educator, author. *Understanding the Bible* (1958); *The Art of Christian Doubt* (1960); *Guide to the Old Testament* (1964); *Introduction to the New Testament* (1965); *The Premature Death of Protestantism* (1967). Prof. religion, Wellesley College, since 1958.

DENBY, EDWIN ORR (Feb. 4, 1903–   ); b. Tientsin, China. Author. *Looking at the Dance* (1949); *Mediterranean Cities* (1956); *Dancers, Buildings, and People in the Streets* (1965); etc. Librettist: *Die Neue Galathee* (1928); *The Second Hurricane* (1937).

DENISON, CHARLES WHEELER (Nov. 11, 1809–Nov. 14, 1881); b. New London, Conn. Editor, clergyman, consul, poet. *Old Slade* (1844); *The American Village, and Other Poems* (1845); *Old Ironsides and Old Adams* (1846); *The Yankee Cruiser* (1848); *Sunshine Castle* (1867); *Out at Sea* (poems, 1867); *The Child Hunters* (1877); also a series of military biographies for boys, which appeared both under his own name and under the pen name "Major Penniman."

DENISON, MARY ANDREWS (Mrs. Charles Wheeler Denison) (May 26, 1826–1911); b. Cambridge, Mass. Pen name, "Clara Vance." Author. *Home Pictures* (1853); *Old Hepsey: A Tale of the South* (1858); *That Husband of Mine* (anon., 1874); etc.

DENISON, T[homas Stewart] (Feb. 20, 1848-1911); b. Marshall Co., Va. (now W.Va.). Publisher, author. *Friday Afternoon Dialogues* (1879); *The Old Schoolhouse, and Other Poems* (1902); *Pomes ov the Peepul* (1904); etc. Founder, publishing firm under own name, in 1878.

DENKER, HENRY (Nov. 25, 1912–); b. New York. Novelist. *I'll Be Right Home, Ma* (1949); *My Son, The Lawyer* (1950); *Salome, Princess of Galilee* (1952); *That First Easter* (1959); *A Far Country* (play, 1961); *A Case of Libel* (1964); *The Director* (1970). Radio scenarist: *The Greatest Story Ever Told.*

DENNES, WILLIAM RAY (Apr. 10, 1898–); b. Healdsburg, Cal. Educator, author. *Conflict* (1946); *Some Dilemmas of Naturalism* (1960); etc. Prof. philosophy, University of California at Berkeley, since 1936.

DENNETT, TYLER (June 13, 1883–Dec. 29, 1949); b. Spencer, Wis. Educator, author. *The Democratic Movement in Asia* (1918); *Americans in Eastern Asia* (1923); *John Hay: From Poetry to Politics* (1933, Pulitzer prize for American biography, 1934); *Lincoln and the Civil War: Hay Diaries* (1939); etc. President, Williams College, 1934–37.

DENNEY, REUEL (1913–). Sociologist, poet. *Connecticut River and Other Poems* (1939); *The Astonished Muse* (1957); *In Praise of Adam* (poems, 1961); *Conrad Aiken* (1964).

DENNIE, JOSEPH (Aug. 30, 1768–Jan. 7, 1812); b. Boston, Mass. Editor, essayist. *The Lay Preacher* (1796); *The Spirit of the Farmer's Museum, and Lay Preacher's Gazette* (1801). Editor, *The Tablet,* 1795; *The Farmer's Weekly Museum,* 1796–99; *The Port Folio,* 1801–12. He used the pen name "Oliver Oldschool, Esq." on the masthead of *The Port Folio,* and this continued after his death. *See* William W. Clapp's *Joseph Dennie* (1880); Milton Ellis's *Joseph Dennie and His Circle* (1915); *The Letters of Joseph Dennie, 1768–1812,* ed. by Laura Green Pedder (1936); and Andrew P. Peabody's *The Farmer's Weekly Museum, in Proc. of Amer. Antiq. Soc., N.J.,* v. 6 (1889–1890). *See also* Dennie's obituary in *The Port Folio,* Feb., 1812.

DENNIS, CHARLES HENRY (Feb. 8, 1860–Sept. 25, 1943); b. Decatur, Ill. Editor, author. *Eugene Field's Creative Years* (1924); *Victor Lawson: His Time and His Work* (1935). With *Chicago Daily News,* 1882–91; and 1901–34; editor, 1925–34.

DENNIS, LAWRENCE (Dec. 25, 1893–); b. Atlanta, Ga. Author. *Is Capitalism Doomed?* (1932); *The Coming American Fascism* (1936); *The Dynamics of War and Revolution* (1940); *A Trial on Trial* (with Maximilian J. St. George, 1946). Editor: *The Arts in Higher Education* (with Renate M. Jacob, 1968).

DENNIS, MORGAN (1891–Oct. 22, 1960). Illustrator, author. *Pup Himself* (1943); *Burlap* (1945); *Skit and Skat* (1951); *Sea Dog* (1958); *Kitten on the Keys* (1961).

Dennis, Patrick. Pen name of Edward Everett Tanner.

DENNISON, GEORGE (1925–). Author. *The Lives of Children* (1969).

DENNY, HAROLD NORMAN (Mar. 11, 1889–July 3, 1945); b. Des Moines, Ia. Correspondent, author. *Dollars for Bullets* (1929); *Behind Both Lines* (1942). In newspaper work from 1913; with *New York Times,* from 1922.

DENNY, LUDWELL (Nov. 18, 1894–); b. Boonville, Ind. Editor, author. *We Fight for Oil* (1928); *America Conquers Britain* (1930). With Scripps-Howard newspapers, 1928–32; editor, *Indianapolis Times,* 1935–39; columnist, Scripps-Howard newspapers, 1939–60.

DENSLOW, WILLIAM WALLACE (May 5, 1856–Mar. 27, 1915); b. Philadelphia, Pa. Illustrator, author. *The Pearl and the Pumpkin* (with Paul West, 1904); *Billy Bounce* (with Dudley A. Bragdon, 1906); *When I Grow Up* (1909); etc.

DENSON, JOHN (July 25, 1905–); b. Arcadia, La. Editor, *Newsweek,* since 1953.

DENTAN, ROBERT CLAUDE (Nov. 27, 1907–); b. Rossville, Ind. Protestant Episcopal clergyman, educator. *The Holy Scriptures* (with others, 1949); *Redemption and Revelation* (1951); *The Apocrypha, Bridge of the Testaments* (1954); *The First and Second Books of the Kings; The First and Second Books of the Chronicles* (1964); *The King and His Cross* (1965); *The Knowledge of God in Ancient Israel* (1968); etc. Prof. Old Testament, General Theological Seminary, since 1954.

Denver Post. Denver, Colo. Newspaper. Founded 1892, and purchased by Frederic G. Bonfils and Harry H. Tammen in 1895. Palmer Hoyt is editor. Stanton Peckham is book-review editor and edits a special book supplement.

DEPEW, CHAUNCEY MITCHELL (Apr. 23, 1834–Apr. 5, 1928); b. Peekskill, N.Y. Lawyer, after-dinner speaker, wit, author. *Orations, Addresses and Speeches,* ed. by J. D. Chaplin, 8v. (1910); *My Memories of Eighty Years* (1922). U.S. senator from New York, 1899–1911.

DERBY, GEORGE HORATIO (Apr. 3, 1823–May 15, 1861); b. Dedham, Mass. Humorist. Wrote for the *Pioneer Magazine* and other California journals, under the pen name of "John Phoenix" and "John P. Squibob." These writers were published as *Phoenixiana* (1856) and the *Squibob Papers* (1859). *See* George R. Stewart's *John Phoenix, Esq., The Veritable Squibob: A Life of Captain H. Derby, U.S.A.* (1937).

DERBY, JAMES CEPHAS (July 20, 1818–1892); b. Little Falls, N.Y. Publisher, author. *Fifty Years among Authors, Books and Publishers* (1884). Began publishing business in 1844.

Dere Mable. By Edward Streeter (1918). Humorous correspondence of an unlettered rookie in the American army.

DERLETH, AUGUST [William] (Feb. 24, 1909–July 4, 1971); b. Sauk City, Wis. Novelist, poet. *Place of Hawks* (1935); *Still Is the Summer Night* (1937); *Hawk on the Wind* (Poems, 1938); *Wind over Wisconsin* (1938); *Restless is the River* (1939); *Country Growth* (1940); *Bright Journey* (1940); *Still Small Voice* (1940); *Mischief in the Lane* (1944); *Edge of Night* (poems, 1945); *Rendezvous in a Landscape* (poems, 1952); *The Country of the Hawk* (1952); *Fell Purpose* (1953); *The Land of Grey Gold* (1954); *Land of Sky-Blue Waters* (1955); *St. Ignatius and the Company of Jesus* (1956); *Country Poems* (1956); *The Return of Solar Pons* (1958); *The Mill Creek Irregulars* (1959); *Sweet Land of Michigan* (1962); *Countryman's Journal* (1963); *The Tent Show Summer* (1963); *Forest Orphans* (1964); *A Wisconsin Harvest* (1966); *Travellers by Night* (1967); *The Beast in Holger's Woods* (1968); *A House above Cuzco* (1969); etc. Editor: *Beyond Time and Space* (1950); *Worlds of Tomorrow* (1953); *Fire and Sleet and Candlelight* (1962); etc.

DERN, PEGGY [Gaddis] (Mrs. John Sherman Dern) (1896–June 14, 1966). Author. Pen names, "Carolina Lee," "Joan Sherman," "Georgia Craig." *House of Yesterday* (1929); *Key to Paradise* (1929); *Eve in the Garden* (1935); *Yaller Gal* (1936); *Unrestrained* (1938); *Song in Her Heart* (1938); *Midnight in Arcady* (1940); *Palm Beach Nurse* (1953); *Nurse Ellen* (1956); *Settlement Nurse* (1959); *Rozalinda* (1961); *Intruders in Eden* (1961); *Nurse Christine* (1962); *Clinic Nurse* (1963); *Betsy Moran, R.N.* (1964); etc.

DEROUNIAN, AVODIS ARTHUR (Apr. 9, 1909–); b. Alexandropolis, Greece. Lecturer, author. Writes under pen name "John Roy Carlson." *Under Cover* (1943); *The Plotters* (1946); *Cairo to Damascus* (1951).

Derrydale Press. New York. Founded 1927, by Eugene V. Connett III. Published fine sporting books and prints. Many old and scarce American sporting books were reprinted by the firm, including the sporting novels of Frank Forester (William Henry Herbert). Besides books on contemporary sports, the Derrydale Press produced many hand-colored prints on rag paper of current sporting scenes. See *The Derrydale Press, 1927–1937. Tenth Anniversary Catalogue* (1937). Acquired by Outlet Book Co., a subsidiary of Crown Publishers.

DERWOOD, GENE (1909–1954). Poet. *Poems* (1955).

Des Moines Register. Des Moines, Ia. Newspaper. Founded 1849, as the *Iowa Star.* In 1855, name changed to the *Iowa Statesman.* In 1862 merged with the *Commonwealth* and called the *Times.* In 1870 it was called the *Iowa State Leader.*

Combined with the *Iowa State Register* in 1902. Owned by Gardner Cowles since 1903. Now combined with the *Des Moines Tribune* (which appears evenings) as a morning and Sunday paper, published under its own name.

Des Moines Tribune. Des Moines, Ia. Newspaper. Founded 1906. Bought by Gardner Cowles in 1908, and combined in 1924 with the *Des Moines Daily News.* Merged with the *Des Moines Capital* in 1927. Now combined with the *Des Moines Register* as an evening paper appearing under its own name.

Descendant, The. Novel by Ellen Glasgow, published anonymously (1897). The author's first novel. The scene is Virginia.

Deseret Book Company. Salt Lake City, Utah. Founded in 1866 by George Q. Cannon as the George Q. Cannon and Sons Book Company. Cannon published a magazine called the *Juvenile Instructor.* In 1901 he sold the magazine to the Deseret Sunday School Union and the bookstore to the *Deseret News,* the daily paper published by the Mormon Church. From this grew the Deseret Sunday School Union Bookstore, managed by Walter K. Lewis, and the Deseret News Book Company, managed by George D. Pyper, William A. Morton, and others. In 1919 the two were combined to form the Deseret Book Company. In 1932 the company was incorporated, and James E. Talmadge became president, followed by Melvin J. Ballard, and by S. O. Bennion. The firm is one of the publishing houses for the Church of Jesus Christ of Latter-day Saints.

Deseret News. Salt Lake City Utah. Newspaper. Founded 1850 by the Church of Jesus Christ of Latter-Day Saints, under Brigham Young's presidency. William B. Smart edits the Sunday book reviews.

Desire Under the Elms. Tragedy by Eugene O'Neill (1925). Grim account of New England decay, centering around old Ephraim Cabot, his third wife Abbie, and his son, Eben, whose greed for the farm, pitted against Abbie's, is dissolved like hers in mutual love.

Désirée's Baby. Short story by Kate Chopin, which appeared in *Vogue,* 1893.

DESMOND, ALICE CURTIS (Sept. 19, 1897–); b. Southport, Conn. Author. *Far Horizons* (1931); *South American Adventures* (1934); *The Lucky Llama* (1939); *Soldier of the Sun* (1939); *For Cross and King* (1941); *Martha Washington* (1942); *The Sea Cats* (1944); *Glamorous Dolly Madison* (1946); *The Talking Tree* (1949); *Alexander Hamilton's Wife* (1952); *Barnum Presents General Tom Thumb* (1954); *Bewitching Betsy Bonaparte* (1958); *Sword and Pen for George Washington* (1964); *This Is Our Land* (1965); *Marie Antoinette's Daughter* (1967); etc.

Desolation Angels. Novel by Jack Kerouac (1965).

Destiny of Man, The. By John Fiske (1884). An account of the theory of evolution and an attempt to reconcile science and religion. This was originally an address before the Concord School of Philosophy.

Detective Story. Play by Sidney Kingsley (prod. 1949). Life in a New York City police station.

Detective Story Magazine. New York. Semi-monthly. Founded 1917. Suspended 1949.

Detroit Free Press. Detroit, Mich. Newspaper. Founded May 5, 1831, by Sheldon McKnight. In 1836 it was sold to L. L. Morse and John S. Bagg, in 1850 to Thornton F. Brodhead, in 1853 to Wilbur F. Storey, in 1863 to William E. Quinby, and to Edward D. Stair and associates in 1906, and to John S. Knight and associates in 1940. William E. Quinby was its leading editor for a long period. Quinby developed two famous columnists, C. B. Lewis ("M. Quad") and Robert M. Barr ("Luke Sharp"). Edgar A. Guest was with the paper after 1895. Malcolm W. Bingay conducted a column, "Good Morning" and John S. Knight wrote a Sunday column, "Editor's Notebook."

Detroit News. Detroit, Mich. Newspaper. Founded Aug. 23, 1873, by James Edmund Scripps, as the *Detroit Evening News.* In 1905 it became the *Detroit News.* George G. Booth became manager in 1888, president in 1906. William Steele Gilmore was editor after 1933. William Silverman is now book critic. See L. A. White's *The Detroit News, 1873–1917* (1918).

Detroit Times. Detroit, Mich. Newspaper. Founded 1900, by James Schermerhorn, as *Detroit Today.* John Creecy was book-review editor before it expired in 1960.

DETT, R[obert] NATHANIEL (Oct. 11, 1882–Oct. 3, 1943); b. Drummondsville, Ont. Composer. Editor: *The Dett Collection of Negro Spirituals,* 4v. (1937); and other books on Negro folk tunes and spirituals.

DETZER, KARL [William] (Sept. 4, 1891–); b. Fort Wayne, Ind. Novelist. *True Tales of the D. C. I.* (1925); *The Broken 3* (1929); *Contrabando* (1936); *Culture Under Canvas* (with H. P. Harrison, 1958); *Myself When Young* (1968); etc. Roving editor, *Reader's Digest,* 1939–42, and since 1946.

DEUTSCH, ALBERT (Oct. 23, 1905–June 18, 1961); b. New York. Author. *The Mentally Ill in America* (1937); *The Shame of the States* (1948); *Our Rejected Children* (1950); *The Trouble with Cops* (1955); etc. Columnist, *PM,* 1941–48; *New York Post,* 1949.

DEUTSCH, BABETTE (Mrs. Avrahm Yarmolinsky) (Sept. 22, 1895–); b. New York. Poet, critic, novelist. *Banners* (poems, 1919); *Honey out of the Rock* (poems, 1925); *A Brittle Heaven* (1926); *In Such a Night* (1927); *Potable Gold: Some Notes on Poetry and This Age* (1929); *Fire for the Night* (poems, 1930); *Epistle to Prometheus* (poems, 1931); *Mask of Silenus* (1933); *This Modern Poetry* (1935); *One Part Love* (poems, 1939); *Walt Whitman* (1941); *The Welcome* (1942); *Rogue's Legacy* (1942); *Take Them, Stranger* (poems, 1944); *The Reader's Shakespeare* (1946); *Poetry in Our Time* (1952); *Animal, Vegetable, Mineral* (poems, 1954); *Poetry Handbook* (1957); *Coming of Age: New and Selected Poems* (1959); *Collected Poems, 1919–1962* (1963); *I Often Wish* (1966). Translator: Rilke's *Poems from the Book of Hours;* Alexander Blok's *The Twelve;* Pushkin's *Eugene Onegin; Two Centuries of Russian Verse;* Elisabeth Borchers' *There Comes a Time;* etc.

DEVEREUX, MARY (Mrs. Mary Devereux Watson) (d. Feb. 19, 1914); b. Marblehead, Mass. Author. *Betty Peach* (1896); *From Kingdom to Colony* (1899); *Up and Down the Sands of Gold* (1901); *Lafitte of Louisiana* (1902).

Devil and Daniel Webster, The. Story by Stephen Vincent Benét (1937).

Devil and Tom Walker, The. Story in *Tales of a Traveller* by Washington Irving (1824).

Devil in Manuscript, The. Sketch by Nathaniel Hawthorne in *New England Magazine,* Nov., 1835, under the pen name "Ashley A. Royce." Reprinted in *The Snow-Image* (1851).

Devil Puzzlers. Short story by Frederic Beecher Perkins (1877).

"Devil's Delight, The." Poetical satire by John R. Thompson, in *The Land We Love,* 1867.

Devil's Dictionary, The. By Ambrose Bierce. First published as *The Cynic's Word Book* (1906). Title changed to *The Devil's Dictionary* in collected works. A lexicon of common terms defined satirically and maliciously.

DEVOE, ALAN [Taylor] (Oct. 13, 1909–Aug. 17, 1955); b. Montclair, N.J. Editor, author. *Phudd Hill* (1937); *Down to Earth* (1940); *Lives Around Us* (1942); *Speaking of Animals* (1947); *This Fascinating Animal World* (1951); *Our Animal Neighbors* (with Mary Berry DeVoe, 1953). Wrote "Down to Earth" department for *American Mercury.* Assoc. editor, *The Writer,* from 1934.

DEWART, LESLIE (Dec. 12, 1922–); b. Madrid, Spain. Educator, author. *Christianity and Revolution* (1963); *The Future of Belief: Theism in a World Come of Age* (1966); *The Foundations of Belief* (1969); *Reality, Language and Belief* (1970).

DEWART, WILLIAM THOMPSON (Jan. 29, 1875–Jan. 27, 1944); b. Fenelon Falls, Ont. Publisher. President of the Frank A. Munsey Co., Sun Printing and Publishing Association; etc. Publisher, New York *Sun.*

DEWEY, BYRD SPILMAN (Mrs.); b. Covington, Ky. Author. *Bruno* (1899); *Peter the Tramp* (1907); *The Tale of Satan* (1913); etc.

Dewey, James. Pen name of Mildred Masterson McNeilly.

DEWEY, JOHN (Oct. 20, 1859–June 2, 1952); b. Burlington, Vt. Educator, philosopher, author. *How We Think* (1910); *Democracy and Education* (1916); *Reconstruction in Philosophy* (1920); *The Quest for Certainty* (1929); *Art as Experience* (1934); *The Theory of Inquiry* (1938); *Education Today* (1940); *Democracy and Education* (1944); *Problems of Man* (1946); *Knowing and the Known* (with A. Bently, 1949); etc. Prof. philosophy, Columbia University, from 1904. See *A Bibliography of John Dewey, 1882–1939,* by Milton Halsey Thomas (1939); John H. Randall's *The Philosophy of John Dewey* (1939); and *The Philosopher of the Common Man: Essays in Honor of John Dewey* (1940); Jerome Nathanson's *John Dewey: The Reconstruction of the Democratic Life* (1951); Charles W. Hendel's *John Dewey and the Experimental Spirit in Philosophy* (1959); Douglas E. Lawson's and Arthur E. Lean's *John Dewey and the World View* (1964); Lowell Nissen's *John Dewey's Theory of Inquiry and Truth* (1966).

DEWEY, MELVIL (Dec. 10, 1851–Dec. 26, 1931); b. Adams Centre, N.Y. Librarian, inventor of the Dewey Decimal System of book classification. He first published his classification scheme in 1876 and revised it until 1929. Librarian, Columbia University Library, 1883–88; director of New York State Library, 1889–1906; founder and director, New York State Library School, 1887–1906; founder, *Library Journal,* 1876; founder, *Library Notes,* 1886; Library Bureau, 1876; the Lake Placid Club, 1895; one of the founders of the American Library Association, 1876. He was an advocate of simplified spelling.

DEWEY, ORVILLE (Mar. 28, 1794–Mar. 21, 1882); b. Sheffield, Mass. Clergyman, author. *Discourses on Various Subjects* (1835); *The Old World and the New* (1836); *The Works of Orville Dewey* (1844); *The Problem of Human Destiny* (1864); *Autobiography and Letters of Orville Dewey,* edited by Mary E. Dewey (1883).

DEWING, ARTHUR STONE (Apr. 16, 1880–Jan. 20, 1971); b. Boston, Mass. Educator, author. *Introduction to History of Modern Philosophy* (1903); *Life As Reality* (1910); *Financial Policy of Corporations* (1920); *The Corporation—A Study of Its Financial Structure* (1934); etc. Economics dept., Harvard University, 1911–33.

DEWOLF, L[otan] HAROLD (Jan. 31, 1905–); b. Columbus, Neb. Educator, author. *Issues Concerning Immortality in Thirty Ingersoll Lectures, 1896–1935* (1935); *The Religious Revolt Against Reason* (1949); *A Theology of the Living Church* (1953); *The Case for Theology in Liberal Perspective* (1959); *Teaching Our Faith in God* (1963); *A Hard Rain and a Cross* (1966); etc. Prof. theology, Boston University, since 1944.

DEXTER, BYRON (Dec. 9, 1900–); b. Newark, N.J. Editor. *The Arabs: A Short History* (with Philip K. Hitti, 1943); *The Years of Opportunity: The League of Nations 1920–1926* (1967). With *Foreign Affairs,* 1943, 1949–55; editor, *Let's Talk About,* 1952–55.

DEXTER, FRANKLIN BOWDITCH (Sept. 11, 1842–Aug. 13, 1920); b. Fairhaven, Mass. Educator, librarian, antiquarian, author. *A Selection from the Miscellaneous Historical Papers of Fifty Years* (1918); and many other papers, especially on Yale. Editor: *Literary Diary of Ezra Stiles, D.D.,* 3v. (1901). Compiler: *Biographical Sketches of the Graduates of Yale College, 1701–1815,* 6v. (1885–1912). Assistant librarian, Yale College Library, 1869–1912.

DEXTER, TIMOTHY (Jan. 22, 1747–Oct. 23, 1806); b. Malden, Mass. Merchant, eccentric, author. *A Pickle for the Knowing Ones* (1802). This book was without punctuation; in 1838, another edition was published by "Peter Quince" containing a page of punctuation marks, and readers were advised to "pepper and salt it as they please." See John P. Marquand's *Lord Timothy Dexter* (1925).

DEY, FREDERICK VAN RENSSELAER (1865–Apr., 1922). Dime novelist. Pen names, "Nicholas Carter," "Varick Vanardy," and "Frederic Ormond." Under own name: *The Magic Story* (1903); *A Gentleman of Quality* (1909); etc. Under pen name, "Nicholas Carter": *In Suspicion's Shadow* (1913); *Not on the Record* (1914); *A Rogue Worth Training* (1914); etc. ["Probably by him"—Library of Congress.] Under pen name, "Varick Vanardy": *Alias the Night Wind* (1913); *The Return of the Night Wind* (1914); *The Night Wind's Promise* (1914); *The Lady of the Night Wind* (1919); *Up Against It* (1920); etc. Under pen name, "Frederic Ormond": *The Three Keys* (1909).

DI DONATO, PIETRO (1911–); b. Hoboken, N.J. Novelist. *Christ in Concrete* (1939); *Immigrant Saint: The Life of Mother Cabrini* (1960); *Three Circles of Light* (1960); *The Penitent* (1962).

Dial, The. Boston, Mass. Magazine. Founded July, 1840. Grew out of the "Transcendental Club" to which Emerson, Margaret Fuller, Bronson Alcott and other New Englanders belonged. It was edited by Miss Fuller until April, 1842; by Emerson after July, 1842. It coincided with the utopian project at Brook Farm. Expired Apr., 1844.

Dial, The. Chicago, Ill. Monthly. Founded by Francis F. Browne, May, 1880. Editors: Francis F. Browne, 1880–1913; Waldo R. Browne, 1913–16; Clinton Joseph Masseck, 1916; George Bernard Donlin, 1917–18; Robert Morss Lovett, 1919; Scofield Thayer, 1919–26; Marianne Moore, 1926–29. It was published in New York, from 1916 to 1929. Translations of foreign writers were a feature during its last years, but American writers such as Sherwood Anderson, Edna St. Vincent Millay, Gertrude Stein, T. S. Eliot, E. E. Cummings, Ezra Pound, Amy Lowell, Edwin Arlington Robinson, Kenneth Burke, Gilbert Seldes, George Santayana, John Dewey, Harold J. Laski, Thorstein Veblen, Randolph Bourne, Charles A. Beard, and Norman Angell were contributors. William Morton Payne was associate editor, 1892–1915. See his *Editorial Echoes* (1902) and other books. Magazine ceased July, 1929. In 1959 another *Dial* was founded in New York to publish fiction only, but it also contained selections from the old *Dial* of the period 1919–29. This new venture was discontinued in 1961. See N. T. Joost's *Years of Transition: The Dial 1912–20* (1967).

Dial Press, The. New York. Founded 1924, by Lincoln MacVeagh, who has president until 1934, when he sold the firm to Max Salop, who sold it in turn to Burton C. Hoffman in 1938. Acquired by Dell Publishing Co. (q.v.) in 1963.

Dialect Notes. New Haven, Conn. Founded 1890, by The American Dialect Society, at Boston. Moved to Norwood, Mass., 1895; and to New Haven, Conn., 1900. Percy Waldron Long was editor, 1912–30. Suspended 1939.

Diamond Lens, The. Classic short story, somewhat in the manner of Poe's tales, by Fitz James O'Brien (1857).

Diario-La Prensa, El. New York. Newspaper. Founded 1913. Published by O. Roy Chalk. Sergio Santelices is editor. Concerned with news of the Puerto Rican community in New York and elsewhere.

DIAZ, ABBY MORTON (1821–Apr. 1, 1904); b. Plymouth, Mass. Author of books for young people. *The School Master's Trunk* (1864); *The King's Lily and Rosebud* (1868); *The Entertaining Story of King Bronde* (1868); *The William Henry Letters* (1870); *William Henry and His Friends* (1871); *Lucy Maria* (1873); *A Domestic Problem* (1875); *A Story Book for the Children* (1875); *Neighborhood Talks* (1876); *The Jimmyjohns, and Other Stories* (1878); *Christmas Morning* (1880); *King Grimalkins and Pussyanite; or, The Cat's Arabian Nights* (1881); *Polly Cologne* (1881); *The Chronicles of the Stimpcett Family and Others* (1882); *Bybury to Beacon Street* (1887); *The John Spicer Letters* (1887); *Only a Flock of Women* (1893).

DIBBLE, R[oy] F[loyd] (Mar. 12, 1887–Dec. 3, 1929); b. Portland, N.Y. Author: *Albion W. Tourgée* (1921); *Strenuous Americans* (1923); *John L. Sullivan* (1925); *Mohammed* (1926).

DICHTER, ERNEST (Aug. 14, 1907–   ); b. Vienna. Consulting psychologist, author. *The Psychology of Everyday Living* (1946); *The Strategy of Desire* (1960); *Handbook of Consumer Motivations* (1964); etc. Pres., Institute for Motivational Research. Introduced "depth interviews" into marketing research.

DICK, PHILIP K. Author. *The World Jones Made* (1956); *The Man Who Japed* (1956); *Eye in the Sky* (1957); *The Cosmic Puppets* (1957); *Time Out of Joint* (1959); *The Three Stigmata of Palmer Eldritch* (1965); *Now Wait for Last Year* (1966); *The Crack in Space* (1966); *Ubik* (1969).

DICKERSON, ROY ERNEST (Apr. 3, 1886–Nov. 8, 1965); b. Versailles, Ind. Director of boys' work, author. *So Youth May Know* (1930); *Growing into Manhood* (1933); *How Character Develops* (with Fritz Kunkel, 1939); etc. Co-editor: *Preinduction Health and Human Relations* (1952). With Y.M.C.A., 1917–23; director activities, Order of De Molay, 1923–40.

DICKEY, HERBERT SPENCER (Feb. 24, 1876–Oct. 28, 1948); b. Highland Falls, N.Y. Explorer, lecturer. Author: *The Misadventures of a Tropical Medico* (with Hawthorne Daniel, 1929); *My Jungle Book* (1932).

DICKEY, JAMES (Feb. 2, 1923–   ); b. Atlanta, Ga. Poet, critic, novelist. *Into the Stone* (1960); *Drowning with Others* (1962); *Interpreter's House* (1963); *Helmets* (1964); *Two Poems of the Air* (1964); *Buckdancer's Choice* (1965; National Book Award, 1966); *The Suspect in Poetry* (1964); *Poems, 1957–67* (1967); *Babel to Byzantium* (1968); *Deliverance* (1970); *The Eyebeaters, Blood, Victory, Madness, Buckhead and Mercy* (1970). Faculty, University of South Carolina.

DICKEY, MARCUS (b. Sept. 26, 1859–); b. near Longwood, Ind. Author: *The Youth of James Whitcomb Riley* (1919); *The Maturity of James Whitcomb Riley* (1922); *Life of James Whitcomb Riley*, 2v. (1923).

DICKINSON, ANNA ELIZABETH (Oct. 28, 1842–1932); b. Philadelphia, Pa. Writer, lecturer. Author: *What Answer* (1868); *A Ragged Register of People, Places, and Opinions* (1879); etc.

DICKINSON, ASA DON (May 15, 1876–Nov. 14, 1960); b. Detroit, Mich. Librarian. Editor: *Drama* (1922); *One Thousand Best Books* (1924); *Best Books of Our Time, 1901–1925* (1928); *The Best Books of the Decade, 1926–1935* (1937); *Great Leaders of the World*, 6v. (1937); *Best Books of the Decade, 1936–1945* (1948); etc.; also children's books. Managing editor, *Doubleday's Encyclopedia*, 10v. (1930). Librarian, Brooklyn College, 1931–44.

DICKINSON, CHARLES MONROE (Nov. 15, 1842–July 3, 1924); b. Lowville, N.Y. Diplomat, editor, poet. Author: *The Children, and Other Verses* (1889); *The Children After Fifty Years* (1915); etc. Editor, *Binghamton* (N.Y.) *Republican*, 1878–1911.

DICKINSON, [Clinton] ROY (Mar. 14, 1888–deceased); b. Newark, N.J. Editor, author. *The Cowards Never Started* (1933); *The Ultimate Frog* (1939); etc. With *Cosmopolitan Magazine*, 1910–15; *Puck*, 1915–16; assoc. editor, *Printers' Ink*, 1919–33; president, Printers' Ink Publishing Co., 1933–42.

DICKINSON, EDWARD (Oct. 10, 1853–Jan. 25, 1946); b. West Springfield, Mass. Musician, author. *The Study of the History of Music* (1905); *The Education of a Music Lover* (1911); *The Spirit of Music* (1925); etc. Prof. of music, Oberlin College, 1893–1922.

DICKINSON, EMILY [Elizabeth] (Dec. 10, 1830–May 15, 1886); b. Amherst, Mass. Poet. Except for a few poems in magazines, all of her poetry was published after her death. *Poems*, 3 series (1890–1896); *Letters*, 2v. (1894); *The Single Hound: Poems of a Lifetime* (1914); *The Complete Poems* (1924); *Further Poems* (1929); *The Poems* (1930); *Unpublished Poems* (1936); *Bolts of Melody: New Poems* (1945); *The Poems of Emily Dickinson*, 3v. (1955). See George F. Whicher's *This Was a Poet* (1938); Martha Dickinson Bianchi's *Life and Letters of Emily Dickinson* (1924), and her editions of the poems; MacGregor Jenkins' *Emily Dickinson, Friend and Neighbor* (1930), and his *Emily Dickinson* (1939); Mabel Loomis Todd's *Letters of Emily Dickinson*, 2v. (1894, enlarged 1931); Thomas H. Johnson's *The Letters of Emily Dickinson*, 3v. (1958). *See also* Richard Chase's *Emily Dickinson* (1951); T. H. Johnson's *Emily Dickinson: An Interpretive Biography* (1955); Charles R. Anderson's *Emily Dickinson's Poetry: Stairway of Surprise* (1960); Clark Griffith's *The Long Shadow: Emily Dickinson's Tragic Poetry* (1964); Douglas Duncan's *Emily Dickinson* (1965); Albert Gelpi's *Emily Dickinson, The Mind of the Poet* (1965); David Higgins' *Portrait of Emily Dickinson* (1967).

DICKINSON, HELENA A[dell Snyder] (Mrs. Clarence Dickinson) (Dec. 5, 1875–Aug. 25, 1957); b. Port Elmsley, Ont. Author. *A Study of Henry D. Thoreau* (1902); *German Masters of Art* (1914); *Excursions in Musical History* (with husband, 1917); *The Troubadours and Their Songs* (1919); *A Treasury of Worship* (1926); *The Choirloft and the Pulpit* (1943). Translator of ancient carols.

DICKINSON, JOHN (Nov. 8, 1732–Feb. 14, 1808); b. in Talbot Co., Md. Statesman. Author: *The Political Writings of John Dickinson, Esq.*, 2v. (1801); *Writings*, 3v. (1895) edited by P. L. Ford. *See* C. J. Stillé's *The Life and Times of John Dickinson* (1891).

Dickinson, Martha Gilbert. See Martha [Gilbert] Dickinson Bianchi.

DICKINSON, THOMAS H[erbert] (Nov. 9, 1877–June 12, 1961); b. in Charlotte Co., Va. Author. *The Insurgent Theatre* (1917); *Playwrights of the New American Theatre* (1925); *An Outline of Contemporary Drama* (1927); *The Making of American Literature* (1932); *The Theatre in a Changing Europe* (1937); etc. Editor: *Chief Contemporary Dramatists*, 3 series (1915, 1921, 1930); *Types of Contemporary Drama*, 2v. (1935); etc.

Dickson, Carr. Pen name of John Dickson Carr.

Dickson, Carter. Pen name of John Dickson Carr.

DICKSON, HARRIS (July 21, 1868–); b. Yazoo City, Miss. Lawyer, historical writer. *The Black Wolf's Breed* (1899); *The Siege of Lady Resolute* (1902); *The Ravanels* (1905); *The Duke of Devil-May-Care* (1905); *Old Reliable* (1912); *Old Reliable in Africa* (1920); *Children of the River* (1928); *Port of Queer Cargoes* (1931); etc. Wrote "Sunlover Sam" stories and "Coffin Club" stories.

Dictionary of American Authors, by Oscar Fay Adams (rev. edition, 1905).

Dictionary of American Biography, 20v. (1928–1937). Index volume (1937). Published by Charles Scribner's Sons under the auspices of the American Council of Learned Societies. Allen Johnson edited vols. 1–3, vols. 4–7 were edited by Johnson with Dumas Malone as associate editor. Johnson died Jan. 18, 1931, and Dumas Malone became editor, Feb. 2, 1931, editing vols. 8–20, assisted by Harris E. Starr. J. Franklin Jameson and John H. Finley were among the early sponsors of the idea of producing in America a biographical dictionary on the order of the British *Dictionary of National Biography.* The work was made possible through the financial assistance of the *New York Times* and its publisher, Adolph S. Ochs. It contains over 14,000 biographical sketches, each written by an authority. Living persons were not included. Supplement One, edited by Harris E. Starr, covered the period until December 31, 1935; Supplement Two, edited by R. L. Schuyler and E. T. James, covered the period until December 31, 1940.

Dictionary of American English. Published at the University of Chicago, with Sir William Alexander Craigie and James R. Hulbert as editors. The work is in four volumes (1936-44).

Dictionary of American English on Historical Principles, A. Edited by Sir William Craigie, James R. Hulbert, and others, 4v. (1936–43). Published by University of Chicago Press. Modeled on the "Oxford English Dictionary," it traces words to their earliest use in presenting the language common to America.

Dictionary of American History, 6v. (1940). Editor-in-chief, James Truslow Adams. R. V. Coleman, managing editor, T. R. Hay, editorial assistant. Contains 6425 signed articles by over 1000 historians. Has an index volume.

Dictionary of Americanisms on Historical Principles, A. Edited by Mitford McLeod Mathews, 2v. (1951). Published by University of Chicago Press.

Dictionary of Books Relating to America, by Joseph Sabin, 29v. (1868–1936). Sabin died before completing this work. It was finished by Wilberforce Eames and R. W. G. Vail. A monumental undertaking noted for its full bibliographical notes. Sabin was a New York bookseller. Eames and Vail were with the New York Public Library during their periods of editorship.

DIDIER, EUGENE LEMOINE (Dec. 22, 1838–Sept. 8, 1913); b. Baltimore, Md. Literary critic. Author. *Life and Poems of Edgar Allan Poe* (1877); *The Life and Letters of Madame Bonaparte* (1879); *A Primer of Criticism* (1883); *The Poe Cult, and Other Poe Papers* (1909); etc. Editor, *Southern Society,* 1867–68.

DIDION, JOAN (Dec. 5, 1934–   ); b. Sacramento, Cal. Novelist, essayist. *Run River* (1963); *Slouching Toward Bethlehem* (1968); *Play It As It Lays* (1970).

DIEHL, CHARLES SANFORD (Aug. 8, 1854–Aug. 19, 1946); b. Flintstone, Md. Journalist, author. *The Staff Correspondent* (1931). With Associated Press, 1883–1911; publisher (with Harrison L. Beach), *San Antonio Light,* 1911–24.

DIEKHOFF, JOHN SIEMON (Oct. 23, 1905–); b. Ann Arbor, Mich. Educator. *Milton on Himself* (1939); *Milton's Paradise Lost: A Commentary* (1946); *Democracy's College* (1950); *The Domain of the Faculty* (1956). Editor: *A Maske at Ludlow: Essays on Milton's Comus* (1968). Dean, Cleveland College, Western Reserve University, since 1956.

DIES, EDWARD JEROME (May 23, 1891–); b. Springfield, Ore. Author. *The Wheat Pit* (1925); *Solving the Farm Riddle* (1926); *Skylines* (1930); *Street of Adventure* (1935); *Titans of the Soil* (1949); *Behind the Wall Street Curtain* (1952); etc.

DIETRICH, JOHN HASSLER (Jan. 14, 1878–); b. Chambersburg, Pa. Unitarian clergyman, author. *The Religion of a Skeptic* (1911); *The Religion of Evolution* (1917); *The Religion of Humanity* (1919); *Humanism* (1925); *The Humanist Pulpit,* 7v. (1926–33); etc.

DIETZ, FREDERICK CHARLES (May 23, 1888–); b. Philadelphia, Pa. Educator, historian. *A Political and Social History of England* (1927); *The Industrial Revolution* (1927); *An Economic History of England* (1942); etc. Prof. history, University of Illinois.

DIETZ, HOWARD (Sept. 8, 1896–); b. New York. Librettist, lyricist. Wrote librettos for: *The Little Show* (prod. 1929); *The Band Wagon* (prod. 1931); *At Home Abroad* (prod. 1935); *Jackpot* (prod. 1944); *Sadie Thompson* (prod. 1944); *Inside U.S.A.* (prod. 1948); *The Gay Life* (1961); *Jenny* (1963); etc. Wrote lyrics for: *Dear Sir* (prod. 1924); *Merry-Go-Round* (prod. 1927); *Between the Devil* (prod. 1937); etc.

Dietz Press. Richmond, Virginia. Publishers. Founded in 1890 by August Dietz, in Goddin Hall, once the Treasury Department of the Confederate States of America. It was later moved to the office of the *Richmond Enquirer.* In 1939 the Dietz Press, headed by F. Meredith Dietz and August Dietz, Jr., revived the publication of the *Southern Literary Messenger.* The Dietz Press publishes Americana, particularly Virginiana, including reprints of old items and works of contemporary Southern writers.

DIFFENDORFER, RALPH EUGENE (Aug. 15, 1879–Jan. 31, 1951); b. Hayesville, O. Methodist missionary executive, author. *Child Life in Mission Lands* (1904); *A Modern Disciple of Jesus Christ: David Livingstone* (1913); *The Church and the Community* (1920); etc.

Digest. See *Literary Digest.*

Digges, Jeremiah. Pen name of Josef Berger.

DILL, [George] MARSHALL, Jʀ. (Aug. 21, 1916–); b. San Francisco, Cal. Educator, author. *Germany: A Modern History* (1961). Dominican College, San Rafael, Cal.

Dill Pickle Club. Chicago theatrical club.

DILLARD, R[ichard] H[enry] W[ilde] (Oct. 11, 1937–); b. Roanoke, Va. Poet. *The Day I Stopped Dreaming About Barbara Steele, and Other Poems* (1966). Contributor: *The Girl in the Black Raincoat* (1966). Faculty, Hollins College, since 1964.

DILLENBERGER, JOHN (July 11, 1918–); b. St. Louis, Mo. United Church of Christ clergyman, educator, author. *God Hidden and Revealed* (1953); *Protestant Christianity Interpreted through Its Development* (with Claude Welch, 1954); *Protestant Thought and Natural Science* (1960); *Contours of Faith* (1969). Chairman, editorial board, *Library of Protestant Thought,* 25v., since 1958. Prof. theology, Drew University, since 1958.

DILLER, ELLIOT VAN NOSTRAND (Oct. 20, 1904–); b. Brooklyn, N.Y. Educator, author. *The Religious Philosophy of Schleiermacher* (1934); *The Mountain and the River* (1938); etc. Prof. philosophy, Mills College, California, since 1949.

DILLINGHAM, CHARLES B[ancroft] (May 30, 1868–Aug. 30, 1934); b. Hartford, Conn. Journalist, drama critic, producer. Drama editor, *New York Evening Sun.*

DILLINGHAM, FRANCES BENT; b. Chelsea, Mass. Educator, author. *A Proud Little Baxter* (1898); *A Christmas Tree Scholar and Other Stories* (1900).

DILLON, CHARLES (Jan. 9, 1873–Aug. 16, 1942); b. Brooklyn, N.Y. Editor, author. *Journalism for High Schools* (1919); *Dillon's Desk Book* (1919); *Since Grover Cleveland's Day* (1935).

DILLON, GEORGE [Hill] (Nov. 12, 1906–Sept. 9, 1968); b. Jacksonville, Fla. Poet. *Boy in the Wind* (1927); *The Flowering Stone* (1931, Pulitzer Prize for poetry, 1932); *Flowers of Evil* (trans., with E. St. V. Millay, 1936). Assoc. editor, *Poetry: A Magazine of Verse, 1925–27;* became editor in 1937.

DILLON, JOHN BROWN (1808–Feb. 27, 1879); b. Wellsburg, W. Va. Librarian, historian. Called "the father of Indiana history." *Historical Notes* (1843); *The History of Indiana,* v.1 (1843), no more published; *A History of Indiana* (1859); *Oddities of Colonial Legislation in America* (1879). State librarian, Indiana, 1845–51.

DILLON, PHILIP ROBERT (Dec. 1, 1868–); b. Savannah, Ga. Editor, author. *The United States Flag* (1917); *American Anniversaries* (1918); and a number of works of fiction including *Judas of Kerioth* (1953). Editor, *Editor and Publisher,* 1901–02, 1906–07, 1909–11; managing editor, *American Penman,* 1912–21.

DILLON, RICHARD HUGH (Jan. 16, 1924–); b. Sausalito, Cal. Librarian, author. *Embarcadero* (1959); *The Gila Trail* (1960); *Shanghaiing Days* (1961); *Meriwether Lewis* (1965); *The Legend of Grizzly Adams* (1966); etc. Head, Sutro Library, San Francisco, since 1953.

DILLON, THOMAS J. (May 20, 1878–Jan. 27, 1949); b. Baldwin, Wis. Editor. Founder, *Portland* (Ore.) *News,* 1906; editor, *Minneapolis Morning and Evening News,* 1920–46.

Dime novels. These "Yellow Backs" and "Blood and Thunder" stories had a sensational vogue in America from 1860 to 1900, inspired by the success of the "Penny Dreadfuls" in England. Prominent publishers of dime novels were Beadle and Adams, George Munro, Robert M. DeWitt, J. S. Ogilvie Co., Frank Starr Co., Frank Tousey, Norman L. Munro, Nickel Library Co., George Sibley Co., Thomas & Talbot, Street & Smith, etc. Among leading dime novelists were Emerson Bennett, George Waldo Brown, Charles Dunning Clark, William Carleton, Sylvanus Cobb, John R. Coryell, Frederick Van Rensselaer Dey, Francis A. Durivage, Edwin Emerson, Edward S. Ellis, Thomas C. Harbaugh, Harry Hazelton, Joseph Holt Ingraham, Prentiss Ingraham, N. C. Irons, W. I. James, George C. Jenks, E. Z. C. Judson, George Lippard, Arthur Messerves, William Gilbert Patten, St. George Henry Rathbone, Mayne Reid, Eugene T. Sawyer, Luis P. Senarens, Mrs. E. D. E. N. Southworth, Edward Stratemeyer, Metta Victoria Victor, etc. For a full list of dime novelists see Ralph F. Cummings's *Dime Novel Authors, 1860–1900* (1933). *See also* Edmund Lester Pearson's *Dime Novels* (1929), and Irvin S. Cobb's *A Plea for Old Cap Collier* (1921). Dime novel series are listed in *Collector's Journal,* v.4, 1934. Stock names such as Nicholas Carter, Bertha M. Clay, John F. Conway, Gale Richards, Horace Paine, William Ward, Alden F. Bradshaw, and W. B. Lawson were often used to hide the identity of the dime novelists, who sometimes wrote more serious work under their real names.

DIMITRY, CHARLES PATTON (July 31, 1837–Nov. 10, 1910); b. Washington, D.C. Journalist, novelist. Author: *The House on Balfour Street* (1868); etc. He wrote many articles under the pen name of "Tobias Guarnerius, Jr." His father, Alexander Dimitry, educator, had written much for literary annuals under the pen name of "Tobias Guarnerius."

Ding, J. N. Pen name of Jay Norwood Darling.

Dinner at Eight. Play by George S. Kaufman and Edna Ferber (prod. 1932). Millicent Jordan invites a number of friends to a dinner in honor of prominent English visitors. Short scenes reveal the current problems of each guest as they prepare for the forthcoming dinner. In the end the guests of honor, when the dinner hour arrives, cannot come.

DINSMOOR, ROBERT (Oct. 7, 1757–Mar. 16, 1836); b. Windham, N.H. Poet. *Incidental Poems* (1828); *Poems of Robert Dinsmoor, "The Rustic Bard"* (1898). The latter is a new compilation.

DINSMORE, CHARLES ALLEN (Aug. 4, 1860–deceased); b. New York City. Congregational clergyman, author. *The Teachings of Dante* (1901); *Aids to the Study of Dante* (1903); *Life of Dante Alighieri* (1919); *The Great Poets and the Meaning of Life* (1937); *The English Bible As Literature* (1931); etc. Lecturer, Yale Divinity School, since 1920.

"Dionysius in Doubt." Poem by Edwin Arlington Robinson (1925). A condemnation of the Eighteenth Amendment.

Direction: A Quarterly of New Literature. Peoria, Ill. Founded 1934. Edited by Kerker Quinn and others. Discontinued 1935. Some of the editors helped establish *Accent* in 1940 as the same type of periodical.

Directory of Little Magazines and Small Presses. El Cerrito, Cal. Yearly. Founded 1965. Published by Dustbooks. Len Fulton, publisher and editor. A comprehensive listing of little magazines. See *Little magazine.* Also lists non-commercial publishers of literary and graphic works.

"Dirge for a Soldier." Poem by George Henry Boker (1862). In memory of Gen. Philip Kearny.

"Dirge for One Who Fell in Battle." Poem by Thomas William Parsons. The subject of the poem was Theodore Winthrop.

"Discordants." Four lyrics by Conrad Aiken in his *Turns and Movies* (1916).

Discourse, The. Address by Daniel Webster at Plymouth, Mass., 1820, on the 200th anniversary of landing of the Pilgrims.

Discourses on Davila. By John Adams (1805). Originally appeared in the *Gazette of the United States,* 1790.

Discovery of America, The. By John Fiske, 2v. (1892). One of the classic accounts of our early history.

Disenchanted, The. Novel by Budd Schulberg (1950). Based on the life of F. Scott Fitzgerald.

DISNEY, DORIS MILES (Mrs. George J. Disney) (Dec. 22, 1907–); b. Glastonbury, Conn. Author. *Family Skeleton* (1949); *Fire at Will* (1950); *Look Back on Murder* (1951); *Prescription: Murder* (1953); *Room for Murder* (1955); *Method in Madness* (1957); *Did She Fall or Was She Pushed* (1959); *Mrs. Meeker's Money* (1961); *Find the Woman* (1962); *Here Lies . . .* (1963); *The Hospitality of the House* (1964); *Money for the Taking* (1968); *Voice from the Grave* (1968); etc.

Dissent. New York. Quarterly. Founded 1954. Edited by Irving Howe. Social and cultural criticism from a Socialist viewpoint.

Dissertations. See *A List of American Doctoral Dissertations,* published annually by the Library of Congress, beginning 1915. The first *List* contains dissertations of 1912–14. Columbia University has listed its dissertations from 1872, Harvard University from 1873, Yale University from 1861, University of Pennsylvania from 1889, all in separate publications which are kept up to date with supplements.

Dissertations in American Literature, 1891–1966. (1968). Edited by James Leslie Woodress.

DISTURNELL, JOHN (Oct. 6, 1801–Oct. 1, 1877); b. Lansingburg, N.Y. Compiler of scores of guide-books, gazetteers, and handbooks. *The Great Lakes* (1863); *Traveller's Guide to the Hudson River* (1864); *New York As It Was and Is* (1876); etc.

DITHMAR, EDWARD AUGUSTUS (May 22, 1854–Oct. 16, 1917); b. New York City. Editor, author. *John Drew: A Biographical Sketch* (1900). With *New York Times,* from 1871; dramatic critic, 1884–1901.

DITMARS, RAYMOND LEE (June 20, 1876–May 20, 1942); b. Newark, N.J. Naturalist, curator, author. *The Reptile Book* (1907); *Snakes of the World* (1931); *Thrills of a Naturalist's Quest* (1932); *Forest of Adventure* (1933); *Confessions of a Scientist* (1934); *The Making of a Scientist* (1937); *The Fight to Live* (1938); *Strange Animals I Have Known* (1939); *Animal Kingdom: The Way of Life in a Zoo* (1941); etc. Curator of reptiles, New York Zoological Society (Bronx Zoo), from 1899; in charge dept. of mammals, from 1910.

DITSON, GEORGE LEIGHTON (Aug. 5, 1812–Jan. 29, 1895); b. Westford, Mass. Novelist. *Circassia; or, A Tour to the Caucasus* (1850); *Crimora; or, Love's Cross* (1852); *The Crescent and French Crusaders* (1859); *The Federati of Italy* (1871); etc.

DITSON, OLIVER (Oct. 20, 1811–Dec. 21, 1888); b. Boston, Mass. Music publisher. Started music publishing business in Boston in 1835. It has continued until this day. He published *Dwight's Journal of Music* from 1858 to 1876. Many of America's leading songs were printed by Oliver Ditson & Company. William Arms Fisher was editor of Ditson publications, 1897–1937. *See* his *One Hundred and Fifty Years of Music Publishing in the United States 1783–1933.*

DIVINE, CHARLES (Jan. 20, 1889–); b. Binghamton, N.Y. Novelist, poet. *City Ways and Company Streets* (poems, 1918); *Gypsy Gold* (poems, 1923); *The Road to Town* (poems, 1925); *Cognac Hill* (1927); *Strangers at Home* (1935); etc.

Divinity School Address. Name usually applied to *An Address Before the Senior Class in Divinity College, Cambridge,* delivered by Ralph Waldo Emerson, July 15, 1838, published 1838. It became the keynote of transcendentalism in America.

DIX, BEULAH MARIE (Mrs. George H. Flebbe) (Dec. 25, 1876–); b. Kingston, Mass. Playwright. *Soldier Rigdale* (1899); *The Fair Maid of Graystones* (1905); *The Road to Yesterday* (1906); *The Lilac Room* (1906); *Young Fernald* (1906); *The Substitute* (1908); *Allison's Lad* (1910); *Fighting Blade* (1912); *Moloch* (1915); *Across the Border* (1915); *Pity of God* (1932); *The Wedding Eve Murder* (1941); etc.

DIX, DOROTHEA LYNDE (Apr. 4, 1802–July 18, 1887); b. Hampden, Mass. Educator, poet, promoter of care for insane. *Conversations on Common Things* (1824); *Hymns for Children* (1825); *Evening Hours* (1825); *The Garland of Flora* (1829); *American Moral Tales for Young Persons* (1832); etc. *See* Helen E. Marshall's *Dorothea Dix, Forgotten Samaritan* (1937).

Dix, Dorothy. Pen name of Elizabeth Meriwether Gilmer.

DIX, EDWIN ASA (June 25, 1860–1911); b. Newark, N.J. Author. *A Midsummer Drive Through the Pyrenees* (1890); *Deacon Bradbury* (1900); *Old Bowen's Legacy* (1901); *Champlain, the Founder of New France* (1903); *Prophet's Landing* (1907).

DIX, MORGAN (Nov. 1, 1827–Apr. 29, 1908); b. New York City. Episcopal clergyman, author. *Memoirs of John Adams Dix,* 2v. (1883); *A History of the Parish of Trinity Church in the City of New York,* 4v. (1898–1906); etc.

"Dixie." Popular song by Daniel Decatur Emmett. Written for Bryant's minstrels in 1859, published by Firth & Pond, in New York, 1860. It was sung by Mrs. John Woods in New Orleans in 1860 and became a hit. It was first called "I Wish I Was in Dixie's Land." The song was pirated and many claimants to authorship arose, but Emmett was the creator of the song.

DIXON, GEORGE WASHINGTON (c. 1808–1861). Minstrel. His best known songs were "Zip Coon" and "The Coal Black Rose." Founder, *The New York Polyanthos,* 1839.

DIXON, HARRY VERNOR (Oct. 30, 1908–); b. Sacramento, Cal. Author. *Laughing Gods* (1935); *Something for Nothing* (1950); *Too Rich to Die* (1953); *Cry Blood* (1955); *A Girl like Marian* (1961); *The Rag Pickers* (1966); etc.

DIXON, JAMES MAIN (Apr. 20, 1856–Sept. 27, 1933); b. Paisley, England. Educator, author. *Matthew Arnold* (1906); *A Survey of Scottish Literature in the Nineteenth Century* (1906); *English Idioms* (1927); etc. Prof. English and Oriental studies, University of Southern California, 1905–33.

DIXON, JEANE [L.] Real estate broker, author. *The Door to the Future* (1962); *My Life and Prophecies* (1969); etc.

DIXON, ROLAND BURRAGE (Nov. 6, 1875–Dec. 19, 1934); b. Worcester, Mass. Educator, folk-lorist, author. *The Racial History of Man* (1923); *The Building of Cultures* (1928); etc. Anthropology dept., Harvard, 1897–1934.

DIXON, ROYAL (May 25, 1885–June 4, 1962); b. Huntsville, Tex. Naturalist, lecturer, novelist. *Signs Is Signs* (1915); *Americanization* (1916); *The Human Side of Animals* (1918); *Mary Elkins* (1925); *Wildwood Friends* (1929); *The Ape of Heaven* (1936); *Half Dark Moon* (1939); *Earth-Hunger* (1940); *Behold Elizabeth Ney* (1953); *The Lost Angel* (1957); etc. Founder, "Wild Flower Day in America," Mar. 29, 1929.

DIXON, THOMAS (Jan. 11, 1864–Apr. 3, 1946); b. Shelby, N.C. Novelist, playwright. *The Leopard's Spots* (1902); *The One Woman* (1903); *The Clansman* (1905); *The Traitor* (1907); *Comrades* (1909); *The Sins of the Father* (1912); *The Southerner* (1913); *The Victim* (1914); *A Man of the People* (1920); *The Man in Gray* (1921); *Companions* (1931); *A Dreamer in Portugal* (1934); *The Flaming Sword* (1939); etc. The play, *The Clansman,* (prod. 1905) was drawn from *The Leopard's Spots* and *The Clansman;* the material was used for the scenario, *The Birth of a Nation* (prod. 1915).

DIXSON, ZELLA ALLEN (Aug. 10, 1858–Jan. 12, 1924); b. Zanesville, O. Librarian, author. *The Comprehensive Subject Index to Universal Prose Fiction* (1897); *Concerning Book Plates: A Hand-Book for Collectors* (1903). University of Chicago Library, 1891–1924.

DOANE, GEORGE WASHINGTON (May 27, 1799–Apr. 27, 1859); b. Trenton, N.J. Episcopal bishop, hymn writer. *Songs by the Way* (1824); *The Life and Writings,* edited by William Croswell Doane, 4v. (1860–61). Among his hymns are "Thou art the Way, to Thee alone," "Lord, should we leave Thy hallowed feet," and "Softly now the light of day." *See* J. Julian's *A Dictionary of Hymnology* (1907).

DOANE, WILLIAM CROSWELL (Mar. 2, 1832–May 17, 1913); b. Boston, Mass. Episcopal bishop, poet. *Rhymes from Time to Time* (1901). Best known hymn is "Ancient of Days."

DOANE, WILLIAM HOWARD (Feb. 3, 1831–Dec. 24, 1915); b. Preston, Conn. Hymn writer, composer. *Sabbath-School Gems* (1862); etc. Editor: *The Baptist Hymnal* (1886); etc. Among his hymns are "Safe in the arms of Jesus," "More like Jesus," and "Draw me nearer."

DOBELL, BYRON [Maxwell] (May 30, 1927–); b. Bronx, N.Y. Editor. Editor: *Life Pictorial Atlas of the World; Life Guide to Paris.* Editor, *Book World, Chicago Tribune* and *Washington Post,* 1967–69; editor-in-chief, book division, McCall Publishing Co., 1969–70; editor, *Time–Life Books,* since 1971.

DOBIE, CHARLES CALDWELL (Mar. 15, 1881–Jan. 11, 1943); b. San Francisco, Cal. Novelist, playwright. *Blood Red Dawn* (1920); *Less Than Kin* (1926); *The Arrested Moment* (1927); *San Francisco: A Pageant* (1933); *Portrait of a Courtezan* (1934); *San Francisco Tales* (1935); *San Francisco's Chinatown* (1936); *San Francisco Adventure* (1937); etc.

DOBIE, J[ames] **FRANK** (Sept. 26, 1888–Sept. 18, 1964); b. in Live Oak Co., Tex. Educator, editor, folklorist, author. *A Vaquero of the Brush Country* (1929); *Coronado's Children*

(1930); *On the Open Range* (1931); *Tongues of the Monte* (1935); *Tales of the Mustang* (1936); *The Flavor of Texas* (1936); *Apache Gold & Yaqui Silver* (1939); *John C. Duval, First Texas Man of Letters* (1939); *In the Shadow of History* (1939); *The Longhorns* (1941); *Guide to Life and Literature of the Southwest* (1943); *A Texan in England* (1945); *The Voice of the Coyote* (1949); *The Ben Lilly Legend* (1950); *The Mustangs* (1952); *Up the Trail from Texas* (1955); *Tales of Old-Time Texas* (1955); *I'll Tell You a Tale* (1960); *Cow People* (1964). Editor: *Texas and Southwestern Lore* (1927); *Spur-of-the-Cock* (1933); *Puro Mexicano* (1935). Editor, Texas Folk-Lore Society. English dept., University of Texas, 1925–47.

DOBRIANSKY, LEV EUGENE (Nov. 9, 1918–); b. New York. Economist, author. *A Philosophico-Economic Critique of Thorstein Veblen* (1943); *Free Trade Ideal* (1954); *Veblenism, a New Critique* (1957); *The Crimes of Krushchev* (1959); *Vulnerabilities of the USSR* (1963); *Nations, Peoples and Countries in the USSR* (1964); etc.

DOBZHANSKY, THEODOSIUS (Jan. 25, 1900–); b. Nemirov, Rus. Educator, author. *Genetics and Origin of Species* (1937); *Evolution, Genetics and Man* (1955); *Man Evolving* (1962). Prof. genetics, California Institute of Technology, 1936–40; prof. zoology, Columbia University, since 1940.

DODD, EDWARD HOWARD (June 18, 1869–June 19, 1965); b. Bloomfield, N.J. Publisher. With Dodd, Mead & Co., New York, from 1893; president, 1916–31; former president, International Encyclopedia Co.

DODD, EDWARD HOWARD, JR. (June 25, 1905–); b. New York. Publisher. *Great Dipper to Southern Cross* (1930); *Of Nature, Time, and Teale* (1960); *Tales of Maui* (1964); *Polynesian Art* (1967). With Dodd, Mead & Co. since 1929; chairman of the board, since 1966.

DODD, FRANK COURTENAY (Jan. 9, 1876–Jan. 4, 1968); b. Winnebago, Minn. Publisher. President, Dodd, Mead & Co., New York, 1931–42; chairman of the board, 1942–59.

DODD, FRANK HOWARD (Apr. 12, 1844–Jan. 10, 1916); b. Bloomfield, N.J. Publisher. Son of Moses W. Dodd, founder of the firm of Dodd, Mead & Company, he succeeded his father in 1870, and took as partner Edward S. Mead. He was succeeded by his son Edward H. Dodd in 1916. Founder, *The Bookman,* 1895; *The New International Encyclopedia,* 20v. (1902–04).

DODD, LEE WILSON (July 11, 1879–May 16, 1933); b. Franklin, Pa. Playwright, novelist, poet. *A Modern Alchemist, and Other Poems* (1906); *The Return of Eve* (prod. 1911); *Speed* (prod. 1911); *The Middle Miles, and Other Poems* (1915); *Pals First* (prod. 1917); *The Book of Susan* (1920); *Lilia Chenoworth* (1922); *The Girl Next Door* (1923); *The Changelings* (prod. 1923); *Pegeen and the Potamus* (1925); *The Golden Complex* (1927); *The Great Enlightenment* (poems, 1928); etc.

Dodd, Mead & Company. New York. Publishers. Founded in 1839 by Moses Woodruff Dodd. The first books published were theological. Charlotte Elizabeth was the firm's first successful author. Cruden's *Concordance to the Bible* was an early best seller. In 1870 Moses W. Dodd retired in favor of his son Frank Howard Dodd (1844–1916), who brought in his cousin, Edward S. Mead, as partner, and the firm name of Dodd & Mead was established. The first nation-wide bestseller under the new partnership was E. P. Roe's *Barriers Burned Away* (1871). Mead himself wrote juvenile fiction under the pen name of Richard Markham. In 1886 the firm launched *The International Encyclopedia.* Robert H. Dodd joined the firm in 1889, and Edward H. Dodd in 1893. The firm also published *The Bookman.* Also inaugurated *American Book Prices Current.* Absorbed Moffat, Yard, 1924. Affiliated with F. S. Crofts Company in 1924. Absorbed Small, Maynard in 1926, Duffield & Green in 1934, Sears in 1934. A Canadian branch was established in 1925 in Toronto. The firm was the

American publisher of Bernard Shaw. Edward H. Dodd, Jr., is chairman of the board. See *The First Hundred Years: A History of the House of Dodd, Mead 1839–1939* (1939); by Edward H. Dodd, Jr.

DODD, WILLIAM E[dward] (Oct. 21, 1869–Feb. 9, 1940); b. Clayton, N.C. Editor, diplomat, author. *The Life of Nathaniel Macon* (1903); *Jefferson Davis* (1907); *Statesmen of the Old South* (1911); *Expansion and Conflict* (1915); *Woodrow Wilson and His Work* (1920); *Lincoln or Lee* (1928); *The Old South* (1937); *Ambassador Dodd's Diary 1933–1938* (1941); etc. Editor: *The Riverside History of the United States,* 4v. (1915). Ambassador to Germany, 1933–37. Prof. history, University of Chicago.

DODDRIDGE, JOSEPH (Oct. 14, 1769–Nov. 9, 1826); b. Bedford, Pa. Episcopal clergyman, physician, pioneer, author. *Logan: The Last of the Race of Shikellemus* (drama, 1823); *Notes on the Settlement and Indian Wars, of the Western Part of Virginia & Pennsylvania, from the Year 1763 until the Year 1783 Inclusive* (1824).

DODDS, HAROLD WILLIS (June 28, 1889–); b. Utica, Pa. Educator, editor. Author: *Out of This Nettle, Danger ...* (1943); *The Academic President* (with Felix C. Robb and R. Robb Taylor, 1962). Editor, *National Municipal Review,* 1920–28. President, Princeton University, 1933–57.

DODGE, CONSTANCE (1896–). Author. *Bitter Waters* (1939); *Dark Stranger* (1940); *Weathercock* (1942); *In Adam's Fall* (1946); *Unrelenting* (1950); etc.

DODGE, DAVID; (b. 1919). Author. *How Green Was My Father* (1947); *The Crazy Glasspecker* (1949); *The Red Tassel* (1950); *The Lights of Skaro* (1954); *Angel's Ransom* (1956); *Loo Loo's Legacy* (1961); *Poor Man's Guide to the Orient* (1965); *Hooligan* (1969); etc.

DODGE, HENRY IRVING (1861–July 28, 1934); b. Kasoag, N.Y. Humorist, playwright. *Skinner's Dress Suit* (1916); *Skinner's Baby* (1917); *Skinner's Big Idea* (1918); etc.

DODGE, HENRY NEHEMIAH (May 19, 1843–July 24, 1937); b. New York City. Dentist, poet. *The Angels of the Tower* (1894); *Christus Victor* (1899); *Mystery of the West* (1906); *John Murray's Landfall* (1911); etc.

DODGE, LOUIS (Sept. 27, 1870–); b. Burlington, Ia. Author. *Bonnie May* (1916); *The Sandman's Forest* (1918); *Children of the Desert* (1917); *The Sandman's Mountain* (1919); *Nancy* (1921); *Tawi Tawi* (1921); *The American* (1934); etc.

Dodge, Mabel. See Mabel Dodge Luhan.

DODGE, MARY ABIGAIL (Mar. 31, 1833–Aug. 17, 1896); b. Hamilton, Mass. Editor, essayist, poet. Pen name "Gail Hamilton." *Country Living and Country Thinking* (1862); *Gala-Days* (1863); *Skirmishes and Sketches* (1866); *Summer Rest* (1866); *Wool-Gathering* (1867); *A Battle of the Books* (1870); *Twelve Miles From a Lemon* (1874); *First Love Is Best* (1877); *Chips, Fragments and Vestiges* (poems, 1902). Editor, *Our Young Folks,* 1865–67.

DODGE, MARY BARKER; b. Bridgewater, Pa. Poet. *Belfry Voices* (1869); *The Gray Masque, and Other Poems* (1885).

DODGE, MARY [Elizabeth] MAPES (Jan. 26, 1831–Aug. 21, 1905); b. New York City. Editor, author. *The Irvington Stories* (1865); *Hans Brinker, or The Silver Skates* (1865); *Rhymes and Jingles* (1874); *Along the Way* (poems, 1879), republished as, *Poems and Verses* (1904); *Theophilus and Others* (1876); *Donald and Dorothy* (1883); *The Land of Pluck* (1894); *The Golden Gate* (1903); etc. Editor, *St. Nicholas Magazine,* 1873–1905.

DODGE, RICHARD IRVING (May 19, 1827–June 16, 1895); b. Huntsville, N.C. Soldier, author. *The Black Hills* (1876); *The Plains of the Great West* (1877); *Our Wild Indians* (1882); etc.

DODGE, THEODORE AYRAULT (May 28, 1842–Oct. 25, 1909); b. Pittsfield, Mass. Army officer, military historian and biographer. *A Chat in the Saddle* (1885); *Alexander* (1890); *Riders of Many Lands* (1893); *Gustavus Adolphus* (1895); *Napoleon,* 4v. (1904–07) etc. Editor: *History of the Art of War,* 12v. (1890–1907).

DODGE, WALTER PHELPS (June 13, 1869–); b. Beirut. Lawyer, author. *Three Greek Tales* (1893); *From Squire to Prince* (1901); *Types (Chiefly Malicious)* (1929); etc.

DODGE, WENDELL PHILLIPS (August 12, 1883–); b. Manchester, N.H. Producer, publicist, explorer, playwright. *Mating* (prod. 1911); *Smoldering Fires* (prod. 1928); *Ballyhooing the Theatre* (1929); *Sweeney Todd* (1959); etc. Editor and author: *Dictionary of Geographical Discoveries* (1959); *Short History of the Artic* (1963). Founder, The World Wide News Service, 1913. Editor, *Wide World Magazine,* 1914–16; *Explorer's Journal,* 1945–54. Founder, "The Tormentors" (drama producing organization) New York, 1923; Boston, 1931; San Francisco, 1938.

DODSON, OWEN (1914–). Author. *Powerful Long Ladder* (poems, 1946); *Box at the Window* (1951).

Dodsworth. Novel by Sinclair Lewis (1929). A successful American businessman tours Europe against his will, to please his ambitious wife. She forms a foolish attachment, and drives her husband into the arms of another woman.

DOERFLINGER, WILLIAM MAIN (July 30, 1910–); b. Brooklyn, N.Y. Editor. *The Middle Passage* (1939). Editor: *Shantymen and Shantyboys* (1951). With E. P. Dutton & Co., 1942, 1945–50, since 1953.

Doesticks, Q. K. Philander, P. B. Pen name of Mortimer Thompson.

Dogood, Silence. Pen name used by Benjamin Franklin for his "Dogood Papers" in the *New England Courant* in 1722.

Dog's Tale, A. Story by Mark Twain, first published in *Harper's Magazine,* Dec., 1903.

DOHERTY, EDWARD J[oseph] (Oct. 30, 1890–); b. Chicago, Ill. Editorial writer, author. *East River* (with Borden Chase, 1935); *Gall and Honey* (autobiography, 1941); *Splendor of Sorrow* (1943); *Tumbleweed* (1948); *Matt Talbot* (1953); *Conquering March of Don John Bosco* (1959); *A Nun with a Gun: Sister Stanislaus* (1960); *King of Sinners* (1964); etc. Editional writer, *Chicago Sun,* since 1941.

DOLBIER, MAURICE [Wyman] (May 5, 1912–); b. Skowhegan, Me. Journalist, author. *Jenny the Bus That Nobody Loved* (1944); *The Magic Shop* (1946); *Nowhere Near Everest* (1955); *All Wrong on the Night* (1966); *Benjy Boone* (1967); etc. Daily book critic, *New York World Journal Tribune,* 1966. Lit. editor, *Providence Journal,* since 1967.

DOLE, HELEN JAMES BENNETT (d. June 9, 1944); b. Worcester, Mass. Translator of the children's books of Spyri, Brentano, Theuriet, Baumbach, etc., Loti's *Iceland Fisherman,* Rostand's *Cyrano de Bergerac,* etc.

DOLE, NATHAN HASKELL (Aug. 31, 1852–May 9, 1935); b. Chelsea, Mass. Poet. *On the Point: A Summer Idyl* (1895); *The Hawthorn Tree, and Other Poems* (1895); *Joseph Jefferson at Home* (1898); *Omar, the Tentmaker* (1899); *The Pilgrims, and Other Poems* (1907); *Alaska* (1909); *Life of Count Tolstoi* (1911); *Maine of the Sea and Pines* (with Irwin Leslie Gordon, 1928); etc. Translator of Tolstoi, Daudet, Voldes, etc. Editor: *Young Folks Library* (with others, 1902); *The Greek Poets* (1904); *The Latin Poets* (1905); *Brevian Treasures,* 10v. (1904–05); *Bartlett's Familiar Quotations* (10th ed.); etc.

DOLLARD, JOHN (Aug. 29, 1900–); b. Menasha, Wis. Psychologist, author. *Class and Caste in a Southern Town* (1937); *Social Learning and Imitation* (with N. E. Miller, 1941); *Personality and Psychotherapy* (with same, 1950); *Scoring Hu-* *man Motives* (with Frank Auld, Jr., 1959); *Children of Bondage* (1964); etc.

Dolliver Romance, The. Unfinished story by Nathaniel Hawthorne (1864), dealing with the mystery of immortality. The manuscript was laid on his coffin at the burial service.

Dolph Heyliger. One of the Dutch tales in *Bracebridge Hall,* by Washington Irving.

Dome of Many-Colored Glass, A. Poems by Amy Lowell (1912).

DONAGHEY, FREDERICK (c. 1865–Nov. 8, 1937); b. Philadelphia, Pa. Drama critic, playwright. *Louisiana Lou* (with M. Hough, prod. 1912); *The Girl at the Gate* (with Addison Burkhart, prod. 1912); etc. Drama, music, and lit. critic, Philadelphia *Public Ledger,* 1902–06; music critic, Chicago *Tribune,* 1915–18; drama critic, 1923–30.

DONAHEY, JAMES HARRISON (Apr. 8, 1875–June 1, 1949); b. Westchester, O. Artist. Cartoonist, *Cleveland Plain Dealer,* since 1899. Drawings from been published as *Sketches in Yucatan, Sketches in Alaska,* etc.

DONAHEY, MARY [Augusta] DICKERSON (Sept. 22, 1876–March 31, 1962); b. New York City. Author. *The Castle of Grumpy Grouch* (1908); *Down Spider Web Lane* (1909); *Through the Little Green Door* (1910); *The Magical House of Zur* (1914); *Peter and Prue* (1924); *Marty Lu* (1929); *The Spanish McQuades* (1931); *Mysterious Mansions* (1932); *Apple Pie Inn* (1942); etc.

DONAHOE, PATRICK (Mar. 17, 1811–Mar. 18, 1901); b. Munnery, Co. Cavan, Ireland. Editor, publisher. Founder, *The Pilot,* a Roman Catholic weekly, Boston, with H. L. Devereaux, 1836; *Donahoe's Magazine,* a monthly, 1878.

Donahoe's Magazine. Boston, Mass. An Irish-American periodical, founded in 1878 by Patrick Donahoe. Ceased 1908.

DONAHUE, JACK CLIFFORD (Dec. 6, 1917–); b. Waco, Tex. Author. *The Confessor* (1963); *Erase My Name* (1964); *Divorce–American Style* (1967).

DONALD, DAVID [Herbert] (Oct. 1, 1920–); b. Goodman, Miss. Educator, author. *Lincoln's Herndon* (1948); *Lincoln Reconsidered* (1956); *Charles Sumner and the Coming of the Civil War* (1960, Pulitzer prize for biography, 1961); *The Politics of Reconstruction, 1863—1867* (1965). Editor: *Divided We Fought* (1952); *Inside Lincoln's Cabinet: The Civil War Diaries of Salmon P. Chase* (1954); *A Rebel's Recollections* (1959); *The Nation in Crisis, 1861-1877*; etc. Prof. history, Columbia University, since 1957.

Donald and Dorothy. Children's book by Mary Mapes Dodge (1883).

DONDO, MATHURIN [Marius] (Mar. 8, 1884–); b. Lorient, France. Educator, author. *French Fairy Plays* (with M. Elizabeth Perley, 1923); *Two Blind Men and a Donkey* (1925); *Modern French Course* (1929); *The French Faust, Henri de Saint-Simon* (1955); and books in French. French dept., University of California, 1922–48.

DONER, MARY FRANCES b. Port Huron, Mich. Author. *Ravenswood* (1948); *Cloud of Arrows* (1950); *The Host Rock* (1952); *The Salvager* (1958); *The Shores of Home* (1961); *The Wind and the Fog* (1963); *Cleavenger versus Castle* (1968); *Pere Marquette—Soldier of the Cross* (1969); etc.

DONIPHAN, ALEXANDER (July 9, 1808–Aug. 8, 1887); b. near Maysville, Ky. Army officer, lawyer. Doniphan's expedition from Missouri to Mexico during the Mexican war is a saga of heroism. *See* John Taylor Hughes's *Doniphan's Expedition* (1848); Jacob S. Robinson's *Sketches of the Great West* (1848), republished as *A Journal of the Santa Fé Expedition Under Colonel Doniphan* (1932); William E. Connelley's *Doniphan's Expedition* (1907); E. Alexander Powell's *The*

Road to Glory (1915); George R. Gibson's *Journal of a Soldier under Kearny and Doniphan* (1935).

DONLEAVY, JAMES P[atrick] (Apr. 23, 1926–); b. Brooklyn N.Y. Author. *The Ginger Man* (1955); *Fairy Tales of New York* (1960); *A Singular Man* (1963); *Meet My Maker, the Mad Molecule* (1964); *The Saddest Summer of Samuel S.* (1966); *The Beastly Beatitudes of Balthazar B* (1968).

Donn-Byrne, Brian Oswald. See Donn Byrne.

DONNELLY, ELEANOR CECILIA (Sept. 6, 1838–Apr. 30, 1917); b. Philadelphia, Pa. Novelist, biographer, poet. *Out of Sweet Solitude* (1873); *Domus Dei* (poems, 1875); *The Children of the Golden Sheaf, and Other Poems* (1884); *Poems* (1892); *A Klondike Picnic* (1898); *The Secret of the Statue, and Other Verses* (1907); etc.

DONNELLY, IGNATIUS (Nov. 3, 1831–Jan. 1, 1901); b. Philadelphia, Pa. Reformer, author. Known as the "Sage of Nininger." *Atlantis: The Antediluvian World* (1882); *Ragnarok: The Age of Fire and Gravel* (1883); *The Great Cryptogram* (1888); *Caesar's Column: A Story of the Twentieth Century* (1891); etc.

Donnelley, R. R., & Sons. Chicago, Ill. Publishers. Founded 1864, by Richard Robert Donnelly, who also founded Lakeside Press, publisher of the "Lakeside Classics." The firm specializes in telephone directories. The Fourteenth Edition of the *Encyclopaedia Britannica* was printed by Donnelly.

DONOVAN, EDWARD FRANCES (d. Jan. 25, 1943); b. Kingston, Ont., Canada. Lexicographer. Editor: *Unabridged New Standard Dictionary* (1909–14). Style editor, *Encyclopaedia Britannica*, 14th edition (1927–29); on editorial staff of other dictionaries and encyclopedias.

DONOVAN, ROBERT JOHN (Aug. 21, 1912–); b. Buffalo, N.Y. Journalist. *The Assassins* (1955); *Eisenhower: The Inside Story* (1956); *John F. Kennedy in World War II* (1961); *The Future of the Republican Party* (1964); etc. With New York *Herald Tribune*, 1937-63; chief, Washington Bureau, 1957–63; chief, Washington bureau, Los Angeles *Times*, since 1963.

DOOB, LEONARD WILLIAM (Mar. 3, 1909–): b. New York. Psychologist. *Propaganda: Its Psychology and Technique* (1935); *Competition and Cooperation* (with M. A. May, 1937); *The Plans of Men* (1940); *Public Opinion and Propaganda* (1948); *Social Psychology* (1952); *Communication in Africa* (1961); *Patriotism and Nationalism* (1964); *Ants Will Not Eat Your Fingers* (1966).

D'OOGE, BENJAMIN LEONARD (1860–Mar. 8, 1940); b. Grand Rapids, Mich. Educator. Editor: *Colloquia Latina* (1888); *Second Year Latin* (with James B. Greenough and M. Grant, 1899); *Cicero, Select Orations* (1901); *Latin Composition* (1901); *Elements of Latin* (1921); etc. Prof. Latin, Michigan State Normal College, 1886–1940.

D'OOGE, MARTIN LUTHER (July 17, 1839–Sept. 12, 1915); b. Zonnemaire, the Netherlands. Educator, classicist, author. *The Acropolis of Athens* (1908). Brother of Benjamin Leonard D'Ooge.

DOOLEY, THOMAS [Anthony] (1927–Jan. 18, 1961). Medical missionary, author. *Deliver Us from Evil* (1956); *The Edge of Tomorrow* (1958); *The Night They Burned the Mountain* (1960); *Before I Sleep* (Ed. by James Monahan), 1961.

DOOLITTLE, HILDA (Mrs. Richard Aldington) (Sept. 10, 1886–Sept. 27, 1961); b. Bethlehem, Pa. Poet. Wrote under initials "H. D." *Sea Garden* (poems, 1919); *Hymen* (poems, 1921); *Heliodora, and Other Poems* (1924); *Collected Poems* (1925); *Palimpsest* (1926); *Hippolytus Temporizes* (play in verse, 1927); *Hedylus* (1928); *Red Roses from Bronze* (1932); *The Hedgehog* (1936); *Collected Poems* (1940); *The Walls Do Not Fall* (1944); *Tribute to the Angels* (1945); *Flowering of the Rod* (1946); *By Avon River* (1949); *Tribute to Freud*

(1956); *Bid Me to Live* (1960); *Helen in Eqypt* (1961). Translator: *Ion of Euripides* (1937).

DOPP, KATHARINE ELIZABETH (1863–); b. Belmont, Wis. Educator, author. *The Tree Dwellers* (1903); *The Early Cave-Men* (1904); *The Early Sea People* (1912); the *Bobby and Betty* series, 4v. (1917–27); *The Early Herdsmen* (1923); etc. Extension division, University of Chicago, 1902–11.

DORFMAN, JOSEPH (Mar. 27, 1904–); b. Ramanovska, Rus. Educator, author. *Thorstein Veblen and His America* (1934); *The Economic Mind in American Civilization*, 5v. (1946–59); *Early American Policy* (with Rexford G. Tugwell, 1960); *Institutional Economics* (with others, 1963); *Types of Economic Theory*, vol. 1 (with W. C. Mitchell, 1967). Prof. economics, Columbia University, since 1948.

DORGAN, THOMAS ALOYSIUS (Apr. 29, 1877–May 2, 1929); b. San Francisco, Cal. Pen name, "Tad." Cartoonist, sports writer, famous for colorful use of slang. Creator of comic strip character "Silk Hat Harry," and the syndicated cartoon "Indoor Sports."

Dormie, M. A. Pen name of Marian Edna Sharrock.

DORN, EDWARD (1929–   ); b. in Illinois. Poet, critic. *What I See in the Maximus Poems* (1960); *The Newly Fallen* (1961); *Hands Up!* (1964); *From Gloucester Out* (1964); *Idaho Out* (1964); *Geography* (1964); *The Shoshoneans* (1966); *Guerilla Poems from Latin America* (1968); etc.

Dorothy. Short story by Erskine Caldwell (1940).

"Dorothy Q." Poem by Oliver Wendell Holmes, in *Atlantic Monthly*, Jan., 1871. Another poem, "Dear Little Dorothy Q," was written in 1882. It appeared in print in *Life and Letters of Oliver Wendell Holmes* (1896).

DORR, JULIA C[aroline] R[ipley] (Feb. 13, 1825–Jan. 18, 1913); b. Charleston, S.C. Poet, novelist. *Farmingdale* (1854); *Poems* (1872); *Afternoon Songs* (1885); *A Cathedral Pilgrimage* (1896); *Afterglow: Later Poems* (1900); *Beyond the Sunset: Latest Poems* (1909); *Last Poems* (1913); etc.

DORR, RHETA [Louise] CHILDE (d. Aug. 8, 1948); b. Omaha, Neb. Journalist, author. *A Woman of Fifty* (autobiography, 1924); *Susan B. Anthony* (1928); etc.

DORRANCE, GORDON (June 14, 1890–Mar. 22, 1957); b. Camden, N.Y. Publisher, author. *The Story of the Forest* (1916); *Broken Shackles* (1920). Editor: *Contemporary Poets: An Anthology of 50* (1927). President, Dorrance & Co. Inc., Philadelphia, 1920–40.

DORRANCE, WARD ALLISON (Apr. 30, 1904–); b. Jefferson City, Mo. Author. *Three Ozark Streams* (1937); *We're from Missouri* (1938); *Where the Rivers Meet* (1939); *The Sundowners* (1942); *The White Hound* (with Thomas Mabray, 1959); etc.

DORSEY, ANNA H[anson McKenney] (Dec. 12, 1815–Dec. 26, 1896); b. Georgetown, D.C. Poet, novelist. *The Student of Blenheim Forest* (1847); *Flowers of Love and Memory* (poems, 1849); *Woodreve Manor (1852); Adrift* (1887); etc.

DORSEY, GEORGE AMOS (Feb. 6, 1868–Mar. 29, 1931); b. Hebron, O. Educator, museum curator, author. *Why We Behave Like Human Beings* (1925); *The Nature of Man* (1927); *The Evolution of Charles Darwin* (1927); *Man's Own Show: Civilization* (1931). Curator, Field Museum of Natural History, Chicago, 1898–1915; dept. anthropology, University of Chicago, 1905-15.

DORSEY, SARAH ANNE ELLIS (Feb. 16, 1829-July 4, 1879); b. Natchez, Miss. Author. Pen name "Filia." *Lucia Dare* (1867); *Agnes Graham* (1869); *Athalie; or, A Southern Villeggiatura* (1872); *Panola: A Tale of Louisiana* (1877). She assisted Jefferson Davis in writing *The Rise and Fall of the Confederate Government*, 2v. (1881).

Dorval; or, The Speculator. Novel by Sarah Sayward Barrell (1801).

Dorymates: A Tale of the Fishing Banks. By Kirk Munroe (1890). Account of the fishing boats out of Gloucester, Mass.

DOS PASSOS, JOHN R[oderigo] (Jan. 14, 1896–Sept. 28, 1970); b. Chicago, Ill. Novelist. *One Man's Initiation—1917* (1920); *Three Soldiers* (1921); *A Pushcart at the Curb* (poems, 1922); *Streets of Night* (1923); *Manhattan Transfer* (1925); *Orient Express* (1927); *The 42nd Parallel (1930); 1919* (1932); *In All Countries* (1934); *The Big Money* (1936); *Journeys Between Wars* (1938); *Adventures of a Young Man* (1939); *The Ground We Stand On* (1941); *Number One* (1943); *State of the Nation* (1944); *Tour of Duty* (1946); *The Grand Design* (1948); *The Prospect Before Us* (1950); *Chosen Country* (1951); *District of Columbia* (1952); *The Head and Heart of Thomas Jefferson* (1954); *Most Likely to Succeed* (1954); *The Theme Is Freedom* (1956); *The Men Who Made Our Nation* (1957); *The Great Days* (1958); *Prospects of A Golden Age* (1959); *Midcentury* (1961); *Brazil on the Move* (1963); *Occasions and Protests* (1964); *World in a Glass* (1966); *The Shackles of Power* (1966); *The Portugal Story* (1969); etc. *See* John H. Wrenn's *John Dos Passos* (1962).

DOTY, DOUGLAS ZABRISKIE (Oct. 15, 1874–Feb. 20, 1935); b. New York City. Editor. Lit. adviser, the *Century Magazine,* 1902–14; editor, 1914–17; *Cosmopolitan* magazine, 1917–18; lit. adviser, Harper & Bros., after 1918.

Double Helix, The. By James D. Watson (1968). A personal account of the discovery of the structure of DNA by a Nobel Prize recipient. Watson was awarded the prize with Francis Crick and Maurice Wilkins in 1962 for achievements in medicine and physiology.

DOUBLEDAY, FRANK NELSON (Jan. 8, 1862–Jan. 30, 1934); b. Brooklyn N.Y. Publisher. Joined publishing firm of Charles Scribner's Sons in 1877. Refounded and edited *The Book Buyer,* and became manager of *Scribner's Magazine* in 1886. In 1897 joined S. S. McClure in founding the publication house of Doubleday & McClure Company. In 1900 organized, with Walter Hines Page, the Doubleday, Page & Co., which was merged with the George H. Doran Company in 1927, to form the Doubleday, Doran Company. Founded *The World's Work,* 1900; *Country Life in America,* 1901; and *The Garden Magazine,* 1905. His wife, Neltje De Graff Doubleday (1865–1918), was the author of several books on birds and gardening.

DOUBLEDAY, RUSSELL (May 26, 1872–June 14, 1949); b. Brooklyn, N.Y. Editor, author. *A Gunner Aboard the "Yankee"* (1898); *Cattle Ranch to College* (1899); *A Year in a Yawl* (1901); *Stories of Inventors and Engineers* (1904); *Long Island* (1939); *Tree Neighbors* (1940). Editor, Doubleday, Page & Co.

Doubleday & Co. Publishers. New York. Founded in 1927. Doubleday & McClure Company founded by Frank Nelson Doubleday and Samuel Sidney McClure in 1897. Doubleday joined with Walter Hines Page in 1899 to form Doubleday, Page & Co. Moved plant to Garden City, L.I., in 1910. Returned to New York in 1938 where editorial and sales offices are now located. Plant in Garden City became Country Life Press Corporation. Garden City Publishing Company, a subsidiary, formed in 1920. The George H. Doran Company was founded in New York in 1908 and merged with Doubleday in 1927 as Doubleday, Doran & Co. John T. Sargent is president and Samuel S. Vaughan is publisher. Departments and subsidiaries of the firm are Anchor Books, Crime Club, Dolphin Books, Hanover House, Image Books, Made Simple Books. Runs many book clubs, such as Literary Guild, Bargain Book Club, Mystery Book Club, Mainstream Book Club, Cook Book Club. Made the first American copyright agreement with the Soviet Union in 1970.

Doubleday Encyclopedia. See *Grolier Encyclopedia.*

Double-Dealer. New Orleans, La, Monthly. Literary review. Founded 1921 to counteract the romantic trend of Southern literature. Contributors were Ernest Hemingway, William Faulkner, Sherwood Anderson, Jean Toomer, Hart Crane, Edmund Wilson, and others. Discontinued 1926.

DOUGHERTY, RICHARD (Aug. 7, 1921–); b. in New York. Novelist. *A Summer World* (1960); *Duggan* (1962); *The Commissioner* (1962); *Fair Game for Lovers,* (1964); etc.

DOUGLAS, ALICE MAY (June 28, 1865–Jan. 6, 1943); b. Bath, Me. Lecturer, poet. *Phlox* (1888); *Guns without Polish* (1890); *The Pine and the Palm; Peace Bells;* etc.

DOUGLAS, AMANDA M[innie] (July 14, 1831–July 18, 1916); b. New York City. Author. *In Trust* (1866); the *Kathi* series, 6v. (1868–70); the *Little Girl* series, 10v. (1897–1909); *Larry* (1897); *Red House Children at Grafton* (1913); etc.

DOUGLAS, CHARLES HENRY (June 10, 1861–Apr. 11, 1954); b. Liberty, N.Y. Editor, author. *The Government of the People in the State of Connecticut* (1896). Editor-in-chief, D.C. Heath & Co., 1895–1925.

DOUGLAS, CHARLES WINFRED (Feb. 15, 1867–Jan. 18, 1944); b. Oswego, N.Y. Episcopal clergyman, musician, author. *The Midnight Mass* (poems, 1933); *Church Music in History and Practice* (1937). Musical editor: *The Order of Matins* (1916); *The American Missal* (1931); *The Plainsong Psalter* (1932); etc.

DOUGLAS, CLARENCE BROWN (Oct. 19, 1864–); b. Jefferson City, Mo. Editor, author. *Prominent Men of Indian Territory* (1904); *A Book of Verse* (1920); *History of Tulsa* (1921); *Life of Tams Bixby* (1928).

DOUGLAS, GEORGE WILLIAM (Apr. 8, 1863-Feb. 17, 1945); b. Liberty, N.Y. Editor, author. *The Many Sided Roosevelt* (1907); *The American Book of Days* (1937). Assoc. editor, *Youth's Companion,* 1902-14; *Philadelphia Public Ledger,* 1914–15; *Evening Public Ledger,* 1915–34; lit. editor, 1917-24.

Douglas, Hudson. Pen name of Robert Aitken.

DOUGLAS, LLOYD C[assel] (Aug. 27, 1877–Feb. 13, 1951); b. Columbia City, Ind. Congregational clergyman, novelist. *Wanted—A Congregation* (1920); *The Minister's Everyday Life* (1924); *These Sayings of Mine* (1926); *Those Disturbing Miracles* (1927); *Magnificent Obsession* (1929); *Forgive Us Our Trespasses* (1932); *Precious Jeopardy* (1933); *Green Light* (1935); *White Banners* (1936); *Home for Christmas* (1937); *Disputed Passage* (1939); *Dr. Hudson's Secret Journal* (1939); *Invitation to Live* (1940); *The Robe* (1942); *The Big Fisherman* (1948); *A Time to Remember* (1951); *The Living Faith* (1955). *See* Edmund Wilson's *Classics and Commercials* (1951).

Douglas, Marian. Pen name of Annie Douglas Green Robinson.

DOUGLAS, MARJORY STONEMAN (Apr. 7, 1890–); b. Minneapolis, Minn. Author. *The Gallows Gate* (1928); *The Everglades: River of Grass* (1947); *Road to the Sun* (1952); *Freedom River* (1953); *Hurricane* (1958); *Alligator Crossing* (1959); etc.

DOUGLAS, PAUL HOWARD (Mar. 26, 1892–); b. Salem, Mass. Former U.S. Senator, educator, author. *American Apprenticeship and Industrial Education* (1921); *Wages and the Family* (1925); *Real Wages in the United States, 1890-1926* (1930); *Ethics in Government* (1952); *America in the Market Place* (1966); etc. U.S. senator, 1948–66; faculty, New School of Social Research, since 1966.

DOUGLAS, STEPHEN A[rnold] (Apr. 23, 1813–June 3, 1861); b. Brandon, Vt. Statesman, orator. *See* his *Autobiography,* ed. by Frank E. Stevens, in the *Journal* of the Illinois State Historical Society, Oct., 1912. Congressman, 1843–47;

U.S. senator, 1847–61. See *Political Speeches and Debates of Abraham Lincoln and Stephen A. Douglas, 1854-1861,* ed. by Alonzo T. Jones (1895); Allen Johnson's *Stephen A. Douglas* (1908); Clark E. Carr's *Stephen A. Douglas* (1909); Henry P. Willis's *Stephen A. Douglas* (1910); Louis Howland's *Stephen A. Douglas* (1920); Gerald M. Caper's *Stephen Douglas: Defender of the Union* (1959); George F. Milton's *Eve of Conflict* (1963).

DOUGLAS, THEODORE WAYLAND (May 29, 1897– March 25, 1961); b. Indianapolis, Ind. Author. *Border Range* (1942); *The Strong Shall Hold* (1943); *Way of the Strong* (1944); *Tropical Maze* (1948); etc.

DOUGLAS, WILLIAM O[rville] (Oct. 16, 1898–); b. Maine, Minn. Supreme Court justice, author. *Of Men and Mountains* (1950); *Strange Lands and Friendly People* (1951); *Beyond the High Himalayas* (1952); *North from Malaya* (1953); *An Almanac of Liberty* (1954); *We the Judges* (1956); *Russian Journey* (1956); *The Right of the People* (1958); *Exploring the Himalaya* (1958); *West of the Indus* (1958); *America Challenged* (1960); *My Wilderness: The Pacific West* (1960); *My Wilderness: East to Katahdin* (1961); *A Living Bill of Rights* (1961); *Muir of the Mountain* (1961); *Democracy's Manifesto* (1962); *Points of Rebellion* (1969); *International Dissent* (1970).

DOUGLASS, FREDERICK (Feb. 1817?–Feb. 20, 1895); b. Tuckahoe, Md. Orator, statesman, author. *The Narrative of the Life of Frederick Douglass, an American Slave* (1845); *My Bondage and My Freedom* (1855); *Life and Times of Frederick Douglass* (1881). See Alain Locke's *Frederick Douglass* (1935); Booker T. Washington's *Life of Frederick Douglass* (1907); *Life and Writings,* 4v., ed. by P. S. Foner (1965).

DOUGLASS, TRUMAN BARTLETT (July 15, 1901–); b. Grinnell, Ia. Congregationalist clergyman, author. *Mission to America* (1951); *Preaching and the New Reformation* (1956); *Why Go to Church?* (1957).

DOUNCE, HARRY ESTY (Apr. 6, 1889–Mar. 26, 1957); b. Syracuse, N.Y. Editor. Book editor, *New York Sun,* 1919–20; *New York Evening Post,* 1926–28; on editiorial staff, *Liberty* magazine, 1928–47.

DOVE, DAVID JAMES (c. 1696–Apr., 1769); b. Portsmouth, England. Educator, pamphleteer. *Labour in Vain* (1757); *The Lottery* (1758); *The Quaker Unmask'd* (under pen name, "Philopatrius," 1764); etc.

Dover Publications, Inc. New York. Publishers. Founded 1945. Specializes in paperback reprints of authoritative works in science, natural history, music, art, popular culture. Also issues recordings.

DOW, DOROTHY [Minerva] (1899–); b. Lockport, Ill. Poet. *Black Babylon* (1924); *Will-o'-the-Wisp* (1925); *Dark Glory* (biography of Poe, 1931); *Time and Love* (poems, 1942); *Sunday Morning* (1947).

DOW, GEORGE FRANCIS (Jan. 7, 1868–June 5, 1936); b. Wakefield, N.H. Antiquarian, author. *The Sailing Ships of New England,* 3 series (1 & 2 with John Robinson, 1922–28); *The Pirates of the New England Coast, 1630–1730* (with John Henry Edmonds, 1923); *Whale Ships and Whaling* (1925); *Slave Ships and Slaving* (1927); *The Arts and Crafts in New England* (1927); *Everyday Life in the Massachusetts Bay Colony* (1935). Director and editor of publications, Essex Institute, Salem, Mass., 1898–1918; Museum of the Society for the Preservation of New England antiquities, Boston, 1919–36.

DOW, LORENZO (Oct. 16, 1777–Feb. 2, 1834); b. Coventry, Conn. Eccentric preacher, author. *Biography and Miscellany* (1834); *History of a Cosmopolite* (1851); etc.

DOW, MOSES A. (1810–June 22, 1886); b. Littleton, N.H. Publisher. Founder, *The Waverly Magazine,* Boston, 1850, which catered to amateur authors and made him a fortune. The magazine ceased publication in 1908.

DOWD, EMMA C. (d. Dec. 21, 1938); b. Meriden, Conn. Author. The *Polly* series, 4v. (1912–21); *The Owl and the Bobolink* (1914); *Doodles, the Sunshine Boy* (1915); etc.

DOWDEY, CLIFFORD [Shirley], JR. (Jan. 23, 1904–); b. Richmond, Va. Novelist. *Bugles Blow No More* (1938); *Gamble's Hundred* (1939); *Sing for a Penny* (1941); *Experiment in Rebellion* (1946); *Weep for My Brother* (1950); *Jasmine Street* (1952); *The Proud Retreat* (1953); *The Land They Fought For: The Story of the South as the Confederacy, 1832-1865* (1955); *The Great Plantation* (1957); *The Death of a Nation* (1958); *Lee's Last Campaign* (1960); *Seven Days: The Emergence of Lee* (1964); *The Virginian Dynasties* (1969).

DOWE, JENNIE ELIZABETH TUPPER (Dec. 11, 1845– Mar. 6, 1919); b. Wilbraham, Mass. Poet. *Purty Molly Rhu* (1902); *Song of the Mountain* (1913); *The Minute Men* (1915); etc.

"Down by the Old Mill Stream." Song by Tell Taylor.

"Down Went McGinty to the Bottom of the Sea." Song by Joe Flynn.

Down-Easters, The. Novel of Maine life by John Neal (1833).

DOWNER, ALAN SEYMOUR (July 15, 1912–); b. Syracuse, N.Y. Educator. *British Drama* (1950); *Fifty Years of American Drama* (1951); *Recent American Drama* (1961); etc. Editor: *American Drama* (1960); *Theatre of Bernard Shaw* (1961); *The Eminent Tragedian: William Charles Macready* (1966); *American Theater Today* (1967); etc. Prof. English, Princeton University, since 1957.

DOWNES, ANNE MILLER (d. May 30, 1964); b. Utica, N.Y. Author. *Heartwood* (1945); *Mary Donovan* (1948); *The Eagle's Song* (1949); *The High Hills Calling* (1951); *The Pilgrim Soul* (1952); *Speak to Me, Brother* (1954); *The Captive Rider* (1956); *Kate Cavanaugh* (1958); *Natalia* (1960); *No Parade for Mrs. Greenia* (1962); etc.

DOWNES, [Edwin] OLIN (Jan. 27, 1886–Aug. 22, 1955); b. Evanston, Ill. Music critic. *The Lure of Music* (1918); *Symphonic Broadcasts* (1932); *Ten Operatic Masterpieces, from Mozart to Prokofieff* (1952); etc. Music critic, *Boston Post,* 1906–24; *New York Times,* 1924–55.

DOWNES, WILLIAM HOWE (Mar. 1, 1854–Feb. 19, 1941); b. Derby, Conn. Art critic. Author. *Life and Works of Winslow Homer* (1911); *John S. Sargent: His Life, and Work* (1925); etc. Art critic *Boston Transcript,* 1883–1922.

DOWNEY, FAIRFAX DAVIS (Nov. 28, 1893–); b. Salt Lake City, Utah. Journalist, author. *A Comic History of Yale* (1924); *Father's First Two Years* (1925); *When We Were Rather Older* (1926); *Young Enough to Know Better* (1927); *The Grande Turke, Suleyman the Magnificent* (1929); *Burton, Arabian Nights Adventurer* (1931); *Richard Harding Davis: His Day* (1933); *Portrait of an Era, as Drawn by C. D. Gibson* (1936); *Disaster Fighters* (1938); *Indian-Fighting Army* (1941); *Our Lusty Forefathers* (1947); *Dogs of Destiny* (1949); *Free and Easy* (1951); *Mascots* (1954); *The Shining Filly* (1954); *Sound of the Guns* (1956); *General Crook, Indian Fighter* (1957); *The Guns of Gettysburg* (1958), *Clash of Cavalry: The Battle of Brandy Station* (1959); *Famous Horses of the Civil War* (1959); *Indian Wars of the U.S. Army, 1776-1865* (1963); *Buffalo Soldiers in the Indian Wars* (1969); etc.

DOWNING, ANDREW JACKSON (Oct. 30, 1815–July 28, 1852); b. Newburgh, N.Y. Horticulturist, landscape gardener, essayist. *Cottage Residences* (1842); *Rural Essays* (1853); etc.

DOWNING, FANNY [Frances] MURDAUGH (1835– 1894); b. Portsmouth, Va. Novelist, poet. *Nameless* (1865); *Pluto* (poem, under pen name, "Frank Dashmore," 1867); etc.

DOWNING, [George] TODD (Mar. 29, 1902–); b. Atoka, Okla. Novelist. *Vultures in the Sky* (1935); *The Last Trumpet* (1937); *Night over Mexico* (1938); *The Lazy Lawrence Murders* (1941); etc.

Downing, J. Pen name of Charles Augustus Davis.

DOWNS, ROBERT BINGHAM (May 25, 1903–); b. Lenoir, N.C. Librarian, author. *The Story of Books* (1935); *Resources of Southern Libraries* (1938); *American Humor* (with Elizabeth C. Downs, 1938); *Resources of New York City Libraries* (1942); *American Library Resources* (1951); *Books That Changed the World* (1956); *Molders of the Modern Mind* (1961); *Famous Books since 1492* (1961); etc. Editor: *Library Specialization* (1941); *Union Catalogs in the United States* (1942); *First Freedom: Liberty and Justice in the World of Books and Reading* (1960); *Bibliography: Current State and Future Trends* (with Frances B. Jenkins, 1967). Director Library and Library School, prof. library science, University of Illinois, 1943–58; dean, library administration, since 1958.

DOWNS, SARAH ELIZABETH (Mrs. George Sheldon Downs) (June 5, 1843–deceased); b. Wrentham, Mass. Novelist. Pen name, "Mrs. Georgie Sheldon." Under married name: *Katherine's Sheaves* (1904); *Step by Step* (1906); *Redeemed* (1911); etc.; and under pen name: *Brownie's Triumph* (1877); *Earle Wayne's Nobility* (1880); *A True Aristocrat* (1882); *Geoffrey's Victory* (1888); *Edric's Legacy* (1892); *Dorothy's Jewels* (1900); etc.

Dow's Patent Sermons. Humorous sermons by "Dow, Jr." (Elbridge Gerry Paige, 1816–1859), which first appeared in the *New York Sunday Mercury* in 1840. They were published as *Short Patent Sermons* (1841), augmented to 2v. (1845), and finally as *Patent Sermons*, 4v. (1857).

DOYLE, EDWARD (b. 1854). Poet. *Cagliostro* (dramatic poem, 1882); *Moody Moments* (poems, 1888); *Laying the Hero to Rest* (poem, 1897); *The Haunted Temple, and Other Poems* (1905); *Ginevra* (1912); *Freedom, Truth and Beauty: Sonnets* (1921); *Gleams, Lyrics and Sonnets* (1921); etc.

DOYLE, HENRY GRATTAN (Sept. 22, 1889–Nov. 3, 1964); b. Somerville, Mass. Educator, editor. Author: *Spanish Studies in the United States* (1926); *A Bibliography of Rubén Darío* (1935); *George Ticknor* (1937); *Education and Its Backgrounds in the U.S. and Overseas* (1959); etc. Editor, *Hispania*, 1942–48. Prof. Romance languages, George Washington University, from 1930.

DOYLE, MARION; b. in Somerset Co., Pa. Lecturer, poet. *Strange Exodus* (1934).

DOYLE, MARTHA CLAIRE MacGOWAN (June 16, 1869–); b. Boston, Mass. Author. Pen name, "Martha James." *Little Miss Dorothy* (1900); *My Friend Jim* (1901); *Mint Julep* (1909); etc.

Dr. Latimer. Novel by Clara Louise Burnham (1893). Story of the Maine coast, chiefly Casco Bay. Dr. Latimer exerts a kindly influence on three orphans, Josephine, Helen, and Vernon Ivison, and helps straighten out their tangled love affairs.

DRACHMAN, BERNARD (June 27, 1861–Mar. 12, 1945); b. New York. Rabbi, Hebraist, author. *From the Heart of Israel* (1905); *Looking at America* (1934); *Unfailing Light: Memoirs of an American Rabbi* (1948); etc. With Jewish Theological Seminary, New York, 1887–1908; later with Yeshiva College, New York.

DRAGO, HARRY SINCLAIR (1888–). Novelist. Pen names, "Kirk Deming," "Will Ermine," "Bliss Lomax," "J. Wesley Putnam," "Grant Sinclair," "Stewart Cross." Under own name: *Suzanna* (1912); *Following the Grass* (1924); *Guardians of the Sage* (1932); *Stagecoach Kingdom* (1943); *The Buckskin Affair* (1958); *Fenced Off* (1959); *Red River Valley* (1962); *Outlaws on Horseback* (1964); *Great American Cattle Trails* (1965); *Many Beavers: The Story of a Cree*

Indian Boy (1967); *Steamboaters, from the Early Side-Wheelers to the Big Packets* (1967); *Roads to Empire, the Dramatic Conquest of the American West* (1968); *Notorious Ladies of the Frontier* (1969); etc. Under pen name "Kirk Deming": *Colt Lightnin'* (1938); etc. Under pen name, "Will Ermine": *Barbed-Wire Empire* (1937); *Boss of the Plains* (1940); *Buckskin Marshal* (1945); *Guns in the Night* (1957); etc. Under pen name "Bliss Lomax": *Closed Range* (1936); *Canyon of Golden Skulls* (1937); *Shadow Mountain* (1948); *Stranger with a Gun* (1957); etc. Under pen name "J. Wesley Putnam": *The Hidden Things* (1915); *Borrowed Reputations* (1928); etc. Under pen name "Grant Sinclair": *The Woman Thou Art* (1925); etc. Under pen name "Stewart Cross": *This Way to Hell* (1933); etc.

DRAKE, ALAN DAVIS (June 5, 1945–   ) b. New York. Poet. *Twenty-Two Plus Three* (1966); *Twenty-Five* (1967); *Eight Sketches of Change* (1970).

DRAKE, ALEXANDER WILSON (1843–Feb. 4, 1915); b. Westfield, N.J. director, collector, author. *Three Midnight Stories* (1916). Art director, *The Century Magazine* and *St. Nicholas.* Co-founder, The Grolier Club.

DRAKE, BENJAMIN (1795–Apr. 1, 1841); b. Mays Lick, Ky. Lawyer, editor, biographer. *The Life and Adventures of Black Hawk* (1838); *Tales and Sketches from the Queen City* (1838); *Life of Tecumseh, and of His Brother, the Prophet* (1841). Editor, *Cincinnati Chronicle*, 1826–34.

DRAKE, DANIEL (Oct. 20, 1785–Nov. 6, 1852); b. near Plainfield, N.J. Physician, scientist, author. *Notices Concerning Cincinnati* (1810); *Natural and Statistical View; or, Picture of Cincinnati and the Miami Country* (1815). See his *Letters,* edited by his son, Charles D. Drake, in *Pioneer Life in Kentucky* (1870); and E. D. Mansfield's *Life and Services of Daniel Drake* (1855); O. Juettner's *Daniel Drake and His Followers* (1909).

DRAKE, FRANCIS SAMUEL (Feb. 22, 1828–Feb 22, 1885); b. Northwood, N.H., son of Samuel Gardner Drake. Historian. *The Town of Roxbury* (1873); *Tea Leaves* (1884); *Indian History for Young Folks* (1885); etc. Editor: *Dictionary of American Biography* (1872).

DRAKE, JAMES FREDERICK (Sept. 13, 1863–Aug. 31, 1933); b. New York City. Dealer in rare books. With Dodd, Mead & Co., 1881–88; book collector, 1888–1900; with George H. Richmond, 1900–03; with J. W. Bouton, 1903–05. In 1905, he established his own business as The Association Book Co., which in 1911 became James F. Drake, Inc. Since his death, the business has been continued by his sons, Marston E. Drake and James H. Drake.

DRAKE, [John Gibbs] ST. CLAIR (Jan. 2, 1911–); b. Suffolk, Va. Educator, anthropologist. *Black Metropolis* (with Horace R. Cayton, 1945). Prof. sociology, Roosevelt College, Chicago, since 1954.

DRAKE, JOSEPH RODMAN (Aug. 17, 1795–Sept. 21, 1820); b. New York City. Critic, poet. *The Culprit Fay, and Other Poems* (1835). His best known poems are "The American Flag," "The Culprit Fay," "Bronx," and "Niagara." See Fitz-Greene Halleck; and *The Croaker Papers.* See also *The Life and Works of Joseph Rodman Drake,* ed. by Frank L. Pleadwell (1935).

DRAKE, SAMUEL ADAMS (Dec. 19, 1833–Dec. 4, 1905); b. Boston, Mass., son of Samuel Gardner Drake. Historian. *Old Landmarks and Historic Personages of Boston* (1873); *Nooks and Corners of the New England Coast* (1875); *The Heart of the White Mountains* (1882); *A Book of New England Legends and Folk Lore* (1884); *The Making of New England, 1580–1643* (1886); *The Making of the Great West, 1512–1883* (1887); *The Making of the Ohio Valley States, 1660–1837* (1894); *The Young Vigilantes* (1904); etc. See S. G. Drake's *Genealogical and Biographical Account of the Family of Drake* (1845).

DRAKE, SAMUEL GARDNER (Oct. 11, 1798–June 14, 1875); b. Pittsfield, N.H. Bookseller, bibliophile, antiquarian, historian. *The History and Antiquities of Boston* (1856); *The Witchcraft Delusion in New England*, 3v. (1866). One of the Founders of the New-England Historic Genealogical Society, and editor of *The New-England Historical and Genealogical Register*, v. 1–15. Became a bookseller in 1824. Opened a shop in Cornhill, Boston, in 1830. He also published books, notably *Indian Biography* (1832); *Indian Captivities* (1839); *Book of the Indians* (1841).

DRAKE, WILLIAM A. (Dec 9, 1899–Oct. 28, 1965); b. Dayton, O. Editor, author. *Contemporary European Writers* (1928). Editor: *American Criticism* (1926). Foreign lit. editor, section of *New York Herald Tribune Books* (1924–27). Adapter of European plays, including *Grand Hotel* (1930); *Lysistrata* (1930).

Drake's Magazine. New York. Humorous magazine. Founded 1882, by John N. Drake. Expired 1893.

Drama. Chicago, Ill. Founded 1911. Edited successively by William Norman Guthrie, Charles Hubbard Sergel, Theodore Ballou Hinckley, and Albert E. Thompson. Renamed *The Drama Magazine*, 1930–31, expired 1931.

Drama League of America. Founded 1910, at Evanston, Ill. Merged 1929 with Church and Drama Association, and the American Theatre Association, to form the Church and Drama League of America.

Drama Review, The. New Orleans, La.; New York. Triennial. Founded 1957, successor to *Carleton Drama Review*, and published at Tulane University as *Tulane Drama Review*. Edited by Robert W. Corrigan. Moved to New York University as *The Drama Review*, edited by Richard Schechner and later Erika Munk.

Dramatic Index. Boston, Mass. Founded 1909 by F. W. Faxon. Annual subject index to articles about the theatre, actors, playwrights, synopses of plays, etc.

Dramatist. Easton, Pa. Quarterly. Founded 1909. Devoted to dramatic technology. Discontinued 1932.

Dramatists Guild of the Authors' League of America. New York. Founded 1921.

DRANSFIELD, JANE (Dec. 9, 1875–); b. Rochester, N.Y. Playwright. *The Lost Pleiad* (1918); *Blood O'Kings* (1924); *Joe: A Hudson Valley Play* (1923); *Marks upon a Stone* (poems, 1940); etc.

DRAPER, ANDREW SLOAN (June 21, 1848–Apr. 27, 1913); b. Westford, N.Y. Educator, author. *American Schools and American Citizenship* (1891); *Public School Pioneering in New York and Massachusetts* (1892); *Holiday Papers* (1912); etc. President, University of Illinois, 1894–1904. *See* Harlan Hoyt Harner's *The Life and Work of Andrew Sloan Draper* (1934).

DRAPER, JOHN (Oct. 29, 1702–Nov. 29, 1762); b. Boston, Mass. Editor, publisher. Became editor, *Boston News-Letter*, Jan. 4, 1733. Printed Ames's *Almanack*.

DRAPER, JOHN WILLIAM (May 5, 1811–Jan. 4, 1882); b. Liverpool, England. Educator, physicist, historian. *History of the Intellectual Development of Modern Europe* (1863); *History of the American Civil War*, 3v. (1867–70); *History of the Conflict between Religion and Science* (1874); etc.

DRAPER, JOHN WILLIAM (July 23, 1893–); b. Hastings-on-Hudson, N.Y. Educator, philologist, author. *Poems* (1913); *Exotics* (1915); *William Mason* (1924); *The Funeral Elegy and the Rise of English Romanticism* (1929); *The Humors and Shakespeare's Characters* (1945); *The Twelfth Night of Shakespeare's Audience* (1949); *Tempo-Patterns of Shakespeare's Plays* (1957); *Stratford to Dogberry* (1961); etc. Prof. of English, University of West Virginia, since 1929. Editor, *The Colonnade*, 1913–17, 1921–25.

DRAPER, LYMAN COPELAND (Sept. 4, 1815–Aug. 26, 1891); b. in New York State. Historian, collector. *Madison. The Capital of Wisconsin* (1857); *King's Mountain and Its Heroes* (1881). As Secretary of the Wisconsin State Historical Society, 1854–86, he built up one of the finest collections of Western manuscripts in existence. He bequeathed his private collection to that society. He obtained as librarian Daniel Steel Durrie (q.v.).

DRAPER, RICHARD (Feb. 24, 1726/7–June 5, 1774); b. Boston, Mass. Printer, editor. Published *The Boston Weekly News-Letter and New England Chronicle*, and changed its title on Apr. 7, 1763, to *The Massachusetts Gazette and Boston News-Letter*. It was continued by his widow until it was suspended on Feb. 22, 1776.

DRAPER, THEODORE (Sept. 11, 1912–   ). Author. *The Six Week's War* (1944); *The Roots of American Communism* (1957); *Castro's Revolution: Myths and Realities* (1962); *Castroism, Theory and Practice* (1965); *Abuse of Power* (1967); *The Rediscovery of Black Nationalism* (1970).

Drayne, George. Pen name of Johnston McCulley.

DRAYTON, GRACE GEBBIE (Oct. 14, 1877–Jan. 31, 1936); b. Philadelphia, Pa. Illustrator. Created several comic strips for newspapers, including "Toodles and Pussy Pumpkins," "Dimples," "Pussy Cat Princess," "The Campbell Kids," "Dolly Dingle," "Bobby Blake," "Dolly Drake," "Peek-a-Boo Dollies," etc. Illustrated many children's books.

Dream Children. By Horace E. Scudder (1863). A make-believe world in which children talk to flowers, birds, and animals, one in which inanimate objects take on human attributes, where fact and fancy mingle, with always the ghost of unattainable ideals haunting the background.

Dream Life. Essays by "Ik Marvel" (Donald G. Mitchell) (1851). Romantic musings over life, love, and kindred topics.

"Dreaming in the Trenches." Civil War poem by William Gordon McCabe (1864).

Dred: A Tale of the Great Dismal Swamp. Novel by Harriet Beecher Stowe (1856).

DREIER, THOMAS (May 5, 1884–); b. near Durand, Wis. Editor, author. *Devil of Fear* (1910); *Vagabond Trail* (1913); *The Mountain Road* (1935); *Men—and the Power of Print* (1936); *We Human Chemicals* (1948); etc.

DREIKURS, RUDOLF (1897–); b. Vienna. Psychiatrist. *The Challenge of Marriage* (1946); *The Challenge of Parenthood* (1948); *Character, Education and Spiritual Values in an Anxious Age* (1952); *Psychology in the Classroom* (1957); *Children: The Challenge* (with Vicki Soltz, 1964); *Logical Consequences, A New Approach to Discipline* (1968).

Dreiser, Paul. See Paul Dresser.

DREISER, THEODORE (Aug. 27, 1871–Dec. 28, 1945); b. Terre Haute, Ind. Journalist, author. *Sister Carrie* (1900); *Jennie Gerhardt* (1911); *The Financier* (1912); *A Traveller at Forty* (1913); *The Titan* (1914); *The "Genius"* (1915); *Plays of the Natural and the Supernatural* (1916); *A Hoosier Holiday* (1916); *Free, and Other Stories* (1918); *The Hand of the Potter* (1918); *Hey Rub-a-Dub-Dub—A Book of Essays and Philosophy* (1920); *A Book About Myself* (1922); *The Color of a Great City* (1923); *An American Tragedy* (1925); *Moods* (poems, 1926); *Dreiser Looks at Russia* (1928); *A Gallery of Women*, 2v. (1929); *My City* (1929); *Epitaph* (1929); *Tragic America* (1931); *Thoreau* (1939); *America Is Worth Saving* (1941); *The Bulwark* (1946); *The Stoic* (1947); *The Tobacco Man: A Novel Based on Notes by Theodore Dreiser and Hy Kraft* (1965). *See* Vrest Orton's *Dreiserana* (1929); F. O. Matthiessen's *Theodore Dreiser* (1951); *Letters of Theodore Dreiser*, ed., Robert H. Elias (1959); W. A. Swanberg's *Dreiser* (1965); Marguerite Tjader's *Theodore Dreiser: A New Dimension* (1965).

DRESBACH, GLENN WARD (Sept. 9, 1889–June 27, 1968); b. Lanark, Ill. Poet. *The Road to Everywhere* (1916); *In the Paths of the Wind* (1918); *Morning, Noon and Night* (1920); *In Colors of the West* (1922); *Enchanted Mesa, and Other Poems* (1924); *Cliff Dwellings, and Other Poems* (1926); *Stardust and Stone* (1928); *This Side of Avalon* (1928); *The Wind in the Cedars* (1930); *Selected Poems* (1931); *Collected Poems (1914–48)* (1950); etc.

DRESSER, DAVIS (1904–). Author. Writes under pen name "Brett Halliday." *The Corpse Came Calling* (1942); *Marked for Murder* (1945); *Dead Man's Diary* (1948); *One Night with Nora* (1953); *The Blonde Cried Murder* (1956); *Die Like a Dog* (1959); *Murder Takes No Holiday* (1960); *The Careless Corpse* (1961); *The Body Came Back* (1963); *A Redhead for Mike Shayne* (1964); etc.

DRESSER, HORATIO WILLIS (Jan. 15, 1866–Mar. 30, 1954); b. Yarmouth, Me. Psychologist, author. *The Power of Silence* (1895); *The Philosophy of the Spirit* (1908); *Handbook of the New Thought* (1917); *A History of the New Thought Movement* (1919); *Ethics in Theory and Application* (1925); *A History of Ancient and Medieval Philosophy* (1926); *A History of Modern Philosophy* (1928); *Knowing and Helping People* (1933); etc.

DRESSER, PAUL (1857–1911); b. Terre Haute, Ind., brother of Theodore Dreiser. Song writer. His best-known song is "On the Banks of the Wabash Far Away" (1897).

DRESSLER, MARIE (Nov. 9, 1873–July 28, 1934); b. Ontario, Canada. Actress, author. *The Life Story of an Ugly Duckling* (1924); *My Own Story As Told to Mildred Harrington* (1934).

DREW, JOHN (Nov. 13, 1853–July 9, 1927); b. Philadelphia, Pa. Actor, author. *My Years on the Stage* (1922). His mother, Mrs. John Drew (1820–1897), was an actress and theatre manager, conducting the Arch Street Theatre in Philadelphia for many years, beginning in 1862. He wrote the introduction to her *Autobiographical Sketch* (1899). The elder John Drew (1827–1862) managed the Arch Street Theatre until his death. *See* Montrose J. Moses's *Famous Actor-Families in America* (1906).

DREWRY, [Guy] CARLETON (May 21, 1901–); b. Stevensburg, Va. Poet. *Proud Horns* (1933); *The Sounding Summer* (1948); *A Time of Turning* (1951); *The Writhen Wood* (1953); *Cloud above Clocktime* (1957); etc.

DREWRY, JOHN ELDRIDGE (June 4, 1902–); b. Griffin, Ga. Educator, author. *Some Magazines and Magazine Makers* (1924); *Concerning the Fourth Estate* (1938); *Contemporary American Magazines* (1938); *Book Reviewing* (1945). Editor: *Journalism in the Mid-Century* (1950); *Journalism Is Communications* (1954); *The What, Why, and How of Communications* (1958); *Better Journalism for a Better Tomorrow* (1963); *Communications Cartography* (1964); *Higher Ground for Journalism* (1965); *Journalistic Escalation* (1968); etc. Prof. journalism, University of Georgia, since 1930; dean, 1940–69.

DREXLER, ROSALYN. Playwright, author. *I Am the Beautiful Stranger* (1965); *Home Movies* (1967); *The Line of Least Existence* (1967); *One or Another* (1970); etc.

D'ri and I. Novel of the War of 1812, by Irving Bacheller (1901). "D'ri" was the nickname of Darius Olen, a courageous and brawny woodsman. Ramon Bell, the son of his employer, is his special charge and he looks after him in many a thrilling war adventure.

"Drifting." Poem by Thomas Buchanan Read (1859).

DRIGGS, HOWARD ROSCOE (Aug. 8, 1873–Feb. 17, 1963); b. Pleasant Grove, Utah. Educator, author. *Wild Roses* (1915); *Our Living Language* (1920); *Deadwood Gold* (with George W. Stokes, 1925); *The Texas Ranger* (with James B.

Gillett, 1927); *The Pioneer Photographer* (with William H. Jackson, 1929); *Living English* (1935); *The Pony Express Goes Through* (1935); *Westward America* (1942); *Ben the Wagon Boy* (1944); *Mormon Trail* (1947); *Pitch Pine Tales* (1951); *The Old West Speaks* (1956); *Red Feather's Homecoming* (with Enoch George Payne, 1963); etc. Co-author of numerous other books on the West and frontier life. English education department, New York University, 1927–42.

DRIGGS, LAURENCE LA TOURETTE (Dec. 1, 1876–May 26, 1945); b. Saginaw, Mich. Aviator, author. *Arnold Adair* (1917); *The Golden Book of Aviation* (1920); *Secret Air Service* (1930); *The Secret Squadron* (1931); *Flight* (1933); etc.

DRINKER, ANNA (b. Dec. 3, 1827–); b. Philadelphia, Pa. Poet. Pen name "Edith May." Author. *Poems by Edith May* (1862); *Tales and Verses for Children* (1855).

Drinkwater, Jennie M[aria]. See Jennie M. Drinkwater Conklin.

DRISCOLL, CHARLES BENEDICT (Oct. 19, 1885–Jan. 15, 1951); b. Witchita, Kan. Editor, lecturer, author. *Doubloons: The Story of Buried Treasure* (1930); *Driscoll's Book of Pirates* (1934); *The Life of O. O. McIntyre* (1938); *Pirates Ahoy!* (1941); *Kansas Irish* (1943); *Country Jake* (1946). Author of syndicated column "New York Day by Day," from 1938, a column started by O. O. McIntyre; syndicated stories "Pirates Ahoy," 1927–38; etc. Executive editor, McNaught's Syndicate, 1925–38.

DRISCOLL, CLARA (Apr. 2, 1881–July 17, 1945); b. St. Mary's, Tex. Novelist. *The Girl of La Gloria* (1905); *In the Shadow of the Alamo* (1906).

DRISCOLL, JOSEPH (Jan. 5, 1902–May 7, 1954); b. St. Louis, Mo. Journalist, author. *Dock Walloper* (with Richard Joseph Butler, 1933); *War Discovers Alaska* (1943); *Pacific Victory* (1945). With *New York Herald Tribune,* 1930–45.

DRISCOLL, LOUISE (Jan. 15, 1875–July 24, 1957); b. Poughkeepsie, N.Y. Poet. *The Garden of the West* (1922); *Garden Grace* (1924).

"Driving Home the Cows." Poem by Kate Putnam Osgood, which appeared in *Scribner's Monthly* (1865).

Droch. Pen name of Robert Bridges.

DROMGOOLE, WILL[iam] ALLEN (Miss) (d. Sept. 1, 1934); b. Murfreesboro, Tenn. Editor, story-writer. *The Heart of Old Hickory, and Other Stories of Tennessee* (1895); *Harum-Scarum Joe* (1899); etc. Lit. editor, *Nashville Daily Banner.*

"Drone, The." Essay department in the *New York Magazine,* 1790–97.

Drop Shot. Pen name used by George Washington Cable in the New Orleans *Picayune.*

DROUGHT, JAMES [William] (Nov. 4, 1931–); b. Aurora, Ill. Publisher, author. *The Gypsy Moths* (1956); *Poems* (1958); *The Secret* (1963); *Mover* (1964); *Memories of a Humble Man* (1964); *The Enemy* (1964); *Drugoth* (1965); *The Master* (1968); etc. Chairman of the board and pres., Skylight Press, since 1963.

DRUCKER, PETER F[erdinand] (Nov. 19, 1909–); b. Vienna. Management consultant, educator, author. *The End of Economic Man* (1939); *The Future of Industrial Man* (1942); *Concept of the Corporation* (1946); *The New Society* (1950); *Practice of Management* (1954); *America's Next Twenty Years* (1957); *The Landmarks of Tomorrow* (1959); *Managing for Results* (1962); *The Effective Executive* (1967); *The Age of Discontinuity* (1969); etc. Prof. philosophy and politics, Bennington College, 1942–49; prof. management, New York University, since 1950.

Druid, The. Essays on "Americanisms," etc., by John Witherspoon, in the *Pennsylvania Journal and the Weekly Advertiser* (1781). The word "Americanism" was coined by Witherspoon in the fifth essay of the *Druid* series.

Drums. Novel by James Boyd (1925). Story of Johnny Fraser, who served during the Revolution with John Paul Jones and General Morgan.

Drums Along the Mohawk. Novel by Walter D. Edmonds (1936). Story of a Mohawk Valley farm during the Indian forays of the American Revolution.

Drum-Taps. Poems by Walt Whitman (1865). Most copies contain *Sequel to Drum-Taps . . . When Lilacs Last in the Door-Yard Bloom'd, and Other Poems* (1865–66). The latter contains the well-known poem of Lincoln, "O Captain! My Captian!"

Drunkard; or, The Fallen Saved, The. Play by William H. Smith (prod. 1844). Most popular temperance play of its day.

DRURY, ALLEN [Stuart] (Sept. 2, 1918–); b. Houston, Tex. Author. *Advise and Consent* (1959); *A Shade of Difference* (1962); *That Summer* (1965); *Three Kids in a Cart* (1965); *Capable of Honor* (1966); *A Very Strange Society* (1967); *Preserve and Protect* (1968); *The Throne of Saturn* (1971).

DRURY, CLIFFORD MERRILL (Nov. 7, 1897–); b. Early, Ia. Presbyterian clergyman, educator, biographer. *Henry Harmon Spalding, Pioneer of Old Oregon* (1936); *Marcus Whitman, M.D., Pioneer and Martyr* (1937); *Mary and Elkanah Walker* (1940); *A Tepee in His Front Yard* (1949); *Presbyterian Panorama* (1952); *Diary of Titian Peale* (1957); *The Diaries and Letters of Henry H. Spalding and Asa Bowen Smith* (1958); *The First White Women over the Rockies,* 3v. (1963–66); *William Anderson Scott, No Ordinary Man* (1967); *Rudolph James Wigg* (1968); etc. Prof. San Francisco Theological Seminary, 1938–63.

DRURY, FRANCIS KEESE WYNKOOP (Feb. 9, 1878– Sept. 6, 1954); b. Ghent, N.Y. Librarian, author. *Viewpoints in Modern Drama* (1925); *Novels Too Good to Miss* (1926); *Book Selection* (1930); *Drury's Guide to Best Plays* (1953); etc. Brown University library, 1919–28; librarian, Nashville, Tenn., public library, 1931–46.

"Dry Salvages, The." Poem by T. S. Eliot published as part of *Four Quartets* (1943).

Dry September. Short story by William Faulkner (1931).

DU BOIS, CONSTANCE GODDARD; b. Zanesville, O. Author. *Martha Corey: A Tale of the Salem Witchcraft* (1890); *A Modern Pagan* (1895); *A Soul in Bronze* (1900); etc.

DU BOIS, GUY PÈNE (Jan. 4, 1884–July 18, 1958); b. Brooklyn, N.Y. Artist, art critic, author. *Artists Say the Silliest Things* (autobiography, 1940). Art critic, New York *American;* New York *Tribune;* New York *Evening Post.* Editor, *Arts and Decoration,* 1913–22.

DU BOIS, MARY CONSTANCE (Mar. 28, 1879–June 19, 1959); b. Philadelphia, Pa. Author. *Elinor Arden, Royalist* (1904); *White Fire* (1923); *Patsy of the Pet Shop* (1937); *Shadow Cove Mystery* (1940); etc.

DU BOIS, THEODORA McCORMICK (Mrs. Delafield Du Bois) (Sept. 14, 1890–); b. Brooklyn, N.Y. Educator, novelist. *The Devil's Spoon* (1930); *Diana's Feathers* (1935); *Diana Can Do It* (1937); *Death Wears a White Coat* (1938); *The Body Goes Round and Round* (1942); *Heroes in Plenty* (1945); *Devil and Destiny* (1948); *High Tension* (1950); *The Cavalier's Corpse* (1952); *The Listener* (1953); *The Emerald Crown* (1955); *The Love of Fingin O'Lea* (1957); *Rich Boy, Poor Boy* (1961); *Tiger Burning Bright* (1964); *High King's Daughter* (1965); etc. Foote School, New Haven, Conn.

DU BOIS, W[illiam] E[dward] B[urghardt] (Feb. 23, 1868– Aug. 29, 1963); b. Great Barrington, Mass. Educator, editor, author. *The Suppression of the African Slave Trade to the United States of America, 1638–1870* (1898); *The Souls of Black Folk* (1903); *John Brown* (1909); *Quest of the Silver Fleece* (1911); *The Negro* (1915); *Darkwater* (1920); *The Gift of Black Folk* (1924); *Dark Princess* (1928); *Black Reconstruction in America* (1935); *Dusk of Dawn* (autobiography, 1940); *Color and Democracy* (1945); *The World and Africa* (1947); *In Battle for Peace* (1952); *The Black Flame: A Trilogy* (1957–61). Editor, *Crisis* magazine, 1910–32; editor-in-chief, *Encyclopedia of the Negro,* 1933–45; editor, *Phylon Quarterly Review,* 1940–44.

DU BOIS, WILLIAM PÈNE (May 9, 1916–); b. Nutley, N.J. Illustrator, author. *Elisabeth, the Cow Ghost* (1936); *Giant Otto* (1936); *Otto at Sea* (1936); *Three Policemen* (1938); *The Great Geppy* (1940); *The Flying Locomotive* (1941); *The Twenty-One Balloons* (1947); *Peter Graves* (1950); *Bear Party* (1951); *Lion* (1956); *Otto in Texas* (1959); *Otto in Africa* (1961); *Porko Von Popbutton* (1969); etc.

DU BOSE, WILLIAM PORCHER (Apr. 11, 1836–Aug. 18, 1918); b. Winnsboro, S.C. Episcopal clergyman, educator, author. *High Priesthood and Sacrifice* (1908); *The Reason of Life* (1911); *Turning Points in My Life* (1912); etc. Prof., University of the South, Sewanee, Tenn., 1871–1918.

DU CHAILLU, PAUL BELLONI (July 31, 1835–Apr. 30, 1903); b. in France. African explorer, author. *Explorations and Adventures in Equatorial Africa* (1861); *Stories of the Gorilla Country* (1868); *Wild Life Under the Equator* (1869); *Lost in the Jungle* (1869); *The Country of the Dwarfs* (1871); *The Land of the Midnight Sun,* 2v. (1881); *The Viking Age* (1889); etc.

DU PONCEAU, PIERRE ÉTIENNE (June 3, 1760–Apr. 1, 1844); b. St. Martin, Ile de Ré, France. Historical writer. Known in America as Peter Stephen Du Ponceau, he came here in 1777 as secretary to Baron Steuben. Author: *A Discourse on the Necessity and the Means of Making Our National Literature Independent of That of Great Britain* (1834), one of the first American attempts at a comparative study of literature.

DU PUY, WILLIAM ATHERTON (Jan. 6. 1876–1941); b. Palestine, Tex. Conservationist, author. *Uncle Sam, Wonder Worker* (1913); *Uncle Sam, Detective* (1915); *Wonders of the Animal World* (1929); *The Nation's Forests* (1938); *The Baron of the Colorados* (1940); *Our Bird Friends and Foes* (1948); etc.

DUANE, WILLIAM (May 17, 1760–Nov. 24, 1835); b. near Lake Champlain, N.Y. Editor, author. *A Visit to Colombia in the Years 1822 & 1823* (1826). Editor, *The Aurora,* Philadelphia, 1798–1822.

DUBERMAN, MARTIN (Aug. 6, 1930–); b. New York. Historian, author. *Charles Francis Adams, 1807– 1886* (1962); *In White America* (1963); *James Russell Lowell* (1966); *The Uncompleted Past* (1969). Editor: *Anti-Slavery Vanguard* (1965). Prof. history, Princeton University, since 1967.

DUBOS, RENÉ [Jules] (Feb. 20, 1901–); b. Saint Brice, Fr. Bacteriologist. *The Bacterial Cell* (1945); *Louis Pasteur: Free Lance of Science* (1950); *The White Plague: Tuberculosis, Man and Society* (with J. P. Dwoos, 1952); *Mirage of Health* (1959); *The Torch of Life* (1962); *The Dreams of Reason: Science and Utopias* (1963); *Health and Disease* (1965); *So Human an Animal* (1968); *Man, Medicine and Environment* (1968); etc.

Dubuque Telegraph-Herald. Dubuque, Ia. Newspaper. Founded 1836, as the *Du Buque Visitor,* first newspaper in Iowa. Merged in 1854 with the *Dubuque Daily Herald,* founded 1851. The *Dubuque Daily Telegraph,* founded 1870, merged with the *Herald* in 1901. James Geladas is editor.

DUCHÉ, JACOB (Jan. 31, 1737/38–Jan. 3, 1798); b. Philadelphia, Pa. Clergyman, Revolutionary patriot, author. *Observations on a Variety of Subjects* (under pen name, "T. Caspipina," 1774); republished as *Caspipina's Letters* (1777), these letters appeared originally in the *Pennsylvania Packet*, 1772; *Discourses on Several Subjects,* 2v. (1779).

DUDLEY, ALBERTUS TRUE (Jan. 19, 1886–Feb. 11, 1955); b. Paris, N.Y. Author. The *Phillips Exeter* series of books for boys; etc., chiefly about hero athletes.

Dudley, Bide. See Walter Bronson Dudley.

DUDLEY, LAVINIA PRATT, B. New York. Editor. With *Encyclopaedia Britannica,* 1925–38; *Encyclopedia Americana,* since 1939, editor, 1948–59; exec. editor, 1959–64; American Peoples Encyclopedia since 1964.

DUDLEY, WALTER BRONSON (Sept. 8, 1877–Jan. 4, 1944); b. Minneapolis, Minn. Drama critic, playwright, humorist. Wrote under name "Bide Dudley." *Odds and Ends of 1917* (with John Godfrey and James Byrnes, prod. 1917); *Oh, Henry* (prod. 1920); *Bolivar Brown* (1921); etc. With New York *World-Telegram,* from 1914.

Duell, Sloan and Pearce. New York. Publishers. Founded 1939 by C. Halliwell Duell, Samuel Sloan, and Charles A. Pearce. Began publishing with Archibald MacLeish's *America Was Promises.* Acquired by Meredith Corporation.

DUER, WILLIAM ALEXANDER (Sept. 8, 1780–May 30, 1858); b. Rhinebeck, N.Y. Jurist, educator. *The Duties and Responsibilities of the Rising Generation* (1848); *New York As It Was* (1849); *Reminiscences of an Old Yorker* (1867); etc. President, Columbia College, 1829–42.

DUFFIELD, PITTS (Jan. 22, 1869–Aug. 12, 1938); b. Detroit, Mich. Publisher, author. *Blind Man's Bluff* (prod. 1918). Lit. editor, Charles Scribner's Sons, 1898–1902; secretary, Fox, Duffield & Co., 1903–05; president, Duffield & Co., 1905–18.

DUFFIELD, SAMUEL AUGUSTUS WILLOUGHBY (Sept. 24, 1843–May 12, 1887); b. Brooklyn, N.Y. Presbyterian clergyman, hymnologist, poet, author. *The Heavenly Land* (1867); *Warp and Woof* (1870); *English Hymns: Their Authors and History* (1886); *The Latin Hymn-Writers and Their Hymns* (unfinished at Duffield's death, but completed by Robert E. Thompson, 1889).

DUFFUS, R[obert] L[uther] (July 10, 1888–); b. Waterbury, Vt. Journalist, author. *Roads Going South* (1921); *The Coast of Eden* (1923); *The American Renaissance* (1928); *Tomorrow Never Comes* (1929); *Books: Their Place in a Democracy* (1930); *The Santa Fé Trail* (1930); *The Arts in American Life* (with Frederick P. Keppel, 1933); *Our Starving Libraries* (1933); *Jornada* (1935); *Democracy Enters College* (1936); *Night between the Rivers* (1937); *Lillian Wald, Neighbour and Crusader* (1938); *L. Emmett Holt: A Pioneer of a Children's Century* (with L. Emmett Holt, Jr., 1940); *The Innocents at Cedro* (1944); *The Valley and Its People* (1944); *Non-Scheduled Flight* (1950); *Williamstown Branch* (memoirs, 1958); *The Tower of Jewels* (1960); *Nostalgia, U.S.A.* (1963); *Adventure in Retirement* (1965); *West of the Dateline* (1968); *Jason Goose* (1969); etc. With *The New York Times* since 1937.

DUFFY, EDMUND (Mar. 1, 1899–Sept., 1962); b. Jersey City, N.J. Cartoonist. Illustrator for *Scribner's, Century, New York Tribune,* etc., 1918–23. Political cartoonist, *Baltimore Sun,* 1924–48.

DUGAN, ALAN (Feb. 12, 1923–   ); b. Brooklyn, N.Y. Poet. *Poems* (1961; National Book Award, 1962; Pulitzer Prize for poetry, 1962; *Poems 2* (1963); *Poems 3* (1967).

DUGANNE, AUGUSTINE JOSEPH HICKEY (1823–Oct. 20, 1884); b. Boston, Mass. Author. *Massachusetts* (1843);

Home Poems (1844); *The Lydian Queen* (prod. 1848); *Parnassus in Pillory* (under pen name, "Motley Manners," 1851); *Poetical Works* (1855); *Ballads of the War* (1865); *Camps and Prisons* (1865); etc.

DUGGER, SHEPERD M[onroe] (b. 1854). Author. *The Balsam Groves of Grandfather Mountain* (1892); *The War Trails of the Blue Ridge* (1932).

DUGUE, CHARLES OSCAR (May 1, 1821–Aug. 29, 1872); b. New Orleans, La. Poet, playwright, author. *Essais Poétiques* (1847); *Le Cygne où Mingo* (1852); *Homo: Poème Philosophique* (1872); etc.

DUJARDIN, ROSAMOND NEAL (July 22, 1902–March 27, 1963); b. Fairland, Ill. Author. *Practically Seventeen* (1949); *Wait for Marcy* (1950); *Boy Trouble* (1953); *Showboat Summer* (1955); *Wedding in the Family* (1958); *Someone to Count On* (1962); etc.

Duke of Stockbridge, The. Novel by Edward Bellamy (1879). Based on Shays's Rebellion.

Duke University Press. Durham, N.C. Founded 1922. Publishes scholarly works.

Dukesborough Tales, The. By Richard Malcolm Johnston (1871). Georgia stories.

DULLES, ALLEN [Welsh] (Apr. 7, 1893–1969); b. Watertown, N.Y. Government official. *Can America Stay Neutral?* (with Hamilton Fish Armstrong, 1939); *Germany's Underground* (1947); *The Craft of Intelligence* (1963); *The Secret Surrender* (1966); etc. Editor: *Great Spy Stories from Fiction* (1969).

DULLES, FOSTER RHEA (Jan. 24, 1900–); b. Englewood, N.J. Journalist, author. *The Old China Trade* (1930); *Eastward Ho!* (1931); *America in the Pacific* (1932); *Lowered Boats: A Chronicle of American Whaling* (1933); *Harpoon* (1935); *Forty Years of American-Japanese Relations* (1937); *Labor in America* (1949); *The American Red Cross: A History* (1950); *America's Rise to World Power* (1955); *The Imperial Years* (1956); *The United States Since 1865* (1959); *Americans Abroad* (1964); *The Imperial Years* (1966); *The United States Since 1865* (1969); etc. Prof. history, Ohio State University, since 1941.

DULLES, JOHN FOSTER (Feb. 25, 1888–May 24, 1959); b. Washington, D.C. Lawyer, government official. *War, Peace and Change* (1939); *War or Peace* (1950); *Spiritual Legacy,* ed. by Henry P. Van Dusen (1960). *See* Frank L. Kluckhohn's *Man Who Kept the Peace* (1968).

DUMMER, JEREMIAH (c. 1679–May 19, 1739); b. Boston, Mass. Colonial agent, author. *A Defense of the New-England Charters* (1721). Instrumental in founding Yale College, and donated several hundred books to form its first library. His father, Jeremiah Dummer (1645–1718) was a noted silversmith and portrait painter. *See* Henry Wilder Foote and H. F. Clarke's *Jeremiah Dummer, Craftsman and Merchant* (1935).

DUMOND, DWIGHT LOWELL (Aug. 27, 1895–); b. Kingston, O. Educator, author. *A History of the United States* (1942); *America in Our Time* (1947); *Antislavery Origins of the Civil War* (1959); *Antislavery: The Crusade for Freedom* (1961); *The Secession Movement, 1860–1861* (1963); *America's Shame and Redemption* (1965); etc. Editor: *Letters of James Gillespie Birney, 1831–1857,* 2v. (1938); etc. Prof. history, University of Michigan, since 1939.

DUNBAR, HELEN FLANDERS (1902–1959). Author. *Symbolism in Medieval Thought and Its Consummation in the Divine Comedy* (1929); *Emotions and Bodily Changes* (1935); *Mind and Body: Psychosomatic Medicine* (1947); *Your Child's Mind and Body* (1947).

DUNBAR, PAUL LAURENCE (June 27, 1872–Feb. 9, 1906); b. Dayton, O. Poet, author. *Oak and Ivy* (poems, 1892); *Majors and Minors* (poems, 1896); *Lyrics of Lowly Life* (1896); *The Uncalled* (1898); *The Love of Landry* (1900); *The Fanatics* (1901); *The Sport of the Gods* (1902); *Lyrics of Sunshine and Shadow* (1905); *The Complete Poems* (1913); See L. K. Wiggins's *The Life and Works of Paul Laurence Dunbar* (1907); Benjamin Griffith Brawley's *Paul Laurence Dunbar, Poet of His People* (1936); Virginia Cunningham's *Paul Laurence Dunbar and His Song* (1947).

DUNCALF, FREDERIC (Mar. 23, 1882–May 29, 1963); b. Lancaster, Wis. Educator, author. *A Brief History of the War* (1918); *Old Europe and Our Nation* (1932); etc. Co-author: *Story of Civilization* (1938); etc. Prof. history, University of Texas, 1914–50.

DUNCAN, DAVID (Feb. 17, 1913–); b. Billings, Mont. Author. *Flower of the Ranch* (play, 1939); *Remember the Shadow* (1944); *The Bramble Bush* (1948); *The Madrone Tree* (1949); *The Serpent's Egg* (1950); *Trumpet of God* (1956); *Yes, My Darling Daughters* (1959); *The Long Walk Home from Town* (1964); etc.

DUNCAN, ISADORA (May 27, 1878–Sept. 14, 1927); b. San Francisco, Cal. Dancer, author. *My Life* (1927); *The Art of the Dance* (1928).

DUNCAN, KUNIGUNDE (Mrs. Bliss Isely) (Aug. 29, 1886–); b. Nescatunga, Kan. Author. *The Land of Little Boys* (1930); *Love Cycle* (1932); *Blue Star* (1938); *Long, Long Ago* (1938); *Mentor Graham: The Man Who Taught Lincoln* (1944); *Tether: Una Grey's Story* (1953); *Lincoln's Teacher* (1958); *On Relief* (1966); *Half a Million Wild Horses* (1968); *In the Laboratory* (1968); etc.

DUNCAN, NORMAN (July 2, 1871–Oct. 18, 1916); b. Brantford, Ont., Canada. Journalist, educator, traveler, author. *Doctor Luke of the Labrador* (1904); *The Adventures of Billy Topsail* (1906); *The Cruise of the Shining Light* (1907); *Australian Byways* (1915); etc.

DUNCAN, ROBERT [Edward] (Jan. 7, 1919–); b. Oakland, Cal. Poet. *Heavenly City, Earthly City* (1947); *The Opening of the Field* (1960); *Roots and Branches* (1964); *Bending the Bow* (1968); *Derivations: Selected Poems, 1950–1956* (1969); *Heavenly City, Earthly City* (1970); etc.

DUNCAN, THOMAS WILLIAM (Aug. 15, 1905–); b. Casey, Ia. Novelist, poet. *O, Chautauqua* (1935); *Elephants at War* (poems, 1935); *We Pluck This Flower* (1937); *Gus the Great* (1947); *Ring Horse* (1952); *Virgo Descending* (1961); *The Labyrinth* (1967).

DUNCAN, WILLIAM CARY (Feb. 6, 1874–Nov. 21, 1945); b. North Brookfield, Mass. Librettist, lyricist, biographer. *Molly Darling* (with Otto A. Harbach, prod. 1922); *The Amazing Madame Jumel* (1935); *Golden Hoofs* (1938); *Dog Training Made Easy for You and Your Dog* (1940); also librettos or lyrics for many musical comedies.

DUNHAM, JAMES HENRY (July 31, 1870–Oct. 20, 1953); b. Bedminster, N.J. Presbyterian clergyman, educator, author. *Freedom and Purpose: The Psychology of Spinoza* (1916); *John Fourteen* (1917); *Principles of Ethics* (1929); *The Religion of Philosophers* (1947). Prof. philosophy, Temple University, 1915–42.

DUNIWAY, ABIGAIL [Jane] SCOTT (Oct. 22, 1834–Oct. 11, 1915); b. Groveland, Ill. Novelist, poet, editor. *Captain Gray's Company; or, Crossing the Plains and Living in Oregon* (1859); *David and Anna Matson* (poems, 1876); *From the West to the West* (1905); etc. Founder, *The New Northwest,* 1871, editor, 1871–87; founder, Woman Suffrage Association, 1873.

DUNLAP, GEORGE T[erry] (1864–June 27, 1956); b. Monongahela City, Pa. Publisher, author. *The Fleeting Years* (autobiography, 1937). Founder, Grosset & Dunlap, 1898.

DUNLAP, JOHN (1747–Nov. 27, 1812); b. Strabane, Ireland. Printer, publisher. Founded and published the *Pennsylvania Packet,* in Philadelphia, Nov., 1777. This weekly became a daily newspaper, Sept. 21, 1784. Dunlap printed the Declaration of Independence. He also printed the Constitution of the United States, which was first published in the *Pennsylvania Packet.* This newspaper, after many changes of name, was absorbed by the *Philadelphia Public Ledger* in 1924. Dunlap was printer to Congress until the federal government was moved to New York.

DUNLAP, KNIGHT (Nov. 21, 1875–Aug. 14, 1949); b. Diamond Spring, Cal. Educator, psychologist, author. *A System of Psychology* (1912); *Social Psychology* (1925); *Habits, Their Making and Unmaking* (1932); *Civilized Life* (1935); *Personal Adjustment* (1946); *Religion, Its Functions in Human Life* (1946); etc. Prof. psychology, University of California at Los Angeles, 1936–47.

DUNLAP, ORRIN ELMER, JR. (Aug. 23, 1896–); b. Niagara Falls, N.Y. Author. *The Story of Radio* (1927); *Radio in Advertising* (1931); *The Future of Television* (1942); *Radio and Television Almanac* (1951); *Communications in Space* (1964); etc.

DUNLAP, WILLIAM (Feb. 19, 1766–Sept. 28, 1839); b. Perth Amboy, N.J. Playwright, historian, artist. *The Father; or, American Shandy-ism* (prod. 1788); *The Fatal Deception;* (prod. 1794), published as *Leicester; The Archers* (prod. 1796); *Ribbemont* (prod. 1796); *Andre* (prod. 1798), revised as *The Glory of Columbia* (prod. 1803); *The Italian Father* (prod. 1799); *The Dramatic Works,* 2v. (1806–16); *The Africans* (prod. 1810); *Yankee Chronology* (prod. 1812); *Life of Charles Brockden Brown,* 2v. (1815); *A Trip to Niagara* (prod. 1828); *A History of the American Theatre* (1832); *Diary,* 3v. (ed. by Dorothy C. Barck, 1930); etc. See Oscar Wegelin's *A Bibliographical Checklist of the Plays and Miscellaneous Writings of William Dunlap* (1916). The Dunlap Society was founded in his honor.

Dunlap Society. New York. Founded in 1885 by Brander Matthews, Laurence Hutton, and others in honor of William Dunlap. It was devoted to the study and preservation of the literature of the American theatre, and many publications were issued under its imprint.

DUNN, ALAN [Cantwell] (Aug. 11, 1900–); b. Belmar, N.J. Cartoonist. *Rejections* (1931); *Who's Paying for This Cab?* (1945); *East of Fifth* (1948); *Should It Gurgle?* (1956); *Is There Any Intelligent Life on Earth?* (1960); *A Portfolio of Social Cartoons 1957–1968* (1968).

DUNN, BYRON ARCHIBALD (b. Aug. 4, 1842–deceased); b. in Hillsdale Co., Mich. Author of books for boys. The *Young Kentuckians* series; the *Young Missourians* series; the *Young Virginians* series; etc.

DUNN, ESTHER CLOUDMAN (May 5, 1891–); b. Portland, Me. Educator, author. *Ben Jonson's Art: Elizabethan Life and Literature as Reflected Therein* (1925); *The Literature of Shakespeare's England* (1936); *Shakespeare in America* (1939); *Pursuit of Understanding* (1945); *The Trollope Reader* (co-editor, 1947).

DUNN, JOSEPH ALLAN [Elphinstone] (Jan. 21, 1872–Mar. 25, 1941); b. London, England. Explorer, editor, novelist. *Jim Morse, Gold-Hunter* (1920); *Rimrock Trail* (1922); *The Water-Bearer* (1924); *The Odyssey of Boru* (1926), also published as *Boru: The Story of an Irish Wolfhound; Death Gamble* (1932); *Outlaws from Nevada* (1936); etc.

DUNN, ROBERT [Steed] (Aug. 16, 1877–Dec. 24, 1955); b. Newport, R.I. Explorer, author. *The Shameless Diary of an Explorer* (1907); *The Youngest World* (1914); *Five Fronts* (1915); *Horizon Fever* (1932); *And Least Love* (poems, 1945); *World Alive* (1956).

DUNN, WALDO HILARY (Oct. 4, 1882–); b. Rutland, O. Educator, author. *English Biography* (1916); *The Life of Donald G. G. Mitchell* (1922); *Froude & Carlyle* (1930); *Three Eminent Victorians* (1932); *George Washington* (with N. W. Stephenson, 1940); *R. D. Blackmore* (1956); *James Anthony Froude: A Biography*, 2v. (1961–63); etc. Co-editor: *Matthew Arnold's Notebooks* (1940); etc. Prof. English, Scripps College, 1934–52.

DUNNE, FINLEY PETER (July 10, 1867–Apr. 24, 1936); b. Chicago, Ill. Humorist. Creator of character "Mr. Dooley." *Mr. Dooley in Peace and in War* (1898); *Mr. Dooley in the Hearts of His Countrymen* (1898); *Mr. Dooley's Philosophy* (1900); *Mr. Dooley's Opinions* (1901); *Observations by Mr. Dooley* (1902); *Dissertations by Mr. Dooley* (1906); *Mr. Dooley Says* (1910); etc. Editor, *Chicago Journal*, 1897–1900. See *Mr. Dooley at His Best* (selections by Elmer Ellis, 1938), and Elmer Ellis's *Mr. Dooley's America* (1941).

DUNNER, JOSEPH (May 10, 1908–); b. Fuerth, Ger. Educator, author. *The Republic of Israel, Its History and Its Promise* (1950); *Baruch Spinoza and Western Democracy* (1955); *Handbook of World History* (1967); etc. Editor: *Dictionary of Political Science* (1964). Prof. political science, Grinnell College, 1946–58.

DUNNING, ALBERT ELIJAH (Jan. 5, 1844–Nov. 14, 1923); b. Brookfield, Conn. Congregational clergyman, author. *Bible Studies* (1886); *Congregationalists in America* (1894); etc.

Dunning, Charlotte. See Charlotte Dunning Wood.

DUNNING, PHILIP [Hart] (Dec. 11, 1892–); b. Meriden, Conn. Playwright, producer. *Dollar Bill* (1915); *Faint Heart* (1919); *Dollars and Horse Sense* (1940); *Broadway* (with George Abbott, prod. 1926); *The Understudy* (with Jack Donohue, prod. 1927); *Night Hostess* (prod. 1928); *Sweet Land of Liberty* (prod. 1929); *Lilly Turner* (with George Abbott, prod. 1932); *Page Miss Glory* (with Joseph Schrank, prod. 1934); *Remember the Day* (with Philo Higley, prod. 1935); *Four Cheers for Joan* (with L. G. Lippman, 1941); etc.

DUNNING, WILLIAM ARCHIBALD (May 12, 1857–Aug. 25, 1922); b. Plainfield, N.J. Educator, historian. *Essays on the Civil War and Reconstruction* (1898); *History of Political Theories*, 3v. (1902–20); *From Luther to Montesquieu* (1905); *From Rousseau to Spencer* (1920); *Truth in History, and Other Essays* (1937); etc. History and political science depts., Columbia University, New York, 1886–1922.

DUNSTER, HENRY (1609–Feb. 27, 1658/59); b. in Lancashire, England. Congregational clergyman, educator. First president of Harvard College, 1640–54. See Jeremiah Chaplin's *Life of Henry Dunster* (1872).

DUNTON, EDITH KELLOGG (Dec. 28, 1875–Dec. 31, 1944); b. Rutland, Vt. Pen name, "Margaret Warde." Author. The *Betty Wales* series, 8v. (1904–10); the *Nancy Lee* series, 4v. (1912–18); *Biddy and Buddy's Holidays* (1930); *Joan Jordan's Job* (1931); etc.

DUNTON, JAMES GERALD (Nov. 19, 1899–); b. Circleville, O. Author. *Wild Asses* (1925); *Murders in Lovers' Lane* (1927); *The Counterfeit Wife* (1930); *The Queen's Harem* (1933); *A Maid and a Million Men* (1940); etc.

DUNTON, WILLIAM HERBERT (Aug. 28, 1878–Mar. 18, 1936); b. Augusta, Me. Illustrator of outdoor scenes, particularly of the West. Illustrated stories for *Harper's*, *Scribner's*, *Everybody's* and many other magazines. Also did murals and lithographs.

DUNWORTH, GRACE; b. Machias, Me. Author. *The Letters of Jennie Allen to Her Friend Miss Musgrove* (1909); *Down Home with Jennie Allen* (1910).

DUPEE, F[rederick] W[ilcox] (June 25, 1904–); b. Chicago, Ill. Educator, author. *Henry James* (1951). Editor: *The Ques-*

tion of Henry James* (1945); *Great French Short Novels* (1952); *Henry James's Autobiography* (1956); *Selected Letters of Charles Dickens* (1960); *Selected Letters of E. E. Cummings* (with George Stade, 1969); etc.

DUPRAT, ALPHONSE. Bibliophile, bookseller. One of the original members of the Book Fellows' Club. He published *Booklover's Almanack* from 1893 to 1897.

Dupratz, Antoine Simon Le Page. See Antoine Simon Le Page du Pratz.

DUPUY, ELIZA ANN (1814–Jan. 15, 1881); b. Petersburg, Va. Novelist, author. *The Conspirator* (1850); *The Huguenot Exiles* (1856); *All for Love* (1873); *The Cancelled Will* (1872); *The Clandestine Marriage* (1875); *The Discarded Wife* (1875). Wrote many short stories for the New York *Ledger* under the pen name, "Annie Young."

DUPUY, RICHARD ERNEST (Mar. 24, 1887–); b. New York. Army officer, author. *With the Fifty-Seventh in France* (1929); *Perish by the Sword* (1939); *St. Vith: Lion in the Way* (1949); *Five Days to War* (1967); *Little Wars of the United States* (with W. H. Baumer, 1968); etc. With T. N. Dupuy: *Military Heritage of America* (1956); *Brave Men and Great Captains* (1959); *The Compact History of the Civil War* (1962); *The Compact History of the Revolutionary War* (1963); *Encyclopedia of Military History* (1965).

Durable Satisfactions of Life, The. Essays and addresses by Charles William Eliot, president of Harvard University (1910).

DURAND, ASHER BROWN (Aug. 21, 1796–Sept. 17, 1886); b. Jefferson, N.J. Engraver, painter. His engravings of heads and landscapes and historical and literary characters earned him the reputation of being America's foremost engraver. He did many engravings for the literary annuals, particularly for *The Gift*, *The Token*, *The Talisman*, *The Magnolia*, and *The Atlantic Souvenir*. One of the founders of the National Academy of Design, 1826, and its president, 1845–61. See John Durand's *The Life and Times of Asher Brown Durand* (1894).

Durand, Mrs. Albert C. See Ruth Sawyer.

DURANT, HENRY FOWLE (Feb. 20, 1822–Oct. 3, 1881); b. Hanover, N.H. Lawyer, philanthropist. Founder, Wellesley College, 1870. See Florence M. Kingsley's *The Life of Henry Fowle Durant* (1923).

DURANT, JOHN (Jan. 10, 1902–); b. Waterbury, Conn. Author. *The Story of Baseball* (1947); *Pictorial History of American Ships* (with A. K. R. Durant, 1953); *Pictorial History of American Presidents* (with same, 1955); *Pictorial History of the American Circus* (with same, 1957); *Heavyweight Champions* (1960); *Highlights of the World Series* (1963); *The Sports of Our Presidents* (1964); etc.

Durant, Mrs. Kenneth. See Genevieve Taggart.

DURANT, WILL[iam James] (Nov. 5, 1885–); b. North Adams, Mass. Lecturer, author. *The Story of Philosophy* (1926); *Transition* (autobiography, 1927); *The Mansions of Philosophy* (1929); *Adventures in Genius* (1931); *The Story of Civilization: Vol. I, Our Oriental Heritage* (1935); *Vol. II, The Life of Greece* (1939); *Vol. III, Caesar and Christ* (1944); *Vol. IV, The Age of Faith* (1950); *Vol. V, The Renaissance* (1953); *Vol. VI, The Reformation* (1957); *Vol. VII, The Age of Reason Begins* (with Ariel Durant, 1961); *Vol. VIII, The Age of Louis XIV* (with same, 1963); *Vol. IX, The Age of Voltaire* (with same, 1965); *Vol. X, Rousseau and Revolution* (with same, 1967); *The Lessons of History* (with same, 1968).

DURANTY, WALTER (May 25, 1884–Oct. 3, 1957); b. in Lancashire, Eng. Correspondent, author. *The Curious Lottery, and Other Tales* (1929); *Duranty Reports Russia* (1934); *I Write As I Please* (autobiography, 1935); *Solomans Cat* (poem, 1937); *One Life, One Kopeck* (1937); *Babies Without*

Tails (1937); *The Gold Train* (1938); *The Kremlin and the People* (1942); *Search for a Key* (1943); *USSR* (1944); *Stalin and Co.* (1949); etc. Foreign correspondent, *New York Times,* 1913–39.

DURBIN, JOHN PRICE (Oct. 10, 1800–Oct. 19, 1876); b. in Bourbon Co., Ky. Methodist clergyman, educator, traveler. Author: *Observations in Europe,* 2v. (1844); *Observations in the East* (1845).

DUREN, WILLIAM LARKIN (Oct. 27, 1870–); b. Carroll Co., Miss. Methodist clergyman, editor, author. *Francis Asbury* (1928); *The Top Sergeant* (1930); *Trail of the Circuit Rider* (1936). Editor, *Christian Advocate,* since 1935.

DURFEE, JOB (Sept. 20, 1790–July 26, 1847); b. Tiverton, N.H. Jurist, author. *The Vision of Petrarch* (poem, 1814); *What Cheer; or, Roger Williams in Banishment* (poem, 1832); *The Complete Works* (1849); etc.

DURIVAGE, FRANCIS ALEXANDER (1814–Feb. 1, 1881); b. Boston, Mass. Editor, novelist, playwright. *Angela* (1843); *Edith Vernon* (1845); *Mike Martin* (1845); *The Mill of Poissy* (in Justin Jones's *The Belle of Boston,* 1849); *Rosalie de Clairville* (in Martha A. Clough's *Paoling,* 1849); *Stray Subjects* (with George P. Burnham, under pen names "Old Un" and "Young Un," 1848); *Monaldi* (with Steele MacKaye, prod. 1872); etc. Compiler: *Life Scenes from the World around Us* (1853).

DURKEE, J[ames] STANLEY (Nov. 21, 1866–); b. Carleton, N.S. Congregational clergyman, educator, author. *In the Footsteps of a Friend* (1916); *In the Meadows of Memory* (1920); *Winds Off Shore* (poems, 1933); *Where Are They Marching?* (1942); etc. President, Howard University, 1918–26.

DURRETT, REUBEN THOMAS (Jan. 22, 1824–Sept. 16, 1913); b. in Henry Co., Ky. Editor, historian, book collector. *John Filson, the First Historian of Kentucky* (1884). Editor, *Louisville Courier,* 1857–59. Founder, the Filson Club in 1884, its president until 1913. Founder, Louisville Public Library. Collected over 50,000 books, chiefly on the subject of the Ohio Valley, which eventually went to the University of Chicago Library.

DURRIE, DANIEL STEELE (Jan. 2, 1819–Aug. 31, 1892); b. Albany, N.Y. Librarian, historian. *Bibliographia Genealogica Americana* (1868); *A History of Madison, the Capital of Wisconsin* (1874). Librarian, The State Historical Society of Wisconsin, 1856–92. *See* Lyman Copeland Draper.

DURSTINE, ROY SARLES (Dec. 13, 1886–Nov., 1962); b. Jamestown, N.D. Advertising executive, author. *This Advertising Business* (1928); *Red Thunder* (1933). On staff, *New York Sun,* 1908–12. President, Batten, Barton, Durstine & Osborn, 1936–39. President, Roy S. Durstine, Inc., from 1939.

DURYEA, NINA LARREY (Mrs. Chester B. Duryea) (Aug. 11, 1874–Nov. 1, 1951); b. Cohasset, Mass. Author. *The House of Seven Gabblers* (1908); *A Sentimental Dragon* (1911); *The Voice Unheard* (1913); *Mallorca the Magnificent* (1927); *The Pride of Maura* (1932).

Dust Which Is God, The. Novel in verse by William Rose Benét (1941).

Dustin, Charles. Pen name of John Ulrich Giesy.

Dutch Treat Club. New York. Founded 1905. Celebrated weekly luncheon club with membership of authors, actors, critics, musicians, painters and others who have made notable contributions to American culture. Dramatic and music skits, etc., are staged from scripts written by the members of the club.

DUTCHER, GEORGE MATTHEW (Sept. 16, 1874–Feb. 22, 1959); b. Pleasant Valley, N.Y. Educator, bibliographer, author. *The Political Awakening of the East* (1925). Co-edi-

tor: *A Guide to Historical Literature* (1931). Prof. history, Wesleyan University, 1905–46. State historian of Connecticut, 1936–41.

Dutchman's Fireside, The. Novel of the Dutch settlements along the Hudson River, by James Kirke Paulding (1831).

DUTTON, CHARLES J[udson] (Aug. 22, 1888–Aug. 21, 1964); b. Fall River, Mass. Unitarian clergyman, novelist, biographer. *The Underwood Mystery* (1921); *The Second Bullet* (1925); *Murder in a Library* (1931); *The Samaritans of Molokai* (1932); *Oliver Hazard Perry* (1935); *Saints and Sinners* (1940); etc. Writer of a column, "The World We Live In," in Albany *Telegram,* 1916–28.

Dutton, E. P. & Co. New York. Publishers and booksellers. Founded in Boston in 1852 by Edward Payson Dutton as Ide & Dutton. Lemuel Ide was the son of the New Hampshire printer, Simeon Ide. In 1858 it was called E. P. Dutton & Company. Dutton bought the Old Corner Book Store in Boston, and Charles A. Clapp, the store's star salesman, joined the Dutton firm. In 1869 the publishing house was moved to New York. E. C. Swayne became a partner in 1878. John Macrae took over the bookstore in 1885 and became a partner in 1900; his son, Elliott B. Macrae succeeded him. John Macrae III is now president. As the American agents of the London firm of J. M. Dent, the firm published the popular "Everyman's Library," "Temple Classics," etc. Many noted English authors have appeared on the Dutton list. See *Seventy-five Years,* a history of the firm published in 1927, edited by George M. Acklom of the Dutton staff.

DUTTON, EDWARD PAYSON (Jan. 4, 1831–Sept. 6, 1923); b. Keene, N.H. Publisher. Founder, E. P. Dutton & Co., publishing house (q.v.). This grew out of a bookstore operated in Boston by Dutton and Charles A. Clapp.

DUVAL, JOHN CRITTENDEN (1816–Jan. 15, 1897); b. in Florida. Surveyor, prospector, author. *The Adventures of Big-Foot Wallace* (1870); *Early Times in Texas* (1892). *See* J. Frank Dobie's *John C. Duval* (1939).

DUVALL, EVELYN MILLIS (July 28, 1906–); b. Oswego, N.Y. Author. *Family Living* (1950); *Family Development* (1957); *Sex Ways: In Fact and Faith* (with S. M. Duvall, 1961); *Love and the Facts of Life* (1963); *Why Wait Till Marriage?* (1965); *Today's Teen-Agers* (1966); *About Sex and Growing Up* (1968); etc.

DUVOISIN, ROGER ANTOINE (Aug. 28, 1904–); b. Geneva, Switz. Artist, illustrator, author. *The Four Corners of the World* (1948); *Petunia* (1950); *Petunia and the Song* (1951); *Petunia Takes a Trip* (1953); *The House of Four Seasons* (1956); *Night and Day* (1959); *Happy Hunter* (1961); *Our Veronica Goes to Petunia's Farm* (1962); *Lonely Veronica* (1963); *The Missing Milkman* (1966); *Veronica's Smile* (1964); *What Is Right for Tulip* (1969); etc.

DUYCKINCK, EVERT AUGUSTUS (Nov. 23, 1816–Aug. 13, 1878); b. New York City. Editor, biographer, compiler. Editor: *Cyclopaedia of American Literature,* 2v. (1855). This work was brought down to the year 1873 by Michael Laird Simons. He edited works by Thackeray, Irving, Freneau, Sydney Smith, and others, and wrote texts for subscription books. Editor, *Arcturus,* 1840–42; *Literary World,* 1847–53. His extensive library was bequeathed to The New York Public Library, together with his correspondence, notebooks, etc.

DUYCKINCK, GEORGE LONG (Oct. 17, 1823–Mar. 30, 1863); b. New York City. Editor, biographer. *The Life of George Herbert* (1858); *The Life of Thomas Ken* (1859); *The Life of Jeremy Taylor* (1860); *The Life of Hugh Latimer* (1861); etc. Editor (with his brother, Evert Duyckinck): *Cyclopaedia of American Literature,* 2v. (1855). Co-editor (with brother): *Literary World,* 1848–53.

DWIGGINS, W[illiam] A[ddison] (June 19, 1880–Dec. 25, 1956); b. Martinsville, O. Illustrator, book designer. Director,

Harvard University Press, 1917–18. Also with Yale University Press and Alfred A. Knopf. Author of several professional books, illustrator, and promoter of the art of book design in America.

DWIGHT, HARRISON GRISWOLD (Aug. 6, 1875–Mar. 24, 1959); b. Constantinople, Turkey. Writer. *Stamboul Nights* (1916); *Persian Miniatures* (1917); *The Emperor of Elam, and Other Stories* (1920); *Art Parade* (with A. M. Frankfurter, 1943); etc.

DWIGHT, HENRY OTIS (June 3, 1843–June 20, 1917); b. Constantinople, Turkey. Missionary, author. *Turkish Life in Wartime* (1881); *Constantinople and Its Problems* (1901); *A Muslim Sir Galahad* (1913); *Centennial History of the American Bible Society* (1916). Editor: *Encyclopedia of Missions* (1904); etc.

DWIGHT, JOHN SULLIVAN (May 13, 1813–Sept. 5, 1893); b. Boston, Mass. Music critic, editor, author. *Select Minor Poems Translated from the German of Goethe and Schiller* (1839). Founder and editor, *Dwight's Journal of Music: A Paper of Literature and Art,* 1852. Sold the *Journal* to Oliver Ditson & Co. in 1858. Music critic, *Harbinger; Boston Transcript; Boston Commonwealth; Sartain's Magazine;* etc. Member of The Transcendental Club and Brook Farm.

DWIGHT, THEODORE (Dec. 15, 1764–June 12, 1846); b. Northampton, Mass. Lawyer, editor. One of the "Hartford Wits." Founder, Albany *Daily Advertiser,* in 1815, New York *Daily Advertiser* in 1817, which he managed until 1836. He wrote verse and essays for the *Connecticut Courant* and the *Connecticut Mirror.*

DWIGHT, THEODORE (Mar. 3, 1796–Oct. 16, 1866); b. Hartford, Conn. Educator. Author: *A Journal of a Tour in Italy in the Year 1821* (1824); *The Northern Traveller* (1825); *Sketches of Scenery and Manners in the United States* (1829); *Things as They Are* (1834); *History of Connecticut* (1841); *Life of General Garibaldi* (1861); etc. Founder, Dwight's *American Magazine and Family Newspaper,* 1845; editor, 1845–52.

DWIGHT, TIMOTHY (May 14, 1752–Jan. 11, 1817); b. Northampton, Mass. Clergyman, educator, poet. One of the "Hartford Wits." *America: A Poem* (1772); *The Conquest of Canaan* (1785); *Greenfield Hill* (1794); *The Triumph of Infidelity, a Poem* (1788); *Theology, Explained and Defended,* 5v. (1818–19); etc. The hymn, "I love Thy kingdom, Lord."

DWYER, JAMES FRANCIS (Apr. 22, 1874–deceased); b. Camden, N.S.W., Australia. Correspondent, traveler, author. *The White Waterfall* (1912); *The Spotted Panther* (1913); *Evelyn* (1929); *Cold Eyes* (1934); *Hespamora* (1935); *Lady with Feet of Gold* (1935); *Leg-Irons on Wings* (1949); etc.

DYER, GEORGE [Bell] (Apr. 12, 1903–); b. Washington, D.C. Author. *The Three-Cornered Wound* (1931); *A Storm Is Rising* (1934); *The Catalyst Club* (1936); *The Long Death* (1937); *Adriana* (1939); *The People Ask Death* (1940); *XII Corps, Spearhead of Patton's Third Army* (with Charlotte Leavitt Dyer, 1947); *The Beginnings of a U.S. Strategic Intelligence System in Latin America* (1950); *A Century of Strategic Intelligence Reporting* (1954); *A Strategic Intelligence Lesson* (1955); *The World Analyst* (1958); *Estimating National Power and Intentions* (1960); *Exercises on an Assumption of Violence* (1962); etc.

DYER, LOUIS (Sept. 30, 1851–July 20, 1908); b. Chicago, Ill. Educator, classicist, author. *Studies of the Gods in Greece* (1891); *Machiavelli and the Modern State* (1904); etc.

DYER, RUTH OMEGA (Mrs. Smith Johns Williams) (Sept. 6, 1885–); b. Herndon, Va. Educator, author. *The Sleepy-Time Story Book* (1915); *What Happened Then Stories* (1918); *The Little People of the Garden* (1922); etc.

DYER, SIDNEY (Feb. 11, 1814–1898); b. Cambridge, Mass. Baptist clergyman, author. *Voices of Nature* (poems, 1850); *Songs and Ballads* (1857); *Home and Abroad* (1872); etc.

DYER, WALTER A[lden] (Oct. 10, 1878–June 20, 1943); b. Roslindale, Mass. Editor, author. *Pierrot, Dog of Belgium* (1915); *Gulliver the Great, and Other Dog Stories* (1916); *The Dogs of Boytown* (1918); *Many Dogs There Be* (1924); *All Around Robin Hood's Barn* (1926); *The Breakwater* (1927); *Sprigs of Hemlock* (1931); etc. Was director, Amherst College Press.

"Dying Cowboy, The." Cowboy song with the familiar refrain "Bury me not on the lone prairie." Authorship unknown. It has been attributed to H. Clemens, circa 1872.

"Dying Indian, The." Poem by Philip Freneau (1784).

Dylan, Bob. See Zimmerman, Robert.

DYOTT, GEORGE M[iller] (Feb. 6, 1883–); b. New York City. Explorer, author. *Silent Highways of the Jungle* (1924); *On the Trail of the Unknown in the Wilds of Ecuador and the Amazon* (1926); *Man Hunting in the Jungle* (1930); etc.

DYSON, VERNE (Jan. 25, 1879–); b. Rolla, Me. Educator, journalist, Sinologist, author. *Black Cloth* (1925); *Forgotten Tales of Ancient China* (1927); *Land of the Yellow Spring* (1937); *A Century of Brentwood* (1950). Editor: *Shanghai Stories* (1925). With *Kansas City Star, Los Angeles Times, China Courier, Manila Daily Bulletin,* etc. Dean, Williams College, Shanghai, 1921; in English dept., University of Philippines, 1928–33; etc.

E

E Pluribus Unum. Motto on the seal of the United States of America. Meaning "From many, one," it was selected by Franklin, Adams, and Jefferson in 1776, to express the union of the many colonies into one confederation.

"Each and All." Poem by Ralph Waldo Emerson (1839).

"Each in His Own Tongue." Poem by William Herbert Carruth (1906). Often-quoted poem on evolution, with the lines, "Some call it evolution, And others call it God."

"Eagle of Corinth, The." Poem by Henry Howard Brownell (1862). Inspired by the flight of an eagle over the battlefield of Corinth.

EAKER, IRA C. (Apr. 13, 1896–); b. in Llano Co., Tex. Air force officer, manufacturing executive. Co-author, with H. H. Arnold: *This Flying Game* (1936); *Winged Warfare* (1941); *Army Flyer* (1942).

EAMES, WILBERFORCE (Oct. 12, 1855–Dec. 6, 1937); b. Newark, N.J. Bibliographer, librarian. *Columbus' Letter to Sanchez* (1892); *John Eliot and the Indians* (1915); *The First Year of Printing in New York* (1928); *The Antigua Press and Benjamin Mecom* (1929); etc. Editor, *Sabin's Dictionary of Books Relating to America,* v. 15–20 (1885–92), later volumes (1927–29), including the articles on *Bay Psalm Book,* Captain John Smith, Columbus, Sir Walter Raleigh, and Ptolemy's *Geography.* With Lenox Library, 1885–95; librarian, 1893–95; librarian, Bibliographical Society of America, 1904–09; chief bibliographer, New York Public Library, 1895–1937. He was the dean of American bibliographers, and began his bibliographical labors as a clerk in a New York bookstore. He trained himself by looking up every reference in Gibbon's *Decline and Fall of the Roman Empire.* He mastered the American Indian languages and collected several libraries of books on the Indians. His books went to the New York Public

Library after his death. See *Bibliographical Essays: a Tribute to Wilberforce Eames* (1924); Victor Hugo Palsits's *Wilberforce Eames* (1935).

Earl, John Prescott. Pen name of Beth Bradford Gilchrist.

EARLE, ALICE MORSE (Apr. 27, 1853–Feb. 16, 1911); b. Worcester, Mass. Antiquarian, author. *The Sabbath in Puritan New England* (1891); *Customs and Fashions in Old New England* (1893); *Colonial Dames and Good Wives* (1895); *Colonial Days in Old New York* (1897); *Child-Life in Colonial Days* (1899); *Stage-Coach and Tavern Days* (1900); *Two Centuries of Costume in America,* 2v. (1903); etc.

EARLE, EDWARD MEAD (May 20, 1894–June 24, 1954); b. New York City. Educator, author. *An Outline of Modern History* (1921); *Turkey, The Great Powers, and the Bagdad Railway* (1923); *Against this Torrent* (1941). Editor and co-author: *Makers of Modern Strategy* (1943); *Modern France* (1951); etc. Prof. Institute for Advanced Studies, Princeton, N.J., from 1934.

Earle, W. J. Pen name of Luis Philip Senarens.

EARLY, ELEANOR (d. Aug. 25, 1969); b. Newton, Mass. Correspondent, author. *And This Is Boston* (1933); *And This Is Cape Cod* (1936); *Ports of the Sun* (1937); *Adirondack Tales* (1939); *Lands of Delight* (1939); *New Orleans Holiday* (1946); *New York Holiday* (1950); *New England Cookbook* (1954); *Caribbean Holiday* (1960); etc.

Early Autumn. Novel by Louis Bromfield (1926). Story of the New England Pentlands, the last of the Puritans, some of their members struggling to hold on to the family traditions, others yearning to be free of them. The whole family portrait gallery passes in review.

Early Western Travels, 1748–1846. Ed. by Reuben Gold Thwaites, 33v. (1904–07). Reprints, with notes, of numerous travel narratives in America in the era of exploration and the penetration of the wilderness.

EARNEST, ERNEST P. (Sept. 19, 1901–   ); b. Hummelstown, Pa. Educator, author. *John and William Bartram* (1940); *A Foreword to Literature* (1945); *S. Weir Mitchell, Novelist and Physician* (1950); *Academic Procession, an Informal History of the American College, 1936–1953* (1954); *The Uses of Prose* (1956); *Expatriates and Patriots: American Scholars, Artists and Writers in Europe* (1967). English dept., Temple University, since 1927.

"Earth." Poem by John Hall Wheelock in his *Dust and Light* (1919).

Earthlings: Tales of a Time and Place. By Grace King (1891). Short stories of Louisiana life.

Easiest Way, The. Play by Eugene Walter (prod. 1909). Realistic play based on a morbid emotionalism.

East Angels. Novel by Constance Fenimore Woolson (1888). Depicts a sleepy town on the southern coast of the United States, with Edgarda Thorne as its heroine.

"East Coker." Poem by T. S. Eliot published as part of *Four Quartets* (1943).

East of Eden. Novel by John Steinbeck (1952). Story of a family spanning the period from the mid-nineteenth century to World War I, concerned with the basic conflict between forces of good and evil. The principal characters are two brothers of opposite tendencies.

East Village. An area east of Greenwich Village (q.v.), which runs roughly from Third Avenue to the East River, and from Houston Street to Fourteenth Street, in New York City. Tompkins Park is its center for group activities. During the 1950's high rents and overcrowding forced many artists and writers to seek apartments and studios farther east, especially

around St. Mark's Place. With the rise of the new bohemianism associated with the hippies (q.v.) in the mid-1960's, the East Village became a center of underground movies; underground presses; street theater, guerilla theater, and off-off-Broadway theater productions; poetry readings against rock music and motion-picture backgrounds; multi-media shows and "light" shows, etc.

East Village Other, The. New York. Weekly. Founded 1966. Edited by Joel Fabrikant, Allan Katzman, and others. The most influential of the underground weeklies published in New York City.

EASTBURN, JAMES WALLIS (Sept. 26, 1797–Dec. 2, 1819); b. London, England. Episcopal clergyman, poet, hymn writer. *Yamoyden: A Tale of the Wars of King Philip* (with Robert Charles Sands, 1820). His best known hymn is "O holy, holy, holy Lord, Bright in Thy deeds."

EASTER, MARGUERITE ELIZABETH (1839–1894); b. Leesburg, Va. Poet. *Clytie, and Other Poems* (1891).

EASTLAKE, WILLIAM [Derry] (July 14, 1917–); b. New York. Novelist. *Go in Beauty* (1955); *The Bronc People* (1958); *Portrait of an Artist with Twenty-Six Horses* (1963); *Castle Keep* (1965); *The Bamboo Bed* (1970).

EASTMAN, CHARLES ALEXANDER (1858–1939); b. Redwood Falls, Minn. Sioux Indian physician, author. Indian name, "Ohiyesa." *Indian Boyhood* (1902); *Wigwam Evenings* (with wife, Elaine Goodale Eastman, 1909); *The Soul of the Indian* (1911); *From the Deep Woods to Civilization* (1916); etc.

EASTMAN, CHARLES GAMAGE (June 1, 1816–Sept. 16, 1860); b. Fryeburg, Me. Journalist, politician, poet. Called "the Burns of New England." *Poems* (1848). Founder, *Spirit of the Age,* Woodstock, Vt., 1840; *Vermont Patriot,* Montpelier, Vt., 1846.

EASTMAN, ELAINE GOODALE (Mrs. Charles Alexander Eastman) (Oct. 9, 1863–Feb. 24, 1948); b. Mt. Washington, Mass., sister of Dora Read Goodale. Author. *Apple Blossoms: Verses of Two Children* (with sister, 1878); *In Berkshire with the Wild Flowers* (poems, with sister, 1879); *All Round the Year Verses from Sky Farm* (with sister, 1881); *Journal of a Farmer's Daughter* (1881); *Wigwam Evenings* (with husband, 1909); *Little Brother o' Dreams* (1910); *Yellow Star* (1911); *Indian Legends Retold* (1919); *The Luck of Oldacres* (1929); *Pratt, the Red Man's Moses* (1935); etc.

EASTMAN, ELIZABETH (Nov. 16, 1905–); b. South Carver, Mass. Novelist. *Sun on Their Shoulders* (1934); *The Mouse with Red Eyes* (1948).

EASTMAN, FRED (July 11, 1886–Apr. 2, 1963); b. Lima, O. Educator, author. *Bread* (play, 1927); *The Menace of the Movies* (1930); *Drama in the Church* (with Louis Wilson, 1933); *Plays of American Life* (1934); *Books That Have Shaped the World* (1937); *Men of Power,* 5v. (1938–40); *Christ in the Drama* (1947); *An American Family* (1951); etc. Editor: *Modern Religious Dramas* (1928); *Ten One Act Plays* (1937); etc. Prof., Chicago Theological Seminary, 1926–52.

EASTMAN, JULIA ARABELLA (July 17, 1837–Jan. 1, 1911); b. Fulton, N.Y. Novelist. *Short Comings and Long Goings* (1869); *Beulah Romney* (1871); *Young Rick* (1875); etc.

EASTMAN, MARY H[enderson] (Mrs. Seth Eastman) (1818–80); b. Warrenton, Va. Author. *Dahcotah; or, Life and Legends of the Sioux Around Fort Snelling* (1849, which inspired Longfellow to write *Hiawatha*); *Aunt Phillis's Cabin; or, Southern Life As It Is* (1852, a Southern answer to *Uncle Tom's Cabin*); *The American Aboriginal Portfolio* (1853); *The American Annual: Illustrative of the Early History of North America* (1853?); *Chicóra and Other Regions of the Conquerors and the Conquered* (1854); *Tales of Fashionable Life* (1856).

EASTMAN, MAX [Forrester] (Jan. 4, 1883–Mar. 25, 1969); b. Canandaigua, N.Y. Editor, essayist, poet. *Enjoyment of Poetry* (1913, revised 1939); *Colors of Life* (poems, 1918); *The Literary Mind: Its Place in an Age of Science* (1931); *Art and the Life of Action* (1934); *Enjoyment of Laughter* (1936); *The End of Socialism in Russia* (1937); *Stalin's Russia and the Crisis in Socialism* (1939); *Marxism: Is It Science?* (1940); *Heroes I Have Known* (1942); *Lot's Wife, a Dramatic Poem* (1942); *Enjoyment of Living* (1948); *The Road to Abundance* (with Jacob Rosin, 1953); *Poems of Five Decades* (1954); *Reflections on the Failure of Socialism* (1955); *Great Companions—Critical Memoirs of Some Famous Friends* (1959); *Love and Revolution: My Journey through an Epoch* (1965); etc. Editor, *The Masses*, 1913–17; *The Liberator*, 1918–22; roving editor, *Reader's Digest*, from 1941. Compiler: *Anthology for the Enjoyment of Poetry.*

EASTMAN, SETH (Jan. 24, 1808–Aug. 31, 1875); b. Brunswick, Me. Army officer, artist. Illustrated Henry R. Schoolcraft's *Information Concerning the History, Condition and Prospects of the Indian Tribes of the United States*, 6v. (1851–57); and several books by his wife, Mary H. Eastman. *See* David I. Bushnell's *Seth Eastman, the Master Painter of the North American Indian* (1932).

EATON, ANNE T[haxter] (May 3, 1881–May 5, 1971); b. Beverly Farms, Mass. Editor, author. *Reading with Children* (1940). Compiler: *Poet's Craft* (with Helen Fern Daringer, poems, 1935); *Animals' Christmas* (1944); *Treasure for the Taking: A Book List for Boys and Girls* (1946); etc. Was editor, children's book dept., *The New York Times Book Review.*

EATON, ARTHUR WENTWORTH HAMILTON (1849–July 11, 1937); b. Kentville, N.S. Episcopal clergyman, author. *The Heart of the Creeds* (1888); *Acadian Legends, and Lyrics* (1889); *The Church of England in Nova Scotia and the Tory Clergy of the Revolution* (1891); *Tales of a Garrison Town* (with Craven Langstroth Betts, 1892); *Acadian Ballads, and De Soto's Last Dream* (1905); *Poems of the Christian Year* (1905); *The Lotus of the Nile, and Other Poems* (1907); *The Famous Mather Byles* (1914); *Acadian Ballads, and Lyrics in Many Moods: Collected Poems* (1930); etc. Editor: *Recollections of a Georgia Loyalist, by Mrs. Elizabeth Lichtenstein Johnston, Written in 1836* (1901).

EATON, CLEMENT (Feb. 23, 1898–); b. Winston-Salem, N.C. Educator, author. *Freedom of Thought in the Old South* (1940); *A History of the Old South* (1949); *A History of the Southern Confederacy* (1954); *Henry Clay and the Art of American Politics* (1957); *The Growth of Southern Civilization, 1790–1860* (1961); *The Mind of the Old South* (1964); *The Waning of the Old South Civilization 1860–1880* (1969). Prof. history, University of Kentucky, since 1946–68.

EATON, CYRUS STEPHEN (December 27, 1883–); b. In Nova Scotia. Industrialist, Banker, Author. *The Third Term "Tradition"* (1940); *Financial Democracy* (1941); *The Engineer as Philosopher* (1961); etc.

EATON, EDWARD DWIGHT (Jan. 12, 1851–June 19, 1942); b. Lancaster, Wis. Educator, author. *Historical Sketches of Beloit College* (1928); *Two Wisconsin Pioneers* (1933); *Thronging Echoes* (1938); *Along Life's Pathway* (1941); etc. President, Beloit College, 1886–1905, 1907–17.

EATON, EVELYN [Sybil Mary] (Dec. 22, 1902–); b. Montreux, Switz. Author. *Stolen Hours* (poems, 1923); *Desire, Spanish Version* (1933); *John—Film Star* (1937); *Pray to the Earth* (1938); *Quietly My Captain Waits* (1940); *Restless Are the Sails* (1941); *The Sea Is So Wide* (1943); *In What Torn Ship* (1944); *Every Month Was May* (autobiography, 1947); *The North Star Is Nearer* (autobiography, 1949); *Give Me Your Golden Hand* (1951); *Flight* (1954); *I Saw My Mortal Sight* (1959); *Go Ask the River* (1969).

EATON, JEANETTE (d. Feb. 19, 1968) b. Columbus, O. Biographer. *A Daughter of the Seine: The Life of Madame Roland* (1929); *The Flame: Saint Catherine of Siena* (1931); *Jeanne d'Arc, the Warrior Saint* (1931); *Young Lafayette* (1932); *Leader by Destiny: George Washington, Man and Patriot* (1938); *Narcissa Whitman* (1941); *Lone Journey* (1944); etc.

Eaton, Peggy. *See* Margaret L. O'Neale.

EATON, WALTER PRICHARD (Aug. 24, 1878–Feb. 27, 1957); b. Malden, Mass. Educator, essayist. *The American Stage of Today* (1908); *At the New Theatre and Others* (1910); *Barn Doors and Byways* (1913); *The Man Who Found Christmas* (1913); *The Idyl of Twin Fires* (1915); *Plays and Players* (1916); *Green Trails and Upland Pastures* (1917); *In Berkshire Fields* (1919); *On the Edge of the Wilderness* (1920); *Penguin Persons and Peppermints* (1922); *The Actor's Heritage* (1924); *A Bucolic Attitude* (1926); *Hawkeye's Room Mate* (1927); *The Theatre Guild: The First Ten Years* (1929); *New England Vista* (1930); *The Drama in English* (1930); *On Yankee Hilltops* (1933); *Romance and Rummage* (one-act play, 1937); etc. Author of many Boy Scout books. Dramatic critic *American Magazine* 1909–18; assoc. prof. play-writing, Yale University, 1933–47.

Eben Holden. Novel by Irving Bacheller (1900). The author's first novel. Its hero is a "hired man" who looks after the orphan boy who is adopted by a Northern family. The boy later becomes associated with Horace Greeley, and fights in the Civil War. The faithful Eben is always in the background, and his homely sayings are a feature of the book. Cf. *D'ri and I,* by the same author.

EBENSTEIN, WILLIAM (May 11, 1910–); b. in Austria. Educator, author. *Fascist Italy* (1939); *Great Political Thinkers: Plato to the Present* (1951); *Introduction to Political Philosophy* (1952); *Modern Political Thought* (1954); *Political Thought in Perspective* (1957); *Totalitarianism: New Perspectives* (1962); *Communism in Theory and Practice* (1964); *American Democracy in World Perspective* (with others, 1967); *American Government in the Twentieth Century* (1968); etc. Prof. politics, Princeton University, since 1949.

EBERHART, MIGNON GOOD (Mrs. Alanson C. Eberhart) (July 6, 1899–); b. Lincoln, Neb. Novelist. *The Patient in Room 18* (1929); *From This Dark Stairway* (1931); *Murder by an Aristocrat* (1932); *The White Cockatoo* (1933); *Case of Susan Dare* (1934); *The Glass Slipper* (1938); *The Chiffon Scarf* (1939); *The Hangman's Whip* (1940); *Five Passengers from Lisbon* (1946); *Another Woman's House* (1947); *House of Storm* (1949); *Never Look Back* (1951); *Dead Man's Plans* (1952); *Unknown Quantity* (1953); *Man Missing* (1954); *Post Mark Murder* (1956); *Another Man's Murder* (1958); *Melora* (1959); *Jury of One* (1960); *Enemy in the House* (1962); *Run Scared* (1963); *Call After Midnight* (1964); *R.S.V.P. Murder* (1965); *Woman on the Roof* (1967); *Message from Hong Kong* (1968); *El Rancho Rio* (1970); etc.

EBERHART, NELLE RICHMOND (1871–Nov. 5, 1944); b. Detroit, Mich. Song writer. *From the Land of the Sky-Blue Water, and Other Songs for Music* (1926). Collaborated with the composer, Charles Wakefield Cadman, writing the words for *From the Land of the Sky-Blue Water* and *At Dawning;* also other lyrics and librettos for Cadman and others.

EBERHART, RICHARD (Apr. 5, 1904–); b. Anstin, Minn. Poet. *A Bravery of Earth* (1930); *Reading the Spirit* (1936); *Song and Idea* (1942); *Poems New and Selected* (1944); *Brotherhood of Men* (1949); *Selected Poems* (1951); *Undercliff: Poems, 1946–53* (1953); *Collected Poems, 1930–60* (1960); *Collected Verse Plays* (1962); *The Quarry* (1964); *Selected Poems* (1965); *Thirty-One Sonnets* (1967); *Shifts of Being* (1968); etc. Editor: *War and the Poet* (with Selden Rodman, 1945).

EBERLE, IRMENGARDE (Nov. 11, 1898–); b. San Antonio, Tex. Author. *Modern Medical Discoveries* (1948); *Big Family of Peoples* (1952); *Evie and Cookie* (1957); *Johnny's Island Ark* (1960); *Foxes Live Here* (1966); *The Dog Who Came to Visit* (1968); etc.

EBERLEIN, HAROLD DONALDSON (d. July 26, 1964); b. Columbia, Pa. Antiquarian, author. *The Architecture of Colonial America* (1915); *The Practical Book of American Antiques* (with Abbot McClure, 1916); *Manor Houses and Historic Homes of the Hudson Valley* (1924); *Manor Houses and Historic Homes of Long Island and Staten Island* (1928); *Little Known England* (1930); *Down the Tiber and Up to Rome* (with Geoffrey J. Marks and Frank A. Wallis, 1930); *The Rabelaisian Princess, Madame Royale of France* (1931); *Portrait of a Colonial City; Philadelphia 1670-1838* (with C. V. D. Hubbard, 1939); *Diary of Independence Hall* (with same, 1948); *American Georgian Architecture* (with same, 1952); *Historic Houses of George-Town and Washington City* (with same, 1958); etc.

Ebony. Chicago, Ill. Monthly. Founded 1945 by John H. Johnson. Picture magazine of Negro interest.

EBY, FREDERICK (Oct. 26, 1874–Feb. 1968); b. Berlin, Ont. Educator, author. *Development of Education in Texas* (1925); *Early Protestant Educators* (1931); *The Development of Modern Education* (with Arrowood, 1934); *The History and Philosophy of Education, Ancient and Medieval* (1940); *Newman, the Church Historian* (1946); etc. Prof. of education, University of Texas, from 1909.

ECCLES, MARRINER STODDARD (Sept. 9, 1890–); b. Logan, Utah. Financier, author. *Economic Balance and a Balanced Budget* (1940); *Beckoning Frontiers* (1951).

Echo, The. Hartford, Conn. Literary paper established by the "Hartford Wits"(q.v.).

ECKARDT, ARTHUR ROY (Aug. 8, 1918–); b. Brooklyn, N.Y. Educator, author. *Christianity and the Children of Israel* (1948); *Religion, Society and the Individual* (1957); *The Surge of Piety in America* (1958); *Jews and Christians* (with others, 1965); *Elder and Younger Brothers: The Encounter of Jews and Christians* (1967); *Encounter with Israel* (with Alice L. Eckardt, 1970). Editor, Journal of the American Academy of Religion since 1961. Prof. religion, Lehigh University, since 1956.

ECKENRODE, HAMILTON JAMES (Apr. 30, 1881–); b. Fredericksburg, Va. Virginia historian. *The Political History of Virginia During the Reconstruction* (1904); *The Revolution in Virginia* (1916); *Life of Nathan B. Forrest* (1918); *Jefferson Davis* (1923); *Rutherford B. Hayes* (1930); *Bottom Rail on Top* (1935); *James Longstreet* (with Bryan Conrad, 1936); *The Randolphs: The Story of A Virginia Family* (1946); etc. Editor: *Southern Historical Society Papers,* V. 43–47, 1920–30. Historian of Virginia since 1927.

ECKSTEIN, GUSTAV (Oct. 26, 1890–); b. Cincinnati, O. Physician, educator, author. *Noguchi* (1931); *Lives* (1932); *Kettle* (1933); *Hokusai* (1935); *Canary* (1936); *Christmas Eve* (1940); *Everyday Miracle* (1948); *The Body Has a Head* (1970); etc.

ECKSTORM, FANNIE HARDY (June 18, 1865–Dec. 31, 1946); b. Brewer, Me. Author. *The Penobscot Man* (1904); *David Libbey* (1907); *Indian Brother* (with H. V. Coryell, 1934); etc. Compiler: *The Minstrelsy of Maine* (with Mary Winslow Smyth, 1927); *British Ballads from Maine* (with Phillips Barry, and Mary Winslow Smyth, 1929); *The Scalp Hunters* (with H. V. Coryell, 1936); *Indian Place-names of Penobscot Valley and the Maine Coast* (1941); *Old John Neptune and Other Maine Indian Shamans* (1945); etc.

Eclectic Magazine of Foreign Literature, Science and Art. New York and Philadelphia. Founded Jan., 1844. Ceased 1907. It grew out of the *Eclectic Museum,* founded by E. Littell in 1843, which was a merger of the *Museum of Foreign Literature and Science,* founded 1822, and the *American Eclectic.* In 1819 Littell founded the *Philadelphia Register,* which became the *National Recorder* the same year, and in July, 1821, the *Saturday Magazine,* and in July, 1822, the *Museum of Foreign Literature and Science,* mentioned above.

Walter Hilliard Bidwell and John Holmes Agnew were editors. The engravings of John Sartain were a feature. *See* F. L. Mott's *A History of American Magazines,* v. 1 (1938).

ED, CARL FRANK LUDWIG (July 16, 1890–Oct. 10, 1959); b. Moline, Ill. Cartoonist for *Chicago Tribune* from 1918. Creator of "Harold Teen."

EDDY, BRAYTON (Jan. 13, 1901–July 17, 1950); b. Providence, R.I. Naturalist, lecturer, author. *Strangeways* (1922); *Rock Bottom* (1923); *The Pick-Up* (1925); *Night Caps* (1928); *A Couple of Brokers* (1929); etc.

EDDY, DANIEL CLARKE (May 21, 1823–July 26, 1896); b. Salem, Mass. Baptist clergyman, traveler, author. *The Percy Family* series of travel books, 5v. (1852); *Walter's Tour in the East* series, 6v. (1861); etc.

EDDY, [George] SHERWOOD (Jan. 19, 1871–Mar. 3, 1963); b. Leavenworth, Kan. Lecturer, traveler, Y.M.C.A. executive, author. *India Awakening* (1911); *The Students of Asia* (1915); *Facing the Crisis* (1920); *Religion and Social Justice* (1928); *Sex and Youth* (1929); *The Challenge of Russia* (1930); *The Challenge of Europe* (1933); *A Pilgrimage of Ideas* (1935); *Revolutionary Christianity* (1939); *God in History* (1947); *You Will Survive After Death* (1950); *Eighty Adventurous Years* (autobiography, 1955); *Why I Believe* (1957); etc.

EDDY, MARY MORSE BAKER GLOVER (July 16, 1821–Dec. 3, 1910); b. Bow, N.H. Founder of the Church of Christ, Scientist, author. *Science and Health* (1875) and many later editions; *Miscellaneous Writings* (1896). Founder and editor of the *Journal of Christian Science,* Apr. 14, 1883. *See* Lyman Pierson Powell's *Christian Science: The Faith and the Founder* (1907) and his *Mary Baker Eddy* (1930); Sibyl Wilbur's *The Life of Mary Baker Eddy* (1908); see also many articles by Clifford P. Smith, editor of the department of history of the First Church of Christ, Scientist, in Boston.

EDDY, WILLIAM ALFRED (Mar. 9, 1896–May 3, 1962); b. Sidon, Syria. Educator, diplomat, author. *Gulliver's Travels: A Critical Study* (1923); *FDR Meets Ibn Saud* (1954). Editor, *Oxford Standard Edition of Jonathan Swift,* 2v. (1932–33). President, Hobart College, Geneva, N.Y., 1936–42.

EDEL, LEON [Joseph] (Sept. 9, 1907–); b. Pittsburgh, Pa. Educator, author. *James Joyce: The Last Journey* (1947); *Henry James: The Untried Years* (1953); *Willa Cather* (with E. K. Brown, 1953); *The Psychological Novel, 1900–1950* (1955); *Literary Biography* (1957); *Henry James: The Middle Years* (1962); *Henry James: The Treacherous Years 1895–1901* (1969); *Henry James: The Master: 1901–1916.* (1972); etc. Editor: *The Ghostly Tales of Henry James* (1949); *Selected Letters of Henry James* (1955); *The Future of the Novel* (1956); *Five World Biographies* (with others, 1961); *The Diary of Alice James* (1964); etc. Prof. English, New York University, since 1955.

EDES, BENJAMIN (Oct. 14, 1732–Dec. 11, 1803); b. Charlestown, Mass. Editor, pamphleteer. Founder, with John Gill, of the *Boston Gazette and Country Journal,* 1755. Wrote political tracts during the Revolution.

EDES, HENRY HERBERT (Mar. 29, 1849–Oct. 13, 1922); b. Charlestown, Mass. Genealogist, biographer. *Documents Concerning the Early History of Yale University* (1902); *John Winthrop* (1902); etc.

EDES, ROBERT THAXTER (Sept. 23, 1838–Jan. 12, 1923); b. Eastport, Me. Physician, educator, author. *The Story of Rodman Heath; or, Mugwumps* (anon., 1894); *Parson Gay's Three Sermons; or, Saint Sacrement* (1908); etc. Harvard Medical School, 1870-86.

Edgar Huntley. Novel by Charles Brockden Brown (1799). A study of a somnambulist who commits suicide.

EDGERTON, ALICE CRAIG (July 25, 1874–Jan. 7, 1946); b. Caldwell, Wis. Lawyer, author. *A Speech for Every Occasion* (1931); *Juvenile Selections and Dialogues* (1931); *More Speeches and Stories for Every Occasion* (1936); etc.

EDGERTON, FRANKLIN (July 24, 1885–Dec. 7, 1963); b. Lemars, Ia. Indologist, *The Panchatantra Reconstructed*, 2v. (1924); *The Baghavad Gita or Song of the Blessed One* (1925); *The Elephant Lore of the Hindus* (1931); *Buddhist Hybrid Sanskrit Language and Literature* (1954); etc. Prof. Sanskrit and comparative philology, Yale University, 1926–53.

EDGERTON, WILLIAM FRANKLIN (Sept. 30, 1893–); b. Binghamton, N.Y. Egyptologist. *Medinet Habu*, Vol. I, *Earlier Historical Records of Ramses III* (with others, 1930); *Notes on Egyptian Marriage, Chiefly in the Ptolemaic Period* (1931); *Medinet Habu Graffiti Facsimiles* (1937); and other works in Egyptology.

EDGETT, EDWIN FRANCIS (Jan. 12, 1867–Mar. 12, 1948); b. Boston, Mass. Editor, critic. *Plays of the Present* (with J. B. Clapp, 1901); *Players of the Present* (with same, 1901); *Slings and Arrows* (1922); *I Speak for Myself* (autobiography, 1940); etc. Dramatic editor, Boston *Transcript*, 1894–99; lit. editor, 1901–38.

EDGREN, AUGUST HJALMAR (Oct. 18, 1840–Dec. 9, 1903); b. in Vermland, Sweden. Lexicographer, Orientalist, poet. *Swedish Literature in America* (1883); *Dikter* (1884); *A Compendious Sanskrit Grammar* (1885); *Blaklint: Ny Diktsamling* (1894); etc. Compiler: *A Compendious German and English Dictionary* (with W. D. Whitney, 1877). Prof. modern languages, University of Nebraska, 1885–1900.

EDINGTON, ARLO CHANNING (Sept. 23, 1890–Nov. 16, 1953); b. Washington, Kan. Novelist. Co-author (with wife, Carmen Ballen Edington): *The Studio Murder Mystery* (1929); *The House of the Vanishing Goblets* (1930); *Tundra* (1930); *The Monk's Hood Murders* (1931).

EDINGTON, CARMEN[cita Alicia Eunice Ursula de] **BALLEN** (Mrs. Arlo Channing Edington) (Dec. 31, 1894–); b. Santa Cruz, Calif. Novelist. Co-author (with husband): *The Studio Murder Mystery* (1929); *The House of the Vanishing Goblets* (1930); *Tundra* (1930); *The Monk's Hood Murders* (1931).

Editha's Burglar. Girls' story by Frances Hodgson Burnett (1888).

Editions Imagi. Baltimore, Md. Founded 1952. Devoted to first volumes of poems by Americans. Thomas Cole is editor.

Editor and Publisher. New York. Weekly journal of the newspaper trade. Founded 1901. Absorbed the *Journalist* (founded 1884), 1911, and became the *Editor and Publisher and Journalist.* Assumed volume numbering of the *Journalist*, Mar. 20, 1915. Resumed original name 1916. Absorbed *Newspaperdom* (founded 1892), 1925; and *Fourth Estate* (founded 1894), 1927. Its *International Year Book Number* contains the names of the leading American newspapers, their publishers, editors, cartoonists, columnists, etc., with a selective bibliography on journalistic subjects.

Editorial Review. New York. Founded Aug., 1909. Expired 1912.

"Editor's Drawer, The." Humorous department in *Harper's Monthly Magazine*, starting with volume three. Lewis Gaylord Clarke was its first editor and in 1853 the Rev. Samuel Irenaeus Prime took charge of it. William A. Seaver, Charles Dudley Warner, and John Kendrick Bangs were also editors.

"Editor's Easy Chair, The." Department begun in 1851 in *Harper's Monthly Magazine.* Donald G. Mitchell conducted it for a while, George William Curtis conducted it for forty years, followed by William Dean Howells (1900–20), E. S. Martin, Bernard De Voto, and John Fischer.

Editors of the Past. By R. W. Hughes (1897).

"Editor's Study, The." Department in *Harper's Monthly Magazine*, started by William Dean Howells, in 1885. Charles Dudley Warner succeeded him in 1894, and Henry Mills Alden took charge in 1898.

"Editor's Table, The." Humorous department in the *Knickerbocker Magazine*, conducted by Lewis Gaylord Clark.

EDMAN, IRWIN (Nov. 28, 1896–Sept. 4, 1954); b. New York City. Educator, philosopher, essayist, poet. *Poems* (1925); *Adam, the Baby, and the Man from Mars* (1929); *On Going to College* (1937); *Philosopher's Holiday* (1938); *Candle in the Dark* (1939); *Arts and the Man* (1939); *I Believe* (1939); *Fountainheads of Freedom* (with H. W. Schneider, 1941); *Philosopher's Quest* (1947); *Under Whatever Sky* (1951); *John Dewey: His Contribution to the American Tradition* (1955); etc. Co-author: *Landmarks in Philosophy* (1941). Editor: *Works of Plato* (1927); *The Philosophy of Santayana* (1936). Prof. philosophy, Columbia University, from 1935.

EDMAN, V[ictor] **RAYMOND** (May 9, 1900–Sept. 22, 1967); b. Chicago, Ill. Educator, author. *The Disciplines of Life* (1948); *The Light in Dark Ages* (1949); *Finney Lives On* (1951); *But God!* (1963); *Then and There* (1964); etc. Pres., Wheaton College, Illinois, since 1941.

EDMANDS, JOHN (Feb. 1, 1820–Oct. 17, 1915); b. Framingham, Mass. Librarian, author. *Subjects for Debate* (1847), a forerunner of *Poole's Index to Periodical Literature; Catalogue of the Mercantile Library of Philadelphia* (1870); etc. Librarian, Mercantile Library, Philadelphia, 1856–1901.

EDMONDS, WALTER (D[umaux] (July 15, 1903–); b. Boonville, N.Y. Author. *Rome Haul* (1929); *The Big Barn* (1930); *Erie Water* (1933); *Mostly Canallers* (1934); *Drums Along the Mohawk* (1936); *Chad Hanna* (1940); *Young Ames* (1942); *Wilderness Clearing* (1944); *In the Hands of the Senecas* (1947); *They Fought with What They Had* (1951); *The Boyds of Black River* (1953); *Uncle Ben's Whale* (1955); *The Musket and the Cross* (1968); *Time to Go House* (1969); etc.

EDMUNDS, ALBERT JOSEPH (Nov. 21, 1857–Dec. 17, 1941); b. Tottenham, Middlesex, England. Librarian, poet. *English and American Poems*, 2v. (1888); *Songs of Asia Sung in America* (1896); *Buddhist and Christian Gospels* (1902); *Hymns of the Faith* (1902); *Fairmount Park, and Other Poems* (1906); *A Duet with Omar* (1913); *Leaves from the Gospel of Mark* (1936); etc. Cataloguer, Historical Society of Pennsylvania, 1891–1936.

EDSON, GUS (Sept. 20, 1901–Sept. 26, 1966); b. Cincinnati, O. Cartoonist. New York *Daily News*, 1931–35. Creator of "Streaky" and "The Gumps." The latter appeared in the *Chicago Tribune* and the *News* from 1935. Creator-author of comic strip "Dondi."

EDSTROM, DAVID (Mar. 27, 1873–Aug. 12, 1938); b. Hvetlanda, Sweden. Sculptor, author. *The Testament of Caliban* (autobiography, 1937).

Education of Henry Adams, The. By Henry Adams (1906, 1918). A revealing autobiography of a man saddened by unrealized potentialities; a record of complete disillusionment, and an indictment of the machine age with its menace to culture. Adams found his genteel Boston background a formidable handicap to his political career, and his attempt to adjust himself to modern life ended in failure.

Educator's Guide to Media and Methods. Philadelphia, Pa. Monthly during the school year. Founded 1966. Formerly *Teachers' Guide to Media and Methods.* Notable for its attempt to adapt media technology, audiovisual imagination, and the nonverbal forms of expression to practical educational use.

EDWARDS, BELA BATES (July 4, 1802–Apr. 20, 1852); b. Southampton, Mass. Congregational clergyman, educator, editor, author. *Biography of Self Taught Men* (1832); *Writings*, 2v. (1853). Editor, *American Quarterly Register*, 1827–43; founder, *American Quarterly Observer*, 1833; cofounder (with Edwards A. A. Park), *Bibliotheca Sacra*, 1842; editor, 1844–52.

EDWARDS, EDWARD B. (Feb. 8, 1873–Feb. 16, 1948); b. Columbia, Pa. Artist, illustrator, author. *Dynamarhythmic Design* (1932). Designer and illustrator of books, magazines, etc., including *A Book of Shakespeare's Songs* (1903); *The Great Chalice of Antioch* (1923); etc.

EDWARDS, GEORGE WHARTON (Mar. 14, 1869–Jan 18, 1950); b. Fair Haven, Conn. Painter, author. *Thumbnail Sketches* (1886); *Break o' Day, and Other Poems* (1889); *Holland of Today* (1909); *Brittany and the Bretons* (1910); *Some Old Flemish Towns* (1911); *The Forest of Arden* (1914); *Vanished Halls and Cathedrals of France* (1917); *London* (1921); *Paris* (1924); *Spain* (1925); *Rome* (1928); *Constantinople* (1929–30); etc. Illustrated Holmes's *The Last Leaf* (1885); Spenser's *Epithalamium* (1895); *Old English Ballads* (1897); etc.

EDWARDS, GUS (Aug. 18, 1881–1945); b. in Germany. Song writer, actor. His best known songs are "School Days," "By the Light of the Silvery Moon," "I Don't Know Why I Love You, But I Do," "Tammany," etc. Discoverer of Earl Carroll, Joe Cook, Eddie Cantor, Mae Murray, George Jessell, Helen Menken, and others, and was the subject of the motion picture, *The Star Maker* (1939).

EDWARDS, HARRY STILLWELL (Apr. 23, 1855–Oct. 22, 1938); b. Macon, Ga. Novelist, poet. *Sons and Fathers* (1896); *The Marbeau Cousins* (1897); *Fifth Dimension* (1912); *Just Sweethearts* (1919); *Eneas Africanus* (1919); *Little Legends of the Land* (poems, 1930); etc.

EDWARDS, JONATHAN (Oct. 5, 1703–Mar. 22, 1758); b. East Windsor, Conn. Presbyterian clergyman, educator, philosopher, author. *A Careful and Strict Enquiry into Modern Prevailing Notions of that Freedom of Will, which is Supposed to be Essential to Moral Agency, Virtue, and Vice, Reward and Punishment, Praise and Blame* (1754); *The Works of President Edwards*, edited by S. Austin, 8v. (1808–09). Third president of Princeton University. His manuscripts are in the library of Yale University. *See* Arthur Cushman McGiffert's *Jonathan Edwards* (1932); Henry Bamford Parkes's *Jonathan Edwards* (1930); Ola E. Winslow's *Jonathan Edwards* (1940); Perry Miller's *Jonathan Edwards* (1949); A. O. Aldridge's *Jonathan Edwards* (1964).

EDWARDS, LOREN McCLAIN (Nov. 14, 1877–July 20, 1945); b. Rising Sun, Ind. Methodist clergyman, author. *The Spectrum of Religion* (1918); *Light of Christmas, and Other Poems* (1923); etc.

Edwards, Samuel. Pen name of Noel B. Gerson.

EELLS, ELSIE [Eusebia] SPICER (Mrs. Burr Gould Eells) (Sept. 21, 1880–May 24, 1963); b. West Winfield, N.Y. Author. *Fairy Tales from Brazil* (1917); *The Islands of Magic* (1922); *The Magic Tooth* (1927); *South America's Story* (1931); *Tales of Enchantment from Spain* (1950); etc.

EELLS, HASTINGS (June 9, 1895–); b. Absecon, N.J. Educator, author. *Martin Bucer* (1931); *Europe Since 1500* (1933). Co-author: *Post War World* (1944). Prof. history, Ohio Wesleyan University, since 1931.

EGAN, JOSEPH B[urke] (Oct. 11, 1879–); b. Omaha, Neb. Publisher, author. *Little People of the Dust* (1913); *Character Chats* (1926); *New Found Tales* (1930); *Prairie Days* (1935); *Mathew Brady, Pioneer* (1941); etc. President, Welles Publishing Co., Inc.

EGAN, MAURICE FRANCIS (May 24, 1852–Jan. 15, 1924); b. Philadelphia, Pa. Diplomat, educator, essayist, poet. *Preludes* (1880); *Modern Novels and Novelists* (1888); *Songs and Sonnets, and Other Poems* (1892); *The Leopard of Lancianus, and Other Tales* (1899); *Studies in Literature* (1899); *The Ghost in Hamlet, and Other Essays in Comparative Literature* (1906); *Ten Years Near the German Frontier* (1919); *Everybody's St. Francis* (1920); *Confessions of a Book-Lover* (1922); *Recollections of a Happy Life* (1924). Editor, *Freeman's Journal*, 1881–88. Prof. English, Notre Dame University, 1888–96. Catholic University of America, 1896–1907. U.S. Minister to Denmark, 1907–18.

Egg and I, The. By Betty MacDonald (1945). Reminiscences of the author's life in mining regions and on a chicken farm. Humorous incidents enliven the story.

EGGLESTON, EDWARD (Dec. 10, 1837–Sept. 2, 1902); b. Vevay, Ind. Methodist clergyman, editor, novelist, historian. *The Hoosier Schoolmaster* (1871); *The Circuit Rider* (1874); *Roxy* (1878); *The Hoosier Schoolboy* (1883); *The Graysons* (1887); *The Faith Doctor* (1891); *Duffels* (1893); *The Beginnings of a Nation* (1896); *The Transit of Civilization* (1901); etc. Editor, *Little Corporal, Hearth and Home*, etc. *See* G. C. Eggleston's *The First of the Hoosiers* (1903); Edward Stone's *Voices of Despair: Four Motifs in American Literature* (1966); *American Literary Realism* (1967).

EGGLESTON, GEORGE CARY (Nov. 26, 1839–Apr. 14, 1911); b. Vevay, Ind. Journalist, novelist. *A Man of Honor* (1873); *The Big Brother* (1875); *A Rebel's Recollections* (1878); *Strange Stories from History* (1886); *Dorothy South* (1902); *The Master of Warlock* (1903); *Evelyn Byrd* (1904); *The History of the Confederate War*, 2v. (1910); *Recollections of a Varied Life* (1910); etc. Compiler: *American War Ballads and Lyrics*, 2v. (1889). Editor, *Hearth and Home; American Homes*; literary editor, New York *Evening Post*, 1875–81.

EGLE, WILLIAM HENRY (Sept. 17, 1830–Feb. 19, 1901); b. in Lancaster Co., Pa. Surgeon, historian. *An Illustrated History of the Commonwealth of Pennsylvania* (1877); *Some Pennsylvania Women During the War of the Revolution* (1898); etc. State librarian of Pennsylvania, 1887–1901. Co-editor, the *Pennsylvania Archives*, 2d series, v. 1–14; editor, v. 15–19, and 3d series, v. 1–26.

Egoists: A Book of Supermen. Critical essays by James Gibbons Huneker (1909).

EHLE, JOHN (1925–); b. Asheville, N.C. Author. *Move Over, Mountain* (1957); *The Survivor* (1958); *Kingstree Island* (1959); *Shepherd of the Streets* (1960); *Lion on the Hearth* (1961); *The Land Breakers* (1964); *The Road* (1967); etc.

EHRLICH, LEONARD (June 19, 1905–); b. New York. Novelist. *God's Angry Man* (1932).

EHRMANN, MAX[imilian] (Sept. 26, 1872–); b. Terre Haute, Ind. Author. *A Farrago* (1898); *The Mystery of Madeline Le Blanc* (1899); *Breaking Home Ties* (poems, 1904); *Poems* (1906); *The Poems of Max Ehrmann* (1910); *The Seasons* (1917); *David and Bathsheba* (1918); *A Virgin's Dream* (1922); *Life of Paul Dresser* (1924); *Be Quiet, I'm Talking* (1926); *Desiderata* (1927); *Worldly Wisdom* (1934); etc.

Eichmann in Jerusalem. By Hannah Arendt (1963). Controversial account of the Eichmann trial in Israel amid a documented historical treatment of the genocide of the Jews, in which the author discusses the reasons for the tragedy and the degree of Eichmann's blame.

EIFERT, VIRGINIA SNIDER (Jan. 23, 1911–June 17, 1966); b. Springfield, Ill. Author. *Three Rivers South* (1953); *The Buffalo Trace* (1955); *Out of the Wilderness* (1956); *With a Task Before Me* (1958); *New Birth of Freedom* (1959); *Delta Queen* (1960); *Louis Jolliet, Explorer of Rivers* (1961); *George Shannon: Young Explorer with Lewis and Clark* (1963); *Journeys in Green Places* (1963); *Of Men and Rivers* (1966); etc.

EIKER, MATHILDE (Jan. 5, 1893–); b. Washington, D.C. Author. *Mrs. Mason's Daughters* (1925); *The Lady of Stainless Raiment* (1928); *My Own Far Towers* (1930); *Brief Seduction of Eva* (1932); *Key Next Door;* etc. Under pen name "March Evermay": *They Talked of Poison* (1938); *Red Light for Murder* (1951); etc.

"Eili, Eili." Jewish lament. Its authorship was claimed by Jacob Koppel Saidler, who said he composed it in 1896. His suit for infringement of copyright was tried before Judge Knox in Apr., 1925, in New York. See *A Judge Comes of Age,* by John C. Knox (1940).

EILSHEMIUS, LOUIS MICHEL (Feb. 4, 1864–Dec. 29, 1941); b. Laurel Hill, Arlington, N.J. Painter, author. *Songs of Spring* (1895); *"Lady Vere," and Other Narratives* (1897); *Sweetbrier* (1900); *Poetical Works* (1901); *Songs of Southern Scenes* (1904); *The Poet; and Elegiac Poems* (1907); *Inspirations* (1907); *Fragments and Flashes of Thought* (1907); *Nannie* (1907); etc. *See* William Schack's *And He Sat Among the Ashes* (1939).

Eimi. Account of a trip to the U.S.S.R., by E. E. Cummings (1933). Written in an impressionistic style with symphonic accumulation of effects found in his poetry. An unmitigated attack on the Soviet stifling of individuality and freedom of the imagination.

EINSELEN, ANNE F. (1900–); b. Philadelphia, Pa. Editor, author. Writes under pen name "Anne Paterson." *Take These Hands* (1939); *Sleepless Candle* (1941); *Queen Street Story* (1949).

EINSTEIN, ALBERT (Mar. 14, 1879–Apr. 18, 1955); b. Ulm a.d. Donau, Ger. Theoretical physicist. *Relativity* (1920); *The Meaning of Relativity* (1923); *Sidelights on Relativity* (1923); *Investigation on the Theory of the Brownian Movement* (1926); *About Zionism* (1931); *Builders of the Universe* (1932); *On the Method of Theoretical Physics* (1933); *The World as I See It* (1934); *Evolution of Physics* (with Leopold Infeld, 1938); *Out of My Later Years* (1950); *Ideas and Opinions* (1954); etc. Nobel prize for physics, 1921.

EINSTEIN, ALFRED (Dec. 30, 1880–Feb. 13, 1952); b. Munich, Bav. Musicologist. *Gluck* (1936); *A Short History of Music* (1936); *Greatness in Music* (1941); *Mozart: His Character, His Work* (1945); *Music in the Romantic Era* (1947); *The Italian Madrigal* (1949); *Schubert: A Musical Portrait* (1951); etc.

EISELEY, LOREN C[orey] (Sept. 3, 1907–); b. Lincoln, Neb. Anthropologist. *The Immense Journey* (1957); *Darwin's Century* (1958); *The Firmament of Time* (1960); *Francis Bacon and the Modern Dilemma* (1963); *The Mind as Nature* (1963); *The Unexpected Universe* (1969). Editor: *Early Man in the Eden Valley* (1951). Co-editor: *An Appraisal of Anthropology Today* (1953). Prof. anthropology, University of Pennsylvania, since 1947.

EISEN, GUSTAVUS AUGUSTUS (Aug. 2, 1847–Oct. 29, 1940); b. Stockholm, Sweden. Archaeologist, author. *The Great Chalice of Antioch,* 2v. (1923), simplified edition (1933); *Glass,* 2v. (1927); *Portraits of Washington,* 3v. (1933); etc.

EISENHOWER, DWIGHT DAVID (Oct. 14, 1890–Mar. 28, 1969); b. Denison, Tex. Thirty-third President of the United States. *Eisenhower's Own Story of the War* (1946); *Crusade in Europe* (1948); *Peace with Justice: Selected Addresses* (1961); *At Ease: Stories I Tell to Friends* (1967). Allied commander in chief in Europe, 1943–45; commander, U.S. occupation forces in Germany, 1945; chief of staff, U.S. Army, 1945–48; pres., Columbia University,1948–52; President of the U.S., 1953–60. *See* Arthur Larsen's *Eisenhower: The President Nobody Knew* (1968); Stephen E. Ambrose's *The War Years of General Dwight D. Eisenhower* (1970).

EISENSCHIML, OTTO (June 16, 1880–Dec. 7, 1963); b. Vienna. Chemist. Author or co-author: *Why Was Lincoln Murdered?* (1937); *In the Shadow of Lincoln's Death* (1940); *Reviewers Reviewed* (1940); *Without Fame* (1942); *The Story of Shiloh* (1946); *The American Iliad* (co-ed., 1947); *As Luck Would Have It* (1948); *Why the Civil War?* (1958); *The Hidden Face of the Civil War* (1961); *The Civil War in Miniature* (1962); etc.

EISNER, WILL (Mar. 6, 1917–); b. New York. Cartoonist, author. *America's Combat Weapons* (1960); *America's Space Vehicles* (1961). Cartoonist, syndicated feature, *The Spirit,* 1940-52.

EKINS, H[erbert] R[oslyn] (May 9, 1901–Oct. 14, 1963); b. Minneapolis, Minn. Correspondent. *Around the World in Eighteen Days and How to Do It* (1936); *China Fights for Her Life* (with Theon Wright, 1938). Foreign manager of United Press in Honolulu, Manila, Shanghai, Peiping, etc., 1927–35; managing editor, Schenectady *Union-Star,* from 1953.

ELBERT, JOHN ALOYSIUS (Mar. 15, 1895–Oct. 1966); b. Brooklyn, N.Y. Educator, author. *Evolution of Newman's Concept of Faith* (1934); *Greater Love* (1937); *Prayer in a Modern Age* (1941); etc. Prof. philosophy, University of Dayton, 1947–48, from 1958.

ELDER, PAUL (Jan. 1, 1872–Jan. 24, 1948); b. Harrisburg, Pa. Publisher, bookseller, author. *Old Spanish Missions of California* (1913). Compiler: *Mosaic Essays* (1906); *California the Beautiful* (1911).

Elder, Paul, & Company. San Francisco. Booksellers, publishers. Founded by Paul Elder in 1898. In 1899 Morgan Shepard went into partnership to form Elder and Shepard. In 1903 Shepard retired and the business was incorporated as Paul Elder and Company. For some years the firm was active in book publishing, and its books were distinguished by their fine printing.

ELDER, SUSAN BLANCHARD (Apr. 19, 1835–Nov. 3, 1923); b. Fort Jessup, La. Biographer, poet. *James the Second* (1874); *Savonarola* (1875); *Ellen Fitzgerald* (1876); *Elder Flowers* (poems, 1912); *Life of the Abbé Adrien Rouquette* (1913); *A Mosaic in Blue and Gray* (1914); etc.

ELDER, WILLIAM (July 23, 1806–Apr. 5, 1885); b. Somerset, Pa. Physician, essayist, economist. *Periscopics* (1854); *The Enchanted Beauty* (1855); *Biography of Elisha Kent Kane* (1858); *Questions of the Day* (1871); etc.

ELDRIDGE, FREDERICK WILLIAM (Aug. 10, 1877–Aug. 9, 1937); b. Alexandria, Va. Editor, novelist, playwright. *A Social Cockatrice* (1903); *The Eternal Triangle* (prod. 1910). Managing editor, *Los Angeles Examiner,* 1908–37.

ELDRIDGE, PAUL (May 5, 1888–); b. Philadelphia, Pa. Educator, novelist, poet. *Vanitas* (poems, 1920); *And the Sphinx Spoke* (1921); *Our Dead Selves* (poems, 1923); *Irony and Pity* (1926); *The Intruder* (1928); *My First Two Thousand Years: The Autobiography of the Wandering Jew* (with George Sylvester Viereck, 1928); *Salome* (with same, 1930); *Cobwebs and Cosmos* (poems, 1930) ; *The Invincible Adam* (with George Sylvester Viereck, 1932); *One Man Show* (1933); *Prince Pax* (with George Sylvester Viereck, 1933); *Men and Women* (1946); *The Crown of Empire* (1957); *The Second Life of John H. Stevens* (1959); *The Tree of Ignorance* (1962); *Maxims for a Modern Man* (1965); *The Homecoming* (1966); *The Story-Tellers* (1969); etc.

ELDRIDGE, SEBA (July 22, 1885–Feb. 16, 1953); b. Johnston Co., N.Y. Sociologist. *Political Action* (1924); *The Organization of Life* (1925); *An Introduction to Sociology* (with others, 1927); *The New Christianity* (1929); *Public Intelligence* (1935); *New Social Horizons* (1941); *Fundamentals of Sociology* (with others, 1950); etc. Prof. sociology, University of Kansas, from 1929.

Electric Kool-Aid Acid Test, The. By Tom Wolfe. (1968). An account of the adventures of Ken Kesey (q.v.) and his Merry Pranksters in their painted bus in search of communal drug experiences, especially with LSD.

ELEGANT, ROBERT SAMPSON (Mar. 7, 1928–); b. New York. Journalist, author. *China's Red Masters* (1951); *The Dragon's Seed* (1959); *The Center of the World* (1964); *A Kind of Treason* (1965); *The Seeking* (1968). Chief, Hong Kong bureau, *Los Angeles Times,* since 1965.

Elegant Extracts. By Vicesimus Knox, 6v. (1825). Edited by James Gates Percival.

Elegies and Epitaphs. Popular verse forms characteristic of the Colonies, written in honor of the dead. The elegy was often written by the minister of the parish and printed in a book or as a broadside. The epitaph was usually written by a nameless poet to be carved on stone. See *Elegies and Epitaphs, 1677–1717,* ed. by James F. Hunnewell (1896); Harriette M. Forbes's *Gravestones of Early New England* (1927).

ELIADE, MIRCEA (Mar. 9, 1907–   ); b. Bucharest, Rumania. Educator, author. *Yoga* (1936); *The Myth of the Eternal Return* (1954); *Birth and Rebirth* (1958); *The Forge and the Crucible* (1962); *Myth and Reality* (1963); *Patterns in Comparative Religion* (1963); *The Two and the One* (1965); *Shamanism* (1964); *From Primitives to Zen: A Thematic Sourcebook* (1967); *Two Tales of the Occult* (1970). Prof. religion, University of Chicago, since 1958.

ELIAS, ROBERT HENRY (Sept. 17, 1914–   ); b. New York. Educator, author. *Theodore Dreiser: Apostle of Nature* (1949). Editor: *Chapters of Erie* (1956); *Letters of Theodore Dreiser* (1959). Associate editor; *Epoch,* 1947–54. Prof. English, Cornell University, since 1959.

ELIOT, ALEXANDER (Apr. 28, 1919–   ); b. Cambridge, Mass. Author. *Proud Youth* (1953); *Three Hundred Years of American Painting* (1957); *Sight and Insight* (1959); *Earth, Air, Fire and Water* (1962); *Greece* (1963); *Love Play* (1966); *Creatures of Arcadia* (1967); *Socrates* (1967); *Everyman's Dream* (1968).

ELIOT, CHARLES WILLIAM (Mar. 20, 1834–Aug. 22, 1926); b. Boston, Mass., son of Samuel Atkins Eliot (1798–1862). Educator, author. *The Happy Life* (1896); *Educational Reform* (1898); *American Contributions to Civilization* (1897); *John Gilley* (1904); *Four American Leaders* (1906); *The Durable Satisfactions of Life* (1910); *A Late Harvest* (1924); etc. Editor, *The Harvard Classics,* 50v. (1909–10). *See* William Allan Neilson's *Charles W. Eliot, the Man and His Beliefs* (1926). President, Harvard University, 1869–1909.

ELIOT, ETHEL COOK (Mrs. Samuel Atkins Eliot, Jr.) (Apr. 15, 1890–); b. North Gage, N.Y. Author. *The Little House in the Fairy Wood* (1918); *The Wind Boy* (1923); *Ariel Dances* (1931); *Her Soul to Keep* (1934); *Angels' Mirth* (1936); etc.

ELIOT, GEORGE FIELDING (June 22, 1894–); b. Brooklyn, N.Y. Army officer, military critic, author. *Eagles of Death* (1930); *Navy Spy Murders* (1937); *If War Comes* (with R. E. Dupuy, 1937); *The Ramparts We Watch* (1938); *Bombs Bursting in Air* (1939); *Hour of Triumph* (1944); *The Strength We Need* (1946); *Hate, Hope and High Explosive* (1948); *If Russia Strikes* (1949); *Caleb Pettengill, USN* (1956); *Victory Without War* (1958); *Reserve Forces and the Kennedy Strategy* (1962); *Franklin Buchanan* (1962).

ELIOT, HENRIETTA R[obins]; b. 1845, Amherst, Mass. Novelist. *Laura's Holidays* (1898); *Laura in the Mountains* (1905).

ELIOT, JOHN (1604–May 21, 1690); b. Widford, England. Clergyman, missionary to the Indians. Translated the Bible into the Indian language: *The New Testament* (1661); *The Holy Bible* (1663). Compiler: *The Indian Primer* (1669); etc. *See* S. E. Morison's *Builders of the Bay Colony* (1930).

Eliot, Mrs. Christian. See Nina Wilcox Putnam.

ELIOT, SAMUEL (Dec. 22, 1821–Sept. 14, 1898); b. Boston, Mass., nephew of Samuel Atkins Eliot (1798–1862). Educator, historian. *The Liberty of Rome,* 2v. (1849), expanded into *The History of Liberty,* 4v. (1853); etc. Compiler: *Selections from American Authors* (1879); *Poetry for Children* (1879). President, Trinity College, Hartford, Conn., 1860–64.

ELIOT, SAMUEL ATKINS (Mar. 5, 1798–Jan. 29, 1862); b. Boston, Mass. Author. *The Life of Josiah Henson, Formerly a Slave* (1843); *Sketch of the History of Harvard College* (1848); etc.

ELIOT, SAMUEL ATKINS, JR. (Mar. 14, 1893–); b. Denver, Colo. Educator, theatre director, editor, translator. Editor, *Little Theatre Classics,* v. 1–4 (1918–22). Translator of several plays by Wedekind, etc. English dept., Smith College, 1918–1961.

ELIOT, T[homas] S[tearns] (Sept. 26, 1888–Jan. 4, 1965); b. St. Louis, Mo. Poet, literary critic, playwright. *Prufrock and Other Observations* (poems, 1917); *Poems* (1919); *Ara Vos Prec* (poems, 1920); *The Sacred Wood* (1920); *The Waste Land* (poem, 1922); *Poems, 1909–1925* (1925); *For Lancelot Andrewes* (1928); *Dante* (1929); *Selected Essays, 1917–1932* (1932); *The Use of Poetry and the Use of Criticism* (1933); *After Strange Gods* (1933); *The Rock* (1934); *Elizabethan Essays* (1934); *Murder in the Cathedral* (prod. 1935); *Essays Ancient & Modern* (1936); *Collected Poems, 1909–1935* (1936); *The Family Reunion* (prod. 1939); *Old Possum's Book of Practical Cats* (poems, 1939); *The Idea of a Christian Society* (1940); *The Classics and the Man of Letters* (1942); *Four Quartets* (poems, 1943); *Notes Toward a Definition of Culture* (1949); *The Cocktail Party* (prod. 1950); *Poetry and Drama* (1951); *Complete Poems and Plays* (1952); *The Three Voices of Poetry* (1954); *Religious Drama: Medieval and Modern* (1954); *The Confidential Clerk* (prod. 1954); *The Cultivation of Christmas Trees* (poem, 1956); *On Poetry and Poets* (1957); *The Elder Statesman* (prod. 1959); *Christianity and Culture* (1960); *Collected Poems, 1909–1963* (1963); *Knowledge and Experience* (1964); etc. Awarded Nobel Prize for Literature, 1948. *See* F. O. Matthiessen's *The Achievement of T. S. Eliot* (1935); Elizabeth Drew's *T. S. Eliot, the Design of His Poetry* (1949); George Williamson's *A Reader's Guide to T. S. Eliot* (1953); Hugh Kenner's *Invisible Poet* (1959); Northrop Frye's *T. S. Eliot* (1963); Genesius Jones's *Approach to the Purpose: A Study of the Poetry of T. S. Eliot* (1965).

ELISOFON, ELIOT (Apr. 17, 1911–); b. New York. Painter, photographer. *Food Is a Four Letter Word* (1948); *The Sculpture of Africa* (with William Fagg, 1958); *The Nile* (1964); *Africa's Animals* (with M. E. Newman, 1967); *Indian Cookbook* (1969); *Java Diary* (1969).

Elizabeth the Queen. Play in blank verse by Maxwell Anderson (prod. 1930).

Elizabethan Club of Yale. Founded by Alexander Smith Cochran in 1911, with the object of collecting rare Elizabethan literature, to provide a club for informal discussions of literature between students and faculty members, and to produce a congenial atmosphere for the promotion of Elizabethan scholarship.

ELKIN, STANLEY [Lawrence] (May 11, 1930–); b. New York. Educator, author. *Boswell* (1964); *Criers and Kibitzers, Kibitzers and Criers* (1966); *A Bad Man* (1967); *The Dick Gibson Show* (1971). Prof. American literature, Washington University, since 1969.

Ellen, The Late Henry. Pen name of James Barron Hope.

Ellery Queen's Mystery Magazine. New York. Monthly. Founded 1941. Published by Davis Publications, Inc. Edited by "Ellery Queen" (Frederic Dannay and Manfred Bennington Lee until 1971; Mr. Dannay now sole editor).

ELLET, ELIZABETH FRIES LUMMIS (Oct., 1818–June 3, 1877); b. Sodus Point, N.Y. Author. *Teresa Contarina* (1835); *Women of the American Revolution* (1848); *Pioneer Women of the West* (1852); *Summer Rambles in the West* (1853); etc.

ELLIN, STANLEY (1916–). Author. *Mystery Stories* (1956); *The Eighth Circle* (1958); *The Winter After This Summer* (1960); *The Blessington Method and Other Strange Tales* (1964); *House of Cards* (1967); *The Valentine Estate* (1968); *The Bind* (1970); etc.

ELLIOT, HENRY RUTHERFORD (Apr. 21, 1849–1906); b. Woodbridge, Conn. Editor, novelist. *The Basset Claim* (1884); *The Common Chord* (1886). Editor, *The Church Economist.*

ELLIOT, SAMUEL HAYES (1809–1869); b. in Vermont. Congregational clergyman, author. *Rolling Ridge* (anon., 1838); *The Sequel to Rolling Ridge* (anon., 1844). *New England's Chattels; or, Life in the Northern Poor-House* (1858), revised as, *A Look at Home; or, Life in the Poor-House of New England* (1860); etc.

ELLIOTT, GEORGE P[aul] (June 16, 1918–). Educator, author. *Parktilden Village* (1958); *Among the Dangs* (1961); *David Knudsen* (1962); *A Piece of Lettuce* (1964); *In the World* (1965); *An Hour of Last Things and Other Stories* (1968); *From the Berkeley Hills* (1969); *Conversions* (1971); etc. Editor: *Fifteen American Poets* (1956); *Types of Prose Fiction* (1964); *New and Selected Poems of W. T. Scott* (1967). Prof. English, Syracuse University, since 1963.

ELLIOTT, G[eorge] R[oy] (Dec. 31, 1883–Oct. 17, 1963); b. London, Ont. Educator, author. *The Cycle of Modern Poetry* (1929); *Humanism and Imagination* (1938); *Scourge and Minister (a Study in Hamlet)* (1951); *Flaming Minister* (1953); *Dramatic Providence in Macbeth* (1958). Editor: *English Poetry of the Nineteenth Century* (with Norman Foerster, 1923). Prof. English, Amherst College, 1925–50.

Elliott, Lillian Elwyn. See Lillian Elwyn Elliott Joyce.

ELLIOTT, MAUD HOWE (Nov. 9, 1854–Mar. 19, 1948); b. Boston, Mass., daughter of Julia Ward Howe. Author. *A Newport Aquarelle* (1883); *The San Rosario Ranch* (1884); *Laura Bridgman* (with Florence Howe Hall, 1902); *Roma Beata* (1904); *Two in Italy* (1905); *Sun and Shadow in Spain* (1908); *Sicily in Shadow and in Sun* (1910); *The Eleventh Hour in the Life of Julia Ward Howe* (1911); *Julia Ward Howe, 1819–1910*, 2v. (with Laura Elizabeth Richards and Florence Howe Hall, 1916, Pulitzer Prize for biography, 1917); *Three Generations* (1923); *Lord Byron's Helmet* (1927); *John Elliott, the Story of an Artist* (1930); *My Cousin, F. Marion Crawford* (1934); *Uncle Sam Ward and His Circle* (1938); *Recollections of the Civil War* (1943); *This Was My Newport* (1944); *What I Saw and Heard in Panama* (1947); etc.

ELLIOTT, OSBORN (Oct. 25, 1924–   ); b. New York. Editor, author. *Men at the Top* (1959). Editor: *The Negro Revolution in America* (1964). Editor, *Newsweek*, since 1961.

ELLIOTT, SARAH BARNWELL (1848–Aug. 30, 1928); b. Georgia. Novelist. *The Felmeres* (1879); *A Simple Heart* (1887); *Jerry* (1891); *John Paget* (1893); *The Durket Sperret* (1898); *Sam Houston* (1900); *The Making of Jane* (1901); etc.

ELLIOTT, WALTER HACKETT ROBERT (Jan. 6, 1842–Apr. 18, 1928); b. Detroit, Mich. Roman Catholic priest, author. *Life of Father Hecker* (1891); *Parish Sermons* (1913); *Mission Sermons* (1926); etc. Founder, *The Missionary,* (1896).

ELLIOTT, WILLIAM (Apr. 27, 1788–Feb. 3, 1863); b. Beaufort, S.C. Planter, poet. *Carolina Sports by Land and Water* (1846); *Fiesco* (drama in verse, 1850); *The Letters of Agricola* (anon., 1852).

ELLIOTT, WILLIAM YANDELL (May 12, 1896–); b. Murfreesboro, Tenn. Educator, author. *The Pragmatic Revolt in Politics* (1928); *The New British Empire* (1932); *The Western Political Heritage* (with N. A. McDonald, 1949); *American Foreign Policy: Organization and Control (1952); Political Economy of the Foreign Policy of the United States* (1955); *The Secretary of State* (1960); etc. Editor: *Television's Impact on American Culture* (1956); *Education and Training in the Developing Countries* (1966). Prof. government, Harvard University, since 1931.

Elliott and Thomes. Boston, Mass. Publishers. Later called Elliott, Thomes and Talbot; and Thomes and Talbot. Publishers of dime novels and popular magazines such as: *The American Union; Flag of Our Union; True Flag; Weekly Novelette; Line-of-Battle Ship.* They were publishers for Frederick Gleason and Maturin M. Ballou.

ELLIS, ALBERT (1913–). Psychologist, author. *The Folklore of Sex* (1951); *The American Sexual Tragedy* (1954); *How to Live with a Neurotic* (1957); *The Art and Science of Love* (1960); *Creative Marriage* (1961); *A Guide to Rational Living* (with Robert A. Harper, 1961); *If This Be Sexual Heresy* (1963); *The Origins and the Development of the Incest Taboo* (1963); *The Intelligent Woman's Guide to Manhunting* (1964); *Homosexuality: Its Causes and Cure* (1965); *The Art of Erotic Seduction* (with Roger O. Conway, 1967); *Nymphomania: A Study of the Oversexed Woman* (with Edward Sagarin, 1968); *Is Objectivism a Religion?* (1968); *The Psychology of Murder and Assassination* (1969); etc. Editor: *The Encyclopedia of Sexual Behavior,* 5v. (with Albert Abarbanel) (1969).

ELLIS, ANNE (1875–1938). Colorado pioneer, author. *The Life of an Ordinary Woman* (autobiography, 1929); *"Plain Anne Ellis": More About the Life of an Ordinary Woman* (1931).

ELLIS, EDITH (Mrs. C. Becker Furness) (June, 1876–Apr. 27, 1960); b. Coldwater, Mich. Playwright. *The Wrong Man* (prod. 1905); *Contrary Mary* (prod. 1905); *Ben of Broken Bow Ranch* (prod. 1905); *Mary Jane's Pa* (prod. 1908); *Zaza's Hit* (prod. 1909); *Whose Little Bride Are You?* (prod. 1921); *Betty's Last Bet* (prod. 1922); *The Judsons Entertain* (prod. 1923); *The Last Chapter* (with Edward Ellis, 1930); etc. Transcriber: *We Knew These Men* by Wilfred Brandon (1942); *Love in the Afterlife* by Wilfred Brandon (1956); etc. See Margaret G. Mayorga's *A Short History of the American Drama* (1934).

ELLIS, EDWARD SYLVESTER (Apr. 11, 1840–June 20, 1916); b. Geneva, O. Novelist, historical writer. *Seth Jones; or, The Captive of the Frontier* (1860); and many other dime novels, including the *Deerfoot Series,* under own and many pen names.

ELLIS, ELMER (July 27, 1901–); b. in McHenry Co., N.D. Educator, historian, author. *Henry Moore Teller, Defender of the West* (1941); *Mr. Dooley's America* (1941). Editor: *Education Against Propaganda* (1937); *Mr. Dooley at His Best* (1938); *Toward Better Teaching in College* (1954). History dept., University of Missouri, since 1930; pres., 1955–66; prof. history, since 1966.

ELLIS, GEORGE EDWARD (Aug. 8, 1814–Dec. 20, 1894); b. Boston, Mass. Unitarian clergyman, historian. *The Puritan Age and Rule in the Colony of Massachusetts Bay, 1629–1685* (1888); etc.

ELLIS, GEORGE WASHINGTON (May 4, 1875–Nov. 26, 1919); b. Weston, Mo. Lawyer, author. *Negro Culture in West Africa* (1914); *Negro Achievements in Social Progress* (1915); *The Leopard's Claw* (1917); etc.

ELLIS, GRIFFITH OGDEN (Nov. 19, 1869–Feb. 4, 1948); b. Urbana, Ill. Publisher. Editor, *American Boy.* President, Sprague Publishing Co., Detroit, Mich., 1908–39; William A. Scripps Co.

ELLIS, [Harold] MILTON (Aug. 2, 1885–May 18, 1947); b. Belfast, Me. Educator, author. *Joseph Dennie and His Circle* (1915); *Philenia: The Life and Works of Sarah Wentworth Morton, 1759–1846* (with Emily Pendleton, 1931). Editor: *The Lay Preacher Essays of Joseph Dennie, Scholars' Facsimiles and Reprints* (1943). English dept., University of Maine, from 1919.

ELLIS, HARRY BEARSE (Dec. 9, 1921–); b. Springfield, Mass. Journalist, author. *Heritage of the Desert* (1956); *Israel and the Middle East* (1957); *The Arabs* (1958); *Challenge in the Middle East* (1960); *The Common Market* (1965). Staff, *Christian Science Monitor,* since 1947.

ELLIS, J[ohn] BRECKENRIDGE (Feb. 11, 1870–Apr. 2, 1956); b. near Hannibal, Mo. Novelist. *In the Days of Jehu* (1898); *Garcilaso* (1901); *Story of a Life* (1910); *Fran* (1912); *Lahoma* (1913); *Little Fiddler of the Ozarks* (1913); *Agnes of the Bad Lands* (1916); *Old Steady* (1932); *Adventure of Living* (autobiography, 1933); *Two Masters* (1936); *Other Things* (1940); etc.

ELLIS, JOHN TRACY (July 30, 1905–); b. Seneca, Ill. Roman Catholic clergyman, educator, author. *Anti-Papal Legislation in Mediaeval England, 1066–1377* (1930); *The Formative Years of the Catholic University of America* (1946); *The Life of James Cardinal Gibbons, Archbishop of Baltimore,* 2v. (1952); *American Catholicism* (1956); *Perspectives in American Catholicism* (1963); *Catholics in Colonial America* (1964); *Essays in Seminary Education* (1967); etc. Editor: *Documents of American Catholic History,* 2v. (1967). Prof. church history, Catholic University of America, 1947–64.

ELLIS, KATHARINE RUTH (May 31, 1879–); b. Charles City, Ia. Author. The *Wide-Awake Girls* series, 3v. (1908–10).

ELLISON, [Earl] JEROME (Oct. 28, 1907–); b. Maywood, Ill. Author. *John Brown's Soul* (1951); *Report to the Creator* (autobiography 1955); *Call to an American (R) Evolution* (1967); etc. Editor-in-chief, *Liberty* magazine, 1942–43; founder, *Best Articles and Stories* magazine, 1957; publisher and editor, since 1957.

ELLISON, RALPH [Waldo] (Mar. 1, 1914–); b. Oklahoma City, Okla. Author. *The Invisible Man* (1952); *Shadow and Act* (1964).

ELLISTON, GEORGE (Miss) (deceased). b. Mt. Sterling, Ky. Poet. *Everyday Poems* (1921); *Changing Moods* (1922); *Through Many Windows* (1924); *Bright World* (1927); *Cinderella Cargoes* (1929); etc. Editor, *Gypsy Poetry Magazine,* 1925–39.

ELLMANN, RICHARD (Mar. 15, 1918–); b. Highland Park, Mich. Educator, author. *Yeats: The Man and the Mask* (1948); *The Identity of Yeats* (1954); *James Joyce* (1959); *Eminent Domain: Yeats Among Wilde, Joyce, Pound, Eliot and Auden* (1967). Editor: *Selected Writings of Henri Michaux* (1951); *My Brother's Keeper* (1958); *The Critical Writings of James Joyce* (with Ellsworth Mason, 1959); *Letters of James Joyce,* vols. 2 and 3 (1967); *The Artist as Critic: Critical Writings of Oscar Wilde* (1969); *Oscar Wilde: A Collection of Critical Essays* (1969); etc. Prof. English, Northwestern University, since 1951.

ELLSBERG, EDWARD (Nov. 21, 1891–); b. New Haven, Conn. Naval officer, engineer, author. *On the Bottom* (1929); *Thirty Fathoms Deep* (1930); *Pigboats* (1931); *S–54, Stories of the Sea* (1932); *Submerged* (1934); *Ocean Gold* (1935); *Spanish Ingots* (1936); *Hell on Ice* (1938); *Men Under the Sea* (1939); *Captain Paul* (1940); *Treasure Below* (1940); *I Have Just Begun to Fight* (1942); *No Banners, No Bugles* (1949); *Passport for Jennifer* (1952); *Mid Watch* (1954); *The Far Shore* (1960); etc.

ELLSWORTH, LINCOLN [W.] (May 12, 1880–May 26, 1951); b. Chicago, Ill. Explorer, author. *The Last Wild Buffalo Hunt* (1915); *Our Polar Flight* (with Roald Amundsen, 1925); *First Crossing of the Polar Sea* (with same, 1926); *Search* (1932); *Beyond Horizons* (1938).

ELLSWORTH, MARY WOLCOTT JANVRIN (1830–Aug. 19, 1870); b. Exeter, N.H. Author. *Peace; or, The Stolen Will* (1857); *An Hour with the Children* (1860). From 1858 she was a regular contributor to *Godey's Lady's Book.*

ELLSWORTH, WILLIAM WEBSTER (Oct. 30, 1855–Dec. 18, 1936); b. Hartford, Conn., great-grandson of Noah Webster. Publisher, lecturer, author. *A Golden Age of Authors* (1919); *Creative Writing* (1929). Editor: *Readings from the New Poets* (1928). Secretary, Century Company, 1881–1913; president, 1913–16. Connected with *St. Nicholas* magazine for many years.

ELLWANGER, GEORGE HERMAN (July 10, 1848–1906); b. Rochester, N.Y. Author. *In Gold and Silver* (1892); *Idyllists of the Country Side* (1896); etc. Compiler: *Love's Demesne,* 2v. (anthology of contemporary love-poems, 1896).

ELLWANGER, WILLIAM DE LANCEY (Sept. 27, 1855–Feb. 16, 1913); b. Rochester, N.Y. Poet, essayist. *A Summer Snowflake and Drift of Other Verse and Song* (1902); *The Oriental Rug* (1903); *A Snuff-Box Full of Trees & Some Apocryphal Essays* (1909).

ELMAN, RICHARD M[artin]. Author. *The Poorhouse State: The American Way of Life on Public Assistance* (1966); *Ill-at-ease in Compton* (1967); *The 28th Day of Elul* (1967); *Lilo's Diary* (1968); *The Reckoning* (1969); *An Education in Blood* (1971).

Elmer Gantry. Novel by Sinclair Lewis (1927). An arraignment of a half-educated, vulgar, dissimulating clergyman, in the Middle West.

ELMSLIE, KENWARD (Apr. 27, 1929–); b. New York. Author. *Pavilions* (poems, 1961); *The Baby Book* (1965); *Power Plant Poems* (1967); *The Champ* (1968). Opera libretti: *Miss Julie* (prod. 1965); *Lizzie Borden* (prod. 1965); *The Sweet Bye and Bye* (1966).

ELSER, FRANK B[all] (Jan. 9, 1885–Feb. 1, 1935); b. Ft. Worth, Tex. Journalist, playwright, novelist. *The Keen Desire* (1926); *Mr. Gilhooley* (prod. 1930); *The Farmer Takes a Wife* (with Marc Connelly, prod. 1934).

Elsie Dinsmore. By Martha Finley (1867). One of the most popular of American juveniles. The first of a long series of "Elsie" books.

Elsie Venner. Novel by Oliver Wendell Holmes (1861). A psychological novel of an unfortunate girl in a New England village, obsessed by a "serpent complex" which is eventually sublimated when she falls in love. The village becomes a psychological symbol and reveals the author's medical background and his insight into hidden depths of New England character.

Elsket, and Other Stories, by Thomas Nelson Page (1891).

ELSON, ARTHUR (Nov. 18, 1873–Mar. 1, 1940); b. Boston, Mass. Music critic. *A Critical History of Opera* (1901); *Modern Composers of Europe* (1904); *The Musician's Guide* (1913); *The Book of Musical Knowledge* (1915); etc.

ELSON, CHARLES (Sept. 5, 1909–); b. Chicago, Ill. Educator, stage designer, author. Editor: *Design in the World Theatre* (1956); *Stage Design Throughout the World,* Vol. 1 (1956), Vol. 2 (1964). Professor, director, theatre workshop, Hunter College, since 1948.

ELSON, HENRY WILLIAM (Mar. 29, 1857–Jan. 29, 1954); b. in Muskingum Co., O. Educator, historian. *Sidelights on American History,* 2v. (1900); *History of the United States,* 5v. (1904); etc. President, Thiel College, 1916–21.

ELSON, LOUIS C[harles] (Apr. 17, 1848–Feb. 14, 1920); b. Boston, Mass. Music critic. *Curiosities of Music* (1880); *European Reminiscences Musical and Otherwise* (1891); *The National Music of America* (1899); *The History of American Music* (1904); *Women in Music* (1918); etc. Music critic, *Boston Advertiser*, 1886–1920. See W. S. B. Matthews's *A Hundred Years of Music in America* (1889).

ELSTON, ALLAN VAUGHAN (1887–). Author. *Eagle's Eye* (1943); *Guns on the Cimarron* (1943); *Hit the Saddle* (1947); *Forbidden Valley* (1957); *Grand Mesa* (1957); *Beyond the Bitterroots* (1960); *Timberline Bonanza* (1961); *The Landseekers* (1964); *The Lawless Border* (1968); *Montana Passage* (1968); etc.

ELWOOD, MURIEL (Apr. 11, 1902–); b. London. Author. *Pauline Frederick: On and Off the Stage* (1939); *So Much as Beauty Does* (1941); *Heritage of the River* (1945); *Deeper the Heritage* (1946); *Towards the Sunset* (1947); *Against the Tide* (1950); *Web of Destiny* (1951); *Haven't We Met Before?* (play, 1956); *The Deluge* (1959); *The Bigamous Duchess* (1960).

ELWYN, ALFRED LANGDON (July 9, 1804–Mar. 15, 1884); b. Portsmouth, N.H. Compiler: *Glossary of Supposed Americanisms* (1859).

ELY, DAVID (1927–   ). Author. *Seconds* (1963); *Trot* (1963); *The Tour* (1967); *Time Out* (1968).

"Embargo, The." First poem of William Cullen Bryant (1808). A political satire.

EMBLER, WELLER BEARDSLEY (Aug. 15, 1906–); b. West Haven, Conn. Educator. *Metaphor and Meaning* (1966). Prof. English, Cooper Union, since 1945.

EMBREE, EDWIN R[ogers] (July 31, 1883–Feb. 21, 1950); b. Osceola, Neb. Ethnologist, author. *Brown America: The Story of a New Race* (1931); *Prospecting for Heaven* (1932); *Island India Goes to School* (1934); *Little Red Schoolhouse* (1938); *Southern Style* (1938); *Indians of the Americas* (1939); *Peoples of the Earth* (1941); etc. Executive staff, Yale University, 1907–17; officer, Rockefeller Foundation, 1917–27, later president Julius Rosenwald Fund.

EMBURY, EMMA CATHERINE (c. 1806–Feb. 10, 1863); b. New York City. Poet, story-writer, essayist. *Guido, a Tale* (under pen name, "Ianthe," 1828); *Constance Latimer; or, The Blind Girl* (1838); *Pictures of Early Life or Sketches of Youth* (1839); *Love's Token Flowers* (1846); *The Waldorf Family* (1848); *Glimpses of Home Life* (1848) also published as *The Home Offering* (n.d.); *The Poems* (1869); *Selected Prose Writings* (1893); etc.

EMERSON, ALICE B. Author of books for girls. The *Betty Gordon* series, 15v.; the *Ruth Fielding* series, 30v.

EMERSON, EDWARD WALDO (July 10, 1844–Jan. 27, 1930); b. Concord, Mass., son of Ralph Waldo Emerson. Author. *Memoirs of the Members of the Social Club in Concord* (1888), republished as *Emerson in Concord* (1889); *Henry Thoreau as Remembered by a Young Friend* (1917); *The Early Years of the Saturday Club, 1855–1870* (1918).

EMERSON, EDWIN. Dime novelist. *Dingle, the Outlaw* (1871); *The Phantom Hunter* (1871); *Dusky Darrell, Trapper* (1871), also published as *The Green Ranger; The Wood Witch* (1871); also published as *Minonee, the Wood Witch; The Mad Horseman* (1872); *Sharp-Shooter Sam* (1890); etc. The dates are not necessarily those of first editions.

EMERSON, EDWIN (Jan 23, 1869–Oct. 2, 1959); b. Dresden, Saxony. Correspondent. *Pepys' Ghost* (1899); *Rough Rider Stories* (1900); *Mexican Notes* (1913); *Adventures of Theodore Roosevelt* (1923); *Benedict Arnold* (1923); *Hoover and His Times* (1932); *German Swordplay* (1936); etc.

EMERSON, ELLEN RUSSELL (Jan. 16, 1837–June 12, 1907); b. New Sharon, Me. Folklorist, author. *Indian Myths* (1884); *Masks, Heads and Faces* (1894); *Nature and Human Nature* (1901); etc.

EMERSON, GEORGE BARRELL (Sept. 12, 1797–Mar. 4, 1881); b. Wells, Me. Educator, author. *Reminiscences of an Old Teacher* (1878); etc.

EMERSON, JOHN (May 29, 1874–Mar. 8, 1956); b. Sandusky, O. Actor, producer, playwright. *Breaking into the Movies* (with wife, Anita Loos, 1921); *The Whole Town's Talking* (with wife, 1923); *The Fall of Eve* (with wife, 1924); *The Social Register* (with wife, prod. 1931).

Emerson, Mrs. John See Anita Loos.

EMERSON, OLIVER FARRAR (May 24, 1860–Mar. 13, 1927); b. Wolf Creek, Ia. Educator, author. *History of the English Language* (1894); etc. Editor: *Memoirs of the Life and Writings of Edward Gibbon* (1898); *Poems of Chaucer* (1911); etc. Prof. English, Western Reserve University, 1896–1927.

EMERSON, RALPH WALDO (May 25, 1803–Apr. 27, 1882); b. Boston, Mass. Essayist, poet, philosopher, editor, lecturer. *Letter . . . to the Second Church and Society* (n.d.); *Nature* (1836); *An Oration, Delivered before the Phi Beta Kappa Society* (1837), later called *The American Scholar; An Address Delivered before the Senior Class in Divinity College, Cambridge* (1838), commonly called the *Divinity School Address; Poems* (publ. 1846, dated 1847); *Representative Men* (cop. 1849, dated 1850); *English Traits* (1856); *The Conduct of Life* (1860); *May-Day and Other Poems* (1867); *Society and Solitude* (1870); *Selected Poems* (1876); *Fortune of the Republic* (1878); *The Complete Works*, ed. by Edward Waldo Emerson, 12v. (1903–04); *Journals*, ed. by same and Waldo Emerson Forbes, 10v. (1909–14); *The Letters*, ed. by Ralph L. Rusk, 6v. (1939); *Early Lectures*, ed. by S. E. Whicher and R. E. Spiller, Vol. 1 (1959), Vol. 2 (1964); *Journals and Miscellaneous Notebooks*, ed. by W. H. Gilman and others (1961). Editor, *The Dial*, 1842–44. See James E. Cabot's *A Memoir of Ralph Waldo Emerson*, 2v. (1887); Oliver W. Holmes's *Ralph Waldo Emerson* (1885); Bliss Perry's *Emerson Today* (1931); Van Wyck Brooks's *The Life of Emerson* (1932); R. L. Rusk's *The Life of Ralph Waldo Emerson*, 2v. (1949); Sherman Paul's *Emerson's Angle of Vision: Man and Nature in American Experience* (1952); S. E. Whicher's *Freedom and Fate* (1953); Jonathan Bishop's *Emerson on the Soul* (1964); Joel Porte's *Emerson and Thoreau: Transcendentalists in Conflict* (1966); Michael H. Cowan's *City of the West: Emerson, America and Urban Metaphor* (1967).

EMERSON, RUPERT (Aug. 20, 1899–); b. Rye, N.Y. Educator, author. *State and Sovereignty in Modern Germany* (1928); *Malaysia* (1937); *The Netherlands Indies and the U.S.* (1942); *Representative Government in Southeast Asia* (1955); *From Empire to Nation* (1960); *Self-Determination Revisited in the Era of Decolonization* (1964); *Malaysia: A Study in Direct and Indirect Rule* (1966); *Africa and United States Policy* (1967). Prof. international relations, Harvard University, since 1946.

EMERTON, EPHRAIM (Feb. 18, 1851–Mar. 3, 1935); b. Salem, Mass. Educator, historian. *Mediaeval Europe, 814–1300* (1894); *An Introduction to the Study of the Middle Ages* (1895); *Desiderio Erasmus of Rotterdam* (1899); *The Beginnings of Modern Europe, 1250–1450* (1917); etc. History dept., Harvard, 1876–1908.

Emigrants, The. Novel by Gilbert Imlay (1793). Laid in Kentucky in the late eighteenth century.

Emily Emmins Papers, The. Humorous sketches by Carolyn Wells (1907).

EMMET, THOMAS ADDIS (May 29, 1828–Mar. 1, 1919); b. Charlottesville, Va. Physician, collector, author. *Ireland* *under English Rule*, 2v. (1903); *Incidents of My Life* (1911); etc. Collector of prints and autographs and extra-illustrated books, most of which are now in the New York Public Library.

EMMETT, CHRIS (1886–). Author. *Texas Camel Tales* (1932); *Texas As It Was Then* (1935); etc.

EMMETT, DANIEL DECATUR (Oct. 29, 1815–June 28, 1904); b. Clinton, O. Minstrel. Author of "Old Dan Tucker" (1830); "Dixie" (1860); "Here We Are; or, Cross Ober Jordan" (1863). Organized the "Virginia Minstrels" in 1842. *See* Charles Burleigh Galbreath's *Daniel Decatur Emmett* (1904); Hans Nathan's *Dan Emmett and the Rise of Early Negro Minstrelsy* (1962).

Emperor Jones, The. Play by Eugene O'Neill (prod. 1920). Brutus Jones, formerly Pullman car porter, makes himself a swaggering emperor of an island in the West Indies, but his ancient fears and his atavistic instincts prove fatal. In a few hours of jungle suspense he is transformed into a frightened coward.

"Emperor of Ice Cream, The." Poem by Wallace Stevens.

EMPEY, ARTHUR GUY (Dec. 11, 1883–Feb. 1963); b. Ogden, Utah. Soldier, author. *"Over the Top"* (1917); *Tales from a Dugout* (1918); *The Madonna of the Hills* (1921); etc.

Emporia Gazette. Emporia, Kan. Newspaper. Published and edited by William Allen White from 1895 to 1944. His son, William L. White, joined the staff in 1914, and is now editor and publisher. Ted McDaniel is book editor.

Encounter. London. Monthly. Founded 1953 as a joint British-American undertaking by the Congress for Cultural Freedom. Stephen Spender and Irving Kristol were respectively the first British and American editors. Later editors were Melvin J. Lasky and Nigel Dennis. One of the most influential literary and cultural periodicals in the English language. Notable writers who have appeared in its pages include Kenneth Tynan, Robert Graves, W. H. Auden, Robert Warshow, Lionel Trilling, James Agee, Edwin Muir.

Encyclopedia Americana, The. Edited by Francis Lieber and E. Wigglesworth, 13v. (1829–33). The work underwent an entire revision in thirty volumes, in 1918–20, and a year book appeared annually after 1923. Editors in recent years have been Lavinia P. Dudley and George A. Cornish.

Encyclopaedia Britannica. Twenty-four volume encyclopedia published by Encyclopaedia Britannica, Inc. and revised annually. The original *Encyclopaedia Britannica* appeared in 1768–71, in Edinburgh, Scotland. In 1897 it was bought by Horace E. Hooper from A. and C. Black, the British publisher, and in 1920 sold to Sears, Roebuck Co., which offered it to the University of Chicago in 1943. William Benton has been publisher and chairman of the board since 1943. *Encyclopaedia Britannica* is especially noted for its ninth (1875–89) and eleventh (1910–11) editions. Encyclopedia Britannica Educational Corp., which produces films and programed materials, is an affiliate. G. and C. Merriam Co. and Frederick A. Praeger, Inc., are subsidiaries. *See* Herman Kogan's *The Great EB: The Story of the Encyclopaedia Britannica* (1958); Harvey Einbinder's *The Myth of the Britannica* (1964).

Encyclopedia International. Edited by Stanely Schindler, 20v. (1970), and published by Grolier, Inc.

Encyclopedia of American History. Edited by Richard B. Morris (1953).

Encyclopedia of Philosophy. Published in eight volumes (1967), it covers both Eastern and Western philosophy in 1500 signed articles. Editor-in-chief is Paul Edwards.

Encyclopaedia of the Social Sciences, The. Edited by E. R. A. Seligman and Alvin Johnson, 15v. (1930–35). Standard reference work, including contributions by scholars in all areas of the study of society.

Encyclopedia of World Art. Comprehensive encyclopedia published by McGraw-Hill in English and simultaneously by Sansone in Italian *(Enciclopedia universale dell'arte)*, 15v. (1959–68). Contents consist of signed articles by noted scholars.

ENDICOTT, CHARLES MOSES (Dec. 6, 1793–Dec. 14, 1863); b. Danvers, Mass. Sea captain, author. *Life of John Endicott* (1847); etc. Wrote for Boston *Gazette* under pen name of "Junius Americanus."

ENDICOTT, ROBERT RANTOUL (Feb. 14, 1905–); b. Detroit, Mich. Editor. Editor, *Family Circle*, 1936–54; *New Homes Guide and Home Modernizing*, 1955–56; *Today's Living*, magazine of New York *Herald Tribune*, 1956–61; *The American Heritage New Illustrated History of the United States*, 1962–63; now publishing consultant.

ENDORE, GUY [Sam] (July 4, 1900–Feb. 12, 1970); b. New York. Author. *Casanova: His Known and Unknown Life* (1929); *The Man from Limbo* (1930); *The Sword of God: Jeanne d'Arc* (1931); *The Werewolf of Paris* (1933); *Babouk* (1934); *Methinks the Lady . . .* (1945); *King of Paris* (1956); *Detour at Night* (1959); *Voltaire! Voltaire!* (1961); *Dumas* (1962); *The Heart and the Mind: The Story of Rousseau and Voltaire* (1963); *Satan's Saint* (1967); *Synanon* (1968).

Eneas Africanus. By Harry Stillwell Edwards (1919). Negro story. It has become a genuine folk-book of Georgia.

ENGEL, LEHMAN (Sept. 14, 1910–   ); b. Jackson, Miss. Composer, conductor, author. *Planning and Producing a Musical Show* (1956); *This Bright Day* (1956); *The American Musical Theatre* (1967). Composed music for numerous stage, film, radio, and television productions.

ENGEL, LEONARD (1916–Dec. 4, 1964). Author. *The Operation* (1958); *The Sea* (1961); *Medicine Makers of Kalamazoo* (1961); *The New Genetics* (1967); *Sea Life* (1969); etc. Editor-in-chief, *Sterling Junior Pictorial Encyclopedia of Science*, 1962.

ENGELS, NORBERT [Anthony] (Sept. 4, 1903–); b. Green Bay, Wis. Educator, author. *Thou Art My Strength* (poems, 1947); *Man Around the House* (1949); *Writing Techniques* (1962); *Experience and Imagination* (1965). Prof. English, University of Notre Dame, 1939–68.

ENGLAND, GEORGE ALLAN (Feb. 9, 1877–June 26, 1936); b. Fort McPherson, Neb. Explorer, novelist. *Underneath the Bough* (poems, 1903); *Darkness and Dawn* (1914); *The Golden Blight* (1916); *Vikings of the Ice* (1924); *Isles of Romance* (1929); etc.

ENGLAND, JOHN (Sept. 23, 1786–Apr. 11, 1842); b. in Ireland. Catholic bishop, author. *The Garden of the Soul* (1845); etc. *The Works*, ed. Ignatius A. Reynolds, 5v. (1840); *The Works*, ed. Sebastian G. Messmer, 7v. (1908). Founder, *United States Catholic Miscellany*, 1822, which expired 1861. *See* Peter Guilday's *The Life and Times of John England* (1927).

ENGLE, PAUL [Hamilton] (Oct. 12, 1908–); b. Cedar Rapids, Ia. Poet. *Worn Earth* (1932); *American Song* (1934); *Break the Heart's Anger* (1936); *Corn: A Book of Poems* (1939); *Always the Land* (1941); *West of Midnight* (1941); *American Child* (1945); *The Word of Love* (1951); *Poems in Praise* (1959); *Prairie Christmas* (1960); *Golden Child* (1962); *Old-Fashioned Christmas* (1964); *A Woman Unashamed, and Other Poems* (1965); *Embrace* (1969). Editor: *West of the Great Water: An Iowa Anthology* (with Harold Cooper, 1931); *Midland* (with others, 1961); *On Creative Writing* (1964). Prof. English, State University of Iowa, since 1937.

ENGLEMAN, JAMES OZRO (Sept. 13, 1873–Sept. 15, 1943); b. Jeffersonville, Ind. Educator, author. *Guide Books to Literature*, 3v. (with Lawrence McTurnan, 1924–26). President, Kent State University (Ohio), 1928–38.

ENGLISH, E[ugene] SCHUYLER (Oct. 12, 1899–); b. New York. Editor, author. *Studies in the Gospel According to Matthew* (1935); *By Life and by Death: Excerpts from the Diary of J. C. Stam* (ed., 1938); *Studies in the Gospel of Mark* (1944); *The Shifting of the Scenes* (1945); *Robert G. Lee, a Chosen Vessel* (1949); *Re-Thinking the Rapture* (1954); *Studies in the Epistle to the Hebrews* (1955). Editor-in-chief, Pilgrim Edition of the *Holy Bible* (1948). Editor, *Revised New Testament Berkeley Bible* (1968). Assoc. editor, *Our Hope* magazine, 1939–45; editor, 1946–58; editor, *The Pilgrim*, since 1944.

ENGLISH, MAURICE (Oct. 21, 1909–   ); b. Chicago, Ill. Editor, poet. *Midnight in the Century* (poems, 1964); Editor: *The Testament of Stone* (1963). Translator: *Selected Poems of Eugenio Montale* (1966). Senior editor, University of Chicago Press, since 1961.

ENGLISH, THOMAS DUNN (June 29, 1819–Apr. 1, 1902); b. Philadelphia, Pa. Editor, playwright, novelist, poet. *1844; or, The Power of the "S. F."* (1847); *Walter Woolfe* (1847); *The Mormons* (prod. 1858); *American Ballads* (1880); *Boy's Book of Battle Lyrics* (1885); *Jacob Schuyler's Millions* (1886); *The Select Poems* (1894); *Fairy Stories and Wonder Tales* (1897). His most famous poem, "Ben Bolt," appeared in *New Mirror*, Sept. 2, 1843. Editor, *The Aristidean*, 1845; co-founder, *John Donkey*, 1848.

ENGLISH, WILLIAM B. Novelist. *Gertrude Howard* (1843); *Rosina Meadows* (1843); *Smiles and Tears* (anon., 1847).

English Journal. Chicago, Ill.; Tallahassee, Fla. Monthly during academic year. Organ of the National Council of Teachers of English. Founded 1912.

English Notebooks. By Nathaniel Hawthorne (1870). A record of Hawthorne's sojourn in England while serving as United States consul at Liverpool; filled with observations on English life and with literary and philosophical reflections.

English Traits. By Ralph Waldo Emerson (1856). Written as the result of trips made to England in 1833 and 1847. These penetrating analyses of English character rank high among Emerson's essays.

ENGSTRAND, STUART DAVID (Mar. 13, 1905–Sept. 9, 1955); b. Chicago, Ill. Novelist. *The Invaders* (1937); *They Sought for Paradise* (1939); *Spring* (1941); *The Sling and the Arrow* (1947); *Beyond the Forest* (1948); *Son of the Giant* (1950); *Husband in the House* (1952); *The Scattering Seed* (1953); *More Deaths Than One* (1955); etc.

Enormous Room, The. By E. E. Cummings (1922). Story of life in a French military prison, during the first World War.

Enough Rope. Collection of poems by Dorothy Parker (1926).

ENRIGHT, ELIZABETH (Mrs. Robert Gillham) (Sept. 17, 1909–June 8, 1968); b. Oak Park, Ill. Author, illustrator. *Thimble Summer* (1938); *The Sea Is All Around* (1940); *Four-Story Mistake* (1942); *Borrowed Summer and Other Stories* (1946); *Spider Web for Two* (1951); *The Moment Before the Rain* (1955); *The Riddle of the Fly and Other Stories* (1959); *Return to Gone-Away* (1961); *Zeee* (1965); *Doublefields* (1966); *Then There Were Five* (1967); etc.

ENRIGHT, WALTER J[oseph Pat] (July 3, 1879–); b. Chicago, Ill. Cartoonist, author. *Once Upon a Time Stories,* 3v. (1926); *Al Alligator and How He Learned to Play the Banjo* (1947); *Sailor Jim's Cave* (1951); etc. Created "Once Upon a Time" strip for McClure Syndicate.

Entailed Hat, The. Novel by George Alfred Townsend (1884). A tale involving the kidnapping of free Negroes in Delaware and Maryland before the Civil War.

ENTERS, ANGNA (Apr. 28, 1907–); b. New York. Dancer, artist, author. *First Person Plural* (1937); *Love Possessed Juana* (play, 1939); *Silly Girl* (1944); *Among the Daughters* (1955); *Artist's Life* (1958); *The Loved and the Unloved* (1961); *On Mime* (1965); etc.

"Envoi." Poem by Ezra Pound.

Ephemera: An Emblem of Human Life, The. By Benjamin Franklin (1778).

Ephrata Press. Established Ephrata, Pa., 1746, by the Dunkers, a religious sect headed by Conrad Beissel. Peter Miller (1709–1790) was in charge of the Press. It printed many religious books in the German language. The original Blaeu hand printing press is now in the possession of the Historical Society of Pennsylvania.

Epic of America, The. By James Truslow Adams (1931). An interpretation of the creative forces in American life which have produced a great civilization in a short space of time, written in a manner calculated to stimulate a wider reading of American history.

Episcopalian, The. Philadelphia, Pa. Monthly magazine of the Protestant Episcopal Church. Founded 1960, to succeed *Forth*. Editor, Henry L. McCorkle.

Epistle to Posterity, An. By Mrs. M. E. W. Sherwood (1897). Autobiographical chapters which throw light on the author's literary life, her visits to Boston, Brook Farm, Wisconsin, Washington, D.C., etc., and her impressions of the great writers, statesmen, and educators of her day.

Epitaphs. See Elegies and Epitaphs.

Epoch. Ithaca, N.Y. Triannual literary magazine. Founded 1947. Published at Cornell University. Edited by Baxter Hathaway and others. Afforded early publication to George P. Elliott, Joyce Carol Oates, Thomas Pynchon, Peter Viereck.

Epoch, The. New York. A literary magazine. Founded Feb. 11, 1887. Expired 1892.

Epos: A Quarterly of Poetry. Crescent City, Fla. Founded 1949. Published and edited by Will Tulos and Evelyn Thorne.

EPSTEIN, SEYMOUR (Dec. 2, 1917–); b. New York. Novelist. *Pillar of Salt* (1960); *The Successor* (1961); *Leah* (1964); *A Penny for Charity* (1965); *Caught in That Music* (1967).

ERDMAN, CHARLES ROSENBURY (July 20, 1866–May 9, 1960); b. Fayetteville, N.Y. Presbyterian clergyman, educator, author. *The Gospel of John* (1916); *The General Epistles* (1918); *The Acts* (1919); and other commentaries; also: *Within the Gateways of the Far East* (1922); *The Work of the Pastor* (1924); *D. L. Moody* (1928); *Remember Jesus Christ* (1958); etc. Prof., Princeton Theological Seminary, 1906–36.

ERDMAN, LOULA GRACE; b. near Alma, Mo. Novelist. *Separate Star* (1944); *Fair Is the Morning* (1945); *The Years of the Locust* (1947); *Lonely Passage* (1948); *The Edge of Time* (1950); *My Sky Is Blue* (1953); *Far Journey* (1955); *Wide Horizon* (1956); *A Short Summer* (1958); *The Good Land* (1959); *Many a Voyage* (1960); *Life Was Simpler Then* (1963); *Wonderful Thing and Other Stories* (1964); *Another Spring* (1966); *Time to Write* (1969); etc.

ERIKSON, ERIK H[omburger] (June 15, 1902–); b. Frankfort-am-Main, Ger. Psychoanalyst, educator, author. *Childhood and Society* (1950); *Young Man Luther* (1958); *Identity and the Life Cycle* (1959); *Insight and Responsibility* (1964); *Identity: Youth and Crisis* (1968); *Gandhi's Truth: On the Origins of Militant Nonviolence* (1969). Editor: *Youth: Change and Challenge* (1963). Professor of human development, Harvard University, since 1960. *See* Robert Coles' *Erik H. Erikson: The Growth of His Work* (1970).

ERNST, CLAYTON HOLT (Dec. 29, 1886–Oct. 15, 1945); b. Franconia, N.H. Editor, author. *Blind Trails* (1919); *The Mark of the Knife* (1920); *The Secret of Coffin Cove* (1926); etc. Editor: *Deep-River Jim's Outdoor Guide* (1947); etc. Assoc. editor, *The Youth's Companion*, 1911–19; president, The Open Road Publishing Company, from 1928.

ERNST, MORRIS L[eopold] (Aug. 23, 1888–); b. Uniontown, Ala. Lawyer, author. *To the Pure* (with William Seagle, 1928); *Censored: The Private Life of the Movie* (with Pare Lorentz, 1930); *America's Primer* (1931); *Hold Your Tongue! Adventures on Libel and Slander* (1932); *The Ultimate Power* (1937); *The Censor Marches On* (with Alexander Lindey, 1940); *Too Big* (1940); *The Best is Yet* (1945); *The First Freedom* (1946); *So Far So Good* (autobiography, 1948); *American Sexual Behavior and the Kinsey Report* (with D. G. Loth, 1948); *For Better or Worse* (with same, 1952); *Report on the American Communist* (with same, 1952); *Utopia 1976* (1955); *Touch Wood* (1960); *How High Is Up* (1964); *Censorship* (with A. Schwartz, 1964); *Lawyers and What They Do* (1965); *A Love Affair with the Law* (1968); etc. Editor: *The Comparative International Almanac* (with Judith A. Posner, 1967).

"Eros Turannos." Poem by Edward Arlington Robinson.

ERRETT, ISAAC (Jan. 2, 1820–Dec. 19, 1888); b. New York City. Disciples clergyman, editor, author. *About Jerusalem: A Search After the Landmarks of Primitive Christianity* (1871); *Evenings with the Bible*, 3v. (1884–89); *Linsey-Woolsey and Other Addresses* (1893); etc. Editor, *The Christian Standard*, 1866–88. See J. T. Brown's *Churches of Christ* (1904).

ERSKINE, DOROTHY (Sept. 11, 1906–); b. Steubenville, O. Novelist. *The Crystal Boat* (1946); *Miss Pettinger's Niece* (1949); *Pink Hotel* (with E. E. Tanner, 1957).

ERSKINE, JOHN (Oct. 5, 1879–June 2, 1951); b. New York City. Educator, critic, novelist, poet. *Actaeon, and Other Poems* (1906); *Leading American Novelists* (1910); *Great American Writers* (with William P. Trent, 1912); *The Moral Obligation to be Intelligent, and Other Essays* (1915); *The Shadowed Hour* (poems, 1917); *Democracy and Ideals* (1920); *The Kinds of Poetry, and Other Essays* (1920); *Collected Poems, 1907–1922* (1922); *The Literary Discipline* (1923); *Sonata, and Other Poems* (1925); *The Private Life of Helen of Troy* (1925); *The Enchanted Garden* (1925); *Galahad* (1926); *Adam and Eve* (1927); *The Delight of Great Books* (1928); *Penelope's Man* (1928); *Sincerity* (1929); *Cinderella's Daughter* (1930); *Unfinished Business* (1931); *Tristan and Isolde* (1932); *Bachelor of Arts* (1934); *Solomon, My Son!* (1935); *The Influence of Woman—and Its Cure* (1936); *Young Love* (1936); *The Brief Hour of François Villon* (1937); *Give Me Liberty* (1940); *Mrs. Doratt* (1941); *Casanova's Women* (1941); *The Voyage of Captain Bart* (1943); *The Philharmonic Symphony Society of New York: Its First Hundred Years* (1943); *What Is Music?* (1944); *Human Life of Jesus* (1945); *The Memory of Certain Persons* (1947); *Venus, the Lovely Goddess* (1949); *My Life in Music* (1950); etc. Prof. English, Columbia University, 1916–37.

ERSKINE, LAURIE YORK (June 23, 1894–); b. Kirkcudbright, Scotland. Educator, author. *The Renfrew* series, 7v. (1922–36); *The Laughing Rider* (1924); *Fine Fellows* (1929); *One Man Came Back* (1938); *Renfrew Flies Again* (1940); etc. One of the organizers of The Solebury School, New Hope, Pa., in 1925.

Escape from Freedom. By Erich Fromm (1941). Study of the meaning of freedom in modern life, interpreting freedom as a function of man's self-awareness and personal spontaneity.

ESENWEIN, JOSEPH BERG (May 15, 1867–Nov. 7, 1946); b. Philadelphia, Pa. Editor, author. *Short Story Masterpieces* (1912); *The Art of Versification* (with Mary E. Roberts, 1913); etc. Editor, *Lippincott's Magazine*, 1905–14; *The Writer's Monthly*, from 1915.

Esquire. New York. Monthly. Founded 1933, and published by David A. Smart and William H. Weintraub, with Arnold Gingrich as editor. Noted for its humorous illustrations and its short stories and more recently for its searching articles on various aspects of modern life and the arts.

Essa on the Muel bi Josh Billings. By Henry W. Shaw (1860). First of a series of humorous sketches.

Essay on Rime. Verse essay by Karl Shapiro (1945).

Essays. By Ralph Waldo Emerson. First Series (1841) included essays on History, Self-Reliance, Compensation, Spiritual Laws, Love, Friendship, Prudence, Heroism, The Over-Soul, Circles, Intellect, and Art. Second Series (1844) included essays on The Poet, Experience, Character, Manners, Gifts, Nature, Politics, Nominalist and Realist, and New England Reformers.

Essays and General Literature Index, 1900–1933. Edited by Minnie Earl Sears and Marian Shaw (1934). Lists essays and similar articles by authors, titles, and subjects. *1934–1936 Supplement* was published in 1937, and annual supplements have appeared since then.

Essays from the Desk of Poor Robert the Scribe. By Charles Miner (1815).

Essence. New York. Monthly. Founded 1970. Magazine devoted to the interests of black women.

ESTES, DANA (Mar. 4, 1840–June 16, 1909); b. Gorham, Me. Publisher, traveler, editor. *Half-Hour Recreations in Popular Science* (1871–79). Compiler: *Chimes for Childhood* (1868); *Echoes from Home* (1870); *Light at Eventide* (1870). Founder of publishing firm of Estes & Lauriat.

ESTES, ELEANOR (May 9, 1906–); b. West Haven, Conn. Author. *The Moffats* (1941); *Rufus M.* (1943); *The Echoing Green* (1947); *The Sleeping Giant* (1948); *A Little Oven* (1955); *Pinky Pye* (1958); *The Witch Family* (1960); *The Alley* (1964); *Miranda the Great* (1967); etc.

Estes & Lauriat. Publishing firm founded in Boston, Mass., in 1872 by Dana Estes and Charles E. Lauriat. The partnership was dissolved in 1898; the publishing firm continued as Dana Estes & Co. and the bookstore became Charles E. Lauriat Company. See George H. Sargent's *Lauriats* (1922).

ETC. San Francisco, Cal. Quarterly. Founded 1943. Published by The International Society for General Semantics. Edited by S. I. Hayakawa. Concerned with the use of language and symbols in human affairs and behavior.

"Eternal Goodness, The." Poem by John Greenleaf Whittier (1865).

Ethan Brand. Short story by Nathaniel Hawthorne. First appeared in the *Dollar Magazine*, Phila., May, 1851, under the title *The Unpardonable Sin*.

Ethan Frome. Novel by Edith Wharton (1911). Ethan's wife, Zeena, is an invalid, and Ethan falls in love with her cousin, Mattie, who comes to live with the Fromes. Zeena demands that Ethan send the girl away, and on his way to the train he stops to have a last sled ride with her down a steep hill. He deliberately runs an elm tree hoping to end it all, but he and Mattie are crippled for life, becoming dependent on Zeena.

"Ethnogenesis." Ode by Henry Timrod, celebrating the meeting of the Confederate Congress in Montgomery, Ala., Feb., 1861. Ethnogenesis, as Timrod used the word, meant the birth of a nation.

ETHRIDGE, WILLIE SNOW [Mrs.] (Dec. 10, 1900–); b. Savannah, Ga. Author. *Mingled Yarn* (1938); *I'll Sing One Song* (1941); *This Little Pig Stayed Home* (1944); *It's Greek to Me* (1948); *Going to Jerusalem* (1950); *Let's Talk Turkey* (1952); *Russian Duet* (1959); *There's Yeast in the Middle East*

(1963); *I Just Happen to Have Some Pictures* (1964); *You Can't Hardly Get There from Here* (1965); etc.

Etiquette. By Emily Post (1922). Practical guide to "gracious modern living." Continually revised, and later edited by Elizabeth L. Post.

Étude. Monthly musical journal founded in 1883 by Theodore Presser, at Lynchburg, Va. In 1884 it was moved to Philadelphia. Discontinued 1957.

EUBANK, EARL[E] Edward (Mar. 20, 1887–Dec. 17, 1945); b. Columbia, Mo. Sociologist. *Lockstep and Corridor* (with C. L. Clark, 1927); *The Concepts of Sociology* (1931); *Fields and Methods of Sociology* (with others, 1934); *Contemporary Social Theory* (1940); etc.

"Euclid alone has looked on beauty bare." Opening line in the first of eight sonnets contributed to *American Poetry, 1922: A Miscellany*, by Edna St. Vincent Millay.

"Eulalie." Poem by Edgar Allan Poe, which appeared in *The American Review*, July, 1845.

Eulogy on Sumner. By Lucius Quintus Cincinnatus Lamar (Apr. 28, 1874). Delivered in Congress, on the occasion of the death of Charles Sumner.

EUNSON, DALE (Aug. 15, 1904–   ); b. Neillsville, Wis. Author. *Homestead* (1935); *The Day They Gave the Babies Away* (1947); *Loco* (play, with Katherine Albert, 1947); etc.

Eureka. Tale by Edgar Allan Poe (1848).

Europeans, The. By Henry James (1878). Novel recounting the experiences of Felix Young and the Baroness Munster, cultured Europeans, on a visit to New England. The contrast between the Old World and the New is not too complimentary to the provincialism of the latter.

Eutaw. Novel by William Gilmore Simms (1856). A sequel to *The Forayers*, celebrates the American military successes of the year 1781, with a distinct backwoods flavor and Indian background.

"Evangeline." Narrative poem by Henry Wadsworth Longfellow (1847). The story of the expulsion of the Acadians from Grand Pré in Nova Scotia. Gabriel Lajeunesse and Evangeline Bellefontaine, lovers, are separated in the confusion of the hasty embarkation, and the poem relates their pathetic search for each other through the long years of exile. Evangeline finds her lover in her old age for one brief moment of reunion before he dies in an almshouse. The original of Evangeline, whose name was Emmerline Labiche, is buried in the cemetery of Saint Martinville in Louisiana.

Evans, Augusta J. See Augusta [Jane] Evans Wilson.

EVANS, BERGEN [Baldwin] (Sept. 19, 1904–); b. Franklin, O. Educator, author. *The Psychiatry of Robert Burton* (with George Mohr, 1944); *Natural History of Nonsense* (1946); *The Spoor of Spooks* (1954); *Dictionary of Contemporary American Usage* (with Cornelia Evans, 1957); *Comfortable Words* (1961); *Word-a-Day Vocabulary Builder* (1963); etc. Editor: *Fifty Essays* (1936); *Essays by Samuel Johnson* (1940); *Boswell's Life of Johnson* (1952); *The World, The Flesh, and H. Allen Smith* (1954); *Dictionary of Quotations* (1968). Writer, "The Skeptic's Corner," *American Mercury*, 1946–50. Prof. English, Northwestern University.

EVANS, CHARLES (Nov. 13, 1850–Feb. 8, 1935); b. Boston, Mass. Librarian, bibliographer, author. *American Bibliography* [1639–1820], 12v. (1903–34). Organized Indianapolis Public Library in 1872, librarian, 1872–80, 1889–92; one of the organizers of the Enoch Pratt Library, Baltimore, in 1884, Classified the Newberry Library, Chicago, 1892–95. Librarian, Chicago Historical Society, 1896–1901.

EVANS, CLEMENT ANSELM (Feb. 25, 1833–July 2, 1911); b. Stewart Co., Ga. Confederate general, historian. *Confederate Military History*, 12v. (1899); *Georgia*, 3v. (with Allen D. Candler, 1906).

EVANS, DONALD (July 24, 1884–May 26, 1921); b. Philadelphia, Pa. Poet. *Discords* (1912); *Sonnets from the Patagonian* (1914); *Two Deaths in the Bronx* (1916); *Nine Poems from a Valetudinarium* (1916); *Ironica* (1919).

EVANS, EDWARD PAYSON (Dec. 8, 1831–Mar. 6, 1917); b. Remsen, N.Y. Scholar, author. *Animal Symbolism in Ecclesiastical Architecture* (1896); *Beitrage zur Amerikanischen Literatur und Kulturgeschichte*, 2v. (1898–1903); *Criminal Prosecution and Capital Punishment of Animals* (1904). Author of text books, and translator of German works, etc. Prof., University of Michigan, 1861–70.

EVANS, ELIZABETH EDSON GIBSON (Mar. 8, 1832–1911); b. Newport, N.H. Author. *The Story of Kaspar Hauser* (1892); *The Story of Louis XVII of France* (1893); *Laura, an American Girl* (1884); etc.

EVANS, FLORENCE WILKINSON (Mrs. Wilfrid Muir Evans); b. Tarrytown, N.Y. Novelist, poet, playwright. *The Lady of the Flag-Flowers* (1899); *Two Is Company* (prod. 1902); *Kings and Queens* (poems, 1903); *The Far Country* (poems, 1906); *The Ride Home* (poems, 1913); *Connecticut* (poems, 1932); etc.

EVANS, FREDERICK WILLIAM (June 9, 1808–Mar. 6, 1893); b. Leominster, Worcestershire, England. Shaker leader, author. *Ann Lee (the Founder of the Shakers): A Biography* (1858); *Autobiography of a Shaker* (1869); etc.

EVANS, HENRY RIDGELY (Nov. 7, 1861–Mar. 29, 1949); b. Baltimore, Md. Author. *The Napoleon Myth* (1905); *Adventures in Magic* (1927); *History of Conjuring and Magic* (1928); *Cagliostro, Sorcerer of the Eighteenth Century* (1931); *Old Georgetown on the Potomac* (1933); *Edgar Allan Poe and Baron von Kempelen's Chess-Playing Automaton* (1939); etc.

Evans, Mrs. J. G. See Claire Spencer.

EVANS, NATHANIEL (June 8, 1742–Oct. 29, 1767); b. Philadelphia, Pa. Clergyman, editor, poet. *Poems on Several Occasions* (1772). See Edgar Legare Pennington's *Nathaniel Evans: A Poet of Colonial America* (1935).

EVANS, RICHARD LOUIS (Mar. 23, 1906–); b. Salt Lake City, Utah. Journalist, author. *At This Same Hour* (1949); *Tonic for Our Times* (1952); *From the Crossroads* (1955); *The Everlasting Things* (1957); *May Peace Be with You* (1961); *Faith in the Future* (1963); *An Open Road* (1968); etc.

EVANS, ROBLEY DUNGLISON (Aug. 18, 1846–Jan. 3, 1912); b. Floyd Court House, Va. "Fighting Bob Evans." Naval officer, author. *A Sailor's Log: Recollections of Forty Years of Naval Life* (1901); *An Admiral's Log: Being Continued Recollections of Naval Life* (1910). See J. H. Brown's *American Naval Heroes* (1899).

EVANS, WALKER (Nov. 3, 1903–   ); b. St. Louis, Mo. Photographer, author. Author: *American Photographs* (1962); *Message from the Interior* (1966); *Many Are Called* (1966). Collaborated as photographer on *Let Us Now Praise Famous Men* (with James Agee, 1941).

EVARTS, HAL GEORGE (Aug. 24, 1887–Oct. 18, 1934); b. Topeka, Kan. Rancher, trapper, novelist. *The Cross Pull* (1920); *The Yellow Horde* (1921); *Passing of the Old West* (1921); *The Bald Face* (1921); *The Settling of the Sage* (1922); *Fur Sign* (1922); *Tumbleweeds* (1923); *Shortgrass* (1932); etc.

EVARTS, WILLIAM MAXWELL (Feb. 6, 1818–Feb. 28, 1901); b. Boston, Mass. Lawyer, editor, orator, author. *Arguments and Speeches of William Maxwell Evarts*, edited by Sherman Evarts, 3v. (1919). One of the founders of the *Yale Literary Magazine*.

EVE, JOSEPH (May 24, 1760–Nov. 14, 1835); b. Philadelphia, Pa. Inventor, poet. *Better to Be* (1823).

Eve of St. Mark. Play by Maxwell Anderson (prod. 1942). An American soldier killed in World War II is the hero.

"Evening Song." Poem by Sidney Lanier. Set to music by a number of composers, including Dudley Buck, as "Sunset"; Reginald De Koven, as "A Love-Song"; and E. E. Freer. The first line is "Look off, dear love, across the sallow sands."

EVEREST, CHARLES WILLIAM (May 22, 1814–Jan. 11, 1877); b. Windsor, Conn. Episcopal clergyman, poet, hymn writer. *Vision of Death: A Poem* (1837); *Babylon: A Poem* (1838); *The Poets of Connecticut* (1843); *Vision of Death, and Other Poems* (1845). His best known hymn is "Take up thy Cross, the Saviour said."

EVERETT, ALEXANDER HILL (Mar. 19, 1790–June 29, 1847); b. Boston, Mass. Editor, diplomat, author. *Europe* (1822); *America* (1827); *Critical and Miscellaneous Essays*, 2v. (1845–46); *Poems* (1845). Editor, *North American Review*, 1830–35.

EVERETT, CHARLES CARROLL (June 19, 1829–Oct. 16, 1900); b. Brunswick, Me. Unitarian clergyman, educator, author. *The Science of Thought* (1869); *Essays on Poetry, Comedy, and Duty* (1888); *Immortality and Other Essays* (1902); etc. Bussey prof. of theology, Harvard, 1869–1900.

EVERETT, DAVID (Mar. 29, 1770–Dec. 21, 1813); b. Princeton, Mass. Lawyer, editor, poet. *Daranzel; or, The Persian Patriot* (prod. 1798, publ. 1800). Best known as the author of

"You'd scarce expect one of my age
To speak in public on the stage."

EVERETT, EDWARD (Apr. 11, 1794–Jan. 15, 1865); b. Dorchester, Mass. Unitarian clergyman, educator, statesman, diplomat, orator, author. *Life of John Stark* (1834); *The Life of George Washington* (1860); *Orations and Speeches*, 4v. (1853–68); etc. Editor, the *North American Review*, 1820–23. President, Harvard University, 1846–49. Congressman, 1825–35; Governor of Massachusetts, 1836–39; Minister to Great Britain, 1841–45; Secretary of State, 1852–53; U.S. Senator, 1853–59. Orator of the day at Gettysburg, Nov. 19, 1863, when Lincoln delivered his *Gettysburg Address*. See Paul R. Frothingham's *Edward Everett, Orator and Statesman* (1925); Orie W. Long's *Literary Pioneers* (1935).

EVERETT, JOHN [Rutherford] (Dec. 27, 1918–); b. Portland, Ore. Educator, author. *Religion in Economics* (1946); *Religion in Human Experience* (1950); *Living Constructively!* (1957). Pres., Hollins College, Virginia, 1950–60; Pres., Council of Higher Educational Institutions in New York City, since 1967.

Everett, Wade. Pen name of Will Cook.

Evergreen, Anthony. Pen name of Washington Irving.

Evergreen Review. New York. Quarterly of literature and the arts. Founded 1956 by Grove Press. Barney Rosset, president. One of the earliest of the new types of paperback periodicals put out by trade publishers. Noted for its receptiveness to avant-garde writing of personal protest. Has published Henry Miller, Jack Kerouac, Terry Southern, Semour Krim, William Jay Smith, Paul Goodman, etc. By the early 1960's *Evergreen Review* had become a mass circulation periodical, mixing experimentalism in the arts with radical social and political opinion.

Evermay, March. Pen name of Mathilde Eiker.

EVERSON, WILLIAM (1912–); b. Sacramento, Cal. Author. Writes under pen name, "Brother Antoninus." *The Residual Years* (1948); *The Crooked Lines of God* (1959); *Robinson Jeffers: Fragments of an Older Fury* (1967).

EVERSULL, HARRY KELSO (Sept. 20, 1893–Sept. 13, 1953); b. Cincinnati, O. Educator, author. *The Congregational Church* (1925); *Education and the Democratic Tradition* (1939); *The Temples in Jerusalem* (1946). President, Marietta College, from 1937.

Every Saturday. Boston. Weekly illustrated journal. Founded 1866, by Ticknor & Fields, the publishers, and edited by Thomas Bailey Aldrich. Illustrated with handsome wood engravings, the work of Winslow Homer, F. O. C. Darley, W. L. Sheppard, Sol Eytinge, W. J. Linton, A. R. Waud, and others. Absorbed by *Littell's Living Age*, 1874.

Everybody's Magazine. New York. Fiction magazine. Founded 1899. Absorbed by *Romance* in 1929.

Everyday Reference Library, The. Edited by Lewis Copeland and Lawrence W. Lamm, 1v. (1953). Formerly *Austin's New Encyclopedia of Usable Information.*

Everyman's Library. Reprints of the world's literary classics. Published in England by J. M. Dent and in America by E. P. Dutton. The series was conceived by Ernest Rhys. *See* his autobiography, *Wales England Wed* (1941). Dutton's paperback line is known as Dutton Everyman Paperbacks.

Everything You Always Wanted to Know about Sex. By David Reuben (1970). Bestseller offering information about sex in question-and-answer form.

Eve's Diary. By Mark Twain (1905). Half humorous, imaginary diary of the world's first woman.

EVISON, FRANCES MILLICENT MARION (Mrs. Frank D. McEntee) (July 7, 1880–); b. Leicester, Eng. Actress, author. *Rainbow Gold* (1920); *Peggy Pretend* (1922); *The Good-for-Nothing Graysons* (1928).

EWBANK, THOMAS (Mar. 11, 1792–Sept. 16, 1870); b. Durham, England. Inventor, author. *Life in Brazil* (1856); *Reminiscences of the Patent Office* (1859); etc.

EWEN, DAVID (Nov. 26, 1907–); b. Lemberg, Aust. Musician, author. *Men and Women Who Make Music* (1939); *Dictators of the Baton* (1943); *Haydn: A Good Life* (1946); *The Story of Irving Berlin* (1950); *The Story of Arturo Toscanini* (1951); *The Story of Jerome Kern* (1953); *Homebook of Musical Knowledge* (1955); *Panorama of American Popular Music* (1957); *The Complete Book of the American Musical Theatre* (1958); *Encyclopedia of Concert Music* (1959); *The World of Great Composers* (1962); *The Complete Book of Classical Music* (1965); *The World of Twentieth-Century Music* (1968); *David Ewen Introduces Modern Music: A History and Appreciation from Wagner to the Avant-Garde* (1969); etc. Editor: *From Bach to Stravinsky* (1933); *Book of Modern Composers* (1942); *American Composers Today* (1949); *Popular American Composers* (1962); *Great Composers: 1300–1900* (1966); *Composers since 1900* (1969); etc.

EWING, HUGH BOYLE (Oct. 31, 1826–June 30, 1905); b. Lancaster, O. Lawyer, diplomat, author. *A Castle in the Air* (1888); *The Black List: A Tale of Early California* (1893).

"Excelsior." Poem by Henry Wadsworth Longfellow (1841).

Exile. Founded 1927. Edited by Ezra Pound from Paris and Rapallo, Italy. Four issues published. Discontinued 1928.

Exit Laughing. By Irvin S. Cobb (1941). The author's experiences as a World War I reporter, and as author and lecturer, told in numerous anecdotes.

Experience As a Minister. By Theodore Parker (1859). A widely discussed book which epitomized the author's unorthodox views on religion and reform. It defended the philosophy of the transcendentalists and exposed the hypocrisy of many preachers and politicians.

Explicator. Fredericksburg, Va.; Lynchburg, Va.; Richmond, Va. Monthly. Founded 1942. Literary magazine. Edited during the years by G. W. Arms, J. P. Kirby, L. G. Locke, J. E. Whitesell.

Explorers and Travelers. By A. W. Greely (1902). Account of the exploits of many American explorers.

"Extra! Extra!" Short story by Robert E. Sherwood (1926).

Extracts in Prose and Verse; by a Lady of Maryland; Together with a Collection of Original Poetry, Never Before Published, by Citizens of Maryland. Published at Annapolis, 2v., 1808.

Extrait de la Lettre du Roi. First example of printing in Louisiana. Printed at New Orleans, by Denis Braud, 1764.

Exurbanites, The. By A. C. Spectorsky (1955). Informal and witty sociological analysis of suburban life among the top-income-bracket people who commute to New York City.

Eye, The. Novel by Vladimir Nabokov (1965).

Eye Witness. Pen name of James O'Donnell Bennett.

EYRE, KATHERINE WIGMORE (Sept. 23, 1901–Feb. 27, 1970); b. Los Angeles, Cal. Author. *Lottie's Valentine* (1941); *Rosa and Randy* (1948); *Song of a Thrush* (1952); *The Lute and the Glove* (1955); *The Chinese Box* (1959); *Monks' Court* (1966); *Sandalwood Court* (1968); etc.

EYRE, LAURENCE (1881–June 6, 1959); b. Chester, Pa. Playwright. *The Things That Count* (1914); *Sazus Matazus* (prod. 1916); *Driftwood* (1917); *The Merry Wives of Gotham* (prod. 1924); *While Doctors Disagree* (1932); etc.

Eyster, Nellie Blessing. See Penelope Anna Margaretta Blessing Eyster.

EYSTER, PENELOPE ANNA MARGARETTA BLESSING (Dec. 7, 1831?–Feb., 1922); b. Frederick, Md. Lecturer, author. Wrote under name "Nellie Blessing Eyster." *Sunny Hours* (1865); *Chincapin Charlie* (1866); *Tom Harding and His Friends* (1869); *Lionel Wintour's Diary* (1882); etc.

EYSTER, WILLIAM R. Dime novelist. *The Luckless Trapper* (1871); *Waving Plume* (1874); *Faro Frank of High Pine* (1881); *Derringer Dick* (1885); *The Dude from Denver* (1888); *Double Cinch Dan* (1891); etc. The dates are not necessarily those of first editions.

EYTINGE, MARGARET WINSHIP (Mrs. Sol Eytinge). Author of stories for children. Pen name, "Madge Elliot." *The Ball of the Fruits* (1872); and many other stories, published in annual collections as *Original Christmas Stories* by Oran S. Baldwin, Clothier, New York. Some of these were illustrated by Sol Eytinge.

EYTINGE, ROSE (Nov. 21, 1835–Dec. 20, 1911); b. Philadelphia, Pa. Actress, playwright. *It Happened This Way* (with S. Ada Fisher, 1890); *The Memories of Rose Eytinge* (1905); etc.

F

F. P. A. Pen name of Franklin Pierce Adams.

Fabius. Pen name of John Dickinson.

Fable, A. Novel by William Faulkner (1954). The Christian story transplanted to World War I as a parable.

Fable for Critics, A. By James Russell Lowell (1848). Caustic essay in verse presenting Lowell's opinions of his literary contemporaries, somewhat in the manner of Alexander Pope's unflattering couplets.

Fables in Slang. By George Ade (1902). Humorous tales written in the vernacular. They set the pattern for stories in slang.

FABRICANT, SOLOMON (Aug. 15, 1906–); b. Brooklyn, N.Y. Economist, educator. *Capital Consumption and Adjustment* (1938); *Trend of Government Activity* (1953); *The Economic Consequences of the Size of Nations* (1960); *Which Productivity* (with others 1962); *Labor Productivity* (1965); *A Primer on Productivity* (1969); etc.

Fabulous Forties: 1840–1850, The. By Meade Minnigerode (1924). A portrait of a decade in America, culled from contemporary records.

Fadette. Pen name of Marian Calhoun Legaré Reeves.

FADIMAN, CLIFTON (May 15, 1904–); b. New York. Author, editor. *Party of One* (1955); *Any Number Can Play* (1957); *Voyages of Ulysses* (1959); *Lifetime Reading Plan* (1960); *The Story of Young King Arthur* (1961); *Enter, Conversing* (1962); etc. Editor: *Living Philosophies* (1931), revised as, *I Believe: The Personal Philosophies of Certain Eminent Men and Women of Our Time* (1939); *Fantasia Mathematica* (1958); *Clifton Fadiman's Fireside Reader* (1961); *Mathematical Magpie* (1964); *Fifty Years* (1965); etc. Book editor, *The New Yorker,* 1933–43. Asst. editor, Simon & Schuster, 1927–29; editor, 1929–35; editorial adviser, 1935. Master of ceremonies of "Information Please" radio program, 1938–48.

FAGAN, JAMES OCTAVIUS (1858–deceased); b. Inverness, Scotland. Railroad signalman, author. *Confessions of a Railroad Signalman* (1908); *Autobiography of an Individualist* (1912).

FAGLEY, FREDERICK LOUIS (May 8, 1879–Aug. 25, 1958); b. Bethel, O. Congregational clergyman, author. *The Congregational Churches* (1926); *An Outline of Church History* (1935); *The Religions of Mankind* (1936); *History of Congregational Christian Churches* (1956); etc.

FAHEY, JOHN H. (Feb 19, 1873–Nov. 19, 1950); b. Manchester, N.H. Publisher. Editor and publisher, *Boston Traveler,* 1903–10; publisher, *Worcester Post,* 1914–37; *New York Evening Post,* 1923. President, The Clarke Press.

Fahnestock, Zephine Humphrey. See Zephine Humphrey.

Fahrenheit 451. Novelette by Ray Bradbury (1953). First appeared in a shorter version, entitled "The Fireman," in *Galaxy Science Fiction* in 1950. The title refers to the temperature at which book-paper will ignite. One of the most famous science-fiction writings to receive acclaim by literary critics for its style and imaginative resources, it describes a future anti-intellectual world in which book burning is the job of firemen.

Fail-Safe. Novel by Eugene Burdick and Harvey Wheeler (1963). Concerns the reciprocal destruction of New York City and Moscow as the result of a technical failure in Strategic Air Command precautions.

FAIN, WILLIAM (July 15, 1917–Apr. 23, 1961); b. New York. Author. *The Lizard's Tail* (1954); *Cheers, Major Barlow* (1958); *A Sporting Life* (1961).

FAINSOD, MERLE (May 2, 1907–); b. McKees Rocks, Pa. Educator, author. *International Socialism and the World War* (1935); *How Russia Is Ruled* (1953); *Smolensk Under Soviet Rule* (1958). Co-author: *The American People and Their Government* (1933); *Government and the American Economy* (1941). Harvard University, since 1946.

Faint Perfume. Novel by Zona Gale (1923). The story of imaginative and artistic Leda Perrin, and her unhappy life with her dull and quarrelsome cousins, the Crumbs. She is denied her true romance, but catches its "faint perfume."

FAIR, RONALD L. (Oct. 27, 1932–); b. Chicago, Ill. Novelist. *Many Thousand Gone* (1965); *Hog Butcher* (1966); *World of Nothing* (1970).

Fair God, The. Novel by Lew Wallace (1873). Romance of Mexico in the time of the Aztec Montezuma, and the Spanish invader Cortez. The action centers in the final battle between the two armies. The title derives from Quetzalcoatl, Aztec diety, which is translated as the "fair god."

"Fair Harvard." Harvard alma mater song, written by Samuel Gilman for the 200th anniversary of Harvard College, Sept. 8, 1836.

FAIRBAIRN, ANN; (d. Feb. 7, 1972); b. Cambridge, Mass. Novelist. *Five Smooth Stones* (1966); *Call Him George* (1969); *That Man Cartwright* (1970).

FAIRBANK, JANET AYER (1879–Dec. 28, 1951); Novelist. Sister of Margaret Ayer Barnes. *At Home* (1910); *The Cortlands of Washington Square* (1923); *The Smiths* (1925); *Idle Hands* (stories, 1927); *The Lions' Den* (1930); *The Bright Land* (1932); *Rich Man, Poor Man* (1936); etc.

FAIRBANK, JOHN KING (May 24, 1907–); b. Huron, S.D. Historian. *Modern China: A Bibliographical Guide to Chinese Works, 1898–1937* (with K. C. Liu, 1950); *Trade and Diplomacy on the China Coast* (1954); *China's Response to the West* (with S. Y. Teng, 1954); *The Great Tradition* (with E. O. Reischauer, 1960); *History of Asian Civilization, Vol. 2: East Asia: The Modern Transformation* (with others, 1965); *China: The People's Middle Kingdom and the U.S.A.* (1967); etc. Editor: *Chinese Thought and Institutions* (1957); *The Chinese World Order* (1968); etc. Prof. history, Harvard University, since 1946.

FAIRCHILD, ASHBEL GREEN (May 1, 1795–1864); b. Hanover, N.J. Presbyterian clergyman, author. *The Great Supper* (1847); etc.

Fairchild, Clarence. Pen name of Edwin Ross Champlin.

FAIRCHILD, DAVID [Grandison] (Apr. 7, 1869–Aug. 2, 1954); b. Lansing, Mich. Agricultural explorer, author. *The World Was My Garden* (autobiography, 1938); *Garden Islands of the Great East* (1945); *The World Grows Round My Door* (1947); and technical books. In charge Foreign Plant Exploration and Introduction, U.S. Dept. of Agriculture, 1906–28.

FAIRCHILD, HENRY PRATT (Aug. 18, 1880–Oct. 2, 1956); b. Dundee, Ill. Educator, sociologist, author. *Immigration* (1913); *Elements of Social Science* (1924); *The Melting-Pot Mistake* (1925); *General Sociology* (1934); *Economics for the Millions* (1940); *Main Street: The American Town, Past and Present* (1941); *Race and Nationality As Factors in American Life* (1947); *Prodigal Century* (1950); etc. Editor: *Immigrant Backgrounds* (1927); *Dictionary of Sociology* (1944). Prof. sociology, New York University, 1919–45.

FAIRCHILD, HOXIE NEALE (Sept. 7, 1894–); b. New York City. Educator, author. *The Noble Savage* (1928); *An Approach to Literature* (1929); *Teaching The Romantic Quest* (1931); *Toward Belief* (1935), *Religious Trends in English Poetry* 6v. (1939–68). Editor: *Religious Perspectives in College Teaching* (1952); etc. Dept. English, Columbia University, 1919–40; prof. English, Hunter College, 1940–60.

FAIRCHILD, JAMES HARRIS (Nov. 25, 1817–Mar. 19, 1902); b. Stockbridge, Mass. Educator, author. *Moral Philosophy on the Science of Obligation* (1869); *Oberlin: The Colony and the College* (1883); etc. President, Oberlin College, 1866–89.

FAIRCHILD, LOUIS W. (Mar. 3, 1901–); b. Glen Ridge, N.J. Publisher. Pres., Fairchild Publications, since 1947.

FAIRCHILD, MARY SALOME CUTLER (June 21, 1855–Dec. 20, 1921); b. Dalton, Mass. Pioneer in special phases of library work and instruction, author. *Children's Home Libraries* (1894); etc. Vice-director, New York State Library School, 1889–1905.

Fairfax, Beatrice. Pen name of Marie Manning.

Fairfax, L. Pen name of Celia Logan Connelly.

Fairfax, Marion. See Marion Fairfax Marshall.

Faith Healer, The. Play by William Vaughn Moody (1909). The story of a man who heals the sick by faith, but who finds that his work is being destroyed by his passion for a woman.

Falkner, William. See William Faulkner.

FALL, BERNARD (Nov. 11, 1926–Feb. 21, 1967); b. Vienna. Author. *The Viet-Minh Regime* (1954); *Education in the Republic of the Congo* (1961); *Street Without Joy: Indo-china at War, 1946–1954* (1961); *Military Developments in Viet Nam* (1962); *The Two Viet-Nams* (1963); *Viet-Nam Witness, 1953–66* (1966); *Hell in a Very Small Place* (1967); *Last Reflections on a War* (1967); etc.

Fall of British Tyranny; or, American Liberty Triumphant, The. Play by John Leacock (1776). Political satire on the first year of the American Revolution.

"Fall of Niagara." Best-known lyric of John G. C. Brainerd.

Fall of the House of Usher, The. Tale by Edgar Allan Poe (1839).

FALLOWS, SAMUEL (Dec. 13, 1835–Sept. 5, 1922); b. Pendleton, Lancashire, England. Methodist bishop, author. *Synonyms and Antonyms* (1884); *Handbook of Briticisms, Americanisms, etc.* (1884); *Past Noon* (1886); *Life of Samuel Adams* (1898); etc.

Falmouth Gazette. Falmouth (now Portland), Me. Newspaper. Founded 1785. First newspaper published in Maine. Name changed to *Cumberland Gazette*, 1786; and to the *Eastern Herald*, 1792. Expired 1804.

Falstaff, Jake. Pen name of Herman Fetzer.

FALSTEIN, LOUIS (May 1, 1909–); b. in Ukraine, Rus. Author. *Face of a Hero* (1950); *Slaughter Street* (1953); *Sole Survivor* (1954); *Spring of Desire* (1958); *Laughter on a Weekday* (1965); *The Man Who Loved Laughter: The Story of Sholom Aleichem* (1968); etc. Editor: *The Martyrdom of Polish-Jewish Physicians* (1963).

Family Circle. Monthly. Founded 1932 by Harry Evans as a women's service magazine distributed by Piggly Wiggly Stores, and later other chains. Merged with *Everywoman's* in 1958.

Family Magazine: Weekly Abstract of General Knowledge. New York. Founded 1833, by Origen Bacheler. Became a monthly in 1834, and sub-title was changed accordingly. Illustrated with wood-cuts. Expired 1841.

Family of Man. By Edward Steichen (1955). Photographs and text representing the diversity of mankind in sixty-eight countries. Originally assembled as a photographic exhibition at the Museum of Modern Art in New York City.

"Fanny." Satirical Poem by Fitz-Greene Halleck (1819). The story in 175 six-line stanzas of the rise and fall of Fanny and her father in wealth and social position.

Fanshawe. By Nathaniel Hawthorne (1828). The story of an ascetic and consumptive young man in a New England college town who turns down a proposal of marriage because of his health and his love of solitude.

Fantasy and Science Fiction. Rockville Center, N.Y.; New York City. Monthly. Founded 1949.

FANTE, JOHN [Thomas] (Apr. 8, 1909–); b. Denver, Colo. Author. *Wait Until Spring, Bandini* (1938); *Ask the Dust* (1939); *Dago Red* (short stories, 1940); *Full of Life* (1952); etc.

"Far Above Cayuga's Waters." Cornell alma mater song. Words by C. K. Urquhart.

Far Country, A. Novel by Winston Churchill (1913). Hugh Paret, lawyer, tires of his stuffy domestic environment and seeks diversion in a clandestine love affair. A political opponent, Hermann Krebs, is the means of reshaping Paret's materialistic outlook on life, and restores him to his family.

Far Cry, A. Short story by Zona Gale (1927).

FARABEE, WILLIAM CURTIS (Feb. 2, 1865–June 24, 1925); b. Washington County, Pa. Anthropologist, explorer, museum curator, author. *The Central Arawaks* (1918); *The Indian Tribes of Eastern Peru* (1923); *The Central Caribs* (1924); etc. Curator, Museum of the University of Pennsylvania, 1913–25.

FARAGO, LADISLAS (Sept. 21, 1906–); b. Csurgo, Hung. Author. *Abyssinia on the Eve* (1935); *Palestine at the Crossroads* (1937); *Behind Closed Doors* (1950); *It's Your Money* (1964); *The Age of Scoundrels* (1965); *The Broken Seal* (1967); *The Game of the Foxes* (1969); etc.

FARALLA, DANA (Aug. 4, 1909–); b. Renville, Minn. Novelist. *Magnificent Barb* (1947); *Dream in the Stone* (1948); *Black Renegade* (1954); *A Circle of Trees* (1955); *Children of Lucifer* (1963); *Swanhilda-of-the-Swans* (1964); *Wonderful Flying-Go-Round* (1965); etc.

FARB, PETER (July 25, 1929–); b. New York. Museum curator, author. *Living Earth* (1959); *The Story of Dams* (1961); *The Insects* (1962); *Face of North America: The Natural History of a Continent* (1963); *The Forest Reader* (1964); *The Land, Wildlife, and Peoples of the Bible* (1967); *Man's Rise to Civilization as Shown by the Indians of North America, from Primeval Times to the Coming of the Industrial State* (1969); etc. Curator, American Indian Cultures, Riverside Museum, New York City, since 1964.

FARBER, MARVIN (Dec. 14, 1901–); b. Buffalo, N.Y. Educator, author. *Phenomenology as a Method and as a Philosophical Discipline* (1928); *The Foundation of Phenomenology* (1943); *Naturalism and Subjectivism* (1959); *The Aims of Phenomenology* (1966); *Phenomenology and Existence* (1967); *Basic Issues in Philosophy* (1967); etc. Editor: *Philosophical Essays in Memory of Edmund Husserl* (1940); *Philosophic Thought in France and the United States* (1950); etc. Editor, *American Lectures in Philosophy*, since 1951. Prof. philosophy, University of Buffalo, since 1930.

Farewell! Farewell! Farewell! Short story by Conrad Aiken (1927).

Farewell to Arms, A. Novel by Ernest Hemingway (1929). Story of Frederick Henry, an American in the ambulance service in Italy during World War I, who falls in love with an English nurse. In the hard realities of the war they do not legalize their marriage and the birth of their child results in the mother's death.

FARIÑA, RICHARD (d. April 30, 1966). Songwriter, novelist. *Been Down So Long It Looks Like Up To Me* (1966); *Long Time Coming and A Long Time Gone* (1969). Wrote music and words to such songs as "Pack Up Your Sorrows" (1965), "Bold Marauder" (1966), "Hard-Lovin' Loser" (1966).

FARIS, JOHN THOMPSON (Jan. 23, 1871–Apr. 13, 1949); b. Cape Girardeau, Mo. Presbyterian clergyman, editor, author. *Winning the Oregon Country* (1911); *The Alaskan Pathfinder* (1913); *Historic Shrines of America* (1918); *On the Trail of the Pioneers* (1920); *Seeing the Far West* (1920); *Seeing the Sunny South* (1921); *The Romance of Forgotten*

Towns (1924); *The Romance of the Rivers* (1927); *Roaming the Rockies* (1930); *Roaming the Eastern Mountains* (1932); *Steamboat Coming* (1936); etc.

FARLEY, FRANK EDGAR (Apr. 25, 1868–Mar. 25, 1943); b. Manchester, N.H. Educator, author. *Scandinavian Influences in the English Romantic Movement* (1903); *An Advanced English Grammar* (with G. L. Kittredge, 1913); etc. Prof. English, Wesleyan University, 1918–36.

FARLEY, HARRIET (Mrs. John Intaglio Donlevy) (Feb. 18, 1817–Nov. 12, 1907); b. Claremont, N.H. Editor, mill-worker, author. *Shells from the Strand of the Sea of Genius* (1847); *Happy Hours at Hazel Nook* (1852); *Fancy's Frolics; or, Christmas Stories* (1880). Editor, *The Lowell Offering*, 1842–45; *The New England Offering*, 1847–50.

Farm Ballads. By Will Carleton (1873). These popular ballads caught the fancy of the public and ran into many editions.

Farman, Ella. Pen name of Eliza Anna Farman Pratt.

FARMER, FANNIE MERRITT (Mar. 23, 1857–Jan. 15, 1915); b. Boston, Mass. Director of Boston Cooking School, and department editor of *Woman's Home Companion*. Author, *The Boston Cooking School Cook Book* (1896); and other books on cookery, etc.

FARMER, HENRY TUDOR (1782–Jan., 1828); b. in England. Poet. *Imagination, the Maniac's Dream, and Other Poems* (1819).

FARMER, JAMES (Jan. 12, 1920–); b. Marshall, Tex. Civil rights official. *Freedom—When?* (1965).

FARMER, JAMES EUGENE (July 5, 1867–1915); b. Cleveland, O. Educator, author. *Essays on French History* (1897); *The Grenadier* (1898); *The Grand Mademoiselle* (1899); *Brinton Eliot* (1902); *Versailles and the Court Under Louis XIV* (1905). Teacher, St. Paul's School.

FARMER, JOHN (June 12, 1789–Aug. 13, 1838); b. Chelmsford, Mass. Antiquarian, editor. Compiler: *A Genealogical Register of the First Settlers of New England* (1829). Editor, *Collections, Historical and Miscellaneous, and Monthly Literary Journal* (with Jacob Bailey Moore), 1822–24; *The New Hampshire Register*, 1824–38. Corresponding secretary, The New Hampshire Historical Society, 1825–38.

FARMER, LYDIA HOYT (1842–Dec. 27, 1903); b. Cleveland, O. Author. *The Boys' Book of Famous Rulers* (1886); *The Girls' Book of Famous Queens* (1887); *The Life of Lafayette* (1888); *A Short History of the French Revolution* (1889); *Aunt Belindy's Points of View* (1895); *The Doom of the Holy City* (1895); etc.

FARMER, PHILIP JOSE (Jan. 26, 1918–); b. Terre Haute, Ind. Author. *The Green Odyssey* (1957); *Strange Relations* (1960); *Flesh, A Woman a Day* (1960); *The Lovers* (1961); *The Alley God* (1962); *Fire and the Night* (1962); *Cache from Outer Space* (1963); *The Celestial Blueprint* (1963); *Inside Outside* (1964); *Dare* (1965); *The Maker of Universes* (1965); *Night of Light* (1966); *The Gates of Creation* (1966); *A Private Cosmos* (1968); etc.

Farmer's Letters, The. By John Dickinson (1767–68). Series of twelve letters which had a great influence on the political thought of America prior to the Revolution.

Farmers' Museum. Walpole, N.H. Weekly newspaper. Founded 1793, by Isaiah Thomas and David Carlisle, Jr., as *The New Hampshire Journal; or, the Farmers' Weekly Museum.* Joseph Dennie was editor, 1796–99. Thomas Green Fessenden and Royal Tyler were contributors, and gave it a literary reputation. Tyler and Dennie formed a literary partnership in 1794 and wrote a column of prose and poetry for the *Farmers' Museum* entitled "Colon and Spondee." Expired 1810. *See* Joseph Dennie's *The Spirit of the Farmers' Museum* (1801); and Milton Ellis's *Joseph Dennie and His Circle* (1915).

FARNHAM, ELIZA WOODSON BURHANS (Nov. 17, 1815–Dec. 15, 1864); b. Rensselaerville, N.Y. Philanthropist, author. *Life in Prairie Land* (1846); *California, Indoors and Out* (1856); *Woman and Her Era,* 2v. (1864); *The Ideal Attained* (1865); etc.

FARNHAM, MATEEL HOWE (Mrs. Dwight Thompson Farnham) (d. May 2, 1957); b. Atchison, Kan. Novelist. *Rebellion* (1927); *Marsh Fire* (1928); *Wild Beauty* (1930); *Battle Royal* (1931); *Lost Laughter* (1933); *Great Riches* (1934); *Ex-Love* (1937); *Tollivers* (1944).

FARNHAM, THOMAS JEFFERSON (1804–Sept. 13, 1848); b. in Vermont. Lawyer, traveler, author. *Travels in the Great Western Prairies, the Anahuac and Rocky Mountains, and in the Oregon Territory* (1841); *Life and Adventures in California* (1847); etc.

FARNHAM, WILLARD EDWARD (Sept. 29, 1891–); b. Wichita, Kan. Educator, author. *The Medieval Heritage of Elizabethan Tragedy* (1936); *Shakespeare's Tragic Frontier* (1950); etc. Editor: *Shakespeare's Troilus and Cressida* (1966); *Twentieth Century Interpretations of Doctor Faustus* (1969). English dept., University of California, 1923–59.

FARNSWORTH, CHARLES HUBERT (Nov. 29, 1859–May 22, 1947); b. Cesarea, Turkey. Professor of music, author. *How to Study Music* (1920); *Short Studies in Musical Psychology* (1929); etc. Editor: *Songs for Schools* (1907); *Folk Songs* (1916); *Singing Youth* (1935). Head, dept. music and speech, Teachers College, Columbia University, 1901–26.

Farquharson, Martha. Pen name of Martha Finley.

FARR, T. J. (Mar. 27, 1902–Apr. 30, 1962); b. Bolton, Miss. Educator, author. *History of Public Elementary and Secondary School System in Mississippi, 1798–1930* (1931). Compiler: *Tennessee Riddles and Superstitions* (1935); *Folk Speech of Tennessee* (1936); and other works on Tennessee folklore. English dept., Tennessee Polytechnic Institute, 1929–33; director, School of Education, 1949–62.

Farrago. Essays by Joseph Dennie, which appeared in *The Port Folio* and other magazines. The series was never published as a unit. See Milton Ellis's *Joseph Dennie and His Circle* (1915).

FARRAND, LIVINGSTON (June 14, 1867–Nov. 8, 1939); b. Newark, N.J., brother of Max Farrand. Educator, author. *The Basis of American History* (1904). President, University of Colorado, 1914–19; president, Cornell University, 1921–37.

FARRAND, MAX (Mar. 29, 1869–June 17, 1945); b. Newark, N.J., brother of Livingston Farrand. Librarian, educator, editor, author. *The Framing of the Constitution* (1913); *The Fathers of the Constitution* (1921); etc. Editor, *The Records of the Federal Convention of 1787,* 4v. (1911; 1937); etc. Director, Henry E. Huntington Library and Art Gallery, 1927–41.

FARRAR, ELIZA WARE (Mrs. John Farrar) (1791–Apr. 22, 1870); b. in Flanders, of American parentage. Author: *The Young Lady's Friend* (anon., 1837); *Congo in Search of His Master* (1854); *Recollections of Seventy Years* (1865); etc.

FARRAR, JOHN CHIPMAN (Feb. 25, 1896–); b. Burlington, Vt. Editor, publisher, author. *Forgotten Shrines* (1919); *Songs for Parents* (1921); *The Magic Sea Shell* (1923); *The Middle Twenties* (1924); *For the Record* (1943); etc. Editor: *The Literary Spotlight* (1924); Editor, *The Bookman,* 1921–1927; editor, George H. Doran Co., 1925; director, Doubleday, Doran & Co., 1927; co-founder, Farrar and Rinehart, 1929; chairman of the board, Farrar, Straus and Giroux, since 1946.

Farrar & Rinehart. New York. Publishers. Founded in 1929 by John Farrar and Stanley M. Rinehart, Jr. Its first big book was Hervey Allen's *Anthony Adverse,* and it initiated the Rivers of America series. The firm became Rinehart & Co. after World War II, upon the separation of Farrar from Rinehart. In 1959 it was merged with Holt and Winston to become Holt, Rinehart & Winston (q.v.). *See* Farrar, Straus & Giroux.

Farrar, Straus & Co. *See* Farrar, Straus and Giroux.

Farrar, Straus & Giroux. New York. Publishers. John Farrar, who had founded Farrar & Rinehart in 1929, and separated from it after World War II, founded Farrar, Straus & Co. in 1946. He was chairman of the board and Roger W. Straus, Jr., was president. In 1950 the firm became known as Farrar, Straus & Young and later as Farrar, Straus and Cudahy. It soon absorbed Hendricks House, publishers of college texts. Farrar is chairman of the board and Straus is president. Robert Giroux is vice-president and editor-in-chief. The firm owns the Noonday Press and L. C. Page and Co. Some of its divisions are *Vision Books,* Catholic juveniles; and *Ariel Books,* juveniles.

FARRELL, GABRIEL (Jan. 30, 1886–) b. Boston, Mass. Episcopal clergyman, educator. *The Story of Blindness* (1956). Director, Perkins Institution and Massachusetts School for the Blind, 1931–51.

FARRELL, JAMES THOMAS (Feb. 27, 1904–); b. Chicago, Ill. Author. *Young Lonigan: A Boyhood in Chicago Streets* (1932); *Gas-House McGinty* (1933); *The Young Manhood of Studs Lonigan* (1934); *Calico Shoes* (1934); *Judgment Day* (1935); *Guillotine Party, and Other Stories* (1935); *A Note on Literary Criticism* (1936); *A World I Never Made* (1936); *Can All This Grandeur Perish?* (1937); *Father and Son* (1940); *Ellen Rogers* (1941); *My Days of Anger* (1943); *To Whom It May Concern* (1944); *The League of Frightened Philistines* (1945); *Bernard Clare* (1946); *Literature and Morality* (1947); *The Life Adventurous* (1947); *The Road Between* (1949); *An American Dream Girl* (1950); *This Man and This Woman* (1951); *Yet Other Waters* (1952); *The Face of Time* (1953); *Reflections at Fifty and Other Essays* (1954); *French Girls Are Vicious* (1955); *A Dangerous Woman and Other Short Stories* (1957); *My Baseball Diary* (1957); *It Has Come to Pass* (1958); *Boarding House Blues* (1961); *The Silence of History* (1963); *What Time Collects* (1964); *Collected Poems* (1965); *When Time Was Born* (1966); *Lonely for the Future* (1966); *Childhood Is Not Forever* (1969). *See* Joseph Warren Beach's *American Fiction, 1920–1940* (1941); W. M. Forhock's *The Novel of Violence in America* (1950).

FARRINGTON, S[elwyn] KIP, JR. (May 7, 1904–); b. Orange, N.J. Sportsman, author. *Ships of the U.S. Merchant Marine* (1947); *Railroads of Today* (1949); *Sport Fishing Boats* (1949); *Railroading the Modern Way* (1951); *Fishing the Pacific* (1953); *Railroads of the Hour* (1958); etc.

FARRISS, CHARLES SHERWOOD (June 1, 1856–Apr. 14, 1938); b. Warrenton, N.C. Educator, author. *The American Soul* (1920); *Robert E. Lee* (drama, 1924); Acting president, Stetson University, 1904 and 1933.

FARROW, JOHN VILLIERS (Feb. 10, 1906–Jan., 1963); b. Sydney, Aus. Motion picture director and producer, author. *Laughter Ends* (1934); *Damien the Leper* (1937); *Pageant of the Popes* (1942); *The Story of Thomas More* (1954); etc.

FARSON, [James Scott] NEGLEY (May 14, 1890–Dec. 13, 1960); b. Plainfield, N.J. Author. *Sailing Across Europe* (1926); *Daphne's in Love* (1927); *There's No End to It* (1929); *Black Bread and Red Coffins* (1930); *The Way of a Transgressor* (1935); *Transgressor in the Tropics* (1937); *Fugitive Love* (1939); *Story of a Lake* (1939); *Behind God's Back* (1941); *Going Fishing* (1943); *Last Chance in Africa* (1950); *The Sons of Noah* (1949); *Caucasian Journey* (1952); *A Mirror for Narcissus* (1957); *The Lost World of the Caucasus* (1958); etc.

Fashion and Famine. Novel by Ann Sophia Stephens (1854).

Fashion; or, Life in New York. Play by Anna Cora Mowatt (prod. 1845). Satire of the efforts of the "new rich" of New York to adopt foreign manners.

FAST, HOWARD [Melvin] (Nov. 11, 1914–); b. New York. Author. *Two Valleys* (1932); *Strange Yesterday* (1933); *A Place in the City* (1937); *Conceived in Liberty* (1939); *Haym Salomon* (1941); *The Last Frontier* (1941); *Lord Baden-Powell of the Boy Scouts* (1941); *The Unvanquished* (1942); *Citizen Tom Paine* (1943); *Freedom Road* (1944); *The American* (1946); *My Glorious Brothers* (1948); *Departure, and Other Stories* (1949); *Literature and Reality* (1949); *The Proud and the Free* (1950); *Spartacus* (1952); *Silas Timberman* (1954); *Thirty Pieces of Silver* (play, 1954); *Moses, Prince of Egypt* (1958); *The Winston Affair* (1959); *April Morning* (1961); *Power* (1962); *Agrippa's Daughter* (1964); *Torquemada* (1966); *The Hunter and the Trap* (1967); *The Jews* (1969). Under pen name "Walter Ericson": *Fallen Angel* (1952). Under pen name "E. V. Cunningham": *Lydia* (1964); *Penelope* (1965); *Margie* (1966); *Cynthia* (1969); *The Assassin Who Gave Up His Gun* (1969).

Fatal Deception, The. Play by William Dunlap (prod. 1794). Later called *Leicester.* One of the first American tragedies.

Fatal Interview. Poems by Edna St. Vincent Millay (1931). A sequence of fifty-two love sonnets.

Fate Magazine. Evanston, Ill. Monthly. Founded 1948. Devoted to the occult and related esoterica.

Fate of Mansfield Humphreys, The. Novel by Richard Grant White (1884). The story of an unsuccessful marriage between an American, Washington Adams, and an English girl, Margaret Duffield. The book places an exaggerated emphasis on the boorishness of American speech and manners and the snobbery of titled Englishmen.

"Father Abbey's Will." Poem by John Seccomb, written in 1730. It was based on the death of Matthew Abdy, bedmaker and sweeper at Harvard College. To these stanzas were added twelve stanzas called "A Letter of Courtship to his virtuous and amiable Widow," supposed to have been written by the sweeper at Yale. These verses were printed in the *Gentleman's Magazine* in 1732, and in the *Massachusetts Magazine* in 1794, and privately printed at Cambridge by John L. Sibley in 1854.

Father Abraham's Speech. Compiled by Benjamin Franklin from twenty-four issues of his *Poor Richard's Almanac,* and published in the almanac for 1758. It was first published separately in 1760; was republished as *The Way to Wealth* (1774); and translated into French as *La Science du Bonhomme Richard* (1777). Many editions have appeared since.

Father; or, American Shandy-ism, The. Play by William Dunlap (prod. 1788). A comedy of manners.

FAUGHT, MILLARD C[lark] (Apr. 11, 1916–); b. Sunset, Ariz. Public relations executive. Author: *Falmouth, Massachusetts* (1945); *The Care and Feeding of Executives* (with Laurence Hammond, 1947); *How To Scratch a Match* (1948).

FAULEY, WILBUR FINLEY (Oct. 15, 1872–Dec. 21, 1942); b. Fultonham, O. Journalist, playwright. Pen name "Wilbur Fawley." *After Midnight* (1904); *Within Four Walls* (1914); *Jenny Be Good* (1919); *Queenie* (1921); *Fires of Fate* (1922); *Princess Charming* (1927); *Virginia* (1931); *Misalliance* (1934); *Burnt Earth* (1936); etc. With *New York Times,* from 1909.

FAULK, JOHN HENRY (Aug. 21, 1913–); b. Austin, Tex. Radio performer. *Fear on Trial* (1964). With Columbia Broadcasting System, 1946–48; conducted John Henry Faulk Show, WCBS, 1951–57.

FAULKNER, GEORGENE (Oct. 6, 1873–); b. Chicago, Ill. Author of children's stories. Known as "The Story Lady." *Old English Tales* (1916); *Tales of Many Folk* (1926); *The White Elephant* (1929); *Melindy's Medal* (with J. L. Becker, 1945); *Hidden Silver* (1952); etc. Wrote stories for *Ladies' Home Journal* under title "The Story Lady," 1915–19.

FAULKNER, HAROLD UNDERWOOD (Feb. 25, 1896–); b. Taylor, Pa. Educator, author. *American Economic History* (1924); *The Quest for Social Justice, 1898–1914* (1931); *American Political and Social History* (1937); *The American Way of Life* (with others, 1941); *Labor in America* (with Mark Starr, 1944); *From Versailles to the New Deal* (1950); *The Decline of Laissez Faire* (1951); *Politics: Reform and Expansion* (1959); etc. Co-editor, *Smith College Studies in History,* 1925–41. Professor of history, Smith College, since 1931.

FAULKNER, VIRGINIA LOUISE (Mar. 1, 1913–); b. Lincoln, Neb. Author. *Friends and Romans* (1934); *The Barbarians* (1935). Editor: *Roundup: A Nebraska Reader* (1957). Under pen name "Princess Tulip Murphy": *Myttey Day* (1940).

FAULKNER, WILLIAM (Sept. 25, 1897–July 6, 1962); b. (Falkner) New Albany, Miss. Novelist. *The Marble Faun* (poems, 1924); *Soldier's Pay* (1926); *Mosquitoes* (1927); *Sartoris* (1929); *The Sound and the Fury* (1929); *As I Lay Dying* (1930); *Sanctuary* (1931); *These Thirteen* (1931); *Idyll in the Desert* (1931); *Miss Zilphia Gant* (1932); *Light in August* (1932); *A Green Bough* (poems, 1933); *Pylon* (1935); *Absalom, Absalom!* (1936); *The Unvanquished* (1938); *The Wild Palms* (1939); *The Hamlet* (1940); *Go Down Moses and Other Stories* (1942); *Intruder in the Dust* (1948); *Knight's Gambit* (1949); *Collected Stories* (1950); *Requiem for a Nun* (1951); *Mirrors of Chartres Street* (1953); *A Fable* (1954; Pulitzer Prize for fiction, 1955; *Big Woods* (1955); *The Town* (1957); *The Mansion* (1959); *The Reivers* (1962); *Essays, Speeches, and Public Letters of William Faulkner* (1965), ed. by James Meriwether; etc. Nobel Prize for literature, 1949. *See* Harry M. Campbell and R. E. Foster's *William Faulkner: A Critical Appraisal* (1951); Irving Howe's *William Faulkner: A Critical Study* (1952); Willian Van O'Connor's *The Tangled Fire of William Faulkner* (1954); Robert Coughlan's *The Private World of William Faulkner* (1954); Hyatt Wagoner's *William Faulkner: From Jefferson to the World* (1960); R. N. Raimbault's *Faulkner* (1963); John W. Hunt's *William Faulkner: Art in Theological Tension* (1965); Murry C. Falkner's *The Falkners of Mississippi* (1967).

FAUNCE, WILLIAM HERBERT PERRY (Jan. 15, 1859–Jan. 31, 1930); b. Worcester, Mass. Baptist clergyman, educator, author. *What Does Christianity Mean* (1912); *Religion and War* (1918); etc. President, Brown University, 1899–1929.

FAURE, RAOUL C[ohen] (Sept. 10, 1909–); b. Cairo, Egypt. Novelist. *The Spear in the Sand* (1946); *Mister St. John* (1947); *Lady Godiva and Master Tom* (1948); *The Cave and the Rock* (1953).

FAUSET, JESSIE REDMON (1884?–Apr. 30, 1961); b. Philadelphia, Pa. Educator, editor, novelist. *There Is Confusion* (1924); *Plum Bun* (1928); *The Chinaberry Tree* (1931); *Comedy, American Style* (1933). Lit. editor, *The Crisis,* 1926–27.

FAUST, ALBERT BERNHARDT (Apr. 20, 1870–Feb. 8, 1951); b. Baltimore, Md. Educator, author. *Charles Sealsfield* (1897); *The German Element in the United States* (1909); *Das Deutschtum in den Vereinigten Staaten,* 2v. (1912); *The Bank War: An American Historical Drama* (1944); etc. German dept., Cornell University, 1904–38.

FAUST, FREDERICK (May 29, 1892–May 11, 1944); b. Seattle, Wash. Novelist, poet. Pen names, "Max Brand," "M. B." and many others. Under own name: *The Village Street, and Other Poems* (1922); *Dionysus in Hades* (poem, 1931); also, under pen name "Max Brand": *The Untamed* (1918); *Trailin'* (1920); *The Seventh Man* (1921); *Alcatraz* (1923); *Destry Rides Again* (1930); *Happy Valley* (1931);

Twenty Notches (1932); *Brothers on the Trail* (1934); *South of the Rio Grande* (1936); *Trouble Trail* (1937); *The Secret of Dr. Kildare* (1940); *Wine in the Desert, and Other Stories,* (1940); etc. also, under pen name "M. B.": *The Thunderer* (1933); etc.

FAUST, IRVIN. Author. *Entering Angel's World* (1963); *Roar Lion Roar* (1965); *The Steagle* (1966); *The File on Stanley Patton Buchta* (1970).

Favelle: or, The Fatal Duel. One-act play by Charles L. Adams (1809).

FAWCETT, EDGAR (May 26, 1847–May 2, 1904); b. New York. Poet, playwright, novelist. *Purple and Fine Linen* (1873); *Fantasy and Passion* (poems, 1878); *A False Friend* (prod. 1880); *Our First Families* (prod. 1880); *Sixes and Sevens* (prod. 1881); *Tinkling Cymbals* (1884); *Song and Story* (poems, 1884); *An Ambitious Woman* (1884); *Rutherford* (1884); *The Adventures of a Woman* (1884); *Romance and Revery* (poems, 1886); *Demoralizing Marriage* (1889); *Songs of Doubt and Dream* (poems, 1891); *New York* (1898); etc.

Fawcett World Library. New York. Founded 1950. Publishers. Includes Crest Books, Premier Books, and Gold Medal Books: paperback fiction and nonfiction.

FAWLEY, WILBUR. Pen name of Wilbur Finley Fauley.

FAXON, HENRY W. (1830–Sept. 11, 1864); b. Buffalo, N.Y. Author. *The Silver Lake Serpent* (1855). This advertising hoax which first appeared in *The Buffalo Republic,* is one of the first American sea-serpent tales.

FAY, CHARLES ERNEST (Mar. 10, 1846–Jan. 25, 1931); b. Roxbury, Mass. Educator, editor, alpinist. Editor, *Appalachia,* 1879–1920; *Alpina Americana,* 1907–14. One of the founders of Modern Language Association of America, 1883; Appalachian Mountain Club, 1876; Round Table Club, Boston, 1885. Wade prof. modern languages, Tufts College, 1871–1928.

Fay, Joseph Dewey (1779–1825). *See* Theodore Sedgwick Fay.

FAY, SIDNEY BRADSHAW (Apr. 13, 1876–Aug. 29, 1967); b. in Washington. Educator, author. *The Records of the Town of Hanover, N.H.* (1905); *The Rise of Brandenburg Prussia to 1786* (1937); etc. Editor: *The Origins of the World War,* 2v. (1928); *A Guide to Historical Literature* (with others, 1931); etc. Co-editor, *Smith College Studies in History,* 1915–29. Translator: *The German Catastrophe* by F. Meinecke (1950). Prof. history, Harvard University, 1929–46.

FAY, THEODORE SEDGWICK (Feb. 10, 1807–Mar. 24, 1898); b. New York City. Diplomat, editor, poet, novelist. *Dreams and Reveries of a Quiet Man, Consisting of The Little Genius and Other Essays,* 2v. (1832); *Norman Leslie* (anon., 1835); *Herbert Wendall* (1835); *Sydney Clifton* (anon., 1839); *The Countess Ida* (anon., 1840); *Hoboken: A Romance of New York* (1843); *Robert Rueful* (1844); *Ulric; or The Voices* (poem, 1851); *The Three Germanys,* 2v. (1889). Co-editor, the *New York Mirror,* 1828. Minister to Switzerland, 1853–61. The essays *The Little Genius,* included in his first book, were begun in the *New York Mirror* by his father, Joseph Dewey Fay, and continued by Theodore S. Fay after his father's death in 1825. Those signed "D" in the books are by the elder Fay.

Fearing, Blanche. *See* Lilian Blanche Fearing.

FEARING, KENNETH [Flexner] (July 28, 1902–June 26, 1961); b. Chicago, Ill. Poet, novelist. *Angel Arms* (poems, 1929); *Poems* (1935); *Dead Reckoning* (poems, 1938); *The Hospital* (1939); *Collected Poems* (1940); *Dagger of the Mind* (mystery novel, 1941); *Clark Gifford's Body* (1942); *The Big Clock* (1946); *Stranger at Coney Island* (poems, 1948); *Loneliest Girl in the World* (1951); *The Generous Heart* (1954); *New and Selected Poems* (1956); *The Crozart Story* (1960); etc.

FEARING, LILIAN BLANCHE (1863–1901); b. Davenport, Ia. Poet. Wrote also as "Lillien Blanche Fearing" and as "Blanche Fearing." *The Sleeping World, and Other Poems* (1887); *In the City by the Lake* (1892); *Asleep and Awake* (under pen name, "Raymond Russell," 1893); *Roberta* (1895).

FEATHER, LEONARD [Geoffrey] (Sept. 13, 1914–); b. London. Composer, music critic, author. *Encyclopedia of Jazz* (1956); *Book of Jazz* (1957); *Laughter from the Hip* (1964); *The Encyclopedia of Jazz in the 60s* (1966); etc.

FEATHER, WILLIAM (Aug. 25, 1889–); b. Jamestown, N.Y. Publisher, author. *As We Were Saying* (1921); *Haystacks and Smokestacks* (1923); *Business of Life* (1949); *Talk about Women* (1960). Editor and publisher, *The William Feather Magazine.* Founder, William Feather Co., printers and publishers, Cleveland, O., in 1916.

FEDDEN, KATHERINE WALDO DOUGLAS (Mrs. Romilly Fedden) (d. Apr. 7, 1939); b. New York City. Author. Wrote also under name "Mrs. Romilly Fedden." *The Sign* (1912); *The Spare Room* (1913); *Shifting Sands* (1914); *The Basque Country* (1921); *The Peacock's Tail* (1925); *1900 A.D.* (1931); *Manor Life in Old France* (1933).

Federal Theatre Project. Established 1935, as a project of the Works Project Administration, with Hallie Flanagan as national director. *See* Hallie Flanagan's *Arena: An Adventure in the American Theatre* (1940).

Federal Writers Project. Established 1934, as a project of the Works Project Administration, with Henry G. Alsberg as national director. Forty-eight state directors were named to assist in the publication of the *American Guide Series* and other books. The first guide published was *Idaho, a Guide in Word and Picture* (1937). The work was supervised by J. D. Newson at the national headquarters, Washington, D.C. The *American Guide Series* was completed in 1941.

Federalist, The. Series of eighty-five papers which first appeared in *The Independent Journal of New York,* Oct. 27, 1787–Apr. 2, 1788. They were signed "Publius," and were written by Alexander Hamilton, James Madison and John Jay. Published in 2v. (1788). J. E. Cooke's complete edition, printed from the original text, with annotations, was published in 1960.

FEE, CHESTER ANDERS (July 26, 1893–May 24, 1951); b. Pendleton, Ore. Author. *Rimes o' Round Up* (1935); *Chief Joseph: The Biography of a Great Indian* (1936); *Wilderness Patriot: A Drama of Marcus Whitman* (1939); *Major General Charles Lee: American Palladium* (1951).

FEENEY, LEONARD (1897–); b. Lynn, Mass. Roman Catholic clergyman, editor, poet, biographer, essayist. *In Towns and Little Towns* (1927); *Riddle and Reverie* (1933); *Fish on Friday* (1934); *Boundaries* (poems, 1935); *Song for a Listener* (poems, 1936); *Elizabeth Seton* (1938); *You'd Better Come Quietly (1939); The Ark and the Alphabet* (with Nathalia Crane, 1939); *Survival Till Seventeen* (1941); *The Leonard Feeney Omnibus* (1943); *London Is a Place* (1951); *Bread of Life* (1952).

FEIBLEMAN, JAMES KERN (July 13, 1904–); b. New Orleans, La. Educator, author. *Death of the God in Mexico* (1931); *In Praise of Comedy* (1939); *The Revival of Realism* (1946); *Philosophers Lead Sheltered Lives* (autobiography, 1952); *Inside the Great Mirror* (1958); *The Foundations of Empiricism* (1962); *Mankind Behaving: Human Needs and Material Culture* (1963); *The Two-Story World* (1966); *Moral Strategy* (1967); *The Reach of Politics* (1969); etc. Head, philosophy dept., Tulane University, since 1951.

FEIFFER, JULES. Cartoonist, author. *Sick, Sick, Sick* (1958); *Passionella and Other Stories* (1959); *Boy, Girl, Boy, Girl* (1959); *The Explainers* (1960); *The Unexpurgated Memoirs of Bernard Mergendeiler* (1965); *Feiffer's Marriage Manual* (1967); *Little Murders* (1967); *God Bless* (1968); etc.

FEIKEMA, FEIKE. See Frederick Feikema Manfred.

FEIN, RICHARD J. (Dec. 5, 1929–); b. Brooklyn, N.Y. Educator, author. *Robert Lowell* (1970). English dept., University of Puerto Rico, 1961–63; State University of New York at New Paltz, since 1963.

FEINBERG, SAMUEL MAURICE (Mar. 28, 1895–); b. in Russia. Physician, author. *Allergy in General Practice* (1934); *The Antihistamines* (1950); *Living with Your Allergy* (1958); *How Do You Manage?* (1965); etc.

FEININGER, ANDREAS (Dec. 27, 1906–); b. Paris. Photographer, author. *New York* (1947); *On Photography* (1949); *The Face of New York* (with Susan Lyman, 1954); *The Anatomy of Nature* (1956); *Man and Stone* (1961); *Total Picture Control* (1962); *Maids, Madonnas and Witches* (1961); *Forms of Nature and Life* (1966); *Trees* (1968); etc.

FEIS, HERBERT (June 7, 1893–); b. New York. Economist, author. *The Changing Pattern of International Economic Affairs* (1940); *Seen from E.A.* (1947); *The Spanish Story* (1948); *The Road to Pearl Harbor* (1950); *Diplomacy of the Dollar: First Era, 1919–32* (1950); *The China Tangle* (1953); *Churchill, Roosevelt, Stalin* (1957); *Between War and Peace: The Potsdam Conference* (1960; Pulitzer prize for history, 1961); *Japan Subdued* (1961); *Foreign Aid and Foreign Policy* (1964); *Characters in Crisis* (1966); *Contest Over Japan* (1967); *The Birth of Israel: The Tousled Diplomatic Bed* (1969).

FELD, ROSE CAROLINE (May 12, 1895–); b. in Rumania, came to the United States in 1898. Journalist, author. *Humanizing Industry* (1920); *Heritage* (1928); *A Young Man of Fifty* (1932); *Sophie Halenczik, American* (1943); *My Aunt Lucienne* (1955); etc. With the *New York Times,* 1916–22.

FELDERMAN, ERIC (1944–   ); b. New York. Poet. *The Dummy's Soliloquy* (1965).

FELDMAN, ABRAHAM J[ehiel] (June 28, 1893–); b. Kiev, Ukraine. Rabbi, author. *Words in Season* (1920); *We Jews* (1927); *The Adventure of Judaism* (1937); *The American Jew* (1937); *The Rabbi and His Early Ministry* (1941); *Remember the Days of Old* (1943); *In Time of Need* (1946); *100 Benedictions* (1948); *Reform Judaism: A Guide* (1953); *The American Reform Rabbi—A Profile of a Profession* (1969); etc.

FELDMAN, IRVING [Mordecai] (Sept. 22, 1928–); b. Brooklyn, N.Y. Poet. *Works and Days* (1961); *The Pripet Marshes, and Other Poems* (1965); *Magic Papers* (1970). Faculty, Kenyon College, since 1958.

Felix, Pastor. Pen name of Arthur John Lockhart.

Felix O'Day. Novel by F. Hopkinson Smith (1915). Story of a financially embarrassed Englishman stranded in New York. He is befriended by a curio dealer and a Catholic priest who realize that he is a gentleman, and who assist him in finding his runaway wife. He turns out to be Sir Felix O'Day.

Fellows-Johnston, Annie See Annie Fellows Johnston.

FELT, JOSEPH BARLOW (Dec. 22, 1789–Sept. 8, 1869); b. Salem, Mass. Congregational clergyman, antiquarian, author. *Annals of Salem* (1827); *The Customs of New England* (1853); *Ecclesiastical History of New England,* 2v. (1851–1862). Librarian of Massachusetts Historical Society, 1842–58.

FELTON, CORNELIUS CONWAY (Nov. 6, 1807–Feb. 26, 1862); b. Newbury, Mass. Educator, classicist, author. *Familiar Letters from Europe* (1865); *Greece, Ancient and Modern* (1867). Greek and Latin dept., Harvard University, 1829–60; president of Harvard, 1860–62.

FELTON, REBECCA LATIMER (June 10, 1835–Jan. 24, 1930); b. Decatur, Ga. Senator, author. *My Memoirs of Georgia Politics* (1911); *Country Life in Georgia in the Days of My Youth* (1919).

Female Quixotism. Novel by Tabitha Gilman Tenney (1801). One of the earliest popular novels in America. It satirizes the current literary tastes in the person of the pretentious and ebullient litterateur, Dorcasina Sheldon. It coincides with the twilight of "Della Cruscan" literature in America.

Feminine Mystique, The. By Betty Friedan (1963). Investigation of attitudes towards femininity and womanhood in modern society.

FENNELL, JAMES (Dec. 11, 1766–June 13, 1816); b. London, England. Actor, adventurer, author. *Lindor and Clara; or, The British Officer* (1791); *An Apology for the Life of James Fennell* (1814); etc.

FENNO, JOHN (Aug. 12, 1751–Sept. 14, 1798); b. Boston, Mass. Editor. Founder, *The Gazette of the United States,* New York, Apr. 11, 1789. It was moved to Philadelphia, Pa., Apr. 14, 1790.

FENOLLOSA, MARY McNEIL (Mrs. Ernest Francisco Fenollosa) (d. Jan. 11, 1954); b. Mobile, Ala. Novelist, poet. Pen name, "Sidney McCall." *Out of the Nest: A Flight of Verses* (1899); *The Dragon Painter* (1906); also, under pen name: *Truth Dexter* (1901); *The Breath of the Gods* (1905); *Red Horse Hill* (1909); *Sunshine Beggars* (1918); *Christopher Laird* (1919).

FENTON, CARROLL LANE (Feb. 12, 1900–Nov. 16, 1970); b. near Parkersburg, Ia. Geologist, lecturer, author. *The World of Fossils* (1933); *Along the Hill* (1935); *Holiday Shore* (with Edith M. Patch, 1935); *Mountain Neighbors* (with same, 1936); *Forest Neighbors* (with same, 1938); *Prairie Neighbors* (with same, 1940); *Worlds in the Sky* (with same, 1950); *Prehistoric World* (1954); *Wild Folk in the Mountains* (1958); *The Fruits We Eat* (with Herminie Kitchen, 1961); *Tales Told by Fossils* (1965); *The Land We Live On* (with Mildred A. Fenton, 1966); *The Plants We Live On* (with Herminie Kitchen, 1969); etc.

FENTON, CHARLES A[ndrews] (1919–July 21, 1960); b. Springfield, Mass. Educator, author. *The Apprenticeship of Ernest Hemingway: The Early Years* (1954); *Stephen Vincent Benét: The Life and Times of an American Man of Letters* (1958). Editor: *The Best Short Stories of World War II* (1957); Stephen Vincent Benét's *Selected Letters* (1960).

Feodor Vladimir Larrovitch: An Appreciation of His Life and Works. By William George Jordon and R. Wright (1918). Celebrated literary hoax perpetrated by members of the Authors Club.

FERBER, EDNA (Aug. 15, 1887–Apr. 16, 1968); b. Kalamazoo, Mich. Novelist, playwright. *Dawn O'Hara* (1911); *Roast Beef Medium* (1913); *Emma McChesney & Co.* (1915); *Fanny Herself* (1917); *Cheerful, by Request* (1918); *The Girls* (1921); *So Big* (1924; Pulitzer prize for fiction, 1925); *Minick* with George S. Kaufman, prod. 1924); *Show Boat* (1926); *Mother Knows Best* (1927); *The Royal Family* (with George S. Kaufman, prod. 1927); *Cimarron* (1930); *American Beauty* (1931); *Dinner at Eight* (with George S. Kaufman, prod. 1932); *They Brought Their Women* (1933); *Stage Door* (with George S. Kaufman, prod. 1936); *A Peculiar Treasure* (autobiography, 1939); *Saratoga Trunk* (1941); *Great Son* (1945); *One Basket* (short stories, 1947); *Giant* (1952); *Ice Palace* (1958).

FERBER, NAT J[oseph] (1889–). Author. *Sidewalks of New York* (1927); *New York* (1929); *A New American* (1938); *I Found Out* (1939).

FERGUSON, CHARLES W[right] (Aug. 23, 1901–); b. Quanah, Tex. Editor, author. *The Confusion of Tongues: A Review of Modern Isms* (1927); *Pigskin* (1928); *A Little Democracy Is a Dangerous Thing* (1948); *Naked to Mine Enemies: The Life of Cardinal Wolsey* (1958); *Getting to Know the U.S.A.* (1963); *The Abecedarian Book* (1964); *The Male Attitude* (1966); *A is for Advent* (1968); *Say It With*

Words (1969); etc. Assoc. editor, *Reader's Digest,* 1934–40; senior editor, 1940–68.

FERGUSON, ELIZABETH GRAEME (Feb. 3, 1737–Feb. 23, 1801); b. Philadelphia, Pa. Poet, letter writer. Her home was a literary gathering place. Her manuscripts are at the Historical Society of Pennsylvania and the Ridgway Library, Philadelphia. See Simon Gratz's *Some Material for a Biography of Mrs. Elizabeth Fergusson,* in *The Pennsylvania Magazine of History and Biography,* v. 39, 1915.

FERGUSON, JOHN DeLANCEY (Nov. 13, 1888–); b. Scottsville, N.Y. Educator, author. *American Literature in Spain* (1916); *Pride and Passion: Robert Burns, 1759–1796* (1939). Editor, *The Letters of Robert Burns,* 2v. (1931); *Men and Moments* (1937); *Mark Twain, Man and Legend* (1943). Editor: *RLS: Letters to Charles Baxter* (with Marshall Waingrow, 1956); etc. Prof. English, Western Reserve University, since 1930.

FERGUSON, MILTON JAMES (Apr. 11, 1879–Oct. 23, 1954); b. Hubbardstown, W.Va. Librarian. Editor: *American Library Laws* (1930). President, American Library Association, 1938–39. Librarian, California State Library, 1917–30; librarian, Brooklyn Public Library, 1930–49.

FERGUSON, WILLIAM BLAIR MORTON (Feb. 4, 1881–Apr. 27, 1967); b. Belfast, Ireland. Novelist. Pen name, "William Morton." *Garrison's Finish* (1907); *A Man's Code* (1915); *The Dumb-Bell* (1927); *Vanishing Men* (1935); *Wyoming Tragedy* (1935); *Somewhere Off Borneo* (1936); *Bobo Marches* (1937); *Dog Fox* (1938); *London Lamb* (1939); etc.

FERGUSON, WILLIAM SCOTT (Nov. 11, 1875–Apr. 28, 1954); b. Marshfield, P.E.I., Can. Educator, author. *The Athenian Secretaries* (1898); *The Athenian Archons* (1899); *Hellenistic Athens* (1911); *Greek Imperialism* (1913); *The Treasures of Athens* (1931); *Athenian Tribal Cycles* (1932). History dept., Harvard University, 1908–1945.

Fergusson, Elizabeth Graeme. See Elizabeth Graeme Fergusson.

FERGUSSON, ERNA (Jan. 10, 1888–); b. Albuquerque, N.M., sister of Harvey and Francis Fergusson. Author. *Dancing Gods* (1931); *Fiesta in Mexico* (1934); *Guatemala* (1937); *Venezuela* (1939); *Our Southwest* (1940); *Albuquerque* (1947); *Let's Read About Hawaiian Islands* (1950); *A Mexican Cookbook* (1961); etc.

FERGUSSON, FRANCIS (Feb. 21, 1904–); b. Albuquerque, N.M. Educator, author. *The Idea of a Theatre* (1949); *Dante's Drama of the Mind* (1953); *The King and the Duke: A Melodramatic Farce from Huckleberry Finn* (prod. 1955); *The Human Image* (1957); *Poems: 1929–1961* (1962); *Dante* (1966); *Shakespeare: The Pattern in His Carpet* (1970). Director, Princeton Seminars in literary criticism, 1949–52; prof. comparative literature, Rutgers University, since 1953.

FERGUSSON, HARVEY (Jan. 28, 1890–); b. Albuquerque, N.M., brother of Erna and Francis Fergusson. Novelist. *The Blood of the Conquerors* (1921); *Wolf Song* (1927); *In Those Days* (1929); *Footloose McGarnigal* (1930); *Rio Grande* (1933); *Followers of the Sun* (1936); *The Life of Riley* (1937); *Home in the West* (1945); *People and Power* (1947); *Grant of Kingdom* (1950); *The Conquest of Don Pedro* (1954). Translator: *Fontamara* by Ignazio Silone (1960). Editor: *The Last Rustler: The Autobiography of Lee Sage* (1930).

FERLINGHETTI, LAWRENCE (1920–); b. New York. Poet. *Pictures of the Gone World* (1955); *A Coney Island of the Mind* (1958); *Her* (1961); *Starting from San Francisco* (1962); *Routines* (1964); *Secret Meaning of Things* (1969); etc.

FERM, VERGILIUS TURE ANSELM (Jan. 6, 1896–); b. Sioux City, Ia. Lutheran clergyman, educator, author. *First Adventures in Philosophy* (1936); *First Chapters in Religious Philosophy* (1937); *What Can We Believe?* (1948); *A Protestant Dictionary* (1951); *Dictionary of Pastoral Psychology* (1955); *Pictorial History of Protestantism* (1957); *A Brief Dictionary of American Superstitions* (1959); *Inside Ivy Walls* (1964); *Toward An Expansive Christian Theology* (1965); *Basic Philosophy for Beginners* (1969); etc. Editor: *Encyclopedia of Religion* (1945); *Religion in the Twentieth Century* (1947); *Forgotten Religions* (1949); *Puritan Sage: The Collected Writings of Jonathan Edwards* (1953); *Encyclopedia of Morals* (1956); *Classics Of Protestantism* (1959); etc. Prof. philosophy, College of Wooster, since 1928.

FERMAN, JOSEPH WOLFE (June 8, 1906–); b. New York. Publisher. Editor: *No Limits* (1964). President, Mercury Publications, since 1954; editor and publisher, *Best-seller Mysteries, Mercury Mystery Magazine;* publisher, *Fantasy and Science Fiction,* etc. 1958–61.

FERMI, LAURA [Capon] (Mrs. Enrico Fermi) (June 16, 1907–); b. Rome. Author. *Atoms in the Family* (1954); *Atoms for the World* (1957); *Mussolini* (1961); *Galileo and the Scientific Revolution* (with Gilberto Bernardini, 1961); *Illustrious Immigrants* (1968).

Fern, Fanny. Pen name of Sara Payson Parton.

FERNALD, CHESTER BAILEY (Mar. 18, 1869–Apr. 10, 1938); b. Boston, Mass. Storywriter, playwright. *The Cat and the Cherub, and Other Stories* (1896); *Chinatown Stories* (1899); *Under the Jackstaff* (1903); *John Kendry's Idea* (1907); *The Married Woman* (prod. 1913); *The White Umbrella* (1919); *The Pursuit of Pamela* (1914); *To-Morrow: A Play* (1928); etc.

FERNALD, JAMES CHAMPLIN (Aug. 18, 1838–Nov. 10, 1918); b. Portland, Me. Baptist clergyman, educator, author. *Synonyms, Antonyms, and Prepositions of the English Language* (1896); *Effective English* (1918); etc. On editorial staff, *Standard Dictionary,* 1893–94, assisted in later abridgments and revisions.

FERNOW, BERTHOLD (Nov. 28, 1837–Mar. 3, 1908); b. Posen, Germany. Historian, editor. *Documents Relating to the Colonial History of the State of New York,* vols. XII, XIII, XIV (1877–83); *The Records of New Amsterdam from 1673 to 1674 anno Domini,* 7v. (1897); etc.

FERRÉ, NELS FREDERICK SOLOMON (June 8, 1908–); b. Lulea, Swed. Congregational clergyman, educator, author. *Swedish Contributions to Modern Theology* (1939); *Faith and Reason* (1946); *The Christian Understanding of God* (1951); *The Sun and the Umbrella* (1953); *God's New Age* (1962); *The Finality of Faith* (1963); *Paul Tillich: Retrospect and Future* (with others, 1967); *Living God of Nowhere and Nothing* (1967); *Universal Word: A Theology for a Universal Faith* (1969); etc. Prof. Christian theology, Andover Newton Theological School, 1939–50; and since 1957.

FERRIL, THOMAS HORNSBY (Feb. 25, 1896–); b. Denver, Colo. Poet. *High Passage* (1926); *Westering* (1934); *Trial by Time* (1944); *I Hate Thursday* (1946); *New and Selected Poems* (1952); *Words for Denver* (1966).

FERRIN, DANA HOLMAN (June 23, 1886–July 19, 1960); b. Keeseville, N.Y. Publisher. With Century Company, New York, since 1908. Vice-president, D. Appleton-Century Co., 1933–41; president, Appleton-Century-Crofts, from 1948.

FERRIS, HELEN JOSEPHINE (Nov. 19, 1890–Sept. 28, 1969); b. Hastings, Neb. Editor, author. *This Happened to Me* (1929); *Dody and Cap-tin Jinks* (1939). Compiler: *Adventure Waits* (1928); *When I Was a Girl* (1930); *Here Comes Barnum* (1932); *Challenge* (1936); *Tommy and His Dog, Hurry* (1944); etc. Editor: *Favorite Poems Old and New* (1957); etc. Editor, *The American Girl,* 1923–28; assoc. ed., *Youth's Companion,* 1928–29; editor-in-chief, Junior Literary Guild, 1929–59.

FERRIS, THEODORE PARKER (Dec. 23, 1908–); b. Port Chester, N.Y. Episcopal clergyman. *This Created World* (1944); *Go Tell the People* (1951); *The Story of Jesus* (1953); *When I Became a Man* (1957); *Book of Prayer for Everyman* (1962); *What Jesus Did* (1963); *The Image of God* (1965); etc.

FESSENDEN, LAURA [Canfield Spencer] DAYTON; (deceased); b. New York. Novelist. *Beth* (1878); *A Puritan Lover* (1887); *A Colonial Dame* (1897); *Dorothy Lee* (1905); etc.

FESSENDEN, THOMAS GREEN (Apr. 22, 1771–Nov. 11, 1837); b. Walpole, N.H. Journalist, poet, satirist. Known as "The American Butler," he was one of the "Walpole Wits." *Terrible Tractoration!!* (poem, under pen name, "Christopher Caustic," (1804); *Democracy Unveiled* (poem, under same pen name, 1805); *Original Poems* (1804); *The Ladies' Monitor* (poem, 1818); *Pills: Poetical, Political, and Philosophical* (poems, under pen name, "Peter Pepper Box," 1809). Founder, *New England Farmer,* 1822; editor, 1822–37. His best known poems are "The Country Lovers" (1795) and "The Rutland Ode" (1798). *See* H. M. Ellis's *Joseph Dennie and His Circle* (1915).

FESSIER, MICHAEL (Nov. 6, 1905–); b. Angel's Camp, Cal. Novelist. *Fully Dressed and in His Right Mind* (1935); *Clovis* (1948).

Festoons of Fancy, Consisting of Compositions Amatory, Sentimental and Humorous in Verse and Prose. By William Littell (1814).

FETTER, FRANK ALBERT (Mar. 8, 1863–Mar. 21, 1949); b. Peru, Ind. Educator, author. *The Principles of Economics* (1904); *Modern Economic Problems* (1916); etc. Prof. political economy, Princeton University, 1911–31.

FETZER, HERMAN (1899–Jan. 17, 1935); b. Akron, O. Columnist, novelist, poet. Pen name, "Jake Falstaff." *The Book of Rabelais* (1928); *The Bulls of Spring* (poems, 1937); *Jacoby's Corners* (1940); etc. Wrote column "Pippins and Cheese" for Akron and Cleveland newspapers.

FEUCHTWANGER, LION (July 7, 1884–Dec. 21, 1958); b. Munich, Bav. Author. *Power* (1926); *The Ugly Duchess* (1928); *Two Anglo-Saxon Plays* (1928); *Pep: J. L. Wetcheek's American Song Book Success* (1930); *Josephus* (1932); *The Oppermanns* (1934); *Three Plays* (1934); *The Jew of Rome* (1935); *Marianne in India* (1936); *Moscow 1937* (1937); *The Pretender* (1937); *The Devil in France* (1941); *Josephus and the Emperor* (1942); *Paris Gazette* (1942); *Double, Double, Toil, and Trouble* (1943); *Simone* (1944); *Proud Destiny* (1947); *This Is the Hour* (1951); *'Tis Folly To Be Wise* (1953); *Raquel* (1956); *Jephta and His Daughter* (1958); etc.

FEUER, LEWIS S[amuel] (Dec. 7, 1912–   ); b. New York. Educator, author. *Psychoanalysis and Ethics* (1955); *Spinoza and the Rise of Liberalism* (1958); *The Scientific Intellectual* (1963); *The Conflict of Generations* (1969). Editor: *Marx and Engels' Basic Writings in Politics and Philosophy* (1959). Prof. philosophy and social sciences, University of California at Berkeley, since 1957.

"Few Figs from Thistles, A." Poem by Edna St. Vincent Millay (1921).

FEWKES, JESSE WALTER (Nov. 14, 1850–May 31, 1930); b. Newton, Mass. Ethnologist, author of many studies on the Hopi Indians. Joined Bureau of American Ethnology in 1895, and was its director, 1918–28.

FIALA, ANTHONY (Sept. 19, 1869–Apr. 8, 1950); b. Jersey City Heights, N.J. Explorer, author. *Troop "C" in Service* (1899); *Fighting the Polar Ice* (1906).

FICKE, ARTHUR DAVISON (Nov. 10, 1883–Nov. 30, 1945); b. Davenport, Ia. Essayist, poet. *From the Isles* (1907); *The Happy Princess, and Other Poems* (1907); *The Earth Passion* (1908); *The Breaking of Bonds* (1910); *Twelve Japa-*

nese Painters (1913); *Mr. Faust* (1913); *Sonnets of a Portrait Painter* (1914); *The Man of the Hill Top, and Other Poems* (1915); *Chats on Japanese Prints* (1915); *An April Elegy* (poems, 1917); *Spectra* (with Witter Bynner, under pen names, "Emanuel Morgan" and "Anne Knish," 1916); *Sonnets of a Portrait Painter* (1922); *Out of Silence, and Other Poems* (1924); *Selected Poems* (1926); *Mountain Against Mountain* (1929); *The Secret, and Other Poems* (1936); *Mrs. Morton of Mexico* (1940).

Fiction Parade. New York. A digest. Founded May, 1935. Edited by Francis Rufus Bellamy. Absorbed *Golden Book Magazine,* Oct., 1935, and became *Fiction Parade and Golden Book Magazine.* Expired Feb., 1938.

Fiddle and the Bow, The. Popular lecture given by Robert Love Taylor, governor of Tennessee. It is published in *Gov. Bob Taylor's Tales* (1896).

FIEDLER, LESLIE A[aron] (Mar. 8, 1917–); b. Newark, N.J. Educator, author. *An End to Innocence* (1955); *The Art of the Essay* (1958); *Love and Death in the American Novel* (1960); *No! in Thunder* (1960); *Pull Down Vanity!* (1962); *Waiting for the End* (1964); *Back to China* (1965); *The Last Jew in America* (1966); *Nude Croquet* (1969); *The Return of the Vanishing American* (1968); *Being Busted* (1970); Prof. English, Montana State University, 1953–64; New York State University at Buffalo, since 1965.

FIELD, BEN (Oct. 15, 1901–   ); b. New York. Novelist. *The Cock's Funeral* (1937); *The Outside Leaf* (1943); *Piper Tompkins* (1946); *The Last Freshet* (1948); *Jacob's Son* (1971).

FIELD, CAROLINE LESLIE WHITNEY (Nov. 16, 1853–Dec. 1, 1902); b. Milton, Mass. Novelist, poet. *High Lights* (1886); *The Unseen King, and Other Verses* (1887).

FIELD, EDWARD (June 7, 1924–   ); b. Brooklyn, N.Y. Poet. *Stand Up, Friend, with Me* (1962); *Variety Photoplays* (1967).

FIELD, EUGENE (Sept. 2, 1850–Nov. 4, 1895); b. St. Louis, Mo. Author. *The Tribune Primer* (1882); *Culture's Garland* (1887); *A Little Book of Western Verse* (1889); *A Little Book of Profitable Tales* (priv. pr. 1889, publ. 1890); *Echoes from the Sabine Farm* (with Roswell Field, 1891); *With Trumpet and Drum* (1892); *Second Book of Verse* (1892); *The Holy Cross, and Other Tales* (1893); *Love Affairs of a Bibliomaniac* (1896); *Sharps and Flats* (1900); *Collected Works,* 10v. (1896). Editor of column, "Sharps and Flats" in the *Chicago Morning News,* 1883–95. With *Denver Tribune* 1881–83. *See* Slason Thompson's *Eugene Field,* 2v. (1901), and his *Life of Eugene Field* (1927); Charles H. Dennis's *Eugene Field's Creative Years* (1924). His best-known poems are: "Just 'fore Christmas," "Little Boy Blue," "Wynken, Blynken and Nod," and "The Little Peach."

FIELD, HENRY (Dec. 15, 1902–); b. Chicago, Ill. Anthropologist. *Arabs of Central Iraq* (1935); *Contributions to the Anthropology of Iran* (1939); *Contributions to the Anthropology of the Caucasus* (1953); *The Track of Man* (1953); *Ancient and Modern Man in Southwestern Asia* 2v. (1956); *Anthropological Reconnaissance in West Pakistan, 1955* (1959); *"M" Project for F.D.R.* (1962); *Anthropology of Iraq* (1940). Editor: *Bibliographies on Southwest Asia, I–VII* (1953–61); etc. Curator, Field Museum of Natural History, Chicago, 1937–41.

FIELD, HENRY MARTYN (Apr. 3, 1822–Jan. 26, 1907); b. Stockbridge, Mass. Brother of Cyrus Field. Presbyterian clergyman, author. *The Irish Confederates and the Rebellion of 1798* (1851); *From Egypt to Japan* (1877); *Among the Holy Hills* (1884); *The Greek Islands and Turkey* (1885); *History of the Atlantic Telegraph* (1866); *The Barbary Coast* (1893); etc.

FIELD, JOSEPH M. (1810–Jan. 28, 1856); b. Dublin, Ireland (?). Actor, journalist, author. Pen name, "Everpoint." *Three Years in Texas* (1836); *The Drama of Pokerville; The Bench and Bar of Jurytown; and Other Stories* (1843); *Taos: A Romance of the Massacre* (1847); etc.

FIELD, KATE [Mary Katherine Keemle] (Oct. 1, 1838–May 19, 1896); b. St. Louis, Mo. Journalist, lecturer, actress, author. *Adelaide Ristori* (1867); *Planchette's Diary* (1868); *Mad on Purpose, a Comedy* (1868); *Pen Photographs of Charles Dickens's Readings* (1868); *Hap-Hazard* (1873); *Ten Days in Spain* (1875); *Charles Albert Fechter* (1882).

FIELD, LOUISE MAUNSELL; b. New York City. Novelist. *Katherine Trevalyan* (1908); *A Woman of Feeling* (1916); *Love and Life* (1923); Editor: *Amagansett* (1948).

FIELD, MAUNSELL BRADHURST (Mar. 26, 1822–Jan. 24, 1875); b. Peekskill, N.Y. Author. *Adrian: or, The Clouds of the Mind* (with G. P. R. James, 1852); *Memories of Many Men and of Some Women* (1874).

FIELD, RACHEL [Lyman] (Mrs. Arthur S. Pederson) (Sept. 19, 1894–Mar. 15, 1942); b. New York City. Novelist, poet, playwright. *Polly Patchwork* (1928); *Hitty, Her First Hundred Years* (1929); *Points East* (poems, 1930); *A Circus Garland* (poems, 1930); *Calico Bush* (1931); *Hepatica Hawks* (1932); *Branches Green* (poems, 1934); *Time Out of Mind* (1935); *Fear Is the Thorn* (poems, 1936); *All This and Heaven Too* (1938); *Ave Maria* (1940); *And Now Tomorrow* (1942); *A Prayer for a Child* (1945); etc. Editor of several collections of fairy tales.

FIELD, ROSWELL MARTIN (Sept. 1, 1851–Jan. 10, 1919); b. St. Louis, Mo., brother of Eugene Field. Journalist, author. *Echoes from the Sabine Farm* (with brother, 1891); *In Sunflower Land: Stories of God's Own Country* (1892); *The Romance of an Old Fool* (1902); *Little Miss Dee* (1904); *Madeline* (1906); etc. Conducted column, "Lights and Shadows" in the Chicago *Post.*

FIELD, SARA BARD (1882–); b. Cincinnati, O. Poet. *The Vintage Festival* (1920); *To a Poet Born on the Edge of Spring* (1925); *The Pale Woman* (1927); *Vineyard Voices* (1930); *Barabbas* (1932); *Darkling Plain* (1936); *Selected Poems* (with C. E. S. Wood, 1937); etc. Editor: *Collected Poems of C. E. S. Wood* (1949).

FIELD, THOMAS WARREN (1821–Nov. 25, 1881); b. near Syracuse, N.Y. Author. *The Minstrel Pilgrim* (poems, 1848); *An Essay Towards an Indian Bibliography* (1873); *The Schoolmistress in History, Poetry and Romance* (1874).

FIELD, WALTER TAYLOR (Feb. 21, 1861–Aug. 18, 1939); b. Galesburg, Ill. Author. *Rome,* 2v. (1905); *The Quest of the Four-Leaved Clover* (1911); *The Changing Year* (1917); etc. Editor: *The Abbey Classics,* 5v. (1907–10); etc.

Field and Stream. New York. Monthly. Founded 1896. Published by Holt, Rinehart & Winston, Inc. Magazine for sportsmen.

"Field of Glory, The." Poem by Edwin Arlington Robinson in his *The Town Down the River* (1910).

"Field of the Grounded Arms, The." Poem by Fitz-Greene Halleck (1831), celebrating an episode at Saratoga in the American Revolution.

Field of Vision. Novel by Wright Morris (1956).

FIELDING, TEMPLE HORNADAY (Oct. 8, 1913–); b. New York. Author numerous guides for tourists, such as *Fielding's Travel Guide to Europe,* since 1948; *Fielding's Currency Guide to Europe,* since 1951; *Fielding's Super-Economy Guide to Europe,* since 1967; etc.

FIELDING, WILLIAM JOHN (Apr. 10, 1886–); b. Wharton, N.J. Editor, author. *Pebbles from Parnassus* (1917); *Prin-*

cipal Poets of the World (1937); *Woman—the Eternal Primitive* (1927); *Boccaccio* (1930); *The Art of Love* (1931); *Strange Customs of Courtship and Marriage* (1942); *Strange Superstitions and Magical Practices* (1945); *Self-Mastery Through Psychoanalysis* (1952); *Autosuggestion You Can Use* (1960); etc.

FIELDS, ANNIE ADAMS (Mrs. James Thomas Fields) (June 6, 1834–Jan. 5, 1915); b. Boston, Mass. Author. *Under the Olive* (1881); *James T. Fields* (1881); *Whittier* (1893); *A Shelf of Old Books* (1894); *Authors and Friends* (1896); *The Life and Letters of Harriet Beecher Stowe* (1897); *Letters of Sarah Orne Jewett* (1911). *See* M. A. De W. Howe, *Memories of a Hostess* (1922).

FIELDS, JAMES THOMAS (Dec. 31, 1817–Apr. 24, 1881); b. Portsmouth, N.H. Editor, publisher, poet. *Poems* (1849), containing the well-known "Ballad of the Tempest": " 'We are lost!' the Captain shouted ..."; *Yesterdays with Authors* (1872); *Hawthorne* (1876); *In and Out of Doors with Charles Dickens* (1876); *Underbrush* (1877); *Ballads and Other Verses* (1881); etc. Member of publishing firm, Ticknor & Fields (q.v.), 1838–70. Editor, *The Atlantic Monthly,* 1861–70. *See* Annie Adams Fields's *James T. Fields* (1881).

FIELDS, JOSEPH (1895–). Playwright. Co-author, with Jerome Chodorov: *My Sister Eileen* (prod. 1940); *Junior Miss* (prod. 1941); *Doughgirls* (1943); *Wonderful Town* (prod. 1952); *Anniversary Waltz* (prod. 1954); *The Ponder Heart* (prod. 1957); etc.

FIFE, GEORGE BUCHANAN (Aug. 9, 1869–Mar. 12, 1939); b. Charlestown, Mass. Editor, author. *The Passing Legions* (1920); *Lindbergh, the Lone Eagle* (1927); *Ask Your Wife* (1929). On staff, New York *Evening World,* 1912–17, 1920–31; and other New York newspapers, and *Harper's Weekly.*

FIFE, ROBERT HERNDON (Nov. 18, 1871–Aug. 1, 1958); b. Charlottesville, Va. Educator, editor, author. *The German Empire Between Two Wars* (1916); *Young Luther* (1928); *The Revolt of Martin Luther* (1957); etc. Editor, *Virginia Historical Magazine,* vols. 11–13; publications of American Committee on Modern Languages, 13v., 1927–30; etc. Prof., German, Columbia University, 1920–46.

"Fifteen men on the dead man's chest, Yo-ho-ho and a bottle of rum." Lines from a song by Young Ewing Allison, set to music by Henry Waller. It was published as a song of three stanzas under the title, *A Piratical Ballad* (1891). The first appearance of the complete poem in six stanzas was in *The Rubric,* Oct., 1901, under the title "The Derelict." It has been frequently published since as "The Derelict," "The Dead Men's Song," etc. It is an amplification of "Cap'n Billy Bones His Song" from Robert Louis Stevenson's *Treasure Island.* *See* Champion Ingraham Hitchcock's *The Dead Men's Song* (1914), a book on Allison and the writing of the song.

Fifties, The. See *Seventies, The.*

Fifty Grand. Short story by Ernest Hemingway, in his *Men Without Women* (1928). About a prize-fighter who is bribed to "throw" a fight.

Fifty-Minute Hour, The. By Robert Lindner (1955). A case history which dramatizes the uses and results of the therapeutic techniques of psychiatry.

Fighting Chance, The. Novel by Robert W. Chambers (1906). First of a trilogy, including *The Younger Set* (1907) and *The Firing Line* (1908), which portrays the problems of divorce and remarriage.

"Fighting Race, The." Poem by Joseph Ignatius Constantine Clarke, published first in the New York *Sun,* Mar. 17, 1898.

Figure in the Carpet, The. Story by Henry James (1896). Several people involved in the search for the principal motif characterizing the work of a brilliant novelist.

Filia. Pen name of Sarah Anne Ellis Dorsey.

Filigree Ball, The. Mystery novel by Anna Katharine Green (1903). The main characters are Veronica Moore and Francis Jeffrey. The scene is Washington, D.C.

FILLMORE, MILLARD (Jan. 7, 1800–Mar. 8, 1874); b. Locke, N.Y. Thirteenth president of the United States. See *Millard Fillmore Papers,* ed. by Frank H. Severance, 2v. (1907). *See also* W. Harvey Wise and J. W. Cronin's *A Bibliography of Zachary Taylor, Millard Fillmore, Franklin Pierce, James Buchanan* (1935); William Griffis's *Millard Fillmore, Constructive Statesman* (1935).

FILLMORE, PARKER [Hoysted] (Sept. 21, 1878–June 5, 1944); b. Cincinnati, O. Author. *The Hickory Limb* (1910); *The Rosie World* (1914); *Czechoslovak Fairy Tales* (1919); *The Shoemaker's Apron* (1920); *Mighty Mikko* (1922); *The Stuffed Parrot* (1931); *Yesterday Morning* (1931); etc.

Film Quarterly. Berkeley, Cal. Founded 1945. Published by University of California Press. Concerned with appreciation and criticism of motion-picture and television presentations.

FILSON, FLOYD VIVIAN (Nov. 15, 1896–); b. Hamilton, Mo. Theologian, author. *Origins of the Gospels* (1938); *Pioneers of the Primitive Church* (1940); *The New Testament Against Its Environment* (1951); *Jesus Christ, the Risen Lord* (1956); *The Bible According to St. Matthew* (1960); *Yesterday* (1967); etc. Co-editor: *Westminster Bible Atlas* (1945); *Westminster Study Bible* (1948). Prof. New Testament literature and history, McCormick Theological Seminary, 1934–54; dean, 1954–67.

FILSON, JOHN (ca. 1747–Oct., 1788); b. East Fallowfield, Pa. Explorer, historian. *The Discovery, Settlement, and Present State of Kentucke* (1784). This, the first history of Kentucky, contains as an appendix, *The Adventures of Colonel Daniel Boon* [sic], written for Boone by Filson, published separately in 1786. The Filson Club, Louisville, Ky., is named after him. It was founded by 1884 by Reuben Thomas Durrett and published a *History Quarterly* beginning Oct., 1926.

Financier, The. Novel by Theodore Dreiser (1912). The life story of Frank Cowperwood carried through this novel and *The Titan,* giving his adventures in search of power and wealth in Philadelphia and Chicago.

FINCH, FRANCIS MILES (June 9, 1827–July 31, 1907); b. Ithaca, N.Y. Jurist, poet. *The Blue and the Gray, and Other Verses* (1909). His best known poems are "Nathan Hale" (1853); and "The Blue and the Gray" (1867).

FINCK, HENRY THEOPHILUS (Sept. 22, 1854–Oct. 1, 1926); b. Bethel, Mo. Music critic. *Romantic Love and Personal Beauty* (1887); *Chopin, and Other Musical Essays* (1889); *Wagner and His Works,* 2v. (1893); *Songs and Song Writers* (1900); *Grieg and His Music* (1909); *Richard Strauss* (1917); *My Adventures in the Golden Age of Music* (1926). Music critic, the *New York Evening Post,* 1881–1924.

FINE, BENJAMIN (Sept. 1, 1905–); b. New York. Educator, journalist, author. *A Giant of the Press* (1933); *Educational Publicity* (1943); *Admission to American Colleges* (1946); *Our Children Are Cheated* (1947); *One Million Delinquents* (1955); *How To Be Accepted by the College of Your Choice* (1957); *Modern Family Guide to Education* (1962); *Profiles of American Colleges* (1964); *Stretching Their Minds: The Exciting New Approach to the Education of the Gifted Child Pioneered by the Sands Point Country Day School* (1964); *Your Child and School* (1965); *Underachievers: How They Can Be Helped* (1966); etc. Education reporter and editor, *The New York Times,* 1937–58. Dean, graduate school of education, Yeshiva University, 1958–60. Headmaster, Sands Point Country Day School Academy, since 1960.

FINE, SYDNEY (Oct. 11, 1920–   ); b. Cleveland, O. Educator, author. *Laissez-Faire and the General Welfare State* (1956); *The American Past,* 2v. (with G. S. Brown, 1961); *Recent America* (1962); *The Automobile under the Blue Eagle* (1963). Prof. history, University of Michigan, since 1959.

Fine Feathers. Play by Eugene Walter (prod. 1913). Deals with contemporary social questions.

Fine Madness, A. Novel by Elliott Baker (1964). Comic adventures of a poet who ends up in the hands of psychologists and psychoanalysts.

FINEBERG, S[olomon] ANDHIL (Nov. 29, 1896–); b. Pittsburgh, Pa. Rabbi, author. *Biblical Myth and Legend* (1929); *Overcoming Anti-Semitism* (1943); *Punishment Without Crime* (1949); *The Rosenberg Case* (1953); *Religion Behind the Iron Curtain* (1962); *Plight of Soviet Jews* (1964); etc.

FINEMAN, IRVING (Apr. 9, 1893–); b. New York City. Educator, author. *This Pure Young Man* (1930); *Lovers Must Learn* (1932); *Hear Ye Sons* (1933); *Doctor Addams* (1938); *Akiba, a Child's Play* (1950); *Fig Tree Madonna* (prod. 1954); *Helen Herself* (1957); *Woman of Valor* (1961).

FINER, HERMAN (Feb. 24, 1898–); b. Herta, Rumania. Educator. *British Civil Service* (1927); *Theory and Practice of Modern Government,* 2v. (1932); *Mussolini's Italy* (1935); *Road to Reaction* (1945); *America's Destiny* (1947); *Major Governments of Modern Europe* (1960); *The Presidency: Crisis and Regeneration* (1960); etc. Prof. political science, University of Chicago, since 1946.

FINERTY, JOHN FREDERICK (Sept. 10, 1846–1908); b. Galway, Ireland. Editor, author. *War-Path and Bivouac; or, The Conquest of the Sioux* (1890). Editor, *The Chicago Citizen,* 1882–1908.

FINGER, CHARLES JOSEPH (Dec. 25, 1869–Jan. 7, 1941); b. Willesden, England. Editor, author. *Highwaymen* (1923); *Bushrangers* (1924); *Tales from Silver Lands* (1924); *Ozark Fantasia* (1927); *Romantic Rascals* (1927); *Tales Worth Telling* (1927); *David Livingstone* (1927); *Courageous Companions* (1929); *Seven Horizons* (autobiography, 1930); *A Paul Bunyan Geography* (1931); *Adventure Under Sapphire Skies* (1931); *Foot Loose in the West* (1932); *The Magic Tower* (1933); *After the Great Compromise* (1934); *A Dog at His Heel* (1936); *Valiant Vagabonds* (1936); *Give a Man a Horse* (1938); *Golden Tales from Far Away* (1940); *Fighting for Fur* (1940); etc. Compiler: *Frontier Ballads* (1927). Editor and proprietor, *All's Well* magazine, 1920–35.

FINKEL, DONALD (Oct. 21, 1929–   ); b. New York. Poet. *Simeon* (1965); *A Joyful Noise* (1966); *Answer Back* (1968); *The Garbage Wars* (1970). Poet in residence, Washington University, since 1960.

FINKELSTEIN, LOUIS (June 14, 1895–); b. Cincinnati, O. Rabbi, educator, author. *Jewish Self-Government in the Middle Ages* (1924); *Akiba, Scholar, Saint and Martyr* (1936); *The Pharisees: The Sociological Background of Their Faith,* 2v. (1938); etc. Editor: *American Spiritual Autobiographies* (1948); etc. Prof. theology, Jewish Theological Seminary, New York; chancellor since 1951.

FINLETTER, THOMAS K[night] (Nov. 11, 1893–); b. Philadelphia, Pa. Lawyer, author. *Principles of Corporate Reorganization* (1937); *Can Representative Government Do the Job?* (1945); *Power and Policy* (1954); *Foreign Policy: The Next Phase* (1958); *Interim Report on the U.S. Search for a Substitute for Isolation* (1968).

FINLEY, JAMES BRADLEY (July 1, 1781–Sept. 6, 1856); b. in North Carolina. Circuit rider, historian. *Autobiography* (1853); *Life Among the Indians* (1857); etc.

FINLEY, JOHN (Jan. 11, 1797–Dec. 23, 1866); b. Richmond, Ind. Poet. *The Hoosier's Nest, and Other Poems* (1860). *See* "The Hoosier's Nest."

FINLEY, JOHN HUSTON (Oct. 19, 1863–Mar. 7, 1940); b. Grand Ridge, Ill. Editor, educator, author. *The French in the Heart of America* (1914); *A Pilgrim in Palestine* (1918); *The Debt Eternal* (1923); *The Mystery of the Mind's Desire* (1936); *The Coming of the Scot* (1940); etc. Associate editor, *The New York Times*, 1921–37; editor in chief, 1937–39. President, Knox College, 1892–99; president, College of the City of New York, 1903–13. Commissioner of education, New York State, 1913–21.

FINLEY, JOHN HUSTON, Jr. (Feb. 11, 1904–); b. New York. Educator, author. *Thalia* (masque in verse, 1929); *Thucydides* (1942); *Pindar and Aeschylus* (1955); *Four Stages of Greek Thought* (1966); *Three Essays on Thucydides* (1967); etc. Prof. Greek literature, Harvard University, 1942–68.

FINLEY, MARTHA (Apr. 26, 1828–Jan. 30, 1909); b. Chillicothe, O. Author. Pen name, "Martha Farquharson." The *Elsie* series, 18v. (1867–1905), the *Mildred* series, 7v. (1878–94); etc. Her best-known book is *Elsie Dinsmore* (1867), the first of the *Elsie* series.

FINLEY, M[oses] I. (May 20, 1912–); b. New York. Educator, author. *Studies in Land and Credit in Ancient Athens* (1952); *The World of Odysseus* (1954); *The Ancient Greeks* (1963); *A History of Sicily*, 3v. (with Denis Mack Smith, 1968). Editor: *The Greek Historians* (1958); *Slavery in Classical Antiquity* (1960); *Josephus* (1965). Faculty, Columbia University, 1933–54; lecturer classics, Cambridge University, England, 1955–64; reader ancient social and economic history, since 1964.

FINLEY, RUTH E[bright] (Mrs. Emmet Finley) (Sept. 25, 1884–Sept. 24, 1955); b. Akron, O. Editor, author. *Old Patchwork Quilts and the Women Who Made Them* (1929); *The Lady of Godey's: Sarah Josepha Hale* (1931).

FINN, FRANCIS JAMES (Oct. 4, 1859–Nov. 2, 1928); b. St. Louis, Mo. Roman Catholic clergyman, author of juveniles. *Percy Wynn* (1890); *Tom Playfair* (1891); etc; also, *Father Finn, S. J.; The Story of His Life Told by Himself,* ed. by Daniel A. Lord (1929).

FINN, HENRY JAMES WILLIAM (June 17, 1787–Jan. 13, 1840); b. Sydney, N.S. Actor, playwright. *Montgomery; or, The Falls of Montmorency* (prod. 1825); *Removing the Deposits* (prod. 1835, not publ.); *Casper Hauser; or, The Down Easter* (prod. 1835, not publ.).

FINNEY, CHARLES GRANDISON (Aug. 29, 1792–Aug. 16, 1875); b. Warren, Conn. Presbyterian clergyman, educator, editor, author. *Lectures on Systematic Theology* (1847); *Memoirs* (1876); etc. Founder, *Oberlin Evangelist,* 1839, which he also edited. President, Oberlin College, 1851–66. See D. C. Seitz's *Uncommon Americans* (1925).

FINNEY, CHARLES GRANDISON (1905–). Novelist. *The Circus of Dr. Lao* (1935); *The Unholy City* (1937); *Past the End of the Pavement* (1939); *The Old China Hands* (1961).

FINNEY, THEODORE MITCHELL (Mar. 14, 1902–); b. Fayette, Ia. Musician, educator, author. *A History of Music* (1935); *Hearing Music* (1941); *We Have Made Music* (1955). Head, music dept., University of Pittsburgh, 1936–68.

"*Finnigin to Flannigan.*" Humorous poem by Strickland Gillilan, which appeared in the Richmond, Ind., *Palladium* in 1897.

FINOTTI, JOSEPH MARIA (Sept. 21, 1817–Jan. 10, 1879); b. Ferrara, Italy. Priest, novelist, bibliographer. *Diary of a Soldier* (1861); *The French Zouave* (1863); *Herman, the Pianist* (1863); *Mystery of the Wizard Clip* (1879); etc. Compiler: *Bibliographica Catholica Americana* (1872), only one volume published.

"*Fire and Ice.*" Poem by Robert Frost (1923).

Fire-Bringer, The. Drama by William Vaughn Moody (1904). In blank verse, dealing with the Promethean theme.

"*Firehead.*" Narrative poem by Lola Ridge (1929), depicting scenes on the day of the Crucifixion.

Fireside Companion, The. New York. Dime novel magazine. Founded 1866, by George P. Munro. Expired 1907.

Fireside Conversation in the Time of Queen Elizabeth. By "Mark Twain," later called *1601.* Imaginary conversation recorded by a supposed Pepys of that period; a pamphlet often surreptitiously reprinted.

FIRESTONE, CLARK B[arnaby] (Sept. 10, 1869–June 3, 1957); b. Lisbon, O. Journalist, author. *The Coasts of Illusion* (1924); *Sycamore Shores* (1936); *The Winding Road* (poems, 1937); *Bubbling Waters* (1938); *Journey to Japan* (1940); *Tower Window* (1949); *The Yesterdays* (verse, 1953).

FIRKINS, OSCAR W• (1864–Mar. 7, 1932); b. Minneapolis, Minn. Critic. *Ralph Waldo Emerson* (1915); *Jane Austen* (1920); *William Dean Howells* (1924); *The Bride of Quietness, and Other Plays* (1932); *Selected Essays* (1933); *Memoirs and Letters* (1934); *Power and Elusiveness in Shelley* (1937); etc. Drama critic, *New York Weekly Review,* 1915–18.

First Book of the American Chronicles of the Times, The. Anonymous humorous record of contemporary events, written in the style of the *Old Testament.* Published in parts (1774–75).

First Christmas Tree, The. Story by Henry van Dyke (1897).

"*First Duel in Boston, The.*" Poem by Frank Wilson Cheney Hersey, on the duel between Benjamin Woodbridge and Henry Phillips, July 3, 1728.

"*First in war, first in peace, first in the hearts of his countrymen.*" These words, applied to George Washington, were first used in resolutions on his death, drawn by Henry Lee (1756–1818) and offered by John Marshall (1799).

First Person. Boston, Mass. Triannual. Founded 1960 by M. D. Elevitch. Literary magazine. Discontinued 1962.

"*First Snow-Fall.*" Poem by James Russell Lowell (1849).

First Stage: A Quarterly of New Drama. Lafayette, Ind. Founded 1962. Published by the Purdue Research Foundation. Devoted to publication of new plays.

"*First Travels of Max.*" Poem by John Crowe Ransom. Account of a small boy's walk in the deep woods.

FISCHEL, WALTER JOSEPH (Nov. 12, 1902–); b. Frankfurt, Ger. Educator, author. *History of the Marrano Community in Central Asia* (1936); *Ibn Khaldun and Tamerlane* (1952); *New Light on the Dead Sea Scrolls* (1956); *The Jews in India, Their Contribution to the Economical and Political Life* (1960); etc. Prof. Semitic languages and literature, University of California, since 1946.

FISCHER, JOHN (Apr. 27, 1910–); b. Texhoma, Okla. Editor, author. *Why They Behave Like Russians* (1947); *Master Plan, U.S.A.* (1951); *The Stupidity Problem* (1964). Assoc. editor, *Harper's,* 1944–47; editor-in-chief, 1953–67; contributing editor, since 1967.

FISCHER, LOUIS (Feb. 29, 1896–Jan. 15, 1970); b. Philadelphia, Pa. Author. *The Soviets in World Affairs,* 2v. (1930); *Soviet Journey* (1935); *The War in Spain* (1937); *Men and Politics, an Autobiography* (1941); *The Great Challenge* (1946); *Gandhi and Stalin* (1947); *The Life of Mahatma Gandhi* (1950); *The Life and Death of Stalin* (1952); *This Is Our World* (1956); *Russia Revisited* (1957); *Russia, America, and the World* (1961); *The Life of Lenin* (1964); *50 Years of Soviet Communism: An Appraisal* (1968); *Russia's Road from Peace to War 1917–1941* (1969); etc. Editor: *Thirteen Who Fled* (1949).

FISCHER, MARJORIE (1903–Nov. 2, 1961). Author. *Street Fair* (1935); *Palaces on Monday* (1936); *The Dog Can't Bark* (1940); *All On A Summer's Day* (1941); *Embarrassment of Riches* (1944); *Red Feather* (1950); *Mrs. Sherman's Summer* (1960); etc.

Fisguill, Richard. Pen name of Richard Henry Wilson.

FISH, CARL RUSSELL (Oct. 17, 1876–July 10, 1932); b. Central Falls, R.I. Educator, author. *American Diplomacy* (1915); *The Path of Empire* (1919); *History of America* (1925); etc. History dept., University of Wisconsin, 1900–32.

FISH, HELEN DEAN; b. Hempstead, L.I., N.Y. Editor, author. *Invitation to Travel* (1937); *The Doll House Book* (1940). Compiler: *The Boy's Book of Verse* (1923); *The Children's Almanac of Books and Holidays* (1934); *When the Root Children Wake Up* (1941); *Invitation to England* (1950); etc. Editor: *Animals of the Bible* (1969).

"Fish, The." Poem by Elizabeth Bishop.

FISH, WILLISTON (Jan. 15, 1858–Dec. 19, 1939); b. Berlin Heights, O. Lawyer. Author of over 600 articles, including verse, in *Puck, Life,* and *Harper's Weekly.* His best known work, *A Last Will and Testament,* first appeared in *Harper's Weekly* in 1898. Sometimes known as *The Last Will of Charles Lounsbury,* it has been repeatedly published in newspapers and in pamphlet form, frequently garbled. A correct edition was printed by The Merrymount Press in 1908.

FISHBACK, MARGARET (Mrs. Alberto G. Antolini); b. Washington, D.C. Poet. *I Feel Better Now* (1932); *Out of My Heart* (1933); *I Take It Back* (1935); *One to a Customer* (1937); *Safe Conduct: When to Behave—And Why* (1939); *Look Who's a Mother* (1945); etc.

FISHBEIN, MORRIS (July 22, 1889–); b. St. Louis, Mo. Pathologist, editor, author. *Medical Follies* (1925); *Mirrors of Medicine* (1925); *Fads and Quackery in Healing* (1933); *Frontiers of Medicine* (1933); *Syphilis* (1937); *Do You Want to Be a Doctor?* (1939); *Popular Medical Encyclopedia* (1946); *Handy Home Medical Adviser* (1952); *Morris Fishbein, M.D.: An Autobiography* (1969); etc. Editor: *Medical Progress* (1953); *Heart Care* (1960); *Modern Home Remedies and How to Use Them* (1966); etc. Editor, *World-Wide Abstracts of General Medicine,* 1958–67; *Medical World News,* since 1960.

FISHER, ANNE BENSON (Feb. 1, 1898–deceased); b. Denver, Col. Author. *Look What Brains Can Do* (1932); *Career for Constance* (1936); *Live with a Man and Love It* (1937); *Brides Are Like New Shoes* (1938); *Wide Road Ahead* (1939); *Cathedral in the Sun* (1940); *The Salinas* (1945); *Bears, Pirates, and Silver Lace* (1944); *No More a Stranger* (1946); *It's a Wise Child* (1949); *The Story of California's Constitution and Laws* (1953); *Stories California Indians Told* (1957); etc.

FISHER, "BUD" [H. C.] (Apr. 3, 1884–Sept. 7, 1954); b. in Illinois. Cartoonist. Creator of the "Mutt and Jeff" comic strip. Fisher started his career as a cartoonist in San Francisco in 1905.

Fisher, Clay. Pen name of Henry Allen.

Fisher, Cyrus. Pen name of Darwin Teilhet.

FISHER, DOROTHY CANFIELD (Dorothea Frances Canfield Fisher) (Feb. 17, 1879–Nov. 9, 1958); b. Lawrence, Kan. Novelist. *Gunhild* (1907); *The Squirrel Cage* (1912); *The Montessori Mother* (1913); *Hillsboro People* (1915); *The Bent Twig* (1915); *Understood Betsy* (1919); *The Brimming Cup* (1921); *Rough-Hewn* (1922); *Her Son's Wife* (1926); *The Deepening Stream* (1930); *Bonfire* (1933); *Fables for Parents* (1937); *Seasoned Timber* (1939); *Our Young Folks* (1943); *American Portraits* (1946); *Four Square* (1949); *Something Old, Something New* (1949); *Paul Revere and the Minute Men* (1950); *Our Independence and the Constitution* (1950); *A Fair World for All* (1952); *Vermont Tradition: The Biogra-*

phy of an Outlook on Life (1953); *A Harvest of Stories* (1956); *Memories of Arlington, Vermont* (1957); etc.

FISHER, [George] CLYDE (May 22, 1878–Jan. 7, 1949); b. near Sidney, O. Curator, author. *Nature's Secrets* (1921); *Exploring the Heavens* (1937); *Marvels and Mysteries of Science* (with others, 1941); *The Story of the Moon* (1943); *The Life of John James Audubon* (1949); etc. Editor: *Nature Encyclopedia,* 5v. (1921–27). Staff, American Museum of Natural History, 1913–49.

FISHER, GEORGE PARK (Aug. 10, 1827–Dec. 20, 1909); b. Wrentham, Mass. Congregational clergyman, educator, author. *Life of Benjamin Silliman* (1866); *The Reformation* (1873); *The Colonial Era* (1892). Prof. divinity, Yale, 1853–1901.

FISHER, HAMMOND EDWARD [Ham] (Sept. 24, 1900–Dec. 27, 1955); b. Wilkes-Barre, Pa. Cartoonist. Creator of the syndicated comic strip "Joe Palooka" in 1930.

FISHER, HAROLD HENRY (Feb. 15, 1890–); b. Morristown, Vt. Educator, author. *The Famine in Soviet Russia* (1927); *The Bolshevik Revolution* (1934); *America and Russia in the World Community* (1946); etc. Editor: *Out of My Past: Memoirs of Count Kokovtsov* (1935); *American Research on Russia* (1959); etc. History dept., Stanford University, 1933–55.

FISHER, HARRISON (July 27, 1875–Jan. 19, 1934); b. Brooklyn, N.Y. Illustrator, artist. Among the popular collections of his illustrations are: *The Harrison Fisher Book* (1907); *A Dream of Fair Women* (1907); *Bachelor Belles* (1908); *American Beauties* (1909); *Pictures in Color* (1910); *American Belles* (1911). Creator of the "American Girl" type, sometimes called the "Fisher Girl."

FISHER, IRVING (Feb. 27, 1867–Apr. 29, 1947); b. Saugerties, N.Y. Educator, political economist, author. *The Nature of Capital and Income* (1906); *How to Live* (with others, 1915); *Prohibition at Its Worst* (1926); *The Money Illusion* (1928), and many other books on economics, mathematics, and money. In dept. economics, Yale University, 1893–1935.

FISHER, MAHLON LEONARD (July 20, 1874–Sept. 25, 1947); b. Williamsport, Pa. Poet. *Sonnets: A First Series* (1917); *Lyrics Between the Years* (1928); *River's Gift* (1928). Founder, *The Sonnet,* 1917; editor, *The Golden Galleon,* from 1924.

FISHER, SIDNEY GEORGE (Mar. 2, 1809–July 25, 1871); b. Philadelphia, Pa. Lawyer, poet. *Winter Studies in the Country* (1856); *Rustic Rhymes* (1859); etc.

FISHER, SOPHIE [Thérèse Ada]; b. Birmingham. Eng. Author. *It Happened This Way* (with Rose Eytinge, 1895); *The Imprudence of Prue* (1911).

FISHER, SYDNEY GEORGE (Sept. 11, 1856–Feb. 22, 1927); b. Philadelphia, Pa. Lawyer, historian. *The Making of Pennsylvania* (1896); *Men, Women, and Manners in Colonial Times* (1898); *The True Benjamin Franklin* (1899); *The True William Penn* (1900); *The Struggle for American Independence,* 2v. (1908); *The True Daniel Webster* (1911); *The Quaker Colonies* (1919); etc.

FISHER, VARDIS [Alvero] (Mar. 31, 1895–July 9, 1968); b. Annis, Ida. Novelist. *Sonnets to an Imaginary Madonna* (1927); *Toilers of the Hills* (1928); *In Tragic Life* (1932); *Passions Spin the Plot* (1934); *No Villain Need Be* (1936); *Odyssey of a Hero* (1937); *Children of God* (1939); *City of Illusion* (1941); *Darkness and the Deep* (1943); *The Mothers* (1943); *The Golden Rooms* (1944); *Intimations of Eve* (1946); *Adam and the Serpent* (1947); *The Divine Passion* (1948); *The Valley of Vision* (1951); *The Island of the Innocent* (1952); *God or Caesar* (1953); *Pemmican* (1956); *Jesus Came Again* (1956); *A Goat for Azazel* (1956); *Peace Like a River* (1957); *Tale of Valor* (1958); *My Holy Satan* (1958); *Love and*

Death (stories, 1959); *Orphans in Gethsemane* (1960); *Suicide or Murder? The Strange Death of Governor Meriwether Lewis* (1962); *Thomas Wolfe as I Knew Him, and other Essays* (1963).

FISHER, WELTHY HONSINGER (Mrs. Frederick Bohn Fisher) (Sept. 18, 1880–); b. Rome, N.Y. Lecturer, author. *Beyond the Moon Gate* (1924); *A String of Chinese Pearls* (1924); *The Top of the World* (1926); *Freedom: a Story of Young India* (1930); *Frederick Bohn Fisher, World Citizen* (1944); *Handbook for Ministers' Wives* (1950); etc.

FISHER, WILLIAM ARMS (Apr. 27, 1861–Dec. 18, 1948); b. San Francisco, Cal. Musician, editor, author. *One Hundred and Fifty Years of Music Publishing in the United States* (1933); etc. Editor, Oliver Ditson Co., 1897–1937.

Fisherman's Luck. Essays by Henry van Dyke (1899).

FISK, WILBUR (Aug. 31, 1792–Feb. 22, 1839). Methodist clergyman, educator, author. *Travels in Europe* (1838). A founder and first president of Wesleyan University, Middletown, Conn., 1830–39. *See* George Prentice's *Wilbur Fisk* (1890).

FISKE, AMOS KIDDER (May 12, 1842–Sept. 18, 1921); b. Whitefield, N.H. Lawyer, essayist, folk-lorist. *Midnight Talks at the Club* (1890); *Beyond the Bourn* (1891); *The Story of the Philippines* (1898); *The West Indies* (1899); *The Great Epic of Israel* (1911); etc. Editor, the *Boston Globe*, 1874–77; with *New York Times* for 22 years.

FISKE, GEORGE WALTER (June 3, 1872–Oct. 10, 1945); b. Holliston, Mass. Congregational clergyman, educator, author. *The Changing Family* (1928); *The Recovery of Worship* (1931); *Studies in Religious Education* (with others, 1931); *In a College Chapel* (1932); etc. Co-author: *Founders of Christian Movements* (1941).

FISKE, HORACE SPENCER (Nov. 4, 1859–June 2, 1940); b. Dexter, Mich. Editor, poet. *The Ballad of Manila Bay, and Other Verses* (1900); *Provincial Types in American Fiction* (1903); *In Stratford and the Plays* (poems, 1917); *Ballads of Peace and War, and Other Verse* (1918); *Poems on Chicago and Illinois* (1927); etc.

Fiske, Isabella Howe. See Isabel Fiske Conant.

FISKE, JOHN (Mar. 30, 1842–July 4, 1901); b. Hartford, Conn. Lecturer, philosopher, historian. *Myths and Myth-Makers* (1872); *Outlines of Cosmic Philosophy*, 2v. (1874); *The Unseen World* (1876); *The American Revolution*, 2v. (1891); *The Discovery of America*, 2v. (1892); *Old Virginia and Her Neighbors*, 2v. (1897); *A Century of Science and Other Essays* (1899); *Through Nature to God* (1899); *Essays, Historical and Literary*, 2v. (1902); etc. *See The Letters of John Fiske*, ed. by his daughter, Ethel F. Fisk (1940) and J. S. Clark's *Life and Letters of John Fiske*, 2v. (1917).

FISKE, NATHAN (Sept. 9, 1733–Nov. 24, 1799); b. Weston, Mass. Congregational clergyman, essayist. *The Moral Monitor*, 2v. (1801), originally written for *The Massachusetts Spy* under the pen name, "The Neighbor."

FISKE, SAMUEL WHEELOCK (1828–1864). Humorist. Pen name, "Dunn Browne." *Mr. Dunn Browne's Experiences in Foreign Ports* (1857); *Mr. Dunn Browne's Experiences in the Army* (1866). These sketches first appeared in the *Springfield Republican*.

FISKE, STEPHEN RYDER (Nov. 22, 1840–Apr. 27, 1916); b. New Brunswick, N.J. Journalist, playwright, drama critic. *English Photographs, by an American* (1869); *Holiday Stories* (1891); *Paddy From Cork, and Other Stories* (1891); *Off-Hand Portraits of Prominent New Yorkers* (1884); etc. Dramatic critic, *New York Herald*, 1862–66; one of the founders, *New York Dramatic Mirror*, 1879.

FISKE, WILLARD (Nov. 11, 1831–Sept. 17, 1904); b. Ellisburg, N.Y. Librarian, book collector, author. *Bibliographical Notices*, 6v. (1886–1907); *Chess Tales & Chess Miscellanies* (1912); *Memorials of Willard Fiske*, 3v. (1920–22). With the Astor Library, New York, 1852–59. Librarian, Cornell University, 1868–83. He gave his magnificent Dante and Petrarch Collections to Cornell University. See *The Dante Library* (1894); and *Catalogue of the Petrarch Collection* (1916).

FITCH, CLYDE (May 2, 1865–Sept. 4, 1909); b. Elmira, N.Y. Playwright. *Beau Brummel* (prod. 1890); *The Moth and the Flame* (prod. 1898); *Nathan Hale* (prod. 1898); *Barbara Frietchie* (prod. 1899); *The Cowboy and the Lady* (with Willis Steell, prod. 1899); *The Climbers* (prod. 1901); *Lover's Lane* (prod. 1901); *Captain Jinks of the Horse Marines* (prod. 1902); *The Girl with the Green Eyes* (prod. 1902); *The Stubbornness of Geraldine* (prod. 1902); *Her Own Way* (prod. 1903); *Her Great Match* (prod. 1905); *The Woman in the Case* (prod. 1905); *The Truth* (prod. 1907); *The City* (prod. 1909); etc. Most of these are in *Plays by Clyde Fitch*, 4v. (1915), ed. by Montrose J. Moses and Virginia Gerson.

FITCH, FLORENCE MARY (Feb. 17, 1875–June 2, 1959); b. Stratford, Conn. Educator, author. *One God: The Ways We Worship Him* (1944); *Their Search for God: Ways of Worship in the Orient* (1947); *Allah, the God of Islam* (1950); *The Child Jesus* (1955); etc. Prof. philosophy, Biblical literature, Oberlin College, 1904–40.

FITCH, GEORGE HAMLIN (Nov. 25, 1852–1915); b. Lancaster, N.Y. Editor, author. *Comfort Found in Good Old Books* (1911); *Modern English Books of Power* (1912); *Great Spiritual Writers of America* (1916); etc. Lit. editor, *San Francisco Chronicle*, 1880–1915.

FITCH, GEORGE [Helgeson] (June 5, 1877–Aug. 9, 1915); b. Galva, Ill. Journalist, humorist. *The Big Strike at Siwash* (1909); *At Good Old Siwash* (1911); *My Demon Motor Boat* (1912); *Homeburg Memories* (1915).

FITCH, JAMES MARSTON, JR. (May 8, 1909–). Author. *American Building* (1948); *Treasury of American Gardens* (with F. F. Rockwell, 1956); *Walter Gropius* (1960); *Architecture and the Esthetics of Plenty* (1961); etc.

FITCH, ROBERT ELLIOTT (Jan. 25, 1902–); b. Ningpo, China. Congregational clergyman, educator, author. *A Certain Blind Man and Other Essays on the American Mood* (1944); *Preface to Ethical Living* (1947); *Kingdom Without End* (1950); *The Limits of Liberty* (1952); *The Decline and Fall of Sex* (1957); *Odyssey of the Self-Centered Self* (1961); etc. Prof. Christian ethics, Pacific School of Religion, since 1949.

FITE, EMERSON DAVID (Mar. 3, 1874–May 10, 1953); b. Marion, O. Educator, author. *The Presidential Campaign of 1860* (1911); *History of the United States* (1916); etc. Professor political science, Vassar College, 1913–44.

FITE, WARNER (Mar. 5, 1867–June 23, 1955); b. Philadelphia, Pa. Educator, author. *Introductory Study of Ethics* (1903); *Individualism* (1911); *Moral Philosophy* (1925); *The Platonic Legend* (1934); *Jesus, the Man—A Critical Essay* (1943); etc. Translator: Unamuno's *Mist* (1928). Professor of ethics, Princeton University, 1915–35.

FITHIAN, PHILIP VICKERS (Dec. 29, 1747–Oct. 8, 1776); b. Greenwich, N.J. Clergyman, diarist. See *Philip Vickers Fithian: Journal and Letters*, ed. John Roger Williams, 2v. (1900–34).

FITTS, DUDLEY (Apr. 28, 1903–July 10, 1968); b. Boston, Mass. Educator, translator, author. *Poems, 1929–36* (1937). Editor: *Ten Introductions* (with Genevieve Taggard, 1934); *Anthology of Contemporary Latin American Poetry* (1942); *Greek Plays in Modern Translation* (1947); *Office Hymns of the Church* (with C. F. Pfatteicher, 1951); etc. Translator: *The Alcestis of Euripides* (with Robert Fitzgerald, 1936); *One*

Hundred Poems from the Palatine Anthology (1938); The Antigone of Sophocles (with Fitzgerald, 1939); Sophocles' Oedipus Rex (with same, 1949); Aristophanes' Lysistrata (1954), The Frogs (1955), The Birds (1957); Poems from the Greek Anthology (1956); Sixty Poems of Martial in Translation (1967); also poems from Spanish, etc. English dept., Phillips Academy, Andover, from 1941.

FITTS, JAMES FRANKLIN (1840–1890). Journalist, novelist. Captain Kidd's Gold (1888); A Modern Miracle (1889); A Bartered Birthright (1890); The Struggle for Maverick (1890); etc.

FITZ-GERALD, JOHN D[riscoll], II (May 2, 1873–June 8, 1946); b. Newark, N.J. Educator, author. Rambles in Spain (1910). Editor and translator of numerous works of Spanish authors. Head of Spanish dept., University of Arizona, 1929–43.

FITZGERALD, EDWARD EARL (Sept. 10, 1919–); b. New York. Educator, author. Player-Manager (with Lous Boudreau, 1949); I Always Wanted to Be Somebody (with Althea Gibson, 1958); The Kingdom Within (with Genevieve Caulfield, 1960); Yogi (with Yogi Berra, 1961); You Can't Beat the Hours (with Mel Allen, 1964); etc. General manager book club divisions, Doubleday & Co., since 1964.

FITZGERALD, F[rancis] SCOTT [Key] (Sept. 24, 1896–Dec. 21, 1940); b. St. Paul, Minn. Novelist. This Side of Paradise (1920); Flappers and Philosophers (1920); The Beautiful and Damned (1922); Tales of the Jazz Age (1922); The Great Gatsby (1925); Tender Is the Night (1934); Taps at Reveille (1935); The Last Tycoon (1941); The Crack-Up (1945). See Arthur Mizener's The Far Side of Paradise (1951); Budd Schulberg's novel The Disenchanted (1950); Alfred Kazin's F. Scott Fitzgerald: The Man and His Work (1951); Andrew Turnbull's Scott Fitzgerald (1961) and The Letters of F. Scott Fitzgerald (1963); Edwin M. Moseley's F. Scott Fitzgerald: A Critical Essay (1967).

FITZGERALD, O[scar] P[enn] (Aug. 24, 1829–Aug. 5, 1911); b. in Caswell Co., N.C. Bishop, editor, author. California Sketches, 2 series (1880–81); Judge Longstreet (1891); Sunset Views (1901); Fifty Years (1903); etc. Editor, Christian Advocate, Nashville, Tenn., 1878–90.

FITZGERALD, ROBERT [Stuart] (Oct. 12, 1910–); b. Geneva, N.Y. Poet, translator. Poems (1935); A Wreath for the Sea (1944); In the Rose of Time: Poems, 1931–56 (1956); etc. Translator: Sophocles' Oedipus at Colonus (1941); also other Greek plays with Dudley Fitts (q.v.); St. John Perse's Chroniques (1961); The Odyssey (1961); etc.

FITZGERALD, THOMAS (Dec. 22, 1819–June 25, 1891); b. New York City. Editor, publisher, playwright. Light at Last (prod. 1867); etc. Founder, The City Item, Philadelphia, a weekly newspaper, 1847, which became the Evening City Item, Sept. 10, 1870.

FITZGERALD, ZELDA [Sayre] (Mrs. F. Scott Fitzgerald) (1899–1948). Author. Save Me the Waltz (1932). See Nancy Milford's Zelda (1970).

FITZGIBBON, [Robert Louis] CONSTANTINE (June 8, 1919–); b. Lenox, Mass. The Arabian Bird (1948); The Iron Hoop (1949); Dear Emily (1952); The Holiday (1953); Miss Finnegan's Fault (1953); Norman Douglas: A Pictorial Record (1953); The Fair Game (1956); The Winter of the Bombs (1958); Paradise Lost and More (1959); When the Kissing Had to Stop (1960); Going to the River (1963); Random Thoughts of a Fascist Hyena (1963); The Life of Dylan Thomas (1965); Through the Minefield: An Autobiography (1967). Editor: Selected Letters of Dylan Thomas (1967).

FITZHUGH, GEORGE (Nov. 4, 1806–July 30, 1881); b. in Prince William Co., Va. Lawyer, sociologist, author. Sociology for the South (1854); Cannibals All! or Slaves Without Masters (1857).

FITZHUGH, PERCY KEESE (Sept. 7, 1876–July 5, 1950); b. Brooklyn, N.Y. Author. Pen name "Hugh Lloyd." The Tom Slade series, 20v. (1915–29); the Roy Blakeley series, 17v. (1918–30); the Pee-Wee Harris series, 13v. (1922–30); Westy Martin series, etc. Editor, Every Girl's Library, 10v. (1909), etc. Many of his books deal with Boy Scouts.

FITZPATRICK, EDWARD AUGUSTUS (Aug. 29, 1884–Sept. 13, 1960); b. New York. Educator, author. Wisconsin (1927); Foundation of Christian Education (1929); Life of the Soul (1931); I Believe in Education (1938); Exploring a Theology of Education (1949); La Salle, Patron of Teachers (1953); etc. Editor: The Autobiography of a College (1939). Editor, Catholic School Journal, from 1929; Highway to Heaven series, from 1931; etc. President, Mount St. Mary's College for Women, Milwaukee, 1929–54.

FITZPATRICK, [James] BENEDICT [Ossory] (Feb. 4, 1881–Feb. 4, 1964); b. Egremont, Eng. Author. Ireland and the Making of Britain (1922); Donjon of Demons (1930); Frail Anne Boleyn, and Her Fateful Loves with Henry VIII (1931); Salad Days of a Prodigal—Prelude and Autobiography (1938); A Literature in Wonderland (1939); etc. Assoc. editor, History of New York State, 1523–1927, 8v. (1927–32).

FITZPATRICK, JOHN CLEMENT (Aug. 10, 1876–Feb. 10, 1940); b. Washington, D.C. Archivist, author. The Spirit of the Revolution (1924); George Washington Himself (1933); Some Historic Houses (1939); etc. Editor, The Diaries of George Washington, 1748–1799, 4v. (1925); The Writings of George Washington, 26v. (1931–38); etc. With Library of Congress, 1897–1928; asst. chief, Manuscript division, 1902–28.

FITZSIMMONS, CORTLAND (June 19, 1893–July 25, 1949); b. Richmond Hill, L.I., N.Y. Novelist. Manville Murders (1930); Crimson Ice (1935); Moving Finger (1937); Sudden Silence (1938); The Girl in the Cage (1939); One Man's Poison (1940); Tied for Murder (1943); If You Can Read You Can Cook (with wife, Muriel S. Fitzsimmons, 1946); etc.

Five Little Peppers and How They Grew. By "Margaret Sidney" (Harriet Mulford Stone Lothrop), appeared first in the juvenile magazine, Wide Awake, in 1880.

FLACK, MARJORIE (Oct. 23, 1897–Aug. 29, 1958); b. Greenport, L.I., N.Y. Author, illustrator. Taktuk, An Arctic Boy (1928); Angus and the Ducks (1930); Wag-Tail-Bess (1933); Humphrey (1934); Topsy (1935); Christopher (1935); The Restless Robin (1937); The Lazy Mouse (1937); Walter, the Lazy Mouse (1937); etc. Illustrator: The Country Bunny and the Little Gold Shoes (1939); Adolphus, the Adopted Dolphin (1941); The Happy Birthday Letter (1947); etc.

Flag of Our Union. Boston, Mass. Fiction weekly. Founded 1846, by Frederick Gleason, and sold in 1854 to Maturin M. Ballou. Expired 1870.

FLAGG, EDMUND (Nov. 24, 1815–Nov. 1, 1890); b. Wiscasset, Me. Editor, traveler, playwright. The Far West; or, A Tour Beyond the Mountains, 2v. (1838); Mary Tudor (1844); Venice: The City of the Sea, 1797–1849, 2v. (1853); De Molai (1888); etc. Editor, Marietta Gazette, 1842–43, St. Louis Evening Gazette, 1844–48, etc.

FLAGG, JAMES MONTGOMERY (June 18, 1877–May 27, 1960); b. Pelham Manor, N.Y. Artist, illustrator. Yankee Girls Abroad (1900); Tomfoolery (1904); All in the Same Boat (1908); City People (1909); The Adventures of Kitty Cobb (1912); Boulevard All the Way—Maybe (1925); Roses and Buckshot (autobiography, 1946); Celebrities (1951); etc. Did illustrations for Life and Judge from 1892.

FLAGG, MILDRED BUCHANAN (Mrs. Francis John Flagg) (May 1, 1886–); b. Moravia, N.Y. Author. Community English (1921); Camera Adventures in Africa (1935); Boy of Salem (1939); Notable Boston Authors (1965); Boston Authors Now and Then (1966); etc.

FLAGG, [Thomas] WILSON (Nov. 5, 1805–May 6, 1884); b. Beverly, Mass. Naturalist, essayist, poet. *Analysis of Female Beauty* (1834); *Mount Auburn* (1861); *The Woods and By-Ways of New England* (1872); *Birds and Seasons of New England* (1875); etc.

FLAHERTY, FRANCES HUBBARD (Mrs. Robert J. Flaherty). Author. *My Eskimo Friends* (with husband, 1924); *Elephant Dance* (1937); *Sabu, the Elephant Boy* (1937).

FLAHERTY, JOE. Journalist. *Managing Mailer* (1970). Writer, *Village Voice.*

FLAHERTY, ROBERT JOSEPH (Feb. 16, 1884–July 23, 1951); b. in Canada. Explorer, producer, author. *My Eskimo Friends* (with wife, Frances Hubbard Flaherty, 1924); *The Captain's Chair: A Story of the North* (1939). Director, motion pictures: *Elephant Boy, Nanook of the North, Man of Aran, Tabu, Louisiana Story;* etc.

"Flammonde." Poem by Edwin Arlington Robinson (1915).

Flanagan, Dorothy Belle. See Dorothy B. Hughes.

FLANDERS, HELEN HARTNESS (May 19, 1890–); b. Springfield, Vt. Ballad collector, author. *Looking Out of Jimmy* (1926). Compiler: *Vermont Folk Songs and Ballads* (with George Brown, 1931); *A Garland of Green Mountain Song* (1934); *New Green Mountain Songster* (with others, 1939); *Vermont Chapbook* (1941); *Ballads Migrant in New England* (1953); *Green Mountain Verse* (1943); *Ancient Ballads Traditionally Sung in New England* (1959); *Country News Items and Other Poems* (1965); etc.

FLANDERS, HENRY (Feb. 13, 1824–Apr. 3, 1911); b. Plainfield, N.H. Lawyer, author. *The Lives and Times of the Chief Justices of the Supreme Court of the United States from Jay to Marshall,* 2v. (1855–58); *The Adventures of a Virginian* (under pen name, "Oliver Thurston," 1881); etc.

FLANDRAU, CHARLES EUGENE (July 15, 1828–Sept. 9, 1903); b. New York City. Jurist, author. *The History of Minnesota and Tales of the Frontier* (1900).

FLANDRAU, CHARLES MACOMB (Dec. 9, 1871–Mar. 28, 1938); b. St. Paul, Minn. Essayist. *Harvard Episodes* (1897); *The Diary of a Freshman* (1901); *Viva Mexico!* (1908); *Prejudices* (1911); *Loquacities* (1931).

FLANDRAU, GRACE [Hodgson]; b. St. Paul, Minn. Novelist. *Cousin Julia* (1917); *Being Respectable* (1923); *Entranced* (1924); *Then I Saw the Congo* (1929); *Indeed This Flesh* (1934); *Under the Sun* (1936); etc.

FLANNER, HILDEGARDE (Mrs. Frederick Monhoff) (June 3, 1899–); b. Indianapolis, Ind. Poet. *This Morning* (1920); *Young Girl* (1920); *A Tree in Bloom, and Other Verses* (1924); *Time's Profile* (1929); *If There Is Time* (1942); etc.

FLANNER, JANET (Mar. 13, 1892–); b. Indianapolis, Ind. Journalist, author. *The Cubical City* (1926); *American in Paris* (1940); *Men and Monuments* (1957); *Paris Journal* (1966); etc. Translator: *Claudine à l'Ecole* and *Chéri* by Colette; *Ma Vie avec Maeterlinck* by Mme. Georgette Le Blanc. Foreign correspondent and writer, under pen name "Genêt," of "Letter from Paris," *New Yorker,* since 1925.

FLAVIN, MARTIN [Archer] (Nov. 2, 1883–Dec. 27, 1967); b. San Francisco, Calif. Playwright, novelist. *Children of the Moon* (prod. 1923); *Lady of the Rose* (prod. 1925); *Service for Two* (prod. 1926); *The Criminal Code* (prod. 1929); *Cross Roads* (prod. 1929); *Broken Dishes* (prod. 1929); *Spindrift* (prod. 1930); *Achilles Had a Heel* (prod. 1935); *Tapestry in Gray* (prod. 1935); *Sunday* (prod. 1936), revised as *Around the Corner* (prod. 1936); *Mr. Littlejohn* (1940); *Corporal Cat* (1941); *Journey in the Dark* (1943; Pulitzer prize for fiction, 1944); *The Enchanted* (1947); *Black and White* (1950); *Cameron Hill* (1957); *Red Poppies and White Marble* (1962); etc.

Flaxie Frizzle Stories, The. By "Sophie May" (Rebecca Sophia Clarke), 6v. (1876–84). Books for girls.

Flebbe, Mrs. George H. See Beulah Marie Dix.

FLEET, THOMAS (Sept. 8, 1685–July 21, 1758); b. Shropshire, England. Printer. Founded Boston *Evening Post,* Aug. 18, 1735. Located on Pudding Lane from ca. 1712 to 1731, he then moved to Cornhill, Boston, where he operated the "Heart and Crown" print-shop until his death. Printed over 250 books, pamphlets, etc., from 1713 to 1758, including *Songs for the Nursery; or, Mother Goose's Melodies for Children* (1719). Publisher, *Weekly Rehearsal,* 1733, which became Boston *Evening Post* in 1735, which he published until 1758.

FLEISCHMANN, RAOUL H. (Aug. 17, 1885–May 11, 1969); b. Ischl, Aust. Publisher. With F-R Publishing Corp. (now The New Yorker Magazine, Inc.), from 1925; president and chairman of board, 1926–69.

FLEMING, BERRY (Mar. 19, 1899–); b. Augusta, Ga. Author. *Siesta* (1935); *To the Market Place* (1938); *Colonel Effingham's Raid* (1943); *The Lightwood Tree* (1947); *The Fortune Tellers* (1951); *Carnival* (1953); *Autobiography of a Colony* (compiler, 1957); *The Winter Rider* (1960).

FLEMING, DENNA FRANK (Mar. 25, 1893–); b. Paris, Ill. Educator, author. *The United States and the League of Nations* (1932); *The United States and World Organization* (1938); *Can We Win the Peace?* (1943); *While America Slept* (1944); *The United States and the World Court* (1945); *The Origins and Legacies of World War I* (1968); *America's Role in Asia* (1969); etc. Political science dept., Vanderbilt University, since 1928.

Fleming, George. Pen name of Julia Constance Fletcher.

FLEMING, THOMAS J[ames] (July 5, 1927–); b. Jersey City, N.J. Author. *Now We Are Enemies* (1960); *All Good Men* (1961); *The Gods of Love* (1963); *One Small Candle* (1964); *King of the Hill* (1966); *A Cry of Whiteness* (1967); *The Man from Monticello: An Intimate Life of Thomas Jefferson* (1969); *Romans, Countrymen, Lovers* (1969); *West Point: The Men and Times of the U.S. Military Academy* (1969); etc.

FLEMING, WALLACE B. (Nov. 22, 1872–June 30, 1952); b. Cambridge, O. Educator, author. *History of the City of Tyre* (1915); *Guide-Posts to Life Work* (1923). President, Baker University, 1922–36.

FLEMING, WILLIAM HANSELL (Aug. 23, 1844–Oct. 1, 1915); b. Philadelphia, Pa. Lecturer, editor, author. *How to Study Shakespeare,* 4v. (1897–1904); *Shakespeare's Plots* (1902).

FLESCH, RUDOLF [Franz] (May 8, 1911–); b. Vienna. Author. *The Art of Plain Talk* (1946); *The Art of Readable Writing* (1949); *The Art of Clear Thinking* (1951); *How to Make Sense* (1954); *Why Johnny Can't Read* (1955); *A New Way to Better English* (1958); *How to Write, Speak, and Think More Effectively* (1960); *How to be Brief* (1962); *The ABC of Style* (1964); *The Book of Surprises* (1965); *The New Book of Unusual Quotations* (1966); etc. Author of syndicated newspaper column "Conversation Piece," since 1959.

FLETCHER, ALICE CUNNINGHAM (Mar. 15, 1838–Apr. 6, 1923); b. in Cuba, of American parentage. Ethnologist, author. *Indian Ceremonies* (1884); *Indian Story and Song* (1900); *The Hako* (1904); *The Omaha Tribe* (1911); *Indian Games and Dances* (1915); etc.

FLETCHER, GRACE [Nies]; b. Townsend, Mass. Author. *In My Father's House* (1955); *Preacher's Kids* (1958); *No Marriage in Heaven* (1960); *I Was Born Tomorrow* (1961); *The Fabulous Flemings of Kathmandu* (1964); *What's Right with Our Young People* (1966); *In Quest of the Least Coin* (1968); etc.

FLETCHER, HARRIS FRANCIS (Oct. 23, 1892–); b. Ypsilanti, Mich. Educator, author. *Milton's Semitic Studies* (1926); *Milton's Rabbinical Readings* (1930); *The Use of the Bible in Milton's Prose* (1929); etc. Editor: *The Complete Poetical Works of John Milton* (1941); *Milton's Poetical Works: Facsimile and Critical Text Edition*, 4v. (1943–48); *The Intellectual Development of John Milton*, 2v. (1956, 1961). Faculty, University of Illinois, since 1926.

FLETCHER, INGLIS (Mrs. John G. Fletcher) (1888–Apr. 30, 1969); b. Alton, Ill. Author. *White Leopard* (1931); *Red Jasmine* (1932); *Raleigh's Eden* (1940); *Men of Albermarle* (1942); *Lusty Wind for Carolina* (1944); *Toil of the Brave* (1946); *Roanoke Hundred* (1948); *Bennett's Welcome* (1950); *Queen's Gift* (1952); *The Scotswoman* (1955); *Pay, Pack, and Follow* (autobiography, 1959); *Cormorant's Brood* (1959).

FLETCHER, JEFFERSON BUTLER (Nov. 13, 1865–Aug. 17, 1946); b. Chicago, Ill. Educator, author. *The Overture, and Other Poems* (1911); *The Religion of Beauty in Woman* (1911); *Dante* (1916); *Symbolism of the Divine Comedy* (1921); *Literature of the Italian Renaissance* (1934); etc. Translator, Dante's *The Divine Comedy* (1931). Prof. comparative literature, Columbia University, 1904–1939.

FLETCHER, JOHN GOULD (Jan. 3, 1886–May 20, 1950); b. Little Rock, Ark. Poet. *Fire and Wine* (1913); *Irradiations: Sand and Spray* (1915); *Goblins and Pagodas* (1916); *Japanese Prints* (1918); *Breakers and Granite* (1921); *Paul Gauguin: His Life and Art* (1921); *Branches of Adam* (1926); *The Black Rock* (1928); *The Two Frontiers* (1930); *XXIV Elegies* (1935); *The Epic of Arkansas* (1936); *Life Is My Song* (autobiography, 1937); *Selected Poems* (1938, Pulitzer Prize for poetry, 1939); *South Star* (1941); *The Burning Mountain* (1946); *Arkansas* (1947); etc.

FLETCHER, JULIA CONSTANCE (1858–June, 1938). Novelist. Pen name, "George Fleming." *A Nile Novel* (1876), republished as *Kismet* (anon., 1877); *Mirage* (anon., 1877); *The Head of Medusa* (1880); *Vestigia* (1884); *Andromeda* (1885); *The Truth About Clement Ker* (1889); *For Plain Women Only* (1885); etc.

FLETCHER, MRS. JOHN GOULD (Aug. 17, 1897–); b. near Monticello, Ark. Pen name "Charlie May Simon." Author. *Robin on the Mountain* (1934); *Lost Corner* (1935); *The Share-Cropper* (1937); *Popo's Miracle* (1938); *Bright Morning* (1939); *The Far Away Trail* (1940); *Straw in the Sun* (1945); *Joe Mason* (1946); *The Royal Road* (1948); *Johnswood* (1954); *All Men Are Brothers* (1958); *A Seed Shall Serve* (1958); *Sun and the Birch* (1960); *The Andrew Carnegie Story* (1965); *The Dag Hammarskjöld Story* (1967); *Martin Buber* (1969); etc.

FLETCHER, ROBERT HOWE (July 21, 1850–deceased); b. Cincinnati, O. Editor, novelist. *The Annals of the Bohemian Club* [of San Francisco], 3v. (1872–95); *A Blind Bargain* (1889); *Marjorie and Her Papa* (1891); etc.

FLEWELLING, RALPH TYLER (Nov. 23, 1871–); b. DeWitt, Mich. Educator, author. *Christ and the Drama of Doubt* (1913); *Personalism and the Problems of Philosophy* (1915); *Bergson and Personal Realism* (1919); *Creative Personality* (1926); *The Basic Ideas of East and West* (1933); *The Destiny of the West* (1937); *The Survival of Western Culture* (1943); *Winds of Hiroshima* (1956); etc. Philosophy dept., University of Southern California, since 1917.

FLEXNER, ABRAHAM (Nov. 13, 1866–Sept. 21, 1959); b. Louisville, Ky. Educator, author. *The American College* (1908); *Medical Education in the United States and Canada* (1910); *A Modern College* (1923); *Universities: American, English, German* (1930); *I Remember* (autobiography, 1940; revised, 1959); *Henry S. Pritchett, A Biography* (1943); *Daniel Colt Gilman* (1946); *Funds and Foundations—Their Policies Past and Present* (with Esther S. Bailey, 1952). With Carnegie Foundation for Advancement of Teaching, New York, from 1908. Director, Institute for Advanced Study, Princeton, N.J., 1930–39.

FLEXNER, ANNE CRAWFORD (Mrs. Abraham Flexner) (June 27, 1874–Jan. 12, 1955); b. Georgetown, Ky. Playwright. *The Marriage Game* (prod. 1913); *The Blue Pearl* (prod. 1918); *All Souls' Eve* (prod. 1920); *Aged 26: A Play About John Keats* (prod. 1936); etc.

FLEXNER, HORTENSE (Mrs. Wyncie King) (Apr. 12, 1885–); b. Louisville, Ky. Poet, playwright. *Clouds and Cobblestones* (poems, 1920); *This Stubborn Root, and Other Poems* (1930); *North Window and Other Poems* (1943); etc.

FLEXNER, JAMES THOMAS (Jan. 13, 1908–); b. New York. Author. *Doctors on Horseback: Pioneers of American Medicine* (1937); *A Short History of American Painting* (1950); *The Traitor and the Spy* (1953); *Gilbert Stuart* (1955); *Mohawk Baronet: Sir William Johnson of New York* (1959); *George Washington: The Forge of Experience, 1732–1775* (1965); *The World of Winslow Homer* (1966); *George Washington in the American Revolution* (1968); *First Flowers of Our Wilderness: American Painting, Colonial Period* (1969); etc.

FLICK, ALEXANDER CLARENCE (Aug. 16, 1869–July 30, 1942); b. Galion, O. Historian. *Loyalism in New York* (1901); *History in Rhyme and Jingles* (1901); *Rise of the Mediaeval Church* (1909); *The American Revolution in New York* (1926); *The Decline of the Mediaeval Church* (1929); *History of the State of New York* (1933–37); *Samuel J. Tilden* (1939); etc. State historian, New York, 1923–39.

FLICKINGER, ROY CASTON (Dec. 17, 1876–July 6, 1942); b. Seneca, Ill. Educator, author. *Plutarch and the Greek Theatre* (1904); *The Greek Theatre and Its Drama* (1918); *Horace's First Bimillennium* (1936). Editor: *Carmina Latina* (1919); etc. Editor, *Iowa Studies in Classical Philology*, from 1934. Editor, *Iowa Studies in Classical Philology*, from 1905. Greek and Latin dept., Northwestern University, from 1905.

FLING, FRED MORROW (1860–June 8, 1934); b. Portland, Me. Educator, author. *Studies in Greek Civilization* (1898); *History of France* (1907); *Mirabeau and the French Revolution* (1908); *The Writing of History* (1920). Prof. European history, University of Nebraska, 1891–1934.

FLINT, AUSTIN (Mar. 28, 1836–Sept. 22, 1915); b. Northampton, Mass. Physician, author. *The Physiology of Man*, 5v. (1867–73); *Collected Essays and Articles on Physiology and Medicine* (1903). His father, Austin Flint (1812–1886), founded the Buffalo Medical College in 1847.

FLINT, LEON NELSON (Oct. 5, 1875–Sept. 30, 1955); b. Thayer, Kan. Educator, author. *The Editorial* (1920); *The Conscience of the Newspaper* (1925); etc. Journalism dept., University of Kansas, from 1906. Editor, *The Kansas Editor*, 1917–41.

FLINT, TIMOTHY (July 11, 1780–Aug. 16, 1840); b. North Reading, Mass. Congregational clergyman, author. *Recollections of the Last Ten Years* (1826); *Francis Berrian; or, The Mexican Patriot*, 2v. (anon., 1826); *The Life and Adventures of Arthur Clenning* (anon., 1828); *George Mason, the Young Backwoodsman; or, "Don't Give Up the Ship"* (anon., 1829); *The Shoshonee Valley*, 2v. (anon., 1830); *Biographical Memoir of Daniel Boone* (1833); etc. Editor, *Western Monthly Review*, 1827–30. See J. E. Kirkpatrick's *Timothy Flint* (1911).

FLIPPIN, PERCY SCOTT (Sept. 19, 1874–); b. Amelia, Va. Archivist, educator, author. *The Royal Government in Virginia* (1919); *The Royal Government in Georgia* (1923); *William Gooch: Successful Royal Governor of Virginia* (1925); *Herschel V. Johnson of Georgia, State Rights Unionist* (1930); *The Archives of the United States Government, 1774–1934* (1938); etc. Prof. history, Mercer College, 1919–27, etc.; chief, division of research, The National Archives, from 1935.

Floating Prince, and Other Fairy Tales, The. By Frank R. Stockton (1881).

FLOHERTY, JOHN JOSEPH (Apr. 28, 1882–Dec. 3, 1964); b. in Ireland. Author. *Fire* (1935); *Aviation from Shop to Sky* (1940); *Flowing Gold* (1945); *Shooting the News* (1949); *Search and Rescue at Sea* (1953); *Forest Ranger* (1955); *Whirling Wings* (1961); etc.

FLOM, GEORGE TOBIAS (Apr. 12, 1871–Jan., 1960); b. Utica, Wis. Educator, philologist, author. *A History of Scandinavian Studies in American Universities* (1907); *A History of Norwegian Immigration to the United States* (1909); *Morphology of the Dialect of Aurland in Sogn, Norway* (1944); etc. Editor, *Scandinavian Studies and Notes,* 1911–20; on editorial staff, *Journal of English and Germanic Philology,* 1902–1940. Prof. Scandinavian languages, University of Illinois, from 1909.

FLOOD, CHARLES BRACELEN (1930–). Author. *Love Is a Bridge* (1953); *A Distant Drum* (1957); *Tell Me, Stranger* (1959); *Monmouth* (1961); *More Lives than One* (1967); etc.

FLOOD, DANIEL J. (Nov. 26, 1904–); b. Hazelton, Pa. Congressman, author. *The Dreyfus Affair* (1925); *Three One-Act Plays* (1936).

"Flood of Years, The." Poem by William Cullen Bryant (1876).

Florence. Pen name of Frances Sargent Locke Osgood.

Florence, Percy. Pen name of Elizabeth Chase Akers.

"Florence Vane." Ballad by Philip Pendleton Cooke, was first published in Burton's *Gentleman's Magazine,* Mar., 1840, and was later translated into many languages.

FLORES, ANGEL (1900–). Editor, author. *Literature and Marxism: A Controversy* (1938). Editor: *Henrik Ibsen* (1937); *The Kafka Problem* (1946); *Great Spanish Stories* (1956); *Franz Kafka Today* (with Homer Swander, 1958); *Nineteenth Century French Tales* (1960); etc.

FLORINSKY, MICHAEL (Dec. 27, 1894–); b. Kiev, Rus. Educator, author. *End of the Russian Empire* (1931); *Saar Struggle* (1934); *Fascism and National Socialism* (1936); *Russia: A History and an Interpretation* (1953); *Integrated Europe?* (1955); *Russia: A Short History* (1964); etc.

Florio. Pen name of James Gordon Brooks.

FLOWER, B[enjamin] O[range] (Oct. 19, 1858–Dec. 24, 1918); b. Albion, Ill. Editor, social reformer, author. *Whittier: Prophet, Seer, and Man* (1896); *Persons, Places, and Ideas* (1896); etc. Founder, *The American Spectator,* Boston, 1886; and later merged it with *The Arena,* which he founded in 1889.

FLOWER, ELLIOTT (Aug. 2, 1863–July 3, 1920); b. Madison, Wis. Author. *Policeman Flynn* (1892); *The Spoilsman* (1903); *Nurse Norah's Up-to-Date Fairy Tales* (1903); *Delightful Dodd* (1904); *Slaves of Success* (1905); *The Best Policy* (1905).

FLOWER, J[ames] HOWARD (May 21, 1883–); b. Hartland, Vt. Poet. *Florentine Sonnets* (1918); *Flowers of the Road* (1919); *Songs of Love and Liberty* (1920). Editor: *Wit and Humour of Poetic Vermont* (1930); *The Yankee Bard: Vermont Ballads* (with Walter J. Coates, 1934).

Flowering Judas. Collection of stories by Katharine Anne Porter (1930).

Flush Times of Alabama and Mississippi, The. By Joseph Glover Baldwin (1853). Humorous stories of a country lawyer riding the circuit.

Flute and Violin. Short stories by James Lane Allen (1891).

FLYNN, ERROL [Leslie] (June 20, 1909–Oct. 14, 1959); b. Hobart, Tasmania. Actor, author. *Beam Ends* (1937); *Showdown* (1946); *My Wicked, Wicked Ways* (1959).

FLYNN, JOHN THOMAS (Oct. 25, 1882–Apr. 14, 1964); b. Bladensburg, Md. Journalist, author. *God's Gold: The Story of Rockefeller and His Times* (1932); *Country Squire in the White House* (1940); *The Fourteen Decisive Fortunes of History* (1940); *Men of Wealth* (1941); *As We Go Marching* (1944); *Meet Your Congress* (1944); *Truth About Pearl Harbor* (1945); *Epic of Freedom* (1946); *The Roosevelt Myth* (1948); *The Road Ahead* (1949); *While You Slept* (1951); *The Lattimore Story* (1953); *The Decline of the American Republic* (1955). Columnist, *New Republic,* 1931–40. Commentator, Mutual Broadcasting System, from 1954.

FOAKES-JACKSON, FREDERICK JOHN (Aug. 10, 1885–1941); b. Ipswich, England. Episcopal clergyman, educator, author. *The History of the Christian Church* (1891); *The Biblical History of the Hebrews* (1903); *Social Life in England, 1750–1850* (1916); *The Life of Saint Paul* (1926); *Peter, Prince of Apostles* (1927); *History of Church Historians* (1939); etc. Editor: *The Faith and the War* (1915); etc. With the Union Theological Seminary, New York, 1916–34.

FODOR, EUGENE (Oct. 14, 1905–   ); b. Léva, Hung. Editor and publisher: Fodor's Modern Guides, Inc., 1949–64; executive chairman of the board, Fodor's Modern Guides, Ltd., London, since 1964.

FOERSTER, NORMAN (Apr. 14, 1887–); b. Pittsburgh, Pa. Educator, critic. *Nature in American Literature* (1923); *American Criticism* (1928); *The American Scholar* (1929); *Toward Standards* (1931); *The Future of the Liberal College* (1938); *The Humanities and the Common Man* (1946). Co-author: *The Reinterpretation of American Literature* (1928); *Literary Scholarship* (1941); *The Humanities After the War* (1944). Editor: *The Chief American Prose Writers* (1916); *American Ideals* (with W. W. Pierson, Jr., 1917); *English Poetry of the Nineteenth Century* (with G. R. Elliott, 1923); *American Poetry and Prose* (1925); *Humanism and America* (1930); *American Critical Essays* (1930). English dept., University of North Carolina, 1914–30; director, School of Letters, University of Iowa, 1930–44.

"Fog." Six-line poem by Carl Sandburg in his *Chicago Poems* (1916). A delicate condensation of the poet's mood as he watches the fog come in from Lake Michigan.

FOGEL, EDWIN MILLER (May 29, 1874–Dec. 16, 1949); b. Fogelsville, Pa. Educator, author. *Beliefs and Superstitions of the Pennsylvania Germans* (1915); *Proverbs of Pennsylvania Germans* (1929); etc. Editor, *German-American Annals,* 1914–17. Co-founder, Pennsylvania Folk-Lore Society; director, from 1935.

Folder Editions. New York. Founded 1958. Poems and poetic prose in English and French published in conjunction with graphic material to achieve a combined artistic effect. Daisy Aldan edited the various works.

FOLEY, MARTHA; b. Boston, Mass. Editor (with Whit Burnett): *A Story Anthology, 1931–1933* (1933). Co-founder (with same), *Story* magazine, Vienna, 1931, brought to U.S., 1933; co-editor, 1931–41. Editor: *The Best American Short Stories* (annually, since 1942). Lecturer, Columbia University, since 1945.

FOLEY, P[atrick] K[evin] (Mar. 14, 1856–Apr. 13, 1937); b. in Co. Cork, Ireland. Boston bookseller and bibliophile. Compiler: *American Authors, 1795–1895: A Bibliography of First and Notable Editions* (1897). He ran a shop on Hamilton Place, and was an authority on American first editions.

FOLGER, PETER (1617–1690); b. Norwich, England. Author. *A Looking-Glass for the Times; or, The Former Spirit of New-England Revived in This Generation* (verse, 1676).

FOLKS, HOMER (Feb. 18, 1867–Feb. 13, 1963); b. Hanover, Mich. Social worker, author. *Care of Destitute, Neglected and Delinquent Children* (1902); *The Human Costs of the War* (1920); *Public Health and Welfare: The Citizens' Responsibility* (1958).

Folks, The. Novel by Ruth Suckow (1934). Realistic picture of contemporary American life on the farm and in the small town.

FOLLEN, CHARLES [Theodore Christian] (Sept. 4, 1796– Jan. 13, 1840); b. Giessen, Hesse-Darmstadt, Germany. Educator, abolitionist, author. See *The Works of Charles Follen, with a Memoir of His Life,* edited by his widow, Eliza Lee Cabot Follen, 5v. (1841–42). German dept., Harvard, 1825– 35, first professor of German at Harvard, 1830–35.

FOLLEN, ELIZA LEE CABOT (Mrs. Charles Theodore Christian Follen) (Aug. 15, 1787–Jan. 26, 1860); b. Boston, Mass. Author. *The Well-Spent Hour* (1827); *The Skeptic* (anon., 1835); *Sketches of Married Life* (1838); *Poems* (1839); *Hymns, Songs, and Fables* (1854); *Home Dramas* (1859); etc. Editor: *Gammer Grethel* (1840); *The Works of Charles Follen, with a Memoir of His Life,* 5v. (1841–42).

FOLLETT, HELEN [Thomas] (Mrs. Wilson Follett) (d. Apr. 21, 1970). Author. *Some Modern Novelists* (with husband, 1918); *Magic Portholes* (1932); *Stars to Steer By* (1934); *Third Class Ticket to Heaven* (1938).

FOLLETT, WILSON (1887–Jan. 7, 1963). Author. *The Modern Novel* (1918); *Some Modern Novelists* (with wife, Helen Thomas Follett, 1918); *No More Sea* (1933). Editor: *The Works of Stephen Crane,* 12v. (1925–26). Translator: Ramon Fernandez' *Molière: The Man Seen Through the Plays* (1958).

FOLSOM, CHARLES (Dec. 24, 1794–Nov. 8, 1872); b. Exeter, N.H. Librarian, editor. Editor (with Andrews Norton): *The Select Journal of Foreign Periodical Literature,* 4v. (1833–34). Librarian, Harvard Library, 1823–26; with the University Press, 1824–40; librarian, Boston Athenaeum, 1846–56.

FOLSOM, GEORGE (May 23, 1802–Mar. 27, 1869); b. Kennebunk, Me. Lawyer, librarian, antiquarian, author. *History of Saco and Biddeford* (1830); *Dutch Annals of New York* (1841); *Mexico in 1842* (1842). Librarian, New York Historical Society. Editor, *Historical Magazine,* 1858–59.

FOLTZ, CHARLES STEINMAN (1859–Jan. 15, 1941); b. Philadelphia, Pa. Editor, author. *Surgeon of the Seas: The Adventurous Life of Surgeon-General Jonathan M. Foltz in the Days of Wooden Ships* (1931). Publisher, the *Lancaster* (Pa.) *Intelligencer;* the *Lancaster News-Journal.*

FOLWELL, ARTHUR HAMILTON (Nov. 22, 1877–July 12, 1962); b. Brooklyn, N.Y. Editor, drama critic. *Monsieur d'Em Brochette* (with Bert Leston Taylor and John Kendrick Bangs, 1905). Editor-in-chief, *Puck,* 1905–16; editor, "Magazine" section, New York *Herald Tribune,* 1921–26; art director, 1926–27; dramatic editor, from 1927.

FOLWELL, WILLIAM WATTS (Feb. 14, 1833–Sept. 19, 1929); b. Romulus, N.Y. Educator, historian. *University Addresses* (1909); *A History of Minnesota,* 4v. (1921–30); *William Watts Folwell: The Autobiography and Letters of a Pioneer of Culture* (1933); etc. President of University of Minnesota, 1869–84.

FONER, PHILIP SHELDON (Dec. 14, 1910–); b. New York. Publisher, author. *Business and Slavery* (1941); *History of the Labor Movement in the United States* (1947); *The Life and Writings of Frederick Douglass* (1949–52); *Mark Twain: Social Critic* (1958); *The Case of Joe Hill* (1965); etc. Editor: *The Autobiographies of the Haymarket Martyrs* (1969). Co-director, editor, Citadel Press, 1945–66. Prof. history, Lincoln University, since 1967.

Fool, The. Play by Channing Pollock (prod. 1922). Story of a young rector who is ousted from his parish because his practical application of Christian living makes his parishioners too uncomfortable.

Fool's Errand, A. Novel by Albion W. Tourgée (1879). Story of Comfort Servosse, a Union colonel who moves to the South after the Civil War and finds old prejudices still alive. He is solicitous for the freedmen. Ku Klux Klan figures in the narrative.

"Fool's Prayer, The." Poem by Edward Rowland Sill (1879).

Foot-Prints. Poems by Richard Henry Stoddard (1849). The author's first volume of verse. He tried to destroy the entire edition, having repented of writing the poems, but a few copies have survived.

FOOTE, GASTON (Sept. 6, 1903–); b. near Comanche, Tex. Methodist clergyman, author. *Living in Four Dimensions* (1953); *Footnotes* (1956); *The Transformation of the Twelve* (1958); *How God Helps* (1966).

FOOTE, HENRY STUART (Feb. 28, 1804–May 20, 1880); b. in Fauquier Co., Va. Governor, author. *Texas and the Texans,* 2v. (1841); *War of the Rebellion; or, Scylla and Charybdis* (1866); *Casket of Reminiscences* (1874); *The Bench and Bar of the South and Southwest* (1876). U.S. Senator, 1847–52; Governor of Mississippi, 1853–54.

FOOTE, HENRY WILDER (1875–Aug. 27, 1964). Unitarian clergyman, author. *The Minister and His Parish* (1923); *Thomas Jefferson, Champion of Religious Freedom* (1947); *The Religion of an Inquiring Mind* (1955); *Three Centuries of American Hymnody* (1961); etc.

FOOTE, HORTON (Mar. 14, 1916–   ); b. Wharton, Tex. Author. *The Chase* (1956). Screen writer: *To Kill a Mockingbird* (1962); *The Chase* (1965); *The Stalking Moon* (1968). Playwright: *Trip to Bountiful* (1953); *The Traveling Lady* (1954); *Three Plays* (1962). Television scenarist: *Young Lady of Property* (1953); *The Oil Well* (1953); *Harrison, Texas* (collected television plays, 1956); *Roots in a Parched Ground* (1961).

FOOTE, JOHN TAINTOR (Mar. 29, 1881–Jan. 29, 1950); b. Leadville, Colo. Author. *Blister Jones* (1913); *Toby's Bow* (prod. 1919); *Trub's Diary* (1928); *Daughter of Delilah* (1936); *Julie the Great* (prod. 1936); *Jing* (1936); *Hell Cat* (1936); *Broadway Angler* (1937); *Sporting Days* (1937); etc.

FOOTE, LUCIUS HARWOOD (Apr. 10, 1826–June 4, 1913); b. Winfield, N.Y. Diplomat, poet. *A Red Letter Day, and Other Poems* (1882); *On the Heights* (1897); *The Wooing of the Rose, and Other Poems* (1911).

FOOTE, MARY HALLOCK (Mrs. Arthur De Wint Foote) (Nov. 19, 1847–June 25, 1938); b. Milton, N.Y. Novelist, illustrator. *The Led-Horse Claim* (1883); *The Chosen Valley* (1892); *In Exile, and Other Stories* (1894); *Coeur d'Alene* (1894); *The Desert and the Sown* (1902); *A Picked Company* (1912); *The Ground Swell* (1919); etc.

FOOTE, SHELBY (Nov. 17, 1916–); b. Greenville, Miss. Author. *Tournament* (1949); *Follow Me Down* (1950); *Love in a Dry Season* (1951); *Shiloh* (1952); *Jordan County* (1954); *The Civil War: A Narrative,* 2v. (1958, 1963).

FOOTNER, HULBERT (Apr. 2, 1879–Nov. 25, 1944); b. Hamilton, Ont. Novelist, playwright. *Two on the Trail* (1911); *Shirley Kaye* (prod. 1916); *The Deaves Affair* (1922); *Ramshackle House* (1922); *The Under Dogs* (1925); *Madame Storey* (1926); *Cap'n Sue* (1928); *The Doctor Who Held Hands* (1929); *The Ring of Eyes* (1933); *Scarred Jungle* (1935); *The Island of Fear* (1936); *The Dark Ships* (1937); *New York, City of Cities* (1937); *Charles' Gift: Salute to a Maryland House of 1650* (1939); *Sinfully Rich* (1940); *Maryland Main and the Eastern Shore* (1942); *The House with the Blue Door* (1942); *The Death of a Saboteur* (1943); *Rivers of the Eastern Shore* (1944); etc.

For Esmé—with Love and Squalor. Short story by J. D. Salinger. Appeared in *Nine Stories* (1953).

For Lancelot Andrewes. Collection of essays, by T. S. Eliot (1928). The subjects include Andrewes, Bramhall, Bradley, Baudelaire, and Crashaw.

For the Major. Novel by Constance Fenimore Woolson (1883). Account of village life in Eastern Appalachians.

For Whom the Bell Tolls. By Ernest Hemingway (1940). Novel of the Spanish Civil War; a chronicle of Robert Jordan, American volunteer, who is assigned the task of blowing up a bridge. Four crowded days furnish the action for a story of love and war.

Forayers; or, The Raid of the Dog-Days, The. Novel by William Gilmore Simms (1855). Revolutionary tale, laid in South Carolina in 1781. *Eutaw* (1856) was a sequel.

Forbes. New York. Semi-monthly. Founded 1917. Business and financial periodical.

FORBES, ANITA P. Editor. *Modern Verse, British and American* (1921); *Essays for Discussion* (1931).

FORBES, EDGAR ALLEN (Sept. 25, 1872–); b. near Gainesville, Ga. Editor, author. *The Land of the White Helmet* (1910); *Twice Around the World* (1912); *The Voyage of Your Dreams* (1922).

FORBES, EDWIN (1839–Mar. 6, 1895); b. New York City. Painter, etcher, author. *Thirty Years After: An Artist's Story of the Great War* (1891). Staff artist with the Army of the Potomac for *Frank Leslie's Illustrated Newspaper.* A collection of his etchings was published as *Life Studies of the Great Army* (1876).

FORBES, ESTHER (Mrs. A. L. Hoskins) (d. Aug. 12, 1967); b. Westborough, Mass. Author. *O Genteel Lady!* (1926); *A Mirror for Witches* (1928); *Miss Marvel* (1935); *Paradise* (1937); *The General's Lady* (1938); *Paul Revere and the World He Lived In* (1942; Pulitzer prize for history, 1943); *Johnny Tremaine* (1943); *The Boston Book* (with Arthur Griffin, 1947); *The Running of the Tide* (1948); *Rainbow on the Road* (1954); etc.

FORBES, HARRIETTE MERRIFIELD (Oct. 22, 1856–Oct. 12, 1951); b. Worcester, Mass. Antiquarian, author. *The Hundredth Town* (1889); *Gravestones of Early New England* (1927). Editor: *The Diary of Rev. Ebenezer Parkman* (1899); *New England Diaries, 1602–1800* (1923).

FORBES, JAMES (Sept. 2, 1871–May 26, 1938); b. Salem, Ont. Playwright. *The Chorus Lady* (prod. 1906); *The Traveling Salesman* (prod. 1908); *The Commuters* (prod. 1910); *A Rich Man's Son* (prod. 1912); *The Show Shop* (prod. 1914); *The Famous Mrs. Fair* (prod. 1919); etc.

Forbes, Kathryn. Pen name of Kathryn MacLean.

FORBES, MRS. A[rmitage] S. C.; b. Everett, Pa. Author. *California Missions and Landmarks* (1903); *Mission Tales in the Days of the Dons* (1909).

FORBES, ROBERT BENNET (Apr. 18, 1804–Nov. 23, 1889); b. Boston, Mass. Ship owner, sea captain, author. *Remarks on China and the China Trade* (1844); *The Forbes Rig* (1862); *Personal Reminiscences* (1876); *Notes on Ships of the Past* (1888); etc. See S. F. Hughes's *Letters and Recollections of John Murray Forbes* (1889).

FORBUSH, BLISS (Jan. 14, 1896–); b. Yarmouth, N.S. Educator, author. *Loyalties* (1930); *Gospel of Mark* (1935); *Toward Understanding Jesus* (1939); *Elias Hicks: Quaker Liberal* (1956); *Moses Sheppard: Quaker Philanthropist of Baltimore* (1968); etc. Headmaster, Friends School, Baltimore, since 1943.

FORBUSH, EDWARD HOWE (Apr. 24, 1858–Mar. 8, 1929); b. Quincy, Mass. Ornithologist, author. *The Gypsy Moth* (1896); *Useful Birds and Their Protection* (1907); *A History of Game Birds, Wild Fowl and Shore Birds* (1912); *Birds of Massachusetts and Other New England States,* 2v. (1925–27); etc.

FORCE, MANNING FERGUSON (Dec. 17, 1824–May 8, 1899); b. Washington, D.C. Jurist, author. *From Fort Henry to Corinth* (1881); *General Sherman* (1899); etc.

FORCE, PETER (Nov. 26, 1790–Jan. 23, 1868); b. Passaic Falls, N.J. Archivist, historian. Editor: *American Archives,* 9v. (1837–53). Publisher, *National Calendar,* 1820–36, an historical annual. His extensive collection of books on American history was sold to the Library of Congress. Founder and editor, *National Journal,* 1823–30.

FORD, CHARLES HENRI. Author. *Garden of Disorder and Other Poems* (1938); *Overturned Lake* (1941); *Sleep in a Nest of Flames* (poems, 1949); etc. Editor: *A Night With Jupiter and Other Fantastic Stories* (1945); etc.

FORD, CLELLAN STEARNS (July 27, 1909–); b. Worcester, Mass. Educator, author. *Smoke from Their Fires* (1941); *A Comparative Study of Human Reproduction* (1945); *Patterns of Sexual Behavior* (with F. A. Beach, 1951). Anthropology dept., Yale University, since 1940.

FORD, COREY (Apr. 29, 1902–July 27, 1969); b. New York. Humorist, parodist. Pen name, "John Riddell." Under own name: *Three Rousing Cheers for the Rollo Boys* (1925); *The Gazelle's Ears* (1926); *Salt Water Taffy* (1929); *Coconut Oil* (1931); *The Horse of Another Color* (1946); *How to Guess Your Age* (1950); *The Office Party* (1951); *Every Dog Should Have a Man* (1952); *Daughter of the Gold Rush* (1958); *You Can Always Tell a Fisherman* (1958); *What Every Bachelor Knows* (1961); *Uncle Perk's Jug* (1964); *A Peculiar Service* (1965); *The Time of Laughter* (1967); *Where the Sea Breaks Its Back* (1966); etc. Under pen name: *Meaning No Offense* (1928); *John Riddell Murder Case* (1930); *In the Worst Possible Taste* (1932).

FORD, DANIEL SHARP (Apr. 5, 1822–Dec. 24, 1899); b. Cambridge, Mass. Editor, publisher, philanthropist. Editor (or co-editor), *Youth's Companion,* 1857–99. President, Perry Mason & Co., publishers, 1867–99.

FORD, EDSEL (Dec. 30, 1928–   ); b. Eva, Ala. Poet. *The Manchild from Sunday Creek* (1956); *A Thicket of Sky* (1961); *Love Is the House It Lives In* (1965); *Looking for Shiloh* (1968).

FORD, GUY STANTON (May 9, 1873–Dec. 29, 1962); b. Salem, Wis. Educator, author. *Hanover and Prussia* (1903); *Science and Civilization* (1933); *Dictatorship in the Modern World* (1935); *On and Off the Campus* (1938); etc. Editor-in-chief, *Compton's Pictured Encyclopedia; Harper's History Series;* etc. Prof. history, University of Minnesota, 1913–38; president, 1939–41.

FORD, HARRIET [French] (Mrs. Forde Morgan) (1868–Oct. 12, 1949); b. Seymour, Conn. Playwright. *The Argyle Case* (with Harvey O'Higgins, prod. 1912); *The Dummy* (with same, prod. 1914); *The Dickey Bird* (with same, prod. 1915); *Mr. Lazarus* (with same, prod. 1916); *On the Hiring Line* (with same, prod. 1919); *In the Next Room* (with Eleanor Robson, prod. 1923); etc.

FORD, HENRY (July 30, 1863–Apr. 7, 1947); b. in Wayne Co., Mich. Automobile manufacturer, author. *My Life and Work* (autobiography, with Samuel Crowther, 1923); *Today and Tomorrow* (with same, 1926); *Edison as I Knew Him* (with same, 1930); *Moving Forward* (with same, 1930). Founder, *The Dearborn Independent,* 1919. See James M. Miller's *The Amazing Story of Henry Ford* (1922); Jonathan N. Leonard's *The Tragedy of Henry Ford* (1932); Ralph H. Graves's *The Triumph of an Idea* (1934); Upton Sinclair's *The Flivver King* (1937).

FORD, HENRY JONES (Aug. 25, 1851–Aug. 29, 1925); b. Baltimore, Md. Educator, editor, historian. *The Scotch-Irish in America* (1915); *Woodrow Wilson* (1916); *Washington and His Colleagues* (1918); *The Cleveland Era* (1919); *Alexander Hamilton* (1920); etc. Editor, *Pittsburgh Gazette,* 1901–05.

FORD, JAMES LAUREN (July 25, 1854–Feb. 26, 1928); b. St. Louis, Mo. Author. *The Literary Shop, and Other Tales* (1894); *Forty-Odd Years in the Literary Shop* (autobiography, 1921); etc.

FORD, JEREMIAH DENIS MATHIAS (July 2, 1873–Nov. 13, 1958); b. Cambridge, Mass. Educator, author. *Spanish Grammar* (1904); *Main Currents of Spanish Literature* (1919); *Portuguese Grammar* (1925); etc. Editor: *A Spanish Anthology* (1901); *Chivalrous Romances in Italian Verse* (1904); *Bibliography of Cervantes* (1931); *Bibliography of Brazilian Belles-Lettres* (1931); *Bibliography of Cuban Belles-Lettres* (1932); etc. Editor-in-chief, *Speculum,* 1927–36. Romance language dept., Harvard University and Radcliffe College, 1895–1943.

FORD, JESSE HILL, JR. (Dec. 28, 1928–   ); b. Troy, Ala. Author. *Mountains of Gilead* (1961); *The Conversion of Buster Drumwright* (1963); *The Liberation of Lord Byron Jones* (1965); *Fishes, Birds and Sons of Men* (1967); *The Feast of St. Barnabas* (1969).

FORD, JOSEPH BRANDON (Jan. 20, 1918–); b. Los Angeles, Cal. Sociologist, author. *Contemporary Sociology* (with others, 1958); *Contemporary American Sociology* (with others, 1961); *Sociology of Change* (with C. C. Zimmermann, 1964); *Bibliographic Introduction to Urban Sociology* (1964); *Comte and Positivism* (1967); etc. Prof. sociology, San Fernando State College, since 1958.

FORD, JULIA ELLSWORTH (Mrs. Simeon Ford) (Apr. 6, 1859); b. New York. Author. *A. E.—A Note of Appreciation* (1908); *The Mist* (prod. 1913); *Imagina* (1914); *Consequences* (1929); etc. Established Julia Ellsworth Ford Foundation in 1934 to encourage the writers of books for young people. An annual prize is awarded.

Ford, Leslie. Pen name of Zenith J. Brown.

FORD, PATRICK (Aug. 12, 1835–Sept. 23, 1913); b. Galway, Ireland. Editor, publisher, author. *The Criminal History of the British Empire* (1881); *The Irish Question and American Statesmen* (1885). Founder, *The Irish World,* 1870; editor, 1870–1913.

FORD, PAUL LEICESTER (Mar. 23, 1865–May 8, 1902); b. Brooklyn, N.Y., brother of Worthington Chauncey Ford. Historian, novelist. *The Honorable Peter Sterling and What People Thought of Him* (1894); *The True George Washington* (1896); *Janice Meredith: A Study of the American Revolution* (1899); etc. Editor: *The Writings of Thomas Jefferson,* 10v. (1892–99). Compiler: *Check-List of American Magazines Printed in the Eighteenth Century* (1889). Editor, *Library Journal,* 1890–93.

FORD, RICHARD CLYDE (May 17, 1870–May 8, 1951); b. Calhoun Co., Mich. Educator, author. *John D. Pierce* (1905); *The White Captive* (1915); *Sandy MacDonald's Man* (1928); *Heroes and Hero Tales of Michigan* (1930); *Red Man or White* (1931). Prof. modern languages, Michigan State Normal School, Ypsilanti, 1903–40.

FORD, SALLY ROCHESTER; (1828–deceased); b. Rochester Springs, Ky. Novelist. *Grace Truman* (1857); *Mary Bunyan* (1860); *Raids and Romance of Morgan and His Men* (1864); *Ernest Quest* (1877).

FORD, SEWELL (Mar. 7, 1868–deceased); b. S. Levant, Me. Author. *Shorty McCabe* (1906); *Cherub Divine* (1909); *Just Horses* (1910); *Torchy* (1911); *Odd Numbers* (1912); *Inez and Trilby May* (1921); and many other books carrying forward the experiences of "Shorty McCabe" and "Torchy."

FORD, WORTHINGTON CHAUNCEY (Feb. 16, 1858–Mar. 7, 1941); b. Brooklyn, N.Y., brother of Paul Leicester Ford. Editor, bibliophile, author. *George Washington,* 2v. (1899); *The Boston Book Market, 1679–1700* (1917); etc. Editor: v. 1–15 of *Journals of the Continental Congress, 1774–1789,* 34v. (1904–37); etc. Chief, division of manuscripts, Library of Congress, 1902–09; editor, Massachusetts Historical Society, 1909–29.

Foregone Conclusion, A. Novel by William Dean Howells (1875). The story of Florida Vervain and her mother in Venice, and of Don Ippolito, a priest and inventor, who is led astray by Florida's meddling in his career.

Foreign Affairs. New York. Quarterly, later semi-monthly. Founded 1922. Successor to *The Journal of Race Development* and *The Journal of International Relations.* Publishes scholarly contributions on international affairs, history, politics, and economics. Edited by Hamilton Fish Armstrong.

Foreign Policy. New York. Quarterly. Founded 1970. Edited by Samuel P. Huntington and Warren D. Manshel. Concerned with United States foreign relations. Has published Adam Yarmolinsky, Leslie H. Gelb, John K. Galbraith.

FOREMAN, GRANT (June 3, 1869–Apr. 21, 1953); b. Detroit, Ill. Lawyer, historian. *Indians and Pioneers: The Story of the American Southwest Before 1830* (1930); *Advancing the Frontier, 1830–1860* (1933); *The Five Civilized Tribes* (1934); *Down the Texas Road* (1936); *The Adventures of James Collier* (1937); *Adventure on Red River* (1937); *Sequoyah* (1938); *Marcy and the Gold Seekers* (1939); *A History of Oklahoma* (1942); *Muskogee* (1943); *Indian Removal* (1953); etc.

FORESMAN, HUGH AUSTIN (July 8, 1867–Jan. 1960); b. Easton, Pa. Publisher. With Silver, Burdett & Co., Chicago, 1891–95; organized Scott, Foresman & Co., publishers of textbooks, in 1895; president, 1929–43; chairman of the board, 1943–55.

Forest and the Fort, The. Novel by Hervey Allen (1943). Part of the trilogy, *The City in the Dawn* (1950).

"Forest Hymn, A." Poem by William Cullen Bryant (1825).

Forest Life and Forest Trees. By John S. Springer (1857). A description of life in the Maine and New Brunswick logging camps.

Forest Rangers: A Poetic Tale of the Western Wilderness in 1794, The. By Andrew Coffinberry (1842).

Forest Rose; or, American Farmers, The. Play by Samuel Woodworth (prod. 1825). A favorite play of the American theatre for forty years, it featured the Yankee character, Jonathan Ploughboy.

FORESTER, C[ecil] S[cott] (Aug. 27, 1899–Apr. 2, 1966); b. Cairo. Author. *Payment Deferred* (1926); *The Shadow of the Hawk* (1928); *Death to the French* (1932); *The African Queen* (1935); *Beat to Quarters* (1937); *Flying Colours* (1938); *A Ship of the Line* (1939); *To the Indies* (1940); *The Captain from Connecticut* (1941); *The Ship* (1943); *Commodore Hornblower* (1945); *The Sky and the Forest* (1948); *Randall and the River of Time* (1950); *The Good Shepherd* (1955); *The Age of Fighting Sail* (1956); *The Last Nine Days of the Bismarck* (1959); *Hornblower and the Hotspur* (1962); *The Indomitable Hornblower* (1963); *The Happy Return* (1964); *Long Before Forty* (1967); etc.

Forester, Fanny. Pen name of Emily Judson.

Forester, Frank. Pen name of Henry William Herbert.

"Foresters, The." Narrative poem by Alexander Wilson (1804). Story of a journey through New York and Pennsylvania to Niagara Falls.

Forever Amber. Novel by Kathleen Winsor (1944). Historical romance about Restoration England, centering on the love affairs of the immoral but ravishing Amber.

Forge, The. Novel by T. S. Stribling (1931). Deals with life in Alabama before and during the Civil War.

Forgotten Man, and Other Essays, The. By William Graham Sumner (1919). The phrase "the forgotten man" was popularized by Franklin D. Roosevelt in the presidential campaign of 1932. See *The Discoverer of the Forgotten Man,* in the *American Mercury,* Nov., 1932.

FORMAN, HARRISON (June 15, 1904–); b. Milwaukee, Wis. Explorer, author. *Through Forbidden Tibet* (1935); *The World Is My Beat* (1940); *Horizon Hunter* (1940); *Report from Red China* (1945); *Changing China* (1948); *Blunder in Asia* (1950); *How to Make Money with Your Camera* (1951); *The Land and the People of Nigeria* (1964); *West Africa and Central Africa* (1965); *Pakistan and Nepal, India* (1969).

FORMAN, HENRY JAMES (Feb. 17, 1879–Jan. 1966); b. in Russia. Editor, author. *In the Footprints of Heine* (1910); *The Captain of His Soul* (1914); *Fire of Youth* (1920); *The Man Who Lived in a Shoe* (1922); *The Enchanted Garden* (1923); *Guilt* (1924); *Grecian Italy* (1924); *The Pony Express* (1925); *Our Movie-Made Children* (1933); *The Story of Prophecy* (1936); *Truth Is One* (with Roland Gammon, 1954); etc.

FORMAN, JUSTUS MILES (Nov. 1, 1875–May 7, 1915); b. Le Roy, N.Y. Novelist, playwright. *The Garden of Lies* (1902); *Journey's End* (1903); *Tommy Carteret* (1905); *Bianca's Daughter* (1910); *The Unknown Lady* (1911); *The Opening Door* (1913); *The Blind Spot* (1914); *The Hyphen* (prod. 1915); etc.

FORMAN, SAMUEL EAGLE (Apr. 29, 1858–1941); b. Brentsville, Va. Author. *The Life and Writings of Thomas Jefferson* (1900); *The Political Activities of Philip Freneau* (1902); *Advanced Civics* (1905); *A History of the United States* (1910); *The American Democracy* (1920); etc. Wrote the "Watch Tower" in *St. Nicholas,* 1915–17.

FORNEY, JOHN WIEN (Sept. 30, 1817–Dec. 9, 1881); b. Lancaster, Pa. Editor, author. *Letters from Europe* (1867); *What I Saw in Texas* (1872); *Anecdotes of Public Men,* 2v. (1873–81); *Forty Years of American Journalism* (1877); etc. Founder, the *Press,* Philadelphia, 1857; *Sunday Morning Chronicle,* Washington, 1861; *Forney's Progress,* Philadelphia, 1878.

Forney's Progress. Philadelphia. Republican weekly. Founded 1878, by John W. Forney. Expired 1885.

FORREST, EARLE R[obert] (June 29, 1883–); b. Washington, Pa. Author. *Missions and Pueblos of the Old Southwest,* 2v. (1929); *California Joe, Noted Scout and Indian Fighter* (with Joe E. Milnor, 1935); *Arizona's Dark and Bloody Ground* (1936); *Wicked Dodge* (1938); *Lone War Trail of Apache Kid* (with Edwin B. Hill, 1947); *Covered Bridges of Washington County, Pa.* (1952); *National Pike in Fayette and Somerset Counties, Pa.* (1956); *With a Camera in Old Navaholand* (1969).

Forrest, Felix C. Pen name of Paul Myron Anthony Linebarger.

FORREST, THOMAS. Playwright. *The Disappointment* (rehearsed 1767, but never produced).

FORRESTAL, JAMES (Feb. 15, 1892–May 22, 1949); b. Beacon, N.Y. Government official. *The Forrestal Diaries* (1951), edited by Walter Millis and E. S. Duffield. First Secretary of Defense, 1947–49. *See* Robert G. Albion's and Robert H. Connery's *Forrestal and the Navy* (1962).

FORRESTER, IZOLA [Louise] (Mrs. Mann Page) (Nov. 15, 1878–); b. Pascoag, R.I. Author. *The Polly Page* series, 4v. (1910–13); *This One Mad Act: The Unknown Story of John Wilkes Booth and His Family* (1937); etc.

FORSTER, ARNOLD (June 25, 1912–); b. New York. Lawyer, author. *Anti-Semitism in the United States* (1947); *A Measure of Freedom* (1950); *The Troublemakers* (with B. R. Epstein, 1952); *Cross-Currents* (1956); *Some of My Best Friends . . .* (1962); *Danger on the Right* (1964); *Report on the John Birch Society* (with Benjamin R. Epstein, 1966); *The Radical Right* (with same, 1967).

Forsythe, Robert. Pen name of Kyle Samuel Crichton.

FORT, CHARLES [Hoy] (1874–May 3, 1932); b. Albany, N.Y. Author. *The Book of the Damned* (1919); *New Lands* (1923); *Lo!* (1931); *Wild Talents* (1932). The Fortean Society, founded in New York City in his honor, has published the *Fortean Society Magazine,* since 1937.

Fort Worth Star-Telegram. Fort Worth, Tex. Newspaper. The *Fort Worth Star* was founded in 1906 and combined with the *Telegram;* founded in 1895. Jack Butler is editor. Leonard Sanders is book-review editor.

FORTESCUE, GRANVILLE ROLAND (Oct. 12, 1875–Apr. 21, 1952); b. New York City. Soldier, editor, playwright. *At the Front with Three Armies* (1914); *Russia, the Balkans, and the Dardanelles* (1915); *Fore-Armed* (1916); *Front Line and Deadline* (1937); etc.; also plays. *Dolores* (1915); *Love and Live* (1921); *The Unbeliever* (1925); etc.

FORTIER, ALCÉE (June 5, 1856–Feb. 14, 1914); b. St. James Parish, La. Educator, author. *Bits of Louisiana Folk-Lore* (1888); *Louisiana Studies* (1894); *Louisiana Folk Tales in French Dialect and English Translation* (1895); *A History of Louisiana,* 4v. (1904); *History of Mexico* (1907); etc., including works in French. Editor: *Encyclopedia of Louisiana* (1908). Prof. Romance languages, Tulane University, 1880–1914. President, Athénée Louisianais, 1892–1914. *See* Grace E. King's *Creole Families of New Orleans* (1921).

Fortnightly Club. Chicago, Ill. Founded 1873. Women's literary society.

Fortune. New York. Monthly magazine. Founded 1930, by Henry Robinson Luce. He edited it until Nov., 1935, when he was succeeded by Russell W. Davenport, who was in turn succeeded in May, 1936, by John Chamberlain. Ralph Ingersoll was managing editor 1930–35. Noted for its elaborately illustrated articles on American industry and the American scene. Merged with *Architectural Forum* in 1964.

FORTUNE, TIMOTHY THOMAS (Oct. 3, 1856–June 2, 1928); b. Mariana, Fla. Editor, author. *Black and White* (1884); *The Negro in Politics* (1885); *Dreams of Life* (poems, 1905). Editor, *The Negro World,* 1925–28.

Fortune Hunter, The. Play by Winchell Smith (prod. 1909).

Fortune's Foot-Ball; or, The Adventures of Mercutio. By James Butler, 2v. (1797–98). Adventure tales in various countries.

47 Workshop. Drama school founded at Harvard University by George Pierce Baker to encourage creative writing. When Baker went to Yale University in 1933, he took the workshop with him.

Forty Years on the Frontier. By Granville Stuart, 2v. (1925).

Forum, The. New York. Magazine. Founded Mar., 1886, by Isaac L. Rice. Lorettus S. Metcalf was first editor. First published by The Forum Publishing Co. From 1910 to 1916 it was published by Mitchell Kennerley. Merged with the *Century Illustrated Monthly Magazine* in 1930. In July, 1940, *Current History* was merged with *Forum and Century.* Expired 1950.

FOSBROKE, GERALD ELTON (Apr. 26, 1876–Jan. 10, 1964); b. Netherton, Eng. Lawyer, author. *Character Revelations of Mind and Body* (1922); *Character Reading through Analysis of the Features* (1933); *Common-Sense Business Leadership* (1946); etc.

FOSDICK, CHARLES AUSTIN (Sept. 16, 1842–Aug. 22, 1915); b. Randolph, N.Y. Author of books for boys. Pen name, "Harry Castlemon." The *Gunboat* series (1864–68); the *Rocky Mountain* series (1868–71); the *Rod and Gun* series (1883–84); etc.

FOSDICK, HARRY EMERSON (May 24, 1878–Oct. 6, 1969); b. Buffalo, N.Y., brother of Raymond Blaine Fosdick. Baptist clergyman, author. *The Second Mile* (1908); *The Meaning of Prayer* (1915); *The Meaning of Faith* (1917); *Adventurous Religion* (1926); *A Pilgrimage to Palestine* (1927); *As I See Religion* (1932); *Successful Christian Living* (1937); *Living Under Tension* (1941); *On Being a Real Person* (1943); *A Great Time to Be Alive* (1944); *On Being Fit to Live With* (1946); *The Man from Nazareth* (1949); *A Faith for Tough Times* (1952); *The Living of These Days* (autobiography, 1956); *Dear Mr. Brown: Letters to a Person Perplexed about Religion* (1961); etc.

FOSDICK, RAYMOND BLAINE (June 9, 1883–); b. Buffalo, N.Y., brother of Harry Emerson Fosdick. Executive, lawyer, author. *European Police Systems* (1915); *American Police Systems* (1920); *The Old Savage in the New Civilization* (1928); *The Story of the Rockefeller Foundation* (1952); *Within Our Power* (1952); *John D. Rockefeller, Jr.: A Portrait* (1956); *A Chronicle of a Generation* (autobiography, 1958); *Adventure in Giving* (1962); *Letters on the League of Nations* (1966); etc. Compiler: *Princeton Verse* (1904). President, The Rockefeller Foundation and General Education Board, 1936–48.

FOSDICK, WILLIAM WHITEMAN (Jan. 28, 1825–Mar. 8, 1862); b. Cincinnati, O. Novelist, poet. *Malmiztic the Toltec* (1851); *Ariel, and Other Poems* (1855).

FOSS, MARTIN MOORE (June 3, 1878–); b. Lewiston, Me. Publisher. With Baker & Taylor Co., New York, 1901–07; one of the founders of McGraw-Hill Book Co., New York, in 1909 and later president.

FOSS, SAM WALTER (June 19, 1858–Feb. 26, 1911); b. Candia, N.H. Librarian, journalist, humorist, poet. *Back Country Poems* (1894); *Whiffs From Wild Meadows* (1895); *Dreams in Homespun* (1897), which contains his best known poem, "The House by the Side of the Road"; *Songs of the Average Man* (1907); etc. Editor, *Yankee Blade*, Boston, Mass., 1887–94. Librarian, Somerville (Mass.) Public Library, 1898–1911.

FOSTER, AGNESS GREENE (1863–Sept. 12, 1933); b. Athens, Ala. Poet. *By the Way: Travel Letters* (1903); *The Weaving of Life's Fabric* (1907); *Your Happy Way, and Other Verse for Occasions* (1924); etc.

FOSTER, ARDEEN [Jones] (Oct. 14, 1862–deceased); b. Franklin, Mich. Author. *The Poetical Works of Ardeen Foster* (1892); *Broken Barriers* (1893); *The Reign of John Rudd* (1906); etc.

FOSTER, CHARLES JAMES (Nov. 24, 1820–Sept. 12, 1883); b. Bicester, Oxford, England. Sports writer. *The White Horse of Wootton* (1878). Editor, *Wilkes' Spirit of the Times*, New York, 1860–74; co-founder, *New York Sportsman*, 1875.

FOSTER, DAVID SKAATS (Jan. 23, 1852–June 23, 1920); b. Utica, N.Y. Novelist, poet. *The Romance of the Unexpected* (1887), republished as *Rebecca the Witch, and Other Tales* (1888); *Casanova the Courier* (1892); *Elinor Fenton* (1893); *Flighty Arethusa* (1910).

FOSTER, EDNA [Abigail] (d. July 11, 1945); b. Sullivan Harbor, Me. Editor, author. *Hortense, a Difficult Child* (1902); *Cordelia's Pathway Out* (1905); *Barbara's Bridge* (1917).

FOSTER, GENEVIEVE [Stump] (1893–). Author. *George Washington's World* (1941); *Abraham Lincoln's World* (1944); *Augustus Caesar's World* (1947); *Abraham Lincoln* (1949); *George Washington* (1949); *Theodore Roosevelt* (1954); *The World of Captain John Smith* (1959); *The World of Columbus and Sons* (1965); *The Year of Columbus, 1492* (1969); *The Year of the Pilgrims, 1620* (1969); etc.

FOSTER, GEORGE G. (d. 1850). Author. *The French Revolution of 1848* (with Thomas Dunn English, 1848); *The Gold Regions of California* (1848); *Memoir of Jenny Lind* (1850); *New York in Slices* (anon., 1850); *Celio; or, New York Above Ground and Under-Ground* (1850); *New York by Gas-Light* (1850); *Fifteen Minutes Around New York* (1854); etc. Editor: *The Poetical Works of Percy Bysshe Shelley* (1845).

FOSTER, HANNAH WEBSTER (1759–Apr. 17, 1840); b. Boston, Mass. Novelist. *The Coquette; or, The History of Eliza Wharton* (anon., 1797); *The Boarding School* (1798). See her daughters, Harriet Vaughan Foster Cheney and Eliza Lanesford Foster Cushing.

FOSTER, HARRY LA TOURETTE (Oct. 31, 1894–Mar. 15, 1932); b. Brooklyn, N.Y. Traveler, author. *The Adventures of a Tropical Tramp* (1922); *A Gringo in Mañana-Land* (1924); *Combing the Caribbees* (1929); etc.

FOSTER, JEANNE ROBERT (Mrs. Matlack Foster) (Mar. 10, 1884–); b. Johnsborough, N.Y. Editor, poet. *Wild Apples* (1916); *Neighbors of Yesterday* (1916); *Rock Flower* (1922). Lit. editor, *Review of Reviews*, 1910–22.

FOSTER, JOHN WATSON (Mar. 2, 1836–Nov. 15, 1917); b. Pike County, Ind. Diplomat, editor, author. *A Century of American Diplomacy . . . 1776–1876* (1900); *American Diplomacy in the Orient* (1904); *Diplomatic Memoirs* (1909); etc. U.S. minister to Mexico, 1873–80; Russia, 1880–81; Spain, 1883–85.

FOSTER, MAXIMILIAN (Feb. 27, 1872–); b. San Francisco, Cal. Journalist, novelist, playwright. *In the Forest* (1902); *The Whistling Man* (1913); *Smoke* (prod. 1919); *Humdrum House* (1924).

FOSTER, STEPHEN COLLINS (July 4, 1826–Jan. 13, 1864); b. Pittsburgh, Pa. Author of songs and ballads. Best known are "Nelly Was a Lady" (1849); "The Old Folks at Home" (1851); "Massa's in the Cold Ground (1852); "My Old Kentucky Home" (1853); "Old Dog Tray" (1853); "Old Black Joe" (1860); "Oh! Susanna" (1848). Many of his songs were popularized by E. P. Christy, the minstrel. See H. V. Milligan's *Stephen Collins Foster* (1920); and John Tasker Howard's *Stephen Foster: America's Troubadour* (1934); Raymond Walters's *Stephen Foster* (1936). Josiah Lilly, of Indianapolis, made a notable collection of Fosteriana, and built a Foster memorial in Pittsburgh.

FOSTER, THEODOSIA MARIA TOLL (1838–deceased); b. Verona, N.Y. Author. Pen name, "Faye Huntington." *Echoing and Re-Echoing* (1878); *Millerton People* (1884); *Lewis Elmore, Crusader* (1898); *A Break in Schedule Time* (1901); *Opportunity Circle* (1901).

FOSTER, W[alter] **BERT**[ram] (Nov. 3, 1869–Apr. 26, 1929); b. Providence, R.I. Author. *The Lost Galleon* (1901); *With Ethan Allen at Ticonderoga* (1903); *The Ocean Express* (1913); etc.

FOSTER, WILLIAM ZEBULON (Feb. 25, 1881–Sept. 1, 1961); b. Taunton, Mass. Communist Party leader, author. *The Great Steel Strike and Its Lessons* (1920); *Toward Soviet America* (1932); *From Bryan to Stalin* (1937); *Pages from a Worker's Life* (1939); *American Trade Unionism* (1947); *History of the Communist Party of the United States* (1952); *History of the Three Internationals* (1955); etc.

FOUGNER, G. SELMER (Aug. 24, 1884–Apr. 2, 1941); b. Chicago, Ill. Journalist, epicure, author. *Along the Wine Trail* (1935); *Dining Out in New York* (1939). Wrote column, "Along the Wine Trail" in the *New York Sun* 1933–41.

FOULKE, WILLIAM DUDLEY (Nov. 20, 1848–May 30, 1935); b. New York City. Poet, novelist. *Maya: A Story of Yucatan* (1900); *Lyrics of War and Peace* (1916); *A Hoosier Autobiography* (1922); *To-Day and Yesterday* (poems, 1920); *Songs of Eventide* (poems, 1928); etc.

Founding of New England, The. By James Truslow Adams (1921). One of the first American histories written from the popular, rather than the formal textbook approach. Won the Pulitzer prize for history (1922).

Fountain, and Other Poems. By William Cullen Bryant (1842).

Fountainhead, The. Novel by Ayn Rand (1943). Concerns the artistic integrity of an architect who fights against the pressures of conventional thinking.

Four Million, The. By O. Henry (1906). A social satire, based on the fashionable set, the exclusive "four hundred," with the inference that the poor and underprivileged be taken into consideration.

Four Quartets. Sequence of poems by T. S. Eliot (1943). It comprises "Burnt Norton," "East Coker," "The Dry Salvages," and "Little Gidding."

Four Saints in Three Acts. Opera, produced in 1934, with libretto by Gertrude Stein and music by Virgil Thomson.

"Four-leaf Clover, The." Poem by Ella Higginson; set to music by Leila M. Brownell. The first line is "I know a place where the sun is like gold."

Fourteen to One. Short stories by Elizabeth Stuart Phelps (1891).

FOWLE, DANIEL (Oct. 1715–June 8, 1787); b. Charlestown, Mass. Printer, pamphleteer. *A Total Eclipse of Liberty* (1755). Printer (with Gamaliel Rogers) of *Boston Weekly Magazine,* beginning Mar. 2, 1743, and the *American Magazine and Historical Chronicle,* 1743–48. Founder, *New Hampshire Gazette,* Portsmouth, Oct. 7, 1756.

FOWLER, CHARLES HENRY (Aug. 11, 1837–Mar. 20, 1908); b. Burford (now Clarendon), Ont. Methodist bishop, educator, editor, author. *Missions and World Movements* (1903); *Addresses on Public Occasions* (1908); *Patriotic Orations* (1910); etc. Editor, the *Christian Advocate,* 1876–80. President, Northwestern University, 1873–76.

FOWLER, GENE (1890–July 2, 1960); b. Denver, Colo. Author. *Trumpet in the Dust* (1930); *Shoe the Wild Mare* (1931); *The Great Mouthpiece* (1931); *Timberline* (1933); *Father Goose* (1934); *Salute to Yesterday* (1937); *Illusion in Java* (1939); *Good Night, Sweet Prince* (1944); *A Solo in Tom-Toms* (1946); *Beau James* (1949); *Schnozzola* (1951).

FOWLER, GENE (Oct. 5, 1931–   ) b. Oakland, Cal. Author. *Field Studies* (1965); *Shaman Songs* (1967).

FOWLER, HENRY THATCHER (Mar. 4, 1867–Jan. 23, 1948); b. Fishkill, N.Y. Educator, author. *Studies in Wisdom Literature of the Old Testament* (1907); *History of the Literature of Ancient Israel* (1912); *Great Leaders of Hebrew History* (1920); *The History and Literature of the New Testament* (1925); *General Knox and His Home in Maine* (1931); etc. Prof. Biblical literature, Brown University, 1901–34.

Fowler and Wells Co. Boston, Mass. Publishers. Founded by Orson Squire Fowler (1809–87) and Lorenzo Niles Fowler (1811–96). In 1844 the Fowlers took in as partner S. R. Wells. Fowler and Wells went out of business in 1863. They published phrenological books. They also published, without their imprint, the second edition of Whitman's *Leaves of Grass,* which bore Emerson's testimonial.

FOWLIE, WALLACE (Nov. 8, 1908–); b. Brookline, Mass. Educator, author. *From Chartered Land* (1938); *Clowns and Angels* (1943); *Spirit of France: Studies in Modern French Literature* (1944); *Rimbaud* (1946); *Jacob's Night* (1947); *The Clown's Grail* (1948); *Sleep of the Pigeon* (1948); *Age of Surrealism* (1950); *Pantomime* (autobiography 1951); *Mallarmé* (1953); *Rimbaud's Illuminations: A Study in Angelism* (1953); *Guide to Contemporary French Literature* (1957); *André Gide: His Life and Art* (1965); *Rimbaud* (1966); *Climate of Violence: The French Literary Tradition from Baudelaire to the Present* (1967); *The French Critic, 1549–1967* (1968); *Stendhal* (1969); etc. Editor: *Mid-Century French Poets* (1956); etc. Translator: *Two Dramas of Claudel* (1960).

FOX, DIXON RYAN (Dec. 7, 1887–Jan. 30, 1945); b. Potsdam, N.Y. Educator, historian. *Caleb Heathcote, Gentleman Colonial* (1926); *Ideas in Motion* (1935); *Yankees and Yorkers* (1940); etc. Co-author: *Aspects of Social History* (1931); *The Completion of Independence* (with J. A. Krout, 1943). Editor: *History of American Life,* 12v. (with A. M. Schleisinger, 1927); *History of the State of New York,* 10v. (1933); *A Quarter Century of Learning* (1931). Editor: *Sources of Culture in the Middle West* (1934); *Columbia University Quarterly,* 1930–34; *Croft's American History Series* from 1932; etc. President, Union College, from 1934.

FOX, FONTAINE [Talbot], JR. (June 4, 1884–Aug. 9, 1964); b. Louisville, Ky. Cartoonist. *Fontaine Fox's Funny Folk* (1917); *Toonerville Trolley and Other Cartoons* (1921); etc. Creator of "Toonerville Folks" and the "Toonerville Trolley" syndicated comic cartoons.

FOX, FRANCES MARGARET (June 23, 1870–); b. S. Framingham, Mass. Author. *Farmer Brown and the Birds* (1900); *The Rainbow Bridge* (1905); the *Little Bear* series, 11v. (1915–28); *The Little Cat That Could Not Sleep* (1941); etc.

FOX, GENEVIEVE (Mrs. Raymond G. Fuller) (d. Oct. 5, 1959); b. Southampton, Mass. Editor, author. *Mountain Girl* (1932); *Mountain Girl Comes Home* (1934); *Lona of Hollybush Creek* (1935); *Susan of the Green Mountains* (1937); *Border Girl* (1939); *Army Surgeon* (1944); *Cynthia of Bee Tree Hollow* (1948); *Bonnie, Island Girl* (1954).

FOX, JOHN [William], JR. (Dec. 16, 1863–July 8, 1919); b. Stony Point, Ky. Novelist. *A Cumberland Vendetta, and Other Stories* (1896); *"Hell fer Sartain," and Other Stories* (1897); *The Kentuckians* (1898); *A Mountain Europa* (1899); *Crittenden* (1900); *Blue Grass and Rhododendron* (1901); *The Little Shepherd of Kingdom Come* (1903); *Christmas Eve on Lonesome, and Other Stories* (1904); *Following the Sun-Flag* (1905); *A Knight of the Cumberland* (1906); *The Trail of the Lonesome Pine* (1908); *The Heart of the Hills* (1913); *In Happy Valley* (1917); *Erskine Dale, Pioneer* (1920).

FOX, NORMAN ARNOLD (May 26, 1911–Mar. 24, 1960); b. Sault Ste Marie, Mich. Author. *Gunsight Kid* (1941); *Six-Gun Syndicate* (1942); *Thundering Trail* (1944); *Dead End Trail* (1946); *Phantom Spur* (1950); *Night Passage* (1956); *Rope the Wind* (1958); etc. The television series "Gunsmoke" was adapted from his novel *Rough Shod* (1951).

FOX, WALTER DENNIS (July 4, 1867–Dec. 8, 1911); b. near Murfreesboro, Tenn. Editor, author. *Sam Davis, the Confederate Scout* (1896); *The Harlequin of Dreams* (1901); *Jean Lafitte* (1903); etc.

FOXCROFT, FRANK (Jan. 21, 1850–Dec. 10, 1921); b. Boston, Mass. Editor, poet. *Transcript Pieces* (poems, 1868). Editor: *Resurgit: A Collection of Hymns and Songs of the Resurrection* (1879); *War Verse* (1918). Editor: *The Boston Journal,* 1871–1904; *Littell's Living Age,* 1896–1918.

FRALEY, OSCAR (1914–). Journalist, author. *Golf in Action* (with Charles Yerkow, 1952); *Pictorial Guide to Casting and Spinning* (with same, 1954); *Untouchables* (with Eliot Ness, 1957); *Complete Handbook of Bowling* (with Charles Yerkow, 1958); *The All-Star Athletes Cook Book* (with David Huntley, 1965); *Four Against the Mob* (1968); etc.

FRANCE, LEWIS (Apr. 8, 1833–1907); b. Washington, D.C. Lawyer, author. *Rod and Line* (1884); *Mountain Trails and Peaks in Colorado* (1887); *Mr. Dido: His Vacation in Colorado; and Other Sketches* (1890); *Pine Valley* (1891); *Over the Old Trail* (1895); *Scraps* (1899); *No Stranger to My Neighbor* (1906).

Francesca. See Francesca Alexander.

Francesca Da Rimini. Play by George Henry Boker (prod. 1855). A tragic love story, based on a brief episode in Dante's "Inferno."

FRANCIS, CHARLES STEPHEN (Jan. 9, 1805–Dec. 1, 1887); b. Boston, Mass. Book-seller and publisher. Son of David Francis, of the Boston publishing firm of Munroe & Francis. Charles S. Francis opened a book store on Broadway, New York, in 1826. Among his patrons was Aaron Burr, DeWitt Clinton and James Audubon. Francis printed the American edition of Audubon's *Birds of America.* He was also the first publisher of Shakespeare's works in America, and of the *Mother Goose Melodies.* A popular success was Mrs. Kirkland's *A New Home—Who'll Follow?* The firm dissolved in 1860.

FRANCIS, JOHN, JR. (May 6, 1875–Jan. 2, 1954); b. Iola, Kans. Author. *The Triumph of Virginia Dale* (1921); *The Successful Mr. Bagley* (1926).

FRANCIS, JOHN WAKEFIELD (Nov. 17, 1789–Feb. 8, 1861); b. New York City. Physician, author. *Old New York; or, Reminiscences of the Past Sixty Years* (1858).

FRANCIS, JOSEPH GREENE (Apr. 21, 1849–deceased); b. Boston, Mass. Author of books for children. *A Book of Cheerful Cats and Other Animated Animals* (1892); *The Joyous Aztecs* (1929).

FRANCIS, ROBERT (1901–). Poet. *Stand With Me Here* (1936); *Valhalla and Other Poems* (1938); *The Sound I Listened For* (1943); *We Fly Away* (1948); *The Orb Weaver* (1960); *Come Out Into The Sun* (1965); *The Satirical Rogue on Poetry* (1968); etc.

FRANCIS, SAMUEL WARD (Dec. 26, 1835–Mar. 25, 1886); b. New York City. Physician, inventor, essayist, novelist. *Inside Out* (1862); *Life and Death: A Novel* (1871); etc.

Francis Berrian; or, The Mexican Patriot. Novel by Timothy Flint, 2v. (1826). An early evangelical tale that mingles pioneer adventure with religious zeal.

FRANCK, FREDERICK SIGFRED (Apr. 12, 1909–); b. Maastricht, Neth. Artist, dental surgeon, author. *Au Pays du Soleil* (with Louise Bégué, 1958); *Days with Albert Schweitzer* (1959); *African Sketchbook* (1961); *My Eye Is in Love* (1963); *Outsider in the Vatican* (1965); *I Love Life* (1967); *Exploding Church* (1968); *Croquis Parisien* (1969).

FRANCK, HARRY ALVERSON (June 29, 1881–Apr. 17, 1962); b. Munger, Mich. Traveler, author. *A Vagabond Journey around the World* (1910); *Four Months Afoot in Spain* (1911); *Zone Policeman 88* (1913); *Tramping through Mexico, Guatemala and Honduras* (1916); *Vagabonding Down the Andes* (1917); *Vagabonding through Changing Germany* (1919); *Roaming through the West Indies* (1920); *Working North from Patagonia* (1921); *Wandering in Northern China* (1923); *Glimpses of Japan and Formosa* (1924); *Roving through Southern China* (1925); *East of Siam* (1926); *The Fringe of the Moslem World* (1928); *I Discover Greece* (1929); *A Scandinavian Summer* (1930); *Marco Polo, Junior* (1930); *Foot-Loose in the British Isles* (1932); *A Vagabond in Sovietland* (1935); *Trailing Cortez through Mexico* (1935); *Roaming in Hawaii* (1937); *Sky Roaming above Two Continents* (1938); *The Lure of Alaska* (1939); *The Pan American Highway* (1940); *Rediscovering South America* (1943).

FRANCKE, KUNO (Sept. 27, 1855–June 25, 1930); b. Kiel, Germany. Educator, historian, essayist, poet. *Social Forces in German Literature* (1896), republished as, *A History of German Literature as Determined by Social Forces* (1901); *A German-American's Confession of Faith* (1915); *The German Spirit* (1916); *Deutsches Schicksal* (poems, 1923); *Deutsche Arbeit in Amerika* (autobiography, 1930); and many books in German. German dept., Harvard University, 1884–1917.

Franco, Harry. Pen name of Charles Frederick Briggs.

FRANK, BRUNO (June 13, 1887–June 20, 1945); b. Stuttgart, Ger. Author. *The Days of the King* (1927); *Trenck* (1928); *Twelve Thousand* (play, 1928); *The Persians Are Coming* (1929); *A Man Called Cervantes* (1934); *Lost Heritage* (1937); *Storm in a Teacup* (1938); *Young Madame Conti* (1938); *One Fair Daughter* (1943); *The Magician* (short stories, 1946); etc.

FRANK, GLENN (Oct. 1, 1887–Sept. 15, 1940); b. Queen City, Mo. Educator, publicist, author. *An American Looks at His World* (1923); *Thunder and Dawn: The Outlook for Western Civilization* (1932); etc. Assoc. editor, *Century Magazine,* 1919–21; editor-in-chief, 1921–25. President, University of Wisconsin, 1925–37.

FRANK, JOSEPH (Dec. 20, 1916–); b. Chicago, Ill. Educator, author. *The Levellers* (1955); *The Beginnings of the English Newspaper* (1961); *The Widening Gyre: Crisis and Mastery in Modern Literature* (1963); *Modern Essays in English* (1966). Editor: *Horizons of a Philosopher* (1963); *Hobbled Pegasus: A Descriptive Bibliography of Minor English Poetry* (1968). Faculty, University of Rochester, since 1948.

FRANK, TENNEY (May 19, 1876–Apr. 3, 1939); b. Clay Center, Kan. Educator, author. *Roman Imperialism* (1914); *Economic History of Rome* (1920); *Vergil: A Biography* (1922); *A History of Rome* (1923); *Catullus and Horace* (1928); *Life and Literature in the Roman Republic* (1930); etc. Prof. Latin, Johns Hopkins University, 1919–38.

FRANK, WALDO [David] (Aug. 25, 1889–Jan. 9, 1967); b. Long Branch, N.J. Critic, novelist. *The Unwelcome Man* (1917); *Our America* (1919); *City Block* (1922); *Salvos* (1924); *Chalk Face* (1924); *Virgin Spain* (1926); *The Re-Discovery of America* (1929); *In the American Jungle* (1937); *The Bridegroom Cometh* (1938); *Chart for Rough Water* (1940); *The Jew in Our Day* (1944); *The Island in the Atlantic* (1946); *The Invaders* (1948); *Not Heaven* (1953); *Bridgehead, the Drama of Israel* (1957); *The Rediscovery of Man* (1958); *Cuba: Prophetic Island* (1961); etc. Co-author, *The American Caravan* (1928); *America and Alfred Stieglitz* (1934). Editor, *Plays of Molière* (1924); *Tales From the Argentine* (1930). Co-founder, *Seven Arts,* 1916; editor, 1916–17.

Frank Leslie's Boys of America. New York. A weekly. Founded 1863. Title later changed to *Frank Leslie's Boys' and Girls' Weekly.* Ceased 1878.

Frank Leslie's Budget of Fun. New York. A comic monthly. Founded 1858. Ceased 1896.

Frank Leslie's Illustrated Newspaper. New York. Founded 1855. Ceased 1922. See *Leslie's Weekly.*

Frank Leslie's Ladies' Gazette of Fashion and Fancy Needlework. New York City. Illustrated monthly. Founded Jan. 1854. Its name was changed to *Frank Leslie's Gazette of Fashions and the Beau Monde* in 1855. Editors: Ann S. Stephens, 1854–56; Frank Leslie, 1856–57. Expired Aug. 1857.

Frank Leslie's New York Journal of Romance, General Literature, Science, and Art. New York. Founded 1853. An outgrowth of *The New York Journal,* which Leslie purchased in 1854. Merged with *Mrs. Stephens Illustrated New Monthly* in 1858.

Frank Leslie's Pleasant Hours. New York. An illustrated fiction monthly. Founded 1866. It grew out of *Frank Leslie's New Monthly,* which in turn had sprung from *Frank Leslie's Ten-Cent Monthly,* founded 1863. Ceased 1896.

Frank Leslie's Popular Monthly. New York. Founded 1876, by Frank Leslie, who by that time had already founded eight other magazines. Name changed in 1904 to *Frank Leslie's Magazine;* in 1905 to *American Illustrated Magazine.* In 1906 it was purchased by a group of Muckrakers, headed by John S. Phillips, and the name was changed to *The American Magazine* (q.v.).

FRANKAU, PAMELA (1908–June 8, 1967); b. in England. Author. *Marriage of Harlequin* (1927); *Three* (1929); *I Find Four People* (1935); *The Devil We Know* (1939); *Appointment with Death* (1940); *Shaken in the Wind* (1948); *A Wreath for the Enemy* (1954); *The Bridge* (1957); *Ask Me No More* (1958); *Road through the Woods* (1960); *Pen to Paper: A Novelist's Notebook* (1962); *Slaves of the Lamp* (1964); etc.

FRANKEL, CHARLES (Dec. 13, 1917–); b. New York. Educator, author. *The Faith of Reason* (1948); *The Case for Modern Man* (1956); *The Power of the Democratic Idea* (1960); *The Love of Anxiety, and Other Essays* (1965); *The Neglected Aspect of Foreign Affairs* (1966); *Education and the Barricades* (1968); *High on Foggy Bottom* (1969); etc. Editor: *The Uses of Philosophy* (1955); *Issues in University Education* (1959); etc. Philosophy dept., Columbia University.

FRANKEN, ROSE [D.] (Mrs. William Brown Meloney) (1898–); b. in Texas. Novelist, playwright. *Pattern* (1925); *Another Language* (prod. 1932); *Mr. Dooley, Jr.* (with Jane Lewis, publ. 1932, prod. 1935); *Twice Born* (1935); *Of Great Riches* (1937); *Claudia* (1939); *Claudia and David* (1940); *Outrageous Fortune* (prod. 1944); *Soldier's Wife* (prod. 1945); *The Hallams* (1947); *From Claudia to David* (1950); *The Fragile Years* (1952); *Rendezvous* (1954); *Third Person Intimate* (1955); *The Antic Years* (1958); *Claudia Omnibus* (1958); *You're Well Out of a Hospital;* etc. Under pen name "Margaret Grant": *Call Back Love* (1938). Under pen name "Franken Meloney": *Strange Victory* (1939); *When Doctors Disagree* (1940); *American Bred* (1941).

FRANKENBERG, LLOYD (Sept. 3, 1907–); b. Mt. Vernon, N.Y. Author. *The Red Kite* (poems, 1939); *Pleasure Dome: On Reading Modern Poetry* (1949). Editor: *Invitation to Poetry* (1956); *James Seumas and Jaques: Unpublished Writings of James Stephens* (1964); etc.

FRANKENSTEIN, ALFRED VICTOR (Oct. 5, 1906–); b. Chicago, Ill. Author. *Two Journeymen Painters* (with A. K. D. Healy, 1950); *After the Hunt: William Harnett and Other American Still Life Painters, 1870–1900* (1953); *Angels Over the Altar* (1962); *The Royal Visitors* (1963); *A Modern Guide to Symphonic Literature* (1967).

FRANKFURTER, FELIX (Nov. 15, 1882–Feb. 22, 1965); b. Vienna. Jurist, educator, author. *The Business of the Supreme Court* (1927); *Law and Politics: Occasional Papers* (1939); *Mr. Justice Holmes and the Supreme Court* (1939); *Of Law and Men* (1956); *Felix Frankfurter Reminisces* (with Harlen B. Phillips, 1960); etc. Editor: *Mr. Justice Holmes* (1931); *Mr. Justice Brandeis* (1932). Prof. Harvard Law School, 1914–39; Associate Justice of the Supreme Court of the United States, 1939–1962.

"Frankie and Johnny." Modern American ballad. The refrain is, "He was her man, but he done her wrong." Frankie avenged the wrong by shooting her lover. See *The American Songbag,* ed. by Carl Sandburg (1927).

FRANKLIN, BENJAMIN (Jan. 17, 1706–Apr. 17, 1790); b. Boston, Mass. Printer, inventor, statesman, diplomat, author. *A Dissertation on Liberty and Necessity, Pleasure and Pain* (1725); *The Autobiography of Benjamin Franklin* (1868); (q.v.); etc. Compiler: *Poor Richard's Almanack,* 26v. (1732–57). See *Memoirs of the Life and Writings of Benjamin Franklin,* ed. by Temple Franklin, 6v. (1818); *The Works of Benjamin Franklin,* ed. by Jared Sparks, 10v. (1836–40); *The Complete Works of Benjamin Franklin,* ed. by John Bigelow, 10v. (1887–88); *The Writings of Benjamin Franklin,* ed. by

Albert Henry Smythe, 10v. (1905–07); *The Papers of Benjamin Franklin,* ed. by Leonard W. Labaree, Vols. I–X (1959–65). The Curtis Collection of Franklin Imprints was given to the University of Pennsylvania by the Curtis Publishing Co. in 1920. See William J. Campbell's *The Collection of Franklin Imprints in the Museum of the Curtis Publishing Co.* (1918). Among early plays based on the life of Franklin are: *The Apotheosis of Franklin* (anon., 1796); *Americana; or, A New Tale of the Genii* (anon., 1798); John Brougham's *Franklin* (prod. 1846). See Paul Leicester Ford's *Franklin Bibliography* (1889); W. Cabell Bruce's *Benjamin Franklin,* 2v. (1918); Bernard Faÿ's *Franklin* (1929); V. W. Crane's *Benjamin Franklin* (1936); Carl Van Doren's *Benjamin Franklin* (1938); Carl Becker's *Benjamin Franklin* (1946); Ralph Ketcham's *Benjamin Franklin* (1965); Paul W. Conner's *Poor Richard's Politics: Benjamin Franklin and his New America* (1965). The *Franklin Papers* are being published by Yale University Press under the editorship of Leonard W. Labaree and others.

FRANKLIN, JAMES (Feb. 4, 1696/7–Feb. 1735); b. Boston, Mass., brother of Benjamin Franklin. Printer. Founder, *The New England Courant,* Boston, Mass., Aug. 7, 1721; editor, 1721–26; founder, the *Rhode Island Gazette,* Newport, Sept., 1732. First printer in the Province of Rhode Island.

FRANKLIN, JOHN HOPE (Jan. 2, 1915–); b. Rentiesville, Okla. Educator, author. *Free Negro in North Carolina* (1943); *From Slavery to Freedom: A History of American Negroes* (1947); *Militant South* (1956); *Reconstruction after the Civil War* (1961); *The Emancipation Proclamation* (1963); *Land of the Free* (1966). Prof. history, Howard University, 1947–56; Brooklyn College, since 1956.

Franklin Evans; or, The Inebriate. Novel by Walt Whitman (1842).

Franklin Inn Club. Philadelphia, Pa. Founded 1902. A literary society limited to one hundred members. S. Weir Mitchell was its first president.

Franklin Square Library. A series of cheap reprints of popular novels, inaugurated by Harper & Brothers, in 1878. Discontinued with No. 759, April, 1895.

Franny and Zooey. Two stories in book form, by J. D. Salinger (1961). Franny Glass, in the first story, spends a week-end college date with her boyfriend. In the second story she is aided to a solution of her problems in life by her brother Zooey.

FRANTZ, JOE BERTRAM (Jan. 16, 1917–); Author. *Gail Borden: Dairyman to a Nation* (1951); *The American Cowboy* (with J. E. Choate, 1955); *6,000 Miles of Fence* (1961); *Readings in American History* (1964); *Three Historians on the American Frontier* (1965); *Violence in America* (1969).

FRASCONI, ANTONIO (Apr. 28, 1919–); b. Montevideo, Uruguay. Artist, author. *See and Say* (1955); *Frasconi Woodcuts* (1957); *The House that Jack Built* (1958); *The Neighboring Shore* (film, 1960); *Known Fables* (1964); *The Cantilever Rainbow* (1965); *Kaleidoscope in Woodcuts* (1968). Art dept., New School for Social Research, 1951–57.

FRASER, CHELSEA CURTIS (Aug. 28, 1876–Nov. 7, 1954); b. New Sarum, Ont. Author. *Good Old Chums* (1911); *The Boy Hikers* (1918); *Boys' Book of Sea Fights* (1920); *Heroes of the Wilds* (1923); *Heroes of the Sea* (1924); *Heroes of the Air* (1926); *Heroes of the Farthest North and Farthest South* (1930); *Famous American Flyers* (1941); *Silver Strings* (1952); etc.

FRASER, RUSSELL ALFRED (May 31, 1927–); b. Elizabeth, N.J. Educator, author. *Shakespeare's Poetics* (1962). Editor: *The Court of Venus* (1955); *The Court of Virtue* (1961); *King Lear* (1963); *Oscar Wilde* (1969). Prof. English, Vanderbilt University, since 1965.

FRAZER, ELIZABETH (d. May 12, 1967); b. Upper Lake, Cal. Novelist. *Old Glory and Verdun, and Other Stories* (1918); *The Secret Partner* (1922); etc.

FRAZER, WILLIAM HENRY (Sept. 10, 1873–June 19, 1953); b. Lafayette, Ala. Educator, author. *The Possumist and Other Stories* (1924); *Fireside Musings of Uncle Rastus and Aunt Randy* (1925); *Challenging Mantles* (1925). President, Queens College, Charlotte, N.C. from 1921.

FRAZIER, EDWARD FRANKLIN (Sept. 24, 1894–May 17, 1962); b. Baltimore, Md. Educator, author. *The Negro Family in Chicago* (1932); *The Negro Family in the United States* (1939); *The Negro in the United States* (1949); *Black Bourgeoisie* (1957).

Freckles. Novel by Gene Stratton Porter (1904). Story of a waif in the Indiana swamplands, who triumphs over adversity.

FREDE, RICHARD (Mar. 20, 1934–); b. Albany, N.Y. Author. *The Interns* (1960); *The Secret Circus* (1967); *Coming Out Party* (1969).

FREDERIC, HAROLD (Aug. 19, 1856–Oct. 19, 1898); b. Utica, N.Y. Journalist, novelist. *Seth's Brother's Wife* (1887); *The Lawton Girl* (1890); *In the Valley* (1890); *The Return of the O'Mahoney* (1892); *The Copperhead* (1893); *Marsens, and Other Stories* (1894); *The Damnation of Theron Ware* (1896); *March Hares* (1896); *Gloria Mundi* (1898); *The Market Place* (1899).

FREDERICK, JOHN TOWNER (Feb. 1, 1893–); b. Corning, Ia. Editor, author. *Druida* (1923); *Green Bush* (1925); *The Darkened Sky: Nineteenth-Century American Novelists and Religion* (1969). Editor: *Stories from the Midland* (1924); *Present-Day Stories* (1941); *Out of the Midwest* (1944). Founder, *The Midland,* 1915; editor, 1915–33.

FREDERICK, J[ustus] GEORGE (Jan. 14, 1882–); b. Reading, Pa. Author. *Modern Sales Management* (1918); *Humanism as a Way of Life* (1930); *The Pennsylvania Dutch and Their Cookery* (1935); *Standard Business Etiquette* (1937); *The New Deal: A People's Capitalism* (1944); *Introduction to Motivation Research* (1957); etc. Compiler, co-editor: *The Technique of Marketing Research* (1937).

Frederick de Algeroy, the Hero of Camden Plains. Novel by "Giles Gazer, Esq." (1825). Author unknown. A story of the American Revolution.

Fredericks, Arnold. Pen name of Frederic Arnold Kummer.

Free Joe and the Rest of the World. Story by Joel Chandler Harris (1884).

Free verse. Often called *"vers libre"* and sometimes "polyrhythmic." verse." A kind of verse without rhyme distinguished by irregular patterns and cadence or rhythm. The unit may be either the typographical phrase or line, the natural breath pause, or the stanza. Ancient Hebrew verse, some French verse, and other types of non-Western verse are often "free" in one of these senses. Heinrich Heine, William Ernest Henley, Matthew Arnold, Stephen Crane, Walt Whitman, wrote early types of free verse. In modern times it is associated with the work of the Imagists (q.v.), notably Ezra Pound, Amy Lowell, and "H. D." Other American writers of free verse are Carl Sandburg, William Carlos Williams, and E. E. Cummings. The work of Charles Olson, which he calls "open-field composition," is also free verse. The poets of the Beat Generation brought free verse into prominence again in the 1950's and 1960's, but it has been practiced by numerous poets ever since the early years of the twentieth century.

Free World. New York. Founded 1941. Published in seven separate international editions. Begun as an organ of opinion on world organization. Merged with *United Nations World,* founded 1946. Converted in 1953 into *World,* a monthly of information about international business and politics.

Free World Forum. Washington, D.C. Bi-monthly. Founded 1959. Magazine of foreign affairs.

Free World Review. New York. Monthly. Founded 1955. Concerned with Europeans living in exile.

Freebetter, Edmund. Pen name of Nathan Daboll.

FREEDLEY, GEORGE [Reynolds] (Sept. 5, 1904–Sept. 11, 1967); b. Richmond, Va. Librarian, drama critic, author. *Theatre Collections in Libraries and Museums* (with Rosamund Gilder, 1936); *A History of the Theatre* (with John A. Reeves, 1940); *The Lunts* (1958); etc. Co-editor: *Performing Arts Collections: An International Handbook* (1961). Theatre editor, *Library Journal,* from 1940; drama critic, *Morning Telegraph,* New York City, 1940–49; book editor, from 1949. Organized theatre collection of the New York Public Library in 1931, and became its first curator, 1938.

FREEDMAN, BENEDICT (Dec. 19, 1919–); b. New York. Co-author (with Nancy Freedman): *Mrs. Mike* (1947); *This and No More* (1950); *The Spark and the Exodus* (1954); *Lootville* (1957); *Tresa* (1959); *The Apprentice Bastard* (1967); *Cyclone of Silence* (1969).

FREEDMAN, NANCY [Mars] (July 4, 1920–); b. Evanston, Ill. Co-author, with Benedict Freedman (q.v.), of several novels.

Freedom and Union. Washington, D.C. Monthly. Founded 1946, by Clarence Streit. Devoted to the cause of world government. Contributors and staff have included Stringfellow Barr, Owen J. Roberts, Herbert Agar, Russell Davenport.

Freedom of the Press; an Annotated Bibliography. Edited by Ralph Edward McCoy (1968). Comprehensive treatment including such subjects as heresy, sedition, blasphemy, obscenity, libel.

Freedom Road. Novel by Howard Fast (1944).

Freedom's Journal. New York. Newspaper. Founded 1827, by Samuel Cornish and J. B. Russworm. The first Negro newspaper in America.

FREEMAN, DOUGLAS SOUTHALL (May 16, 1886–June 13, 1953); b. Lynchburg, Va. Editor, author. *Virginia—A Gentle Dominion* (1924); *The Last Parade* (1932); *R. E. Lee,* 4v. (1934–1935, Pulitzer Prize for American biography, 1935); *The South to Posterity* (1939); *Lee's Lieutenants,* 3v. (1942–44); *George Washington* (1948–1957), completed by J. A. Carroll and M. W. Ashworth; Pulitzer Prize for biography, 1958; etc. Editor: *A Calendar of Confederate Papers* (1908); *Lee's Dispatches* (1914). Editor, *The News-Leader,* Richmond, Va. from 1915.

FREEMAN, IRA MAXIMILIAN (1905–). Author. *Invitation to Experiment* (1940); *Fun with Figures* (with Mae B. Freeman, 1946); *Theoretical Physics* (with Georg Joos, 1950); *Modern Introductory Physics* (1950); *Fun with Your Camera* (with Mae B. Freeman, 1955); *Fun with Scientific Experiments* (with Mae B. Freeman, 1960); *All about Light and Radiation* (1965); *The Science of Sound and Ultrasonics* (1968); *The Look-It-Up Book of Space* (1969); *The Water Book: Where It Comes From and Where It Goes* (with Sean Morrison, 1970); etc.

FREEMAN, JOSEPH (Oct. 7, 1897–Aug. 8, 1965); b. in the Ukraine. Editor, author. *Dollar Diplomacy: A Study in American Imperialism* (with Scott Nearing, 1925); *Voices of October* (with others, 1930); *An American Testament* (autobiography, 1936); *Never Call Retreat* (1943); *The Long Pursuit* (1947); etc. Co-founder, *New Masses,* 1926; *Partisan Review,* 1934; editorial board, radio program "Information Please," 1943–45.

FREEMAN, JULIA DEANE. Author. Pen name, "Mary Forrest." *Women of the South Distinguished in Literature* (1861); *Poems* (n.d.).

FREEMAN, LEWIS RANSOME (Oct. 4, 1878–); b. Genoa Junction, Wis. Correspondent. *Stories of the Ships* (1919); *In the Tracks of the Trades* (1920); *Down the Columbia* (1921); *When Cassi Blooms* (1922); *The Colorado River* (1923); *Down the Grand Canyon* (1924); *On the Roof of the Rockies* (1925); *Waterways of Westward Wandering* (1927); *The Nearing North* (1928); *Marquesan Nocturne* (1936); *Mary Rivers* (1937); *Discovering South America* (1937); etc.

FREEMAN, LUCY (Dec. 13, 1916–); b. New York. Author. *Fight Against Fears* (1951); *Hope for the Troubled* (1953); *Before I Kill More* (1955); *Hospital in Action* (1956); *Troubled Women* (1959); *All the Way* (with Ted Atkinson, 1961); *The Abortionist* (1962); *The Wandering Husband* (1964); *Why People Act That Way* (1965); *Lords of Hell* (1967); *The Available Woman* (1968); *The Cry for Love* (1969); etc.

FREEMAN, MARGARET B[arss] (1905–); b. West Orange, N.J. Museum curator, author. *Herbs for the Mediaeval Household* (1943); *The Story of the Three Kings* (1955); *Saint Martin Embroideries* (1968).

FREEMAN, MARY E[leanor] WILKINS (Oct. 31, 1862– Mar. 13, 1930); b. Randolph, Mass. Novelist. *The Adventures of Ann* (1886); *A Humble Romance, and Other Stories* (1887); *A New England Nun, and Other Stories* (1891); *The Pot of Gold, and Other Stories* (1892); *Young Lucretia, and Other Stories* (1892); *Giles Corey* (1892); *Jane Field* (1892); *Pembroke* (1894); *Madelon* (1896); *Jerome* (1897); *Silence, and Other Stories* (1898); *The Jameson's* (1899); *The Heart's Highway* (1900); *The Love of Parson Lord, and Other Stories* (1900); *Understudies* (1901); *The Portion of Labor* (1901); *Six Trees* (1903); *The Wind in the Rose Bush, and Other Stories* (1903); *The Givers* (1904); *"Doc" Gordon* (1906); *By the Light of the Soul* (1907); *The Shoulders of Atlas* (1908); *The Winning Lady, and Others* (1909); *The Green Door* (1910); *The Butterfly House* (1912); *The Yates Pride* (1912); *The Copy-Cat, and Other Stories* (1914); *Edgewater People* (1914); *An Alabaster Box* (with Florence Morse Kingsley, 1917); *The Best Stories*, ed. by Henry W. Lanier (1927); etc.

Freeman, The. New York. Irvington-on-Hudson, N.Y. Monthly. Founded 1920. Edited by Francis Neilson and Albert Jay Nock. Published weekly. Discontinued 1924 but reestablished in 1950 as a biweekly, by Alfred Kohlberg. Suzanne LaFollette and Henry Hazlitt were on its editorial board in the early 1950's. Taken over by the Foundation of Economic Education in 1954. Paul L. Poirot is editor. A journal of ideas about liberty.

FREIDEL, FRANK BURT, JR. (May 22, 1916–); b. Brooklyn, N.Y. Educator, author. *Francis Lieber: Nineteenth-Century Liberal* (1948); *Franklin D. Roosevelt: The Apprenticeship* (1952); *Roosevelt: The Ordeal* (1954); *Roosevelt: The Triumph* (1956); *The Splendid Little War* (1958); *America in the Twentieth Century* (1960); *Over There* (1964); *F. D. R. and the South* (1965); *Our Country's Presidents* (1966). Editor: *Union Pamphlets of the Civil War* (1967). Prof. history, Harvard University, since 1955.

FREIDIN, SEYMOUR KENNETH (Apr. 27, 1917–); b. New York. Columnist, author. *The Forgotten People* (1962); *The Experts* (1968). Co-author: *The Fatal Decisions* (1956). Syndicated foreign affairs columnist, since 1966.

FREMANTLE, ANNE [Jackson] (June, 1910–); b. in Savoy, Fr. Author. *Poems* (1931); *George Eliot* (1931); *Loyal Enemy* (1938); *Come to Dust* (1941); *James and Joan* (1948); *Desert Calling* (1949); *This Little Band of Prophets: The British Fabians* (1959); *Age of Faith* (1965); *The Pilgrimage to People* (1968); etc. Translator: *Lives of the Saints* (1951); etc. Editor: *The Age of Belief* (1955); *Christmas Is Here* (1966); *Christian Conversion: Catholic Thought for Every Day in the Year* (1967); etc.

FREMLIN, CELIA (1914–). Author. *The Hours Before Dawn* (1959); *Uncle Paul* (1960); *Wait for the Wedding* (1961); *Troublemakers* (1963); *The Jealous One* (1965); *Prisoner's Base* (1967); *Possession* (1969).

FRÉMONT, JESSIE BENTON (Mrs. John C. Frémont) (May 31, 1824–Dec. 27, 1902); b. Lexington, Va. Author. *A Year of American Travel* (1878); *The Story of the Guard: A Chronicle of the War* (1863); *Souvenirs of My Time* (1887); *Far-West Sketches* (1890); *The Will and the Way Stories* (1891). See Allan Nevins's *Frémont*, 2v. (1928).

FRÉMONT, JOHN CHARLES (Jan. 21, 1813–July 13, 1890); b. Savannah, Ga. Army officer, explorer, author. *Report of the Exploring Expedition to the Rocky Mountains in the Year 1842, and to Oregon and Northern California in the Years 1843–44* (1845); *Memoirs of My Life* (1887). See Allan Nevins's *Frémont*, 2v. (1928); John Bigelow's *Memoir of the Life and Public Services of John Charles Frémont* (1856); F. S. Dellenbaugh's *Frémont and '49* (1914); LeRoy R. Hafen's and A. W. Hafen's *Frémont's Fourth Expedition* (1960); Fredrika S. Smith's *Frémont: Soldier, Explorer, Statesman* (1966).

Frémont, Mrs. John Charles. See Jessie Benton Frémont.

FRENCH, ALICE (Mar. 19, 1850–Jan. 9, 1934); b. Andover, Mass. Novelist. Pen name, "Octave Thanet." *Knitters in the Sun* (1887); *Expiation* (1890); *Stories of a Western Town* (1893); *Otto the Knight* (1893); *A Book of True Lovers* (1897); *Missionary Sheriff* (1897); *The Heart of Toil* (1898); *A Slave to Duty* (1900); *The Man of the Hour* (1905); *The Lion's Share* (1907); *By Inheritance* (1910); *Stories That End Well* (1911); *A Step on the Stair* (1913); *And the Captain Answered* (1917); etc.

FRENCH, ALLEN (Nov. 28, 1870–Oct. 6, 1946); b. Boston, Mass. Author. *The Junior Cup* (1901); *The Colonials* (1902); *Heroes of Iceland* (1905); *Friend Tim* (1906); *Old Concord* (1915); *At Plattsburgh* (1917); *The Day of Concord and Lexington* (1925); *General Gage's Informers* (1932); *The First Year of the American Revolution* (1934); *The Drama of Concord* (1935); *The Lost Baron* (1940); *Historic Concord* (1942); etc.

French, Anne Warner. See Anne Warner.

FRENCH, JOSEPH LEWIS (Aug. 16, 1858–Dec. 13, 1936); b. New York City. Author. *A Breath of Desire* (poems, 1901); *The Pioneer West* (1923). Editor or compiler: *Great Ghost Stories* (1918); *Great Pirate Stories* (1922); *The Book of the Rogues* (1926); etc.

FRENCH, J[oseph] MILTON (Mar. 7, 1895–Apr. 11, 1962); b. Randolph, Mass. Educator, author. *George Wither's History of the Pestilence* (1932); *Milton in Chancery* (1939); *The Life Records of John Milton*, 5v. (1949–58). Head, English dept., Rutgers University, from 1940.

FRENCH, LILLIE HAMILTON (May 17, 1854–June 3, 1939); b. Washington, D.C. Author. *Hezekiah's Wives* (1902); *My Old Maid's Corner* (1903); *The Joy of Life* (1905); *Mrs. Van Twiller's Salon* (1905).

FRENCH, L[ucy] VIRGINIA SMITH (Mar. 16, 1825–Mar. 31, 1881); b. in Accomac Co., Va. Editor, novelist, poet, essayist. Pen name, "L'Inconnue." *Wind Whispers* (poems, 1856); *Istalixo, the Lady of Tula* (1856); *Legends of the South* (1867); *My Roses* (1872); *Darlingtonia* (1879); *One or Two?* (poems, anon., with sister, Lida Smith Meriwether, 1883).

French, Paul. Pen name of Isaac Asimov.

French, Samuel. Publisher of plays. New York. Firm founded 1830, by Samuel French. Later called S. French & Son. Now Samuel French.

French Traits. Essays by William C. Brownell (1889). A study of the racial and national characteristics of the French people.

FRENEAU, PHILIP [Morin] (Jan. 2, 1752–Dec. 19, 1832); b. New York. Editor, mariner, poet. *The American Village* (1772); *A Poem on the Rising Glory of America* (with Hugh

Henry Brackenridge, anon., 1772); *American Liberty* (anon., 1775); *A Voyage to Boston* (anon., 1775); *General Gage's Confession* (1775); *The British Prison-Ship* (anon., 1781); *The Poems* (1786), republished as *Poems on Various Subjects* (1861); *The Miscellaneous Works* (1788); *Poems Written Between the Years 1768 & 1794* (1795); *Poems Written and Published During the American Revolutionary War*, 2v. (1809); *A Collection of Poems, on American Affairs ... Written Between the Years 1797 and the Present Time*, 2v. (1815); etc. See *Poems Relating to the American Revolution*, ed. by Evert A. Duyckinck (1865); *The Poems of Philip Freneau*, ed. by Fred L. Pattee, 3v. (1902–07); *Poems of Freneau*, ed. by Harry Hayden Clark (1929). Editor: *The National Gazette*, 1791–93; *The Jersey Chronicle*, 1795–96; *The Time-Piece, and Literary Companion*, 1797–98. See Lewis Leary's *That Rascal Freneau: A Study in Literary Failure* (1941); Philip M. Marsh's *Philip Freneau, Poet and Journalist* (1967).

"Frescoes for Mr. Rockefeller's City." Poem by Archibald MacLeish (1933).

Fresno Bee. Fresno, Cal. Newspaper. Founded 1922. O. M. Shelton is editor. Verne H. Cole is book-review editor.

FREUND, PHILIP (Feb. 5, 1909–); b. Vancouver, B.C. Author. *The Merry Communist* (1934); *The Show* (1935); *The Evening Heron* (1937); *Book of Kings* (1938); *The Dark Shore* (1941); *The Young Greek and The Creole* (stories, 1944); *Three Exotic Tales* (1946); *Edward Zoltan* (1946); *Easter Island* (1947); *How to Become a Literary Critic* (1947); *A Man of Taste* (1949); *Private Speech* (poems, 1952); *Prince Hamlet* (play, 1953); *The Beholder* (1961); *The Spymaster* (1965); *Myths of Creation* (1966); *Three Off-Broadway Plays: The Peons, The Fire Bringers, The Brooding Angel* (1968); etc.

FRIAR, KIMON. Translator, author. Editor: *Modern Poetry, American and British* (with John Malcolm Brinnin, 1951). Translator: Kazantzakis's *The Odyssey: A Modern Sequel* (1958); *Saviors of God: Spiritual Exercises* (1960).

"Friar Jerome's Beautiful Book." Poem by Thomas Bailey Aldrich (1864).

Friars, The. New York. Theatrical club. Founded 1904; incorporated 1907.

FRIEDAN, BETTY (Feb. 4, 1921–); b. Peoria, Ill. Feminist leader, author. *The Feminine Mystique* (1963).

FRIEDENBERG, EDGAR Z[odiag] (Mar. 18, 1921–); b. New York. Educator, author. *The Vanishing Adolescent* (1959); *Coming of Age in America* (1965); *The Dignity of Youth and Other Atavisms* (1965); *Society's Children* (with Carl Nordstrom and A. Hilary Gold, 1967). Prof. education, Dalhousie University, Can.

FRIEDERICH, WERNER P[aul] (June 2, 1905–); b. Thun, Switz. Educator, author. *Outline-History of German Literature* (1948); *Dante's Fame Abroad, 1350–1850* (1950); *Outline of Comparative Literature from Dante Alighieri to Eugene O'Neill* (with David H. Malone, 1954); *Australia in Western Imaginative Prose Writings* (1967); *The Challenge of Comparative Literature and Other Addresses* (1970); etc. Prof. German and comparative literature, University of North Carolina, since 1948.

FRIEDLANDER, ISRAEL (Sept. 8, 1876–July 5, 1920); b. Kovel, Russian Poland. Educator, Semitist, Zionist leader. Author. *The Jews of Russia and Poland* (1915); *Past and Present* (1919). Prof. Biblical history and literature, Jewish Theological Seminary, New York, 1903.

FRIEDMAN, B[ernard] H[arper] (July 27, 1926–); b. New York. Author. *Circles* (1962); *Robert Goodnough* (with Barbara Guest, 1962); *Yarborough* (1964); *One-Man Show* (1967).

FRIEDMAN, BRUCE JAY (Apr. 26, 1930–); b. New York. Editor, author. *Stern* (1962); *Far From the City of Class* (1963); *A Mother's Kisses* (1964); *Black Angels* (1966); *Scuba Duba* (play, 1968); *The Dick* (1970); *Steambath* (play, 1971). Editorial director, Magazine Management Co., 1953–66.

FRIEDMAN, ISAAC KAHN (Nov. 3, 1870–deceased); b. Chicago, Ill. Journalist, traveler, author. *The Lucky Number* (1896); *The Autobiography of a Beggar* (1903); etc.

FRIEDMAN, MILTON (July 31, 1912–); b. Brooklyn, N.Y. Economist, author. *Taxing to Prevent Inflation* (with Carl Shoup and Ruth P. Mack, 1943); *Sampling Inspection* (with others, 1948); *Essays in Positive Economics* (1953); *A Theory of the Consumption Function* (1957); *A Program for Monetary Stability* (1960); *Price Theory* (1962); *Capitalism and Freedom* (with Rose D. Friedman, 1962); *A Monetary History of the United States, 1867–1960* (with Anna J. Schwartz, 1963); *Inflation: Causes and Consequences* (1963); *The Great Contraction* (with Anna J. Schwartz, 1965); *The Balance of Payments* (with Robert Roosa, 1967); *Dollars and Deficits* (1968); *The Optimum Quantity of Money and Other Essays* (1969). Prof. economics, University of Chicago, since 1948.

FRIEDMAN, WILLIAM FREDERICK (Sept. 24, 1891–); b. Kishinev, Rus. Cryptologist, author. *The Shakespearean Ciphers Examined* (with Elizabeth S. Friedman, 1957); also War Dept. publications on cryptology.

FRIEDMANN, HERBERT (Apr. 22, 1900–); b. Brooklyn, N.Y. Ornithologist, author. *The Cowbirds: A Study in the Biology of Social Parasitism* (1929); *The Symbolic Goldfinch* (1946); *Parasitic Cuckoos of Africa* (1949); *Birds of Mexico*, 2v. (with others, 1950, 1957); *Parasitic Weaverbirds* (1960); *Host Relations of Parasitic Cowbirds* (1963); *The Evolutionary History of the Avian Genus Chrysococcyx* (1968); etc.

FRIEDRICH, CARL JOACHIM (June 5, 1901–); b. Leipzig, Ger. Educator, author. *Responsible Bureaucracy* (1932); *Foreign Policy in the Making* (1938); *The New Belief in the Common Man* (1942); *Inevitable Peace* (1948); *The Age of the Baroque* (1952); *The Philosophy of Law in Historical Perspective* (1958); *Man and His Government* (1963); *Transcendant Justice* (1964); *An Introduction to Political Theory* (1967); *Trends of Federalism in Theory and Practice* (1968); *An Emergent Nation?* (1969); etc. Government dept., Harvard University, since 1926.

FRIEDRICH, OTTO ALVA (Feb. 3, 1929–); b. Boston, Mass. Editor, author. *The Poor in Spirit* (1952); *The Loner* (1954). Co-author, with wife, Priscilla Boughton: *The Easter Bunny that Overslept* (1957); *Clean Clarence* (1959); *The League of Unusual Animals* (1965).

FRIEL, ARTHUR O[lney] (May 31, 1885–Jan. 27, 1959); b. Detroit, Mich. Novelist. *King of Kearsarge* (1921); *Tiger River* (1923); *The River of Seven Stars* (1924); *Renegade* (1926); *Forgotten Island* (1931).

FRIEND, OSCAR JEROME (Jan. 8, 1897–Jan 19, 1963); b. St. Louis, Mo. Novelist. *The Round-Up* (1924); *Bloody Ground* (1928); *The Range Doctor* (1933); *The Kid from Mars* (1949); etc. Under pen name "Owen Fox Jerome": *The Hand of Horror* (1927); *The Red Kite Clue* (1928); *The Murder at Avalon Arms* (1930); *Murder: As Usual* (1940); *The Five Assassins* (1958); etc. Under pen name "Ford Smith": *Mavericks* (1959); *Buzzard's Roost* (1961); *Action at Powder River* (1963); etc.

Friend Olivia. Novel by Amelia E. Barr (1890). A tale of the Quakers in the last months of Cromwell's rule of England.

FRIENDLY, FRED W.; b. New York. Television consultant. *Due to Circumstances Beyond Our Control* (1967). Collaborated with Edward R. Murrow on *I Can Hear It Now*, aural history of 1932–45, produced by Columbia Records. Consultant with Ford Foundation, since 1966.

Friendly Club, The. New York. Late eighteenth century club. William Dunlap, James Kent, Noah Webster, Anthony Bleecker, E. H. Smith, Charles Brockden Brown, and W. W. Woolsey were among its members.

Friends' Library, The. 14v. (1837–50). A collection of historical and literary remains of Quaker writers.

Friendship Village Love Stories. By Zona Gale (1908).

FRIES, ADELAIDE LISETTA (Nov. 12, 1871–Nov. 29, 1949); b. Salem, N.C. Archivist of Moravian church, author. *The Moravians in Georgia, 1735–1740* (1905); *The Moravian Church Yesterday and Today* (with J. Kenneth Pfohl, 1926); *Records of the Moravians in North Carolina,* 4v. (1922–30); *Moravian Customs* (1936); *Some Moravian Heroes* (1936); *The Road to Salem* (1944); etc.

FRIES, CHARLES CARPENTER (Nov. 29, 1887–); b. Reading, Pa. Educator, author. *The Teaching of Literature* (with others, 1925); *Studies in Shakespeare, Milton and Donne* (with others, 1925); *The Teaching of the English Language* (1927); *The Inflections and Syntax of American English* (1939); *American English Grammar* (1940); *What Is Good English?* (1940); *English for Latin-American Students,* 6v. (with staff of English Language Institute, 1942–44); *Teaching and Learning English as a Foreign Language* (1945); *The Structure of English* (1952); *Linguistics and Reading* (1963); etc. English dept. University of Michigan, 1915–58.

FRINGS, KETTI [Katherine Hartley], b. Columbus, O. Author. *Hold Back the Dawn* (1940); *Mr. Sycamore* (play, 1943); *God's Front Porch* (1945); *Look Homeward Angel* (adaptation, prod. 1957; Pulitzer prize for drama, 1958). Also screen plays.

FRISBIE, ROBERT DEAN (Apr. 16, 1896–deceased); b. Cleveland, O. Trader, traveler, author. *Book of Puka-Puka* (1929); *A Kanaka Voyage* (1930); *My Tahiti* (1937); *Mr. Moonlight's Island* (1939); *The Island of Desire* (1944); *Amaru* (1945); etc.

FRISBIE, WILLIAM ALBERT (Dec. 12, 1867–deceased); b. Danbury, Conn. Journalist. Author of children's books. *Tale of the Bandit Mouse* (1900); *Pirate Frog, and Other Tales* (1901); *Puggery Wee* (1902); *The Other Man* (1904); *ABC Mother Goose* (1905); *The Private Life of Samson* (1929).

FROHMAN, DANIEL (Aug. 22, 1851–Dec. 26, 1940); b. Sandusky, O. Theatrical producer, author. *Daniel Frohman Presents* (1935). In 1874 he became advance agent for Callender's Original Georgia Minstrels. In 1879 he joined Steele MacKaye in New York and soon became a theatre manager. He formed the Lyceum Theatre Stock Company, and developed many Broadway stars. He was known as the dean of American theatrical producers.

FROHOCK, WILBER MERRILL (June 20, 1908–); b. South Thomaston, Me. Educator, author. *The Novel of Violence in America* (1950); *André Malraux and the Tragic Imagination* (1952); *Strangers to This Ground* (1962); *Rimbaud's Poetic Practice* (1963); *French Literature, an Approach through Close Reading* (1964); *Style and Temper* (1967). Romance languages dept., Harvard University, since 1956.

"From Greenland's Icy Mountains." Hymn composed by Lowell Mason (1823).

From Here to Eternity. Novel by James Jones (1951). One of the most forceful and most popular of World War II novels. Army frustrations and conflicts on Hawaii just before the Japanese attack. Noted for its naturalistic vigor.

From Immigrant to Inventor. By Michael Pupin (1922). Autobiography of a Serbian peasant boy who came to America and became a great inventor.

From the Easy Chair. By George William Curtis (1891). Essays which appeared in *Harper's Magazine* in department "Easy Chair."

"From the Land of the Sky-blue Water." Song of Nelle Richmond Eberhart; set to music by Charles Wakefield Cadman.

Frome, David. Pen name of Zenith J. Brown, used in England. "Leslie Ford" is used by the same author in America.

FROMM, ERICH (Mar. 23, 1900–); b. Frankfurt, Ger. Psychoanalyst, author. *Escape from Freedom* (1941); *Man for Himself* (1947); *Psychoanalysis and Religion* (1950); *The Forgotten Language* (1951); *The Sane Society* (1955); *The Art of Loving* (1956); *Sigmund Freud's Mission* (1959); *May Man Prevail?* (1961); *The Heart of Man* (1964); *The Dogma of Christ* (1966); *The Revolution of Hope* (1968); etc. Editor: *Zen Buddhism and Psychoanalysis* (with others, 1960).

Front Page, The. Play by Ben Hecht and Charles MacArthur (prod. 1928). A comedy based on the activities and drama of a newspaper office.

Front Yard, and Other Italian Stories, The. By Constance Fenimore Woolson (1895).

Frontier, The. Missoula, Mont. Quarterly magazine. Founded May, 1920, as *The Montanan,* its name was changed with the second number to *The Frontier.* Absorbed *The Midland,* Nov., 1933, and changed its name to *The Frontier and Midland.* It expired 1939. Editor, Harold Guy Merriam.

Frontier Index. Triweekly newspaper, published by Frederick Kemper Freeman (1841–1928). Founded May, 1866, at Kearney City, Neb., it was moved westward with the advance of the Union Pacific Railroad. It appeared in numerous towns, including Platte, Neb., Laramie, Wyo., and Corinne, Utah, where it came to rest and was renamed *Freeman's Farmer.* Freeman was assisted in operating this "press on wheels" by his brother Lewis.

Frontier Scout. Fort Union, N.D. Newspaper. Founded July 7, 1864. First newspaper published in North Dakota; printed for Company I, 30th Wisconsin Volunteers.

Frontier Times. Austin, Tex. Bimonthly. Founded 1958. Published by Western Publications, Inc. Devoted to articles about the Old West.

FROST, ARTHUR BURDETT (Jan. 17, 1851–June 22, 1928); b. Philadelphia, Pa. Illustrator, humorist. *Stuff & Nonsense* (1884); *Carlo* (1913). Illustrated many articles in *Scribner's Magazine, Harper's Magazine,* and *Collier's;* and books by Thomas Nelson Page, Mark Twain, Joel Chandler Harris, H. C. Bunner, John Kendrick Bangs, etc. *See* Henry W. Lanier's *A. B. Frost, the American Sportsman's artist* (1933).

FROST, ELIZABETH HOLLISTER; b. Rochester, N.Y. Poet, novelist. *The Lost Lyrist* (poems, 1928); *Hovering Shadow* (poems, 1929); *The Closed Gentian* (poems, 1931); *The Wedding Ring* (1939); *This Side of Land* (1942); *Mary and the Spinner* (1946).

FROST, FRANCES M. (Aug. 3, 1905–Feb. 11, 1959); b. St. Albans, Vt. Poet, novelist. *Hemlock Wall* (poems, 1929); *Blue Harvest* (poems, 1931); *These Acres* (poems, 1932); *Pool in the Meadow* (poems, 1933); *Woman of This Earth* (poem, 1934); *Innocent Summer* (1936); *Road to America* (poems, 1937); *Yoke of Stars* (1939); *Uncle Snowball* (1940); *Kate Triumphant* (1940); *Windy Foot at the County Fair* (1947); *Little Whistler* (poems, 1949); *Maple Sugar for Windy Foot* (1950); *Then Came Timothy* (1950); *The Cat that Went to College* (1951); *Little Fox* (1952); *Rocket Away* (1953); *Star of Wonder* (1953); *This Rowdy Heart* (1954); *Fireworks for Windy Foot* (1956). Editor, *American Poetry Journal,* 1933–35.

FROST, JOHN (Jan. 26, 1800–Dec. 28, 1859); b. Kennebunk, Me. Compiler: *Pictorial History of the United States of America,* 4v. (1844); and many similar historical compilations. He sometimes used the pen name "Robert Ramble."

FROST, ROBERT [LEE] (Mar. 26, 1874–Jan. 29, 1963); b. San Francisco, Calif. Poet. *A Boy's Will* (1913); *North of Boston* (1914); *Mountain Interval* (1916); *New Hampshire* (1923, Pulitzer Prize for poetry, 1924); *West-Running Brook* (1928); *A Way Out* (Play, 1929); *The Lovely Shall Be Choosers* (1929); *Collected Poems* (1930, Pulitzer Prize for poetry, 1931), augmented edition (1939); *The Lone Striker* (1933); *A Further Range* (1936, Pulitzer Prize for poetry, 1937); *From Snow to Snow* (1936); *The Witness Tree* (1942, Pulitzer Prize for poetry, 1943); *A Masque of Reason* (1945); *A Masque of Mercy* (1947); *Steeple Bush* (1947); *Complete Poems* (1949); *The Road Not Taken* (1951); *Hard Not To Be King* (1951); *Aforesaid* (1954); *And All We Call American* (1958); *You Come Too* (1959); *The Gift Outright* (1961); *In the Clearing* (1962); *Selected Poems* (1963); etc. Co-founder, Bread Loaf School of English, Middlebury College, 1920; prof. English, Amherst College, 1916–20; 1923–25; 1926–38. *See* Lawrence R. Thompson's *Fire and Ice* (1942), *Selected Letters* (1964); *The Early Years, 1874–1915* (1966), and *The Years of Triumph, 1915–1938* (1970); Elizabeth S. Sergeant's *Robert Frost* (1960); Reuben Brower's *The Poetry of Robert Frost* (1963).

FROST, WALTER ARCHER (Dec. 18, 1876–March 11, 1964); b. Amenia, N.Y. Editor, novelist. *The Man Between* (1913); *No Questions Asked* (1926); *The Marworth Mystery* (1927); *Cape Smoke* (prod. 1926). Assoc. editor, *Munsey's* magazines, 1912–13; etc.

FROTHINGHAM, ARTHUR LINCOLN (June 21, 1859–July 28, 1923); b. Boston, Mass. Educator, archeologist, editor, author. *The Monuments of Christian Rome* (1908); *A History of Architecture*, v. 3 & 4 (1915), sequel to v. 1 & 2, by Russell Sturgis; etc. Founder, *American Journal of Archaeology,* 1885; editor, 1885–96; co-founder, the *Princeton College Bulletin,* 1889.

FROTHINGHAM, EUGENIA BROOKS (Nov. 17, 1874–); b. Paris. Author. *The Turn of the Road* (1901); *The Evasion* (1906); *The Finding of Norah* (1918); *Youth and I* (autobiography, 1938).

FROTHINGHAM, JESSIE PEABODY (d. Jan. 17, 1949); b. Boston, Mass. Author. *Sea Fighters from Drake to Farragut* (1902); *Sea Wolves of Seven Shores* (1904); *Running the Gantlet* (1906).

FROTHINGHAM, NATHANIEL LANGDON (July 23, 1793–Apr. 4, 1870); b. Boston, Mass. Unitarian clergyman, poet, hymn writer. *Metrical Pieces, Translated and Original,* 2v. (1855–70); etc.

FROTHINGHAM, OCTAVIUS BROOKS (Nov. 26, 1822–Nov. 27, 1895); b. Boston, Mass. Unitarian clergyman, biographer, hymn-writer. *Theodore Parker* (1874); *Transcendentalism in New England* (1876); *Gerrit Smith* (1877); *George Ripley* (1882); *Memoir of William Henry Channing* (1886); *A Study of the Life and Work of Nathaniel Langdon Frothingham* (1890); *Recollections and Impressions* (1891). His best known hymn is "The Lord of Hosts, Whose guiding hand."

FROTHINGHAM, PAUL REVERE (July 6, 1864–Nov. 27, 1926); b. Jamaica Plain, Mass. Unitarian clergyman, biographer, essayist. *William Ellery Channing* (1903); *The Temple of Virtue* (1907); *A Confusion of Tongues* (1917); *Edward Everett* (1925); *All These* (1927); etc. *See* Howard Chandler Robbins's *The Life of Paul Revere Frothingham* (1935).

FROTHINGHAM, RICHARD (Jan. 31, 1812–Jan. 29, 1880); b. Charlestown, Mass. Historian. *The History of Charlestown, Mass.,* 7 parts (1845–49); *Life and Times of Joseph Warren* (1865); *The Rise of the Republic* (1872); etc. Owner, *Boston Post,* and its managing editor, 1852–65.

FROTHINGHAM, ROBERT (Mar. 22, 1865–Dec. 7, 1937); b. Galesville, Wis. Traveler, lecturer, author. *The Pioneer* (1920); *Around the World* (1925); *Arctic Walrus Hunting with the Eskimos* (1931); *Trails through the Golden West* (1932). Compiler: *Songs of Men* (1918); *Songs of Dogs* (1920); *Songs of Horses* (1920); *Songs of the Sea* (1924); *Songs of Adventure* (1926); etc.

FROTHINGHAM, THOMAS GODDARD (July 9, 1865–Mar. 17, 1945); b. Boston, Mass. Naval and military historian. *A Guide to the Military History of the World War, 1914–18* (1920); *A True Account of the Battle of Jutland* (1920); *The Naval History of the World War: Offensive Operations, 1914–15* (1924); *The Naval History of the World War: The Stress of Sea Power, 1915–16* (1925); *The Naval History of the World War: The United States in the War, 1917–18* (1926); *George Washington* (1930); etc.

FRUCHTER, NORMAN (1937–   ); b. Philadelphia, Pa. Author. *Coat Upon a Stick* (1963).

Fruits of Philosophy, The. Essays by Charles Knowlton (1832). Pioneer publication on limiting human reproduction.

FRUMKIN, GENE (Jan. 29, 1928–   ); b. New York. Poet. *The Hawk and the Lizard* (1963); *The Orange Tree* (1964). Co-founder, *Coastlines,* 1955.

FRY, JAMES BARNETT (Feb. 28, 1827–July 4, 1894); b. Carrollton, Ill. Army officer, military writer. *Army Sacrifices* (1879); *Military Miscellanies* (1889); etc.

FRY, JOSEPH REESE (d. 1865). Librettist, biographer. *A Life of General Z. Taylor* (with Robert T. Conrad, 1847); *Leonora* (opera, prod. 1845); and *Notre Dame of Paris* (opera, prod. 1864); the music for both composed by his brother, William Henry Fry.

FRY, WILLIAM HENRY (Aug. 10, 1815–Dec. 21, 1864); b. Philadelphia, Pa. Editor, music critic, composer. Wrote the music for the operas *Leonora* (prod. 1845); and *Notre Dame of Paris* (prod. 1864); the librettos for both written by his brother, Joseph Reese Fry (q.v.). Editor, the Philadelphia *Public Ledger,* 1844; music critic, the *New York Tribune,* 1852–61.

FRYE, ALEXIS EVERETT (Nov. 2, 1859–July 1, 1936); b. N. Haven, Me. Educator, geographer, author. *Complete Geography* (1895); and many graded geographies.

FRYE, NORTHROP (July 14, 1912–   ); b. Sherbrooke, Que., Can. Educator, author. *Fearful Symmetry* (1947); *Anatomy of Criticism* (1957); *Fables of Identity: Studies in Poetic Mythology* (1963); *The Well-Tempered Critic* (1963); *T. S. Eliot* (1963); *The Educated Imagination* (1964); *The Return of Eden* (1965); *A Natural Perspective: The Development of Shakesperean Comedy and Romance* (1965); *Fools of Time: Studies in Shakesperean Tragedy* (1967); *The Stubborn Structure: Essays on Criticism and Society* (1970). Editor: *Romanticism Reconsidered* (1963); *Blake: A Collection of Critical Essays* (1966). Prof. English, Victoria College, University of Toronto, since 1947.

FRYE, PEARL (Mrs. Lowell Sanford Rau) (1917–). Author. *Narrow Bridge* (1947); *Game for Empires* (1950); *Gallant Captain: A Biographical Novel Based on the Life of John Paul Jones* (1956); etc.

FRYE, RICHARD NELSON (Jan. 10, 1920–); b. Birmingham, Ala. Orientalist, author. *Iran* (1953); etc. Translator: *History of Bukhara* (1954); *The Heritage of Persia* (1963); *Persia* (1968); etc. Editor: *Islam and the West* (1957); *The Near East and the Great Powers* (1969); etc. Prof. Iranian, Harvard University, since 1957.

FUCHS, DANIEL (1909–). Author. *Summer in Williamsburg* (1934); *Homage to Blenholt* (1936); *Low Company* (1937); *The Comic Spirit of Wallace Stevens* (1963); *How to Reach the Jew for Christ* (1965); etc.

FUESS, CLAUDE MOORE (Jan. 12, 1885–Sept. 9, 1963); b. Waterville, N.Y. Educator, author. *An Old New England*

School (1917); *The Life of Caleb Cushing* (1923); *The Andover Way* (1926); *Rufus Choate* (1927); *Men of Andover* (1928); *Daniel Webster* (1930); *Amherst, Story of a New England College* (1935); *Carl Schurz* (1932); *Amherst* (1935); *Creed of a Schoolmaster* (1939); *Calvin Coolidge* (1940); *The College Board: Its First Fifty Years* (1950); *Stanley King of Amherst* (1955); etc. Editor: *Selected Short Stories* (1914); *A Little Book of Familiar Verse* (1922); *In My Time: A Medley of Andover Reminiscences* (1959); etc. Editor, *Phillips Bulletin*, 1908–33. Headmaster of Phillips Academy, Andover, Mass., 1933–48.

Fugitive: A Magazine of Verse. Nashville, Tenn. Bi-monthly magazine. Founded April, 1922, by John Crowe Ransom, Donald Davidson, Walter Clyde Curry, Allen Tate, Robert Penn Warren, Merrill Moore, William Y. Elliott, William Frierson, Jesse Wills, Alec B. Stevenson, Sidney M'ttron Hirsch, James Marshall Frank, and Stanley Johnson. Nineteen numbers were published. Expired Dec., 1925. See *Fugitives: An Anthology of Verse* (1928); and *The Fugitive: Clippings and Comment*, comp. by Merrill Moore (1939).

Fugitives: An Anthology of Verse. Selected poems by eleven of the contributors to *Fugitive*. Published 1928.

FULBRIGHT, J[ames] WILLIAM (Apr. 9, 1905–   ); b. Sumner, Mo. U.S. Senator, author. *Prospects for the West* (1963); *Old Myths and New Realities* (1964); *The Arrogance of Power* (1967); *The Pentagon Progaganda Machine* (1970). U.S. Senator, since 1945. *See* K. E. Meyer's *Fulbright of Arkansas* (1963).

FULCHER, PAUL MILTON (Nov. 10, 1895–Jan, 1958); b. Eureka, Ill. Educator, author. *Guests of Summer* (1930). Editor, *Descriptive Passages* (1928); *Short Narratives* (1928); etc. English dept., University of Wisconsin, 1920–58.

FULLER, EDMUND (1914–). Author. *Pageant of the Theater* (1941); *John Milton* (1944); *Star Pointed North* (1946); *Brothers Divided* (1951); *Tinkers and Genius: The Story of Yankee Inventors* (1955); *Successful Calamity* (1966); *God in the White House: The Faiths of the American Presidents* (with David Green, 1968). Editor: *The Christian Idea of Education* (1957); *Man in Modern Fiction* (1958); *Four American Novels* (1959); *Four American Biographies* (with O. B. Davis, 1961); etc.

FULLER, HENRY BLAKE (Jan. 9, 1857–July 28, 1929); b. Chicago, Ill. Author. *The Chevalier of Pensieri-Vani* (1890); *The Chatelaine of La Trinité* (1892); *The Cliff-Dwellers* (1893); *The New Flag* (1899); *The Last Refuge* (1900); *Gardens of this World* (1929); *Not on the Screen* (1930); etc.

FULLER, JOHN GRANT (Nov. 30, 1913–   ); b. Philadelphia, Pa. Columnist, author. *The Pink Elephant* (1953); *Love Me Little* (1959); *Gentlemen Conspirators* (1962); *The Money Changers* (1962); *Incident at Exeter* (1966); *Interrupted Journey* (1966); *Games for Insomniacs* (1966); *The Day of St. Anthony's Fire* (1970). Columnist, "Trade Winds," in *Saturday Review*, 1957–67.

FULLER, MARGARET, MARCHIONESS OSSOLI (May 23, 1810–July 19, 1850); b. Cambridgeport, Mass. Journalist, social reformer, critic. *Summer on the Lakes in 1843* (1844); *Woman in the Nineteenth Century* (1845); *Papers on Literature and Art* (1846); republished as *Literature and Art* (1852); *At Home and Abroad* (1856); *Life Without and Life Within* (1859); *Love Letters, 1845–1846* (1903). Editor, *The Dial*, 1840–43; first lit. critic of the *New York Tribune*, 1844–46. See *The Memoirs of Margaret Fuller Ossoli*, ed. by Ralph W. Emerson, William H. Channing, and James F. Clarke, 2v. (1852); Katharine Anthony's *Margaret Fuller: A Psychological Biography* (1921); Mason Wade's *Margaret Fuller, Whetstone of Genius* (1940), and his *The Writings of Margaret Fuller* (1941).

FULLER, MARGARET [Witter] (1872–Feb. 1, 1954); b. Brooklyn, N.Y. Poet. *A New England Childhood* (1916); *One*

World at a Time (1922); *Alma* (1927); *Her Son* (1929); *The Golden Roof* (1930); *The Complete History of the Deluge, in Verse and Pictures* (1936); *It Is All So Simple* (1947); *This Awakening* (1948); *Sonnets and Songs* (1955).

Fuller, Metta Victoria. See Metta Victoria Victor.

Fuller, Roger. Pen name of Don Tracy.

FULLER, SAMUEL RICHARD, Jr. (Feb. 19, 1879–); b. Corning, N.Y. Manufacturer. Pen name, "Norman Brainerd." *Winning His Shoulder Straps* (1909); *Winning the Junior Cup* (1911); *The Cadet Sergeant* (1929); etc.

FULLER, TIMOTHY (1914–   ). Novelist. *Harvard Has a Homicide* (1936); republished as, *J for Jupiter* (1937); *Three Thirds of a Ghost* (1941); *This Is Murder, Mr. Jones* (1943); *Keep Cool, Mr. Jones* (1950); etc.

FULLER, WALTER DEANE (June 5, 1882–Nov. 12, 1964); b. Corning, Ia. Publisher. With Curtis Publishing Co., Philadelphia, since 1908; president, 1934–50; chairman of the board, 1950–57. President, Walter D. Fuller Company, since 1957.

FULLER, WILLIAM OLIVER (Feb. 3, 1856–deceased); b. Rockland, Me. Newspaperman. *What Happened to Wigglesworth* (1901); *An Old Town by the Sea* (1910); *A Night with Sherlock Holmes* (1929). Editor, *Rockland Courier-Gazette*, Rockland, Me.

FULLERTON, GEORGE STUART (Aug. 18, 1859–Mar. 23, 1925); b. Fatehgarh, India. Episcopal clergyman, educator, philosopher, author. *Philosophy of Spinoza* (1894); *System of Metaphysics* (1904); *The World We Live In* (1912); *A Handbook of Ethics* (1922); etc. Prof. philosophy, Columbia University, 1904–25.

FÜLÖP-MILLER, RENÉ (Mar. 17, 1891–May 7, 1963); b. Caransebes, Rumania. Author. *Lenin and Gandhi* (1928); *The Unknown Tolstoy* (1930); *The Imagination Machine* (1931); *Leo XIII* (1935); *The Motion Picture in America* (1938); *Saints that Moved the World* (1945); *Fyodor Dostoevsky* (1950); *The Web* (1950); *The Night of Time* (1955); *Silver Bacchanal* (1960); *The Russian Theatre* (with Joseph Gregor, 1968).

"Funeral Song." Poem by Samuel Wigglesworth (1709).

FUNK, CHARLES EARLE (Apr. 4, 1881–Apr. 16, 1957); b. Springfield, O. Lexicographer, author. *What's the Name, Please?* (1936); *A Hog on Ice, and Other Sayings* (1948); *Thereby Hangs a Tale* (1950); *Heavens to Betsy: and Other Sayings* (1955); *Horsefeathers* (1958). Assoc. editor, *New Standard Dictionary*, and its abridgments, 1921–27, 1931–38, editor from 1939; assoc. editor, *New International Year Books*, 1932–38, editor 1939–47.

FUNK, ISAAC KAUFFMAN (Sept. 10, 1839–Apr. 4, 1912); b. Clifton, O. Publisher, editor. In 1877 he joined with Adam Willis Wagnalls to form the publishing firm of I. K. Funk & Company, New York, known later as Funk & Wagnalls Company. He founded the *Literary Digest* in 1890, and was its first editor. He directed the work on *A Standard Dictionary of the English Language*, 1890–93. He published *The Jewish Encyclopedia*, 12v. (1901–06), and many other standard works.

FUNK, WILFRED [John] (Mar. 20, 1883–June 1, 1965); b. Brooklyn, N.Y. Publisher, author. *Manhattans, Bronxes and Queens* (poems, 1931); *Light Lines and Dears* (poems, 1932); *"So You Think It's New"* (1937); *It Might Be Verse* (poems, 1938); *When the Merry-Go-Round Breaks Down* (1938); *If You Drink* (1940); *30 Days to a More Powerful Vocabulary* (with N. Lewis, 1942); *Word Origins and Their Romantic Stories* (1950); *Six Weeks to Words of Power* (1953); *Twenty-five Magic Steps to Word Power* (1959). With Funk & Wagnalls Co., since 1909; president 1925–40; resigned to found Wilfred Funk, Inc.; editor in chief, *Literary Digest*, 1936–37.

Funk and Wagnalls. New York. Publishers. Founded 1877. Publishes reference books and general nonfiction. Acquired by Reader's Digest Books, Inc., in 1967. Emile Capouya is executive editor.

FUNKE, LEWIS (Jan. 25, 1912–); b. New York. Drama editor. *Max Gordon Presents* (with Max Gordon, 1963); *A Gift of Joy* (with Helen Hayes, 1965). Editor: *Actors Talk about Acting* (with John E. Booth, 1962). Sportswriter, *The New York Times,* 1928–44; drama editor, since 1944.

FURBAY, JOHN HARVEY (Sept. 23, 1903–); b. Mt. Gilead, O. Educator, author. *A History of Sex Education* (1928); *Nature Chats* (1934); *It Has Been Debunked* (1936); *Folklore of the Native Tribes in Liberia* (1939); etc. President, College of West Africa, Monrovia, Liberia, 1935–38.

Furioso. New Haven, Conn.; Northfield, Minn. Founded 1939. Published poetry and criticism and was known for its satirical articles. Edited by James Angleton and Reed Whittemore, and later by others including the original editors, Arthur Mizener, and Howard Nemerov. Published Edmund Wilson, Howard Nemerov, Arthur Mizener, Robie Macauley, Emma Swan. Suspended 1953.

FURMAN, BESS (Mrs. Robert B. Armstrong, Jr.) (Dec. 2, 1894–); b. Danbury, Neb. Journalist, author. *Washington Byline* (1949); *White House Profile: A Social History of the White House* (1951). Washington bureau, *The New York Times,* since 1943.

FURMAN, LUCY (d. Aug., 1958); b. Henderson, Ky. Author. *Stories of a Sanctified Town* (1896); *Mothering on Perilous* (1913); *Sight to the Blind* (1914); *The Quare Women* (1923); *The Glass Window* (1925); *The Lonesome Road* (1927).

FURNAS, CLIFFORD COOK (Oct. 24, 1900–); b. Sheridan, Ind. Educator, chemist, author. *America's Tomorrow* (1932); *The Next Hundred Years* (1936); *Man, Bread and Destiny* (1937); *The Storehouse of Civilization* (1939); *The Engineer* (1966). Editor: *Research in Industry* (1948). Dept. of clinical engineering, Yale University, 1931–42; chancellor, University of Buffalo, since 1954.

FURNAS, JOSEPH CHAMBERLAIN (Nov. 24, 1905–); b. Indianapolis, Ind. Author. *The Prophet's Chamber* (1937); *Many People Prize It* (1938); *So You're Going to Stop Smoking* (1939); *Anatomy of Paradise* (1948); *Voyage to Windward* (1951); *Goodbye to Uncle Tom* (1956); *The Road to Harper's Ferry* (1959); *The Devil's Rainbow* (1962); *The Life and Times of the Late Demon Rum* (1966); *Lightfoot Island* (1968); *The Americans: A Social History of the United States* (1969); etc. Co-author: *Sudden Death and How to Avoid It* (1935); *How America Lives* (1941).

FURNAS, MARTHEDITH (Mar. 18, 1904–   ); b. Indianapolis, Ind. Novelist. *The Night Is Coming* (1939); *A Serpent's Tooth* (1946); *The Far Country* (1947).

FURNESS, HORACE HOWARD (Nov. 2, 1833–Aug. 13, 1912); b. Philadelphia, Pa. Shakespearean scholar. Editor: v. 1–15 of the *New Variorum Shakespeare,* 1871 until his death. This monumental work grew out of the Shakespeare Society of Philadelphia, founded in 1851. After his death the editorship was taken over by his son, Horace Howard Furness, Jr. The Horace Howard Furness Memorial Library of Shakespeareana is now in the University of Pennsylvania Library.

FURNESS, WILLIAM HENRY (Apr. 20, 1802–Jan. 30, 1896); b. Boston, Mass. Unitarian clergyman, author. *Remarks on the Four Gospels* (1836); *A History of Jesus* (1850); *The Veil Partly Lifted* (1864); etc.

FURNISS, GRACE LIVINGSTON (1864–Apr. 20, 1938); b. New York City. Playwright. *A Colonial Girl* (with Abby Sage Richardson, prod. 1898); *The Pride of Jennico* (with same, prod. 1900); *Mrs. Jack* (prod. 1902); *Gretna Green* (prod.

1903); *The Man on the Case* (prod. 1907); *The Man on the Box* (prod. 1915); etc.

Further Range, A. Collection of poems, by Robert Frost (1937).

FUTRELLE, JACQUES (Apr. 9, 1875–Apr. 15, 1912); b. in Pike Co., Ga. Novelist. *The Chase of the Golden Plate* (1906); *The Simple Case of Susan* (1908); *The High Hand* (1910); etc.

FYLES, FRANKLIN (1847–July 4, 1911); b. Troy, N.Y. Drama critic, playwright, author. *The Girl I Left Behind Me* (with David Belasco, prod. 1893); *The Governor of Kentucky* (prod. 1896); *Cumberland '61* (prod. 1897); *A Ward of France* (with Eugene W. Presbrey, prod. 1897); *Kit Carson* (prod. 1901); *Drusa Wayne* (prod. 1906); *The Theatre and Its People* (1900); etc. Drama critic, *The Sun,* New York, 1885–1903.

G

GABELEIN, FRANK ELY (Mar. 31, 1899–); b. Mt. Vernon, N.Y. Educator, author. *Down Through the Ages* (1924); *The Hollow Queen* (1933); *From A Headmaster's Study* (1935); *Philemon: The Gospel of Emancipation* (1939); etc. Headmaster, Stony Brook School, Stony Brook, L.I.

GABLE, J. HARRIS [Jacob Henry] (Feb. 20, 1902–); b. Denison, Ia. Author. *The Boys' Book of Astronomy* (with G. D. Swezey, 1929); *Bibliography of Robin Hood* (1939); *Complete Introduction to Photography* (1940); etc.

GABRIEL, GILBERT WOLF (Jan. 18, 1890–Sept. 3, 1952); b. Brooklyn, N.Y. Drama critic. *The Seven Branched Candlestick* (1916); *Jiminy* (1922); *Brownstone Front* (1924); *Famous Pianists and Composers* (1927); *I, James Lewis* (1931); *Great Fortune* (1933); *I Got a Country* (1944); *Love from London* (1946); *I Thee Wed* (1948); etc. With *New York Sun* 1912–37; drama critic *New York American* 1929–37; *Cue* magazine, from 1949.

GABRIEL, RALPH HENRY (Apr. 29, 1890–); b. Watkins Glen, N.Y. Educator, editor, historian. *The Evolution of Long Island* (1921); *The Rise of American Democracy* (with Mabel B. Casner, 1938); *The Course of American Democratic Thought* (1940); *Religion and Learning at Yale* (1958); etc. General editor: *The Pageant of America,* 15v. (1925–29), to which he contributed: v. 2, *The Lure of the Frontier* (1929); v. 3, *Toilers of Sea and Land* (1920); and v. 6, *The Winning of Freedom* (with W. C. H. Wood, 1927). History dept., Yale University, 1915–58; prof. American civilization, School of International Service, American University, since 1958.

Gabriel Conroy. Novel by Bret Harte (1876). The scene is laid in California during the gold-rush era, and gives a graphic picture of a mining camp.

GADDIS, PEGGY. See Peggy Dern.

GADDIS, WILLIAM (1922–   ); b. New York. Novelist. *The Recognitions* (1955).

GADE, JOHN ALLYNE (Feb. 10, 1875–Aug. 16, 1955); b. Cambridge, Mass. Diplomat, biographer. *Book Plates Old and New* (1898); *Cathedrals of Spain* (1911); *Charles the Twelfth, King of Sweden* (1916); *Christian IV, King of Denmark and Norway* (1928); *The Life of Cardinal Mercier* (1934); *All My Born Days* (1942); *Life and Times of Tycho Brahe* (1947); *Luxemburg in the Middle Ages* (1951); *Under the Golden Lilies* (1955).

GAEBELEIN, ARNO CLEMENS (Aug. 27, 1861–Dec. 25, 1945); b. in Germany. Methodist clergyman, author. *Studies in Prophecy* (1917); *Half a Century* (autobiography, 1930); *The Conflict of the Ages* (1933); *The Hope of the Ages* (1938);

What Will Become of Europe? (1941); *Gabriel and Michael the Archangel* (1945); etc. Editor: *The Annotated Bible,* 9v. (1913–20).

GAER, JOSEPH (Mar. 16, 1897–); b. in Russia. Publisher, author. *The Magic Flight* (1926); *How the Great Religions Began* (1930); *Bret Harte: Bibliography and Biographical Data* (1935); *Men and Trees* (1939); *Everybody's Weather* (1944); *Lore of the Old Testament* (1951); *Lore of the New Testament* (1952); *The Fables of India* (1955); *The Wisdom of the Living Religions* (1956); *What the Great Religions Believe* (1963); etc. Editor: *Our Federal Government and How It Functions* (1939); etc. President, Gaer Associates Publishing Co., 1946–49.

GAFFNEY, CORNELIA, b. Utica, N.Y. Author. *The Blue Jingle Book* (1908); *The Travellings of Nanny Goat* (1908); *The Art of Conversation* (1909); *The Tiny Aces* (1918); *The Cuties* (1919).

GÁG, WANDA (Mar. 11, 1893–June 27, 1946); b. New Ulm, Minn. Artist, author and illustrator of children's books. *Millions of Cats* (1928); *Snippy and Snappy* (1931); *The Funny Thing* (1929); *The ABC Bunny* (1933); *Gone Is Gone* (1935); *Growing Pains* (autobiography, 1940); *Nothing at All* (1941). Translator and illustrator of several books of Grimm's tales.

GAGE, FRANCES DANA [Barker] (Oct. 12, 1808–Nov. 10, 1844); b. Marietta, O. Reformer, author. Pen name "Aunt Fanny." *Elsie Magoon; or, The Old Still-House in the Hollow* (1867); *Poems* (1867); *Gertie's Sacrifice* (1869); *Steps Upward* (1870); etc.

GAILOR, THOMAS FRANK (Sept. 17, 1856–Oct. 3, 1935); b. Jackson, Miss. Episcopal bishop, author. *The Divine Event of All Time* (1900); *Things New and Old* (1891); *The Puritan Reaction* (1897); etc. Chancellor, University of the South, Sewanee, Tenn., 1908–35.

GAINE, HUGH (1726/7–Apr. 25, 1807); b. Belfast, Ireland. Printer, bookseller. Founder, the *New York Mercury,* a weekly publication, Aug., 1752. His bookshop was called the "Bible & Crown." See *The Journals of Hugh Gaine, Printer,* edited by Paul Leicester Ford, 2v. (1902). Official printer, Province of New York, 1768.

GAINES, CHARLES KELSEY (Oct. 21, 1854–Jan. 2, 1944); b. Royalton, N.Y. Educator, author. *Gorgo: A Romance of Old Athens* (1903); *Echoes of Many Moods* (poems, 1926). Prof. Greek, St. Lawrence University, 1876–1895, and from 1900.

GAINES, FRANCIS PENDLETON (Apr. 21, 1892–Dec. 31, 1963); b. Due West, S.C. Educator, author. *The Southern Plantation* (1924); *Lee: The Final Achievement* (1933); *Southern Oratory* (1946); etc. President, Washington and Lee University, since 1930.

GAINES, RUTH [Louise] (1877–); b. Litchfield, Conn. Social worker, author. *Little Light* (1911); *The Village Shield* (1917); *A Village in Picardy* (1918); *Ladies of Grécourt* (1920); *Treasure Flower* (1940); etc.

GAINHAM, SARAH. Author. *Appointment in Vienna* (1957); *Night Falls on the City* (1967); *A Place in the Country* (1969).

GAITHER, FRANCES ORMOND JONES (Mrs. Rice Gaither) (May 21, 1889–Oct. 28, 1955); b. Somerville, Tenn. Author. *The Painted Arrow* (1931); *The Fatal River: The Life and Death of La Salle* (1931); *The Scarlet Coat* (1934); *Little Miss Cappo* (1937); *Follow the Drinking Gourd* (1940); *The Red Cock Crows* (1944); *Double Muscadine* (1949).

GALANTIÈRE, LEWIS (Oct. 10, 1895–); b. Chicago, Ill. Translator, author. *And Be My Love* (prod. 1932); etc. Editor: *America and the Mind of Europe* (1952). Editor, translator: *The Goncourt Journals, 1851–70* (1937). Translator: Saint Exupéry's *Wind, Sand and Stars* (1939), *Flight to Arras* (1942); Anouilh's *Antigone* (1951); etc.

Galaxy, The. New York. Literary monthly (semi-monthly during first year). Founded 1866 by William Conant Church and Francis Pharcellus Church. Among its contributors were "Mark Twain," Henry James, John Burroughs, and Edmund Clarence Stedman. Artists who illustrated its papers were Sol Eytinge and Winslow Homer; in 1872 it ceased to be illustrated. Expired 1878. See Frank L. Mott's *A History of American Magazines,* v. 3 (1938).

Galaxy Magazine. New York. Bimonthly. Founded 1950. Edited by Horace L. Gold, later by Frederik Pohl. A magazine of science fiction.

GALBRAITH, JOHN KENNETH (Oct. 15, 1908–); b. Iona Station, Ont. Economist, author. *American Capitalism* (1952); *A Theory of Price Control* (1952); *The Great Crash, 1929* (1955); *Economics and the Art of Controversy* (1955); *The Affluent Society* (1958); *The Liberal Hour* (1960); *Economic Development* (1963); *The Scotch* (1964); *The New Industrial State* (1967); *Indian Painting* (1968); *How to Control the Military* (1969); *Ambassador's Journal* (1969); etc. Prof. economics, Harvard University, since 1949. Ambassador to India, 1961–63.

GALBREATH, CHARLES BURLEIGH (Feb. 25, 1858–Feb. 23, 1934); b. near Leetonia, O. Librarian, author. *Daniel Decatur Emmet* (1904); *Benjamin Russell Hanby* (1905); *Will L. Thompson* (1905); *Alexander Coffman Ross* (1905); *This Crimson Flower* (poems, 1919); *History of Ohio,* 5v. (1925); etc. State librarian of Ohio, 1896–1911, 1915, 1918, 1927.

GALE, MARY ELIZABETH, b. Wood Ridge, N.J. Author of children's books, playwright. *How the Animals Came to the Circus* (1917); *The Romance Hunters* (1917); *Little Sonny Sunfish* (1923); *Circus Babies* (1930); *Katrina van Ost and the Silver Rose* (1934); *Seven Beads of Wampum* (1936); etc.

GALE, ZONA (Aug. 26, 1874–Dec. 27, 1938); b. Portage, Wis. Novelist, playwright. *Romance Island* (1905); *Friendship Village Love Stories* (1909); *Mothers to Men* (1911); *When I Was a Little Girl* (1913); *Neighborhood Stories* (1914); *Heart's Kindred* (1915); *A Daughter of the Morning* (1917); *Birth* (1918); *Peace in Friendship Village* (1919); *Miss Lula Bett* (1920), dramatized (prod. 1921; Pulitzer Prize for drama, 1921); *The Secret Way* (poems, 1921); *Mister Pitt* (prod. 1921); *Faint Perfume* (1923); *Preface to a Life* (1926); *Yellow Gentians and Blue* (1927); *Portage, Wisconsin* (1929); *Old-Fashioned Tales* (1933); *Papa LaFleur* (1933); *Light Woman* (1937); *Magna* (1939); etc. See August Derleth's *Still Small Voice* (1940).

GALES, JOSEPH (Feb. 4, 1761–Aug. 24, 1841); b. Eckingham, England. Editor, reformer. Founder the *Raleigh Register,* Raleigh, N.C., Oct. 22, 1799. Compiler, v. 1–2, of the *Annals of Congress* (1834). His son, Joseph (1786–1860), became proprietor of the *National Intelligencer,* Wash., D.C., in 1810. With William W. Seaton he published a *Register of Debates of Congress,* 29v. (1825–37); and the *Annuals of Congress,* v. 3–42 (1849–56) and the *American State Papers,* 38v. (1832–61). See J. Seaton's *William Winston Seaton* (1871).

GALL, ALICE [Crew] (d. 1949). Co-author, with Fleming Crew (q.v.), of children's books.

GALLAGHER, BUELL GORDON (Feb. 4, 1904–); b. Rankin, Ill. Educator, author. *American Caste and the Negro College* (1938); *Portrait of a Pilgrim* (1946); *Color and Conscience* (1946); etc. President, Talladega College, Ala., 1933–43; prof. Christian ethics, Pacific School of Religion, 1944–49; pres., City College of New York, 1952–69.

GALLAGHER, WILLIAM DAVIS (Aug. 21, 1808–June 27, 1894); b. Philadelphia, Pa. Editor, poet. *Erato No. I* (1835); *Erato No. II* (1835); *Erato No. III* (1837); *Miami Woods, A Golden Wedding, and Other Poems* (1881). Editor: *Selections from the Poetical Literature of the West* (1841). Editor, *The Cincinnati Mirror,* 1832–36; *The Western Monthly Maga-*

zine, 1837; founder, *The Hesperian*, 1838; co-editor, 1838–39; on staff of *Cincinnati Gazette*, 1840–50, and other Western newspapers and magazines. See E. Venable's *Poets of Ohio* (1909).

GALLATIN, [Abraham Alphonse] ALBERT (Jan. 29, 1761–Aug. 12, 1849); b. Geneva, Switzerland. Statesman, diplomat, ethnologist. Called "The Father of American Ethnology." *The Writings of Albert Gallatin*, ed. by Henry Adams, 3v. (1879). Secretary of the Treasury, 1801–14; minister to France, 1816–23; minister to England, 1826–27. Co-founder, New York University, 1831. Founder, The American Ethnological Society, 1842. See Henry Brooks Adams's *Life of Albert Gallatin* (1879); Raymond Walters, Jr.'s *Albert Gallatin: Jeffersonian Financier and Diplomat* (1969).

GALLATIN, ALBERT EUGENE (July 23, 1881–June 15, 1952); b. Villanova, Pa. Art critic, collector. *Whistler's Art Dicta* (1904); *Certain Contemporaries* (1916); *Portraits of Whistler* (1918); *Modern Fine Printing in America* (1921); *American Water-Colourists* (1922); *Gallatin Iconography* (1934); *George Braque* (1943); *Sir Max Beerbohm: Bibliographical Notes* (1944); *Aubrey Beardsley—Catalogue of Drawings and Bibliography* (1945); etc.

GALLAUDET, THOMAS HOPKINS (Dec. 10, 1787–Sept. 10, 1851); b. Philadelphia, Pa. Educator, author. *Discourses* (1818). In 1817 founded at Hartford the first free deaf-mute institute in the United States. Gallaudet College, Washington, D.C. is named in his honor; his son, Edward Miner Gallaudet, was one of its founders. Prof. education, New York University, 1832–33. See Edward M. Gallaudet's *Life of Thomas Hopkins Gallaudet*.

Gallegher, and Other Stories. By Richard Harding Davis (1891). The title story records the adventures of an office boy on a metropolitan newspaper who turns reporter and detective.

Gallery, The. Novel by John Hornes Burns (1947). Concerned with Americans living in Italy.

GALLICO, PAUL [William] (July 26, 1897–); b. New York. Journalist, author. *Farewell to Sport* (1938); *Adventures of Hiram Holliday* (1939); *The Secret Front* (1940); *The Snow Goose* (1941); *Golf Is a Friendly Game* (1942); *Lou Gehrig* (1942); *Confessions of a Story Writer* (1946); *The Abandoned* (1950); *Trial by Terror* (1952); *Small Miracle* (1952); *The Foolish Immortals* (1953); *Snowflake* (1953); *Love of Seven Dolls* (1954); *Thomasina* (1958); *Mrs. 'Arris Goes to Paris* (1958); *Ludmila* (1955); *Too Many Ghosts* (1959); *Mrs. 'Arris Goes to New York* (1960); *The Hurricane Story* (1960); *Further Confessions of a Story Writer* (1961); *Scruffy* (1962); etc. With New York *Daily News*, 1922–36. *Love, Let Me Not Hunger* (1963); *The Golden People* (1965); *The Man Who Was Magic* (1966); *The Story of Silent Night* (1967); *Manxmouse* (1968); *The Poseidon Adventure* (1969). With Suzanne Szasz - Ed. *The Silent Miaow* (1964).

GALLOWAY, GEORGE BARNES (Jan. 9, 1898–); b. Brooklyn, N.Y. Political scientist, author. *Congress at the Crossroads* (1946); *Congress and Parliament* (1955); *History of the House of Representatives* (1962); etc. Editor, co-author: *Internal Debts of the United States* (with Evans Clark, 1933); *Planning for America* (1941); etc.

GALLUP, DONALD CLIFFORD (May 12, 1913–); b. Sterling, Conn. Educator, author. *T. S. Eliot Bibliography* (1953); *Ezra Pound Bibliography* (1963). Editor: *The Flowers of Friendship* (1953); *Eugene O'Neill Inscriptions* (1960); *Eugene O'Neill: More Stately Mansions* (1964). Curator, American literature collection, Jonathan Edwards College, since 1947.

GALLUP, GEORGE HORACE (Nov. 18, 1901–); b. Jefferson, Ia. Public opinion statistician, author. *The Pulse of Democracy* (with S. F. Rae, 1940); *Guide to Public Opinion Polls* (1944); *The Secrets of Long Life* (with Evan Hill, 1960).

Founder, American Institute of Public Opinion, 1935; British Institute of Public Opinion, 1936; Audience Research Institute, 1939; pres., since 1939. Supervises compilation of numerous polls of public opinion on current affairs, particularly of political questions and national elections.

GAMBRELL, HERBERT PICKENS (July 15, 1898–); b. Tyler, Tex. Educator, historian. *A Social and Political History of Texas* (with L. W. Newton, 1932); *Mirabeau Buonaparte Lamar* (1934); *Anson Jones, the Last President of Texas* (1948); *Texas Yesterday and Today* (with L. W. Newton, 1948); *Pictorial History of Texas* (with wife, Virginia Gambrell, 1960). History dept., Southern Methodist University, since 1923; curator, Dallas Historical Society, 1934–38; director of its museum, 1938–48.

GAMBRILL, J[ohn] MONTGOMERY (May 9, 1880–Jan. 13, 1953); b. Baltimore, Md. Educator, historian. *Leading Events of Maryland History* (1903); etc. Co-editor: *The Westward Movement* (1939). History dept., Teachers College, Columbia University, from 1913.

Games People Play. Analysis of psychological "character" types, by Eric Berne (1964).

Gamesters; or, Ruins of Innocence, The. Novel by Caroline Matilda Warren (1805).

GAMOW, GEORGE (Mar. 4, 1904–Aug. 19, 1968); b. Odessa, Rus. Educator, author. *Structure of Atomic Nuclei and Nuclear Transformations* (1931); *The Birth and Death of the Sun* (1940); *Biography of the Earth* (1941); *One, Two, Three . . . Infinity* (1947); *Creation of the Universe* (1952); *The Moon* (1953); *Puzzle-Math* (1958); *Matter, Earth and Sky* (1958); *The Atom and Its Nucleus* (1961); *Planet Called Earth* (1963); *Mr. Tompkins in Paperback* (1965); *Thirty Years that Shook Physics* (1966); etc. Prof. physics, George Washington University, 1934–56; University of Colorado, from 1956.

GANN, ERNEST K[ellogg] (Oct. 13, 1910–); b. Lincoln, Neb. Author. *Island In the Sky* (1944); *Blaze of Noon* (1946); *Fiddler's Green* (1950); *The High and the Mighty* (1953); *Soldier of Fortune* (1954); *Twilight for the Gods* (1956); *Fate Is the Hunter* (1961); *In the Company of Eagles* (1966); *Song of the Sirens* (1968); etc.

GANNETT, FRANK ERNEST (Sept. 15, 1876–Dec. 3, 1957); b. Bristol, N.Y. Editor, publisher. *Winging Round the World* (1947). Owner of *Rochester Democrat and Chronicle*, *Rochester Times-Union*, *Albany Knickerbocker*, *Albany News*, *Elmira Advertiser*, *Elmira Telegram*, *Elmira Star-Gazette*, *Utica Observer-Dispatch*, *Utica Press*, *Ithaca Journal*, *Hartford Times*, *Plainfield* (N.J.) *Courier-News*, *Danville* (Ill.) *Commercial-News*, and other newspapers, chiefly in New York State. See S. T. Williamson's *Frank Gannett* (1940).

GANNETT, HENRY (Aug. 24, 1846–Nov. 5, 1914); b. Bath, Me. Geographer, author. *A Manual of Topographic Methods* (1893); *Physiographic Types*, 2v. (1898–1900); *Gazetteer of Texas* (1902); *Origin of Certain Place Names in the United States* (1902); *Commercial Geography* (with others, 1905); etc. One of the founders of the National Geographic Society in 1883. He was called the "Father of American Map Making."

GANNETT, LEWIS STILES (Oct. 3, 1891–Feb. 4, 1966); b. Rochester, N.Y. Journalist, author. *Young China* (1926); *Sweet Land* (1934); *Cream Hill* (1949). Editor: *The Family Book of Verse* (1961). On staff of *The Nation*, 1919–1928; New York *Herald Tribune*, 1928–1956; author of daily column, "Books and Things," 1931–56.

GANNETT, WILLIAM CHANNING (Mar. 13, 1840–Dec. 15, 1923); b. Boston, Mass. Unitarian clergyman, author. *Ezra Stiles Gannett* (1875); *Studies in Longfellow, Whittier, Holmes and Lowell* (1898); etc. Compiler (with Frederick L.

Hosmer): *The Thought of God in Hymns and Poems,* 3 series (1885, 1894, 1918).

GANOE, WILLIAM ADDLEMAN (May 14, 1881–); b. Mifflintown, Pa. Army officer, author. *The English of Military Communications* (1918); *Soldiers Unmasked* (1935); *History of the United States Army* (1942); *My Heart Remembers* (1950); etc.

GARBER, PAUL NEFF (July 27, 1899–); b. New Market, Va. Methodist bishop, educator, author. *The Romance of American Methodism* (1931); *John Carlyle Kilgo* (1937); *The Methodists Are One People* (1939); *The Methodists of Continental Europe* (1949); *The Gadsden Treaty* (1960); Contributor: *Dictionary of American Biography.* History dept., Duke University, 1924–44.

GARD, WAYNE [Sanford] (1899–). Author. *Book Reviewing* (1927); *Sam Bass* (1936); *Frontier Justice* (1949); *The Chisholm Trail* (1954); *The Great Buffalo Hunt* (1959); *Rawhide Texas* (1965); etc.

GARDENER, HELEN H[amilton] (Mrs. Charles Selden Smart; Mrs. Selden Allen Day) (June 21, 1853–July 26, 1925); b. (Alice Chenoweth) Winchester, Va. Essayist. *Men, Women, and Gods* (1885); *A Thoughtless Yes* (1890); *Facts and Fictions of Life* (1893); *An Unofficial Patriot* (1894), dramatized by James A. Herne as *Griffith Davenport, Circuit Rider* (prod. 1899); etc.

GARDINER, DOROTHY (Nov. 5, 1894–); b. Naples, Italy. Author. *The Transatlantic Ghost* (1933); *A Drink for Mr. Cherry* (1934); *The Golden Lady* (1935); *Snow-Water* (1939); *The Great Betrayal* (1949); *What Crime Is It?* (1956); *The Seventh Mourner* (1958); etc.

GARDINER, HAROLD CHARLES (Feb. 6, 1904–Sept. 3, 1969); b. Washington, D.C. Roman Catholic clergyman, author. *Mysteries' End* (1946); *The Great Books: A Christian Appraisal,* 4v. (1949–51); *Norms for the Novel* (1953); *Edmund Campion* (1957); *Catholic Viewpoint on Censorship* (1958); *Movies, Morals and Art* (1961); etc. Literary editor, *America,* 1940–62.

GARDNER, ERLE STANLEY (July 17, 1889–Mar. 11, 1970); b. Malden, Mass. Lawyer, novelist. Writes under own name and pen name "A. A. Fair." *The Case of the Velvet Claws* (1933); *The Case of the Sulky Girl* (1933); *The Case of the Counterfeit Eye* (1935); *The Case of the Caretaker's Cat* (1935); *The Case of the Curious Bride* (1935); *The Case of the Stuttering Bishop* (1937); *The Case of the Perjured Parrot* (1939); *The Case of the Silent Partner* (1940); *The Case of the Buried Clock* (1943); *The Case of the Golddigger's Purse* (1945); *The Land of Shorter Shadow* (1947); *The Case of the Dubious Bridegroom* (1949); *The Case of the Fiery Fingers* (1951); *The Case of the Hesitant Hostess* (1953); *The Case of the Glamorous Ghost* (1955); *The Case of the Daring Decoy* (1957); *The Case of the Mythical Monkeys* (1959); *The Case of the Bigamous Spouse* (1961); *The Desert Is Yours* (1963); *The Case of the Beautiful Beggar* (1965); *The Case of the Worried Waitress* (1966); *Mexico's Magic Square* (1968); *The Case of the Amorous Aunt* (1969); *Drifting Down the Delta* (1969); *Mexico's Magic Square* (1969); etc.

GARDNER, GILSON (Mar. 16, 1869–Aug. 16, 1935); b. Chicago, Ill. Journalist, author. *A New Robinson Crusoe* (1920). With Chicago *Journal,* 1895–1905.

GARDNER, ISABELLA (Sept. 7, 1915–); b. Newton, Mass. Poet. *Birthdays from the Ocean* (1955); *The Looking Glass* (1961); *West of Childhood* (1965); etc.

GARDNER, JOHN W[illiam] (Oct. 8, 1912–); b. Los Angeles, Cal. Government official, foundation executive, author. *Excellence: Can We Be Equal and Excellent Too?* (1961); *Self-Renewal* (1964); *No Easy Victories* (1968); *The Recovery of Confidence* (1970). Editor: *To Turn the Tide* (1961). Vice-president, Carnegie Corporation of New York, 1949–55; pres.

1955–65; Secretary of Health, Education and Welfare, 1965–68; fellow, Kennedy Institute of Politics, Harvard University, since 1968; chairman, Urban Coalition, since 1968.

GARDNER, MARTIN (1914–). Author. *In the Name of Science* (1952); *Fads and Fallacies* (1957); *Logic, Machines, and Diagrams* (1958); *Scientific American Book of Mathematical Puzzles and Diversions* (1959); *The Second Scientific American Book of Mathematical Puzzles and Diversions* (1961); *The Ambidextrous Universe* (1964); *Archimedes* (1965); *Never Make Fun of a Turtle, My Son* (1969); etc. Editor: *The Annotated Alice* (1962); *The Annotated Ancient Mariner* (1965); *The Annotated Casey at the Bat* (1967); etc.

GARDNER, RICHARD [orginally Richard Orth] (Aug. 26, 1931–   ); b. Bremerton, Wash. Author. *The Impossible* (1962); *Scandalous John* (1963). Under pen name "Dic Gardner", self-illustrated juveniles: *Your Backyard Circus* (1959); *Before TV* (1960); *Danny and the Ape, Komba* (1962); *Is My Job for You* (1962); *The Bridge* (1963). Under pen name "John Carver": *The Sex Twist* (1962); *That Motorcycle Boy* (1966); *Wolverine* (1967). Under pen name "Richard Orth": *The Pad Upstairs* (1960); *Girl in a Go-Go Cage* (1967). Under pen name "Richard Commings": *101 Hand Puppets* (1962); *The Alchemist* (1966); *101 Masks* (1967). Under pen name "Clifford Anderson": *The Hollow Hero* (with Clifford Irving and Robert Anderson, 1959).

GARDNER, RICHARD NEWTON (July 9, 1927–); b. New York. Educator, author. *Sterling Dollar Diplomacy* (1956); *New Directions in U.S. Foreign Economic Policy* (1959); *In Pursuit of World Order* (1964); *Blueprint for Peace* (1966). Prof. law and international relations, Columbia University, since 1966.

GARFIELD, JAMES ABRAM (Nov. 19, 1831–Sept. 19, 1881); b. Orange, O. Twentieth president of the United States, author. *The Works of James Abram Garfield,* 2v. (1882–83); *The Diary of James A. Garfield,* ed. by H. J. Brown and F. D. Williams (1967). *See* Theodore C. Smith's *The Life and Letters of James Abram Garfield,* 2v. (1925); R. G. Caldwell's *James A. Garfield, Party Chieftain* (1931).

GARIS, HOWARD R. (Apr. 25, 1873–Nov. 6, 1962); b. Binghamton, N.Y. Author of books for children. *With Force of Arms* (1902); the *Uncle Wiggily* series, 35v.; the *Curlytops* series, 10v.; the *Daddy* series, 10v.; the *Buddy* series, 10v.; *Teddy* series, 7v. *Rocket Riders* series, 4v.; and many other books for children.

GARIS, LILIAN [C. McNamara] (Mrs. Howard R. Garis) (1873–Apr. 19, 1954); b. Cleveland, O. Author. *Two Little Girls* (1901); the *Girl Scout* series, 5v.; the *Make Believe Books,* 4v.; *The Melody Lane Mystery Stories,* 9v.; etc.; also other series under various pen names.

GARLAND, HAMLIN (Sept. 16, 1860–Mar. 4, 1940); b. West Salem, Wis. Novelist, playwright, author. *Main Traveled Roads* (1891); *A Spoil of Office* (1892); *Prairie Folks* (1893); *Prairie Songs* (1893); *Crumbling Idols* (1894); *Rose of Dutcher's Coolly* (1895); *Boy Life on the Prairie* (1899); *Her Mountain Lover* (1901); *Other Main Traveled Roads* (1910); *A Son of the Middle Border* (1917); *A Daughter of the Middle Border* (1921, Pulitzer prize for American biography, 1922); *Trail-Makers of the Middle Border* (1926); *Back Trailers from the Middle Border* (1928); *Roadside Meetings* (1930); *Companions on the Trail* (1931); *My Friendly Contemporaries* (1932); *Afternoon Neighbors* (1934); *Forty Years of Psychic Research* (1936); etc. For bibliography *see* Fred B. Millett's *Contemporary American Authors* (1940); H. Wayne Morgan's *American Writers in Rebellion from Twain to Dreiser* (1965); *Political Literature of the Progressive Era* ed. by G. L. Groman (1966).

GARLAND, JOSEPH (Jan. 1, 1893–); b. Gloucester, Mass. Physician, author. *The Story of Medicine* (1949); *All Creatures Here Below* (1954); etc.

GARLAND, ROBERT (Apr. 29, 1895–Dec. 27, 1955); b. Baltimore, Md. Critic, playwright, author. *The Double Miracle* (1915); *The Importance of Being a Roughneck* (1921); *At Night All Cats Are Grey* (1933); *Calling All Men* (with Leonard Sillman, 1937); etc. Drama critic, *New York World-Telegram*, 1928-1937.

GARNER, JAMES WILFORD (Nov. 22, 1871–Dec. 9, 1938); b. in Pike County, Miss. Educator, author. *The History of the United States*, 4v. (with Henry Cabot Lodge, 1906); *Government in the United States* (1911); *International Law and the World War*, 2v. (1920); *Political Science and Government* (1928); *American Foreign Policies* (1928); etc. Prof. political science, University of Illinois, 1904–38.

GARNETT, ARTHUR CAMPBELL (Oct. 20, 1894–); b. Port Victoria, South Australia. Educator, author. *Instinct and Personality* (1928); *The Mind in Action* (1931); *Reality and Value* (1937); *Freedom and Planning in Australia* (1949); *The Moral Nature of Man* (1952); *Religion and the Moral Life* (1955); *The Perpetual Process* (1965). Philosophy dept., University of Wisconsin, since 1937.

GARNETT, JAMES MERCER (Apr. 24, 1840–Feb. 18, 1916); b. in Virginia. Educator, philologist, author. *The University of Virginia*, 2v. (1904). His metrical translation of *Beowulf* (1882) was the first American translation of the poem. Editor: *Selections in English Prose* (1891).

GARNETT, LOUISE AYRES (Mrs. Eugene H. Garnett) (d. Oct. 31, 1937); b. Plymouth, Ind. Musician, composer, author. *The Muffin Shop* (1908); *Master Will of Stratford* (1916); *Eve Walks in Her Garden* (poems, 1926); *The Joyous Pretender* (1928); etc.

GARNETT, PORTER (Mar. 12, 1871–Mar. 20, 1951); b. San Francisco, Calif. Printer, author. *The Bohemian Jinks* (1908); *The Ideal Book* (with Francis P. Dill, 1931); *Letters to Bill* (1932); *Paucism and Beaumanence; or, The Culture of Fewness* (1937); etc. Editor: *The Grove Plays of the Bohemian Club*, 3v. (1918). Producer of Bohemian Grove plays, journalist, exponent of fine printing.

GARREAU, EMILE HENRY (Feb. 4, 1891–); b. Centerville, Conn. Editor, author. *Hot News* (1931); *The Scandal Monger* (1932); *What So Proudly We Hailed* (1935); Managing editor, *New York Daily Mirror* and *Sunday Mirror*, 1929–35.

GARRETSON, JAMES EDMUND (Oct. 18, 1828–Oct. 26, 1895); b. Wilmington, Del. Dentist, oral surgeon, educator, author. Pen name, "John Darby." *Old Hours of a Physician* (1871); *Thinkers and Thinking* (1873); *Two Thousand Years After* (1876); *Nineteenth Century Sense* (1887); etc.

GARRETT, EDMUND HENRY (Oct. 19, 1853–Apr. 2, 1929); b. Albany, N.Y. Painter, illustrator, author. *Romance and Reality of the Puritan Coast* (1897); *The Pilgrim Shore* (1897). Illustrated Keats, Lowell, Dumas, Bulwer, Merimée, etc.

GARRETT, EILEEN JEANETTE (d. Sept. 15, 1970); b. Beau Park, Co. Meath, Ire. Publisher, author. *My Life, As a Search for the Meaning of Mediumship* (1939); *Man the Maker* (1946); *Life Is the Healer* (1957); *Many Voices: The Autobiography of a Medium* (1968); etc. Under pen name "Jean Lyttle": *Today the Sun Rises* (1942); etc. Owner, *Tomorrow* magazine, Garrett Publications.

GARRETT, ERWIN CLARKSON (Mar. 28, 1879–Oct., 1954); b. Germantown, Philadelphia, Pa. Poet. *My Bunkie, and Other Ballads* (1907); *The Dyak Chief, and Other Verses* (1915); *Army Ballads, and Other Verses* (1916); *Jenghiz Khan, and Other Verses* (1924); *Io Triumphe, and Other Verses* (1928); *Arcturus, and Other Verses* (1955).

GARRETT, GARET (Feb. 19, 1878–Nov. 6, 1954); b. (Edward Peter Garrett) Pana, Ill. Author. *Where the Money Grows* (1911); *The Driver* (1921); *Harangue* (1927); *A Bub-*

ble That Broke the World (1932); *A Time Is Born* (1944); *The People's Pottage* (1952); *Wild Wheel* (1952); *The American Story* (1955); etc.

GARRETT, GEORGE [Palmer], Jʀ. (June 11, 1929–); b. Orlando, Fla. *The Reverend Ghost: Poems* (1957); *King of the Mountain* (1958); *The Sleeping Gypsy, and Other Poems* (1958); *The Finished Man* (1959); *In The Briar Patch* (1961); *The Cold Ground Was My Bed Last Night* (1964); *Do Lord Remember Me* (1965); *A Wreath for Garibaldi* (1969).

GARRIGUE, JEAN (Dec. 8, 1914–); b. Evansville, Ind. Poet. *The Ego and the Centaur* (1947); *The Monument Rose* (1953); *Water Walk by Villa d'Este* (1959); *Country without Maps* (1964); *New and Selected Poems* (1967).

GARRISON, FIELD HUDSON (Nov. 5, 1870–Apr. 18, 1935); b. Washington, D.C. Army officer, editor, librarian, author. *Josiah Willard Gibbs and His Relation to Modern Science* (1909); *An Introduction to the History of Medicine* (1913); *John Shaw Billings* (1915); etc. Compiler (with Casey A. Wood): *A Physician's Anthology* (1920). Editor, *Index Medicus*, 1903–27. Librarian, Surgeon General's Office, Washington, D.C., 1889–1922.

GARRISON, THEODOSIA (Mrs. Frederic J. Faulks) (1874–); b. Newark, N.J. Poet. *Joy o' Life, and Other Poems* (1909); *Earth Cry, and Other Poems* (1910); *The Dreamers, and Other Poems* (1917); *As the Larks Rise* (1921).

GARRISON, WENDELL PHILLIPS (June 4, 1840–1907); b. Cambridgeport, Mass., son of William Lloyd Garrison. Editor, author. *William Lloyd Garrison* (with Francis Jackson Garrison, 1894); *Parables for School and Home* (1897); *The New Gulliver* (1898). Compiler: *Bedtime Poetry* (1887). Lit. editor, *The Nation*, (1865–1906). See *Letters and Memorials of Wendell Phillips Garrison* (1908).

GARRISON, WILLIAM LLOYD (Dec. 10, 1805–May 24, 1879); b. Newburyport, Mass. Editor, abolitionist, author. *Thoughts on African Colonization* (1832); *Sonnets and Other Poems* (1843); etc. Founder, *The Liberator*, Jan. 1, 1831. See *William Lloyd Garrison, 1805–1879: The Story of His Life Told by His Children*, 4v. (1885–89); John L. Thomas's *Liberator: William Lloyd Garrison* (1963); G. Fredrickson's *William Lloyd Garrison* (1968).

GARRISON, WINFRED ERNEST (Oct. 1, 1874–); b. St. Louis, Mo. Educator, author. *Wheeling through Europe* (1900); *Catholicism and the American Mind* (1928); *The March of Faith: Religion in America since 1856* (1933); *Religion Follows the Frontier* (1931); *A Protestant Manifesto* (1952); *Twenty Centuries of Christianity* (with Paul Hutchinson, 1959); *Heritage and Destiny* (1963); *Thy Sea So Great* (1965); etc. Literary editor, *Christian Century*, 1923–55. Prof. church history, Disciples Divinity House and University of Chicago, 1935–43; prof. philosophy and religion, University of Houston, since 1951.

"Garrison of Cape Ann, The." Poem by John Greenleaf Whittier (1857).

GARRITY, DEVIN ADAIR (Nov. 26, 1905–); b. Staten Island, N.Y. Editor, publisher. Editor: *New Irish Poets* (1948); *Forty-four Irish Short Stories* (1955); *Mentor Book of Irish Poetry* (1965). Pres., Devin Adair Co., since 1939.

GARSIDE, EDWARD BALLARD (1907–). Author. *Cranberry Red* (1938); *The Man from Brazil* (1953); *Whirligig* (1955); etc. Translator: *Dream of Philip II* by Edgar Maass (1944); *Gods, Graves and Scholars* by C. W. Ceram (1953); etc.

GARSON, BARBARA (1942–). Author. *MacBird* (1966).

Garth. Novel by Julian Hawthorne (1875). The story revolves around an Indian curse placed upon a New Hampshire family because one of its founders had violated a sacred Indian grave.

Garth, Will. Pen name of Henry Kuttner.

GARTHOFF, RAYMOND LEONARD (Mar. 26, 1929–); b. Cairo, Egypt. Foreign service officer, author. *Soviet Military Doctrine* (1953); *Soviet Strategy in the Nuclear Age* (1958); *The Soviet Image of Future War* (1959); *Sino-Soviet Military Relations* (1966). Co-author, editor, and translator of other books on Soviet military and political affairs.

GARVIN, MARGARET ROOT (d. Dec. 4, 1949); b. New York City. Poet. *A Walled Garden, and Other Poems* (1913); *Peacocks in the Sun, and Other Poems* (1925).

GARWOOD, IRVING (Nov. 28, 1883–June 8, 1957); b. Ada, O. Educator, author. *Questions and Problems in American Literature* (1927); *The American Periodicals from 1850 to 1860* (1931); *New Studies in American Literature* (1937). Head, English dept., Western Illinois State Teachers College, 1924–46.

GASKIN, CATHERINE (Apr. 2, 1929–); b. Dundalk, Ire. Author. *This Other Eden* (1948); *With Every Year* (1946); *All Else Is Folly* (1951); *Sara Dane* (1954); *Blake's Reach* (1958); *Corporation Wife* (1960); *I Know My Love* (1962); *The File on Devlin* (1965); *Edge of Glass* (1967); etc.

GASS, PATRICK (June 12, 1771–Apr. 30, 1870); b. Sherman's Creek Valley, Pa. Explorer, author. *A Journal of the Voyages and Travels of a Corps of Discovery, Under the Command of Capt. Lewis and Captain Clarke* (1807).

GASS, SHERLOCK BRONSON (Oct. 17, 1878–Aug. 31, 1945); b. Mansfield, O. Educator, author. *A Lover of the Chair* (1919); *Criers of the Shops* (1925); *A Tap on the Shoulder* (1929); *Irons in the Fire* (1939); *Family Crisis* (1940); etc. Prof. English, University of Nebraska, from 1917.

GASS, WILLIAM H. (July 30, 1924–   ); b. Fargo, N.D. Author. *Omensetter's Luck* (1966); *In the Heart of the Country* (stories, 1967); *The Clairvoyant* (1968); *Willie Master's Lonesome Wife* (1968); *Tunnel* (1970). Faculty, Purdue University.

GASSNER, JOHN (Waldhorn) (Jan. 30, 1903–April 2, 1967); b. Sziget, Hung. Educator, drama critic. *Producing the Play* (1941); *The Theatre in Our Times* (1954); *Form and Idea in the Modern Theatre* (1956); *Directions in Modern Theatre and Drama* (1965); *Dramatic Soundings: Evaluations and Retractions Culled from 30 Years of Dramatic Criticism* (1968); etc. Editor: *Masters of the Drama* (1940); *Treasury of the Theatre*, 3v. (1951); *Twenty Best European Plays on the American Stage* (1957); *Best American Plays* series, 6v. (1939–61); *Reader's Encyclopedia of World Drama* (with Edward Quinn, 1969); etc. Drama critic, *The Forum*, 1941–49; *Educational Theatre Journal*, from 1951; *The Survey*, 1951–52; etc. Sterling prof. playwriting and dramatic literature, Yale University, from 1956.

GASTER, THEODORE H[erzl] (July 21, 1906–); b. London. Archeologist. *Passover, Its History and Traditions* (1949); *The Oldest Stories in the World* (1952); *Thespis: Ritual, Myth, and Drama in the Ancient Near East* (1950); *Festivals of the Jewish Year* (1953); *The Holy and the Profane* (1955); *Myth, Legend and Custom in the Old Testament* (1969); etc. Prof. comparative religion, Dropsie College, 1944–59; prof. religion, Barnard College, since 1966.

GATES, ELEANOR (Mrs. Richard Walton Tully; Mrs. Frederick Ferdinand Moore) (Sept. 26, 1875–Mar. 7, 1951); b. Shakopee, Minn. Playwright, novelist. *The Biography of a Prairie Girl* (1902); *We Are Seven* (1915); *The Poor Little Rich Girl* (1916); *Phoebe* (1919); etc.

GATES, JOSEPHINE SCRIBNER (Sept. 12, 1859–Aug 21, 1930); b. Mt. Vernon, O. Author of books for children. *The Story of Live Dolls* (1901); and numerous other *Live Doll* stories; *Little Red, White and Blue* (1906); *Sunshine Annie* (1910); *The Story of the Mince Pie* (1916); etc.

GATES, PAUL WALLACE (Dec. 4, 1901–); b. Nashua, N.H. Educator, author. *Frontier Landlords and Pioneer Tenants* (1945); *Fifty Million Acres* (1954); *Agriculture and the Civil War* (1965); *California Ranchos and Farms* (1967); *History of Public Land Law Development* (1968); *The Farmer's Age: Agriculture 1815–1860* (1968); *The Frontier in American Development* (1969); etc. Prof. history, Cornell University, since 1936.

Gates Ajar, The. Novel by Elizabeth Stuart Phelps (1868, but dated 1869). The author's best known book. Its purpose was to comfort parents whose sons had been killed in the Civil War, by revising the stern theological opinions then current. The dead would retain their family characteristics and continue the work left unfinished on earth. Sequels to it were *Beyond the Gates* (1883); *The Gates Between* (1887); and *Within the Gates* (1901).

Gath. Pen name of George Alfred Townsend.

"Gathering Shells from the Sea Shore." Song by Will L. Thompson.

GATTI, ATTILIO (1896–); b. in Italy. *Mediterranean Spotlights* (1944); *Here Is the Veld* (1948); *Africa Is Adventure* (1959); *New Africa* (with Ellen Gatti, 1960); *Sangoma* (1962); etc.

GATZKE, HANS WILHEIM (Dec. 10, 1915–); b. Duelken, Ger. Educator. *Germany's Drive to the West* (1950); *The Present in Perspective* (1957); *The Course of Civilization* (1961); Editor, translator: Karl von Clausewitz' *Principles of War* (1942). History dept., Johns Hopkins University, 1947–64; prof. history, Yale University, since 1964.

GAUSS, CHRISTIAN (Feb. 2, 1878–Nov. 1, 1951); b. Ann Arbor, Mich. Educator. *Through College on Nothing a Year* (1915); *The German Emperor* (1915); *Why We Went to War* (1918); *Life in College* (1930); *A Primer for Tomorrow* (1934); etc. Co-author: *America Now* (1938); *The City of Man* (1940); *American Thought* (1947); *Modern Princeton* (1947). Modern language dept., Princeton University, from 1905; dean of the college, 1925–45.

GAUSS, MARIANNE (1885–); Author. *Danae* (1925); *Five Animals* (1926); *Book of the Woods* (1931); *Kickapoo, the Fighting Bronco* (with Charlotte Wilhelmina Gauss, 1938); *Smasher and Kickup* (with same, 1939); *Adventure in the West* (1944).

GAVER, JACK (1906–); b. Tolono, Ill. Drama critic. *There's Laughter in the Air* (with David Dacks, 1945); *Curtain Calls* (1949). With United Press Association, since 1929; drama critic, columnist, since 1930.

GAVIN, CATHERINE IRVINE. Author. *Louis Phillipe, King of the French* (1933); *Liberated France* (1955); *Madeleine* (1957); *The Cactus and the Crown* (1962); etc.

GAVIN, FRANK STANTON BURNS (Oct. 31, 1890–Mar. 20, 1938); b. Cincinnati, O. Episcopal clergyman, educator, theologian, author. *The Jewish Antecedents of the Christian Sacraments* (1928); *Selfhood and Sacrifice* (1932); *Seven Centuries of the Problem of Church and State* (1938); etc. Prof., ecclesiastical history, General Theological Seminary, New York, 1923–38.

GAVIN, JAMES M[aurice] (Mar. 22, 1907–); b. New York. Army officer. *Airborne Warfare* (1948); *War and Peace in the Space Age* (1958); *A Civil War Album of Paintings by the Prince de Joinville* (with André Maurois, 1964); *Crisis Now* (1968).

GAVIT, JOHN PALMER (July 1, 1868–Oct. 27, 1954); b. Albany, N.Y. Editor, author. *Reporter's Manual* (1903); *Americans by Choice* (1922); *College* (1924); *Opium* (1927); etc. Managing editor, *New York Evening Post*, 1913–18; director, 1920–22, etc.

GAW, ALLISON (May 23, 1877–May 17, 1954); b. Philadelphia, Pa. Educator, author. *Sir Samuel Tuke's Adventures of Five Hours* (1917); *Studying the Play* (1921); *Pharoah's Daughter* (with wife, Ethelean Tyson Gaw, prod. 1925); *Time in Shakespeare* (1946); etc. Editor and owner, *The Lyric West,* from 1925. English dept., University of Southern California, from 1911.

GAW, ETHELEAN TYSON (Mrs. Allison Gaw); b. in Pennsylvania. Playwright. *Pharoah's Daughter* (with husband, prod. 1927); etc. Co-editor, *The Lyric West,* from 1925.

GAY, PETER (June 20, 1923–   ); b. Berlin. Educator, author. *The Dilemma of Democratic Socialism: Eduard Bernstein's Challenge to Marx* (1952); *Voltaire's Politics: The Poet as Realist* (1959); *The Party of Humanity: Essays in the French Enlightenment* (1964); *A Loss of Mastery: Puritan Historians in Colonial America* (1966); *The Enlightenment: An Interpretation:* vol. I, *The Rise of Modern Paganism* (1966); vol. II, *The Science of Freedom* (1969); *Weimar Culture* (1968). Prof. history, Yale·University, since 1969.

GAY, ROBERT MALCOLM (Feb. 15, 1879–July 21, 1961); b. Brooklyn, N.Y. Educator, author. *Emerson: A Study of the Poet as Seer* (1928); *Reading and Writing* (1935); etc. Compiler: *The Riverside Book of Verse, 1250–1925* (1927); *College Book of Verse* (1927); *College Book of Prose* (1929); *Words into Type* (with Marjorie E. Skillin, 1948); *The Timid Sex* (1952); etc. Director, Bread Loaf Writers Conference 1929–31. Prof. English, Simmons College, from 1918.

GAY, SYDNEY HOWARD (May 22, 1814–June 25, 1888); b. Hingham, Mass. Editor, abolitionist, author. *James Madison* (1884). Editor, *Anti-Slavery Standard,* 1844–58.

GAYARRÉ, CHARLES ÉTIENNE ARTHUR (Jan. 9, 1805–Feb. 11, 1895); b. New Orleans, La. Jurist, historian, novelist. *Histoire de la Louisane,* 2v. (1846–47); *History of Louisiana,* 3v. (1854–66); *Philip II of Spain* (1866); *Fernando de Lemos* (1872); *Albert Dubayet* (1882); etc. See Edward Larocque Tinker's *Charles Gayarré,* in Bibliographical Society of America *Papers,* v. 27, 1933.

Gayle, Newton. Pen name of Muna Lee and Maurice Guiness.

GAYLER, CHARLES (Apr. 1, 1820–May 28, 1892); b. New York City. Journalist, novelist, playwright. *The Buckeye Gold Hunters* (prod. 1849); *The Son of the Night* (prod. 1857); *Bull Run; or, The Sacking of Fairfax Courthouse* (prod. 1861); *Out of the Streets* (1869); *Lights and Shadows* (prod. 1888); *Fritz, Our Cousin German* (prod. 1870).

GAYLEY, CHARLES MILLS (Feb. 22, 1858–July 26, 1932); b. Shanghai, China. Educator, author. *Methods and Materials of Literary Criticism,* 2v. (v. 1, with Fred Newton Scott, 1899, v. 2, with Benjamin Putnam Kurtz, 1920); *English Poetry: Its Principles and Progress* (with Clement Calhoun Young and Benjamin Putnam Kurtz, 1904); *Plays of Our Forefathers* (1907); *Beaumont, the Dramatist* (1914). Editor: *The Classic Myths in English Literature* (1893); *Representative English Comedies,* 4v. (1914–36). Prof. English, University of California, 1889–1923.

Gaylord, Glance. Pen name of Warren Ives Bradley.

Gazette of the United States. New York City. Semiweekly. First news journal devoted to official government intelligence. Founded Apr. 15, 1789, by John Fenno and Alexander Hamilton. It grew out of the opening of the First Session of Congress, Mar. 4, 1789. Moved to Philadelphia Nov. 3, 1790; suspended Sept. 18, 1793; resumed Dec. 11, 1793, as a daily. Name changed Feb. 20, 1804, to the *United States Gazette.* Merged Mar. 9, 1818, with the *True American* to form *The Union.*

GEBHARD, PAUL HENRY (July 3, 1917–); b. Rocky Ford, Colo. Anthropologist, author. *Sexual Behavior in the Human Female* (with Alfred Kinsey, 1953); *Sex Offenders* (1965). Co-author: *Pregnancy, Birth, and Abortion* (1958); Executive director, Institute for Sexual Research, University of Indiana, since 1956; prof. anthropology, since 1967.

GÉBLER, ERNEST (1915–). *Plymouth Adventure* (1950); *A Week in the Country* (1957); *The Love Investigator* (1960); *Hoffman* (1969); *Old Man and the Girl* (1969); etc.

GEDDES, JAMES, Jr. (July 29, 1858–Sept. 30, 1948); b. Boston, Mass. Educator, author. *Canadian French: The Language and Literature* (1902); *Study of an Acadian French Dialect* (1908); *Memoirs of a College Professor* (1945); etc. Romance language dept., Boston University, 1887–1937.

GEDDES, VIRGIL (May 14, 1897–); b. in Dixon, Co., Neb. Playwright. *Forty Poems* (1926); *The Frog* (1928); *The Earth Between, and Beyond the Night* (1930); *Beyond Tragedy* (1930); *Native Ground, The Plowshare's Gleam, As the Crow Flies* (1932); *Pocahontas and the Elders* (1933); *Towards Revolution in the American Theatre* (1933); *Decisions Before Battle* (poems, 1939); *Country Postmaster* (1952); etc.

GEE, WILSON [Parham] (Sept. 18, 1888–Feb. 1, 1961); b. Union, S.C. Rural economist, author. *The Place of Agriculture in American Life* (1930); *Research Barriers in the South* (1932); *The Gist Family of South Carolina* (1934); etc. Editor: *Economic and Social Survey of Warren County* (1943); *Social Science Research Methods* (1950). Prof. rural economics, University of Virginia, from 1923.

GEER, WALTER (Aug. 19, 1857–Feb 23, 1937); b. Williamstown, Mass. Author. *Napoleon the Third* (1920); *The French Revolution* (1922); *Napoleon and His Family,* 3v. (1927–29); etc.

Geese Flying South. Short story by August Derleth (1940).

GEIGER, GEORGE RAYMOND (May 8, 1903–); b. New York. Educator, author. *The Philosophy of Henry George* (1933); *Towards an Objective Ethics* (1938); *Philosophy and the Social Order* (1947); *John Dewey in Perspective* (1958); *Science, Folklore and Philosophy* (1966); etc. Prof. philosophy, Antioch College, since 1937.

GEIL, WILLIAM EDGAR (1865–Apr. 1925); b. near Doylestown, Pa. Explorer, author. *The Isle Called Patmos* (1898); *Laodicea* (1898); *A Yankee on the Yangtze* (1904); *The Men on the Mount* (1905); *A Yankee in Pigmy Land* (1905); *The Great Wall of China* (1909); *Eighteen Capitals of China* (1911); etc.

GEIRINGER, KARL (Apr. 26, 1899–); b. Vienna. Educator, musician, author. *Brahms* (1936); *Musical Instruments* (1945); *The Bach Family* (with I. S. Geiringer, 1954); *Music of the Bach Family* (1955); *The Structure of Beethoven's Diabelli Variations* (1964); *Johann Sebastian Bach* (1966); etc. Prof. history and theory of music, Boston University, since 1941.

Geis, Bernard, Associates. New York. Publishers. Founded 1958 by Bernard Geis, who is director and editor. Books include general fiction and nonfiction.

GEISEL, THEODOR SEUSS (Mar. 2, 1904–); b. Springfield, Mass. Cartoonist, author. Pen names, "Dr. Seuss" and Theo. Le Seig. *And to Think That I Saw It on Mulberry Street* (1937); *The 500 Hats of Bartholomew Cubbins* (1938); *The Seven Lady Godivas* (1939); *The King's Stilts* (1939); *Horton Hatches the Egg* (1940); *McElligot's Pool* (1947); *If I Ran the Zoo* (1950); *Scrambled Eggs, Super!* (1953); *On Beyond Zebra* (1955); *If I Ran the Circus* (1956); *The Cat in the Hat* (1957); *Green Eggs and Ham* (1960); *Dr. Seuss's Sleep Book* (1962); *I Wish I Had Duck Feet* (1965); *Fox in Socks* (1966); *The Foot Book* (1968); *My Book about Me* (1969); *I Can Draw It Myself* (1970); *Mr. Brown Can Moo! Can You?* (1970); etc.

Under pen name "Theo Le Seig": *The Eye Book* (1968); *The Foot Book* (1968).

Geisha, The. Musical comedy by James Davis (1848–1907) under the pen name "Owen Hall" (prod. 1896). Lyrics by Harry Greenbank, music by Sidney Jones.

GEISMAR, MAXWELL DAVID (Aug. 1, 1909–); b. New York. Critic. *Writers in Crisis* (1942); *The Last of the Provincials* (1947); *Rebels and Ancestors* (1953); *American Moderns: From Rebellion to Conformity* (1958); *Henry James and the Jacobites* (1965); etc. Editor: *A Whitman Reader* (1955); *The Ring Lardner Reader* (1963); etc.

GELB, IGNACE JAY (Oct. 14, 1907–); b. Tarnow, Pol. Educator, author. *Hittite Hieroglyphs,* 3v. (1931–42); *Inscriptions from Alishar* (1935); *Hurrians and Subarians* (1944); *Study of Writing* (1952); *Glossary of Old Akkadian* (1955); etc. Editor: *Chicago Assyrian Dictionary,* since 1947. Dept. of Assyriology, University of Chicago, since 1941.

GELBART, LARRY (Feb. 25, 1928–   ); b. Chicago, Ill. Playwright, screenwriter, radio and television writer. Playwright: *My L.A.* (1950); *The Conquering Hero* (1960); *A Funny Thing Happened on the Way to the Forum* (with Burt Shevelove, 1961). Screenwriter: *The Notorious Landlady* (1960); *The Wrong Box* (with Burt Shevelove, 1966); *Not With My Wife You Don't!* (1966).

GELBER, JACK (April 12, 1932–   ); b. Chicago, Ill. Playwright. *The Connection* (1960); *The Apple* (prod. 1961); *On Ice* (1964); *The Cuban Thing* (1968); *Square in the Eye* (1969).

Geldert, Mrs. Louis Napoleon. See Grace Duffie Boylan.

GELLHORN, MARTHA ELLIS (1908–); b. St. Louis, Mo. Author. *What Mad Pursuit* (1934); *The Trouble I've Seen* (1936); *A Stricken Field* (1940); *The Heart of Another* (1941); *Liana* (1944); *Wine of Astonishment* (1948); *The Honeyed Peace* (1953); *Two by Two* (1958); *The Face of War* (1959); *His Own Man* (1961); *Pretty Tales for Tired People* (1965); *The Lowest Trees Have Tops* (1969); etc. Foreign correspondent, *Collier's Weekly,* 1937–46.

GELLHORN, WALTER (Sept. 18, 1906–); b. St. Louis, Mo. Educator, author. *Administrative Law: Cases and Comments* (1940); *Security, Loyalty, and Science* (1950); *Individual Freedom and Governmental Restraints* (1956); *Ombudsmen and Others* (1966); *When Americans Complain* (1966); etc. Faculty of law, Columbia University, since 1933; political science dept., since 1937.

Gem of the Prairie. Chicago, Ill. Weekly literary magazine. Founded 1844. In 1852, it was absorbed by the *Chicago Tribune,* which its publishers had founded in 1847, and became the Sunday edition of the *Tribune.*

General Magazine, and Historical Chronicle for All the British Plantations in America. Philadelphia, Pa. Monthly magazine. Founded Jan. 1741, by Benjamin Franklin, in imitation of the *Gentleman's Magazine,* the *London Magazine,* and other English magazines. Second magazine to be published in the United States, following Andrew Bradford's *American Magazine* by three days. Only six numbers were issued and it expired June 1741. *See* Frank L. Mott's *A History of American Magazines,* v. I (1938).

General Respository and Review. Boston, Mass. Quarterly. Founded Jan., 1812, and edited by Andrews Norton. Expired Oct., 1813.

"General William Booth Enters into Heaven." Poem by Vachel Lindsay (1913). A poem to be chanted with dramatic fervor, often recited by its author. It was inspired by the leader of the Salvation Army, which suggested the use of tambourines as an accompaniment.

Genesis of the United States, The. By Alexander Brown, 2v. (1890). An often cited study of our early history, by a Virginia historian who lost his hearing in the Civil War and took up a literary career as a result.

Genêt. Pen name of Janet Flanner.

GENIN, THOMAS HEDGES (Mar. 23, 1796–Oct. 19, 1868); b. near Aquebogue, L.I., N.Y. Lawyer, poet. *The Napolead, in Twelve Books* (1833); *Selections* (1869).

Genius, The. Novel by Theodore Dreiser (1915). Story of the Bohemian artist, Eugene Witla, and his love affairs, and his quest for a satisfying philosophy in a world of change.

Genius of the West. Cincinnati, O. Monthly. Founded 1853, by Howard Durham, who took into partnership the poet Coates Kinney and the librarian and anthologist William Turner Coggeshall. Expired 1856.

GENOVESE, EUGENE DOMINICK (May 19, 1930–); b. Brooklyn, N.Y. Educator, author. *The Political Economy of Slavery* (1965); *The World the Shareholders Made* (1969). Prof. history, University of Rochester, since 1969.

Genteel tradition. Defined by George Santayana as a "New England disease," a literary and social tradition which reflected austerity of mind and rigid mental discipline as opposed to a freer paganism which released the emotions. This tradition is satirized in Santayana's *The Last Puritan,* and John P. Marquand's *The Late George Apley,* novels with a Boston setting.

GENTHE, ARNOLD (Jan. 8, 1869–Aug. 8, 1942); b. Berlin, Germany, came to the United States in 1895. Photographer, author. *Old Chinatown* (with Will Irwin, 1913); *The Book of the Dance* (1916); *Impressions of Old New Orleans* (1926); *Isadora Duncan* (1929); *As I Remember* (1936); *Highlights and Shadows* (1937); etc.

Gentle Art of Making Enemies, The. By James McNeill Whistler (1890). A provocative reply to his critics and an original presentation of his ideas on art.

Gentle Reader. Essays by Samuel McChord Crothers (1903).

Gentleman from Indiana, The. First novel by Booth Tarkington (1899). Story of John Harkless, who disappoints his college friends by turning his back on ambition and settling down in a small Indiana town to edit a country newspaper.

Gentleman's Agreement. Novel by Laura Z. Hobson (1947). Deals with the politer forms of anti-Semitism under which Jews are tacitly excluded from middle-class social acceptance.

Gentleman's Magazine, The. See Burton's Gentleman's Magazine.

Gentlemen Prefer Blondes. Novel by Anita Loos (1925). Satire on flappers and their pursuit of moneyed men in the 1920's.

GENTRY, HELEN (Nov. 21, 1897–). Book designer, author. *Chronology of Books & Printing* (with David Greenhood, 1933). Worked for the Grabhorn Press, San Francisco before coming East. Designer of children's books in the publishing firm, Holiday House, New York.

GENUNG, JOHN FRANKLIN (Jan. 27, 1850–Oct. 1, 1919); b. Wilseyville, N.Y. Baptist clergyman, educator, author. *Epic of the Inner Life* (1891); *Outlines of Rhetoric* (1893); *Stevenson's Attitude to Life* (1901); *The Life Indeed* (1921); etc. Editor, *Amherst Graduates' Quarterly,* 1911–18. English dept., Amherst College, 1882–1919.

GEORGE, ALBERT JOSEPH (Jan. 7, 1913–Jan. 7, 1968); b. Cambridge, Mass. Educator, author. *Lamartine and Romantic Unanimism* (1940); *The Cap'n's Wife: The Diary of Didama Kelley Doane* (1946); *The Development of French Romanticism* (1955); *Short Fiction in France* (1964); etc. Prof. Romance languages, Syracuse University, from 1942.

GEORGE, HENRY (Sept. 2, 1839–Oct. 29, 1897); b. Philadelphia, Pa. Economist, single-taxer, author. *Progress and Poverty* (1879); *The Complete Works*, 10v. (1871–97); etc. See Henry George, Jr.'s *The Life of Henry George* (1900); George R. Geiger's *The Philosophy of Henry George* (1933); Albert Jay Nock's *Henry George* (1939); Steven B. Cord's *Henry George, Dreamer or Realist?* (1965); and the Henry George collection at The New York Public Library.

GEORGE, HENRY (Nov. 3, 1862–Nov. 14, 1916); b. Sacramento, Calif., son of Henry George (1839–1897). Editor, correspondent, author. *The Life of Henry George* (1900); *The Romance of John Bainbridge* (1906).

GEORGE, JEAN CRAIGHEAD (July 2, 1919–); b. Washington, D.C. Artist, author. *Vulpes, the Red Fox* (1948); *Vison, the Mink* (with John L. George, 1949); *The Masked Prowler* (1950); *Meph, The Pet Skunk* (1952); *Dipper of Copper Creek* (1956); *My Side of the Mountain* (1959); *Summer of the Falcon* (1962); *Gull Number 737* (1964); *Spring Comes to the Ocean* (1965); *Hold Zero!* (1966); *Moon of the Bears* (1967); *Moon of the Monarch Butterflies* (1968); *Coyote in Manhattan* (1968); *Moon of the Alligators* (1969); *Moon of the Grey Wolves* (1969); *Moon of the Moles* (1970); etc.

GEORGE, JOHN. Author, with Jean Craighead George (q.v.), of children's books.

George Balcombe. Novel by Nathaniel Beverly Tucker (1836), published anonymously. Considered by Edgar Allan Poe the best novel by an American up to that time.

George Mason, the Young Backwoodsman; or, "Don't Give Up the Ship." By Timothy Flint (1829). A book of adventure for boys.

Georgia Gazette. Savannah, Ga. Newspaper founded 1763, by James Johnston. First newspaper in Georgia.

"Georgia Land." Poem by Frank Lebby Stanton, often referred to as the unofficial state song of Georgia.

Georgia Review. Athens, Ga. Quarterly. Founded 1947. Published at the University of Georgia. A regional magazine devoted to poetry, stories, and articles.

Georgia Scenes, Characters, Incidents, &c., in the First Half Century of the Republic. by Augustus Baldwin Longstreet (1835). Classic of Georgia humor, portraying the robust and homely life of the poor whites. It ran into many editions. These sketches first appeared in the *Southern Recorder*, Milledgeville, Ga., and in the *Augusta State Rights Sentinel*, beginning in 1827.

"Georgia Volunteer, A." Civil War poem by Mary Ashley Townsend.

GEPHART, JOSEPH CURTIN (Sept. 7, 1902–); b. Bedford, Pa. Editor: *New York Handbook and Guide* (1932–42); *The New York Times Index*, since 1943.

GERARD, JAMES WATSON (1867–Dec. 6, 1951); b. Geneseo, N.Y. Lawyer, ambassador, author. *My Four Years in Germany* (1917); *Face to Face With Kaiserism* (1918); *My First Eighty-Three Years in America* (1951). Ambassador to Germany, 1913–17.

Geraud, Saint. Pen name of Bill Knott.

GEREN, PAUL FRANCIS (Dec. 5, 1913–); b. El Dorado, Ark. Author. *Burma Diary* (1943); *The Pilgrimage of Peter Strong* (1948); *New Voices, Old Worlds* (1958).

German Element in the United States, The. By A. B. Faust, 2v. (1909).

GERNSBACK, HUGO (Aug. 16, 1884–Aug. 19, 1967); b. Luxembourg. Editor, publisher, author. *The Wireless Telephone* (1908); *Radio for All* (1922); *Ralph 124C 41 Plus* (1925). Founder, *Modern Electrics* [the first radio magazine,

now incorporated with *Popular Science*] (1908); *Radio News* (1919); *Amazing Stories* (1926); *Everyday Science and Mechanics* (1931); *Sexology* (1933); etc.

"Gerontion." Poem by T. S. Eliot, from *Poems* (1920).

GEROULD, GORDON HALL (Oct. 4, 1877–1953); b. Goffstown, N.H. Educator, author. *Sir Guy of Warwick* (1905); *The Grateful Dead: The History of a Folk Story* (1908); *Saints' Legends* (1916); *Peter Sanders, Retired* (1917); *Youth in Harley* (1920); *Filibuster* (1924); *A Midsummer Mystery* (1925); *The Ballad of Tradition* (1932); *Patterns of English and American Fiction* (1942); etc. Editor: *Contemporary Short Stories* (1927); etc. English dept., Princeton University, 1905–46.

GEROULD, JAMES THAYER (Oct. 3, 1872–June 8, 1951); b. Goffstown, N.H. Librarian, editor. *Sources of English History of the Seventeenth Century, 1603–1689* (1921); *A Guide to Trollope* (1948). Literary editor, *The Bellman*, 1916–18. Librarian, Princeton University, 1920–38.

GEROULD, KATHARINE FULLERTON (Mrs. Gordon Hall Gerould) (Feb. 6, 1879–July 27, 1944); b. Brockton, Mass. Novelist, essayist. *Vain Oblations* (1914); *The Great Tradition, and Other Stories* (1915); *Hawaii: Scenes and Impressions* (1916); *A Change of Air* (1917); *Modes and Morals* (1920); *Lost Valley* (1922); *Valiant Dust* (1922); *Conquistador* (1923); *The Aristocratic West* (1925); *The Light That Never Was* (1931); *Ringside Seats* (1937).

GERRY, MARGARITA SPAULDING (July 28, 1870–); b. Washington, D.C. Author. *The Toy Shop* (1908); *As Caesar's Wife* (1912); *The Sound of Water* (1914); *Philippa's Fortune* (1921); *Philippa of the Chateau* (1922); *Philippa's Experiments* (1923); etc.

GERSCHENKRON, ALEXANDER (Oct. 1, 1904–); b. Odessa, Rus. Educator, author. *Bread and Democracy in Germany* (1943); *Economic Relations with the U.S.S.R.* (1945); *The Progress of Underdeveloped Areas* (with others, 1952); *Economic Backwardness in Historical Perspective* (1962); *Continuity in History and Other Essays* (1968); etc. Prof. economics, Harvard University, since 1948.

GERSHOY, LEO (Sept. 27, 1897–); b. Krivoi Rog, Rus. Educator, author. *The French Revolution, 1789–99* (1932); *The French Revolution and Napoleon* (1933); *From Despotism to Revolution, 1763–1789* (1944); *The Era of the French Revolution, 1789–1799, Ten Years That Shook the World* (1957); *Bertrand Barére: A Reluctant Terrorist* (1962). Editor: *A Survey of European Civilization* (with others, 1969). Prof. history, New York University, since 1946.

GERSHWIN, IRA (Dec. 6, 1896–); b. New York. Lyricist. Wrote lyrics for music of his brother, George Gershwin, in the following: *A Dangerous Maid* (prod. 1921); *Lady, Be Good* (prod. 1924); *Tip Toes* (prod. 1925); *Oh, Kay* (prod. 1926); *Funny Face* (prod. 1927); *Rosalie* (with P. G. Wodehouse, prod. 1927); *Strike Up The Band* (prod. 1929); *Girl Crazy* (prod. 1930); *Of Thee I Sing* (prod. 1932); *Let 'Em Eat Cake* (prod. 1933); *Porgy and Bess* (with DuBose Heyward, prod. 1935). Also lyrics for the following: *Be Yourself* (with Kaufman and Connelly, prod. 1924); *Ziegfeld Follies* (prod. 1936); *Lady in the Dark* (1940); etc. See *The George and Ira Gershwin Songbook* (1960).

GERSON, NOEL B[ertram] (Nov. 6, 1914–); b. Chicago, Ill. Under own name: *Mohawk Ladder* (1951); *Golden Eagle* (1953); *The Highwayman* (1955); *The Conqueror's Wife* (1957); *Daughter of Eve* (1958); *The Hittite* (1961); *Old Hickory* (1964); *The Slender Reed* (1965); *Anthem* (1967); *Sam Houston* (1968); *Jefferson Square* (1968); *The Golden Ghetto* (1969); *Mirror, Mirror* (1970); etc. Under pen name "Samuel Edwards": *Savage Gentleman* (1950); *Scimitar* (1955); *Naked Maja* (1959); *The Whole Plume* (1961); *Theodora* (1968); etc. Under pen name "Carter A. Vaughn": *Dragon Cove* (1964); *Roanoke Warrior* (1965); *Fortress Fury* (1966); *The River*

Devils (1969). Under pen name "Paul Lewis": *Yankee Admiral: A Biography of David Dixon Porter* (1968); etc.

GERSTENBERG, ALICE (Aug. 2, 1885–); b. Chicago, Ill. Novelist, playwright. Author or co-author: *A Little World* (1908); *Unquenched Fire* (1912); *The Conscience of Sarah Platt* (1915); *Four Plays for Four Women* (1924); *Ten One-Act Plays* (1928); *Comedies All: Short Plays* (1930); *When Chicago Was Young* (1934); *Within the Hour* (1934); *Victory Belles* (1943); *The Hourglass* (1955); *Our Calla* (1956); etc. Founder and director, Alice Gerstenberg Experimental Theatre Workshop.

GERVASI, FRANK [Henry] (Feb. 5, 1908–); b. Baltimore, Md. Journalist, author. *War Has Seven Faces* (1942); *Big Government* (1949); *The Case for Israel* (1968); etc. Foreign correspondent, *Collier's Weekly*, 1939–45; Washington correspondent, 1945–50; with Washington *Post*, 1950–53.

GESELL, ARNOLD LUCIUS (June 21, 1880–May 29, 1961); b. Alma, Wis. Child specialist, author. *The Normal Child and Primary Education* (with wife, 1912); *Guidance of Mental Growth in Infant and Child* (1930); *The First Five Years of Life* (with others, 1940); *Wolf Child and Human Child* (1941); *How a Baby Grows* (1945); *The Child From Five to Ten* (with others, 1946); *Studies in Child Development* (1948); *Vision: Its Development in Infant and Child* (with others, 1949); *Infant Development* (1952); *Youth: The Years from 10 to 16* (with others, 1956); etc. Prof. child hygiene, Yale University School of Medicine, 1915–48.

GESSLER, CLIFFORD FRANKLIN (Nov. 9, 1893–); b. Milton Junction, Wis. Editor, author. *Slants* (poems, 1924); *Kanaka Moon* (poems, 1927); *Road My Body Goes* (1937); *Hawaii: Isles of Enchantment* (1937); *Pattern of Mexico* (1941); *Tropic Landfall: The Port of Honolulu* (1942); *The Leaning Wind* (1943); *Tropic Earth* (verse, 1944); *The Reasonable Life* (1950). Lit. editor, Honolulu *Star-Bulletin*, 1924–34, with *Oakland* (Calif.), *Tribune* since 1937.

GESSNER, ROBERT (Oct. 23, 1907–Jan. 16, 1968); b. Escanaba, Mich. Educator, author. *Here is My Home* (1941); *Treason* (1944); *Youth is the Time* (1945); *The Moving Image: A Guide to Cinematic Literacy* (1968); etc. Editor: *Democratic Man* (1956). Prof. motion pictures, New York University, since 1945.

Get-Rich-Quick Wallingford. Novel by George Randolph Chester (1908), dramatized by George M. Cohan (prod. 1910). Popular story of American business and high pressure methods of salesmanship, touched with humor.

GETLEIN, FRANK (Mar. 6, 1921–   ); b. Ansonia, Conn. Art critic, author. *Christianity in Art* (with wife, Dorothy Woolen, 1959); *Christianity in Modern Art* (1961); *The Bite of the Print* (1964); *Georges Rouault's Miserere* (1964); etc. Editor: *Ten French Impressionists* (1966). Art critic, *Washington Star*, since 1961.

GETTELL, RAYMOND GARFIELD (Mar. 4, 1881–Oct. 9, 1949); b. Shippensburg, Pa. Educator, author. *History of Political Thought* (1924); *History of American Political Thought* (1928); *Political Science* (1933); etc. Prof. political science, University of California, from 1923.

"Ghetto, The." Poem by Lola Ridge (1918).

GHISELIN, BREWSTER (June 13, 1903–   ); b. Webster Groves, Mo. Poet, critic. *Against the Circle* (1946); *The Nets* (1955); etc. Editor: *The Creative Process* (1952); *Country of the Minotaur* (1969). Prof. English, University of Utah.

Giant. Novel by Edna Ferber (1952). Modern-day ranch life in Texas.

Giants in the Earth. Novel by Ole Edvart Rölvaag (1927). Translated from his *I de Dage* (1925) by Lincoln Colcord and the author. Grim saga of a Norwegian family in the Dakota farm lands in the pioneering days of the 1870's. The hero is Per Hansa, who struggles to master the soil. His wife, Beret, becomes very devout, and part of the tragedy of the story springs from her almost fanatical zeal.

GIBBES, ROBERT WILSON (July 8, 1809–Oct. 15, 1866); b. Charleston, S.C. Physician, author. *A Memoir of James De Veaux* (1846); *Documentary History of the American Revolution*, 3v. (1853–57).

GIBBONS, EUELL [Theophilus] (Sept. 8, 1911–   ); b. Clarksville, Texas. Naturalist, author. *Stalking the Wild Asparagus* (1962); *Stalking the Blue-Eyed Scallop* (1964); *Stalking the Healthful Herbs* (1966); *Euell Gibbons' Beachcomber's Handbook* (1967); *Feast on a Diabetic Diet* (with brother, Joe Gibbons, 1969); *Stalking the Good Life* (1971).

GIBBONS, FLOYD [Phillips] (July 16, 1887–Sept. 24, 1939); b. Washington, D.C. Correspondent, author. *The Red Knight of Germany* (1927); *The Red Napoleon* (1929); etc. With the Chicago Tribune, 1912–39. See Douglas Wilbert's *Floyd Gibbons, Knight of the Air* (1930).

GIBBONS, HELEN DAVENPORT (Mrs. Herbert Adams Gibbons) (Dec. 2, 1882–Sept. 1, 1960); b. Philadelphia, Pa. Author. *The Red Rugs of Tarsus* (1917); *A Little Gray Home in France* (1919); *Paris Vistas* (1919); *Four Little Pilgrims* (1926).

GIBBONS, HERBERT ADAMS (Apr. 9, 1880–Aug. 7, 1934); b. Annapolis, Md. Correspondent, author. *The Foundation of the Ottoman Empire* (1916); *France and Ourselves* (1920); *Riviera Towns* (1920); *An Introduction to World Problems* (1922); *Europe Since 1918* (1923); *John Wanamaker*, 2v. (1926); *Ports of France* (1926); *Wider Horizons* (1930); *Nationalism and Internationalism* (1930); etc.

GIBBONS, JAMES CARDINAL (July 23, 1834–Mar. 24, 1921); b. Baltimore, Md. Roman Catholic archbishop, author. *The Faith of Our Fathers* (1877); *Our Christian Heritage* (1889); *A Retrospect of Fifty Years*, 2v. (1916); etc. He was made a cardinal in 1886. See J. J. Walsh's *Our American Cardinals* (1926); J. T. Ellis's *The Life of James Cardinal Gibbons*, 2v. (1952).

GIBBONS, JAMES SLOAN (July 1, 1816–Oct. 17, 1892); b. Wilmington, Del. Banker, abolitionist. Author of the song, "We are coming, Father Abraham, three hundred thousand strong."

GIBBONS, ROBERT (May 1, 1915–); b. Tuscaloosa, Ala. Author. *Bright Is the Morning* (1943); *The Patchwork Time* (1948).

GIBBS, A[rthur] **HAMILTON** (Mar. 9, 1888–May 24, 1964); b. London, England. Author. *The Complete Oxford Man* (1910); *Cheadle and Son* (1911); *Rowlandson's Oxford* (1911); *The Hour of Conflict* (1913); *The Persistent Lovers* (1914); *Gun Fodder* (1919); *Bluebottles* (poems, 1919); *Soundings* (1925); *Labels* (1926); *Meredew's Right Hand* (1927); *Harness* (1928); *Chances* (1930); *Undertow* (1932); *Rivers Glide On* (1934); *The Need We Have* (1936); *The Young Prince* (1937); *A Half Inch of Candle* (1939); *A Way of Life* (1947); *One Touch of France* (poems, 1953); *Obedience to the Moon* (1956).

GIBBS, GEORGE (July 17, 1815–Apr. 9, 1873); b. Sunswick, L.I., N.Y. Ethnologist, author. *A Dictionary of the Chinook Jargon; or Trade Language of Oregon* (1863); and other books on Indians and the Northwest.

GIBBS, GEORGE FORT (Mar. 8, 1870–Oct. 10, 1942); b. New Orleans, La. Artist, novelist. *Pike and Cutlass* (1900); *The Medusa Emerald* (1907); *Madcap* (1913); *The Flaming Sword* (1914); *The Golden Bough* (1918); *The Black Stone* (1919); *The Splendid Outcast* (1920); *Youth Triumphant* (1921); *Sack Cloth and Scarlet* (1924); *Mad Marriage* (1925);

The Joyous Conspirator (1927); *The Isle of Illusion* (1929); *Old Philadelphia,* 4v. (1931); *Foul Weather* (1932); *The Yellow Diamond* (1934); *Out of the Dark* (1935); *The Vanishing Idol* (1936); *Hunted* (1937); *The Road to Bagdad* (1938); *The Silver Death* (1940); *The Sleeper Wakes* (1941); etc.

GIBBS, JEANNETTE [Clarke] **PHILLIPS** (Mrs. A. Hamilton Gibbs) (Dec. 23, 1892–); b. Lynn, Mass. Lawyer, novelist. *Portia Marries* (1926); *Humdrum House* (1928); *French Leave* (1930); *Copy for Mother* (1934).

GIBBS, JOSIAH WILLARD (Apr. 30, 1790–Mar. 25, 1861); b. Salem, Mass. Educator, Orientalist, author. *Hebrew and English Lexicon of the Old Testament* (1824); etc. Prof. sacred literature, Yale Divinity School, 1826–61.

GIBBS, WILLA (Sept. 25, 1917–); b. Hanna, Alberta, Can. *Tell Your Sons* (1946); *The Tender Men* (1948); *The Seed of Mischief* (1953); *The Twelfth Physician* (1954); *All the Golden Doors* (1957); *Dedicated* (1959); *According to Mary* (1962); *The Shadow of His Wings* (1964).

GIBBS, WOLCOTT (Mar. 15, 1902–Aug. 16, 1958); b. New York. Editor, critic, author. *Bed of Neuroses* (1937); *Season in the Sun* (1946); dramatized (prod. 1950); *More in Sorrow* (1958). Staff, *New Yorker,* from 1927; drama critic, 1940–58.

GIBRAN, KAHLIL (1883–Apr. 10, 1931); b. Bechari, Lebanon. Artist, author. *The Forerunner* (1920); *The Prophet* (1923); *Sand and Foam* (1926); *Jesus the Son of Man* (1928); *The Earth Gods* (1931); *The Garden of the Prophet* (1933); *Tears and Laughter* (1947); *Nymphs of the Valley* (1948); *Tears and a Smile* (1950); etc.

GIBSON, CHARLES [Hammond] (Nov 21, 1874–Nov. 17, 1954); b. Boston, Mass. Traveler, poet. *Two Gentlemen in Touraine* (under pen name of "Richard Sudbury," 1900); *Among French Inns* (1905); *The Spirit of Love and Other Poems* (1906); *The Wounded Eros: Sonnets* (1908); *The Prisoner's Hymn* (1914); *At Lincoln's Memorial* (1924); *England: A Pindaric Ode* (1930).

GIBSON, CHARLES DANA (Sept. 4, 1867–Dec. 23, 1944); b. Roxbury, Mass. Artist. Creator of the "Gibson Girl." His many illustrations in books and magazines both reflect, and set, the fashions and manners of the 1890's and the early years of the 20th century. Among the collections of his drawings are: *The Education of Mr. Pipp* (1899); *The Gibson Book,* 2v. (1906); and *Other People* (1911); *National Academician* (1932). See Fairfax Downey's *Portrait of an Era* (1936).

GIBSON, EVA KATHERINE CLAPP (deceased); b. Bradford, Ill. Novelist, poet. *Her Bright Future* (1884); *A Dark Secret* (1888); *Songs of Red Rose Land* (1901); *Zauberlinda, the Wise Witch* (1902); etc.

Gibson, Katharine. See Katharine Gibson Wicks.

GIBSON, PRESTON (Mar. 13, 1879–Feb. 15, 1937); b. Washington, D.C. Playwright. *Mrs. Erskine's Devotion* (prod. 1904); *The Vacuum* (prod. 1908); *The Turning Point* (prod. 1909); etc.

GIBSON, WALKER (1919–). Poet. *The Reckless Spenders* (poems, 1954); *Come As You Are* (poems, 1958); *Seeing and Writing* (1959); *Poems in the Making* (1963); *Tough, Sweet and Stuffy* (1966); etc. Editor: *Limits of Language* (1962); *Persona: A Study for Readers and Writers* (1969).

GIBSON, WILLIAM HAMILTON (Oct. 5, 1850–July 16, 1896); b. Sandy Hook, Conn. Artist, author. *Highways and Byways; or, Saunterings in New England* (1883); *Sharp Eyes* (1892); *Eye Spy* (1897); *My Studio Neighbors* (1898); etc. His nature drawings appeared in *Harper's Magazine, Scribner's Magazine,* and the *Century.*

GIBSON, WILLIAM W. (Nov. 13, 1914–). Playwright. *Cobweb* (play, 1954); *The Seesaw Log: a Chronicle of the Stage Production, with the Text of Two for the Seesaw* (1959);

Dinny and the Witches and *The Miracle Worker: Two Plays* (1960); *Golden Boy* (musical, with Clifford Odets, 1964); *A Mass for the Dead* (1968); *A Cry of Players* (1969); etc.

GIDDINGS, FRANKLIN HENRY (Mar. 23, 1855–June 11, 1921); b. Sherman, Col. Educator, sociologist. *The Theory of Sociology* (1894); *The Principles of Sociology* (1896); *The Responsible State* (1918); etc. Prof. sociology, Columbia University, 1894–1931.

GIDDINGS, JOSHUA REED (Oct. 6, 1795–May 27, 1864); b. Tioga Point, Pa. Abolitionist, intimate friend of Lincoln, author. *The Exiles of Florida* (1858); *History of the Rebellion* (1864).

GIDEONSE, HARRY DAVID (May 17, 1901–); b. Rotterdam, The Netherlands. Educator, author. *The Higher Learning in a Democracy* (1937); *Organized Scarcity and Public Policy* (1939); *Against the Running Tide* (1967); etc. President, Brooklyn College, 1939–66; Chancellor, New School for Social Research, since 1966.

GIESY, JOHN ULRICH (Aug. 6, 1877–Sept. 8, 1947); b. Chillicothe, O. Physician, novelist. *All for His Country* (1914); *The Other Woman* (with Octavus Roy Cohen, 1917); *Mimi* (1918); etc. Under pen name "Charles Dustin": *Bronco Men* (1940); *Riders of the Desert Trail* (1942); etc.

GIFFORD, EDWARD WINSLOW (Aug. 14, 1887–); b. Oakland, Calif. Anthropologist, author. *Tongan Myths and Tales* (1924); *California Indian Nights Entertainments* (1930); *The Cacopa* (1933); *Apache-Pueblo Culture Element Distribution* (1940); *California Shell Artifacts* (1947); *Central Miwok Ceremonies* (1955); *Archaeological Excavations in Yap* (with D. S. Gifford, 1958); etc. With University of California, since 1912, and curator of its anthropology museum since 1925.

GIFFORD, FANNIE STEARNS DAVIS (Mrs. Augustus McKinstry Gifford) (Mar. 6, 1884–); b. Cleveland, O. Poet. *Myself and I* (1913); *Crack O'Dawn* (1915); *The Ancient Beautiful Things* (1923).

Gift of the Magi, The. Short story by "O. Henry" (1905).

GILBERT, ALLAN H. (Mar. 18, 1888–); b. Rushford, N.Y. Educator, author. *Dante's Conception of Justice* (1925); *Machiavelli's Prince and Its Forerunners* (1938); *Literary Criticism from Plato to Dryden* (1940); *On the Composition of Paradise Lost* (1947); *Principles and Practice of Criticism* (1959); etc. Compiler: *A Geographical Dictionary of Milton* (1919). Translator: Ariosto's *Orlando Furioso* (1954); *The Letters of Machiavelli* (1961); *Dante's Inferno, a New Translation* (1967); etc. Editor, *Renaissance Studies* 1954–56. Prof. English, Duke University, 1921–57; Prof. literature, Drew University, since 1963.

GILBERT, CREIGHTON (June 6, 1924–); b. Durham, N.C. Art educator, author. *Paintings by Raphael* (1957); *Seventeenth-Century Paintings from the Low Countries* (1966); *Michelangelo* (1967); *Renaissance Art* (1970). Translator: *Complete Poems and Selected Letters of Michelangelo* (1963). Prof. art history, Brandeis University, since 1965.

GILBERT, DOUGLAS. Journalist, author. *Floyd Gibbons* (1930); *American Vaudeville* (1940). Feature writer, the *New York World-Telegram.*

GILBERT, EDWIN (1907–). Author. *Squirrel Cage* (1947); *Damion's Daughter* (1949); *The Hot and the Cool* (1953); *Native Stone* (1956); *Silver Spoon* (1957); *The New Ambassadors* (1961); *American Chrome* (1965); *Beautiful Life* (1967); *Jamey: Novel of a Period, 1967–1968* (1969).

GILBERT, KENNETH (June 10, 1889–); b. Chetek, Wis. Novelist. *Fighting Hearts of the Wild* (1928); *Red Meat Country* (1929); *Boru, Wolf Dog* (1929); *Bird Dog Bargain* (1947); *Triple-Threat Patrol* (1953); *Wolf Dog Valley* (1956); *The Mystery of Z-Canyon* (1969); etc.

GILBRETH, FRANK B[unker] JR. (1911–). *I'm a Lucky Guy* (1951); *Held's Angels* (1952); *Inside Nantucket* (1954); *Of Whales and Women* (1956); *Loblolly* (1959); *He's My Boy* (1962); etc. Co-author with Ernestine G. Carey: *Cheaper by the Dozen* (1949); *Belles on Their Toes* (1950).

GILCHRIST, ANNIE SOMERS. Author. *Rosehurst* (1884); *Harcourt* (1886); *A Souvenir of the Tennessee Centennial* (poems, 1897); *Some Representative Women of Tennessee* (1902); *Katherine Somerville; or, The Southland Before and After the Civil War* (1906); *The Night-Rider's Daughter* (1910).

GILCHRIST, BETH BRADFORD (Apr. 14, 1879–Apr. 23, 1957); b. Peacham, Vt. Author. *The Life of Mary Lyon* (1910); the *Helen* series, 4v. (1912–15); *Trails End* (1925); etc. Under pen name "John Prescott Earl" wrote a series of boys' prep-school stories.

Gilded Age, The. Novel by Mark Twain and Charles Dudley Warner (1874). A satire on the times, with the character Col. Mulberry Sellers playing the leading part.

GILDER, JEANNETTE LEONARD (Oct. 3, 1849–Jan. 17, 1916); b. Flushing, L.I., N.Y., sister of Richard Watson Gilder. Editor, critic, playwright. *Quits* (prod. 1876); *Taken by Siege* (1887); *The Autobiography of a Tomboy* (1900); *The Tomboy at Work* (1904). Editor: *Essays from the Critic* (with brother, Joseph B. Gilder, 1882); *Pen Portraits of Literary Women* (with Helen Gray Cone, 1887); *Authors at Home* (with brother, 1888). Compiler: *Representative Poems of Living Poets* (1886). Founder (with brother), *The Critic*, New York, 1881; editor, 1881–1906.

GILDER, JOSEPH B. (June 29, 1858–Dec. 9, 1936); b. Flushing, L.I., N.Y., brother of Richard Watson Gilder. Editor. Author (with sister, Jeannette L. Gilder): *Essays from the Critic* (1883); *Authors at Home* (1888). Founder (with sister), *The Critic*, 1881; co-editor, 1881–1906; *Putnam's Monthly,* 1906–09.

GILDER, RICHARD WATSON (Feb. 8, 1844–Nov. 18, 1909); b. Bordertown, N.J. Editor, poet. *The New Day* (1876); *The Poet and His Master* (1878); *The Celestial Passion* (1887); *Two Worlds, and Other Poems* (1891); *Five Books of Song* (1900); *In the Heights* (1905); *The Fire Divine* (1907); *The Poems* (1908); *Letters,* ed. by Rosamond de Kay Gilder, 1916; etc. Assoc. editor, *Scribner's Monthly,* 1870–81; editor, *The Century,* 1881–1909.

GILDER, RODMAN (Jan. 8, 1877–Sept. 30, 1953); b. New York City, son of Richard Watson Gilder. Publisher, author. *Joan, the Maiden* (1933); *The Battery, New York: A History* (1935).

GILDER, ROSAMOND DE KAY; b. Marion, Mass., daughter of Richard Watson Gilder. Author. *Enter the Actress: The First Women in the Theatre* (1931); *A Theatre Library* (1932); *John Gielgud's Hamlet* (1937); Editor: *Letters of Richard Watson Gilder* (1916); *Theatre Arts Anthology* (with others, 1961); *Theatre Collections in Libraries and Museums* (with George Freedley, 1936). Translator: Emma Calvé's *My Life* (1922). Drama critic, *Theatre Arts,* 1938–48; editor, 1945–48.

GILDERSLEEVE, BASIL LANNEAU (Oct. 23, 1831–Jan. 9, 1924); b. Charleston, S.C. Educator, classicist, editor, author. *Essays and Studies* (1890); *Hellas and Hesperia* (1909); *The Creed of the Old South, 1865–1915* (1915). Founder, *American Journal of Philology,* 1880; editor, 1880–1924. Prof. Greek, University of Virginia, 1856–76; Johns Hopkins University, 1876–1915.

GILDERSLEEVE, VIRGINIA CROCHERON (Oct. 3, 1877–July 7, 1965); b. New York City. Educator, author. *Government Regulation of the Elizabethan Drama* (1908); *Many a Good Crusade* (1954); etc. With Barnard College, Columbia University, New York, since 1900; dean, 1911–47.

GILES, CHAUNCEY (May 11, 1813–Nov. 6, 1893); b. Charlemont, Mass. Swedenborgian clergyman, editor, author. *The Magic Spectacle* (1868); *The Wonderful Pocket, Chestnutting, and Other Stories* (1868); *The Gate of Pearl* (1869); etc.

GILES, HENRY (Nov. 1, 1809–July 10, 1882); b. Crokford, Co. Wexford, Ireland. Unitarian clergyman, lecturer, essayist. *Lectures and Essays,* 2v. (1850); *Illustrations of Genius* (1854); *Human Life in Shakespeare* (1868); etc.

GILES, H[ermann] HARRY (Oct. 6, 1901–); b. Oberlin, O. Educator, author. *Teacher-Pupil Planning* (1941); *Human Dynamics* (1954); *The Integrated Classroom* (1959); etc. Prof. education, New York University, 1947–56.

GILES, JANICE [Holt] (1905–). Author. *Enduring Hills* (1950); *The Kentuckians* (1953); *The Plum Thicket* (1954); *Hannah Fowler* (1956); *The Believers* (1957); *Land Beyond the Mountains* (1958); *Johnny Osage* (1960); *Savanna* (1961); *Voyage to Santa Fe* (1962); *Run Me a River* (1964); *Great Adventure* (1966); *Shady Grove* (1968); *Six-Horse Hitch* (1969); etc.

Giles Goat-Boy. Novel by John Barth (1966). Satirical fantasy about the world as a university, distinguished by the author's linguistic inventiveness and comic imagination.

Gilkyson, Mrs. Walter. See Bernice Kenyon.

GILKYSON, [Thomas] WALTER (Dec. 18, 1880–); b. Phoenixville, Pa. Novelist. *Oil* (1924); *The Lost Adventurer* (1927); *Lights of Fame* (1930); *Tomorrow Never Comes* (1933); *Toward What Bright Land* (1947).

GILL, BRENDAN (Oct. 4, 1914–); b. Hartford, Conn. Playwright. *The Trouble of One House* (prod. 1950); *The Day the Money Stopped* (with Maxwell Anderson, 1957). Contributor: *The New Yorker,* since 1936.

GILL, RICHARD COCHRAN (Nov. 22, 1901–July 7, 1958); b. Washington, D.C. Explorer, author. *Manga* (1937); *The Volcano of Gold* (1938); *Kalu* (1939); *White Water and Black Magic* (1940); *Paco Goes to the Fair* (with Helen L. Hoke, 1940); *The Flying Death (Curare): A Manga Book* (1942); and other books and articles on curare.

GILL, ROBERT SUTHERLAND (Nov. 5, 1886–); b. near Sault Ste. Marie, Mich. Publisher, author. *Dramatic Personality of Jesus* (with Knight Dunlap, 1933); *Author, Publisher, Printer Complex* (1940).

GILL, TOM [Thomas Harvey] (Jan. 21, 1891–); b. Philadelphia, Pa. Forester, author. *Gay Bandit of the Border* (1930); *Tropical Forests of the Caribbean* (1931); *Death Rides the Mesa* (1934); *Starlight Pass* (1935); *Red Earth* (1937); *Heartwood* (1937); *Firebrand* (1939); *No Place for Women* (1946); *Land Hunger in Mexico* (1951); etc. Compiler: *The Forestry Directory* (with E. C. Dowling, 1943 and 1949).

GILLETT, CHARLES RIPLEY (Nov. 27, 1855–1948); b. New York. Educator, librarian, author. *Burned Books: Neglected Chapters in British History and Literature* (1932); etc. Compiler of catalogues of numerous collections of antiquities for the Metropolitan Museum in New York. With Union Theological Seminary, New York, 1883–1929, librarian, 1883–1908; dean of students, 1913–29.

GILLETT, EZRA HALL (July 15, 1823–Sept. 2, 1875); b. Colchester, Conn. Presbyterian clergyman, educator, author. *The Life and Times of John Huss,* 2v. (1863–64); *England Two Hundred Years Ago* (1866); *Ancient Cities and Empires* (1867); etc. Prof. political science, New York University, 1870–75.

GILLETTE, WILLIAM [Hooker] (July 24, 1855–Apr. 29, 1937); b. Hartford, Conn. Actor, playwright. *The Professor* (prod. 1881); *Too Much Johnson* (prod. 1894); *Clarice* (prod. 1905); etc.

GILLIGAN, EDMUND (June 7, 1899–); b. West Newton, Mass. Novelist. *One Lives to Tell the Tale* (1931); *Boundary against the Night* (1938); *White Sails Crowding* (1939); *Strangers in the Vly* (1941); *The Gaunt Woman* (1943); *The Ringed Horizon* (1943); *Voyage of the Golden Hind* (1945); *I Name Thee Mara* (1946); *Storm at Sable Island* (1948); *Sea Dog* (1954); *Shoe the Wild Mare* (1956); *My Earth, My Sea* (1959).

GILLILAN, STRICKLAND (Oct. 9, 1869–Apr. 25, 1954); b. Jackson, O. Journalist, humorous poet. *Including Finnigin* (1908); *Including You and Me* (1917); *Laugh It Off* (1924); *Danny and Fanny* (1928); *Gillilan, Finnigin & Co.* (1940); etc. His best-known poem, "Finnigin to Flannigan," first appeared in *The Palladium* (Richmond, Ind.) in 1897.

GILLIN, JOHN LEWIS (Oct. 12, 1871–Dec. 8, 1958); b. Hudson, Ia. Educator, author. *A History of Legislation for the Relief of the Poor in Iowa* (1914); *Wholesome Citizens and Spare Time* (1918); *Poverty and Dependency* (1920); *Criminology and Penology* (1925); *Social Pathology* (1933); *The Wisconsin Prisoner* (1946); *Cultural Sociology* (with John P. Gillin, 1948); etc. Prof. sociology, University of Wisconsin, 1912–42.

GILLIN, JOHN (Philip) (Aug. 1, 1907–); b. Waterloo, Ia. Educator, author. *Archaeological Investigations in Nine Mile Canyon* (1938); *Archaeological Investigations in Central Utah* (1941); *The Ways of Men* (1948); *The Culture of Security in San Carlos* (1951); *San Luis Jilotepeque* (1958); *Social Change in Latin America Today* (1961); *Human Ways* (1969); etc. Editor, co-author: *For a Science of Social Man* (1954).

GILLIS, JAMES MARTIN (Nov. 12, 1876–Mar. 14, 1957); b. Boston, Mass. Roman Catholic clergyman, editor, author. *False Prophets* (1925); *The Catholic Church and the Home* (1928); *Christianity and Civilization* (1932); *The Paulists* (1932); *So Near Is God* (1953); *On Almost Everything* (1955); *This Mysterious Human Nature* (1956); *My Last Book* (1958); etc. Editor, *Catholic World,* 1922–48.

GILLISS, WALTER (May 17, 1855–Sept. 24, 1925); b. Lexington, Ky. Printer, author. *A Printers' Sun Dial* (1913); *A Few Verses and Songs by Walter Gilliss* (1916); *Recollections of the Gilliss Press* (1926). Founder, the Gilliss Press, New York, 1871; retired from the printing business in 1908. Gillis Brothers printed the first numbers of *Life;* Lew Wallace's *Ben Hur* (1891); Henry James's *Daisy Miller* (1892); G. W. Curtis's *Prue and I* (1892); and *Vogue* (1892). The Gilliss books were noted for their fine design. The masterpiece of bookmaking designed by Walter Gilliss was *The Iconography of Manhattan Island,* by I. N. Phelps Stokes.

GILLMOR, FRANCES (May 21, 1903–); b. Buffalo, N.Y. Novelist. *Thumbcap Weir* (1929); *Windsinger* (1930); *Traders to the Navajos* (with Louisa Wade Wetherill, 1934); *Fruit Out of the Rock* (1940); *Flute of the Smoking Mirror: A Portrait of Nezahualcoyotl, Poet-King of the Aztecs* (1949); *The King Danced in the Market Place* (1964). Prof. English, University of Arizona, since 1934.

GILLMORE, RUFUS HAMILTON (Apr. 30, 1879–Jan. 22, 1935); b. Chelsea, Mass. Novelist. Wrote under name "Rufus Hamilton." *The Mystery of the Second Shot* (1912); *The Opal Pin* (1914); *The Alster Case* (1914).

GILMAN, ARTHUR (June 22, 1837–Dec. 27, 1909); b. Alton, Ill. Educator, editor, author. *Kings, Queens and Barbarians* (1871); *Boston, Past and Present* (1873); *Tales of the Pathfinders* (1884); *The Story of Rome* (1886); *The Colonization of America* (1887); etc. Editor: *The Poetical Works of Geoffrey Chaucer,* 3v. (1879); *Lothrop's Library of Entertaining History,* 6v. (1880–85); *Library of Religious Poetry* (1887); etc. Founder, the "Harvard Annex," 1878, known as Radcliffe College, after 1893.

GILMAN, CAROLINE HOWARD (Mrs. Samuel Gilman) (Oct. 8, 1794–Sept. 15, 1888); b. Boston, Mass. Poet, essayist, novelist. *Recollections of a Housekeeper* (under pen name, "Mrs. Clarissa Packard," 1834); *The Poetry of Travelling in the United States* (1838); *Recollections of a Southern Matron* 1838); *Love's Progress* (anon., 1840); *Tales and Ballads* (1839); *Verses of a Life-Time* (1849). Editor: *Oracles from the Poets* (1844); etc.

GILMAN, CHANDLER ROBBINS (Sept. 6, 1802–Sept. 26, 1865); b. Marietta, O. Physician, author. *Legends of a Log Cabin* (anon., 1835); *Life on the Lakes,* 2v. (anon., 1836). These are attributed to Gilman by the Library of Congress; by others attributed to Margaret Fuller, and to Charles Lanman, and to Thomas Bangs Thorpe.

GILMAN, CHARLOTTE PERKINS [Stetson] (July 3, 1860–Aug. 11, 1935); b. Hartford, Conn. Lecturer, author. *In This Our World, and Other Poems* (1895); *Women and Economics* (1898); *The Man-Made World* (1911); *The Living of Charlotte Perkins Gilman: An Autobiography* (1935).

GILMAN, DANIEL COIT (July 6, 1831–Oct. 13, 1908); b. Norwich, Conn. Educator, editor, author. *James Monroe* (1883); *The Launching of a University* (1906); etc. Editor-in-chief, *The New International Encyclopedia* (1902). President, Johns Hopkins University, 1875–1901. First president of the University of California, 1872–75.

GILMAN, DOROTHY FOSTER (Feb. 3, 1891–); b. Concord, N.H. Novelist. *The Bloom of Youth* (1916); *Surprising Antoine* (1922); *Lorraine* (1923); *The Unexpected Mrs. Pollifax* (1966); *Uncertain Voyage* (1967).

GILMAN, LAWRENCE (July 5, 1878–Sept. 8, 1939); b. Flushing, L.I., N.Y. Editor, music critic. *Wagner's Operas* (1937); *Stories of Symphonic Music* (1937); *Toscanini and Great Music* (1938); etc. Music critic, *Harper's Weekly,* 1901–13; asst. editor, 1903–11; managing editor, 1911–13; on editorial staff, *Harper's Magazine,* 1913–15; music, drama, and literary critic, *North American Review,* 1915–23; music critic, New York *Herald Tribune,* 1923–39.

GILMAN, MARGARET (Aug. 14, 1896–May 27, 1958); b. Meadville, Pa. Educator, author. *Othello in French* (1923); *Baudelaire the Critic* (1943); *The Idea of Poetry in France* (1958). French dept., Bryn Mawr College, from 1923.

GILMAN, NICHOLAS PAINE (Dec. 21, 1849–Jan. 23, 1912); b. Quincy, Ill. Unitarian clergyman, educator, author. *Socialism and the American Spirit* (1893); etc. Editor, *The Literary World,* Boston, Mass., 1888–95; *The New World,* 1892–1900. Prof. theology, Meadville Theological Seminary, 1895–1912.

GILMAN, SAMUEL (Feb. 16, 1791–Feb. 9, 1858); b. Gloucester, Mass. Congregational clergyman, author. *Memoirs of a New England Village Choir* (anon., 1829); *Pleasures and Pains of the Student's Life* (poems, 1852); *Contributions to Literature* (1856). Wrote "Fair Harvard" for the Harvard Bi-centennial in 1836. Editor: *The Poetical Remains of the Late Mary Elizabeth Lee* (1851).

GILMER, ALBERT HATTON (Dec. 31, 1878–June 5, 1950); b. Loraine, Ill. Educator, playwright. *The Edge of the World* (1912); *Old John Brown* (1913); *A Wake for a Wedding* (1936); *A Voice for Freedom* (prod. 1950); etc. English dept., Lafayette College, 1928–47.

GILMER, ELIZABETH MERIWETHER (Mrs. George O. Gilmer) (Nov. 18, 1870–Dec. 16, 1951); b. in Montgomery Co., Tenn. Journalist, author. Pen name, "Dorothy Dix." *Fables of the Elite* (1902); *Mirandy* (1912); *Mirandy Exhorts* (1922); *Dorothy Dix: Her Book* (1926); etc. Editor, woman's dept., New Orleans *Picayune,* 1896–1901; on staff, New York *Journal,* 1901–17; Wheeler Syndicate, 1917–23; Ledger Syndicate, from 1923; Bell Syndicate, from 1933.

GILMORE, JAMES ROBERTS (Sept. 10, 1822–Nov. 16, 1903); b. Boston, Mass. Novelist, abolitionist. Pen name, "Edmund Kirke." *Among the Pines* (1862); *Down in Tennessee* (1863); *Adrift in Dixie* (1863); *On the Border* (1867); *The Rear-Guard of the Revolution* (1886); *Personal Recollections of Abraham Lincoln* (1898); etc.

GILMORE, JOSEPH HENRY (Apr. 29, 1834–July 23, 1918); b. Boston, Mass. Baptist clergyman, critic, hymnwriter. *The Art of Expression* (1875); *He Leadeth Me, and Other Religious Poems* (1877); *Familiar Chats About Books and Reading* (1892). His best-known hymn is "He Leadeth Me."

GILPATRIC, GUY (Jan. 21, 1896–July 6, 1950); b. New York City. Novelist. *Scotch and Water* (1931); *French Summer* (1933); *Mr. Glencannon* (1935); *Three Sheets in the Wind* (1936); *The Gentleman with the Walrus Mustache* (1938); *The Compleat Goggler* (1939); *Glencannon Afloat* (1941); *Action in the North Atlantic* (1943); *Mr. Glencannon Ignores the War* (1944); *Flying Stories* (1945); *Glencannon Meets Tugboat Annie* (with N. R. Raine, 1950); etc.

GILPIN, HENRY DILWORTH (Apr. 14, 1801–Jan. 29, 1860); b. Lancaster, England. Lawyer, editor. Editor: *The Papers of James Madison,* 3v. (1840). Editor, the *Atlantic Souvenir,* 1825. Attorney-General, 1840–41.

GILROY, FRANK D[aniel] (Oct. 13, 1925–   ); b. New York. Playwright. *Who'll Save the Plowboy* (1957, prod. 1962); *The Subject Was Roses* (1962, prod. 1964); *Private* (1970). Also television plays.

GILSON, ROY ROLFE (Aug. 12, 1875–Aug. 2, 1933); b. Clinton, Ia. Episcopal clergyman, novelist. *When Love Is Young* (1901); *The Flower of Youth* (1904); *The Wistful Years* (1909); *The Legend of Jerry Ladd* (1912); etc.

Gin Mill Club, The. New York. Founded in 1877 by four members of the Law School of Columbia University. They and their friends met for luncheon the Saturday before Christmas for forty-nine consecutive years, first in Great Jones Street, then at the Downtown Association, The Century Club, and the Lotos Club. Andrew F. West, Nicholas Murray Butler, Robert E. Annin, William E. Annin, and Henry Fairfield Osborn were later members. The founders were Moses Taylor Pyne, Francis Speir, John B. Pine, and William J. Forbes.

GINGRICH, ARNOLD (Dec. 5, 1903–); b. Grand Rapids, Mich. Editor, author. *Cast Down the Laurel* (1935); *The Well Tempered Angler* (1965); *Toys of a Lifetime* (1966); *Business and the Arts* (1969); *A Thousand Mornings of Music* (1970); *Nothing But People* (1971). Editor, *Esquire,* 1935–45; *Coronet,* 1936–45; publisher and senior vice-president, Esquire, Inc., since 1952.

GINN, EDWIN (Feb. 14, 1838–Jan. 21, 1914); b. Orland, Me. Publisher. Founded Ginn Brothers, Boston, in 1865. In 1876, D. C. Heath joined the firm, and in 1881 the name was changed to Ginn, Heath & Company. In 1885, after Heath left the company, the name was changed to Ginn & Company.

Ginn & Co. Boston, Mass. Publishers. Founded 1865 by Edwin Ginn and Frederick Ginn. It was called Ginn Brothers until 1870, then Ginn Brothers & Co., Ginn, Heath & Co., in 1881, and Ginn & Co., since 1885. In 1873 Daniel Collamore Heath joined the firm and became a partner in 1876. He left in 1885 to found his own publishing house. In 1896 he founded the Athenaeum Press. Specializing in educational textbooks, the firm expanded rapidly and opened branches in New York, Chicago, and other cities. It published the Allen and Greenough Latin Series, Wentworth's textbooks in mathematics, Goodwin's Greek grammars, Myer's histories, the Robinson and Breasted histories, etc. It also printed the *Philosophical Review,* the *Yale Review,* the *Political Science Quarterly,* etc. Bought out by Xerox Education Division in 1968. *See* Thomas B. Lawler's *Seventy Years of Textbook Publishing: A History of Ginn & Co.* (1938).

GINOTT, HAIM G. (1922–); Author. *Between Parent and Child: New Solutions to Old Problems* (1965); *Between Parent and Teenager* (1969).

GINSBERG, ALLEN (June 3, 1926–); b. Paterson, N.J. Poet. *Howl and Other Poems* (1956); *Empty Mirror* (1961); *Kaddish* (1960); *Reality Sandwiches* (1963); *Planet News* (1968); etc. *See* Jane Kramer's *Allen Ginsberg in America* (1969).

GINTHER, MRS. PEMBERTON (d. Aug. 7, 1959); b. Philadelphia, Pa. Artist, author of books for young people. The *Miss Pat* series, 9v. (1915); the *Beth Anne* series, 4v. (1915); the *Hilda of Grey Cot* series, 4v. (1922–25); *The Secret Stair* (1928); *The Jade Necklace* (1929); *The Thirteenth Spoon* (1930); etc.

GINZBERG, ELI (Apr. 30, 1911–); b. New York. Economist, educator, author. *The House of Adam Smith* (1934); *The Unemployed* (with others, 1943); *The Labor Leader* (1948); *Agenda for American Jews* (1950); *What Makes an Executive* (with others, 1955); *The Negro Potential* (with others, 1956); *Human Resources* (1958); *The American Worker in the Twentieth Century* (1963); *The Negro Challenge to the Business Community* (1964); *The Pluralistic Economy* (1965); *Keeper of the Law: Louis Ginzberg* (1966); *The Middle-Class Negro in the White Man's World* (1967); *Business Leadership and the Negro Crisis* (1968); *Manpower Strategy for the Metropolis* (with others, 1968); etc. Editor: *Values and Ideals of American Youth* (1961). Prof. economics, Columbia University, since 1935.

GINZBERG, LOUIS (Nov. 28, 1873–Nov. 11, 1953); b. Kovno, Russia. Educator, author. *The Legends of the Jews,* 6v. (1909–28); *Students, Scholars and Saints* (1928); *On Jewish Law and Lore* (1955); *The Legends of the Bible* (1956); etc. Prof. Talmud and Rabbinics, Jewish Theological Seminary, New York, from 1902.

GIOVANNITTI, ARTURO (1884–); b. Campobasso, Italy. Poet. *Arrows in the Gale* (1914); and books in Italian.

GIPSON, FRED (1908–). Author. *Fabulous Empire* (1946); *Hound-dog Man* (1947); *Cowhand* (1953); *Recollection Creek* (1955); *Old Yeller* (1956); *Savage Sam* (1962); etc.

GIPSON, JAMES HERRICK (June 18, 1885–Feb. 19, 1965); b. Greeley, Colo. Printer, publisher. Founder, Caxton Printers, Ltd., Caldwell, Idaho, in 1904. Publisher of books by Western authors.

GIPSON, LAWRENCE HENRY (Dec. 7, 1880–); b. Greeley, Colo. Educator, author. *Jared Ingersol* (1920); *Lewis Evans* (1939); *The British Empire before the American Revolution,* 14v. (1936–69, Pulitzer prize for history, 1962, for Vol. 10: *Triumphant Empire: Thunder-Clouds Gather in the West, 1763–66*); etc. Head, history dept., Lehigh University, 1924–52.

Girl of the Golden West. Play by David Belasco (prod. 1905). In 1910 it was produced as an opera, with music by Giacomo Puccini. The scene is a California mining camp. Minnie, an orphan who runs a bar, gives shelter to Johnson the outlaw, who falls in love with her. She saves him from a posse.

Girl of the Limberlost, A. Novel by Gene Stratton Porter (1909). Popular story of the hard life of the Indiana swamp lands and a girl's triumph over such an environment.

Girl With the Green Eyes, The. Play by Clyde Fitch (prod. 1902). A study of feminine jealousy and the havoc caused by this "green-eyed monster."

"Give Me Your Hand, Johnny Bull." Civil War poem by W. A. Devon, in a bid for British sympathy.

GIVLER, ROBERT CHENAULT (Dec. 1, 1884–); b. Ft. Scott, Kan. Educator, psychologist, author. *Psycho-physiological Effect of Speech Elements in Poetry* (1916); *Psychology, the Science of Human Behavior* (1922); *The Ethics* *of Hercules* (1924); *Insight* (1935); etc. Philosophy dept., Tufts College, since 1919.

Gizycka, Eleanor M. Pen name of Eleanor Medill Patterson.

GIZYCKA, FELICIA (1905–); b. Blansco, Austria, daughter of Eleanor Medill Patterson. Novelist. *Flower of Smoke* (1939).

GJERSET, KNUT (Sept. 15, 1865–Oct. 29, 1936); b. Romsdal, Norway. Educator, author. *History of the Norwegian People*, 2v. (1915); *History of Iceland* (1923); *Norwegian Sailors on the Great Lakes* (1927); *Norwegian Sailors in American Waters* (1933); etc.

GLADDEN, WASHINGTON (Feb. 11, 1836–July 2, 1918); b. Pottsgrove, Pa. Congregational clergyman, author. *Plain Thoughts on the Art of Living* (1868); *From the Hub to the Hudson* (1869); *Art and Morality* (1897); *Where Does the Sky Begin?* (1904); *Recollections* (1909); *Ultima Veritas and Other Verses* (1912); etc.

Gladiator, The. Play by Robert Montgomery Bird (prod. 1831). Written for Edwin Forrest.

GLAENZER, RICHARD BUTLER (Dec. 15, 1876–Apr. 15, 1937); b. Paris, France. Editor, poet. *Beggar and King* (1917); *Literary Snapshots* (1920). Editor, Robert M. McBride & Co., 1929–1934.

Glamour. New York. Monthly. Founded 1939 by Condé Nast. Popular women's magazine featuring fashions, beauty articles, career advice, in conversational style. Incorporated *Charm* in 1959.

GLASGOW, ELLEN [Anderson Gholson] (Apr. 22, 1874–Nov. 21, 1945); b. Richmond, Va. Novelist. *The Descendant* (anon., 1897); *Phases of an Inferior Planet* (1898); *The Voice of the People* (1900); *The Freeman, and Other Poems* (1902); *The Battle-Ground* (1902); *The Deliverance* (1904); *The Wheel of Life* (1906); *The Ancient Law* (1908); *The Romance of a Plain Man* (1909); *The Miller of Old Church* (1911); *Virginia* (1913); *Life and Gabriella* (1916); *The Builders* (1919); *One Man in His Time* (1922); *The Shadowy Third, and Other Stories* (1923); *Barren Ground* (1925); *The Romantic Comedians* (1926); *They Stooped to Folly* (1929); *The Sheltered Life* (1932); *Vein of Iron* (1935); *In This Our Life* (1941); *A Certain Measure: An Interpretation of Prose Fiction* (1943); *The Woman Within* (autobiography, 1954). *See* Maxwell Geismar's *Rebels and Ancestors* (1953); Blair Rouse's *Ellen Glasgow* (1962). Her collected works have been published as *The Old Dominion Edition of the Works*, 8v. (1929–33); and *Virginia Edition*, 12v. (1938).

GLASPELL, SUSAN (Mrs. George Cram Cook; Mrs. Norman H. Matson) (July 1, 1882–July 27, 1948); b. Davenport, Ia. Playwright, novelist. *The Glory of the Conquered* (1909); *The Visioning* (1911); *Lifted Masks* (1912); *Fidelity* (1915); *Trifles* (1916); *Suppressed Desires* (with George Cram Cook, prod. 1915); *Plays* (1920); *Inheritors* (1921); *Verge* (1922); *The Road to the Temple* (1926); *Fugitive's Return* (1929); *Alison's House* (prod. 1930, Pulitzer Prize play, 1931); *Ambrose Holt and Family* (1931); *The Morning Is Near Us* (1940); *Norma Ashe* (1942); *Judd Rankin's Daughter* (1945). *See* Arthur E. Waterman's *Susan Glaspell* (1966).

GLASS, MONTAGUE [Marsden] (July 23, 1877–Feb. 3, 1934); b. Manchester, England. Humorist, playwright. *Potash and Perlmutter* (1910), dramatized (with Charles Klein, prod. 1913); *Abe and Mawruss* (1911), dramatized (with R. C. Megrue, prod. 1915); *Object: Matrimony* (1912); *Potash and Perlmutter Settle Things* (1919); *The Truth about Potash and Perlmutter, and Five Other Stories* (1924); *Y'Understand* (1925); *Lucky Numbers* (1927); *You Can't Learn 'Em Nothin'* (1930); etc.

Glass Menagerie, The. Play by Tennessee Williams (prod. 1947). Concerns a crippled girl who escapes from reality by fixing her feelings on her collection of glass animals. The incidents are reflections of a Southern family's incapacity to adapt to the modern world.

GLASSCOCK, CARL BURGESS (May 4, 1884–Nov. 13, 1942); b. Ferndale, Calif. Journalist, author. *Bandits and the Southern Pacific* (1929); *The Big Bonanza* (1931); *Gold in Them Hills* (1932); *Lucky Baldwin* (1933); *A Golden Highway* (1934); *The War of the Copper Kings* (1935); *The Gasoline Age* (1937); *Then Came Oil* (1938); *Here's Death Valley* (1940).

GLATZER, NAHUM NORBERT (Mar. 25, 1903–); b. Lemberg, Aust. Educator, historian. *In Time and Eternity* (1946); *Language of Faith* (1947); *A Midrash Reader* (1948); *Franz Rosenzweig* (1953); *Hillel the Elder* (1956); *Leopold and Adelheid Zunz* (1958); etc. Editor: *Days of Awe* (1948); *On Jewish Learning* (1955); *The Way of Response* (1966); *Buber on Judaism* (1967); *Buber on the Bible* (1968); *The Dimensions of Job* (1969); etc. Editor and translator: *The Passover Haggadah* (1969). Prof. Jewish history, Brandeis University, since 1956.

GLAZER, NATHAN (Feb. 25, 1923–). Author. *The Lonely Crowd* (with David Riesman and others, 1950); *American Judaism* (1957); *The Social Basis of American Communism* (1961); *Beyond the Melting Pot* (1964); etc. Editor: *The Judaic Tradition* (1969).

GLAZIER, WILLARD (Aug. 22, 1841–1905); b. Fowler, N.Y. Soldier, traveler, author. *Capture, Prison-Pen and Escape* (1865); *Battles for the Union* (1874); *Peculiarities of American Cities* (1883); *Down the Great River* (1887); etc.

GLEASON, FREDERICK. Editor, publisher. Founder, *The Flag of Our Union*, (1846); *Gleason's Pictorial Drawing-Room Companion* (1851); *Gleason's Literary Companion* (1860); *Gleason's Monthly Companion* (1872).

GLEASON, SARELL EVERETT (Mar. 14, 1905–); b. Brooklyn, N.Y. Educator, author. *The Challenge to Isolation* (with W. L. Langer, 1952); *The Undeclared War* (1953); etc. History dept., Amherst College, 1938–46. Cultural attaché, American Embassy, London, 1959–61. Historian, Dept. of State since 1962.

Gleason's Pictorial Drawing-Room Companion. Boston, Mass. Founded 1851 by Frederick Gleason, modeled after the *London Illustrated News*. Editor, Maturin M. Ballou. Sylvanus Cobb, Jr., Frances A. Durivage, Ben Perley Poore, and other popular writers of fiction, furnished serials. Horatio Alger, Jr., contributed to it, but he had not begun his serials of juveniles which were to prove so popular. Sold to Ballou 1854, and from 1855 the name was changed to *Ballou's Pictorial Drawing-Room Companion*. Expired 1859. *See* Frank L. Mott's *A History of American Magazines*, v. 2 (1938).

GLENN, ISA (Mrs. S. J. Bayard Schindel) b. Atlanta, Ga. Novelist. *Heat* (1926); *Little Pitchers* (1927); *Southern Charm* (1928); *Transport* (1929); *A Short History of Julia* (1930); *East of Eden* (1932); *Mr. Darlington's Dangerous Age* (1933); *The Little Candle's Beam* (1935); *According to Mac Tavish* (1938).

GLICK, CARL (Sept. 11, 1890–); b. Marshalltown, Ia. Playwright. *The Devil's Host* (1934); *The Laughing Buddha* (1937); *The Unconquered* (1937); *Shake Hands With the Dragon* (1941); *Three Times I Bow* (1943); *Swords of Silence: The Secret Societies of China* (with Hong Sheng-Hun, 1947); *The Secret of Serenity* (1951); *Death Sits In* (1954); *The Story of Our Flag* (with Ollie Rogers, 1964). Director of little theatres in San Antonio, Tex., Sarasota, Fla., York, Pa., Columbia, S.C., etc. Member drama department, California Western University, since 1955.

GLOAG, JULIAN. Author. *Our Mother's House* (1963); *A Sentence of Life* (1966); *Maundy* (1968).

"Glory Trail, The." Cowboy poem by Charles Badger Clark Jr., in his *Sun and Saddle Leather* (1915). The poem is also called "High Chin Bob."

GLOSTER, HUGH (May 11, 1911–); b. Brownsville, Tenn. Author. *Negro Voices in American Fiction* (1948). Editor: *My Life, My Country, My World* (with others, 1952).

"Gloucester Moors." Poem by William Vaughn Moody (1900).

GLOVER, JULIA LESTARJETTE (Sept. 25, 1866–); b. Chester, S.C. Author of books for young people. *Hilda's Sowings and Harvest* (1920); *Children of Greycourt* (1928); *When Janey May Was a Little Girl* (1929); *When Janey May Was Twelve* (1930); *The Christmas Castle* (1932); *Mystery on the Mountain Top* (1935); *Silver Trumpets* (1938); *True to Her King* (1946); etc.

GLUECK, ELEANOR T[ouroff] (Mrs. Sheldon Glueck) (Apr. 12, 1898–); b. New York. Criminologist, author. *The Community Use of Schools* (1927); *Evaluative Research in Social Work* (1936); *Physique and Delinquency* (1956); etc. Co-author (with Sheldon Glueck): *500 Criminal Careers* (1930); *500 Delinquent Women* (1938); *Juvenile Delinquents Grown Up* (1940); *After-Conduct of Discharged Offenders* (1945); *Unraveling Juvenile Delinquency* (1950); *Delinquents and Nondelinquents in Perspective* (1968); etc. Research in criminology, Harvard University Law School, since 1930.

GLUECK, NELSON (June 4, 1900–Feb. 12, 1971); b. Cincinnati, O. Archaeologist, educator, author. *Explorations in Eastern Palestine,* 5v. (with others, 1934–51); *The Other Side of the Jordan* (1940); *The River Jordan* (1946); *Rivers in the Desert: A History of the Negev* (1959); *Deities and Dolphins* (1965); *Hesed in the Bible* (1967); *Dateline: Jerusalem* (1968); etc. Prof. Bible and Biblical archaeology, Hebrew Union College, from 1936; pres., from 1947.

GLUECK, SHELDON (Aug. 15, 1896–); b. Warsaw, Pol. Criminologist, author. *Mental Disorder and the Criminal Law* (1925); *Crime and Justice* (1936); *War Criminals: Their Prosecution and Punishment* (1944); *Crime and Correction: Selected Papers* (1952); *Law and Psychiatry* (1962); etc. Co-author, with Eleanor T. Glueck: *Family Environment and Delinquency* (1962); *Ventures in Criminology* (1964); etc. Dept. of criminology, Harvard University Law School, since 1929.

Glyndon, Howard. Pen name of Laura Catherine Redden Searing.

Go Down, Moses. Novel by William Faulkner (1942). A saga about the McCaslin, Edmonds and Beauchamps families loosely connected as stories. The novelette, *The Bear,* also appears in this work.

Go Tell It on the Mountain. Novel by James Baldwin (1953). John, a fourteen-year-old Harlem Negro, experiences religious conversion. The vitality of the story derives from flashbacks into the past of the boy's family.

"Go West, young man, go West." First used by J. L. B. Soule in the *Terre Haute* (Ind.) *Express,* in 1851. Horace Greeley in an editorial in the *New York Tribune,* July 13, 1865, used the phrase and it gained wide circulation.

"God be with you, till we meet again." Hymn by Jeremiah Eames Rankin (1885).

"God Save the South." Confederate battle song, words and music by George Henry Miles (1863).

GODCHARLES, FREDERIC ANTES (June 3, 1872–Dec. 30, 1944); b. Northumberland, Pa. Librarian, author. *Daily Stories of Pennsylvania,* 2v. (1924–27); *Pennsylvania Past and Present* (1926); etc. Director, Pennsylvania State Library and Museum, 1927–31.

GODDARD, CHARLES WILLIAM (Nov. 26, 1879–Jan. 11, 1951); b. Portland, Me. Playwright. *The Misleading Lady* (with Paul Dickey, prod. 1913); etc. Author of many motion picture serials, including *The Perils of Pauline.* On staff, *American Weekly,* from 1923.

GODDARD, GLORIA (Feb. 18, 1897–); b. Philadelphia, Pa. Author. *Backyard* (1926); *A Dictionary of American Slang* (with Clement Wood, 1926); *These Lords' Descendants* (1930); *A Breadline for Souls* (poems, 1930); *The Last Knight of Europe* (1932); *If You Can Wait* (1933); *Bargain Basement* (1934); *Better to Burn* (1935); etc. Susan Merton series, under pen name "Louise Logan."

GODDARD, PLINY EARLE (Nov. 24, 1869–July 12, 1928); b. Lewiston, Me. Ethnologist, museum curator, author. *Life and Culture of the Hupa* (1903); *Indians of the Southwest* (1913); *Indians of the Northwest Coast* (1922); etc. Editor: *Hupa Texts* (1904); *Kato Texts* (1909); etc. Editor, *American Anthropologist,* 1915–20. Curator of anthropology and ethnology, American Museum of Natural History, New York, 1909–28.

GODEY, LOUIS ANTOINE (June 6, 1804–Nov. 29, 1878); b. New York City. Publisher, editor. Founder, *The Lady's Book,* Philadelphia, 1830, later called *Godey's Lady's Book; The Saturday News and Literary Gazette,* Philadelphia, 1836. His insistence on moral rectitude was so great that he boasted that nothing ever entered the pages of his magazine which might offend the sensibilities of the subscribers.

Godey's Lady's Book. Philadelphia, Pa. Monthly magazine for women. Founded 1830, by Louis A. Godey, as the *Lady's Book.* Godey's name was added to the title in 1840. Sarah J. Hale (q.v.) became co-editor in 1837, and remained with the magazine until 1877, when Godey himself retired from active control. Other editors were Lydia H. Sigourney, Morton McMichael, J. Hannum Jones, A. E. Brown, J. H. Haulenbeek, Eleanor Moore Hiestand, Mrs. D. G. Croly. Many of the leading authors wrote for Godey's, including Poe, and it was a particular haven for women with literary pretensions. Leading engravers, such as Sartain and Rothermel, did some of their best work for the magazine. It featured moral tales and poems, and was noted for its colored fashion plates, now prized by collectors. Moved to New York, 1892. Expired 1898. *See* Frank L. Mott's *A History of American Magazines,* v. 1 (1938).

Godfather, The. Novel by Mario Puzo (1968). Bestseller fictional treatment of the Mafia.

GODFREY, THOMAS (Dec. 4, 1736–Aug. 3, 1763); b. Philadelphia, Pa. Poet, playwright, author. *The Court of Fancy: A Poem* (1762); *Juvenile Poems on Various Subjects; with The Prince of Parthia* (1765); *The Prince of Parthia* (prod. 1767).

GODKIN, EDWIN LAWRENCE (Oct. 2, 1831–May 21, 1902); b. in Ireland. Editor, author. *The History of Hungary and the Magyars* (1853); *Reflections and Comments, 1865–1895* (1895); *Life and Letters,* 2v. (1907); etc. Founder, *The Nation,* July 6, 1865; editor, 1865–81; editor, the New York *Evening Post,* 1883–1900. *See* Allan Nevins' *The Evening Post* (1922).

GODMAN, JOHN DAVIDSON (Dec. 20, 1794–Apr. 17, 1830); b. Annapolis, Md. Anatomist, naturalist, author. *American Natural History,* 3v. (1826–28); *Rambles of a Naturalist* (1833). *See* H. A. Kelly and W. L. Burrage's *Dictionary of American Medical Biography* (1928).

God's Country and Mine. By Jacques Barzun (1954). Acute analysis of the nature of American life, its manners, morals, and intellectual climate.

God's Little Acre. Novel by Erskine Caldwell (1933). A Georgia mountaineer family entangled in their economic circumstances, sexual lusts, and religious superstitions.

God's Protecting Providence. Narrative by Jonathan Dickinson (1699). Story of the hardships of a band of shipwreck survivors on the Florida coast and a six weeks' hazardous journey to St. Augustine, in 1696.

"God's World." Poem by Edna St. Vincent Millay, in her *Renascence and Other Poems* (1917).

GODWIN, PARKE (Feb. 25, 1816–Jan. 7, 1904); b. Paterson, N.J. Editor, author. *Handbook of Universal Biography* (1852); *Political Essays* (1856); *Out of the Past* (1870); *A Biography of William Cullen Bryant,* 2v. (1883); *A New Study of the Sonnets of Shakespeare* (1900). Co-editor, *Putnam's Monthly,* 1853–57; editor, 1870. Associated intermittently with his father-in-law, William Cullen Bryant on the New York *Evening Post,* 1837–81.

GOERTZ, ARTHÉMISE (Mrs. Hector Alfonso) (Nov. 9, 1905–); b. New Orleans, La. Novelist. *South of the Border* (1940); *Give Us Our Dream* (1947); *The Moon is Mine* (1948); *New Heaven, New Earth* (1953); *Dream of Fuji* (1958).

Goetchius, Marie Louise. See Marie Louise Gibson Hale.

Goetz, George. See V. F. Calverton.

GOETZ, PHILIP BECKER (July 20, 1870–Dec. 1, 1950); b. Buffalo, N.Y. Educator, poet. *Poems* (1898); *Interlude* (1904); *Lyrics and Meditations* (1925); etc. Columnist for *Buffalo Evening News.* With University of Buffalo, 1913–26.

GOHDES, CLARENCE L[ouis] F[rank] (July 2, 1901–); b. San Antonio, Tex. Educator, author. *The Periodicals of American Transcendentalism* (1931); *American Literature in Nineteenth Century England* (1944); *The Literature of the American People* (with others, 1951); etc. Editor: *Uncollected Lectures by Ralph Waldo Emerson* (1932); *Faint Clews and Indirections by Walt Whitman* (with Rollo G. Silver, 1949); *Hunting in the Old South* (1967); *Russian Studies of American Literature: A Bibliography* (with Valentina A. Libman, 1969); *American Short Story Series;* etc. Managing editor, *American Literature,* 1931–54; editor-in-chief, 1954–69. Prof. English, Duke University, 1930–61; James B. Duke prof., since 1961.

GOHEEN, ROBERT FRANCIS (Aub. 15, 1919–); b. Vengurla, India. Educator. *The Imagery of Sophocles' Antigone* (1951). Classics dept., Princeton University, since 1948; pres., 1957–71.

GOING, CHARLES BUXTON (April 5, 1863–); b. Westchester, N.Y. Editor, author. *Summer-Fallow* (poems, 1892); *Urchins of the Sea* (with Marie Overton Corbin, 1900); *Urchins at the Pole* (with same, 1901); *Precarious Paradise and Other Plays* (1904); *Star-Glow and Song* (poems, 1909); *David Wilmot, Free-Soiler* (1924); *Folklore and Fairy Plays* (1927); *Château and Hill-Towns of Provence* 1936). On staff, *Engineering Magazine,* 1896–1915; editor, 1912–15.

Gold. Novel by Stewart Edward White (1913). Adventures of a group of young men in the California gold rush. *See also* the same author's *The Forty Niners* (1918).

GOLD, H. L. Editor, author. *The Enormous Room* (with R. W. Krepps, 1954); *The Old Die Rich and Other Science Fiction Stories* (1955). Editor: *Five Galaxy Short Novels* (1958); etc.

GOLD, HERBERT (Mar. 9, 1924–); b. Cleveland, O. Author. *Birth of a Hero* (1951); *The Prospect before Us* (1954); *The Man Who Was Not with It* (1956); *The Optimist* (1959); *Love and Like* (1960); *Therefore Be Bold* (1960); *The Age of Happy Problems* (1962); *Salt* (1963); *Fathers* (1967); *The Great American Jackpot* (1970); *The Magic Will* (1971); etc. Editor: *Fiction of the Fifties* (1961); etc.

GOLD, IVAN (May 12, 1932–   ); b. New York. Author. *Nickel Miseries* (1963); *Sick Friends* (1969).

Gold, Michael. Pen name of Irving Granich.

Gold-Bug, The. Short story by Edgar Allan Poe (1843), first published in the *Dollar Magazine,* Philadelphia, June 21–28, 1843. It deals with the discovery of hidden treasure through the ingenious solution of a mysterious cryptogram.

GOLDBERG, ARTHUR J[oseph] (Aug. 8, 1908–); b. Chicago, Ill. Lawyer, author. *AFL-CIO: Labor United* (1956); *Defenses of Freedom* (1966). Secretary of Labor, 1961–62; Associate Justice of the Supreme Court of the United States, 1962–65; U.S. representative to the United Nations, 1965–68.

GOLDBERG, GERALD JAY. Author. *Notes from the Diaspora* (short stories, 1962); *The Lynching of Orin Newfield* (1970). Editor: *The Fate of Innocence* (1965).

GOLDBERG, ISAAC (Nov. 1, 1887–July 14, 1938); b. Boston, Mass. Critic, editor, author. *Sir William G. Gilbert* (1913); *Studies in Spanish-American Literature* (1920); *Brazilian Literature* (1922); *The Drama of Transition* (1922); *The Man Mencken* (1925); *Havelock Ellis* (1926); *The Theatre of George Jean Nathan* (1926); *The Story of Gilbert and Sullivan* (1928); *Tin Pan Alley* (1930); *George Gershwin* (1931); *Queen of Hearts: The Passionate Pilgrimage of Lola Montez* (1936); *The Wonder of Words* (1929); etc. Lit. editor, *American Freeman,* 1923–32.

GOLDBERG, ISRAEL (1887–Aug. 1, 1964); b. in Poland. Author (under pen name of "Rufus Learsi"): *Kasriel the Watchman and Other Stories* (1925); *Outline of Jewish Knowledge,* 3v. (with Samson Benderly, 1929–31); *The Wedding Song: A Book of Chasidic Ballads* (1938); *Shimmele* (1940); *Shimmele and His Friends* (1949); *Israel: A History of the Jewish People* (1949); *Filled with Laughter* (1961); etc.

GOLDBERG, REUBEN LUCIUS [Rube] (July 4, 1883–Dec. 7, 1970); b. San Francisco, Cal. Cartoonist, author. *Foolish Questions* (1909); *Is There A Doctor in the House?* (1929); *Plan for the Post-War World* (1944); *Rube Goldberg's Guide to Europe* (text by Sam Boal, 1954); *I Made My Bed* (1968); etc. Cartoons syndicated from 1921. Winner of Pulitzer prize for best editorial cartoon, 1948.

GOLDEN, HARRY [Lewis] (May 6, 1902–); b. New York. Editor, author. *Jews in American History* (with Martin Rywell, 1950); *Only in America* (1958); *For 2¢ Plain* (1959); *Carl Sandburg* (1961); *You're Entitle'* (1962); *A Little Girl Is Dead* (1965); *Eat, Eat, My Child* (1966); *The Right Time: An Autobiography* (1969); etc. Editor and publisher, *The Carolina Israelite,* since 1942.

GOLDEN, JOHN (June 27, 1874–June 17, 1955); b. New York City. Playwright, producer, song writer. *Eva the Fifth* (with Kenyon Nicholson, prod. 1928); *Stage-Struck John Golden* (with Viola Brothers Shore, 1930); *After Tomorrow* (with Hugh Stangé, prod. 1931); *The Divine Drudge* (with Vicki Baum, prod. 1933); etc. Wrote or composed over 1000 songs, including "Poor Butterfly."

Golden Age. Lewiston, Ida. Newspaper. Founded 1862, by Alexander S. Gould. First newspaper published in Idaho. Expired 1865.

Golden Apples. Novel by Marjorie Kinnan Rawlings (1935). Story of an Englishman and a young girl of the Florida back country, with a background of mystery.

Golden Argosy. See *Argosy.*

Golden Book. New York. Monthly magazine. Founded 1925. Editors: Henry W. Lanier, 1925–28; Edith O'Dell, 1929–30; Frederic P. Field, 1930–33. Until its last few years, it was devoted almost entirely to reprinting stories and articles from world literature. Absorbed by *Fiction Parade,* 1935.

Golden Books. Inexpensive books for children, launched 1942, by Simon and Schuster in cooperation with Artists and

Writers Guild, a branch of Western Printing and Lithographing Co. Now owned as Golden Press by Western Publishing Co. *Golden Books,* especially in the formats *Little Golden Books* and *Giant Golden Books,* became the most popular type of children's books in the United States for two decades. Periodicals include *Gold Key Comics* and *Golden Magazine for Boys and Girls.*

Golden Bowl, The. Novel by Henry James (1905). Story of the marriage of an Italian prince to Maggie Verver, daughter of an American millionaire. Their idyllic happiness in England is suddenly marred by the appearance of Charlotte Stant, Maggie's old school chum.

Golden Boy. Play by Clifford Odets (prod. 1937). An Italian-American boy who plays the violin becomes a professional boxer in order to achieve wealth and success. He is killed in an automobile accident.

Golden Day, The. By Lewis Mumford (1926). Study of American culture in New England from 1830 to 1860, as reflected in the thought of Emerson, Hawthorne, Melville, Whitman, William James, and others. The machine age and the "Gilded Age," with their implications of political and industrial changes hostile to culture, are anticipated at the end of the book.

Golden Dog, The. Novel by William Kirby (1877). Story of life in Quebec around 1748, when war was being waged between the French and the British.

Golden Galleon. Kansas City, Mo. Quarterly magazine of poetry. Founded 1924. Expired 1925.

Golden House, The. Novel by Charles Dudley Warner (1894). A satire on the vulgar manners of the newly rich who seek to purchase prestige.

"Golden Legend, The." Poem by Henry Wadsworth Longfellow (1851). Based on a 12th century German story by Hartmann von der Auë. Prince Henry of Hoheneck, a leper, can only be cured if a girl sacrifices her life. He is filled with remorse at the last moment, but is miraculously cured by the relics of St. Matthew.

Golden Multitudes. By Frank Luther Mott (1947). Best sellers from 1662 to 1945.

Golden Wedding. Short story by Ruth Suckow (1926).

Golden Wedding. Short story by Ring Lardner. In his *How to Write Short Stories* (1924).

Golden Whales of California, The. Poems by Vachel Lindsay (1920).

GOLDENWEISER, ALEXANDER (Jan. 29, 1880–deceased); b. Kiev, Russia. Anthropologist, author. *Totemism* (1910); *Early Civilization* (1922); *Robots or Gods* (1932); *History, Psychology and Culture* (1933); *Anthropology* (1937); etc. Co-author: *Our Changing Morality* (1924); *Sex in Civilization* (1929); etc. Lecturer on anthropology, New School for Social Research, New York, 1919–26. etc.

GOLDIN, JUDAH (Sept. 14, 1914–   ); b. New York. Educator, author. *The Two Versions of Abot de Rabbi Nathan* (1945); *Hillel the Elder* (1946); *The Period of the Talmud* (1949); *The Contemporary Jew and His Judaism* (1952); *The Fathers* (1955); *The Living Talmud* (1957); *The End of Ecclesiastes* (1966); etc. Prof. Jewish studies, Yale University, 1958–62; prof. classical Judaica, since 1962.

GOLDMAN, ALBERT (April 15, 1927–   ); b. Dormont, Pa. Educator, author. *The Mine and the Mint: Sources for the Writings of Thomas De Quincey* (1965). Editor-in-chief, *Cultural Affairs.* Faculty, Columbia University, since 1963.

GOLDMAN, ERIC FREDERICK (June 17, 1915–); b. Washington, D.C. Educator, author. *Charles J. Bonaparte* (1943); *Rendezvous with Destiny* (1952); *The Crucial Decade, America, 1945–55* (1956); *The Crucial Decade—and After: America 1945–1960* (1961); *The Tragedy of Lyndon Johnson* (1969); etc. History dept., Princeton University, since 1943.

GOLDMAN, JAMES (June 30, 1927–   ); b. Chicago, Ill. Playwright. *Blood, Sweat and Stanley Poole* (with William Goldman, 1961); *Family Affair* (with William Goldman and John Kander, 1962); *The Lion in Winter* (1966); *Father's Day* (1971); etc.

GOLDMAN, RICHARD FRANK (Dec. 7, 1910–); b. New York. Conductor, composer, author. *The Band's Music* (1938); *The Concert Band* (1946); *The Wind Band* (1961); *Harmony in Western Music* (1965); Translator: Eca de Queriroz' *The Mandarin and Other Stories* (1965). Conductor, Goldman Band, since 1956.

GOLDMAN, SOLOMON (Aug. 18, 1893–May 14, 1953); b. Kozin, Russia. Rabbi, Zionist, editor, author. *A Rabbi Takes Stock* (1931); *A Jew and the Universe* (1936); *Crisis and Decision* (1938); *Undefeated* (1940); *The Words of Justice Brandeis* (1953); *The Ten Commandments* (1956); etc.

GOLDMAN, WILLIAM (Aug. 12, 1931–   ); b. Chicago, Ill. Author. *The Temple of Gold* (1957); *Your Turn to Curtsy, My Turn to Bow* (1958); *Soldier in the Rain* (1960); *Boys and Girls Together* (1964); *Harper* (screenplay, 1966); *The Thing of it Is* (1967); *The Season* (1969); *Butch Cassidy and the Sundance Kid* (screenplay, 1970). Under pen name "Harry Longbaugh": *No Way to Treat a Lady* (1964). Author of plays with James Goldman (q.v.) and John Kander.

GOLDSTEIN, ISRAEL (June 18, 1896–); b. Philadelphia, Pa. Rabbi, Zionist, author. *A Century of Judaism in New York* (1930); *Brandeis University* (1951); *American Jewry Comes of Age* (1955).

GOLDSTON, ROBERT CONROY (July 9, 1927–); b. New York. Author. *The Eighth Day* (1956); *The Catafalque* (1957); *The Shore Dimly Seen* (1963); *The Last of Lazarus* (1966). Also author of numerous juveniles and television documentary films.

GOLDWATER, BARRY M[ORRIS] (Jan. 1, 1909–); b. Phoenix, Ariz. Senator, author. *Arizona Portraits,* (1941); *Conscience of a Conservative* (1960); *How Do You Stand, Sir?* (1962); *People and Places* (1967); *The Conscience of a Majority* (1970); etc. U. S. Senator, 1953–64, since 1968.

GOLFFING, FRANCIS (Nov. 10, 1910–); b. Vienna. Author. *Selected Poems* (1961). Translator: Nietzschev's *Birth of Tragedy* (1956).

GOLLOMB, JOSEPH (Nov. 15, 1881–May 23, 1950); b. St. Petersburg, Russia. Author. *The Girl in the Fog* (1923); *Master Man Hunters* (1926); *The Subtle Trail* (1929); *The Curtain of Storm* (1932); *Unquiet* (1935); *Armies of Spies* (1939); *Captains of Labor* (1940); *What's Democracy to You?* (1940); *Young Heroes of the War* (with Alice Taylor, 1943); *Up at City High* (1945); *Tiger at City High* (1946); *Window on the World* (1947); *Albert Schweitzer: Genius in the Jungle* (1949); etc.

Gombo, the Creole Dialect of Louisiana. By Edward Larocque Tinker (1936).

GOMPERS, SAM[uel] (Jan. 27, 1850–Dec. 13, 1924); b. London, England; came to the United States in 1863. Labor leader, author. *Labor in Europe and America* (1910); *Labor and the Common Welfare* (1919); *Seventy Years of Life and Labor* (autobiography, 1925); etc. President, the American Federation of Labor, 1886–1895, 1896–1924.

Gone With the Wind. Novel by Margaret Mitchell (1936). Story of the Civil War in Georgia, and Scarlett O'Hara's fight to restore her father's plantation, destroyed in Sherman's march. Stepping out of her lady's role, she fights her way through the business world, becoming obligated to Rhett Butler, who does not share her patriotism, but who understands her motives and makes the most of his opportunity. Their marriage ends in tragedy. The most successful of modern best-sellers. The motion picture made from it was equally a spectacular success.

GONZALES, AMBROSE ELLIOT (May 28, 1857–July 11, 1926); b. Colleton Co., S.C. Publisher, author. *The Black Border* (1922); *With Aesop Along the Black Border* (1922); *The Captain* (1924); *Laguerre, a Gascon of the Black Border* (1924); all dealing with the Gullah Negro. Editor and publisher, *The State,* Charleston, S.C., 1891–1926.

GOOD, JAMES ISAAC (Dec. 31, 1850–Jan. 22, 1924); b. York, Pa. German Reformed clergyman, educator, historian. *The Origin of the Reformed Church in Germany* (1887); *History of the Reformed Church in the United States* (1899); etc. Prof. Ursinus School of Theology, 1890–1924; Central Theological Seminary, 1907–24.

Good Bye, Wisconsin. Short stories by Glenway Wescott (1928).

Good Earth, The. Novel by Pearl Buck (1931). First of a trilogy, including *Sons* (1932) and *A House Divided* (1935), which follows the family of Wang through its rise and triumph, and its conflicts in the modern world. The trilogy was republished as a unit under the title *House of Earth* (1935).

Good Housekeeping. New York. Monthly. Founded 1885. Sold in 1900 to the Phelps Publishing Co., headed by Herbert Myrick. It was acquired by William Randolph Hearst in 1911. James Eaton Power was editor, 1900–13; William Frederick Bigelow, 1913–40. Wade H. Nichols is present editor. One of the most popular of general family magazines.

Good Morning, America. Book of poems by Carl Sandburg (1928).

Good News from New England. By Edward Winslow (1625), reprinted in the *Collections of the Massachusetts Historical Society,* v.8, 1832, and ser. 2, v.9, 1856. Recounts the daily life of the Plymouth colonists.

"Good Old Rebel." Humorous Southern song of Reconstruction days. Written by Innes Randolph. First line is "Oh, I'm a good old Rebel, And that's just what I am."

GOODALE, DORA READ (Oct. 29, 1866–deceased); b. Mt. Washington, Mass., sister of Elaine Goodale Eastman. Poet. *Apple Blossoms: Verses of Two Children* (with sister, 1878); *In Berkshire with the Wild Flowers* (with sister, 1879); *All Round the Year Verses from Sky Farm* (with sister, 1880); *Test of the Sky* (1926); *Mountain Dooryards* (1946); etc.

Goodale, Elaine. See Elaine Goodale Eastman.

GOODE, CLEMENT TYSON (d. Nov. 8, 1943); b. Mooresboro, N.C. Educator, author. *Byron as Critic* (1923); *An Atlas of English Literature* (with E. F. Shannon, 1925); *Composition and Rhetoric* (with T. P. Cross and R. A. Law, 1932); *A Literary Map of the British Isles* (1941); etc. Prof. English, University of Richmond, 1924–41.

GOODELL, WILLIAM (Feb. 14, 1792–Feb. 18, 1867); b. Templeton, Mass. Congregational missionary, author. *Forty Years in the Turkish Empire* (memoirs, 1876); *The Old and the New; or, The Change of Thirty Years in the East* (1853).

GOODENOUGH, ERWIN RAMSDELL (Oct. 24, 1893–March 20, 1965); b. Brooklyn, N.Y. Educator, editor, historian. *The Theology of Justin Martyr* (1923); *The Church in the Roman Empire* (1930); *Religious Tradition and Myth* (1937); *Jewish Symbols in the Greco-Roman Period,* 10v. (1953–58); *Toward a Mature Faith* (1955); *The Psychology of Religious Experiences* (1965); etc. Editor, *Journal of Biblical*

Literature, 1934–42. History dept., Yale University, from 1923.

GOODFRIEND, ARTHUR (June 2, 1907–); b. New York. Foreign service officer, author. *The Only War We Seek* (1951); *What Can a Man Do?* (1954); *What Is America?* (1954); *Stand Fast in Liberty* (1959); *The Twisted Image* (1963); *Tomtoms and Transistors* (1966); *The Cognoscent Abroad* (1969); etc.

GOODHUE, WILLIS MAXWELL (1873–Nov. 22, 1938); b. Akron, O. Playwright. *All Wet* (prod. 1925); *Betty, Be Careful* (prod. 1931); etc.

GOODIN, PEGGY (May 18, 1923–); b. Kansas City, Mo. Novelist. *Clementine* (1946); *Take Care of My Little Girl* (1950); *The Lie* (1953); *Dede O'Shea* (1957).

GOODIS, DAVID (1917–Jan. 7, 1967); b. Philadelphia, Pa. Novelist. *Retreat from Oblivion* (1939); *Dark Passage* (1946); *Nightfall* (1947); *Behold This Woman* (1947); *Of Missing Persons* (1950).

GOODLOE, A[bbie] CARTER (1867–); b. Versailles, Ky. Author. *Antinoüs* (1891); *College Girls* (1896); *Calvert of Strathore* (1903); *At the Foot of the Rockies* (1905); *The Star Gazers* (1910).

GOODLOE, DANIEL REAVES (May 28, 1814–Jan. 18, 1902); b. Louisburg, N.C. Southern abolitionist, historical writer. *The Southern Platform* (1858); and many controversial books and pamphlets.

GOODMAN, DANIEL CARSON (Aug. 24, 1883–May 16, 1957); b. Chicago, Ill. Novelist. *Unclothed* (1912); *The Taker* (1918); *Kaleidoscope,* 2v. (1935); *Fan Dance at Cockcrow* (1941); *The Dead Came to Life* (1943); *They Came to See Dr. Arkady* (1943); etc.

GOODMAN, GEORGE J. W. (Aug. 10, 1930–); b. St. Louis, Mo. Author. *The Bubble Makers* (1955); *A Time for Paris* (1957); *A Killing in the Market* (1958); *Bascomb, the Fastest Hound Alive* (1958); *The Wheeler Dealers* (1959; also screenplay, 1963); *The Money Game* (under pen name "Adam Smith," 1968). Editor: *Institutional Investor,* since 1967.

GOODMAN, JULES ECKERT (Nov. 2, 1876–July 10, 1962); b. Gervais, Ore. Playwright. *The Man Who Stood Still* (prod. 1908); *Mother* (prod. 1910); *The Silent Voice* (prod. 1914); *Pietro* (with Maud Skinner, prod. 1919); *Chains* (prod. 1924); *The Great Romancer* (prod. 1937); *Many Mansions* (with Eckert Goodman, prod. 1937). He also dramatized many of Montague Glass's stories of "Potash and Perlmutter."

GOODMAN, KENNETH SAWYER (Sept. 19, 1883–Nov. 29, 1918); b. Chicago, Ill. Playwright. *Quick Curtains* (1915); *More Quick Curtains* (1923); *The Wonder Hat* (with Ben Hecht, 1925); all collections of one-act plays.

GOODMAN, NATHAN GERSON (Jan. 9, 1899–Aug. 22, 1953); b. Philadelphia, Pa. Historian. *Benjamin Rush* (1934); *Benjamin Franklin's Own Story* (1937); etc. Co-author: *Famous Explorers* (1942); *Famous Pioneers* (1945); etc. Editor, *The Ingenious Dr. Franklin* (1931); *Profile of Genius: The Poor Richard Pamphlets* (1938); *A Benjamin Franklin Reader* (1945); etc.

GOODMAN, NELSON (Aug. 7, 1906–); b. Somerville, Mass. Educator, author. *The Structure of Appearance* (1951); *Fact, Fiction, and Forecast* (1955); *Languages of Art* (1968). Philosophy dept., University of Pennsylvania, since 1946.

GOODMAN, PAUL (Sept. 9, 1911–); b. New York. Author. *Stop Light* (poems, 1942); *The Grand Piano* (1942); *The Facts of Life* (1946); *The State of Nature* (1946); *Art and Social Nature* (1946); *Communitas* (with Percival Goodman, 1947); *Kafka's Prayer* (1947); *Faustina* (play, 1949); *The Break-up of Our Camp* (stories, 1950); *The Structure of Liter-*

ature (1954); *The Empire City* (1959); *Growing Up Absurd* (1960); *Utopian Essays and Practical Proposals* (1962); *Compulsory Mis-education* (1964); *People or Personnel* (1965); *Hawkweed* (1967); *The New Reformation* (1970); etc.

GOODMAN, PERCIVAL (Jan. 13, 1904–   ); b. New York. Architect, author. *Communitas* (with Paul Goodman, 1947). Prof. architecture, Columbia University, since 1966.

GOODRICH, ARTHUR [Frederick] (Feb. 18, 1878–); b. New Britain, Conn. Novelist, playwright. *The Balance of Power* (1906); *The Yardstick Man* (1910); *The Man with an Honest Face* (1911); *So This Is London* (prod. 1922); *The Ring of Truth* (prod. 1923); *The Joker* (prod. 1925); *The Plutocrat* (prod. 1929); *Richelieu* (prod. 1930); *Dr. Grant* (1934); *A Journey by Night* (1935); *You Wouldn't Believe It* (1936); *I Can't Help It* (1938); *The Sound of Wings* (1941); etc.

GOODRICH, CHAUNCEY ALLEN (Oct. 23, 1790–Feb. 25, 1860); b. New Haven, Conn. Congregational clergyman, educator, lexicographer. He revised and abridged a number of editions of the *American Dictionary*, compiled by his father-in-law, Noah Webster, in 1828. These revisions were continued by his son, Chauncey Allen Goodrich (1817–1868). Prof. pastoral theology, Yale, 1838–60.

GOODRICH, FRANCES (Mrs. Albert M. Hackett), b. Belleville, N.J. Playwright. Co-author (with Albert M. Hackett): *Up Pops the Devil* (prod. 1930); *The Great Big Doorstep* (prod. 1943); *Diary of Anne Frank* (adaptation, prod. 1955, Pulitzer Prize for drama, 1956); *The Third Adam* (1967); etc. Also many screenplays.

GOODRICH, FRANK BOOTT (Dec. 14, 1826–Mar. 15, 1894); b. Boston, Mass., son of Samuel Griswold Goodrich. Journalist, playwright. *Tri-Colored Sketches in Paris* (anon., 1855), first published in the *New York Times* under the pen name "Dick Tinto"; *Man Upon the Sea* (1858), republished as *Ocean's Story* (1873), and as *Remarkable Voyages* (1873); *Women of Beauty and Heroism* (1859); republished as *World Famous Women* (1871).

GOODRICH, LELAND MATTHEW (Sept. 1, 1899–); b. Lewiston, Me. Educator, author. *Korea: A Study of United States Policy in the United Nations* (1956); *The United Nations* (1959); *The United Nations in the Balance* (with Norman J. Padelford, 1965); etc. Political science dept., Brown University, 1926–50; Columbia University, since 1950.

GOODRICH, LLOYD (July 10, 1897–); b. Nutley, N.J. Museum officer, author. *Thomas Eakins* (1933); *Winslow Homer* (1944); *Yasuo Kuniyoshi* (1948); *Max Weber* (1949); *Edward Hopper* (1950); *John Sloan* (1952); *Albert Ryder* (1959); *Young America* (1965); *Edwin Dickinson* (1966); *Raphael Soyer* (1967); *Winslow Homer's America* (1969); etc.

GOODRICH, SAMUEL (Aug. 19, 1793–May 9, 1860); b. Ridgefield, Conn. Publisher, author. Pen name, "Peter Parley." *The Tales of Peter Parley in America* (1827), and many sequels; *The Outcast, and Other Poems* (1836); *Poems* (1851); *Recollections of a Lifetime*, 2v. (1856); etc. Publisher and editor, *Parley's Magazine*, 1833–34; *Robert Merry's Museum*, 1841–50.

GOODSELL, DANIEL AYRES (Nov. 5, 1840–Dec. 5, 1909); b. Newbury, N.Y. Editor, author. *Nature and Character at Granite Bay* (1901). Lit. editor, the *Christian Advocate*, 1880–87.

GOODSPEED, EDGAR JOHNSON (Oct. 23, 1871–Jan. 13, 1962); b. Quincy, Ill. Educator, author. *Things Seen and Heard* (1925); *Buying Happiness* (1932); *The Story of the Bible* (1936); etc. Editor: *Index Patristicus* (1907); *Chicago Literary Papyri* (1908); *Index Apologeticus* (1912); *Catalogue of the University of Chicago Manuscripts* (with M. Sprengling, 1912); *The Story of the New Testament* (1916);

The Complete Bible: An American Translation (with J. M. P. Smith, 1939); *How to Read the Bible* (1946); *As I Remember* (1953); *The Twelve: The Story of Christ's Apostles* (1957); *Matthew, Apostle and Evangelist* (1959); *Paul* (1959); *The Apocrypha: An American Translation* (1959); etc. Dept. Bible literature, University of Chicago, 1898–1937.

GOODSPEED, THOMAS WAKEFIELD (Sept. 4, 1842–Dec. 16, 1927); b. Glens Falls, N.Y. Baptist clergyman, biographer. *The University of Chicago Biographical Sketches*, 2v. (1922–25); *The Story of the University of Chicago* (1925); *Ernest De Witt Burton* (1926); *William Rainey Harper* (1928). *See* Allan Nevins's *John D. Rockefeller*, 2v. (1940).

GOODWIN, CARDINAL (Leonidas) (May 1, 1880–June 23, 1944); b. Pine Bluff, Ark. Educator, author. *A Larger View of the Yellowstone Expedition* (1918); *The Trans-Mississippi West from 1803 to 1853* (1922); *John Charles Frémont* (1930); etc. Editor: *New Spain and the Anglo-American West*, 2v. (1932). Prof. history, Mills College, from 1918.

GOODWIN, HANNAH ELIZABETH BRADBURY (Mrs. H. B. Goodwin; Mrs. Goodwin Talcott) (1827–1893); b. in Massachusetts. Author. Wrote also under initials, "H. B. G." *Roger Deane's Work* (1863); *Madge; or, Night and Morning* (1863); *Sherbrook* (1866); *Dr. Howell's Family* (1868); *The Fortunes of Miss Follen* (1876); *Christine's Fortune* (1881); *One among Many* (1884); *Our Party of Four* (1887); *Dorothy Gray* (1891); etc.

GOODWIN, J[ohn] CHEEVER (July 14, 1850–Dec. 18, 1912); b. Boston, Mass. Playwright. He wrote the librettos for *Evangeline* (prod. 1874); *The Merry Monarch* (prod. 1890); *Panjandrum* (prod. 1893); *The Monks of Malabar* (prod. 1900); etc.

GOODWIN, MAUD WILDER (Mrs. Almon Goodwin) (June 5, 1856–Feb. 5, 1935); b. Ballston Spa, N.Y. Novelist, biographer. *The Colonial Cavalier* (1894); *White Aprons* (1896); *Dolly Madison* (1896); *Flint* (1897); *Sir Christopher* (1901); *Claims and Counter Claims* (1905); *Veronica Playfair* (1909); etc.

GOODYEAR, WILLIAM HENRY (Apr. 21, 1846–Feb. 19, 1923); b. New Haven, Conn. Archeologist, author. *Ancient and Modern History* (1883); *A History of Art* (1888); *Roman and Medieval Art* (1893); *Renaissance and Modern Art* (1894); etc. Curator, Metropolitan Museum of Art, 1882–88; curator of fine arts, Brooklyn Institute of Arts and Sciences, 1899–1923.

GOODYKOONTZ, COLIN BRUMMITT (Dec. 14, 1885–Jan. 6, 1958); b. Atlanta, Ind. Educator, historian. *Home Missions on the American Frontier* (1939). Editor: *The Trans-Mississippi West* (1930); etc. History dept., University of Colorado, 1921–54.

GOOKIN, DANIEL (1612–Mar. 19, 1686); b. in Kent, England, or Co. Cork, Ireland. American colonist, author. *Historical Collections of the Indians in New England* (published by the Massachusetts Historical Society, 1792); *An Historical Account of the Doings and Sufferings of the Christian Indians of New England* (published by the American Antiquarian Society, 1836).

Goose Pond School, The. Story by Richard Malcolm Johnston (1857).

Goose-Quill Papers. Essays by Louise Imogen Guiney (1885).

GOOSSEN, EUGENE COONS (Aug. 6, 1920–); b. Gloversville, N.Y. Educator, author. *Ellsworth Kelly* (1958); *Three American Sculptors* (1959); *Stuart Davis* (1959); *The Art of the Real: U.S.A. 1948–1968* (1968). Prof. art, Hunter College, since 1961.

GORDIS, ROBERT (Feb. 6, 1908–); b. Brooklyn, N.Y. Rabbi, author. *The Biblical Text in the Making* (1937); *Conservative Judaism: An American Philosophy* (1945);

Koheleth, The Man and His World (1951); *The Song of Songs* (1954); *The Book of God and Man* (1965); *Judaism in a Christian World* (1966); *Leave a Little to God* (1967); *Poet, Prophet and Sage* (1969); etc.

GORDON, ARMISTEAD CHURCHILL (Dec. 20, 1855–Oct. 21, 1931); b. in Albemarle Co., Va. Lawyer, author. *Maje: A Love Story* (1914); *Jefferson Davis* (1918); *Memories and Memorials of William Gordon McCabe*, 2v. (1925); *Allegra: The Story of Byron and Miss Clairmont* (1926); etc.

GORDON, ARMISTEAD CHURCHILL, Jr. (July 1, 1897–May 12, 1953); b. Staunton, Va., Educator. Editor: *Virginian Writers of Fugitive Verse* (1923). English dept., University of Virginia, from 1919.

GORDON, CAROLINE (Oct. 6, 1895–); b. in Todd Co., Ky. Author. *Penhally* (1931); *Aleck Maury, Sportsman* (1934); *The Garden of Adonis* (1937); *The Green Centuries* (1941); *The Woman on the Porch* (1944); *The Forest of the South* (stories, 1945); *The House of Fiction* (ed., with Allen Tate, 1950); *The Strange Children* (1951); *The Malefactors* (1956); *How to Read a Novel* (1957); *Old Red and Other Stories* (1963).

Gordon, Col. H. R. Pen name of Edward S. Ellis.

GORDON, DOROTHY (Apr. 4, 1893–); b. Odessa, Rus. Broadcaster, author. *Around the World in Song* (1929); *Treasure Bag of Game Songs* (1939); *All Children Listen* (1941); *You and Democracy* (1951); *Who Has the Answer?* (1965); etc.

GORDON, ELIZABETH (Aug. 8, 1907–); b. Logansport, Ind. Editor. Co-author: *More House for Your Money* (1937). Editor-in-chief, *House Beautiful*, 1941–64.

GORDON, GEORGE ANGIER (Jan. 2, 1853–Oct. 25, 1929); b. in Scotland. Congregational clergyman, author. *The New Epoch for Faith* (1901); *Religion and Miracle* (1913); *Humanism in New England Theology* (1920); *My Education and Religion* (autobiography, 1925); etc.

GORDON, GEORGE BYRON (Aug. 4, 1870–Jan. 30, 1927); b. New Perth, P.E.I. Archeologist, author. *In the Alaska Wilderness* (1917); *Baalbek* (1919); *Rambles in Old London* (1924); etc. Curator of anthropology, University of Pennsylvania, 1904–27.

GORDON, IRWIN LESLIE (Oct. 24, 1888–July 21, 1954); b. Lowell, Mass. Journalist, author. *The Log of the Ark* (with A. J. Frueh, 1915); *What Allah Wills* (1917); *Maine of the Sea and Pines* (with Nathan Haskell Dole, 1928). With *Philadelphia Evening Ledger*, 1914–21.

GORDON, JAMES LINDSAY (Jan. 9, 1860–Nov. 30, 1904); b. "Longwood," Louisa Co., Va. Lawyer, poet. *Ballads of the Sunlit Years* (1904).

GORDON, JOHN B[rown] (Feb. 6, 1832–Jan. 9, 1904); b. in Upson Co., Ga. Confederate general, author. *Reminiscences of the Civil War* (1903).

Gordon, Julien. Pen name of Julie Grinnell Chance.

GORDON, MARGARET (Nov. 27, 1868–deceased); b. Arlington, Mass. Editor, author. *The Free-Lance Writer's Handbook* (with William D. Kennedy, 1926). Editor, *The Writer*, 1920–1925).

GORDON, PATRICIA (1904–). Author. Writes under pen name "Joan Howard." *The Boy Jones* (1943); *Rommany Luck* (1946); *Summer Is Magic* (1952); *The Story of Louisa May Alcott* (1955); *Light in the Tower* (1957); etc.

GORDON, RUTH (Mrs. Garson Kanin) (Oct. 30, 1896–); b. Wollaston, Mass. Actress, playwright. *Over Twenty-One* (1944); *Years Ago* (1947); *The Leading Lady* (1949); *Myself among Others* (1971).

GORDON, WILLIAM (1728–Oct. 19, 1807); b. Hitchin, Hertfordshire, England. Congregational clergyman, author. *The History of the Rise, Progress, and Establishment of the Independence of the United States of America*, 3v. (1789).

Gordon Keith. Novel of the Civil War by Thomas Nelson Page (1903). The Keith estate "Elphinestone" is lost after the war and falls into the hands of an unfeeling Northerner. Gordon attempts to regain the family's wealth and prestige.

GORDONE, CHARLES. Playwright. *No Place to be Somebody* (1970). Pulitzer Prize for Drama, 1970.

GORDY, WILBUR FISK (June 14, 1854–Dec. 23, 1929); b. near Salisbury, Md. Educator, historian. *American Leaders and Heroes* (1901); *Stories of American Explorers* (1906); *Colonial Days* (1907); *Stories of Early American History* (1913); *Stories of Later American History* (1915); *Abraham Lincoln* (1917); *Leaders in Making America* (1923); etc.

GOREN, CHARLES H[enry] (Mar. 4, 1901–); b. Philadelphia, Pa. Author. *Contract Bridge in a Nutshell* (1946); *Point Count Bidding* (1950); *Contract Bridge Complete* (1951); *An Evening of Bridge with Charles Goren* (1959); *Winning Partnership Bridge* (1961); *Goren's Bridge Complete* (1963); *Play Winning Bridge with Any Partner, Even a Stranger* (1965); *Goren's Bridge Quizzes* (1966); etc. Author, column "Goren on Bridge," Chicago *Tribune* syndicate, since 1944.

GORHAM, CHARLES ORSON (Sept. 25, 1911–); b. Philadelphia, Pa. Novelist. *The Gilded Hearse* (1948); *The Future Mr. Dolan* (1948); *Trial by Darkness* (1952); *Gold of Their Bodies* (1955); *The Wine of Life* (1958); *Carlotta McBride* (1959); *McCaffery* (1961); *The Lion of Judah* (1966).

GORKIN, JESS (Oct. 23, 1913–); b. Rochester, N.Y. Editor. Editor, *Parade* magazine, since 1947.

GORMAN, HERBERT SHERMAN (Jan. 1, 1893–Oct. 28, 1954); b. Springfield, Mass. Biographer, poet. *The Fool of Love* (1920); *The Barcarole of James Smith* (1922); *The Procession of Masks* (1923); *James Joyce: His First Forty Years* (1924); *A Victorian American: Henry Wadsworth Longfellow* (1926); *Hawthorne: A Study in Solitude* (1927); *The Place Called Dagon* (1927); *The Incredible Marquis: Alexandre Dumas* (1929); *The Scottish Queen* (1932); *Suzy* (1934); *James Joyce* (1940); *Brave General* (1942); *The Wine of San Lorenzo* (1945); *The Cry of Dolores* (1947); *The Breast of the Dove* (1950); etc. Editor (with wife, Jean Wright Gorman): *The Peterborough Anthology* (1923).

GORSLINE, DOUGLAS W. (May 24, 1913–); b. Rochester, N.Y. Artist, author. *Farm Boy* (1950); *What People Wore: A Visual History of Dress* (1952).

GOSNELL, HAROLD FOOTE (Dec. 24, 1896–); b. Lockport, N.Y. Educator, author. *Boss Platt and His New York Machine* (1924); *Why Europe Votes* (1930); *Machine Politics* (1937); *Grass Roots Politics* (1942); *Democracy* (1948). *Champion Campaigner: Franklin D. Roosevelt* (1952); etc. Prof. political science, American University, since 1946.

Gospel of Wealth, and Other Timely Essays, The. By Andrew Carnegie (1900).

GOSS, MADELEINE [Binkley] (1892–). Author. *Beethoven* (1931); *Bolero* (1940); *Unfinished Symphony* (1941); *Brahms* (1943); *Modern Music Makers* (1952); *Yoga for Today* (with Clara Spring, 1959); etc.

GOSS, WARREN LEE (Aug. 19, 1835–Nov. 20, 1925); b. Brewster, Mass. Author. *The Soldier's Story of Captivity at Andersonville* (1866); *Jed* (1889); *Tom Clifton* (1892); *Jack Alden* (1895); *Jed's Boy* (1919); etc.

GOTSHALK, D[ilman] W[alter] (Sept. 11, 1901–); b. Trenton, N.J. Educator, author. *Structure and Reality* (1937); *Metaphysics in Modern Times* (1940); *Art and the Social Order* (1947); *Patterns of Good and Evil* (1963); *Human*

Aims in Modern Perspective (1966). Philosophy dept., University of Illinois, since 1927.

GOTTEHRER, BARRY H[ugh] (Jan. 25, 1935–); b. Bronx, N.Y. Government official, journalist, author. *Football Stars of 1962* (1962); *Basketball Stars of 1964* (1964); *Football Stars of 1964* (1964); *Giants of New York* (1964); *New York City in Crisis* (1965). Sports editor *Newsweek* magazine, 1960–63; editorial staff, New York *Herald Tribune,* 1964–65; assistant to mayor of New York City, since 1965.

GOTTFRIED, MANFRED (May 7, 1900–); b. Chicago, Ill. Editor, novelist. *Prelude to Battle* (1928). With *Time Magazine,* since 1923; assoc. ed. *Fortune,* 1930–33.

GOTTHEIL, RICHARD JAMES HORATIO (Oct. 13, 1862–May 22, 1936); b. Manchester, England. Semitic scholar, author. *Zionism* (1914). Editor: *Selections from the Syriac Julian Romanes* (1906); *The Syriac-Arabic Glosses of Isha bar Ali* (1910); etc. Editor, *Jewish Quarterly Review;* co-editor, *Jewish Encyclopedia.* Prof. Semitic languages, Columbia University, 1887–1936. Head, Oriental dept., New York Public Library, 1896–1936.

Gottschalk, Laura Riding. See Laura Riding.

GOTTSCHALK, LOUIS ([Reichenthal]) (Feb. 21, 1899–); Brooklyn, N.Y. Educator, historian. *Jean Paul Marat* (1927); *The Era of the French Revolution* (1929); *Lafayette Comes to America* (1935); *Lafayette Joins the American Army* (1937); *Lady-in-Waiting* (1939); *The Letters of Lafayette to Washington* (1945); *Lafayette between the American and the French Revolution 1783–1789* (1950); *Understanding History* (1950); *Europe and the Modern World,* 2v. (with D. F. Lach, 1951, 1954); *Lafayette in the French Revolution through the October Days* (with Margaret Maddox, 1969); etc. History dept., University of Chicago, 1925–64.

GOUCHER, JOHN FRANKLIN (June 7, 1845–July 19, 1922); b. Waynesburg, Pa. Methodist clergyman, philanthropist, author. *True Education* (1904); *The Growth of the Missionary Concept* (1911); etc. President, Woman's College of Baltimore (now Goucher College), 1890–1908.

GOUDY, FREDERICK WILLIAM (Mar. 8, 1865–May 11, 1947); b. Bloomington, Ill. Printer, type-designer, author. *The Alphabet* (1918); *Elements of Lettering* (1921); *Typologia* (1940); etc. Editor, *Ars Typographica* magazine, 1918–34. Founder (with wife, Bertha M. Sprinks), the Village Press and Letter Foundry, at Park Ridge, Ill., 1903; this was later moved to Deepdene, Marlborough-on-Hudson, N.Y., and was destroyed by fire in 1939.

GOUGH, JOHN BARTHOLOMEW (Aug. 22, 1817–Feb. 18, 1886); b. Sandgate, England. Prohibitionist, lecturer, author. *An Autobiography* (1845, expanded 1859, and again 1869); *Sunshine and Shadow* (1880); *Platform Echoes* (1885).

GOULD, BEATRICE BLACKMAR (Mrs. Charles Bruce Gould); b. Emmetsburg, Ia. Editor, playwright. *Man's Estate* (with husband, prod. 1929); *The Terrible Turk* (with same, prod. 1934). Co-editor (with husband), *Ladies' Home Journal,* 1935–62.

GOULD, CHARLES BRUCE (July 28, 1898–); b. Luana, Ia. Editor, author. *Sky Larking* (1929); *Flying Dutchman: The Life of Anthony Fokker* (with Anthony H. G. Fokker, 1931); *Man's Estate* (with wife, Beatrice Blackmar Gould, prod. 1929); *The Terrible Turk* (with same, prod. 1934); etc. Editor, *Ladies' Home Journal,* 1935–62.

GOULD, EDWARD SHERMAN (May 11, 1805–Feb. 18, 1885); b. Litchfield, Conn. Author. *The Sleep-Rider; or, The Old Boy in the Omnibus: by the Man in the Claret-Colored Coat* (1843); *The Very Age* (1850); *John Doe and Richard Roe; or, Episodes of Life in New York* (1862); *Good English* (1867); etc. Edited: *Forecastle Yarns,* written by his brother, John W. Gould (1850).

GOULD, GEORGE MILBRY (Nov. 8, 1848–Aug 8, 1922); b. Auburn, Me. Physician, author. *Borderland Studies,* 2v. (1896–1908); *An Autumn Singer* (poems, 1897); *Biographic Clinics,* 6v. (1903–09); *Concerning Lafcadio Hearn* (1908); *The Infinite Presence* (1910). Editor (with Laura Stedman): *Life and Letters of Edmund Clarence Stedman,* 2v. (1910). Compiler: *A New Medical Dictionary* (1890); etc. Founder, *American Medicine,* 1901.

GOULD, HANNAH FLAGG (Sept. 3, 1789–Sept. 5, 1865); b. Lancaster, Mass. Poet. *Poems* (1832, augmented to 2v. 1836, and again to 3v. 1841); *The Golden Vase* (1843); *Gathered Leaves* (1846); *New Poems* (1850); *The Youth's Coronal* (1851); *Hymns and Other Poems for Children* (1854); *Poems for Little Ones* (1863); etc.

GOULD, JACK [John Ludlow] (Feb. 5, 1914–); b. New York. Journalist. *All about Radio and Television* (1953). Drama department, *New York Times,* 1937–42; radio and television department, since 1942; radio and television critic, 1944–71.

GOULD, JOHN THOMAS (Oct. 22, 1908–); b. Brighton, Mass. Farmer, author. *New England Town Meeting* (1940); *Farmer Takes a Wife* (1945); *Neither Hay nor Grass* (1951); *The Fastest Hound Dog in the State of Maine* (1953); *Monstrous Depravity* (1963); *Parables of Peter Partout* (1964); *You Should Start Sooner* (1965); *Last One In* (1966); *Europe on Saturday Night* (1968); *The Jonesport Raffle* (1969); etc. Weekly column, "Dispatch from the Farm," *The Christian Science Monitor.*

GOULD, KENNETH MILLER (May 13, 1895–Mar. 12, 1969); b. Cleveland, O. Editor, author. *Windows on the World* (1938). Editor, *Scholastic Magazine,* 1940–63.

Gould, Laura Stedman. See Laura Stedman.

GOULD, LOIS. Author. *Such Good Friends* (1970).

GOULDING, FRANCIS ROBERT (Sept. 28, 1810–Aug. 22, 1881); b. Midway, Ga. Presbyterian clergyman, author of books for boys. *Little Josephine* (1844); *Robert and Harold; or, The Young Marooners on the Florida Coast* (1852), republished as *The Young Marooners on the Florida Coast; or, Robert and Harold* (1866); *Marooner's Island* (1869); *Frank Gordon* (1869); *Woodruff Stories* (1870); *Nacoochee* (1871); etc.

Gourmet. New York. Monthly. Founded 1941. Concerned with the pleasures of good living as typified by knowledgeable cuisine.

Gousha, Mrs. Joseph R. See Dawn Powell.

GOVAN, MARY CHRISTINE NOBLE (Dec. 12, 1898–); b. New York. Author. *Jennifer's House* (1945); *The Pink Maple House* (1950); *Mystery at Shingle Rock* (1955); *Mystery at the Haunted House* (1959); *Mystery at Snowed-in Cabin* (1961); *Mystery at Echoing Cave* (1965); *Curious Clubhouse* (1967); *Phinny's Fine Summer-World* (1968); *Mr. Alexander and the Witch* (1969); *Mystery of the Missing Wallpaper* (1970); etc.

GOVER, ROBERT (Nov. 2, 1929–); b. Philadelphia, Pa. Author. *One Hundred Dollar Misunderstanding* (1962); *The Maniac Responsible* (1963); *Here Goes Kitten* (1964); *Poorboy at the Party* (1966); *J. C. Saves* (1968).

GOWANS, ALAN (Nov. 30, 1923–); b. Toronto, Can. Educator, author. *Church Architecture in New France* (1955); *The Face of Toronto* (1960); *Images of American Living* (1964); *The Restless Art; A Study of Painting and Painters, 1750–1950* (1966); etc. Prof. art history, University of Delaware, since 1960.

GOWANS, WILLIAM (Mar. 29, 1803–Nov. 27, 1870); b. in Lanarkshire, Scotland. Bibliophile, publisher, bookseller. Assisted by James Harper, he opened a bookstall in New York City, where he took lodgings in the home of Edgar Allan Poe.

From 1863 he was known as the "Antiquarian of Nassau Street." Published *Gowans' Bibliotheca Americana*, 5v. (1845–69). *See* William L. Andrews *The Old Booksellers of New York* (1895); *Catalogue of the Books Belonging to the Estate of the Late Mr. William Gowans*, 16 parts (1871).

GOWEN, (SAMUEL) EMMETT (Sept. 10, 1902–); b. La Vergne, Tenn. Journalist, author. *Racketeers: An Expose* (1930); *Mountain Born* (1932); *Dark Moon of March* (1933); *The Brass Face* (1935); *The Joys of Fishing* (1961); *Expedition Holy Book* (1967); etc.

GOYEN, [Charles] WILLIAM (Apr. 25, 1915–); b. Trinity, Tex. Author. *The House of Breath* (1950); *In a Farther Country* (1955); *The Faces of Blood Kindred* (1960); *Ghost and Flesh* (short stories, 1962); *The Fair Sister* (1963). Playwright: *The House of Breath* (1956); *The Diamond Rattler* (1960); *Christy* (1964).

GRABO, CARL HENRY (Aug. 1881–); b. Chicago, Ill. Educator, author. *The Art of the Short Story* (1913); *The Amateur Philosopher* (1917); *The Technique of the Novel* (1928); *The Cat in Grandfather's House* (1929); *The Creative Critic* (1948); *Shelley's Eccentricities* (1950); *The Technique of the Novel* (1964); and many books on the poet Shelley, juveniles, etc.

GRAEBNER, NORMAN ARTHUR (Oct. 19, 1915–); b. Kingman, Kan. Educator, author. *Empire on the Pacific* (1955); *The New Isolationism* (1956); *Cold War Diplomacy* (1962). Editor: *The Enduring Lincoln* (1959); *An Uncertain Tradition* (1961); *Manifest Destiny* (1967); etc. Prof. history, University of Illinois, 1956–67; prof. modern American history, University of Virginia, since 1967.

GRAF, OSKAR MARIA (July 22, 1894–Apr. 28, 1967); b. Berg am Starnberger See, Ger. Author. *Prisoners All* (autobiography, 1928); *The Life of My Mother* (1940); also many other books in German.

GRAFF, HENRY F[ranklin] (Aug. 11, 1921–); b. New York. Educator, author. *Bluejackets with Perry in Japan* (1952); *The Modern Researcher* (with Jacques Barzun, 1962); *American Themes* (with Clifford Lord, 1963); *The Adventure of the American People* (with John A. Krout, 1966); *The Free and the Brave* (1967). Prof. history, Columbia University, since 1961.

GRAFTON, SAMUEL (Sept. 4, 1907–); b. New York. Journalist, author. *All Out!* (1940); *An American Diary* (1943); *A Most Contagious Game* (1955). Daily column, "I'd Rather Be Right," 1939–49.

GRAHAM, AELRED (Sept. 15, 1907–); b. Liverpool, Eng. Roman Catholic clergyman, author. *The Love of God* (1940); *The Christ of Catholicism* (1947); *Christian Thought and Action* (1958); etc.

GRAHAM, BESSIE (1883–Oct. 1, 1966). Author. *The Bookman's Manual* (1921); *Famous Literary Prizes and Their Winners* (1935).

GRAHAM, DOROTHY (Dec. 13, 1893–June 22, 1959); b. New Rochelle, N.Y. Author. *Through the Moon Door* (1926); *Lotus of the Dusk* (1927); *Brush Strokes on the Fan of a Courtesan* (poems, with James Bennett, 1927); *The French Wife* (1928); *The China Venture* (1929); *Candles in the Sun* (1930); *Chinese Gardens* (1938); *Wind Across the World* (1947); etc.

GRAHAM, FRANK (Nov. 12, 1894–March 9, 1965); b. New York. Journalist, author. *Lou Gehrig, a Quiet Hero* (1942); *McGraw of the Giants* (1944); *Al Smith, American* (1945); *Baseball Extra* (1954); etc. Sport columnist, New York *Journal American*, from 1945.

GRAHAM, GEORGE ADAMS (Dec. 23, 1904–); b. Cambridge, N.Y. Educator, author. *Regulatory Administration* (with Henry Reining, 1943); *Morality in American Politics*

(1952); *America's Capacity to Govern* (1960); etc. Director of governmental studies, Brookings Institution, since 1958.

GRAHAM, GEORGE REX (Jan. 18, 1813–July 13, 1894); b. Philadelphia, Pa. Publisher, editor. Publisher, *Atkinson's Casket*, 1839–41; founder and publisher, *Graham's Weekly*, 1841; he sold it in 1853.

GRAHAM, GWETHALYN. Pen name of Gwethalyn Graham Erichsen Brown.

GRAHAM, MALBONE WATSON (Mar. 26, 1898–Oct. 16, 1965); b. Bogota. Educator, author. *New Governments of Central Europe* (1924); *The Soviet Security System* (1929); *In Quest of a Law of Recognition* (1933); *Czechoslovakia: Twenty Years of Independence* (with others, 1940); *Yugoslavia* (with others, 1949); etc. Political science dept., University of California at Los Angeles, 1924–63.

GRAHAM, PHILIP (Aug. 27, 1894–); b. Comanche, Tex. Educator, author. *Life and Poems of Mirabeau B. Lamar* (1938); *Showboats: The History of an American Institution* (1951). Editor: *Early Texas Verse* (1936); etc. Compiler: *A Concordance to the Poems of Sidney Lanier* (with J. Jones, 1939). English dept., University of Texas, since 1923.

GRAHAM, SHEILAH. Columnist. *Beloved Infidel* (with Gerold Frank, 1958); *The Rest of the Story* (1964); *College of One* (1967); *Confessions of a Hollywood Columnist* (1969); *The Garden of Allah* (1971). Writer of syndicated motion-picture column.

GRAHAM, SHIRLEY (Nov. 11, 1907–); b. Indianapolis, Ind. Author. *Dr. George Washington Carver, Scientist* (with G. Lipcombe, 1944); *There Was Once a Slave* (1947); *Your Most Humble Servant* (1949); *Jean Baptiste Pointe de Sale* (1953); *Booker T. Washington* (1955); etc.

GRAHAM, WILLIAM FRANKLIN [Billy] (Nov. 7, 1918–); b. Charlotte, N.C. Baptist clergyman, author. *Calling Youth to Christ* (1947); *Revival in Our Times* (with others, 1950); *America's Hour of Decision* (1951); *Peace with God* (1953); *The Secret of Happiness* (1955); *My Answer* (1960); *World Aflame* (1965); *The Quotable Billy Graham*, ed. by Cort Flint and Quote Magazine, 1966); *The Faith of Billy Graham*, ed. by T. S. Settel (1968); etc.

Graham's Magazine. See *The Casket*.

GRAMATKY, HARDIE (Apr. 12, 1907–); b. Dallas, Tex. Artist, author. Author, illustrator: *Little Toot* (1939); *Loopy* (1941); *Creepers Jeep* (1948); *Homer and the Circus Train* (1957); *Sparky* (1960); *Nikos and the Sea God* (1963); *Little Toot on the Thames* (1964); *Little Toot on the Grand Canal* (1968); etc.

GRANBERRY, EDWIN PHILLIPS (Apr. 18, 1897–); b. Meridian, Miss. Author. *The Ancient Hunger* (1927); *Strangers and Lovers* (1928); *The Erl King* (1930).

GRANBERY, JOHN COWPER (June 15, 1874–May 5, 1953); b. Richmond, Va. Educator, author. *Introduction to the History of Civilization* (with others, 1930); *Students' Prolegomena to Philosophy* (1931); etc. Founder and editor, *The Emancipator*, 1938. Head dept. of philosophy, Southwestern University, 1935–38.

Grand Design, The. Novel by John Dos Passos (1949). Last of the trilogy which includes *Adventures of a Young Man* (1939) and *Number One* (1943).

Grandfather Stories. By Samuel Hopkins Adams (1955).

Grandfather's Chair. Stories by Nathaniel Hawthorne (1841). Historical tales for young people, drawn from New England in colonial and revolutionary times.

"Grandfather's Clock." Song composed by Samuel L. Milady (1878); wrongly attributed to Henry Clay Work.

GRANDGENT, CHARLES HALL (Nov. 14, 1862–Sept. 11, 1939); b. Dorchester, Mass. Educator, philologist, author. *Dante* (1916); *The Ladies of Dante's Lyrics* (1917); *Old and New* (1920); *Discourses on Dante* (1924); *Prunes and Prisms* (1928); *Imitation and Other Essays* (1933); *Musketeers of the Mountains* (1932); etc. Prof. Romance languages, Harvard University, 1896–1932.

Grandissimes, The. Novel by George W. Cable (1880). Story of Creole life. The Grandissimes, whose fortunes are here told, are one of the leading families in Louisiana. The head of the family is Honoré, a banker.

Grandmother Brown's Hundred Years, 1827–1927. By Harriet Connor Brown (1929). Account of pioneer days in Iowa.

Grandmothers, The. Novel by Glenway Westcott (1927). Family life in Wisconsin, beginning with the pioneer days.

"Grandmother's Story of Bunker Hill Battle." Poem by Oliver Wendell Holmes (1875).

Granger's Index to Poetry and Recitations. Compiled by Edith Granger (revised ed. 1930). Contains over 50,000 titles. Has title index, author index, index to first lines, and a bibliography. Includes English translations of foreign poetry and prose. First edition was called *An Index to Poetry and Recitations* (1904). The fourth edition, called *Index to Poetry*, was edited in 1953 by Raymond J. Dixon, who also edited the 1957 supplement. The fifth edition was completely revised and enlarged by William F. Bernhardt (1962), who also issued a *Supplement* with Kathryn W. Sewny (1967).

GRANICH, IRVING (Apr. 12, 1896–May 14, 1967); b. New York. Author. Pen name "Michael Gold." *120 Million* (1929); *Jews without Money* (1930); *Battle Hymn* (play, with Michael Blankfort, 1936); *Change the World* (1937); etc. Successively editor, *The Masses, The New Masses.*

Granite Monthly. Concord, N.H. Literary and historical magazine. Founded Apr. 1877, by Henry Harrison Metcalf, who published it 1877–1919. Expired Dec. 1930.

GRANNISS, ANNE J[ane] (b. Apr. 23, 1856); b. Berlin, Conn. Poet. *Skipped Stitches* (1893); *Sandwort* (1897); *Speedwell* (1900); *A Christmas Snowflake* (1904); etc.

GRANNISS, RUTH S.; b. Old Saybrook, Conn. Librarian, bibliographer. *An American Friend of Southey* (1913); *A Descriptive Catalogue of the First Editions—of the Writings of Percy Bysshe Shelley* (1922); *The Book in America* (with Helmut Lehmann-Haupt and Lawrence C. Wroth, 1939); etc. Librarian, Grolier Club, New York, from 1905.

Grant, Charles. Pen name of William Charles Lengel.

GRANT, DOROTHY FREMONT (Mrs. Douglas Grant) (Oct. 8, 1900–); b. New York. Author. *What Other Answer* (1943); *Margaret Brent, Adventurer* (1944); *War Is My Parish* (1944); *Night of Decision* (1946); *So! You Want to Get Married!* (1947); *John England: American Christopher* (1949); *Devil's Food* (1949); *Born Again* (1950); *The Fun We've Had* (1954); *Rose Greenhow, Confederate Secret Agent* (1961); etc.

Grant, Douglas. Pen name of Isabel Ostrander.

GRANT, ELIHU (July 12, 1873–Nov. 2, 1942); b. Stevensville, Pa. Methodist clergyman, educator, author. *The Orient in Bible Times* (1920); *The People of Palestine* (1921); *Ain Shems Excavations,* 5v. (1931–39); *Palestine Today* (1938); *Palestine, Our Holy Land* (1940); etc. Prof. Biblical literature, Haverford College, 1917–38.

Grant, Ethel Watts Mumford. See Ethel Watts Mumford.

GRANT, FREDERICK CLIFTON (Feb. 2, 1891–); b. Beloit, Wis. Episcopal clergyman, educator. *The Life and Times of Jesus* (1921); *The Early Days of Christianity* (1922); *New Horizons of the Christian Faith* (1928); *The Practice of Religion* (1946); *An Introduction to New Testament Thought* (1950); *Hellenistic Religions* (ed., 1953); *Ancient Roman Religion* (1957); *The Gospels, Their Origin and Growth* (1957); *Ancient Judaism and the New Testament* (1959); *Translating the Bible* (1961); etc. Editor, *Anglican Theological Review,* 1924–55. President, Seabury-Western Theological Seminary, 1927–38; prof. New Testament, Union Theological Seminary, since 1938.

GRANT, GEORGE HOOK (Aug. 1, 1896–); b. Thornliebank, Scotland. Mariner, author. *The Half Deck* (1933); *Consigned to Davy Jones* (1934); *The Heels of a Gale* (1937); *Take to the Boats* (1938); *Boy Overboard!* (1961).

GRANT, GORDON H. (June 7, 1875–May 6, 1962); b. San Francisco, Calif. Illustrator, author. *The Story of the Ship* (1919); *Sail Ho!* (1931); *Greasy Luck* (1932); *Ships Under Sail* (1939); *The Book of Old Ships* (1936); *Secret Voyage* (1942); *Sketchbook* (1960).

GRANT, JESSE R. (Feb. 6, 1858–June 8, 1934); b. St. Louis, Mo., son of Ulysses Simpson Grant. Author. *In the Days of My Father, General Grant* (with Henry Francis Granger, 1925).

Grant, Julia Dent. See Princess Cantacuzene.

GRANT, MADISON (Nov. 19, 1865–May 30, 1937); b. New York City. Lawyer, author. *The Passing of the Great Race* (1916); *The Conquest of a Continent* (1933); etc.

Grant, Margaret. Pen name of Rose Franken.

GRANT, PERCY STICKNEY (May 13, 1860–Feb. 13, 1927); b. Boston, Mass. Episcopal clergyman, author. *Ad Matrem, and Other Poems* (1905); *The Search of Belisarius* (1907); *Essays* (1922); *A Fifth Avenue Parade, and Other Poems* (1922); etc.

GRANT, ROBERT (Jan. 24, 1852–May 19, 1940); b. Boston, Mass. Novelist, essayist, poet. *The Confessions of a Frivolous Girl* (1880); *The Lambs* (1882); *Yankee Doodle* (1883); *An Average Man* (1883); *The Knave of Hearts* (1885); *The Oldest School in America* (1885); *The Carletons* (1886); *A Romantic Young Lady* (1886); *Primulas and Pansies* (poems, anon., 1886); *Face to Face* (1886); *Jack Hall* (1887); *Jack in the Bush* (1888); *Mrs. Harold Stagg* (1889); *The Reflections of a Married Man* (1892); *The Opinions of a Philosopher* (1893); *The Art of Living* (1895); *The Bachelor's Christmas, and Other Stories* (1895); *Search-Light Letters* (1899); *Unleavened Bread* (1900); *The Undercurrent* (1901); *The Orchid* (1905); *The Law-Breakers, and Other Stories* (1906); *The Chippendales* (1909); *The Convictions of a Grandfather* (1912); *The High Priestess* (1915); *Their Spirit* (1916); *The Bishop's Granddaughter* (1925); *Occasional Verses* (1926); *Vanneck* (1927); *Shorn!* (1928); *The Dark Horse* (1931); *Fourscore: An Autobiography* (1934).

GRANT, ROBERT M[cQueen] (Nov. 25, 1917–); b. Evanston, Ill. Episcopal clergyman, educator, author. *Second-Century Christianity* (1946); *Miracle and Natural Law in Graeco-Roman and Early Christian Thought* (1952); *The Sword and the Cross* (1955); *Gnosticism and Early Christianity* (1959); *U-Boats Destroyed* (1964); *The Formation of the New Testament* (1966); etc. Federated Theological Faculty, University of Chicago, since 1953.

GRANT, ULYSSES SIMPSON (Apr. 27, 1822–July 23, 1885); b. Point Pleasant, O. Eighteenth president of the United States, Union general, author. *Personal Memoirs* 2v. (1885–86); *Grant's Personal Memoirs, 1885–86,* ed. by E. B. Long (1952). See Adam Badeau's *Military History of Ulysses S. Grant,* 3v. (1868–81); Louis A Coolidge's *The Life of Ulysses S. Grant* (1922); William E. Woodward's *Meet General Grant* (1928); Horace Green's *General Grant's Last Stand* (1936); Helen Todd's *A Man Named Grant* (1940); Kenneth Powers Williams' *Lincoln Finds a General,* 5v. (1952).

Granville-Barker, Helen. See Helen Huntington.

Grapes of Wrath. Novel by John Steinbeck (1939). The wanderings of the Joad family from the dust bowl of Oklahoma to the expected paradise in California which turns out to be a hostile region which extends no welcome to the homeless underprivileged.

Grass Harp, The. Novel by Truman Capote (1951). Two sisters and their young cousin in legal conflict—sister Dolly and cousin Collin against sister Verena. Amusingly and ironically, the two gather reinforcements in a retired judge, a young dandy, and a child evangelist to oppose Verena, who has the law on her side.

GRASTY, CHARLES HENRY (Mar. 3, 1863–Jan. 19, 1924); b. Fincastle, Va. Editor, publisher, author. *Flashes from the Front* (1918). Editor and publisher, *Baltimore News,* 1892–1908; *The Sun,* Baltimore, Md., 1910–14; correspondent, *New York Times,* 1916–21. Also with *Kansas City Times,* and *St. Paul Dispatch.*

GRATTAN, C[linton] HARTLEY (Oct. 19, 1902–); b. Wakefield, Mass. Critic, essayist. *Bitter Bierce* (1929); *The Three Jameses: A Family of Minds* (1932); *Preface to Chaos* (1936); *The Deadly Parallel* (1939); *Introducing Australia* (1942); *In Quest of Knowledge* (1955); *The United States and the Southwest Pacific* (1961); etc. Editor: *The Critique of Humanism* (1930); *Molders of American Thought* (1934); *Australia* (U.N. series, 1947); *American Ideas About Adult Education* (1959); *The Southwest Pacific,* 2v. (1961–1963); etc.

GRATZ, REBECCA (Mar. 4, 1781–Aug. 29, 1869); b. Philadelphia, Pa. Philanthropist. Original of Scott's "Rebecca" in *Ivanhoe.* Author: *Letters of Rebecca Gratz* (1929). *See* Beatrice T. Mantel's *Rebecca Gratz* (1929); Rollin Gustav Osterweis's *Rebecca Gratz: A Study in Charm* (1935).

GRATZ, SIMON (1838–1925); b. Philadelphia, Pa. Lawyer, collector, author. *A Book About Autographs* (1920). His manuscript collection is in the Pennsylvania Historical Society.

GRAU, SHIRLEY ANN (July 8, 1929–) b. New Orleans, La. Author. *The Black Prince and Other Stories* (1955); *The Hard Blue Sky* (1958); *The House on Coliseum Street* (1961); *The Keepers of the House* (1964); etc.

Graustark. Novel by George Barr McCutcheon (1901). Grenfall Lorry's quest for the Princess of Graustark takes him from America to Europe and through perilous adventures. His lack of noble blood, a barrier to marriage, is overcome by his feats of heroism, and he wins the Princess.

GRAVES, FRANK PIERREPONT (July 23, 1869–Sept. 13, 1956); b. Brooklyn, N.Y. Educator, author. *A History of Education before the Middle Ages* (1909); *A History of Education during the Middle Ages* (1910); *Great Educators of Three Centuries* (1912); *Peter Ramus* (1912); *A History of Education in Modern Times* (1913); *Addresses and Papers,* 4 series (1926–40); etc. President, University of Wyoming, 1896–98; University of Washington, 1898–1903; dean, School of Education, University of Pennsylvania, 1913–21; chancellor, University of the State of New York, 1921–40.

GRAVES, JACKSON ALPHEUS (Dec. 5, 1852–Feb. 13, 1933); b. Hauntown, Ia. Lawyer, author. *My Seventy Years in California, 1857–1927* (1927); *California Memories, 1857–1930* (1930).

GRAVES, JOHN TEMPLE (Apr. 25, 1892–May 19, 1961); b. Rome, Ga. Editor, lecturer, author. *Two Bubbles* (1920); *The Shaft in the Sky* (1923); *The Book of Alabama and the South* (1933); *Tonight in the South* (1935); *The Fighting South* (1943); etc. Editorial staff, *Birmingham Age-Herald,* 1929–1946; *Birmingham Post,* from 1946.

GRAVES, RALPH [Augustus] (Oct. 17, 1924–); b. Washington, D.C. Journalist. *Thanks for the Ride* (1949); *The Lost Eagles* (1955). Staff, *Life* magazine, since 1948.

GRAVES, RALPH H[enry] (July 11, 1878–Dec. 1, 1939); b. Chapel Hill, N.C. Editor, author. *Triumph of an Idea: The Story of Henry Ford* (1934). Sunday editor, *New York Times,* 1917–23; syndicate editor, Doubleday, Doran Co., 1923–1936; editor his own syndicate, 1936–39.

GRAY, ARTHUR IRVING (b. May 26, 1859); b. Madison, Wis. Author. Compiler: *Bath Robes and Bachelors* (1897); *Over the Black Coffee* (1902); *The Little Tea Book* (1903); *Toasts and Tributes* (1904); etc.

GRAY, ASA (Nov. 18, 1810–Jan. 30, 1888); b. Sanquoit, N.Y. Botanist, author. *Botanical Text-Book* (1842); *Letters of Asa Gray,* 2v. (1893); etc. Gray was one of the first Americans to support Charles Darwin's theory of evolution. Prof. natural history, Harvard University, 1842–88.

Gray, Barry. Pen name of Robert Barry Coffin.

GRAY, CHARLES WRIGHT. Anthologist. Editor: *The Sporting Spirit: An Anthology* (1925); *"Dawgs!" An Anthology of Stories about Them* (1925); *"Hosses": An Anthology of Short Stories* (1927); *Deep Waters: An Anthology of Stories of the Sea* (1928).

GRAY, DAVID (Aug. 8, 1870–Apr. 11, 1968); b. Buffalo, N.Y. Diplomat, playwright. *Gallops* (prod. 1906); *The Best People* (with Avery Hopwood, prod. 1923); *The Hitchcock Edition of David Gray,* 3v. (1929); etc. Minister to Ireland, 1940–47.

Gray, Elizabeth. See Elizabeth Gray Vining.

GRAY, GEORGE WILLIAM (Dec. 8, 1886–Dec. 29, 1960); b. Caldwell, Tex. Author. *New World Picture* (1936); *The Advancing Front of Science* (1937); *Education on an International Scale* (1941); *Science at War* (1943); *Frontiers of Flight* (1948); etc.

GRAY, HAROLD [Lincoln] (Jan. 20, 1894–); b. Kankakee, Ill. Cartoonist. Creator of the comic strip, "Little Orphan Annie," and assistant to Sidney Smith in the comic strip, "Andy Gump."

GRAY, HENRY DAVID (Nov. 6, 1873–); b. Plainfield, N.J. Educator, author. *Hannibal: A Tragedy* (1893); *Emerson: A Statement of New England Transcendentalism* (1917). Editor: *Selections from Old Testament Literature* (1929); *Theology for Christian Youth* (1941); *The Christian Doctrine of Grace* (1950); etc. English dept., Stanford University, from 1905.

GRAY, JAMES (June 30, 1899–); b. Minneapolis, Minn. Critic, novelist. *The Penciled Frown* (1925); *Shoulder the Sky* (1935); *Wake and Remember* (1936); *Wings of Great Desire* (1938); *The Illinois* (1940); *Pine, Stream and Prairie* (1945); *On Second Thought* (1946); *Business without Boundary* (1954); *Open Wide the Door: The Story of the University of Minnesota* (1958); etc. With St. Paul *Pioneer Press and Dispatch,* 1920–46; literary editor, Chicago *Daily News,* 1946–48. Prof. English, University of Minnesota, 1948–56.

GRAY, JOSEPH M. M. (Aug. 31, 1877–Jan. 9, 1957); b. Montgomery, Pa. Methodist clergyman, educator, author. *The Contemporary Christ* (1921); *An Adventure in Orthodoxy* (1923); *Concerning the Faith* (1928); *Prophets of the Soul* (1936); *The Post-War Strategy of Religion* (1944); etc. President, American University, Washington, D.C. 1934–40.

GRAY, JOSLYN, b. Brattleboro, Vt. Novelist. *Kathleen's Probation* (1918); *Rusty Miller* (1919); *Rosemary Greenaway* (1919); *Bouncing Bet* (1921); etc.

"Gray, Walter T." Kirk's *Supplement* to Allibone's *Dictionary* attributes a number of books to this name, including *Blunders of a Bashful Man* (1881); *Miss Simmens' Boarding House* (1882); and *Abijah Beanpole in New York* (1884). These are by Metta Victoria Victor. "Walter T. Gray" was probably a stock name used for cheap reprints of anonymous books.

GRAY, WILLIAM SCOTT (June 5, 1885–Sept. 8, 1960); b. Coatburg, Ill. Educator, author. *Reading Interests and Habits of Adults* (1929); *What Makes a Book Readable?* (1935); *The Teaching of Reading and Writing* (1950); etc. Prof. education, University of Chicago, from 1921.

GRAYDON, ALEXANDER (Apr. 10, 1752–May 21, 1818); b. Bristol, Pa. Revolutionary soldier, author. *Memoirs of a Life* (1811).

Grayson, David. Pen name of Ray Stannard Baker.

Grayson, Eldred. Pen name of Robert Hare.

GRAYSON, WILLIAM JOHN (Nov. 1788–Oct. 4, 1863); b. Beaufort, S.C. Lawyer, biographer, poet. *The Hireling and the Slave* (poem, 1854); *The Hireling and the Slave, Chicora, and Other Poems* (1856); *James Louis Petigru* (1866); *Selected Poems* (1907).

Graysons, The. Novel by Edward Eggleston (1887). Story of Illinois in pioneer Days. The young Abraham Lincoln is introduced into the story.

Great Awakening. The spiritual awakening in opposition to the formalism of Puritanism, which began in New England under Jonathan Edwards (q.v.) in 1734 and reached its culmination in the Middle and Southern colonies in the Middle and Southern colonies under George Whitefield (q.v.) in 1740. It led among other things to the establishment of four colleges: Princeton, Brown, Dartmouth, and Rutgers. *See* Charles H. Maxson's *The Great Awakening in the Middle Colonies* (1920); Wesley M. Gewehr's *The Great Awakening in Virginia* (1930).

"Great Bell Roland, The." Civil War poem by Theodore Tilton, in the *Independent,* April 18, 1861.

Great Books. Educational movement centering in the use of classic writings as the basis of a sound humanistic and scientific modern education. Associated with John Erskine's program of readings at Columbia University after World War I, but more specifically with the Great Books program of St. John's College, Annapolis, which made use of one hundred books thought most influential in shaping Western civilization. Somewhat the same program was adopted at the University of Chicago. The Great Books Foundation was organized in 1947 in Chicago, with Robert M. Hutchins as chairman.

Great Books of the Western World. Under the supervision of Robert M. Hutchins, editor-in-chief, and Mortimer J. Adler, associate editor, 54v. (1952). Contains the selected works of 71 authors, from Homer to Freud. Volume I is a description of the Great Books movement; volumes II and III constitute the Syntopicon, an index of 102 Great Ideas.

Great Chain of Being, The. By A. O. Lovejoy (1948). Study of the idea of Being in all phases of Western thought and philosophy.

Great Divide, The. Play by William Vaughn Moody (1906). Ruth Jordan, of New England, falls into the hands of a rough miner in the Arizona desert and is forced to share his life. She finally is rescued by her brother who takes her back East. Later, Ghent, the miner, comes for her and she returns with him to the desert, discovering that she had learned to love him.

Great Gatsby, The. Novel by F. Scott Fitzgerald (1925). The story of riotous living on Long Island with the mysterious Jay Gatsby as the main character. His lavish expenditure on parties ends in ironic tragedy, and he fails to win the girl he has squandered his life for, and no one mourns his passing.

Great God Brown, The. Play by Eugene O'Neill (prod. 1926). Symbolical study of the multiple personalities which fight for dominance in human beings. The players wear masks, which they take off from time to time as their hidden characteristics appear.

Great Meadow, The. Historical novel of Kentucky by Elizabeth Madox Roberts (1930). It describes the early settlement of Kentucky and the effects of the wilderness on the philosophically-minded Diony Hall.

Great Rehearsal, The. By Carl Van Doren (1948). The story of the making and ratifying of the Constitution.

Great South, The. By Edward King (1875). A personal travel description of the post-war South, which first appeared serially in *Scribner's Monthly,* 1873–74. Illustrated by J. Wells Champney.

Great Train Robbery, The. Scenario by Edwin S. Porter (prod. 1903). The first American story picture, made in the fall of 1903 and shown that year.

Greaves, Richard. Pen name of George Barr McCutcheon.

GREBANIER, BERNARD D. N. (Mar. 8, 1903–); b. New York. Educator, author. *Fauns, Satyrs, and a Few Sages* (poems, 1945); *Mirrors of the Fire* (poems, 1946); *The Other Love, A Triptych* (poems, 1957); *The Heart of Hamlet* (1960); *Playwriting* (1961); *The Great Shakespeare Forgery* (1965); *The Uninhibited Byron* (1970); etc. Prof. English, Brooklyn College, since 1954.

Greek Club. New York. A club of classical scholars. Founded 1857, by Henry Drisler (1818–1897) and Howard Crosby (1826–1891). Disbanded 1897.

Greek Way, The. By Edith Hamilton (1930). Lively discussion of the Greek way of life. The author also wrote *The Roman Way* (1932).

GREELEY, HORACE (Feb. 3, 1811–Nov. 29, 1872); b. Amherst, N.H. Editor, reformer, author. *Glances at Europe* (1851); *An Overland Journey from New York to San Francisco in the Summer of 1859* (1860); *Recollections of a Busy Life* (1868). Founder (with Jonas Winchester), the *New Yorker,* a weekly, Mar. 22, 1834, later absorbed by the *New York Tribune;* founder, the *New York Tribune,* Apr. 10, 1841; editor, 1841–72. Greeley was an advocate of Fourierism, a social movement headed in America by Albert Brisbane. "Go West, young man" is one of his best-known phrases. He was a presidential candidate in 1872. *See* James Parton's *The Life of Horace Greeley* (1855); William A. Linn's *Horace Greeley* (1903); Don C. Seitz's *Horace Greeley* (1926); E. D. Ross's *Horace Greeley and the West* (1933); Wilbur J. Granberg's *Spread the Truth: The Life of Horace Greeley* (1959); G. Van Deusen's *Horace Greeley* (1964).

GREELY, ADOLPHUS WASHINGTON (Mar. 27, 1844–Oct. 20, 1935); b. Newburyport, Mass. Army officer, polar explorer, author. *Explorers and Travellers* (1893); *True Tales of Arctic Heroism* (1912); *Reminiscences of Adventure and Service* (1927); etc.

GREEN, ADOLPH (Dec. 2, 1915–); b. New York. Playwright. Co-author, (with Betty Comden): *On the Town* (prod. 1944); *Billion Dollar Baby* (prod. 1945); *Two on the Aisle* (prod. 1951); *The Bells Are Ringing* (prod. 1957); *Do Re Mi* (1960); *Subways Are for Sleeping* (1962); *Fade Out, Fade In* (1964); etc.

GREEN, ALLEN AYRAULT (Mar. 11, 1878–); b. Williamsport, Pa. Author. *My Painted Tree and Other Poems* (1904); *The Making of a Steam Engine* (1904); *The Good Fairy and the Bunnies* (1906); *The Land of Lost* (1908); *Runaway Teds* (1909); *Rhymes of the Woods* (1911).

GREEN, ANNA KATHARINE (Mrs. Charles Rohlfs) (Nov. 11, 1846–Apr. 11, 1935); b. Brooklyn, N.Y. Novelist. *The Leavenworth Case* (1878); *A Strange Disappearance* (1880); *The Mill Mystery* (1886); *The Old Stone House* (1891); *That Affair Next Door* (1897); *The Filigree Ball* (1903); *The House in the Mist* (1905); *The Chief Legatee* (1906); *The House of Whispering Pines* (1910); *The Golden Slipper* (1915); *The Step on the Stair* (1923).

GREEN, ANNE (Nov. 11, 1899–); b. Savannah, Ga., sister of Julian Green. Novelist. *The Selbys* (1930); *A Marriage of Convenience* (1932); *Fools Rush In* (1934); *Paris* (1938); *The Silent Duchess* (1939); *The Lady in the Mask* (1942); *Just Before Dawn* (1943); *The Old Lady* (1947); *With Much Love* (autobiography, 1948); etc. Translator: *A Certain Smile* (1956); etc.

GREEN, CONSTANCE MCLAUGHLIN (1898–); b. Ann Arbor, Mich. Author. *Washington, Village and Capital, 1800–1878* (1963); *Washington, Capital City* (1963); *American Cities in the Growth of the Nation* (1965); *Eli Whitney and the Birth of American Technology* (1965); *The Secret City: A History of Race Relations in the Nation's Capital* (1967).

GREEN, DUFF (Aug. 15, 1791–June 10, 1875); b. in Woodford Co., Ky. Editor, publisher, author. *Facts and Suggestions* (1886). Purchased the *United States Telegraph*, Washington, D.C., in 1825; founder, the New York *Republic*, 1844.

GREEN, EDWIN LUTHER (Dec. 13, 1870–Aug. 8, 1948); b. Milton, Fla. Educator, author. *Indians of South Carolina* (1904); *History of the University of South Carolina* (1916); etc. Dept. of ancient languages, University of South Carolina, from 1900.

GREEN, ELEANOR (Feb. 8, 1911–); b. Milwaukee, Wis. Author. *The Hill* (1936); *Pastoral* (1937); *Ariadne Spinning* (1941); *Dora* (1948).

GREEN, FITZHUGH (Aug 16, 1888–Dec. 2, 1947); b. St. Joseph, Mo. Naval officer, author. *Arctic Duty* (1917); *Midshipmen All* (1925); *Our Naval Heritage* (1925); *I'll Never Move Again* (1926); *Some Famous Sea Fights* (with Holloway Frost, 1927); *We* (with Charles A. Lindbergh, 1927); *Dick Byrd, Air Explorer* (1928); *Martin Johnson, Lion Hunter* (1928); *Bob Bartlett, Master Mariner* (1929); etc.

GREEN, FRANCIS HARVEY (May 19, 1861–Jan. 23, 1958); b. Booth's Corner, Pa. Educator, author. *Notes on Rhetoric* (1909); etc. Compiler: *Quotations from Great Authors* (1912); *What They Say Day by Day* (1916); etc. Prof. English, West Chester Normal School, 1888–1920; headmaster, Pennington School, Pennington, N.J., from 1921.

GREEN, GERALD (1922–). Novelist. *The Last Angry Man* (1956); *The Lotus Eaters* (1959); *The Heartless Light* (1961); *The Portofino PTA* (1962); *The Legion of Noble Christians* (1965); *To Brooklyn with Love* (1969); *The Artists of Terezin* (1969).

GREEN, HORACE (Oct. 13, 1885–Nov. 14, 1943); b. New York City. Publisher, author. *The Log of a Non-Combatant* (1915); *The Life of Calvin Coolidge* (1924); *General Grant's Last Stand* (1936). Editor: *Contemporary Statesmen* series. With Duffield & Co., later Duffield & Green, publishers, 1923–34; president, 1925–34.

GREEN, JAMES FREDERICK (Nov. 17, 1910–); b. Kansas City, Mo. Government official, author. *The British Empire Under Fire* (1940); *The United States and Human Rights* (1956). Consul general, Leopoldville, 1956–58; Bureau of African Affairs, since 1958.

GREEN, JOSEPH (1706–Dec. 11, 1780); b. Boston, Mass. Merchant, satiric poet. *Entertainment for a Winter's Evening* (1750); *The Grand Arcanum Detected* (1755); etc. He wrote "The Poet's Lamentation for the Loss of His Cat, Which He Used to Call His Muse"; this poem, which appeared in *The London Magazine*, Nov., 1733, is a satire directed at Mather Byles, and is better known as "Doctor Byles' Cat."

GREEN, JULIAN (Sept. 6, 1900–); b. Paris, of American parentage, brother of Anne Green. Novelist. Writes in French, as "Julien Green." His books have been translated as follows: *Avarice House* (1927); *The Closed Garden* (1928); *The Dark Journey* (1929); *Christine, and Other Stories* (1930); *The Strange River* (1932); *The Dreamer* (1934); *Midnight* (1936);

Personal Record (1939); *Memories of Happy Days* (autobiography, 1942); *If I Were You* (1949); *Moira* (1951); *The Transgressor* (1957); *Each in His Darkness* (1961); *Diary, 1928–1957* (1964); *To Leave Before the Dawn* (1967).

GREEN, PAUL [Eliot] (Mar. 17, 1894–); b. Lillington, N.C. Educator, playwright, novelist. *The Lord's Will, and Other Carolina Plays* (1925); *Lonesome Road* (1926), which contains *In Abraham's Bosom* (prod. 1926, Pulitzer prize play, 1927); *In the Valley, and Other Carolina Plays* (1928); *The House of Connelly, and Other Plays* (1931); *The Laughing Pioneer* (1932); *Shroud My Body Down* (1935); *This Body the Earth* (1935); *Johnny Johnson* (1937); *The Lost Colony* (pageant, prod. 1937); *Out of the South* (1939); *The Highland Call* (1939); *The Enchanted Maze* (1939); *America in Action* (with others, 1941); *Native Son* (play, 1941); *Salvation on a String* (stories, 1946); *The Common Glory* (play, 1948); *Dog on the Sun* (stories, 1949); *Peer Gynt* (adaptation, 1951); *Dramatic Heritage* (1953); *Wilderness Road* (1955); *The Founders* (play, 1957); *Drama and the Weather* (1958); *The Confederacy* (1959); *The Stephen Foster Story* (1960); *Cross and Sword* (1964); *Texas* (1966); *Home to My Valley* (1969); etc. Editor, *The Reviewer*, 1925. Prof. dramatic art, University of North Carolina, 1939–44.

GREEN, SAMUEL SWETT (Feb. 20, 1837–Dec. 8, 1918); b. Worcester, Mass. Librarian, author. *The Public Library Movement in the United States* (1913). Librarian, Worcester Free Library, 1871–1909; librarian emeritus, 1909–18.

GREEN, THOMAS EDWARD (Dec. 27, 1857–Jan. 24, 1940). Lecturer, author. *The Mantraps of the City* (1884); *The Salt of the Earth* (1919); *The Dream of the Ages* (1921); etc.

Green Bay Tree, The. Novel by Louis Bromfield (1924). Lily Shane's story beginning with a small Middle Western town and ending in Paris, with the World War as the climax. A contrast of two civilizations and cultures.

Green Mountain Boy, The. Play by Joseph Stevens Jones (prod. 1833).

Green Mountain Boys, The. Novel by Daniel Pierce Thompson (1839). This Vermont classic deals with the American Revolution. Ethan Allen's capture of Fort Ticonderoga is a feature.

Green Pastures. Play by Marc Connelly (prod. 1930), based on *Ol' Man Adam and His Chillun* by Roark Bradford. Won the Pulitzer Prize in 1930.

Green Room Book. New York. Annual dramatic register. Four volumes were published, 1906–09.

Green Room Club. New York. Theatrical club. Founded 1902. Absorbed the Theatrical Business Men's Club, 1903.

GREENBERG, CLEMENT (Jan. 16, 1909–); b. New York. Art critic. *Joan Miró* (1948); *Art and Culture* (1961); *Post Painterly Abstractions* (1964); *Avant-Garde Attitudes* (1968). Art criticism for *Partisan Review, Nation*, etc. Associate editor, *Commentary*.

GREENBERG, JOANNE (Sept. 24, 1932–   ); b. Brooklyn, N.Y. Author. *The King's Persons* (1963); under pen name "Hannah Green," *I Never Promised You a Rose Garden* (1964); *The Monday Voices* (1965); *Summering* (1966).

GREENBERG, SAMUEL (1893–1917). Poet. *Poems* (1947).

GREENBIE, MARJORIE [Latta] BARSTOW (Mrs. Sydney Greenbie) (Aug. 4, 1891–); b. Jersey City, N.J. Author. *Memories* (poems, 1914); *Wordsworth's Theory of Poetic Diction* (1917); *In the Eyes of the East* (1921); *Ashes of Roses* (poems, 1924); *Gold of Ophir* (with husband, 1925); *The Arts of Leisure* (1935); *American Saga* (1938); *My Dear Lady* (1940); *Lincoln's Daughters of Mercy* (1944); *Castine* (with husband, 1948); *Grow Up But Don't Grow Old* (1958); etc.

GREENBIE, SYDNEY (June 28, 1889–June 5, 1960); b. in Dakota Territory. Educator, author. *The Pacific Triangle* (1921); *Frontiers and the Fur Trade* (1929); *The Romantic East* (1930); *Furs to Furrows* (1939); *Asia Unbound* (1943); *An American Boy Visits the Orient* (1946). Co-author (with wife, Marjorie Greenbie): *This We Inherit* (play, 1946); *The General Was a Lady* (play, 1949); *Dancer from Heaven* (play, 1953); *Hoofbeats to Heaven* (1954); *The Suit with Red Lining* (1958); etc.

GREENBURG, DAN (June 20, 1936–   ); b. Chicago, Ill. Author. *How to Be a Jewish Mother* (1964); *Kiss My Firm But Pliant Lips* (1965); *How to Make Yourself Miserable* (with Marcia Jacobs, 1966); *Chewsday* (1968); *Porno-Graphics: The Shame of Our Art Museums* (1969); etc.

GREENE, ALBERT GORTON (Feb. 10, 1802–Jan. 3, 1868); b. Providence, R.I. Poet, jurist, book-collector. His most famous poems were: "Old Grimes" (q.v.); "To the Weathercock on Our Steeple"; "The Baron's Last Banquet"; and "Song of the Windmill Spirits." Editor, *The Literary Journal and Register of Science and Arts, Providence, R.I.,* 1833–34. His literary remains are now in The Harris Collection of American Poetry at Brown University.

GREENE, ANNE BOSWORTH (1878–July 25, 1961); b. Chippenham, Wiltshire, Eng. Artist, author. *The Lone Winter* (1923); *Greylight* (1924); *Dipper Hill* (1925); *The White Pony in the Hills* (1927); *Lambs in March, and Other Essays* (1928); *Lighthearted Journey* (1930); *Sunshine and Dust* (1936); *Punch, the Cruising Dog* (1939).

GREENE, CHARLES WARREN (Aug. 17, 1840–d.); b. Belchertown, Mass. Author. *Birds: Their Homes and Habits* (1886); etc. Editor, *Lippincott's Gazeteer, Lippincott's Biographical Dictionary,* etc.

GREENE, CLAY MEREDITH (Mar. 12, 1850–Sept. 5, 1933); b. San Francisco, Calif. Playwright, poet. *The Dispensation, and Other Plays* (1914); *Verses of Love, Sentiment, and Friendship* (1921); etc.

GREENE, EVARTS BOUTELL (July 8, 1870–June 27, 1947); b. Kobe, Japan. Educator, author. *Provincial America* (1905); *Foundations of American Nationality* (1922); *A New Englander in Japan* (1927); etc. Compiler: *Guide to Sources for Early American History in New York City* (with R. B. Morris, 1929); *Religion and the State in America* (1941); *The Revolutionary Generation, 1763–1790* (1943); etc. History dept., Columbia University, 1923–39.

GREENE, FRANCES NIMMO b. Tuscaloosa, Ala. Author. *Legends of King Arthur and His Court* (1901); *With Spurs of Gold* (with Dolly Williams Kirk, 1905); *Into the Night* (1909); *The Right of the Strongest* (1913); *One Clear Call* (1914); *American Ideals* (1921); etc.

GREENE, GEORGE WASHINGTON (Apr. 8, 1811–Feb. 2, 1883); b. East Greenwich, R.I. Educator, historian. *The Life of Nathaniel Greene* (1846); *Biographical Studies* (1860); *Historical View of the American Revolution* (1865); *The Life of Nathaniel Greene,* 3v. (1867–71); *A Short History of Rhode Island* (1877); etc. Modern language dept., Brown University, 1848–52.

GREENE, HENRY COPLEY (Nov. 21, 1871–Dec. 29, 1951); b. Vienna. Author. *Théophile: A Miracle Play* (1898); *Plains and Uplands of Old France: A Book of Verse and Prose* (1898); *Pontius Pilate, Saint Ronan of Brittany, Théophile* (plays in verse, 1903); *The Father* (1904). Secretary, History Reference Council, Harvard University, 1926–40.

GREENE, HERBERT EVELETH (Aug. 27, 1858–Sept. 3, 1942); b. Newton, Mass. Educator, editor. Editor of Shakespearean texts in the *Tudor and Arden* editions; etc. Prof. English, Johns Hopkins University, 1893–1925.

GREENE, HOMER (Jan. 10, 1853–Nov. 26, 1940); b. Lake Ariel, Pa. *Burnham Breaker* (1887); *Pickett's Gap* (1902); *Handicapped* (1914); *The Unhallowed Harvest* (1917); *The Guardsman* (1919); *What My Lover Said, and Other Poems* (1931); etc. His best known poem is "What My Lover Said."

GREENE, JOSIAH E. (Mar. 22, 1911–); b. Duluth, Minn. Novelist. *Madmen Die Alone* (1938); *The Laughing Loon* (1939); *Not In Our Stars* (1945); *A Bridge at Branfield* (1948); *The Man with One Talent* (1951).

GREENE, SARAH PRATT [McLean] (July 3, 1856–Dec. 29, 1935); b. Simsbury, Conn. Author. Wrote also as "Sally Platt McLean." Author. *Cape Cod Folks* (1881); *Some Other Folks* (1882); *Towhead* (1883); *Lastchance Junction* (anon., 1889); *Leon Pontifex* (1890); *Vesty of the Basins* (1892); *Stuart and Bamboo* (1897); *The Moral Imbeciles* (1898); *Flood-Tide* (1901); *Winslow Plain* (1902); *Deacon Lysander* (1904); *Power Lot* (1906); *Everbreeze* (1913).

GREENE, THEODORE MEYER (Jan. 25, 1897–Aug. 13, 1969); b. Constantinople, Turkey. Educator, author. *The Arts and the Art of Criticism* (1940); *Liberal Education Re-examined* (1943); *Liberalism* (1957); *Moral, Aesthetic, and Religious Insight* (1958); etc. Editor: *The Meaning of the Humanities* (1938). Prof. philosophy, Yale University, 1946–55; Scripps College, from 1955.

GREENE, WARD (Dec. 23, 1892–Jan. 22, 1956); b. Asheville, N.C. Author. *Cora Potts* (1929); *Ride the Nightmare* (1930); *Weep No More* (1932); *Death in the Deep South* (1936); *Honey* (1937); *What They Don't Know* (1944); *Blue Bonnets* (1945); *Lady and the Tramp* (1954). Under pen name "Jean Greene": *Forgetful Elephant* (1945). Under pen name "Frank Dudley": *King Cobra* (1940). Editor, King Features Syndicate, from 1921.

GREENE, WILLIAM BATCHELDER (b. 1851). Poet, essayist. *Imogen, and Other Poems* (1871); *Three Vows* (poems, 1881); *Reflections and Modern Maxims* (1886); *Cloudrifts at Twilight* (poems, 1888).

GREENE, WILLIAM CHASE (June 14, 1890–); b. Brookline, Mass. Educator, author. *Richard I Before Jerusalem* (Newdigate prize poem, 1912); *The Achievement of Greece: A Chapter in Human Experience* (1923); *The Achievement of Rome: A Chapter in Civilization* (1933); *Moira: Fate, Good and Evil, in Greek Thought* (1944); etc. Editor: *Scholia Platonica* (1938); etc. Greek and Latin dept., Harvard University, since 1927.

"Greenfield Hill." Poem by Timothy Dwight (1794). Inspired by the plundering of New Haven and the burning of Fairfield by the British in 1779.

Greenhorn. Pen name of George Thompson.

GREENLEAF, THOMAS (1755–Sept. 14, 1798); b. Abington, Mass. Printer. Publisher, *The New-York Journal,* 1787–93; *Greenleaf's New-York Journal, 1793–98; The Argus, 1795–1798.*

GREENOUGH, CHESTER NOYES (June 29, 1874–Feb. 26, 1938); b. Wakefield, Mass. Educator, author. *A History of Literature in America* (with Barrett Wendell, 1904); etc. English dept., Harvard, 1910–35. *See* Ruth Hornblower Greenough's *Chester Noyes Greenough* 2v. (1940).

GREENOUGH, HENRY (Oct. 5, 1807–Oct. 31, 1883); b. Newburyport, Mass. Painter, novelist. *Ernest Carroll* (1859); *Apelles* (1860).

GREENOUGH, HORATIO (Sept. 6, 1805–Dec. 18, 1852); b. Boston, Mass. Sculptor, author. *Aesthetics in Washington* (1851); *Form and Function: Remarks on Art,* ed. by H. A. Small (1957). See *Letters of Horatio Greenough to his Brother Henry Greenough,* ed. by F. B. Greenough (1887).

GREENOUGH, JAMES BRADSTREET (May 8, 1833–Oct. 11, 1901); b. Portland, Me. Educator, classical philologist, playwright. *A Latin Grammar* (with Joseph Henry Allen, 1873); *Queen of Hearts* (1875), and other plays for amateurs; *Words and Their Ways in English Speech* (with George L. Kittredge, 1901); etc. He translated Theodore Roosevelt's *The Strenuous Life* into Ciceronian Latin. Co-founder, *Harvard Studies in Classical Philology.* Latin dept., Harvard University, 1865–1901; prof. 1883–1901.

GREENSLET, FERRIS (June 30, 1875–Nov. 19, 1959); b. Glens Falls, N.Y. Editor, author. *Joseph Glanvill* (1900); *Walter Pater* (1903); *James Russell Lowell* (1905); *The Life of Thomas Bailey Aldrich* (1908); *Under the Bridge* (1943); *The Practical Cogitator* (with C. P. Curtis, 1945); *The Lowells and Their Seven Worlds* (1946). Assoc. editor, *Atlantic Monthly,* 1902–07; literary advisor to Houghton Mifflin & Co., from 1907; director, from 1910.

GREENWALD, HAROLD (1910–). Author. *The Call Girl* (1958); *Emotional Maturity in Love and Marriage* (with Lucy Freeman, 1961); etc. Editor: *The Prostitute in Literature* (with Aron Krich, 1960); *Active Psychotherapy* (1967).

Greenwich Village. New York. The old section of New York radiating from Washington Square. Haunt of bohemian artists and writers. It enjoyed a literary revival in the 1920's when Edna St. Vincent Millay, Floyd Dell, Theodore Dreiser, Carl Van Vechten, E. E. Cummings, John Cowper Powys, and others were living there. Robert Frederick Blum, the artist, established a studio at 90 Grove Street, around 1893, which brought an influx of artists to the neighborhood. *See* Thomas A. Janvier's *Color Studies* (1885); Owen Johnson's *Max Fargus* (1906); Anna Alice Chapin's *Greenwich Village* (1917); Floyd Dell's *Love in Greenwich Village* (1926); Clement Wood's *The Greenwich Village Blues* (1926); Jule Brousseau's *Episode on West 8th Street* (1941); Henry W. Lanier's *Greenwich Village, Today and Yesterday* (1949); Allen Churchill's *The Improper Bohemians* (1959); Caroline Farrar Ware's *Greenwich Village, 1920–1930* (1965). See also *Bohemians; Bruno's Chap Books; Bruno's Weekly; East Village; Little Review;* etc.

Greenwood, Grace. Pen name of Sara Jane Clarke Lippincott.

GREER, HILTON ROSS (Dec. 10, 1879–Nov. 26, 1949); b. Hawkins, Tex. Editor, poet. *Sun Gleams and Gossamers* (1903); *The Spiders, and Other Poems* (1906); *A Prairie Prayer, and Other Poems* (1912); *Ten and Twenty Aprils: Selected Verse* (1935); *An Introduction to Texas Literature* (1941). Editor: *Voices of the Southwest* (1923); *Best Short Stories from the Southwest,* 2 series (1928–31); *New Voices of the Southwest* (with Florence Elberta Barns, 1934). Editorial writer, *Dallas Journal,* 1914–33; lit. editor, 1935–38; columnist, *Dallas Morning News,* 1938–42.

GREER, SCOTT A. (Oct. 25, 1922–   ); b. Sweetwater, Tex. Sociologist, author. *Social Organization* (1955); *The Last Man In* (1959); *Exploring the Metropolitan Community* (with others, 1960); *The Emerging City* (1962); *Metropolitics* (1962); *Via Urbana* (1964); *Urban Renewal and American Cities* (1965); *The Logic of Social Inquiry* (1968); etc. Faculty, Northwestern University, since 1957.

GREER-PETRIE, CORDIA, b. "Merry Oaks," Barren Co., Ky. Author: the *Angeline* series, 11v. (1930–31).

GREET, WILLIAM CABELL (Jan. 28, 1901–); b. El Paso, Tex. Educator. *World Words* (1944); *In Other Words, a Beginning Thesaurus* (1968); *My Second In Other Words* (1969). Chairman of advisory committee, Thorndike-Barnhart dictionaries, since 1949. Dept of English, Barnard College, since 1926.

GREGG, JOHN ROBERT (June 17, 1867–Feb. 23, 1948); b. Rockcorry, Ireland. Educator, author. *Gregg Shorthand Manual* (1888) and numerous later editions, and other books on shorthand. Editor, *The Gregg Writer,* monthly magazine, from 1900. President, Gregg Publishing Co.

GREGG, JOSIAH (July 19, 1806–Feb. 25, 1850); b. in Overton Co., Tenn. Author. *Commerce of the Prairies; or, The Journal of a Santa Fé Trader* (1844), a classic of the West. *Diary and Letters,* edited by M. G. Fulton, 1941.

GREGOR, ELMER RUSSELL (Dec. 23, 1878–Apr. 4, 1954); b. New York City. Author. *The Red Arrow* (1915); *White Otter* (1917); *The White Wolf* (1920); *Three Sioux Scouts* (1922); *Captain Jim Mason* (1924); *Mason and His Rangers* (1926); *The Oswego Trail* (1928); *The Spoiled Pony* (1928); etc.

GREGORY, DANIEL SEELYE (Aug. 21, 1832–Apr. 14, 1915); b. Carmel, N.Y. Presbyterian clergyman, educator, editor, author. *Why Four Gospels?* (1877); *The Church in America* (with S. B. Halliday, 1896); etc. Managing editor, *Standard Dictionary;* co-editor, the *Homiletic Review,* 1895–1904. Prof., University of Wooster, Ohio, 1871–78; president, Lake Forest University, 1878–86.

GREGORY, DICK (1932–   ); b. St. Louis, Mo. Comedian, public speaker, author. *From the Back of the Bus* (1962); *nigger,* ed. by R. Lipsyte (1964); *What's Happening?* (1965); *The Shadow that Scares Me,* ed. by James R. McGraw (1968); *No More Lies* (1970); etc.

GREGORY, ELIOT (Oct. 13, 1854?–June 1, 1915); b. New York City. Painter, essayist. *Worldly Ways and Byways* (1898); *The Ways of Men* (1900).

GREGORY, HORACE (Apr. 10, 1898–); b. Milwaukee, Wis. Poet. *Chelsea Rooming House* (1930); *No Retreat* (1933); *Pilgrim of the Apocalypse: A Critical Study of D. H. Lawrence* (1933); *Chorus for Survival* (1935); *Poems: 1930–1940* (1941); *The Shield of Achilles* (1944); *A History of American Poetry, 1900–1940* (with Marya Zaturenska, 1946); *Selected Poems* (1951); *Amy Lowell: Portrait of the Poet in Her Times* (1958); *The World of James McNeill Whistler* (1959); *The Dying Gladiators* (1961); *Medusa in Gramercy Park* (poems, 1961); *Collected Poems* (1964); *The Silver Swan* (with Marya Zaturenska, 1966); *Dorothy Richardson: An Adventure in Self-Discovery* (1967); etc. Translator: *Poems of Catullus* (1931). Editor: *The Triumph of Life* (1943); *The Portable Sherwood Anderson* (1949); *Selected Poetry of Robert Browning* (1956); etc.

GREGORY, JACKSON (Mar. 12, 1882–June 12, 1943); b. Salinas, Calif. Novelist. *The Outlaw* (1916); *Wolf Breed* (1917); *Man to Man* (1920); *Desert Valley* (1921); *Timber-Wolf* (1923); *Redwood and Gold* (1928); *A Case for Mr. Paul Savoy* (1933); *Valley of Adventure* (1935); *Mountain Men* (1936); *Dark Valley* (1937); *I Must Ride Alone* (1940); *The Secret of Secret Valley* (1939); *Girl at the Crossroads* (1940); *The Far Call* (1940); *Guardians of the Trail* (1940); *Ace in the Hole* (1941); etc.

GREGORY, JOHN GOADBY (July 11, 1856–Apr. 12, 1947); b. Milwaukee, Wis. Journalist, historian, poet. *A Beauty of Thebes, and Other Verses* (1892); *History of Milwaukee,* 4v. (1931); *Southeastern Wisconsin,* 4v. (1932); *Southwestern Wisconsin* 4v. (1932); *West Central Wisconsin,* 4v. (1933). Editor, *Evening Wisconsin,* Milwaukee, 1905–18.

GREGORY, WINIFRED (Oct. 14, 1885–); b. Independence, Ia. Bibliographer. Editor: *Union List of Serials in Libraries of the United States and Canada* (1927); *Union List of Newspaper Files in Libraries of the United States and Canada* (1936); *Guide To Trollope* (1948); etc. Research editor for the Bibliographical Society of America and the American Library Association.

GREIG, MAYSIE (1902–). Author. Writes under various pen names and one other name. *Debutante Uniform* (1938); *Diplomatic Honeymoon* (1942); *At the Same Time Tomorrow* (1944); *Yours Ever* (1948); *After Tomorrow* (1951); *The Winds of Fear* (1956); *Love on Wings* (1958); *Her Heart's Desire* (1961); *The Doctor and the Dancer* (1965); *Doctor on Wings* (1966); *The Doctor Takes a Holiday* (1969).

Grenstone Poems (1917). By Witter Bynner (1917). A series of nearly 200 short lyrics.

GRESHAM, WILLIAM LINDSAY (Aug. 20, 1909–Sept. 14, 1962); b. Baltimore, Md. Author. *Nightmare Alley* (1946); *Limbo Tower* (1949); *Monster Midway* (1953); *Book of Strength* (1961); etc.

GREW, JOSEPH CLARK (May 27, 1880–May 25, 1965); b. Boston, Mass. Diplomat, author. *Sport and Travel in the Far East* (1910); *Report from Tokyo* (1942); *Ten Years in Japan* (1944); *Turbulent Era: A Diplomatic Record of Forty Years* (1952). United States foreign-service officer, 1904–45; ambassador to Turkey, 1927–32; Japan, 1931–41.

Grey, Donald. Pen name of Eugene Thomas.

GREY, ZANE (Jan. 31, 1875–Oct. 23, 1939); b. Zanesville, O. Author. *Betty Zane* (1904); *The Spirit of the Border* (1905); *The Last of the Plainsmen* (1908); *The Heritage of the Desert* (1910); *Riders of the Purple Sage* (1912); *Desert Gold* (1913); *The Light of the Western Stars* (1914); *The Lone Star Ranger* (1915); *The Border Legion* (1916); *Wildfire* (1917); *U.P. Trail* (1918); *Tales of Fishes* (1919); *The Man of the Forest* (1920); *The Mysterious Rider* (1921); *To the Last Man* (1922); *Tales of Lonely Trails* (1922); *The Wanderer of the Wasteland* (1923); *The Call of the Canyon* (1924); *Tales of Southern Rivers* (1924); *The Thundering Herd* (1925); *Tales of Fishing* (1925); *Virgin Seas* (1925); *Tales of Swordfish and Tuna* (1927); *Forlorn River* (1927); *Wild Horse Mesa* (1928); *Sunset Pass* (1931); *Robbers' Roost* (1932); *Code of the West* (1934); *Thunder Mountain* (1935); *The Trail Driver* (1936); *West of the Pecos* (1937); *Western Union* (1939); *Twin Sombreros* (1941); *Majesty's Rancho* (1942); *Stairs of Sand* (1943); *Wilderness Trek* (1944); *Shadow on the Trail* (1946); *Valley of Wild Horses* (1947); *Rogue River Feud* (1948); *Maverick Queen* (1950); *Dude Ranger* (1951); *Captives of the Desert* (1952); *Adventures in Fishing* (1952); *Wyoming* (1953); *Lost Pueblo* (1954); etc.

Greyfriars Bobby. Dog story by Eleanor Atkinson (1912).

Greyslaer. Novel by Charles Fenno Hoffman (1840). A tale of the Mohawk region of New York in the time of the Revolution.

GRIERSON, FRANCIS (Sept. 18, 1848–May 20, 1927); b. ([Benjamin Henry] Jesse [Francis] Shepard) Birkenhead, England. Musician, essayist. *Modern Mysticism, and Other Essays* (1899); *The Valley of the Shadows: Recollections of the Lincoln Country, 1858–1863* (1909); *The Celtic Temperament, and Other Essays* (1911); etc.

GRIFFIN, APPLETON P[rentiss] C[lark] (July 24, 1852–Apr. 16, 1926); b. Wilton, N.H. Librarian, bibliographer. Compiler: *Bibliography of American Historical Societies* (1896); *Catalogue of the Washington Collection* (1897), prepared for the Boston Athenaeum; etc. With Boston Public Library, 1871–94; with Boston Athenaeum, 1895–1908; chief asst. librarian, Library of Congress, 1908–26.

GRIFFIN, CLARE ELMER (Mar. 22, 1892–); b. Allegan, Mich. Educator, author. *Principles of Foreign Trade* (1924); *Life History of Automobiles* (1926); *Enterprise in a Free Society* (1949); *The Free Society* (1965); etc. Prof. business economics, University of Michigan, since 1943.

GRIFFIN, JOHN HOWARD (June 16, 1920–); b. Dallas, Tex. Photographer, author. *Devil Rides Outside* (1952); *Nuni* (1956); *Land of the High Sky* (1959); *Black Like Me* (1961); *The Church and The Black Man* (1968).

GRIFFIS, JOSEPH K. (b. 1852); b. in U.S.A. Indian scout, lecturer, author. Indian name, "Tahan." *Tahan: Out of Savagery Into Civilization* (autobiography, 1915); *Indian Story Circle Stories* (1928).

GRIFFIS, WILLIAM ELLIOT (Sept. 17, 1843–Feb. 5, 1928); b. Philadelphia, Pa. Congregational clergyman, educa-

tor, author. *The Mikado's Empire* (1876); *Japanese Fairy World* (1880); *Corea: The Hermit Nation* (1882); *Matthew Calbraith Perry* (1887); *Japan: In History, Folk-lore and Art* (1892); *Townsend Harris* (1895); *America in the East* (1899); *Sunny Memories of Three Pastorates* (1903); *The Fire-Fly's Lovers, and Other Fairy Tales of Old Japan* (1908); *China's Story* (1911); *The Unmannerly Tiger, and Other Korean Tales* (1911); *Millard Fillmore* (1915); etc.

GRIFFITH, HELEN SHERMAN (Mrs. W. O. Griffith) (1873–July 14, 1961); b. Des Moines, Ia. Author. *Her Wilful Way* (1902); *Her Father's Legacy* (1904); the *Letty* series, 10v. (1909–1918); *Rosemary for Remembrance* (1911); *For Love or Money* (1916); the *Virginia* series, 6v. (1920–30); *The Lane* (1925); etc.

GRIFFITH, RICHARD (Oct. 6, 1912–); b. Winchester, Va. Motion picture critic. *The Film Till Now: A Survey of World Cinema* (with Paul Rotha, 1950); *Documentary Film* (with Paul Rotha and Sinclair Reed, 1952); *The World of Robert Flaherty* (1953); *The Movies* (with Arthur Mayer, 1957); *The Anatomy of a Motion Picture* (1959).

GRIFFITH, THOMAS (Dec. 30, 1915–); b. Tacoma, Wash. Editor. *The Waist High Culture* (1959). Staff, *Time* magazine, 1943–63; editor, *Life*, since 1968.

GRIFFITH, WILLIAM (Feb. 15, 1876–Apr. 1, 1936); b. Memphis, Mo. Poet. *Trialogues* (1896); *The House of Dreams, and Other Poems* (1899); *History of Kansas City and the Louisiana Purchase* (1899); *City Views and Visions* (1911); *City Pastorals, and Other Poems* (1918); *Candles in the Sun* (1921); *Greek Gestures* (1929); etc. Compiler: *Bermuda Troubadours* (1935); etc. Editor, *Travel Magazine*, 1910; *McCall's Magazine*, 1911–12; etc.

GRIGGS, EARL LESLIE (Apr. 15, 1899–); b. New York. Educator, author. *Hartley Coleridge: His Life and Work* (1929); *Thomas Clarkson, The Friend of Slaves* (1938); *Coleridge Fille, A Biography of Sara Coleridge* (1940). Editor: *Unpublished Letters of Samuel Taylor Coleridge*, 2v. (1932); *Wordsworth and Coleridge* (1939); *Collected Letters of Samuel Taylor Coleridge*, Vols. I–VI, (1956–69); etc. English dept., University of California, 1947–62. Director, Education Abroad Program in Ireland and U.K., 1968–69.

GRIGGS, EDWARD HOWARD (1868–June 6, 1951); b. Owatonna, Minn. Educator, lecturer, author. *The New Humanism* (1900); *Moral Education* (1904); *The Philosophy of Art* (1913); *American Statesmen* (1924); *Socrates* (1932); *The Story of an Itinerant Teacher* (autobiography, 1934); *Earl Barnes* (1935); *Great Leaders in Human Progress* (1939); *Moral Leaders* (1940); etc. Prof. ethics, Stanford University, 1891, 1893–98.

GRIMBALL, ELIZABETH BERKELEY (d. Aug. 30, 1953); b. Union, S.C. Producer, author. *The Snow Queen* (1920); *The Waif* (1924); *Costuming a Play* (with, Rhea Wells, 1925).

GRIMKÉ, ANGELINA EMILY (Mrs. Theodore Dwight Weld) (Feb. 20, 1805–Oct. 26, 1879); b. Charleston, S.C. Anti-slavery and woman's rights advocate, author. *Appeal to the Christian Women of the South* (1836); *Letters to Catherine E. Beecher* (1838); etc. Sister of Sarah Moore Grimké (Nov. 26, 1792–Dec. 23, 1873), author of anti-slavery tracts; and of Thomas Smith Grimké (Sept. 26, 1786–Oct. 12, 1834), peace advocate and reformer. See Catherine H. Birney's *The Grimké Sisters, Sarah and Angelina Grimké* (1885); *Letters of Theodore Dwight Weld, Angelina Grimké Weld and Sarah Grimké* (1934), ed. by G. H. Barnes and D. L. Dumond.

GRIMKÉ, ANGELINA WELD (Feb. 27, 1880–deceased); b. Boston, Mass. Educator, playwright. *Rachel* (1920).

GRIMKÉ, ARCHIBALD HENRY (Aug. 17, 1849–Feb. 25, 1930); b. near Charleston, S.C. Lawyer, publicist, author. *William Lloyd Garrison, the Abolitionist* (1891); *The Life of*

Charles Sumner, the Scholar in Politics (1892); *Right on the Scaffold* (1901); *The Ultimate Criminal* (1915); *The Shame of America* (1924).

Gringo, Harry. Pen name of Henry Augustus Wise.

GRINNELL, GEORGE BIRD (Sept. 20, 1849–Apr. 11, 1938); b. Brooklyn, N.Y. Author. *Pawnee Hero Stories and Folk-Tales* (1889); *Blackfoot Lodge Tales* (1892); the *Jack* series, 7v. (1899–1913); *Travels of the Pathfinders* (1911); *Beyond the Old Frontier* (1913); *Blackfeet Indian Stories* (1913); *The Cheyenne Indians*, 2v. (1923); *By Cheyenne Campfires* (1926); etc. Editor, *Forest and Stream*, 1876–1911.

GRISWOLD, A[lfred] WHITNEY (Oct. 27, 1906–Apr. 19, 1963); b. Morristown, N.J. Educator, author. *The Far Eastern Policy of the U.S.* (1938); *Farming and Democracy* (1948); *Essays on Education* (1954); *In the University Tradition* (1957); *Liberal Education and the Democratic Ideal* (1959). Depts. of history, political science, Yale University, 1933–50; former pres.

GRISWOLD, FLORENCE K. b. Philadelphia, Pa. Lecturer, author. *Hindu Fairy Tales* (1918); *Trees and Heart Strings* (poems, 1932).

GRISWOLD, FRANCES IRENE BURGE (1826-1900); b. Wickford, R.I. Author. *Elm Tree Tales* (1856); *Nina; or, Life's Caprices* (1861); *Stained Hand* (1861); *Missionary Kite* (1861); *Curious Eyes* (1861); *Maddie and Lollie* (1861); *Hetty Baker* (1861); *Miriam's Reward* (1861); *Little Mary's Three Homes* (1861); *Fairfax Stories* (1863); *Our Birds* (1864); *Asleep* (1871); *Sister Eleanor's Brood* (under pen name, "Mrs. S. B. Phelps," 1872); *The Bishop and Nannette* (1874); *Miss Bent* (1881); *Old Wickford* (1900); etc. Editor, the *Ladies' Wreath* annual, 1860–61.

GRISWOLD, FRANCIS (1902–); b. Albany, N.Y. Novelist. *The Tides of Malvern* (1930); *Sea Island Lady* (1939).

GRISWOLD, F[rank] GRAY (Dec. 21, 1854–Mar. 30, 1937); b. New York City. Merchant, sportsman, author. *Sport on Land and Water*, 7v. (1913–33); *Race Horses and Racing* (1925); *Horses and Hounds* (1926); *Clipper Ships and Yachts* (1927); *El Greco* (1930); *Memoirs of a Salmon* (1931); *Plantation Days* (under pen name, "Anthony Ashley, Jr.," 1935); *After Thoughts* (1936); *The Horse and Buggy Days* (autobiography, 1936); etc.

GRISWOLD, LATTA (Feb. 4, 1876–Aug. 16, 1931); b. Lancaster, O. Episcopal clergyman, educator, author. *Deering of Deal* (1912); *Deering at Princeton* (1913); *The Winds of Deal* (1914); *The Episcopal Church* (1916); *The Inn at the Red Oak* (1917); *The Tides of Deal* (1922); *Values of Catholic Faith* (1926); etc.

GRISWOLD, RUFUS WILMOT (Feb. 15, 1815–Aug. 27, 1857); b. Benson, Vt. Journalist, anthologist. Compiler: *The Poets and Poetry of America* (1842); *The Poets and Poetry of England in the Nineteenth Century* (1844); *The Prose Works of John Milton*, 2v. (1845–47); *The Prose Writers of America* (1847); *The Female Poets of America* (1848); *The Republican Court; or, American Society in the Days of Washington* (1855). Editor, *Graham's Magazine*, 1842–43; *International Monthly Magazine*, 1850–52; P. T. Barnum's *Illustrated News*, 1852–53. *See* William M. Griswold's *Passages from the Correspondence and Other Papers of Rufus W. Griswold* (1898).

GRISWOLD, WILLIAM McGRILLIS (Oct. 9, 1853–Aug. 3, 1899); b. Bangor, Me., son of Rufus Wilmot Griswold. Bibliographer, author. *A Directory of Writers for the Literary Press in the United States* (1884); *Descriptive List of Novels and Tales* (1890–92); *Passages from the Correspondence and Other Papers* (1898). Compiler of many periodical indexes, including *A General Index to the Nation, Volumes I–XXX* (1880); *Q. P. Index Annual* (1882–85); *Annual Index to Periodicals* (1886–89).

Grit. Williamsport, Pa. Weekly newspaper. Founded 1882, by Dietrick Lamade.

Grolier Club. New York. Society for bibliophiles. Founded Feb. 5, 1884, by William Loring Andrews, Theodore De Vinne, Alexander W. Drake, Robert Hoe, Brayton Ives, Edward S. Mead, Albert Gallup, Arthur B. Turnure, and Samuel W. Marvin. Robert Hoe was its first president. It was named in honor of Jean Grolier, Vicomte d'Aquisy, Treasurer of France under Francis I, and a noted bibliophile. Interested in all phases of book arts, this club has collected a large library, and has held numerous exhibitions relating to books. A club bindery has been organized to produce artistic book bindings. *See* John T. Winterich's *The Grolier Club: An Informal History* (1950).

Grolier Encyclopedia. Ten-volume encyclopedia first published by The Grolier Society in 1944. Previously it had appeared as the *Doubleday Encyclopedia* (1931–43). Annual yearbook since 1947. It went out of print in 1963 but most of the material was incorporated in the *Unified Encyclopedia*, which went out of print in 1966.

Grolier Society, Inc. New York. Publishers of subscription books. Founded 1894; as Grolier Society, at Boston; moved to New York, 1900. Named in honor of Jean Grolier. Among the Grolier Society's many educational sets have been *The Book of Knowledge, The New Book of Knowledge, The Grolier Encyclopedia, The Book of Popular Science.* A subsidiary of Grolier Incorporated.

GROPIUS, WALTER ADOLF (May 18, 1883–July 5, 1969); b. Berlin. Architect. *The New Architecture and the Bauhaus* (1935); *Rebuilding Our Communities* (1945); *Scope of Total Architecture* (1955); etc. Co-editor: *The Bauhaus, 1919–28* (1938). Chairman, School of Architecture, Harvard University, after 1938.

GROPPER, WILLIAM (Dec. 3, 1897–); b. New York. Artist, author. *The Golden Land* (1927); *56 Drawings of the U.S.S.R.* (1928); *Alay-Oop* (1930); *Gropper* (1938); *Portfolio of Caucasian Sketches* (1950); *American Folklore Lithographs* (1953); *The Little Tailor* (1954); *The Lost Conscience* (1955); *Capricios* (1957). Illustrator of numerous works by other authors.

GROSECLOSE, ELGIN (Nov. 25, 1899–); b. Waukomis, Okla. Author. *The Persian Journey of the Reverend Ashley Wishard and His Servant Fathi* (1937); *Ararat* (1939); *The Firedrake* (1942); *Introduction to Iran* (1947); *The Carmelite* (1955); *The Scimitar of Saladin* (1956); *Money and Man* (1961); *Fifty Years of Managed Money* (1965).

GROSS, BEN SAMUEL (Nov. 24, 1891–); b. Birmingham, Ala. Journalist, author. *Husbands* (play, 1927); *What This Town Needs* (play, with Charles Perner, 1937); *I Looked and I Listened* (1954). Staff, New York *Daily News*, since 1925; now radio-television editor.

GROSS, BERTRAM MYRON (Dec. 25, 1912–); b. Philadelphia, Pa. Educator, government official, author. *Legislative Struggle* (1953); *The Hard Money Crusade* (with Will Lumer, 1954); *The Managing of Organizations*, 2v. (1964); *The State of the Nation* (1966); *Social Intelligence for America's Future* (1969); etc. Editor: *Social Goals and Indicators for American Society*, 2v. (1967); *Action under Planning* (1967); *A Great Society?* (1968). Prof. administration, Syracuse University, since 1960.

GROSS, CHAIM (Mar. 17, 1904–); b. in Austria. Sculptor. *A Sculptor's Progress: An Autobiography* (1938); *Fantasy Drawings* (1956); *Technique of Wood Carving* (1957). Illustrated a number of children's books. Teacher of sculpture, Museum of Modern Art, New School for Social Research, etc.

GROSS, CHARLES (Feb. 10, 1857–Dec. 3, 1909); b. Troy, N.Y. Educator, historian. *The Gild Merchant*, 2v. (1890); *Sources and Literature of English History from the Earliest*

Times to About 1485 (1900); etc. History dept., Harvard University, 1888–1909; prof. 1901–09.

GROSS, MILT (Mar. 4, 1895–Nov. 29, 1953); b. New York City. Cartoonist, humorist. Creator of "Nize Baby" and "Gross Exaggerations." *Nize Baby* (1926); *Hiawatta with No Odder Poems* (1926); *Dunt Esk* (1927); *De Night in de Front From Chreesmas* (1927); *Famous Fimales from Heestory* (1928); etc. Cartoonist, *New York Evening Journal, New York Tribune, New York World,* etc.

GROSS, RONALD (Nov. 27, 1935–   ); b. New York. Author. *Learning by Television* (1966); *Pop Poems* (1967); *High School* (1971). Editor: *The Teacher and the Taught* (1963); *The Revolution in the Schools* (1964); *Homo Faber: Work Through the Ages* (1964).

Grosset & Dunlap. New York. Publishers. Founded 1898, by George T. Dunlap and Alexander Grosset. First called Dunlap & Grosset, but changed to Grosset & Dunlap in 1900. Popular books by other publishers are reprinted in cheaper format by Grosset & Dunlap, making the books available to a larger public. Bantam Books was organized in 1946 by Ian Ballantine for Grosset & Dunlap. Acquired by National General Corp., film producers and exhibitors, in 1968. *See* George T. Dunlap's *The Fleeting Years: A Memoir* (1927).

GROSSMAN, ALLEN R. (Jan. 7, 1932–   ); b. Minneapolis, Minn. Educator, author. *A Harlot's Hire* (1961); *The Recluse and Other Poems* (1965); *Poetic Knowledge in the Early Yeats* (1969); etc. Faculty, Brandeis University.

Grossman Publishers. New York. Founded 1962 by Richard L. Grossman. Orion Press is an imprint. Publishes general fiction and nonfiction, and art books. A subsidiary of Viking Press (q.v.).

GROSVENOR, ABBIE JOHNSTON (Sept. 21, 1865–deceased); b. Richmond, Ind. Author. *Merrie May Tyme* (1916); *Strange Stories of the Great Valley* (1917); *Strange Stories of the Great River* (1918); *Boy Explorer* (1926); *Winged Moccasins* (1933).

GROSVENOR, GILBERT HOVEY (Oct. 28, 1875–Feb. 4, 1966); b. Constantinople, Turkey. Editor, author. *Young Russia* (1914); *The Hawaiian Islands* (1924); *Discovery and Exploration* (1924); *The National Geographic Society and Its Magazine* (1936); etc. Editor: *Scenes From Every Land,* 4 series (1907–17); *Stalking Birds with Color Camera* (1951); etc. Editor, *National Geographic Magazine,* 1903–1954.

GROSVENOR, MELVILLE BELL (Nov. 26, 1901–); b. Washington, D.C. Editor. Staff, *National Geographic Magazine,* since 1924; editor since 1957.

GROSZ, GEORGE (July 26, 1893–July 6, 1959); b. Berlin, Germany. Painter, illustrator. *A Little Yes and a Big No* (1946); also collections of drawings. Illustrated *O. Henry Short Stories* for Limited Ediitons Club (1935); *Interregnum* (1936); etc. Author of about forty books, mostly in German.

Ground We Stand On, The. By John Dos Passos (1941). The work comprises various biographies of Americans who have devoted themselves to the principles of intellectual and political liberty.

"Groundhog, The." Poem by Richard Eberhart.

Group, The. Novel by Mary McCarthy (1963). Follows the lives of Vassar graduates.

Grove Press. New York. Founded 1952 by Barney Rosset. Publishes various series, such as Evergreen Books, quality paperbacks; Black Cat Books, mass-market paperbacks; Profile Books, pictorial paperbacks; Evergreen Pilot Books, guides to the "masters of modern literature," etc. Issues *Evergreen Review,* paperback periodical of literature and the arts. Notable for publishing books hitherto banned in the United States,

such as the unexpurgated edition of D. H. Lawrence's *Lady Chatterley's Lover* and Henry Miller's *Tropic of Cancer.*

GROVER, EDWIN OSGOOD (June 4, 1870–); b. Mantorville, Minn. Educator, librarian, editor, author. *I Wish You Joy* (1909); *The Gift of Friendship* (1910); *Never-Grow-Old Stories* (1925); *The Nature Lover's Knapsack* (1927); *The Roadmakers* (1931); *The Romance of the Book* (1932); *Annals of an Era* (1932); *Down East and Up Along* (1937); etc. With Prang Co., Boston, 1911–38, president, 1911–25; founder, Angel Alley Press, at Winter Park, Fla., 1926; prof. of books, Rollins College, from 1926.

GROVER, EULALIE OSGOOD (June 22, 1873–); b. Mantorville, Minn. Author of children's books. The *Sunbonnet Babies* series; the *Overall Boys* series; *Robert Louis Stevenson, Teller of Tales* (1940); etc. Editor: *My Caravan: A Book of Poems for Boys and Girls in Search of Adventure* (1931); *Benjamin Franklin: The Story of Poor Richard* (1953); etc.

GROVES, ERNEST RUTHERFORD (May 6, 1877–Aug. 28, 1946); b. Framingham, Mass. Educator, sociologist, author. *Social Problems and Education* (1925); *Social Problems of the Family* (1927); *The Marriage Crisis* (1928); *Marriage* (1933); *The American Woman* (1937); *Our Changing Social Order* (1938); *The Family and Its Social Functions* (1940); *Christianity and the Family* (1942); etc. Co-author of many books on family life, with wife, Gladys Hoagland Groves. Prof. sociology, University of North Carolina, from 1927.

GROVES, GLADYS [Hoagland] (Apr. 3, 1894–); b. Boston, Mass. Author or co-author: *Wholesome Childhood* (1924); *Parents and Children* (1929); *Sex in Marriage* (1931); *The Married Woman* (1936); *Sex Fulfillment in Marriage* (1942); *The Contemporary American Family* (1947); etc. Editor, *Marriage and Family Living,* 1950–53.

Growing Up Absurd. By Paul Goodman (1961). Discussion of the nature of "growing up" in modern American society, the difficulties that lie in the way of youth in forming principles, ideals, and objectives in the process of becoming responsible adults. A radical viewpoint involving the fullest and most searching examination of democratic, progressive, and libertarian ideas in all areas of psychological, social, and political life.

GROWOLL, ADOLF (1850–1909); b. New York City. Bibliographer, author. *American Book Clubs* (1897); *Book-Trade Bibliography in the United States in the XIXth Century* (1898); *Three Centuries of English Booktrade Bibliography* (1903); etc. He was assisted in his bibliographical work by Wilberforce Eames. Many of his scrapbooks, etc., are now in the possession of *Publishers' Weekly.*

GRUBB, DAVIS (1919–). Author. *Night of the Hunter* (1955); *Watchman* (1961); *A Tree Full of Stars* (1965); *Shadow of My Brother* (1966); *The Golden Sickle* (1968); *Fools Parade* (1969); etc.

GRUBER, FRANK (Feb. 2, 1904–Dec. 9, 1969); b. Elmer, Minn. Book collector, novelist. *Peace Marshal* (1939); *The French Key* (1940); *The Laughing Fox* (1940); *The Talking Clock* (1941); *Simon Lash: Private Detective* (1941); *Fighting Man* (1948); *The Highway Man* (1955); *The Lonesome River* (1957); *The Town Tamer* (1958); *Twenty Plus Two* (1961); *Brothers of Silence* (1962); *The Greek Affair* (1964); *Little Hercules* (1965); *The Life and Times of the Pulp Story* (1966); *The Gold Gap* (1968); *The Etruscan Bull* (1969); etc.

GRUBER, L[evi] FRANKLIN (d. Dec. 5, 1941); b. near Reading, Pa. Lutheran clergyman, educator, author. *The Creative Days* (1919); *The Freedom of the Will* (1923); etc. President, Chicago Lutheran Theological Seminary, from 1927. Assoc. editor, *Bibliotheca Sacra,* 1920–34.

GRUELLE, JOHNNY [John Barton] (Dec. 24, 1880–Jan. 9, 1938); b. Arcola, Ill. Author of children's books. Creator of "Raggedy Ann," "Raggedy Andy," and "Beloved Belindy."

My Very Own Fairy Stories (1917); *Raggedy Ann* (1918); *Raggedy Andy* (1920); and others of the *Raggedy Ann* series.

GRUENBERG, SIDONIE [Matsner] (Mrs. Benjamin C. Gruenberg) (June 10, 1881–); b. in Austria. Author: *Sons and Daughters* (1916); *New Parents for Old* (part IV, *The New Generation*, 1930); *The Wonderful Story of How You Were Born* (1952); etc. Co-author: *Parents, Children and Money* (1933); *The Many Lives of Modern Woman* (1952); *Children for the Childless* (1954). Editor: *Parents' Questions* (1936); *Favorite Stories Old and New* (1942); etc. Editor and co-author: *Parents' Guide to Everyday Problems of Boys and Girls* (1958); *Let's Hear a Story* (1961); *All Kinds of Courage* (1962); etc. Editor-in-chief: *Encyclopedia of Child Care and Guidance* (1954).

GRUENING, ERNEST (Feb. 6, 1887–); b. New York. Senator, editor, author. *Mexico and Its Heritage* (1928); *The Public Pays* (1931); *The State of Alaska* (1954); *An Alaskan Reader* (1967). Founder, Portland (Me.) *Evening News*, 1927. U.S. Senator, 1956–58; 1958–69.

GRUMBINE, HARVEY CARSON (May 1, 1869–Dec. 24, 1941); b. Fredericksburg, Pa. Educator, author. *Stories from Browning* (1914); *The Web* (poems, 1929); *The Chase* (poems, 1928); etc. Prof. English, West Virginia University, 1919–25.

GRUNWALD, HENRY ANATOLE (Dec. 3, 1922–): b. Vienna. Editor, author. *Salinger, a Critical and Personal Portrait* (1962); *Churchill, The Life Triumphant* (1965); *The Age of Elegance* (1966). Editorial staff, *Time* Magazine, since 1945.

Guard of Honor. Novel by James Gould Cozzens (1948). The scene is an Air Force establishment during World War II. The characters come into conflict over the difficulty of acting comprehensively as sensitive human beings as well as men of war.

Guardian, The. New York. Independent radical news weekly. Founded 1948 as *The National Guardian*.

Guardian Angel, The. Novel by Oliver Wendell Holmes (1867). Myrtle Hazard, an orphan from the tropics, is brought up by a New England professor who watches over her mental development, which turns out to be quite alien to the New England temperament. Under his patient tutelage she overcomes traits which threaten to wreck her life.

GUDDE, ERWIN GUSTAV (Feb. 23, 1889–); b. Schippenbeil, Ger. Author: *Social Conflicts in Medieval Poetry* (1934); *Sutter's Own Story* (1936); *California Place Names: A Geographical Dictionary* (1949); etc. Editor and translator: *Edward Vischer's First Visit to California* (1940); *Exploring with Fremont* (with E. K. Gudde, 1958); etc. Co-editor: *Poems of Lupold Hornburg* (1945); etc.

GUE, BENJAMIN F. (Dec. 25, 1828–June 1, 1904); b. Greene County, N.Y. Journalist, author. *Iowa Homestead* (1871); *History of Iowa from the Earliest Times to the Beginning of the Twentieth Century*, 4v. (1903). Editor, *Fort Dodge Republican*, 1864–71.

GUÉRARD, ALBERT JOSEPH (Nov. 2, 1914–); b. Houston, Tex. Educator, author. *The Past Must Alter* (1937); *Robert Bridges* (1942); *The Hunted* (1944); *Maquisard* (1945); *Joseph Conrad* (1947); *Thomas Hardy* (1949); *Night Journey* (1950); *André Gide* (1951); *Conrad the Novelist* (1958); *The Bystander* (1958); *The Exiles* (1963). English dept., Harvard University, 1938–61; prof. English, Stanford University, since 1961.

GUÉRARD, ALBERT LÉON (Nov. 3, 1880–Nov. 12, 1959); b. Paris. Educator, author. *Five Masters of French Romance* (1916); *French Civilization* (1920); *The Napoleonic Legend* (1923); *Beyond Hatred* (1925); *Life and Death of an Ideal* (1928); *Literature and Society* (1935); *Art for Art's Sake* (1936); *Preface to World Literature* (1940); *The France of*

Tomorrow (1942); *Napoleon III* (1943); *Europe Free and United* (1945); *France: A Short History* (1946); *Napoleon I* (1956); *Fossils and Presences* (1957); *Joan of Arc* (1957); *France: The Biography of a Nation* (1959). Prof. general literature, Stanford University, 1925–46.

GUERNSEY, ALFRED HUDSON (1825–Jan. 16, 1902); b. Brandon, Vt. Editor, author. *Thomas Carlyle* (1879); *Ralph Waldo Emerson* (1881); etc. Editor: *Harper's Pictorial History of the Great Rebellion*, 2v. (with Henry M. Alden, 1866–68), republ. as *Harper's Pictorial History of the Civil War*, 2v. (1894–96); etc. Editor, *Harper's Magazine*, 1856–69.

GUERNSEY, LUCY ELLEN (Aug. 12, 1826–Nov. 3, 1899); b. Rochester, N.Y. Novelist. *Irish Amy* (anon., 1854); *Kitty Maynard* (anon., 1857); *Winifred* (1869); *Only in Fun* (1871); *Lady Betty's Governess* (1872); *Lady Rosamond's Book* (1874); *The Foster Sisters* (1882); *Oldham* (1886); etc.

GUERNSEY, OTIS LOVE, Jr. (Aug. 9, 1918–); b. New York. Critic, editor. Editor: *The Best Plays* series, since 1965. Staff, New York *Herald Tribune*, 1941–60: drama critic and senior editor, *Show* magazine, 1963–64.

GUEST, BARBARA (Sept. 6, 1920–); b. Wilmington, N.C. Author. *The Ladies Choice* (play, 1953); *The Location of Things* (poems, 1960); *The Office* (play, 1961); *Poems* (1963); *Port* (play, 1965); *The Blue Stars* (poems, 1968); *I Ching: Poems and Lithographs* (with Sheila Isham, 1969).

GUEST, EDGAR A[lbert] (Aug. 20, 1881–Aug. 5, 1959); b. Birmingham, England. Journalist, poet. *A Heap o' Livin'* (1916); *Just Folks* (1917); *Over Here* (1918); *Path to Home* (1918); *When Day Is Done* (1921); *All That Matters* (1922); *The Passing Throng* (1923); *Rhymes of Childhood* (1924); *The Light of Faith* (1926); *Harbor Lights of Home* (1928); *The Friendly Way* (1931); *Collected Verse* (1934); *Life's Highway* (1933); *All in a Lifetime* (1938); *Poems of Patriotism* (1942); *Living the Years* (1949); etc. With *Detroit Free Press*, from 1895.

Guggenheim Fellowships. Awarded by the John Simon Guggenheim Memorial Foundation, in New York, founded 1924. Several American men and women are selected each year to receive a stipend to enable them to carry on research in any field of creative knowledge, the award being made on the basis of the candidate's demonstrated knowledge and ability and need of financial assistance. A great many of the awards are for literary projects.

Guide to Reference Books. By Isadore Gilbert Mudge (1917). An outgrowth of Alice Bertha Kroeger's *Guide to the Study and Use of Reference Books* (1902). Revisions were made in 1923 and 1929, and supplements and further revisions have kept this reference guide up to date. Latest edition appeared in 1967, edited by Constance Mabel Winchell. It is the standard text for library schools, and gives detailed descriptions of all the better reference tools used in libraries. Includes reference works in foreign languages.

Guideposts. Carmel, N.Y. Monthly. Founded 1947. Edited by Norman Vincent Peale. Religious and inspirational magazine.

GUILD, CURTIS (Jan. 13, 1827–Mar. 12, 1911); b. Boston, Mass. Editor, author. *Over the Ocean* (1869); *From Sunrise to Sunset* (poems, 1894); *A Chat About Celebrities* (1897); etc. Founder, *Commercial Bulletin* (1859). In 1857 he merged the *Boston Evening Traveler*, the *Boston Daily Atlas*, the *Daily Evening Telegraph*, and the *Boston Chronicle* under the name of the *Boston Morning Traveler* and *Evening Traveler*. Founder, the Bostonian Society, 1881; and was president of The Club of Odd Volumes.

GUILD, REUBEN ALDRIDGE (May 4, 1822–May 13, 1899); b. West Dedham, Mass. Librarian, author. *The Librarian's Manual* (1858); *History of Brown University* (1867); etc. Librarian, Brown University, 1848–93.

GUILDAY, PETER (Mar. 25, 1884–July 31, 1947); b. Chester, Pa. Roman Catholic clergyman, educator, author. *The Life and Times of John Carroll* (1922); *The Life and Times of John England* (1927); *A History of the Councils of Baltimore* (1932); etc. Editor: *Church Historians* (1926). Founder and editor, *Catholic Historical Review*, 1915. Founder, *Catholic Historical Association*, 1919. History dept., Catholic University of America, Washington, D.C., from 1914.

GUILFORD, NATHAN (July 19, 1786–Dec. 18, 1854); b. Spencer, Mass. Educator, author. *A Letter on Free Education* (1822); *The Western Spelling Book* (1831); *The Juvenile Arithmetic* (1836); etc. A pioneer in promoting free education in Ohio.

GUINESS, MAURICE. Co-author, with Muna Lee (q.v.), under pen name "Newton Gayle," (of detective fiction).

GUINEY, LOUISE IMOGEN (Jan. 7, 1861–Nov. 2, 1920); b. Boston, Mass. Essayist, poet. *Songs at the Start* (1884); *Goose-Quill Papers* (1885); *The White Sail, and Other Poems* (1887); *Brownies and Bogles* (1888); *"Monsieur Henri"* (1892); *A Roadside Harp* (poems, 1893); *A Little English Gallery* (1894); *Robert Louis Stevenson* (1895); *Lover's Saint Ruth's, and Three Other Tales* (1895); *Nine Sonnets Written at Oxford* (1895); *Patrins* (1897); *"England and Yesterday"* (poems, 1898); *The Martyr's Idyl, and Shorter Poems* (1899); *Robert Emmet* (1904); *The Princess of the Tower* (1906); *Blessed Edward Campion* (1908); *Happy Ending: The Collected Lyrics* (1909); *Letters*, 2v. (1926). *See* Alice Brown's *Louise Imogen Guiney* (1921).

GUINZBURG, HAROLD K. (1899–Oct. 18, 1961). Publisher. Co-founder, Viking Press, 1925; director, after 1925. Founder, Literary Guild, 1927.

GUITERMAN, ARTHUR (Nov. 20, 1871–Jan. 11, 1943); b. Vienna, of American parentage. Poet. *Betel Nuts* (1907); *The Laughing Muse* (1915); *Ballads of Old New York* (1920); *Chips of Jade* (1920); *I Sing the Pioneer* (1926); *Wildwood Fables* (1927); *Death and General Putnam, and 101 Other Poems* (1935); *Gaily the Troubadour* (1936); *Lyric Laughter* (1939); *A Man Without a Country* (opera libretto, prod. 1937); etc.

GULICK, LUTHER HALSEY (Dec. 4, 1865–Aug. 13, 1918); b. Honolulu, T.H. Educator, author. *The Efficient Life* (1907); *Mind and Work* (1908); etc. Pioneer in physical education publicity; founder, Camp Fire Girls.

GULICK, SIDNEY LEWIS (Apr. 10, 1860–Dec. 20, 1945); b. in the Marshall Islands. Congregational missionary, author. *The White Peril in the Far East* (1905); *America and the Orient* (1916); *Problems of the Pacific and the Far East* (1921); *Towards Understanding Japan* (1935); *Mixing the Races in Hawaii* (1937); etc. Missionary to Japan, 1887–1913.

Gullible's Travels. By Ring Lardner (1917).

GULLIVER, LUCILE (1882–Mar. 20, 1964); b. Somerville, Mass. Literary agent, editor, author. *Over the Nonsense Road* (1910); *The Friendship of Nations* (1912); *Daniel Boone* (1916). Head children's book dept., Little Brown & Co., 1927–33; editor, Lothrop, Lee & Shepard, 1933–35; editor, *American Childhood*, 1937–38.

GUMMERE, AMELIA MOTT (Mrs. Francis Barton Gummere) (July 17, 1859–Oct. 7, 1937); b. Burlington, N.J. Author. *The Quaker: A Study in Costume* (1902); *Witchcraft and Quakerism* (1908); *The Quaker in the Forum* (1910); etc.

GUMMERE, FRANCIS BARTON (Mar. 6, 1855–May 30, 1919); b. Burlington, N.J. Educator, philologist, critic, folklorist. *A Handbook of Poetics* (1885); *Germanic Origins: A Study in Primitive Culture* (1892); *The Beginnings of Poetry* (1908); *Democracy and Poetry* (1911); etc. Editor: *Old English Ballads* (1894). Prof. English, Haverford College, 1887–1919.

Gunmaker of Moscow, The. Novel by Sylvanus Cobb, Jr. (1856). The story of Ruric Nevel and his love for Rosalind Valdai, a duchess, whose guardian opposes the match. The Emperor, Peter the Great, captivated by Ruric's swordsmanship, secretly aids him in adventures and makes possible his marriage to Rosalind.

GUNN, BILL [William Harrison] (July 15, 1934–); b. Philadelphia, Pa. *Marcus in the High Grass* (1960); *All the Rest Have Died* (1964).

GUNN, THOM (Aug. 29, 1929–); b. Gravesend, Eng., son of William Gunn. Poet. *Fighting Terms* (1954); *The Sense of Movement* (1957); *My Sad Captains* (1961); *Selected Poems* (with Ted Hughes, 1962); *Geography* (1966); *Positives* (with Ander Gunn, 1966); *Touch* (1967).

GUNSAULUS, FRANK W[akely] (Jan. 1, 1856–Mar. 17, 1921); b. Chesterville, O. Congregational clergyman, bibliophile, author. *Phidias, and Other Poems* (1887); *Loose Leaves of Song* (1888); *Monk and Knight: An Historical Study in Fiction*, 2v. (1891); *Songs of Night and Day* (1896); *The Higher Ministries of Recent English Poetry* (1907); etc. He presented his collection of incunabula to the University of Chicago. He was a frequenter of the "Saints and Sinners' Corner" in McClurg's bookstore, celebrated by Eugene Field.

GUNTER, ARCHIBALD CLAVERING (Oct. 25, 1847–Feb. 27, 1907); b. Liverpool, England. Playwright, novelist. *Found the True Vein* (1872); *Prince Karl* (prod. 1886); *Mr. Barnes of New York* (1887); *Mr. Potter of Texas* (1888); *That Frenchman!* (1889); *Miss Nobody of Nowhere* (1890); *A Princess of Paris* (1904); etc.

GUNTHER, JOHN (Aug. 30, 1901–May 29, 1970); b. Chicago, Ill. Foreign correspondent, author. *The Red Pavilion* (1926); *Eden for One* (1927); *The Golden Fleece* (1929); *The Bright Nemesis* (1932); *Inside Europe* (1936); *Inside Asia* (1939); *The High Cost of Hitler* (1940); *Inside Latin America* (1941); *D-Day* (1944); *The Troubled Midnight* (1945); *Inside U.S.A.* (1947); *Death Be Not Proud* (1949); *Roosevelt in Retrospect* (1950); *The Riddle of MacArthur* (1951); *Eisenhower: The Man and the Symbol* (1952); *Inside Africa* (1955); *Inside Russia Today* (1958); *Meet the Congo* (1959); *The Golden Fleece* (1959); *Taken at the Flood* (1961); *Inside Europe Today* (1961); *The Lost City* (1964); *Procession* (1965); *Inside South America* (1967); *Chicago Revisited* (1968); *Twelve Cities* (1969); etc. With *Chicago Daily News*, 1922–36.

Gurney, Antoinette. *See* Allen Chaffee.

GUROWSKI, ADAM (Sept. 10, 1805–May 4, 1866); b. Kalisz, Poland. Linguist, translator, author. *Russia As It Is* (1854); *America and Europe* (1857); *Diary*, 3v. (1862–66); etc.

GUSTAFSON, ALRIK (Apr. 23, 1903–Mar. 24, 1970); b. Sioux City, Ia. Educator, author. *Six Scandinavian Novelists* (1940); *A History of Swedish Literature* (1961). Editor: *Scandinavian Plays of the 20th Century*, 2v. (1944–46). Prof. Scandinavian literature, University of Minnesota, from 1939.

Gustavus Vasa. Play said by tradition to have been written by Benjamin Colman, and produced at Harvard College in 1690. If tradition is correct, this may have been the first play by an American playwright.

GUTERMUTH, CLINTON RAYMOND (Aug. 16, 1900–); b. Fort Wayne, Ind. Conservationist, naturalist. *Where to Go in Indiana, Official Lake Guide* (1938); etc. Co-author: *The Fisherman's Encyclopedia* (1950); *The Standard Book of Fishing* (1950).

GUTHEIM, FREDERICK [Albert] (Mar. 3, 1908–); b. Cambridge, Mass. Author: *The Potomac* (1949); *One Hundred Years of Architecture in America* (1957); *Alvar Aalto* (1960); etc. Editor: *Frank Lloyd Wright on Architecture* (1941).

GUTHRIE, A[lfred] B[ertram], JR. (Jan 13, 1901–); b. Bedford, Ind. Novelist. *The Big Sky* (1947); *The Way West* (1949; Pulitzer Prize for fiction, 1950); *These Thousand Hills* (1956); *The Big It* (1960); *The Blue Hen's Chick* (1965).

GUTHRIE, ARLO (1947–   ); Songwriter and performer. *This Is the Arlo Guthrie Book* (1969). Composed words and music: *"Alice's Restaurant," "Ring-around-the-Rosy Rag," "Now and Then," "I'm Going Home," "The Motorcycle Song," "Highway in the Wind,"* etc.

GUTHRIE, RAMON (Jan. 14, 1896–); b. New York City. Educator, poet, novelist. *Trobar Clus* (poems, 1923); *Marcabrun* (1926); *A World Too Old* (poems, 1927); *Graffiti* (poems, 1959); *Asbestos Phoenix* (1968); etc. Co-editor: *French Literature and Thought since the Revolution* (1942). Prof. Romance languages, Dartmouth College.

GUTHRIE, WILLIAM NORMAN (Mar. 4, 1868–Dec. 9, 1944); b. Dundee, Scot. Episcopal clergyman, author. *Love Conquereth* (1890); *Modern Poet Prophets* (1897); *Songs of American Destiny* (1899); *The Old Hemlock, and Other Symbols* (poems, 1902); *Orpheus Today, Saint Francis of the Trees, and Other Verse* (1907); *The Vital Study of Literature* (1911).

GUTHRIE, WOODY [Woodrow Wilson] (July 14, 1912– Oct. 3, 1967); b. Okemah, Okla. Folk singer, ballad composer, author. *Bound for Glory* (1943). Composer-lyricist of numerous songs including *"Pastures of Plenty," "This Land Is Your Land," "Roll On, Columbia," "The Reuben James," "So Long, It's Been Good to Know You," "Tom Joad," "Hard Traveling," "This Train Is Bound for Glory."*

GUTWILLIG, ROBERT (1931?–). Editor, novelist. *After Long Silence* (1958); *Fugitives* (1959).

Guy Rivers. Novel by William Gilmore Simms (1834). The adventures of a border bandit in Georgia.

GWATHMEY, EDWARD MOSELEY (Oct. 13, 1891–June 7, 1956); b. Richmond, Va. Educator, author. *John Pendleton Kennedy* (1931). English dept., College of William and Mary, 1921–33; president, Converse College, Spartanburg, S.C., 1933–55.

GWATHMEY, JOHN H[astings] (Feb. 15, 1886–); b. Richmond, Va. Journalist, historical writer. *Legends of Virginia Courthouses* (1933); *Legends of Virginia Lawyers* (1934); *Justice John* (1934); *The Love Affairs of Captain John Smith* (1935); *Twelve Virginia Counties* (1937); etc.

Gypsy. Cincinnati, O. Quarterly. Poetry journal. Founded 1925. Discontinued 1937.

H

H. D. See Hilda Doolittle Aldington.

H. M. Pulham, Esq. Novel by J. P. Marquand (1941).

H. T. P. Pen name of Henry Taylor Parker.

HABBERTON, JOHN (Feb. 24, 1842–Feb. 24, 1921); b. Brooklyn, N.Y. Editor, author. *Helen's Babies* (1876); *Other People's Children* (1877); *Budge and Toddie* (1878); *The Worst Boy in Town* (1880); *The Chautauquans* (1891); *Caleb Wright* (1901); etc. Lit. and drama critic, the *New York Herald*, 1876–93.

HABERLEY, LOYD (Dec. 9, 1896–); b. Ellsworth, Ia. Educator, author. *Collected Poems* (1931); *Medieval English Paving-tiles* (1937); *Silent Fame* (1945); *Pursuit of the Hori-*

zon (1948); etc. Prof. English, Fairleigh Dickinson University, 1948–59; dean, arts and sciences, 1959–66.

HACK, ELIZABETH JANE MILLER (Aug. 17, 1878–Aug. 18, 1961); b. New Ross, Ind. Author. *The Yoke* (1904); *Saul of Tarsus* (1906); *The City of Delight* (1907); *Daybreak, a Story of the Age of Discovery* (1915); *The Science of Christopher Columbus* (1922).

HACKER, LOUIS MORTON (Mar. 17, 1899–); b. New York. Editor, author. *The United States Since 1865* (with Benjamin B. Kendrick, 1932); *The United States: A Graphic History* (1937); *American Problems of Today* (1938); *The Triumph of American Capitalism* (1940); *Shaping of the American Tradition* (1947); *Alexander Hamilton in the American Tradition* (1957); *Major Documents in American History*, 2v. (1961); *Larger View of the University* (1961); *The World of Andrew Carnegie, 1865–1901* (1968); etc. Prof. economics, Columbia University, 1948–67.

HACKETT, ALBERT (Feb. 16, 1900–); b. New York. Actor, author. Co-author of plays with Frances Goodrich (q.v.).

HACKETT, E[dmond] BYRNE (June 8, 1879–Nov. 10, 1953); b. Kilkenny, Ireland. Publisher. With Doubleday Page & Co., New York, 1901–07; Baker & Taylor Co., 1907–09; director, Yale University Press, from 1909. Founder, Brick Row Bookshop, New York.

HACKETT, FRANCIS (Jan. 21, 1883–Apr. 25, 1962); b. Kilkenny, Ireland. Critic. *Horizons: A Book of Criticism* (1918); *Henry the Eighth* (1929); *A Personal History* (1929); *Francis the First* (1934); *The Green Lion* (1936); *Queen Anne Boleyn* (1938); *I Chose Denmark* (1940); *What "Mein Kampf" Means to America* (1941); *The Senator's Last Night* (1943); *On Judging Books* (1947); etc. Assoc. editor, the *New Republic*, 1914–22; book editor, *The New York Times*, 1944–45.

HACKETT, JAMES HENRY (Mar. 15, 1800–Dec. 28, 1871); b. New York. Actor, author. *Notes and Comments Upon Certain Plays and Actors of Shakespeare* (1863).

"Hadad: A Dramatic Poem." By James Abraham Hillhouse (1825).

HADAS, MOSES (June 25, 1900–Aug. 17, 1966); b. Atlanta, Ga. Educator, translator, author. *A History of Greek Literature* (1950); *A History of Latin Literature* (1952); *Ancilla to Classical Reading* (1954); *Hellenistic Culture: Fusion and Diffusion* (1959); *Imperial Rome* (1965); *Living Tradition* (1967); etc. Editor: *Complete Works of Tacitus* (1942); *Basic Works of Cicero* (1951); *The Greek Poets* (1953); etc. Translator: Burckhardt's *The Age of Constantine the Great* (1949); Otto's *The Homeric Gods* (1954); *A History of Rome, as told by the Roman Historians* (1961). Prof. Greek, Columbia University, from 1953.

HADER, BERTA HOERNER (Mrs. Elmer Stanley Hader); b. San Pedro, Coahuila, Mex. Author (or co-author, with husband), of children's books. *Two Funny Clowns* (1929); *Farmer in the Dell* (1931); *Spunky* (1933); *Green and Gold* (1936); *Little Stone House* (1944); *Rainbow's End* (1945); *Little White Foot* (1952); *Wish on the Moon* (1954); *Ding Dong Bell* (1957); *Mr. Billy's Gun* (1960); *Snow in the City* (1963); *Two Is Company, Three's a Crowd* (1965); etc.

HADER, ELMER STANLEY (Sept. 7, 1889–); b. Pajaro, Calif. Author and illustrator of children's books. *See* Berta H. Hader.

HADLEY, ARTHUR TWINING (Apr. 23, 1856–Mar. 6, 1930); b. New Haven, Conn. Educator, political economist, author. *Railroad Transportation* (1885); *Some Influences in Modern Philosophic Thought* (1913); *The Moral Basis of Democracy* (1919); etc. President, Yale University, 1899–1921.

HADZSITS, GEORGE DEPUE (Jan. 30, 1875–June 9, 1954); b. Detroit, Mich. Educator, author. *Lucretius and His*

Influence (1935); etc. Editor-in-chief: *Our Debt to Greece and Rome* series. Classics dept., University of Pennsylvania, 1906–43.

HAENIGSEN, HARRY WILLIAM (July 14, 1900–); b. New York. Cartoonist, author. *Jive's Like That: Being the Life and Times of Our Bill* (1947); *Penny* (1953); *Penny's Party Book* (1954). Creator of comics "Our Bill" (1939) and "Penny" (1943), New York *Herald Tribune* syndicate.

HAFEN, LEROY R. (Dec. 8, 1893–); b. Bunkerville, Nev. Editor, historian. *The Overland Mail* (1926); *Colorado* (1933); *Fort Laramie* (with F. M. Young, 1938); *Western America* (with C. C. Rister, 1941); *The Colorado Story* (with Ann W. Hafen, 1953); *Relations with Plains Indians, 1857–61* (1959); *To the Rockies and Oregon 1839–42* (1960); *Mountain Men and Fur Trade of the Far West,* 7 v. (1965); etc. Editor: *History of Colorado,* 3v. (with J. H. Baker, 1927); *Life in the Far West* (1951); etc. Editor, *Colorado Magazine,* 1925–54.

HAGEDORN, HERMANN (July 18, 1882–July 27, 1964); b. New York. Novelist, poet, biographer. *The Woman of Corinth* (1908); *A Troop of the Guard, and Other Poems* (1909); *Poems and Ballads* (1912); *The Heart of Youth* (1915); *Ladders Through the Blue* (poems, 1925); *The Rough Riders* (1927); *The Book of Courage* (1929); *Leonard Wood* (1931); *Edwin Arlington Robinson (1938); This Darkness and This Light* (poems, 1938); *Americans—A Book of Lives* (1946); *Prophet in the Wilderness—the Story of Albert Schweitzer* (1947); *The Roosevelt Family of Sagamore Hill* (1954); *Hyphenated Family* (1960). Editor: *The Works of Theodore Roosevelt,* 20v. (1926). Co-founder, *The Vigilantes,* 1916.

HAGEN, OSKAR FRANK LEONARD (Oct. 14, 1888–Oct. 4, 1957; b. Wiesbaden, Germany. Educator, author. *Vincent Van Gogh* (1920); *Art Epochs and Their Leaders* (1927); *Patterns and Principles of Spanish Art* (1934); *The Birth of the American Tradition in Art* (1940); etc. Prof. history of art, University of Wisconsin, from 1924.

HAGER, ALICE ROGERS (1894–); Peoria, Ill. Author. *Brazil, Giant to the South* (1945); *Wings for the Dragon* (1945); *Janice, Air Line Hostess* (1948); *Dateline: Paris* (1954); *Wonderful Ice Cream Cart* (1955); *Washington Secretary* (1958); *Love's Golden Circle* (1962); *Cathy Whitney, President's Daughter* (1966); etc.

HAGGARD, HOWARD WILCOX (July 19, 1891–Apr. 22, 1959); b. La Porte, Ind. Physician, educator, author. *Are You Intelligent?* (1926); *Devils, Drugs and Doctors* (1929); *Mystery, Magic and Medicine* (1933); *The Doctor in History* (1934); *The Anatomy of Personality* (1935); *Man and His Body* (1938); *Alcohol Explored* (with E. M. Jellinek, 1942); etc. Dept. physiology, Yale University, from 1914.

Haggard, Paul. Pen name of Stephen Longstreet.

HAHN, EMILY (Jan. 14, 1905–); b. St. Louis, Mo. Author. *The Soong Sisters* (1941); *Hong Kong Holiday* (1946); *Raffles of Singapore* (1946); *Miss Jill* (1947); *England to Me* (1949); *Purple Passage* (1950); *Love Conquers Nothing* (1952); *Chiang Kai-shek* (1955); *Diamond* (1956); *The Tiger House Party* (1959); *China Only Yesterday* (1963); *Indo* (1964); *Animal Gardens* (1967); *Cooking of China* (1968); etc.

HAIGHT, GORDON S[herman] (Feb. 6, 1901–); b. Muskegon, Mich. Educator, biographer. *Mrs. Sigourney, the Sweet Singer of Hartford* (1930); *George Eliot and John Chapman* (1940); *George Eliot: A Biography* (1968). Editor: *George Eliot's Letters* (1954–55); etc. English dept., Yale University, since 1933.

"Hail, Columbia." Patriotic song, the words of which were written by Joseph Hopkinson, and published as *Song [Hail, Columbia!]* Adapted to the *President's March* (c.1793).

"Hail! Hail! the Gang's All Here." Popular song (1897). Words by D. A. Estrom, sung to an air from Gilbert and Sullivan's *The Pirates of Penzance.*

HAILEY, ARTHUR (Apr. 5, 1920–); b. Luton, Eng. Author. *The Final Diagnosis* (1959); *Close-Up on Writing for Television* (1960); *In High Places* (1962); *Hotel* (1965); *Airport* (1968); *The Final Diagnosis* (1969); *Wheels* (1971); etc.

HAILMANN, WILLIAM NICHOLAS (Oct. 20, 1836–May 13, 1920); b. Glarus, Switzerland. Educator, pioneer in kindergarten work in America, author. *Outlines of a System of Object-Teaching* (1867); *Kindergarten Culture in the Family and Kindergarten* (1873); *Letters to a Mother* (1876); *Kindergarten Guide,* 2v. (with Maria Kraus Boelté, 1877); *Early Education* (1878); etc. Founder, kindergarten school in Louisville, Ky., 1865.

HAILPERIN, HERMAN (Apr. 6, 1899–); b. Newark, N.J. Rabbi, author. *A Rabbi Teaches* (1939); *Nicolas De Lyra and Rashi* (1940); *Rashi and the Christian Scholars* (1963); etc. Editor: J. S. Raisin's *Gentile Reactions to Jewish Ideals* (1953). Columnist for *Jewish Criterion* and *American Jewish Outlook.*

HAINES, C[harles] **GROVE** (Dec. 10, 1906–); b. Abbottstown, Pa. Educator, author. *The Development of Western Civilization* (with W. B. Walsh, 1941); *The Origins and Background of the Second World War* (with R. J. S. Hoffman, 1943); *Role of the Supreme Court in American Government and Politics, 1789–1835* (1961); *The Revival of Natural Law Concepts* (1965); *Africa Today* (1968); etc. Prof. diplomatic history, School of Advanced International Studies, Johns Hopkins University, since 1945.

HAINES, JOHN (June 29, 1924–); b. Norfolk, Va. Poet. *Winter News* (1966).

HAINES, WILLIAM WISTER (Sept. 1908–); b. Des Moines, Ia. Novelist. *Slim* (1934); *High Tension* (1938); *Command Decision* (1947); *The Honorable Rocky Slade* (1957); *The Winter War* (1961); *Target* (1964); *The Image* (1968).

HAINS, THORNTON JENKINS (Nov. 14, 1866–deceased); b. Washington, D.C. Navigator, author. *Captain Gore's Courtship* (1896); *Mr. Trunnell: Mate of the Ship* (1900); *The Cruise of the Petrel* (1901); *The Black Barque* (1905); *Bahama Bill* (1908); *The Chief Mate's Yarns* (1912); etc.

HAIRSTON, WILLIAM. Playwright. *Walk in Darkness* (1962); *World of Carlos* (1967).

Hairy Ape, The. Play by Eugene O'Neill (prod. 1922). Realistic story of a stoker on a transatlantic liner whose beast-like appearance makes him a social outcast.

HALBERSTAM, DAVID (Apr. 10, 1934–); b. New York. Editor, author. *The Noblest Roman* (1961); *The Making of a Quagmire* (1965); *Ho* (1971). Contributing editor, *Harper's* magazine, 1967–71.

HALDEMAN, SAMUEL STEHMAN (Aug. 12, 1812–Sept. 10, 1880); b. Locust Grove, Pa. Educator, philologist, naturalist, author. *Rhymes of the Poets* (under pen name, "Felix Ago," 1868); *Pennsylvania Dutch* (1872); *Word-Building* (1881); etc. Prof. philology, University of Pennsylvania, 1868–80.

HALDEMAN-JULIUS, E[manuel] (July 30, 1889–July 31, 1951); b. Philadelphia, Pa. Publisher, author. *The Color of Life* (1920); *Dust* (with wife, Marcet Haldeman-Julius, 1921); *The Art of Reading* (1922); *Literary Essays* (1923); *An Agnostic Looks at Life* (1926); *The First Hundred Million* (1928); etc. Founded the "Little Blue Books," reprints, sometimes in abridged form, of well-known books, published at Girard, Kansas.

HALE, EDWARD EVERETT (Apr. 3, 1822–June 10, 1909); b. Boston, Mass. Unitarian clergyman, author. *Ten Times One Is Ten* (1870); *A New England Boyhood* (1893); *James Russell Lowell and His Friends* (1899); *Memories of a Hundred Years,* 2v. (1902). His best known short stories are: *The Man Without a Country,* first published in *The Atlantic Monthly* for Dec., 1863; and *My Double and How He Undid Me,* *Atlantic Monthly* (1859). See: *The Life and Letters of Edward Everett Hale,* 2v. edited by E. E. Hale, Jr. (1917).

HALE, EDWARD EVERETT (Feb. 18, 1863–Aug. 19, 1932); b. Boston, Mass., son of Edward Everett Hale. Educator, author. *James Russell Lowell* (1899); *William H. Seward* (1910); *Dramatists of To-Day* (1911); etc. Editor: *Ballads and Ballad Poetry* (1902); *Life and Letters of Edward Everett Hale* (1917).

Hale, Garth. Pen name of Albert Benjamin Cunningham.

HALE, LOUISE CLOSSER (Oct. 13, 1872–July 26, 1933); b. Chicago, Ill. Actress, author. *A Motor Car Divorce* (1906); *The Actress* (1909); *The Married Miss Worth* (1911); *We Discover New England* (1915); *We Discover the Old Dominion* (1916); *Home Talent* (1926).

HALE, LUCRETIA P[eabody] (Sept. 2, 1820–June 12, 1900); b. Boston, Mass. Author. *The Peterkin Papers* (1880); *The Last of the Peterkins* (1886); etc. In these two books she created the character "The Lady from Philadelphia." See *Letters of Susan Hale* (1919).

HALE, MARIE LOUISE GIBSON (Mrs. Morgan Goetchius; Mrs. Edmond Van Saanen Algi; Mrs. Gardner Hale) (Nov. 24, 1886–); b. New York City. Novelist. Pen names, "Marice Rutledge," "Maryse Rutledge." *Anne of Tréboul* (1910); *The Blind Who See* (1911); *Wild Grapes* (1913); *Children of Fate* (1917); *The Sad Adventurers* (1924); *The Silver Peril* (1931); etc.

HALE, NANCY (Mrs. Fredson Thayer Bowers) (May 6, 1908–); b. Boston, Mass., granddaughter of Edward Everett Hale. Novelist. *The Young Die Good* (1932); *Never Any More Joy* (1934); *The Earliest Dreams* (1936); *The Prodigal Woman* (1942); *Between the Dark and the Daylight* (1943); *The Sign of Jonah* (1950); *The Empress's Ring* (1955); *Heaven and Hardpan Farm* (1957); *New England Girlhood* (autobiography, 1958); *Dear Beast* (1959); *Pattern of Perfection* (1960); *The Realities of Fiction* (1962); *Black Summer* (1963); *The Life in the Studio* (1969).

HALE, NATHAN (Aug. 16, 1784–Feb. 8, 1863); b. Westhampton, Mass. Journalist, author. *The Wars of the Gulls* (with Jacob Bigelow, anon., 1812); *An Epitome of Universal Geography* (1830). Purchased the *Boston Daily Advertiser* in 1814 and edited it until 1854. One of the founders of the *North American Review* and the *Christian Examiner.* Publisher and editor, the *Monthly Chronicle,* 1840–46.

HALE, RALPH TRACY (Dec. 29, 1880–Sept., 1951); b. Newburyport, Mass. Publisher, editor, author. *The Last Voyage of the Karluk* (with Robert A. Bartlett, 1916). Editor, Bobbs-Merrill Co., 1904–07; Small Maynard Co., 1907–20; Medici Society of America, 1920–29; president, Hale, Cushman & Flint, publishers, Boston, 1927–42, Ralph T. Hale & Co., 1942–47; president, Boston Authors' Club.

HALE, SARAH JOSEPHA BUELL (Oct. 24, 1788–Apr. 30, 1879); b. Newport, N.H. Editor, author. *The Genius of Oblivion* (1823); *Northwood: A Tale of New England* (1827); *Sketches of American Character* (1829); *Poems for Our Children* (1830); *Traits of American Life* (1835); etc. Editor, the *Juvenile Miscellany,* 1826–28; the *Ladies' Magazine* (Boston), 1828–37; co-editor, *Godey's Lady's Book,* 1837–77. Her best known poem is "Mary Had a Little Lamb," which appeared in the *Juvenile Miscellany,* Sept., 1830, and in her *Poems for Our Children* (1830). See Ruth E. Finley's *The Lady of Godey's: Sarah Josepha Hale* (1931).

HALE, WILLIAM HARLAN (July 21, 1910–); b. New York. Editor, author. *Challenge to Defeat* (1932); *Hannibal Hooker* (1939); *The March of Freedom* (1947); *Horace Greeley, Voice of the People* (1950); *Innocence Abroad* (1957); *The Horizon Book of Ancient Greece* (1965); *The Horizon History of Eating and Drinking Through the Ages* (1968); etc.

Founder (with Selden Rodman), the *Harkness Hoot,* 1930; co-editor, 1930–31; managing editor, *Horizon,* 1958–61; editor, 1961–63; editor, Horizon Books, 1963–67; senior writer, 1967–68.

HALECKI, OSCAR (May 26, 1891–); b. Vienna. Educator, author. *Limits and Divisions of European History* (1950); *Borderlands of Western Civilization* (1952); *History of Poland* (1956); *From Florence to Brest, 1439–1596* (1959); and other books published in Europe. Prof. history, Fordham University, since 1944.

HALEY, J[ames] Evetts (July 5, 1901–); b. Belton, Texas. Author. *The XIT Ranch of Texas and the Early Days of the Llano Estacado* (1929); *Charles Goodnight: Cowman and Plainsman* (1936). Editor: *A Log of the Texas-California Cattle Trail* (1932); *Jeff Milton, a Good Man with a Gun* (1948); *Life on the Texas Range* (1952); *A Texan Looks at Lyndon* (1964).

HALEY, MOLLY [Whitford] ANDERSON (Mrs. Frank LeRoy Haley) (Jan. 19, 1888–); b. Waterford, N.Y. Poet. *Heritage, and Other Poems* (1925); *Gardens and You* (1925); *The Window Cleaner, and Other Poems* (1930).

Half-Dime Library. New York. Fiction weekly published by Beadle, 1877–98.

HALL, A[braham] OAKEY (July 26, 1826–Oct. 7, 1898); b. Albany, N.Y. Lawyer, journalist, author. *The Manhattaner in New Orleans* (1851); *Sketches of Travel* (1859); *The Crucible* (prod. 1878); *Ballads of Hans York* (1880); etc. Mayor of New York City 1868–72.

HALL, AMANDA BENJAMIN (Mrs. John Angell Brownell) (July 12, 1890–); b. Hallville, O. Novelist, poet. *The Little Red House in the Hollow* (1918); *Blind Wisdom* (1920); *The Heart's Justice* (1922); *The Dancer in the Shrine, and Other Poems* (1923); *Afternoons in Eden* (poems, 1932); *Cinnamon Saint* (poem, 1937); *Honey Out of Heaven* (poems, 1938); *Unweave a Rainbow* (poems, 1942); *The Frosty Harp* (poems, 1954); *The View from the Heart* (poems, 1964).

HALL, ANSEL FRANKLIN (May 6, 1894–Mar. 28, 1962); b. Oakland, Calif. Naturalist, national park official. *Guide to Yosemite* (1920); *Handbook of Yosemite National Park* (1921); *Guide to Yosemite Valley* (1929); *Guide to Mesa Verde National Park* (1937); *Mesa Verde (1952);* etc.

HALL, ARETHUSA (Oct. 13, 1802–May 24, 1891); b. Norwich (now Huntington), Mass. Author. *The Literary Reader* (1858); *Life and Character of the Rev. Sylvester Judd* (1854); *Memorabilia of Sylvester Judd, Sr.* (1882); *Arethusa Hall: A Memorial* (autobiography, 1892).

HALL, BAYNARD RUSH (Jan. 28, 1798–Jan. 23, 1863); b. Philadelphia, Pa. Presbyterian clergyman, educator, novelist. Pen name, "Robert Carlton." *The New Purchase* (1843); *Something for Everybody* (1846); *Frank Freeman's Barber Shop* (1852); etc.

HALL, CALVIN SPRINGER, JR. (Jan. 18, 1909–); b. Seattle, Wash. Educator. *The Meaning of Dreams* (1953); *A Primer of Freudian Psychology* (1954); *Psychology* (1960); etc. Co-author: *Theories of Personality* (1957). Prof. psychology, Western Reserve University, 1937–57; Syracuse University, since 1957.

HALL, CHARLES FRANCIS (1821–Nov. 8, 1871); b. Rochester, N.H. Arctic explorer, author. *Arctic Researches and Life among the Esquimaux* (1865).

HALL, CLARENCE W[ilbur] (Dec. 16. 1902–); b. Anna Maria, Fla. Editor, author. *Out of the Depths* (1930); *Samuel Logan Brengle, Portrait of a Prophet* (1933); *Protestant Panorama* (with Desider Holisher, 1951); *Adventurers for God* (1959). Editor-in-chief, Salvation Army publications, 1935–39; founder, *The Link* and *The Chaplain,* 1942; editor, 1942–45; with *Christian Herald,* 1946–56; senior editor,

Reader's Digest, since 1956; editorial director, *Lifetime Living*.

HALL, COLBY DIXON (Dec. 29, 1875–); b. Madisonville, Ky. Disciples of Christ clergyman, educator, author. *History of Texas Christian University* (1947); *Texas Disciples* (1953); *The Gay Nineties* (1961); etc. With Brite College of the Bible, 1914–47.

HALL, DONALD (Sept. 20, 1928–); b. New Haven, Conn. Author. *Exiles and Marriages* (poems, 1955); *Dark Houses* (poems, 1958); *Andrew the Lion Farmer* (1959); *String Too Short to Be Saved* (autobiography, 1961); *The Alligator Bride: Poems New and Selected* (1969); etc. Editor: *New Poets of England and America* (with others, 1957); *Contemporary American Poetry* (1962); *A Poetry Sampler* (1962); *Poetry in English* (1963); *Henry Moore* (1966); *The Modern Stylists* (1968); *Man and Boy: An Anthology* (1968); *American Poetry* (1969); etc.

HALL, EDWARD TWITCHELL (May 16, 1914–); b. Webster Groves, Mo. Anthropologist, author. *Early Stockaded Settlements in Governador, New Mexico* (1942); *The Silent Language* (1959); *The Hidden Dimension* (1966). Prof. anthropology, Northwestern University, since 1967.

HALL, EVERETT WESLEY (Apr. 4, 1901–June 17, 1960); b. Janesville, Wis. Educator. *What Is Value?* (1952); *Modern Science and Human Values* (1956); *Categorical Analysis* (1964). Prof. philosophy, State University of Iowa, 1941–52; University of North Carolina, since 1952.

HALL, FITZEDWARD (Mar. 21, 1825–Feb. 1, 1901); b. Troy, N.Y. Sanskrit scholar, philologist, author. *Benares, Ancient and Medieval* (1868); *Recent Exemplifications of Falsu Philology* (1872); *Modern English* (1873); etc. He edited numerous Sanskrit texts, including *The Vishñu Duráná*.

HALL, FLORENCE MARION HOWE (Aug. 25, 1845–Apr. 10, 1922); b. Boston, Mass. Biographer, lecturer. *Laura Bridgman* (with sister, Maud Howe Elliott, 1902); *Julia Ward Howe, 1819–1910,* 2v. (with Laura Elizabeth Richards and Maud Howe Elliott, 1915, Pulitzer Prize for American biography, 1917); *Memories Grave and Gay* (autobiography, 1918); also numerous books on etiquette.

Hall, Gertrude. See Gertrude Hall Brownell.

Hall, Holworthy. Pen name of Harold Everett Porter.

HALL, HOWARD JUDSON (Feb. 6, 1869–Dec. 14, 1942); b. Lansingburgh, N.Y. Educator. Editor: *Three Centuries of American Poetry and Prose* (with Alphonso Gerald Newcomer and Alice E. Andrews, 1917); *Types of Poetry* (1927); *Twelve Centuries of English Poetry and Prose* (with Alphonso G. Newcomer and Alice E. Andrews, 1929). English dept., Stanford University, 1905–35.

HALL, JAMES (Aug. 19, 1793–July 5, 1868); b. Philadelphia, Pa. Jurist, banker, editor, historian, poet. *Letters from the West* (1828); *Winter Evenings* (anon., 1829); *Legends of the West* (1832); *The Harpe's Head* (1833); *The Soldier's Bride, and Other Tales* (1833); *Tales of the Border* (1835); *Sketches of History, Life, and Manners in the West,* 2v. (1834–35); *The Wilderness and the War Path* (1836); etc. Founder, the *Illinois Monthly Magazine*, 1830; editor, 1830–32; the *Western Monthly Magazine*, 1832–36. See *The Colophon*, 1936. *See* Ralph L. Rusk's *Literature of the Middle Western Frontier,* 2v. (1925).

HALL, JAMES NORMAN (Apr. 22, 1887–July 5, 1951); b. Colfax, Ia. Author. *Kitchener's Mob* (1916); *High Adventure* (1918); *Mid-Pacific* (1928); *Flying with Chaucer* (1930); *The Friends* (poem, 1934); *The Tale of a Shipwreck* (1935); *Lost Island* (1944); *A Word for His Sponsor* (poem, 1949); *The Far Lands* (1950); *My Island Home* (autobiography, 1952). Co-author, with Charles Bernard Nordhoff: *Falcons of France* (1929); *Mutiny on the Bounty* (1933); *Men Against the Sea*

(1934); *Pitcairn's Island* (1934); *The Hurricane* (1936); *The Dark River* (1938); *Botany Bay* (1941); *Men without Country* (1942); *The High Barbaree* (1945).

Hall, Jarvis. Pen name of Helen F. Bagg.

HALL, JEROME (Feb. 4, 1901–); b. Chicago, Ill. Educator, author. *Readings in Jurisprudence* (1938); *General Principles of Criminal Law* (1947); *Living Law of Democratic Society* (1949); *Studies in Jurisprudence and Criminal Theory* (1958); *Comparative Law and Social Theory* (1963); etc. Prof. law, Indiana University, since 1939.

HALL, JOHN ELIHU (Dec. 27, 1783–June 12, 1829); b. Philadelphia, Pa. Lawyer, editor, author. *Memoirs of Eminent Persons* (1827). Compiler: *The Philadelphia Souvenir: A Collection of Fugitive Pieces from the Philadelphia Press* (1826). Founder and publisher, the *American Law Journal,* Baltimore, 1808–17; editor, the *Port Folio,* 1816–27.

HALL, JOSEF WASHINGTON (Feb. 27, 1894–Nov. 13, 1960); b. Kelso, Wash. Lecturer, author. Pen name, "Upton Close." Author: *In the Land of the Laughing Buddha* (1924); *The Revolt of Asia* (1927); *Moonlight* (1927); *Challenge: Behind the Face of Japan* (1934); *Son of Mine* (1936); *Workbook in World History* (1948); etc. Co-author: *Ladder of History* (with Merle Burke, 1945).

HALL, LELAND (July 20, 1883–Feb. 8, 1957); b. Malden, Mass. Educator, author. *Sinister House* (1919); *Timbuctoo* (1927); *Salah and His American* (1934); *They Seldom Speak* (1936); *Listeners' Music* (1937). Prof. music, Smith College, 1930–52.

HALL, ROBERT ANDERSON, Jr. (Apr. 4, 1911–); b. Raleigh, N.C. Educator, author. *Bibliography of Italian Linguistics* (1941); *Melanesian Pidgin English* (1943); *Hungarian Grammar* (1944); *Leave Your Language Alone!* (1950); *Haitian Creole* (with others, 1953); *Hands Off Pidgin English* (1955); *Italian for Modern Living* (1959); *Italian Stories* (1961); *Cultural Symbolism in Literature* (1963); *Introductory Linguistics* (1964); *New Ways to Learn a Foreign Language* (1965); *Pidqin and Creole Languages* (1966); etc. Prof. linguistics, Cornell University, since 1950.

HALL, ROBERT KING (Mar. 13, 1912–); b. Kewanee, Ill. Educator, author. *Kokutai No Hongi* (ed., 1949); *Education for a New Japan* (1949); *Shūshin: the Ethics of a Defeated Nation* (1949); *A Strategy for the Inner City* (1963).

HALL, RUTH (b. Apr. 10, 1858); b. Schoharie, N.Y. Novelist. *In the Brave Days of Old* (1898); *The Boys of Scrooby* (1899); *The Black Gown* (1900); *The Pine Grove House* (1903); etc.

HALL, SAMUEL (Nov. 2, 1740–Oct. 30, 1809); b. Medford, Mass. Printer, publisher, pamphleteer. Partner of Ann Franklin in 1762, and assisted her in publishing the *Newport Mercury.* Founder, the *Essex Gazette,* Salem, Mass., Aug. 2, 1768; the *New England Chronicle or Essex Gazette,* Cambridge, Mass., May, 1775, which he moved to Boston in 1776; the *Massachusetts Gazette,* Boston, Nov. 28, 1785.

HALL, SAMUEL S. Dime novelist. Pen name, "Buckskin Sam." *Kit Carson, Jr.* (1878); *Arizona Jack* (1882); *The Brazos Tigers* (1882); *Diamond Dick, the Dandy from Denver* (1882); *Desperate Duke* (1883); *The Bayou Bravo* (1883); *Rocky Mountain Al* (1883); *Snap-Shot Sam* (1890); etc. The dates are not necessarily those of first editions.

HALL, SARAH EWING (Oct. 30, 1761–Apr. 8, 1830); b. Philadelphia, Pa. Essayist. *Conversations on the Bible* (1818); *Selections from the Writings of Mrs. Sarah Hall* (1833). Wrote for the *Port Folio* under pen names, "Constantia" and "Florepha."

HALL, VERNON, Jr. (Nov. 30, 1913–); b. Atlanta, Ga. Educator, author. *Renaissance Literary Criticism* (1945); *Life of Julius Caesar Scaliger* (1950); *Byzantine Gold Coins in the*

Dartmouth Collection (with J. B. Stearns, 1952); *Literary Criticism: Plato through Johnson* (1969); etc. Foreign Language editor, *explicator,* since 1948. Prof. comparative literature, Dartmouth College, 1950–64; University of Wisconsin, since 1964.

HALL, WALTER PHELPS (May 5, 1884–); b. Newburgh, N.Y. Educator, author. *Empire to Commonwealth* (1928); *Mr. Gladstone* (1931); *History of England and the British Empire* (with R. G. Albion, 1937); *Iron Out of Calvary* (1946); *Europe in the Twentieth Century* (1957); etc. History dept., Princeton University, since 1913.

Hall of Fame. Erected on the campus of New York University. Founded 1900, by Henry Mitchell MacCracken. Famous Americans, chosen every five years by a board of electors, are commemorated in the Hall of Fame by tablets and busts. Among the literary men and women so honored are: Ralph Waldo Emerson, Henry Wadsworth Longfellow, Washington Irving, Harriet Beecher Stowe, Nathaniel Hawthorne, James Russell Lowell, John Greenleaf Whittier, William Cullen Bryant, John Lothrop Motley, Oliver Wendell Holmes, James Fenimore Cooper, Edgar Allan Poe, Francis Parkman, Mark Twain and Walt Whitman. Robert Underwood Johnson was director, 1919–37, and was succeeded by John H. Finley, who was succeeded by William Lyon Phelps. *See* H. M. MacCracken's *The Hall of Fame* (1901); R. U. Johnson's *Your Hall of Fame* (1935). See also *World Almanac* for full list of names included in the Hall of Fame.

HALL-QUEST, ALFRED LAWRENCE; b. New York. Educator, author. *The Textbook, How to Use and Judge It* (1917); *The University Afield* (1926); *It's Not Our Fault* (1929); *Teaching Through the Elementary School Library* (with M. K. Walraven, 1948); etc. Editor: Supervised Study Series, since 1917. Prof. education, New York University, since 1932.

HALLE, LOUIS JOSEPH, Jr. (Nov. 17, 1910–); b. New York City. Author. *Transcaribbean* (1936); *Birds Against Men* (1938); *River of Rains* (1941); *Spring in Washington* (1947); *On Facing the World* (1950); *Civilization and Foreign Policy* (1955); *Choice for Survival* (1958); *Dream and Reality* (1959); *The Society of Man* (1965); *The Cold War as History* (1967).

HALLECK, FITZ-GREENE (July 8, 1790–Nov. 19, 1867); b. Guilford, Conn. Poet. *Fanny* (1819); *Alnwick Castle, with Other Poems* (1827); *The Poetical Works* (1847). His best-known poems are "On the Death of Joseph Rodman Drake," and "Marco Bozzaris." *See* Joseph Rodman Drake; and *The Croaker Papers.* See also *The Life and Letters of Fitz-Greene Halleck* (1869), and *The Poetical Writings of Fitz-Greene Halleck* (1869), both ed. by James G. Wilson; and Nelson F. Adkins's *Fitz-Greene Halleck* (1930).

HALLECK, REUBEN POST (Feb. 8, 1859–Dec. 24, 1936); b. Rocky Point, L.I., N.Y. Lecturer, author. *History of English Literature* (1900); *History of American Literature* (1911); *New English Literature* (1913); *The Romance of American Literature* (1934); etc.

HALLET, RICHARD MATTHEWS (July 21, 1887–Sept. 14, 1967); b. Bath, Me. Author. *The Lady Aft* (1915); *Trial by Fire* (1916); *The Rolling World* (1938); *Foothold of Earth* (1944).

HALLETT, GEORGE HERVEY, Jr. (May 24, 1895–); b. Philadelphia, Pa. Editor, author. *Proportional Representation* (with C. G. Hoag, 1926); *Proportional Representation–The Key to Democracy* (1937). Editor: Proportional representation dept. of the *National Municipal Review,* 1932–53; legislative representation dept., since 1967.

HALLGREN, MAURITZ ALFRED (June 18, 1899–Nov. 10, 1956); b. Chicago, Ill. Editor, author. *Seeds of Revolt* (1933); *The Gay Reformer* (1935); *The Tragic Fallacy* (1937); *Landscape of freedom* (1941). Assoc. editor, *The Nation,* 1930–34; the *Baltimore Sun,* 1934–38.

HALLIBURTON, RICHARD (Jan. 9, 1900–Mar. 21/22, 1939); b. Brownsville, Tenn. Lost at sea. Author. *The Royal Road to Romance* (1925); *The Glorious Adventure* (1927); *New Worlds to Conquer* (1929); *The Flying Carpet* (1932); *Seven League Boots* (1935); *A Book of Marvels* (1937); *Second Book of Marvels* (1938). See *Richard Halliburton: His Story of His Life's Adventures* (1940).

Halliday, Brett. Pen name of Davis Dresser.

HALLOCK, CHARLES (May 13, 1834–Dec. 2, 1917); b. New York City. Editor, author. *The Recluse of the Oconee* (1854); *The Fishing Tourist* (1873); *Vacation Rambles in Northern Michigan* (1877); *Peerless Alaska* (1908). Compiler: *American Club List and Sportsman's Glossary* (1878). Founder, *Forest and Stream,* 1873.

Hallowell, Mrs. Robert. See Charlotte Rudyard.

HALPER, ALBERT (Aug. 3, 1904–); b. Chicago, Ill. Novelist. *Union Square* (1933); *On the Shore* (1934); *The Foundry* (1934); *The Chute* (1937); *Sons of the Fathers* (1940); *The Little People* (1942); *Only an Inch from Glory* (1943); *The Golden Watch* (1953); *Atlantic Avenue* (1956); *The Fourth Horseman of Miami Beach* (1966); etc. Editor: *This Is Chicago* (1952); *Chicago Crime Book* (1968).

HALPERN, MARTIN (Oct. 3, 1929–); b. New York. Educator, author. *Two Sides of an Island and Other Poems* (1963); *William Vaughn Moody* (1964). Assoc. prof. theater arts, Brandeis University, since 1966.

HALPINE, CHARLES GRAHAM (Nov. 20, 1829–Aug. 3, 1868); b. Oldcastle, Co. Meath, Ireland. Journalist, poet. *Lyrics by the Letter H* (1854); *The Life and Adventures, Songs, Services, and Speeches of Private Miles O'Reilly* (1864); *Baked Meats of the Funeral* (1866); *The Poetical Works* (1869). Private secretary to P. T. Barnum. Co-editor, with B. P. Shillaber, of the *Carpet-Bag,* Boston, 1852.

HALSEY, FORREST (Nov. 9, 1878–); b. Roseville, N.J. Novelist, playwright. *Fate and the Butterfly* (1909); *The Stain* (1910); *The Question* (1911); *The Bawlerout* (1912); *A Term of Silence* (1913); *The Shadow on the Hearth* (1914); *His Chinese Wife* (with Clara Branger, prod. 1920); etc.

HALSEY, FRANCIS WHITING (Oct. 15, 1851–Nov. 24, 1919); b. Unadilla, N.Y. Editor, author. *Two Months Abroad* (1878); *The Old New York Frontier* (1901); *Our Literary Deluge* (1902); etc. Editor: *American Authors and Their Homes* (1901); etc. With the *New York Tribune,* 1875–80; the *New York Times,* 1880–1902; D. Appleton & Co., 1902–05; Funk & Wagnalls Co., 1905–19.

HALSEY, FRANK D[avis] (Mar. 1, 1890–Apr. 8, 1941); b. Elizabeth, N.J. Editor, author. *The Last Mile* with Coleman McAlister, under joint pen name "Frank A. McAlister," (1922). Editor: *Goal Lines: An Anthology of Princeton Verse* (with A. C. M. Azoy, 1922). Asst. director, Princeton University Press, 1922–41.

HALSEY, MARGARET [Frances] (Feb. 13, 1910–); b. Yonkers, N.Y. Author. *With Malice Towards Some* (1938); *Some of My Best Friends Are Soldiers* (1944); *Color Blind* (1946); *Folks at Home* (1952); *This Demi-Paradise: A Westchester Diary* (1960); *Corrupted Giant* (1963).

HALSMAN, PHILIPPE (May 2, 1906–); b. Riga, Latvia. Photographer, author. *The Frenchman: A Photographic Interview* (1949); *Piccoli* (1953); *Dali's Moustache* (with S. Dali, 1954); *Jump Book* (1959); *Halsman on the Creation of Photographic Ideas* (1961).

HALSTEAD, MURAT (Sept. 2, 1829–July 2, 1908); b. in Butler Co., O. Editor, author. *Caucuses of 1860* (1860); *Our Country in War and Relations with All Nations* (1898); *The World on Fire* (1902); etc. With the *Cincinnati Commercial* from 1853; became owner in 1865; became editor-in-chief of the *Cincinnati Commercial-Gazette* upon the 1881 merger of the two papers.

"Halyard, Harry." Real name unknown. Novelist. *The Heroine of Tampico* (1847); *The Chieftain of Churubusco* (1848); *The Doom of the Dolphin* (1848); *The Haunted Bride* (1848); *The Mexican Spy* (1848); *The Ocean Monarch* (1848); *The Rover of the Reef* (1848); *The Spectre of the Woods* (1848); *Wharton the Whale-Killer* (1848); etc.

HAMBERLIN, LAFAYETTE RUPERT (Feb. 25, 1861–Apr. 24, 1902); b. Clinton, Miss. Educator, poet. *Lyrics* (1880); *Seven Songs* (1887); *Alumni Lilts, and Other Lines* (1892); *A Batch of Rhymes* (1893); *In Colorado* (1895); *Rhymes of the War* (1899). English dept., Vanderbilt University, 1900–02.

HAMBIDGE, GOVE (Nov. 17, 1890–); b. Kansas City, Mo. International official, author. *Time to Live* (1933); *Your Meals and Your Money* (1934); *Enchanted Acre* (1935); *Six Rooms Make a World* (1938); *New Aims in Education* (1940); *Prime of Life* (1942); *The Story of FAO* (1955); *Dynamics of Development* (1964). Editor, *International Development Review,* since 1958.

HAMBLEN, EDWIN CROWELL (Aug. 23, 1900–Nov. 24, 1963); b. Greenville, Miss. Gynecologist, endocrinologist, author. *Endocrine Gynecology* (1939); *Facts for Childless Couples* (1942); *Endocrinology of Woman* (1945); *Facts About the Change of Life* (1949); etc.

HAMBLEN, HERBERT ELLIOTT (b. Dec. 24, 1849); b. Ossippe, N.H. Engineer, author. *On Many Seas* (under pen name, "Frederick Benton Williams," 1897); *Tom Benton's Luck* (1898); *The General Manager's Story* (1898); *The Story of a Yankee Boy* (1898); *The Yarn of a Bucko Mate* (1899); *The Red Shirts* (1902); etc.

HAMBURGER, PHILIP [Paul] (July 2, 1914–); b. Wheeling, W.Va. Author. *The Oblong Blur, and Other Odysseys* (1949); *J. P. Marquand, Esquire* (1952); *Mayor Watching and Other Pleasures* (1958); *Our Man Stanley* (1963); *An American Notebook* (1965). Staff member, *New Yorker,* since 1939.

HAMELE, OTTAMAR (Apr. 19, 1878–Feb. 12, 1964); b. E. Otto, New York. Lawyer, author. *Federal Reclamation Laws Annotated* (1920); *When Destiny Called* (1948); *Your Desire to Feel Important* (1955).

HAMER, PHILIP MAY (Nov. 7, 1891–); b. Marion, S.C. Historian. *The Secession Movement in South Carolina, 1847–52* (1918); *Tennessee: A History* (1933). Editor: *Guide to Archives and Manuscripts in the United States* (1961); *The Papers of Henry Laurens, Vol. 1, 1746–1755* (with others, 1968). With the National Archives, 1935–51; executive director, National Historical Publications Commission, 1951–61.

HAMILTON, ALEXANDER (Jan. 11, 1757–July 12, 1804); b. in Nevis, B.W.I. Revolutionary officer, statesman, author. *The Federalist,* 2v. (with James Madison and John Jay, 1788); *The Works,* ed. by his son, John C. Hamilton, 7v. (1850–51); *The Works,* ed. by Henry Cabot Lodge, 9v. (1885–88), augmented, 12v. (1904); *The Papers,* ed. by Harold C. Syrett, 2v. (1961). Secretary of the Treasury, 1789–95. His papers are in the Library of Congress. *See* John C. Hamilton's *The Life of Alexander Hamilton,* 2v. (1834–40); Henry C. Lodge's *Alexander Hamilton* (1882); Henry J. Ford's *Alexander Hamilton* (1920); Claude G. Bower's *Jefferson and Hamilton* (1925); Gertrude Atherton's *The Conqueror* (1902); Broadus Mitchell's *Alexander Hamilton,* 2v. (1962); Jacob E. Cooke's *Alexander Hamilton: A Profile* (1967).

Hamilton, Betsy. Pen name of Idora McClellan Moore.

HAMILTON, CHARLES VERNON (Oct. 19, 1929–); b. Muskogee, Okla. Educator, author. *Minority Politics in Black Belt Alabama* (1962); *Black Power: The Politics of Liberation in America* (with Stokely Carmichael, 1967). Prof. political science, Roosevelt University, since 1967.

HAMILTON, CLAYTON [Meeker] (Nov. 14, 1881–Sept. 17, 1946); b. Brooklyn, N.Y. Drama critic, playwright. *The Love That Blinds* (with Grace Isabel Colbron, prod. 1906); *Materials and Methods of Fiction* (1908); *The Stranger at the Inn* (prod. 1913); *Studies in Stagecraft* (1914); *The Big Idea* (with A. E. Thomas, prod. 1914); *The Better Understanding* (with Albert E. Thomas, prod. 1917); *Thirty Days* (with A. E. Thomas, prod. 1919); *Seen on the Stage* (1920); *Friend Indeed* (with Bernard Voigt, prod. 1926); etc. Drama editor, *The Forum,* 1907–09; *The Bookman,* 1910–18; *Vogue,* 1912–20.

HAMILTON, DONALD (1916–). Author. *Date with Darkness* (1947); *Steel Mirror* (1948); *Murder Twice Told* (1950); *The Menacers* (1967); *The Ravagers* (1969); etc.

HAMILTON, EDITH (Aug. 12, 1867–May 31, 1963); b. Dresden, Ger. Author. *The Greek Way* (1930); *The Roman Way* (1932); *The Prophets of Israel* (1936); *Mythology* (1942); *Witness to the Truth* (1948); *Spokesmen for God* (1949); *Introduction to Plutarch, Selected Lives and Essays* (1951); *The Echo of Greece* (1957). Editor: *Three Greek Plays (The Trojan Women, Prometheus, Agamemnon)* (1937).

HAMILTON, EDMOND (Oct. 21, 1904–); b. Youngstown, O. Author. *The Horror on the Asteroid* (1936); *The Star Kings* (1949); *City at World's End* (1951); *The Star of Life* (1959); *The Haunted Stars* (1960); *Battle for the Stars* (1961); *Outside the Universe* (1964); *Fugitive of the Stars* (1965).

Hamilton, Gail. Pen name of Mary Abigail Dodge.

HAMILTON, JAMES ALEXANDER (Apr. 14, 1788–Sept. 24, 1878); b. New York City, son of Alexander Hamilton. Lawyer, author. *Reminiscences* (1869); etc.

HAMILTON, JOHN CHURCH (Aug. 22, 1792–July 25, 1882); b. Philadelphia, Pa., son of Alexander Hamilton. Biographer, editor. *The Life of Alexander Hamilton,* 2v. (1834–40). Editor: *The Works of Alexander Hamilton,* 7v. (1850–51).

HAMILTON, J[ohn] TAYLOR (b. Aug. 30, 1859); b. in Antigua, B.W.I. Moravian bishop, educator, historian of the Moravians. *History of the Moravian Church in the United States* (1895); *A History of the Moravian Church during the Eighteenth and Nineteenth Centuries* (1900); *The Contacts of the Moravian Church with the Iroquois League* (1931); etc. Prof., Moravian College and Theological Seminary, Bethlehem, Pa., 1886–1903; president, 1918–28.

HAMILTON, J[oseph] G[régoire] DE ROULHAC (Aug. 6, 1878–); b. Hillsboro, N.C. Educator, historian. *Reconstruction in North Carolina* (1914); *Party Politics in North Carolina, 1835–1860* (1916); *North Carolina Since 1860* (1919); etc. Editor: *The Papers of Jonathan Worth,* 2v. (1909); *The Papers of Thomas Ruffin,* 4v. (1918–21); etc. Prof. history, University of North Carolina, since 1906.

HAMILTON, KATE W[aterman] (b. 1841); b. Schenectady, N.Y. Novelist. *Chinks of Crannyford* (1872); *We Three* (1877); *Rachel's Share of the Road* (1882); *Wood, Hay and Stubble* (1886); *The Hand with the Keys* (1890); *The Parson's Proxy* (1896); *The Kinkaid Venture* (1900); etc.

Hamilton, Rufus. See Rufus Hamilton Gillmore.

HAMILTON, WILLIAM JOHN, Jr. (Dec. 11, 1902–); b. Corona, N.Y. Zoologist. *Conservation in the United States* (with others, 1939); *American Mammals* (1939); *Mammals of the Eastern United States* (1943). Zoology dept., Cornell University, since 1930.

HAMILTON, WILLIAM WISTAR (Dec. 9, 1868–Nov. 19, 1960); b. near Hopkinsville, Ky. Baptist clergyman, author. *Helping Hand* (1908); *Worldly Amusements* (1909); *Bible Evangelism* (1919); *Fine Art of Soul-Winning* (1935); etc.

"Hamiltoniad." Bitter anti-federalist poem by John Williams (1761–1818), published in Boston, 1804, under the pen name of "Anthony Pasquin."

Hamlet of A. MacLeish, The. Long poem by Archibald MacLeish (1928). A modern version of the Hamlet story.

HAMLIN, ALFRED DWIGHT FOSTER (Sept. 5, 1855–Mar. 21, 1926); b. Constantinople, Turkey, of American parentage. Architect, educator, author. *A Text-Book of the History of Architecture* (1896); *A History of Ornament,* 2v. (1916, 1923). Architecture dept., Columbia University, 1887–1926; prof. history of architecture, 1904–26.

HAMLIN, JOHN H. (Jan. 16, 1880–June 13, 1951); b. Verdi, Nev. Author of western juveniles. *Beloved Acres* (1925); *Tales of an Old Lumber Camp* (1936); *The Death Rider* (1939); *The Phanton Rider* (1940); *By Paddle Wheel and Pack Train* (1941); *Flying Horses* (1942).

HAMLIN, TALBOT FAULKNER (June 16, 1889–Oct. 7, 1956); b. New York. Architect, author. *The Enjoyment of Architecture* (1916); *The American Spirit in Architecture* (1926); *Architecture through the Ages* (1940); *Greek Revival Architecture in America* (1944); *Architecture: An Art for All Men* (1947); *Benjamin Henry Latrobe* (1955; Pulitzer prize for biography, 1956); etc. Editor: *Forms and Functions of Twentieth Century Architecture,* 4v. (1952); Columbia University School of Architecture, 1916–54. Librarian, Avery Library, Columbia University, 1933–45.

HAMM, MARGHERITA ARLINA (Apr. 29, 1871–1907); b. St. Stephens, N.B. Author. *Chinese Legends* (1893); *Corean Journeys* (1893); *Christmas Poems* (1900); *Ghetto Silhouettes* (1902); etc.

HAMMERSTEIN, OSCAR II (July 12, 1895–Aug. 23, 1960); b. New York. Librettist. *Wildflower* (prod. 1923); *Rose Marie* (prod. 1924); *The Desert Song* (prod. 1926); *Show Boat* (adaptation, prod. 1927); *The New Moon* (prod. 1927); *Sweet Adeline* (prod. 1929); *May Wine* (prod. 1935); *Oklahoma!* (prod. 1943; special Pulitzer Prize award, 1944); *Carmen Jones* (prod. 1943); *Carousel* (prod. 1945); *South Pacific* (prod. 1949; Pulitzer Prize for drama, 1950); *The King and I* (prod. 1951); *Flower Drum Song* (prod. 1958); etc.

HAMMETT, SAMUEL ADAMS (Feb. 4, 1816–Dec. 24, 1865); b. Jewett City, Conn. Merchant, author. Under pen name, "Philip Paxton": *A Stray Yankee in Texas* (1853); *The Wonderful Adventures of Captain Priest* (1855); *Piney Woods Tavern; or, Sam Slick in Texas* (1858); and under pen name, "Sam Slick, Jr.": *The Courtship and Adventures of Johnathan Homebred* (1860).

HAMMETT, [Samuel] DASHIELL (May 27, 1894–Jan. 10, 1961); b. in St. Mary's Co., Md. Author. *Red Harvest* (1929); *The Dain Curse* (1929); *The Maltese Falcon* (1930); *The Glass Key* (1931); *The Thin Man* (1934); *Adventures of Sam Spade* (1944); *Omnibus* (1950); etc. Editor: *Creeps by Night* (1931). Compiler: *Modern Tales of Horror* (1932). *See* William F. Nolan's *Dashiell Hammett: A Casebook* (1968).

HAMMON, JUPITER (c. 1720–c. 1800). African slave, first American Negro poet, essayist. *An Evening Thought* (broadside, 1761); *An Essay on the Ten Virgins* (1779); *A Winter Piece* (1782); *An Address to the Negroes of the State of New York* (1787); *An Evening's Improvement* (1790). *See* Oscar Wegelin's *Jupiter Hammon* (1915).

HAMMOND, BRAY (Nov. 20, 1886–July 20, 1968); b. Springfield, Mo. Author. *Banks and Politics in America from the Revolution to the Civil War* (1957; Pulitzer prize for history, 1958).

HAMMOND, CALEB [Dean], JR. (June 24, 1915–); b. Orange, N.J. Publisher, cartographer. Pres., C. S. Hammond & Co., 1948–67; chairman of the board since 1967.

HAMMOND, GEORGE PETER (Sept. 19, 1896–); b. Hutchinson, Minn. Educator, historian. *Don Juan de Oñate and the Founding of New Mexico* (1927); *The Story of New Mexico* (with Thomas C. Donnelly, 1936); *Adventure of Don Francisco Vasquez de Coronado* (with E. F. Goad, 1938); *Coronado's Seven Cities* (1940); etc. Editor: *Narratives of the Coronado Expedition* (with Agapito Rey, 1940); *The Larkin Papers for the History of California,* 11v. (1951–64); etc. History dept., University of New Mexico, 1929–38; prof. history, University of California at Berkeley, since 1946.

HAMMOND, HENRIETTA HARDY (1854–1883); b. in Virginia. Novelist. *Her Waiting Heart* (under pen name, "Lou Capsadell," 1875); *The Georgians* (anon., 1881); *A Fair Philosopher* (under pen name, "Henri Daugé, 1882); etc.

HAMMOND, WILLIAM ALEXANDER (Aug. 28, 1828–Jan. 5, 1900); b. Annapolis, Md. Neurologist, novelist. *Robert Severne* (1867); *Doctor Grattan* (1884); *Lal* (1884); *Mr. Oldmixon* (1885); *A Strong-Minded Woman* (1885); *The Son of Perdition* (1898); and many medical books.

HAMMONDS, CARSIE (May 16, 1894–); b. Ono, Ky. Author. *Your Farming Program* (with W. R. Tabb, 1945); *Farming Handbook* (with same, 1947); *Teaching Agriculture* (1950); *Everybody's Agriculture* (1956); etc.

HAMP, SIDFORD FREDERICK (Mar. 10, 1855–Sept. 3, 1919); b. Liverpool, England. Author. *Treasure of Mushroom Rock* (1899); *Dale and Fraser, Sheepmen* (1906); *The Boys of Crawford's Basin* (1907); *Coco Bolo* (1910); *Sheridan's Twins* (1917); etc.

HANAFORD, PHEBE A[nn Coffin] (May 6, 1829–June 2, 1921); b. on Nantucket Island, Mass. Universalist minister, author. *My Brother* (1852); *Frank Nelson, the Runaway Boy* (1865); *From Shore to Shore, and Other Poems* (1871); *Women of the Century* (1877); *Daughters of America* (1882); etc.

HANBY, BENJAMIN RUSSEL (July 22, 1833–Mar. 16, 1867); b. Rushville, O. Songwriter. His best-known song is "Darling Nelly Gray." With George F. Root, he published a juvenile musical periodical, *Our Song Birds,* 1866–67.

HANCOCK, RALPH LOWELL (Nov. 23, 1903–); b. Plainville, Ind. Author. *Rainbow Republics: Central America* (1947); *Magic Land: Mexico* (1948); *Fabulous Boulevard* (1949); *Forest Lawn Story* (1955); *Puerto Rico: A Success Story* (1960); *A Traveler's Guide* (1961); *Mexico* (1964); *The Compleat Swindler* (1968); etc.

HAND, HAROLD CURTIS (Jan. 5, 1901–); b. Piper City, Ill. Educator, author. *What People Think About Their Schools* (1948); *Principles of Public Secondary Education* (1958); etc. Prof. education, University of Illinois, since 1946.

HAND, LEARNED (Jan. 27, 1872–Aug. 18, 1961); b. Albany, N.Y. Judge. *The Spirit of Liberty* (1951); *The Bill of Rights* (1958).

HANDFORTH, THOMAS (Sept. 16, 1897–Oct. 19, 1948); b. Tacoma, Wash. Artist, illustrator, author. *Mei Li* (1938); *Faraway Meadow* (1939); etc.

HANDLIN, OSCAR (Sept. 29, 1915–); b. Brooklyn, N.Y. Educator, author. *Boston's Immigrants* (1941); *Commonwealth* (1947); *The Uprooted* (1951; Pulitzer Prize for history, 1952); *The American People in the Twentieth Century* (1954); *Race and Nationality in American Life* (1957); *Al Smith and His America* (1958); *Immigration as a Factor in American Life* (ed., 1959); *The Newcomers—Negroes and Puerto Ricans in a Changing Neighborhood Metropolis* (1959); *The Dimensions of Liberty* M. F. M.F. Handlin, 1961); *The Americans* (1963); *Fire-Bell in the Night* (1964); *Children of the Uprooted* (1966); *Popular Sources of Political Authority* (1967); *The History of the United States,* 2v. (1967, 1968); *America: A History* (1968); *Facing Life: Youth and the Fam-*

ily in American History (with Mary Handlin, 1971); *A Pictorial History of Immigration* (1972); etc. Prof. history, Harvard University, since 1954.

HANDY, WILLIAM CHRISTOPHER (Nov. 16, 1873–Mar. 28, 1958); b. Florence, Ala. Composer, author. *Negro Authors and Composers of the United States* (1937); *Father of the Blues* (autobiography, 1941); *Unsung American Sung* (1944). Editor: *Blues: An Anthology* (1926). Composer of "St. Louis Blues," "Memphis Blues," "Beale Street Blues," etc.

HANES, FRANK BORDEN. Author. *Abel Anders* (1951); *Bat Brothers* (poems, 1953); *The Fleet Rabble* (1961); *Jackknife John* (1964).

HANES, LEIGH [Buckner] (Dec. 24, 1893–); b. Montvale, Va. Poet. *Song of the New Hercules, and Other Poems* (1930); *Green Girdle* (1939); *Wide the Gate* (1957). Editor, *The Lyric*, 1929–49.

HANFORD, JAMES HOLLY (Mar. 19, 1882–Apr. 28, 1969); b. Rochester, N.Y. Educator, author. *A Milton Handbook* (1926); *The Teaching of Literature* (with C. C. Fries, 1926); *John Milton, Englishman* (1949). Editor: *The Great Tradition* (1919); *Milton's Poems* (1936); *A Restoration Reader* (1954). Prof. English, Western Reserve University, 1928–52.

HANGEN, PUTNAM WELLES (Mar. 22, 1930–); b. New York. Journalist, author. *After Nehru, Who?* (1963); *The Muted Revolution–East Germany's Challenge to Russia and the West* (1966). With *New York Herald Tribune*, 1948–49; *The New York Times*, 1949–56; National Broadcasting Company, since 1956.

HANKE, LEWIS ULYSSES (Jan. 2, 1905–); b. Oregon City, Ore. Historian. *The First Social Experiments in America* (1935); *The Spanish Struggle for Justice in the Conquest of America* (1949); *Bartolomé de Las Casas: Bookman, Scholar, and Propagandist* (1952); *Bartolomé de Las Casas: Historian* (1952); *Aristotle and the American Indian: A Study in Race Prejudice in the Modern World* (1959); *The Spanish Struggle for Justice in the Conquest of America* (1966); *A History of Latin American Civilization* (1967); *Contemporary Latin America* (1968); etc.

HANKINS, JOHN ERSKINE (Jan. 2, 1905–); b. Lake View, S.C. Educator, author. *Life and Works of George Turbervile* (1940); *The Character of Hamlet and Other Essays* (1941); *Shakespeare's Derived Imagery* (1953); *Lincoln the Writer* (1962); etc. Prof. English, University of Maine, since 1956.

"Hannah Binding Shoes." Poem by Lucy Larcom, in her first book of verse, *Poems* (1869). It had appeared earlier in *The Knickerbocker*, and also in *The Crayon*. Set to music by A. B. Hutchinson, it became a popular song.

Hannah Thurston. Novel by Bayard Taylor (1863). A story of village life in Pennsylvania. Maxwell Woodberry returns from his travels to fall in love with the Quakeress, Hannah Thurston.

HANNUM, ALBERTA PIERSON (Aug. 3, 1906–); b. Condit, O. Author. *Thursday April* (1931); *The Hills Step Lightly* (1934); *The Gods and One* (1941); *Spin a Silver Dollar* (1946); *Roseanna McCoy* (1947); *Paint the Wind* (1958); *Look Back with Love: A Memoir of the Blue Ridge* (1969); etc.

"Hans Breitmann's Barty." First ballad by Charles Godfrey Leland, in *Graham's Magazine*, May, 1857, later included in his *Hans Breitmann's Party, with Other Ballads* (Philadelphia, 1868), also published as *Hans Breitmann's Barty, and Other Ballads* (London, 1869).

Hans Brinker; or, The Silver Skates. Juvenile classic by Mary Mapes Dodge (1865). Inspired by reading Motley's *Rise of the Dutch Republic*.

HANSBERRY, LORRAINE (1930–Jan. 12, 1965). Playwright. *A Raisin in the Sun* (prod. 1959); *The Movement* (1964); *The Sign in Sidney Brustein's Window* (1965).

HANSEN, ALVIN HARVEY (Aug. 23, 1887–); b. Viborg, S.D. Educator, author. *Cycles of Prosperity and Depression* (1921); *Business Cycle Theory* (1927); *Full Recovery or Stagnation?* (1938); *Economic Policy and Full Employment* (1947); *Business Cycles and National Income* (1951); *A Guide to Keynes* (1953); *The American Economy* (1957); *Economic Issues of the 1960's* (1960); *The Dollar and the International Monetary System* (1965); etc. Prof. political economy, Harvard University, 1937–57.

HANSEN, HARRY (Dec. 26, 1884–); b. Davenport, Ia. Editor, author. *The Adventures of the Fourteen Points* (1919); *Midwest Portraits* (1923); *Your Life Lies before You* (1935); *North of Manhattan* (1950); *Old Ironsides: The Fighting Constitution* (1955); *The Story of Illinois* (1956); *California* (1967); *New England Legends and Folklore* (1967); etc. Editor: *First Prize Stories from the O. Henry Memorial Awards, 1919–1966* (1967); *Texas: A Guide to the Lone Star State* (1968); etc. *World Almanac*, since 1949. Literary editor, *Chicago Daily News*, 1920–26; *New York World*, 1926–31; *New York World-Telegram*, 1931–48 book reviewer, *Harper's*, 1923–39; *Redbook* 1940–50; *Survey*, 1940–52. Vice-president, Special Projects, Hastings House.

HANSEN, MARCUS LEE (Dec. 8, 1892–May 11, 1938); b. Neenah, Wis. Sociologist. *Old Fort Snelling: 1819–58* (1918); *Welfare Work in Iowa* (1921); *The Atlantic Migration, 1607–1860: A History of the Continuing Settlement of the U.S.* (1940; Pulitzer prize for history, 1941); *The Immigrant in American History* (1940); *The Mingling of the Canadian and American Peoples* (1940); etc. History dept., University of Illinois, from 1928.

HANSON, EARL PARKER (Mar. 16, 1899–); b. Berlin. Engineering geographer, author. *Journey to Manaos* (1938); *Stefansson, Prophet of the North* (1941); *New Worlds Emerging* (1949); *Puerto Rico: Land of Wonders* (1960); *Puerto Rico, Ally for Progress* (1962); *South from the Spanish Main* (1967); etc.

HANSON, HALDORE (Apr. 22, 1912–); b. Virginia, Minn. Government official, author. *Humane Endeavor, Story of the China War* (1939); etc.

HANSON, JOSEPH MILLS (July 20, 1876–); b. Yankton, S.D. Historical writer. *The Conquest of the Missouri* (1909); *Frontier Ballads* (1910); *With Carrington on the Bozeman Road* (1912); *The Trail to El Dorado* (1913); *America's Battles in the Great War* (1920); *Bull Run Remembers* (1953); etc.

HANSON, KITTY; b. Chicago, Ill. Journalist, author. *Special Events* (with husband, Hal Golden, 1960); *Working with the Working Press* (1962); *Rebels in the Streets* (1964); *The High Cost of Getting Married* (1967). Reporter and feature writer, *New York Daily News*, since 1954.

HANTZ, HAROLD DONOVAN (June 17, 1911–); b. Thermopolis, Wyo. Educator. *Index of Congressional Committee Hearings* (with others, 1935; supplement, 1937); *Science, Folklore and Philosophy* (with others, 1966); etc. Prof. philosophy, University of Arkansas, since 1948.

HAPGOOD, HUTCHINS (May 21, 1869–Nov. 19, 1944); b. Chicago, Ill. Journalist, author. *Paul Jones* (1901); *The Spirit of the Ghetto* (1902); *The Autobiography of a Thief* (1903); *Types from City Streets* (1910); *Enemies* (with Neith Boyce, 1916); *The Story of a Lover* (1919); *A Victorian in the Modern World* (autobiography, 1939); etc.

HAPGOOD, ISABEL FLORENCE (Nov. 21, 1850–June 26, 1928); b. Boston, Mass. Journalist, author. *The Epic Songs of Russia* (1886); *Russian Rambles* (1895); etc. Translator of many Russian books.

HAPGOOD, NEITH BOYCE (Mrs. Hutchins Hapgood) (Mar. 21, 1872–Dec. 2, 1951); b. Franklin, Ind. Novelist. Wrote under maiden name. *The Forerunner* (1903); *The Eternal Spring* (1906); *Proud Lady* (1923); *Harry* (1923); *Winter's Night* (1927); etc.

HAPGOOD, NORMAN (Mar. 28, 1868–Apr. 29, 1937); b. Chicago, Ill. Editor, author. *Literary Statesmen and Others* (1897); *Abraham Lincoln: The Man of the People* (1899); *The Stage in America* (1901); *The Changing Years* (reminiscences, 1930); etc. Editor, *Collier's Weekly,* 1903–12; *Harper's Weekly,* 1913–16; *Hearst's International Magazine,* 1923–25.

Hapless Orphan; or, Innocent Victim of Revenge, The; By an American Lady, 2v. (1793). Anonymous novel laid in Philadelphia.

Happening. A performance conceived according to a prepared scheme, using materials of any and all kinds (movies, dance, music, readings, etc.), in which whatever "happens" during the fulfillment of the scheme constitutes all that was meant to happen. The term was first used in *18 Happenings in 6 Parts,* by Allan Kaprow, presented in 1959, and afterwards became loosely applied to all forms of non-scripted presentations to which the terms *play, improvisation, tableau, skit,* etc. would not seem to apply. Claes Oldenburg, Robert Whitman, Dick Higgins, Jackson MacLow, and Allan Kaprow are most notably associated with the form. Although Happenings have no fixed verbal forms, schemes and prescriptions have been published in periodicals and books. See *Tulane Drama Review* (Winter, 1965); *Happenings,* ed. by Michael Kirby (1966).

Happy Hawkins. Novel by Robert Alexander Wason (1909). A famous Western.

Happy Mountain. Novel by Maristan Chapman (1928). Laid among the hill-folk of the Tennessee Mountains. Waits Lowe is the central character.

HARBACH, OTTO ABELS (Aug. 18, 1873–Jan. 24, 1963); b. Salt Lake City, Utah. Librettist, lyricist. Lyrics for: *Three Twins* (prod. 1907); *Bright Eyes* (prod. 1908). Librettos, alone or in collaboration, for: *The Girl of My Dreams* (prod. 1909); *Madame Sherry* (prod. 1909); *The Firefly* (prod. 1912); *High Jinks* (prod. 1913); *Katinka* (prod. 1915); *The Silent Witness* (prod. 1915); *Up in Mabel's Room* (prod. 1919); *Jimmie* (prod. 1920); *Kid Boots* (prod. 1923); *No! No! Nanette* (prod. 1924); *Rose Marie* (prod. 1924); *Song of the Flame* (1925); *The Desert Song* (prod. 1926); *The Cat and the Fiddle* (prod. 1931); *Roberta* (prod. 1933); *Gentlemen Unafraid* (prod. 1938); *Meet Miss April* (prod. 1945); etc.

HARBAGE, ALFRED (July 18, 1901–); b. Philadelphia, Pa. Educator, author. *Thomas Killigrew, Cavalier Dramatist* (1930); *Sir William Davenant, Poet-Venturer* (1935); *Cavalier Drama* (1936); *Annals of English Drama, 975–1700* (1940); Shakespeare's *Audience* (1941); *As They Liked It* (1947); *Shakespeare and the Rival Traditions* (1952); *A Theatre for Shakespeare* (1955); *William Shakespeare: A Reader's Guide* (1963); *Conceptions of Shakespeare* (1966); etc. Prof. English, Harvard University, since 1952.

HARBAUGH, HENRY (Oct. 28, 1817–Dec. 28, 1867); b. Franklin Co., Pa. German Reformed clergyman, poet, hymnwriter. *Poems* (1860); *The Golden Censer* (1860); etc. He also wrote some poems in Pennsylvania-German, published as *Harbaugh's Harfe* (1870), which included "Das alt Schulhaus an der Krick," "Die Schlofschtub" and "Der Pihwie."

HARBAUGH, THOMAS CHALMERS (Jan. 13, 1849–Oct. 28, 1924); b. Middletown, Md. Dime novelist, poet. Pen name, "Capt. Howard Holmes." *Judge Lynch, Jr.* (1880); *Navajo Nick* (1881); *The Pampas Hunters* (1882); *The Boy Exiles of Siberia* (1882); *Velvet Foot* (1884); *Maple Leaves* (poems, 1884); *The Silken Lasso* (1885); *The Desperate Dozen* (1885); *The Lost Bonanza* (1886); *Dodger Dick* (1887); *Captain Cobra* (1889); *Ballads of the Blue* (1892); *The White Squadron*

(1896); *Stories of Ohio* (1903); *The Withered Hand* (1911); *Kit Carson's Chum* (1913); *The Leopard Woman* (1914). The dates are not necessarily those of first editions.

HARBEN, WILL[iam] N[athaniel] (July 5, 1858–Aug. 7, 1919); b. Dalton, Ga. Novelist. *White Marie: A Story of Georgian Plantation Life* (1889); *The Land of the Changing Sun* (1894); *Northern Georgia Sketches* (1900); *Ann Boyd* (1906); *The Inner Law* (1915); etc.

Harbinger, The. New York and Boston. Weekly magazine. Founded June 14, 1845, at Brook Farm by Albert Brisbane. This magazine grew out of the communistic movement of Fourier. Brisbane had established *The Phalanx* in New York in Oct., 1843, to promote the new social reformation promised by Fourierism. When the New England group established Brook Farm at West Roxbury, Mass., Brisbane moved *The Phalanx* there. He discontinued it in May, 1845, to make way for *The Harbinger.* George Ripley became its chief editor. Horace Greeley and other leaders in the Fourier movement contributed articles. Although edited at Brook Farm, it was published simultaneously in Boston and New York. Expired Feb. 10, 1849.

HARBISON, E[lmore] HARRIS (Apr. 28, 1907–July 14, 1964); b. Sewickley, Pa. Educator, author. *Rival Ambassadors at the Court of Queen Mary, 1553–57* (1940); *The Age of Reformation* (1955); *The Christian Scholar in the Age of the Reformation* (1956); *The Course of Civilization* (1961). Prof. history, Princeton University, from 1945.

Harbor, The. Novel by Ernest Poole (1915). A symbolical novel of New York harbor as seen by a resident of Brooklyn Heights. Has a sociological background and describes the conditions of the laboring class.

Harbor Press. New York. Printers, publishers. Founded 1925, by Roland A. Wood, its first president. The press specialized in fine printing. Included in the firm's publications were *The Cries of New York* (1931); Robert Frost's *A Way Out* (1929); *Dante's Divine Comedy,* translated by Louis Howe, 3v. (1934–40).

HARBOUR, JEFFERSON LEE (Mar. 31, 1857–Feb. 25, 1931); b. Oskaloosa, Ia. Editor. Author of more than 700 short stories. Assoc. editor, *The Youth's Companion,* 1884–1901.

HARBY, ISAAC (Nov. 9, 1788–Dec. 14, 1828); b. Charleston, S.C. Editor, playwright. *Alexander Severus* (1805); *The Gordian Knot; or, Causes and Effects* (prod. 1810); *Alberti* (prod. 1819); *A Selection from the Miscellaneous Writings,* ed. by Henry L. Pinckney and Abraham Moise (1829). See Lucius C. Moise's *Biography of Isaac Harby* (1931).

HARCHAR, HARRY A. (June 3, 1912–); b. Bethlehem, Pa. Editor. Editor, *Boys' Life,* 1952–64. National director, Editorial Services, *Boy Scouts of America,* since 1964.

HARCOURT, ALFRED (Jan. 31, 1881–June 20, 1954); b. New Paltz, N.Y. Publisher. Compiler (with Crosby Gaige) *Books and Reading* (1908). Founded publishing firm of Harcourt, Brace & Howe, New York, in 1919. Was with Henry Holt & Co., from 1904 to 1919. Also a founder of Blue Ribbon Books, Inc.

Harcourt, Brace & World. New York. Publishers. Founded 1919, by Alfred Harcourt, Donald Brace, and Will D. Howe, as Harcourt, Brace & Howe. The firm became Harcourt, Brace & Co. in 1921, when Will D. Howe left to enter the firm of Charles Scribner's Sons. In 1948 Harcourt, Brace & Co. absorbed Reynall & Hitchcock. In 1960 the firm merged with the World Book Co. Now known as Harcourt Brace Jovanovich. William Jovanovich is chairman; Paul D. Corbett is president. Among its most famous books have been *Main Street,* Carl Sandburg's *Abraham Lincoln,* and Lincoln Steffens' *Autobiography. See* William Jovanovich's *Now, Barabbas* (1964).

HARD, WALTER [R.] (May 3, 1882–May 21, 1966); b. Manchester, Vt. Poet. *Some Vermonters* (1928); *Salt of Vermont* (1931); *Vermont Vintage* (1937); *Vermont Valley* (1939); *Connecticut* (1947); *A Matter of Fifty Houses* (1952); *Vermont Neighbors* (1960); etc.

Hard Times. By Studs Terkel (1970). Interviews with 160 witnesses of the Depression period of the 1930's in America.

HARDEN, WILLIAM (Nov. 11, 1844–Jan. 4, 1936); b. Savannah, Ga. Librarian, author. *A History of Savannah and South Georgia*, 2v. (1913); *Recollections of a Long and Satisfactory Life* (1934). Librarian, Georgia Historical Society, 1869–1936.

Hardin, Clement. Pen name of Dwight Bennett Newton.

HARDING, ALFRED (May 10, 1892–); b. Washington, D.C. Author. *Tropical Fruit* (1928); *The Revolt of the Actors* (1929); etc.

HARDING, BERTITA [Carla Camille Leonarz de] (Nov. 1, 1907–); b. Nuremberg, Germany. Lecturer, author. *Phantom Crown* (1934); *Royal Purple* (1935); *Golden Fleece* (1937); *Farewell 'Toinette* (1938); *Imperial Twilight* (1939); *Hungarian Rhapsody* (1940); *Age Cannot Wither* (1947); *Magic Fire* (1953); *Concerto* (1961).

HARDING, JESPER (Nov. 5, 1799–Aug. 21, 1865); b. Philadelphia, Pa. Publisher. Purchased the Pennsylvania *Inquirer* in 1829, and the *National Gazette*, Jan. 1, 1842. Some of Charles Dickens's novels ran serially in the *Inquirer*, their first appearance in America. He became the largest publisher of Bibles in the United States. His business was continued by his son, William White Harding.

HARDING, JOHN WILLIAM (b. Oct. 30, 1864); b. London. Editor, novelist. *An Art Failure* (1896); *The Strolling Piper of Brittany* (1897); *A Conjurer of Phantoms* (1898); *The Gate of the Kiss* (1902); *The City of Splendid Night* (1909); etc. With the *New York Times*.

HARDING, WARREN GAMALIEL (Nov. 2, 1865–Aug. 2, 1923); b. Caledonia (now Blooming Grove), O. Twenty-ninth president of the United States, author. *Rededicating America* (1920); *Our Common Country* (1921). See Joe Mitchell Chapple's *Life and Times of Warren G. Harding* (1924); Samuel H. Adams's *Incredible Era* (1930); Elizabeth Jaffray's *Secrets of the White House* (1927); Irwin Hood (Ike) Hoover's *Forty-Two Years in the White House* (1934); Francis Russell's *The Shadow of Blooming Grove* (1968).

HARDWICK, ELIZABETH (July 27, 1916–); b. Lexington, Ky. Author. *The Ghostly Lover* (1945); *The Simple Truth* (1955); *A View of My Own* (1962); etc. Editor: *Selected Letters of William James* (1961). Contributor, *New York Review of Books.*

HARDY, ARTHUR SHERBURNE (Aug. 13, 1847–Mar. 13, 1930); b. Andover, Mass. Educator, engineer, editor, diplomat, novelist, poet. *Francesca of Rimini* (poem, 1878); *But Yet a Woman* (1883); *The Wind of Destiny* (1886); *Passé Rose* (1889); *Songs of Two* (poems, 1900); *Helen* (1916); *Things Remembered* (1923); etc. Co-editor, *Cosmopolitan* magazine, 1893–95. Prof. mathematics, Dartmouth College, 1878–93; U.S. minister to Persia, Greece, Rumania, Serbia, Switzerland, and Spain, 1899–1905.

HARDY, JOHN EDWARD (Apr. 3, 1922–   ); b. Baton Rouge, La. Educator, author. *Poems of Mr. John Milton* (with Cleanth Brooks, 1951); *The Curious Frame* (1962); *Man in the Modern Novel* (1964); etc. Editor: *The Modern Talent* (1964). Prof. English, Notre Dame University, since 1964.

HARE, AMORY (Mrs. James Pemberton Hutchinson) (Aug. 30, 1885–); b. Philadelphia, Pa. Poet. *Tossed Coins* (1920); *The Swept Hearth* (1922); *The Olympians and Other Poems* (1925); *Sonnets* (1927); *Deep Country* (1933); *Between Wars: Sonnets and Road Songs* (1955).

HARE, ROBERT (Jan. 17, 1781–May 15, 1858); b. Philadelphia, Pa. Chemist, novelist. Pen name, "Eldred Grayson." *Standish, the Puritan* (1850); *Overing; or, the Heir of Wycherly* (1852).

HARGROVE, MARION (1919–). Author. *See Here, Private Hargrove* (1942); *The Girl He Left Behind* (1956).

HARING, CLARENCE HENRY (Feb. 9, 1885–Sept. 4, 1960); b. Philadelphia, Pa. Educator, author. *The Buccaneers of the West Indies in the Seventeenth Century* (1910); *South American Progress* (1934); *The Spanish Empire in South America* (1947); *Empire in Brazil* (1958); *Trade and Navigation between Spain and the Indies* (1964); etc. Prof. Latin American history, Harvard University, 1923–53.

HARING, DOUGLAS GILBERT (Aug. 6, 1894–); b. Watkins Glen, N.Y. Anthropologist. *The Land of Gods and Earthquakes* (1929); *Blood on the Rising Sun* (1943); etc. Editor, *Personal Character and Cultural Milieu*, 1948–56.

HARKNESS, GEORGIA [Elma] (Apr. 21, 1891–); b. Harkness, N.Y. Methodist minister, educator, author. *John Calvin* (1931); *Holy Flame* (verse, 1935); *The Recovery of Ideals* (1937); *Religious Living* (1937); *Understanding the Christian Faith* (1947); *The Gospel and Our World* (1949); *Toward Understanding the Bible* (1954); *Foundations of Christian Knowledge* (1955); *Christian Ethics* (1957); *Beliefs that Count* (1961); *The Church and Its Laity* (1962); *Our Christian Hope* (1964); *The Fellowship of the Holy Spirit* (1966); *Disciples of the Christian Life* (1967); *A Devotional Treasury from the Early Church* (1968); *Stability Amid Change* (1969); etc. Prof. applied theology, Garrett Biblical Institute, Evanston, Ill., 1939–50; Pacific School of Religion, since 1950.

HARLAN, CALEB (1814–1902). Physician, poet. *Ida Randolph of Virginia* (anon. 1860); *Elflora of the Susquehanna* (1879); *The Fate of Marcel* (1883); etc.

HARLAND, HENRY (Mar. 1, 1861–Dec. 20, 1905); b. New York City. Editor, novelist. Pen name, "Sidney Luska." *As It Was Written* (1885); *The Yoke of Thorah* (1887); *A Latin-Quarter Courtship* (1889); *Grandison Mather* (1889); *Mea Culpa* (1891); *Comedies and Errors* (1898); *The Cardinal's Snuff-Box* (1900); *The Lady Paramount* (1902); *My Friend Prospero* (1904); etc. With John Lane and Aubrey Beardsley he founded and edited the *Yellow Book*, Apr., 1894–Apr., 1897.

HARLAND, JAMES PENROSE (Feb. 5, 1891–); b. Wenonah, N.J. Archeologist. *Peloponnesos in the Bronze Age* (1923); *Prehistoric Aigina* (1925); etc. Prof. archeology, University of North Carolina, since 1929.

Harland, Marion. Pen name of Mary Virginia Terhune.

HARLEY, JOHN EUGENE (Nov. 17, 1892–); b. Mt. Vernon, Mo. Educator, author. *The League of Nations and the New International Law* (1921); *World-Wide Influences of the Cinema* (1940); *Woodrow Wilson Still Lives* (1944); *Documentary Textbook on the United Nations: Humanity's March Towards Peace* (1947); etc. Prof. political science, University of Southern California, since 1921.

HARLOW, ALVIN FAY (Mar. 10, 1875–Nov. 17, 1963); b. Sedalia, Mo. Author. *Old Towpaths* (1926); *Clowning through Life* (with Edwin Foy, 1927); *Old Post Bags* (1928); *Old Bowery Days* (1931); *Old Waybills* (1934); *Paper Chase* (1940); *Joel Chandler Harris* (1941); *Theodore Roosevelt, Strenuous American* (1943); *The Serene Cincinnatians* (1950); *Treasury of Railroad Folklore* (ed., with Benjamin A. Botkin, 1953); *Henry Bergh: Founder of the A.S.P.C.A.* (1957); etc.

HARLOW, RALPH VOLNEY (May 4, 1884–Oct. 3, 1956); b. Claremont, N.H. Educator, author. *Samuel Adams* (1923); *Story of America* (1937); *Gerrit Smith* (1939); *The United States: From Wilderness to World Power* (1949); etc. Prof. history, Syracuse University, 1929–48.

HARLOW, REX [Francis] (June 19, 1892–); b. Winfield, Mo. Editor, author. *Successful Oklahomans* (1927); *Oklahoma Leaders* (1928); *A Biography of Everett Wentworth Hill* (1930); *Oklahoma City's Younger Leaders* (1931); *Public Relations in War and Peace* (1942); *Social Science in Public Relations* (1957); etc. Editor and publisher, *The Social Science Reporter,* since 1953; *Public Relations Research Review,* since 1958.

HARLOW, VICTOR EMMANUEL (Nov. 23, 1876–Oct. 6, 1958); b. Chantilly, Mo. Publisher, author. *The Nations* (poems, 1895); *A Bibliography and Genetic Study of American Realism* (1931); *Oklahoma: A History* (1934); *The Destroyer of Jesus: The Life of Herod Antipas* (1953); Founder, *Harlow's Weekly,* 1912; editor, since 1912.

HARMON, DANIEL WILLIAMS (Feb. 19, 1778–Mar. 26, 1845); b. Bennington, Vt. Fur trader, explorer, author. *A Journal of Voyages and Travels in the Interiour of North America,* ed. by Daniel Haskel (1820).

HARMON, GEORGE DEWEY (Aug. 23, 1896–); b. Pittsboro, N.C. Historian. *Sixty Years of Indian Affairs, 1789–1850* (1941); etc. History dept., Lehigh University, 1927–64.

HARMON, NOLAN BAILEY (July 14, 1892–); b. Meridian, Miss. Methodist bishop, editor. Editor: *Methodist Book of Discipline* (1940). Editor, Abingdon-Cokesbury Press, 1940–56; *Religion in Life,* 1940–56. Faculty, Brevard College, 1957–64; American University, since 1964.

Harmonium. Poems by Wallace Stevens (1923).

HARNACK, CURTIS (1927–). Author. *The Work of an Ancient Hand* (1960); *Love and be Silent* (1962); *Persian Lions, Persian Lambs* (1965).

HARNEY, JOHN MILTON (Mar. 9, 1789–Jan. 15, 1825); b. in Sussex Co., Dela. Poet. *Crystalina* (anon. 1816).

HAROUTUNIAN, JOSEPH (Sept. 18, 1904–); b. Marash, Turk. Educator. *Piety versus Moralism* (1932); *Wisdom and Folly in Religion* (1940); *Lust for Power* (1949); *God Within Us* (1965); etc. Editor, translator: Calvin's *Commentaries* (1958). Prof. theology, McCormick Theological Seminary, since 1940.

Harp, The. Learned, Kan. Magazine of verse. Founded 1925, by Israel Newman. May Williams Ward became editor in 1926. Expired 1932.

Harp of a Thousand Strings, The. Travesty on a pioneer frontier sermon by William P. Brannan. It appeared in *The Spirit of the Times,* Sept. 29, 1855, but was reprinted from some earlier source.

Harp of a Thousand Strings, The. Compiled by "Spavery" (i.e., Samuel Putnam Avery) (1858). Selections from American humorists.

Harp-Weaver, and Other Poems, The. By Edna St. Vincent Millay (1923). Awarded the Pulitzer prize for poetry in 1923.

HARPER, FLETCHER (Jan. 31, 1806–May 29, 1877); b. Newtown, L.I., N.Y. Editor, printer, publisher. Founder, *Harper's Magazine,* 1850; *Harper's Weekly,* 1857; *Harper's Bazar,* 1867. Joined the publishing firm of J. & J. Harper in 1825.

HARPER, FLOYD ARTHUR (Feb. 7, 1905–); b. Middleville, Mich. Economist, educator. *High Prices* (1948); *Liberty: A Path to Its Recovery* (1949); *Why Wages Rise* (1957); etc. Prof. marketing, Cornell University, 1935–46.

HARPER, GEORGE McLEAN (Dec. 31, 1863–July 14, 1947); b. Shippensburg, Pa. Educator, author. *The Legend of the Holy Grail* (1893); *Masters of French Literature* (1901); *Life of Charles Augustin Sainte-Beuve* (1909); *William Wordsworth: His Life, Works and Influence,* 2v. (1916); *John

Morley, and Other Essays (1920); *Wordsworth's French Daughter* (1921); *Dreams and Memories* (1922); *Spirit of Delight* (1928); *Literary Appreciations* (1937). Editor: Standard Oxford Edition of the Poetical Works of Wordsworth (1933); etc. With Princeton University, 1889–1932.

HARPER, HENRY HOWARD (1871–). Bibliophile, novelist. *Book-Lovers, Bibliomaniacs and Book Clubs* (1904); *The Stumbling Block* (1912); *The Codicil* (1915); *The Tides of Fate* (1918); *Library Essays* (1924); *The Devil's Nest* (1923); *Boëthius and Dante* (1930); *Letters from an Outsider to an Insider* (1932); *Pain Discovers Me* (1950); etc. Editor: *The Personal Letters of John Fiske* (1939); etc.

HARPER, IDA HUSTED (Feb. 18, 1851–Mar. 14, 1931); b. Fairfield, Ind. Journalist, woman suffragist, author. *The Life and Work of Susan B. Anthony,* 3v. (1899–1908); etc.

HARPER, JAMES (Apr. 13, 1795–Mar. 27, 1869); b. Newtown, L.I., N.Y. Publisher, eldest of four brothers (James, John, Wesley, Fletcher) who founded Harper & Brothers, 1833. Founder, *Harper's New Monthly Magazine,* 1850. See J. Henry Harper's *The House of Harper* (1912).

HARPER, LAWRENCE A[verell] (May 18, 1901–); b. Oakland, Calif. Educator, lawyer, author. *The English Navigation Laws* (1939); etc. Prof. history, University of California, since 1947.

HARPER, ROBERT S[tory] (Oct. 30, 1899–Dec. 12, 1962); b. Greenfield, O. Editor, author. *Trumpet in the Wilderness* (1940); *The Road to Baltimore* (1942); *Lincoln and the Press* (1951). Editorial staff, *Ohio State Journal,* Columbus, 1928–46.

HARPER, THEODORE ACLAND (Dec. 17, 1871–May 6, 1942); b. Christchurch, N.Z., Australia. Author. *The Mushroom Boy* (1924); *Siberian Gold* (with wife, Winifred Mary Hunter-Brown, 1927); *Kubrik the Outlaw* (with wife, 1928); *Forgotten Gods* (with wife, 1929); *Windy Island* (with wife, 1931); *Red Sky* (1935); *Seventeen Chimneys* (1938); etc.

HARPER, WILHELMINA; b. Farmington, Me. Librarian. Compiler: *The Magic Fairy Tales* (1926); *Far Away Hills* (1928); *A Little Book of Necessary Ballads* (1930); *The Selfish Giant, and Other Stories* (1935); *Ghosts and Goblins* (1936); *The Gunniwolf, and Other Merry Tales* (1936); *The Lonely Little Pig, and Other Animal Tales* (1938); *Flying Hoofs* (1939); *Merry Christmas to You* (1965); and other school readers and children's books. Librarian, Redwood (Calif.) Public Library, 1930–54.

HARPER, WILLIAM ALLEN (Apr. 27, 1880–May 11, 1942); b. Berkley, Va. Educator, author. *The Making of Men* (1915); *The New Church for the New Time* (1917); *Personal Religious Beliefs* (1937); *The Minister of Education* (1939); etc. Prof. religious education, Vanderbilt University, from 1932.

HARPER, WILLIAM RAINEY (July 24, 1856–Jan. 10, 1906); b. New Concord, O. Educator, Hebraist, author. *Religion and the Higher Life* (1904); *The Trend in Higher Education* (1905); etc. President, University of Chicago, 1891–1906. See Thomas W. Goodspeed's *William Rainey Harper* (1928); Allan Nevins's *John D. Rockefeller,* 2v. (1940).

Harper & Row, Publishers. New York. The printing business of J. and J. Harper was started in 1817 by James Harper (1795–1869) and John Harper (1797–1875). The first book printed was *Seneca's Morals,* for Evert Duyckinck. Joseph Wesley Harper (1801–70) joined the firm in 1825; Fletcher Harper (1806–77) joined his three brothers in 1825. In 1833 the firm changed its name to Harper & Brothers. In 1850 *Harper's Magazine* was founded, and in 1857 *Harper's Weekly.* In 1867 came *Harper's Bazar* and in 1879, *Harper's Young People.* Always one of the largest New York publishing houses, it has issued thousands of books by leading American and European writers. Members of the Harper family had always headed, the house until 1931 when Cass Canfield became president. John Cowles, Jr., is now chairman of the board. Besides its trade list, the firm has a large religious book department with paperback reprints known as Torchbooks, and publishes many textbooks and medical books. Bought out Basic Books, Inc., Publishers (q.v.) by 1969.

Harper's Bazaar. New York. A magazine for women. Founded Nov. 2, 1867, by Harper & Brothers. Weekly from 1867 to 1901, monthly since then. Name changed from *"Bazar"* to *"Bazaar"* in 1929. Notable editors have been Mary Louise Booth, 1867–89; Margaret Sangster, 1889–99; Elizabeth Jordan, 1900–13; Harford Powell; Henry Blackman Sell; Charles Hanson Towne; Arthur H. Samuels; Carmel Snow; Nancy White. The early numbers included contributions by George William Curtis, Thomas Wentworth Higginson, William Dean Howells, and Mary E. Wilkins. John Kendrick Bangs contributed many humorous articles. Purchased by the International Magazine Company, controlled by William Randolph Hearst, in 1913. Noted for its trend-setting fashion and beauty articles, and in recent years for its interest in new writers of fiction.

Harper's Library of Select Novels. This series, in brown paper covers, began in 1842; 615 titles, mostly foreign, were published.

Harper's Magazine. New York. Founded June, 1850, by the publishing firm of Harper & Brothers. Editors have included Henry J. Raymond, 1850–56; Alfred H. Guernsey, 1856–69; Henry Mills Alden, 1869–1919; Thomas B. Wells, 1919–31, Lee Foster Hartman, Frederick Lewis Allen, and John Fischer. Willie Morris was editor-in-chief from 1967–1971. Novels by leading English writers ran serially in the early issues. American writers became more frequent contributors in later years. Its stories during the Civil War were outstanding, and its illustrations vied with those of *Scribner's* and *Century* for many years. One of the early successful serials was John S. C. Abbott's *History of Napoleon Bonaparte.* In recent years illustrations were dropped and the appearance of the magazine altered to fit the modern trend in magazines. Famous departments in the magazine have been "The Editor's Drawer," "The Editor's Table," "The Editor's Easy Chair," "The Editor's Study," conducted by such writers as E. P. Whipple, William Dean Howells, Samuel Osgood, John Kendrick Bangs, Theodore Sedgwick, Donald G. Mitchell, Charles Dudley Warner, Henry Mills Alden, George William Curtis, Edward S. Martin and more recently, Bernard De Voto. In 1950 it celebrated its hundredth anniversary with a special three-hundred-page issue. *See* J. Henry Harper's *The House of Harper* (1912); historical articles in *Harper's Monthly Magazine,* May, 1900, and June, 1910; Henry Seidel Canby's *Harper's Magazine* (1925); A. R. Hyde's *The Story of Harper's Magazine* (1931); Frank L. Mott's *History of American Magazines,* v.2 (1938).

Harper's Round Table. See *Harper's Young People.*

Harper's Weekly. New York. Founded 1857, by Fletcher Harper. Editors: Theodore Sedgwick, 1857–58; John Bonner, 1858–63; George William Curtis, 1863–92; Carl Schurz, 1892–94; Henry Loomis Nelson, 1894–98; John Kendrick Bangs, 1898–1901; George Harvey, 1901–13; Norman Hapgood, 1913–16. Noted for its woodcut illustrations of contemporary men and events. Serial fiction was always a feature. Thomas Nast did his best cartoons for it, retiring in 1887. Dickens, Reade, Kipling, Henry James, Owen Wister, Richard Harding Davis, William Dean Howells and many other leading authors were contributors. In 1913 the magazine was sold to the McClure organization, and in 1916 was merged with *The Independent.*

Harper's Young People. New York. Weekly. Founded 1879, by Harper & Bros. Kirk Munro was its first editor. Name changed in 1895 to *Harper's Round Table;* in 1897 it became a monthly. Expired 1899.

HARRÉ, T[homas] EVERETT (Dec. 17, 1884–deceased); b. Marietta, Pa. Author. *The Eternal Maiden* (1913); *Behold the Woman!* (1916); *One Hour and Forever* (1925); *Beware after Dark* (1929); *The Heavenly Sinner: The Romance of Lola Montez* (1935); etc. Editor: *Bedside Treasury of Love* (1945); *Treasures of the Kingdom* (1947).

HARRER, GUSTAVE ADOLPHUS (May 14, 1886–Nov. 26, 1943); b. Brooklyn, N.Y. Educator, compiler. *Roman Literature in Translation* (with George Howe, 1924); *Greek Literature in Translation* (1924); *A Handbook of Classical Mythology* (1929); etc. Latin dept., University of North Carolina, from 1915.

HARRIGAN, EDWARD (Oct. 26, 1845–June 6, 1911); b. New York City. Actor, playwright. *The Blue and the Grey* (prod. 1875); *Pete* (prod. 1887); *Reilly and the Four Hundred* (prod. 1890); *Under Cover* (prod. 1903); etc. Teamed with Tony Hart in vaudeville, beginning in 1871. Their many popular songs were published by William A. Pond & Co., New York. For full list of plays, *see* Margaret G. Mayorga's *A Short History of the American Drama* (1934).

HARRIMAN, JOHN (Sept. 29, 1904–Jan. 23, 1960); b. Purchase, N.Y. Author. *Winter Term* (1940); *The Career of Philip Hazen* (1941); *The Magnate* (1946); *It's Your Business* (1960). Financial columnist, *Boston Globe.*

HARRIMAN, KARL EDWIN (Dec. 29, 1875–Oct. 1, 1935); b. Ann Arbor, Mich. Editor, author. *Ann Arbor Tales* (1902); *The Girl and the Deal* (1905); etc. Editor, *Red Book* and *Blue Book* magazines, 1919–1927.

HARRIMAN, MARGARET CASE [Morgan] (d. Aug. 7, 1966). Author. *Take Them Up Tenderly* (1944); *Vicious Circle* (1951); *Blessed Are the Debonair* (1956); *And the Price Is Right* (1958).

HARRINGTON, ALAN (1919–   ). Author. *The Secret Swinger* (1966); *The Immoralist* (1969).

HARRINGTON, FRED HARVEY (June 24, 1912–); b. Watertown, N.Y. Educator, author. *God, Mammon and the Japanese: Dr. Horace N. Allen and Korean-American Relations, 1884–1905* (1944); *Fighting Politician: Major General N. P. Banks* (1948); *Hanging Judge* (1951); etc. Prof. history, University of Wisconsin, since 1947.

Harrington, George F. Pen name of William Mumford Baker.

HARRINGTON, KARL POMEROY (June 13, 1861–1953); b. Somersworth, N.H. Educator, classicist, author. *The Roman Elegiac Poets* (1914); *Catullus and His Influence* (1923); *Walks and Climbs in the White Mountains* (1926); *Richard Alsop: A Hartford Wit* (1939). Compiler of college song books and hymnals, including *Songs of All the Colleges* (with David B. Chamberlain, 1900). Prof. Latin, Wesleyan University, Middletown, Conn., 1905–29.

HARRINGTON, MICHAEL (Feb. 24, 1928–); b. St. Louis, Mo. Author. *The Other America: Poverty in the United States* (1962); *The Retail Clerks* (1962); *Conference on Poverty-in-Plenty: The Poor in Our Affluent Society* (1964); *The Accidental Century* (1965); *Toward a Democratic Left: A Radical Program for a New Majority* (1968); *Why We Need Socialism in America* (1970). Editor: *Labor in a Free Society* (with Paul Jacobs, 1959).

HARRINGTON, WILLIAM (Nov. 21, 1931–); b. Marietta, O. Lawyer, author. *Which the Justice, Which the Thief* (1963); *The Power* (1964); *One Over One* (1970); *Trial;* etc.

Harriott, Clara Morris. See Clara Morris.

HARRIS, AMANDA BARTLETT (Aug. 15, 1824–Jan. 13, 1917); b. Warner, N.H. Author. *Dooryard Folks; and A Winter Garden* (1883); *Old School-Days* (reminiscences, 1886); *American Authors for Young Folks* (1887); etc.

HARRIS, BENJAMIN (fl. 1673–1716); b. London, England. Publisher, bookseller. Opened a bookshop in Boston in 1686. His first publication was *John Tulley's Almanach for 1687.* He also published America's first newspaper, *Publick Occurrences Both Foreign and Domestick,* Sept. 25, 1690; and the *New England Primer,* some time before 1690.

HARRIS, BERNICE KELLY (Mrs. Herbert Kavanaugh Harris) (Oct., 1894–); b. in Wake Co., N.C. Author. *Purslane* (1939); *Folk Plays of Eastern Carolina* (1940); *Portulaca* (1941); *Sweet Beulah Land* (1943); *Sage Quarter* (1945); *Janey Jeens* (1946); *Hearthstones* (1948); *Wild Cherry Tree Road* (1951). Editor: *Southern Home Remedies* (1968).

HARRIS, CHARLES KASSELL (May 1, 1865–Dec. 22, 1930); b. Poughkeepsie, N.Y. Publisher, song-writer. *After the Ball: Forty Years of Melody* (autobiography, 1926); etc. Among his best-known songs are: "After the Ball" (1892); "Break the News to Mother" (1897); "Hello Central, Give Me Heaven" (1901).

HARRIS, CORRA MAY (Mrs. Lundy Howard Harris) (Mar. 17, 1869–Feb. 9, 1935); b. Farm Hill, Ga. Novelist. *A Circuit Rider's Wife* (1910); *My Book and Heart* (1924); *The Happy Pilgrimage* (1927); etc.

HARRIS, CREDO FITCH (d. Apr. 4, 1956); b. in Jefferson Co., Ky. Author. *Toby: A Novel of Kentucky* (1912); *Motor Rambles in Italy* (1912); *Sun Light Patch* (1915); *Where the Souls of Men Are Calling* (1918); *Wings of the Wind* (1920); *Microphone Memoirs* (1937).

HARRIS, CYRIL (1891–); b. in Nova Scotia, came to the United States in 1905. Novelist. *Trumpets at Dawn* (1938); *Richard Pryne* (1941); *One Braver Thing* (1942); *Trouble at Hungerfords* (1953); etc. English dept., Bard College, Annandale, N.Y.

HARRIS, GEORGE WASHINGTON (Mar. 20, 1814–Dec. 11, 1869); b. Allegheny City, Pa. Humorist. Pen name, "Sugartail." *Sut Lovingood* (1867). Wrote his first "Sut Lovingood" sketch for the *Spirit of the Times* in 1854, and followed it with others in the Knoxville, Chattanooga, and Nashville newspapers.

HARRIS, JOEL CHANDLER (Dec. 9, 1848–July 3, 1908); b. Eatonton, Ga. Editor, author. *Uncle Remus: His Songs and Sayings* (1880); *Nights with Uncle Remus* (1883); *Mingo, and Other Sketches in Black and White* (1884); *Free Joe, and Other Georgian Sketches* (1887); *Uncle Remus and His Friends* (1892); *On the Plantation: A Story of a Georgia Boy's Adventures during the War* (1892); *Little Mr. Thimblefinger and His Queer Country* (1894); *The Chronicles of Aunt Minervy Ann* (1899); *On the Wing of Occasions* (1900); *The Tar Baby and Other Rhymes of Uncle Remus* (1904); *Uncle Remus and Brer Rabbit* (1906); *Uncle Remus Returns* (1918); etc. On staff of *Atlanta Constitution,* 1876–1900; editor, *Uncle Remus's Magazine,* June, 1907–July, 1908. *See* Julia Collier Harris's *The Life and Letters of Joel Chandler Harris* (1918); Ivy L. Lee's *"Uncle Remus": Joel Chandler Harris as Seen and Remembered by a Few of His Friends* (1908); Robert L. Wiggin's, *The Life of Joel Chandler Harris* (1918); S. B. Brooks's *Joel Chandler Harris, Folklorist* (1950); Paul M. Cousins' *Joel Chandler Harris* (1968).

HARRIS, JULIA COLLIER (Mrs. Julian La Rose Harris) (Nov. 11, 1875–); b. Atlanta, Ga. Editor: *The Life and Letters of Joel Chandler Harris* (1918); *Joel Chandler Harris: Editor and Essayist* (1931).

HARRIS, LAURA B. Author. *Ring in the New* (1950); *Bride of the River* (1956).

HARRIS, MARK (Nov. 19, 1922–); b. Mt. Vernon, N.Y. Author. *Trumpet to the World* (1946); *City of Discontent* (1952); *Something about a Soldier* (1957); *Wake Up, Stupid* (1959); *Friedman and Son* (1962); *Glove Boy* (1964); *Twenty-one Twice: A Journal* (1966); etc. Under pen name "Henry W.

Wiggen": *The Southpaw* (1953); *Bang the Drum Slowly* (1956).

HARRIS, MARVIN (Aug. 18, 1927–   ); b. Brooklyn, N.Y. Anthropologist, author. *Town and Country in Brazil* (1956); *Minorities in the New World* (with Charles Wagley, 1958); *Patterns of Race in the Americas* (1964); *The Nature of Cultural Things* (1964). Prof. anthropology, Columbia University, since 1963.

HARRIS, M[attie] VIRGINIA. Author. *Weddin' Trimmin's* (1949).

HARRIS, MIRIAM COLES (July 7, 1834–Jan. 23, 1925); b. Dosoris, L.I., N.Y. Novelist. *Rutledge* (anon., 1860); *Frank Warrington* (1863); *Missy* (1880); *Phoebe* (1884); *An Utter Failure* (1891); etc.

HARRIS, SEYMOUR EDWIN (Sept. 8, 1897–); b. New York. Economist. *Exchange Depreciation* (1936); *Economics of Social Security* (1941); *Inflation and the American Economy* (1945); *The European Recovery Program* (1948); *Economic Planning* (1949); *Economics of Mobilization and Inflation* (1951); *Economics of New England* (1952); *Keynes: Economist and Policy Maker* (1955); *International and Interregional Economics* (1957); *American Economic History* (1961); *Economics of the Kennedy Years* (1964); *Challenge and Change in American Education* (1965); etc. Editor: *Foreign Economic Policy for the United States* (1948); *Schumpeter, Social Scientist* (1951); *Higher Education in the United States: The Economic Problems* (with others, 1960); etc. Prof. economics, Harvard University, since 1945.

HARRIS, SYDNEY JUSTIN (Sept. 14, 1914–); b. London. Journalist, author. *Strictly Personal* (1953); *A Majority of One* (1957); *Last Things First* (1961); *On the Contrary* (1964); *Leaving the Surface* (1967). With Chicago *Daily News,* since 1941; writer of syndicated column "Strictly Personal," since 1950.

HARRIS, THADDEUS MASON (July 7, 1768–Apr. 3, 1842); b. Charlestown, Mass. Unitarian clergyman, librarian. Author. *Minor Encyclopedia,* 4v. (1803); *The Journal of a Tour into the Territory Northwest of the Alleghany Mountains* (1805); *Biographical Memorials of James Oglethorpe* (1841); and numerous other books on religion and on Freemasonry. Editor, *The Massachusetts Magazine,* 1795–1796.

HARRIS, THOMAS LAKE (May 15, 1823–Mar. 23, 1906); b. Fenny Stratford, England. Poet, mystic. *The Epic of the Starry Heaven* (1854); *The Great Republic* (1867); *Star Flowers* (1886); *God's Breath in Man* (1891); *The Brotherhood of the New Life* (1891); *The Song of Theos* (1903); etc.

HARRIS, WILLIAM TORREY (Sept. 10, 1835–Nov. 5, 1909); b. North Killingly, Conn. Philosopher, educator, editor, author. *Psychologic Foundations of Education* (1898); *The Spiritual Sense of Dante's Divina Commedia* (1889). Founder, *The Journal of Speculative Philosophy* (1867); editor, 1867–1909. Editor-in-chief, *Webster's International Dictionary,* 1900–09. Chief organizer of the Concord School of Philosophy. See *The St. Louis Movement in Philosophy,* ed. by Charles Milton Perry (1930); and *Studies in Honor of William Torrey Harris* (1935).

HARRIS, ZELLIG S[abbettai] (Oct. 12, 1909–); b. Balta, Rus. Educator, author. *Development of the Canaanite Dialects* (1939); *Methods in Structural Linguistics* (1951); *String Analysis of Sentence Structure* (1962); *Discourse Analysis Reprints* (1963); *Mathematical Structures of Language* (1968). Prof. linguistics, University of Pennsylvania, 1947–67.

HARRISON, BENJAMIN (Aug. 20, 1833–Mar. 13, 1901); b. North Bend, O. Twenty-third president of the United States, author. *Speeches* (1892); *This Country of Ours* (1897); *Views of an Ex-President,* comp. by M. L. Harrison (1901). *See* Lew Wallace's *Life of Gen. Ben Harrison* (1888).

HARRISON, CHARLES YALE (June 16, 1898–Mar. 17, 1954); b. Philadelphia, Pa. Author. *Generals Die in Bed* (1930); *Clarence Darrow* (1931); *A Child Is Born* (1931); *There Are Victories* (1933); *Meet Me on the Barricades* (1938); *Nobody's Fool* (1948); *Thank God for My Heart Attack* (1949); etc.

Harrison, Constance Cary. See Mrs. Burton Harrison.

HARRISON, EDITH OGDEN (Mrs. Carter H. Harrison) (d. May 22, 1955); b. New Orleans, La. Author. *Prince Silverwings* (1902); *Ladder of Moonlight* (1909); *Lady of the Snows* (1912); *Enchanted House and Other Fairy Tales* (1913); *All the Way 'Round* (1922); *Lands of the Sun* (1925); *The Scarlet Riders* (1930); *Strange to Say—Recollections of Persons and Events in New Orleans and Chicago* (1949); etc.

HARRISON, ELIZABETH (Sept. 1, 1849–Oct. 31, 1927); b. Athens, Ky. Pioneer in kindergarten work. Author. *A Study in Child Nature* (1890); *Montessori, and the Kindergarten* (1913); *Sketches along Life's Road* (autobiography, 1930).

HARRISON, GABRIEL (Mar. 25, 1818–Dec. 15, 1902); b. Philadelphia, Pa. Theatrical manager, playwright. *The Life and Writings of John Howard Payne* (1875); *Edwin Forrest* (1889); *Melanthia* (prod. 1866).

HARRISON, G[eorge] B[agshawe] (July 14, 1894–); b. Hove, Eng. Educator, author. *The Elizabethan Journals, 1591–1603,* 3v. (1928–33); *The Jacobean Journal, 1603–1606* (1941); *Shakespeare's Tragedies* (1951); *A Second Jacobean Journal, 1607–1610* (1958); *Profession of English* (1962); *The Fires of Arcadia* (1965); etc. Editor: *Shakespeare: The Complete Works* (1952). Prof. English, University of Michigan, 1949–64. Prof. Emeritus from 1964.

HARRISON, GILBERT A. (May 8, 1915–); b. Detroit, Mich. Publisher, *New Republic,* since 1953. Editor: *Gertrude Stein's America* (1965).

HARRISON, HENRY SYDNOR (Feb. 12, 1880–July 14, 1930); b. Sewanee, Tenn. Journalist, novelist. *Captivating Mary Carstairs* (under pen name, "Henry Second," 1910); *Queed* (1911); *V. V.'s Eyes* (1913); *Angela's Business* (1915); *Saint Teresa* (1922); *Andrew Bride of Paris* (1925); etc. Wrote "Rhymes for the Day" for the *Richmond Times-Dispatch,* Richmond, Va.

HARRISON, JAMES ALBERT (Aug. 21, 1848–Jan. 31, 1911); b. Pass Christian, Miss. Educator, philologist, author. *A Group of Poets and Their Haunts* (1875); *Greek Vignettes* (1878); *Spain in Profile* (1879); *Autrefois: A Collection of Creole Tales* (1885); etc. Editor: *The Complete Works of Edgar Allan Poe,* 17v. (1902). Compiler: *A Dictionary of Anglo-Saxon Poetry* (1900). Prof. Germanic languages, University of Virginia, 1895–1911.

HARRISON, JIM (Dec. 11, 1937–   ); b. Grayling, Mich. Author. *Plainsong* (1965); *Walking* (1967).

HARRISON, JOSEPH LE ROY (Oct. 12, 1862–May 19, 1950); b. North Adams, Mass. Librarian. Compiler: *Cap and Gown* (1893); *With Pipe and Book* (1897); *In College Days* (1901); and other anthologies of college verse. Librarian, Forbes Library, Northampton, Mass., from 1912.

HARRISON, MARGUERITE E[lton]; b. Baltimore, Md. Author. *Marooned in Moscow* (1921); *Asia Reborn* (1928); *Saints Run Mad* (1934); *There's Always Tomorrow* (autobiography, 1935); etc.

HARRISON, Mrs. BURTON (Constance Cary Harrison) (Apr. 25, 1843–Nov. 21, 1920); b. Fairfax Co., Va. Novelist, essayist. *Golden Rod* (1880); *Bar Harbor Days* (1887); *The Anglomaniacs* (1890); *Flower de Hundred: the Story of a Virginia Plantation* (1890); *A Daughter of the South* (1892); *Sweet Bells Out of Tune* (1893); *A Bachelor Maid* (1894); *Recollections Grave and Gay* (autobiography, 1911); etc.

HARRISON, WILLIAM HENRY (Feb. 9, 1773–Apr. 4, 1841); b. "Berkeley," Charles City Co., Va. Ninth president of the United States. See *Governors Messages and Letters: Messages and Letters of William H. Harrison,* ed. by Logan Esarey, in the *Indiana Historical Collections,* 2v. (1922). His letters are in the Manuscripts Division of the Library of Congress. *See* Dorothy B. Goebel's *William Henry Harrison* (1926); Freeman Cleave's *Old Tippecanoe* (1939).

HARRISSE, HENRY (Mar. 24, 1829–May 13, 1910); b. (Herisse) Paris, France, came to the United States c. 1847. Bibliographer, historian. *Notes on Columbus* (1866); *The Diplomatic History of America: Its First Chapter* (1892); *The Discovery of America* (1892); *Jean Cabot* (1896); etc. Compiler: *Bibliotheca Americana Vetustissima,* 2v. (1866, 1872); *Excerpta Colombiniana* (1887); etc. *See* Randolph G. Adams's *Three Americans* (1939).

HARSCH, JOSEPH C. (May 25, 1905–); b. Toledo, O. Journalist, author. *Pattern for Conquest* (1941); *The Curtain Isn't Iron* (1950). With *Christian Science Monitor,* since 1929.

HARSHA, DAVID ADDISON (Sept. 15, 1827–1895); b. Argyle, N.Y. Author. *The Life of Charles Sumner* (1856); *Life and Choice Works of Isaac Watts* (1857); *The Golden Age of English Literature* (1872); etc.

HART, ABRAHAM (Dec. 15, 1810–July 23, 1885); b. Philadelphia, Pa. Publisher. Became partner in publishing house of Carey and Hart, Philadelphia, in 1829; retired from firm in 1854. *See* Carey and Hart.

HART, ADOLPHUS M[ordecai] (1813–1879); b. in Canada. Author. Pen name, "Hampden." *History of the Discovery of the Valley of the Mississippi* (1852); *History of the Valley of the Mississippi* (1853); *Uncle Tom in Paris* (1854); *The Impending Crisis* (1855); *Life in the Far West; or, the Comical, Original, and Tragical Adventures of a Hoosier* (1860); etc.

HART, ALBERT GAILORD (Mar. 9, 1909–); b. Oak Park, Ill. Economist. *Money, Debt and Economic Activity* (1948); *Defense Without Inflation* (1951); *Defense and the Dollar* (1953); *Economic Order* (1958); *International Compensation for Fluctuations in Commodity Trade* (1961); *Anticipations, Uncertainty, and Dynamic Planning* (1965); etc.

HART, ALBERT BUSHNELL (July 1, 1854–June 16, 1943); b. Clarksville, Pa. Educator, historian, editor. *Formation of the Union* (1892); *Essentials of American History* (1905); *The Southern South* (1911); *Monroe Doctrine* (1915); *America at War* (1917); *New American History* (1917); *We and Our History* (1923). Editor: *Epochs of American History,* 4v. (1891–1921); *American History Told by Contemporaries,* 5v. (1898–1929); *Source Book of American History* (1899); *The American Nation,* 28v. (1904–18); *American Year Book,* 1911–20, 1926–32, etc. History dept., Harvard University, 1883–1926.

HART, CHARLES HENRY (Feb. 4, 1847–July 29, 1918); b. Philadelphia, Pa. Art critic, author. *Catalogue of the Engraved Portraits of Washington* (1904); *Frauds in Historical Portraiture,* in the *Annual Report of the American Historical Association,* 1913; etc.

HART, FRANCES NOYES (Aug. 10, 1890–Oct. 25, 1943); b. Silver Springs, Md. Author. *Mark* (1913); *The Bellamy Trial* (1927); *Pigs in Clover* (1931); *The Crooked Lane* (1934); etc.

HART, HENRY HERSCH (Sept. 27, 1886–); b. San Francisco, Calif. Lecturer, traveler. Author or translator: *A Chinese Market* (poems, 1931); *The Hundred Names* (poems, 1933); *The West Chamber* (play, 1936); *Seven Hundred Chinese Proverbs* (1937); *A Garden of Peonies* (poems, 1938); *Sea Road to the Indies* (1950); etc.

HART, HORNELL [Norris] (Aug. 2, 1888–Feb. 1967); b. St. Paul, Minn. Sociologist. *The Great Debate on American For-*

eign *Policy* (ed., 1951); *Autoconditioning: The New Way to a Successful Life* (1956); *Your Share of God* (1958); *The Enigma of Survival* (1959).

HART, JAMES MORGAN (Nov. 2, 1839–Apr. 18, 1916); b. Princeton, N.J. Educator, author. *German Universities: A Narrative of Personal Reminiscences* (1874); *Essentials of Prose Composition* (1902); etc. Book reviewer, *The Nation.* Prof. rhetoric and English philology, Cornell University, 1890–1907.

HART, JEROME ALFRED (Sept. 6, 1854–Jan. 3, 1937); b. San Francisco, Calif. Editor, author. *Argonaut Letters* (1900); *Two Argonauts in Spain* (1904); *A Levantine Log-Book* (1905); *The Golconda Bonanza* (1923). Editor: *Argonaut Stories* (1906). Assoc. editor, *San Francisco Argonaut,* 1880–91; editor, 1891–1907.

HART, JOHN LEWIS (Feb. 18, 1931–); b. Endicott, N.Y. Cartoonist. *Hey! B.C.* (1959); *Back to B.C.* (1960); *B.C. Strikes Back* (1961); *The Sunday Best of B.C.* (1964). Cartoonist, Syndicated comic strips *B.C.,* since 1958; *The Wizard of Id,* since 1964.

HART, JOHN SEELY (Jan. 28, 1810–Mar. 26, 1877); b. Stockbridge, Mass. Educator, editor, author. *The Female Prose Writers of America* (1857); *A Manual of American Literature* (1872); *A Manual of English Literature* (1872); etc. Founder, the *Sunday School Times,* 1859; editor, 1859–71. Prof. rhetoric and English literature, Princeton, 1872–74.

HART, JOSEPH C. (d. 1855). Novelist. *Miriam Coffin; or, The Whale-Fishermen,* 2v. (anon. 1834); *The Romance of Yachting* (1848).

HART, JOSEPH KINMONT (Feb. 16, 1876–Mar. 10, 1949); b. Columbia City, Ind. Educator, author. *Critical Studies of Current Theories of Moral Education* (1910); *Democracy in Education* (1918); *The Discovery of Intelligence* (1924); *Inside Experience* (1927); *Education for an Age of Power* (1935); *Mind in Transition* (1938); etc. Prof. education, Columbia University, 1934–40.

HART, JULIA CATHERINE BECKWITH (1796–1867). Author. *Tonnewonte; or, The Adopted Son of America,* 2v. (anon., 1824–25).

HART, MOSS (Oct. 24, 1904–Dec. 20, 1961); b. New York. Playwright. *The Hold-Up Man* (prod. 1923); *Once in a Lifetime* (with George S. Kaufman, 1930); *As Thousands Cheer* (prod. 1933); *Merrily We Roll Along* (with George Kaufman, prod. 1934); *You Can't Take It With You* (with same, prod. 1936, Pulitzer Prize play, 1937); *The Fabulous Invalid* (with same, prod. 1938); *The American Way* (with George S. Kaufman, prod. 1938); *The Man Who Came to Dinner* (with same, prod. 1939); *Lady in the Dark* (1941); *Winged Victory* (prod. 1943); *Christopher Blake* (prod. 1946); *Light Up the Sky* (prod. 1948); *The Climate of Eden* (prod. 1952); *Act One: An Autobiography* (1959); etc.

HART, WALTER MORRIS (Nov. 23, 1872–); b. Philadelphia, Pa. Educator, author. *Ballad and Epic: A Study in the Development of the Narrative Art* (1907); *Kipling, the Story Writer* (1918); *High Comedy in the Odyssey* (1943); *Five Gayley Lectures* (1954); etc. Editor: *English Popular Ballads* (1916). English dept., University of California, since 1895.

HART, WILLIAM S. (Dec. 6, 1872–June 23, 1946); b. Newburgh, N.Y. Motion picture actor, author. *A Lighter of Flames* (1923); *My Life East and West* (autobiography, 1929); *Hoofbeats* (1933); *The Law on Horseback, and Other Stories* (1935); *And All Points West* (1940).

HARTE, BRET [Francis Brett] (Aug. 25, 1839–May 5, 1902); b. Albany, N.Y. Short story writer, poet, novelist. *The Lost Galleon, and Other Tales* (verse, 1867); *Condensed Novels,* 2 series (1867, 1902); *The Luck of Roaring Camp, and Other Sketches* (1870); *Poems* (1871); *Mrs. Skagg's Husbands*

(1873); *Tales of the Argonauts* (1875); *Gabriel Conroy,* 3v. (1876); *Maruja* (1885); *Cressy* (1889); *Susy* (1893); *Clarence* (1895); *Tales of Trail and Town* (1898); *From Sand Hill to Pine* (1900); *Trent's Toast* (1903); *Sketches of the Sixties* (1926); *Complete Works,* 10v. (1929); etc. Editor: *Outcroppings* (verse, 1866). Editor, the *Overland Monthly,* 1868–70. Among his best known short stories is *The Outcasts of Poker Flat* (q.v.); his best known poem is "The Heathen Chinee" (q.v.). For complete bibliography, *see* Merle Johnson's *American First Editions,* 3rd edition rev. by Jacob Blanck (1936). *See* T. E. Pemberton's *Life of Bret Harte* (1903); George R. Stewart's *Bret Harte* (1931); Stanley Walker's *San Francisco's Literary Frontier* (1939); Richard O'Connor's *Bret Harte* (1966).

HARTFORD, HUNTINGTON (Apr. 18, 1911–); b. New York. Publisher, editor, financier, art patron, author. *Jane Eyre* (play, 1958); *Art or Anarchy* (1964). Publisher and editor, *Show* Magazine.

Hartford Courant. Hartford, Conn. Newspaper. Founded 1764, as the *Connecticut Courant,* by Thomas Green. Became a daily in 1837. Its editors have included Joseph R. Hawley, Charles Dudley Warner, and Charles Hopkins Clark. The *Connecticut Courant Supplement,* which carried fiction, ran from 1825 to 1878. Elizabeth A. McSherry edits the Sunday book review.

Hartford Times. Hartford, Conn. Newspaper. Founded 1817, as a weekly, by Frederick Dunton Bolles and John M. Niles. Became a daily in 1841. Alfred E. Burr founded the daily edition and headed the paper until 1900. His son, Willie O. Burr, succeeded him. Gideon Welles became editor in 1826. Nat A. Sestero is the present editor. Theodore L. Holden is book review editor.

Hartford Wits. Name given to a distinguished literary group in Hartford, Conn. The leading members were John Trumbull, Joel Barlow, Theodore Dwight, Lemuel Hopkins, Elihu Smith, Richard Alsop, and David Humphreys. This group brought new life to the solemn-toned New England literature which had prevailed for generations. Sometimes called "The Connecticut Wits" and the "Pleiades." See: *The Anarchiad;* Henry A. Beers's *The Connecticut Wits* (1920); Vernon L. Parrington's *The Connecticut Wits* (1926); and Annie R. Marble's *The Hartford Wits* (1936).

HARTLEY, GEORGE INNESS (May 21, 1887–); b. Montclair, N.J. Artist, author. *The Boy Hunters in Demerara* (1921); *The Last Parrakeet* (1923); *The Lost Flamingo* (1924).

HARTLEY, HELENE WILLEY; b. Freeville, N.Y. Educator, author. *Tests in the Interpretive Reading of Poetry* (1930). Editor: *Interest Trails in Literature,* 3v. (1935); etc. Dept. of education, Syracuse University, after 1934.

HARTMAN, GERTRUDE (d. May 12, 1955); b. Philadelphia, Pa. Editor, author. *The Child and the School* (1921); *Creative Expression* (1931); *These United States* (1932); *Machines* (1939); *The Making of a Democracy* (1940); *America —Land of Freedom* (1946); *In Bible Days* (1948); etc. Editor, *Progressive Education,* 1924–30.

HARTMAN, LEE FOSTER (Oct. 2, 1879–deceased); b. Ft. Wayne, Ind. Editor. With Harper & Brothers, New York, from 1904; vice president, from 1936; with *Harper's Magazine* from 1908; editor, since 1931.

HARTMANN, SADAKICHI (Nov. 8, 1869–1944); b. Nagasaki, Japan. Author. *Shakespeare in Art* (1901); *A History of American Art,* 2v. (1902); *Japanese Art* (1904); *Drifting Flowers of the Sea* (poems, 1906); *The Whistler Book* (1910); *My Rubaiyat* (poems, 1913); *Passport to Immortality* (1927); *Seven Short Stories* (1930); etc.

HARTSHORNE, CHARLES (June 5, 1897–); b. Kittanning, Pa. Educator, author. *The Philosophy and Psychology of Sen-*

sation (1934); *Beyond Humanism* (1937); *Man's Vision of God and the Logic of Theism* (1941); *The Divine Relativity* (1948); *Reality as Social Process* (1953); *The Logic of Perfection* (1962); *Anselm's Discovery* (1965); *A Natural Theology for Our Time* (1967); etc. Editor: *Collected Papers of Charles S. Peirce* (1931–35). Prof. philosophy, Emory University, 1955–62. Prof. of philosophy, Univ. of Texas, since 1963.

HARTSHORNE, HENRY (Mar. 16, 1823–Feb. 10, 1897); b. Philadelphia, Pa. Pen name "Corinne L'Estrange." Novelist, poet, physician. *Woman's Witchcraft* (1854); *Summer's Songs* (1865); etc.

HARTSHORNE, HUGH (Nov. 13, 1885–Dec. 13, 1967); b. Lawrence, Mass. Congregational clergyman, educator, author. *Childhood and Character* (1919); *Standards and Trends in Religious Education* (with others, 1933); *Ethical Dilemmas of Ministers* (with F. F. Mueller, 1937); etc. Editor: *From School to College* (1939). With Yale Divinity School, since 1929.

HARTSOCK, ERNEST (May 5, 1903–Dec. 14, 1930); b. in Georgia. Editor, poet. *Strange Splendor* (1930); *Romance and Stardust* (1925); *Narcissus and Iscariot* (1927). Editor: *Patterns for Pan* (1928). Founder, *Bozart*, 1927; editor, 1927–30.

HARTT, ROLLIN LYNDE (Nov. 20, 1869–June 17, 1946); b. Ithaca, N.Y. Congregational clergyman, journalist, author. *Understanding the French* (1914); *Confessions of a Clergyman* (anon., 1915); etc.

HARTWICK, HARRY. Educator, author. *The Foreground of American Fiction* (1934); *A History of American Letters* (with Walter Fuller Taylor, 1936).

Harvard Classics, The. Ed. by Charles W. Eliot, 50v. (1909–10). Known as the "Five-Foot Shelf." Includes literary classics of all nations. William Allan Neilson was assoc. editor.

Harvard University Press. Cambridge, Mass. Founded 1913. Dumas Malone became director in 1936; Mark Carroll is now director. Harvard University had its own printing press as early as 1872. In 1933 it took over the Loeb Classical Library.

Harvardiana. Cambridge, Mass. Founded 1835. James Russell Lowell was one of the editors. Expired 1838. This magazine was similar to the *Harvard Register,* Mar., 1827–Feb., 1828, and *The Collegian,* 1830, to which O. W. Holmes contributed.

Harvester, The. Novel by Gene Stratton Porter (1911). David Langston, herb gardener and dreamer, idealizes his wife who does not return his love. Illness and separation awaken her latent affections, and her life is saved by David's herb medicines.

Harvey. Play by Mary Coyle Chase (prod. 1944). Comic fantasy about a man whose drinking turns up an imaginary friend, the oversize rabbit Harvey.

HARVEY, ALEXANDER (Dec. 25, 1868–Nov. 20, 1949); b. Brussels, Belgium. Editor, author. *The Toe, and Other Tales* (1913); *William Dean Howells* (1917); *Shelley's Elopement* (1918); etc. Assoc. editor, *Current Opinion*, 1905–22; *American Monthly,* 1922–29.

HARVEY, GEORGE BRINTON McCLELLAN (Feb. 16, 1864–Aug. 20, 1928); b. Peacham, Vt. Editor, diplomat, author. *Henry Clay Frick* (1928). Editor: *The North American Review,* 1899–1926; *Harper's Weekly,* 1901–13; *The Washington Post,* 1924–25. Ambassador to England, 1921–23.

HARVEY, GEORGE COCKBURN (1858–deceased); b. Thornby, Eng. Editor, author. *The Light That Lies* (1894); *Famous Four-Footed Friends* (1916); etc. Editor: *Robin Hood* (1924).

Harvey, Paul. Pen name of Paul Harvey Aurandt.

HARWELL, RICHARD BARKSDALE (June 6, 1915–); b. Washington, Ga. Librarian, author. *Confederate Belles-Lettres* (1941); *Confederate Music* (1950); *Cornerstones of Confederate Collecting* (1953); *The Union Reader* (1958); etc. Editor: *The War They Fought* (1960); *A Confederate Marine* (1963); *Hawthorne and Longfellow* (1966). Librarian, Bowdoin College, since 1961.

HASBROUCK, LOUISE SEYMOUR (Mrs. Louise Hasbrouck Zimm) (May 5, 1883–); b. Ogdensburg, N.Y. Author. *La Salle* (1916); *Israel Putnam* (1916); *The Hall with Doors* (1920); *Those Careless Kincaids* (1928); *At the Sign of the Wild Horse* (1929); etc. Compiler: *Southeastern New York* (with others, 1946).

Hasheesh Eater, The. By Fitz Hugh Ludlow (1859). Account of the author's struggles against the narcotic hashish. *Cf.* Thomas De Quincey's *Confessions of an English Opium-Eater* (1822).

HASKEL, DANIEL (1784–Aug. 9, 1848); b. Preston, Conn. Congregational clergyman, educator, author. *A Chronological View of the World* (1845); etc. Compiler: *A Complete Descriptive and Statistical Gazetteer of the United States of America* (1843). President, University of Vermont, 1821–24.

HASKELL, DANIEL C. (Jan. 12, 1883–); b. Vernon, Vt. Bibliographer. Compiler: *List of Works Relating to the West Indies* (1912); *Checklist of Newspapers and Official Gazettes in the New York Public Library* (1915); *List of American Dramas* (1916); *Foreign Plays in English* (1920); *Provençal Language and Literature* (1925); *Manhattan Maps* (1931); *American Historical Prints* (with I. N. Phelps Stokes, 1932); *The Shorthand Collection in the New York Public Library* (with Karl Brown, 1935); *Tentative Check-list of Early European Railway Literature* (1955); etc. Editor: *On Reconnaissance for the Great Northern* (1948). With New York Public Library, since 1908; chief bibliographer, since 1938.

HASKELL, HELEN EGGLESTON (1871–); b. Fairwater, Wis. Author. *Billy's Princess* (1907); *Katrinka* (1915); *Katrinka Grows Up* (1932); *Nadya Makes Her Bow* (1938); etc.

HASKINS, CHARLES HOMER (Dec. 12, 1870–May 14, 1937); b. Meadville, Pa. Educator, author. *The Normans in European History* (1915); *The Rise of Universities* (1923); *The Renaissance of the Twelfth Century* (1927); *Studies in Medieval Culture* (1929); etc. Prof. history, Harvard University, 1902–31.

HASSARD, JOHN ROSE GREENE (Sept. 4, 1836–Apr. 18, 1888); b. New York. Journalist, author. *Richard Wagner at Bayreuth* (1877); *A History of the United States of America* (1878); *A Pickwickian Pilgrimage* (1881). Editor, *The Catholic World,* 1865.

Hastings, Elizabeth. Pen name of Margaret Pollock Sherwood.

HASTINGS, THOMAS (Oct. 15, 1784–May 15, 1872); b. Washington, Conn. Hymn-writer, composer. *Dissertation on Musical Taste* (1822); *Devotional Hymns and Religious Poems* (1850). Compiler: *Musical Miscellany,* 2v. (1836); *The Sacred Lyre* (1840); *Selah* (1856); and many other hymnals. See F. J. Metcalf's *American Writers and Compilers of Sacred Music* (1925).

"Hasty Pudding, The." Poem by Joel Barlow (1793). Long mock-heroic poem about cornmeal-mush as food for man. Dedicated to Mrs. Washington.

Hasty Pudding Club. A dramatic organization founded in 1770 at Harvard College. It was called the Hasty Pudding Institute at first. The Hasty Pudding Club library was founded in 1807.

HASWELL, ALANSON MASON (June 29, 1847–deceased); b. Maulmain, Burma, of American parentage. Author. *Wayside Verses* (1910); *A Daughter of the Ozarks* (1921); *A*

Drama of the Hills (1923); *An Ozark Oligarchy* (1927), republished as *The Revolt* (1931); *Autobiography* (1929); *Virginia Justice* (1931); etc.

HASWELL, ANTHONY (Apr. 6, 1756–May 22, 1816); b. Portsmouth, England. Editor, printer, ballad writer. Editor, *The Massachusetts Spy*, 1777-78; founder, with Elisha Babcock, of the *Massachusetts Gazette; or, The Springfield and Northampton Weekly Advertiser*, May 14, 1782; founder, *The Vermont Gazette, or Freeman's Depository*, June 5, 1783, which he ran until 1816. See John Spargo's *Anthony Haswell* (1925).

HATCH, ALDEN (Sept. 28, 1898–); b. New York. Author. *Gaming Lady* (1931); *Glass Walls* (1933); *Bridlewise* (1942); *Glenn Curtiss* (1942); *Heroes of Annapolis* (1943); *Young Willkie* (1944); *Franklin D. Roosevelt* (1947); *Woodrow Wilson* (1947); *General Patton* (1950); *Red Carpet for Mamie* (1954); *Ambassador Extraordinary: Clare Boothe Luce* (1956); *The Wadsworths of the Genesee* (1959); *The De Gaulle Nobody Knows* (1960); *Edith Bolling Wilson* (1961); *Bernhard, Prince of the Netherlands* (1962); *A Man Named John: Pope John XXIII* (1963); *Apostle of Peace* (1965); *The Mountbattens* (1966); *We Nehrus* (1967); etc. Editor: *Thank You Twice* (1941).

HATCH, ERIC STOW (Oct. 31, 1901–); b. New York. Author. *A Couple of Quick Ones* (1928); *Domestic Animal* (1929); *Road Show* (1934); *Fly by Night* (1935); *My Man Godfrey* (1935); *Good Old Jack* (1936); *The Captain Needs a Mate* (1937); *June Remembers* (1938); *Unexpected Uncle* (1941); *Words and Music* (1943); *Unexpected Warrior* (1947); *A Beautiful Bequest* (1950); *Spousery: Her Edition* (1956); *The Year of the Horse* (1965); *Two and Two Is Six* (1969).

HATCH, LOUIS CLINTON (Sept. 1, 1872–Dec. 2, 1931); b. Bangor, Me. Historian. *The History of Bowdoin College* (1927); *A History of the Vice-Presidency* (1934). Editor-in-chief: *Maine: A History*, 3v. (1919).

HATCH, MARY R. PLATT (b. June 19, 1848); b. Stratford, N.H. Novelist. *The Upland Mystery* (1887); *The Bank Tragedy* (1890); *The Missing Man* (1893); *The Strange Disappearance of Eugene Comstocks* (1895); *The Berkeley Street Mystery* (1928); etc.

HATCH, RICHARD WARREN (Apr. 1, 1898–); b. Framingham, Mass. Author. *Into the Wind* (1929); *Old New England Ships* (1931); *This Bright Summer* (1933); *The Fugitive* (1938); *All Aboard the Whale* (1942); *Lobster Books* (1951); etc.

HATCH, WILLIAM HENRY PAINE (Aug. 2, 1875– deceased); b. Camden, N.J. Episcopal clergyman, educator. Compiler, *The Gospel Manuscripts of the General Theological Seminary* (with C. C. Edmunds, 1918); *The Greek Manuscripts of the New Testament at Mount Sinai* (1932); *The Greek Manuscripts of the New Testament in Jerusalem* (1934); *The Principal Uncial Manuscripts of the New Testament* (1939); *Album of Dated Syriac Manuscripts* (1947); *Facsimiles and Descriptions of Minuscule Manuscripts of the New Testament* (1951); etc. Prof. New Testament, Episcopal Theological School, Cambridge, Mass., since 1919.

HATCHER, HARLAN [Henthorne] (Sept. 9, 1898–); b. Ironton, Ohio. Educator, author. *Tunnel Hill* (1931); *Patterns of Wolfpen* (1934); *Creating the American Novel* (1935); *Central Standard Time* (1937); *The Buckeye Country* (1940); *The Great Lakes* (1944); *The Western Reserve* (1949); *A Century of Iron and Men* (1950); *Giant from the Wilderness* (1955); *A Pictorial History of the Great Lakes* (1963); *Creating the Modern American Novel* (1965); *The Western Reserve* (1966). English dept., Ohio State University, 1922–44; pres. University of Michigan, 1951–1967; pres. emeritus since 1967.

HATFIELD, CLARENCE E. Novelist. *Waglets* (under pen name, "Takkie Caution," 1902); *The Echo of Union Chapel* (1912); *The Tug of the Millstone* (1915); *One Man's Destiny* (1937).

HATFIELD, EDWIN FRANCIS (Jan. 9, 1807–Sept. 22, 1883); b. Elizabeth, N.J. Presbyterian clergyman, hymn-writer. Author: *St. Helena and the Cape of Good Hope* (1852); *The Poets of the Church* (1884); etc. Compiler: *The Church Hymn Book* (1872).

HATFIELD, HENRY CARAWAY (June 3, 1912–); b. Evanston, Ill. Educator, author. *Winckelmann and His German Critics* (1943); *Thomas Mann* (1951); *Schnitzler, Kafka, Mann* (with J. M. Stein, 1953); *Goethe: A Critical Introduction* (1963); *Aesthetic Paganism in General Literature* (1964); *Modern German Literature* (1967). Editor: *The Lichtenberg Reader* (with F. H. Mautner, 1959); *Thomas Mann: A Collection of Critical Essays* (1964). General editor, *Germanic Review*, 1947–53. Prof. German, Harvard University, 1956–67. Prof. German Art, Culture since 1967.

HATFIELD, JAMES TAFT (June 15, 1862–Oct. 3, 1945); b. Brooklyn, N.Y. Educator, editor, author. *From Broom to Heather* (1903); *New Light on Longfellow* (1933); *German Culture in the U.S.* (1936); etc. Editor: *German Lyrics and Ballads* (1900); *Shorter German Poems* (1915). Prof. German language and literature, Northwestern University, 1890–1934.

HATHAWAY, BAXTER L. (Dec. 4, 1909–   ); b. Cincinnati, O. *The Stubborn Way* (1937); *Writing Mature Prose* (1952); *The Age of Criticism* (1962). Editor, *Epoch*, since 1947. English dept., Cornell University, since 1946.

HATHAWAY, BENJAMIN (b. Sept. 30, 1822); b. in Cayuga Co., N.Y. Farmer, nurseryman, poet. *Art-Life, and Other Poems* (1877); *The League of the Iroquois, and Other Legends* (1880); *The Finished Creation, and Other Poems* (1892).

HATTON, FANNY [Cottinet Locke] (Mrs. Frederic Hatton) (b. c. 1870–Nov. 27, 1939); b. Chicago, Ill (?). Playwright. Author (with husband): *Years of Discretion* (prod. 1912); *Lombardi, Ltd.* (prod. 1917); *The Indestructible Wife* (prod. 1918); *Playthings* (prod. 1925); *Treat 'Em Rough* (prod. 1926); etc.

HATTON, FREDERIC (July 30, 1879–); b. Peru, Ill. Critic, playwright. Author (with wife, Fanny Hatton): *Years of Discretion* (prod. 1912); *Lombardi, Ltd.* (prod. 1917); *The Indestructible Wife* (prod. 1918); *Playthings* (prod. 1925); *Treat 'Em Rough* (prod. 1926); *We Girls* (1937); etc. Drama critic, *Chicago Evening Post*, since 1909.

HAUCK, LOUISE PLATT (Aug. 15, 1883–Dec. 10, 1943); b. Argentine, Kan. Novelist. Pen names, "Lane Archer," "Louise Landon," "Peter Ash," and "Jean Randall." *Missouri Yesterdays* (1920); *The Gold Trail* (1929); *Partners* (1929); *Sylvia* (1931); *The Green Light* (1931); *Mystery Mansion* (1931); *Lucky Shot* (1931); *Untarnished* (1931); *Wild Grapes* (1931); *The Pink House* (1933); *The Story of Nancy Meadows* (1933); *Blackberry Winter* (1934); *Friday's Child* (1934); *Bridesmaid* (1936); *Beloved Buff* (1940); *Peppertree Inn* (1941); *Soft as Silk* (1942); *Gardenias for Sue* (1942); *The Little Secretary* (1942); *A Woman Will or Won't* (1942); *Careless Rapture* (1943); *Evergreen House* (1943); *Cary Fordyce* (1943); *Traveler's End* (1943); *No Sweeter Woman* (1943).

Haupt, William Ayres. See William Ayres Mestayer.

HAVELOCK, ERIC ALFRED (June 3, 1903–); b. London. Educator, author. *Lyric Genius of Catullus* (1939); *Crucifixion of Intellectual Man* (1950); *The Liberal Temper in Greek Politics* (1957); *Preface to Plato* (1963). Prof. Greek and Latin, Harvard University, 1951–63.

HAVEN, ALICE BRADLEY NEAL (Mrs. Joseph C. Neal; Mrs. Samuel L. Haven) (Sept. 13, 1827–Aug. 23, 1863); b.

(Emily Bradley) Hudson, N.Y. Novelist. Pen name, "Cousin Alice." *Helen Morton's Trial* (1849); *The Gossips of Rivertown* (1850); *"All's Not Gold That Glitters"; or, The Young Californian* (1853); *Out of Debt, Out of Danger* (1855); etc. Editor, *Saturday Gazette,* Philadelphia, 1847–53.

HAVENS, GEORGE REMINGTON (Aug. 25, 1890–); b. Shelter Island Heights, N.Y. Educator, author. *The Abbé Prévost and English Literature* (1921); *The Age of Ideas* (1955). Editor: *Selections from Voltaire* (1925); *Voltaire's Marginalia on Rousseau* (1933); and other books on Voltaire. French dept., Ohio State University, 1919–61. Emeritus since 1961.

HAVENS, RAYMOND DEXTER (July 25, 1880–1958); b. Rochester, N.Y. Educator, editor, author. *The Influence of Milton on English Poetry* (1922); *The Mind of a Poet* (1941); etc. Joint editor, *Modern Language Notes.* Prof. English, Johns Hopkins University, 1925–47.

HAVERLY, CHRISTOPHER (June 30, 1837–Sept. 28, 1901); b. Boiling Springs, Pa. Theatrical manager, minstrel. Compiler, *Haverly's Genuine Georgia Minstrels' Songster* (1879).

HAVIGHURST, WALTER [Edwin] (Nov. 28, 1901–); b. Appleton, Wis. Educator, author. *Pier 17* (1935); *The Quiet Shore* (1937); *Upper Mississippi: A Wilderness Saga* (1937); *The Winds of Spring* (1940); *The Long Ships Passing* (1942); *Land of Promise* (1946); *The Signature of Time* (1949); *Wilderness for Sale* (1956); *The Miami Years* (1958); *Vein of Iron* (1959); *Land of the Long Horizons* (1960); *The Heathland* (1962); *Voices on the River* (1964); *The Midwest* (1965); *The Great Lakes Reader* (1966); *Three Flags at the Straits* (1966); *Alexander Sportwood: Portrait of a Governor* (1967); etc. English dept., Miami University, Oxford, O., since 1928.

HAVILAND-TAYLOR, KATHARINE; b. Mankato, Minn. Novelist. *Cecilia of the Pink Roses* (1917); *Cross Currents* (1922); *The Family Failing* (1931); etc.

HAVILL, EDWARD (Nov. 29, 1907–   ); b. Rochester, N.Y. Novelist. *Tell It to the Laughing Stars* (1942); *The Low Road* (1944); *Big Ember* (1947); *Pinnacle* (1951).

HAWES, CHARLES BOARDMAN (Jan. 24, 1889–July 15, 1923); b. Clifton Springs, N.Y. Author. *The Mutineers* (1920); *The Great Quest* (1921); *The Dark Frigate* (1923); *Gloucester, by Land and Sea* (1923); *Whaling* (1924).

HAWES, CHARLES HENRY (Sept. 30, 1867–Dec. 13, 1943); b. New Southgate, Eng. Anthropologist. *In the Uttermost East* (1903); *Crete, the Forerunner of Greece* (with Harriet Boyd Hawes, 1909); etc. With Museum of Fine Arts, Boston, 1919–34, assoc. director, 1924–34.

HAWES, WILLIAM POST (Feb. 4, 1803–1842); b. New York City. Lawyer, author. *Sporting Scenes and Sundry Sketches: Being the Miscellaneous Writings of J. Cypress, Jr.: Edited by Frank Forester* [i.e., Henry William Herbert], 2v. (1842).

HAWKES, CLARENCE (Dec. 16, 1869–Jan. 19, 1954); b. Goshen, Mass. Blind poet. *Pebbles and Shells* (poems, 1895); *Idyls of Old New England* (poems, 1897); *Master Frisky* (1902); *Hitting the Dark Trail* (autobiography, 1915); *Silversheen* (1924); *Jungle Joe* (1926); *Bing* (1929); *The Light That Did Not Fail* (autobiography, 1935); *Igloo Stories* (1937); *Notes of a Naturalist* (1938); *Christmas All the Year* (1938); *Holiday Hopes* (1939); *My Country (The America I Know)* (1940); *The Strange Adventures of Mr. Turtle* (1944); etc.

HAWKES, ERNEST WILLIAM (July 19, 1881–); b. Ashfield, Mass. Educator, biologist, poet. *Eskimo Land* (1914); *Dance Festivals of the Alaskan Eskimo* (1914); *Wood Gods* (poems, 1935); *Interpretations* (1936); *Songs of the Redwood Highway* (1939); *Paths of Peace* (1952); etc. Prof. biology, Glendale Junior College, Glendale, Calif., since 1928.

HAWKES, JOHN (Aug. 17, 1925–); b. Stamford, Conn. Author. *Cannibal* (1950); *Beetle Leg* (1951); *Goose on the Grave* (1954); *The Lime Twig* (1961); *Second Skin* (1964); *The Innocent Party* (1966); etc.

HAWKINS, MICAH (Jan. 1, 1777–July 29, 1825); b. Stony Brook, L.I., N.Y. Grocer, poet, playwright. *Mynehieur von Herrick Heimelman, the Dancing Master; or, The Confluence of Nassau-Street and Maiden-Lane, As It Was Whilom* (poem, 1824); *The Saw-Mill; or, A Yankee Trick* (prod. 1824).

HAWKINS, RUSH CHRISTOPHER (Sept. 14, 1831–Oct. 25, 1920); b. Pomfret, Vt. Book collector, author. *Titles of the First Books from the Earliest Presses* (1884). His collection of incunabula is now in the Annmary Brown Memorial, Providence, R.I., which he erected in memory of his wife. During the Civil War he was the leader of "Hawkins' Zouaves."

HAWKS, FRANCIS LISTER (June 10, 1798–Sept. 27, 1866); b. New Bern, N.C. Episcopal clergyman, editor, book collector, author. *Early History of the Southern States* (1832); *History of North Carolina,* 2v. (1857–58); *Romance of Biography* (1855); *The English Language* (1867); *Poems Hitherto Uncollected* (1873); etc. He also wrote books for children under the pen names, "Uncle Philip" and "Lambert Lilly." President, University of Louisiana, 1844–49. The American history library collected by Hawks was purchased by William Niblo, the theatrical manager, and presented to the New York Historical Society. *See* E. A. Duyckinck's *A Memorial of Francis Lister Hawks* (1871).

Hawks of Hawk Hollow, The. Novel by Robert Montgomery Bird (1835). The scene is Pennsylvania during the American Revolution.

HAWLEY, CAMERON (Sept. 19, 1905–Feb. 9, 1969); b. Howard, S.D. Author. *Executive Suite* (1952); *Cash McCall* (1955); *The Lincoln Lords* (1960); *The Hurricane Years* (1968).

HAWORTH, PAUL LELAND (Aug. 28, 1876–Mar. 24, 1938); b. W. Newton, Ind. Educator, historian. *The Path of Glory* (1911); *George Washington: Farmer* (1915); *Trailmakers of the Northwest* (1921); etc. Prof. history, Butler College, 1922–38.

HAWTHORNE, HILDEGARDE (Mrs. John Milton Oskison) (d. 1952); b. New York City, dau. of Julian Hawthorne. Author. *A Country Interlude* (1904); *Poems* (1904); *Essays* (1907); *Women and Other Women* (1908); *Old Seaport Towns of New England* (1916); *Girls in Bookland* (1917); *Rambles in Old College Towns* (1917); *Makeshift Farm* (1925); *Deedah's Wonderful Years* (1927); *Romantic Rebel: The Story of Nathaniel Hawthorne* (1932); *Lone Rider* (1933); *Romantic Cities of California* (1934); *Youth's Captain: The Story of Ralph Waldo Emerson* (1935); *Enos Mills of the Rockies* (with E. B. Mills, 1935); *Poet of Craigie House: The Life of Longfellow* (1936); *Rising Thunder: The Life of Jack Jouett* (1937); *The Happy Autocrat: The Life of Oliver Wendell Holmes* (1939); *Romantic Cities of California* (1939); *No Road Too Long* (1940); *Williamsburg* (1941); *Matthew Fontaine Maury, Trail Maker of the Seas* (1943); *Give Me Liberty, the Story of Patrick Henry* (1945); *Westward the Course* (1946); *Born to Adventure* (1947); *His World Was the Country, A Life of Thomas Paine* (1949); etc.

HAWTHORNE, JULIAN (June 22, 1846–July 14, 1934); b. Boston, Mass., son of Nathaniel Hawthorne. Novelist, biographer. *Bressart* (1873); *Idolatry* (1874); *Garth* (1877); *Sebastian Strome* (1880); *Fortune's Fool* (1883); *Beatrice Randolph* (1884); *Nathaniel Hawthorne and His Wife,* 2v. (1884); *Noble Blood* (1885); *John Parmalee's Curse* (1886); *Confessions and Criticisms* (1887); *A Dream and a Forgetting* (1888); *American Literature* (1891); *The Golden Fleece* (1892); *The Story of Oregon,* 2v. (1892); *A Fool of Nature* (1896); *Hawthorne and His Circle* (1903); *The Subterranean Brotherhood* (1914); *Shapes That Pass* (1928); *The Memoirs,* ed. by his wife, Edith Garrigues Hawthorne (1938); etc. Editor: *The Lock and Key Library,* 10v. (1909–15).

HAWTHORNE, NATHANIEL (July 4, 1804–May 18/19, 1864); b. Salem, Mass. Author. *Fanshawe* (anon., 1828); *Twice-Told Tales* (1837); *Grandfather's Chair* (1841); *Famous Old People* (1842); *Liberty Tree* (1842); *The Celestial Rail-Road* (1843); *Mosses from an Old Manse* (1846); *The Scarlet Letter* (1850); *The House of the Seven Gables* (1851); *A Wonder-Book* (1852); *The Snow-Image, and Other Twice-Told Tales* (1852); *The Blithedale Romance* (1852); *Tanglewood Tales* (1853); *The Marble Faun* (1860); *Our Old Home* (1863); *Septimus Felton* (1872); *The Dolliver Romance, and Other Pieces* (1876); *Fanshawe, and Other Pieces* (1876); *Dr. Grimshawe's Secret* (1883); *The Complete Works*, ed. by George P. Lathrop, 12v. (1883); etc. *See* Julian Hawthorne's *Nathaniel Hawthorne and His Wife*, 2v. (1884); Frederick B. Sanborn's *Hawthorne and His Wife* (1908); Herbert S. Gorman's *Hawthorne: A Study in Solitude* (1927); Newton Arvin's *The Heart of Hawthorne's Journals* (1929); Hildegarde Hawthorne's *Romantic Rebel* (1932); Edward Mather's *Nathaniel Hawthorne* (1940); Arlin Turner's *Hawthorne as Editor* (1941); Mark Van Doren's *Nathaniel Hawthorne* (1949); R. R. Male's *Hawthorne's Tragic Vision* (1957); Terence Martin's *Nathaniel Hawthorne* (1965); Mary Rohrberger's *Hawthorne and the Modern Short Story* (1966); Jac Tharpe's *Nathaniel Hawthorne: Identity and Knowledge* (1967).

Hawthorne, Rose. See Rose Hawthorne Lathrop.

Hay, Elzey. Pen name of Eliza Frances Andrews.

HAY, JAMES, JR. (Jan. 28, 1881–May 7, 1936); b. Harrisonburg, Va. Novelist. *The Man Who Forgot* (1915); *Mrs. Marden's Ordeal* (1918); *The Unlighted House* (1921); etc.

HAY, JOHN (Aug. 31, 1915–   ); b. Ipswich, Mass. Author. *A Private History* (poems, 1947); *The Run* (1959); *Nature's Year* (1961); *A Sense of Nature* (with Arlene Strong, 1962); *The Great Beach* (1963); *The Atlantic Shore* (with Peter Farb, 1966); *In Defense of Nature* (1969).

HAY, JOHN [Milton] (Oct. 8, 1838–July 1, 1905); b. Salem, Ind. Statesman, diplomat, journalist, historian, poet. *Pike County Ballads, and Other Pieces* (1871); *Castilian Days* (1871); *The Bread-Winners* (anon., 1884); *Poems* (1890); *Abraham Lincoln: A History*, 10v. (with John Nicolay, 1890); *Addresses of John Hay* (1907); *The Complete Poetical Works* (1916); etc. His best known poems are "Jim Bludso" and "Little Breeches." Ambassador to England, 1897–98; Secretary of State, 1898–1905. *See* W. R. Thayer's *Life and Letters of John Hay*, 2v. (1916).

HAY, SARA HENDERSON (Mrs. Raymond Holden) (Nov. 13, 1906–); b. Pittsburgh, Pa. Poet. *Field of Honor* (1933); *This, My Letter* (1939); *Delicate Balance* (1951); *Stone and the Shell* (1959); *A Footing on This Earth* (1966); etc.

HAY, THOMAS ROBSON (Oct. 2, 1888–); b. Fort Sam Houston, Tex. Historian. *Hood's Tennessee Campaign* (1929); *The Admirable Trumpeter: Life of James Wilkinson* (with M. R. Werner, 1941); *Politician, Office Holder, and Writer* (1952); *Pat Cleburne, Stonewall Jackson of the West* (1959). Assoc. editor: *Dictionary of American History*, 6v. (1940).

HAYAKAWA, S[amuel] I[chiye] (July 18, 1906–); b. Vancouver, B.C. Educator, author. *Language in Action* (1939); *Symbol, Status and Personality* (1963). Editor: *Oliver Wendell Holmes* (with Howard Mumford Jones, 1939); *Language, Meaning and Maturity* (1954); *Our Language and Our World* (1959); Columnist, Chicago *Defender*, 1942–47; editor, *ETC: A Review of General Semantics*, since 1943. Prof. language arts, San Francisco State College, 1955–68; acting president since 1968.

HAYCOX, ERNEST (Oct. 1, 1899–Oct. 13, 1958); b. Portland, Ore. Novelist. *Free Grass* (1929); *Whispering Range* (1930); *Riders West* (1934); *The Silver Desert* (1935); *Deep West* (1937); *Sundown Jim* (1938); *The Border Trumpet* (1939); *Saddle and Ride* (1940); *Rim of the Desert* (1941);

Trail Town (1941); *Alder Gulch* (1942); *Action by Night* (1943); *The Wild Bunch* (1943); *Bugles in the Afternoon* (1944); *Canyon Passage* (1945); *Long Storm* (1946); etc.

HAYCRAFT, HOWARD (July 24, 1905–); b. Madelia, Minn. Publisher, author. Author, editor, or co-editor: *Authors Today and Yesterday* (1933); *Junior Book of Authors* (1934); *Boys' Sherlock Holmes* (1936); *British Authors of the Nineteenth Century* (1936); *American Authors: 1600–1900* (1938); *Crime Club Encore* (1942); *Twentieth Century Authors* (1942); *Art of the Mystery Story* (1944); *British Authors Before 1800* (1952); *Treasury of Great Mysteries* (1957); *Ten Great Mysteries* (1959); *Five Spy Novels* (1962); *Three Times Three, Mystery Omnibus* (1964); *Books for the Blind: A Postscript and an Appreciation* (1965). Pres., H. W. Wilson, 1953–67; Chairman of the Board from 1967.

HAYDEN, HORACE EDWIN (Feb. 18, 1837–Aug. 22, 1917); b. Catonsville, Md. Episcopal clergyman, librarian, editor, author. *A Biographical Sketch of Capt. Oliver Pollock* (1882); *The Weitzel Memorial* (1883); *Virginia Genealogies* (1891); *The Massacre of Wyoming* (1895); etc. Co-editor: *Genealogical and Family History of the Wyoming and Lackawanna Valleys, Pennsylvania*, 2v. (1906). Librarian, Wyoming Historical and Geological Society, Wilkes-Barre, Pa., 1900–17.

HAYDEN, ROBERT EARL. (Aug. 4, 1913–). Poet. *Heartshape in the Dust* (poems, 1940); *Selected Poems* (1966). Assoc. Prof. English, Fiske University, since 1946.

HAYDEN, THOMAS EMMETT (1940?–   ). Political activist, author. *Revolution in Mississippi* (1962); *The Dixiecrats and Changing Southern Power from Bourbon to Bourbon* (1963); *Liberal Analysis and Federal Power* (1964); *Rebellion in Newark* (1967); *The Other Side* (with Staughton Lynd, 1967); *Trial* (1970).

HAYDN, HIRAM [Collins] (Nov. 3, 1907–); b. Cleveland, O. Editor, author. *By Nature Free* (1943); *Manhattan Furlough* (1945); *The Time Is Noon* (1948); *The Counter-Renaissance* (1950); *The Hands of Esau* (1962). Co-editor: *A World of Great Stories* (1947); *C.F. Gauss's Papers* (1959); *The Makers of the American Tradition series* (1953–60); *Report from the Red Windmill* (1967). Editor, *American Scholar*, since 1944; editor in chief, Random House, 1956–59; pres. Atheneum Publishers, 1959–64. Co-publisher, Harcourt, Brace and Jovanovich.

HAYDN, HIRAM COLLINS (Dec. 11, 1831–July 31, 1913); b. Pompey, N.Y. Congregational clergyman, educator, author. *American Heroes in Mission Fields* (1890); *Brightening the World* (1893); *Western Reserve University* (1905); etc. President, Western Reserve University, 1887–90.

HAYES, ALFRED (1911–   ); b. London. Author. *The Big Time* (poems, 1944); *All Thy Conquests* (1946); *Shadow of Heaven* (1947); *The Girl on the Via Flaminia* (1949); *Welcome to the Castle* (poems, 1950); *In Love* (1953); *My Face for the World to See* (1958); *The Temptation of Don Volpi* (1960); *End of Me* (1968); *Just Before the Divorce* (1968). Co-author: *Journeyman* (adaptation of Erskine Caldwell's novel, prod. 1938); *'Tis of Thee* (prod. 1940).

HAYES, AUGUSTUS ALLEN (1837–Apr. 18, 1892); b. Boston, Mass. Historian, novelist. *New Colorado and the Santa Fé Trail* (1880); *The Jesuit's Ring* (1887); *The Denver Express;* etc.

HAYES, CARLTON JOSEPH HUNTLEY (May 16, 1882–Sept. 3, 1964); b. Afton, N.Y. Educator, historian. *A Political and Social History of Modern Europe*, 2v. (1924); *These Eventful Years* (1924); *Essays on Nationalism* (1926); *Essays in Intellectual History* (1929); *France, a Nation of Patriots* (1930); *The Historical Evolution of Modern Nationalism* (1931); *A Quarter Century of Learning* (1931); *World History* (with Parker Thomas Moon and John W. Wayland, 1932); *Political and Cultural History of Modern Europe*, 2v. (1932–

36); *A Generation of Materialism* (1941); *Wartime Mission in Spain* (1945); *The U.S. and Spain* (1951); *Christianity and Western Civilization* (1954); *Contemporary Europe since 1870* (1958); *History of Western Civilization* (1962); *Modern Times* (with Margareta Faissler, 1965); etc. History dept., Columbia University, 1907–50. U.S. ambassador to Spain, 1942–45.

HAYES, DORSHA; b. Galesburg, Ill. Author. *The American Primer* (1941); *Mrs. Heaton's Daughter* (1943); *Chicago: Crossroads of American Enterprise* (1944); *Who Walk with the Earth* (1945).

HAYES, ISAAC ISRAEL (Mar. 5, 1832–Dec. 17, 1881); b. in Chester Co., Pa. Physician, arctic explorer, author. *An Arctic Boat-Journey* (1860); *The Open Polar Sea* (1867); *Cast Away in the Cold: a Story of Arctic Adventure for Boys* (1868); *The Land of Desolation* (1872).

HAYES, JOHN (d.1815). Presbyterian clergyman, educator, poet. *Rural Poems, Moral and Descriptive* (1807). Prof. languages, Dickinson College, 1807–09.

HAYES, JOHN RUSSELL (June 25, 1866–Dec. 29, 1945); b. West Chester, Pa. Librarian, author. *The Old-Fashioned Garden, and Other Verses* (1895); *Brandywine Days* (1910); *In Memory of Whittier* (1910); *Molly Pryce* (1913); *Roger Morland: A Quaker Idyll* (1915); *Collected Poems* (1916); etc. With Swarthmore College, 1893–1936; librarian Friends Historical Library, 1927–36.

HAYES, JOSEPH [Arnold] (1918–Aug. 2, 1968). Author. *The Desperate Hours* (1954), dramatization (prod. 1955). Co-author, with Marrijane Hayes: *Change of Heart: A 3-Act Comedy for High Schools* (1948), and other plays; *Bon Voyage!* (1957); *The Hours after Midnight* (1959); *Calculated Risk* (1962); *Don't Go Away Mad* (1963); *The Third Day* (1964); *The Deep End* (1967); etc.

HAYES, MARJORIE; b. Newton Center, Mass. Author. *The Little House on Wheels* (1934); *Wampum and Sixpence* (1936); *Alice-Albert Elephant* (1938); *The Little House on Runners* (1939); *Homer's Hill* (1944); *Robin on the River* (1950); *Robin and Company* (1952); etc.

HAYES, PETER LIND (June 25, 1915–); b. San Francisco, Cal. Actor. *Twenty-five Minutes from Broadway* (1961).

HAYES, RUTHERFORD BIRCHARD (Oct. 4, 1822–Jan. 17, 1893); b. Delaware, O. Nineteenth president of the United States, author. *Diary and Letters* ed. by Charles R. Williams, 5v. (1922–26). *See* Charles R. Williams's *Life of Rutherford Birchard Hayes*, 2v. (1914); H. J. Eckenrode's *Rutherford B. Hayes* (1930).

HAYES, WILLIAM EDWARD (Jan. 27, 1897–); b. Muncie, Ind. Railways executive, author. *The Black Doll* (1936); *Before the Cock Crowed* (1937); *Black Chronicle* (1938); *Iron Road to Empire* (1953).

HAYGOOD, ATTICUS GREEN (Nov. 19, 1839–Jan. 19, 1896); b. Watkinsville, Ga. Methodist bishop, educator, editor, author. *Our Brother in Black* (1881); *Sermons and Speeches* (1883); *The Man of Galilee* (1889); *Pleas for Progress* (1889); *Jack Knife and Brambles* (1893); *The Monk and the Prince* (1895); etc. Editor, the *Wesleyan Christian Advocate*, 1878–82. President, Emory College, 1876–84. *See* Elam F. Dempsey's *Atticus Green Haygood* (1940).

HAYNE, PAUL HAMILTON (Jan. 1, 1830–July 6, 1886); b. Charleston, S.C. Editor, poet. *Poems* (1855); *Sonnets and Other Poems* (1857); *Avolio: A Legend of the Island of Cos* (1860); *Legends and Lyrics* (1872); *The Mountain of the Lovers* (1875); *Loves of Robert Young Hayne and Hugo Swinton Legare* (1878); *The Broken Battalions* (1885). Editor, *Russell's Magazine*, Charleston, S.C., 1857–60.

HAYNES, CARLYLE BOYNTON (May 24, 1882–Mar. 11, 1958); b. Bristol, Conn. Adventist clergyman, author. *The Other Side of Death* (1916); *Our Times and Their Meaning* (1929); *Spiritism and the Bible* (1931); *Earth's Last Hour* (1937); *The Blackout of Civilization and Beyond* (1941); *When God Splits the Atom* (1946); *When a Man Dies* (1948); *The Book of All Nations* (1950); *The Legion of the Tenth* (1957); etc.

HAYNES, GEORGE EDMUND (1880–Jan. 8, 1960). Sociologist. *Africa, Continent of the Future* (1951).

HAYNES, [Nathan Gallup] WILLIAMS (July 29, 1886–); b. Detroit, Mich. Editor, publisher, author. *Casco Bay Yarns* (1916); *Sandhills Sketches* (1916); etc. Compiler: *Fisherman's Verse* (1918); *Winter Sports Verse* (1919); *Men, Money and Molecules* (1935); *The Stone That Burns* (1942); *American Chemical Industry, a History*, 6v. (1945–52); *Cellulose, the Chemical That Grows* (1952); *Captain George and Lady Ann Denison* (1959). Publisher, *Chemical Industries*, 1920–39; pres., Pequot Press, since 1945.

HAYNIE, [James] HENRY (July 19, 1841–May 15, 1912); b. Winchester, Ill. Journalist, author. *Paris: Past and Present*, 2v. (1902); *The Captains and the Kings* (1904).

HAYS, ARTHUR GARFIELD (Dec. 12, 1881–Dec. 14, 1954); b. Rochester, N.Y. Lawyer, author. *Let Freedom Ring* (1928); *Don't Tread on Me* (with others, 1928); *Trial by Prejudice* (1933); *Democracy Works* (1939); *City Lawyer* (1942); etc.

HAYS, ELINOR RICE. Author. *Morning Star: A Biography of Lucy Stone* (1961).

HAYS, H[offman] R[eynolds] (Mar. 25, 1904–); b. New York. Author. *Stranger on the Highway* (1943); *Lie Down in Darkness* (1944); *The Takers of the City* (1946); *The Envoys* (1953); *From Ape to Angel* (1958); *The Dangerous Sex* (1966); etc.

HAYS, WILLIAM SHAKESPEARE (July 19, 1837–July 23, 1907); b. Louisville, Ky. Ballad-writer. *The Modern Meeting House, and Other Poems* (1874); *Songs and Poems* (1886); *Poems and Songs* (1895). Among his best known ballads are "Mollie Darling" and "Little Ones at Home." He wrote the Civil War song "The Union Forever" in 1861. He was on the staff of the *Louisville Courier-Journal.*

HAYWARD, WALTER BROWNELL (Aug. 3, 1877–); b. St. George's, Bermuda. Journalist, author. *Bermuda Past and Present* (1910); *The Last Continent of Adventure* (1930); etc. With New York *Evening Post*, 1917–24; *New York Times*, since 1924.

HAYWOOD, CAROLYN (1898–). Author. *"B" Is for Betsy* (1939); *Betsy and the Boys* (1945); *Betsy and Billy* (1951); *Eddie and His Big Deals* (1955); *Annie Pat and Eddie* (1960); *Here's a Penny* (1965); *Eddie the Dog Holder* (1966); etc.

HAZARD, CAROLINE (June 10, 1856–Mar. 19, 1945); b. Peace Dale, R.I. Educator, poet, essayist. *Narragansett Ballads* (1894); *A Scallop Shell of Quiet* (poems, 1908); *The Yosemite, and Other Verse* (1917); *Songs in the Sun* (1927); *Threads from the Distaff* (1934); *The Golden State* (1939); etc. President, Wellesley College, 1899–1910.

HAZARD, LUCY LOCKWOOD (Mrs. Bertram Martin Adams) (Dec. 9, 1890–); b. New Haven, Conn. Educator, author. *The Frontier in American Literature* (1927); *In Search of America* (1930). English dept., Mills College, since 1920.

HAZARD, SAMUEL (May 26, 1784–May 22, 1870); b. Philadelphia, Pa. Editor, antiquarian, author. *Annals of Pennsylvania* (1850). Editor: *Colonial Records of Pennsylvania*, 16v. (1838–53); *Pennsylvania Archives*, 12v. (1852–56). Founder, the *Register of Pennsylvania*, a Philadelphia weekly, Jan., 1828.

HAZARD, THOMAS ROBINSON (Jan. 3, 1797–Mar. 26, 1886); b. South Kingstown, R.I. Author. Known as, "Shepherd Tom." *The Jonny-Cake Letters* (1882); *Miscellaneous Essays and Letters* (1883). *See* Caroline E. Robinson's *The Hazard Family of Rhode Island* (1895).

Hazard of New Fortunes, A. Novel by William Dean Howells (1890): Chronicle of a German family in New York, showing the contrasting social strata of a metropolis.

Hazel, Harry. Pen name of Justin Jones.

HAZEL, ROBERT (1921–   ); b. in Indiana. Poet, novelist. *The Lost Year* (1953); *A Field Full of People* (1954); *Poems 1951–1961* (1961); *American Elegies* (1968).

"Hazel Dell, The." Song by George Frederick Root under the pen name "Wurzel" (1853).

Hazel Kirke. Play by Steele MacKaye (prod. 1880).

HAZELTINE, MARY EMOGENE (May 5, 1868–June 16, 1949); b. Jamestown, O. Librarian, bibliographer. Compiler: *Anniversaries and Holidays* (1928); *One Hundred Years of Wisconsin Authorship* (1937); etc. Principal, Library School, University of Wisconsin, 1906–38.

HAZELTINE, MAYO WILLIAMSON (Apr. 24, 1841–Sept. 14, 1909); b. Boston, Mass. Critic. *Chats About Books: Poets and Novelists* (1883); etc. Lit. editor, *New York Sun,* 1878–1909. One of the characters in William Tucker Washburn's *Harvard: A Story of American College Life* (1869), was based on Hazeltine.

HAZELTON, GEORGE COCHRANE (Jan. 20, 1868–June 24, 1921); b. Boscobel, Wis. Lawyer, actor, novelist, playwright. *The Raven* (prod. 1895); *Mistress Nell* (prod. 1901); *Captain Molly* (prod. 1902); *The Cracksman* (prod. 1908); *The Yellow Jacket* (with J. Henry Benrimo, prod. 1912).

HAZELTON, ROGER (1909–). Author. *The Root and Flower of Prayer* (1943); *The God We Worship* (1946); *On Proving God* (1952); *God's Way with Man* (1956); *New Accents in Contemporary Theology* (1960); *Christ and Ourselves* (1965); *God: the Creator and Governor* (1966); *A Theological Approach to Art* (1967); *Knowing the Living God* (1968); etc.

HAZEN, CHARLES DOWNER (Mar. 17, 1868–Sept. 18, 1941); b. Barnet, Vt. Educator, historian. *Europe Since 1815* (1910); *Modern European History* (1917); *The French Revolution,* 2v. (1932); etc. Editor: *The Letters of William Roscoe Thayer* (1926); etc. Prof. history, Columbia University, 1916–38.

HAZLITT, HENRY (Nov. 28, 1894–); b. Philadelphia, Pa. Editor, author. *Thinking As a Science* (1916); *The Anatomy of Criticism* (1933); *A New Constitution Now* (1942); *Will Dollars Save the World?* (1947); *The Great Idea* (1951); *The Free Man's Library* (1956); *The Failure of the New Economics* (1959); *What You Should Know About Inflation* (1960); *The Foundations of Morality* (1964); *Life and Death of the Welfare State* (1968); *Man vs. the Welfare State* (1969). Staff, *New York Times,* 1934–46; writer of column "Business Tides," *Newsweek,* since 1946; co-editor, *The Freeman,* 1950–52.

HAZZARD, SHIRLEY (Jan. 30, 1931–   ); b. Sydney, Australia. Author. *Cliffs of Fall* (1963); *The Evening of the Holiday* (1966); *People in Glass Houses* (1967); *The Bay of Noon* (1970).

He and She. Play by Rachel Crothers (prod. 1911), also called *The Herfords.* The struggle of a woman who tries to manage her home and have a career at the same time.

Head, Matthew. Pen name of John E. Canaday.

Head, Mrs. Cloyd. See Eunice Tietjens.

HEAD, ROBERT. (1942–); b. Memphis, Tenn. Author. *Sanctity* (1963).

HEADLAND, ISAAC TAYLOR (Aug. 16, 1859–Aug. 2, 1942); b. Freedom, Pa. Methodist clergyman, educator, author. *Chinese Heroes* (1902); *Court Life in China* (1909); *Home Life in China* (1914); *Chinese Rhymes for Children* (1933); etc. Missionary to China; with Mt. Union REP,1532/6 1915–); College, 1914–37.

HEADLEY, JOEL TYLER (Dec. 30, 1813–Jan. 16, 1897); b. Walton, N.Y. Traveler, author. *Italy and the Italians* (1844); *Napoleon and His Marshals,* 2v. (1846); *Washington and His Generals,* 2v. (1847); *Sacred Mountains* (1847); *The Adirondacks; or, Life in the Woods* (1849); etc. *Napoleon and His Marshals* was the first publishing success of the new firm of Charles Scribner, and over fifty editions were printed in eight years.

HEADLEY, PHINEAS CAMP (June 24, 1819–Jan. 5, 1903); b. Walton, N.Y. Presbyterian clergyman, author. *The Life of the Empress Josephine* (1850); *The Life of Napoleon Bonaparte* (1859); *Young Folks' Heroes of the Rebellion* series; etc.

HEALY, PAUL FRANCIS (Mar. 1, 1915–   ); b. Chicago, Ill. Journalist. *Yankee From the West* (with Burton K. Wheeler, 1962); *Cissy: A Biography of Eleanor M. Patterson* (1966). Washington correspondent and political columnist, *New York Daily News,* since 1945.

"Heap o' Livin', A." Poems by Edgar A. Guest (1916). The title poem is probably the author's most quoted poem.

HEARD, FRANKLIN FISKE (Jan. 17, 1825–Sept. 29, 1889); b. East Sudbury, Mass. Lawyer, author. *Oddities of the Law* (1881); *Shakespeare as a Lawyer* (1883); and other books on legal *curiosa.*

HEARD, GERALD (Oct. 6, 1889–1971); b. London. Author. *Narcissus* (1924); *Ascent of Humanity* (1929); *These Hurrying Years* (1934); *The Source of Civilization* (1937); *The Code of Christ* (1941); *The Great Fog, and Other Weird Tales* (1944); *The Eternal Gospel* (1946); *Dopplegangers* (1947); *Lost Cavern* (1948); *Is God in History?* (1950); *Notched Hairpin* (1949); *Black Fox* (1951); *Is Another World Watching?* (1951); *Morals Since 1900* (1950); *Gabriel and the Creatures* (1952); *Human Venture* (1955); *Kingdom Without God* (with others, 1956); *Five Ages of Man* (1970); etc.

HEARD, NATHAN CLIFF (Nov. 7, 1936–   ); b. Newark, N.J. Musician, author. *To Reach a Dream* (1967); *Howard Street* (1968).

HEARN, [Patricio] LAFCADIO [Tessima Carlos] (June 27, 1850–Sept. 26, 1904); b. Santa Maura Island, Greece. Author, translator. Japanese name, "Yakuma Koizumi." *Stray Leaves from Strange Literature* (1884); *Some Chinese Ghosts* (1887); *Chita* (1899); *Youma* (1890); *Out of the East* (1895); *Kokoro* (1896); *In Ghostly Japan* (1899); *A Japanese Miscellany* (1901); *Kotto* (1902); *Kwaidan* (1904); *Japan* (1904); *The Romance of the Milky Way, and Other Studies and Stories* (1905); *The Writings,* 16v. (1922). Translator of French and Japanese authors. With the *Cincinnati Enquirer,* 1872–75; the *Cincinnati Commercial,* 1876–77; assoc. editor, the *New Orleans Item,* 1878–81; with the *New Orleans Times-Democrat,* 1881–87. Prof. English literature, Imperial University of Tokyo, 1894–1903. *See* Elizabeth Bisland's *The Life and Letters,* 2v. (1906); George M. Gould's *Concerning Lafcadio Hearn* (1908); Yone Noguchi's *Lafcadio Hearn in Japan* (1910); Edward L. Tinker's *Lafcadio Hearn's American Days* (1924); Elizabeth Stevenson's *Lafcadio Hearn* (1961).

HEARST, WILLIAM RANDOLPH (Apr. 29, 1863–Aug. 14, 1951); b. San Francisco, Calif. Newspaper publisher, collector. Publisher, *San Francisco Call-Bulletin, San Francisco Examiner, Los Angeles Examiner, Los Angeles Herald and*

Express, Baltimore Sunday American, Baltimore News-Post, New York Journal-American, New York Mirror, Boston American, Boston Sunday Advertiser, Boston Record, Chicago Herald and Examiner, Chicago American, Pittsburgh Sun-Telegraph, Detroit Times, Seattle Post-Intelligencer, Albany Times-Union, Syracuse Journal and Sunday American, Atlanta Georgian, Oakland Post-Enquirer, San Antonio Light; Harper's Bazaar, Good Housekeeping, Hearst's International Combined with Cosmopolitan, Town and Country, House Beautiful, etc. The Hearst collection of works of art was sold in New York in 1941, comprising the largest single private collection ever offered for sale. See Ferdinand Lundberg's Imperial Hearst (1936); Mrs. Fremont Older's William Randolph Hearst (1936); Oliver Carlson and Ernest S. Bates's Hearst, Lord of San Simeon (1936); W. A. Swanberg's Citizen Hearst (1961).

HEARST, W[illiam] R[andolph], Jr. (Jan. 27, 1908–); b. New York. Editor. Publisher, New York Journal-American, 1937–56; now editor-in-chief, Hearst newspapers.

Heart Is a Lonely Hunter, The. Novel by Carson McCullers (1940). A deaf-mute's friendship with a number of bizarre characters in a Southern town. His closest friend is another deaf-mute whose death in an insane asylum brings on the main character's suicide.

Heart of the Hills, The. Novel by John Fox, Jr. (1913). The scene of this story is Kentucky and it deals for the most part with the lives of the mountaineers. The principal character is Jason Hawn.

Heart Throbs. Anthology of sentimental poetry comp. by Joseph M. Chapple (1906).

Hearth and Home. New York City. Magazine. Founded 1868, by Pettingill, Bates & Co. Donald G. Mitchell, Harriet Beecher Stowe, Mary Mapes Dodge, and Edward Eggleston were among its editors. The latter's The Hoosier Schoolmaster appeared in its pages. Expired 1875.

HEATH, [Charles] MONROE (1899–). Author. Beyond This Hour (poems, 1953); Our Fifty States at a Glance (1959); Our American Indians at a Glance (1961); etc.

Heath, D. C., & Co. Boston. Publishers of textbooks. Founded 1885 by Daniel Collamore Heath. (1843–1908), who had formerly been connected with Ginn Brothers. It has published innumerable textbooks in many languages, representing the work of the world's foremost educators. Charles Henry Douglas was editor in chief, 1895–1925. Dean M. Laux is now president. Acquired by Raytheon Education Co. in 1966.

HEATH, JAMES EWELL (July 8, 1792–June 28, 1862); b. in Virginia. Author. Edge-Hill; or, The Family of the Fitzroyals, 2v. (anon., 1828); Whigs and Democrats; or, Love of Politics (publ. 1839, prod. 1844).

HEATHCOTE, CHARLES WILLIAM (Apr. 19, 1882–Aug. 5, 1963); b. Glen Rock, Pa. Presbyterian clergyman, educator, author. Battle of the Brandywine (1923); Outlines of Modern Government (1923); Story of Valley Forge (1924); Luke's Gospel (1925); History of Chester County (1927); and other works on early American history. Editor, Chester County Historical Bulletin, 1922–36. Prof. history dept., West Chester State Normal School, 1922–55.

"Heathen Chinee, The." Poem by Bret Harte, which first appeared in the Overland Monthly, Sept., 1870, under the title "Plain Language from Truthful James." See Robert Ernest Cowan's Bibliographical Notes on Certain of the Earlier Editions of Bret Harte's "Heathen Chinee" (1934).

HEATON, JOHN LANGDON (Jan. 29, 1860–Feb. 21, 1935); b. Canton, N.Y. Editor, author. The Story of Vermont (1889); The Book of Lies (1896); The Quilting Bee, and Other Rhymes (1896); The Story of a Page (1913). Editor: Cobb of "The World" (1924). With the New York World, 1899–1931.

"Heaven Will Protect the Working Girl." Song, words by Edgar Smith and music by A. Baldwin Sloane, published by Charles Kassel Harris in 1909, and sung by Marie Dressler in Tillie's Nightmare.

"Heavy Bear Who Goes With Me, The." Poem by Delmore Schwartz, from In Dreams Begin Responsibilities (1938).

Hebrews in America. By Isaac Markens (1888). One of the early studies of the Jewish contribution to American life.

HECHINGER, FRED MICHAEL (July 7, 1920–); b. Nuremberg, Ger. Journalist, author. An Adventure in Education (1956); The Big Red Schoolhouse (1959); Teenage Tyranny (1963); Pre-School Education Today (1966); The New York Times Guide to Pre-School Education Today (1966); etc. Education columnist, Washington Post, 1947–50; education editor, New York Herald Tribune, 1950–56; New York Times, since 1959.

HECHLER, KEN (Sept. 20, 1914–); b. Roslyn, New York. Congressman, author. Insurgency: Personalities and Policies of the Taft Era (1940); The Bridge at Remagen (1957); West Virginia Memories of President Kennedy (1965).

HECHT, ANTHONY [Evan] (Jan. 16, 1923–); b. New York City. Poet. A Summoning of Stones (1954); The Seven Deadly Sins (1958); A Bestiary (1960); The Hard Hours (1968, Pulitzer Prize, 1969). Co-author and co-editor with John Ashbery, Jiggery-Pokery (1967). English department, University of Rochester, since 1967.

HECHT, BEN (Feb. 28, 1894–Apr. 18, 1964); b. New York City. Novelist, playwright. The Wonder Hat (with Kenneth Sawyer Goodman, prod. 1920); Erik Dorn (1921); Fantazius Mallare (1922); Gargoyles (1922); A Thousand and One Afternoons in Chicago (1922); The Egotist (prod. 1922); The Florentine Dagger (1923); Humpty Dumpty (1924); The Kingdom of Evil (1924); Count Bruga (1926); Broken Necks (1926); The Front Page (play, with Charles MacArthur, prod. 1928); A Jew in Love (1931); Champion from Far Away (1931); The Great Magoo (with Gene Fowler, prod. 1932); Actor's Blood (1936); To Quito and Back (prod. 1937); A Book of Miracles (1939); A Guide for the Bedevilled (1945); A Flag Is Born (prod. 1946); A Child of the Century (autobiography, 1954); Charlie (1957); The Sensualists (1959); Perfidy (1961); Gaily, Gaily (1963); Letters from Bohemia (1964); etc. With the Chicago Daily News, 1914–23; founder, the Chicago Literary Times, 1923; publisher, 1923–25.

HECKER, ISAAC THOMAS (Dec. 18, 1819–Dec. 22, 1888); b. New York City. Roman Catholic clergyman, founder of the Paulist order, author. Questions of the Soul (1852); Aspirations of Nature (1857); etc. Founder, Catholic World, 1865; and Young Catholic, 1870. See Walter Elliott's The Life of Father Hecker (1891).

HECKSCHER, AUGUST (Sept. 16, 1913–); b. Huntington, N.Y. Journalist, author. These Are the Days (1936); A Pattern of Politics (1947); Diversity of Worlds (with Raymond Aron, 1957); The Public Happiness (1962). Editor: Woodrow Wilson's Politics (1956). Chief editorial writer, New York Herald Tribune, 1948–56.

HECKSCHER, ROBERT VALANTINE (Nov. 19, 1883–); b. Philadelphia, Pa. Poet. Through Dust to Light (1911); Rose Windows (1912).

HEDDEN, WORTH TUTTLE (Jan. 10, 1896–); b. Raleigh, N.C. Novelist. Wives of High Pasture (1944); The Other Room (1947); Love Is a Wound (1952).

HEDGE, FREDERIC HENRY (Dec. 12, 1805–Aug. 21, 1890); b. Cambridge, Mass. Unitarian clergyman, poet. Prose Writers of Germany (1848); Martin Luther, and Other Essays (1888); Metrical Translations and Poems (1888); etc. Co-editor, The Christian Examiner, 1857–61.

HEERMANS, FORBES (Oct. 25, 1856–Sept. 18, 1928); b. Syracuse, N.Y. Journalist, novelist, playwright. *Thirteen: Stories of the Far West* (1887); *Between Two Foes* (1899); *Twin Star* (1907); *Tales of the West and East* (1922); etc.

HEGGEN, THOMAS O[rle] (Dec. 23, 1919–May, 1949); b. Fort Dodge, Ia. Author. *Mr. Roberts* (1946).

HEIDEL, WILLIAM ARTHUR (Mar. 10, 1868–Jan. 15, 1941); b. Burlington, Ia. Educator, author. *Pseudo-Platonica* (1896); *The Logic of the Pre-Socratic Philosophy* (1903); *The Day of Yahweh* (1929); *The Heroic Age of Science* (1933); *Hippocratic Medicine* (1941); etc. Prof. Greek, Wesleyan University. Middletown, Conn., 1905–36.

HEILBRONER, ROBERT LOUIS. Author. *The Worldly Philosophers* (1953); *The Quest for Wealth* (1956); *The Future as History* (1960); *The Making of Economic Society* (1962); *Great Ascent* (1963); *Understanding Macroeconomics* (1965); *The Limits of American Capitalism* (1966); etc. Editor: *Economic Means and Social Ends* (with others, 1969).

HEILMAN, ROBERT BECHTOLD (July 18, 1906–); b. Philadelphia, Pa. Educator, author. *The American in English Fiction, 1760–1800* (1937); *This Great Stage* (1948); *Magic in the Web: Action and Language in Othello* (1956); *Conrad's Lord Jim* (1957); *Hardy's Mayor of Casterbridge* (1962); *Shakespeare's Cymbeline* (1964); *Euripides' Alcestis* (1965); *Hardy's Jude the Obscure* (1966). Prof. English, University of Washington, since 1948.

HEILPRIN, ANGELO (Mar. 31, 1853–July 17, 1907); b. Sátoralja-Ujhely, Hungary. Geologist, explorer, artist, author. *Town Geology* (1885); *The Geological Evidences of Evolution* (1888); *The Earth and Its Story* (1896); *Alaska and the Klondike* (1899); *The Tower of Pelée* (1904); etc. Editor-in-chief: *Lippincott's Pronouncing Gazetteer* (1905).

HEILPRIN, MICHAEL (1823–May 10, 1888); b. Piotrkow, Poland. Scholar, cyclopedist. *The Historical Poetry of the Ancient Hebrews*, 2v. (1879–80). Revised the *American Cyclopaedia* (1872–76). *See* Gustav Pollak's *Michael Heilprin and His Sons* (1912).

HEINLEIN, ROBERT A[nson] (1907–). Author. *Rocket Ship Galileo* (1947); *Beyond This Horizon* (1948); *The Green Hills of Earth* (1951); *Time for the Star* (1956); *Stranger in a Strange Land* (1961); *Farnham's Freehold* (1965); *The Moon is a Harsh Mistress* (1966); and many other science-fiction novels.

HEISER, VICTOR GEORGE (Feb. 1873–); b. Johnstown, Pa. Physician, author. *An American Doctor's Odyssey* (1936); *You're the Doctor* (1939).

HEISKELL, ANDREW (Sept. 13, 1915–); b. Naples, Italy. With *Life*, since 1937; publisher, since 1946; president, *Time*, Inc., 1949–60; chairman of the board 1960–69; chief executive officer from 1969.

HELBURN, THERESA (Mrs. John Baker Updycke) (d. Aug. 18, 1959). Stage director, producer, playwright, author. *Crops and Croppers* (prod. 1918), published as *Allison Makes Hay* (1919); *Denbigh* (1921); *Other Lives* (with Edward Goodman, prod. 1921); *A Hero Is Born* (1937); *Little Dark Horse* (adaptation, prod. 1941); *The Wayward Quest* (autobiography, 1960); etc.

HELD, JOHN, JR. (Jan. 10, 1889–Mar. 2, 1958); b. Salt Lake City, Utah. Artist, author. *Grim Youth* (1930); *Dog Stories* (1930); *Saga of Frankie and Johnny* (1931); *Women Are Necessary* (1931); *The Flesh Is Weak* (1932); *The Works of John Held, Jr.* (1931); *A Bowl of Cherries* (1933); *Crosstown* (1934); *The Gods Were Promiscuous* (1937); *Danny Decoy* (1942); etc.

Held by the Enemy. Civil War play by William Gillette (prod. 1886).

Helen's Babies. By John Habberton (1876). Popular and humorous record of the author's mischievous boys whose questions and antics kept the household constantly on the defensive.

Helfenstein, Ernest. Pen name of Elizabeth Oakes Smith.

Hell-Bent for Heaven. Play by Hatcher Hughes (prod. 1924). Story of Rufe Pryor, a religious fanatic who is driven from his community when the mountain folk discover that he is a dangerous, scheming hypocrite. Pulitzer Prize play, 1924.

Hell-Fire Club. The group of essayists and wits who contributed to James Franklin's *The New England Courant* in 1721.

HELLENTHAL, JOHN ALBERTUS (Sept. 17, 1874–May 25, 1945); b. Allegan Co., Mich. Lawyer, author. *The Alaskan Melodrama* (1936); etc.

HELLER, EDMUND (May 21, 1875–July 18, 1939); b. Freeport, Ill. Naturalist, explorer, author. *Life-Histories of African Game Animals*, 2v. (with Theodore Roosevelt, 1914); etc. Director, Milwaukee Zoological Gardens, 1928–35.

HELLER, ERICH (Mar. 27, 1911–   ); b. Komotau, Bohemia. Educator, author. *The Disinherited Mind* (1952); *The Ironic German* (1958); *The Artist's Journey into the Interior and Other Essays* (1965). Editor: *Kafka's Letter to his Fiancée* (1967). Editor, *Studies in Modern European Literature and Thought,* since 1950. Prof. German, Northwestern University, 1960–66; prof. humanities, since 1966.

HELLER, JOSEPH (May 1, 1923–   ); b. Brooklyn, New York. Author. *Catch-22* (1961); *We Bombed in New Haven* (play, 1968).

HELLER, RICHARD H. (Oct. 16, 1924–   ); b. Yonkers, N.Y. Editor, author. *The Helm* (1951); *Who's Who in TV* (1967). Editor: *The President Speaks* (1964). Editor, Hillman Periodicals, 1952–53; Sterling Group, 1954–62; Dell Publishing Co. and *Modern Screen* Magazine, since 1962.

HELLINGER, MARK (Mar. 21, 1903–Dec. 21, 1947); New York City. Journalist, author, film producer. *Moon Over Broadway* (1931); *The Ten Million* (1934); *I Meet a Lot of People* (1940). Columnist, *New York Daily Mirror,* 1930–38.

HELLMAN, GEOFFREY T[heodore] (Feb. 13, 1907–); b. New York. Editor, writer. With *New Yorker,* 1929–31; staff writer, since 1938. *The Smithsonian* (1967); *Bankers, Bones and Beetles: The First Century of the Museum of Natural History* (1969). Writer of numerous "Profiles" for *New Yorker* and satirical articles for magazines.

HELLMAN, GEORGE SIDNEY (Nov. 14, 1878–July 16, 1958); b. New York City. Author. *The Hudson, and Other Poems* (1909); *Washington Irving* (1925); *Lanes of Memory* (1927); *Persian Conqueror* (1935); *Benjamin N. Cardozo* (1940). Editor or co-editor of various collections of unpublished writings of R. L. Stevenson and Washington Irving. His collection of Irvingiana is now in the New York Public Library.

HELLMAN, LILLIAN (June 20, 1905–); b. New Orleans, La. Playwright. *The Children's Hour* (prod. 1934); *Days to Come* (prod. 1936); *The Little Foxes* (prod. 1939); *Watch on the Rhine* (prod. 1941); *The Searching Wind* (prod. 1944); *Another Part of the Forest* (prod. 1946); *The Autumn Garden* (prod. 1951); *Toys in the Attic* (prod. 1960); *An Unfinished Woman–A Memoir* (1969); etc.

HELLMAN, SAM (July 4, 1885–); b. San Francisco, Calif. Humorist. *Low Bridge and Punk Pungs* (1924); *Toll Bridge* (1930).

"Hello Central, Give Me Heaven." Song, words and music by Charles K. Harris (1901).

HELMERICKS, CONSTANCE (Jan. 4, 1918–); b. Binghamton, N.Y. Explorer, author. *Hunting in North America* (1957); *Down the Wild River North* (1969). Co-author with husband, Harmon Helmericks, of numerous books on the Arctic.

HELMERICKS, HARMON (Jan. 18, 1918–); b. Gibson City, Ill. Explorer, author. *Oolak's Brother* (1953); *Arctic Hunter* (1956); etc. Co-author, with Constance Helmericks: *We Live in the Arctic* (1947); *Our Summer with the Eskimos* (1948); *Flight of the Arctic Tern* (1952); *The Last of the Bush Pilots* (1968); etc.

HELMUTH, WILLIAM TOD (Oct. 30, 1833–May 15, 1902); b. Philadelphia, Pa. Surgeon, essayist, poet. *Medical Pomposity; or, The Doctor's Dream* (1866); *"Scratches" of a Surgeon* (1879); *With the "Pousse Café"* (poems, 1892); *Various Verses* (1901); etc.

HELPER, HINTON ROWAN (Dec. 27, 1829–Mar. 8, 1909); b. in Rowan (now Davie) Co., N.C. Anti-slavery writer. *The Land of Gold* (1855); *Impending Crisis of the South* (1857); *Nojoque* (1867); *The Negroes in Negroland* (1868); *Noonday Exigencies* (1871); etc.

HELSER, ALBERT D. (July 10, 1897–); b. Thornville, O. Church of the Brethren clergyman, missionary, author. *In Sunny Nigeria* (1926); *African Stories* (1930); *The Glory of the Impossible* (1940); *The Hand of God in the Sudan* (1946); *Africa's Bible* (1950). Translator of books into the Bura language of Nigeria.

HELTON, ROY ADDISON (Apr. 3, 1886–); b. Washington, D.C. Lecturer, poet, novelist. *Youth's Pilgrimage* (poems, 1914); *Outcasts in Beulah Land, and Other Poems* (1918); *Jimmy Sharswood* (1924); *The Early Adventures of Peacham Grew* (1925); *Lonesome Water* (poems, 1930); *Nitchey Tilley* (1934); *Come Back to Earth* (poems, 1946); etc.

HEMINGWAY, ERNEST (July 21, 1899–July 2, 1961); b. Oak Park, Ill. Novelist. *In Our Time* (1925); *The Sun Also Rises* (1926); *The Torrents of Spring* (1926); *Men without Women* (1927); *A Farewell to Arms* (1929); *Death in the Afternoon* (1932); *Winner Take Nothing* (1933); *Green Hills of Africa* (1935); *To Have and Have Not* (1937); *The Fifth Column, and the First Forty-Nine Stories* (1938); *The Spanish Earth* (1938); *For Whom the Bell Tolls* (1940); *Across the River and into the Trees* (1950); *The Old Man and the Sea* (1952; Pulitzer Prize for fiction, 1953); *A Moveable Feast* (1964); *By-Line: Ernest Hemingway*, ed. by William White (1967); *Islands in the Stream* (1970). Editor: *Men at War* (1942). Nobel Prize in literature, 1954. *See* Carlos Baker's *Hemingway: The Writer as Artist* (1952); Philip Young's *Ernest Hemingway* (1952); Leicester Hemingway's *My Brother, Ernest Hemingway* (1962); Lillian Ross's *Portrait of Ernest Hemingway* (1962); Sheridan Baker's *Ernest Hemingway* (1967); Carlos Baker's *Ernest Hemingway: A Life Story* (1969).

Hemispheres. Brooklyn, N.Y. Founded 1943. Published French and American poetry. Edited by Yvan Goll. Discontinued 1945.

HEMLEY, CECIL (July 21, 1914–Mar. 9, 1966); b. New York. Editor, author. *Porphyry's Journey* (1951); *Twenty Poems* (1956); *In the Midnight Wood* (1960); *The Experience* (1960); *Young Crankshaw* (1963); *Dimensions of Midnight* (1967). Founder Noonday Press, 1951; co-director 1951–60; director and editor, Ohio University Press, 1964–66.

HEMPSTEAD, FAY (Nov. 24, 1847–Apr. 24, 1934); b. Little Rock, Ark. Poet. *Random Arrows* (1878); *A Pictorial History of Arkansas* (1890); *Poems* (1898); *Laureate Poems* (1908); *Historical Review of Arkansas*, 3v. (1911); *Poems* (1922); etc.

HEMSTREET, CHARLES (Sept. 20, 1866–deceased); b. New York City. Journalist, author. *Nooks and Corners of Old New York* (1899); *When Old New York Was Young* (1902); *Literary New York* (1903); etc.

HENDERSON, ALICE CORBIN (1881–); b. St. Louis, Mo. Author. *The Spinning Woman of the Sky* (poems, 1912); *Red Earth* (poems, 1920); *The Sun Turns West* (poems, 1933); *Brothers of Light: the Penitentes of the Southwest* (1937); etc. Compiler, *The Turquoise Trail: An Anthology of New Mexico Poetry* (1926). Assoc. editor, *Poetry*, 1912–16.

HENDERSON, ARCHIBALD (June 17, 1877–Dec. 6, 1963); b. Salisbury, N.C. Educator, mathematician, author. Pen name, "Erskine Steele." *Mark Twain* (1911); *George Bernard Shaw: His Life and Works* (1911); *Interpreters of Life and the Modern Spirit* (1911); *The Changing Drama* (1914); *The Conquest of the Old Southwest* (1920); *Contemporary Immortals* (1930); *Bernard Shaw: Playboy and Prophet* (1932); *North Carolina, the Old North State and the New* (1941); *Campus of the First State University* (1949); *George Bernard Shaw: Man of the Century* (1956); etc. Mathematics dept., University of North Carolina, 1899–1948.

HENDERSON, C[harles] HANFORD (Dec. 30, 1861–Jan. 9, 1941); b. Philadelphia, Pa. Educator, author. *John Percyfield* (1903); *The Lighted Lamp* (1908); *The Charioteer* (1933); etc.

HENDERSON, CHARLES RICHMOND (Dec. 17, 1848–Mar. 29, 1915); b. Covington, Ind. Baptist clergyman, educator, author. *The Social Spirit in America* (1896); *Social Settlements* (1897); *Social Elements* (1898); etc. Sociology dept., University of Chicago, 1892–1915.

HENDERSON, DANIEL [MacIntyre] (May 27, 1880–Nov. 12, 1955); b. Baltimore, Md. Editor, poet, novelist. *Life's Minstrelsy* (poems, 1919); *Boone of the Wilderness* (1921); *A Harp in the Wind* (poems, 1924); *The Crimson Queen: Mary Tudor* (1933); *Frontiers* (poems, 1933); *The Russian March to Alaska and California* (1944); *Americans in China* (1945); *The Hidden Coasts: Life of Admiral Charles Wilkes, U.S.N.* (with B. J. Hendrick, 1953). With Hearst Magazines, Inc., 1924–48.

HENDERSON, DANIEL McINTYRE (July 10, 1851–Sept. 8, 1906); b. Glasgow, Scotland. Bookseller, poet. *Poems, Scottish and American* (1888); *A Bit Bookie of Verse* (1905). Best known poems, "The Heather" and "Daisies in Baltimore."

HENDERSON, GEORGE WYLIE (1904–); b. Warrior's Stand, Ala. Author. *Ollie Miss* (1935); *Jule* (1946).

HENDERSON, HELEN WESTON (Sept. 23, 1874–); b. Philadelphia, Pa. Journalist, author. *A Loiterer in New York* (1917); *A Loiterer in New England* (1919); *A Loiterer in Paris* (1921); *A Loiterer in London* (1924); *The Enchantress* (1928); *Cathedrals of France* (1929). On staff, *Philadelphia Inquirer*, since 1904.

HENDERSON, ISAAC (Feb. 13, 1850–1909); b. Brooklyn, N.Y. Publisher, novelist. *The Prelate* (1886); *Agatha Page* (1888); etc.

HENDERSON, ROBERT WILLIAM (Dec. 25, 1888–); b. South Shields, England. Librarian, bibliographer of sports, author. *Tennis Origins and Mysteries* (with Malcolm D. Whitman, 1932); *How Old is the Game of Racquets?* (1936); *Early American Sport: A Bibliography* (1937); *Baseball and Rounders* (1940); *Six Hundred Years of Sport* (1940); *Ball, Bat and Bishop* (1947); *Early American Sport* (1953); etc. With New York Public Library, since 1910; librarian, Racquet & Tennis Club, New York, since 1916.

HENDERSON, W[alter] B[rooks] DRAYTON (Aug. 4, 1887–July 10, 1939); b. Brown's Town, Jamaica, B.W.I. Educator, author. *Swinburne and Landor* (1918); *The New Argonautica* (poem, 1928); *Castle in Spain* (1942). English dept., Dartmouth College, from 1925.

HENDERSON, WILLIAM JAMES (Dec. 4, 1855–June 5, 1937); b. Newark, N.J. Music critic. *Richard Wagner: His Life and His Dramas* (1901); *Pipes and Timbrels* (poems, 1905); etc. Music critic, *The New York Sun*, 1902–37.

Henderson the Rain King. Novel by Saul Bellow (1959). A Connecticut millionaire of tremendous physical and moral energy goes to Africa. After several ironic and amazing adventures he becomes a tribal god.

HENDRICK, BURTON J[esse] (Dec. 8, 1870–Mar. 23, 1949); b. New Haven, Conn. Editor, biographer. *The Victory at Sea* (with William Sowden Sims, 1920, Pulitzer Prize for American history, 1921); *The Life and Letters of Walter H. Page,* 3v. (1922–25; vol. I, Pulitzer Prize for American biography, 1923); *The Jews in America* (1923); *The Training of an American* (1928, Pulitzer Prize for American biography, 1929); *William Crawford Gorgas* (with Marie Doughty Gorgas, 1924); *The Life of Andrew Carnegie,* 2v. (1932); *The Lees of Virginia* (1935); *Bulwark of the Republic: A Biography of the Constitution* (1937); *Statesmen of the Lost Cause* (1939); *Lincoln's War Cabinet* (1946). Assoc. editor, *World's Work,* 1913–27.

HENDRICK, ELLWOOD (Dec. 19, 1861–Oct. 29, 1930); b. Albany, N.Y. Chemist, author. *Percolator Papers* (1919); *Lewis Miller* (1925); *Modern Views of Physical Science* (1925); etc.

HENDRICKS, ELDO LEWIS (Oct. 2, 1866–Nov. 22, 1938); b. Rossville, Ind. Educator, author. *A Study in Reading* (1911); *Rimming the Mediterranean* (1935); etc. President, Central Missouri State Teachers College, from 1915.

HENDRYX, JAMES B[eardsley] (Dec. 9, 1880–Mar. 1, 1963); b. Sauk Center, Minn. Author. The *Connie Morgan* series, 7v. (1916–29); *Oak and Iron* (1925); *The Yukon Kid* (1934); *Outlaws of Hafaday Creek* (1935); *Blood of the North* (1938); *Edge of Beyond* (1939); *Saga of Halfaday Creek* (1947); *Good Men and Bad* (1954); etc.

HENKLE, HENRIETTA (1909–); b. Cleveland, Ohio. Author. Writes under pen name "Henrietta Buckmaster." *Tomorrow Is Another Day* (1934); *His End Was His Beginning* (1936); *Let My People Go* (1941); *Deep River* (1944); *Fire in the Heart* (1948); *Bread From Heaven* (1952); *And Walk in Love* (1956); *Flight to Freedom* (1958); *Raleigh* (1965); *Women Who Shaped History* (1966); etc.

HENNEMAN, JOHN BELL (Jan. 2, 1864–1908); b. Spartanburg, S.C. Educator, editor, author. Editor: *Best American Tales* (with William P. Trent, 1907); etc. Editor, the *Sewanee Review,* 1907–08. Prof. English, University of the South, Sewanee, Tenn., 1900–08.

HENNESSY, ROLAND BURKE (Jan. 30, 1870–Feb. 1, 1939); b. Milford, Mass. Editor, poet. *Tales of the Heart and Tales of Broadway* (1897); *Motherland* (poem, 1915); *Liberty Aflame, and Other Verses* (1925).

HENNEY, NELLA [Braddy] (Nov. 28, 1894–); b. in Sumter Co., Ga. Editor, author. *Anne Sullivan Macy: The Story Behind Helen Keller* (1933). Editor: *Masterpieces of Adventure* (1921); *Standard Book of British and American Verse* (1933); *The Business Encyclopedia* (under pen name "Henry Marshall," 1939); *The New Business Encyclopedia* (under same pen name, 1952); etc.

HENNINGSEN, CHARLES FREDERICK (Feb. 21, 1815–June 14, 1877); b. in Belgium (?). Soldier, biographer, historian, poet. *The Last of the Sophis* (poem, 1831); *Revelations of Russia,* 2v. (1844); *Analogies and Contrasts,* 2v. (1848); *Kossuth and the Times* (1851); etc.

HENRI, FLORETTE. Author. *Kings Mountain* (1950).

HENRICKS, NAMÉE (Mrs. Walter A. Henricks) (Nov. 12, 1890–); b. Harrington, Del. Lecturer, author. Adopted by the Tonawanda Senecas as "Sah-nee-weh." *Legends of the Long House* (with Jesse J. Cornplanter, 1938); etc.

Henrietta, The. Popular play by Bronson Howard (prod. 1887). Based on the business and family life of Nicholas Van Alstyne, called the "Napoleon of Wall Street," and his two sons Nick and Bertie. "The Henrietta" was the name of a mine.

HENRY, ARTHUR (Nov. 27, 1867–deceased); b. Pecatonica, Ill. Novelist. *Nicholas Blood, Candidate* (1890); *An Island Cabin* (1902); *The Unwritten Law* (1905); etc.

HENRY, C[aleb] S[prague] (Aug. 2, 1804–Mar. 9, 1884); b. Rutland, Mass. Episcopal clergyman, educator, editor, author. *Doctor Oldham at Greystones* (1860); *About Men and Things* (1873); etc. Co-founder, the *New York Review,* 1837; editor, the *Churchman,* 1847–50. Prof. philosophy, New York University, 1838–52.

HENRY, GEORGE WILLIAM (June 13, 1889–May 23, 1964); b. Oswego, N.Y. Psychiatrist. *Essentials of Psychiatry* (1925); *Sex Variants* (1941); *All the Sexes, a Study of Masculinity and Femininity* (1955); etc.

HENRY, MARGUERITE (1902–); b. Milwaukee, Wis. Author. *Auno and Tauno* (1940); *Geraldine Belinda* (1942); *A Boy and a Dog* (1944); *Always Reddy* (1947); *Misty of Chincoteague* (1947); *Born to Trot* (1950); *Brighty of the Grand Canyon* (1953); *Black Gold* (1957); *Five O'Clock Charlie* (1962); *Stormy, Misty's Foal* (1963); *White Stallion of Lipizza* (1964); *Mustang, Wild Spirit of the West* (1966); etc.

Henry, O. Pen name of William Sidney Porter.

HENRY, PATRICK (May 29, 1736–June 6, 1799); b. in Hanover, Co., Va. Statesman, orator. Known as "The Mill-Boy of the Slashes." His best-known orations were those made in the "Parsons' Case," 1763; and before the Virginia Assembly, May 20, 1775, with its famous closing words, "Give me liberty, or give me death." See *Patrick Henry: Life, Correspondence and Speeches,* ed. by William Wirt Henry, 3v. (1891). Governor of Virginia, 1776–79, 1784–86. See William Wirt's *Sketches of the Life and Character of Patrick Henry* (1817); Moses C. Tyler's *Patrick Henry* (1887); George Morgan's *The True Patrick Henry* (1907), republished as *Patrick Henry* (1929); George F. Willison's *Patrick Henry and His World* (1965); Robert D. Meade's *Patrick Henry,* 2v. (1969).

HENRY, SAREPTA MYRENDA IRISH (Nov. 4, 1839–Jan. 16, 1900); b. Albion, Pa. Temperance worker, poet. *One More Chance* (1885); *Victoria, with Other Poems* (1888); *Beforehand* (1888); *Afterward* (1891); etc. See Mary Henry Rossiter's *My Mother's Life* (1900).

HENRY, STUART (Sept. 17, 1860–Feb., 1953); b. Clifton Springs, N.Y. Author. *Paris Days and Evenings* (1896); *Hours with Famous Parisians* (1897); *Villa Elsa* (1920); *French Essays and Profiles* (1921); *Conquering Our Great American Plains* (1930); etc.

Henry, Will. Pen name of Henry Allen.

HENRY, WILLIAM WIRT (Feb. 14, 1831–Dec. 5, 1900); b. Charlotte Co., Va., grandson of Patrick Henry. Lawyer, historical writer. Editor: *Patrick Henry: Life, Correspondence, and Speeches,* 3v. (1891).

HENSON, JOSIAH (June 15, 1789–May 5, 1881); b. in Charles Co., Md. Methodist clergyman, author. Said to have been the original of Uncle Tom in Harriet Beecher Stowe's *Uncle Tom's Cabin. The Life of Josiah Henson* (1849), augmented as *Truth Stranger Than Fiction* (autobiography, with preface by Mrs. Stowe, 1858).

HENTOFF, NATHAN IRVING (June 10, 1925–); b. Boston, Mass. Editor, author. *The Jazz Life* (1961); *The Peace Agitator* (1963); *The New Equality* (1964); *Jazz Country* (1964); *Our Children Are Dying* (1966); *Onwards!* (1967); *Journey Into Jazz* (1968); *A Political Life: The Education of John V. Lindsay* (1969). Editor: *The Jazz Makers* (1957); *Jazz* (with Albert McCarthy, 1959). Assoc. editor, *Down Beat,* 1953–57; co-founder, *Jazz Review,* 1958; co-editor, since 1958.

HENTZ, CAROLINE LEE [Whiting] (June 1, 1800–Feb. 11, 1856); b. Lancaster, Mass. Novelist, playwright. *De Lara; or, The Moorish Bride* (prod. 1831); *Werdenberg; or, The Forest League* (prod. 1832); *Lamorah; or, The Western Wild* (prod. 1833); *Lovell's Folly* (1833); *Aunt Patty's Scrap Bag* (1846); *Linda; or, The Young Pilot of the Belle Creole* (1850); *Rena; or, The Snow Bird* (1851); *The Planter's Northern Bride*, 2v. (1854); *Robert Graham: A Sequel to Linda* (1855); *Ernest Linwood* (1856); etc.

HEPBURN, ELIZABETH NEWPORT; b. Media, Pa. Author. *The Wings of Time* (1921); *Fulfillment* (1924); *Alison Vail* (1926).

HEPWORTH, GEORGE HUGHES (Feb. 4, 1833–June 7, 1902); b. Boston, Mass. Unitarian clergyman, editor, author. *The Whip, Hoe and Sword* (1864); *Rocks and Shoals* (1870); *Starboard and Port* (1876); *!!!* (1881); *Through Armenia on Horseback* (1898); etc. His sermons in the *New York Herald* were published in four volumes (1894–1904).

Her Great Match. Play by Clyde Fitch (prod. 1905). Story of the German crown prince who is willing to yield his right to the throne in order to marry an American girl.

Herald International Tribune. Paris, France. Newspaper. Published with the *New York Times* and the *Washington Post.* When the *New York Herald Tribune* was suspended in 1966, the *Paris Herald* (q.v.) changed its name to the *Herald Tribune/Washington Post International.* In 1967 the *New York Times International,* founded in 1949, merged with the *Herald Tribune/Washington Post International.* The *Herald International Tribune* became the name of the new publication.

Herald of Gospel Liberty. Portsmouth, N.H. First religious weekly. Founded 1808, by Elias Smith. Suspended 1930. *See* J. Prester Barrett's *The Centennial of Religious Journalism* (1908).

Heralds of a Liberal Faith. Ed. by Samuel Atkins Eliot, 4v. (1910).

HERBERG, WILL (Aug. 4, 1908–); b. New York. Author. *Judaism and Modern Man* (1951); *Protestant, Catholic, Jew* (1955); *The Writings of Martin Buber* (1956); *Community State and Church* (1960). Editor: *Four Existentialist Theologians* (1958); etc.

HERBERMANN, CHARLES GEORGE (Dec. 8, 1840–Aug. 24, 1916); b. Saerbeck, Westphalia, Germany. Editor-in-chief: *The Catholic Encyclopedia,* 16v. (1907–14).

HERBERT, DONALD JEFFRY [Don] (July 10, 1917–); b. Wauconia, Minn. Television producer and performer, author. *Mr. Wizard's Science Secrets* (1955); *Mr. Wizard's Experiments for Young Scientists* (1959); *Beginning Science with Mr. Wizard* (1960); *Kilauea, Case History of a Volcano* (1968); *Secret in the White Cell* (1969).

HERBERT, FRANK (1920–   ); b. in Washington state. Author. *Dune* (1965); *Dune Messiah* (1969); *Destination Void; The Eyes of Heisenberg.*

HERBERT, F[rederick] HUGH (1897–May 17, 1958); b. Vienna. Playwright, novelist. *There You Are!* (1925); *A Lover Would Be Nice* (1935); *The Revolt of Henry* (1939); *Kiss and Tell* (prod. 1943); *Meet Corliss Archer* (short stories, 1944); *For Love or Money* (prod. 1947); *The Moon Is Blue* (prod. 1951); *A Girl Can Tell* (prod. 1953); *I'd Rather Be Kissed* (1954); etc. Also screenplays.

HERBERT, HENRY WILLIAM (Apr. 7, 1807–May 17, 1858); b. London, England. Novelist, sports writer. Pen name "Frank Forester." *The Brothers: A Tale of the Fronde* (anon., 1835); *Cromwell* (anon., 1838); under own name: *The Roman Traitor* (1846); *The Cavaliers of England* (1852); *The Cavaliers of France* (1852); *Poems* (1888); etc; under pen name: *The Warwick Woodlands* (1845); *My Shooting Box* (1846);

The Deerstalkers (1849); *Field Sports of the United States and British Provinces of North America* (1849); *The Quorndon Hounds* (1852); *The Complete Manual for Young Sportsmen* (1856); *Horse and Horsemanship of the United States and British Provinces of North America,* 2v. (1857); *Fugitive Sporting Sketches,* ed. by "Will Wildwood" (i.e. Fred E. Pond) (1879); etc. Founder (with A. D. Patterson) the *American Monthly Magazine,* 1833. *See* David W. Judd's *Life and Writings of Frank Forester,* 2v. (1882); William Southworth Hunt's *Frank Forester* (1927); *Henry William Herbert: A Bibliography of His Writings* (1936), comp. by William Mitchell Van Winkle and David A. Randall.

HERBST, JOSEPHINE [Frey] (Mar. 5, 1897–Jan. 28, 1969); b. Sioux City, Ia. Novelist. *Nothing Is Sacred* (1928); *Money for Love* (1929); *Pity Is Not Enough* (1933); *The Executioner Waits* (1934); *Rope of Gold* (1939); *Satan's Sergeants* (1941); *Somewhere the Tempest Fell* (1947); *New Green World* (1954); etc.

Herder and Herder, Inc. New York. Publishers. Founded 1957. Justus G. Lawler is vice-president and editor-in-chief. Specializes in history, theology, philosophy, sociology, art.

Herder Book Co., B. St. Louis, Mo. Booksellers and publishers. Founded in 1801 by Bartholomew Herder, at Freiburg, Baden. The St. Louis branch was founded in 1873 by Joseph Gummersbach (d. 1924). Joseph J. Gummersbach is now president. The firm publishes Catholic books chiefly in the English language including: religion, canon law, history, biography, fiction, and textbooks for schools and colleges.

HERFORD, OLIVER (Dec. 1863–July 5, 1935); b. in England. Artist, humorist. *The Bashful Earthquake, and Other Fables and Verses* (1898); *Alphabet of Celebrities* (1899); *Rubaiyat of a Persian Kitten* (1904); *Cupid's Fair Weather Book* (1909); *Happy Days* (with J. Cecil Clay, 1911); *Confessions of a Caricaturist* (1917); *The Herford Æsop* (1921); *Neither Here Nor There* (1922); *The Deb's Dictionary* (1931); etc.

HERGESHEIMER, JOSEPH (Feb. 15, 1880–Apr. 25, 1954); b. Philadelphia, Pa. Novelist. *The Lay Anthony* (1914); *The Three Black Pennys* (1917); *Gold and Iron* (1918); *Java Head* (1919); *The Happy End* (1919); *Linda Condon* (1919); *Cytherea* (1922); *The Bright Shawl* (1922); *The Presbyterian Child* (autobiography, 1923); *Balisand* (1924); *From an Old House* (autobiography, 1925); *Tampico* (1926); *Swords & Roses* (1929); *The Party Dress* (1930); *The Limestone Tree* (1931); *The Foolscap Rose* (1934); etc. *See* E. T. C. Balch's *Ingénue among the Lions* (1965); R. E. Martin's *The Fiction of Joseph Hergesheimer* (1965).

HERLIHY, JAMES LEO (Feb. 27, 1927–); b. Detroit, Mich. Playwright. *Blue Denim* (play, with W. A. Noble, 1958); *The Sleep of Baby Filbertson, and Other Stories* (1959); *All Fall Down* (1960); *Midnight Cowboy* (1965); *A Story That Ends With a Scream, and Eight Others* (1967).

HERMANNSSON, HALLDOR (Jan. 6, 1878–Aug. 28, 1958); b. Völlur, Iceland. Educator, author. *The Northmen in America* (1909); *Icelandic Authors of Today* (1913); *Bibliography of the Eddas* (1920); *Old Icelandic Literature* (1933); *The Problem of Wineland* (1936); *Sagas of the Kings of Norway and the Mythical-Heroic Sagas* (1937); etc. Curator, Fiske Icelandic collection, Cornell University, 1905–48; Scandinavian language dept., 1905–46.

HERMENS, FERDINAND ALOYS (Dec. 20, 1906–); b. Niehelm, Ger. Political scientist, economist. *Democracy or Anarchy?* (1941); *The Tyrants' War and the Peoples' Peace* (1944); *Europe Between Democracy and Anarchy* (1951); *The Representative Republic* (1958); *The Fifth Republic* (1960); etc. Prof. political science, University of Notre Dame, since 1945.

HERNDON, WILLIAM HENRY (Dec. 25, 1818–Mar. 18, 1891); b. Greensburg, Ky. Law partner of Abraham Lincoln.

Author: *Lincoln: The True Story of a Great Life,* 3v. (with Jesse W. Weik, 1889). *See* Carl Sandburg's *Abraham Lincoln,* 6v. (1926–39).

HERNE, JAMES A. (Feb. 1, 1839–June 2, 1901); b. Cohoes, N.Y. Actor, playwright. *Hearts of Oak* (with David Belasco, prod. 1879); *Drifting Apart* (prod. 1888); *Margaret Fleming* (prod. 1890); *Shore Acres* (prod. 1892); *Sag Harbor* (prod. 1900); etc.

HERNTON, CALVIN C. (Apr. 28, 1932–   ); b. Chattanooga, Tenn. Author. *The Coming of Chronos to the House of Night-song* (poetry, 1963); *Sex and Racism in America* (1965); *White Papers for White America* (1966).

Heroes of the Nations 1889–June Series. Ed. by Evelyn Abbott, 52v. (1890–1931).

HEROLD, DON (July 9, 1889-June 1, 1966); b. Bloomfield, Ind. Artist, author. *So Human* (1924); *Bigger and Better* (1925); *There Ought to Be a Law* (1926); *Strange Bedfellows* (1930); *Doing Europe–and Vice Versa* (1931); *Love that Golf* (1952); *Drunks Are Driving Me to Drink* (1953); *Adventures in Golf* (1965); etc.

HEROLD, JEAN CHRISTOPHER (May 11, 1919–Dec. 10, 1964); b. Brünn, Czech. Editor, author. *The Swiss Without Halos* (1948); *Joan, Maid of France* (1952); *Mistress to an Age: A Life of Madame de Staël* (1958); *Love in Five Temperaments* (1961). Editor and translator: *The Mind of Napoleon* (1955); Editor in chief, Stanford University Press, from 1956.

HERRICK, CHEESMAN ABIAH (July 21, 1866–Feb., 1956); b. Redwood, N.Y. Educator. *Outstanding Days* (1920); etc. Editor: *History of Girard College* (1927); etc. President, Girard College, Philadelphia, 1910–36.

HERRICK, FRANCIS HOBART (Nov. 19, 1858–1940); b. Woodstock, Vt. Naturalist, author. *Home Life of Wild Birds* (1902); *Audubon, the Naturalist,* 2v. (1917); *The American Eagle: A Study in Natural and Civil History* (1934); *Wild Birds at Home* (1935); *Audubon the Naturalist* (1938); etc.

HERRICK, ROBERT (Apr. 26, 1868–Dec. 23, 1938); b. Cambridge, Mass. Educator, novelist. *The Man Who Wins* (1897); *The Gospel of Freedom* (1898); *The Web of Life* (1900); *The Common Lot* (1904); *The Master of the Inn* (1908); *Together* (1908); *A Life for a Life* (1910); *One Woman's Life* (1913); *Clark's Field* (1914); *Chimes* (1926); *The End of Desire* (1932); *Sometime* (1933); etc. English dept., University of Chicago, 1893–1923. *See* Fred B. Millett's *Contemporary American Authors* (1940).

HERRICK, SOPHIA McILVAINE BLEDSOE (Mar. 26, 1837–Oct. 9, 1919); b. Gambier, O. Editor, author. *A Century of Sonnets* (1902); and several scientific books. Assoc. editor, the *Southern Review,* Baltimore, 1875–78; joined editorial staff of *Scribner's,* 1879, and continued with its successor, *The Century,* for twenty-five years.

HERRMANN, LAZAR (1896–Nov. 9, 1961); b. in Russia. Writes under pen name "Leo Lania." *The Darkest Hour* (1941); *Today We are Brothers* (1942); *The Nine Lives of Europe* (1950); *Foreign Minister* (1956); *Hemingway: A Pictorial Biography* (1961); etc.

HERSCH, [Helen] VIRGINIA [Davis] (Mrs. Lee Hersch) (May 31, 1896–); b. San Francisco, Calif. Author. *Bird of God: The Romance of El Greco* (1929); *Woman Under Glass: St. Teresa of Avila* (1930); *The Carvalhos* (1932); *Storm Beach* (1933); *The Seven Cities of Gold* (1946); *To Seize a Dream* (1948); etc.

HERSCHBERGER, RUTH [Margaret] (Jan. 30, 1917–); b. Philipse Manor, N.Y. Author. *A Way of Happening* (poems, 1948); *Adam's Rib* (1948); etc.

HERSEY, HAROLD BRAINERD (Mar., 1893–); b. Bozeman, Mont. Editor, poet. *The Singing Flame* (1917); *Gestures in Ivory* (1919); *Night* (1923); *Cylinders* (1925); *Singing Rawhide* (1926); *Bubble and Squeak* (1927); *Pulpwood Editor* (1937); *Verse,* 2v. (1939). Editor: *G.I. Laughs* (1944). For his editorial connections, see his *Pulpwood Editor.*

HERSEY, JOHN (June 17, 1914–); b. Tientsin, China. Author. *Men on Bataan* (1942); *Into the Valley* (1943); *A Bell for Adano* (1944; Pulitzer prize for fiction, 1945); *Hiroshima* (1946); *The Wall* (1950); *The Marmot Drive* (1953); *A Single Pebble* (1956); *The War Lover* (1959); *The Child Buyer* (1960); *Here to Stay* (1963); *White Lotus* (1965); *Too Far to Walk* (1966); *Under the Eye of the Storm* (1967); *The Algiers Motel Incident* (1968).

HERSH, SEYMOUR, Journalist, author. *Chemical and Biological Warfare: America's Hidden Arsenal* (1968); *My Lai 4: A Report on the Massacre and its Aftermath* (1970).

HERSHEY, BURNET (Dec. 13, 1898–); b. in Roumania. Journalist, author. *It's a Small World: All About Midgets* (with Walter Bodin, 1934); *World of Midgets* (1935); *The Air Future* (1943); *Skyways of Tomorrow* (1944); *The Bloody Record of Nazi Atrocities* (1945); *Trial by Fire* (1964); *From A Reporter's Little Black Book* (1966); *You Can't Go to Heaven on a Roller Skate* (1969).

HERSKOVITS, MELVILLE JEAN (Sept. 10, 1895–Feb. 25, 1963); b. Bellefontaine, O. Anthropologist, author. *The American Negro* (1928); *Suriname Folklore* (with Frances S. Herskovits, 1936); *Life in a Haitian Valley* (1937); *Dahomey* (1938); *The Economic Life of Primitive Peoples* (1940); *The Myth of the Negro Past* (1941); *Man and His Works* (1948); *Franz Boas* (1953); *Dahomean Narrative: A Cross-Cultural Analysis* (with Frances S. Herskovits, 1958); *The Human Factor in Changing Africa* (1962); *Economic Transition in Africa* (with M. Harwitz, 1964); etc. Anthropology dept., Northwestern University, from 1927.

HERTS, BENJAMIN RUSSELL (May 27, 1888–Nov. 3, 1954); b. New York City. Interior decorator, editor, author. *A Female of the Species* (prod. 1914); *The Son of Man* (1917); *Grand Slam* (1933). Editor, *Moods,* 1908–09; *Forum,* 1909–10; etc.

HERTZ, EMANUEL (Sept. 2, 1870–May 23, 1940); b. Butka, Austria. Lawyer, collector of Lincolniana, author. *Abraham Lincoln: A New Portrait* (1931); *The Hidden Lincoln* (1938); etc. His collection of Lincolniana was considered to be the largest in existence; much of it was given to the Library of Congress.

HERTZLER, ARTHUR EMANUEL (July 26, 1870–Sept. 12, 1946); b. West Point, Ia. Surgeon, author. *The Horse and Buggy Doctor* (1938); *The Doctor and His Patients* (1940); *Grounds of an Old Surgeon's Faith* (1944); *Ventures in Science of a Country Surgeon* (1944); *Always the Child* (1944); etc.

HERVEY, HARRY CLAY (Nov. 5, 1900–Aug. 12, 1951); b. Beaumont, Tex. Explorer, author. *Caravans by Night* (1922); *The Black Parrot* (1923); *Where Strange Gods Call* (1924); *Ethan Quest* (1925); *Congai* (1927); *King Cobra* (1927); *Travels in French Indo-China* (1928); *Red Ending* (1929); *The Iron Widow* (1931); *Red Hotel* (1932); *The Damned Don't Cry* (1939); *School for Eternity* (1941); *The Veiled Fountain* (1947); *Barracoon* (1950).

Hervey, Mrs. Mayo D. See Frances Lester Warner.

HERZBERG, MAX J[ohn] (Mar. 29, 1886–Jan. 21, 1958); b. New York City. Editor. Compiler: *Stories of Adventure* (1927); *Myths and Their Meaning* (1928); *Outline of Contemporary American and British Literature* (1928); *Off to Arcady* (1933); *Mark Twain Omnibus* (1935); *Albert Payson Terhune Omnibus* (1937); *Happy Landings* (1942); *Humor of America* (1945); etc. Lit. editor, the *Newark Evening News,* since 1914.

HERZOG, MARGARET GUION, b. Cincinnati, O. Author. *Two's Company* (1934); *Three to Get Ready* (1938); etc.

HESCHEL, ABRAHAM JOSHUA (1907–   ); b. Warsaw, Poland. Educator, author. *The Earth is the Lord's* (1950); *Man is Not Alone: A Philosophy of Religion* (1951); *The Sabbath* (1952); *Man's Quest for God* (1954); *God in Search of Man* (1955); *The Prophets* (1962); *Ancient Jewish Theology*, 2v. (1962, 1963); *Israel: An Echo of Eternity* (1969). Professor, Jewish Theological Seminary of America, since 1945.

HESS, FJERIL (Aug. 27, 1893–); b. Omaha, Neb. Author. *High Adventure* (1925); *Buckaroo* (1931); *Sandra's Cellar* (1933); *The House of Many Tongues* (1934); *Saddle and Bridle* (1935); *Castle Camp* (1938); *Toplofty* (1939); *Fly Away Home* (1947); etc.

HESS, THOMAS BAER (July 14, 1920–   ); b. Rye, N.Y. Editor, author. *Abstract Painting: Background and American Phase* (1951); *William De Kooning* (1959). Editor *Art News* Magazine, since 1965.

HESSELTINE, WILLIAM BEST (Feb. 21, 1902–Dec. 8, 1963); b. Brucetown, Va. Educator, author. *Civil War Prisons* (1930); *History of the South* (1936); *Lincoln and the War Governors* (1948); *Confederate Leaders in the New South* (1950); *Ulysses S. Grant, Politician* (1957); *The Blue and the Gray on the Nile* (with H. C. Wolf, 1961); *Tragic Conflict* (1962); *Lincoln's Plan of Reconstruction* (1963); etc. Co-editor: *In Support of Clio* (1958). Prof. history, University of Wisconsin, 1940–63.

HESTER, HUBERT INMAN (Mar. 17, 1895–); b. Lyons, Ga. Educator, author. *The Christian College* (1940); *The Heart of the New Testament* (1950); etc. Vice president, William Jewell College, Missouri, since 1943.

HETH, EDWARD HARRIS (Sept. 13, 1909–Apr. 26, 1963); b. Milwaukee, Wis. Novelist. *Some We Loved* (1935); *Told with a Drum* (1937); *Light Over Ruby Street* (1940); *Any Number Can Play* (1945); *We Are the Robbers* (1947); *If You Lived Here* (1949); *My Life on Earth* (1953); *The Wonderful World of Cooking* (1956); *Country Kitchen Cookbook* (1968).

Hetty's Strange History. Novel by Helen Hunt Jackson, published anonymously in 1877.

HEWES, AGNES DANFORTH (Mrs. Laurence Ilsley Hewes), b. Tripoli, Syria, of American parentage. Author. *A Boy of the Lost Crusade* (1923); *Swords on the Sea* (1928); *Spice and the Devil's Cave* (1930); *Glory of the Seas* (1933); *The Codfish Musket* (1936); *The Golden Sleeve* (1937); *The Sword of Roland Arnot* (1939); *The Iron Doctor* (1940).

HEWES, HENRY (Apr. 9, 1917–); b. Boston, Mass. Drama critic. *Accounting for Love* (adaptation, prod. 1954). Drama editor, *Saturday Review*, since 1954.

HEWETT, EDGAR LEE (Nov. 23, 1865–Dec. 31, 1946); b. in Warren Co., Ill. Educator, archeologist, author. *Ancient Life in the American Southwest* (1930); *Ancient Life in Mexico and Central America* (1936); *Ancient Andean Life* (1939); *From Cave Dwelling to Mount Olympus* (1943); *Man and the State* (1944); *Man and Culture* (1945). Prof. archeology and anthropology, University of New Mexico, 1927–40.

HEWETT, WATERMAN THOMAS (Jan. 10, 1846–Sept. 13, 1921); b. Miami, Mo. Educator, editor, author. *The Frisian Language and Literature* (1879). Editor of many textbooks in German. German dept., Cornell University, 1870–1910; prof., 1883–1910.

HEWETT-THAYER, HARVEY WATERMAN (Sept. 21, 1873–June 16, 1960); b. Woolwich, Me. Educator, author. *Laurence Sterne in Germany* (1905); *The Modern German Novel* (1924); *Hoffman, Author of Tales* (1948); etc. Modern language dept., Princeton University, 1905–43.

HEWITT, ARTHUR WENTWORTH (June 22, 1883–); b. West Berlin, Vt. Methodist clergyman, poet. *Harp of the North* (1916); *Bubbles* (1920); *Songs of the Sea* (1923); *Steeples among the Hills* (autobiography, 1926); *The City of Joy* (1926); *God's Back Pasture* (1941); *The Shepherdess* (1943); *Jerusalem the Golden* (1944); *The Bridge* (1948); *The Mountain Troubadour* (1962); *The Old Brick Manse* (1966).

HEWITT, JOHN H[ill] (July 11, 1801–Oct. 7, 1890); b. New York. Editor, poet. Sometimes called "The Father of American Ballad Poetry." *Miscellaneous Poems* (1838); *Shadows on the Wall; or, Glimpses of the Past* (1877). Editor, Baltimore, *Minerva and Saturday Post,* 1830–32; *Baltimore Saturday Visitor,* 1812–35; *Baltimore Clipper,* 1839–40. Wrote the ballads, "Rock Me to Sleep, Mother" "Carry Me Back to the Sweet Sunny South," etc.

HEWITT, MARY E[lizabeth] [Moore] (b. 1818); b. Malden, Mass. Poet. *The Songs of Our Land, and Other Poems* (1846); *Poems* (1854); *Heroines of History* (1856); etc. Editor: *The Gem of the Western World* (1850); *The Memorial: Written by Friends of the Late Mrs. Osgood* (1851), republished as *Laurel Leaves* (1854).

HEWLETT, JOHN (May 30, 1905–   ); b. Conyers, Ga. Author. *Thunder Beats the Drum* (1944); *Like Moonlight on the Snow* (1947); *Cross on the Moon* (1946); *Wild Grape* (1947); *Harlem Story* (1948); *Devil's Thumb* (1950).

HEYLIGER, WILLIAM (Mar. 22, 1884–); b. Hoboken, N.J. Author. *Bucking the Line* (1912); *Don Strong of the Wolf Patrol* (1916); *Dan's Tomorrow* (1922); *Quinby and Son* (1925); *Macklin Brothers* (1928); the *Jerry Hicks* series, 4v. (1929–30); *Silver Run* (1934); *Brave Years* (1937); *Riverman* (1938); *Home Is a One Way Street* (1945); etc.

HEYM, STEFAN (Apr. 10, 1913–   ); b. Chemnitz, Ger. Editor, author. *Hostages* (1942); *Of Smiling Peace* (1944); *The Crusaders* (1948); *The Eyes of Reason* (1951); *Goldsborough* (1954). Editor, *Deutsche Volkseche,* 1937–39.

HEYWARD, DOROTHY (Mrs. DuBose Heyward) (June 6, 1890–Nov. 19, 1961); b. Wooster, O. Playwright, novelist. *Nancy Ann* (prod. 1924); *Porgy* (with husband, prod. 1927); *Three-a-Day* (1930); *The Pulitzer Prize Murders* (1932); *Mamba's Daughters* (with husband, prod. 1939); *South Pacific* (with Howard Rigsby, prod. 1944); *Set My People Free* (prod. 1948).

HEYWARD, DuBOSE (Aug. 31, 1885–June 16, 1940); b. Charleston, S.C. Novelist, playwright, poet. Author: *Carolina Chansons* (with Hervey Allen, 1922); *Skylines and Horizons* (poems, 1924); *Porgy* (1925); dramatized (with wife, Dorothy Heyward, prod. 1927), made into opera, *Porgy and Bess* (music by George Gershwin, prod. 1935); *Angel* (1926); *Mamba's Daughters* (1929), dramatized (with wife, prod. 1939); *Jasbo Brown, and Selected Poems* (1931); *Brass Ankles* (prod. 1931); *Peter Ashley* (1932); *Lost Morning* (1936); *Star Spangled Virgin* (1939); etc. See Fred B. Millett's *Contemporary American Authors* (1940).

"Hiawatha." Long poem by Henry Wadsworth Longfellow (1855). Based on the hero myths and customs of the American Indians. It has remained one of the most popular of Longfellow's poems. Dozens of parodies appeared, since the verse pattern was so easy to imitate. Among these is Mortimer N. Thompson's *Plu-ri-bus-tah* (1856).

HIBBARD, [Clarence] ADDISON (Aug. 29, 1887–May 17, 1945); b. Racine, Wis. Educator, critic. *A Handbook to Literature* (with William Flint Thrall, 1936). Editor: *The Lyric South* (1929); *The Book of Poe* (1929); *Stories of the South* (1931); *Writers of the Western World* (1942). Author of syndicated column called "The Literary Lantern." English dept., Northwestern University, since 1930.

HIBBARD, GEORGE A[biah] (Jan. 8, 1858–July 3, 1928); b. Buffalo, N.Y. Artist, writer of fiction. *Iduna, and Other Stories* (1891); *The Governor, and Other Stories* (1892); *Nowadays, and Other Stories* (1893); *Eyes of Affection* (1906).

HIBBEN, JOHN GRIER (Apr. 19, 1861–May 16, 1933); b. Peoria, Ill. Educator, philosopher, author. *The Problems of Philosophy* (1898); *The Philosophy of the Enlightenment* (1910); *A Defence of Prejudice, and Other Essays* (1911); President, Princeton University, 1912–33.

HIBBEN, PAXTON PATTISON (Dec. 5, 1880–Dec. 15, 1928); b. Indianapolis, Ind. Correspondent, biographer. *Constantine I and the Greek People* (1920); *Henry Ward Beecher: An American Portrait* (1927); *The Peerless Leader, William Jennings Bryan* (1929); etc.

HIBBETT, HOWARD S[cott] (July 27, 1920–); b. Akron, O. Educator, author, translator. *The Floating World in Japanese Fiction* (1959); *Modern Japanese: A Basic Reader* (with Gen. Itasaka, 1965). Translator: J. Tanizaki's *The Key* (1961); *Seven Japanese Tales* (1963); *Diary of a Mad Old Man* (1965). Prof. Japanese literature, Harvard University, since 1963.

HIBBS, BEN (July 23, 1901–); b. Fontana, Kans. Editor, *Country Gentleman*, 1940–42; *Saturday Evening Post*, 1942–61; *Reader's Digest*, since 1963.

HICK, JOHN HARWOOD (Jan. 20, 1922–   ); b. Scarborough, Eng. Educator, author. *Faith and Knowledge* (1957); *Philosophy of Religion* (1963); *Classical and Contemporary Readings in the Philosophy of Religion* (1964); *Faith and the Philosophers* (1964); *The Existence of God* (1964); *Evil and the Love of God* (1965). Prof. Christian philosophy, Princeton Theological Seminary, since 1959.

HICKOK, LAURENS PERSEUS (Dec. 29, 1798–Mar. 6, 1888); b. Bethel, Conn. Presbyterian clergyman, educator, philosopher, author. *A System of Moral Science* (1853); *The Logic of Reason* (1875); etc. Vice-president, Union College, 1852–66; president, 1866–68.

HICKS, CLIFFORD BYRON (Aug. 10, 1920–); b. Marshalltown, Ia. Magazine editor, author. *Do-It-Yourself Materials Guide* (1955); *First Boy on the Moon* (1958); *The Marvelous Inventions of Alvin Fernald* (1960); *Alvin's Secret Code* (1963); *The World Above* (1965); *Alvin Fernald, Mayor for a Day* (1969). Editorial staff, *Popular Mechanics* magazine, since 1945.

HICKS, ELIAS (Mar. 19, 1748–Feb. 27, 1830); b. in Hempstead Twp., L.I., N.Y. Author. *Observations on the Slavery of the Africans* (1811); *The Quaker*, 4v. (1827–28); *Journal* (1832); etc. Founder of the so-called "Hicksite" branch of Quakers, 1828. See Henry W. Wilbur's *The Life and Labors of Elias Hicks* (1910).

HICKS, FREDERICK CHARLES (Oct. 14, 1875–Apr. 30, 1956); b. Auburn, N.Y. Librarian, educator, writer on legal subjects. *Men and Books Famous in the Law* (1921); *William Howard Taft, Yale Professor of Law and New Haven Citizen* (1945); etc. Editor: *Bermuda in Poetry* (1915); *Materials and Methods of Legal Research* (1923); *Famous American Jury Speeches* (1925); *Famous Speeches by Eminent American Statesmen* (1929); *Arguments and Addresses of Joseph Hodges Choate* (1926). Law librarian, Columbia University, 1915–28; law librarian, Yale University, 1928–44; prof. law, Yale University, 1929–44.

HICKS, GRANVILLE (Sept. 9, 1901–); b. Exeter, N.H. Editor, author. *The Great Tradition: An Interpretation of American Literature Since the Civil War* (1933); *I Like America* (1938); *Figures of Transition: A Study of British Literature at the End of the Nineteenth Century* (1939); *Only One Storm* (1942); *Behold Trouble* (1944); *Small Town* (1946); *There Was a Man in Our Town* (1952); *Where We Came Out* (1954); *Part of the Truth: An Autobiography* (1965); *James*

Gould Cozzens (1967); etc. Editor: *Proletarian Literature in the United States* (1935); *The Letters of Lincoln Steffens*, 2v. (with Ella Winter, 1938). With *New Masses*, 1934–39; with *New Leader*, 1951–58.

HICKS, JOHN DONALD (Jan. 25, 1890–); b. Pickering, Mo. Educator, author. *The Populist Revolt* (1931); *The Federal Union* (1937); *The American Nation* (1941); *Agricultural Discontent in the Middle West, 1900–1939* (1951); *The American Tradition* (1955); *Rehearsal for Disaster* (1961). History dept., University of Wisconsin, 1932–42; University of California, 1942–57, Emeritus since 1957.

HICKS, WILSON (Jan. 7, 1897–July 5, 1970); b. Sedalia, Mo. Editor. *Words and Pictures* (1952). Editor: *This Is Ike* (1952). Editorial staff, *Life* magazine, 1937–50. Lecturer, photo journalism, University of Miami.

Hidden best-sellers. Books which have tremendous sales but which do not appear on best-seller lists. *The Bible*, school books, *The Boy Scout Manual*, cook books, and dime novels are examples.

Hidden Persuaders, The. By Vance Packard (1957). Lively presentation of the uses of motivational research in persuading consumers to buy products. An exposé of current commercial attitudes.

HIEBERT, RAY ELDON (May 21, 1932–   ); b. Freeman, S.D. Educator, author. *Books in Human Development* (1965); *The Press in Washington* (1966); *Courtier to the Crowd* (1966). Editor, *Government and Communication*, since 1966. Head dept. journalism, University of Maryland, since 1967.

HIGBY, CHESTER PENN (Oct. 27, 1885–June 26, 1966); b. Farm Ridge, Ill. Educator, author. *History of Europe, 1492–1815* (1927); *History of Modern Europe* (1932); etc. Prof. history, University of Wisconsin, since 1927.

HIGGINS, AILEEN CLEVELAND (Mrs. John Archibald Sinclair) (Dec. 7, 1882–); b. Perry, Ill. Author. *Thekla* (1907); *Dream Blocks* (1908); the *Little Princess* series, 5v.

HIGGINS, MARGUERITE (d. Jan. 3, 1966); b. Hong Kong. Journalist, author. *War in Korea: The Report of a Woman Combat Correspondent* (1951); *News Is a Singular Thing* (1955); *Red Plush and Black Bread* (1955); *Our Vietnam Nightmare* (1965). With New York *Herald Tribune*, 1942–66.

HIGGINS, RICHARD C. (Mar. 15, 1938–   ); b. Cambridge, England. Publisher, author. *What are Legends?* (1960); *Jefferson's Birthday* (plays, 1964); *Postface* (1964); *A Book About Love and War and Death, Canto One* (1965); *Act. Ed 912* (1968); *FOEW&OMBWHNW* (1968). Designer and manager of Something Else Press.

HIGGINSON, ELLA [Rhoades] (1862–deceased); b. Council Grove, Kan. Novelist, poet. *The Flower That Grew in the Sand, and Other Stories* (1896); *When the Birds Go North Again* (poems, 1898); *The Voice of April-Land, and Other Poems* (1903); *Alaska, the Great Country* (1908); *The Vanishing Race, and Other Poems* (1912); etc.

HIGGINSON, FRANCIS (1586–Aug. 6, 1630); b. Claybrooke (?), Leicestershire, England. Congregational clergyman, author. *New-Englands Plantation* (1630).

HIGGINSON, MARY [Potter] THACHER (Mrs. Thomas Wentworth Higginson) (Nov. 26, 1844–deceased); b. Machias, Me. Poet, biographer. *Sea Shore and Prairie* (1876); *Room for One More* (1879); *Such As They Are* (poems, with husband, 1894); *The Playmate Hours* (poems, 1904); *Thomas Wentworth Higginson: the Story of His Life* (1914); *Fugitives* (poems, 1929). Editor, *Letters and Journals of Thomas Wentworth Higginson* (1921).

HIGGINSON, THOMAS WENTWORTH (Dec. 22, 1823–May 9, 1911); b. Cambridge, Mass. Unitarian clergyman, critic, poet. *Outdoor Papers* (1963); *Malbone* (1869); *Army Life in a Black Regiment* (1870); *Atlantic Essays* (1871); *Oldport Days* (1873); *Short Studies of American Authors* (1879); *Margaret Fuller Ossoli* (1884); *Such As They Are* (poems, with wife, Mary Thacher Higginson, 1894); *Cheerful Yesterdays* (1898); *Contemporaries* (1899); *Henry Wadsworth Longfellow* (1902); *John Greenleaf Whittier* (1902); *A Reader's History of American Literature* (with Henry Walcott Boynton, 1903); *Letters and Journals*, ed. by wife, Mary Thacher Higginson (1921); etc. *See* Mary T. Higginson's *Thomas Wentworth Higginson* (1914); Anna Mary Wells's *Preceptor: The Life and Times of Thomas Wentworth Higginson* (1963).

HIGH, STANLEY [Hoflund] (Dec. 30, 1895–Feb. 3, 1961); b. Chicago, Ill. Editor, author. *China's Place in the Sun* (1922); *The Revolt of Youth* (1923); *Europe Turns the Corner* (1925); *A Waking World* (1928); *The New Crisis in the Far East* (1932); *Roosevelt–And Then* (1937); *Billy Graham, The Personal Story of the Man, His Message, and His Mission* (1956). Editor, *Christian Herald*, 1928–30; senior editor, *Reader's Digest*, from 1952.

High Fidelity and Audiocraft. Great Barrington, Mass. Monthly. Founded 1951, as *High Fidelity;* changed name in 1958 after it absorbed *Audiocraft.* Concerned with radio and phonograph equipment, and recordings; features book reviews.

"High Tide at Gettysburg, The." Poem by Will Henry Thompson (1888). Delivered at Gettysburg, July 4, 1888, the twenty-eighth anniversary of the battle, by the author, a former Confederate soldier.

HIGHET, GILBERT ARTHUR (June 22, 1906–); b. Glasgow, Scot. Educator, author. *The Classical Tradition* (1949); *The Art of Teaching* (1950); *Peoples, Places and Books* (1953); *Man's Unconquerable Mind* (1954); *Migration of Ideas* (1954); *A Clerk of Oxenford* (1954); *Juvenal the Satirist* (1954); *Talents and Geniuses: The Pleasures of Appreciation* (1957); *Poets in a Landscape* (1957); *The Powers of Poetry* (1960); *The Anatomy of Satire* (1961); etc., including Latin textbooks. Translator: Werner Jaeger's *Paideia* (1939–45). Chairman editorial board, *Horizon*, since 1959. Prof. Greek and Latin, Columbia University, 1938–50.

HIGINBOTHAM, JOHN U. (Nov. 5, 1867–deceased); b. Manhattan, Kan. Author: The *Three Weeks* series of travel books, 4v. (1904–12).

HILBERSEIMER, LUDWIG KARL (Sept. 14, 1885–May 6, 1967); b. Karlsruhe, Ger. City planner, author. *The New City* (1944); *The New Regional Pattern* (1949); *The Nature of Cities* (1955); *Mies van der Rohe* (1956); *Contemporary Architecture–Its Roots and Trends* (1964).

HILDEBRAND, JESSE RICHARDSON (Feb. 3, 1888–Sept. 18, 1951); b. Smithsburg, Mo. Author. *The Columbus of the Pacific* (1927); *The World's Greatest Overland Explorer* (1928); *California's Coastal Redwood Realm* (1939); *Glass "Goes to Town"* (1943); etc. Editorial staff, *National Geographic Magazine*, from 1919; assistant editor from 1931.

HILDRETH, CHARLES LOTIN (Aug. 28, 1858–Aug. 19, 1896); b. New York City. Novelist, poet. *Judith* (1876); *The New Symphony, and Other Stories* (1878); *The Masque of Death, and Other Poems* (1889); *Oo: Adventures in Orbello Land* (1889); *The Mysterious City of Oo* (1893); etc. On staff, the *New York World; Bedford's Magazine; Demorest's Magazine.*

HILDRETH, RICHARD (June 28, 1807–July 11, 1865); b. Deerfield, Mass. Lawyer, editor, author. *The Slave; or, Memoirs of Archy Moore* (anon., 1836); *Despotism in America* (1840); *The History of the United States of America*, 6v. (1849–52); etc. Founder, the *Boston Daily Atlas*, 1832; editor, 1832–38.

HILDRETH, SAMUEL PRESCOTT (Sept. 30, 1783–July 24, 1863); b. Methuen, Mass. Physician, naturalist, historian. *Pioneer History: Being an Account of the First Examinations of the Ohio Valley* (1848); *Biographical and Historical Memoirs of the Early Pioneer Settlers in Ohio* (1852); etc.

HILL, ADAMS SHERMAN (Jan. 30, 1833–1910); b. Boston, Mass. Educator, author. *Principles of Rhetoric* (1878); *Our English* (1889); etc. Prof. rhetoric, Harvard University, 1876–1904.

HILL, "BILLY" [William Joseph] (1898–Dec. 24, 1940); b. Boston, Mass. Song writer. Writer of many popular songs, including "The Last Round-up," "Wagon Wheels," "They Cut Down the Old Pine Tree," "Colorado Moon," "The Old Spinning Wheel," "Chapel in the Moonlight," "Cabin in the Carolinas," "Empty Saddles," "For Molly and Me," "Sleepy Head," "Peaceful Valley," "The Call of the Canyon," etc.

HILL, DANIEL HARVEY (July 12, 1821–Sept. 24, 1889); b. York District, S.C. Confederate general, editor, educator. Founder, the *Land We Love*, 1866; the *Southern Home*, 1869. President, University of Arkansas, 1877–84.

HILL, DAVID JAYNE (June 10, 1850–Mar. 2, 1932); b. Plainfield, N.J. Educator, diplomat, biographer. *Washington Irving* (1879); *William Cullen Bryant* (1879); *The People's Government* (1915); etc. President, Bucknell University, 1879–88; University of Rochester, 1888–96. Minister to Switzerland, 1903–05; to The Netherlands, 1905–08; ambassador to Germany, 1908–11.

HILL, EDWIN C[onger] (Apr. 23, 1884–Feb. 12, 1958); b. Aurora, Ind. Radio commentator, author. *The Iron Horse* (1925); *The American Scene* (1933); *The Human Side of the News* (1934).

HILL, FRANK ERNEST (Aug. 29, 1888–d. 1970); b. San Jose, Calif. Editor, author. *The Winged Horse* (with Joseph Auslander, 1927); *Stone Dust* (poems, 1928); *What Is American* (1933); *The Westward Star* (poem, 1934); *To Meet Will Shakespeare* (1949); *Ford: The Times, the Man, the Company* (with A. Nevins, 1954); *Ford: Expansion and Challenge, 1915–33* (with same, 1957); *Famous Historians* (1966). Translator: *The Canterbury Tales* (into modern verse, 1930). Editor: *The Winged Horse Anthology* (with Joseph Auslander, 1929). Editor, Longmans Green & Co., New York, 1925–31.

HILL, FRANK PIERCE (Aug. 22, 1855–deceased); b. Concord, N.H. Librarian, editor. Editor and compiler: *Lowell* [Mass.] *Illustrated* (1884); *Books, Pamphlets and Newspapers Printed at Newark, New Jersey* (with Varnum Lansing Collins, 1902); *American Plays Printed* (1934); etc. Librarian, Brooklyn Public Library, 1901–30.

HILL, FREDERIC STANHOPE (1805–Apr. 7, 1851); b. Boston, Mass. Actor, playwright, poet. *The Harvest Festival, with Other Poems* (1826). Founder, the *Boston Lyceum*, 1827.

HILL, FREDERICK STANHOPE (Aug. 4, 1829–1913); b. Boston, Mass., son of Frederic Stanhope Hill. Author. *Twenty Years at Sea* (1893); *Twenty-Six Historic Ships* (1903); *The Romance of the American Navy* (1910); etc.

HILL, FREDERICK TREVOR (May 5, 1866–Mar. 17, 1930); b. Brooklyn, N.Y. Lawyer, novelist. *The Case and Exceptions* (1900); *The Minority* (1902); *The Web* (1903); *The Accomplice* (1905); *Lincoln the Lawyer* (1906); *The Story of a Street* (1908); etc.

HILL, GEORGE (1796–Dec. 15, 1871); b. Guilford, Conn. Poet. *The Ruins of Athens, with Other Poems* (anon., 1831); revised and augmented as, *The Ruins of Athens; Titania's Banquet, a Mask; and Other Poems* (1839); and again as, *Titania's Banquet, Pictures of Women, and Other Poems* (1870).

HILL, GRACE LIVINGSTON (Apr. 16, 1865–Feb. 23, 1947); b. Wellsville, N.Y. Novelist. Pen name, "Marcia Mac-Donald." Under own name: *A Chatauqua Idyl* (1887); *Katherine's Yesterday* (1896); *The Girl From Montana* (1907); *Phoebe Dean* (1909); *The Man of the Desert* (1914); *The Enchanted Barn* (1918); *Exit Betty* (1920); *Coming Through the Rye* (1926); *Kerry* (1931); *Rainbow Cottage* (1934); *Marigold* (1938); *Head of the House* (1940); *The Street of the City* (1942); *A Girl to Come Home To* (1945); etc.; and under pen name: *The Honor Girl* (1927); *Found Treasure* (1928); *Out of the Storm* (1929); etc.

HILL, HERBERT WYNFORD (Aug. 14, 1875–Feb. 16, 1943); b. Stanstead, P.Q. Educator, author. *Sidney's Arcadia and the Elizabethan Drama* (1909); *La Calprenède and the Restoration Drama* (1911); etc. Prof. English, University of Nevada, 1907–27; University of Southern California, from 1927.

HILL, HOWARD COPELAND (Dec. 20, 1878–1940); b. St. Louis, Mo. Educator, author. *Reading and Living,* 2v. (with Rollo L. Lyman, 1924); *Literature and Living,* 3v. (with same, 1925); *Roosevelt and the Caribbean* (1927); etc. Co-editor: *American Literature* (1937); *English Literature* (1937); *World Literature* (1938); *Contemporary Literature* (1938). With University of Chicago, from 1924.

HILL, JIM DAN (Feb. 4, 1897–); b. Leon County, Tex. Educator, author. *Sea Dogs of the Sixties* (1935); *The Texas Navy* (1936); etc. President, State Teachers College, Superior, Wis., since 1931.

HILL, ROSCOE R. (Feb. 22, 1880–Oct. 26, 1960); b. Lilly, Ill. Archivist. Compiler: *Descriptive Catalogue of the Documents Relating to the History of the United States in the Papeles Procedentes de Cuba, Deposited in the Archivo General de Indias at Seville* (1916); and numerous other archives, the latest of which is *American Missions in European Archives* (1951). Chief of classification division, the National Archives, Washington, D.C., 1935–41; Department of State division, 1941–46.

HILL, THEOPHILUS HUNTER (Oct. 31, 1836–June 29, 1901); b. near Raleigh, N.C. Poet. *Hesper, and Other Poems* (1861); *Poems* (1869); *Passion Flower, and Other Poems* (1883).

HILL, THOMAS (Jan. 7, 1818–Nov. 21, 1891); b. New Brunswick, N.J. Unitarian clergyman, educator, author. *Christmas, and Poems on Slavery* (1843); *Geometry and Faith* (1849); *The True Order of Studies* (1876); *In the Woods, and Elsewhere* (poems, 1888); etc. President, Antioch College, 1859–62; Harvard University, 1862–68.

HILL, WELDON (pseud.). *Onionhead* (1957); *The Long Summer of George Adams* (1961); *Rafe* (1966).

HILL, WILLIAM BANCROFT (Feb. 17, 1857–Jan. 23, 1945); b. Colebrook, N.H. Educator, author. *Guide to the Lives of Christ* (1905); *Life of Christ* (1917); *The Apostolic Age* (1922); etc. Prof. Biblical literature, Vassar College, 1902–21.

Hill and Wang. New York. Publishers. Founded 1956, by Lawrence Hill and Arthur W. Wang. Publishes Dramabooks and American Century Series. Developed a notable list of books on Afro-American literature and history. A division of Farrar, Straus and Giroux since 1971.

HILLARD, GEORGE STILLMAN (Sept. 22, 1808–Jan. 21, 1879); b. Machias, Me. Lawyer, author. *Six Months in Italy* (1853); *Life, Letters, and Journal of George Ticknor,* 2v. (1876); etc. Editor: *The Poetical Works of Edmund Spenser,* 5v. (1839); also the *Franklin* readers; etc.

HILLCOURT, WILLIAM [Bjerregaard-Jensen, Vilhelm Hans] (Aug. 6, 1900–); b. Aarhus, Denmark. Editor, author. *Handbook for Patrol Leaders* (1929); *Hand-*

book for Scoutmasters (1936); *Scout Field Book* (1944); *Field Book of Nature Activities* (1950); *Boy Scout Handbook* (1959); *Field Book of Nature Activities and Conservation* (1961); *Baden-Powell, The Two Lives of a Hero* (with Olive, Lady Baden-Powell, 1967). *Physical Fitness for Boys* (1967); *Physical Fitness for Girls* (1967). Editor: *The 1929 World Jamboree Book* (1929); *Scouting for Boys* (1946). With *Boys' Life,* since 1932.

HILLEBRAND, HAROLD NEWCOMB (Jan. 1, 1887–Jan. 26, 1953); b. Washington, D.C. Educator, author. *The Child Actors: A Chapter on Elizabethan Stage History,* 2v. (1926); *Edmund Kean* (1933); etc. English dept., University of Illinois, from 1914; head, 1939–46.

HILLHOUSE, JAMES A[braham] (Sept. 26, 1789–Jan. 4, 1841); b. New Haven, Conn. Poet. *Percy's Masque* (anon., 1819); *The Judgment: A Vision* (anon., 1821); *Hadad* (1825); *Sachem's-Wood* (1838); *Demetria* (1839); *Dramas, Discourses, and Other Pieces,* 2v. (1839).

HILLIARD, HENRY WASHINGTON (Aug. 4, 1808–Dec. 17, 1892); b. Fayetteville, N.C. Lawyer, author. *De Vane* (1865); *Politics and Pen Pictures of Home and Abroad* (1892).

HILLIS, MARJORIE (May 25, 1890–d. 1971); b. Peoria, Ill. Editor, author. *Live Alone and Like It* (1936); *Orchids on Your Budget* (1937); *Corned Beef and Caviar* (1937); *Work Ends at Nightfall* (poems, 1938); *You Can Start All Over* (1951); etc. On editorial staff, *Vogue,* since 1918; exec. editor, 1932–37.

HILLIS, NEWELL DWIGHT (Sept. 2, 1858–Feb. 25, 1929); b. Magnolia, Ia. Congregational clergyman, author. *A Man's Value to Society* (1896); *Great Books As Life-Teachers* (1899); As *The Quest of John Chapman* (1904); etc.

HILLMAN, ALEX L. (Sept. 16, 1900–Mar. 25, 1968); b. Chicago, Ill. Publisher. Pres., William Godwin, 1927–31; founder, Hillman-Curl, 1931; pres., 1931–38; pres., Hillman Periodicals, from 1938.

Hillsboro People. By Dorothy Canfield Fisher (1915). Collection of short stories, including occasional verse by Sarah N. Cleghorn.

HILLYER, ROBERT [Silliman] (June 3, 1895–Dec. 24, 1961); b. East Orange, N.J. Poet, novelist. *Sonnets and Other Lyrics* (1917); *Alchemy: A Symphonic Poem* (1920); *The Five Books of Youth* (1920); *The Hills Give Promise* (1923); *The Halt in the Garden* (1925); *The Happy Episode* (1927); *The Seventh Hill* (1928); *The Gates of the Compass* (1930); *Riverhead* (1932); *The Collected Verse* (1933, Pulitzer prize for poetry, 1934); *A Letter to Robert Frost and Others* (1937); *First Principles of Verse* (1938); *In Times of Mistrust* (1939); *Pattern of a Day* (1940); *Poems for Music* (1947); *The Death of Captain Nemo* (1949); *The Suburb by the Sea* (1952); *The Relic, and Other Poems* (1957); *In Pursuit of Poetry* (1960); *Collected Poems* (1961); etc. Editor: *Eight Harvard Poets* (1917); *Eight More Harvard Poets* (with S. Foster Damon, 1923); *Prose Masterpieces of English and American Literature* (with others, 1931). English dept., Harvard University, 1919–45; University of Delaware, from 1954.

HILLYER, VIRGIL MORES (Sept. 2, 1875–Dec. 21, 1931); b. Weymouth, Mass. Educator, author. *A Child's History of the World* (1924); *A Child's Geography of the World* (1929); *A Child's History of Art* (with Edward Greene Huey, 1933); etc.

HILSMAN, ROGER (Nov. 29, 1919–); b. Waco, Tex. Educator, author. *Strategic Intelligence and National Decisions* (1956); *To Move a Nation* (1967). Co-author: *Military Policy and National Security* (1956); *Alliance Policy in the Cold War* (1959); *NATO and American Security* (1959); *Foreign Policy in the Sixties* (1965). Prof. government, Columbia University, since 1964.

HILTMAN, JOHN WOLFE (Feb. 27, 1862–Apr. 15, 1941); b. Manchester, England. Publisher. With Edward Thompson Co., law book publishers, Northport, L.I., N.Y., 1897–1912. With D. Appleton Co., New York, 1912–41; president, 1919–33; board of directors, Appleton-Century Co., 1933–41.

HILTON, HENRY HOYT (Apr. 17, 1868–Apr. 10, 1948); b. Cambridge, Mass. Publisher. With Ginn & Co., publishers, 1890–1946.

HIMES, CHESTER B[omar] (July 29, 1909–); b. Jefferson City, Mo. Author. *If He Hollers Let Him Go* (1945); *Lonely Crusade* (1947); *Cast the First Stone* (1953); *The Third Generation* (1954); *Cotton Comes to Harlem* (1965); *The Primitive Harlem* (1968); *Blind Man with a Pistol* (1969).

HIMMELFARB, GERTRUDE (Aug. 8, 1922–); b. New York. Educator, author. *Lord Acton: A Study in Conscience and Politics* (1952); *Darwin and the Darwinian Revolution* (1959); *Victorian Minds* (1968). Prof. history, Brooklyn College.

HINCKLEY, GEORGE WALTER (July 27, 1853–Aug. 10, 1961); b. Guilford, Conn. Baptist clergyman, educator, author. *The Story of Good Will Farm* (1892); *Story of Dan McDonald* (1904); *Letters from Applehurst* (1923); *As I Remember It,* 2v. (1935–36); and other books. Founder, *The Good Will Record,* 1888.

HINCKLEY, JULIAN (Feb. 6, 1884–); b. Lawrence, L.I., N.Y. Novelist. *E: The Complete and Somewhat Mad History of the Family of Montague Vincent* (1914); *The Family Tradition* (1918).

HINDLEY, HOWARD L[ister] (July 23, 1870–May 10, 1943); b. Frome, Ont. Editor, author. *The Gentlemen from Hayville* (1908). Editor, *Rutland* (Vt.) *Herald,* from 1905.

HINDUS, MAURICE [Gershon] (Feb. 27, 1891–July 8, 1969); b. Bolshoye Bikovo, Russia. Author. *The Russian Peasant and the Revolution* (1920); *Broken Earth* (1926); *Red Bread* (1931); *Moscow Skies* (1936); *Green Worlds* (autobiography, 1938); *We Shall Live Again* (1939); *Sons and Fathers* (1940); *To Sing with the Angels* (1941); *Mother Russia* (1943); *The Cossacks* (1945); *Bright Passage* (1947); *In Search of a Future* (1949); *Magda* (1951); *Christ in the Kremlin* (1953); *House Without a Roof* (1961); etc.

HINE, DARYL [William] (Feb. 24, 1936–   ); b. New Westminster, B.C., Can. Author. *Five Poems* (1955); *The Carnal and the Crane* (1957); *The Devil's Picture Book* (1960); *The Prince of Darkness and Co.* (novel, 1961); *The Wooden Horse* (1965); *Minutes* (1968); *The Death of Seneca* (play, 1967); etc. Faculty, University of Chicago, since 1967. Editor, *Poetry,* 1968.

HINES, DUNCAN (Mar. 26, 1880–Mar. 15, 1959); b. Bowling Green, Ky. Businessman, author. *Adventures in Good Eating* (1936); *Lodging for a Night* (1938); *Adventures in Good Cooking* (1939); *Food Odyssey* (1955).

HINKE, WILLIAM JOHN (Mar. 24, 1871–Jan. 1, 1947); b. Giershofen, Germany. Educator, librarian. Compiler: *Bibliography of the Reformed Church in the United States* (1901); *Pennsylvania German Pioneers,* 3v. (1934); etc. Prof. Semitic languages, Auburn Theological Seminary, 1907–39; librarian 1923–39.

HINKLE, THOMAS CLARK (June 12, 1876–May 13, 1949); b. Laclede, Ill. Author of children's books about dogs: *Split-Ear* (1925); *Bugle* (1929); *Bing* (1932); *King* (1936); *Dusty* (1940); *Blackjack* (1946); *Wolf* (1948); etc.; and about horses: *Black Storm* (1929); *Silver* (1934); *Cinchfoot* (1938); *Buckskin* (1939); *Mustang* (1942); etc.

HINMAN, WILBUR F. Author. *Corporal Si Klegg and His "Pard"* (1887); *The Story of the Sherman Brigade* (1897). Compiler: *Camp and Field* (1892).

HINSDALE, BURKE AARON (Mar. 31, 1837–Nov. 29, 1900); b. Wadsworth, O. Educator, editor, author. *The Old Northwest* (1888); *The Art of Study* (1900); etc. Editor: *The Works of James Abram Garfield* 2v. (18–). President, Hiram College, Hiram, O., 1870–82; prof. education, University of Michigan, 1888–1900.

Hinterland, The. Des Moines, Ia. Literary magazine. Founded 1934, by Dale D. Kramer, at Cedar Rapids, Iowa. Beginning with the second number, it was published at Des Moines. Expired 1939.

HINTZ, HOWARD WILLIAM (June 10, 1903–Oct. 19, 1964); b. Brooklyn, N.Y. Presbyterian clergyman, educator, author. *Basic Necessity for Spiritual Reconstruction* (1936); *Modern American Vistas* (with B. D. N. Grebanier, 1940); *Religion and Higher Education* (1955); *The Quaker Influence in American Literature* (1965); etc. Prof. English, Brooklyn College, from 1951.

Hippies. In one respect, the successors to the Beat Generation (q.v.) of the 1950's in the bohemian tradition of writers and artists, but with one radical difference. Many are specifically either nonverbal or antiliterary. They deny the primacy of verbal and written communication, and base their ideals of expression on visual and aural imagery; on the sensuous experiences of touching, tasting, and smelling; on revery and hallucination induced by various drugs; and on occult and Oriental forms of mystical knowledge. In general, the young people usually called hippies recognize an ideal of hedonism that equates peace and love with the pleasure of being alive, preferring to live for the moment rather than to act purposefully. The term "hippie" came into prominence during the early 1960's and is connected with "hep," "hip," and "hipster," which derive from the metropolitan Negro jazz and drug culture. *See* Harold Wentworth's and Stuart Flexner's *Dictionary of American Slang.* Hippies were called Flower Children until about 1968, and have been discussed under such terms as Youth Revolution, Counter Culture, Alternate Culture, Generation Gap, and Street People. Of those called hippies, many write poetry and prose that stems from Beat Generation, Black Humor (q.v.) and Absurdist styles; compose words and music to rock, folk-rock, and other popular, neo-primitive modes; make movies; write in theatrical forms; produce and participate in happenings; edit and write for Underground newspapers and periodicals; etc. In the mid-1960's the term "yippies" came into use to describe those hippies who developed public forms of theatrical improvisation to gain exposure in the mass media as a means of political protest. Among authors who have anticipated, shared, or discussed hippie views in their writings are Paul Goodman, Kenneth Rexroth, Leslie Fiedler, Allen Ginsberg, Herbert Marcuse, Norman Mailer, Edgar Z. Friedenberg, Paul Krassner, Ken Kesey, Abbie Hoffman, Jerry Rubin, Marshall McLuhan, Buckminster Fuller, John Cage, Norman O. Brown, Timothy Leary. *See McLuhanism, Pop Poetry. See also* John Gruen's *The New Bohemia* (1966); Nicholas Von Hoffman's *We Are the People Our Parents Warned Us Against* (1967); Lewis Yablonsky's *The Hippie Trip* (1968); Theodore Roszak's *The Making of a Counter Culture* (1969); Don McNeill's *Moving Through Here* (1970); Charles Reich's *The Greening of America* (1970).

Hippisley, George. See "George Herbert Westley."

"Hippopotamus, The." Poem by T. S. Eliot (1920). An ironical poem on the Church as an institution.

"Hireling and Slave, The." Long narrative poem by William John Grayson (1854).

Hiroshima. By John Hersey (1946). An account of the effects upon the inhabitants of Hiroshima, Japan, of the atomic bombing of that city by the U.S. Air Force during World War II. First appeared in the *New Yorker,* which devoted an entire issue to its publication in 1946.

HIRSCHFELD, ALBERT (June 21, 1903–); b. St. Louis, Mo. Artist, author. *Manhattan Oases* (1932); *Harlem as Seen by Hirschfeld* (with William Saroyan, 1942); *Sweet Bye and Bye* (musical comedy, 1946); *Westward Ha!* (with S. J. Perelman, 1948); *Show Business Is No Business* (1951); *The American Theatre as Seen by Hirschfeld* (1961); *Hirschfeld Folio* (1964). Theatre caricaturist for *New York Times,* since 1925.

HIRST, HENRY BECK (Aug. 23, 1817–Mar. 30, 1874); b. Philadelphia, Pa. Lawyer, poet. *The Coming of the Mammoth; and Funeral of Time; and Other Poems* (1845); *Endymion* (1848); *The Penance of Roland . . . and Other Poems* (1849). Hirst steadfastly maintained that he, and not Poe, was the author of "The Raven."

His Father's Son. Novel by Brander Matthews (1896). A story of Wall Street.

Hispanic American Historical Review. Durham, N.C. Quarterly. Founded 1918, at Baltimore, Md. It was suspended in 1922, and revived at Durham in 1926. Expired 1934.

Historic Americans. Essays by Theodore Parker (1878). On Franklin, Washington, Jefferson, and John Adams.

Historical Magazine and Notes and Queries. Morrisania, N.Y. Founded 1857, by C. B. Richardson, at Boston. Moved to New York, and later to Morrisania. Expired 1875.

Historical Sketch of the Greek Revolution. By Samuel Gridley Howe (1828). It shows the influence of the Greek revival on American poetry, architecture, etc.

History of American Letters, A. By Walter F. Taylor, with bibliographies by Harry Hartwick (1936).

History of American Magazines, A. Edited by Frank Luther Mott, 4v. (1930–57). Volume 5 appeared in 1968. Covers the period beginning in 1741.

History of American Verse. By James L. Onderdonk (1901). Covers the period, 1610–1900.

History of Constantius & Pulchera; or, Constancy Rewarded. Anonymous novel of the American Revolution (1795).

History of Maria Kittle. Novel by Mrs. Ann Eliza Bleecker, written in 1781, and published in 1793. The earliest American treatment in fiction of an Indian captive.

History of New York, A. By "Diedrich Knickerbocker" (Washington Irving) (1809). The story of New Amsterdam's discovery, growth, and community life, told by an imaginary historian with a sense of humor. Many legends are woven into the narrative. Irving's first important writing.

History of Plymouth Plantation, A. By William Bradford (1630). Enlarged in 1856. One of the earliest first-hand chronicles of the hardships of the little band of Pilgrims from the time they fled from Holland until 1648. The original manuscript was owned by Thomas Prince, who left it to the Old South Church in Boston. It found its way to London and came into the possession of the Bishop of London. Rediscovered around 1850 it was published in full in 1856 by the Massachusetts Historical Society. In 1896 by an act of parliament it was restored to America.

History of Spanish Literature, The. By George Ticknor (1849). A classic work written during a period of twenty years.

History of the American Drama from the Civil War to the Present Day, A. By Arthur Hobson Quinn, 2v. (1927).

History of the American Frontier. By Frederic L. Paxton (1924).

History of the Conquest of Mexico. By William Hickling Prescott, 3v. (1843). A classic history of the Spanish conquest and colonization of Mexico related in the manner of the author's *History of the Conquest of Peru.*

History of the Conquest of Peru. By William Hickling Prescott, 2v. (1847). Classic study of Peru noted for its scholarship and literary style. It begins with the high civilization of the Incas, and treats of the Spanish conquest and colonization.

History of the Dividing Line Between Virginia and North Carolina. By William Byrd. Record of the surveying party which established the line in 1728–29.

History of the Rise, Progress and Establishment of the Independence of the United States of America, The. By William Gordon, 3v. (1789).

HITCHCOCK, ALFRED MARSHALL (May 7, 1868–Apr. 14, 1941); b. Troy, N.Y. Educator, author. *A New England Boyhood* (1934); *Lucy, Perhaps* (1935); *Drill* (1935).

HITCHCOCK, CURTICE (Mar. 4, 1892–May 3, 1946); b. Pittsford, Vt. Publisher. With Macmillan Co., 1924–31; the Century Co., 1932–33; president, Reynal and Hitchcock, Inc., New York, from 1934.

HITCHCOCK, ENOS (Mar. 7, 1744–Feb. 26, 1803); b. Springfield, Mass. Congregational clergyman, chaplain in the Continental Army, author. *Memoirs of the Bloomsgrove Family,* 2v. (1790); *The Farmer's Friend; or, The History of Mr. Charles Worthy* (1793); *Discourse on the Dignity and Excellence of the Human Character, Illustrated in the Life of General George Washington* (1800); etc.

HITCHCOCK, ETHAN ALLEN (May 18, 1798–Aug. 5, 1870); b. Vergennes, Vt. Soldier, author. *Swedenborg: A Hermetic Philosopher* (1858); *Remarks on the Sonnets of Shakespeare* (1865); *Notes on the Vita Nuova and Minor Poems of Dante* (1866); *Fifty Years in Camp and Field* (diary, 1909); etc.

HITCHCOCK, FREDERICK HILLS (July 4, 1867–July 10, 1928); b. Boston, Mass. Publisher, editor. Editor: *The Building of a Book* (1906). With D. Appleton & Co., 1891–1901; founder (with Robert Grier Cooke), The Grafton Press, 1901; president, 1901–28.

HITCHCOCK, [James] RIPLEY [Wellman] (July 3, 1857–May 4, 1918); b. Fitchburg, Mass. Journalist, art critic. *Etching in America* (1886); *The Louisiana Purchase* (1903); *The Lewis and Clark Expedition* (1905); etc. Editor: *The Story of the West* series, 7v. (1895–1902). Art critic, *New York Tribune,* 1882–90; lit. adviser, D. Appleton & Co., 1890–1902; Harper & Brothers, 1906–18.

HITCHCOCK, ROSWELL DWIGHT (Aug. 15, 1817–June 16, 1887); b. East Machias, Me. Congregational clergyman, educator, author. *Socialism* (1879); *The Eternal Atonement* (1888); etc. Compiler: *Hymns and Songs of Praise* (with others, 1874); *Carmina Sanctorum* (with others, 1886). Editor, *American Theological Review,* 1863–70. Prof. Church history, Union Theological Seminary, New York, 1855–87.

HITREC, JOSEPH GEORGE (Feb. 28, 1912–); b. Zagreb, Yugoslavia. Author. *Son of the Moon* (1948); *Angel of Gaiety* (1951); etc.

HITTELL, JOHN SHERTZER (Dec. 25, 1825–Mar. 8, 1901); b. Jonestown, Pa. Journalist, statistician, author. *The Resources of California* (1863); *A History of the City of San Francisco, and Incidentally of the State of California* (1878); etc. With *Alta California,* 1852–80.

HITTELL, THEODORE HENRY (Apr. 5, 1830–Feb. 23, 1917); b. Marietta, Pa. Lawyer, author. *The Adventures of James Capen Adams* (1861); *History of California,* 4v. (1885–97); etc. Editor, *San Francisco Bulletin.*

HITTI, PHILIP K[huri] (June 24, 1886–); b. Shimlau, Mt. Lebanon, Syria. Educator, Orientalist, author. *The Origin of the Islamic State* (1916); *Syria and the Syrians* (1926); *The Origin of the Druze People and Religion* (1929); *History of the Arabs* (1937); *History of Syria, Lebanon, Palestine* (1950);

Syria: A Short History (1959); *The Near East in History* (1961); *A Short History of Lebanon* (1965); *A Short History of the Near East* (1966). Semitic literature dept., Princeton, 1926–54.

Hitty, Her First Hundred Years. By Rachel Field (1929). A book for children which won the Newbery Medal in 1930.

HOAGLAND, EDWARD (Dec. 21, 1932–   ); b. New York. Author. *Cat Man* (1958); *The Circle Home* (1960); *The Peacock's Tail* (1965); *Notes From the Century Before* (1969).

HOAR, GEORGE FRISBIE (Aug. 29, 1826–Sept. 30, 1904); b. Concord, Mass. Senator, author. *Autobiography of Seventy Years,* 2v. (1903). Congressman, 1869–77; U.S. Senator, 1877–1904.

HOBART, ALICE TISDALE (Mrs. Earle Tisdale Hobart) (Jan. 28, 1882–Mar. 14, 1967); b. Lockport, N.Y. Author. *Pidgin Cargo* (1929), republished as *River Supreme* (1934); *Oil for the Lamps of China* (1933); *Yang and Yin* (1936); *Their Own Country* (1940); *The Cup and the Sword* (1942); *The Peacock Sheds His Tail* (1945); *The Cleft Rock* (1948); *The Serpent-Wreathed Staff* (1951); *Venture Into Darkness* (1955); *Gusty's Child* (autobiography, 1959); *The Innocent Dreamers* (1964); etc.

HOBART, GEORGE V[ere] (June 16, 1867–Jan. 31, 1926); b. Cape Breton, N.S. Journalist, humorist, playwright. Pen name, "Hugh McHugh." Under own name: *Many Moods and Many Meters* (poems, 1899); *D. Dinkelspiel: His Conversationings* (1900), and its sequels; etc.; under pen name: *John Henry* (1901); *It's Up to You* (1902); and other "John Henry" books.

Hobbes, John Oliver. Pen name of Pearl Mary Teresa Craigie.

HOBBIE, ALFRED M. (d.1881); b. in Georgia(?). Author. *Life and Times of David G. Burnet* (1871); *The Frontier from the Saddle* (1875); *The Sentinel's Dream* (poems). See *The Frontier Times,* Aug. 1935.

HOBBS, WILLIAM HERBERT (July 2, 1864–Jan. 1, 1953); b. Worcester, Mass. Geologist, author. *Leonard Wood* (1920); *Cruises along By-ways of the Pacific* (1923); *Exploring about the North Pole of the Winds* (1930); *Peary* (1936); *Explorers of the Antarctic* (1941); *Fortress Islands of the Pacific* (1945); *An Explorer-Scientist's Pilgrimage* (autobiography, 1952), etc., and books on geology. Prof. geology, University of Michigan, 1906–34.

HOBERECHT, EARNEST (Jan. 1, 1918–); b. Watonga, Okla. Newspaper executive, author. *Tokyo Romance* (1947); *Asia Is My Beat* (1961). Vice-president, United Press International, 1953–66. Pres. American Suppliers, Inc. since 1966.

Hoboken. Novel by Theodore Sedgwick Fay (1843). Written against dueling.

Hobomok. First novel by Lydia Maria Child (1821). The scene is early Salem and Plymouth.

HOBSON, [Francis] THAYER (Sept. 4, 1897–Oct. 19, 1967); b. Denver, Colo. Publisher. Pres., William Morrow and Co., 1931–58; chairman of the board, 1958–67.

HOBSON, HARRIET MALONE, b. Nashville, Tenn. Author. *Jinks' Inside* (1911); *Sis Within* (1914); *Comrade of Navarre* (1914).

HOBSON, LAURA Z[ametkin], b. New York. Author. *A Dog of His Own* (1941); *The Trespassers* (1943); *Gentleman's Agreement* (1947); *The Other Father* (1950); *The Celebrity* (1951); *First Papers* (1964); *"I'm Going to Have a Baby"* (1967); *The Tenth Month* (1971). Writer of monthly book page, *Good Housekeeping,* 1953–56.

HOBSON, RICHMOND PEARSON (Aug. 17, 1870–Mar. 16, 1937); b. Greensboro, Ala. Naval officer, reformer, author. *The Sinking of the Merrimac* (1899); *Buck Jones of Annapolis* (1907); *In Line of Duty* (1910); etc.

HOBSON, WILDER (Feb. 18, 1906–May 24, 1964); b. Brooklyn, N.Y. Journalist, author. *American Jazz Music* (1939); *All Summer Long* (1945). With *Time,* 1928–30; *Fortune,* 1932–37; *Newsweek,* from 1954.

HOCHMAN, SANDRA (Sept. 11, 1936–   ); b. New York. Poet. *Voyage Home* (1960); *Manhattan Pastures* (1963); *Love Poems* (1966); *The Vaudeville Marriage* (1966); *Earthworks, selected poetry, 1960–70* (1970).

HOCHWALT, ALBERT FREDERICK (Dec. 24, 1869–July 24, 1938); b. Dayton, O. Publisher, author. *Arrows of Ambition* (1907); *Dogcraft* (1907); *Bird Dogs and Their History* (1922); *Greymist* (1925); etc. President, A. F. Hochwalt Co., publishers.

HOCKETT, HOMER CAREY (Dec. 11, 1875–); b. Martinsville, O. Educator, author. *A Political and Social History of the United States, 1492–1928* (1928); *Introduction to Research in American History* (1931); *The Political and Social Growth of the United States, 1492–1852* (1933); *The Constitutional History of the United States, 1776–1786,* 2v. (1939); etc. History dept., Ohio State University, since 1909.

HOCKING, WILLIAM ERNEST (Aug. 10, 1873–June 12, 1966); b. Cleveland, O. Educator, author. *The Meaning of God in Human Experience* (1912); *Morale and Its Enemies* (1918); *Man and the State* (1926); *The Self: Its Body and Freedom* (1928); *Types of Philosophy* (1929); *Thoughts on Death and Life* (1937); *Living Religion and World Faith* (1940); *Lectures on Recent Trends in American Philosophy* (1941); *What Man Can Make of Man* (1942); *Freedom of the Press* (1947); *Experiment in Education* (1954); *The Coming World Civilization* (1956); *Strength of Men and Nations: A Message to USA vis-a-vis USSR* (1959); etc. Prof. philosophy, Harvard University, 1914–43.

HODGE, ARCHIBALD ALEXANDER (July 18, 1823–Nov. 11, 1886); b. Princeton, N.J., son of Charles Hodge. Presbyterian clergyman, educator, author. *Outlines of Theology* (1860); *The Life of Charles Hodge* (1880); *Popular Lectures* (1887). Prof., Princeton Theological Seminary, 1877–86.

HODGE, CHARLES (Dec. 27, 1797–June 19, 1878); b. Philadelphia, Pa. Presbyterian clergyman, educator, author. *The Constitutional History of the Presbyterian Church,* 2v. (1839–40); *Systematic Theology,* 4v. (1872–73); etc. Founder, *Biblical Repertory,* 1825, which became in 1836 the *Biblical Repertory and Princeton Review.* Prof., Princeton Theological Seminary, 1820–78.

HODGE, FREDERICK WEBB (Oct. 28, 1864–Sept. 28, 1956); b. Plymouth, England. Ethnologist. Author of books on the American Indian. Editor: *Handbook of American Indians North of Mexico,* 2v. (1907–10); *Handbook of Indians of Canada* (1913); etc. Editor, *American Anthropologist,* 1899–1910, 1912–14. With Museum of the American Indian, New York, 1918–31; director, Southwest Museum, Los Angeles, Calif.

HODGES, GEORGE (Oct. 6, 1856–May 27, 1919); b. Rome, N.Y. Episcopal clergyman, educator, author. *William Penn* (1901); *The Battles of Peace* (1914); *Henry Codman Potter* (1915); etc. Dean, Episcopal Theological School, Cambridge, Mass., 1894–1919.

HODGES, LEIGH MITCHELL (July 9, 1876–Apr. 4, 1954); b. Denver, Colo. Journalist, author. *The Great Optimist, and Other Essays* (1903); etc. Compiler: *Poems We Love* (1907). Author of column, "The Optimist" in the Philadelphia *North American,* 1902–25; and in the Philadelphia *Evening Bulletin* from 1925.

HODGINS, ERIC (Mar. 2, 1899–Jan. 7, 1971); b. Detroit, Mich. Editor, publisher, author. *A History of Aircraft* (1931); *Behemoth* (1932); *Mr. Blanding Builds His Dream House* (1946); *Blanding's Way* (1950); etc. With *Fortune*, 1934–41; publisher, 1937–41; vice-president, Time, Inc., from 1938.

HODGKINS, LOUISE MANNING (Aug. 5, 1846–Nov. 28, 1935); b. Ipswich, Mass. Educator, author. *A Guide to the Study of Nineteenth Century Authors* (1889); etc. Prof. English literature, Wellesley College, 1877–91.

HODNETT, EDWARD (Oct. 15, 1901–); b. Sag Harbor, N.Y. Public relations executive, author. *Plain English* (1931); *The Art of Problem Solving* (1955); *The Art of Working with People* (1959); *Which College for You* (1960); *The Cultivated Mind* (1963); *Effective Presentations* (1967); *Marcus Cheeraerts the Elder* (1969); etc. Editor: *Poems to Read Aloud* (1957).

HOE, ROBERT (Mar. 10, 1839–Sept. 22, 1909); b. New York City, grandson of Robert Hoe (1784–1833). Manufacturer and improver of the printing press, and one of the world's leading book collectors. Author. *A Short History of the Printing Press* (1902). See *Catalogue of the Library of Robert Hoe of New York,* 8v. (1911–12); and other catalogues of special collections. Hoe was one of the founders and the first president of The Grolier Club.

HOFER, PHILLIP (Mar. 14, 1898–); b. Cincinnati, O. Librarian, collector. With the New York Public Library, 1929–34; the Pierpont Morgan Library, 1934–38; Harvard University Library, since 1938. The Hofer Typographical Collection was deposited in The New York Public Library, 1932.

HOFF, SYD[ney] (Sept. 4, 1912–); b. New York. Cartoonist, author. *Muscles and Brains* (1940); *Feeling No Pain* (1944); *Oops! Wrong Party!* (1951); *It's Fun Learning Cartooning* (1952); *Danny and the Dinosaur* (1958); *Sammy the Seal* (1959); *Little Chief* (1961); *Twix the Cup and the Lipton* (1962); *So This is Matrimony* (1963); *Mrs. Switch* (1967); *Irving and Me* (1968); *Roberto and the Bull* (1969).

HOFFENSTEIN, SAMUEL [Goodman] (Oct. 8, 1890–Oct., 1949); b. in Lithuania. Author. *Life Sings a Song* (1916); *Poems in Praise of Practically Nothing* (1928); *Year In, You're Out* (1930); *Pencil in the Air* (poems, 1947).

HOFFMAN, ABBIE [Abbott] (Nov. 30, 1936–); b. Worcester, Mass. Youth leader. *Revolution for the Hell of It* (1968); *Woodstock Nation* (1970). Leader of the Yippie youth movement.

HOFFMAN, ARTHUR SULLIVANT (Sept. 28, 1876–); b. Columbus, O. Editor, author. *Fundamentals of Fiction Writing* (1922); *The Writing of Fiction* (1934); etc. Editor: *Fiction Writers on Fiction Writing* (1923). On staff, *The Chautauquan; The Smart Set; Watson's; Delineator; Fiction Writing Self-Taught* (1939); etc. Editor, *Adventure,* 1911–27; *Romance,* 1919–20; *McClure's Magazine,* 1927–28; etc.

HOFFMAN, CHARLES FENNO (Feb. 7, 1806–June 7, 1884); b. New York City. Editor, poet, novelist. *A Winter in the West,* 2v. (1835); *Greyslaer: A Romance of the Mohawk* (1840); *The Vigil of Faith, and Other Poems* (1842); *Wild Scenes in the Forest and Prairie,* 2v. (1843); *The Echo* (poems, 1844); *Love's Calendar, Lays of the Hudson, and Other Poems* (1850); *The Poems* (1873). Editor: *The New York Book of Poetry,* 1837; *Knickerbocker Magazine,* 1833; *American Monthly Magazine,* 1835–37; *Literary World,* 1847–48. See H. F. Barnes's *Charles Fenno Hoffman* (1930).

HOFFMAN, DANIEL GERARD (Apr. 3, 1923–); b. New York. Author. *An Armada of Thirty Whales* (poems, 1954); *The Poetry of Stephen Crane* (1958); *Little Geste and Other Poems* (1960); *Form and Fable in American Fiction* (1961); *The City of Satisfactions* (1963); *Barbarous Knowledge* (1967); *Striking the Stones* (1968).

HOFFMAN, DAVID (Dec. 24, 1784–Nov. 11, 1854); b. Baltimore, Md. Lawyer, educator, historian. Pen name, "Anthony Grumbler." *Miscellaneous Thoughts on Men, Manners, and Things* (1837); *Viator; or, a Peep Into My Note-Book* (1839); *Chronicles Selected from the Originals of Cartaphilus, the Wandering Jew,* 3v. (under own name, 1853–54); etc. Prof. law, University of Maryland, 1816–43.

HOFFMAN, FREDERICK J[ohn] (Sept. 21, 1909–); b. Port Washington, Wis. Author. *The Little Magazine* (with others, 1947); *The Twenties* (1955); *Freudianism and the Literary Mind* (1957); *William Faulkner* (1961); *Samuel Beckett: The Language of Self* (1962); *Art of Southern Fiction* (1967); etc.

HOFFMAN, MALVINA (Mrs. Malvina Grimson) (June 15, 1887–July 10, 1966); b. New York. Sculptor, author. *Heads and Tales* (autobiography, 1930); *Sculpture Inside and Out* (1939); *American Sculpture Series* (1948); *Yesterday is Tomorrow* (1965).

HOFFMAN, ROSS JOHN [Swado] SWARTZ (Feb. 2, 1902–); b. Harrisburg, Pa. Historian, educator. *The Spirit of Politics and the Future of Freedom* (1951); *Edmund Burke, New York Agent* (1956); *Man and His History* (with others, 1958); etc. Editor: The Christendom Series (1940–42); The Christian Democracy Series (1955). Prof. history, Fordham University, since 1944.

HOFFMAN, STANLEY (Nov. 27, 1928–   ); b. Vienna. Political scientist, author. *Organisations Internationales et Pouvoirs Politiques des États* (1954); *Le Mouvement Poujade* (1956); *The State of War* (1965). Co-author: *In Search of France* (1963). Editor: *Contemporary Theory in International Relations* (1960). Prof. government, Harvard University, since 1963.

HOFFMAN, WILLIAM (1925–   ). Author. *The Dark Mountains* (1963); *Yancey's War* (1966); *A Walk to the River* (1970); etc.

HOFFMAN, W[illiam] D[awson] (July 11, 1884–Mar. 10, 1952); b. Johnstown, Pa. Novelist. *Knights of the Desert* (1927); *Westward to Paradise* (1927); *Bravo Jim* (1928); *The Saddle Wolf* (1928); *Santone* (1929); *Tremaine of Texas* (1929); *The Canyon of No Return* (1931); *The Range Ghost* (1937); *Feudists of the Outlands* (1937); *Range Rebellion* (1938); *Gun-Johnnies of Texas* (1944); etc.

HOFSTADTER, RICHARD (Aug. 6, 1916–Oct. 24, 1970); b. Buffalo, N.Y. Educator, author. *Social Darwinism in American Thought* (1944); *The American Political Tradition* (1948); *The Development and Scope of Higher Education in the United States* (with C. D. Hardy, 1952); *The Age of Reform* (1955; Pulitzer Prize for history, 1956); *The Development of Academic Freedom in the United States* (with W. P. Metzger, 1955); *The Paranoid Style in American Politics, and Other Essays* (1965); *Anti-Intellectualism in American Life* (1966); etc. Editor: *Great Issues in American History* 2v. (1958); *American Higher Education,* 2v. (with Wilson Smith, 1961). Prof. history, Columbia University, from 1952.

HOGE, PEYTON HARRISON (Jan. 6, 1858–deceased); b. Hampden-Sydney, Va. Presbyterian clergyman, author. *Moses Drury Hoge* (1899); *The Divine Tragedy* (drama in verse, 1905). Editor: *Poems in Florida* (1933).

HOGNER, DOROTHY CHILDS, b. New York City. Author. *South to Padre* (1936); *Santa Fé Caravans* (1937); *Summer Roads to Gaspé* (1939); *Barnyard Family* (1948); *Frogs and Polliwogs* (1956); *Conservation in America* (1958); *Water Over the Dam* (1960); *A Fresh Herb Platter* (1961); *A Book of Snakes* (1966); etc.

HOHENBERG, JOHN (Feb. 17, 1906–   ); b. New York City. Educator, author. *The Pulitzer Prize Story* (1959); *The Professional Journalist* (1960); *Foreign Correspondence: The Great Reporters and Their Times* (1964); *The New Front Page* (1965); *Between Two Worlds* (1967); *The*

News Media: A Journalist Looks at His Profession (1968); *Free Press and Free People* (1969). Staff, *New York Journal-American,* 1933–42; prof. journalism, Columbia University, since 1950.

HOKE, RUSSELL ALLEN (June 17, 1896–); b. Harrisburg, Pa. Publisher, editor, short story writer. With *Youth's Companion,* 1920–21; Little Brown & Co., 1921–26; publisher, *The Town Crier,* Newton Centre, Mass., 1928–36; president, Bellman Publishing Co., until 1948.

HOKE, TRAVIS HENDERSON (Oct. 28, 1892–June 14, 1947); b. St. Louis, Mo. Editor, author. *Weather* (with E. E. Free, 1929); *The Short Story Builder* (with Stewart Beach, 1935); etc. With *The Dial,* 1916–17, *American Weekly,* 1920–29; editor, *Popular Science Monthly,* 1929–30, etc.

HOLAND, HJALMAR RUED (Oct. 20, 1872–Aug. 8, 1963); b. near Oslo, Nor. Author. *History of the Norwegian Settlements* (1908); *Old Peninsula Days* (1925); *History of Coon Prairie* (1927); *Coon Valley* (1928); *The Last Migration* (1931); *The Kensington Stone* (1932); *Westward from Vinland* (1940); *America, 1355–1364* (1946); *Explorations in America Before Columbus* (1956); *My First Eighty Years* (1957).

HOLBROOK, RICHARD THAYER (Dec. 13, 1870–July 31, 1934); b. Windsor Locks, Conn. Educator, author. *Boys and Men* (1900); *Dante and the Animal Kingdom* (1902); *Portraits of Dante from Giotto to Raffael* (1911). Prof. Italian, Bryn Mawr College, 1906–16; prof. French, University of California, 1919–34.

HOLBROOK, SILAS PINCKNEY (June 1, 1796–May 26, 1835); b. Pineville, S.C. Lawyer, traveler, editor, author. *Sketches by a Traveller* (1834), originally published in the *New England Galaxy* and the *Boston Courier* under the pen name "Jonathan Fabrick." Editor, the *Boston Tribune.*

HOLBROOK, STEWART HALL (Aug. 22, 1893–Sept. 3, 1964); b. Newport, Vt. Author. *Holy Old Mackinaw* (1938); *Let Them Live* (1938); *Iron Brew* (1939); *Ethan Allen* (1940); *Burning an Empire: America's Great Forest Fires* (1943); *The Story of America's Railroads* (1947); *The Yankee Exodus* (1950); *Far Corner* (1952); *The Age of the Moguls* (1953); *Down on the Farm* (1954); *The Golden Age of Quackery* (1959); *The Columbia River* (1965).

HOLCOMBE, ARTHUR NORMAN (Nov. 3, 1884–); b. Winchester, Mass. Educator, author. *State Government in the United States* (1916); *The Political Parties of Today* (1924); *The Chinese Revolution* (1930); *Human Rights in the Modern World* (1948); *Our More Perfect Union* (1950); *The Middle Classes in American Politics* (1965). Prof. government, Harvard University until 1955.

HOLCOMBE, WILLIAM HENRY (May 29, 1825–Nov. 28, 1893); b. Lynchburg, Va. Physician, author. *Poems* (1860); *Southern Voices* (1872); *Song Novels* (1873); *A Mystery of New Orleans* (1890); etc.

Hold, Mrs. Roland. See Constance D'Arcy Mackay.

HOLDEN, MARTHA EVERTS (1844–1896). Author. Pen name, "Amber." *A String of Amber Beads* (1893); *Rosemary and Rue* (1896); *Amber Glints* (1897).

HOLDEN, OLIVER (Sept. 18, 1765–Sept. 4, 1844); b. Shirley, Mass. Carpenter, preacher, composer. Compiler: *The American Harmony* (1792); *Sacred Dirges, Hymns and Anthems* (1800); *Charlestown Collection of Sacred Songs* (1803); etc. His best known hymn-tune is "Coronation."

HOLDEN, RAYMOND PECKHAM (Apr. 7, 1894–); b. New York City. Poet, novelist, biographer. *Granite and Alabaster* (poems, 1922); *Abraham Lincoln: The Politician and the Man* (1929); *The Penthouse Murders* (1931); *Chance Has a Whip* (1935); *Death on the Border* (1937); *Believe the Heart* (poems, 1939); *The Arrow at the Heel* (poems, 1940); *Selected Poems* (1946); *Famous Scientific Expeditions* (1955); *The Merrimack* (1958); *Famous Fossil Finds* (1966); *All About Fire* (1964); etc. Assoc. director, the Book of the Month Club; retired 1957.

HOLDEN, WILLIAM CURRY (July 19, 1896–); b. near Cooledge, Texas. Educator, author. *Alkali Trails* (1930); *The Spur Ranch* (1934); *Studies of the Yaqui Indians* (1935); etc. Depts. history and anthropology, Texas Technological College, Lubbock, Tex., 1929–39; dean graduate school, 1945–51.

HOLDER, CHARLES FREDERICK (Aug. 5, 1851–Oct. 10, 1915); b. Lynn, Mass. Naturalist, sportsman, author. *Marvels of Animal Life* (1885); *Charles Darwin* (1891); *Louis Agassiz* (1893); *Stories of Animal Life* (1899); *Life in the Open* (1906); *The Quakers in Great Britain and America* (1913); *Angling Adventures Around the World* (1914); etc.

HOLDING, ELISABETH SANXAY (June 8, 1889–Feb. 7, 1955); b. Brooklyn, N.Y. Novelist. *Invincible Minnie* (1920); *Rosaleen among the Artists* (1921); *Angelica* (1921); *The Unlit Lamp* (1922); *The Silk Purse* (1928); *Miasma* (1929); *The Unfinished Crime* (1935); *The Obstinate Murderer* (1938); *The Girl Who Had to Die* (1940); *The Old Battle-Ax* (1942); *The Blank Wall* (1947); *The Widow's Mite* (1953); etc.

Holiday. New York. Monthly. Founded 1946. Published by Curtis Publishing Co. Picture magazine of travel with articles by noted writers.

Holiday. Play by Philip Barry (prod. 1928). Conflict of ideals between Johnny Chase, who believes in holidays in youth, and his fiancee, Julia, and her father, who believe in success first and holidays later. Julia's sister, Linda, agrees with Johnny, who eventually marries her.

HOLL, ADELAIDE. Author. *Sylvester, the Mouse with the Musical Ear* (1961); *Mrs. McGarrity's Peppermint Sweater* (1966); *The Rain Puddle* (1966); *Have You Seen My Puppy?* (1968); *Moon Mouse* (1969).

HOLLAND, CLAUDIA (Mrs. Bernard P. Holland, Jr.) (Dec. 8, 1903–   ); b. Portsmouth, Va. Author. *Primrose Path* (1947); *Center Aisle* (1949).

HOLLAND, EDWIN CLIFFORD (c. 1794–Sept. 11, 1824); b. Charleston, S.C. Editor, poet, essayist. *Odes, Naval Songs, and Other Occasional Poems* (1813); *Essays; and a Drama in Five Acts* (1852); etc. Editor, the *Charleston Times.*

HOLLAND, JOSIAH GILBERT (July 24, 1819–Oct. 12, 1881); b. Belchertown, Mass. Editor, poet, novelist. *The Bay-Path* (1857); *Titcomb's Letters to Young People, Single and Married* (under pen name of "Timothy Titcomb," 1858); *Bitter Sweet: A Poem in Dramatic Form* (1858); *Kathrina: Her Life and Mine in a Poem* (1867); *Garnered Sheaves* (1873); *Arthur Bonnicastle* (1873); *The Mistress of the Manse* (1874); *Sevenoaks* (1875); *Nicholas Minturn* (1877); *Collected Poems* (1873). Founder (with Roswell Smith), *Scribner's Monthly,* 1870; editor, 1870–81. With *Springfield Republican,* 1850–57. See Harry H. Peckham's *Josiah Gilbert Holland in Relation to His Times* (1940).

HOLLAND, KATRIN. Pen name of Heidi Huberta Loewengard.

HOLLAND, RAY[mond] P[runty] (Aug. 20, 1884–); b. Atchison, Kan. Editor, conservationist. *My Gun Dogs* (1929); *Nip and Tuck* (1939); *Good Shot!* (1946); *The Master* (1946); *Bird Dogs* (1948); *Scattergunning* (1951); *Seven Grand Gun Dogs* (1961); etc. Author of shooting stories under pen name of "Bob White." Editor, *Field and Stream,* 1924–41.

HOLLAND, WILLIAM J[acob] (Aug. 16, 1848–Dec. 13, 1932); b. in Jamaica, B.W.I. Educator, naturalist, author. *The Butterfly Book* (1898); *The Moth Book* (1903); *To the River Plate and Back* (1913); etc. Chancellor, Western University of Pennsylvania (now University of Pittsburgh), 1891–1901. Director, Carnegie Institute, Pittsburgh, 1898–1922.

HOLLANDER, JOHN (Oct. 28, 1929–); b. New York. Author. *A Crackling of Thorns* (poems, 1958); *The Untuning of the Sky: Ideas of Music in English Poetry, 1500–1700* (1961); *Movie Going* (poems, 1962); *Various Owls* (1963); *Visions from the Ramble* (1965); *The Quest of the Cole* (1966); *Images of Voices* (1968); *Types of Shape* (poems, 1969).

Holland's: The Magazine of the South. Dallas, Tex. Monthly. Founded 1876, as *Street's Weekly.* Name changed in 1904. Ceased publication.

HOLLEY, HORACE (Apr. 7, 1887–July 12, 1960); b. Torrington, Conn. Editor, author. *The Inner Garden* (poems, 1912); *The Stricken King* (poems, 1912); *The Modern Social Religion* (1914); *Bahai* (1921); *Religion for Mankind* (1956); etc. Editor, *World Unity,* 1927–35; co-editor, *World Order,* 1935–47.

HOLLEY, MARIETTA (July 16, 1836–Mar. 1, 1926); b. in Jefferson Co., N.Y. Humorist, novelist, poet, essayist. Creator of character "Josiah Allen's Wife, Samantha." *My Opinions and Betsy Bobbet's* (1873); *Josiah Allen's Wife as a P. A. and P. I.: Samantha at the Centennial* (1877); *Poems* (1887); *Samantha among the Brethren* (1890); *Josiah Allen on Women's Rights* (1914); etc.

HOLLIDAY, CARL (Mar. 2, 1879–Aug. 16, 1936); b. Hanging Rock, O. Educator, author. *A History of Southern Literature* (1906); *The Cotton-Picker, and Other Poems* (1907); *The Literature of Colonial Virginia* (1909); *Once Upon a Time Stories* (1909); *The Cavalier Poets* (1911); *The Wit and Humor of Colonial Days* (1912); *Woman's Life in Colonial Days* (1922); *The Dawn of Literature* (1931); etc. Editor: *Three Centuries of Southern Poetry* (1908). Prof. English, University of Toledo, 1917–29; California State College, San José, 1929–36.

HOLLIDAY, ROBERT CORTES (July 18, 1880–Jan., 1947); b. Indianapolis, Ind. Editor, essayist, biographer. *Booth Tarkington* (1918); *Walking-Stick Papers* (1918); *Joyce Kilmer: A Memoir* (1918); *Broome Street Straws* (1919); *Men and Books and Cities* (1920); *Literary Lanes and Other Byways* (1925); *Unmentionables* (1933); etc. With the *Bookman,* 1918–23; editor, 1919–20.

HOLLING, HOLLING C[LANCY] (1900–). Author. *Book of Cowboys* (1936); *Paddle to the Sea* (1941); *Seabird* (1948); *Minn of the Mississippi* (1951); *Pagoo* (1957); etc.

HOLLINGWORTH, HARRY LEVI (May 26, 1880–Sept. 17, 1956); b. De Witt, Ia. Educator, psychologist, author. *Studies in Judgment* (1913); *Outlines for Experimental Psychology* (1914); *Outlines for Applied and Abnormal Psychology* (1914); *Applied Psychology* (1917); *Mental Growth and Decline* (1927); *Abnormal Psychology* (1930); *Educational Psychology* (1932); *Psychology and Ethics* (1949); etc. Prof. psychology, Columbia University, 1921–46.

HOLLISTER, GIDEON HIRAM (Dec. 14, 1817–Mar. 24, 1881); b. Washington, Conn. Lawyer, author. *Mount Hope; or, Philip, King of the Wampanoags* (1851); *The History of Connecticut,* 2v. (1855); *Thomas à Becket, a Tragedy, and Other Poems* (1866); *Kinley Hollow* (1882).

HOLLISTER, MARY BREWSTER (Aug. 31, 1891–); b. Foochow, China, of American parentage. Author. *Lady Fourth Daughter of China* (1932); *South China Folk* (1934); *River Children* (1938); *Mulberry Village* (1936); *Pagoda Anchorage* (1939); *Dike Against The Sea* (1948); etc.

HOLLON, WILLIAM EUGENE (May 28, 1913–); b. Commerce, Tex. Historian, author. *The Lost Pathfinder: Zebulon Pike* (1949); *History of Pre-flight Training in the USAF, 1917–52* (1953); *William Bollaert's Texas* (1956); *Outline History of the United States* (with Berthrong and Owings, 1957); *The Southwest Old and New* (1961); *The Great American Desert* (1966); etc. Prof. history, University of Oklahoma, since 1956.

"Hollow Men, The." Poem by T. S. Eliot (1925).

HOLLOWAY, EMORY (Mar. 16, 1885–); b. Marshall, Mo. Educator, author. *Whitman—An Interpretation in Narrative* (1926, Pulitzer Prize for American biography, 1927); *Janice in Tomorrow-Land* (1936). Editor: *The Uncollected Poetry and Prose of Walt Whitman,* 2v. (1921); *Free and Lonesome Heart: The Secret of Walt Whitman* (1960); and other Whitmaniana. English dept., Adelphi College, Garden City, L.I., N.Y., 1914–37; Queens College, since 1937.

Holm, Saxe. Pen name of Helen Hunt Jackson.

HOLMAN, HUGH (Feb. 24, 1914–); b. Cross Anchor, S.C. Educator, author. Pen name "Clarence Hunt". *Death Like Thunder* (1942); *Trout in the Milk* (1945); *Up This Crooked Way* (1946); *Slay the Murderer* (1946); *Another Man's Poison* (1947); *Small Town Corpses* (under pen name, 1951); etc. Editor: *The Short Novels of Thomas Wolfe* (1961); *Three Modes of Modern Fiction* (1966). Prof. English, University of North Carolina, since 1958.

HOLMAN, LOUIS ARTHUR (July 13, 1866–Dec. 14, 1939); b. Summerside, P.E.I. Illustrator, author. *Old Maps and Their Makers* (1925); *The Graphic Processes* (1926); etc. Illustrator: *Boston, the Place and the People* (1903); *Boston Common* (1910); etc. Art editor, *New England Magazine,* 1890–96; asst. art editor, *Youth's Companion,* 1896–1914.

HOLMES, ABIEL (Dec. 24, 1763–June 4, 1837); b. Woodstock, Conn. Congregational clergyman, historian, poet. *The Life of Ezra Stiles* (1798); *American Annals,* 2v. (1805); *A Family Tablet* (poems, with others, 1796).

HOLMES, ARTHUR (May 5, 1872–Sept. 20, 1965); b. Cincinnati, O. Educator, author. *The Decay of Rationalism* (1909); *Controlled Power* (1924); *Mind of St. Paul* (1929); etc. President, Drake University, 1918–22; prof. psychology, University of Pennsylvania, 1922–33; Butler University, since 1933.

HOLMES, DANIEL HENRY (July 16, 1851–Dec. 15, 1908); b. New York City. Poet. *Under a Fool's Cap* (1884); *A Pedlar's Pack* (1906); *Hempen Homespun Songs* (1906).

HOLMES, DWIGHT OLIVER WENDELL (Nov. 15, 1877–deceased); b. Lewisburg, W.Va. Educator, author. *The Evolution of the Negro College* (1934); etc. With Howard University, 1919–37; president, Morgan College, Baltimore, from 1937.

HOLMES, [Elias] BURTON (Jan. 8, 1870–July 22, 1958); b. Chicago, Ill. Travel-lecturer, author. *The Burton Holmes Travelogues,* 15v. (1901–22); *The Burton Holmes Lectures,* 10v. (1905).

HOLMES, FREDERICK LIONEL (May 9, 1883–July 27, 1946); b. Waukau, Wis. Author. *Abraham Lincoln Traveled This Way* (1930); *George Washington Traveled This Way* (1935); *Alluring Wisconsin* (1937); *Badger Saints and Sinners* (1939); *Old World Wisconsin* (1944); etc. Editor, *Wisconsin Blue Book,* 1923, 1925–27; *Wisconsin: Stability, Progress and Beauty* (1945).

Holmes, H. H. Pen name of William Anthony Parker White.

HOLMES, HENRY ALFRED (Aug. 15, 1883–Aug. 15, 1963); b. Alfred, Me. Educator, author. *Martin Fierro* (1923); *Spanish America in Song and Story* (1932); *Spanish America at Work* (1936); etc. Editor: *Contemporary Spanish Americans* (1942). Translator: *Martín Fierro: The Argentine Gaucho Epic* (1948). Romance language dept., College of the City of New York, 1928–51.

HOLMES, JOHN ALBERT (Jan. 6, 1904–June 22, 1962); b. Somerville, Mass. Educator, poet. *Address to the Living* (1937); *Fair Warning* (1939); *Map of My Country* (1943); *The Double Root* (1950); *The Symbols* (1955); *The Fortune Teller* (1961); etc. English dept., Tufts College, since 1950.

HOLMES, JOHN CLELLON (Mar. 12, 1926–); b. Holyoke, Mass. Author. *Go* (1952); *Horn* (1958); *Get Home Free* (1964); *Nothing More to Declare* (1967).

HOLMES, JOHN HAYNES (Nov. 29, 1879–Apr. 3, 1964); b. Philadelphia, Pa. Unitarian clergyman, author. *Marriage and Divorce* (1913); *Religion for Today* (1917); *New Churches for Old* (1922); *Palestine Today and Tomorrow* (1929); *The Sensible Man's View of Religion* (1933); *If This Be Treason* (with Reginald Lawrence, prod. 1935); *Rethinking Religion* (1938); *The Second Christmas* (1943); *The Affirmation of Immortality* (1947); *My Gandhi* (1953); *I Speak for Myself* (autobiography, 1959); *Collected Hymns* (1960); etc. Editor: *The Life and Letters of Robert Collyer* (1917). Compiler: *Readings From Great Authors* (with others, 1918); *The Grail of Life: An Anthology* (1919). Editor, *Unity,* 1921–46.

Holmes, Margret. See Margret Holmes Bates.

HOLMES, MARJORIE [Rose] (Mrs. Lynn Burton Mighell) (Sept. 22, 1910–   ); b. Storm Lake, Ia. Novelist. *World by the Tail* (1943); *Ten O'Clock Scholar* (1948); *Saturday Night* (1959); *Cherry Blossom Princess* (1960); *Follow Your Dream* (1961); *I've Got to Talk to Somebody, God* (1969).

HOLMES, MARY J[ane Hawes] (Apr. 5, 1825–Oct. 6, 1907); b. Brookfield, Mass. Novelist. *Tempest and Sunshine* (1854); *Lena Rivers* (1856); *Rosamond* (1860); *Marian Gray* (1863); *Millbank* (1871); *Mildred* (1877); *The Tracy Diamonds* (1899); etc.

HOLMES, OLIVER WENDELL (Aug. 29, 1809–Oct. 7, 1894); b. Cambridge, Mass. Physician, educator, essayist, poet, wit. *Poems* (1836); *The Autocrat of the Breakfast Table* (1858); *The Professor at the Breakfast Table* (1860); *Elsie Venner* (1861); *Songs in Many Keys* (1862); *Soundings from the Atlantic* (1864); *The Guardian Angel* (1867); *The Poet at the Breakfast Table* (1872); *Songs of Many Seasons* (1875); *John Lothrop Motley: A Memoir* (1879); *The Iron Gate, and Other Poems* (1880); *Pages from an Old Volume of Life* (1883); *A Mortal Antipathy* (1885); *Ralph Waldo Emerson* (1885); *Over the Teacups* (1891); *Works of Oliver Wendell Holmes,* 13v. (1891); etc. His best known poems are "The Deacon's Masterpiece; or, The Wonderful One-Hoss Shay"; "The Boys"; "Bill and Joe"; "Old Ironsides"; "The Chambered Nautilus"; and his best known hymn, "Lord of all being! Throned afar." *See* John Torrey Morse's *Life and Letters of Oliver Wendell Holmes,* 2v. (1896); M. A. DeWolfe Howe's *Holmes of the Breakfast Table* (1939); E. M. Tilton's *Amiable Autocrat* (1947); Miriam Small's *Oliver Wendell Holmes* (1962).

HOLMES, OLIVER WENDELL (Mar. 8, 1841–Mar. 6, 1935); b. Boston, Mass., son of Oliver Wendell Holmes. Jurist, author. *The Common Law* (1881); *Speeches,* 2 series (1891, 1913); *Collected Legal Papers* (1920). See *Holmes-Pollock Letters,* ed. by M. A. DeWolfe Howe, 2v. (1941). Assoc. justice, U.S. Supreme Court, 1882–99; chief justice, 1899–1932. *See* Felix Frankfurter's *Mr. Justice Holmes and the Constitution* (1927); Catherine Drinker Bowen's *Yankee from Olympus* (1944); Mark D. Howe's *Justice Oliver Wendell Holmes,* 2v. (1963); Arthur E. Sutherland's *Apology for Uncomfortable Change, 1865–1965* (1965).

HOLMES, ROBERT SHAILOR (Feb. 8, 1870–July 24, 1939); b. Unadilla, Mich. Traveler, author. *Builders, and Other Poems* (1925); *Our Heritage, and Other Poems* (1928).

HOLMES, SAMUEL JACKSON (Mar. 7, 1868–); b. Henry, Ill. Educator, zoologist, author. *The Trend of the Race* (1921); *Studies in Evolution and Eugenics* (1923); *Louis Pasteur* (1924); *A Bibliography of Eugenics* (1924); *The Negro's Struggle for Survival* (1937); *Life and Morals* (1948); etc. Zoology dept., University of California.

HOLST, HERMANN EDWARD von (June 19, 1841–Jan. 20, 1904); b. Fellin, Russia. Educator, historian. *The Constitu-*

tional and Political History of the United States, 3v. (1876–92); *John C. Calhoun* (1882); *The French Revolution Tested by Mirabeau's Career,* 2v. (1894). Prof. history, University of Chicago, 1893–1900.

HOLT, ALFRED HUBBARD (Oct. 15, 1897–); b. Oconto, Wis. Author. *Phrase Origins* (1936); *You Don't Say!* (1937); *American Place Names* (1938); *Hubbard's Trail* (1952); etc. With Williams College, 1930–36.

HOLT, FELIX (1898?–1954). Author. *The Gabriel Horn* (1951); *Dan'l Boone Kissed Me* (1954).

HOLT, GUY (Jan. 18, 1892–Apr. 21, 1934); b. Boston, Mass. Publisher. With Doubleday, Page & Co., 1909–14; mng. editor, *Lippincott's Magazine,* 1914–15; *McBride's Magazine,* 1915–16; with Robert McBride & Co., 1917–26; The John Day Co., 1926–30; director, Whittlesey House, 1930–34.

HOLT, HAMILTON (Aug. 19, 1872–Apr. 26, 1951); b. Brooklyn, N.Y. Educator. Editor: *The Life Stories of Undistinguished Americans as Told by Themselves* (1906). Managing editor and editor, *The Independent,* 1897–1921. President, Rollins College, Winter Park, Fla., from 1925.

HOLT, HENRY (Jan. 3, 1840–Feb. 13, 1926); b. Baltimore, Md. Publisher, author. *Calmire: Man and Nature* (anon. 1892); *Sturmsee: Man and Man* (anon. 1905); *Garrulities of an Octogenarian Editor* (1923); etc. Founder, Henry Holt & Co. Founder, the *Unpopular Review,* later called the *Unpartizan Review.*

HOLT, ISABELLA (Sept. 2, 1892–Mar. 12, 1962); b. Chicago, Ill. Novelist. *The Marriotts and the Powells* (1921); *Golden Legend* (1935); *Aunt Jessie* (1942); *My Son and Heir* (1949); *Rampole Place* (1952); *Midpoint* (1955); *The Golden Moment* (1959); etc.

HOLT, JOHN [Caldwell]. Educator, author. *How Children Fail* (1964); *How Children Learn* (1967); *The Underachieving School* (1969); *What Do We Do Monday Morning?* (1970).

HOLT, JOHN (1721–Jan. 30, 1784); b. Williamsburg, Va. Printer, journalist. Founder, *The Connecticut Gazette,* Apr. 12, 1755; *The New-York Gazette and Weekly Post-Boy,* July 31, 1760; *The New-York Journal, or General Advertiser,* May 29, 1766.

HOLT, LUCIUS HUDSON (Jan. 16, 1881–Jan. 20, 1953); b. Atchison, Kan. Educator, author. *The History of Europe from 1862 to 1914* (with Alexander W. Chilton, 1917); *English Analysis and Exposition* (with same, 1923); etc. Editor: *The Leading English Poets* (1915). Prof., U.S. Military Academy, 1910–30; with G. & C. Merriam Co., 1932–46.

HOLT, L[uther] EMMETT, JR. (Mar. 20, 1895–); b. New York. Physician, author. *Diseases of Infancy and Childhood* (ed., with R. McIntosh, 1933); *Pioneer of a Children's Century* (with others, 1939); *Good Housekeeping Book of Baby and Child Care* (with R. L. Duffus, 1957).

Holt, Rinehart & Winston, Inc. New York. Publishers. Founded 1866, as Leypoldt & Holt. Called Leypoldt, Holt & Williams in 1868, and Henry Holt & Company in 1873. In 1959 the firm was merged with Rinehart & Co. and the John C. Winston Co. Edgar T. Rigg, formerly president of Henry Holt & Co., was first president; Stanley M. Rinehart, Jr., formerly president of Rinehart & Co., and Charles F. Kindt, Jr., formerly president of the John C. Winston Co., were senior vice-presidents. Acquired by Columbia Broadcasting System in 1967.

HOLT, VICTORIA (pseud.). *Mistress of Mellyn* (1960); *Kirkland Revels* (1962); *The Legend of the Seventh Virgin* (1965); *Menfreya in the Morning* (1966); *The King of the Castle* (1967); *Bride of Pendorric* (1969).

HOLT, WINIFRED (Mrs. Rufus Graves Mather) (d. June 14, 1945); b. New York. Sculptor, author. *A Short Life of*

Henry Fawcett (1911); *The Beacon for the Blind* (1914); *The Light Which Cannot Fail* (1922). Founder, New York Association for the Blind and "The Lighthouse." Founder, *The Searchlight,* first Braille magazine for children.

"Holy Earth, The." Poem by John Hall Wheelock (1925).

HOLYOKE, SAMUEL (Oct. 15, 1762–Feb. 21, 1820); b. Boxford, Mass. Composer, teacher. Compiler: *Harmonia Americana* (1791); *The Christian Harmonist* (1804); etc. His best known hymn tune is "Arnheim."

HOLZMAN, ROBERT STUART (Nov. 18, 1907–); b. Paterson, N.J. Educator, tax consultant, author. *Corporate Reorganizations: Their Federal Tax Status* (1948); *Stormy Ben Butler* (1954); *General Baseball Doubleday* (with others, 1955); *The Romance of Fire Fighting* (with others, 1956); *Arm's Length Transactions* (1958); *Sound Business Purposes* (1958); *Federal Income Taxation* (1960); *Tax Basis for Managerial Decisions* (1965); etc. *The Manager's Letter* (1968); *Guide to Pension and Profit Sharing Plans* (1969). Editor: *Tax Practitioner's Library,* 15v. (1956–60). Prof. taxation, New York University, since 1953.

Homage to Clio. Collection of poems by W. H. Auden (1960).

HOMAN, HELEN WALKER (1893–). Author. *Letters to St. Francis and His Friars* (1935); *Letters to the Martyrs* (1951); *By Post to the Apostles* (1952); *Star of Jacob* (1953); *St. Thérèse and the Roses* (1955).

"Home, Sweet Home." Song by John Howard Payne. It was set to music by Sir Henry Bishop. The song was a part of his opera *Clari* (prod. 1823). The original MS is in the Sibley Music Library at the University of Rochester.

Home Book of Verse, 1580–1918. Comp. by Burton E. Stevenson (1918). *See also* his *Home Book of Modern Verse* (1925), and *Poems of American History* (1908).

Home Companion. See *Woman's Home Companion.*

Home Journal, The. New York City. Founded by Nathaniel Parker Willis and George Pope Morris, Feb. 14, 1846. It was first called *The National Press; A Home Journal.* Simply called *The Home Journal* beginning Nov. 21, 1846. In 1901 it was called *Town and Country* and has continued under that name. Both Willis and Morris were brilliant writers, and made voluminous contributions. Poe wrote poems and essays for it.

Home of the Brave, The. Play by Arthur Laurents (prod. 1946). A shell-shocked Jewish soldier in World War II encounters anti-Semitism.

"Home on the Range." A cowboy song. The words have been attributed to Dr. Brewster Highley, of Smith County, Kan., and the music to Dan Kelly, of Harlan, Kan., but the song's origin is still a matter of dispute.

HOMES, MARY SOPHIE SHAW ROGERS (Mrs. Norman Rogers; Mrs. Luther Homes) (b. 1830?); b. Frederick, Md. Poet, novelist. Pen name "Millie Mayfield." *Carrie Harrington; or, Scenes in New Orleans* (1857); *Progression; or, The South Defended* (1860); *A Wreath of Rhymes* (1869); etc.

"Homesick in Heaven." Poem by Oliver Wendell Holmes (1872).

Hon. Peter Sterling, The. Novel by Paul Leicester Ford (1894). Story of politics and society in New York City, and the rise of a benevolent "boss," the gentlemanly Peter Sterling.

HONCE, CHARLES [Ellsworth] (Nov. 18, 1895–); b. Keokuk, Ill. Journalist, author. *Songs of the Seasons* (1918); *Sunlight* (1926); *Books and Ghosts* (1948); etc. Editor: *The APME Red Book,* 1948–52; *Uplands of Dream* (1969). With Associated Press, 1919–53.

HONE, PHILIP (Oct. 25, 1780–May 5, 1851); b. New York City. Diarist, friend of famous men of his day. His MS diary in twenty-eight quarto volumes is in the New York Historical Society library. Two selections from it have been published: *The Diary of Philip Hone, 1828–1851,* ed. by Bayard Tuckerman, 2v. (1889); and *The Diary of Philip Hone, 1828–1851,* ed. by Allan Nevins, 2v. (1927). He was one of the founders of the Union Club.

Honest John Vane. Political novel by John William De Forest (1875).

Honey in the Horn. Novel by H. L. Davis (1935). Pulitzer Prize novel, 1936.

HONEYWOOD, ST. JOHN (Feb. 7, 1763–Sept. 1, 1798); b. Leicester, Mass. Poet. *Poems* (1801).

HONIG, EDWIN (Sept. 3, 1919–). Poet, critic. *Garcia Lorca* (1945); *Dark Conceit: The Making of Allegory* (1959); *Gazabos* (poems, 1960); *The Mentor Book of Major American Poets* (1961); *Cervantes Interludes* (1964); *Spring Journal: Poems* (1968).

Honolulu Star-Bulletin. Honolulu, Hawaii. Newspaper. The *Evening Bulletin* founded 1882; the *Star,* 1893. Merged 1912. Now published with *Honolulu Advertiser,* founded 1856. The *Advertiser* is a morning paper; the *Star-Bulletin and Advertiser* is the Sunday edition.

HOOD, MARGARET PAGE. Author. *Tequila* (1950); *Silent Women* (1954); *Scarlet Thread* (1956); *In the Dark Night* (1957); *Bell on Lonely* (1959); *Drown the Wind* (1961).

HOOK, SIDNEY (Dec. 20, 1902–); b. New York. Educator, author. *The Metaphysics of Pragmatism* (1927); *Towards the Understanding of Karl Marx* (1933); *From Hegel to Marx* (1936); *John Dewey* (1939); *Hero in History* (1943); *Education for Modern Man* (1946); *Heresy, Yes—Conspiracy No* (1953); *Marx and the Marxists: The Ambiguous Legacy* (1955); *Common Sense and the Fifth Amendment* (1957); *Political Power and Personal Freedom* (1959); *The Quest for Being* (1961); *The Paradoxes of Freedom* (1962); *Art and Philosophy* (1966); *The Place of Religion in a Free Society* (1968); etc. Prof. philosophy, New York University, 1939–48. Head philosophy dept., 1948–69.

HOOKER, FORRESTINE C[ooper] (Mar. 8, 1867–Mar. 21, 1932); b. Philadelphia, Pa., dau. of Brig. Gen. Charles Lawrence Cooper, who organized Theodore Roosevelt's "Rough Riders." Novelist. *The Long Dim Trail* (1920); *Prince Jan, St. Bernard* (1921); *Star* (1922); *When Geronimo Rode* (1924); *Cricket* (1925); *Just George* (1926); *Civilizing Cricket* (1927); *The Garden of the Lost Key* (1929); etc.

HOOKER, ISABELLA BEECHER (Feb. 22, 1822–Jan. 25, 1907); b. Litchfield, Conn. Suffragist, author. *Womanhood: Its Sanctities and Fidelities* (1874).

HOOKER, KATHARINE [Putnam] (b. 1849); b. Milwaukee, Wis. Author. *Wayfarers in Italy* (1902); *Byways in Southern Tuscany* (1918); *Through the Heel of Italy* (1927).

HOOKER, RICHARD (Feb. 20, 1878–Nov. 25, 1967); b. Augusta, Ga. Editor, author. *The Story of an Independent Newspaper* (1924). With the *Springfield Republican,* since 1900; lit. editor, 1911–15; editor, 1915–22; president, 1915–32. Director, Associated Press, 1927–34.

HOOKER, THOMAS (1586?–July 7, 1647); b. Marfield, Leicestershire, England (?). Congregational clergyman, author. *The Soules Humiliation* (1637); *The Soules Vocation* (1638); *The Soules Implantation* (1640); etc. *See* G. L. Walker's *Thomas Hooker* (1891).

HOOKER, [William] BRIAN (Nov. 2, 1880–Dec. 28, 1946); b. New York City. Author. *The Right Man* (1908); *Mona* (opera, 1911); *The Professor's Mystery* (with Wells Hastings, 1911); *Fairyland* (opera, 1915); *Morven and the Grail* (opera, 1915); *Poems* (1915); *The White Bird* (opera, 1924); etc.

HOOKER, WORTHINGTON (Mar. 3, 1806–Nov. 6, 1867); b. Springfield, Mass. Physician, author. *The Child's Book of Nature* (1857); *The Child's Book of Common Things* (1858); *Natural History* (1860); etc.

"Hooker's Across." Civil War poem by George Henry Boker (1863).

HOOPER, FRANKLIN HENRY (Jan. 28, 1862–Aug. 14, 1940); b. Worcester, Mass. Editor. With Century Co., 1883–96; editorial staff, American edition of the *Encyclopedia Britannica,* 1899–1940; editor in chief, American edition of the 10th, 11th, 12th, 13th, and 14th editions of the *Encyclopedia Britannica;* editor, *The World Today,* 1933–38.

HOOPER, JOHNSON JONES (June 9, 1815–June 7, 1862); b. Wilmington, N.C. Humorist, creator of the character, "Simon Suggs." *Some Adventures of Captain Simon Suggs, Late of the Tallapoosa Volunteers* (anon., 1845); *The Widow Rugby's Husband, a Night at the Ugly Man's, and Other Tales of Alabama* (anon., 1851).

HOOPER, LUCY (Feb. 4, 1816–Aug. 1, 1851); b. Newburyport, Mass. Poet. *Scenes from Real Life* (1840); *Poetical Remains* (1842); *Complete Poetical Works* (1848). Editor: *The Lady's Book of Flowers and Poetry* (1842).

HOOPER, LUCY HAMILTON (Jan. 20, 1835–Aug. 31, 1893); b. Philadelphia, Pa. Editor, novelist, poet, playwright. *Poems* (1864); augmented (1871); *Under the Tricolor* (1880); *The Tsar's Window* (anon., 1881); *Those Pretty St. George Girls* (1883); *Her Living Image* (with Paul Aimé Chapelle, called Laurencin, 1886); *Helen's Inheritance* (prod. 1889), later called *Inherited.* Assoc. editor, *Lippincott's Magazine,* 1868–70; correspondent, *Appleton's Journal,* Philadelphia *Evening Telegraph,* etc.

HOOPER, OSMAN CASTLE (Apr. 10, 1858–deceased); b. Alexandria, O. Educator, journalist, author. *The Joy of Things* (1910); *The Shepherd Wind, and Other Verses* (1916); *History of Columbus, Ohio* (1919); *History of Ohio State University* (1925); *History of Ohio Journalism* (1933); etc. Editorial writer, the *Columbus Dispatch,* 1893–1917, editor, the *Ohio Newspaper,* 1919–33. Prof. journalism, Ohio State University, 1918–32.

Hoosier Chronicle, A. Novel by Meredith Nicholson (1912). The scene of this story is laid in Montgomery, the seat of Madison College, in Indiana. Professor Kelton, retired, lives a quiet life with his granddaughter Sylvia.

Hoosier School-Master, The. Novel by Edward Eggleston (1871). It appeared originally in *Hearth and Home,* 1870. It is the story of a country school teacher, Ralph Hartsock, and his experiences in Indiana in the days before the Civil War. Filled with homely observation, humor, and country charm. The author's *The Hoosier School-Boy* (1883) rounds out the picture of this adventure in education.

"Hoosier's Nest, The." Poem by John Finley (1883). This poem, in which the word "Hoosier" as applied to a native of Indiana first found currency, was printed as a carrier's address of the *Indianapolis Journal,* Jan. 1, 1833. It is included in Finley's *The Hoosier's Nest, and Other Poems* (1860).

HOOTON, EARNEST ALBERT (Nov. 20, 1887–May 3, 1954); b. Clemansville, Wis. Educator, anthropologist. *Up from the Ape* (1931); *Apes, Men and Morons* (1937); *Why Men Behave Like Apes and Vice Versa* (1940); *Man's Poor Relations* (1942); *"Young Man, You Are Normal"* (1945); *Non-Human Primates and Human Evolution* (1955); etc. Anthropology dept., Harvard University, from 1913.

HOOVEN, HERBERT NELSON (Jan. 31, 1898–); b. Hazelton, Pa. Artist, poet. *Rig Veda* (1933); *Pencilled Hands* (1934); *The Laughing One* (1937).

HOOVER, HERBERT [Clark] (Aug. 10, 1874–Oct. 20, 1964); b. West Branch, Ia. Thirty-first president of the United States, author. *American Individualism* (1922); *The Challenge to Liberty* (1934); *The State Papers,* ed. by William Starr Myers, 2v. (1934); *Addresses Upon the American Road,* 7v. (1938–55); *America's First Crusade* (1941); *The Problems of Lasting Peace* (with Hugh Gibson, 1942); *The Hoover Commission Report on Organization of the Executive Branch of the Government* (1949); *Memoirs,* Vols. I, II, III (1951–52); *The Ordeal of Woodrow Wilson* (1958); *The American Epic,* 3v. (1959–61); *Addresses Upon the American Road, 1955–60* (1961); *Fishing for Fun—and to Wash Your Soul,* ed. by William Nichols (1963). Translator (with wife, Lou Henry Hoover): *Georgius Agricola de Re Metallica* (1912); See Rose Wilder Lane's *The Making of Herbert Hoover* (1920); Will Irwin's *Herbert Hoover* (1928); William Starr Myer's *The Foreign Policies of Herbert Hoover* (1940); Joseph Brandes' *Herbert Hoover and Economic Diplomacy* (1962); Eugene Lyons' *Herbert Hoover: A Biography* (1964); Albert U. Romasco's *Poverty of Abundance: Hoover, The Nation, The Depression* (1965); C. G. Wilson's *Herbert Hoover* (1968).

HOOVER, J[ohn] EDGAR (Jan. 1, 1895–May 2, 1972); b. Washington, D.C. Government official. *Persons in Hiding* (1938); *Masters of Deceit* (1958); *A Study in Communism* (1962); *Crime in the United States* (1965); *J. Edgar Hoover on Communism* (1969). Director, Federal Bureau of Investigation, U.S. Department of Justice, from 1924.

Hopalong Cassidy. Novel by Clarence Edward Mulford (1910). Hopalong Cassidy, created by Mulford, is one of the most popular Western characters in fiction. His first appearance in book form was in *Bar-20* (1907).

HOPE, BOB [Leslie Towne], b. London, Eng. Radio, motion-picture, and television comedian, author. *I Never Left Home* (1944); *So This Is Peace* (1946); *Have Tux, Will Travel* (1954); *I Owe Russia $1200* (1963).

Hope, Edward. Pen name of Edward Hope Goffe, Jr.

HOPE, JAMES BARRON (Mar. 23, 1829–Sept. 15, 1887); b. Norfolk, Va. Poet. Pen name "The Late Henry Ellen, Esq." *Leoni di Monota, and Other Poems* (1857); *A Collection of Poems* (1859); *Arms and the Man* (1882); *A Wreath of Virginia Bay Leaves* (1895).

Hope Leslie. Novel by Catherine M. Sedgwick (1827). Laid in Massachusetts in colonial days.

HOPKINS, ALPHONSO ALVA (Mar. 27, 1843–Sept. 25, 1918); b. Burlington Flats, N.Y. Reformer, author. *Geraldine* (poem, 1882); *Ballads of Brotherhood* (1900); etc.

HOPKINS, ARTHUR [Melancthon] (Oct. 4, 1878–Mar. 22, 1950); b. Cleveland, O. Producer, author. *How's Your Second Act?* (1918); *The Glory Road* (1935); *To a Lonely Boy* (1937); *Reference Point* (1948); etc.

HOPKINS, JOHN HENRY (Jan. 30, 1792–Jan. 9, 1868); b. Dublin, Ireland. Episcopal bishop, author. *The Primitive Church* (1836); *The American Citizen* (1857); *Autobiography in Verse* (1866); etc.

HOPKINS, LEMUEL (June 19, 1750–Apr. 14, 1801); b. Waterbury, Conn. Physician, satirist. *The Democratiad* (1795); *The Guillotine; or, A Democratic Dirge* (1796). See *The Anarchiad: A New England Poem.*

HOPKINS, LOUISE VIRGINIA MARTIN (b. Oct. 2, 1861); b. Nebraska City, Neb. Author. *Signal Lights* (1906); *Frontier Days at Cheyenne* (1908); *Ranch Life in Wyoming* (1909); etc.

HOPKINS, MARGARET SUTTON BRISCOE (b. Dec. 7, 1864); b. Baltimore, Md. Humorist. Writes under maiden name. *Perchance to Dream, and Other Stories* (1892); *Jimty and Others* (1898); *The Image of Eve* (1909); etc.

HOPKINS, MARK (Feb. 4, 1802–June 17, 1887); b. Stockbridge, Mass. Educator, Congregational clergyman, essayist. *Miscellaneous Essays and Discourses* (1847); *Lectures on Moral Science* (1862); *Baccalaureate Sermons and Occasional Discourses* (1862); etc. The quotation "A pine bench, with Mark Hopkins at one end of it and me at the other, is a good enough college for me!" is from a speech by James Abram Garfield (1831–1881) made at Delmonico's in New York, Dec. 28, 1871. President, Williams College, 1836–72. *See* Franklin Carter's *Mark Hopkins* (1892); J. H. Denison's *Mark Hopkins, Biography* (1935).

HOPKINS, MARY ALDEN (1876–Nov. 8, 1960). Author. *Hannah More and her Circle* (1947); *Dr. Johnson's Lichfield* (1952); etc.

Hopkins, Pauline Mackie. See Pauline Bradford Mackie.

Hopkins, Puffer. Pen name of Cornelius Mathews.

HOPKINS, SAMUEL (Sept. 17, 1721–Dec. 20, 1803); b. Waterbury, Conn. Congregational clergyman, author. *The Life and Character of the Late Rev. Jonathan Edwards* (1765); *A Dialogue, Concerning the Slavery of the Africans* (1776); *The System of Doctrines,* 2v. (1793); *A Discourse upon the Slave Trade* (1793); *The Works,* ed. by Sewall Harding, 3v. (1854); etc. Said to have inspired Harriet Beecher Stowe's novel *The Minister's Wooing.*

HOPKINS, SAMUEL (Apr. 11, 1807–Feb. 10, 1887); b. Hadley, Mass. Congregational clergyman, author. *The Youth of the Old Dominion* (1856); *The Puritans,* 3v. (1859–61), republished as *The Puritans and Queen Elizabeth,* 3v. (1875); etc.

HOPKINS, WILLIAM JOHN (June 10, 1863–Nov. 24, 1926); b. New Bedford, Mass. Author. *The Sandman* series, 4v. (1902–08); *The Meddlings of Eve* (1910); *She Blows! And Sparm at That* (1922); etc.

HOPKINSON, FRANCIS (Oct. 2, 1737–May 9, 1791); b. Philadelphia, Pa. Jurist, musician, essayist, pamphleteer. *The Miscellaneous Essays and Occasional Writings,* 3v. (1792). Wrote many Revolutionary pamphlets. His best known work is his poem, "The Battle of the Kegs" (1778). In 1777 he designed the American flag. *See* George E. Hasting's *The Life and Works of Francis Hopkinson* (1926).

HOPKINSON, JOSEPH (Nov. 12, 1770–Jan. 15, 1842); b. Philadelphia, Pa. Jurist. Author of "Hail Columbia" (1798).

HOPPE, ARTHUR WATTERSON (Apr. 23, 1925–); b. Honolulu, Hawaii. Journalist, author. *Love Everybody Crusade* (1962); *Dreamboat* (1962); *The Perfect Solution to Absolutely Everything* (1968). Staff, *San Francisco Chronicle,* since 1949.

HOPPER, HEDDA (June 2, 1890–Feb. 1, 1966); b. Hollidaysburg, Pa. Radio, television, and newspaper columnist. *From Under My Hat* (autobiography, 1952); *The Whole Truth and Nothing But* (1963). Syndicated columnist, Chicago Tribune–New York News, Inc.

HOPPER, JAMES MARIE (July 23, 1876–Aug. 28, 1956); b. Paris, France. Author. *Caybigan* (1906); *What Happened in the Night* (1913); *Medals of Honor* (1929); etc.

HOPPER, STANLEY ROMAINE (Mar. 22, 1907–); b. Fresno, Cal. Educator, author. *The Crisis of Faith* (1944). Contributor: *Interpreter's Bible* (1956). Editor: *Spiritual Problems in Contemporary Literature* (1952). Co-editor: *Interpretation: The Poetry of Meaning* (1967). Dean, graduate school, Drew University, 1954–1968. Prof. Religion, Syracuse University since 1968.

HOPPER, [William] DE WOLF (Mar. 30, 1858–Sept. 23, 1935); b. New York City. Comedian. Starred in Gilbert and Sullivan operas. His recitation of "Casey at the Bat" was a classic. Author: *Once a Clown, Always a Clown* (reminiscences, with Wesley Winans Stout, 1927).

HOPPIN, AUGUSTUS (July 13, 1828–Apr. 1, 1896); b. Providence, R.I. Illustrator, satirist and caricaturist of manners. *Carrot-Pomade* (1864); *Ups and Downs on Land and Water* (1871); *Crossing the Atlantic* (1872); *On the Nile* (1874); *A Fashionable Sufferer* (1883); *Married for Fun* (1885); etc. In the 1850's his illustrations began to appear in *Putnam's Magazine, Yankee Notions,* and other periodicals. He also illustrated Holmes's *The Autocrat of the Breakfast Table;* William Allen's *Nothing to Wear;* and G. W. Curtis's *Potiphar Papers.*

HOPPIN, JAMES MASON (Jan. 17, 1820–Nov. 15, 1906); b. Providence, R.I. Educator, art critic. *Old England* (1867); *Sermons on Faith, Hope and Love* (1891); *Art Subjects* (1892); etc. Prof., Yale Divinity School, 1861–79; prof. history of art, Yale University, 1879–99.

HOPWOOD, AVERY (May 28, 1882–July 1, 1928); b. Cleveland, O. Playwright. *Clothes* (with Channing Pollock, prod. 1906); *Fair and Warmer* (prod. 1915); *The Gold Diggers* (prod. 1919); *The Bat* (with Mary Roberts Rinehart, 1920); *Spanish Love* (with same, 1920); *Ladies' Night* (with Carlton Andrews, 1920); *The Demi-Virgin* (prod. 1921); *Little Miss Bluebeard* (prod. 1923); etc. By his will the University of Michigan received an endowment, the income of which is used for prizes in creative literary work, fiction, poetry, essays, and plays.

"Horace in Baltimore: Odes and Epodes." By Peter Hoffman Cruse, published in *The Portico,* 1818–19.

HORAN, JAMES D[avid] (July 27, 1914–); b. New York. Journalist, author. *Action Tonight* (1945); *Desperate Men* (1949); *Confederate Agent* (1954); *Mathew Brady, Historian with a Camera* (1955); *The DA's Man* (1957); *The Great American West* (1959); *The Shadow Catcher* (1961); *The Desperate Years* (1962); *The Seat of Power* (1965); *America's Forgotten Photographer: Timothy O'Sullivan* (1966); *The Right Image* (1967); *The Pinkertons: The Detective Dynasty That Made History* (1968); *The Life and Art of Charles Schreyvogel* (1969); *The Blue Messiah* (1971); etc. Staff, New York *Journal American.*

HORAN, KENNETH [O'Donnell] (Mrs. John William Rogers) (1890–); b. Jackson, Miss. Author. *The Longest Night* (1933); *It's Later Than You Think* (1934); *Remember the Day* (1937); *Oh, Promise Me* (1938); *Night Bell* (1940); *I Give Thee Back* (1942); *A Bashful Woman* (1944); *Papa Went to Congress* (1946); *Mama Took Up Travel* (1948); etc.

HORD, PARKER (Dec. 28, 1883–); b. in Mason Co., Ky. Playwright. *A Mix-Up* (prod. 1914); *Suite 16* (prod. 1919); *Tyndale* (1925); *A Youth Goes Forth* (1938).

HORGAN, PAUL (Aug. 1, 1903–); b. Buffalo, N.Y. Librarian, novelist. *Men of Arms* (1931); *The Fault of Angels* (1933); *No Quarter Given* (1935); *Main Line West* (1936); *A Lamp on the Plains* (1937); *Figures in a Landscape* (1940); *The Habit of Empire* (1939); *Yours, A. Lincoln* (play, 1942); *One Red Rose for Christmas* (1952); *Great River: The Rio Grande in North American History* (1954; Pulitzer prize for history, 1955); *The Centuries of Santa Fe* (1956); *Give Me Possession* (1957); *Rome Eternal* (1959); *The Distant Trumpet* (1960); *Mountain Standard Time* (1962); *Conquistadors in North American History* (1963); *Things as They Are* (1964); *Songs After Lincoln* (1965); *Memories of the Future* (1966); *The Peach Stone* (1967); *Everything to Live For* (1968); etc. Librarian, New Mexico Military Institute, Roswell, N.M., 1926–42.

Horizon. New York. Bimonthly. Founded 1958 by the American Heritage Publishing Co. Hard-cover periodical devoted to the arts and containing excerpts from books. Bought by McGraw-Hill in 1969.

HORN, STANLEY FITZGERALD (May 27, 1889–); b. near Nashville, Tenn. Editor, publisher. *Boy's Life of Robert E. Lee* (1935); *The Hermitage: Home of Andrew Jackson* (1938);

Invisible Empire (1939); *The Army of Tennessee* (1941); *This Fascinating Lumber Business* (1943); *Gallant Rebel* (1947); *Robert E. Lee Reader* (1949); *The Decisive Battle of Nashville* (1957). Editor and co-owner, *Southern Lumberman,* Nashville, Tenn., since 1917; with J. W. Baird Publishing Co., since 1908.

Horn Book. Boston, Mass. Bimonthly magazine about juvenile literature. Founded 1924 as *Horn Book Magazine.*

HORNADAY, WILLIAM TEMPLE (Dec. 1, 1854–Mar. 6, 1939); b. Plainfield, Ind. Zoölogist, author. *Two Years in the Jungle* (1885); *The American Natural History* (1904); *A Wild Animal Round-Up* (1908); *Old-Fashioned Verses* (1919); *Thirty Years' War for Wild Life* (autobiography, 1931); etc. Director, New York Zoölogical Society (Bronx Zoo), 1896–1926.

HORNBLOW, ARTHUR (June 6, 1865–May 6, 1941); b. Manchester, England. Editor, playwright. *The End of the Game* (1907); *The Easiest Way* (with Eugene Walter, prod. 1908); *The Third Degree* (with Charles Klein, prod. 1908); *By Right of Conquest* (1909); *The Gamblers* (with Charles Klein, prod. 1910); *Kindling* (with Charles Kenyon, prod. 1911); *Bought and Paid For* (with George H. Broadhurst, prod. 1911); *The Argyle Case* (with Harriet Ford and Harvey O'Higgins, prod. 1912); *Training for the Stage* (1916); *A History of the Theatre in America,* 2v. (1919); etc. Editor, *Theatre Magazine,* 1901–26.

HORNE, CHARLES FRANCIS (Jan. 12, 1870–Sept. 14, 1942); b. Jersey City, N.J. Educator, editor, author. *The Birth of the Novel* (1897); *History of the College of the City of New York* (1907); *The Technique of the Novel* (1908); etc. Editor: *The Great Events by Famous Historians,* 20v. (1904–05); *Great Men and Famous Women,* 8v. (1894); *The Story of the Greatest Nations,* 10v. (with Edward S. Ellis, 1901–06); *The World's Famous Events,* 10v. (1914); *Sacred Books and Early Literature of the East,* 14v. (1917); *World Epochs,* 12v. (1936); etc. English dept., College of the City of New York, 1897–1940; head dept., 1935–40.

Horne, Howard. Pen name of Robert Payne.

HORNE, MARY TRACY EARLE (b. Oct. 21, 1864); b. Cobden, Ill. Author. *The Wonderful Wheel* (1896); *The Man Who Worked for Collister* (1898); *Through Old-Rose Glasses* (1900); *The Flag on the Hill-Top* (1902).

HORNEY, KAREN (Sept. 16, 1885–Dec., 1952); b. Hamburg, Ger. Psychiatrist, author. *Neurotic Personality of Our Time* (1936); *New Ways in Psychoanalysis* (1939); *Self-Analysis* (1942); *Our Inner Conflicts* (1945); *Neurosis and Human Growth* (1950); etc.

HORNIBROOKE, ISABEL; b. in Ireland, of English parentage. Author of books for young people. *Camp and Trail* (1897); *From Keel to Kite* (1908); *The Camp Fire Girls and Mount Greylock* (1917); *Anne of Seacrest High* (1924); etc.

HORRWITZ, ERNEST PHILIP (Aug. 27, 1866–); b. Gruenberg, Silesia. Educator, Sanskrit scholar, author. *A Short History of Indian Literature* (1907); *The Indian Theatre* (1912); *Rose Petals and Gorse Bloom* (1920); etc.

Horse-shoe Robinson: A Tale of the Tory Ascendancy. Novel by John Pendleton Kennedy (1835). Story of the Revolutionary War, centering about the exploits of Horse-shoe Robinson, an American spy. The locale is Virginia and North Carolina. The hero resembles Harvey Birch in Cooper's *The Spy,* but the romantic tale of Kennedy's is considered to be superior to its model in style. The story ends with the Battle of King's Mountain.

HORTON, DOUGLAS (July 27, 1891–); b. Brooklyn, N.Y. Congregational clergyman, author. *Out Into Life* (1925); *A Legend of the Graal* (1926); *The Art of Living Today* (1935); *Congregationalism: A Study in Church Polity* (1952); etc. Dean, Harvard Divinity School, 1955–59.

HORTON, GEORGE (Oct. 11, 1859–Jan. 5, 1942); b. Fairville, N.Y. Editor, diplomat, author. *Songs of the Lowly* (1891); *In Unknown Seas* (poems, 1895); *Like Another Helen* (1901); *In Argolis* (1902); *The Long Straight Road* (1902); *Recollections Grave and Gay* (1927); *Poems of an Exile* (1931); etc.

HORTON, WALTER MARSHALL (Apr. 7, 1895–April 22, 1966); b. Somerville, Mass. Baptist clergyman, educator, author. *Theism in the Modern World* (1930); *Contemporary American Theology* (with others, 1932); *Realistic Theology* (1934); *The Church through Half a Century* (with others, 1936); *God* (1937); *Revelation* (with others, 1937); *The Authority of the Faith* (with others, 1939); *Christianity Today* (with others, 1947); *The Churches Witness to God's Design* (with others, 1949); *Protestant Thought in the Twentieth Centuries* (with others, 1951); *Christian Theology: An Ecumenical Approach* (1955); *The God We Trust* (1960); etc. Prof. theology, Oberlin College, since 1926.

HORWICH, FRANCES R[appaport] (July 16, 1908–); b. Ottawa, O. Educator, author. *Ding Dong School Books* series, since 1954; *Miss Frances' All-Day-Long Book* (with Reinald Werrenrath, 1954); *Have Fun with Your Children* (with same, 1954); *Miss Frances' Story Book of Manners for the Very Young* (1955); *Miss Frances' Story Book of Pets for the Very Young* (1956); *The Magic of Bringing Up Your Child* (1959); *Story Book of Manners* (1960); *Stories and Poems to Enjoy* (1962); *From Miss Frances' Desk* (1964); etc. Prof. education, Roosevelt University, 1947–52. Television program, "Ding Dong School of the Air," since 1952.

HORWITZ, JULIUS (Aug. 18, 1920–   ); b. Cleveland, Ohio. Author. *The City* (1953); *The Inhabitants* (1960); *Can I Get There by Candlelight?* (1964); *The W.A.S.P.* (1967). Consultant to New York State Majority Leader on Public Welfare.

HOSHOUR, SAMUEL KLINEFELTER (Dec. 9, 1803–Nov. 29, 1883); b. Heidelburg Twp., York Co., Pa. Disciples clergyman, educator, author. *Letters to Esq. Pedant in the East by Lorenzo Altisonant, an Emigrant to the West* (1844); *Autobiography* (1884). President, Butler University, 1858–61; prof. languages, 1861–73.

HOSIC, JAMES FLEMING (Oct. 11, 1870–Jan. 13, 1959); b. Henry, Ill. Educator, editor, author. *Empirical Studies in Reading* (1921); *Pathway to Reading* (with Bessie B. Coleman and Willis L. Uhl, 1926); *Introductory Studies in Literature* (with W. W. Hatfield, 1927); etc. Founder and editor, *English Journal,* 1912–21. With Teachers College, Columbia University, 1921–36.

HOSKINS, HALFORD LANCASTER (Mar. 25, 1891–Sept. 14, 1967); b. near Carmel, Ind. Educator, author. *Preliminaries of the World War* (1918); *Guide to Latin-American History* (1922); *An Outline of Modern European History* (1925); *British Routes to India* (1928); *The Atlantic Pact* (1949); *The Middle East: Problem Area in World Politics* (1954); etc. History dept., Tufts College, 1920–44; director, School of Advanced International Studies, Washington, D.C., 1944–49; with Legislative Reference Service, Library of Congress, since 1949.

HOSKINS, KATHARINE DE MONTALANT (May 25, 1909–); b. Indian Head, Md. Author. *A Penitential Primer* (1945); *Villa Narcisse* (1956); *Out in the Open* (1959).

Hoskins, Mrs. A. L. See Esther Forbes.

HOSMER, FREDERICK LUCIAN (Oct. 16, 1840–June 7, 1929); b. Framingham, Mass. Unitarian clergyman, hymnwriter. Author (with William Channing Gannett): *The Thought of God in Hymns and Poems,* 3v. (1885, 1904, 1918). Compiler (with William Channing Gannett and J. Vila Blake): *Unity Hymns and Carols* (1880).

HOSMER, GEORGE WASHINGTON (1830–1914). Author. *The People and Politics* (1883); *As We Went Marching On* (1885); etc.

HOSMER, HEZEKIAH LORD (Dec. 10, 1814–Oct. 31, 1893); b. Hudson, N.Y. Jurist, author. *Early History of the Maumee Valley* (1858); *Adela, the Octoroon* (1860). Became editor and part owner of the *Toledo Blade*, 1844.

HOSMER, JAMES KENDALL (Jan. 29, 1834–Mar. 11, 1927); b. Northfield, Mass., son of George Washington Hosmer (1814–93). Educator, librarian, historian, novelist. *The Color-Guard* (1864); *The Thinking Bayonet* (1865); *Samuel Adams* (1885); *The Story of the Jews* (1885); *How Thankful Was Bewitched* (1894); *The History of the Louisiana Purchase*, 2v. (1902); *The Last Leaf* (recollections, 1912); etc. Prof. history, University of Missouri, 1872–74; Washington University, 1874–92; librarian, Minneapolis Public Library, 1892–1904.

HOSMER, JOHN ALLEN (Sept. 15, 1850–1907); b. Toledo, O., son of Hezekiah Lord Hosmer. Author. *A Trip to the States* (1867). This was the second book published in Montana.

HOSMER, MARGARET KERR (1830–Feb. 3, 1897); b. Philadelphia, Pa. Author. *Ten Years of a Lifetime* (1866); *Grandma Merritt's Stories* (anon., 1868); *Juliet, the Heiress* (1869); *Rich and Poor* (1869); *Lenny, the Orphan* (1869); *Little Rosie in the Country* (1869); *Three Times Lost* (1870); *John Hartman* (1872); *A Rough Boy's Story* (1873); *Chambo's Hut* (1879); etc.

HOSMER, WILLIAM HOWE CUYLER (May 24, 1814–May 23, 1877); b. Avon, N.Y. Poet, embodying in verse the legends of the Seneca Indians. *The Fall of Tecumseh* (1830); *Yonnondio; or, Warriors of the Genesee* (1844); *The Months* (1847); *Indian Traditions and Songs* (1850); *Legend of the Senecas* (1850); *Poetical Works*, 2v. (1854); *Later Lays and Lyrics* (1873); etc.

HOSPERS, JOHN (1918–). Author. *Meaning and Truth in the Arts* (1947); *Introduction to Philosophical Analysis* (1953); *Human Conduct* (1961). Editor: *Readings in Ethical Theory* (with W. S. Sellars, 1952). Compiler: *Readings in Introductory Philosophical Analysis* (1969).

Hot Corn: Life Scenes in New York: Tales of Slum Life. By Solon Richardson (1854). These stories of New York night life were very popular. A similar popular work was George G. Foster's *New York by Gas-Light.*

"Hot Time in the Old Town, A." Song by Joe Hayden and Theodore A. Metz (1896). Popularized by the American soldiers during the Spanish-American War, 1898.

HOTCHKISS, CHAUNCEY CRAFTS (Oct. 28, 1852–Dec., 1920); b. New York City. Author. *In Defiance of the King* (1895); *A Colonial Free-Lance* (1897); *Betsy Ross* (1901); etc.

HOTCHNER, AARON EDWARD (June 28, 1919–); b. St. Louis, Mo. Author. *The Dangerous American* (1958); *The White House* (play, 1964); *Papa Hemingway: A Personal Memoir* (1966); *The Hemingway Hero* (1967); *Treasure* (1970). Author of television adaptations of Hemingway's works, such as *For Whom the Bell Tolls* (1958) and *The Killers* (1959).

HOTSON, [John] LESLIE (Aug. 16, 1897–); b. in Ontario. Educator, author. *The Death of Christopher Marlowe* (1925); *The Commonwealth and Restoration Stage* (1928); *Shelley's Lost Letters to Harriet* (1930); *Shakespeare Versus Shallow* (1931); *I, William Shakespeare* (1937); *The First Night of Twelfth Night* (1954); *Shakespeare's Wooden O* (1960); *Mr. W. H.* (1964); etc. Prof. English, Haverford College, since 1931.

HOUGH, CLARA SHARPE (Aug. 26, 1893–); Monterey, N.L., Mexico, of American parentage. Author. *Leif, the*

Lucky (1926); *Not for Publication* (1927); *The Lone Star of Carbajal* (under the pen name "C. Sharpe," 1928); *The Charming Chest* (1932).

HOUGH, DONALD (June 29, 1895–May 11, 1965); b. St. Paul, Minn. Author. *Snow Above Town* (1943); *Captain Retread* (1944); *The Camelephamoose* (1946); *Darling, I Am Home* (1946); *The Cocktail Hour in Jackson Hole* (1956); *Streetcar House* (1960); *The Poet* (1963); etc.

HOUGH, EMERSON (June 28, 1857–Apr. 30, 1923); b. Newton, Ia. Journalist, author. *The Story of the Cowboy* (1897); *The Girl at the Half-Way House* (1900); *The Mississippi Bubble* (1902); *The Law of the Land* (1904); *The Sowing* (1909); the *Young Alaskans* series, 4v. (1910–18); *The Magnificent Adventure* (1916); *The Man Next Door* (1917); *The Passing of the Frontier* (1918); *The Covered Wagon* (1922); etc.

HOUGH, HENRY BEETLE (1896–). Editor, publisher, author. *Martha's Vineyard* (1936); *Country Editor* (1940); *That Lofty Sky* (1941); *Roosters Crow in Town* (1945); *Long Anchorage* (1947); *Once More the Thunderer* (1950); *Whaling Wives* (with Emma Whiting, 1953); *Thoreau of Walden* (1956); *Great Days of Whaling* (1958); *Lament for a City* (1960); *The Port* (1963). Editor and publisher, the *Vineyard Gazette*, since 1920.

HOUGH, LYNN HAROLD (Sept. 10, 1877–July 14, 1971); b. Cadiz, O. Methodist clergyman, editor, educator, author. *Athenasius, the Hero* (1906); *The Lure of Books* (1911); *The Theology of a Preacher* (1912); *The Men of the Gospels* (1913); *In the Valley of Decision* (1916); *The Little Old Lady* (1917); *The Opinions of John Clearfield* (1920); *The Artist and the Critic* (1930); *The Church and Civilization* (1934); *Forest Essays*, 3v. (1934–39); *Patterns of the Mind* (1942); *The Meaning of Human Experience* (1945); *The Dignity of Man* (1950); *Great Humanists* (1952); *The Great Argument* (1953); *The Living Church* (1959); etc. Prof. homiletics, Drew University, 1930–47.

HOUGHTON, [Charles] NORRIS (Dec. 26, 1909–); b. Indianapolis, Ind. Stage director, author. *Moscow Rehearsals* (1936); *Advance from Broadway* (1941); *But Not Forgotten* (1952); *Return Engagement* (1962). Assoc. editor, *Theatre Arts*, 1945–48. Prof. theatre arts, State University of N.Y., since 1967.

HOUGHTON, EDWARD RITTENHOUSE (Mar. 13, 1871–May 16, 1955); b. Norristown, Pa. Publisher. With Houghton Mifflin Co., since 1893; president, 1922–39.

HOUGHTON, [George] WASHINGTON WRIGHT (Aug. 12, 1850–91); b. Cambridge, Mass. Poet. *Poems* (1872); *Songs from Over the Sea* (1874); *The Legend of St. Olaf's Kirk* (1880); *Niagara and Other Poems* (1882).

HOUGHTON, HENRY OSCAR (Apr. 30, 1823–Aug. 25, 1895); b. Sutton, Vt. Publisher. Founder, H. O. Houghton & Co., and the Riverside Press, Cambridge, Mass., 1852. See Horace E. Scudder's *Henry Oscar Houghton* (1897).

Houghton, Mifflin Co. Boston, Mass. Publishers. Founded 1852, by Henry Oscar Houghton in Cambridge, Mass. In 1864 he joined with Melancthon Hurd to form Hurd & Houghton. In 1867 George Harrison Mifflin joined the firm, and was president for many years. Stephen W. Grant is now president. In 1878 the name was changed to Houghton, Osgood & Co., and in 1880 to Houghton, Mifflin & Co. In 1878 the firm absorbed Ticknor & Fields, giving it an enviable list of authors, including Longfellow, Emerson, Holmes, Lowell, Thoreau and Hawthorne. The firm publishes many textbooks in addition to its trade list, and has a line of paperbound reprints called Riverside Editions.

HOUGHTON, WALTER EDWARDS (Sept. 21, 1904–); b. Stamford, Conn. Educator, author. *The Formation of Thomas Fuller's Holy and Profane States* (1938); *The Art of New-*

man's Apologia (1945); *The Victorian Frame of Mind,
1830–70* (1957); *The Wellesley Index to Victorian Periodicals,
1824–1900,* v.1 (1966). Co-editor: *Victorian Poetry and Poetics* (1959).

Hound and Horn. New York City. Critical quarterly.
Founded Sept., 1927 at Cambridge, Mass. Moved to New
York in 1930. Lincoln Kirstein, Bernard Bandler, R. F. Black-
mur, Varian Fry, and A. Hyatt Mayor, were editors. Expired
Sept., 1934.

Hours at Home. New York City. Monthly magazine.
Founded May, 1865, by Charles Scribner & Co. Editors:
James Manning Sherwood, 1867–69; Richard Watson Gilder,
1869–70. It was somewhat evangelical in tone. Discontinued
1870, to make way for *Scribner's Monthly.*

HOUSE, BOYCE (Nov. 29, 1896–Dec. 30, 1961); b. Piggott,
Ark. Author. *Were You in Ranger?* (1935); *Oil Boom* (1941);
Tall Talk From Texas (1944); *Cub Reporter* (1947); *Laugh
Parade of the States* (1948); *Texas Rhythms* (poems, 1950);
Roaring Ranger, the World's Biggest Boom (1951); *Oil Field
Fury* (1954); *As I Was Saying* (1957); *Friendly Feudin':
Alaska vs. Texas* (1959); *I Give You Texas!* (1961); etc.

HOUSE, EDWARD HOWARD (Sept. 5, 1836–Dec. 17,
1901); b. Boston, Mass. Journalist, musician, Japanophile, author. *Japanese Episodes* (1881); *Yone Santo, a Child of Japan*
(1889); *Midnight Warning, and Other Stories* (1892).

HOUSE, EDWARD MANDELL (July 26, 1858–Mar. 28,
1938); b. Houston, Tex. Diplomat, author. *Philip Dru* (1919);
The Intimate Papers, ed. by Charles Seymour, 4v. (1926–28);
Riding for Texas (1936). Personal representative of President
Woodrow Wilson in Europe during the First World War. *See*
A. D. H. Smith's *Mr. House of Texas* (1940).

HOUSE, HOMER CLYDE (June 23, 1871–Aug. 28, 1939);
b. Manson, Ia. Educator, author. *A Theory of the Genetic
Basis of Appeal in Literature* (1909); *Handbook of Correct
English* (1926); *College Rhetoric* (1934); *Sun Dance* (poems,
1935); etc. Head, English dept., University of Maryland,
1920–39.

HOUSE, JAY ELMER (Apr. 3, 1872–Jan. 5, 1936); b. Plymouth, Ill. Journalist. *On Second Thought* (1937). Syndicated
newspaper columnist, 1901–36.

HOUSE, ROY TEMPLE (May 26, 1878–Dec. 4, 1963); b.
Lexington, Neb. Educator, editor. Editor and translator of
many foreign plays. Editor, *Books Abroad,* since 1927. Modern language dept., University of Oklahoma, since 1911.

House and Garden. New York. Monthly. Founded 1901.
Incorporated *Living for Young Homemakers.* Published by
Condé Nast.

House Beautiful. New York. Monthly. Founded 1896. Published by Hearst Corp.

"House by the Side of the Road, The." Poem by Sam Walter
Foss, in his *Dreams in Homespun* (1897).

House of a Thousand Candles. Novel by Meredith Nicholson (1905). A mystery story laid on an Indiana estate, which
must be inhabited by the heir for one year in order for him to
obtain possession.

House of Mirth, The. Novel by Edith Wharton (1905). Satire
on the vanities of fashionable life in New York. The heroine,
Lily Bart, a poor relation of an aristocratic family, finds herself
enmeshed in its way of life even though she dislikes it for its
emptiness.

House of the Far and Lost, The. Short story by Thomas
Wolfe, in *Scribner's Magazine,* July, 1934.

House of the Seven Gables, The. Novel by Nathaniel Hawthorne (1851). One of the best-known tales of New England,

centering around the Pyncheon family. An old curse rests on
the house of the seven gables, and an air of tragedy haunts it.
Clifford Pyncheon, just released from prison, is persecuted by
Judge Pyncheon, who wishes to have him declared insane.
Hepzibah Pyncheon struggles to shield her brother Clifford.
Phoebe Pyncheon, Hepzibah's cousin, relieves the tension of
the story with her simple sweetness.

Houseboat on the Styx, The. Story by John Kendrick Bangs
(1896). Humorous account of a reunion of the great shades of
the past.

HOUSTON, DAVID FRANKLIN (Feb. 17, 1866–
deceased); b. Monroe, N.C. Educator, cabinet officer, author.
A Critical Study of Nullification in South Carolina (1902);
Eight Years with Wilson's Cabinet (1926). With University of
Texas, 1894–1902; president, 1905–08; chancellor, Washing-
ton University, 1908–16. Secretary of Agriculture, 1913–20;
Secretary of the Treasury, 1920–21.

HOUSTON, MARGARET BELL (d. June 22, 1966); b.
Houston, Tex. Author. *Prairie Flowers* (poems, 1907); *The
Little Straw Wife* (1914); *The Witch Man* (1922); *The Singing
Heart, and Other Poems* (1926); *Moon of Delight* (1931);
Lanterns in the Dusk (poems, 1930); *Hurdy-Gurdy* (1932);
Magic Valley (1934); *Gypsy Weather* (1935); *Window in
Heaven* (1936); *Pilgrim in Manhattan* (1940); *Dark of the
Moon* (1943); *The Bride's Island* (1951); *Yonder* (1955); *Cot-
tonwoods Grow Tall* (1958); etc.

HOUSTON, PERCY HAZEN (Feb. 3, 1882–); b. Chicago,
Ill. Educator, author. *Doctor Johnson* (1921); *Main Currents
of English Literature* (1926); Editor: *Types of Great Literature* (with John Kester Bonnell, 1919); *Types of World Literature* (with R. M. Smith, 1930); *Our Educational Discontents*
(1951). With Occidental College, La Jolla, Calif.

HOUSTON, SAM[uel] (Mar. 2, 1793–July 26, 1863); b. near
Lexington, Va. Soldier, statesman, author. *The Writings of
Sam Houston, 1821–1847,* ed. by Amelia W. Williams and
Eugene C. Barker, 6v. (1938–40). President, Republic of
Texas, 1836–44; U.S. Senator, 1846–59; Governor of Texas,
1859–61. *See* Marquis James's *The Raven* (1929); John M.
Oskison's *Texas Titan* (1929); Flora W. Seymour's *Sam Hous-
ton, Patriot* (1930); Amelia W. Williams's *Following General
Sam Houston from 1793 to 1863* (1935); Llerena Friend's *Sam
Houston: The Great Designer* (1954).

Houston Chronicle. Houston, Tex. Newspaper. Founded
1901. John W. Thomason, novelist, was once on the staff.
Everett Collier is editor. Jo Wostendiek edits the book reviews.

Houston Post. Houston, Tex. Newspaper. Founded 1880, by
Gail Borden Johnson. Suspended, but re-established 1885 by
J. L. Watson. "O. Henry" began his short-story writing on the
Post. W. P. Hobby, Jr. is editor. Diana Hobby is book review
editor. Bought *Galveston News, Galveston Tribune,* and
Texas City Sun in 1963.

HOVEY, RICHARD (May 4, 1864–Feb. 24, 1900); b. Normal, Ill. Poet. *The Laurel* (1889); *Launcelot and Guenevere,*
4v. (1891–1907); *Seaward* (1893); *Songs from Vagabondia*
(with Bliss Carman, 1894); *More Songs from Vagabondia*
(with same, 1896); *Along the Trail* (1898); *Last Songs from
Vagabondia* (with Bliss Carman, 1900); *The Holy Grail,* ed.
by his wife, Henriette Russell Hovey (1907); *To the End of the
Trail* (1908). *See* A. H. MacDonald's *Richard Hovey* (1957).

HOVEY, RICHARD BENNETT (1917–). Author. *John Jay
Chapman, an American Mind* (1959); *Hemingway: The Inward Terrain* (1968).

HOW, LOUIS (Feb. 14, 1873–Oct. 3, 1947); b. St. Louis, Mo.
Novelist, poet. *The Penitentes of San Rafael* (1900); *James E.
Eads* (1900); *Lyrics and Sonnets* (1911); *The Youth Replies,
and Other Verses* (1912); *Barricades* (1914); *A Hidden Well*
(poems, 1916); *Nursery Rhymes of New York City* (1919);
Ruin and Gold (1924); *Narcissus, and Other Poems* (1928);

The Other Don Juan (poem, 1932); *The Years Relent* (1936); *Regional Rhymes of New York City* (1937). Translator of Dante's *Divine Comedy* (1934–40).

How Children Fail. By John Holt (1967). Deals with the reasons for the dissatisfaction of children with school and the extent to which failure is caused and insured by the attitudes of the educational establishment.

"How Long?" Poem by Emma Lazarus (1871).

"How the Women Went to Dover." Poem by John Greenleaf Whittier which first appeared in the *Atlantic Monthly*, June, 1883. It is included in his *The Bay of Seven Islands, and Other Poems* (1883). Describes the whipping of three Quaker women in 1662 at Dover, N.H.

How to Win Friends and Influence People. By Dale Carnegie (1936). On being a successful extrovert.

HOWARD, BAILEY KNEIRIEM (Oct. 25, 1914–); b. Jamestown, Mo. Publisher. Pres. World Book Encyclopedia, since 1957.

HOWARD, BLANCHE WILLIS (Mrs. Julius von Teuffel) (July 21, 1847–Oct. 7, 1898); b. Bangor, Me. Author. *One Summer* (anon., 1875); *Aunt Serena* (1881); *Guenn: A Wave on the Breton Coast* (1883); *Dionysius the Weaver's Heart's Dearest* (1899); etc.

HOWARD, BRONSON [Crocker] (Oct. 27, 1842–Aug. 4, 1908); b. Detroit, Mich. Playwright. *Saratoga* (prod. 1870); *Lillian's Last Love* (prod. 1873), revived as, *The Banker's Daughter* (prod. 1878); *Old Love Letters* (prod. 1878); *Young Mrs. Winthrop* (prod. 1882); *One of Our Girls* (1885); *The Henrietta* (prod. 1887); *Shenandoah* (prod. 1888); *Aristocracy* (prod. 1892); etc. Founder, American Dramatists Club, later called the Society of American Dramatists and Composers. *See* H. P. Mawson's *In Memoriam: Bronson Howard* (1910).

HOWARD, CLIFFORD (Oct. 12, 1868–May 19, 1942); b. Bethlehem, Pa. Author. *Twigs, Leaves and Blossoms* (1892); *Thoughts in Verse* (1895); *Tenatsali* (poems, 1912).

HOWARD, DELTON THOMAS (Mar. 23, 1883–); b. South Bend, Ind. Educator, author. *John Dewey's Logical Theory* (with R. H. Gault, 1918); *An Outline of General Psychology* (1924); *Analytical Syllogistics* (1946); etc. Philosophy dept., Northwestern University, since 1916.

HOWARD, ELIZABETH METZGER (Mrs. Frank Liddon-Howard), b. Wilkes-Barre, Pa. Novelist. *Before the Sun Goes Down* (1946).

HOWARD, ERIC (May 18, 1895–May 17, 1943); b. Baltimore, Md. Biographer, playwright. *Famous California of Today and Yesterday* (1923); *The Alien* (with George Bronson Howard, 1927); *Pretty Fast* (with same, 1927); *These Artists* (with same, 1929).

HOWARD, FLORENCE RUTH (Mrs. Philip MacDonald) (1902–); b. Wolford, N.D. Author. *Green Entry* (1940); *View from a Window* (1942); *Sailmaker* (1948).

HOWARD, GEORGE [Fitzalan] **BRONSON** (Jan. 7, 1884–Nov. 20, 1922); b. "The Relay," Howard Co., Md. Journalist, novelist, playwright. *The Snobs* (prod. 1911); *The Red Light of Mars* (1913); *God's Man* (1915); *Birds of Prey* (1918); *The Black Book* (1920); *The Devil's Chaplain* (1922); *The Alien* (with Eric Howard, 1927); *Pretty Fast* (with same, 1927); *These Artists* (with same, 1929); etc.

HOWARD, GEORGE ELLIOTT (Oct. 1, 1849–June 9, 1928); b. Saratoga, N.Y. Educator, historian. *A History of Matrimonial Institutions*, 3v. (1904); *Preliminaries of the Revolution* (1905); etc. Prof. science and sociology, University of Nebraska, 1906–28.

HOWARD, H. R. Author. *The History of Virgil A. Stewart* (1836); *The Life and Adventures of John A. Murrell, the Great Western Land Pirate* (1847); *The Life and Adventures of Joseph T. Hare, the Bold Robber and Highwayman* (anon., 1847); *The Life and Adventures of Henry Thomas, the Western Burglar and Murderer* (anon., 1848).

HOWARD, HARRY NICHOLAS (Feb. 19, 1902–); b. Excelsior Springs, Mo. Educator, government official, author. *The Partition of Turkey* (1931); *Study in the Recent History of the Balkan and Near Eastern Peoples* (1936); and other books mainly concerning the Balkan area. History dept., Miami University, Oxford, O. 1930–42; with Department of State, since 1942. Prof. Middle East Affairs, American University, since 1968. Assoc. editor, *Middle East Journal.*

HOWARD, JAMES QUAY (1836–Nov. 15, 1912); b. Newark, N.J. Librarian, journalist, author. *The Life, Public Services and Select Speeches of Rutherford B. Hayes* (1876); *History of the Louisiana Purchase* (1902); etc. Reference librarian, Library of Congress, 1897–1912.

HOWARD, J[ohn] **GORDON** (Dec. 3, 1899–); b. Tokyo. Clergyman of the Evangelical United Brethren Church, author. *When Youth Worship* (1940); *A Catechism for Youth* (1942); *Christian Belief for Christian Youth* (1950); *Small Windows in a Big World* (1969).

HOWARD, JOHN RAYMOND (May 25, 1837–Dec. 29, 1926); b. Brooklyn, N.Y. Publisher, editor, author. *Henry Ward Beecher* (1891); *Remembrance of Things Past* (1925); etc. Editor: *Best American Essays* (1910); *Poems of Friendship* (1911); *The Changing Year* (1913); *Poems of Heroism* (1922); etc.

HOWARD, JOHN TASKER (Nov. 30, 1890–Nov. 20, 1964); b. Brooklyn, N.Y. Music critic, composer. *Our American Music* (1931); *Stephen Foster, America's Troubadour* (1934); *Ethelbert Nevin* (1935); *The World's Great Operas* (1948); *A Short History of American Music* (with James Lyons, 1957); etc. Music editor, *McCall's Magazine*, 1928–30; *Cue* magazine, 1937–38.

HOWARD, JOSEPH KINSEY (1906–Aug. 25, 1951); b. in Iowa. Editor, author. *Montana—High, Wide and Handsome* (1943); *Strange Empire* (1952). Editor: *Montana Margins* (1946). News editor, Great Falls (Mont.) *Leader.*

HOWARD, LEON (Nov. 8, 1903–); b. Talladega, Ala. Educator, author. *The Connecticut Wits* (1943); *Herman Melville, a Biography* (1951); *Victorian Knight-Errant: A Study of the Early Literary Career of James Russell Lowell* (1952); *Literature and the American Tradition* (1960); *The Mind of Jonathan Edwards* (1963). Prof. English, Northwestern University, since 1943.

HOWARD, OLIVER OTIS (Nov. 8, 1830–Oct. 26, 1909); b. Leeds, Me. Army officer, author. *General Taylor* (1892); *Autobiography* (1907); *My Life and Experiences among Our Hostile Indians* (1907); *Famous Indian Chiefs I Have Known* (1908); etc.

HOWARD, PHILIP EUGENE (Apr. 1, 1870–June 22, 1946); b. Lynn, Mass. Editor, author. *The Life Story of Henry Clay Trumbull* (1905); *Boy-Talks* (1920); *Father and Son* (1922); *Living through These Days* (1930); *Charles G. Trumbull* (1944); etc. With *Sunday School Times*, Philadelphia, from 1891; president, Sunday School Times Co.

Howard, Police Captain. Pen name of Luis Philip Senarens.

HOWARD, RICHARD (1929–   ); b. Cleveland, O. Poet. *Quantities* (1962); *The Damages* (1967); *Untitled Subjects* (1969, Pulitzer prize, 1970).

HOWARD, ROBERT WEST (Apr. 7, 1908–); b. Addison, N.Y. Editor, author. *Two Billion Acre Farm* (1945); *The Real Book about Farms* (1952); etc. Editor: *This Is the West* (1957); *This Is the South* (1959); *The Great Iron Trail* (1962);

The Wagonmen (1964); *The Flag of the Dreadful Bear* (1965); *Eli Whitney* (1966); *The Boatmen* (1967); *First Book of Farms* (1968); *Niagara Falls* (1969). Editor, *Pathfinder*, 1943–45.

HOWARD, ROY W[ilson] (Jan. 1, 1883–Nov. 20, 1964); b. Gano, O. Publisher, editor. Head of Scripps-Howard chain of newspapers, including New York *Telegram*, purchased 1927, New York *World*, purchased 1931; and New York *Sun*, purchased 1950; pres., New York *World-Telegram and Sun*, since 1950. An executive officer of the United Press, The Newspaper Enterprise Assn., etc.

HOWARD, SIDNEY [Coe] (June 26, 1891–Aug. 23, 1939); b. Oakland, Calif. Playwright. *Swords* (prod. 1921); *They Knew What They Wanted* (prod. 1925, Pulitzer prize play, 1926); *Lucky Sam McCarver* (prod. 1925); *Ned McCobb's Daughter* (prod. 1926); *The Silver Cord* (prod. 1926); *Salvation* (with Charles MacArthur, prod. 1928); *Yellow Jack* (publ. 1928, prod. 1934); *Alien Corn* (publ. 1931, prod. 1933); *The Late Christopher Bean* (prod. 1932); *Paths of Glory* (with Humphrey Cobb, prod. 1935); *The Ghost of Yankee Doodle* (prod. 1937); *Lute Song* (with Will Irwin, prod. 1946); *Madam, Will You Walk?* (prod. 1953); etc. See Fred B. Millett's *Contemporary American Authors* (1940).

Howard, Warren. Pen name of James Noble Gifford.

HOWE, DELIA AKELEY (Dec. 5, 1875–); b. Beaver Dam, Wis. Explorer, author. *J. T. Jr.: The Biography of an African Monkey* (1928); *Jungle Portraits* (1930); *All True* (1931).

HOWE, EDGAR WATSON (May 3, 1853–Oct. 3, 1937); b. Treaty, Ind. Editor, author. Known as the "Sage of Potato Hill." *The Story of a Country Town* (1883); *The Anthology of Another Town* (1920); *Plain People* (autobiography, 1929); etc. Editor, *Atchison Daily Globe*, 1877–1911; publisher, *E. W. Howe's Monthly*, 1911–33.

HOWE, GEORGE (Sept. 22, 1881–); b. New Orleans, La. Real estate businessman, author. *Mathematics for the Practical Man* (1908); *Economics for the Practical Man* (1948); *Memoirs of a Westchester Realtor* (1959).

HOWE, GEORGE [Locke] (Apr. 19, 1898–   ); b. Bristol, R.I. Novelist. *Slaves' Cottage* (1935); *Call It Treason* (1949); *Heart Alone* (1953).

HOWE, HELEN HUNTINGTON (Jan. 11, 1905–); b. Boston, Mass. Author. *The Whole Heart* (1943); *We Happy Few* (1946); *The Circle of the Day* (1950); *The Success* (1956); *The Fires of Autumn* (1959); *The Gentle Americans* (1965).

HOWE, HENRY (Oct. 11, 1816–Oct. 14, 1893); b. New Haven, Conn. Historian. Compiler: *Historical Collections of the Great West* (1851); *Travels and Adventures of Celebrated Travelers* (1853); *Adventures and Achievements of Americans* (1859); and other similar works.

HOWE, IRVING (1920–); b. New York. Educator, author. *The UAW and Walter Reuther* (with B. J. Widick, 1949); *Sherwood Anderson* (1951); *Politics and the Novel* (1957); *The American Communist Party* (1958); etc. Editor: *Modern Literary Criticism* (1959); *Steady Work* (1966). Co-editor: *A Treasury of Yiddish Stories* (1954). English dept., Brandeis University, 1953–61. Prof. English, Hunter College. Editor, *Dissent* Magazine.

HOWE, JULIA WARD (May 27, 1819–Oct. 17, 1910); b. New York. Reformer, author. *Passion Flowers* (poems, anon., 1854); *The World's Own* (play, 1857); *Later Lyrics* (1866); *Margaret Fuller* (1883); *From Sunset Ridge* (poems, 1898); *Reminiscences* (1899); etc. Editor: *Sex and Education* (1878); *Sketches of Representative New England Women* (1904). Her best-known poem is "The Battle Hymn of the Republic" (q.v.). Assoc. editor, the *Woman's Journal*. See Laura E. Richards's and Maude Elliott's *Julia Ward Howe*, 2v. (1915).

HOWE, MARK ANTONY DE WOLFE (Aug. 28, 1864–Dec. 6, 1960); b. Bristol, R.I. Author: *Shadows* (poems, 1897); *American Bookmen* (1898); *Phillips Brooks* (1899); *Life and Letters of George Bancroft*, 2v. (1908); *Harmonies* (poems, 1909); *Life and Labors of Bishop Hare, Apostle to the Sioux* (1911); *The Atlantic Monthly and Its Makers* (1919); *George von Lengerke Meyer: His Life and Public Services* (1919); *Memories of a Hostess* (1922); *Barrett Wendell and His Letters* (1924, Pulitzer Prize for American biography, 1925); *Causes and Their Champions* (1926); *Classic Shades* (1928); *James Ford Rhodes, American Historian* (1929); *Yankee Ballads* (1930); *Portrait of an Independent: Moorfield Storey, 1845–1929* (1932); *The Children's Judge: Frederick Pickering Cabot* (1932); *Songs of September* (1934); *A Venture in Remembrance* (1941); *Boston Landmarks* (1946); *Personae Gratae* (1953); *Sundown: Later and Earlier Selected Poems* (1955); etc. Editor: *The Beacon Biographies*, 31v. (1899–1910); *Letters of C. E. Norton*, 2v. (with Sarah Norton, 1913); *New Letters of James Russell Lowell* (1932); *John Jay Chapman and His Letters* (1937); *The Articulate Sisters* (1946); *The Scholar-Friends: Letters of Francis Jane Child and James Russell Lowell* (with G. W. Cottrell, Jr., 1952). Assoc. editor, *Youth's Companion*, 1888–93, 1899–1913; editor, *Harvard Alumni Bulletin*, 1913–19; etc.

HOWE, MARK DE WOLFE (May 22, 1906–Feb. 28, 1967); b. Boston, Mass. Lawyer, author, editor. Editor: *Holmes-Pollock Letters*, 2v. (1941); *Touched with Fire: Civil War Letters of Oliver Wendell Holmes, Jr.* (1946); *Readings in American Legal History* (1949); *Holmes-Laski Letters, 1916–1935*, 2v. (1953); *Justice Oliver Wendell Holmes: The Shaping Years, 1841–1870* (1957); *Justice Holmes: The Proving Years 1870–1882* (1963).

HOWE, QUINCY (Aug. 17, 1900–); b. Boston, Mass., son of Mark Antony de Wolfe Howe. Editor, author. *World Diary: 1929–1934* (1934); *England Expects Every American to Do His Duty* (1937); *Blood Is Cheaper Than Water* (1939); *The News and How to Understand It* (1940); *A World History of Our Own Times*, 2v. (1949–53); etc. Editor, *Living Age*, 1929–35; with Atlantic Monthly Co., 1922–28; with Simon & Schuster, 1935–42; news analyst, American Broadcasting Co., 1954–63.

HOWE, SAMUEL GRIDLEY (Nov. 10, 1801–Jan. 9, 1876); b. Boston, Mass. Philanthropist, educator. Husband of Julia Ward Howe. *Letters and Journals*, ed. by his daughter, Laura E. Richards, 2v. (1906–09). Director, Massachusetts School for the Blind, 1831–76. See Franklin B. Sanborn's *Dr. S. G. Howe, the Philanthropist* (1891); Julia Ward Howe's *Memoir of Dr. Samuel Gridley Howe* (1876).

HOWE, WILL D[avid] (Aug. 25, 1873–Dec. 6, 1946); b. Charlestown, Ind. Educator, editor. Co-author: *The Howe Readers* (1909); *Gate to English* (1915); *Modern Student's Book of English Literature* (1924); *The Literature of America*, 2v. (1929); *American Authors and Books* (1943); *Charles Lamb and His Friends* (1944). Editor: *Modern Student's Library; How to Know the Great Authors* series; etc. English dept., Indiana University, 1906–19; with Harcourt, Brace & Howe, 1919–21; editor and director, Charles Scribner's Sons, 1921–42.

HOWE, WILLIAM THOMAS HILDRUP (1874–Aug. 19, 1939); b. Boston, Mass. Book collector. President, American Book Co., 1931–39. His large library of nineteenth and twentieth century English and American literature was bought by Dr. Albert A. Berg and presented to The New York Public Library in 1940.

HOWE, WILLIAM WIRT (1833–1909); b. Canandaigua, N.Y. Lawyer, author. *The Pasha Papers* (under pen name, "Mohammed Pasha," 1859); *Municipal History of New Orleans* (1889).

Howell, Soskin & Co. New York. Publishers. Founded 1940. William Soskin, literary critic, was one of the founders. Frank

Mannheim was president. In 1948 the house was acquired by Crown Publishers, Inc.

HOWELL, WILBUR SAMUEL (Apr. 22, 1904–); b. Wayne, N.Y. Educator, author. *The Rhetoric of Alcuin and Charlemagne* (ed. and translator, 1941); *Problems and Styles of Communication* (ed., 1945); Fenelon's *Dialogues on Eloquence* (translator, 1951); *Logic and Rhetoric in England: 1500–1700* (1956). Editor, *Quarterly Journal of Speech,* 1954–56. Prof. rhetoric and oratory, Princeton University, since 1955.

HOWELLS, WILLIAM DEAN (Mar. 1, 1837–May 11, 1920); b. Martin's Ferry, O. Critic, novelist, poet, playwright. *Venetian Life* (1866); *Their Wedding Journey* (1872); *A Chance Acquaintance* (1873); *Poems* (1873); *A Foregone Conclusion* (1875); *The Parlor Car* (1876); *A Counterfeit Presentment* (1877); *The Lady of the Aroostook* (1879); *The Undiscovered Country* (1880); *A Modern Instance* (1882); *A Woman's Reason* (1883); *The Rise of Silas Lapham* (1885); *Indian Summer* (1886); *The Minister's Charge* (1887); *April Hopes* (1888); *Annie Kilburn* (1889); *The Mouse-Trap, and Other Farces* (1889); *A Boy's Town* (1890); *A Hazard of New Fortunes* (1890); *Criticism and Fiction* (1891); *The Quality of Mercy* (1892); *The Coast of Bohemia* (1893); *The Unexpected Guests* (1893); *A Traveler from Altruria* (1894); *Stops of Various Quills* (poems, 1894); *My Literary Passions* (1895); *Impressions and Experiences* (1896); *The Landlord and the Lion's Head* (1897); *Their Silver Wedding Journey* (1899); *Literary Friends and Acquaintances* (1900); *The Smoking Car* (1900); *Heroines of Fiction* (1901); *The Kentons* (1902); *Literature and Life* (1902); *Through the Eye of the Needle* (1907); *Fennel and Rue* (1908); *Imaginary Interviews* (1910); *My Mark Twain* (1910); *New Leaf Mills* (1913); *The Leatherwood God* (1916); *Years of My Youth* (1916); *Eighty Years and After* (1921); *Selected Writings,* ed. by Henry Steele Commager (1950); *Complete Plays,* ed. by W. J. Meserve (1960). Editor, the *Atlantic Monthly,* 1866–81; *Cosmopolitan* magazine, 1891–92. Wrote the "Easy Chair" department in *Harper's Monthly,* 1900–21. See Mildred Howells's *Life in Letters of William Dean Howells,* 2v. (1928); Van Wyck Brooks's *Howells: His Life and Work* (1959); Clara M. Kirk's *W. D. Howells and Art in His Time* (1965).

HOWELLS, WILLIAM WHITE (Nov. 27, 1908–); b. New York. Educator, anthropologist. *Mankind So Far* (1944); *The Heathens* (1948); *Back of History* (1954); *Mankind in the Making* (1959). Prof. anthropology, Harvard University, since 1954. Editor, *American Naturalist,* since 1967.

HOWES, BARBARA (Mrs. William Jay Smith) (May 1, 1914–); b. New York. Poet. *The Undersea Farmer* (1948); *In the Cold Country* (1954); *Light and Dark* (1959); *Looking up at Leaves* (poems, 1966); *From the Green Antilles* (1966); etc.

HOWES, ROYCE B. (Jan. 3, 1901–); b. Minneapolis, Minn. Author. *Death on the Bridge* (1935); *The Callao Clue* (1936); *Night of the Garter Murder* (1937); *Death Dupes a Lady* (1937); *Murder at Maneuvers* (1938); *Nasty Names Murders* (1939); *Death Rides a Hobby* (1939); *Case of the Copy Hook Killing* (1945); *Edgar A. Guest, a Biography* (1953); etc.

HOWISON, GEORGE HOLMES (Nov. 29, 1834–Dec. 31, 1916); b. Montgomery Co., Md. Educator, philosopher, author: *The Limits of Evolution and Other Essays* (1901); and other books on philosophy.

"Howl." Poem by Allen Ginsberg (1956). Best-known poem by the leading poet of the Beat Generation. Noted for its expressive cry of outrage against a world whose spiritual degradation is stifling the "best minds" of the young author's generation.

HOWLAND, ARTHUR CHARLES (Dec. 24, 1869–Mar. 28, 1952); b. Danby, N.Y. Educator, author. *World History Today* (1927); etc. Editor: Lea's *Materials Towards a History of Witchcraft,* 3v. (1939); Lea's *Minor Historical Writings and Other Essays* (1942); etc. Henry Charles Lea professor of European history, University of Pennsylvania, 1934–40.

HOWLAND, FRANCES LOUISE MORSE (b. Jan. 5, 1855); b. Lockport, N.Y. Author. Pen name, "Kenyon West." *Onward* (1877); *Broken Bonds* (1889); *The Laureates of England* (1895); *Cliveden* (1903); etc.

HOWLAND, HAROLD [Jacobs] (June 29, 1877–June 19, 1966); b. Chatham, N.Y. Writer, author. *Theodore Roosevelt and His Times* (1925). On editorial staff, *The Outlook,* 1902–13; assoc. editor, *The Independent,* 1913–20; with Ginn and Co., from 1952.

HOWLAND, HEWITT HANSON (Oct. 8, 1863–May 10, 1944); b. Indianapolis, Ind. Editor, author. *Dwight Whitney Morrow* (1930). Editor, The Bobbs-Merrill Co., 1900–25; editor, *The Century,* 1925–31.

HOWLAND, LOUIS (June 13, 1857–1934); b. Indianapolis, Ind. Editor, author. *Day unto Day* (1911); *Stephen A. Douglas* (1920); *The Mind of Jesus* (1926). Editor *Indianapolis News,* 1911–1934.

HOWLETT, DUNCAN (May 15, 1906–); b. Newton, Mass. Unitarian clergyman, author. *Man Against the Church* (1954); *The Essenes and Christianity* (1957); *The Fourth American Faith* (1964); *Contemporary Accents in Liberal Religion* (1960); *No Greater Love* (1966).

HOWLEY, FRANK LEO (Feb. 4, 1903–); b. Hampton, N.J. Educator, author. *Berlin Command* (1950); *Your War for Peace* (1953); *Peoples and Policies* (1959); *An African Alamo* (1962); *Berlin and the Western Cause; The African State That Tried to Help Itself* (1964); etc. Vice-president, New York University, 1952–67. Vice-President: Bache and Co. since 1967.

HOYT, CHARLES HALE (July 26, 1860–Nov. 20, 1900); b. Concord, N.H. Playwright. *A Bunch of Keys* (with W. Edouin, prod. 1882; *Cezalia* (prod. 1882); *A Parlor Match* (prod. 1884); *A Tin Soldier* (prod. 1886); *A Hole in the Ground* (prod. 1887); *A Brass Monkey* (prod. 1888); *A Midnight Bell* (prod. 1889); *A Texas Steer* (prod. 1890); *A Trip to Chinatown* (prod. 1891); *A Temperance Town* (prod. 1893); *A Milk White Flag* (prod. 1893); *A Black Sheep* (1896); *A Contented Woman* (prod. 1897); *A Stranger in New York* (prod. 1897); etc. Hoyt's manuscript plays are deposited in The New York Public Library.

HOYT, NANCY (Oct. 1, 1902–); b. Washington, D.C. Novelist. *Roundabout* (1926); *Unkind Star* (1927); *Bright Intervals* (1929); *Cupboard Love* (1930); *Three Cornered Love* (1932); *Career Man* (1933); *Susan Errant* (1934); *Elinor Wylie: The Portrait of an Unknown Lady* (1935); etc.

HOYT, RALPH (Apr. 18, 1806–Oct. 11, 1878); b. New York City. Episcopal clergyman, poet. *A Chant of Life, and Other Poems, with Sketches and Essays,* in parts (1844–45); *Sketches of Life and Landscape,* in parts (1846–47); *Echoes of Memory and Emotion* (anon., 1859); etc.

HOYT, VANCE JOSEPH (Apr. 27, 1889–); b. Arkansas City, Kan. Naturalist, author. *Silver Boy* (1929); *Malibu* (1931); *Bar-Rac: The Biography of a Raccoon* (1931); *Zorra* (1932); *Song Dog* (1939); *Yankee Doodle Goes West* (1940); etc. Wrote nature column, "Rob Wagner's Script," 1930–39.

HRDLICKA, ALEŠ (Mar. 29, 1869–Sept. 5, 1943); b. Humpolec, Bohemia. Anthropologist, author. *The Old Americans* (1925); etc. Founder, *American Journal of Physical Anthropology,* 1918; editor, from 1918. Curator of anthropology, United States National Museum, from 1910.

HSU, FRANCIS LANG KWANG (Oct. 28, 1909–); b. Chuang Ho, China. Educator, author. *Under the Ancestors' Shadow* (1948); *Religion, Science, and Human Crises* (1952); *Americans and Chinese: Two Ways of Life* (1953). Editor: *Aspects of Culture and Personality* (1954); *Kinship and Culture* (1968); *The Study of Literate Civilizations* (1969). Prof. anthropology, Northwestern University, since 1955.

HUBBARD, BERNARD ROSECRANS (Nov. 24, 1888–May 28, 1962); b. San Francisco, Calif. Roman Catholic clergyman, explorer, author. *Mush, You Malemutes!* (1932); *Cradle of the Storms* (1935); and reports of surveys of Alaska area. With University of Santa Clara, Calif., from 1926.

HUBBARD, ELBERT (June 19, 1856–May 7, 1915); b. Bloomington, Ill. Editor, publisher, author. *One Day: A Tale of the Prairies* (1893); *Forbes of Harvard* (1894); *A Message to Garcia* (1899); also numerous *Little Journeys;* etc. Founder, *The Philistine,* 1895; editor, 1895–1915; founder, *The Fra,* 1908; editor, 1908–15. Founder the Roycroft Shop, East Aurora, N.Y. *See* Felix Shay's *Elbert Hubbard of East Aurora* (1926).

HUBBARD, "KIN" [Frank McKinney] (Sept. 1, 1868–Dec. 26, 1930); b. Bellefontaine, O. Humorist, caricaturist. Created character of "Abe Martin." *Abe Martin, Brown County Indiana* (1906) and twenty-five other "Abe Martin" books (1907–30). *Short Furrows* (1911) and *Abe Martin's Wisecracks* (1930) are selections from them. The first "Abe Martin" sketch appeared in the *Indianapolis News,* Dec. 31, 1904. On staff, the *Indianapolis News,* 1891–1930, except for a short interval. *See* Blanche Stillson's *Abe Martin—Kin Hubbard* (1939).

HUBBARD, WILLIAM (c. 1621–Sept. 14, 1704); b. in England. Congregational clergyman, historian. *Narrative of the Troubles with the Indians in New England* (1677); *A General History of New England from the Discovery to MDCLXXX* (published by the Massachusetts Historical Society, 1815); etc.

HUBBARD, WYNANT DAVIS (Aug. 28, 1900–Dec. 9, 1961); b. Kansas City, Mo. Naturalist, author. *Wild Animals* (1925); *Bong'kwe* (1930); *The Thousandth Frog* (1934); *Fiasco in Ethiopia* (1936); *Wild Animal Hunter* (1958).

HUBBELL, JAY BROADUS (May 8, 1885–); b. in Smyth Co., Va. Educator, editor, author. *An Introduction to Poetry* (with John Owen Beaty, 1922); *An Introduction to Drama* (with same, 1927); *The Enjoyment of Literature* (1936); *The South in American Literature, 1607–1900* (1954); *Southern Life in Fiction* (1960); *South and Southwest* (1965); Editor: *The Last Years of Henry Timrod, 1864–1867* (1941). Editor, *Southwest Review,* 1924–27; chairman, board of editors, *American Literature;* 1928–54. Prof. English, Duke University, 1927–54.

HUBBELL, LINDLEY WILLIAMS (June 3, 1901–); b. Hartford, Conn. Librarian, poet. *Dark Pavilion* (1927); *The Tracing of a Portal* (1931); *Winter-Burning* (1938); *Long Island Triptych* (1947); *Lectures on Shakespeare* (1958); *Seventy Poems* (1965). Co-editor, *The Measure,* 1926. With The New York Public Library, since 1925.

HUBBELL, MARTHA STONE (1814–1856); b. Oxford, Conn. Author. *The Shady Side; or, Life in a Country Parsonage* (1853); *The Memorial; or, The Life and Writings of an Only Daughter,* ed. by A. L. Stone (1857); etc.

HUBBELL, MARY ELIZABETH (Dec. 5, 1833–June 10, 1854); b. Mt. Carmel, Hamden, Conn., daughter of Martha Stone Hubbell. Author. *See* Martha Stone Hubbell's *The Memorial; or, The Life and Writings of an Only Daughter* (1857).

HUBER, MIRIAM BLANTON; b. Lynchburg, Tenn. Educator, editor. Author or co-author: *Skags, the Milk Horse* (1931); *Cinder, the Cat* (1931); the *Wonder Story* books, 3v. (1938); *The Painted Calf* (1939); etc. Editor: *The Poetry Book,* 9v. (with others, 1926); *The Work-Play Books,* 12v. (1930); *Story and Verse for Children* (1940); etc. Prof. education, Arizona State Teachers College, 1935–37.

HUBLER, RICHARD GIBSON (Aug. 20, 1912–); b. Scranton, Pa. Editor, author. *Lou Gehrig* (1941); *Flying Leathernecks* (with J. A. DeChant, 1944); *I've Got Mine* (1946); *The Quiet Kingdom* (1948); *The Chase* (1952); *In Darkest Childhood* (1954); *The Man in the Sky* (1956); *SAC: Strategic Air Command* (1958); *True Love, True Love* (1959); *Straight Up* (1961); *The Christianis* (1966); etc. Departmental editor, *Newsweek,* 1935–39; *PM,* 1940–42.

HUBNER, CHARLES WILLIAM (Jan. 16, 1835–Jan. 3, 1929); b. Baltimore, Md. Librarian, poet. *Wild Flowers* (poems, 1876); *Poems and Essays* (1881); *War Poets of the South* (1896); *Representative Southern Poets* (1906); *Poems* (1906); *Poems of Faith and Consolation* (1927). Asst. librarian, Carnegie Library, Atlanta, Ga., 1899–1919.

HUCKEL, OLIVER (Jan. 11, 1864–Feb. 3, 1940); b. Philadelphia, Pa. Congregational clergyman, author. *The Larger Life* (poems, 1900); *Through England with Tennyson* (1913); *A Dreamer of Dreams* (1916); etc.

Huckleberries Gathered from New England Hills. Short stories by Rose Terry Cooke (1891). Contains what is perhaps the author's best story, "The Town and Country Mouse."

HUDDLESTON, JOHN HOMER (Feb. 9, 1869–); b. Cleveland, O. Educator, author. *Essentials of New Testament Greek* (1895); *Attitude of the Greek Tragedians Towards Art* (1897); *Lessons From Greek Pottery* (1902); etc. With University of Maine, from 1899.

HUDSON, ARTHUR PALMER (May 4, 1892–); b. Palmer's Hall, Attala Co., Miss. Educator, author. *Folksongs of Mississippi and Their Background* (1936); *The Singing South* (1936); *Folklore in America* (with John T. Flanagan, 1958); *Folklore Keeps the Past Alive* (1962). Editor: *Specimens of Mississippi Folklore* (1928); *Humor of the Old Deep South* (1936); *Folk Tunes from Mississippi* (with others, 1937); etc. Editor, *North Carolina Folklore,* since 1954. English dept., University of North Carolina, since 1930.

HUDSON, CHARLES (Nov. 14, 1795–May 4, 1881); b. Marlboro, Mass. *A History of the Town of Westminster* (1832); *Doubts Concerning the Battle of Bunker Hill* (1857); *History of the Town of Marlborough* (1862); etc. Editor, the *Boston Daily Atlas.*

HUDSON, HELEN. Author. *Tell the Time to None* (1966); *Meyer Meyer* (1967).

HUDSON, HENRY NORMAN (Jan. 28, 1814–Jan. 16, 1886); b. Cornwall, Vt. Episcopal clergyman, Shakespearean scholar, editor, author. *Lectures on Shakespeare,* 2v. (1848); *A Chaplain's Campaigns with General Butler* (1865); *Shakespeare: His Life, Art, and Characters,* 2v. (1872); *Studies in Wordsworth* (1884); *Essays on English Studies* (1906); etc. Editor: "Harvard Edition" of Shakespeare, 20v. (1880–81). Editor, the *Churchman,* 1852–55; the *American Church Monthly,* 1857–58.

HUDSON, JAY WILLIAM (Mar. 12, 1874–May 11, 1958); b. Cleveland, O. Educator, author. *The College and the New America* (1920); *The Truths We Live By* (1921); *Abbé Pierre* (1922); *Nowhere Else in the World* (1923); *The Eternal Cycle* (1925); *Abbé Pierre's People* (1928); *The Old Faiths Perish* (1939); *Prayers of Aspiration* (1950); etc. Philosophy dept., University of Missouri, 1908–44.

Hudson, Mary Clemmer Ames. See Mary Clemmer Ames.

HUDSON, WILLIAM CADWALADER (Nov. 14, 1843–Oct. 16, 1915); b. New Brunswick, N.J. Journalist, novelist. *The Diamond Button* (1888); *The Dugdale Millions* (1892); *Random Recollections of an Old Political Reporter* (1911); etc.

HUDSON, WINTHROP STILL (Aug. 28, 1911–); b. Schoolcraft, Mich. Baptist clergyman, author. *John Ponet: Advocate of Limited Monarchy* (1942); *The Great Tradition of the American Churches* (1953); *The Story of the Christian Church* (1958); *Understanding Roman Catholicism* (1959); *American Protestantism* (1961); *Religion in America* (1965).

Hudson Review, The. New York. Literary quarterly. Founded 1948. Edited by Frederick Morgan. Published articles, stories, and verse by such writers as Saul Bellow, R. P. Blackmur, Ezra Pound, Allen Tate, Eudora Welty, Mark Schorer, Herbert Gold, Harold Rosenberg, W. D. Snodgrass, Louis Simpson, and Robert Lowell.

HUESTON, ETHEL (Dec. 3, 1887–); b. Cincinnati, O. Author. The *Prudence* series, 3v. (1915–24); the *Ginger* series, 3v. (1927–30); *Star of the West: The Romance of the Lewis and Clark Expedition* (1935); *Calamity Jane of Deadwood Gulch* (1937); *High Bridge* (1938); *The Honorable Uncle Lancy* (1939); *Preacher's Wife* (1941); *Drink to Me Only* (1943); *No Shortage of Men* (1945); *The Family Takes a Wife* (1950); etc.

HUGGENVIK, THEODORE (Oct. 22, 1889–); b. Mandal, Nor. Lutheran clergyman, educator, author. *Fourteen Men Who Knew Christ* (1931); *The Approach to Jesus* (1934); *An Outline of Church History* (1935); *Search the Scriptures* (1936); *Your Key to the Bible* (1944); *We Believe* (1950); *Victory by the Cross* (1954); *A God Who Likes Me* (1956). Dept. religion, St. Olaf College, since 1926.

"Hugh Selwyn Mauberley." Poem by Ezra Pound (1920). T. S. Eliot called it "a document of an epoch . . . genuine tragedy and comedy."

Hugh Wynne, Free Quaker. Novel by S. Weir Mitchell (1897). Story of Philadelphia during the American Revolution. Told in the form of an autobiography of Hugh Wynne, who becomes an officer on General George Washington's staff. He engages in most of the stirring battles, and while he is away other gallants try to win the hand of his sweetheart. A grim old merchant father figures in the story.

HUGHES, AGNES LOCKHART; b. Halifax, N.S. Editor, music critic, poet. *Gems from Scotia's Crown* (1898); *Told in the Garden* (1901). Music critic and assoc. editor, *Seattle Mail and Herald*, since 1903.

HUGHES, CHARLES EVANS (Apr. 11, 1862–Aug. 27, 1948); b. Glens Falls, N.Y. Jurist, author. *Conditions of Progress in Democratic Government* (1909); *The Pathway of Peace and Other Addresses* (1925); *The Supreme Court of the United States* (1927); etc. Governor of New York, 1907–10; assoc. justice, U.S. Supreme Court, 1910–16; Secretary of State, 1921–25; chief justice, U.S. Supreme Court, 1930–41. *See* Merlo John Pusey's *Charles Evans Hughes,* 2v. (1951).

HUGHES, DOROTHY B[elle Flanagan] (1904–); b. Kansas City, Mo. Author. *Dark Certainty* (poems, 1931); *The So Blue Marble* (1940); *The Cross-Eyed Bear* (1940); *The Fallen Sparrow* (1942); *The Bamboo Blonde* (1943); *The Delicate Ape* (1944); *Ride the Pink Horse* (1946); *In a Lonely Place* (1947); *The Candy Kid* (1950); *The Davidian Report* (1952); etc.

HUGHES, EDWIN HOLT (Dec. 7, 1866–Feb. 12, 1950); b. Moundsville, W.Va. Methodist bishop, author. *Letters on Evangelism* (1907); *A Boy's Religion* (1914); *Christianity and Success* (1928); *Evangelism and Change* (1938); *I Was Made a Minister* (autobiography, 1943); etc.

HUGHES, ELINOR L[ambert] (Mar. 3, 1906–); b. Cambridge, Mass. Drama editor and reviewer. *Famous Stars of Filmdom* (1932); etc. Drama and film editor and reviewer, Boston *Herald-Traveler, 1934–66.*

HUGHES, EMMET JOHN (Dec. 26, 1920–); b. Newark, N.J. Editor, author. *The Church and the Liberal Society* (1943); *Report from Spain* (1947); *America the Vincible* (1959); *The Ordeal of Power* (1963). With *Time, Life, Fortune,* 1946–63; *Newsweek* and *Washington Post* 1963–68.

HUGHES, GLENN [Arthur] (Dec. 7, 1894–); b. Cozad, Neb. Educator, playwright, poet. *Souls, and Other Poems* (1917); *Broken Lights* (poems, 1920); *The Story of the Theatre* (1928); *Imagism & the Imagists* (1931); *What Do You Think?*

(1932); *Dollars to Doughnuts* (1934); *Say It With Flowers* (1935); *Miss Millions* (1937); *Spring Fever* (1937); *Running Wild* (1939); *Imagism and the Imagists* (1941); *Fresh Air* (play, 1946); *Mrs. Carlyle* (play, 1950); *A History of the American Theatre, 1700–1950* (1951); *Notion Counter* (poems, 1953); *Trivia* (poems, 1956); etc. Prof. drama, University of Washington, since 1930.

HUGHES, HATCHER (Feb. 12, 1881–Oct. 17, 1945); b. Polkville, N.C. Educator, playwright. *A Marriage Made in Heaven* (1918); *Wake Up, Jonathan* (with Elmer Rice, prod. 1921); *Hell-Bent for Heaven* (prod. 1924, Pulitzer prize play, 1924); *Ruint* (prod. 1925); etc. English dept., Columbia University, from 1910.

HUGHES, H[enry] STUART (May 7, 1916–); b. New York. Educator, author. *An Essay for Our Times* (1950); *Oswald Spengler: A Critical Estimate* (1952); *The United States and Italy* (1953); *Consciousness and Society* (1958); *Contemporary Europe: A History* (1961); *An Approach to Peace* (1962); *History as Art and Science* (1965); *Contemporary Europe* (1966); *The Obstructed Path* (1968). Prof. history, Harvard University, since 1957.

HUGHES, JOHN [Joseph] (June 24, 1797–Jan. 3, 1864); b. Annaloghan, Co. Tyrone, Ireland. Roman Catholic archbishop, author. *Complete Works of the Most Rev. John Hughes,* ed. by Lawrence Kehoe, 2v. (1866). Founder: *Catholic Herald* (1833). In 1839 he purchased the Rose Hill estate near Fordham and established a seminary there, which became St. John's College in 1841, and eventually Fordham University.

HUGHES, LANGSTON [James] (Feb. 1, 1902–May 22, 1967); b. Joplin, Mo. Poet, novelist, playwright. *The Weary Blues* (poems, 1926); *Fine Clothes to the Jew* (poems, 1927); *Not Without Laughter* (1930); *Dear Lovely Death* (poems, 1931); *Popo and Fifina* (1932); *The Dream Keeper* (poems, 1932); *Scottsboro Limited* (plays and poems, 1932); *The Ways of White Folk* (stories, 1934); *Mulatto* (prod. 1935); *A New Song* (1938); *The Big Sea* (autobiography, 1940); *Freedom's Plow* (poems, 1943); *Shakespeare in Harlem* (poems, 1942); *Fields of Wonder* (poems, 1947); *One-Way Ticket* (poems, 1949); *Simple Speaks His Mind* (1950); *Montage of a Dream Deferred* (poems, 1951); *Laughing to Keep from Crying* (1952); *First Book of Negroes* (1952); *Simple Takes a Wife* (1953); *Famous American Negroes* (1954); *First Book of Rhythms* (1954); *First Book of Jazz* (1954); *Famous Negro Music Makers* (1955); *The Sweet Flypaper of Life* (1955); *First Book of the West Indies* (1956); *I Wonder as I Wander: An Autobiographical Journey* (1956); *A Pictorial History of the Negro in America* (with Milton Meltzer, 1956); *Simple Stakes a Claim* (1957); *Tambourines to Glory* (1958); *Famous Negro Heroes of America* (1958); *Selected Poems* (1959); *First Book of Africa* (1960); *Ask Your Mama* (1961); *The Best of Simple* (1961). Editor: *The Poetry of the Negro* (with Arna Bontemps, 1949); *The Book of Negro Folklore* (with same, 1958); *An African Treasury* (1960); *Simple Uncle Sam* (1967); etc. Translator: Lorca's *Gypsy Ballads* (1951); etc.

HUGHES, RUPERT (Jan. 31, 1872–Sept. 9, 1956); b. Lancaster, Mo. Novelist, playwright. *American Composers* (1900); *Gyges Ring* (poems, 1901); *The Whirlwind* (1902); *Alexander the Great* (prod. 1903); *Love Affairs of Great Musicians* (1903); *The Bridge* (prod. 1909); *The Cat Bird* (prod. 1910); *Uncle Zeb* (prod. 1913); *What Will People Say?* (1914); *The Thirteenth Commandment* (1916); *The Cup of Fury* (1919); *The Unpardonable Sin* (1919); *Souls for Sale* (1922); *Destiny* (1925); *The Old Home Town* (1926); *George Washington,* 3v. (1926–30); *The Lovely Ducklings* (1928); *Love Song* (1934); *Stately Timber* (1939); *City of Angels* (1941); *The Giant Wakes* (1950); *The War of the Mayan King* (1952); etc.

HUGHES, THOMAS ALOYSIUS (b. Jan. 24, 1849); b. Liverpool, Eng. Educator, author. *History of the Society of Jesus in North America,* 3v. (1907–17). Prof. literature and philosophy, St. Xavier College, Cincinnati, O.; St. Louis University; Detroit College.

HUIE, WILLIAM BRADFORD (Nov. 13, 1910–); b. Hartselle, Ala. Lecturer, author. *Mud on the Stars* (1942); *The Fight for Air Power* (1942); *Can Do: The Story of the Seabees* (1944); *From Omaha to Okinawa* (1945); *The Case Against the Admirals* (1946); *The Revolt of Mamie Stover* (1951); *The Execution of Private Slovik* (1954); *Ruby McCollum: Woman in the Suwanee Jail* (1956); *Wolf Whistle* (1959); *The Americanization of Emily* (1959); *The Hero of Iwo Jima* (1960); *Hotel Mamie Stover* (1963); *The Hiroshima Pilot* (1964); *Three Lives for Mississippi* (1965); *The Klansman* (1967). Editor and publisher, *The American Mercury,* 1951–52.

HUIZINGA, ARNOLD van C[outhen] P[iccardt] (Sept. 10, 1876–Sept. 3, 1953); b. Groningen, The Netherlands. Congregational clergyman, lecturer, author. *American Philosophy Critically Considered in Relation to Present Day Theology* (1911); *Authority of Might and Right* (1911); *Theological Essays* (1917); *Dutch Contributions to and Influence on America* (1924); etc.

HUIZINGA, HENRY (Jan. 8, 1873–Dec. 3, 1945); b. New Groningen, Mich. Baptist clergyman, educator, editor, author. *Missionary Education in India* (1909); *I Say Unto You, being the Sermon on the Mount according to Luke* (1942); etc. Compiler: *Modern Short Stories* (1922); *The World's Best Short Stories* (1924); *The Best Modern Short Stories* (1927); *The Best English Essays,* 2v. (1931–35); *The Best Long Plays* (1931). Prof. English, University of Shanghai, China, from 1917.

HULBERT, ARCHER BUTLER (Jan. 26, 1873–Dec. 24, 1933); b. Bennington, Vt. Educator, author. *Red Men's Roads* (1900); *The Queen of Quelparte* (1902); *Historic Highways of America,* 16v. (1902–05); *Frontiers* (1929); *The Forty-Niners* (1931); etc. Editor: *The Call of the Columbia* (1934); *Ohio in the Time of the Confederation* (1918); etc. Prof. American history, Marietta College, 1904–18; Colorado College, 1920–33.

HULL, EDNA MAYNE. Author. *Out of the Unknown* (stories, with husband, A. E. Van Vogt, 1948); *Planets for Sale* (1954); *The Church Not Made with Hands* (1965).

Hull, H. Braxton. Pen name of Helen Hull Jacobs.

HULL, HELEN ROSE (1888–July 15, 1971); b. Albion, Mich. Novelist. *Quest* (1922); *Labyrinth* (1923); *The Surry Family* (1925); *Islanders* (1927); *Hardy Perennial* (1933); *Morning Shows the Day* (1934); *Uncommon People* (1936); *Candle Indoors* (1936); *Frost Flower* (1939); *Through the House Door* (1940); *Hawk's Flight* (1946); *Octave* (1947); *Wind Rose* (1958); *A Tapping on the Wall* (1960); *Close Her Pale Blue Eyes* (1963). Editor: *The Writer's Book* (1950); *Landfall* (1953); *Writer's Roundtable* (1959). With Columbia University, 1916–58. Emeritus.

HULL, WILLIAM I[saac] (Nov. 19, 1868–Nov. 14, 1939); b. Baltimore, Md. Educator, historian. *William Penn and the Dutch Quaker Migration to Pennsylvania* (1935); *Eight First Biographies of William Penn* (1936); *William Penn: A Topical Biography* (1937); etc. Prof. history, Swarthmore College, 1894–1939.

HULME, EDWARD MASLIN (Sept. 17, 1871–); b. London, England. Educator, historian. *Renaissance and Reformation* (1914); *A History of the British People* (1924); *The Middle Ages* (1929). Prof. medieval history, Stanford University, 1921–37.

HULME, KATHRYN CAVARLY (Jan. 6, 1900–); b. San Francisco, Calif. Author. *Arab Interlude* (1931); *Desert Night* (1933); *We Lived as Children* (1938); *The Wild Place* (1953); *The Nun's Story* (1956); *Annie's Captain* (1961); *Undiscovered Country* (1966).

HULT, GOTTFRIED EMANUEL (Mar. 14, 1869–June 28, 1950); b. Chicago, Ill. Educator, poet. *Reveries, and Other Poems* (1909); *Outbound* (poems, 1920); *Inverted Torches* (two plays, 1940); etc. Prof. classics, University of North Dakota, from 1907.

Human Behavior: An Inventory of Effects. By Gary Steiner and Bernard Berelson (1964). Comprehensive survey of knowledge about human behavior as studied in the behavioral sciences.

Human Comedy, The. Novel by William Saroyan (1943). Story of the lovable Macauley family, after the death of the elder Macauley.

Human Sexual Inadequacy. By William H. Masters and Virginia E. Johnson (1970). Results of eleven years of research into and treatment of sexual disorders.

Human Sexual Response. By William H. Masters and Virginia E. Johnson (1966). A scientific study based upon experiments performed on volunteers who participated in sexual intercourse.

Human Use of Human Beings, The: Cybernetics and Society. By Norbert Wiener (1950). Study of the social implications of the newest electronic computers and their likelihood of affecting men's lives profoundly.

Humanist, The. San Francisco, Cal. Bimonthly. Founded 1941. Published by the American Humanist Association. Devoted to philosophy, liberal religion, science, and literature as they are concerned with scientific humanism.

Humanizing of Knowledge, The. By James Harvey Robinson (1924). A plea for the popularization of science, literature, education, and philosophy.

"Humble-Bee." Poem by Ralph Waldo Emerson (1839).

HUME, CYRIL (Mar. 16, 1900–Mar. 3, 1966); b. New Rochelle, N.Y. Novelist. *Wife of the Centaur* (1923); *The Golden Dancer* (1926); *Myself and the Young Bowman* (1932); etc.

HUMES, H[arold] **L.** (Apr. 30, 1926–   ); b. Douglas, Ariz. Author. *Underground City* (1958); *Men Die* (1959); *Memoirs of Dorsey Slade.* Founder, with Peter Matthiessen, *Paris Review,* 1952; editor, *Film Culture.*

HUMMEL, GEORGE FREDERICK (Sept. 3, 1882–Dec. 20, 1952); b. Southold, L.I., N.Y. Novelist, playwright. *After All* (1923); *Subsoil* (1924); *A Good Man* (1925); *Evelyn Grainger* (1927); *Lazy Isle* (1927); *Summer Lightning* (1928); *The World Waits* (prod. 1933); *Heritage* (1935); *Tradition* (1936); *Adriatic Interlude* (1938); *The Eternal Mother* (1945).

HUMPHREY, GRACE (Sept. 3, 1882–); b. Springfield, Ill. Author. *Women in American History* (1919); *The Story of the Catherines* (1927); *The Story of Krakow* (1934); *Hungary, Land of Contrasts* (1936); *Pilsudski, Builder of Poland* (1936); *The Story of the Annes* (1937); etc.

HUMPHREY, [Harriette] ZEPHINE (Mrs. Wallace Weir Fahnestock) (Dec. 15, 1874–); b. Philadelphia, Pa. Author. *The Calling of the Apostle* (1900); *Uncle Charley* (1902); *Over Against Green Peak* (1908); *Recollections of My Mother* (1912); *The Edge of the Woods* (1912); *Grail Fire* (1917); *The Homestead* (1919); *The Sword of the Spirit* (1920); *Mountain Verities* (1923); *The Story of Dorset* (1924); *Winterwise* (1927); *Chrysalis* (1929); *The Beloved Community* (1930); *Green Mountains to Sierras* (1936); *Cactus Forest* (1938); *'Allo Goodby* (1940).

HUMPHREY, WILLIAM (1924–). Author. *The Last Husband and Other Stories* (1953); *Home from the Hill* (1958); *The Ordways* (1965); *A Time and a Place* (1968); *The Spawning Run* (1970).

HUMPHREYS, DAVID (July 10, 1752–Feb. 21, 1818); b. Derby, Conn. Revolutionary soldier, statesman, poet. *The Miscellaneous Works of Colonel Humphreys* (1790). See *The Anarchiad: A New England Poem*. Member of the "Hartford Wits." See F. L. Humphreys's *Life and Times of David Humphreys*, 2v. (1917).

HUMPHREYS, JAMES (Jan. 15, 1748–Feb. 2, 1810); b. Philadelphia, Pa. Loyalist printer, publisher. Founder, *The Pennsylvania Ledger*, Philadelphia, Jan., 1775.

HUMPHRIES, [George] ROLFE (Nov. 20, 1894–Apr. 23, 1969); b. Philadelphia, Pa. Educator, poet, translator. *Europe and Other Poems and Sonnets* (1929); *Out of the Jewel* (poems, 1942); *The Summer Landscape* (poems, 1944); *Forbid Thy Ravens* (poems, 1947); *The Wind of Time* (poems, 1949); *Poems, Collected and New* (1954); *Green Armor on Green Ground* (poems, 1956). Translator: Lorca's *Poet in New York* (1940); Virgil's *The Aeneid* (1951); *Gypsy Ballads of Lorca* (1953); Ovid's *Metamorphoses* (1955); Ovid's *Art of Love* (1957); *Satires of Juvenal* (1958). Latin dept., Hunter College, since 1957.

Hundred Boston Orators, The. By J. S. Loring (1852).

HUNEKER, JAMES GIBBONS (Jan. 31, 1860–Feb. 6, 1921); b. Philadelphia, Pa. Musician, critic, author. *Mezzotints in Modern Music* (1899); *Chopin: The Man and His Music* (1900); *Melomaniacs* (1902); *Overtones* (1904); *Iconoclasts* (1905); *Visionaries* (1905); *Egoists* (1909); *Franz Liszt* (1911); *Old Fogy* (1913); *The Pathos of Distance* (1913); *Ivory, Apes and Peacocks* (1915); *Unicorns* (1917); *Bedouins* (1920); *Painted Veils* (1920); *Steeplejack*, 2v. (autobiography, 1920); *Letters of James Gibbons Huneker* (1922); *Intimate Letters* (1924); etc. Music critic, New York *Evening Recorder*, New York *Sun*, New York *Times*, New York *World*, *Philadelphia Press*. See Benjamin de Casseres's *James Gibbons Huneker* (1925).

Hungerfield and Other Poems. By Robinson Jeffers (1954).

HUNGERFORD, EDWARD (Dec. 21, 1875–July 29, 1948); b. Dexter, N.Y. Author. *Little Corky* (1912); *Gertrude* (1913); *Personality of American Cities* (1913); *Men and Iron* (1938); *Daniel Willard Rides the Line* (1938); *Men of Erie* (1946); *Wells Fargo* (1948); and many books on railroads.

HUNNINGHER, BENJAMIN (Apr. 15, 1903–); b. Vlissingen, Neth. Educator, author. *The Origin of the Theater* (1955); *The Idea in American Drama* (1963); *The Mirror of Baroque Theatre* (1964); etc. Prof. drama, Columbia University, 1948–64. History of Theatre Arts Dept. University of Amsterdam since 1964.

HUNT, CLARA WHITEHILL (1871–Jan. 10, 1958); b. Utica, N.Y. Librarian, author. *The Little House in the Woods* (1918); *The Little House in Green Valley* (1932); etc. Children's librarian, Brooklyn Public Library, 1903–39.

HUNT, ERLING MESSER (Mar. 18, 1901–) b. Charlestown, N.H. Educator. Editor: *America Organizes to Win the War* (1942); *Citizens for a New World* (1944); etc. Head dept. social science teaching, Teachers College, Columbia University, since 1938.

HUNT, [Everette] HOWARD, Jr. (Oct. 9, 1918–); b. Buffalo, N.Y. Editor, novelist. *East of Farewell* (1942); *Limit of Darkness* (1944); *Stranger in Town* (1947); *Maelstrom* (1948); *Bimini Run* (1949). Editor, *March of Time;* war correspondent, *Life*. Department of State, Washington, D.C., since 1968.

HUNT, FRAZIER (Dec. 1, 1885–Dec. 24, 1967); b. Rock Island, Ill. Correspondent, author. *This Bewildered World* (1934); *Bachelor Prince* (1935); *One American, and His Attempt at Education* (1938); *Little Doc: the Story of Allan Roy Dafoe* (1939); *MacArthur and the War* (1944); *The Tragic Days of Billy the Kid* (1956); etc. Foreign correspondent for the *New York Sun, Chicago Tribune*, etc.

HUNT, FREEMAN (Mar. 21, 1804–Mar. 2, 1858); b. Quincy, Mass. Publisher, editor, author. *American Anecdotes: Original and Select*, 2v. (1830); *Letters About the Hudson River* (1836); *Lives of American Merchants*, 2v. (1856–57). Founder, the *Ladies' Magazine*, Boston, with Sarah Josepha Hale, 1828; the *Merchants Magazine and Commercial Review*, N.Y., 1839; editor, 1839–55. Putnam and Hunt published the *Juvenile Miscellany*, Boston, ed. by Lydia Maria Child, in 1828.

HUNT, GAILLARD (Sept. 8, 1862–Mar. 20, 1924); b. New Orleans, La. Historical writer. *The Life of James Madison* (1902); *John C. Calhoun* (1907); *Life in America One Hundred Years Ago* (1914). Editor: *The Writings of James Madison*, 9v. (1900–10). Chief, manuscripts division, Library of Congress, 1909–17.

HUNT, ISAAC (c. 1742–1809); b. Bridgetown, Barbados. Anglican clergyman, loyalist, author. Father of Leigh Hunt. *A Humble Attempt at Scurrility* (1765); *The Political Family* (1775); etc.

HUNT, MABEL LEIGH (Nov. 1, 1892–); b. Coatesville, Ind. Author. *Double Birthday Present* (1947); *Matilda's Buttons* (1948); *The Wonderful Baker* (1950); *Better Known as Johnny Appleseed* (1950); *Ladycake Farm* (1952); *Cristy at Skippinghills* (1958); *Cupola House* (1961); *Beggar's Daughter* (1963); etc.

HUNT, THEODORE WHITEFIELD (Feb. 19, 1844–Apr. 12, 1930); b. Metuchen, N.J. Educator, critic. *Representative English Prose and Prose Writers* (1887); *American Meditative Lyrics* (1896); *English Literary Miscellany*, 2v. (1914); etc. With English dept., Princeton University, 1873–1918; professor, 1881–1918.

HUNT, WILLIAM SOUTHWORTH (Jan. 17, 1879–Jan. 26, 1940); b. Newark, N.J. Publisher, editor, author. *Frank Forester: A Tragedy in Exile* (1927); On staff, *Newark Call*, 1903–19, 1924–40; managing editor, 1924–32; president, 1932–40; editor, *Newark Star-Eagle*, 1919–24.

Hunter, Clingham, M. D. One of the pen names of William Taylor Adams.

HUNTER, DARD (Nov. 29, 1883–Feb. 20, 1966); b. Steubenville, O. Printer, papermaker, author. *The Art of Bookmaking* (1915); *Primitive Papermaking* (1927); *Old Papermaking in China and Japan* (1932); *Old Papermaking* (1923); *The Literature of Papermaking, 1390–1800* (1925); *Papermaking Through Eighteen Centuries* (1929); *A Papermaking Pilgrimage to Japan, Korea and China* (1936); *The Story of Paper* (1937); *Papermaking in Pioneer America* (1952); *My Life with Paper* (autobiography, 1958); etc. Art director, The Roycroft Shop, East Aurora, N.Y., 1903–10; established own press in Chillicothe, O., in 1919, where he makes his own paper, designs his type, and prints books by hand. Founder, Dard Hunter Paper Museum, Massachusetts Institute of Technology, 1939, now located in Appleton, Wis.

HUNTER, EDWARD (July 2, 1902–); b. New York. Journalist, author. *Brain-Washing in Red China* (1951); *Brainwashing: The Story of Men Who Defied It* (1956); *The Story of Mary Liu* (1957); *The Black Book on Red China* (1958); *The Past Present: A Year in Afghanistan* (1959); *In Many Voices: Our Fabulous Foreign Language Press* (1960); *Attack by Mail* (1963). With International News Service, 1931–36. Chairman Anti-Communist Liaison, Inc. since 1962.

HUNTER, EVAN (1926–). Author. *Find the Feathered Serpent* (1952); *The Blackboard Jungle* (1954); *Strangers When We Meet* (1958); *A Matter of Conviction* (1959); *The Remarkable Harry* (1961); *Mothers and Daughters* (1961); *Happy New Year, Herbie* (1963); *Buddwing* (1964); *The Paper Dragon* (1966); *A Horse's Head* (1967); *Last Summer* (1968); *Sons* (1969). Writes detective stories under pen names "Ed McBain"; "Hunt Collins"; "Richard Marsten."

HUNTER, FRED. Novelist. *The Child of the Wreck* (1848); *The Blue Velvet Bonnet* (1849); *The Daguerreotype; or, Love at First Sight* (1849); *Lady Alice; or, The New Una* (1849); etc.

HUNTER, [James] GRAHAM; b. LaGrange, Ill. Cartoonist. Creator of "Jolly Jingles," "Motor Laffs," "Biceps Brothers," and other cartoons.

HUNTER, JOHN DUNN (c. 1797–1827); b. west of the Mississippi River. Adventurer, author. *Manners and Customs of Several Indian Tribes Located West of the Mississippi* (1823), described by scholars as the work of an impostor. Duponceau and General Cass exposed Hunter's ignorance of the Indian languages he professed to know.

HUNTER, THOMAS LOMAX. Journalist, poet. *Forbidden Fruit, and Other Ballads* (1923); *Columns from the Cavalier* (1935). Has conducted column "As It Appears to the Cavalier" in the *Richmond Times-Dispatch,* since 1929.

HUNTER, WALTER SAMUEL (Mar. 22, 1889–Aug. 3, 1954); b. Decatur, Ill. Educator, psychologist, editor, author. *General Psychology* (1919); *Human Behavior* (1928); etc. Assoc. editor, *Psychological Bulletin,* 1916–34; *American Journal of Psychology,* from 1940; etc.; editor, *Psychological Index,* 1925–36; *Psychological Abstracts,* 1926–46. Prof. psychology, Brown University, from 1936.

HUNTER, WILLIAM C. (1812–June 25, 1891); b. in Kentucky, or New York City. China merchant, author. *The 'Fan-Kwae' at Canton before Treaty Days, 1825–1844* (1822); *Bits of Old China* (1885); See P. de Varges's *William C. Hunter's Books on the Old Canton Factories,* in the *Yenching Journal of Social Studies,* Peking, China, July, 1939.

HUNTING, [Henry] GARDNER (Sept. 2, 1872–Nov. 21, 1958); b. Kilbourn City, Wis. Novelist, playwright. *The Senator's Vindication* (prod. 1906); *A Hand in the Game* (1911); *The Vicarion* (1926); *Sunrise Calling* (1929); *The Volunteer Wife* (with Edward C. Marsh, 1933); *Great Reward* (1942); *Prove Me Now* (1953); *The Word Beyond Words* (1955); also the *Sandsy* series and other books for boys.

HUNTINGTON, ARCHER MILTON (Mar. 10, 1870–Dec. 11, 1955); b. New York City. Editor, Hispanic scholar, art collector, poet. *A Notebook in Northern Spain* (1898); *Lace Maker of Segovia* (poems, 1928); *The Ladies of Vallbona* (poems, 1931); *The Lady of Elche* (poems, 1933); *Rimas* (1936); *Recuerdos* (poems, 1949); *Collected Verse* (1952); *The Torch Bearers* (1955); etc. Founder, the Hispanic Society of America, 1904.

HUNTINGTON, ARRIA SARGENT (June 22, 1848–deceased); b. Roxbury, Mass. Author. *Under a Colonial Roof-Tree* (1891); *Memoirs and Letters of Frederic Dan Huntington* (1906); etc.

HUNTINGTON, ELLSWORTH (Sept. 16, 1876–Oct. 17, 1947); b. Galesburg, Ill. Educator, geographer, author. *Explorations in Turkestan* (1905); *The Pulse of Asia* (1907); *Civilization and Climate* (1915); *Red Man's Continent* (1919); *Principles of Human Geography* (with S. W. Cushing, 1920); *The Character of Races* (1924); *West of the Pacific* (1925); *The Builders of America* (with L. F. Whitney, 1927); *The Human Habitat* (1927); *Season of Birth* (1938); *Mainsprings of Civilization* (1945); etc. Geography dept., Yale University, 1907–45.

Huntington, Faye. Pen name of Theodosia Toll Foster.

Huntington, Frances Carpenter. See Frances Carpenter.

HUNTINGTON, FREDERICK DAN (May 28, 1819–July 11, 1904); b. Hadley, Mass. Episcopal bishop, author. *Christian Believing and Living* (1859); *Lectures on Human Society* (1860); *Unconscious Tuition* (1878); etc. Editor, the *Monthly Religious Magazine,* 1845–58.

HUNTINGTON, HARRIETE (1909–). Author. *Let's Go Outdoors* (1939); *Tune Up: The Instruments of the Orchestra and Their Players* (1942); *Let's Go to the Desert* (1949); *The Praying Mantis* (1957); *California Harbors* (1964); *Let's Go to the Woods* (1968); *Let's Look at Flowers* (1969).

HUNTINGTON, HELEN [Manchester Gates] (Mrs. Harley Granville-Barker) (d. Feb. 16, 1950). Poet, novelist. *The Solitary Path* (poems, 1902); *The Days That Pass* (poems, 1906); *From the Cup of Silence, and Other Poems* (1909); *Eastern Red* (1918); *Songs in Cities and Gardens* (1919); etc.

HUNTINGTON, JEDEDIAH VINCENT (Jan. 20, 1815–Mar. 10, 1862); b. New York City. Editor, novelist, poet. *Poems* (1843); *Lady Alice; or, The New Una* (anon., 1849); *Alban: A Tale of the New World* (anon., 1851); *The Forest: A Sequel to Alban* (1852); *St. Vincent de Paul* (1852); *Rosemary* (1860); etc.

HUNTINGTON, SAMUEL PHILLIPS (Apr. 18, 1927–); b. New York. Educator, author. *The Soldier and the State* (1957); *The Common Defense* (1961). Co-author: *Political Power: USA-USSR* (1964). Editor: *Changing Patterns of Military Politics* (1967). Prof. government, Harvard University, since 1967.

HUNTINGTON, TULEY FRANCIS (Sept. 23, 1870–May 4, 1938); b. near Barrington, Ill. Typographical authority, author. *The Acre of the Earth Turned* (1929); *Iron Rain and Green* (1929); *Jacqueline of Very Near* (1931).

HUNTINGTON, WILLIAM REED (Sept. 20, 1838–July 26, 1909); b. Lowell, Mass. Episcopal clergyman, author. *Twenty Years of a Massachusetts Rectorship* (autobiography, 1883); *Sonnets and a Dream* (1899); *Twenty Years of a New York Rectorship* (autobiography, 1903); etc.

HUNTON, WILLIAM LEE (Feb. 16, 1864–Oct. 12, 1930); b. Morrisburg, Ont. Lutheran clergyman, editor, author. *Favorite Hymns* (1917); *I Believe* (1922); *Facts of Our Faith* (1925); etc. Editor, the *Lutheran Messenger,* 1908–18; *Lutheran Young Folks,* 1908–30.

Huntress, The. Washington, D.C. Weekly journal. Founded 1836, by Anne Newport Royall. Expired at her death, 1854.

HURD, CHARLES (May 11, 1903–May 16, 1968); b. Tonkawa, Okla. Publicist, author. *The White House: A Biography* (1940); *The Veterans' Program* (1946); *Washington Cavalcade* (1948); *The Compact History of the American Red Cross* (1959); *When the New Deal was Young and Gay* (1965). Editor: *Treasury of Great American Quotations* (1968). Staff, *New York Times,* 1929–49.

HURD, MELANCTHON M. New York publisher. He joined with H. O. Houghton in 1864 to found the firm of Hurd & Houghton. Merged with James R. Osgood & Co. in 1878, as Houghton, Osgood and Company. In 1880 it became Houghton, Mifflin & Co., in 1908 Houghton Mifflin Company.

HURLBERT, WILLIAM HENRY (July 3, 1827–Sept. 4, 1895); b. (Hurlbut) Charleston, S.C. Editor, author. *Gen-Eden or Pictures of Cuba* (1854); *Americans in Paris; or A Game of Dominoes* (prod. 1858); *Ireland under Coercion,* 2v. (1888); *England under Coercion* (1893); etc. Editor-in-chief, the *New York World,* 1876–83.

HURLBUT, WILLIAM [James] (July 13, 1883–); b. Belvidere, Ill. Playwright. *The Fighting Hope* (prod. 1908); *The Writing on the Wall* (prod. 1909); *New York* (1911); *Chivalry* (1925); *Bride of the Lamb* (1926); *On the Stairs* (1931); *Recessional* (1931); etc.

HURST, FANNIE (Oct. 19, 1889–Feb. 23, 1968); b. Hamilton, O. Novelist. *Just Around the Corner* (1914); *Every Soul Hath Its Song* (1916); *Gaslight Sonatas* (1918); *Humoresque* (1919); *Star-Dust* (1921); *The Vertical City* (1922); *Lummox* (1923); *Appasionata* (1926); *Mannequin* (1926); *Song of Life* (1927); *A President Is Born* (1928); *Five and Ten* (1929);

Procession (1929); *Back Street* (1931); *Imitation of Life* (1933); *Anitra's Dance* (1934); *Great Laughter* (1936); *We Are Ten* (1937); *Lonely Parade* (1942); *Hallelujah* (1944); *Any Woman* (1950); *The Man with One Head* (1953); *Anatomy of Me* (autobiography, 1958); *Family!* (1960); *God Must Be Sad* (1961); *Fool—Be Still* (1964); etc.

HURSTON, ZORA NEALE (Jan. 7, 1903–Jan. 28, 1960); b. Eatonville, Fla. Educator, author. *Jonah's Gourd Vine* (1934); *Mules and Men* (1935); *Their Eyes Were Watching God* (1937); *Tell My Horse* (1938); *Moses, Man of the Mountain* (1939); *Dust Tracks on a Road* (autobiography, 1942); *Seraph on the Suwanee* (1948). Prof. drama, North Carolina College for Negroes.

HURT, HUBER WILLIAM (Nov. 3, 1883–Nov. 24, 1966); b. Princeton, Mo. Author. *Handbook for Scout Masters* (1919); *Handbook of Cub Masters* (1931); *Adventuring for Senior Scouts* (1938); *Scouting for Rural Boys* (1939); *Hints to Squandron Leaders* (1942); etc. Co-editor, *The College Blue Book,* for many years.

HUSBAND, JOSEPH (July 25, 1885–Sept. 21, 1938); b. Rochester, N.Y. Author. *A Year in a Coal Mine* (1911); *The Story of the Pullman Car* (1917); *A Year in the Navy* (1919); *On the Coast of France* (1919); *Americans by Adoption* (1920); *High Hurdles* (1923); *Citadel* (1924); etc.

HUSE, HOWARD RUSSELL (July 20, 1890–); b. Omaha, Neb. Educator. *Psychology of Foreign Language Study* (1931); *Illiteracy of the Literate* (1933); *Reading and Speaking Foreign Languages* (1945). Translator: Dante's *Divine Comedy* (1954). Prof. Romance languages, University of North Carolina, since 1931.

HUSSLEIN, JOSEPH (June 10, 1873–Oct. 19, 1952); b. Milwaukee, Wis. Roman Catholic clergyman, educator, editor, author. *Evolution and Social Progress* (1920); *The Reign of Christ* (1928); *The Spirit World about Us* (1934); etc. Editor: *Social Wellsprings* 2v. (1940, 1942); *Our Great Devotions* (1951); etc. Assoc. editor, *America,* 1911–27; etc. Dean, school of sociology, St. Louis University, 1930–33; social service, 1933–40.

HUSTON, McCREADY (Mar. 11, 1891–); b. Brownsville, Pa. Journalist, writer. *Huling's Quest* (1925); *The Big Show* (1927); *Dear Senator* (1928); *The King of Spain's Daughter* (1930); *Solid Citizen* (1933); etc. On editorial staff of several newspapers, since 1912; editor, *Frontiers,* since 1940.

HUTCHENS, JOHN KENNEDY (Aug. 9, 1905–); b. Chicago, Ill. Journalist, critic. Editor: *The American Twenties* (1952). With *New York Times Book Review,* 1944–48; editor, 1946–48; book columnist, *New York Herald Tribune,* 1948–56; daily book Reviewer, 1956–63; editorial board: Book-of-the Month Club since 1963.

Hutchings' Illustrated California Magazine. San Francisco, Calif. Founded 1856, by James M. Hutchings. Contains his well-known "The Miner's Ten Commandments," and articles by pioneers. Expired 1861.

HUTCHINS, MAUDE PHELPS MCVEIGH; b. New York. Sculptor, author. *Diagrammatics* (with M. J. Adler, 1932); *Georgiana, A Diary of Love* (1962); *Victorine: The Elevator* (1962); *Honey on the Moon* (1964); *Blood on the Doves* (1965); *The Unbelievers Downstairs* (1968); etc.

HUTCHINS, ROBERT MAYNARD (Jan. 17, 1899–); b. Brooklyn, N.Y. Educator, fund executive, author. *No Friendly Voice* (1936); *The Higher Learning in America* (1936); *Education for Freedom* (1943); *The Conflict in Education* (1953); *Some Observations on American Education* (1956); *The Two Faces of Federalism* (1961); *The Learning Society* (1968); etc. President, University of Chicago, 1929–45; chancellor, 1945–51; with Ford Foundation, 1951–54; pres., Fund for the Republic, since 1954.

HUTCHINS, WILLIAM J[ames] (July 5, 1871–Feb. 20, 1958); b. Brooklyn, N.Y. Educator, author. *The Preacher's Inspiration and Ideals* (1917); *The Religious Experience of Israel* (1919); etc. President, Berea College, 1920–39.

HUTCHINSON, EDWARD PRINCE (Jan. 3, 1906–); b. Auburn, Me. Educator, demographer. *Immigrants and Their Children, 1850–1950* (1956); *The Population Debate* (1967); etc. Department of sociology, University of Pennsylvania, since 1945.

HUTCHINSON, FRANCES KINSLEY (b. Sept. 17, 1857); b. Baltimore, Md. Author. *Our Country Home* (1907); *Motoring in the Balkans* (1909); *Our Country Life* (1912); *Wychwood, The History of an Idea* (1928).

HUTCHINSON, G[eorge] EVELYN (Jan. 30, 1903–); b. Cambridge, Eng. Educator, biologist. *The Clear Mirror* (1936); *The Itinerant Ivory Tower* (1953); *A Treatise on Limnology,* Vol. I (1957); *The Ecological Theatre and the Evolutionary Play* (1965); etc. Prof. zoology, Yale University, since 1928.

Hutchinson, Mrs. James Pemberton. See Amory Hare.

HUTCHINSON, PAUL (Aug. 10, 1890–Apr. 15, 1956); b. Madison, N.J. Editor, author. *The Spread of Christianity* (1922); *China's Real Revolution* (1924); *The Story of Methodism* (with H. E. Luccock, 1926); *Men Who Made the Churches* (1930); *Storm Over Asia* (1932); *The New Leviathan* (1946); *The New Ordeal of Christianity* (1957); etc. Editor, *China Christian Advocate,* Shanghai, 1916–21; managing editor, editor, *Christian Century* from 1924.

HUTCHINSON, THOMAS (Sept. 9, 1711–June 3, 1780); b. Boston, Mass. Royal governor, historian. *The History of the Colony of Massachusetts-Bay,* 3v. (1764–1828); *Diary and Letters of His Excellency Thomas Hutchinson, Esq.,* ed. by P. O. Hutchinson, 2v. (1884–86). Compiler: *A Collection of Original Papers Relative to the History of the Colony of Massachusetts-Bay* (1769). Governor of Massachusetts Bay, 1771–74.

HUTCHISON, JOHN ALEXANDER (Mar. 2, 1912–); b. Cedar Grove, N.J. Educator, author. *We Are Not Divided* (1941); *Ways of Faith* (with J. A. Martin, 1953); *Faith, Reason and Existence* (1955); *The Two Cities* (1957). Editor: *Christian Faith and Social Action* (1953); *Paths of Faith* (1969). Prof. religion, Columbia University, since 1955.

HUTSON, CHARLES WOODWARD (b. Sept. 23, 1840–); b. McPhersonville, S.C. Artist, author. *Out of a Besieged City* (1887); etc. Editor of several collections of Lafcadio Hearn.

HUTSON, HAROLD HORTON (Jan. 14, 1914–); b. Spring Hill, S.C. Educator. *New Testament Life and Literature* (with Donald W. Riddle, 1946); *Survey of the New Testament* (1949).

HUTTON, JOSEPH (1787–1828); b. Philadelphia, Pa. Actor, playwright. *The School for Prodigals* (prod. 1808); *The Wounded Hussar* (prod. 1809); *The Orphan of Prague* (1810); *The Fall of York, and the Death of General Pike* (prod. 1813); *Fashionable Follies* (prod. 1809); etc.

HUTTON, LAURENCE (Aug. 8, 1843–June 10, 1904); b. New York City. Bibliophile, editor, author. *Plays and Players* (1875); *Literary Landmarks of London* (1885), followed by similar works on the landmarks of Edinburgh (1891), Jerusalem (1895), Venice (1890), Rome (1897), Florence (1897), Oxford (1903), Scottish Universities (1904); *Stars and Actresses of Great Britain and the United States* (1886); *Curiosities of the American Stage* (1891); *Edwin Booth* (1893); *Other Times and Other Seasons* (1895); *A Boy I Knew* (with Brander Matthews, 1898); *Talks in a Library* (1905); etc. Conducted department of "Literary Notes" in *Harper's Magazine,* 1886–98.

HUXLEY, ALDOUS [Leonard] (July 26, 1894–Nov. 22, 1963); b. Godalming, Eng. Author. *The Burning Wheel* (poems, 1916); *Jonah* (poems, 1917); *The Defeat of Youth* (poems, 1918); *Leda* (poems, 1920); *Limbo* (1920); *Crome Yellow* (1921); *Mortal Coils* (1922); *On the Margin* (1923); *Antic Hay* (1923); *Young Archimedes and Other Stories* (1924); *Those Barren Leaves* (1925); *Along the Road* (1925); *Jesting Pilate* (1926); *Two or Three Graces* (1926); *Proper Studies* (1927); *Point Counter Point* (1928); *Do What You Will* (1929); *Brief Candles* (1930); *Vulgarity in Literature* (1930); *The Cicada and Other Poems* (1931); *The World of Light* (play, 1931); *Music at Night and Other Essays* (1931); *Brave New World* (1932); *Rotunda* (1932); *Texts and Pretexts* (1932); *Beyond the Mexique Bay* (1934); *Eyeless in Gaza* (1936); *The Olive Tree and Other Essays* (1936); *Ends and Means* (1937); *After Many a Summer Dies the Swan* (1939); *Gray Eminence* (1941); *The Art of Seeing* (1942); *Time Must Have a Stop* (1944); *The Perennial Philosophy* (1945); *Ape and Essence* (1948); *Themes and Variations* (1950); *The Devils of Loudun* (1952); *The Doors of Perception* (1954); *The Genius and the Goddess* (1955); *Heaven and Hell* (1956); *Tomorrow and Tomorrow and Tomorrow* (1956); *Collected Short Stories* (1957); *Brave New World Revisited* (1958); *Collected Essays* (1959); *On Art and Artists* (1960); *Island* (1962); *Letters of Aldous Huxley,* ed. by Grover Smith (1970).

HUXLEY, LAURA ARCHERA, b. Turin, Italy. Psychotherapist, author. *You Are Not the Target* (1963); *The Timeless Moment: A Personal View of Aldous Huxley* (1968).

HYAMS, JOE (June 6, 1923–); b. Cambridge, Mass. Author. *My Life with Cleopatra* (with Walter Wanger, 1963); *A Weekend Gambler's Handbook* (with Maj. Riddle, 1963); *How to Dress for Success* (with Edith Head, 1966); *Seller's Market* (with Peter Sellers, 1964); *Bogie* (1966); *A Field of Buttercups* (1968).

HYATT, JAMES PHILIP (Feb. 16, 1909–); b. Monticello, Ark. Educator. *Prophetic Religion* (1947); *Jeremiah: Prophet of Courage and Hope* (1958); *The Heritage of Biblical Faith* (1964). etc. Archaeological editor, *Journal of Bible and Religion,* 1939–48; editor, *Journal of Biblical Literature,* 1948–49.

HYDE, GRANT MILNOR (Apr. 8, 1889–); b. The Dalles, Ore. Educator, author. *Newspaper Reporting and Correspondence* (1912); *Newspaper Editing* (1915); *Handbook for Newspaper Workers* (1921); *Newspaper Reporting* (1952); etc. Prof. journalism, University of Wisconsin, since 1910; editor, University Press Bureau, 1915–27.

HYDE, HENRY MORROW (b. Oct. 6, 1866); b. Freeport, Ill. Journalist, author. *One Forty-Two: The Reformed Messenger Boy* (1901); *The Buccaneers* (1904); *The Upstart* (1906); etc.

HYDE, MILES GOODYEAR (b. June 12, 1842); b. Cortland, N.Y. Physician, author. *The Story of a Day in London* (1888); *The Girl from Mexico, and Other Stories* (1900); *Mary Markham* (1903); *The Confessions and Letters of Terence Quinn McManus* (1911); etc.

HYDE, WALTER WOODBURN (May 14, 1870–); b. Ithaca, N.Y. Educator, author. *Thessaly and the Vale of Tempe* (1912); *Monasteries of Meteora and Greek Monasticism* (1913); *Mountains of Greece* (1915); *Greek Religion and Its Survivals* (1923); *Paganism to Christianity in the Roman Empire* (1946); *Ancient Greek Mariners* (1947); etc. Greek dept., University of Pennsylvania, 1910–40.

HYER, JULIEN CAPERS (Apr. 1, 1894–); b. Greenville, S.C. Lawyer, author. *The Land of Beginning Again* (1952); *The Shepherd* (poems, 1955); *Texas Lions 1917–67* (1969).

HYLANDER, CLARENCE JOHN (1897–deceased). Author. *Out of Doors in Spring* (1942); *Sea and Shore* (1950); *Animals in Armor* (1954); *Insects on Parade* (1957); *Feathers and Flight* (1959); etc.

HYMA, ALBERT (Mar. 18, 1893–); b. Groningen, The Netherlands. Educator, author. *The Christian Renaissance* (1924); *A Short History of Europe, 1500–1815* (1928); *Erasmus and the Humanists* (1930); *The Youth of Erasmus* (1930); *Europe from the Renaissance to 1815* (1931); *Christianity and Politics* (1938); *The Growth of European Civilization,* 2v. (with others 1938); *An Outline of the Growth of Western Civilization,* 2v. (1938–39); *Dynamic Citizenship* (1950); *New Light on Martin Luther* (1958); *A Survey of Ancient Civilization* (1959); *A Survey of Medieval Civilization* (1960); *The Christian Renaissance: A History of the Devotio Modern* (1965); *The Youth of Erasmus* (1968); etc. History dept., University of Michigan, since 1924.

HYMAN, MAC (1923–July 17, 1963). Author. *No Time for Sergeants* (1954).

HYMAN, STANLEY EDGAR (June 11, 1919–July 29, 1970); b. New York. Literary critic. *The Armed Vision* (1948); *Poetry and Criticism: Four Revolutions in Literary Taste* (1961); *The Tangled Bank: Darwin, Marx, Frazer, and Freud* (1962); *The Promised End* (1963); *Flannery O'Conner* (1966). Editor: *The Critical Performance* (1956).

HYNEMAN, CHARLES S[hang] (May 5, 1900–); b. in Gibson Co., Ind. Educator, author. *The First American Neutrality* (1935); *Bureaucracy in a Democracy* (1950); *The Study of Politics* (1959); *The Supreme Court on Trial* (1963); *Popular Government in America* (1968); etc. Prof. government, Indiana University, 1956–61.

HYNES, SAMUEL (Aug. 29, 1924–); b. Chicago, Ill. Educator, author. *Further Speculations by T. E. Hulmes* (1955); *The Pattern of Hardy's Poetry* (1961); *William Golding* (1964); *The Edwardian Turn of Mind* (1968). Prof. English literature, Swarthmore College, since 1965.

HYNSON, GEORGE BESWICK. Humorist, poet. *Down Yan and Thereabout* (poems, 1920). Wrote the lyric for "Our Delaware," adopted as the State song of Delaware in 1925.

"Hyperion." Romantic poem by Henry Wadsworth Longfellow (1839). The journey of a young man in search of his soul. Longfellow's European tour was the germ of the poem.

HYSLOP, JAMES HERVEY (Aug. 18, 1854–June 17, 1920); b. Xenia, O. Philosopher, psychologist, author. *Elements of Logic* (1892); *Democracy* (1899); *Problems of Philosophy* (1905); etc.

I

I. F. Stone's Weekly. Washington, D.C. Founded in 1953 by I. F. Stone and edited and published by him. Concerned with political analysis. A one-man job of research and writing, known for its scholarly ingenuity, daring exposure of information unpublicized by most other news media, and methodical thinking.

"I Have a Rendezvous with Death." Poem by Alan Seeger (1916).

"I Heard a Fly Buzz When I Died." Poem by Emily Dickinson (1896).

"I Like to See It Lap the Miles." Poem by Emily Dickinson (1891).

'I Lost It at the Movies.' Collection of motion picture reviews and critiques by Pauline Kael (1965).

"I Love Thy Kingdom, Lord." Hymn by the elder Timothy Dwight.

"I Love to Tell the Story." Hymn by William Gustavus Fischer.

"I Love You Truly." Song by Carrie Jacobs Bond (1901).

"I shot an arrow into the air." Opening line of "The Arrow and the Song" by Henry Wadsworth Longfellow, in his *The Belfry of Bruges, and Other Poems* (1846).

"I stood on the bridge at midnight." First line of "The Bridge" by Henry Wadsworth Longfellow, in his *Poems* (1845).

"I Taste a Liquor Never Brewed." Poem by Emily Dickinson (1861).

"I Would Not Live Always." Popular hymn by William Augustus Muhlenberg (1824). He also wrote "Saviour, Who Thy Flock Art Feeding" (1826).

IAMS, JACK (Samuel H. Iams, Jr.) (Nov. 15, 1910–); b. Baltimore, Md. Journalist, author. *Countess to Boot* (1941); *Girl Meets Body* (1947); *Prematurely Gay* (1948); *Death Draws the Line* (1949); *What Rhymes with Murder* (1950); *Into Thin Air* (1952); etc. With *Newsweek* since 1956.

Icebound. Play by Owen Davis (prod. 1922). A New England version of the prodigal son motif. "Icebound" in the play means a cold, undemonstrative type of New England character. Pulitzer prize play, 1923.

Iceman Cometh, The. Play by Eugene O'Neill (1946). A number of beaten Bowery characters discuss their disillusion and disgust with life. The iceman, who is Death, lies in wait for them all.

"Ichabod." Poem by John Greenleaf Whittier (1850). A rebuke to Daniel Webster on his Seventh of March Speech, in which he supported the Missouri Compromise and the Fugitive Slave Law.

ICKES, HAROLD L[e Claire] (Mar. 15, 1874–Feb. 3, 1952); b. Frankstown Township, Pa. Cabinet official, author. *The New Democracy* (1934); *The Third Term Bugaboo* (1940); *Autobiography of a Curmudgeon* (1943); *My Twelve Years with F.D.R.* (1948); *The Secret Diary of Harold L. Ickes,* 3v. (1953–54); etc. U.S. Secretary of the Interior, 1933–46.

Iconoclasts. By James Gibbons Huneker (1905). Series of dramatic essays which first appeared in the New York *Sun.*

Ida May. Novel by "Mary Langdon" (Mary Hayden Green Pike) (1854). Deals with a child of wealthy parents who was sold into slavery.

IDE, FRANCES OTIS OGDEN (Mrs. Charles W. Ide) (Dec. 27, 1853–July 2, 1927); b. Brooklyn, N.Y. Author of books for children. Pen name, "Ruth Ogden." *A Loyal Little Red-Coat* (1890); *"Courage"* (1891); *A Little Queen of Hearts* (1893); *Little Homespun* (1897); *His Little Royal Highness* (1898); *Loyal Hearts and True* (1899); *Little Pierre and Big Peter* (1915); etc.

Idea of a Theater, The. By Francis Fergusson (1949). A study of ten great plays from the Greeks to modern times, showing the changing purposes and conceptions of the play as a form of theater.

Ideas of Order. Collection of poems by Wallace Stevens (1935).

IDELL, ALBERT E[dward] (June 21, 1901–July 7, 1958); b. Philadelphia, Pa. Novelist. *Pug* (1941); *Cross in the Caribbean* (1941); *Centennial Summer* (1943); *Bridge to Brooklyn* (1944); *Stag Night* (pen name "Phillips Rogers," 1946); *The Sea Is Woman* (1947); *The Great Blizzard* (1948); *Stephen Hayne* (1951); *Mighty Milo* (1954); *Rogers' Folly* (1957); etc.

Ides of March, The. Historical novel by Thornton Wilder (1948). Reconstruction of the assassination of Julius Caesar through imaginary documents.

Idiot's Delight. Play by Robert Sherwood (prod. 1936). An American theatrical group touring Europe is caught in the meshes of a world war. Pulitzer Prize play, 1936.

Idle Man. New York City. Essay magazine. Founded 1821 by Richard Henry Dana, who edited it until 1823, when it expired.

Iduna, and Other Stories. By George A. Hibbard (1891).

"If at first you don't succeed, try, try again." Line from a poem by T. H. Palmer, in *The Village Reader* (1841). It may have been written earlier. It has been wrongly attributed to William E. Hickson.

"If I Should Die Tonight." Poem by Arabella Eugenie Smith (1844–1916), in the *Christian Union,* June 18, 1873. Attributed also to others. The parody by Ben King, with the same title, has almost eclipsed the original. See Burton Stevenson's *Famous Single Poems* (1923).

If: Science Fiction. New York. Bimonthly. Published by Digest Productions Corp. Editor is H. L. Gold; feature editor is Frederick Pohl.

IGNATOW, DAVID (Feb. 7, 1914–   ); b. Brooklyn, N.Y. Poet. *Poems* (1948); *The Gentle Weight Lifter* (1955); *Say Pardon* (1962); *Figures of the Human* (1964); *Earth Hard* (1967); *Poems 1934–69* (1970).

ILES, GEORGE (b. June 20, 1852); b. Gibraltar, came to the United States in 1887. Author. *Leading American Inventors* (1912); *Canadian Stories* (1918); etc. Editor: *Little Masterpieces of Science,* 6v. (1902); *Little Masterpieces of Autobiography,* 6v. (1908).

ILG, FRANCES L. (Oct. 11, 1902–); b. Oak Park, Ill. Educator. Co-author: *The Child from Five to Ten* (with Arnold Gesell and others, 1946); *Youth: The Years from Ten to Sixteen* (with same, 1956); *The Gesell Institute Party Book* (with others, 1959); *Parents Ask* (with Louise Bates Ames, 1962); *Child Behavior* (1966); etc. Director, Gesell Institute for Child Development, since 1950.

I'll Take My Stand: The South and the Agrarian Tradition, by Twelve Southerners (1930). A symposium by J. C. Ransom, Donald Davidson, F. L. Owsley, J. G. Fletcher, L. H. Lanier, Allen Tate, H. C. Nixon, A. N. Lytle, R. P. Warren, J. D. Wade, H. B. Kline, Stark Young.

"I'll Take You Home Again, Kathleen." Song by Thomas Paine Westendorf (1876).

Illinois Herald. Kaskaskia, Ill. Newspaper. Founded 1814, by Matthew Duncan. First newspaper published in Illinois. Later renamed the *Illinois Intelligencer.* Expired c. 1834.

Illinois Intelligencer. See *Illinois Herald.*

Illinois Monthly Magazine. Vandalia, Ill. Founded Oct., 1830, by James Hall. It later moved to Cincinnati, and then to Louisville, Ky., where it expired June, 1837.

ILSLEY, CHARLES P[arker] (1807–1887); b. in Maine. Publisher, author. *Forest and Shore; or, Legends of the Pine-Tree State* (1856), republished as *The Wrecker's Daughter, and Other Tales* (1860). Founder, the *Portland* (Me.) *Transcript,* 1837.

ILSLEY, SAMUEL MARSHALL (b. June 26, 1863); b. Milwaukee, Wis. Author. *By the Western Sea* (1898); *The Whole World* (prod. 1907); *Teacher* (1928).

Imagi. Baltimore, Md. Published irregularly. Founded 1945. Literary magazine. T. Cole has been editor.

Imagists. School of poets headed by Ezra Pound, beginning in 1914. *Des Imagistes* (1914) was the first study of the group. *Some Imagist Poets,* 3v. (1915–17) was an anthology of their poems. Amy Lowell, "H.D.," Richard Aldington, William Carlos Williams, Allen Upward, and John Cournos were among those associated with Pound in a movement to create new patterns of verse, particularly through new and bold images. It was a revolt against conventional poetry. *See* Glenn Hughes's *Imagism & the Imagists* (1931); Stanley Coffman's *Imagism: A Chapter for the History of Modern Poetry* (1951).

IMBS, BRAVIG (Oct. 8, 1904–1946); b. Milwaukee, Wis. Author. *Eden: Exit This Way* (poems, 1927); *The Professor's Wife* (1928); *Chatterton* (1934); *The Cats* (1935); *Confessions of Another Young Man* (1937).

IMLAY, GILBERT (c. 1754–Nov. 20, 1828?); b. in Monmouth Co., N.J. (?). Revolutionary soldier, adventurer, author. *Topographical Description of the Western Territory of North America* (1792); *The Emigrants,* 3v. (1793).

Impending Crisis of the South, The. By Hinton Rowan Helper (1857). An economic appeal to the nonslaveholders of the South. It was refuted by Southern newspapers and orators; copies were publicly burned, and persons possessing copies were jailed. Samuel W. Wolfe wrote a reply to it, *Helper's Impending Crisis Dissected* (1860).

Imperial Purple, The. By Edgar Saltus (1892). Chronicle of the Roman emperors from Julius Caesar to Heliogabalus, showing the extravagance and splendor and vices of the imperial court.

In Abraham's Bosom. Play by Paul Green (prod. 1926), included in his *Lonesome Road* (1926). Abraham McCranie, a mulatto, realizes that the future of his people depends on education. He opens a school financed by his white father. Upon the latter's death, the school has to be abandoned. When McCranie's shiftless son fails him and his own white half-brother refuses financial assistance, McCranie kills him. Pulitzer Prize play, 1927.

"In an Atelier." Poem by Thomas Bailey Aldrich (1875).

In Cold Blood. By Truman Capote (1966). A reportorial account of the murder of a family by two young men who were caught, tried, and executed for the crime. The basic material was written up by the author reflecting the attitudes of the young men and the involvement of the author with them as a result of his interviewing them in prison. Often referred to as a "nonfiction novel."

In Defense of Reason. Work of literary criticism by Yvor Winters (1947). It includes three previous books: *Primitivism and Decadence* (1937), *Maule's Curse* (1938), and *Anatomy of Nonsense* (1943).

In Fact. Long Island City, N.Y. Monthly. Founded 1940, by George Seldes. Devoted to freedom in reporting of the news.

"In Harbor." Civil War poem by Paul Hamilton Hayne.

In His Name. Novel by Edward Everett Hale (1873). Deals with the Waldenses, persecuted religious group in France.

In His Steps. By Charles Monroe Sheldon (1896). Describes a congregation which followed consistently the teachings of Jesus. It sold millions of copies and was translated into many languages, but brought little profit to the author or his publishers because of defective copyright.

"In Memory of W. B. Yeats." Poem by W. H. Auden.

In My Youth. By "Robert Dudley" (James Baldwin) (1914). The book is based on the author's boyhood in Indiana during pioneer days. Baldwin's authorship was kept secret for many years.

In Old Kentucky. Play by Charles Turner Dazey (prod. 1893). The story of a horse race, it was popular as a road show for over a quarter of a century.

In Ole Virginia. Short stories by Thomas Nelson Page (1887). Tales of Virginia, including "Marse Chan" and "Meh Lady," written in Negro dialect.

"In Praise of Johnny Appleseed." Poem by Vachel Lindsay (1921).

"In School-Days." Poem by John Greenleaf Whittier (1870).

In the American Grain. By William Carlos Williams (1925). Imaginative interpretation of historical figures who have helped create the idea of America.

"In the Baggage Coach Ahead." Song by the composer Gussie L. Davis (1896). Popularized by Imogene Comer, known as the "Queen Regent of Song."

In the Bishop's Carriage. Light novel by Miriam Michelson (1904). A best seller of the day.

In the Clouds. Novel by "Charles Egbert Craddock" (Mary Noailles Murfree) (1887). Story of the "poor whites" in the cloudlands of the Big Smoky Mountains in Tennessee, with illicit distilling, court room scenes, and warped romance furnishing the drama.

"In the Evening by the Moonlight." Song by James A. Bland (1880). Known also as "Southern Melodies." Bland also composed "Carry Me Back to Old Virginny."

"In the Good Old Summer Time." Song, words by Ren Shields, music by George "Honey Boy" Evans, the black-face comedian (1902).

In the Midst of Life. Short stories by Ambrose Bierce (1898), originally published as *Tales of Soldiers and Civilians* (1891). Contains his celebrated ghost story, *The Damned Thing.*

"In the Shade of the Old Apple Tree." Song, words by Henry Williams, music by Egbert Van Alstyne (1905).

In the Valley. Novel by Harold Frederic (1890). Narrative of adventure in the Mohawk Valley in New York during the French and Indian wars.

In This Our Life. Novel by Ellen Glasgow (1941). A family of aristocratic background forced to face loneliness and the loss of former values.

In Tune with the Infinite. By Ralph Waldo Trine (1919). A popular book which applies religious psychology to the solution of personal problems.

Inchiquin the Jesuit's Letters, During a Late Residence in the United States of America. By Charles J. Ingersoll, published anonymously (1810). An effort to refute English criticism of American literature and manners.

Inconnue, L'. Pen name of L. Virginia Smith French.

Incunabula. Books printed before 1501. Sometimes the term is applied loosely to the early period of printing in any country, *e.g.,* to books printed in America before 1750.

Incunabula and Americana. By Margaret Bingham Stillwell (1931). A handbook for collectors and librarians based on a study of book rarities in America.

Independent, The. New York City. Weekly magazine. Founded Dec. 7, 1848. Editors: Leonard Bacon, Joseph P. Thompson, Richard S. Storrs, 1848–61; Henry Ward Beecher, 1861–63; Theodore Tilton, 1863–70; Henry Chandler Bowen, 1870–96; William Hayes Ward, 1896–1914; Hamilton Holt, 1914–20; Harold DeWolf Fuller, 1921–24; Richard E. Danielson and Christian A. Herter, 1924–28. It began as a religious publication with Congregationalist leanings. It later became noted for its literary articles. Moved to Boston in 1923. Merged with *The Outlook* in 1928. *See* Frank Luther Mott's *History of American Magazines* vol. 2 (1938).

Index to One-Act Plays, An. Compiled by Hannah Logasa and Winifred Ver Nooy (1924), with supplements in 1932 and 1941. Standard compilation in this field.

Index to Plays, 1800–1926. Compiled by Ina Ten Eyck Firkins (1927). *Supplement* (1935).

Indian Bible. Name commonly applied to the *Holy Bible* translated by John Eliot into the dialect of the Naticks, a tribe of the Algonquins, and printed at Cambridge, Mass., by Samuel Green and Marmaduke Johnson, 1663. First Indian translation of the Bible, and a noted landmark in the history of American printing.

"Indian Burying Ground." Poem by Philip Freneau (1788).

Indian Princess; or, La Belle Sauvage, The. Play by James Nelson Barker (prod. 1808). The first play dealing with the Indian to be produced by an American. It was also the first play based on the story of Pocahontas.

Indian Summer. Novel by William Dean Howells (1886). Story of an American colony in Italy, and the love affairs of a man of forty in a romantic setting.

Indiana Gazette. Vincennes, Ind. Newspaper. Founded 1804, by Elihu Stout. First newspaper published in Indiana. Later called the *Western Sun.* Expired c. 1925.

Indiana University Press. Bloomington, Ind. Founded 1950. Midland Books is an imprint of the press.

Indianapolis News. Indianapolis, Ind. Newspaper. Founded 1869, by John Hampden Holliday, who published and edited it until 1892. "Kin" Hubbard's "Abe Martin" first appeared in the *News.* Roy Wilson Howard began his career as a reporter on the *News* in 1902. Now combined with the *Indianapolis Star;* the *News* appears evenings; the *Star,* mornings and Sunday.

Indianapolis Star. Indianapolis, Ind. Newspaper. Founded 1903. See *Indianapolis News.*

Indians. Play by Arthur Kopit (prod. 1969). Ironic farce about the systematic persecution of the Indians during the course of American history.

Infant and Child Care in the Culture of Today. By Arnold Gesell and Frances Ilg (1943). The most influential scientific study of the development of children during their early years. It was followed by *The Child from Five to Ten* (1946) and *Youth: The Years from Ten to Sixteen* (1956).

INFELD, LEOPOLD (Aug. 20, 1898–Jan. 16, 1968); b. Krakow, Poland. Author. *Quest: The Evolution of a Scientist* (1941); *Whom the Gods Love* (1948); *Albert Einstein* (1950); *Motion and Relativity* (with J. Plebansky, 1961); etc.

Information. Until the 1950's the word "information" generally meant the acquisition of data and intelligence largely by means of reading and study, through published material. In mathematical communication theory it now means a property of all signals and refers to the statistical rarity of signs. The information content of signals lies in their syntactic relations, in their potentiality, and not in their actual value or significance. This change in meaning from a semantic term to a statistical one accompanies a tendency in modern communication studies to conceive of education and learning as deriving from information sources that include words and print but no longer rely on them exclusively. See *McLuhanism.*

INGALLS, JOHN JAMES (Dec. 29, 1833–Aug. 16, 1900); b. Middleton, Mass. Senator, author. *A Collection of the Writings,* ed. by William E. Connelley (1902). His most famous poem is "Opportunity." U.S. Senator, 1873–91. *See* William E. Connelley's *Ingalls of Kansas* (1909).

INGE, WILLIAM (May 3, 1913–); b. Independence, Kans. Playwright. *Farther Off from Heaven* (prod. 1947); *Come Back, Little Sheba* (prod. 1950); *Picnic* (prod. 1953, Pulitzer prize for drama, 1953); *Bus Stop* (prod. 1955); *The Dark at the Top of the Stairs* (prod. 1957); *Splendor in the Grass* (1961); *Natural Affection* (1963); *Where's Daddy?* (1966).

Ingenue. New York. Monthly. Founded 1959. A magazine for teen-age girls.

INGERSOLL, CHARLES JARED (Oct. 3, 1782–May 14, 1862); b. Philadelphia, Pa. Lawyer, author. *Edwy and Elgiva; A Tragedy* (prod. 1801); *Inchiquin the Jesuit's Letters* (anon., 1810); *Julian: A Tragedy* (1831); *Historical Sketch of the Second War between the United States of America and Great Britain,* 2v. (1845–49); *History of the Second War between the United States of America and Great Britain: Second Series,* 2v. (1852); *Recollections* (1861); etc.

INGERSOLL, ERNEST (Mar. 13, 1852–Nov. 13, 1946); b. Monroe, Mich. Naturalist, author. *Knocking 'Round the Rockies* (1882); *Country Cousins* (1884); *The Strange Ventures of a Stowaway* (1885); *Wild Life in Orchard and Field* (1902); *The Wit of the Wild* (1906); *Birds in Legend, Fable and Folklore* (1923); *Dragons and Dragon Lore* (1928); etc.

INGERSOLL, RALPH McALLISTER (Dec. 8, 1900–); b. New Haven, Conn. Editor, author. *In and Under Mexico* (1923); *Report on England* (1940); *The Battle Is the Payoff* (1943); *Top Secret* (1946); *The Great Ones* (1948); *Wine of Violence* (1951); *Point of Departure* (1961); etc. With the *New Yorker,* 1925–30; managing editor, *Fortune,* 1930–35; vice president Time, Inc., 1935–38; founder, *PM,* 1939.

INGERSOLL, ROBERT GREEN (Aug. 11, 1833–July 21, 1899); b. Dresden, N.Y. Orator, agnostic, author. *The Gods* (1872); *Some Mistakes of Moses* (1879); *Why I Am an Agnostic* (1896); *The Works of Robert G. Ingersoll,* 12v. (1900); etc. *See* H. E. Kittredge's *Ingersoll* (1911); Cameron Rogers's *Colonel Bob Ingersoll* (1927).

INGLIS, ALEXANDER JAMES (Nov. 24, 1879–Apr. 12, 1924); b. Middletown, Conn. Educator, influential in reorganization of secondary schools, author. *Principles of Secondary Education* (1918); *Virginia Public Schools* (1919). Dept. education, Harvard University, 1914–24.

INGOLD, ERNEST (Mar. 26, 1885–); b. Chicago, Ill. Business executive, author. *Tales of a Peddler* (1942); *The House in Mallorca* (1950).

INGRAHAM, JOSEPH HOLT (Jan. 25/26, 1809–Dec. 18, 1860); b. Portland, Me. Episcopal clergyman, novelist. *The South-West* (anon. 1835); *Lafitte, the Pirate of the Gulf* (anon. 1836); *Burton; or, The Sieges,* 2v. (anon. 1838); *The American Lounger* (anon. 1839); *Captain Kyd* (anon. 1839); *The Quadroone* (anon. 1841); *Edward Austin* (1842); *Jemmy Daily* (1843); *Morris Graeme* (1843); *Arnold; or, The British Spy* (1844); *The Corsair of Casco Bay* (1844); *The Midshipman* (1844); *The Spanish Galleon* (1844); *Rafael* (1845); *The Slave King* (1846); *The Spectre Steamer, and Other Tales* (1846); *Blanche Talbot* (1847); *The Treason of Arnold* (anon. 1847); *The Prince of the House of David* (1855); *The Pillar of Fire* (1859); *The Throne of David* (1860); etc. *See* Lyle H. Wright's *American Fiction* (1939).

INGRAHAM, PRENTISS (Dec. 22, 1843–Aug. 16, 1904); b. near Natchez, Miss., son of Joseph Holt Ingraham. Confederate soldier, adventurer, dime novelist. *Wild Madge* (1881); *The Beautiful Rivals* (1884); *Saratoga* (1885); *Darkie Dan* (1888); *Zuleikah: A Story of Crete* (1887); *Cadet Carey of West Point* (1890); *An American Monte Cristo* (1891); *The Girl Rough Riders* (1903); *Lafitte, the Pirate of the Gulf* (1931); *La Fitte's Lieutenant* (1931); etc. The dates are not necessarily those of first editions. Over two hundred of his dime novels had "Buffalo Bill" (William F. Cody) as their hero. *See* Edmund L. Pearson's *Dime Novels* (1929).

Inland. Salt Lake City, Utah. Literary quarterly. Founded 1957. Incorporated with *Interim.* Edited by John Rackham.

INMAN, ARTHUR CREW (May 11, 1895–); b. Atlanta, Ga. Poet. *Red Autumn* (1920); *American Silhouettes* (1925); *Bubbles of Gold* (1923); *The Night Express* (1927); *None Now Are Quietly Wise* (1939); etc.

INMAN, HENRY (July 30, 1837–Nov. 13, 1899); b. New York City. Author. *The Old Santa Fé Trail* (1897); *Tales of the Trail* (1898); *The Great Salt Lake Trail* (with William F. Cody, 1898); *The Delahoydes* (1899); etc. Editor: *Buffalo Jones's Forty Years of Adventure* (1899).

INMAN, SAMUEL GUY (June 24, 1877–Feb. 19, 1965); b. Trinity, Tex. Latin Americanist, author. *Through Santo Domingo and Haiti* (1919); *South America Today* (1921); *Trailing the Conquistadores* (1930); *Latin America: Its Place in World Life* (1937); *History of Latin America for Schools* (with C. E. Casteñeda, 1954); *History of Inter-American Conferences* (1963); etc. Prof. international relations, University of Pennsylvania 1937–42; University of Mexico, from 1952.

INNES, HAMMOND (1913–). Author. *Trapped* (1940); *Attack Alarm* (1942); *Blue Ice* (1948); *Campbell's Kingdom* (1952); *The Wreck of the Mary Deare* (1956); *The Land God Gave to Cain* (1958); *Harvest of Journeys* (autobiography, 1960); *Atlantic Fury* (1962); *The Strode Venturer* (1965); *The White South* (1966); *Sea and Islands* (1967); *The Conquistadors* (1969); *Levkas Man* (1971).

Innocents Abroad. By "Mark Twain" (1869). Record of a trip to Europe, Egypt, and the Holy Land, made on the steamer "Quaker City." Filled with humorous incidents and observations of places and peoples not found in any conventional guide book, and with many a new and unorthodox slant on history.

Inside Europe. Journalistic account of European politics and society, by John Gunther (1936). First of a series of "inside" reports, followed by *Inside Asia* (1939), *Inside Latin America* (1941), *Inside U.S.A.* (1947), *Inside Africa* (1955); etc.

Inside the Cup. Novel by Winston Churchill (1913). Story of John Hodder, preacher from a small New England parish who is called to a fashionable city church to combat the trend toward modernism, but the urgency of the modern problems he faces revolutionizes his ideas.

International Conciliation. New York. Five issues yearly. Founded 1907. Published by Carnegie Endowment for International Peace.

International Episode, An. Novelette by Henry James (1879). Lord Lambeth, on a visit to America, falls in love with Bessie Alden, and she visits England and meets him again. Although his family disapproves, he proposes to her, but she, thoughtfully, refuses.

International Index to Periodicals. New York City. Quarterly. Founded 1904. Cumulative author and subject index of periodicals, with annual and two-, three-, and four-year volumes. Now known as *Social Sciences and Humanities Index.*

International Monthly Magazine of Literature, Science and Art. New York City. Founded July, 1850, with Rufus Griswold as editor. It was published by Stringer and Townsend. Merged with *Harper's Monthly Magazine* in 1852.

International Review. New York. Magazine. Founded 1874, by John McD. Leavitt. One of its editors was Henry Cabot Lodge. Among its contributors were Henry James, Brander Matthews, John Fiske, Oliver Wendell Holmes, John Greenleaf Whittier. Expired 1883.

Interpreter's Bible, The. The Holy Scriptures in the King James and Revised Standard versions, with general articles and introduction, exegesis, and exposition for each book of the Bible. Edited by George Arthur Buttrick and others in twelve volumes and published 1951–57.

Intext Educational Publishers. Scranton, Pa. Publishers. Ballantine Books, the John Day Co., and the Steck-Vaughn Co. are all subsidiaries. Acquired Abelard-Schuman in 1969.

Intruder in the Dust. Novel by William Faulkner (1948). A white boy grows in moral stature as he faces the legal trial of a Negro who behaves proudly under duress.

INVERARITY, ROBERT BRUCE (1909–). Author, editor. *Movable Masks and Figures of the North Pacific Coast Indians* (1941); *Art of the Northwest Coast Indians* (1950); etc. Editor: *Winslow Homer in the Adirondacks* (1959).

Invisible Man, The. Novel by Ralph Ellison (1952). The moral progress of a Negro from accommodation to life in a Southern town to horror at life after a race riot in Harlem. A brutal but probing analysis of the relations not only between whites and Negroes but between Negroes and others of their own race.

Invitation to Learning. New York. Quarterly. Founded 1951. Devoted to discussions of classics in literature.

IOOR, WILLIAM (1780?–1830); b. Dorchester, S.C. Playwright. *Independence; or, Which Do You Like Best, the Peer or the Farmer?* (prod. 1805); *The Battle of Eutaw Springs and Evacuation of Charleston* (prod. 1813).

Iowan, The. Shenandoah, Ia. Bimonthly. Founded 1952. Published by Sentinel Publishing Co. Devoted to Iowa life and culture.

IRELAND, JOSEPH NORTON (Apr. 24, 1817–Dec. 29, 1898); b. New York City. Historian of the stage. *Records of the New York Stage, from 1750 to 1860,* 2v. (1866–67); *Mrs.* [Mary Ann] *Duff* (1882); etc.

IRELAND, THOMAS SAXTON (Dec. 16, 1895–); b. Cleveland. O. Lawyer, author. *The Great Lakes–St. Lawrence Deep Waterway to the Sea* (1934); *War Clouds in the Skies of the Far East* (1935); *Ireland Past and Present* (1942); *The Great Lakes–St. Lawrence Seaway and Power Project* (1946); etc.

Irish, William. Pen name of Cornell Woolrich.

Irish American. New York City. Roman Catholic weekly. Founded 1849. Expired 1915.

Irish World and American Industrial Liberator. New York. Founded 1870 by Patrick Ford, who was editor, 1870–1913.

Iron Woman, The. Novel by Margaret Deland (1911). Sequel to her *The Awakening of Helena Ritchie* (1906).

Ironquill. Pen name of Eugene Fitch Ware.

IRVINE, WILLIAM (June 9, 1906–Oct. 8, 1964); b. Carson Hill, Calif. Educator, author. *Walter Bagehot* (1939); *The Universe of G.B.S.* (1949); *Apes, Angels and Victorians* (1955); etc. Prof. English, Stanford University, from 1948.

IRVING, JOHN TREAT (Dec. 2, 1812–Feb. 27, 1906); b. New York City. Author. *Indian Sketches,* 2v. (1835); *The Hunters of the Prairie; or, The Hawk Chief* (1837); *The Quod Correspondent; or, The Attorney,* 2v. (1842); *Harry Harson* (1844); *The Van Gelder Papers, and Other Sketches* (1887); etc. Wrote for the *Knickerbocker Magazine* under the pen name of "John Quod."

Irving, Minna. Pen name of Minnie Odell.

IRVING, PETER (Oct. 30, 1771–June 27, 1838); b. New York City. Author. *Giovanni Sbogarro: A Venetian Tale,* 2v. (under pen name "Percival G——," 1820). He assisted his brother, Washington Irving, in the preparation of his *A History of New York* (1809).

Irving, Robert. Pen name of Irving Adler.

IRVING, WASHINGTON (Apr. 3, 1783–Nov. 28, 1859); b. New York City. Author. *A History of New York,* 2v. (under pen name "Diedrich Knickerbocker," 1809); *The Sketch Book of Geoffrey Crayon, Gent.,* 7 pts. (1819–20); *Bracebridge Hall,* 2v. (1822); *Tales of a Traveller* (1824); *A History of the Life and Voyages of Christopher Columbus,* 3v. (1828); *A Chronicle of the Conquest of Granada,* 2v. (1829); *The Alhambra,* 2v. (1832); *A Tour on the Prairies* (1835); *Astoria,* 2v. (1836); *The Adventures of Captain Bonneville,* 2v. (1837); *The Life of Oliver Goldsmith,* 4v. (1849); *Mahomet and His Successors,* 2v. (1850); *Wolfert's Roost* (1855); *Life of George Washington,* 5v. (1855–59); etc. There are many editions of his collected works. See *The Works of Washington Irving,* 40v. (1891). *The Journals of Washington Irving* (1919), ed. by W. P. Trent and G. S. Hellman; *Journal of Washington Irving* (1931), ed. by S. T. Williams; *Letters of Washington Irving to Henry Brevoort* (1915), ed. by G. S. Hellman; *Letters of Henry Brevoort to Washington Irving* (1916), ed. by G. S. Hellman. *See also* P. M. Irving's *The Life and Letters of Washington Irving,* 4v. (1862–64); H. W. Boynton's *Washington Irving* (1901); George S. Hellman's *Washington Irving* (1925); Claude G. Bowers's *The Spanish Adventures of Washington Irving* (1940); Edward Wagenknecht's *Washington Irving* (1962); William L. Hedges, *Washington Irving, An American Study* (1965). For complete bibliographies see William R. Langfeld and Philip C. Blackburn's *Washington Irving: A Bibliography* (1933); S. T. Williams and M. E. Edge's *A Bibliography of the Writings of Washington Irving* (1936). See also *Salmagundi,* Astor Library. Among the pen names used by Irving were "Geoffrey Corson," "Anthony Evergreen," "Jonathan Oldstyle." Large collections of Irving books and manuscripts are in the New York Public Library (Hellman collection), and Yale University Library.

IRWIN, FLORENCE (1869–); b. Philadelphia, Pa. Author. *The Road to Mecca* (1916); *The Mask* (1917); *Poor Dear Theodora* (1920); and many books on bridge.

IRWIN, INEZ HAYNES (Mar. 2, 1873–); b. Rio de Janeiro, Brazil. Author. *June Jeopardy* (1908); the *Maida* series; *Janey* (1911); *Angel Island* (1914); *The Californiacs* (1916); *The Happy Years* (1919); *Out of the Air* (1921); *Family Circle* (1931); *Angels and Amazons* (1933); *Murder Masquerade* (1935); *A Body Rolled Downstairs* (1938); *Women Swore Revenge* (1946).

Irwin, Mrs. Wallace. See Laetitia McDonald.

IRWIN, THEODORE (Sept. 17, 1907–   ); b. New York. Author. *Collusion* (1932); *Strange Passage* (1935); *Accident of Birth* (1937); *Holland: Fantastic Land Below the Sea* (1961); *Modern Birth Control* (1961); *Better Health After Fifty* (1964); *What Executives Should Know about Tension* (1965).

IRWIN, VIOLET [Mary] (1881–); b. Toronto, Ont. Author. *The Human Desire* (1913); *Wits and the Woman* (1919); *Kak, the Copper Eskimo* (with Vilhjalmur Stefansson, 1924); *The Shaman's Revenge* (1925); *The Mountain of Jade* (1926); *The Short Sword* (1928).

IRWIN, WALLACE [Admah] (Mar. 15, 1876–Feb. 14, 1959); b. Oneida, N.Y. Author. *The Love Sonnets of a Hoodlum* (1904); *Chinatown Ballads* (1905); *Random Rhymes and Odd Numbers* (1906); *Letters of a Japanese Schoolboy* (1909); *Mr. Togo, Maid of All Work* (1913); *Venus in the East* (1918); *Seed of the Sun* (1921); *Mated* (1926); *The Days of Her Life* (1931); *Young Wife* (1936); *Yankee Doctor in Paradise* (with S. M. Lambert, 1941); etc.

IRWIN, WILL[iam Henry] (Sept. 14, 1873–Feb. 24, 1948); b. Oneida, N.Y. Editor, author. *Stanford Stories* (with C. K. Field, 1900); *The Reign of Queen Isyl* (with Gelett Burgess, 1903); *The Picaroons* (with same, 1903); *The Hamadryads* (1904); *Old Chinatown* (1908); *The House of Mystery* (1910); *Beating Back* (with Al Jennings, 1914); *A Reporter in Armageddon* (1918); *Christ or Mars* (1923); *Youth Rides West*

(1925); *Highlights of Manhattan* (1927); *Herbert Hoover: A Reminiscent Biography* (1928); *Lute Song* (play, with Sidney Howard, 1930); *The Making of a Reporter* (1942); etc. Editor, *The Wave,* 1900; with *McClure's Magazine,* 1906–07; *Collier's Weekly,* 1907–08; etc.

Is There a Santa Claus? Editorial by Frances Pharcellus Church, in the New York *Sun,* Sept. 21, 1897. Frequently reprinted.

ISAACS, ASHER (Mar. 13, 1902–Sept. 3, 1963); b. Cincinnati, O. Educator, editor. *International Trade: Tariff and Commercial Policies* (1948); *Selected Readings in Modern Economics* (co-ed., 1952); etc. Editor, *American Jewish Outlook,* 1934–46. Prof. economics, University of Pittsburgh, 1946–63.

ISAACS, EDITH J[uliet] R[ich] (Mrs. Lewis Montefiore Isaacs) (Mar. 27, 1878–Jan. 10, 1956); b. Milwaukee, Wis. Editor, author. *Theatre* (1927); *Plays of American Life and Fantasy* (1929); *Architecture for the New Theatre* (1935); *The Negro in the American Theatre* (1947). Editor, *Theatre Arts Magazine* (now *Theatre Arts Monthly*), 1924–46.

ISAACS, HAROLD ROBERT (Sept. 13, 1910–); b. New York. Author. *The Tragedy of the Chinese Revolution* (1938); *No Peace for Asia* (1947); *Two-Thirds of the World* (1950); *Scratches on Our Minds: American Images of China and India* (1958); *Emergent Americans: A Report on Crossroads Africa* (1961); *The New World of Negro Americans* (1963); *India's Ex-Untouchables* (1965); *American Jews in Israel* (1967).

ISELY, BLISS (Feb. 10, 1881–); b. Fairview, Kan. Author. *Early Days in Kansas* (1927); *Blazing the Way West* (1939); *Our Careers as Citizens* (with W. M. Richards, 1943); *The Presidents: Men of Faith* (1953); *The Kansas Story* (with Richards, 1961); *Bird People* (1965).

ISHAM, FREDERIC STEWART (Mar. 29, 1866–Sept. 8, 1922); b. Detroit, Mich. Novelist. *The Strollers* (1902); *Under the Rose* (1903); *Aladdin from Broadway* (1913); *Nothing But the Truth* (1915); *Three Live Ghosts* (1918); etc.

ISHAM, SAMUEL (May 12, 1855–June 12, 1914); b. New York City. Artist, author. *The History of American Painting* (1905).

ISHERWOOD, CHRISTOPHER (Aug. 26, 1904–); b. High Lane, Eng. Author. *All The Conspirators* (1928); *Mr. Norris Changes Trains* (1935); *Goodbye to Berlin* (1939); *Prater Violet* (1945); *The Condor and the Cows* (1949); *The World in the Evening* (1954); *Down There on a Visit* (1962); *A Single Man* (1964); *Ramakrishna and His Disciples* (1965); *Exhumations* (1966); *A Meeting by the River* (1967). Co-author, with W. H. Auden: *The Dog Beneath the Skin* (play, 1935); *Ascent of F6* (play, 1936); *On the Frontier* (play, 1938); *Journey to a War* (1939). Translator: *The Intimate Journals of Charles Baudelaire* (1947); *The Bhagavad Gita* (with Swami Prabhavananda, 1944); *The Crest—Jewel of Discrimination* (with same, 1947); *How to Know God: The Yoga Aphorisms* (with same, 1953).

Israel Potter. Novel by Herman Melville (1855). Based on the career of a Revolutionary soldier at the Battle of Bunker Hill, and his escape from a British ship and subsequent adventures with John Paul Jones.

"Israfel." Poem by Edgar Allan Poe (1831).

Israfel: The Life and Times of Edgar Allan Poe. By Hervey Allen, 2v. (1926). A biography of Poe.

It Is. New York. Triannual. Founded 1958. Published by Second-Half Publishing Co., Inc. Devoted to reproductions of and written work concerning abstract art.

It Pays to Advertise. Play by Roi Cooper Megrue and Walter Hackett (prod. 1914). A story of business success.

Italian Journeys. By William Dean Howells (1867). Record of leisurely trips to the famed centers of Italy and the impact of ancient culture on a literary American.

It's a Great Life. Autobiography by John Charles Nugent (1940). A chronicle of theatrical life in America since 1880.

IVES, BURL [Icle Ivanhoe] (June 14, 1909–); b. Hunt, Ill. Singer, actor. *Wayfaring Stranger* (autobiography, 1948); *Burl Ives Song Book* (1953); *Tales of America* (1954); *Irish Songs* (1958); *Albad the Oaf* (1965); etc.

Ives, James Merritt. See Currier & Ives.

IVES, SARAH NOBLE (1864–); b. Grosse Ile, Mich. Author of children's books. *Songs of the Shining Way* (1895); *The Story of a Little Bear* (1908); *The Key to Betsy's Heart* (1916); *Dog Heroes of Many Lands* (1922); *Altadena* (1938).

Ivory Tower, The. Unfinished novel by Henry James (1917).

J

J. A. K. Pen name of Anna Bolles Williams.

J. S. of Dale. Pen name of Frederic Jesup Stimson.

JACCACI, AUGUSTO FLORIANO (Jan. 28, 1856–July 22, 1930); b. Fontainebleau, France. Artist, illustrator. Author: *On the Trail of Don Quixote* (1896). Art director, *McClure's Magazine*, and *Scribner's Magazine.* Founder, August F. Jaccaci Co., New York.

JACK, THEODORE HENLEY (Dec. 30, 1881–Sept. 20, 1964); b. Bellevue, Ala. Educator, author. *Sectionalism and Party Politics in Alabama, 1816–42* (1919); *The Story of America* (with Smith Burnham, 1933); etc. President, Randolph-Macon Woman's College, 1933–52.

Jack Cade. Play by Robert Taylor Conrad (prod. 1835), under the title of *Aylmere.* Story of the insurrections in England in 1431 and 1450. The hero seeks to abolish serfdom. For further changes of title, *see* Robert Taylor Conrad.

Jack Lafaience Book. By James J. McLoughlin (1922). A collection of letters written in Creole dialect for New Orleans newspapers over a period of some thirty years.

JACKS, LEO VINCENT (Mar. 14, 1896–); b. Grand Island, Neb. Author. *Xenophon, Soldier of Fortune* (1939); *La Salle* (1931); *Mother Marianne of Molokai* (1935); *Claude Dubuis, Bishop of Galveston* (1946); *Wires West* (1957); *Prairie Venture* (1958).

JACKSON, A[braham] V[alentine] WILLIAMS (Feb. 9, 1862–Aug. 8, 1937); b. New York City. Educator, Orientalist, author. *Persia Past and Present* (1906); *From Constantinople to the Home of Omar Khayyam* (1911); *Early Persian Poetry* (1920); and other books on Iran [Persia], its history, language, and religion. Editor: *History of India*, 9v. (1906–1907). Prof. Indo-Iranian languages, Columbia University, 1895–1935.

JACKSON, ANDREW (Mar. 15, 1767–June 8, 1845); b. Waxhaw Settlement, S.C. Seventh president of the United States. Known as "Old Hickory." *Correspondence*, ed. by John S. Bassett, 6v. (1926–35). *See* James Parton's *Life of Andrew Jackson*, 3v. (1860); W. G. Sumner's *Andrew Jackson* (1882); John S. Bassett's *The Life of Andrew Jackson* (1911); Frederic A. Ogg's *The Reign of Andrew Jackson* (1919); Claude G. Bowers's *The Party Battles of the Jackson Period* (1922); Gerald W. Johnson's *Andrew Jackson* (1927); Meredith Nicholson's *The Cavalier of Tennessee* (1928); Marquis James's *Andrew Jackson*, 2v. (1933–37); Erich Brandeis's *Andrew Jackson, Old Hickory* (1936); Sister Grace Madelei-

ne's *Monetary and Banking Theories of Jacksonian Democracy* (1943); Arthur Schlesinger, Jr.'s, *The Age of Jackson* (1945); Marquis James's *Andrew Jackson: Border Captain* (1959); James L. Bugg's *Jacksonian Democracy: Myth or Reality* (1962); Robert V. Remini's *Andrew Jackson* (1966); Peter Temin's *Jacksonian Economy* (1969); Ronald E. Shaw's *Andrew Jackson, 1767–1845: Chronology, Documents, Bibliographical Aids* (1969).

JACKSON, CHARLES [Reginald] (Apr. 6, 1903–Sept. 21, 1968); b. Summit, N. J. Author. *The Lost Weekend* (1944); *The Fall of Valor* (1946); *The Outer Edges* (1948); *Sunnier Side* (1950); *Earthly Creatures* (1953); *How To Buy A Used Car* (1967).

JACKSON, CHARLES TENNEY (Oct. 15, 1874–); b. St. Louis, Mo. Journalist, novelist. *Loser's Luck* (1905); *John the Fool* (1915); *Captain Sazarac* (1922); *Buffalo Wallow* (1953); *New Orleans Adventure* (1955); etc.

JACKSON, FREDERICK. Novelist. *A Week in Wall Street* (1841); *The Victim of Chancery* (1841); *The Effinghams* (1841); *Riches and Honor* (1847); all anonymous.

JACKSON, FREDERICK (Sept. 21, 1886–May 22, 1953); b. Pittsburgh, Pa. Playwright, novelist. Pen name, "Victor Thorne." Under own name: *The Hidden Princess* (1910); *A Full House* (prod. 1915); *The Diamond Necklace* (1930); *The School for Husbands* (prod. 1932;) *The Bishop Misbehaves* (prod. 1935); *The Ghost Flies South* (1937); etc.; also, under pen name: *Anne Against the World* (1925); *The Man Who Married for Money* (1925); *Golden Temptation* (1926); *Quicksands* (1926); *Open Your Eyes* (prod. 1929); *The Ninth Man* (prod. 1931); *The Bishop Misbehaves* (1934); *Ghost Flies South* (play, 1937); *Man Bites Dog* (play, 1939); etc.

Jackson, Frederick John Foakes. See Frederick John Foakes-Jackson.

JACKSON, GABRIELLE E[milie Snow] (b. Oct. 13, 1861); b. New York City. Author of children's books. *Pretty Polly Perkins* (1900); *Little Miss Sunshine* (1902); *The Dawn of Womanhood* (1908); *Dixie School Girl* (1939); etc.

JACKSON, GEORGE PULLEN (Aug. 20, 1874–Jan. 19, 1953); b. Monson, Me. Educator, musicologist, author. *White Spirituals in the Southern Uplands* (1933); *Spiritual Folk Songs of Early America* (1937); *Down-East Spirituals* (1940); *White and Negro Spirituals* (1943); *Another Sheaf of White Spirituals* (1952). German dept., Vanderbilt University, 1918–43.

JACKSON, HELEN [Maria Fiske] HUNT (Oct. 15, 1830–Aug. 12, 1885); b. Amherst, Mass. Novelist, poet. Wrote under initials, "H.H"; also used pen name, "Saxe Holm." *Bathmendi* (1867); *Verses* (1870); *Saxe Holm's Stories*, 2 series (1874, 1878); *Mercy Philbrick's Choice* (anon., 1876); *Hetty's Strange History* (anon., 1877); *Nelly's Silver Mine* (1878); *A Century of Dishonor* (1881); *Ramona* (1884); *Zeph* (1885); *Sonnets and Lyrics* (1886); *Poems* (1891); etc. *See* Ruth Odell's *Helen Hunt Jackson (H.H)* (1931); Thomas Wentworth Higginson's *Contemporaries* (1899).

JACKSON, HENRY ROOTES (June 24, 1820–May 23, 1898); b. Athens, Ga. Lawyer, editor, poet. *Tallulah, and Other Poems* (1850). His best known poems are "My Wife and Child" and "The Red Old Hills of Georgia." *See* C. C. Jones's *History of Savannah, Georgia* (1890).

JACKSON, JOSEPH [Francis Ambrose] (May 20, 1867–Mar. 4, 1946); b. Philadelphia, Pa. Editor, bibliographer, author. *Dickens in Philadelphia* (1912); *Market Street, Philadelphia* (1918); *Encyclopedia of Philadelphia*, 4v. (1931–33); *Literary Landmarks of Philadelphia* (1939); etc. On staff, *Philadelphia Evening Ledger*, 1888–1918. Editor, *The Pennsylvania Architect*, from 1938.

JACKSON, JOSEPH HENRY (July 21, 1894–July 15, 1955); b. Madison, N.J. Editor, literary critic. *Mexican Interlude* (1936); *Notes on a Drum: Travel Sketches in Guatemala* (1937); *Tintypes in Gold* (1939); *Anybody's Gold* (1941); *My San Francisco* (1953); *The Girl in the Belfry* (1955); etc. Editor: *Portable Murder Book* (1945); *The Gold Rush Album* (1949); etc. Wrote daily column, "A Bookman's Notebook," in *San Francisco Chronicle,* from 1930. Began first radio broadcasts of book reviews, May 22, 1924.

Jackson, Laura Riding. See Laura Riding.

JACKSON, MARGARET DOYLE (b. Jan. 7, 1868); b. in Bermuda, B. W. I. Author. *A Daughter of the Pit* (1903); *The Horse-Leech's Daughter* (1904); *When Love Is King* (1905).

JACKSON, MARGARET WEYMOUTH (Feb. 11, 1895–); b. Eureka Springs, Ark. Novelist. *Elizabeth's Tower* (1926); *Jenny Fowler* (1930); *First Fiddle* (1932); *Sarah Thornton* (1933); etc.

JACKSON, PHYLLIS WYNNE. Author. *Victorian Cinderella* (1948); *Golden Footlights* (1949).

JACKSON, SAMUEL MACAULEY (June 19, 1851–Aug. 2, 1912); b. New York City. Presbyterian clergyman, editor. Assoc. editor: *A Religious Encyclopedia,* 3v. (1882–84), popularly known as the "Schaff-Herzog Encyclopedia"; editor-in-chief: *New Schaff-Herzog Encyclopedia of Religious Knowledge,* 13v. (1908–14); etc.

JACKSON, SHIRLEY (Dec. 14, 1919–Aug. 8, 1965); b. San Francisco, Cal. Author. *The Road Through the Wall* (1948); *The Lottery* (1949); *Hangsaman* (1951); *Life Among the Savages* (1953); *The Bird's Nest* (1954); *The Witchcraft of Salem Village* (1956); *The Sundial* (1958); *The Haunting of Hill House* (1959); *We Have Always Lived in the Castle* (1962).

JACKSON, WILLIAM HENRY (Apr. 4, 1843–June 30, 1942); b. Keeseville, N.Y. Photographer, explorer, author. *The Pioneer Photographer: Rocky Mountain Adventures with a Camera* (with Howard R. Driggs, 1929); *Time Exposure* (autobiography, 1940).

JACOBS, CHARLES MICHAEL (Dec. 5, 1875–Mar. 30, 1938); b. Gettysburg, Pa. Lutheran clergyman, educator, author. *The Story of the Church* (1925); *Help on the Road* (1933); *The Faith of the Church* (1938); etc. Prof. church history, Lutheran Theological Seminary, Philadelphia, 1913–38; president, 1927–38.

JACOBS, HELEN HULL (Aug. 6, 1908–); b. Globe, Ariz. Tennis player, author. *Modern Tennis* (1932); *Beyond the Game* (autobiography, 1936); *Gallery of Champions* (1949); *Judy, Tennis Ace* (1951); *Proudly She Serves* (1953); *Famous Women Athletes* (1964); *The Young Sportsman's Guide to Tennis* (1965); *Courage to Conquer* (1967); etc. Under pen name "H. Braxton Hull": *Barry Cort* (1938).

JACOBS, JANE (May 4, 1916–); b. Scranton, Pa. Author. *The Death and Life of Great American Cities* (1961); *The Economy of Cities* (1969). Associate editor, *Architectural Forum.*

JACOBS, JOSEPH (Aug. 29, 1854–Jan. 30, 1916); b. Sydney, N.S.W. Editor, author. *Indian Fairy Tales* (1892); *Celtic Fairy Tales* (1892); *The Jews of Angevin England* (1893); *As Others Saw Him* (1895); *Europa's Fairy Book* (1916); etc. Founder, *The Jewish Year Book,* (1896); editor, *American Hebrew,* 1913–16.

JACOBS, MELVILLE (1902–). Anthropologist, author. *Northwest Sahaptin Texts* (1929); *Coos Myth Texts* (1940); *Kalapuya Texts* (1945); *Content and Style of an Oral Literature: Clackamas Chinook Myths and Tales* (1959); *The People Are Coming Soon* (1960); *Pattern in Cultural Anthropology* (1964); *The Anthropologist Looks at Myth* (1966).

JACOBS, PAUL (Aug. 24, 1918–   ); b. New York. Author. *Old Age and Political Behavior* (with others, 1959); *Labor in a Free Society* (with M. Harrington, 1959); *The State of the Unions* (1963); *Is Curly Jewish?* (1965); *The New Radicals* (with S. Landau, 1966); *Prelude to Riot* (1968); *Between the Rock and the Hard Place* (1970).

JACOBS, THORNWELL (Feb. 15, 1877–Aug. 4, 1956); b. Clinton, S.C. Presbyterian clergyman, educator, editor. *The Law of the White Circle* (1908); *Midnight Mummer* (poems, 1911); *Life of William Plumer Jacobs* (1918); *The New Science and the Old Religion* (1927); *Islands of the Blest, and Other Poems* (1928); *Story of Christmas* (1941); *Step Down, Dr. Jacobs* (1945); etc. Founder, the *Westminster Magazine,* 1912. Founder, Oglethorpe University, Atlanta, Ga., and president from 1915.

JACOBS, WILBUR RIPLEY (June 30, 1918–); b. Chicago, Ill. Historian. *Diplomacy and Indian Gifts* (1950); *Indians of the Southern Colonial Frontier* (1954); *Letters of Francis Parkman,* 2v. (1960); *Frederick Jackson Turner's Legacy* (1965); *The Paxton Riots and the Frontier Theory* (1967). Prof. American history, University of California at Santa Barbara, since 1960.

Jacobs-Bond, Carrie. See Carrie Jacobs Bond.

JACOBY, OSWALD (Dec. 8, 1902–   ); b. Brooklyn, N.Y. Actuary, author. *Oswald Jacoby on Poker* (1940); *How to Figure the Odds* (1946); *Gin Rummy* (1946); *How to Win at Canasta* (1949); *Oswald Jacoby's Complete Canasta* (1950); *Winning Poker* (1950); *What's New in Bridge?* (1953); *Mathematics for Pleasure* (with William H. Benson, 1962); *Oswald Jacoby on Gambling* (1963).

JAEGER, WERNER [Wilhelm] (July 30, 1888–Oct. 20, 1961); b. Lobberich, Ger. Educator, author. *Aristotle: Fundamentals of the History of His Development* (1934); *Demosthenes: The Origin and Growth of His Policy* (1938); *Paideia: The Ideals of Greek Culture,* 3v. (1939–44); *Two Rediscovered Works of Ancient Christian Literature* (1954); *Early Christianity and Greek Paideia* (1961). Prof. classics, Harvard University, from 1939.

JAEKEL, FREDERIC BLAIR (May 6, 1882–Feb. 9, 1943); b. Hollidaysburg, Pa. Editor, author. *The Land of the Tamed Turk* (1910); *Windmills and Wooden Shoes* (1912). Editor, the *Bucks County Daily News,* Doylestown, Pa., 1921–24; etc.

JAFFE, RONA. Author. *The Best of Everything* (1958); *Mr. Right Is Dead* (1965); *The Cherry in the Martini* (1966); *The Fame Game* (1969).

JAKOBSON, ROMAN (Oct. 11, 1896–   ); b. Moscow. Linguist, literary historian. *Kindersprache, Aphasie und Allgemeine Lautgesetze* (1941); *La Geste d'Igor* (with others, 1948); *Russian Epic Studies* (with E. J. Simmons, 1949); *Preliminaries to Speech Analysis* (with others, 1952); *Fundamentals of Language* (1956); *Selected Writings* (1962–68).

JAMES, ALICE ARCHER SEWALL (1870–Sept. 20, 1955); b. Glendale, O. Illustrator, poet. *Ode to Girlhood, and Other Poems* (1899); *The Ballad of the Prince* (1900); *The Morning Moon (1941); A Biography of Frank Sewall* (1952).

JAMES, BESSIE [Williams] ROWLAND (Mrs. Marquis James) (July 29, 1895–); b. Imporia, Tex. Author. *For God, for Country, for Home* (1920); *Six Feet Six* (with husband, 1931); *Happy Animals of Atagahi* (1935); *The Courageous Heart* (with husband, 1934); *Biography of a Bank* (with same, 1954).

JAMES, EDWIN (Aug. 27, 1797–Oct. 28, 1861); b. Weybridge, Vt. Explorer, naturalist, author. *Account of an Expedition from Pittsburgh to the Rocky Mountains Performed in the Years 1819 and '20,* 2v. (1823), based on the notes of

Major Stephen H. Long and others; *A Narrative of the Captivity and Adventures of John Tanner* (1830).

JAMES, FLEMING (Jan. 11, 1877–Sept. 11, 1959); b. Gambier, O. Episcopal clergyman, educator, author. *Thirty Psalmists* (1938); *Personalities of the Old Testament* (1939). Prof. Old Testament literature, Yale University, 1921–40; University of the South, 1940–47.

JAMES, GEORGE WHARTON (Sept. 27, 1858–Nov. 8, 1923); b. Gainsborough, England. Editor, author. *The Wonders of the Colorado Desert* (1905); *In and Out of the Old Missions of California* (1905); *Our American Wonderlands* (1915); etc. Editor, *Out West*, 1912–14. His library of Americana is now in the Southwest Museum at Los Angeles.

JAMES, HENRY (June 3, 1811–Dec. 18, 1882); b. Albany, N.Y. Lecturer, author. Father of Henry and William James. *Substance and Shadow* (1863); *Society the Redeemed Form of Man* (1879); *The Literary Remains*, ed. by his son, William James (1885). *See* J. A. Kellogg's *The Philosophy of Henry James* (1885); C. Hartley Grattan's *The Three Jameses* (1932).

JAMES, HENRY (Apr. 15, 1843–Feb. 28, 1916); b. New York City. Novelist, letter writer. *A Passionate Pilgrim, and Other Tales* (1875); *Roderick Hudson* (1876); *The American* (1877); *The Europeans* (1878, but dated 1879); *Daisy Miller* (1879); *Washington Square* (1881); *The Portrait of a Lady*, 3v. (1881); *Tales of Three Cities* (1884); *The Bostonians*, 3v. (1886); *The Princess Casamassima*, 3v. (1886); *The Tragic Muse*, 2v. (1890): *The Spoils of Poynton* (1897); *What Maisie Knew* (1897); *The Two Magics, the Turn of the Screw, Covering End* (1898); *The Awkward Age* (1899); *The Wings of the Dove*, 2v. (1902); *The Ambassadors* (1903); *The Golden Bowl*, 2v. (1904); *The American Scene* (1907); *The Novels and Tales of Henry James*, 26v. (1907–17); *A Small Boy and Others* (autobiography, 1913); *Notes of a Son and Brother* (autobiography, 1914); *The Middle Years* (autobiography, 1917); *The Ivory Tower* (1917); *The Sense of the Past* (1917). The prefaces which James wrote for the collected edition were published separately as *The Art of the Novel: Critical Prefaces* (1934). The complete works and letters have appeared as *The Letters*, 2v. (1920); *The Art of the Novel, Critical Prefaces* (1943); *The Notebooks* (1947); *Complete Plays* (1949); *Complete Tales*, 8v. (1964). *See* Rebecca West's *Henry James* (1916); Ford Madox Hueffer's *Henry James* (1916); Van Wyck Brooks's *The Pilgrimage of Henry James* (1925); Pelham Edgar's *Henry James: Man and Author* (1927); C. Hartley Grattan's *The Three Jameses* (1932); Edith Wharton's *A Backward Glance* (1934); F. O. Matthiessen's *Henry James: The Major Phase* (1944); Leon Edel's *Henry James: The Untried Years* (1953); *The Conquest of London, 1870–81; The Middle Years, 1882–95* (1962); *The Treacherous Years* (1969); *The Master: 1901–16* (1972); Robert Gale's *The Caught Image* (1964); Edward Stone's *The Battle and the Books* (1964); Peter Buitenhuis's *The Grasping Imagination* (1970).

JAMES, HENRY (May, 1879–Dec. 13, 1947); b. Boston, Mass., son of William James. Biographer. *Richard Olney* (1923); *Charles W. Eliot* (1930, Pulitzer Prize for American Biography, 1931). Editor: *The Letters of William James*, 2v. (1920).

JAMES, JAMES ALTON (Sept. 17, 1864–Feb. 12, 1962); b. Hazel Green, Wis. Educator, biographer, historian. *The Life of George Rogers Clark* (1928); *Oliver Pollock; The Life and Times of an Unknown Patriot* (1937); *The First Scientific Exploration of Russian America and the Purchase of Alaska* (1942). Editor: *George Rogers Clark Papers*, 2v. (1912–24). Prof. history, Northwestern University, 1897–1935.

JAMES, MARQUIS (Aug. 29, 1891–Nov. 19, 1955); b. Springfield, Mo. Author. *A History of the American Legion* (1923); *The Raven: A Biography of Sam Houston* (1929, Pulitzer Prize for biography, 1930); *Six Feet Six* (with wife,

Bessie Rowland James, 1931); *Andrew Jackson: The Border Captain* (1933); *They Had Their Hour* (1934); *The Courageous Heart* (with wife, 1935); *Andrew Jackson: Portrait of a President* (1937, Pulitzer Prize for biography, 1938); *Mr. Garner of Texas* (1939); *The Cherokee Strip* (1945); *The Texaco Story* (1953).

James, Martha. Pen name of Martha Claire MacGowan Doyle.

JAMES, NEILL (Miss), (1902–); b. in Mississippi. Traveler, author. *Petticoat Vagabond: Up and Down the World* (1937); *Petticoat Vagabond: Among the Nomads* (1939); *White Reindeer* (1940); *Dust on My Heart* (1946).

James, Paul. Pen name of James Paul Warburg.

JAMES, SAMUEL HUMPHREYS (b. Dec. 12, 1857); b. "Cottage Oaks Plantation," La. Author. *A Woman of New Orleans* (1889); *A Prince of Good Fellows* (1891).

JAMES, WILLIAM (Jan. 11, 1842–Aug. 26, 1910); b. New York City. Educator, psychologist, author. *The Principles of Psychology*, 2v. (1890); *The Will to Believe, and Other Essays* (1897); *Talks to Teachers on Psychology* (1899); *The Varieties of Religious Experience* (1902); *Memories and Studies* (1911); *Letters*, 2v. (1920); *Collected Essays and Reviews* (1920); etc. With Harvard University, 1872–1907; prof. philosophy, 1885–1907. *See* Henry James's *Notes of a Son and Brother* (1914); Ralph Barton Perry's *Annotated Bibliography of the Works of William James* (1920), his *The Thought and Character of William James* (1935), and his *In the Spirit of William James* (1939); C. Hartley Grattan's *The Three Jameses* (1932); Lloyd R. Morris's *William James: The Messages of a Modern Mind* (1950); G. W. Allen's *William James* (1967).

JAMES, WILL[iam Roderick] (June 6, 1892–Sept. 3, 1942); b. Great Falls, Mont. Artist, author. *Smoky, the Cowhorse* (1926); *Lone Cowboy* (autobiography, 1930); *Big Enough* (1931); *Sun Up* (1931); *Uncle Bill* (1932); *All in the Day's Riding* (1932); *Flint Spears* (1938); *My First Horse* (1940); *Horses I've Known* (1940); etc.

JAMESON, JOHN FRANKLIN (Sept. 19, 1859–Sept. 26, 1937); b. Boston, Mass. Editor, author. *The History of Historical Writing in America* (1891); etc. General editor: *Original Narratives of Early American History*, 19v. (1906–19). Chairman of committee of management, *Dictionary of American Biography* (q.v.). Director of research, Carnegie Institution, 1905–28; chief of manucripts division, Library of Congress, 1928–37.

JAMISON, CECILIA VIETS DAKIN (Mrs. George Hamilton; Mrs. Samuel Jamison) (1837–Apr. 11, 1909); b. Yarmouth, N.S. Artist, author. *Something to Do* (anon., 1871); *Ropes of Sand, and Other Stories* (anon. 1876); *My Bonnie Lass* (1877); *The Story of an Enthusiast* (1888); *Lady Jane* (1889); *Toinette's Philip* (1894); *Thistledown* (1903); *The Penhallow Family* (1905); etc.

Jan Vedder's Wife. Novel by Amelia Barr (1885). The scene is laid in the Shetland Islands. The sailor, Jan Vedder, and his stingy wife have many a domestic clash due to Jan's easy-going and spendthrift ways.

JANEWAY, ELIOT (Jan. 1, 1913–); b. New York. Economist. *The Struggle for Survival* (1951); *The Economics of Crisis* (1968); *What Shall I Do With My Money?* (1970).

JANEWAY, ELIZABETH [Hall] (Oct. 7, 1913–); b. Brooklyn, N.Y. Author. *The Walsh Girls* (1943); *Daisy Kenyon* (1945); *The Question of Gregory* (1949); *The Vikings* (1951); *Leaving Home* (1953); *Early Days of the Automobile* (1956); *The Third Choice* (1959); *Angry Kate* (1963); *Accident* (1964); *Ivanov Seven* (1967); *Man's World, Woman's Place* (1971).

Janice Meredith. Novel by Paul Leicester Ford (1899). Popular romance based on incidents in New Jersey during the

American Revolution, filled with stirring adventures experienced by Janice and her courageous and gallant lover, John Brereton. George Washington plays a role in the novel.

JANIS, SIDNEY (July 8, 1896–); b. Buffalo, N.Y. Art dealer, author. *They Taught Themselves* (1940); *Abstract and Surrealist Art in America* (1942); *Picasso: Recent Years* (with wife, Celia Cohn, 1946).

JANNEY, RUSSELL (Apr. 14, 1884–July 1963); b. Wilmington, Ohio. Theatrical producer, author. *The Miracle of the Bells* (1946); *The Vision of Red O'Shea* (poem, 1949); *So Long as Love Remembers* (1953); *Curtain Call* (1957). Producer, *White Eagle, June Love, Sancho Panza,* etc. Producer and co-author, *The Vagabond King* (1925).

JANNEY, SAMUEL McPHERSON (Jan. 11, 1801–Apr. 30, 1880); b. in Loudoun Co., Va. Historian of the Friends, biographer, poet. Author: *The Last of the Lenape, and Other Poems* (1839); *The Life of William Penn* (1852); *The Life of George Fox* (cop. 1853); *History of the Religious Society of Friends.* 4v. (1859–67); *Memoirs* (1881).

JANOWITZ, MAURICE (Oct. 22, 1919–); b. Paterson, N.J. Educator, author. *The Professional Soldier* (1960); *Social Change and Prejudice* (1964). Professor sociology, University of Chicago, since 1962.

JANSEN, REINER (d. Mar. 6, 1706); b. Alkmar, Holland. Printer. He came to America in 1698 and set up a printing press. From 1698 to 1706 he was Pennsylvania's only printer. *See* Joseph Smith's *Short Biographical Notices of William Bradford, Reiner Jansen, Andrew Bradford, and Samuel Keimer, Early Printers in Pennsylvania* (1891).

JANVIER, CATHARINE ANN (Mrs. Thomas Allibone Janvier) (May 1, 1841–July 17, 1923); b. Philadelphia, Pa. Artist, author. *London Mews* (poems, 1904). Translator of Provençal literature. Her collection of Provençal books is now in The New York Public Library.

JANVIER, FRANCIS DE HAES (1817–1885); b. in Pennsylvania. Poet. *The Skeleton Monk, and Other Poems* (1860); *The Sleeping Sentinel* (1863); *Patriotic Poems* (1866).

JANVIER, MARGARET THOMSON (Feb. 1844–Feb. 1913); b. New Orleans, La. Poet. Pen name, "Margaret Vandegrift." *Clover Beach* (1880); *Doris and Theodora* (1884); *Ways and Means* (1886); *Little Helpers* (1889); *The Dead Doll and Other Verses* (1889); *Umbrellas to Mend* (1905); etc.

JANVIER, MEREDITH (1872–1936). Author. *Baltimore in the Eighties and Nineties* (1933); *Baltimore Yesterdays* (1937).

JANVIER, THOMAS ALLIBONE (July 16, 1849–June 18, 1913); b. Philadelphia, Pa. Journalist, author. *Color Studies* (1885); *The Aztec Treasure House* (1890); *Stories of Old New Spain* (1891); *In Old New York* (1894); *In the Sargasso Sea* (1898); *Henry Hudson* (1909); *Legends of the City of Mexico* (1910); etc.

Japanese Schoolboy. See Hashimura Togo.

JARRELL, RANDALL (May 6, 1914–Oct. 14, 1965); b. Nashville, Tenn. Poet, critic, novelist. *Blood for a Stranger* (poems, 1942); *Little Friend, Little Friend* (poems, 1945); *Losses* (poems, 1948); *The Seven-League Crutches* (poems, 1951); *Poetry and the Age* (1953); *Pictures from an Institution* (1954); *Selected Poems* (1955); *The Woman at the Washington Zoo* (poems, 1960); *A Sad Heart at the Supermarket* (1962); *The Gingerbread Rabbit* (1963); *The Bat Poet* (1964); *The Lost World* (1965).

JARRETT, CORA HARDY (Feb. 21, 1877–); b. Norfolk, Va. Novelist. *Peccadilloes* (1929); *Night Over Fitch's Pond* (1933); *Pattern in Black and Red* (under pen name of "Faraday Keene," 1934); *The Ginkgo Tree* (1935); *Strange Houses* (1936); *I Asked No Other Thing* (1937); *The Silver String* (1937); *Return in December* (1951).

JARVES, JAMES JACKSON (Aug. 20, 1818–June 28, 1888); b. Boston, Mass. Editor, author. *History of the Hawaiian or Sandwich Islands* (1843); *Scenes and Scenery in the Sandwich Islands* (1843); *Italian Rambles* (1883); and many books on art. Founder, *The Polynesian,* Honolulu, T. H., 1840, the first newspaper on the Hawaiian Islands; editor, 1840–48.

JASTROW, JOSEPH (Jan. 30, 1863–Jan. 8, 1944); b. Warsaw, Poland. Educator, psychologist, author. *Fact and Fable in Psychology* (1900); *The Subconscious* (1906); *The Qualities of Men* (1910); *Keeping Mentally Fit* (1928); *Freud, His Dream and Sex Theories* (1948); etc. Prof. psychology, University of Wisconsin, 1888–1927.

Java Head. Novel by Joseph Hergesheimer (1919). Story of Salem in the days of the China trade and the clipper ships. Jerry Ammidon, wealthy merchant, names his house "Java Head."

JAVITS, JACOB KOPPEL (May 18, 1904–); b. New York City. U.S. Senator, author. *A Proposal to Amend the Anti-Trust Laws* (1939); *Discrimination U.S.A.* (1960); *Order of Battle: A Republican's Call to Reason* (1964).

JAY, JOHN (Dec. 12, 1745–May 17, 1829); b. New York City. Statesman, jurist, diplomat, best known as negotiator of "Jay's Treaty." He wrote some of the articles in the *Federalist* (q.v.). President of the Continental Congress, 1778–79; minister to Spain, 1779–82; Secretary of Foreign Affairs, 1784–89; Chief Justice, U.S. Supreme Court, 1790–95; Governor of New York, 1795–1801. See *Correspondence and Public Papers of John Jay,* ed. by Henry P. Johnston, 4v. (1890–93); William Jay's *The Life of John Jay,* 2v. (1833); George Pellew's *John Jay* (1890); Richard B. Morris's *John Jay, the Nation and the Court* (1967); Donald L. Smith's *John Jay: Founder of a State and Nation* (1968).

Jay, W. L. M. Pen name of Julia Louisa Matilda Woodruff.

JAY, WILLIAM (June 16, 1789–Oct. 14, 1858); b. New York City. Jurist, reformer, author. *The Life of John Jay,* 2v. (1833); *War and Peace* (1842); *Miscellaneous Writings on Slavery* (1853); etc.

Jayhawkers: A Tale of the Border War, The. By Thompson B. Ferguson (1892). One of the first works of fiction published in Oklahoma.

Jayne, Lieut. R. H. Pen name of Edward S. Ellis.

Jaynes, Clare. Pen name of Jane Rothschild Mayer and Clara Spiegel.

Jazz Age. Assigned to the period of the World War and the years which immediately followed; characterized by reckless youth and a wildly syncopated music which originated with Negro orchestras in New Orleans and other southern cities. Another Negro influence was the singing of "Blues." *See* William Christopher Handy's *Blues: An Anthology* (1926); and for jazz age slang *see* W. J. Burke's *The Literature of Slang* (1939). *See also* Leonard Feather's *The Encyclopedia of Jazz* (rev. 1962); Samuel Barclay Charter's *Jazz: A History of the New York Scene* (1962).

Jazz Review. New York. Monthly. Founded 1958. Concerned with jazz and related subjects; features book reviews. Edited by Nat Hentoff and Martin Williams.

"Jealous Lover, The." American ballad. Lorella is stabbed to death by her lover. The ballad is also known as "Poor Lorella," "Loretta," "The Weeping Willow," "Floella," "Flora Ella," "Poor Lurella," "Poor Lora," etc.

Jed: A Boy's Adventures in the Army of '61–'65. By Warren Lee Goss (1889). One of the early successes of Thomas Y. Crowell's publishing firm.

JEFFERIS, BARBARA. Author. *Undercurrent* (1953); *Beloved Lady* (1955); *Half Angel* (1959); *Solo for Several Players* (1961); etc.

JEFFERS, LeROY (Aug. 1878–July 25, 1926); b. Ipswich, Mass. Librarian, lecturer, author. *The Call of the Mountains* (1922). With the New York Public Library, 1905–14.

JEFFERS, ROBINSON (Jan. 10, 1887–Jan. 21, 1962); b. Pittsburgh, Pa. Poet. *Flagons and Apples* (1912); *Californians* (1916); *Tamar, and Other Poems* (1924); *Roan Stallion, Tamar, and Other Poems* (1925); *The Women at Point Sur* (1927); *Cawdor, and Other Poems* (1928); *Dear Judas, and Other Poems* (1929); *Stars* (1930); *Descent to the Dead* (1931); *Thurso's Landing, and Other Poems* (1932); *Give Your Heart to the Hawks, and Other Poems* (1933); *Solstice, and Other Poems* (1935); *Such Counsels You Gave to Me, & Other Poems* (1937); *The Selected Poetry* (1938); *Be Angry at the Sun* (1941); *Medea* (play, 1946); *The Double Axe* (1948); *Hungerfield and Other Poems* (1954); *De Rerum Virtute* (1953); *The Cretan Woman* (play, 1954); *Loving Shepherdess* (1955); *Themes in My Poems* (1956); *The Beginning and the End, and other Poems* (1963). His manuscripts are in the library of Occidental College. *See* Rudolph Gilbert's *Shine, Perishing Republic* (1936); William Van Wyck's *Robinson Jeffers* (1938); Lawrence Clark Powell's *Robinson Jeffers, the Man and His Work* (1940); R. Squires's *Loyalties of Robinson Jeffers* (1956); M. C. Monjian's *Robinson Jeffers* (1958); Frederic I. Carpenter's *Robinson Jeffers* (1962).

JEFFERSON, JOSEPH (Feb. 20, 1829–Apr. 23, 1905); b. Philadelphia, Pa. Actor, author. *The Autobiography of Joseph Jefferson* (1890). *See* William Winter's *The Life and Art of Joseph Jefferson* (1894).

JEFFERSON, THOMAS (Apr. 2/13, 1743–July 4, 1826); b. "Shadwell," Goochland (now Albemarle) Co., Va. Third president of the United States, architect, scientist, scholar, author. *Notes on the State of Virginia* (1785); *The Writings,* ed. by Henry A. Washington, 9v. (1853–54); *The Writings,* ed. by Paul L. Ford, 10v. (1892–99), revised in 20v. (1903–04); *The Papers,* ed. by Julian P. Boyd, 16v. of projected 52v. (1950–61). Author of the Declaration of Independence, 1776; and of the Virginia Statute for Religious Freedom, 1779. Founder of the University of Virginia, 1819. His library, which he sold to the United States government in 1814 for $23,000, became the nucleus of the Library of Congress. *See* Henry S. Randall's *The Life of Thomas Jefferson,* 3v. (1858); *The Jefferson Cyclopedia,* ed. by John P. Foley (1900); John S. Patton's *Jefferson, Cabell, and the University of Virginia* (1906); David G. Muzzey's *Thomas Jefferson* (1919); Philip A. Bruce's *History of the University of Virginia,* 5v. (1920–22); Claude G. Bowers's *Jefferson and Hamilton* (1925); Francis W. Hirst's *Life and Letters of Thomas Jefferson* (1926); Albert J. Nock's *Jefferson* (1926); James T. Adams's *The Living Jefferson* (1936); John Dewey's *The Living Thoughts of Thomas Jefferson* (1940); Claude G. Bowers's *Thomas Jefferson,* 3v. (1945); Dumas Malone's *Jefferson the Virginian* (1948), *Jefferson and the Rights of Man* (1952) and *Jefferson and the Ordeal of Liberty* (1962); Merrill D. Peterson's *Thomas Jefferson: A Profile* (1967) and *Thomas Jefferson and the New Nation: A Biography* (1970). See also *The Papers of Thomas Jefferson,* edited by Julian P. Boyd, expected to comprise about fifty volumes, under publication by Princeton University Press.

JEFFERYS, WILLIAM HAMILTON (July 3, 1871–May 14, 1945); b. Philadelphia, Pa. Missionary, surgeon, author. *The Great Mystery* (1900); *Life of Bishop Ingle* (1913); *The Shuffling Coolie, and Other Plays* (1913); etc. Prof. surgery, St. John's University, Shanghai, China, 1905–13; head Philadelphia City Mission, 1917–43.

JEFFREY, ROSA [Griffith] **VERTNER JOHNSON** (Mrs. Claude M. Johnson; Mrs. Alexander Jeffrey) (1828–Oct. 6, 1894); b. Natchez, Miss. Poet, novelist. *Poems* (1857); *Woodburn* (1864); *Daisy Dare and Baby Power* (1871); *The Crimson Hand, and Other Poems* (1881); *Marah* (1884); etc.

JENISON, MADGE (1874–June 6, 1960); Author. *Sunwise Turn; A Human Comedy of Bookselling* (1923); *Dominance* (1928); *Roads* (1948); etc. Founder (1917), Women's National Book Association.

JENKINS, BURRIS ATKINS (Oct. 2, 1869–Mar. 13, 1945); b. Kansas City, Mo. Disciples clergyman, educator, editor, author. *Heroes of Faith* (1896); *Princess Salome* (1921); *The Bracegirdle* (1922); *Torrent* (1932); *Hand of Bronze* (1934); *Fresh Furrow* (1936); *Where My Caravan Has Rested* (autobiography, 1939); etc. Editor, the *Kansas City Post,* 1919–21; publisher, *The Christian,* 1926–34. President, Kentucky University (now Transylvania College), 1901–07.

JENKINS, CHARLES FRANCIS (Dec. 17, 1865–July 2, 1951); b. Norristown, Pa. Publisher, compiler, editor. *Tortola* (1923); *Button Gwinnett* (1926); etc. Editor: *Quaker Poems* (1893); *The Guidebook to Historic Germantown* (1902); *Jefferson's Germantown Letters* (1906); etc.

JENKINS, DEADERICK FRANKLIN. Author. *It Was Not My World* (1942); *Letters to My Son* (1947).

JENKINS, HOWARD MALCOLM (Mar. 30, 1842–Oct. 11, 1902); b. Gwynedd, Pa. Editor. Editor: *Pennsylvania, Colonial and Federal,* 3v. (1903); etc. Founder, The *Wilmington Daily Commercial,* 1866; editor, the *Philadelphia American,* the *Friend's Intelligencer,* etc.

JENKINS, JOHN STILWELL (Feb. 15, 1818–Sept. 20, 1852); b. Albany, N.Y. (?) Biographer, historian. Compiler: *Lives of the Governors of the State of New York* (1851); *The Heroines of History* (1851); and many other biographical and historical collections.

JENKINS, MacGREGOR (Apr. 14, 1869–deceased); b. Amherst, Mass. Publisher, author. *The Reading Public* (1914); *Literature with a Large L* (1919); *Bucolic Beatitudes* (1925); *Shiner Watson* (1929); *The Last Cruise of the Panther* (1929); *Emily Dickinson, Friend and Neighbor* (1930); *Emily* (1930); *Sons of Ephraim: The Spirit of Williams College* (1934); *Emily Dickinson* (1939); etc. With Houghton Mifflin Co., 1890–1908; with Atlantic Monthly Co., 1908–28; publisher, the *Atlantic Monthly* until 1928.

JENKINS, WILL[iam] F[itzgerald] (June 16, 1896–); b. Norfolk, Va. Author of mystery and adventure stories, under pen name "Murray Leinster," 1915–32. Author of science-fiction stories under same pen name: *The Last Space Ship* (1949); *Sidewise in Time and Other Stories* (1950); *Space Platform* (1953); *Forgotten Planet* (1954); *Colonial Survey* (1957); *War with the Gizmos* (1958); etc. Author under own name: *The Man Who Feared* (1942); *Guns for Achin* (1943); *Murder of the U.S.A.* (1947).

JENKS, ALBERT ERNEST (Nov. 28, 1869–June 6, 1953); b. Ionia, Mich. Educator, anthropologist, author. *The Childhood of Jishib, the Ojibwa* (1900); *The Wild Rice Gatherers of the Upper Lakes* (1901); *The Bontoc Igorot* (1905); *Ba-Long-Long, the Igorot Boy* (1907); *Indian-White Amalgamation* (1916); *Pleistocene Man in Minnesota* (1936); etc. Anthropology dept., University of Minnesota, 1906–1938.

JENKS, GEORGE CHARLES (Apr. 13, 1850–Sept. 12, 1929); b. London, England. Journalist, novelist. Creator of character "Diamond Dick," used in many dime novels. Pen name, "W. B. Lawson." Under own name: *The Demon Doctor* (1887); *The Giant Horseman* (1887); *The Deserters* (with Anna A. Chapin, 1911); *Stop Thief!* (with Carlyle Moore, 1913); etc. Under pen name: *Diamond Dick's Decoy Duck* (1891); *The Dalton Boys in California* (1893); *Out with the Apache Kid* (1894); *Rube Burrow's Pard* (1895); etc. Under same pen name wrote many numbers of *Diamond Dick Jr.: The Boys' Best Weekly,* 1896–1911. Wrote also many "Nick Carter" books. With the *Pittsburgh Press,* 1889–95; thereafter New York correspondent for the *Pittsburgh Dispatch* and the *Pittsburgh Gazette-Times. See* his *Dime Novel Makers,* in the *Bookman,* Oct. 1904.

JENKS, TUDOR [Storrs] (May 7, 1857–Feb. 11, 1922); b. Brooklyn N.Y. Editor, author. *Captain John Smith* (1904); *In the Days of Chaucer* (1904); *The Book of Famous Sieges* (1909); and many other books for young people. Asst. editor, *St. Nicholas,* 1887–1902.

Jennie Gerhardt. Novel by Theodore Dreiser (1911). The story of a woman who lived outside the conventional code of morality, but whose love for her child mitigated her transgressions. The book was withdrawn by the publishers after review copies had been sent out.

Jennifer Lorn. Novel by Elinor Wylie (1923). An eighteenth-century story in which Gerald Poynyard, a smug Englishman, is satirized through the quips of his witty wife as they travel about the world.

JENNINGS, DEAN SOUTHERN (June 30, 1905–); b. Rochester, N.Y. Author. *The Man Who Killed Hitler* (1939); *Leg Man* (1940); *The San Quentin Story* (with Clinton T. Duffy, 1950); *My First Hundred Years in Hollywood* (with Jack L. Warner, 1965); *We Only Kill Each Other* (1967).

JENNINGS, HERBERT SPENCER (Apr. 8, 1868–Apr. 14, 1947); b. Tonica, Ill. Educator, zoologist, author. *Behavior of the Lower Organisms* (1906); *Prometheus; or, Biology and the Advancement of Man* (1925); *The Biological Basis of Human Nature* (1930); *The Universe and Life* (1933); *Genetics* (1935); *Scientific Aspects of the Race Problem* (with others, 1941); etc. Zoology dept., Johns Hopkins University, 1906–38.

JENNINGS, JOHN EDWARD, JR. (Dec. 30, 1906–); b. Brooklyn, N.Y. Author. *Next to Valour* (1939); *Call the New World* (1941); *Gentleman Ranker* (1942); *Wheel of Fortune* (1943); *The Shadow and the Glory* (1943); *The Salem Frigate* (1946); *The Sea Eagles* (1950); *Rogue's Yarn* (1953); *The Wind in His Fists* (1956); *Blood on the Moon* (1957); *Golden Eagle* (1958); *The Raider* (1963); *Tattered Ensign* (1966); etc.

JENNISON, KEITH WARREN (Dec. 12, 1911–); b. Winnipeg, Can. Editor, publisher, author. *Vermont Is Where You Find It* (1941); *The Maine Idea* (1943); *New Hampshire* (1944); *New York and the State It's In* (1949); *The Half Open Road* (1953); *The Green Place* (1954); *The Boys and Their Mother* (1956); *Remember Maine* (1964). Editor, Viking Press, 1949–58. Vice-president and editor-in-chief, David McKay Co., 1959–62.

JENSEN, MERRILL [Monroe] (July 16, 1905–); b. Elkhorn, Ia. Historian, author. *The New Nation: A History of the United States during the Confederation* (1950); *American Colonial Documents to 1776* (1955); *The Making of the American Constitution* (1964); *Tracts of the American Revolution* (1967). Editor: *Regionalism in America* (1951). Prof. history, University of Wisconsin, since 1946.

JERAULD, CHARLOTTE A. FILLE-BROWN (Apr. 16, 1820–Aug. 2, 1845); b. Cambridge, Mass. Author. *Poetry and Prose* (1850).

JERNEGAN, MARCUS WILSON (Aug. 5, 1872–Feb. 19, 1949); b. Edgartown, Mass. Educator, historian. *The American Colonies, 1492–1750* (1929); *Growth of the American People* (1934); etc. History dept., University of Chicago, 1908–37.

Jerome, Owen Fox. Pen name of Oscar Jerome Friend.

Jersey Street and Jersey Lane. By H. C. Bunner (1896). A description of New York City, with a chapter on the Bohemian quarter of artists and writers.

JERVEY, CAROLINE HOWARD GILMAN GLOVER (1823–1877); b. in South Carolina, daughter of Samuel and Caroline Howard Gilman. Novelist, poet. *Vernon Grove* (anon., 1859); *Helen Courtenay's Promise* (anon., 1866); *Stories and Poems* (with her mother, 1872).

JESSEY, CORNELIA (Mrs. Irving Sussman) (Feb. 9, 1910–); b. Jeannette, Pa. Novelist. *The Growing Roots* (1947); *Teach the Angry Spirit* (1949); *Treasures of Darkness* (1953); *The Plough and the Harrow* (1961).

JESSUP, PHILIP C. (Jan. 5, 1897–); b. New York. Lawyer, educator, author. *The Law of Territorial Waters and Maritime Jurisdiction* (1927); *The United States and the World Court* (1929); *Elihu Root* (1938); *A Modern Law of Nations* (1948); *Transitional Law* (1956); *Use of International Law* (with J. H. Taubenfeld, 1959); etc. Law dept. Columbia University, since 1925; prof. international law and diplomacy, since 1946. U.S. representative, U.N. General Assembly, 1948–52; ambassador at large 1949–53. Judge, International Court of Justice, since 1961.

JESSUP, RICHARD. (1925–) Author. *The Cincinnati Kid* (1964); *The Recreation Hall* (1967); *A Quiet Voyage Home* (1970); *Sailor: A Novel of the Sea* (1969).

"Jest 'Fore Christmas." Poem by Eugene Field, in his *Love Songs of Childhood* (1894).

Jesuit Relations. The annual reports of the successive superiors of the Jesuit mission in New France (now Canada), which were published in France from 1632 to 1673. These important sources for American history have been translated as *Jesuit Relations and Allied Documents: Travels and Explorations of the Jesuit Missionaries in New France, 1610–1791,* ed. by Reuben Gold Thwaites, 73v. (1896–1901). *See* Lawrence C. Wroth's *The Jesuit Relations from New France,* in the Bibliographical Society of America *Papers,* vol. 30, 1936; and James C. McCoy's *Jesuit Relations of Canada, 1632–1673: A Bibliography* (1937).

"Jesus loves me, this I know. For the Bible tells me so." First lines of hymn by Susan Warner, in *Say and Seal,* 1860.

JEWELL, EDWARD ALDEN (Mar. 10, 1888–Oct. 11, 1947); b. Grand Rapids, Mich. Art critic, novelist. *The Charmed Circle* (1921); *The White Kami* (1922); *The Moth Decides* (1922); *Americans* (1930); *Have We an American Art?* (1939); *Cézanne* (1944); *Rouault* (1945); *Van Gogh* (1946); etc. Art critic, the *New York Times.*

JEWELL, LOUISE POND (d. Dec. 26, 1943); b. Oberlin, O. Author. *The Great Adventure* (1911); *The Conqueror* (1916).

JEWETT, CHARLES COFFIN (Aug. 12, 1816–Jan. 9, 1868); b. Lebanon, Me. Librarian, bibliographer, author. *Notices of Public Libraries in the United States of America* (1851); *Facts and Considerations Relative to Duties on Books* (1846); etc. Compiler: *Catalogue of the Library of Brown University* (1843). Librarian, Brown University, 1841–45; the Smithsonian Institution, 1848–54; the Boston Public Library, 1858–68.

JEWETT, JOHN HOWARD (Jan. 19, 1843–Sept. 18, 1925); b. Hadley, Mass. Author. Pen name, "Hannah Warner." *Fugitive Verses* (1889); *The Bunny Stories* (1890); *More Bunny Stories* (1900); the *Little Mother* stories, 10v. (1906); the *Grandmother Goose* stories, 4v. (1907); etc.

JEWETT, SARAH ORNE (Sept. 3, 1849–June 24, 1909); b. South Berwick, Me. Author. *Deephaven* (1877); *Country By-Ways* (1881); *A Country Doctor* (1884); *The King of Folly Island and Other People* (1888); *Betty Leicester* (1889); *Tales of New England* (1890); *The Life of Nancy* (1895); *The Country of the Pointed Firs* (1896); *The Tory Lover* (1901); *Letters* (1911); *The Best Stories,* 2v. (1925); etc. *See* M. A. DeWolfe Howe's *Memories of a Hostess* (1922); Francis O. Matthiessen's *Sarah Orne Jewett* (1929); Louis Auchincloss's *Pioneers and Caretakers* (1965); *Letters of Sarah Orne Jewett,* rev. ed., by Richard Cary (1967).

JEWETT, SOPHIE (June 3, 1861–1909); b. Moravia, N.Y. Poet. Pen name "Ellen Burroughs." *The Pilgrim, and Other Poems* (1896); *The Poems* (1910).

Jewish Daily Forward. New York. Newspaper. Founded 1897, by the Jewish Socialist Press Federation. Edited for many years by Abraham Cahan. Lazar Fogelman is now editor. Printed in Yiddish. Prints editions for Boston, Chicago, Detroit, Los Angeles, Philadelphia.

Jewish Exponent. Philadelphia, Pa. Weekly. Founded 1887. Devoted to Jewish interests. Book review editors have included Mortimer J. Cohen, Charles Angoff, Harold V. Ribalow.

Jewish Publication Society of America. Philadelphia, Pa. Founded 1888.

Jews in America, The. By Madison Clinton Peters (1905).

JILLSON, WILLARD ROUSE (May 28, 1890–); b. Syracuse, N.Y. Geologist, author. *Songs and Satires* (1920); *The Kentuckie Country* (1931); *Rare Kentucky Books* (1939); and other books on Kentucky and on geology, latest being *A Tour Down Stream* (1959). Editor: *Filson's Kentucke* (1929). State geologist of Kentucky, since 1919.

"Jim Bludso of the Prairie Bell." Poem by John Hay, in his *Pike County Ballads* (1871). It describes the heroism of a Mississippi steamboat pilot who lost his life saving passengers from a fire.

"Jim Crow." Popular minstrel song by Thomas Davenport Rice, first sung in 1828. It was accompanied by a hopping and shuffling dance which became the hit of America and England. "Jim Crow" is also a term used in some Southern states for separate cars, restaurants, theatres, etc., for Negroes.

"Jinny." Stories and poems by Bret Harte, first published in London (1878).

JOB, THOMAS (1900–July 31, 1947). Playwright. *Uncle Harry* (prod. 1942). Adapter: *Barchester Towers* (1938); *Therese* (1947).

"Joe Bowers." Ballad based on the legendary hero of the "Forty-niners," who was supposedly a "Piker" from Missouri.

JOHN, WILLIAM MESTREZAT (Oct. 3, 1888–Nov. 30, 1962); b. Trinidad, Col. Author. *Seven Women* (1929); *Every Wise Woman* (1931); *Mingled Yarn* (1933); *Circumstance* (1936).

John Brent. Novel by Theodore Winthrop (1862). Narrative of adventures in the Far West, with a horse, Don Fulano, as the hero.

"John Brown's Body." Narrative poem by Stephen Vincent Benét (1928).

John Bull in America; or, The New Munchausen. By James Kirke Paulding (1825). Allegorical satire on English opinion as reflected in the accounts of America written by English travelers.

"John Deth." Long poem by Conrad Aiken (1930).

John Harvey: A Tale of the Twentieth Century. Utopian novel by A. Ridgeley (1897). America during the years 1935–50. Foretells conscription, union of England and America, etc.

John March, Southerner. Novel by George W. Cable (1894), which was first published in *Scribner's Magazine,* beginning Jan., 1894. A portrait of the old South and its plantation life, which reflects the spirit and philosophy of the true Southern gentleman. Contains considerable Negro dialect.

John Marr and Other Sailors. Collection of poems by Herman Melville (1888).

John Martin's Book. New York City. Monthly children's magazine. Founded 1913, by "John Martin" (Morgan van Roorbach Shepard). Expired 1932.

John Ward, Preacher. Novel by Margaret Deland (1888). The conflict between a Calvinist minister and his more liberal wife.

John-Donkey. New York and Philadelphia. Comic weekly. Founded Jan. 1, 1848, by Thomas Dunn English, George C. Foster, and George Zieber. F. O. C. Darley was its most distinguished illustrator. One of its chief objects of satire was Edgar Allan Poe. Expired July 15, 1848. *See* Frank L. Mott's *History of American Magazines,* v. 1 (1938).

Johnny Appleseed. See John Chapman.

Johnny Tremaine. Novel by Esther Forbes (1943). An apprentice silversmith becomes a dispatch rider during the American Revolution and meets Hancock, Revere, the Adamses, and other notable people.

JOHNS, ORRICK (1887–); b. St. Louis, Mo. Poet. *Asphalt, and Other Poems* (1917); *Black Branches* (1920); *Time of Our Lives: The Story of My Father and Myself* (1937); etc.

Johns Hopkins Press, The. Baltimore, Md. Founded 1878. Publishes scholarly books, paperbacks, and professional journals.

JOHNSON, ALEXANDER BRYAN (May 29, 1786–Sept. 9, 1867); b. Gosport, Eng. Banker, philosophical writer. *The Philosophy of Human Knowledge* (1828); revised as *A Treatice on Language* (1836); and other books, mainly on banking.

JOHNSON, ALLEN (Jan. 29, 1870–Jan. 18, 1931); b. Lowell, Mass. Educator, historian, biographer. *Stephen A. Douglas* (1908); *Union and Democracy* (1915); *Jefferson and His Colleagues* (1921); *The Historian and Historical Evidence* (1926); etc. Editor: *The Chronicles of America* series, 50v. (1918–21); *Dictionary of American Biography,* v. 1–7 (1928–31); v. 4–7, with Dumas Malone. Learned professor American history, Yale University, 1910–26.

JOHNSON, ALVIN SAUNDERS (Dec. 18, 1874–June 7, 1971); b. Homer, Neb. Educator, economist, author. *The Professor and the Petticoat* (1914); *John Stuyvesant, Ancestor; and Other People* (1919); *Spring Storm* (1936); *Clock of History* (1946); *Pioneers' Progress* (autobiography, 1952); *The Battle of the Wild Turkey and Other Tales* (1961); etc. Editor, the *New Republic,* 1917–23. Director, New School for Social Research, New York, from 1923; prof. economics, Yale University, from 1938.

JOHNSON, AMANDUS (Oct. 27, 1877–); b. in Sweden. Educator, explorer, author. *The Swedish Settlements on the Delaware,* 2v. (1911); *The Journal and Biography of Nicholas Collin* (1936); *Swedish Contributions to American Freedom 1776–1783* (1953); and numerous other books on Swedish-American history. Editor: *Instruction for John Printz* (1930); *Naval Campaigns of Count de Grasse During the American Revolution* (1942). Scandinavian language dept., University of Pennsylvania, 1910–22.

JOHNSON, ANDREW (Dec. 20, 1808–July 31, 1870); b. Raleigh, N.C. Seventeenth president of the United States. *See* John Savage's *The Life and Public Services of Andrew Johnson* (1866); James S. Jones's *Life of Andrew Johnson* (1901); W. Archibald Dunning's *Reconstruction, Political and Economic* (1907); Robert W. Winston's *Andrew Johnson* (1928); Claude G. Bowers's *The Tragic Era* (1929); Lloyd Stryker's *Andrew Johnson* (1929); George F. Milton's *The Age of Hate* (1930). The Johnson papers in the Library of Congress have been under publication by the University of Tennessee Press since 1967 under the editorial direction of LeRoy P. Graf and Ralph W. Haskins.

JOHNSON, ANNA (July 11, 1860–deceased); b. in Bradford Co., Pa. Author. Pen name "Hope Daring." *To the Third Generation* (1901); *Agnes Grant's Education* (1902); *Madeline, the Island Girl* (1906); *Father John* (1907); *A Virginian Holiday* (1909); *The Gordons* (1912); *Sowing and Reaping* (1922); *Harvest of the Years* (1938); etc.

JOHNSON, ANNABEL (1921–). Author. *As a Speckled Bird* (1956). Co-author (with husband, Edgar Johnson): *Big Rock Candy* (1958); *Black Symbol* (1959); *Torrie* (1960); *The Secret Gift* (under pen name "A. E. Johnson," 1961); *A Peculiar Magic* (1965); etc.

JOHNSON, BURGES (Nov. 9, 1877–); b. Rutland, Vt. Educator, poet, humorist. *Rhymes of Little Boys* (1905); *Beastly Rhymes* (1906); *Bashful Ballads* (1911); *The Well of English and the Bucket* (1917); *Parodies for Housekeepers* (with wife, 1921); *As I Was Saying* (1923); *Essaying an Essay* (1927); *A Little Book of Necessary Nonsense* (1929); *More Necessary Nonesense* (1931); *New Rhyming Dictionary and Poets' Handbook* (1931); *Sonnets from the Pekinese, and Other Doggerel* (1935); *Professor at Bay* (1937); *Rubaiyat of Omar Ki-yi* (1938); *Ladder to the Moon* (1939); *As Much As I Dare* (1944); *Campus Versus Classroom* (1946); *The Lost Art of Profanity* (1948); etc. Editor, *Judge*, 1908–09; *Bulletin of the Author's League of America*, 1919–25, etc. With E. P. Dutton Co., 1913–19. Prof. English, Vassar College, 1915–26.

JOHNSON, CHARLES FREDERICK (May 8, 1836–June 9, 1931); b. New York City. Educator, poet. *Three Americans and Three Englishmen* (1886); *What Can I Do for Brady? and Other Verse* (1897); *Elements of Literary Criticism* (1898); *Shakespeare and His Critics* (1909); etc. Prof. English literature, Trinity College, 1883–1907.

JOHNSON, CHARLES SPURGEON (July 24, 1893–Oct. 29, 1956); b. Bristol, Va. Educator, author. *The Negro in American Civilization* (1930); *Shadow of the Plantation* (1934); *The Negro College Graduate* (1936); *Growing Up in the Black Belt* (1941); *Education and the Cultural Crisis* (1951); etc. Co-editor: *Race and Culture* (1950). Director, social science dept., Fisk University, 1928–47; president, from 1946.

JOHNSON, CLIFTON (Jan. 25, 1865–Jan. 22, 1940); b. Hadley, Mass. Editor, illustrator, author. *The New England Country* (1892); *Among English Hedgerows* (1899); *The Isle of the Shamrock* (1901); *New England and Its Neighbors* (1902); *The Land of Heather* (1903); *American Highways and Byways*, 7v. (1904–15); *The Country School* (1907); *The Farmer's Boy* (1907); *The Picturesque Hudson* (1909); *What to See in America* (1919); *John Burroughs' Talks* (1922); *Historic Hampshire in the Connecticut Valley* (1932). Illustrator of many children's books, etc.

JOHNSON, CONSTANCE FULLER WHEELER (Mrs. Burges Johnson) (Sept. 16, 1879–); b. on Staten Island, N.Y. Author. The *When Mother Lets Us* series, 4v. (1908–12); *Mary in New Mexico* (1921); *Mary in California* (1922); etc.

JOHNSON, EDGAR (Dec. 1, 1901–); b. New York. Educator, author. *Unweave a Rainbow* (1931); *One Mighty Torrent* (1937); *Praying Mantis* (1937); *Charles Dickens* (1952); *The Black Symbol* (with Annabel Johnson, 1959); *The Rescued Heart* (with same, 1961); *Sir Walter Scott: the Great Unknown* (1969); etc. English dept., City College of New York, since 1927.

JOHNSON, EDWARD (Sept., 1598–Apr. 23, 1672); b. Canterbury, Eng. Author. *A History of New England* (publ. 1653, dated 1654), frequently referred to by its running-title, *Wonder-Working Providence of Sion's Saviour in New England*.

JOHNSON, ELIZABETH WINTHROP (b. Jan. 12, 1850); b. New York. Author. *Yesterday* (1882); *Two Loyal Lovers* (1890); *Orchard Folk* (1898); etc.

JOHNSON, GEORGE METCALF (Feb. 13, 1885–); b. Yankton, S.D. Novelist. Writes under name, "George Metcalf." *The Gun Slinger* (1927); *Squatter's Rights* (1929); *Riders of the Trail* (1932); *Jerry Rides the Range* (1932); *The Texas Range Rider* (1933); *Open Range* (1934); *The Saddle Bum* (1936); *Gun Smoke* (1938); etc.

JOHNSON, GERALD WHITE (Aug. 6, 1890–); b. Riverton, N.C. Journalist, essayist. *Andrew Jackson: An Epic in Homespun* (1927); *Randolph of Roanoke: A Political Fantastic* (1929); *The Wasted Land* (1937); *The Sunpapers of Baltimore* (with Frank R. Kent, Henry L. Mencken, and Hamilton Owens, 1937); *America's Silver Age* (1939); *Roosevelt: Dictator or Democrat?* (1941); *American Heroes and Hero Worship* (1943); *Woodrow Wilson* (1944); *An Honorable Titan* (1946); *The First Captain* (1947); *Liberal's Progress* (1948); *Our English Heritage* (1949); *Incredible Tale* (1950); *This American People* (1951); *Pattern for Liberty* (1952); *Lunatic Fringe* (1957); *Peril and Promise* (1958); *The Lines Are Drawn* (1958); *America Is Born* (1959); *The Man Who Feels Left Behind* (1961); *The Cabinet* (1966); *Communism: An American's View* (1967); *The British Empire: An American View of Its History from 1776 to 1945* (1969). With *Baltimore Evening Sun*, 1926–43.

JOHNSON, HAYNES BONNER (July 9, 1931–); b. New York. Journalist, author. *Duck at the Mountain* (1963); *The Bay of Pigs* (1964); *Fulbright: The Dissenter* (with Bernard Gwertzman, 1968). With *Washington Star* since 1957.

JOHNSON, HELEN [Louise] **KENDRICK** (Mrs. Rossiter Johnson) (Jan. 4, 1844–Jan. 3, 1917); b. Hamilton, N.Y. Editor, author. The *Roddy Books*, 3v. (1874–76); *Raleigh Westgate* (1889); *Women and the Republic* (1897); etc. Editor: the *Nutshell* series, 6v. (1884); *Our Familiar Songs and Those Who Made Them* (1889); *A Dictionary of Terms, Phrases, and Quotations* (with Henry Percy Smith, 1895); etc. Editor, the *American Woman's Journal*, 1894–96. See Rossiter Johnson's *Helen Kendrick Johnson* (1917).

JOHNSON, HENRY (June 25, 1855–Feb. 7, 1918); b. Gardiner, Me. Educator, poet, translator of Dante. *Where Beauty Is, and Other Poems* (1898); *The Seer* (1910); etc. Prof. modern languages, Bowdoin College, 1877; librarian, 1880–83; curator, Bowdoin Art Collection, 1894–1918.

JOHNSON, HERBERT (Oct. 30, 1878–Dec. 4, 1946); b. Sutton, Neb. Cartoonist for the *Saturday Evening Post*, 1912–41.

JOHNSON, HOWARD (1888–May 1, 1941); b. Waterbury, Conn. Song writer. Wrote "When the Moon Comes over the Mountain," "Ireland Must Be Heaven," "Where Do We Go from Here," "M-o-t-h-e-r," etc. Wrote lyrics for musical comedy, *Tangerine*, in 1921.

JOHNSON, HUGH S. (Aug. 5, 1882–Apr. 15, 1942); b. Ft. Scott, Kan. Army officer, columnist. Columnist for the Scripps-Howard newspapers, from 1934.

JOHNSON, JAMES WELDON (June 17, 1871–June 26, 1938); b. Jacksonville, Fla. Novelist, poet. *The Autobiography of an Ex-Colored Man* (anon., 1912); *Fifty Years, & Other Poems* (1917); *God's Trombones* (poems, 1927); *Black Manhattan* (1930); *St. Peter Relates an Incident of the Resurrection Day* (1930); *Along This Way* (autobiography, 1933); *Negro Americans, What Now?* (1934). Editor: *The Book of American Negro Poetry* (1922); *The Book of American Negro Spirituals* (1925); *The Second Book of Negro Spirituals* (1926). See Fred B. Millett's *Contemporary American Authors* (1940).

JOHNSON, JOSEPH FRENCH (Aug. 24, 1853–Jan. 22, 1925); b. Hardwick, Mass. Educator, editor. Wrote several books on currency. Founder and editor, *The Spokesman*, Spokane, Wash., 1890. Dean, school of commerce, New York University, 1901–25.

JOHNSON, JOSEPHINE [Winslow] (June 20, 1910–); b. Kirkwood, Mo. Novelist, poet. *Now in November* (1934, Pulitzer prize novel, 1935); *Winter Orchard, and Other Stories* (1935); *Jordanstown* (1937); *Year's End* (poems, 1937); *Wildwood* (1946); *The Dark Traveler* (1963); *The Sorcerer's Son, and Other Stories* (1965); *The Inland Island* (1969); etc.

JOHNSON, LYNDON BAINES (Aug. 27, 1908–); b. near Stonewall, Tex. Thirty-sixth president of the United States, author. *My Hope for America* (1964); *A Time for Action: A Selection from the Speeches and Writings of Lyndon B. Johnson, 1953–64* (1964); *The Johnson Humor,* ed. by Bill Adler (1965); *This America* (1966); *The Choices We Face* (1969). Congressman, 1937–48; senator, 1948–61; vice-president, 1961–63; president, 1964–69. See Harry Provence's *Lyndon B. Johnson, a Biography* (1964); William S. White's *The Professional: Lyndon B. Johnson* (1964); Tom Wicker's *JFK and LBJ* (1968); Eric F. Goldman's *The Tragedy of Lyndon Johnson* (1969).

JOHNSON, MARGARET (b. Apr. 5, 1860); b. Boston, Mass. Illustrator, author. *A Bunch of Keys* (1904); *Polly and the Wishing-Ring* (1918).

JOHNSON, MARMADUKE (d. Dec. 25, 1674); b. in England. Printer. He and Samuel Green printed Eliot's *Indian Bible* in 1663.

JOHNSON, MARTIN [Elmer] (Oct. 9, 1884–Jan. 12/13, 1937); b. Rockford, Ill. Explorer, author. *Through the South Seas with Jack London* (1913); *Cannibal-Land* (1917); *Camera Trails in Africa* (1924); *Safari: A Saga of the African Blue* (1928); *Lion: African Adventures with the King of Beasts* (1929); *Congorilla* (1931); *Over African Jungles* (1935).

JOHNSON, MERLE DE VORE (Nov. 24, 1874–Sept. 1, 1935); b. Oregon City, Ore. Illustrator, bibliographer. Compiler: *Bibliography of Mark Twain* (1910); *American First Editions* (1929); *High Spots of American Literature* (1929); *You Know These Lines* (1934); etc.

Johnson, Mrs. Rossiter. See Helen Kendrick Johnson.

JOHNSON, NICHOLAS (Sept. 23, 1934–   ); b. Iowa City, Ia. Government official. *How to Talk Back to Your Television* (1970). Commissioner, Federal Communications Commission, since 1966.

JOHNSON, NUNNALLY (Dec. 5, 1897–   ); b. Columbus, Ga. Author. *There Ought to Be a Law* (short stories, 1930). Writer of stories and articles for *Saturday Evening Post* and other magazines, and of such screenplays as *The House of Rothschild, The Grapes of Wrath, How to Marry a Millionaire, The Dirty Dozen.*

JOHNSON, OLIVER (Dec. 27, 1809–Dec. 10, 1889); b. Peacham, Vt. Editor, abolitionist, author. *William Lloyd Garrison and His Times* (1880). Founder, the *Christian Soldier,* 1831; assoc. editor, the *Independent,* 1865–70; the New York *Weekly Tribune,* 1870–73; managing editor, the *Christian Union,* 1873–76; assoc. editor, the *New York Evening Post,* 1881–89; etc.

JOHNSON, OSA [Helen Leighty] (Mrs. Martin Johnson) (Mar. 14, 1894–Jan. 7, 1953); b. Chanute, Kan. Explorer, author. *Jungle Babies* (1930); *Jungle Pets* (1932); *Osa Johnson's Jungle Friends* (1939); *I Married Adventure* (1940); *Bride in the Solomons* (1944); *Last Adventure* (1966); etc. Collaborated with Martin Johnson in his explorations and in writing his books.

JOHNSON, OWEN [McMahon] (Aug. 27, 1878–Jan. 27, 1952); b. New York. Author. *Arrows of the Almighty* (1901); *In the Name of Liberty* (1905); *Max Fargus* (1906); *The Eternal Boy* (1909); *The Humming Bird* (1910); *The Varmint* (1910); *The Tennessee Shad* (1911); *Stover at Yale* (1911); *A Comedy for Wives* (1911); *The Sixty-first Second* (1912); *The Salamander* (1913); *The Woman Gives* (1915); *The Spirit of France* (1915); *Virtuous Wives* (1917); *The Wasted Generation* (1921); *Skipper Bedelle* (1923); *Blue Blood* (1923); *Children of Divorce* (1927); *Sacrifice* (1929); *Prodigious Hickey: A Lawrenceville Story* (1946); etc.

JOHNSON, PHILANDER CHASE (Feb. 6, 1866–May 18, 1939); b. Wheeling, W.Va. Editor, author. *Sayings of Uncle*

Eben (1897); *Now-a-Day Poems* (1900); *Senator Sorghum's Primer of Politics* (1906); etc. Wrote daily verse under caption "Shooting Stars" for the *Washington Star,* 1891–1939.

JOHNSON, RAY[mond Edward] (Oct. 16, 1927–); b. Detroit, Mich. Artist, author. *Book of the Month* (1957); *The Paper Snake* (1965).

JOHNSON, ROBERT IVAR (Aug. 18, 1933–); b. Chicago, Ill. Museum director, author. *Astronomy—Our Solar System and Beyond* (1963); *The Story of the Moon* (1963); *Celestial Planetarium Guide Book* (1964); *Sundials* (1967).

JOHNSON, ROBERT UNDERWOOD (Jan. 12, 1853–Oct. 14, 1937); b. Washington, D.C. Author, poet. *The Winter Hour, and Other Poems,* (1891); *Songs of Liberty, and Other Poems* (1897); *Poems of War and Peace* (1916); *Remembered Yesterdays* (1923); *Poems of the Longer Flight* (1928); *Poems of Fifty Years* (1931); *Heroes, Children, and Fun* (1934); *Your Hall of Fame* (1935); etc. With the *Century Magazine,* 1873–1913; assoc. editor, 1881–1909; editor, 1909–13. Director, Hall of Fame, 1919–37.

Johnson, Rosa Vertner. See Rosa Vertner Johnson Jeffrey.

JOHNSON, ROSSITER (Jan. 27, 1840–Oct. 3, 1931); b. Rochester, N.Y. Editor, author. *Phaeton Rogers* (1881); *Idler and Poet* (poems, 1883); *A History of the War of Secession* (1888); *Campfire and Battlefield* (1896); *Three Decades* (poems, 1895); *Captain John Smith* (1914); etc. Editor: *Little Classics,* 18v. (1875–80); *Single and Famous Poems* (1877); *The World's Great Books,* 40v. (1898–1901); *The Great Events, by Famous Historians,* 20v. (1905); *The Literature of Italy,* 16v. (with Dora K. Ranous, 1907); *The Author's Digest,* 20v. (1908); also *Liber Scriptorum* (q.v.); etc. Editor, *Appleton's Annual Cyclopaedia,* 1883–1902. Conducted "The Literary Queries" department for Scribner's *The Book Buyer* for many years.

JOHNSON, SAMUEL (Oct. 14, 1696–Jan. 6, 1772); b. Guilford, Conn. Anglican clergyman, educator, philosopher, author. *An Introduction to the Study of Philosophy* (1731); *Ethics Elementa* (1746), republished by Benjamin Franklin in augmented form as *Elementa Philosophica* (1752); etc. President, King's College (now Columbia University), 1754–72. See *Samuel Johnson, President of King's College: His Career and Writings,* ed. by Herbert and Carl Schneider, 4v. (1929).

JOHNSON, THOMAS MARVIN (June 20, 1889–); b. Buffalo, N.Y. Author. *Without Caesar* (1928); *Our Secret War* (1929); *The Lost Battalion* (with Fletcher Pratt, 1938); *Unlocking Adventure* (1942); etc. Co-author: *What You Should Know About Spies and Saboteurs* (1943); *American Legion Reader* (1953); *Great True Spy Adventures* (1957); etc.

JOHNSON, VIRGINIA ESHELMAN (Feb. 11, 1925–); b. Springfield, Mo. Psychologist, author. *Human Sexual Response* (with William H. Masters, 1966); *Human Sexual Inadequacy* (with same, 1970).

JOHNSON, VIRGINIA WALES (Dec. 28, 1849–Jan. 16, 1916); b. Brooklyn, N.Y. Author of children's books, novelist. The *Kettle Club* series (1860–70); the *Doll's Club* series (1871); *Joseph, the Jew* (1874); *A Sack of Gold* (1874); *The Calderwood Secret* (1875); *Miss Nancy's Pilgrimage* (1876); *Two Old Cats* (1882); *The Fainalls of Tipton* (1884); *The Lily of the Arno* (1891); *Genoa, the Superb* (1892); *A Lift on the Road* (1913); etc.

JOHNSON, WENDELL A. L. (Apr. 16, 1906–); b. Roxbury, Kans. Speech pathologist, author. *People in Quandaries* (1946); *Your Most Enchanted Listener* (1956); *Stuttering and What You can Do About It* (1960); *Diagnostic Methods in Speech Pathology* (1963); etc.

JOHNSON, WILLIAM SAMUEL (Dec. 1, 1859–Mar. 2, 1937); b. Ellicottville, N.Y. Author. *Glamourie* (1911); *Prayer for Peace, and Other Poems* (1915); *Buttadeus* (1916); etc.

JOHNSON, WILLIAM SAMUEL (Oct. 7, 1727–Nov. 14, 1819); b. Stratford, Conn., son of Samuel Johnson. Statesman, jurist, educator. President, Columbia College, 1787–1800. U.S. Senator from Connecticut, 1789–91. *See* E. Edwards Beardsley's *Life and Times of William Samuel Johnson* (1876); George C. Grace's *William Samuel Johnson* (1937).

JOHNSON, WILLIAM W. (Dec. 18, 1909–); b. Mattoon, Ill. Author. *Sam Houston, The Tallest Texan* (1953); *Kelly Blue* (1960); *Birth of Texas* (1960); *Captain Cortes Conquers Mexico* (1960); *Mexico* (1961); *The Andean Countries* (1965).

JOHNSON, WILLIS FLETCHER (Oct. 7, 1857–Mar. 28, 1931); b. New York City. Editor, author. *History of the Johnstown Flood* (1889); *George Harvey* (1929); etc. Political and literary editor, the *New York Tribune,* 1880–1931.

Johnson & Warner. Philadelphia, Pa. Publishers. Founded c. 1780 by Jacob Johnson. The firm was later known as McCarty & Davis. William McCarty retired in 1831, and Moses Polock acquired the business in 1851 on the death of Thomas Davis. Polock ran a bookstore as a part of the business and it was often frequented by Poe, Cooper, Melville, Charles Godfrey Leland, and Noah Webster. Polock later specialized in rare books.

Johnson of Boone, Benj. Pen name of James Whitcomb Riley.

JOHNSTON, ALEXANDER (Apr. 29, 1849–July 20, 1889); b. Brooklyn, N.Y. Educator, author. *History of American Politics* (1879); *A History of Connecticut* (1887); *American Political History* (1905); etc. Editor: *Representative American Orations,* 3v. (1884). Prof. jurisprudence, Princeton, 1883–89.

JOHNSTON, ANNIE FELLOWS (May 15, 1863–Oct. 5, 1931); b. Evansville, Ind. Author. *Big Brother* (1893); *The Little Colonel* series, 12v. (1895–1912); *The Land of the Little Colonel: Reminiscence and Autobiography* (1929); etc.

JOHNSTON, CHARLES HAVEN LADD (July 17, 1877–July 9, 1943); b. Washington, D.C. Author. *Little Pilgrimages among the Women Who Have Written Famous Books* (1901); *Famous Indian Chiefs* (1909); *Famous Scouts* (1910); *Famous Privateersmen* (1911); *Famous Frontiersmen and Heroes of the Border* (1913); etc.

JOHNSTON, DAVID CLAYPOOLE (Mar. 1799–Nov. 8, 1865); b. Philadelphia, Pa. Engraver, actor. He published a series of humorous plates, beginning in 1830, which he called *Scraps.* He also illustrated Fanny Kemble's *Journal* and Joseph C. Neal's *Charcoal Sketches.*

JOHNSTON, HENRY PHELPS (Apr. 19, 1842–Feb. 28, 1923); b. Trebizond, Turkey. Educator, historian. *The Yorktown Campaign* (1881); *The Battle of Harlem Heights* (1897); *Nathan Hale* (1901); etc. Editor: *Correspondence and Public Papers of John Jay,* 4v. (1890–93). Prof. history, College of the City of New York, 1883–1916.

JOHNSTON, J[ames] WESLEY (b. 1850). Methodist clergyman, author. *Dwellers in Gotham* (under pen name, "Annan Dale," 1898); *Philip Yoakley* (1901); *The Riddle of Life* (1902); *The Mystery of Miriam* (1904); etc.

JOHNSTON, MARY (Nov. 21, 1870–May 9, 1936); b. Buchanan, Va. Novelist. *Prisoners of Hope* (1898); *To Have and to Hold* (1900); *Audrey* (1902); *Sir Mortimer* (1904); *Lewis Rand* (1908); *The Long Roll* (1911); *Cease Firing* (1912); *The Witch* (1914); *The Wanderers* (1917); *Michael Forth* (1919); *Sweet Rocket* (1920); *Silver Cross* (1922); *Croatan* (1923); *The Slave Ship* (1924); *The Exile* (1927); *Hunting Shirt* (1931); *Drury Randall* (1934); etc.

JOHNSTON, RICHARD JAMES HUMPHREYS (May 20, 1910–   ); b. New York. Journalist, author. *Off the Record* (with others, 1952); *Around the U.S.A. in 1000 Pictures* (with others, 1955); *The Two Koreas* (1965); *How I Got That Story* (with others, 1967). Staff, *New York Times,* since 1934.

JOHNSTON, RICHARD MALCOLM (Mar. 8, 1822–Sept. 23, 1898); b. "Oak Grove," near Powelton, Ga. Educator, novelist, essayist. *Dukesborough Tales* (1871); *Mr. Billy Downs and His Likes* (1872); *Old Mark Langston* (1884); *Studies, Literary and Social,* 2 series (1891–92); *Autobiography* (1900). Founder, Pen Lucy School, Baltimore, 1867.

JOHNSTON, ROBERT MATTESON (Apr. 11, 1867–Jan. 28, 1920); b. Paris, France. Educator, historian. *The Roman Theocracy and the Republic* (1901); *Napoleon* (1904); *Leading American Soldiers* (1907); *The French Revolution* (1909); *The Corsican* (1910); *The Holy Christian Church* (1912); *Bull Run* (1913); etc. History dept., Harvard, 1908–20.

JOHNSTON, WILLIAM [Andrew] (Jan. 26, 1871–Feb. 16, 1929); b. Pittsburgh, Pa. Journalist, author. *History Up to Date* (1899); *The Yellow Letter* (1911); *Limpy* (1917); *The Apartment Next Door* (1919); *The Fun of Being a Fat Man* (1922); *Waddington Cipher* (1923); etc. On editorial staff *New York Herald,* 1897–1900; *New York World,* 1900–29.

JOLINE, ADRIAN HOFFMAN (June 30, 1850–Oct. 15, 1912); b. Sing Sing (now Ossining), N.Y. Lawyer, autograph collector, essayist. *Meditations of an Autograph Collector* (1902); *The Diversions of a Book Lover* (1903); *At the Library Table* (1910); *Edgehill Essays* (1911); *Rambles in Autograph Land* (1913); etc.

"Jolly Old Pedagogue, The." Best-known poem of George Arnold, author of the "McArone" papers.

JONAS, CARL (May 22, 1913–); b. Omaha, Neb. Author. *Beachhead on the Wind* (1945); *Snowslide* (1950); *Jefferson Selleck* (1952); *Riley McCullough* (1954); *Our Revels Now Are Ended* (1957); *Lillian White Deer* (1964); *The Observatory* (1966).

"Jonathan to John." Poem by James Russell Lowell (1862). A satire expressing the resentment of the North toward England as a result of the "Trent Affair."

JONES, ADAM LEROY (July 2, 1873–Mar. 2, 1934); b. Dunlap, Ill. Educator, author. *Early American Philosophers* (1898); *Logic* (1909). Philosophy dept., Columbia University, 1898–1905, 1909–34.

JONES, AMANDA THEODOSIA (Oct. 19, 1835–Mar. 31, 1914); b. East Bloomfield, N.Y. Inventor, poet, song writer. *Ulah, and Other Poems* (1861); *Poems* (1867); *A Prairie Idyl* (1882); *Poems, 1854–1906* (1906); *A Psychic Autobiography* (1910); etc.

JONES, BAYARD HALE (1887–1957). Author. *American Lectionary* (1944); *Dynamic Redemption* (1961); etc.

JONES, CHARLES COLCOCK (Oct. 28, 1831–July 19, 1893); b. Savannah, Ga. Historian of Georgia. *Monumental Remains of Georgia* (1861); *Antiquities of the Southern Indians* (1873); *The History of Georgia,* 2v. (1883); etc. Bancroft called him "the Macaulay of the South."

JONES, EDGAR DeWITT (Dec. 5, 1876–Mar. 26, 1956); b. Hearne, Tex. Disciples clergyman, author. *The Inner Circle* (1914); *Roses of Bethany* (1936); *Lords of Speech* (1937); *Lincoln and the Preachers* (1948); *Sermons I Love to Preach* (1953); etc.

JONES, E[li] STANLEY (Jan. 3, 1884–); b. Clarksville, Md. Methodist clergyman, author. *The Christ of the Indian Road* (1925); *The Christ on the Mount* (1931); *The Choice Before Us* (1937); *Along the Indian Road* (1939); *Abundant Living* (1942); *Mahatma Gandhi: An Interpretation* (1948); *Growing Spiritually* (1953); *Mastery* (1955); *Conversion* (1959); *In Christ* (1961); *Victory through Surrender* (1966); *A Song of Ascents* (1968).

JONES, EVAN (1915–). Author. *Trappers and Mountain Men* (1961); *The Minnesota: Forgotten River* (1962). Editor: *The Fathers: Letters to Sons and Daughters* (1960); *Citadel in the Wilderness* (1966).

JONES, EVAN (1927–). Author. *Protector of the Indians* (1958).

JONES, [Everett] LEROI (Oct. 7, 1934–   ); b. Newark, N.J. Author. *Preface to a Twenty Volume Suicide Note* (1961); *Blues People: Negro Music in White America* (1963); *The Moderns* (1963); *The Dead Lecturer* (1964); *Dutchman and the Slave* (1964); *The System of Dante's Hell* (1965); *Home* (1966); *The Toilet* and *The Baptism* (1967); *Striptease* (1967); *Tales* (1967); *Black Magic* (1968). Co-editor: *Black Fire: An Anthology of Afro-American Writing* (1969). Founder, *Yugen* magazine 1958.

JONES, FREDERICK LAFAYETTE (Dec. 5, 1901–); b. Spartanburg, S.C. Educator, editor. *An Examination of the Shelley Legend* (with others, 1962). Editor: *The Letters of Mary W. Shelley,* 2v. (1944); *Mary Shelley's Journal* (1947); *Maria Gisborne and E. E. Williams, Their Journals and Letters* (1952); *Percy Bysshe Shelley, Selected Poems* (1956); *The Letters of Percy Bysshe Shelley,* 2v. (1964). Prof. English, University of Pennsylvania, since 1947.

JONES, GEORGE (July 30, 1800–Jan. 22, 1870); b. York, Pa. Episcopal clergyman, Naval chaplain, author. *Sketches of Naval Life,* 2v. (1829); *Excursions to Cairo, Jerusalem, Damascus, and Balbec* (1836); *Life-Scenes from the Four Gospels* (1865); *Life-scenes from the Old Testament* (1868).

JONES, GROVER (1893–Sept. 24, 1940); b. West Terre Haute, Ind. Scenarist, book collector, short-story writer. He wrote scenarios for over four hundred motion picture plays. His recollections appeared in *The Saturday Evening Post,* and he wrote many short stories for *Collier's* and other magazines.

JONES, HERSCHEL V[espasian] (Aug. 30, 1861–May 24, 1928); b. Jefferson, N.Y. Editor, book collector, author. *Adventures in Americana,* 2v. (1928). Editor and publisher, the *Minneapolis Journal* 1908–1928. His notable collection of Americana was sold in Dec. 1939 to Dr. A. S. W. Rosenbach.

JONES, HOWARD MUMFORD (Apr. 16, 1892–); b. Saginaw, Mich. Author: *A Little Book of Local Verse* (1915); *Gargoyles, and Other Poems* (1918); *America and French Culture, 1750–1848* (1927); *The Romanesque Lyric* (with Philip Schuyler Allen, 1927); *The Life of Moses Coit Tyler* (1933); *The Harp That Once—: A Chronicle of the Life of Thomas Moore* (1937); *Ideas in America* (1944); *Education and World Tragedy* (1946); *The Theory of American Literature* (1948); *The Bright Medusa* (1952); *The Pursuit of Happiness* (1953); *American Humanism* (1957); *One Great Society* (1959); *O Strange New World* (1964); *Jeffersonianism and the American Novel* (1966); *Belief and Disbelief in American Literature* (1967); *The Literature of Virginia in the Seventeenth Century* (1968); *Violence and Reason* (essays, 1969). Editor: *Poems of Edgar Allan Poe* (1929); *Major American Writers* (with Ernest E. Leisy, 1935); *Modern Minds* (with others, 1949); etc. Lit. editor, Boston *Evening Transcript,* 1938–41. Prof. English, Harvard University, since 1936.

JONES, IDWAL (Dec. 8, 1892–Nov. 14, 1964); b. Festinion, Wales. Author. *Whistlers' Van* (1936); *Black Bayou* (1941); *High Bonnet* (1945); *The Sierra* (1947); *Vines in the Sun* (1949); *Chef's Holiday* (1952); etc.

JONES, JAMES (Nov. 6, 1921–); b. Robinson, Ill. Author. *From Here to Eternity* (1951); *Some Came Running* (1957); *The Pistol* (1959); *The Thin Red Line* (1962); *Go to the Widow-Maker* (1967); *Ice-Cream Headache and Other Stories* (1968).

JONES, JAMES ATHEARN (June 4, 1791–Aug. 1854); b. Tisbury, Mass. Editor, author. *Tales of an Indian Camp* (1820), revised as *Traditions of the North American Indians* (1830); *The Refugee; A Romance,* 2v. (under pen name "Murgatroyd," 1825); *Haverhill; or, Memoirs of an Officer in the Army of Wolfe,* 2v. (1831); etc.

JONES, JENKIN LLOYD (Nov. 14, 1843–Sept. 12, 1918); b. in Cardiganshire, Wales. Unitarian clergyman, editor, reformer, author. *Jess: Bits of Wayside Gospel,* 2 series (1899, 1901); *Nuggets from a Welsh Mine* (1902); *An Artilleryman's Diary* (1914); etc. Editor, *Unity,* 1880–1918.

JONES, JOHN BEAUCHAMP (Mar. 6, 1810–Feb. 4, 1866); b. Baltimore, Md. Editor, novelist, poet. *The Western Merchant* (under pen name "Luke Shortfield," 1840); *Books of Vision* (1847); *The Life and Adventures of a Country Merchant* (1854); *Freaks of Fortune; or, The History of Ned Lorn* (1854); *Wild Western Scenes,* 2 series (1841, 1856); *Rural Sports: A Poem* (1849); *Wild Southern Scenes* (1859); *A Rebel War Clerk's Diary* (1866); etc. Founder, the *Southern Monitor,* Philadelphia, 1857.

JONES, JOHN PAUL (July 6, 1747–July 18, 1792); b. (John Paul) Kirkbean, Kirkcudbrightshire, Scotland. Naval officer, author. *Memoirs,* 2v. (1830). See Alexander S. Mackenzie's *The Life of Paul Jones,* 2v. (1841); Anna F. de Koven's *The Life and Letters of John Paul Jones,* 2v. (1913); *Paul Jones,* ed. by Don Carlos Seitz (1917); Phillips Russell's *John Paul Jones* (1927); Valentine Thomson's *Knight of the Seas* (1939). See also J. Fenimore Cooper's *The Pilot* (1823); Allan Cunningham's *Paul Jones: A Romance,* 3v. (1827); *Paul Jones: A Tale of the Sea* (anon., 1843); Frederick Whitaker's *The Sea-King; or, The Two Corvettes* (1873); Winston Churchill's *Richard Carvel* (1899); Samuel Spewack's *Mon Paul: The Private Life of a Privateer* (under pen name, "A. A. Abbott," 1928); Edward Ellsberg's *Captain Paul* (1941). See also Dixon Wecter's *The Hero in America* (1941).

JONES, JOHN RICHTER (Oct. 2, 1803–May 23, 1863); b. Salem, N.Y. Lawyer, author. *The Quaker Soldier* (anon., 1858).

JONES, JOSEPH STEVENS (Sept. 28, 1809–Dec. 29, 1877); b. Boston, Mass. Actor, playwright. *The Liberty Tree* (prod. 1832); *The Green Mountain Boy* (prod. 1833); *Moll Pitcher* (prod. 1839); *The Silver Spoon* (prod. 1852); *Solon Shingle; or, The People's Lawyer* (prod. 1839); *Paul Revere and the Sons of Liberty* (1875); *Life of Jefferson S. Batkins* (1871); etc. See Margaret G. Mayorga's *A Short History of the American Drama* (1934).

JONES, JUSTIN. Novelist. Pen name, "Harry Hazel." *The Belle of Boston* (1844); *The Nun of St. Ursula* (1845); *The West Point Cadet* (1845); *Big Dick* (1846); *The Corsair* (1846); *Osmond, the Avenger* (1847); *The Pirate's Daughter* (1847); *Jessie Manton* (1848); *The Light Dragoon* (1848); *Hasserac* (1849); *Mad Jack and Gentleman Jack* (1850); *Red King* (1850); *The Flying Artillerist* (1853); *The Rebel and the Rover* (1860); *The Light Dragoon* (1864); *The Yankee Middy* (1865); *Old Put* (1866); *Virginia Graham* (1867); etc.

JONES, LLEWELLYN (July 13, 1884–May 18, 1961); b. Castletown, Isle of Man. Editor, critic. *First Impressions: Essays on Poetry, Criticism, and Prosody* (1925); *How to Criticize Books* (1928); *How to Read Books* (1930). Compiler: *Gems of the World's Best Classics* (with C. C. Gaul, 1939). Lit. editor, the *Chicago Evening Post,* 1914–32; editor, the *Christian Register,* 1938–41.

JONES, NARD [Maynard Benedict] (Apr. 12, 1904–); b. Seattle, Wash. Author. *Oregon Detour* (1930); *The Petlands* (1931); *Wheat Women* (1933); *All Six Were Lovers* (1934); *Sun Tan* (1935); *West, Young Man!* (1937); *Swift Flows the River* (1940); *Evergreen Land* (1941); *Still to the West* (1946); *The Island* (1948); *Great Command* (1959); *Pacific Northwest* (1962).

JONES, RICHARD FOSTER (July 7, 1886–); b. Solado, Tex. Educator, author. *Lewis Theobald* (1919); *The Background of the Battle of the Books* (1920); *Ancients and Moderns* (1936); etc. Editor: *Seventeenth Century Literature* (1930); *Eighteenth Century Literature* (1930); *Triumph of the English Language* (1953); etc. English dept., Washington University, St. Louis, since 1919.

JONES, RUFUS MATTHEW (Jan. 25, 1863–June 16, 1948); b. S. China, Me. Educator, author. *Life of Eli and Sibyl Jones* (1899); *Quakerism, a Religion of Life* (1908); *The Story of George Fox* (1919); *Later Periods of Quakerism* (1921); *New Studies in Mystical Religion* (1927); *Haverford College* (1933); *The Flowering of Mysticism* (1939); *A Small-Town Boy* (1941); etc. Philosophy dept., Haverford College, 1893–34.

JONES, THOMAS SAMUEL, JR. (Nov. 6, 1882–Oct. 16, 1932); b. Boonville, N.Y. Poet. *The Path of Dreams* (1905); *From Quiet Valleys* (1908); *Interludes* (1908); *Ave Atque Vale* (1909); *From the Heart of the Hills* (with Clinton Scollard, 1909); *The Rose-Jar* (1906); *Sonnets* (1909); *The Voice in the Silence* (1911); *Leonardo da Vinci, and Other Sonnets* (1930); *The Unicorn, and Other Sonnets* (1931); *Shadow of the Perfect Rose: Collected Poems* (1937).

JONES, TOM (Feb. 17, 1928–); b. Littlefield, Tex. Playwright, lyricist. Author books and lyrics: *The Fantasticks* (1961); *110 in the Shade* (1963); *I Do, I Do* (1966).

JONES, VIRGIL CARRINGTON (1906-). Author. *Ranger Mosby* (1944); *The Hatfields and the McCoys* (1948); *Grey Ghosts and Rebel Raiders* (1956); *Eight Hours Before Richmond* (1957); *The Civil War at Sea*, 2v. of projected 3v. (1960–61).

JONES, WILLIAM (Mar. 28, 1871–Mar. 29, 1909); b. Sac and Fox Reservation, Ind. Terr. (now Okla.). Fox Indian, ethnologist, author. *Ethnography of the Fox Indians*, ed. by Margaret W. Fisher (1912); and many papers on the Fox tribe. With the Field Museum, Chicago, 1906–09. *See* Henry M. Rideout's *William Jones* (1912).

JONES, WILLIAM ALFRED (June 26, 1817–May 6, 1900); b. New York City. Librarian, essayist. *The Analyst: A Collection of Miscellaneous Papers* (1840); *Literary Studies*, 2v. (1847); *Essays Upon Authors and Books* (1849); *Characters and Criticism*, 2v. (1857), which includes most of the contents of the first three books. Librarian, Columbia College, 1851–65.

JONES, WILLIS KNAPP (Nov. 27, 1895–); b. Matteawan, N.Y. Educator, author. *Songs from Hypnia* (with Henry C. Fenn, 1915); *The Hammon Twins* (1926); *The Nightingale* (1930); *Storm Before Sunset* (1931); *Latin America through Drama in English* (1950); *Rigoberto* (1954); etc. Prof. Romance languages, Miami University, Oxford, O., since 1923.

Jonny-Cake Letters, The. By Thomas Robinson Hazard (1882), which appeared first in the *Providence Journal*.

JOOST, NICHOLAS TEYNAC (May 28, 1916–); b. Jacksonville, Fla. Educator, author. *Fifty Years of the American Novel* (1951); *The Authorship of the Free Thinker: Studies in the Early English Periodical* (1957); *Scofield Thayer and The Dial* (1964); *Years of Transition: The Dial, 1912–20* (1967); etc. Staff, *Poetry* magazine, 1951–54. Prof. English, Southern Illinois University, since 1960.

JORDAN, CORNELIA J[ane] M[atthews] (Mrs. Francis H. Jordan) (Jan. 11, 1830–1898); b. Lynchburg, Va. Poet. *Flowers of Hope and Memory* (1861); *Corinth, and Other Poems of the War* (1865); *Richmond: Her Glory and Her Graves* (1867); *Echoes from the Cannon* (1899); etc.

JORDAN, DAVID STARR (Jan. 19, 1851–Sept. 19, 1931); b. Gainesville, N.Y. Educator, author. *The Voice of the Scholar* (1903); *Life's Enthusiasms* (1906); *Fishes* (1907); *The Human Harvest* (1907); *The Days of a Man*, 2v. (autobiography, 1922); *The Higher Foolishness* (1927); *The Trend of the American University* (1929); etc. President, Stanford University, 1891–1916.

JORDAN, ELIZABETH (May 9, 1867–Feb. 24, 1947); b. Milwaukee, Wis. Critic, novelist, playwright. *Tales of the City Room* (1898); *May Iverson: Her Book* (1904); *The Lady from Oklahoma* (prod. 1911); *The Lady of Pentlands* (1923); *Miss*

Nobody from Nowhere (1927); *The Night Club Mystery* (1929); *Playboy* (1931); *The Life of the Party* (1935); *The Trap* (1936); *Three Rousing Cheers* (autobiography, 1937); *First Port of Call* (1940); *Herself* (1943); *The Real Ruth Arnold* (1945); etc. Lit. adviser, Harper & Brothers, 1913–18; drama critic, *America*.

JORDAN, JOHN WOOLF (Sept. 14, 1840–June 11, 1921); b. Philadelphia, Pa. Librarian, editor. Editor: *Encyclopedia of Pennsylvania Biography*, vols. 1–13 (1914–21); etc. Editor, *Pennsylvania Magazine of History and Biography*, 1887–1921. Librarian, Historical Society of Pennsylvania, 1903–21.

JORDAN, KATE (Mrs. Frederick M. Vermilye) (Dec. 23, 1862–June 20, 1926); b. Dublin, Ireland. Novelist, playwright. *The Other House* (1892); *A Circle on the Sand* (1898); *A Luncheon at Nick's* (1903); *The Pompadour's Protégé* (1903); *Mrs. Dakon* (1909); *Time the Comedian* (1909); *The Right Road* (1911); *The Creeping Tides* (1913); *Trouble-the-House* (1921); etc.

JORDAN, MARY AUGUSTA (July 5, 1855–Apr. 14, 1941); b. Ironton, O. Educator. Editor: Goldsmith's *Vicar of Wakefield*; Milton's *Minor Poems*; etc. English dept., Smith College, 1884–1921.

JORDAN, MILDRED A. (Mrs. J. Lee Bausher) (Mar. 18, 1901–); b. Chicago, Ill. Author. *One Red Rose Forever* (1941); *Apple in the Attic* (1942); *The Shoo-Fly Pie* (1944); *"I Won't," Said the King* (1945); *Asylum for the Queen* (1948); *Miracle in Brittany* (1950); *Echo of the Flute* (1958); *Proud To Be Amish* (1968).

JORDAN, WILLIAM GEORGE (Mar. 6, 1864–Apr. 20, 1928); b. New York City. Editor, author. *The Kingship of Self-Control* (1899); *The Trusteeship of Life* (1921); etc. Editor, *Book Chat*, 1886–87; *Saturday Evening Post*, 1898–99.

JORGENSON, THEODORE (Nov. 2, 1894–); b. Narvestad, Nor. Educator, author. *History of Norwegian Literature* (1933); *Ole Edvart Rölvaag* (with Nora O. Solum, 1939); *Henrik Ibsen* (1945); *Norwegian Literature in Medieval and Early Modern Times* (1952); *Brand* (1957); *Tr. Arne Garborg, The Teacher of Righteousness* (1960); etc., and other books on Norwegian culture and literature. Norwegian dept., St. Olaf College, Northfield, Minn., since 1925.

JOSAPHARE, LIONEL (May 26, 1876–); b. St. Louis, Mo. Author. *The Lion at the Well* (poems, 1901); *Turquoise and Iron* (poems, 1902); *Christopher* (1921).

JOSEPH, DONALD (Apr. 22, 1898–); b. Cuero, Tex. Educator, editor, novelist. *October's Child* (1929); *Long Bondage* (1930); *Four Blind Mice* (1932); *Straw in the South Wind* (1946); *Lud Dangerfield* (1956). Editor: Hewitt L. Ballowe's *The Lawd Sayin' the Same* (1946) and *Creole Folk Tales* (1947). Translator: *Champ D'Asile* (1969).

JOSEPH, RICHARD (Apr. 24, 1910–); b. New York. Travel commentator, author. *Your Trip Abroad* (1950); *Your Trip to Britain* (1951); *Richard Joseph's World Wide Travel Guide* (1952); *A Letter to the Man Who Killed My Dog* (1956); *Richard Joseph's Comprehensive Guide to Europe* (1956); etc. Travel editor, *Esquire* magazine, since 1947.

JOSEPHSON, MATTHEW (Feb. 15, 1899–); b. Brooklyn, N.Y. Author. *Galimathias, and Other Poems* (1923); *Zola and His Time* (1928); *Portrait of the Artist as American* (1930); *Jean-Jacques Rousseau* (1931); *The Robber Barons* (1934); *The Politicos, 1865–1896* (1938); *The President Makers* (1940); *Victor Hugo* (1942); *Empire of the Air* (1944); *Stendhal; or, The Pursuit of Happiness* (1946); *Sidney Hillman, Statesman of American Labor* (1952); *Union House, Union Bay* (1956); *Edison* (1959); *Life Among the Surrealists* (1962); *The Infidel in the Temple* (1967).

Josiah Allen's Wife. Pen name of Marietta Holley.

JOSSELYN, JOHN (fl. 1630–1675); b. in Essex, Eng. Traveler, author. *New-England's Rarities Discovered* (1672); *An Account of Two Voyages to New-England* (1674).

Journal of Aesthetics and Art Criticism. Cleveland, Ohio. Quarterly. Founded 1946. Published by the American Society for Aesthetics.

Journal of American History. Salt Lake City. Quarterly. Founded 1914 as *Mississippi Valley Historical Review.* Published at the University of Utah by the Organization of American Historians.

Journal of Black Studies. Los Angeles, Cal. Quarterly. Founded 1970. Concerned with current scholarship on a broad range of questions involving black people. Edited by Arthur L. Smith.

Journal of Economic History. Chapel Hill, N.C. Quarterly. Founded 1941. Published at the University of North Carolina.

Journal of Philosophy. New York. Biweekly. Founded 1940. Published at Columbia University.

Journal of Southern History. Baton Rouge, La.; Lexington, Ky; New Orleans, La. Quarterly. Founded 1935. Published by the Southern Historical Association.

Journal of Speculative Philosophy. St. Louis, Mo. Philosophical quarterly. Founded 1867, and edited by William Torrey Harris. Noted for its translations of German philosophy, and for its essays on aesthetics. The American philosophers William James, Josiah Royce, Charles S. Peirce, and John Dewey wrote some of their first articles for this journal. Moved to New York in 1880, and published by D. Appleton & Co., until it expired in 1893.

Journalism Quarterly. Grand Forks, N.D.; Minneapolis, Minn. Founded 1924, as the *Journalism Bulletin,* by Lawrence William Murphy, who was its first editor. Present name adopted 1928. Frank Luther Mott was editor, 1930–34.

Journals of Madam Knight and Rev. Mr. Buckingham, The. By Sarah Kemble Knight, published posthumously in 1825. Record of a tour from Boston to New York in 1704. One of the classic travel journals in American literature.

Journey in the Dark. Novel by Martin Flavin (1943). Sam Braden rises to fame and affluence in Chicago but remains unfulfilled in his attempt to cope with life.

Journey in the Seaboard Slave States, A. By Frederick Law Olmsted (1856). A significant series of sketches written for the *New York Times,* which did much to create unfavorable public opinion in the North against the institution of slavery.

"Journey of the Magi." Poem by T. S. Eliot, from *Collected Poems 1909–1935* (1936).

Journeyman. Pen name of Albert Jay Nock.

JOY, JAMES RICHARD (Oct. 16, 1863–July 1, 1957); b. Groton, Mass. Editor, librarian, author. *The Greek Drama* (1887); *Grecian History* (1890); *Twenty Centuries of English History* (1898); *John Wesley's Awakening* (1937); etc. Asst. editor, the *Christian Advocate,* New York, 1904–15; editor, 1915–36. Librarian, New York Methodist Historical Society, 1936–52.

JOYCE, JOHN ALEXANDER (July 4, 1840–Jan. 18, 1915); b. Shraugh, Ireland. Author. *A Checkered Life* (1883); *Peculiar Poems* (1885); *Zig-Zag* (1888); *Jewels of Memory* (1895); *Complete Poems* (1899); *Oliver Goldsmith* (1901); *Edgar Allan Poe* (1901); *Brickbats and Bouquets* (1902); *Robert Burns* (1909); etc.

JOYCE, LILLIAN ELWYN ELLIOTT, b. London, England. Traveler, author. Also wrote under maiden name. *Brazil Today and Tomorrow* (1917); *Chile Today and Tomorrow* (1922); *The Argentine of To-Day* (1926); etc.

JOYCE, ROBERT DWYER (Sept. 1836–Oct. 23, 1883); b. in Co. Limerick, Ire. Poet. *Ballads, Romances, and Songs* (1872); *Deirdré* (1876); *Blanid* (1879); etc.

Juba. Pen name of Benjamin Allen.

Jubilee. New York. Monthly. Founded 1953. Devoted to Catholic and Christian thought and ideas, including articles, fiction, and poetry. Has been edited by Edward Rice, Robert Lax, and Wilfred Sheed.

Jubilee Jim. By Robert H. Fuller (1828). Story of James Fisk (1934–1872), the railroad magnate and stock-market figure.

JUDAH, SAMUEL BENJAMIN HELBERT (c.1799–July 21, 1876); b. New York City. Playwright, poet. *The Mountain Torrent* (prod. 1820); *The Rose of Arragon* (prod. 1822); *A Tale of Lexington* (prod. 1822); *Odofriede, the Outcast* (1822); *Gotham and the Gothamites* (poems, 1823); *The Buccaneers* (under pen name, "Terentius Phlogobombos," 1827); *The Maid of Midian* (drama in verse, 1833); etc.

JUDD, CHARLES HUBBARD (Feb. 20, 1873–July 18, 1946); b. Bareilly, India. Educator, psychologist, author. *Psychology* (1907); *The Evolution of a Democratic School System* (1918); *The Psychology of Social Institutions* (1926); *Problems of Education in the United States* (1933); *Educational Psychology* (1939); *The Teacher and Educational Administration* (with W. C. Reavis, 1942); etc. Department of education, Chicago University, 1909–38.

JUDD, SYLVESTER (July 23, 1813–Jan. 26, 1853); b. Westhampton, Mass. Unitarian clergyman, author. *Margaret* (anon., 1845); *Richard Edney and the Governor's Family* (anon., 1850); *Philo: An Evangeliad* (anon., 1850). See Arethusa Hall's *Life and Character of the Rev. Sylvester Judd* (1854).

Judge. New York City. Comic weekly. Founded Oct. 29, 1881, as *The Judge,* by James Albert Wales and a group of artists who had left *Puck.* In 1886, it dropped the "the" from its title. Editors: James Albert Wales, 1881–85; Isaac M. Gregory, 1886–1907; Burges Johnson, 1908; James Melvin Lee, 1909–12; Carleton G. Garretson, 1912–17; Douglas H. Cooke, 1922–27; Norman Anthony, 1927–28; Jack Shuttleworth, 1929–36, 1937–38; Monte Bourjaily, 1936–37; Robert T. Gebler, 1938–39. Noted for its cartoons and political satire. Expired 1939.

JUDGE, WILLIAM QUAN (Apr. 13, 1851–Mar. 21, 1896); b. Dublin, Ireland, came to the United States in 1864. Theosophist leader, editor, author. *The Yoga Aphorisms* (1889); *Echoes from the Orient* (1890); *The Ocean of Theosophy* (1893); *Notes on the Bhagavad-Gita* (1918). Founder, *The Path,* 1886; editor, 1886–96.

Judith of Bethulia. Play by Thomas Bailey Aldrich (1904).

JUDSON, ADONIRAM (Aug. 9, 1788–Apr. 12, 1850); b. Malden, Mass. Baptist clergyman, missionary to Burma. Compiler: *A Dictionary, English and Burmese* (1850). Translator (with his first wife, Ann Hasseltine Judson) of the Bible into Burmese. See Edward Judson's *Life of Adoniram Judson* (1883); Honoré W. Morrow's *The Splendor of God* (1929).

JUDSON, ANN HASSELTINE JUDSON (Mrs. Adoniram Judson) (Dec. 22, 1789–Oct. 24, 1826); b. Bradford, Mass. Baptist missionary to Burma, author. *A Particular Relation of the American Baptist Mission to the Burman Empire* (1823). See J. D. Knowles's *Memoir of Ann H. Judson* (1829); Arabella W. Stuart's *Lives of the Three Mrs. Judsons* (1872).

JUDSON, CLARA INGRAM (May 4, 1879–May 24, 1960); b. Logansport, Ind. Author of children's books. *Flower Fairies* (1915); the "Mary Jane" series, 19v.; *People Who Work near Our House* (1942); *They Came from France* (1943); *Petar's*

Treasure (1945); *City Neighbor: The Story of Jane Addams* (1951); *Thomas Jefferson: Champion of the People* (1952); *The Mighty Soo* (1955); *Mr. Justice Holmes* (1956); *St. Lawrence Seaway* (1959); etc.

JUDSON, EDWARD ZANE CARROLL (Mar. 20, 1820–July 16, 1886); b. Philadelphia, Pa. First of the dime novelists. Pen name, "Ned Buntline." *Magdalena, the Beautiful Mexican Maid: A Story of Buena Vista* (1847); *The Black Avenger* (1847); *The Virgin of the Sun* (1847); *The Volunteer* (1847); *The Mysteries and Miseries of New York* (1848); *The B'hoys of New York* (1848); *The Gals of New York* (1848); *Cruisings Afloat and Ashore* (1848); *The Red Revenger* (1848); *Norwood; or, Life on the Prairie* (1849); *Ned Buntline's Life Yarn* (under own name, 1849); *Navigator Ned* (1860); *The Scouts of the Plains* (prod. 1873); and other dime novels, 400 in all. He met William Frederick Cody in 1869, nicknamed him "Buffalo Bill," and began a series of dime novels about him; he wrote the play *The Scouts of the Plains* for Cody; it was later called *Scouts of the Prairies.* Founder, *Ned Buntline's Own,* a magazine, New York City, 1848. *See* Frederick E. Pond's *Life and Adventures of "Ned Buntline"* (1919).

JUDSON, EMILY CHUBBUCK (Mrs. Adoniram Judson) (Aug. 22, 1817–June 1, 1854); b. Eaton, N.Y. Author. Pen name, "Fanny Forester." Anonymously: *Charles Linn* (1841); *The Great Secret* (1842); *Allen Luce* (1843), the three republished in one volume as *How to Be Great, Good, and Happy;* and other Sunday School stories. Under pen name, she wrote many tales for the *New York Mirror,* which were collected into: *Lilias Fane, and Other Stories* (unauthorized edition, 1846); *Trippins in Author-Land* (1846), revised and augmented as *Alderbrook,* 2v. (1847). Under own name: *An Olio of Domestic Verses* (1852); *The Kathayan Slave, and Other Papers* (1853); *My Two Sisters* (1854); etc. *See* A. C. Kendrick's *The Life and Letters of Mrs. Emily C. Judson* (1860); Arabella W. Stuart's *Lives of the Three Mrs. Judsons* (1872).

JUDSON, HARRY PRATT (Dec. 20, 1849–Mar. 4, 1927); b. Jamestown, N.Y. Educator, historian. *Caesar's Army: A Study of the Military Art of the Romans* (1888); *Europe in the Nineteenth Century* (1894); *The Growth of the American Nation* (1895); etc. Pres., University of Chicago, 1907–23.

JUDSON, SARAH HALL BOARDMAN (Mrs. George Dana Boardman; Mrs. Adoniram Judson) (Nov. 4, 1803–Sept. 1, 1845); b. Alstead, N.H. Baptist missionary to Burma. Translated Bunyan's *The Pilgrim's Progress* into Burmese. *See* Emily C. Judson's *Memoir of Sarah B. Judson* (1848); Arabella W. Stuart's *Lives of the Three Mrs. Judsons* (1872).

Julia and the Illuminated Baron. Novel by Sarah Wood (1800). One of the earliest examples of the Gothic novel in America, a vogue started in England by Mrs. Ann Radcliffe, whose *The Mysteries of Udolpho* was the best known example of this type of horror fiction.

Jumping Frog of Calaveras County, The. See Celebrated Jumping Frog of Calaveras County, The.

June, Jennie. Pen name of Jane Cunningham Croly.

Jungle, The. By Upton Sinclair (1906). A realistic picture of life in the Chicago stockyards, and the opposition of the workingman against trade unions. The book led to a government investigation of conditions in the stockyards.

Junior Book of Authors, The. Ed. by Stanley J. Kunitz and Howard Haycraft (1935). Autobiographical sketches of writers and illustrators of children's books, with photographs and drawings of the persons included. A second edition appeared in 1951.

Junior Libraries—Jr. Books Appraised. New York. Founded 1954. Reviews by school and public librarians of new books for children and young people.

Junior Reviewers. Aspen, Colo. Bimonthly. Founded 1942. Reviews of children's books, recordings, and films. Discontinued 1960.

Junius. Pen name of Calvin Colton.

Junius Americanus. Pen name of Arthur Lee.

JUNKINS, DONALD (1931–   ); b. Saugus, Mass. Poet. *The Sunfish and the Partridge* (1965); *And Sandpipers She Said* (1970).

Junto, The. A debating society founded by Benjamin Franklin in Philadelphia in 1727. Out of it grew the Library Company of Philadelphia, founded in 1731, and the American Philosophical Society, founded in 1743.

Jupiter Lights. Novel by Constance Fenimore Woolson (1889). A tale of southern Georgia.

Jurgen. Novel by James Branch Cabell (1919). Chronicle of the fanciful Jurgen, lover and philosopher, who moves in a mythological company including Helen of Troy, Guinevere, the Devil, and other figures of passion and evil, expounding his subtle views on love and life.

"Just a-Wearyin' For You." Song, words by Frank L. Stanton, music by Carrie Jacobs Bond (1901).

Just and the Unjust, The. Novel by James Gould Cozzens (1948). The life of a small town as affected by a murder trial. Written with meticulous documentation in an analytical style.

"Just before the Battle, Mother." Civil War song by George Frederick Root (1863).

Just Folks. Collection of verse by Edgar A. Guest (1917).

"Just for Today." Popular hymn by Horatio Richard Palmer, which first appeared in his *Book of Gems for the Sunday School* (1887).

JUSTICE, DONALD [Rodney] (Aug. 12, 1925–); b. Miami, Fla. Poet. *The Summer Anniversaries* (1959); *A Local Storm* (1963); *Night Light* (1967); etc. Co-editor: *Midlands* (1961). Faculty, Syracuse University.

JUSTUS, MAY (May 12, 1898–). Author of children's books. *Peter Pocket* (1927); *Betty Lou of Big Log Mountain* (1928); *Gabby Gaffer* (1929); *At the Foot of Windy Low* (1930); *The Other Side of the Mountain* (1931); *Honey Jane* (1935); *Near-Side-and-Far* (1936); *The House in No-End Hollow* (1938); *Mr. Songcatcher and Company* (1940); *Cabin on Kettle Creek* (1941); *Bluebird, Fly Up* (1943); *Sammy* (1946); *Luck for Lihu* (1950); *Peter Pocket and His Pickle Pup* (1953); *Use Your Head* (1956); *Big Log Mountain* (1958); *Barney, Bring Your Banjo* (1959); *A New Name for Billy* (1966); *It Happened in No-End Hollow* (1969).

Juvenile Miscellany. Boston, Mass. Bi-monthly children's magazine. Founded 1826. Editor, Lydia Maria Francis Child. Expired 1834.

Juvenile Port Folio. Philadelphia, Pa. Children's weekly. Founded Oct. 30, 1812, by Thomas G. Condie, Jr., aged 14. Expired Dec. 7, 1816.

K

"K." Novel by Mary Roberts Rinehart (1915). Story of a surgeon who makes a fatal error and gives up his profession, followed by a struggle to rehabilitate himself.

KAEL, PAULINE (June 19, 1919–   ); b. Petaluma, Cal. Motion picture critic, author. *I Lost It at the Movies* (1965); *Kiss Kiss Bang Bang* (1968); *Going Steady* (1970). Critic, *New Republic* magazine, *Cosmopolitan, New Yorker.*

KAFKA, JOHN (Dec. 26, 1905–); b. Vienna. Author. *Das Grenzenlose* (*No Limits,* 1925); *Geschichte einer Grossen Liebe* (*The Story of a Great Love,* 1935); *The Apple Orchard* (1947); *Sicilian Street* (1949).

KAGEY, RUDOLF (Sept. 5, 1904–1946); b. Tuscola, Ill. Educator, novelist. Pen name, "Kurt Steel." *Murder of a Dead Man* (1935); *Murder Goes to College* (1936); *Murder for What?* (1936); *Murder in G-Sharp* (1937); *Crooked Shadow* (1939); *Judas Incorporated* (1939); *Dead of Night* (1940); *The Imposter* (1942). Philosophy dept., Washington Square College, New York University, from 1928.

KAHLER, HUGH [Torbert] MacNair (Feb. 25, 1883–); b. Philadelphia, Pa. Author. *Babel* (1921); *The East Wind* (1922); *The Collector's What-Not* (with Kenneth L. Roberts and Booth Tarkington, 1923); *Father Means Well* (1930); *Hills Were Higher Then* (1931); *The Big Pink* (1932); *Bright Danger* (1942); etc.

KAHN, E[ly] **J**[acques], **Jr.** (Dec. 4, 1916–); b. New York. Author. *This Is the Army* (1942); *G.I. Jungle* (1943); *McNair: Educator of an Army* (1945); *The Voice* (1947); *Who, Me?* (1949); *The Peculiar War* (1952); *The Merry Partners: The Age and Stage of Harrigan and Hart* (1955); *A Reporter Here and There* (1961); *The World of Swope* (1965); *A Reporter in Micronesia* (1966); *The Separated People* (1968); *A Building Goes Up* (1969). With *New Yorker* since 1937.

KAHN, HERMAN (Feb. 15, 1922–); b. Bayonne, N.J. Author. *On Thermonuclear War* (1960); *Thinking About the Unthinkable* (1962); *On Escalation Metaphors and Scenarios* (1965); *The Year 2000* (1967); *Can We Win in Viet Nam?* (1968).

KALASHNIKOFF, NICHOLAS (1888–Aug. 17, 1961); b. Minusisk, Rus. *They That Take the Sword* (1939); *Jumper, A Story of a Siberian Horse* (1944); *Toyon* (1950); *My Friend Yakub* (1953); etc.

KALB, MARVIN LEONARD (June 9, 1930–); radio and television correspondent, author. *Eastern Exposure* (1958); *Dragon in the Kremlin* (1961); *The Volga, a Political Journey Through Russia* (1967). Correspondent CBS News since 1960.

KALER, JAMES OTIS (Mar. 19, 1848–Dec. 11, 1912); b. Winterport, Me. Author of over one hundred books for children. Pen name "James Otis." *Toby Tyler* (1880); *Silent Pete* (1886); *Braganza Diamond* (1891); *At the Siege of Quebec* (1897); *Life Savers* (1899); *Among the Fur Traders* (1906); *The Light Keepers* (1906); etc., including the *Minute Boys Series,* the *Colonial Series,* the *Pioneer Series,* etc.

KALLEN, HORACE MEYER (Aug. 11, 1882–); b. Berenstadt, Silesia, Ger. Educator, author. *Culture and Democracy in the United States* (1924); *Frontiers of Hope* (1929); *Individualism: An American Way of Life* (1933); *Art and Freedom,* 2v. (1942); *Modernity and Liberty* (1947); *The Liberal Spirit* (1948); *Ideals and Experience* (1948); *The Education of Free Men* (1949); *Patterns of Progress* (1950); *Democracy's True Religion* (1951); *Secularism Is the Will of God* (1954); *Cultural Pluralism and the American Idea* (1956); *Utopians at Bay* (1958); *The Book of Job as Greek Tragedy* (1959); *A Study of Liberty* (1959); *Philosophical Issues in Adult Education* (1962); *Freedom, Tragedy and Comedy* (1963); *Liberty, Laughter and Tears* (1968); etc. Editor: *The Bertrand Russell Case* (with John Dewey, 1941). Faculty, New School for Social Research, 1919–52.

KALLMAN, CHESTER S. (Jan. 7, 1921–); b. Brooklyn, N.Y. Poet, librettist, translator. *The Rake's Progress* (with W. H.

Auden, prod. 1951; music by Igor Stravinsky); *Storm at Castelfranco* (poems, 1956); *The Tuscan Players* (prod. 1957; music by Carlos Chavez); *Elegy for Young Lovers* (with W. H. Auden, prod. 1961; music by Hans Henze); *Absent and Present* (poems, 1962). Libretto translations: *Bluebeard, Coronation of Poppea, Falstaff, Anne Boleyn, Don Giovanni.* Libretto translations, with W. H. Auden: *The Magic Flute, The Seven Deadly Sins.*

Kaloolah. By William Starbuck Mayo (1849). A romance which gives an imaginary account of an African Utopia visited by the Yankee hero Jonathan Romer.

KALTENBORN, H[ans] **V.** (July 9, 1878–June 14, 1965); b. Milwaukee, Wis. Editor, radio news commentator, author. *We Look at the World* (1930); *Kaltenborn Edits the News* (1937); *I Broadcast the Crisis* (1938); *Kaltenborn Edits the War News* (1942); *Europe Now* (1945); *Fifty Fabulous Years* (1950); *It Seems Like Yesterday* (1956); etc. With *Brooklyn Eagle,* 1910–30; with Columbia Broadcasting Co., 1929–40; with National Broadcasting Co., from 1940.

Kandy-Kolored Tangerine-Flake Streamline Baby, The. Collection of periodical pieces on popular culture, by Tom Wolfe (1965).

KANE, FRANK (1912–Nov. 29, 1968). Author. *About Face* (1947); *Dead Weight* (1951); *Poisons Unknown* (1953); *Red Hot Ice* (1955); *Real Gone Guy* (1956); *Trigger Mortis* (1958); *Stacked Deck* (1968).

KANE, HARNETT T[homas] (Nov. 8, 1910–); b. New Orleans, La. Author. *Louisiana Hayride* (1941); *Bayous of Louisiana* (1943); *New Orleans Woman* (1946); *Pathway to the Stars* (1950); *The Lady of Arlington* (1953); *The Gallant Mrs. Stonewall* (1957); *Have Pen, Will Autograph* (1959); *Gone Are the Days* (1960); *The Amazing Mrs. Bonaparte* (1963); *Young Mark Twain and the Mississippi* (1966); etc.

KANE, HENRY (1918–); Author. *Halo for Nobody* (1947); *Armchair in Hell* (1948); *Until You Are Dead* (1951); *The Death of a Flack* (1961); *A Picture Story of the Confederacy* (1965); etc.

KANG, YOUNGHILL (1903–); b. Song-Dune-Chi, Korea, came to the United States in 1920. Author. *The Grass Roof* (1931); *The Happy Grove* (1933); *East Goes West* (1937). Translator: Michiro Maruyama's *Anatahan* (1954).

KANIN, GARSON (Nov. 24, 1912–); b. Rochester, N.Y. Director, playwright, author. *Born Yesterday* (prod. 1946); *Smile of the World* (prod. 1949); *The Rat Race* (prod. 1949); *The Live Wire* (prod. 1950); *Do Re Mi* (1955); *Blow Up a Storm* (1959); *The Rat Race* (1960); *Remembering Mr. Maugham* (1966); *Cast of Characters: Stories of Broadway and Hollywood* (1969). Also author or co-author (with wife, Ruth Gordon) of screen plays.

Kansas City Journal-Post. Kansas City, Mo. Founded 1854, by Robert Van Horn as the *Kansas City Enterprise,* a weekly. It became a daily in 1858. It had many changes of name, including the *Daily Kansas City Journal of Commerce,* and in 1878 the *Kansas City Daily Journal.* The *Kansas City Post* was founded in 1906, and was merged with the *Journal* in 1928. Eugene Field, Albert Johnson, and Walt Disney were at one time on the staff. Expired 1941.

Kansas City Star. Kansas City, Mo. Founded Sept. 8, 1880. The *Kansas City Times* (founded 1868) was acquired in 1901 as the morning edition. The united papers achieved prominence under the ownership and direction of William Rockhill Nelson. W. W. Baker is editor. Thorpe Menn is book review editor. *See* I. F. Johnson's *William Rockhill Nelson and the Kansas City Star* (1935).

Kansas Magazine. Manhattan, Kan. Annual. Founded 1872, at Topeka, as a monthly. Expired 1873. Revived 1886, at Kansas City, Kan. Expired 1888. Revived 1909, at Wichita.

Expired 1912. Revived 1933 at Manhattan, Kan. Edited by W. R. Moses.

Kansas Weekly Herald. Leavenworth, Kan. Newspaper. Founded Sept. 15, 1854, by William H. Adams. Became the *Weekly Leavenworth Herald* 1859. First newspaper published in English in Kansas, though the *Siwinowe Kesibwi (Shawnee Sun)* in the Shawnee language began publication Mar. 1, 1835. The *Herald* expired 1861.

KANTOR, MacKINLAY (Feb. 4, 1904–); b. Webster City, Ia. Novelist. *Diversey* (1928); *El Goes South* (1930); *The Jaybird* (1932); *Long Remember* (1934); *Turkey in the Straw* (poems, 1935); *The Voice of Bugle Ann* (1935);*Arouse and Beware* (1936); *The Romance of Rosy Ridge* (1937); *Here Lies Holly Springs* (1938); *The Noise of Their Wings* (1938); *Cuba Libre* (1940); *Gentle Annie* (1942); *Happy Land* (1943); *Glory for Me* (1945); *Midnight Lace* (1948); *Wicked Water* (1949); *Signal Thirty-Two* (1950); *Don't Touch Me* (1951); *The Daughter of Bugle Ann* (1953); *God and My Country* (1954); *Andersonville* (1955; Pulitzer prize for fiction, 1956); *Lobo* (1957); *The Work of St. Francis* (1958); *Spirit Lake* (1961); *Mission with LeMay* (1965); *Story Teller* (1967); *Beauty Beast* (1968).

KAPELNER, ALAN. Author. *Lonely Boy Blues* (1947); *All the Naked Heroes* (1960).

KAPLAN, ABRAHAM (June 11, 1918–   ); b. Odessa, Russia. Educator, author. *Power and Society* (with H. D. Lasswell, 1950); *The New World of Philosophy* (1961); *American Ethics and Public Policy* (1963); *The Conduct of Inquiry* (1964). Prof. philosophy, University of Michigan, since 1963.

KAPLAN, HAROLD J. (July 29, 1918–); b. Newark, N.J. Novelist. *The Plenipotentiaries* (1949); *The Spirit and the Bride* (1951); *The Passive Voice* (1966); etc.

KAPLAN, JUSTIN (Sept. 5, 1925–   ); b. New York. Author. *Mr. Clemens and Mark Twain* (1966: National Book Award and Pulitzer Prize Award, 1967); *Mark Twain: A Profile* (1967). Editor: *Dialogues of Plato* (1950); *With Malice Toward Women* (1952); *The Pocket Aristotle* (1958); *The Gilded Age* (1964); *Great Short Works of Mark Twain* (1967).

KAPLAN, MORDECAI [Menahem] (June 11, 1881–); b. Swenziany, Lith. Rabbi, educator, author. *The Meaning of God in Modern Jewish Religion* (1937); *The Future of the American Jew* (1948); *Questions Jews Ask* (1956); *Judaism Without Supernaturalism* (1958); *A Greater Judaism in the Making* (1960); *Not So Random Thoughts* (1966); *Judaism as a Civilization* (1967); etc. Editor, *The Reconstructionist,* since 1935. Faculty, Jewish Theological Seminary, since 1909.

KAPROW, ALLAN (Aug. 23, 1927–   ); b. Atlantic City, N.J. Artist. *Assemblages, Environments and Happenings* (1966). Devised the first "happenings." Prof. fine arts, State University at Stony Brook, N.Y., since 1966.

KARDINER, ABRAM (Aug. 17, 1891–); b. New York. Psychiatrist, author. *The Individual and His Society* (1939); *The Psychological Frontiers of Society* (with others, 1945); *Sex and Morality* (1954); *They Studied Man* (with Edward Preble, 1961); etc.

KARIEL, HENRY (July 7, 1924–   ); b. Plauen, Ger. Educator, author. *The Decline of American Pluralism* (1961); *In Search of Authority* (1964); *Sources in Twentieth Century Political Thought* (1964); *The Promise of Politics* (1966). Faculty Harvard University, 1955–58; Bennington College, 1958–64; University of Hawaii, since 1964.

KARIG, WALTER (Nov. 13, 1898–Sept. 30, 1956); b. New York. Editor, author. *The Magic Acorn* (with wife, Eleanor Keating Freye Karig, 1928); *Hungry Crawford, Legionnaire* (1929); *Death Is a Tory* (under pen name, "Keats Patrick,"

1935); *Asia's Good Neighbor* (1937); *Lower than Angels* (1945); *War in the Atomic Age* (1946); *Zotz* (1947); etc. Co-author: *Battle Report,* 6v. (1944–51); *Don't Tread on Me* (with Horace V. Bird, 1954); etc; also juvenile mystery stories under various pen names. With the Newark *Evening News,* 1921–42; Washington correspondent, from 1934.

KARP, DAVID (May 5, 1922–); b. New York. Author. *One* (1953); *Day of the Monkey* (1955); *All Honorable Men* (1956); *Leave Me Alone* (1957); *Enter, Sleeping* (1960); *The Last Believers* (1964); etc.

KARSNER, DAVID (Mar. 22, 1889–Feb. 20, 1941); b. Baltimore, Md. Journalist, author. *Debs: His Authorized Life and Letters* (1919); *Horace Traubel* (1919); *Talks with Debs in Terre Haute* (1922); *Sixteen Authors to One* (1928); *Andrew Jackson, the Gentle Savage* (1929); *Silver Dollar: The Story of the Tabors* (1932); *John Brown, Terrible "Saint"* (1934).

"Kathrina: Her Life and Mine in a Poem." By Josiah Gilbert Holland (1867). This long poem was exceeded in popularity only by Longfellow's "Hiawatha."

KATKOV, NORMAN (July 26, 1918–); b. in U.S.S.R. Novelist. *Eagle at My Eyes* (1948); *A Little Sleep, a Little Slumber* (1949); *Fabulous Fanny* (1953).

Katrinka. By Helen Eggleston Haskell (1915). The first and most popular of the "Katrinka" books for children.

KAUFFMAN, REGINALD WRIGHT (Sept. 8, 1877–1959); b. Columbia, Pa. Editor, war correspondent, novelist. *Jarvis of Harvard* (1901); *The Bachelor's Guide* (1907); *My Heart and Stephanie* (1910); *The House of Bondage* (1910); *Jim* (1915); *The Mark of the Beast* (1916); *Spanish Dollars* (1925); *Seventy-six* (1926); *The Overland Trail* (1927); *Pirate Jean* (1929); *Mad Anthony's Drummer* (1929); *Front Porch* (1933); etc. Editor, *Hampton's Magazine,* 1909.

KAUFFMAN, RUTH [Hammitt] (Mrs. Reginald Wright Kauffman) (d. Aug. 13, 1952); b. New York City. Author. *High Stakes* (1914); *Three Little Kittens* (1922); *Stars for Sale* (1930); *Tourist Third* (1933); *Spun Gold* (1936); *Narcotics* (1938); etc. Editor: *Unfamiliar Quotations* (1949).

KAUFFMANN, STANLEY (Apr. 24, 1916–   ); b. New York. Playwright, novelist. *Altogether Reformed* (play, 1936); *The King of Proxy Street* (1941); *Bobino* (prod. 1944); *This Time Forever* (1945); *The Hidden Hero* (1949); *A Change of Climate* (1954); *Man of the World* (1956); *A World on Film* (1966). Author of numerous one-act plays.

KAUFMAN, BEL, b. Berlin, Ger. Educator, author. *Up the Down Staircase* (1965). Teacher of English, New York City high schools; English faculty, Manhattan Community College, New York.

KAUFMAN, GEORGE S. (Nov. 16, 1889–June 2, 1961); b. Pittsburgh, Pa. Playwright. *Dulcy* (with Marc Connelly, prod. 1921); *To the Ladies* (with same, prod. 1922); *The Beggar on Horseback* (with same, prod. 1924); *The Butter and Egg Man* (prod. 1925); *The Royal Family* (with Edna Ferber, prod. 1927); *Once in a Lifetime* (with Moss Hart, prod. 1930); *Of Thee I Sing* (with Morris Ryskind and Ira Gershwin, prod. 1931, Pulitzer Prize play, 1932); *Dinner at Eight* (with Edna Ferber, prod. 1932); *First Lady* (with Katharine Dayton, prod. 1935); *Stage Door* (with Edna Ferber, prod. 1936); *You Can't Take It with You* (with Moss Hart, prod. 1936); *The American Way* (with same, prod. 1939); *The Man Who Came to Dinner* (prod. 1939); *George Washington Slept Here* (prod. 1940); *The Late George Apley* (with J. P. Marquand, prod. 1944); *Park Avenue* (with Nunnally Johnson, prod. 1946); *Bravo!* (with Edna Ferber, prod. 1948); *The Small Hours* (with Leueen MacGrath prod. 1951); *Silk Stockings* (with same, prod. 1955); etc. See George Scott Meredith's *George S. Kaufman: A Biography* (1965).

KAUFMAN, HERBERT (Mar. 6, 1878–Sept. 6, 1947); b. Washington, D.C. Editor, author. *Poems* (1913); *Neighbors* (1916); *The Splendid Gamble* (1939); etc. Editor and owner, *McClure's Magazine,* 1919–21; founder, Herbert Kaufman Newspaper Syndicate, New York.

KAUFMAN, KENNETH CARLYLE (Apr. 30, 1887–Apr. 29, 1945); b. Leon, Kan. Educator, editor, poet. *Level Land: A Book of Western Verse* (1935). Managing editor, *Books Abroad;* literary editor, *Daily Oklahoman.* Modern language dept., University of Oklahoma, from 1929.

KAUFMAN, LENARD (Aug. 20, 1913–); b. New York. Novelist. *The Lower Part of the Sky* (1948); *Tender Mercy* (1949); *Jubel's Children* (1950); *Diminishing Return* (1952); *An Apple a Day* (1955); *Color of Green* (1956).

KAUFMAN, PAUL (July 29, 1886–); b. Providence, R.I. Educator, author. *Outline Guide to Shakespeare* (1924); *Heralds of Original Genius* (1926). Editor: *Essays in Memory of Barrett Wendell* (with W. R. Castle, 1926); etc. Prof. English, American University, Washington, D.C., 1920–30, etc.

KAUFMANN, WALTER A[rnold] (July 1, 1921–); b. Freiburg, Ger. Educator, author. *Nietzsche: Philosopher, Psychologist, Antichrist* (1950); *Existentialism from Dostoevsky to Sartre* (ed., 1956); *The Faith of a Heretic* (1961); *Ethics and Business* (1962); *Martin Buber* (1963); *Of Poetry and Power* (1964); *Hegel* (1965); *The Will to Power* (1967); etc. Philosophy dept., Princeton University, since 1954.

KAUP, ELIZABETH BARTOL DEWING (Nov. 26, 1885–); b. New York. Author. *Other People's Houses* (1909); *A Big Horse to Ride* (1911); *My Son John* (1926); *Eagles Fly High* (1929); *So Refined* (1937); *Not for the Meek* (1941); *Seed of the Puritan* (1943); *Repeat with Laughter* (1948).

KAY, GERTRUDE ALICE (d. Dec. 18, 1939); b. Alliance, O. Author and illustrator of children's books. *When the Sandman Comes* (1914); *The Book of Seven Wishes* (1917); *Adventures in Our Street* (1925); *Us Kids and the Circus* (1927); *Peter, Patter & Pixie* (1931); etc.

KAYE, FREDERICK BENJAMIN (Apr. 20, 1892–Feb. 28, 1930); b. (Kugelman) New York City. Educator. Editor: *A Census of British Newspapers and Periodicals, 1620–1800* (with Ronald S. Crane, 1927); etc. English dept., Northwestern University, 1917–30.

Kaye, Philip B. Pen name of Alger Adams.

KAZAR. Novel by James Oliver Curwood (1914). Story of an Arctic dog which was part wolf.

KAZIN, ALFRED (June 5, 1915–); b. Brooklyn, N.Y. Author. *On Native Grounds* (1942); *The Inmost Leaf* (1955); *A Walker in the City* (1968). Editor: *The Viking Portable William Blake* (1946); *F. Scott Fitzgerald: The Man and His Work* (1951); *The Open Form* (1961); *Contemporaries* (1962); etc.

KEAN, CHARLES DUELL (Feb. 22, 1910–Oct. 16, 1963); b. West Point, N.Y. Episcopal clergyman, author. *Christianity and the Cultural Crisis* (1945); *The Meaning of Existence* (1947); *The Christian Gospel and the Parish Church* (1953); *God's Word to His People* (1956); *The Road to Reunion* (1958); *That Hearing They Shall Perceive* (1963); etc.

KEATING, JOHN McLEOD (June 12, 1830–Aug. 15, 1906); b. in Kings Co., Ireland. Editor, author. *History of the Yellow Fever* (1879); *History of the City of Memphis,* 3v. (1888); etc. Founder, the *Memphis Daily Commercial,* 1865; editor, the *Memphis Appeal,* 1868–89; the *Memphis Daily Commercial,* 1889–91.

KEATS, JOHN C. (1920–); Author. *The Crack in the Picture Window* (1957); *The Insolent Chariots* (1958); *Schools Without Scholars* (1958); *The Sheepskin Psychosis* (1965); *Howard Hughes* (1966).

Keats, Myron. Pen name of Charles Stanley Strong.

KEELER, CHARLES (Augustus) (Oct. 7, 1871–July 31, 1937); b. Milwaukee, Wis. Poet. *A Light Through the Storm* (1894); *The Promise of the Ages* (1896); *Sequoia Sonnets* (1919); etc.

KEELER, HARRY STEPHEN (Nov. 3, 1894–Jan. 22, 1967); b. Chicago, Ill. Editor, author. *Find the Clock* (1927); *Sing Sing Nights* (1928); *Thieves' Nights* (1929); *The Spectacles of Mr. Cagliostro* (1929); *The Green Jade Hand* (1930); *The Box from Japan* (1932); *The Face of the Man from Saturn* (1933); *The Five Silver Buddhas* (1934); *The Case of the Barking Clock* (1947); *The Strange Case of Alfred Crofts-Hartley* (1955); *Hangman's Nights* (1959); and other detective fiction.

KEELER, RALPH OLMSTEAD (Aug. 29, 1840–Dec. 17, 1873); b. northern Ohio. Journalist, author. *Gloverson and His Silent Partners* (1869); *Vagabond Adventures* (1870); etc. On staff, *Alta California; Golden Era; Atlantic Monthly; New York Tribune;* etc.

KEELEY, EDMUND LEROY (Feb. 5, 1928–); b. Damascus, Syria. Educator, author. *The Libation* (1958); *Six Poets of Modern Greece* (with Philip Sherrard, 1960). Translator: *George Seferis, Collected Poems, 1924–1955* (1967). English dept., Princeton University, since 1954.

KEELEY, JAMES (Oct. 14, 1867–June 7, 1934); b. London, England. Editor. Editor, the *Chicago Tribune,* 1898–1914; the *Chicago Herald,* 1914–18. See James W. Linn's *James Keeley, Newspaperman* (1937).

KEELEY, JOSEPH CHARLES (Aug. 10, 1907–); b. Wilkes-Barre, Pa. Editor, author. *They Sold Themselves* (with Howard Stephenson, 1937); *Making Inventions Pay* (1950); *Taking It Easy with Your Camera* (1957); *Photography for Your Family* (1964); *Chiva Lobby Man* (1969). Editor, *American Legion Magazine,* since 1949.

KEENAN, HENRY FRANCIS (b. May 4, 1850); b. Rochester, N.Y. Novelist. *The Money-Makers* (1885); *Trajan* (1885); *The Aliens* (1886); *The Iron Game* (1891); etc.

"Keenan's Charge." Civil War ballad by George Parsons Lathrop.

Keene, Carolyn. Pen name of Harriet S. Adams. Author of mystery stories for girls. *The Secret of the Old Clock* (1930); *The Secret of Shadow Ranch* (1931); *The Sign of the Twisted Candles* (1933); *The Mystery of the Ivory Charm* (1936); *The Mystery of the Brass Bound Trunk* (1940); and others of the Nancy Drew Mystery Stories. Also: *By the Light of the Study Lamp* (1934); *The Three Cornered Mystery* (1935); *The Mystery of the Locked Room* (1938); *The Secret at the Gatehouse* (1940); and others of the Dana Girls Mystery Stories.

KEENE, DONALD (1922–). Educator, author. *Japanese Literature* (1955); *Living Japan* (1959); etc. Editor: *Anthology of Japanese Literature* (1955); *Modern Japanese Literature* (1956). Translator: Dazai's *No Longer Human* (1958); Dazai's *The Setting Sun* (1956); *Bunraku* (1965); etc.

Keep Cool: A Novel Written in Hot Weather by Somebody. By John Neal (1817).

KEESE, JOHN (Nov. 24, 1805–May 30, 1856); b. New York City. Editor, auctioneer. Editor: *The Poets of America,* 2v. (1840–1842); *The Forest Legendary* (poems, 1845); *The Floral Keepsake* (1850); etc.

KEESING, FELIX MAXWELL (Jan. 5, 1902–Apr. 22, 1961); b. Taiping, Straits Settlements. Anthropologist. *The Changing Maori* (1928); *Taming Philippine Headhunters* (1934); *Hawaiian Homesteading on Molokai* (1936); *The South Seas in the Modern World* (1941); *Cultural Anthropology: The Science of Custom* (1958); etc. Prof. anthropology, Stanford University, 1942–61.

KEEZER, DEXTER MERRIAM (Aug. 24, 1896–); b. Acton, Mass. Economist, educator. *The Light That Flickers* (1947); *Making Capitalism Work* (with others, 1950); *New Forces in American Business* (1959). Pres., Reed College, Portland, Ore., 1934–42.

KEFAUVER, ESTES (July 26, 1903–Aug. 10, 1963); b. Madisonville, Tenn. Senator. *Crime in America* (1951); *In a Few Hands: Monopoly Power in America* (ed. by Irene Till, 1965).

KEGLEY, CHARLES WILLIAM (Feb. 17, 1912–); b. Chicago, Ill. Lutheran clergyman, educator. Editor: *The Theology of Paul Tillich* (1952); *Reinhold Niebuhr: His Religious, Social, and Political Thought* (1956); *Protestantism in Transition* (1965); *The Theology of Rudolf Bultmann* (1966); etc. Prof. philosophy, Wagner College, since 1949.

KEIMER, SAMUEL (Feb. 11, 1688–c. 1739); b. London, England. Printer, author. Associated with Benjamin Franklin. *A Brand Pluck'd from the Burning* (1718); *Elegy on the Much Lamented Death of . . . Aquila Rose* (1723); etc. Founder, *Universal Instructor in All Arts and Science and Pennsylvania Gazette*, Dec. 24, 1728. *See* Carl Van Doren's *Benjamin Franklin* (1938).

KEISER, ALBERT (Dec. 7, 1887–Dec. 5, 1959); b. in East Friesia, Ger. Educator, author. *The Indian in American Literature* (1933); *College Names: Their Origin and Significance* (1940); *The Way Up* (autobiography, 1962); etc. Head, English dept., Lenoir-Rhyne College, Hickory, N.C., from 1925.

KEITH, AGNES NEWTON (1901–); b. Oak Park, Ill. Author. *Land Below the Wind* (1939); *Three Came Home* (1947); *White Man Returns* (1951); *Bare Feet in the Palace* (1955); *Children of Allah* (1966).

Keith, David. Pen name of Francis Steegmuller.

KEITH, HAROLD VERNE (Apr. 8, 1903–); b. Lambert, Okla. Author. *Boy's Life of Will Rogers* (1937); *Oklahoma Kickoff* (1948); *A Pair of Captains* (1951); *Rifles for Watie* (1957); etc.

Keith, Mrs. Oscar L. See Frances Guiguard Gibbes.

KELLAND, CLARENCE BUDINGTON (July 11, 1881–Feb. 18, 1964); b. Portland, Mich. Author. The *Mark Tidd* series, 6v. (1913–18); *Sudden Jim* (1916); *Scattergood Baines* (1921); *Contraband* (1922); *The Great Crooner* (1933); *Catspaw* (1934); *Roxana* (1936); *Arizona* (1939); *Valley of the Sun* (1940); *Sugarfool* (1942); *Archibald the Great* (1943); *Land of the Torreones* (1946); *Double Treasure* (1946); *Merchant of Valor* (1947); *Stolen Goods* (1950); *The Great Mail Robbery* (1951); *No Escape* (1951); *Dangerous Angel* (1953); *Murder Makes an Entrance* (1955); *Case of the Nameless Corpse* (1957); *West of the Law* (1958); *The Lady and the Giant* (1959); *The Counterfeit Gentleman* (1960); *Mark of Treachery* (1961); *The Artless Heiress* (1962); etc. Editor, *American Boy,* 1907–15.

KELLER, ALBERT GALLOWAY (Apr. 10, 1874–Oct. 31, 1956); b. Springfield, O. Educator, author. *Homeric Society* (1902); *Man's Rough Road* (1932); *Reminiscences of William Graham Sumner* (1933); etc. Editor: *Essays of William Graham Sumner,* 2v. (with Maurice R. Davie, 1934); and many other works by Sumner; *All of Us* (1944). Social science dept., Yale University, 1900–42.

KELLER, ARTHUR IGNATIUS (July 4, 1867–Dec. 2, 1924); b. New York City. Artist, illustrator. *Figure Studies from Life,* 2v. (1920). Illustrated books by Bret Harte, Longfellow, Irving, F. Hopkinson Smith, S. Weir Mitchell, etc.

KELLER, ETHEL MAY (1878–); b. West Harwick, Mass. *When I Was Little* (1915); *Elizabeth: Her Friends* (under pen name, "Barbara Kay," 1920); *Elizabeth: Her Folks* (under same pen name, 1920); *Beauty and Mary Blair* (1921); *Home, James* (1927); *Through My Open Door* (under pen name, "Lucia Whitney," 1935); etc.

KELLER, HELEN [Adams] (June 27, 1880–June 1, 1968); b. Tuscumbia, Ala. Blind author, lecturer. *The Story of My Life* (1902); *Out of the Dark* (1913); *Midstream: My Later Life* (1930); *Helen Keller's Journal, 1936–1937* (1938); *Let Us Have Faith* (1940); *Teacher* (1955); *The Open Door* (1957); etc.

KELLER, JAMES G. (June 27, 1900–); b. Oakland, Cal. Roman Catholic clergyman, author. *You Can Change the World* (1948); *Three Minutes a Day* (1949); *Government Is Your Business* (1951); *All God's Children* (1953); *A Day at a Time* (1957); etc.

KELLEY, FRANCIS CLEMENT (Oct. 23, 1870–Feb. 1, 1948); b. Vernon River, P.E.I. Roman Catholic bishop, author. *The Last Battle of the Gods* (1907); *Letters to Jack* (1917); *Charred Wood* (1917); *Dominus Vobiscum* (1922); *Mexico the Land of Blood-Drenched Altars* (1935); *Problem Island* (1937); *The Bishop Jots It Down* (1939); etc.

KELLEY, JAMES DOUGLAS JERROLD (b. Dec. 25, 1847); b. New York City. Naval officer, author. *A Desperate Chance* (1886); *The Ship's Company* (1897); etc. He wrote the U.S. Naval Academy song, "God Bless Sweethearts and Wives."

KELLEY, WILLIAM MELVIN (1937–   ); b. Author. *A Different Drummer* (1962); *Dancers on the Shore* (1964); *A Drop of Patience* (1965); *dem* (1967); *Dunfords Travels Everywheres* (1970).

KELLOGG, CHARLOTTE HOFFMAN (Mrs. Vernon L. Kellogg). Author. *Women of Belgium* (1917); *Mercier, the Fighting Cardinal of Belgium* (1920); *Jadwiga, Queen of Poland* (1936); *Pacific Light* (poems, 1939); *Paderewski* (1956); etc.

KELLOGG, EDWARD (Oct. 18, 1790–Apr. 29, 1858); b. Norwalk, Conn. Economist, author. *Remarks upon Usury* (under pen name, "Whitehook," 1841); *Currency: The Evil and the Remedy* (under pen name, "Godek Gardwell," 1843), revised as *Labor and Other Capital* (1849), republished by his daughter, Mary Kellogg Putnam, as *A New Monetary System* (1861).

KELLOGG, ELIJAH (May 20, 1813–Mar. 17, 1901); b. Portland, Me. Congregational clergyman, author. The *Elm Island* series, 6v. (1869–70); the *Pleasant Cove* series, 6v. (1870–74); the *Whispering Pine* series, 6v. (1871–73); the *Forest Glen* series, 6v. (1874–78); the *Good Old Times* series, 4v. (1878–83); etc. He also wrote the popular declamation "Spartacus to the Gladiators," which first appeared in the *School Reader* of Epes Sargent (1846). *See* Wilmot Brookings Mitchell's *Elijah Kellogg: The Man and His Work* (1903).

KELLOGG, LOUISE PHELPS (d. July 11, 1942); b. Milwaukee, Wis. Historian. *The French Regime in Wisconsin and the Northwest* (1925); *The British Regime in Wisconsin and the Northwest* (1935); *Historic Wisconsin* (1939); and other books on Wisconsin in history. Editor: *Early Narratives of the Northwest* (1917); etc. Assisted Reuben Gold Thwaites in editing *Early Western Travels,* 30v. (1904–06), etc. Research associate, State Historical Society of Wisconsin, from 1901.

KELLOGG, MARJORIE. Playwright. *Tell Me That You Love Me, Junie Moon* (1969).

KELLOGG, PAUL UNDERWOOD (Sept. 30, 1879–Nov. 1, 1958); b. Kalamazoo, Mich. Editor. Editor, the *Survey* (now the *Survey-Graphic),* 1912–42.

KELLOGG, VERNON LYMAN (Dec. 1, 1867–Aug. 8, 1937); b. Emporia, Kan. Educator, zoologist, author. *Insect Stories* (1908); *In and Out of Florence* (under pen name, "Max Vernon," 1910); *Headquarters Nights* (1917); *Nuova, the New Bee* (1921); *Herbert Hoover* (1920); *Human Life as the Biologist Sees It* (1922); etc. Prof. entomology, Stanford University, 1894–1920.

Kelly, Eleanor Mercein. See Eleanor Mercein.

KELLY, ERIC PHILBROOK (Mar. 16, 1884–Jan., 1960); b. Amesbury, Mass. Educator, novelist. *The Trumpeter of Krakow* (1928); *The Blacksmith of Vilno* (1930); *The Golden Star of Halich* (1930); *Treasure Mountain* (1937); *At the Sign of the Golden Compass* (1938); *A Girl Who Would Be Queen* (1939); *On the Staked Plain* (1940); *From Star to Star* (1944); *A Hand in the Picture* (1947); *Amazing Journey of David Ingram* (1949); *In Clean Hay* (1953). English dept., Dartmouth College, 1921–29; prof. journalism, 1929–54.

KELLY, FLORENCE FINCH (Mar. 27, 1858–Dec. 17, 1939); b. Girard, Ill. Journalist, novelist. *The Delafield Affair* (1909); *Rhoda of the Underground* (1909); *Emerson's Wife, and Other Western Stories* (1911); *Fate of Felix Brand* (1913); *The Dixons* (1921); *Flowing Stream: the Story of Fifty-Six Years in American Newspaper Life* (1938); etc. On staff, the *New York Times Book Review,* 1906–1936.

KELLY, FRED C[harters] (Jan. 27, 1882–May 23, 1959); b. Xenia, O. Journalist, author. *The Wisdom of Laziness* (1924); *You and Your Dog* (1926); *But on the Other Hand* (1928); *The Wright Brothers* (biography, 1943); *The Life and Times of Kin Hubbard* (1952); etc. Wrote syndicated column, "Statesmen, Real and Near," 1910–18. Author of syndicated editorials known as "Kelly-grams."

KELLY, GEORGE [Edward] (1887–Apr. 3, 1943); b. Philadelphia, Pa. Playwright. *The Torch Bearers* (prod. 1922); *The Show-Off* (prod. 1924); *Craig's Wife* (prod. 1925, Pulitzer Prize play, 1926); *Behold the Bridegroom* (prod. 1927); *Philip Goes Forth* (prod. 1931); *Reflected Glory* (prod. 1936); *The Deep Mrs. Sykes* (prod. 1945); *The Fatal Weakness* (prod. 1946); etc.

Kelly, Glenn. Pen name of Mildred Masterson McNeilly.

KELLY, HAROLD EDWARD (b. July 18, 1864); b. Belfast, Ireland. Correspondent, author. *The Fate of Sheumas O'Shea* (1897); *A Newspaper Correspondent's Diary* (1902); *With the Japanese Army at the Front* (1906); etc. Wrote *The Wanderers* series of books for boys, 5v. (1907–12).

KELLY, JAMES (1912–). Author. *The Insider* (1958).

KELLY, JOHN (1913–Mar. 16, 1966); b. Jersey City, N.J. Novelist. *All Souls' Night* (1947); *Alexander's Feast* (1949).

KELLY, JOHN BERNARD (Jan. 12, 1888–); b. New York City. Roman Catholic clergyman, author. Friend of Joyce Kilmer, and spiritual director of Catholic Writers Guild of America. *The Son of Man, and Other Poems and Essays* (1927); *The Romance of Truth* (1935); *Cardinal Hayes* (1940).

KELLY, JONATHAN FALCONBRIDGE (1818–1854); b. Philadelphia, Pa. Publisher, author. *The Humors of Falconbridge* (1856). Publisher, the New York *Arena;* the Boston *Traveller;* the *Aurora Borealis.*

KELLY, LUTHER S[age] (July 27, 1849–Dec. 17, 1928); b. Geneva, N.Y. Army scout. Known as "Yellowstone Kelly." See *"Yellowstone Kelly": The Memoirs of Luther S. Kelly,* ed. by Milo M. Quaife (1926).

KELLY, MYRA (Aug. 26, 1875–Mar. 30, 1910); b. Dublin, Ire. Author. *Little Citizens: The Humours of School Life* (1904); *The Isle of Dreams* (1907); *Little Aliens* (1910); etc.

KELLY, THOMAS (b. 1863); Novelist. *General Sullivan's Great War Trail; or, Heroes and Heroines of 1779* (1913); and its sequel, *The Big Tree Treaty; or, The Last Council on the Genesee* (1916).

KELLY, T[homas] HOWARD (June 26, 1895–); b. Fernandina, Fla. Author. *What Outfit Buddy?* (1920); *The Unknown Soldier* (1929); *A Doughboy Goes Back* (1930); *Roll Call from On High* (1936); etc. On staff, *McClure's, Smart Set, Cosmopolitan,* Hearst magazines, etc.

KELLY, WALT (Aug. 25, 1913–); b. Philadelphia, Pa. Cartoonist, author. *Pogo* (1951); *I Go Pogo* (1952); *Incompleat Pogo* (1954); *Pogo Party* (1956); *Beau Pogo* (1960); *East of Berlin and Short of the Moon* (1962); *The Return of Pogo* (1965); etc.

KELSEY, FRANCIS WILLEY (May 23, 1858–May 14, 1927); b. Ogden, N.Y. Educator, classicist, editor. Author of Greek and Latin textbooks. Editor: *Latin and Greek in American Education* (1911); a symposium. Founder, *Humanistic Series,* University of Michigan, the *University of Michigan Studies,* etc. Prof. Latin, University of Michigan, 1889–1927.

KEMBLE, FRANCES ANNE (Nov. 27, 1809–Jan. 15, 1893); b. London. Actress, author. Grandmother of Owen Wister. *Journal of a Residence in America,* 2v. (1835); *Poems* (1844); *Journal of a Residence on a Georgian Plantation* (1863); *Records of a Girlhood,* 2v. (1878); *Far Away and Long Ago* (1889); *Further Records* (1891); etc.

KEMELMAN, HARRY (Nov. 24, 1908–   ); b. Boston, Mass. Author. *Friday the Rabbi Slept Late* (1964); *Saturday the Rabbi Went Hungry* (1966); *The Nine Mile Walk* (1968); *Sunday the Rabbi Stayed Home* (1969); *Common Sense in Education* (1970).

KEMLER, EDGAR J. (1906–Dec. 1, 1960). Author. *The Irreverent Mr. Mencken* (1950).

KEMP, HARRY [Hibbard] (Dec. 15, 1883–Aug. 8, 1960); b. Youngstown, O. Author. *Judas* (1910); *The Cry of Youth* (poems, 1914); *Chanteys and Ballads* (1920); *Tramping on Life* (1922); *The Sea and the Dunes* (poems, 1926); *More Miles* (1927); *Love among the Cape-Enders* (1931); *Mabel Tarner* (1936); *Poet's Life of Christ* (1946); etc.

KEMP, LYSANDER (1920–). Poet. *Northern Stranger* (poems, 1946). Translator: Juan Rulfo's *Pedro Páramo* (1959); Octavio Paz's *The Labyrinth of Solitude* (1962).

KEMPTON, [James] MURRAY (Dec. 16, 1918–); b. Baltimore, Md. Journalist. *Part of Our Time* (1955); *America Comes to Middle Age* (1962). With N.Y. *Post* since 1942; columnist, 1949–69; with *New York Review of Books* from 1969.

KENDALL, AMOS (Aug. 16, 1789–Nov. 12, 1869); b. Dunstable, Mass. Editor, cabinet officer, author. *Life of Andrew Jackson* (1843–1844, only 7 of 15 parts published); *Secession Letters* (1861); *Autobiography* (1872). Co-editor, the *Argus of Western America,* 1816–29. Postmaster General, 1835–40.

KENDALL, GEORGE WILKINS (Aug. 22, 1809–Oct. 21, 1867); b. Mount Vernon, N.H. Editor, author. *Narrative of the Texas Santa Fé Expedition,* 2v. (1844); *The War between the United States and Mexico* (1851); etc. Founder (with Francis Lumsden), the *New Orleans Picayune,* Jan., 1837.

KENDALL, JOHN SMITH (Apr. 9, 1874–); b. Ocean Springs, Miss. Educator, author. *Seven Mexican Cities* (1906); *Picayune Guide to New Orleans* (1908); *History of New Orleans,* 3v. (1922). Lit. editor, the New Orleans *Picayune,* 1901–13. Prof. Spanish, Tulane University, 1914–39.

Kendall, Lace. Pen name of Adrien Stoutenburg.

KENDALL, W. S. (d. 1876). Called the "Mad Poet of California."

KENDRICK, ASAHEL CLARK (Dec. 7, 1809–Oct. 21, 1895); b. Poultney, Vt. Educator, classicist, author. *Echoes* (1855); etc. Compiler: *Our Poetical Favorites,* 3v. (1871–81). Wrote Greek textbooks, edited Biblical commentaries, etc. Prof. languages, Madison (now Colgate) University, 1831–50; prof. Greek, University of Rochester, 1850–88.

KENDRICK, BAYNARD HARDWICK (Apr. 8, 1894–); b. Philadelphia, Pa. Author. *Blood on Lake Louisa* (1934); *The Iron Spiders* (1936); *The Whistling Hangman* (1937); *The*

Odor of Violets (1941); *Blind Man's Bluff* (1943); *Lights Out* (1945); *Flames of Time* (1948); *You Die Today* (1952); *Blind Allies* (1954); *Reservations for Death* (1957); *Hot Red Money* (1959); *The Aluminum Turtle* (1960); *Frankincense and Murder* (1961); etc.

KENISTON, KENNETH (Jan. 6, 1930–   ); b. Chicago, Ill. Educator, psychologist. *The Uncommitted: Alienated Youth in American Society* (1965); *The Young Radicals: Notes on Committed Youth* (1968). Faculty, Yale Medical School, since 1962.

KENLY, JULIE WOODBRIDGE TERRY (Mar. 26, 1869–Jan. 8, 1943); b. Cleveland, O. Author. *Strictly Personal* (1929); *Green Magic* (1930); *Wild Wings* (1933); *Cities of Wax* (1935); *Little Lives* (1938); etc.

KENNAN, GEORGE (Feb. 16, 1845–May 10, 1924); b. Norwalk, O. Explorer, journalist, author. *Tent Life in Siberia* (1870); *Siberia and the Exile System*, 2v. (1891); *A Russian Comedy of Errors* (1915); *E. H. Harriman*, 2v. (1922); and other books on Russia.

KENNAN, GEORGE F[rost] (Feb. 16, 1904–); b. Milwaukee, Wis. Diplomat, author. *American Diplomacy, 1900–1950* (1951); *Realities of American Foreign Policy* (1954); *Russia Leaves the War* (1956, Pulitzer Prize for history, 1957); *Decision to Intervene* (1958); *Russia and the West under Lenin and Stalin* (1961); *On Dealing with the Communist World* (1964); *Memoirs 1925–1950* (1967, Pulitzer Prize, 1968); *Democracy and the Student Left* (1968); etc. Ambassador to U.S.S.R., 1952; Yugoslavia, since 1961.

KENNARD, JOSEPH SPENCER (May 20, 1859–1944); b. Bridgeton, N.J. Author. *The Fallen God, and Other Essays* (1900); *Some Early Printers and Their Colophons* (1902); *Italian Romance Writers* (1906); *Goldoni and the Venice of His Times* (1920); *The Friar in Fiction, Sincerity in Art, and Other Essays* (1923); *Swiss Legends* (1930); *The Italian Theatre*, 2v. (1932); *Masks and Marionettes* (1935); *A Literary History of the Italian People* (1941); *Dante and His Precursors* (1944); etc.

KENNAWAY, JAMES (1928–1968). Author. *Tunes of Glory* (1956); *Household Ghosts* (1961); *The Cost of Living Like This* (1969).

KENNEDY, ARTHUR GARFIELD (June 29, 1880–Apr. 21, 1954); b. Weeping Water, Neb. Educator, philologist, author. A *Bibliography of Writings on the English Language* (1927); *Current English* (1935); *English Usage* (1942); and other books on English. Co-founder, *American Speech*, 1925. Prof. English, Stanford University, 1914–45.

KENNEDY, CHARLES RANN (Feb. 14, 1871–Feb. 16, 1950); b. Derby, Eng. Playwright. *The Servant in the House* (1908); *The Winterfeast* (1908); *The Terrible Meek* (1911); *The Necessary Evil* (1913); *The Idol-Breaker* (1914); *The Rib of the Man* (1916); *The Army with Banners* (1917); *The Fool from the Hills* (1919); *The Chastening* (1922); *The Admiral* (1923); *The Salutation* (1925); *Old Nobody* (1927); *Crumbs* (1931); *Flaming Ministers* (1932); *Face of God* (1935); *Beggar's Gift* (1935); *Isles of the Blest* (1940); *Sonnets for Armageddon* (1943).

KENNEDY, CHARLES WILLIAM (Jan. 13, 1882–July 13, 1969); b. Port Richmond, S.I. Educator, poet. *Pausanias* (with James S. Wilson, poem, 1902); *The Walls of Hamelin* (poems, 1922); *Beowulf* (1940); *The Earliest English Poetry* (1943); *Early English Christian Poetry* (1952); *An Anthology of Old English Poetry* (1960). Translator into English verse: *The Poems of Cynewulf* (1910); *The Caedmon Poems* (1916); *Old English Elegies* (1936). English dept., Princeton University, 1906–44.

KENNEDY, CRAMMOND (Dec. 29, 1842–Feb. 20, 1918); b. North Berwick, Scotland. Lawyer, author. *James Stanley* (anon., 1859); *Corn in the Blade* (poems, 1860); *The Liberty of the Press* (1876); *The Capture of Aquinaldo* (1902); etc. Editor, the *Church Union*, 1869–70; the *Christian Union*, 1870.

KENNEDY, HOWARD. Pen name of Josiah Pitts Woolfolk.

KENNEDY, JOHN FITZGERALD (May 29, 1917–Nov. 22, 1963); b. Brookline, Mass. Thirty-fifth president of the United States, author. *Why England Slept* (1940); *Profiles in Courage* (1956; Pulitzer Prize for biography, 1957); *The Strategy of Peace* (1960); *Let Us Begin* (1961); *The New Frontier: Major Address and Messages* (1961); *To Turn the Tide* (1962). Victor Lasky's *J.F.K.: The Man and the Myth* (1963); T. C. Sorenson's *Kennedy* (1965); Arthur M. Schlesinger's *A Thousand Days* (1965); Pierre Salinger's *With Kennedy* (1966); Roger Hilsman's *To Move a Nation* (1967); Edmund Ion's *The Politics of John F. Kennedy* (1967); William Manchester's *Portrait of a President* (1967) and *Death of a President* (1967); Tom Wicker's *J. F. K. and L. B. J.* (1968); etc.

KENNEDY, JOHN PENDLETON (Oct. 25, 1795–Aug. 18, 1870); b. Baltimore, Md. Cabinet officer, educator, editor, author. *Swallow Barn; or, A Sojourn in the Old Dominion*, 2v. (anon., 1832); *Horse-Shoe Robinson: A Tale of the Tory Ascendancy*, 2v. (anon., 1835); *Rob of the Bowl; A Legend of St. Inigoe's* (anon., 1838); *Quodlibet* (under pen name, "Solomon Second-thoughts," 1840); *Memoirs of the Life of William Wirt*, 2v. (1942); *Mr. Ambrose's Letters on the Rebellion* (1865). Editor, the *Red Book*, Baltimore, 1848–49. Secretary of the Navy, 1853–57. *See* Edward M. Gwathmey's *John Pendleton Kennedy* (1931); Henry T. Tuckerman's *The Life of John Pendleton Kennedy* (1871).

KENNEDY, R[obert] EMMET (1877–); b. Gretna, La. Author. *Black Cameos* (1924); *Mellows: A Chronicle of Unknown Singers* (1925); *Runes and Cadences* (1926); *Gritny People* (1927); *Red Bean Row* (1929); *More Mellows* (1931); *Songs of an Alien Spirit* (1940).

KENNEDY, ROBERT FRANCIS (Nov. 20, 1925–June 6, 1968). Lawyer. *The Enemy Within* (1960); *Just Friends and Brave Enemies* (1962); *Pursuit of Justice* (1964). Attorney general of the United States 1961–64. *See* Victor Lasky's *Robert F. Kennedy: The Myth and the Man* (1968); *American Journey: The Times of Robert Kennedy*, based on interviews by Jean Stein, ed. by George Plimpton (1970).

KENNEDY, SARA BEAUMONT (d. Mar. 12, 1921); b. Somerville, Tenn. Novelist, poet. *Joscelyn Cheshire* (1901); *The Wooing of Judith* (1902); *Cicely* (1911); *One Wish* (poems, 1915); *Poems* (1919).

KENNEDY, WILLIAM SLOANE (Sept. 26, 1850–Aug. 4, 1929); b. Brecksville, O. Author. *Henry W. Longfellow* (1882); *John G. Whittier* (1892); *Reminiscences of Walt Whitman* (1896); *In Portia's Gardens* (1897); *The Flight of a Book for the World: A Companion Volume to Leaves of Grass* (1926); *Autolycus Pack, or What You Will* (1927); etc. Editor: *Walt Whitman's Diary in Canada* (1904).

KENNEDY, X. J[oseph] (Aug. 21, 1929–   ); b. Dover, N.J. Educator, poet. *Nude Descending a Staircase* (1961); *Mark Twain's Frontier* (with J. E. Camp, 1963); *An Introduction to Poetry* (1966). Faculty, Woman's College, University of North Carolina, since 1962. Poetry editor, *Paris Review*, since 1961.

Kennedy Square. Novel by F. Hopkinson Smith (1911). A story of life in the South in the 1850's, centering around the Temple mansion on genteel Kennedy Square where life was lived easily. The story began serially in *Scribner's Magazine* in 1910.

KENNELLY, ARDYTH, b. Glenada, Ore. Author. *The Peaceable Kingdom* (1949); *The Spur* (1951); *Good Morning, Young Lady* (1953); *Up Home* (1955); *Marry Me, Carry Me* (1956).

KENNERLEY, MITCHELL (Aug. 14, 1878–); b. Burslem, England. Publisher. Founded own publishing business in New York in 1905. Director, Printing House of William Edwin Rudge, since 1931. Founder, the Little Book Shop Around the Corner, 1907; the *Reader Magazine,* 1901; editor, 1901–04; publisher, the *Forum,* 1910–16. President, The Anderson Galleries, 1916–29. Frederick W. Goudy, type designer, named one of his type faces "Kennerley."

KENNICOTT, DONALD (Sept. 30, 1881–Sept. 11, 1965); b. Chicago, Ill. Editor. Assoc. editor, *Red Book, Blue Book,* and *Green Book* magazines, 1910–29; editor, *Blue Book,* 1929–51, and *Red Book,* 1937–52.

KENNY, NICHOLAS NAPOLEON [Nick] (Feb. 3, 1895–); b. Astoria, N.Y. Columnist. *Day Unto Day* (1943); *Collected Poems* (1952); *Poems to Inspire* (1959); etc. Also lyrics for songs, including "There's a Gold Mine in the Sky," "Carelessly," "In My Cabin of Dreams," "While a Cigarette Was Burning," "Undertow." Radio columnist, *N.Y. Daily Mirror,* 1930–63; writer, syndicated column, "Nick Kenny Speaking," 1930–63.

KENRICK, FRANCIS PATRICK (Dec. 3, 1796–July 8, 1863); b. Dublin, Ire. Roman Catholic archbishop, author. *Theologia Dogmatica,* 4v. (1839–40); *Theologia Moralis,* 3v. (1841–43); etc. Revised the Challoner edition of the Rheims-Douai translation of the Bible for use of Roman Catholics in the United States.

KENT, CHARLES FOSTER (Aug. 13, 1867–May 2, 1925); b. Palmyra, N.Y. Educator, biblical scholar, author. *A History of the Jewish People* (1899); *The Great Teachers of Judaism and Christianity* (1911); and numerous books on Hebrew history and Bible subjects. Editor: *The Student's Old Testament,* 6v. (1904–27); *The Historical Bible,* 6v. (1908–16); *The Shorter Bible,* 2v. (1918–21); etc. Prof. Biblical literature, Yale, 1901–25.

KENT, CHARLES WILLIAM (Sept. 27, 1860–Oct. 5, 1917); b. Louisa C.H., Va. Educator. Editor: *Idylls of the Lawn* (poems, 1899); *The Book of the Poe Centenary* (1909); *Southern Poems* (1913). Lit. editor, *Library of Southern Literature,* 15v. (1909–10). Prof. English literature, University of Virginia, 1893–1917.

KENT, CORITA (also known as "Sister Corita") (Nov. 20, 1918–   ); b. Ft. Dodge, Ia. Artist, author. *Footnotes and Headlines* (1967); *Damn Everything but the Circus* (1970).

KENT, FRANK RICHARDSON (May 1, 1877–Apr. 14, 1958); b. Baltimore Md. Editor, author. *The Story of Maryland Politics* (1911); *Without Gloves* (1934); *The Story of Alexander Brown & Sons* (1950); etc. With the *Baltimore Sun,* 1898–1921. Wrote syndicated political column.

KENT, IRA RICH (Oct. 28, 1876–Nov. 9, 1945); b. Calais, Vt. Publisher. On editorial staff, *Youth's Companion,* 1900–25; editor, Houghton Mifflin Co., from 1926.

KENT, JACK [John Wellington] (Mar. 10, 1920–); b. Burlington, Ia. Cartoonist. Created comic strip "King Aroo," 1950. Author-illustrator: *Only John* (1968); *Fly Away Home* (1969); *Clotilda* (1969).

KENT, JAMES (July 31, 1763–Dec. 12, 1847); b. Fredericksburgh (now Southeast), N.Y. Jurist, author. *Commentaries on American Law,* 4v. (1826–30), which has gone through at least 14 editions. See *Memoirs and Letters of James Kent,* ed. by William Kent (1898). *See also* W. Draper Lewis's *Great American Lawyers,* v. 2 (1907).

KENT, LOUISE ANDREWS (May 25, 1886–Aug. 6, 1969); b. Brookline, Mass. Author of children's books. *Douglas of Porcupine* (1931); *Two Children of Tyre* (1932); *The Red Rajah* (1933); *He Went with Marco Polo* (1935); *Paul Revere Square* (1939); *Mrs. Appleyard's Year* (1941); *He Went with*

Magellan (1943); *Country Mouse* (1945); *Village Greens of New England* (1948); *With Kitchen Privileges* (1953); *The Brookline Trunk* (1955); *He Went with Drake* (1961); *The Vermont Year Round Cookbook* (1965).

KENT, ROCKWELL (June 21, 1882–Mar. 13, 1971); b. Tarrytown Heights, N.Y. Artist, author. *Wilderness* (1920); *Voyaging Southward from the Strait of Magellan* (1924); *N. by E.* (1930); *Salamina* (1935); *This Is My Own* (1940); *It's Me O Lord* (1955); *Of Men and Mountains* (1959); *Greenland Journal* (1963); etc. Illustrated Casanova's *Memoirs;* Chaucer's *Canterbury Tales;* Melville's *Moby-Dick;* Whitman's *Leaves of Grass;* etc.

KENTON, SIMON (Apr. 3, 1755–Apr. 29, 1836); b. in Virginia. Indian fighter, and one of Daniel Boone's scouts. *See* Edna Kenton's *Simon Kenton* (1930); J. A. McClung's *Sketches of Western Adventure* (1832).

Kentuckians, The. Novel by John Fox, Jr. (1898). A picture of the aristocratic families of the blue-grass country, who are contrasted with the unlettered mountaineers who still cling to Elizabethan speech and backwoods manners and superstitions.

Kentucky Cardinal, A. Novel by James Lane Allen (1895). The story of Adam Moss, a recluse and nature-lover who lives an idyllic life among his birds and flowers. *The Aftermath* (1896) was a sequel.

Kentucky Gazette. Lexington, Ky. Newspaper. Founded 1787, as the *Kentucke Gazette.* First newspaper in Kentucky. Name changed to present spelling in 1789. Expired 1848.

Kentucky Miscellany, The. Poems by Thomas Johnson (1789). Published at Lexington, Ky. This is the first book of verse written and printed in Kentucky.

KENYON, BERNICE LESBIA (Mrs. Walter Gilkyson) (Sept. 21, 1897–); b. Newton, Mass. Author. *Songs of Unrest* (1923); *Meridian* (poems, 1933); *Night Sky* (poems, 1951). On staff, *Scribner's Magazine,* 1920–24.

KENYON, CHARLES [Arthur] (Nov. 2, 1880–); b. San Francisco, Calif. Playwright. *Kindling* (prod. 1911); *Husband and Wife* (prod. 1915); *The Claim* (prod. 1917); etc.

KENYON, JAMES BENJAMIN (Apr. 26, 1858–May 11, 1924); b. Frankfort, N.Y. Poet. *The Fallen, and Other Poems* (1876); *Out of the Shadows* (1880); *Songs in All Seasons* (1885); *In Realms of Gold* (1887); *At the Gate of Dreams* (1892); *An Oaten Pipe* (1896); *Poems* (1901); *Remembered Days* (essays, 1902); *Reed Voices* (1917); *The Harvest Home: Collected Poems* (1919); *Spring Flowers, and Rowen* (with daughter, Doris Kenyon, 1922); etc.

KENYON, THEDA, b. Brooklyn, N.Y. Author. *Jeanne* (1928); *Witches Still Live* (1929); *Certain Ladies* (poems, 1930); *Scarlet Anne* (poems, 1939); *Pendulum* (1942); *That Skipper from Stonington* (1946); *Something Gleamed* (1948); etc.

Kenyon Review, The. Gambier, O. Quarterly. Founded 1939. Published at Kenyon College. Edited successively by John Crowe Ransom, Robie Macauley, and George Lanning. One of the most influential literary magazines in the United States since its founding. It became the organ of the New Criticism during the 1940's and 1950's.

KEOGH, ANDREW (Nov. 14, 1869–Feb. 13, 1953); b. Newcastle-upon-Tyne, Eng. Librarian. With Yale University Library, 1899–1938, librarian, 1916–38.

KEPES, GYORGY (Oct. 4, 1906–); b. Selyp, Hung. Designer, educator. *Language of Vision* (1945); *The New Landscape* (1956). Prof. visual design, Massachusetts Institute of Technology, since 1946. Editor: *Visual Arts Today* (1960); *Vision and Value Series* (1965).

KEPHART, HORACE (Sept. 8, 1862–Apr. 2, 1931); b. East Salem, Pa. Author. *Book of Camping and Woodcraft* (1906), later editions called *Camping and Woodcraft; Our Southern Highlanders* (1913); etc. Editor: *Captives among the Indians* (1915).

KEPLER, THOMAS SAMUEL (Sept. 20, 1897–May 2, 1963); b. Mount Vernon, Ia. Theologian, author. *Why Was Jesus Crucified?* (1937); *Journey with the Saints* (1951); *A Spiritual Journey with Paul* (1953); *Jesus' Design for Living* (1955); *The Book of Revelation: Commentary for Laymen* (1957); *Leaves from My Spiritual Notebook* (1960); *The Evelyn Underhill Reader* (1962); *Dreams of the Future* (1963); etc. Prof. New Testament, Graduate School of Theology, Oberlin College, from 1946.

KEPPEL, FREDERICK (Mar. 22, 1845–Mar. 7, 1912); b. in Ireland. Importer of works of art, particularly engravings, author. *Christmas in Art* (1909); *The Golden Age of Engraving* (1910); *The Gentle Art of Resenting Injuries* (1904); etc.

KEPPEL, FREDERICK PAUL (July 2, 1875–Sept. 8, 1943); b. on Staten Island, N.Y. Director of philanthropies, author. *Columbia University* (1913); *Education for Adults* (1926); *The Arts in American Life* (with R. L. Duffus, 1933); *Philanthropy and Learning* (1936). Secretary, Columbia University, 1902–10; dean of the College, 1910–18. President, Carnegie Corporation, 1923–41.

KEPPLER, JOSEPH (Feb. 1, 1838–Feb. 19, 1894); b. Vienna. Illustrator, magazine publisher. Founder, *Die Vehme,* humorous weekly, St. Louis, Mo., 1869; *Puck, Illustrierte Wochenschrift,* St. Louis, 1871; *Puck, Humoristisches Wochenblatt,* with Adolph Schwarzmann, New York, 1876. In 1877, these men started their English edition of *Puck,* in New York, which lasted until 1918. Keppler introduced the lithographic cartoon to take the place of the cartoons cut in wood. His political cartoons in *Puck* were famous.

KERLIN, ROBERT THOMAS (Mar. 22, 1866–Feb. 21, 1950); b. Newcastle, Mo. Educator, author. *Mainly for Myself* (poems, 1897); *Theocritus in English Literature* (1909); *Negro Poets and Their Poems* (1923); etc. Prof. literature, Virginia Military Institute, 1910–21, etc.

KERMAN, JOSEPH WILFRED (Apr. 3, 1924–); b. London. Musicologist, author. *Opera As Drama* (1956); *The Elizabethan Madrigal* (1962); *The Beethoven Quartets* (1967). Prof. music, University of California at Berkeley, since 1960.

KERNER, FRED (Feb. 15, 1921–); b. Montreal, Can. Publisher, author. *Eat, Think and Be Slender* (with Leonard Kotkin, 1954); *The Magic Power of Your Mind* (with Walter M. Germain, 1956); *Ten Days to a Successful Memory* (with Joyce Brothers, 1957); *Stress and Your Heart* (1961); *Watch Your Weight Go Down* (pen name Frederick Kerr, 1962); *What's Best for Your Child—and You* (with David Goodman, 1966); *Buy High, Sell Higher* (with Jesse Reid, 1966). Editor: *Love Is a Man's Affair* (1958); *Treasury of Lincoln Quotations* (1965). Pres. and editor-in-chief, Hawthorn Books, since 1964.

Kerner, Fred/Publishing Projects. New York. Publishers. Founded 1968 by Fred Kerner, who is managing director. Books of general trade, reference, juvenile, and religious interest.

KERNER, ROBERT JOSEPH (Aug. 26, 1887–Nov. 29, 1956); b. Chicago, Ill. Educator, author. *The Foundations of Slavic Bibliography* (1916); *Bohemia in the Eighteenth Century* (1932); *Northeastern Asia,* 2v. (1939); *The Russian Adventure* (1943); etc. History dept., University of Missouri, 1916–26; prof. history, University of California, 1928–54.

KEROUAC, JACK (1922–Oct. 21, 1969). Novelist. *The Town and the City* (1950); *On the Road* (1957); *The Subterraneans* (1958); *The Dharma Bums* (1958); *Doctor Sax* (1959); *Mexico City Blues* (poems, 1959); *Book of Dreams* (1961); etc.

KERR, ALVAH MILTON (July 22, 1858–Sept. 26, 1924); b. Athens, O. Editor, author. *Trean; or, The Mormon's Daughter* (1889); *An Honest Lawyer* (1892); *The Diamond Key* (1907); etc. Editor, *Iroquois Magazine,* etc.

KERR, CLARK (May 17, 1911–); b. Reading Pa. Educator. *Migration to the Seattle Labor Market Area* (1942); *The Uses of the University* (1963); *Labor and Management in Industrial Society* (1964); etc. Editor (with E. Wight Bakke): *Unions, Management and the Public* (1948). Pres., University of California at Berkeley, 1958–67; head, Carnegie Foundation for the Advancement of Teaching, since 1967.

KERR, JEAN [Collins] (July, 1923–); b. Scranton, Pa. Playwright, author. *Jenny Kissed Me* (prod. 1949); *Please Don't Eat the Daisies* (1957); *The Snake Has All the Lines* (1962). Co-author: *King of Hearts* (with Eleanor Brooke, prod. 1954); *Goldilocks* (with Walter Kerr, prod. 1958); *Mary, Mary* (1965); *Poor Richard* (play, 1964).

KERR, ORPHEUS C. Pen name of Robert Henry Newell.

KERR, SOPHIE (Mrs. Sophie Kerr Underwood) (Aug. 23, 1880–Feb. 6, 1965); b. Denton, Md. Novelist. *Love at Large* (1916); *Painted Meadows* (1920); *Confetti* (1927); *Mareea-Maria* (1929); *Adventure with Women* (1938); *Curtain Going Up* (1940); *Michael's Girl* (1942); *Jenny Devlin* (1943); *Love Story Incidental* (1946); *Wife's Eye View* (1947); *The Sound of Petticoats* (1948); *The Man Who Knew the Date* (1951); *The Best I Ever Ate* (with June Platt, 1953); etc.

KERR, WALTER F. (July 8, 1913–); b. Evanston, Ill. Drama critic, playwright. *Sing Out, Sweet Land* (prod. 1944); *Touch and Go* (prod. 1949); *How Not to Write a Play* (1955); *Criticism and Censorship* (1956); *Pieces at Eight* (1957); *The Decline of Pleasure* (1962); *The Theatre In Spite of Itself* (1963); *Tragedy and Comedy* (1967); *Thirty Plays Hath November* (1969). Co-author: *Goldilocks* (with Jean Kerr, prod. 1958). Drama Critic, *Commonweal,* 1950–52; N.Y. *Herald Tribune,* 1951–66; *New York Times* since 1966. Speech and drama dept., Catholic University, Washington, 1938–49.

KERSHNER, HOWARD ELDRED (Nov. 17, 1891–); b. Tescott, Kan. Author. *The Menace of Roosevelt and His Policies* (1936); *One Humanity* (1943); *Quaker Service in Modern War* (1950); *God, Gold and Government* (1957); *Diamonds, Persimmons and Stars* (1964); etc. Editor: *James W. Ellsworth* (1929); *Lincoln Ellsworth* (1930).

KESEY, KEN [Elton] (Sept. 17, 1935–); b. La Junta, Colo. Author. *One Flew Over the Cuckoo's Nest* (1962); *Sometimes a Great Nation* (1964). See Thomas Wolfe's *The Electric Kool-Aid Acid Test* (1968).

KESSELRING, JOSEPH O[tto] (June 21, 1902–Nov. 5, 1967); b. New York City. Playwright. *Aggie Appleby, Maker of Men* (1933); *There's Wisdom in Women* (1935); *Arsenic and Old Lace* (1941); *Maggie McGilligan* (1942); *Four Twelves Are Forty-eight* (1949); *Accidental Angel* (1955); *A Frog in His Pocket* (1958); *Mother of That Wisdom* (1963); etc.

KESTER, PAUL (Nov. 2, 1870–June 20, 1933); b. Delaware, O. Playwright, novelist. *Zamar* (prod. 1893); *Tales of the Real Gypsy* (1897); *The Cousin of the King* (with Vaughn Kester, prod. 1898); *Sweet Nell of Old Drury* (prod. 1901); *Mademoiselle Mars* (prod. 1902); *His Own Country* (1917); *Diana Dauntless* (1929); *The Course of True Love* (1930); etc.

KESTER, VAUGHAN (Sept. 12, 1869–July 4, 1911); b. New Brunswick, N.J. Journalist, novelist. *The Manager of the B. & A.* (1901); *John O'Jamestown* (1907); *The Prodigal Judge* (1911); *The Hand of the Mighty, and Other Stories* (1913).

KETCHAM, HENRY KING [Hank] (Mar. 14, 1920–); b. Seattle, Wash. Cartoonist. *Dennis the Menace* (1952); *More Dennis the Menace* (1953); *Dennis the Menace vs. Everybody* (1956); *In This Corner: Dennis the Menace* (1958); *I Wanna Go Home* (1965); etc.

KETCHUM, ANNIE CHAMBERS (Nov. 8, 1824–1904); b. in Scott Co., Ky. Poet. *Nellie Bracken* (1855); *Benny: A Christmas Ballad* (1869); *Lotos-Flowers* (1877); *Christmas Carillons, and Other Poems* (1888).

KETTELL, SAMUEL (Aug. 5, 1800–Dec. 3, 1855); b. Newburyport, Mass. Editor, anthologist, author. *Yankee Notions: A Medley* (under pen name of "Timo. Titterwell," 1838); *Daw's Doings; or, The History of the Late War in the Plantations* (under pen name "Sampson Short-and-Fat," 1842); *Quozziana; or, Letters from Great Goslington, Mass.* (under same pen name, 1842); etc. Editor: *Specimens of American Poetry,* 3v. (1829). He assisted S. G. Goodrich in compiling the "Peter Parley" books. In 1848 he succeeded Joseph Tinker Buckingham as editor of the *Boston Courier.*

KEY, FRANCIS SCOTT (Aug. 1, 1779–Jan. 11, 1843); b. "Terra Rubra," Frederick (now Carroll) Co., Md. Lawyer, poet. Author of "The Star Spangled Banner" (q.v.). *Poems of the Late Francis S. Key, Esq.* (1857). One of his poems is used as a hymn, "Lord, with glowing heart I'd praise thee." *See* Francis Scott Key Smith's *Francis Scott Key* (1911); Edward S. Delaplaine's *Francis Scott Key* (1937).

KEY, PIERRE VAN RENSSELAER (Aug. 28, 1872–Nov. 28, 1945); b. Grand Haven, Mich. Music editor, author. *John McCormack: His Own Life Story* (1918); *Enrico Caruso: A Biography* (with Bruno Zirato, 1922). Music editor, the *New York World,* 1907–19; editor, the *Musical Digest,* from 1919. Publisher, *Pierre Key's Musical Who's Who,* every four years.

KEY, TED (Aug. 25, 1912–); b. Fresno, Cal. Cartoonist, author. *Hazel* (1946); *Many Happy Returns* (1951); *If You Like Hazel* (1952); *Phyllis* (1957); *All Hazel* (1958); *Hazel Time* (1962); *Life with Hazel* (1965); *Squirrels in the Feeding Station* (1967); etc.

KEYES, FRANCES PARKINSON (Mrs. Henry Wilder Keyes) (July 21, 1885–); b. University, Va. Author. *The Old Gray Homestead* (1919); *Letters from a Senator's Wife* (1924); *Queen Anne's Lace* (1930); *Silver Seas and Golden Cities* (1931); *The Happy Wanderer* (poems, 1935); *Honor Bright* (1936); *Parts Unknown* (1938); *The Great Tradition* (1939); *The Sublime Shepardess* (1940); *Fielding's Folly* (1940); *Crescent Carnival* (1942); *Also the Hills* (1943); *The River Road* (1945); *Dinner at Antoine's* (1948); *Joy Street* (1950); *The Royal Box* (1954); *Victorine* (1958); *The Rose and the Lily* (1961); *Madame Castel's Lodger* (1962); *Three Ways of Love* (1963); *The Explorer* (1964); *Tongues of Fire* (1966); *Heritage* (1968); etc.

KEYHOE, DONALD EDWARD (June 20, 1897–); b. Ottumwa, Ia. Author. *Flying with Lindbergh* (1928); *The Flying Saucer Conspiracy* (1955); etc.

Keys of the Kingdom, The. Novel by A. J. Cronin (1941). The life of a Scottish priest who becomes a missionary in China.

KIDDER, DANIEL PARISH (Oct. 18, 1815–July 29, 1891); b. South Pembroke, N.Y. Methodist clergyman, author. *Mormonism and the Mormons* (1942); *Sketches of Residence and Travels in Brazil,* 2v. (1845); *Brazil and the Brazilians* (1857); etc.

KIDDER, FREDERIC (Apr. 16, 1804–Dec. 19, 1885); b. New Ipswich, N.H. Antiquarian, author. *The Expeditions of Captain John Lovewell* (1865); *History of the Boston Massacre* (1870); etc.

KIERAN, JOHN FRANCIS (Aug. 2, 1892–); b. New York. Sports writer, naturalist. *Nature Notes* (1941); *American Sporting Scene* (1941); *Footnotes on Nature* (1947); *Introduction to Birds* (1950); *Introduction to Trees* (1954); *The Story of the Olympic Games* (with Arthur Daley, 1957); *The Natural History of New York City* (1959); etc. With the *New York Times* 1915–43. On board of experts on radio program "Information Please."

KILBOURNE, CHARLES EVANS (Dec. 23, 1872–Nov. 12, 1963); b. Fort Whipple, Va. Educator, author. The *Army Boy* series, 4v. (1913–16); the *Baby Animal Books,* 10v. (1913–17). Supt., Virginia Military Institute, Lexington, Va., since 1937.

KILBOURNE, FANNIE (Mrs. Henry Allen Schubert) (Nov. 28, 1890–); b. Minneapolis, Minn. Author. *Betty Bell* (1919); *Paul and Rhoda The Horton Twins* (1926); *Dot and Will* (1929); *But Never Be Denied* (1941); etc.

KILBOURNE, PAYNE KENYON (July 26, 1815–July 19, 1859); b. Litchfield, Conn. Antiquarian, poet. *Harp of the Vale: A Collection of Poems* (1843) also called *The Skeptic, and Other Poems;* also several books on Connecticut history.

KILDARE, OWEN [Frawley] (June 11, 1864–1911); b. New York City. Editor, author. *My Mamie Rose* (autobiography, 1903); *The Wisdom of the Simple* (1905); etc. Assoc. editor, *Pearson's Magazine.*

Killers, The. Short story by Ernest Hemingway (1928). About gunmen who are hunting a pugilist who took money to lose a fight.

KILLIKELLY, SARAH HUTCHINS (Jan. 1, 1840–May 14, 1912); b. Vincennes, Ind. Author. *Curious Questions in History, Literature, Art, and Social Life,* 3v. (1886–1900); *The History of Pittsburgh* (1907).

KILMER, ALINE [Murray] (Mrs. Joyce Kilmer) (Aug. 1, 1888–Oct. 1, 1941); b. Norfolk, Va. Poet. *Candles That Burn* (1919); *Vigils* (1921); *Hunting a Hair Shirt, and Other Spiritual Adventures* (1923); *The Poor King's Daughter, and Other Poems* (1925); *Selected Poems* (1929); etc.

KILMER, ANNIE KILBURN (d. Jan. 1, 1932); b. Albany, N.Y. Mother of Joyce Kilmer. Composer, author. *Memories of My Son Sergeant Joyce Kilmer* (1920); *Leaves from My Life* (autobiography, 1925); *Whimsical Whimsies* (1927); *More Whimsies* (1929).

KILMER, JOYCE (Dec. 6, 1886–July 30, 1918); b. New Brunswick, N.J. Poet. *Summer of Love* (1911); *Trees, ana Other Poems* (1914); *The Circus, and Other Essays* (1916); *Main Street and Other Poems* (1917). Editor: *Literature in the Making* (1917); *Dreams and Images: An Anthology of Catholic Poets* (1917). His best-known poem is "Trees." *See* Robert C. Holliday's *Joyce Kilmer,* 2v. (1918).

KILPATRICK, JAMES JACKSON, JR. (Nov. 1, 1920–); b. Oklahoma City, Okla. Journalist, author. *The Sovereign States* (1957); *The Smut Peddlers* (1960); *The Southern Case for School Segregation* (1962). Editor: *We the States* (1964). Co-editor: *The Lasting South* (1957). Editor, Richmond, Va., *News Leader,* since 1951.

KILPATRICK, WILLIAM HEARD (Nov. 20, 1871–Feb. 15, 1965); b. White Plains, Ga. Educator, author. *Source Book in the Philosophy of Education* (1923); *Education for a Changing Civilization* (1926); *How We Learn* (1928); *Remaking the Curriculum* (1936); *Selfhood and Civilization* (1941); *Philosophy of Education* (1951). Co-author and co-editor: *Intercultural Attitudes in the Making* (1947); *Philosophy of Education* (1951). Prof. education, Teachers College, Columbia University, 1915–38.

KILVERT, MARGARET CAMERON. *See* Margaret Cameron.

KIMBALL, FISKE (Dec. 8, 1888–Aug. 14, 1955); b. Newton, Mass. Architect, museum director, author. *Thomas Jefferson, Architect* (1916); *A History of Architecture* (with G. H. Edgell, 1918); *Domestic Architecture of the American Colonies* (1922); *American Architecture* (1928); *The Creation of the Rococo* (1943); etc. Director, Philadelphia Museum of Art from 1925.

KIMBALL, HARRIET McEWEN (Nov., 1834–Sept. 3, 1917); b. Portsmouth, N.H. Poet, hymn-writer. *Hymns*

(1866); *Swallow-Flights* (1874); *The Blessed Company of All Faithful People* (1879); *Poems* [collected] (1889).

KIMBLE, GEORGE HERBERT TINLEY (Aug. 2, 1908–); b. London. Geographer. *Geography of the Middle Ages* (1938); *The Way of the World* (1953); *Our American Weather* (1955); etc. Chairman, geography dept., Indiana University, since 1957.

KIMBROUGH, EDWARD (Aug. 15, 1918); b. Meridian, Miss. Novelist. *From Hell to Breakfast* (1941); *Night Fire* (1946); *The Secret Pilgrim* (1949).

KIMBROUGH, EMILY [Emily Kimbrough Wrench] (Oct. 23, 1899–); b. Muncie, Ind. Author. *Our Hearts Were Young and Gay* (with Cornelia Otis Skinner, 1942); *We Followed Our Hearts to Hollywood* (1943); *It Gives Me Great Pleasure* (1948); *The Innocents from Indiana* (1950); *Forty Plus and Fancy Free* (1954); *And a Right Good Crew* (1958); *Pleasure by the Busload* (1961); *Forever Old; Forever New* (1964); *Floating Island* (1968); etc.

KINARD, JAMES PINCKNEY (July 17, 1864–June, 1951); b. Kinard, S.C. Educator, author. *English Language and Literature* (1912); *Our Language* (1927); etc. Editor: *Old English Ballads* (1902); etc. Prof. English, Winthrop College, Rock Hill, S.C., 1895–1913; prof. psychology, 1917–29, president, 1929–34.

Kindergarten Messenger. Cambridge, Mass. Magazine. Founded 1873, by Elizabeth Palmer Peabody. First kindergarten journal in America.

KINDLEBERGER, CHARLES P., II (Oct. 12, 1910–); b. New York City. Economist. *The Dollar Shortage* (1950); *International Economics* (1953); *The Terms of Trade* (with others, 1956); *Economic Development* (1958); *Foreign Trade and the National Economy* (1962); *International Short-Term Capital Movements* (1965); *Europe and the Dollar* (1966); *Postwar European Growth* (1967); *American Business Abroad* (1969). Economics dept., Massachusetts Institute of Technology, 1948–51. Prof. M.I.T. since 1951.

Kindling. Play by Charles Kenyon (prod. 1911). Life in a New York tenement. Maggie turns burglar in order to go West where her unborn child will have a chance in life.

KING, ALAN (Dec. 26, 1927–   ); b. Brooklyn, N.Y. Entertainer, author. Co-author: *Anybody Who Owns His Own Home Deserves It* (1962); *Help! I'm a Prisoner in a Chinese Bakery* (with J. Shurman, 1964). Cafe, vaudeville, television entertainer, since 1957.

KING, ALEXANDER (Nov. 13, 1900–Nov. 15, 1965); b. Vienna. Artist, author. *Mine Enemy Grows Older* (1958); *May This House Be Safe from Tigers* (1960); *I Should Have Kissed Her More* (1961). Editor: *Peter Altenberg's Evocations of Love* (1960); *The Great Ker-Plunk* (1962); *Rich Man, Poor Man, Freud and Fruit* (1965); *Memoirs of a Certain Mouse* (1966).

KING, BASIL (Feb. 26, 1859–June 22, 1928); b. Charlottetown, P.E.I. Episcopal clergyman, author. *Griselda* (1900); *The Steps of Honor* (1904); *The Inner Shrine* (anon., 1909); *The Wild Olive* (1910); *The Street Called Straight* (1912); *The Side of the Angels* (1916); *The Dust Flower* (1922); *The Happy Isles* (1923); *Adventures in Religion* (1929); and books on spiritualism.

KING, BEN[jamin Franklin] (Mar. 17, 1857–Apr. 7, 1894); b. St. Joseph, Mich. Poet. *Ben King's Verse* (1894). His best-known poem is "If I Should Die Tonight," a parody on the poem of the same name by Arabella Eugenie Smith.

KING, CHARLES (Oct. 12, 1844–Mar. 17, 1933); b. Albany, N.Y. Army officer, novelist. *The Colonel's Daughter* (1883); *Marion's Faith* (1886); *Captain Blake* (1892); *Cadet Days* (1894); *An Army Wife* (1896); *To the Front* (1908); *The True Ulysses S. Grant* (1914); etc.

KING, CHARLES DALY (Feb. 17, 1895–); b. New York. Author. *Beyond Behaviorism* (1923); *Psychology of Consciousness* (1932); *Obelists at Sea* (1932); *The Curious Mr. Tarrant* (1935); *Bermuda Burial* (1940); *States of Human Consciousness* (1963); etc.

KING, CLARENCE (Jan. 6, 1842–Dec. 24, 1901); b. Newport, R.I. Geologist, mining engineer, author. *Mountaineering in the Sierra Nevada* (1872); etc. George Strong, in Henry James's *Esther*, is based on the life of King. See Thurman Wilkins's *Clarence King* (1958).

KING, DAN (Jan. 27, 1791–Nov. 13, 1864); b. Mansfield, Conn. Physician, pamphleteer. *Spiritualism* (1867); *Quackery Unmasked* (1858); *Tobacco: What It Is and What It Does* (1861); *The Life and Times of Thomas Wilson Dorr* (1859); etc. Reputed author of *The Draft; or, Conscription Reviewed by the People* (1863).

KING, EDWARD [Smith] (Sept. 8, 1848–Mar. 27, 1896); b. Middlefield, Mass. Journalist. Discovered George W. Cable, and launched him on his literary career. Author: *My Paris* (1868); *Kentucky's Love* (1873); *The Great South* (1875); *Echoes from the Orient* (1880); *The Gentle Savage* (1883); *Descriptive Portraiture of Europe* (reminiscences, 1885), also published as *Europe in Storm and Calm; A Venetian Lover* (1887); *Joseph Zalmonah* (1893); etc. On staff, the *Springfield Republican.*

KING, FRANK O. (April 9, 1883–June 24, 1969); b. Cashton, Wis. Cartoonist, author. *Skeezix and Uncle Walt* (1924); *Skeezix and Pal* (1925); etc. Creator of comic strips, "Skeezix and Uncle Walt" and "Gasoline Alley," the latter in 1919. Cartoonist, *Chicago Tribune*, from 1909.

KING, GEORGE CONGDON (1893–1930). Author. *Horatio's Story* (1923); *The Ostriches: A Political Fantasy* (1926); *The Rise of Rome* (1932); etc.

KING, GEORGIANA GODDARD (Aug. 5, 1871–May 4, 1939); b. West Columbia, W. Va. Author. *The Way of Perfect Love* (1909); *George Edmund Street* (1916); *The Military Orders in Spain* (1923); *Sardinian Painting* (1923); *Pre-Romanesque Churches of Spain* (1924); *Mudéjar* (1927); etc. Art dept., Bryn Mawr College.

KING, GRACE ELIZABETH (Nov. 29, 1851–Jan. 14, 1932); b. New Orleans, La. Novelist, short story writer, essayist. *Monsieur Motte* (1888); *Balcony Stories* (1892); *Tales of a Time and Place* (1892); *The Pleasant Ways of St. Medard* (1916); *New Orleans, the Place and the People* (1895); *De Soto and His Men in the Land of Florida* (1898); *Madame Girard* (1922); *La Dame de Sainte Hermine* (1924); *Memories of a Southern Woman* (1932); etc.

KING, HENRY (May 11, 1842–Mar. 15, 1916); b. Salem, O. Editor, author. *American Journalism* (1871); etc. Editor, the *St. Louis Globe-Democrat*, 1897–1915. Also editor, the *Topeka Daily Capital*, the *Kansas Magazine*, etc.

KING, HENRY CHURCHILL (Sept. 18, 1858–Feb. 27, 1934); b. Hillsdale, Mich. Educator, author. *The Appeal of the Child* (1900); *Rational Living* (1905); *The Ethics of Jesus* (1909); *Religion as Life* (1913); *A New Mind for the New Age* (1920); *Seeing Life Whole* (1923); etc. President, Oberlin College, 1902–27.

KING, HORATIO (June 21, 1811–May 20, 1897); b. Paris, Me. Cabinet officer, traveler, author. *Sketches of Travel* (1878); *Turning on the Light* (1895); etc. With Post Office Department, 1839–61; Postmaster general, Feb. 1–Mar. 8, 1861.

KING, MARIAN, b. Washington, D.C. Author. *ABC Game Book* (1928); *Kees* (1930); *Kees and Kleintje* (1934); *Elizabeth: The Tudor Princess* (1940); *The Coat of Many Colors* (1950); *A Gallery of Children* (1955); *A Gallery of Mothers and Their Children* (1958); *The Star of Bethlehem* (1968); etc.

KING, MARTIN LUTHER, Jr. (Jan. 15, 1929–April 4, 1968); b. Atlanta, Ga. Baptist clergyman. *Stride Toward Freedom* (1958). See L. Bennett's *What Manner of Man* (1964).

King, Mrs. Wyncie. See Hortense Flexner.

KING, RUFUS (Mar. 24, 1755–Apr. 29, 1827); b. Scarboro, Me. Statesman, diplomat. U.S. Senator 1789–1796, 1813–25; Minister to England, 1796–1803, 1825–27. See *The Life and Correspondence of Rufus King*, ed. by Charles R. King, 6v. (1894–1900).

KING, RUFUS [Frederick] (Jan. 3, 1893–); b. New York. Novelist. *North Star* (1925); *Whelp of the Winds* (1926); *Murder in the Willett Family* (1931); *Invitation to a Murder* (1934); *The Case of the Constant God* (1936); *Murder Masks Miami* (1939); *Holiday Homicide* (1940); *The Deadly Dove* (1945); *Duenna to a Murder* (1951); *Malice in Wonderland* (1958); etc.

KING, STODDARD (Aug. 19, 1889–June 13, 1933); b. Jackson, Wis. Columnist, author. *What the Queen Said* (1926); *Listen to the Mocking Bird* (1928); *The Raspberry Tree* (1930); etc. Wrote column, "Facetious Fragments," for the *Spokesman-Review*, Spokane, Wash., 1916–33. Wrote words of song, "There's a Long, Long Trail," etc.

KING, THOMAS STARR (Dec. 17, 1824–Mar. 4, 1864); b. New York. Universalist clergyman, orator, author. *The White Hills; Their Legends, Landscape, and Poetry* (1860, cop. 1859); *Substance and Show, and Other Lectures*, ed. by Edwin P. Whipple (1877); etc.

King Features Syndicate. New York. News-gathering organization. Founded 1916, by Moses Koenigsburg, who had founded the Newspaper Feature Service in 1913. See his *King News* (1940). E. B. Thompson is editor.

King of the Khyber Rifles. Best-known novel by Talbot Mundy (1916).

"Kingdom Coming." Song by Henry C. Work (1862).

King's Henchman, The. By Edna St. Vincent Millay (1927). Lyric drama in three acts. Story of King Eadgar and the beautiful but faithless Aelfrida, the Thane of Devon's daughter. Aethelwold, the king's favorite henchman, kills himself on discovering Aelfrida's perfidy.

Kings Row. Novel by Henry Bellamann (1940). Life in a Midwestern town at the turn of the century. The central character is a psychiatrist.

Kingsblood Royal. Novel by Sinclair Lewis (1947). A banker discovers that he is partly of Negro ancestry and must cope with race prejudice.

KINGSLEY, FLORENCE MORSE (Mrs. Charles R. Kingsley); (July 14, 1859–Oct. 26, 1937); b. near Medina, O. Author. *Titus* (1894); *The Singular Miss Smith* (1904); *Truthful Jane* (1907); *Balm in Gilead* (1907); *Those Queer Browns* (1907); *And So They Were Married* (1908); *Those Brewster Children* (1910); *Francesca* (1911); *The Heart of Philura* (1915); *Neighbors* (1917); *The Life of Henry Fowle Durant* (1923); etc.

KINGSLEY, SIDNEY (Oct. 18, 1906–); b. New York City. Playwright. *Men in White* (prod. 1933, Pulitzer Prize play, 1934); *Dead End* (prod. 1935); *Ten Million Ghosts* (prod. 1936); *The World We Make* (prod. 1939); *The Patriots* (prod. 1943); *Detective Story* (prod. 1949); *Darkness at Noon* (adaptation, prod. 1951); *Lunatics and Lovers* (prod. 1954); *Night Life* (1962); etc.

KINKEAD, CLEVES (Mar. 4, 1882–Oct. 1955); b. Louisville, Ky. Playwright. *Common Clay* (prod. 1915).

KINKEAD, ELEANOR TALBOT (Mrs. Thompson Short), b. in Kentucky. Novelist. *'Gainst Wind and Tide* (1892);

Florida Alexander (1898); *The Invisible Bond* (1906); *The Spoils of the Strong* (1920); etc.

KINNAIRD, CLARK (May 4, 1901–); b. Louisville, Ky. Journalist. *This Must Not Happen Again!* (1945). Editor: *The Real F.D.R.* (1945); *A Treasury of Damon Runyon* (1958); etc. Associate editor, King Features Syndicate, 1930–37, and since 1939; syndicated column, "Parade of Books," since 1949.

KINNELL, GALWAY (Feb. 1, 1927–); b. Providence, R.I. Author. *What a Kingdom It Was* (1960); *Flower Herding on Mount Monadnock* (poems, 1964); *Black Light* (novel, 1966); *Body Rags* (1968). Translator: *The Poems of François Villon* (1965).

KINNEY, COATES (Nov. 24, 1826–1904); b. near Penn Yan, N.Y. Poet. *Ke-u-Ka and Other Poems* (1855); *Lyrics of the Ideal and the Real* (1887); *Mists of Fire* (1899), which includes his best-known poem, "Rain on the Roof."

KINNEY, ELIZABETH C[lementine Dodge Stedman] (Dec. 18, 1810–Nov. 19, 1889); b. New York City. Poet. *Felicità* (1855); *Poems* (1867); *Bianca Cappello* (1873).

KINNEY, HENRY WALSWORTH (1879–); b. Wailuku, T.H. Correspondent, author. *The Island of Hawaii* (1913); *The Code of the Carstens* (1923); *Broken Butterflies* (1924); *Earthquake* (1928); *Manchuria Today* (1931); etc.

KINNEY, TROY (Dec. 1, 1871–Jan. 29, 1938); b. Kansas City, Mo. Artist, author. *The Dance: Its Place in Art and Life* (with wife, Margaret West Kinney, 1914).

KINSEY, ALFRED CHARLES (June 23, 1894–Aug. 25, 1956); b. Hoboken, N.J. Zoologist. *An Introduction to Biology* (1926); *Methods in Biology* (1937); *Sexual Behavior in the Human Male* (with others, 1948); *Sexual Behavior in the Human Female* (1953); etc. Prof. zoology, Indiana University, 1929–56.

Kinsey Report, The. See *Sexual Behavior in the Human Male.*

Kinsmen, The. New York City. An international social club. Founded 1882 by Brander Matthews, E. A. Abbey, Laurence Hutton, and others. W. D. Howells, Thomas Bailey Aldrich, Charles Dudley Warner, and others were later members.

KINSOLVING, SALLY BRUCE (Feb. 14, 1876–Apr. 27, 1962); b. Richmond, Va. Author. *Depths and Shallows* (1921); *David and Bathsheba, and Other Poems* (1922); *Gray Heather* (1930); *Many Waters* (1942).

KIP, LEONARD (Sept. 13, 1826–1906); b. New York. Lawyer, author. *California Sketches* (1850); *The Volcano Diggings* (1851); *Under the Bells* (1879); etc.

KIP, WILLIAM INGRAHAM (Oct. 3, 1811–Apr. 7, 1893); b. New York City. Episcopal bishop, author. *The Double Witness* (1843); *The Church of the Apostles* (1877); etc.

KIPLINGER, AUSTIN HUNTINGTON (Sept. 19, 1918–); b. Washington, D.C. Publisher, editor. Co-author with W. M. Kiplinger: *Boom and Inflation Ahead* (1958). Editor *Kiplinger Washington Letter*, since 1961; publisher, *Changing Times* magazine, since 1959.

KIPLINGER, WILLARD MONROE (Jan. 8, 1891–Aug. 6, 1967); b. Bellefontaine, O. Journalist, author. *Inflation Ahead* (with Frederick Shelton, 1935); *Washington Is Like That* (1942); *Boom and Inflation Ahead* (with Austin Kiplinger, 1958); *Your Guide to a Higher Income* (1959). Editor, *Kiplinger Washington Letters*, from 1923; *Changing Times, the Kiplinger Magazine*, from 1947.

KIRBY, ROLLIN (Sept. 4, 1875–May 9, 1952); b. Galva, Ill. Cartoonist, illustrator. Illustrations have appeared in *Scribner's, Century, Collier's, Harper's,* etc. Cartoonist for the *New York World*, 1914–31; the *New York World-Telegram*, 1931–39; the *New York Post*, 1939–42; *Look*, from 1942.

KIRCHWEY, FREDA. Editor. With *The Nation* since 1918; editor since 1932.

Kirk, Eleanor. Pen name of Eleanor Maria Ames.

KIRK, ELLEN WARNER OLNEY (Mrs. John Foster Kirk) (b. Nov. 6, 1842); b. Southington, Conn. Novelist. Pen name, "Henry Hayes." Anonymously: *His Heart's Desire* (1878); *Clare and Bébé* (1879); etc.; also under own name: *Love in Idleness* (1877); *Through Winding Ways* (1880); *A Midsummer Madness* (1884); *Walford* (1890); *Ciphers* (1891); *The Story of Lawrence Garthe* (1894); *Dorothy Deane* (1899); *Good-Bye, Proud World* (1903); *Marcia* (1907); etc.; also under pen name: *The Story of Margaret Kent* (1886); *Sons and Daughters* (1887); *A Daughter of Eve* (1889); etc.

KIRK, GRAYSON LOUIS (Oct. 12, 1903–); b. Jeffersonville, O. Educator. *Philippine Independence* (1936); *The Study of International Relations* (1947). Editor: *War and National Policy, a Syllabus* (with R. P. Stebbins, 1942). Prof. government, Columbia University, 1943–47; pres. 1953–68.

KIRK, HARRIS ELLIOTT (Oct. 12, 1872–Nov. 6, 1953); b. Pulaski, Tenn. Presbyterian clergyman, author. *The Consuming Fire* (1919); *One Generation to Another* (1924); *The Spirit of Protestantism* (1930); *A Design for Living* (1939); etc. Prof. Biblical literature, Goucher College, from 1928.

KIRK, JOHN FOSTER (Mar. 22, 1824–Sept. 21, 1904); b. Frederiction, N.B. Editor, author. *History of Charles the Bold*, 3v. (1864–68); etc. Editor: *A Supplement to Allibone's Critical Dictionary of English Literature*, 2v. (1891). Editor, *Lippincott's Magazine*, 1870–86. He was William H. Prescott's literary secretary.

KIRK, RUSSELL AMOS (Oct. 19, 1918–); b. Plymouth, Mich. Author. *Randolph of Roanoke* (1951); *The Conservative Mind from Burke to Santayana* (1953); *Old House of Fear* (1961); *The Surly Sullen Bell* (1962); *Confessions of a Bohemian Tory* (1963); *The Intemperate Professor, and Other Cultural Splenetics* (1965); *A Creature of the Twilight* (1966); *Edmund Burke* (1967); *Enemies of the Permanent Things* (1969); etc.

KIRKBRIDE, RONALD [de Levington] (Feb. 1, 1912–); b. Victoria, British Columbia. Author. *Letters of an Unknown* (1931); *The Private Life of Guy de Maupassant* (1932); *Dark Surrender* (1933); *River of Souls* (poems, 1934); *Armerdale* (1941); *Broken Melody* (1942); *Winds, Blow Gently* (1945); *Spring Is Not Gentle* (1949); *Only the Unafraid* (1953); *A Girl Named Tamiko* (1959); *An Innocent Abroad* (1961); *The Secret Journey* (1965); etc.

Kirke, Edmund. Pen name of James Roberts Gilmore.

KIRKHAM, STANTON DAVIS (Dec. 7, 1868–Jan. 6, 1944); b. Nice, Fr. Author. *Where Dwells the Soul Serene* (1899); *As Nature Whispers* (1900); *Mexican Trails* (1908); *East and West* (1911); *Outdoor Philosophy* (1912); *North and South* (1913); *Half-True Stories* (1916); *Animal Nature, and Other Stories* (1926); *Cruising* (1927); *Shut-In* (1936); *The Pearl Ship* (1937); etc.

KIRKLAND, CAROLINE MATILDA STANSBURY (Jan. 12, 1801–Apr. 6, 1864); b. New York. Educator, editor, author. Pen name, "Mrs. Mary Clavers." *A New Home: Who'll Follow?* (1839); *Forest Life*, 2v. (anon., 1842); *Western Gleanings* (1845); *Holidays Abroad*, 2v. (1849); etc. Founder, the *Union Magazine of Literature and Art*, 1847; editor, 1847–51.

KIRKLAND, JAMES HAMPTON (Sept. 9, 1859–Aug. 5, 1939); b. Spartanburg, S.C. Educator, classicist. Editor: *Satires and Epistles of Horace* (1893). Chancellor, Vanderbilt University, 1893–1937. *See* Edwin Mims's *Chancellor Kirkland of Vanderbilt* (1940).

KIRKLAND, JOHN THORNTON (Aug. 17, 1770–Apr. 26, 1840); b. Little Falls, N.Y. Educator. One of the early members of the Boston Athenaeum and of the Anthology Society. President, Harvard University, 1810–28.

KIRKLAND, JOSEPH (Jan. 7, 1830–Apr. 29, 1894); b. Geneva, N.Y., son of Caroline Matilda Stansbury Kirkland. Novelist. *Zury, the Meanest Man in Spring County* (1885); *The McVeys* (1888); *The Captain of Company K* (1891).

KIRKLAND, WINIFRED MARGARETTA (Nov. 25, 1872–May 14, 1943); b. Columbia, Pa. Author. *Polly Pot's Parish* (1907); *Christmas Bishop* (1913); *Chaos and Creed* (under pen name "James Priceman," 1925); *Portrait of a Carpenter* (1931); *As Far As I Can See* (1936); *Star in the East* (1938); *Are We Immortal?* (1941); etc.

KIRKMAN, MARSHALL MONROE (July 10, 1842–Apr. 18, 1921); b. Morgan Co., Ill. Railroad executive, author. *The Science of Railways*, 12v. (1894); *Classical Portfolio of Primitive Carriers* (1895); *The Romance of Gilbert Holmes* (1900); *Iskander* (1903); *History of Alexander the Great* (1911); etc.

KIRKUS, VIRGINIA (Mrs. Frank Glick) (Dec. 7, 1893–); b. Meadville, Pa. Book specialist, author. *A House for the Week Ends* (1940); etc. Founder, Virginia Kirkus's Bookshop Service, issuing bimonthly bulletins to the book trade which provide reviews of forthcoming books. Editorial staff, *Pictorial Review*, 1920–23; *McCall's Magazine*, 1924–25; *Harper's Magazine*, 1925–33.

KIRSCH, ROBERT (Oct. 18, 1922–); b. Coney Island, N.Y. Critic, author. *Do Not Go Gentle* (1958); *In the Wrong Rain* (1959); *Madeleine Austrian* (1960); *The Wars of Pardon* (1965); *The Restless Lovers* (under pen name Robert Dundee, 1960); *Pandora's Box* (1961); *Inferno* (1962); *Knight of the Scimitar* (1965). Literary editor and book columnist *Los Angeles Times*, since 1952.

KIRSTEIN, GEORGE GARLAND (Dec. 10, 1909–); b. Rochester, N.Y. Publisher, *The Nation*, 1955–65. Executive vice-president, Montefiore Hospital and Medical Center, 1966–69.

KIRSTEIN, LINCOLN (May 4, 1907–); b. Rochester, N.Y. Ballet manager, author. *Dance: A Short History of Theatrical Dancing* (1935); *Low Ceiling* (poems, 1935); *Blast at Ballet* (1938); *Ballet Alphabet* (1939); *The Classic Ballet* (with others, 1952); *Rhymes and More Rhymes of a PFC* (1965); *Movement and Metaphor: Four Centuries of Ballet* (1969). Editor: *Pavel Tchelitchew Drawings* (1947); *Elie Nadelman Drawings* (1949). Founder, *Hound and Horn*, 1927; editor, 1927–34. Director, N.Y. City Ballet. Dir. Gen., American Ballet.

KIRTLAND, LUCIAN SWIFT (Oct. 13, 1881–Oct. 10, 1965); b. Poland, O. Author. *Samurai Trails* (1918); *Finding the Worth While in the Orient* (1926); etc.

KISER, SAMUEL ELLSWORTH (1862–Jan. 30, 1942); b. Shippensville, Pa. Author. *Georgie* (1900); *Love Sonnets of an Office Boy* (1902); *Charles the Chauffeur* (1905); *Sonnets of a Chorus Girl* (1909); *It Is to Laugh* (1927); etc.

Kismet. First novel of Constance Julia Fletcher (1877), published anonymously. It had been published previously as *A Nile Novel* (1876).

Kismet. Popular play by Edward Knoblock (prod. 1911). The story of Haji, the begger of Bagdad, and his amazing crimes and exploits. The role was created by Otis Skinner.

Kiss of Gold, The. Story by Kate Jordan, which appeared in *Lippincott's Monthly Magazine*, Oct. 1892. One of her most popular stories.

KISSINGER, HENRY ALFRED (May 27, 1923–); b. Fuerth, Ger. Educator, author. *Nuclear Weapons and Foreign Policy* (1957); *A World Restored* (1957); *The National Purpose* (1960); *The Necessity for Choice* (1961); *The Troubled Partnership* (1965); *Problems of National Strategy* (1966);

American Foreign Policy (1969). Assoc. prof. government, Harvard University, since 1959.

"Kit Carson's Ride." Poem by Joaquin Miller, in his *Songs of the Sierras* (1871).

KITCHEN, KARL KINGSLEY (Mar. 2, 1885–June 21, 1935); b. Cleveland, O. Correspondent, columnist, author. *The Night Side of Europe* (1914); *After Dark in the War Capitals* (1916); *Pleasure—If Possible* (1928); etc. Wrote column "Man About Town" for the New York *Evening World.* With the *Evening World* and the *New York Sun,* 1908–33.

KITMAN, MARVIN (Nov. 24, 1929–); b. Pittsburgh. Pa. Editor, author. *The Number-One Best Seller* (1966); *The RCAF (Red Chinese Air Force Exercise, Diet and Sex Book)* (under pen name William Randolph Hirsch, with Richard Lingeman, 1967); *George Washington's Expense Account* (1970). Editor, *Monocle,* since 1963.

KITTREDGE, GEORGE LYMAN (Feb. 28, 1860–July 23, 1941); b. Boston, Mass. Educator, author. *The Mother Tongue* (with Sarah L. Arnold, 1900); *Words and Their Ways in English Speech* (with James B. Greenough, 1901); *The Old Farmer and His Almanack* (1904); *English Witchcraft and James the First* (1912); *Chaucer and His Poetry* (1915); *A Study of Gawain and the Green Knight* (1916); *Sir Thomas Malory* (1925); *Doctor Robert Child, the Remonstrant* (1919); *Witchcraft in Old and New England* (1929). Editor: *Athenaeum Press Series of English Classics,* 29v. (with C. T. Winchester, 1890–1905); *Albion Series of Anglo-Saxon and Middle English Poetry,* 5v. (with J. W. Bright, 1900–07); *English and Scottish Popular Ballads* (with H. C. Sargent, 1904); *Ballads and Songs* (1917); *The Complete Works of Shakespeare* (1936). English dept., Harvard University, 1888–1936; prof. from 1894.

Kitty Foyle. Novel by Christopher Morley (1939). Story of an Irish office girl who falls in love with the scion of a snobbish Philadelphia family. Torn between two loyalties, he follows Kitty to New York only after it is too late to heal the breach.

"K-K-K-katy." Song by Geoffrey O'Hara. Popular with the American soldiers in the First World War.

KLAEBER, FRIEDERICH (b. Oct. 1, 1863–); b. Beetzendorf, Prussia. Educator, author. Editor: *Old English Historical Texts* (1896); *The Later Genesis* (1913); *Beowulf* (1922); etc. English dept., University of Minnesota, 1893–1931; prof., 1898–1931.

KLAVER, MARTIN ARNOLD (Dec. 13, 1900–); b. Grand Haven, Mich. Editor. Asst. editor, the *American Boy,* 1927–30; the *Wilmington Morning News,* 1935–39; editor, *News-Journal* papers, 1939–55.

KLEEMAN, RITA HALLE (Mrs. Arthur S. Kleeman) (May 23, 1887–May 22, 1971); b. Chillicothe, O. Author. *Which College?* (1928); *Gracious Lady: Life of Sara Delano Roosevelt* (1935); *A Bible for Freshmen* (1937); *Young Franklin Roosevelt* (1946); etc.

KLEIN, ALEXANDER (1918–). Editor, author. *Counterfeit Traitor* (1958); *Rebels, Rogues, and Rascals* (1961); etc. Editor: *Courage Is the Key* (1953); *The Grand Deception* (1955); *The Empire City* (1955); *That Pellet Woman!* (autobiography, with Elizabeth Pellet, 1965); etc.

KLEIN, CHARLES (Jan. 7, 1867–May 7, 1915); b. London, England. Playwright. *The District Attorney* (with Harrison Gray Fiske, prod. 1895); *Heartsease* (with J. I. C. Clarke, prod. 1897); *The Auctioneer* (1901); *The Music Master* (with David Belasco, prod. 1904); *The Lion and the Mouse* (prod. 1905); *Daughters of Men* (prod. 1906); *The Third Degree* (prod. 1908); *The Gamblers* (prod. 1910); *Maggie Pepper* (prod. 1911); etc.

KLEISER, GRENVILLE (July 15, 1868–Oct., 1953); b. Toronto, Canada. Author. *How to Speak in Public* (1906);

Training for Authorship (1925); *Everyday Poems* (1941); *Make Your Life Worth Living* (1949); and numerous books on public speaking. Compiler: *The World's Great Sermons* (1909); *Fifteen Thousand Useful Phrases* (1917); etc.

KLEMPNER, JOHN (Aug. 4, 1898–); b. New York. Novelist. *No Stork at Nine* (1938); *Once Around the Block* (1939); *Another Night, Another Day* (1941); *Letter to Five Wives* (1946); *Hurry, Hurry Home* (1948).

KLINE, BURTON, b. Williamsport, Pa. Journalist, author. *An Onslaught of Fame* (1901); *The Embarrassment of Mr. Perkins* (1912); *The End of the Flight* (1917); *Canardin* (1920); *The Puppet-Show on the Potomac* (under pen name, "Rufus Dart II," 1933); *The Gallant Rogue* (1921); etc. With the *Boston Transcript,* 1904–18; etc.

KLINE, GEORGE (c. 1757–Nov. 12, 1820); b. in Germany. Editor, publisher. Publisher, the *Allied Mercury,* Philadelphia, 1781; founder, the *Carlisle* (Pa.) *Gazette,* 1785, which merged with the *Carlisle Spirit of the Times* in 1817. He also published books.

KLINEBERG, OTTO (Nov. 2, 1899–); b. Quebec, Can. Educator. *Race Differences* (1935); *Social Psychology* (1940); *Tensions Affecting International Understanding* (1950). Editor: *Characteristics of the American Negro* (1944). Psychology dept., Columbia University, since 1931.

KLUBERTANZ, GEORGE PETER (June 29, 1912–); b. near Columbus, Wis. Roman Catholic clergyman, author. *The Discursive Power* (1952); *Introduction to the Philosophy of Being* (1955); *St. Thomas Aquinas on Analogy* (1960); *Being and God* (1963); *Habits and Virtues* (1965); etc. Philosophy dept., St. Louis University, since 1968.

KLUCKHOHN, CLYDE KAY MABEN (Jan. 11, 1905–July 29, 1960); b. Le Mars, Ia. Anthropologist. *To the Foot of the Rainbow* (1927); *Beyond the Rainbow* (1933); *The Navaho* (with Dorothea Leighton, 1946); *Mirror for Man* (1949); *Anthropology and the Classics* (1961); *Culture and Behavior* (1962); etc. Anthropology dept., Harvard University, from 1935.

KLUGE, ALEXANDER. Author. *Attendance List for a Funeral* (short stories, 1966); *The Battle* (novel, 1967).

KNAPLUND, PAUL ALEXANDER (Feb. 5, 1885–April 8, 1964); b. Straumen i Boden, Nor. Educator. Author: *Gladstone and Britain's Imperial Policy* (1927); *The British Empire, 1815–1939* (1941); *James Stephen and the British Colonial System, 1813–1847* (1953); *Britain, Commonwealth and Empire, 1901–1955* (1957); etc. Editor: *Speeches on Foreign Affairs by Sir Edward Grey, 1904–14* (1931); *British Opinion on Norwegian-Swedish Problems, 1880–1895* (with C. M. Clewes, 1952); *Moorings Old and New* (1963); etc. History dept., University of Wisconsin, 1916–55.

KNAPP, GEORGE LEONARD (Apr. 6, 1872–); b. Dover, Minn. Journalist, author. *The Face of Air* (1912); *Brigham Young* (with Frank J. Cannon, 1913); *The Boys' Book of Annapolis* (1930); *The Boys' Book of West Point* (1931); etc. With the *Chicago Journal,* 1912–25.

KNAPP, SAMUEL LORENZO (Jan. 19, 1783–July 8, 1838); b. Newburyport, Mass. Editor, orator, author. *Letters of Shahcoolen, a Hindu Philosopher . . . to His Friend El Hassan* (anon., 1802); *Extracts from a Journal of Travels in North America* (under pen name, "Ali Bey," 1818); *Biographical Sketches of Eminent Lawyers, Statesmen and Men of Letters* (1821); *Memoirs of General Lafayette* (anon., 1824); *Lectures on American Literature* (1829); *Sketches of Public Characters* (under pen name, "Ignatius Loyola Robertston," 1830); *A Memoir of the Life of Daniel Webster* (1831); *Advice in the Pursuit of Literature* (1832); *American Biography* (1833); *Female Biography* (1834); *Tales of the Garden of Kosciuszko* (1834); *The Life of Aaron Burr* (1835); *Andrew Jackson* (1835); *The Picturesque Beauties of the Hudson River,* 2v.

(1835–36); *The Bachelors, and Other Tales* (1836); etc. Editor, the *Boston Gazette,* 1824–26; founder and editor, the *Boston Monthly Magazine,* 1825–26; founder and editor, the *Boston National Republican,* 1826–27.

KNAPP, WILLIAM IRELAND (Mar. 10, 1835–Dec. 6, 1908); b. Greenport, N.Y. Educator, author. *Life, Writings and Correspondence of George Borrow,* 2v. (1899). Editor: George Borrow's *Lavengro* (1900), and his *The Romany Rye* (1900); etc. Street prof., modern languages, Yale University, 1880–92; prof. Romance languages, University of Chicago, 1892–95.

KNEBEL, FLETCHER (Oct. 1, 1911–); b. Dayton, Ohio. Author. *No High Ground* (with Charles Bailey, 1960); *Seven Days in May* (1962); *Convention* (1964); *Night of Camp David* (1965); *The Zinzin Road* (1966).

"Knee-Deep in June." Poem by James Whitcomb Riley (1887).

KNEELAND, SAMUEL (Jan. 31, 1697–Dec. 14, 1769); b. Boston, Mass. Printer, publisher. Publisher, the *Boston Gazette,* 1727–41; the *New England Weekly Journal,* 1741–52.

KNEELAND, SAMUEL (Aug. 1, 1821–Sept. 27, 1888); b. Boston, Mass. Educator, physician, zoölogist, author. *The Wonders of the Yosemite Valley and of California* (1871); *An American in Iceland* (1876); *The Philippine Islands* (1883); etc. Prof. zoölogy, Massachusetts Institute of Technology, 1869–78.

KNEELAND, STILLMAN FOSTER (May 17, 1845–Aug. 30, 1926); b. South Stukely, P.Q. Lawyer, author. *Law, Lawyers and Lambs* (1910); *Random Rhymes of a Busy Barrister* (1914).

KNEIPPLE, EDITH ELIZABETH (Mrs. George Wiswell) (Aug. 4, 1902–); b. Marion, Ind. Author. *Candle in the Sun* (1937); *Reap the Whirlwind* (1938); *Tamarack* (1940); *This Marriage* (1941); *Little Hell, Big Heaven* (1942); *That Hagen Girl* (1946); *The Divorce of Marcia Moore* (1948); *That Loring Woman* (1950). Before 1936, wrote children's stories under name "Elizabeth Kneipple Van Deusen"; afterward, adopted pen name "Edith Roberts."

KNEVELS, GERTRUDE (Apr. 2, 1881–Apr. 6, 1962); b. Fishkill-on-Hudson, N.Y. Author. *The Wonderful Bed* (1911); *Dragon's Glory* (1925); *Octagon House* (1926); *The Diamond Rose Mystery* (1928); *Of Love Beware* (1936); *Twelfth Night at Moulderby Hall* (1936); *Death on the Clock* (1940); etc.

KNIBBS, HARRY HERBERT (Oct. 24, 1874–May 17, 1945); b. Clifton, Ont. Poet, novelist. *First Poems* (1908); *Lost Farm Camp* (1912); *Stephen March's Way* (1913); *Songs of the Outlands* (1914); *Overland Red* (1914); *Sundown Slim* (1915); *Riders of the Stars* (poems, 1916); *The Ridin' Kid from Powder River* (1919); *Songs of the Trail* (1920); *Saddle Songs, and Other Verse* (1922); *Wild Horses* (1924); *Sunny Mateel* (1927); *The Tonto Kid* (1936); etc.

KNICKERBOCKER, CHARLES H[errick (1922–). Author. *Juniper Island* (1958); *The Boy Came Back* (1961); *The Dynasty* (1962); *The Hospital War* (1966).

Knickerbocker, Cholly. Pen name of Igor Loiewski Cassini.

Knickerbocker, Cholly. Pen name of Maury Henry Biddle Paul.

Knickerbocker, Diedrich. Pen name of Washington Irving.

KNICKERBOCKER, HUBERT RENFRO (Jan. 31, 1898–July 13, 1949); b. Yoakum, Tex. Correspondent. *The Red Trade Menace* (1931); *The German Crisis* (1932); *The Siege of Alcazar* (1936); etc. Correspondent, the International News Service, 1925–41; foreign service chief, *Chicago Sun,* 1941–45.

KNICKERBOCKER, WILLIAM SKINKLE (Jan. 7, 1892–); b. New York. Educator, editor, author. *Creative Oxford* (1925); *Victorian Education and Concept of Culture* (1949); etc. Editor, the *Sewanee Review,* 1926–42. Prof. English, University of the South, Sewanee, Tenn. 1926–43; Newton Junior College, since 1957.

Knickerbocker Magazine. New York City. Monthly. Founded Jan., 1833. Editors: Charles Fenno Hoffman, 1833; Samuel Daly Langtree, 1833–34; Timothy Flint, 1834; Lewis Gaylord Clark, 1834–60; Charles Godfrey Leland, 1861–62; Kinahan Cornwallis, 1862–63 (with L. G. Clark, 1863); John Holmes Agnew, 1863–65. Willis Gaylord Clark was associate editor, 1834–41. "Old Knick," as it was popularly called, flourished under the able hands of Lewis Gaylord Clark, and his twin brother, Willis Gaylord Clark. Among the contributors were Washington Irving, Cooper, Bryant, Longfellow, Holmes, Bayard Taylor, Robert Montgomery Bird, Mathew Carey, Charles Godfrey Leland, Joseph C. Neal, James Hall, Albert Pike, H. R. Schoolcraft, and George Horatio Derby. A literary feature was "The Editor's Table," a humorous department conducted for many years by Lewis Gaylord Clark. Expired Oct., 1865. *The Knickerbocker Gallery* (1855) is an anthology of selections from the magazine. *See* F. L. Mott's *History of American Magazines,* v. 1 (1938).

Knickerbocker's History of New York. See *A History of New York,* by "Diedrich Knickerbocker" (Washington Irving) (1809).

Knight, Adam. Pen name of Lawrence Lariar.

KNIGHT, CLIFFORD [Reynolds] (Dec. 7, 1886–); b. Fulton, Kan. Author. *Tommy of the Voices* (1918); *The Affair of the Scarlet Crab* (1938); *The Affair on the Painted Desert* (1939); *The Affair of the Crimson Gull* (1941); *The Affair of the Jade Monkey* (1943); *The Affair of the Corpse Escort* (1946); *Dark Abyss* (1948); *Death and Little Brother* (1952); and many other mystery novels.

KNIGHT, EDGAR WALLACE (Apr. 9, 1886–Aug. 7, 1953); b. in Northampton Co., N.C. Educator, author. *The Influence of Reconstruction on Education in the South* (1913); *Education in the South* (1924); *Among the Danes* (1927); *Culture in the South* (with others, 1934); *Twenty Centuries of Education* (1941); *Fifty Years of American Education* (1952); etc. Prof. education, University of North Carolina, from 1919.

KNIGHT, GRANT COCHRAN (April 15, 1893–Mar. 15, 1956); b. Williamsport, Pa. Educator, author. *Superlatives* (1925); *The Novel in English* (1931); *American Literature and Culture* (1932); *James Lane Allen and the Genteel Tradition* (1935); *The Sealed Well* (poems, 1943); *The Strenuous Age in American Literature* (1954); etc. English dept., University of Kentucky, since 1921.

KNIGHT, HELEN C[ross]. Author. *City Cousins* (anon., 1846); *A New Memoir of Hannah More; or, Life in Hall and Cottage* (1851), republished as *Hannah More; or, Life in Hall and Cottage; Hugh Fisher* (anon., 1851); *Kitty King* (anon., 1861); *Taking a Stand* (anon., 1865); etc.

KNIGHT, HENRY COGSWELL (Jan. 29, 1789–Jan. 10, 1835); b. Newburyport, Mass. Author. *The Cypriad* (poems, 1809); *The Broken Harp* (poems, 1815); *Letters from the South and West* (under pen name "Arthur Singleton," 1824); etc.

KNIGHT, LUCIAN LAMAR (Feb. 9, 1868–Nov. 19, 1933); b. Atlanta, Ga. Editor, historian. *Reminiscences of Famous Georgians,* 2v. (1907–08); *Georgia's Landmarks, Memorials and Legends,* 2v. (1913–14); *Standard History of Georgia and Georgians,* 6v. (1916); *Memorials of Dixieland* (1919); etc. Lit. editor, Martin & Hoyt Co., Atlanta, Ga., 1910–33; State Historian of Georgia, 1919–33. Founder, Department of Archives and History, State of Georgia; founder and first president, Georgia Historical Association, 1917.

KNIGHT, SARAH KEMBLE (Apr. 19, 1666–Sept. 25, 1727); b. Boston, Mass. Diarist. *The Journals of Madam Knight and Rev. Mr. Buckingham* (1825).

KNIGHT, WILLIAM ALLEN (Oct. 20, 1863–Feb. 11, 1957); b. Milton, Mo. Disciples clergyman, author. *The Song of Our Syrian Guest* (1904); *No Room in the Inn* (1910); *On the Way to Bethlehem* (1912); *A Bedouin Lover* (1913); *Wartime over Here* (1918); *Our Bethlehem Guests* (1944); etc. Associate editor, *Framingham News,* from 1934.

Knight's Gambit. Collection of stories by William Faulkner (1949).

KNIPE, ALDEN ARTHUR (June 26, 1870–May 22, 1950); b. Philadelphia, Pa. Author. *Captain of the Eleven* (1910); *The Last Lap* (1911); *Bunny Plays the Game* (1925); *Sarah and Son* (1929); *Everybody's Washington* (1931); *The Cowboy and the Duchess* (1932). Co-author (with wife, Emilie Benson Knipe): *Little Miss Fales* (1910); *The Lucky Sixpence* (1912); *A Maid of '76* (1915); *A Maid of Old Manhattan* (1917); *Girls of '64* (1918); *A Cavalier Maid* (1919); *Diantha's Quest* (1921); *A Continental Dollar* (1923); *Treasure Trove* (1927); *The Story of Old Ironsides* (1928); *The Pirate's Ward* (1929); etc.

KNIPE, EMILIE BENSON (Mrs. Alden Arthur Knipe) (June 12, 1870–Oct. 25, 1958); b. Philadelphia, Pa. Artist, author. Under pen name "Therese Benson": *The Unknown Daughter* (1929); *The Go-Between* (1930); *Strictly Private* (1931); *Fools Gold* (1932); *Gallant Adventuress* (1933); *Death Wears a Mask* (1935); etc. Co-author (with husband): *Little Miss Fales* (1910); *The Lucky Sixpence* (1912); *A Maid of '76* (1915); *A Maid of Old Manhattan* (1917); *Girls of '64* (1918); *A Cavalier Maid* (1919); *Diantha's Quest* (1921); *A Continental Dollar* (1923); *Treasure Trove* (1927); *The Story of Old Ironsides* (1928); *The Pirate's Ward* (1929); etc.

Knish, Ann. Pen name of Arthur Davison Ficke.

KNOBLOCK, EDWARD (Apr. 7, 1874–1945); b. New York. Playwright. Became an English citizen in 1916. *Kismet* (prod. 1911); *Milestones* (with Arnold Bennett, prod. 1912); *My Lady's Dress* (prod. 1914); *Marie-Odile* (prod. 1915); *A War Committee* (prod. 1915); *Tiger! Tiger!* (prod. 1918); *The Lullaby* (prod. 1923); *Round the Room* (autobiography, 1939); etc. See Margaret G. Mayorga's *A Short History of the American Drama* (1934).

Knock on Any Door. Novel by Willard Motley (1947). A boy who grows up on the Chicago streets turns into a murderer.

KNOLES, GEORGE HARMON (Feb. 20, 1907–); b. Los Angeles, Cal. Educator. *The Presidential Campaign and Election of 1892* (1942); *The Jazz Age Revisited* (1955); *The New United States* (1959). Editor: *The Responsibilities of Power, 1900–1929* (1967). History dept., Stanford University, since 1935.

KNOLLENBERG, BERNHARD (Nov. 26, 1892–); b. Richmond, Ind. Librarian, author. *Washington and the Revolution* (1940); *Whitewater Valley* (1946); *Samuel Ward* (1952); *Origin of the American Revolution* (1960); *George Washington: The Virginia Period* (1964). Librarian, Yale University, 1938–44.

KNOPF, ALFRED A. (Sept. 12, 1892–); b. New York. Publisher. With Doubleday Page & Co., 1912–13; with Mitchell Kennerley, 1914. Founder, publishing house of Alfred A. Knopf, New York, 1915.

Knopf, Alfred A. New York. Publisher. Founded 1915, by Alfred A. Knopf. Books by outstanding European authors have always been featured, and the Knopf books, called Borzoi Books, are noted for their type design and layout; W. A. Dwiggins was consultant to the firm for many years. Alfred A. Knopf is chairman of the board. In 1960 Random House acquired an interest in the firm, but it continues to publish

under its own imprint. It also publishes Vintage Books, paperback reprints.

KNOPF, BLANCHE [Wolf] (d. June 4, 1966); b. New York. Publisher. Vice-president, Alfred A. Knopf, Inc., 1921–57; president, from 1957.

KNOTT, BILL. (1940–   ); b. Grindel, Ohio. Author. Under pen name "Saint Geraud": *The Naomi Poems* (1968).

KNOTT, THOMAS ALBERT (Jan. 12, 1880–Aug. 16, 1945); b. Chicago, Ill. Educator, editor, author. *Elements of Old English* (with S. Moore, 1919); etc. Editor, Webster's *New International Dictionary,* 2d edition (1934); editor, *Middle English Dictionary.* Co-editor with John S. Kenyon: *Pronouncing Dictionary of American English* (1943). Prof. English, University of Michigan, from 1935.

KNOTT, WILLIAM CECIL, JR. (Aug. 7, 1927–); b. Boston, Mass. Author. *Junk Pitcher* (1963); *They Work and Serve* (1967); *The Dwarf on Black Mountain* (1967); etc. Under pen name "Bill Knott": *Night Pursuit* (1966); *The Secret of the Old Brownstone* (1969); etc. Under pen name "Bill J. Carol": *Backboard Scrambles* (1963); *Circus Catch; Clutch Single* (1964); *Full-Court Pirate* (1965); *Hit Away!* (1965); *Hard Smash to Third* (1966); *Crazylegs Merrill* (1969); etc.

KNOWLES, JOHN (Sept. 16, 1926–); b. Cheyenne, Wyoming. Author. *A Separate Peace* (1960); *Morning in Antibes* (1962); *Double Vision* (1964); *Indian Summer* (1966); *Phineas* (1968); *The Paragon* (1970).

KNOX, FRANKLIN. (Jan. 1, 1874–1944); b. Boston, Mass. Cabinet member, publisher. Publisher, *Chicago Daily News,* from 1931. Secretary of the Navy, from 1940.

KNOX, JOHN (Dec. 30, 1900–); b. Frankfort, Ky. Methodist clergyman, educator, author. *He Whom a Dream Hath Possessed* (1932); *Marcion and the New Testament* (1942); *On the Meaning of Christ* (1947); *Chapters in a Life of Paul* (1950); *The Early Church and the Coming Great Church* (1955); *The Death of Christ* (1958); *The Church and the Reality of Christ* (1962); *Myth and Truth* (1964); *The Integrity of Preaching* (1966); *The Humanity and Divinity of Christ* (1967); etc. Associate editor: *The Interpreter's Bible,* 12v. (1951–57). Prof. sacred literature, Union Theological Seminary, since 1943.

KNOX, JOHN CLARK (Oct. 13, 1881–Aug. 23, 1966); b. Waynesburg, Pa. Jurist, author. *A Judge Comes of Age* (autobiography, 1940); *Order in the Court* (1943).

KNOX, ROSE BELL (Dec. 16, 1879–); b. Talladega, Ala. Author of children's books. *The Boys and Sally Down on a Plantation* (1930); *Gray Caps* (1932); *Marty and Company on a Carolina Farm* (1933); *Patsy's Progress* (1935); *Footlights Afloat* (1937); *Cousins' Luck* (1940); *Marty and Company on a California Farm* (1946); etc.

KNOX, THOMAS WALLACE (June 26, 1835–Jan. 6, 1896); b. Pembroke, N.H. Journalist, author. *Camp-Fire and Cotton-Field* (1865); *Overland through Asia* (1870); etc. Wrote many travel books for boys, including the *Boy Travellers* series, the *Young Nimrods* series, etc.

Knoxville Gazette. Knoxville, Tenn. Newspaper. Founded 1791; printed at nearby Rogersville until 1792. With several suspensions, continued until 1808. First newspaper in Tennessee.

Knoxville Journal. Knoxville, Tenn. Newspaper. Founded 1885. Merged with the *Knoxville Tribune* (founded 1876) in 1898. See *Knoxville News-Sentinel.*

Knoxville News-Sentinel. Knoxville, Tenn. Newspaper. The *Sentinel* founded 1886; the *News,* 1921. The Scripps-Howard organization bought both papers and merged them in 1926. Now combined with the *Knoxville Journal.* The *News-Senti-*

nel appears evenings and Sundays; the *Journal* appears mornings, except Sundays. Ralph L. Millet is editor. F. Gunby Rule is book-review editor.

KOBBÉ, GUSTAV (Mar. 4, 1857–July 27, 1918); b. New York. Music critic, author. *The New Jersey Coast and Pines* (1889); *Wagner's Life and Work,* 2v. (1890); *New York and Its Environs* (1891); *My Rosary, and Other Poems* (1896); *Miriam* (1898); *Opera Singers* (1901); *Famous Actors & Actresses and Their Homes* (1903); *The Loves of Great Composers* (1905); *Opera Singers* (1901); *Famous American Songs* (1906); *Portrait Gallery of Great Composers* (1911); *The Complete Opera Book* (1919); etc. Founder and editor, *The Lotus* magazine, 1909.

KOBER, ARTHUR (Aug. 25, 1900–); b. Brody, Aust.-Hung. Author. *Thunder over the Bronx* (1935); *Having Wonderful Time* (1937); *Pardon Me for Pointing* (1939); *My Dear Bella* (1941); *That Man Is Here Again* (1946); *Bella, Bella Kissed a Fella* (1951); *Ooh, What You Said!* (1958); *A Mighty Man Is He* (with George Oppenheimer, 1959).

KOBRIN, LEON (Mar. 15, 1873–Mar. 31, 1946); b. Vitebsk, Russia. Yiddish novelist, playwright. Translations of his books have been published as: *Yankel Boila, and Other Tales* (1898); *A Lithuanian Village* (1920); *The Reminiscences of a Yiddish Dramatist,* 2v. (1925); *Homeless* (1937); etc.

KOCH, ADRIENNE (1912–). Historian. *Jefferson and Madison: the Great Collaboration* (1950); *The Philosophy of Thomas Jefferson* (1957); *Power, Morals, and the Founding Fathers* (1961); *The American Enlightenment* (1965); *Madison's Advice to My Country* (1966). Editor: *Philosophy for a Time of Crisis* (1959).

KOCH, FREDERICK HENRY (Sept. 12, 1877–Aug. 16, 1944); b. Covington, Ky. Educator, editor, playwright. Editor: *Carolina Folk-Plays,* 4 series (1922–31); *American Folk-Plays* (1939). Editor, *Carolina Play-Book;* etc. Founder, The Dakota Playmakers, 1910; the Carolina Playmakers, 1918. English dept., University of North Dakota, 1905–18; prof. dramatic literature, University of North Carolina, from 1918.

KOCH, HOWARD, b. New York. Playwright. *Give Us This Day* (1933); *In Time to Come* (with John Huston, prod. 1941).

KOCH, KENNETH (Feb. 27, 1925–   ); b. Cincinnati, O. Poet. *Poems* (1953); *Ko, or a Season on Earth* (1959); *Permanently* (1961); *Thank You and Other Poems* (1962); *Bertha and Other Plays* (1966); *Interlocking Lives* (with Alex Katz, 1970). Assoc. prof. English and comparative literature, Columbia University, since 1966.

KOCH, THEODORE WESLEY (Aug. 4, 1871–Mar. 23, 1941); b. Philadelphia, Pa. Librarian, translator, author. *Dante in America* (1896); *A Book of Carnegie Libraries* (1917); *Reading, a Vice or a Virtue* (1926); *Tales for Bibliophiles* (1929); etc. Translator: Flaubert's *Bibliomania* (1929); Zweig's *The Old Book Peddler, and Other Tales for Bibliophiles* (1937); etc. Librarian, University of Michigan, 1905–16; Northwestern University, from 1919.

KOCH, VIVIENNE (Mrs. John F. Day) (1914–Nov. 29, 1961). Author. *William Carlos Williams* (1950); *W. B. Yeats: The Tragic Phase* (1952); *Change of Love* (1960).

KOEHLER, SYLVESTER ROSA (Feb. 11, 1837–Sept. 15, 1900); b. Leipzig, Ger. Museum curator, author. *Original Etchings by American Artists* (1883); *American Art* (1886); *Frederick Juengling* (1890); etc. With L. Prang & Co., Boston, 1868–78; curator, Boston Museum of Fine Arts, 1887–1900.

KOENIGSBERG, MOSES (Apr. 16, 1878–Sept. 21, 1945); b. New Orleans, La. Syndicate executive, author. *Southern Martyrs* (1898); *The Elk and the Elephant* (1899); *King News* (autobiography, 1941); etc. Organized Newspaper Feature Service, 1913; King Features Syndicate, 1916.

KOHL, HERBERT R. Educator, author. *36 Children* (1967); *Teaching the Unteachable* (1967); *The Open Classroom* (1970). Editor: *Stuff* (with Victor Cruz, 1970).

KOHLER, JULILLY HOUSE (Mrs. John M. Kohler) (Oct. 18, 1908–); b. Cincinnati, O. Author. *You and the Constitution of the United States* (with P. A. Witty, 1948); *Daniel in the Cub Scout Den* (1951); *The Boy Who Stole the Elephant* (1952); *Crazy As You Look!* (1954); *Razzberry Jamboree* (1957); etc.

KOHLER, KAUFMANN (May 10, 1843–Jan. 28, 1926); b. Fürth, Bavaria. Rabbi, educator. *Backwards or Forwards* (1885); *Jewish Theology Systematically and Historically Considered* (1918); *Studies, Addresses and Personal Papers* (1931); etc. President, Hebrew Union College, Cincinnati, 1903–22.

KÖHLER, WOLFGANG (Jan. 21, 1887–June 11, 1967); b. Reval, Est. Psychologist. *The Mentality of Apes* (1925); *Gestalt Psychology* (1929); *The Place of Value in a World of Facts* (1938); *Dynamics in Psychology* (1940); etc. Prof. psychology, Swarthmore College, 1935–58. Research prof., Dartmouth College, 1958–67.

KOHLSAAT, HERMAN HENRY (Mar. 22, 1853–Oct. 17, 1924); b. Albion, Ill. Restaurateur, editor, author. *From McKinley to Harding: Personal Recollections of the Presidents* (1923). Editor and publisher, the *Chicago Times-Herald* (later *Record-Herald*), 1895–1902, 1910–11.

KOHN, HANS (Sept. 15, 1891–Mar. 17, 1971); b. Prague. Educator, author. *A History of Nationalism in the East* (1929); *Nationalism in the Soviet Union* (1933); *Force or Reason* (1937); *Revolutions and Dictatorships* (1938); *Not by Arms Alone* (1940); *The Idea of Nationalism* (1944); *The Twentieth Century: A Midway Account of the Western World* (1949); *Pan-Slavism* (1953); *American Nationalism* (1957); *The Mind of Germany* (1960); *The Age of Nationalism* (1962); *Reflections on Modern History* (1963); *Living in a World Revolution* (1964); *Absolutism and Democracy* (1965); *Nationalism and Realism* (1967); *Europe in Crisis* (1969). Prof. history, City College of New York, 1949–71.

KOHNER, FREDERICK. Author. *Gidget* (1957); *Cher Papa* (1960).

KOHUT, ALEXANDER (Apr. 22, 1842–May 25, 1894); b. Félégyháza, Hungary. Rabbi, lexicographer, orator. *Aruch,* 8v. (1878–92); etc. His family established in his memory the Alexander Kohut Research Fellowship in Semitics at Yale, and left to Yale his library of Hebrew and Rabbinic books. *See* Rebekah Kohut's *My Portion* (1925).

KOLARZ, WALTER (d. 1962). Author. *Stalin and Eternal Russia* (1944); *Myths and Realities in Eastern Europe* (1946); *Russia and Her Colonies* (1953); *Religion in the Soviet Union* (1962).

KOLLOCK, SHEPARD (Sept. 1750–July 28, 1839); b. Lewes, Del. Publisher, editor. Founder, the *New Jersey Gazette,* Chatham, N.J., Feb. 16, 1779; the *New York Gazetteer,* New York City, Dec. 3, 1783; the *Political Intelligencer,* New Brunswick, N.J., Oct. 14, 1783. He also published books and pamphlets.

KOLODIN, IRVING (Feb. 22, 1908–); b. New York. Music critic. *Metropolitan Opera* (1936); *The Kingdom of Swing* (with Benny Goodman, 1939); *Guide to Recorded Music* (1941); *Story of the Metropolitan Opera* (1953); *The Musical Life* (1958); *Metropolitan Opera* (1966); *The Continuity of Music* (1969). Program annotator, New York Philharmonic Orchestra, since 1953. Music editor and critic, *New York Sun,* 1945–50; music editor, *Saturday Review of Literature,* 1950–52; associate editor, *Saturday Review,* since 1952.

KOMAROVSKY, MIRRA (Mrs. Marcus A. Heyman) (Feb. 4, 1906–); b. in Russia. Educator. *Leisure: A Suburban Study* (with others, 1934); *The Unemployed Man and His Family* (1940); *Women in the Modern World: Their Education and Their Dilemmas* (1953); *Blue Collar Marriage* (1964). Editor: *Common Frontiers of the Social Sciences* (1957). Sociology dept., Barnard College, since 1936.

KOMROFF, MANUEL (Sept. 7, 1890–); b. New York. Editor, author. *The Grace of Lambs* (1925); *The Travels of Marco Polo* (1926); *Coronet* (1930); *Two Thieves* (1931); *Waterloo* (1936); *The Magic Bow: A Romance of Paganini* (1940); *In the Years of Our Lord* (1942); *The One Story: The Life of Christ* (1943); *Feast of the Jesters* (1947); *How to Write a Novel* (1950); *Jade Star* (1951); *Marco Polo* (1952); *Napoleon* (1954); *Mozart* (1956); *Abraham Lincoln* (1959); *Beethoven and the World of Music* (1961); *The Third Eye* (1962); *Disraeli* (1963); *Charlemagne* (1964); *Talleyrand* (1965); *Heroes of the Bible* (1966); *The Whole World is Outside* (1968); etc. Editor: *Contemporaries of Marco Polo* (1928); *Tales of the Monks, from the Gesta Romanorum* (1928); etc. Editor, *Modern Library,* 1921–26.

KONINGSBERGER, HANS (July 12, 1921–); b. Amsterdam, Holland. Author. *Golden Keys* (1956); *The Affair* (1958); *An American Romance* (1961); *A Walk with Love and Death* (1961); *I Know What I'm Doing* (1964); *Love and Hate in China* (1966); *The Revolutionary* (1967); *Along the Roads of the New Russia* (1968).

Koningsmarke, the Long Finne. Novel by James Kirke Paulding (1823). It deals with the Swedish settlers on the Delaware. Contains the famous jingle, "Peter Piper picked a peck of pickled peppers."

KONKLE, BURTON ALVA (Apr. 25, 1861–Oct. 24, 1944); b. Albion, Ind. Author. *George Bryan and the Constitution of Pennsylvania* (1922); *Joseph Hopkinson, 1770–1842* (1931); *Life of Andrew Hamilton, 1676–1741* (1941); etc. Editor: *The Life and Speeches of Thomas Williams,* 2v. (1905); *Life and Letters of Chief Justice Benjamin Chew* (1932); etc.

KONVITZ, MILTON RIDVAS (Mar. 12, 1908–); b. Safad, Pal. Educator. Author: *On the Nature of Value: The Philosophy of Samuel Alexander* (1946); *The Constitution and Civil Rights* (1947); *Civil Rights in Immigration* (1953); *Fundamental Liberties of a Free People* (1957); *A Century of Civil Rights* (1961); *First Amendment Freedoms* (1963); *Expanding Liberties* (1966); *Religious Liberty and Conscience* (1968); etc. Editor: *Freedom and Experience* (with Sidney Hook, 1947); *Liberian Code of Laws,* 4v. (1957–58); etc. Prof. law, Cornell Law School, since 1956.

KOOPMAN, HARRY LYMAN (July 1, 1860–Dec. 28, 1937); b. Freeport, Me. Librarian, author. *Orestes: A Dramatic Sketch, and Other Poems* (1888); *The Mastery of Books* (1896); *Morrow-Songs, 1880–1898* (1898); *At the Gates of the Century* (poems, 1905); *My Summer in Europe* (1910); *The Booklover and His Books* (1917); *Hesperia,* 2v. (poem, 1919–24); etc. Librarian, Brown University, 1893–1930.

KOPIT, ARTHUR (May 10, 1937–); b. New York. Playwright, author. *Oh Dad, Poor Dad, Mamma's Hung You in the Closet and I'm Feelin' So Sad* (prod. 1962; film 1967); *The Day the Whores Came Out to Play Tennis, and Other Plays* (1956); *Indians* (1969).

KOPKIND, ANDREW DAVID (Aug. 24, 1935–); b. New Haven, Conn. Journalist, author. *America: The Mixed Curse* (1969). Founder, *Mayday* and *Hard Times,* weeklies, Washington, D.C., 1968; editor, since 1968.

KÖRMENDI, FERENC (Feb. 12, 1900–); b. Budapest. Author. editor. *Martyr* (1921); *Escape to Life* (1932); *Via Bodenbach* (1933); *The Happy Generation* (1934); *Serenade* (1935); *Sinners* (1936); *The Island* (1937); *That One Mistake* (1938); *Weekday in June* (1943); *Years of Eclipse* (1951). Editor, *A Hét,* 1919–22; literary correspondent, Budapest *Pesti Napló,* 1933–38.

KORN, BERTRAM WALLACE (Oct. 6, 1918–); b. Philadelphia, Pa. Rabbi, author. *American Jewry and the Civil War* (1951); *The American Reaction to the Mortara Case* (1957); *Jews and Negro Slavery in the Old South* (1962); *Early Jews of New Orleans* (1969); etc. Editor: Carvalho's *Incidents of Travel and Adventure in the Far West* (1954).

KORZYBSKI, ALFRED (July 3, 1879–Mar. 1, 1950); b. Warsaw. Semanticist. *Manhood of Humanity: The Science and Art of Human Engineering* (1921); *Time-Binding: The General Theory* (1926); *Science and Sanity: An Introduction to Non-Aristotelian Systems and General Semantics* (1933). Pres. and director, Institute of General Semantics, from 1938.

KOSINSKI, JERZY NIKODEM (June 14, 1933–); b. Lodz, Poland. Author. *The Future Is Ours, Comrade* (pen name Joseph Novak, 1960); *No Third Path* (1962); *The Painted Bird* (1965); *Steps* (1968, National Book Award, 1969); *Being There* (1971).

KOSTELANETZ, RICHARD C[ory] (May 14, 1940–); b. New York. Author. *The Theatre of Mixed Means* (1968); *Possibilities of Poetry* (1970). Editor: *On Contemporary Literature* (1964); *The New American Arts* (1965).

KOUWENHOVEN, JOHN ATLEE (1909–); b. Yonkers, N.Y. Educator, editor. *Adventures of America, 1857–1900* (1938); *Made in America: The Arts in Modern Civilization* (1948); *The Columbia Historical Portrait of New York* (1953); *The Beer Can by the Highway* (1961); *Partners in Banking* (1968). Staff, *Harper's,* 1941–54. English dept., Barnard College, since 1948.

KOVACS, ERNIE (Jan. 23, 1919–Jan. 13, 1962); b. Trenton, N.J. Actor, producer-director, author. *Zoomar* (1957); *Talk at Gin* (1962); *You'll Excuse It Please, the Pencil* (1962).

KOZLENKO, WILLIAM (1908–). Editor, author of one-act plays. Editor: *Contemporary One-Act Plays* (1938); *The Best Short Plays of the Social Theatre* (1939); *Open Door* (one-act play, 1942). Compiler: *One Hundred Non-Royalty One-Act Plays* (1947). Editor, *One Act Play Magazine,* since 1937.

KOZLOFF, MAX (June 21, 1933–); b. Chicago, Ill. Art critic, author. *Jasper Jones* (1968); *Modern Art and the Process of Criticism* (1968).

KOZOL, JONATHAN (Sept. 5, 1936–); b. Boston, Mass. Teacher, author. *Death at an Early Age* (1967, National Book Award, 1968). Teacher, Boston Public Schools, 1964–65; Newton Public Schools, 1966–68.

KRAFT, JOSEPH (Sept. 4, 1924–); b. S. Orange, N.J. Journalist, author. *The Struggle for Algeria* (1961); *The Grand Design* (1962); *Profiles in Power* (1966). Syndicated columnist since 1963.

KRAMER, DALE (1911–Nov. 30, 1966). Author. *Heywood Broun* (1949); *Ross and the New Yorker* (1951); *The Heart of O. Henry* (1954); *Wild Jackasses: The American Farmer in Revolt* (1956); etc.

KRAMER, SAMUEL NOAH (Sept. 28, 1897–); b. in Russia. Assyriologist, author. Author or editor: *Lamentation over the Destruction of Ur* (1940); *Sumerian Literary Texts from Nippur* (1944); *From the Tablets of Sumer* (1956); *Sumerian Mythology* (1961); etc. Curator, tablet collections, University of Pennsylvania.

KRAMER, SIMON PAUL (Aug. 17, 1914–); b. Cincinnati, O. Consultant, author. *Lord Acton and the Present Crisis in Latin America* (1962); *The Last Manchu* (1967). Consultant on Latin American affairs, since 1962.

KRAMM, JOSEPH, b. South Philadelphia, Pa. Actor, director, playwright. *The Shrike* (prod. 1952; Pulitzer Prize for drama, 1952); *Giants, Sons of Giants* (prod. 1962).

KRANS, HORATIO SHEAFE (Dec. 9, 1872–July 28, 1952); b. Boston, Mass. Author. *Irish Life in Irish Fiction* (1903); *William Butler Yeats, and the Irish Literary Revival* (1904). Assoc. editor: *The World's Wit and Humor,* 10v. (1906).

KRAPP, GEORGE PHILIP (Sept. 1, 1872–Apr. 21, 1934); b. Cincinnati, O. Educator, author. *The Kitchen Porch* (1923); *America, the Great Adventure* (1924); *The English Language in America,* 2v. (1925); *The Knowledge of English* (1927); *Anglo-Saxon Reader* (1929); etc. Prof. English, Columbia University, 1910–34.

KRASNA, NORMAN (Nov. 7, 1909–); b. New York. Playwright. *Louder Please* (prod. 1931); *Small Miracle* (prod. 1934); *Dear Ruth* (prod. 1944); *John Loves Mary* (prod. 1947); *Time for Elizabeth* (with Groucho Marx, prod. 1948); *Kind Sir* (prod. 1953); *Who Was That Lady I Saw You With?* (prod. 1958); *Sunday in New York* (1961); *Love in E Flat* (1967); also screen plays.

KRASSNER, PAUL (Apr. 9, 1932–   ); b. Brooklyn, N.Y. *Impolite Interviews* (1961). Founder, *The Realist,* 1958; editor, since 1958.

KRAUS, ROBERT (June 21, 1925–   ); b. Milwaukee, Wis. Publisher, cartoonist, author. *Miranda's Beautiful Dream* (1964); *Juniper* (1965); *The First Robin* (1965); *Amanda Remembers* (1965); *The Little Giant* (1967); etc. Cartoonist, *New Yorker,* since 1952; founder, Windmill Books, 1966.

KRAUSE, HERBERT ARTHUR (May 25, 1905–); b. Fergus Falls, Minn. Educator, poet, novelist. *Wind Without Rain* (1939); *Neighbor Boy* (poems, 1939); *The Thresher* (1946); *Oxcart Trail* (1954). Head English dept., Augustana College, since 1938.

KRAUSE, LYDE FARRINGTON (b. 1864–); b. St. Croix, Danish W.I. Author. Pen name "Barbara Yechton." *Gentle Heart Stories* (1894); *Scaramouch* (1897); *Toinette* (1897); *A Young Savage* (1899); *Molly* (1902); *Two Young Americans* (1912); etc.

KRAUSS, RUTH (Mrs. Crocket Johnson); b. Baltimore, Md. Author. *The Carrott Seed* (1945); *Bears* (1948); *The Happy Day* (1949); *I Can Fly* (1950); *A Hole Is to Dig* (1952); *Monkey Day* (1957); *If Only* (poem, 1960); etc.

KRAVETZ, NATHAN (Feb. 11, 1921–   ); b. New York. Educator, author. *Two for a Walk* (1954); *A Horse of Another Color* (1962); *Tips to Teachers* (with Ted Gordon, 1962); *A Monkey's Tale* (1964); *The Dog on Ice* (with Muriel Farrell, 1967). Director, National Teachers' Corps, Hunter College, since 1966.

KREHBIEL, HENRY EDWARD (Mar. 10, 1854–Mar. 20, 1923); b. Ann Arbor, Mich. Music critic, author. *A Book of Operas* (1909); *Chapters of Opera* (1909); *Afro-American Folksongs* (1914); *A Second Book of Operas* (1917); *More Chapters on Opera* (1919). Editor: Alexander Wheelock Thayer's *The Life of Ludwig van Beethoven,* 3v. (1921). Music critic, New York *Tribune,* 1880–1923, succeeding John R. G. Hassard.

KRETZMANN, PAUL EDWARD (Aug. 24, 1883–); b. in Dearborn Co., Ind. Lutheran clergyman, author. *Christian Art* (1921); *Popular Commentary of the Bible,* 4v. (1921–24); *Heroes of Missions and Their Work* (1927); *The Mountain School* (1928); *Great Missionary Women* (1930); *The God of the Bible and other "Gods"* (1943); *Jesus Only* (sermons, 1955); etc. Prof. theology, Concordia Seminary, St. Louis, 1923–46.

KREY, AUGUST CHARLES (June 29, 1887–July 28, 1961); b. in Germany. Educator, author. *Founding of Western Civilization* (with G. C. Sellery, 1929); *The Meaning of the Humanities* (1938); etc. Editor: *The First Crusade* (1921); *History of Deeds Done Beyond the Sea* (with E. A. Babcock, 1943);

History and the Social Web (1955); *The First Crusade: The Accounts of Eye-Witnesses and Participants* (1958); etc. Prof. history, University of Minnesota, 1913–61.

KREY, LAURA [Lettie Smith] (Mrs. August Charles Krey) (Dec. 18, 1890–); b. Galveston, Tex. Novelist. *And Tell of Time* (1938); *On the Long Tide* (1940).

KREYMBORG, ALFRED (Dec. 10, 1883–Aug. 14, 1966); b. New York. Author. *Love and Life, and Other Studies* (1908); *Mushrooms* (poems, 1916); *Blood of Things* (poems, 1920); *Puppet Plays* (1923); *Troubadour* (autobiography, 1925); *Our Singing Strength: An Outline of American Poetry, 1620–1930* (1929); *Manhattan Men* (poems, 1929); *I'm No Hero* (1933); *The Four Apes, and Other Fables of Our Day* (1939); *Selected Poems, 1912–44* (1945); *Man and Shadow* (1946); *No More War and Other Poems* (1950); etc. Editor: *Others,* 3v. (1916–20); *The American Caravan,* 4v. (with others, 1927–31); *Lyric America: An Anthology of American Poetry, 1630–1930* (1930); *The New Caravan* (with others, 1936).

KRIEGER, LEONARD (Aug. 28, 1918–   ); b. Newark, N.J. Educator, author. *The German Idea of Freedom* (1957); *The Politics of Discretion* (1965); *History* (with J. Higham and F. Gilbert, 1965). Professor of history, University of Chicago, since 1962.

KRIEGER, MURRAY (Nov. 27, 1923–   ); b. Newark, N.J. Educator, author. *The New Apologists for Poetry* (1956); etc. Editor: *Eliseo Vivas, The Problems of Aesthetics* (with Eliseo Vivas, 1953); *Northrup Frye in Modern Criticism* (1966). Prof. English, University of Illinois, 1958–63; prof. literary criticism, University of Iowa, 1963–66; prof. English, University of California, at Irvine, since 1966.

KRISTELLER, PAUL OSKAR (May 22, 1905–); b. Berlin. Educator, author. *The Philosophy of Marsilio Ficino* (1943); *The Classics and Renaissance Thought* (1954); *Studies in Renaissance Thought and Letters* (1956); *Eight Philosophers of the Italian Renaissance* (1964); *Renaissance Thought II* (1965); *Renaissance Philosophy and the Medieval Tradition* (1966); etc. Philosophy dept., Columbia University, since 1939.

KROCK, ARTHUR (Nov. 16, 1886–); b. Glasgow, Ky. Journalist, author. *In the Nation* (1966); *Sixty Years on the Firing Line* (1968). Editor: *The Editorials of Henry Watterson* (1923). Washington correspondent, the New York *Times,* 1932–53; Washington commentator, since 1953.

KROEBER, ALFRED L[ouis] (June 11, 1876–Oct. 5, 1960); b. Hoboken, N.J. Anthropologist. *Anthropology* (1923); *Configurations of Culture Growth* (1944); *Nature of Culture* (1952); *Anthropology Today* (1953); *Style and Civilization* (1957); etc. Prof. anthropology, University of California, 1919–46.

KROEBER, THEODORA [Kracaw Brown] (Mrs. Alfred Louis Kroeber). Author. *The Inland Whale* (1959); *Ishi in Two Worlds* (1961).

KROLL, HARRY HARRISON (Feb. 18, 1888–); b. nr. Hartford City, Ind. Author. *Comparative Study of Southern Folk Speech* (1925); *The Cabin in the Cotton* (1931); *The Ghosts of Slave Driver's Bend* (1937); *The Usurper* (1941); *Waters over the Dam* (1944); *Lost Homecoming* (1950); *Summer Gold* (1955); *My Heart's in the Hills* (1956); *For Cloi, with Love* (1958); *Riders in the Night* (1965).

KRONENBERGER, LOUIS (Dec. 9, 1904–); b. Cincinnati, O. Drama critic, author. *The Grand Manner* (1929); *Kings and Desperate Men* (1942); *Grand Right and Left* (1952); *The Thread of Laughter: Chapters on English Stage Comedy* (1952); *Company Manners* (1954); *Marlborough's Duchess* (1958); *A Month of Sundays* (1961); *The Cart and the Horse* (1964). Editor: *An Anthology of Light Verse* (1935); *An Eighteenth Century Miscellany* (1936); *The Maxims of La Rouch-*

foucauld (1937); *Reader's Companion* (1945); *The Pleasure of Their Company* (1946); *G.B.S.: A Survey* (1953); *The Best Plays of 1960–1961* (1961); *Quality: Its Image in the Arts* (1969). Drama critic, *Time* magazine, 1938–61.

KROUT, CAROLINE VIRGINIA (1853–Oct. 9, 1931); b. Crawfordsville, Ind. Author. Pen name, "Caroline Brown." *Knights in Fustian: A War Time Story of Indiana* (1900); *On the We-a Trail* (1903); *Bold Robin and His Forest Rangers* (1905); *Dionis of the White Veil* (1911).

KROUT, JOHN ALLEN (Oct. 3, 1896–); b. Tiffin, O. Educator, author. *The Origins of Prohibition* (1925); *Annals of American Sport* (1929); *An Outline History of the United States,* 2v. (1934); *The Completion of Independence* (with D. R. Fox, 1944); *The Adventure of the American People* (with Henry F. Graff, 1959). Co-editor: *The Greater City* (with Allan Nevins, 1948). History dept., Columbia University, since 1922; dean, graduate faculty, 1949–63.

KRUTCH, JOSEPH WOOD (Nov. 25, 1893–May 22, 1970); b. Knoxville, Tenn. Educator, editor, literary critic, naturalist. *Our Changing Morals* (1925); *Edgar Allan Poe* (1926); *The Modern Temper* (1929); *Five Masters* (1930); *Experience and Art* (1932); *The American Drama Since 1918* (1939); *Samuel Johnson* (1944); *Henry David Thoreau* (1948); *The Twelve Seasons* (1949); *The Desert Year* (1952); *The Best of Two Worlds* (1953); *Modernism in Modern Drama* (1953); *The Measure of Man* (1954); *The Voice of the Desert* (1955); *The Great Chain of Life* (1957); *The Grand Canyon: Today and All Its Yesterdays* (1958); *Human Nature and the Human Condition* (1959); *The Gardener's World* (1959); *The Forgotten Peninsula* (1961); *More Lives Than One* (1962); *Herbal* (1965); *Even If You Do* (1967); *The Most Wonderful Animals That Never Were* (1969). Editor: *Representative American Dramas* (1941); *Selected Letters of Thomas Gray* (1952). Drama critic and assoc. editor, *The Nation,* 1924–32; editor, 1932–37; drama critic, 1937–52. Prof. English, Columbia University, 1937–52.

KUBIE, LAWRENCE S[chlesinger] (Mar. 17, 1896–); b. New York. Neurologist, psychiatrist. *Practical Aspects of Psychoanalysis* (1936); *Practical and Theoretical Aspects of Psychoanalysis* (1950); *Neurotic Distortion of the Creative Process* (1958). Prof. psychiatry, University of Maryland Medical School, since 1961.

KUBLY, HERBERT (Apr. 26, 1915–); b. New Glarus, Wis. Author. *Men to the Sea* (play, 1944); *Inherit the Wind* (play, 1946); *The Cocoon* (play, 1954); *American in Italy* (1955); *Beautiful Dreamer* (play, 1956); *Easter in Sicily* (1956); *Italy* (1961); *Switzerland* (1964); *Gods and Heroes* (1969).

KUGELMASS, JOSEPH ALVIN (Sept. 25, 1910–); b. New York. Author. *Louis Braille: Windows for the Blind* (1951); *Ralph J. Bunche* (1952); *History of the Institute for Advanced Studies* (1952); *J. Robert Oppenheimer and the Atomic Story* (1953); *Roald Amundsen: Saga of the Polar Seas* (1955); *Earl Warren: Crusader for the People* (1967).

KUH, KATHARINE (July 15, 1904–); b. St. Louis, Mo. Art curator. *Art Has Many Faces* (1951); *Léger* (1953); *The Artist's Voice* (1962); *Break-Up* (1963). With Chicago Art Institute, since 1937; curator of painting and sculpture, since 1957. Art critic, *Saturday Review,* since 1959.

KUHLMAN, AUGUSTUS FREDERICK (Sept. 3, 1889–); b. Hubbard, Ia. Librarian, bibliographer. Compiler: *A Guide to Material on Crime and Criminal Justice* (1929); and inventories of regional libraries. Assoc. director, University of Chicago libraries, 1929–36; librarian, Vanderbilt University, since 1936.

KUHN, FERDINAND (Apr. 10, 1905–). b. New York. Journalist. *Commodore Perry and the Opening of Japan* (1955); *The Story of the Secret Service* (1957); *Borderlands* (1962); *The Philippines* (1966). Staff, *New York Times,* 1925–40.

KUHN, RENE LEILANI (Mar. 2, 1932–); b. Honolulu, Hawaii. Novelist. *34 Charlton* (1945); *Cornelia* (1948).

KUHNS, OSCAR (Feb. 21, 1856–Aug. 20, 1929); b. Columbia, Pa. Educator, author. *The German and Swiss Settlements of Colonial Pennsylvania* (1901); *Dante and the English Poets from Chaucer to Tennyson* (1904); *The Great Poets of Italy* (1904); *Switzerland* (1910); *The Love of Books and Reading* (1910); *A One-Sided Autobiography* (1913); etc. Prof., Romance languages, Wesleyan University, 1890–1929.

KUIST, HOWARD TILMAN (July 30, 1895–May 14, 1964); b. Highland Park, Ill. Evangelical clergyman, author. *The Pedagogy of Saint Paul* (1925); *How to Enjoy the Bible* (1939); *These Words upon Thy Heart* (1947); *The Book of Jeremiah;* etc. Prof. Biblical theology, Princeton Theological Seminary, 1943–56.

KUMIN, MAXINE WINOKUR (June 6, 1925–); b. Philadelphia, Pa. Author. *Sebastian and the Dragon* (1960); *Halfway* (1961); *No One Writes a Letter to the Snail* (1962); *Archibald the Travelling Poodle* (1963); *Paul Bunyan* (1966); *The Passions of Uxport* (1968); *Wonderful Babies of 1809* (1968); *The Nightmare Factory* (1970).

KUMMER, CLARE [Rodman Beecher]. Song writer, playwright. *Good Gracious, Annabelle!* (prod. 1916); *The Rescuing Angel* (prod. 1917); *A Successful Calamity* (prod. 1917); *Be Calm, Camilla* (prod. 1918); *Rollo's Wild Oat* (prod. 1920); *Bridges* (prod. 1921); *Chinese Love* (prod. 1921); *The Robbery* (prod. 1921); *Pomeroy's Past* (prod. 1922); *Her Master's Voice* (1934); etc. Author of many songs, the best known of which is "Dearie" (1905). *See* Margaret G. Mayorga's *A Short History of the American Drama* (1934); Fred B. Millett's *Contemporary American Authors* (1940).

KUMMER, FREDERIC ARNOLD (Aug. 5, 1873–Nov. 22, 1943); b. Catonsville, Md. Novelist, playwright. Pen name, "Arnold Fredericks." Under own name: *Mr. Buttles* (prod. 1910); *The Green God* (1911); *The Brute* (1912); *The Diamond Necklace* (prod. 1912); *A Song of Sixpence* (1913); *The Painted Woman* (1917); *The Web* (1919); *The Bonehead* (prod. 1920); *The Pipes of Yesterday* (with Mary Christian, 1921); *Plaster Saints* (1922); *Ladies in Hades* (1928); *Maypoles and Morals* (1929); *Red Clay* (1933); *The Great Road* (1938); *The Captive* (prod. 1938); etc.; also under pen name: *One Million Francs* (1912); *The Ivory Snuff Box* (1912); *The Little Fortune* (1915); *The Blue Lights* (1915); *The Film of Fear* (1917); *The Mark of the Rat* (1929); *The Spanish Lady* (1933); etc.

KUNITZ, STANLEY J[asspon] (July 29, 1905–); b. Worcester, Mass. Poet, editor. *Intellectual Things* (1930); *Passport to the War* (1944); *Selected Poems* (1958); *Poems of John Keats* (1964); *The Testing-Tree* (1971). Editor or co-editor: *Living Authors* (under pen name "Dilly Tante," 1931); *Authors Today and Yesterday* (1933); *The Junior Book of Authors* (1934); *British Authors of the Nineteenth Century* (1936); *American Authors, 1600–1900* (1938); *Twentieth Century Authors* (1942); *British Authors Before 1800* (1952); *Twentieth Century Authors—First Supplement* (1955). With H. W. Wilson Co., 1928–43; director, poetry workshop, YMHA, New York, since 1958.

KUNSTLER, WILLIAM MOSES (July 7, 1919–); b. New York. Educator, lawyer, author. *Our Pleasant Vices* (1941); *The Law of Accidents* (1954); *First Degree* (1960); *Beyond a Reasonable Doubt* (1961); *The Case for Courage* (1962); *And Justice for All* (1963); *The Minister and the Choir Singer* (1964); *Deep in My Heart* (1966). Lecturer, The New School, since 1966. Defense attorney, trial of the Chicago Eight, 1969–70.

KUPFERBERG, TULI [Naphtali] (Sept. 28, 1923–); b. New York. Composer, singer, author. *Boating* (1959); *Selected Fruits and Nuts from One Crazy Month in Spring Not So Long Ago* (cartoons, 1959); *Snow Job: Poems, 1946–1959*

(1959); *Stimulants: An Exhibition* (1960); *Beatniks, or the War Against the Beats* (1961); *Kill for Peace* (1965); *1001 Ways to Beat the Draft* (with Robert Bashlow, 1966); *1001 Ways to Make Love* (1969); etc. Co-editor: *Children as Authors, a Big Bibliography* (1959). Composer, lyricist, and performer with The Fugs rock group: "Supergirl," "Seize the Day," "Nothing," "Kill for Peace," "Morning, Morning," "Life Is Strange," etc.

KURTZ, BENJAMIN PUTNAM (Dec. 12, 1878–Oct. 18, 1950); b. Maui, T.H. Educator, author. *Studies in the Marvellous* (1910); *Methods and Materials of Literary Criticism* (with Charles Mills Gayley, 1920); *Twelve Andamanese Songs* (1922); *Gifer the Worm* (1929); *The Pursuit of Death: A Study of Shelley's Poetry* (1933); *William Caxton* (1938); *Charles Mills Gayley* (biography, 1943); etc. English dept., University of California, 1903–49.

KURTZ, STEPHEN GUILD (Sept. 9, 1926–); b. Buffalo, N.Y. Historian, author. *The Presidency of John Adams* (1957); *America's Ten Greatest Presidents* (1960). Prof. history, College of William and Mary, since 1964.

KURTZMAN, HARVEY. Cartoonist, editor. *Playboy's Little Annie Fanny* (with Will Elder, 1966). Editor: *Who Said That?* (with others, 1962); *Fun and Games* (1965). Founder: *Mad*, 1952; *Trump*, 1957; *Help*, 1960.

KURZMAN, DAN (Mar. 27, 1922–); b. San Francisco, Cal. Journalist, author. *Kishi and Japan: The Search for the Sun* (1960); *Subversion of the Innocents* (1963); *Santo Domingo: Revolt of the Damned* (1965). Foreign correspondent, *Washington Post,* since 1962.

KUTTNER, HENRY. Author. *The Time Axis* (1948); *The Well of the Worlds* (1952); *Return to Otherness* (1961). Under pen name "Will Garth": *Dr. Cyclops; Lawless Guns.* Under pen name "Jack Vance": *The Dying Earth* (1950); *Vandals of the Void* (1953); *Big Planet* (1957); *The Dragon Masters* (1962); *The Star King* (1962); *The Killing Machine* (1964); *Space Opera* (1965); *The Palace of Love* (1967); *City of the Chasch* (1968); etc.

KYNE, PETER BERNARD (Oct. 12, 1880–Nov. 25, 1957); b. San Francisco, Calif. Novelist. *Cappy Ricks* (1916); *The Valley of the Giants* (1918); *Kindred of the Dust* (1920); *The Pride of Palomar* (1921); *The Go-Getter* (1922); *Cappy Ricks Retires* (1922); *Outlaws of Eden* (1930); *Thunder God* (1931); *Cappy Ricks Comes Back* (1934); *Dude Woman* (1940); etc.

L

LA BARGE, JOSEPH (Oct. 1, 1815–Apr. 3, 1899); b. St. Louis, Mo. Pioneer navigator of the Mississippi and a famous Indian trader. His adventures were recorded by Hiram Martin Chittenden in his *History of Early Steamboat Navigation on the Missouri River,* 2v. (1903).

LA BORDE, MAXIMILIAN (June 5, 1804–Nov. 6, 1873); b. Edgefield, S.C. Physician, author. *History of South Carolina College* (1859); *Story of Lethea and Verona* (1860); *A Suburban House and an Old Lady* (1861); etc.

LA FARGE, CHRISTOPHER [Grant] (Dec. 10, 1897–Jan. 5, 1956); b. New York. Artist, poet. *Hoxie Sells His Acres* (1934); *Each to the Other* (1939); *Poems and Portraits* (1940); *The Wilsons* (1941); *East by Southwest* (1944); *Mesa Verde* (1945); *The Sudden Guest* (1946); *All Sorts and Kinds* (1949); *Beauty for Ashes* (1953).

LA FARGE, JOHN (Mar. 31, 1835–Nov. 14, 1910); b. New York. Painter, author. *An Artist's Letters from Japan* (1897); *Great Masters* (1903); *Reminiscences of the South Seas* (1912); etc. See Royal Cortissoz's *John La Farge* (1911).

LA FARGE, JOHN (Feb. 13, 1880–Nov. 24, 1963); b. Newport, R.I. Roman Catholic clergyman, editor, author. *Jesuits in Modern Times* (1927); *Interracial Justice* (1937); *The Race Question and the Negro* (1943); *No Postponement* (1950); *The Manner Is Ordinary* (autobiography, 1954); *An American Amen* (1958); *Reflections on Growing Old* (1963). Staff, *America,* from 1926; editor in chief, 1944–48.

LA FARGE, OLIVER [Hazard Perry] (Dec. 19, 1901–Aug. 2, 1963); b. New York. Ethnologist, novelist. *Laughing Boy* (1929, Pulitzer prize novel, 1930); *Sparks Fly Upward* (1931); *Long Pennant* (1933); *All the Young Men* (1935); *The Enemy Gods* (1937); *The Copper Pot* (1942); *Raw Material* (1945); *Santa Eulalia* (1947); *The Eagle in the Egg* (1949); *Cochise of Arizona* (1953); *The Mother Ditch* (1954); *Behind the Mountains* (1956); *A Pictorial History of the American Indian* (1956); *A Pause in the Desert* (1957); *Santa Fe* (1959); *The Door in the Wall* (1965); *The Man with the Calabash Pipe* (1966); etc. Editor: *The Changing Indian* (1942).

LA FLESCHE, FRANCIS (1857?–Sept. 5, 1932); b. on Omaha Reservation, Neb. Omaha Indian, ethnologist, historian of the Omaha tribe. Adopted son of Alice Cunningham Fletcher (q.v.). *The Middle Five: Indian Boys at School* (1900); *The Omaha Tribe* (with Alice Cunningham Fletcher, 1907); etc.

LA FLESCHE, SUZETTE (Mrs. Thomas H. Tibbles) (1854–May 26, 1903); b. on Omaha Reservation, Neb., sister of Francis La Flesche. Omaha Indian, educator, lecturer, author. Indian name, "Inshtatheanba" or "Bright Eyes." Editor: *Ploughed Under: The Story of an Indian Chief* (anon., 1881).

LA GORCE, JOHN OLIVER (Sept. 22, 1879–Dec. 23, 1959); b. Scranton, Pa. Editor. *Book of Fishes* (rev. ed., 1939). With National Geographic Society, from 1905; pres., 1954–57; former editor, *National Geographic.*

LA MASTER, SLATER (June 25, 1890–); b. Big Bone Springs, Ky. Author. *Luckett of the Moon* (1927); *The Phantom of the Rainbow* (1928); *Memory Lane: Life Story of Gus Hill* (1933); *Cupid Napoleon* (1934); etc.

LA RUE, MABEL GUINNIP, b. Honesdale, Pa. Author. *Under the Story Tree* (1924); *The Billy Bang Book* (1927); *The Toy Mule* (1932); *The Tooseys* (1938); *Letter to Popsey* (1942); *Dicky and the Indians* (1948); *Tiny Toosey's Birthday* (1952); etc.

LA VARRE, WILLIAM JOHANNE (Aug. 4, 1898–); b. Richmond, Va. Journalist, author. *Up the Mazaruni* (1919); *Johnny Round the World* (1934); *Gold, Diamonds and Orchids* (1935); *Dry Guillotine* (1938); *Southward Ho!* (1940).

LABAREE, LEONARD WOODS (Aug. 26, 1897–); b. Urumia, Persia. Educator, editor, author. *Royal Government in America* (1930); *Milford, Connecticut* (1933); *Conservatism in Early American History* (1948). Co-editor: *Mr. Franklin* (1956). Editor, *Yale Historical Publications,* 40v. (1933–46). Hist. dept., Yale University, since 1924.

LACY, ALEXANDER LESLIE ALEXANDER. Author. *Cheer the Lonesome Traveler: The Life of W. E. B. du Bois* (1970); *The Rise and Fall of a Proper Negro* (autobiography, 1970).

LACY, ED. Author. *The Best That Ever Did It* (1955); *The Men from the Boys* (1956); *Lead with Your Left* (1957); *Be Careful How You Live* (1959); *Double Trouble* (1965); *The Hotel Dwellers* (1966); etc.

LACY, ERNEST (Sept. 19, 1863–June 17, 1916); b. Warren, Pa. Poet, playwright. *Chatterton* (prod. 1894); *Rinaldo* (prod. 1895); *The Ragged Earl* (prod. 1899); *Plays and Sonnets*

(1900); *The Bard of Mary Redcliffe* (drama in verse, 1910); etc.

LADD, ANNA COLEMAN (Mrs. Maynard Ladd) (July 15, 1878–June 3, 1939); b. Philadelphia, Pa. Sculptor, author. *Hieronymus Rides* (1912); *The Candid Adventure* (1912).

LADD, GEORGE TRUMBULL (Jan. 19, 1842–Aug. 8, 1921); b. Painesville, O. Educator, author. *Elements of Physiological Psychology* (1887); *Philosophy of Mind* (1891); *Philosophy of Knowledge* (1897); *A Theory of Reality* (1899); *Philosophy of Conduct* (1902); *Philosophy of Religion* (1905); *In Korea with Marquis Ito* (1908); *Rare Days in Japan* (1910); *The Secret of Personality* (1918); *Intimate Glimpses of Life in India* (1919); etc. Prof. philosophy, Yale, 1881–1905, where he founded the psychology laboratory.

LADD, JOSEPH BROWN (July 7, 1764–Nov. 2, 1786); b. Newport, R.I. Physician, poet. *The Poems of Arouet* (1786); etc. See *Literary Remains of Joseph Brown Ladd, M.D.,* ed. by Elizabeth Haskins (1832).

LADER, LAWRENCE (Aug. 6, 1919–   ); b. New York. Author. *Margaret Sanger* (1955); *The Bold Brahmins* (1961); *Abortion* (1966).

Ladies' Companion. New York. Magazine. Founded May, 1834, by William W. Snowden, who edited the first numbers. Mrs. Lydia H. Sigourney and Mrs. Emma C. Embury were later editors. Poe's "The Mystery of Marie Roget" appeared in it in 1842–43. Expired Oct., 1844.

Ladies Home Journal. Philadelphia, Pa. Monthly magazine. Founded Dec., 1883, by Cyrus H. K. Curtis. Mrs. Curtis (Kate Stanwood Pillsbury) edited the first few volumes under the pen name "Mrs. Louisa Knapp." She resigned in 1889 and Edward Bok became editor, remaining in that position for thirty years. Subsequent editors have included Loring A. Schuler, Charles Bruce Gould, and Beatrice Blackmar Gould. Curtiss Anderson became editor in 1962. Now edited by John Mack Carter. Noted for its short stories. Many American novels made their first appearance in its pages in serial form. Franklin Baldwin Wiley was literary editor, 1899–1930. Sold by Curtis Publishing Co. to Downe Communications, Inc. in 1968.

Ladies' Repository. Cincinnati, O. Fashion and literary monthly. Founded Jan., 1841, by Samuel Williams, and published by the Western agents of the Methodist Book concern. Alice and Phoebe Cary were frequent contributors. Emily C. Huntington, Virginia I. Townsend, Charles Nordhoff, and Frances E. Willard, founder of the Women's Christian Temperance Union, were also contributors. Expired Dec., 1876.

Lady Baltimore. Novel by Owen Wister (1906). Story laid in the South in a town called Kings Port. John Mayrant is about to marry Hortense Rieppe against the wishes of his family. The sudden appearance of a stranger called "Charley" and an incident on a yacht disrupt the match. John shares his wedding cake, called "Lady Baltimore," with Eliza La Heu.

Lady in the Dark. Play by Moss Hart (prod. 1941). The editor of a fashion magazine discovers through psychoanalysis the man she really loves. Famous for its dream sequences.

Lady of Fort St. John, The. Novel by Mary Hartwell Catherwood (1892). The scene is Acadia in 1645, Marie de la Tour defends in vain the fort against the attack of D'Aulnay de Charnisay who has come to confiscate her husband's estate.

Lady of Maine. Pen name of Sarah Sayward Barrell.

Lady of Massachusetts. Pen name of Sarah Sayward Barrell.

Lady of Quality, A. Novel by Frances Hodgson Burnett (1896). England in the reign of Queen Anne. Clorinda, a pathetic, mistreated waif, grows up to be a beautiful and refined woman. Her adventures are continued in a sequel, *His Grace of Osmonde* (1897).

Lady of the Aroostook, The. Novel by William Dean Howells (1879). Story of a young New England school teacher, Lydia Blood, who takes a trip to Venice, meeting on the ship a young man by the name of Staniford. Discovering in this farm girl all the qualities of a true lady, he marries her.

Lady or the Tiger, The. Novelette by Frank Stockton (1884). Story in which a prisoner has the choice of opening two doors. Behind one is a tiger, behind the other is a beautiful woman. If the prisoner opens the latter door, he will be pronounced innocent and will win a bride. The Princess, who loves the prisoner, discovers which door leads to the beautiful woman, her rival. She secretly advises her lover to open the right-hand door. The story ends there and the reader never knows whether the Princess doomed her lover to death or gave him his freedom.

LAFFAN, WILLIAM MACKAY (Jan. 22, 1848–Nov. 19, 1909); b. Dublin, Ire. Art critic, editor, author. *Engravings on Wood* (1887); *Oriental Ceramic Art* (1897); etc. Editor and owner, *Baltimore Daily Bulletin.* Drama and art critic, *New York Sun,* 1877–1909; became publisher of the *Sun* in 1884, and started the *Evening Sun* in 1887.

LAFORE, LAURENCE DAVIS (Sept. 15, 1917–); b. Narberth, Pa. Educator, author. *Modern Europe* (with Paul Beik, 1958); *Learner's Permit* (1962); *The Devil's Chapel* (1964); *The Long Fuse* (1965); *Philadelphia, the Unexpected City* (with Sarah L. Lippincott, 1965); *Stephen's Bridge* (1968). Prof. history, U. of Iowa, since 1969.

LAHEE, HENRY CHARLES (b. July 2, 1856); b. London. Author of books on music. *Famous Singers of To-Day and Yesterday* (1898); *Grand Opera in America* (1901); *Grand Opera Singers of To-Day* (1912); *Annals of Music in America* (1922); etc.

LAHR, JOHN. Drama critic, author. *Notes on a Cowardly Lion* (1969); *Up Against the Fourth Wall: Essays in Modern Theater* (1970). Drama critic, *Village Voice.*

LAING, ALEXANDER [Kinnan] (Aug. 7, 1903–); b. Great Neck, L.I., N.Y. Librarian, author. *Hanover Poems* (with Richmond Lattimore, 1927); *Fool's Errand* (poems, 1928); *End of Roaming* (1930); *The Sea Witch* (1933); *The Cadaver of Gideon Wyck* (1933); *The Flowering Thorn* (poems, 1933); *Wine and Physics* (1934); *Dr. Scarlett* (1936); *The Motives of Nicholas Holtz* (with Thomas Painter, 1936); *The Methods of Dr. Scarlett* (1937); *Sailing In* (1937); *Clipper Ship Men* (1944); *Jonathan Eagle* (1955); *Matthew Early* (1957); *American Sail* (1961); *Clipper Ships and their Makers* (1966); *The Pacific World* (1969); etc. Editor: *The Life and Adventures of John Nicol, Mariner* (1936); *The Haunted Omnibus* (1937). Asst. librarian, Dartmouth College, 1937–50.

LAISTNER, MAX LUDWIG WOLFRAM (Oct. 10, 1890–Dec. 10, 1959); b. London. Educator, author. *A Survey of Ancient History* (1929); *Thought and Letters in Western Europe, A.D., 500 to 900* (1931); *Greek History* (1932); *Christianity and Pagan Culture in the Later Roman Empire* (1951); *The Intellectual Heritage of the Early Middle Ages* (1957); etc. Prof. history, Cornell University, from 1925.

LAIT, JACK [Jacquin L.] (Mar. 13, 1883–Apr. 1, 1954); b. New York. Editor, author. *Help Wanted* (1914); *Short Stories* (1916); *One of Us* (1919); *Gus the Bus* (1920); *The White Way* (1921); *Spice* (1922); *Broadway Melody* (1928); *The Big House* (1929); *Gangster Girl* (1931); *Our Will Rogers* (1935); etc. Co-author (with Lee Mortimer): *New York: Confidential* (1948); etc. Editor, *New York Mirror,* 1936–1954.

LAKE, KIRSOPP (Apr. 7, 1872–Nov. 10, 1946); b. Southampton, England. Educator, author. *The Early Epistles of St. Paul* (1911); *The Beginnings of Christianity,* 5v. (with F. J. Foakes-Jackson, 1920–33); *Immortality and the Modern Mind* (1922); *The Religion of Yesterday and To-Morrow* (1925); etc. Editor: *Codex Sinaiticus,* 2v. (1911–22); and other biblical texts. Prof. Christian literature and history, Harvard, 1914–38.

Lakeside Monthly. Chicago, Ill. Magazine. Founded Jan., 1869, by H. V. Reed, as the *Western Monthly.* Name changed to the *Lakeside Monthly* in 1871. Edited by Reed until Apr., 1869, and then by Francis Fisher Browne. The publishing plant was destroyed in the Chicago fire of 1871, but in Jan., 1872 the famous "fire number" of the magazine appeared. Moses Coit Tyler was its chief literary critic. Expired Feb., 1874.

LALIBERTE, NORMAN (Nov. 24, 1925–   ); b. Worcester, Mass. Artist, author. *The History of the Cross* (1960); *Banners and Hangings* (1966); *Wooden Images* (1966); *Painting with Crayon* (1967); *Silhouettes* (1967).

LAMANTIA, PHILIP (1927–   ). Poet. *Erotic Poems* (1946); *Ekstasis* (1959); *Narcotica* (1959); *One Touch of the Marvelous* (1966); *Selected Poems, 1943–1966* (1967).

LAMAR, MIRABEAU BUONAPARTE (Aug. 16, 1798–Dec. 19, 1859); b. Louisville, Ga. Second president of the Republic of Texas, author. *The Life and Poems,* ed. by Philip Graham (1938); *The Papers of Mirabeau Buonaparte Lamar,* 6v. (1920–27); etc. *See* Herbert Pickens Gambrell's *Mirabeau Buonaparte Lamar, Troubadour and Crusader* (1934). Vice-President of Texas, 1836–38; President of Texas, 1838–41; U.S. Minister to Nicaragua and Costa Rica, 1858–59.

LAMB, HAROLD ALBERT (Sept. 1, 1892–Apr. 9, 1962); b. Alpine, N.J. Author. *Ghengis Khan* (1927); *Tamerlane* (1928); *The Crusades: Iron Men and the Saints* (1930); *The Crusades: The Flame of Islam* (1931); *Nur-Mahal* (1932); *Kirdy* (1933); *Omar Khayyam* (1934); *The March of the Barbarians* (1940); *Alexander of Macedon* (1946); *A Garden to the Eastward* (1947); *The March of Muscovy* (1948); *The City and the Tsar* (1948); *Suleiman the Magnificent* (1951); *Theodora and the Emperor* (1952); *Charlemagne: The Legend and the Man* (1954); *New Found World* (1955); *Constantinople* (1957); *Hannibal, One Man Against Rome* (1958); *Cyrus the Great* (1960); *Babur the Tiger* (1961).

LAMB, MARTHA JOANNA READE NASH (Aug. 13, 1829–Jan. 2, 1893); b. Plainsfield, Mass. Editor, author. *Spicey: A Novel* (1873); *History of the City of New York,* 2v. (1877–81); etc. Editor, *Magazine of American History,* 1883–93. Wrote several children's books.

LAMBERTON, JOHN PORTER (Oct. 22, 1839–July 26, 1917); b. Philadelphia, Pa. Librarian, editor, author. *English Literature* (1905); etc. Editor: *Historic Characters and Famous Events,* 12v. (1894–96); *Literature of All Ages,* 10v. (1897–99); *Literature of the Nineteenth Century* (1900); etc. With University of Pennsylvania Library, 1902–17.

Lamberton-Becker, May. See May Lamberton Becker.

Lambs, The. A New York Club. Organized 1874. Incorporated in 1877. Its membership is largely made up of actors, dramatists, artists, and patrons of the theatre. It stages an annual show, called the Lambs Gambol.

LAMERS, WILLIAM M[athias] (1900–). Author. *The Makings of a Speaker* (with M. E. Smith, 1937); *Thunder Maker: General Thomas Meagher* (1959); *The Edge of Glory* (1961); etc.

LAMON, WARD HILL (Jan. 6, 1828–May 7, 1893); b. in Frederick Co., Va. Law partner of Abraham Lincoln, author. *The Life of Abraham Lincoln* (1872); *Recollections of Abraham Lincoln, 1847–1865* (with Dorothy Lamon Teillard, 1911). He collected much material on Lincoln, including copies of the W. H. Herndon data. The Lamon collection is now in the Henry E. Huntington Library, San Marino, Calif.

LAMONT, CORLISS (Mar. 28, 1902–); b. Englewood, N.J. Author. *Issues of Immortality* (1932); *The Illusion of Immortality* (1935); *The Peoples of the Soviet Union* (1946); *Humanism as a Philosophy* (1949); *The Independent Mind* (1951); *Freedom Is As Freedom Does: Civil Liberties Today* (1956); *Freedom of Choice Affirmed* (1967); etc.

LAMONT, HAMMOND (Jan. 19, 1864–May 6, 1909); b. Monticello, N.Y. Educator, editor, author. *English Composition* (1906); etc. English depts., Harvard and Brown Universities. Managing editor, the *New York Evening Post,* 1900–06; editor, *The Nation,* 1906–09.

LAMONT, LANSING (Mar. 13, 1930–   ); b. New York. Journalist, author. *Day of Trinity* (1965). Reporter, *Time* magazine, since 1961.

LAMPELL, MILLARD (Jan. 10, 1919–); b. Paterson, N.J. Novelist, librettist, radio playwright. *The Lonesome Train* (cantata, music by Earl Robinson, 1943); *Morning Star* (cantata, 1946); *The Long Way Home* (1946); *The Hero* (1948); *Journey to the Cape* (1960); *The Inheritance* (1964); *The Idol* (1965); *The Whistle* (1966). Radio plays published in *Radio's Best Plays, Radio Drama in Action,* etc.

Lamplighter, The. Novel by Maria Susanna Cummins (1854), published anonymously. This story, very popular in its day, is about an old lamplighter, Trueman Flint, and Gerty, the waif of the streets whom he adopts into his humble family. Gerty rises to wealth and position. James A. Maitland's *The Watchman* (1855) is a sequel.

LAMPORT, FELICIA (Jan. 4, 1916–   ); b. New York. Author. *Mink on Weekdays* (1950); *Scrap Irony* (1961); *Cultural Slag* (1966).

LAMPREY, LOUISE (Apr. 17, 1869–Jan. 13, 1951); b. Alexandria, N.H. Author of children's books. *In the Days of the Guild* (1918); *Masters of the Guild* (1920); *The Alo Man* (1921); *Children of Ancient Britain* (1921); *Days of the Discoverers* (1921); *Children of Ancient Rome* (1922); *Days of the Colonists* (1922); *Days of the Commanders* (1923); *Children of Ancient Greece* (1924); *Days of the Pioneers* (1924); *Days of the Leaders* (1925); *Children of Ancient Egypt* (1926); *Children of Ancient Gaul* (1927); *The Tomahawk Trail* (1934); *The Story of Weaving* (1939); *The Story of Cookery* (1940); *Building a Republic* (1942); etc.

LAMPSON, ROBIN (Feb. 2, 1900–); b. Mokelunne Hill, Calaveras Co., Calif. Poet, novelist. *Laughter Out of the Ground* (novel in verse, 1935); *Terza Rima Sonnets* (1935); *Death Loses a Pair of Wings* (novel in verse, 1939); etc.

LAMSON, DAVID ALBERT, b. Cupertino, Calif. Author. *We Who Are About to Die* (1935); *Whirlpool* (1937); *Once in My Saddle* (1940).

LAMSON, ROY (Feb. 7, 1908–); b. New Haven, Conn. Educator. Compiler: *The Golden Hind* (with H. D. Smith, 1942); *Elizabethan and Shakespearean Musicke for the Recorder* (with Claude Simpson, 1941); *Renaissance England* (with H. D. Smith, 1956); etc. English dept., Williams College, 1938–57; Massachusetts Institute of Technology, since 1957.

LANCASTER, BRUCE (Aug. 22, 1896–June 29, 1963); b. Worcester, Mass. Novelist. *Wide Sleeve of Kwannon* (1938); *Bride of a Thousand Cedars* (with Lowell Brentano, 1939); *Guns of Burgoyne* (1939); *For Us the Living* (1940); *Bright to the Wanderer* (1942); *Trumpet to Arms* (1944); *The Scarlet Patch* (1947); *The Phantom Fortress* (1950); *Venture in the East* (1951); *The Secret Road* (1952); *Guns in the Forest* (1952); *The Blind Journey* (1953); *From Lexington to Liberty* (1955); *Roll, Shenandoah* (1956); *The American Revolution* (1957); *Night March* (1958); *Ticonderoga: The Story of a Fort* (1959); *Big Knife* (1963).

LANCASTER, HENRY CARRINGTON (Nov. 10, 1882–Jan. 29, 1954); b. Richmond, Va. Educator, author. *The French Tragi-Comedy* (1907); *A History of French Dramatic Literature in the Seventeenth Century,* 9v. (1929–42); *Saül* (1931); *The Comédie Française, 1680–1701* (1941); *1701–74* (1951); *French Tragedy in the Time of Louis XV and Voltaire* (1950); *Actors Roles at the Comédie Française* (1953); etc. Prof. French literature, Johns Hopkins University, 1919–52.

LANCASTER, LANE W. (Dec. 9, 1892–); b. Bellaire, O. Educator. *Government in Rural America* (1937); *Masters of Political Thought: Hegel to Dewey* (1959). Prof. political science, University of Nebraska, since 1930.

Land and the Book, The. By William McClure Thomson, 2v. (1858). Description of Palestine and Southern Syria in the form of a travel journal. It was extremely popular, and in England sold more copies than any other American book except *Uncle Tom's Cabin.*

Land of Little Rain, The. By Mary Austin (1903). Sketches of life and landscape in the Southwest.

Land of Poco Tiempo, The. By Charles F. Lummis (1893). A record of travel in New Mexico, steeped in folklore and legend.

Land We Love. Baltimore, Md. Monthly literary magazine. Founded May, 1865, by Gen. Daniel H. Hill. Contained many articles on the Civil War from the Southern point of view. Name changed in 1871 to the *Southern Magazine.* Expired 1875.

"Land Where We Were Dreaming, The." Best known poem of Daniel Bedinger Lucas, which he wrote on the occasion of Lee's surrender at Appomattox, Apr. 9, 1865.

LANDA, LOUIS A. (Nov. 6, 1901–); b. Hallettsville, Tex. Educator. *Swift and the Church of Ireland* (1954). Editor: *English Literature, 1660–1800: A Bibliography,* 2v. (with others, 1952); *Annual Eighteenth Century Bibliography* (1942–54); etc. English dept., Princeton University, since 1946.

LANDERS, ANN (July 4, 1918–   ); b. Sioux City, Ia. Columnist. *Since You Asked Me* (1962); *Teen-Agers and Sex* (1964). Syndicated columnist *Sun-Times* Syndicate-Field Enterprises, since 1955.

LANDES, DAVID SAUL (Apr. 29, 1924–   ); b. New York. Historian, author. *Bankers and Pashas* (1958); *Technological Change and Industrial Development in Western Europe, 1750–1914* (1965). Editor: *Reader in the Rise of Capitalism* (1965). Chairman, Council on Research Economic History, since 1963.

LANDI, ELISSA (Dec. 6, 1905–Oct. 21, 1948); b. (Elizabeth Marie Zanardi-Landi) Venice, Italy. Actress, lecturer, novelist. *Neilson* (1926); *The Helmers* (1929); *House for Sale* (1932); *The Ancestor* (1934).

LANDIS, FREDERICK (Aug. 18, 1872–Nov. 15, 1934); b. Seven Mile, Ohio. Congressman, novelist, playwright. *The Glory of His Country* (1910); *The Angel of Lonesome Hill* (1910); *The People Are Coming* (1913); etc. Editor, *The Hoosier Editor,* 1933–34.

LANDMAN, ISAAC (Oct. 24, 1880–Sept. 3, 1946); b. Sudilkov, Russia. Rabbi, editor, author. *Luzatto, First Hebrew Playwright* (1907); *Stories of the Prophets* (1912); etc. Editor: *Universal Jewish Encyclopedia* (1928–43); the *American Hebrew,* 1918–37.

LANDON, HERMAN (May 7, 1882–Mar. 22, 1960); b. Stockholm, Sweden. Author. *Hands Unseen* (1924); *Gray Magic* (1925); *The Green Shadow* (1927); *Death on the Air* (1929); *The Silver Chest* (1932); *The Picaroon, Knight-Errant* (1933); etc.

Landon, Louise. Pen name of Louise Platt Hauck.

LANDON, MARGARET [Dorothea Mortenson] (Sept. 7, 1903–); b. Somers, Wis. Author. *Anna and the King of Siam* (1944); *Never Dies the Dream* (1949); etc.

LANDON, MELVILLE DE LANCEY (Sept. 7, 1839–Dec. 6, 1910); b. Eaton, N.Y. Humorist. Pen name "Eli Perkins." *Saratoga in 1901* (1872); *Eli Perkins (At Large): His Sayings and Doings* (1875); *Wit, Humor, and Pathos* (1884); *Thirty*

Years of Wit and Reminiscences of Witty, Wise, and Eloquent Men (1891); etc.

LANDRY, ROBERT JOHN (June 14, 1903–); b. East Haddam, Conn. Editor. *Who, What, Why Is Radio?* (1942); *This Fascinating Radio Business* (1946); *The Performing Arts* (1967). Radio editor, *Variety,* 1932–42; now managing editor.

LANE, ARTHUR BLISS (June 16, 1894–Aug. 12, 1956); b. Bay Ridge, N.Y. Diplomat, author. *I Saw Poland Betrayed* (1948); etc.

LANE, CARL DANIEL (1899–). Author. *Boatowner's Sheet Anchor* (1941, rev. 1968); *The Fleet in the Forest* (1943); *River Dragon* (1948); *Black Tide* (1952); *Cruiser's Manual* (1969); etc.

LANE, ELINOR MACARTNEY (d. 1909); b. in Maryland. Author. *Mills of God* (1901); *Nancy Stair* (1904); *All for the Love of a Lady* (1906); *Katrine* (1909); *The Apple-Tree Cottage* (1910).

LANE, FERDINAND COLE (1885–); b. in Minnesota. Geographer, author. *The Mysterious Sea* (1947); *The World's Great Lakes* (1948); *The Earth's Grandest Rivers* (1949); *The Story of Mountains* (1950); *The Story of Trees* (1952); *All About the Sea* (1953); *All About the Insect World* (1954); *All About the Flowering World* (1956); etc.

LANE, FREDERIC CHAPIN (Nov. 23, 1900–); b. Lansing, Mich. Educator. *Venetian Ships and Shipbuilders of the Renaissance* (1934); *Andrea Barbarigo, Merchant of Venice, 1418–1449* (1944); *Venice and History* (1966). Editor, *Journal of Economic History,* 1943–51. History dept., Johns Hopkins University, since 1928.

LANE, ROSE WILDER (Dec. 5, 1887–Oct. 30, 1968); b. De Smet, S.D. Author. *Diverging Roads* (1919); *White Shadows in the South Seas* (with Frederick O'Brien, 1919); *The Making of Herbert Hoover* (1920); *The Peaks of Shala* (1923); *He Was a Man* (1925); *Hill-Billy* (1926); *Cindy* (1928); *Old Home Town* (1935); *Free Land* (1938); *Discovery of Freedom* (1943); etc.

LANG, DANIEL (May 30, 1915–); b. New York. Author. *Early Tales of the Atomic Age* (1948); *The Man in the Thick Lead Suit* (1954); *A Summer's Duckling* (1963); *An Inquiry into Enoughness* (1965); *Casualties of War* (1969). Staff writer, *New Yorker* magazine.

LANG, PAUL HENRY (Aug. 28, 1901–); b. Budapest. Musicologist, critic. *Music in Western Civilization* (1941); *Pictorial History of Music* (with O. L. Bettmann, 1960); *Creative World of Mozart* (1963); *Ceremony and Celebration* (1965); *George Frederic Handel* (1966); *Symphony 1800–1900* (1969); *Concerto 1800–1900* (1970). Editor: *The Musical Quarterly.* Music critic, *New York Herald Tribune,* since 1954. Prof. musicology, Columbia University, since 1933.

LANGDON, COURTNEY (Jan. 18, 1861–Nov. 19, 1924); b. Rome, of American parents. Educator, poet. *Sonnets on the War* (1917). Translator: *The Divine Comedy of Dante Alighieri,* 3v. (1918–21). Prof. Romance languages, Brown University, 1899–1924.

Langdon, Mary. Pen name of Mary Hayden Green Pike.

LANGDON, WILLIAM CHAUNCY (Apr. 21, 1871–Apr. 11, 1947); b. Florence, of American parents. Antiquarian, author. *Everyday Things in American Life,* 2v. (1937–41). Writer and director of many historical pageants.

LANGE, DIETRICH (June 2, 1863–Nov. 18, 1940); b. Bonstorf, Ger. Educator, naturalist, author of boys' books. *On the Trail of the Sioux* (1912); *Lost in the Fur Country* (1914); *The Lure of the Black Hills* (1916); *The Shawnee's Warning* (1919); *The Raid of the Ottawa* (1921); *Nature Trails* (1927); *Birds of the Midwest* (1939); etc.

LANGE, VICTOR (July 13, 1908-); b. Leipzig, Ger. Educator. Author: *Modern German Literature* (1945, rev. 1967); etc. Editor: Goethe's *The Sorrows of Young Werther* (1949); *German Short Stories* (1952); *Lessing's Hamburg Dramaturgy* (1962); *German Classical Drama* (1962); *American Scholarship in Modern Languages* (1962); *Modern Literature, Vol. 2* (Princeton Study Series) (1968); etc. German dept., Cornell University, 1938-57; Princeton University, since 1957.

LANGER, SUSANNE K[atherina Knaut] (1894-); b. New York. Philosopher, author. *The Practice of Philosophy* (1930); *Introduction to Symbolic Logic* (1937); *Philosophy in a New Key* (1942); *Feeling and Form* (1953); *Problems of Art* (1957); *Philosophical Sketches* (1962); *Mind: An Essay on Human Feeling, Vol. I* (1967). Philosophy dept., Columbia University, 1945-50. Prof. philosophy, Connecticut College, 1954-62. Emeritus since 1962.

LANGER, WILLIAM LEONARD (Mar. 16, 1896-); b. Boston, Mass. Historian. *The Franco-Russian Alliance* (1929); *European Alliances and Alignments* (1931); *The Diplomacy of Imperialism, 1890-1902,* 2v. (1935); *Our Vichy Gamble* (1947). Co-author, with S. Everett Gleason: *The Challenge of Isolation (1937-40)* (1952); *The Undeclared War (1940-41)* (1953). Editor: *Encyclopedia of World History* (1940); etc. History dept., Harvard University, since 1927.

LANGFORD, NATHANIEL PITT (Aug. 9, 1832—1911); b. Westmoreland, N.Y. Explorer, author. *Vigilante Days and Ways* (1890). With Washburn party that discovered geysers in Yellowstone region in 1870; superintendent, Yellowstone National Park, 1872-77.

LANGLEY, ADRIA [Locke], b. in Iowa. Author. *A Lion Is in the Streets* (1945).

Langley, Dorothy. Pen name of Dorothy Richardson.

LANGNER, LAWRENCE (May 30, 1890-Dec. 26, 1962); b. Swansea, Wales, came to the United States in 1911. Playwright. *The Family Exit* (prod. 1917); *Moses* (1924); *Henry Behave* (prod. 1926); *The Pursuit of Happiness* (with wife, Armina Marshall, under pen names, "Alan Child" and "Isabelle Loudon," prod. 1933); *On to Fortune* (with same, 1936); *Susanna and the Elders* (with same, 1939); *The Magic Curtain* (autobiography, 1951); *The Importance of Wearing Clothes* (1959); etc. Founder, Theatre Guild, New York, 1918, and director since 1919. Owner and director (with wife, Armina Marshall) of the Westport Country Playhouse, Westport, Conn. Founder, American Shakespeare Festival Theater and Academy, Stratford, Conn., 1950. *See* Walter Prichard Eaton's *The Theatre Guild* (1929).

LANGSTAFF, JOHN MEREDITH (Dec. 24, 1920-); b. Brooklyn, N.Y. Musician, author. *Frog Went a-Courtin'* (1955); *Over in the Meadow* (1957); *Swapping Boy* (1960). Compiler: *On Christmas Day in the Morning* (1959); *Ol' Dan Tucker* (1963); *Hi Ho the Rattlin' Bog and other Folk Songs for Group Singing* (1969).

Language as Gesture. By R. P. Blackmur (1952). Twenty-one critical essays about poetry.

Language in Thought and Action. By S. I. Hayakawa (rev. ed., 1949). One of the most influential works of semantic analysis in wide circulation. Brings to light the need for social action through the understanding of meaning in language.

LANHAM, EDWIN [Moultrie] (Oct. 11, 1904-); b. Weatherford, Tex. Novelist. *Sailors Don't Care* (1930); *The Wind Blew West* (1935); *Another Ophelia* (1938); *The Stricklands* (1939); *Thunder in the Earth* (1941); *Slug It Slay* (1946); *Politics Is Murder* (1947); *One Murder Too Many* (1952); *Death of a Corinthian* (1953); *Death in the Wind* (1955); *Murder on My Street* (1958); *Double Jeopardy* (1959); *Six Black Camels* (1961); *Passage to Danger* (1962); *Monkey on a Chain* (1963); *Speak Not Evil* (1964); *The Paste-Pot Man* (1967); etc.

Lania, Lee. Pen name of Lazar Herrmann.

LANIER, CLIFFORD ANDERSON (Apr. 24, 1844-Nov. 3, 1908); b. Griffin, Ga., brother of Sidney Lanier. Author. *Thorn-Fruit* (1867); *Apollo & Keats on Browning: A Fantasy; and Other Poems* (1902); *Sonnets to Sidney Lanier, and Other Lyrics* (1915); etc. Several poems written jointly with his brother are included in the latter's *Poems* (1884).

LANIER, HENRY WYSHAM (June 1873-May 10, 1958); b. Milledgeville, Ga., son of Sidney Lanier. Editor, publisher, author. *The Romance of Piscator* (1904); *O Rare Content* (1933); *A. B. Frost* (1933); *Secret Life of a Secret Agent* (1938); *The First English Actresses* (1942); *Greenwich Village: Today and Yesterday* (1949). Editor: *The Book of Bravery,* 3 series (1918-20); *The Book of Giants* (1923). Editor, the *Golden Book Magazine,* 1925-28. With Charles Scribner's Sons, 1896-97; Doubleday Page & Co., 1900-12.

LANIER, SIDNEY (Feb. 3, 1842-Sept. 7, 1881); b. Macon, Ga. Critic, musician, poet, novelist. *Tiger-Lilies* (1867); *Poems* (1876); *The Science of English Verse* (1880); *The English Novel* (1883); *Poems* (1884); *Music and Poetry* (1898); *Bob: The Story of Our Mocking Bird* (1899); *Letters* (1899); *Retrospect and Prospect* (1899); *Shakspeare and His Forerunners* (1902); *Poem Outlines* (1908); etc. Editor: *The Boy's Froissart* (1879); *The Boy's King Arthur* (1880); *The Boy's Mabinogion* (1881); *The Boy's Percy* (1882). His best known poems are "The Song of the Chattahoochee," "Sunrise," and "The Marshes of Glynn." *See* Edwin Mims's *Sidney Lanier* (1905); Aubrey H. Starke's *Sidney Lanier* (1932); Lincoln Lorenz's *The Life of Sidney Lanier* (1935); Edwin R. Coulson's *Sidney Lanier* (1941).

LANIGAN, GEORGE THOMAS (Dec. 10, 1845-Feb. 5, 1886); b. St. Charles, P.Q. Journalist, humorist. *Canadian Ballads* (1864); *Fables by G. Washington Aesop* (1878); etc. Best known for his "Akhoond of Swat" and "The Amateur Orlando." On staff *New York World,* 1874-83.

LANKES, JULIUS J. (Aug. 31, 1884-Apr. 22, 1960); b. Buffalo, N.Y. Illustrator, author. *A Woodcut Manual* (1932). Illustrator of Robert Frost's *New Hampshire,* Selma Lagerlöf's *Marbacka,* Lizette Woodworth Reese's *A Victorian Village,* Roark Bradford's *John Henry,* etc.

LANMAN, CHARLES (June 14, 1819-Mar. 4, 1895); b. Monroe, Mich. Explorer, librarian, artist, author. *Essays for Summer Hours* (1842); *Letters from a Landscape Painter* (1845); *A Summer in the Wilderness* (1847); *Letters from the Alleghany Mountains* (1849); *Haw-ho-no; or, Records of a Tourist* (1850); *Adventures in the Wilds of America* (1854); *Biographical Annals of the Civil Government of the United States* (1887); etc. Librarian of House of Representatives, and secretary to Daniel Webster.

LANMAN, CHARLES ROCKWELL (July 8, 1850-Feb. 20, 1941); b. Norwich, Conn. Educator, Orientalist, author. *Sanskrit Reader* (1884); *Beginnings of Hindu Pantheism* (1890); etc. Editor, *Harvard Oriental Series,* etc. Prof. Sanskrit, Harvard University, 1880-1941.

Lanny Budd. Hero of a series of novels by Upton Sinclair. *World's End* (1940); *Between Two Worlds* (1941); *Dragon's Teeth* (1942); *Wide Is the Gate* (1943); *Presidential Agent* (1944); *Dragon Harvest* (1945); *A World to Win* (1946); *Presidential Mission* (1947); *One Clear Call* (1948); and *O Shepherd, Speak!* (1949). These novels describe Lanny Budd's meetings with the foremost historical personages in international politics during the period from 1913 to the end of World War II. The hero serves to explain Sinclair's attitudes toward world events during this period of world crises.

LANSDALE, MARIA HORNOR (b. 1860); b. Philadelphia, Pa. Author. *Paris: Its Sites, Monuments and History* (1899); *Scotland, Historic and Romantic* (1901); *The Châteaux of Touraine* (1906).

LANSING, MARION FLORENCE (June 10, 1883–); b. Waverley, Mass. Author. *The Story of the Great Lakes* (with Edward Channing, 1907); *Life in the Greenwood* (1909); *Great Moments in Science* (1926); *Great Moments in Exploration* (1928); *Man's Long Climb* (1933); *Mary Lyon through Her Letters* (1937); *Liberators and Heroes of South America* (1941); *Calling South America* (1945); *Makers of the Americas* (1947); *America in the World* (1949); *Liberators and Heroes of the West Indian Islands* (1953); *When Washington Traveled* (1954); etc. Editor: *The Open Road Library,* 7v. (1907–12); *The New Wonder World,* 11v. (1932); etc.

LANSING, ROBERT (Oct. 17, 1864–Oct. 30, 1928); b. Watertown, N.Y. Cabinet officer, author. *The Peace Negotiations: A Personal Narrative* (1921); *The Big Four and Others of the Peace Conference* (1921); *Notes on Sovereignty* (1921). Secretary of State, 1915–20.

LAPIERE, RICHARD TRACY (Sept. 15, 1899–); b. Beloit, Wis. Educator, author. *Son of Han* (1937); *Collective Behavior* (1938); *When the Living Strive* (1941); *Sociology* (1946); *A Theory of Social Control* (1954); *The Freudian Ethic* (1959); *Social Change* (1965). Sociology dept., Stanford University, since 1932.

LAPP, RALPH E[ugene] (Aug. 24, 1917–); b. Buffalo, N.Y. Physicist, author. *Must We Hide?* (1949); *The New Force* (1953); *Nuclear Radiation Physics* (1954); *Atoms and People* (1956); *The Voyage of the Lucky Dragon* (1958); *Roads to Discovery* (1960); *Man and Space* (1961); *Kill and Overkill* (1962); *Matter* (1963); *The New Priesthood* (1965); *The Weapons Culture* (1968); etc.

LAPRADE, WILLIAM THOMAS (Dec. 27, 1883–); b. in Franklin Co., Va. Educator, author. *England and the French Revolution* (1909); *British History for American Students* (1926); etc. Editor, *South Atlantic Quarterly,* since 1944. Prof. history, Duke University, 1909–53. Emeritus since 1953.

LAQUEUR, WALTER Z[e'ev] (Mar. 26, 1921–); b. Breslau, Germany. Educator, author. *Communism and Nationalism in the Middle East* (1956); *The Soviet Union and the Middle East* (1959); *Russia and Germany* (1965); *The Fate of the Revolution* (1967). Editor: *The Future of Communist Society* (with Leopold Labedz, 1962); *Literature and Politics in the Twentieth Century* (with G. L. Mosse, 1968); *The Israel-Arab Reader: A Documentary History of the Middle East Conflict* (1969).

LARCOM, LUCY (Mar. 5, 1824–Apr. 17, 1893); b. Beverly, Mass. Poet, editor, author. *Similitudes* (1854); *Poems* (1869); *Wild Roses of Cape Ann* (1880); *A New England Girlhood Outlined from Memory* (1889); etc. Compiler, *Child Life* (with John G. Whittier, 1871); *Songs of Three Centuries* (with same, 1883); etc. Editor, *Our Young Folks,* 1865–73. Among her best known poems are "Hannah Binding Shoes" and "Call to Kansas."

LARDNER, JOHN [Abbott] (May 4, 1912–Mar. 24, 1960); b. Chicago, Ill., son of Ring Lardner. Author. *The Crowning of Technocracy* (1933); *The Yanks in the Pacific* (1943); *It Beats Working* (1947); *White Hopes and Other Tigers* (1951); *Strong Cigars and Lovely Women* (1951). With *New York Herald Tribune,* 1931–33; sports columnist, North American Newspaper Alliance, 1933–48; columnist, *Newsweek,* 1939–57; critic and reviewer, *New Yorker,* 1957–60. See Roger Kahn's *The World of John Lardner* (1961).

LARDNER, REX (Sept. 3, 1881–June 23, 1941); b. Niles, Mich., brother of Ring Lardner. Journalist, editor. *Out of the Bunker and Into the Trees* (1961); *The Lardner Report* (1961). On editorial staff of *Liberty,* and *Cosmopolitan.* With Chicago *Inter-Ocean* for many years, and on editorial staff of the *New York Times,* 1929–41.

LARDNER, RING[gold] W[ilmer] (Mar. 6, 1885–Sept. 25, 1933); b. Niles, Mich. Humorist. *Bib Ballads* (1915); *You Know Me Al* (1916); *Gullible's Travels* (1917); *Regular Fel-*

lows I Have Met (poems, 1919); *The Big Town* (1921); *How to Write Short Stories* (1924); *The Love Nest, and Other Stories* (1926); *The Story of a Wonder Man* (autobiography, 1927); *Round Up* (1929); *June Moon* (with George S. Kaufman, prod. 1929); etc. See Fred B. Millett's *Contemporary American Authors* (1940); Donald Elder's *Ring Lardner* (1956).

LARIAR, LAWRENCE (Dec. 25, 1908–); b. Brooklyn, N.Y. Cartoonist, editor, author. *Cartooning for Everybody* (1941); *Death Paints the Picture* (1943); *Army Fun Book* (1943); *Oh! Dr. Kinsey* (1953); *You've Got Me in Stitches* (1954); *Hunt and Be Damned* (1956); etc. Under pen name "Adam Knight": *Kiss and Kill* (1953); etc. Editor: *Bed and Bored* (1945); *Easy Way to Cartooning* (1950); *The Salesman* (1955); *Best Cartoons of the Year,* series since 1942; *The Teen Scene* (1966); etc. Free lance illustrator and political cartoonist since 1933.

Lark, The. San Francisco, Calif. A bibelot. Founded May, 1895, by Gelett Burgess and Bruce Porter. Burgess's celebrated "Purple Cow" appeared in it in 1895. Expired Apr., 1897.

LARKIN, OLIVER WATERMAN (Aug. 17, 1896–); b. Medford, Mass. Educator, author. *Art and Life in America* (1949, rev. 1960; Pulitzer Prize for history, 1949); *Samuel F. B. Morse* (1954); *Daumier: A Man of His Time* (1966).

LARNED, AUGUSTA (b. Apr. 16, 1835). b. Rutland, N.Y. Suffragist, poet, author of children's books. The *Home Story* series, 6v. (1873); *Old Tales Retold from Grecian Mythology* (1877); *Tales from the Norse Grandmother* (1881); *In Woods and Fields* (poems, 1895); etc. Wrote the *Roundabout Road* series for the New York *Evening Post.*

LARNED, JOSEPHUS NELSON (May 11, 1836–Aug. 15, 1913); b. Chatham, Ont. Librarian, editor, author. *Talks about Labor* (1877); *Books, Culture and Character* (1906); *A Study of Greatness in Men* (1911); *A History of Buffalo* (1911). Compiler: *History for Ready Reference,* 5v. (1894–95); *History of the World* (1915); *The Literature of American History: A Bibliographical Guide* (1902); etc. Librarian, Buffalo Public Library, 1877–97. On editorial staff, the *Buffalo Express,* 1859–72.

LARNER, JEREMY (Mar. 20, 1937–   ); b. Olean, N.Y. Author. *Drive, He Said* (1964); *The Addict in the Street* (with Ralph Tefferviller, 1965); *The Answer* (1968); *Poverty: Views from the Left* (with Irving Howe, 1969); *Nobody Knows: Reflections on the McCarthy Campaign of 1968* (1970).

LARRABEE, ERIC (Mar. 6, 1922–); b. Melrose, Mass. Editor. *The Self-Conscious Society* (1960); *Museums and Education* (1968). Editor: *American Panorama* (1957); *Mass Leisure* (with Rolf Meyersohn, 1958). Editorial consultant for Doubleday & Co. 1964. Associate editor, *Harper's,* 1946–58; executive editor, *American Heritage,* since 1958.

LARRABEE, HAROLD ATKINS (Aug. 20, 1894–); b. Melrose, Mass. Educator. *What Philosophy Is* (1928); *Rhymes about College* (1936); *Reliable Knowledge* (1945); *Senation: The Origin of Life* (1960). Editor: *Selections from Bergson* (1949); *Bentham's Handbook of Political Fallacies* (1952). Philosophy dept., Union College, since 1925.

Larrimore, Lida. See Lida Larrimore Turner.

"Lars; A Pastoral of Norway." Poem by Bayard Taylor (1893). Norse adventure tale, featuring a thrilling knife duel between doughty warriors.

LARSEN, HANNA ASTRUP (Sept. 1, 1873–Dec. 3, 1945); b. Decorah, Ia. Editor, author. *Knut Hamsun* (1922); *Selma Lagerlöf* (1935); etc. Editor: *Told In Norway* (1927); *Sweden's Best Stories* (1928); *Denmark's Best Stories* (1928); etc. Translator of major works of Jens Peter Jacobsen: *Marie*

Grubbe (1917); *Niels Lyhne* (1919). Translator: *Twelve Stories* (by Steen S. Blicher, 1945). Lit. editor, *American Scandinavian Review,* New York, 1913–21; editor, from 1921.

LARSEN, NELLA. Author. *Quicksand* (1928); *Passing* (1929).

LARSON, ARTHUR (July 4, 1910–); b. Sioux Falls, S.D. Educator, author. *The Law of Workmen's Compensation,* 2v. (1952); *Know Your Social Security* (1955); *A Republican Looks at His Party* (1956); *What We Are For* (1959); *When Nations Disagree* (1961); *Preventing World War III: Some Proposals* (1962); *A Warless World* (1964); *Eisenhower: The President Nobody Knew* (1968). Co-author: *Sovereignty Within the Law* (with C. W. Jenks and others, 1965); *Vietnam and Beyond* (with Don R. Larson, 1965). Director, U.S. Information Agency, 1956–57. Prof. law, Duke University, since 1958.

LASCH, CHRISTOPHER (June 1, 1932–   ); b. Omaha, Neb. Educator, author. *The American Liberals and the Russian Revolution* (1962); *The New Radicalism in America* (1965); *The Agony of the American Left* (1969). Prof. history, Northwestern University, since 1966.

LASKY, JESSE L[enard] JR. (Sept. 19, 1910–); b. New York. Novelist. *No Angels in Heaven* (1938); *Spindrift* (1948); *Naked in a Cactus Garden* (1961).

LASKY, VICTOR (Jan. 7, 1918–   ); b. Liberty, N.Y. Columnist, author. *Seeds of Treason* (with Ralph de Toledano, 1950); *J.F.K., The Man and the Myth* (1963); *The Ugly Russian* (1965); *Robert F. Kennedy: The Myth and the Man* (1968); *Arthur J. Goldberg: The Old and the New* (1970). Editor: *The American Legion Reader* (1953). News Columnist, North American Newspaper Alliance, since 1962.

LASSWELL, HAROLD DWIGHT (Feb. 13, 1902–); b. Donnellson, Ill. Political scientist. *Propaganda Technique in the World War* (1927); *Psychopathology and Politics* (1930); *Politics: Who Gets What, When, How* (1936); *Democracy Through Public Opinion* (1941); *Power and Personality* (1948); *National Security and Individual Freedom* (1950); *World Revolution of Our Time* (1951); *World Politics and Personal Insecurity* (1965); *The Sharing of Power in a Psychiatric Hospital* (with R. Rubenstein and others, 1966); *Language of Politics: Studies in Qualitative Semantics* (with others, 1968). Editor: *Propaganda and Promotional Activities* (1969); etc. Dept. of political science, University of Chicago, 1922–38; prof. law, Yale University, since 1946.

LASSWELL, MARY [Clyde Grayson Lubbock] (Feb. 8, 1905–); b. Glasgow, Scot. *Suds in Your Eye* (1942); *Mrs. Rasmussen's Book of One-Arm Cookery* (1946); *Bread for the Living* (1948); *Wait for the Wagon* (1951); *Tooner Schooner* (1953); *I'll Take Texas* (with Bob Pool, 1958); *John Henry Kirby, Prince of the Pines* (1967); etc.

Last Day in the Field, The. Short story by Caroline Gordon (1935).

Last Exit to Brooklyn. By Hubert Selby, Jr. (1965). Six short stories set in the wastelands and slum areas of Brooklyn. The themes and moods are underlined by sexual aggression and physical violence.

Last Frontier, The. By Howard Fast (1941).

"Last Leaf, The." Poem by Oliver Wendell Holmes (1831). Inspired by the sight of Major Thomas Melville, of Boston, dressed in knee breeches and a cocked hat, after such costume had been outmoded.

Last Mile, The. Play by John Wexley (prod. 1930), expanded from an earlier one-act play, *Rules.* Story of a prison mutiny fomented by Killer Mears, who dies in the attempt.

Last of the Mohicans, The. Novel by James Fenimore Cooper (1826). A chronicle of the author's favorite character, Natty

Bumppo, who in this novel is called Hawkeye. Cora and Alice, daughters of Colonel Monroe, fleeing from besieged Fort William Henry, are to be betrayed by their guide, but Hawkeye, Chingachgook and Uncas, save their lives. In a later capture, Cora is slain.

Last of the Provincials, The. By Maxwell Geismar (1942). A study of the American novel between World Wars I and II.

Last Puritan, The. Novel by George Santayana (1936). A philosophical narrative of two generations of Boston aristocrats, showing the slow decay of a way of life which had flourished on Beacon Hill for over a hundred years. Cf. John P. Marquand's *The Late George Apley* (1937).

Last Time I Saw Paris, The. By Elliot Paul (1942). Paris through the eyes of a long-time American resident.

Last Tycoon, The. Novel by F. Scott Fitzgerald (1941). About a motion-picture producer. Unfinished at the author's death in 1940.

"Last Walk in Autumn, The." Poem by John Greenleaf Whittier (1857).

Last Will and Testament, A. *See* Williston Fish.

Last Words, Real and Traditional, of Distinguished Men and Women, The. By Frederic Rowland Marvin (1901).

Late George Apley, The. Novel by John P. Marquand (1937). A satire on the traditional, conventional life of the Boston brahmins as represented in the person of George Apley, whose habits and sayings are herein recorded.

LATHAM, EARL (Oct. 28, 1907–); b. New Bedford, Mass. Political scientist. *Group Basis of Politics: A Study in Basing-Point Legislation* (1952); *The Politics of Railroad Coordination, 1933–36* (1959); *Teaching Political Science* (1965); *The Communist Controversy in Washington* (1966, received David Demarest Lloyd prize from Harry S. Truman Library Institute, 1967). Editor: *Philosophy and Policies of Woodrow Wilson* (1958). Political science dept., Amherst College, since 1948.

LATHAM, HAROLD STRONG (Feb. 14, 1887–Mar. 6, 1969); b. Marlboro, Conn. Editor, author. *Under Orders* (1918); *Marty Lends a Hand* (1919); *Jimmy Quigg, Office Boy* (1920); *At the Sign of the Feather* (1924); *My Life in Publishing* (1965); etc. With The Macmillan Co., New York, since 1909; head of trade dept., 1919–52.

LATHAM, JEAN LEE (Apr. 19, 1902–); b. Buckhannon, W. Va. Author. *The Blue Teapot* (play, 1932); *Do's and Don'ts of Drama* (1935); *Señor Freedom* (play, 1941); *The Nightmare* (play, 1953); *The Story of Eli Whitney* (1953); *Carry On, Mr. Bowditch* (1955); *This Dear-Bought Land* (1957); *On Stage, Mr. Jefferson!* (1958); *Young Man in a Hurry: The Story of Cyrus W. Field* (1958); *The Story of Eli Whitney* (1963); *Sam Houston: Hero of Texas* (1965); *Anchors Aweigh: The Story of David G. Farragut* (1968); etc.

LATHBURY, MARY ARTEMISIA (Aug. 10, 1841–Oct. 20, 1913); b. Manchester, N.Y. Artist, poet, hymn writer. *Fleda and the Voice* (1876); *Out of Darkness into Light* (1878); *Seven Little Maids* (1882); *Idyls of the Months* (1885); *From Meadow Sweet to Mistletoe* (1888); etc. Her best known hymns are "Break Thou the Bread of Life," and "Day is Dying in the West."

LATHROP, DOROTHY P[ulis] (Apr. 16, 1891–); b. Albany, N.Y. Author and illustrator. *The Fairy Circus* (1931); *The Little White Goat* (1933); *The Lost Merry-Go-Round* (1934); *Who Goes There?* (1935); *Bouncing Betty* (1936); *The Colt From Moon Mountain* (1941); *Puppies for Keeps* (1943); *Angel in the Woods* (1947); *Let Them Live* (1951); *The Littlest Mouse* (1955); *Follow the Brook* (1960); *Dog in the Tapestry Garden* (1962); *Let Them Live* (1966); etc. Illustrator of Walter de la Mare's *Crossings;* W. H. Hudson's *A Little*

Boy Lost; Jean Ingelow's *Mopsa the Fairy;* Rachel Field's *Hitty,* Sara Teasdale's *Stars To-night,* etc.

LATHROP, GEORGE PARSONS (Aug. 25, 1851–Apr. 19, 1898); b. Honolulu, T.H. Editor, author. *Rose and Roof-Tree* (poems, 1875); *A Study of Hawthorne* (1876); *A Masque of Poets* (1877); *An Echo of Passion* (1882); *In the Distance* (1882); *Spanish Vistas* (1883); *Dreams and Days* (poems, 1892); etc. Editor, *Boston Sunday Courier,* 1877–79; asst. editor, *Atlantic Monthly,* 1875–77; etc. Founder, American Copyright League, 1883.

LATHROP, JOHN (Jan. 13, 1772–Jan. 30, 1820; b. Boston, Mass. Lawyer, poet. *The Speech of Caunonicus* (Calcutta, 1802, Boston, 1803). Contributed series of essays, "The Moral Censor" to the *Polyanthos,* 1812–14.

LATHROP, ROSE HAWTHORNE (Mother Mary Alphonsa) (May 20, 1851–July 9, 1926); b. Lenox, Mass., daughter of Nathaniel Hawthorne. Philanthropist, author. *Along the Shore* (poems, 1888); *A Story of Courage* (with George Parsons Lathrop, 1894); *Memories of Hawthorne* (1897); etc. Founder, the Servants of Relief for Incurable Cancer, and of their Rosary Hill Home, Hawthorne, N.Y. *See* James Joseph Walsh's *Mother Alphonsa* (1930); J. B. Code's *Great American Foundress* (1929).

LATIMER, JONATHAN WYATT (Oct. 23, 1906–); b. Chicago, Ill. Author. *Murder in the Madhouse* (1935); *The Lady in the Morgue* (1936); *The Dead Don't Care* (1937); *Red Gardenias* (1939); *Sinners and Shrouds* (1955); *Black Is the Fashion for Dying* (1959); *The Mink-Lined Coffin* (1960); etc.

LATIMER, MARY ELIZABETH WORMELEY (July 26, 1822–Jan. 4, 1904); b. London. Author. *Amabel: a Family History* (1853); *Our Cousin Veronica* (1855); *France in the Nineteenth Century* (1892); etc.

Latin Quarter. Section around Telegraph Hill, in San Francisco. It is filled with foreign restaurants and is a gourmet's paradise.

LATOURETTE, KENNETH SCOTT (Aug. 9, 1884–Dec. 24, 1968); b. Oregon City, Ore. Baptist clergyman, educator, author. *Development of China* (1917); *Development of Japan* (1918); *A History of Christian Missions in China* (1929); *A History of the Expansion of Christianity* 7v. (1937–45); *Anno Domini* (1940); *Prospect for Christianity* (1949); *American Record in the Far East, 1945–1951* (1952); *A History of Christianity* (1953); *A History of Modern China* (1954); *Challenge and Conformity* (1955); *Christianity in a Revolutionary Age,* 4v. of projected 5v. (1958–62); etc. Religion dept., Yale University, since 1921.

LATROBE, JOHN HAZELHURST BONEVAL (May 4, 1803–Sept. 11, 1891); b. Philadelphia, Pa. Lawyer, philanthropist, artist, author. *The History of Mason and Dixon's Line* (1855); *The Baltimore and Ohio Railroad: Personal Recollections* (1858); *Odds and Ends* (poems, 1876); *Recollections of West Point* (1887); etc. President of the American Colonization Society, 1853–91, the work of which is described in his *Maryland in Liberia* (1885).

LATTIMORE, ELEANOR FRANCES (Mrs. Robert Armstrong Andrews) (June 30, 1904–); b. Shanghai, China. Artist, author. *Johnny* (1939); *Peachblossom* (1943); *Bayou Boys* (1946); *Christopher and His Turtle* (1950); *Diana in the China Shop* (1955); *Fair Bay* (1958); *Chinese Daughter* (1960); *The Mexican Bird* (1965); *The Search for Christina* (1966); etc. Co-author, with Owen Lattimore: *Silks, Spices, and Empire* (1968); *The Girl on the Deer* (1969).

LATTIMORE, OWEN (July 29, 1900–); b. Washington, D.C. Editor, author. *The Desert Road of Turkestan* (1929); *High Tartary* (1930); *Manchuria* (1932); *The Mongols of Manchuria* (1934); *Inner Asian Frontiers of China* (1940); *Mongol Journeys* (1941); *China: A Short History* (with Elea-

nor Lattimore, 1947); *Solution in Asia* (1945); *The Situation in Asia* (1949); *Ordeal by Slander* (1950); *Pivot of Asia* (1950); *Nationalism and Revolution in Mongolia* (1955); *Nomads and Commissars* (1962); *Studies in Frontier History* (1963); *Silks, Spices and Empire,* (with Eleanor Lattimore, 1968); etc. Editor, *Pacific Affairs,* 1934–41. Lecturer, Johns Hopkins University, since 1938.

LATTIMORE, RICHMOND [Alexander] (May 6, 1906–); b. Paotingfu, China. Educator, author. *Themes in Greek and Latin Epitaphs* (1942); *Poems* (1957); *The Poetry of Greek Tragedy* (1958); *The Stride of Time* (1966). Translator: *The Odes of Pindar* (1947); *The Iliad of Homer* (1951); *The Oresteia of Aeschylus* (1953); *Greek Lyrics* (1955); *Hesiod* (1959); *Aristophanes' The Frogs* (1962). Editor: *The Complete Greek Tragedies* (with David Grene, 1959); *The Revelation of John* (1962); *Story Patterns in Greek Tragedy* (1969). Prof. Greek, Bryn Mawr College, since 1948.

LAUFER, CALVIN WEISS (Apr. 6, 1874–Sept. 20, 1938); b. Brodheadsville, Pa. Presbyterian clergyman, hymnologist. *Hymn Lore* (1932); Compiler: *Songs for Men* (1928); *The* [Presbyterian] *Hymnal* (1933); etc.

LAUFERTY, LILIAN (Mrs. James Wolfe); b. Fort Wayne, Ind. Author. *A Pair of Sixes* (1914); *The Street of Chains* (1929); *The Crimson Thread* (1942); *The Hungry House* (1943); *Baritone* (1948); *God Keeps an Open House* (1952). Hearst chain newspaper columnist, "The Girl Reporter," "Advice to the Lovelorn."

"Laugh and the world laughs with you, weep and you weep alone." Lines from the poem "Solitude" by Ella Wheeler Wilcox in her *Poems of Passion* (1883).

Laughing Boy. Novel by Oliver La Farge (1929). Story of a Navaho Indian lad seen in relation to his tribal customs.

Laughing Horse: A Magazine of Satire from the Pacific Slope. Berkeley, Cal.; Guadalajara, Mexico, and Taos, New Mexico. Founded 1922. Edited by Roy E. Chanslor, James T. Van Renssalaer, Jr., and Willard Johnson. Discontinued 1939.

LAUGHLIN, CLARA ELIZABETH (Aug. 3, 1873–Mar. 3, 1941); b. New York. Author. *Stories of Author's Loves,* 2v. (1902); *Miladi* (1903); *Felicity* (1907); *The Death of Lincoln* (1909); *The Gleaners* (1911); *Reminiscences of James Whitcomb Riley* (1916); *The Martyred Towns of France* (1919); *So You're Going to Paris* (1924); and similar books for *Italy* (1925), *England* (1926), *France* (1927), *Rome* (1928), *Germany and Austria* (1930), *Spain* (1931), *Ireland and Scotland* (1932), *Mediterranean* (1935), *Scandinavia* (1937); *Traveling through Life* (autobiography, 1934); *So You're Seeing New England* (1940); *So You're Seeing the South* (1940).

LAUGHLIN, JAMES (Oct. 30, 1914–); b. Pittsburgh, Pa. Publisher, author. *Some Natural Things* (1945); *A Small Book of Poems* (1948); *The Wild Anemone and Other Poems* (1957); *Selected Poems* (1960). Founder, New Directions, 1936; editor, pres., since 1936.

LAUMER, [John] KEITH (June 9, 1925–); b. Syracuse, N.Y. Author. *How to Design and Build Flying Machines* (1960); *Worlds of the Imperium* (1962); *Envoy to New Worlds* (1963); *A Trace of Memory* (1963); *The Great Time Machine Hoax* (1964); *A Plague of Demons* (1965); *Galactic Diplomat* (1965); *Embassy* (1965); *The Other Side of Time* (1965); *Catastrophe Planet* (1966); *The Monitors* (1966).

LAURENCE, WILLIAM L[eonard] (Mar. 7, 1888–); b. Salantai, Lith. Journalist. *Dawn Over Zero: The Story of the Atomic Bomb* (1946); *The Hell Bomb* (1951); *Men and Atoms* (1959); *New Frontiers of Science* (1964). Translator and adapter: Gorky's *At the Bottom* (prod. 1930); Andreyev's *Devil in the Mind* (prod. 1931). Science reporter, *New York Times,* from 1930; science editor, from 1956; Pulitzer Prize for reporting, 1937, 1946.

LAURENTS, ARTHUR (July 14, 1920–); b. New York. Playwright. *Home of the Brave* (prod. 1945); *The Bird Cage* (prod. 1950); *The Time of the Cuckoo* (prod. 1952); *A Clearing in the Woods* (prod. 1956); *West Side Story* (prod. 1957); *Gypsy* (prod. 1959); *I Can Get It for You Wholesale* (1962); *Anyone Can Whistle* (1965); also radio and screen plays.

"Laus Deo." Poem by John Greenleaf Whittier (1865). Written upon hearing the bells ringing when news came that the amendment abolishing slavery had been passed.

LAUT, AGNES (Feb. 11, 1871–Nov. 15, 1936); b. Ontario, Can. Author. *Lords of the North* (1900); *The Story of the Trapper* (1902); *Freebooters of the Wilderness* (1910); *Through Our Unknown Southwest* (1913); *The Fur Trade of America* (1921); *The Blazed Trail of the Old Frontier* (1926); *The Conquest of Our Western Empire* (1927); *Romance of the Rails*, 2v. (1928); *The Overland Trail* (1929); *Cadillac, Knight Errant of the Wilderness* (1931); *Pilgrims of the Santa Fé* (1931); etc.

LAUTERBACH, JACOB ZALLEL (Jan. 6, 1873–Mar. 21, 1942); b. in Galicia, Aust. Educator. *Midrash and Mishnah* (1916); *The Pharisees and Their Teachings* (1929); etc. Translator: *The Mekilta*, 3v. (1933). Prof. Talmud, Hebrew Union College, Cincinnati, from 1911.

LAVELL, CECIL FAIRFIELD (Nov. 28, 1872–May 2, 1948); b. Kingston, Ont. Author. *Italian Cities* (1905); *Imperial England* (with Charles E. Payne, 1918); *A Biography of the Greek People* (1934); etc. Prof. history, Grinnel College, 1917–43.

Lavender and Old Lace. Novel by Myrtle Reed (1902). The love story of Ruth Thorne and Carl Winfield told against the background of the broken romance of Miss Ainslie.

LAVERY, EMMET [Godfrey] (Nov. 8, 1902–); b. Poughkeepsie, N.Y. Playwright. *The First Legion* (prod. 1934); *The Magnificent Yankee* (prod. 1946); *Fénelon* (prod. 1956); *Hail to the Chief* (prod. 1958); etc.; also screen plays.

LAVINE, HAROLD (Feb. 19, 1915–); b. New York. Editor, author. *Fifth Column in America* (1940); *War Propaganda and the United States* (with James A. Wechsler, 1940). Senior editor for national affairs, *Newsweek,* since 1956.

LAW, FREDERICK HOUK (Sept. 7, 1871–Sept. 7, 1957); b. New York. Author. *The Heart of Sindhra* (1898); *The Life of the World, and Other Poems* (1899); *Modern Great Americans* (1926); *Civilization Builders* (1929); *Great Lives* (1952); *Great Adventures* (1956); etc. Editor: *Modern Plays, Short and Long* (1924); etc.

LAW, ROBERT ADGER (Mar. 8, 1879–Aug. 16, 1961); b. Spartansburg, S.C. Educator, editor, author. *Written English* (with others, 1932); *Ideas and Models* (with others, 1935). Editor: Shakespeare's *Henry VI* (1913); *Romeo and Juliet* (1913); etc. Editor, the *Texas Review,* 1915–24. English dept., University of Texas, 1906–57.

LAWES, LEWIS E. (Sept. 13, 1883–Apr. 23, 1947); b. Elmira, N.Y. Prison warden, author. *Life and Death in Sing Sing* (1928); *20,000 Years in Sing Sing* (1932); *Stone and Steel* (1941); etc.

LAWLER, THOMAS BONAVENTURE (July 14, 1864–July 20, 1945); b. Worcester, Mass. Publisher, author. *The Story of Columbus and Magellan* (1905); *Builders of American History* (1927); *Standard History of America* (1933); *Seventy Years of Textbook Publishing* (1938). With Ginn & Co., publishers, from 1906.

LAWRENCE, ALBERTA (1875–); b. Cleveland, O. Editor, author. *Travels of Phoebe Ann* (1918); *Customs in Many Lands* (1939); etc. Editor, *Who's Who among North American Authors,* 7v. (1921–39); lit. editor, *Pasadena Star-News,* etc.

LAWRENCE, DAVID (Dec. 25, 1888–); b. Philadelphia, Pa. Newspaperman. *The True Story of Woodrow Wilson* (1924); *Beyond the New Deal* (1934); *Diary of a Washington Correspondent* (1942); etc. President, *United States Daily,* Washington, D.C., 1926–33; president and editor, *United States News,* 1933–48; president and editor, *U.S. News and World Report,* since 1948. Writes daily syndicated column "Today in Washington."

LAWRENCE, HILDA, b. Baltimore, Md. Author. *Blood upon the Snow* (1944); *A Time to Die* (1945); *The Pavilion* (1946); *Death of a Doll* (1947); *Duet of Death* (1949); etc.

LAWRENCE, JEROME (July 14, 1915–); b. Cleveland, O. Playwright. Editor: *Off Mike* (1944). Co-author, with Robert E. Lee (q.v.) of a number of plays.

LAWRENCE, JOSEPHINE, b. Newark, N.J. Author. *Rosemary* (1922); the *Linda Lane* series, 6v. (1925–29); the *Two Little Fellows* series, 5v. (1927–29); *Head of the Family* (1932); *Years Are So Long* (1934); *If I Had Four Apples* (1935); *The Sound of Running Feet* (1937); *Bow Down to Wood and Stone* (1938); *But You Are Young* (1940); *Double Wedding Ring* (1946); *My Heart Shall Not Fear* (1949); *The Picture Window* (1951); *The Web of Time* (1953); *The Gates of Living* (1955); *The Prodigal* (1957); *All Our Tomorrows* (1959); *The Amiable Meddlers* (1961); *I Am in Urgent Need of Advice* (1962); *In the Name of Love* (1963); *Not a Cloud in the Sky* (1964); *In All Walks of Life* (1968). On staff, *Newark Sunday News.*

LAWRENCE, WILLIAM (May 30, 1850–1941); b. Boston, Mass. Episcopal bishop, author. *Life of Amos A. Lawrence* (1889); *Life of Roger Wolcott* (1902); *Fifty Years* (1923); *Henry Cabot Lodge* (1925); *Memories of a Happy Life* (1926); *The New American* (1929); *Phillips Brooks* (1930); etc.

LAWSON, JAMES (Nov. 9, 1799–Mar. 24, 1880); b. Glasgow, Scot. Author. *Ontwa, the Son of the Forest* (poem, 1822); *Giordano* (prod. 1828); *Tales and Sketches by a Cosmopolite* (1830); *Poems* (1857); *Liddesdale; or, the Border Chief* (1874); *The Maiden's Oath* (1877); all anonymous. Co-editor, the *Literary Gazette,* 1827–29; the *Mercantile Advertiser,* 1829–33.

LAWSON, JAMES GILCHRIST (Sept. 10, 1874–June 17, 1946); b. Cleveland, Tenn. Compiler: *The World's Best Humorous Anecdotes* (1923); *Cyclopedia of Religious Anecdotes* (1923); *The World's Best Epigrams* (1924); *Best Loved Religious Poems* (1933); etc.

LAWSON, JOHN (d. 1711); b. in Scotland. Traveler, author. *A New Voyage to Carolina* (1709), republished as *The History of Carolina* (1714), and plagiarized by John Brickell as *The Natural History of North Carolina* (1737).

LAWSON, JOHN HOWARD (Sept. 25, 1895–); b. New York. Playwright. *Roger Bloomer* (1923); *Processional* (prod. 1925); *Loud Speaker* (prod. 1927); *Success Story* (prod. 1932); *The Pure in Heart* (prod. 1934); *Theory and Technique of Playwriting* (1936); *Marching Song* (prod. 1937); *The Hidden Heritage* (1950); *Film in the Battle of Ideas* (1953); etc. Also motion picture scenarios.

LAWSON, ROBERT (Oct. 4, 1892–May 26, 1957); b. New York. Illustrator, author. *Ben and Me: A New and Astonishing Life of Benjamin Franklin as Written by His Good Mouse Amos* (1939); *They Were Strong and Good* (1941); *Rabbit Hill* (1945); *McWhinney's Jaunt* (1951); *Great Wheel* (1957); etc. Illustrator Munro Leaf's *The Story of Ferdinand,* Arthur Mason's *Roving Lobster,* Ella Young's *Silver Shoes,* etc.

LAWSON, THOMAS WILLIAM (Feb. 26, 1857–Feb. 8, 1925); b. Charlestown, Mass. Stockbroker, author. *The Lawson History of the America's Cup* (1902); *Frenzied Finance* (1905); *Friday, the Thirteenth* (1907); *The Remedy* (1912); *The Leak* (1919); etc.

LAWSON, VICTOR FREMONT (Sept. 9, 1850–Aug. 19, 1925); b. Chicago, Ill. Newspaper publisher. Bought the *Chicago Daily News* in 1876, and took as partner, Melville E. Stone. He bought Stone's interest in 1888. He remained as publisher until 1925. *See* Charles H. Dennis's *Victor Lawson* (1935).

Lawton, Mrs. Raymond C. *See* Vingie Eve Roe.

LAWTON, WILLIAM CRANSTON (b. May 22, 1853); b. New Bedford, Mass. Educator, author. *Folia Dispersa* (poems, 1895); *The New England Poets* (1898); *Introduction to the Study of American Literature* (1902); and books on Greek literature. Prof. literature, Hobart College, 1914–18; etc.

LAY, MARGARET REBECCA; b. near Sugar Valley, Ga. Novelist. *Ceylun* (1947); *Thornblossoms* (1948).

Lay Preacher, The. Essays by Joseph Dennie (1796). Dennie wrote 118 of these essays which were published in various magazines from 1795 to 1818. Forty are included in the above collection.

LAYMON, CHARLES MARTIN (Aug. 11, 1904–); b. Dayton, O. Methodist clergyman, educator, author. *The Life and Teachings of Jesus* (1955); *Christ in the New Testament* (1958); *The Book of Revelation* (1960); *The Use of the Bible in Teaching Youth* (1962); *Thy Kingdom Come* (1964); *New Testament Guide* (1964); *Old Testament Guide* (1964); *The Lord's Prayer in Its Biblical Setting* (1968). Dean, prof. Bible history, Scarritt College, 1943–50.

LAZAROVICH-HREBELIANOVICH, PRINCESS (d. Jan. 9, 1957); b. Eleanor Calhoun, at Visalia, Cal. Author. *The Serbian People*, 2v. (with husband, Prince Lazar Eugene Lazarovich-Hrebelianovich, 1910); *Pleasures and Palaces* (memoirs, 1915); etc.

Lazarre. Novel by Mary Hartwell Catherwood (1901). Founded on the legend that the Dauphin was spirited from France at the time of the French Revolution and taken to America. The foundation in fact for *Lazarre* is the life of Eleazar Williams.

LAZARSFELD, PAUL FELIX (Feb. 13, 1901–); b. Vienna. Sociologist. *Radio and the Printed Page* (1940); *The People's Choice* (with others, 1944); *Radio Listening in America* (with Patricia Kendall, 1948); *Personal Influence* (with E. Katz, 1955); *Latent Structure Analysis* (with Neil Henry, 1967); etc. Editor: *Mathematical Thinking in the Social Sciences* (1954); *Readings in Mathematical Social Science* (with others, 1968). Prof. sociology, Columbia University, since 1940.

LAZARUS, EMMA (July 22, 1849–Nov. 19, 1887); b. New York City. Poet, essayist. *Poems and Translations* (1866); *Admetus, and Other Poems* (1871); *Alide: An Episode of Goethe's Life* (1874); *Spagnolello* (1876); *Songs of a Semite: The Dance to Death, and Other Poems* (1882); *Complete Poems* (1888); *Letters to Emma Lazarus*, ed. by R. L. Rusk, (1939); etc.

Lazarus Laughed. Play by Eugene O'Neill (1927). Based on the Bible story of the raising of Lazarus from the dead. The play opens just after his resurrection, and Lazarus tells his friends that the message he brings back from the grave is that there is no death.

LE GALLIENNE, EVA (Jan. 11, 1899–); b. London. Actress, author. *At Thirty-three* (autobiography, 1934); *Flossie and Bossie* (1949); *With a Quiet Heart* (autobiography, 1953); *The Mystic in the Theatre: Eleonora Duse* (1966). Translator, editor: Ibsen's *Hedda Gabler* (1955), and *The Master Builder* (1955). Founder and director, Civic Repertory Theatre, 1926–33.

LE MAY, ALAN (June 3, 1899–Apr. 27, 1964); b. Indianapolis, Ind. Novelist. *Painted Ponies* (1927); *Pelican Coast* (1929); *Gunsight Trail* (1931); *Winter Range* (1932); *Cattle Kingdom* (1933); *Thunder in the Dust* (1934); *Deepwater*

Island (1936); *San Antonio* (1945); *Cheyenne* (1947); *Gun Fighters* (1947); *Tap Roots* (1948); *Rocky Mountain* (1950); *Jeannie* (1951); *Blackbeard* (1952); *Flight Nurse* (1953); *The Searchers* (1954); *The Unforgiven* (1957); *By Dim and Flaring Lamps* (1962); etc. Also motion picture scenarios.

"Le Monocle de Mon Oncle." Poem by Wallace Stevens (1923).

LE PAGE DU PRATZ, ANTOINE SIMON (ca. 1690–1775); b. in the Low Countries. Louisiana historian. *Histoire de la Louisiane*, 3v. (1758), translated anonymously as, *The History of Louisiana, or of the Western Parts of Virginia and Carolina*, 2v. (1763).

LEA, FANNY HEASLIP (Oct. 30, 1884–Jan. 13, 1955); b. New Orleans, La. Novelist. *Quicksands* (1911); *The Jaconetta Stories* (1912); *Sicily Ann* (1914); *Chloe Malone* (1916); *With This Ring* (1925); *Good-Bye Summer* (1931); *Half Angel* (1932); *Summer People* (1933); *The Four Marys* (1936); *Not For Just An Hour* (1938); *Sailor's Star* (1944); *Devil Within* (1948); etc.

LEA, HENRY CHARLES (Sept. 19, 1825–Oct. 24, 1909); b. Philadelphia, Pa. Publisher, author. *Superstition and Force* (1866); *Studies in Church History* (1869); *Translations, and Other Rhymes* (1882); *A History of the Inquisition in the Middle Ages*, 3v. (1888); *The Moriscos of Spain* (1901); *A History of the Inquisition in Spain*, 4v. (1906–07); *Materials Toward a History of Witchcraft*, ed. by Arthur Charles Howland, 3v. (1939); etc. In 1851 he succeeded his father as a partner in Blanchard & Lea, publishers, Philadelphia. The Henry C. Lea library of medieval history, 15,000 volumes, is now in the University of Pennsylvania library and a chair in history is named in his honor. *See* Edward S. Bradley's *Henry Charles Lea* (1931). *See also* Carey & Lea and Lea & Lebiger.

LEA, HOMER (Nov. 17, 1876–Nov. 1, 1912); b. Denver, Colo. Novelist. *The Vermilion Pencil* (1908); *The Valor of Ignorance* (1909); *The day of the Saxon* (1912).

LEA, TOM (July 11, 1907–); b. El Paso, Tex. Artist, author. *The Brave Bulls* (1949); *The Wonderful Country* (1952); *The King Ranch*, 2v. (1957); *The Primal Yoke* (1960); *The Hands of Cantú* (1964); *A Picture Gallery* (1968); etc. Artist-correspondent, *Life*, 1941–45.

Lea & Febiger. Philadelphia, Pa. Publishers. Founded as Carey & Lea in 1785 by Mathew Carey. It has had many changes in names, including Carey, Lea & Carey; Carey, Lea & Blanchard; Henry C. Lea; Henry C. Lea's Son & Co; Lea Brothers & Co.; and the present name. William A. Blanchard retired in 1865. His son, Henry Blanchard, succeeded him. This firm published the works of Sir Walter Scott, James Fenimore Cooper, and Washington Irving. In 1851 the firm began to publish medical books. Mathew Carey was succeeded by his son, Henry Carey, and his son-in-law, Isaac Lea. Henry C. Lea succeed him in 1851. Christian C. Febiger and James M. Barnes were active in the firm. Mason Locke Weems was an agent for Mathew Carey for over thirty years. *See* the firm's *One Hundred Years of Publishing*, and Edward S. Bradley's *Henry Charles Lea* (1931).

LEACH, HENRY GODDARD (July 3, 1880–); b. Philadelphia, Pa. Author, editor. *Scandinavia and the Scandinavians* (1915); *Angevin Britain and the Scandinavians* (1915); *Pageant of Old Scandinavia* (1946); *The Fire's Center* (1950); *My Last Seventy Years* (1956); *American-Scandinavian Foundation* (1965); *Echoes of Childhood* (1966). Editor, The Forum, 1923–40. Curator, Scandinavian history and literature, Harvard University, 1921–31; president, American-Scandinavian Foundation, 1926–47.

LEACH, HOWARD SEAVOY (May 14, 1887–Nov. 17, 1948); b. Penobscot, Me. Librarian, bibliographer. Compiler: *Lists of Collections of English Drama in American Libraries* (1916); *Bibliography of Woodrow Wilson, 1875–1924;* etc. Librarian, Lehigh University, from 1924.

LEACOCK, JOHN. Playwright. *The Fall of British Tyranny; or, American Liberty Triumphant* (1776).

LEAF, MUNRO (Dec. 4, 1905–); b. Hamilton, Md. Artist, author. *Lo, the Poor Indian* (under pen name, "Mun," 1934); *Grammar Can Be Fun* (1934); *Manners Can Be Fun* (1936); *The Story of Ferdinand* (1936); *The Watchbirds* (1936); *Wee Gillis* (1938); *Safety Can Be Fun* (1938); *Fair Play* (1939); *John Henry Davis* (1940); *Arithmetic Can Be Fun* (1949); *History Can Be Fun* (1950); *Geography Can Be Fun* (1951); *Three Promises to You* (1957); *Science Can Be Fun* (1958); *Being an American Can Be Fun* (1964); *Turnabout: An Animal Story* (1967); *Noodle: Pictures by Ludwig Bemelmans* (1969); etc. Director, Frederick A. Stokes Co., 1932–39.

Leah and Rachel; or, The Two Faithful Sisters, Virginia and Maryland. By John Hammond (1656). A criticism by a Marylander, of judicial procedure in Maryland and Virginia.

LEAHY, WILLIAM AUGUSTINE (July 18, 1867); b. Boston, Mass. Author. *The Siege of Syracuse* (drama in verse, 1889); *The Incendiary* (1896); *History of the Catholic Church in New England* (1899); etc. Editor: *The Story of the Films* (1927); etc.

LEAHY, WILLIAM DANIEL (May 6, 1875–July 20, 1959); b. Hampton, Ia. Fleet admiral. *I Was There* (1950).

LEAKE, CHAUNCEY D[epew] (Sept. 5, 1896–); b. Elizabeth, N.J. Educator, author. *Letheon* (1947); *Can We Agree?* (with Patrick Romanell, 1950); *Old Egyptian Medical Papyri* (1952); *Some Founders of Physiology* (1956); *The Amphetamines* (1958); *Alcoholic Beverages in Clinical Medicine* (with M. M. Silverman, 1966); etc. Prof. pharmacology, University of California, 1928–42.

Leaning Tower, The. Collection of short stories by Katherine Anne Porter (1944).

LEAR, JOHN (Aug. 10, 1909–   ); b. near Allen, Pa. Editor, author. *Forgotten Front* (1942); *Kepler's Dream* (1965). Editorial staff, *Collier's* Magazine, 1949–53; science editor, *Saturday Review,* since 1956.

LEARNED, WALTER (June 22, 1847–Dec. 11, 1915); b. New London, Conn. Poet. *Between Times* (poems, 1889). Editor: *Treasury of Favorite American Poems* (1897); etc.

LEARNED, WILLIAM SETCHEL (June 5, 1876–Jan. 3, 1950); b. Alpena, Mich. Educator, author. *Education in the Maritime Provinces* (1922); *The American Public Library and the Diffusion of Knowledge* (1924); *The Student and His Knowledge* (1938); *An Experiment in Responsible Learning* (1940); etc. With Carnegie Foundation for the Advancement of Teaching, New York, from 1913.

Learsi, Rufus. Pen name of Israel Goldberg.

LEARY, DANIEL BELL (June 16, 1886–Apr. 30, 1946); b. New York. Educator, psychologist, author. *Philosophy of Education* (1920); *Applied Psychology* (1921); *That Mind of Yours* (1927); *Modern Psychology* (1928); *Living and Learning* (1931); etc. Head, dept. psychology, University of Buffalo, from 1919.

LEARY, LEWIS GASTON (Aug. 3, 1877–May 27, 1951); b. Elizabeth, N.J. Presbyterian clergyman, author. *The Christmas City* (1911); *Andorra, the Hidden Republic* (1912); *Syria, the Land of Lebanon* (1913); *For Them That Mourn* (1938); *The Service Book of Scripture and Prayer* (1941); etc.

LEARY, LEWIS GASTON (Apr. 18, 1906–); b. Blauvelt, N.Y. Educator, author. *That Rascal Freneau: A Study in Literary Failure* (1941); *The Literary Career of Nathaniel Tucker* (1951); *Mark Twain's Wound* (1962); *The Essential Longfellow* (1963); *Modern Chivalry* (1964); *The Teacher and American Literature* (1965); etc. Editor: *The Last Poems of Phillip Freneau* (1946); *Method and Motive in the Cantos of Ezra Pound* (1954); *The Unity of Knowledge* (1955); *Mark*

Twain's Correspondence with Henry Huttleston Rogers, 1893–1909 (1969); etc. Faculty, Duke University, 1941–52. Prof. English, Columbia University, since 1952.

LEARY, TIMOTHY FRANCIS (Oct. 22, 1920–); b. Springfield, Mass. Psychologist, author. *Social Dimensions of Personality* (1950); *Interpersonal Diagnosis of Personality* (1950); *Multi-level Assessment of Personality* (1951); *The Psychedelic Experience* (with others, 1964); *Psychedelic Prayers* (1966); *High Priest* (1968); *Politics of Ecstasy* (1968); *Psychology of Pleasure* (1969). Faculty, Harvard University, 1959–63.

Leather-Stocking Tales. A series of five novels of frontier life by James Fenimore Cooper. *The Pioneers* (1823), *The Last of the Mohicans* (1826), *The Prairie* (1827), *The Pathfinder* (1840), and *The Deerslayer* (1841).

Leave Her to Heaven. Novel by Ben Ames Williams (1944). The malevolent influence of a psychopathic woman on a man she pursues and drives to his death.

Leavenworth Case, The. Mystery novel by Anna Katharine Greene (1878). The author's first novel. Ebenezer Gryce is the name of the detective.

Leaves from Margaret Smith's Journal in the Province of Massachusetts Bay, 1678–9. Novel by John Greenleaf Whittier, published anonymously (1849). It had appeared serially in the *National Era* in 1848. Imaginary observations of a young woman from England on a visit to New England in the colonial period, with an account of witch-hunting, Indian warfare, etc.

Leaves of Grass. Poems by Walt Whitman (1855). A literary landmark, this volume has influenced both verse and prose in the twentieth century, being a clear-cut break with the New England school of poetry and expressing the new democracy of a nation finding itself, and the metaphysical bond of man with his kind as they participate in the vigor of life, each appreciating both his own uniqueness and his feelings of engagement with others.

LEAVITT, DUDLEY (May 23, 1772–Sept. 15, 1851); b. Exeter, N.H. Almanac-maker. Compiler: *Leavitt's Farmer's Almanack* (with various changes of name), 1797–1851; and *New Hampshire Register,* 1811–17.

LEAVITT, EZEKIEL (May 2, 1878–); b. Tolotchin, Russia. Rabbi, author. *Education and Psychology* (1908); *Parrot Gods* (1920); *Spinoza* (1926); *Satan Laughed* (1932); etc.; also poems in Russian, Hebrew, and Yiddish.

LECHLITNER, RUTH N. (Mrs. Paul F. Corey) (Mar. 1901–); b. Mishawaka, Ind. Poet. *Tomorrow's Phoenix* (1937); *Only the Years* (poems, 1945).

Lectures in America. Collection of lectures by Gertrude Stein (1935).

Led-Horse Claim, The. Novel by Mary Hallock Foote (1883). The scene of this romance is a mining town in Colorado during boom days.

LEDERER, WILLIAM JULIUS (b. May 31, 1912–); Author. *All the Ship's at Sea* (1950); *Spare-Time Article Writing for Money* (1954); *Ensign O'Toole and Me* (1957); *The Ugly American* (with E. L. Burdick, 1958); *A Nation of Sheep* (1961); *Timothy's Song* (1965); *Pink Jade* (1966); *Our Own Worst Enemy* (1967); *The Mirages of Marriage* (with Dr. Donald Jackson, 1968); etc.

LEDOUX, LOUIS VERNON (June 6, 1880–Feb. 25, 1948); b. New York. Author. *Songs from the Silent Land* (1905); *The Soul's Progress, and Other Poems* (1906); *Yzdra: A Tragedy* (1909); *The Shadow of Aetna* (poems, 1914); *The Story of Eleusis* (1916); *George Edward Woodberry* (1917); *The Art of Japan* (1927); *Japanese Prints* (1936); *Harunobu and Shunsho* (1945); etc.

LEE, AGNES (Mrs. Otto Freer) (1868–July 23, 1939); b. Chicago, Ill. Poet. *The Border of the Lake* (1910); *The Sharing* (1914); *Faces and Open Doors* (1922); *New Lyrics and a Few Old Ones* (1930); etc.

LEE, ALBERT (May 11, 1868–Dec. 10, 1946); b. New Orleans, La. Editor, author. *Tommy Todddles* (1896); *The Knave of Hearts* (1897); etc. Editor, *Harper's Round Table*, 1895–99; managing editor, *Collier's Weekly*, 1903–11; *Vanity Fair*, 1915–19, etc.

LEE, ALICE LOUISE (Feb. 13, 1868–); b. Brooklyn, Pa. Author of children's books. The *Co-ed* series, 4v. (1910–13); the *Ross Grant* series of cowboy books, 4v. (1915–18); etc.

Lee, Andrew. Pen name of Louis Auchincloss.

Lee, Anne S. Pen name of Mabel Ansley Murphy.

LEE, ARTHUR (Dec. 21, 1740–Dec. 12, 1792); b. "Stratford," Westmoreland Co., Va. Diplomat, author. *The Political Detection* (under pen name, "Junius Americanus," 1770); *An Appeal to the Justice and Interests of the People of Great Britain* (anon., 1774); *A Second Appeal . . .* (anon., 1775); *The American Wanderer* (anon., 1783). Wrote "The Monitor's Letters" in the *Virginia Gazette*, 1768. Confidential agent of Continental Congress in Europe, 1775–79.

Lee, Carolina. Pen name of Peggy Gaddis Dern.

LEE, CHARLES (1731–Oct. 2, 1782); b. Cheshire, Eng. Revolutionary general, author. *The Lee Papers*, in the *Collections of the New York Historical Society for 1871–1874*, 4v. (1872–75).

LEE, CHARLES (Jan. 2, 1913–); b. Philadelphia, Pa. Educator, author: *Exile: A Book of Verse* (1936); *How to Enjoy Reading* (1939); *Almanac of Reading* (1940); *Weekend at the Waldorf* (1945); *The Hidden Public* (1958); etc. Editor: *North, East, South, West* (with others, 1945); *Snow, Ice and Penguins* (1950). Lit. editor, *Philadelphia Record*, 1940–47. Prof. English, University of Pennsylvania, since 1959.

LEE, ELIZA BUCKMINSTER (c. 1788–June 22, 1864); b. Portsmouth, N.H. Author. *Sketches of a New England Village* (anon., 1838); *Delusion; or, The Witch of New England* (anon., 1840); *Naomi; or, Boston Two Hundred Years Ago* (1848); *Florence, the Parish Orphan* (1852); *Parthenia; or, The Last Days of Paganism* (1858); etc.

LEE, GERALD STANLEY (Oct. 4, 1862–Apr. 3, 1944); b. Brockton, Mass. Congregational clergyman, critic. *The Lost Art of Reading* (1902); *Crowds* (1913); etc.

LEE, GUY CARLTON (1862–Dec. 26, 1936); b. in Massachusetts, as John Ayer; changed name in his youth. Author. *Robert E. Lee* (1905); etc. Editor: *The World's Orators*, 10v. (1899–1901); *The History of Woman*, 10v. (1902–03); *The History of North America*, 20v. (1903–05); etc.

LEE, GYPSY ROSE [Rose Louise Hovick] (Jan. 9, 1914–Apr. 25, 1970); b. in Washington state. Actress, author. *The G-String Murders* (1941); *Mother Finds a Body* (1942); *The Naked Genius* (1943); *Gypsy* (1957, musical comedy 1959).

LEE, HANNAH FARNHAM SAWYER (1780–Dec. 27, 1865); b. Newburyport, Mass. Author. *Grace Seymour* (anon., 1830); *The Backslider* (anon., 1835); *The Harcourts* (anon., 1837); *Rich Enough* (anon., 1837); *Three Experiments of Living* (anon., 1837); *Elinor Fulton* (anon., 1837); *The Contrast* (anon., 1838); *Historical Sketches of the Old Painters* (1838); *Rosanna; or, Scenes in Boston* (anon., 1839); *Tales* (anon., 1842); *The Huguenots in France and America*, 2v. (anon., 1843); *The Log Cabin* (anon., 1844); etc.

LEE, HARPER (April 28, 1926–); b. Monroe, Ala. Novelist. *To Kill a Mockingbird* (1960; Pulitzer Prize for fiction, 1961).

LEE, HENRY (Jan. 29, 1756–Mar. 25, 1818); b. "Leesylvania," Prince William Co., Va. Revolutionary officer, statesman, author. Known as "Light-Horse Harry Lee." *Memoirs of the War in the Southern Department of the United States*, 2v. (1812); *See* Thomas Boyd's *Light-Horse Harry Lee* (1931); John Torrey Morse's *Life and Letters of Col. Henry Lee* (1905).

LEE, HENRY (May 28, 1787–Jan. 30, 1837); b. "Stratford," Westmoreland Co., Va., son of Henry Lee (1758–1818). Soldier, author. *The Campaign of 1781 in the Carolinas* (1824); *The Life of the Emperor Napoleon* (1835).

LEE, JAMES MELVIN (May 16, 1878–Nov. 17, 1929); b. Port Crane, N.Y. Editor, author. *History of American Journalism* (1917); *America's Oldest Daily Newspaper: The New York Globe* (1918); etc. Editor, the *Bohemian Magazine*, 1906–07; *Judge*, 1908–12; lit. editor, *Editor and Publisher*, 1911–29; director, dept. of journalism, New York University, 1911–29.

LEE, JENNETTE [Barbour Perry] (Nov. 10, 1860–Oct. 10, 1951); b. Bristol, Conn. Novelist. *Kate Wetherill* (1900); *A Pillar of Salt* (1901); *The Ibsen Secret* (1907); *Simeon Tetloe's Shadow* (1909); *Happy Island* (1910); *Aunt Jane* (1915); *The Air-Man and the Tramp* (1918); *This Magic Body* (1946); etc.

LEE, JOHN CLARENCE (Oct. 15, 1856–Sept. 16, 1940); b. Woodstock, Vt. Universalist, clergyman, educator, author. *The Beginnings of St. Lawrence University* (1913); etc. President, St. Lawrence University, 1896–99.

LEE, JOHN M. (1907–). Author. *Counter-Clockwise* (1940).

LEE, LAWRENCE (Jan. 3, 1903–); b. Gadsden, Ala. Editor, poet. *Summer Goes On* (1933); *Monticello, and Other Poems* (1937); *The Tomb of Thomas Jefferson* (1940); *American As Faust* (1965); *Stained Glass* (1967); *Cretan Flute* (1968). With Street and Smith, 1925–30. Editor, the *Virginia Quarterly Review*, since 1938.

LEE, MANFRED BENNINGTON (Jan. 11, 1905–Apr. 3, 1971); Novelist. Co-author with Frederic Dannay (q.v.), using together the pen names "Ellery Queen" and "Barnaby Ross."

LEE, MARGARET (Nov. 27, 1841?–Dec. 24, 1914); b. New York. Novelist. *Dr. Wilmer's Love* (1868); *Lorimer and Wife* (1881); *A Brighton Knight* (1884); *A Brooklyn Bachelor* (1886); *Divorce* (1889); *Lizzie Adriance* (1889); *One Touch of Nature* (1892); *Lovers and Shekels* (1906); *The Wanderer* (1913); etc.

LEE, MARJORIE (June 28, 1921–); b. Long Island, N.Y. Author. *Dance With Me* (1949); *The Lion House* (1959); *The Eye of Summer* (1961).

LEE, MUNA (Jan. 29, 1895–Apr. 3, 1965); b. Raymond, Miss. Author. *Sea-Change* (poems, 1923); *Art in Review* (1940); *American Story Handbook* (1944); *Pioneers of Puerto Rico* (1945). Co-author, with Maurice Guinness, under pen name "Newton Gayle": *Death Follows a Formula* (1934); *The Sentry-Box Murder* (1935); *Death in the Glass* (1936); *Murder at 28:10* (1937); *Sinister Crag* (1938). Co-author, with Ruth McMurry: *The Cultural Approach—Another Way in International Relations* (1947).

LEE, ROBERT (Apr. 28, 1929–); b. San Francisco, Cal. Educator, author. *Social Sources of Church History* (1960); *Religion and Leisure in America* (1964); *Stranger in the Land* (1967). Editor: *Cities and Churches* (1962); *Religion and Social Conflict* (with Martin E. Marty, 1964); *The Church and the Exploding Metropolis* (1965). Prof. social ethics, San Francisco Theological Seminary, since 1961.

LEE, ROBERT E[dward] (Jan. 19, 1807–Oct. 12, 1870); b. "Stratford," Westmoreland Co., Va., son of Henry Lee (1758–1818). Confederate general, educator. Superintendent, U.S. Military Academy, 1852–55; president, Washington College (now Washington and Lee University), 1865–70. *See* Armistead L. Long's *Memoirs of Robert E. Lee* (1886); William P. Trent's *Robert E. Lee* (1899); his son Robert E. Lee's *Recollections and Letters of General Robert E. Lee* (1924); Ethel M. Armes's *Stratford Hall* (1930); William J. Johnston's *Robert E. Lee* (1933); Robert W. Winston's *Robert E. Lee* (1934); Douglas S. Freeman's *Robert E. Lee,* 4v. (1934–35); *The Wartime Papers of Robert E. Lee* (1961).

LEE, ROBERT EDWIN (Oct. 15, 1918–); b. Elyria, O. Playwright. Author: *Television: The Revolution* (1945). Coauthor: *Look Ma, I'm Dancin'* (prod. 1948); *Inherit the Wind* (prod. 1955); *Auntie Mame* (prod. 1956); *Shangri-La* (prod. 1956); *The Gang's All Here* (prod. 1959); *Only in America* (prod. 1959); *Dear World* (1968); *Incomparable Max* (1969).

LEE, UMPHREY (Mar. 23, 1893–June 23, 1958); b. Oakland City, Ind. Methodist clergyman, educator, author. *Jesus the Pioneer* (1926); *Historical Backgrounds of Early Methodist Enthusiasm* (1931); *John Wesley and Modern Religion* (1936); *Render Unto the People* (1947); *Our Fathers and Us* (1958); etc. President, Southern Methodist University, 1939–54; chancellor, from 1954.

Lee and Shepard. Publishing firm. Boston, Mass. Founded 1862, by William Lee and Charles Augustus Billings Shepard. Lee had formerly been a junior partner in the firm of Phillips, Sampson & Co., who had published Emerson's *Essays.* Shepard was a senior member of Shepard, Clark & Brown, which suspended business in 1859. There was also a New York branch of Lee, Shepard & Dillingham. Children's books and Sunday School literature were featured. They published the works of Oliver Optic and Sophie May. Merged with D. Lothrop & Co., in 1904 to become Lothrop, Lee and Shepard Company.

LEECH, MARGARET [Kernochan] (Mrs. Ralph Pulitzer) (Nov. 7, 1893–); b. Newburgh, N.Y. Author. *The Back of the Book* (1924); *Tin Wedding* (1926); *Anthony Comstock* (with Heywood Broun, 1927); *The Feathered Nest* (1928); *Reveille in Washington* (1941, Pulitzer Prize for history, 1942); *In the Days of McKinley* (1959, Bancroft Prize, 1960, Pulitzer Prize for history, 1960).

Leedle Yawcob Strauss. Humorous poems in German dialect by Charles Follen Adams.

LEEDS, DANIEL (1652–Sept. 28, 1720), b. in England. Almanac-maker, author. *The Temple of Wisdom for the Little World* (anon., 1688); *News of a Trumpet Sounding in the Wilderness* (1697); etc. His first almanac was printed by William Bradford, in Philadelphia, 1687. His son, Titan Leeds, computed the almanacs from 1714 to 1726, and another son, Daniel Leeds, computed them for the years 1727–30.

Lee's Lieutenants: A Study in Command. By Douglas Southall Freeman, 3v. (1942–44).

LEETCH, DOROTHY LYMAN (Mrs. Langford Wheaton Smith) (Aug. 26, 1895–); b. Washington, D.C. Librarian, author. *Tommy Tucker on a Plantation* (1925); *Annetje and Her Family* (1926); *Benito and Loreta Delfin* (1932); etc. Children's librarian, Library of the District of Columbia, 1919–24.

LEETE, FREDERICK DeLAND (Oct. 1, 1866–Feb. 16, 1958); b. Avon, N.Y. Methodist bishop, author. *Francis Asbury* (1916); *Palestine, Land of the Light* (1932); *Palestine: Its History, Peoples and Scenery* (1932); *New Testament Windows* (1939); *Adventures of a Traveling Preacher* (1952); etc.

LEFEVRE, EDWIN (Jan. 23, 1871–Feb. 22, 1943); b. Colon, Colombia. Journalist, author. *Wall Street Stories* (1901); *Sampson Rock of Wall Street* (1907); *H.R.* (1915); *Simonetta* (1919); *Reminiscences of a Stock Operator* (1923); etc. One of his best known stories is *The Woman and Her Bonds.*

LEFEVRE, LAURA ZENOBIA, b. Strasburg, Pa. Author. Pen name "Zenobia Bird." *Under Whose Wings* (1928); *Eyes in the Dark* (1930); *The Return of the Tide* (1932); *Sally Jo*

(1934); *Stoke of Brier Hill* (1936); *Muffy, the Tale of a Muskrat* (1941); *Through Winding Ways* (1946); etc.

LEFEVRE, PERRY DEYO (July 12, 1921–); b. Kingston, N.Y. Clergyman, educator, author. *The Prayers of Kierkegaard* (1956); *The Christian Teacher* (1958); *Introduction to Religious Existentialism* (1961); *Understandings of Man* (1966); *Philosophical Resources for Christian Thought* (1968). Dean of faculty, Chicago Theological Seminary, since 1961.

LEFLER, HUGH TALMAGE (Dec. 8, 1901–); b. Cooleemee, N.C. Educator. Author: *Hinton Rowan Helper: Advocate of a "White America"* (1935); *History of North Carolina,* 2v. (1956); etc. Co-author: *Colonial America* (1958); etc. Editor: *North Carolina History Told by Contemporaries* (1934); *John Lawson's New Voyage to Carolina* (1968). Prof. history, University of North Carolina, since 1935.

LEGARÉ, HUGH SWINTON (Jan. 2, 1797–June 20, 1843); b. Charleston, S.C. Statesman, editor. *Writings,* ed. by his sister, Mary Swinton Legaré, 2v. (1845–46). Co-editor (with Stephen Elliott), the *Southern Review,* 1828–32. Chargé d'affaires in Belgium, 1832–36; Congressman, 1837–39; Attorney-General of the United States, 1841–43. See Linda Rhea's *Hugh Swinton Legaré* (1934).

LEGARÉ, JAMES MATHEWS (1823–1859); b. Charleston, S.C. Poet. *Orta-Undis, and Other Poems* (1848).

Legend of Sleepy Hollow, The. Famous story by Washington Irving, in his *The Sketch Book.*

LEGGETT, JOHN [Ward] (Nov. 11, 1917–); b. New York. Author. *The Gloucester Branch* (1964); *Wilder Stone* (1960); *Who Took the Gold Away?* (1969). Faculty, University of Iowa.

LEGGETT, WILLIAM (Apr. 30, 1802–May 29, 1839); b. New York City. Editor, author. *Leisure Hours at Sea* (poems, 1825); *Journals of the Ocean* (1826); *Tales and Sketches: By a Country Schoolmaster* (anon., 1829); *Naval Stories* (1834); *A Collection of the Political Writings,* 2v. (1840); etc. Founder, *The Critic,* 1828, part owner and associate editor, *New York Evening Post,* 1829–36. See Allen Nevins's *The Evening Post: A Century of Journalism* (1922).

LEGLER, HENRY EDUARD (June 22, 1861–Sept. 13, 1917); b. Palermo, It. Librarian, author. *Chevalier Henry de Tonty* (1896); *A Moses of the Mormons* (1897); *Leading Events of Wisconsin History* (1898); *James Gates Percival* (1901); *Early Wisconsin Imprints* (1903); *The Genesis of Poe's Raven* (1907); *Of Much Love and Some Knowledge of Books* (1912). Librarian, Chicago Public Library, 1909–17.

LEHMAN, BENJAMIN HARRISON (Oct. 20, 1889–); b. Mullan, Idaho. Educator, novelist. *Wild Marriage* (1925); *The Lordly Ones* (1927); etc. English dept., University of California, since 1920.

LEHMANN, KARL (Sept. 27, 1894–Dec. 17, 1960); b. Rostock, Ger. Educator. Author. *Dionysiac Sarcophagi in Baltimore* (with E. C. Olsen, 1942); *Thomas Jefferson, American Humanist* (1947); *Samothrace* (1955); also a number of archaeological works in German. Editor: *Samothrace: The Ancient Literary Sources* (1959). Prof., Institute of Fine Arts, New York University, from 1935.

LEHRER, THOMAS ANDREW (Apr. 9, 1928–); b. New York. Songwriter, entertainer, educator. *Tom Lehrer Song Book* (1954); *More of Tom Lehrer* (1959); *Tom Lehrer Revisited* (1960); *That Was the Year That Was* (1965). Lecturer political science, Massachusetts Institute of Technology, since 1962.

LEIBER, FRITZ (1910–). Author. *Gather, Darkness!* (1943); *The Swords of Lankhm* (1968); *The Secret Songs* (1968); *A Specter is Haunting Texas* (1968); *The Wanderer* (1969); etc.

LEIDING, HARRIETTE KERSHAW (Mrs. Herman G. Leiding) (June, 1878–Mar. 20, 1948); b. Sewanee, Tenn. Author. *Street Cries of a Southern City* (1911); *A Walk Around Ye Old Historic Charleston* (1912); *Historic Houses of South Carolina* (1921); *Charleston, Historic and Romantic* (1931).

LEIGHTON, CLARE [Veronica Hope] (Apr. 12, 1901–); b. London. Artist, author. *How To Do Wood Engraving and Woodcuts* (1932); *The Musical Box* (1932); *The Farmer's Year* (1933); *The Wood That Came Back* (1934); *Four Hedges* (1935); *Wood Engraving of the 1930's* (1936); *Country Matters* (1937); *Sometime—Never* (1939); *Southern Harvest* (1942); *Give Us This Day* (1943); *Tempestuous Petticoat: The Story of an Invincible Edwardian* (1947); *Where Land Meets Sea* (1954); etc. Illustrator of many books.

LEIGHTON, JOSEPH ALEXANDER (Dec. 2, 1870–June 17, 1954); b. Orangeville, Ont., Can. Educator, author. *The Field of Philosophy* (1918); *Man and the Cosmos* (1922); *Religion and the Mind of Today* (1924); *Individuality and Education* (1928); *The Diversities of Cultures and the Unity of Mankind* (1949); etc. Prof. philosophy, Ohio State University, 1910–41.

LEIGHTON, MARGARET [Carver] (Dec. 20, 1896–); b. Oberlin, O. Author. *Junior High School Plays* (1938); *The Secret of the Old House* (1941); *Twelve Bright Trumpets* (1942); *The Singing Cave* (1945); *Judith of France* (1948); *The Story of Florence Nightingale* (1952); *Who Rides By?* (1955); *The Secret of Smuggler's Cove* (1959); *Journey for a Princess* (1960); *Bride of Glory* (1962); *Voyage to Coromandel* (1965); *The Canyon Castaways* (1966); *A Hole in the Hedge* (1968); *Cleopatra, Sister of the Moon* (1969).

Leinster, Murray. Pen name of William Fitzgerald Jenkins.

LEIPER, HENRY SMITH (Sept. 17, 1891–); b. Belmar, N.J. Congregational clergyman, editor, author. *The Ghost of Caesar Walks* (1935); *World Chaos or World Christianity* (1938); *Blind Spots* (1944); etc. Editor: *Christianity Today* (1947). Editor, the *Potter's Wheel;* assoc. editor, the *Congregationalist,* 1927–30.

LEISY, ERNEST ERWIN (Dec. 22, 1887–); b. Moundridge, Ga. Educator, editor, author. *American Literature* (1929); etc. Editor: *Facts and Ideas,* 2v. (with others, 1930–39); *Major American Writers* (with H. M. Jones, 1935); *Voices of England and America* (with others, 1939); Mark Twain's *Letters of Quintus Curtius Snodgrass* (1946); *The American Historical Novel* (1950); etc. Prof. English, Southern Methodist University, since 1927.

LEITCH, MARY SINTON (Sept. 8, 1876–Aug. 20, 1954); b. New York. Poet. *The Wagon and the Star* (1922); *The Unrisen Morrow* (1926); *The Black Moon* (play, 1929); *Two Mile Tree* (1931); *Spider Architect* (1937); *From Invisible Mountains* (1943); etc. Editor: *Lyric Virginia To-Day* (1932).

LEKACHMAN, ROBERT (May 12, 1920–   ); b. New York. Educator, author. *A History of Economic Ideas* (1959); *The Age of Keynes* (1966). Editor: *Keynes and the Classics* (1964). Prof. economics, State University of New York at Stony Brook, since 1965.

LELAND, CHARLES GODFREY (Aug. 15, 1824–Mar. 20, 1903); b. Philadelphia, Pa. Editor, humorist, essayist. *Meister Karl's Sketch-Book* (1855); *Legends of Birds* (1864); *Hans Breitmann's Ballads* (1871); *English Gipsies and Their Language* (1873); *Abraham Lincoln and the Abolition of Slavery* (1879); *The Gypsies* (1882); *The Algonquin Legends of New England* (1884); *Memoirs* (1893); *Songs of the Sea and Lays of the Land* (1895); etc. Compiler: *Dictionary of Slang,* 2v. (with Albert Barrere, 1889). Editor, the *New York Illustrated News,* the *Philadelphia Evening Bulletin,* etc. Founder, the *Continental Magazine,* Boston, 1865. *See* Joseph Jackson's *Bibliography of the Works of Charles Godfrey Leland* (1927); Elizabeth Robins Pennell's *Charles Godfrey Leland* (1906).

LELAND, JOHN ADAMS. Author. *Othneil Jones* (1956).

LELAND, WALDO GIFFORD (July 17, 1879–Oct. 19, 1966); b. Newton, Mass. Educator, author. *Guide to the Archives of the Government of the United States* (with C. H. Van Tyne 1904); *Guide to Materials for American History in the Archives and Libraries of Paris,* 4v. (1932–60). Dept. historical research, Carnegie Institution, 1903–32; director, American Council of Learned Societies, 1927–46.

LEMAÎTRE, GEORGES ÉDOUARD (Nov. 26, 1898–); b. Algiers. Educator, author. *Four French Novelists: Marcel Proust, André Gide, Jean Giraudoux, Paul Morand* (1938, rev. ed., 1969); *From Cubism to Surrealism in French Literature* (1941); *Beaumarchais* (1949); *Maurois: The Writer and His Work* (1968). Prof. Romanic languages, Stanford University, since 1939.

LEMMON, ROBERT STELL (June 26, 1885–Mar. 3, 1964); b. Englewood, N.J. Editor, author. *Training the Dog* (1914); *Old Doc Lemmon* (1930); *How to Attract the Birds* (1947); *Our Amazing Birds* (1952); *All About Moths and Butterflies* (1956); *All About Monkeys* (1958); *Wildflowers of North America* (with C. C. Johnson, 1961); etc. Managing editor, *House and Garden,* 1918–37; *The Home Garden,* 1943–51.

Lena Rivers. Popular novel by Mary Jane Holmes (1856).

LENGEL, WILLIAM C[harles] (June 27, 1888–Oct. 11, 1965); b. Durango, Calif. Editor, author. Pen names, "Warren Spencer" and "Charles Grant." *Forever and Ever* (1932); *Mad Melody* (1932); *Torch Singer* (1933); *More Money* (with Katharine Hill, 1934); *Candles in the Wind* (1933). Editorial dept., *Hearst's International Magazine, Smart Set, Liberty, Cosmopolitan,* etc. Editor-in-chief, Gold Medal Books, Fawcett Publications Inc., 1942–54; Fawcett World Library, from 1955.

L'ENGLE, MADELEINE (Mrs. Hugh Franklin) (Nov. 28, 1918–); b. New York. Author. *18 Washington Square* (play, 1944); *The Small Rain* (1945); *Ilsa* (1946); *And Both Were Young* (1949); *Camilla Dickinson* (1951); *Winter's Love* (1957); *Meet the Austins* (1961); *A Wrinkle in Time* (1962); *The Love Letters* (1966); *Journey with Jonah* (1967); *The Young Unicorns* (1968); *Dance in the Desert* (1969); *Lines Scribbled on an Envelope* (1969).

LENGYEL, EMIL (Apr. 26, 1895–); b. Budapest, Hung. Educator, author. *Cattle Car Express* (1931); *The Cauldron Boils* (1932); *Hitler* (1932); *The New Deal in Europe* (1934); *Millions of Dictators* (1936); *The Danube* (1939); *Siberia* (1943); *America's Role in World Affairs* (1946); *Americans from Hungary* (1948); *World Without End: The Middle East* (1953); *Egypt's Role in World Affairs* (1957); *1,000 Years of Hungary* (1958); *The Changing Middle East* (1960); *The Land and the People of Hungary* (1965); *India, Pakistan, Ceylon* (1961); *Krishna Menon: A Biography* (1962); *Scenario: World in Revolt: From Prison to Power* (1964); *Mahatma Gandhi: The Great Soul* (1966); *Jawaharlal Nehru: The Brahmin from Kashmir* (1968); *Lajos Kossuth, Hungary's Great Patriot* (1969); etc. Prof. history, Brooklyn Polytechnic Institute, 1935–42; New York University School of Education, since 1951.

LENNOX, CHARLOTTE RAMSAY (1720–Jan. 4, 1804); b. New York. Novelist, biographer, poet. *Poems on Several Occasions* (1747); *The Life of Harriot Stuart* (1750); *The Female Quixote; or, The Adventures of Arabella,* 2v. (1752); *Philander* (1758); *The History of Henrietta* (1758); *Memoirs of the Duke of Sully* (1761); *The Sister* (1769); *Euphemia,* 4v. (1790); etc. She was a friend of Samuel Johnson. *See* Gustavus H. Maynadier's *The First American Novelist?* (1940).

LENNOX, PATRICK JOSEPH (Aug. 12, 1862–Dec. 15, 1943); b. Nurney, Co. Kildare, Ire. Educator, author. *Early Printing in Ireland* (1909); *Addison and the Modern Essay* (1912); *History of Panama* (1915); etc. Prof. English, Catholic University, 1907–39. On editorial staff, the *Washington Post,* 1909–29.

"Lenore." Poem by Edgar Allan Poe (1831).

LENOX, JAMES (Aug. 19, 1800–Feb. 17, 1880); b. New York. Philanthropist, book collector, library founder. Founder, Lenox Library, New York, 1870. His first librarian was Samuel Austin Allibone. *See* Henry Stevens's *Recollections of Mr. James Lenox of New York and the Foundation of His Library* (1886); H. M. Lydenberg's *History of The New York Public Library* (1923). *See also* New York Public Library.

LENSKI, LOIS (Mrs. Arthur S. Covey) (Oct. 14, 1893–); b. Springfield, O. Artist, author. *A Little Girl of Nineteen Hundred* (1928); *The Wonder City* (1929); *Grandmother Tippy-Toe* (1931); *The Little Family* (1932); *Arabella and Her Aunts* (1932); *Gooseberry Garden* (1934); *Sugarplum House* (1935); *Ocean-Born Mary* (1939); *Strawberry Girl* (1945); *Blue Ridge Billy* (1946); *Boom Town Boy* (1948); *Cowboy Small* (1949); *I Like Winter* (1950); *Prairie School* (1951); *Papa Small* (1951); *On a Summer Day* (1953); *Project Boy* (1954); *Corn-farm Boy* (1954); *San Francisco Boy* (1955); *We Live By the River* (1956); *Houseboat Girl* (1957); *Davy and His Dog* (1957); *Little Sioux Girl* (1958); *We Live in the Country* (1961); *We Live in the North* (1965); *High-Rise Secret* (1966); *Debbie and Her Grandma* (1967); *Deer Valley Girl* (1968); *Adventure in Understanding: Talks to Parents, Teachers and Librarians 1944–1966* (1968); etc.

LENZEN, VICTOR F[ritz] (Dec. 14, 1890–); b. San Jose, Cal. Physicist, educator, author. *The Nature of Physical Theory* (1931); *Procedures of Empirical Science* (1938); *The Figure of Dionysos on the Siphnian Frieze* (1946); *Casualty in Natural Science* (1954); etc. Contributor: *Twentieth Century Philosophy* (1943); *Albert Einstein: Philosopher-Scientist* (1949); etc. Dept. of physics, University of California, 1918–58. Emeritus since 1958.

Leonard, Baird. Pen name of Mrs. Harry St. Clair Zogbaum.

LEONARD, DANIEL (May 18, 1740–June 27, 1829); Tory lawyer, writer. *Massachusettensis* (1775), also published as *The Origin of the American Contest with Great-Britain* (1775). He wrote a brilliant series of weekly letters from Dec. 12, 1774 to Apr. 3, 1775, under the pen name "Massachusettensis," addressed to the inhabitants of Massachusetts Bay.

LEONARD, JOHN. Book reviewer, author. *The Naked Martini* (1964); *Wyke Regis* (1966); *Crybaby of the Western World* (1969). Book reviewer, *New York Times.*

LEONARD, MARY FINLEY (b. Jan. 11, 1862); b. Philadelphia, Pa. Author. *Half a Dozen Thinking Caps* (1900); *The Spectacle Man* (1901); *The Pleasant Street Partnership* (1903); *Everyday Susan* (1912); *The Little Red Chimney* (1914); *The Ways of Jane* (1917); etc.

LEONARD, WILLIAM ELLERY (Jan. 25, 1876–May 2, 1944); b. Plainfield, N.J. Educator, poet, playwright. *Sonnets and Poems* (1906); *The Poet of Galilee* (1909); *The Vaunt of Man, and Other Poems* (1912); *Socrates, Master of Life* (1915); *Poems, 1914–16* (1916); *The Lynching Bee, and Other Poems* (1920); *Two Lives: A Poem* (anon., 1922); *Tutankhamen and After* (poems, 1924); *The Locomotive God* (autobiography, 1927); *A Son of Earth: Collected Poems* (1930); *This Midland City* (poems, 1930); *Lucretius, the Man, the Poet, the Times* (1941); *Byron and Byronism in America* (1965); etc. Translator of Lucretius, *Beowulf,* Empedocles, etc. English dept., University of Wisconsin, from 1906.

LEONARD, ZENAS (Mar. 19, 1809–July 14, 1857); b. Clearfield, Pa. Trapper, author. *Narrative of the Adventures of Zenas Leonard* (1839), republished, ed. by Milo M. Quaife (1934).

LEOPOLD, RICHARD WILLIAM (Jan. 6, 1912–); b. New York. Educator. *Robert Dale Owen: A Biography* (1940); *Elihu Root and the Conservative Tradition* (1954); *The Growth of American Foreign Policy* (1962); etc. Contributor

to *Change and Continuity in Twentieth Century America* (1964). Dept. of history, Northwestern University, since 1948.

LERNER, ALAN JAY (Aug. 31, 1918–); b. New York. Playwright. Author, book and lyrics: *The Day Before Spring* (prod. 1945); *Brigadoon* (prod. 1947); *Love Life* (prod. 1948); *Paint Your Wagon* (prod. 1951); *My Fair Lady* (prod. 1956); *Camelot* (prod. 1961); *On a Clear Day You Can See Forever* (prod. 1965); etc.

LERNER, DANIEL (Oct. 30, 1917–); b. New York. Sociologist, author. *Sykewar: Psychological Warfare Against Germany* (1949); *The Nazi Elite* (with others, 1951); *The Passing of Traditional Society* (1958); *The Transfer of Institutions* (with others, 1964); *Communication and Change in the Developing Countries* (1967); *Euratlantica: Changing Perspectives of the European Elites* (1969); etc. Editor: *Propaganda in War and Crisis* (1951); *Quantity and Quality* (1962); etc. Prof. sociology, Massachusetts Institute of Technology, since 1953.

LERNER, LEO ALFRED (Sept. 20, 1907–Mar. 6, 1965); b. Chicago, Ill. Editor, author. *Continental Journey* (1947); *The Itch of Opinion* (1956); *The Italics Are Mine* (1960).

LERNER, MAX (Dec. 20, 1902–); b. Minsk, Russia. Educator, editor, author. *It Is Later Than You Think* (1938); *Ideas Are Weapons* (1939); *Ideas for the Ice Age* (1941); *Actions and Passions* (1949); *America as a Civilization* (1957); *The Unfinished Country* (1959); *Beyond the Power Principle* (1961); *The Age of Overkill* (1962); *The Revolutionary Theme in Contemporary America* (with others, 1965); *Tocqueville and American Civilization* (1969); etc. Editor: *The Mind and Faith of Justice Holmes* (1943). Prof. political science, Williams College, 1938–43; prof. American civilization, Brandeis University, since 1949.

LERRIGO, CHARLES HENRY (Sept. 12, 1872–Dec. 4, 1955); b. Birmingham, Eng. Author. *Doc Williams: A Tale of the Middle West* (1913); *The Boy Scout Treasure Hunters* (1917); *Boy Scouts to the Rescue* (1919); *Boy Scouts on Special Service* (1922); *The Castle of Cheer* (1925); *A Son of John Brown* (1937); *The Better Half of Your Life* (1951); etc.

LESLEY, PETER (Sept. 17, 1819–June 1, 1903); b. Philadelphia, Pa. Geologist, author. *Man's Origin and Destiny* (1868); *Paul Dreifuss: His Holiday Abroad* (1882). He directed the second geological survey of Pennsylvania, the results of which were published in 77 volumes.

Leslie, Amy. Pen name of Lillie West.

LESLIE, ELIZA (Nov. 15, 1787–Jan. 1, 1858); b. Philadelphia, Pa. Author. Wrote as "Miss Leslie." *Pencil Sketches,* 3 series (1833–37); *Laura Lovel* (1834); *Althea Vernon* (1838); *Mr. & Mrs. Woodbridge* (1841); *Mrs. Worthington Potts, and Mrs. Smith* (1843); *Leonilla Lynmore* (1847); *Amelia* (1848); *The Behavior-Book* (1853); and many books on etiquette, cook books, children's stories, etc. Editor, *The Gift,* and *The Violet,* etc. Founder and editor, *Miss Leslie's Magazine,* 1843.

LESLIE, FRANK (Mar. 29, 1821–Jan. 10, 1880); b. Ipswich, Eng. Came to America in 1848. Wood-engraver, publisher, editor. Founder, *Frank Leslie's Illustrated Newspaper* (later *Leslie's Weekly*), Dec. 15, 1855. He also founded *Frank Leslie's Ladies' Gazette,* 1854; *Frank Leslie's New York Journal,* 1855; *Frank Leslie's New Family Magazine,* 1857; *Frank Leslie's Budget of Fun,* 1858; *Frank Leslie's Boys of America,* 1863; *Frank Leslie's Ten-Cent Magazine,* 1863; *Frank Leslie's Popular Monthly,* 1876, and many other magazines. Born Henry Carter, he changed his name by legal action in 1857 to Frank Leslie. When he first came to America, he was associated with P. T. Barnum. His wife continued to edit and publish his magazines after his death. *See* F. L. Mott's *A History of American Magazines,* 3 v. (1938). *See also* Miriam Florence Folline Leslie.

LESLIE, MIRIAM FLORENCE FOLLINE (Mrs. Frank Leslie) (1836–Sept. 18, 1914); b. New Orelans, La. Editor, author. *Are Men Gay Deceivers, and Other Sketches* (1893); *California: A Pleasure Trip* (1877); *Rents in Our Robes* (1888); *A Social Mirage* (1899); etc. Editor, *Frank Leslie's Popular Monthly,* etc. In 1882 she changed her name to Frank Leslie by court order, since her magazines were published under that name.

Leslie, Miss. *See* Eliza Leslie.

Leslie, Mrs. Madeline. Pen name of Harriette Newall Woods Baker.

Leslie's Weekly. New York. Newspaper. Founded Dec. 15, 1855, by Frank Leslie, under the name *Frank Leslie's Illustrated Newspaper.* Its first editor was Thomas Powell. It stressed sensational news, and was noted for its illustrations. In later years it modified its treatment of news to conform to new trends in journalism. Expired June 24, 1922.

LESSING, BRUNO (Dec. 6, 1870–Apr. 29, 1940); b. (Rudolph Edgar Block) New York City. Columnist, author. *Children of Men* (1903); *With the Best Intention* (1914); *Lapidowitz* (1915). With Hearst newspapers, 1896–1940, editing their comic supplements for twenty-eight years. Began column "Vagabondia" in 1928, and traveled over the world to find material for it.

Lesson of the Master, The. Collection of short stories by Henry James (1892).

LESTER, CHARLES EDWARDS (July 15, 1815–Jan. 29, 1890); b. Griswold, Conn. Author. *Chains and Freedom* (1839); *My Consulship* (1853); *Life and Voyages of Americus Vespucius* (with Andrew Foster, 1846); *The Light and Dark of the Rebellion* (1863); etc. U.S. Consul at Genoa, 1842–47.

LESTER, JULIUS B. (Jan. 27, 1939–); b. St. Louis, Mo. Journalist, radio and television performer, commentator and interviewer, author. *The Twelve-String Guitar as Played by Leadbelly* (with Pete Seeger, 1965); *To Be a Slave* (1968); *Look Out, Whitey! Black Power's Gon' to Get Your Mama!* (1968); *Search for a New Land* (1969); *Revolutionary Notes* (1970); etc. Associate editor, *Singout,* since 1964; regular weekly program, WBAI–FM, New York City, since 1968; regular participant on "Free Time," NET, New York City.

L'Estrange, Corinne. Pen name of Henry Hartshorne.

"Let Her Go, Gallagher." Song by William W. Delaney (1887).

Let Us Be Gay. Play by Rachel Crothers. (prod. 1929). Kitty Brown divorces her husband for infidelity, and later has an opportunity to warn a young girl against a serious love affair with an older man, only to discover that this man is her former husband. Copying his tactics, she shames him into a final reconciliation.

"Let us go then, you and I." First line of "The Love Song of J. Alfred Prufrock," by T. S. Eliot. It continues: "When the evening is spread out against the sky Like a patient etherised upon a table ..."

Let Us Now Praise Famous Men. By James Agee (1941). Photographs by Walker Evans. A probing look at the life led by Southern tenant farmers. Begun as a documentary on commission from *Life,* the book was continued by Agee as an expression of personal outrage at the degradation of the farmers' lives. It is written in a mixed style that ranges from the lyrical to the ironic matter-of-fact.

Letter G, The. Best known short story of Elizabeth Barrow (1864).

Letters from a Cat. By Helen Hunt Jackson (1879). A book for children.

Letters from a Farmer in Pennsylvania, to the Inhabitants of the British Colonies. Published anonymously (1768). Written by John Dickinson and first published anonymously in the *Pennsylvania Chronicle,* 1767–68. A defense of the right of colonial self-government and self-taxation, setting forth the legal basis therefor.

Letters of a Japanese Schoolboy. By Wallace Irwin (1909).

Letters of the British Spy, The. By William Wirt (1803). Ten papers which originally appeared anonymously in the *Virginia Argus* in 1803. In book form it became a best-seller, running into many editions.

Letters of William James. Ed. by Henry James, 2v. (1920). William James was one of the great letter writers of the day, and his letters, written in an easy style, touch on a wide range of subjects. *The Letters of Henry James,* ed. by Percy Lubbock, 2v. (1920), read in connection with his brother's letters, give a portrait of the James family and of the intellectual life of the times. See also *Letters of Charles Eliot Norton,* ed. by M. A. DeWolfe Howe, 2v. (1913), which were written at the same time.

LEUBA, JAMES HENRY (Apr. 9, 1868–Dec. 8, 1946); b. Neuchâtel, Switz. Psychologist, author. *The Psychological Origin and the Nature of Religion* (1909); *The Beliefs in God and Immortality* (1916); *The Psychology of Religious Mysticism* (1925); etc. Prof. psychology, Bryn Mawr College, 1889–1933.

LEUCHTENBURG, WILLIAM EDWARD (Sept. 28, 1922–); b. New York. Historian, author. *Flood Control Politics* (1953); *The Perils of Prosperity* (1958); *Franklin D. Roosevelt and the New Deal* (1963); *New Deal and Global War* (1964); *The Great Age of Change* (1964). Editor: *Theodore Roosevelt: The New Nationalism* (1961); *Walter Lippmann: Drift and Mastery* (1961); *Franklin D. Roosevelt: A Profile* (1967). Dept. of political science, Columbia University, since 1952.

LEUPP, FRANCIS ELLINGTON (Jan. 2, 1849–Nov. 19, 1918); b. New York. Journalist, Indian agent, author. *The Man Roosevelt* (1904); *In Red Man's Land* (1914); *Walks about Washington* (1915); etc. Asst. editor, under William Cullen Bryant, of the *New York Evening Post,* and its Washington correspondent, 1889–1904.

LEVANT, OSCAR (Dec. 27, 1906–); b. Pittsburgh, Pa. Pianist, actor, author. *A Smattering of Ignorance* (1940); *The Memoirs of an Amnesiac* (1965); *The Unimportance of Being Oscar* (1968).

LEVERTOV, DENISE (Oct. 1923–); b. Ilford, Essex, Eng. Poet. *The Double Image* (1946); *Overland to the Islands* (1958); *With Eyes at the Back of Our Heads* (1959); *The Jacob's Ladder* (1961); *O Taste and See* (1964); *The Sorrow Dance* (1967); etc.

LEVI, HARRY (Aug. 7, 1875–June 13, 1944); b. Cincinnati, O. Rabbi, author. *Jewish Characters in Fiction: English Literature* (1899); *A Rabbi Speaks* (1930).

LEVI, WERNER (Mar. 23, 1912–); b. Halberstadt, Ger. Educator. *American-Australian Relations* (1947); *Fundamentals of World Organization* (1950); *Free India in Asia* (1952); *Modern China's Foreign Policy* (1953); *Australia's Outlook on Asia* (1959); *The Challenge of World Politics in South and Southeast Asia* (1968). Faculty, University of Michigan, since 1943.

LEVIN, HARRY (Tuchman) (July 18, 1912–); b. Minneapolis, Minn. Educator, author. *The Broken Column: A Study in Romantic Hellenism* (1931); *James Joyce: A Critical Introduction* (1941); *Toward Stendhal* (1945); *Toward Balzac* (1948); *The Overreacher: A Study of Christopher Marlowe* (1952); *Symbolism and Fiction* (1956); *The Power of Blackness: Hawthorne, Poe, Melville* (1958); *The Question of Ham-*

let (1959); *Hawthorne's Scarlet Letter* (1960); *Irving Babbitt and the Teaching of Literature* (1961). *Shakespeare's Comedy of Errors* (1965). Dept. of English and comparative literature, Harvard University, since 1939.

LEVIN, IRA (Aug. 27, 1929–); b. New York. Author. *A Kiss Before Dying* (1953); *No Time for Sergeants* (1956); *Interlock* (prod. 1958); *Critic's Choice* (prod. 1960); *Rosemary's Baby* (1967); *This Perfect Day* (1970); etc.

LEVIN, JACK (June 23, 1898–); b. Portland, Ore. Lawyer, political scientist. *Power Ethics* (1931); *Valuation and Regulation of Public Utilities* (with John H. Gray, 1933); *A 20th Century Congress* (with Estes Kefauver, 1947; rev. ed. 1969).

LEVIN, MEYER (Oct. 7, 1905–); b. Chicago, Ill. Author. *Yehuda* (1931); *Golden Mountain* (1932); *New Bridge* (1933); *Old Bunch* (1937); *Citizens* (1940); *My Father's House* (1946); *In Search* (1950); *Compulsion* (1956); *Eva* (1959); *The Fanatic* (1964); *The Stronghold* (1965); *Gore and Igor* (1968); *The Story of Israel* (1966).

LEVINE, IRVING RASKIN (Aug. 26, 1922–); b. Pawtucket, R.I. Commentator, author. *Main Street, U.S.S.R.* (1959); *Travel Guide to Russia* (1960); *Main Street, Italy* (1963). Correspondent, NBC, since 1950.

LEVINE, ISAAC DON (Feb. 1, 1892–); b. Mozir, Russia. Author. *The Russian Revolution* (1917); *The Man Lenin* (1924); *Red Smoke* (1932); *Mitchell: Pioneer of Air Power* (1943); *Stalin's Great Secret* (1956); *The Mind of an Assassin* (1959); *I Rediscover Russia* (1964); *Intervention* (1969); *The Causes and Consequences of the Czechoslovakian Invasion* (1969).

LEVINGER, ELMA [C.] EHRLICH (Mrs. Lee J. Levinger) (Oct. 6, 1867–Jan. 27, 1958); b. Chicago, Ill. Author. *Jewish Holy-Day Stories* (1918); *The New Land* (1920); *Tales Old and New* (1926); *Wonder Tales of Bible Days* (1929); *Grapes of Canaan* (1931); *More Stories of the New Land* (1938); *Albert Einstein* (1949); *Elijah, Prophet of the One God* (1956); etc.

LEVINGER, LEE JOSEPH (Mar. 4, 1890–July 1, 1966); b. Burke, Idaho. Rabbi, educator, author. *A History of the Jews in the United States* (1930); *Anti-Semitism Yesterday and Tomorrow* (1936); *The Jewish Student in America* (1937); *The Story of the Jew for Young People* (with Elma E. Levinger, 1928); *Mr. Smith, Meet Mr. Cohen* (with J. W. Wise, 1940); etc. Director, B'nai B'rith Hillel Foundation, Ohio State University, 1925–35.

LEVY, LEONARD WILLIAMS (Apr. 9, 1923–); b. Toronto, Can. Educator, author. *The Law of the Commonwealth and Chief Justice Shaw* (1957); *Legacy of Suppression* (1960); *Jefferson and Civil Liberties* (1963); *Origins of the Fifth Amendment* (1968, Pulitzer Prize, 1969). Editor: *Major Crises in American History* (1962); *The American Political Process* (1963); *The Presidency* (1964); *American Constitutional Law* (1966); *Judicial Review and the Supreme Court* (1967); etc. Dean of faculty of arts and sciences, Brandeis University, since 1963.

LEVY, NEWMAN (Nov. 30, 1888–Mar., 1966); b. New York. Lawyer, author. *$1200 a Year* (with Edna Ferber, 1920); *Opera Guyed* (1923); *Gay but Wistful* (poems, 1925); *Saturday to Monday* (1930); *Theatre Guyed* (1933); *My Double Life: Adventures in Law and Letters* (1958); *The Nan Patterson Case* (1959); *F. P. A.* (1961); etc.

Lewars, Mrs. Harold. See Elsie Singmaster.

LEWIN, LEONARD C[ase] (Oct. 2, 1916–   ); b. New York. Author. *Report from Iron Mountain* (1967). Editor: *A Treasury of American Political Humor* (1964).

LEWIS, ALFRED HENRY (c. 1858–Dec. 23, 1914); b. Cleveland, O. Editor, author. Pen name, "Dan Quin." *Wolfville* (1897); *Sandburrs* (1900); *Wolfville Nights* (1902); *Wolf-*

ville Days (1902); *The Boss* (1903); *Confessions of a Detective* (1906); *Wolfville Folks* (1908); *The Apaches of New York* (1912); *Faro Nell and Her Friends* (1913); etc. Created the character of the "Old Cattleman" who relates the *Wolfville* stories, the first of which appeared in the *Kansas City Times* in 1890. Founder, *The Verdict* magazine, 1898; editor, 1898–1914.

LEWIS, ALONZO (1794–1861); b. Lynn, Mass. Poet. Known as the "Lynn Bard." *The History of Lynn* (1829); *Love, Forest Flowers, and Sea-Shells* (poems, 1845); etc.

LEWIS, B[enjamin] ROLAND (Dec. 3, 1884–); b. St. Marys, O. Educator, author. *Creative Poetry* (1930); etc. Editor: *Contemporary One-Act Plays* (1922); *University of Utah Plays* (1928); *Shakespeare Documents*, 2v. (1941); etc. Prof. English, University of Utah, since 1915.

LEWIS, CHARLES BERTRAND (Feb. 15, 1842–Aug. 21, 1924); b. Liverpool, O. Humorist, playwright, dime novelist, journalist. Pen name "M. Quad." *Bugler Ben* (1872); *Mad Dan, the Spy of 1776* (1873); *"Quad's Odds"* (1875); *Goaks and Tears* (1875); *Brother Gardner's Lime-Kiln Club* (1882); *Sawed-Off Sketches* (1884); *Yakie* (prod. 1884); *Under Five Lakes* (1886); *Mr. and Mrs. Bowser* (1899); *The Life and Troubles of Mr. Bowser* (1902); etc. On staff *Detroit Free Press*, 1869–91; *New York World*, etc.

LEWIS, CHARLES LEE (Mar. 7, 1886–); b. Doyle, Tenn. Educator, author. *Famous American Naval Officers* (1924); *Life of Matthew Fontaine Maury* (1927); *Famous Old World Sea Fighers* (1929); *Admiral Franklin Buchanan* (1930); *The Romantic Decatur* (1937); *Books of the Sea* (1943); *Famous American Marines* (1950); and many other naval biographies. English dept., United States Naval Academy, since 1916.

LEWIS, CHARLTON MINER (Mar. 4, 1866–Mar. 12, 1923); b. Brooklyn, N.Y. Educator, editor, author. *Gawayne and the Green Knight* (poem, 1904); *The Principles of English Verse* (1906); *Poems* (1924); etc. Editor, *The Yale Series of Younger Poets*. English dept., Yale, 1895–1923, prof., 1899–1923.

LEWIS, EDWIN HERBERT (Nov. 28, 1866–June 6, 1938); b. Westerly, R.I. Educator, poet, novelist. *An Introduction to the Study of Literature* (1899); *Almost Fairy Children* (1908); *White Lightning* (1923); *University of Chicago Poems* (1923); *Sallie's Newspaper* (1924); etc. Prof. English, Lewis Institute, Chicago, 1899–1935.

LEWIS, ELIZABETH FOREMAN (May 24, 1892–Aug. 7, 1958); b. Baltimore, Md. Author. *Young Fu of the Upper Yangtze* (1933); *Ho-Ming, Girl of New China* (1934); *China Quest* (1937); *Portraits from a Chinese Scroll* (1938); *When the Typhoon Blows* (1942); *To Beat a Tiger One Needs a Brother's Help* (1956); etc.

LEWIS, ESTELLE ANNA [Blanche Robinson] (Apr. 1824–Nov. 24, 1850); b. Baltimore, Md. Poet. Pen names "Sarah Anna Lewis," "S. Anna Lewis," and "Stella." Under first pen name: *Records of the Heart* (1844); under second pen name: *Child of the Sea, and Other Poems* (1844); under own name: *Myths of the Minstrel* (1852); those three with additions published under own name as *Records of the Sea, and Other Poems* (1857); under pen name "Stella": *The King's Stratagem* (drama in verse, 1869); *Sappho* (drama in verse, 1875).

LEWIS, FRANK GRANT (July 18, 1865–Nov. 19, 1945); b. Gang Mills, N.Y. Librarian, author. *How the Bible Grew* (1919); *Church and State* (1928); *A Critique of Conduct* (1930); etc. Compiler: *Biographical Catalogue of the Crozer Theological Seminary, 1855–1933* (with R. Neisser, 1933); etc. Librarian, American Baptist Historical Society, 1912–35, Crozer Theological Seminary, 1909–35.

Lewis, Henry Clay. See Louisiana Swamp Doctor.

LEWIS, JANET (Mrs. Yvor Winters) (Aug. 17, 1899–); b. Chicago, Ill. Author. *Adventures of Ollie Ostrich* (1923); *The Wheel in Midsummer* (poems, 1927); *The Wife of Martin Guerre* (1941); *The Earth-Bound* (poems, 1946); *Good-bye, Son, and Other Stories* (1946); *The Trial of Sören Qvist* (1947); *The Ghost of Monsieur Scarron* (1959); etc.

LEWIS, JOSEPH (June 11, 1889–); b. Montgomery, Ala. Author. *The Tyranny of God* (1921); *Voltaire: The Incomparable Infidel* (1929); *Burbank: The Infidel* (1939); *The Ten Commandments* (1946); *In the Name of Humanity!* (1949); *The Tragic Patriot* (play, 1954); *Ingersoll the Magnificent* (1957); *The Serpents of Religion* (1959); *The Fable of Jesus Christ* (1969); etc.

LEWIS, [Joseph] ANTHONY (Mar. 27, 1927–); b. New York. Journalist, author. *Gideon's Trumpet* (1964); *Portrait of a Decade: The Second American Revolution* (1964). Chief, London bureau, *New York Times,* since 1965.

LEWIS, JUDD MORTIMER (Sept. 13, 1867–July 25, 1945); b. Fulton, N.Y. Columnist, editor, poet. *Sing the South* (1905); *Lilt o' Love* (1906); *Toddle-Town Trails* (1914); etc. Poet laureate of Texas. Author of the syndicated story series "Jubilee's Pardner," "Patsy Kildare," "Outlaw," etc. With the *Houston Post,* from 1900, writing column "Tampering with Trifles."

LEWIS, LLOYD [Downs] (May 2, 1891–Apr. 21, 1949); b. Pendleton, Ind. Drama critic, author. *Myths After Lincoln* (1929); *Chicago: The History of Its Reputation* (with Henry Justin Smith, 1929); *Sherman, Fighting Prophet* (1932); *Jayhawker* (with Sinclair Lewis, prod. 1934); *Oscar Wilde Discovers America* (with Henry Justin Smith, 1936); *It Takes All Kinds* (1947); *Captain Sam Grant* (1949); etc. Drama critic, sports editor, managing editor, *Chicago Daily News,* 1930–45; columnist, *Chicago Sun-Times,* from 1945.

Lewis, Margaret Cameron. See Margaret Cameron.

LEWIS, MERIWETHER (Aug. 18, 1774–Oct. 11, 1809); b. in Albemarle Co., Va. Explorer, soldier. See *History of the Expedition Under the Command of Captain Lewis and Clark,* 2v. (1814), ed. by Nicholas Biddle and Paul Allen. *See also* edition ed. by Elliott Coues, 4v. (1893); that ed. by John B. McMaster, 3v. (1904); the definitive one ed. by Reuben Gold Thwaites, 8v. (1904–05); that ed. by Bernard DeVoto (1953); etc. Lewis and Clark led the exploring expedition from Missouri to Oregon in 1803–06. *See* Emerson Hough's *The Magnificent Adventure* (1916); Charles Morrow Wilson's *Meriwether Lewis* (1934); R. H. Dillon's *Meriwether Lewis* (1965).

Lewis, Mrs. Sinclair. See Dorothy Thompson.

LEWIS, OSCAR (May 5, 1893–); b. San Francisco, Calif. Author. *Hearn and His Biographers* (1930); *A History of San Francisco* (with Lewis Francis Byinton, 1931); *Frank Norris of the Wave* (1931); *California in 1846* (1934); *Lola Montez* (1938); *The Big Four* (1938); *Bonanza Inn* (with Carroll Douglas Hall, 1939); *I Remember Christine* (1942); *Uncertain Journey* (1945); *Silver Kings* (1947); *Sea Routes to the Gold Fields* (1949); *California Heritage* (1949); *The Lost Years* (1951); *Sagebrush Casinos: The Story of Legal Gambling in Nevada* (1953); *Hawaii: Gem of the Pacific* (1954); *George Davidson: Pioneer West Coast Scientist* (1954); *The Town That Died Laughing* (1955); *High Sierra Country* (1955); *Bay Window Bohemia* (1956); *Here Lived the Californians* (1957); *The Way in the Far West: 1861–1865* (1961). Editor: *The Autobiography of the West* (1958).

LEWIS, OSCAR (Dec. 25, 1914–Dec. 16, 1970). Sociologist. *Life in a Mexican Village* (1951); *Five Families: Mexican Case Studies in the Culture of Poverty* (1959); *The Children of Sánchez* (1961); *Pedro Martinez* (1964); *Village Life in Northern India* (1965); *La Vida* (1966); *A Death in the Sanchez Family* (1969).

LEWIS, R[ichard] W[arrington] B[aldwin] (Nov. 1, 1917–); b. Chicago, Ill. Educator, author. *The American Adam* (1955); *The Picaresque Saint* (1959); *Trails of the World* (1965). Editor: *Herman Melville* (1962); *The Presence of Walt Whitman* (1962); *Malraux* (1964). Prof. English and American Studies, Yale University, since 1960.

LEWIS, SAM, b. New York City. Song writer. Wrote lyrics for over 800 songs, including "Mammy," "Dinah," "In a Little Spanish Town," "Tuck Me to Sleep in My Old 'Tucky Home," "Mellow Melody," "How You Gonna Keep 'Em Down on the Farm After They've Seen Paree?," and many others, some with George Meyer and Joe Young.

Lewis, Sarah Anne. Pen name of Estelle Anna Blanche Robinson Lewis.

LEWIS, SINCLAIR (Feb. 7, 1885–Jan. 10, 1951); b. Sauk Center, Minn. Novelist. *Our Mr. Wrenn* (1914); *The Trail of the Hawk* (1915); *The Innocents* (1917); *The Job* (1917); *Free Air* (1919); *Main Street* (1920); *Babbitt* (1922); *Arrowsmith* (1925); *Mantrap* (1926); *Elmer Gantry* (1927); *The Man Who Knew Coolidge* (1928); *Dodsworth* (1929); *Ann Vickers* (1933); *Work of Art* (1934); *Jayhawker* (with Lloyd Lewis, prod. 1935); *It Can't Happen Here* (1935); *Selected Short Stories* (1935); *The Prodigal Parents* (1938); *Bethel Merriday* (1940); *Gideon Planish* (1943); *Cass Timberlane* (1945); *Kingsblood Royal* (1947); *The God-Seeker* (1949); *World So Wide* (1951); *The Man from Main Street* (1953); *From Main Street to Stockholm: Letters of Sinclair Lewis, 1919–1930* (1952), ed. by Harrison Smith. Won Nobel Prize in literature, 1930. *See* Maxwell Geismar's *The Last of the Provincials* (1947); Grace Hegger Lewis's *With Love from Sinclair Lewis, 1912–1925* (1956); Mark Schorer's *Sinclair Lewis: An American Life* (1961); Vincent Sheean's *Dorothy and Red* (1963); D. J. Dooley's *The Art of Sinclair Lewis* (1967).

LEWIS, WILLIAM STANLEY (July 21, 1876–); b. Hamden, N.Y. Lawyer, author. *The Case of Spokane Gardy* (1917); *Early Days in the Big Bend Country* (1921).

LEWIS, WILMARTH SHELDON (Nov. 14, 1895–); b. Alameda, Calif. Editor, author. *Tutor's Lane* (1922); *Three Tours Through London in the Years 1748, 1776, and 1797* (1941); *The Yale Collections* (1946); *Collector's Progress* (1951); *Horace Walpole's Library* (1958); *Horace Walpole* (1960). Editor: *Miscellaneous Antiquities,* 11v. (1927–37); *The Yale Edition of Horace Walpole's Correspondence,* 26v. (with others, 1937–60); *The Castle of Ontranto* (1964).

LEWISOHN, LUDWIG (May 30, 1883–Dec. 31, 1955); b. Berlin, Germany. Critic, novelist. *The Broken Snare* (1908); *The Modern Drama* (1915); *Upstream* (autobiography, 1922); *Don Juan* (1923); *The Creative Life* (1924); *The Case of Mr. Crump* (1926); *Cities and Men* (1927); *Mid-Channel* (autobiography, 1929); *Stephen Escott* (1930); *Expression in America* (1932); *The Permanent Horizon* (1934); *Trumpet of Jubilee* (1937); *The Answer* (1939); *Haven* (with wife, Edna Manley Lewisohn, 1940); *Renegade* (1942); *Breathe Upon These* (1944); *Anniversary* (1948); *The American Jew, Character and Destiny* (1950); *Magic Word* (1950); *In a Summer Season* (1955); etc. *See* Fred B. Millett's *Contemporary American Authors* (1940).

LEY, WILLY (Oct. 2, 1906–June 24, 1969); b. Berlin. Author. *The Lungfish and the Unicorn* (1940); *Bombs and Bombing* (1941); *The Days of Creation* (1941); *Rockets* (1944); *Conquest of Space* (1949); *Dragons in Amber* (1951); *Salamanders and Other Wonders* (1955); *The Exploration of Mars* (with Wernher von Braun, 1956); *Willy Ley's Exotic Zoology* (1959); *Beyond the Solar System* (1964); *Inside the Orbit of the Earth* (1968); *The Meteorite Craters* (1968); *Another Look at Atlantis and Fifteen Other Essays* (1969); *Events in Space* (1969); *Visitors from Afar: The Comets* (1969); *Watchers of the Skies* (1969); etc.

LEYBURN, JAMES GRAHAM (Jan. 17, 1902–); b. Hedgesville, W. Va. Sociologist. *Handbook of Ethnography* (1931);

Frontier Folkways (1935); *The Haitian People* (1941); *A Social History* (1962); etc. Prof. sociology, Washington and Lee University, since 1956.

LEYDA, JAY (1910–). Author. *Sergei Rachmaninoff* (with S. Bertensson, 1956); *Kino: A History of the Russian and Soviet Film* (1960); *The Years and Hours of Emily Dickinson*, 2v. (1960); *Films Beget Films* (1964). Editor: *The Melville Log*, 2v. (1951); *The Portable Melville* (1968). Editor, translator: Eisenstein's *Film Sense* (1942); *The Musorgsky Reader* (with S. Bertensson, 1947).

LEYS, WAYNE ALBERT RISSER (June 29, 1905–); b. Bloomington, Ill. Educator. *The Religious Control of Emotion* (1932); *Ethics and Social Policy* (1941); *Ethics for Policy Decisions* (1952, rev. ed. 1968). Prof. philosophy, Roosevelt University, since 1945.

L'HOMMEDIEU, DOROTHY [Keasbey] (1885–Mar. 16, 1964). Author. *Scampy, the Little Black Cocker* (1939); *Skippy, the Little Skye Terrier* (1944); *Togo, the Little Husky* (1951); *Pompon* (1955); *Topper and Madame Pig* (1956); *Little Black Chaing* (1958); etc.

LIBBEY, LAURA JEAN (Mar. 22, 1862–Oct. 25, 1924); b. New York. Novelist. *A Fatal Wooing* (1883); *Madolin Rivers* (1885); *Junie's Love Test* (1886); *Miss Middleton's Lover* (1888); *That Pretty Young Girl* (1889); *A Mad Betrothal* (1890); *Parted by Fate* (1890); *We Parted at the Altar* (1892); etc. *See* Edna Kenton's *Parted on Her Bridal Tour and Other Novels*, in *The Trend*, Aug. 1914; Louis Gold's *Laura Jean Libbey*, in the *American Mercury*, Sept. 1931.

Liber Scriptorum. New York. Publication of the Authors Club. Two have been issued: *The First Book of the Authors Club: Liber Scriptorum* (1893); *The Second Book of the Authors Club: Liber Scriptorum* (1921). Both were edited by Rossiter Johnson. Members of the club wrote the text.

Liberal Imagination, The. By Lionel Trilling (1950). Essays on literature and society.

Liberation. New York. Monthly. Founded 1956. Devoted to pacifism and non-violent action. Has been edited by A. J. Muste and Dave Dellinger.

Liberation News Service. Founded 1968 by Marshall Bloom and Raymond Mungo. Supplies over 200 subscribers, mainly New Left, underground, and student newspapers with material overlooked by ordinary news sources.

Liberator. Boston, Mass. Abolitionist journal. Founded Jan. 1, 1831, by William Lloyd Garrison, who was also the editor. It was noted for its brilliant articles against slavery. Expired Dec. 29, 1865.

Liberator. New York. Monthly. Black nationalist magazine, founded 1960. Edited by Daniel Watts.

Liberator, The. New York. See *The Masses*.

Liberty. New York. Weekly magazine. Founded 1924, by the *Chicago Tribune* organization. Max Annenberg became general manager in 1926. In 1931 it was purchased by MacFadden Publications, headed by Bernarr MacFadden. Fulton Oursler was editor after 1931. This illustrated magazine featured short stories and articles on world events. It was discontinued in 1951.

"Liberty Enlightening the World." Poem by Edmund Clarence Stedman (1888). Written about the Statue of Liberty, which had been unveiled Oct. 28, 1886. It begins: "Warden at Ocean's gate, Thy feet on sea and shore."

"Liberty Enlightening the World." Poem by Henry van Dyke (1917). Written on the entry of the United States into the First World War. The first line is "Thou warden of the Western gate, above Manhattan Bay."

"Liberty Song, The." By John Dickinson. It first appeared in the Boston *Gazette*, July 18, 1768, and was published as the first separate sheet-music to appear in the Colonies in 1768. The first line is "Come join hand in hand, brave Americans all." There was a Loyalist parody, also 1768, beginning, "Come shake your dull noddles, ye bumkins, and bawl."

"Liberty's Call." Poem by John Mason (1775). It first appeared in the *Pennsylvania Packet;* then was published as a broadside. Attributed also to Francis Hopkinson.

Library Journal. New York. Founded 1876, by R. R. Bowker, Frederick Leypoldt, and Melvil Dewey, who became editors. Other editors have been C. A. Cutter, Paul Leicester Ford, Frederic G. Melcher, and Bertine E. Weston.

Library of American Literature, A. Ed. by Edmund Clarence Stedman and E. M. Hutchinson, 11v. (1888–90). Selections from the writings of American authors, with biographies. Has a general index.

Library of Congress. Washington, D.C. Established Apr. 24, 1800. Begun with the library of Thomas Jefferson as a nucleus, it now contains over 58,000,000 items. Present building erected 1897. Librarians: John Beckley, 1802–07; Patrick Magruder, 1807–15; George Watterston, 1915–29; John Silva Meehan, 1829–61; John G. Stephenson, 1861–64; Ainsworth Rand Spofford, 1864–97; John Russell Young, 1897–99; Herbert Putnam, 1899–1939; Archibald MacLeish, 1939–45; Luther Evans 1945–53; L. Quincy Mumford, since 1954. The Library houses the personal papers of James Michener, Felix Frankfurter, Edna St. Vincent Millay, Karl Shapiro, Clare Booth Luce, Owen Wister, Bill Mauldin, among others. It is also the repository for the Walt Whitman collection of Charles Feinberg; holograph scores of compositions by Igor Stravinsky, Aaron Copland, Howard Hanson, and George Gershwin; early silent motion pictures; original drawings of *New Yorker* cartoons.

Library of Southern Literature, 17v. (1908–23). Editors in chief: Edwin Anderson Alderman, Joel Chandler Harris. Lit. editor, Charles William Kent. Biographical and critical sketches of Southern authors with selections from their works, with bibliographies. Vol. 16 contains reading courses, charts, etc. Vol. 15 is a biographical dictionary of 3800 subjects, edited by Lucian Lamar Knight.

Library of the World's Best Literature, 31v. (1896–97). Edited by Charles Dudley Warner and others. Enlarged as *The Warner Library*, 30v. (1917), ed. by John W. Cunliffe and Ashley H. Thorndike. Contains a general index volume, a *Students Course in Literature*, and the *Reader's Digest of Books*, edited by Helen Rex Keller.

Library Quarterly. Chicago, Ill. Founded 1930. Covers the field of library science. Howard W. Winger is editor and book review editor.

LIDDELL, MARK HARVEY (Apr. 1, 1866–July 28, 1936); b. Clearfield, Pa. Educator, editor, author. *An Introduction to the Study of Poetry* (1902); *A New Theory of Sound* (1935); etc. Editor of various works of Chaucer and Shakespeare. English dept., Purdue University, 1913–32.

Lie Down in Darkness. Novel by William Styron (1951). The disintegration of spirit in a Southern family. Written in stream-of-consciousness style.

LIEBER, FRANCIS (Mar. 18, 1800–Oct. 2, 1872); b. Berlin, Ger. Educator, political scientist, author. *The Stranger in America* (1835); *Political Ethics*, 2v. (1838–39); *The West* (poem, 1848); *On Civil Liberty and Self-Government*, 2v. (1853); *Miscellaneous Writings*, ed. by Daniel C. Gilman, 2v. (1881); etc. Founder: *Encyclopedia Americana*, 13v. (1829–33). *See* T. S. Perry's *The Life and Letters of Francis Lieber* (1882). His manuscripts are in the Johns Hopkins Library and the Henry E. Huntington Library. Prof. history, University of South Carolina, 1835–56; Columbia University, 1856–65; prof. political science, Columbia University, 1865–72.

LIEBER, LILLIAN R[osanoff] (July 26, 1886–); b. Nicolaiev, Rus. Educator, author. *Non-Euclidean Geometry* (1931); *The Einstein Theory of Relativity* (1936); *The Education of T. C. Mits* (1942); *Take a Number: Mathematics for the Two Billion* (1946); *Mits, Wits and Logic* (1947); *Infinity* (1953); *Lattice Theory: The Atomic Age in Mathematics* (1959); etc. Head, dept. of mathematics, Long Island University, 1945–54.

LIEBERMAN, ELIAS (Oct. 30, 1883–July 13, 1969); b. St. Petersburg, Russia. Author. *The American Short Story* (1912); *The Awakening of Narradin* (with Gustav Blum, prod. 1916); *Paved Streets* (poems, 1917); *Hand Organ Man* (poems, 1930); *Man in the Shadows* (poems, 1939); *Unions Before the Bar* (1950); *To My Brothers Everywhere* (poems, 1954).

LIEBLING, A[bbott] J[oseph] (Oct. 18, 1904–Dec. 28, 1963); b. New York. Journalist, author. *Back Where I Came From* (1938); *The Telephone Booth Indian* (1942); *The Road Back to Paris* (1944); *The Wayward Pressman* (1947); *Mink and Red Herring: The Wayward Pressman's Casebook* (1949); *The Honest Rainmaker* (1953); *The Sweet Science* (1956); *Normandy Revisited* (1958); *The Earl of Louisiana* (1961); *The Press* (1961); etc. Staff, *The New Yorker,* from 1935.

LIEBMAN, JOSHUA LOTH (Apr. 7, 1907–June 9, 1948); b. Hamilton, Ohio. Rabbi, author. *The Religious Philosophy of Aaron Ben Elijah* (1939); *God and the World Crisis* (1941); *Peace of Mind* (1946); etc.

LIEDER, PAUL ROBERT (Sept. 18, 1889–May 14, 1956); b. Brooklyn, N.Y. Educator, editor. *Scott and Scandinavian Literature* (1920); Editor: *Poems by Tegnér* (1914); *The Chief British Dramatists* (with Brander Matthews, 1924); *British Poetry and Prose* (with others, 1928); *Eminent British Poets of the Nineteenth Century,* 2v. (1938); *The Art of Literary Criticism* (with Robert Withington, 1941); etc. English dept., Smith College, 1915–54.

Life. New York. Satiric weekly. Founded Jan. 4, 1883, by John Ames Mitchell, who was publisher, 1883–1918. Charles Dana Gibson was publisher, 1920–28; Clair Maxwell, 1928–36. Edward Sandford Martin was editor for the first few months, and was editorial writer 1887–1906. Later editors include: Henry Guy Carleton, 1883–87; Tom Masson, 1893–1922; Robert E. Sherwood, 1924–28. John Kendrick Bangs was assoc. editor, 1884–88. Robert Bridges was book editor, 1883–1900. Among the drama editors were "Alan Dale" (Alfred J. Cohen), 1885–88; James Stetson Metcalfe, 1888–1920; Robert C. Benchley, 1920–29; George Jean Nathan, 1934–36. It became a monthly in Jan., 1932, and in 1936 was sold to Time, Inc. See *Life's Jubilee Number,* Jan., 1893, *Anniversary Number,* Jan. 2, 1908, and *Fiftieth Anniversary Number,* Jan., 1933; chap. 5 in Francis Hyde Bangs's *John Kendrick Bangs* (1941).

Life. New York. Weekly picture magazine. Founded 1936, by Time, Inc. Henry Robinson Luce was editor until his death in 1967; succeeded by Hedley W. Donovan. A new venture in pictorial journalism, it has maintained its popularity ever since. Notable features have been comprehensive popular articles of encyclopedic nature, reproductions of paintings, and serialized fiction or memoirs of outstanding importance.

Life Against Death. By Norman O. Brown (1959). A study of the relation of psychoanalysis to history which argues that repression is the source of man's social neurosis throughout the centuries.

Life at the South; or, "Uncle Tom's Cabin" As It Is. Novel by W. L. G. Smith (1852). Written in answer to *Uncle Tom's Cabin* by Harriet Beecher Stowe.

Life in the Iron Mills. Short story by Rebecca Harding Davis (1861). An early attempt at realism.

Life of Reason, The. By George Santayana, 5v. (1905–06). A philosophical study of the modern mind, written in a polished literary style by a philosopher who is also a poet.

Life on the Mississippi. By Mark Twain (1883). An autobiographical narrative of the author's early days as a pilot, with an introductory account of the Mississippi river's scenery and history. An epic of steamboat life in the early days of the West.

"Life on the Ocean Wave, A." Poem by Epes Sargent. It first appeared in the *New York Mirror,* May 19, 1838, and was published the same year with music by Henry Russell.

Life with Father. By Clarence Day (1935), dramatized by Russel Crouse and Howard Lindsay (prod. 1939). Humorous account of a noted New York family, centering around a conceited and domineering father and a pious mother.

Life's Minor Collisions. By Francis Lester Warner and Gertrude Chandler Warner (1921). A volume of popular essays.

LIFTON, ROBERT JAY (1926–). Psychiatrist, author. *Thought Reform and the Psychology of Totalism* (1963); *Death in Life: Survivors of Hiroshima* (1968, National Book Award, 1969); *Revolutionary Immortality* (1968); *History and Human Survival* (1970). Editor: *The Woman in America* (1965). Research professor of psychiatry, Yale University.

Ligeia. Tale by Edgar Allan Poe (1838).

LIGGETT, WALTER WILLIAM (Feb. 14, 1886–Dec. 9, 1935); b. Benson, Miss. Editor, author. *The Frozen Frontier* (1926); *The River Riders* (1927); *Pioneers of Justice* (1930); etc. Editor and publisher, the *Austin* (Minn.) *American,* and the *Rochester* (Minn.) *American.*

Light in August. Novel by William Faulkner (1932).

Lightnin'. Play by Frank Bacon and Winchell Smith (1918). The story of Lightnin' Bill Jones, who owns a hotel, part of which is in Nevada and part in California. The law is frustrated when John Marvin jumps from one state to another. This play enjoyed a long run. The leading role, that of Bill Jones, was played by Frank Bacon, from 1918 to 1922. The role in the movie version was played by Will Rogers.

LIGHTON, WILLIAM RHEEM (b. July 13, 1866); b. in Lycoming Co., Pa. Author. *Sons of Strength: A Romance of the Kansas Border Wars* (1899); *Lewis and Clark* (1901); *Billy Fortune* (1912); *Happy Holly Farm* (1916); etc.

LILIENTHAL, DAVID ELI (July 8, 1899–); b. Morton, Ill. Industrialist, government official. *TVA: Democracy on the March* (1944); *This I Do Believe* (1949); *Big Business: A New Era* (1953); *The Multi-National Corporation* (1960); *Change, Hope, and the Bomb* (1963); *Journals of David E. Lilienthal,* Vols. I and II (1964), Vol. III (1966), Vol. IV (1969); etc.

LILJENCRANTZ, OTTILIE ADALINE (Jan. 19, 1876–1910); b. Chicago, Ill. Author. *The Scrape That Jack Built* (1896); *The Thrall of Leif the Lucky* (1902); *The Ward of King Canute* (1904); *The Vinland Champions* (1904); *Randvar, the Songsmith* (1906).

LILLIE, LUCY C[ecil White] (b. 1855); b. New York. Author. *The Story of English Literature for Young Readers* (1878); *Prudence: A Story of Esthetic London* (1882); *Mildred's Bargain* (1883); *The Colonel's Money* (1888); *Esther's Fortune* (1889); *The Squire's Daughter* (1891); *Alison's Adventures* (1894); *Elinor Belden* (1896); etc.

LILLY, ELI (Apr. 1, 1885–); b. Indianapolis, Ind. Manufacturing chemist, philanthropist, historian. *Prehistoric Antiquities of Indiana* (1937); *The Little Church on the Circle* (1957); *Early Wawasee Days* (1960); *Schliemann in Indianapolis* (1961). President, Indiana Historical Society, 1933–40; Eli Lilly Co., Indianapolis, 1932–48; chairman of the board since 1948.

Lily: A Ladies' Journal Devoted to Temperance and Literature, The. Seneca Falls, N.Y. Founded January, 1849, by Amelia Bloomer. Moved to Mt. Vernon, O., 1854; and to

Richmond, Ind., 1855. Expired 1856. A similar magazine, *The Sibyl* (1856–64) was published at Middletown, N.Y., under the editorship of Drs. Lydia Sayer, the "Drs." standing for "Doctoress."

Limited Editions Club. New York. Founded 1929, by George Macy. See its *Ten Years and William Shakespeare* (1941), which gives a history of the club and a bibliography of its publications.

LIN YUTANG (Oct. 10, 1895–); b. Changchow, Fukien Prov., China. Author. *Letters of a Chinese Amazon* (1927); *My Country and My People* (1935); *Essays about Nothing* (1936); *The Importance of Living* (1937); *Moment in Peking* (1939); *With Love and Irony* (1940); *A Leaf in the Storm* (1941); *Wisdom of China and India* (1942); *Between Tears and Laughter* (1943); *The Gay Genius* (1947); *Wisdom of Laotse* (1948); *On the Wisdom of America* (1950); *Widow, Nun and Courtesan: Three Novelettes from the Chinese* (1951); *Vermilion Gate* (1953); *The Secret Name* (1958); *From Pagan to Christian* (1959); *Imperial Peking* (1961); *Lady Wu* (1965); *Chinese Theory of Art* (1967); *A History of the Press and Public Opinion in China* (1968); etc. Chancellor, Nanyang University, Singapore.

LINCOLN, ABRAHAM (Feb. 12, 1809–Apr. 15, 1865); b. "Sinking Spring Farm," Hardin Co., Ky. Sixteenth president of the United States. *A Memorial Lincoln Bibliography*, comp. by Andrew Boyd and Charles Henry Hart (1870); *A List of Lincolniana in the Library of Congress*, comp. by Thomas Ritchie (1903); *Complete Works of Abraham Lincoln*, ed. by J. G. Nicolay and John Hay, 12v. (1905); *Abraham Lincoln: His Speeches and Writings*, ed. by Roy P. Basler (1946); *The Collected Works of Abraham Lincoln*, ed. by Roy P. Basler and others, 9v. (1953). See William Henry Herndon's *Lincoln*, 3v. (with Jesse W. Weik, 1889); John G. Nicolay's and John Hay's *Abraham Lincoln: A History*, 10v. (1890); Ward Hill Lamon's *The Life of Abraham Lincoln* (1872), and his *Recollections of Abraham Lincoln* (with Dorothy Lamon Teillard, 1911); Albert J. Beveridge's *Abraham Lincoln*, 2v. (1928); Emanuel Herts's *Abraham Lincoln: A New Portrait* (1931), and his *The Hidden Lincoln* (1938); James G. Randall's *Abraham Lincoln*, in *Dictionary of American Biography*, v. II (1933); Paul Angle's *Lincoln* (1933), and his *Here I Have Lived: A History of Lincoln's Springfield* (1935); Carl Sandburg's *Abraham Lincoln: The Prairie Years*, 2v. (1926), and his *Abraham Lincoln: The War Years*, 4v. (1939); George S. Bryan's *The Great American Myth* (1940); Alan Nevins' *The Emergence of Lincoln*, 2v. (1950); Herbert Agar's *Abraham Lincoln* (1952); Benjamin P. Thomas' *Abraham Lincoln* (1952); Norman A. Graebner's *Enduring Lincoln* (1959); Denis W. Brogan's *Abraham Lincoln* (1963); William B. Catton's and Bruce Catton's *Two Roads to Sumter* (1963); Roy P. Basler's *Lincoln Legend* (1969). Among the better known poems on Lincoln are: William Cullen Bryant's "Abraham Lincoln"; James Russell Lowell's "Commemoration Ode"; Walt Whitman's "O Captain! My Captain!" and his "When Lilacs Last in the Dooryard Bloom'd"; Edwin Arlington Robinson's "The Master"; Edwin Markham's "Lincoln, the Man of the People"; Witter Bynner's "A Farmer Remembers Lincoln"; Maurice Thompson's "Lincoln's Grave"; Vachel Lindsay's "Abraham Lincoln Walks at Midnight"; Percy MacKaye's "Ode on the Centenary of Abraham Lincoln"; Richard Watson Gilder's "On the Life Mask of Abraham Lincoln"; R. H. Stoddard's "Lincoln"; etc.

LINCOLN, C[harles] ERIC (June 23, 1924–   ); b. Athens, Ala. Educator, author. *The Black Muslims in America* (1961); *My Face Is Black* (1964); *The Negro Pilgrimage in America* (1967). Prof. social relations, 1961–65, Portland Oregon State College, prof. sociology, 1965–67; prof. sociology and religion, Union Theological Seminary, since 1967.

LINCOLN, ELLIOTT C[urtis] (1884–); Poet. *Rhymes of a Homesteader* (1920); *The Ranch: Poems of the West* (1924).

LINCOLN, JEANIE [Thomas] GOULD (1846–Aug. 8, 1921); b. Troy, N.Y. Author. *A Chaplet of Leaves* (poems, 1869); *An Unwilling Maid* (1897); *A Pretty Tory* (1899); *The Luck of Rathcoole* (1911); etc.

LINCOLN, JOSEPH CROSBY (Feb. 13, 1870–Mar. 10, 1944); b. Brewster, Mass. Author. *Cape Cod Ballads* (1902); *Cap'n Eri* (1904); *Partners of the Tide* (1905); *The Old Home House* (1907); *Cy Whitaker's Place* (1908); *Our Village* (1909); *Keziah Coffin* (1909); *The Woman Haters* (1911); *The Postmaster* (1912); *Cap'n Dan's Daughter* (1914); *Mary 'Gusta* (1916); *The Portygee* (1919); *Galusha the Magnificent* (1921); *Fair Harbor* (1922); *Rugged Water* (1924); *Queer Judson* (1925); *Blowing Clear* (1930); *Head Tide* (1932); *Cape Cod Yesterdays* (1935); *Storm Girl* (1937); *Christmas Days* (1938); *Out of the Fog* (1940); etc.

LINCOLN, [Joseph] FREEMAN (July 16, 1900–Feb. 11, 1962); b. Hackensack, N.J. Editor. Co-author of books with father, Joseph C. Lincoln: *Blair's Attic* (1929); *Ownley Inn* (1939); *New Hope* (1941); etc. Staff, *Fortune* magazine, from 1946.

LINCOLN, NATALIE SUMNER (Oct. 4, 1881–Aug. 31, 1935); b. Washington, D.C. Novelist. *The Trevor Case* (1912); *The Man Inside* (1914); *The Moving Finger* (1918); *I Spy* (1916); *The Red Seal* (1920); etc.

LINCOLN, VICTORIA ENDICOTT (Oct. 23, 1904–); b. Fall River, Mass. Author. *The Swan Island Murders* (1930); *February Hill* (1934); *Grandmother and the Comet* (1944); *The Wind at My Back* (1946); *Celia Amberley* (1949); *Out from Eden* (1951); *The Wild Honey* (1953); *A Dangerous Innocence* (1958); *Charles* (1962); *Everyhow Remarkable* (1967); *Private Disgrace: Lizzie Borden by Daylight* (1967); etc.

Lincoln Library of Essential Information, The. First issued in 1924 by M. J. Kinsella, founder of The Frontier Press, which still publishes it. A compendium of reference information and helpful instruction.

Lincoln's Doctor's Dog, and Other Famous Best Sellers. By George Stevens (1939). A book explaining how books become best sellers. The author points out that any book with "Lincoln" in the title, or about a dog or a doctor is bound to sell, hence the title.

Linda Condon. Novel by Joseph Hergesheimer (1919). A study of the disintegration of surface beauty which reveals woman's need for a corresponding inner beauty and strength of character. The setting is made up of the fashionable life of Florida in winter, and Lake George in summer.

LINDBERGH, ANNE [Spencer] MORROW (Mrs. Charles Augustus Lindbergh) (1907–). Author. *North to the Orient* (1935); *Listen! the Wind* (1938); *The Wave of the Future* (1940); *The Steep Ascent* (1944); *Gift from the Sea* (1955); *Unicorn and Other Poems* (1956); *Dearly Beloved* (1962).

LINDBERGH, CHARLES A[ugustus] (Feb. 4, 1902–); b. Detroit, Mich. Aviator. Author. *We* (1926); *Of Flight and Life* (1948); *The Spirit of St. Louis* (1953, Pulitzer prize for biography, 1954). *The Wartime Journals of Charles A. Lindbergh* (1970).

LINDEMAN, JACK (Dec. 31, 1924–   ); Philadelphia, Pa. Poet. *Twenty-One Poems* (1963); *The Conflict of Convictions* (1968).

LINDERMAN, FRANK BIRD (Sept. 25, 1869–May 12, 1938); b. Cleveland, O. Trapper, journalist, author. *Indian Why Stories* (1915); *On a Passing Frontier* (1920); *How It Came About Stories* (1921); *Indian Old-Man Stories* (1926); *Kootenai Why Stories* (1926); *American: The Life Story of a Great Indian, Plenty-Coups* (1930); *Old Man Coyote* (1931); *Blackfeet Indians* (1935).

LINDEY, ALEXANDER (May 15, 1896–). Lawyer, author. *Hold Your Tongue* (with Morris L. Ernst, 1932); *The Censor Marches On* (with Morris L. Ernst, 1940); *Motion Picture Agreements Annotated* (1947); *Plagiarism and Originality* (1952); etc.

LINDLEY, ERNEST KIDDER (July 14, 1899–); b. Richmond, Ind. Journalist, author. *Franklin D. Roosevelt: A Career in Progressive Democracy* (1931); *Half Way with Roosevelt* (1936); *How War Came* (with Forrest Davis, 1942); etc. Editor: *Winds of Freedom,* by Dean Rusk (1963). Political commentator, Washington *Post,* 1938–48.

LINDLEY, HARLOW (May 31, 1875–Aug. 20, 1959); b. Sylvania, Ind. Educator, author. *The Quakers of the Old Northwest* (1912); *The Indiana Centennial* (1919); etc. Editor: *Indiana As Seen by Early Travelers* (1916); *Ohio in the Twentieth Century,* 6v. (1941–44); etc. Prof. history, Earlham College, 1905–28; librarian, 1898–1928.

LINDSAY, HOWARD (Mar. 29, 1889–Feb. 11, 1968); b. Waterford, N.Y. Actor, producer, playwright. Co-author: with Bertrand Robinson: *Your Uncle Dudley* (prod. 1929); with Damon Runyon: *A Slight Case of Murder* (prod. 1935); with Russell Crouse: *Anything Goes* (prod. 1934); *Red, Hot and Blue* (prod. 1936); *Hooray for What?* (prod. 1937); *Life With Father* (from stories by Clarence Day, prod. 1939); *State of the Union* (prod. 1945, Pulitzer Prize for drama, 1946); *Life With Mother* (from stories by Clarence Day, 1948); *Call Me Madam* (prod. 1950); *Remains To Be Seen* (prod. 1951); *The Prescott Proposals* (prod. 1953); *Happy Hunting* (prod. 1956); *The Sound of Music* (prod. 1959); etc.

LINDSAY, [Nicholas] VACHEL (Nov. 10, 1879–Dec. 5, 1931); b. Springfield, Ill. Poet. *The Village Magazine* (1910); *Rhymes to Be Traded for Bread* (1912); *General William Booth Enters into Heaven, and Other Poems* (1913); *The Congo, and Other Poems* (1914); *The Chinese Nightingale, and Other Poems* (1917); *Collected Poems* (1923); *Johnny Appleseed, and Other Poems* (1928); etc. His best-known poems are "The Congo," and "Abraham Lincoln Walks at Midnight." *See* Fred B. Millett's *Contemporary American Authors* (1940); and Eleanor Ruggles' *The West-Going Heart: A Life of Vachel Lindsay* (1959); *Friendship's Garland,* ed. by V. Gabrieli (1966).

LINDSEY, BEN[jamin] B[arr] (Nov. 25, 1869–Mar. 26, 1943); b. Jackson, Tenn. Jurist, author. *The Beast* (with Harvey Jerrold O'Higgins, 1910); *The Revolt of Modern Youth* (1925); *The Companionate Marriage* (1927); *The Dangerous Life* (with Rube Borrough, autobiography, 1931); etc.

LINDSEY, WILLIAM (Aug. 12, 1858–Nov. 25, 1922); b. Fall River, Mass. Manufacturer, novelist, poet. *Apples of Istakhar* (poems, 1895); *Cinder Path Tales* (1896); *The Severed Mantle* (1909); *Red Wine of Rousillon* (drama in verse, 1915); *The Backsliders* (1922); *The Curtain of Forgetfulness* (poems, 1923); etc.

"Line-o'-Type or Two, A." Column conducted by Bert Leston Taylor in the *Chicago Daily Tribune. See* his *Line-o'-Type Lyrics* (1902). He signed the column with the initials B. L. T. The column contained many stories about "Bunn, the Baker of Baraboo," who in real life is John Bunn, of Baraboo, Wis. He and his wife ran a small bakery shop for many years, and became famous through B. L. T.'s column. Richard Henry Little has conducted the column since 1920.

LINEBARGER, PAUL MYRON ANTHONY (July 11, 1913–Aug. 6, 1966); b. Milwaukee, Wis. Novelist. Under pen name "Felix C. Forrest:" *Ria* (1947); *Carola* (1948). Under pen name "Charmichael Smith:" *Atomsk* (1949). Under own name: *Psychological Warfare* (1948).

LINEBARGER, PAUL MYRON WENTWORTH (June 15, 1871–Feb. 20, 1939); b. Warren, Ill. Lawyer, author. Pen name "Paul Myron." *Bugle Rhymes from France* (1916); *Chinese Interpretive Lyrics* (1920); *Sun Yat Sen and the Chinese Republic* (1925); etc.

LINK, ARTHUR STANLEY (Aug. 8, 1920–); b. New Market, Va. Educator. *Wilson: The Road to the White House* (1947); *Woodrow Wilson and the Progressive Era* (1954); *The American Epoch* (1955); *Wilson: The New Freedom* (1956); *Wilson the Diplomatist* (1957); *Wilson: The Struggle for Neutrality* (1960); *Our American Republic* (with D. S. Muzzey, 1963); *Our Country's History* (1964); *Woodrow Wilson, A Brief Biography* (1963); *Wilson: Confusions and Crisis* (1915–1916) (1964); *Wilson: Campaigns for Progressivism and Peace* (1916–1917) (1965); *The Growth of American Democracy* (1968); *The Impact of World War I* (1969); etc. Faculty, Princeton University.

LINK, HENRY CHARLES (Aug. 27, 1889–Jan. 9, 1952); b. Buffalo, N.Y. Author. *Employment Psychology* (1919); *The Return to Religion* (1936); *The Rediscovery of Man* (1938); *The Way to Security* (1951); etc.

LINKLETTER, ART [Arthur Gordon] (July 17, 1912–); b. Moose Jaw, Sask. Radio and television broadcaster. *People Are Funny* (1947); *Kids Say the Darndest Things* (1957); *The Secret World of Kids* (1959); *A Child's Garden of Misinformation* (1965); *I Wish I'd Said That* (1968); *Linkletter Down Under* (1969); *Oops* (1970).

LINN, EDWARD ALLEN (Nov. 14, 1922–   ); b. Boston, Mass. Author. *Veeck—as in Wreck* (1962); *The Last Loud Roar* (1964); *The Hustler's Handbook* (1965); *Koufax* (1966).

LINN, JAMES WEBER (May 11, 1876–July 16, 1939); b. Winnebago, Ill. Educator, author. *The Second Generation* (1902); *The Chameleon* (1903); *Jane Addams: A Biography* (1935); *A Foreword to Fiction* (with Houghton Wells Taylor, 1935); *This Was Life* (1936); *Wind Over the Campus* (1936); *James Keeley, Newspaperman* (1937). Prof. English, University of Chicago.

LINN, JOHN BLAIR (Mar. 14, 1777–Aug. 30, 1804); b. Shippensburg, Pa. Presbyterian clergyman, poet, playwright. Brother-in-law of Charles Brockden Brown. *Miscellaneous Works, Prose and Poetical* (anon., 1795); *The Poetical Wanderer* (1796); *Bourville Castle; or, The Gallic Orphan* (prod. 1797); *The Death of Washington* (poem, 1800); *The Powers of Genius* (poem, 1801); *Valerian,* ed. by Charles Brockden Brown (poem, 1805); etc.

LINNINGTON, ELIZABETH. Author. *The Long Watch* (1956); *Greenmask* (1964); *Date with Death* (1966); *Something Wrong* (1967); *Policeman's Lot* (1968); etc.

LINTHICUM, RICHARD (b. Mar. 30, 1859); b. Libertytown, Md. Journalist, author. *Rocky Mountain Tales* (1892); *Boer and Britisher in South Africa* (1900); etc. News editor, the *Chicago Chronicle,* beginning in 1904.

LINTON, RALPH (Feb. 27, 1893–Dec. 24, 1953); b. Philadelphia, Pa. Anthropologist, author. *The Material Culture of the Marquesas Islands* (1923); *The Tanala, A Hill Tribe of Madagascar* (1933); *The Study of Man* (1936); *The Individual and His Society* (with A. Kardiner, 1939); *The Cultural Background of Personality* (1945); *The Tree of Culture* (1955); etc. Co-author, with Adelin Linton: *Man's Way from Cave to Skyscraper* (1947); *The Lore of Birthdays* (1951); etc. Editor: *The Science of Man in the World Crisis* (1945); etc. Dept. anthropology, Columbia University, 1937–46; Yale University, 1946–53.

LINTON, WILLIAM JAMES (Dec. 7, 1812–Dec. 29, 1897); b. London. Wood-engraver, printer, author. *Life of Paine* (1839); *Claribel, and Other Poems* (1865); *The Flower and the Star* (1868); *History of Wood-Engraving in America* (1882); *Love Lore* (poems, 1887); *The Life of John Greenleaf Whittier* (1893); *Three-score and Ten Years* (autobiography, 1894); reissued as *Memories* (1895). Editor: *English Verse,* 5v. (with R. H. Stoddard, 1883); *The Poetry of America, 1776–1876* (1878). Editor, *London Illuminated Magazine,* 1845. He came to America in 1866 and worked on *Frank Leslie's Illustrated*

News. He illustrated Bryant's "Thanatopsis," "The Flood of Years," Whittier's "Snow-Bound," etc. He founded the Appledore Press, in New Haven, Conn., in 1878 and printed beautifully illustrated books. He contributed illustrations to *Scribner's, The Century,* etc.

LIONNI, LEO (May 5, 1910–); b. Amsterdam, Holland. Designer, painter, author. *Little Blue and Little Yellow* (1959); *Inch by Inch* (1960); *On My Beach There Are Many Pebbles* (1961); *Swimmy* (1963); *Tico* (1964); *Frederick* (1967); *The Alphabet Tree* (1968); *Alexander and the Wind-up Mouse* (1969); etc.

LIPPARD, GEORGE (Apr. 10, 1822–Feb. 9, 1854); b. in Chester Co., Pa. Editor, novelist. *The Battle-Day of Germantown* (1843); *Herbert Tracy* (1844); *The Ladye Annabel* (anon., 1844); *The Quaker City; or, The Monks of Monk Hall* (anon., 1844); *Blanche of Brandywine* (1846); *The Nazarene; or, The Last of the Washington* (1846); *The Rose of Wissahikon* (1847); *Washington and His Generals* (1847); *Legends of Mexico* (1847); *'Bel of Prairie Eden* (1848); *Paul Ardenheim, the Monk of Wissahikon* (1848); *Washington and His Men* (1850); *The Empire City; or, New York by Night* (1853); *New York: Its Upper Ten and Lower Million* (1854). *See* Joseph Jackson's *A Bibliography of the Works of George Lippard,* in the *Pennsylvania Magazine of History and Biography,* Apr., 1930.

LIPPHARD, WILLIAM BENJAMIN (Oct. 29, 1886–Apr. 14, 1971); b. Evansville, Ind. Author. *The Ministry of Healing* (1920); *The Second Century* (1926); *Communing with Communism* (1931); *Out of the Storm in China* (1932); *Fifty Years an Editor* (1963); *A History of the Associated Church Press* (1965); *Disillusioned World* (1967). Editor, American Baptist Missions, 1932–52.

LIPPINCOTT, HORACE MATHER (Apr. 20, 1877–Jan. 12, 1967); b. Philadelphia, Pa. Author. *Pennsylvania* (1910); *Early Philadelphia* (1917); *The University of Pennsylvania* (1919); *Philadelphia* (1926); *Old York Road* (1937); *Chelten Hills* (1938); *Narrative of Chestnut Hill* (1948); etc. Editor: *Through a Quaker Archway* (1959), and many other studies of Philadelphia and the Quakers.

Lippincott, J. B., Company. Philadelphia, Pa. Publishers. Founded in 1836 by Joshua Ballinger Lippincott (1816–1886). After his death, his son Craig, assisted by two other sons, Walter (d. 1927) and Joshua Bertram (1857–1940) took over the management. In 1849 Lippincott had absorbed the firm of Grigg & Elliott, jobbers. In 1850 the firm was called Lippincott, Grambo & Company. The present name was adopted in 1855. In Jan., 1868, *Lippincott's Magazine* was launched. A London branch of J. B. Lippincott & Co., was established in 1876. In 1855 *Lippincott's Pronouncing Gazetteer* was first published. It was compiled by Joseph Thomas (1811–1891), who was a Lippincott editor, 1854–71. Allibone's *Critical Dictionary of English Literature and British and American Authors,* was a Lippincott standard work, as were editions of Worcester's dictionaries, etc. In 1941 the firm absorbed the New York publishing house, Carrick & Evans, and bought controlling interest in the Frederick A. Stokes Co., New York. J. W. Lippincott, Jr., is president.

LIPPINCOTT, JOSEPH WHARTON (Feb. 28, 1887–); b. Philadelphia, Pa. Publisher, author. *Bun, A Wild Rabbit* (1918); *Gray Squirrel* (1921); *The Wolf King* (1933); *Chisel-Tooth the Beaver* (1943); *Black Wings* (1948); *Red Roan Pony* (1951); *Phantom Deer* (1954); *Old Bill the Whooping Crane* (1958); etc.

LIPPINCOTT, JOSHUA BALLINGER (Mar. 18, 1813–Jan. 5, 1886); b. Burlington Co., N.J. Publisher. Founded publishing house J. B. Lippincott and Co., Philadelphia, in 1836. Established *Lippincott's Magazine* in 1868.

LIPPINCOTT, J[oshua] BERTRAM (Aug. 24, 1857–Jan. 19, 1940); b. Huntington Valley, Pa. Publisher. Entered J. B. Lippincott Publishing Company (founded by his father) in 1875;

vice-president, 1886–1911; president, 1911–26; chairman of the board of directors, 1926–40.

LIPPINCOTT, MARTHA SHEPARD (d. Aug. 10, 1949); b. Moorestown, N.J. Poet. Known as "The Quaker Poetess." *Visions of Life* (1901); also many poems and songs.

LIPPINCOTT, SARA JANE CLARKE (Mrs. Leander L. Lippincott) (Sept. 23, 1823–Apr. 20, 1904); b. Pompey, N.Y. Editor, author. Pen name, "Grace Greenwood." *Greenwood Leaves: A Collection of Sketches and Letters,* 2 series (1850, 1852); *Poems* (1851); *Recollections of My Childhood* (1852); *Haps and Mishaps of a Tour in Europe* (1854); *Merrie England* (1855); *Bonnie Scotland* (1861); *Queen Victoria* (1883); etc. Editor, *Little Pilgrim,* juvenile magazine.

Lippincott's Magazine. Philadelphia, Pa. Monthly. Founded Jan., 1868, by J. B. Lippincott & Company. Editors: John Foster Kirk, 1868–84; J. Bird, 1885; William Shepherd Walsh, 1885–89; Henry Stoddart, 1889–96; Frederic M. Bird, 1896–98; Harrison S. Morris, 1899–1905; J. Berg Esenwein, 1905–14; Louise Bull, 1914; Edward Frank Allen, 1914–16. Illustrated, from 1869 to 1885. Notable for the variety and excellence of its literary contributions, and for its encouragement of Southern writers, although leading Northern writers were equally represented. McBride, Nast & Co. bought the magazine in Dec., 1914, moved it to New York, and changed its name to *McBride's Magazine.* Merged with *Scribner's Magazine* May, 1916. *See* Frank L. Mott's *A History of American Magazines,* v. 3 (1938).

LIPPMAN, JULIE MATHILDE (1864–Apr. 10, 1952); b. Brooklyn, N.Y. Author. *Jock o' Dreams* (1891); *Dorothy Day* (1898); *Martha By-the-Day* (1912); *Making Over Martha* (1913); *The Mannequin* (1917); etc.

Lippmann, WALTER (Sept. 23, 1889–); b. New York. Journalist, author. *A Preface to Politics* (1913); *Public Opinion* (1922); *Men of Destiny* (1927); *A Preface to Morals* (1929); *Interpretations,* 2 series (1932, 1936); *The New Imperative* (1935); *The Good Society* (1937); *Some Notes on War and Peace* (1940); *U.S. Foreign Policy: Shield of the Republic* (1943); *The Cold War: A Study in U.S. Foreign Policy* (1947); *Isolation and Alliances: An American Speaks to the British* (1952); *Essays in the Public Philosophy* (1955); *The Communist World and Ours* (1959); *Drift and Mastery: An Attempt to Diagnose the Present Unrest* (1961); *The Coming Test with Russia* (1961); *Western Unity and the Common Market* (1962); *The Essential Lippmann* (1963); *Conversations with Walter Lippmann* (1965); etc. Syndicated columnist, *New York Herald Tribune,* and other papers, from 1931. *See* W. E. Leuchtenberg's *Walter Lippmann: Drift and Mastery* (1961).

"Lips That Touch Liquor Must Never Touch Mine, The." Poem by George Young, in his *Standard Recitations* (1884), although probably of earlier date.

LIPSET, SEYMOUR MARTIN. Author. *Mobility in the United States* (with Reinhard Bendix, 1955); *Union Democracy* (with others, 1956); *Social Mobility in Industrial Society* (with Reinhard Bendix, 1959); *Culture and Social Character* (with Leo Lowenthal, 1961); *The Berkeley Student Revolt* (1965); *Class, Status and Power in Comparative Perspective* (1966); *Elites in Latin America* (1967); *Revolution and Counter Revolution: Change and Persistence in Social Structures* (1969); etc.

LIPSKY, ELEAZAR (1911–). Author. *Murder One* (1948); *The People Against O'Hara* (1950); *Lincoln McKeever* (1953); *The Scientists* (1959); *Devil's Daughter* (1969); etc.

LISKA, GEORGE (June 30, 1922–   ); b. Pardubice, Czechoslovakia. Educator, author. *International Equilibrium* (1957); *The New Statecraft* (1960); *Nations in Alliance* (1962); *Europe Ascendant* (1964); *Imperial America* (1967). Prof. political science, Johns Hopkins University, since 1964.

"Listen to the Mocking Bird." Popular song by "Alice Hawthorne" (Septimus Winner), melody by Richard Milburn (1855).

LITCHFIELD, GRACE DENIO (Nov. 19, 1849–Dec. 4, 1944); b. New York. Poet, novelist. *Only Incidents* (1883); *The Knight of the Black Forest* (1885); *A Hard Won Victory* (1888); *Little Venice, and Other Stories* (1890); *Mimosa Leaves* (poems, 1895); *The Letter D* (1904); *Vita* (drama in verse, 1904); *The Nun of Kent* (drama in verse, 1911); *Collected Poems* (1913); *As a Man Sows, and Other Stories* (1926); etc.

Literary Advertiser. Cincinnati, O. Semi-monthly. Founded 1851, as the *Western Literary Advertiser and Record.* Contents largely biographical. Expired 1856.

Literary and Library Prizes. Published by R. R. Bowker Co. since 1935. Contains history, conditions, and rules of national and international literary prizes and lists winning entries.

Literary and Scientific Repository. New York City. Founded June, 1821. Charles K. Gardner was editor. It contained Fitz-Greene Halleck's elegy "On the Death of Joseph Rodman Drake." Expired May, 1822.

Literary Budget. Chicago, Ill. Magazine. Founded 1852, by the bookseller W. W. Danenhower. Benjamin F. Taylor became editor in 1854. Expired 1855.

Literary Bulletin. New York City. Founded 1868, by Frederick Leypoldt. One of the forerunners of *Publishers' Weekly.* Expired 1869.

Literary Confederacy. New York. Club founded by Robert Charles Sands, James Eastburn, and others. In 1821 it established *St. Tammany's Magazine,* under the editorship of C. S. Van Winkle. Only five numbers were issued.

Literary Digest. New York. Weekly digest magazine. Founded Mar. 1, 1890, by Isaac Kauffman Funk, who edited it until 1905. William Seaver Woods was editor, 1905–33; Authur Stimson Draper, 1933–35; Wilfred J. Funk, 1936–37; Albert Shaw, 1937; David P. Page, 1937–38. Current events and personalities were featured, and a poetry department contained a selection from the representative poems currently published in newspapers and magazines. Merged July 1937 with *Review of Reviews* as *The Digest.* Original title resumed Nov. 13, 1937. Suspended publication Feb. 19, 1938, and absorbed by *Time,* May 23, 1938.

Literary History of the American Revolution, The. By Moses Coit Tyler, 2 v. (1897). Classic study of early American literature, noted for its scholarship and fullness. Reprinted by Barnes & Noble in 1941, in their Facsimile Library.

Literary History of the United States. Three-volume critical survey edited by Robert E. Spiller, Willard Thorp, Thomas H. Johnson, and Henry Seidel Canby (1948).

Literary Life. New York. Magazine. Founded 1884, by A. P. T. Elder, at Cleveland, O. Moved to Chicago in 1885, and to New York in 1889. Expired 1903.

Literary Magazine and American Register. Philadelphia, Pa. Monthly. Founded Oct., 1803, by Charles Brockden Brown, who was its only editor. Expired Dec., 1807.

Literary News. New York City. Monthly. Founded 1875, by Frederick Leypoldt, as a revival of his *Monthly Book Trade Circular* (1869–72). Expired 1904.

Literary Pioneers. By Orie William Long (1935). Studies of George Ticknor, Edward Everett, Joseph Green Cogswell, George Bancroft, H. W. Longfellow, John Lothrop Motley, with particular reference to their European travels and researches.

Literary Review, The. Teaneck, N.J. Quarterly. Founded 1957. Published by Fairleigh Dickinson University. Editors have been Clarence R. Decker and Charles Angoff.

Literary Situation, The. By Malcolm Cowley (1954). Discussion of the problems and preoccupations of writers and the nature of the literary world at the time.

Literary World. New York City. Weekly. Founded Feb., 1847, by Osgood & Co., and edited by Evert A. Duyckinck, George L. Duyckinck, and Charles Fenno Hoffman. The brothers Duyckinck, with Hoffman, were distinguished literary men in New York, and the literati of the day were contributors to the magazine. Expired Dec., 1853.

Literary World: A Review of Current Literature. Boston, Mass. Monthly. Founded June, 1870, by S. R. Crocker. Editors were: S. R. Crocker, 1870–77; Edward Abbott, 1877–88, 1895–1903; N. P. Gilman, 1888–95; Bliss Carman, 1903–04. W. J. Rolfe, the Shakespearean editor, conducted a department of Shakespeareana for several years. There was a special Whittier number, Dec., 1877, and a special Emerson number, May, 1880. Starting as a monthly, the magazine became a fortnightly in 1879. Absorbed by *The Critic* in 1904. From 1879 to 1900, it was a fortnightly and was called the *Fortnightly Literary World. See* Frank L. Mott's *History of American Magazines,* v. 2 (1938).

Literati, The. By Edgar Allan Poe (1850). Critical essays on thirty-eight literary contemporaries in America. These essays appeared originally in *Godey's Lady's Book,* May–Oct., 1846.

Literature and Theater of the States and Regions of the U.S.A. A historical bibliography, by Clarence L. F. Gohdes (1967).

Literature of the Middle-Western Frontier, The. By Ralph L. Rusk, 2v. (1925). Comprehensive survey of the literary beginnings of the Middle West, with an analysis of books and magazines of the period, with selected bibliographical references.

LITSEY, EDWIN CARLILE (June 3, 1874–); b. Beechland, Ky. Novelist, poet. *The Man from Jericho* (1911); *A Maid of the Kentucky Hills* (1913); *Spindrift* (poems, 1915); *A Bluegrass Cavalier* (1922); *Grist* (1927); *The Filled Cup* (poems, 1935); *Stones for Bread* (1940); etc.

LITTELL, ELIAKIM (Jan. 2, 1797–May 17, 1870); b. Burlington, N.J. Editor, publisher. Founder, the *Philadelphia Register and National Recorder,* 1819, which eventually led to the establishment of the *Eclectic Magazine of Foreign Literature, Science and Art* (q.v.); founder, *Littell's Living Age,* 1844.

LITTELL, PHILIP (Aug. 6, 1868–Oct. 31, 1943); b. Brookline, Mass. Author. *Books and Things* (1919); *This Way Out* (1928). On staff the *New Republic,* 1914–23.

LITTELL, ROBERT (May 15, 1896–Dec. 5, 1963); b. Milwaukee, Wis. Critic, editor, author. *Read America First* (1926); *Candles in the Storm* (1934); *Gather Ye Rosebuds* (with Sidney Howard, 1934). Drama critic, the New York *Evening Post,* 1927–29; the New York *World,* (1929–31; assoc. editor, the *New Republic,* 1922–27; *Reader's Digest,* since 1937.

LITTELL, WILLIAM (1768–Sept. 26, 1824); b. in New Jersey. Lawyer, satirist. *Epistles . . . to the People of the Realm of Kentucky* (1806); *A Narrative of the Settlement of Kentucky* (1806); *Political Transactions in and Concerning Kentucky* (1806); *Festoons of Fancy, Consisting of Compositions Amatory, Sentimental and Humorous, in Verse and Prose* (1814), also law books.

Littell's Living Age. See Living Age.

LITTEN, FREDERIC NELSON (May 26, 1885–July 26, 1951); b. Chicago, Ill. Educator, author of boys' adventure stories. *Rhodes of the Flying Cadets* (1929); *Rhodes of the 94th* (1934); *Rhodes of the Leathernecks* (1936); *Pilot of the High Sierras* (1936); *Mission to Algiers* (1943); *Air Mission Red* (1951); etc.

Little, Brown & Co. Boston, Mass. Publishers. Founded 1847, by Charles Coffin Little and James Brown. In 1821 Little had entered the bookstore of Carter, Hilliard & Co., and in 1827 became a member of the firm, then called Hilliard Gray & Co. Little became senior partner and in 1837 took James Brown into the firm. Brown began his career in 1818 with William Hilliard, in Cambridge, Mass. Since 1847 the name has been Little, Brown & Co. Towards the close of the century the firm absorbed another Boston house, Roberts Brothers, the publishers of Louisa May Alcott, Edward Everett Hale, Helen Hunt Jackson, and other popular authors. James McIntyre was director of Little, Brown & Co., for many years, and his son, Alfred McIntyre, was president from 1926 to 1948. Arthur H. Thornhill, Jr., is now president. In the early days the firm published Bancroft, Prescott, Parkman, Dana, Child, Story, Bowditch, and other great writers of New England. Its longest-lived best sellers are *Bartlett's Familiar Quotations* and *The Boston Cooking-School Cook Book*. It has published books of the Atlantic Monthly Press since 1925. *See* G. S. Hillard's *A Memoir of James Brown* (1856); *Books from Beacon Hill* (1927); and *One Hundred and Twenty-five Years of Publishing, 1837–1962* (1962). Acquired by Time Inc. in 1968.

LITTLE, CHARLES COFFIN (July 25, 1790–Aug. 9, 1869); b. Kennebunk, Me. Publisher. *See* Little, Brown & Co.

LITTLE, CLARENCE COOK (Oct. 6, 1888–); b. Brookline, Mass. Educator, biologist, author. *The Awakening College* (1930); *Civilization Against Cancer* (1939); *Genetics, Medicine, and Man* (with others, 1947); *Genetics, Biological Individuality, and Cancer* (1954); *Inheritance of Coat Color in Dogs* (1957; rev. ed. 1967); etc. President, University of Maine, 1922–25; president, University of Michigan, 1925–29; head, Roscoe B. Jackson Memorial Laboratory, Bar Harbor, Me. Managing director, American Society for Control of Cancer, 1929–56.

Little, Frances. Pen name of Fannie Caldwell Macaulay.

LITTLE, JOSEPH JAMES (June 5, 1841–Feb. 11, 1913); b. Bristol, Eng. came to the United States in 1841. Printer. Founder, J. J. Little & Co., printers, in New York, in 1867. Now known as J. J. Little & Ives. A son, Arthur W. Little, entered the firm in 1891.

LITTLE, MALCOLM [Malcolm X] (May 19, 1925–Feb. 21, 1965); b. Omaha, Neb. Black leader, author. *The Autobiography of Malcolm X* (1965); *Malcolm X Speaks* (ed. by G. Breitman, 1965); *Malcolm X on Afro-American History* (1967); *The Speeches of Malcolm X at Harvard*, ed. by Archie Epps (1970). *See* J. Henrick Clarke's *Malcolm X, the Man and his Times* (1970).

LITTLE, RICHARD HENRY (Aug. 25, 1869–Apr. 27, 1946); b. Le Roy, Ill. Columnist, author. *The Line Book* (annual, 1924); *Better Angels* (1928). Editor, "Line-o'-Type or Two" column in the Chicago *Tribune,* from 1920. *See* Bert Leston Taylor.

Little Big Man. Novel by Thomas Berger (1964).

Little Book Shop Around the Corner. Founded 1907, by Mitchell Kennerley on E. 29 Street, in New York City. Frederic Goudy, the type designer, occupied the rear of the shop. Later, Laurence J. Gomme became manager, and continued the business until 1917. The store was a literary rendezvous for such men as Bliss Carman, Joyce Kilmer, Gordon Craig, Lincoln Steffens, Charles Hanson Towne, Richard Le Gallienne, Edgar Saltus and others.

"Little Boy Blue." Poem by Eugene Field, in his *A Little Book of Western Verse* (1889). It was set to music by Ethelbert Nevin.

"Little Breeches." Poem by John Hay, in his *Pike County Ballads* (1871).

"Little Brown Church in the Vale, The." Song by William S. Pitts (1857). Inspired by the little church in Bradford, Iowa, where it was written.

Little Caesar. Novel by W. R. Burnett (1929). Deals with the intimate life of a gangster.

Little Colonel Series. A group of children's books by Annie Fellows Johnston, 12v. (1895–1929).

Little Corporal, The. Chicago. Juvenile magazine. Founded July, 1865, by Alfred L. Sewell. The editors were Sewell, Edward Eggleston, and Emily Huntington Miller. It absorbed *Work and Play* in 1872, and in turn was absorbed by *St. Nicholas* in 1875.

Little Foxes. By Harriet Beecher Stowe (1866). Moral essays for the young written under the pen name of "Christopher Crowfield."

Little Foxes, The. Play by Lillian Hellman (prod. 1939). Regina Giddens allows her husband to die without calling in medical aid, and joins in a family intrigue to gain the controlling interest in a cotton mill.

Little French Girl, The. Novel by Anne Douglas Sedgwick (1924). Story of a French girl, Alix de Mouveray, who comes to England to live with Captain Owen Bradley, one of her mother's lovers. Two English boys fall in love with Alix, presenting her with the problem of choosing between a marriage for love or a marriage of convenience.

Little Friend, Little Friend. Collection of poems by Randall Jarrell (1945).

"Little Gidding." Poem by T. S. Eliot published as part of *Four Quartets* (1943).

Little Giffen of Tennessee." Poem by Dr. Francis O. Ticknor, in the *Land We Love,* Oct., 1867.

Little Lord Fauntleroy. By Frances Hodgson Burnett (1886). Story of a beautifully dressed and beautifully mannered child, Cedric Errol, who goes from New York to England, to assume his proper station as heir to his English grandfather, an English earl. This sentimental tale with its emphasis on good manners became a model for mothers wishing to impress their sons with the proper mode of dress and behavior. Mark Twain achieved the opposite effect with his *Tom Sawyer* and *Huckleberry Finn.*

"Little Lost Child, The." Sentimental song by Joseph William Stern and Edward B. Marks (1894).

Little magazine. Type of periodical of limited circulation, usually concerned with literature, the arts, and cultural analysis or criticism. Since the period shortly before World War I, the little magazine has served to publish avant-garde, politically and socially radical, and, in general, commercially unacceptable work. Among the most famous have been *Poetry: A Magazine of Verse, The Little Review, Hound and Horn, The Dial,* and *Partisan Review.* The various kinds of little magazine include the college quarterlies, such as *Kenyon Review* or *Sewanee Review,* which are academic in orientation; the experimental type of periodical, such as *Furioso* or *Big Table,* devoted to poetry and fiction primarily; the paperback periodical issued by book publishers, such as *Evergreen Review, The Noble Savage,* or *New American Writing;* and the "little" little magazine, such as *The Blue Guitar* or *Imagi. The International Guide,* published in England, lists all the important little magazines in print throughout the world. Beginning with Gertrude Stein, Ezra Pound, and T. S. Eliot, most of the now established writers of modernistic fiction and poetry have appeared at the beginning of their careers in the little magazines. The *Directory of Little Magazines,* published by Len Fulton, and *Trace,* edited by James Boyer May, both publish periodical lists of little magazines in print and small presses in operation.

Little Men. Novel by Louisa May Alcott (1871). A counterpart to the author's successful novel, *Little Women.* A happy chronicle of New England village life. The background is a school kept at Plumfield by Jo, one of the heroines of *Little Women,* and her husband, Professor Baer. *Jo's Boys* (1886) is a sequel.

Little Murders. Play by Jules Feiffer (prod. 1969).

"Little Orphant Annie". Poem by James Whitcomb Riley (1885). First printed under title, "The Elf Child."

Little Pilgrim. Philadelphia, Pa. Juvenile magazine. Founded 1854. Edited by "Grace Greenwood" (Sarah J. Lippincott). Expired 1875.

Little Review. Chicago, Ill. Founded 1914 by Margaret Anderson, who moved it to New York three years later, and then to Paris. James Joyce's *Ulysses* first appeared in the magazine, causing a literary sensation. Discontinued 1929.

Little Rivers. By Henry van Dyke (1895). An account of the author's outings to the Adirondacks, and the rivers of Canada, long walks and fishing adventures in Scotland, the Austrian Tyrol, etc. Expresses the idyllic philosophy of a nature lover.

Little Room. Chicago, Ill. Founded 1894. Meeting place of the Chicago literati, artists, and musicians.

Little Shepherd of Kingdom Come. Novel by John Fox, Jr. (1903). Kentucky romance, with Chadwick Buford, a homeless boy, as the chief character. Chad grows to manhood just in time to fight in the Civil War. Having fought in the Union army, he has to overcome the estrangement of his Kentucky friends, including Margaret Dean, whom he loves.

"Little While I Fain Would Linger Yet, A." Poem by Paul Hamilton Hayne.

Little Women. Novel by Louisa May Alcott, 2v. (1868–69). One of the best loved of all American novels. It recounts the intimate joys and sorrows of the March family, with the four daughters, Jo, Meg, Beth and Amy, as the heroines. The character of each girl is finely drawn. The story is continued in *Little Men* (1871), and *Jo's Boys* (1886). In reality the story is based on the author's own family life in Concord, Mass.

LITTLEFIELD, GEORGE EMERY (Aug. 29, 1844–Sept. 4, 1915); b. Boston, Mass. Bookseller, author. *Early Boston Booksellers, 1642–1711* (1900); *Early Schools and School-Books of New England* (1904); *The Early Massachusetts Press, 1638–1711,* 2v. (1907); etc.

LITTLEFIELD, WALTER (Mar. 17, 1867–Mar. 25, 1948); b. Boston, Mass. Journalist, author. *The Truth about Dreyfus* (1927); *When France Went Mad* (1936); etc. Editor: *Early Prose Writings of James Russell Lowell* (1902); *Love Letters of Famous Men and Women,* 4v. (with Lionel Strachey, 1909–10); etc. On editorial staff, the *New York Times,* 1897–1942.

Littlepage Manuscripts, The. A trilogy of novels by J. Fenimore Cooper dealing with the life of a New York family, the Littlepages, through three generations. They were *Satanstoe* (1845); *The Chainbearer* (1845); and *The Redskins* (1846).

Littleton, Mark. Pen name of John Pendleton Kennedy.

LITWAK, LEO E. (May 28, 1924–   ); b. Detroit, Mich. Novelist. *To the Hanging Gardens* (1964); *In O'Brien's House* (1969). Faculty, San Francisco State College, since 1961.

Liveright Publishing Corporation. New York. Publishers. Founded 1917, by Albert Boni and Horace Liveright, as Boni & Liveright. The partners separated in 1918 but the firm name was continued until 1928, when it became Horace Liveright, and later Liveright Publishing Corporation. It made publishing history with its moderately priced Modern Library series, which was sold to Bennett Cerf in 1925. Liveright Publishing Corp. publishes the Black and Gold Library of Great Books. Arthur Pell is now president. *See* Lester Cohen's *The Fabulous World of Horace Liveright* (1962); Walker Gilmer's *Horace Liveright: Publisher of the Twenties* (1970).

LIVERMORE, MARY ASHTON RICE (Dec. 19, 1820–May 23, 1905); b. Boston, Mass. Editor, reformer, author. *My Story of the War: A Woman's Narrative of Four Years' Personal Experience* (1888); *The Story of My Life; or, the Sunshine and Shadow of Seventy Years* (1897); etc. Editor: *American Women,* 2v. (with Frances E. Willard, 1897). Founder, *The Agitator,* 1869.

Living Age, The. Magazine. Founded at Boston, May 11, 1844, by Eliakim Littell, under the name *Littell's Living Age.* The present name was adopted in 1897. Eliakim Littell was editor until 1870. Robert S. Littell was editor, 1870–96, Frank Foxcroft, 1896–1918, and in recent years it has been edited by Henry B. Sheahan, Victor Selden Clark, Varian Fry, Joseph Hilton Smyth, and others. In 1919 it was sold to the Atlantic Monthly Company. It was a weekly until 1927, and became a monthly afterward. Discontinued in 1941. Joseph Hilton, who had bought it and *North American Review* in 1938, was financially supported by the Japanese government to utilize both periodicals for Japanese propaganda.

Living Church, The. Milwaukee, Wis. Weekly news magazine. National publication of the Protestant Episcopal Church. Publishes special book numbers quarterly.

LIVINGSTON, FLORENCE BINGHAM, b. Burlington, Vt. Author. *The Custard Cup* (1921); *Under a Thousand Eyes* (1923); *This Man and This Woman* (1928).

Livingston, Grace. See Grace Livingston Hill.

LIVINGSTON, LUTHER SAMUEL (1864–1914). Editor, *American Book-Prices Current.* With rare book firm of Dodd & Livingston, New York. First librarian of the Harry Elkins Widener Collection of the Harvard College Library.

LIVINGSTON, MYRA COHN. Author. *Whispers, and Other Poems* (1958); *Wide Awake, and Other Poems* (1959); *See What I Found* (1962); *The Moon and a Star, and Other Poems* (1965); *I'm Waiting* (1966); *A Crazy Flight and Other Poems* (1969); *Old Mrs. Twindlytart and Other Rhymes* (1967); etc.

LIVINGSTON, WILLIAM (Nov., 1723–July 25, 1790); b. Albany, N.Y. Governor, lawyer, author. *Philosophic Solitude* (poem, 1747). He contributed to the *Independent Reflector,* and to the "Watch Tower" column of the *New York Mercury.* Governor of New Jersey, 1776–90.

LLOYD, ALFRED HENRY (Jan. 3, 1864–May 11, 1927); b. Montclair, N.J. Educator, author. *Citizenship and Salvation* (1897); *Dynamic Idealism* (1898); *Philosophy of History* (1899); *The Will to Doubt* (1907); *Leadership and Progress* (1922). Philosophy dept., University of Michigan, 1891–1927.

LLOYD, DAVID DEMAREST (1851–1889); b. New York. Playwright. *For Congress* (prod. 1884); *The Woman Hater* (prod. 1887); *The Dominie's Daughter* (prod. 1887); *The Senator* (with Sydney Rosenfeld, prod. 1890).

LLOYD, EVERETT (Oct. 20, 1881–); b. Italy, Texas. Editor, author. *Law West of the Pecos: The Story of Roy Bean* (1931). Founder and editor, *Everett Lloyd's Magazine,* San Antonio, Tex., 1924, a monthly literary and historical magazine; founder, *The Vagabond,* a magazine issued from a different city each month.

LLOYD, HENRY DEMAREST (May 1, 1847–Sept. 28, 1903); b. New York. Journalist, author. *Wealth Against Commonwealth* (1894); *Man, the Social Creature* (1906); *A Sovereign People* (1907); *Lords of Industry* (1910); etc. His *Story of a Great Monopoly* in the *Atlantic Monthly*, Mar. 1881, is considered to be the first of the so-called "muck-raking" articles. With the *Chicago Tribune*, 1872–85. *See* Louis Filler's *Crusaders for American Liberalism* (1939). *See also* Muckrakers.

Lloyd, Hugh. Pen name of Percy Keese Fitzhugh.

LLOYD, JOHN URI (Apr. 19, 1849–Apr. 9, 1936); b. West Bloomfield, N.J. Pharmacist, editor, historian of medicine, author. *Etidorhpa; or, The End of Earth* (1896); *The Right Side of the Car* (1897); *Stringtown on the Pike* (1900); *Warwick of the Knobs* (1901); *Red Head* (1903); *Scroggins* (1904); *Our Willie: A Folklore Story* (1934); and many books on pharmacy and medicine, etc. President, Lloyd Library and Museum.

LLOYD, NELSON McALLISTER (Dec. 18, 1873–Feb. 8, 1933); b. Philadelphia, Pa. Journalist, author. *The Chronic Loafer* (1900); *The Soldier of the Valley* (1904); *Six Stars* (1906); *David Malcolm* (1913); etc. With the *New York Sun*, 1892–1909.

Lo. Musical comedy by Franklin P. Adams and "O. Henry," with music by A. Baldwin Stearns (prod. 1909).

LOBANOV-ROSTOVSKY, PRINCE A[ndrei Anatolievich] (May 5, 1892–); b. Yokohama, Japan. Educator, author. *Russia and Asia* (1933); *The Grinding Mill: Reminiscences of War and Revolution in Russia, 1913–20* (1935); *Russia and Europe, 1789–1825* (1947; rev. ed. 1968); *Russia and Europe, 1825–1878* (1954). Prof. history, University of Michigan, since 1945.

LOBSENZ, NORMAN MITCHELL (1919–). Author. *The Minister's Complete Guide to Successful Retirement* (1955); *Emergency!* (1958); *First Book of National Parks* (1959); *First Book of Ghana* (1960); *Is Anybody Happy? A Study of the American Search for Pleasure* (1962); *First Book of East Africa* (1964); *Peace Corps* (1968); *How to Stay Married: A Modern Approach to Sex, Money and Emotions in Marriage* (with C. W. Blackburn, 1969); etc.

LOCKE, ALAIN [Leroy] (Sept. 13, 1886–June, 1954); b. Philadelphia, Pa. Educator, author. *The New Negro* (1925); *Four Negro Poets* (1927); *The Negro in American Literature* (1929); *Frederick Douglass* (1935); *The Negro and His Music* (1936); *Negro Art, Past and Present* (1937). Editor, *Plays of Negro Life* (1927); *The Negro in Art* (1940); *When Peoples Meet* (with B. J. Stern, 1946); etc. Philosophy dept., Howard University, Wash., D.C., from 1912; prof. from 1928.

LOCKE, CHARLES EDWARD (Sept. 9, 1858–Mar. 4, 1940); b. Pittburgh, Pa. Methodist bishop, author. *The Typical America* (1902); *First Christmas Story* (1915); *Daybreak Everywhere* (1919); etc.

LOCKE, DAVID ROSS (Sept. 20, 1833–Feb. 15, 1888); b. Vestal, N.Y. Editor, humorist. Pen name "Petroleum V. Nasby." *The Nasby Papers* (1864); *Eastern Fruit on Western Dishes: The Morals of Abou Ben Adhem* (1875); *The Demagogue* (1891); etc. Editor, the *Toledo Blade*, 1865–87. The first Petroleum V. Nasby paper appeared in the *Jeffersonian*, Findlay, O., Mar. 21, 1861. *See* Cyril Clemens's *Petroleum Vesuvius Nasby* (1936).

LOCKE, EDWARD (Oct. 18, 1869–March 1, 1945); b. Stourbridge, Worcs., Eng. Actor, playwright. *The Climax* (prod. 1909); *The Case of Beckey* (prod. 1912); *The Silver Wedding* (prod. 1913); *The Revolt* (prod. 1915); *The Bubble* (prod. 1915); *57 Bowery* (prod. 1928); etc.

LOCKE, GLADYS EDSON (1887–); b. Boston, Mass. Author. *Queen Elizabeth* (1913); *Ronald o' the Moors* (1919);

The Red Cavalier (1922); *The Scarlet Macaw* (1923); *The Purple Mist* (1924); *The House on the Downs* (1925); *The Golden Lotus* (1927); *Grey Gables* (1929); *The Fenwood Murders* (1931); *The Ravensdale Mystery* (1935); etc.

LOCKE, JANE ERMINA (Apr. 25, 1805–Mar. 8, 1859); b. Worthington, Mass. Author. *Poems* (1842); *Boston* (poem, 1846); *The Recalled; or, Voices of the Past* (1855); etc.

LOCKE, JOHN STAPLES (1836–1906); b. Biddeford, Me. Educator, author. *Old Orchard, Maine* (1879); *Shores of Saco Bay* (1880); *The Art of Correspondence* (1883); *A Brave Struggle; or, The Orphans' Inheritance* (1887); etc.

LOCKE, RICHARD ADAMS (Sept. 22, 1800–Feb. 16, 1871); b. East Brent, Som., Eng. Journalist. He came to America in 1832 and joined the staff of the *New York Sun* in 1835, perpetrating in Aug. 1835, the famous *Moon Hoax*, an anticipation of Poe's *Hans Phaall*. Leaving the *Sun* in 1836, he founded, with Joseph Price, the *New Era*, in which appeared his *The Lost Manuscript of Mungo Park*.

LOCKE, ROBINSON (1856–1920). Critic and collector. Drama critic, the *Toledo Blade*. He left his magnificent dramatic collection to The New York Public Library. It covered American theatrical life from 1870 to 1925, and included almost 500 bound scrapbooks and nearly 5,000 portfolios of unmounted material.

LOCKE, WALTER (March 16, 1875–Oct. 23, 1957); b. St. Marys, W. Va. Editor, author. *Whistling Post, Ohio* (1934); *Halcyon Days* (1949); etc. Editor, the *Dayton Daily News*, from 1927.

Locke Amsden. Novel by Daniel Pierce Thompson (1847). A picture of life in Vermont.

LOCKHART, ARTHUR JOHN (May 5, 1850–July 29, 1926); b. Lockhartville, Kings Co., N.S. Methodist clergyman, author. Pen name "Pastor Felix." *Beside the Narraguagus, and Other Poems* (1895); *The Papers of Pastor Felix* (1903); etc. He lived in Maine, 1872–1926.

LOCKHART, CAROLINE (1875–); b. Eagle Point, Ill. Novelist. *Me: Smith* (1911); *The Lady Doc* (1912); *Full of the Moon* (1914); *The Man from the Bitter Roots* (1915); *The Dude Wrangler* (1921); *Old West and New* (1933).

LOCKLEY, FRED (Mar. 19, 1871–Oct. 15, 1958); b. Leavenworth, Kan. Author. *Oregon's Yesterdays* (1928); etc. Editor: *History of the Columbia River Valley*, 3v. (1928). Columnist, *Oregon Journal*, from 1911.

LOCKRIDGE, FRANCES (d. Feb. 17, 1963); b. Kansas City, Mo. Author. *Adopting a Child* (1947). Co-author (with Richard Lockridge): *The Norths Meet Murder* (1940); *A Pinch of Poison* (1941); *Death on the Aisle* (1942); *Killing the Goose* (1944); *Payoff for the Banker* (1945); *Cats and People* (1950); *Dead as a Dinosaur* (1952); *The Faceless Adversary* (1956); *Catch as Catch Can* (1958); *Murder Has its Points* (1961); *Quest of the Bogeyman* (1964); *Four Hours to Fear* (1965); etc.

LOCKRIDGE, RICHARD (Orson) (Sept. 26, 1898–); b. St. Joseph, Mo. Drama critic, author. *Darling of Misfortunes: Edwin Booth* (1932); *Die Laughing* (1969); *Murder in False Face* (1969); *A Risky Way to Kill* (1969). Co-author, with Frances Lockridge (q.v.): *Mr. and Mrs. North* (1936); and other mystery novels. Under pen name, "Francis Richards": *A Plate of Red Herrings* (1969). Drama critic, *New York Sun*, from 1928.

LOCKRIDGE, ROSS, JR. (Apr. 25, 1914–Mar. 6, 1948); b. Bloomington, Ind. Novelist. *Raintree Country* (1948).

LOCKWOOD, CHARLES ANDREWS (1890–Feb. 11, 1968). Co-author with Hans Christian Adamson (q.v.) of adventure stories.

LOCKWOOD, FRANCIS CUMMINS (May 22, 1864–Jan. 12, 1948); b. Mt. Erie, Ill. Educator, author. *Emerson as a Philosopher* (1896); *Robert Browning* (1906); *Arizona Characters* (1928); *Pioneer Days in Arizona* (1932); *Story of the Spanish Missions* (1934); *The Apache Indians* (1938); *The Old English Coffee House* (1939); *Life in Old Tucson—1854–64* (1943); etc. Prof. literature, University of Arizona, 1916–18; dean, College of Letters, Arts and Sciences, 1920–30.

LOCKWOOD, INGERSOLL (Aug. 2, 1841–Sept. 30, 1918); b. Ossining, N.Y. Lawyer, editor, author. Pen name, "Irwin Longman." *Washington: A Heroic Drama of the Revolution* (1875); *The P. G.; or, Perfect Gentleman* (1887); *How to be Witty* (1887); *The Travels and Adventures of Little Baron Trump* (1890); *The Wonderful Deeds and Doings of Little Giant Boab* (1891); *Extraordinary Experiences of Little Captain Doppelkopp* (1891); *Baron Trump's Marvellous Underground Journey* (1893); *1900; or, The Last President* (1896); *In Varying Mood* (poems, 1912); etc. Editor, the *Book Lover*, 1888–90.

LOCKWOOD, RALPH INGERSOLL (July 8, 1789–Apr. 12, 1855); b. Greenwich, Conn. Lawyer, novelist. Pen name, "Mr. Smith." *Rosine Laval* (1833); *The Insurgents* (anon. 1835).

Locomotive-God, The. Autobiography of William Ellery Leonard (1927). The self-scrutiny revealed by this work is based on psychoanalysis.

LODGE, GEORGE CABOT (Oct. 10, 1873–Aug. 21, 1909); b. Boston, Mass. Poet. *The Song of the Wave, and Other Poems* (1898); *Poems, 1899–1902* (1902); *Cain: A Drama* (1904); *Herakles* (drama in verse, 1908); *The Soul's Inheritance, and Other Poems* (1909); *Poems and Dramas*, 2v. (1911). Best known for his sonnets. *See* Henry Adams's *The Life of George Cabot Lodge* (1911).

LODGE, HENRY CABOT (May 12, 1850–Nov. 9, 1924); b. Boston, Mass. Senator, biographer, essayist. *Life and Letters of George Cabot* (1877); *Alexander Hamilton* (1882); *Daniel Webster* (1882); *George Washington*, 2v. (1889); *Boston* (1891); *The Story of the Revolution*, 2v. (1898); *Early Memories* (1912). Editor, the *North American Review*, 1873–76. U.S. Senator, 1893–1924. *See* Henry Brooks Adams's *Life of Henry Cabot Lodge* (1911); William Lawrence's *Life of Henry Cabot Lodge* (1925).

LOEWENGARD, HEIDI HUBERTA (Sept. 8, 1911–); b. Rostock, Mecklenburg, Ger. Novelist. Pen names "Martha Albrand," "Alberta Albrand," "Katrin Holland." *No Surrender* (1942); *Without Orders* (1943); *Endure No Longer* (1944); *None Shall Know* (1945); *Remembered Anger* (1946); *Whispering Hill* (1947); *After Midnight* (1949); *Wait for the Dawn* (1950); *Desperate Moment* (1951); *The Mask of Alexander* (1955); *The Obsession of Emmet Booth* (1957); *A Day in Monte Carlo* (1959); *Meet Me Tonight* (1960); *Call from Austria* (1963); *A Door Fell Shut* (1966); *Rhine Replica* (1969); etc.

LOEWENSTEIN, KARL (Nov. 9, 1891–); b. Munich, Ger. Educator, author. *Hitler's Germany* (1939); *Brazil under Vargas* (1942); *Political Reconstruction* (1946); *Political Power and the Governmental Process* (1957); *British Cabinet Government* (1967); etc. Prof. political science and jurisprudence, Amherst College, 1936–61. Emeritus since 1961.

LOFLAND, JOHN (Mar. 9, 1798–Jan. 22, 1849); b. Milford, Del. Poet. Known as the "Milford Bard." *The Harp of Delaware* (1828); *The Poetical and Prose Writings* (1846); etc. *See* William W. Smithers's *The Life of John Lofland* (1894).

LOFTING, HUGH (Jan. 14, 1886–Sept. 26, 1947); b. Maidenhead, Berks., Eng., came to the United States in 1912. Illustrator, author. Creator of the character "Dr. Dolittle." *The Story of Dr. Dolittle* (1920); and other "Dr. Dolittle" books for children, the last being *Dr. Dolittle and the Green Canary* (1950).

LOGAN, ALGERNON SYDNEY (May 17, 1849–Dec. 11, 1925); b. Philadelphia, Pa. Poet, novelist. *The Last Crusade* (poem, 1870); *The Mirror of a Mind* (poem, 1875); *The Image of Air, and Other Poems* (1878); *Saul: A Dramatic Poem* (1883); *A Feather from the World's Wing* (poem, 1885); *Jesus in Modern Life* (1888); *Messalina* (drama in verse, 1890); *Not on the Chart* (1899); *Amy Warren* (1900); *Vestigia* (poems, 1913); *Vistas from the Stream*, ed. by his son, Robert Restalrig Logan (journal, 1934).

LOGAN, ANDY. Author. *The Man Who Robbed the Robber Barons* (1965); *Against the Evidence: The Becker-Rosenthal Affair* (1970).

Logan, Celia. *See* Celia Logan Connelly.

LOGAN, CORNELIUS AMBROSIUS (May 4, 1806–Feb. 22, 1853); b. Baltimore, Md. Actor, playwright. *Yankee Land* (prod. 1840); *The Way of Maine* (prod. 1834); *The Vermont Wool Dealer* (prod. 1840); *Chloroform; or, New York One Hundred Years Hence* (prod. 1849).

Logan, Ford. Pen name of Dwight Bennett Newton.

LOGAN, JAMES (Oct. 20, 1674–Oct. 31, 1751); b. Lurgan, County Armagh, Ireland. Pennsylvania statesman, scholar, philanthropist. *The Logan Papers*, 45v., the *Logan Letter Books*, 7v., and Deborah Logan's *Selections*, 5v., are now in the Historical Society of Pennsylvania. His letters to William Penn were published in the *Memoirs of the Historical Society of Pennsylvania*, v. 9–10, (1870–72).

LOGAN, JOHN (1923–). Poet. *Cycle for Mother Cabrini* (poems, 1955); *Ghosts of the Heart* (poems, 1960); *Spring of the Thief* (1963); *Zigzag Walk: Poems 1963–1968* (1969); etc. Editor, *Choice*. English dept., State University of New York, at Buffalo.

LOGAN, JOHN ALEXANDER (Feb. 9, 1826–Dec. 26, 1886); b. in Jackson Co., Ill. Army officer, senator, author. *The Great Conspiracy* (1886); *The Volunteer Soldier of America* (1887). Congressman, 1859–63, 1867–71; U.S. Senator, 1871–77, 1879–86.

LOGAN, JOSEPHINE HANCOCK (d. Nov. 1, 1943); b. Chicago, Ill. Author. *Lights and Shadows* (poems, 1932); *Heights and Depths* (poems, 1935); *Sanity in Art* (1937); *Collected Poems* (1941).

LOGAN, JOSHUA (Oct. 5, 1908–); b. Texarkana, Tex. Director, playwright. *Wisteria Trees* (prod. 1950). Co-author: *Higher and Higher* (prod. 1939); *Mister Roberts* (prod. 1948); *South Pacific* (prod. 1949); *Fanny* (prod. 1954); *Camelot* (prod. 1967); *Ensign Pulver* (prod. 1969).

Logan, Louise. Pen name of Gloria Goddard.

LOGAN, OLIVE (Mrs. Wirt Sikes) (Apr. 22, 1839–Apr. 29, 1909); b. Elmira, N.Y. Actress, journalist, playwright. *Eveleen* (prod. 1864); *Apropos of Women and Theatres* (1869); *Surf* (prod. 1870); *Before the Footlights and Behind the Scenes* (1870); *The Mimic World* (1871); *Get Thee Behind Me, Satan* (1872); etc.

LOGAN, RAYFORD WHITTINGHAM (Jan. 7, 1897–); b. Washington, D.C. Educator, author. *The Diplomatic Relations of the U.S. with Haiti, 1776–1891* (1941; rev. ed. 1969); *The Senate and the Versailles Mandate System* (1945); *The African Mandates in World Politics* (1948); *The Negro in American Life and Thought: The Nadir, 1877–1901* (1954); *The Negro in the United States* (1957); *Four Took Freedom: The Lives of Harriet Tubman, Frederick Douglass, Robert Smalls, and Blanche K. Bruce* (with Philip Sterling, 1967); etc. Editor: *What the Negro Wants* (1944; rev. ed. 1969); *Memoirs of a Monticello Slave* (1951); etc. Prof. history, Howard University, since 1938.

LOGGINS, VERNON (Jan. 10, 1893–Oct 3, 1968); b. Hempstead, Tex. Educator, author. *The Negro Author: His Devel-*

opment in America (1931); *Visual Outline of American Literature* (1933); *I Hear America ...: Literature in the United States Since 1900* (1937); *Two Romantics* (1946); *The Hawthornes* (1951); *Where the Word Ends* (1955). English dept., Columbia University.

LOHRKE, EUGENE WILLIAM (Apr. 8, 1897–May 17, 1953); b. East Orange, N.J. Author. *Overshadowed* (1929); *Deep Evening* (1931); *The First Bus Out* (1935); *The Long Exile* (1936); *Night Raid* (1941). Co-author with Arline Lohrke: *Night over England* (1939); *The Long Watch in England* (1940). Editor: *Armageddon: The World War in Literature* (1930).

Lolita. Novel by Vladimir Nabokov (1955). An erotic comedy with symbolic overtones about the European Humbert Humbert who has a passion for pre-adolescent girls, in particular Lolita, with whom he engages in madcap wanderings by automobile through the United States.

LOMAX, ALAN (Jan. 31, 1915–); b. Austin, Tex. Folklorist. *Mister Jelly Roll* (1950). Editor: *Folk Song Style and Culture* (1968). Co-editor, compiler (with John A. Lomax): *American Ballads and Folk Songs* (1934); *Cowboy Songs* (1937); *Folk Song: U.S.A.* (1947); *Folk Songs of North America* (1960); etc. Editor: World Library Folk and Primitive Music, Columbia Records, 17v. (1951–57).

LOMAX, JOHN AVERY (Sept. 23, 1872–Jan. 26, 1948); b. Goodman, Miss. Folklorist. *The Adventures of a Ballad Hunter* (1947). Compiler: *Cowboy Songs, and Other Frontier Ballads* (1910); *Songs of the Cattle Trail and Cow Camp* (1916); *American Ballads and Folk Songs* (with son, Alan Lomax, 1934); *Negro Folk Songs as Sung by Lead Belly* (with son, 1936); *The One Hundred and One Best American Ballads* (with son, and Mr. and Mrs. Charles Seeger, 1947); etc.

LOMAX, LOUIS E. (1922–). Author. *The Reluctant African* (1960); *The Negro Revolt* (1962); *Thailand: The Way That Is the War That Will Be* (1967).

LOMBARD, LOUIS (Dec. 15, 1861–1927); b. Lyons, Fr. Composer, author. *Observations of a Musician* (1889); *Observations of a Bachelor* (1897); *Observations of a Traveler* (1897); *The Art Melodious* (1897); *The Vicious Virtuoso* (1898); etc.

LONDON, CHARMIAN KITTREDGE (Mrs. Jack London), b. Los Angeles, Calif. Author. *The Log of the Snark* (1915); *Our Hawaii* (1917); *The Book of Jack London,* 2v. (1921); etc.

LONDON, JACK [John Griffith] (Jan. 12, 1876–Nov. 22, 1916); b. San Francisco, Calif. Novelist. *The Son of the Wolf* (1900); *The Call of the Wild* (1903); *The People of theAbyss* (1903); *The Sea-Wolf* (1904); *White Fang* (1905); *The Road* (1907); *Martin Eden* (1909); *The Cruise of the Snark* (1911); *John Barleycorn* (1913); *The Strength of the Strong* (1914); *The Works,* 12v. (1917); *See* I. Stone's *Sailor on Horseback* (1939); Charmian London's *The Book of Jack London,* 2v. (1921); Richard O'Connor's *Jack London* (1964); Philip S. Foner's *Jack London: American Rebel* (1969). Most of London's original manuscripts are in the Huntington Library, San Marino, Calif.

LONDON, KURT (Sept. 12, 1900–   ); b. Berlin, Ger. Political scientist, author. *Film Music* (1936); *The Seven Soviet Arts* (1938); *Backgrounds of Conflict* (1945); *How Foreign Policy Is Made* (1949); *The Permanent Crisis* (1962); *New Nations in a Divided World* (1963); *Eastern Europe in Transition* (1966). Prof. international affairs; director, Institute of Sino-Soviet Studies, George Washington University, since 1962.

Lone Star Bo-Peep, and Other Tales of Texas Life. By Howard Seely (1885). Stories of the Texas cow country.

Lonely Crowd, The. By David Riesman, Nathan Glazer, Reuel Denney (1950). Intricately argued analysis of modern American life in terms of "other-direction," the individual's looking toward his peers for the values and objectives of his own existence. Attempts to demonstrate that this tendency partly compensates in social advantages for the abandonment of personal decisiveness. This work made the concept of other-direction one of the key ideas in recent sociological theory.

LONG, ARMISTEAD LINDSAY (Sept. 3, 1825–Apr. 29, 1891); b. Campbell Co., Va. Military secretary and biographer of General Robert E. Lee. *Memoirs of Robert E. Lee. His Military and Personal History* (1886).

LONG, CLARENCE D[ickinson], JR. (Dec. 11, 1908–); b. South Bend, Ind. Educator, author. *Building Cyles and the Theory of Investment* (1940); *The Labor Force in Wartime America* (1944). Co-author (with Frederick C. Mills): *Statistical Agencies of the Federal Government* (1949); *The Labor Force Under Changing Income and Employment* (1958); etc. Prof. economics, Johns Hopkins University, since 1947.

LONG, E[ugene] HUDSON (Nov. 4, 1908–); b. Waco, Tex. Educator, author. *O. Henry: The Man and His Work* (1949); *Mark Twain Handbook* (1958); *Twain's Pudd'nhead Wilson* (1964); *Anna Karenina* (1966); *O. Henry: The Man and His Work* (1969). Prof. American literature, Baylor University, since 1949.

LONG, HANIEL [Clark] (Mar. 9, 1888–Oct. 17, 1956); b. Rangoon. Educator, author. *Poems* (1920); *Notes for a New Mythology* (1926); *Atlantides* (poems, 1933); *Pittsburgh Memoranda* (poems, 1935); *Interlinear to Cabeza de Vaca* (1936); *Walt Whitman and the Springs of Courage* (1938); *Malinche* (1939); *The Grist Mill* (1945); *Spring Returns* (1958); etc. English dept., Carnegie Institute of Technology, 1910–29.

LONG, JOHN CUTHBERT (Aug. 22, 1892–); b. Babylon, L.I., N.Y. Author. *Bryan, the Great Commoner* (1928); *Lord Jeffrey Amherst: A Soldier of the King* (1933); *Mr. Pitt and America's Birthright* (1940); *Long's Bible Quiz* (1943); *The Liberal Presidents* (1948); *Soldier for the King—A Story of Amherst in America* (1954); *Maryland Adventure* (1956). Correspondent for several newspapers; with the *New Yorker,* 1927–30; etc.

LONG, JOHN DAVIS (Oct. 27, 1838–Aug. 28, 1915); b. Buckfield, Me. Governor, cabinet officer, author. *After-Dinner and Other Speeches* (1895); *The New American Navy,* 2v. (1903). Long's journal from 1848 to 1915, filling 25 vols. in manuscript, form the basis of Lawrence Shaw Mayo's *America of Yesterday, as Reflected in the Journal of John Davis Long* (1923). Governor of Massachusetts, 1880–82; Congressman, 1883–89; Secretary of the Navy, 1897–1902.

LONG, JOHN LUTHER (Jan. 1, 1861–Oct. 31, 1927); b. Hanover, Pa. Novelist, playwright. *Madame Butterfly; Purple Eyes; A Gentleman of Japan and a Lady* (1898); *The Darling of the Gods* (with David Belasco, prod. 1902); *Naughty Nan* (1902); *Adrea* (with David Belasco, prod. 1904); *The Dragon Fly* (with Edward C. Carpenter, prod. 1909); *Billy-Boy* (1906); *Dolce* (prod. 1906); *Felice* (1908); *Kassa* (prod. 1909); *Baby Grand* (1912); *Crowns* (prod. 1922); etc.

LONG, MAE VAN NORMAN, b. Effingham, Ill. Author. *The Wonder Woman* (1917); *Whimsy of Whispering Hill* (1918); *The Flute in the Forest* (1930); *Rose of Sharon* (1937).

LONG, ORIE WILLIAM (May 25, 1882–Sept. 14, 1955); b. Millersburg, Ky. Educator, author. *Literary Pioneers* (1935); *Frederic Henry Hedge, A Cosmopolitan Scholar* (1940); etc. German dept., Williams College, 1916–50.

LONG, PERCY WALDRON (Sept. 21, 1876–Oct. 2, 1952); b. Boston, Mass. Educator, author. *Studies in the Technique of Prose Style* (1915); *Comparison* (1921); *The Greek Element in English* (1931); etc. Editor, *Dialect Notes,* 1912–30;

Publications of the Modern Language Association, 1932–47. English dept., New York University, 1934–47.

LONG, RAY (Mar. 23, 1878–July 9, 1935); b. Lebanon, Ind. Editor: *As I Look at Life* (1925); etc. Editor, *The Red Book, The Blue Book, The Green Book* magazines, 1912–1918; president and editor-in-chief *International Magazine Co.,* 1919–1931; chairman of board, Ray Long & Richard Smith, Inc., publishers, 1931–35.

LONG, STEPHEN HARRIMAN (Dec. 30, 1784–Sept. 4, 1864); b. Hopkinton, N.H. Explorer. *See* Edwin James's *Account of an Expedition from Pittsburgh to the Rocky Mountains, Performed in the Years 1819 and '20,* 2v. (1822–23), and W. H. Keating's *Narrative of an Expedition to the Source of St. Peter's River, Lake Winnepeck, Lake of the Woods . . . Performed in the Year 1823,* 2v. (1824).

LONG, WILLIAM J[oseph] (Apr. 3, 1866–1952); b. Attleboro, Mass. Congregational clergyman, naturalist, author. *Ways of Wood Folk* (1899); *Beasts of the Field* (1901); *School of the Woods* (1902); *Brier-Patch Philosophy* (1906); *English Literature* (1909); *American Literature* (1913); *Mother Nature* (1923); *Spirit of the Wild* (1956); etc.

Long Beach Independent. Long Beach, Cal. Newspaper. Founded 1938. Published by Ridder Publications. Appears mornings; the *Independent-Press-Telegram* appears Sundays; the *Press-Telegram,* founded 1888, appears evenings.

Long Beach Press-Telegram. See *Long Beach Independent.*

Long Day's Journey into Night. Play by Eugene O'Neill (prod. 1956). Setting is 1912 in the life of the Tyrone family. The tragic quality is achieved through psychological revelation of the characters' motives.

Long Hunt, The. Novel by James Boyd (1930). Story of a trapper in early pioneering days as he pushes westward from North Carolina to the wilderness of Tennessee. The scenes and experiences recall the adventures of such hunters as Daniel Boone and Davy Crockett.

Long Roll, The. Novel by Mary Johnston (1911). Virginia during the Civil War, from the beginning to the Battle of Chancellorsville, with Stonewall Jackson as chief character.

Long Valley, The. Collection of stories by John Steinbeck (1938).

LONGAKER, JOHN MARK (Aug. 17, 1900–); b. Newport, Ky. Educator, author. *Contemporary Biography* (1934); *English Biography in the Eighteenth Century* (1931); *Ernest Dowson, A Biography* (1944); *Contemporary English Literature* (with Edwin C. Bolles, 1953). English dept., University of Pennsylvania, since 1919.

Longbaugh, Harry. Pen name of William Goldman.

LONGFELLOW, HENRY WADSWORTH (Feb. 27, 1807–Mar. 24, 1882); b. Portland, Me. Poet, editor, educator. *Elements of French Grammar* (anon., 1830); *Outre-Mer,* 2v. (1833–34); *Hyperion,* 2v. (1839); *Voices of the Night* (1839); *Poems on Slavery* (1842); *Ballads and Other Poems* (1841, dated 1842); *The Spanish Student* (1843); *Poems* (1845); *The Belfry of Bruges, and Other Poems* (1845, dated 1846); *Evangeline* (1847); *Kavanaugh: A Tale* (1849); *The Seaside and Fireside* (1849, dated 1850); *The Golden Legend* (1851); *The Song of Hiawatha* (1855); *Prose Works,* 2v. (1857); *The Courtship of Miles Standish* (1858); *The New England Tragedy* (1860); *Tales of a Wayside Inn* (1863); *Household Poems* (1865); *The Divine Comedy of Dante Alighieri,* 3v. (1865–67); *Flower-de-Luce* (1866, dated 1867); *The New England Tragedies* (1868); *Christus: A Mystery,* 3v. (1872); *Three Books of Song* (1872); *Aftermath* (1873); *The Hanging of the Crane* (1874); *The Masque of Pandora, and Other Poems* (1875); *Keramos, and Other Poems* (1878); *Ultima Thule,* 2 parts (1880–82); *Michael Angelo,* 3 parts (1882–83); *Final Memorials* (1887); *Complete Poetical and Prose Works,*

11v. (Riverside Edition, 1886); etc. Editor, *Poems of Places,* 3Iv. (1876–79); etc. Prof. modern languages, and librarian, Bowdoin College, 1829–35; Smith prof. modern languages and belles lettres, Harvard University, 1835–54. *See* L. S. Livingston's *A Bibliography of the First Editions in Book Form of the Writings of Henry Wadsworth Longfellow* (1908); D. Gilbert Dexter's *Life and Work of Henry Wadsworth Longfellow* (1882); W. Sloane Kennedy's *Henry Wadsworth Longfellow* (1882); Blanche Roosevelt Tucker-Macchetta's *The Home Life of Henry Wadsworth Longfellow* (1882); E. S. Robertson's *Life of Henry Wadsworth Longfellow* (1887); Samuel Longfellow's *Life of Henry Wadsworth Longfellow,* 3v. (1891); F. R. Carpenter's *Henry Wadsworth Longfellow* (1901); Thomas Wentworth Higginson's *Henry Wadsworth Longfellow* (1902); Herbert S. Gorman's *A Victorian American* (1926); Lawrance Thompson's *Young Longfellow* (1938); Edward Wagenknecht's *Longfellow: A Full Length Portrait* (1955); Newton Arvin's *Longfellow: His Life and Work* (1963); Andrew Hilen's *The Letters of Henry Wadsworth Longfellow,* 2v. (1966).

LONGFELLOW, SAMUEL (June 18, 1819–Oct. 3, 1892); b. Portland, Me., brother of Henry Wadsworth Longfellow. Unitarian clergyman, poet. *Thalatta: a Book for the Seaside* (with Thomas Wentworth Higginson, poems, 1853); *Vespers* (1859); *A Book of Hymns and Tunes* (1860); *Life of Henry Wadsworth Longfellow,* 2v. (1866); *Final Memorials of Henry Wadsworth Longfellow* (1887); *Hymns and Verse,* ed. by Edith Longfellow (1894).

Longman, Irwin. Pen name of Ingersoll Lockwood.

Longmans, Green & Co. Publishers. Now merged with David McKay Co. (q.v.). The New York branch was established in 1887. The London firm was founded in 1724 by Thomas Longman. Two of the managers of the American branch were Charles J. Mills and his son Edward S. Mills Since 1935 the business offices of Longmans, Green & Co. have been affiliated with those of the Oxford University Press. Many classic English books were published by the firm, which still specializes in works by English authors, but since the founding of the American branch many American authors have been added, especially in the field of education. Among the early authors on the list were Coleridge, Macaulay, John Stuart Mill, Disraeli, Cardinal Newman, H. Rider Haggard, Andrew Lang, etc. Among the notable series published by the firm have been the *Historic Towns, Epochs of American History, American Citizen* series, *Living Thoughts Library, Our Debt to Greece and Rome* series, etc.

LONGSTREET, AUGUSTUS BALDWIN (Sept. 22, 1790–July 9, 1870); b. Augusta, Ga. Methodist clergyman, educator, author. *Georgia Scenes, Characters, Incidents, &c., in the First Half Century of the Republic* (1835); *Master William Mitten* (1864); *Stories with a Moral* (1912). Founder, the *State Rights Sentinel,* Augusta, Ga., 1834; editor, 1834–36. President, Emory College, 1839–48; Centenary College, 1849; University of Mississippi, 1849–56; South Carolina College, 1857–61. *See* John D. Wade's *Augustus Baldwin Longstreet* (1924).

LONGSTREET, HELEN DORTCH (Mrs. James Longstreet), b. in Franklin Co., Ga. Journalist, author. *Lee and Longstreet at High Tide* (1904); *In the Path of Lee's Old War Horse* (1914).

LONGSTREET, JAMES (Jan. 8, 1821–Jan. 2, 1904); b. Edgefield District, S.C. Confederate general, author. *Annals of the War* (1879); *Battles and Leaders of the Civil War,* 2v. (1887–88); *From Manassas to Appomattox* (1896). *See* Helen D. Longstreet's *Lee and Longstreet at High Tide* (1904); H. J. Eckenrode's *James Longstreet* (with B. Conrad, 1936).

LONGSTREET, RUPERT JAMES (Sept. 28, 1892–); b. Mt. Dora, Fla. Educator, ornithologist. *Florida Birds* (1931); *Stories of Florida* (1931); *The Story of Mount Dora, Florida* (1960); etc. Editor, *Florida Naturalist,* since 1927. Lecturer, Stetson University, since 1935.

LONGSTREET, STEPHEN (Apr. 18, 1907–); b. New York. Author. *Decade* (1940); *The Last Man Around the World* (1941); *The Gay Sisters* (1942); *Nine Lives with Grandfather* (1944); *Stallion Road* (1945); *The Sisters Liked Them Handsome* (1946); *The Pedlocks* (1951); *The Beach House* (1952); *The World Revisited* (1953); *The Lion at Morning* (1954); *The Boy in the Model-T* (autobiography, 1956); *The Promoters* (1957); *Crime* (1959); *Gettysburg* (1961); *The Wilder Shore* (1968); *Eagles Where I Walk* (1966); *A Salute to American Cooking* (with Ethel Longstreet, 1968). Under pen name "Thomas Burton": *Bloodbird* (1941); etc. Under pen name "Paul Haggard": *Dead Is the Doornail* (1938); etc. Under pen name "David Ormsbee": *Chico Goes to the Wars* (1943).

LONGSTRETH, T[homas] MORRIS (1886–). Author. *The Adirondacks* (1917); *The Catskills* (1918); *Mac of Placid* (1920); *The Laurentians* (1922); *Sons of the Mounted Police* (1928); *In Scarlet and Plain Clothes* (1933); *To Nova Scotia* (1935); *Trial by Wilderness* (1940); *Tad Lincoln, the President's Son* (1944); *Two Rivers Meet in Concord* (1946); *The Great Venture* (1948); *Showdown* (1950); *Elephant Toast* (1952); *The Scarlet Force* (1953); *Time Flight* (1954); *Dangerline* (1955); *Doorway in the Dark* (1956); *The MacQuarrie Boys* (1957); *Bull Session* (1958); *Trouble Guaranteed* (1960); *Henry Thoreau: American Rebel* (1963); *The Comeback Catcher* (1965); etc.

LONGWORTH, ALICE [Lee] ROOSEVELT (Feb. 12, 1884–); b. New York City, daughter of Theodore Roosevelt. Author. *Crowded Hours: Reminiscences* (1933). Compiler: *Desk Drawer Anthology* (with Theodore Roosevelt, Jr., 1937).

Look. New York. Biweekly. Founded 1937 and published by Cowles Magazines, Inc. Pictorial journalism aimed at a mass audience interested in personalities, photographic quizzes and mysteries, and other spectacular features. *Look* has been known for its journalistic daring. It published in 1964 the first three-dimensional photograph to be reproduced in any periodical. In 1967 it serialized William A. Manchester's controversial account of the death of President John F. Kennedy, *The Death of a President.* Expired 1971.

Look Homeward, Angel. Novel by Thomas Wolfe (1929). Story of the revolt of youth against provincial barriers. Eugene Gant seeks freedom in Europe, but finds that too much of America is in his blood and bones for him to become an expatriate, and the urge to express the glory and the tragedy of his age becomes an obsession. The novel is a thinly disguised autobiography.

LOOKER, EARLE (Feb. 11, 1895–); b. Washington, D.C. Author. *The White House Gang* (1929); *Colonel Roosevelt, Private Citizen* (1932); *The American Way* (1933); *Revolt* (with Antonina Looker, 1968); etc.

Looking Backward. By Edward Bellamy (1888). Julian West, a wealthy young Bostonian, is put into hypnotic sleep in 1887 and wakes up in the year 2000. The Utopian state of society in this new world is a commentary on the social evils of the nineteenth century.

Looking Forward. Novel by John Rankin Rogers, first published as *The Graftons; or, Looking Forward* (1893). It had appeared as a serial in the *Kansas Commoner* in 1889. A novel on Populism.

"Looking Glass for the Times, A." Poem by Peter Folger (1677).

LOOMIS, ALFRED F[ullerton] (Aug. 23, 1890–Mar. 26, 1968); b. Brooklyn, N.Y. Yachtsman, author. *The Cruise of the Hippocampus* (1922); *The Sea Bird's Quest* (1923); *Sea Legs* (1927); *Troubled Waters* (1929); *Yachts under Sail* (1933); *Paradise Cove* (1933); *Ocean Racing: The Great Blue-Water Yacht Races, 1866–1935* (1936); *Ranging the Maine Coast* (1939); *The Hotspur Story* (1954); *What Price Dory* (with C. Day, 1955).

LOOMIS, CHARLES BATTELL (Sept. 16, 1861–Sept. 23, 1911); b. Brooklyn, N.Y. Humorist, author. *Just Rhymes* (1899); *Yankee Enchantment* (1900); *Cheerful Americans* (1903); *More Cheerful Americans* (1904); *Minerva's Maneuvers* (1905); *Cheer Up* (1906); *A Holiday Touch* (1907); *A Bath in an English Tub* (1907); etc.

LOOMIS, CHARLES PRICE (Oct. 26, 1905–); b. Bloomfield, Colo. Educator. *Studies of Rural Social Organization in the United States, Latin America and Germany* (1945). Co-author, with J. A. Beegle: *Rural Social Systems* (1950); *Rural Sociology* (1957). Head, dept. of sociology and anthropology, Michigan State University, since 1944.

LOOMIS, EDWARD (1924–). Author. *End of a War* (1958); *The Charcoal Horse* (1959); *The Hunter Deep in Summer* (1961); *The Mothers* (1962); *On Fiction: Critical Essays and Notes* (1966); etc.

LOOMIS, LOUISE ROPES (May 3, 1874–Jan. 2, 1958); b. Yokohama, Jap. Educator, author. *Medieval Hellenism* (1906); *The Book of the Popes* (1916); *The See of Peter* (with James T. Shotwell, 1927); etc. Editor: *Readings in Aristotle* (1943); etc. Prof. history, Wells College, 1921–40.

LOOMIS, ROGER SHERMAN (Oct. 31, 1887–Oct. 11, 1966); b. Yokohama, Jap. Educator, author. *The Romance of Tristram and Ysolt* (rev., 1951); *Celtic Myth and Arthurian Romance* (1927); *Arthurian Legends in Medieval Art* (with Laura H. Loomis, 1938); *Arthurian Tradition and Chrétien de Troyes* (1949); etc. Editor: *Arthurian Literature in the Middle Ages* (1959); etc. English dept., Columbia University, since 1920.

LOOS, ANITA (Mrs. John Emerson) (Apr. 26, 1893–); b. Sisson, Calif. Author. *Breaking into the Movies* (with husband, 1921); *The Whole Town's Talking* (with husband, 1923); *Gentlemen Prefer Blondes* (1925), dramatized (with husband, prod. 1926); *But Gentlemen Marry Brunettes* (1928); *The Social Register* (with husband, prod. 1931); *Happy Birthday* (prod. 1946); *A Mouse is Born* (1950); *Gigi* (prod. 1951); *This Brunette Prefers Work* (1956); *No Mother to Guide Her* (1961); *A Girl Like I* (1966).

LOOVIS, DAVID (1926–). Author. *Try for Elegance* (1959); *The Last of the Southern Winds* (1961).

LORANT, STEFAN (Feb. 22, 1901–); b. Budapest. *I Was Hitler's Prisoner* (1935); *Lincoln: His Life in Photographs* (1941); *F.D.R.: A Pictorial Biography* (1950); *The Presidency* (1951); *The Life of Abraham Lincoln* (1954); *The Life and Times of Theodore Roosevelt* (1959); *The Story of an American City* (1964); *Fighting for the New World* (1967); *Presidential Elections* (1968); *The Glorious Burden: The American Presidency* (1968); etc.

LORD, DANIEL ALOYSIUS (Apr. 27, 1888–Jan. 15, 1955); b. Chicago, Ill. Roman Catholic clergyman, editor, author. *Armchair Philosophy* (1918); *Our Nuns* (1924); *Six One-Act Plays* (1925); *My Mother: The Story of an Uneventful Life* (1934); *Our Part in the Mystical Body* (1935); *Some Notes for the Guidance of Parents* (1944); *Christ in Me* (1952); etc.

LORD, ELEAZAR (Sept. 9, 1788–June 3, 1871); b. Franklin, Conn. Railroad executive, author. *Principles of Currency and Banking* (1829), republished as *Credit, Currency, and Banking* (1834); *Geological Cosmogony* (1943); *A Historical Review of the New York and Erie Railroad* (1855); etc. Co-founder, New York University, 1831.

LORD, JAMES (1922–). Author. *No Traveler Returns* (1956); *The Joys of Success* (1958); *A Giacometti Portrait* (1965).

LORD, JOHN (Dec. 27, 1810–Dec. 15, 1894); b. Portsmouth, N.H. Lecturer, author. *The Life of Emma Willard* (1873). Editor: *Beacon Lights of History,* 8v. (1884–96).

LORD, LOUIS ELEAZER (July 14, 1875–Jan. 24, 1956); b. Ravenna, O. Educator, author. *Literary Criticism of Euripides* (1908); *Aristophanes* (1925); *Thucydides and the World War* (1945); *History of the American School of Classical Studies* (1947); etc. Classics dept., Oberlin College, 1903–41.

LORD, PHILLIPS HAYNES (July 13, 1902–); b. Hartford, Vt. Radio dramatist, author. Pen name, "Seth Parker." *Seth Parker's Album* (1930); *Sunday at Seth Parker's* (1930); *Uncle Hosie* (1930); *Way Back Home* (1932); *Seth Parker's Scrap Book* (1935).

LORD, RUSSELL (July 21, 1895–); b. Baltimore, Md. Editor, author. *Captain Boyd's Battery* (1920); *Men of Earth* (1931); *To Hold This Soil* (1938); *Behold Our Land* (1938); *The Agrarian Revival* (1939); *The Wallaces of Iowa* (1947); *The Care of the Earth* (1962). Editor: *Voices from the Fields* (1937); *A Place on Earth, Subsistence Homestead Study* (1942); *Forever the Land: A Country Chronicle and Anthology* (with Kate Lord, 1949). Contrib. editor, the *Country Home*, 1924–38; *The Progressive Farmer*, since 1942.

LORD, WALTER (1917–). Author. *A Night To Remember* (1955); *Day of Infamy* (1957); *The Good Years* (1960); *A Time To Stand* (1961); *Peary to the Pole* (1963); *The Past That Would Not Die* (1965); *Incredible Victory* (1967); etc.

LORD, WILLIAM WILBERFORCE (Oct. 28, 1819–Apr. 22, 1907); b. in Madison Co., N.Y. Episcopal clergyman, poet. *Poems* (1845); *Christ in Hades* (1851); *André* (drama in verse, 1856); *The Complete Poetical Works*, ed. by Thomas O. Mabbott (1938). *See* Edgar Allan Poe's *The Literati* (1850).

LORD, WILLIAM SINCLAIR (Aug. 24, 1863–Sept. 24, 1925); b. Sycamore, Ill. Poet. *Beads of Morning* (1888); *Blue and Gold* (1895); *The Rock-a-Bye* (1905). Editor: *This Is for You: Love Poems of the Saner Sort* (1908).

"Lord of All Being Throned Afar." Hymn by Oliver Wendell Holmes (1859). Also known as "The Sun-Day Hymn."

Lord Weary's Castle. Collection of poems by Robert Lowell (1946).

"Lorena." Song, words by H. D. L. Webster, music by J. P. Webster (1857). Of Northern origin, it became very popular in the South during the Civil War.

LORENZ, KONRAD ZACHARIAS (Nov. 7, 1903–); b. Vienna. Zoologist, author. *King Solomon's Ring* (1952); *Man Meets Dog* (1954); *On Aggression* (1966); *Evolution and Modification of Behavior* (1966). Vice-director, Max Planck Foundation, 1954–61; director, since 1961.

LORIMER, FRANK (July 1, 1894–); b. Bradley, Me. Sociologist. *The Making of Adult Minds in a Metropolitan Area* (1934); *Population of the Soviet Union: History and Prospects* (1946); *Culture and Human Fertility* (1955); *Demographic Information on Tropical Africa* (1961); etc. Prof. sociology, Graduate School, American University, since 1938.

LORIMER, GEORGE HORACE (Oct. 6, 1868–Oct. 22, 1937); b. Louisville, Ky. Editor, publisher, author. *Letters from a Self-Made Merchant to His Son* (anon. 1902); *Old Gorgon Graham* (1904); *The False Gods* (1906); *Jack Spurlock, Prodigal* (1908); etc. Editor-in-chief, *Saturday Evening Post*, 1899–1937; vice-president, Curtis Publ. Co., 1927–32; president, 1932–34; chairman, 1934–37.

LORIMER, GRAEME (Feb. 9, 1903–); b. Wyncote, Pa. Editor. Author (with wife, Sarah Moss Lorimer): *Men Are Like Street Cars* (1932); *Stag Line* (1934); *Heart Specialist* (1935); *After* (1938); *First Love, Farewell* (1940); etc. Assoc. editor, *Saturday Evening Post*, 1932–38; fiction editor, *Ladies' Home Journal*, 1939–44.

LORIMER, SARAH MOSS (Mar. 25, 1906–); b. Bala, Pa. Author of books with husband, Graeme Lorimer (q.v.).

LORING, EMILIE [Baker] (Mrs. Victor J. Loring) (d. Mar., 1951); b. Boston, Mass. Author. *The Trail of Conflict* (1922); *Swift Water* (1929); *Uncharted Seas* (1932); *Hilltops Clear* (1933); *We Ride the Gale!* (1934); *It's a Great World* (1935); *Give Me One Summer* (1936); *As Long As I Live* (1937); *Across the Years* (1939); *There Is Always Love* (1940); *Where Beauty Dwells* (1941); *When Hearts Are Light* (1943); *Beyond the Sound of Guns* (1945); *Bright Skies* (1946); *Beckoning Trails* (1947); *Love Came Laughing By* (1949); etc.

LORING, FREDERICK WADSWORTH (Dec. 12, 1848–Nov. 5, 1871); b. Boston, Mass. Journalist, playwright, poet. *Wild Rose* (prod. 1870); *The Boston Dip, and Other Verses* (1871); *Two College Friends* (1871). His best known poem, "In the Churchyard at Fredericksburg," first appeared in the *Atlantic Monthly*, Sept. 1870.

LORING, J[ohn] ALDEN (Mar. 6, 1871–May 8, 1947); b. Cleveland, O. Naturalist, author. *Young Folks' Nature Field Book* (1907); *African Adventure Stories* (1914); etc.

Los Angeles Free Press. Los Angeles, Cal. Newspaper. Founded 1963. Edited by Arthur Kunkin. Tabloid format. One of the most important Underground newspapers on the west coast.

Los Angeles Herald and Express. Los Angeles, Cal. Newspaper. Founded 1871, as the *Los Angeles Express*. The *Herald* was founded in 1873. Merged 1931. Owned by Hearst Publishing Co. See *Los Angeles Herald-Examiner*.

Los Angeles Herald-Examiner. Los Angeles, Cal. Newspaper. Founded 1903 as *Examiner*. Later combined with *Herald* of *Herald and Express*. Publishes Sunday supplement, "Pictorial Living." George R. Hearst, Jr., is publisher. Frederick Shroyer edits the book reviews.

Los Angeles Times. Los Angeles, Cal. Newspaper. Founded 1881. In 1882 Harrison Gray became editor. Bailey Millard (1859–1941) was a special writer, 1924–41. Nick Williams is editor. Digby Diehl is book review editor.

LOSSING, BENSON JOHN (Feb. 12, 1813–June 3, 1891); b. Beekman, N.Y. Wood-engraver, author, editor, more than 40 titles on popular subjects in American history. *Pictorial Field-Book of the Revolution*, 2v. (1850–52); *Our Countrymen* (1855); *The Life and Times of Philip Schuyler*, 2v. (1860–73); *Pictorial History of the Civil War*, 3v. (1866–68); *The Hudson, from the Wilderness to the Sea* (1866); *Pictorial Field-Book of the War of 1812* (1868); *The Empire State* (1887); etc. Editor, the *Family Magazine*, N.Y., 1839–41; *American Historical Record and Repertory of Notes and Queries*, 1872–74.

Lost generation. Term derived from a statement made by Gertrude Stein to Ernest Hemingway—"You are all a lost generation"—referring to the disillusionment of the young writers and artists who could find no substitute for their loss of idealism during the period after World War I. Hemingway's early novel, *The Sun Also Rises*, typifies the attitudes of the lost generation.

Lost Lady, A. Novel by Willa Cather (1923). Story of the Middle West, depicting the Forrester family.

"Lost Occasion, The." Poem by John Greenleaf Whittier (1880). It expresses regret over the death of Daniel Webster, who had been castigated in Whittier's "Ichabod."

Lost Phoebe, The. Short story by Theodore Dreiser (1918).

Lost Virgin of the South; A Tale of Truth, Connected with the History of the Indian War in the South, in the Years 1812-13–14 and 15, The. Novel by "Dom Pedro Casender" (Michael Smith) (1831).

Lost Weekend, The. Novel by Charles Jackson (1944). Struggle of an alcoholic to redeem his life from his addiction.

LOTH, DAVID GOLDSMITH (Dec. 7, 1899–); b. St. Louis, Mo. *The Brownings* (1929); *Lorenzo the Magnificent* (1929); *Charles II* (1930); *Philip II* (1932); *Public Plunder* (1938); *Woodrow Wilson: The Fifteenth Point* (1941); *Chief Justice* (1949); *The People's General* (1951); *A Long Way Forward* (1957); *The Erotic in Literature* (1961); etc. Co-author: *Voluntary Parenthood* (1949); *I Was a Drug Addict* (1953); *Peter Freuchen's Book of the Seven Seas* (1957); *The Frigid Wife* (1962); *How High is Up* (1964); *The Emotional Sex* (1964); *Ivan Sanderson's Book of the Jungles* (1965); *The City within a City: the Romance of Rockefeller Center* (1966); etc.

LOTHAR, ERNST (Oct. 25, 1890–); b. Bruenn, Aust. Author. *The Warlord* (1917); *The Clairvoyant* (1931); *Little Friend* (1933); *The Loom of Justice* (1935); *A Woman Is Witness* (1941); *Beneath Another Sun* (1943); *The Angel with the Trumpet* (1944); *The Prisoner* (1945); *Return to Vienna* (1949). Drama critic, *Neue Freie Presse.*

Lothrop, Amy. Pen name of Anna Bartlett Warner.

LOTHROP, DANIEL (Aug. 11, 1831–Mar. 18, 1892); b. Rochester, N.Y. Publisher. Founder, D. Lothrop & Co., 1868. Founded the juvenile magazine *Wide Awake,* Boston, 1875. He was the husband of Harriet Mulford Stone Lothrop ("Margaret Sidney").

LOTHROP, HARRIET MULFORD STONE (Mrs. Daniel Lothrop) (June 22, 1844–Aug. 2, 1924); b. New Haven, Conn. Author of children's books. Pen name, "Margaret Sidney." *Five Little Peppers and How They Grew* (1880); *Old Concord: Her Highways and Byways* (1888); *Five Little Peppers Midway* (1890); *Rob: A Story for Boys* (1891); *Five Little Peppers Grown Up* (1892); *A Little Maid of Concord Town* (1898); *The Judges' Cave* (1900); *A Little Maid of Boston Town* (1910); *Our Davie Pepper* (1916); etc.

Lothrop, Lee & Shepard Company. New York. Publishers. Founded 1850, in Boston, by Daniel Lothrop as the D. Lothrop & Co. Incorporated 1887 as D. Lothrop Co. In 1894 the name was changed to Lothrop Publishing Co. In 1861 Lee & Shepard was founded by William Lee and Charles A. B. Shepard. In 1904 it was consolidated with the Lothrop Publishing Co., to form Lothrop, Lee & Shepard Co. In 1943 it was purchased by Crown Publishing, Inc., and sold to Scott, Foresman in 1966. Now a division of William Morrow & Co.

LOTHROP, SAMUEL KIRKLAND (July 6, 1892–Jan. 10, 1965); b. Milton, Mass. Anthropologist, explorer, author. *Tulum: An Archaeological Study of Eastern Yucatan* (1924); *Indians of Tierra del Fuego* (1928); *Indians of the Parana* (1931); *Inca Treasure as Depicted by Spanish Historians* (1938); *Archaeology of Southern Veraguas, Panama* (1947); *The Cenote of Sacrifice, Chichen Itza—Metals* (1951); *Chancey Style Graves at Zapallan, Peru* (with Joy Mahler, 1957); *Pre-Colombian Art* (with others, 1957); *Archeology of the Diquis Delta Costa Rica* (1963).

Lottery, The. Story by Shirley Jackson (1949). Gruesome story of the acceptance of sadism as a convention, told in terms of a meticulously worked-out fantasy.

LOUDON, SAMUEL (1727–Feb. 24, 1813); b. in Scotland. New York bookseller, printer, author. *The Deceiver Unmasked* (1776), a reply to Paine's *Common Sense.* Founder, The *New York Packet, and the American Advertiser,* Jan. 4, 1776. Started a circulating library in 1774. In 1786 he printed Noah Webster's periodical, the *American Magazine. See* Alexander J. Wall's *Samuel Loudon* (1922).

LOUGHBOROUGH, MARY WEBSTER (Aug. 27, 1836–Aug. 27, 1887); b. New York. Editor, diarist. *My Cave Life in Vicksburg* (anon., 1864). Founder, the *Southern Ladies' Journal,* Little Rock, Ark., 1883; editor, 1883–87. Wrote stories on early St. Louis history for the *Land We Love.*

LOUGHEAD, FLORA HAINES [Apponyi] (b. July 12, 1855); b. Milwaukee, Wis. Author. *The Man Who Was Guilty* (1886); *Dictionary of Given Names* (1934).

Louisiana State University Press. Baton Rouge, La. Founded 1935. Devoted to Southern history and literature, and scholarly paperbacks.

Louisiana Swamp Doctor. By Henry Clay Lewis, under the pen name "Madison Tensas, M.D." (1843). Humorous sketches of life in the Mississippi Delta. The book has three titles: *Louisiana Swamp Doctor* is the cover title; *Odd Leaves from the Life of a Louisiana "Swamp Doctor"* is on the title page; *Odd Leaves from the Note Book of a Louisiana Swamp Doctor* is on an added title page. It was reissued in 1846 and 1850. In 1858 it was reissued, bound with *Streaks of Squatter Life, and Far-West Scenes,* by John S. Robb, under the pen name "Solitaire" (q.v.), each with its original title page, but with an added title page, reading *The Swamp Doctor's Adventures in the South-West* [etc.]

Louisville Courier-Journal. Louisville, Ky. Newspaper. The *Louisville Daily Journal* was founded Nov. 24, 1830. George D. Prentice was editor and publisher until 1868, when he was succeeded by Henry Watterson. The *Louisville Democrat* was founded in 1843, and the *Louisville Courier* in 1844. Watterson acquired these two papers in 1868 and merged them with the *Journal* as the *Louisville Courier-Journal,* which he conducted until his death in 1918. Robert Worth Bingham then acquired the paper and was succeeded at his death in 1937 by his son Harry Bingham. Bruce Haldeman was editor, 1885–95, president, 1902–18, succeeding his father, Walter Newman Haldeman. Harrison Robertson joined the staff in 1879 and became editor in 1929. Herbert Agar became editor in 1940. Barry Bingham is now editor. Cary Robertson is book review editor of the *Courier-Journal.* The Sunday book page features Mortimer Adler's column "Great Ideas from the Great Books." See *Louisville Times.*

Louisville Times. Louisville, Ky. Newspaper. Founded 1884. Acquired by the *Louisville Courier-Journal* as an evening edition.

LOUNSBERRY, ALICE (Nov. 6, 1872–Nov. 21, 1949); b. New York City. Author. *A Guide to the Wild Flowers* (1899); *A Guide to the Trees* (1900); *Gardens Near the Sea* (1911); *Sir William Phips* (1941); etc.

Lounsbury, Charles. See Williston Fish.

LOUNSBURY, THOMAS RAYNESFORD (Jan. 1, 1838–Apr. 9, 1915); b. Ovid, N.Y. Educator, philologist, author. *History of the English Language* (1879); *James Fenimore Cooper* (1882); *Shakespeare and Voltaire* (1902); *The Standard of Usage in English* (1908); *The Life and Times of Tennyson* (1915); etc. Editor: *The Tab Book of American Verse* (1912); *The Yale Book of American Verse* (1912); etc. Editor, *Yale Literary Magazine.* Prof. language and literature, Yale University, 1870–1916.

LOUTHAN, HATTIE HORNER (Feb. 5, 1865–); b. Quincy, Ill. Educator, author. *Poems* (1885); *Not at Home* (1889); *Collection of Kansas Poetry* (1891); *Thoughts Adrift* (poems, 1902); *In Passion's Dragnet* (1904); *This Was a Man* (1907); *A Rocky Mountain Feud* (1910); *Short Story Craftsman* (1930); *The Holy Shadow* (1938). Prof. English, University of Denver, since 1910.

LOVE, EDMUND G. (1912–). Author. *Subways Are for Sleeping* (1957); *War Is a Private Affair* (1959); *Arsenic and Red Tape* (1960); *The Situation in Flushing* (1965).

LOVE, ROBERTUS DONNELL (Jan. 6, 1867–May 7, 1930); b. Irondale, Mo. Journalist, poet. *Poems All the Way from Pike* (1904); *The Rise and Fall of Jesse James* (1926). Lit. editor, the *St. Louis Post Dispatch,* 1926–28; *St. Louis Globe Democrat,* 1928–30. Wrote "Rhymes Along the Road" for the *St. Louis Republic,* 1913–16.

Love Affairs of a Bibliomaniac. By Eugene Field (1896). Field, who was a book-lover, and who started the "Saints and Sinners Corner" in a Chicago bookstore, wrote this book to show how far the passions of a bibliomaniac could carry him if allowed to develop unchecked.

Love Among the Cannibals. Novel by Wright Morris (1957). A satirical view of Hollywood writers and their girl friends.

Love and Death in the American Novel. Major work of literary criticism, by Leslie Fiedler (1960). Ranges over the entire history of a literary form emphasizing the ways in which the themes of love and death are qualified by American social and psychological experience.

Love and Will. By Rollo May (1970). A discussion of sex and civilization.

Love in '76. Play by Oliver Bell Bunce (prod. 1857). Social comedy with historical background.

"Love Me and the World Is Mine." Song, words by David Reed, music by Ernest R. Ball (1906).

Love of Life, and Other Stories, The. By Jack London (1907). Volume of short stories.

"Love Song of J. Alfred Prufrock, The." Poem by T. S. Eliot (1917). Famous for having popularized the French symbolist technique in Engish. An ironic poem in free verse about a man growing older who finds himself too weak to face the importunities of his own life.

Love Sonnets of a Hoodlum. By Wallace Irwin (1902).

Love Story. Novel by Erich Segal (1970). Two college students fall in love and marry. The young man is disinherited by his wealthy, socially prominent father for marrying beneath his station. The wife dies of leukemia at the age of twenty-five. The novel, written after a motion picture based on the same plot was in production, became a best-seller.

LOVECRAFT, HOWARD PHILLIPS (1890–1937); b. Providence, R.I. Author. *The Outsider and Others* (1939); *Beyond the Wall of Sleep* (1943); *Marginalia* (1945); *Something About Cats* (1949). *See* August William Derleth's *H.P.L.: A Memoir* (1945).

LOVEJOY, ARTHUR ONCKEN (Oct. 10, 1873–Dec. 1962); b. Berlin. Educator, author. *The Revolt against Dualism* (1930); *Primitivism and Related Ideas in Antiquity* (with George Boas, 1935); *The Great Chain of Being* (1936); *Essays in the History of Ideas* (1948); *The Reason, the Understanding and Time* (1961); *Reflections on Human Nature* (1961). Prof. philosophy, Johns Hopkins University, 1910–38.

LOVEJOY, CLARENCE EARLE (June 26, 1894–); b. Waterville, Me. Journalist, editor. *The Story of the Thirty-Eighth* (1919); *So You're Going to College* (1940); *Lovejoy's Complete Guide to American Colleges and Universities* (1948); *Lovejoy's College Guide* (1968); *Lovejoy's Prep School Guide* (1969); etc. With the *New York Times*, 1915–20, and since 1934; founder, the *Bronxville Press*, 1925. Editor, *Columbia Alumni News*, 1927–47.

LOVELACE, DELOS WHEELER (Dec. 2, 1894–Jan. 17, 1967); b. Brainerd, Minn. Journalist, author. *Rockne of Notre Dame* (1931); *General Ike Eisenhower* (1944); *Journey to Bethlehem* (1953); *That Dodger Horse* (1953). Co-author (with Maud H. Lovelace): *One Stayed at Welcome* (1934); *Gentleman from England* (1937); *The Golden Wedge* (1942).

LOVELACE, MAUD HART (Mrs. Delos Wheeler Lovelace) (Apr. 25, 1892–); b. Mankato, Minn. *The Black Angels* (1926); *Early Candlelight* (1929); *The Charming Sally* (1932); *Betsy-Tacy* (1940); *Betsy, in Spite of Herself* (1946); *The Tune Is in the Tree* (1950); *Winona's Pony Cart* (1953); *What Cabrillo Found* (1958); *The Valentine Box* (1966); etc. Also co-author of several books with husband, Delos Wheeler Lovelace (q.v.).

LOVEMAN, AMY (May 16, 1881–Dec. 11, 1955); b. New York. Editor. *I'm Looking for a Book* (1936). Associate editor, *Saturday Review,* from 1924. With Book-of-the-Month Club, from 1938; member board of judges, from 1951.

LOVEMAN, ROBERT (Apr. 11, 1864–July 10, 1923); b. Cleveland, O. Poet. *Poems* (1893); *A Book of Verses* (1900); *The Gates of Silence* (1903); *The Blushful South and Hippocrene* (1909); *On the Way to Willowdale* (1912); *Verses* (1912).

Love's Body. By Norman O. Brown (1966).

LOVETT, ROBERT MORSS (Dec. 25, 1870–Feb. 8, 1956); b. Boston, Mass. Educator, author. *A History of English Literature* (with W. V. Moody, 1902); *Richard Gresham* (1904); *A Winged Victory* (1907); *Edith Wharton* (1925); *Preface to Fiction* (1930); *History of the Novel in England* (with Helen S. Hughes, 1932); *All Our Years* (autobiography, 1948); etc. English dept., University of Chicago, 1893–1936.

"Lovewell's Fight." Anonymous ballad (1724).

Lovey Mary. By Alice Hegan Rice (1903). Sequel to *Mrs. Wiggs of the Cabbage Patch.* Lovey Mary was a foundling, and becomes the heroine of the novel.

LOVING, BOYCE. Playwright. *Gay* (1933); *Handicap* (1934); *Swappers* (1934); *Without Benefit of Relatives* (1934); *Tomboy* (1935); *Galahad Jones* (1937); *Treadmill* (1937); *Little Geraldine* (1938); *Mainstreet Princess* (1941); etc.

LOVING, PIERRE (Sept. 5, 1893–); b. New York. Author. *Revolt in German Drama* (1925); *The Cat of Heaven* (London, 1930), republished as *Gardener of Evil* (New York, 1931); etc. Editor: *Fifty Contemporary One-Act Plays* (with Frank Shay, 1920); *Ten-Minute Plays* (1923); etc.

LOW, BENJAMIN R[obbins] C[urtis] (June 22, 1880–June 22, 1941); b. Fairhaven, Mass. Lawyer, poet, biographer. *The Sailor Who Has Sailed, and Other Poems* (1911); *The House That Was* (1915); *Broken Music: Selected Verse* (1920); *Seth Low* (1925); *Darkening Sea* (1925); *Winged Victory* (1927); *Roland* (1930); *Off Soundings* (1932); *King Philip* (1933); *Brooklyn Bridge* (1933); *Symphony in D Minor* (1937); *Poems, 1910–1940* (1940).

LOW, SETH (Jan. 18, 1850–Sept. 17, 1916); b. Brooklyn, N.Y. Educator, mayor, author. *Addresses and Papers on Municipal Government* (1891). Mayor of Brooklyn, 1881–85; of New York City, 1901–03. President, Columbia University, 1890–1901. *See* Benjamin R. C. Low's *Seth Low* (1925).

LOW, WILL H[icok] (May 31, 1853–Nov. 27, 1932); b. Albany, N.Y. Painter, illustrator, author. *A Chronicle of Friendships* (1908); *A Painter's Progress* (1910).

LOWE, MARTHA ANN PERRY (Mrs. Charles Lowe) (Nov. 21, 1829–1902); b. Keene, N.H. Author. *The Olive and the Pine* (poems, 1859); *Love in Spain, and Other Poems* (1867); *The Story of Chief Joseph* (1881); *Memoir of Charles Lowe* (1884); *The Immortals* (poems, 1899); *Bessie Gray, and Our Stepmother* (1891).

LOWELL, A[bbott] LAWRENCE (Dec. 13, 1856–Jan. 16, 1943); b. Boston, Mass. Educator, author. *Governments and Parties in Continental Europe*, 2v. (1896); *The Government of England*, 2v. (1908); *Public Opinion and Popular Government* (1913); *Public Opinion in War and Peace* (1923); *At War with Academic Traditions in America* (1934); *Biography of Percival Lowell* (1935); *What a University President Has Learned* (1938); etc. President, Harvard University, 1909–33.

LOWELL, AMY (Feb. 9, 1874–May 12, 1925); b. Brookline, Mass. Poet, critic. *A Dome of Many-Coloured Glass* (1912); *Sword Blades and Poppy Seeds* (1914); *Men, Women, and Ghosts* (1916); *Tendencies in Modern American Poetry* (1917); *Can Grande's Castle* (1918); *Pictures of the Floating World* (1919); *Legends* (1921); *A Critical Fable* (1922); *John*

Keats, 2v. (1925); *What's O'Clock* (1925; Pulitzer Prize for poetry, 1926); *East Wind* (1926); *Ballads for Sale* (1927); *The Madonna of Carthagena* (1927); *Selected Poems* (1928); *Poetry and Poets* (1930); etc. Miss Lowell gave her Keats collection to Harvard University. *See* Howard Willard Cook's *Amy Lowell* (1923); G. H. Sargents's *Amy Lowell* (1926); S. Foster Damon's *Amy Lowell* (1935); Fred B. Millett's *Contemporary American Authors* (1940); Horace Gregory's *Amy Lowell* (1958).

LOWELL, EDWARD JACKSON (Oct. 18, 1845–May 11, 1894); b. Boston, Mass. Historian. *The Hessians and the Other German Auxiliaries of Great Britain in the Revolutionary War* (1884); *The Era of the French Revolution* (1892).

LOWELL, JAMES RUSSELL (Feb. 22, 1819–Aug. 12, 1891); b. Cambridge, Mass. Poet, critic, diplomat, educator. *Class Poem* (1838); *A Year's Life* (1841); *Poems,* 2 series (1844–48); *Conversations on Some of the Old Poets* (1845); *A Fable for Critics* (1848); *The Biglow Papers,* 2v. (1848–69); *The Vision of Sir Launfal* (1848); *Poems,* 2v. (1849); *Fireside Travels* (1864); *Under the Willows and Other Poems* (1869); *Among My Books,* 2 series (1870–76); *My Study Windows* (1871); *Three Memorial Poems* (1877); *On Democracy* (1884); *Democracy, and Other Addresses* (1887); *Heartsease and Rue* (1888); *Political Essays* (1888); *Latest Literary Essays and Addresses* (1891); *The Old English Dramatists* (1892); *Last Poems* (1895); *Letters,* ed. by Charles Eliot Norton, 2v. (1894); *Anti-Slavery Papers* (1902); *New Letters,* ed. by M. A. DeWolfe Howe (1932); *The Writings,* 12v. (1890–92); *The Complete Writings,* 16v. (Elmwood Edition, 1904); etc. Editor (with Robert Carter), *The Pioneer,* 1843; the *Atlantic Monthly,* 1857–61; co-editor, the *North American Review,* 1864–72. U.S. minister to Spain, 1877–80; to England, 1880–85. Smith prof. French and Spanish languages, Harvard University, 1855–86. His best known poem was "Ode Recited at the Harvard Commemoration." His Cambridge, Mass., home was known as "Elmwood." *See* L. S. Livingston's *A Bibliography of the First Editions in Book Form of the Writings of James Russell Lowell* (1914); Edward Everett Hale's *James Russell Lowell and His Friends* (1899); Edward Everett Hale, Jr's. *James Russell Lowell* (1899); William Dean Howells's *Literary Friends and Acquaintances* (1900); Horace E. Scudder's *James Russell Lowell,* 2v. (1901); Ferris Greenslet's *James Russell Lowell* (1905); William C. Brownell's *American Prose Writers* (1909); Richard Croome Beatty's *James Russell Lowell* (1950); Martin Duberman's *James Russell Lowell* (1966). *See also* Maria White Lowell.

"Lowell, Joan". (pen name) (Nov. 23, 1902–Nov. 14, 1967); b. Berkeley, Calif. Real name unknown. Actress, author. *The Cradle of the Deep* (1929); *Kicked Out of the Cradle* (1930); *Gal Reporter* (1933); *Promised Land* (1952).

LOWELL, JULIET (Aug. 7, 1901–); b. New York. *Dumb-Belles Lettres* (1933); *Dear Sir* (1944); *Dear Mr. Congressman* (1948); *Dear Doctor* (1955); *Dear Justice* (1958); *Dear Man of Affairs* (1961); *Dear VIP* (1963); *It Strikes Me Funny* (1964); *Boners in the News* (1967); *Humor U.S.A.* (1968); etc.

LOWELL, MARIA WHITE (Mrs. James Russell Lowell) (July 8, 1821–Oct. 27, 1853); b. Watertown, Mass. Poet. *The Poems,* ed. by her husband (1855); augmented edition, ed. by Hope Jillson Vernon (1936). Her best known poems are "The Alpine Shepherd" and "The Morning Glory."

LOWELL, PERCIVAL (Mar. 13, 1855–Nov. 2, 1916); b. Boston, Mass., brother of Amy Lowell. Astronomer, poet. *Chosön, the Land of the Morning Calm* (1886); *The Soul of the Far East* (1888); *Noto, an Unexplored Corner of Japan* (1891); *Mars* (1895); *Occult Japan* (1895); etc.; also books on Mars, etc. Established the Lowell Observatory, Flagstaff, Ariz., 1894. *See* A. Lawrence Lowell's *Biography of Percival Lowell* (1935).

LOWELL, ROBERT Jr. [Traill Spence] (Mar. 1, 1917–); b. Boston, Mass. Poet. *Land of Unlikeness* (1944); *Lord Weary's*

Castle (1946; Pulitzer Prize for poetry, 1947); *The Mills of the Kavanaughs* (1951); *Life Studies* (1959); *Imitations* (1961); *For the Union Dead* (1964); *The Old Glory* (prod. 1965); *Near the Ocean* (1967); *Prometheus Bound* (prod. 1967); *Notebook 1967–68* (1969); etc. *See* Hugh B. Stapler's *Robert Lowell: The First Twenty Years* (1962); Jerome Mazzaro's *The Poetic Themes of Robert Lowell* (1965); Richard J. Fein's *Robert Lowell* (1970).

LOWELL, ROBERT TRAILL SPENCE (Oct. 8, 1816–Sept. 12, 1891); b. Boston, Mass., brother of James Russell Lowell. Episcopal clergyman, novelist, poet. *The New Priest in Conception Bay* (1858); *Poems* (1864); *Antony Brade, A Story of a School* (1874); *A Story or Two from an Old Dutch Town* (1878); etc. His best poem is "The Defense of Lucknow."

Lowell Offering. Lowell, Mass. Founded Oct., 1840. Harriet Jane Hanson, later Mrs. Harriet H. Robinson, author of *Loom and Spindle,* was editor. The working girls in the woolen mills were the contributors. The magazine ended in 1845. The magazine was published by Abel C. Thomas and Thomas Baldwin Thayer, who also collaborated in writing the *Lowell Tracts,* a defense of Universalism, and the editing of the Universalist Magazine, *The Star of Bethlehem.*

LOWENFELS, WALTER (1897–   ); b. New York. Author, editor. *The Suicide* (1934); *Sonnets of Love and Liberty* (1955); *American Voices* (1959); *To An Imaginary Daughter* (1964); *Some Deaths* (1964); *Land of Roseberries* (1965); etc. Editor: *Walt Whitman's Civil War* (1960); *Poets of Today* (1964); *Where is Vietnam?* (1967); *In A Time of Revolution* (1970).

LOWENTHAL, MARVIN (Oct. 6, 1890–Mar. 16, 1969); b. Bradford, Pa. Author. *A World Passed By* (1933); *The Autobiography of Montaigne* (1935); *The Jews of Germany: A Story of Sixteen Centuries* (1936). Editor and translator: *Henrietta Szold's Life and Letters* (1942); Theodor Herzl's *Diaries* (1956).

LOWERY, WOODBURY (Feb. 17, 1853–Apr. 11, 1906); b. New York. Editor, historian. *The Spanish Settlements within the Present Limits of the United States,* 2v. (1901–1905). His collection of early Spanish maps of the present United States is now in the Library of Congress.

LOWES, JOHN LIVINGSTON (Dec. 20, 1867–Aug. 15, 1945); b. Decatur, Ind. Educator, author. *Convention and Revolt in Poetry* (1919); *The Road to Xanadu* (1927); *Of Reading Books* (1929); *Geoffrey Chaucer, and the Development of His Genius* (1934); *Essays in Appreciation* (1936). Editor: *Selected Poems of Amy Lowell* (1928). Prof. English, Harvard University, 1918–39.

LOWIE, ROBERT HARRY (June 12, 1883–Sept. 21, 1957); b. Vienna. Anthropologist, author. *Culture and Ethnology* (1917); *Primitive Society* (1920); *Primitive Religion* (1924); *Origin of the State* (1927); *Are We Civilized?* (1929); *An Introduction to Cultural Anthropology* (1934); *The Crow Indians* (1935); *Social Organization* (1948); *Toward Understanding Germany* (1954); *Indians of the Plains* (1954); etc. Prof. anthropology, University of California, 1925–50.

LOWNDES, MARY E[lizabeth] (1864–March 19, 1947); b. Wallasey, Eng., came to the United States in 1909. Educator, author. *Michel de Montaigne* (1898); *The Nuns of Port Royal* (1910).

LOWREY, JANETTE SEBRING (Mrs. Fred V. Lowrey); b. Orange, Tex. Author. *Annunciata and the Shepherds* (1938); *Tap-a-tan* (1942); *A Day in the Jungle* (1943); *The Bird* (1947); *Margaret* (1950); *Mr. Heff and Mr. Ho* (1952); *Love, Bid Me Welcome* (1964); etc.

LOWRIE, WALTER (Apr. 26, 1868–1959); Philadelphia, Pa. Episcopal clergyman, author. *The Doctrine of St. John* (1899); *Monuments of the Early Church* (1901); *Gaudium Crucis* (1905); *Religion or Faith* (1930); *Kierkegaard* (1937);

SS. *Peter and Paul in Rome* (1940); *The Lord's Supper and the Liturgy* (1943); *Ministers of Christ* (1946); *The Enchanted Island* (1953); *A Short Life of Kierkegaard* (1958); etc.

LOWRY, HOWARD FOSTER (July 26, 1901–July 4, 1967); b. Portsmouth. O. Educator. Author: *The Poetry of Matthew Arnold* (with C. B. Tinker, 1940); *Matthew Arnold and the Modern Spirit* (1941). Editor: *The Letters of Matthew Arnold to Arthur Hugh Clough* (1932); *Emerson-Clough Letters* (with Ralph Leslie Rusk, 1934); *An Oxford Anthology of English Poetry* (with Willard Thorp, 1935); *An Oxford Anthology of English Prose* (with Arnold Whitridge and John Wendell Dodds, 1935); *Matthew Arnold's Note-Books* (with Ken Young and W. H. Dunn, 1938). English dept., College of Wooster, 1923–25; 1929–40; president since 1944.

LOWRY, ROBERT (Mar. 12, 1826–1899); b. Philadelphia, Pa. Baptist clergyman, hymn writer. Compiler: *Chapel Melodies* (1868); *Chautauqua Carols* (1878); *Glad Refrains* (1886); etc. His best known hymns are "Shall We Gather at the River" and "Where Is My Wandering Boy To-Night."

LOWRY, ROBERT JAMES (Mar. 28, 1910–); b. Cincinnati, O. Author. *Casualty* (1946); *Find Me in Fire* (1948); *The Big Cage* (1949); *The Wolf that Fed Us* (stories, 1949); *The Violent Wedding* (1953); *Happy New Year, Kamerades!* (stories, 1954); *What's Left of April* (1956); *That Kind of Woman* (1959); *The Prince of Pride Starring* (1959); *Party of Dreamers* (1962); etc.

LOY, MATTHIAS (Mar. 17, 1828–Jan. 26, 1915); b. in Cumberland Co., Pa. Lutheran clergyman, educator, editor, author. *Essay on the Ministry* (1870); *Sermons on the Gospels* (1888); *The Christian Church* (1898); *The Story of My Life* (1905); etc. Editor, the *Lutheran Standard,* 1864–91; etc. Prof. theology, Capital University, Columbus, O., 1865–1915.

Loyalty of Free Men, The. By Alan Barth (1951). Critical investigation of the political loyalty program as it interferes with individual freedom.

LUBELL, SAMUEL (Nov. 3, 1911–); b. in Poland. Journalist, author. *The Future of American Politics* (1952); *Revolution in World Trade* (1955); *Revolt of the Moderates* (1956); *White and Black* (1964). Syndicated column "The Voters Speak."

LUCAS, CURTIS. Author. *Flour Is Dusty* (1943); *Third Ward, Newark* (1946).

LUCAS, DANIEL BEDINGER (Mar. 16, 1836–July 28, 1909); b. Charlestown, W.Va. Jurist, poet. Known as "The poet of the Shenandoah Valley." *The Wreath of Eglantine, and Other Poems* (with Virginia Lucas, 1869); *The Maid of Northumberland: A Dramatic Poem* (1879); *Ballads and Madrigals* (1884); *Dramatic Works* (1913); *The Land Where We Were Dreaming, and Other Poems* (1913).

Lucas, Victoria. Pen name of Sylvia Plath.

LUCCOCK, HALFORD EDWARD (Mar. 11, 1885–Nov. 5, 1960); b. Pittsburgh, Pa. Methodist clergyman, educator, author. *Fares, Please!* (1916); *The Story of Methodism* (with Paul Hutchinson, 1926); *Contemporary American Literature and Religion* (1934); *Christianity and the Individual* (1937); *American Mirror* (1940); *In the Minister's Work Shop* (1944); *Endless Line of Splendor* (1951); *Marching Off the Map* (1952); *Like a Mighty Army: Selected Letters of Simeon Stylites* (1954); *Unfinished Business* (1956); *Living Without Gloves: More Letters of Simeon Stylites* (1957); *365 Windows* (1960); etc. Prof. homiletics, Yale Divinity School, from 1928.

Luce, Clare Boothe. See Clare Boothe.

LUCE, GAY GAER (Oct. 2, 1930–); b. Berkeley, Cal. Author. *Current Research in Sleep and Dreams* (1965); *Sleep* (with Julius Segal, 1966).

LUCE, HENRY ROBINSON (Apr. 3, 1898–Feb. 28, 1967); b. in Shantung Province, China. Editor, publisher. Founder, 1923, with Briton Hadden, of *Time,* a weekly magazine; editor and publisher since 1923; publisher, *Fortune,* from 1930, *Life,* from 1936, and *Sports Illustrated,* from 1954. See John Kubler's *Luce: His Time, Life and Fortune* (1968).

Luce, Mrs. Henry Robinson. See Clare Boothe.

LUCEY, THOMAS ELMORE (Jan. 15, 1874–June 1, 1947); b. Monroe, N.C. Lyceum entertainer, actor, author. Known as "the poet entertainer of the Ozarks." *Etchings by an Optimist* (1894); *Through Prairie Meadows* (poems, 1904).

Lucinda; or, The Mountain Mourner: Being Recent Facts, in a Series of Letters from Mrs. Manvill, in the State of New York, to Her Sister in Pennsylvania. By Mrs. P. D. Manvill (1807). Fictional letters describing events in Saratoga Co., N.Y.

Luck of Roaring Camp, The. By Bret Harte (1870). A series of stories based on incidents in the Far West during the gold rush. Besides the *Luck of Roaring Camp,* the book includes *The Outcasts of Poker Flat, Tennessee's Partner,* and *Miggles,* stories that established the fame of the author, and are often reprinted in anthologies of American literature.

LÜDERS, CHARLES HENRY (1858–1891); b. Philadelphia, Pa. Poet. *Hallo, My Fancy* (with S. Decatur Smith, 1887); *The Dead Nymph, and Other Poems* (1892).

LUDLOW, FITZ HUGH (Sept. 11, 1836–Sept. 12, 1870); b. New York City. Editor, author. *The Hasheesh Eater* (1857); *Little Brother, and Other Genre-Pictures* (1867); *The Heart of the Continent* (1870). Editor, *Vanity Fair,* 1858–60. Drama critic, *New York Evening Post,* 1861–62.

LUDLOW, JAMES MEEKER (Mar. 15, 1841–Oct. 4, 1932); b. Elizabeth, N.J. Presbyterian clergyman, author. *A Man for A' That* (1880); *Captain of the Janizaries* (1886); *A King of Tyre* (1890); *The Age of the Crusades* (1897); *Deborah* (1901); *Sir Raoul* (1905); *Judge West's Opinions* (1908); *Avanti!* (1912); *Along the Friendly Way: Reminiscences and Impressions* (1919).

LUDLOW, NOAH MILLER (July 3, 1795–Jan. 9, 1886); b. New York. Actor, author. *Dramatic Life as I Found It* (1880).

Ludlow, Park. Pen name of Theron Brown.

LUHAN, MABEL [Ganson] DODGE (Feb. 26, 1879–Aug. 13, 1962); b. Buffalo, N.Y. Author. *Lorenzo in Taos* (1932); *Intimate Memories,* 4v. (1933–37); *Winter in Taos* (1935); *Taos and Its Artists* (1947).

LUKAS, J. ANTHONY (Apr. 25, 1933–); b. New York. Journalist, author. *The Barnyard Epithet and Other Obscenities* (1970); *Don't Shoot, We Are Your Children!* (1971). Staff, *New York Times,* since 1962.

"Luke Havergal." Poem by Edwin Arlington Robinson (1897).

LUKENS, HENRY CLAY (b. Aug. 18, 1838); b. Philadelphia, Pa. Editor, author. *The Marine Circus at Cherbourg, and Other Poems* (1865); *Story of the Types* (1881); *Jets and Flashes* (under pen name, "Erratic Enrique," 1883). Editor: *The Journalist: A Pictorial Souvenir* (1887). Assoc. editor, the *New York Daily News,* 1877–84; managing editor, the *Journalist.*

LUMLEY, FREDERICK ELMORE (June 7, 1880–July 26, 1954); b. Iona, Ont., Can. Educator, author. *Principles of Sociology* (1928); *Ourselves and the World* (with Boyd H. Bode, 1931); *The Propaganda Menace* (1933); etc. Editor, *The Ohio Valley Sociologist,* 1930–44. Prof. sociology, Ohio State University, 1920–40.

LUMMIS, CHARLES FLETCHER (Mar. 1, 1859–Nov. 25, 1928); b. Lynn, Mass. Editor, librarian, author. *Birch Bark Poems* (1879); *A New Mexico David, and Other Stories* (1891); *A Tramp Across the Continent* (1892); *Some Strange Corners of Our Country* (1892); *The Land of Poco Tiempo* (1893); *The Spanish Pioneers* (1893); *The Man Who Married the Moon, and Other Pueblo Indian Folk-Stories* (1894); *The Gold Fish of Gran Chimú* (1896); *The King of the Broncos* (1897); *The Enchanted Burro* (1897); *Spanish Songs of Old California,* 2v. (1923–28); *A Bronco Pegasus* (poems, 1928); *Flowers of Our Lost Romance* (1929). Founder and editor of *Out West Magazine,* 1894–1909. Librarian, Los Angeles Public Library, 1905–10.

Lummox. By Fannie Hurst (1925). The story of Bertha, a Scandinavian servant girl, in New York, who leads a hard life but who manages to help people solve their problems.

LUMPKIN, GRACE, b. in Georgia. Novelist. *To Make My Bread* (1932); *A Sign for Cain* (1935); *The Wedding* (1939).

Lunch, The. A club in New York founded by James Fenimore Cooper. Bryant, Morse, Sands, Durand, Vanderlyn, Hillhouse, Halleck, Dunlap, and Jarvis were among its members.

LUNDBERG, FERDINAND (1902–). Author. *Imperial Hearst: A Social Biography* (1936); *America's 60 Families* (1937); *Treason of the People* (1954); *Modern Woman: The Lost Sex* (with M. L. F. Farnham, 1959); *Scoundrels All* (1968).

LUNT, GEORGE (Dec. 31, 1803–May 16, 1885); b. Newburyport, Mass. Poet, journalist. *The Grave of Byron, with Other Poems* (1826); *Poems* (1839); *The Age of Gold, and Other Poems* (1843); *The Dove and the Eagle* (1851); *Lyric Poems, Sonnets, and Miscellanies* (1854); *Eastford; or, Household Sketches* (under pen name, "Wesley Brooke," 1855); *Poems* (1884). Editor: *Old New England Traits* (1873).

LUNT, WILLIAM EDWARD (June 13, 1882–Nov. 10, 1956); b. Lisbon, Me. Educator, author. *History of England* (1928); *Financial Relations of the Papacy with England to 1327* (1939); etc. Prof. history, Haverford College, 1917–52.

Luska, Sidney. Pen name of Henry Harland.

LUTES, DELLA T[hompson] (d. July 13, 1942); b. Jackson, Mich. Editor, novelist. *Just Away* (1906); *Home Grown* (autobiography, 1937); *Millbrook* (1938); *Gabriel's Search* (1940); *The Country Schoolma'am* (1941). Editor, *American Motherhood Magazine,* 1912–23; housekeeping editor, *Modern Priscilla,* 1923–30.

LUTHER, FRANK (Francis Luther Crow) (Aug. 4, 1905–); b. Lakin, Kan. Song writer, author. *Americans and Their Songs* (1942). Has written over one thousand songs, including "Barnacle Bill the Sailor."

LUTHER, MARK LEE (Jan. 5, 1872–); b. Knowlesville, N.Y. Author of mystery novels. *The Favor of Princes* (1899); *The Mastery* (1904); *The Crucible* (1907); *Presenting Jane McRae* (1920); *The Boosters* (1924); *The Saranoff Murder* (1930); etc.

Lutheran, The. Philadelphia, Pa. Weekly. Founded 1918. Published by Board of Publication, United Lutheran Church in America. News magazine of the church.

Lutheran Intelligencer. Frederick, Md. Founded 1826, by David Frederick Schaeffer, who edited it until 1831. This was the first Lutheran church paper in the United States to be published in English.

Lutz, Grace Livingston Hill. See Grace Livingston Hill.

LUTZ, RALPH HASWELL (May 18, 1886–Apr. 18, 1968); b. Circleville, O. Educator, author. *The German Revolution, 1818–1919* (1922); *Fall of the German Empire,* 2v. (1932); *Bibliography of the Paris Peace Conference* (with Nina Al-

mond, 1935); *Dictatorship in the Modern World* (1935); *The Organization of American Relief in Europe, 1918–1919* (with Suda Bane, 1943); *Biographical Sketch of Hanssen* (1955); etc. History dept., University of Washington, 1916–20; Stanford University, 1920–52.

Lyceum. The first proposal for a lyceum appeared in the *Journal of Education,* in 1826. One was formed in Milbury, Mass., in 1826. The idea spread throughout New England and prominent authors were asked to lecture before lyceum audiences. Lyceum bureaus were organized to make arrangements for these appearances, among them being the one founded in Boston by James Redpath and a similar organization founded by James Burton Pond. *See* Charles F. Horner's *The Life of James Redpath and the Development of the Modern Lyceum* (1926); Carl Bode's *The American Lyceum* (1956). *See also* Chautauqua.

LYDENBERG, HARRY MILLER (Nov. 18, 1874–Apr. 16, 1960); b. Dayton, O. Librarian, author. *History of The New York Public Library* (1923); *John Shaw Billings* (1924); *The Care and Repair of Books* (with John Archer, 1931); *Crossing the Line* (1957). Editor: *Archibald Robertson, Lieutenant-General, Royal Enginners, His Diaries and Sketches in America, 1762–1780* (1930). Translator: André Blum's *The Origins of Printing and Engraving* (1940). With The New York Public Library, 1896–1941, director 1934–41.

LYLE, EUGENE P., Jr. (Dec. 31, 1873–); b. Dallas, Tex. Author of Western novels. *The Missourian* (1905); *The Lone Star* (1907); *Blaze Derringer* (1910); *Castaway's Island* (1925); etc.

Lyle Stuart, Inc. New York. Founded 1956. Publishes general fiction and nonfiction. Lyle Stuart is president.

LYMAN, EUGENE WILLIAM (Apr. 4, 1872–Mar. 15, 1948); b. Cummington, Mass. Educator, author. *Theology and Human Problems* (1910); *The Meaning of Selfhood* (1928); *The Kingdom of God and History* (with others, 1938); *Religion and the Issues of Life* (1943); etc. Prof. philosophy of religion, Union Theological Seminary, New York, 1918–40.

LYMAN, GEORGE D[unlap] (Dec. 12, 1882–July 26, 1949); b. Virginia City, Nev. Physician, book collector, author. *John Marsh, Pioneer* (1930); *Saga of the Comstock Lode* (1934); *Ralston's Ring* (1937); *A Friend to Man* (1938).

LYMAN, ROLLO LA VERNE (Mar. 4, 1878–Dec. 22, 1937); b. Windsor, Wis. Educator, author. *The Mind at Work* (1924). Editor: *Reading and Living, Treasury of Life and Literature, Daily-Life Language* series, etc.

LYMAN, THEODORE (Feb. 20, 1792–July 18, 1849); b. Boston, Mass. Philanthropist, mayor, author. *The Diplomacy of the United States with Foreign Nations* (1826), augmented, 2v. (1828); etc.

LYNCH, GERTRUDE, b. New London, Conn. Author. *The Fighting Chance: The Romance of an Ingénue* (1903); *The Wanderers* (1905); *Winds of the World* (1906).

Lynch, Laurence L. Pen name of Emma Murdoch Van Deventer.

LYNCH, MAUDE BARROWS DUTTON (Nov. 1880–); b. Plantsville, Conn. Author of children's books. *Little Stories of France* (1906); *Little Stories of England* (1911); *The Magic Clothes-Pins* (1926); *Billy Gene and His Friends* (1929); *Billy Gene's Play Days* (1932); *Henry the Navigator* (1935); *I'm Busy* (1933); *Christopher Columbus* (1938); etc.

LYNCH, WILLIAM FRANCIS (Apr. 1, 1801–Oct. 17, 1865); b. Norfolk, Va. Naval officer, author. *Naval Life; or, Observations Afloat and on Shore* (1851).

LYND, ROBERT S[taughton] (Sept. 26, 1892–Nov. 1, 1970); b. New Albany, Ind. Educator, author. *Middletown: A Study in Contemporary American Culture* (with Helen Merrell

Lynd, 1929); *Middletown, in Transition* (with same, 1937); *Knowledge for What?* (1939). Editor, *Publishers' Weekly*, 1914–18. Prof. sociology, Columbia University, since 1931.

LYND, STAUGHTON [Craig] (Nov. 22, 1929–); b. Philadelphia, Pa. Educator, author. *Nonviolence in America* (1966); *The Other Side* (with Tom Hayden, 1966); *Class Conflict, Slavery and the United States Constitution* (1967); *Intellectual Origins of American Radicalism* (1968). Editor: *Reconstruction* (1967).

LYNDE, FRANCIS (Nov. 12, 1856–May 16, 1930); b. Lewiston, N.Y. Novelist. *A Fool for Love* (1905); *Empire Builders* (1907); *David Vallory* (1919); *The Wreckers* (1920); *Blind Man's Buff* (1928); *Young Blood* (1929).

LYNES, [Joseph] RUSSELL, JR. (Dec. 2, 1910–); b. Great Barrington, Mass. Editor, author. *Snobs* (1950); *Guests* (1951); *Tastemakers* (1954); *A Surfeit of Honey* (1957); *Cadwallader* (1959); *Confessions of a Dilettante* (1966). Assistant editor, *Harper's,* 1944–47; managing editor, since 1947.

LYNN, KENNETH SCHUYLER (June 17, 1923–); b. Cleveland, O. Educator, author. *Dream of Success* (1955); *Mark Twain and Southwestern Humor* (1959). Editor: *The Comic Tradition in America* (1958); *The American Society* (1963); *World in a Glass* (1966). Prof. English, Harvard University, since 1963.

LYNN, MARGARET, b. Tarkio, Mo. Educator, author. *A Stepdaughter of the Prairie* (1914); *Free Soil* (1920); *The Land of Promise* (1927). Editor: *Eighteenth Century Verse* (1907). English dept., University of Kansas, from 1901.

LYON, HARRIS MERTON (Dec. 22, 1883–June 2, 1916); b. Santa Fé, N.M. Author. *Sardonics* (1908); *Graphics* (1913). Theodore Dreiser called him "De Maupassant, Junior" in his *Twelve Men* (1919).

LYON, LEVERETT SAMUEL (Dec. 14, 1885–Sept. 9, 1959); b. in Will Co., Ill. Economist, executive. Author or co-author: *Elements of Debating* (1913); *Our Economic Organization* (1921); *Making a Living* (1926); *The Economics of Free Deals* (1933); *Government and Economic Life*, 2v. (1939–40); *Nothing but Nonsense* (poems, 1954); etc.

LYON, QUINTER M[arcellus] (June 10, 1898–); b. Washington, D.C. Educator, author. *Three Typical Views of Progress* (1933); *The Great Religions* (1957); *Quiet Strength from World Religions* (1960); *Meditations from World Religions* (1966); etc. Chairman, philosophy dept., University of Mississippi, since 1946.

LYONS, DOROTHY MARAWEE (Dec. 4, 1907–); b. Fenton, Mich. *Silver Birch* (1939); *Midnight Moon* (1941); *Golden Sovereign* (1946); *Harlequin Hullabaloo* (1949); *Blue Smoke* (1953; rev. ed. 1968); *Bright Wampum* (1958); *Dark Sunshine* (1965); etc.

LYONS, EUGENE (July 1, 1898–); b. Uzlian, Rus. Editor, author. *The Life and Death of Sacco and Vanzetti* (1927); *Moscow Carrousel* (1935); *The Red Decade* (1941); *Our Secret Allies: The Peoples of Russia* (1954); *Workers Paradise Lost: 50 Years of Soviet Communism* (1967); *David Sarnoff, a Biography* (1966); etc. Editor, *American Mercury,* 1939–44; staff, *Reader's Digest,* since 1946.

Lyric, The. Norfolk, Va.; Bremo Bluff, Va. Quarterly poetry magazine. Founded 1920, by John Richard Moreland. Monthly, 1920–29; bi-monthly, 1930; quarterly, since 1931. Moreland was editor, 1920–23. Other editors have included Virginia Taylor McCormick, Leigh Hanes, Ruby A. Roberts.

Lyric Virginia To-Day. Ed. by Sinton Leitch (1932).

Lyric Year, The. Ed. by Ferdinand Earle (1912). One hundred lyric poems by American writers, published by Mitchell Kennerley.

Lyrics of Lowly Life. Poems by Paul Lawrence Dunbar (1896).

LYTLE, ANDREW NELSON (Dec. 26, 1902–); b. Murfreesboro, Tenn. Author. *Bedford Forrest and His Critter Company* (1931); *The Long Night* (1936); *At the Moon's Inn* (1941); *A Name for Evil* (1947); *The Velvet Horn* (1957); *A Novel, Novella and Four Stories* (1958); *Hero with the Private Parts* (1966).

LYTLE, WILLIAM HAINES (Nov. 2, 1826–Sept. 20, 1863); b. Cincinnati, O. Soldier, poet. *Poems of William Haines Lytle,* ed. by William H. Venable (1894). His best known poem is "Anthony and Cleopatra," which was published in the *Cincinnati Commercial,* July 29, 1858.

Lyttle, Jean. Pen name of Eileen Jeanette Garrett.

M

M. E. W. S. Pen name of Mary Elizabeth Wilson Sherwood.

M. Quad. Pen name of Charles Bertrand Lewis.

M: One Thousand Autobiographical Sonnets. By Merrill Moore (1938). The beginning of a projected collection of 50,-000 sonnets.

MAAS, PETER (June 27, 1929–); b. New York. Author. *The Rescuer* (1967); *The Valachi Papers* (1969).

MAAS, WILLARD (1911–Dec., 1970). Poet, critic. *Concerning the Young* (1938); etc.

MAASS, EDGAR (1896–); b. Hamburg, Ger. Novelist. *Don Pedro and the Devil* (1942); *The Dream of Philip II* (1944); *Imperial Venus* (1946); *The Queen's Physician* (1948); *The World and Paradise* (1950); *Lady at Bay* (1953); *Magnificent Enemies* (1955).

MABBOTT, THOMAS OLIVE (July 6, 1898–1968); b. New York City. Educator, editor. Editor: *Poe's Brother: The Poems of William Henry Leonard Poe* (1926); *Whitman's Half Breed, and Other Stories* (1927); *The Complete Poetical Works of W. W. Lord* (1938); *William Cullen Bryant's Embargo* (1955); *Collected Works of Edgar Allan Poe Vol. I* (1969) (poems); etc. English dept., Hunter College, New York, since 1929.

MABEE, [Fred] CARLETON (1914–); b. Shanghai, China. Educator, author. *The American Leonardo* (1943; Pulitzer Prize for biography, 1944); *The Seaway Story* (1961); *Black Freedom: The Nonviolent Abolitionists from 1830 to the Civil War* (1970). Professor of history, State University of New York at New Paltz, from 1965.

MABIE, HAMILTON WRIGHT (Dec. 13, 1846–Dec. 31, 1916); b. Coldspring, N.Y. Editor, critic. *My Study Fire* (1890); *Essays in Literary Interpretation* (1892); *Nature and Culture* (1896); *Books and Culture* (1896); *The Life of the Spirit* (1899); *William Shakespeare* (1900); *Works and Days* (1902); *Myths* (1905); *Legends* (1906); *Heroes* (1906); *Heroines that Every Child Should Know* (1908); *American Ideals, Character and Life* (1913); *Japan To-day and To-morrow* (1914); etc. On staff, *Christian Union* (which became the *Outlook* in 1893), 1879–1916; assoc. editor, 1884–1916. See Edwin W. Morse's *The Life and Letters of Hamilton Wright Mabie* (1920).

MACARTHUR, CHARLES (Nov. 5, 1895–Apr. 21, 1956); b. Scranton, Pa. Playwright. *War Bugs* (1926); *Lulu Belle* (with Edward Sheldon, prod. 1926); *Salvation* (with Sidney Howard, prod. 1928); *The Front Page* (with Ben Hecht, prod.

1928); *Twentieth Century* (with same, prod. 1932); *Ladies and Gentlemen* (with same, prod. 1939); *Swan Song* (with same, prod. 1946); etc.

MACARTHUR, JAMES (Feb. 18, 1866–1909); b. Glasgow, Scot. Editor. Co-editor, the *Bookman,* 1894–1900; lit. adviser, Dodd, Mead & Co.; Harper & Brothers.

MACARTHUR, RUTH [Alberta] **BROWN** (Nov. 14, 1881–); b. Searsmont, Me. Author. *Tabitha at Ivy Hall* (1911); *Little Mother* (1916); *The Gingerbread House* (1920); *The Story of Harriet Beecher Stowe* (1922); etc.

MACARTNEY, CLARENCE EDWARD NOBLE (Sept. 18, 1879–Feb. 19, 1957); b. Northwood, O. Presbyterian clergyman, author. *Lincoln and His Generals* (1925); *Highways and Byways of the Civil War* (1926); *Putting off Immortality* (1926); *Lincoln and His Cabinet* (1931); *Sermons from Life* (1932); *Little Mac: The Life of General George B. McClellan* (1939); *Christianity and the Spirit of the Age* (1940); *Strange Texts but Grand Truths* (1953); *Mr. Lincoln's Admirals* (1956); etc. Compiler: *Great Sermons of the World* (1927).

MACARTNEY, WILLIAM N. (Feb. 25, 1862–June 15, 1940); b. Fort Covington, N.Y. Physician, author. *Fifty Years a Country Doctor* (autobiography, 1938).

MACAULAY, FANNIE CALDWELL (Nov. 22, 1863–Jan. 6, 1941); b. Shelbyville, Ky. Author. Pen name "Frances Little." *The Lady of the Decoration* (1906); *Little Sister Snow* (1909); *The Lady and Sada San* (1912); *The House of the Misty Star* (1914); *Camp Jolly* (1917); etc.

MACAULEY, ROBIE. Author. *The End of Pity and Other Stories* (1957); *Technique in Fiction* (1964).

MacBird. Play by Barbara Garson (prod. 1967). Mock-Shakespearean farce about the assassination of President John F. Kennedy and the succession of President Lyndon B. Johnson.

MACCAULEY, CLAY (May 8, 1843–Nov. 15, 1925); b. Chambersburg, Pa. Unitarian clergyman, missionary to Japan, author. *Christianity in History* (1891); *Memories and Memorials* (1914); *Looking Before and After* (1919); etc. Translated the Japanese classic, *Jyaku-nin-issiu; or, Single Songs of a Hundred Poets* (1899).

MACCONNELL, SARAH WARDER, b. Springfield, O. Author. *Why Theodora* (1915); *Many Mansions* (1918); *One* (1922); etc.

MACCRACKEN, HENRY MITCHELL (Sept. 28, 1840–1918); b. Oxford, O. Presbyterian clergyman, educator, author. *Cities and Universities* (1882); *The Scotch Irish in America* (1884); *John Calvin* (1888); *Educational Progress in the United States* (1893); *The Three Essentials* (1901); *Hall of Fame* (1901). Chancellor, Western University of Pennsylvania (now University of Pittsburgh), 1881–84; New York University, 1891–1910.

MACCRACKEN, HENRY NOBLE (Nov. 19, 1880–); b. Toledo, O., son of Henry Mitchell MacCracken. Educator, author. *First Year English* (1903); *An Introduction to Shakespeare* (with others, 1910); *Family on Gramercy Park* (1949); *Hickory Limb* (1950); *Old Dutchess Forever!* (1957); etc. Editor: *The Minor Poems of John Lydgate,* 2v. (1911–34, for 1910–33); *The Principal Plays of Shakespeare* (1914); *Ten Plays of Shakespeare* (1927); etc. President, Vassar College, 1915–46.

MACCRACKEN, JOHN HENRY (Sept. 30, 1875–Feb. 1, 1948); b. Rochester, Vt., son of Henry Mitchell MacCracken. Educator, author. *College and Commonwealth* (1920). President, Westminster College, Fulton, Mo., 1899–1903; prof. politics, New York University, 1903–15; president, Lafayette College, 1915–26.

MACCREAGH, GORDON (Aug. 8, 1886–1953); b. Perth, Ind. Explorer, author. *Big Game in the Shan States* (1909); *White Waters and Black* (1926); *The Last of Free Africa* (1928).

MACCURDY, GEORGE GRANT (Apr. 17, 1863–Nov. 15, 1947); b. Warrensburg, Mo. Educator, anthropologist, author. *Human Origins: A Manual of Prehistory,* 2v. (1924); *Prehistoric Man* (1928); *The Coming of Man* (1932); etc. Anthropology dept., Yale University, 1898–1931.

MACDONALD, AUGUSTIN SYLVESTER (Apr. 19, 1865–); b. San Francisco, Calif. Book collector, author. *California* (1902); *Little Literary Lights* (1915). Compiler: *A Collection of Verse by California Poets* (1914). His collection of books relating to California was acquired by Henry E. Huntington in Apr. 1916. It numbered about 1,500 volumes.

MACDONALD, BETTY [Bard] (Mar. 26, 1908–Feb. 7, 1958); b. Boulder, Colo. Author. *The Egg and I* (1945); *Mrs. Piggle-Wiggle* (1947); *The Plague and I* (1948); *Anybody Can Do Anything* (1950); *Nancy and Plum* (1952); *Onions in the Stew* (1955); *Who, Me?* (1959); etc.

MACDONALD, DUNCAN BLACK (Apr. 9, 1863–Sept. 6, 1943); b. Glasgow, Scotland. Educator, Semitist, author. *Aspects of Islam* (1911); *Hebrew Philosophical Genius: A Vindication* (1935); etc. Head, Mohammedan dept., Kennedy School of Missions, Hartford, Conn., 1911–25.

MACDONALD, DWIGHT (1906–). Author, critic. *Henry Wallace, the Man and the Myth* (1948); *The Ford Foundation* (1956); *Memoirs of a Revolutionist* (1957); *Against the American Grain* (1965); *Dwight MacDonald on Movies* (1969). Editor: *Parodies* (1961).

MACDONALD, EDWINA LeVIN (May 10, 1878–); b. Campti, La. Author. *A Lady of New Orleans* (1925); *Blind Windows* (1927); *Heart Strings* (1930); *Star Jasmine* (1933); *Somebody's Got To Want Me* (1938).

MACDONALD, JOHN D[ann] (1916–). Author. *Wine of Dreamers* (1951); *Cancel All Our Vows* (1953); *Contrary Pleasure* (1954); *The Executioners* (1958); *The End of the Night* (1959); *Bullet for Cinderella* (1960); *One Monday We Killed Them All* (1962); *A Flash of Green* (1962); *The House Guests* (1965); *The Last One Left* (1967); *Bright Orange for the Shroud* (1967); *A Key to the Suite* (1968); *No Deadly Drug* (1968); *One Fearful Yellow Eye* (1968); *Pale Gray for Guilt* (1969); *Cry Hard, Cry Fast* (1969); etc.

MacDonald, Marcia. Pen name of Grace Livingston Hill.

MACDONALD, PHILIP (189?–); b. in England. Author. *The Rasp* (1924); *Patrol* (1928); *Persons Unknown: An Exercise in Detection* (1930); *Escape* (1932); *Warrant for X* (1938); *Something to Hide* (stories, 1952); *Guest in the House* (1955); *The List of Adrian Messenger* (1959); *The White Crow* (1966); *The Wraith* (1968).

MacDonald, Mrs. Reed Inness. See Jessica Nelson North.

MACDONALD, WILLIAM (July 31, 1863–Dec. 15, 1938); b. Providence, R.I. Educator, editor, author. *History and Government of Maine* (1902); *Jacksonian Democracy* (1905); *Three Centuries of American Democracy* (1923); *The Intellectual Worker and His Work* (1923); etc. Editor: *Documentary Source Book of American History* (1908); etc. Prof. history, Brown University, 1901–17. Editorial staff, *The Nation,* 1918–31.

MACDONNELL, JAMES FRANCIS CARLIN (Apr. 7, 1881–); b. Bay Shore, L.I., N.Y. Poet. Writes under name, "Francis Carlin." *My Ireland* (1917); *The Cairn of Stars* (1920).

MACDOWELL, KATHERINE SHERWOOD BONNER (Feb. 26, 1849–July 22, 1894); b. Holly Springs, Miss. Novelist, short story writer. Wrote under name "Sherwood Bonner." *Like unto Like* (1878); *Dialect Tales* (1883); *Suwanee River Tales* (1884). Private secretary to Henry Wadsworth Longfellow for many years.

MacDowell Colony. Peterboro, N.H. Founded 1908, by Marian Nevins MacDowell in memory of her husband, Edward MacDowell, the composer. As early as 1896, Edward Mac-Dowell made his home at Peterboro, and after his death in 1908 his home was made into a workshop for musicians and writers. Edwin Arlington Robinson, Stephen Vincent Benét, Willa Cather, Thornton Wilder, Hervey Allen, Maxwell Bodenheim, Padraic Colum, Allen Seeger, Frances Frost, Margaret Widdemer, and many other prominent writers have worked at MacDowell Colony.

MACE, FRANCIS PARKER LAUGHTON (Jan. 15, 1836–1899); Orono, Me. Poet. *Legends, Lyrics and Sonnets* (1883); etc.

MACE, WILLIAM H[arrison] (Nov. 27, 1852–Aug. 10, 1938); b. Lexington, Ind. Educator, author. *Stories of Heroism* (1907); *American History* (1925); and many textbooks. Prof. history, Syracuse University, 1891–1916.

MACFADDEN, BERNARR (Aug. 16, 1868–Oct. 12, 1955); b. Mill Springs, Mo. Physical culturist, publisher. Founder and publisher, *Physical Culture Magazine,* 1898; *True Story,* 1919; *True Romances,* 1923; *True Detective Mysteries Magazine,* 1925; *Master Detective Magazine,* 1929; etc.; publisher, *Liberty, Photoplay, Movie Mirror, True Detective,* and other magazines; president, Macfadden Publications until 1941, being succeeded by O. J. Elder.

MACFARLAND, CHARLES STEDMAN (Dec. 12, 1866–Oct. 26, 1956); b. Boston, Mass. Congregational clergyman, author. *Chaos in Mexico* (1935); *Contemporary Christian Thought* (1936); *Across the Years* (1936); *Trends of Christian Thinking* (1937); *I Was in Prison* (1939); *Peace through Religion* (1945); *Christian Unity in the Making* (1949); etc.

MACGAHAN, JANUARIUS ALOYSIUS (June 12, 1844–June 9, 1878); b. Perry Co., O. Journalist, author. *Campaigning on the Oxus* (1874); *The Turkish Atrocities in Bulgaria* (1876). Correspondent of the *London Daily News.*

MACGOWAN, ALICE (b. Dec. 10, 1858); b. Perrysburg, O. Author. *The Last Word* (1903); *Huldah* (1905); *Judith of the Cumberland* (1908); *The Sword in the Mountains* (1910); *The Million-Dollar Suitcase* (with Perry Newberry, 1922); etc.

MACGOWAN, KENNETH (Nov. 30, 1888–Apr. 27, 1963); b. Winthrop, Mass. Theatrical producer, author. *The Theatre of Tomorrow* (1921); *Continental Stagecraft* (1922); *Masks and Demons* (1923); *Footlights across America* (1929); *What's Wrong with Marriage* (with Dr. G. V. Hamilton, 1929); *Early Man in the New World* (1950); *A Primer of Playwriting* (1951); *Theater Pictorial* (1953); *The Living Stage* (with William Melnitz, 1955); *Behind the Screen* (1965); etc. Drama critic, *New York Globe,* 1919–23; *Vogue,* 1920–24; *Theatre Arts Magazine,* 1919–25; director, Provincetown Players, 1924–25; Greenwich Village Theatre, 1925–27. Prof. theater arts, University of California at Los Angeles, 1947–56.

MACGRATH, HAROLD (Sept. 4, 1871–Oct. 29, 1932); b. Syracuse, N.Y. Novelist. *Arms and the Woman* (1899); *The Man on the Box* (1904); *Hearts and Masks* (1905); *Half a Rogue* (1906); *The Enchanted Hat* (1908); *The Lure of the Mask* (1908); *The Goose Girl* (1909); *Place of Honeymoon* (1912); *The Voice in the Fog* (1915); *The Drums of Jeopardy* (1920); *The Cellini Plaque* (1925); *The Blue Rajah Murder* (1930); etc.

MACGREGOR, FRANK SILVER (Jan. 13, 1897–Jan. 11, 1971); b. Lunenburg, N.S. Publisher. With Harper and Brothers, since 1924; chairman of board, 1955–61.

MACGREGOR, [John] GEDDES (Nov. 13, 1909–); b. Glasgow, Scot. Educator, author. *Aesthetic Experience in Religion* (1947); *Christian Doubt* (1952); *From a Christian Ghetto* (1954); *The Tichborne Impostor* (1957); *The Bible in the Making* (1959); *The Coming Reformation* (1960); *The Hemlock and the Cross* (1963); *God Beyond Doubt* (1966); *The Sense of Absence* (1967); etc. Dept of philosophy, Bryn Mawr College, since 1949.

MacGrom, John. Pen name of Guy Humphreys McMaster.

MACHARG, WILLIAM [Briggs] (Sept. 18, 1872–Feb. 21, 1951); b. Dover Plains, N.Y. Author. *The Achievements of Luther Trant* (with Edwin Balmer, 1910); *Surakarta* (1913); *The Blind Man's Eyes* (1916); *The Indian Drum* (with Edwin Balmer, 1917); *Peewee* (1921); *The Affairs of O'Malley* (1940); etc.

MACHETANZ, FREDERICK (Feb. 20, 1908–); b. Kenton, O. Artist, author. *Panuck, Eskimo Sled Dog* (1939); *On Arctic Ice* (1940). Has illustrated Renick's *Tommy Carries the Ball* (1940); *Barney Hits the Trail* (with wife, 1950); etc.

MACHLIN, MILTON ROBERT (June 26, 1924–); b. New York. Editor, author. *Ninth Life* (1961); *Private Hell of Hemingway* (1962); *MacArthur—A Fighting Man* (1965). Editor, *Argosy* magazine, since 1960.

MACHUGH, AUGUSTIN (1877–Aug. 24, 1928). Actor, playwright. *Officer 666* (prod. 1912); *The Meanest Man in the World* (prod. 1920); *It's Up to You* (with others, prod. 1921); *True to Form* (prod. 1921); etc.

MACINNES, HELEN (Mrs. Gilbert Highet) (Oct. 7, 1907–); b. Glasgow, Scot. Author. *Above Suspicion* (1941); *Assignment in Brittany* (1942); *While Still We Live* (1944); *Horizon* (1946); *Friends and Lovers* (1947); *Rest and Be Thankful* (1949); *Neither Five nor Three* (1951); *I and My True Love* (1953); *Pray for a Brave Heart* (1955); *North from Rome* (1958); *Decision at Delphi* (1960); *Suspense* (1961); *The Venetian Affair* (1963); *Home is the Hunter* (1964); *The Double Image* (1966); *The Salzburg Connection* (1969).

MACINTOSH, DOUGLAS CLYDE (Feb. 18, 1877–July 6, 1948); b. Breadalbane, Ont., Can. Educator, author. *The Reaction against Metaphysics in Theology* (1911); *The Problem of Knowledge* (1915); *The Reasonableness of Christianity* (1925); *Social Religion* (1939); *Personal Religion* (1942); etc. Prof. theology, Yale, 1916–38.

MAC INTYRE, CARLYLE FERREN (July 16, 1890–June 30, 1967); b. in the Midwest. Poet. *The Brimming Cup* (1930); *Poems* (1936); *Cafés and Cathedrals* (1939); *The Black Bull* (1942); etc. Translator: *French Symbolist Poetry* (1950); also works of Rilke, Baudelaire, Verlaine and other poets.

MACISAAC, FRED[erick] (Mar. 22, 1886–deceased); b. Cambridge, Mass. Playwright, novelist. *Tin Hats* (1926); *The Vanishing Professor* (1927); *Mental Marvel* (1931); *The Yellow Shop* (1936); *Nothing but Money* (prod. 1937); *The Alligator Ring* (1939); *The Hothouse World* (1965).

MACIVER, ROBERT MORRISON (Apr. 17, 1882–June 15, 1970); b. Stornoway, Scotland. Educator, author. *Community: A Sociological Study* (1917); *Labor in the Changing World* (1919); *The Modern State* (1926); *Leviathan and the People* (1939); *Social Causation* (1942); *Toward an Abiding Peace* (1943); *The Web of Government* (1947); *The More Perfect Union* (1949); *The Ramparts We Guard* (1950); *Democracy and the Economic Challenge* (1952); *Academic Freedom in Our Time* (1955); *The Pursuit of Happiness* (1955); *Life: Its Dimensions and Its Bounds* (1960); *The Challenge of the Passing Years* (1962); *Power Transforms* (1964); etc. Lieber prof. political philosophy and sociology, Columbia University, 1929–50.

MACK, GERSTLE (May 21, 1894–); b. San Francisco, Calif. Architect, author. *Paul Cézanne* (1935); *Toulouse-Lautrec*

(1938); *Land Divided: A History of the Panama Canal and Other Isthmian Canal Projects* (1944); *Gustave Courbet* (1951); etc.

MACK, MAYNARD (Oct. 27, 1909–); b. Hillsdale, Mich. Educator. *Tragic Themes in Western Literature* (1955); *Jacobean Theatre* (1960); *Essays in Honor of Hardin Craig* (1962); *King Lear In Our Time* (1966); *Essays in Honor of A. D. McKillop* (1963); *Essays in Honor of F. A. Pottle* (1965); etc. Editor: Pope's *Essay on Man* (vol. 3, part 1, Twickenham edn., 1951). Contributor: *Pope and His Contemporaries* (1950). Prof. English, Yale University, since 1948.

MACKALL, LAWTON (May 23, 1888–Mar. 26, 1968); b. Chestnut Hill, Pa. Lecturer, author. *Scrambled Eggs* (1920); *Poodle Oodle of Doodle Farm* (with Ruth Mackall, 1929); *Portugal for Two* (1931); *Bizarre* (1933); *Restaurateur's Handbook* (with C. A. Faissole, 1938); *Knife and Fork in New York* (1948).

MACKALL, LEONARD LEOPOLD (Jan. 29, 1879–May 19, 1937); b. Baltimore, Md. Bibliographer. Editor, "Notes for Bibliophiles," in the *New York Herald Tribune Books,* 1924–37. Librarian, De Renne Georgia Library, Savannah, Ga., 1916–18.

MACKAY, CONSTANCE D'ARCY (Mrs. Roland Holt); (d. Aug. 21, 1966); b. St. Paul, Minn. Playwright. *The House of the Heart, and Other Plays for Children* (1909); *Patriotic Plays and Pageants* (1912); *Children's Theatres and Plays* (1927); etc.

MACKAY, HELEN [Gansevoort Edwards] (Mrs. Archibald Mackay) (Aug. 10, 1876–May, 1966); b. in Livingston Co., New York. Author. *Half Loaves* (1911); *Accidentals* (1915); *Chill Hours* (1920); etc.

MACKAY, MARGARET [Mackprang] (Nov. 19, 1907–Oct. 14, 1968); b. Oxford, Neb. Author. *Like Water Flowing* (1938); *Homeward the Heart* (1944); *The Flowered Donkey* (1950); *I Live in a Suitcase* (1953); *The Four Fates* (1955); *The Wine Princess* (1958); *Dolphin Boy* (1963); *Angry Island* (1964); *Island Boy* (1969); *The Violent Friend* (1969); etc.

MACKAYE, ARTHUR LORING (b. Dec. 19, 1863); b. Perth Amboy, N.J. Author. *The Slave Prince* (1926); *The Viking Prince* (1928); *The Pirate Prince* (1929).

MACKAYE, PERCY [Wallace] (Mar. 16, 1875–Aug. 31, 1956); b. New York, son of Steele Mackaye. Poet, playwright. *The Canterbury Pilgrims* (prod. 1903); *The Scare-Crow* (1908); *Poems* (1909); *Jeanne d'Arc* (1906); *Uriel, and Other Poems* (1912); *To-Morrow* (1912); *Poems and Plays,* 2v. (1916); *Rip Van Winkle* (music by Reginald De Koven, prod. 1919); *George Washington* (1920); *Dogtown Common* (poems, 1921); *The Skippers of Nancy Gloucester* (poems, 1924); *This Fine-Pretty World* (1924); *Tall Tales of the Kentucky Mountains* (1926); *Epoch: The Life of Steele Mackaye,* 2v. (1927); *Kentucky Mountain Fantasies* (1928); *Weathergoose —Woo!* (1929); *The Far Familiar* (poems, 1938); *What Is She?* (1942); *The Mystery of Hamlet, King of Denmark: A Tetralogy for the Theatre* (1945); *Poog's Pasture: The Mythology of a Child* (1951); etc. Editor: *Letters to Harriet by William Vaughn Moody* (1935). See Fred B. Millett's *Contemporary American Authors* (1940).

MACKAYE, STEELE (June 6, 1842–Feb. 25, 1894); b. Buffalo, N.Y. Playwright. *Won at Last* (prod. 1877); *Hazel Kirke* (prod. 1879); *Paul Kauvar* (1887); *An Arrant Knave* (prod. 1889); etc. See Percy Mackaye's *Epoch: The Life of Steele Mackaye,* 2v. (1927).

MACKELLAR, THOMAS (Aug. 12, 1812–Dec. 29, 1899); b. New York. Printer, type founder, poet. *Tam's Fortnight Ramble* (1847); *Drippings from the Heart* (poems, 1844); *The American Printer* (1866); *Rhymes atween Times* (1873); *Hymns and a Few Metrical Psalms* (1883); *Faith, Hope, Love, These Three* (poems, 1893); etc. Founder, the *Typographic*

Advertiser, 1855, editor, 1855–84; head, MacKellar, Smith & Jordon Co., typefounders, Philadelphia. This business grew out of the typefoundry started by Archibald Binny and James Ronaldson in Philadelphia, a firm which issued a specimen book of their types as early as 1806.

MACKENDRICK, PAUL LACHLAN (Feb. 11, 1914–); b. Taunton, Mass. Educator. *The Ancient World* (with V. M. Scramuzza, 1958); *The Roman Mind at Work* (1958); *The Mute Stones Speak* (1960); *The Greek Stones Speak* (1966); *The Iberian Stones Speak* (1969); *The Athenian Aristocracy 399 to 31 B.C.* (1969); etc.

MACKENZIE, ALEXANDER SLIDELL (Apr. 6, 1803–Sept. 13, 1848); b. New York City. Naval officer, author. *A Year in Spain* (1829); *The American in England* (1836); *The Life of Paul Jones,* 2v. (1841); *Life of Stephen Decatur* (1846); etc.

MACKENZIE, DeWITT [T.]; b. West Burke, Vt. Journalist, author. *The Awakening of India* (1917); *The Girl in the Mask* (1925); *Not Passed by Censor* (1929). Editor: *Hell's Kitchen: the Story of the London Underworld as Related by the Notorious Ex-Burglar, George Ingram* (1929); *India's Problem Can Be Solved* (1943). With Associated Press, since 1910.

MACKENZIE, DONALD. (1908–   ). Author. *Cool Sleeps Balaban* (1964); *The Lonely Side of the River* (1965); *Dead Man* (1966); *Death Is a Friend* (1967); *The Kyle Contract* (1970).

MACKENZIE, JEAN KENYON (Jan. 6, 1874–Sept. 2, 1936); b. Elgin, Ill. Missionary, author. *African Adventures* (1917); *African Clearings* (1924); *An African Trail* (1917); *The Venture* (poems, 1925).

MACKENZIE, ROBERT SHELTON (June 22, 1809–Nov. 21, 1881); b. Drew's Court, Ireland. Journalist, editor, author. *Lays of Palestine* (1828); *Mornings at Matlock,* 3v. (1850); *Life of Charles Dickens* (1870); *Sir Walter Scott* (1871); etc. Editor: *Brougham's Dramatic Works* (1856); *Noctes Ambrosianae,* 5v. (1854); *Miscellaneous Writings of the Late Dr. Maginn,* 5v. (1855–57); etc.

MACKENZIE, WILLIAM ROY (Feb. 14, 1883–Sept. 27. 1957); b. River John, N.S. Educator, author. *The English Moralities from the Point of View of Allegory* (1914); *The Quest of the Ballad* (1919); etc. Compiler: *Ballads and Sea Songs from Nova Scotia* (1928). English dept., Washington University, St. Louis, 1910–52.

MACKIE, JOHN MILTON (Dec. 19, 1813–1894); b. Wareham, Mass. Author. *Cosas de España; or, Going to Madrid via Barcelona* (1848); *Life of Schamyl* (1856); *Life of Tai-Ping-Wang* (1857); *From Cape Cod to Dixie and the Tropics* (1864).

MACKIE, PAULINE BRADFORD (Mrs. Herbert Müller Hopkins; Mrs. Harry Cavendish) (July 6, 1874–); b. Fairfield, Conn. Novelist. *Ye Little Salem Maide* (1898); *The Washingtonians* (1899); *The Girl and the Kaiser* (1904); etc.

MACKINNON, MARY LINEHAM. Author. *One Small Candle* (1956); *Black Racer* (1958).

MACLANE, MARY (May 2, 1881–Aug. 7, 1929); b. Winnipeg, Man. Author. *The Story of Mary MacLane* (1902); *My Friend Annabel Lee* (1903); *I, Mary MacLane* (1917); etc.

MACLAY, EDGAR STANTON (Apr. 18, 1863–Nov. 2, 1919); b. Foochow, China. Author. *A History of American Privateers* (1899); *A History of the United States Navy,* 3v. (1894–1902).

MACLAY, WILLIAM (June 27, 1734–Apr. 16, 1804); b. in Chester Co., Pa. Jurist, senator, diarist. *Journal,* ed. by Edgar S. Maclay (1890); *The Journal,* ed. by Charles A. Beard (1927). U.S. Senator, 1789–91.

MACLEAN, KATHRYN [Anderson] (Mar. 10, 1909–); b. San Francisco, Cal. Author. Writes under pen name "Kathryn Forbes." *Mama's Bank Account* (1943); *Transfer Point* (1947).

MACLEAR, ANNE BUSH (1873–1938); b. Wilmington, Del. Educator, author. *Early New England Towns* (1908); etc. History dept., Hunter College, New York, 1910–38.

MACLEISH, ARCHIBALD (May 1892–); b. Glencoe, Ill. Educator, poet, playwright. *Tower of Ivory* (poems, 1917); *The Happy Marriage and Other Poems* (1924); *The Pot of Earth* (poems, 1925); *Nobodaddy* (verse play, 1925); *Streets in the Moon* (poems, 1926); *The Hamlet of A. MacLeish* (poem, 1928); *New Found Land* (poems, 1930); *Conquistador* (1932; Pulitzer Prize for Poetry, 1933); *Frescoes for Mr. Rockefeller's City* (poems, (1933); *Union Pacific—A Ballet* (1934); *Panic* (verse play, 1935); *Public Speech* (poems, 1936); *The Fall of the City* (verse play, 1937); *Land of the Free* (poems, 1938); *Air Raid* (verse play, 1938); *America Was Promises* (poems, 1939); *The Irresponsibles* (1940); *The American Cause* (1941); *American Opinion and the War* (1942); *A Time to Act* (1943); *American Story* (1944); *Act Five* (poems, 1948); *Poetry and Opinion* (1950); *Freedom Is the Right to Choose* (1951); *Collected Poems 1917–52* (1952; Pulitzer Prize for poetry, 1953); *This Music Crept by Me upon the Waters* (play, 1953); *Sons of Eve* (poems, 1954); *J.B.* (1958; Pulitzer Prize for drama, 1959); *Poetry and Experience* (1961); *Eleanor Roosevelt Story* (1965); *Herakles* (prod. 1967); *Magic Prison* (libretto, 1967); *An Evening's Journey to Conway, Mass.* (prod. 1967); *A Continuing Journey* (1968); *The Wild Old Wicked Men and Other Poems* (1968); etc. Librarian of Congress, 1934–44; assistant secretary of state, 1944–45; prof. rhetoric, Harvard University, 1949–62; Simpson lecturer, Amherst College, after death of Robert Frost, 1963–67. *See* Oscar Cargill's *Intellectual America; Ideas on the March* (1941); Warren Bush's *The Dialogues of Archibald MacLeish and Mark Van Doren* (1964); Signi Falk's *Archibald MacLeish* (1965).

MACLEOD, NORMAN (1906–); Poet. *Horizons of Death* (poems, 1934); *German Lyric Poetry* (1936); *Thanksgiving before November* (1936); *Bitter Roots* (1941); *Man in Midpassage* (poems, 1947); *Pure as Nowhere* (poems, 1952); etc.

MACMANUS, SEUMAS (1869–Oct. 23, 1960); b. in Co. Donegal, Ire. Lecturer, author. *The Leading Road to Donegal* (1895); *The Bewitched Fiddle* (1900); *Irish Nights* (1905); *Yourself and the Neighbors* (1914); *Top o' the Mornin'* (1920); *The Story of the Irish Race* (1921); *Bold Blades of Donegal* (1935); *Dark Patrick* (1939); *Well o' the World's End* (1939); *Heavy Hangs the Golden Grain* (1950); *Bold Heroes of Hungry Hill* (1951); *The Little Mistress of the Eskar Mor* (1959).

MACMILLAN, DONALD BAXTER (Nov. 10, 1874–Sept. 7, 1970); b. Provincetown, Mass. Explorer, author. *Four Years in the White North* (1918); *Etah and Beyond* (1927); *Kah-da* (1930); *How Peary Reached the Pole* (1932).

MACMILLAN, MIRIAM. Author. *Green Seas and White Ice* (1948); *Etuk, the Eskimo Hunter* (1950); *Kudla and His Polar Bear* (1953).

Macmillan Company, The. New York. Publishers. The parent firm in London was founded in 1843. In 1870 an American branch was opened in New York, under the management of George Edward Brett. At his death he was succeeded by George Platt Brett, in 1890. In 1896 the company was made a distinct publishing house instead of being a branch of the London firm. In 1931 George Platt Brett, Jr., became president; he was succeeded by his son, Bruce Y. Brett, in 1958. In 1959 the company merged with the Crowell-Collier Publishing Co., of which it is now a division. See Crowell Collier and Macmillan, Inc. Warren Sullivan is president. Crowell-Collier, publishers of *Collier's Encyclopedia* and *Harvard Classics,* had already absorbed the Free Press of Glencoe and

P. F. Collier. Among the many series of books published by Macmillan have been the English Men of Letters series and the Modern Readers' series. Margaret Mitchell's *Gone with the Wind* was one of the firm's greatest successes.

MACNAIR, FLORENCE [Wheelock] AYSCOUGH (Mrs. Harley Farnsworth MacNair) (1878–Apr. 24, 1942); b. Shanghai, China. Lecturer, author. Wrote under maiden name. *A Chinese Mirror* (1925); *Firecracker Land* (1932); *The Travels of a Chinese Poet* (1934); etc. *See* Harley F. MacNair (ed.): *Florence Ayscough and Amy Lowell: Correspondence of a Friendship* (1947).

MACNAIR, HARLEY FARNSWORTH (July 22, 1891–June 21, 1947); b. Greenfield, Pa. Educator, author. *The Chinese Abroad* (1924); *China's New Nationalism, and other Essays* (1926); *China in Revolution* (1931); *The Real Conflict between China and Japan* (1938); etc. Co-author and editor: *Voices from Unoccupied China* (1944); *Florence Ayscough and Amy Lowell, The Correspondence of a Friendship* (1945); etc. History dept., University of Chicago, from 1928.

MACNEAL, ROBERT E[rnst] (Aug. 24, 1903–); b. Medford, N.J. Publisher. With Curtis Publishing Company, since 1923; president, since 1950; director, Bantam Books.

MACNEIL, NEIL (Feb. 6, 1891–); b. Boston, Mass. Editor, author. *Without Fear or Favor* (1940); *How to Be a Newspaperman* (1942); *The Highland Heart in Nova Scotia* (1948); *The Hoover Report* (with Harold W. Metz, 1956); *Chester Dale and His Pictures* (1963); *Forge of Democracy* (1964); *Tales from a Ball Pen* (1964); etc. Staff, *New York Times,* 1918–51.

MACNEILL, BEN DIXON (d. May 27, 1960). Journalist, author. *The Hatterasman* (1958).

MACNICHOL, KENNETH (Nov. 3, 1887–); b. Canton, O. Author. *The Night Shift* (1919); *Freight* (1923); *The Nose of Papa Hilaire* (1925); *The Piper of Kerimor* (1927); *An Idiot Looks at It* (1934); *Twelve Lectures on the Technique of Fiction Writing* (1929); etc.

MACRAE, DURANT LOOMIS (Apr. 19, 1883–Aug. 4, 1968); b. Winooski, Vt. Publisher. Organizer, Macrae Smith Co., 1925; pres., from 1925.

MACRAE, ELLIOTT BEACH (June 13, 1900–Feb. 13, 1968); b. Staten Island, N.Y. Publisher. With E. P. Dutton & Co., from 1922; pres., from 1944.

MACRAE, JOHN (Aug. 25, 1867–Feb. 18, 1944); b. Richmond, Va. Publisher. With E. P. Dutton & Co., from 1885; pres., 1923–44.

Macrae Smith Company. Philadelphia, Pa. Publishers. Founded 1893, by George W. Jacobs. The first book Jacobs published was by S. Weir Mitchell. In 1925, Allan M. Smith and Durant L. Macrae, who had been with Mr. Jacobs for many years, took over the business under the name Macrae Smith Company. Donald P. Macrae is president.

MACVANE, EDITH (1880–); b. Boston, Mass. Author. *The Adventures of Joujou* (1906); *The Thoroughbred* (1909); *The Black Flier* (1909); *Tarantella* (1911); *Her Word of Honor* (1912); etc.

MACVEAGH, LINCOLN (Oct. 1, 1890–); b. Narragansett Pier, R.I. Publisher, diplomat, author. *Greek Journey* (with Margaret MacVeagh, 1937). Editor: *New Champlin Cyclopedia for Young Folks* (1924), and subsequent editions; *Poetry from the Bible* (1925). With Henry Holt Co., 1915–17, and 1919–23; president, Dial Press, Inc., 1923–33. Minister to Greece, 1933–41; to Iceland, 1941; to Union of South Africa, 1943; Ambassador to Greece and Yugoslavia, 1943; to Greece, 1944; to Portugal, 1948; to Spain, 1952–53.

Macveigh, Sue. Pen name of Elizabeth Custer Nearing.

MACY, GEORGE (May 12, 1900–May 20, 1956); b. New York. Publisher. Founder and president of the Limited Editions Club, New York, and publisher of beautifully printed and illustrated books. Founder and president of the Heritage Press and The Readers Club.

MACY, JESSE (June 21, 1842–Nov. 3, 1919); b. Knightstown, Ind. Educator, political scientist, author. *The English Constitution* (1897); *Political Parties in the United States, 1841–1861* (1900); *Jesse Macy: An Autobiography* (1933); etc. Prof. political science, Grinnell College, 1885–1912.

MACY, JOHN ALBERT (Apr. 10, 1877–Aug. 26, 1932); b. Detroit, Mich. Literary critic, poet. *Edgar Allan Poe* (1907); *The Spirit of American Literature* (1913); *The Critical Game* (1922); *The Story of the World's Literature* (1925); *About Women* (1930). Editor: *American Writers on American Literature* (1931). Became lit. editor of the *Boston Herald* in 1913; *The Nation*, 1922–23.

Mad. New York. Monthly. Founded 1952 by Harvey Kurtzman. Noted for its topical humor and satire, especially its lampoons on the whole area of mass culture and communications. William Gaines is publisher.

Madame Butterfly. Short story by John Luther Long, which appeared first in the *Century Magazine,* Jan., 1898. David Belasco produced it as a play, in New York, Mar. 5, 1900, with Blanche Bates in the leading role. Made into an opera by Puccini, it had its first New York performance, Nov. 12, 1906, with Henry William Savage as producer. It is the story of the deserted Japanese wife of an American naval officer.

Madame Delphine. By George W. Cable (1881). The tragic story of a quadroon mother.

MADDEN, EVA ANNE (b. Oct. 26, 1863); b. Trimble County, Ky. Correspondent, author. *Stephen; or, The Little Crusaders* (1901); *The Soldiers of the Duke* (1904); *Two Royal Foes* (1907); etc. Foreign correspondent, the *New York Herald,* 1901–15.

MADDEN, MAUDE WHITMORE (June 8, 1867–); b. Sandwich, Ill. Missionary, author. *In the Land of the Cherry Blossom* (1915); *When the East Is in the West* (1923); *Chopsticks and Clogs* (1927); *Where Day Dawns* (1930); *Pen Pictures of Japan: In Verse* (1939); etc.

Madeleine: An Autobiography. Novel by Agnes Sears (1919).

MADELEVA, SISTER M[ary] (Mary Evaline Wolff) (May 24, 1887–July 25, 1964); b. Cumberland, Wis. Educator, author. *Knights Errant, and Other Poems* (1923); *Chaucer's Nuns, and Other Essays* (1925); *Penelope, and Other Poems* (1927); *Gates, and Other Poems* (1938); *Selected Poems* (1939); *American Twelfth Night* (1955); *My First Seventy Years* (1959); *The Four Last Things* (1959); *Conversations with Cassandra* (1961); etc. President, St. Mary-of-the-Wasatch, Salt Lake City, 1926–33; St. Mary's College, Notre Dame, since 1934.

Mademoiselle. New York. Monthly. Founded 1935. Published by Street & Smith Publications, later Condé Nast Publications. Edited by Betsy Talbot Blackwell. Fashion magazine, noted for its cultural and literary features aimed at women between the ages of seventeen and thirty.

MADISON, CHARLES A[llan] (Apr. 16, 1895–); b. near Kiev, Rus. Editor, author. *Critics and Crusaders* (1947); *American Labor Leaders* (1950); *Leaders and Liberals in 20th Century America* (1961); *Book Publishing in America* (1966); *Owl Among Colophons* (1966); *Yiddish Literature: Its Scope and Major Writers* (1968). With Holt, Rinehart & Winston from 1924.

MADISON, DOLLY PAYNE (Dorothy Payne Todd Madison) (May 20, 1768–July 12, 1849); b. Guilford Co., N.C. Wife of President James Madison. Diarist. *Memoirs and Letters* (1886). *See* A. C. Clark's *Life and Letters of Dolly Madison*

(1914); Katherine Anthony's *Dolly Madison: Her Life and Times* (1949).

MADISON, JAMES (Mar. 5, 1750/51–June 28, 1836); b. Port Conway, Va. Fourth president of the United States, author. *Writings of James Madison,* 9v. (1900–10); etc. *See* W. C. Rives's *History of the Life and Times of James Madison,* 3v. (1859–68); S. H. Gay's *James Madison* (1884); Gaillard Hunt's *The Life of James Madison* (1902); *The Papers of James Madison,* Vols. I and II (1962). *The Papers of James Madison* are being published by the University of Chicago Press, edited by William T. Hutchinson and W. M. E. Rachal.

Madonna of the Future, The. Story by Henry James (1879). The painter plans for twenty years to paint a perfect madonna —his hand loses its cunning and the end is failure.

Madonna of the Tubs. Best-known short story by Harriet Prescott Spofford.

MAGALANER, MARVIN (Nov. 6, 1920–); b. New York. Educator, author. *Joyce: The Man, the Work, the Reputation* (with Richard M. Kain, 1962); *The Time of the Apprenticeship* (1960). Editor: *A James Joyce Miscellany* (1957); *Twelve Short Short Stories* (with others, 1969).

MAGARET, HELENE (May 18, 1906–); b. Omaha, Neb. Educator, author. *The Trumpeting Crane* (poem, 1934); *The Great Horse* (poem, 1937); *Change of Season* (1941); *Who Walk in Pride* (1945); *Giant in the Wilderness* (1952); *The Head on London Bridge* (1956); *A Kingdom and a Cross* (1958); *Felipe* (1962); etc. Dept. of English, Marymount College (Tarrytown, N.Y.), since 1944.

Magazine of American History. New York and Chicago. Founded 1877. Suspended 1894–1900. Expired 1917. Martha J. Lamb, historian of the City of New York, became editor and owner in 1883.

Magazine Subject Index. Boston, Mass. Founded 1907, by F. W. Faxon. Annual magazine subject index. Discontinued.

MAGEE, JOHN BENJAMIN (July 19, 1887–Apr. 6, 1943); b. Albion, Ia. Methodist clergyman, educator, author. *Runes of the Night* (poems, 1916); *The Silent Shepherd* (1930); etc. President, Cornell College, Mt. Vernon, Ia., from 1939.

Maggie: A Girl of the Streets. By Stephen Crane (privately printed 1893, published 1896). Probably the first bit of naturalism in the American novel.

Magic Barrel, The. Stories by Bernard Malamud (1958). All the stories are about aspects of Jewish tradition or feeling.

MAGIDOFF, ROBERT (1905–). Author. *In Anger and Pity* (1949); *The Kremlin vs. the People* (1953); *Yehudi Menuhin* (1955); *Guide to Russian Literature* (1964); *Russian Science Fiction* (1969); etc.

MAGILL, FRANK NORTHEN (Nov. 21, 1907–); b. Atlanta, Ga. Editor. *Masterplots* (four series, 1949, 1953, 1960, 1968); *Cyclopedia of World Authors* (1958); *Masterpieces of World Philosophy* (1961); *Masterpieces of Christian Literature* (1963); *Cyclopedia of Literary Characters* (1963); *Masterpieces of Catholic Literature* (1965); *Great Events and Their Interpretations,* 6v. (1968); *The Contemporary Reader's Bible,* 8v. (1968).

MAGNA, EDITH SCOTT (Mrs. Russell William Magna) (Nov. 15, 1885–); b. Boston, Mass. Club woman, author. *We Traveled Together* (1925); *Camp Rustle* (1928); *Collected Verse* (1934); etc.

Magnalia Christi Americana. By Cotton Mather (1702). The standard ecclesiastical history of New England from 1620 to 1628.

MAGNER, JAMES ALOYSIUS (Oct. 23, 1901–); b. Wilmington, Ill. Roman Catholic clergyman. *This Catholic Religion* (1930); *Men of Mexico* (1942); *Mental Health in a Mad World* (1953); *The Catholic Priest in the Modern World* (1957); etc.

Magnificent Ambersons, The. Novel by Booth Tarkington (1918). The picture of a snob.

Magnificent Obsession. Novel by Lloyd Douglas (1930). A brain specialist continues the secret philanthropies of the late Dr. Hudson and also invents a surgical device which helps save the life of the woman he loves.

Magnolia, or Southern Appalachian. Macon, Ga. Magazine. Founded Jan., 1840, by George F. Pierce and Philip C. Pendleton. Moved to Savannah, Ga., in 1841, and called *The Magnolia, or Southern Monthly.* In 1842 it was moved to Charleston, S.C., and William Gilmore Simms became editor. Augustus B. Longstreet published some of his *Georgia Scenes* in its pages. Expired June, 1843.

MAGOFFIN, RALPH VAN DEMAN (Aug. 8, 1874–May 15, 1942); b. in Rice Co., Kan. Educator, archaeologist, author. *The Roman Forum* (1928); *The Lure and Lore of Archaeology* (1930); *5000 Years Ago* (1937); etc. Prof. classics, New York University, 1923–39.

MAGOON, ELIAS LYMAN (Oct. 20, 1810–Nov. 25, 1886); b. Lebanon, N.H. Baptist clergyman, book collector, author. *The Eloquence of the Colonial Times* (1847); *Orators of the American Revolution* (1848); *Living Orators in America* (1849); etc. He gave his large collection of books to several American colleges.

MAGOUN, F. ALEXANDER (Mar. 4, 1896–); b. Oberlin, O. Educator, author. *The Frigate Constitution and Other Historic Ships* (1928); *Sky High: The Story of Aviation* (with Eric Hodgkins, 1929); *A History of Aircraft* (with same, 1931); *Love and Marriage* (1948); *The Teaching of Human Relations* (1959); *Finding Yourself and Your Job* (1959); *Living a Happy Life* (1960); *Amos Fortune's Choice* (1964). Naval architecture dept., Massachusetts Institute of Technology, 1920–30; human relations dept., 1930–50.

MAGOUN, FRANCIS PEABODY, Jr. (Jan. 6, 1895–); b. New York. Educator. *The Gests of King Alexander of Macedon* (1929); *History of Football* (1938); *A Chaucer Gazetteer* (1961); etc. Prof. English, Harvard University, since 1951.

MAGRUDER, JULIA (Sept. 14, 1854–June 9, 1907); b. Charlottesville, Va. Novelist. *Across the Chasm* (1885); *A Magnificent Plebeian* (1888); *The Princess Sonia* (1895); *A Manifest Destiny* (1900); etc. Charles Dana Gibson illustrated most of her books.

MAHAN, ALFRED THAYER (Sept. 27, 1840–Dec. 1, 1914); b. West Point, N.Y. Naval officer, historian. *The Influence of Sea Power upon History, 1660–1783* (1890); *The Influence of Sea Power upon the French Revolution and Empire, 1793–1812,* 2v. (1892); *Admiral Farragut* (1892); *The Life of Nelson,* 2v. (1897); *From Sail to Steam* (autobiography, 1907); etc. See W. D. Puleston's *Mahan* (1939); and C. C. Taylor's *The Life of Admiral Mahan* (1920); etc.

MAHAN, ASA (Nov. 9, 1799–Apr. 4, 1889); b. Vernon, N.Y. Congregational clergyman, philosopher. *A System of Intellectual Philosophy* (1845); *Autobiography* (1882); *A Critical History of Philosophy* (1883); etc.

MAHONEY, JOHN THOMAS [Tom] (Dec. 3, 1905–); b. Dallas, Tex. Author. *The Great Merchants* (1955); *The Merchants of Life* (1959); *The Story of George Romney* (1960); etc.

MAIER, WILLIAM (Nov. 3, 1901–   ); b. Schenectady, N.Y. Novelist. *Spring Flight* (1943); *Pleasure Island* (1949); *The Wonderful Sibleys* (1956); *The Temper of the Days* (1961).

MAILER, NORMAN (Jan. 31, 1923–   ); b. Long Branch, N.J. Author. *The Naked and the Dead* (1948); *Barbary Shore* (1951); *The Deer Park* (1955); *The Man Who Studied Yoga* (1956); *The White Negro* (1958); *Advertisements for Myself* (essays, 1959); *Death for the Ladies and Other Disasters* (1962); *The Presidential Papers* (1963); *The American Dream* (1965); *Cannibals and Christians* (1966); *Why Are We in Vietnam?* (1967); *Miami and the Siege of Chicago* (1968); *Armies of the Night* (1968); *Prisoner of Sex* (1971). (National Book Award, 1969, co-recipient, Pulitzer Prize, 1969); etc. See John W. Aldridge's *After the Lost Generation* (1951); *Writers at Work: The Paris Review Interviews* (1967); Barry H. Leeds' *The Structured Vision of Norman Mailer* (1969).

Main Currents in American Thought. By Vernon Louis Parrington, 3v. (1927–30). Vol. 1, *The Colonial Mind,* and vol. 2, *The Romantic Revolution in America,* won the Pulitzer Prize for American history in 1928. The unfinished vol. 3, *The Beginnings of Critical Realism in America,* was ed. by E. H. Eby, and published in 1930. A one-volume edition was published in 1939.

Main Street. Novel by Sinclair Lewis (1920). This literary landmark is regarded as one of the first realistic portrayals of small town life in America. The chief character, Carol Kennicott, is filled with a desire to bring culture to Gopher Prairie, and in so doing she alienates herself from the smug leaders of the town who like their way of life. In the end Carol has to compromise with them.

Main-Travelled Roads. Short stories by Hamlin Garland (1891). These sketches of agrarian life in the Middle West are based on the author's boyhood experiences. Realistic, they stand in sharp relief against the romantic myths of the frontier. The same type of stories appear in his *Prairie Folks* (1893).

Maine Spelling Book, The. By Thomas Mellen Prentiss (1799).

Maine Woods, The. By Henry D. Thoreau (1864). A philosophic retrospect of delightful days spent in the Maine woods, written in the latter part of the author's life.

Mainstream: A Literary Quarterly. New York. Founded 1947 and edited by Samuel Sillen. An organ of Marxist-Communist opinion. Combined with *The New Masses* in 1948 to form *Masses and Mainstream.*

MAINWARING, MARION J., b. Boston, Mass. Author. *Murder at Midyears* (1953); *Murder in Pastiche* (1954); etc.

MAITLAND, JAMES A. Novelist. *The Watchman* (1855); *The Wanderer* (1856); *The Cousins; or, The Captain's Ward* (1857); *The Lawyer's Story; or, The Orphan's Wrongs* (1858); etc. *The Watchman* was a sequel to Maria Susanna Cummins's *The Lamplighter.*

MAJOR, CHARLES (July 25, 1856–Feb. 13, 1913); b. Indianapolis, Ind. Novelist, lawyer. *When Knighthood Was in Flower* (under pen name, "Edwin Caskoden," 1898); *The Bears of Blue River* (1901); *Dorothy Vernon of Haddon Hall* (1902); *Yolanda, Maid of Burgundy* (1905); *A Gentle Knight of Old Brandenburg* (1909).

MAJOR, JAMES RUSSELL (Jan. 7, 1921–   ); b. Riverton, Va. Historian, author. *The Estates General of 1560* (1951); *Representative Institutions in Renaissance France, 1421–1559* (1960); *The Deputies to the Estates General of Renaissance France* (1960); *The Western World: Renaissance to the Present* (1966). Faculty, Emory University, since 1949.

Major Jones's Courtship. By William Tappan Thompson (1840). Southern humor.

Makers and Finders. Series of studies of American literature by Van Wyck Brooks which comprises *The Flowering of New England* (1936); *New England's Indian Summer* (1940); *The World of Washington Irving* (1944); *The Times of Melville and Whitman* (1947); and *The Confident Years* (1952).

Making It. Autobiographical work about the ways in which the author schemed his way toward a successful career as a literary power, by Norman Podhoretz (1968).

Making of American Civilization, The. By Charles and Mary Beard (1937). A well-rounded presentation of American history designed for high-school students.

Making of Americans, The. Novel by Gertrude Stein (1925). The history of a family during three generations. Gertrude Stein wrote it in 1906–08 as an experiment in making the present progressive verbal quality of the language reflect the psychological nature of the changes in family life.

Making of an American, The. By Jacob A. Riis (1901). Autobiography of the Danish immigrant who came to New York and became a leader in welfare work and civic affairs. The author's friendship with Theodore Roosevelt is an important feature. Appeared originally in *The Outlook.*

Malaeska: The Indian Wife of the White Hunter. By Ann Sophia Stephens (1860). It was published by Irwin P. Beadle and Company, as no. 1 of the *Beadle Dime Novels.*

MALAMUD, BERNARD (Apr. 26, 1914–); b. Brooklyn, N.Y. Author. *The Natural* (1952); *The Assistant* (1957); *The Magic Barrel and Other Stories* (1958); *A New Life* (1961); *The Fixer* (1966, Pulitzer Prize, 1967); *Pictures of Fidelman: An Exhibition* (1969); etc. Dept. of English, Oregon State College, since 1949.

MALCOLM, J[ames] P[eller] (Aug., 1767–Apr. 5, 1815); b. Philadelphia, Pa. Engraver, antiquary, author. *Anecdotes of the Manners and Customs of London during the Eighteenth Century,* 2v. (1810); *Anecdotes of the Manners and Customs of London from the Roman Invasion to the Year 1700,* 3v. (1811).

Malcolm X. See Malcolm Little.

MALCOLM-SMITH, GEORGE (Dec. 8, 1901–); b. Poultney, Vt. Author. *Slightly Perfect* (1941); *The Grass Is Always Greener* (1947); *Square Peg* (1952); *The Trouble with Fidelity* (1957); *If a Body Meet a Body* (1959); *Come Out, Come Out* (1965); *Dividend of Death* (1966). Author of the juvenile series "Professor Peckham."

Male and Female: A Study of the Sexes in a Changing World. By Margaret Mead (1949). Study of sexual differences from the biological and social viewpoints as they are affected by changes in modern society.

Male Animal, The. Play by James Thurber and Elliot Nugent (prod. 1940). @634/1 4–7

MALIN, JAMES CLAUDE (Feb. 8, 1893–); b. near Edgeley, N.D. Educator, author. *The United States after the World War* (1930); *John Brown and the Legend of Fifty-six* (1942); *The Grassland of North America* (1947); *On the Nature of History* (1955); *The Contriving Brain and the Skillful Hand* (1955); *Nebraska Question 1852–1854* (1968); etc. Prof. history, University of Kansas, since 1938.

MALLOCH, DOUGLAS (May 5, 1877–July 2, 1938); b. Muskegon, Mich. Poet. *In Forest Land* (1906); *Resawed Fables* (1911); *The Woods* (1913); *Tote-Road and Trail* (1917); *Come on Home* (1923); etc.

MALLOCH, THOMAS ARCHIBALD (Aug. 10, 1887–); b. Hamilton, Ont. Physician, librarian, author. *Finch and Baines: A Seventeenth Century Friendship* (1917); *William Harvey* (1929); *Short Years: The Life and Letters of John Bruce MacCallum* (1938); etc. Librarian, New York Academy of Medicine, since 1926; curator, Osler Library, McGill University, since 1929.

MALOFF, SAUL (Sept. 6, 1922–   ); b. New York. Educator, author. *Happy Families* (1968). Editor: *The Young Readers' Treasury of British and American Verse* (1963). Professor of English, Hunter College, since 1968.

MALONE, DUMAS (Jan. 10, 1892–); b. Coldwater, Miss. Historian, educator, editor, publisher, author. *The Public Life of Thomas Cooper, 1783–1839* (1926); *Saints in Action* (1939); *Jefferson the Virginian* (1948) and *Jefferson and the Rights of Man* (1951), v. 1 and 2 of projected 5 v. work *Jefferson and His Time. Thomas Jefferson as Political Leader* (with Basil Rauch, 1963). Co-editor (with Allen Johnson): *Dictionary of American Biography,* v. 4–7 (1930–31); editor, v. 8–20 (1932–36). History dept., University of Virginia, 1923–29. Director, Harvard University Press, 1936–43. Prof. history, Columbia University, 1945–59; University of Virginia since 1959. 1962 Biographer in Residence.

MALONE, KEMP (Mar. 14, 1889–); b. Minter, Miss. Educator, philologist, editor, author. *The Literary History of Hamlet* (1923); *The Dodo and the Camel* (1938); *Chapters on Chaucer* (1951); *Studies in Heroic Legend* (1959); etc. Co-author: *Literary History of England* (1948); *Literary Masterpieces of the Western World* (1953). Editor: *Studies in English Philology* (1929); *Deor* (1933); *Widsith* (1936); *Thorkelin Transcripts of Beowulf* (1951); *Random House Dictionary of the English Language* (with others, 1966); *The Middle Ages* (with others, 1967). Co-founder and managing editor, *American Speech,* 1925–32, etc. English dept., Johns Hopkins University, since 1924.

MALONE, WALTER (Feb. 10, 1866–May 18, 1915); b. in De Soto Co., Miss. Jurist, poet. *Claribet, and Other Poems* (1882); *The Outcast, and Other Poems* (1886); *Songs of Dusk and Dawn* (1894); *Songs of December and June* (1896); *The Coming of the King* (1897); *Songs of North and South* (1900); *Poems* (1904); *Songs of East and West* (1906); *Hernando de Soto* (1914); *Selected Poems* (1919).

Maltese Falcon, The. Detective novel, by Dashiell Hammett (1930).

MALTZ, ALBERT (b. 1908). Playwright. *Merry-Go-Round* (with George Sklar, 1931); *Peace on Earth* (with same, prod. 1933); *The Black Pit* (prod. 1935); *Private Hicks* (1935); *The Way Things Are, and Other Stories* (1938); *The Underground Stream* (1940); *The Cross and the Arrow* (1944); *The Journey of Simon McKeever* (1949); *The Citizen Writer* (1950); *A Long Day in a Short Life* (1957); *A Tale of One January* (1966); and several motion-picture scenarios.

MALVERN, GLADYS. Author. (d. Nov. 16, 1962). *Rusty, the Pup Who Wanted Wings* (1939); *Dancing: The Story of Anna Pavlova* (1942); *Jonica's Island* (1945); *According to Thomas* (1947); *Eric's Girls* (1949); *Behold Your Queen* (1951); *Dear Wife* (1953); *Saul's Daughter* (1956); *Great Garcias* (1958); *Patriot's Daughter* (1960); *Wilderness Island* (1961); *World of Lady Jane Grey* (1964); etc.

Mamba's Daughters. Novel by Du Bose Heyward (1929). Life story of Negro women in South Carolina.

Mammon of Unrighteousness, The. By Hjalmar H. Boyesen (1891). Sociological novel of American life portrayed with realism.

"Man against the Sky, The." Poem by Edwin Arlington Robinson (1916).

Man from Home, The. Play by Booth Tarkington and Harry Leon Wilson (prod. 1905). A Hoosier in Europe, convinced of the superior way of life in Indiana, finds continental civilization rather preposterous.

Man of the Hour, The. Novel by Octave Thanet (1905). Deals with the labor problem and the socialistic efforts to solve it.

Man on the Box, The. Popular novel by Harold MacGrath (1904). It is the story of Robert Warburton who resigns from the U.S. Army and goes to France where he becomes involved in a romance which brings him home again.

Man Who Corrupted Hadleyburg, The. By Mark Twain (1900). Story of small town greed and complacency. *Cf.* E. W. Howe's *The Story of a Country Town.*

"Man Who Died Twice, The." Poem by Edwin Arlington Robinson (1924).

Man Who Saw through Heaven, and Other Stories, The. By Wilbur Daniel Steele (1927).

Man with the Blue Guitar, The. Collection of poems by Wallace Stevens (1937).

Man with the Golden Arm, The. Novel by Nelson Algren (1949). A picaresque novel of the underworld in Chicago.

Man with the Good Face, The. Short Story by Frank Luther Mott (1920).

"Man with the Hoe, The." Poem by Edwin Markham (1899). Based on a well-known painting by Millet, as an inspired lyrical protest against human degradation. It appeared originally in the *San Francisco Examiner.*

Man without a Country, The. Story by Edward Everett Hale, in the *Atlantic Monthly,* Dec., 1863. Philip Nolan, court martialed and exiled from his country for a hasty denunciation of its government, spends his sad years at sea, repentant, but unable to return to his native shores. The character is not to be confused with the real Philip Nolan (c. 1771–1801), the contraband trader.

MANATT, JAMES IRVING (Feb. 17, 1845–Feb. 13, 1915); b. Millersburg, O. Educator, author. *The Mycenaean Age* (with Chrestos Tsountas, 1897); *Aegean Days* (1914); etc. Prof. Greek literature, Brown University, 1892–1915; chancellor, University of Nebraska, 1884–89.

MANCHESTER, EARL NORTHUP (July 12, 1881–Nov. 11, 1954); b. Factoryville, Pa. Librarian. With Brown University library, 1903–11; University of Chicago library, 1911–21; librarian, University of Kansas, 1921–28; Ohio State University, 1928–52.

MANCHESTER, WILLIAM RAYMOND (April 1, 1922–); b. Attleboro, Mass. Author. *Disturber of the Peace* (1951); *City of Anger* (1953); *Shadow of the Monsoon* (1956); *Beard the Lion* (1958); *Rockefeller Family Portrait* (1959); *The Long Gainer* (1961); *Portrait of a President* (1962); *Death of a President* (1967); *The Arms of Krupp* (1968).

Manchild in the Promised Land. Autobiography by Claude Brown (1965). A convicted criminal attains consciousness of a black man's predicament in the Harlem corner of the Land of Opportunity.

MANCUR, JOHN HENRY. Novelist. *Christine: A Tale of the Revolution* (1843); *The Deserter* (1843); *Jasper Crowe* (1843); *Wilfred Lovel* (1843); etc.

MANDELBAUM, MAURICE H. (Dec. 9, 1908–); b. Chicago, Ill. Educator, author. *The Problem of Historical Knowledge* (1938); *The Phenomenology of Moral Experience* (1955); *Philosophy, Science and Sense Perception* (1964). Faculty, Johns Hopkins University, since 1957.

"Mandy Lee." Song by Thurland Chattaway (1899).

MANFRED, FREDERICK FEIKEMA (Jan. 6, 1912–); b. Rock Rapids, Ia. Novelist. Pen name "Feike Feikema," 1944–51. *The Golden Bowl* (1944); *Boy Almighty* (1945); *This Is the Year* (1947); *The Chokecherry Tree* (1948); *The Primitive* (1949); *The Brother* (1950); *The Giant* (1951); *Lord Grizzley* (1954); *Riders of Judgment* (1957); *Conquering Horse* (1959); *Arrow of Love* (1961); *The Man Who Looked Like the Prince of Whales* (1965); *King of Spades* (1966); *Scarlett Plume* (1966); *Winter Count* (1966); *Eden Prairie* (1968).

MANGIONE, JERRE [Gerlando] (Mar. 20, 1909–); b. Rochester, N.Y. Author. *Mount Allegro* (1943); *The Ship and the Flame* (1948); *Reunion in Sicily* (1950); *Mount Allegro* (1963); *Night Search* (1965); *Life Sentences for Everybody* (1966); *Passion for Sicilians: The World Around Danilo Dolci* (1968); *America Is Also Italian* (1969).

Manhattan. New York City. Fraternal magazine. Founded Jan., 1883, by John W. Orr. During its short life it assembled such notable writers as Julian Hawthorne, Julia Ward Howe, Kate Field, Brander Matthews, Louise Chandler Moulton, and Edgar Fawcett. Orr was a noted commercial engraver on wood. Expired Sept., 1884.

Manhattan Transfer. Novel by John Dos Passos (1925). Involves numerous characters in an attempt to represent the complexity of New York City.

MANIATES, BELLE KANARIS, b. Marshall, Mich. Author. *David Dunne* (1912); *Amarilly of Clothesline Alley* (1916); *Penny of Top Hill Trail* (1919); *Sand Holler* (1920); etc.

MANKIEWICZ, DON M. (Jan. 20, 1922–). Author. *See How They Run* (1951); *Trial* (1955); *It Only Hurts a Minute* (1966).

Mankind. Los Angeles, Cal. Bimonthly. Founded 1967. Devoted to popular history. Edited by Raymond Friday Locke.

MANLY, CHESLY (Oct. 9, 1905–); b. in Jones Co., Tex. Newspaperman. *The Twenty-Year Revolution, From Roosevelt to Eisenhower* (1954); *The UN Record, Ten Fateful Years for America* (1955). Staff, Chicago *Tribune,* since 1929.

MANLY, JOHN MATTHEWS (Sept. 2, 1865–Apr. 2, 1940); b. in Sumter Co., Ala. Educator, Chaucerian scholar, author. *A Manual for Writers* (with J. A. Powell, 1914); *The Writing of English* (with Edith Rickert, 1919); *Contemporary British Literature* (with same, 1921); *Contemporary American Literature* (with same, 1922); *The Text of the Canterbury Tales,* 8v. (with others, 1940); etc. Head, English dept., University of Chicago, 1899–1933.

MANN, ARTHUR [William] (Sept. 11, 1901–); b. Stamford, Conn. Author. *The Jackie Robinson Story* (1951); *Baseball Confidential* (1951); *Branch Rickey* (1957); etc. Under pen name "A. R. Thurman": *The Money Pitcher* (1952); *Goal in Sight* (1953); etc.

MANN, EDWARD BEVERLY (Jan. 31, 1902–); b. Hollis, Kan. Author of Western novels. *The Man from Texas* (1931); *The Blue-Eyed Kid* (1932); *Stampede* (1934); *Rustlers' Round-up* (1935); *El Sombra* (1936); *Comanche Kid* (1936); *With Spurs* (1937); *The Mesa Gang* (1939); *Troubled Range* (1940); *Gunsmoke Trail* (1941); *The Whistler* (1953); *New Mexico: Land of Enchantment* (with others, 1955); etc.

MANN, HELEN R. Author. *Gallant Warrior* (1954); *Plenty, Priscilla* (1956).

MANN, HORACE (May 4, 1796–Aug. 2, 1859); b. Franklin, Mass. Educator, author. *Lectures on Education* (1845); Founder, the *Common School Journal,* 1838. Secretary, Massachusetts Board of Education, 1837–48. President, Antioch College, 1852–59. See Mary Peabody Mann's *Life and Works of Horace Mann,* 3v. (1865–68); Edward I. F. Williams's *Horace Mann, Educational Statesman* (1937).

MANN, MARY TYLER PEABODY (Mrs. Horace Mann) (Nov. 16, 1806–Feb. 11, 1887); b. Cambridge, Mass. Educator, author. *The Flower Book* (1838); *Life and Works of Horace Mann,* 3v. (1865–68); *Juanita: A Romance of Real Life in Cuba Fifty Years Ago* (1887).

MANNERS, J[OHN] HARTLEY (Aug. 10, 1870–Dec. 19, 1928); b. London, England. Actor, playwright. *The House Next Door* (prod. 1909); *Peg-o'-My-Heart* (prod. 1912); *The Woman Intervenes* (prod. 1912); *Just as Well* (prod. 1914); *The Day of Dupes* (prod. 1914); *The Harp of Life* (prod. 1916); *Happiness* (prod. 1917); *Out There* (prod. 1917); *The Wooing of Eve* (prod. 1917); *One Night in Rome* (prod. 1919); *The National Anthem* (prod. 1920); etc.

MANNES, MARYA (Nov. 14, 1904–); b. New York. Journalist, author. *Message from a Stranger* (1948); *More in An-*

ger (1958); *Subverse* (1959); *Who Owns the Air?* (1960); *The New York I Know* (1961); *But Will It Sell?* (1964); *They* (1968). Editorial staff, *Reporter*, from 1952.

MANNING, CLARENCE A[ugustus] (Apr. 1, 1893–); b. New York. Educator, author. *A Study of Archaism in Euripides* (1916); *Ukrainian Literature* (1944); *Soldier of Liberty, Casimir Pulaski* (1945); *The Forgotten Republics* (1952); *Russian Influence on Early America* (1953); *Hetman of the Ukraine, Ivan Mazeppa* (1957); etc. Editor: *Ivan Franko, The Poet of Western Ukraine* (1968). Dept. of East European languages, Columbia University, since 1935.

MANNING, MARIE (Mrs. Herman E. Gasch) (d. Nov. 29, 1945); b. Washington, D.C. Author. Wrote under pen name "Beatrice Fairfax." *Lord Alingham, Bankrupt* (1902); *Judith of the Plains* (1903); *The Prophecies of the Land of No-Smoke* (1906); *Truce* (1906); *Under the Sunset* (with others, 1906); *Crete: The Beginnings* (1924).

MANO, D. KEITH. Author. *Bishop's Progress* (1968); *Horn* (1969); *War Is Heaven* (1970).

Man's Search for Himself. By Rollo May (1953).

Mansfield, Blanche McManus. See Blanche McManus.

MANSFIELD, EDWARD DEERING (Aug. 17, 1801–Oct. 27, 1880); b. New Haven, Conn. Editor, author. *The Life of General Winfield Scott* (1846); *The Mexican War* (1848); *Memoirs of the Life and Services of Daniel Drake* (1855); *Personal Memories* (1879); etc. Editor, the *Cincinnati Daily Gazette,* 1857–80.

MANSFIELD, MILBURG FRANCISCO (Feb. 14, 1871–); b. Lynn, Mass. Traveler, author. Pen name, "Francis Miltoun." *Dickens' London* (1903); *The Cathedrals of Southern France* (c. 1904); *Romantic Ireland,* 2v. (with wife, Blanche McManus Mansfield, 1905); etc. Editor: *Kiplingiana* (1899); etc. He was a pioneer in travel by automobile.

Mansion, The. Novel by William Faulkner (1959). Last of the trilogy about the Snopes family. The other novels are *The Hamlet* (1940) and *The Town* (1957).

MANTLE, [Robert] BURNS (Dec. 1873–Feb. 9, 1948); b. Watertown, N.Y. Editor, critic. *American Playwrights of Today* (1929); *Contemporary American Playwrights* (1938). Editor: *The Treasury of the Theatre* (with others, 1935). Editor: *The Best Plays . . . and the Year Book of the Drama in America,* from 1919. Drama critic, the New York *Evening Mail,* 1911–22; the New York *Daily News,* 1922–43.

MAPES, VICTOR (Mar. 10, 1870–Sept. 27, 1943); b. New York. Playwright, dramatic critic. Pen names, "Maveric Post," "Sidney Sharp." *Duse and the French* (1897); *Don Caesar's Return* (prod. 1901); *The Undercurrent* (prod. 1907); *Partners Three* (1909); *The New Henrietta* (with Winchell Smith, prod. 1913); *The Lassoo* (prod. 1917); *The Boomerang* (with Winchell Smith, prod. 1915); *The Hottentot* (with William Collier, prod. 1920); *The Kangaroos* (prod. 1921); *The Streak* (prod. 1923); etc.

MARBLE, ANNIE RUSSELL (Mrs. Charles F. Marble) (Aug. 10, 1864–Nov. 23, 1936); b. Worcester, Mass. Author. *Heralds of American Literature: A Group of Patriot Writers of the Revolutionary and National Periods* (1907); *The Nobel Prize Winners in Literature* (1925); *A Study of the Modern Novel, British and American, Since 1900* (1928); *Pen Names and Personalities* (1930); *From Boston to Boston* (1930); *From 'Prentice to Patron: The Life Story of Isaiah Thomas* (1935); *The Hartford Wits* (1936); etc.

MARBLE, MANTON [Malone] (Nov. 15, 1835–July 24, 1917); b. Worcester, Mass. Editor, publisher, publicist. Became editor and owner of the New York *World* in 1862, and sold it in 1876. He was also on the staff of the *Boston Traveler,* the New York *Evening Post,* etc.

Marble Faun, The. Novel by Nathaniel Hawthorne (1860). The scene is laid in Rome and involves the romance and tragedy of three American artists and an Italian, Count Donatello. Kenyon, the sculptor, and Hilda and Miriam, art students, become entangled in the affairs of Count Donatello, who resembles the famous faun of Praxiteles.

Marbourg, Dolores. Pen name of Mary Schell Bacon.

MARBURY, ELIZABETH (June 19, 1856–Jan. 22, 1933). Author's representative, author. *My Crystal Ball: Reminiscences* (1923).

March, Anne. Pen name of Constance Fenimore Woolson.

MARCH, CHARLES WAINWRIGHT (Dec. 15, 1815–Jan. 24, 1864); b. Portsmouth, N.H. Lawyer, journalist, author. *Daniel Webster and His Contemporaries* (1850); *Reminiscences of Congress* (1850); *Sketches in Madeira, Portugal and Spain* (1856); etc.

MARCH, FRANCIS ANDREW (Oct. 25, 1825–Sept. 9, 1911); b. Sutton, Mass. Educator, philologist, editor, author. *A Comparative Grammar of the Anglo-Saxon Language* (1870); etc. Editor: *Latin Hymns* (1874); *Eusebius* (1874); *Thesaurus Dictionary of the English Language* (with F. A. March, Jr., 1903). Consulting editor: *The Standard Dictionary,* 2v. (1893–95); etc. Prof. English language, Lafayette College, 1856–1911.

MARCH, FRANCIS ANDREW (Mar. 2, 1863–Feb. 28, 1928); b. Easton, Pa., son of Francis Andrew March. Philologist, editor, educator. *History of the World War* (1918); etc. Editor, *A Thesaurus Dictionary of the English Language* (with F. A. March, 1903); etc. Editorial staff, *The Standard Dictionary,* 2v. (1893–95); etc. English literature dept., Lafayette College, 1882–1928.

MARCH, HAROLD M. (1896–). Author. *The Two Worlds of Marcel Proust* (1948); *Gide and the Hound of Heaven* (1952).

MARCH, JOSEPH MONCURE (1899–); b. New York. Journalist, poet. *The Wild Party* (1928); *The Set-Up* (1928); *A Certain Wilderness* (1968); etc.

March, William. See William Edward March Campbell.

"Marching Along." Civil War song, words adapted by Mrs. M. A. Kidder, music by William Batchelder Bradbury (1862).

Marching On. Novel by James Boyd (1927). Novel which takes much of the romance out of the Civil War by showing the hardships of the soldiers. James Fraser, the central character, sees the war as endless marching and fighting with never a respite.

"Marching Through Georgia." Civil War song by Henry Clay Work (1865).

MARCIN, MAX (May 6, 1879–d. March 30, 1948); b. Province of Posen, Germany. Playwright, producer. *The Substitute Prisoner* (1911); *See My Lawyer* (prod. 1915); *The House of Glass* (with George M. Cohan, prod. 1915); *Cheating Cheaters* (prod. 1916); *Eyes of Youth* (with Charles Guernon, prod. 1916); *Here Comes the Bride* (with Roy Atwell, prod. 1916); *The Woman in Room 13* (with Samuel Shipman, prod. 1917); *The Night Cap* (with Guy Bolton, prod. 1921); *Silence* (prod. 1924); *Los Angeles* (with Donald Ogden Stewart, prod. 1927).

"Marco Bozzaris." Poem by Fitz-Greene Halleck, which first appeared in *The New York Review,* June, 1825.

Marco Millions. Play by Eugene O'Neill (prod. 1928). Based on the travels of Marco Polo.

MARCOSSON, ISAAC FREDERICK (Sept. 13, 1877–Mar. 14, 1961); b. Louisville, Ky. Editor, author. *The Autobiography of a Clown* (1910); *Adventures in Interviewing* (1919–20); *An African Adventure* (1921); *The Black Golconda*

(1924); *David Graham Phillips and His Times* (1932); *Turbulent Years* (1938); *Wherever Men Trade: The Romance of the Cash Register* (1945); *Colonel Deeds, Industrial Builder* (1947); *Marse Henry, the Biography of Henry Watterson* (1951); *Industrial Main Street* (1953); *Copper Heritage* (1955); *Anaconda* (1957); *Before I Forget* (1959); *A Pilgrimage to the Past* (1959).

MARCUS, JACOB RADER (Mar. 5, 1896—); b. Connellsville, Pa. Educator. *The Rise and Destiny of the German Jew* (1934); *Communal Sick-Care in the German Ghetto* (1947); *On Love, Marriage, Children . . . and Death, Too* (1966); *Studies in American Jewish History* (1969); etc. Editor: *Memoirs of American Jews,* 3v. (1955–56); etc. Dept. Jewish history, Hebrew Union College, since 1926.

MARCUS, STEVEN (Dec. 13, 1928–); b. New York. Educator, author. *Dickens: From Pickwick to Dombey* (1965); *The Other Victorians* (1966). Editor: *The World of Modern Fiction* (1966). Department of English, Columbia University.

MARCUSE, HERBERT (July 19, 1898–); b. Berlin, Ger. Educator, author. *Reason and Revolution* (1941); *Eros and Civilization* (1954); *Soviet Marxism* (1958); *One-Dimensional Man* (1964); *Negatives: Essays in Critical Theory* (1968).

MARCY, RANDOLPH BARNES (Apr. 9, 1812–Nov. 22, 1887); b. Greenwich, Mass. Author. *The Prairie Traveler* (1859); *Thirty Years of Army Life on the Border* (1866); *Border Reminiscences* (1872); *Adventure on Red River* (with George B. McClellan, 1937), ed. by Grant Foreman. *See* W. B. Parker's *Notes Taken During the Expedition Commanded by Capt. R. B. Marcy, U.S.A., through Unexplored Texas, in the Summer and Fall of 1854* (1856).

MARDEN, ORISON SWETT (1850–Mar. 10, 1924); b. Thornton, N.H. Journalist, author. *Pushing to the Front* (1894); *Masterful Personality* (1921); etc. Founder, *Success* magazine, 1879.

MARDEN, PHILIP SANFORD (Jan. 12, 1874–July, 1963); b. Lowell, Mass. Editor, author. *Greece and the Aegean Islands* (1907); *Travels in Spain* (1909); *Egyptian Days* (1912); *Sailing South* (1921); *A Wayfarer in Portugal* (1927); *In Times Like These* (1942); etc. Editor, *Lowell Courier-Citizen*, from 1902.

Mardi. By Herman Melville (1849). South Sea romance.

MAREK, KURT W. (Jan. 20, 1915–); b. Berlin, Ger. Author under pen name "C. W. Ceram": *Gods, Graves and Scholars* (1951); *The Secret of the Hittites* (1956); *The March of Archeology* (1958); *Yestermorrow: Notes on Man's Progress* (1961); *Archaeology of the Cinema* (1965); *Hands on the Past* (1966).

Margaret. Novel by Sylvester Judd (1845). Philosophical and bucolic picture of rural Massachusetts just after the American Revolution, noted for its fidelity to nature and its character drawing, but tinged with the emergent transcendentalism of the period and a Unitarian point of view. The edition illustrated by F. O. C. Darley is noteworthy.

Margaret Howth. Novel by Rebecca Harding Davis (1862). Story with a sociological background, one of the earlier attempts at realism in American fiction. It appeared in the *Atlantic Monthly* under the title *A Short Story of Today.*

MARION, ELIZABETH (Jan. 31, 1916–); b. in Spokane County, Wash. Novelist. *The Day Will Come* (1939); *Ellen Spring* (1941); *The Keys to the House* (1941); *Life in a Big City* (with Z. Baxter, 1967).

MARION, FRANCES (Nov. 18, 1890–); b. San Francisco, Calif. Scenarist, author. *Minnie Flynn* (1925); *Valley People* (1935); *Molly, Bless Her* (1937); *How to Write and Sell Film Stories* (1937); *Westward the Dream* (1948); *Powder Keg* (1953).

Maritime History of Massachusetts, 1783–1860, The. By Samuel Eliot Morison (1921). A classic history of the great days of the sailing ships. A similar work for New York is Robert Greenhalgh Albion's *The Rise of New York Port* (1939).

Marjorie Daw. Novel by Thomas Bailey Aldrich (1873). The story is developed through the correspondence of two men, John Flemming and Edward Delaney. The latter seeks to relieve the tedium of his friend's sickroom by a description of his neighbor, Marjorie Daw.

Marjorie Morningstar. Novel by Herman Wouk (1955). A Jewish girl, enticed by romantic and artistic possibilities, confirms the levelheadedness of her own practical temperament by settling down to the sound virtues of family life.

Mark Twain. Pen name of Samuel Langhorne Clemens.

Marketing/Communications. New York. Journal of the printing trade, originally *Printers' Ink.* Founded 1888, by George P. Rowell. Published by Decker Communications, Inc.

MARKEY, GENE (Dec. 11, 1895–); b. Jackson, Mich. Journalist, playwright, motion picture producer. *Literary Lights* (1923); *Men About Town* (1924); *Stepping High* (1929); *The Road to Rouen* (1930); *His Majesty's Pyjamas* (1934); *The Great Companions* (1949); *Kingdom of the Spur* (1953); *Kentucky Pride* (1956); *That Far Paradise* (1960); *Women, Women Everywhere* (1964); etc.

MARKEY, LAWRENCE MORRIS (Jan. 10, 1899–July 10, 1950); b. Alexandria, Va. Author. *The Band Plays Dixie* (1927); *That's New York* (with Johan Bull, 1927); *This Country of Yours* (1932); *Manhattan Reporter* (1935); *Unhurrying Chase* (1946); *Dr. Jeremiah* (1950); etc. On staff, the *New Yorker*, 1925–33.

MARKFIELD, WALLACE (Aug. 12, 1926–); b. Brooklyn, N.Y. Author. *To An Early Grave* (1964); *Teitlebaum's Widow* (1970).

MARKHAM, EDWIN (Apr. 23, 1852–Mar. 7, 1940); b. Oregon City, Ore. Poet. *The Man with the Hoe, and Other Poems* (1899); *Lincoln, and Other Poems* (1901); *The Shoes of Happiness, and Other Poems* (1915); *California, the Wonderful* (1915); *Gates of Paradise* (1920); *The Ballad of the Gallows Bird* (1926); *New Poems: Eighty Songs at Eighty* (1932); *The Star of Araby* (1937); Editor: *The Book of Poetry,* 2v. (1927); *California in Song and Story* (1930); etc. *See* William Le Roy Stidger's *Edwin Markham* (1933); Louis Filler's *The Unknown Edwin Markham: His Mystery and Its Significance* (1966).

MARKHAM, VIRGIL (Apr. 2, 1899–); b. Oakland, Calif. Novelist. *The Scamp* (1926); *Death in the Dusk* (1928); *Inspector Rusby's Finale* (1923); *The Deadly Jest* (1935); *Snatch* (1936); etc.

MARKOE, PETER (1753–Jan. 30, 1792); b. St. Croix, West Indies (now American Virgin Islands). Poet. *The Patriot Chief: A Tragedy* (1784); *The Algerine Spy in Pennsylvania* (anon. 1787); *Miscellaneous Poems* (1787); *The Storm: A Poem* (1788); *The Times: A Poem* (1788); *The Reconciliation* (comic opera, 1790).

MARKS, HENRY KINGDON (1883–Sept. 1, 1942); b. San Francisco, Calif. Physician, author. *Peter Middleton* (1919); *Undertow* (1923); and several books in French.

MARKS, JEANNETTE (Aug. 16, 1875–Mar. 15, 1964); b. Chattanooga, Tenn. Educator, author. *The Cheerful Cricket* (1907); *Through Welsh Doorways* (1909); *The End of a Song* (1911); *Early English Hero Tales* (1915); *Willow Pollen* (poems, 1921); *Genius and Disaster* (1925); *The Merry Cuckoo, and other Welsh Plays* (1927); *The Family of the Barrett* (1938); *The Life and Letters of Mary Emma Woolley* (1955); etc. English dept., Mt. Holyoke College, 1901–39.

MARKS, PERCY (Sept. 9, 1891–Dec. 27, 1956); b. Covelo, Calif. Educator, author. *The Plastic Age* (1924); *Martha* (1925); *Which Way Parnassus?* (1926); *The Craft of Writing* (1932); *Tree Grown Straight* (1936); *And Points Beyond* (1937); *Days Are Fled* (1939); *No Steeper Wall* (1940); *Between Two Autumns* (1941); *Full Flood* (1942); *Knave of Diamonds* (1943); *Blair Marriman* (1949); etc.

MARLETT, MELBA [Grimes] (Mrs. Norval W. Marlett, Jr.) (1909–). Author. *Death Has a Thousand Doors* (1941); *The Devil Builds a Chapel* (1942); *Another Day Toward Dying* (1943); *Escape While I Can* (1944); *Tomorrow Will Be Monday* (1946); *The Garden Path* (with Schuyler Watts, play, 1947); *In Name Only* (1947); *Death Is in the Garden* (1951); *The Frightened Ones* (1956).

MARMUR, JACLAND (Feb. 14, 1901–); b. Sosnowiec, Poland. Author. *Ecola!* (1928); *Wind Driven* (1932); *The Golden Medallion* (1934); *The Sea and the Shore* (1941); *Sea Duty* (1944); *Andromeda* (1947); etc. Also motion-picture scenarios.

MARQUAND, ALLAN (Dec. 10, 1853–Sept. 24, 1924); b. New York. Educator, archeologist, author. *Greek Architecture* (1909); *Andrea della Robbia,* 2v. (1922); etc. Art dept., Princeton University, 1881–1924.

MARQUAND, JOHN PHILLIPS (Nov. 10, 1893–July 16, 1960); b. Wilmington, Del. Novelist. *The Unspeakable Gentleman* (1922); *Four of a Kind* (1923); *The Black Cargo* (1925); *Lord Timothy Dexter* (1925); *Warning Hill* (1930); *Haven's End* (1933); *Ming Yellow* (1934); *No Hero* (1935); *Thank You, Mr. Moto* (1936); *The Late George Apley* (1937, Pulitzer Prize novel, 1938); *Wickford Point* (1939); *H. M. Pulham, Esquire* (1941); *Last Laugh, Mr. Moto* (1942); *So Little Time* (1943); *The Late George Apley* (play, with George S. Kaufman, prod. 1944); *Repent in Haste* (1945); *B.F.'s Daughter* (1946); *Point of No Return* (1949); *Melville Goodwin, U.S.A.* (1951); *Thirty Years* (1954); *Sincerely, Willis Wade* (1955); *Stopover; Tokyo* (1957); *Life at Happy Knoll* (1957); *Women and Thomas Harrow* (1958); *Timothy Dexter Revisited* (1960). *See* Philip Paul's *J. P. Marquand, Esquire: A Portrait in the Form of a Novel* (1952).

MARQUIS, ALBERT NELSON (d. Dec. 21, 1943); b. Brown County, O. Editor, publisher. Founder and publisher, *Who's Who in America,* 1899; editor-in-chief, 1899–1940. Founder, A. N. Marquis Co., Cincinnati, which moved to Chicago in 1884; president 1926–37.

MARQUIS, DON[ald Robert Perry] (July 29, 1878–Dec. 29, 1937); b. Walnut, Ill. Journalist, essayist, poet, playwright, humorist. *Dreams & Dust* (1915); *Hermione and Her Little Group of Serious Thinkers* (1916); *The Old Soak, and Hail and Farewell* (1921); *Poems and Portraits, The Awakening, and Other Poems* (1924); *Archy and Mehitabel* (1927); *Archys Life of Mehitabel* (1933); *Archy Does His Part* (1935); etc. *See* Benjamin De Casseres's *Don Marquis* (1938); Edward Anthony's *O Rare Don Marquis* (1962).

MARRIOTT, ALICE LEE (1910–). Author. *Ten Grandmothers* (1945); *Indians of the Four Corners* (1952); *Sequoyah: Leader of the Cherokees* (1956); *Black Stone Knife* (1957); *First Comers: Indians of America's Dawn* (1960); *Winter Telling Stories* (1969); *Greener Fields* (1969); *American Epic: The Story of the American Indian* (with C. K. Rachlin, 1969).

MARRIOTT, CRITTENDEN (Mar. 20, 1867–); b. Baltimore, Md. Journalist, author. *Uncle Sam's Business* (1908); *Isle of Dead Ships* (1909); *Sally Castleton, Southerner* (1913); *Ward of Tecumseh* (1914); *Via Berlin* (1917); etc. Correspondent for several newspapers.

Marse Chan. Best known dialect story of Thomas Nelson Page, which first appeared in the *Century Magazine,* Apr., 1884.

MARSH, DANIEL L. (Apr. 12, 1880–May 20, 1968); b. West Newton, Pa. Educator, author. *The Faith of the People's Poet* (1920); *Eliot and Warren* (1931); *The Founders of Boston University* (1932); *Highways in the Mind* (1937); *Beginnings* (1938); *The American Canon* (1939); *The House of Seven Pillars* (1950); *Life's Most Arresting Question* (1950); *The True Church* (1958); *History of the Massachusetts Bible Society* (1958); etc. President, Boston University, 1925–51; chancellor, since 1951.

MARSH, ELLEN (Feb. 19, 1922–); b. Coblenz, Ger. Author. *Drink to the Hunted* (1945); *Dull the Sharp Edge* (1947); *Unarmed in Paradise* (1959).

MARSH, GEORGE LINNAEUS (Feb. 1871–); b. in Iowa. Educator, author. *Sources and Analogues of the Flower and the Leaf* (1906); *Good English* (with others, 1906); *John Hamilton Reynolds* (1928); etc. English dept., University of Chicago.

MARSH, GEORGE PERKINS (Mar. 15, 1801–July 23, 1882); b. Woodstock, Vt. Philologist, diplomat, author. *The Goths in New England* (1843); *Lectures on the English Language* (1860); *The Origin and History of the English Language* (1862); *Man and Nature* (1865); etc. Minister to Turkey, 1849–53; to Italy, 1861–82.

MARSH, GEORGE TRACY (Aug. 9, 1876–Aug. 10, 1945); b. Lansingburgh, N.Y. Lawyer, novelist. *Toilers of the Trails* (1921); *The Whelps of the Wolf* (1922); *Flash, the Lead Dog* (1927); *Under the Frozen Stars* (1928); *The River of Skulls* (1936); *White Silence* (1938); *Ask No Quarter* (1945); etc.

Marshall, Armina (Mrs. Lawrence Langner). *See* Lawrence Langner.

MARSHALL, EDISON (Aug. 28, 1894–Oct. 29, 1967); b. Rensselaer, Ind. Explorer, novelist. *The Voice of the Pack* (1920); *The Strength of the Pines* (1921); *The Snowshoe Trail* (1921); *Shepherds of the Wild* (1922); *The Heart of Little Shikara, and Other Stories* (1922); *The Isle of Retribution* (1923); *The Land of Forgotten Men* (1923); *Seward's Folly* (1924); *The Far Call* (1928); *The Missionary* (1930); *The Splendid Quest* (1934); *White Brigand* (1937); *The Upstart* (1945); *Shikar and Safari* (1947); *The Infinite Woman* (1950); *The Viking* (1951); *The Bengal Tiger* (under pen name "Hall Hunter," 1952); *American Captain* (1954); *The Gentleman* (1956); *The Inevitable Hour* (1958); *The Pagan King* (1959); *West with the Vikings* (1961); etc.

MARSHALL, GEORGE CATLETT (Dec. 31, 1880–Oct. 16, 1959); b. Uniontown, Pa. Army officer. *The Winning of the War in Europe and the Pacific* (1945). Army chief of staff, 1939–45. Ambassador to China, 1945–47; secretary of state, 1947–49. *See* F. C. Pogue's *George C. Marshall: Education of a General,* vol. 1 (1963), *Ordeal and Hope* vol. 2 (1966).

Marshall, Henry. Editorial pen name of Nella Braddy Henney.

MARSHALL, HENRY RUTGERS (July 22, 1852–May 3, 1927); b. New York. Psychologist, author. *Aesthetic Principles* (1895); *Instinct and Reason* (1898); *War and the Ideal of Peace* (1915); *Mind and Conduct* (1919); *The Beautiful* (1924); etc.

MARSHALL, JOHN (Sept. 24, 1755–July 6, 1835); b. Germantown, Pa. Chief Justice of the United States, biographer. *The Life of George Washington,* 5v. (1804–07). *See* A. J. Beveridge's *The Life of John Marshall,* 4v. (1916–19); Charles Warren's *The Supreme Court in the United States,* 3v. (1922).

MARSHALL, KATHARINE TUPPER (Mrs. George C. Marshall) (1882–). *Together: Annals of an Army Wife* (1946).

MARSHALL, LENORE [Guinzburg] (Sept. 7, 1897–Sept. 23, 1971); b. New York City. Editor, novelist. *Only the Fear* (1935); *Hall of Mirrors* (1937); *No Boundary* (poems, 1943); *Other Knowledge* (poems, 1956); *Latest Will: New and Se-*

lected Poems (1969). Editor, Cape and Smith, publishers, 1929–32.

MARSHALL, MARGUERITE MOOERS (Mrs. Sidney Walter Dean) (Sept. 9, 1887–May, 1964); b. Kingston, N.H. Novelist. *None but the Brave* (1934); *Salt of the Earth* (1935); *The Golden Height* (1936); *Not in Our Stars* (1937); *Land of Their Fathers* (1938); *Her Soul to Keep* (1940); *Arms and the Girl* (1942); *We Fell in Love with Quebec* (with Sidney W. Dean, 1950); *Ward Nurse* (1952); etc.

MARSHALL, MARION FAIRFAX (Mrs. Tully Marshall); b. Richmond, Va. Playwright. Writes under maiden name. *The Builders* (prod. 1907); *The Chaperon* (prod. 1909); *The Talker* (prod. 1911); *The Modern Girl* (with Ruth Mitchel, prod. 1914); *Mrs. Boltay's Daughter* (prod. 1915); etc. Also screenplays.

MARSHALL, PAULE. Author. *Brown Girl, Brownstones* (1959); *Soul Clap Hands and Sing* (1961); *The Chosen Place, The Timeless People* (1970).

MARSHALL, ROSAMOND [Van der Zee] (Oct. 17, 1900–Nov. 13, 1957); b. New York. Novelist. *None But the Brave* (1942); *Kitty* (1943); *Duchess Hotspur* (1946); *The Treasure of Shafto* (1946); *Celeste* (1949); *Laird's Choice* (1951); *Bond of the Flesh* (1952); *The Loving Meddler* (1954); *The Bixby Girls* (1957). Author of several novels written in French and published in France.

MARSHALL, SAMUEL LYMAN ATWOOD (July 18, 1900–); b. Catskill, N.Y. Military critic, author. *Blitzkrieg* (1940); *Men Against Fire* (1947); *Pork Chop Hill* (1956); *Sinai Victory* (1958); *Night Drop: The American Airborne Invasion of Normandy* (1962); *Heritage History of World War I* (1964); *The Officer as a Leader* (1966);ʼ *War to Free Cuba* (1966); *West to Cambodia* (1968); *Bird, the Christmas Tide Battle* (with D. H. Hackworth, 1968); *Ambush: The Battle of Dau Tieng* (1969). Chief editorial writer, Detroit News, since 1927.

MARSHALL, [Sarah] CATHERINE [Wood] (Sept. 27, 1914–); b. Johnson City, Tenn. Author. *Mr. Jones, Meet the Master* (1949); *A Man Called Peter* (1951); *To Live Again* (1957); *Beyond Our Selves* (1961); *John Doe, Disciple* (1963); *Christy* (1967); etc. Editor: *The Prayers of Peter Marshall* (1954); *The Heart of Peter Marshall's Faith* (1956). Woman's editor, *Christian Herald*, since 1958.

MARSHALL, THOMAS R[iley] (Mar. 14, 1854–June 1, 1925); b. North Manchester, Ind. Statesman, author. *Recollections* (1925). Governor of Indiana, 1909–13; Vice-President of the United States, 1913–21.

"Marshes of Glynn." Poem by Sidney Lanier (1879).

Martin, Allan Langdon. Pen name used jointly by Jane Cowl and Jane Murfin.

MARTIN, ASA EARL (Nov. 15, 1885–Sept. 16, 1962); b. Johnson County, Mo. Educator, historian. *Pennsylvania History as Told by Contemporaries* (with H. H. Jenks, 1925); *History of the United States, 1783–1865*, 2v. (1928–31); *History of the United States, 1492–1865* (1934); *After the White House* (1951); etc. History dept., Pennsylvania State College, from 1915.

MARTIN, CHARLES EMANUEL (Sept. 11, 1891–); b. Corsicana, Tex. Educator, author. *An Outline of the American Government* (1924); *American Government and Citizenship* (1927); *Politics of Peace* (1929); etc. Editor: *Problems of the Peace* (with R. B. von Klein Smid, 1945); *Prospects for World Stability* (with Bryant M. French, 1950). Head, political science dept., University of Washington, 1925–51.

MARTIN, EDWARD SANDFORD (Jan. 2, 1856–June 13, 1939); b. Owasco, N.Y. Editor, author. *Sly Ballads in Harvard China* (1882); *Windfalls of Observation* (1893); *Lucid Intervals* (1900); *Poems and Verses* (1902); etc. One of the

founders of the *Harvard Lampoon,* 1876; first editor of *Life,* 1883; wrote the "Easy Chair" department in *Harper's Magazine,* 1920–35.

Martin, Edward Winslow. Pen name of James Dabney McCabe.

MARTIN, EVERETT DEAN (July 5, 1880–May 10, 1941); b. Jacksonville, Ill. Educator, author. *The Behavior of Crowds* (1920); *The Meaning of A Liberal Education* (1926); etc. Head, philosophy dept., Cooper Union, New York, 1918–38.

MARTIN, FRANK LEE (July 7, 1881–July 18, 1941); b. Benedict, Neb. Educator, editor. *The Practice of Journalism* (with Walter Williams, 1929); etc. Editor, *Quill,* 1917–22. With School of Journalism, University of Missouri, 1909–1941.

MARTIN, FREDERICK ROY (Nov. 17, 1871–Apr. 27, 1952); b. Stratford, N.H. Editor, publisher. With the *Providence Journal,* 1893–1912, editor, 1902–12; general manager, Associated Press, 1920–25; with D. Appleton-Century Co., New York, from 1925.

MARTIN, FREDERICK TOWNSEND (Dec. 6, 1849–Mar. 8, 1914); b. Albany, N.Y. Author. *The Passing of the Idle Rich* (1911); *Things I Remember* (1913).

MARTIN, GEORGE (Jan. 25, 1926–   ); b. New York. Author. *The Opera Companion, A Guide for the Casual Operagoer* (1961); *The Battle of the Frogs and Mice, An Homeric Fable* (1962); *Verdi, His Music, Life and Times* (1963); *The Red Shirt and the Cross of Savoy* (1969).

MARTIN, GEORGE MADDEN (Mrs. Attwood Reading Martin) (May 3, 1866–Nov. 30, 1946); b. Louisville, Ky. Author. *The Angel of the Tenement* (1897); *Emmy Lou: Her Book and Heart* (1902); *Abbie Ann* (1907); *Emmy Lou's Road to Grace* (1916); *Warwickshire Lad* (1916); *Children in the Mist* (1920); *Made in America* (1935); etc.

MARTIN, GEORGE VICTOR (Dec. 16, 1900–); b. Chicago, Ill. Novelist. *Our Vines Have Tender Grapes* (1940); *The Bells of St. Mary's* (1946); *Mark It with a Stone* (1947).

MARTIN, HELEN REIMENSNYDER (Oct. 18, 1868–1939); b. Lancaster, Pa. Author. *Tillie, a Mennonite Maid* (1904); *Sabina: A Story of the Amish* (1905); *The Crossways* (1910); *Barnabetta* (1914), dramatized as *Erstwhile Susan;* *The Snob* (1924); *The Lie* (1928); *Yoked With a Lamb* (1930); *Tender Talons* (1930); *From Pillar to Post* (1933); *Deliverance* (1935); *The Ordeal of Minnie Schultz* (1939); etc.

Martin, John. Pen name of Morgan van Roorbach Shepard.

MARTIN, JOHN BARTLOW (Aug. 4, 1915–); b. Hamilton, O. Author. *Adlai Stevenson* (1952); *Why Did They Kill?* (1953); *Break Down the Walls* (1954); *The Deep South Says Never* (1957); *The Pane of Glass* (1959); *Overtaken by Events* (1966); etc.

MARTIN, JOHN [Joseph] (June 2, 1893–); b. Louisville, Ky. Dance critic, author. *Yniard* (1922); *The Modern Dance* (1933); *America Dancing* (1936); *The Dance* (1945); etc. Dance critic, *New York Times,* since 1927.

MARTIN, MABEL WOOD (d. June 13, 1956); b. Toronto, Ont. Author. *The Green God's Pavilion* (1920); *The Lingering Faun* (1927).

MARTIN, PERCY ALVIN (Aug. 20, 1879–Mar. 8, 1942); b. Jamestown, N.Y. Educator, author. *The Republics of Latin America* (with H. G. James, 1923); *Simon Bolívar* (1931); etc. Compiler, *Who's Who in Latin America* (1935). History dept., Stanford University, from 1908.

MARTIN, RALPH G[uy] (Mar. 4, 1920–   ); b. Chicago, Ill. Editor, author. *Boy from Nebraska* (1946); *The Best is None Too Good* (1948); *Eleanor Roosevelt: Her Life in Pictures* (with R. Harrity, 1958); *The Human Side of FDR* (with R. Harrity, 1959); *Front Runner Dark Horse* (with E. Plant, 1960); *Money, Money, Money, Money* (1961); *Man of Destiny: Charles de Gaulle* (with R. Harrity, 1962); *Man of the Century: Winston Churchill* (with R. Harrity, 1962); *The Three Lives of Helen Keller* (with R. Harrity, 1962); *Ballots and Bandwagons* (1964); *The Bosses* (1964); *President from Missouri: Harry S. Truman* (1964); *Skin Deep* (1964); *The Wizard of Wall Street: The Story of Gerald M. Loeb* (1965); *World War II: A Photographic Record of the War in the Pacific* (1965); *Jennie: The Life of Lady Randolph Churchill* (1969); etc.

MARTIN, WILLIAM ALEXANDER PARSONS (Apr. 10, 1827–Dec. 17, 1916); b. Livonia, Ind. Presbyterian missionary to China, educator, author. *Hamlin Papers* (1880); republished as *The Chinese* (1881); *Hamlin Papers: Second Series* (1894); *A Cycle of Cathay* (1896); *The Love of Cathay* (1901); etc. President, Tung Wen College, Peking, China, 1868–94; president, Imperial University of China, 1898–1900.

Martin Eden. Autobiographical novel by Jack London (1909).

MARTINEK, FRANK V[ictor] (June 15, 1895–); b. Chicago, Ill. Author. *Don Winslow in Ceylon* (1934); *Know Your Man* (1936); *Don Winslow of the Navy* (1940); etc. Created "Don Winslow of the Navy," newspaper adventure strips, 1934.

MARTYN, SARAH TOWNE SMITH (Aug. 15, 1805–Nov. 22, 1879); b. Hopkinton, N.H. Reformer, editor, author. *Margaret, the Pearl of Navarre* (1867); *Daughters of the Cross* (1868); etc. Editor, the *Ladies' Wreath*, 1846–50.

MARTYN, WYNDHAM (July 6, 1875–); b. London, England. Novelist. *Anthony Trent, Master Criminal* (1918); *The Secret of the Silver Car* (1920); *The Recluse of Fifth Avenue* (1925); *Christopher Bond, Adventurer* (1932); *Nightmare Castle* (1935); *The House of Secrets* (1936); *The Ghost City Crimes* (1940); *Manhunt in Murder* (1950); etc.

Marvel, Ik. Pen name of Donald Grant Mitchell.

MARVIN, DWIGHT EDWARDS (Feb. 22, 1851–Feb. 28, 1940); b. Greenwich, N.Y. Congregational clergyman, poet. *The Castle of the Soul* (poems, 1924); *Cloud Islands* (1929); *Sakira, and Other Poems* (1930); *Devotional Lyrics, and Other Poems* (1933); etc. Collector of books on folklore.

MARVIN, WALTER TAYLOR (Apr. 28, 1872–May 26, 1944); b. New York. Educator, author. *Introduction to Systematic Philosophy* (1903); *The History of European Philosophy* (1917); etc. Prof. philosophy, Rutgers University, from 1910.

MARX, GROUCHO [Julius] (Oct. 2, 1895–); b. New York. Comedian. *Many Happy Returns* (1942); *Time for Elizabeth* (with Norman Krasna, prod. 1948); *Groucho and Me* (1959).

"Mary had a little lamb." Popular poem by Sarah Josepha Buell Hale, which appeared in the *Juvenile Miscellany* in 1830 and also in *Poems for Our Children*, 1830. The district school, scene of the poem, was in Sterling, Mass.

Mary of Scotland. Play by Maxwell Anderson (prod. 1933).

Maryland Gazette. Annapolis, Md. Newspaper. Founded 1727, by William Parks. First newspaper in Maryland. Expired 1734.

"Maryland! My Maryland!" Song by James Ryder Randall (1861). Set to music by Charles Ellerbock to the air of "O Tannenbaum."

Maryland Quarterly. College Park, Md. Founded 1944 and name later changed to *Briarcliff Quarterly.* Literary magazine.

Mascot. New Orelans, La. Comic journal. Founded 1881. Expired 1900.

MASLOW, ABRAHAM HAROLD (April 1, 1908–Sept. 4, 1970); b. Brooklyn, N.Y. Educator, author. *Principles of Abnormal Psychology* (with B. Mittelmann, 1941); *Motivation and Personality* (1954); *Toward a Psychology of Being* (1962); *Religion, Values and Peak-Experiences* (1964); *Eupsychian Management: A Journal* (1965); *The Psychology of Science: A Reconnaissance* (1966); *The Healthy Personality* (1969). Faculty, Brandeis University, after 1951.

MASON, ALPHEUS THOMAS (Sept. 18, 1899–); b. Snow Hill, Md. Educator, author. *Organized Labor and the Law* (1925); *Brandeis: Lawyer and Judge in the Modern State* (1933); *Bureaucracy Convicts Itself* (1941); *Brandeis: A Free Man's Life* (1946); *The Supreme Court in a Free Society* (with W. M. Beaney, 1959); *The Supreme Court: Palladium of Freedom* (1962); *The States Rights Debate* (1964); *Free Government in the Making* (1965); *William Howard Taft* (1965); *Harlan Fiske Stone: Pillar of the Law* (1968); etc. Dept. of politics, Princeton University, since 1925.

MASON, ARTHUR (Mar. 14, 1876–); b. Strangford, Co. Down, Ireland. Author. *The Flying Bo'sun* (1920); *Ocean Echoes: An Autobiography* (1922); *The Ship that Waited* (1926); *Salt Horse* (1927); *Swansea Dan* (1929); *From the Horn of the Moon* (1931); *Come Easy, Go Easy* (1933); etc.

MASON, BERNARD STERLING (June 2, 1896–Apr. 11, 1953); b. Warren, Mich. Author. *Camping and Education* (1930); *Primitive and Pioneer Sports* (1937); *Drums, Tom-toms and Rattles* (1938); *Woodcraft* (1939); *Dances and Stories of the American Indian* (1943); *Cabins, Cottages and Summer Homes* (1947); etc. Editor, *Camping Magazine*, 1935–43.

MASON, CAROLINE ATHERTON BRIGGS (1823–1890); b. Marblehead, Mass. Poet, hymn writer. *Utterance; or, Private Voices to the Public Heart* (1852); *The Lost Ring, and Other Poems*, (1891). Best known poem, "Do They Miss Me at Home."

MASON, CAROLINE ATWATER (July 10, 1853–May 2, 1939); b. Providence, R.I. Author. *A Lily of France* (1901); *Lux Christi* (1902); *The Spell of Italy* (1909); *The Spell of France* (1912); *The Spell of Southern Shores* (1914); *Challenged* (1932); etc.

MASON, DANIEL GREGORY (Nov. 20, 1873–Dec. 4, 1953); b. Brookline, Mass. Composer, author. *From Grieg to Brahms* (1903); *Beethoven and His Forerunners* (1904); *The Romantic Composers* (1906); *Contemporary Composers* (1919); *Music in My Time* (1938); *The Quartets of Beethoven* (1947); etc.

MASON, EMILY VIRGINIA (Oct. 15, 1815–1909); b. Lexington, Ky. Author. *Life of General Robert E. Lee* (1871). Editor: *The Southern Poems of the War* (1867); *Journal of a Young Lady of Virginia, 1782* (1871).

MASON, F[rancis] VAN WYCK (Nov. 11, 1897); b. Boston, Mass. Novelist. *Seeds of Murder* (1930); *Shanghai Bund Murders* (1931); *Sulu Sea Murders* (1932); *Washington Legation Murders* (1934); *Murder in the Senate* (under pen name, "Geoffrey Coffin," with Helen Brawner, 1935); *Captain Nemesis* (1936); *Castle Island Case* (1937); *Singapore Exile Murders* (1938); *Stars on the Sea* (1940); *Rivers of Glory* (1942); *Eagle in the Sky* (1948); *Valley Forge, 24 December 1777* (1950); *Proud New Flags* (1951); *Himalayan Assignment* (1952); *Golden Admiral* (1953); *Blue Hurricane* (1954); *Silver Leopard* (1955); *Our Valiant Few* (1956); *The Gracious Lily Affair* (1957); *The Young Titan* (1959); *Manila Galleon* (1961); *Siege of Quebec* (1965); *Macaibo Mission* (1965); *Wild Horizon* (1966); *Deadly Orbit Mission* (1967); *The Maryland Colony* (1969); etc.

MASON, GEORGE CHAMPLIN (1820–1894). Author. *The Life and Works of Gilbert Stuart* (1879); *Reminiscences of Newport* (1884); and other books on Newport.

MASON, GRACE SARTWELL (1877–); b. Port Allegheny, Pa. Author. *The Car and the Lady* (1909); *The Godparents* (1910); *His Wife's Job* (1919); *The Shadow of Rosalie Byrnes* (1919); *Women are Queer* (1932); etc.

MASON, GREGORY (July 3, 1889–Nov. 29, 1968); b. New York City. Anthropologist, author. *Silver Cities of Yucatan* (1927); *Columbus Came Late* (1931); *Mexican Gallop* (with Richard Carroll, 1937); *Remember the Maine* (1939); *September Remember* (with Ruth Mason, under joint pen name "Eliot Taintor," 1945); *The Golden Archer* (1956); *Lemon Pie, and Other Stories* (1961). Editorial staff, the *Outlook,* 1914–20. Head, journalism dept., New York University, from 1941.

MASON, JOHN (1586–1635); b. Norfolk, Eng. Founder of New Hampshire. *A Brief Discourse of the New-Found-Land* (1620).

MASON, JOHN (1600–Jan. 30, 1672); b. in England. Historian. *A Brief History of the Pequot War* (1736), first published in Increase Mather's *A Relation of Troubles by the Indians* (1677). Founder of Windsor, Conn.

MASON, J[oseph] W[arren] T[eets] (Jan. 3, 1879–May 13, 1941); b. Newburgh, N.Y. Correspondent, columnist, author. *Creative Freedom* (1926); *The Creative East* (1928); *The Meaning of Shinto* (1935); *The Spirit of Shinto Mythology* (1939); etc. European editor and manager for Scripps-McRae, 1899–1907; United Press writer on foreign affairs, 1918–30; etc.

MASON, LOWELL (Jan. 8, 1792–Aug. 11, 1872); b. Medfield, Mass. Hymn-writer. Called "The Father of American Church Music." Compiler: *Juvenile Lyre* (1830); *Lyra Sacra* (1832); *Boston Anthem Book* (1839); *Cantica Laudis* (1850); *New Carmina Sacra* (1850); etc. Among his better known hymns are "Nearer My God to Thee," "From Greenland's Icy Mountains," and "My Faith Looks Up to Thee." His musical library was presented to Yale University. *See* John Tasker Howard's *Our American Music* (1930).

MASON, MARY AUGUSTA, b. Windsor, N.Y. Poet. *With the Seasons* (1877).

MASON, MIRIAM EVANGELINE (Jan. 23, 1900–); b. Goshen, Ind. Author. *Smiling Hill Farm* (1937); *Susannah, the Pioneer Cow* (1941); *Mark Twain, Boy of Old Missouri* (1942); *Little Jonathan* (1944); *Happy Jack* (1945); *Middle Sister* (1947); *Pony Called Lightning* (1948); *Mary Mapes Dodge* (1949); *Broomtail* (1952); *Miss Posy Longlegs* (1955); *Freddy* (1957); *Herman, the Brave Pig* (1959); *Daniel Boone* (1961); *Trailblazers of American History* (1966); *Caroline and the Seven Little Words* (1967); etc.

MASON, OTIS TUFTON (Apr. 10, 1838–Nov. 5, 1908); b. Eastport, Me. Curator, ethnologist, author. *Woman's Share in Primitive Culture* (1894); *Origin of Inventions* (1895); *Aboriginal American Basketry,* 2v. (1904); etc. Curator ethnology, National Museum, 1884–1908.

MASON, WALT (May 4, 1862–June 22, 1939); b. Columbus, Ont. Humorist, writer of verse. *Uncle Walt* (1911); *Rippling Rhymes* (1913); *Horse Sense* (1915); etc. With the *Emporia Gazette,* 1907–39.

MASON [-Manheim], MADELINE (Jan. 24, 1913–); b. New York. Author. *Hill Fragments* (1925); *Riding for Texas* (with Colonel E. M. House, 1936); *The Cage of Years* (1949); *At the Ninth Hour* (1958); etc.

Masque of Mercy, A. Blank verse dramatic poem by Robert Frost (1947) which followed *A Masque of Reason* (1945). Characters from the Bible in modern circumstances.

Masque of Poets, A. Anthology edited by Thomas Niles (1878). It contained Emily Dickinson's poem "Success." *See* article by Aubrey H. Starke in *The Colophon,* 1934.

Masque of Reason, A. Blank verse dramatic poem by Robert Frost (1945). Followed by *A Masque of Mercy* (1947). Both are concerned with Biblical themes.

Masque of the Red Death, The. Horror tale by Edgar Allan Poe (1841).

Mass Culture: The Popular Arts in America. The earliest comprehensive collection of articles on mass culture and the mass media, edited by David Manning White (1957).

Mass Media and Violence. By the Task Force for the National Commission on the Causes and Prevention of Violence (1970). Sociological investigation of the relation between the mass media and violence.

Massachusettensis. Pen name of Daniel Leonard.

Massachusetts Institute of Technology Press, The. *See* MIT Press, The.

Massachusetts Magazine. Salem, Mass. Historical quarterly. Founded 1908. Editors: Thomas F. Waters, 1908–12; George Sheldon, Frank Gardner, and others, 1913–16; Charles A. Flagg and others, 1917–18. Expired 1918.

Massachusetts Magazine; or, Monthly Museum of Knowledge and Rational Entertainment. Boston, Mass. Magazine. Founded Jan. 1789, by Isaiah Thomas. Stories and essays were frequent, and women contributed a great part of the articles. Samuel Hill engraved a frontispiece for several numbers. Expired Dec., 1796.

Massachusetts Quarterly Review. Boston, Mass. Founded Dec., 1847. Editors: Ralph Waldo Emerson, Theodore Parker, J. Elliot Cabot. Expired Sept., 1850.

Massachusetts Review, The. Amherst, Mass. Quarterly. Founded 1959. Published with the support and co-operation of Amherst College, Mount Holyoke College, Smith College, and the University of Massachusetts. Contributors have included Cleanth Brooks, Jean-Paul Sartre, and Richard Wilbur. Devoted to public affairs, the arts, philosophy, film, and dance.

Massachusetts Spy. Boston, Mass. Newspaper. Founded 1770. Moved to Worcester, Mass., in 1775. Expired 1904.

Masses, The. New York City. Proletarian monthly. Founded 1911. Superseded 1918 by *The Liberator,* which was absorbed in 1924 by the *Labor Herald,* later the *Workers' Monthly,* published in Chicago, later *The Communist.* John Reed was on the staff, 1913–18 and such contributors as Carl Sandburg, Sherwood Anderson, Walter Lippmann, and Wilbur Daniel Steele appeared in its pages. See *New Masses.*

Masses and Mainstream. New York Monthly. Founded 1948. Edited by Samuel Sillen. Title changed to *Mainstream,* 1956.

MASSEY, MARY ELIZABETH (Dec. 15, 1915–); b. Morrilton, Ark. Educator, author. *Ersatz in the Confederacy* (1952); *Refugees in the Confederacy* (1964); *Bonnet Brigades: American Women and the Civil War* (1966). Faculty, Winthrop College, since 1950.

MASSON, TOM [Thomas Lansing] (July 21, 1866–June 18, 1934); b. Essex, Conn. Editor, author. *Yankee Navy* (1899); *The Von Blumers* (1906); *The New Plato* (1905); *Our American Humorists* (1922); etc. Compiler: *Humorous Masterpieces of American Literature* (1904); *The Best Stories in the World* (1913); *Short Stories from Life* (1916); *Best Short Stories* (1918). Lit. and managing editor, *Life,* 1893–1922; assoc. editor, *Saturday Evening Post,* 1922–30.

MASTEROFF, JOE (Dec. 11, 1919–   ); b. Philadelphia. Playwright. *The Warm Peninsula* (1959); *She Loves Me* (1963); *Cabaret* (1966; Tony Award, New York Drama Critics Circle Award, 1967).

MASTERS, EDGAR LEE (Aug. 23, 1869–Mar. 5, 1950); b. Garnett, Kan. Poet. *A Book of Verses* (1898); *Spoon River Anthology* (1915); *The Great Valley* (1916); *Songs and Satires* (1916); *Toward the Gulf* (1918); *Starved Rock* (1919); *Domesday Book* (1920); *Mitch Miller* (1920); *The Open Sea* (1921); *Children of the Market Place* (1922); *Skeeters Kirby* (1923); *The New Spoon River* (1924); *Lee* (1926); *Jack Kelso* (1928); *The Fate of the Jury* (1929); *Lichee Nuts* (1930); *Lincoln, the Man* (1931); *The Serpent in the Wilderness* (1933); *Vachel Lindsay* (1935); *Invisible Landscapes* (1935); *Poems of People* (1936); *Across Spoon River* (autobiography, 1936); *Whitman* (1937); *Mark Twain* (1938); *More People* (1939); *Emerson* (1940); *Illinois Poems* (1941); *The Sangamon* (1942). *See* Fred B. Millett's *Contemporary American Authors* (1940).

MASTERSON, KATE (1870–); b. Newburg, N.Y. Author. *The Dobleys* (1900); *The Thirteenth Apostle* (1904); *A Yellow Primrose* (1906); etc.

Masterson, Whit. Pen name of Bob Wade and Bill Miller.

MASTON, THOMAS BUFFORD (Nov. 26, 1897–); b. in Jefferson Co., Tenn. Educator, author. *A World in Travail* (1954); *Christianity and World Issues* (1957); *Segregation and Desegregation* (1959); *Isaac Backus: Pioneer of Religious Liberty* (1962); *God's Will and Your Life* (1964); *Biblical Ethics* (1967); *The Christian, the Church and Contemporary Problems* 1968). Prof., Southwestern Baptist Theological Seminary, since 1937.

MATHER, COTTON (Feb. 12, 1662/3–Feb. 13, 1727/8); b. Boston, Mass., son of Increase Mather. Congregational clergyman, scholar, translator, author. *Memorable Providences, Relating to Witchcraft and Possessions* (1689); *The Present State of New-England* (1690); *The Wonders of the Invisible World* (1693); *Pietas in Patriam* (1697); *Magnalia Christi Americana* (1702); *Corderius Americanus: An Essay Upon the Good Education of Children* (1708); etc. *See* Robert Calef's *More Wonders of the Invisible World* (1700). *See also*, Barrett Wendell's *Cotton Mather* (1891); T. J. Holmes's *The Mather Literature* (1927); *Selections from Cotton Mather*, edited by Kenneth B. Murdock (1926).

MATHER, FRANK JEWETT, JR. (July 6, 1868–Nov. 11, 1953); b. Deep River, Conn. Educator, author. *The Collectors* (1912); *Homer Martin: Poet in Landscape* (1912); *Estimates in Art*, 2 series (1916, 1931); *Ulysses in Ithaca* (1926); *Modern Painting* (1927); *The American Spirit in Art* (1927), in *Pageant of America; Concerning Beauty* (1935); *Venetian Painters* (1936); *Western European Painting of the Renaissance* (1939); etc. Co-editor, *Art Studies*, from 1923. Prof. art and archaeology, Princeton University, 1910–33.

MATHER, FRED (Aug. 2, 1833–Feb. 14, 1900); b. Greenbush, N.Y. Author. *In the Louisiana Lowlands* (1900).

MATHER, INCREASE (June 21, 1639–Aug. 23, 1723); b. Dorchester, Mass., son of Richard Mather. Congregational clergyman, educator, author. *A Brief History of the War with the Indians* (1676); *An Essay for the Recording of Illustrious Providences* (1684); etc. President, Harvard College, 1685–1701. *See* Kenneth B. Murdock's *Increase Mather* (1925); T. J. Holmes's *Increase Mather: A Bibliography*, 2v. (1931).

MATHER, RICHARD (1596–Apr. 22, 1669); b. Lancashire, Eng. Congregational clergyman, author. *Church-Government and Church-Covenant Discussed* (1643); *An Heart-Melting Exhortation* (1650); etc. Co-editor: *The Whole Book of Psalmes* (1640) better known as the *Bay Psalm Book; The Summe of Certain Sermons* (1652); etc. *See* Increase Mather's *The Life and Death of that Reverend Man of God, Mr. Richard Mather* (1670).

MATHER, SAMUEL (Oct. 30, 1706–June 27, 1785); b. Boston, Mass., son of Cotton Mather. Congregational clergyman, author. *Life of the Very Reverend and Learned Cotton Mather* (1729); *The Sacred Minister* (poem, 1773); etc.

MATHES, WILLIAM. Author. *Minotaur, Minotaur ...* (1967).

MATHEWS, ALBERT (Sept. 8, 1820–Sept. 9, 1903); b. New York. Lawyer, novelist, poet, essayist. Pen name "Paul Siogvolk." *Walter Ashwood: A Love Story* (1860); *A Bundle of Papers* (1879); *Ruminations* (1893); *A Few Verses* (1896).

MATHEWS, CHARLES THOMPSON (Mar. 31, 1863–Jan. 11, 1934); b. Paris. Architect, author. *The Renaissance under the Valois* (1893); *The Story of Architecture* (1896).

MATHEWS, CORNELIUS (Oct. 28, 1817–Mar. 25, 1889); b. Port Chester, N.Y. Editor, playwright, novelist, poet. *The Motley Book* (under pen name, "The Late Ben Smith," 1838); *Behemoth: A Legend of the Mound-Builders* (anon., 1839); *The Career of Puffer Hopkins* (1842); *Poems on Man* (1843); *The Various Writings* (1863, error for 1843); *Big Abel and the Little Manhattan* (anon., 1845); *Witchcraft; or, The Martyrs of Salem* (prod. 1846); *Jacob Leisler; or, New York in 1690* (prod. 1848); *Chanticleer* (anon., 1850); *Moneypenny* (1850); *False Pretences* (prod. 1855); etc. Editor: *The Indian Fairy Book* (1854). Editor, *Arcturus*, New York, 1840–42; *Yankee Doodle*, 1846–47.

MATHEWS, FRANCES AYMAR, b. New York. Playwright, novelist. *To-Night at Eight* (plays, 1889); *The New Yorkers and Other People* (1900); *My Lady Peggy Goes to Town* (1901); *A Little Tragedy in Tien-Tsin* (1904); *The Marquise's Millions* (1905); etc.

Mathews, Gertrude Singleton. See Gertrude Mathews Shelby.

MATHEWS, HARRY (Feb. 14, 1930–   ); b. New York. Poet, translator, novelist. *The Conversions* (1962); *Tlooth* (1966). Co-editor: *Locus/Solus*, 1960–62.

MATHEWS, JOHN JOSEPH (1895–). Author. *Wah'kon-tah* (1932); *Talking to the Moon* (1945); *The Life and Death of an Oilman* (1951); *The Osages* (1961); etc.

MATHEWS, MITFORD McLEOD, SR. (1891–). Editor, author. *The Beginnings of American English* (1931); *A Survey of English Dictionaries* (1933); *Some Sources of Southernisms* (1948); *A Dictionary of Americanisms* (1951); *Words: How To Know Them* (1956). Asst. editor, Craigie's *A Dictionary of American English on Historical Principles*, since 1936; dictionary editor, University of Chicago Press, 1944–56; staff *Webster New World Dictionary*, since 1957.

MATHEWS, SHAILER (May 26, 1863–Oct. 23, 1941); b. Portland, Me. Educator, editor, author. *The Church and the Changing Order* (1907); *The Social Gospel* (1909); *The French Revolution* (1922); *The Faith of Modernism* (1924); *Creative Christianity* (1935); *New Faith for Old* (autobiography, 1936); *The Church and the Christian* (1938); *Is God Emeritus?* (1940); etc. Compiler: *A Dictionary of Religion and Ethics* (with Gerald B. Smith, 1921). Editor, *The World Today*, 1903–11; the *Biblical World*, 1913–20. Prof. theology, Divinity School, University of Chicago, 1894–1933; dean, 1908–33.

MATHEWS, WILLIAM (July 28, 1818–Feb. 14, 1909); b. Waterville, Me. Editor, author. *Getting On in the World* (1873); *Words: Their Use and Abuse* (1876); *Hours with Men and Books* (1877); *Oratory and Orators* (1879); *Literary Style, and Other Essays* (1881); *Wit and Humor* (1888); *Nugae Litterariae* (1896); etc. Founder, the *Yankee Blade.*

MATHEWS, WILLIAM SMYTHE BABCOCK (May 8, 1837–Apr. 1, 1912); b. London, N.H. Editor, musician, author. *How to Understand Music*, 2v. (with William Mason, 1880–88); *The Great in Music*, 3v. (1900–03); etc. Founder, *Music* magazine, 1891; editor, 1891–1902.

MATSCHAT, CECILE [Hulse]; b. Binghampton, N.Y. Author. *Mexican Plants for American Gardens* (1935); *Shrubs and Trees* (1937); *Preacher on Horseback* (1940); *Tavern in the Town* (1942); *Murder at the Black Crook* (1943); *Ladd of the Big Swamp* (1954); etc.

MATSON, NORMAN HÄGHEJM (1893–Oct. 19, 1965); b. in the Midwest. Novelist. *Flecker's Magic* (1926); *The Comic Artist: A Play in Three Acts* (with Susan Glaspell, 1927); *Day of Fortune* (1928); *Doctor Fogg* (1929); *The Log of the Coriolanus* (1930); *Bats in the Belfry* (1943); *The Enchanted Beggar* (1959); etc.

Matthew Arnold. Critical analysis by Lionel Trilling (1939).

MATTHEWS, BRANDER (Feb. 21, 1852–Mar. 31, 1929); b. New Orleans, La. Educator, critic, playwright. *The Theatres of Paris* (1880); *French Dramatists of the 19th Century* (1881); *Margery's Lovers* (prod. 1884); *In Partnership* (with H. C. Bunner, 1884); *Actors and Actresses of Great Britain and the United States,* 5v. (with Lawrence Hutton, 1886); *Tom Paulding* (1892); *Vignettes of Manhattan* (1894); *Studies of the Stage* (1894); *His Father's Son* (1895); *Aspects of Fiction* (1896); *An Introduction to the Study of American Literature* (1896); *Outlines in Local Color* (1897); *A Confident To-Morrow* (1899); *Peter Stuyvesant* (with Bronson Howard, prod. 1899); *The Historical Novel* (1901); *The Development of the Drama* (1903); *Inquiries and Opinions* (1907); *A Study of the Drama* (1910); *Vistas of New York* (1912); *A Book about the Theatre* (1916); *These Many Years* (autobiography, 1917); *The Principles of Playmaking* (1919); *Essays on English* (1921); *Rip Van Winkle Goes to the Play* (1926); etc. One of the founders of the Dunlap Society, the Actors' Club, the Kinsmen, the American Copyright League, and the Players. Prof. English and dramatic literature, Columbia University, 1891–1924. *See* Roger Howson's *Book Shelf of Brander Matthews* (1931).

MATTHEWS, HERBERT LIONEL (Jan. 10, 1900–); b. New York. Journalist, author. *Eyewitness in Abyssinia* (1937); *Two Wars and More to Come* (1938); *The Fruits of Fascism* (1943); *The Education of a Correspondent* (1946); *Assignment to Austerity* (with wife, Edith Matthews, 1950); *The Yoke and the Arrows* (1957); *The Cuban Story* (1961); *Cuba* (1964); *Fidel Castro* (1969). With *New York Times,* since 1922; editorial staff, since 1949.

MATTHEWS, THOMAS STANLEY (Jan. 16, 1901–); b. Cincinnati, O. Journalist. *To the Gallows I Must Go* (1931); *The Moon's No Fool* (1936); *The Sugar Pill* (1957); *Name and Address* (autobiography, 1960); *O My America* (1962); *The Worst Unsaid* (verse) (1962); *Why So Gloomy?* (1966); etc. Staff, *Time,* 1929–53; editor, 1949–53.

MATTHEWS, WASHINGTON (July 17, 1843–Apr. 29, 1905); b. Killiney, Co. Dublin, Ire. Army surgeon, ethnologist, author. *Navajo Legends* (1897); and many important studies of the Navajo and other Indians.

MATTHEWS, WILLIAM (Mar. 29, 1822–Apr. 15, 1896); b. Aberdeen, Scot. Bookbinder, author. *A Short Historical Sketch of the Art of Bookbinding* (with William Loring Andrews, 1895). Head of bindery department, D. Appleton & Co., 1854–90. His son, Alfred, succeeded him at Appleton's. His library was sold Feb. 10–11, 1897. *See* Brander Matthew's *Bookbindings Old and New* (1895).

"Matthias at the Door." Poem by Edwin Arlington Robinson (1931).

MATTHIESSEN, FRANCIS OTTO (Feb. 19, 1902–Apr. 1, 1950); b. Pasadena, Cal. Educator, author. *Sarah Orne Jewett* (1929); *Translation: An Elizabethan Art* (1931); *The Achievement of T. S. Eliot* (1935); *American Renaissance* (1941); rev. ed. 1968); *Henry James: The Major Phase* (1944); *The James Family* (1947); *From the Heart of Europe* (1948); *Theodore Dreiser* (1951); *The Responsibilities of the Critic* (1952). Editor: Melville's *Selected Poems* (1944); Henry James's *Ameri-*

can Novels and Stories (1947); *Notebooks* (with K. Murdock, 1947); *Oxford Book of American Verse* (1950). History and literature depts., Harvard University, from 1929.

MATTHIESSEN, PETER (May 22, 1927–   ); b. New York. Author. *Race Rock* (1954); *Partisans* (1955); *Wildlife in America* (1959); *Raditzer* (1960); *The Cloud Forest* (1961); *Under the Mountain Wall* (1963); *At Play in the Fields of the Lord* (1965); *Blue Meridian* (1971).

MATTINGLY, GARRETT (May 6, 1900–Dec. 19, 1962); b. Washington, D.C. Educator, author. *Catherine of Aragon* (1941); *Renaissance Diplomacy* (1955); *The Armada* (1959). Prof. history, Columbia University, from 1948.

MATTSON, HANS (Dec. 23, 1832–Mar. 5, 1893); b. Skane, Swe. Publisher, editor, author. *Reminiscences: The Story of an Emigrant* (1891). Editor, *Svenska Amerikanaren,* Chicago, Ill., 1866–67; founder, *Minnesota Stats Tidning,* 1877.

MATTSON, MORRIS (c. 1809–1885). Editor, author. *Paul Ulric; or, The Adventures of an Enthusiast,* 2v. (anon., 1835); and several medical works. Editor, the *Philadelphia Botanic Sentinel,* 1837–39.

MATURIN, EDWARD (1812–May 25, 1881); b. Dublin, Ire. Author. *Sejanus, and Other Roman Tales* (anon., 1839); *Montezuma: The Last of the Aztecs,* 2v. (1845); *Benjamin, the Jew of Granada* (1848); *Lyrics of Spain and Erin* (1850); *Viola* (1858); etc.

MAULDIN, WILLIAM H. [Bill] (Oct. 29, 1921–); b. Mountain Park, N.M. Cartoonist, author. *Star Spangled Banter* (1944); *Up Front* (1945); *Back Home* (1947); *A Sort of a Saga* (1949); *Bill Mauldin's Army* (1951); *What's Got Your Back Up?* (1961); *I've Decided I Want My Seat Back* (1965); etc. Pulitzer Prize for cartoons, 1945, 1959.

MAULE, MARY KATHERINE (b. 1861); b. Pekin, Ill. Author. *The Little Knight of the X Bar B* (1910); *A Prairie-Schooner Princess* (1920).

Maule's Curse. Critical work by Yvor Winters (1938).

Maum Guinea and Her Plantation Children; or, Christmas among the Slaves. By Metta Victoria Victor (1861). A dime novel which had a short vogue, but which was overshadowed by *Uncle Tom's Cabin.*

MAURICE, ARTHUR BARTLETT (Apr. 10, 1873–May 31, 1946); b. Rahway, N.J. Editor, author. *New York in Fiction* (1901); *The History of the Nineteenth Century in Caricature* (with F. T. Cooper, 1904); *The New York of the Novelists* (1916); *Bottled Up in Belgium* (1917); *Fifth Avenue* (1918); *The Paris of the Novelists* (1919); *A Child's Story of American Literature* (with Algernon Tassin, 1923); *The Caliph of Bagdad* (with Robert H. Davis, 1931); *The Riddle of the Rovers* (1942); etc. Assoc. editor, the *Bookman,* 1899–1907; editor, 1907–16.

MAURY, DABNEY HERNDON (May 21, 1822–Jan. 11, 1900); b. Fredericksburg, Va. Army officer, author. *Recollections of a Virginian in the Mexican, Indian, and Civil Wars* (1894); *A Young People's History of Virginia and Virginians* (1896).

MAURY, MATTHEW FONTAINE (Jan. 14, 1806–Feb. 1, 1873); b. near Fredericksburg, Va. Known as "The Pathfinder of the Seas." Naval officer, oceanographer, geographer, author. *The Physical Geography of the Sea* (1855); *The World We Live In* (1868); *Manual of Geography* (1870); etc. Editor, *Southern Literary Messenger,* 1840–43. He wrote sketches for the *Messenger* under the pen name "Harry Bluff." *See* C. L. Lewis, *Matthew Fontaine Maury: The Pathfinder of the Seas* (1927); J. W. Wayland's *The Pathfinder of the Seas* (1930).

Mauve Decade, The. By Thomas Beer (1926). A picture of the "Gay Nineties."

MAVITY, NANCY BARR (Oct. 22, 1890–); b. Lawrenceville, Ill. Journalist, author. *A Dinner of Herbs* (poems, 1923); *The Tule Marsh Murder* (1929); *The Case of the Missing Sandals* (1930); *The Modern Newspaper* (1930); *Sister Aimee* (1931); *The State Versus Elna Jepson* (1938); etc. Editorial and feature writer, *Oakland Tribune*, since 1925.

MAWSON, CHRISTOPHER ORLANDO SYLVESTER (1870–Nov. 4, 1938); b. in England. Editor, lexicographer. *Geographical Manual and New Atlas* (1917); *Professional Book Editing* (1926); *The Roget Dictionary of Synonyms and Antonyms* (1931); *The International Book of Names* (1933); *Dictionary of Foreign Terms* (1934); *The Complete Desk Book* (1939); etc.

Max Fargus. Novel by Owen Johnson (1906). A sordid tale of New York's Greenwich Village.

MAXFIELD, EZRA KEMPTON (Apr. 23, 1881–Jan. 8, 1941); b. Winthrop, Me. Educator, editor of textbooks. Prof. English, Washington and Jefferson College, 1920–41.

MAXWELL, BALDWIN (Aug. 1, 1893–); b. Charlotte, N.C. Educator, editor, author. *Studies in Beaumont, Fletcher and Massinger* (1939); *Studies in the Shakespeare Apocrypha* (1956). etc. Editor, the *Philological Quarterly,* 1928–53. Prof. English, State University of Iowa, since 1926.

MAXWELL, PERRITON (1868–May 2, 1947); b. New York. Editor, author. *Masterpieces of Art and Nature* (1895); *American Art and Artists* (1896); *A Third of Life* (1921); etc. Editor, *Metropolitan* magazine, 1900–06; *Cosmopolitan* magazine, 1906–10; *Hearst's Magazine,* 1913–14; *Judge and Leslie's Weekly,* 1917–21; the *Theatre Magazine,* 1927–29; etc.

MAXWELL, WILLIAM (Aug. 16, 1908–); b. Lincoln, Ill. Novelist. *Bright Center of Heaven* (1934); *They Came Like Swallows* (1937); *The Folded Leaf* (1945); *The Heavenly Tenants* (1946); *Time Will Darken It* (1948); *The Château* (1961); *The Old Man at the Railroad Crossing* (1966).

MAY, ARTHUR JAMES (Jan. 2, 1899–June 17, 1968); b. Rockdale, Pa. Educator. *The Age of Metternich* (1933); *Europe and Two World Wars* (1947); *A History of Civilization: The Mid-Seventeenth Century to Modern Times* (1956); *The Passing of the Hapsburg Monarchy* (1966); *Vienna in the Age of Franz Joseph* (1966); *Europe since 1939* (1966); etc. Dept. of history, University of Rochester, from 1925.

MAY, CAROLINE (b. 1820); b. in England. Poet. *Poems* (1865); *Lays of Memory and Affection* (1888). Editor: *The American Female Poets* (1848), republished as *Pearls from the American Female Poets* (1869); *Treasured Thoughts from Favorite Authors* (1850).

MAY, EARL CHAPIN (Oct. 23, 1873–Nov. 11, 1960); b. Rochelle, Ill. Author. *Cuddy of the White Tops* (1924); *2000 Miles Through Chile* (1924); *Just Circus People* (1930); *The Circus from Rome to Ringling* (1932); *The Prairie Pirates* (1933); *The Canning Clan* (1937); *Model Railroads in the Home* (1939); *The Railroad Trackwalker* (1943); *Principio to Wheeling* (1945); *A Century of Silver* (1947); *Prudential* (1950); *History of the Union League Club of New York* (with others, 1952); etc.

MAY, ERNEST RICHARD (Nov. 19, 1928–); b. Ft. Worth, Texas. Author. *The World War and American Isolation, 1914–1917* (1959); *Imperial Democracy* (1961); *Land of the Free* (1966). Editor: *Ultimate Decision: The President as Commander in Chief* (1960).

MAY, HERBERT GORDON (Dec. 26, 1904–); b. Fair Haven, Vt. Congregational clergyman, educator. Author: *Material Remains of the Megiddo Cult* (with R. M. Engberg, 1935); *Our English Bible in the Making* (1952). Co-author: *Culture and Conscience* (1936); *Remapping the Bible World* (1949). Editor: *Abingdon Maps of Bible Lands* (1966). Prof. Old Testament, Oberlin College, since 1946.

MAY, JAMES BOYER (Dec. 30, 1904–); b. Red Granite, Wis. Poet, editor. *Eight Years* (1946); *For a New Era of Hate* (1947); *Twigs as Varied Bent* (1954); *Selected Poems, 1950–1955* (1955); *Selected Fiction* (1957); *Collected Poems* (1957); *Selected Essays and Criticism* (1957). Editor: *8 American Poets* (1952); *Poetry Los Angeles* (1958). Director, Villiers Publications; editor, *Trace,* since 1952.

MAY, ROLLO (April 21, 1909–); b. Ada, O. Psychologist, author. *Meaning of Anxiety* (1950); *Man's Search for Himself* (1953); *Psychology and the Human Dilemma* (1967); *Love and Will* (1969). Editor: *Existence— A New Dimension in Psychiatry and Psychology* (1958); *Symbolism in Religion and Literature* (1960).

MAY, SAMUEL JOSEPH (Sept. 12, 1797–July 1, 1871); b. Boston, Mass. Unitarian clergyman, abolitionist, author. *Revival of Education* (1855); *Recollections of the Anti-Slavery Conflict* (1869); etc.

May, Sophie. Pen name of Rebecca Sophia Clarke.

MAY, STELLA BURKE (Mrs. Earl Chapin May) (1877–Dec. 11, 1961); b. Des Moines, Ia. Author. *Men, Maidens, and Mantillas* (1923); *Chico, the Circus Cherub* (1928); *The Conqueror's Lady: Ines Suarez* (1930); *Children of Japan* (1935); *Children of Mexico* (1939); *They Helped Make America* (1940); *My Neighbor, Mexico* (1941); *My Neighbor, Brazil* (1947); *Utopia in the Hills* (1949); *Ireland All the Way* (1955); etc.

MAYER, ARTHUR L[oeb] (May 28, 1886–); b. Demopolis, Ala. Motion picture executive. *Merely Colossal* (1953); *The Movies* (with Richard Griffith, 1957).

MAYER, BRANTZ (Sept. 27, 1809–Feb. 23, 1879); b. Baltimore, Md. Lawyer, historian, editor. *Mexico as It Was and as It Is* (1844); *Tah-Gah-Jute; or, Logan and Captain Michael Cresap* (1851); *Baltimore: Past and Present* (1871); etc. Editor: *Captain Canot; or, Twenty Years of an African Slaver* (1854). Founder, Maryland Historical Society; established *Archives of Maryland,* etc.

MAYER, FREDERICK (Aug. 11, 1921–); b. Frankfurt, Ger. Educator, author. *History of Ancient Philosophy* (1950); *History of Modern Philosophy* (1951); *New Directions for the American University* (1957); *History of Educational Thought* (1960); *Web of Hate* (1961); *American Ideas and Education* (1964); *Our Troubled Youth* (1959); *Man, Morals and Education* (1962); *Great Ideas of Education,* 3v. (1966); *The Great Teachers* (1967). Faculty, University of California at Los Angeles, since 1963.

MAYER, "HY" [Henry] (July 18, 1868–Sept. 27, 1954); b. Worms-on-Rhine, Ger. Caricaturist, author. *Autobiography of a Monkey* (1896); *In Laughland* (1899); *A Trip to Toyland* (1900); etc. Illustrator, *Puck Album of Caricatures* (1915); etc. Illustrations appeared in *Life, Judge, Collier's, Century, Puck,* etc. Cartoonist, *New York Times,* 1904–14; editor, *Puck,* 1914.

MAYER, JANE ROTHSCHILD (1903–); b. Kansas City, Mo. Author. *Getting Along in the Family* (1949); *Dolly Madison* (1954); *The Year of the White Trees* (1963); etc. Co-author with Clara Spiegel under pen name "Clare Jaynes": *Instruct My Sorrows* (1942); *This Eager Heart* (1947); *The Early Frost* (1952); etc.

MAYER, MARTIN PRAGER (Jan. 14, 1928–); b. New York. Author. *The Experts* (1954); *Wall Street: Men and Money* (1955); *Madison Avenue, U.S.A.* (1958); *The Voice That Fills the House* (1959); *The Schools* (1961); *Where, When and Why, Social Studies in American Schools* (1963); *All You Know Is Facts* (1968); *Diploma* (1968); *The Lawyers* (1968); *New Breed on Wall Street* (1969); *The Teachers Strike: New York* (1969); etc. Editorial staff, *Esquire.*

MAYES, HERBERT RAYMOND (Aug. 11, 1900–); b. New York. Editor. *Editor's Choice* (1956); *An Editor's Treasury: A Continuing Anthology of Prose, Verse and Literary Curiosa* (1968). Editor, *McCall's* 1959 to 1969.

MAYFIELD, JULIAN (1928–); b. in South Carolina. *The Hit* (1957); *The Long Night* (1958); *The Grand Parade* (1961).

Mayfield Deer, The. Long poem by Mark Van Doren (1941).

MAYHEW, EXPERIENCE (Feb. 5, 1673–Nov. 29, 1758); b. Chilmark, Mass. Missionary, translator of books into the Indian language. *Indian Converts* (1927); *Observations on the Indian Language,* ed. by John S. H. Fogg (1884). Translated the *Psalms* into the Indian language as *The Massachuset Psalter* (1709). The editorship of *The Indian Primer* (1720) has been attributed to him.

MAYHEW, JONATHAN (Oct. 8, 1720–July 9, 1766); b. Chilmark, Martha's Vineyard, Mass. Congregational clergyman, author. *Seven Sermons* (1749); *Practical Discourses* (1760); *Christianity Sobriety* (1763); etc.

MAYLEM, JOHN (Apr. 30, 1739–c.1762); b. Newport, R.I. Poet. *Gallic Perfidy* (1758); *The Conquest of Louisburg* (1758). See *Publications* of the Colonial Society of Massachusetts, v. 32, 1937.

MAYNARD, CHARLES JOHNSON (May 6, 1845–Oct. 15, 1929); b. West Newton, Mass. Naturalist, author. *Naturalist's Guide* (1870); *The Birds of Florida* (1872–78); *The Birds of Eastern North America* (1872–81); *Walks and Talks with Nature,* 12v. (1908–21).

MAYNARD, THEODORE (Nov. 3, 1890–Oct. 18, 1956); b. Madras, India. Educator, author. *Poems* (1919); *Exile, and Other Poems* (1928); *De Soto and the Conquistadores* (1930); *Man and Beast* (1936); *The World I Saw* (1938); *Apostle of Charity: The Life of St. Vincent de Paul* (1939); *Queen Elizabeth* (1940); *Great Catholics in American History* (1957); etc. Compiler: *The Book of Modern Catholic Verse* (1926); *The Book of Modern Catholic Prose* (1928); etc.

MAYO, AMORY DWIGHT (Jan. 31, 1823–Apr. 8, 1907); b. Warwick, Mass. Unitarian clergyman, educator, author. *The Balance* (1847); *Symbols of the Capital; or, Civilization in New York* (1859); *Talks with Teachers* (1881); etc. Assoc. editor, the *Journal of Education,* 1880–85. Prof. church polity and administration, Meadville Theological Seminary, 1863–98.

MAYO, BERNARD (Feb. 13, 1902–); b. Lewiston, Me. Author. *Henry Clay* (1937); *Jefferson and the Way of Honor* (1951); etc. Editor: *Thomas Jefferson and His Unknown Brother Randolph* (1942); *Myths and Men: Patrick Henry, George Washington, Thomas Jefferson* (1959); *Instructions to the British Ministers to the U.S. 1791–1813* (1969).

MAYO, EARL WILLIAMS (May 5, 1873–Oct. 10, 1957); b. Springville, N.Y. Editor, author. *In the Land of the Loon* (with F. K. Scribner, 1899); *Cape Cod Folks* (1906). With various New York papers and magazines.

MAYO, ELEANOR R. (Dec. 27, 1920–); b. Everett, Mass. Novelist. *Turn Home* (1945); *Loom of the Land* (1946); *October Fire* (1951); *Swan's Harbour* (1953); *Forever Strangers* (1958).

MAYO, KATHERINE (Jan. 24, 1867–Oct. 9, 1940); b. Ridgeway, Pa. Author. *Justice to All* (1917); *Mounted Justice* (1922); *The Isles of Fear* (1925); *Mother India* (1927); *The Face of Mother India* (1935); *General Washington's Dilemma* (1938); etc.

MAYO, LAWRENCE SHAW (June 26, 1888–); b. Newton, Mass. Educator, editor, author. *Jeffrey Amherst* (1916); *John Wentworth* (1921); *John Endicott* (1936); *John Langdon of New Hampshire* (1937). Editor, the *New England Quarterly,* since 1928. History dept., Harvard University, since 1911; asst. editor, Graduate School of Arts and Sciences, since 1927.

MAYO, MARGARET (Nov. 19, 1882–Feb. 25, 1951); b. (Lilian Clatten) in Illinois. Actress, playwright. *Polly of the Circus* (prod. 1907); *Baby Mine* (prod. 1910); *Twin Beds* (with Salisbury Field, prod. 1915); *Trouping for the Troops* (1919); etc.

MAYO, SARAH CARTER EDGARTON (Mrs. Amory Dwight Mayo) (Mar. 17, 1819–July 9, 1848); b. Shirley Village, Mass. Editor, author. *The Palfreys* (c.1838); *Ellen Clifford* (c.1839); *Spring Flowers* (1840); *The Poetry of Woman* (1841); *The Flower Vase* (1844); *The Floral Fortune Teller* (1846); *Selections from the Writings,* ed. by her husband (1849). Editor: *Fables of Flora* (1844); etc. Editor, the Universalist annual, the *Rose of Sharon,* 1840–48; assoc. editor, the *Universalist and Ladies' Repository,* 1839–42.

MAYO, WILLIAM STARBUCK (Apr. 15, 1811–Nov. 22, 1895); b. Ogdensburg, N.Y. Author. *Kaloolah; or, Journeyings from the Djebel Kumri* (1849); *The Berber; or, The Mountaineer of the Atlas* (1850); *Romance Dust from the Historic Placer* (1851); republished as *Flood and Field* (1855); *Never Again* (1873); etc.

MAYS, DAVID J[ohn] (May 22, 1896–Feb. 17, 1971); b. in Virginia. Lawyer. *Edmund Pendleton, 1721–1803,* 2v. (1952; Pulitzer Prize for biography, 1953). Editor: *The Letters and Papers of Edmund Pendleton,* 2v. (1967).

MAZO, EARL (July 7, 1919–   ); b. Warsaw, Poland. Author. *Richard Nixon: A Political and Personal Portrait* (1959); *The Mindreaders* (1964); *Nixon, A Political Portrait* (with Stephen Hess, 1968).

MAZOUR, ANATOLE G[regory] (May 24, 1900–); b. Kiev, U.S.S.R. Educator, author. *The First Russian Revolution, 1825* (1937); *An Outline of Modern Russian Historiography* (1938); *Russia: Past and Present* (1952); *Finland Between East and West* (1955); *Men and Nations: A World History* (with John Peoples, 1958); *Modern Russian Historiography* (1959); *Rise and Fall of the Romanovs* (1960); *Russia: Tsarist and Communist* (1962); *Economic Development of the Soviet Union* (1966). Prof. history, Stanford University, 1947–66.

McAFEE, CLELAND BOYD (Sept. 25, 1866–Feb. 4, 1944); b. Ashley, Mo. Presbyterian clergyman, educator, author. *Mosaic Law in Modern Life* (1906); *The Greatest English Classic* (1912); *The Christian Conviction* (1926); *The Uncut Nerve of Missions* (1932); *Studies in the Philippines* (1943); etc. Prof. theology, McCormick Theological Seminary, Chicago, 1912–30.

McAFEE, THOMAS (1928–   ). Poet, novelist. *Poems and Stories* (1960); *I'll Be Home Late Tonight* (1967); *Rover Youngblood* (1969); etc.

McALLISTER, J[ames] GRAY (Nov. 27, 1872–Jan. 22, 1970); b. Covington, Va. Presbyterian clergyman, educator, author. *Studies in Old Testament History* (1925); *Borderlands of the Mediterranean* (1925); etc. Co-author: *Edward O. Guerrant: Apostle to the Southern Highlanders* (1950). Editor: *The Life and Letters of Walter W. Moore* (1939); etc. President, Hampden-Sydney College, 1905–08; prof. English Bible, Union Theological Seminary, Richmond, Va., 1925–43.

McALLISTER, WARD (Dec. 1827–Jan. 31, 1895); b. Savannah, Ga. Social arbiter, author. *Society as I Have Found It* (1890). He coined the term "The Four Hundred" on the occasion of Mrs. William Astor's ball, Feb. 1, 1892.

McALMON, ROBERT [Menzies] (1895–1956). Author. *Explorations* (1921); *Village: As It Happened Through a Fifteen Year Period* (1924); *The Portrait of a Generation* (1926); *North America, Continent of Conjecture* (1929); *Not Alone Lost* (1937); *Being Geniuses Together* (autobiography, 1938); etc.

McANALLY, DAVID RICE (Feb. 17, 1810–July 11, 1895); b. Grainger Co., Tenn. Methodist clergyman, educator, author. *History of Methodism in Missouri* (1881); etc. Editor, the *St. Louis Christian Advocate,* 1851–95.

McArone Papers. By George Arnold. They appeared originally in *Vanity Fair,* beginning Nov. 24, 1860, continued in the *Leader,* and were concluded in the *Weekly Review,* Oct. 14, 1865. Burlesque on the war correspondence of newspapers.

McBRIDE, HENRY (1867–Mar. 31, 1962); b. West Chester, Pa. Art critic. *Florine Stettheimer* (1946); etc. Art critic, *New York Sun, the Dial.*

McBRIDE, MARY MARGARET (Nov. 16, 1899–); b. Paris, Mo. Author. *Jazz: A Story of Paul Whiteman* (with Paul Whiteman, 1926); *Paris Is a Woman's Town* (with Helen Josephy, 1929); *London Is a Man's Town* (with same, 1930); *The Story of Dwight Morrow* (1930); *New York Is Everybody's Town* (with Helen Josephy, 1931); *Beer and Skittles: A Friendly Modern Guide to Germany* (with same, 1932); *How Dear to My Heart* (1940); *America for Me* (1941); *Tune in for Elizabeth* (1945); *Harvest of American Cooking* (1957); *A Long Way from Missouri* (1959); *Out of the Air* (autobiography, 1960); etc. Radio columnist, since 1937.

McBride, Robert M., Company. New York. Publishers. Founded 1909 as McBride, Winston and Company to publish *House and Garden.* In 1911 *Travel Magazine* was taken over and the corporation's name changed to McBride, Nast & Company. In 1912 the firm began to publish books. In 1915 the name was changed to Robert M. McBride and Company.

McBRIDE, ROBERT MEDILL (Aug. 24, 1879–); b. McKeesport, Pa. Author and publisher. *A Little Book of Brittany* (1913); *Sweden and Its People* (1924); *Finland and Its People* (1925); *Romantic Czechoslovakia* (1930); *Hilltop Cities of Italy* (1936); *Towns and Peoples of Modern Poland* (1938); *Horses and Dogs of Great Men* (under pen name "Marshall Reid," 1952). Editor: *Great Hoaxes of All Time* (with Neil Pritchie, 1956). Founder and president of Robert M. McBride & Co., New York, publishers.

McCABE, GIBSON (Mar. 11, 1911–); b. Brooklyn, N.Y. Publisher. With *Newsweek,* since 1942; publisher, since 1959.

McCABE, JAMES DABNEY (July 30, 1842–Jan. 27, 1883); b. Richmond, Va. Author. Pen name, "Edward Winslow Martin." Under own name: *The Aide-de-Camp* (1863); *Lights and Shadows of New York Life* (1872); *New York by Sunlight and Gaslight* (1882); etc.; also under pen name: *The Secrets of the Great City* (1868); *Behind the Scenes in Washington* (1873); *The History of the Great Riots* (1877); etc.

McCABE, LIDA ROSE (1865–Dec. 9, 1938); b. Columbus, O. Author. *Don't You Remember?* (1884); *Ardent Adrienne: The Life of Madame de la Fayette* (1930).

McCABE, WILLIAM GORDON (Aug. 4, 1841–June 1, 1920); b. Richmond, Va. Educator, scholar, raconteur, author of popular lyrics on the Civil War. Compiler: *Ballads of Battle and Bravery* (1879). *See* Armistead C. Gordon's *Memories and Memorials of William Gordon McCabe,* 2v. (1925).

McCALEB, WALTER FLAVIUS (Oct. 17, 1873–); b. Benton, Tex. Author. *The Aaron Burr Conspiracy* (1903); *Winnowings of the Wind* (1910); *Ring, a Frontier Dog* (1921); *Theodore Roosevelt* (1931); *Conquest of the West* (1947); *The Spanish Missions of Texas* (1954); *Bigfoot Wallace* (1956); *S. F. Austin* (1957); etc.

McCALL, MARY CALDWELL (April 4, 1904–); b. New York. Author. *The Goldfish Bowl* (1933).

McCall, Sidney. Pen name of Mary McNeil Fenollosa.

McCall's Magazine. New York. Monthly magazine for women. Founded 1870, as *Queen of Fashion.* Name changed Sept., 1897. Published by The McCall Corp.

McCARDELL, ROY LARCUM (June 30, 1870–); b. Hagerstown, Md. Author. *Conversations of a Chorus Girl* (1903); *Old Love and Lavender, and Other Verses* (1900); *The Diamond from the Sky* (1916); etc.

McCARROLL, JAMES (Aug. 3, 1814–Apr. 10, 1892); b. Lanesboro, Co. Longford, Ire. Journalist, poet, playwright. *The Terry Finnegan Letters* (1864); *The Adventures of a Night* (1865); *Almost a Tragedy: A Comedy* (1874); *Madeline, and other Poems* (1889).

McCARTER, MARGARET HILL (May 2, 1860–Aug. 31, 1938); b. Charlottesville, Ind. Author. *The Cottonwood's Story* (1903); *In Old Quivira* (1908); *The Price of the Prairie* (1910); *The Peace of the Solomon Valley* (1911); *A Wall of Men* (1912); *Winning of the Wilderness* (1914); *Vanguards of the Plains* (1917); *The Reclaimers* (1918); *Homeland* (1922); *The Candle in the Window* (1925); etc.

McCARTHY, CORMAC (July 20, 1933–   ); b. Providence, R.I. Author. *The Orchard Keeper* (1965); *Outer Dark* (1968).

McCARTHY, EUGENE JOSEPH (Mar. 29, 1916–); b. Watkins, Minn. U.S. Senator, author. *Frontiers in American Democracy* (1960); *Dictionary of American Politics* (1962); *A Liberal's Answer to the Conservative Challenge* (1964); *Limits of Power* (1967); *The Year of the People* (1969). U.S. Senator, since 1958.

McCARTHY, JOSEPH W[eston] (Mar. 6, 1915–); b. Cambridge, Mass. Author. *The Remarkable Kennedys* (1960); *In One Ear* (1962); *Ireland* (1964); *New England* (1967). Editor: *Fred Allen's Letters* (1965).

McCARTHY, MARY [Therese] (June 21, 1912–); b. Seattle, Wash. Author. *The Company She Keeps* (1942); *The Oasis* (1949); *Cast a Cold Eye* (1950); *The Groves of Academe* (1952); *A Charmed Life* (1955); *Sights and Spectacles* (1956); *Venice Observed* (1956); *Memories of a Catholic Girlhood* (1957); *The Stones of Florence* (1959); *On the Contrary* (1961); *The Group* (1963); *Vietnam* (1967); *Hanoi* (1968); *Birds of America* (1971).

McCARTY, LOUIS HENRY. Author. *Same Tree, Different Author* (1964).

McCHESNEY, DORA GREENWELL (Oct. 1, 1871–1912); b. Chicago, Ill. Author. *Kathleen Clare: Her Book, 1637–1641* (1895); *Miriam Cromwell, Royalist* (1897); *Beatrix Infelix* (1898); *Rupert* (1899); etc.

McCLELLAN, GEORGE BRINTON (Dec. 3, 1826–Oct. 29, 1885); b. Philadelphia, Pa. Army officer, author. *McClellan's Own Story* (1887); *Mexican War Diary,* ed. by William S. Myers (1917). *See* George S. Hillard's *Life and Correspondence of George B. McClellan* (1864); William Starr Myers's *General George B. McClellan* (1934); Clarence E. N. Macartney's *Little Mac: The Life of General George B. McClellan* (1939).

McCLELLAN, GEORGE BRINTON (Nov. 23, 1865–Nov. 29, 1940); b. Dresden, Germany, son of George Brinton McClellan. Educator, author. *The Oligarchy of Venice* (1904); *Venice and Bonaparte* (1931); *Modern Italy* (1933); etc. Congressman, 1895–1903; Mayor, New York City, 1903–09. History dept., Princeton University, 1908–31.

McCLELLAND, DAVID C[larence] (May 20, 1917–); b. Mt. Vernon, N.Y. Educator. *Personality* (1951); *The Achievement Motive* (with others, 1953); *The Achieving Society* (1961). Editor: *Studies in Motivation* (1955). Prof. psychology, Harvard University, since 1956.

McCLOSKEY, ROBERT (Sept. 15, 1914–Aug. 4, 1969); b. Hamilton, O. Artist, author. *Lentil* (1940); *Make Way for Ducklings* (1942); *Homer Price* (1943); *Centerburg Tales* (1951); *One Morning in Maine* (1952); *Time of Wonder* (1957); *Bert Dow, Deep Water Man* (1963); etc.

McCLOY, HELEN [Worrell Clarkson]. Art critic, novelist. *Dance of Death* (1938), published in England as *Design for Dying* (1938); *The Man in the Moonlight* (1940); *The Deadly Truth* (1941); *Do Not Disturb* (1943); *Through a Glass Darkly* (1950); *He Never Came Back* (1954); *Two-Thirds of a Ghost* (1956); *The Slayer and the Slain* (1957); etc.

McCLUNG, ALEXANDER. (d. 1855). Editor, orator. Known as "The Black Knight of the South." Founder, the *True Issue,* Jackson, Miss., 1840.

McCLUNG, JOHN A. (Sept. 25, 1804–Aug. 7, 1859); b. Washington, Ky. Presbyterian clergyman, author. *Camden: A Tale of the South* (anon., 1830); *Sketches of Western Adventure* (1832).

McCLURE, ALEXANDER K[elly] (Jan. 9, 1828–June 6, 1909); b. Sherman's Dale, Pa. Editor, author. *Three Thousand Miles through the Rocky Mountains* (1869); *Abraham Lincoln and Men of War-Times* (1892); *Recollections of Half a Century* (1902); *Old Time Notes of Pennsylvania,* 2v. (1905). Editor: *Famous American Statesmen and Orators,* 6v. (1902); Founder (with Frank McLaughlin), the *Philadelphia Times,* 1873; editor, 1873–1901.

McCLURE, ALEXANDER WILSON (May 8, 1808–Sept. 1865); b. Boston, Mass. Congregational clergyman, editor, author. *Lives of the Chief Fathers of New England,* 2v. (1846); *The Translators Reviewed* (1953); etc. Editor, the *Christian Observatory,* 1847–50.

McCLURE, JAMES BAIRD (1832–1895). Editor, author. *Edison and His Inventions* (1879). Editor: *Stories and Sketches of Chicago* (1880); *Popular Anecdotes* (1881); *Pearls from Many Seas* (1898); etc.

McCLURE, JAMES GORE KING (Nov. 24, 1848–Jan. 18, 1932); b. Albany, N.Y. Presbyterian clergyman, educator, author. *Possibilities* (1896); *For Hearts That Hope* (1900); *The Growing Pastor* (1904); *Grandfather's Stories,* 2 series (1926–28); *The Story of England's First Library* (1929); *The Supreme Book of Mankind* (1930); etc. President, Lake Forest University, 1897–1901; president, Presbyterian Theological Seminary, Chicago, 1905–28.

McCLURE, JOHN PEEBLES (Dec. 19, 1893–Feb. 8, 1956); b. Ardmore, Okla. Journalist, poet. *Airs and Ballads* (1918); *The Stag's Hornbook* (1918).

McCLURE, MARJORIE BARKLEY (Mrs. Franklyn Evans McClure) (1882–Nov., 1967); b. Newark, N.J. Author. *High Fires* (1924); *A Bush That Burned* (1925); *The Price of Wisdom* (1926); *Many Waters* (1928); *The Marriage of King Paulinus* (1930); *John Dean's Journey* (1932).

McCLURE, MICHAEL (Oct. 20, 1932–   ); b. Marysville, Kan. Author. *Passage* (1956); *For Artaud* (1959); *The New Book: A Book of Torture* (1961); *Hymns to St. Geryon, and Other Poems* (1959); *Dark Brown* (1961); *Meat Science Essays* (1963); *Ghost Tantras* (1964); *Thirteen Mad Sonnets* (1964); *Dream Table* (1965); *Poisoned Wheat* (1965); *Unto Caesar* (1965); *Freewheelin' Frank* (with F. Reynolds, 1967); *Mammals* (1968); *Love Lion Book* (1968). Plays: *The Feast* (prod. 1960); *Pillow* (prod. 1961); *The Blossom, or Billy the Kid* (prod. 1964); *The Beard* (prod. 1965). Editor: *Sermons of Jean Harlow and the Curse of Billy the Kid* (1968).

McCLURE, ROBERT E[merson] (June 12, 1896–); b. Columbus, O. Author. *The Dominant Blood* (1924); *Some Found Adventure* (1926); *Lady in Marble* (1928); *A Fable for Wives* (1932); *Harry Pickering* (1938).

McCLURE, SAMUEL SIDNEY (Feb. 17, 1857–March 21, 1949); b. in Co. Antrim, Ire. Editor, author. *My Autobiography* (1914); *What Freedom Means to Man* (1938); etc. Founder and editor, *McClure's Magazine,* 1893. Founder, McClure Syndicate, 1884; McClure, Phillips & Co., publishers, New York, 1899.

McClure's Magazine. New York. Monthly. Founded 1893, by Samuel Sidney McClure. Merged 1929 with the *New Smart Set.* See *Tales from McClure's,* 5v. (1897).

McClurg, A. C., & Co. Chicago, Ill. Booksellers. Founded in 1848, as Griggs, Bross & Co. In 1872, Egbert L. Jansen and Alexander Caldwell McClurg (Sept. 9, 1832–Apr. 15, 1901), who had entered the firm, took it over and renamed it Jansen, McClurg & Co. In 1886, McClurg became the principal owner, and the firm became A. C. McClurg & Co. Ogden T. McClurg (Sept. 8, 1879–Apr. 20, 1926) entered the firm and was its president, 1911–26. The old English Book Department, started in 1877, was called the "Saints and Sinners Corner" by Eugene Field. *The Dial* was founded by the firm in 1880. The retail part of the business was sold in 1930.

McCONAUGHY, JAMES LUKENS (Oct. 21, 1887–Mar. 7, 1948); b. New York. Educator. *The School Drama* (1913). President, Wesleyan University, Middletown, Conn., 1925–43.

McCONKEY, JAMES R. (Sept. 2, 1921–   ); b. Lakewood, Ohio. Critic, educator. *The Novels of E.M. Forster* (1957); *Night Stand* (1965); etc. Editor: *The Structure of Prose* (1963); etc. English Department, Cornell University, since 1956.

McCONNEL, JOHN LUDLUM (Nov. 11, 1826–Jan. 17, 1862); b. in Morgan (now Scott) Co., Ill. Author. *Grahame; or, Youth and Manhood* (anon., 1850); *Talbot and Vernon* (anon., 1850); *The Glenns: A Family History* (1851); *Western Characters; or, Types of Border Life in the Western States* (1853).

McCONNELL, FRANCIS JOHN (Aug. 18, 1871–Aug. 18, 1953); b. Trinway, O. Methodist bishop, author. *The Diviner Immanence* (1906); *Religious Certainty* (1910); *Personal Christianity* (1914); *Understanding the Scriptures* (1917); *Public Opinion and Theology* (1920); *Borden Parker Bowne* (1929); *John Wesley* (1939); *By the Way: An Autobiography* (1952); etc. President, De Pauw University, 1909–12.

McCONNELL, GRANT (June 27, 1915–   ); b. Portland, Ore. Educator, author. *The Decline of Agrarian Democracy* (1953); *The Steel Seizure of 1952* (1960); *Steel and the Presidency, 1962* (1963); *Private Power and American Democracy* (1965). Professor of political science, University of Chicago, since 1957.

McCOOK, HENRY CHRISTOPHER (July 3, 1837–Oct. 31, 1911); b. New Lisbon, O. Presbyterian clergyman, naturalist, author. *Tenants of an Old Farm: Leaves from the Notebook of a Naturalist* (1885); *The Latimers: A Tale of the Western Insurrection of 1794* (1897); *The Ant Communities and How They are Governed* (1909), and many other books on ants; *Quaker Ben* (1911); etc.

McCORD, DAVID [Thompson Watson] (Nov. 15, 1897–); b. New York. Poet. *Oddly Enough* (1926); *Floodgate* (1927); *Stirabout* (1928); *The Crows* (1934); *Bay Window Ballads* (1935); *Twelve Verses from XII Night* (1938); *On Occasion* (1943); *About Boston* (1948); *A Star by Day* (1950); *Poet Always Next but One* (1951); *The Camp at Lockjaw* (1952); *Far and Few* (1952); *The Old Bateau* (1953); *Odds Without Ends* (1954); *Selected Poems* (1957); *Take Sky* (1962); *The Fabrick of Man: Fifty Years of Peter Bent Brigham* (1963); *In Sight of Sever* (Harvard Essays) (1963); *New England: with Notes and Observations* (1969). Editor: *Once and For All* (1929); *What Cheer* (1945); *The Pocket Book of Humorous Verse* (1946); etc.

McCORD, JOSEPH (July 21, 1880–Jan. 27, 1943); b. Moline, Ill. Novelist. *Silver Linings* (1932); *Bugles Going By* (1933); *Magnolia Square* (1936); *Dreams to Mend* (1940); *His Wife the Doctor* (1941); etc.

McCORD, LOUISA S[usanna Cheves] (Dec. 3, 1810–Nov. 23, 1879); b. Charleston, S.C. Poet. *My Dreams* (1848); *Caius Gracchus: A Tragedy* (1851); etc.

McCORD, WILLIAM MAXWELL (Oct. 24, 1930–); b. St. Louis, Mo. Educator, author. *Psychopathy and Delinquency* (1956); *Origins of Crime* (1959); *Origins of Alcoholism* (1960); *The Psychopath* (1964); *The Springtime of Freedom* (1965); *Mississippi: The Long Hot Summer* (1965). Professor of sociology, Rice Institute, since 1965.

McCORMICK, ANNE O'HARE (1882?–May 29, 1954); b. in Yorkshire, Eng. Journalist. *The Hammer and the Scythe* (1928). With *New York Times* from 1921, member of editorial board from 1936 (Pulitzer Prize for foreign correspondence, 1937).

McCORMICK, JAY (Oct. 1, 1919–   ); b. Harbor Beach, Mich. Novelist. *November Storm* (1943); *Nightshade* (1948).

McCORMICK, JOSEPH MEDILL (May 16, 1877–Feb. 25, 1925); b. Chicago, Ill., grandson of Joseph Medill. Newspaper publisher. Joined staff of the *Chicago Tribune* in 1900, and became owner in 1908. U.S. Senator, 1919–25.

McCORMICK, ROBERT R[utherford] (July 30, 1880–Apr. 1, 1955); b. Chicago, Ill. Editor, publisher, author. *Ulysses S. Grant* (1934); *Freedom of the Press* (1936); *The American Revolution and Its Influence on World Civilization* (1945); *The War Without Grant* (1950); *American Empire* (1952); etc. Editor and publisher, the *Chicago Tribune.*

McCORMICK, VIRGINIA (Taylor) (1873–); b. Berryville, Va. Editor, author. *Star Dust and Gardens* (poems, 1920); *Voices of the Wind* (1924); *Charcoal and Chalk* (1926); *Jericho's Christmas* (1928); *Radio to Daedalus* (poems, 1931); *Winter Apples* (poem, 1942). Editor, The *Lyric* magazine, 1921–29.

McCOSH, JAMES (Apr. 1, 1811–Nov. 16, 1894); b. Carskeoch, Scot. Educator, author. *The Laws of Discursive Thought* (1870); *The Scottish Philosophy* (1875); *Realistic Philosophy Defended in a Philosophic Series,* 2v. (1887); etc. President, College of New Jersey (now Princeton University), 1868–88. *See* William Milligan Sloane's *Life of James McCosh* (1896).

McCOWN, CHESTER CHARLTON (Nov. 26, 1877–1958); b. Orion, Ill. Methodist clergyman, educator, author. *The Promise of His Coming* (1921); *Genesis of the Social Gospel* (1929); *The Search for the Real Jesus* (1940); *Ladder of Progress in Palestine* (1943); *Remapping the Bible World* (ed., with H. G. May, 1949); *Man, Morals and History* (1958); etc. Prof. New Testament literature, Pacific School of Religion, 1914–36.

McCOY, HORACE (Apr. 14, 1897–1955); b. Pegram, Tenn. Editor, novelist. *They Shoot Horses, Don't They?* (1935); *No Pockets in a Shroud* (1937); *I Should Have Stayed Home* (1938); *Kiss Tomorrow Good-Bye* (1948); *Scalpel* (1952). Sports editor, Dallas *Journal,* 1919–30.

McCOY, SAMUEL [Duff] (Apr. 17, 1882–Apr. 7, 1964); b. Burlington, Ia. Journalist, author. *Tippecanoe* (1916); *Merchants of the Morning* (poems, 1919); *This Man Adams* (1928); *Nor Death Dismay* (1944); *Mystery at Pickle Point* (1948); *Mystery at Robber's Rock* (1950); etc.

McCRACKEN, HAROLD (Aug. 31, 1894–); b. Colorado Springs, Col. Explorer, lecturer, author. *Iglaome* (1930); *God's Frozen Children* (1930); *Alaska Bear Trails* (1931); *Pershing: The Story of a Great Soldier* (1931); *Beyond the Frozen Frontier* (1935); *Frederick Remington—Artist of the Old West* (1947); *Caribou Traveler* (1949); *Pirate of the North* (1953); *Winning of the West* (1955); *Story of Alaska* (1956); *Hoofs, Claws, and Antlers* (1958); *George Catlin and the Old Frontier* (1959); *Frederick Remington Book* (1966); *Roughnecks and Gentlemen* (1968); etc.

McCRADY, EDWARD (Apr. 8, 1833–Nov. 1, 1903); b. Charleston, S.C. Lawyer, historian. *The History of South Carolina,* 4v. (1897–1902).

McCROSSEN, VINCENT A[loysius] (Nov. 21, 1908–); b. Meshoppen, Pa. Educator. *The New Renaissance of the Spirit* (1949); *The Empty Room* (1955); etc. Prof. comparative literature and Russian, Boston College, since 1949.

McCULLAGH, JOSEPH BURBRIDGE (Nov. 1842–Dec. 31, 1896); b. Dublin, Ire. Editor, correspondent. With the *St. Louis Democrat,* 1859–60; the *Cincinnati Daily Gazette,* 1860–62; the *Cincinnati Commercial,* 1862–68; managing editor, the *Cincinnati Enquirer,* 1868; the *Chicago Republican,* 1868–71; editor, the *St. Louis Democrat,* 1871–73; the *St. Louis Daily Globe,* 1873–75; the *St. Louis Globe-Democrat,* 1875–96. *See* Walter B. Stevens's *Joseph B. McCullagh* in *Missouri Historical Review,* v. 25–28 (1930–34).

McCULLERS, CARSON [Mrs. Smith] (Feb. 19, 1917–Sept. 29, 1967). Novelist. *The Heart Is a Lonely Hunter* (1940); *Reflections in a Golden Eye* (1941); *The Member of the Wedding* (1946; play, 1950); *The Ballad of the Sad Cafe* (1951); *The Square Root of Wonderful* (play, 1958); *Clock Without Hands* (1961).

McCULLEY, JOHNSTON (Feb. 2, 1883–Nov. 23, 1958); b. Ottawa, Ill. Author. Pen names, "Harrington Strong," "George Drayne," "Raley Brien," "Frederic Phelps," "Rowena Raley." *Land of Lost Hope* (1908); *Captain Fly-By-Night* (1915); *The Mark of Zorro* (1920); *The Curse of Capistrano* (1920); *The Avenging Twins* (1923); *The Crimson Clown* (1927); *A Range Cavalier* (1933); *Rangeland Justice* (1934); *Canyon of Peril* (1935); *Don Peon* (1937); *Rose of the Rio Grande* (1937); *The Saga of Smoky Sarn* (1940); *Iron Horse Town* (1952); *Texas Showdown* (1953); etc. Has written more than fifty screenplays.

McCULLOCH, HUGH (Dec. 7, 1808–May 24, 1895); b. Kennebunk, Me. Statesman, author. *Men and Measures of Half a Century* (1888). Secretary of the Treasury, 1865–69; 1884–85.

McCULLOCH, HUGH (Mar. 9, 1869–Mar. 27, 1902); b. Fort Wayne, Ind. Poet. *The Quest of Heracles, and Other Poems* (1894); *Written in Florence: The Last Verses* (1902).

McCullough, Myrtle Reed. See Myrtle Reed.

McCURDY, IRWIN POUNDS (Mar. 23, 1856–1916); b. in Westmoreland Co., Pa. Presbyterian clergyman, educator, editor, author. *A Philological Discussion of the Works, Style and Language of Edgar Allan Poe* (1880); *Sacra Trinitas* (1881); *Lovely Lafayette, and Other Poems* (1889); etc. Compiler: *Centennial Hymns* (1888); *Christmas Carols and New Year Hymns* (1892); etc. Editor, the *Southwestern Observer,* 1885–87; etc. Prof. religion, Temple University, 1910–16.

McCUTCHEON, BEN FREDERICK (May 31, 1875–Aug. 27, 1934); b. Lafayette, Ind. Author. Pen name, "Benjamin Brace." *Sunrise Acres* (1905); *The Seventh Person* (1906).

McCUTCHEON, GEORGE BARR (July 26, 1886–Oct. 23, 1928); b. Lafayette, Ind. Novelist. *Graustark* (1901); *Castle Craneycrow* (1902); *Brewster's Millions* (under pen name, "Richard Greaves," 1902); *The Sherrods* (1903); *Beverly of Graustark* (1904); *Nedra* (1905); *Mary Midthorne* (1911); *The Prince of Graustark* (1914); *The Merivales* (1929).

McCUTCHEON, JOHN TINNEY (May 6, 1870–June 10, 1949); b. South Raub, Ind. Cartoonist, author. *Cartoons* (1903); *Bird Center Cartoons* (1904); *Congressman Pumphrey* (1907); *T. R. in Cartoons* (1910); *An Heir at Large* (1923); *Drawn from Memory* (autobiography, 1950); etc. Cartoonist, the *Chicago Tribune,* from 1903 (Pulitzer prize for cartoons, 1932).

McDONALD, CORNELIA [Peake] (1822–1909). Diarist. *A Diary with Reminiscences of the War and Refugee Life in the Shenandoah Valley, 1860–1865,* ed. by Hunter McDonald (1935).

McDONALD, ETTA AUSTIN BLAISDELL (Mar. 20, 1872–); b. Manchester, N.H. Author. *Child Life* (with Mary Frances Blaisdell, 1899); *Child Life in Many Lands* (1900); *Boy Blue and His Friends* (1907); *Manuel in Mexico* (1909); *Kathleen in Ireland* (1909); *Gerda in Sweden* (1910); *Betty in Canada* (1910); *The Kelpies* (1924); *My Garden of Stories* (1929); etc.

McDONALD, LAETITIA (Mrs. Wallace Irwin) (1890–); b. Louisville, Ky. Author. *A Lady Alone* (prod. 1927); *Young and Fair* (1933); *Silver Platter* (1934); *Golden Hammock* (1951).

McDOUGALD, ROMAN (d. June 3, 1960). Novelist. *The Deaths of Lora Karen* (1944); *Purgatory Street* (1946); *Lady Without Mercy* (1948); *Women under the Mountain* (1950); *The Blushing Monkey* (1953); etc.

McDougall, Frances Harriet Green. See Frances Harriet Whipple Green.

McDOUGALL, WILLIAM (1871–Nov. 28, 1938); b. in Lancashire, Eng. Educator, psychologist, author. *Physiological Psychology* (1905); *Social Psychology* (1908); *Pagan Tribes of Borneo* (1911); *Psychology* (1912); *Group Mind* (1920); *Janus* (1927); *Character and the Conduct of Life* (1927); *World Chaos: The Responsibility of Science* (1931); etc. Prof. psychology, Harvard University, 1920–27; Duke University, 1927–38.

McELHENEY, JANE (1836–Mar. 4, 1874); b. Charleston, S.C. Actress, author. Pen name, "Ada Clare." Known as "The Queen of Bohemia." *Only a Woman's Heart* (1866). *See* Albert Parry's *The Queen of Bohemia,* in the *American Mercury,* Sept. 1930, and his *Garrets and Pretenders* (1933).

McElrath & Bangs. New York. Publishers. Founded by Thomas McElrath and Lemuel Bangs. Published school texts and religious books. In 1841, McElrath became business manager of the *New York Tribune,* under Horace Greeley.

McELROY, JOHN (Aug. 25, 1846–Oct. 12, 1929); b. in Greenup Co., Ky. Soldier, editor, author. *Andersonville* (1879); *Si Klegg: His Development from a Raw Recruit to a Veteran* (anon., 1897); and other "Si Klegg" books; *The Struggle for Missouri* (1909). Editor, the *Toledo Blade,* 1874–84; the *National Tribune,* Washington, D.C., 1884–1929.

McELROY, MARGARET JULIA (July 27, 1889–); b. Newton, Ia. Author of children's books. *The Adventures of Johnny T. Bear* (1926); *Squirrel Tree* (with Jessica O. Younge, 1927); *Tatters* (with same, 1929); *Toby Chipmunk* (with same, 1931); etc.

McELROY, ROBERT M[cNutt] (Dec. 28, 1872–June 16, 1959); b. Perryville, Ky. Educator, author. *The Winning of the Far West* (1914); *Grover Cleveland: The Man and the Statesman,* 2v. (1923); *Levi Parsons Morton* (1930); *Jefferson Davis: The Unreal and the Real,* 2v. (1937); etc. Co-editor, *The Unfortified Boundary: A Diary of the First Survey of the Canadian-American Boundary* (1943). History dept., Princeton University, 1898–1925; Harmsworth prof., American history, Oxford University, 1925–38.

McEVOY, JOSEPH PATRICK (Jan. 10, 1895–Aug. 8, 1958); b. New York. Author. *Slams of Life* (poems, 1919); *Father Meets Son* (1937); *Charlie Would Have Loved This* (1956); etc.

McFARLAND, J[ohn] HORACE (Sept. 24, 1859–Oct. 2, 1948); b. McAlister, Pa. Printer, editor. Founder, Mt. Pleasant Press, Harrisburg, Pa., 1889, incorporated 1891 as the J. Horace McFarland Co., a press specializing in the printing of garden books. Editor, the *American Rose Annual,* 1916–43; the *American Rose Magazine,* 1933–42; and author of several books on roses and gardening subjects.

McFARLAND, RAYMOND (Apr. 15, 1872–); b. Lamoine, Me. Author. *Skipper John of the Nimbus* (1918); *Sons of the Sea* (1920); *The Sea Panther* (1928); *On the Roof of Labrador* (1935); *The Masts of Gloucester* (1937); *Sea Adventure* (1938); etc.

McFARLANE, ARTHUR EMERSON (Feb. 25, 1876–Apr. 11, 1945); b. Islington, Ont. Author. *Redney McGraw* (1909); *Great Bear Island* (1911); *Behind the Bolted Door* (1915).

McFEE, INEZ N. (Mrs. M. M. McFee) (Feb. 14, 1879–); b. Quasqueton, Ia. Author. *Little Tales of Common Things* (1918); *Boy Heroes in Fiction* (1920); *Girl Heroes in Fiction* (1920); etc.

McFEE, WILLIAM [Morley Punshon] (June 15, 1881–July 2, 1966); b. at sea. Marine engineer, novelist. *Ocean Tramp* (1908); *Aliens* (1914); *Casuals of the Sea* (1916); *Captain Macedoine's Daughter* (1920); *Command* (1922); *Race* (1924); *Sunlight in New Granada* (1925); *Pilgrims of Adversity* (1928); *The Life of Sir Martin Frobisher* (1928); *Sailors of Fortune* (1929); *North of Suez* (1930); *The Harbourmaster* (1931); *No Castle in Spain* (1933); *The Reflections of Marsyas* (poems, 1933); *The Beachcomber* (1935); *Sailor's Bane* (1936); *Derelicts* (1938); *Watch Below* (1940); *Spenlove in Arcady* (1940); *Ship to Shore* (1944); *In the First Watch* (autobiography, 1946); *The Adopted* (1952); etc.

"McFingal." Long poem by John Trumbull (1775–82). Burlesque on the Loyalists, and an espousal of Whig principles, written in Hudibrastic verse, with the Scotch Tory, McFingal, as the main character. Trumbull revised and augmented the poem for seven years, and it ran into many editions, including more than thirty pirated editions.

McGAFFEY, ERNEST (b. 1861); b. London, Ont. Lawyer, poet. *Poems of Gun and Rod* (1883); *Poems* (1895); *A California Idyl* (1899); *Sonnets to a Wife* (1901), augmented (1922); *Ballades and Idyls* (1931); *War* (1937); *Ballades* (1938).

McGARVEY, JOHN WILLIAM (Mar. 1, 1829–Oct. 6, 1911); b. Hopkinsville, Ky. Disciples clergyman, author. *Lands of the Bible* (1881); *Evidences of Christianity,* 2v. (1886–91); *The Standard Bible Commentary,* 4v. (with P. Y. Pendleton, 1905–08). Co-founder, *Apostolic Times,* 1868; conducted dept. in the *Christian Standard.*

McGIFFERT, ARTHUR CUSHMAN (Mar. 4, 1861–Feb. 25, 1933); b. Sauquoit, N.Y. Congregational clergyman, educator, author. *A History of Christianity in the Apostolic Age* (1897); *Protestant Thought before Kant* (1911); *Martin Luther* (1911); *A History of Christian Thought,* 2v. (1931–32); etc. Prof. church history, Union Theological Seminary, New York, 1893–1927; president, 1917–26.

McGIFFERT, ARTHUR CUSHMAN JR. (Nov. 27, 1892–); b. Cincinnati, O., son of Arthur Cushman McGiffert. Congregational clergyman, educator, author. *Jonathan Edwards* (1932). Editor: *Christianity as History and Faith* (1934); *Young Emerson Speaks* (1938); etc. President, Pacific School of Religion, Berkeley, Calif., 1939–45; Chicago Theological Seminary, 1946–58.

McGillycuddy Agent. By Julia B. McGillycuddy (1941). Biography of Dr. Valentine T. McGillycuddy, Indian agent and Western pioneer. Calamity Jane, Crazy Horse, California Joe, Custer, and Sitting Bull are among the many persons described in the narrative.

McGINLEY, PHYLLIS [Louise] (Mrs. Charles Hayden) (Mar. 21, 1905–); b. Ontario, Ore. Poet, author of children's books. *On the Contrary* (poems, 1934); *One More Manhattan* (poems, 1937); *Pocketful of Wry* (poems, 1940); *Husbands Are Difficult* (poems, 1941); *The Horse Who Lived Upstairs* (1944); *The Plain Princess* (1945); *Stones from a Glass House* (poems, 1946); *All Around the Town* (1948); *Small Wonder* (lyrics for revue, 1948); *The Most Wonderful Doll in the World* (1950); *Blunderbus* (1951); *The Emperor's Nightingale* (film narration, 1951); *The Horse Who Had His Picture* *in the Paper* (1951); *Make-Believe Twins* (1953); *Love Letters* (1954); *The Year Without a Santa Claus* (1957); *Merry Christmas, Happy New Year* (poems, 1958); *Times Three: Selected Verses from Three Decades* (1960; Pulitzer prize for poetry, 1961; *Boys are Awful* (1962); *The B Book* (1963); *A Little Girl's Room* (1963); *Sixpence in Her Shoe* (1964); *Wonderful Time* (1966); *A Wreath of Christmas Legends* (1967); *Saint-Watching* (1969); *Wonders and Surprise* (1968); etc.

McGINNIS, JOHN HATHAWAY (Dec. 21, 1883–); b. Carmichaels, Pa. Educator, editor. Editor, the *Southwest Review*, since 1927; lit. editor, the *Dallas News*, since 1923; Prof. English, Southern Methodist University, since 1916.

McGINNISS, JOE. Journalist, author. *Selling of the President, 1968* (1970).

McGIVERN, WILLIAM PETER. Author. *But Death Runs Faster* (1948); *Crooked Frame* (1952); *Seven File* (1956); *Night Extra* (1957); *Savage Streets* (1959); *The Road to the Snail* (1961); *The Caper of the Golden Bulls* (1966); *Lie Down I Want to Talk to You* (1967); etc.

McGlasson, Eva Wilder. See Eva Wilder Brodhead.

McGOVERN, JOHN (Feb. 18, 1850–Dec. 17, 1917); b. Troy, N.Y. Journalist, poet. *A Pastoral Poem, and Other Pieces* (1882); *David Lockwin, the People's Idol* (1891); *Poems* (1902); *The Right of Way* (1903); etc. Chief editorial writer, the *Chicago Herald*, 1887–89.

McGOVERN, JOHN TERENCE (Dec. 9, 1876–May 26, 1960); b. Albany, N.Y. Lawyer, sociologist, author. *Your Son and Mine* (1931); *Diogenes Discovers Us* (1933); *Lord Reading and His Cases* (1935); *Shrines in America* (1937).

McGOVERN, WILLIAM MONTGOMERY (Sept. 28, 1897–Dec. 12, 1964); b. New York. Educator, explorer, author. *To Lhasa in Disguise* (1924); *Jungle Paths and Inca Ruins* (1927); *The Early Empires of Central Asia* (1924); *The Early Empires of Central Asia* (1938); *From Luther to Hitler* (1941); *Radicals and Conservatives* (1958); etc. Co-author: *Essays on Individuality* (1958). Political science dept., Northwestern University, since 1929; prof., since 1936.

McGrant, Terence. Pen name of George Wilbur Peck.

McGRATH, THOMAS (Nov. 20, 1916–   ); b. near Sheldon, N.D. Author. *First Manifesto* (1940); *To Walk A Crooked Mile* (1947); *A Garland of Practical Poesy* (1949); *Witness to the Times* (1954); *Figures from a Double World* (1955); *The Gates of Ivory, The Gates of Horn* (1957); *Clouds* (1959); *Letter to an Imaginary Friend* (1962); *New and Selected Poems* (1964).

Mc GRAW, ELOISE JARVIS (Dec. 9, 1915–); b. Houston, Tex. Author. *Sawdust in His Shoes* (1950); *Crown Fire* (1951); *Moccasin Trail* (1952); *Pharaoh* (1958); *The Golden Goblet* (1961); *Greensleeves* (1968); etc.

McGraw-Hill Book Co. New York. Publishers. Founded in 1909 through the merger of the McGraw Publishing Company and the Hill Publishing Company. Whittlesey House, a subsidiary, was founded in 1930 to publish books of a literary nature; the imprint is now used for the firm's children's books. (Whittlesey was the family name of Mrs. James Herbert McGraw.) John A. Hill sold his printing establishment to Hal Marchbanks when he withdrew to join with McGraw, and this became the Marchbanks Press, devoted to fine printing. Harold W. McGraw, Jr. is president of McGraw-Hill. The firm publishes many technical and engineering books and school and college textbooks. In 1966 McGraw-Hill combined with the National Broadcasting Company and the American Broadcasting Company to enter the new field of educational technology. Bought *American Heritage* and *Horizon* in 1969.

McGUFFEY, WILLIAM HOLMES (Sept. 23, 1800–May 4, 1873); b. Claysville, Pa. Educator. Widely known for his *Eclectic Readers* for schools, which reached the fabulous sale

of 122,000,000 copies and had a great influence on the entire country. The printers of the McGuffey readers, all in Cincinnati, Ohio, have been: Truman and Smith, 1834–41; W. B. Smith, 1841–52; W. B. Smith & Co., 1852–63; Sargent, Wilson & Hinkle, 1863–68; Wilson, Hinkle & Co., 1868–77; Van Antwerp, Bragg & Co., 1877–90; American Book Co., after 1890. *See* Mark Sullivan's *Our Times*, v.2 (1932); Harvey C. Minnick's *William Holmes McGuffey and His Friends* (1936), and his *Old Favorites from the McGuffey Readers* (1936); Henry Ford's bibliography of his McGuffey collection in the *Colophon*, Spring 1936; *Publishers' Weekly*, Sept. 19, 1936.

McGUIRE, WILLIAM ANTHONY (July 9, 1885–Sept. 16, 1940); b. Chicago, Ill. Playwright. *The Walls of Wall Street* (prod. 1908); *The Divorce Question* (prod. 1912); *The Man Without a Country* (prod. 1916); etc. He wrote the scripts for the "Ziegfeld Follies," besides many movie scenarios, including "The Great Ziegfeld," "Lillian Russell," etc.

McHENRY, JAMES (Dec. 20, 1785–July 21, 1845); b. Larne, Ire. Poet, critic, novelist. Pen name "Solomon Secondsight." *The Pleasures of Friendship* (1822); *The Spectre of the Forest* (anon., 1823); *The Wilderness; or, Braddock's Times* (anon., 1823); *O'Halloran; or, The Insurgent Chief* (anon., 1824); *The Hearts of Steel* (anon., 1825); *The Usurper* (prod. 1827); *The Betrothed of Wyoming* (anon., 1830); *Meredith; or, The Mystery of Meschianza* (anon., 1831); etc. Founder, the *American Monthly Magazine*, Philadelphia, 1824. He wrote extensively for the *American Quarterly Review*.

McHugh, Hugh. Pen name of George Vere Hobart.

McHUGH, VINCENT (1904–). Author. *Touch Me Not* (1930); *Sing Before Breakfast* (1933); *Caleb Catlum's America* (1936); *I Am Thinking of My Darling* (1943); *Victory* (1947); *Primer of the Novel* (1950); *Edge of the World* (1953).

McILWAIN, CHARLES HOWARD (Mar. 15, 1871–); b. Saltsburg, Pa. Educator, author. *The American Revolution* (1923; Pulitzer Prize for American history, 1924); *The Growth of Political Thought in the West from the Greeks to the Middle Ages* (1932); *Constitutionalism and the Changing World* (1939); *Constitutionalism, Ancient and Modern* (1940); etc. Editor: *Wraxall's Abridgement of the New York Indian Records, 1678-1751* (1915); *Lombarde's Archeion* (with Paul L. Ward, 1956). History and government depts., Harvard University, from 1911; prof., 1916–46.

McILWAINE, SHIELDS (1902–). Author. *Southern Poor-White* (1939); *Memphis Down in Dixie* (1948); etc.

McINTOSH, MARIA JANE (1803–Feb. 25, 1878); b. Sunbury, Ga. Author. Pen name, "Aunt Kitty." *Blind Alice* (1841); *Conquest and Self-Conquest* (anon., 1843); *Woman an Enigma* (anon., 1843); *Praise and Principle* (anon., 1845); *Two Lives; or, To Seem and To Be* (1846); *Aunt Kitty's Tales* (1847); *Charms and Counter-Charms* (1848); etc.

McINTYRE, ALFRED ROBERT (Aug. 22, 1886–Nov. 28, 1948); b. Hyde Park, Mass. Publisher. With Little, Brown & Co., Boston, publishers, from 1907; president, from 1926.

McINTYRE, JOHN T[homas] (Nov. 26, 1871–May 21, 1951); b. Philadelphia, Pa. Novelist. *The Ragged Edge* (1902); *Street Singer* (1908); *Ashton-Kirk, Investigator* (1910); *Blowing Weather* (1923); *A Young Man's Fancy* (1925); *Shot Towers* (1926); *Slag* (1927); *Drums in the Dawn* (1932); *Steps Going Down* (1936); *Ferment* (1937); *Young Patriots at Lexington* (1949); etc.

McINTYRE, O[scar] O[dd] (Feb. 18, 1884–Feb. 14, 1938); b. Plattsburg, Mo. Journalist, short story writer, columnist. *White Light Nights* (1924); *Twenty-three Selected Stories* (1929); *Another Odd Book* (1931); *The Big Town* (1935). Conducted syndicated daily newspaper column "New York Day by Day," 1912–38, continued by Charles B. Driscoll, author of *The Life of O. O. McIntyre* (1938).

McKAY, CLAUDE (Sept. 15, 1890–May 22, 1948); b. Sunny Ville, Jamaica, B.W.I. Poet, novelist. *Spring in New Hampshire, and Other Poems* (1920); *Harlem Shadows* (collected poems, 1922); *Banjo* (1929); *Gingertown* (1932); *A Long Way from Home* (travel autobiography, 1937); *Harlem: Negro Metropolis* (1940); etc.

McKay, David, Company. New York. Publishers. Founded 1883, by David McKay (June 24, 1860–Nov. 21, 1918). He began his publishing career while still associated with Rees Welsh, retail booksellers, bringing out an edition of Walt Whitman's *Leaves of Grass*, which had been rejected by James R. Osgood & Co. In 1885 he published a set of Shakespeare's works. In 1888 he took over the business of H. C. Watts & Co., and in 1896 the publishing business of Charles De Silver & Sons. In the same year he absorbed the business of Edward Meeks, who had succeeded to the firm of E. Claxton & Co. In 1903 he purchased the American branch of George Routledge & Sons. The David McKay Company was incorporated, April 23, 1919. David McKay was succeeded by Alexander McKay. Kennett L. Rawson is now president. The firm has always featured beautifully illustrated children's books, by such artists as N. C. Wyeth and Willy Pogany. Now merged with Longmans, Green and Co. (q.v.).

McKAY, DONALD COPE (Feb. 14, 1902–Apr. 2, 1959); b. Salt Lake City, Utah. Educator. *The National Workshops* (1933); *The United States and France* (1951). Editor, translator: Alfred and Pierre Dreyfus: *The Dreyfus Case* (1937). Editor: *Essays on the History of Modern Europe* (1936); "Makers of Modern Europe," Harvard University Press series; "American Foreign Policy Library," etc.

McKAY, GEORGE L[eslie] (1895–); b. Columbus Grove, O. Bibliographer. *A Bibliography of the Writings of Sir Rider Haggard* (1930), augmented (1939); *A Bibliography of Robert Bridges* (1933); *American Book Auction Catalogues, 1713–1934* (1937); *A Register of Artists, Booksellers, Printers and Publishers in New York City, 1801–1810, 1811–1820* (1939–40); *Early American Currency* (1944). Compiler: *A Stevenson Library*, 5v. (1953–61). Curator of the Grolier Club since 1923; editor, publications of the Bibliographical Society of America, since Jan. 1940.

McKay, Kelvin. Pen name of Charles Stanley Strong.

McKAY, VERNON (Oct. 8, 1912–); b. Independence, Kan. Educator, author. *Africa in World Politics* (1962); *African Diplomacy* (1966). Professor of African Studies, Johns Hopkins University, since 1956.

McKEAN, THOMAS (Apr. 29, 1869–Feb. 7, 1942); b. Philadelphia, Pa. Playwright. *The Mermaid* (1907); *The Master Influence* (1907); *The Punishment* (1909); *The Mercy of Fate* (1910); *The Wife Decides* (1911).

McKEE, RUTH ELEANOR (Aug. 6, 1903–); b. Bardsdale, Calif. Author. *The Lord's Anointed* (1934); *After a Hundred Years* (1935); *Under One Roof* (1936); *Christopher Strange* (1941); *Storm Point* (1942); *Wartime Handling of Evacuee Property and Wartime Exile* (1946); etc.

McKEEVER, HARRIET BURN (Aug. 28, 1807–Feb. 7, 1886); b. Philadelphia, Pa. Educator, author. *Twilight Musings, and Other Poems* (1857); and numerous Sunday school stories.

McKELWAY, ST. CLAIR (Feb. 13, 1905–); b. Charlotte, N.C. Journalist, author. *Gossip: The Life and Times of Walter Winchell* (1940); *True Tales from the Annals of Crime and Rascality* (1954); *The Edinburgh Caper* (1962); *The Big Little Man from Brooklyn* (1969); etc. Editor and writer, *The New Yorker*.

McKENNEY, RUTH (Nov. 18, 1911–); b. Mishawaka, Ind. Author. *My Sister Eileen* (1938); *Industrial Valley* (1939); *The McKenneys Carry On* (1940); *Jake Home* (1943); *Loud Red Patrick* (1947); *Love Story* (1950); *Here's England* (with

Richard Bransten, 1950); *All About Eileen* (1952); *Far, Far from Home* (1954); *Mirage* (1956); etc.

McKEON, RICHARD PETER (Apr. 26, 1900–); b. Union Hall, N.J. Educator, author. *The Philosophy of Spinoza* (1928); *Freedom and History* (1952); *Thought, Action, and Passion* (1954); *The Freedom to Read* (with others, 1957); etc. Editor and translator: *Selections from Medieval Philosophers*, 2v. (1929–30); etc. Prof. philosophy, and dean, division of humanities, University of Chicago.

McKILLOP, ALAN DUGALD (May 24, 1892–); b. Lynn, Mass. Educator. Author: *Samuel Richardson, Printer and Novelist* (1936); *The Background of Thomson's "Seasons"* (1942); *The Early Masters of English Fiction* (1956); *The Castle of Indolence and Other Poems* (1961); etc. Editor: *James Thomson: Letters and Documents* (1958); etc. Dept. of English, Rice Institute, since 1930.

McKINLEY, CARLYLE (Nov. 22, 1847–Aug. 24, 1904); b. Newman, Ga. Editor, essayist, poet. *An Appeal to Pharaoh* (1889); *Selections from the Poems* (1904); etc. With the *Charleston News and Courier*, 1875–1904; assoc. editor, 1881–1904.

McKINLEY, WILLIAM (Jan. 29, 1843–Sept. 14, 1901); b. Niles, O. Twenty-fifth president of the United States. *See* Charles S. Olcott's *The Life of William McKinley* (1916). The greater part of his official papers are in the Library of Congress.

McKNIGHT, CHARLES (1826–1881). Author. *Old Fort Duquesne; or, Captain Jack, the Scout* (1873), republished as *Captain Jack, the Scout* (1878); *Our Western Border... One Hundred Years Ago* (1875); *Simon Girty, "The White Savage"* (1880).

McKNIGHT, GEORGE HARLEY (Apr. 24, 1871–); b. Sterling Valley, N.Y. Educator, author. *St. Nicholas* (1917); *English Words and Their Background* (1923); *Modern English in the Making* (1928); *Grammar of Living English* (with others, 1939); etc. Prof. English, Ohio State University, since 1907.

McKUEN, ROD (Apr. 29, 1933–); b. Oakland, Cal. Poet, composer, singer. *And Autumn Came* (1954); *Seasons in the Sun* (album, 1966); *Stanyan Street and Other Sorrows* (1966); *Listen to the Warm* (1967); *In Someone's Shadow* (1969); etc.

McLAUGHLIN, ANDREW CUNNINGHAM (Feb. 14, 1861–Sept. 24, 1947); b. Beardstown, Ill. Educator, author. *Lewis Cass* (1891); b. Beardstown, Ill. *A History of the American Nation* (1899); *America and Britain* (1918); *A Constitutional History of the United States* (1935); etc. Assoc. editor, *American Historical Review*, 1898–1914. Prof. history, University of Chicago, 1906–29.

McLaughlin, Charles W. *See* Willard Mack.

McLAUGHLIN, J[ames] FAIRFAX (Mar. 15, 1839–Dec. 1903); b. Alexandria, Va. Lawyer, author. *Bombastes Furioso Buncombe* (1862); *The American Cyclops* (poem, under pen name "Pasquino," 1868); *College Days at Georgetown, and other Papers* (1899); *Matthew Lyon* (1900); etc.

McLAUGHLIN, ROBERT (1908–); b. Chicago, Ill. Editor, author. *The Axe Fell* (1939); *The Side of the Angels* (1947); *Gayden* (with wife, prod. 1949); *The Walls of Heaven* (1961); *Heartland* (1967); etc. Staff, *Time*, since 1947.

McLAURIN, KATE L. (Mrs. Frederick Calvin). Actress, playwright. *The Least Resistance* (1916); *The Six-Fifty* (1921); etc.

McLAWS, LAFAYETTE (Miss). b. Augusta, Ga. Author. *Jezebel* (1902); *Maid of Athens* (1906); *The Welding* (1907); etc.

McLean, Sally Pratt. See Sarah Pratt Greene.

McLELLAN, C[harles] M[orton] S[tewart] (1865–Sept. 21, 1916); b. in Maine, moved to England in 1897. Playwright. Wrote the librettos to: *The Belle of New York* (under pen name, "Hugh Morton," prod. 1897); *The Pink Lady* (prod. 1911); *Oh! Oh! Delphine* (prod. 1912); *Around the Map* (prod. 1915); etc.

McLELLAN, ISAAC (May 21, 1806–Aug. 20, 1899); b. Portland, Me. Sportsman, poet. *The Fall of the Indian, with Other Poems* (1830); *Mount Auburn, and Other Poems* (1843); *Poems of the Rod and Gun; or, Sports by Flood and Field,* ed. by Frederick E. Pond (1886); *Haunts of Wild Game; or, Poems of Woods, Wilds, and Waters,* ed. by Charles Barker Bradford (1896).

McLoughlin Brothers. New York. Publishers. Founded 1828. Publishers of children's books until consolidated with Grosset and Dunlap.

McLUHAM, MARSHALL (July 21, 1911–); b. Edmonton, Alta. Communications specialist, educator, writer. *The Mechanical Bride* (with E. S. Carpenter, 1951); *Studies in Communications* (1960); *The Gutenberg Galaxy* (1962; Gov. General's literary award for critical prose, 1963); *Understanding Media, the Extensions of Man* (1964); *The Medium is the Massage: An Inventory of Effects* (with Quentin Fiore, 1967). Co-Editor, *Explorations,* 1953–59, editor, 1964–.

McLuhanism. A term derived from the name of Marshall McLuhan (q.v.), author of several works on mass media and informational technology (see *Information*). It came into use shortly after the publication of McLuhan's *Understanding Media* (q.v.), and refers to an attitude, rather than a doctrine or movement, which stresses the superiority, in a time of rapid technological change, of auditory, visual, kinetic, and tactile communication to conceptual communication through the printed word alone. The use of the term "McLuhanism" generally assumes that we are entering a post-industrial age, one based on the production and consumption not of goods and services but of information. Man is considered to be passing through a stage in evolution in which the electronic processing of non-verbal data has become part of his nature. The term is also popularly used to imply the end of five centuries of book culture.

McMAHAN, ANNA BENNESON (July 24, 1846–Nov. 1919); b. Quincy, Ill. Editor, author. *With Shelley in Italy* (1905); *With Byron in Italy* (1906); *Shakespeare's Christmas Gift to Queen Bess* (1907); etc. Editor: *Best Letters of Horace Walpole* (1890); *Best Letters of William Cowper* (1893); etc.

McMAHON, AMOS PHILIP (Aug. 14, 1890–June 21, 1947); b. Warren, O. Educator, author. *The Meaning of Art* (1930); *The Art of Enjoying Art* (1938); *Preface to an American Philosophy of Art* (1945); etc. Dept. of fine arts, New York University, from 1926.

McMANUS, BLANCHE (Mrs. Milburg Francisco Mansfield); b. in Louisiana. Artist, author. *The Voyage of the Mayflower* (1897); *Romantic Ireland,* 2v. (with husband, 1905); *Our Little Cousin* series, 8v. (1905–11); *American Women Abroad* (1911); etc. Compiler: *Bachelor Ballads* (1898); etc.

McMASTER, GUY HUMPHREYS (Jan. 31, 1829–Sept. 13, 1887); b. Clyde, N.Y. Jurist, poet, local historian. Pen name "John MacGrom." His best known poem was "Carmen Bellicosun ¹. His collected verse has never been published. See *Dictionary of American Biography,* v.12.

McMASTER, JOHN BACH (June 29, 1852–May 24, 1932); b. Brooklyn, N.Y. Historian. *History of the People of the United States,* 8v. (1883–1912); *Benjamin Franklin as a Man of Letters* (1887); *With the Fathers: Studies in American History* (1896); *Daniel Webster* (1902); *Life and Times of Stephen Girard* (1917); etc. Prof. American history, University of Pennsylvania, 1883–1920. He spent most of his life on his scholarly history of the American people.

McMeekin, Clark. Pen name used jointly by Dorothy Park Clark and Isabella McLennan McMeekin.

McMEEKIN, ISABELLA McLENNAN (Nov. 19, 1895–); b. Louisville, Ky. Poet, novelist. Co-author with Dorothy Park Clark, using together the pen name "Clark McMeekin": *Show Me a Land* (1940); *Reckon with the River* (1941); *Welcome Soldier* (1942); *Red Raskall* (1943); *Black Moon* (1945); *Gaudy's Ladies* (1948); *City of the Flags* (1950). Author: *Journey Cake* (1942); *Louisville, The Gateway City* (1946); *Kentucky Derby Winner* (1949); etc.

McMICHAEL, MORTON (Oct. 20, 1807–Jan. 6, 1879); b. Bordentown, N.J. Editor. Editor, the *Saturday Evening Post,* 1826–31; *Godey's Lady's Book,* 1842–46; also editor for short periods of the *Saturday Courier* and *Neal's Gazette.* Founder (with Joseph C. Neal and Louis A. Gody), the *Saturday News and Literary Gazette,* 1837. He and George R. Graham purchased the *Philadelphia North American* in 1847, and merged the *United States Gazette* with it.

McMILLEN, WHEELER (Jan. 27, 1893–); b. Ada, O. Author. *The Farming Fever* (1924); *The Young Collector* (1928); *Too Many Farmers* (1929); *New Riches from the Soil* (1946); *Land of Plenty* (1961); *Why the United States is Rich* (1963); *Possums, Politicians and People* (1964); *Bugs or People* (1965); *Fifty Useful Americans* (1965); *Farmers in the United States* (1966); etc. Editor: *Harvest: An Anthology of Farm Writing* (1964).

McMURRY, LIDA BROWN (b. Feb. 6, 1853); b. Kiantone, N.Y. Author of children's books. *Classic Stories for the Little Ones* (1892); etc. Editor: *Fifty Famous Fables* (1910); *Sunshine* (1920); etc.

McMURTRIE, DOUGLAS CRAWFORD (July 20, 1888–Sept. 29, 1944); b. Belmar, N.J. Typographer, bibliographer, historian of printing. *American Type Design* (1924); *The First Printers of Chicago* (1927); *The Golden Book* (1927); revised as *The Book* (1937); *Early Printing in New Orleans* (1929); *Jonathan Meeker, Pioneer Printer of Kansas* (1930); *The Beginnings of Printing in Utah* (1931); *Early Printing in Michigan* (1931); *Early Printing in Wisconsin* (1931); *Early Printing in Tennessee* (1933); *The Beginnings of Printing in Virginia* (1935); *A History of Printing in the United States* (1936); *The Beginnings of Printing in Arizona* (1937); *Indiana Imprints, 1804–1849* (1937); *Montana Imprints, 1864–1889* (1937); *Eighteenth Century North Carolina Imprints, 1749–1800* (1938); *Early Printing in Colorado* (1935); *Wings for Words: The Story of the Gutenberg Documents* (1941); *Louisiana Imprints* (1942); etc. National editor, American Imprints Inventory, 1937–41.

McMURTRY, LARRY [Jeff] (June 3, 1936–); b. Wichita Falls, Texas. Author. *Leaving Cheyenne* (1963); *Horseman, Pass By* (1961, filmed as *Hud*); *Moving On* (1970).

McNALLY, WILLIAM J[ames] (June 8, 1891–Apr. 23, 1967); b. New Richmond, Wis. Author. *The Barb* (1923); *Ink* (with T. J. Dillon, prod. 1927); *House of Vanished Splendor* (1932); *The Roofs of Elm Street* (1936); *Prelude to Exile* (prod. 1936).

McNAMARA, ROBERT CHARLES (May 28, 1881–Sept. 23, 1967); b. Redfield, N.Y. Publisher. With Scott, Foresman & Co., since 1908; pres., 1943–55.

McNaught's Monthly. New York. Magazine. Founded 1923, by Virgil V. McNitt, who had founded McNaught's Syndicate in 1920.

McNEAL, THOMAS ALLEN (Oct. 14, 1853–Aug. 7, 1942); b. in Marion Co., O. Author. *Tom McNeal's Fables* (1900); *When Kansas Was Young* (1922); *Stories by Truthful James* (1925).

McNEER, MAY YONGE (1902–). Author. *Covered Wagon* (1944); *The Story of Florida* (1947); *California Gold Rush*

(1950); *Little Baptiste* (1954); *America's Abraham Lincoln* (1957); *The Alaska Gold Rush* (1960); *America's Gold Rush* (1963); *America's Mark Twain* (1962); *Give Me Freedom* (1964); etc. Co-author (with husband, Lynd Kendall Ward): *Martin Luther* (1953); *Armed with Courage* (1957).

McNEILLY, MILDRED MASTERSON (Mrs. Glenn McNeilly) (May 28, 1910–); b. in Kittitas County, Wash. Author. *Heaven Is Too High* (1944); *Praise at Morning* (1947); *Each Bright River* (1950). Magazine mystery-story writer under pen names "Glenn Kelly" and "James Dewey."

McPHERSON, JAMES ALAN (1943–   ). Author. *Hue and Cry* (1969).

McPHERSON, JAMES LOWELL (Jan. 25, 1921–); b. Cincinnati, Ohio. Author. *Goodbye, Rosie* (1965).

McQuill, Thursty. Pen name of Wallace Bruce.

McRAE, MILTON ALEXANDER (June 13, 1858–Oct. 11, 1930); b. Detroit, Mich. Publisher, author. *Forty Years in Newspaperdom* (1924). Joined with Edward Wyllis Scripps in 1897 to found the Scripps-McRae League of Newspapers, now known as the Scripps-Howard Newspapers. He retired in 1908.

McSORLEY, EDWARD (July 6, 1902–Dec. 22, 1966); b. Providence, R.I. Novelist. *Our Own Kind* (1946); *The Young McDermott* (1949); *Kitty, I Hardly Knew You* (1959).

McSPADDEN, JOSEPH WALKER (May 13, 1874–Feb. 9, 1960); b. Knoxville, Tenn. Editor, author. *Light Opera and Musical Comedy* (1936); *Beautiful Hawaii* (1939). Editor: *Book of Holidays* (1917); *Famous Dogs in Fiction* (1921); *Indian Heroes* (1928); *Pioneer Heroes* (1929); *Storm Center* (1947); *How They Blazed the Way* (1959); etc.

McTeague. Novel by Frank Norris (1899). A significant contribution to naturalism in American literature. Story of the slow-witted McTeague, and his wife Trina, whose passion for thrift leads to domestic strife. Both are caught in sordid circumstances beyond their control. The villain of the story is Marcus Schouler.

McWILLIAMS, CAREY (Dec. 13, 1905–); b. Steamboat Springs, Colo. Editor, author. *Ambrose Bierce: a Biography* (1929); *Factories in the Field* (1939); *Brothers under the Skin* (1943); *Prejudice* (1944); *A Mask for Privilege: Anti-Semitism in America* (1948); *North from Mexico: The Spanish-Speaking People of the United States* (1949); *Witch Hunt: The Revival of Heresy* (1950); etc. Editor, *The Nation,* since 1955. Contributor, *Dictionary of American Biography.*

MEAD, EDWARD SHEPHERD (Apr. 26, 1914–); b. St. Louis, Mo. Author. *The Magnificent MacInnes* (1949); *Tessie, the Hound of Channel One* (1951); *How to Succeed in Business Without Really Trying* (prod. as musical comedy, Pulitzer Prize, 1952); *The Big Ball of Wax* (1954); *How to Get Rich in TV—Without Really Trying* (1956); *How to Succeed With Women Without Really Trying* (1957); *The Admen* (1958); *The Four Window Girl, or How to Make Money from Men* (1959); *Dudley, There is No Tomorrow; Then How About This Afternoon?* (1963).

MEAD, EDWIN DOAK (Sept. 29, 1849–Aug. 17, 1937); b. Chesterfield, N.H. Lecturer, author. *The Philosophy of Carlyle* (1881); *Martin Luther* (1884); *The Influence of Emerson* (1903); etc. Editor, the *New England Magazine,* 1889–1901.

MEAD, MARGARET (Dec. 16, 1901–); b. Philadelphia, Pa. Anthropologist, author. *Coming of Age in Samoa* (1928); *Growing Up in New Guinea* (1930); *Sex and Temperament in Three Primitive Societies* (1935); *From the South Seas* (1939); *And Keep Your Powder Dry* (1942); *Male and Female* (1949); *Soviet Attitudes Toward Authority* (1951); *Growth and Culture* (with Frances MacGregor, 1951); *Primitive Heritage* (with Nicholas Calas, 1953); *Themes in a French Culture* (1954); *Childhood in Contemporary Cultures* (with Martha

Wolfenstein, 1955); *People and Places* (1959); *Family* (with Ken Heyman, 1965); *Wagon and the Star: A Study of American Community Initiative* (with Muriel Brown, 1967); *The Small Conference: An Innovation in Communication* (with Paul Byers, 1968). Editor: *An Anthropologist at Work* (with Ruth Benedict, 1958).

MEAD, WILLIAM LEON (b. Apr. 27, 1861); b. Margaretville, N.Y. Author. *Sky Rockets* (poems, 1883); *How Words Grow* (1897), republished as *Word-Coinage* (1902); etc.

MEADER, STEPHEN WARREN (May 2, 1892–); b. Providence, R.I. Author. *The Black Buccaneer* (1920); *Longshanks* (1928); *King of the Hills* (1933); *Trap-Lines North* (1936); *The Long Trains Roll* (1944); *Jonathan Goes West* (1946); *Whaler Round the Horn* (1950); *Sabre Pilot* (1956); *Everglades Adventure* (1957); *The Voyage of the Javeline* (1959); *Snow on Blueberry Mountain* (1961); *A Blow for Liberty* (1965); *Topsail Island Treasure* (1966); *Keep 'Em Rolling* (1967); *The Cape May Packet* (1969); etc.

Meadow Grass. By Alice Brown (1895). Stories of New Hampshire.

MEADOWCROFT, WILLIAM HENRY (May 29, 1853–Oct. 14, 1937); b. Manchester, Eng. Aide and biographer of Edison. *The Boy's Life of Edison* (1911); *Edison: His Life and Inventions,* 2v. (with Frank Lewis Dyer and Thomas Commerford Martin, 1929).

Meaning of Truth, The. Essays on pragmatism by William James (1909).

MEANS, ELDRED KURTZ (Mar. 11, 1878–Feb. 19, 1957); b. in Taylor Co., Ky. Methodist clergyman, author. *The Squeeze Wheel* (1917); *E. K. Means* (1918); *More E. K. Means* (1919); *Further E. K. Means* (1921); *Tarrapin Toes* (1924); *Black Fortune* (1931); etc.

MEANS, FLORENCE CRANNELL (May 15, 1891–); b. Baldwinsville, N.Y. Author. *A Candle in the Mist* (1931); *Penny for Luck* (1935); *Tangled Waters* (1936); *The Singing Wood* (1937); *Adella Mary in Old New Mexico* (1939); *Across the Fluted Plain* (1940); *Whispering Girl* (1941); *Teresita of the Valley* (1943); *Peter of the Mesa* (1944); *Assorted Sisters* (1947); *The House Under the Hill* (1949); *Hetty of the Grande Deluxe* (1951); *Alicia* (1953); *Sagebrush George* (1956); *Borrowed Brother* (1958); *Emmy and the Blue Door* (1959); *Us Maltbys* (1966); *Our Cup Is Broken* (1969); etc.

MEANS, GARDINER COIT (June 8, 1896–); b. Windham, Conn. Economist. Author or co-author: *The Holding Company* (1932); *The Modern Corporation and Private Property* (1932); *The Structure of the American Economy* (1939); *Jobs and Markets* (1946); etc. Co-author: *Pricing Power and the Public Interest* (1962).

MEANS, PHILIP AINSWORTH (Apr. 3, 1892–Nov. 24, 1944); b. Boston, Mass. Educator, archaeologist, author. *A Survey of Ancient Peruvian Art* (1917); *Ancient Civilizations of the Andes* (1931); *Fall of the Inca Empire* (1932); *The Spanish Main* (1935); *Newport Tower* (1942); etc. Anthropology dept., Peabody Museum, Harvard University, 1921–27, etc.

MEARNS, DAVID C[hambers] (Dec. 31, 1899–); b. Washington, D.C. Librarian. *Largely Lincoln* (1961); *Long Remembered* (with Lloyd A. Dunlap, 1963); *Lincoln and the Gettysburg Address* (with others, 1964); etc. Editor: *The Lincoln Papers* (1948). Staff, Library of Congress, since 1918.

MEARNS, HUGHES (Sept. 28, 1875–Mar. 3, 1965); b. Philadelphia, Pa. Educator, author. *Richard, Richard* (1916); *The Vinegar Saint* (1919); *Creative Youth* (1925); *Lions in the Way* (1927); *The Creative Adult* (1940); etc. Education dept., New York University, from 1925.

MEARS, JOHN WILLIAM (Aug. 10, 1825–Nov. 10, 1881); b. Reading, Pa. Presbyterian clergyman, educator, editor, author. *The Beggars of Holland and the Grandees of Spain* (1867); *Heroes of Bohemia* (1874); etc. Co-editor, the *American Presbyterian,* 1860–65; editor and publisher, 1865–70. Prof. intellectual and moral philosophy, Hamilton College, 1871–81.

MEARS, LOUISE WILHELMINA (Mar. 12, 1874–); b. Beatrice, Neb. Educator, author. *The Hills of Peru* (1912); *America's Fairyland: The Hawaiian Islands* (1922); *The Life and Times of a Midwest Educator* (1944); *They Come and Go* (1955). Prof. geography, State Teachers College, Milwaukee, Wis., since 1912.

MEARS, MARY MARTHA (1876–); b. Oshkosh, Wis. Author. *Emma Lou: Her Book* (1896); *Breath of the Runners* (1906); *The Bird in the Box* (1910); *Rosamond the Second* (1910); etc.

MEARSON, LYON (Dec. 6, 1888–Jan. 9, 1966); b. Montreal, P.Q. Editor, novelist, playwright. *The Whisper on the Stair* (1924); *Footsteps in the Dark* (1927); *People Don't Do Such Things* (with Edgar M. Schoenberg, prod. 1927); *Phantom Fingers* (1928); *The French They Are a Funny Race* (1931); *Our Wife* (with Lillian Day, prod. 1933); *Murder by Appointment* (with Burnet Hershey, prod. 1936); etc.

Measure: A Critical Journal. Chicago. Quarterly. Founded 1949. Edited by Daniel J. Boorstin, David Grene, Robert M. Hutchins and others. Superseded *Human Affairs Pamphlets* (1945–47). Discontinued 1951.

Measure: A Journal of Poetry. New York. Monthly. Founded Mar., 1921. Expired June, 1926.

MECOM, BENJAMIN (b. Dec. 29, 1732); b. Boston, Mass., nephew of Benjamin Franklin. Printer. Manager of Benjamin Franklin's press at St. John, Antigua, B. W. I., 1752–56. Established his own business in Boston, 1757; moved to New York, 1763, and to New Haven, 1764. He printed *Father Abraham's Speech.* He also printed an enlarged edition of the New England Primer (1757); etc. *See* Wilberforce Eames's *The Antigua Press and Benjamin Mecom, 1748–1765* (1929).

Medea. Dramatic adaptation of Euripides' *Medea,* by Robinson Jeffers (1946).

Mediaeval Academy of America. Boston, Mass. Founded 1925, by the American Council of Learned Societies. Has published the quarterly *Speculum,* since 1926.

Medieval Mind, The. By Henry Osborn Taylor, 2v. (1911). Best known work of the author, noted for its literary style and scholarship. It re-creates the personalities and happenings which shaped the trend of medieval history, with emphasis on the Church.

MEDILL, JOSEPH (Apr. 6, 1823–Mar. 16, 1899); b. near St. John, N.B. Journalist. He bought an interest in the *Chicago Tribune* in 1855, and in 1874 obtained a majority of the stock, directing the newspaper until his death.

MEDINA, HAROLD RAYMOND (Feb. 16, 1888–); b. Brooklyn, N.Y. Judge. *Pleading and Practice under the New Civil Practice Act* (1922); *Cases and Materials on Jurisdiction of Courts* (1931); *Judge Medina Speaks* (1954); *Anatomy of Freedom* (1959); etc.

"Mediterranean, The." Poem by Allen Tate (1936).

Medium is the Message, The. A print and picture demonstration of the effects of modern mass media, by Marshall McLuhan and Quentin Fiore (1967).

MEDNICK, MURRAY (Aug. 24, 1939–); b. Brooklyn, N.Y. Playwright, poet. *Five plays* (1968); *The Hawk: An Improvisational Play* (with Tony Barsha, 1968); *The Hunter* (1968); *The Shadow Ripens* (1969).

MEDSGER, OLIVER PERRY (Nov. 1, 1870–); b. Jacob's Creek, Pa. Educator, naturalist, author. *Nature Rambles,* 4v. (1931–32); *Edible Wild Plants* (1939). Editor: Alice Rich Northrop's *Through Field and Woodland* (1924). Prof. nature education, Pennsylvania State College, 1934–37.

MEEK, ALEXANDER BEAUFORT (July 17, 1814–Nov. 1, 1865); b. Columbia, S.C. Editor, orator, essayist, poet. *The South West* (1840); *The Red Eagle: A Poem of the South* (1855); *Songs and Poems of the South* (1857); *Romantic Passages in Southwestern History* (1857); etc. His best known poem is "Balaklava."

MEEK, S[terner St.] P[aul] (Apr. 8, 1894–); b. Chicago, Ill. Author. *Jerry: The Adventures of an Army Dog* (1932); *Frog, the Horse That Knew No Master* (1933); *Frank, a Dog of the Police* (1935); *Dignity, a Springer Spaniel* (1937); *Rusty, a Cocker Spaniel* (1938); *Gustav, a Son of Franz* (1940); *Surfman* (1950); *Pagan, A Border Patrol Horse* (1951); *Rip, A Game Protector* (1952); *Pierre of the Big Top* (1956); *The Drums of Tapajos* (1961); *Troyana* (1961); etc.

MEEKER, ARTHUR (Nov. 3, 1902–); b. Chicago, Ill. Author. *American Beauty* (1929); *Strange Capers* (1931); *Vestal Virgin* (1934); *Sacrifice to the Graces* (1937); *The Ivory Mischief* (1942); *The Far Away Music* (1945); *Prairie Avenue* (1949); *The Silver Plume* (1952); *Chicago, with Love* (1955).

MEEKER, EZRA (Dec. 29, 1830–Dec. 3, 1928); b. Huntsville, O. Western pioneer, author. *Reminiscences of Puget Sound* (1906); *The Ox-Team; or, The Old Oregon Trail, 1852–1906* (1906), revised as *Ox-Team Days on the Oregon Trail* (1922); *Ventures and Adventures of Ezra Meeker; or, Sixty Years of Frontier Life* (1909), revised as *The Busy Life of Eighty-Five Years of Ezra Meeker* (1916); *Seventy Years of Progress in Washington* (1921); *Kate Mulhall: A Romance of the Oregon Trail* (1926); etc.

MEEKER, NATHAN COOK (July 12, 1817–Sept. 29, 1879); b. Euclid, O. Journalist, Indian agent, author. *Life in the West* (1868). Backed by Horace Greeley, he founded Union Colony in Colorado, a socialistic community.

MEERLOO, JOOST A[braham Maurits] (1903–). Psychoanalyst, author. *The Aftermath of Peace* (1946); *Patterns of Panic* (1950); *Conversation and Communication* (1952); *The Rape of the Mind* (1956); *Dance: From Ritual to Rock and Roll, Ballet to Ballroom* (1960); *That Difficult Peace* (1961); *Justice and Injustice* (with Edmund Bergler, 1963); *Illness and Cure* (1964); *Unobtrusive Communication* (1965); *Mental First Aid* (1966); *Suicide and Mass Suicide* (1968); *Creativity and Eternization: Essays on the Creative Instinct* (1968); etc.

MEGRUE, ROI COOPER (June 12, 1883–Feb. 27, 1927); b. New York. Playwright. *Under Cover* (prod. 1914); *It Pays to Advertise* (with Walter Hackett, prod. 1914); *Under Fire* (prod. 1915); *Potash and Perlmutter in Society* (with Montague Glass, prod. 1915); *Seven Chances* (prod. 1916); *Honors Are Even* (prod. 1921); etc.

MEHDEVI, ANNE [Sinclair] Author. *Persian Adventure* (1953); *From Pillar to Post* (1956); *Don Chato* (1959); *The Leather Hand* (1961); *Rubies of the Red Sea* (1963); *Persia Revisited* (1964); *Persian Folk and Fairy Tales* (1965); *Parveen* (1969).

MEIGS, CORNELIA [Lynde] (Dec. 6, 1884–); b. Rock Island, Ill. Author. *Kingdom of the Winding Road* (1915); *Master Simon's Garden* (1916); *Rain on the Roof* (1925); *The Trade Wind* (1927); *Swift Rivers* (1932); *Invincible Louisa: The Story of Little Women* (1933); *The Covered Bridge* (1936); *The Scarlet Oak* (1939); *The Violent Men* (1949); *The Dutch Colt* (1952); *A Critical History of Children's Literature* (with others, 1953); *Fair Wind to Virginia* (1955); *Wild Geese Flying* (1957); etc.

MEIGS, JOSIAH (Aug. 21, 1757–Sept. 4, 1822); b. Middletown, Conn. Lawyer, editor. Founder (with Daniel Bowen and Eleutheros Dana), the *New Haven Gazette,* 1784; co-editor, 1784–87; editor, 1787–88. Prof. mathematics, Yale College, 1794–1800; University of Georgia, 1800–11; president, 1801–11. See William M. Meigs's *Life of Josiah Meigs* (1882).

MEIGS, WILLIAM MONTGOMERY (Aug. 12, 1852–Dec. 30, 1929); b. Philadelphia, Pa., great-grandson of Josiah Meigs. Lawyer, historian, biographer. *The Life of Josiah Meigs* (1881); *The Life of Charles Jared Ingersoll* (1897); *The Life of Thomas Hart Benton* (1904); *The Life of John Caldwell Calhoun,* 2v. (1917); *The Constitution and the Courts* (with Thomas H. Calvert, 3v. (1924); etc.

MEIKLEJOHN, ALEXANDER (Feb. 3, 1872–Sept. 14, 1964); b. Rochdale, Eng. Educator. *The Liberal College* (1920); *Freedom and the College* (1923); *The Experimental College* (1932); *What Does America Mean?* (1935); *Education Between Two Worlds* (1942); *Inclinations and Obligations* (1948); *Political Freedom* (1960); etc. Prof. philosophy, Brown University, 1897–1912; pres., Amherst College, 1912–1924.

MEIN, JOHN. Bookseller, author. *Sagittarius's Letters and Political Speculations* (anon., 1775); etc. Founder (with John Fleming), the *Boston Chronicle,* Dec. 21, 1767. His bookstore in Boston boasted 10,000 volumes long before the Revolution. He started a circulating library in 1765.

MEINE, FRANKLIN JULIUS (1896–). Author. *Mike Fink, King of the Mississippi Keelboatmen* (with Walter Blair, 1933). Editor: *Tall Tales of the Southwest* (1930); *Great Leaders* (with H. G. Warren, 1938); *Half Horse, Half Alligator: The Growth of the Mike Fink Legend* (with Walter Blair, 1956). Editor in chief: *American People's Encyclopedia,* 20v. (1952).

MEISSNER, SOPHIE RADFORD (b. Nov. 17, 1854); b. Morristown, N.J. Author. *The Terrace of Mon Désir* (1889); *A Tcherkess Prince* (1892); *Old Naval Days* (1920); etc.

MELCHER, FREDERIC GERSHOM (Apr. 12, 1879–Mar. 4, 1963); b. Malden, Mass. Editor, lecturer. With Lauriat & Co., Boston, 1895–1913; W. K. Stewart Co., Indianapolis, 1913–18; co-editor, *Publishers' Weekly,* 1918–58; chairman, R. R. Bowker & Co., since 1959. A founder, Children's Book Week, in 1919; established John Newbery Medal, Caldecott Medal.

MELINE, JAMES FLORANT (1811–Aug. 14, 1873); b. Sackett's Harbor, N.Y. Critic, author. *Two Thousand Miles on Horseback* (1867); *Mary Queen of Scots and Her Latest English Historian* (1872); etc.

MELISH, JOHN (June 13, 1771–Dec. 30, 1822); b. Methven, Perth., Scot. Cartographer, traveler, author. *Travels in the United States of America in the Years 1806 & 1807, and 1809, 1810 & 1811,* 2v. (1812); *Description of the Roads in the United States* (1814); etc.

MELLEN, GRENVILLE (June 19, 1799–Sept. 5, 1841); b. Biddeford, Me. Poet. *Sad Tales and Glad Tales* (under pen name, "Reginald Reverie," 1828); *The Martyr's Triumph; Buried Valley; and Other Poems* (1833). His manuscripts are in the Maine Historical Society Library.

MELLEN, IDA M. (Jan. 9, 1877–); b. New York. Biologist, author. *Fishes in the Home* (1927); *The Young Folks' Book of Fishes* (1927); *A Practical Cat Book* (1931); *The Science and the Mystery of the Cat* (1940); *Twenty Little Fishes* (1942); *The Wonder World of Fishes* (1951); *The Natural History of the Pig* (1952); etc. Aquarist, New York Aquarium, 1916–29.

MELLETT, JOHN CALVIN (Aug. 4, 1888–); b. Elwood, Ind. Author. Pen name, "Jonathan Brooks." *High Ground* (1928); *Ink: A Novel* (1930); *Varsity Jim* (1939); etc.

MELMAN, SEYMOUR (Dec. 30, 1907–); b. New York. Educator, author. *Decision Making and Productivity* (1958); *Peace Race* (1962); *Our Depleted Society* (1965); *Pentagon Capitalism: The Political Economy of War* (1970). Editor: *Dynamic Factors in Industrial Productivity* (1956); *Inspection for Disarmament* (1958); *Disarmament, its Politics and Economics* (1963); etc. Professor of industrial engineering, Columbia University.

Meloney, Franken. Pen name used jointly by William Brown Meloney and his wife, Rose Franken.

MELONEY, MARIE MATTINGLY (Mrs. William Brown Meloney); (d. June 23, 1943); b. Bardstown, Ky. Editor, *Woman's Magazine,* 1914–20; *The Delineator,* 1920–26; the *New York Herald Tribune Sunday Magazine,* from 1926; *This Week* magazine, from 1934.

MELONEY, WILLIAM BROWN (June 6, 1878–Dec. 7, 1925); b. San Francisco, Calif. Editor, author. *Graft* (prod. 1911); *The Girl of the Golden Gate* (1913); *The Heritage of Tyre* (1916); *Where Do We Go from Here?* (1919); etc. With the *New York World,* 1901–08; also several other San Francisco and New York newspapers.

MELONEY, WILLIAM BROWN (May 3, 1905–May 4, 1971); b. New York, son of William Brown Meloney and Marie Mattingly Meloney. Author. *Rush to the Sun* (1937); *In High Places* (1939); also, with wife, Rose Franken, using the joint pen name "Franken Meloney": *Call Back Love* (1937); *Strange Victory* (1939); *When Doctors Disagree* (1940); *American Bred* (1941); *Mooney* (1952); *Many Are the Travelers* (1954).

MELTON, WIGHTMAN FLETCHER (Sept. 26, 1867–Nov. 10, 1944); b. Ripley, Tenn. Educator, author. *The Preacher's Son* (1894); *The Rhetoric of John Donne's Verse* (1903); *Chimes of Oglethorpe* (poems, 1933); etc. Editor: *Poems of Trees,* 8v. (1932–40). Editor, *Bozart,* 1933–35. Prof. English language, Emory University, 1908–24.

MELVILLE, HERMAN (Aug. 1, 1819–Sept. 28, 1891); b. New York. Author. *Typee* (1846); *Omoo* (1847); *Mardi* (1849); *Redburn* (1849); *White-Jacket* (1850); *Moby-Dick* (1851), published in England as *The Whale; Pierre* (1852); *Israel Potter* (1855); *The Piazza Tales* (1856); *The Confidence Man* (1857); *Battle-Pieces* (1866); *Clarel: A Poem and a Pilgrimage in the Holy Land,* 2v. (1876); *John Marr and Other Sailors* (1888); *Timoleon* (1891); *The Works,* 16v. (1922–24); *The Apple-Tree Table* (1922); *Journal Up the Straits,* ed. by Raymond M. Weaver (1935); *Journal of a Visit to London and the Continent* (1948); *Journal of a Visit to Europe and the Levant* (1955); *The Complete Writings of Herman Melville,* known as the Northwestern-Newbury Edition, is under the editorship of Harrison Hayford and Hershel Parker. See Raymond M. Weaver's *Herman Melville* (1921); Lewis Mumford's *Herman Melville* (1929); *Family Correspondence of Herman Melville, 1830–1904,* ed. by Victor Hugo Palsits (1929); Richard Chase's *Herman Melville: A Critical Study* (1949); Newton Arvin's *Herman Melville* (1950); Jay Leyda's *The Melville Log,* 2v. (1951); Lawrence R. Thompson's *Melville's Quarrel with God* (1952); Warner Berthoff's *The Example of Melville* (1962); Hershel Parker's *The Recognition of Herman Melville* (1967).

Member of the Wedding, A. Novel by Carson McCullers (1946). A pre-adolescent Southern girl vibrant with anticipation before the wedding of her brother. The wedding means, however, her isolation from his life.

Memoirs of a Superfluous Man. By Albert Jay Nock (1943). Essays on the economic, political, and sociological problems of the times.

Memoirs of Hecate County. Collection of stories by Edmund Wilson (1946). The lives of various people in the intellectual circles of New York and its suburbs.

Memoirs of the Administrations of Washington and John Adams. By Oliver Wolcott, 2v. (1846). Important for history of the Federalist party and of early American politics.

"Memoranda." A department in *The Galaxy,* conducted by "Mark Twain."

Memphis Commercial Appeal. Memphis, Tenn. Newspaper. Founded 1840, by Henry Van Pelt, as the *Appeal.* Moved to Mississippi and Georgia during the Civil War, returning to Memphis in 1865. In 1894, absorbed the *Avalanche;* in the same year, it was bought by the *Commercial* and became the *Commercial-Appeal.* Purchased by the Scripps-Howard chain in 1936. F. R. Ahlgren is editor. Paul Flowers is book review editor.

Memphis Press-Scimitar. Memphis, Tenn. Newspaper. The weekly *Scimitar,* founded 1880; became a daily in 1883. Merged with the *News* (founded 1902) in 1904, as the *News-Scimitar.* The *Press* founded 1906, merged with the *News-Scimitar* in 1926 under present name. Charles H. Schneider is editor. Edwin Howard is book review editor.

Men, Women, and Dogs. By James Thurber (1943).

Men of the Old Stone Age. By Henry Fairfield Osborn (1915). Popular account of man's slow development from anthropoid progenitors to the crude society which existed just before the dawn of the modern European races. It ran into many editions.

Men Who Make Our Novels. By C. C. Baldwin (1924). A study of contemporary American novelists.

Men without Women. Short stories by Ernest Hemingway (1927). Contains *The Undefeated,* story of a bullfighter past his prime; *The Killers,* a gangster story; and *Fifty Grand,* the story of a boxer who agrees to a dishonest transaction.

MENCKEN, H[enry] L[ouis] (Sept. 12, 1880–Jan. 29, 1956); b. Baltimore, Md. Editor, essayist, critic. *Ventures into Verse* (1903); *George Bernard Shaw: His Plays* (1905); *The Philosophy of Friedrich Nietzsche* (1908); *A Book of Prefaces* (1917); *The American Language* (1919; supplements, 1945, 1948); *Prejudices,* 6 series (1919–1927); *The American Credo* (with George Jean Nathan, 1920); *Treatise on Right and Wrong* (1934); *Happy Days, 1880–1892* (autobiography, 1940); *Newspaper Days, 1899–1906* (1941); *Heathen Days, 1890–1936* (1943); *Generally Political* (1944); *A Mencken Crestomathy* (1949); *A Carnival of Buncomb* (1956); *Notebooks* (1956); *Prejudices: A Selection* (1958). On staff of the *Baltimore Sun,* 1906–10; the *Baltimore Evening Sun,* 1910–16, 1918–35; both papers, from 1936; lit. critic, the *Smart Set,* 1908–23; co-editor, 1914–23; editor, the *American Mercury,* 1924–33. *See* William R. Manchester's *Disturber of the Peace: The Life of H. L. Mencken* (1951); Charles Angoff's *H. L. Mencken* (1956); *Letters,* ed. by Guy J. Forgue (1961); M. K. Singleton's *H. L. Mencken and The American Mercury* (1962); William H. Nolte's *H. L. Mencken, Literary Critic* (1966); Sara Mayfield's *The Constant Circle: H. L. Mencken and His Friends* (1968).

MENCKEN, SARA POWELL HAARDT (Mrs. Henry Louis Mencken) (Mar. 1, 1898–May 31, 1935); b. Montgomery, Ala. Author. *The Making of a Lady* (1931).

"Mending Wall." Poem by Robert Frost in his *North of Boston* (1915).

MENKEN, ADAH ISAACS (June 15, 1835–Aug. 10, 1868); b. New Orleans, La. Actress, poet. *Infelicia* (1868). Her salons in London and San Francisco drew such personages as Dickens, Swinburne, Charles Reade, Burne-Jones, Mark Twain, Bret Harte, and Joaquin Miller.

MENNINGER, KARL AUGUSTUS (July 22, 1893–); b. Topeka, Kan. Psychiatrist. *Why Men Fail* (with others, 1918); *The Human Mind* (1930); *Man Against Himself* (1938); *Love Against Hate* (with wife, 1942); *Manual for Psychiatric Case Study* (1952); *Theory of Psychoanalytic Technique* (1958); *A Psychiatrist's World* (1959); *The Vital Balance* (1963); *The Crime of Punishment* (1968); etc.

MENNINGER, WILLIAM CLAIRE (Oct. 15, 1899–Sept. 6, 1966); b. Topeka, Kan. Psychiatrist. *Handbook for Skippers* (1934); *Psychiatry in a Troubled World* (1948); *You and Psychiatry* (with Munro Leaf, 1948); *Psychiatry: Its Evolution and Present Status* (1948); etc.

Menorah. New York. Jewish monthly. Founded 1886, by Benjamin Franklin Peixotto. Expired 1907.

Mentor, The. New York. Weekly magazine. Founded 1913. William David Moffat was editor, 1912–29. In June, 1930, it absorbed the *World Traveler* and became the *Mentor and World Traveler.* Expired 1931.

Mercantile libraries. Around 1820 a number of libraries were founded for the benefit of working men, apprentices and merchants. They were designed to promote education, and lectureships were a part of the program. Mercantile libraries were founded in Boston, 1820 (absorbed by the Boston Public Library in 1877); in New York, 1820; in Philadelphia, 1821; in Cincinnati, 1835; in Baltimore, 1839; in St. Louis, 1846; in Pittsburgh, 1845 (expired c. 1899); in Brooklyn, 1857 (absorbed by the Brooklyn Public Library in 1902). Those in New York and San Francisco have grown into large institutions.

MERCEIN, ELEANOR (Mrs. Robert Morrow Kelly, Jr.) (Aug. 30, 1880–); b. Milwaukee, Wis. Novelist. *Kildares of Storm* (1916); *The Mansion House* (1925); *Basquerie* (1927); *The Book of Bette* (1928); *Nacio* (1931); *Sounding Harbors* (1935); etc.

MERCER, CHARLES E. (July 12, 1917–). Author. *Narrow Ledge* (1951); *Here Comes a Time* (1955); *Rachel Cade* (1956); *The Drummond Tradition* (1957); *Enough Good Men* (1960); *Pilgrim Strangers* (1961); *Beyond Bojador* (1965); *Promise Morning* (1966); *Let's Go to Europe* (1968); *The Minister* (1969); etc.

Mercersburg Review. Philadelphia, Pa. Theological and literary periodical. Founded 1849, as a bi-monthly at Marshall (now Franklin and Marshall) College. Became quarterly in 1853. Expired 1926.

"Merchants from Cathay." Poem by William Rose Benét (1913).

MERCIER, ALFRED (June 3, 1816–May 12, 1894); b. McDonogh, La. Author of poems, novels, plays in French. *L'Habitation Saint-Ybars* (1881); *Lidia* (1887); *Émile des Ormiers* (1891). He founded, Jan. 12, 1876, a French literary society in New Orleans called *L'Athénée Louisianais,* which published *Compte Rendus,* a periodical which contains the best of the French literature written in Louisiana of the period.

MERCIER, HENRY JAMES. Author. *Life in a Man-of-War; or, Scenes in "Old Ironsides" during Her Cruise in the Pacific* (with William Gallop, 1841).

Mercy Philbrick's Choice. Novel by Helen Hunt Jackson (1876), published anonymously as the first in the *No Name Series.* Part of the story is set in Amherst, Mass., and was thought by many to be based on the life of Emily Dickinson, friend of the author's.

MEREDITH, SCOTT (Nov. 24, 1923–   ); b. New York. Authors' representative, editor, author. *Writing to Sell* (1950); *Writing for the American Market* (1960); *The Face of Comedy* (1961); *George S. Kaufman: A Biography* (1965). Editor of several anthologies.

MEREDITH, WILLIAM MORRIS (1919–). Poet. *Love Letters from an Impossible Land* (1944); *Ships and Other Figures* (1948); *Open Sea and Other Poems* (1958); *Shelley* (1962); *The Wreck of the Thresher and Other Poems* (1964); Translator: *Alcools* (1964); etc.

Meredith Corporation. Des Moines, Ia. Publishers. Founded 1961. Acquired Channel Press, a religious publishing house, in 1964. Also owns Better Homes and Gardens Books; New Century, learning and information systems; Meredith Press Books; Appleton-Century-Crofts; Duell, Sloan and Pearce; and other concerns.

MERGENDAHL, CHARLES [Henry] (Feb. 23, 1919–1959); b. Lynn, Mass. Novelist. *Don't Wait Up for Spring* (1944); *His Days Are as Grass* (1946); *This Spring of Love* (1948); *It's Only Temporary* (1950); *With Kisses Four* (1954); *Bramble Bush* (1958); *The Next Best Thing* (1960).

MERINGTON, MARGUERITE, b. Stoke Newington, Eng. Playwright, novelist. *Captain Lettarblair* (prod. 1891); *Daphne; or, The Pipes of Arcadia* (1896); *Love Finds the Way* (prod. 1898); *Scarlet of the Mounted* (1906); *Holiday Plays* (1910); etc.

MERIWETHER, ELIZABETH AVERY (1824–Nov. 4, 1917); b. Bolivar, Tenn. Mother of Lee Meriwether. Author. *The Ku-Klux Klan* (1877); *The Master of Red Leaf* (1880); *Black and White* (1883); *The Sowing of Swords* (1910); etc.

MERIWETHER, LEE (Dec. 25, 1862–Mar. 12, 1966); b. Columbus, Miss. Lawyer, author. *A Tramp Trip* (1887); *The Tramp at Home* (1889); *Afloat and Ashore on the Mediterranean* (1892); *Miss Chunk* (1899); *Seeing Europe by Automobile* (1911); *War Diary of a Diplomat* (1919); *My Yesteryears: An Autobiography* (1942); *Afterthoughts* (1945); *Jim Reed—Senatorial Immortal* (1948); etc. Special agent of the United States in Europe during the First World War.

MERK, FREDERICK (Aug. 15, 1887–); b. Milwaukee, Wis. Educator. *List of References on the History of the West* (with Frederick J. Turner, 1922); *Albert Gallatin and the Oregon Problem* (1950); *Manifest Destiny and Mission in American History* (1963); *The Monroe Doctrine and American Expansionism 1843–1849* (1966); *The Oregon Question* (1967); etc. Editor: *Fur Trade and Empire—George Simpson's Journal* (1931); etc. Dept. of history, Harvard University, since 1921.

"Merlin." Poem by Ralph Waldo Emerson (1847). An expression of the author's creed.

MERRIAM, CHARLES EDWARD (Nov. 15, 1874–Jan. 8, 1953); b. Hopkinton, Ia. Educator, author. *History of American Political Theories* (1903); *American Party System* (1922); *The Making of Citizens* (1931); *Political Power* (1934); *The Role of Politics in Social Change* (1936); *Prologue to Politics* (1939); *What Is Democracy?* (1941); *Systematic Politics* (1945); etc. Dept. political science, University of Chicago, from 1900.

MERRIAM, CHARLES (Nov. 31, 1806–July 9, 1887); b. West Brookfield, Mass. Publisher. Founder, with brother, George, of the G. and C. Merriam Company (q.v.).

MERRIAM, C[linton] **HART** (Dec. 5, 1855–Mar. 19, 1942); b. New York. Naturalist, author. *Totemism in California* (1908); *G. K. Gilbert, Geologist* (1918); *Baird, the Naturalist* (1924); *William Healey Dall* (1927); and many books on natural history, geology, American Indians, etc.

MERRIAM, EVE (July 19, 1916–   ); b. Philadelphia, Pa. Poet, author. *Family Circle* (1946); *Tomorrow Morning* (1951); *Real Book About Franklin D. Roosevelt* (1952); *Montgomery, Alabama, Money, Mississippi and Other Places* (1956); *The Double Bed from the Feminine Side* (1958); *The Voice of Liberty* (1959); *Figleaf* (1960); *The Trouble with Love* (1961); *Basics* (1962); *After Nora Slammed the Door* (1964); *The Nixon Poems* (1970). Juveniles: *A Gaggle of Geese* (1960); *Mommies at Work* (1961); *There is No Rhyme for Silver* (1962); *It Doesn't Always Have to Rhyme* (1964); *A Little Rhyme* (1965). Recipient, Yale Younger Poets award, 1946.

Merriam, G. & C., Company. Springfield, Mass. Founded 1831, by George and Charles Merriam, who had been printers in West Brookfield, Mass. When Noah Webster died in 1843, the Merriams bought the exclusive rights to his *An American Dictionary of the English Language*, first published in 1828 in two volumes. A second edition appeared in 1840; this one came into the possession of the firm. A one-volume edition came out in 1847. In 1859 illustrations were introduced for the first time. In 1864 the famous Webster's "Unabridged" edition was published. The next complete revision was in 1890. Another revision appeared in 1909, called *Webster's New International Dictionary*, edited by William T. Harris, assisted by F. Sturges Allen, George Lyman Kittredge, John Livingston Lowes, and others. In 1934 William Allan Neilson, Thomas A. Knott, and others edited the "Second Edition" of this dictionary. The "Third Edition" appeared in 1961, edited by Philip B. Gove and others. This edition created a controversy because of the wide range of usage denoted acceptable. The *Webster's Collegiate Dictionary*, published in various editions since 1916, is based on the "Unabridged." The firm's name was changed to G. & C. Merriam & Company in 1882, and in 1892 incorporated as G. & C. Merriam Company. Gordon J. Gallan is president. A subsidiary of Encyclopaedia Britannica, Inc.

MERRIAM, GEORGE (Jan. 19, 1803–June 22, 1880); b. West Brookfield, Mass. Publisher. Founder, with brother, Charles, of the G. and C. Merriam Company (q.v.).

MERRIAM, JOHN CAMPBELL (Oct. 20, 1869–Oct. 30, 1945); b. Hopkinton, Ia. Paleontologist, educator, author. *Cave Exploration* (1906); *The Research Spirit in the Everyday Life of the Average Man* (1920); *Common Aims of Culture and Research in the University* (1922); *The Living Past* (1930); *Spiritual Values and Constructive Life* (1933); *The Carnegie Institution of Washington* (1938); etc. Paleontology dept., University of California, 1894–1920; president, Carnegie Institution, Washington, D.C., 1920–38.

MERRICK, ELLIOTT (May 11, 1905–); b. Montclair, N.J. Author. *True North* (1933); *From the Hill Look Down* (1934); *Ever the Winds Blow* (1936); *Frost and Fire* (1939); *Passing By* (1947).

MERRILL, FLORA, b. New York. Author. *Flush of Wimpole Street and Broadway* (1933); *Kippy of the Cavendish* (1934).

MERRILL, FRANCIS ELLSWORTH (May 21, 1904–); b. Ft. Dodge, Ia. Educator. *Social Problems on the Home Front* (1948); *Courtship and Marriage* (1949); *Society and Culture* (with H. W. Eldredge, 1957; rev. ed. 1969); etc. Prof. sociology, Dartmouth College, since 1935.

MERRILL, JAMES [Ingram] (Mar. 3, 1926–); b. New York. Author. *First Poems* (1951); *The Seraglio* (1957); *The Country of a Thousand Years of Peace* (1959); *Water Street* (1962); *Nights and Days* (1966, National Book Award, 1967); *The (Diblos) Notebook* (1965); *Violent Pastoral* (1965); *The Fire Screen* (1970). Plays: *The Immortal Husband* (1956); *The Bait* (1960).

MERRILL, STUART [Fitzrandolph] (Aug. 1, 1863–Dec. 1, 1915); b. Hempstead, L.I., N.Y. Author, poet, bohemian. *Poèmes* (1897); *Les Quatre Saisons* (1940); *Une Voix dans la Foule* (1909); *Prose et Vers* (1925); etc. Translator: *Pastels in Prose* (1890); See *Dictionary of American Biography*, v. 12 (1933).

MERRILL, WILLIAM PIERSON (Jan. 10, 1867–June 19, 1954); b. Orange, N.J. Presbyterian clergyman, author. *Faith and Sight* (1900); *Christian Internationalism* (1919); *Liberal Christianity* (1925); *Prophets of Dawn* (1927); *The Way* (1941); etc.

Merriman, Charles Eustace. Pen name used jointly by Wilder Dwight Quint and George Tilton Richardson.

MERRIMAN, ROGER BIGELOW (May 24, 1876–Sept. 7, 1945); b. Boston, Mass. Educator, historian. *Life and Letters of Thomas Cromwell*, 2v. (1902); *The Rise of the Spanish Empire*, 4v. (1918–34); *Six Contemporaneous Revolutions* (1938); *Suleiman the Magnificent* (1944). History dept., Harvard University, 1902–42.

MERRITT, ABRAHAM (Jan. 20, 1884–Aug., 1943); b. Beverly, N.J. Editor, author. *The Moon Pool* (1919); *The Ship of Ishtar* (1926); *The Face in the Abyss* (1931); *Dwellers in the Mirage* (1932); *Creep, Shadow* (1934); *The Story Behind the Story* (1942); *Black Wheel* (1948); etc. Editor, the *American Weekly,* from 1937.

Merry-Mount: A Romance of the Massachusetts Colony. By John Lothrop Motley, 2v. (1849). Published anonymously.

Merryman's Monthly. New York. Comic magazine. Founded 1863. Published by Jesse Haney. Expired 1877.

Merry's Museum. Boston, Mass. Monthly magazine for children. Founded 1841, by "Peter Parley" (Samuel G. Goodrich), as *Robert Merry's Museum.* Name changed 1851 to *Merry's Museum and Parley's Magazine.* Illustrated with woodcuts. Louisa M. Alcott edited the magazine, 1867–70. After several changes of subtitle, it expired in 1872.

MERSAND, JOSEPH (July 30, 1907–); b. Zbaraz, Austria. Author. *Your Vocabulary* (1934); *The Inferiority of Women, and Other Fairy Tales* (1937); *Lavender and Lipstick* (1938); *Contemporary American Dramatists* (1938); *Traditions in American Literature: A Study of Jewish Characters and Authors* (1939); *A Decade of Biographical Plays, 1928–1938* (1939); *American Drama* (1941); *The Play's the Thing* (1948); *Attitudes Toward English Teaching* (1961); *Index to Plays with Suggestions for Teaching* (1966); *Teaching the Drama in Secondary Schools,* 3v. (1969); etc. Editor: *Stories for Teen-agers* (with E. A. Burton, 1959).

MERTINS, [Marshall] LOUIS (Dec. 7, 1885–); b. in Jackson Co., Mo. Baptist clergyman, lecturer, autograph collector, poet. *The Wishing Gate* (1919); *The Sumac Trail* (1919); *The Covered Wagon* (1921); *The Baratarians* (1924); *The Intervals of Robert Frost* (with Esther Mertins, 1947); *Robert Frost: Life and Talks-Walking* (1965); etc. Owner of annotated collection of Robert Frost's works.

MERTON, ROBERT KING (July 5, 1910–); b. Philadelphia, Pa. Educator, author. *Social Theory and Social Structure* (1949; rev. ed., 1968); *The Focused Interview* (1956); *On the Shoulders of Giants* (1965); etc. Co-author: *Mass Persuasion* (1946). Editor: *Reader in Bureaucracy* (1965). Sociology dept., Columbia University, since 1941.

MERTON, THOMAS (Jan. 31, 1915–Dec. 10, 1968); b. Prades, Fr. Roman Catholic clergyman, author. *Thirty Poems* (1944); *A Man in the Divided Sea* (poems, 1946); *Figures for an Apocalypse* (poems, 1947); *The Seven Storey Mountain* (autobiography, 1948); *Exile Ends in Glory* (1948); *Seeds of Contemplation* (1949); *Waters of Siloe* (1949); *Tears of the Blind Lions* (poems, 1949); *What Are These Wounds?* (1950); *The Ascent to Truth* (1951); *Sign of Jonas* (1953); *Bread in the Wilderness* (1953); *Last of the Fathers* (1954); *No Man Is an Island* (1955); *The Living Bread* (1956); *The Silent Life* (1957); *The Strange Islands* (poems, 1957); *Thoughts in Solitude* (1958); *Secular Journal* (1959); *Selected Poems* (1959); *Disputed Questions* (1960); *The Behavior of Titans* (1961); *The New Man* (1961); *The Original Child Bomb* (1962). *See* Edward Rice's *The Man in the Sycamore Tree: The Good Times and Hard Life of Thomas Merton* (1970).

Merton of the Movies. Novel by Harry Leon Wilson (1922), dramatized for the stage by George Kaufman and Marc Connelly (prod. 1922). Merton Gill, grocery clerk in Illinois, goes to Hollywood to become a movie star. He finally plays the part of a cowboy, to him an ignoble role.

MERWIN, SAMUEL (Oct. 6, 1874–Oct. 17, 1936); b. Evanston, Ill. Novelist. *The Short Line War* (with Henry Kitchell Webster, 1899); *Calumet K* (with same, 1901); *The Road to Frontenac* (1901); *The Whip Hand* (1903); *The Citadel* (1912); *Anthony the Absolute* (1914); *Henry is Twenty* (1918); *The Passionate Pilgrim* (1919); *In Red and Gold* (1921); *Goldie Green* (1922); *Old Concord* (1922); *Silk* (1923); *Moment of Beauty* (1924); *Anabel at Sea* (1927); *Bad Penny* (1933); etc. Assoc. editor, *Success Magazine,* 1905–09; editor, 1909–11.

MERWIN, WILLIAM STANLEY (1927–). Poet. *A Mask for Janus* (1952); *Dancing Bears* (1954); *Green With Beasts* (1956); *Drunk in the Furnace* (1960); *Moving Target* (1963); *The Lice* (1969); etc.

MERZ, CHARLES (Feb. 23, 1893–); b. Sandusky, O. Editor, author. *The Great American Band Wagon* (1928); *The Dry Decade* (1931). Editor: *Days of Decision* (1941). With *The New York Times,* since 1931; editor, since 1938.

Message to Garcia, A. By Elbert Hubbard (1899). Inspirational essay based on the visit of Lieut. Andrew Summers Rowan, U.S.A., to Gen. Calixto Garcia in May, 1898, to obtain information about the Cuban Army.

MESSENGER, LILLIAN ROZELL (1843–1921); b. near Milburn, Ky. Poet. *Threads of Fate* (1874); *Fragments from an Old Inn* (1885); *The Vision of Gold, and Other Poems* (1886).

Messer Marco Polo. Short novel by Donn Byrne (1921). Story of the love of the young Marco Polo and the Chinese princess Golden Bells.

Messner, Julian, Inc. New York. Publishers. Founded 1933, by Julian Messner and his wife, Kathryn G. Messner. Julian Messner was associated with Horace Liveright for many years. The firm's juvenile literature department is a feature. Now a division of Simon and Schuster (q.v.).

MESTAYER, WILLIAM AYRES (June 8, 1844–Nov. 21, 1896); b. (Haupt or Houpt) Philadelphia, Pa. Actor, playwright. *The Tourists in a Pullman Palace Car* (prod. 1879?); *We, Us and Co.* (prod. 1884); *The Kitty;* etc.

METALIOUS, GRACE (d. Feb. 25, 1964). Novelist. *Peyton Place* (1956); *Return to Peyton Place* (1959); *The Tight White Collar* (1960); etc.

Metamora; or, the Last of the Wampanoags. A play by John Augustus Stone (prod. 1829). It was burlesqued by John Brougham in his *Metamora; or, The Last of the Pollywogs* (prod. 1847).

Metaphysical Club. Founded at Cambridge, Mass. in the 1870's. It met fortnightly and had among its members, Oliver Wendell Holmes the younger, John Fiske, Francis E. Abbot, and Charles Sanders Peirce. The latter's philosophy, known as pragmatism, grew out of the discussions of the Metaphysical Club.

Metcalf, George. See George Metcalf Johnson.

METCALF, JOHN CALVIN (Aug. 7, 1865–Sept. 9, 1949); b. in Christian Co., Ky. Educator, author. *History of English Literature* (1912); *American Literature* (1914); *The Stream of English Biography* (1930); *De Quincey: A Portrait* (1940); *Know Your Shakespeare* (1949); etc. Editor: *The Literary World,* 3v. (1919); *The Enchanted Years: A Book of Contemporary Verse* (with James S. Wilson, 1921); etc. Prof. English, University of Virginia, 1917–40; dean, Graduate School, 1923–37.

METCALF, KEYES DeWITT (Apr. 13, 1889–); b. Elyria, O. Librarian. With The New York Public Library, 1913–37; chief, reference dept., 1928–37; director, Harvard University Libraries, 1937–55; library consultant, Rutgers University, since 1955.

METCALFE, JAMES STETSON (June 27, 1858–May 26, 1927); b. Buffalo, N.Y. Dramatic critic. *Mythology for Moderns* (1900); *The American Slave* (1900); *Another Three Weeks* (1908); *The Diary of a District Messenger* (1909); *Jane Street* (1921); etc. Drama editor, *Life,* 1888–1920; lit. editor, 1890–93.

Metcalfe, Mrs. John. See Evelyn Scott.

Methodist Book Concern. New York. Publishers. Founded 1789, at Philadelphia, Pa. Moved to New York in 1804. In 1927 the press was moved to Dobbs Ferry, N.Y. In 1914 the Abingdon Press was established to publish books of an undenominational character. Upon the union in 1939 of the Methodist Episcopal Church and the Methodist Episcopal Church South, the Methodist Book Concern of the former absorbed the Publishing House of the latter and became known as the Methodist Publishing House. At the same time the Abingdon Press absorbed the Cokesbury Press of the Southern Church, becoming the Abingdon-Cokesbury Press. The Methodist Publishing House is now known as the Abingdon Press (q.v.). Besides the *Christian Advocate* the firm published the *Youth's Instructor,* 1823, *Our Youth,* 1888, and the *Methodist Magazine. See* W. F. Whitlock's *The Story of the Book Concerns* (1903); Abel Stevens's *Life and Times of Nathan Bangs* (1863); F. A. Archibald's *Methodism and Literature* (1883); Henry C. Jennings's *The Methodist Book Concern* (1924).

Methodist Review. New York. Bimonthly. Founded 1818, as the *Methodist Magazine,* a revival of the old *Methodist Magazine* (1797–98). Name changed in 1830 to the *Methodist Magazine and Quarterly Review;* in 1841 to the *Methodist Quarterly Review;* in 1885 to the *Methodist Review.* Among its editors have been Joshua Soule, Thomas Mason, Nathan Bangs, John Emory, George Peck, John McClintock, D. D. Whedon, Daniel Curry, James W. Mendenhall, William V. Kelley, and George Elliott. Discontinued 1931.

Metropolitan Magazine. New York City. Founded 1895. Perriton Maxwell was editor, 1900–06; Henry James Whigham was editor and publisher, 1912–22. In 1924 it was absorbed by *Macfadden's Fiction Lover's Magazine* (founded 1923, expired 1925).

MEYER, ADOLPH E[rich] (Oct. 15, 1897–); b. New York. Educator. *Education in Modern Times* (1931); *Development of Education in the Twentieth Century* (1939); *Voltaire: Man of Justice* (1945); *An Educational History of the American People* (1957; rev. ed., 1967); etc. Co-author: *Becoming an Educator* (1963). Prof. education, New York University, since 1948.

MEYER, ANNIE NATHAN (Feb. 19, 1867–Sept. 23, 1951); b. New York. Founder of Barnard College, author. *Woman's Work in America* (1891); *Helen Brent, M.D.* (1893); *Robert Annys* (1901); *The Dominant Sex* (1911); *The Dreamer* (1912); *The District Attorney* (prod. 1920); *Black Souls* (prod. 1932); *Barnard Beginnings* (1935); *It's Been Fun* (autobiography, 1951); etc.

MEYER, FRANK STRAUS (May 9, 1909–); b. Newark, N.J. Editor, author. *The Moulding of Communists* (1961); *In Defense of Freedom* (1962). Co-author: *What is Conservatism?* (1964). Editor: *The African Nettle* (1965). Editor, *National Review,* since 1955.

MEYER, H[erman] H[enry] B[ernard] (Oct. 17, 1864–Jan. 16, 1937); b. New York. Bibliographer. Compiler: *Brief Guide to the Literature of Shakespeare* (1915); *The European War* (checklist, 1918); and numerous bibliographies for the Library of Congress. Chief bibliographer, Library of Congress, 1908–23. He owned a large collection of books which exemplified fine printing in America.

MEYER, KARL ERNEST (May 22, 1928–   ); b. Madison, Wis. Journalist, author. *The New America* (1961); *The Cuban Invasion* (with Tad Szulc, 1962); *Fulbright of Arkansas* (1963).

MEYER, MAX [Friedrich] (June 15, 1873–); b. Danzig, Ger. Educator, psychologist, author. *Psychology of the Other One* (1921); *Abnormal Psychology* (1927); *Fitting into a Silent World* (1934); *How We Hear: How Tones Make Music* (1950); etc. Prof. psychology, University of Missouri, 1900–29.

MEYER, ZOE (Apr. 26, 1888–); b. Metamora, Ill. Author. *Under the Blue Sky* (1917); *The Little Green Door* (1921); *Followers of the Trail* (1926); *The Sunshine Book* (1932); *Children's Stories From the Dawn-Breakers* (1955); etc.

MEYERS, ROBERT CORNELIUS V. (May 1, 1858–1917); b. Philadelphia, Pa. Author. *The Colonel's Christmas Morning* (1900); *Victoria, Empress and Queen* (1901); *Battles and Heroes of the American Navy* (1902); *Theodore Roosevelt* (1902); etc.

MEYNIER, GIL (Dec. 31, 1902–); b. Pau, France. Author. *Conducted Tour* (1931); *Stranger at the Door* (1948).

MEZEY, ROBERT (1935–   ); b. Philadelphia, Pa. Author. *The Lovemaker* (1961); *Poems* (1961); *White Blossoms* (1965); *Favors* (1968).

Miami and the Siege of Chicago. Description and analysis of the Republican and Democratic Conventions of 1968, by Norman Mailer (1968). Noted for the author's novelistic inclusion of his own thoughts and actions while participating in the events.

Miami Herald. Miami, Fla. Newspaper. Founded 1910. J. S. Knight is editor. Jay Clarke is book review editor.

MICHAELS, SIDNEY RAMON (Aug. 17, 1927–); b. New York. Playwright. *The Plaster Bambino* (1959); *Tchin Tchin* (1962); *Dylan* (1964); *Ben Franklin in Paris* (1964); *The Night They Raided Minsky's* (1969).

MICHAUD, RÉGIS (May 1, 1880–Feb. 7, 1939); b. Montélimar, France. Educator, author. *The American Novel To-Day* (1928); *Emerson, the Enraptured Yankee,* translated from the French by George Boas (1930); *Modern Thought and Literature in France* (1934). Prof. French, University of California, since 1919.

MICHEAUX, OSCAR (1884–). Author. *The Conquest* (1913); *The Forged Note* (1915); *The Case of Mrs. Wingate* (1944); *The Story of Dorothy Stanfield* (1946); *The Homesteader* (1969); etc.

MICHELSON, MIRIAM (1870–May 28, 1942); b. Calaveras, Calif. Novelist. *In the Bishop's Carriage* (1904); *The Madigans* (1904); *Petticoat King* (1929); *The Wonderlode of Silver and Gold* (1934); etc.

MICHELSON, TRUMAN (Aug. 11, 1879–July 26, 1938); b. New Rochelle, N.Y. Ethnologist, author. *Kickapoo Tales* (with William Jones, 1915); *The Autobiography of a Fox Indian Woman* (1925); *Fox Miscellany* (1937); and numerous other books on the Fox Indians. Ethnologist, U.S. Bureau of Ethnology, 1910–38; prof. ethnology, George Washington University, 1917–32.

MICHENER, JAMES A[lbert] (Feb. 3, 1907–); b. New York. Author. *Tales of the South Pacific* (1947, Pulitzer Prize for fiction, 1948); *The Fires of Spring* (1949); *Return to Paradise* (1951); *The Voice of Asia* (1951); *The Bridges at Toko-ri* (1953); *Floating World* (1954); *Sayonara* (1954); *The Bridge at Andau* (1957); *Rascals in Paradise* (with A. Grove Day, 1957); *Selected Writings* (1957); *The Hokusai Sketch-books* (1958); *Japanese Prints* (1959); *Hawaii* (1959); *Report of the County Chairman* (1961); *The Source* (1965); *Iberia* (1968); *Presidential Lottery* (1969); *Quality of Life* (1970); *Kent State: What Happened and Why* (1971); *The Drifters* (1971); etc. *See* Arthur Grove Day's *James A. Michener.*

Michigan Quarterly Review. Ann Arbor, Mich. Founded 1962. Published at the University of Michigan. Edited by

Sheridan Baker. Has published Thurgood Marshall, U Thant, Alfred Kazin, and Denise Levertov, indicating a wide scope of literary and public affairs material.

Mickey Finn Idylls. By Ernest Jarrold (1899). Irish stories of New York City. See also the same author's *Mickey Finn's New Irish Yarns* (1902).

Microbe Hunters. By Paul de Kruif (1926). Biographical sketches of twelve scientists who have led the war on disease-producing bacteria.

Mid-West Quarterly. Lincoln, Neb. Magazine. Founded 1913, by the University of Nebraska. Editor, Prosser Hall Frye. Expired 1918.

Mid-West Quarterly. Pittsburgh, Kans. Founded 1959. Published at Kansas State College. A journal of contemporary thought.

Middle of the Journey, The. Novel by Lionel Trilling (1947). Conflict between personal loyalty and political responsibility.

Middle Years, The. Autobiographical work by Henry James (1917).

MIDDLETON, DREW (Oct. 14, 1913–); b. New York. Journalist, author. *Our Share of Night* (1946); *The Struggle for Germany* (1949); *The Defense of Western Europe* (1952); *These Are the British* (1957); *The Sky Suspended: The Story of the Battle of Britain* (1961); *The Supreme Choice* (1963); *The Atlantic Community* (1965); etc. Chief London correspondent, *New York Times*, since 1953.

MIDDLETON, GEORGE (Oct. 27, 1880–Dec. 23, 1967); b. Paterson, N.J. Playwright. *The Cavaliers* (with Paul Kester, prod. 1902); *The Wife's Strategy* (prod. 1905); *The Sinner* (with Leonidas Westerveldt, prod. 1907); *Embers, and Other Plays* (1911); *Tradition, and Other Plays* (1913); *Possession, and Other Plays* (1915); *Polly with a Past* (with Guy Bolton, prod. 1917); *Adam and Eva* (with same, prod. 1919); *Masks, and Other Plays* (1920); *Circles* (prod. 1922); *That Was Balzac* (1936); *These Things Are Mine* (autobiography, 1947); etc.

Middletown. Sociological analysis of a typical American town, by Robert Lynd and his wife, Helen Merrell Lynd (1929). It was followed by *Middletown in Transition* (1937).

Midge, The. Story by H. C. Bunner (1886).

Midland, The. Iowa City, Ia. Literary magazine. Founded 1915, by John T. Frederick. Frank Luther Mott was assistant editor. Absorbed Nov. 1933 by *The Frontier*.

Midland Monthly. Des Moines, Ia. Literary magazine. Founded 1894, by Johnson Brigham. Expired 1899.

Midstream. New York. Quarterly. Founded 1955. Published by The Theodore Herzl Foundation, Inc. Edited by Shlomo Katz. A review of political, social, and literary subjects pertaining to Judaism and general interest.

Midway: Magazine of Discovery in the Arts and Sciences. Chicago, Ill. Quarterly. Founded 1960; published by University of Chicago Press.

Midwest Journal. Jefferson City, Mo. Quarterly. Published at Lincoln University. Discontinued 1956.

MIERS, EARL SCHENK (May 27, 1910–); b. Brooklyn, N.Y. Editor, author. *The Chronicles of Colonel Henry* (with Ernest E. McMahon, 1936); *Backfield Feud* (1936); *Career Coach* (1941); *Grass Roots* (1944); *Touchdown Trouble* (1953); *Web of Victory* (1955); *Ball of Fire* (1956); *The Great Rebellion* (1958); *America and Its Presidents* (1959); *The American Civil War* (1961); *Golden Book of American History* (1963); *Wild and Woolly West* (1964); *New Jersey and the Civil War* (1964); *Freedom* (1965); *Men of Valor* (1965); *The Capital and Our Lawmakers* (1965); *The Night We*

Stopped the Trolley (1965); *The Trouble Bush* (1966); *The Bill of Rights* (1968). Director, Rutgers University Press, 1944–49; editor, Alfred A. Knopf, 1949–51; World Publishing Co., 1951–54.

MIFFLIN, GEORGE HARRISON (May 1, 1845–Apr. 5, 1921); b. Boston, Mass. Publisher. Joined publishing firm of Hurd & Houghton in 1867, admitted as a partner in 1872. President of Houghton, Mifflin & Co., 1908–1921. President of Riverside Press.

MIFFLIN, LLOYD (Sept. 15, 1846–July 16, 1921); b. Columbia, Pa. Printer, poet. *The Hills* (1895); *At the Gates of Song* (1897); *The Slopes of Helicon, and Other Poems* (1898); *Echoes of Greek Idyls* (1899); *The Fields of Dawn, and Later Sonnets* (1900); *Castalian Days* (1903); *The Fleeing Nymph, and Other Verse* (1905); *Collected Sonnets* (1905); *My Lady of Dream* (1906); *Toward the Upland: Later Poems* (1908); *The Flower and Thorn* (1909); *As Twilight Falls* (1916); etc.

MIGHELS, ELLA STERLING (Mrs. Philip Verrill Mighels) (May 5, 1853–1934); b. in mining camp near Folsom, Calif. Author. *The Story of the Files* (1893); *Wawona* (1921); *Life and Letters of a Forty-Niner's Daughter* (under pen name, "Aurora Esmeralda," 1929). Compiler: *Literary California* (1918).

MIGHELS, HENRY RUST (Nov. 3, 1830–May 28, 1879); b. Norway, Me. Editor, author. *Sage Brush Leaves* (1879). With the *Butte Record*, Oroville, Calif.; the *Sacramento Bee;* the *Marysville Appeal;* editor, the *Carson* (Nev.) *Appeal,* 1865–79.

MIGHELS, PHILIP VERRILL (1869–1911). Author. *Out of a Silver Flute* (poems, 1896); *The Crystal Sceptre* (1901); *Bruvver Jim's Baby* (1904); *The Ultimate Passion* (1905); *The Furnace of Gold* (1910); *Thurley Buxton* (1911).

"Mighty Lak' a Rose." Song, words by Frank L. Stanton, music by Ethelbert Nevin (1901).

MIHANOVICH, CLEMENT SIMON (Apr. 3, 1913–); b. St. Louis, Mo. Educator. *Principles of Juvenile Delinquency* (1950); *Guide to Catholic Marriage* (with others, 1955); *Papal Pronouncements on Marriage and Family* (1956); *Glossary of Sociological Terms* (1957); etc. Editor: *Social Theorists* (1953). Prof. sociology, St. Louis University, since 1947.

MILBURN, GEORGE (Apr. 27, 1906–Sept. 22, 1966); b. Coweta, Indian Ter. (now Okla.). Author. *Oklahoma Town* (1931); *No More Trumpets, and Other Stories* (1933); *Catalogue* (1936); *Flannigan's Folly* (1947).

MILBURN, WILLIAM HENRY (Sept. 26, 1823–Apr. 10, 1903); b. Philadelphia, Pa. Methodist clergyman, author. *The Rifle, Axe, and Saddle-Bags* (1857), republished as *The Pioneer Preacher* (1859); *Ten Years of Preacher-Life* (1859); *The Pioneers, Preachers and People of the Mississippi Valley* (1860); *The Lance, Cross, and Canoe; the Flatboat, Rifle, and Plough in the Valley of the Mississippi* (1892).

MILES, CARLTON WRIGHT (June 12, 1884–deceased); b. Fergus Falls, Minn. Journalist, playwright. *Portrait of Gilbert* (prod. 1934); etc. With the *Minneapolis Journal,* 1907–28.

MILES, DUDLEY [Howe] (July 16, 1881–Sept. 5, 1954); b. Milwaukee, Wis. Educator, author. *History of English Literature* (1935); *History of American Literature* (1936); etc. Editor: *Poetry and Eloquence of the Civil War* (1911); etc.

MILES, GEORGE HENRY (July 31, 1824–July 24, 1871); b. Baltimore, Md. Educator, poet, playwright, novelist. *Mohammed* (1850); *Hernando De Soto* (prod. 1857); *Señor Valiente* (prod. 1859); *Christine* (poems, 1866). *The Truce of God*, a novel, appeared anonymously in the *United States Catholic Magazine* in 1847.

MILES, JOSEPHINE (June 11, 1911–); b. Chicago, Ill. Educator, poet. *Lines at Intersection* (poems, 1939); *Poems on*

Several Occasions (1941); *Local Measures* (poems, 1946); *The Vocabulary of Poetry* (1946); *The Continuity of English Poetic Language* (1951); *Prefabrications* (poems, 1955); *Eras and Modes in English Poetry* (1957); *Poems, 1930–60* (1960); *Ralph Waldo Emerson* (1964); *Wordsworth and the Vocabulary of Emotion* (1965); *Pathetic Fallacy in the Nineteenth Century* (1965); *Style and Proportion: The Language of Prose and Poetry* (1967). Prof. English, University of California, since 1952.

MILES, NELSON A[ppleton] (Aug. 8, 1839–May 15, 1925); b. Westminster, Mass. Army officer, author. *Personal Recollections* (1896); *Military Europe* (1898); *Observations Abroad* (1899); *Serving the Republic* (autobiography, 1911).

MILHOUS, KATHERINE (1894–). Author. *Lavinia* (1940); *Corporal Keeperupper* (1943); *Snow Over Bethlehem* (1945); *The Egg Tree* (1950); *Appolonia's Valentine* (1954); *With Bells On* (1955); *Through These Arches: The Story of Independence Hall* (1964); etc.

Military Journal During the American Revolutionary War, 1775–1783. By James Thacher (1823).

Milk for Babes, Drawn Out of the Breasts of Both Testaments. By John Cotton (1646). Prepared for the religious instruction of children.

MILLAR, KENNETH (Dec. 13, 1915–); b. Los Gatos, Cal. Author. Writes under pen names "John Macdonald," "John Ross Macdonald," "Ross Macdonald." *The Dark Tunnel* (1944); *Trouble Follows Me* (1946); *Blue City* (1947); *The Three Roads* (1948); *The Drowning Pool* (1950); *Ivory Grin* (1952); *Find a Victim* (1954); *Barbarous Coast* (1956); *The Doomsters* (1958); *The Wycherly Woman* (1961); *The Zebra-Striped Hearse* (1962); *The Chill* (1964); *The Far Side of the Dollar* (1965); *Black Money* (1966); *The Instant Enemy* (1968); *The Goodbye Look* (1969); *The Underground Man* (1971); etc.

MILLAR, MARGARET [Ellis] (Feb. 5, 1915–); b. Kitchener, Ont. Author. *The Invisible Worm* (1941); *Fire Will Freeze* (1944); *Experiment in Springtime* (1947); *Do Evil in Return* (1950); *Vanish in an Instant* (1952); *Beast in View* (1955); *The Listening Walls* (1959); *A Stranger in My Grave* (1960); *How Like An Angel* (1962); *The Fiend* (1964); *Birds and the Beasts Were There* (1968); *Beyond this Point Are Monsters* (1971); etc.

MILLARD, BAILEY (Oct. 2, 1859–Mar. 20, 1941); b. Markesan, Wis. Editor, author. *Great American Novel* (1899); *She of the West* (1900); *Songs of the Press* (1902); *The Lure o' Gold* (1904); *The Sea Hawk* (1910); *Sunland Song* (1932); etc. Editor, *Cosmopolitan Magazine*, 1905–07; etc. As city editor of the *San Francisco Call* he published Edwin Markham's "The Man with the Hoe" and started Joaquin Miller on his career. He was special writer for the *Los Angeles Times, 1924–41.*

MILLAY, EDNA ST. VINCENT (Feb. 22, 1892–Oct. 19, 1950); b. Rockland, Me. Poet. *Renascence and Other Poems* (1917); *A Few Figs from Thistles* (1920); *Second April* (1921); *The Lamp and the Bell* (1921); *The Harp-Weaver, and Other Poems* (1923, Pulitzer Prize for poetry, 1923); *Poems* (1923); *The King's Henchman* (1927); *The Buck in the Snow, and Other Poems* (1928); *Fatal Interview* (1931); *Wine from These Grapes* (1934); *Conversation at Midnight* (1937); *Huntsman, What Quarry?* (1939); *Make Bright the Arrows* (1940); *There Are No Islands Any More* (1940); *Collected Sonnets* (1941); *Collected Lyrics* (1943); *The Murder of Lidice* (1942); *Mine the Harvest* (1954); *Collected Poems* (1956); etc. See Fred B. Millett's *Contemporary American Authors* (1940); Elizabeth Atkins' *Edna St. Vincent Millay and Her Times* (1936); the *Letters* (1952); Toby Shafter's *Edna St. Vincent Millay* (1957); Miriam Gurko's *Restless Spirit* (1962).

MILLAY, KATHLEEN [Kalloch] (d. Sept. 21, 1943); b. Union, Me., sister of Edna St. Vincent Millay. Author. *Wayfarers* (1926); *The Evergreen Tree* (poems, 1927); *The Hermit Thrush* (poems, 1929); *Against the Wall* (1929); *The Beggar at the Gate* (poems, 1931); *Persephone* (1932); *Black of the Moon* (1934); *The Very Little Giant* (1934); *Hollywood Wife* (1939).

MILLER, ALEXANDER (1908–). Author. *Biblical Politics* (1943); *The Christian Significance of Karl Marx* (1947); *The Renewal of Man* (1955); *Man in the Mirror* (1958); *Faith and Learning* (1960).

MILLER, Alice Duer (1874–Aug. 22, 1942); b. New York. Author. *Poems, by Caroline Duer and Alice Duer* (1896); *The Modern Obstacle* (1903); *Less than Kin* (1909); *Blue Arch* (1910); *The Charm School* (1919); *Priceless Pearl* (1924); *Are Parents People?* (1925); *Forsaking All Others* (1930); *Come Out of the Pantry* (1933); *Death Sentence* (1934); *Not for Love* (1937); *Barnard College: The First Fifty Years* (with Susan Myers, 1939); *The White Cliffs* (1941); etc.

MILLER, ARTHUR (1915–); b. New York. Author. *The Man Who Had All the Luck* (prod. 1944); *Situation Normal · · ·* (1944); *Focus* (1945); *All My Sons* (prod. 1947); *Death of a Salesman* (prod. 1949; Pulitzer Prize for drama, 1949); *The Crucible* (prod. 1953); *View from the Bridge* (prod. 1955); *Collected Plays* (1957); *The Misfits* (1961); *After the Fall* (1963); *Incident at Vichy* (1965); *I Don't Need You Anymore* (1967); *Theatre One: American Theatre* (with others, 1967–68); etc.

MILLER, BILL (1920–Aug. 21, 1961). Co-author with Bob Wade, under pen name "Wade Miller," of mystery novels: *Deadly Weapon* (1946); *Guilty Bystander* (1947); *Fatal Step* (1948); *Uneasy Street* (1948); *Devil on Two Sticks* (1949); *Shoot to Kill* (1951); *All Through the Night* (1955); *711-Officer Needs Help* (1965); *Killer With a Badge* (1966); etc. Also books with same under pen names "Whit Masterson" and "Dale Wilmer."

MILLER, BROWN. Poet. *Fertilized Brains* (1968); *Lung Socket* (1968); *Whiskeytown, Iron Mountain, Triptych* (1968).

MILLER, CAROLYN (Mrs. William D. Miller; Mrs. Clyde H. Ray) (Aug 26, 1903–); b. Waycross, Ga. Novelist. *Lamb In His Bosom* (1933, Pulitzer Prize novel, 1934); *Lebanon* (1944).

Miller, Cincinnatus Hiner. See Joaquin Miller.

MILLER, DOUGLAS PHILLIPS (1892–). Author. *You Can't Do Business with Hitler* (1941); *Via Diplomatic Pouch* (1944).

MILLER, EMILY CLARK HUNTINGTON (Oct. 22, 1833–Nov. 2, 1913); b. Brooklyn, Conn. Editor, poet. *For the Beloved* (poems, 1892); *From Avalon, and Other Poems* (1896); etc. Author of the *Kirkwood Series*, and numerous other books for children. Editor, the *Little Corporal*, Chicago, 1871–75.

MILLER, FRANCIS TREVELYAN (Oct. 8, 1877–Nov. 7, 1959); b. Southington, Conn. Editor, author. *American Hero Tales* (1909); *History of the American People*, 10v. (1911–12); *American Wonder Stories* (1913); *The World's Crisis* (1914); *World Religions*, 6v. (1927); *The Life of Thomas A. Edison* (1931); *General Douglas MacArthur, Soldier-statesman* (1942); *Eisenhower: Man and Soldier* (1944); *A History of World War Two* (1945); *War in Korea and the Complete History of World War Two* (with others, 1952); etc. Editor: *Photographic History of the Civil War*, 5v. (1957). Editor, *Connecticut Magazine*, 1902–08; founder, *Jounal of American History*, 1907.

MILLER, FRANK JUSTUS (Nov. 26, 1858–Apr. 24, 1938); b. Clinton, Tenn. Educator, classicist, author. *Dido: An Epic*

Tragedy (1901); *Studies in Roman Poetry* (1901). Translated several Latin classics. Latin dept., University of Chicago, 1892-1925; prof., 1909-25.

MILLER, GEORGE AMOS (July 8, 1868-); b. Mendon, Ill. Methodist bishop, author. *Interesting Manila* (1905); *China Inside Out* (1915); *Prowling About Panama* (1918); *Peggy Ann in Latin America* (1926); *Mexico and the Mexicans* (1927); etc.

MILLER, HARRIET MANN (June 25, 1831-Dec. 25, 1918); b. Auburn, N.Y. Pen name "Olive Thorne Miller." Naturalist, author. *Little Folks in Feathers and Fur, and Others in Neither* (1875); *True Bird Stories* (1903); and many other books on birds and outdoor life, mostly for children.

MILLER, HEATHER ROSS (Sept. 15, 1939-); b. Albemarle, N.C. Author. *The Edge of the Woods* (1964); *Tenants of the House* (1966); *Wind Southerly* (poems, 1967); *Gone a Hundred Miles* (1967).

MILLER, HELEN MARKLEY (Dec. 4, 1899-); b. Cedar Falls, Iowa. Author. *Promenade All* (1953); *Dust in the Gold Sack* (1957); *Miss Gail* (1959); *Ski Fast, Ski Long* (1960); *Westering Women* (1961); *Blades of Grass* (1963); *Ski the Mountain* (1965); *Julie* (1966); *Beloved Monster* (1968); *George Rogers Clark, Frontier Fighter* (1968); etc.

MILLER, HELEN TOPPING (Dec. 8, 1884-Feb. 4, 1960); b. Fenton, Mich. Novelist. *Sharon* (1931); *White Peacock* (1932); *Splendor of Eagles* (1935); *Song After Midnight* (1939); *The Mulberry Bush* (1940); *Who Is This Girl?* (1941); *Desperate Angel* (1942); *Last Lover* (1944); *Spotlight* (1946); *The Sound of Chariots* (1947); *The Horns of Capricorn* (1950); *Slow Dies the Thunder* (1955); *Sing One Song* (1956); *After the Glory* (1958); *Nightshade* (1960); etc.

MILLER, HENRY (Dec. 26, 1891-   ); b. New York. Author. *Tropic of Cancer* (1931); *Max and the White Phagocytes* (1938); *Tropic of Capricorn* (1939); *Black Spring* (1939); *The Cosmological Eye* (1939); *The Wisdom of the Heart* (1941); *The Colossus of Maroussi* (1941); *Hamlet: A Philosophical Correspondence* 2v. (with M. Fraenkel, 1939-41); *Sunday After the War* (1944); *The Air-Conditioned Nightmare,* 2v.; Vol. II, *Remember to Remember* (1945-47); *The Smile at the Foot of the Ladder* (1948); *The Books in My Life* (1952); *A Devil in Paradise* (1956); *Big Sur and the Oranges of Hieronymus Bosch* (1957); *Stand Still Like the Hummingbird* (1962); *A Letter* (1962); *Watercolors* (1962); *Greece* (1964); *To Paint Is to Love Again* (1968); *Henry Miller Miscellanea* (1970). See Nicholas Moore's *Henry Miller* (1943); Bernard H. Porter's *The Happy Rock: A Book About Henry Miller* (1945); William A. Gordon's *The Mind and Art of Henry Miller* (1967).

MILLER, HENRY RUSSELL (May 12, 1880-Dec. 16, 1955); b. Sidney, O. Author. *The Man Higher Up* (1910); *The Ambition of Mark Truitt* (1913); *The House of Toys* (1914); etc.

MILLER, JOAQUIN [Cincinnatus Hiner] (Mar. 10, 1839-Feb. 17, 1913); b. Liberty, Ind. Poet, playwright. *Specimens* (1868); *Joaquin et al* (1869); *Songs of the Sierras* (1871); *Songs of the Sun-lands* (1873); *Life amongst the Modocs* (1873); *The Ship in the Desert* (1875); *Shadows of Shasta* (1881); *The Danites in the Sierras* (prod. 1881); *Memoire and Rime* (1884); *The Complete Poetical Works* (1897); etc. One of his best-known poems is "Columbus." See the *Overland Monthly,* Feb. 1920; Stuart P. Sherman's introduction to *The Poetical Works of Joaquin Miller* (1923); Harr Wagner's *Joaquin Miller and His Other Self* (1929); Merritt P. Allen's *Joaquin Miller, Frontier Poet* (1932); Martin S. Peterson's *Joaquin Miller* (1937); M. Marion Marberry's *Splendid Poseur* (1953); O. W. Frost's *Joaquin Miller* (1967).

MILLER, JOHN ANDERSON (1895-Feb. 25, 1964). Author. *Master Builders of Sixty Centuries* (1938); *Fares, Please!* (1941); *Men and Volts at War* (1947); *Modern Jupiter: The*

Story of Charles Proteus Steinmetz (1958); *At the Touch of a Button* (1962); *Coolidge: Yankee Scientist* (1963); *Atoms and Epochs* (1966).

MILLER, JOHN HENRY (Mar. 12, 1702-Mar. 31, 1782); b. Rheden, Waldeck, Ger., of Swiss parentage. Printer, publisher, editor. Founder (with Samuel Holland), *Die Lancastersche* (Pa.) *Zeitung,* 1751, in both German and English; founder, *Der Wöchentliche Staatsbote,* 1762. Established his own press in Philadelphia, 1760. The first printed announcement of the *Declaration of Independence* was in *Heinrich Miller's Pennsylvanische Staatsbote,* July 5, 1776, and the text was printed in full in its issue for July 9, 1776. See Charles F. Dapp's *The Evolution of an American Patriot, Being an Intimate Study of the Patriotic Activities of John Henry Miller* (1924).

MILLER, J[oseph] CORSON (Nov. 13, 1883-); b. Buffalo, N.Y. Poet. *Veils of Samite* (1921); *A Horn from Caerleon* (1927); *Cup of the Years* (1934); *Finger at the Crossroads* (poems, 1942).

MILLER, JOSEPH DANA (July 1, 1864-May 8, 1939); b. New York. Editor, publisher, poet. *Verses from a Vagrant Muse* (1894); *Thirty Years of Verse Making* (1926). Founder, the *Single Tax Review* (later, *Land and Freedom),* 1901.

MILLER, KEITH (1927?-   ); Author. *A Second Touch* (1967); *A Taste of New Wine* (1965); *Habitation of Dragons* (1970).

MILLER, LEO EDWARD (May 11, 1887-Oct. 6, 1952); b. Huntingburg, Ind. Explorer, author. *In the Wilds of South America* (1918); *The Hidden People* (1920); *Tiger's Lair* (1921); *The Black Phantom* (1922); *Adrift on the Amazon* (1923); *The Jungle Pirates* (1925); etc.

MILLER, LEWIS B[ennett] (b. May 27, 1861-); b. in Cooke Co., Tex. Novelist. *The White River Raft* (1910); *Saddles and Lariats* (1912); *Fort Blocker Boys* (1917); *Pike's Peak or Bust* (1922); *Big Smoke Mountain* (1930); etc.

MILLER, MARY BRITTON (Aug. 1883-); b. New London, Conn. Author. *Songs of the Infancy, and Other Poems* (1928); *Menagerie* (1928); *Without Sanctuary* (1932); *Intrepid Bird* (1934); *In the Days of Thy Youth* (1943); *The Crucifixion* (poem, 1944). Under pen name "Isabel Bolton": *Do I Wake or Sleep?* (1946); *The Christmas Tree* (1949); *Many Mansions* (1952); *Give a Guess* (1957); *All Aboard* (1958); *A Handful of Flowers* (1959); *Jungle Journey* (1959); *Under Gemini* (1966); *Whirligig of Time* (1971).

MILLER, MAX (Feb. 9, 1901-Dec. 27, 1967); b. Traverse City, Mich. Author. *I Cover the Waterfront* (1932); *The Beginning of a Mortal* (1933); *The Man of the Barge* (1935); *The Great Trek* (1935); *Mexico around Me* (1937); *Harbor of the Sun* (1940); *Reno* (1941); *It Must Be the Climate* (1941); *Land Where Time Stands Still* (1943); *It's Tomorrow Out Here* (1943); *I'm Sure We've Met Before* (1951); *The Cruise of the Cow* (1952); *Speak to the Earth* (1955); *Shinny on Your Own Side* (1958); *And Bring All Your Folks* (1959); *Holladay Street* (1962); etc.

MILLER, MERLE (May 17, 1919-); b. Montour, Ia. Author. *Island 49* (1945); *We Dropped the A-Bomb* (with Abe Spitzer, 1946); *That Winter* (1948); *The Sure Thing* (1949); *The Judges and the Judged* (1952); *Reunion* (1954); *A Secret Understanding* (1956); *A Gay and Melancholy Sound* (1961); *The Warm Feeling* (1968); etc.

MILLER, MINNIE WILLIS BAINES (b. 1845); b. Lebanon, N.H. Author. *The Silent Land* (1890); *His Cousin, the Doctor* (1891); *The Pilgrim's Vision* (poem, 1891); *Mrs. Cherry's Sister* (1909); etc.

MILLER, MRS. ALEX[ander] McVEIGH. Novelist. *The Bride of the Tomb* (1883); *Bonnie Dora* (1883); *Brunette and Blonde* (1887); *Lynette's Wedding* (1896); etc.

Miller, Mrs. Friend H. See Grace Miller White.

MILLER, NELLIE BURGET (Mrs. L. A. Miller) (June 6, 1875–June 4, 1952); b. Fayette, Ia. Poet. *The Fleece of Gold* (1921); *The Flame of God* (1924); *In Earthen Bowls* (collected poems, 1924); *The Living Drama* (1924); *Sun Drops Red* (collected poems, 1947); *In the Tents of the Shepherd Prince* (play, 1950). Appointed poet laureate of Colorado, 1923.

MILLER, NOLAN (May 4, 1915–); b. Kalida, O. Novelist. *Moth of Time* (1946); *The Merry Innocents* (1947); *Why I Am So Beat* (1954). Co-editor, *New Campus Writing*, 1957–59.

MILLER, OLIVE [Kennon] BEAUPRE. Publisher, editor, author of children's books. *Sunny Rhymes for Happy Children* (1917); *Engines and Brass Bands* (1933); *Heroes, Outlaws, & Funny Fellows of American Popular Tales* (1939); *Heroes of the Bible* (1940); etc. Editor: *My Bookhouse*, 6v. (1920–35); *My Travelship*, 3v. (1925–26); *Picturesque Tales of Progress*, 8v. (with H. N. Baum, 1935).

Miller, Olive Thorne. Pen name of Harriet Mann Miller.

MILLER, PARK HAYS (Dec. 21, 1879–); b. Allegheny, Pa. Presbyterian clergyman, editor, author. *The Abundant Life* (1920); *Heroes of the Church* (1922); *Christian Doctrine for Sunday School Teachers* (1947); *How to Study and Use the Bible* (1949); *Why I Am a Presbyterian* (1956); etc. Editor, Board of Christian Education of the Presbyterian Church.

MILLER, PERRY [Gilbert Eddy] (Feb. 25, 1905–Dec. 9, 1963); b. Chicago, Ill. Educator, author. *Orthodoxy in Massachusetts* (1933); *The New England Mind* (1939); *Jonathan Edwards* (1949); *Roger Williams* (1953); *The Raven and the Whale* (1956); *The Life of the Mind in America* (1965); etc. Prof. American literature, Harvard University, from 1946.

Miller, Wade. Pen name of Billy Miller and Bob Wade.

MILLER, WALTER MICHAEL JR. (Jan. 23, 1923–); b. New Smyrna Beach, Fla. Author. *A Canticle for Leibowitz* (1960); *Conditionally Human* (1962); *The View from the Stars* (1965); and numerous stories for science fiction magazines.

MILLER, WALTER (May 5, 1864–July 28, 1949); b. Ashland Co., O. Educator, editor, author. *Daedalus and Thespis*, 3v. (1929–32); *Greece and the Greeks* (1941); also textbooks. Translator of Greek and Latin classics. Assoc. editor, the *Classical Journal*, 1905–33; editor, 1933–35. Prof. classical languages, University of Missouri, 1911–36.

MILLER, WARREN. Author. *The Sleep of Reason* (1956); *The Way We Live Now* (1958); *The Cool World* (1959); *Ninety Miles From Home* (1961); etc. Under pen name "Amanda Vail": *Love Me Little* (1957); etc.

MILLER, WARREN E. (Mar. 26, 1924–Apr. 20, 1966); b. Hawarden, Ia. Educator, author. *The American Voter* (1960); *The Lost Plantation: The Face of Cuba Today* (1961); *The Siege of Harlem* (1964); *The Cool World* (1964); *Elections and the Political Order* (1966). Co-author: *The Voter Decides* (1954). Professor of political science, University of Michigan, 1963–66.

MILLER, WARREN HASTINGS (Aug. 21, 1876–Apr. 20, 1966); b. Honesdale, Pa. Editor, author. *Camp Craft* (1915); *Sea Fighters* (1920); *In Darkest New Guinea* (1921); *Across Borneo* (1922); *Red Mesa* (1923); *On Tiger Trails in Burma* (1925); *Pirate Archipelago* (1926); *All Around the Mediterranean* (1926); *Sahara Sands* (1927); *Tiger Bridge* (1937); *Boys of 1917* (1939); *Home-Builders* (1946); etc.

MILLER, WEBB (Feb. 10, 1892–May 8, 1940); b. Pokagon, Mich. Correspondent, author. *I Found No Peace* (1936). Foreign correspondent, United Press, 1916–40.

MILLET, FRANCIS DAVIS (Nov. 3, 1846–Apr. 15, 1912); b. Mattapoisett, Mass. Artist, correspondent, author. *A Capillary Crime, and Other Stories* (1892); *The Danube from the Black Forest to the Black Sea* (1893); *The Expedition to the Philippines* (1899). War correspondent, the *New York Herald*, 1877; the *New York Sun*, 1898; etc.

MILLETT, FRED B[enjamin] (Feb. 19, 1890–); b. Brockton, Mass. Educator, author. *The Art of the Drama* (with Gerald E. Bentley, 1935); *Contemporary American Authors* (1940); *The Rebirth of Liberal Education* (1945); *Reading Fiction* (1950); *Professor: Problems and Rewards in College Teaching* (1961). Editor: *The Play's the Thing* (with Gerald E. Bentley, 1936). English dept., University of Chicago, 1927–37; Wesleyan University, since 1937.

MILLETT, KATE (1934–   ); Author. *Sexual Politics* (1970).

MILLIKAN, ROBERT ANDREWS (Mar. 22, 1868–Dec. 19, 1953); b. Morrison, Ill. Educator, physicist, author. *Science and Life* (1923); *Science and the New Civilization* (1930); *Cosmic Rays* (1939); *Autobiography* (1950); also many books on physics. Nobel Prize in physics, 1923. Prof. physics, University of Chicago, 1896–1921; director Norman Bridge Laboratory of Physics, California Institute of Technology, Pasadena, Calif., 1921–45.

MILLIS, WALTER (Mar. 16, 1899–Mar. 17, 1968); b. Atlanta, Ga. Journalist, author. *The Martial Spirit* (1931); *Why Europe Fights* (1940); *This is Pearl!* (1947); *Arms and Men* (1956); etc. Editor: James Forrestal's *Diaries* (1951). Staff writer, New York *Herald Tribune*, 1924–54.

MILLS, C[harles] WRIGHT, (1916–Mar. 20, 1962); b. Waco, Tex. Educator, author. *The New Men of Power: America's Labor Leaders* (with Helen Schneider, 1948); *White Collar: The American Middle Classes* (1951); *The Power Elite* (1956); *The Causes of World War Three* (1958); *The Sociological Imagination* (1959); *Listen, Yankee: The Revolution in Cuba* (1960); etc. Sociology dept., Columbia University, since 1946.

MILLS, EDWARD S. (Mar. 3, 1883–); b. Orange, N.J. Publisher. Pres., Longmans, Green & Co., 1927–57.

MILLS, ENOS A[bijah] (Apr. 22, 1870–Sept. 21, 1922); b. near Kansas City, Kan. Guide, hunter, author. *The Spell of the Rockies* (1911); *In Beaver World* (1913); *The Grizzly* (1919); *The Adventures of a Native Guide* (1920); *Bird Memories of the Rockies* (1931); *Waiting in the Wilderness,* (1932); etc.

MILLS, LENNOX A[lgernon] (July 30, 1896–); b. Vancouver, B.C. Educator. *British Rule in Ceylon* (1933); *British Rule in Eastern Asia* (1942); *Malaya: A Political and Economic Appraisal* (1958); *Southeast Asia: Illusion and Reality in Politics and Economics* (1964); etc. Prof. political science, University of Minnesota, since 1928.

MILLS, WEYMER JAY (Aug. 26, 1880–May 26, 1938); b. Jersey City, N.J. Editor, novelist. *Caroline of Courtlandt Street* (1905); *Through the Gates of Old Romance* (1903); *The Van Rensselaers of Old Manhattan* (1907).

MILLSPAUGH, CLARENCE ARTHUR (Aug. 12, 1908–July 15, 1961); b. Kalamazoo, Mich. Poet, novelist. *In Sight of Mountains* (poems, 1936); *Men are Not Stars* (1938). English dept., University of Chicago, 1938–40.

MILN, LOUISE [Jordan] (Mar. 5, 1864–Sept. 22, 1933); b. Macomb, Ill. Author. *When We Were Strolling Players in the East* (1894); *Little Folk of Many Lands* (1899); *A Woman and Her Talent* (1905); *Mr. Wu* (1918); *The Feast of Lanterns* (1920); *In A Shantung Garden* (1924); *It Happened in Peking* (1926); *Red Lily and Chinese Jade* (short stories, 1928); *Rice* (1930); *Anne Zu-Zan* (1932); etc.

MILNE, LORUS JOHNSON (Sept. 12, 1912–); b. Toronto, Can. Naturalist, author. Co-author with M. J. G. Milne: *Famous Naturalists* (1952); *The Mating Instinct* (1954); *The World of Night* (1956); *Paths Across the Earth* (1958); *Animal Life* (1959); *Plant Life* (1959); *The Lower Animals: Living Invertebrates of the World* (1960); *Senses of Animals and Men* (1962); *The Mountains* (1962); *Water and Life* (1964); *The Crab That Crawled Out of the Past* (1965); *Gift from the Sky* (1967); *Patterns of Survival* (1967); *Living Plants of the World* (1967); *Montanges* (1968); *Phoenix Forest* (1968); *The Nature of Animals* (1969); etc. Prof. zoology, University of New Hampshire, since 1948.

MILNE, MARGERY JOAN GREENE (Mrs. Lorus Johnson Milne) (1914–). Author. Co-author, with husband (q.v.), of numerous books.

MILTON, GEORGE FORT (Nov. 19, 1894–Nov. 12, 1955); b. Chattanooga, Tenn. Editor, author. *The Age of Hate: Andrew Johnson and the Radicals* (1930); *The Eve of Conflict: Stephen A. Douglas and the Needless War* (1934); *Abraham Lincoln and the Fifth Column* (1942); *Use of Presidential Power* (1944); etc. Editor, the *Chattanooga News*, (1924–39; the *Chattanooga Evening Tribune*, from 1940.

Miltoun, Francis. Pen name of Milburg Francisco Mansfield.

Milwaukee Journal. Milwaukee, Wis. Newspaper. Founded Nov. 16, 1882, by Lucius W. Nieman. Zona Gale, Edna Ferber, M. Lyle Spencer, M. K. Scott have been on the staff. Richard Leonard is editor. Leslie Cross is book review editor.

Milwaukee Sentinel. Milwaukee, Wis. Newspaper. Founded 1837, as a weekly. Became a daily in 1844. Rufus King was editor until 1861. Harvey Schwander is now editor; book reviews and book supplement are edited by Dorothy Kincaid.

MIMS, EDWIN (May 27, 1872–Sept. 15, 1959); b. Richmond, Ark. Educator, author. *Sidney Lanier* (1905); *The Advancing South* (1926); *Adventurous America* (1929); *Life of Chancellor Kirkland* (1940); *Great Writers as Interpreters of Religion* (1945); *Christ of the Poets* (1948); etc. Editor: *Southern Prose and Poetry* (1910); etc. Head, English dept., Vanderbilt University, 1912–42.

"Mind Is an Enchanting Thing, The." Poem by Marianne Moore.

Mind of the South, The. By W. J. Cash (1941). Critical examination of the Southern mind. Probes the reasons for its historical characteristics and attempts to predict the probable future of Southern thinking.

MINEAR, PAUL S[evier] (Feb. 17, 1906–); b. Mt. Pleasant, Ia. Educator. *An Introduction to Paul* (1936); *The Choice* (1948); *The Kingdom and the Power* (1950); *Jesus and His People* (1956); *The Gospel of Mark* (1962); *Images of the Church in the New Testament* (1960); *Eves of Faith* (1966); *I Saw a New Earth: An Introduction to the Visions of the Apocalypse* (1968). Editor: *The Nature of the Unity We Seek* (1963). Prof. New Testament, Yale Divinity School, since 1956.

MINER, CHARLES (Feb. 1, 1780–Oct. 26, 1865); b. Norwich, Conn. Editor, congressman, author. *Essays from the Desk of Poor Robert the Scribe* (1815); *History of Wyoming* [Valley] (1845). He wrote the ballad "James Bird" (1814). Publisher (with brother, Asher Miner, until 1804), the *Luzerne Federalist and Susquehannah Intelligencer*, Wilkes-Barré, Pa., 1802–09, 1810–11; the *Gleaner and Luzerne Intelligencer*, 1811–16; the *True American*, Philadelphia, 1816–17; the *Chester and Delaware Federalist* (later the *Village Record*), West Chester, Pa., 1817–25, 1829–32. Congressman, 1825–29. Largely responsible for the introduction of anthracite coal. *See* C. F. and E. M. T. Richardson's *Charles Miner, a Pennsylvania Pioneer* (1916).

MINER, WILLIAM HARVEY (Mar. 5, 1877–deceased); b. New Haven, Conn. Journalist, author. *George Catlin: A Short Memoir* (1900); *Daniel Boone* (1901); *The Lewis and Clark Expedition* (1901).

Mingo and Other Sketches. By Joel Chandler Harris (1883).

Minister's Wooing, The. Novel by Harriet Beecher Stowe (1859). A study in New England morality. Mary Scudder, who loves James Marvyn, decides to marry her pastor, Dr. Hopkins, when she is convinced that James has been lost at sea. Just before the wedding James comes back and the minister graciously steps aside, sacrificing his own happiness.

"Miniver Cheevy." Poem by Edwin Arlington Robinson (1907).

Minneapolis Morning Tribune. See *Minneapolis Star.*

Minneapolis Star. Minneapolis, Minn. Newspaper. Founded 1878, as the *Journal;* combined 1939 with the *Star* (founded 1924). John Cowles, Jr., is editor. Sunday edition shared with the Morning *Tribune* (founded 1867) as the *Sunday Tribune and Star-Journal.* Robert Sorenson is the *Tribune* book review editor.

Minnesota Pioneer. See *St. Paul Pioneer Press.*

MINNIGERODE, MEADE (June 19, 1887–Oct. 27, 1967); b. London of American parentage. Author. *Laughing House* (1920); *The Big Year* (1921); *The Queen of Sheba* (1922); *The Fabulous Forties* (1924); *Lives and Times* (1925); *Some American Ladies* (1926); *Cockades* (1927); *Certain Rich Men* (1927); *Marie Antoinette's Henchman* (1936); *Black Forest* (1937); etc. Editor: *Some Personal Letters of Herman Melville, and a Bibliography* (1922).

MINOR, BENJAMIN BLAKE (Oct. 21, 1818–Aug. 1, 1905); b. Tappanhannock, Essex Co., Va. Lawyer, educator, editor, author. *The Southern Literary Messenger, 1834-1864* (1905). Editor, *Southern Literary Messenger,* Aug. 1843–Oct., 1847.

MINOR, LUCIAN (Apr. 24, 1802–July 8, 1858); b. in Louisa Co., Va. Temperance advocate, writer. His best known writing was *Letters from New England,* first published in the *Southern Literary Messenger,* 1834–35. Part of his journal was printed by James Russell Lowell in the *Atlantic Monthly* in 1870–71.

MINOT, JOHN CLAIR (Nov. 30, 1872–Oct. 3, 1941); b. Belgrade, Me. Editor, local historian. *Tales of Bowdoin* (1901); *Rhymes of Freckle Days* (1933); and books on history of Maine towns. Editor: *Bowdoin Verse* (1907); *The Best College Stories I Know* (1931). With *Youth's Companion,* 1909–18; lit. editor, the *Boston Herald,* 1919–38.

Minton, Balch & Co. New York. Publishers. Founded 1924, by Melville Minton and Earl H. Balch. Later merged with G. P. Putnam's Sons.

MINTON, WALTER JOSEPH (Nov. 13, 1923–); b. New York. Publisher. With G. P. Putnam's Sons, since 1947; pres., since 1955.

Miracle Man, The. Novel by Frank L. Packard (1914). Story of a group of city crooks who exploit an elderly "faith-healer," but in turn succumb to his spiritual influence.

Miriam Coffin; or, the Whale-Fishermen. Novel by Joseph C. Hart, 2v. (1834), published anonymously. The first American novel of whaling, and a whaling classic. Nantucket and New Bedford figure prominently in the setting.

Mirror, The. Augusta, Ga. Magazine. Founded 1838, by William Tappan Thompson. In 1842 it was merged with the *Macon Family Companion,* as the *Family Companion and Ladies' Mirror.* Although this magazine expired in 1843, it lasted long enough to receive the first of Thompson's famous "Major Jones" letters.

Mirror for Witches. By Esther Forbes (1928). A novel based on the witchcraft trials in Salem, Mass.

MIRSKY, JEANNETTE (Sept. 3, 1903–); b. Bradley Beach, N.J. Author. *To the North!* (1934); *The Westward Crossings* (1944); *To the Arctic!* (1946); *The World of Eli Whitney* (with Allan Nevins, 1952); *Elisha Kane and the Seafaring Frontier* (1954); *Balboa, Discoverer of the Pacific* (1964); *Houses of God* (1965); etc. Editor: *The Great Chinese Travelers* (1964).

MIRVISH, ROBERT FRANKLIN (July 17, 1921–); Author. *House of Her Own* (1953); *Red Sky at Midnight* (1955); *Two Women, Two Worlds* (1960); *Dust on the Sea* (1960); *Point of Impact* (1961); *Cleared Narvick 2000* (1962); *The Last Capitalist* (1963); *Business is People* (1963); *Holy Loch* (1964); *There You Are, But Where Are You?* (1965); etc.

Miss Leslie's Magazine. Philadelphia, Pa. Magazine. Founded Jan., 1843. Edited by Eliza Leslie and T. S. Arthur. In 1845 it became *Arthur's Ladies' Magazine of Elegant Literature and the Fine Arts.* Longfellow's "The Village Blacksmith" appeared in the Aug., 1844 number. Merged with *Godey's Lady's Book* in July, 1846.

Miss Lonelyhearts. Novel by Nathanael West (1933). A newspaperman conducts a love-advice column and becomes tragically involved in the affairs of his readers. The comedy that arises from the pathetic nature of the emotions exploited by the columnist is raised to ironic levels through symbolism.

Miss Lucinda. Short story by Rose Terry Cooke (1861). Pathetic story of a woman whose yearning to be a heroine was never fulfilled.

Miss Lulu Bett. Novel by Zona Gale (1920). The story of a naïve small-town girl who is fascinated by Ninian Deacon, who tricks her into a mock marriage, and leaves her when he discovers that his first wife is still living. Lulu's life was one of frustration and bewilderment. The dramatization of this novel won the Pulitzer Prize in 1921.

Miss Minerva and William Green Hill. By Frances Boyd Calhoun (1867–1909), published in 1909. Amusing sketches of a little boy who comes to live with his elderly spinster aunt. Emma Speed Sampson has written a number of sequels.

Miss Ravenel's Conversion from Secession to Loyalty. By John W. De Forest (1867). Civil War novel with Lillie Ravenel, a secessionist, as the chief character. John Carter and Edward Colburne marry her in turn but the war makes her twice a widow. Most of the story is laid in New Orleans, and the manners of the time are faithfully mirrored.

Missouri Gazette. St. Louis, Mo. Newspaper. Founded July 12, 1808. First newspaper in Missouri. Expired 1822.

Mister Roberts. Novel by Thomas O. Heggen (1946). Life on a cargo vessel during World War II.

MIT Press, The. Cambridge, Mass. Publishers. Founded 1932. Publishes scholarly and experimental textbooks, trade books in architecture, the humanities, social sciences, science, engineering.

MITCHEL, FREDERICK AUGUSTUS (Dec. 4, 1839–1918); b. Cincinnati, O. Editor, novelist, biographer. *Ormsby MacKnight Mitchel* (1887); *Chattanooga* (1891); *Chickamauga* (1892); *The Twenty Million Ransom* (1890); *Sweet Revenge* (1897).

MITCHELL, BROADUS (Dec. 27, 1892–); b. Georgetown, Ky. Economist, author. *The Rise of the Cotton Mills in the South* (1921); *Industrial Revolution in the South* (with George S. Mitchell, 1930); *Depression Decade, 1929–1941* (1947); *Heritage from Hamilton* (1957); *A Biography of the Constitution of the United States* (1964); *William Gregg, Factory Master of the Old South* (1966); *Postscripts to Economic History* (1967); etc. Prof. economics, Rutgers University, since 1949.

MITCHELL, DODSON LOMAX (1868–June 2, 1939); b. Memphis, Tenn. Actor, playwright. *Cornered* (prod. 1920); *In Times Square* (with Clyde Fitch, prod. 1931).

MITCHELL, DONALD GRANT (Apr. 12, 1822–Dec. 15, 1908); b. Norwich, Conn. Agriculturist, author. Pen name "Ik Marvel." *Fresh Gleanings* (1847); *The Lorgnette; or, Studies of the Town by an Opera Goer,* 24 nos. (1850); *Reveries of a Bachelor* (1850); *Dream Life* (1851); *My Farm at Edgewood* (1863); *Wet Days at Edgewood* (1865); *Rural Studies* (1867); *Woodbridge Record* (1883); *English Lands, Letters and Kings,* 4v. (1889–97); *American Lands and Letters,* 2v. (1897–99); *The Works,* 15v. (1907); etc. See Waldo H. Dunn's *The Life of Donald G. Mitchell* (1922).

MITCHELL, EDMUND (Mar. 19, 1861–1917); b. Glasgow, Scot. Journalist, author. *The Temple of Death* (1894); *Chickabiddy Stories* (1899); *The Despoilers* (1904); *In Desert Keeping* (1905); *El Moko* (1909); *Tales of Destiny* (1913); etc.

MITCHELL, EDWARD PAGE (Mar. 24, 1852–Jan. 22, 1927); b. Bath, Me. Editor, author. *Memoirs of an Editor* (1924). On staff of the *New York Sun,* 1875–1927; editor, 1903–20.

MITCHELL, EDWIN VALENTINE (1890–Nov. 26, 1960); b. Hartford, Conn. Editor, author. *The Horse and Buggy Age in New England* (1937); *Maine Summer* (1939); *It's an Old New England Custom* (1946); *The Romance of New England Antiques* (1950); etc. Edited new editions of the Lincoln Library of Essential Information.

MITCHELL, GEORGE [William] (Nov. 25, 1873–); b. New York. Artist, author. *Little Babs* (1919); *Kernel Cob* (1920); *King Kuriosity* (1926); *Sergeant Giggles* (1929); etc.

MITCHELL, ISAAC (1759–Nov. 26, 1812); b. Albany, N.Y. Editor, novelist. *The Asylum; or, Alonzo and Melissa,* 2v. (1811). This was first published serially in his paper, the *Political Barometer,* Poughkeepsie, N.Y., during 1804. Shortly after the appearance of the book, it was plagiarized by Daniel Jackson (b. 1790), as *Alonzo and Melissa; or, The Unfeeling Father* (1811), republished many times under varying titles. See Edmund Pearson's *Queer Books* (1928). See also *Book Notes,* 1905; and *The Nation,* Dec. 8, 1904, Feb. 2, 1905, Feb. 25, 1908.

MITCHELL, JOHN AMES (Jan. 17, 1845–June 29, 1918); b. New York. Artist, editor, author. *A Romance of the Moon* (1886); *The Last American* (1889); *Amos Judd* (1895); *The Pines of Lory* (1901); *The Villa Claudia* (1904); *Pandora's Box* (1911); etc. Founder, *Life,* New York, Jan. 4, 1883; publisher, 1883–1918.

MITCHELL, JOHN KEARSLEY (May 12, 1793–Apr. 4, 1858); b. Shepherdstown, Va. Physician, poet. *Helena* (1821); *Indecision . . . and Other Poems* (1839).

MITCHELL, LANGDON ELWYN (Feb. 17, 1862–Oct. 21, 1935); b. Philadelphia, Pa., son of S. Weir Mitchell. Poet, playwright. *Poems* (1894); *The New York Idea* (prod. 1906); *Understanding America* (1927); etc.

MITCHELL, MARGARET [Munnerlyn] (Mrs. John Robert Marsh). (Nov. 8, 1900–Aug. 16, 1949); b. Atlanta, Ga. Novelist. *Gone With the Wind* (1936, Pulitzer Prize novel 1937).

MITCHELL, RONALD ELWY (June 1, 1905–); b. London. Educator, author. *America: A Practical Handbook* (1935); *Deep Waters* (1937); *Design for November* (1947); *Dan Owen and the Angel Joe* (1948); *Three Men Went to Mow* (1951); also plays. Speech dept., University of Wisconsin, since 1939.

MITCHELL, RUTH COMFORT (Mrs. Sanborn Young) (1882–Feb. 17, 1953); b. San Francisco, Calif. Author. *The Night Court, and Other Verse* (1916); *Narratives in Verse* (1923); *Call of the House* (1927); *Army with Banners* (1928); *Old San Francisco* (1933); *Of Human Kindness* (1940); *They Shall Come Again* (1944); etc.

MITCHELL, SAMUEL AUGUSTUS (Mar. 20, 1792–Dec. 18, 1868); b. Bristol, Conn. Author and publisher of geographies. *A New American Atlas* (1831); *Mitchell's Traveller's Guide through the United States* (1832); *A General View of the World* (1842); etc.

MITCHELL, S[ilas] WEIR (1829–1914); b. Philadelphia, Pa. Physician, poet, novelist. *The Hill of Stones* (1882); *In War Time* (1885); *Roland Blake* (1886); *Far in the Forest* (1889); *A Psalm of Deaths, and Other Poems* (1890); *Characteristics* (1891); *Collected Poems* (1896); *Hugh Wynne* (1897); *The Adventures of François* (1899); *Dr. North and His Friends* (1900); *The Autobiography of a Quack* (1900); *Circumstance* (1901); *Little Stories* (1903); *Constance Trescot* (1905); *The Red City* (1907); *A Venture in 1777* (1908); *The Comfort of the Hills* (poems, 1909); *Westways* (1913); *Complete Poems* (1914); etc. See Anna Robeson Burr's *Weir Mitchell* (1929); Ernest P. Erneast's *S. Weir Mitchell, Novelist and Physician* (1950).

MITCHELL, WALTER (Jan. 22, 1826–Apr. 15, 1908); b. Nantucket, Mass. Episcopal clergyman, author. *Bryan Maurice* (1867); *Two Strings to His Bow* (1894).

MITFORD, JESSICA (Sept. 11, 1917–   ); b. Batsford Mansion, England. Author. *Daughters and Rebels* (1960); *The American Way of Death* (1963); *The Trial of Dr. Spock* (1969).

MITGANG, HERBERT. (Jan. 20, 1920–); b. New York. Journalist, author. *Lincoln as They Saw Him* (1956); *The Return* (1959); *The Man Who Rode the Tiger: The Life and Times of Judge Samuel Seabury* (1963); etc. Editor: *The Letters of Carl Sandburg* (1968); *America at Random: Topics of the Times* (1969). With the editorial board of the *New York Times* since 1967.

MIZENER, ARTHUR MOORE (Sept. 3, 1907–); b. Erie, Pa. Educator, author. *The Far Side of Paradise: A Biography of F. Scott Fitzgerald* (1951; rev. ed. 1969); *The Sense of Life in the Modern Novel* (1964); *Twelve Great American Novels* (1967). Editor: F. Scott Fitzgerald's *Afternoon of an Author* (1957); *The Fitzgerald Reader* (1963); *The Last Chronicle of Barset* (1964). Prof. English, Cornell University, since 1951.

MIZNER, WILSON (May 19, 1876–Apr. 6, 1933); b. Benicia, Calif. Playwright. *The Only Law* (with G. Bronson Howard, prod. 1909); *The Deep Purple* (with Paul Armstrong, prod. 1910); *The Greyhound* (with same, prod. 1912). *See* Edward Dean Sullivan's *The Fabulous Wilson Mizner* (1935).

M'liss. Short story by Bret Harte (1867).

Moby-Dick. Novel by Herman Melville (1851). The masterpiece of the whaling era, giving an account of Captain Ahab's grim search for a hugh white whale called Moby Dick, which had attacked him on an earlier expedition causing the loss of one leg. Besides being an accurate study of whales and whaling, and a thrilling sea adventure, it is also a symbolic book reflecting the author's philosophic outlook. See *Mocha Dick.*

Mocha Dick; or, The White Whale. Story by J. N. Reynolds, which appeared in the *Knickerbocker Magazine*, May 1839, twelve years before Melville's *Moby-Dick.*

"Mocking Bird, The." Poem by Sidney Lanier (1877). Other well-known poems with the same title were written by Alexander Beaufort Meek and Frank Lebby Stanton.

MODELL, MERRIAM (1908–); b. New York. Novelist. *The Sound of Years* (1946); *My Sister, My Bride* (1948). Under pen name "Evelyn Piper:" *Motive* (1950); *Plot* (1951); *The Lady and Her Doctor* (1956); etc.

Modern Age: A Conservative Review. Chicago, Ill. Quarterly. Founded 1957. Published by the Institute for Philosophical and Historical Studies. Eugene Davidson is editor.

Modern Age Books. New York. Publishers. Founded 1937. Published regular trade books, and *The Modern Age Reprints*, the latter a popular price series of outstanding modern authors.

Modern American Poetry and **Modern British Poetry.** By Louis Untermeyer. The first appeared in 1919 and the second in 1920; they were later combined in one volume. New poets were added in subsequent editions. One of the most influential anthologies in popularizing the work of modern poets.

Modern Chivalry. By Hugh Henry Brackenridge, 4v. (1792–97). First important literary work of the backwoods; a broad satire on coonskin democracy and political upstarts, with discursive sidelights on the humor and foibles of the times. Often called the American counterpart of *Don Quixote* on account of its characters Captain John Farrago and his foil, Teague O'Regan. Vols. 1–2 published at Philadelphia, 1792; vol. 3, at Pittsburgh, 1793; and vol. 4, at Philadelphia, 1797. Revised in four volumes (Philadelphia, 1815), the last volume containing new material. A critical edition was edited by C. M. Newlin in 1937.

Modern Fiction Studies. Lafayette, Ind. Quarterly. Founded 1955. Concerned with critical, scholarly, and bibliographical contributions to the study of modern prose fiction since 1860. Every other issue deals with a single writer and contains a checklist of criticism with an index to studies of individual works. Edited at Purdue University by Maurice Beebe; later by William T. Stafford.

Modern Instance, A. Novel by William Dean Howells (1881). Story of Bartley Hubbard, a young newspaper editor in Maine who moves to Boston to further his career. His wife, Marcia, does not adapt herself to the new environment, and after a scene Bartley leaves her and goes West, where he is killed in a brawl.

Modern Language Association of America. Baltimore, Md. Founded 1883, by A. Marshall Elliott (1844–1910), who was editor of its *Publications* from 1884 to 1892, and by Henry Alfred Todd (1854–1925).

Modern Language Journal. Milwaukee, Wis. Monthly during the academic year. Founded 1916. Published by the National Federation of Modern Language Teachers.

Modern Language Notes. Baltimore, Md. Founded Jan., 1886, by A. Marshall Elliott, who printed it on his own private press for seventeen years, assisted by Henry Alfred Todd.

Modern Library. Reprint series of ancient and modern literary classics of all countries. The series was inaugurated by Boni & Liveright shortly after the firm was founded in 1917. In 1925 Bennet A. Cerf founded Modern Library, Inc., and became its president, continuing the publication of the pocket-sized Modern Library series of Boni & Liveright. Exceptions in the format were made to accommodate such longer works as Gibbons's *Decline and Fall of the Roman Empire,* Tolstoi's *War and Peace,* etc. These are known as Modern Library Giants.

Modern Philology. Chicago, Ill. Quarterly. Founded 1905 by John Matthews Manly. Published by the University of Chicago Press.

Modern Quarterly. Baltimore, Md. Founded 1923, by Victor F. Calverton, who edited it until his death in 1940. From 1933 to 1938 it was called the *Modern Monthly.*

MOELLER, PHILIP (Aug. 26, 1880–Apr. 26, 1958); b. New York. Playwright. *Helena's Husband* (prod. 1915); *Madame Sand* (prod. 1917); *Five Somewhat Historical Plays* (1918); *Molière* (prod. 1919); *Sophie* (1919); etc. A founder of the Washington Square Players, and a sponsor of the Little Theatre movement.

MOERS, ELLEN (Dec. 9, 1928–   ); b. New York. Author. *The Dandy: Brummel to Beerbohm* (1960); *The Two Dreisers* (1969).

MOFFAT, JAMES C[lement] (May 30, 1811–June 7, 1890); b. Glencree, Scot., came to the United States in 1833. Presbyterian clergyman, educator, author. *An Introduction to the Study of Aesthetics* (1858); *A Comprehensive History of Religion,* 2v. (1871–73); *Song and Scenery; or, A Summer Ramble in Scotland* (1874); *Alwyn: A Romance of Study* (1875); etc. Prof. Church history, Princeton Theological Seminary, 1861–88.

MOFFAT, JESSIE [Emerson] (Mrs. Joseph Alpheus Moffat; Mrs. Francis Duncan Bailey) (Aug. 22, 1880–); b. Fredonia, N.Y. Novelist, playwright. *A Friend at Court* (1904); *The Mirror of Miyama* (prod. 1907); *Bridge Across Hell* (1942); *Mrs. Gilbert Lancaster, 3rd* (1951).

MOFFAT, WILLIAM DAVID (Jan. 17, 1865–Oct. 1, 1946); b. Princeton, N.J. Publisher, editor, author. *Not Without Honor* (1896); *The Crimson Banner* (1907). On staff, *The Book Buyer,* and *Scribner's Magazine,* 1897–1905. Editor, *The Mentor,* 1912–29. President, Moffat, Yard & Co., publishers, 1905–22; vice-president, Gardner, Moffat Co., 1916–29. *See* Robert Sterling Yard.

MOFFATT, JAMES (July 4, 1870–June 27, 1944); b. Glasgow, Scotland. Educator, author. *An Introduction to the Literature of the New Testament* (1911); *The Moffatt New Testament* (trans., 1913); *Everyman's Life of Jesus* (1924); *Presbyterianism* (1928); *The First Five Centuries of the Church* (1938); etc. Prof. church history, Union Theological Seminary, New York, from 1927.

MOFFETT, CLEVELAND LANGSTON (Apr. 27, 1863–Oct. 14, 1926); b. Boonville, N.Y. Journalist, playwright, author of mystery stories. *True Detective Stories from the Archives of the Pinkertons* (1897); *A King in Rags* (1907); *Money Talks* (prod. 1906); *Through the Wall* (1907); *The Battle* (prod. 1908); *For Better, For Worse* (prod. 1910); *Greater Than the Law* (prod. 1912); *The Bishop's Purse* (with Oliver Herford, 1913); etc.

"Mogg Megone." Poem by John G. Whittier (1834). Depicts the border strife of the early Eastern New England settlers.

MOÏSE, PENINA (Apr. 23, 1797–Sept. 13, 1880); b. Charleston, S.C. Poet. *Fancy's Sketch-Book* (1833); *Hymns Written for the Use of Hebrew Congregation* (1856); *Secular and Religious Works* (1911).

MOLEY, RAYMOND (Sept. 27, 1886–); b. Berea, O. Journalist, educator, author. *Lessons in American Citizenship* (1917); *The Outline of Government* (1922); *After Seven Years* (1939); *The Hays Office* (1945); *Twenty-Seven Masters of Politics* (1949); *How to Keep Our Liberty* (1952); *The American Century of John C. Lincoln* (1962); *The First New Deal* (1966); etc. Editor, *Today,* 1933–37; *Newsweek,* since 1937. Prof. law, Columbia University, 1928–54.

MOLL, ERNEST GEORGE (Aug. 25, 1900–); b. Murtoa, Vict., Austl. Educator, author. *Sedge Fire* (poems, 1927); *Native Moments* (poems, 1930); *Appreciation of Poetry* (1934); *Brief Waters* (poems, 1945); *The Lifted Spear* (poems, 1953); *Poems 1940–55* (1957); *The Rainbow Serpent* (1962); *Briseis* (1965); etc. Prof. emeritus of English, University of Oregon, since 1965.

MOLLENHOFF, CLARK RAYMOND (Apr. 16, 1921–); b. Burnside, Iowa. Journalist, author. *Washington Cover-up* (1962); *Tentacles of Power* (1965); *Despoilers of Democracy* (1965); *The Pentagon* (1967).

MOLLOY, ROBERT (Jan. 9, 1906–); b. Charleston, S.C. Editor, novelist. *Pride's Way* (1945); *Uneasy Spring* (1946); *The Best of Intentions* (1949); *Pound Foolish* (1950); *A Multitude of Sins* (1953); *An Afternoon in March* (1958); *The Reunion* (1959); *The Other Side of the Hill* (1962). Literary editor, *New York Sun,* 1943–45.

MOLLOY, SISTER MARY ALOYSIUS (June 14, 1880–Sept. 28, 1954); b. Sandusky, O. Educator, author. *The Lay Apostolate* (1915); *Catholic Colleges for Women* (1918); etc. Dean, College of Saint Teresa, Winona, Minn., 1911–28; president, 1928–46.

Molly Make-Believe. Novel by Eleanor Hallowell Abbott (1912).

MOMADAY, N[orman] SCOTT (Feb. 27, 1934–); b. Lawton, Okla. Educator, author. *The Complete Poems of Frederick Goddard Tuckerman* (1965); *House Made of Dawn* (1968; Pulitzer Prize, 1969); *The Way to Rainy Mountain* (1969). Professor, University of California at Berkeley, since 1969.

MOMBERT, JACOB ISIDOR (Nov. 6, 1829–Oct. 7, 1913); b. Cassel, Ger. Episcopal clergyman, author. *An Authentic History of Lancaster County in the State of Pennsylvania* (1869); *A History of Charles the Great* (1888); *A Short History of the Crusades* (1894); etc.

MONAGHAN, FRANK (Nov. 4, 1904–Apr. 17, 1969); b. Uniontown, Pa. Educator, author. *French Travellers in the United States, 1765–1932* (1933); *John Jay* (1935); *World War Two: An Illustrated History* (1943); *Heritage of Freedom* (1947); etc. History dept., New York University, 1931–33; Yale University. Archivist, New York World's Fair, 1940.

MONAGHAN, JAMES [Jay], IV (Mar. 19, 1891–); b. West Chester, Pa. Author. *Diplomat in Carpet Slippers: Lincoln Deals with Foreign Affairs* (1945); *The Last of the Bad Men* (1946); *The Overland Trail* (1947); *The Great Rascal: The Life and Adventures of Ned Buntline* (1952); *The Civil War on the Western Border* (1955); *Swamp Fox of the Confederacy* (1956); *The Life of General George Armstrong Custer* (1959); *Australians and the Gold Rush* (1966); etc. Editor: *American Trails* series, since 1947; *The Book of the American West* (1963); *A Tenderfoot in Colorado* (1968).

Monahan, Deane. Pen name of James Steele.

MONAHAN, MICHAEL (Apr. 6, 1865–Nov. 22, 1933); b. in Co. Cork, Ire. Editor, poet. *Youth … and Other Poems* (1895); *Heinrich Heine* (1902); *Adventures in Life and Letters* (1912). Founder, *Papyrus,* a magazine, 1903.

Monday Evening Club. Hartford, Conn. A literary organization which has had as members Horace Bushnell, Calvin E. Stowe, J. Hammond Trumbull, Charles Dudley Warner, Joseph Twichell and "Mark Twain."

MONETTE, JOHN WESLEY (Apr. 5, 1803–Mar. 1, 1851); b. Staunton, Va. Physician, author. *History of the Discovery and Settlement of the Valley of the Mississippi,* 2v. (1846); etc.

Moneysworth. New York. Founded 1970. Consumer newsletter. Published by Frank Brady. Editor-in-chief is Ralph Ginzburg.

Monfort, Mrs. William N. *See* Grace May North.

Moniteur de la Louisiane. New Orleans, La. Newspaper. Founded 1794, by Louis Duclot, the printer. First newspaper in Louisiana. Expired 1814.

MONK, MARIA (1816–1849). Author. *Awful Disclosures of Maria Monk* (1836); *Further Disclosures* (1837). *See* William Leete Stone's *Maria Monk and the Nunnery of the Hôtel Dieu* (1836), an exposé; Laughton Osborn's *The Vision of Rubeta* (1838), a reply in satirical verse; Justin Jones's *The Nun of St. Ursula* (1845). *See also* Ralph Thompson's *The Maria Monk Affair,* in the *Colophon,* pt. 17, 1934.

Monocle: A Leisurely Journal of Political Satire. New York. Founded 1957. Published and edited by Victor S. Navasky.

MONROE, ANNE SHANNON (1877–July 27, 1945); b. Bloomington, Mo. Author. *Eugene Norton* (1900); *The World I Saw* (1929); *Feelin' Fine! Bill Hanley's Book* (1930).

MONROE, HARRIET (Dec. 23, 1860–Sept. 26, 1936); b. Chicago, Ill. Editor, poet. *Valeria, and Other Poems* (1891); *You and I* (1914); *The Difference, and Other Poems* (1924); *Poets and Their Art* (1926); *Chosen Poems* (1935); *A Poet's Life: Seventy Years in a Changing World* (1938). *The New Poetry: An Anthology* (with Alice Corbin Henderson, 1917). Founder, *Poetry: A Magazine of Verse,* 1912; editor, 1912–36.

MONROE, JAMES (Apr. 28, 1758–July 4, 1831); b. in Westmoreland Co., Va. Fifth president of the United States, author. *The Writings of James Monroe,* ed. by S. M. Hamilton, 7v. (1898–1903). *See* Daniel C. Gilman's *James Monroe* (1883); George Morgan's *The Life of James Monroe* (1921); Dexter Perkins's *The Monroe Doctrine* (1927); Edwin P. Hoyt's *James Monroe* (1968); N. Gerson's *James Monroe* (1969). The best collections of his papers are in the Library of Congress and the New York Public Library.

MONROE, PAUL (June 7, 1869–Dec. 6, 1947); b. North Madison, Ind. Educator, author. *Thomas Platter and the Educational Renaissance of the Sixteenth Century* (1904); *Principles of Secondary Education* (1914); *China: A Nation in Evolution* (1927); *Essays in Comparative Education,* 2v. (1927–32); *Founding of the American Public School System* (1940); etc. Editor: *A Cyclopedia of Education,* 5v. (1910–15); etc. Dept. of education, Teachers College, Columbia University, 1897–1923; Barnard prof. of education, 1925–38.

Monsieur Beaucaire. Novel by Booth Tarkington (1900). A best seller of its day, which recounts incidents in the life of Louis Phillippe de Valois who, masquerading as Monsieur Beaucaire, seeks love and adventure in England, but being mistreated as a man of low degree, reveals his true identity.

Mont-Saint-Michel and Chartres. By Henry Adams (1904). A classic study of the French people of the Middle Ages who could express their great love in the stones of a cathedral, the flowering of Medieval Christian art.

MONTAGU, [Montague Francis] **ASHLEY** (June 28, 1905–); b. London. Anthropologist, author. *Man's Most Dangerous Myth: The Fallacy of Race* (1942); *Introduction to Physical Anthropology* (1945); *On Being Human* (1950); *On Being Intelligent* (1951); *Darwin: Competition and Cooperation* (1952); *The Natural Superiority of Women* (1953); *The Direction of Human Development* (1955); *Immortality* (1955); *Biosocial Nature of Man* (1956); *Anthropology and Human Nature* (1957); *Man: His First Million Years* (1957); *The Reproductive Development of the Female* (1957); *Education and Human Relations* (1958); *The Cultured Man* (1958); *Human Heredity* (1959); *Prenatal Influences* (1962); *Race, Science and Humanity* (1963); *The Human Revolution* (1965); *The American Way of Life* (1967); *Sex, Man and Society* (1969); etc. Chairman, Anthropology dept., Rutgers University, 1949–55.

MONTAGUE, CHARLES HOWARD (1858–1889); b. in Massachusetts. Editor, author. *The Romance of Lilies* (1886); *The Face of Rosenfel* (1888); etc. Editor, the *Boston Globe.*

MONTAGUE, MARGARET PRESCOTT (Nov. 29, 1878–Sept. 26, 1955); b. White Sulphur Springs, W.Va. Author. *The Poet, Miss Kate and I* (1905); *The Sowing of Alderson Cree* (1907); *Linda* (1912); *Closed Doors* (1915); *The Gift* (1919); *England to America* (1920); *Uncle Sam of Freedom Ridge* (1920); *Deep Channel* (1923); *Leaves From a Secret Journal* (1926); *Up Eel River* (1928); *The Lucky Lady* (1933); etc.

MONTAGUE, WILLIAM PEPPERELL (Nov. 24, 1873–Aug. 1, 1953); b. Chelsea, Mass. Educator, author. *The Ways of Knowing; or, The Methods of Philosophy* (1925); *Belief Unbound: A Promethean Religion for the Modern World* (1930); *Knowledge, Nature and Value* (1940); *Great Visions of Philosophy* (1950); etc. Philosophy dept., Barnard College, Columbia University.

Montana As It Is. By Granville Stuart (1865). One of the rare books on Montana.

Montanan, The. See *The Frontier.*

Montcalm and Wolfe. Historical study by Francis Parkman, 2v. (1884). Thorough account of the conflict between the French and English for the North American continent, culminating in the fall of Quebec.

"Monterey." Poem by Charles Fenno Hoffman.

MONTEZ, LOLA (Marie Dolores Eliza Rosann Gilbert, countess of Landsfeld) (1818–June 30, 1861); b. Limerick, Ire. Actress, adventuress, author. *The Arts of Beauty* (1858); *Anecdotes of Love* (1858); *Lectures of Lola Montez* (actually written by Chauncey Burr, 1858); etc. *See* Francis Lister Hawks's *The Story of a Penitent* (anon., 1867); Edmund B. d'Auvergne's *Lola Montez* (1909); Horace Wyndham's *The Magnificent Montez* (1935); T. Everett Harré's *The Heavenly Sinner* (1935); Isaac Goldberg's *Queen of Hearts* (1936); Oscar Lewis's *Lola Montez: The Mid-Victorian Bad Girl in California* (1938).

MONTGOMERY, DAVID HENRY (Apr. 7, 1837–May 28, 1928); b. Syracuse, N.Y. Historian, writer of text-books. *The Leading Facts of English History* (1886); *The Leading Facts of French History* (1889); *The Leading Facts of American History* (1890); etc.

MONTGOMERY, GEORGE WASHINGTON (1804–June 5, 1841); b. Alicante, Sp. Translator, author. *Tareas de un Solitario* (1829), a translation of some of Washington Irving's stories; *El Bastardo de Castilla* (1832); *Narrative of a Journey to Guatemala* (1839). Translator in the United States legation in Madrid while Washington Irving was Minister.

MONTGOMERY, RUTHERFORD GEORGE (Apr. 12, 1896–); b. Freeborn, N.D. Jurist, author. *Troopers Three* (1932); *Call of the West* (1933); *Broken Fang* (1935); *High Country* (1938); *Iceblink* (1940); *Big Brownie* (1945); *Kildee House* (1950); *Wapiti* (1952); *McGonnigle's Lake* (1953); *Seecatch* (1955); *Happy Hollow* (1958); *White Trail* (1958); *The Stubborn One* (1965); *Thornbush Jungle* (1966); *Into the Groove* (1967); *Corey's Sea Monster* (1969); etc. Under pen name "Al Avery": *A Yankee Flier in the R.A.F.* (1940); etc.

MONTGOMERY, VAIDA STEWART (Mrs. Whitney Montgomery) (Aug. 28, 1888–July 24, 1959); b. in Childress Co., Tex. Editor, poet. *Locoed, and Other Poems* (1930). Editor: *Bright Excalibur* (with husband, 1933); *A Century with Texas Poets and Poetry* (1934); *Merry-Go-Round* (with husband, 1935); *Moon in the Steeple* (with husband, 1937); *Blood and Dust* (with husband, 1939); etc. Co-editor (with husband), *Kaleidograph: A National Magazine of Poetry,* 1929–59.

MONTGOMERY, WHITNEY MAXWELL (Sept. 14, 1877–Dec. 7, 1966); b. Eureka, Tex. Publisher, editor, poet. *Corn Silks and Cotton Blossoms* (1928); *Brown Fields and Bright Lights* (1930); *Hounds in the Hills* (1934). Editor (with wife, Vaida Stewart Montgomery): *Bright Excalibur* (1933); *Merry-Go-Round* (1935); *Moon in the Steeple* (1937); *Blood and Dust* (1939); *Joseph's Coat: Ballads, Lyrics, Sonnets* (1946); etc. Publisher and editor (with wife), *Kaleidograph: A National Magazine of Poetry,* from 1929.

Montgomery Advertiser. Montgomery, Ala. Newspaper. Founded 1829, as the weekly *Planter's Gazette* which about 1836 became the weekly *Montgomery Advertiser.* Established as a daily c. 1850. Grover Cleveland Hall was editor 1926–41. Harold E. Martin is now editor and Sunday book review editor.

Monthly Anthology and Boston Review. Boston, Mass. Founded Nov., 1803, by Phineas Adams, who wrote for it under the pen name of "Sylvanus per Se." In 1804 William Emerson, father of Ralph Waldo Emerson, became editor. In 1805 the Anthology Society was organized to edit and finance the magazine. This distinguished literary journal became the nucleus of the *North American Review.* Expired June, 1811.

Monthly Magazine, and American Review. New York. Founded Apr., 1799. Editor: Charles Brockden Brown. Expired Dec., 1800.

Monthly Register and Review of the United States. Charleston, S.C., Magazine. Founded Jan., 1805, by Stephen C. Carpenter, who moved it to New York in Nov., 1806. John Bristed became assoc. editor at that time, and editor in June, 1807. Bristed was the son-in-law of John Jacob Astor and the father of Charles Astor Bristed ("Carl Benson"). Expired Dec., 1807.

Monthly Review. New York. Monthly. Founded 1949. Editors are Harry Magdoff and Paul M. Sweezy. An independent socialist magazine.

MONTI, LUIGI (1830–1903); b. Palcomo, Sicily, came to the United States in 1850. Educator, consul, author. *The Adventures of a Consul Abroad* (under pen name, "Samuel Sampleton," 1878); *Leone* (anon., 1882); etc. Longfellow introduced him as the young Sicilian in his *Tales of a Wayside Inn.* With Harvard University, 1854–59. U.S. Consul at Palermo, 1861–73.

MONTROSS, LOIS SEYSTER (Apr. 27, 1897–Sept. 12, 1961); b. Kempton, Ill. Author. *Town and Gown* (with husband, 1923); *The Crimson Cloak* (poems, 1924); *Fraternity Row* (with husband, 1926); *Wind before Dawn* (1932); *No Stranger to My Heart* (1937); *If the Bough Breaks* (1938); *With Land in Sight* (1939); etc.

MONTROSS, LYNN (Oct. 17, 1895–Jan. 28, 1961); b. Battle Creek, Neb. Author. *Town and Gown* (with wife, Lois Seyster Montross, 1923); *Half Gods* (1924); *East of Eden* (1925); *Fraternity Row* (with wife, 1926); *War Through the Ages* (1944); *The Reluctant Rebels* (1950); *Rag, Tag and Bobtail* (1951); *Cavalry of the Sky* (1954); etc. Editor and co-author: *U.S. Marine Operations in Korea* (1959); *The U.S. Marines: A Pictorial History* (1959).

MOODY, DWIGHT LYMAN (Feb. 5, 1837–Dec. 22, 1899); b. Northfield, Mass. Evangelist, founder of religious conferences and institutes. Published eighteen volumes of sermons and addresses. See Gamaliel Bradford's *D. L. Moody, a Worker in Souls* (1927); W. R. Moody's *D. L. Moody* (1930); Richard K. Curtis's *They Called Him Mister Moody* (1966); James F. Findlay's *Dwight L. Moody: American Evangelist, 1837–1899* (1969).

MOODY, JOHN (May 2, 1868–Feb. 16, 1958); b. Jersey City, N.J. Financial analyst. *The Truth about the Trusts* (1904); *Masters of Capital* (1919); *The Remaking of Europe* (1921); *The Long Road Home* (1933); *Fast By the Road* (1942); *John Henry Newman* (1945). Founder and editor, *Moody's Magazine,* 1905; president and founder, Moody's Investment Service; publisher, *Moody's Manual,* since 1909.

MOODY, WILLIAM VAUGHN (July 8, 1869–Oct. 17, 1910); b. Spencer, Ind. Educator, poet, playwright. *The Masque of Judgment* (1900); *Gloucester Moors, and Other Poems* (1901); *Poems* (1901); *The Fire-Bringer* (1904); *A First View of English Literature* (1904); *The Sabine Woman* (prod. 1906), renamed *The Great Divide* (prod. 1906); *The Faith Healer* (prod. 1909); *Some Letters of William Vaughn Moody* (1913); *Selected Poems* (1931); *Letters to Harriet* (1935); etc. The Moody collection of American literature is now owned by the University of Chicago. With English dept., University of Chicago, 1895–99, 1901–07. See David D. Henry's *William Vaughn Moody* (1934); Martin Halpern's *William Vaughn Moody* (1964).

MOODY, WINFIELD SCOTT (b. 1856); b. New York. Editor, author. *Pickwick Ladle, and Other Collectors' Stories* (1907). Editor, *The Book Buyer,* 1894–1902. On staff, *New York Sun, New York Times,* etc.

MOON, BUCKLIN (May 13, 1911–); b. Eau Claire, Wis. Editor, author. *Brother* (1943); *The Darker: The High Cost of Prejudice* (1947); *Without Magnolias* (1949). Editor: *Primer for White Folks* (1945).

MOON, CARL (Oct. 5, 1879–June 24, 1948); b. Wilmington, O. Artist, author of children's books. *Lost Indian Magic* (with wife, Grace Moon, 1918); *Wongo and the Wise Old Crow* (with same, 1927); *Painted Moccasin* (1931); *Book of Nah-Wee* (with same, 1940); etc. Has illustrated other books by his wife.

MOON, GRACE (Mrs. Carl Moon) (d. Sept. 6, 1947); b. Indianapolis, Ind. Author of children's books. *Indian Legends in Rhyme* (1916); *Lost Indian Magic* (with husband, 1918); *Chi-Wee* (1925); *Nadita* (1927); *The Arrow of Teemay* (1931); *Shanty Ann* (1935); *Solita* (1938); *Daughter of Thunder* (1942); etc.

Moon Calf. Novel by Floyd Dell (1920). Felix, a young dreamer in a small town in Illinois, tries a number of jobs, falls in love several times, and finally goes to Chicago, determined to be a writer, believing that he has outgrown his childhood sweetheart, Rose. In *The Briary-Bush* (1921), a sequel, he and Rose are married.

Moon Hoax, The. By Richard Adams Locke (1859). The original hoax took place in 1835 when a series of articles was published in the New York *Sun* under the title, *Great Astronomical Discoveries, Lately Made by Sir John Herschel,* which announced that a vast human population had been discovered on the moon. It was believed by thousands. Augustus De Morgan in his *Budget of Paradoxes* (1872) attributed the hoax to Jean Nicolas Nicollet, but Edgar Allan Poe, who knew Locke intimately, substantiated his claim to the authorship and even said it anticipated his own story *Hans Phaall.*

MOONEY, CHARLES PATRICK JOSEPH (Sept. 15, 1865–Nov. 22, 1926); b. Bardstown Junction, Ky. Editor. City editor, the *Memphis Scimitar,* 1891–96; managing editor, the *Memphis Commercial Appeal,* 1896–1902; the New York *Daily News,* 1902–03; the *New York American,* 1903–05; the *Chicago Examiner,* 1905–08; the *Memphis Commercial Appeal,* 1908–26. President, the Commercial Publishing Co.

MOORE, ANNE (1872–); b. Wilmington, N.C. Poet, novelist. *Children of God and Winged Things* (poems, 1921); *A Misty Sea* (poems, 1937); *Wayfarers in Toodlume* (1939); etc.

MOORE, ANNE CARROLL (1871–Jan. 20, 1961); b. Limerick, Me. Librarian, author. *Roads to Childhood* (1920); *New Roads to Childhood* (1923); *Nicholas: A Manhattan Christmas Story* (1924); *The Three Owls,* 3v. (1925–31); *Cross-Roads to Childhood* (1926); *Seven Stories High* (1932); *Nicholas and the Golden Goose* (1932); *Reading for Pleasure* (1935); *My Roads to Childhood* (1939); *A Century of Kate Greenaway* (1946). Editor: *Writing and Criticism* (with B. E. Mahony, 1951); Washington Irving's *Knickerbocker's History of New York* (1959). Supt. of work for children, The New York Public Library, 1906–41. Critic of children's books, *The Bookman,* 1918–27; the *New York Herald Tribune Books,* 1924–30; the *Atlantic Monthly,* from 1930. Pioneer in organization of children's book departments in public libraries.

MOORE, BARRINGTON, JR. (1913–   ). Political scientist, author. *Terror and Progress, USSR* (1954); *Political Power and Social Theory* (1958); *Soviet Politics: The Dilemma of Power* (1965); *Social Origins of Dictatorship and Democracy* (1966). Editor: *The Critical Spirit* (1967). Co-editor: *A Critique of Tolerance* (1965). Research fellow, Russian Research Center, Harvard University.

MOORE, CHARLES (Oct. 20, 1855–Sept. 26, 1942); b. Ypsilanti, Mich. Librarian, historian. *The Gladwin Manuscripts* (1897); *The Northwest under Three Flags* (1900); *History of Michigan,* 4v. (1915); *The Family Life of George Washington* (1926); *Life and Letters of Charles Follen McKim* (1929); *Washington Past and Present* (1929); etc. Acting chief, Division of Manuscripts, Library of Congress, 1918–27.

MOORE, CHARLES HERBERT (Apr. 10, 1840–Feb. 15, 1930); b. New York. Artist, educator, author. *Development & Character of Gothic Architecture* (1890); *Character of*

Renaissance Architecture (1905); etc. Dept. fine arts, Harvard University, 1880–1909; prof., 1896–1909; director, the Fogg Art Museum, 1895–1909.

MOORE, CHARLES LEONARD (b. 1854); b. Philadelphia, Pa. Lawyer, poet. *Atlas* (1881); *Poems, Antique and Modern* (1883); *Book of Day-Dreams* (1888); *Banquet of Palacios* (1889); *Odes* (1896); *Incense & Iconoclasm* (1915).

MOORE, CLARA SOPHIA JESSUP (Mrs. Bloomfield H. Moore) (Feb. 16, 1824–1899); b. Philadelphia, Pa. Author. Pen names, "Clara Moreton" and "Mrs. H. O. Ward"; also wrote as Mrs. Bloomfield H. Moore and Mrs. Bloomfield-Moore. *Frank and Fannie* (1851); *The Diamond Cross* (1857); *Miscellaneous Poems* (anon., 1875); *On Dangerous Ground* (1876); *Tales from Ariosto* (anon., 1880); *The Young Lady's Friend* (1880); *Gondaline's Lesson . . . and Other Poems* (1881); etc.

MOORE, CLEMENT CLARKE (July 15, 1779–July 10, 1863); b. New York. Educator, Hebraist, poet. *A Compendious Lexicon of the Hebrew Language,* 2v. (1809); *Poems* (1844); *George Castriot, Surnamed Scanderbeg, King of Albania* (1850); Best known for his ballad "The Night Before Christmas." Biblical teacher, General Theological Seminary, New York, 1823–50.

MOORE, CLIFFORD HERSCHEL (Mar. 11, 1866–Aug. 31, 1931); b. Sudbury, Mass. Educator, classicist, author. *The Religious Thought of the Greeks, from Homer to the Triumph of Christianity* (1916). Translated the *Histories of Tacitus,* the *Medea* of Euripides, the *Odes* of Horace, etc. Classics dept., Harvard University, 1898–1931; prof. Latin, 1905–31.

MOORE, DOUGLAS STUART (Aug. 10, 1893–July 25, 1969); b. Cutchogue, L.I. Educator, composer. *Listening to Music* (1932); *From Madrigal to Modern Music* (1942).

MOORE, EDWARD CALDWELL (Sept. 1, 1857–Mar. 26, 1943); b. West Chester, Pa. Presbyterian clergyman, educator, author. *History of Christian Thought Since Kant* (1912); *West and East* (1919); *The Nature of Religion* (1936); etc. Plummer prof. Christian morals, Harvard University, 1915–29.

MOORE, FRANK (Dec. 17, 1828–Aug. 10, 1904); b. Concord, N.H. Editor, compiler. Editor: *Songs and Ballads of the American Revolution* (1856); *American Eloquence,* 2v. (1857); *Diary of the American Revolution,* 2v. (1860); *Rebel Rhymes and Rhapsodies* (1864); *Anecdotes, Poetry, and Incidents of the War* (1866), reissued as *The Civil War in Song and Story* (1882); *Songs and Ballads of the Southern People, 1861–65* (1886); *The Rebellion Record,* 11v. (1861–68).

MOORE, FREDERICK FERDINAND (Dec. 24, 1877–); b. Concord, N.H. Editor, author. *The Devil's Admiral* (1913); *Siberia To-Day* (1919); *Sailor Girl* (1920); *Isle o' Dreams* (1920); *The Samovar Girl* (1921); With the *San Francisco Examiner,* 1905–13; editor, *The Argosy,* 1913–15; founder, the *Book Dealers' Weekly,* 1925.

MOORE, GEORGE FOOT (Oct. 15, 1851–May 16, 1931); b. West Chester, Pa. Presbyterian clergyman, educator, author. *The Literature of the Old Testament* (1913); *History of Religions,* 2v. (1913–19); *Judaism,* 2v. (1927); etc. Prof. Andover Theological Seminary, 1883–1904; prof. history of religion, Harvard, 1904–28.

MOORE, GEORGE HENRY (Apr. 20, 1823–May 5, 1892); b. Concord, N.H. Librarian, historian, bibliographer. *"Mr. Lee's Plan—March 29, 1777": The Treason of Charles Lee* (1860); *Notes on the History of Slavery in Massachusetts* (1866); *Notes on the History of Witchcraft in Massachusetts* (1883); *Washington as an Angler* (1887); *Typographiae Neo-Eboracensis Primitiae* (1888). The sale of his collection was one of the noted book auctions of the day, 1893. Librarian, New York Historical Society, 1849–72; Lenox Library, 1876–92. *See* H. M. Lydenberg's *History of The New York Public Library* (1923).

MOORE, HARRY T[hornton] (Aug. 2, 1908–); b. Oakland, Cal. Educator, author. *The Novels of John Steinbeck* (1939); *Life and Works of D.H. Lawrence* (1951); *The Intelligent Heart* (1955); *Poste Restante* (1956); *Edward Morgan Foster* (1965); *20th Century German Literature* (1967); *20th Century French Literature* (1969). Editor: D.H. Lawrence's *Sex, Literature and Censorship: Essays* (1953); Rilke, *Selected Letters* (1960); *Letters of D.H. Lawrence* (1962); *The World of Lawrence Durrell* (1962); *Contemporary American Novelists* (1964); *Elizabethan Age* (1965); etc.

MOORE, HORATIO NEWTON (1814–Aug. 26, 1859); b. in New Jersey. Author. *Orlando; or, A Woman's Virtue* (1835); *Life and Services of Gen. Anthony Wayne* (1845); *The Life and Times of Gen. Francis Marion* (1845); *Fitzgerald and Hopkins* (1847); etc.

MOORE, IDORA McCLELLAN (Oct. 31, 1843–Feb. 1929); b. Talladega, Ala. Author. Pen name, "Betsy Hamilton." Contributed Southern character sketches to the *Atlanta Constitution* for thirty years. Some of these were edited and published by her daughter, Julia Moore Smith, as *Southern Character Sketches* (1937).

MOORE, JACOB BAILEY (Oct. 3, 1797–Sept. 1, 1853); b. Andover, N.H. Editor, printer, librarian, author. *Collections, Historical and Miscellaneous,* 3v. (1822–24); *Memoirs of American Governors* (v. 1 only, 1846), republished as *Lives of the Governors of New Plymouth and Massachusetts Bay* (1848); etc. Founder, the *New Hampshire Journal,* Concord, N.H., Sept. 11, 1826. Librarian, New York Historical Society, 1848–49.

MOORE, JOHN BASSETT (Dec. 3, 1860–Nov. 12, 1947); b. Smyrna, Del. Jurist, educator, author. *Extradition and Interstate Rendition,* 2v. (1891); *History and Digest of International Arbitration,* 6v. (1898); *American Diplomacy* (1905); *Digest of International Law,* 8v. (1906); *Collected Papers* (1945); etc. Editor, *The Works of James Buchanan,* 12v. (1908). Prof. international law, Columbia University, 1891–1924; Judge, Permanent Court of International Justice, 1921–28.

MOORE, JOHN ROBERT (July 27, 1890–Oct. 14, 1969); b. Pueblo, Col. Educator, author. *Symphonies and Songs* (1923); *Defoe in the Pillory, and Other Studies* (1938); *A Checklist of the Writings of Daniel Defoe* (1960); etc. Editor: *Representative Essays, English and American* (1930); *Defoe's A Brief History of the Poor Palatine Refugees* (1964); etc. Prof. emeritus, English dept., Indiana University, from 1961.

MOORE, JOHN TROTWOOD (Aug. 26, 1858–May 10, 1929); b. Marion, Ala. Editor, author. He added the "Trotwood" to his name, from Dickens's *David Copperfield,* and then used it as his pen name. *Songs and Stories from Tennessee* (1897), republished as *Ole Mistis, and Other Songs and Stories from Tennessee* (1925); *A Summer Hymnal* (1901); *The Bishop of Cottontown* (1906); *Uncle Wash: His Stories* (1910); *The Gift of the Grass* (1911); *Hearts of Hickory* (1926); etc. Founder, *Trotwood's Monthly,* 1905, which in 1906 became the *Taylor-Trotwood Magazine;* editor, 1905–11.

MOORE, JOHN WEEKS (Apr. 11, 1807–Mar. 23, 1889); b. Andover, N.H. Musical editor. Editor: *Complete Encyclopaedia of Music* (1854); *The Songs and Song-Writers of America,* in 200 parts (1859–80); *Moore's Historical, Biographical, and Miscellaneous Gatherings in the Form of Disconnected Notes Relative to Printers, Printing, Publishing, and Editing of Books, Newspapers, Magazines and Other Literary Productions* (1886); etc. Editor, *Bellows Falls* (Vt.) *Gazette,* 1838–55.

MOORE, MARIANNE [Craig] (Nov. 15, 1887–Feb. 5, 1972); b. St. Louis, Mo. Editor, poet. *Poems* (1921); *Observations* (1924); *Selected Poems* (1935); *The Pangolin, and Other Verse* (1936); *What Are Years?* (1941); *Nevertheless* (1944); *Collected Poems* (1951; Pulitzer Prize for poetry, 1952); *The*

Fables of La Fontaine (trans., 1954); Predilections (1955); Like a Bulwark (poems, 1956); O To Be a Dragon (poems, 1959); Marianne Moore Reader (1961); The Absentee (1962); Three Classic Tales (transl., 1963); The Arctic Ox (1964); Tell Me, Tell Me (1966); Complete Poems (1968). Editor, The Dial, 1925–29. See E. P. Sheehy's and A. Lohf's The Achievement of Marianne Moore: A Bibliography, 1907–1957 (1958); B. F. Engel's Marianne Moore (1963); Jean Garrigue's Marianne Moore (1965).

MOORE, MERRILL (Sept. 11, 1903–Sept. 20, 1957); b. Columbia, Tenn., son of John Trotwood Moore. Psychiatrist, poet. The Noise That Times Makes (1929); It is a Good Deal Later Than You Think (1934); Six Sides to a Man (1935); Poems from the Fugitive (1936); M: One Thousand Autobiographical Sonnets (1938); Clinical Sonnets (1949); Illegitimate Sonnets (1950); Case Record from a Sonnetorium (1952); More Clinical Sonnets (1952); A Doctor's Book of Hours (1954); Dance of Death (1957); The Phoenix and the Bees (poems, 1958).

Moore, Mrs. Bloomfield H. See Clara Sophia Jessup Moore.

Moore, Mrs. Frederick Ferdinand. See Eleanor Gates.

MOORE, ROBERT LOWELL, JR. (Oct. 31, 1925–); b. Boston. Pen name "Robin Moore". Author. Pitchman (1956); The Devil To Pay (1961); The Green Berets (1965); The Country Team (1967); Fiedler (1968); The French Connection (1969); The Khaki Mafia (1971).

MOORE, RUTH [Ellen] (1908–); b. St. Louis, Mo. Journalist, author. Man, Time and Fossils (1953); Charles Darwin: A Great Life in Brief (1955); The Earth We Live On (1956); The Coil of Life (1961); Evolution (1962); The Sea Flower (1965); Niels Bohr: His Life, His Science and the World They Changed (1966). Staff writer, Chicago Sun-Times, since 1943.

MOORE, RUTH, b. in Maine. Novelist. The Weir (1943); Spoonhandle (1946); The Fire Balloon (1948); A Fair Wind Home (1953); Candlemas Bay (1951); Second Growth (1962); etc.

MOORE, SAMUEL TAYLOR (June 1893–); b. Westfield, Mass. Author. Hetty Green (with Boyden Sparkes, 1930); Fighting Aces (1931); Under-Sea Heroes (1931); America and the World War (1939); U.S. Airpower (1958); etc.

MOORE, VIRGINIA (July 11, 1903–); b. in Nebraska. Critic, poet, novelist, biographer. Not Poppy (poems, 1926); Sweet Water and Bitter (poems, 1928); Rising Wind (1928); Distinguished Women Writers (1934); Homer's Golden Chain (poems, 1936); The Life and Eager Death of Emily Brontë (1936); Virginia Is a State of Mind (1942); Ho for Heaven! (1946); The Unicorn: William Butler Yeats' Search For Reality (1954); The Whole World, Stranger (1957).

MOORE, WARD (Aug. 10, 1903–); b. Madison, N.J. Novelist. Breathe the Air Again (1942); Greener Than You Think (1947); Bring the Jubilee (1953); Cloud By Day (1956); etc.

MOORE, WILBERT E[llis] (Oct. 26, 1914–); b. Elma, Wash. Sociologist. Industrial Relations and the Social Order (1946); Industrialization and Labor (1951); The Conduct of the Corporation (1962); The Impact of Industry (1965); Order and Change: Essays in Comparative Sociology (1967); etc. Co-editor: Twentieth Century Sociology (1945); Indicators of Social Change (1968); etc.

MOOS, MALCOLM CHARLES (Apr. 19, 1916–); b. St. Paul, Minn. Educator, author. Politics, Presidents, and Coattails (1952); The Republicans: A History of Their Party (1956); Dwight D. Eisenhower (1964). Co-author: A Grammar of American Politics (1949); The Campus and the State (1959); Hats in the Ring (1960); etc. President, University of Minnesota, since 1967.

MORE, BROOKES (Mar. 29, 1859–June 9, 1942); b. Dayton, O. Publisher, poet. The Lover's Rosary (1918); Songs of a Red

Cross Nurse (1918); Hero and Leander (1926); Adventured Values (1929); etc. President, Cornhill Publishing Co., Boston, from 1922; president, Jordan & More Press, 1933–39. See Wilmon Brewer's Life and Poems of Brookes More (1940).

MORE, PAUL ELMER (Dec. 12, 1864–Mar. 9, 1937); b. St. Louis, Mo. Editor, author. Helena, and Occasional Poems (1890); Benjamin Franklin (1900); Shelburne Essays, 11 series (1904–21); Platonism (1917); The Religion of Plato (1921); Hellenistic Philosophies (1923); The Christ of the New Testament (1924); Christ the Word (1927); New Shelburne Essays, 3v. (1928–1936); The Catholic Faith (1931); Pages from an Oxford Diary (1937); etc. Lit. editor, The Independent, 1901–03; New York Evening Post, 1903–09; The Nation, 1909–14. See Fred B. Millett's Contemporary American Authors (1940); Myron Simon's and Thornton H. Parsons' Transcendentalism and Its Legacy (1966).

More Wonders of the Invisible World. By Robert Calef (1700). A plea for tolerance in the New England Witchcraft trials, and a reply and a rebuke to Cotton Mather's Wonders of the Invisible World. Increase Mather had Calef's book burned in the Harvard College yard. Giles Corey and Martha Corey and Sarah Good appear in this work which furnished material for the opening chapter of Hawthorne's The House of the Seven Gables.

Morecamp, Arthur. Pen name of Thomas Pilgrim.

MOREHEAD, ALBERT HODGES (Aug. 7, 1909–Oct. 5, 1966); b. Chattanooga, Tenn. Editor, author. The Modern Hoyle (1944). Co-author, editor: Official Rules of Card Games (1946–59); etc.

MOREHOUSE, CLIFFORD PHELPS (Apr. 18, 1904–); b. Milwaukee, Wis., son of Frederic Cook Morehouse. Editor, author. Origins of Episcopal Church Press (1942); Wartime Pilgrimage (1942); A Layman Looks at the Church (1964). Co-author: Outline Life of Christ (1947). Editor: Episcopal Church Annual. With Morehouse (now Morehouse-Barlow) Publishing Co., New York, since 1925; editor, the Living Church, 1932–52.

MOREHOUSE, FREDERIC COOK (May 19, 1868–June 25, 1932); b. Milwaukee, Wis. Editor, author. Some American Churchmen (1892); The Evolution of Parties in the Anglican Communion (1905); etc. Editor, the Living Church, 1899–32. President, Morehouse Publishing Co., Milwaukee, Wis.

MOREHOUSE, WARD (Nov. 24, 1899–Dec. 7, 1966); b. Savannah, Ga. Journalist, author. Gentlemen of the Press (prod. 1928); Miss Quis (prod. 1937); Forty-Five Minutes Past Eight (1939); U.S. 90 (prod. 1941); American Reveille (1942); George M. Cohan: Prince of the American Theatre (1943); Matinee Tomorrow: Fifty Years of Our Theater (1949); Just the Other Day (1953). Columnist, North American Newspaper Alliance.

Morehouse-Barlow Co. New York. Publishers. Founded 1884, by Linden H. Morehouse, as the Young Churchman Co. Name changed 1918 to the Morehouse Publishing Co. Absorbed Edwin S. Gorham, Inc. in 1938 and took the name Morehouse-Gorman. Took present name in 1959. Specializes in publication for the Episcopal Church.

MORELAND, JOHN RICHARD (Nov. 28, 1880–Nov. 12, 1947); b. Norfolk, Va. Author. Red Poppies in the Wheat (1921); The Sea and April (1928); The Moon Mender (1933); A Blue Wave Breaking (1938); What of the Night? (1942); Shadow at My Heel (1946); etc. Founder, The Lyric, 1920; editor, 1920–23.

MORELAND, PATRICK D[acus] (Mar. 8, 1897–); b. Unaka, N.C. Poet. Arrow Unspent (1931); Slumber at Noon (1934); Seven Songs (1936).

MORENO, J[acob] L. (May 20, 1892–); b. Bucharest. Psychiatrist. Who Shall Survive? (1934); The Words of the Father

(1941); *Psychodrama*, (1946); *Sociometry, Experimental Method and the Science of Society* (1951); *Psychodrama,* Vol. II (1959); Vol. I, enlarged (1964); Vol. III (1969). Editor: *Sociometry and the Science of Man* (1956); *International Handbook of Group Psychotherapy* (1966). Founded *Sociometry, A Journal of Interpersonal Relations*, 1937.

MORFORD, HENRY (Mar. 10, 1823–Aug. 4, 1881); b. New Monmouth, N.J. Editor, poet, novelist, playwright, author of many popular travel guides. *Music of the Spheres* (poems, 1840); *Rhymes of Twenty Years* (1859); *The Rest of Don Juan* (poem, 1846); *Shoulder-Straps* (1863); *The Days of Shoddy* (1863); *Sprees and Splashes* (1863); *The Coward* (1864); *Over-Sea* (1867); *The Bells of Shandon* (with John Brougham, prod. 1867); *Morford's Short-Trip Guide to Europe* (1868); *Rhymes of an Editor* (1873); *John Jasper's Secret: Sequel to Charles Dickens' Mystery of Edwin Drood* (1872); etc.

MORGAN, ALBERT (1920–). Author. *The Great Man* (1955); *Cast of Characters* (1957); *One Star General* (1959); *A Small Success* (1960); *Minor Miracle* (1961).

MORGAN, ANGELA (d. Jan. 24, 1957); b. Washington, D.C. Poet. *The Hour Has Struck* (poems, 1914); *Because of Beauty* (poems, 1922); *Selected Poems* (1927); *Creator Man* (1929); *Awful Rainbow* (1932); *Gold on Your Pillow* (1936); *Drum Beats Out of Heaven* (1941); *Whirlwind Vision* (poems, 1943); *Rockets to the Sun* (1948); etc.

Morgan, Appleton. See James Appleton Morgan.

MORGAN, ARTHUR ERNEST (June 20, 1878–); b. Cincinnati, O. Civil engineer, educator, author. *My World* (1927); *The Seedman* (1933); *The Long Road* (1936); *The Small Community* (1942); *Edward Bellamy* (1944); *Nowhere Was Somewhere* (1946); *Search for Purpose* (1955); *The Community of the Future* (1957); *It Can Be Done in Education* (1962); etc. Pres., Antioch College, 1920–36.

MORGAN, EDMUND SEARS (Jan. 17, 1916–Jan. 31, 1966); b. Minneapolis, Minn. Historian. *The Puritan Family* (1944); *The Stamp Act Crisis* (with Helen M. Morgan, 1953); *The Birth of the Republic* (1956); *The Puritan Dilemma: The Story of John Winthrop* (1958); *Visible Saints* (1965); *Roger Williams* (1967); etc. Sterling prof. of history, Yale University, since 1965.

MORGAN, EDWARD P. (June 23, 1910–   ); b. Walla Walla, Wash. Journalist, broadcaster, author. Co-author: *Candidates* (1960); *The Press in Washington* (1966). Editor: *This I Believe* (v. 1, 1952; v. 2,.1954); *Clearing the Air* (1963). News commentator, ABC, Washington, D.C., 1955–67; newspaper columnist, Newsday Syndicate, since 1966; senior correspondent, Public Broadcasting Laboratory, since 1967.

Morgan, Emanuel. Pen name of Witter Bynner.

MORGAN, FORREST (Mar. 20, 1852–Feb. 24, 1924); b. Rockville, Conn. Librarian. Editor: *Connecticut as a Colony and as a State,* 4v. (1904); etc. Asst. librarian, Watkinson Library, Hartford, Conn.

MORGAN, GEORGE (Oct. 10, 1854–Jan. 8, 1936); b. Concord, Del. Author. *John Littlejohn, of J* (1895); *The Issue* (1904); *The True Patrick Henry* (1907); *The True Lafayette* (1919); *The Life of James Monroe* (1921); *The City of Firsts: Being a Complete History of the City of Philadelphia* (1926).

MORGAN, JAMES (1861–May 12, 1955); b. Fleming Co., Ky. Journalist, author. *Theodore Roosevelt: The Boy and the Man* (1907); *Abraham Lincoln: The Boy and the Man* (1908); *Charles H. Taylor, Builder of the Boston Globe* (1923); *Our Presidents* (1924); *The Birth of the American People* (1930); etc. On editorial staff, the *Boston Globe.*

MORGAN, JAMES APPLETON (Oct. 2, 1845–Aug. 15, 1928); b. Portland, Me. Shakespearean scholar, author. Wrote later books as Appleton Morgan. *The Law of Literature,* 2v.

(1875); *The Shakespearean Myth* (1881); *Shakespeare in Fact and in Criticism* (1888); etc. Compiler: *Macaronic Poetry* (1872); *Digesta Shakespeareana,* 2v. (1886–87). Founder, The Shakespeare Society of New York, 1885; president, 1885–1910.

MORGAN, JAMES MORRIS (Mar. 10, 1845–Apr. 21, 1928); b. New Orleans, La. Confederate naval officer, author. *Prince and Boatswain: Sea Tales from the Recollections of Rear-Admiral Charles E. Clark* (with J. P. Marquand, 1915); *Recollections of a Rebel Reefer* (autobiography, 1917).

MORGAN, JOY ELMER (Dec. 11, 1889–); b. Calloway, Neb. Editor, author. *The Great Transition* (1932); *The Planning of Your Life* (1936); *Horace Mann: His Ideas and Ideals* (1937); *The School That Built a Nation* (1954); *Planning Your Retirement* (1958); *A Philosophy of Life* (1963); etc. Editor: *American Citizens Handbook* (1941; rev. ed. 1968). Editor, *Journal of N.E.A.,* 1920–54.

MORGAN, LEWIS HENRY (Nov. 21, 1818–Dec. 17, 1881); b. Aurora, N.Y. Ethnologist, anthropologist, author. Adopted into the Seneca tribe. Indian name, "Tayadawahkugh." *League of the Ho-dé-no-san-nee; or, Iroquois* (1851); *The American Beaver and His Works* (1868); *Ancient Society* (1877); *House and House-Life of the American Aborigines* (1881). He was called the "Father of American Anthropology," his writings on the Iroquois being the first scientific account in America of an Indian tribe.

MORGAN, MORRIS HICKY (Feb. 8, 1859–Mar. 16, 1910); b. Providence, R.I. Educator, classicist, author. *Addresses and Essays* (1910). Editor and translator of works of Xenophon, Terence, Lysias, Vitrurius, and Persius. He left his Persius collection to the Harvard College Library. Classics dept., Harvard University, 1887–1910; prof. Latin, 1896–99; prof. classical philology, 1899–1910.

MORGAN, MURRAY (Feb. 16, 1916–); b. Tacoma, Wash. Author. *Day of the Dead* (pen name "Cromwell Murray," 1947); *Bridge to Russia: Those Amazing Aleutians* (1947); *Dixie Raider* (1948); *The Columbia: Powerhouse of the West* (1949); *The Viewless Winds* (1949); *Skid Road* (1951); *Dam* (1954); *Doctors to the World* (1958); *Century Twenty One* (1962); *Northwest Corner* (1962); *One Man's Gold* (1967); *Love Letters to My Beloved* (1968).

MORGAN, NEIL (Feb. 27, 1924–   ); b. Smithfield, N.C. Author. *My San Diego* (1951); *It Began with a Roar* (1953); *Know Your Doctor* (1954); *Crosstown* (1955); *My San Diego* (1960); *Westward Tilt* (1963); *Neil Morgan's San Diego* (1964); *The Pacific States* (1967).

MORGAN, SUSAN RIGBY DALLAM (Mrs. L. F. Morgan). Author. *The Swiss Heiress; or, The Bride of Destiny* (anon., 1836); *The Polish Orphan; or, Vicissitudes* (anon., 1838); *The Haunting Shadow* (1848); etc.

MORGAN, WILLIAM THOMAS (May 19, 1883–June 9, 1946); b. Dell Roy, O. Educator, author. *A Guide to the Study of English History* (1926); *A Bibliography of British History, 1700–1715,* 5v. (1934–42); etc. History dept., Indiana University, from 1919.

MORGENTHAU, HANS JOACHIM (Feb. 17, 1904–); b. Coburg, Ger. Educator, author. *The International Jurisdiction* (1929); *Scientific Man vs. Power Politics* (1946); *Politics Among Nations* (1948); *In Defense of the National Interest* (1951); *Dilemmas of Politics* (1958); *Politics in the 20th Century* (1968); *Vietnam and the United States* (1965); *A New Foreign Policy for the United States* (1969); etc. Dept. of political science, University of Chicago, since 1945.

MORGENTHAU, HENRY (Apr. 26, 1856–Nov. 25, 1946); b. Mannheim, Ger. Diplomat, author. *All in a Life-Time* (1922); *My Trip around the World* (1928); etc. U.S. Ambassador to Turkey, 1913–16.

MORISON, ELTING ELMORE (Dec. 14, 1909–); b. Milwaukee, Wisc. Educator. *Admiral Sims and the Modern American Navy* (1942); *Turmoil and Tradition, a Study of the Life and Times of Henry L. Stimson* (1960); *Men, Machines and Modern Times* (1966); etc. Editor: *Theodore Roosevelt's Letters,* 8v. (1951–54). Prof. history, Massachusetts Institute of Technology, since 1953.

MORISON, SAMUEL ELIOT (July 9, 1887–); b. Boston, Mass. Historian. *The Life of Harrison Gray Otis* (1913); *Maritime History of Massachusetts* (1921); *Oxford History of the United States* (1927); *Builders of Bay Colony* (1930); *Tercentennial History of Harvard University,* 5v. (1930–36); *Puritan Pronaos* (1936); *Growth of the American Republic* (with Henry Steele Commager, 1942); *Admiral of the Ocean Sea: A Life of Christopher Columbus* (1942, Pulitzer Prize for biography, 1943); *History of United States Naval Operations in World War II,* 14v. (1947–60); *By Land and by Sea* (1953); *Christopher Columbus, Mariner* (1955); *Freedom in Contemporary Society* (1956); *The Story of the Old Colony of New Plymouth* (1956); *Strategy and Compromise* (1958); *John Paul Jones* (1959); *The Story of Mt. Desert Island* (1960); *The Two-Ocean War* (1963); *Spring Tides* (1965); *H. G. Otis, Urbane Federalist* (1969); etc. Prof. history, Harvard University, 1915–55.

MORLEY, CHRISTOPHER [Darlington] (May 5, 1890–Mar. 28, 1957); b. Haverford, Pa. Poet, essayist. Author: *Parnassus on Wheels* (1917); *Shandygaff* (1918); *The Haunted Book Shop* (1919); *Mince Pie* (1919); *Pipefuls* (1920); *Chimneysmoke* (poems, 1921); *Tales from a Rolltop Desk* (1921); *Where the Blue Begins* (1922); *Translations from the Chinese,* 3v. (1922, 1927, 1933); *Inward Ho!* (1923); *The Powder of Sympathy* (1923); *Pandora Lifts the Lid* (with Don Marquis, 1924); *Thunder on the Left* (1925); *The Romany Stain* (1926); *The Haverford Edition* [collected works], 12v. (1927); *Essays* (1928); *Poems* (1929); *John Mistletoe* (1931); *The Trojan Horse* (1937); *Kitty Foyle* (1939); *Letters of Askance* (1939); *The Middle Kingdom* (poems, 1944); *The Old Mandarin* (poems, 1947); *The Ironing Board* (1949); *The Ballad of New York* (poems, 1950); *Gentlemen's Relish* (1955); etc. Editor-in-chief: *Bartlett's Familiar Quotations,* revised edition (1937). Founder (with William Rose Benét), the *Saturday Review of Literature,* 1924.

MORLEY, FELIX [Muskett] (Jan. 6, 1894–); b. Haverford, Pa., brother of Christopher Morley. Educator, editor, author. *The Society of Nations* (1932); *The Power in the People* (1949); *The Foreign Policy of the United States* (1951); *Gumption Island* (1956); *Freedom and Federalism* (1959). Editor, *Washington Post,* 1933–40; pres. and editor, *Human Events,* 1945–50; Washington correspondent, *Barron's Weekly,* 1950–54. Pres. Haverford College, 1940–45.

MORLEY, FRANK VIGOR (Jan. 4, 1899–); b. Haverford, Pa., brother of Christopher Morley. Publisher, author. *Travels in East Anglia* (1923); *River Thames* (1926); *Whaling North and South* (with J. S. Hodgson, 1926); *Lamb Before Elia* (1932); *The Wreck of the Active* (1936); *My One Contribution to Chess* (1946); *Death in Dwelly Lane* (1952); etc. Editor: *Everybody's Boswell* (1930). With the Century Co., publishers, 1924–29; now a director, Harcourt, Brace & Co.

MORLEY, MARGARET WARNER (Feb. 17, 1858–Dec. 12, 1923); b. Montrose, Iowa. Author. *A Song of Life* (1891); *The Honey Makers* (1899); *The Bee People* (1899); *Little Mitchell: The Story of a Mountain Squirrel* (1904); *The Carolina Mountains* (1913); etc.

Morley, Ralph. Pen name of Howard Hinton.

MORLEY, S[ylvanus] GRISWOLD (Feb. 23, 1878–); b. Templeton, Mass. Educator, editor, author. *The Covered Bridges of California* (1938). Editor: *Spanish Ballads* (1911); *Modern Spanish Lyrics* (with E. C. Hills, 1913); *Spanish Humor in Story and Essay* (1921); *Pseudonyms and Literary Disguises of Lope de Vega* (1951); etc. Spanish dept., University of California, since 1914; prof., from 1923.

MORLEY, SYLVANUS GRISWOLD (June 7, 1883–Sept. 2, 1948); b. Chester, Pa. Archaeologist, author. *Introduction to the Study of Maya Hieroglyphs* (1915); *Inscriptions at Copan* (1920); *The Inscriptions of Peten* (1937–38); *Ancient Maya* (1946); etc. Director Chichen Itza project, Carnegie Institution, 1924–40.

Morning Courier and New York Enquirer. New York. Newspaper. The *New York Enquirer* was founded 1826, by Mordecai Manuel Noah. The *Morning Courier* was founded 1827. Merged 1829. In 1861, it was merged with the *New York World.* James Watson Webb was editor from 1829 to 1861.

MORRELL, BENJAMIN (July 5, 1795–1839); b. Rye, N.Y. Sealing captain, explorer, author. *A Narrative of Four Voyages to the South Sea* (1832). *See* Thomas J. Jacob's *Scenes, Incidents, and Adventures in the Pacific Ocean ... under Captain Benjamin Morrell* (1844).

MORRIS, CHARLES (Oct. 1, 1833–Sept. 6, 1922); b. Chester, Pa. Compiler, dime-novelist. *Bob Rockett, the Boy Dodger* (1880); *Dick, the Stowaway* (1882); *Cop Colt, the Quaker City Detective* (1885); *Handsome Harry, the Bootblack Detective* (1886); *Mike Merry, the Harbor Police Boy* (1886); *The Street Arab Detective* (1890); *New York Tim* (1896); etc. The dates are not necessarily those of first editions. Compiler: *Tales from the Dramatists,* 4v. (1893); *Half-Hours with the Best American Authors,* 4v. (1887); *The Handy Dictionary of Biography* (1901); *Famous Orators of the World* (1903); etc.

MORRIS, CHARLES [William] (May 23, 1901–); b. Denver, Colo. Educator. *Six Theories of Mind* (1932); *Paths of Life* (1942); *The Open Self* (1948); *Varieties of Human Value* (1956); *Signification and Significance* (1964); *Festival* (1966); etc. Dept. of philosophy, University of Florida, since 1958.

MORRIS, CLARA (Mrs. Frederick C. Harriott) (Mar. 17, 1848–Nov. 20, 1925); b. Toronto, Ont. Actress, author. *A Silent Singer* (1899); *Life on the Stage* (1901); *Stage Confidences* (1902); *The Life of a Star* (1906); *The New "East Lynne"* (1908); etc.

MORRIS, CONSTANCE LILY (d. May 12, 1954); b. New York. Author. *On Tour with Queen Marie* (1926); *Maria Theresa, the Last Conservative* (1937); *Heritage from My Father* (1947).

MORRIS, EARL J. Author. *The Cop* (1951).

MORRIS, EDITA (Mrs. Ira V. Morris) (Mar. 5, 1903–); b. Orebro, Sweden. Author. *My Darling from the Lions* (1943); *Three Who Loved* (1945); *Charade* (1948); *Flowers of Hiroshima* (1959); *Echo in Asia* (1961); *The Seeds of Hiroshima* (1965); *Dear Me* (1967); *Love to Vietman* (1969); etc.

MORRIS, E[dward] JOY (July 16, 1815–Dec. 31, 1881); b. Philadelphia, Pa. Diplomat, traveler, translator, author. *Notes of a Tour through Turkey, Greece, Egypt, Arabia Petraea, to the Holy Land,* 2v. (1842); etc. Congressman, 1843–45; 1856–58; U.S. Minister to Turkey, 1861–70.

MORRIS, ELISABETH WOODBRIDGE (Mrs. Charles Gould Morris) (June 16, 1870–); b. Brooklyn, N.Y. Author. *The Jonathan Papers* (1912); *More Jonathan Papers* (1915); *Days Out, and Other Papers* (1917); etc.

MORRIS, GEORGE POPE (Oct. 10, 1802–July 6, 1864); b. Philadelphia, Pa. Editor, poet, playwright. *Brier Cliff* (prod. 1826); *The Deserted Bride, and Other Poems* (1838); *The Little Frenchman and His Water Lots* (1839); *The Songs and Ballads* (1844); *Poems* (1854); etc. Compiler: *American Melodies* (1840). Founder, the *New York Mirror and Ladies' Literary Gazette,* 1823; founder, the *Home Journal,* 1846. His best known poems are "Woodman, Spare That Tree," and "Near the Lake."

MORRIS, GEORGE SYLVESTER (Nov. 15, 1840–Mar. 23, 1889); b. Norwich, Vt. Educator, philosopher, author. *British

Thought and Thinkers (1880); Kant's Critique of Pure Reason (1882); Hegel's Philosophy of the State and of History (1887); etc. Prof. modern language and literature, University of Michigan, 1870–81; prof. philosophy, 1881–89.

MORRIS, GOUVERNEUR (Jan. 31, 1752–Nov. 6, 1816); b. Morrisania, N.Y. Statesman, diplomat, author. The Diary and Letters of Gouverneur Morris, ed. by Anne Carey Morris, 2v. (1888); A Diary of the French Revolution, ed. by Beatrix C. Davenport, 2v. (1939). Minister to France, 1792–94; U.S. Senator, 1800–03. See Theodore Roosevelt's Gouverneur Morris (1888).

MORRIS, GOUVERNEUR (Feb. 7, 1876–Aug. 14, 1953); b. New York. Author. A Bunch of Grapes (1897); The Footprint, and Other Stories (1908); Putting on the Screws (1909); Spread Eagle, and Other Stories (1910); It, and Other Stories (1912); The Wild Goose (1919); Tiger Island (1934); etc.

MORRIS, HARRISON SMITH (Oct. 4, 1856–Apr. 12, 1948); b. Philadelphia, Pa. Editor, author. Madonna, and Other Poems (1894); Lyrics and Landscapes (1908); Hannah Bye (1920); Odes (1938); etc. Editor, Lippincott's Magazine, 1899–1905.

MORRIS, IRA VICTOR (Nov. 11, 1903–); b. Chicago, Ill. Author. Covering Two Years (1934); Marching Orders (1938); Liberty Street (1944); The Tree Within (1948); The Chicago Story (1952); The Bombay Meeting (1955); The Paper Wall (1960); Road to Spain (1965); Dictionary of Selected Forms in Classical Japanese Literature (1966).

MORRIS, JOHN GOTTLIEB (Nov. 14, 1803–Oct. 10, 1895); b. York, Pa. Lutheran clergyman, author. Life Reminiscences of an Old Lutheran Minister (1896); etc.

MORRIS, LLOYD R. (Sept. 23, 1893–Aug. 8, 1954); b. New York. Author. The Celtic Dawn (1917); The Poetry of Edwin Arlington Robinson (1923); The Rebellious Puritan: Portrait of Mr. Hawthorne (1927); Procession of Lovers (1929); This Circle of Flesh (1932); The Damask Cheek (with John van Druten, prod. 1942); A Threshold in the Sun (autobiography, 1943); Postscript to Yesterday (1947); William James (1950); Curtain Time: Story of the American Theatre (1953); etc.

MORRIS, RICHARD B[randon] (July 24, 1904–); b. New York. Educator, author. Government and Labor in Early America (1946); Fair Trial (1952); The American Revolution: A Short History (1955); Great Presidential Decisions (1960); A Nation Is Born (1963); The Peacemakers (1965); The American Revolution Reconsidered (1967); U.S.A.: The History of a Nation (with William Greenleaf, 1969); etc. Editor: Encyclopedia of American History (1953); Hamilton and the Founding of the Nation (1957); The Spirit of 'Seventy-Six (with H. S. Commager, 1958); etc. Prof. history, Columbia University, since 1949.

MORRIS, ROBERT (Aug. 31, 1818–July 31, 1888); b. near Boston, Mass. Author of books on Free-masonry. The Lights and Shadows of Freemasonry (1852); The Poetry of Freemasonry (1895); etc.

MORRIS, ROBERT CLARK (Nov. 19, 1869–Oct. 13, 1938); b. Bridgeport, Conn. Lawyer, author. "The Pursuit of Happiness" (1930); The Spirit of Liberty (1931); The Autobiography of a Son of New England (1938).

MORRIS, WILLIAM (Apr. 13, 1913–); b. Boston, Mass. Editor. It's Easy to Increase Your Vocabulary (1957); The Word Game Book (with Mary Morris, 1959); Dictionary of Word and Phrase Origins, with wife, vol. I (1962); vol. II (1967). Editor: Berlitz Self-Teacher language books (1949–53); Little Music Library (1947–50); William Morris Vocabulary Enrichment Program (1964); etc. Editor in chief, Grosset & Dunlap, since 1953.

MORRIS, WRIGHT (Jan. 6, 1910–); b. Central City, Neb. Author. My Uncle Dudley (1942); The Man Who Was There

(1945); The Inhabitants (1946); The Home Place (1948); The World in the Attic (1949); Man and Boy (1951); The Works of Love (1952); The Deep Sleep (1953); The Huge Season (1954); The Field of Vision (1956); Love Among the Cannibals (1957); The Territory Ahead (1958); Ceremony in Lone Tree (1960); The Mississippi River Reader (1961); What a Way to Go (1962); Cause For Wonder (1963); One Day (1965); In Orbit (1967); A Bill of Rites, a Bill of Wrongs, a Bill of Goods (1968); God's Country and My People (1968).

MORRISON, JOSEPH L[ederman] (May 28, 1918–); b. New York. Author. Josephus Daniels Says . . . An Editor's Political Odyssey from Bryan to Wilson and F.D.R., 1894-1913 (1962); Josephus Daniels: The Small-d Democrat (1966); W. J. Cash: Southern Prophet (1967).

MORRISON, SARAH E[lizabeth]. Author. The Chilhowee Boys series, 4v. (1893–98).

MORRISON, SARAH PARKE (b. 1833). Author. Among Ourselves, 3v. (1901–04); Sicily: A Poem (1910).

MORRISON, THEODORE (Nov. 4, 1901–); b. Concord, N.H. Educator, author. The Serpent in the Cloud (1931); Notes of Death and Life (1935); The Devious Way (1944); The Dream of Alcestis (poem, 1950); The Stones of the House (1953); To Make a World (1957); The Whole Creation (1962); etc. Editor: The Portable Chaucer (1949). English dept., Harvard University, since 1931.

MORRISON, WILLIAM BROWN (June 12, 1877–Mar. 20, 1944); b. Lexington, Va. Educator, author. An Oklahoman Abroad (1928); The Red Man's Trail (1931); Out in Oklahoma (poems, 1934); Military Posts and Camps in Oklahoma (1936). President, Oklahoma Presbyterian College for Girls, 1910–20; history dept., Southeastern State College, Durant, Okla., from 1922.

MORROW, ELIZABETH [Reeve Cutter] (Mrs. Dwight Whitney Morrow) (May 29, 1873–Jan. 23, 1955); b. Cleveland, O. Author. The Painted Pig (1930); Quatrains for My Daughter (1931); Casa Mañana (1932); The Rabbit's Nest (1940); My Favorite Age (1943); A Pint of Judgment (1960); etc.

MORROW, HONORÉ WILLSIE (Mrs. William Morrow) (1880–Apr. 12, 1940); b. Ottumwa, Ia. Novelist, biographer. The Heart of the Desert (1913); Still Jim (1915); Benefits Forgot (1917); We Must March (1925); Forever Free (1927); With Malice Toward None (1928); The Last Full Measure (1930, reissued, together with the preceding two, in one volume, Great Captain, 1935); Black Daniel (1931); Argonaut (1933); Yonder Sails the Mayflower (1934); Let the King Beware! (1936); also, the following biographies: The Father of "Little Women" (1927); Mary Todd Lincoln (1928); Tiger! Tiger! The Life of John B. Gough (1930); etc. Editor, The Delineator, 1914–19. See Felicia Morrow's Demon Daughter (1939).

MORROW, WILLIAM (June 15, 1873–Nov. 11, 1931); b. Dublin, Ire. Publisher. With McClure's Magazine and Leslie's Popular Monthly. Joined Frederick A. Stokes & Co., in 1906. Founded publishing house of William Morrow & Co., New York, in 1926.

MORROW, WILLIAM CHAMBERS (1853–Apr. 3, 1923). Author. The Ape, the Idiot, and Other People (1897); Bohemian Paris of To-day (1900); Lentala of the South Seas (1908); etc.

Morrow, William & Co. New York. Publishers. Founded 1926, by William Morrow. Has absorbed M. Barrows & Co., M. S. Mill Co., and William Sloane Associates, among other firms. Acquired by Scott, Foresman and Co. in 1967.

MORSE, JEDIDIAH (Aug. 23, 1761–June 9, 1826); b. Woodstock, Conn. Geographer, author. Called the "Father of American Geography." The American Geography (1789);

Annals of the American Revolution (1824); etc. Founder, the *Mercury and New England Palladium,* Boston, 1801; the *Panoplist,* Boston, 1805.

MORSE, JOHN TORREY (Jan. 9, 1840–Mar. 27, 1937); b. Boston, Mass. Author. *Famous Trials* (1874); *The Life of Alexander Hamilton,* 2v. (1876); *Abraham Lincoln,* 2v. (1893); *Life and Letters of Oliver Wendell Holmes,* 2v. (1896); etc. Editor: *American Statesmen,* 24v. (1882–1899).

MORSE, LUCY GIBBONS (1893–July 13, 1936); b. New York, daughter of James Sloan Gibbons. Abolitionist, author. *The Chezzles* (1888); *Rachel Stanwood* (1894).

MORSE, SAMUEL FRENCH (1916–May 11, 1969). Poet. *The Time of Year* (1944); *Scattered Causes* (1955). Editor: Wallace Stevens' *Opus Posthumous* (1957).

MORSE, SIDNEY EDWARDS (Feb. 6, 1794–Dec. 23, 1871); b. Charlestown, Mass., son of Jedidiah Morse. Editor, inventor, geographer, author. *A New System of Modern Geography* (1823); *Premium Questions on Slavery* (1860). Founder, the *Boston Recorder,* 1816; the *New York Observer,* 1823; editor, 1823–58.

MORTIMER, LEE (d. Mar. 1, 1963); b. Chicago, Ill. Journalist. Author: *Around the World Confidential* (1956); etc. Co-author (with Jack Lait): *New York: Confidential!* (1948); *U.S.A. Confidential* (1952); *Washington Confidential* (1960); etc. Columnist, New York *Mirror,* from 1932.

MORTON, CHARLES (c. 1627–Apr. 11, 1698); b. in Cornwall, Eng. Congregational clergyman, author. *The Spirit of Man* (1693); etc.

MORTON, CHARLES W. (Feb. 10, 1899–Sept. 23, 1967); b. Omaha, Neb. Editor, author. *Frankly, George* (1951); *How to Protect Yourself Against Women and Other Vicissitudes* (1951); *A Slight Sense of Outrage* (1955); etc.

MORTON, DAVID (Feb. 21, 1886–June 13, 1957); b. Elkton, Ky. Educator, poet. *Ships in Harbour* (1921); *Harvest* (1924); *Nocturnes and Autumnals* (1928); *The Renaissance of Irish Poetry* (1929); *A Man of Earth* (1930); *Spell against Time* (1936); *All in One Breath* (1939); *A Letter to Youth* (1942); *Poems, 1920–1945* (1945); *New England Devotional* (1952); *Chimes at Lages* (1955); etc. Compiler: *Amherst Undergraduate Verse, 1925–29* (1929); *Shorter Modern Poems, 1900–31* (1932). Prof. English, Amherst College, 1924–45.

MORTON, FREDERIC (Oct. 5, 1924–   ); b. Vienna. Novelist. *The Hound* (1947); *The Darkness Below* (1949); *Asphalt and Desire* (1952); *The Witching Ship* (1960); *The Rothschilds* (1962); *The Schatten Affair* (1965); *Snow Gods* (1969).

MORTON, HOWARD E. (Oct. 2, 1878–Dec. 23, 1938); b. San Francisco, Calif. Editor, playwright. *The Dream Maker* (with William Gillette, prod. 1921). With the Hearst newspapers, 1900–38; Sunday editor, the *New York Journal and American,* 1928–38.

MORTON, LOUIS (Dec. 30, 1913–   ); b. New York. Educator, author. *Robert Carter of Nomini Hall: A Virginia Tobacco Planter of the Eighteenth Century* (1941); *The Fall of the Philippines* (1953); *War in the Pacific: Strategy and Command* (1963). Co-author: *Command Decisions* (1960); *Total War and Cold War* (1962); *Theory and Practice in American Politics* (1964); *Schools for Strategy* (1965). Editor: *War in the Pacific, U.S. Army in World War II,* 11 v. (1949–63); *Wars and Military Institutions of the United States,* 17 v., since 1963.

MORTON, NATHANIEL (1613–June 29, 1685, O. S.); b. Leyden, Neth. Pilgrim father, author. *New Englands Memoriall* (1669).

MORTON, RICHARD LEE (Sept. 20, 1889–); b. in Prince Edward Co., Va. Historian. *The Negro in Virginia Politics* (1919); *History of Virginia since 1861* (1924). Editor: Hugh Jones's *The Present State of Virginia* (1956). Dept. of history, College of William and Mary, since 1919.

MORTON, ROSALIE SLAUGHTER (Oct. 28, 1876–); b. Lynchburg, Va. Surgeon, author. *A Woman Surgeon* (autobiography, 1937); *A Doctor's Holiday in Iran* (1940).

MORTON, SARAH WENTWORTH APTHORP (1759–May 14, 1846); b. Boston, Mass. Poet, novelist. *Ouabi; or, The Virtues of Nature, an Indian Tale* (anon., 1790); *Beacon Hill* (poem, anon., 1797); *The Virtues of Society* (poem, 1799); *My Mind and Its Thoughts* (1823); etc. *The Power of Sympathy* (1789), the first American novel, formerly attributed to her, is now attributed to William Hill Brown. She was one of the Della Cruscan poets and wrote for the *Massachusetts Magazine* under the name "Philenia." *See* Milton Ellis's *Philenia: The Life and Works of Sarah Wentworth Morton* (1931).

MORTON, THOMAS (c. 1575–1647); b. in England. Adventurer, author. *New English Cannaan; or, New Canaan, Containing an Abstract of New England* (1632). His conduct at Merry Mount so shocked the Puritans that they cut down his maypole. The adventures of Morton supplied material for Hawthorne's story *The Maypole of Merry Mount,* and Motley's novels *Morton's Hope* and *Merry-Mount.*

Morton, William. Pen name of William Blair Morton Ferguson.

MOSCOW, ALVIN (Dec. 31, 1925–). Author. *Collision Course* (1959); *Tiger on a Leash* (1961); *City at Sea* (1962); *Merchants of Heroin* (1968); etc.

MOSER, EDWA (Aug. 9, 1899–   ); b. St. Louis, Mo. Author. *The Mexican Touch* (1940); *Wedding Day* (1944); *Roundelay* (1948); *Bell Tower* (1959).

MOSES, BELLE, b. Savannah, Ga. Author. *Life of Louisa May Alcott* (1909); *Louisa May Alcott, Dreamer and Worker* (1909); *Lewis Carroll in Wonderland and at Home* (1910); *Charles Dickens and His Girl Heroines* (1911); etc.

MOSES, BERNARD (Aug. 27, 1840–Mar. 4, 1930); b. Burlington, Conn. Educator, historian. *The Establishment of Spanish Rule in America* (1898); *The Spanish Dependencies in South America,* 2v. (1914). History dept., University of California, 1876–1930.

MOSES, MONTROSE JONAS (Sept. 2, 1878–Mar. 29, 1934); b. New York. Drama critic, editor. *Famous Actor-Families in America* (1906); *Henrik Ibsen* (1908); *The Literature of the South* (1909); *Maurice Maeterlinck* (1911); *The American Dramatist* (1911); *The Fabulous Forrest* (1929); etc. Editor: *Memorial Edition of the Plays of Clyde Fitch* (1915); *Representative Plays by American Dramatists,* 3v. (1918); *Representative Continental Dramas* (1924); *Representative American Dramas* (1925); *British Plays from the Restoration to 1820* (1929); *Dramas of Modernism and Their Forerunners* (1931); *The American Theatre as Seen by Its Critics* (with John Mason Brown, 1934); etc. Drama critic, *The Independent,* 1908–18; *The Bellman,* 1910–19; etc.

MOSHER, THOMAS BIRD (Sept. 11, 1852–Aug. 31, 1923); b. Biddeford, Me. Publisher, printer, editor, author. *Amphora,* 2v. (1912–26). Founder, *The Bibelot,* Jan. 1895. He printed the first of the "Mosher Books" at Portland, Me., in 1891. The fine editions of literary classics which he published and the monthly periodical, *The Bibelot,* which he edited, are noteworthy examples of the graphic arts in America.

MOSKIN, JOHN ROBERT (May 9, 1923–   ); Editor, author. *Morality in America* (1966). Co-author: *The Decline of the American Male* (1958).

MOSS, HOWARD (Jan. 22, 1922–). Editor, poet. *Toy Fair* (1954); *Swimmer in the Air* (1957); *The Folding Green* (1958); *A Winter Come, a Summer Gone: Poems, 1946–1960* (1960); *The Magic Lantern of Marcel Proust* (1962); *The*

Nonsense Books of Edward Lear (1964); *Finding Them Lost* (1965); *Second Nature* (1968); *Writing Against Time: Critical Essays and Reviews* (1969); etc. Poetry editor, *New Yorker,* since 1948.

Mosses from an Old Manse. Short stories by Nathaniel Hawthorne (1846). In the opening of this book Hawthorne describes the Old Manse in Concord, Mass., which he inhabited for some time.

Mother Goose. In 1786 Isaiah Thomas issued the first American edition of the *Mother Goose's Melody. See* William Henry Whitmore's *The Original Mother Goose's Melody, as First Issued by John Newbery* (1889); Adeline Dutton Train's *Mother Goose for Grown Folks* (1860); etc. For a list of Mother Goose rhymes see Bertha E. Mahony and Elinor Whitney's *Realms of Gold in Children's Books* (1937).

Mother India. By Katharine Mayo (1927). A realistic study of modern India, showing the evils of the caste system and the status of women and children under such a system. The book was controversial and brought forth replies by Hindu authors.

"Mother Machree." Song by Ernest Ball and Chauncey Olcott.

Mother's Kisses, A. Novel by Bruce Jay Friedman (1964). Comic novel about a Jewish boy's family life.

Motive. Nashville, Tenn. Monthly. Founded 1940. Published by the University Christian Movement. Directed toward a youthful readership, stressing the religious and moral seriousness of many current ideas in the arts, mass media, and popular music.

MOTLEY, JOHN LOTHROP (Apr. 15, 1814–May 29, 1877); b. Dorchester, Mass. Historian, diplomat. *Morton's Hope* (anon., 1839); *Merry-Mount* (anon., 1849); *The Rise of the Dutch Republic,* 3v. (1856); *The History of the United Netherlands,* 4v. (1861–68); *The Life and Death of John of Barneveld,* 2v. (1874); *The Correspondence of John Lothrop Motley,* ed. by George W. Curtis, 2v. (1889); etc. Minister to Austria, 1861–67; to Great Britain, 1869–70. *See* Oliver Wendell Holmes's *John Lothrop Motley* (1879); Orie William Long's *Literary Pioneers* (1935).

MOTLEY, WILLARD FRANCIS (July 14, 1912–Mar. 4, 1965); b. Chicago, Ill. Author. *Knock on Any Door* (1947); *We Fished All Night* (1951); *Let No Man Write My Epitaph* (1958); *Let Noon Be Fair* (1966).

MOTON, ROBERT RUSSA (Aug. 26, 1867–May 31, 1940); b. in Amelia Co., Va. Educator, author. *Racial Good Will* (1916); *Finding a Way Out* (autobiography, 1920); *What the Negro Thinks* (1929). Succeeded Booker T. Washington as principal, Tuskegee Institute, in 1915.

MOTT, FRANK LUTHER (Apr. 4, 1886–Oct. 23, 1964); b. in Keokuk Co., Ia. Educator, editor, author. *Six Prophets Out of the Middle West* (1917); *The Man with the Good Face* (1921); *The Literature of Pioneer Life in Iowa* (1923); *Rewards of Reading* (1926); *A History of American Magazines,* 3v. (1938, Pulitzer Prize for American history, 1939); *American Journalism* (1941); *Jefferson and the Press* (1943); *Golden Multitudes* (1947); *The News in America* (1952); *Five Stories* (1957); *A History of American Magazines,* Vol. IV (1957); etc. Joint editor and publisher, *The Midland,* 1925–30; assoc. ed., 1930–33; editor, *Journalism Quarterly,* 1930–34; etc. Dean, school of journalism, University of Missouri, 1942–51.

MOTT, LAWRENCE (Aug. 15, 1881–); b. New York. Author. *Jules of the Great Heart* (1905); *The White Darkness, and Other Stories* (1907); *To the Credit of the Sea* (1907); *Prairie, Sea and Snow* (1910).

MOULTON, CHARLES WELLS (Sept. 22, 1859–1913); b. Alexander, N.Y. Publisher, editor. Editor: *The Library of Literary Criticism of English and American Authors,* 8v. (1901–05). Founder, *Literature* magazine, 1881; editor, the *Magazine of Poetry,* 1889–96.

MOULTON, ELLEN LOUISE CHANDLER (Apr. 10, 1835–Aug. 10, 1908); b. Pomfret, Conn. Editor, author. Wrote as Ellen Louise, Ellen Louise Chandler, and Louise Chandler Moulton. *This, That and the Other* (1854); *My Third Book* (1859); *Bed-Time Stories* (1874); *Firelight Stories* (1883); *Miss Eyre from Boston and Others* (1889); *In the Garden of Dreams* (poems, 1890); *Lazy Tours in Spain and Elsewhere* (1896); *The Poems and Sonnets,* ed. by Harriet P. Spofford (1909); etc. Her Friday salon in Boston drew such guests as Longfellow, Holmes, Whittier, and Lowell. Her library was given to the Boston Public Library. *See* Lilian Whitney's *Louise Chandler Moulton* (1910).

MOULTON, HAROLD GLENN (Nov. 7, 1883–Dec., 1966); b. Le Roy, Mich. Economist. Author: *Waterways vs. Railways* (1912); *Financial Organization of Society* (1921); *The Formation of Capital* (1935); *The New Philosophy of Public Debt* (1943); *Can Inflation Be Controlled* (1958); etc. Co-author: *America's Capacity to Consume* (1934); *The Dynamic Economy* (1950); etc.

MOULTON, RICHARD GREEN (May 5, 1849–Aug. 15, 1924); b. Preston, Eng. Educator, editor, author. *Shakespeare as a Dramatic Artist* (1885); *World Literature and Its Place in General Culture* (1911); *The Modern Study of Literature* (1915). Editor: *The Modern Reader's Bible,* 20v. (1896–1906). Prof. English literature, University of Chicago, 1892–1919. *See* W. F. Moulton's *Richard Green Moulton* (1926).

Mountaineering in the Sierra Nevada. By Clarence King (1872). Written as a scientific study of the geology and geography of the Sierra Nevada Mountains, this work is now read for its literary charm and its western humor.

Mourning Becomes Electra. Play by Eugene O'Neill (prod. 1931). The theme of an old Greek tragedy applied to a New England setting in the days following the Civil War. It depicts the lives of the Mannon family, tragic and tangled, obsessed with the evil aspects of the Puritan conscience. The drama is made up of three plays: *Homecoming, The Hunted,* and *The Haunted,* presented in a sequence of 13 acts.

Mourt's Relation. Popular title for a journal first published as *A Relation or Journall of the Beginning and Proceedings of the English Plantation Settled at Plymouth in New England* (1622). The preface was signed G. Mourt, but it is probable that Governor Bradford, Edward Winslow, and others helped to write the journal.

Moviegoer, The. Novel by Walker Percy (1963).

MOWAT, FARLEY [McGill] (May 12, 1921–); b. Belleville, Ont. Author. *People of the Deer* (1952); *The Regiment* (1955); *Lost in the Barrens* (1956); *The Dog Who Wouldn't Be* (1957); *The Grey Seas Under* (1958); *Desperate People* (1959); *Owls in the Family* (1961); *The Black Joke* (1962); *The Serpent's Coil* (1962); *Never Cry Wolf* (1963); *Westviking* (1965); *Curse of the Viking Grave* (1966); *Canada North* (1967); *Polar Passion* (1967); *This Rock Within the Sea* (1968); *The Boat That Wouldn't Float* (1969). Editor: *Coppermine Journey* (1958); *Ordeal by Ice* (1961).

MOWATT, ANNA CORA [Ogden] (Mrs. James Mowatt; Mrs. William Foushee Ritchie) (Mar. 5, 1819–July 21, 1870); b. Bordeaux, Fr. Actress, playwright, novelist, biographer. *Pelayo; or, The Cavern of Covadonga* (under pen name, "Isabel," 1836); *The Fortune Hunter* (under pen name, "Helen Berkley," 1844); *Fashion; or, Life in New York* (prod. 1845); *Armand, the Child of the People* (prod. 1847); *Autobiography of an Actress* (1854); *Mimic Life; or, Before and Behind the Curtain* (1856); *Twin Roses* (1857); etc.

MOWERY, WILLIAM BYRON (Aug. 15, 1899–Apr. 2, 1957); b. Adelphia, O. Novelist. *The Silver Hawk* (1929); *Heart of the North* (1931); *Singer of the Wilderness* (1931); *Forbidden Valley* (1933); *Challenge of the North* (1933); *The Phantom Canoe* (1934); *The Valley Beyond* (1937); *The Smoke Tree* (1943); *Sagas of the Mounted Police* (1953); *Swift in the Night* (1956); etc.

MOWRER, EDGAR ANSEL (Mar. 8, 1892–); b. Bloomington, Ill., brother of Paul Scott Mowrer. Correspondent, author. *Immortal Italy* (1922); *This American World* (1928); *Germany Puts the Clock Back* (1933); *The Dragon Wakes* (1939); *Global War* (with Martha Rajchman, 1942); *The Nightmare of American Foreign Policy* (1948); *Challenge and Decision* (1950); *A Good Time to Be Alive* (1960); *An End to Make Believe* (1961); *Triumph and Turmoil—A Personal History of Our Time* (1968); etc. Foreign correspondent, the *Chicago Daily News;* American editor, *Western World,* since 1956.

MOWRER, PAUL SCOTT (July 14, 1887–d. 1971); b. Bloomington, Ill., brother of Edgar Ansell Mowrer. Editor, author. *Hours of France* (poems, 1918); *The Good Comrade and Fairies* (poems, 1923); *Poems Between Wars* (1941); *The House of Europe* (1945); *On Going to Live in New Hampshire* (poems, 1953); *And Let the Glory Go* (poems, 1955); *Twenty-one and Sixty-five* (poems, 1958); *Mothering Land* (poems, 1960); *High Mountain Pond* (poems, 1962); *School for Diplomats* (poems, 1964); *This Teeming Earth* (poems, 1965); *The Island Ireland* (1966); *Poems* (complete, 1968); *Six Plays* (1968); etc. Editor: *The Golden Quill Anthology* (with Clarence G. Garrar, 1968). With *Chicago Daily News,* since 1905; editor 1935–44; European editor, *New York Post,* since 1945.

Mowry, Blanche Swett. See Blanche Swett Buggelli.

MOWRY, GEORGE E[dwin] (Sept. 5, 1909–); b. Washington, D.C. Educator, author. *Theodore Roosevelt and the Progressive Movement* (1946); *California Progressives* (1951); *The Era of Theodore Roosevelt* (1958); *The Church and the New Generation* (1968); etc. Prof. American history, University of California at Los Angeles, 1950–67; Kenan prof. American history, University of North Carolina, Chapel Hill, since 1967.

MOWRY, WILLIAM AUGUSTUS (Aug. 13, 1829–May 22, 1917); b. Uxbridge, Mass. Educator, author. *Talks With My Boys* (1885); *The Uxbridge Academy* (1897); *Recollections of a New England Educator* (1908). President, Martha's Vineyard Summer Institute, 1887–1905.

MOXOM, PHILIP STAFFORD (Aug. 10, 1848–Aug. 13, 1923); b. Markham, Ont. Congregational clergyman, author. *The Aim of Life* (1894); *From Jerusalem to Nicaea* (1896); *The Religion of Hope* (1896); *Two Masters: Browning and Turgenief* (1912).

MOYNIHAN, DANIEL PATRICK (Mar. 16, 1927–); b. Tulsa, Okla. Educator, government official, author. *Maximum Feasible Misunderstanding: Community Action in the War on Poverty* (1969). Co-author: *Beyond the Melting Pot* (1963). Ass't Sec., U.S. Dep't of Labor, 1963–65; director, Joint Center for Urban Studies, Harvard University and M.I.T., since 1966; Ass't for Urban Affairs to President of the U.S., 1969–70.

Mr. Barnes of New York. Novel by Archibald Clavering Gunter (1887). This, his first novel, had one of the most sensational successes in the history of American publishing.

Mr. Crewe's Career. Novel by Winston Churchill (1908). A political novel showing the effects upon a man's character of material and selfish motives.

Mr. Dooley in Peace and War. By Finley Peter Dunne (1898). The quaint opinions of the genial Irishman of Archey Road, imparted for the benefit of Mr. Hennessy. For the origin of "Mr. Dooley" see the introduction of *Mr. Dooley At His Best,* ed. by Elmer Ellis (1938).

"Mr. Flood's Party." Poem by Edward Arlington Robinson (1920).

Mr. Pope and Other Poems. Collection of poems by Allen Tate (1928).

Mr. Potter of Texas. By Archibald Clavering Gunter (1888). Series of humorous adventures in the Orient, Australia, and Paris.

Mr. Salt. By Will Payne (1903). A sympathetic study of a coal baron who is caught in the panic of 1893.

Mr. Smith. Pen name of Ralph Ingersoll Lockwood.

Mrs. Wiggs of the Cabbage Patch. By Alice Hegan Rice (1901). Mrs. Wiggs, a widow with five children to support, looks on the bright side of life in an environment normally considered to be depressing. The scene is laid in the poorer quarters of Louisville, Ky.

MS. Found in a Bottle, The. Story by Edgar Allan Poe, which first appeared in the *Saturday Visitor,* Oct. 19, 1833.

Muckrakers. This term derives from Bunyan's *Pilgrim's Progress,* but its modern application stems from Theodore Roosevelt's use of it in 1906 to describe those writers who were revealing corrupt practices in the national life. Among them were Ida M. Tarbell, Lincoln Steffens, Ray Stannard Baker, Finley Peter Dunne, and William Allen White.

MUDGE, ISADORE GILBERT (Mar. 14, 1875–May 1957); b. Brooklyn, N.Y. Librarian, bibliographer. Compiler: *A Thackeray Dictionary* (with Minnie E. Sears, 1910); *Bibliography* (1915); *A George Eliot Dictionary* (with Minnie E. Sears, 1924); *Guide to Reference Books* (1917, and later revisions); etc. Librarian, Bryn Mawr College, 1903–08; reference librarian, Columbia University, 1911–41; assoc. prof. bibliography, 1927–38.

MUDGE, JAMES (Apr. 5, 1844–May 7, 1918); b. West Springfield, Mass. Methodist clergyman, missionary, editor, poet. *Faber* (1885); *China* (1900); *Fenelon: The Mystic* (1906); *The Perfect Life* (1911). Compiler, *The Best of Browning* (1898); *Hymns of Trust* (1912); etc. Editor, *Lucknow Witness,* Lucknow, India, 1873–83; book editor, *Zion's Herald,* 1908–12.

MUDGE, ZACHARIAH ATWELL (July 2, 1813–1888); b. Orrington, Me. Methodist clergyman, author. *Gracie Goodwin; or, Love Lightens Labor* (n.d.); *The Forest Boy: A Sketch of the Life of Abraham Lincoln* (1867); the *Casket* library, 6v. (1867), the *Rustic* library, 6v. (1867), the two forming the *Pure Gold* series, 12v. (1867); *Views from Plymouth Rock* (1869); *Witch Hill: A History of Salem Witchcraft* (1870); *The Boat-Builder's Family* (1871); *Arctic Heroes* (1874); *Fur-Clad Adventures* (1880); etc.

"Mug Books." Name given to hundreds of county histories compiled during the era 1870–1900. They were promoted by men who took photographs of business men and farmers who desired to have their pictures in a book.

MÜHLEN, NORBERT. Author. *Schacht: Hitler's Magician* (1939); *The Return of Germany* (1953); *The Incredible Krupps* (1959); etc.

MUHLENBERG, WILLIAM AUGUSTUS (Sept. 16, 1796–Apr. 6, 1877); b. Philadelphia, Pa. Episcopal clergyman, hymn writer. *Church Poetry* (1823); etc. His best known hymns are "I Would Not Live Always" (c. 1824), and "Saviour, Who Thy Flock Art Feeding" (1826). See Anne Ayres's *The Life and Works of William Augustus Muhlenberg* (1889).

MUIR, JOHN (Apr. 21, 1838–Dec. 24, 1914); b. Dunbar, Scot. Naturalist, explorer, author. *The Mountains of California* (1894); *Our National Parks* (1901); *Stickeen* (1909); *My First Summer in the Sierra* (1911); *The Yosemite* (1912); *The Story of My Boyhood and Youth* (1913); *A Thousand Mile Walk to the Gulf,* ed. by William F. Badé (1916); *The Cruise of the Corwin* (1917); *Steep Trails* (1918); etc. See William F. Badé's *The Life and Letters of John Muir,* 2v. (1923–24); Herbert F. Smith's *John Muir* (1964).

MUIR, MALCOLM (July 19, 1885–); b. Glen Ridge, N.J. Editor, publisher. With *Newsweek,* since 1937.

MUIR, MALCOLM, JR. (July 27, 1915–); b. Stamford, Conn. Editor. Editor, *Newsweek,* 1947–62; *Atlas Magazine,* since 1964.

MULFORD, CLARENCE EDWARD (Feb, 3, 1883–May, 1956); b. Streator, Ill. Author. *Bar-20* (1907); *The Orphan* (1908); *Hopalong Cassidy* (1910); *The Coming of Cassidy and Others* (1913); *The Man from Bar-20* (1918); *Rustlers' Valley* (1924); *Cottonwood Gulch* (1925); *Mesquite Jenkins* (1928); *The Round-Up* (1933); *Trail Dust* (1934); *Hopalong Cassidy Serves a Writ* (1941); etc.

MULFORD, ELISHA (Nov. 19, 1833–Dec. 9, 1885); b. Montrose, Pa. Episcopal clergyman, educator, author. *The Nation* (1870); *The Republic of God* (1880). Lecturer in theology and apologetics, Episcopal Theological School, Cambridge, Mass., 1880–85.

MULFORD, PRENTICE (Apr. 5, 1834–c. May 27, 1891); b. Sag Harbor, L.I., N.Y. Journalist, hermit, author. *Your Forces and How to Use Them,* 6v. (1887), a collection of essays known as the *White Cross Library,* expounding a philosophy which came to be known as "New Thought"; *The Swamp Angel* (1888); *Prentice Mulford's Story* (1889); etc. Wrote for the *Union Democrat,* Sonora, Calif., under pen name of "Dogberry."

MULHOLLAND, JOHN (June 9, 1898–); b. Chicago, Ill. Magician, collector of books on magic, editor, author. *Magic in the Making* (with Milton Smith, 1925); *Quicker Than the Eye* (1932); *Story of Magic* (1935); *Beware Familiar Spirits* (1938); *The Art of Illusion* (1944); *Practical Puppetry* (1962); *Book of Magic* (1963); *Magic of the World* (1965); *The Magical Mind* (with Dr. George N. Gordon, 1967); etc. Editor, *The Sphinx.*

Mullany, Patrick Francis. See Brother Azarias.

MULLER, HERBERT J[oseph] (July 7, 1905–); b. Mamaroneck, N.Y. Educator, author. *Modern Fiction* (1937); *Science and Criticism* (1943); *Thomas Wolfe* (1947); *The Uses of the Past* (1952); *The Spirit of Tragedy* (1956); *The Loom of History* (1958); *Issues of Freedom* (1960); *Freedom in the Ancient World* (1961); *Freedom in the Western World* (1962); *Religion and Freedom in the Modern World* (1963); *The Individual in a Revolutionary World* (1964); *Freedom in the Modern World* (1966); *Adlai Stevenson: A Study in Values* (1968); *The Uses of English* (1968); etc. Prof. English and government, Indiana University, since 1956.

MULLINS, EDGAR YOUNG (Jan. 5, 1860–Nov. 23, 1928); b. in Franklin Co., Miss. Baptist clergyman, educator, author. *The Axioms of Religion* (1908); *The Life of Christ* (1917); *Christianity at the Cross Roads* (1924); etc. President, Southern Baptist Theological Seminary, Louisville, Ky., 1899–1928. *See* Isla May Mullins's *Edgar Young Mullins* (1929).

MULLINS, HELENE (July 12, 1899–); b. New Rochelle, N.Y. Poet, novelist. *Paulus Fy* (1924); *Earthbound, & Other Poems* (1929); *Convent Girl* (1929); *Balm in Gilead* (poems, 1930); *Streams from the Source* (poems, 1938).

MULLINS, ISLA MAY (Mrs. Edgar Young Mullins) (Apr. 30, 1859–Feb. 6, 1936); b. Summerfield, Ala. Author. *When Yesterday Was Young* (1926); *Edgar Young Mullins* (1929); etc.

MUMFORD, ETHEL WATTS (Mrs. George Dana Mumford; Mrs. Peter Geddes Grant) (1878–May 2, 1940); b. New York. Author. *Dupes* (1901); *The Complete Cynic's Calendar* (with Oliver Herford and Addison Mizner annually, 1905, and sequels); *Out of the Ashes* (1913); *Sick A-bed* (prod. 1918); *The Pageant of the Seven Seas* (1925); etc.

MUMFORD, JAMES GREGORY (Dec. 2, 1863–Oct. 18, 1914); b. Rochester, N.Y. Surgeon, author. *A Doctor's Table Talk* (1912); *Surgical Memoirs, and Other Essays* (1908); etc.

MUMFORD, LEWIS (Oct. 19, 1895–); b. Flushing, N.Y. Educator, editor, author. *The Story of Utopias* (1922); *Sticks and Stones* (1924); *The Golden Day* (1926); *Herman Melville* (1929); *American Taste* (1929); *The Brown Decades* (1931); *Technics and Civilization* (1934); *The Culture of Cities* (1938); *Men Must Act* (rev. ed., 1939); *Faith for Living* (1940); *The South in Architecture* (1941); *The Condition of Man* (1944); *City Development* (1945); *Values for Survival* (1946); *Green Memories: The Story of Geddes Mumford* (1947); *The Conduct of Life* (1951); *Art and Technics* (1952); *The Transformation of Man* (1956); *The City in History* (1961); *The Highway and the City* (1963); *The Myth of the Machine* (1967); *The Urban Prospect* (1968); *Myths of Machines: Pentagon of Power* (1970). Editor: *American Caravan,* 1927–36. Prof. humanities, Stanford University, 1942–44; city and regional planning, University of Pennsylvania, 1951–59.

MUNDT, ERNEST [Karl] (Oct. 30, 1905–); b. Bleicherode, Ger. Educator, author. *A Primer of Visual Art* (1950); *Art, Form, and Civilization* (1952); *The Birth of a Cook* (1956). Dept. of art, San Francisco State College, since 1955.

MUNDY, TALBOT (Apr. 23, 1879–Aug. 5, 1940); b. London, England, came to the United States in 1911. Novelist. *Rung Ho!* (1914); *Winds of the World* (1915); *King of the Khyber Rifles* (1916); *Hira Singh* (1918); *The Ivory Trail* (1919); *Om* (1923); *The Devil's Guard* (1925); *Jimgrim* (1931); *Purple Pirate* (1935); *Full Moon* (1936); *Old Ugly-Face* (1940); etc.

MUNFORD, ROBERT (d. 1784); b. in Prince George Co., Va. Revolutionary soldier, playwright, poet. *The Patriots* (1776); *The Candidates; or, The Humours of a Virginia Election* (1798); *A Collection of Plays and Poems* (1798); etc.

MUNGER, THEODORE THORNTON (Mar. 5, 1830–Jan. 11, 1910); b. Bainbridge, N.Y. Congregational clergyman, author. *On the Threshold* (1881); *The Freedom of Faith* (1883); *Horace Bushnell, Preacher and Theologian* (1899); etc.

Municipal Report, A. Short story by "O. Henry," which first appeared in *Hampton's Magazine,* Nov., 1909. A Negro story with Nashville, Tenn., as the setting, written to disprove a remark by Frank Norris that nothing worth writing about could happen in Nashville.

MUNKITTRICK, RICHARD KENDALL (1853–1911); b. Manchester, Eng. Editor, poet. *Farming* (1891); *The Moon Prince, and Other Nabobs* (1893); *The Acrobatic Muse* (1897). With *Puck,* 1881–89; editor, *Judge,* 1901–05.

MUNN, CHARLES CLARK (May 11, 1848–July 8, 1917); b. Southington, Conn. Novelist. *Uncle Terry: A Story of the Maine Coast* (1900); *Rockhaven* (1902); *The Hermit* (1904); *The Castle Builders* (1910); *Camp Castaway* (1916); etc.

MUNRO, DANA CARLETON (June 7, 1866–Jan. 13, 1933); b. Bristol, R.I. Educator, author. *The Middle Ages* (1902); *The Kingdom of the Crusaders* (1935). Editor: *L. J. Paetow's A Guide to the Study of Medieval History* (1931). Prof. European history, University of Wisconsin, 1902–15; prof. medieval history, Princeton University, 1915–33. *See* memorial volume, *The Crusades, and Other Historical Essays,* ed. by L. J. Paetow (1928).

MUNRO, GEORGE P. (Nov. 12, 1825–Apr. 23, 1896); b. West River, N.S. Publisher. In 1866 he left the firm of Beadle & Adams (q.v.), New York, and went into partnership with Irwin P. Beadle. Under the latter's name they began the publication of the *New Dime Novels.* Forbidden by injunction to use the name Beadle, the firm became George P. Munro. It published Harlan P. Halsey's *Old Sleuth, the Detective* (1872), first of the *Old Sleuth* series of over two hundred titles; the *Old Cap Collier* series; *Munro's Ten Cent Novels;* and the *Seaside Series* of reprints, including over 2,000 titles. Founder, the *Fireside Companion,* a magazine, 1866. George Munro's brother Norman began the Riverside Library in 1877. *See* Edmund L. Pearson's *Dime Novels* (1929).

MUNRO, WILFRED HAROLD (Aug. 20, 1849–Aug. 9, 1934); b. Bristol, R.I. Educator, historian. *Picturesque Rhode Island* (1881); *The Most Successful American Privateer* (1913); *Legends of Mount Hope* (1915); *Tales of an Old Sea Port* (1917); etc. History dept., Brown University, 1891–1911; prof., 1899–1911.

MUNRO, WILLIAM BENNETT (Jan. 5, 1875–Sept. 4, 1957); b. Almonte, Ont. Educator, author. *The Government of American Cities* (1912); *The Government of the United States* (1919); *Municipal Government and Administration*, 2v. (1923); *Personality in Politics* (1924); etc. Editor, *Harvard Graduates Magazine*, 1908–29; editorial writer, *Boston Herald*, 1907–21. Government and history dept., Harvard, 1904–29.

MUNROE, KIRK (Sept. 15, 1850–June 16, 1930); b. near Prairie du Chien, Wis. Author. *The Flamingo Feather* (1887); *The Golden Days of '49* (1889); *Dory Mates* (1890); *Under Orders* (1890); *Canoemates* (1893); *Rick Dale* (1896); *The Painted Desert* (1897); *In Pirate Waters* (1898); *Under the Great Bear* (1901); *Campmates* (1903); *The Blue Dragon* (1904); *The Outcast Warrior* (1905). Editor, *Harper's Young People*, 1879–82. Founder, the League of American Wheelmen, 1880.

MUNSELL, JOEL (Apr. 14, 1808–Jan. 15, 1880); b. Northfield, Mass. Printer, antiquarian. Compiler: *Outline of the History of Printing* (1839); *The Typographical Miscellany* (1850); *The Annals of Albany*, 10v. (1850–59); etc. He published the *Lady's Magazine*, the *American Literary Magazine*, the *Spectator*, the *State Register*, the *Unionist*, and several other newspapers and magazines, chiefly in Albany, N.Y. One of the founders of the Albany Institute. See *Bibliotheca Munselliana* (1872), a catalogue of Munsell imprints.

MUNSEY, FRANK A[ndrew] (Aug. 21, 1854–Dec. 22, 1925); b. Mercer, Me. Publisher, novelist. *Afloat in a Great City* (1887); *The Boy Broker* (1888); *Derringforth* (1894); *A Tragedy of Errors* (1899); *The Founding of the Munsey Publishing House* (1907); etc. Founder, the *Golden Argosy*, 1882; *Munsey's Weekly* (later *Munsey's Magazine*), 1889. Publisher of the *Baltimore News;* the *Washington Times;* the *New York Sun;* the *New York Herald;* the *New York Telegram;* the *All-Story Weekly;* etc. *See* George Britt's *Forty Years—Forty Millions* (1935).

Munsey's Magazine. New York. Monthly. Founded Feb., 1889, as *Munsey's Weekly*, by Frank A Munsey. Name changed Oct., 1891. Merged 1929 with *Argosy All-Story Weekly* to form *All-Story Combined with Munsey's.*

MUNSON, GORHAM B[ert] (May 26, 1896–Aug. 15, 1969); b. Amityville, N.Y. Editor, author. Author or co-author: *Waldo Frank* (1923); *Robert Frost* (1927); *Destinations: A Canvass of American Literature Since 1900* (1928); *Style and Form in American Prose* (1929); *The Dilemma of the Liberated* (1930); *New Directions* (1936); *Aladdin's Lamp* (1945); *The Written Word* (1949); *The Writer's Workshop Companion* (1951); *Penobscot: Down East Paradise* (1959); etc.

MÜNSTERBERG, HUGO (June 1, 1863–Dec. 16, 1916); b. Danzig, Ger. Educator, psychologist, author. *Psychology and Life* (1899); *Principles of Art Education* (1905); *The Eternal Values* (1908); *Psychology and the Teacher* (1909); *Psychology and Social Sanity* (1914); *Psychology, General and Applied* (1914); etc. Prof. psychology, Harvard University, 1892–1916. See Margaret Münsterberg's *Hugo Münsterberg* (1922).

MURCHIE, GUY (Jan. 25, 1907–); b. Boston, Mass. Author. *Men on the Horizon* (1932); *Mutiny of the Bounty* (1936); *Soldiers of Darkness* (1937); *Saint Croix: The Sentinel River* (1947); *Song of the Sky* (1954); *World Aloft* (1960); *Music of the Spheres* (1961); etc.

Murder in the Cathedral. Poetic drama by T. S. Eliot (prod. 1935). A play based on the martyrdom of Saint Thomas à Becket, Archbishop of Canterbury.

Murders in the Rue Morgue, The. Horror tale by Edgar Allan Poe, which first appeared in *Graham's Magazine*, Apr., 1841. First modern detective story. *See* Philip Van Doren Stern's *The Case of the Corpses in the Blind Alley*, in the *Virginia Quarterly Review*, spring issue, 1941.

MURDOCH, FRANK HITCHCOCK (Mar. 11, 1843–Nov. 13, 1872); b. Chelsea, Mass. Actor, playwright. *Davy Crockett* (1872); *Bohemia; or, The Lottery of Art* (prod. 1872); *Only a Jew* (prod. 1873); etc.

MURDOCK, HAROLD (1862–Apr. 5, 1934); b. Boston, Mass. Banker, author. *The Reconstruction of Europe* (1889); *Earl Paercy's Dinner Table* (1907); *Bunker Hill* (1927); etc.

MURDOCK, KENNETH BALLARD (June 22, 1895–); b. Boston, Mass. Educator, editor, author. *The Portraits of Increase Mather* (1924); *Increase Mather, the Foremost American Puritan* (1925); *The Sun at Noon* (1929); *Literature and Theology in Colonial New England* (1949); *The Literature of the American People*, Part I (1951); etc. Editor: *Handkerchiefs from Paul* (1927); *A Leaf of Grass from Shady Hill* (1938); *The Notebooks of Henry James* (with F. O. Matthiessen, 1947); etc. Editor, *Publications*, Colonial Society of Massachusetts, 1925–30; *New England Quarterly*, 1928–38, since 1939; *Graduates' Magazine*, 1929–31; *American Literature*, 1929–49. English dept., Harvard University, since 1916.

MURFREE, MARY NOAILLES (Jan. 24, 1850–July 31, 1922); b. Murfreesboro, Tenn. Novelist, short-story writer. Pen name "Charles Egbert Craddock." *In the Tennessee Mountains* (1884); *When the Battle Was Fought* (1884); *The Prophet of the Great Smoky Mountains* (1885); *Down the Ravine* (1885); *In the Clouds* (1887); *The Story of Keedon Bluffs* (1888); *The Despot of Broomsedge Cove* (1889); *In the "Stranger People's" Country* (1891); *His Vanished Star* (1894); *The Mystery of Witch-Face Mountain, and Other Stories* (1895); *The Phantoms of the Foot-Bridge, and Other Stories* (1895); *The Juggler* (1897); *The Young Mountaineers* (1897); *The Story of Old Fort Loudon* (1899); *The Bushwhackers, and Other Stories* (1899); *The Champion* (1902); *A Spectre of Power* (1903); *The Frontiersman* (1904); *The Storm Centre* (1905); *The Amulet* (1906); *The Windfall* (1907); *The Fair Mississippian* (1908); *The Ordeal* (1912); *The Raid of the Guerilla, and Other Stories* (1912); *The Story of Duciehurst* (1914). *See* E. W. Parks's *Charles Egbert Craddock* (1941).

Murgaytroyd, Matthew. Pen name of James Athearn Jones.

MURPHY, EDWARD FRANCIS (July 21, 1892–1967); b. Salem, Mass. Roman Catholic clergyman, educator, author. *The Goal* (1911); *Just Jack* (1918); *St. Thomas' Political Theories and Democracy* (1921); *New Psychology and Old Religion* (1933); *Handclasps with the Holy* (1934); *The Tenth Man* (1936); *Scarlet Lily* (1944); *Song of the Cave* (1950); *Yankee Priest* (1952); *Angel of Delta* (1958); etc. Dean philosophy and religion, Xavier University, New Orleans, La., since 1932.

MURPHY, FRED P. (Apr. 17, 1889–); b. Stamford, N.Y. Publisher. With Grolier Society, since 1913; executive committee chairman, since 1967; chairman, Americana Corporation, 1947–52; chairman, Grolier International, since 1964.

MURPHY, GARDNER (July 8, 1895–); b. Chillicothe, O. Psychologist. *General Psychology* (1933); *In the Minds of Men* (1953); *Human Potentialities* (1958); *The Challenge of Psychical Research* (1961); *Freeing Intelligence Through Teaching* (1961); *Encounter with Reality* (with H. E. Spohn, 1968); *Psychological Thought from Pythagoras to Freud* (1968); etc.

MURPHY, HENRY CRUSE (July 5, 1810–Dec. 1, 1882); b. Brooklyn, N.Y. Lawyer, book collector, editor, author. *Henry Hudson in Holland* (1859); *The Voyage of Verrazzano* (1875). Editor: *Anthology of New Netherland; or, Translations from the Early Dutch Poets of New York* (1865). Editorial writer, the *Brooklyn Advocate;* founder, the *Brooklyn Eagle,* Oct. 1841.

MURPHY, MABEL ANSLEY (Feb. 21, 1870–); b. Plumville, Pa. Author. Pen name, "Anne S. Lee." *American Leaders* (1920); *Timoleon, a Friend of Paul* (1921); *The Torchbearers* (1924); *When Rome Reigned* (1926); *Trails* (1934); *They Were Little Once* (1942); *When America was Young* (1948); etc.

Murphy, Princess Tulip. Pen name of Virginia Louise Faulkner.

MURRAY, AUGUSTUS TABER (Oct. 29, 1866–Mar. 8, 1940); b. New York. Educator, editor, translator. Editor: *The Religious Poems of Whittier* (1934); etc. Translator: *The Odyssey of Homer* (1919); *The Iliad* (1925); *Four Plays of Euripides* (1931); *Private Orations of Demosthenes,* 3v. (1939); etc. Prof. Greek, Stanford University, 1892–1932.

MURRAY, CHARLES THEODORE (b. Mar. 30, 1843); b. Goshen, Ind. Journalist, author. *Sub Rosa* (1880); *A Modern Gypsy* (1897); *Mlle. Fonchette* (1902). One of the founders of the Gridiron Club, 1885.

Murray, Cromwell. Pen name of Murray Morgan.

MURRAY, DONALD M. (Sept. 16, 1924–); b. Boston, Mass. Author. *Men Against Earth* (1961); *The Man Who Had Everything* (1964); *The World of Sound Recording* (1965).

MURRAY, JOHN (Dec. 10, 1741–Sept. 3, 1815); b. Alton, Hampshire, Eng. Universalist clergyman, author. Founder of Universalism in the United States. *Letters and Sketches of Sermons,* 3v. (1812–13). See *Records of the Life of the Rev. John Murray* (1816), a memoir left unfinished by Murray and completed by his wife, Judith Sargent Stevens Murray.

MURRAY, JOHN O'KANE (Dec. 12, 1847–July 30, 1885); b. Glenariffe, Co. Antrim, Ire. Physician, author. *Lives of the Catholic Heroes and Heroines of America* (1880); *Little Lives of the Great Saints* (1880); *The Catholic Pioneers of America* (1882); *Lessons in English Literature* (1884). Editor: *The Prose and Poetry of Ireland* (1877).

MURRAY, JUDITH SARGENT STEVENS (Mrs. John Murray) (May 1, 1751–July 6, 1820); b. Gloucester, Mass. Playwright, poet, essayist. Pen name "Constantia." *The Medium; or, A Happy Tea-Party* (prod. 1795); *The Traveller Returned* (prod. 1796); *The Gleaner,* 3v. (collected works, 1798). See Vena B. Field's *Constantia: A Study of the Life and Works of Judith Sargent Murray* (1931).

Murray, Lieut. Pen name of Maturin Murray Ballou.

MURRAY, LINDLEY (June 7, 1745–Jan. 16, 1826); b. in Dauphin Co., Pa. Grammarian, author. *The Sentiments of Pious and Eminent Men, on the Pernicious Tendency of Dramatic Entertainments and Other Vain Amusements* (c.1789); *English Grammar* (1795), and numerous later editions which made it the most widely used grammar in the United States; *Memoirs* (1826); etc. Editor: *The English Reader* (1799).

MURRAY, PAUL [Cooper] (Aug. 12, 1920–); b. Kennewick, Wash. Novelist. *Once There Was a Waltz* (1947); *The Heart Is a Stranger* (1949); *Free Agent* (1952); etc.

MURRAY, W. W. Novelist. *Isadore; or, The Captives of the Norridgwock* (1846); *Robert and Jane; or The Village Dress-Maker, and the Rejected Son Restored* (1849).

MURRAY, WILLIAM HENRY HARRISON (Apr. 26, 1840–Mar. 3, 1904); b. Guilford, Conn. Congregational clergyman, sportsman, author. Known as "Adirondack." *Adventures in the Wilderness; or, Camp Life in the Adirondacks* (1869); *Adirondack Tales* (1877); *Holiday Tales* (1897); etc.

MURTAGH, JOHN MARTIN (Feb. 26, 1911–); b. New York. Judge. *Cast the First Stone* (with Sara Harris, 1957); *Who Live in Shadow* (with same, 1959). Justice of the Supreme Court of N.Y. State, since 1966.

"Musée des Beaux Arts." Poem by W. H. Auden.

Music in Western Civilization. By Paul Henry Lang (1941). A scholarly one-volume work written in a sprightly style.

Music Master, The. Play by Charles Klein (prod. 1904). Written for David Warfield, and produced by David Belasco.

MUSICK, JOHN ROY (Feb. 28, 1848–1901); b. in St. Louis Co., Mo. Journalist, author. *The Bad Boy and His Sister* (under pen name, "Benjamin Broadaxe," 1887); *Brother against Brother* (1887); *Calamity Row* (1887); *Columbia* (1891); *The Columbian Historical Novels,* 14v. (1892–1900), republished as *The Real America in Romance,* 14v. (1907); *Mysterious Mr. Howard* (1896); *Stories of Missouri* (1897); *His Brother's Crime* (1898); *Hawaii* (1898); etc.

MUSMANNO, MICHAEL ANGELO (1897–Oct. 12, 1968); b. near Pittsburgh, Pa. Judge, author. *Jan Wolkanik: Black Fury* (1935); *After Twelve Years* (1939); *Ten Days to Die* (1950); *Across the Street from the Courthouse* (1954); *Justice Musmanno Dissents* (1956); *Verdict!* (1958); *The Eichmann Kommandos* (1961); etc.

MUSSER, BENJAMIN FRANCIS (Feb. 3, 1889–1951); b. Lancaster, Pa. Editor, essayist, poet. *Bucolics and Caviar* (poems, 1930); *Bensbook* (1931); *Straws on the Wind* (1931); *The End of Singing* (1935); *Bird Below the Waves* (collected poems, 1938); *Beloved Mendicant* (1943); *Margent of the World* (poems, 1956); etc. Editor, *The Trend,* 1920–21; *Contemporary Verse,* 1927–30; the *Poetry Weekly,* 1928–30.

MUZZEY, ARTEMAS BOWERS (Sept. 21, 1802–1892); b. Lexington, Mass. Unitarian clergyman, author. *The Young Man's Friend* (1836); *The Young Maiden* (1840); *The Fireside* (1849); *The Blade and the Ear* (1864); *The Battle of Lexington* (1877); etc.

MUZZEY, DAVID SAVILLE (Oct. 9, 1870–Apr. 14, 1965); b. Lexington, Mass. Educator, author. *Rise of the New Testament* (1900); *The Spiritual Franciscans* (1907); *An American History* (1911); *Life of Thomas Jefferson* (1918); *History of the American People* (1927); *James G. Blaine* (1934); *Ethics as a Religion* (1951); etc. Dept. of history, Columbia University, 1923–40.

My Antonia. Novel by Willa Cather (1918). Story of pioneer life in Nebraska.

My Bookhouse. A graded series of books for young children, edited and published by Olive Beaupré Miller.

"My candle burns at both ends." First line of the opening poem by Edna St. Vincent Millay in her *A Few Figs from Thistles* (1920).

"My country, 'tis of thee." First line of America (q.v.).

My Double and How He Undid Me. Short story by Edward Everett, in the *Atlantic Monthly,* 1859.

"My Faith Looks Up to Thee." Hymn by Ray Palmer, first published in *Spiritual Songs for Social Worship* by Thomas Hastings and Lowell Mason (1832).

"My Gal Sal." Song by Paul Dresser (1905).

My Life and Hard Times. Collection of humorous sketches, by James Thurber (1933).

"My Life Is Like the Summer Rose." Poem by Richard Henry Wilde, which appeared originally in the *Analectic Magazine*, Apr., 1819. Later its authorship was claimed by the Irish poet, Patrick O'Kelly. Anthony Barclay of Savannah translated it into Greek as a hoax and claimed it was written by Alcaeus. Sidney Lanier set Wilde's poem to music. *See* Anthony Barclay's *Wilde's Summer Rose* (1871).

My Life on the Plains. By George Armstrong Custer (1873), which was first published serially in *The Galaxy,* 1872–74. Later republished, with additional material, as *Wild Life on the Plains and Horrors of Indian Warfare* (1883).

"My Lost Youth." Poem by Henry Wadsworth Longfellow, in *Putnam's Magazine,* Aug., 1855.

My Mortal Enemy. Novel by Willa Cather (1926). Myra Henshawe's domestic happiness is shattered by the conviction that she does not fit into the scheme of things. In spite of her husband's devotion she comes to the point where she considers him a mortal enemy.

"My Mother Was a Lady; or If Jack Were Only Here." Popular song, words by Edward B. Marks, music by Joseph William Stern (1896).

My Name Is Aram. Novel by William Saroyan (1940).

"My Old Kentucky Home." Song by Stephen Collins Foster (1853).

My Study Windows. Familiar essays by James Russell Lowell (1874). Biographical, critical, and poetical essays written at "Elmwood."

"My Sweet Old Etcetera." Poem by E. E. Cummings (1926).

"My Sweetheart's The Man In the Moon." Popular song by James Thornton.

"My Wild Irish Rose." Song by Chauncey Olcott (1899).

MYERS, ALBERT COOK (Dec. 12, 1874–Apr. 2, 1960); b. York Springs, Pa. Editor, author. Editor: *Sally Wister's Journal, 1777–1778* (1902); *Narratives of Early Pennsylvania, West New Jersey and Delaware* (1911); *William Penn's Early Life in Brief* (1937); and many books on Pennsylvania history, William Penn, etc.

MYERS, GUSTAVUS (Mar. 20, 1872–Dec. 7, 1942); b. Trenton, N.J. Author. *The History of Tammany Hall* (1901); *The History of the Great American Fortunes* (1910); *The History of American Idealism* (1925); *Sources of Bigotry in the United States* (1943); etc.

MYERS, JEROME (Mar. 20, 1867–June 19, 1940); b. Petersburg, Va. Painter, author. *Artist in Manhattan* (autobiography, 1940).

MYERS, JOHN MYERS (Jan. 11, 1906–   ); b. Northport, N.Y. Author. *The Harp and the Blade* (1941); *Out on Any Limb* (1942); *The Wild Yazoo* (1947); *The Alamo* (1948); *Silverlock* (1949); *The Last Chance: Tombstone's Early Years* (1950); *Doc Holliday* (1955); *I, Jack Swilling, Founder of Phoenix, Arizona* (1961); *San Francisco's Reign of Terror* (1966); *The Westerner: A Roundup of Pioneer Reminiscences* (1969); etc.

MYERS, PETER HAMILTON (Aug. 4, 1812–Oct. 30, 1878); b. Herkimer, N.Y. Author. *Ensenore: A Poem* (1840), augmented as, *Ensenore, and Other Poems* (1875); *The First of the Knickerbockers: A Tale of 1673* (anon., 1848); *The Young Patroon: or, Christmas in 1690* (anon., 1849); *The King of the Hurons* (anon., 1850), republished in England as *Blanche Montaigne; The Prisoner of the Border* (1857).

MYERS, PHILIP VAN NESS (Aug. 10, 1846–Sept. 20, 1937); b. Tribes' Hill, N.Y. Educator, historian. *Remains of Lost Empires* (1875); *Ancient History* (1904); *Mediaeval and Modern History,* 2v. (1902–03); *History as Past Ethics*

(1913); *Ancient and Mediaeval History* (1927); etc. Prof. history, University of Cincinnati, 1890–1900.

MYERS, ROLLO H[ugh] (1892–). Music critic. *Music in the Modern World* (1939); *Debussy* (1949); *Ravel: Life and Works* (1960); etc. Editor: *Twentieth Century Music* (1961; rev. ed. 1969); *Correspondence, Together with Fragments from the Diary of Romain Rolland, and Other Essays* (1968).

MYERS, SARAH ANN IRWIN (1800–Dec. 11, 1876); b. Wilmington, Del. Artist, author. *Fitz Harold* (1853); *Faithful Nicolette* (1859); *Self-Sacrifice; or, The Pioneers of Fuegia* (1861); *Poor Nicholas* (1863); *Margaret Gordon* (1869); etc.

MYERS, WILLIAM STARR (June 17, 1877–Jan. 28, 1956); b. Baltimore, Md. Educator, author. *American Democracy Today* (1924); *The Republican Party: A History* (1928); *General George B. McClellan* (1934); *The Foreign Policies of Herbert Hoover* (1940); etc. Editor, *The State Papers of Herbert Hoover,* 2v. (1934). Prof. politics, Princeton, 1918–43.

Myra Breckenridge. Novel by Gore Vidal (1968). Myra, once a male, Myron, seduces both a young man and his girl, and later reverts to her original sex. The sexual changes highlight a sharp satire on American conventions about the roles of the sexes.

MYRDAL, GUNNAR KARL (Dec. 6, 1898–); b. Gustafs, Sweden. Swedish economist and author. *Population: A Problem for Democracy* (1940); *An American Dilemma: The Negro Problem and Modern Democracy* (1944); *Beyond the Welfare State* (1960); *Challenge to Affluence* (1963); *Asian Drama: An Inquiry into the Poverty of Nations* (1968); *The Challenge of World Poverty* (1970); etc.

MYRICK, HERBERT (Aug. 20, 1860–July 6, 1927); b. Arlington, Mass. Editor, publisher, author. *Ode to the Organ, and Other Poems by Mother and Son* (with mother, Lucy Caroline Myrick, 1926). Publisher of *Farm and Home; Current Events; Good Housekeeping,* etc. Founder, Good Housekeeping Institute.

Myron, Paul. See Paul Myron Wentworth Linebarger.

Mysteries of the Backwoods. By Thomas Bangs Thorpe (1846). Collection of stories of Southern wilderness adventure.

Mysterious Stranger, The. By Mark Twain (1916), written in 1898. Bitter reflections on the hopeless struggle of the human race. Philip Traum, a reincarnation of Satan, appears in the book to lure the unsuspecting by confusing the moral issues of life.

Mythology. By Edith Hamilton (1942). Brief retellings of the ancient classical myths.

N

N. E. A. See National Education Association.

NABOKOV[-Sirin], VLADIMIR [Vladimirovich] (Apr. 23, 1899–); b. St. Petersburg, Rus. Educator, author. *Camera Obscura* (1938); *The Real Life of Sebastian Knight* (1941); *Nicolai Gogol* (1944); *Nine Stories* (1947); *Bend Sinister* (1947); *Conclusive Evidence: A Memoir* (1950); *Lolita* (1955); *Pnin* (1957); *Nabokov's Dozen* (1958); *Invitation to a Beheading* (1959); *Poems* (1959); *Laughter in the Dark* (1960); *Pale Fire* (1962); *The Gift* (1963); *The Defense* (1964); *The Eye* (1965); *Despair* (1966); *The Waltz Invention* (1966); *Nabokov's Quartet* (1966); *King, Queen, Knave* (1968); *Ada* (1969). Translator: *Three Russian Poets: Selections from Pushkin, Lermontov and Tyutchev* (1945); *Song of Igor's Campaign* (1960); etc. *See* Page Stegner's *Escape into Aesthetics: The*

Art of Vladimir Nabokov (1966); Andrew Field's *Nabokov: His Life in Art* (1970).

NACK, JAMES [M.] (Jan. 4, 1809–Sept. 23, 1879); b. New York. Poet. Known as the "Deaf and dumb poet." *The Legend of the Rocks, and Other Poems* (1827); *Earl Rupert, and Other Tales and Poems* (1839); *Poems* (1852); *The Romance of the Ring, and Other Poems* (1859); etc.

NADAL, EHRMAN SYME (Feb. 13, 1843–July 26, 1922); b. in Greenbrier Co., Va. (now W.Va.). Essayist. *Impressions of London Social Life* (1875); *Essays at Home and Elsewhere* (1882); *Notes of a Professional Exile* (1895); *A Virginian Village, and Other Papers, together with some Autobiographical Notes* (1917).

NADER, RALPH (Feb. 27, 1934–   ); b. Winsted, Conn. Lawyer, author. *Unsafe at Any Speed* (1965). Also: *The Chemical Feast: The Ralph Nader Study Group Report on Food Protection and the Food and Drug Administration* by James S. Turner (1970); *The Vanishing Air: The Ralph Nader Study Group Report on Air Pollution* by John C. Esposito and Larry J. Silverman (1970); *The Interstate Commerce Omission: The Ralph Nader Study Group Report on the I.C.C. and Transportation* by Robert C. Fellmeth (1970).

NAGEL, ERNEST (Nov. 16, 1901–); b. Nove Mesto, Czech. Educator. *Sovereign Reason* (1954); *Logic Without Metaphysics* (1957); *Gödel's Proof* (with J. R. Newman, 1958); *Mind Power* (1960); etc. Philosophy dept., Columbia University, since 1931.

NAGLE, URBAN (Sept. 10, 1905–May 11, 1965); b. Providence, R.I. Roman Catholic clergyman, playwright. *Barter* (play, 1929); *Savonarola* (play, 1940); *Uncle George and Uncle Malachy* (1946); *Lady of Fatima* (play, 1948); *Behind the Masque* (1951); etc.

NAHM, MILTON C. (Dec. 12, 1903–); b. Las Vegas, N.M. Philosopher, educator. *Aesthetic Experience and Its Presuppositions* (1946); *The Artist as Creator* (1956); *Selections from Early Greek Philosophy* (1964); *Las Vegas and Uncle Joe: The New Mexico I Remember* (1964); *Genius and Creativity* (1965); *Aesthetics and Criticism* (1965).

Naked and the Dead, The. Novel by Norman Mailer (1948). An infantry platoon during World War II on a Pacific island. Notable for its contrapuntal themes as expressed by a variety of characters, from the slightly effeminate but highly capable general to the sergeant without nerves and the privates doomed within the limited circles of their army lives.

Naked Came the Stranger. Novel by "Penelope Ashe" (1969). Actually an elaborately prepared literary hoax devised by Long Island *Newsday* columnist Mike McGrady, who arranged to have more than twenty different "authors" write a chapter apiece from a story outline he patterned after the best-selling *Valley of the Dolls* (q.v.) by Jacqueline Susann.

Naked Lunch. By William Burroughs (1959). Adventures of underworld characters involved in crime, homosexuality, and drug addiction, depicted in a surrealistic, stream-of-consciousness style as creatures symbolic of our modern spiritual degradation.

Names on the Land. Historical work by George R. Stewart (1945).

Napoleon and His Marshals. By Joel Tyler Headley, 2v. (1846). The success of this book launched the publishing firm of Charles Scribner.

Narraganset Chief; or, The Adventures of a Wanderer, The. By Isaac Peirce (1832), published anonymously.

Narrative and Critical History of America. Ed. by Justin Winsor, 8v. (1884–89). A standard work, particularly valuable for the history of New England.

Narrative of Colonel Ethan Allen's Captivity, A. By Ethan Allen (1779). Description of treatment of prisoners held by the British in the American Revolution.

Narrative of Four Voyages to the South Sea, A. By Benjamin Morrell (1832). Valuable for its account of American maritime progress in the days of sail.

Narrative of the Troubles with the Indians of New England. By William Hubbard (1677).

Narrative of Voyages and Commercial Enterprises. By Richard Jeffry Cleveland, 2v. (1842). Mirror of American business in the days of the great clipper fleets.

Nasby, Petroleum V. Pen name of David Ross Locke.

NASH, BRADLEY DE LAMATER (Apr. 7, 1900–); b. Boston, Mass. Government official. *Investment Banking in England* (1924); *A Hook in Leviathan* (1950); *Staffing the Presidency* (1952); etc.

NASH, ELEANOR ARNETT (Jan. 23, 1892–Oct. 3, 1969); b. Louisville, Ky. Novelist. *Footnote to Life* (1944); *Bachelors Are Made* (1946); *It Was Mary* (1947); *Lucky Miss Spaulding* (1952); *Beauty Is Not an Age* (1953); *Kit Corelli: TV Stylist* (1955).

NASH, MANNING (May 4, 1924–   ); b. Philadelphia, Pa. Anthropologist, educator, author. *The Golden Road to Modernity* (1965); *Primitive and Peasant Economic Systems* (1966); *Machine Age Maya* (1967). Professor of anthropology, University of Chicago, since 1962.

NASH, OGDEN (Aug. 19, 1902–May 19, 1971); b. Rye, N.Y. Writer of humorous verse. *Free Wheeling* (1931); *Hard Lines* (1931); *Happy Days* (1933); *The Primrose Path* (1935); *The Bad Parents' Garden of Verse* (1936); *I'm a Stranger Here Myself* (1938); *The Face Is Familiar* (1940); *Good Intentions* (1942); *One Touch of Venus* (with S. J. Perelman, prod. 1943); *Many Long Years Ago* (1945); *Versus* (1949); *Parents Keep Out* (1951); *The Private Dining Room* (1953); *You Can't Get There from Here* (1957); *The Christmas That Almost Wasn't* (1957); *Verses from 1929 On* (1959); *Everyone But Thee and Me* (1962); *Marriage Lines—Notes of a Student Husband* (1964); *Animal Garden* (1965); *Cruise of the Aardvark* (1967); *There's Always Another Windmill* (1968); *Santa Go Home: A Case History for Parents* (1968); etc.

NASH, RAY (Feb. 27, 1905–); b. Milwaukie, Ore. Graphic arts historian. *Writing: Some Early American Writing Books and Masters* (1943); *Printing as an Art* (1955); *American Writing Masters and Copybooks* (1959); *American Penmanship 1800–1850* (1967); etc. Art dept., Dartmouth College, since 1937.

Nashville Banner. Nashville, Tenn. Newspaper. Founded 1876. Edward Bushrod Stahlman was president from 1885 to 1930. His son, James G. Stahlman, has been with the paper since 1913; president since 1930. Alvand C. Dunkleberger is editor. Mary Stahlman Douglas is book review editor.

Nashville Tennessean. Nashville, Tenn. Newspaper. Founded 1907, by Luke Lea. Absorbed *Nashville American* in 1910. Donald Davidson and Grantland Rice were formerly on the staff. John Siegenthaler is editor; Mrs. Floy Beatty, book review editor.

NASON, ARTHUR HUNTINGTON (Feb. 3, 1887–Apr. 22, 1944); b. Augusta, Me. Educator, author. *James Shirley, Dramatist* (1915); etc. Director, New York University Press, 1916–33. English dept., New York University, 1905–42.

NASON, ELIAS (Apr. 21, 1811–June 17, 1887); b. Wrentham, Mass. Congregational clergyman, educator, editor, author. *Sir Charles Henry Frankland, Baronet; or, Boston in the Colonial Times* (1865); *A Memoir of Mrs. Susannah Rowson* (1870); *The Life and Times of Charles Sumner* (1874).

NASON, LEONARD HASTINGS (Sept. 28, 1895–); b. Somerville, Mass. Author. *Chevrons* (1926); *Three Lights from a Match* (1927); *The Top Kick* (1928); *Among the Trumpets* (1932); *I Spy Strangers* (1940); *Approach to Battle* (1941); *Contact Mercury* (1946); etc. Contributes verse to the *Chicago Tribune* under pen name "Steamer."

NASSAU, ROBERT HAMILL (Oct. 11, 1835–May 6, 1921); b. Norristown, Pa. Presbyterian clergyman, missionary, recorder of African folk-stories. *Corisco Days* (1910); *Tales Out of School* (1911); *In an Elephant Corral* (1912); *My Ogowe* (1914); *Batanga Tales* (1915).

NAST, CONDÉ (Mar. 26, 1874–Sept. 19, 1942); b. New York. Publisher. President and publisher of *Vogue,* from 1909; president Condé Nast Press, and publisher of *House and Garden, Glamour, Hollywood Patterns,* etc.

NATHAN, GEORGE JEAN (Feb. 14, 1882–Apr. 8, 1958); b. Ft. Wayne, Ind. Drama critic, editor, author. *Another Book on the Theatre* (1916); *Mr. George Jean Nathan Presents* (1917); *The Popular Theatre* (1918); *Comedians All* (1919); *The American Credo* (with H. L. Mencken, 1920); *Heliogabalus* (with same, 1920); *The Theatre, the Drama, the Girls* (1921); *The Critic and the Drama* (1922); *The World in Falseface* (1923); *Materia Critica* (1924); *The House of Satan* (1926); *Land of the Pilgrim's Pride* (1927); *Art of the Night* (1928); *Monks Are Monks* (1929); *Testament of a Critic* (1931); *The Intimate Notebooks* (1932); *Since Ibsen* (1933); *Passing Judgments* (1934); *The Theatre of the Moment* (1936); *The Morning After the First Night* (1938); *The Encyclopedia of the Theatre* (1940); *The Bachelor Life* (1941); *The Entertainment of a Nation* (1942); *Beware of Parents* (1943); *The Theatre Book of the Year* (annual, 1943–51); *The Theatre in the Fifties* (1953); *The Magic Mirror* (1960); etc. Drama critic, *Smart Set,* 1908–23; *Puck,* 1915–16; *Judge,* 1922–35; *Life,* 1935–36; *Vanity Fair,* 1930–35; *Saturday Review of Literature,* 1937; *Esquire,* 1935–46; *Newsweek,* 1937–40; *The American Mercury,* 1940–51. Editor, *Smart Set,* 1914–23; Founder, *The American Mercury,* 1924; editor, 1924–25; contrib. editor, 1925–30; co-founder, *The American Spectator,* 1932; co-editor, 1932.

NATHAN, ROBERT [Gruntal] (Jan. 2, 1894–); b. New York. Novelist, poet. *Peter Kindred* (1919); *Autumn* (1921); *Youth Grows Old* (poems, 1922); *The Puppet Master* (1923); *Jonah* (1925); *The Fiddler in Barly* (1926); *The Woodcutter's House* (1927); *The Bishop's Wife* (1928); *There Is Another Heaven* (1929); *A Cedar Box* (poems, 1929); *The Orchid* (1931); *One More Spring* (1933); *Road of Ages* (1935); *Selected Poems* (1935); *The Enchanted Voyage* (1936); *Journey of Tapiola* (1938); *Winter in April* (1938); *Portrait of Jennie* (1940); *They Went on Together* (1941); *Tapiola's Regiment* (1941); *The Seagull Cry* (1942); *Journal for Josephine* (1943); *But Gently Day* (1943); *Morning in Iowa* (1944); *The Darkening Meadows* (poems, 1945); *Mr. Whittle and the Morning Star* (1947); *A Family Peace* (play, 1947); *Long After Summer* (1948); *River Journey* (1949); *The Innocent Eve* (1951); *Jezebel's Husband* (play, 1951); *The Sleeping Beauty* (play, 1950); *Susan and the Stranger* (play, 1954); *The Rancho of Little Loves* (1956); *The Snowflake and the Starfish* (1959); *The Weans* (1960); *The Wilderness-Stone* (1961); *A Star in the Wind* (1962); *The Devil with Love* (1963); *The Fair* (1964); *The Mallot Diaries* (1965); *One More Spring* (1966); *Stonecliff* (1967); etc. *See* C. K. Sandelin's *Robert Nathan* (1968).

NATION, CARRY [Amelia Moore] (Nov. 25, 1846–June 9, 1911); b. Garrard Co., Ky. Temperance agitator, author. *The Use and Need of the Life of Carry A. Nation* (1904). *See* Herbert Asbury's *Carry Nation* (1929).

Nation, The. New York. Weekly magazine. Founded July 6, 1865, by Frederick Law Olmsted, Edwin Lawrence Godkin, James Miller McKim, Charles Eliot Norton, and others. Its editors have included Wendell Phillips Garrison, Paul Elmer More, Oswald Garrison Villard, Joseph Wood Krutch, Max Lerner, and the present editor, Carey McWilliams. It has been notably liberal in its political and literary views.

National Academy of Sciences. Washington, D.C. Incorporated by Act of Congress, Mar. 3, 1863. It first published its *Memoirs* in 1866, its *Proceedings* in 1877; and its *Biographical Memoirs* in 1877. It established the National Research Council in 1916 and the National Academy of Engineering in 1964. Publishes scientific and technical reports, abstracts, bibliographies, catalogues.

National Amateur Journalist. See *National Printer Journalist.*

National Archives. Washington, D.C. Organized by Congress 1934. The building in Washington contains the records of the history of our national government in the most improved concrete vaults.

National Book Awards. Literary awards honoring the year's best work in fiction, nonfiction, and poetry. Founded 1950 by the American Book Publishers Council, American Booksellers Association, and Book Manufacturers Institute.

The following have received the awards for fiction: Nelson Algren's *The Man with the Golden Arm* (1950); William Faulkner's *The Collected Stories of William Faulkner* (1951); Brendan Gill's *The Trouble of One House* (special award, 1951); James Jones's *From Here to Eternity* (1952); Ralph Ellison's *Invisible Man* (1953); Saul Bellow's *The Adventures of Augie March* (1954); William Faulkner's *A Fable* (1955); John O'Hara's *Ten North Frederick* (1956); Wright Morris's *The Field of Vision* (1957); John Cheever's *The Wapshot Chronicle* (1958); Bernard Malamud's *The Magic Barrel* (1959); Philip Roth's *Good-by Columbus* (1960); Conrad Richter's *The Waters of Kronos* (1961); Walker Percy's *The Moviegoer* (1962); J. F. Powers' *Morte D'Urban* (1963); John Updike's *The Centaur* (1964); Saul Bellow's *Herzog* (1965); Katherine Anne Porter's *Collected Stories* (1966), Bernard Malamud's *The Fixer* (1967); Thornton Wilder's *The Eighth Day* (1968); Jerzy Kosinski's *Steps* (1969); Joyce Carol Oates' *Them* (1970); Saul Bellow's *Mr. Sammler's Planet* (1971).

The following have received the awards for nonfiction: Ralph L. Rusk's *Ralph Waldo Emerson* (1950); Newton Arvin's *Herman Melville* (1951); Rachel L. Carson's *The Sea Around Us* (1952); Bernard De Voto's *The Course of Empire* (1953); Bruce Catton's *A Stillness at Appomattox* (1954); Joseph Wood Krutch's *The Measure of Man* (1955); Herbert Kubly's *American in Italy* (1956); George F. Kennan's *Russia Leaves the War* (1957); Catherine Drinker Bowen's *The Lion and the Throne* (1958); J. Christopher Herold's *Mistress to an Age: A Life of Madame de Staël* (1959); Richard Ellman's *James Joyce: A Biography* (1960); William L. Shirer's *The Rise and Fall of the Third Reich* (1961); Lewis Mumford's *The City in History* (1962); Leon Edel's *Henry James: The Conquest of London* and *Henry James: The Middle Years* (1963).

The following have received awards in science, philosophy or religion: Christopher Tunnard's and Boris Pushkarev's *Man-Made America: Chaos or Control?* (1964); Norbert Wiener's *God and Golem, Inc.* (1965); no award (1966); Oscar Lewis's *La Vida* (1967); Jonathan Kozol's *Death at an Early Age* (1968); Robert Jay Lifton's *Death in Life: Survivors of Hiroshima* (1969); Erik H. Erikson's *Gandhi's Truth: On the Origins of Militant Nonviolence* (1970); Raymond Phineas Stearns' *Science and the British Colonies of America* (1971).

The following have received awards in history or biography: William H. McNeill's *The Rise of the West* (1964); Louis Fischer's *The Life of Lenin* (1965); Arthur M. Schlesinger's *A Thousand Days* (1966); Peter Gay's *The Enlightenment* (1967); George M. Kennan's *Memoirs* (1968); Winthrop D. Jordan's *White Over Black: American Attitudes Toward the Negro, 1550–1812* (1969); T. Harry Williams' *Huey Long* (1970); James McGregor Burns' *Roosevelt: The Soldier of Freedom* (1971).

The following have received awards in arts and letters: Aileen Ward's *John Keats: The Making of a Poet* (1964); Eleanor Clark's *The Oysters of Locmariaquer* (1965); Janet Flanner's *Paris Journal 1944–65* (1966); Justin M. Kaplan's *Mr. Clemens and Mark Twain* (1967); William Troy's *Se-*

lected Essays (1968); Norman Mailer's *Armies of the Night* (1969); Lillian Hellman's *An Unfinished Woman* (1970); Francis Steegmuller's *Cocteau* (1971).

The following have received the awards for poetry: William Carlos Williams' *Patterson III* and *Selected Poems* (1950); Wallace Stevens' *The Auroras of Autumn* (1951); Marianne Moore's *Collected Poems* (1952); Archibald MacLeish's *Collected Poems: 1917–1952* (1953); Conrad Aiken's *Collected Poems* (1954); Wallace Stevens' *Collected Poems of Wallace Stevens* (1955); E. E. Cummings' *Poems: 1923–1954* (special award, 1955); W. H. Auden's *The Shield of Achilles* (1956); Richard Wilbur's *Things of This World* (1957); Robert Penn Warren's *Promises: Poems, 1954–1956* (1958); Theodore Roethke's *Words for the Wind* (1959); Robert Lowell's *Life Studies* (1960); Randall Jarrell's *The Women at the Washington Zoo* (1961); Alan Dugan's *Poems* (1962); William Stafford's *Traveling through the Dark* (1963); John Crowe Ransom's *Selected Poems* (1964); Theodore Roethke's *The Far Field* (1965); James Dickey's *Buckdancer's Choice* (1966); James Merrill's *Nights and Days* (1967); Robert Bly's *The Light Around the Body* (1968); John Berryman's *His Toy, His Dream, His Rest* (1969); Elizabeth Bishop's *The Complete Poems* (1970); Mona Van Duyn's *To See, To Take* (1971).

The following have received awards for translation: Willard Trask's *History of My Life,* by Casanova, and Gregory Rabassa's *Hopscotch,* by Julio Cortazar (1967); Howard and Edna Hong's *Journals and Papers of Soren Kierkegaard* (1968); William Weaver's *Cosmocomics,* by Italo Calvino (1969); Ralph Manheim's *Castle to Castle,* by Louis-Ferdinand Céline (1970); Bertolt Brecht's play, translated by Frank Jones, *Saint Joan of the Stockyards,* and Yusunari Kawabata's novel, translated by Edward G. Seidensticker, *The Sound of the Mountain* (1971).

National Cyclopaedia of American Biography, The. Published by James T. White & Co., New York, 28v. (1892–1940). With supplementary *Conspectus* (1906). Contains accounts of living persons. A continuing series, the 1965 edition contained forty-seven volumes.

National Education Association Journal. Washington, D.C. Monthly, except June, July, August. Founded 1913. Published by the National Education Association.

National Era. Washington, D.C. Abolitionist paper. Founded 1847, by Gamaliel Bailey. Hawthorne and Whittier wrote for the *National Era,* and from 1851 to 1852, *Uncle Tom's Cabin* by Harriet Beecher Stowe appeared in it serially. Expired 1860.

National Foundation on the Arts and the Humanities. Washington, D.C. Founded 1965 as an independent agency in the Executive Branch of Government to develop a broadly conceived national policy of support for the humanities and the arts. It consists of National Endowment for the Arts, National Endowment for the Humanities, National Council on the Arts, National Council on the Humanities, and Federal Council on the Arts and the Humanities.

National Gazette. Philadelphia, Pa. Newspaper. Founded Oct. 31, 1791, by Philip Freneau. Expired Oct. 26, 1793.

National Geographic Magazine. Washington, D.C. Monthly. Founded 1889 as the chief publication of the National Geographic Society. Gilbert Grosvenor became its first editor in 1900. It is noted for its illustrated travel articles.

National Institute of Arts and Letters. Washington, D.C. Founded 1898. Incorporated by an Act of Congress, Jan. 19, 1910.

National Intelligencer. Washington, D.C. Newspaper. Founded by Samuel Harrison Smith, Oct. 31, 1800, as a tri-weekly, under the name *National Intelligencer and Washington Advertiser.* It became a daily in 1813. Joseph Gales became sole proprietor Aug. 31, 1810, and editor in 1812, with William Winston Seaton as associate editor. Seaton retired in

1826. William Winston was an associate editor, 1812–60. It reported the proceedings of Congress and was the chief source of information for such reports until the *Congressional Globe* was established in 1834 by Blair and Rives. It was a noted Whig organ, and had the support of Thomas Jefferson and Daniel Webster.

National Library Week. Observed April 8 to April 14 every year since 1958 to direct public attention to the work done by libraries in making publications of all kinds available to everyone. Organized by the National Book Committee and the American Library Association.

National Magazine. Cleveland, O. (1884–88); New York (1888–94). Historical monthly. Founded 1884, as the *Magazine of Western History.* Name changed 1891. Editors: William W. Williams, 1884–87; James Harrison Kennedy, 1887–91. Expired 1894.

National Medal for Literature. Conferred yearly since 1965 by the National Book Committee in recognition of a living American writer in the amount of $5000. Endowed by the Guinzburg Fund, in memory of Harold K. Guinzburg, late president of Viking Press. Awards have been made to Thornton Wilder (1965), Edmund Wilson (1966), W. H. Auden (1967), Marianne Moore (1968), Conrad Aiken (1969), Robert Penn Warren (1970).

National Police Gazette. New York. Weekly journal, monthly since 1935. Founded Sept. 14, 1845, by George Wilkes, and Enoch E. Camp. It was purchased in 1857 by George W. Matsell, and in 1877 by Richard Kyle Fox. Before it became a sports magazine, it featured lurid literature. Its illustrations were considered "naughty," and for many years it was printed on pink paper. Copies could always be found in barber shops. It was discontinued in 1932 and revived in 1933. It was sold in 1935 to Harold H. Roswell. Similar publications were the *California Police Gazette, San Francisco,* 1859–77, and the *Illustrated Police News,* Boston, 1860–1904.

National Portrait Gallery of Distinguished Americans, The. By James Herring and James B. Longacre, 4v. (1834–39).

National Quarterly Review. New York City. Founded June, 1860, by Edward I. Sears, and often referred to as "Sears' Review." David A. Gorton became editor in 1876, and was succeeded by C. H. Woodman in 1880. Expired Oct., 1880.

National Research Council. Washington, D.C. Established by the National Academy of Sciences in 1916 for the encouragement of research in the natural sciences and for its application to the public welfare.

National Review. New York. Biweekly. Founded 1955. Edited by William F. Buckley, Jr. The chief organ of conservatism as an intellectual, social, and political movement.

National Tribune. Washington, D.C. Weekly journal of the Grand Army of the Republic. Founded 1877. George Lemmon was editor until 1885, and was followed by John McElroy, 1885–1929. The latter's *Ki Klegg* stories appeared in it. Kate Sherwood edited the woman's department, 1883–98. Name later changed to *National Tribune-Stars and Stripes.*

National Writers Club. Denver, Colo. Founded 1937. Organization of North American free-lance writers.

Native Son. Novel by Richard Wright (1940). Life story of "Bigger Thomas," a Chicago Negro, showing in dramatic manner the problems involved in racial discrimination.

Natural History of Nonsense, The. By Bergen Evans (1946). A history of erroneous thinking, long-lived legends, and superstitions.

Nature. Essays by Ralph Waldo Emerson, published anonymously (1836). The beginning of Emerson's Transcendentalism.

Nature and Elements of Poetry, The. By Edmund Clarence Stedman (1892), Turnbull lectures at Johns Hopkins University, 1891.

Nature and Science. New York. Seventeen issues yearly. Founded 1963. Published by the American Museum of Natural History. Simple, clearly written, intelligent explanations to young people of many scientific topics.

NAYLOR, JAMES BALL (Oct. 4, 1860–Apr. 1, 1945); b. Pennsville, O. Physician, novelist, poet. *Current Coin* (1893); *Goldenrod and Thistledown* (1896); *The Sign of the Prophet* (1901); *The Kentuckian* (1905); *The Scalawags* (1907); *The Misadventures of Marjory* (1908); *A Book of Buckeye Verse* (1927); *Vagrant Verse* (1935).

Nazarene: A Tale of the Christ, The. By Shalom Asch (1939).

Neal, Alice B. See Alice Bradley Neal Haven.

NEAL, JOHN (Aug. 25, 1793–June 20, 1876); b. Portland, Me. Editor, novelist, poet. *Keep Cool* (under pen name, "Somebody, M. D. C.," 1817); *The Battle of Niagara* (under pen name, "John O'Cataract," 1818); *Otho* (drama in verse, 1819); *Logan* (anon., 1822); *Randolph* (anon., 1823); *Seventy-Six* (anon., 1823); *Rachel Dyer* (1828); *Authorship* (anon., 1830); *The Down-Easters* (1833); *True Womanhood* (1859); *The White Faced Pacer* (1863); *The Moose-Hunter* (1864); *Wandering Recollections of a Somewhat Busy Life* (1869). *American Writers: A Series of Papers Contributed to Blackwood's Magazine, 1824–1825* (1937); etc. Co-author, with Tobias Watkins, of *A History of the American Revolution,* 2v. (1819), projected by Paul Allen, but written by Neal and Watkins. Editor, *Brother Jonathan, New England Galaxy, Yankee, The Portico,* etc.

NEAL, JOSEPH CLAY (Feb. 3, 1807–July 17, 1847); b. Greenland, N.H. Editor, humorist, author. *Charcoal Sketches,* 2 series (1838, 1848); *In Town and About* (1843); *Petter Ploddy, and Other Oddities* (1844); *The Misfortunes of Peter Faber, and Other Sketches* (1856). See *Neal's Saturday Gazette and Ladies' Literary Museum.*

NEALE, WALTER (Jan. 21, 1873–Sept. 28, 1933); b. Eastville, Va. Publisher, author. *The Betrayal* (1910); *The Sovereignty of the States* (1910); *Life of Ambrose Bierce* (1929). Compiler: *Masterpieces of the Southern Poets* (1911). Founder, Neale Publishing Co. 1911, president, 1911–33.

Neal's Saturday Gazette and Ladies' Literary Museum. Philadelphia, Pa. Founded 1836, by Joseph C. Neal, Morton McMichael and Louis A. Godey, as the *Saturday News and Literary Gazette.* Neal was editor, 1836–47. In it appeared Neal's *Charcoal Sketches* and Frances M. Whitcher's *The Widow Bedott Papers.* Expired 1853.

NEARING, ELIZABETH CUSTER (Mrs. Max Nearing) (Jan. 9, 1900–   ); b. Philadelphia, Pa. Novelist. *Grand Central Murder* (pen name "Sue McVeigh," 1939); *The Lancasters* (1947).

NEARING, SCOTT (Aug. 6, 1883–); b. Morris Run, Pa. Sociologist, author. *Social Religion* (1913); *Poverty and Riches* (1916); *The Next Stage* (1924); *Whither China?* (1927); *Black America* (1929; rev. ed. 1969); *Twilight of Empire* (1930); *Democracy Is Not Enough* (1945); *Economics for the Power Age* (1952); *Man's Search for the Good Life* (1954); *Freedom: Promise and Menace* (1961); *The Conscience of a Radical* (1965); *Dollar Diplomacy: A Study in American Imperialism* (with Joseph Freeman, 1969); etc.

Nebraska Folklore. Lincoln, Neb. Magazine. Founded 1937. Contains many historical studies on cowboy songs, Indian legends, ballads, tall tales, dance calls, children's games, etc.

Ned Myers. Novel by James Fenimore Cooper (1843). Story of a sailor's experiences before the mast.

NEESER, ROBERT WILDEN (July 16, 1884–); b. Seabright, N.J. Author. *Statistical and Chronological History of the United States Navy, 1775–1907,* 2v. (1909); etc. Editor: *American Naval Songs & Ballads* (1938).

NEF, JOHN ULRIC (July 13, 1899–); b. Chicago, Ill. Educator, author. *Industry and Government in France and England, 1540–1640* (1940); *The United States and Civilization* (1942); *War and Human Progress* (1950; rev. ed. 1968); *Cultural Foundations of Industrial Civilization* (1958); *A Search for Civilization* (1962); *Bridges of Human Understanding* (1964); *Conquest of the Material World* (1964); etc. Prof. economic history, University of Chicago, since 1936.

NEFF, EMERY (Mar. 23, 1892–); b. Delaware, O. Educator, author. *Carlyle and Mill* (1924; rev. ed. 1964); *Carlyle* (1932); *Revolution in European Poetry* (1940); *The Poetry of History* (1947); *Edward Arlington Robinson* (1948; rev. ed. 1968). Prof. English, Columbia University, since 1942.

NEFF, WANDA FRAIKEN (Mrs. Emery Neff) (May 6, 1889–); b. Minneapolis, Minn. Author. *We Sing Diana* (1928); *Lone Voyagers* (1929); *Victorian Working Women* (1929).

NEIDEG, WILLIAM JONATHAN (d. Feb. 7, 1955); b. Western College, Ia. Author. *The First Wardens* (poems, 1905); *The Fire Flingers* (1919); *Wild Rice* (1932); *Slug Seven* (1935); *Water's Edge* (1941); etc. Sub-editor, *The Argonaut,* 1898–99; book editor, *The Wave,* 1899–1901. English dept., Stanford University, 1901–04; University of Wisconsin, 1905–11.

NEIDER, CHARLES (1915–). Author. *The Frozen Sea* (1948); *The White Citadel* (1954); *The Authentic Death of Henry Jones* (1956); etc. Editor: *Great Shipwrecks and Castaways* (1952); Mark Twain's *Life as I Find It* (1961); *Suzy* (1966); etc.

Neighbor Jackwood. By John T. Trowbridge (1856). Antislavery novel based on the forced return of the slave, Anthony Burns, from Boston to Virginia.

NEIHARDT, JOHN G[neisenau] (Jan. 8, 1881–); b. near Sharpsburg, Ill. Editor, poet, novelist. *The Divine Enchantment* (poems, 1900); *The Lonesome Trail* (1907); *A Bundle of Myrrh* (poems, 1907); *Man-Song* (1909); *The River and I* (1910); *The Dawn-Builder* (1911); *The Stranger at the Gate* (poems, 1912); *Life's Lure* (1914); *The Song of Hugh Glass* (poem, 1915); *The Song of Three Friends* (1919); *The Splendid Wayfaring* (1920); *Poetic Values* (1925); *The Song of the Indian Wars* (1925); *Collected Poems,* 2v. (1926); *Indian Tales and Others* (1926); *Black Elk Speaks* (1932); *The Song of the Messiah* (poem, 1935); *The Song of Jed Smith* (1940); *A Cycle of the West* (1949); *When the Tree Flowered* (1951); *Eagle Voice* (1953); *Lyric and Dramatic Poems* (1965); etc. Poet laureate of Nebraska, 1921. Lit. editor, the *St. Louis Post Dispatch,* 1926–38. Poet in residence, University of Missouri, since 1948. See Fred B. Millett's *Contemporary American Authors* (1940).

NEILL, EDWARD DUFFIELD (Aug. 9, 1823–Sept. 26, 1893); b. Philadelphia, Pa. Reformed Episcopal clergyman, educator, author. *Terra Mariae; or, Threads of Maryland Colonial History* (1867); *History of the Virginia Company of London* (1869); *The English Colonization of America During the Seventeenth Century* (1871); etc. President, Macalester College, Minneapolis, Minn., 1874–84; prof. history, etc., 1885–93.

NEILL, ESTHER [Waggaman] (Mrs. Charles P. Neill) (1873–); b. Washington, D.C. Author. *The Red Ascent* (1914); *Barbara's Marriage and the Bishop* (1925); *Miss Princess* (1929); *Tragic City* (1932).

NEILSON, FRANCIS (Jan. 26, 1867–Apr. 3, 1961); b. Birkenhead, Eng. Playwright, author. *Manabozo* (1899); *The Bath Road* (1902); *A Butterfly's Wheel* (play, 1911); *How Diplomats Make War* (1915); *The Desire for Change* (prod.

1925); *Eleventh Commandment* (play, 1933); *Tragedy of Europe* (1940); *Roots of Our Learning* (essays, 1946); *My Life in Two Worlds*, 2v. (1952); *Poems* (1956); *Shakespeare and the Tempest* (1956); *The Cultural Tradition and Other Essays* (1957); *From Ur to Nazareth* (1959). Wrote librettos for Victor Herbert's *La Vivandière*, *Prince Ananias*.

NEILSON, WILLIAM ALLAN (Mar. 28, 1869–Feb. 13, 1946); b. Doune, Scot. Educator, editor, author. *Essentials of Poetry* (1912); *The Facts about Shakespeare* (with Ashley H. Thorndike, 1913); *Robert Burns: How to Know Him* (1917); *A History of English Literature* (1920); *Intellectual Honesty, and Other Addresses* (1956); etc. Assoc. editor: *The Harvard Classics*, 50v. (1909–10); editor: *Roads to Knowledge* (1932); editor-in-chief: *Webster's New International Dictionary*, 2d edition (1934); editor or co-editor of many texts in English literature. Prof. English, Harvard University, 1906–17; president, Smith College, 1917–39. *See* Margaret Thorp's *Neilson of Smith* (1956).

NELL, WILLIAM COOPER (Dec. 20, 1816–May 25, 1874); b. Boston, Mass. Journalist, author. *Services of Colored Americans in the Wars of 1776 and 1812* (1851); *The Colored Patriots of the American Revolution* (1855).

NELSON, ANNIE GREENE. Author. *After the Storm* (1942); *The Dawn Appears* (1944).

NELSON, CHARLES ALEXANDER (Apr. 14, 1839–Jan. 12, 1933); b. Calais, Me. Librarian, bibliographer, poet. *Selected Poems* (1933). Compiled *Catalogue of the Astor Library*, 4v. (1886–88), a continuation of the Cogswell catalogue; and numerous bibliographies for the Columbia University Library, etc.

NELSON, HENRY LOOMIS (Jan. 5, 1846–Feb. 29, 1908); b. New York. Editor, educator, author. *John Rantoul* (1885); *The Money We Need* (1895). Editor, *Harper's Weekly*, 1894–98. Prof. political science, Williams College, 1902–08.

NELSON, JOHN HERBERT (July 29, 1897–); b. in Rutherford Co., N.C. Educator. *The Negro Character in American Literature* (1926); *Chief Modern Poets of England and America* (with G. D. Sanders, 1929); *Contemporary Trends* (1933). Prof. English, University of Kansas, since 1930.

Nelson, Joseph. Pen name of Isaac Mitchell.

Nelson, Thomas & Sons. New York; Camden, N.J. Publishers. Founded 1798, by Thomas Nelson at Edinburgh, Scotland. The New York branch was established in 1854. Among the outstanding publications of the American firm are the *American Standard Version of the Bible* and *Nelson's Loose Leaf Encyclopedia.* The latter was first published in 1911, and its editor was John H. Finley, assisted by Sir Henry Newbolt in England and Sir Robert Falconer in Canada.

NELSON, WALTER HENRY (Mar. 23, 1928–); b. Munich, Ger. Author. *Small Wonder: The Amazing Story of the Volkswagen* (1965); *The Great Discount Delusion* (1965).

NELSON, WILLIAM (Jan. 18, 1908–   ); b. New York. Educator, author. *John Skelton, Laureate* (1939); *Out of the Crocodile's Mouth* (1949); *Barclay's Life of St. George* (1955); *A Fifteenth Century School Book* (1956); *The Poetry of Edmund Spenser* (1963). Professor of English, Columbia University, since 1953.

NEMEROV, HOWARD (Mar. 1, 1920–); b. New York. Educator, author. *The Image and the Law* (poems, 1947); *The Melodramatists* (1949); *Guide to the Ruins* (poems, 1950); *Federigo, or The Power of Love* (1954); *The Salt Garden* (poems, 1955); *The Homecoming Game* (1957); *Mirrors and Windows* (poems, 1958); *A Commodity of Dreams* (stories, 1959); *New and Selected Poems* (1960); *Journal of the Fictive Life* (1965); *Poets on Poetry* (with others, 1966); *The Blue Swallows* (1967); etc. Assoc. editor, 1946–57. 1846–57. Faculty literature and languages, Bennington College, since 1948.

NESBIT, WILBUR D[ick] (Sept. 16, 1871–Aug. 20, 1927); b. Xenia, O. Poet. *The Trail to Boyland, and Other Poems* (1904); *The Gentleman Ragman* (1906); *A Book of Poems* (1906); *Who's Hoosier*, 2v. (1912); *The Paths of Long Ago* (poems, 1926); *Sermons in Song* (1929); *As Children Do* (poems, 1929); etc.

NESMITH, JAMES ERNEST (1856–1898); b. in Massachusetts. Artist, poet. *Monadnoc, and Other Sketches in Verse* (1888); *Philoctetes, and Other Poems and Sonnets* (1894); *The Life and Work of Frederic Thomas Greenhalge, Governor of Massachusetts* (1897).

NETHERCOT, ARTHUR HOBART (Apr. 20. 1895–); b. Chicago, Ill. Educator, author. *Sir William D'Avenant* (1938); *The Road to Tryermaine* (1939); *Men and Supermen: The Shavian Portrait Gallery* (1954; rev. ed. 1966); *The First Five Lives of Annie Besant* (1960); *The Last Four Lives of Annie Besant* (1963); etc. English dept., Northwestern University, since 1919.

Nets to Catch the Wind. By Elinor Wylie (1921). Her first volume of verse. It attracted immediate attention.

NETTELS, CURTIS PUTNAM (Aug. 25, 1898–); b. Topeka, Kan. Historian. *The Money Supply of the American Colonies* (1934); *The Roots of American Civilization* (1938); *George Washington and American Independence* (1951); *The Emergence of A National Economy 1775–1815* (1969). Prof. American history, Cornell University, since 1944.

NETTLETON, GEORGE HENRY (July 16, 1874–Feb. 5, 1959); b. Boston, Mass. Educator, author. *English Drama of the Restoration and Eighteenth Century* (1914); etc. Editor: *Specimens of the Short Story* (1901); *British Dramatists from Dryden to Sheridan* (1939); etc. English dept., Yale University, 1899–30, dean, Yale College, 1937–39.

NEUBERGER, RICHARD LEWIS (Dec. 26, 1912–Mar. 9, 1960); b. Portland, Ore. Senator, author. *An Army of the Aged* (with Kelley Loe, 1936); *Integrity: The Life of George W. Norris* (with Stephen B. Kahn, 1937); *Our Promised Land* (1938); *The Lewis and Clark Expedition* (1951); *Royal Canadian Mounted Police* (1953); *Adventures in Politics: We Go to the Legislature* (1954).

NEUGEBOREN, JAY (May 30, 1938–   ); b. Brooklyn, N.Y. Author. *Big Man* (1966).

NEUMANN, SIGMUND (May 1, 1904–Oct. 22, 1962); b. Leipzig, Ger. Educator, author. Author: *Permanent Revolution* (1942); *The Future in Prospective* (1946); etc. Editor: *Modern Political Parties* (1956). Prof. social science, Wesleyan University, since 1944.

NEUTRA, RICHARD JOSEPH (Apr. 8, 1892–); b. Vienna. Architect, author. Author: *How America Builds* (1926); *America: New Building in the World* (1929); *Buildings and Projects* (1950); *Mystery and Realities of the Site* (1951); *Survival through Design* (1954); *Life and Human Habitat* (1956); *World and Dwelling* (1962); *Life and Shape* (1962); etc.

NEVIN, ROBERT PEEBLES (July 31, 1820–June 28, 1908); b. Shippensburg, Pa. Father of Ethelbert Nevin, the composer. Journalist, author. *Black-Robes* (1872); *The "Beautiful River," and Other Poems* (1899).

NEVIN, WILLIAM CHANNING (Jan. 1, 1844–Apr. 10, 1920); b. New Athens, O. Lawyer, journalist, poet. *Legends of Martha's Vineyard* (1905); etc. Founder, the *Evening Express*, Philadelphia, 1874.

NEVINS, ALLAN (May 20, 1890–Mar. 4, 1971); b. Camp Point, Ill. Educator, editor, historian, biographer. *The Evening Post: A Century of Journalism* (1922); *The Emergence of Modern America* (1927); *Frémont, the West's Greatest Adventurer*, 2v. (1928); *Henry White: Thirty Years of American Diplomacy* (1930); *Grover Cleveland: A Study in Cour-*

age (1932, Pulitzer prize for biography, 1933); *Hamilton Fish: The Inner History of the Grant Administration* (1936, Pulitzer prize for biography, 1937); *John D. Rockefeller,* 2v. (1940); *America in World Affairs* (1942); *A Short History of the United States* (with H. S. Commager, 1945); *The Ordeal of the Union,* 2v. (1947); *The Emergence of Lincoln,* 2v. (1950); *Statesmanship of the Civil War* (1953); *Ford: The Times, the Man, the Company* (with Frank E. Hill, 1954); *The War for the Union,* 2v. (1959–60); *The State Universities and Democracy* (1962); *A History of the American People from 1492* (1965). Editor: *The Diary of Philip Hone* (1927); *The Diary of John Quincy Adams* (1928); *The Letters and Journals of Brand Whitlock* (1936); *The Diary of George Templeton Strong* (1952); *The Letters of James Truslow Adams* (1967); *American Press Opinion: Washington to Coolidge: A Documentary Record of Editorial Leadership and Criticism 1785-1927,* 2v. (1969). With the *New York Evening Post,* 1913–23; *Nation,* 1913–18; *New York Sun,* 1924–25; *New York World,* 1925–31. Prof. American history, Columbia University, 1931–58; research scholar, Huntington Library, San Marino, Cal., from 1958.

New American Bible, The. Translated by members of the Catholic Biblical Association of America (1970). Intended to replace the Douay-Rheims version of 1609. Originally named "Confraternity Version of the Bible."

New American Cyclopaedia, The. Ed. by George Ripley and Charles A. Dana, 16v. (1858–63). Later published under title, *The American Cyclopaedia.*

New American Library, Inc., The. New York. Publishers. Founded 1948 as New American Library of World Literature. Victor Weybright was chairman of the board; later, Martin P. Levin. Imprints have included *Signet Books, Signet Key Books, Signet Classics,* and *Mentor Books.* A subsidiary of The Times Mirror Co. (q.v.).

New American Poetry, The. Anthology of recent verse, edited by Donald M. Allen (1960). From Charles Olson to the youngest of the Beat Generation, covering the period 1945–1960. The poets represented are the free-verse-writing, non-academic poets following the tradition of Whitman and William Carlos Williams.

New American Review. New York. Three times a year. Founded 1967. Published by the New American Library. Edited by Theodore Solotaroff. Devoted to new ideas and writings in continuation of *New World Writing,* a similar kind of literary paperback magazine, published between 1952 and 1959. Has published Anne Sexton, William H. Gass, Kate Millett, John Ashbery, Richard Eberhardt.

New Book of Knowledge: The Children's Encyclopedia. Twenty volume encyclopedia published in 1966 by Grolier Society.

New Catholic Encyclopedia. Edited by a staff of scholars of the Catholic University of America, 15v. (1967). The first new comprehensive encyclopedia of its kind to appear in the United States in fifty years. William J. McDonald is editor-in-chief. See *Catholic Encyclopedia.*

New Century Cyclopedia of Names. Edited by Clarence L. Barnhart, 3v. (1954). Information on all kinds of subjects under proper-name entries.

New Challenge. Boston, Mass. Literary quarterly. Founded 1937, as a reorganization of *Challenge,* but discontinued shortly afterward. Richard Wright was associate editor.

New Colophon. New York. Monthly. Founded 1947, by Elmer Adler, John T. Winterich, and F. B. Adams, Jr. Superseded *Colophon* (q.v.).

New Criticism. Type of literary analysis associated especially with the magazines *Kenyon Review* and *Sewanee Review.* It concentrated on the imaginative coherence of a work, mainly the lyric poem as conveyed by symbols, metaphor, rhythm, and "texture"—organic unity of form and content. The New Critics, notably John Crowe Ransom, Cleanth Brooks, and Allen Tate, derived some of their emphasis from the criticism of I. A. Richards, Robert Graves, T. S. Eliot, and Ezra Pound. *See* John Crowe Ransom's *The New Criticism* (1941); Richard Foster's *The New Romantics* (1962).

New Directions. New York. Publishers. Founded 1936, by James Laughlin, then a Harvard undergraduate. Has published works by writers in experimental literature and an annual anthology, *New Directions in Prose and Poetry.* James Laughlin heads the firm. Laughlin opened a college text department with Richard Smyth.

New England Legends. By Harriet Elizabeth Prescott Spofford (1871).

New England Nun, A. By Mary E. Wilkins Freeman (1891). Story of an old maid betrothed to an absent fortune-hunting lover. She rejoices when he returns and chooses another woman.

New England Primer, The. (1690). This religious instructor for children was printed in Boston and ran through many editions. It contains the alphabet and syllabarium, alphabet rhymes, illustrated with crude woodcuts, the Lord's Prayer, the Creed, the Shorter Catechism, and a few hymns. The 1775 edition, printed at Providence, R.I., contains the childhood prayer, "Now I lay me down to sleep." The earliest known copy is dated 1727 and is owned by The New York Public Library. It was printed in Boston by S. Kneeland and T. Green. A 1735 edition is owned by the Henry E. Huntington Library. Bibliographers have found traces of an edition going back as far as 1690, but no copies have been located. The Frank J. Hogan collection in the Library of Congress contains ten early editions of the book. *See* Paul L. Ford's *The New England Primer* (1897).

New England Quarterly. Brunswick, Me. Historical magazine. Founded 1928, at Cambridge, Mass. Moved to Orono in 1938 and later to Brunswick.

New Englander, The. Boston, Mass. Magazine. Founded January, 1843, by Edward Royall Tyler, son of the famous playwright, Royall Tyler. In 1885 its name was changed to the *New Englander and Yale Review.* Expired in 1892, and was replaced by the *Yale Review.*

"New England's Crisis." Poem by Benjamin Thompson (1676). About King Philip's War.

New England's Memorial. By Nathaniel Morton (1669). A history of Plymouth Colony.

New England's Rarities Discovered. By John Josselyn (1672). First systematic account of the animals and plants of North America.

New English Canaan. By Thomas Morton (1637). Sets forth the origins of the Indians, describes their customs, and satirizes the dress, speech, and religion of the Puritans.

"New Hampshire." Poem by Robert Frost (1923).

New Hampshire Journal; or, The Farmer's Weekly Museum. See *Farmers' Museum.*

New Home–Who'll Follow, A. By Caroline Matilda Stansbury Kirkland (1839). Letters on the frontier life in Michigan, then a part of Northwest Territory.

New Humanism, The. A philosophically oriented movement of cultural criticism that flourished during the 1920's. Irving Babbitt and Paul Elmer More were the most influential exponents of its ideas, which expressed the need for man's adherence to universal ethical human values. The New Humanists were classically oriented and anti-romantic and stressed intellectual as opposed to religious principles.

New Industrial State, The. Analysis of modern American economy, by John Kenneth Galbraith (1967).

New International Encyclopaedia. Ed. by Harry Thurston Peck, 17v. (1902–04), published by Dodd, Mead & Co., New York, who had published it first in 1886, as the *International Encyclopedia,* an outgrowth of the *Library of Universal Knowledge,* which was a reprint of *Chambers's Encyclopaedia.* A new edition in 23v. was published 1914–16. Frank Moore Colby and Talcott Williams followed Peck in the editorship. The *International Year Book,* an annual supplement, began in 1899, and was succeeded by the *New International Year Book* in 1907.

New Leader, The. New York. Bi-weekly magazine of news and opinion. Founded 1923. Published by the American Labor Conference on International Affairs. It is noted for its literary articles and reviews. Regular contributors include William Henry Chamberlin, Sidney Hook, Reinhold Niebuhr, Leslie Fiedler.

New London Gazette. See *New London Summary.*

New London Summary. New London, Conn. Newspaper. Founded 1758, by Timothy Green. First newspaper in Connecticut. Expired 1763. Green's son, Timothy Green, established the *New London Gazette* the same year. From 1773 to 1823 it was called the *Connecticut Gazette.* Expired 1844.

New Masses. New York. Weekly. Founded 1926 as a monthly, becoming a weekly in 1934. Devoted to social criticism and literature from the Marxist viewpoint. Edited by Joseph Freeman, Michael Gold, and others. Merged in 1948 with the Marxist periodical *Mainstream* as *Masses and Mainstream.*

New Mexico Quarterly. Albuquerque, N.M. Review of literature and the arts. Founded 1931.

New Orleans Poetry Journal. New Orleans, La. Quarterly of poetry. Founded 1955. Edited by Richard Ashmore. Discontinued 1958.

New Orleans States-Item. New Orleans, La. Newspaper. Founded 1877 as the *Daily City Item.* Lafcadio Hearn joined it in 1878. The *Daily States,* founded 1879, later merged with it. The *New Orleans Tribune* was started in 1924 as the *Item's* morning paper. George W. Healy, Jr. is the present editor. Now published by the Times-Picayune Publishing Co. See *New Orleans Times-Picayune.*

New Orleans Times-Picayune. New Orleans, La. Newspaper. The *Daily Picayune,* founded 1836, sold for a picayune, a small silver coin then worth about 6-1/2 cents. In 1876, at the death of the editor, A. M. Holbrook, his wife, "Pearl Rivers," became editor. "Dorothy Dix" (Mrs. Elizabeth B. Gilmer) started her column of advice to the lovelorn in the *Picayune* in 1896. The *Times* (founded 1863) merged with the *Democrat* (founded 1875) in 1904 as the *Times-Democrat,* which merged with the *Picayune* in 1914 under the present name. The *Daily States,* founded 1879, was taken over in 1933. At present the *States* is published evenings, except Sunday, with the *Item,* as the *New Orleans States-Item;* the latter is owned by the Times-Picayune Publishing Co. George W. Healy, Jr., is editor of the *Times-Picayune.* Mabel Simmons edits the Sunday book review.

New Republic. New York; Washington D.C. Founded 1914, by Willard Dickerman Straight, with Herbert D. Croly as editor. Bruce Bliven became editor in 1930. One of the longest-lived organs of liberal political opinion, noted also for its literary contributions; Randolph Bourne, Stark Young, Edmund Wilson, John Dewey, Alvin Johnson, George Soule, and Walter Lippmann were among its early editors or contributors. After World War II, the magazine under Henry A. Wallace was for a time associated with the Progressive Party. Gilbert A. Harrison is now editor and publisher. Contributing editors have included Robert Brustein, B. H. Haggin, Irving Howe, Gerald W. Johnson, and Michael Straight.

New Voices. Periodical paperback of new writing published by Permabooks.

New Voyage to Carolina, A. By John Lawson (1709).

New World. New York. Fiction weekly. Founded June 6, 1840, by Park Benjamin, Rufus W. Griswold, and Jonas Winchester. Expired May 10, 1845.

New World Review. New York. Monthly. Founded 1932. Magazine of Russian interests.

New World Writing. See *New American Review.*

New York American. See *New York Journal-American.*

New York Amsterdam News. New York. Newspaper. Founded 1909. Principal Negro newspaper in New York. C. B. Powell is editor.

New York Citizen and Round Table. New York. Weekly. Formed 1869, by a merger of *The Citizen* and the *Round Table.* Expired c. 1873.

New York Clipper. New York. Sporting journal. Founded 1853, by Frank Queen. Absorbed by *Variety,* in 1923.

New York Commercial Advertiser. See *New York Globe.*

New York Corsair. New York. Magazine. Founded in 1839 by Nathaniel Parker Willis. "A gazette of literature, art, dramatic criticism, fashion and novelty."

New York Courier. New York. Sunday newspaper. Founded Mar. 20, 1825. The first Sunday newspaper in New York. Expired c. 1826.

New York Daily Graphic. New York. First illustrated newspaper in the world; founded 1873. The first halftone was made for it by Stephen Henry Horgan, Mar. 4, 1880. Expired 1889.

New York Daily Graphic. New York. Newspaper. Founded 1924, by Bernarr Macfadden, as a tabloid. Edited by Emile Gauvreau. After a period of scandal concerned with its sensational methods of reporting various criminal trials, it expired in 1932.

New York Daily News. New York. Newspaper. Founded 1919, by Robert Rutherford McCormick and Joseph Medill Patterson, as the *New York Illustrated Daily News.* Later the same year the *"Illustrated"* was dropped. First successful tabloid newspaper in America. Patterson directed the paper from the beginning and added a Sunday edition in 1922. By 1924 it had attained the largest circulation of any newspaper in the United States: 750,000 readers. It is still the largest, with a daily circulation of over 2,000,000. Noted for its frank sensationalism, sports, comics, and direct and personal editorial manner. F. M. Flynn is publisher and Floyd Barger is executive editor. Acquired the *New York Mirror* in 1963.

New York Dramatic Mirror. New York. Weekly. Founded 1879, as the *New York Mirror,* by Ernest Harvier, who was succeeded by G. W. Hamersly. Harrison Grey Fiske was editor until 1911, followed by Frederick F. Shrader. In 1889, the name was changed to the *New York Dramatic Mirror;* and in 1917, to the *Dramatic Mirror.* In later years Burns Mantle was a regular contributor. Expired 1922.

New York Evening Express. See *New York Evening Mail.*

New York Evening Journal. See *New York Journal-American.*

New York Evening Mail. New York. Newspaper. Founded Sept. 21, 1867. Absorbed the *New York Evening Express,* founded June 20, 1836 by James Brooks, in 1881, to form the *Mail and Express.* In 1904, the original name was resumed. In 1924, the *Evening Mail* was absorbed by the *New York Evening Telegram.* See *New York World-Telegram and Sun.*

New York Evening Post. See *New York Post.*

New York Evening Star. New York. Newspaper. Founded 1833. The *Times and Commercial Intelligencer* was founded 1838. Merged 1840 as the *New York Times and Evening Star,* which merged 1841 with the *Commercial Advertiser,* later the *New York Globe.*

New York Evening Telegram. See *New York World-Telegram and Sun.*

New York Gazette and General Advertiser. New York. Newspaper. Founded Dec. 29, 1788, as the *New-York Daily Gazette,* becoming the *New York Gazette and General Advertiser* in 1795. Merged 1840 with the *New York Journal of Commerce.*

New York Globe. New York. Newspaper. Founded 1797. It grew out of the *American Minerva,* founded Dec. 9, 1793, by Noah Webster and George Bunce, with the support of Alexander Hamilton. It became the *Commercial Advertiser,* Oct. 7, 1797. Webster bought out Bunce in 1796, and retired as editor in 1803. Zachariah Lewis was editor, 1803–13. Lewis retired from the staff in 1820. William Leete Stone was editor, 1820–44. John Inman and Robert Charles Sands were Stone's assistants, and this brilliant trio gave the *Commercial Advertiser* a distinct literary flavor. Francis Hall was editor, 1844–63. William Henry Hurlbert was editor, 1863–67, followed by Thurlow Weed, 1867–68. Hugh J. Hastings was editor, 1868–85. Henry J. Wright was editor from 1885 to 1923, when the paper was merged with the New York *Sun.* In 1904 it had been renamed the *Globe and Commercial Advertiser.* Jason Rogers became publisher in 1910. Allan Dawson, Pitts Sanborn, J. H. Pearsall, L. J. Wight, W. A. Gramer, Percy T. Ayers, S. P. West, J. B. Lander, Charles D. Losee and Mrs. J. Allan Dawson were on the staff in its latter days. *See* James Melvin Lee's *America's Oldest Newspaper: The New York Globe* (1918).

New York Herald Tribune. New York. Newspaper. The *New York Herald* was founded 1835, by James Gordon Bennett. Other prominent members of the staff included Frederic Hudson, George F. Williams, Henry M. Stanley, Januarius A. MacGahan, Charles Nordhoff, Charles A. Hart, George R. Miner, Arthur H. Fowler. Frank Munsey bought the *Herald* in 1920 and merged it with the *Sun.* In 1924 it was merged with the *Tribune* to form the *Herald Tribune. See* I. C. Clarke's *My Life and Memories* (1925). The *Tribune* had been founded by Horace Greeley in 1841, and was edited by him until 1872. Whitelaw Reid was editor, 1872–1905. Ogden Mills Reid succeeded him in 1913. A Sunday edition appeared in 1861. It was discontinued but revived in 1879. Its coverage of the Civil War was noteworthy. The *Tribune* was the first to use curved stereotyped plates in 1860, and linotype in 1886. Among the paper's foreign correspondents were Joel Tyler Headley, Wilbur Forrest, and Richard Harding Davis. Margaret Fuller became the first literary critic in 1844. Elmer Davis, Heywood Broun, and Burton Rascoe were later literary critics. Lewis Gannett conducted the column "Books and Things" after 1930. Those associated with the paper have included John Hay, Rebecca Harding Davis, Stuart Sherman, Walter Millis, Geoffrey Parsons, and Nicholas Roosevelt. Walter Lippmann, Mark Sullivan, John Crosby, Art Buchwald, Clementine Paddleford, David Lawrence, and Roscoe Drummond have been columnists. The Sunday edition of the paper included "Today's Living," the "Herald Tribune TV and Radio Magazine," and the "Herald Tribune Books." Merged with *New York Journal-American* and *New York World-Telegram and Sun* (qq.v.) as *New York World Journal Tribune* (q.v.) in 1966. Expired 1967. *See* Harry W. Baehr's *The New York Tribune Since the Civil War* (1936); and Joseph G. Herzberg's *Late City Edition* (1947). See *Paris Herald.*

New York Herald Tribune Books. New York. Sunday literary section of the *New York Herald Tribune.* It was founded in 1924 with Stuart P. Sherman as editor. Irita Van Doren

became editor in 1926. It grew out of the Sunday section established in 1879. In 1902 a *Saturday Book Page* was printed. In 1922 a Sunday section called *Tribune Magazine and Books* was edited by Burton Rascoe. Margaret Fuller was the *Tribune's* first literary critic. She was employed by Horace Greeley in 1844. In 1849 George Ripley succeeded her, and filled the post until 1880. Ellen Mackay Hutchinson was literary editor, 1880–97. Became *Book Week* in 1963. See *Book World.*

New York Journal of Commerce and Commercial. New York. Newspaper. The *Journal of Commerce* was founded 1827. Conrad Hallock was editor, 1828–61; William Cowper Prime, 1861–69. The *General Shipping and Commercial List* was founded in 1815, becoming, after many changes of name, the *Commercial* in 1898. Merged 1926 under present title. Eric Ridder is publisher; H. E. Luedicke is editor.

New York Journal-American. New York. Newspaper. The *New York Morning Journal* was founded in 1882 by Albert Pulitzer. John R. McLean bought it in 1884 and William Randolph Hearst became the owner in 1895. In 1902 it was called the *New York American,* retaining that name until 1937 when it was merged with the *New York Evening Journal* to form the *New York Journal-American.* The *Evening Journal* was founded by William Randolph Hearst in 1896, with Foster Coates as managing editor and John L. Eddy as city editor. Arthur Brisbane was chief editorial writer, 1897–1921. John Vincent Smith was drama editor until his death in 1941. Among those associated with the paper have been Richard Harding Davis, Dorothy Dix, Beatrice Fairfax, Damon Runyon, Benjamin de Casseres, Louella Parsons, George Rothwell Brown, M. S. Rukeyser, Paul Mallon, Edwin C. Hill, "Bugs" Baer, Bill Corum, Dorothy Kilgallen, Louis Sobol, George E. Sololsky, and Bob Considine. Merged with *New York Herald Tribune* and *New York World-Telegram and Sun* (qq.v.) in 1966 as *New York World Journal Tribune* (q.v.).

New York Ledger. New York. Illustrated weekly. Founded 1847, as the *Merchant's Ledger;* changed name in 1855 to *New York Ledger.* Robert Bonner, who had bought it in 1850, added fiction and verse; contributors included Sarah Payson Parton, Sylvanus Cobb, Jr., and E. D. E. N. Southworth. Became the *Ledger Monthly* in 1898. Expired 1903.

New York Magazine. New York. Weekly. Founded 1968. Edited by Clay Felker. Contributing editors have included Peter Blake, John Simon, Gloria Steinem, Jimmy Breslin, Tom Wolfe. Lively treatment of all current aspects of sophisticated New York City culture. Originally a *World Journal Tribune* supplement.

New York Mirror. New York. Tabloid newspaper. Founded June 24, 1924, by William Randolph Hearst. Arthur Brisbane and Phil Payne were among its early editors. Columnists who have been connected with the *Mirror* are Walter Winchell, Dan Parker, Herbert Kaufman, Howard Brubaker, Mark Hellinger, etc. Acquired by *New York Daily News* in 1963.

New York Mirror, and Ladies' Literary Gazette. New York. Weekly. Founded Aug. 2, 1823, by George Pope Morris, with Samuel Woodworth as editor. Morris became editor in 1823. Nathaniel Parker Willis was associated with him, 1831–35, 1843–45. In 1843 the name was changed to the *New Mirror;* in 1844, to the *Weekly Mirror;* 1845, to the *New York Mirror,* and in 1847, to the *American Literary Gazette and Weekly Mirror.*

New York Morning Telegraph. New York. Newspaper. Founded 1836. Devoted chiefly to music, the theatre, and sports, particularly racing news. Among the writers who have been on the staff are Ring Lardner, Bide Dudley, Louella Parsons, Walter D. Shackelton, Westbrook Pegler, Gene Fowler, G. D. Eaton, Heywood Broun, Theodore Sterns, S. Jay Kaufman, George Jean Nathan, Aileen St. John Brenon, Charles D. Isaacson, Harry Acton, Regina Crewe. S. D. Rosen is editor; Whitney Bolton is book critic. Now published by Triangle Publications, Inc.

New York Observer. New York. Presbyterian literary magazine. Founded Jan., 1823, by Sidney E. Morse. Expired May 30, 1912. Charles Augustus Stoddard was editor, 1885–1902.

New York Packet, and the American Advertiser. New York. Newspaper. Founded Jan. 4, 1776, by Samuel Loudon. Published in Fishkill, N.Y., during the British occupation of New York, 1777–83. Name changed to the *Diary; or, Loudon's Register* in 1792. Expired 1798.

New York Picayune. New York. Comic weekly. Founded 1847, by a Dr. Hutchings. Robert H. Lenson's burlesque Negro sermons by "Professor Julius Caesar Hannibal" appeared in it and were very popular. Expired 1860.

New York Post. New York. Newspaper. Founded Nov. 16, 1801, by William Coleman, with the backing of Alexander Hamilton. Coleman was editor, 1801–29. William Cullen Bryant was editor, 1828–78. William Leggett became part owner and junior editor in 1827. John Bigelow was literary critic in 1849, became a proprietor and junior editor in 1848, and assoc. editor, 1849–60. John R. Thompson was literary editor, 1868–73. George Cary Eggleston joined the staff in 1875. Wendell Phillips Garrison was literary editor, 1881–1903. Bryant was followed in the editorship by Parke Godwin in 1878, who was editor until 1881, when the paper was bought by Carl Schurz, Horace White and Edwin L. Godkin, for Henry Villard. Schurz was editor, 1881–83, Godkin was editor, 1883–99; White was assoc. editor, 1881–99, and editor, 1900–03. Later editors have included Rollo Ogden, Harry Truax Saylor, Theodore O. Thackrey, and James Wechsler, the present editor. Dorothy Schiff is now publisher. Among well-known staff members have been Lincoln Steffens, Norman Hapgood, Charles Nordhoff, Charleton Lewis, Christopher Morley, Allan Nevins, Henry S. Canby, Oswald Garrison Villard, Arthur Pound, Leonard Lyons, Franklin P. Adams, Samuel Grafton, Sidney Skolsky, Max Lerner, Murray Kempton, Eric Sevareid, Joseph Barry. Formerly called the *New York Evening Post;* became the *New York Post* after 1934. In 1948 it was merged with the *Bronx Home News.* In recent years it has been known for its shrewd combination of tabloid sensationalism and crusading liberalism.

New York Press. New York. Newspaper. Founded 1887, by Robert Percival Porter and Frank Hatton. Merged with the *New York Sun* in 1916 to form the *Sun and New York Press,* which shortened its name to the *Sun* after a month.

New York Public Library, The. New York. Founded May 23, 1895. It grew out of the consolidation of the Astor Library, founded 1848, the Lenox Library, founded 1870, and the Tilden Trust, created by the will of Samuel J. Tilden, who died in 1886. John Shaw Billings of the Surgeon General's Library at Washington, D.C., became the first librarian of the newly consolidated library. *The Bulletin of the New York Public Library,* chiefly devoted to describing the many treasures of the library, began its monthly publication in 1897. The library has its own printing and binding department and publishes books. Its Rare Book room, Print Collection, Manuscript Division, Spencer Collection, American History Division, Children's Room, Economics Division, Newspaper Division, Science and Technology Division, Jewish Division, Oriental Division, Slavonic Division, Theatre Collection, Periodicals Division, Music Division, Art Division, and Picture Collection are all outstanding in their fields. The Library holds many exhibitions including the annual formal opening of the Fifty Books of the Year exhibit, sponsored by the American Institute of Graphic Arts. The Richard Rogers Bowker Memorial Lectures have been sponsored by the Library since 1935. Its circulation department has 80 branches and 4 bookmobiles in the boroughs of Manhattan, the Bronx, and Richmond. The Reference Department contains about 4,000,000 books.

New York Quarterly, The. New York. Founded 1970. Literary magazine, edited by William Packard.

New York Review. New York. Quarterly. Founded Mar., 1837, by Caleb Sprague Henry. Prominent literary men contributed to it during its brief but distinguished life. Joseph G. Cogswell, who became librarian of The Astor Library, was one of its editors. Expired Apr., 1842.

New York Review and Atheneum. See the *Atlantic Magazine.*

New York Review of Books, The. New York. Biweekly. Founded 1963. Edited by Robert Silvers and Barbara Epstein. Established during a strike against the *New York Times* and other city newspapers, in order to fill the gap created by the absence of the *New York Times Book Review.* The editors' long-term intention was to provide a forum for discussion of books given limited space in weekly reviews. Contributors have included some of the most distinguished authors and scholars in both the United States and England who ordinarily published in monthlies and quarterlies. Barrington Moore, Denis Donoghue, W. H. Auden, Mary McCarthy, F. W. Dupee, V. S. Pritchett, Francis Yates, Ernest Gombrich have regularly reviewed books. Articles are often published of topical cultural or political interest not occasioned by the publication of a book.

New York Sun. New York. Newspaper. Founded Sept. 3, 1883, by Benjamin Day. George W. Wisner and Richard Adams Locke were associated with Day. In 1838 the paper was sold to Moses Yale Beach, who was owner until 1848. Alfred Ely Beach was part owner, 1845–52. Moses Sperry Beach was owner, 1852–68. Charles A. Dana became owner and editor in 1868, remaining in active control until 1897. It was Dana who made the *Sun* a dominating force in American journalism. He discovered that light fiction was popular and obtained the services of such writers as Horatio Alger, John Vance, H. Warren Trowbridge, and Mary J. Holmes. Paul Dana owned and edited the paper, 1898–1902. William Mackay Laffan, with the paper from 1877, became publisher in 1884, and was the owner, 1902–1909. He started the *Evening Sun* in 1887. Edward P. Mitchell was a distinguished editor, 1903–20. Frank M. O'Brien and William C. Reick were notable editors. William Mackay Laffan was dramatic critic, 1877–1909. Ward Morehouse and Richard Lockridge were later dramatic critics. Will Irwin, Frank Ward O'Malley, Julian Ralph, Amos J. Cummings, Chester S. Lord, John B. Bogart, William J. Henderson, Mayo W. Hazeltine, Francis P. Church, John Swinton, Henry Hazlitt, Chester Sanders Lord, Laurence Hill, Franklyn Fyles, S. M. Clarke, were members of the staff. In 1923 the *Sun* absorbed the *New York Globe.* See Frank M. O'Brien's *The Story of the Sun* (1918); Edward P. Mitchell's *Memoirs of an Editor* (1924); Charles J. Rosebault's *When Dana Was the Sun* (1931); Candace Stone's *Dana and the Sun* (1938). Merged with the *New York World-Telegram* in 1950. See *New York World-Telegram and Sun.*

New York Times. New York. Newspaper. Founded Sept. 18, 1851, by Henry J. Raymond and George Jones as the *New York Daily Times.* In 1857 the word "Daily" was dropped. Among its editors have been: Louis J. Jennings, John Foord, Charles R. Miller, Rollo Ogden, John H. Finley, Charles Merz, Turner Catledge, and James Reston. Edward Cary was assoc. editor, 1871–1917. Noted members of the editorial staff have included Carr Van Anda, F. C. Mortimer, F. T. Birchall, Edward M. Kingsbury, John Corbin, Ralph H. Graves, Osmond Phillips, Elmer H. Davis, Charles Marshall Graves, E. A. Bradford, Henry E. Armstrong, Louis Wiley, Alden March, Lester Markel, Edwin Leland James, Florence Finch Kelly, Simeon Strunsky, Arthur Krock, Anne O'Hare McCormick, Meyer Berger, Harrison Salisbury, Clifton Daniels, C. L. Sulzberger. Adolph Ochs bought the newspaper in 1896 and developed it into one of the largest newspapers in the world, with the slogan "All the News That's Fit to Print." He was publisher until his death in 1935. Arthur O. Sulzberger is now publisher. John Leonard, Christopher Lehmann-Haupt, and Thomas Lask are daily book reviewers. The *New York Times* founded *Mid-Week Pictorial* in 1914 and *Current History* in 1915. The *New York Times Index* was begun in 1913.

The *New York Times Book Review* and the *New York Times Magazine* were founded in 1896. *See* Elmer Davis's *History of the New York Times, 1851–1921* (1921); *The Newspaper and Its Meaning,* by members of the *Times* staff (1945); Meyer Berger's *The Story of the New York Times, 1851–1951* (1951); Gay Talese's *The Kingdom and the Power* (1969).

New York Times Book Review. New York. Section of the Sunday edition of the New York Times. Founded 1896. Francis Brown, editor for many years, was succeeded by John Leonard in 1970. J. Donald Adams wrote a regular column, "Speaking of Books," which is now open to contributors. Lewis Nichols discusses book news in "In and Out of Books." Other regular feature writers have included Anthony Boucher, Martin Levin, Marc Slonim, Allen J. Hubin.

New York Times Current History. See *Current History.*

New York Times Index. New York. Founded 1913. A quarterly index to the daily and Sunday issues of *The New York Times.*

New York Times Magazine. New York. Section of the Sunday edition of the *New York Times.* Founded 1896. Publishes articles of topical interest by outstanding authorities, as well as regular features on the home, child-rearing, food, etc. Noted for its crossword puzzle, for many years edited by Margaret Farrar.

New York Tribune. See *New York Herald Tribune.*

New York Tribune Index. New York. Founded 1875. Expired 1906. An index to each issue of the *New York Tribune* for the period covered.

New York University Press. New York. Founded 1916. Arthur Huntington Nason was director, 1916–33. Chris W. Kentera is now director.

New York World. New York. Newspaper. Founded 1860, by Alexander Cummings, who sold it to August Belmont and Fernando Wood. Manton Malone Marble, the editor, became part owner in 1862, and sold his interest to Jay Gould, who in turn sold the paper to Joseph Pulitzer in 1883. The *Evening World* was established in 1887. The fame of the *World* was achieved under Pulitzer's vigorous editorship. Frank Irving Cobb was editor, 1904–23. John O'Hara Cosgrave was Sunday editor, 1912–27. Herbert Bayard Swope was city editor for many years, followed by James W. Barrett. Prominent staff members were David Graham Phillips, Harold Stanley Pollard, Arthur Brisbane, Irvin S. Cobb, James G. Huneker, Heywood Broun, Deems Taylor, William Bolitho, Franklin P. Adams, Alexander Woollcott, Don C. Seitz, John L. Heaton, Rollin Kirby, Margaret Leech, James M. Tuohy, John Lloyd Balderston, John O'Hara Cosgrave, Charles M. Lincoln, Robert Hunt Lyman, William Henry Merrill, Charles S. Hand, Herbert Pulitzer, Ralph Pulitzer, Robert Littell, Frank Sullivan, Elsie McCormick, Dudley Nichols, L. R. E. Paulin, William Henry Hurlbert. In 1931 the *World* was merged with the *New York Evening Telegram,* as the *New York World-Telegram.* See *New York World-Telegram and Sun. See Also* John L. Heaton's *The Story of a Page* (1913); *Cobb of "The World,"* ed. by John L. Heaton (1924); James W. Barrett's *The World, the Flesh, and Messrs. Pulitzer* (1931), and his *Pulitzer and His World* (1941).

New York World Journal Tribune. New York. Newspaper. Founded 1966. Result of a merger of *New York Herald Tribune, New York Journal-American,* and *New York World-Telegram and Sun* (qq.v.). Edited by Frank Cunniff. Expired in 1967.

New York World-Telegram and Sun. New York. Newspaper. Founded 1867, as the *Evening Telegram.* In 1931 it acquired the *New York World,* assuming the name *New York World-Telegram.* Roy W. Howard was editor and president. Ray Allen Huber was publisher, 1931–38. Columnists have included Westbrook Pegler, Raymond Clapper, Eleanor Roose-

velt, Hugh S. Johnson, Ernie Pyle, Al Williams, and Joe Williams. Lee B. Word is editor. Absorbed the *New York Sun* in 1950 and assumed the present name. Merged with *New York Herald Tribune* and *New York Journal-American* (qq.v.) in 1966 as *New York World Journal Tribune* (q.v.). Ceased publication 1967, after eight months.

New Yorker, The. New York. Weekly magazine. Founded 1925. Noted for its cartoons, cover designs, short stories, poems, and features. E. B. White, James Thurber, Wolcott Gibbs, Robert Benchley, Edmund Wilson, Clifton Fadiman, Peter De Vries are among those who have been or are most notably associated with it. Its "profiles" are renowned for their factual accuracy, incisiveness, and adept revelation of the character of those interviewed. Its stories, notably by John Cheever and John O'Hara, are sometime referred to as a "type," in the Chekhov-Katherine Mansfield tradition. It has published the poetry of W. H. Auden, Marianne Moore, Theodore Roethke, Howard Nemerov, John Ciardi, and many others. Harold Wallace Ross became the first editor, in 1925. William Shawn is now editor. *See* James Thurber's *The Years With Ross* (1960). In the 1960's and 1970 *The New Yorker* published numerous serialized pieces that enhanced its reputation for serious journalism, notably by Rachel Carson on environmental pollution, by Hannah Arendt on the Eichmann Trial, and by Charles Reich on the Youth Culture. In 1969, for the first time in its 44-year existence, the magazine published a table of contents and began advertising itself in various mass media. *See* Jane Grant's *Ross, The New Yorker and Me* (1968).

New-England Courant. Boston, Mass. Newspaper. Founded Aug. 14, 1721. Edited by James Franklin who, in 1723, because of trouble with the General Court, substituted the name of his brother, Benjamin Franklin, as editor. Expired June 4, 1726.

New-England Magazine. Boston, Mass. Monthly. Founded July, 1831, by Joseph T. Buckingham. The better-known New England writers contributed. *The Autocrat of the Breakfast Table* by Holmes began in this magazine, but was left unfinished. Years later it was finished in *The Atlantic Monthly,* and began with the amusing line, "As I was just going to say, when I was interrupted." Park Benjamin was its last editor and he conducted a department called the "Cabinet Council" modelled after the "Noctes Ambrosianae." Hawthorne wrote many stories for it. Expired Dec., 1835.

New-England Weekly Journal. Boston, Mass. Newspaper. Founded 1727, by Samuel Kneeland. Edited by Matthew Byles. Merged with the *Boston Gazette* in 1741.

New-Hampshire Gazette. Portsmouth, N.H. Newspaper. Founded 1756, by Daniel Fowle. First Newspaper in New Hampshire. Now the oldest continuously issued newspaper in the United States, surviving as the *Portsmouth Herald*'s weekly picture supplement.

New-York Gazette. New York. Weekly newspaper. Founded Nov. 8, 1725, by William Bradford. First newspaper published in New York City. Expired probably Nov. 19, 1744.

New-York Magazine; or, Literary Repository. New York. Monthly. Founded Jan., 1790, by Thomas and James Swords. Illustrated with copperplates. Expired Dec., 1797.

New-York Morning Post, and Daily Advertiser. New York. First New York daily newspaper. Founded Feb. 23, 1785. Published by William Morton and Samuel Horner. Expired June 12, 1792. These same men had begun the *Evening Post,* a New York weekly, in Sept. 1782. The second New York daily newspaper, published by Francis Childs, was called the *Daily Advertiser;* its first issue was Mar. 1, 1785, and its last, Aug. 30, 1806.

New-Yorker, The. New York. Weekly journal. Founded 1834, by Horace Greeley. Assisting Greeley were Park Benjamin, R. W. Griswold, and Henry J. Raymond. When Greeley founded *The Tribune* in 1841, the *New-Yorker* became the weekly edition of that newspaper. *See* Don Seitz's *Horace Greeley* (1927).

Newark News. Newark, N.J. Newspaper. Founded 1883, by Wallace McIlvane Scudder and others; Scudder was publisher until his death in 1931. Succeeded by his son, Edward Wallace Scudder. Richard B. Scudder is now publisher. William Clark is editor. Alan Branigan edits book reviews.

Newark Star-Ledger. Newark, N.J. Newspaper. The *Newark Star* developed from the defunct *Newark Daily Advertiser* (founded 1832) and merged with the *New Jersey Eagle* (founded 1820); became the *Star-Ledger* in 1916. S. I. Newhouse is publisher. Philip Hochstein is editor.

NEWBERRY, PERRY (Oct. 16, 1870–Dec. 6, 1938); b. Union City, Mich. Editor, novelist. *Tom Westlake's Golden Luck* (1913); *Castaway Island* (1917); *Black Boulder Claim* (1921); *Forward Ho!* (1927); *The Houseboat Mystery* (1935); etc. Co-author (with Alice MacGowan): *The Million-Dollar Suitcase* (1922); *Mystery Woman* (1924); *The Seventh Passenger* (1926); etc. Owner and editor, *The Wave,* San Francisco, 1901.

Newbery Medal. Awarded annually, since 1922, for the most distinguished contribution to literature for American children. It takes its name from John Newbery (1713–67), a London bookseller. The bronze medal, the gift of Frederic G. Melcher of the R. R. Bowker Co., was designed by the American sculptor René Chambellan. For a list of award winners, see the most recent revision of *Literary and Library Prizes,* published by R. R. Bowker Co. since 1935.

NEWBOLD, WILLIAM ROMAINE (Nov. 20, 1865–Sept. 26, 1926); b. Wilmington, Del. Educator, psychologist, Orientalist, author. Famous for his deciphering of the Roger Bacon manuscript. *The Cipher of Roger Bacon* (1928); etc. Philosophy dept., University of Pennsylvania, 1889–1926.

NEWBURGER, GABRIEL F. (c. 1867–July 31, 1939); b. Rock Island, Ill. Poet. Known as the "Poet of the Ozarks." *Oriental Sketches, and Other Themes,* ed. by O. E. Rölvaag (1930); *Ozark Anthology,* ed. by Paul Engle (1938).

NEWCOMB, COVELLE (1908–); Author. *Black Fire* (1940); *Silver Saddles* (1943); *Secret Door* (1946); *Running Waters* (1947); *Broken Sword* (1955); *Brother Zero* (1959); *Christopher Columbus: The Sea Lord* (1963); *Leonardo da Vinci, Prince of Painters* (1965); *Explorer with a Heart: The Story of Giovanni da Verrazzano* (1969); etc.

NEWCOMB, REXFORD (Apr. 24, 1886–); b. Independence, Kan. Educator, author. *Outlines of the History of Architecture,* 4 parts (1922–39); *The Old Mission Churches and Historic Houses of California* (1925); *In the Lincoln Country* (1928); *The Colonial and Federal House* (1933); *Spanish-Colonial Architecture in the United States* (1937); *Old Kentucky Architecture,* (1940); *Architecture of the Old Northwest Territory* (1950); etc. Prof. history of architecture, University of Illinois, 1921–54.

NEWCOMB, RICHARD FAIRCHILD (June 6, 1913–); b. Rutherford, N.J. Editor, author. *Abandon Ship* (1958); *Savo* (1961); *Iwo Jima* (1965).

NEWCOMB, SIMON (Mar. 12, 1835–July 11, 1909); b. Wallace, N.S. Astronomer. *Popular Astronomy* (1878); *The Stars* (1901); *Astronomy for Everybody* (1902); *The Reminiscences of an Astronomer* (1903); etc.

NEWELL, CHARLES MARTIN (b. 1821). Novelist. Pen name, "Captain Robert Barnacle." Under own name: *Kalani of Oahu* (1881); *Kaméhaméha, the Conquering King* (1885); *The Voyage of the Fleetwing* (1886); *The Wreck of the Greyhound* (1889); etc.; also, under pen name: *The Cruise of the Graceful* (1847); *The Fair and the Brave* (1849); *A Sailor's Love* (1849); *Leaves from an Old Log* (1877); etc.

NEWELL, HOPE [Hockenberry] (1896–1965); Author. *Steppin and Family* (1942); *The Old Woman Carries On* (1947); *A Cap for Mary Ellis* (1953); *Mary Ellis, Student Nurse* (1958); etc.

NEWELL, PETER [Sheaf Hersey] (Mar. 5, 1862–Jan. 15, 1924); b. Bushnell, Ill. Illustrator, author. *Topsys and Turvys,* 2v. (1893); *The Hole Book* (1908); *Jungle Jangle* (1909); *The Slant Book* (1910); *The Rocket Book* (1912); etc. Illustrated books by John Kendrick Bangs, Clifton Johnson, Frank Stockton, Guy Wetmore Carryl, etc. Made many drawings for *Harper's Weekly,* etc.

NEWELL, ROBERT HENRY (Dec. 13, 1836–July, 1901); b. New York. Editor, humorist. Pen name "Orpheus C. Kerr." *The Orpheus C. Kerr Papers,* 3v. (1862–65); *The Palace Beautiful, and Other Poems* (1865); *Avery Glibun* (under pen name, 1867); *Versatilities* (1871); *The Walking Doll; or, The Asters and Disasters of Society* (1872); *There Was Once A Man* (1884); etc. Editor, *Hearth and Home,* 1874–76; New York *Daily Graphic,* etc. On staff *New York World,* 1869–74. *See* Robert Ford's *American Humorists* (1897); Jennette Tandy's *Crackerbox Philosophers in American Humor and Satire* (1925).

NEWELL, WILLIAM WELLS (Jan. 24, 1839–Jan. 21, 1907); b. Cambridge, Mass. Scholar, folklorist, editor, author. *Words for Music* (poems, 1895); *King Arthur and the Table Round,* 2v. (1897); *The Legend of the Holy Grail* (1902); *Isolt's Return* (1907). Compiler: *Games and Songs of American Children* (1883). Co-founder, the American Folk-Lore Society, 1888; editor, its *Journal of American Folk-Lore,* 1888–1900 and *Memoirs.* He ran a private press at Wayland, Mass.

NEWFIELD, JACK (Feb. 18, 1939–   ); b. New York. Journalist, author. *A Prophetic Minority* (1966); *Robert Kennedy: A Memoir* (1969). Assistant editor, *The Village Voice.*

NEWHOUSE, EDWARD (Nov. 10, 1911–); b. Budapest. Author. *You Can't Sleep Here* (1934); *Anything Can Happen* (short stories, 1941); *The Hollow of the Wave* (1949); *Many Are Called* (short stories, 1951); *The Temptation of Roger Heriott* (1954); etc.

NEWKIRK, NEWTON (Aug. 29, 1870–May 15, 1938); b. Bentleyville, Pa. Journalist, author. *Recollections of a Gold Cure Graduate* (1906); etc. Columnist, the *Boston Post,* 1901–34. Creator of humorous newspaper features, "All Sorts" and the "Bingville Bugle."

NEWMAN, EDWARD MANUEL (Mar. 16, 1872– deceased); b. Cleveland, O. Traveler, lecturer. Author of the *Newman Traveltalks* series: *Seeing Italy* (1927); *Seeing Egypt and the Holy Land* (1928); *Seeing Russia* (1928); *Seeing Germany* (1929); *Seeing England and Scotland* (1930); *Seeing France* (1930); *Seeing Spain and Morocco* (1930); *Seeing Paris* (1931); *Seeing London* (1932); etc.

NEWMAN, FRANCES (Sept. 13, 1883–Oct. 22, 1928); b. Atlanta, Ga. Novelist. *The Hard Boiled Virgin* (1926). Editor: *The Short Story's Mutations from Petronius to Paul Morand* (1924). *See* Emily Clark's *Innocence Abroad* (1931).

NEWMAN, JAMES ROY (Aug. 3, 1907–May 28, 1966); b. New York. Editor, author. *The Tools of War* (1942); *What Is Science?* (1955); *The World of Mathematics,* 4v. (1956); *Science and Sensibility* (1961); *The Rule of Folly* (1962); etc. Editor: W. K. Clifford's *Common Sense of the Exact Sciences* (1955); *Harper Encyclopedia of Science* (rev. ed. 1967); board of editors, *Scientific American,* from 1948.

NEWMAN, JOHN PHILIP (Sept. 1, 1826–July 5, 1899); b. New York. Methodist bishop, author. *"From Dan to Beersheba"* (1864); *Sermons* (1876); *The Thrones and Palaces of Babylon and Nineveh* (1876); *Christianity Triumphant* (1884); etc.

NEWMAN, JOSEPH SIMON (1891–Nov. 10, 1960). Journalist, author. *It Could Be Verse* (1948); *Perishable Poems* (1952); *Verse Yet!* (1959); *One Summer Day* (1962); etc. Columnist, Cleveland Press, "Frying Pan" and "It Could Be Verse."

NEWMAN, LOUIS ISRAEL (Dec. 20, 1893–); b. Providence, R.I. Rabbi, Zionist, author. *Richard Cumberland* (1919); *Joyful Jeremiads* (poems, 1926); *Richard J. H. Gottheil* (1937); *A Chief Rabbi of Rome Becomes a Catholic* (1945); *Search for Serenity* (1954); *Pangs of the Messiah and Other Plays, Pageants and Cantatas* (1957); *The Woman at The Wall* (play, 1958); *The Little Zaddik* (play, 1961); *Maggidim and Hasidum: Their Wisdom* (1962); *The Jewish People, Faith, and Life* (1965); etc. Compiler: *The Hasidic Anthology* (1934); *The Talmudic Anthology* (1939); etc. Dept. apologetics, Jewish Institute of Religion, New York, 1922–24; 1931–33.

NEWMAN, RALPH GEOFFREY (Nov. 3, 1911–); b. Chicago, Ill. Bookseller, editor, author. *The American Iliad* (with O. Eisenschiml, 1947); *999 Questions and Answers on American History* (1966). Editor: *The Diary of a Public Man* (1945); *The Railsplitter* (1950); *The Civil War* (with O. Eisenschiml and E. B. Long, 1956); *Lincoln for the Ages* (1960); *Eyewitness* (with O. Eisenschiml, 1960); *The Civil War Digest* (with E. B. Long, 1960); *Pictorial Autobiography of Abraham Lincoln* (1962).

Newman, Richard Brinsley. Pen name of Franklin Kent Gifford.

NEWQUIST, ROY ARVID (July 14, 1925–); b. Ashland, Wis. Literary critic, author. *Counterpoint* (1964); *Showcase* (1966); *Conversations* (1967). Book editor, *Chicago's American*, since 1963.

"News from Virginia." Ballad by Richard Rich, written in 1610, but not published until 1865.

Newsday. Garden City, Long Island, N.Y. Newspaper. Founded 1940 by Alicia Patterson. Bill Moyers became publisher in 1967. Harry Guggenheim is editor-in-chief. Harold R. Burton edits books reviews.

NEWSOM, CARROLL VINCENT (Feb. 23, 1904–); b. Buckley, Ill. Educator. Author: *An Introduction to Mathematics: A Study of the Nature of Mathematics* (1936); *Mathematical Discourses* (1964); etc. Editor: *Television Policy for Education* (1952). Editor, *American Mathematical Monthly*, 1947–52. Pres., New York University, 1956–61. Chairman of board, Hawthorne Books, since 1964.

Newsweek. New York. Weekly news magazine. Founded 1933, as *News-Week*, by Thomas J. C. Martyn, formerly associated with *Time*. Merged in 1937, with *Today*, founded 1933, a New Deal publication. The name was changed to *Newsweek* in 1937 when Malcolm Muir became president and publisher. *Newsweek* is devoted to reportage, background information on the news, and interpretation of the significance of events. Raymond Moley was a columnist for it since its earliest years. Gibson McCabe is now president.

NEWTON, ALFRED EDWARD (Aug. 26, 1863–Sept. 29, 1940); b. Philadelphia, Pa. Essayist, bibliophile, author. *The Amenities of Book-Collecting and Kindred Affections* (1918); *A Magnificent Farce, and Other Diversions of a Book-Collector* (1921); *This Book-Collecting Game* (1928); *A Tourist in Spite of Himself* (1930); *End Paper* (1933); *Doctor Johnson* (play, 1933); etc. See George Henry Sargent's *The Writings of A. Edward Newton, a Bibliography* (1927). See *A Tribute to A. Edward Newton*, published by the Library of Congress (1940). Newton's library was sold at auction in New York in 1941.

NEWTON, DWIGHT BENNETT (1916–). Novelist. Writes under pen names "Dwight Bennett," "Clement Hardin," and "Ford Logan." *Shotgun Guard* (1950); *Stormy Range* (1951);

Six-Gun Gamble (1951); *Range Feud* (1953); *Rainbow Rider* (1954); *Cherokee Outlet* (1961); etc.

NEWTON, EARLE WILLIAMS (Apr. 10, 1917–); Cortland, N.Y. Editor, author. *Before Pearl Harbor* (1942); *The Vermont Story: A History* (1949); etc. Founder, editor, *American Heritage*, 1949–54.

NEWTON, JOHN EDWARD. Author. *The Rogue and the Witch* (1955).

NEWTON, JOSEPH FORT (July 21, 1880–Jan. 24, 1950); b. Decatur, Tex. Episcopal clergyman, author. *David Swing* (1909); *Abraham Lincoln* (1910); *Lincoln and Herndon* (1910); *Wesley and Woolman* (1914); *Some Living Masters of the Pulpit* (1922); *The New Preaching* (1929); *Living Every Day* (1937); *The Stuff of Life* (1939); *Live, Love, and Learn* (1943); *River of Years* (autobiography, 1946); *The One Great Church* (1947); *Life Victorious* (1948); etc.

NEWTON, RICHARD HEBER (Oct. 31, 1840–Dec. 19, 1914); b. Philadelphia, Pa. Episcopal clergyman, author. *Studies of Jesus* (1880); *Womanhood* (1883); *Philistinism* (1885); *Parsifal* (1904); etc.

NEWTON, WILLIAM WILBERFORCE (Nov. 4, 1843–June 25, 1914); b. Philadelphia, Pa. Episcopal clergyman, novelist, essayist. *Pilgrim Series* of sermons for children, 6v. (1877–90); *Essays of To-day* (1879); *The Voice of St. John, and Other Poems* (1881); *The Priest and the Man; or, Abelard and Heloisa* (1883); *The Vine Out of Egypt* (poems, 1887); *Dr. Muhlenberg* (1891); *Philip MacGregor* (1895); etc.

Nicholas Minturn. Novel by J. G. Holland (1876). Study of a young man of wealth who desires to be of service to mankind.

NICHOLL, LOUISE TOWNSEND, b. Scotch Plains, N.J. Editor, poet. *The Blossom-Print* (1938); *Water and Light* (poems, 1939); *Dawn in Snow* (poems, 1941); *Life Is the Flesh* (poems, 1947); *The Explicit Flower* (poems, 1952); *Collected Poems* (1953); *The Curious Quotient* (poems, 1956); *The World's One Clock* (poems, 1959); *The Blood That Is Language* (1967); etc.

NICHOLS, ANNE (d. Sept. 14, 1966). Playwright. *Linger Longer Letty* (1919); *The Gilded Cage* (1920); *Love Dreams* (1921); *Just Married* (with Adelaide Matthews, 1921); *Abie's Irish Rose* (prod. 1922).

NICHOLS, CHARLES LEMUEL (May 29, 1851–Feb. 19, 1929); b. Worcester, Mass. Physician, bibliographer, bibliophile. *Some Notes on Isaiah Thomas and His Worcester Imprints* (1900); *Isaiah Thomas, Printer, Writer and Collector* (1912); etc. Compiler: *Checklist of Maine, New Hampshire and Vermont Almanacs* (1929); etc. President, American Antiquarian Society, 1927–29.

NICHOLS, EGBERT RAY (May 6, 1884–Apr. 5, 1958); b. Mt. Ayr, Ind. Educator, editor. Co-author: *Modern Debating* (1936). Compiler, *Intercollegiate Debates*, since 1912. Editor, *The Forensic*, 1914–20. English dept., University of Redlands, Redlands, Calif., 1913–52.

NICHOLS, GEORGE WARD (June 21, 1831–Sept. 15, 1855); b. Mount Desert, Me. Soldier, author. *The Story of the Great March* (1865); etc.

NICHOLS, JAMES HASTINGS (Jan. 18, 1915–); b. Auburn, N.Y. Educator. *Primer for Protestants* (1947); *Democracy and the Churches* (1951); *History of Christianity, 1650–1950* (1956); *Romanticism in American Theology* (1961); *The Mercersburg Theology* (1966); *Corporate Worship in the Reformed Tradition* (1968); etc. Federated theological faculty, University of Chicago, since 1943.

NICHOLS, JEANNETTE P[addock] (Mrs. Roy F. Nichols); b. Rochelle, Ill. Educator, author. *History of Alaska* (1924); *James Styles of Kingston, New York, and George*

Stuart of Schoolcraft, Michigan (1936); *Mostly People* (1966); *Emblems of Passage* (poems, 1968); etc. Co-author (with Roy F. Nichols): *Growth of American Democracy* (1939); etc. History dept., University of Pennsylvania, since 1957.

NICHOLS, LEWIS. Journalist. Columnist, "In and Out of Books," *New York Times Book Review.*

NICHOLS, MARY SARGEANT NEAL (Mrs. Hiram Gove; Mrs. Thomas Low Nichols) (Aug. 10, 1810–May 30, 1884); b. Goffstown, N.H. Reformer, author. *Marriage* (with husband, 1854); *Mary Lyndon; or, Revelations of a Life* (autobiography, 1855). Included in Poe's *The Literati* (1850).

NICHOLS, ROY FRANKLIN (Mar. 3, 1896–); b. Newark, N.J. Educator, author: *Franklin Pierce* (1931); *Disruption of the American Democracy* (1948; Pulitzer prize for history, 1949); *Advance Agents of American Destiny* (1956); *Religion and American Democracy* (1959); *Stakes of Power 1845–1877* (1961); *Blueprints for Leviathan, American Style* (1963). Coauthor (with Jeannette P. Nichols): *A Short History of American Democracy* (1943); History dept., University of Pennsylvania, since 1925.

NICHOLS, THOMAS LOW (1815–1901); b. Orford, N.H. Physician, reformer, novelist. *Journal in Jail* (1840); *Ellen Ramsay* (1843); *The Lady in Black* (1844); *Raffle for a Wife* (1845); *Women, in All Ages and Nations* (1849); *Esoteric Anthropology* (1853); *Marriage* (with wife, Mary Sargeant Nichols, 1854); *Forty Years of American Life*, 2v. (1864); etc.

NICHOLS, WILLIAM ICHABOD (June 27, 1905–); b. Brooklyn, N.Y. Editor, publisher. Editor and publisher, *This Week* magazine, since 1955. Editor: *Words to Live By* (1948); *A New Treasury of Words to Live By* (1959); *The Third Book of Words to Live By* (1962); *On Growing Up* (by Herbert Hoover, 1965); *Fishing for Fun* (by Herbert Hoover, 1967).

NICHOLSON, ELIZA JANE POITEVENT (Mrs. Alvah Morris Holbrook; Mrs. George Nicholson) (Mar. 11, 1849–Feb. 15, 1896); b. Pearlington, Miss. Editor, poet. Pen name, "Pearl Rivers." *Lyrics* (1873). Editor, *New Orleans Picayune,* 1876–96. See James H. Harrison's *Pearl Rivers, Publisher of the Picayune* (1932).

NICHOLSON, JAMES BARTRAM (Jan. 28, 1820–Mar. 4, 1901); b. St. Louis, Mo. Bookbinder, author. *A Manual of the Art of Bookbinding* (1856). Founded bookbinding firm of Pawson & Nicholson, in Philadelphia, in 1848, which was carried on by the family until 1911.

NICHOLSON, [John] KENYON (May 21, 1894–); b. Crawfordsville, Ind. Playwright. *Honor Bright* (with Meredith Nicholson, prod. 1921); *Garden Varieties* (1924); *Sally and Company* (1925); *The Meal Ticket* (1926); *The Barker* (prod. 1927); *Tell Me Your Troubles* (1928); *Taxi* (1929); *Swing Your Lady* (with Charles Robinson, prod. 1936); *Flying Gerardos* (with same, 1941); *Apple of His Eye* (with same, 1946); etc. Compiler: *The Appleton Book of Short Plays,* 2 series (1925, 1927); etc.

NICHOLSON, MEREDITH (Dec. 9, 1866–Dec. 20, 1947); b. Crawfordsville, Ind. Novelist, diplomat. *Short Flights* (poems, 1891); *The Main Chance* (1903); *The House of a Thousand Candles* (1905); *Poems* (1906); *The Port of Missing Men* (1907); *Rosalind at Red Gate* (1907); *The Little Brown Jug at Kildaire* (1908); *The Lords of High Decision* (1909); *A Hoosier Chronicle* (1912); *The Provincial American* (1913); *Otherwise Phyllis* (1913); *The Poet* (1914); *The Proof of the Pudding* (1916); *Lady Larkspur* (1919); *Blacksheep! Blacksheep!* (1920); *The Man in the Street* (1921); *Best Laid Schemes* (1922); *Broken Barriers* (1922); *The Cavalier of Tennessee* (1928); *Old Familiar Faces* (1929); etc. Minister to Paraguay, 1933–34, Venezuela, 1935–38, Nicaragua, 1938–41.

NICHOLSON, WATSON (Sept. 23, 1866–Dec. 2, 1951); b. Pendleton, Ind. Author. *The Struggle for a Free Stage in London* (1906); *The Historical Sources of Defoe's Journal of the Plague Year* (1919); *Anthony Aston, Stroller and Adventurer* (1920).

Nick Nax for All Creation. New York. Comic magazine. Founded 1856. Published by M. A. Levison and J. C. Haney. Expired 1875.

Nick of the Woods; or, The Jibbenainosay. By Robert Montgomery Bird (1837). A tale of Kentucky in olden times, centering about the exploits of Nick, who seeks to avenge his relatives who have been killed by marauding Indians.

NICKERSON, HOFFMAN (Dec. 6, 1888–Mar. 24, 1965); b. Paterson, N.J. Author. *The Inquisition* (1923); *The Turning Point of the Revolution* (1928); *The American Rich* (1930); *Armed Horde, 1793–1939* (1941); *Arms and Policy, 1939–1944* (1945); *New Slavery* (1947); *The Loss of Unity* (1961); etc.

NICOLAY, HELEN (Mar. 9, 1866–Sept. 12, 1954); b. Paris, daughter of John G. Nicolay. Author of boys' books, especially American biographies. *The Boys' Life of Abraham Lincoln* (1906); *The Boys' Life of Ulysses S. Grant* (1909); *Peter and Paul and Their Friends* (1922); *The Boys' Life of Alexander Hamilton* (1927); *The Boys' Life of Washington* (1931); *The Boys' Life of Thomas Jefferson* (1933); *The Boys' Life of Benjamin Franklin* (1935); *The Bridge of Water* (1940); *Decatur of the Old Navy* (1942); *Born to Command* (1945); *Lincoln's Secretary* (1949); etc.

NICOLAY, JOHN GEORGE (Feb. 26, 1832–Sept. 26, 1901); b. Essingen, Bavaria. Private secretary and biographer of Lincoln, author. *The Outbreak of Rebellion* (1881); *Abraham Lincoln: A History,* 10v. (with John Hay, 1890).

NICOLSON, J[ohn] U[rban] (Oct. 9, 1885–); b. Alma, Kan. Poet. *King of the Black Isles* (1924); *The Painted Courtezan and Other Poems* (1924); *The Drums of Ylyle* (1925); *The Road to Antioch* (1926); *Sonnets of a Minnesinger, and Other Lyrics* (1926); *Fingers of Fear* (1937). Translator: *Canterbury Tales* (1943).

NICOLSON, MARJORIE HOPE (Feb. 18, 1894–); b. Yonkers, N.Y. Educator, author. *The Art of Description* (1926); *The Microscope and English Imagination* (1935); *A World in the Moon* (1937); *Newton Demands the Muse* (1946); *Voyages to the Moon* (1948); *The Breaking of the Circle* (1950); *Science and Imagination* (1956); *Mountain Gloom and Mountain Glory* (1959); *Milton: Poems and Selected Prose* (1962); *A Reader's Guide to Milton* (1963); *Pepys Diary and the New Science* (1965); *This Long Disease, My Life: Alexander Pope and the Sciences* (1968); etc. Editor: *Conway Letters* (1930). Prof. English, Columbia University, since 1940.

NIEBUHR, H[elmut] RICHARD (Sept. 3, 1894–July 5, 1962); b. Wright City, Mo. Evangelical and Reformed clergyman, author. *The Social Sources of Denominationalism* (1929); *The Kingdom of God in America* (1937); *The Meaning of Revelation* (1941); *Christ and Culture* (1951); *The Purpose of the Church and Its Ministry* (1956); *Radical Monotheism and Western Culture* (1960); *The Responsible Self* (1963); etc. Prof. Christian ethics, Yale University Divinity School, from 1938.

NIEBUHR, REINHOLD (June 21, 1892–June 1, 1971); b. Wright City, Mo. Evangelical clergyman, educator, author. *Leaves from the Notebook of a Tamed Cynic* (1929); *Moral Man and Immoral Society* (1932); *Reflections on the End of an Era* (1934); *An Interpretation of Christian Ethics* (1935); *Beyond Tragedy* (1937); *The Nature and Destiny of Man* (1941); *The Children of Light and the Children of Darkness* (1944); *Christian Realism and Political Problems* (1953); *The Self and the Dramas of History* (1955); *Pious and Secular America* (1958); *The Structure of Nations and Empires* (1963); *Man's Nature and His Communities* (1965); *Christianity and Power Politics* (1969); *The Democratic Experience: Past and Prospects* (with P. E. Sigmund, 1969); etc. Editor, *Christianity and Crisis.* Prof. applied Christianity, Union Theological Seminary, New York, from 1930.

Nigger Heaven. Novel by Carl Van Vechten (1926). Depicts life in Harlem, New York City's Negro center. A picture of the jazz era.

NIGGLI, JOSEPHINA (1910–); b. Monterrey, Mex. Novelist. *Mexican Village* (1945); *Step Down, Elder Brother* (1948). Author of play collection and textbooks on radio writing and playwriting.

"Night before Christmas, The." Ballad by Clement Clarke Moore, first written in 1822, but first published in the *Troy Sentinel,* Dec. 23, 1823. It is also known under the title "A Visit from St. Nicholas."

Night of the Hunter, The. Novel by Davis Grubb (1953). A psychological thriller about a fanatic who attempts to murder two children.

Nightwood. By Djuna Barnes (1936). A novel in the stream-of-consciousness mode, about a man caught in a triangular relationship to three women, his mother, his wife, and his mistress.

NILES, BLAIR (Mrs. Robert Niles) (d. Apr. 13, 1959); b. Coles Ferry, Va. Explorer, author. *Casual Wanderings in Ecuador* (1923); *Colombia, Land of Miracles* (1924); *Black Haiti* (1926); *Free* (1930); *Strange Brother* (1931); *Maria Paluna* (1934); *Peruvian Pageant* (1937); *Day of Immense Sun* (1936); *The James* (1939); *East by Day* (1941); *Passengers to Mexico: The Last Invasion of the Americas* (1943); *Martha's Husband: An Informal Portrait of George Washington* (1951); etc.

NILES, HEZEKIAH (Oct. 10, 1777–Apr. 2, 1839); b. Chester Co., Pa. Publisher, editor. Editor, *Baltimore Evening Post,* 1805–11. Founder, *Weekly Register,* Baltimore, 1811, later known as *Niles' Weekly Register* (q.v.). See Richard G. Stone's *Hezekiah Niles as an Economist* (1933).

NILES, JOHN JACOB (Apr. 28, 1892–); b. Louisville, Ky. Song writer. *Singing Soldiers* (1927; rev. ed. 1968); *Songs My Mother Never Taught Me* (1929); *One Man's War* (1929); *Songs of the Hill-Folk* (1934); *Ballads, Carols, and Tragic Legends from the Southern Appalachian Mountains* (1937); *Anglo-American Ballad Study Book* (1945); *Folk Ballads for Young Actors* (1962); *Folk Carols for Young Actors* (1962). Editor: *The Ballad Book of John Jacob Niles* (1961).

NILES, SAMUEL (May 1, 1674–May 1, 1762); b. Block Island, R.I. Episcopal clergyman, author. *Tristitiae Ecclesiarum* (1745); *A Brief and Plain Essay on God's Wonder-Working Providence for New England in the Reduction of Louisburg* (poem, 1747); *A Vindication of Divers Important Gospel-Doctrines* (1752); etc. See *Collections* of the Massachusetts Historical Society, Ser. 3, v. 6 (1837), Ser. 4, v. 5 (1861).

NILSSON, VICTOR (Mar. 10, 1867–Apr. 7, 1942); b. Trelleborg, Swe. Author. *Sweden* (1899); *A Bayreuth Pilgrimage* (1925); *A Pilgrimage to Bonn and Its Beethoven House* (1927); *Absaroka* (1938). Music editor, the *Minneapolis Journal,* 1907–38.

NIMKOFF, MEYER F[rancis] (Apr. 16, 1904–); b. New York. Educator. *The Child* (1933); *The Family* (1935); *Parent-Child Relations* (1936); *Marriage and the Family* (1947); *Technology and the Changing Family* (with W. F. Ogburn, 1955); *Comparative Family Systems* (1965); etc. Head, sociology dept., Florida State University, since 1950.

NIMS, JOHN FREDERICK (Nov. 10, 1913–); b. Muskegon, Mich. Educator, poet. *The Iron Pastoral* (1947); *A Fountain in Kentucky* (1950); *Knowledge of the Evening: Poems, 1950–1960* (1960); *Of Flesh and Bone* (1967). Faculty, University of Notre Dame, 1939–45; University of Illinois at Urbana, 1961–65; University of Illinois at Chicago from 1965.

NIN, ANAÏS (1903–); b. Paris. Author. *The House of Incest* (1936); *Winter of Artifice* (1939); *This Hunger* (1945); *Ladders to Fire* (1946); *Children of the Albatross* (1947); *The Four-Chambered Heart* (1950); *Solar Barque* (1958); *The Seduction of the Minotaur* (1961); *The Diary of Anaïs Nin, 1931–1934* (1966); *The Novel of the Future* (1968); *Under a Glass Bell* (rev. ed. 1968); etc.

Nine Stories. Collection of stories by J. D. Salinger (1953). Notably includes "A Perfect Day for Banana Fish" and "For Esmé—with Love and Squalor," which appeared originally in the *New Yorker.*

Nine Worthies. Group of literary men, including Washington Irving, who met at Cockloft Hall, the mansion of Gouverneur Kemble, in Newark, N.J. Also known as "The Lads of Kilkenny."

Nineteenth Century Fiction. Berkeley, Cal. Quarterly. Founded 1945. Published by the University of California Press. Bradford A. Booth is editor.

NININGER, HARVEY HARLOW (Jan. 17, 1887–); b. Conway Springs, Kan. Meteoriticist. *Our Stone-Pelted Planet* (1933); *Out of the Sky* (1952); *Arizona's Meteorite Crater* (1957); *Ask A Question About Meteorites* (1962); etc.

NIRDLINGER, CHARLES FREDERIC (1862–May 13, 1940); b. Fort Wayne, Ind. Playwright. *Masques and Mummers* (1899); *The First Lady of the Land* (prod. 1911); *The Convalescents* (1923); etc.

NISBET, ROBERT A. (Sept. 30, 1913–   ); b. Los Angeles, Cal. Educator, author. *The Quest for Community* (1953); *Human Relations in Administration* (1956); *Emile Durkheim* (1965); *The Sociological Tradition* (1965). Co-editor: *Contemporary Social Problems* (1961).

NITZE, WILLIAM ALBERT (Mar. 20, 1876–July 5, 1957); b. Baltimore, Md. Educator, author. *A History of French Literature* (with Edwin P. Dargan, 1922); *Lancelot and Guinevere* (with Tom Peete Cross, 1930); *Arthurian Romance and Modern Poetry and Music* (1940); *Perceval and the Holy Grail* (1949); etc. Prof. Romance languages, University of Chicago, from 1909.

NIXON, RICHARD MILHOUS (Jan. 9, 1913–); b. Yorba Linda, Calif. Lawyer, government official. *Six Crises* (1962). Senator, 1951–53. Vice President of the U.S., 1953–61. President of the U.S. 1969–.

Nix's Mate. By Rufus Dawes, 2v. (1939). Extravagant tale of New England witchcraft.

No Name Series. Published by Roberts Brothers, Boston. A well-known series of books, prose and poetry, written anonymously. The First Series, 14v., was issued in black and red bindings, 1876–78. The Second Series was issued in green and gold in 12v., 1879–81. The Third Series, in brown and gold, was issued in 11v., 1882–87. Thomas Niles was the editor. The first novel in the Series was *Mercy Philbrick's Choice,* by Helen Hunt Jackson.

NOAH, MORDECAI MANUEL (July 19, 1785–Mar. 22, 1851); b. Philadelphia, Pa. Lawyer, editor, playwright. *Travels in England, France, Spain, and the Barbary States* (1819); *She Would Be a Soldier* (prod. 1819); *The Siege of Tripoli* (prod. 1820); *Marion; or, The Hero of Lake George* (prod. 1821); *The Grecian Captive* (prod. 1822); *Gleanings from a Gathered Harvest* (1845); etc. Editor, the *National Advocate,* New York, 1817–26; founder, the *New York Enquirer,* 1826; the *New York Evening Star,* 1833.

"Noah an' Jonah an' Cap'n John Smith," poem by Don Marquis (1921).

Nobel Prize. Founded 1901, by Alfred Bernhard Nobel, Swedish munitions maker, in Stockholm, Sweden. It is awarded to men and women judged to have made outstanding contributions to the cause of peace, science, literature, etc. Americans who have won the Nobel Prize in literature are Sinclair Lewis, 1930; Eugene O'Neill, 1936; Pearl Buck, 1938; T. S. Eliot, 1948; William Faulkner, 1950; Ernest Hemingway, 1954; John Steinbeck, 1962.

NOBLE, ANNETTE LUCILE (July 12, 1844–Nov. 27, 1932); b. Albion, N.Y. Author. *Eleanor Willoughby* (1870); *Silas Gower's Daughters* (1878); *The Crazy Angel* (1901); etc.

NOBLE, LOUIS LEGRAND (Sept. 26, 1813–Feb. 6, 1882); b. Lisbon, N.Y. Poet. *Ne-Ma-Min: An Indian Story,* in three cantos (1852); *The Lady Angeline, A Lay of the Appalachians; The Hours, and Other Poems* (1857).

Noble Savage, The. New York. Semiannual. Founded 1960. Published by Meridian Books, The World Publishing Co. A periodical of literature, reportage, and opinion, edited by Saul Bellow and Keith Botsford. Published Ralph Ellison, Harold Rosenberg, Wright Morris, Howard Nemerov, and Louis Gallo.

NOCK, ALBERT JAY (d. Aug. 19, 1945). Editor, author. *Jefferson* (1926); *Francis Rabelais, the Man and His Work* (with C. R. Wilson, 1929); *The Book of Journeyman* (1930); *A Journey into Rabelais's France* (1934); *Free Speech and Plain Language* (1937); *Henry George: An Essay* (1939); *Memoirs of a Superfluous Man* (1943); *Journal of Forgotten Days: May 1934–October 1935* (1948); *Theory of Education in the United States* (1949). Editor: *Selected Works of Charles F. Brown* (1924); etc. On staff, *New Republic,* for many years, writing a column under pen name "Journeyman"; editor, *The Freeman,* etc.

NOLAN, JEANNETTE COVERT (Mar. 31, 1897–); b. Evansville, Ind. Author. *Second Best* (1933); *The Gay Poet* (1940); *Treason at the Point* (1944); *Poet of the People* (with Horace Gregory and James T. Farrell, 1951); *Dolley Madison* (1958); *Spy for the Confederacy* (1960); *John Marshall* (1962); *The Shot Heard Round the World* (1963); *John Hancock: Friend of Freedom* (1966); *Belle Boyd, Secret Agent* (1967); *Indiana* (States of the Nation series); etc.

NOLDE, OTTO FREDERICK (June 30, 1899–); b. Philadelphia, Pa. Educator. *Yesterday, Today, Tomorrow* (1933); *Christian World Action* (1942); *Power for Peace* (1946); etc. Prof., Lutheran Theological Seminary, Philadelphia, since 1931.

NOLTE, VINCENT [Otto] (1779–1856). Lived in New Orleans from 1808 to 1838. Author. *Fifty Years in Both Hemispheres* (1854), republished as, *The Memoirs of Vincent Nolte: Reminiscences in the Period of Anthony Adverse* (1934). Nolte's life was romanticized in *Anthony Adverse* by Hervey Allen.

NOMAD, MAX (pseud.). *Apostles of Revolution* (1933); *A Sceptic's Political Handbook* (1953); *Aspects of Revolt* (1959); etc.

Noname. Pen name of Luis Philip Senarens.

Nones. Collection of poems by W. H. Auden (1952).

NORBORG, CHRISTOPHER SVERRE (May 1, 1902–); b. Oslo, Nor. Lutheran clergyman. *Josiah Royce* (1935); *From Plato to Hitler* (1940); *Christ on Main Street* (1959); *Sixty Fascinating Years* (1962); etc.

NORDHOFF, CHARLES (Aug. 31, 1830–July 14, 1901); b. Erwitte, Prussia. Journalist, editor, author. *Man-of-War Life* (1856); *The Merchant Vessel* (1956); *Whaling and Fishing* (1856); the three combined as *Nine Years a Sailor* (1857), and republished as *Life on the Ocean* (1874); *Cape Cod and All along Shore* (1868); *Communistic Societies of America* (1870); etc. *In Yankee Windjammers,* ed. by his son, Charles Bernard Nordhoff (1940). Editor, Harper & Brothers, 1857–61.

NORDHOFF, CHARLES BERNARD (Feb. 1, 1887–Apr. 11, 1947); b. London, son of Charles Nordhoff. Author: *The Fledgling* (1919); *Picaro* (1924); *The Pearl Lagoon* (1924); *The Derelict* (1925). Co-author, with James Norman Hall: *Faery Lands in the South Seas* (1921); *Falcons of France* (1929); *Mutiny on the Bounty* (1932); *Men Against the Sea* (1934); *Pitcairn's Island* (1934); *The Hurricane* (1935); *The Dark River* (1938); *Out of Gas* (1939); *Botany Bay* (1941); *Men without Country* (1942); *The High Barbaree* (1945); etc.

NORDSTROM, URSULA; b. New York. Editor, author. *The Secret Language* (1960); Children's Book Department, Harper & Row, since 1940.

Norfolk Journal and Guide. Norfolk, Va. Newspaper. Founded 1901. One of the most influential Negro newspapers in the South.

Norfolk Virginian Pilot and Sunday Star. Norfolk, Va. Newspaper. Founded 1865, as the *Norfolk Virginian.* The *Norfolk Daily Pilot* was founded in 1894, and became the *New Daily Pilot* in 1895. The two merged in 1898 as the *Virginian-Pilot,* which merged in 1911 with the *Norfolk Landmark* (founded 1873) as the *Virginian-Pilot and Norfolk Landmark.* The *Virginian Pilot* appears as the morning edition, except Sunday. The *Norfolk Ledger-Dispatch* (founded 1876), now combined with the *Portsmouth Star,* appears as the evening edition, except Sunday, under the name *Norfolk Ledger-Dispatch and the Portsmouth Star.* The *Virginian Pilot and the Portsmouth Star* appears as the Sunday edition.

NORMAN, CHARLES (May 9, 1904–); b. in Russia. Artist, author. *Poems* (1929); *The Bright World* (poems, 1930); *The Savage Century* (poems, 1942); *A Soldier's Diary* (poems, 1944); *The Muse's Darling: The Life of Christopher Marlowe* (1946); *The Case of Ezra Pound* (1948); *The Well of the Past* (1949); *Mr. Oddity: Samuel Johnson, LL.D.* (1951); *The Pundit and the Player: Dr. Johnson and Mr. Garrick* (1951); *Rake Rochester* (1954); *The Magic-Maker: E. E. Cummings* (1959); *Selected Poems* (1962); *The Long Bows of Agincourt* (1963); *Come Live With Me* (1966); *Discoverers of America* (1968); *Ezra Pound: A Biography* (1968); etc.

NORRIS, CHARLES G[ILMAN] (Apr. 23, 1881–July 25, 1945); b. Chicago, Ill. Author. *The Amateur* (1916); *Salt; or, The Education of Griffith Adams* (1918); *Brass* (1921); *Bread* (1923); *Pig Iron* (1926); *Zelda Marsh* (1927); *Seed* (1931); *Zest* (1933); *Hands* (1935); *Bricks without Straw* (1938); *Flint* (1944); and plays for the Bohemian Grove; etc.

NORRIS, FRANK (Benjamin Franklin) (Mar. 5, 1870–Oct. 25, 1902); b. Chicago, Ill. Journalist, novelist. *Moran of the Lady Letty* (1898); *McTeague* (1899); *Blix* (1899); *The Octopus* (1901); *The Pit* (1903); *The Responsibilities of the Novelist* (1903); *Vandover and the Brute* (1914); etc. On staff, *The Wave,* San Francisco, *McClure's Magazine,* etc. Editorial dept., Doubleday, Page & Co. See Franklin Walker's *Frank Norris* (1932); Vernon L. Parrington's *Main Currents in American Thought,* v.3 (1930); Ernest Marchand's *Frank Norris, a Study* (1942).

NORRIS, FRANK CALLAN (1907–Aug. 8, 1967). Author. *Nutro 29* (1950); *Tower in the West* (1957); *At Last to Kiss Amanda* (1961).

NORRIS, KATHLEEN (Mrs. Charles Gilman Norris) (July 16, 1880–Jan. 18, 1966); b. San Francisco, Calif. Novelist. *Mother* (1911); *Saturday's Child* (1914); *The Story of Julia Page* (1915); *The Heart of Rachel* (1916); *Undertow* (1917); *Harriet and the Piper* (1920); *Certain People of Importance* (1922); *Butterfly* (1923); *The Callahans and the Murphys* (1924); *Noon* (1925); *The Black Flemings* (1926); *Hildegarde* (1926); *The Sea Gull* (1927); *Barberry Bush* (1927); *Beauty and the Beast* (1928); *The Foolish Virgin* (1928); *Red Silence* (1929); *Mother and Son* (1929); *Passion Flower* (1930); *Second Hand Wife* (1932); *My San Francisco* (1932); *My California* (1933); *Manhattan Love Song* (1934); *The American Flaggs* (1936); *You Can't Have Everything* (1937); *Bakers'*

Dozen (1938); *The Runaway* (1939); *Lost Sunrise* (1939); *The World is Like That* (1940); *These I Like Best* (1941); *One Nation Indivisible* (1942); *Corner of Heaven* (1943); *Burned Fingers* (1945); *High Holiday* (1949); *Morning Light* (1950); *Shadow Marriage* (1952); *Miss Harriet Townsend* (1955); *Through a Glass Darkly* (1957); *Family Gathering* (1959); etc.

NORRIS, LOUIS W[illiam] (Feb. 3, 1906–); b. Columbus, O. Educator. *Polarity: A Philosophy of Tensions Among Values* (1956); *The Good New Days* (1956). Pres., MacMurray College, Ill., 1952–60; Albion College from 1960.

NORRIS, MARY HARRIOTT (Mar. 16, 1848–Sept. 14, 1919); b. Boonton, N.J. Author. *Fraulein Mina; or, Life in a North American German Family* (1873); *School Life of Ben and Bentie* (1874); *Phebe* (1890); *Lakewood* (1895); *The Gray House of the Quarries* (1898); *The Grapes of Wrath* (1901); *The Veil* (1907); *The Golden Age of Vassar* (1915); etc.

NORSE, HAROLD. Poet. *Undersea Mountain* (poems, 1953); *The Dancing Beasts* (1962).

North, Andrew. Pen name of Alice Mary Norton.

NORTH, ERNEST DRESSEL (b. Feb. 19, 1858); b. New York. Bibliophile, bookseller, author. *The Wit and Wisdom of Charles Lamb* (1892); etc. Editor: *Addison's Sir Roger de Coverley Papers* (1892); contributed bibliographies to Ferris Greenslet's *Life of T. B. Aldrich* (1905); B. E. Martin's *In the Footprints of Charles Lamb* (1890). Lit. editor, *Christian Advocate*, for twenty years; wrote rare book notes for *The Book Buyer*, etc. Founded bookselling business in New York, Nov., 1902, which was transferred to Summit, N.J., in 1934. Joined Charles Scribner's Sons, 1877. Owns large Charles Lamb collection.

NORTH, GRACE MAY (Mrs. William N. Monfort) (1876–); b. Utica, N.Y. Author. The *Adele Doring* series, 5v. (1919–23); *Virginia Davis Ranch Stories* (1924); *Rilla of the Lighthouse* (1926); *Sisters* (1927); *The Phantom Town* (1931); etc.

NORTH, JESSICA NELSON (Mrs. Reed Inness MacDonald) (1894–); b. Madison, Wis. Editor, author. *A Prayer Rug* (poems, 1923); *The Long Leash* (poems, 1928); *Arden Acres* (novel, 1935); *Morning in the Land* (1941); etc. On editorial staff, *Poetry*.

NORTH, SIMEON (Sept. 7, 1802–Feb. 9, 1884); b. Berlin, Conn. Educator, author. *Anglo-Saxon Literature* (1847); *The College System of Education* (1839); etc. President, Hamilton College, 1839–57.

NORTH, STERLING (Nov. 4, 1906–); b. Edgerton, Wis. Editor, author. *Plowing on Sunday* (1934); *The Five Little Bears* (1935); *Night Outlasts the Whippoorwill* (1936); *Seven Against the Years* (1939); *So Dear to My Heart* (1947); *Reunion on the Wabash* (1952); *Son of the Lampmaker* (1956); *Mark Twain and the River* (1963); *Rascal* (1963); *Hurry Spring* (1966); *Raccoons Are the Brightest People* (1966); etc. Lit. editor, the *Chicago Daily News*, 1933–43; *New York World Telegram and Sun*, 1949–56.

North American Review. New York City. Magazine. Founded May, 1815, at Boston, by William Tudor and others, and first published by Wells & Lilly. Tudor was its first editor. Other successive editors have been: Jared Sparks, Edward Tyrrel Channing, Edward Everett, Alexander Hill Everett, John Gorham Palfrey, Francis Bowen, Andrew Preston Peabody, James Russell Lowell, Charles Eliot Norton, E. W. Gurney, Henry Adams, Allen Thorndike Rice, Lloyd Bryce, David A. Munro, George B. M. Harvey, Walter Butler Mahony, John H. G. Pell, Joseph Hilton Smyth. Two of its noted assistant editors were Thomas Sergeant Perry and Henry Cabot Lodge. It began as a bimonthly, and changed to a quarterly, then to a monthly, and after many other changes in periodicity became a quarterly. In 1878 it moved from Boston to New York. George Harvey owned the magazine from 1899 to 1926. William Cushing compiled an *Index* to the magazine for the years 1815–80. It was discontinued in 1940. See *Living Age.*

North of Boston. By Robert Frost (1914). A picture of rural New England in a volume of poetry which contains many of the author's best known poems.

North-Carolina Gazette. New Bern, N.C. Newspaper. First newspaper in North Carolina; founded 1751. Expired 1804.

NORTHROP, F[ilmer] **S**[tuart] **C**[uckow] (Nov. 27, 1893–); b. Janesville, Wis. Educator, author. *Science and First Principles* (1931); *The Meeting of East and West* (1946); *The Logic of the Sciences and the Humanities* (1947); *The Taming of the Nations* (1952); *European Union and United States Foreign Policy* (1954); *The Complexity of Legal and Ethical Experience* (1959); *Philosophical Anthropology and Practical Politics* (1960); *Man, Nature and God* (1962); etc. Dept. philosophy, Yale University, 1923–47. Prof. Philosophy and Law, Sterling College, 1947–62. Emeritus since 1962.

Northwest Magazine. St. Paul, Minn. Founded, 1883, by Eugene Virgil Smalley, who edited it until 1899. V. H. Smalley was editor, 1900–03. Expired 1903.

Northwest Passage. Novel by Kenneth Roberts (1937). Story of Rogers' Rangers during the French and Indian wars. These picked woodsmen went from Crown Point at Lake Champlain into the Canadian wilderness, fighting and pillaging.

Northwest Review. Eugene, Ore. Triannual. Founded 1957. Published at the University of Oregon. Primarily a literary magazine.

NORTON, ALICE MARY; b. Cleveland, O. Librarian, editor, author. Pen names "Andre Norton" and "Andrew North." *Moon of Three Rings* (1966); *Catseye* (1961); *Witch World; Web of the Witch World; Judgement on Janus* (1963); *Three Against the Witch World; Warlock of the Witch World;* etc.

NORTON, ANDREWS (Dec. 31, 1786–Sept. 18, 1853); b. Hingham, Mass. Biblical scholar, author. Father of Charles Eliot Norton. *Evidences of the Genuineness of the Gospels,* 3v. (1837–44); *Verses* (1953); etc. Founder and editor, the *General Repository,* Boston, 1812–13, a connecting link between the *Monthly Anthology* and the *North American Review;* editor, the *Select Journal of Foreign Periodical Literature,* 1833–34.

Norton, Carol. Pen name of Grace May North.

NORTON, CHARLES ELIOT (Nov. 16, 1827–Oct. 21, 1908); b. Cambridge, Mass. Educator, editor, author. *Notes of Travel and Study in Italy* (1860); *Historical Studies of Church Building in the Middle Ages* (1880); *History of Ancient Art* (1891). Translator: Dante's *The Divine Comedy,* 3v. (1891–92). Editor: *The Poems of John Donne,* 2v. (1895). Co-founder, *The Nation,* New York, 1865; editor (with James Russell Lowell), the *North American Review,* 1864–68. Prof. history of art, Harvard, 1874–98. The Charles Eliot Norton Lectureship of Poetry, at Harvard was established in his honor. See Sara Norton and M. A. DeWolfe Howe's *Letters of Charles Eliot Norton, with Biographical Comment,* 2v. (1913); and E. W. Emerson and W. F. Harris's *Charles Eliot Norton* (1912); and Kermit Vanderbilt's *Charles Eliot Norton: Apostle of Culture in a Democracy* (1959).

NORTON, GRACE (Apr. 7, 1834–May 5, 1926); b. Cambridge, Mass. Author. *Studies in Montaigne* (1904); *The Early Writings of Montaigne, and Other Papers* (1904); etc. Compiler: *The Spirit of Montaigne* (1908); etc.

NORTON, GRACE FALLOW (Oct. 29, 1876–); b. Northfield, Mass. Poet. *Little Gray Songs from St. Joseph's* (1912); *The Sister of the Wind* (1914); *Roads* (1916); etc.

NORTON, HENRY KITTREDGE (Oct. 14, 1884–Oct. 14, 1965); b. Chicago, Ill. Business executive, author. *Story of California* (1913); *The Far Eastern Republic of Siberia* (1923); *China and the Powers* (1927); *The Coming of South America* (1932); etc.

NORTON, JOHN (May 6, 1606–Apr. 5, 1663); b. in Hertfordshire, Eng. Congregational clergyman, author. *A Discussion of that Great Point in Divinity, the Sufferings of Christ* (1653); *The Orthodox Evangelist* (1654); *Abel Being Dead Yet Speaketh; or, The Life and Death of John Cotton* (1658); etc.

NORTON, ROY (Sept. 30, 1869–June 28, 1942); b. Kewanee, Ill. Engineer, novelist. *The Vanishing Fleets* (1907); *The Toll of the Sea* (1909); *Mary Jane's Pa* (1909); *The Moccasins of Gold* (1913); *The Mediator* (1913); *The Scamps* (1917); *The Shaman* (1926); *The Lone Rider* (1932); *Below the Rio Grande* (1933); *The Blossom Belle* (1936); etc.

Norton, W. W. & Co. New York. Publishers. Founded 1924, by William Warder Norton. The firm publishes books on science, government, psychology, medicine, and education chiefly, but it also publishes books in the field of travel, biography, fiction, etc. *Seagull Editions* is an imprint of the firm.

NORTON, WILLIAM WARDER (Sept. 17, 1891–Nov. 7, 1945); b. Springfield, O. Publisher. Founder W. W. Norton Co., publishing firm, New York, in 1924, of which he was president until his death.

NORVAL, JAMES (1765–May 8, 1847). Author. *The Generous Chief* (1792); *Popular Lectures on the Solar System and Fixed Stars* (1834); etc. *See* Robert M. Lawrance's *James Norval, M.A., Schoolmaster, Playwright, and Author* (1926).

Norwood. Novel by Henry Ward Beecher (1867). Said to be the first novel to introduce the figure of Abraham Lincoln.

NORWOOD, EDWIN P. (Apr. 20, 1881–Oct. 13, 1940); b. Cucamonga, Calif. Author. *The Adventures of Diggeldy Dan* (1922); *The Friends of Diggeldy Dan* (1924); *Davy Winkle in Circusland* (1926); *The Other Side of the Circus* (1926); *The Circus Menagerie* (1929). Director of publicity, Ringling Brothers Circus, 1917–27.

NORWOOD, ROBERT WINKWORTH (Mar. 27, 1874–Sept. 28, 1932); b. New Ross, N.S. Episcopal clergyman, poet. *The Heresy of Antioch* (1928); *The Man Who Dared to be God* (1929); *His Lady of the Sonnets* (1915); *The Witch of Endor* (1916); *The Piper and the Reed* (1917); *The Man of Kerioth* (1919); *Bill Boram* (1921); *Mother and Son* (1925); *The Steep Ascent* (1928); *Issa* (1931).

Not So Deep As a Well. Collection of poems by Dorothy Parker (1936).

Notes of a Native Son. Essays by James Baldwin (1955). Acute discussion of the moral condition of the Negro in modern America and of the deficiencies in quality in American life.

Notes of a Son and Brother. Autobiographical work by Henry James (1914).

Nothing to Wear. Long, humorous poem by William Allen Butler (1857), which had appeared anonymously in *Harper's Weekly.* It was parodied by Mortimer Neal Thompson in his *Nothing to Say* (1857). *See* John A. Kouwenhoven's *Some Ado about Nothing,* in the *Colophon,* Autumn 1936.

NOTT, ELIPHALET (June 25, 1773–Jan. 29, 1866); b. Ashford, Conn. Educator, author. *A Discourse ... Occasioned by the Ever to be Lamented Death of General Alexander Hamilton* (1804); *Miscelleaneous Works* (1810); *Lectures on Temperance* (1847). President, Union College, 1804–66.

NOTT, HENRY JUNIUS (Nov. 4, 1797–Oct. 9, 1837); b. Union District, S.C. Humorist. *Novellettes of a Traveller; or, Odds and Ends from the Knapsack of Thomas Singularity, Journeyman Printer,* 2v. (1834).

NOURSE, JAMES. Novelist. *Uncle Hugh; or, "Twenty Years Ago"* (1841); *The Forest Knight; or, Early Times in Kentucky* (1846); *Leavenworth: A Story of the Mississippi and the Prairies* (1848); etc.

NOVAK, SONIA (Mme. Sonia Ruthele Novak) (July 15, 1900–deceased); b. Madisonville, Tenn. Poet. *Winds from the Moon* (1928); *Strange Thoroughfare* (1931); etc.

"Now I lay me down to sleep." Opening line of the child's prayer which first appeared in the 1775 edition of the *New England Primer* (q.v.).

NOYES, CARLETON [Eldredge] (Oct. 1, 1872–1950); b. Boston, Mass. Author. *The Enjoyment of Art* (1903); *The Gate of Appreciation* (1907); *An Approach to Walt Whitman* (1910); *The Genius of Israel* (1924).

NOYES, GEORGE RAPALL (Apr. 2, 1873–1952); b. Cambridge, Mass. Educator, translator of Russian plays and novels, editor, author. *Tolstoy* (1918); *Essay Upon Satyr ... London ... Dring ... 1680* (with H. R. Mead, 1948). Editor: *Dryden's Poetical Works* (1909); *Masterpieces of the Russian Drama* (1933). With University of California, since 1901; prof. Slavic languages, since 1919.

NOYES, JOHN HUMPHREY (Sept. 3, 1811–Apr. 13, 1886); b. Brattleboro, Vt. Perfectionist, reformer, author. *The Berean* (1847); *Male Continence* (1848); *Scientific Propagation* (c. 1873); *Home Talks* (1875); *History of American Socialisms* (1870). Founder, Perfectionist cult at Putney, Vt.; founder of Oneida Community. Founder and editor of *The Perfectionist,* 1834. See *Religious Experience of John Humphrey Noyes* (1923) and *John Henry Noyes: The Putney Community* (1931), both ed. by G. W. Noyes; Robert Allerton Parker's *A Yankee Saint: John Humphreys Noyes and the Oneida Community* (1935).

Nugae, by Nugator; or, Pieces in Prose and Verse. By St. Leger L. Carter (1844).

NUGENT, ELLIOTT (Sept. 29, 1899–); b. Dover, O. Actor, playwright. *Of Cheat and Charmer* (1962); *Events Leading up to Comedy* (1965). Co-author: *Kempy* (play, with J. C. Nugent, 1922); *The Poor Nut* (play, with same, 1925); *The Male Animal* (play, with James Thurber, 1940). ⊙

NUHN, FERNER. Author. *The Wind Blew from the East: A Study in the Orientation of American Culture* (1942).

Number One. Novel by John Dos Passos (1943). Second novel in the trilogy which begins with *Adventures of a Young Man* (1939) and ends with *The Grand Design* (1949).

NUTTALL, THOMAS (Jan. 5, 1786–Sept. 10, 1859); b. Settle, York., Eng. Botanist, ornithologist, author. *A Journal of Travels into the Arkansa Territory, During the Year 1819* (1821); *A Manual of the Ornithology of the United States and Canada* (1832). He wrote vols. IV–VI of F. A. Michaux's *The North American Sylva* (1842–49).

NUTTING, WALLACE (Nov. 17, 1861–July 19, 1941); b. Marlboro, Mass. Congregational clergyman, antiquarian, author. *Vermont Beautiful* (1922); *Massachusetts Beautiful* (1923); *Connecticut Beautiful* (1923); *New Hampshire Beautiful* (1923); *Maine Beautiful* (1924); *Pennsylvania Beautiful* (1924); *Ireland Beautiful* (1925); *New York Beautiful* (1927); *England Beautiful* (1928); *Virginia Beautiful* (1930); *Wallace Nutting's Biography* (1936); etc.

NYBURG, SIDNEY LAUER (Dec. 8, 1880–June 19, 1957); b. Baltimore, Md. Lawyer, author. *The Chosen People* (1917); *The Buried Rose: Legends of Old Baltimore* (1932).

NYE, BILL [Edgar Wilson] (Aug. 26, 1850–Feb. 22, 1896); b. Shirley, Me. Journalist, humorist, lecturer, author. *Bill Nye and Boomerang* (1881); *Forty Liars and Other Lies* (1882); *Baled Hay* (1884). Founder, the *Laramie Boomerang,* 1881. Joined staff of New York *World* in 1887. Appeared in joint lectureships with James Whitcomb Riley, 1886–90. See *Bill Nye: His Own Life Story,* comp. by his son, F. W. Nye (1926).

NYE, RUSSEL BLAINE (Feb. 17, 1913–); b. Viola, Wis. Author. *George Bancroft: Brahmin Rebel* (1944; Pulitzer prize for biography, 1945); *Fettered Freedom: Civil Liberties and the Slavery Controversy* (1948); *A Baker's Dozen* (1956); *Cultural Life of the New Nation* (1960); *Midwestern Progressive Politics* (1965); *This Almost Chosen People* (1966); etc.

Nye and Riley's Railway Guide. By Bill Nye and James Whitcomb Riley (1888). A guide "which will not be cursed by a plethora of facts or poisoned by information."

"Nym Crinkle's Feuilleton," weekly column by Andrew Carpenter Wheeler in the *New York Dramatic Mirror,* 1889.

O

"O Captain! My Captain!" Poems by Walt Whitman on Abraham Lincoln (1965).

O. Henry. Pen name of William Sidney Porter.

O. Henry Memorial Prize Stories. Founded 1919. An annual collection of American stories. Editors have included Blanche Colton Williams, Harry Hansen, Herschel Brickell, and Richard Poirier.

"O Little Town of Bethlehem." Carol by Phillips Brooks, written in Philadelphia for the Sunday school and sung for the first time at Christmas, 1868.

Oak Openings. By J. Fenimore Cooper (1848). Inspired by a journey which Cooper made to the West in 1847. A tale of bee-hunting and Indian fighting on Lake Michigan.

OAKES, GEORGE WASHINGTON [Ochs] (Oct. 27, 1861–Oct. 26, 1931); b. Cincinnati, O. Editor, publisher. Named changed from Ochs to Oakes in 1917. His brother, Adolph S. Ochs, was publisher of the *New York Times.* Managing editor, the *Chattanooga Daily Times,* and general manager of the *Philadelphia Times.* In 1902 the *Times* was merged with the *Public Ledger* and Oakes became publisher. Editor, *New York Times Current History,* 1915–31; *Mid-Week Pictorial,* 1915.

OAKES, URIAN (c. 1631–July 25, 1681); b. London. Educator, poet. *New-England Pleaded With* (1673); *Elegie Upon the Death of the Reverend Mr. Thomas Shepard* (1677). President, Harvard College, 1679/80–81.

Oakland Tribune. Oakland, Cal. Newspaper. Founded 1874. W. F. Knowland is editor. J. F. Knowland is publisher. John Moreland edits the book reviews weekdays and Sundays.

OAKLEY, AMY (Mrs. Thornton Oakley) (Jan. 21, 1882–); b. Bryn Mawr, Pa. Author: *Hill-Towns of the Pyrenees* (1923); *Cloud-lands of France* (1927); *Enchanted Brittany* (1930); *The Heart of Provence* (1936); *Scandinavia Beckons* (1938); *Behold the West Indies* (1941); *Kaleidoscopic Quebec* (1947); *Our Pennsylvania: Keys to the Keystone State* (1950). Many of her books were illustrated by her husband, Thorton Oakley.

OATES, JOYCE CAROL (June 16, 1938–); b. Lockport, N.Y. Author. *By the North Gate* (1963); *With Shuddering Fall* (1965); *Upon the Sweeping Flood* (1966); *A Garden of Earthly Delights* (1967); *Expensive People* (1968); *Them* (1969; National Book Award, 1970); *Anonymous Sins* (1969); *Wheel of Love* (1970); *Love and its Derangements* (1970); etc.

OATES, WHITNEY J[ennings] (Mar. 26, 1904–); b. Evanston, Ill. Educator, author. *Aristotle and the Problem of Value* (1963). Editor: *The Complete Greek Drama* (with Eugene O'Neill, Jr., 1938); *The Stoic and Epicurean Philosophers* (1940); *Basic Writings of St. Augustine* (1948); etc. Classics dept., Princeton University, since 1927.

OATMAN, JOHNSON (Apr. 21, 1856–Sept. 25, 1922); b. Medford, N.J. Hymn writer. His best known hymns are "No, not one," "Count your blessings," "Sweeter than all."

OBENCHAIN, ELIZA [Caroline] CALVERT HALL (b. 1856); b. Bowling Green, Ky. Author. *Sally Ann's Experience* (1907); *Aunt Jane of Kentucky* (1908); *The Land of Long Ago* (1909); etc. Wrote novels under maiden name, Eliza Calvert Hall, and suffrage pamphlets as Mrs. Lida Calvert Obenchain.

OBER, FREDERICK A[lbion] (Feb. 13, 1849–June 1, 1913). Author. *Camps in the Caribbees* (1879); *Travels in Mexico* (1884); *Montezuma's Gold Mines* (1887); *Columbus the Discoverer* (1906); *Amerigo Vespucci* (1907); etc. Wrote the *Knockabout Club* series.

OBERHOLTZER, ELLIS PAXSON (1868–Dec. 8, 1936); b. near West Chester, Pa. Historian. *Robert Morris, Patriot and Financier* (1903); *Abraham Lincoln* (1904); *The Literary History of Philadelphia* (1906); *Jay Cooke, Financier of the Civil War,* 2v. (1907); *A History of the United States Since the Civil War,* 5v. (1917–37); and many books on Pennsylvania history.

OBERHOLTZER, SARA LOUISA VICKERS (May 20, 1841–Feb. 2, 1930); b. Uwchlan, Pa. Poet, novelist. *Violet Lee, and Other Poems* (1873); *Come for Arbutus* (poem, 1882); *Daisies of Verse* (1886); *Hope's Heart Bells* (1884); *Souvenirs of Occasions* (poems, 1892); etc.

Obolensky, Ivan, Inc. New York. Founded 1957, by Ivan Obolensky and David McDowell, as McDowell, Obolensky Inc.; later Ivan Obolensky, Inc. Ivan Obolensky was president. Publishes general trade books, including art books. Now known as Astor-Honor Inc., with juveniles under the Astor imprint, paperbacks under the Honor imprint, and adult titles under the Obolensky imprint. John Ledes is publisher.

OBOLER, ARCH (Dec. 6, 1909–); b. Chicago, Ill. Playwright. *Fourteen Radio Plays* (1940); *Night of the Auk* (prod. 1956); etc. Also radio and screen plays.

O'BRIEN, EDWARD J[oseph Harrington] (Dec. 10, 1890–Feb. 25, 1941); b. Boston, Mass. Poet, editor. *White Fountains* (poems, 1917); *Son of the Morning* (1932); etc. Editor: *The Best Short Stories,* 26v. (1915–40); *The Great Modern English Stories* (1919); *The Best British Short Stories,* 20v. (1921–40); *The Fifty Best American Short Stories, 1914–1939* (1939); etc.

O'BRIEN, FITZ-JAMES (c. 1828–Apr. 6, 1862); b. in Co. Limerick, Ire. Journalist, playwright. *A Gentleman from Ireland* (prod. 1858); *The Poems and Stories of Fitz-James O'Brien,* ed. by William Winter (1881). His best-known story is *The Diamond Lens* in the *Atlantic Monthly* (1857). Drama editor, *Saturday Press,* New York, 1858.

O'BRIEN, FRANK MICHAEL (Mar. 31, 1875–Sept. 22, 1943); b. Dunkirk, N.Y. Editor, author. *The Story of the Sun* (1918); *New York Murder Mysteries* (1932); etc. Editor, *New York Sun,* from 1926. His Beadle Collection of dime novels is in the New York Public Library. Another collection of his Beadle books is in the Huntington Library, San Marino, Calif.

O'BRIEN, FREDERICK (June 16, 1869–Jan. 9, 1932); b. Baltimore, Md. Journalist, author. *White Shadows in the South Seas* (1919); *Mystic Isles of the South Seas* (1921); *Atolls of the Sun* (1922).

O'BRIEN, HOWARD VINCENT (July 11, 1888–Sept. 30, 1947); b. Chicago, Ill. Columnist, author. *New Men for Old* (1912); *Thirty* (1914); *Trodden Gold* (1922); *The Thunderbolt* (under pen name "Clyde Perrin," 1923); *The Terms of Conquest* (1923); *The Green Scarf* (1924); *Wine, Women and*

War (1926); *P. S.* (1928); *Folding Bedouins* (1936); *Memoirs of a Guinea Pig* (1942); *So Long, Son* (1944); *All Things Considered* (1948); etc. Lit. editor, *Chicago Daily News,* 1928–32; columnist, from 1932.

O'BRIEN, JUSTIN McCORTNEY (Nov. 26, 1906–Dec. 7, 1968), b. Chicago, Ill. Educator, translator, author. *The Novel of Adolescence in France* (1937); *Portrait of André Gide* (1953). Editor, translator: *The Journals of André Gide,* 4v. (1947–51); *The Maxims of Marcel Proust* (1948); Gide's *Madeleine* (1952); Camus's *The Myth of Sisyphus* (1955); *The Fall* (1957); *Exile and the Kingdom* (1958); Gide's *So Be It* (1959); *Pretexts* (1959). French dept., Columbia University, since 1931.

O'Brien, Mrs. Joseph. See Mary Heaton Vorse.

O'BRIEN, P[atrick] J[oseph] (1892–June 10, 1938); b. Penfield, Pa. Journalist, author. *The Lindberghs* (1935); *Will Rogers* (1935).

O'CALLAGHAN, E[dmund] B[ailey] (Feb. 28, 1797–May 29, 1880); b. Mallow, Ire. Editor, author. *History of New Netherland,* 2v. (1846–48); etc. Editor: *The Documentary History of the State of New York,* 4v. (1849–51); *Documents Relative to the Colonial History of the State of New-York,* 11v. (1853–61); etc.

O'Cataract, Jehu. Pen name of John Neal.

OCCOM, (or Ockum), **SAMSON** (1723–July 14, 1792); b. near New London, Conn. Mohegan Indian missionary, hymn writer, author. *A Choice Collection of Hymns and Spiritual Songs* (1774). His best known hymn in English is "Awaked by Sinai's Awful Sound." *See* Harold W. Blodgett's *Samson Occom* (1935).

Occurrence at Owl Creek Bridge. By Ambrose Bierce. Civil War ghost story which appeared in the author's *Tales of Soldiers and Civilians* (1895).

OCHS, ADOLPH S[imon] (Mar. 12, 1858–Apr. 8, 1935); b. Cincinnati, O. Publisher, philanthropist. Publisher, the *Chattanooga Daily Times,* 1878–1935; the *New York Times,* 1896–1935; *New York Times Current History,* 1915–35; *Mid-Week Pictorial;* etc. Bought the Philadelphia *Times,* 1901, and the Philadelphia *Ledger,* 1902, both of which he sold to Cyrus H. K. Curtis in 1912. He gave $500,000 on behalf of the *New York Times* to aid in the publication of the *Dictionary of American Biography* (q.v.). *See* George Washington Ochs Oakes; *New York Times, Chattanooga Daily Times.*

O'Conner, Mrs. Larry. See Barrett Willoughby.

O'CONNOR, EDWIN (July 29, 1918–Mar. 23, 1968); b. Providence, R.I. Author. *The Oracle* (1951); *The Last Hurrah* (1956); *Benjy* (1957); *The Edge of Sadness* (1961).

O'CONNOR, FLANNERY (1925–Aug. 2, 1964). Author. *Wise Blood* (1952); *A Good Man Is Hard to Find, and Other Stories* (1955); *Artificial Nigger, and Other Tales* (1957); *The Violent Bear It Away* (1960); *Five Plays* (1961); *A Memoir of Mary Ann* (1961); *Everything That Rises Must Converge* (1965); etc.

O'CONNOR, FRANK [Michael O'Donovan] (1903–Mar. 10, 1966); b. Cork, Ire. Author. *Dutch Interior* (1940); *Towards an Appreciation of Literature* (1945); *Irish Miles* (1947); *Stories of Frank O'Connor* (1952); *The Mirror in the Roadway* (1956); *Domestic Relations* (1957); *An Only Child* (autobiography, 1961); etc.

O'CONNOR, HARVEY (Mar. 29, 1897–); b. Minneapolis, Minn. Author. *Mellon's Millions* (1933); *Steel-Dictator* (1935); *The Guggenheims* (1937); *The Astors* (1941); *History of the Oil Workers' International Union* (1950); *The Empire of Oil* (1955); *World Crisis in Oil* (1962); *Revolution in Seattle* (1964).

O'CONNOR, JACK (Jan. 22, 1902–); b. Nogales, Ariz. Author. *Conquest* (1930); *Boom Town* (1938); *Game in the Desert* (1939); *Hunting in the Rockies* (1947); *Big Game Rifle* (1952); *Complete Book of Rifles and Shotguns* (1961); *The Complete Book of Shooting* (with others, 1966); etc.

O'CONNOR, JOHN PATRICK (Jan. 18, 1892–); b. New York. Publisher. Pres., Grosset & Dunlap, from 1944. Retired.

O'CONNOR, JOHN WOOLF [Jack] (Jan. 22, 1902–); b. Nogales, Ariz. Author. *Conquest* (1930); *Boom Town* (1938); *Hunting in the Southwest* (1945); *The Rifle Book* (1949); *Game in the Desert* (1939); *Arms and Ammunition* (1952); *The Big Game Rifle* (1952); *Shotguns and Rifles* (1961); *Big Game on North America* (1962); *The Complete Book of Shooting* (with others, 1966); *The Art of Hunting* (1967); *Horse and Buggy West* (1969); etc.

O'CONNOR, JOHNSON (Jan. 22, 1891–); b. Chicago, Ill. Psychometrician. *Born That Way* (1928); *Psychometrics* (1934); *Unsolved Business Problems* (1940); *Aptitudes and the Languages* (1944); *The Unique Individual* (1948); *Science Vocabulary Builder* (1956); etc. Co-author: *Ginn Vocabulary Building Program* (1966).

O'CONNOR, RICHARD (Mar. 10, 1915–   ); b. La Porte, Ind. Journalist, author. *Bat Masterson* (1957); *Hell's Kitchen* (1958); *Black Jack Pershing* (1961); *Gould's Millions* (1962); *Jack London* (1964); *Bret Harte* (1966); *The Lost Revolutionary* (1967); *Ambrose Bierce* (1967); etc.

O'CONNOR, WILLIAM DOUGLAS (Jan. 2, 1832–May 9, 1889); b. Boston, Mass. Journalist, author. *Harrington* (1860); *The Good Gray Poet* (1866); *Three Tales* (1892). He was a close friend of Walt Whitman. *See* Sumner Increase Kimball's *Heroes of the Storm* (1904).

O'CONNOR, WILLIAM VAN (Jan. 10, 1915–Sept. 26, 1966); b. Syracuse, N.Y. Educator, author. *The New Woman of the Renaissance* (1942); *Sense and Sensibility in Modern Poetry* (1948); *The Shaping Spirit: A Study of Wallace Stevens* (1950); *The Tangled Fire of William Faulkner* (1954); *Campus on the River* (1959); *The Grotesque: An American Genre* (1962); etc. Editor: *Forms of Modern Fiction: Essays Collected in Honor of Joseph Warren Beach* (1948); etc. English dept., University of Minnesota, since 1946.

O'CONOR, NORREYS JEPHSON (Dec. 31, 1885–Oct. 24, 1958); b. New York. Author. *Celtic Memories, and Other Poems* (1914); *The Fairy Bride* (1916); *There Was Magic in Those Days* (1929); *Late Offerings* (1952); etc.

Octopus, The. Novel of California by Frank Norris (1901). The central theme is the importance of wheat-growing in the lives of men. For some it meant power and wealth; for others, labor and suffering.

Octoroon, The. Play by Dion Boucicault (prod. 1859). Story of a woman of mixed blood who is sold into slavery.

Odd Couple, The. Play by Neil Simon (prod. 1965).

"Ode to the Confederate Dead." Poem by Allen Tate, which first appeared in *The American Caravan* (1927). Reprinted, with revisions, in his *Selected Poems* (1937).

O'DEA, JAMES (Dec. 25, 1871–Apr. 12, 1914); b. Hamilton, Ont. Songwriter, poet. *Daddy Longlegs* (poems, 1900); *Jingleman Jack* (poems, 1901); etc.

ODEGARD, PETER H. (Apr. 5, 1901–Dec. 6, 1966); b. Kalispell, Mont. Educator. *The American Public Mind* (1930); *Prologue to November* (1940); etc. Prof. political science, University of California, since 1948.

ODELL, GEORGE C[linton] D[ensmore] (Mar. 19, 1866–Oct. 17, 1949); b. Newburgh, N.Y. Educator, historian of the stage. *Shakespeare from Betterton to Irving,* 2v. (1920); *Annals of the New York Stage,* 15v. (1927–49). English dept.,

Columbia University, from 1895; prof. dramatic literature, 1924–39.

ODELL, JONATHAN (Sept. 25, 1737–Nov. 25, 1818); b. Newark, N.J. Loyalist, satirist. In 1779 he wrote the poetic satires "The Word of Congress," "The Congratulation," "Feu de Joie," "The American Times." The latter has also been attributed to George Cockings and to Jonathan Boucher. Many of his verses are included in *The Loyal Verses of Joseph Stansbury and Doctor Jonathan Odell, Relating to the American Revolution,* ed. by Joel Munsell (1860).

O'DELL, SCOTT (1901–   ); b. Los Angeles, Cal. Author. *Woman of Spain* (1934); *Hill of the Hawk* (1947); *Country of the Sun* (1957); *Island of the Blue Dolphins* (1960); *King's Fifth* (1966); *The Black Pearl* (1967); etc.

ODETS, CLIFFORD (July 18, 1906–Aug. 15, 1963); b. Philadelphia, Pa. Playwright. *Awake and Sing* (prod. 1935); *Till the Day I Die* (prod. 1935); *Paradise Lost* (prod. 1935); *Waiting for Lefty* (prod. 1935); *Golden Boy* (prod. 1938); *The Silent Partner* (1938); *Rocket to the Moon* (prod. 1938); *Night Music* (prod. 1940); *Clash by Night* (prod. 1941); *The Big Knife* (prod. 1948); *The Country Girl* (prod. 1950); *The Flowering Peach* (1954); and several movie scenarios. *See* Joseph Wood Krutch's *The American Drama Since 1918* (1939).

ODLAND, MARTIN W[endell] (Jan. 2, 1875–); b. Meckling, S.D. Author. *The Saga of the Norsemen in America* (1925); *The Life of Knute Nelson* (1926); etc.

O'DONNELL, CHARLES LEO (Nov. 15, 1884–June 4, 1934); b. Greenfield, Ind. Roman Catholic clergyman, poet. *The Dead Musician, and Other Poems* (1916); *Cloister, and Other Poems* (1922); *A Rime of the Road, and Other Poems* (1928).

O'DONNELL, DANIEL KANE (1838–Sept. 8, 1871); b. Philadelphia, Pa. Journalist, poet. *The Song of Iron and the Song of Slaves, with Other Poems* (1863). Editorial staff, *The Press,* Philadelphia, 1862–64; the *New York Tribune,* 1866–67.

O'DONNELL, MARY KING (Mrs. Edwin P. O'Donnell; Mrs. Michael Quin) (Mar. 2, 1909–); b. Angleton, Tex. Novelist. *Quincie Bolliver* (1941); *Those Other People* (1946).

ODUM, HOWARD WASHINGTON (May 24, 1884–Nov. 8, 1954); b. Bethlehem, Ga. Educator, author. *The Negro and His Songs* (with Guy B. Johnson, 1925); *Negro Workaday Songs* (with same, 1926); *American Masters of Social Science* (1927); *Rainbow Round My Shoulder* (1928); *Wings on My Feet* (1929); *An American Epoch* (1930); *Cold Blue Moon* (1931); *American Social Problems* (1939); *Race and Rumors of Race* (1943); *Understanding Society* (1947); *American Sociology: The Study of Sociology in the United States through 1950* (1951); etc. Social science dept., University of North Carolina, from 1924.

Odyssey Review. New York. Founded 1962, by the Latin American and European Literary Society. Devoted to writings and writers of Latin America, in particular.

OEMLER, MARIE CONWAY (May 29, 1879–June 6, 1932); b. Savannah, Ga. Novelist. *Slippy McGee* (1917); *The Purple Heights* (1920); *Two Shall Be Born* (1922); *Johnny Reb* (1929); *Flower of Thorn* (1931); etc.

Of Mice and Men. Novel by John Steinbeck (1937). Story of George and Lennie, the latter a helpless Moron who is dependent on George, and who destroys the things he loves with fierce passion and unintentional cruelty.

Of Thee I Sing. Musical comedy by George S. Kaufman and Morrie Ryskind (prod. 1931). Lyrics by Ira Gershwin and music by George Gershwin. A burlesque on an American presidential election. Pulitzer prize play, 1932.

Of Time and the River. Novel by Thomas Wolfe (1935). It is a sequel to *Look Homeward, Angel* (1929). Eugene Gant studies play writing at Harvard, has several love affairs, and goes through an apprenticeship to life and experience that takes him to Europe and returns him disillusioned to the U.S.

Off Broadway. Refers to the numerous New York halls and theatres away from the Broadway district, ranging from Greenwich Village and the lower east side to the upper east and west sides of New York, where plays, musical comedies, and other forms of theatre are presented at prices lower than those on Broadway. These productions are often avant-garde, experimental dramas, or revivals of theatre classics, which would not be feasible under Broadway financial conditions. Since the 1950's off-Broadway presentations have received regular critical notice in the press. Although the distinction is not always clear, some theatres are referred to as Off-Off Broadway, especially if they stage productions in very small halls at cheaper prices, almost always experimental, avant-garde, or improvisatory in style.

OFFORD, C. R. Author. *The White Face* (1943).

OGBURN, CHARLTON (Aug. 19, 1882–Feb. 23, 1962); b. Butler, Ga. Lawyer, author. *The Lawyer and Democracy* (1915); *National Labor Relations Act: Its Constitutionality* (1935); *The Renaissance Man of England* (1949); *This Star of England* (with Dorothy Stevens Ogburn, 1952); *Economic Plan and Action* (1959); etc.

OGBURN, CHARLTON, JR. (Mar. 15, 1911–); b. Atlanta, Ga. Author. *The White Falcon* (1955); *The Bridge* (1957); *Big Caesar* (1958); *The Marauders* (1959); *The Gold of the River Sea* (1965); *The Winter Beach* (1966); *Down, Boy, Down, Blast You* (1967); *The Foraging of Our Continent* (1968). Co-author: *Shakespeare: The Man Behind the Name* (1962).

OGBURN, DOROTHY STEVENS (June 8, 1890–); b. Atlanta, Ga. Author. *Death on the Mountain* (1913); *Ra-ta-plan!* (1930); *The Will and the Deed* (1935); *This Star of England* (with Charlton Ogburn, 1952); *The Renaissance Man of England* (1955); *The Queen and Shakespeare: England's Power and Glory* (1959).

OGBURN, WILLIAM FIELDING (June 29, 1886–Apr. 27, 1959); b. Butler, Ga. Sociologist. *Progress and Uniformity in Child Labor Legislation* (1912); *The Economic Development of Post-War France* (with W. Jaffe, 1929); *You and Machines* (1935); *Sociology* (with N. F. Nimkoff, 1940); *The Social Effects of Aviation* (1946); *Technology and the Changing Family* (with same, 1955); etc. Editor: *Social Sciences and Their Interrelations* (1927); *American Society in Wartime* (1943); etc. Sociology dept., University of Chicago, 1927–51.

OGDEN, GEORGE WASHINGTON (Dec. 9, 1871–Mar. 31, 1966); b. in Kansas. Author. *Tennessee Todd* (1903); *The Duke of Chimney Butte* (1920); *The Trail Rider* (1924); *The Road to Monterey* (1925); *West of Dodge* (1926); *Sooner Land* (1929); *The Guard of Timberline* (1934); *There Were No Heroes* (1940); *West of the Rainbow* (1942); etc.

OGDEN, ROLLO (Jan. 19, 1856–Feb. 22, 1937); b. Sand Lake, N.Y. Editor, author. *William Hickling Prescott* (1904). With the New York *Evening Post,* 1891–1920; editor, 1903–20; editor, the *New York Times,* 1922–37.

Ogden, Ruth. Pen name of Francis Otis Ide.

OGDON, INA DULEY (Apr. 3, 1872–); b. Rossville, Ill. Hymn writer. *Keepsake from the Old House* (poems, 1937). Wrote words for "Brighten the Corner Where You Are," and hundreds of other hymns, poems, etc.

OGG, FREDERIC AUSTIN (Feb. 8, 1878–Oct. 23, 1951); b. Solsberry, Ind. Educator, author. *The Opening of the Mississippi* (1904); *Governments of Europe* (1913); *Life of Daniel Webster* (1914); *Introduction to American Government* (with

P. O. Ray, 1921); *Essentials of American Government* (with same, 1932); etc. Political science dept., University of Wisconsin, 1914–37.

OGILVIE, ELISABETH (May 20, 1917–); b. Boston, Mass. Novelist. *High Tide at Noon* (1944); *Storm Tide* (1945); *The Ebbing Tide* (1947); *Rowan Head* (1949); *My World Is an Island* (1950); *Drawing of the Day* (1954); *No Evil Angel* (1956); *Fabulous Year* (1958); *Witch Door* (1959); *Becky's Island* (1961); *The Pigeon Pair* (1967); etc.

OGILVIE, J[ohn] S[tuart] (1843–1910). Publisher. Founded his publishing firm in New York in 1858, and became the largest distributor of so-called "railroad literature," cheap humor, sex books, and sensational fiction. He sold his business to the United States Book Company in 1890.

O'GORMAN, NED (1929–). Poet. *The Night of the Hammer* (1959); *Adam Before His Mirror* (1961). Editor: *Prophetic Voices: Ideas and Words on Revolution* (1969).

"Oh Dad, Poor Dad, Mamma's Hung You in the Closet and I'm Feeling So Sad. Play by Arthur Kopit (1962).

"Oh, Promise Me" (1890) a song by Reginald De Koven, from the comic opera "Robin Hood," first sung by Jessie Bartlett Davis in Chicago, June, 1890.

O'HARA, FRANK (June 27, 1926–July 25, 1966); b. Baltimore, Md. Poet. *A City Winter, and Other Poems* (1952); *Meditations in an Emergency* (1956); *Hartigan and Rivers with O'Hara* (1959); *Jackson Pollock* (1959); *Second Avenue* (1960); *Odes* (1960); *Lunch Poems* (1964); *Love Poems* (1966). Assistant curator, The Museum of Modern Art, after 1955. *See* Bill Berkson's *Frank O'Hara: In Memory of My Feelings* (1967).

O'HARA, FRANK HURBURT (Feb. 2, 1888–Oct. 9, 1965); b. Berrien Springs, Mich. Author. *A Handbook of Drama* (with Marguerite Harmon Bro, 1938); *To-Day in American Drama* (1939); *Invitation to the Theater* (with Marguerite Harmon Bro, 1951); etc. English dept., University of Chicago, from 1924; director of drama, 1927–38.

O'HARA, GEOFFREY (Feb. 2, 1882–Jan. 31, 1967); b. Chatham, Ont. Composer, author. *Give a Man a Horse He Can Ride, and Other Poems* (1940); etc. Editor, *Canadian Folk Songs* (with J. Murray Gibbon, 1927). Composer: *Peggy and the Pirate* (1927); *The Smiling Sixpence* (1930); *Rogues and Vagabonds* (prod. 1930); *Harmony Hall* (1933); *Little Women* (1939); and other operettas. Among his songs are "K-K-K-Katy," "Wreck of the Julie Plante," "There Is No Death," etc.

O'HARA, JOHN [Henry] (Jan. 31, 1905–Apr. 11, 1970); b. Pottsville, Pa. Novelist. *Appointment in Samarra* (1934); *The Doctor's Son, and Other Stories* (1935); *Butterfield 8* (1935); *Hope of Heaven* (1938); *Files on Parade* (1939); *Pal Joey* (1940); *Pipe Night* (1945); *Here's O'Hara* (1946); *Hellbox* (1947); *A Rage to Live* (1949); *The Farmer's Hotel* (1951); *Sweet and Sour* (essays, 1954); *Ten North Frederick* (1955); *A Family Party* (1956); *From the Terrace* (1958); *Ourselves to Know* (1960); *Assembly* (1961); *Five Plays* (1961); *The Cape Cod Lighter* (1962); *The Big Laugh* (1962); *Elizabeth Appleton* (1963); *The Hat on the Bed* (1963); *The Horse Knows the Way* (1964); *The Lockwood Concern* (1965); *My Turn* (essays, 1966); *Waiting for Winter* (1966); *The Instrument* (1967); *And Other Stories* (1968); etc.

O'HARA, MARY (Mrs. Helge Sture-Vasa) (July 10, 1885–); b. Cape May Point, N.J. Composer, author. *My Friend Flicka* (1941); *Thunderhead* (1943); *Green Grass of Wyoming* (1946); *Son of Adam Wyngate* (1952); *Novel in the Making* (autobiography, 1954); *Wyoming Summer* (1963); *A Musical in the Making* (1966). Composer, "Esperan" (1943); "May God Keep You" (1946); *The Catch Colt* (a musical play, 1961); etc.

O'HARA, NEAL [Russell] (June 19, 1893–Oct. 4, 1962); b. Middleboro, Mass. Columnist, author. *Take It from Me* (1939); *Thoughts While Shaving* (1946). Columnist, *New York Evening World,* 1919–31; columnist for McNaught syndicate, from 1931.

O'HARA, THEODORE (Feb. 11, 1820–June 6, 1867); b. Danville, Ky. Soldier, journalist, poet. He is best known for his poem "The Bivouac of the Dead" (1847) and his eulogy on William Taylor Barry. *See* George W. Ranck's *O'Hara and His Elegies* (1875); and Edgar Erskine Hume's *Colonel Theodore O'Hara* (1936).

O'HIGGINS, HARVEY (Nov. 14, 1876–Feb. 28, 1929); b. London, Ont. Novelist, journalist, playwright. *The Smoke Eaters* (1905); *Don-a-Dreams* (1906); *Old Clinkers* (1909); *The Argyle Case* (with Harriet Ford 1913); *The Dummy* (with same, prod. 1914); *Mr. Lazarus* (with same, prod. 1916); *On the Hiring Line* (with same, prod. 1919); *Some Distinguished Americans* (1922); *The American Mind in Action* (with Edward H. Reade, 1924); *Julie Cane* (1924); *Clara Barron* (1926).

Ohiyesa. See Charles Alexander Eastman.

O'KANE, WALTER COLLINS (Nov. 10, 1877–); b. Columbus, O. Entomologist, author. *Jim and Peggy at Meadowbrook Farm* (1917); *Jim and Peggy at Apple-top Farm* (1923); *Trails and Summits of the White Mountains* (1925); *Trails and Summits of the Green Mountains* (1926); *Trails and Summits of the Adirondacks* (1928); *The Hopis: Portrait of a Desert People* (1953); *Cabin* (1955); *Beyond the Cabin Door* (1957); etc.

Oklahoma! Musical comedy by Richard Rodgers and Oscar Hammerstein II (1943).

Oklahoma City Oklahoman. Oklahoma City, Okla. Newspaper. Founded 1894. The *Oklahoma City Times,* founded 1889, absorbed the *Oklahoma Journal* (founded 1889) in 1891, as the *Oklahoma Times.* The *Times* merged later with the *Oklahoman.* The *Oklahoman* appears mornings; the *Times* appears evenings, except Sunday. E. K. Gaylord edits both; Edith Copeland is book review editor.

Oklahoma City Times. See *Oklahoma City Oklahoman.*

Ol' Man Adam an' His Chillun. By Roark Bradford (1928). Tales of Negro life based on their religious beliefs. These stories became the basis of the play *Green Pastures* by Marc Connelly.

O'LAUGHLIN, JOHN CALLAN (Jan. 11, 1873–Mar. 14, 1949); b. Washington, D.C. Author. *From the Jungle through Europe with Roosevelt* (1910); *Imperiled America* (1916); etc.

OLCOTT, CHARLES SUMNER (Feb. 20, 1864–May 3, 1935); b. Cambridge, Mass. Publisher, author. *George Eliot: Scenes and People in Her Novels* (1910); *The Country of Sir Walter Scott* (1913); *The Life of William McKinley* (1916); etc. General manager, private library dept., Houghton, Mifflin Co., Boston, 1891–1933.

OLCOTT, CHAUNCEY [Chancellor John] (July 21, 1860–Mar. 18, 1932); b. Buffalo, N.Y. Actor, singer, song-writer, minstrel, author. *The Irish Artist* (1894). Wrote the popular song "My Wild Irish Rose." He introduced the song "Mother Machree" to American audiences. One of his star performances was in Rida J. Young's *Macushla* (prod. 1912).

OLCOTT, FRANCES JENKINS, b. Paris. Compiler: *The Children's Reading* (1912); *Good Stories for Great Holidays* (1914); *Book of Elves and Fairies* (1918); *Story Telling Ballads* (1920); *Wonder Tales from China Seas* (1925); *Good Stories for Great Birthdays* (1927); *Wonder Tales from Pirate Isles* (1927); *Good Stories for Anniversaries* (1937); *The Bridge of Caravans* (1940); *In the Bright Syrian Land* (1946); etc. Weekly contributor, *New York Evening Post,* 1916–20.

OLCOTT, HENRY STEEL (Aug. 2, 1832–Feb. 17, 1907); b. Orange, N.J. Theosophist leader, author. *People from the Other World* (1875); *Theosophy, Religion and Occult Languages* (1885); *Old Diary Leaves,* 3v. (1895, 1900, 1904); etc. President, the Theosophical Society, Sept., 1875; editor of the *Theosophist,* 1879–1907.

OLCOTT, VIRGINIA, b. Albany, N.Y. Author. *Jean and Fanchon, Children of France* (1931); *Erik and Britta, Children of Flowery Sweden* (1937); and similar books for children on national types. Compiler: *Everyday Plays* (1916); *Holiday Plays* (1917); *Patriotic Plays* (1918); *Household Plays* (1928); etc.

OLCOTT, WILLIAM TYLER (Jan. 11, 1873–July 6, 1936); b. Chicago, Ill. Author. *Star Lore of All Ages* (1911); and other popular books on astronomy.

Old and New. Boston, Mass. Magazine. Founded Jan., 1870. Edward Everett Hale, Jr. was editor, 1870–75. Charles Dudley Warner's "Sorrento" was serialized in its pages in 1872. Robert Dale Owen and Julia Ward Howe were also contributors. Absorbed by *Scribner's Monthly,* 1875.

"Old Armchair, The." Poem by Eliza Cook (1840). It was first published in England in 1839.

Old Bachelor, An. Pen name of George William Curtis.

Old Bachelor, The. Addisonian essays by William Wirt (1812).

"Old Black Joe." Song by Stephen Foster (1860).

Old Block. Pen name of Alonzo Delano.

Old Chester Tales. By Margaret Deland (1895). Short stories of the Pennsylvania Presbyterians.

"Old Clock on the Stairs." Poem by Henry Wadsworth Longfellow (1845).

Old Creole Days. By George W. Cable (1879). Collection of eight stories depicting the life of the Creoles in Louisiana.

"Old Dan Tucker." Minstrel song by Daniel Decatur Emmett (1830).

"Old Folks at Home, The." Song by Stephen Foster (1851). First line is "Way down upon the Suwanee River."

"Old Grimes." Humorous poem by Albert Gorton Greene, which first appeared in the *Providence Gazette,* Jan. 16, 1822.

Old Guard. New York. "Copperhead" monthly. Founded 1862. Editor, C. Chauncey Burr. Expired 1870.

Old Homestead, The. Novel by Ann S. Stephens (1855). Dramatized by George L. Aiken (prod. 1856).

Old Homestead, The. Play by Denman Thompson (prod. 1886). Based on a character sketch first presented 1875, and then augmented to a three-act comedy, *Joshua Whitcomb* (prod. 1877). Thompson played the leading role, and the play ran for many years as a popular road show.

Old Judge Priest. Stories by Irvin S. Cobb (1915). Small town life in Kentucky as revealed by the wise and humorous old judge.

Old Jules. Biography by Mari Sandoz (1935). Chronicle of Nebraska farm life in pioneer days. "Old Jules" was Jules Sandoz, the author's father.

Old Maid, The. Novel by Edith Wharton (1924), dramatized by Zoë Akins (prod. 1935). Story of Tina, illegitimate daughter of Charlotte Lovell, who is brought up by Charlotte's sister Delia, in complete ignorance of her parentage. She looks upon Charlotte as an old maid. Pulitzer Prize play, 1935.

"Old Man and Jim, The." Civil War poem by James Whitcomb Riley (1888).

Old Man and the Sea, The. Novelette by Ernest Hemingway (1952). An old Cuban fisherman rows into the Gulf Stream in quest of marlin. He catches an enormous marlin after a tremendous struggle but is forced to fight off sharks that attack the fish lashed to his boat. When he returns to land, the marlin is nothing but a shark-stripped skeleton. The novelette ends on a note of pride as the exhausted old man sleeps off his weariness dreaming of his prowess as a youth.

Old New York. By Edith Wharton (1924). Four novelettes, each dealing with a decade, from 1840 to 1880.

"Old Oaken Bucket, The." Poem by Samuel Woodworth. It first appeared in the New York *Republican-Chronicle* in 1817, under the title "The Bucket." Set to music c. 1834, it became one of America's most popular songs, and was often parodied.

Old School, Oliver. Pen name used by Joseph Dennie as editor of the *Port Folio,* and continued by his successor.

"Old Sergeant, The." Poem by Forceythe Willson (1863). Death scene of a nameless soldier wounded at Shiloh in the Civil War.

Old Soak, The. By Don Marquis (1920). A pleasant satire on the Prohibition Era, the story of a chronic but genial alcoholic.

Old Stager. Pen name of William Taylor Adams.

"Old Sweetheart of Mine, An." Poem by James Whitcomb Riley (1877).

Old Swimmin'-Hole, and 'Leven More Poems, The. By James Whitcomb Riley (1883). Dialect poems which marked the beginning of Riley's popularity as the poet of the people.

Old Town Folks. By Harriet Beecher Stowe (1869). A story of Colonial life in Natick, Mass.

Old West. Austin, Tex. Quarterly. Founded 1964. Published by Western Publications, Inc. Concerned with Western Americana.

"Old Zip Coon." Popular minstrel song first sung by Bob Farrell at the Bowery Theatre, New York, Aug. 11, 1834.

OLDENBURG, CLAES [Thure] (Jan. 28, 1929–); b. Stockholm, Sweden. Artist. *Store Days and Ray Gun Theatre* (1967); *Claes Oldenburg: Proposals for Monuments and Buildings, 1965–69* (1969).

OLDER, CORA MIRANDA [Baggery] (Mrs. Fremont Older); b. Clyde, N.Y. Author. *Esther Damon* (1911); *Savages and Saints* (1936); *William Randolph Hearst, American* (1936); *California Missions and Their Romances* (1938); *Love Stories of Old California* (1940); *San Francisco, Magic City* (1961); etc.

OLDS, ELIZABETH (Dec. 10, 1897–); b. Minneapolis, Minn. Artist, author. Author, illustrator: *The Big Fire* (1946); *Riding the Rails* (1948); *Feather Mountain* (1951); *Deep Treasure* (1958); *Plop Plop Ploppie* (1962); *Little Una* (1963); etc.

Oldstyle, Jonathan. Pen name of Washington Irving.

"Ole Shady: The Song of the Contraband." Poem by Benjamin R. Hanby (1861).

OLIN, STEPHEN (Mar. 2, 1797–Aug. 16, 1851); b. Leicester, Vt. Methodist clergyman, educator, author. *Travels in Egypt, Arabia, Petraea, and the Holy Land,* 2v. (1843); *The Works,* 2v. (1852); *The Life and Letters of Stephen Olin,* 2v. (1853–54); *Greece and the Golden Horn* (1854); etc. President, Randolph-Macon College, 1834–37; president, Wesleyan University, 1842–51.

OLIVER, DOUGLAS LLEWELLYN (Feb. 10, 1913–); b. Ruston, La. Anthropologist. *Studies in the Anthropology of Bougainville* (1949); *The Pacific Islands* (1951); *A Solomon Island Society* (1955); *Invitation to Anthropology* (1964); *Ancient Tahitian Society* (1969); etc. Anthropology dept., Harvard University, since 1950.

OLIVER, GRACE A[tkinson] (Sept. 24, 1844–99); b. Boston, Mass. Author. *Life and Works of Anna L. Barbauld* (1873); *A Study of Maria Edgeworth* (1882); *Arthur Penrhyn Stanley* (1885).

OLIVER, JOHN RATHBONE (Jan. 4, 1872–Jan. 21, 1943); b. Albany, N.Y. Episcopal clergyman, educator, psychiatrist, author. *Fear* (1927); *Victim and Victor* (1928); *Four square* (1929); *Rock and Sand* (1930); *Article Thirty-Two* (1931); *Priest or Pagan* (1933); *Spontaneous Combustion* (1937); etc. Prof. history of medicine, Johns Hopkins University, from 1930.

OLIVER, PETER (Mar. 26, 1713–Oct., 1791); b. Boston, Mass. Loyalist, author. *Poem Sacred to the Memory of the Honorable Josiah Willard* (1757); *The Scripture Lexicon* (1787); etc.

Oliver Optic's Magazine. Boston, Mass. Juvenile magazine. Founded Jan. 5, 1867. Published by Lee & Shepard. Noted for its serials for young readers, mostly written by William T. Adams ("Oliver Optic"), who was its editor. Expired Dec., 1875.

Oliver Wiswell. Novel by Kenneth Roberts (1940). Story of the Loyalists during the American Revolution, purporting to show their cultural superiority over the rabble that made up a large part of the forces opposed to England.

Olivia Delaplaine. Novel by Edgar Fawcett (1888). A satire on Anglomania.

OLMSTEAD, A[lbert] T[en Eyck] (Mar. 23, 1880–Apr. 11, 1945); b. Troy, N.Y. Educator, historian. *Travels and Studies in the Nearer East* (1911); *History of Assyria* (1923); *History of Palestine and Syria* (1931); *Jesus in the Light of History* (1942); etc. Prof. history, University of Illinois, 1917–29; Oriental Institute, University of Chicago, from 1929.

OLMSTEAD, FLORENCE, b. Beaulieu, Ga. Author. *Mrs. Eli and Policy Ann* (1912); *A Cloistered Romance* (1915); *Father Bernard's Parish* (1916); *On Furlough* (1918); *Stafford's Island* (1920).

OLMSTED, FREDERICK LAW (Apr. 26, 1822–Aug. 28, 1903); b. Hartford, Conn. Landscape architect, traveler, author. *Walks and Talks of an American Farmer in England* (1852); *A Journey in the Seaboard Slave States* (1856); *A Journey through Texas* (1857); *A Journey in the Back Country* (1860). The latter three books were condensed and published as *The Cotton Kingdom*, 2v. (1861–62). He helped lay out Central Park in New York, designed Prospect Park in Brooklyn, Franklin Park in Boston, the World's Fair in Chicago in 1893, and many other parks and private estates. *See* F. L. Olmsted, Jr., and Theodora Kimball's *Frederick Law Olmsted, Landscape Architect, 1822–1903*, 2v. (1922–28); Broadus Mitchell's *Frederick Law Olmsted* (1924, 1968); Julius Fabos' and others', *Frederick Law Olmsted: Founder of Landscape Architecture in America* (1968).

OLMSTED, MILLICENT (d. June 3, 1939); b. Cleveland, O. Author. *The Land That Never Was* (1908); *The Land of Really True* (1909); *Harmony Wins* (1913); etc.

Olney, Ellen Warner. See Ellen Warner Olney Kirk.

OLSON, CHARLES (Dec. 27, 1910–Jan. 10, 1970); b. Worcester, Mass. Poet, critic. *Call Me Ishmael* (1947); *Y & X* (poems, 1950); *The Maximus Poems 1–10* (1953); *The Maximus Poems 11–22* (1956); *The Maximus Poems* (1960); *The Distances* (1961); *Apellez-Moi Ishmael* (1962); *Human Universe* (1965); *Selected Writings* (1967); *Letters for Origin* (1969); etc. *See* Edward Dorn's *What I See in the Maximus Poems* (1960).

OLSON, ELDER [James] (Mar. 9, 1909–); b. Chicago, Ill. Educator, author. *The Poetry of Dylan Thomas* (1954); *Scarecrow Christ, and Other Poems* (1954); *Plays and Poems, 1948–58* (1958); etc. English dept., University of Chicago, since 1942.

OLSON, ERNST WILLIAM (Mar. 16, 1870–Oct. 6, 1958); b. in Sweden. Editor, author. *History of the Swedes of Illinois*, 2v. (1908); *The Augustana Book Concern: A History* (1934); etc. With Augustana Book Concern, Rock Island, Ill., 1911–49.

OLSON, JAMES CLIFTON (Jan. 23, 1917–); b. Bradgate, Iowa. Educator, author. *J. Sterling Morton* (1942); *History of Nebraska* (1955); *Nebraska is my Home* (with V. F. Olson, 1956); *This Is Nebraska* (1960); *Red Cloud and the Sioux Problem* (1965).

OLSON, TED (Apr. 18, 1899–); b. Laramie, Wyo. Journalist, poet. *A Stranger and Afraid* (1928); *Hawk's Way* (poems, 1941). Editor, the *Republican-Boomerang*, Laramie, Wyo., 1928–38.

Omaha World-Herald. Omaha, Neb. Newspaper. The *Omaha Daily Herald*, founded 1865; the *Omaha Daily World*, founded 1885. Merged 1889. Published by the World Publishing Co. W. E. Christenson is editor. Victor P. Hass is book review editor.

O'MALLEY, FRANK WARD (Nov. 30, 1875–Oct. 19, 1932); b. Pittston, Pa. Journalist, playwright. *The Head of the House* (with E. W. Townsend, prod. 1909); *A Certain Party* (with same, prod. 1910); *The War-Whirl in Washington* (1918); *The Swiss Family O'Malley* (1928); etc. With *New York Sun*, 1906–20. *See* Frederick M. O'Brien's *The Story of the Sun* (1918). Irvin S. Cobb calls him "Malley of the Sun" in his *Judge Priest* stories.

O'MEARA, WALTER ANDREW (Jan. 29, 1897–); b. Minneapolis, Minn. Author. *The Trees Went Forth* (1947); *The Grand Portage* (1951); *Tales of the Two Borders* (1952); *The Spanish Bride* (1954); *Minnesota Gothic* (1956); *The Devil's Cross* (1957); *Savage Country* (1960); *The Last Portage* (1962); *Guns at the Forks* (1965); *The Duke of War* (1966); *Mountain Men* (1968); etc.

Omnibook. New York. Monthly digest of books. Founded 1938. Discontinued 1957.

Omoo. Romance by Herman Melville (1847). Story of Tahiti in the days of the whaling ships.

On Architecture. By Frank Lloyd Wright (1941). Selected writings on architecture of the years 1894–1940.

On Being a Real Person. By Harry Emerson Fosdick (1943). Understanding oneself through the moral application of psychology to everyday life.

"On Board the Cumberland." Civil War poem by George Henry Boker (1862). Describes the attack made upon the *Cumberland* by the *Merrimac*.

On Borrowed Time. Novel by Lawrence Edward Watkins (1937), dramatized by Paul Osborn (prod. 1937). Story of an old man, Gramps, and his grandson, Pud. Death, disguised as Mr. Brink, comes to call for Gramps, who imprisons him in an apple tree.

On Literature Today. Critical work by Van Wyck Brooks (1941).

On National Literature. Significant critical article by William Ellery Channing in the *Christian Examiner* (1830).

On Native Grounds. Critical survey of modern American literature, by Alfred Kazin (1942).

"On Retirement." Poem by Philip Freneau (1786), written under the pen name "Hezekiah Salem."

"On the Banks of the Wabash, Far Away." Song by Paul Dresser (1896).

"On the Death of Joseph Rodman Drake." Poem by Fitz-Greene Halleck which first appeared in the *Literary and Scientific Repository*, Jan., 1821. It was written shortly after Drake's death on Sept. 21, 1820.

On the Freedom of the Will. By Jonathan Edwards (1754). The book which, probably more than any other, was responsible for the development of strict Calvinism in American religious thought.

On the Road. Novel by Jack Kerouac (1957). First novel on the Beat Generation to win wide attention. The characters are morally hedonistic, though they have a strong sense of camaraderie, and find their fulfillment in sex, physical speed, uninhibited talk, and philosophical generalizations. They refuse to join the "rat race" of the workaday world in a time characterized by fear of nuclear warfare and desperate clinging to economic security. Kerouac's other novels treat these themes in different circumstances.

On the Transient and Permanent in Christianity. Sermon by Theodore Parker (1841). This sermon is a landmark in the history of Unitarianism.

"On to Richmond." Civil War poem by John R. Thompson.

ONDERDONK, HENRY (June 11, 1804–June 22, 1886); b. North Hempstead, L.I., N.Y. Historian of Long Island. *Queens County in Olden Times* (1865); etc. Compiler: *The Bibliography of Long Island* (1866); etc.

ONDERDONK, HENRY USTICK (Mar. 16, 1789–Dec. 6, 1858); b. New York. Episcopal bishop, hymn writer, author. *An Appeal to the Religious Public of Canandaigua* (1813), and a number of books on the Episcopacy.

One-Dimensional Man (1965). A critique relying upon Marxist and Freudian theory and concerned with the essentially repressive nature of modern "post-industrial" society, by Herbert Marcuse (1965).

One Flew over the Cuckoo's Nest. Novel by Ken Kesey (1962).

One Hundred Dollar Misunderstanding, The. Novel by Robert Gover (1962). Southern white sexual racism and smugness revealed in an encounter with a Southern black teenage prostitute.

One Magazine. Los Angeles, Calif. Founded 1952. Deals with the viewpoint of the homosexual in modern society, in articles, fiction, poetry, art, and humor. Also publishes *One Institute Quarterly of Homophile Studies,* founded 1958. This quarterly has been devoted to scientific, historical, and moral studies on the significance and nature of homosexuality.

One Man's Meat. Essays by E. B. White (1942).

One More Spring. Novel by Robert Nathan (1933). The story of an unemployed man who spends a winter in Central Park, New York, and helps a pair of lovers find unexpected happiness.

One Woman's Life. Novel by Robert Herrick (1913). Milly Ridge, selfish and ambitious, pursues her ends regardless of the consequences to her friends.

One World. By Wendell Willkie (1943). The internationalist philosophy of a former liberal Republican nominee for the presidency.

One-Dimensional Man (1965). A critique relying upon Marxist and Freudian theory and concerned with the essentially repressive nature of modern "post-industrial" society, by Herbert Marcuse (1965).

O'NEALE, MARGARET L. (Mrs. John B. Timberlake; Mrs. John Henry Eaton) (1796–Nov. 8, 1879); b. Washington, D.C. Known as "Peggy O'Neale" and "Peggy Eaton." Author of *The Autobiography of Peggy Eaton* (1932). *See* Alfred H. Lewis's *Peggy O'Neal* (1903); Channing Pollock's *Peggy Eaton, Democracy's Mistress* (1931); and Samuel Hopkins Adams's *The Gorgeous Hussy* (1934).

O'NEILL, CHARLES KENDALL (1909–). Author. *Morning Time* (1949); *Wild Train* (1956).

O'NEILL, EUGENE [Gladstone] (Oct. 16, 1888–Nov. 27, 1953); b. New York. Playwright. The following dates are those of production. *Thirst* (1916); *The Moon of the Caribbees* (1918); *Beyond the Horizon* (1920, Pulitzer Prize play, 1920); *The Emperor Jones* (1920); *Diff'rent* (1920); *Gold* (1921); *Anna Christie* (1921, Pulitzer Prize play, 1922); *The Straw* (1921); *The First Man* (1922); *The Hairy Ape* (1922); *The Fountain* (1923); *Desire under the Elms* (1924); *The Great God Brown* (1926); *Lazarus Laughed* (1927); *Marco Millions* (1928); *Strange Interlude* (1928, Pulitzer Prize play, 1928); *Dynamo* (1929); *Mourning Becomes Electra* (1931); *Ah, Wilderness* (1933); *Days without End* (1933); *The Iceman Cometh* (1946); *A Moon for the Misbegotten* (1952); *Long Day's Journey Into Night* (1956); *A Touch of the Poet* (1957); etc. His collected plays were published as *The Plays*, 12v. (1934–35), followed by *Lost Plays* (1950); *Ten "Lost" Plays* (1963). O'Neill was awarded the Nobel Prize in literature, 1936. *See* Barrett H. Clark's *Eugene O'Neill* (1936); Edwin A. Engel's *The Haunted Heroes of Eugene O'Neill* (1953); Arthur and Barbara Gelb's *O'Neill* (1962); Clifford Leech's *Eugene O'Neill* (1963); John Raleigh's *The Plays of Eugene O'Neill* (1965); Jordan Miller's *Playwright's Progress: O'Neill and the Critics* (1965).

O'NEILL, ROSE CECIL (Mrs. Rose Cecil O'Neill Wilson) (1874–Apr. 7, 1944); b. Wilkes-Barré, Pa. Illustrator, inventor of the "Kewpie," author. *The Loves of Edwy* (1904); *The Lady in the White Veil* (1909); *The Master-Mistress* (poems, 1922).

ONG, WALTER JACKSON (Nov. 30, 1912–); b. Kansas City, Mo. Roman Catholic clergyman, educator. *Frontiers in American Catholicism* (1957); *Ramus and Talon Inventory* (1959); *American Catholic Crossroads* (1959); *In the Human Grain: Further Explorations of Contemporary Culture* (1967); etc. English dept., St. Louis University, since 1953.

Only in America. By Harry Golden (1958). Collection of essays and editorials from the author's unique periodical, *The Carolina Israelite.* Politics, race relations, social friction, and other topics are pungently and wryly commented on from the viewpoint of a Jew who was brought up on the Lower East Side of New York and later moved to the South.

Only Yesterday. History of recent events, happenings, fads, and fancies by F. L. Allen (1931).

Onoto Watanna. Pen name of Winnifred Babcock.

OPDYCKE, JOHN BAKER (Feb. 28, 1878–Nov. 3, 1956); b. Doylestown, Pa. Author. Pen name "Oliver Opdyke." *The Lure of Life* (poems, 1910); *The Unfathomable Sorrow* (poems, 1910); *Amor Vitaque* (poems, 1912); *The Literature of Letters* (1925); *Telling Types in Literature* (1939); *Say What You Mean* (1944); *Lexicon of Word Selection* (1950); and books on business English, etc.

Opdyke, Oliver. Pen name of John Baker Opdyke.

Open Boat, The. Story by Stephen Crane (1898). It describes a shipwreck off the coast of Florida in 1896.

Open Court. Chicago, Ill. Monthly magazine. Founded 1887 by Edward C. Hegeler. Editor, Paul Carus, 1887–1919. Devoted to an effort to put religion and ethics on a purely scientific basis. Hegeler also founded *The Monist,* a quarterly, in 1890, with Carus as editor. Edward Leroy Schaub was editor,

1926–36. Both magazines expired in 1936. The Open Court Publishing Co. was established to publish the magazines and many books of similar nature.

Operation Sidewinder. Play by Sam Shepard (prod. 1970). Fantasy about a computer that starts a war.

OPPEN, GEORGE (Apr. 24, 1908–); b. New Rochelle, N.Y. Author. *Discrete Series* (1934); *The Materials* (1962); *This in Which* (1965); *On Being Numerous* (1968; Pulitzer Prize 1969).

OPPENHEIM, JAMES (May 24, 1882–Aug. 4, 1932); b. St. Paul, Minn. Poet, novelist. *Monday Morning, and Other Poems* (1909); *Doctor Rast* (1909); *Wild Oats* (1910); *The Pioneers* (1910); *The Nine-Tenths* (1911); *Songs for the New Age* (1914); *The Beloved* (1915); *War and Laughter* (1916); *The Book of Self* (1917); *Golden Bird* (1923); *The Sea* (1924); etc.

OPPENHEIMER, GEORGE (Feb. 7, 1900–); b. New York. Drama critic, author. *The View from the Sixties* (1966); *Here Today* (play, 1932). Editor: *The Passionate Playgoer* (1958). Critic, *Newsday,* since 1955.

OPPENHEIMER, JOEL [Lester] (Feb. 18, 1930–); b. Yonkers, N.Y. Poet. *The Dancer* (1952); *The Dutiful Son* (1957); *The Love Bit* (1962); *The Great American Desert; In Tune: Poems, 1962–1968* (1969). Editor: *Kulchur 5.*

OPPER, FREDERICK BURR (Jan. 2, 1857–Aug. 29, 1937); b. Madison, O. Cartoonist, author. *Our Antediluvian Ancestors* (1902); *Happy Hooligan* (1902); *Alphonse and Gaston* (1902); *John Bull* (1903); etc. Illustrator of works by "Mark Twain," "Bill Nye," George Vere Hobart, Finley Peter Dunne, and others.

"Opportunity." Sonnet by John J. Ingalls (1891). It begins with the lines: "Master of human destiny am I! Fame, love and fortune on my footsteps wait." Republished in *A Collection of the Writings of John James Ingalls* (1902). Often confused with "Opportunity" by Walter Malone, which appeared in his *Songs of East and West* (1906), with "Opportunity" by Charles Warren Stoddard, and with "Opportunity" by Edward Rowland Sill.

Optic, Oliver. Pen name of William Taylor Adams.

Options. Short stories by "O. Henry" (1909).

Oralloosa, Son of the Incas. Play by Robert Montgomery Bird (prod. 1832). A tragedy of Peru.

ORCUTT, WILLIAM DANA (Apr. 18, 1870–Nov. 28, 1953); b. Lebanon, N.H. Book and type designer, book collector, author. *The Flower of Destiny* (1905); *The Moth* (1912); *The Author's Desk Book* (1914); *In Quest of the Perfect Book* (1926); *The Kingdom of Books* (1927); *Master Makers of the Book* (1928); *The Gorgeous Adventures of Benvenuto Cellini* (1931); *Celebrities off Parade* (1925); *Escape to Laughter* (1942); *From My Library Walls* (1945); *Mary Baker Eddy and Her Books* (1950); and many books on books and bookmaking. Associated with the Plimpton Press, etc.

Ordeal by Hunger. By George Stewart (1936). Story of the Donner catastrophe south of the Great Salt Lake.

Ordeal of the Union. Historical study by Allen Nevins, 2v. (1947). Treats the period 1847–1857. Its sequel is *The Emergence of Lincoln,* 2v. (1950).

Ordways, The. Novel by William Humphrey (1965). An epic study of four generations of a family in East Texas.

Oregon Journal. Portland, Ore. Newspaper. Founded 1902, as the *Portland Evening Journal;* name soon changed to present one. Fred Lockley, historical writer, joined the staff in 1911. Arden X. Pangborn is editor. Ed Goetzel is book review editor.

O'REILLY, JOHN BOYLE (June 28, 1844–Aug. 10, 1890); b. Castle Dowth, Ire. Editor, poet. *Songs from the Southern Seas, and Other Poems* (1873); *Songs, Legends, and Ballads* (1878); *The Statues in the Block, and Other Poems* (1881); *In Bohemia* (1886); *Moondyne* (1879); *The King's Men* (1884); *Selected Poems* (1913); etc. Co-owner and editor of the *Pilot,* Boston, beginning in 1876. See J. J. Roche's *Life of John Boyle O'Reilly* (1891); E. P. Mitchell's *Memoirs of an Editor* (1924).

Organization Man, The. By William H. Whyte, Jr. (1956). Spirited analysis of the new cooperative spirit in business and industry in which talent becomes subordinated to the desire to belong to a group. As the "rugged individualism" of business leaders has been softened through greater social consciousness, so the ambition of the white-collar job seeker has been diluted into the need to "get along with others" through greater security consciousness.

ORGANSKI, A[bramo] F[imo] K[enneth] (May 17, 1923–); b. Rome, Italy. Educator, author. *World Politcs* (1958); *Population and World Power* (with K. Organski, 1961); *Stages of Population Development* (1965). Professor of political science, University of Michigan, since 1964.

Origin. Dorchester, Mass. Quarterly of literature. Founded 1951. Expired 1957.

Original Narratives of Early American History. Ed. by J. Franklin Jameson, 19v. (1906–19), published by Charles Scribner's Sons. Texts of various early travels and explorations from the year 985 to 1708.

Orion Press, The. New York. Founded 1957 by Howard Greenfeld. Publishes books of serious interest, both fiction and nonfiction, including translations. Noted for book design and typography. Now merged with Grossman Publishers (q.v.).

ORLOVSKY, PETER (July 8, 1933–); b. New York. Poet. Contributor to *Beatitude Anthology* (1960); *The New American Poetry: 1945–1960* (1960).

Ormond. Novel by Charles Brockden Brown (1799). Constantia Dudley is pursued by a philosophical villain, Ormond, and she is forced to kill him in self-defense.

Ormond, Frederic. Pen name of Frederic Van Rensselaer Dey.

Ormsbee, David. Pen name of Stephen Longstreet.

ORMSBEE, THOMAS HAMILTON (Aug. 25, 1890–Aug. 4, 1969); b. Brooklyn, N.Y. Author. *Early American Furniture Makers* (1930); *The Story of American Furniture* (1934); *Care and Repair of Antiques* (1949); *Know Your Heirlooms* (1956); etc.

ORNITZ, SAMUEL [Badisch] (Nov. 15, 1890–Mar., 1957); b. New York. Author. *Haunch, Paunch, and Jowl* (1923); *Bride of the Sabbath* (1951); etc.

O'ROURKE, FRANK (1916–). Author. *Action at Three Peaks* (1945); *Never Come Back* (1952); *High Dive* (1954); *Last Ride* (1958); *Window in the Dark* (1960); *Springtime Fancy* (1961); *Swift Runner* (1969); *Abduction of Virginia Lee* (1970); etc.

Orphan Angel, The. Story by Elinor Wylie (1926). An imaginary tale of the supposed wanderings in foreign lands of the poet Shelley, whom the author calls Shiloh. *Mr. Hodge and Mr. Hazard* is a sequel in which Mr. Hazard (Shelley) comes back to England as Shelley might have done had he lived.

Orpheus C. Kerr Papers, The. By Robert Henry Newell, 3v. (1862–65). Collection of the author's newspaper sketches in the civil War, chiefly the exploits of the "Mackerel Brigade," a pun on the name of General McClellan. "Orpheus C. Kerr" was a pun for office-seeker.

Orphic Sayings. Essays contributed by Bronson Alcott to the *Dial,* 1839–42.

ORR, MYRON DAVID. Author. *Cathedral of the Pines* (1938); *The Citadel of the Lake* (1952); *Mission to Mackinac* (1956); *The Outlander* (1959); etc.

Orth, Richard. See Richard Gardner.

ORTON, HELEN FULLER (Mrs. Jesse F. Orton) (Nov. 1, 1872–Feb. 16, 1955); b. Pekin, N.Y. Author. *The Cloverfield Farm* series, 4v. (1921–26); *The Gold-Laced Coat: A Story of Niagara* (1934); *The Secret of the Rosewood Box* (1937); *A Lad of Old Williamsburg* (1938); *The Winding River* (1944); *Mystery of the Apple Orchard* (1954); etc.

ORTON, JAMES (Apr. 21, 1830–Sept. 22, 1877). Zoologist, explorer, educator, author. *The Andes and the Amazon* (1870). Compiler: *The Proverbialist and the Poet* (1852).

ORTON, JASON ROCKWOOD (1806–Feb. 13, 1867); b. Hamilton, N.Y. Author. *Poetical Sketches* (1829); *Arnold, and Other Poems* (1854); *Camp-Fires and the Red Men* (1855); etc.

ORTON, VREST TEACHOUT (Sept. 3, 1897–); b. Hardwick, Vt. Typographer, printer, editor, publisher. *Dreiserana* (1929); *A Line of Men 100 Years Long* (1936); *Mary Fletcher Comes Back* (1939); *Vermont Academy Way* (1945). Contributor: *A Treasury of Vermont Life* (1956). Founder, *Vermont Life;* founder, the Stephen Daye Press, 1930; co-founder, *The Colophon,* 1930; president and editor, the Countryman Press. Columnist for the *Rutland (Vt.) Herald.* Formerly with *American Mercury, Saturday Review of Literature,* Limited Editions Club, Merrymount Press, etc.

ORTON, WILLIAM AYLOTT (Feb. 9, 1889–Aug. 13, 1952); b. Bromley, Kent, Eng. Economist, author. *Prelude to Economics* (1932); *America in Search of Culture* (1933); *The Last Romantic* (1937); *The Twenty Years' Armistice, 1918–38* (1938); *The Liberal Tradition* (1945); *The Challenge of Christian Liberalism* (1946); *The Economic Role of the State* (1950); etc. Prof. economics, Smith College, 1922–52.

ORWIG, CLARA B., b. Mifflinburg, Pa. Playwright. *Black and Blue* (1926); *The Charley Horse* (1931); *Clearing Skies* (with Joseph C. McMullen, 1936).

Osander. Pen name of Benjamin Allen.

OSBON, BRADLEY SILLICK (Aug. 16, 1828–May 6, 1912); b. Rye, N.Y. Naval officer, journalist, editor, author. *Osbon's Handbook of the United States Navy* (1863); *A Sailor of Fortune* (1906). Founder and editor, *The Nautical Gazette,* 1871. Naval correspondent for *New York World* and *New York Herald* during the Civil War. His eyewitness account of the fall of Fort Sumter, written for the *World,* was a celebrated newspaper "scoop." He was signal officer for Admiral Farragut.

OSBORN, FAIRFIELD (Jan. 15, 1887–Sept. 16, 1969); b. Princeton, N.J. Naturalist, author. *Our Plundered Planet* (1948); *The Limits of the Earth* (1953). Editor: *Pacific World* (1946).

OSBORN, HENRY FAIRFIELD (Aug. 8, 1857–Nov. 6, 1935); b. Fairfield, Conn. Educator, paleontologist, author. *From the Greeks to Darwin (1894);* *The Age of Mammals* (1910); *Huxley and Education* (1910); *Men of the Old Stone Age* (1915); *Impressions of Great Naturalists* (1924); *Creative Education* (1927); *Man Rises to Parnassus* (1927); *Fifty-Two Years of Research* (1930); *Cope, Master Naturalist* (1931); etc. Prof. biology and zoology, Columbia University, 1891–1935. With the American Museum of Natural History, New York, 1891–1935.

OSBORN, LAUGHTON (c. 1800–Dec. 14, 1878); b. New York. Poet, playwright. *Sixty Years of the Life of Jeremy Levis,* 2v. (anon., 1831); *Confessions of a Poet,* 2v. (anon.,

1835); *The Vision of Rubeta* (1838); *The Dream of Alla-Ad-Deen* (under pen name, "Charles Erskine White, D.D.," 1838); *Arthur Carryl* (anon., 1841); *Alice; or, The Painter's Story* (1867); *Dramatic Works,* 4v. (1868–70); etc.

OSBORN, NORRIS GALPIN (Apr. 17, 1858–May 6, 1932); b. New Haven, Conn. Editor, author. *A Glance Backward: Editorial Reminiscences* (1905). Editor: *Men of Mark in Connecticut,* 5v. (1906–10); *History of Connecticut,* 5v. (1925); etc. Editor, the *New Haven Journal-Courier,* 1907–32.

OSBORN, PAUL (1901–); b. Evansville, Ind. Playwright. *Hotbed* (prod. 1928); *The Vinegar Tree* (prod. 1930); *Morning's At Seven* (prod. 1939); *A Bell for Adano* (play, 1945); *Innocent Voyage* (play, 1947); *Point of No Return* (1952); *East of Eden* (1955); *Sayonara* (1957); *South Pacific* (1958); *Wild River* (1960); *Maiden Voyage* (1960); *John Brown's Body* (1967); etc. Also motion picture scripts.

OSBORN, ROBERT CHESLEY (Oct. 26, 1904–   ); b. Oshkosh, Wis. Artist, author. *War is No Damn Good* (1946); *Low and Inside* (1953); *Osborn on Leisure* (1957); *The Vulgarians* (1960); *Dying to Smoke* (1964).

OSBORN, SELLECK (c. 1782–Oct., 1826); b. Trumbull, Conn. Editor, poet. *Poems* (1823). Editor, the *Suffolk Gazette Herald,* Sag Harbor, N.Y., 1802–03; *The Witness,* Litchfield, Conn., 1805–08; the *American Watchman,* Wilmington, Del., 1817–20; the *New York Patriot,* 1823–24.

OSBORN, STELLANOVA [Brunt] (July 31, 1894–); b. Hamilton, Can. Author. *Eighty and On* (1941); *A Tale of Possum Poke in Possum Lane* (1946); *Balsam Boughs* (poems, 1949); etc. Co-author, with Chase S. Osborn: *The Conquest of a Continent* (1939); *Hiawatha with Its Original Indian Legends* (1944); *Jasmine Springs* (1953); *Polly Cadotte* (1955); *Beside the Cabin* (1956); *Iron and Arbutus* (1962); etc.

OSBORNE, DUFFIELD (June 20, 1858–Nov. 20, 1917); b. Brooklyn, N.Y. Author: *The Spell of Ashtaroth* (1888); *The Robe of Nessus* (1890); *The Secret of the Crater* (1900); *The Lion's Brood* (1901); *The Angels of Messer Ercole* (1907); *Engraved Gems* (1912); *The Authors Club: An Historical Sketch* (1913); etc.

OSBORNE, LETITIA PRESTON (Aug. 9, 1894–); b. Union, W. Va. Lecturer, novelist. *They Change Their Skies* (1945); *Through Purple Glass* (1946); *The Little Voyage* (1949).

OSBOURNE, LLOYD (Apr. 7, 1868–May 22, 1947); b. San Francisco, Calif. Author. *The Wrong Box* (with Robert Louis Stevenson, 1889); *The Wrecker* (with same, 1892); *The Ebb Tide* (with same, 1894); *The Motormaniacs* (1905); *Wild Justice* (1906); *Schmidt, the Adventurer* (1907); *Infatuation* (1909); *Person of Some Importance* (1911); etc.

OSGOOD, CHARLES GROSVENOR (May 4, 1871–July 27, 1964); b. Wellsboro, Pa. Educator, author. *Boccaccio on Poetry* (1930); *Vergil and the English Mind* (1930); *The Voice of England* (1935); *Poetry as a Means of Grace* (1941); *Lights in Nassau Hall* (1951). Editor: *Variorum Edition of the Works of Edmund Spenser,* 6v. (1932–38); etc. Prof. English, Princeton University, 1913–37.

OSGOOD, FRANCES SARGENT [Locke] (June 18, 1811–May 12, 1850); b. Boston, Mass. Pen name "Florence." Poet. *A Wreath of Wild Flowers from New England* (1838); *The Casket of Faith* (1840); *The Poetry of Flowers and the Flowers of Poetry* (1841); *The Rose: Sketches in Verse* (1842); *Puss in Boots* (1844); *The Cries of New York* (1846); *Poems* (1846); etc. She was a friend of Edgar Allan Poe, who included her in his *The Literati* (1850). She wrote a requiem for Poe called "Labor." *See* Mary E. Hewitt's *The Memorial: Written by Friends of the Late Mrs. Osgood* (1851).

OSGOOD, HERBERT LEVI (Apr. 9, 1855–Sept. 11, 1918); b. Canton, Me. Educator, historian. *The American Colonies in the Seventeenth Century,* 3v. (1904–07); *The American*

Colonies in the Eighteenth Century, 4v. (1924); etc. History dept., Columbia University, 1890–1918; professor, 1896–1918. See Dixon Ryan Fox's *Herbert Levi Osgood: An American Scholar* (1924).

OSGOOD, IRENE, b. (de Belot) in Virginia. Author. *An Idol's Passion* (1895); *The Chants of a Lonely Soul* (1896); *Servitude* (1908); *Where Pharoah Dreams* (1909); *The Indelicate Duellist* (1913); etc.

OSGOOD, JAMES R[ipley] (b. Feb. 22, 1836). Brother of Kate Putnam Osgood. Publisher. With James T. Fields he established in 1868 the Boston firm of Fields, Osgood & Co. In 1871, the firm became R. Osgood & Co., with Osgood and Benjamin H. Ticknor as partners. In 1878, the firm merged with H. O. Houghton, Cambridge publisher, to form Houghton, Osgood and Company. In 1880, the firm became Houghton, Mifflin & Co. In 1908, the name was changed to Houghton, Mifflin Company (q.v.). These firms were successively publishers of the *Atlantic Monthly,* 1868–1908.

OSGOOD, KATE PUTNAM (b. May 25, 1841); b. Fryeburg, Me., sister of James R. Osgood. Poet. She wrote the poem "Driving Home the Cows," which appeared anonymously in *Harper's Magazine,* Mar., 1865.

OSGOOD, SAMUEL (Aug. 30, 1812–Apr. 14, 1880); b. Charlestown, Mass. Episcopal clergyman, editor, author. *Studies in Christian Biography* (1851); *The Hearth-Stone* (1854); *Mile-Stones in Our Life-Journey* (1855); *American Leaves* (1867); etc. Editor, *Western Messenger,* Louisville, Ky., 1836–37; co-editor, *Christian Inquirer,* New York, 1850–54.

O'SHAUGHNESSY, EDITH [Coues] (Mrs. Nelson O'Shaughnessy) (d. Feb. 18, 1939); b. Columbia, S.C., daughter of Elliott Coues. Author. *A Diplomat's Wife in Mexico* (1916); *My Lorraine Journal* (1928); *Alsace in Rust and Gold* (1920); *Intimate Pages of Mexican History* (1920).

O'SHEEL, SHAEMAS (Sept. 19, 1886–1954); b. New York. Author. *The Blossomy Bough* (poems, 1911); *The Dear Old Lady of Eighty-Sixth Street* (1912); *The Light Feet of Goats* (poems, 1915); *Jealous of Dead Leaves* (poems, 1928); *It Never Could Happen* (1932); etc.

OSKISON, JOHN MILTON (Sept. 21, 1874–Feb. 25, 1947); b. Vinita, Okla. Author. *Black Jack Davy* (1926); *A Texas Titan: The Story of Sam Houston* (1929); *Brothers Three* (1935); *Tecumseh and His Times* (1938); etc.

OSLER, SIR WILLIAM, BART. (July 12, 1849–Dec. 29, 1919); b. Bond Head, Upper Canada (now Ont.). Physician, educator, author. *Aequanimitas* (1889); *Principles and Practice of Medicine* (1891); *The Student Life* (1905); *Man's Redemption of Man* (1910); *The Old Humanities and the New Science* (1910); *A Way of Life* (1914); etc. *See* Harvey Cushing's *The Life of Sir William Osler,* 2v. (1925). His library was bequeathed to McGill University and is catalogued in *Bibliotheca Osleriana* (1929).

Ossoli, Margaret Fuller, Marchesa d'. See Margaret Fuller.

OSTENSO, MARTHA (Sept. 17, 1900–Nov. 24, 1963); b. Bergen, Norway. Novelist, poet. *A Far Land* (poems, 1924); *Wild Geese* (1925); *The Dark Dawn* (1926); *The Mad Carews* (1927); *The Young May Moon* (1929); *Waters under the Earth* (1930); *There's Always Another Year* (1933); *White Reef* (1934); *The Stone Field* (1937); *The Mandrake Root* (1938); *O River, Remember!* (1943); *And They Shall Walk* (with Sister E. Kenney, 1943); *Milk Route* (1948); *Sunset Tree* (1949); *Man Had Tall Sons* (1958); etc.

OSTRANDER, ISABEL (Sept. 14, 1885–Apr. 23, 1924); b. New York. Novelist. *The Single Track* (under pen name, "Douglas Grant," 1919); *The Trigger of Conscience* (under pen name, "Robert Orr Chipperfield," 1921); *The Doom Dealer* (under pen name, "David Fox," 1923); *Annihilation* (1924); etc.

O'SULLIVAN, JOHN LOUIS (Nov., 1813–Feb. 24, 1895); b. Gibraltar. Journalist. Founder (with Samuel Daly Langtree), the *United States Magazine and Democratic Review,* 1837; co-editor, 1837–39; editor, 1841–46; founder (with Samuel J. Tilden), the *New York Morning News,* 1844; editor, 1844–46. See *Democratic Review.* Coined the political phrase, "Manifest Destiny," in 1845.

O'SULLIVAN, VINCENT (Nov. 28, 1872–1940); b. New York. Author. *Poems* (1896); *The Green Window* (1899); *Sentiment, and Other Stories* (1913); *Aspects of Wilde* (1936); *Opinions* (1959); etc.

OSWALD, JOHN CLYDE (July 11, 1872–June 22, 1938); b. Fort Recovery, O. Printer, publisher, editor, author. *Benjamin Franklin, Printer* (1917); *A History of Printing* (1928); *Printing in the Americas* (1937). Editor, the *American Printer,* 1897–1925.

OTERO, MIGUEL ANTONIO (Oct. 17, 1859–Aug. 7, 1944); b. St. Louis, Mo. Governor, author. *Conquistadores of Spain and Buccaneers of England, France and Holland* (1925); *My Life on the Frontier, 1864–1882* (1925); *The Real Billy the Kid* (1935); *My Nine Years as Governor of the Territory of New Mexico, 1897–1906* (1936); *My Life on the Frontier, 1882–1897* (1939); etc. Governor of New Mexico, 1897–1906.

Other America, The. A study of poverty in the United States, by Michael Harrington (1964).

Other Voices, Other Rooms. Novel by Truman Capote (1948). A homosexual boy faces his future.

OTIS, ARTHUR SINTON (July 28, 1886–Dec. 31, 1963); b. Denver, Colo. Psychologist. *Otis Group Intelligence Scale* (1918); *Statistical Method in Educational Measurement* (1925); *Elements of Aeronautics* (with Francis Pope, 1942); *Added Revenue Without Burden* (1958); etc.

OTIS, HARRISON GRAY (Oct. 6, 1765–Oct. 28, 1848); b. Boston, Mass. Statesman, orator, author. *Letters Developing the Character and Views of the Hartford Convention* (1820); etc. Otis bought and developed the land now known as Beacon Hill in Boston. Charles Bullfinch designed three houses for him. *See* Samuel E. Morison's *The Life and Letters of Harrison Gray Otis, Federalist, 1765–1848,* 2v. (1913).

OTIS, JAMES (Feb. 5, 1725–May 23, 1783); b. West Barnstable, Mass. Politician, pamphleteer. *A Vindication of the Conduct of the House of Representatives of the Province of Massachusetts Bay* (1762); *The Rights of the British Colonies Asserted and Proved* (1764); etc. His pamphlets, edited by C. F. Mullett, were reprinted in the *University of Missouri Studies,* 1929. *See* William Tudor's *The Life of James Otis* (1823).

Otis, James. Pen name of James Otis Kaler.

OTIS, MRS. HARRISON GRAY (Eliza Henderson Bordman) (July 27, 1796–Jan. 21, 1873); b. Boston, Mass. Author. *The Barclays of Boston* (1854). Wrote for *Boston Transcript* under pen name "One of the Barclays." She was responsible for making Washington's birthday a legal holiday.

OTIS, RAYMOND. Novelist. *Fire in the Night* (1934); *Miguel of the Bright Mountain* (1936); *Little Valley* (1937); all with a New Mexico setting.

OTTLEY, ROI (Aug. 2, 1906–Oct. 1, 1960); b. New York. Columnist, author. *New World A-Coming* (1943); *Black Odyssey: The Story of the Negro in America* (1948); *No Green Pastures* (1951); *Lonely Warrior* (1955). Columnist, *Amsterdam News,* 1932–38.

Our Country. By Josiah Strong (1885). Pioneer sociological treatise pointing out the dangers of capitalism, and exhorting the churches to become more active in social reform. It was translated into many languages.

Our Home and Fireside Magazine. Portland, Me. Founded 1873. Published by H. Hallett & Company. Expired 1888.

"Our Left." Civil War poem by Francis O. Ticknor. Inspired by the carnage of the Confederate left wing at the first battle of Bull Run.

Our Plundered Planet. By Fairfield Osborn (1948). The author argues that the balance of nature depends on man's foresight, and that if man continues to remain heedless of his assaults upon natural resources, our planet will become uninhabitable.

Our Press Gang. By Lambert A. Wilmer (1859). An attack on the cheap press of the day, including the magazines *Cytherean Miscellany, Alligator, Flash,* and *Libertine.*

Our Times; The United States, 1900-1925. By Mark Sullivan, 6v. (1926–35). Informal history based on newspaper records and other contemporary sources. Vol. 1, *The Turn of the Century;* 2, *America Finding Herself;* 3, *Pre-War America;* 4, *The War Begins;* 5, *Over Here;* 6, *The Twenties.*

Our Town. Play by Thornton Wilder (prod. 1938). Evokes the supernatural by having the characters return to earlier years. The scene is Grover's Corners, a small New Hampshire town. The stage manager bridges the gap between audience and actors by explaining characters and situations as they are introduced. Pulitzer prize play, 1938.

Our Young Folks. Boston, Mass. Illustrated juvenile magazine. Founded Jan., 1865. Published by Ticknor & Fields. Editors: J. J. Trowbridge, Lucy Larcom, Mary Abigail Dodge. Mayne Reid, "Oliver Optic," William T. Adams, Horatio Alger, and Thomas Bailey Aldrich were contributors. Merged with *St. Nicholas,* Oct., 1873.

OURSLER, [Charles] FULTON (Jan. 22, 1893–May 24, 1952); b. Baltimore, Md. Editor, novelist. *Behold This Dreamer* (1924); *Sandalwood* (1925); *Poor Little Fool* (1928); *Joshua Todd* (1935); *The Precious Secret* (1947); *Modern Parables* (1950); etc. Writer of numerous mystery novels under pen name "Anthony Abbott." Editor, *Cosmopolitan,* 1923–24; *Liberty* magazine, 1931–42.

OURSLER, GRACE PERKINS (Mrs. Fulton Oursler) (d. Dec. 16, 1955); b. Boston, Mass. Novelist. *Ex-Mistress* (1930); *Night Nurse* (1930); *Boy Crazy* (1931); *No More Orchids* (1932); etc.

OURSLER, WILL[iam Charles] (July 12, 1913–); b. Baltimore, Md. Author. *The Trial of Vincent Doon* (1941); *Folio on Florence White* (1942); *Departure Delayed* (1947); *Father Flanagan of Boys Town* (with F. Oursler, 1949); *The Prudential* (with E. C. May, 1950); *Murder Memo* (1950); *Narcotics: America's Peril* (with L. D. Smith, 1952); *N.Y., N.Y.* (1954); *The Boy Scout Story* (1955); *The Healing Power of Faith* (1957); *The Road to Faith* (1960); *The Murderers* (with H. J. Anslinger, 1961); *Family Story* (1963); *The Atheist* (1965); etc.

"Out of the Cradle Endlessly Rocking." Poem by Walt Whitman, which appeared in the *Saturday Press,* New York, in 1859, under the title "A Child's Reminiscence."

Out of the Hurly Burly. By Charles Heber Clark (1874). Humorous sketches. A. B. Frost's first illustrations appeared in this book, and it was the first book published by J. M. Stoddart, Philadelphia publisher.

Outcasts of Poker Flat, The. Short story by Bret Harte, in the *Overland Monthly,* Jan., 1869.

OUTCAULT, R[ichard] F[elton] (Jan. 14, 1863–Sept. 25, 1928); b. Lancaster, O. Cartoonist. Created the comic strip "Hogan's Alley" in the *New York World* in 1895, the "Yellow Kid" in the *New York Journal* in 1896, and "Buster Brown" in the *New York Herald* in 1902.

Outdoor Life. Denver, Colo. Monthly magazine. Founded 1898, by John A. McGuire, who was also its editor. Expired Sept., 1927.

OUTHWAITE, LEONARD (July 12, 1892–); b. Sierra Madre, Calif. Anthropologist, author. *Atlantic Circle* (1931); *Unrolling the Map* (1935); *Atlantic—History of an Ocean* (1957); *The Century of Oil* (1959); *Museums of the Future* (1967); etc.

Outing. New York. Monthly magazine. Founded 1882, at Albany, N.Y. In 1884, it was moved to Boston and merged with *The Wheelman,* as *Outing and The Wheelman.* In 1885 the name *Outing* was restored, and in 1886 it was moved to New York. Subtitle varies. Expired 1923.

Outlook, The. New York. Religious and literary weekly. Founded Jan. 1, 1870, by J. B. Ford & Co. Editors: Henry Ward Beecher, 1870–75; Charles L. Norton and John Habberton, 1875–76; Lyman Abbott, joint editor, 1876–81, editor, 1881–1923; Hamilton Wright Mabie, associate editor, 1884–1916; Ernest Hamlin Abbott, 1923–28; Frances R. Bellamy, 1928–32; Alfred E. Smith, 1932–34; Francis Walton, 1934–35. It grew out of the *Christian Union,* founded 1869, which had emerged from the *Church Union.* At the start it was religious in tone, but later became noted for its literary contributions by Harriet Beecher Stowe, Edward Eggleston, Thomas Nelson Page, Theodore Roosevelt, Helen Hunt Jackson, etc. It expired June, 1935. *See* Lyman Abbott's *Reminiscences* (1915); Frank L. Mott's *A History of American Magazines,* v. 3 (1938).

Outre-Mer. By Henry Wadsworth Longfellow, 2v. (1833–34). Prose account of the author's travels and observations in Europe as a young man.

"Over the Hill to the Poor-House." Poem by Will Carleton, from his *Farm Ballads* (1873). First published in *Harper's Weekly,* June 17, 1871.

Over the Teacups. By Oliver Wendell Holmes (1890). The author's last book. Written in the manner of the "Autocrat" series.

"Over There." World War I song written by George M. Cohan (1917).

Overall Boys. Series of books for boys by Eulalie Osgood Grover.

OVERHOLSER, WAYNE D. Author. *Buckaroo's Code* (1947); *Draw or Drag* (1950); *Cast a Long Shadow* (1955); *The Desperate Man* (1957); *Hearn's Valley* (1958); *The Bitter Night* (1961); *Red Is the Valley* (1967); etc. Also books under pen names "John S. Daniels," "Joseph Wayne," etc.

Overland Monthly. San Francisco Calif. Magazine. Founded July, 1868, by Anton Roman, bookseller and publisher. Editors: Bret Harte, 1868–70; W. C. Bartlett, 1871; Benjamin P. Avery, 1872–73; Walt M. Fisher, 1874–75; Millicent W. Shinn, 1883–94; Rounsevell Wildman, 1894–97; James Howard Bridge, 1897–1900; Frederick Marriott, 1900–03; Florence Jackman, 1903; P. N. Beringer, 1903–05; Thomas B. Wilson, 1905; P. N. Beringer, 1906–11; Frederick Marriott, 1911–20; Herbert Bashford, 1921; Almira Guild McKeon, 1921–22; D. R. Lloyd and Mabel Moffitt, 1923; Harry Noyre Pratt and Mabel Mofitt, 1924–25; V. V. Taylor and Hamilton Wayne, 1925; B. Virginia Lee and S. Bret Cooksley, 1925–26; R. D. Hart, 1926–28; Arthur H. Chamberlain, 1928–35. The *Overland Monthly* was to the West what the *Atlantic Monthly* was to the East. Bret Harte's "The Luck of Roaring Camp" appeared in its second number, and Mark Twain was a contributor. Most of Harte's early work appeared here for the first time. Charles Warren Stoddard contributed some of his *South Sea Idylls* and Benjamin P. Avery his *Sierra Pictures. The Californian* was founded in 1880 and took the place of the *Overland Monthly,* but it expired in 1882 and the second series of the *Overland Monthly* was started. In 1923 it absorbed *Out West Magazine* and was thenceforth known as *Overland Monthly and Out West Magazine.* In 1931 it moved to Los Angeles. Expired July, 1935. *See* Frank L. Mott's *A History of American Magazines,* v. 3 (1938).

OVERSTREET, BONARO WILKINSON (Oct. 30, 1902–); b. Geyserville, Cal. Author. *Poetic Way of Release* (1931); *Search for a Self* (1938); *Freedom's People* (1945); *Understanding Fear in Ourselves and Others* (1951); etc. Co-author, with H. A. Overstreet: *The War Called Peace: Krushchev's Communism* (1961); *The Strange Tactics of Extremism* (1964); *The FBI in Our Open Society* (1969); etc.

OVERSTREET, H[arry] A[llen] (Oct. 25, 1875–Aug. 17, 1970); b. San Francisco, Cal. Educator, author. *Influencing Human Behavior* (1925); *The Enduring Quest* (1931); *A Guide to Civilized Loafing* (1934); *Let Me Think* (1939); *Our Free Minds* (1941); *The Mature Mind* (1949); *The Great Enterprise: Relating Ourselves to Our World* (1954); etc. Co-author, with Bonaro W. Overstreet: *Leaders for Adult Education* (1940); *Where Children Come First* (1949); *The Mind Alive* (1954); *What We Must Know About Communism* (1958); *The War Called Peace: Krushchev's Communism* (1961); *The Strange Tactics of Extremism* (1964); *The FBI in Our Open Society* (1969); etc. Prof. philosophy, College of the City of New York, 1911–39.

OVERTON, GRANT MARTIN (Sept. 19, 1887–July 4, 1930); b. Patchoque, N.Y. Critic, author. *The Women Who Make Our Novels* (1918); *The Mermaid* (1920); *World Without End* (1921); *The Island of the Innocent* (1923); *The Thousand and First Night* (1924); *The Philosophy of Fiction* (1928); etc. Book review editor, *New York Sun;* fiction editor, *Collier's* magazine, 1924–30.

OVINGTON, MARY WHITE (Apr. 11, 1865–July, 1951); b. Brooklyn, N.Y. Author. *Half a Man* (1911); *Hazel* (1913); *Portraits in Color* (1927); etc.

OWEN, GORONWY (Jan. 13, 1722–ca. 1770); b. Anglesea, North Wales. Anglican clergyman, poet. *The Poetical Works,* 2v., ed. by Robert Jones (1876). Came to the United States in 1757 to become a teacher at the College of William and Mary.

OWEN, MARIE BANKHEAD (Mrs. Thomas McAdory Owen) (1869–Mar. 2, 1958); b. in Noxubee Co., Miss. Author. *Yvonne of Braithwaite* (1927); *Our Home Lana* (1935); *Children of the Night* (1937); *Alabama: A Social and Economic History of the State* (1937); *The Story of Alabama* (1949); etc. With Alabama State Dept. of Archives and History, from 1920.

OWEN, MARY ALICIA (b. Jan. 29, 1858); b. St. Joseph, Mo. Author. *Voodoo Tales* (1893); *Folk-Lore of the Mississippi Indians* (1904); etc.

OWEN, ROBERT DALE (Nov. 9, 1801–June 24, 1877); b. Glasgow, Scot. Social reformer, author. *Pocahontas: A Historical Drama* (1837); *The Future of the North-West* (1863); *The Wrong of Slavery* (1864); *Beyond the Breakers* (1870); *Threading My Way* (autobiography, 1874); etc. Editor: *New Harmony Gazette,* 1826–27. One of the founders of the New Harmony Community, New Harmony, Ind., a communal experiment. *See* Richard W. Leopold's *Robert Dale Owen* (1940).

OWEN, RUSSELL (Jan. 8, 1889–Apr. 3, 1952); b. Chicago, Ill. Correspondent, author. *South of the Sun* (1934); *The Antarctic Ocean* (1941); *Conquest of the North and South Poles* (1952); etc. With the Byrd Antarctic Expedition, 1929–30; correspondent, the *New York Times,* from 1920.

OWEN, RUTH BRYAN (Mrs. Borge Rohde) (Oct. 2, 1885–1954); b. Jacksonville, Ill., daughter of William Jennings Bryan. Diplomat, author. *Leaves from a Greenland Diary* (1935); *Denmark Caravan* (1936); *Look Forward, Warrior* (1942); *Caribbean Caravel* (1949). Minister to Denmark, 1933–36.

OWENS, WILLIAM A. (Nov. 2, 1905–   ); b. Blossom, Tex. Educator, author. *Swing and Turn: Texas Play-Party Games* (1936); *Texas Folk Songs* (1950); *Slave Mutiny* (1953); *Walking on Borrowed Land* (1954); *Fever in the Earth* (1958); *Pocantico Hills, 1609–1959* (1960); *Look to the River* (1963); *This Stubborn Soil* (1966). Editor: 1609–1959 (1960); *Look to the River* (1963); *This Stubborn Soil* (1966). Editor: *Energy and Man* (1960). Faculty, Columbia University, since 1947. *Energy and Man* (1960). Faculty, Columbia University, since 1947.

Owl in the Attic, The. Humorous sketches by James Thurber (1931).

OWSLEY, FRANK LAWRENCE (Jan. 20, 1890–Oct. 21, 1956); b. in Montgomery Co., Ala. Educator, author. *State Rights in the Confederacy* (1925); *King Cotton Diplomacy: Educator, author. State Rights in the Confederacy* (1925); *King Cotton Diplomacy: Foreign Relations of the Confederate States of America* (1931); etc. History dept., Foreign Relations of the Confederate States of America (1931); etc. History dept., Vanderbilt University, 1920–49; prof. history, University of Alabama, 1949–54. Vanderbilt University, 1920–49; prof. history, University of Alabama, 1949–54.

Ox-Bow Incident, The. Novel by Walter Van Tilburg Clark (1940). A Western acclaimed for its literary treatment of a "pulp" theme.

Oxford Companion to American Literature, The. Compiled and edited by J. D. Hart (1941). Contains biographies of authors, plots of literary works, and other entries on the backgrounds of American literature.

Oxford University Press. Oxford and London, England, and New York. Publishers. Founded 1478. For many years Oxford publications in America were handled through the Macmillan Company, but in 1896, when that company became a separate American firm, a separate Oxford branch was opened in New York under John Armstrong. In 1935 the business offices were consolidated with those of Longmans, Green & Co. The American branch has specialized in Bibles, prayer books, and liturgical books; anthologies of verse, and scholarly books. Among its better known publications have been *The Oxford Dictionary;* Fowler's *Dictionary of modern Usage;* the *Early English Text Society* publications; the *Oxford Tudar and Stuart Library;* the *Oxford History of Music; The World's Classics;* the *S.P.E. Tracts;* the *Oxford Poets;* the *Oxford Shakespeare.* John R. B. Brett-Smith is now president.

OXNAM, Garfield BROMLEY (Aug. 14, 1891–); b. Sonora, Cal. Methodist bishop, author. *The Mexican in Los Angeles* (1920); *The Ethical Ideals of Jesus in a Changing World* (1941); *Labor and Tomorrow's World* (1945); *The Church and Contemporary Change* (1950); *I Protest* (1954); *A Testament of Faith* (1958); etc.

P

P. E. N. An international club of writers. Founded 1921.

PS, Denver, Colo. Irregularly issued. Founded 1954, by Alan Swallow. Poems and stories constitute its only material.

PAAR, JACK (May 1, 1918–); b. Canton, Ohio. Television performer. *I Kid You Not* (1960); *My Saber Is Bent* (with John Reddy, 1961).

PACH, WALTER (July 11, 1883–Nov. 27, 1958); b. New York. Painter, illustrator, translator, author. *The Masters of Modern Art* (1924); *Modern Art in America* (1928); *Ananias; or, The False Artist* (1928); *Vincent Van Gogh* (1936); *Queer*

Thing Painting: Forty Years in the World of Art (1938); *Ingres* (1939); *The Art Museum in America* (1948); etc. Translated *History of Art*, by Elie Faure, 5v. (1920–30).

PACHTER, HENRY M[aximilian] (Feb. 22, 1907–); b. Berlin. Educator, author. *The Axis Grand Strategy* (With L. Farago, 1942); *German Radio Propaganda* (with E. Kris, 1944); *Nazi-Deutsch* (1944); *Paracelsus: Magic Into Science* (1951); *Collision Course: The Cuban Missile Crisis* (1963); *Chruschtschow-Kennedy-Castro* (1963); etc. Co-editor, *Dissent.* Professor of history, New School for Social Research, since 1952.

Pacific, The. San Francisco, Calif. Congregationalist magazine. Founded 1851. Expired 1928.

Pacific Explicator. North Long Beach, Calif. Triannual. Founded 1953. Devoted to essays, criticism, poems and explications.

Pacific Spectator. Palo Alto, Calif. Founded 1947. Edited by John W. Dodds and others. Published quarterly, by Stanford University Press, for the Pacific Coast Committee for the Humanities of the American Council of Learned Societies.

PACK, ROBERT (1929–). Poet. *Irony of Joy* (1955); *Wallace Stevens: An Approach to His Poetry and Thought* (1958); *Forgotten Secret* (1959); *Stranger's Privilege* (1959); *Then What Did You Do?* (1961); *Guarded Women* (1963); *How To Catch A Crocodile* (1964); etc.

PACKARD, ALPHEUS SPRING (Dec. 23, 1798–July 13, 1884); b. Chelmsford, Mass. Congregational clergyman, educator, author. *History of Bowdoin* (1882). Prof. Classics, 1824–65; Bowdoin College; prof. religion, 1865–84; librarian, 1869–84. See *Memorial: Alpheus Spring Packard* (1886); L. C. Hatch's *The History of Bowdoin College* (1927).

PACKARD, ALPHEUS SPRING (Feb. 19, 1839–Feb. 14, 1905); b. Brunswick, Me., son of Alpheus Spring Packard. Educator, entomologist, author. *Guide to the Study of Insects* (1869); *Half-Hours with Insects* (1877); *Insects of the West* (1877); *Monograph of the Bombycine Moths*, 3v. (1895–1914); *Lamarck, His Life and Work* (1901); etc. A founder and editor, *American Naturalist*, 1862–86. Prof. zoology, Brown University, 1878–1905. See Samuel Henshaw's *The Entomological Writings of Dr. Alpheus Spring Packard* (1887).

PACKARD, FRANK L[ucius] (Feb. 2, 1877–Feb. 17, 1942); b. Montreal, P.Q. Author. *On the Iron at Big Cloud* (1911); *Greater Love Hath No Man* (1913); *The Miracle Man* (1914); *The Beloved Traitor* (1916); *The Sin That Was His* (1917); the Jimmie Dale series, 5v. (1917–35); *From Now On* (1920); *The White Moll* (1920); *Pawned* (1921); *Doors of the Night* (1922); *The Four Stragglers* (1923); *Running Special* (1925); *Two Stolen Idols* (1927); *Shanghai Jim* (1928); *Tiger Claws* (1928); *The Big Shot* (1929); *The Gold Skull Murders* (1931); *The Hidden Door* (1932); *The Purple Ball* (1933); *More Knaves than One* (1938); etc.

PACKARD, FREDERICK ADOLPHUS (Sept. 26, 1794–Nov. 11, 1869); b. Marlboro, Mass. Lawyer, editor. *The Union Bible Dictionary* (1837); *The Rock* (1866); *Life of Robert Owen* (1866); etc. Editor of publications, American Sunday School Union, 1828–67.

PACKARD, HANNAH J. Poet. *The Choice: A Tragedy; With Other Miscellaneous Poems* (1832).

PACKARD, VANCE [Oakley] (May 22, 1914–); b. Summit, Pa. Author. *How to Pick a Mate* (with C. R. Adams, 1946); *Animal IQ* (1950); *The Hidden Persuaders* (1957); *The Status Seekers* (1959); *The Waste Makers* (1960); *The Pyramid Climbers* (1962); *The Naked Society* (1964); *The Sexual Wilderness* (1968); etc.

PACKARD, WINTHROP (Mar. 7, 1862–Apr. 1, 1943); b. Boston, Mass. Naturalist, author. *Wild Pastures* (1909);

Florida Trails (1910); *Literary Pilgrimages of a Naturalist* (1911); *White Mountain Trails* (1912); *Old Plymouth Trails* (1920); *He Dropped into Poetry* (poems, 1940); etc.

PACKER, PETER (Jan. 22, 1908–); b. London. Novelist. *White Crocus* (1947); *The Inward Voyage* (1948).

"Paddle Your Own Canoe." Poem by Sarah Tittle Bolton (1897).

PADELFORD, FREDERICK MORGAN (Feb. 27, 1875–Dec. 3, 1942); b. Haverhill, Mass. Educator, author. *Samuel Osborne, Janitor* (1913); *George Dana Boardman Pepper: A Biographical Sketch* (1914); etc. Editor: *Early Sixteenth Century Lyrics* (1906); *The Poems of Henry Howard, Earl of Surrey* (1920); and of various textbook editions of English authors. Prof. English, University of Washington, from 1901.

PADELFORD, NORMAN JUDSON (Nov. 18, 1903–); b. Haverhill, Mass. Educator. Author: *Peace in the Balkans* (1935); *International Law and Diplomacy in the Spanish Civil Strife* (1939); *International Politics* (with G. A. Lincoln, 1954); *United Nations in the Balance* (with L. M. Goodrich, 1965); *Public Policy and the Use of the Seas* (1968); *The Dynamics of International Politics* (with G. A. Lincoln, 1967); etc. Prof. international relations, Massachusetts Institute of Technology, since 1945.

PADOVER, SAUL K[ussiel] (Apr. 13, 1905–); b. in Austria. Educator, historian. Author: *The Revolutionary Emperor: Joseph II* (1934, rev. ed. 1967); *Jefferson* (1942); *Experiment in Germany: The Story of an American Intelligence Officer* (1946); *The Living U.S. Constitution* (1953); *The Genius of America* (1960). *Foreign Affairs* (1964); *Thomas Jefferson and American Freedom* (1965); etc. Editor: *Wilson's Ideals* (1942); *The Washington Papers* (1955); *A Jefferson Profile* (1956); *Confessions and Self-Portraits* (1957); *The World of the Founding Fathers* (1960), Lecturer, The New School for Social Research, since 1947.

PAGANO, JO (Feb. 5, 1906–); b. Denver, Col. Novelist. *The Paesanos* (1940); *Golden Wedding* (1943); *The Condemned* (1947). Also screenplays.

PAGE, CURTIS HIDDEN (Apr. 4, 1870–Dec. 12, 1946); b. Greenwood, Mo. Educator. Editor: *British Poets of the Nineteenth Century* (1904); *The Chief American Poets* (1905); *The Golden Treasury of American Songs and Lyrics* (1907); *Japanese Poetry: An Historical Essay* (with 230 translations, 1923); etc. Translator of French plays, etc. Prof. English, Dartmouth College, from 1911.

PAGE, ELIZABETH (Aug. 27, 1889–); b. Castleton, Vt. Author. *Wagons West: A Story of the Oregon Trail* (1930); *Wild Horses and Gold: From Wyoming to the Yukon* (1932); *The Tree of Liberty* (1939); *Wilderness Adventure* (1946).

PAGE, ELIZABETH FRY; b. Hillsville, Va. Author. *Vagabond Victor* (1908); *Edward MacDowell: His Works and Ideals* (1910).

PAGE, EMILY REBECCA (b. May 5, 1834); b. Bradford, Vt. Poet. *Lily of the Valley* (1859); etc. Wrote for the *Carpet-Bag, Ladies' Repository,* and other magazines for many years, and was an editorial assistant to Maturin M. Ballou, magazine publisher

PAGE, KIRBY (Aug. 7, 1890–Dec. 16, 1957); b. Tyler Co., Tex. Disciples clergyman, editor, author. *The Sword or the Cross* (1921); *War: Its Causes, Consequences, and Cure* (1923); *Makers of Freedom* (with Sherwood Eddy, 1926); *Living Courageously* (1936); *Creative Pioneers* (1937); *The Light Is Still Shining in the Darkness* (1946); etc. Editor, *The World Tomorrow,* 1926–34; *Christian Century,* from 1935.

Page, L. C. & Company. Boston, Mass. Publishers. Founded 1892, as Joseph Knight Company, a subsidiary of Estes & Lauriat, with Lewis C. Page as an officer. The Joseph Knight Company was reorganized in 1895 with Lewis C. Page as president, George A. Page as treasurer, and Charles F. Page as secretary. Changed to L. C. Page & Company in 1896. In 1914 it was known as the Page Company. In 1914 it purchased the publishing business of Dana Estes & Co. In 1923, it assumed its old name of L. C. Page & Company. Among the best-selling books of the firm have been Eleanor H. Porter's *Pollyanna*, L. M. Montgomery's *Anne of Green Gables*, Annie Fellows Johnston's *The Little Colonel* series, the poems of Bliss Carman, the nature fiction of Charles G. D. Roberts, and the historical romances of Robert Heilson Stephens. The firm was later bought by Farrar, Straus and Cudahy.

PAGE, ROSEWELL (Nov. 21, 1858–Jan. 1, 1939); b. "Oakland," Hanover Co., Va., brother of Thomas Nelson Page. Lawyer, author. *Thomas Nelson Page* (1923); *Government in Virginia* (1924); *Hanover County* (1926); *The Iliads of the South* (poem, 1932).

PAGE, THOMAS NELSON (Apr. 23, 1853–Nov. 1, 1922); b. "Oakland," Hanover Co., Va. Diplomat, author. *In Ole Virginia* (1887); *Two Little Confederates* (1888); *Befo' de War* (with A. C. Gordon, 1888); *Elsket, and Other Stories* (1891); *Among the Camps* (1891); *The Old South* (1892); *The Burial of the Guns* (1894); *The Old Gentleman of the Black Stock* (1897); *Social Life in Old Virginia* (1897); *Red Rock* (1898); *Santa Claus's Partner* (1899); *Gordon Keith* (1903); *Bred in the Bone* (1904); *The Negro, the Southerner's Problem* (1904); *The Coast of Bohemia* (1906); *Under the Crust* (1907); *The Old Dominion* (1908); *John Marvel, Assistant* (1909); *Robert E. Lee, Man and Soldier* (1911); *The Novels, Stories, and Sketches and Poems* (Plantation edition), 18v. (1906–12); *Italy and the World War* (1920); etc. His best-known dialect story is *Marse Chan* (1884). U. S. Ambassador to Italy, 1913–20. *See* Rosewell Page's *Thomas Nelson Page* (1923); T. L. Gross's *Thomas Nelson Page* (1966).

PAGE, WALTER HINES (Aug. 15, 1855–Dec. 21, 1918); b. Cary, N.C. Journalist, diplomat, publisher, author. *The Rebuilding of Old Commonwealths* (1902); *A Publisher's Confessions* (1905); *The Southerner* (under pen name "Nicholas Worth," 1909); etc. On staff of *Forum*, 1887–95; editor, 1890–95; editor, *Atlantic Monthly*, 1896–99 founder, *World's Work*, 1900; editor, 1900–13. Became a partner in publishing firm of Doubleday, Page & Company, 1899. Ambassador to England, 1913–18. *See* Burton J. Hendrick's *The Life and Letters of Walter Hines Page*, 3v. (1922–25).

Pageant. New York. Monthly. Founded 1944. Published by Macfadden-Bartell Corp. Material of general family interest.

Pageant of America. Ed. by Ralph Henry Gabriel, 15v. (1925–29). Copiously illustrated popular survey of American history from the earliest period to the twentieth century, with many facsimiles of historical documents, title pages of rare books, etc. Each volume was prepared by a special board of editors. V. 1, *Adventures in the Wilderness;* v. 2, *The Lure of the Frontier;* v. 3, *Toilers of Land and Sea;* v. 4, *The March of Commerce;* v. 5, *The Epic of Industry;* v. 6, *The Winning of Freedom,* v. 7, *The Defense of Liberty;* v. 8, *Builders of the Republic;* v. 9, *Makers of a New Nation;* v. 10, *American Idealism;* v. 11, *The American Spirit in Letters;* v. 12, *The American Spirit in Art;* v. 13, *The American Spirit in Architecture;* v. 14, *The American State;* v. 15, *Annals of American Sport.*

PAHLOW, GERTRUDE CURTIS BROWN (1881–Jan. 29, 1937); b. Reading, Mass. Author. *The Gilded Chrysalis* (1914); *The Cross of Heart's Desire* (1916); *The Glory of Going On* (1919); *Murder in the Morning* (1931); *Honeymoon Trail* (1931); *The Bright Torch* (1933); *Hermitage Island* (1934); *Cabin in the Pines* (1935).

PAINE, ALBERT BIGELOW (July 10, 1861–Apr. 9, 1937); b. New Bedford, Mass. Editor, author. *Rhymes by Two Friends* (with William Allen White, 1893); *The Mystery of Evelin Delorme* (1894); *Gobolinks* (With Ruth McEnery Stuart, 1896); *The Dumpies* (1897); *The Hollow Tree* (1898);

The Arkansas Bear (1898); *The Deep Woods* (1899); *The Bread Line* (1900); *The Van Dwellers* (1901); *The Great White Way* (1901); *The Commuters* (1904); *Th. Nast: His Period and His Pictures* (1904); *The Lucky Piece* (1906); *A Sailor of Fortune* (1906); *From Van Dweller to Commuter* (1907); *The Tent Dwellers* (1908); *Captain Bill McDonald, Texas Ranger* (1909); *Elsie and the Arkansas Bear* (1909); *The Ship Dwellers* (1910); *Mark Twain: A Biography* (1912); *Hollow Tree Nights and Days* (1916); *The Boy's Life of Mark Twain* (1916); *Dwellers in Arcady* (1919); *George Fisher Baker* (1919); *A Short Life of Mark Twain* (1920); *The Car That Went Abroad* (1921); *In One Man's Life* (1921); *Single Reels* (1923); *Joan of Arc* (1925); *The Girl in White Armor* (1927); etc. Editor: *Mark Twain's Autobiography*, 2v. (1924); *Mark Twain's Letters*, 2v. (1917); *Mark Twain's Notebook* (1935; etc. Literary executor of Mark Twain. With *St. Nicholas Magazine*, 1899–1909.

PAINE, JOHN KNOWLES (Jan. 9, 1839–Apr. 25, 1906); b. Portland, Me. Educator, composer, author. In 1881 he wrote the music for a Harvard presentation of Sophocles's *OEdipus Tyrannus,* perhaps his best known compositon. He was a noted teacher of music at Harvard University, 1862–1905. *See* John Tasker Howard's *Our American Music* (1930).

PAINE, RALPH DELAHAYE (Apr. 28, 1871–Apr. 29, 1925); b. Lemont, Ill. Journalist, author. *The Praying Skipper, and Other Stories* (1906); *The Stroke Oar* (1908); *The Ships and Sailors of Old Salem* (1909); *The Book of Buried Treasure* (1911); *Sandy Sawyer* (1911); *Campus Days* (1912); *The Judgements of the Sea, and Other Stories* (1912); *The Adventures of Captain O'Shea* (1913); *The Steam-Shovel Man* (1913); *The Wall Between* (1914); *The Twisted Skein* (1915); *The Long Road Home* (1916); *Sons of Eli* (1917); *Old Merchant Marine* (1919); *Roads of Adventure* (1922); *Privateers of '76* (1923); etc.

PAINE, ROBERT TREAT (Dec. 9, 1773–Nov. 13, 1811); b. Taunton, Mass. Editor, orator, poet. *The Works, in Verse and Prose, of the Late Robert Treat Paine,* ed. by Charles Prentiss (1812). Founder, the *Federal Orrery,* Boston, 1794. His best known poems are "Adams and Liberty" and "The Ruling Passion."

PAINE, ROBERT TREAT, Jr. (Dec. 15, 1900–July 11, 1965); b. Boston, Mass. Museum curator. *Japanese Screen Paintings* (1935); *The Art and Architecture of Japan* (with Alexander Soper, 1955); etc. With Museum of Fine Arts, from 1932; associate curator, from 1956.

PAINE, THOMAS (Jan. 29, 1737–June 8, 1809); b. Thetford, Eng. Political philosopher, author. *Common Sense* (1776); *The Crisis* (1776); *Public Good* (1780); *The Rights of Man* (1791); *The Age of Reason,* 2v. (1794–96); *The Writings of Thomas Paine,* ed. by Moncure D. Conway, 4v. (1894–99); etc. *See* Moncure D. Conway's *The Life of Thomas Paine,* 2v. (1892); *The Living Thoughts of Tom Paine,* ed. by John Dos Passos (1940); Alfred O. Aldridge's *Man of Reason* (1959).

Painted Veils. Novel by James Gibbons Huneker (1920). A candid record of the art world in New York.

PAINTER, SIDNEY (Sept. 23, 1902–Jan. 12, 1960); b. New York. Historian. Author: *William Marshall* (1933); *French Chivalry* (1940); *Studies in the History of the English Feudal Barony* (1943); *Rise of the Feudal Monarchies* (1951); *Mediaeval Society* (1952); *A History of the Middle Ages* (1953); *Feudalism and Liberty* (1961); *The Reign of King John* (1966); etc. Dept. of history, Johns Hopkins University, from 1931.

Pal Joey. Novel by John O'Hara (1940). In the form of letters written by a night-club singer. It was dramatized by O'Hara as a musical comedy in the same year.

Pale Horse, Pale Rider. Collection of novelettes by Katherine Anne Porter (1939).

PALEN, LEWIS STANTON (July 28, 1878–); b. Monticello, N.Y. Author. *The White Devil of the Black Sea* (1924); *Man and Mystery in Asia* (1924); *The Lost Sword of Shamyl* (1927); *The Red Dragon* (1927). Editor: *The White Devil's Mate* (1926); *Water and Gold, as Told to the Author by Charles G. Hedlund* (1930).

PALEY, GRACE. Novelist. *The Little Disturbances of Man* (1958).

PALFREY, JOHN GORHAM (May 2, 1796–Apr. 26, 1881); b. Boston, Mass. Unitarian clergyman, editor, author. *Lowell Lectures on the Evidences of Christianity*, 2v. (1843); *Relation between Judaism and Christianity* (1854); *History of New England*, 4v. (1858–75); etc. He purchased the *North American Review* in 1835 and conducted it until 1843, selling it to Francis Bowen. He contributed to the magazine, 1817–59. Prof. sacred literature, Harvard University, 1831–39.

PALLEN, CONDÉ BENOIST (Dec. 5, 1858–May 26, 1929); b. St. Louis, Mo. Editor, lecturer, author. *The Philosophy of Literature* (1897); *Epochs of Literature* (1898); *Collected poems* (1915); *Crucible Island* (1919); *Ghost House* (1928); etc. A founder and managing editor, the *Catholic Encyclopedia*, 16v. (1907–14), with *Supplement* (1922). Editor, Universal Knowledge Foundation.

PALMER, ALICE [Elvira] FREEMAN (Feb. 21, 1855–Dec. 6, 1902); b. Colesville, N.Y. Educator, poet. *A Marriage Cycle* (poems, 1915). President, Wellesley College, 1882–87. *See* George Herbert Palmer and Alice Freeman Palmer's *The Teacher: Essays and Addresses on Education* (1908); George Herbert Palmer's *The Life of Alice Freeman Palmer* (1908).

PALMER, ANNA CAMPBELL (Mrs. George Archibald Palmer) (Feb. 3, 1854–June 18, 1928); b. Elmira, N.Y. Author. Pen Name "Mrs. George Archibald." *Verses from Mother's Corner* (1889); *Lady Gay* (1898); *In the Blue Country* (1910); etc.

PALMER, FANNY PURDY (1839–1923). Author. *Sonnets* (1909); *Dates and Days in Europe* (poems, 1915); *Three Plays* (1928). Compiler: *A List of Rhode Island Literary Women, 1726–1892, with Some Account of Their Work* (1893).

PALMER, FRANCIS STERNE (d. Aug. 21, 1938); b. Belmont N.Y. Poet. Co-author: *Strange Stories of 1812* (1907); etc.

PALMER, FREDERICK (Jan. 29, 1873–Sept. 2, 1958); b. Pleasantville, Pa. Correspondent, author. *Going to War in Greece* (1897); *The Ways of the Service* (1901); *The Vagabond* (1903); *With Kuroki in Manchuria* (1904); *Central America and Its Problems* (1910); *Over the Pass* (1912); *The Last Shot* (1914); *My Year of War* (1915); *America in France* (1918); *Our Greatest Battle* (1919); *The Folly of Nations* (1921); *Clark of the Ohio* (1929); *Newton D. Baker* (1931); *With My Own Eyes* (1933); *Bliss, Peacemaker* (1934); *The Man With A Country* (1935); *Our Gallant Madness* (1937); *It Can Be Done* (1944); *Life of John Pershing* (1948); etc. Foreign correspondent from 1897.

PALMER, GEORGE HERBERT (Mar. 19, 1842–May 7, 1933); b. Boston, Mass. Educator, author. *Self Cultivation in English* (1897); *The Field of Ethics* (1901); *The Nature of Goodness* (1903); *The Life of Alice Freeman Palmer* (1908); *The Teacher* (1909); *The Problem of Freedom* (1911); *Formative Types of English Poetry* (1918); *Altruism: Its Nature and Varieties* (1919); *The Autobiography of a Philosopher* (1930); etc. Editor: *The English Works of George Herbert* (1905); etc. Translator: *The Odyssey of Homer* (1893). Philosophy dept., Harvard University, 1872–1913.

PALMER, HORATIO RICHARD (Apr. 26, 1834–Nov. 15, 1907); b. Sherburne, N.Y. Composer, author. *Palmer's Theory of Music* (1876); etc. Compiler: *The Song Queen* (1867); *The Song King* (1872); *Life-Time Hymns* (1896); *The Song Herald* (1904); etc. His best known hymns are "Just for Today" and "Yield Not to Temptation."

PALMER, HOWARD (Nov. 28, 1883–Oct. 24, 1944); b. Norwich, Conn. Explorer, author. *Mountaineering and Exploration in the Selkirks* (1914); *Edward W. D. Holway: A Pioneer of the Canadian Alps* (1931); etc. Editor: *Life on a Whaler* (1929).

PALMER, JOEL (Oct. 4, 1810–June 9, 1881); b. in Ontario, Can. Pioneer, author, negotiator of treaties with Indians. *Journal of Travels over the Rocky Mountains* (1847).

PALMER, JOHN WILLIAMSON (Apr. 4, 1825–Feb 26, 1906); b. Baltimore, Md. Author. *The Golden Dagon; or, Up and Down the Irrawaddi* (1856); *The Queen's Heart* (prod. 1858); *The New and the Old; or, California and India in Romantic Aspects* (1859); *After His Kind* (under pen name, "John Coventry," 1886); *For Charlie's Sake, and Other Lyrics and Ballads* (1901); etc. Editor: *Folk Songs* (1866), republished as four books: *Songs of Life* (1870); *Songs of Home* (1871); *Songs of the Heart* (1872); *Songs of Nature* (1873). His best known poem is "Stonewall Jackson's Way."

PALMER, NORMAN DUNBAR (June 25, 1909–); b. Hinckley, Me. Educator. *The Irish Land League Crisis* (1940); *Sun Yat-sen and Communism* (with Shao Chuan Leng, 1961); *The United States and the United Nations* (1964); *Problems of Defense of South and East Asia* (with others, 1969); etc. Dept. of political science, University of Pennsylvania, since 1947.

PALMER, RAY (Nov. 12, 1808–Mar. 29, 1887); b. Little Compton, R.I. Congregational clergyman, Hymn writer, author. *Closet Hours* (1851); *Hymns and Sacred Pieces* (1865); *Remember Me* (1865); *Hymns of My Holy Hours, and Other Pieces* (1868); *The Poetical Works of Ray Palmer* (1876); etc. His best known hymns were "My Faith Looks Up To Thee," "Take Me, O My Father, Take Me," and "Away From Earth My Spirit Turns." *See* E. S. Ninde's *The Story of the American Hymn* (1921); F. J. Metcalf's *American Hymn Writers and Compilers of Sacred Music* (1925).

PALMER, ROBERT ROSWELL (Jan. 11, 1909–); b. Chicago, Ill. *Twelve Who Ruled* (1941); *The Age of the Democratic Revolution* Vol. I (1959), Vol. II (1964); Editor: *Rand McNally Atlas of World History* (1957). Prof. history, Yale University, since 1969.

PALMER, STUART (June 21, 1905–Feb. 4, 1968); b. Baraboo, Wis. Author. *The Penguin Pool Murder* (1931); *Puzzle of the Happy Hooligan* (1941); *Four Lost Ladies* (1949); *Cold Poison* (1954); *Unhappy Hooligan* (1956); etc.

PALMER, WILLIAM PITT (Feb. 22, 1805–May 2, 1884); b. Stockbridge, Mass. Poet. *Echoes of Half a Century* (1880).

Palmetto Leaves. By Harriet Beecher Stowe (1873). Written at Mandarin, on the St. Johns River in Florida.

PALTSITS, VICTOR HUGO (July 12, 1867–Oct. 3, 1952); b. New York. Librarian, historian, bibliographer, editor. *The Almanacs of Roger Sherman* (1907); *Founding of New Amsterdam in 1626* (1925); *Wilberforce Eames* (1925); *The New York Tercentenary, 1524–1674* (1926); *Judge Augustus Porter, Pioneer of Niagara Falls* (1937); etc. Editor: *Charleston* (1898); *Bibliography of the Works of Father Louis Hennepin* (1902); *A Bibliography of the Separate & Collected Works of Philip Freneau* (1903); *A Bibliography of the Writings of Baron Lahontan* (1905); *Across the Plains to California in 1852: Journal of Mrs. Lodisa Frizzell* (1915); *Cruise of the U.S. Brig Argus in 1813: Journal of Surgeon James Inderwick* (1917); *Family Correspondence of Herman Melville, 1830–1904* (1929); etc. On editorial staff, *Jesuit Relations and Allied Documents*, 73v. (1896–1901). With Lenox Library, New York, 1888–1907; keeper of manuscripts, New York Public Library, 1914–41; chief of the American History Division, New York Public Library, 1916–41. New York State Historian, 1907–11.

Pamphleteer Monthly. New York. Founded May, 1940. Alvin F. Levin is editor. An annotated index to current pamphlets of all kinds.

"Pan in Wall Street." Poem by Edmund Clarence Stedman (1867).

PANCOAST, HENRY SPACKMAN (Aug. 24, 1858–Mar. 25, 1928); b. Germantown, Pa. Author. *An Introduction to American Literature* (1898); *A First Book in English Literature* (with Percy Van Dyke Shelly, 1924); etc. Editor: *A Vista of English Verse* (1911); etc.

PANGBORN, FREDERIC WERDEN (Mar. 7, 1855–); b. St. Albans, Vt. Author. *Alice* (1883); *Perdida* (1899); *Pascack* (1915); *In Varied Moods* (poems, 1917); etc. Editor, *Jersey City Evening Journal,* 1877–95; *Godey's Magazine,* 1895–99.

PANGBORN, GEORGIA WOOD (Aug. 29, 1872–); b. Malone, N.Y. Author. *Roman Biznet* (1902); *Interventions* (1911); *Blencka* (1924).

Panic. Play in verse by Archibald MacLeish (prod. 1935).

PANOFSKY, ERWIN (Mar. 30, 1892–Mar. 14, 1968); b. Hanover, Ger. Art historian. *Studies in Iconology* (1939); *Albrecht Dürer* (1943); *Gothic Architecture and Scholasticism* (1951); *Early Netherlandish Painting,* 2v. (1954); *Meaning in the Visual Arts* (1955); *Renaissance and Renascences in Western Art,* 2v. (1960); etc. Prof., Institute for Advanced Study, from 1935.

Pansy. Pen name of Isabella Alden.

Pansy. Boston, Mass. Juvenile magazine. Founded 1874, by Daniel Lothrop. Edited by Isabella Alden, under the pen name "Pansy." Expired 1896.

Pantheon Books. New York. Founded 1942, by Kurt Wolff. Noted for high standards of taste in publishing books of intellectual interest and cultural importance. Published the *Bollingen Series,* founded by Mary Mellon and devoted to philosophy, anthropology, art, comparative religion, and symbolism. Pantheon merged with Random House in 1961.

PAPASHVILY, GEORGE (Aug. 23, 1898–); b. Kobiankari, Georgia, Rus. Co-author with wife, Helen Waite: *Anything Can Happen* (1945); *Yes and No Stories* (1946); *Thanks to Noah* (1951); *Dogs and People* (1954).

PAPASHVILY, HELEN [Waite] (Dec. 19, 1906–); b. Stockton, Cal. Co-author of books with husband, George Papashvily (q.v.).

Paperback books. Books bound in soft covers for mass distribution, sometimes called "paperbound" or "pocket" books. The earliest paperbacks were the dime novels issued by Erastus Beadle, the first of which, *Malaeska, the Indian Wife,* appeared in 1860. In other well-known paperback series were such imports from England as the *Tauchnitz, Albatross,* and *Penguin* editions. The first modern, mass-distribution paperback line of reprints was *Pocket Books,* which appeared in 1939 with ten titles, selling at twenty-five cents each. During World War II, the Armed Services Editions, consisting of classic and modern reprints, were distributed to American servicemen throughout the world. After the war such editions as *Avon, Dell, New American Library,* and *Bantam* were among the leaders in paperback books. In 1952, Doubleday and Company launched *Anchor Books,* the first of a new type of paperback, under the editorship of Jason Epstein, who conceived the idea of reprinting scholarly books and relatively inaccessible works of literature, which would appeal to the growing numbers of college-educated people. Since 1952, many other publishers of hardbound books, as well as firms publishing only paperbacks, have entered the paperback field. The market for paperbacks, both "quality" and "popular," has increased so greatly during the past decades that bookstores selling only paperbacks have appeared throughout the country; paperbacks are sold not only in bookstores but also in drugstores, supermarkets, stationery stores, at newsstands, and in vending machines. Paperbacks are making substantial inroads into the textbook market, not only on the college, but also on the high-school and elementary-school, level. Such periodicals as *Paperbound Books in Print,* issued three times a year list all the latest additions to the stock of paperbacks currently available.

Paperback Review. New York. Semiannual. Founded 1956. Published by Book Report Service, Inc. Edited by Alan C. Gillespie. A review of the latest in paperback books.

Paperbound Books in Print. New York. Monthly, nine issues a year; cumulative issues, three times a year. Founded 1955. Edited by Olga S. Weber.

Parade. New York. Founded 1941. Distributed every Sunday with numerous newspapers throughout the United States. Articles of timely interest for family reading.

PARADIS, MARJORIE [Bartholomew] b. Montclair, N.J. (d. July 2, 1970); Author. *A Dinner of Herbs* (1928); *The Caddis* (1929); *The New Freedom* (1931); *It Happened One Day* (1932); *Timmy and the Tiger* (1952); *Midge Bennett of Duncan Hall* (1953); *Maid of Honor* (1959); etc.

Parents' Magazine. New York. Monthly. Founded 1926. Published by Parents' Magazine Enterprises. Concerned with responsibilities of parents to children and general family matters.

Paris Herald. Paris, France. Newspaper. Founded 1887, by James Gordon Bennett, Jr. Bennett also published the *London Herald* 1889–90. The *Paris Herald* furnished news to its parent paper, the *New York Herald,* later the *Herald Tribune.* Notable for the many American writers living in Europe who were connected with it. Laurence Hills edited the *Paris Herald,* 1924–39. *See* Al Laney's *The Paris Herald: Incredible Newspaper* (1947). See also *Herald International Tribune.*

Paris Review. Paris, France. Quarterly of literature. Founded 1953. International in scope but printed in English and edited by Americans. Noted for its interviews with famous writers. Sadruddin Aga Khan is the publisher. George A. Plimpton and others are editors. Has published Philip Roth, Mac Hyman, Jack Kerouac, Denise Levertov, John Hollander, Clancy Sigal. *Best Short Stories from the Paris Review,* ed. by William Styron, appeared in 1959. Viking Press has published several volumes of interviews entitled *Writers at Work.*

PARISH, ELIJAH (1762–1825). Congregational clergyman, author. *A Compendious History of New England* (with Jedediah Morse, 1804).

PARK, FRANCES (Oct. 16, 1895–July 24, 1950); b. Nutley, N.J. Editor, author. *This Day's Rapture* (1934); *Walls Against the Wind* (1935); etc. Assoc. editor, the *Theatre Guild Magazine,* 1928–32.

PARK, J[ohn] EDGAR (May 7, 1879–Mar. 4, 1956); b. Belfast, Ire. Congregational clergyman; educator, author. *The Keen Joy of Living* (1907); *The Sermon on the Mount* (1908); *The Man Who Missed Christmas* (1911); *The Dwarf's Spell* (1912); *The Rejuvenation of Father Christmas* (1914); *Bad Results of Good Habits* (1917); *The Merrie Adventures of Robin Hood and Santa Claus* (1922); *New Horizons* (1929); *The Miracle of Preaching* (1936); etc. President, Wheaton College, Norton Mass. 1926–44.

PARK, JULIAN (Nov. 6, 1888–July 17, 1965); b. Buffalo, N.Y. Educator, author. *History of the University of Buffalo* (1917); *The Evolution of a College* (1938); *The Government of France* (1950); *A Soldier of Napoleon* (1955); etc. Editor: *A Williams Anthology* (1910); *Unpublished Poems of John Clare* (1937); *Letters of George Bernard Shaw* (1939); *The Culture of Canada* (1957); etc. Editor and co-author: *The Culture of France* (1954). University of Buffalo, 1913; dean, 1914–1954.

PARK, ROSWELL (Oct. 1, 1807–July 16, 1869); b. Lebanon, Conn., Episcopal clergyman, educator, editor, poet, hymn writer. *Selections of Juvenile and Miscellaneous Poems* (1836); *A Sketch of the History and Topography of West Point* (1840); *Pantology* (1841); *A Handbook for American Travellers in Europe* (1853); *Jerusalem, and Other Poems* (1857); etc. President, Racine College, Racine, Wis., 1852–63.

PARK, ROSWELL (May 4, 1852–Feb. 15, 1914); b. Pomfret, Conn. son of Roswell Park. Surgeon, author. *An Epitome of the History of Medicine* (1897); *The Evil Eye, Thanatology, and Other Essays* (1912); etc.

PARKE, JOHN (Apr. 7, 1754–Dec. 11, 1789); b. Dover, Del. Poet. *Virginia* (1784); *The Lyric Works of Horace . . . to Which are Added, a Number of Original Poems, by a Native of America* (1786).

PARKER, ARTHUR CASWELL (Apr. 5, 1881–Jan. 1, 1955); b. on Cattaraugus Reservation, N.Y. Seneca Indian archeologist, editor, author. Indian name, "Gawaso Wanneh." *The Life of General Ely S. Parker, Last Grand Sachem of the Iroquois* (1919); *Seneca Myths and Folk Tales* (1923); *Skunny Wundy, and Other Indian Tales* (1926); *Rumbling Wings, and Other Indian Tales* (1928); *Gustango Gold* (1930); *Manual for History Museums* (1935); *Red Streak of the Iroquois* (1950); *Red Jacket* (1952); etc. Editor, the *Quarterly Journal of the Society of American Indians* (later the *American Indian Magazine*), 1913–18. State archeologist of New York, 1906–25. Director, Rochester Museum, 1923–46.

PARKER, CORNELIA STRATTON (Sept. 1, 1885–Feb. 4, 1972); b. Oakland, Calif. Author. *An American Idyll* (1919); *Jenny the Joyous* (1924); *Ports and Happy Places,* 2v. (1924–26); *English Summer* (1931); *German Summer* (1932); *Wanderer's Circle* (autobiography, 1934); *Your Child Can Be Happy In Bed* (1952); *Fabulous Valley* (1956); etc.

PARKER, De WITT HENRY (Apr. 17, 1885–June 21, 1949); b. New York. Educator, author. *The Self and Nature* (1917); *The Principles of Aesthetics* (1920); *The Analysis of Art* (1924); *The Analysis of Beauty* (1926); *Human Values* (1931); *Experience and Substance* (1941). Prof. philosophy, University of Michigan, 1925–49.

PARKER, DOROTHY [Rothschild] (Aug. 22, 1893–June 7, 1967); b. West End, N.J. Satirist, poet, *Enough Rope* (poems, 1926); *Sunset Gun* (poems, 1928); *Laments for the Living* (1930); *Death and Taxes* (poems, 1931); *After Such Pleasures* (1933); *Collected Poems: Not So Deep as a Well* (1936); *Here Lies: The Collected Stories* (1939); *Sunset Guns* (poems, 1939); *Collected Poetry* (1944); etc. Co-author: *Close Harmony* (plays with Elmer Rice, 1924); *Ladies of the Corridor* (play, with Arnaud D'Usseau, 1953). Drama critic, *Vanity Fair,* 1917–20; book reviewer, *Esquire;* etc.

PARKER, FRANCIS WAYLAND (Oct. 9, 1837–Mar. 2, 1902); b. in Bedford Township, N.H. Educational reformer, author. *How to Study Geography* (1889); *Talks on Pedagogies* (1889); *Uncle Robert's Geography,* 4v. (with Nellie L. Helm, 1897–1904).

PARKER, FRANKLIN (June 2, 1921–   ); b. New York. Educator, author. *African Development and Education in Southern Rhodesia* (1960); *Africa South of the Sahara* (1966). Professor of education, University of Oklahoma, since 1964.

PARKER, H[elen Eliza] F[itch] (Mrs. Henry Webster Parker) (1827–1874); b. Auburn, N.Y. Author. *Morning Stars of the New World* (1854), republished as *Discoverers and Pioneers of America* (1856); *Constance Aylmer* (1869); etc.

PARKER, HENRY TAYLOR (Apr. 29, 1867–Mar. 31, 1934); b. Boston, Mass. Dramatic critic. Correspondent for a number of newspapers; drama and music critic, the *Boston Transcript,* 1905–34, signing his articles "H.T.P." *See* David McCord's *H.T.P.: Portrait of a Critic* (1935).

PARKER, HORATIO WILLIAM (Sept. 15, 1863–Dec. 18, 1919); b. Auburndale, Mass. Educator, composer. His best-known composition was *Hora Novissima.* Prof. music, Yale University, 1894–1919, dean, school of music, 1903–04. See *Musical Quarterly,* Apr., 1930, for a list of his works. *See also* G. W. Chadwick's *Horatio Parker* (1921).

PARKER, JAMES (c. 1714–July 2, 1770); b. Woodbridge, N.J. Printer. Founder, the *Connecticut Gazette* at New Haven, Conn., Apr. 12, 1755. Printed the *New American Magazine,* at Woodbridge, Jan., 1758–Mar., 1760. In New York he printed the *Independent Reflector;* the *Occasional Reverberator; John Englishman;* the *Instructor;* the *New-York Weekly Post-Boy,* etc.

PARKER, JAMES REID (June 2, 1909–); b. Jersey City, N.J. Author. *Academic Procession* (1937); *Attorneys at Law* (1941); *The Pleasure Was Mine* (1946); *Open House* (1951); *The Merry Wives of Massachusetts* (1959); etc. Columnist, "Small World," in *Woman's Day,* 1947–64.

PARKER, JANE MARSH (June 16, 1836–Mar. 13, 1913); b. Milan, N.Y. Author. *Barley Wood* (1860); *Dick Wortley* (1862); *The Midnight Cry* (1886); etc.

PARKER, JOEL (Jan. 25, 1795–Aug. 17, 1875); b. Jaffrey, N.H. Jurist, author. *Daniel Webster as a Jurist* (1852); *International Law* (1862); *Revolution and Reconstruction* (1866); etc. Royall prof. law, Harvard University, 1847–68.

PARKER, LOTTIE BLAIR (c. 1858–Jan. 5, 1937); b. Oswego, N.Y. Actress, playwright. *Way Down East* (prod. 1898); *Homespun* (1909); etc.

PARKER, MAUDE (Mrs. Edmund W. Pavenstedt) (d. Nov. 13, 1959); b. Galveston, Tex. Author. *The Social Side of Diplomatic Life* (1926); *Secret Envoy* (1930); *Impersonation of a Lady* (1934); *The Intriguer* (1952); *Along Came a Spider* (1959); *Death Us Do Part* (1960).

PARKER, RICHARD GREEN (Dec. 25, 1798–Sept. 25, 1869); b. Boston, Mass. Educator, author. *Progressive Exercises in English Composition* (1832); *Progressive Exercises in Rhetorical Reading* (1835); *A Tribute to the Life and Character of Jonas Chickering* (1854); *The National Fifth Reader* (with James M. Watson, 1858); etc. With the Boston public school system, 1825–53.

PARKER, SAMUEL (1779–1866). Congregational clergyman. *Journal of an Exploring Tour Beyond the Rocky Mountains* (1838).

Parker, Seth. Pen name of Phillips H. Lord.

PARKER, THEODORE (Aug. 24, 1810–May 10, 1860); b. Lexington, Mass. Unitarian clergyman, abolitionist, author. *A Discourse on Matters Pertaining to Religion* (1842); *Ten Sermons of Religion* (1853); *Theism, Atheism, and Popular Theology* (1853); *The Collected Works,* ed. by Frances P. Cobbe, 14v. (1863–72); and the Centenary Edition, 15v. (1907–11); etc. Founder, *Massachusetts Quarterly Review,* 1849. *See* John Weiss's *Life and Correspondence of Theodore Parker* (1864); Henry Steele Commager's *Theodore Parker* (1936).

PARKER, THOMAS (1595–1677); b. in England. Protestant clergyman, educator. *True Copy of a Letter Written by Mr. T. Parker . . .* (1644); *The Visions and Prophecies of Daniel Expounded* (1646).

PARKER, W[alter] COLEMAN. Playwright. *The Bank Cashier* (prod. 1893); *All a Mistake* (prod. 1898); *Brother Josiah* (prod. 1903); *Lovers and Lunatics* (prod. 1905); etc.

PARKER, WILLIAM BELMONT (Sept. 9, 1871–Oct. 6, 1934); b. Hasbury, Eng. Author. *The Wisdom of Emerson* (1909); *Life of Edward Rowland Sill* (1915); *Peruvians of Today* (1919); *Cubans of Today* (1919); *Argentines of Today* (1920); *Chileans of Today* (1920); *Paraguayans of Today*

(1920); *Bolivians of Today* (1920); *Uruguayans of Today* (1921); etc. Assoc. editor, *Atlantic Monthly,* 1898–1902; with Baker & Taylor Co., booksellers, 1902–12.

PARKER, WILLIAM HARWAR (Oct. 8, 1826–Dec. 30, 1896); b. New York. Naval officer, author. *Elements of Seamanship* (1864); *Recollections of a Naval Officer, 1841–1865* (1883); *Familiar Talks on Astronomy* (1889).

Parker House. Boston, Mass. Famous hostelry. Here on May 5, 1857, Emerson, Lowell, Holmes, Longfellow, Motley, Phillips, Cabot, and Underwood formulated plans for a new magazine, the *Atlantic Monthly.* (q.v.).

PARKES, HENRY BAMFORD (Nov. 13, 1904–Jan. 7, 1972); b. Sheffield, Eng. Author. *Jonathan Edwards* (1930); *A History of Mexico* (1938); *Recent America: A History of the United States Since 1900* (1941); *The Pragmatic Test* (1941); *The World After War* (1942); *The American Experience* (1947); *The United States of America* (1953); *God and Men* (1959); *The Divine Order* (1969); etc. History department, New York University, 1930–68.

PARKHURST, CHARLES HENRY (Apr. 17, 1842–Sept. 8, 1933); b. Framingham, Mass. Presbyterian clergyman, reformer, author. *The Swiss Guide* (1889); *Our Fight with Tammany* (1895); *A Little Lower Than the Angels* (1909); *The Pulpit and the Pew* (1913); *My Forty Years in New York* (autobiography, 1923); etc.

PARKHURST, HELEN (Mar. 8, 1892–); b. Durand, Wis. Educator. *Education on the Dalton Plan* (1922); *Work Rhythms in Education* (1935); *Exploring the Child's World* (1951); etc. Started Dalton School, New York; headmistress to 1942.

PARKMAN, FRANCIS (Sept. 16, 1823–Nov. 8, 1893); b. Boston, Mass. Historian, author. *The California and Oregon Trail* (1849); *History of the Conspiracy of Pontiac,* 2v. (1851); *Vassall Morton* (1856); *Pioneers of France in the New World* (1865); *The Book of Roses* (1866); *The Jesuits in North America* (1867); *The Discovery of the Great West* (1869), republished as *La Salle and the Discovery of the Great West* (1879); *The Old Regime in Canada* (1874); *Count Frontenac and New France under Louis XIV* (1877); *Montcalm and Wolfe* (1884); *A Half Century of Conflict* (1892); *The Works of Francis Parkman,* 20v. (1897–98); *Francis Parkman's Works,* 12v. (1899); etc. *See* Charles H. Farnham's *A Life of Francis Parkman* (1900); Howard N. Doughty's *Francis Parkman* (1962); W. R. Jacobs' *The Letters of Francis Parkman,* 2v. (1960); Otis A. Pease's *Parkman's History* (1953, 1968).

PARKS, EDD WINFIELD (Feb. 25, 1906–); b. Newbern, Tenn. Educator, author. *Segments of Southern Thought* (1939); *Long Hunter* (1942); *Predestinate Iron* (poems, 1948); *Little Long Rifle* (1949); *Safe on Second* (1953); *Backwater* (1957); *William Gilmore Simms as Literary Critic* (1960); *Thomas MacDonagh: the Man, the Patriot, the Writer* with Allen Wells Parks (1967); etc. English dept., University of Georgia, since 1935.

Parks, Elizabeth Robins. See Elizabeth Robins.

PARKS, GORDON ALEXANDER BUCHANAN (Nov. 30, 1912–   ); b. Ft. Scott, Kans. Author, photographer, composer. *The Learning Tree* (1963); *A Choice of Weapons* (1966); etc.

PARKS, JOSEPH HOWARD (Dec. 16, 1903–); b. in Lincoln Co., Tenn. Author. *Felix Grundy* (1940); *John Bell of Tennessee* (1950); *General Edmund Kirby Smith, C.S.A.* (1954); *Leonidas Polk: The Fighting Bishop* (1962); etc. Chairman, history dept., University of Georgia, since 1958.

PARKS, LEIGHTON (Feb. 10, 1852–Mar. 21, 1938); b. New York. Episcopal clergyman, author. *The Crisis of the Churches* (1922); *What is Modernism?* (1924); *Turnpikes and Dirt Roads* (reminiscences, 1927); etc.

PARKS, WILLIAM (c. 1698–Apr. 1, 1750); b. in Shropshire, Eng. Colonial printer and publisher. Founder, the *Maryland Gazette* (1727); the *Virginia Gazette* (1736). *See* Lawrence C. Wroth's *William Parks, Printer and Journalist of England and Colonial America* (1926).

Parley, Peter. Pen name of Samuel Griswold Goodrich.

Parley's Magazine. Boston, Mass. Founded Mar. 16, 1833, by Samuel G. Goodrich, known as "Peter Parley." A favorite magazine among children. Illustrated with woodcuts. Hannah F. Gould and Lydia Sigourney were regular contributors. Expired Dec., 1844. *See* Samuel G. Goodrich's *Recollections of a Life Time,* 2v. (1857).

PARMENTER, CHRISTINE WHITING (Mrs. Kenneth R. Parmenter) (Dec. 21, 1877–Mar. 3, 1953); b. Plainfield, N. J. Author. *Jean's Winter with the Warners* (1924); *The Treasure at Shady Vale* (1925); *The Unknown Port* (1927); *One Wide River to Cross* (1928); *The Dusty Highway* (1929); *So Wise We Grow* (1930); *Miss Alladin* (1932); *Shining Palace* (1933); *The Wind Blows West* (1934); *The Kings of Beacon Hill* (1935); *Swift Waters* (1937); *Stories of Courage and Devotion* (1939); *As the Seed is Sown* (1940); *A Golden Age* (1942); *Fair Were the Days* (1947); *Stronger Than Law* (1948); etc.

Parnassuss on Wheels. By Christopher Morley (1917). Story of a perambulating library.

"Parrhasius." Poem by Nathaniel Parker Willis (1831).

PARRINGTON, VERNON LOUIS (Aug. 3, 1871–June 16, 1929); b. Aurora, Ill. Educator, philologist, author. *Main Currents in American Thought,* 3v. (1927–30), Vol. I, *The Colonial Mind,* won the Pulitzer prize for history, 1928; *Sinclair Lewis, Our Own Diogenes* (1927); etc. Editor: *The Connecticut Wits* (1926). English dept., University of Washington, 1908–29, prof. 1912–29.

PARRISH, ANNE (Mrs. Josiah Titzell) (Nov. 12, 1888–Sept. 5, 1957); b. Colorado Springs, Colo. Novelist. *Pocketful of Poses* (1923); *Knee High to a Grasshopper* (with Dillwyn Parrish, 1923); *The Dream Coach* (with same, 1924); *Lustres* (with same, 1924); *Semi-Attached* (1924); *The Perennial Bachelor* (1925); *Tomorrow Morning* (1926); *All Kneeling* (1928); *The Methodist Faun* (1929); *Floating Island* (1930); *Loads of Love* (1932); *Sea Level* (1934); *Golden Wedding* (1936); *Mr. Despondency's Daughter* (1938); *Pray for a Tomorrow* (1941); *Poor Child* (1945); *A Clouded Star* (1948); *The Story of Appleby Capple* (1950); *And Have Not Love* (1954); etc.

PARRISH, MAXFIELD (July 25, 1870–Mar. 30, 1966); b. Philadelphia, Pa. Artist, illustrator. Illustrator of Eugene Field's *Poems of Childhood,* Kenneth Grahame's *Golden Age* and *Dream Days, The Arabian Nights,* Palgrave's *The Golden Treasury,* etc. He made many illustrations for *Scribner's Magazine* and other periodicals. His paintings are noted for their rich blues.

PARRISH, PHILIP HAMMON (Sept. 5, 1896–1956); b. Constantine, Mich. Journalist, author. *Before the Covered Wagon* (1931); *Historic Oregon* (1937); etc. Editorial staff, *The Oregonian,* Portland, Ore., from 1928.

PARRISH, RANDALL (June 10, 1858–Aug. 9, 1923); b. in Henry Co., Ill. Author. *A Sword of the Old Frontier* (1900); *When Wilderness Was King* (1904); *My Lady of the North* (1904); *Historic Illinois* (1905); *The Great Plains* (1907); *Don MacGrath* (1910); *Keith of the Border* (1910); *Love under Fire* (1911); *My Lady of Doubt* (1911); *Molly McDonald* (1912); *The Mystery of the Silver Dagger* (1920); etc.

PARROTT, THOMAS MARC (Dec 22, 1866–Feb. 5, 1960); b. Dayton, O. Educator, author. *Studies of a Book-Lover* (1904); *A Short View of Elizabethan Drama* (with R. H. Ball, 1943); *Shakespearean Comedy* (1949). Editor: *English Poems, from Chaucer to Kipling* (with A. W. Long, 1902); *Chap-*

man's Tragedies (1910); *Chapman's Comedies* (1914); *William Shakespeare: A Handbook* (1934); *Shakespeare: Twenty-Three Plays and the Sonnets* (1938); and many separate plays of Shakespeare. English dept., Princeton University, 1896–1935. *See* Harry Clemon's *Published Writings of Professor Parrott* (1935).

PARROTT, URSULA (Mar. 26, 1902–); b. Boston, Mass. Novelist. *Ex-Wife* (1929); *Strangers May Kiss* (1930); *Love Goes Past* (1931); *The Tumult and the Shouting* (1933); *Next Time We Live* (1935); *For All Our Lives* (1938); *Life Is for the Living* (1939); *One More Such Victory* (1942); *Even in a Hundred Years* (1944); etc.

PARRY, ALBERT (Feb. 24, 1901–); b. Rostov-on-the-Don, Russia. Author. *Tattoo: The Secrets of a Strange Art* (1933); *Garrets and Pretenders: A History of Bohemianism in America* (1933); *Whistler's Father* (1939); *Russian Cavalcade* (1944); *Russia's Rockets and Missiles* (1960); *America Learns Russian* (1967); etc. Under pen name "Victor Leclerc;" *The Scandalous Mrs. Blackford* (with H. T. Kane, 1951).

PARRY, HUGH JONES (Mar. 10, 1916–); b. London. Government official, author. Writes under pen name "James Cross." *Root of Evil* (1957); *The Dark Road* (1959); *The Grave of Heroes* (1961); *To Hell for Half a Crown* (1967); etc.

PARRY, JOHN HORACE (Apr. 26, 1914–   ); b. Handsworth, Eng. Educator, author. *The Spanish Theory of Empire* (1940); *The Audiencia of New Galicia* (1949); *Europe and a Wider World* (1949); *The Sale of Public Office in the Spanish Indies* (1953); *A Short History of the West Indies* (1956); *The Age of Reconnaissance* (1963); *The Spanish Seaborne Empire* (1965). Professor oceanic history and affairs, Harvard University, since 1965.

PARSHLEY, HOWARD MADISON (Aug. 7, 1884–May 19, 1953); b. Hallowell, Me. Zoologist, educator. *Science and Good Behavior* (1928); *Science of Human Reproduction* (1933); *Survey of Biology* (1940); etc. Translator: *The Second Sex* by Simone de Beauvoir (1953); *The Life and Habits of Wild Mammals* by F. Bourlière (1954). Zoology dept., Smith College, 1917–52.

PARSON, DONALD (1882–Dec. 28, 1961); b. Washington, D.C. Author. *Glass Flowers* (poems, 1936); *Surely the Author* (poems, 1944); *Portraits of Keats* (1954); *Fall of the Cards* (1959); etc.

PARSONS, ALICE BEAL (Oct. 8, 1886–Apr. 14, 1962); b. Rockford, Ill. Author. *Woman's Dilemma* (1926); *The Insider* (1929); *John Merrill's Pleasant Life* (1930); *A Lady Who Lost* (1932); *The Mountain* (stories, 1944); *The World Around the Mountain* (stories, 1947); etc.

PARSONS, EDWARD ALEXANDER (Mar. 28, 1878–) b. New Orleans, La. Lawyer, book collector, author. *English as a World Literature* (1916); *The Latin City* (1921); *Dante Alighieri* (1924); *500 Years of Printing* (1940); *The Diplomatic Story of the Louisiana Purchase* (1943); *The Alexandrian Library, Amsterdam* (1952); *Original Letters of Robert R. Livingston* (1953); etc. The Bibliotheca Parsoniana, New Orleans, contains over 50,000 books, manuscripts, and prints.

PARSONS, ELSIE [Worthington] Clews (Mrs. Herbert Parsons) (1875–Dec. 19, 1941). Folklorist, author. *The Family* (1906); *The Old-Fashioned Woman* (1913); *Notes on Zuñi* (1917); *The Pueblo of Jemez* (1925); *Mitla, Town of Souls* (1936); *Taos Tales* (1940); etc. Editor: *American Indian Life* (1922); *Folk-Lore of the Sea Islands, South Carolina* (1923); *Folk-Lore from the Cape Verde Islands,* 2v. (1924); etc.

PARSONS, EUGENE (June 14, 1855–June 22, 1933); b. Henderson, N.Y. Author. *George Washington* (1898); *The Making of Colorado* (1908); *History of Colorado* (1917); etc.

PARSONS, GEOFFREY (Sept. 5, 1879–Dec. 8, 1956) b. Douglaston, N.Y. Journalist, author. *The Land of Fair Play* (1919); *The Stream of History* (1928). With the *New York Evening Sun,* 1906–13; the *New York Tribune, 1913–24;* chief editorial writer, the *New York Herald Tribune,* 1924–52.

PARSONS, GEORGE FREDERIC (Jan. 15, 1840–July 19, 1893); b. Brighton, Eng. Editor, journalist, author. *Life of James Marshall* (1871); *Middle Ground: A Novel* (1874); etc. With *New York Tribune.*

PARSONS, LOUELLA O[ettinger] (Aug. 6, 1893–); b. Freeport, Ill. Columnist. *How to Write for the Movies* (1914); *The Gay Illiterate* (autobiography, 1944); *Tell It to Louella* (1961). With Hearst Publications, 1922–65.

PARSONS, TALCOTT (Dec. 13, 1902–); b. Colorado Springs, Colo. Sociologist, author. *The Structure of Social Action* (1937); *Toward a General Theory of Action* (1951); *The Social System* (1951); *Structure and Process in Modern Societies* (1960); *Social Structure and Personality* (1964); *Sociological Theory and Modern Society* (1968); etc. Co-author: *Economy and Society* (1956); *Economy and Society* (1956); *Societies: Evolutionary and Comparative Perspectives* (1966); etc. Translator: Max Weber's *The Protestant Ethic and the Spirit of Capitalism* (1930).

PARSONS, THEOPHILUS (May 17, 1797–Jan. 26, 1882); b. Newburyport, Mass. Educator, author. *The Constitution* (1861); *Essays,* 3v. (1845–62); *The Law of Conscience* (1853); *Deus Homo* (1867); *Outlines of the Religion and Philosophy of Swedenborg* (1875); etc. Prof of law, Harvard University, 1847–69.

PARSONS, THOMAS WILLIAM (Aug. 18, 1819–Sept. 3, 1892); b Boston, Mass. Dentist, poet, translator. *Poems* (1854); *The Magnolia* (1866); *The Shadow of the Obelisk, and Other Poems* (1872); *The Willey House, and Sonnets* (1875); *Poems* (1893); *The Old House of Sudbury* (1870); etc. Translator: Dante's *Inferno* (1867). He published the first ten cantos of the *Inferno* in 1843, and seventeen cantos in 1865. Fragments of the *Purgatorio* and *Paradiso* were published in 1893. His best-known lyrics are "On a Bust of Dante" and "Paradisi Gloria." *See* Richard Hovey's poem, "Seward: an Elegy on the Death of Thomas William Parsons" (1893), and Longfellow's *Tales of a Wayside Inn,* in which the "poet" is based on Parsons.

PARSONS, WILFRID (Mar. 17, 1887–Oct. 28, 1958); b. Philadelphia, Pa. Roman Catholic clergyman, editor, educator, author. *Mexican Martyrdom* (1936); *The First Freedom* (1948); etc. Editor, *America,* 1925–36. Compiler: *Early Catholic Americana* (1939). Prof. political science, Georgetown University, 1936–40; dean, 1939–40; prof. political science, Catholic University from 1940.

Partisan Leader, The. By Nathaniel Beverley Tucker (under pen name "Edward William Sidney," 1836, deliberately dated 1856). An influential book which foretold the Civil War. It sought to popularize the doctrine of secession. It was suppressed, but during the Civil War was revived by both sides for propaganda purposes.

Partisan Review. New York. Founded 1934 under the auspices of the John Reed Club of New York and edited, since 1934, by Nathan Adler, Edward Dahlberg, Joseph Freeman, Philip Rahv. William Phillips, Delmore Schwartz, Dwight MacDonald, and others. At various times published quarterly, bimonthly, and monthly. Contributors have included T. S. Eliot, Edmund Wilson, W. H. Auden, Saul Bellow, Allen Tate, Sidney Hook, Mary McCarthy. Notable for introducing European writers in translation and for its uncompromising social criticism. Avon Books has published paperback anthologies of selections taken from past issues. *Partisan Review* has been one of the most influential literary magazines in the United States since its inception. Richard Poirier and Steven Marcus recently joined the editorial board.

PARTON, ETHEL (Dec. 1, 1862–); b. New York, daughter of Mortimer Thompson, niece of James Parton (whose name she took legally), grand-daughter of Sarah Payson Parton, and great grand-daughter of Nathaniel Willis. Author. *Melissa Ann, a Little Girl of the Eighteen Twenties* (1931); *Tabitha Mary, a Little Girl of 1810* (1933); *Penelope Ellen and Her Friends: Three Little Girls of 1840* (1936); *Vinny Applegay: Her First Year in New York: A Story of the 1870's* (1937); *The Lost Locket: The Newburyport of 1830* (1940); *The Year Without a Summer* (1945); etc. On staff of the *Youth's Companion* for many years.

PARTON, JAMES (Feb. 9, 1822–Oct. 17, 1891); b. Canterbury, Eng. Biographer. Husband of Sara Payson Parton. *The Life of Horace Greeley* (1855); *The Life and Times of Aaron Burr* (1857); *Life of Andrew Jackson,* 3v. (1859–60); *Life and Times of Benjamin Franklin,* 2v. (1864); *Famous Americans of Recent Times* (1867); *Fanny Fern: A Memorial Volume* (1873); *Life of Thomas Jefferson* (1874); *Life of Voltaire, 2v.* (1881); etc.

PARTON, JAMES (Dec. 10, 1912–); b. Newburyport, Mass. Publisher. Staff, *Time* magazine, 1935–47; founder, American Heritage Publishing Co., 1954.

PARTON, LEMUEL FREDERICK (d. Jan. 30, 1943); b. Platteville, Colo. Journalist. On staff, the *Chicago Tribune;* the *Los Angeles Herald; San Francisco Bulletin;* etc. Author of syndicated column, "Who's News Today," from 1931.

PARTON, SARA PAYSON [Willis] (Mrs. Charles H. Eldredge; Mrs. Samuel H. Farington; Mrs. James Parton) (July 9, 1811–Oct. 10, 1872); b. Portland, Me., sister of Nathaniel Parker Willis. Author. Pen name "Fanny Fern." *Fern Leaves from Fanny's Portfolio,* 2 series (1853–54); *Little Ferns for Fanny's Little Friends* (1854); *Ruth Hall* (1855); *Rose Clark* (1856); *Fresh Leaves* (1857); *Ginger-Snaps* (1870); *Caper-Sauce* (1870); etc. Wrote weekly for Bonner's *New York Ledger,* 1856–72, being the highest paid author of her day. See James Parton's *Fanny Fern: A Memorial Volume* (1873); *The Colophon,* part 18, 1934.

PARTRIDGE, BELLAMY (1878–July 5, 1960); b. Phelps, N.Y. Author. *Sube Cain* (1917); *Cousins* (1925); *Splendid Norseman* (1929); *A Pretty Pickle* (1930); *Sir Billy Howe* (1932); *Pure and Simple* (1934); *The Roosevelt Family in America* (1936); *Thunder Shower* (1936); *Horse and Buggy* (1937); *Get a Horse* (1937); *Country Lawyer* (1939); *Big Family* (1941); *Excuse My Dust* (1943); *January Thaw* (1945, dramatized and prod. 1946); *As We Were* (with Otto Bettmann (1946); *The Big Freeze* (1948); *The Old Oaken Bucket* (1949); *Salad Days* (1951); *Fill'er Up! The Story of Fifty Years of Motoring* (1952); *The Ainsley Case* (1955); *Going, Going, Gone!* (1958); etc. Editor, *Brentano's Book Chat,* 1925–29; editor, Arcadia House publications, 1934–36.

PARTRIDGE, HELEN LAWRENCE DAVIS (Mrs. Bellamy Partridge) (Oct. 22, 1902–); b. Sandy Hill, N.Y. Author. *If the Sky Fall* (1935); *No Moon But This* (1935); *The Windy Hill* (1936); *Idle Rainbow* (under pen naem "Phoebe Sheldon," 1936); *Sing Once More* (1937); *Time Is Forever* (1938); *But Once a Year* (1941).

PARTRIDGE, WILLIAM ORDWAY (Apr. 11, 1861–May 22, 1930); b. Paris. Sculptor, author. *Art for America* (1894); *Song-Life of a Sculptor* (1894); *The Angel of Clay* (1900); *The Czar's Gift* (1906); etc.

PASCAL, ERNEST (Jan. 11, 1896–); b. London. Novelist. *The Dark Swan* (1924); *The Virgin Flame* (1925); *Cynthia Codentry* (1926); *The Marriage Bed* (1927) *The Age for Love* (1930); *Woman at Thirty* (1934).

Pasquin. Pen name of Paul Allen.

Passionate Pilgrim, A. Story by Henry James (1871).

PASTOR, TONY (May 28, 1837–Aug. 26, 1908); b. New York. Actor, manager, song-writer. Introduced "legitimate" vaudeville. Founded Tony Pastor's Theatre in New York, 1888. Wrote several songs, and discovered Lillian Russell and many others of America's stage stars. See *Tony Pastor's New Union Song Book* (1862).

PASTORIUS, FRANCIS DANIEL (Sept. 26, 1651–1719); b. Sommerhausen, Ger. Lawyer, author. *A New Primmer or Methodical Directions to Attain the True Spelling, Reading & Writing of English* (n.d.). *The Beehive,* his commonplace book left in a compendious manuscript, is a mine of information. He was the founder of Germantown, Pa., Oct., 1683. See Oswald Seidensticker's *The First Century of German Printing in America, 1728–1830* (1893); *Americana Germanica,* v. 1-2 (1897–98).

"Pasture, The." Poem of invocation in Robert Frost's *North of Boston* (1915).

PATCH, EDITH MARION (July 27, 1876–Sept. 28, 1954); b. Worcester, Mass. Naturalist, author. *Hexapod Stories* (1920); *Bird Stories* (1921); *First Lessons in Nature Study* (1926); *Holiday Hill* (1931); *Outdoor Visits* (1932); *Through Four Seasons* (1933); *Mountain Neighbors* (1936); *Desert Neighbors* (1937); *Forest Neighbors* (1938); *Prairie Neighbors* (1940).

PATCH, HOWARD ROLLIN (Aug. 7, 1889–); b. Lake Linden, Mich. Educator, author. *The Goddess Fortuna in Medieval Literature* (1927); *The Tradition of Boethius* (1935); *On Rereading Chaucer* (1939); *Cupid on the Stair* (1942); *The Other World; According to Descriptions in Medieval Literature* (1950); etc. English dept., Smith College, 1917–57.

PATCH, KATE WHITING (Aug. 22, 1870–1909); b. Elizabeth, N.J. Author. *Middleway* (1897); *Old Lady and Young Laddie* (1900); *Prince Yellowtop* (1903); etc.

PATCHEN, KENNETH (Dec. 13, 1911–Jan. 8, 1972); b. Niles, O. Artist, poet. *Before the Brave* (1936); *First Will and Testament* (1939); *The Journal of Albion Moonlight* (1941); *The Dark Kingdom* (1942); *Memoirs of a Shy Pornographer* (1945); *Sleepers Awake* (1946); *Red Wine and Yellow Hair* (1949); *The Famous Boating Party* (1954); *Hurrah for Anything* (1957); *Because It Is* (1959); *Don't Look Now* (1950); *But Even So* (1963); *Doubleheader* (1966); *Hallelujah Anyway* (1967); *Collected Poems* (1968).

PATCHIN, FRANK GLINES (Dec. 19, 1861–Mar. 22, 1925); b. Wayland, N.Y. Author. The *Pony Rider Boys* series; the *Circus Boys* series; the *Battleship Boys* series; the *Meadowbrook Girls* series; the *Grace Harlowe Overseas* series; the *Grace Harlowe Overland Riders* series; the *Ted Jones* series; *Uncle Jim's Bible Stories,* 3v. (1923); etc. Wrote several boys' and girls' books a year for many years, the dates of which are difficult to determine on account of reprints.

Paterson. Long poem by William Carlos Williams, 4v. (1946–51).

Patterson, Anne. Pen name of Anne F. Einselen.

PATERSON, ISABEL (1885–Jan. 10, 1961); b. on Manitoulin Island, Lake Huron, Ont. Critic, novelist. *The Shadow Riders* (1916); *The Magpie's Nest* (1917); *The Singing Season* (1924); *The Fourth Queen* (1926); *The Road of the Gods* (1930); *Never Ask the End* (1932); *Golden Vanity* (1934); *If It Prove Fair Weather* (1940); *The God of the Machine* (1943); etc. Wrote column for *New York Herald Tribune Books* entitled "Turns With a Bookworm," 1926–49.

Pathfinder. Washington, D.C. Weekly news magazine. Founded 1894, as *Pathfinder Magazine,* by George D. Mitchell. Bought by Sevellon Brown in 1936, by James L. Bray in 1938, and by Emil Hurja in 1939. Graham C. Patterson bought it in 1943 although Hurja remained on the staff until 1945. Its name was changed to *Pathfinder* in 1954. Before publication was suspended in 1957, the name was changed to *Town Journal*.

PATRI, ANGELO (Nov., 1877–Sept. 12, 1965); b. in Italy. Educator, author. *White Patch* (1911); *A School Master of the Great City* (1917); *Spirit of America* (1924); *Problems of Childhood* (1926); *The Questioning Child* (1930); *Your Children in War Time* (1943); *How to Help Your Child Grow Up* (1948); *Biondino* (1951); etc. Author of syndicated articles on education of children. With public school system, New York City, 1898–1944.

PATRICK, JOHN (full name John Patrick Goggan) (May 17, 1905–); b. Louisville, Ky. Playwright. *Hell Freezes Over* (prod. 1936); *The Hasty Heart* (prod. 1945); *Curious Savage* (prod. 1950); *Lo and Behold!* (prod. 1951); *Teahouse of the August Moon* (prod. 1953, Pulitzer Prize for drama, 1954); *Good as Gold* (1957); *Everybody Loves Opal* (1961); *Everybody's Girl* (1967); *Scandal Point* (1968); *Love Is a Time of Day* (1969); etc.

Patrick, Keats. Pen name of Walter Karig.

"Patrick, Mind the Baby." Barroom ballad in the comedy *Doyle Brothers* by Edward Harrigan (prod. 1874).

Patrick, Q. Pen name of Hugh Callingham Wheeler and R. Wilson Webb.

PATRICK, TED (Sept. 3, 1901–Mar. 11, 1964); b. Rutherford, N.J. Editor. Editor, *Holiday Magazine*, from 1946.

Patrick Henry Literary Society. Richmond, Va. This society flourished around 1845–60, and two of its leading members, John M. Daniel and Robert William Hughes, edited the *Richmond Examiner*.

Patrins. By Louise Imogen Guiney (1897). A collection of twenty essays. "Patrins" is a Romany word, signifying the scattered leaves which gipsies throw on the road to mark their trail so that other gipsies may follow. Similar to the woodsman's tree blazing.

Patriot Chief, The. Play by Peter Markoe (1784).

PATTEE, FRED LEWIS (Mar. 22, 1863–May 6, 1950); b. Bristol, N.H. Literary critic, educator, author. *The Wine of May and Other Lyrics* (1893); *A History of American Literature* (1896); *The Foundations of English Literature* (1900); *Mary Garvin* (1902); *Compelled Men* (1913); *The Development of the American Short Story* (1923); *Tradition and Jazz* (1924); *The New American Literature* (1930); *Mark Twain* (1935); *The Feminine Fifties* (1940); *Penn State Yankee* (autobiography, 1954); etc. Prof. American literature, Pennsylvania State College, 1894–1928.

PATTEN, GEORGE WASHINGTON (Dec 25, 1808–Apr. 28, 1882); b. Newport, R.I. *Voices of the Border* (poems, 1867).

PATTEN, SIMON NELSON (May 1, 1852–July 24, 1922); b. in De Kalb County, Ill. Economist, author. *The Premises of Political Economy* (1885); *The Development of English Thought* (1899); *The New Basis of Civilization* (1907); *Folk Lore* (poems, 1919); *Mud Hollow* (1922); etc. Prof. political economy, University of Pennsylvania, 1888–1917.

PATTEN, WILLIAM (Nov. 27, 1868–July 27, 1936); b. New York. Illustrator, editor. Compiler: *Short Story Classics, American,* 5v. (1905); *Great Short Stories,* 3v. (1906); *Short Story Classics, Foreign,* 5v. (1907). Managing editor: *Harvard Classics,* 50v. (1909–10).

PATTEN, WILLIAM GILBERT (Oct. 25, 1866–Jan. 16, 1945); b. Corinna, Me. Pen name "Burt L. Standish." Creator of character "Frank Merriwell." The *Meriwell* series, 208v. (1900–33); the *Rockspur* series, 3v. (1900); the *Cliff Sterling* series, 5v. (1910–16); the *College Life* series, 6v. (1913–28); the *Big League* series, 14v. (1913–28); the *Rex*

Kingdon series, 5v. (1916–25); the *Oakdale* series, 6v. (1916–25); *Mr. Frank Merriwell* (1941); etc. See John Levi Cutler's *Gilbert Patten and His Frank Merriwell Saga* (1934), in *University of Maine Studies,* 2d series, no. 31.

"Patterns." Poem by Amy Lowell (1912).

Patterns. By Rod Serling (1957). Four long television dramas by one of the few authors whose plays in this medium are also notable as literary works.

Patterns of Culture. By Ruth Benedict (1934). Anthropological discussion of the cultural values of three primitive societies. The author extends the results of her analysis to our modern world.

PATTERSON, ADA, b. Mount Joy, Pa. Author. *Maude Adams: A Biography* (1907); *Love's Lightning* (with Robert Edenson, prod. 1918); etc.

PATTERSON, ALICIA (Mrs. Harry F. Guggenheim) (d. July 2, 1963); b. Chicago, Ill. Editor, publisher. Founder with husband, *Newsday,* Long Island daily, 1940; editor and publisher from 1940 to 1963.

PATTERSON, ELEANOR MEDILL (Mar. 7, 1884–July 24, 1948); b. Chicago, Ill. Editor, author. Pen name "Eleanor M. Gizycka." *Glass Houses* (1926); *Fall Flight* (1928). Editor and publisher, *Washington Times-Herald. See* Paul Francis Healy's *Eleanor M. Patterson* (1966).

PATTERSON, FRANK ALLEN (Aug. 14, 1878–Aug. 4, 1944); b. Allen's Hill, Ontario Co., N.Y. Educator, author. *The Middle English Penitential Lyric* (1911). Editor: *The Complete Works of John Milton,* 18v. (1931); etc. English dept., Columbia University, 1912–43.

PATTERSON, JOSEPH M[edill] (Jan. 6, 1879–May 26, 1946); b. Chicago, Ill. Editor, author. *Little Brother of the Rich* (1908); *Rebellion* (1911); etc. Co-editor and co-publisher, *Chicago Tribune,* 1914–25. Editor, *New York Daily News.*

PATTERSON, MARJORIE, b. Baltimore, Md. Author. *Fortunata* (1911); *The Dust of the Road* (1913); *A Woman's Man* (1919).

PATTERSON, NORMA; b. in Texas. Author. *Jenny* (1930); *The Gay Procession* (1930); *The Sun Shines Bright* (1932); *Give Them Their Dream* (1938); *Love Is Forever* (1941); *When The Lights Go Up Again* (1943); etc.

PATTERSON, ROBERT MAYNE (July 17, 1832–Apr. 5, 1911); b. Philadelphia, Pa. Presbyterian clergyman, editor, author. *Character of Abraham Lincoln* (1864); *Our National Religion* (1876); *Isaiah and the Higher Critics* (1889); *William Blackwood* (1894); *American Presbyterianism* (1896). Editor, *The Presbyterian,* 1870–80; the *Presbyterian Journal,* 1880–93.

PATTERSON, SAMUEL WHITE (Dec. 25, 1883–); b. New York. Educator, author. *Famous Men and Places in the History of New York City* (1923); *Teaching the Child to Read* (1930); *Old Chelsea and St. Peter's Church* (1935); *Etchings in Verse* (1939); *Poet of Christmas Eve: A Life of Clement Clarke Moore* (1956); *When Saint Nicholas Got Back* (1959); etc. Faculty, Hunter College, since 1930.

PATTIE, JAMES OHIO (1804–c. 1850); b. in Bracken Co., Ky. Trapper, author. *Personal Narrative,* ed. by Timothy Flint (1831); plagiarized and abridged by B. Bilson in *The Hunters of Kentucky; or, The Trials and Toils of Trappers and Traders* (1847). Pattie's narrative was reprinted in 1930 by Milo M. Quaife. See *Early Western Travels,* ed. by Reuben G. Thwaites, v. 18 (1905).

PATTON, CORNELIUS HOWARD (Dec. 25, 1860–Aug. 17, 1939); b. Chicago, Ill. Congregational clergyman, author. *The Lure of Africa* (1917); *The Re-Discovery of Wordsworth*

(1935); etc. He gave his large collection of Wordsworthiana to Amherst College.

PATTON, FRANCES GRAY (1906–). Author. *The Finer Things of Life* (1951); *Good Morning, Miss Dove* (1954); *A Piece of Luck* (1955).

PATTON, FRANCIS LANDEY (Jan. 22, 1843–Nov. 25, 1932); b. Warwick, Bermuda. Presbyterian clergyman, educator, author. *Fundamental Christianity* (1926); *A Summary of Christian Doctrine* (1926). Prof. of ethics, Princeton University, 1886–1913; president, 1888–1902; president, Princeton Theological Seminary, 1902–13.

PATTON, JACOB HARRIS (May 20, 1812–1903); b. in Fayette Co., Pa. Author. *The History of the United States of America* (1860), republished as *A Concise History of the American People* (1876); *Yorktown, 1781–1881* (1881); *The Democratic Party* (1884); etc.

PATTON, JOHN SHELTON (Jan. 10, 1857–Oct. 1, 1932); b. in Augusta Co., Va. Librarian, author. *Jefferson, Cabell and the University of Virginia* (1906); *Jefferson's University* (1915); *Monticello and Its Master* (with Sallie J. Doswell, 1925); *Verses* (1922); etc. Editor: *Poems of John R. Thompson* (1920). Librarian, University of Virginia Library, 1903–27).

PATTON, MARION (Mrs. Webb Waldron), b. Oberlin, O. Novelist, illustrator, poet. *Dance on the Tortoise* (1930); etc.

PATTON, WILLIAM (Aug. 23, 1798–Sept. 9, 1879); b. Philadelphia, Pa. Presbyterian clergyman, author. *The Judgment of Jerusalem Predicted in Scripture, Fulfilled in History* (1877); *The Cottage Bible* (revision of Thomas Williams's book of the same name, 1834); etc. Compiler: *The Christian Psalmist* (with Thomas Hastings, 1839).

PATTULLO, GEORGE (Oct. 9, 1879–July 30, 1967); b. Woodstock, Ont. Author. *The Untamed* (1911); *The Sheriff of Badger* (1912); *One Man's War: The Diary of a Leatherneck* (with Joseph Edward Rendinell, 1928); *Horrors of Moonlight* (1939); *All Our Yesterdays* (1948); *Always New Frontiers* (1951); *Era of Infamy* (1952); *The Morning After Cometh* (1954); *How Silly Can We Get?* (1956); *Some Men in Their Time* (1959).

PAUCK, WILHELM (Jan. 31, 1901–); b. Laasphe, Westphalia, Ger. Educator, author. *Karl Barth—Prophet of a New Christianity?* (1931); *The Heritage of the Reformation* (1951). Co-author: *The Church Against the World* (1935); *Religion and Politics* (1946); *The Ministry in Historical Perspective* (1956); etc. Editor: *Luther's Lectures on Romans* (1961); *Melanchthon and Bucer* (1969). Prof. church history, Union Theological Seminary, since 1953.

PAUL, ELLIOT [Harold] (Feb. 13, 1891–Apr. 7, 1958); b. Malden, Mass. Editor, author. *Indelible* (1922); *Low Run Tide* (1928); *The Life and Death of a Spanish Town* (1937); *The Last Time I Saw Paris* (1942); *I'll Hate Myself in the Morning* (1945); *My Old Kentucky Home* (1949); *Springtime in Paris* (1950); *Understanding the French* (1955); *That Crazy American Music* (1957); etc. *See* Robert Van Gelder's *Writers on Writing* (1946).

PAUL, HOWARD (Nov. 16, 1835–1905); b. Philadelphia, Pa. Actor, playwright, compiler. *Dashes of American Humor* (1852); *My Neighbor Opposite* (prod. 1854); *Patchwork* (1858); *Dinners with Celebrities* (1896); etc. Compiler: *The Book of American Songs* (1857); *The Book of Modern Anecdotes* (with others, 1873); *Smart Sayings of Bright Children* (1886); *The Stage and Its Stars Past and Present*, in parts (with George Gebbie, cop. 1887); etc.

Paul, John. Pen name of Charles Henry Webb.

PAUL, LOUIS (Dec. 4, 1901–1970); b. Brooklyn, N.Y. Author. *The Pumpkin Coach* (1935); *Apart from Others* (1936); *Emma* (1937); *The Man Who Left Home* (1938); *A Passion

for Privacy (1940); *The Reverend Ben Pool* (1941); *The Ordeal of Sergeant Smoot* (1943); *This Is My Brother* (1943); *Breakdown* (1946); *Cup of Trembling* (1948); *Summer Storm* (1949); *A Husband for Mama* (1950); *Heroes, Kings and Men* (1955); *Dara the Cypriot* (1959); *Papa Luige's Marionettes* (1963); *The Way Art Happens* (1963).

PAUL, MAURY HENRY BIDDLE (Apr. 14, 1890–July 17, 1942); b. Philadelphia, Pa. Journalist. Pen name "Cholly Knickerbocker." Society editor, the *New York Evening Mail,* 1918–23; the *New York American,* 1919–37; The *New York Journal-American* from 1937.

PAUL, SHERMAN (Aug. 26, 1920–   ); b. Cleveland, O. Educator, author. *Emerson's Angle of Vision* (1952); *The Shores of America* (1958); *Louis Sullivan* (1962); *Edmund Wilson* (1965); *Randolph Bourne* (1966). Professor of English, University of Iowa, since 1967.

PAULDING, HIRAM (Dec. 11, 1797–Oct. 20, 1878); b. In Westchester Co., N.Y. Naval officer, author. *Journal of the Cruise of the United States Schooner Dolphin* (1831); *Bolivar in His Camp* (1834); etc.

PAULDING, JAMES KIRKE (Aug. 22, 1778–Apr. 6, 1860); b. Great Nine Partners, N.Y. Editor, author. *The Diverting History of John Bull and Brother Jonathan* (under pen name "Hector Bull-Us," 1812); *Letters from the South,* 2v. (1817); *The Backwoodsman: A Poem* (anon., 1818); *Salmagundi: Second Series* (under pen name "Launcelot Langstaff," 1819–20); *A Sketch of Old England* (anon., 1822); *Koningsmarke, the Long Finne* (anon., 1823); *John Bull in America* (anon., 1825); *Tales of the Good Woman* (anon., 1829); *Chronicles of the City of Gotham* (anon., 1830); *The Dutchman's Fireside* (anon., 1831); *Westward Ho!* (anon., 1832); *The Book of Saint Nicholas* (anon., 1836); *The Old Continental; or, The Price of Liberty* (anon., 1846); *The Puritan and His Daughter* (1849); etc. *See* Amos L. Herold's *James Kirke Pauling* (1926).

PAULI, HERTHA (Sept. 4, 1909–   ); b. Vienna. Author. *Alfred Nobel* (1942); *Silent Night* (1943); *The Story of the Christmas Tree* (1944); *St. Nicholas' Travels* (1945); *I Lift My Lamp* (with E. B. Ashton, 1948); *The Most Beautiful House* (1949); *The Golden Door* (1949); *Lincoln's Little Correspondent* (1952); *Three Is a Family* (1955); *Bernadette and the Lady* (1956); *Christmas and the Saints* (1956); *Cry of the Heart* (1957); *The First Easter Rabbit* (1961); *The Trumpeters of Vienna* (1961); *The First Christmas Tree* (1961); *Her Name was Sojourner Truth* (1962); *America's First Christmas* (1962); *Little Town of Bethlehem* (1963); *The First Christmas Gifts* (1965); *Gateway to America* (1966); *The Secret of Sarajevo* (1965).

PAULING, LINUS CARL (Feb. 28, 1901–); b. Portland, Ore. Chemist, educator. *Introduction to Quantum Mechanics* (with E. Bright Wilson, Jr., 1935); *No More War!* (1958); *The Chemical Bond: A Brief Introduction to Modern Structural Chemistry* (1967). Nobel Prize in chemistry, 1954, Nobel Peace Prize (1962). Prof. chemistry, Stanford University, since 1969.

PAULLIN, CHARLES OSCAR (d. Sept. 1, 1944); b. Jamestown, O. Naval historian. *The Navy of the American Revolution* (1906); *Guide to Materials for United States History, Since 1783, in London Archives* (with Frederic L. Paxson, 1914); etc. Editor of various naval documents, etc. Research staff, Carnegie Institution, 1912–36.

Paul's Case. Short story by Willa Cather (1920).

Pavenstedt, Mrs. Edmund W. See Maude Parker.

Pavilion of Women. Novel by Pearl Buck (1946). A forty-year-old Chinese woman of the upper class leaves her husband to attain greater freedom and selects a concubine for him. A detailed picture of old-fashioned Chinese manners.

Pawnbroker, The. Novel by Edward L. Wallant (1964). Jewish refugee from the Nazis recovers his faith in man.

Pawnee Bill. See Gordon W. Lillie.

PAXSON, FREDERIC LOGAN (Feb. 23, 1877–Oct. 24, 1948); b. Philadelphia, Pa. Educator, author. *The Last American Frontier* (1910); *The American Civil War* (1911); *Recent History of the United States* (1921); *History of the American Frontier, 1763–1893* (1924, Pulitzer Prize for history, 1925); *When the West Is Gone* (1929); etc. Prof. history, University of California, from 1932.

Paxton, Philip. Pen name of Samuel Adams Hammett.

Paying too Dear for One's Whistle. By Benjamin Franklin (1778). One of the group known as *The Bagatelles,* printed by Franklin on his hand press at Passy, France.

PAYNE, ELISABETH STANCY (d. Jan. 10, 1944); b. Brooklyn, N.Y. Novelist. *All the Way by Water* (1922); *Singing Waters* (1925); *Painters of Dreams* (1928); *Hedges* (1929); *The Steadfast Light* (1939); etc.

PAYNE, GEORGE HENRY (Aug. 13, 1876–Sept. 11, 1941); b. New York. Critic, author. *A Great Part, and Other Stories of the Stage* (1901); *History of the Child in Human Progress* (1915); *History of Journalism in the United States* (1920); *England: Her Treatment of America* (1931); etc. Assoc. editor, the *Criterion Magazine,* 1896–99; drama critic, the *New York Evening Telegram,* 1903–07; etc.

PAYNE, JOHN HOWARD (June 9, 1791–Apr. 9, 1852); b. New York. Actor, playwright, editor, poet. *Brutus; or, The Fall of Tarquin* (prod. 1818); *Love in Humble Life* (prod. 1822); *Ali Pacha; or, The Signet Ring* (prod. 1822); *Clari; or, The Maid of Milan* (prod. 1823); *Mrs. Smith; or, The Wife and the Widow* (prod. 1823); *The Fall of Algiers* (prod. 1825); *'Twas I; or, The Truth of a Lie* (prod. 1825); *The Lancers* (prod. 1827); and other plays and adaptations. His most famous poem is "Home Sweet Home."

PAYNE, KENNETH WILCOX (Oct. 3, 1890–Oct. 19, 1962); b. Cleveland, O. Editor. Assoc. editor, the *People's Home Journal,* 1919–20; editor, 1925–26; managing editor, *McClure's Magazine,* 1923–24; the *Reader's Digest,* 1931–40; executive editor, since 1940.

PAYNE, LEONIDAS WARREN, JR. (July 12, 1873–June 16, 1945); b. Auburn, Ala. Educator, author. *History of American Literature* (1919); *Fifty Famous Southern Poems* (1920); *A Survey of Texas Literature* (1928). Editor: *Southern Literary Readings* (1913); *Selections from American Literature* (1919); *Texas Poems* (with others, 1936); etc. English dept., University of Texas, from 1906.

PAYNE, PHILIP (Dec. 14, 1867–); b. Dayton, O. Author. *The Shadow of the Millionaire* (1891); *The Mills of Man* (1903); *Duchess of Few Clothes* (1904); *The Furnace* (1907); *Saviours of Society* (1909).

PAYNE, [Pierre Stephen] ROBERT (Dec. 4, 1911–July 6, 1969); b. Saltash, Corn., Eng. Author. *Torrents of Spring* (1946); *The Rose Tree* (poems, 1947); *A Bear Coughs at the North Pole* (1947); *Zero, the Story of Terrorism* (1950); *The Fathers of the Western Church* (1951); *The Great God Pan: A Biography of the Tramp Played by Charles Chaplin* (1952); *Journey to Persia* (1952); *Alexander the God* (1954); *A House in Peking* (1956); *The Gold of Troy: The Story of Heinrich Schliemann* (1958); *The Shepherd* (1959); *Dostoyevsky: A Human Portrait* (1961); *The Christian Centuries: From Christ to Dante* (1967); *The Rise and Fall of Stalin (1966); The Fortress* (1967); etc. Under pen name "Valentin Tikhonov": *The Mountains and the Stars* (1938); etc. Also books under pen names "Robert Young," "Richard Cargoe," and "Howard Horne." Editor: *The White Pony* (anthology of Chinese poetry, 1947).

PAYNE, STEPHEN. Novelist *Lawless Range* (1934); *Riders of the Rocker K* (1935); *Black Aces* (1936); *Beyond the Badlands* (1937); *Across the Dead Line* (1940); *Teenage Stories of the West* (1947); *Young Hero of the Range* (1954); *The Raiders of Rimrock* (1956).

PAYNE, WILL (Jan. 9, 1865–May 20, 1954); b. in Whiteside, co., Ill. Journalist, author. *Jerry the Dreamer* (1896); *The Money Captain* (1898); *The Story of Eva* (1901); *On Fortune's Road* (1902); *Mr Salt* (1903); *When Love Speaks* (1906); *The Losing Game* (1909); *Overlook House* (1920); etc. With the *Chicago Daily News,* 1890–96.

PAYNE, WILLIAM MORTON (Feb. 14, 1858–July 11, 1919); b. Newburyport, Mass. Educator, editor, author. *Little Leaders* (1895); *Editorial Echoes* (1902); *Various Views* (1902); all three being reprints of his essays in *The Dial; The Greater English Poets of the Nineteenth Century* (1907); *Leading American Essayist* (1910); etc. Editor: *American Literary Criticism* (1904). Assoc. editor, *The Dial,* 1892–1915; lit. editor, the *Chicago Daily News,* 1884–88; the *Chicago Evening Journal,* 1888–92.

PAYSON, WILLIAM FARQUHAR (Feb. 18, 1876–Apr. 15, 1939); b. New York. Publisher, playwright, author. *The Copy-Maker* (1897); *John Vytal* (1901); *Debonnaire* (1904); *The Joker* (prod. 1925); *Candles in the Sky* (prod. 1931); *Give Me Tomorrow* (1935). Pres. Payson & Clarke, Ltd., 1924–28; William Farquhar Payson, Inc., 1931.

PEABODY, ANDREW PRESTON (Mar. 19, 1811–Mar. 10, 1893); b. Beverly, Mass. Unitarian clergyman, educator, editor, author. *Conversation: Its Faults and Graces* (1856); *Reminiscences of European Travel* (1868); *Christianity and Science* (1874); *Harvard Reminiscences* (1888); *King's Chapel Sermons* (1891). Editor, *North American Review,* 1853–63. Prof. Christian morals, Harvard University, 1860–81.

PEABODY, ELIZABETH PALMER (May 16, 1804–Jan. 3, 1894); b. Billerica, Mass. Educator, author. Pupil of Ralph Waldo Emerson, sister-in-law of Nathaniel Hawthorne and Horace Mann. *Record of a School* (1835); *Kindergarten Culture* (1870); *Last Evening with Allston and Other Papers* (1886). Editor, the *Kindergarten Messenger,* 1873–75; *Reminiscences of Rev. William Ellery Channing, D.D.* (1880). Founder of the first American kindergarten school, Boston, 1860.

PEABODY, FRANCIS GREENWOOD (Dec. 4, 1847–Dec. 28, 1936); b. Boston, Mass. Unitarian clergyman, educator, author. *Mornings in the College Chapel,* 2 series (1896, 1909); *Afternoons in the College Chapel* (1898); *A New England Romance* (1920); *Reminiscences of Present Day Saints* (1927); *The Privilege of Old Age* (1931); *The Rhythm of Life* (1932); etc. Parkman prof. of theology, Harvard University, 1881–86, Plummer prof. Christian morals, 1886–1913.

PEABODY, JOSEPHINE PRESTON (Mrs. Lionel S. Marks) (May 30, 1874–Dec. 4, 1922); b. Brooklyn N.Y. Poet, playwright. *The Wayfarers* (poems, 1898); *Fortune and Men's Eyes: New Poems with a Play* (1900); *Marlowe* (1901); *The Singing Leaves* (1903); *Pan: A Choric Idyl* (1904); *The Piper* (prod. 1910); *The Wings* (prod. 1912); *The Wolf of Gubbio* (1913); *Harvest Moon* (poems, 1916); *Diary and Letters* (1925); *The Collected Plays* (1927); *The Collected Poems* (1927).

Peabody, Mrs. Mark. Pen name of Metta Victoria Victor.

PEABODY, OLIVER WILLIAM BOURN (July 9, 1799–July 5, 1848); b. Exeter, N.H., twin brother of William Bourn Oliver Peabody. Unitarian clergyman, lawyer, editor. Editor: *Dramatic Works of William Shakespeare,* 7v. (1836). On staff of the *North American Review* and the *Boston Daily Advertiser.*

PEABODY, WILLIAM BOURN OLIVER (July 9, 1799–May 28, 1847); b. Exeter, N.H., twin brother of Oliver William Bourn Peabody. Unitarian clergyman, poet. *Poetical Catechism* (1823); *Sermons* (1849); *Literary Remains* (1850).

Peace of Mind. By Joshua Loth Liebman (1946). Insights into man's nature gleaned from psychology and religion.

Peace of Soul. By Fulton J. Sheen (1949). Analysis of the spiritual state of modern man, making use of arguments taken from an examination of Freud and Marx to buttress the author's religious views.

PEAKE, ELMORE ELLIOT (Mar. 25, 1871–); b. Decatur, O. Author. *The Darlingtons* (1900); *The Pride of Tellfair* (1903); *The House of Hawley* (1905); *The Little King of Angel's Landing* (1906).

PEALE, NORMAN VINCENT (May 31, 1898–); b. Bowersville, O. Reformed Church clergyman, author. *The Art of Living* (1948); *You Can Win* (1948); *A Guide to Confident Living* (1948); *The Power of Positive Thinking* (1952); *The Coming of the King* (1956); *Stay Alive All Your Life* (1957); *The Tough-Minded Optimist* (1961); *Adventures in the Holy Land* (1963); *Sin, Sex and Self-Control* (1965); *Enthusiasm Makes the Difference* (1967). Syndicated newspaper column, "Confident Living."

PEALE, REMBRANDT (Feb. 22, 1778–Oct. 3, 1860); b. near Richboro, Bucks Co., Pa. Painter, author. *Notes on Italy* (1831); *Graphics* (1835); *Portfolio of an Artist* (containing poems, 1839). He was the son of the portrait painter Charles Wilson Peale (1741–1827) and a brother of Raphael Peale, painter (1774–1825), and Titian Peale, naturalist (1780–98); a half-brother of Titian Ramsay Peale, naturalist (1799–1885); and a nephew of James Peale, painter (1749–1831).

PEARL, RAYMOND (June 3, 1879–Nov. 17, 1940); b. Farmington, N.H. Educator, biologist, author. *The Biology of Death* (1922); *To Begin With* (1927); *The Ancestry of the Long-lived* (with Ruth D. Pearl, 1934); *The Natural History of Population* (1938); etc. Prof. biology, Johns Hopkins University, 1918–40.

Pearl of Orr's Island, The. By Harriet Beecher Stowe (1862). Story of a Maine fishing village.

PEARSON, ALFRED JOHN (Sept. 29, 1869–Aug. 10, 1939); b. Landskrona, Swe. Educator, author. *The Rhine and Its Legends* (1919); *The Moselle in History and Legend* (1919); *The Land of a Thousand Lakes* (1932). Dean, college of liberal arts, Drake University, 1930–39.

PEARSON, DREW [Andrew Russell] (Dec. 13, 1897–Sept. 1, 1969); b. Evanston, Ill. Journalist, author. *Washington Merry-Go-Round* (with Robert S. Allen, 1931); *More Washington Merry-Go-Round* (with same, 1932); *The Nine Old Men* (with same, 1936); *USA—Second Class Power?* (1958); *The Case Against Congress* (1968); *The Senator* (1968); etc. Wrote daily syndicated newspaper column, with Robert S. Allen, entitled "Daily Washington Merry-Go-Round."

PEARSON, EDMUND LESTER (Feb. 11, 1880–Aug. 8, 1937); b. Newburyport, Mass. Editor, author. *The Librarian at Play* (1911); *The Believing Years* (1911); *Voyage of the Hoppergrass* (1913); *Theodore Roosevelt* (1920); *Books in Black or Red* (1923); *Studies in Murder* (1926); *Queer Books* (1928); *Five Murders* (1928); *Dime Novels* (1929); *Investigation of the Devil* (1930); *More Studies in Murder* (1936). Editor: *Life of Henry Tufts* (1930). Editor, *Bulletin of The New York Public Library,* 1914–27.

PEARSON, HENRY GREENLEAF (Dec. 26, 1870–Dec. 29, 1939); b. Portland, Me. Educator, author. *The Life of John A. Andrew,* 2v. (1905); *James S. Wadsworth of Geneseo* (1913); *William Howe McElwain* (1917); *Richard Cockburn Maclaurin* (1937); etc. English dept., Massachusetts Institute of Technology, 1893–1939.

PEARSON, JAMES LARKIN (Sept. 13, 1879–); b. Moravian Falls, N.C. Poet. *Castle Gates* (1908); *Pearson's Poems* (1924); *Fifty Acres, and Other Poems* (1933); *Early Harvest* (1952); *Selected Poems* (1960). Editor and publisher, the *Fool-Killer,* humorous monthly, 1910–29.

PEARSON, NORMAN HOLMES (Apr. 13, 1909–); b. Gardner, Mass. Educator. Editor: *Complete Novels of Hawthorne* (1937); *The Oxford Anthology of American Literature* (with W. R. Benét, 1938); *Poets of the English Language,* 5v. (with W. H. Auden, 1950); *Four Studies* (1962); *American Literature* (1964); *Some American Studies* (1964). Editor: *Decade* (1969). Dept of English, Yale University, since 1951.

PEARSON, PETER HENRY (b. Mar., 1864–); b. Landskrona, Swe. Educator, author. *The Study of Literature* (1913); *Prairie Vikings* (1927); *Subjects and Story Plots* (1940); etc. Prof. education, Upsala College, East Orange, N.J.

PEARY, JOSEPHINE DIEBITSCH (Mrs. Robert Peary; d. Dec. 19, 1955); b. Washington, D.C. Mother of Marie Ahnighito Peary Stafford, the "Snow Baby." Author. *My Arctic Journal* (1893); *The Snow Baby* (1901).

PEARY, ROBERT EDWIN (May 6, 1856–Feb. 20, 1920); b. Cresson, Pa. Arctic explorer, author. First to reach the North Pole, Apr. 6, 1909. *Northward over the "Great Ice,"* 2v. (1898); *Nearest the Pole* (1907); *The North Pole* (1910). *See* Josephine Diebitsch Peary's *My Arctic Journal* (1893); Fitzhugh Green's *Life of Robert E. Peary* (1926); William H. Hobbs's *Peary* (1936).

Peasant Bard, The. Pen name of Josiah Dean Canning.

"Peasant of Auburn; or, The Emigrant, The." By Thomas Coombe (1783). Loyalist poem in imitation of Goldsmith's *Deserted Village,* recounting unhappy fortunes of an immigrant on the banks of the Ohio.

PEASE, HOWARD (Sept. 6, 1894–); b. Stockton, Calif. Author. *The Tattooed Man* (1926); *The Jinx Ship* (1927); *The Gypsy Caravan* (1930); *Secret Cargo* (1931); *Wind in the Rigging* (1935); *Foghorns* (1937); *The Ship without a Crew* (1937); *Jungle River* (1938); *Captain Binnacle* (1938); *Long Wharf* (1939); *High Road to Adventure* (1939); *The Black Tanker* (1941); *Night Boat* (1942): *Thunderbolt House* (1944); *Heart of Danger* (1946); *Bound for Singapore* (1948); *The Dark Adventure* (1950); *Captain of the Araby* (1953); *Shipwreck* (1957); *Mystery on Telegraph Hill* (1959).

PEASLEE, AMOS JENKINS (Mar. 24, 1887–Aug. 29, 1969); b. Clarksboro, N.J. Lawyer. *Three Wars with Germany* (with Sir William Reginald Hall, 1944); *United Nations Government* (1945); *Constitutions of Nations,* 3v. (1950); etc.

PEATTIE, DONALD CULROSS (June 21, 1898–Nov. 16, 1964); b. Chicago, Ill. Botanist, novelist. Author: *Bounty of Earth* (with wife, Louise Redfield Peattie, 1926); *Up Country* (with wife, 1928); *Down Wind* (with wife, 1929); *Port of Call* (1932); *Sons of the Martian* (1932); *The Bright Lexicon* (1934); *The Happy Kingdom* (with wife, 1935); *Singing in the Wilderness* (1935); *An Almanac for Moderns* (1935); *Green Laurels* (1936); *A Book of Hours* (1937); *Flowering Earth* (1939); *Audubon's America* (1940); *The Road of a Naturalist* (1941); *Forward the Nation* (1942); *Journey into America* (1943); *Immortal Village* (1945); *American Heartwood* (1949); *A Cup of Sky* (with Noel Peattie, 1950); *A Natural History of Trees of Eastern and Central America* (1950); *Sportsman's Country* (1952); *A Natural History of Western Trees* (1953); *Lives of Destiny* (1954); *Parade with Banners* (1957).

PEATTIE, ELIA WILKINSON (Jan. 15, 1862–July 12, 1935); b. Kalamazoo, Mich. Journalist, author. *With Scrip and Staff* (1891); *A Mountain Woman* (1896); *Pippins and Cheese* (1897); *Castle, Knight and Troubadour* (1903); *Edda and the Oak* (1911); *Azalea* (1912); *Lotta Embury's Career* (1915); etc.

PEATTIE, LOUISE REDFIELD (Mrs. Donald Culross Peattie) (June 14, 1900–Feb. 19, 1965); b. "Windy Pines," Glenview, Ill. Author. *Bounty of Earth* (with husband, 1926); *Up Country* (with husband 1928); *Down Wind* (with husband, 1929); *The Happy Kingdom* (with husband, 1935); *Tomorrow Is Ours* (1938); *Lost Daughter* (1938); *Star at Noon* (1939); *The Californians* (1940); *Ring Finger* (1943); etc.

PEATTIE, RODERICK (Aug. 1, 1891–); b. Omaha, Neb. Geographer, author. *Rambles in Europe* (1934); *Geography in Human Destiny* (1940); *The Incurable Romantic* (1941); *Look to the Frontiers* (1944); *Struggle on the Veld* (1947); etc. Editor, American Mountain Series. Geography dept., Ohio State University, since 1919.

PECK, ANNE MERRIMAN (1884–); b. Piermont, N.Y. Illustrator, author. *Roundabout Europe* (1931); *Storybook Europe* (1929); *A Vagabond's Province* (1929); *Young Germany* (1931); *Roundabout America* (with Enid Johnson, 1933); *Roundabout South America* (1940); *Pageant of Middle American History* (1947); *Jo Ann of the Border Country* (1952); etc.

PECK, ANNIE SMITH (Oct. 19, 1850–July 18, 1935); b. Providence, R.I. Alpinist, author. *A Search for the Apex of America* (1911); *The South American Tour* (1913); *Flying over South America* (1932).

PECK, ELLEN. Author. Pen name, "Cuyler Pine." *Mary Brandegee* (1865); *Renshawe* (1867); *Ecce Femina* (anon., 1874), republished as *Ecce Femina; or, The Woman Zoe* (1875).

PECK, EPAPHRODITUS (May 20, 1860–Oct. 29, 1938); b. Bristol, Conn. Jurist, author. *Law of Persons and Domestic Relations* (1913); *A History of Bristol, Connecticut* (1932).

PECK, GEORGE (Aug. 8, 1797–May 20, 1876); b. in Otsego Co., N.Y. Methodist clergyman, editor, author. *Sketches and Incidents; or, A Budget from the Saddlebags of a Superannuated Itinerant,* 2v. (1849); *Wyoming* [Valley]: *Its History* (1858); *The Life and Times of Rev. George Peck, D.D.* (1874). Editor, *Methodist Quarterly Review,* 1840–47; *Christian Advocate,* New York, 1847–52. His daughter, Mrs. Jonathan Townley Crane, was the mother of Stephen Crane.

PECK, GEORGE CLARKE (b. 1865–). Author. *Side-Stepping Saints* (1918); *Forgotten Faces* (1919); *Cross-Lots, and Other Essays* (1921); *The Pot of Gold* (1922); *Flashes of Silence* (1924); etc.

PECK, GEORGE WASHINGTON (Dec. 4, 1817–June 6, 1859); b. Rehoboth, Mass. Journalist, music critic. *Aurifodina; or, Adventures in the Gold Region* (under pen name "Cantell A. Bigly," 1849); *Melbourne and the Chincha Islands* (1854); etc. Founder, *Boston Musical Review,* 1845; on staff *American Whig Review,* etc.

PECK, GEORGE WILBUR (Sept. 28, 1840–Apr. 16, 1916); b. Henderson, N.Y. Governor, editor, author. *Adventures of One Terence McGrant* (1871); *Peck's Bad Boy and His Pa* (1883); *The Grocery Man and Peck's Bad Boy* (1883); the *Peck's Bad Boy* series, 4v. (1883–1907); *How Private Geo. W. Peck Put Down the Rebellion* (1887); *Peck's Uncle Ike and the Red Headed Boy* (1899); *Sunbeams: Humor, Sarcasm, and Sense* (1900); *Peck's Red Headed Boy* (1901); *Peck's Bad Boy Abroad* (1905); *Peck's Bad Boy with the Circus* (1906); *Peck's Bad Boy with the Cowboys* (1907). Founder, *The Sun,* Lacrosse, Wis., 1874, which he moved to Milwaukee in 1878 and called *Peck's Sun.* Governor of Wisconsin, 1891–95.

PECK, HARRY THURSTON (Nov. 24, 1856–Mar. 23, 1914); b. Stamford, Conn. Educator, editor, poet. *The Adventures of Mabel* (1896); *The Personal Equation* (1897); *What Is Good English?* (1899); *Greystone and Porphyry* (poems, 1899); *William Hickling Prescott* (1905); *Twenty Years of the Republic* (1906); *Literature* (1908); *Studies in Several Literatures* (1909); *The New Baedeker* (1910); *Hilda and the Wishes*

(1907); *A History of Classical Philology* (1911); etc. Editor: *The International Encyclopedia* (1892); *New International Encyclopedia,* 1900–03; *Harper's Dictionary of Classical Literature and Antiquities,* 1897. Editor, *Acta Columbiana,* 1892–1903; *The Bookman,* 1895–1902; etc. Prof. classics, Columbia University, 1882–1910. See Thomas Beer's *The Mauve Decade* (1926); *American Mercury,* Sept., 1933; Joel E. Spingarn's poem "The Fate of a Scholar."

PECK, JOHN MASON (Oct. 31, 1789–Mar. 14, 1858); b. Litchfield, Conn. Baptist clergyman, editor, author. *Gazetteer of Illinois* (1834); *Life of Daniel Boone* (1847); *Father Clark; or, The Pioneer Preacher* (1855). Editor, The *Pioneer,* 1829–39; the *Western Watchman* (1849).

PECK, SAMUEL MINTURN (Nov. 1, 1854–May 3, 1938); b. Tuscaloosa, Ala. Poet. *Cap and Bells* (1886); *Rings and Love Knots* (1892); *Rhymes and Roses* (1895); *Fair Women of To-day* (1896); *The Golf Girl* (1899); *Maybloom and Myrtle* (1910); *The Autumn Trail* (1925); and several volumes of prose including: *Alabama Sketches* (1902); *Swamp Tales* (1912). Among his songs are the "Grape Vine Swing" and the Yale song "The Knot of Blue."

PECK, THEODORA AGNES (Oct. 25, 1882–); b. Burlington, Vt. Author. *Hester of the Grants* (1905); *The Sword of Dundee* (1908); *White Dawn* (1914).

PECK, WALTER EDWIN (Feb. 15, 1891–Jan. 16, 1954); b. Ashtabula, O. Author. *Shelley: His Life and Work,* 2v. (1927). Editor: *The Complete Works of Percy Bysshe Shelley,* 10v. (with Roger Ingpen, 1926–30).

PECK, WILLIAM HENRY (Dec. 30, 1830–1892); b. Augusta, Ga. Educator, novelist. *The Confederate Flag on the Ocean* (1867); *The M'Donalds; or, The Ashes of Southern Homes* (1867); *The Stone-Cutter of Lisbon* (1889); *The Fortune-Teller of New Orleans* (1889); etc. President, Masonic Female College, Greenville, Ga.

PECKHAM, HOWARD HENRY (July 13, 1910–); b. Lowell, Mich. Librarian, educator, author. *Invitation to Book Collecting* (with C. Storm, 1947); *William Henry Harrison* (1951); *Nathanael Greene* (1956); *The War for Independence* (1958); *The Colonial Wars* (1964); *Pontiac: Young Ottawa Leader* (1963); *The Making of the University of Michigan* (1967). etc. Editor: *Revolutionary War Journals of Henry Dearborn* (with L.A. Brown, 1939); etc. Director, Clements Library, dept. of history, University of Michigan, since 1953.

Peck's Bad Boy and His Pa. By George Wilbur Peck (1883). Humorous chronicle of a boy who plays practical jokes on his father. These stories appeared originally in *Peck's Sun,* Milwaukee, a paper founded and edited by Peck.

PEDDER, JAMES (July 29, 1775–Aug. 27, 1859); b. Newport, Isle of Wight, Eng. Agriculturist, editor, author. *The Yellow Shoestrings* (1814); *The Farmer's Land Measurer, or Pocket Companion* (1842).

PEEBLES, MARY LOUISE (1833–Apr. 25, 1915); b. Troy, N.Y. Author. Pen name, "Lynde Palmer." *The Little Captain* (1861); *John-Jack* (1869); *Two Blizzards* (1889); *A Question of Honour* (1893); *Where Honour Leads* (1894); and many Sunday School and temperance novels for young people.

PEEL, DORIS [Anne] (Feb. 27, 1909–); b. London. Author. *Children of the Wind* (1927); *Five on Parade* (1930); *Aunt Margot, and Other Stories* (1935); *Inward Journey* (1953).

Peep at the Pilgrims, A. A fictitious narrative by Harriet Vaughan Foster Cheney (1824).

PEET, STEPHEN DENISON (Dec. 2, 1831–May 24, 1914); b. Euclid, O. Congregational clergyman, archeologist, author. *Prehistoric America,* 5v., comprising: *Emblematic Mounds and Animal Effigies* (1890); *The Mound Builders* (1892); *The Cliff Dwellers and Pueblos* (1899); *Ancient Monuments and Ruined Cities* (1904); and *Myths and Symbols* (1905); etc.

Founder, the *American Antiquarian* and *Oriental Journal,* 1878; editor, 1878–1910. Co-founder, the Ohio Archaeological Society, 1875.

PEFFER, NATHANIEL (June 30, 1890–Apr. 12, 1964); b. New York. Author. *The White Man's Dilemma* (1927); *China: The Collapse of a Civilization* (1930); *A Basis for Peace in the Far East* (1942); *America's Place in the World* (1945); *The Far East: A Modern History* (1958); etc.

PEFFER, WILLIAM ALFRED (Sept. 10, 1831–Oct. 7, 1912); b. Cumberland Co., Pa. Senator, editor, author. *The Carpet-Bagger in Tennessee* (1869); *The Farmer's Side* (1891); *Rise and Fall of Populism in the United States* (1900); etc. Founder, *Fredonia Journal,* and *Coffeyville Journal,* both in Kansas; editor, *Kansas Farmer,* 1881–1912. U.S. Senator from Kansas, 1891–97.

Peg o' My Heart. Popular play by J. Hartley Manners (prod. 1912). The story of an American girl who goes to England to live with aristocratic relatives—a study in social backgrounds.

PEGLER, WESTBROOK [James] (Aug. 2, 1894–June 24, 1969); b. Minneapolis, Minn. Columnist, author. *'Taint Right* (1936); *The Dissenting Opinions of Mister Westbrook Pegler* (1938); *George Spelvin, American* (1942). Sports writer, *Chicago Tribune,* 1925–33; with New York *World-Telegram,* Chicago *Daily News,* and other papers, 1933–44; with King Features Syndicate, from 1944.

PEI, MARIO (1901–); b. Rome. Linguist, author. *The Italian Language* (1941); *Languages for War and Peace* (1943); *The American Road to Peace* (1945); *French Precursors of the Chanson de Roland* (1948); *The Story of Language* (1949); *The Story of English* (1952); *Swords of Anjou* (1953); *All About Language* (1954); *The Consumer's Manifesto* (1960); *Invitation to Linguistics* (1965); *The Story of the English Language* (1967); *Talking Your Way Around the World* (1967); *The Many Hues of English* (1967); *Words in Sheep's Clothing* (1969); etc. Romance languages dept., Columbia University, since 1937.

PEIRCE, BENJAMIN (Sept. 30, 1778–July 26, 1831); b. Salem, Mass. Librarian, author. *A Catalogue of the Library of Harvard University,* 4v. (1830–31); *A History of Harvard University* (1833); etc. Librarian, Harvard University, 1826–31.

PEIRCE, BRADFORD KINNEY (Feb. 3, 1819–Apr. 19, 1889); b. Royalton, Vt. Methodist Episcopal clergyman, author. *Life in the Woods; or, The Adventures of Audubon* (1863); *Trials of an Inventor: Life and Discoveries of Charles Goodyear* (1866); *A Half Century with Juvenile Delinquents* (1869); etc. Editor, *Zion's Herald,* Boston, 1872–88.

PEIRCE, CHARLES SANDERS (Sept. 10, 1839–Apr. 19, 1914); b. Cambridge, Mass. Philosopher, author. *Collected Papers of Charles Sanders Peirce,* 5v. (1931–34). Founder of the American school of philosophy known as pragmatism. In later life Peirce adopted the middle name "Santiago." His manuscripts were purchased by Harvard University.

PEIRCE, THOMAS (Aug., 1786–1850); b. in Chester Co., Pa. Poet. *Horace in Cincinnati* (1822); *The Muse of Hesperia* (1823); *Knowledge Is Power* (1827). Wrote "Billy Moody" for the *National Republican* in 1825.

PEIRCE, WILLIAM (c. 1590–1641); b. in England. Shipmaster, compiler of first almanac in America. *An Almanac for the Year of Our Lord 1639* (1638), printed at Cambridge, Mass., by Stephen Day. *See* R. F. Roden's *The Cambridge Press, 1638–92* (1905).

PEIXOTTO, ERNEST [Clifford] (Oct. 15, 1869–Dec. 6, 1940); b. San Francisco, Calif. Artist, author. *By Italian Seas* (1906); *Through the French Provinces* (1910); *Romantic California* (1910); *Pacific Shores from Panama* (1913); *Our Historic Southwest* (1916); *A Revolutionary Pilgrimage* (1917);

The American Front (1919); *Through Spain and Portugal* (1922); *A Bacchic Pilgrimage* (1932). Illustrated books by Theodore Roosevelt, Henry Cabot Lodge, Clayton Hamilton, and others.

PELIKAN, JAROSLAV JAN, (1923–). Educator, author. *From Luther to Kierkegaard* (1950); *Fools for Christ* (1955); *The Riddle of Roman Catholicism* (1959); *The Shape of Death* (1961); *The Light of the World* (1962); *Obedient Rebels* (1964); *The Christian Intellectual* (1966); *Historical Theology* (1969); etc. Prof. ecclesiastical history, Yale University since 1962.

PELL, JOHN L[eggett] E[veritt] (Nov. 16, 1876–); b. New York. Author. *Hell's Acres* (with "Clay Perry," i.e. Clair Willard Perry, 1938); etc. Wrote scenario for the motion picture "Down to the Sea in Ships," etc.

PELTZ, MARY ELLIS (May 4, 1896–); b. New York. Editor, author. *The Plowshare* (1934); *The Metropolitan Opera Guide* (with Robert Lawrence, 1939); *Behind the Gold Curtain* (1950); *The Magic of the Opera* (1960); etc. Editor: *Opera Lover's Campanion* (1948); *Introduction to Opera* (1956). Founder, *Opera News,* 1936; editor to 1958.

PELZER, LOUIS (Feb. 4, 1879–June 28, 1946); b. Griswold, Ia. Educator, author. *Augustus Caesar Dodge* (1907); *Henry Dodge* (1911); *The Cattlemen's Frontier* (1936); etc. History dept., State University of Iowa, from 1911.

Pembroke. Novel by Mary E. Wilkins Freeman (1894). Story showing that there is an affinity between the sturdy New England character and the granite which crops out of the New England soil.

Pencillings by the Way. By Nathaniel Parker Willis (1835). Sketches written during the author's tour of Europe.

PENDELL, ELMER (July 28, 1894–); b. Waverly, N.Y. *Population on the Loose* (1951). Editor, author: *Society under Analysis* (with others, 1942); *The Next Civilization* (1960); *Sex Versus Civilization* (1967); etc. Dept. of economics, State College, Jacksonville, Alabama, since 1957.

PENDEXTER, HUGH (Jan. 15, 1875–June 12, 1940); b. Pittsfield, Me. Author. *Tiberius Smith* (1907); *Young Trappers* (1913); *Young Loggers* (1917); *Red Belts* (1920); *Virginia Scout* (1922); *Old Misery* (1924); *Harry Idaho* (1926); *The Red Road* (1927); *Border Breed* (1933); *Trail of Pontiac* (1933); *Red Man's Courage* (1934); *Blazing West* (1934); *Bushfighters* (1935); *Woods Runner* (1936); *Long Knives* (1937); *The Vigilante of Alder Gulch* (1955); the *Camp and Trail* series; etc.

Pendle Hill Pamphlets. Wallingford, Pa. Founded 1934. Publishes religious, economic, literary essays. Directed by Ernest Peter Docili.

PENDLETON, JOHN B. (1798–Mar. 10, 1866); b. New York. Lithographer, bookseller, publisher. Founded firm of W. S. and J. B. Pendleton, in Boston, 1825, the first commercial lithographers in America. In 1829 he founded the firm of Pendleton, Kearny & Childs in Philadelphia.

PENDLETON, LOUIS [Beauregard] (Apr. 2, 1861–May 13, 1939); b. Tebeauville, Ga. Author. *In the Wire-Grass* (1889); *In the Okefenokee* (1893); *The Wedding Garment* (1894); *Corona of the Natahalas* (1895); *The Sons of Ham* (1895); *Lost Prince Almon* (1898); *Carita: A Cuban Romance* (1898); *The Assyrian Tents* (1904); *Alexander H. Stephens* (1908); *The Invisible Police* (1932); etc.

PENFIELD, EDWARD (June 2, 1866–Feb. 8, 1925); b. Brooklyn, N.Y. Painter, illustrator, author. *Country Carts* (1900); *Holland Sketches* (1907); *Spanish Sketches* (1911); etc. He drew magazine covers, illustrated many books, and made many sketches for the Beck Engraving Co. Art director *Harper's Magazine* and *Harper's Weekly.*

PENHALLOW, SAMUEL (July 2, 1665–Dec. 2, 1726); b. St. Mabyn, Eng. Merchant, judge, historian. *The History of the Wars of New-England, with the Eastern Indians* (1726).

PENINGTON, JOHN (Aug. 1, 1799–Mar. 18, 1867); b. in Monmouth Co., N.J. Scholar, bookseller. *Scraps, Osteologic and Archaeological* (1841); etc. He founded his rare book shop in Philadelphia in 1841. He was for many years one of the leading importers of foreign books.

PENN, ARTHUR A. (1880–Feb. 6, 1941); b. London. Composer, author. *Yokohama Maid* (1915); *Captain Crossbones* (1918); *Mam'zelle Taps* (1919); etc. His best-known light opera composition was *Smilin' Through*.

PENN, WILLIAM (Oct. 14, 1644–July 30, 1718); b. London. Founder of Pennsylvania, Quaker leader, author. *The Sandy Foundation Shaken* (1668); *No Cross, No Crown* (1669); *Some Fruits of Solitude* (1693); *Essay Toward the Present and Future Peace of Europe by the Establishment of an European Dyet, Parliament or Estates* (1693); *A Collection of the Works of William Penn* (1726); *The Select Works of William Penn*, 5v. (1782); *Correspondence Between William Penn and James Logan*, ed. by Deborah Logan and Edward Armstrong, 2v. (1870–72). *See* Richard P. Smith's *William Penn* (prod. 1829; S. M. Janney's *The Life of William Penn* (1852); H. M. Jenkin's *The Family of William Penn* (1899); S. G. Fisher's *The True William Penn* (1900); J. W. Graham's *William Penn, Founder of Pennsylvania* (1917); William C. Braithwaite's *The Second Period of Quakerism* (1919); M. A. Best's *Rebel Saints* (1925); Mabel R. Brailsford's *The Making of William Penn* (1930); Arthur Pound's *The Penns of Pennsylvania and England* (1932); M. K. Spence's *William Penn: A Bibliography* (1932); Bonamy Dobree's *William Penn, Quaker and Pioneer* (1932); C. E. Vulliamy's *William Penn* (1934); Mary Maples Dunn's *William Penn: Politics and Conscience* (1967).

Penn Club. Philadelphia, Pa. Founded 1875, as a literary adjunct to the *Penn Monthly*. Chartered 1889. *See* Charles Joseph Cohen's *The Penn Club* (1924).

Penn Monthly. Philadelphia, Pa. Magazine. Founded Jan., 1870, by Wharton Baker and Robert Ellis Thompson. H. W. Furness, S. Weir Mitchell, and Henry C. Lea were contributors. Expired July, 1882.

PENNELL, ELIZABETH ROBINS (Mrs. Joseph Pennell), b. Philadelphia, Pa. Author. *Life of Mary Wollstonecraft* (1884); *Charles Godfrey Leland* (1906); *The Life of James McNeill Whistler*, 2v. (with husband, 1908); *Our Philadelphia* (1914); *The Whistler Journal* (with husband, 1921); *The Life and Letters of Joseph Pennell*, 2v. (1929).

PENNELL, JOSEPH (July 4, 1857–Apr. 23, 1926); b. Philadelphia, Pa. Artist, author. *A Canterbury Pilgrimage* (1885); *Pen Drawing and Pen Draughtsmen* (1889); *Lithography and Lithographers* (1898); *The Life of James McNeill Whistler*, 2v. (with Elizabeth Pennell, 1908); *The Whistler Journal* (with same, 1921); *The Adventures of an Illustrator* (1925); etc. Illustrated many books, and was illustrator for *Century, Harper's*, etc. *See* Elizabeth Robins Pennell's *The Life and Letters of Joseph Pennell* (1929).

PENNELL, JOSEPH STANLEY (July 4, 1908–Sept. 26, 1963); b. Junction City, Kan. Author. *The History of Rome Hanks* (1944); *The History of Nora Beckham* (1948); etc.

PENNIMAN, JAMES HOSMER (Nov. 8, 1860–Apr. 6, 1931); b. Alexandria, Va. Educator, bibliophile, author. *The School Poetry Book* (1894); *Books, and How to Make the Most of Them* (1911); *George Washington as Commander-in-Chief* (1917); *George Washington as Man of Letters* (1918); *The Alley Rabbit* (1920); *George Washington at Mount Vernon* (1921); *The Children and Their Books* (1921); *Philadelphia in the Early Eighteen Hundreds* (1923); etc. With Delancey School, Philadelphia, 1885–1913.

Penniman, Major. Pen name of Charles Wheeler Denison.

PENNINGTON, JAMES W. C. (1809–Oct., 1870); b. on the Eastern Shore of Maryland. Author. *Text Book of the Origin and History . . . of the Colored People* (1841); *The Fugitive Blacksmith* (1849).

Pennsylvania Evening Post. Philadelphia, Pa. Newspaper. Founded Jan. 24, 1775, by Benjamin Towne. Published at first three times a week, it became a semi-weekly on Jan. 7, 1779. Beginning with the issue of Aug. 3, 1781, the name was changed to the *Pennsylvania Evening Post, and Public Advertiser*. On June 17, 1783, it became the first daily paper in the United States, under the title of the *Pennsylvania Evening Post, and Daily Advertiser*. Expired Oct. 26, 1784.

Pennsylvania Gazette. Philadelphia, Pa. Newspaper. Founded Dec. 24, 1728, by Samuel Keimer, as the *Universal Instructor in All Arts and Sciences and Pennsylvania Gazette*. With the issue of Oct. 2, 1729, it passed into the hands of Benjamin Franklin and Hugh Meredith, who shortened the title to the *Pennsylvania Gazette*. Franklin withdrew from the paper in 1766. Expired Oct. 11, 1815.

"Pennsylvania Georgics." Poem by Henry Hamilton Cox (1817).

Pennsylvania Magazine. Philadelphia, Pa. Founded Jan., 1775. Editors: Robert Aitken, Thomas Paine. John Witherspoon contributed his celebrated philological essays to the magazine in a series entitled *The Druid*. David Rittenhouse and Benjamin Rush were contributors. The vignette for the title page was designed by Pierre Eugene du Simitière (1736–84). Expired July, 1776.

Pennsylvania Packet. Philadelphia, Pa. Newspaper. Founded Nov., 1771, by John Dunlap, as the weekly *Pennsylvania Packet, or the General Advertiser*. David C. Claypoole, Dunlap's partner, assisted in the publication. On Sept. 21, 1784, it became a daily, under the name of the *Pennsylvania Packet, and Daily Advertiser*, sometimes called *Dunlap and Claypoole's American Daily Advertiser*. Zachariah Poulson bought it in 1800, and renamed it *Poulson's American Daily Advertiser*. Poulson edited it until 1839, when it was acquired by the owners of the *North American Review*. In 1924 it was absorbed by the *Philadelphia Public Ledger*.

PENNYBACKER, ANNA J. HARDWICKE (Mrs. Percy V. Pennybacker) (May 7, 1861–Feb. 4, 1938); b. Petersburg, Va. Author. *A New History of Texas for Schools* (1888); etc.

PENNYPACKER, ISAAC RUSLING (Dec. 11, 1852–Sept. 23, 1935); b. Phoenixville, Pa. Editor, author. *Gettysburg, and Other Poems* (1890); *General Meade* (1901); *Bridle Paths* (1911); *The Valley Campaign* (1911); *The Gettysburg Campaign* (1913); *The Snow-Shoe Trail, and Other Poems* (1913). On editorial staff, the *Philadelphia Press* and the *Philadelphia Inquirer*, 1883–99.

PENNYPACKER, SAMUEL WHITAKER (Apr. 9, 1843–Sept. 2, 1916); b. Phoenixville, Pa. Governor, lawyer, bibliophile, historian. *Autobiography of a Pennsylvanian* (1918). President, Philobiblon Club, 1898–1916; president, Pennsylvania Historical Society, 1900–16. Governor of Pennsylvania, 1903–07.

Penrod. By Booth Tarkington (1914). The story of a boy of twelve who has a series of adventures and mishaps reminiscent of the childhood of the typical American boy. His experiences were continued in *Penrod and Sam* (1916).

People's Lawyer, The. Play by Joseph Stevens Jones. See *Solon Shingle; or, The People's Lawyer*.

People's Literary Companion. Augusta, Me. Magazine. Founded Sept., 1869. Expired Nov., 1907.

Pepaction. By John Burroughs (1881). Collection of outdoor sketches. The title of the book derives from the name of a tribe of the Delaware Indians.

PEPLE, EDWARD HENRY (Aug. 10, 1869–July 28, 1924); b. Richmond, Va. Novelist, playwright. *A Broken Rosary* (1903); *The Prince Chap* (prod. 1904); *Richard the Brazen* (with Cyrus Townsend Brady, 1906); *The Spitfire* (1908); *The Littlest Rebel* (1911); *The Cur and the Coyote* (1913); *A Pair of Sixes* (prod. 1914); *Her Birthright* (prod. 1921); etc.

PEPPER, STEPHEN COBURN (Apr. 29, 1891–); b. Newark, N.J. Educator, author. *Modern Color* (1919); *Knowledge and Society* (1938); *Aesthetic Quality: A Contextualist Theory of Beauty* (1938); *The Basis of Criticism in the Arts* (1945); *A Digest of Purposive Values* (1947); *Principles of Art Appreciation* (1949); *The Work of Art* (1955); *The Sources of Value* (1958); *Ethics* (1960); etc. Prof. philosophy, University of California, 1930–58.

Pepper Box, Peter. Pen name of Thomas Green Fessenden.

PERCE, ELBERT (1831–1869); b. New York. Author. *Old Carl the Cooper* (1854); *The Last of the Name* (1854); *The Battle Roll* (1857); etc.

PERCIVAL, JAMES GATES (Sept. 15, 1795–May 2, 1856); b. Kensington, Conn. Editor, geologist, poet. *Poems* (1821); *Clio I and II* (1822); *Prometheus, Part II, with Other Poems* (1822); *Clio III* (1827); *The Dream of a Day, and other Poems* (1843); *Poetical Works*, ed. by L. W. Fitch (1859); etc. Editor, the *Connecticut Herald*, and *American Athenaeum. See* J. A. Ward's *The Life and Letters of James Gates Percival* (1866); Henry E. Legler's *James Gates Percival* (1901).

Percy, Florence. Pen name of Elizabeth Chase Akers.

PERCY, WALKER (May 18, 1916–); b. Birmingham, Ala. Doctor, author. *The Moviegoer* (1961); *The Last Gentleman* (1966); *Love in the Ruins* (1971).

PERCY, WILLIAM ALEXANDER (May 14, 1885–Jan. 21, 1942); b. Greenville, Miss. Lawyer, poet. *Sappho in Levkas, and Other Poems* (1915); *In April Once* (1920); *Enzio's Kingdom, and Other Poems* (1924); *Selected Poems* (1930); *Lanterns on the Levee* (autobiography, 1941); *Collected Poems* (1943); etc.

Père Antoine's Date-Palm. Short story by Thomas Bailey Aldrich (1862).

Père Marquette, Priest, Pioneer and Adventurer. Biography by Agnes Repplier (1929). Account of the exploration of the Mississippi.

PEREIRA, I[rene] RICE (Aug. 5, 1907–); b. Boston, Mass. Artist, author. *Lapis* (1957); *Crystal of the Rose* (1959); *The Simultaneous Ever-Coming "To Be"* (1961); *The Transcendental Formal Logic of the Infinite* (1966); etc.

PERELMAN, S[idney] J[oseph] (Feb. 1, 1904–); b. Brooklyn, N.Y. Playwright, humorist. *Dawn Ginsbergh's Revenge* (1929); *Parlor, Bedlam and Bath* (1930); *All Good Americans* (play, with Laura Perelman, 1934); *Strictly from Hunger* (1937); *Look Who's Talking* (1940); *The Night Before Christmas* (play, with Laura Perelman, 1941); *The Dream Department* (1943); *One Touch of Venus* (with Ogden Nash, prod. 1943); *Crazy Like a Fox* (1944); *Keep It Crisp* (1946); *Acres and Pains* (1947); *Westward Ha!* (1948); *Listen to the Mocking Bird* (1949); *The Swiss Family Perelman* (1950); *The Ill-Tempered Clavichord* (1952); *Perelman's Home Companion* (1955); *The Road to Miltown* (1957); *The Rising Gorge* (1961); *The Beauty Part* (1963); *Chicken Inspector No. 23* (1966).

Perennial Bachelor, The. Novel by Anne Parrish (1925). A picture of the distintegration of the Campion family, beginning just before the Civil War and coming down to the present day. The younger generation is intolerant of the older, more aristocratic Campions, and the novel is filled with bitter irony.

Perfect Day for Bananafish, A. Short story by J. D. Salinger. Appeared in *Nine Stories* (1953). The suicide of Seymour, one of the prodigies of the Glass family who people the author's fiction.

Perfect Tribute, The. By Mary Raymond Shipman Andrews (1906). Popular story of Abraham Lincoln's preparation of his *Gettysburg Address* and his incognito visit the next day to a Washington hospital where he heard a dying Confederate soldier read the speech and give it perfect tribute.

Perfectionists. *See* John Humphrey Noyes.

Perils of Pearl Street, The. By Asa Green (1834). Humorous account of a country boy who comes to New York to make his fortune.

PERKINS, BRADFORD (Mar. 6, 1925–   ); b. Rochester, N.Y. Educator, author. *The First Rapprochement, England and the United States, 1795–1805* (1955); *Youthful America* (1960); *Prologue to War, England and the United States, 1805–1812* (1961); *Causes of the War of 1812* (1962); *Castlereagh and Adams, England and the United States, 1812–1823* (1964). Professor of history, University of Michigan, since 1962.

PERKINS, CHARLES CALLAHAN (Mar. 1, 1823–Aug. 25, 1886); b. Boston, Mass. Etcher, art critic. *Tuscan Sculptors* (1864); *Italian Sculptors* (1868); *Art in Education* (1870); *Raphael and Michelangelo* (1878); *Historical Handbook of Italian Sculpture* (1883); *Ghiberti and His School* (1885); etc.

PERKINS, CLARENCE (Aug. 17, 1878–Oct. 13, 1946); b. Syracuse, N.Y. Educator, author. *An Outline of Recent European History* (1912); *History of European Peoples* (1927); *Man's Advancing Civilization* (1934); *History of European Civilization* (with others, 1940); etc. Prof. history, University of North Dakota, from 1920.

PERKINS, DEXTER (June 20, 1889–); b. Boston, Mass. Educator, author. *Hands Off: The History of the Monroe Doctrine* (1941); *The U.S. and the Caribbean* (1947); *The American Approach to Foreign Policy* (1952); *The New Age of Franklin Roosevelt* (1957); *America's Quest for Peace* (1961); *The American Democracy, Its Rise to Power* (1964); *The Diplomacy of a New Age: Major Issues in U.S. Policy Since 1945* (1967); *The Yield of the Years* (1969); etc. Prof. American civilization, Cornell University, 1954–59.

Perkins, Eli. Pen name of Melville de Lancey Landon.

PERKINS, FREDERICK BEECHER (Sept. 27, 1823–Jan. 27, 1899); b. Hartford, Conn. Editor, librarian, author. *Charles Dickens* (1870); *The Best Reading* (1872); *Scrope; or, The Lost Library* (1874); *Devil Puzzlers, and Other Studies* (1877); etc. Office editor, *The Galaxy;* assistant editor, *Old and New;* assoc. editor, *Library Journal,* 1877–80. Librarian, Connecticut Historical Society, 1857–61; San Francisco Public Library, 1880–87.

PERKINS, JAMES BRECK (Nov. 4, 1847–Mar. 11, 1910); b. St. Croix Falls, Wis. Lawyer, congressman, author. *France Under Mazarin, with A Review of the Administration of Richelieu, 2v. (1886); France under the Regency, with A Review of the Administration of Louis XIV (1892); France under Louis XV, 2v. (1897); France in the American Revolution* (1911); etc. Congressman, 1901–10.

PERKINS, JAMES HANDASYD (July 31, 1810–Dec. 14, 1849); b. Boston, Mass. Author. *Annals of the West* (1846); *The Memoir and Writings of James Handasyd Perkins,* ed. by William Henry Channing, 2v. (1851).

PERKINS, KENNETH BRETT (May 15, 1898–); b. Koda Kanal, India, of American parentage. Author. *The Beloved Brute* (1923); *Ride Him Cowboy* (1924); *Wild Paradise* (1927); *The Starlit Trail* (1927); *Buccaneer Blood* (1936); *The Bulldogger* (under pen name "Kim Knight," 1939); etc.

Perkins, Louise Saunders. *See* Louise Saunders.

PERKINS, LUCY FITCH (July 12, 1865–Mar. 18, 1937); b. Maples, Ind. Author, illustrator. *A Book of Joys* (1907); *The Belgian Twins* (1917); *The Italian Twins* (1920); *The American Twins of the Revolution* (1926); and many others of the Twins series; etc. Edited and illustrated the *Dandelion Classics;* etc.

PERKINS, MAXWELL EVARTS (Sept. 20, 1884–June 17, 1947); b. New York. Editor, *Editor to Author: Letters of Maxwell E. Perkins* (ed. by John H. Wheelock, 1950). On staff, the *New York Times,* 1907–10; with Charles Scribner's Sons, publishers, from 1910; editor, director; vice president, from 1935.

Perley. Pen name of Benjamin Perley Poore.

PERLEY, SIDNEY (Mar. 6, 1858–June 9, 1928); b. Boxford, Mass. Lawyer, antiquarian, author. *History of Boxford, Massachusetts* (1880); *Poets of Essex County, Massachusetts* (1889); *Historic Storms of New England* (1891); *The History of Salem, Massachusetts,* 3v. (1924–28); etc.

PERLMAN, SELIG (Dec. 9, 1888–Aug. 14, 1959); b. Bialystok, Pol. Economist, educator. Author: *A History of Trade Unionism in the United States* (1922); *A Theory of the Labor Movement* (1928); etc. Co-author: *Labor Movements, 1896–1932* (1935); etc. Prof. economics, University of Wisconsin, 1927–59.

PERREAULT, JOHN (1938–   ); b. New York. Art critic, poet. *Camouflage* (1966). Art critic, *Village Voice;* associate editor, *Art News.*

PERRIN, [Edwin] NOEL (Sept. 18, 1927–); New York. Author. *Dr. Bowdler's Legacy: A History of Expurgated Books in England and America* (1969).

PERRINE, LAURENCE (Oct. 13, 1915–   ); b. Toronto, Canada. Educator, author. *Sound and Sense: An Introduction to Poetry* (1963); *Story and Structure* (1966); *Poetry: A Closer Look* (with J. M. Reid and J. Ciardi, 1963); *100 American Poems of the Twentieth Century* (with J. M. Reid, 1966). Professor of English, Southern Methodist University, since 1960.

PERRY, ARTHUR LATHAM (Feb. 27, 1830–July 9, 1905); b. Lyme, N.H. Educator, political economist, antiquarian, author. *Elements of Political Economy* (1866); *Origins in Williamstown* (1894); *Williamstown and Williams College* (1899); etc. Prof. history and political economy, Williams College, 1854–91. *See* Carroll Perry's *A Professor of Life* (1923), and Bliss Perry's *And Gladly Teach* (1935). Arthur Latham Perry was father of Carroll, Bliss, and Lewis Perry.

PERRY, BLISS (Nov. 25, 1860–Feb. 13, 1954); b. Williamstown, Mass. Educator, editor, author. *The Broughton House* (1890); *Salem Kittredge, and Other Stories* (1894); *The Plated City* (1895); *The Powers at Play* (1899); *A Study of Prose Fiction* (1902); *The Amateur Spirit* (1904); *Walt Whitman* (1906); *Whittier* (1907); *Park Street Papers* (1908); *The American Mind* (1912); *Thomas Carlyle: How to Know Him* (1915); *The American Spirit in Literature* (1918); *A Study of Poetry* (1920); *Life and Letters of Henry Lee Higginson* (1921); *The Praise of Folly and Other Papers* (1923); *Pools and Ripples* (1927); *Emerson Today* (1931); *Richard Henry Dana* (1933); *And Gladly Teach* (autobiography, 1935); Editor, *Atlantic Monthly,* 1899–1909. Prof. English, Harvard University, 1907–30.

PERRY, CARROLL (Feb. 2, 1869–Oct. 2, 1937); b. Williamstown, Mass. Episcopal clergyman, author. *Bill Pratt, Sawbuck Philosopher* (with John Sheridan Zelie, 1895); *A Professor of Life: A Sketch of Arthur Latham Perry* (1923).

PERRY, CHARLES MILTON (Nov. 10, 1876–June 11, 1942); b. North Batavia, Mich. Educator, author. *The Ironic Humanist* (1924); *Henry Philip Tappan* (1933); *Toward a*

Dimensional Realism (1939); etc. Editor: *The St. Louis Movement in Philosophy* (1930); etc. Prof. philosophy, University of Oklahoma, from 1932.

PERRY, CLAIR WILLARD (Apr. 13, 1887–Nov. 19, 1961); b. Waupaca, Wis. Author. Pen name, "Clay Perry." *Heart of Hemlock* (1920); *Roving River* (1921); *The Two Reds of Travoy* (1926); *Hell's Acres* (with John L. E. Pell, 1938); *Underground New England* (1939); *Underground Empire* (1948); etc.

Perry, Clay. Pen name of Clair Willard Perry.

PERRY, GEORGE SESSIONS (May 5, 1910–Dec. 13, 1956); b. Rockdale, Tex. Author, *The Walls Rise Up* (1939); *Hold Autumn in Your Hand* (1941); *Texas, A World in Itself* (1942); *Hackberry Cavalier* (1944); *Cities of America* (1947); *Families of America* (1949); *My Granny Van* (1949); *Tale of a Foolish Farmer* (1951); *The Story of Texas* (1952); etc.

PERRY, LAWRENCE (Nov. 10, 1875–Sept. 5, 1954); b. Newark, N.J. Journalist, author. *Dan Merrithew* (1910); *Holton of the Navy* (1913); *The Fullback* (1916); *The Big Game* (1918); *Our Navy in the War* (1918); *The Romantic Liar* (1919); *Old First* (1931); etc. Editor, *Yachting,* 1906–10; with *New York Evening Post,* 1897–1904, 1912–20.

PERRY, LILLA CABOT (Jan. 13, 1848–Feb. 28, 1933); b. Boston, Mass. Poet. *The Heart of the Weed* (1886); *Garden of Hellas* (1891); *Impressions* (1898); *The Jar of Dreams* (1923); etc.

PERRY, NORA (1831–May 13, 1896); b. Dudley, Mass. Poet, journalist. *After the Ball, and Other Poems* (1875); *Her Lover's Friends, and other Poems* (1880); *The Tragedy of the Unexpected and Other Poems* (1880); *New Songs and Ballads* (1887); *Brave Girls* (1889); *Lyrics and Legends* (1891); *Hope Benham: A Story for Girls* (1894); *Cottage Neighbors* (1899); *Mary Bartlett's Step-Mother* (1900); etc. Her best-known poems were "After the Ball" and "Tying Her Bonnet Under Her Chin." She wrote many books for girls.

PERRY, RALPH BARTON (July 3, 1876–Jan. 22, 1957); b. Poultney, Vt. Educator, editor, author. *The Approach to Philosophy* (1905); *The Moral Economy* (1909); *Present Philosophical Tendencies* (1912); *The New Realism* (1912); *The Thought and Character of William James,* 2v. (1935, Pulitzer Prize for American biography, 1936); *In the Spirit of William James* (1938); *Puritanism and Democracy* (1944); *General Theory of Value* (1950); *The Humanity of Man* (1956); etc. Editor: *William James's Collected Essays and Reviews* (1920); etc. Compiler: *Annotated Bibliography of the Works of William James* (1920). Philosophy dept., Harvard University, 1902–46.

PERRY, STELLA GEORGE STERN (b. 1877); b. New Orleans, La. Author. *Go-to-Sleep* (1911); *Melinda* (1912); *Palmetto* (1920); *Barbara of Telegraph Hill* (1925); *The Defenders* (1927); *Extra Girl* (1929); etc.

PERRY, THOMAS SERGEANT (Jan. 23, 1845–May 7, 1928); b. Newport, R.I. Lecturer, educator, author. *The Life and Letters of Francis Lieber* (1882); *English Literature in the Eighteenth Century* (1883); *From Opitz to Lessing* (1885); *The Evolution of the Snob* (1887); *A History of Greek Literature* (1890); *John Fiske* (1906); etc. Editor: *Selections from the Letters of Thomas Sergeant Perry* (1929); etc. English dept., Harvard University, 1877–82.

PERRY, WILLIAM STEVENS (Jan. 22, 1832–May 13, 1898); b. Providence, R.I. Episcopal bishop, author. *Historical Collections Relating to the American Colonial Church,* 5v. (1870–78); *The History of the American Episcopal Church, 1587–1883* (1885); etc.

PERSHING, JOHN JOSEPH (Sept. 13, 1860–July 15, 1948); b. in Linn County, Mo. Army officer, author. *My Experiences in the World War* (1931). General in command of the American Expeditionary Force in France during World War I. *See* Richard O'Connor's *Black Jack Pershing* (1961).

Personal History. Autobiographical work by Vincent Sheean (1935).

Personal Recollections of Joan of Arc. By Mark Twain (1896). The author considered this to be his best work.

Personne. Pen name of Felix Gregory de Fontaine.

Persons and Places. Autobiography of George Santayana. It appeared in the volumes *The Backgrounds of My Life* (1944); *The Middle Span* (1945); and *My Host the World* (1953).

Perspective. St. Louis, Mo. Quarterly of arts and letters. Founded 1947. Has published critical issues on William Faulkner, Wallace Stevens, W. C. Williams, and other American writers. Also devoted to poetry, stories, and articles.

Perspectives U.S.A. New York. Quarterly. Founded 1953. Published under the auspices of the Ford Foundation by Intercultural Publications, Inc. Devoted to presenting the thought, art, and letters of the United States. Discontinued 1956.

Peter Ashley. Novel by Dubose Heyward (1932). South Carolina during the Civil War, with a thrilling account of the bombardment of Fort Sumter.

Peter Pauper Press. Larchmont, N.Y; Mt. Vernon, N.Y. Private press. Founded 1927, by Peter Beilenson and Sidney W. Wallach. Devoted to fine printing.

"Peter Piper pick'd a peck of pickled peppers." This tonguetwister first appeared in James Kirke Paulding's *Konigsmarke* (1823).

"Peter Quince at the Clavier." Poems by Wallace Stevens, in his *Harmonium* (1923).

Peter Rugg, the Missing Man. By William Austin (1824). This story appeared originally in the *New England Galaxy*, Sept. 10, 1824. It relates the story of Peter Rugg, who was driving to Boston with his small daughter during a storm. He swore that he would reach home that night or never see it again. For fifty years he drove about the countryside seeking his home, and his old-fashioned chaise was a common sight on the roads. Louise Imogen Guiney wrote a poem entitled "Peter Rugg, the Bostonian."

Peter Whiffle. By Carl Van Vechten (1922). An imaginary biography of an American aesthete living among real people in Paris, Florence, and New York.

PETERKIN, JULIA [Mood] (Oct. 31, 1880–); b. in Laurens Co., S.C. Author. *Green Thursday* (1924); *Black April* (1927); *Scarlet Sister Mary* (1928, Pulitzer Prize novel, 1929); *Bright Skin* (1932); *Roll, Jordan, Roll* (1933); *A Plantation Christmas* (1934).

Peterkin Papers, The. By Lucretia P. Hale (1882). Humorous sketches of the Peterkins and "The Lady from Philadelphia" who solved all their problems. *The Last of the Peterkins* (1886) is a sequel.

PETERS, DeWITT C[linton]. Army surgeon, author. *The Life and Adventures of Kit Carson, the Nestor of the Rocky Mountains, from Facts Narrated by Himself* (1858). This book established Kit Carson as a romantic figure and gave rise to many similar books.

PETERS, HARRY T[wyford] (1881–June 2, 1948). Book and print collector, author. *Currier and Ives, Printmakers to the American People*, 2v. (1929–31); *America on Stone: The Other Printmakers to the American People* (1931).

PETERS, JOHN PUNNETT (Dec. 16, 1852–Nov. 10, 1921); b. New York. Episcopal clergyman, archeologist, author. *A Political History of Recent Times* (1882); *Nippur*, 2v. (1897); *The Old Testament and the New Scholarship* (1901); *Early Hebrew Story* (1904); *Bible and Spade* (1922); etc.

PETERS, MADISON CLINTON (Nov. 6, 1859–Oct. 12, 1918); b. in Lehigh Co., Pa. Presbyterian clergyman, author. *The Birds of the Bible* (1901); *The Jews in America* (1905); *Haym Salomon* (1911); *The Masons as Makers of America* (1917); etc.

Peters, Phillis Wheatley. See Phillis Wheatley.

PETERS, SAMUEL ANDREW (Nov. 20, 1735–Apr. 19, 1826); b. Hebron, Conn. Anglican clergyman, loyalist, author. *A General History of Connecticut* (1781), which invented the story of the so-called "Blue Laws" of the New Haven Colony. *See* J. H. Trumbull's *The Reverend Samuel Peters: His Defenders and Apologists* (1877).

PETERS, WILLIAM (July 30, 1921–); b. San Francisco. Television producer, author. *Passport to Friendship–the Story of the Experiment in International Living* (1957); *The Southern Temper* (1959); *For Us, The Living* (with Mrs. Medgar Evers, 1967).

PETERSHAM, MAUDE [Mrs. Miska Petersham] (Aug. 5, 1889–Nov. 29, 1971); b. Kingston, N.Y. Illustrator, author. Co-author, with husband: *Get-a-Way and Háry János* (1933); *The Story Book of Food* (1933); *Miki and Mary* (1934); *The Story of Aircraft* (1935); *The Story Book of Trains* (1935); *The Story Book of Ships* (1935); *The Story Book of Corn* (1936); *The Story Book of Wheat* (1936); *Joseph and His Brothers* (1938); *America's Stamps* (1947); *Circus Baby* (1950); *Off to Bed* (1954); *Silver Mace* (1956); *Peppernuts* (1958); *Let's Learn About Silk* (1967); etc.

PETERSHAM, MISKA (Sept. 20, 1888–May 15, 1960); b. in Hungary. Illustrator, author. Co-author of many books with wife, Maude Petersham (q.v.).

PETERSON, CHARLES JACOBS (July 20, 1819–Mar. 4, 1887); b. Philadelphia, Pa. Publisher, editor, novelist, author. *The Oath of Marion* (1847); *The Military Heroes of the Revolution* (1848); *Grace Dudley; or, Arnold at Saratoga* (1849); *The Naval Heroes of the United States* (1850); *Kate Aylesford* (1855); *The Old Stone Mansion* (1859); *Bessie's Lovers* (1877); etc. Editor, *Atkinson's Casket* (later *Graham's Magazine*); *Saturday Evening Post; Saturday Gazette;* etc. Founder, *Ladies' National Magazine* (later *Peterson's Magazine*), 1842; editor (with Ann S. Stephens), 1842–87.

PETERSON, FREDERICK (Mar. 1, 1859–July 9, 1938); b. Faribault, Minn. Neurologist, poet. *Poems and Swedish Translations* (1883); *In the Shade of Ygdrasil* (1893); *Chinese Lyrics* (under the pen name "Pai Ta-shun," 1916); etc. His best-known poem is "The Sweetest Flower that Blows."

PETERSON, HENRY (Dec. 17, 1818–Oct. 10, 1891); b. Philadelphia, Pa. Publisher, editor, novelist, poet. *Poems* (1863); *The Modern Job* (poem, 1869); *Pemberton* (1873); *Helen* (drama in verse, 1876); *Caesar: a Dramatic Study* (1879); *Columbus* (poem, 1893); etc. Editor, *Saturday Evening Post*, 1846–74. His publishing firm, Deacon & Peterson, bought the *Saturday Evening Post*, Feb., 1848, and Peterson sold his interest in 1873. Deacon & Peterson published the *Lady's Friend*, edited by Peterson's wife, Sarah Webb, from 1864 to 1874.

PETERSON, HOUSTON (Dec. 11, 1897–); b. Fresno, Cal. Educator, author. *Havelock Ellis: Philosopher of Love* (1928); *The Melody of Chaos* (1931); *Huxley, Prophet of Science* (1932); *The Lonely Debate* (1938). Editor: *Great Teachers* (1946); *Essays in Philosophy* (with J. Bayley, 1959); etc. Prof. philosophy, Rutgers University, since 1938.

PETERSON, LOUIS [Stamford], JR.; (b. June 17, 1922). Playwright. *Take a Giant Step* (prod. 1953); *Entertain a Ghost* (1962).

PETERSON, ROGER TORY (Aug. 28, 1908–); b. Jamestown, N.Y. Ornithologist, author. *Field Guide to the Birds* (1934); *How to Know the Birds* (1949); *Wild America* (with

James Fisher, 1955); etc. Co-author: Houghton Mifflin's Field Guide Series, since 1946. Editor: American Naturalist series, since 1965.

PETERSON, VIRGILIA (Mrs. Gouverneur Paulding) (May 16, 1904–Dec. 24, 1966); b. New York. Author. *A Matter of Life and Death* (autobiography, 1961). As Virgilia Sapieha (Princess Paul Sapieha): *Polish Profile* (1940); *Beyond This Shore* (1942).

Peterson's Magazine. Philadelphia, Pa. Monthly literary and fashion magazine. Founded Jan., 1842, by Charles Jacob Peterson as the *Ladies National Magazine.* In 1848 its name was changed to *Peterson's Magazine.* Peterson was editor, 1842–87, assisted by Ann S. Stephens, 1842–53. It was a rival of *Graham's Magazine,* and *Godey's Lady's Book.* Frank A. Munsey bought it in 1898 and merged it with the *Argosy. See* Frank L. Mott's *A History of American Magazines,* v. 2 (1938).

Petit, Lizzie. See Lizzie Petit Cutler.

PETRAKIS, HARRY MARK (June 5, 1923–); b. St. Louis, Mo. Author. *Lion at My Heart* (1959); *The Odyssey of Kostas Volakis* (1963); *Pericles on 31st Street* (1965); *The Founder's Touch* (1965); *A Dream of Kings* (1966); *The Waves of Light and Other Stories* (1969); *Stelmark: A Family Recollection* (1970).

Petrified Forest, The. Play by Robert Sherwood (prod. 1935). Disillusioned Alan Squire stops at a restaurant in Arizona and dies at the hands of gangsters, meanwhile deeding his life insurance policy to the restaurant owner's daughter who yearns to see the world Alan has gladly renounced.

PETRY, ANN (Oct. 12, 1912–); b. Old Saybrook, Conn. Author. *The Street* (1946); *Country Place* (1947); *The Drugstore Cat* (1949); *The Narrows* (1953); *Harriet Tubman* (1954); *Tituba of Salem Village* (1964).

PEYRE, HENRI MAURICE (Feb. 21, 1901–); b. Paris. Educator, author. *Writers and Their Critics* (1944); *The Contemporary French Novel* (1955); *Observations on Life, Literature and Learning in America* (1961); *French Novelists of Today* (1967); *Historical and Critical Essays* (1968); etc. Editor: *Essays in Honor of Albert Feuillerat* (1943); etc. Prof. graduate center, City University, N.Y., since 1969.

PEYSER, ETHEL R. (1887–Sept. 12, 1961); b. New York. Music critic, author. *Cheating the Junk Pile* (1927); *How to Enjoy Music* (1931); *The Home That Music Built* [Carnegie Hall] (1935); Co-author: *Music through the Ages* (1932); *How Opera Grew* (1956); etc. Editor, *Good Housekeeping Magazine,* 1912–14.

PEYTON, JOHN LEWIS (Sept. 15, 1824–May 21, 1896); b. near Staunton, Va. Confederate agent, author. *The American Crsis; or, Pages from the Note-Book of an American Agent during the Civil War in America* 2v. (1867); *Over the Alleghanies and across the Prairies: Personal Recollections of the Far West* (1869); *Rambling Reminiscences of a Residence Abroad* (1888); etc.

Peyton Place. Novel by Grace Metalious (1956). Beneath the exterior propriety of life in a small town lurks vice, perversion, and crime. The novel was followed by *Return to Peyton Place* (1959).

Pfaff's Cellar. New York. Chophouse conducted by Charles Ignatius Pfaff, at 653 Broadway, which became a celebrated literary rendezvous. Its frequenters called themselves "Bohemians." Numbered among them were Thomas Bailey Aldrich, Fitz-James O'Brien, George Arnold, Charles Gayler, William Winter, Lola Montez, Walt Whitman, "Artemus Ward," Henry Clapper, and Thomas Powell.

PFORZHEIMER, CARL H[oward] (Jan. 29, 1879–Apr. 4, 1957); Book collector. The Carl H. Pforzheimer Library, Purchase, N.Y., is noted for its rarities, particularly English books and manuscripts from 1475 to 1700, a catalogue of which is to be published in three volumes. The library also contains incunabula, European literature of the 16th century and English books and manuscripts of the 18th, 19th, and 20th centuries, including a notable Shelley collection.

Phaedra, Inc. New York. Publishers. Founded 1965. Publishes modern literature, poetry, and criticism.

Phalanx, The. See The Harbinger.

PHELAN, JAMES (Dec. 7, 1856–Jan. 30, 1891); b. Aberdeen, Miss. Publisher, congressman, author. *History of Tennessee* (1888); etc. Publisher, the *Memphis Avalanche,* 1881–91. Congressman, 1887–91.

PHELPS, ALMIRA HART LINCOLN (July 15, 1793–July 15, 1884); b. Berlin, Conn. Educator, author. *Lectures to Young Ladies* (1833); *Caroline Westerley; or, The Young Traveller from Ohio* (anon., 1833); *Lectures on Natural Philosophy* (1836); *Ida Norman; or, Trials and Their Uses* (1848); etc. She wrote many textbooks on botany, chemistry, geology, etc., and was one of the first to popularize science in America. With Patapsco Female Institute, Ellicott City, Md., 1841–56.

PHELPS, AUSTIN (Jan. 7, 1820–Oct. 13, 1890); b. West Brookfield, Mass. Father of Elizabeth Stuart Phelps Ward. Congregational clergyman, essayist, author. *The Still Hour* (1860); *My Portfolio: A Collection of Essays* (1882); *Men and Books* (1882); *English Style in Public Discourse* (1883); *My Study, and Other Essays* (1886); etc.

PHELPS, CHARLES EDWARD DAVIS (b. Mar. 28, 1851); b. Homer, N.Y. Author. *The Baliff of Tewkesbury* (with "Leigh North," i.e., Elizabeth Steward Phelps, 1893); *Echoes from the Mountain* (1896); *The Accolade* (1903).

PHELPS, ELIZABETH STEWARD (Mrs. Charles Edward Davis Phelps) (d. 1920). Author. Pen name, "Leigh North" *The Bailiff of Tewkesbury* (with Charles Edward David Phelps, 1893); *Predecessors of Cleopatra* (1906); etc.

PHELPS, ELIZABETH STUART (Mrs. Austin Phelps) (Aug. 13, 1815–Nov. 30, 1852); b. Andover, Mass. Author. Pen name "H. Trusta." The *Kitty Brown* series (1850); *A Peep at Number Five* (1851); *The Sunny Side* (1851); *The Angel Over the Right Shoulder* (1851); *The Tell-Tale* (1852); *Litte Mary* (1853); *The Last Sheaf from Sunny Side* (1853).

Phelps, Elizabeth Stuart. See Elizabeth Stuart Phelps Ward.

Phelps, Frederic. Pen name of Johnston McCulley.

PHELPS, JOHN WOLCOTT (Nov. 13, 1813–Feb. 2, 1885); b. Guilford, Vt. Soldier, author. *Sibylline Leaves* (1858); *Secret Societies, Ancient and Modern* (1873); *History of Madagascar* (1884); etc.

PHELPS, WILLIAM LYON (Jan. 2, 1865–Aug. 21, 1943); b. New Haven, Conn. Essayist, educator, author. *The Beginnings of the English Romantic Movement* (1893); *A Dash at the Pole* (1909); *Essays on Modern Novelists* (1910); *Essays on Russian Novelists* (1911); *Essays on Books* (1914); *Robert Browning: How to Know Him* (1915); *The Advance of the English Novel* (1916); *The Advance of English Poetry* (1918); *The Twentieth Century Theatre* (1918); *Essays on Modern Dramatists* (1920); *Human Nature in the Bible* (1922); *Some Makers of American Literature* (1923); *As I Like It* (3 series, 1923, 1924, 1926); *Howells, James, Bryant, and Other Essays* (1924); *Adventures and Confessions* (1926); *Essays on Things* (1930); *What I Like in Poetry* (1934); *What I Like in Prose* (1934); *Wm. Lyon Phelps Yearbook* (1935); *Autobiography, with Letters* (1934). English dept., Yale University, 1892–1933; Lampson professor, 1901–33.

PHENIX, PHILIP HENRY (Mar. 1, 1915–); b. Denver, Colo. Educator. *Intelligible Religion* (1954); *Religious Concerns in Contemporary Education* (1959); *Education and the*

Worship of God (1966); etc. Dean, Carleton College, since 1958.

Phi Beta Kappa Orations. See *Phi Beta Kappa Orations,* ed. by Clark S. Northrup, 2 series (1915, 1927). Many significant orations have been given under the auspices of this honorary scholastic fraternity, including Ralph Waldo Emerson's *The American Scholar,* Wendell Phillips's *The Scholar in a Republic,* Edward Everett's *The Circumstances Favorable to the Progress of Literature,* George William Curtis's *The American Doctrine of Liberty,* Bliss Perry's *The Amateur Spirit,* Woodrow Wilson's *The Spirit of Learning,* Henry van Dyke's *Democratic Aristocracy,* and Edward Everett Hale's *What Is the American People?*

Philadelphia Bulletin. Philadelphia, Pa. Newspaper. Founded 1847, by Alexander Cummings, publisher of *Neal's Saturday Gazette.* Cummings purchased the *American Centinel and Mercantile Advertiser* (founded 1816) and changed the title to *Cummings' Telegraphic Evening Bulletin.* Title shortened to the *Evening Bulletin* in 1870, and later to the *Bulletin.* Walter Lister is editor. William P. Dickinson is managing editor and David Kusheloff serves as book reviewer. Acquired *Santa Barbara News Press* in 1964.

Philadelphia Inquirer. Philadelphia, Pa. Newspaper. Founded 1829 and called the *Pennsylvania Inquirer* until 1859, when it was merged with the *Democratic Press* as the *Philadelphia Inquirer.* Bought out its rivals, the *Morning Journal* and *Morning Courier.* In 1840 the paper scooped all others when it bought the rights to Dickens's novels. Walter A. Annenberg is publisher and editor. David Appel edits the book reviews. Sold to Knight Newspapers in 1969.

Philadelphia News. Philadelphia, Pa. Newspaper. Founded 1925. J. Ray Hunt is managing editor and book critic. Sold to Knight Newspapers in 1969.

Philadelphia Public Ledger. Philadelphia, Pa. Newspaper. Founded Mar. 25, 1836, by Arunah Shepherdson Abell, William M. Swain, and Azariah Simmons. In 1864 it was sold to George W. Childs and Drexel & Company. It was purchased by Adolph S. Ochs in 1902, who placed his brother, George Washington Oakes, in charge. It was shortly thereafter consolidated with the *Philadelphia Times.* In 1913 it was bought by Cyrus H. K. Curtis, who founded the *Evening Public Ledger,* Sept. 14, 1914. Russel Jarvis (1791–1853), was editor, 1836–39. William V. McKean was editor, 1864–92; L. Clarke Davis, 1893–1904; Charles Munro Morrison, 1930–39; George Fairchild Kearny, 1940–41. Robert Cresswell was publisher. Joseph Jackson, Philadelphia historian, was on the staff, 1888–1918. Ellis Porter was chief editorial writer. Aubrey Thomas was book critic. In 1925 the paper absorbed the *North American.* Earlier it had absorbed the *Evening Telegraph,* 1918, and *The Press,* 1920. Expired 1941.

Philadelphia Story, The. Play by Philip Barry (prod. 1939). The escapades of a modern girl who finds the aristocratic and conservative family traditions rather restricting and boring. Sharp wit is the weapon used frequently in the play.

Philenia. Pen name of Sarah Wentworth Apthrop Morton.

PHILES, GEORGE PHILIP (Apr. 15, 1828–1913); b. Ithaca, N.Y. Bookseller, bibliographer. Compiler: *Bibliotheca Curiosa: Catalogue of the Library of Andrew J. Odell,* 2v. (1878–79); etc. Editor, *Philobiblion,* New York, 1861–63. He assisted Henry Harrisse in his bibliographies. He opened a bookstore in New York in 1854, and his knowledge of old books was extraordinary.

PHILIPSON, MORRIS (June 23, 1926–   ); b. New Haven, Conn. Publisher, author. *Outline of Jungian Aesthetics* (1963); *Bourgeois Anonymous* (1964); *The Count Who Wished He Were a Peasant: A Life of Leo Tolstoy* (1967). Editor: *Aldous Huxley on Arts and Artists* (1960); *Aesthetics Today* (1961); *Automation: Implications for the Future* (1962); etc. Director, University of Chicago Press, since 1967.

Philistines, The. Novel by Arlo Bates (1889). Satire on Boston society.

PHILLIPS, AGNES LUCAS (Sept. 4, 1907–); b. Lucama, N.C. Poet. *On Things Inferior, and Other Poems* (1936); *Within These Gates* (1938); *One Clear Call* (novel, 1955).

PHILLIPS, CATHERINE COFFIN (Mrs. Lee Allen Phillips) (Dec. 6, 1874–Dec. 9, 1942); b. Oakland, Ill. Author. *Cornelius Cole* (1929); *Portsmouth Plaza, the Cradle of San Francisco* (1932); *Jessie Benton Frémont* (1935); *Through the Golden Gate* (1938); etc.

PHILLIPS, DAVID GRAHAM (Oct. 31, 1867–Jan. 24, 1911); b. Madison, Ind. Novelist. *The Great God Success* (under pen name "John Graham," 1901); *Golden Fleece* (1903); *The Cost* (1904); *The Deluge* (1905); *The Plum Tree* (1905); *Light-Fingered Gentry* (1907); *The Worth of a Woman* (1908); *The Fashionable Adventures of Joshua Craig* (1909); *The Husband's Story* (1910); *The Conflict* (1911); *George Helm* (1912); *The Price She Paid* (1912); *Susan Lenox: Her Fall and Rise,* 2v. (1917); etc. See I. F. Marcosson's *David Graham Phillips and His Times* (1932).

Phillips, Dorothy Sanburn. Pen name of Dorothy Phillips Huntington.

PHILLIPS, DUNCAN (June 26, 1886–May 12, 1966); b. Pittsburgh, Pa. Museum director, author. *The Enchantment of Art* (1914); *A Collection in the Making* (1926); *The Artist Sees Differently* (1931); *The Leadership of Giorgione* (1937); etc.

PHILLIPS, ETHEL CALVERT (d. Feb. 6, 1947); b. Jersey City, N.J. Author. *Wee Ann* (1919); *Black-Eyed Susan* (1921); *The Popover Family* (1927); *Ride-the-Wind* (1933); *Calico* (1937); *Belinda and the Singing Clock* (1938); *Peter Peppercorn* (1939); etc.

PHILLIPS, HENRY (Sept. 6, 1838–June 6, 1895); b. Philadelphia, Pa. Philologist, translator, folk-lorist, librarian. Translator of Adalbert von Chamisso's *Faust,* etc. Officer of the American Folk-Lore Society, librarian of the American Philosophical Society, 1885–95; etc.

PHILLIPS, HENRY ALBERT (Jan. 28, 1880–Jan. 28, 1951); b. Brooklyn, N.Y. Author: *The Photodrama* (1914); *Other People's Lives* (1924); *Meet the Germans* (1929); *Meet the Spaniards* (1931); *Meet the Japanese* (1932); *White Elephants in the Caribbean* (1936); *New Designs for Old Mexico* (1938); *Brazil: Bulwark of Inter-American Relations* (1945); etc.

PHILLIPS, HENRY IRVING (Nov. 26, 1887–); b. New Haven, Conn. Humorist, columnist, author. *The Globe Trotter* (1922); *The Foolish Question Book* (1927); *Calvin Coolidge* (1933); *On White or Rye* (1941). Wrote column for the New York *Sun* called the "Sun Dial."

PHILLIPS, HENRY WALLACE (Jan 11, 1869–May 23, 1930); b. New York. Author. *Red Saunders* (1902); *Plain Mary Smith: A Romance of Red Saunders* (1905); *Mr. Scraggs: Introduced by Red Saunders* (1906); *Red Saunders' Pets, and Other Critters* (1906); *The Mascot of Sweet Briar Gulch* (1908); *Trolley Folly* (1909); etc.

PHILLIPS, JOHN CHARLES (Nov. 5, 1876–Nov. 14, 1938); b. Boston, Mass. Naturalist, author. *A Sportsman's Scrapbook* (1928); *American Game Mammals and Birds: A Catalogue of Books, 1582 to 1925* (1930); *A Sportsman's Second Scrapbook* (1933); *Quick-Water and Smooth* (1935); etc.

PHILLIPS, JOHN SANBURN (July 2, 1861–Feb. 28, 1949); b. Council Bluffs, Ia. Editor, publisher, author. *The Papers: Occasional Pieces* (1936). Editor, *American Magazine,* 1906–15, advisory editor, 1915–38; editor, *Red Cross Magazine,* 1917–20. Manager, *McClure's Magazine,* 1893–1906.

PHILLIPS, LEROY (May 28, 1870–); b. Columbus, O. Publisher, editor. Editor: *Views and Reviews by Henry James* (1908); *Shakespeare for Today* (with M. M. Crawford, 1940); etc. Compiler: *Bibliography of the Writings of Henry James* (1906). With Ginn & Co., Boston, 1899–1918.

PHILLIPS, MARIE TELLO (Mrs. Charles J. Yaegle) (1874–June 6, 1962); b. Toronto, Can. Poet, novelist. *Book of Verses* (1922); *Stella Marvin* (1927); *Bound in Shallows* (1930); *The Honeysuckle and the Rose* (poems, 1933); *More Truth than Poetry* (1934); *There's a Divinity* (1937); *Pittsburgh Saga* (1951); etc.

PHILLIPS, MARY ELIZABETH (1857); b. Chicago, Ill. Author. *William Wetmore Story* (1897); *Laureled Leaders for Little Folk* (1908); *James Fenimore Cooper* (1913); *Tommy Tregennis* (1913); *Edgar Allan Poe, the Man*, 2v. (1926); etc.

PHILLIPS, PAUL CHRISLER (Nov. 15, 1883–Dec. 23, 1956); b. Bloomfield, Ind. Editor, educator, author. *Forty Years on the Frontier* (with S. Dubar, 1925); *Life in the Rocky Mountains* (1939); *Fur Trade in Montana* (1955); etc. Editor: *The Journal of John Work* (with William S. Lewis, 1923); *The Journals and Letters of Major John Owen*, 2v. (1927); *Scenery of the Plains, Mountains, and Mines*, by Franklin Langworthy (1932); etc. Prof. history, University of Montana, 1911–37.

PHILLIPS, PAULINE FRIEDMAN (July 4, 1918–); b. Sioux City, Ia. Newspaper columnist, author. Pen name "Abigail Van Buren." *Dear Abby* (1957); *Dear Teen Ager* (1959); *Dear Abby On Marriage* (1962); etc. Nationally syndicated newspaper columnist since 1956; radio advice program, Columbia Broadcasting System, since 1963.

PHILLIPS, PHILIP (Aug. 13, 1834–June 25, 1895); b. Cassadaga, N.Y. Hymn writer, compiler, author. *Song Pilgrimage around the World* (1882); etc. Compiler: *Early Blossoms* (1860); *The Singing Pilgrim* (1866); *New Hymn and Tune Book* (1867); *American Sacred Songster* (1868); etc.

PHILLIPS, ULRICH BONNELL (Nov. 4, 1877–Jan. 21, 1934); b. La Grange, Ga. Educator, historian. *Georgia and State Rights* (1901); *The Life of Robert Toombs* (1913); *Life and Labor in the Old South* (1929); *The Course of the South to Secession*, ed. by E. Merton Coulter (1939); etc. Prof. American history, University of Michigan, 1910–29, Yale University, 1929–34.

PHILLIPS, W[alter] S[helley] (1867–Sept. 1, 1940). Artist, author. Pen name, "El Comancho." *Totem Tales* (1896), republished as *Indian Fairy Tales* (1902); *Just about a Boy* (1899); *Two Young Crusoes* (1906); *The Chinook Book* (1913); *Three Boys in the Indian Hills* (1918); *Teepee Tales* (1927); etc. He was adopted by the Sioux, and given the name "Wi-chash-ta Ish-nah-nah."

PHILLIPS, WALTER POLK (June 14, 1846–Jan. 31, 1920); b. near Grafton, Mass. Journalist, author. *Oakum Pickings* (1876), republished as *Sketches, Old and New; My Debut in Journalism* (1892); etc. Compiler, *Songs of the Wheel* (1897). He devised the "Phillips Telegraphic Code" in 1879. He was general manager of the United Press.

PHILLIPS, WENDELL (Nov. 29, 1811–Feb. 2, 1884); b. Boston, Mass. Orator, abolitionist, author. *Speeches, Lectures, and Letters*, 2 series (1863, 1891). He was the foremost lecturer of his day; among his most popular lectures were *The Lost Arts; Street Life in Europe; The Scholar in a Republic; Toussaint L'Ouverture*. See Lorenzo Sears's *Wendell Phillips* (1909).

PHILLIPS, WILLARD (Dec. 19, 1784–Sept. 9, 1873); b. Bridgewater, Mass. Lawyer, editor. *Manual of Political Economy* (1828); *The Inventor's Guide* (1837); etc. In 1828 he and Theophilus Parsons bought the *New-England Galaxy* and conducted it for six years.

Philo-Bellum. Pen name of John Maylem.

Philobiblon Club. Philadelphia, Pa. Founded 1893. A club for lovers of the book arts. Samuel W. Pennypacker was president, 1898–1916.

Philogical Quarterly. Iowa City, Ia. Founded 1922. Hardin Craig was editor, 1922–28.

Philopatrius. Pen name of David James Dove.

"Philosophic Solitude; or, the Choice of a Rural Life." Poem by William Livingston (1747).

Philosophical Review. Boston, Mass; Ithaca, N.Y. Founded 1892, under the editorship of Jacob Gould Schurman and James Edwin Creighton. The latter was editor in chief, 1902–24. Now published at Cornell University.

Philosophy 4. Novel by Owen Wister (1903). Undergraduate life at Harvard College.

Philosophy in a New Key. Philosophical work by Susanne Langer (1942).

Phoenix, John. Pen name of George Horatio Derby.

Phoenix Gazette. Phoenix, Ariz. Newspaper. Founded 1880. Now merged with the *Arizona Republic*. The *Republic* appears mornings and Sunday; the *Gazette*, evenings. Eugene C. Pulliam is publisher. Anna Walsh reviews books for the *Gazette;* Ray Walter, for the *Republic*.

Phoenixiana. By George Horatio Derby (under pen name "John Phoenix," 1855). Humorous sketches of frontier life in California.

Phunny Phellow. New York. Comic magazine. Founded 1859. Published by Ross & Tousey, and Street & Smith. Thomas Nast was its leading cartoonist. Expired 1876.

PHYFE, WILLIAM HENRY PINKNEY (June 13, 1855–Mar. 7, 1915); b. New York. Author. *Napoleon: The Return from St. Helena* (1907). Compiler: *Seven Thousand Words Often Mispronounced* (1892), and later augmented editions, and similar compilations.

Phylon. Atlanta, Ga. Quarterly. Founded 1939, at Atlanta University. Devoted to material concerning race and culture. Edited by Tilman C. Cothran.

Physiocratic Group. The followers of Quesnay, Mirabeau, Condorcet, and Du Pont de Nemours, who advocated a political doctrine based on agriculture. They opposed the Manchester school of industrialists. Benjamin Franklin and Thomas Jefferson were physiocrats in America. John Adams, Fisher Ames, and Alexander Hamilton were opposed to the doctrine, and from this cleavage of political thought grew the Democrats and Republicans. *See* Vernon L. Parrington's *The Colonial Mind* (1927).

PIATT, DONN (June 29, 1819–Nov. 12, 1891); b. Cincinnati, O. Journalist, essayist, poet. *Memories of the Men Who Saved the Union* (1887); *The Lone Grave of the Shenandoah, and Other Tales* (1888); *Poems and Plays* (1893); *The Reverend Melancthon Poundex* (1893); etc. Editor of the "Club Room" department in the *Galaxy* in 1871. Co-founder (with George Alfred Townsend), the weekly *Capital*, Washington, D.C., 1871; editor, 1871–80.

PIATT, JOHN JAMES (Mar. 1, 1835–Feb. 16, 1917); b. James' Mills, Ind. Poet, journalist, editor. *Poems of Two Friends* (with William Dean Howells, 1860); *Poems in Sunshine and Firelight* (1866); *Western Windows, and Other Poems* (1869); *Pencilled Fly-Leaves: A Book of Essays in Town and Country* (1880); *Idyls and Lyrics of the Ohio Valley* (1881); *A Book of Gold, and Other Sonnets* (1889); *Odes in Ohio, and Other Poems* (1895); etc. His best-known poems are "The Night Train," "The Western Pioneer," and "The Morning Street." Lit. editor, *Cincinnati Commercial*, 1869–78; editor, *The Midland* (later *Uncle Remus's Home Magazine*), 1907–09.

PIATT, SARAH MORGAN BRYAN (Mrs. John James Piatt) (Aug. 11, 1836–Dec. 22, 1919); b. Lexington, Ky. Poet. *Selected Poems (1886); An Enchanted Castle, and Other Poems* (1893); *Complete Poems*, 2v. (1894); *The Nests of Washington, and Other Poems* (with husband, 1864); *The Children Out of Doors* (with same, 1885).

Piazza Tales, The. By Herman Melville (1856). Short stories of the South Seas.

PICARD, GEORGE H[enry] (Aug. 3, 1850–Oct. 7, 1916); b. Berea, O. Author. *A Matter of Taste* (1884); *Old Boniface* (1886); *Madame Noël* (1900); *The Bishop's Niece* (1905); etc.

"Piccadilly." Poem by Ezra Pound in his *Provença* (1911).

PICKARD, SAMUEL THOMAS (Mar. 1, 1828–Feb. 12, 1915); b. Rowley, Mass. Printer, editor, author. *Life and Letters of John Greenleaf Whittier* (1894); *Hawthorne's First Diary* (1897); *Whittier-Land* (1904); etc. Associated with Benjamin P. Shillaber in the publication of the *Carpet Bag*, Boston. Editor, *The Portland (Me.) Transcript*, for nearly forty years.

PICKENS, WILLIAM (Jan. 15, 1861–Apr. 6, 1954); b. Anderson County, S.C. Educator, author. *Abraham Lincoln* (1909); *The Heir of Slaves* (1910); *Frederick Douglass* (1912); *Fifty Years of Emancipation* (1913); *The New Negro* (1916); *The Vengeance of the Gods* (1921); *Bursting Bonds* (1923); *American Aesop* (1926); etc. Prof. classics, Talladega College, Wiley University, Morgan College, 1904–20; field secretary, National Association for the Advancement of Colored People, from 1920.

PICKERING, HENRY (Oct. 8, 1781–May 8, 1831); b. Newburgh, N.Y. Poet. *The Ruins of Paestum, and Other Compositions in Verse* (1822); *Athens, and Other Poems* (1824); etc.

PICKERING, JOHN (Feb. 7, 1777–May 5, 1846); b. Salem, Mass. Diplomat, philologist, compiler. *A Vocabulary; or, Collection of Words and Phrases Which Have Been Supposed to be Peculiar to the United States of America (1816); Comprehensive Lexicon of the Greek Language* (1826); etc. U.S. minister to Portugal, 1797–99; to Great Britain, 1799–1801. *See* Noah Webster's *A Letter to the Honorable John Pickering on the Subject of His Vocabulary* (1817).

PICKERING, TIMOTHY (July 17, 1745–Jan. 29, 1829); b. Salem, Mass. Soldier, politician, author. *Political Essays* (1812); *A Review of the Correspondence between the Hon. John Adams . . . and the Late Wm. Cunningham, Esq.* (1824); etc. Most of the Pickering's manuscripts are owned by the Massachusetts Historical Society. He was secretary of state, 1795–1800. *See* Octavius Pickering and C. W. Upham's *The Life of Timothy Pickering*, 4v. (1867–73).

"Picket Guard, The." Poem by Ethel Lynn Beers (1861).

PICKETT, ALBERT JAMES (Aug. 13, 1810–Oct. 28, 1858); b. in Anson Co., N.C. Historian. *History of Alabama and Incidentally of Georgia and Mississippi from the Earliest Period*, 2v. (1851).

PICKETT, LA SALLE CORBELL (Mrs. George Edward Pickett) (May 16, 1848–Mar. 22, 1931); b. in Nansemond Co., Va. Writer of Negro dialect stories. *Pickett and His Men* (1899); *Ebil Eye* (1901); *Jinny* (1901); *Literary Hearthstones of Dixie* (1912); *The Bugles of Gettysburg* (1913); *Across My Path: Memories of People I Have Known* (1916); *What Happened to Me* (reminiscences, 1917).

Pickle for the Knowing Ones, A. By Timothy Dexter (1802). A bizarre production printed without punctuation, and with the advice to the reader to punctuate it according to taste.

Picnic. Play by William Inge (prod. 1953). An attractive homeless man produces various effects on the women of a small town in Kansas.

PICTON, THOMAS (May 16, 1822–Feb. 20, 1891); b. Thomas Picton Milner, at New York. Journalist, soldier of fortune, sports writer, playwright. Pen name "Paul Preston." *Acrostics from Across the Atlantic, and Other Poems* (anon., 1869); *A Tempest in a Teapot* (prod. 1871); *Rose Street: Its Past, Present, and Future* (1873); etc. Compiler: *The Fireside Magician* (1870). He was associated with William Henry Herbert and Edward Z. C. Judson. *See* his *Reminiscences of a Sporting Journalist* in the *Spirit of the Times* (1881).

Pictorial Review. New York. Monthly. Founded 1899. Absorbed *The Delineator* in 1937, as *Pictorial Review Combined with the Delineator.* Expired 1939.

"Picture That Is Turned toward the Wall, The." Song by Charles Graham.

Picturesque America; or, The Land We Live In. Ed. by William Cullen Bryant, 2v. (1872–74). Written mainly by Oliver B. Bunce.

PIDGIN, CHARLES FELTON (Nov. 11, 1844–June 3, 1923); b. Roxbury, Mass. Inventor, novelist. *Quincy Adams Sawyer* (1900); *Blennerhasset; or, The Decrees of Fate* (1901); *The Climax* (1902); *Little Burr, the Warwick of America* (1905); *The Hidden Man* (1906); *Theodosia* (1907); *Labor or the Money God! Which?* (1908); etc.

PIER, ARTHUR STANWOOD (Apr. 2, 1874–Aug. 14, 1966); b. Pittsburgh, Pa. Educator, author. *The Pedagogues* (1899); *Boys of St. Timothy's* (1904); *Story of Harvard* (1913); *The Hilltop Troop* (1919); *The Rigor of the Game* (1929); *History of St. Paul's School* (1934); *The Young Man from Mount Vernon* (1940); *Forbes, Telephone Pioneer* (1953); etc.

PIERCE, BESSIE LOUISE (Apr. 20, 1890–); b. Caro, Mich. Educator, author. *As Others See Chicago* (1933); *A History of Chicago*, 3v. to date (1927–47); also books on education. American history dept., University of Chicago, since 1926.

PIERCE, EDWARD LILLIE (Mar. 29, 1829–Sept. 5, 1897); b. Stoughton, Mass. Lawyer. Editor: *Memoir and Letters of Charles Sumner*, 4v. (1877–93); etc.

PIERCE, FRANK RICHARDSON (Oct. 21, 1887–); b. Greenfield, Mass. Author. *Chuck Ryan, Logger* (1928); *Spruce Valley* (1929); *Black Placer* (1929); *Rugged Alaska Stories* (1950); etc.

PIERCE, FRANKLIN (Nov. 23, 1804–Oct. 8, 1869); b. Hillsboro, N.H. Fourteenth president of the United States. *See* Nathaniel Hawthorne's *Life of Franklin Pierce* (1852); R. F. Nichols's *Franklin Pierce* (1931); Irving Sloan's *Franklin Pierce: Chronology, Documents, Bibliographical aids* (1968). Pierce's Mexican War diary is in the Henry E. Huntington Library, San Marino, Calif. There is an extensive collection of his manuscripts in the Library of Congress, particularly in the Marcy colleciton.

PIERCE, GILBERT ASHVILLE (Jan. 11, 1839–Feb. 15, 1901); b. East Otto, N.Y. Governor, senator, publisher, playwright, novelist. *The Dickens Dictionary* (1872); *Zachariah, the Congressman* (1876); *One Hundred Wives* (prod. 1880); *A Dangerous Woman* (1883); etc. On editorial staff, *Inter Ocean*, and *Chicago Daily News*. Governor of Dakota Territory, 1884–86; U. S. Senator from North Dakota, 1889–91. Publisher (with W. J. Murphy,) the *Minneapolis Tribune*, 1891.

PIERCE, OVID WILLIAMS (1910–). Author. *The Plantation* (1953); *On a Lonesome Porch* (1960); *Devil's Half* (1968); etc.

PIERCY, MARGE; b. Detroit, Mich. Author. *Breaking Camp* (1968); *Going Down Fast* (1969); *Dance the Eagle to Sleep* (1970); etc.

PIERPONT, JOHN (Apr. 6, 1785–Aug. 27, 1866); b. Litchfield, Conn. Unitarian clergyman, poet, reformer. *Airs of Palestine* (1816); *The American First Class Book* (1823); *The National Reader* (1827), these last two textbooks being the first in America to include readings from Shakespeare; *The Anti-Slavery Poems* (1843); etc. His best-known poem was "Warren's Address to His Soldiers at Bunker Hill." *See* S. A. Eliot's *Heralds of a Liberal Faith*, v. 2 (1910). Pierpont was the grandfather of John Pierpont Morgan, the financier.

Pierpont Morgan Library, The. New York. Founded by J. Pierpont Morgan (1837–1913). His son, John Pierpont Morgan, erected the building and placed his magnificent collection of rare books in it in 1924. A feature is its collection of illuminated manuscripts.

Pierrot. Pen name of George Arnold.

PIERROT, GEORGE FRANCIS (Jan. 11, 1898–); b. Chicago, Ill. Editor, author. *Yea, Sheriton* (1925); *The Vagabond Trail* (1935). Editor, the *American Boy*, 1924–36; *American Boy-Youth's Companion*, 1924–36.

PIERSON, DAVID LAWRENCE (Feb. 3, 1865–July 11, 1938); b. Orange, N.J. Author. *History of the Oranges to 1921*, 4v. (1922); etc. Originator of "Constitution Day," Sept. 17.

PIERSON, HAMILTON WILCOX (Sept. 22, 1817–Sept. 7, 1888); b. Bergen, N.Y. Presbyterian clergyman, author. *Jefferson at Monticello* (1862); *In the Brush; or, Old-Time Social, Political, and Religious Life in the Southwest* (1881); etc. He was an agent of the American Bible Society for many years, and traveled extensively in the backwoods country.

Pietas et Gratulatio Collegii Cantabrigiensis apud Novanglos. Poems contributed by a number of Harvard writers, including John Lovell (1761).

Pigs Is Pigs. Popular story by Ellis Parker Butler, which first appeared in *Leslie's Monthly*, 1905.

PIKE, ALBERT (Dec. 29, 1809–Apr. 2, 1891); b. Boston, Mass. Lawyer, soldier, author. Pen name "Casca." *Prose Sketches and Poems, Written in the Western Country* (1834); *Hymns to the Gods, and Other Poems* (1872); *Poems* (1900); *Lyrics and Love Songs* (1916); etc. His version of the song "Dixie" is among his better-known pieces.

PIKE, JAMES ALBERT (Feb. 14, 1913–Sept. 3, 1969); b. Oklahoma City, Okla. Episcopal bishop, educator. *Cases and Other Materials on the New Federal and Code Procedure* (1938); *Beyond Anxiety* (1953); *Doing the Truth* (1956); *The Next Day* (1957); *Our Christmas Challenge* (1961); etc. Co-author: *The Faith of the Church* (1951); etc.

PIKE, JAMES SHEPHERD (Sept. 8, 1811–Nov. 29, 1882); b. Calais, Me. Editor, diplomat, author. *The Financial Crisis* (1867); *Horace Greeley in 1872* (1873); etc. With the *New York Tribune*, 1850–60. Minister to the Netherlands, 1861–66.

PIKE, MARY HAYDEN GREEN (Nov. 30, 1824–Jan. 15, 1908); b. Eastport, Me. Novelist. *Ida May* (under pen name "Mary Langdon," 1854); *Caste* (under pen name, "Sydney A. Story," 1856); *Agnes* (1858); etc.

PIKE, ZEBULON [Montgomery] (Jan. 5, 1779–Apr. 27, 1813); b. Lamberton, N.J. Soldier, explorer, author. *An Account of Expeditions to the Sources of the Mississippi and through the Western Parts of Louisiana* (1810). He sighted the peak in Colorado which is now called Pike's Peak in his honor. *See* Elliot Coues *The Expeditions of Zebulon Montgomery Pike*, 3v. (1895).

Pike County Ballads. By John Hay (1871). These poems achieved a great popularity, being an accurate reflection of the Middle Western character and language. Perhaps the best-known poem in the collection is "Jim Bludso of the Prairie Bell."

PILAT, OLIVER RAMSAY (1903–); b. New York. Seaman, journalist, novelist. *Sea-Mary* (1936); *The Mate Takes Her Home* (1939); *Sodom by the Sea: An Affectionate History of Coney Island* (with Jo Ranson, 1941); *Atom Spies* (1952); *Lindsay's Campaign: A Behind-the-Scenes Diary* (1968); etc. On staff, *The Brooklyn Daily Eagle*, the *New York Post*.

PILCH, FREDERICK HENRY (Nov. 5, 1842–Dec. 3, 1889); b. Newark, N.Y. Poet. *Homespun Verses* (1889).

Pilgrim Hawk, The. Novel by Glenway Wescott (1940). The love life of three couples in Paris during the 1920's.

PILLSBURY, PARKER (1809–1898). Abolitionist and woman suffrage leader. *Acts of the Anti-Slavery Apostles* (1883). Editor, *National Anti-Slavery Standard*.

Pilot, The. Novel by James Fenimore Cooper (1823). A sea story inspired by reading *The Pirate* by Sir Walter Scott. The mysterious pilot bears a resemblance to John Paul Jones.

Pilot, The. Boston, Mass. Catholic weekly. Founded 1836, by Patrick Donahoe and H. L. Devereaux. It was an outgrowth of the *Jesuit; or, Catholic Sentinel*, founded in 1829 by Bishop B. J. Fenwick, and published by George Pepper, which was reorganized in 1832 and expired in 1834. The poet John Boyle O'Reilly became editor in 1870 and part owner in 1876. He made the *Pilot* the most influential Irish-American paper of the day. *See* Paul J. Foik's *Pioneer Efforts of Catholic Journalism in the United States* (1912).

PINCHOT, ANN (Mrs. Ben Pinchot) (1910–); b. New York. Novelist. *Hour upon the Stage* (1929); *Shrine of Fair Women* (1932); *Talk of the Town* (1941); *Hear This Woman!* (with Ben Pinchot, 1949); *Hagar* (with same, 1952); *Rival to My Heart* (1954); *Calling Nurse Adams* (1958); *Lillian Gish: The Movies, Mr. Griffith and Me* (with Lillian Gish, 1969); etc.

PINCHOT, GIFFORD (Aug. 11, 1865–Oct. 4, 1946); b. Simsbury, Conn. Governor, forester, author. *To the South Seas* (1930); *Just Fishing Talk* (1936); *Breaking New Ground* (1946); and many books on forestry. Governor of Pennsylvania, 1923–27, 1931–35. Prof. forestry, Yale University, 1903–36.

PINCKNEY, CHARLES (Oct. 26, 1757–Oct. 29, 1824); b. Charleston, S.C. Governor, diplomat, author. *Speeches* (1800). Wrote the "Pinckney Draught" of the *Constitution*. Governor of South Carolina, 1789–92, 1796–98, 1807–08; U.S. Senator, 1799–1801; Minister to Spain, 1801–05. *See* Charles C. Nott's *The Mystery of the Pinckney Draught* (1908); *The Records of the Federal Convention of 1787*, ed. by Max Farrand, 3v. (1911); Andrew J. Bethea's *The Contribution of Charles Pinckney to the Formation of the American Union* (1937); Marvin R. Zahniser's *Charles Cotesworth Pinckney: Founding Father* (1967).

PINCKNEY, HENRY LAURENS (Sept. 24, 1794–Feb. 3, 1863); b. Charleston, S.C., son of Charles Pinckney. Congressman, editor. Editor, the *Charleston Mercury*, 1823–32. Congressman, 1833–37.

PINCKNEY, JOSEPHINE [Lyons Scott] (Jan. 25, 1895–Oct. 4, 1957); b. Charleston, S.C. Novelist. *Sea-Drinking Cities* (poems, 1927); *Hilton Head* (1941); *Three O'Clock Dinner* (1945); *Great Mischief* (1948); *My Son and Foe* (1952); *Splendid in Ashes* (1958).

PINDAR, SUSAN (b. c. 1820); b. near Tarrytown, N.Y. Poet. *Fireside Fairies* (1850); *Midsummer Fays* (1850); both combined as *Susan Pindar's Story-Book* (1858); *Legends of the Flowers* (1851); etc. She wrote chiefly for the *Knickerbocker Magazine*.

Pine, Cuyler. Pen name of Ellen Peck.

PINKERTON, A. FRANK. Author. *Dyke Darrel, the Railroad Detective* (1886); *Jim Cummings; or, The Great Adams Express Robbery* (1887); *Saved at the Scaffold; or, Nic Brown, the Chicago Detective* (1888); *The Whitechapel Murders* (1889); etc.

PINKERTON, ALLAN (Aug. 25, 1819–July 1, 1884); b. Glasgow, Scot. Detective, author. *The Expressman and the Detective* (1874); *The Detective and the Somnambulist* (1875); *The Molly Maguires and the Detectives* (1877); *Criminal Reminiscences and Detective Sketches* (1879); *The Spy of the Rebellion* (1883); *Bank Robbers and Detectives* (1883); *Thirty Years a Detective* (1884); etc. *See* R. W. Rowan's *The Pinkertons* (1931). Pinkerton, with E. G. Rucker, established a detective agency in Chicago in 1850, the first in America.

PINKERTON, ROBERT E[ugene] (Mar. 12, 1882–Feb. 16, 1970); b. Arena, Wis. Author. *The Canoe* (1914); *The Long Traverse* (with Kathren Pinkerton, 1920); *The Fourth Norwood* (1925); *White Water* (1926); *Spring Tides* (1927); *Hudson's Bay Company* (1931); *The First Overland Mail* (1953); *Nature Roundup* (1955); etc.

Pinkey Perkins. By Harold Hammond (1905). Boy's book relating the humorous adventures of a schoolboy.

PINKNEY, EDWARD COOTE (Oct. 1, 1802–Apr. 11, 1828); b. London. Editor, poet. *Look Out upon the Stars, My Love* (1823); *Rodolph: A Fragment* (1823); *Poems* (1825); etc. Editor, *The Marylander,* 1827–28. His best-known lyrics are "A Health" and "Serenade." *See* T. O. Mabbott and F. L. Pleadwell's *The Life and Works of Edward Coote Pinkney* (1926).

PINSKI, DAVID (Apr. 5, 1872–Aug. 13, 1959); b. Mohilev, Rus. Playwright, novelist. *The Treasure* (prod. 1920); *Three Plays* (1918); *Temptations* (1919); *Ten Plays* (1919); *The Final Balance* (prod. 1928); *Arnold Levenberg* (1931); etc., and many volumes of plays and stories in Yiddish.

PINTO, ISAAC (June 12, 1720–Jan. 17, 1791). Merchant, scholar. He translated into English the first Jewish prayer book printed in America, entitled: *Evening Service of Roshashanah and Kippur* (1761).

Pioneer, The. Boston, Mass. Literary magazine. Founded Jan. 1843, by James Russell Lowell and Robert Carter. Expired Mar., 1843.

Pioneer Lyceum and Literary Club. Oregon City, Ore. Founded 1843.

Pioneer Magazine. San Francisco, Cal. Founded 1854, by Ferdinand Ewer. George Derby ("John Phoenix") was the chief contributor. Expired 1856.

PIPER, EDWIN FORD (Feb. 8, 1871–May 14, 1939); b. Auburn, Neb. Educator, poet. *Barbed Wire, and Other Poems* (1917); *Paintrock Road* (1927); *Canterbury Pilgrims* (1935); etc. English dept., State University of Iowa, 1905–39.

PIPER, MARGARET REBECCA (Dec. 16, 1879–); b. Ashby, Mass. Author. *Sylvia's Experiment* (1914); *The Princess and the Clan* (1915); *House on the Hill* (1917); *Wild Wings* (1921); etc.

Piper, The. Play by Josephine Preston Peabody (prod. 1911). Dramatization of the old German legend of the Pied Piper of Hamelin.

Pipes of Pan. Play by Edward Childs Carpenter (1917). Romantic and sentimental challenge to the newer realism.

PISE, CHARLES CONSTANTINE (Nov. 22, 1801–May 26, 1866); b. Annapolis, Md. Roman Catholic clergyman, novelist, poet, historian. *Father Rowland* (anon., 1829); *The Indian Cottage* (1829); *History of the Church,* 5v. (1827–30); *The*

Pleasures of Religion, and Other Poems (1833); *Saint Ignatius* (1845); etc. Founder (with Felix Varela), the *Catholic Expositor and Literary Magazine,* 1841.

Pistols at Ten Paces. By William Oliver Stevens (1904). History of dueling in America. *See also* Lorenzo Sabine's *Notes on Duels and Duelling* (1855), and Don C. Seitz's *Famous American Duels* (1929).

Pit, The. Novel by Frank Norris (1903). Based on the speculative frenzy of the Chicago wheat market, known in financial circles as "the pit."

Pit and the Pendulum, The. Tale by Edgar Allan Poe (1830).

PITKIN, WALTER BOUGHTON (Feb. 6, 1878–Jan. 25, 1953); b. Ypsilanti, Mich. Educator, author. *How to Write Short Stories* (1922); *The Art of Rapid Reading* (1929); *The Art of Learning* (1931); *Short Introduction to the History of Human Stupidity* (1932); *Life Begins at Forty* (1932); *The Best Years* (1946); etc. Prof. journalism, Columbia University, from 1912.

PITTENGER, WILLIAM NORMAN (July 23, 1905–); b. Bogota, N.J. Episcopal clergyman, educator, author. *Historic Faith and the Changing World* (1950); *Christ in the Haunted Wood* (1953); *Christian Affirmations* (1954); *Episcopalian Way of Life* (1957); *The Pathway to Believing* (1960); *The Christian Understanding of Human Nature* (1964); *God's Way with Men* (1969); etc. Lecturer on the Divinity Faculty, Cambridge University, England, since 1966.

PITTMAN, H[annah] D[aviess] (b. Nov. 18, 1840); b. Harrodsburg, Ky. Author. *Americans of Gentle Birth and Their Ancestors,* 2v. (1903–07); *The Belle of the Bluegrass Country* (1906); *The Heart of Kentucky* (1907); *Go Forth and Find* (1910); etc.

Pittsburgh Post-Gazette. Pittsburgh, Pa. Newspaper. The *Pittsburgh Gazette* was founded as a weekly in 1786; became a daily in 1833, and later changed its name to the *Pittsburgh Commercial Gazette.* Merged in 1906 with the *Pittsburgh Times* (founded 1831; became a daily in 1879), as the *Pittsburgh Gazette-Times.* The *Pittsburgh Post* was founded in 1842; merged in 1927 with the *Gazette-Times,* as the *Pittsburgh Post-Gazette. See* J. Cutler Andrews' *The Pittsburgh Post-Gazette* (1936). Now merged with the *Pittsburgh Sun Telegraph.* Frank Hawkins is editor; James E. Alexander, book-review editor.

Pittsburgh Press. Pittsburgh, Pa. Newspaper. Founded 1884, as the *Evening Penny Press.* Name changed 1888. Ruth Ayers, Jack Iams, Cy King have been associated with it. Joan Troan is editor-in-chief; Sylvia Sachs edits book reviews.

Pittsburgh Sun Telegraph. Pittsburgh, Pa. Newspaper. The *Pittsburgh Telegraph* was founded 1847 as a weekly; its daily edition was established 1873, as the *Evening Telegraph.* The *Pittsburgh Morning Chronicle* had been founded in 1841; it later became the *Evening Chronicle.* The *Telegraph* and the *Chronicle* merged 1884, as the *Chronicle-Telegraph.* The *Pittsburgh Sun,* founded 1908, merged with the *Chronicle-Telegraph* as the *Sun Telegraph.* Now combined with the *Pittsburgh Post-Gazette.*

PITZ, HENRY C[larence] (June 16, 1895–); b. Philadelphia, Pa. Illustrator. *The Practice of Illustration* (1947); *Pen, Brush and Ink* (1949); *Drawing Trees* (1956); *Ink Drawing Techniques* (1957); *Illustrating for Children's Books* (1963); *The Brandywine Tradition* (1968); etc. Has illustrated Bennett's *Master Skylark;* Twain's *A Connecticut Yankee in King Arthur's Court;* De Foe's *Robinson Crusoe;* and many other books, besides illustrations for *Scribner's, Harper's, Cosmopolitan,* etc.

PLAGEMANN, BENTZ (July 27, 1913–   ); b. Springfield, O. Author. *William Walter* (1941); *All for the Best* (1946); *Into the Labyrinth* (1948); *My Place to Stand*

(1949); *This Is Goggle* (1955); *The Steel Cocoon* (1958); *Half the Fun* (1961); *The Heart of Silence* (1967).

Plain Talk. New York. Founded 1946 by Isaac Don Levine and edited by him. Strongly anti-Communist in opinion. Among those associated with it were Ralph de Toledano, Suzanne LaFollette, and Louis Fischer. Sold only by subscription. Discontinued in 1949.

"Planting of the Apple Tree, The." Poem by William Cullen Bryant (1864).

Plastic Age, The. Novel by Percy Marks (1924). Portrayal of the flexible morals of American youth of college age during the jazz era.

PLATH, SYLVIA (Oct. 27, 1932–Feb. 11, 1963); b. Boston, Mass. Poet. *The Colossus* (1960); *Ariel* (1965); *Uncollected Poems* (1965); *A Bell Jar* (novel, under pen name Victoria Lucas, 1963). Editor, *American Poetry Now* (1961).

Play in the Fields of the Lord, At. Novel by Peter Matthiesen (1965). American missionaries in the Amazon are forced to question their institutional purpose. Remarkable for its descriptions of nature and for its satirical view but sympathetic understanding of missionary activities.

Playboy. Chicago, Ill. Monthly. Founded 1953. Published and edited by Hugh Hefner. Emphasizing sex appeal in stories, articles, and photographs, *Playboy* became outstanding for its imaginative social analysis and its intelligent exploration of male interests.

Player Piano. First novel by Kurt Vonnegut Jr. (1951). Science-fiction satire about the computer-programmed future in which men attempt to revolt against machine domination.

Players, The. New York club. Founded Jan. 7, 1888. The club house at 16 Gramercy Park, New York, was formerly the home of the celebrated actor, Edwin Booth, and was dedicated Dec. 3, 1888. His bedroom and working quarters are preserved exactly as he left them at the time of his death. The club membership is made up of actors, playwrights, and men of letters. The club owns a notable collection of portraits, prints, books, and manuscripts on the theatre.

Plays—The Drama Magazine for Young People. Boston, Mass. Eight issues yearly. Founded 1941. Edited by A. S. Burack.

Playwright as Thinker, The. By Eric Bentley (1955). Analysis of the modern drama as represented by Cocteau, Ibsen, Pirandello, Sartre, Shaw, and Strindberg.

Playwrights' Company. New York. Founded 1938, to produce plays by its members.

Pleasant Valley. By Louis Bromfield (1945). Reminiscences of the author's childhood, his years in France, and his life on a farm in Ohio, mingled with theories of farming.

PLEASANTS, HENRY. Music critic. *The Agony of Modern Music* (1962); *The Great Singers* (1966); *Serious Music and All That Jazz* (1969).

PLIMPTON, GEORGE ARTHUR (July 13, 1855–July 1, 1936); b. Walpole, Mass. Publisher, book collector, author. *The Education of Shakespeare, Illustrated from the Schoolbooks in Use in His Time* (1933); *The Education of Chaucer, Illustrated from the Schoolbooks Used in His Times* (1935); etc. He owned the largest collection of textbooks in the world. His collection of first editions of Italian authors was given to Wellesley College. Head of Ginn & Co., publishers, 1914–31.

PLISCHKE, ELMER (July 15, 1914–); b. Milwaukee, Wis. Educator. *Conduct of American Diplomacy* (1950); *American Foreign Relations: A Bibliography of Official Sources* (1955); *Summit Diplomacy: Personal Diplomacy of the President of the United States* (1958); *Government and Politics of*

Contemporary Berlin (1963); *International Relations: Basic Documents* (1967); etc. Head, dept. of government and politics, University of Maryland, 1954–1968.

PLOWHEAD, RUTH GIPSON (Mrs. E. H. Plowhead) (Dec. 11, 1877–); b. Greeley, Colo. Author. *Lucretia Ann on the Oregon Trail* (1931); *Josie and Joe* (1938); *Mile High Cabin* (1945); etc.

"Plu-Ri-Bus-Tah." Poem by Mortimer Thompson (1856). A burlesque on Longfellow's "Hiawatha."

Plumed Horn, The. See *Corno Emplumado, El.*

PLUMLEY, BENJAMIN RUSH (Mar. 1, 1816–Dec. 9, 1887); b. Newton, Pa. Soldier, author. *Kathleen McKinley, the Kerry Girl; Rachel Lockwood;* and *Lays of the Quakers*, published in the *Knickerbocker Magazine;* and *Oriental Ballads*, published in the *Atlantic Magazine.* None of these has been published in book form.

PLUMMER, JONATHAN (July 13, 1761–Sept. 13, 1819); b. Newbury, Mass. Ballad-monger, peddler, poet. *The Author's Congratulatory Address to Citizen Timothy Dexter on His Attaining an Independent Fortune* (1793); *Parson Pidgin; or, Holy Kissing . . . Occasioned by a Report that Parson Pidgin Had Kissed a Young Woman* (1807); etc. Timothy Dexter employed Plummer as his "poet laureate." See the *New England Quarterly*, Mar., 1935.

PLUMMER, MARY WRIGHT (Mar. 8, 1856–Sept. 27, 1916); b. Richmond, Ind. Librarian, poet. *Hints to Small Libraries* (1894); *Verses* (1896); *Roy and Ray in Mexico* (1907); *Roy and Ray in Canada* (1908); *The Seven Joys of Reading* (1915); etc. Librarian, Pratt Institute, Brooklyn, 1894–1904; head, library school, 1896–1911.

Plutocrat, The. Novel by Booth Tarkington (1927). Earl Tinker, American millionaire, with his wife and daughter Olivia, is touring the Mediterranean. Laurence Ogle, a young playwright, is on the same cruise. The story revolves around the romance between Ogle and Olivia, and the vulgarity and pomposity of Tinker.

PLUTZIK, HYAM (1911–Jan. 9, 1962); b. Brooklyn, N.Y. Poet. *Aspects of Proteus* (1949); *Apples from Shinar* (1959); *Horatio* (1961).

PLYMPTON, A[lmira] G[eorge], b. Boston, Mass. Illustrator, author. *Dear Daughter Dorothy* (1891); *Penelope Prig, and Other Stories* (1894); *Betty, a Butterfly* (1894); *Dorothy and Anton* (1895); etc.

PM. New York Newspaper. Founded 1940. Ralph Ingersoll was its first editor and publisher. Ben Hecht, Robert Rice, Tom Meany, Tom O'Reilly were columnists; Roger Pippett was book critic; Louis Kronenberger, drama critic; and Max Lerner, editorial writer. It was a tabloid newspaper which until 1946 carried no advertising. Marshall Field, III owned the controlling stock. Expired 1949.

POCHMANN, HENRY AUGUST (Jan. 5, 1901–); b. Round Top, Tex. Educator. *New England Transcendentalism and St. Louis Hegelianism* (1948); *German Culture in America* (with others, 1957); etc. Editor: *Washington Irving: Representative Selections* (1934); etc. General editor *The Complete Writings of Washington Irving,* 28v., since 1866. Prof. English, University of Wisconsin, since 1938.

Pocket Books Inc. New York. Publishers of reprints and reference books. Founded 1939, by Robert F. de Graff. The firm launched a new trend in publishing with twenty-five cent paperback books. In ten years it issued 600 titles which sold 260,000,000 copies. Its leading titles have been *How to Win Friends and Influence People, The Pocket Book of Baby and Child Care, The Pocket Cook Book,* and *The Merriam-Webster Pocket Dictionary.* In 1944 Marshall Field acquired a substantial interest in the company. Philip Van Doren Stern and Donald Porter Geddes were successively editors. Permabooks is a division. Acquired Washington Square Press in 1959, shortly after its founding. Now a division itself of Simon and Schuster (q.v.). Leon Shimkin is president of both Pocket Books and Simon and Schuster.

Pocket Magazine. New York. Monthly bibelot. Founded Nov., 1895. Editor, Irving Bacheller. Expired Jan., 1897.

PODHORETZ, NORMAN (Jan. 16, 1930–   ); b. Brooklyn, N.Y. Editor, author. *Doings and Undoings; The Fifties and After in American Writing* (1964); *Making It* (1968). Editor: *The Commentary Reader: Two Decades of Articles and Stories* (1966). Editor, *Commentary* magazine, since 1960.

POE, EDGAR ALLAN (Jan. 19, 1809–Oct. 7, 1849); b. Boston, Mass. Poet, critic, short story writer, editor. *Tamerlane, and Other Poems* (under pen name "A Bostonian," 1827); *Al Aaraaf, Tamerlane, and Minor Poems* (1829); *Poems by Edgar A. Poe* (1831); *The Narrative of Arthur Gordon Pym* (1838); *Tales of the Grotesque and Arabesque,* 2v. (1840); *The Prose Romances of Edgar A. Poe* (1943); *Tales* (1845); *The Raven and Other Poems* (1845); *Eureka: A Prose Poem* (1848); *The Literati* (1850). *The Works of Edgar Allan Poe* edited by E. C. Stedman and G. E. Woodberry, 10v. (1894–95). Editorial staff, *Southern Literary Messenger,* 1835–37; *Graham's Magazine,* 1841–42; co-editor, *Burton's Gentleman's Magazine,* 1839–40; on staff *New York Mirror,* 1845; editor, *Broadway Journal,* 1845–46. See J. H. Ingram's *Edgar Allan Poe, His Life, Letters, and Opinions,* 2v. (1880); J. A. Harrison's *The Life and Letters of Edgar Allan Poe,* 2v. (1903); George E. Woodberry's *The Life of Edgar Allan Poe,* 2v. (1909); Frederick C. Prescott's *Critical Writings of Edgar Allan Poe* (1909); J. W. Robertson's *Edgar Allan Poe: A Psychopathic Study* (1922); Mary E. Phillips's *Edgar Allan Poe, the Man,* 2v. (1926); Hervey Allen's *Israfel,* 2v. (1926); Joseph Wood Krutch's *Edgar Allan Poe, A Study in Genius* (1926); C. P. Cambiare's *The Influence of Edgar Allan Poe in France* (1927); Thomas Olive Mabbott's *Poe's Doings of Gotham* (1929); Killis Campbell's *The Mind of Poe and Other Studies* (1933); John W. Robertson's *Bibliography of the Writings of Edgar A. Poe,* 2v. (1934); *Edgar Allan Poe. Letters and Documents in the Enoch Pratt Free Library,* edited by Arthur H. Quinn and Richard H. Hart (1941); Arthur H. Quinn's *Edgar Allan Poe: A Critical Biography* (1941); *The Letters of Edgar Allan Poe,* 2v. (1948); E. Wagenknecht's *Edgar Allan Poe, The Man Behind the Legend* (1963); E. W. Parks' *Edgar Allan Poe* (1964); Robert Regan's *Poe: A Collection of Critical Essays* (1967).

Poems by Several Hands. (1774). Includes poems by Mather Byles, Joseph Green, and John Adams.

Poems of the War. By George Henry Boker (1864). This collection contains the celebrated poem "Dirge for a Soldier," inspired by the death of General Kearny.

Poems on Several Occasions, with Some Other Compositions. By Nathaniel Evans (1772).

"Poet and His Book, The." Poem by Edna St. Vincent Millay (1921).

Poet at the Breakfast Table, The. By Oliver Wendell Holmes (1872). First printed in a series of papers in the *Atlantic Monthly.* Rambling conversations on a variety of subjects, some humorous, some philosophic and scientific.

Poet Lore. Boston, Mass. Founded 1888, at Philadelphia, by Archibald Clarke and Charlotte Endymion Porter. It was moved to Boston in 1892. In 1903 the magazine was sold to Richard G. Badger, but Clarke and Porter continued their editorship. Later edited by Edmund R. Brown.

Poetic Principle, The. By Edgar Allan Poe (1850). Expression of the author's theory of criticism.

"Poetry." Poem by Marianne Moore.

Poetry: A Magazine of Verse. Chicago, Ill. Monthly. Founded 1912, by Harriet Monroe. Many American poets received their first encouragement from this magazine, notably through the "roving editorship" of Ezra Pound. Harriet Monroe was editor until her death in 1936, and was succeeded by Morton D. Zabel, George Dillon, Karl Shapiro, Henry Rago, among others. Henry Blake Fuller was an assistant and adviser, 1912–29. The magazine awards the Helen Haire Levinson Prize, founded 1914. *Poetry* has been the most influential magazine in the United States in spreading the modern movement associated with T. S. Eliot, Ezra Pound, W. C. Williams, Wallace Stevens, etc.

Poetry and Drama. By T. S. Eliot (1951). The Theodore Spencer memorial lecture at Harvard University, 1950, in which Eliot discusses his own plays and his theory of poetic drama.

Poetry Society of America. New York. Founded 1910. Gustav Davidson is secretary. The society has awarded the Poetry Society of America Annual Award, since 1916; the William Rose Benét Memorial Award, since 1952; the Alexander Droutzkoy Memorial Award, since 1951; the Edna St. Vincent Millay Memorial Award, since 1952; the Shelley Memorial Award, since 1930; and other awards.

Poets and Poetry of the West, The. Ed. by William Turner Coggeshall (1860). Anthology of poetry of the Middle Western States. Contains biographical and critical notes.

Poets of America, The. By Edmund Clarence Stedman (1885). Chiefly on Bryant, Emerson, Poe, Longfellow, Whittier, Holmes, Lowell, Whitman, and Taylor.

Poets of America, The. By John Keese, 2v. (1840–42).

Poets of the Church, The. By Edwin F. Hatfield (1884).

Poets of the English Language. Compiled by W. H. Auden and Norman H. Pearson, 5v. (1950). Anthology ranging from Langland to Yeats. The most extensive and selective compilation in recent years.

POFFENBARGER, LIVIA [Nye] SIMPSON (Mrs. George Poffenbarger) (Mar. 1, 1862–Oct. 27, 1937); b. Pomeroy, O. Publisher, author. *Ann Bailey* (1907); *Fort Randolph* (1907); *The Battle of Point Pleasant* (1909); *Romantic and Historic Virginia* (1932); etc. Owner, *Stage Gazette,* Point Pleasant, W. Va., 1888–1913.

Pogo. By Walt Kelly (1951). The first collection of cartoon strips and humorous nonsense verses by the originator of the comic-strip character "Pogo." Many other collections appeared in subsequent years.

POGUE, FORREST CARLISLE (Sept. 17, 1912–); b. Eddyville, Ky. Historian, author. *The Supreme Command* (1954); *George C. Marshall: Education of a General* (vol. 1, 1963; vol. 2, 1966). Co-author: *The Meaning of Yalta* (1956). Director, George C. Marshall Research Library, since 1964.

POHL, FREDERICK (1919?–). Author. *Alternating Currents* (1956); *Slave Ship* (1957); *Undersea City* (with Jack Williamson, 1958); *Drunkard's Walk* (1960); etc. With Cyril M. Kornbluth: *The Space Merchants* (1953); *Gladiator-at-Law* (1955); *Presidential Year* (1956); *Starchild* (with Jack Williamson, 1966); *Undersea Quest* (with same, 1966); etc. *Galaxy Reader* (1967); *The Frederick Pohl Omnibus* (1967); *The Wonder Effect* with C. M. Kornbluth (1967); Recipient International Science Fiction Achievement Award (1966).

Point of No Return. Novel by J. P. Marquand (1949). A banker, no longer young, finds himself committed to the way of life his vocation entails, with no possibility for any imaginative release.

POIRIER, RICHARD (Sept. 9, 1925–); b. Gloucester, Mass. Educator, writer. *The Comic Sense in Henry James* (1960); *In Defense of Reading* (1962); *A World Elsewhere* (1966). Prof. English, Rutgers University, since 1963. Editor, *Partisan Review,* since 1963.

POLACHEK, VICTOR H. (Aug. 24, 1876–June 11, 1940); b. Chicago, Ill. Publisher, editor. With Hearst newspapers, 1899–1939; publisher, the *New York American,* 1918–19; on managerial staff, Hearst newspapers, 1931–39.

POLANYI, KARL [Paul] (Oct. 25, 1886–Apr. 23, 1964); b. Vienna. Educator. *The Great Transformation* (1944). Editor: *Christianity and the Social Revolution* (1935); *Trade and Market in the Early Empires* (with others, 1957).

Police Captain Howard. Pen name of Luis Philip Senarens.

Police Gazette. See *National Police Gazette.*

POLIER, JUSTINE WISE (Apr. 12, 1903–); b. Portland, Ore. Judge. *Everyone's Children, Nobody's Child* (1941); *Back to What Woodshed* (1956); *The Rule of Law and the Role of Psychiatry* (1968). Co-editor: Stephen S. Wise's *Personal Letters* (1956).

POLING, DANIEL ALFRED (Nov. 30, 1884–Feb. 7, 1968); b. Portland, Ore. Reformed Church clergyman, editor, author. *Mothers of Men* (1914); *What Men Need Most* (1923); *John of Oregon* (1926); *The Heretic* (1928); *Youth Marches* (1937); *A Preacher Looks at War* (1943); *Faith Is Power for You* (1950); *Mine Eyes Have Seen* (1959); *Jesus Says to You* (1961); etc. Editor, *Christian Herald.*

Political Novel, The. By Morris Edmund Spears (1924).

Political Science Quarterly. New York. Quarterly. Founded 1886. Published by the Academy of Political Science, Columbia University.

Politician Outwitted, The. Play by Samuel Low (1789). Probably the first American play to use Negro dialect.

Politics. New York. Founded in 1942 and edited by Dwight MacDonald. Published weekly, monthly, and then irregularly. Discontinued 1949. An attempt among radical but anti-communist intellectuals of the left to explore the possibilities for a new political orientation based on moral responsibility and social justice.

Politics: Who Gets What, When, How? By Harold Lasswell (1958). A cross-section analysis of political motives and underlying purposes.

POLK, JAMES K[nox] (Nov. 2, 1795–June 15, 1849); b. in Mecklenburg, Co., N.C. Eleventh president of the United States. See *The Diary of James K. Polk,* ed. by Milo M. Quaife, 4v. (1910); E. I. McCormac's *James K. Polk: A Political Biography* (1922); *The Diary of a President,* ed. by Allan Nevins (1929).

POLK, WILLIAM ROE (Mar. 7, 1929–); b. Fort Worth, Texas. Educator, author. *Perspective of the Arab World* (1956); *Backdrop to Tragedy: The Struggle for Palestine* (1957); *Generations, Classes and Politics* (1962); *The Opening of South Lebanon* (1963); *The Developmental Revolution* (1964); *The United States and the Arab World* (1965). Editor: *Studies on the Civilization of Islam* (with S. Shaw) 1962. Prof. Middle Eastern History, University of Chicago, since 1965.

POLLACK, JACK HARRISON; b. Philadelphia. Author. *A Psychology Outline* (1938); *Croiset the Clairvoyant* (1964).

POLLAK, GUSTAV (May 4, 1849–Nov. 1, 1919); b. Vienna. Editor, author. *Franz Grillparzer and the Austrian Drama* (1907); *International Perspective in Literary Criticism* (1914); *Fifty Years of American Idealism* (1915); etc. Contributor to *The Nation,* 1874–1919.

POLLARD, EDWARD ALBERT (Feb. 27, 1831–Dec. 16, 1872); b. in Albemarle Co., Va. Editor, author. *The Southern Spy; or, Curiosities of Negro Slavery in the South* (1859); *Letters of the Southern Spy* (1861); *Southern History of the War* (1863), augmented, 2v. (1866); *The Lost Cause* (1866); *Life of Jefferson Davis* (1869); etc. Editor, the *Daily Richmond Examiner,* 1861–67. Founder, *Southern Opinion,* 1867.

POLLARD, HAROLD STANLEY (May 28, 1878–Sept. 21, 1953); b. Hyde Park, Mass. Chief editorial writer, *New York Evening World,* 1911–18, editor, 1918–31; editorial writer, *New York World-Telegram,* from 1931.

POLLARD, JOSEPH PERCIVAL (Jan. 29, 1869–Dec. 17, 1911); b. Griefswald, Pomerania. Critic, playwright, novelist. *Figaro Fiction* (1892); *Cape of Storms* (1895); *The Imitator* (1901); *Lingo Dan* (1903); *Nocturnes* (with Leo Ditrichstein, prod. 1906); *The Ambitious Mrs. Alcott* (with same, prod. 1907); *Their Day in Court* (1909); etc. Lit. reviewer, *Town Topics,* 1897–1911.

POLLARD, JOSEPHINE (c. 1840–1892); b. New York. Poet. The *Gypsy* series, 6v. (1873–74); *A Piece of Silver* (1876); *The Burden Lifted* (1882); *Vagrant Verses* (1886); etc.

POLLOCK, CHANNING (Mar. 4, 1880–Aug. 17, 1946); b. Washington, D.C. Drama critic, playwright. *Stage Stories* (1901); *The Footlights Fore and Aft* (1909); *Such a Little Queen* (prod. 1909); *Roads to Destiny* (prod. 1918); *The Fool* (prod. 1922); *The Enemy* (prod. 1925); *Mr. Moneypenny* (prod. 1928); *The House Beautiful* (prod. 1931); *The Adventures of a Happy Man* (1939); *Harvest of My Years* (autobiography, 1943); etc. Drama critic, the *Washington Post;* the *Washington Times; Ainslee's; The Smart Set; The Green Book;* etc.

POLLOCK, EDWARD (Sept. 2, 1823–Dec. 13, 1856); b. Philadelphia, Pa. Poet. *Poems* (1876); etc.

POLLOCK, THOMAS CLARK (Mar. 31, 1902–); b. Monmouth, Ill. Educator, author. *The Philadelphia Theatre in the Eighteenth Century* (1933); *The Nature of Literature* (1942). Editor: *Thomas Wolfe at Washington Square* (with Oscar Cargill, 1954); etc. English dept., New York University, since 1947.

Polly Peaseblossom's Wedding, and Other Tales. Ed. by Thomas A. Burke (1848). An anthology of American humor of the frontier days, similar to Longstreet's *Georgia Scenes.*

"Polly-Wolly-Doodle." One of the most popular of American nonsense songs. Its authorship is unknown.

Pollyanna. Novel by Eleanor H. Porter (1913). The optimism and good cheer radiated by Pollyanna has made her name a part of the American language; excessive optimism is perhaps the connotation most often given. *See also* Harriet Lummis Smith.

POLOCK, WILLIAM GUSTAVE (Dec. 7, 1890–); b. Wausau, Wis. Educator, author. *John Eliot* (1925); *Shegonaba* (1925); *The Missionary of the Forests* (1927); *David Livingstone* (1929); *Famous Hymns, and Their Story* (1930); *Fathers and Founders* (1938); *Stories of Our Favorite Hymns* (1938). Prof. theology, Concordia Seminary, St. Louis.

Polyanthos. Boston, Mass. Theatrical magazine. Founded Dec., 1805, by Joseph T. Buckminster. Royall Tyler was a contributor. Expired 1814.

POMEROY, EARL SPENCER (Dec. 27, 1915–); b. Capitola, Cal. Educator, author. *The Territories and the United States, 1861–1890* (1947); *In Search of the Golden West: The Tourist in Western America* (1957); *The Pacific Slope: a History* (1965); etc. History dept., University of Oregon, since 1949.

POMEROY, MARCUS M[ills] (Dec. 25, 1833–May 30, 1896); b. Elmira, N.Y. Printer, publisher, humorist. Pen name

"Brick Pomeroy." *Sense* (1868); *Nonsense* (1868); *Our Saturday Nights* (1870); *Gold-Dust* (1871); *Brick-Dust* (1871); *Home Harmonies* (1876); *Journey of Life* (autobiography, 1890); etc. Editor, *Pomeroy's Democrat*, etc.

POMEROY, RALPH (1926–). Poet. *The Canaries as They Are* (1965); *In the Financial District* (1968); etc. Staff, *Art News.*

POMFRET, JOHN EDWIN (Sept. 21, 1898–); b. Philadelphia, Pa. Educator. *The Struggle for Land in Ireland* (1930); *The Geographic Pattern of Mankind* (1935). Editor: *California Gold Rush Voyages* (1954); *The Province of West New Jersey, 1609–1702* (1956); *The New Jersey Proprietors and their Lands, 1664–1776* (1964); etc. Pres., College of William and Mary, 1942–51.

POND, ENOCH (July 29, 1791–Jan. 21, 1882); b. Wrentham, Mass. Congregational clergyman, educator, author. *The Young Pastor's Guide* (1844), republished as *Lectures on Pastoral Theology* (1866); *The Lives of Increase Mather and Sir William Phipps* (1847); *The Seals Opened* (1871); *The Autobiography of Enoch Pond* (1883); etc. With Bangor Theological Seminary, 1832–82.

POND, FREDERICK EUGENE (Apr. 8, 1856–Nov. 1, 1925); b. Packwaukee, Wis. Writer on field sports. Pen name "Will Wildwood." *Handbook for Young Sportsmen* (1876); *Memoirs of Eminent Sportsmen* (1878); *Life and Adventures of Ned Buntline* (1888); etc. Editor: Henry William Herbert's *Sporting Scenes and Characters,* 2v. (1881); Isaac McLellan's *Poems of the Rod and Gun* (1886); Charles Halpine's *An Angler's Reminiscences* (1913); etc. Editor, *Wildwood's Magazine; Sportsman's Review; American Angler; Turf, Field, and Farm;* etc.

POND, GEORGE EDWARD (Mar. 11, 1837–Sept. 22, 1899); b. Boston, Mass. Editor, author. *The Shenandoah Valley in 1864* (1883). Editor, the *Philadelphia Record,* 1870–77; editorial writer, the *New York Sun,* 1880–99. Wrote "Driftwood Essays" in the *Galaxy* under the pen name "Philip Quilibet," May, 1868–Jan., 1878.

POND, JAMES BURTON (June 11, 1838–June 21, 1903); b. Cuba, N.Y. Lecture manager, author. *A Summer in England with Henry Ward Beecher* (1887); *Eccentricities of Genius* (1900). In 1875 Pond and George H. Hathaway bought James Redpath's interest in a Boston lyceum bureau, and in 1879 Pond opened a bureau of his own in New York. Among the lecturers he sponsored were Henry Ward Beecher, Mark Twain, "Bill Nye," Conan Doyle, Ralph Waldo Emerson.

POND, SAMUEL WILLIAM (Apr. 10, 1808–Dec. 12, 1891); b. New Preston, Conn. Congregational missionary to the Indians, poet. *Dakota Dowanpi Kin: Hymns in the Dakota or Sioux Language* (1842); *Legends of the Dakotas, and Other Selections from the Poetical Works of Reverend Samuel William Pond* (1911).

Ponder Heart, The. Novel by Eudora Welty (1954). Rural life in Mississippi, with bizarre incidents and an ingenious blend of the comical and terrifying.

"Pondy Woods." Poem by Robert Penn Warren (1929).

Ponkapog Papers. By Thomas Bailey Aldrich (1903). Miscellaneous notes and essays from a small Massachusetts settlement.

PONTE, LORENZO DA (Mar. 10, 1749–Aug. 17, 1838); b. near Venice, Italy, came to the United States in 1805. Educator, librettist, poet. *Memorie,* 2v. (1823), translated by Elizabeth Abbott as *Memoirs* (1929); and many other books in Italian. He wrote the librettos for Mozart's operas *Le Nozze di Figaro* (prod. 1786), *Don Giovanni* (prod. 1787), and *Cosi Fan Tutte* (prod. 1790). He was licensed to teach Italian to the students at Columbia College, 1825–38. *See* Joseph L. Russo's *Lorenzo da Ponte, Poet and Adventurer* (1922).

Ponteach; or, The Savages of America. Play by Robert Rogers (1766). The first play by an American about the American scene. It was never acted.

POOL, BETTIE FRESHWATER. Author. *The Eyrie, and Other Southern Stories* (1905); *Under Brazilian Skies* (1908); *Carolina* (poem, 1909); *Literature in the Albemarle* (1915).

POOL, DAVID DE SOLA (May 16, 1885–Dec. 1, 1970); b. London. Rabbi, author. *Hebrew Learning among the Puritans of New England* (1911); *Portraits Etched in Stone* (1952); *An Old Faith in the New World* (with Tamar de Sola Pool, 1955); *Why I Am a Jew* (1957); *Is There An Answer? An Inquiry Into Some Human Dilemmas* (with same, 1966); etc. Editor and translator: *The Traditional Prayer Book for Sabbath and Festivals* (1960).

POOL, ITHIEL DE SOLA (Oct. 26, 1917–   ); b. New York. Educator, author. *The Comparative Study of Symbols* (1952); *Symbols of Internationalism* (1951); *Symbols of Democracy* (1952); *Satellite Generals* (1955); *American Business and Public Policy* (1963); *The People Look at Educational Television* (1963); *Candidates, Issues and Strategies* (1964). Prof. political science, Massachusetts Institute of Technology, since 1953.

POOL, MARIA LOUISE (Aug. 20, 1841–May 19, 1898); b. Rockland, Mass. Novelist, humorist. *Dally* (1891); *Roweny in Boston* (1892); *Against Human Nature* (1895); *In Buncombe County* (1896); *Boss and Other Dogs* (1896); *In a Dike Shanty* (1896); *A Golden Sorrow* (1898); *A Widower & Some Spinsters* (1899); *The Meloon Farm* (1900); etc.

POOLE, ERNEST (Jan 23, 1880–Jan. 10, 1950); b. Chicago, Ill. Novelist. *The Voice of the Street* (1906); *The Harbor* (1915); *His Family* (1917, Pulitzer Prize novel, 1918); *His Second Wife* (1918); *Blind* (1920); *Beggars' Gold* (1921); *Millions* (1922); *Danger* (1923); *The Avalanche* (1924); *The Hunter's Moon* (1925); *With Eastern Eyes* (1926); *Silent Storms* (1927); *The Car of Croesus* (1930); *The Destroyer* (1931); *Great Winds* (1933); *One of Us* (1934); *The Bridge* (autobiography, 1940); *Giants Gone: Men Who Made Chicago* (1943); *The Great White Hills of New Hampshire* (1946); *The Nancy Flyer: A Stagecoach Epic* (1949); etc.

POOLE, FITCH (June 13, 1803–Aug. 19, 1873); b. South Danvers, Mass. Journalist, poet, librarian, humorist. Editor, the *Danvers Courier,* and on staff of the *Wizard,* 1859–69. Among his humorous poems are: "Giles Corey & Goodwyfe Corey," "Lines to a Mouse in the Peabody Institute," "The Librarian's Epitaph."

POOLE, LYNN (Aug. 11, 1910–); b. Eagle Grove, Ia. Public relations executive. *Science Via Television* (1950); *Science, the Super Sleuth* (1954); *Ballooning in the Space Age* (1958); etc.

Poole, Mrs. Abram. See Mercedes de Acosta.

POOLE, WILLIAM FREDERICK (Dec. 24, 1821–Mar. 1, 1894); b. Salem, Mass. Librarian, compiler, author. *The Battle of the Dictionaries* (1856); *Cotton Mather and Salem Witchcraft* (1869). Compiler: *An Alphabetical Index to Subjects Treated in the Reviews and Other Periodicals* (1848), the beginning of the well-known *Poole's Index.* Librarian, Boston Mercantile Library, 1852–56; Boston Athenaeum, 1856–69; Cincinnati Public Library, 1871–73; Chicago Public Library, 1874–87; Newberry Library, Chicago, 1887–94. One of the founders of the American Library Association, 1876.

Poole's Index to Periodical Literature. Ed. by William Frederick Poole, first edition (1848); second edition (1853); third edition, ed. by Poole and William Isaac Fletcher (1882); fourth edition, ed. by Fletcher (1891). *Supplements,* ed. by Fletcher, 5v. (1887–1908), covering the years 1882–1906. These indexes contain subject entries only. An abridged edition was published by Fletcher and Mary Poole in 1901, with a *Supplement* (1905).

POOR, AGNES BLAKE (d. Feb. 28, 1922). Author. Pen name "Dorothy Prescott." *Brothers and Strangers* (1894); *Boston Neighbours in Town and Out* (1898); etc. Compiler: *Pan-American Poems* (1918).

POOR, HENRY VARNUM (Dec. 8, 1812–Jan. 4, 1905); b. Andover, Me. Editor, economist, author. *Money and Its Laws* (1877); *Twenty-Two Years of Protection* (1888); *The Tariff* (1892); etc. Editor, the *American Railroad Journal*, 1849–62. With his son, Henry William Poor, he formed the firm of H. V. & H. W. Poor, which published *Poor's Manual of Railroads* annually, beginning in 1868; with the 1925 issue, this became Poor's Railroad Section. Out of this grew other manuals and handbooks.

POOR, HENRY WILLIAM (June 16, 1844–Apr. 13, 1915); b. Bangor, Me., son of Henry Varnum Poor. Banker, editor, book collector. See *American Bookbindings in the Library of Henry William Poor, Described by Edward Henri Pène du Bois* (1903); *Catalogue of the Library of Henry W. Poor* (1908). *See* Henry Varnum Poor.

Poor Little Rich Girl, The. Play by Eleanor Gates (prod. 1913).

Poor Richard's Almanack. By Benjamin Franklin. Published annually, 1732–57. Most popular of early almanacs. They were filled with proverbs and witty sayings which have passed into the common speech of America. *See* Carl Van Doren's *Benjamin Franklin* (1938).

Poor White. Novel by Sherwood Anderson (1920). Hugh McVey, springing from a poor white group, fights to achieve a higher station in life in the new industrial era which has turned his agricultural community into a manufacturing center.

POORE, BENJAMIN PERLEY (Nov. 2, 1820–May 29, 1887); b. Newburyport, Mass. Editor, author. *Life of Gen. Zachary Taylor* (1848); *Life of U. S. Grant* (1885); *Perley's Reminiscences*, 2v. (1886); *The Mameluke; or, The Sign of the Mystic Tie* (1852); etc. Editor, the *Boston Daily Bee*, 1848; editor, first issue of the *Congressional Directory*, 1869. For more than thirty years he wrote newspaper columns under the pen name "Perley." Washington correspondent, *Boston Journal*, 1854–84.

POORE, CHARLES [Graydon] (Aug. 20, 1902–d. 1971); b. Monterrey, N.L., Mexico. Critic, author. *Goya* (1938). Editor: *The Hemingway Reader* (1953). On the staff of the *New York Times*, from 1926. Wrote book reviews for the daily *New York Times* and the *New York Times Book Review.*

POORE, HENRY RANKIN (Mar. 21, 1859–Aug. 15, 1940); b. Newark, N.J. Artist, author. *The Conception of Art* (1913); *The New Tendency in Art* (1915); *Modern Art* (1931); *Art's Place in Education* (1934); etc.

"Pop Goes the Weasel." Popular song (1862). Authorship unknown.

Pop poetry. Usually, the lyrics written to certain kinds of popular music known as rock, folk, folk-rock, folk-blues. Unlike the lyrics written to musical-comedy, popular-jazz, or dance-band tunes, pop poetry is literary enough to be considered by itself although its distinctive character is inseparable from musical performance. Most examples since the 1950's, when such lyrics became noteworthy, have been the products of composer-lyricists who perform their own work. The literary influences stem from the words of jazz, blues, Country and Western, and other indigenous forms; from Symbolist, Dadaist, and Surrealist verse techniques; and from colloquial speech. The most notable American pop poets have been Woody Guthrie, Chuck Berry, Paul Simon, Bob Dylan, Richard Fariña, Jim Morrison, Arlo Guthrie, Tuli Kupferberg, Buffy Sainte-Marie, and Rod McKuen. *See* Richard Goldstein's *The Poetry of Rock,* Paul Williams' *Outlaw Blues,* and Lilian Roxon's *Rock Encyclopedia.*

POPE, ARTHUR UPHAM (Feb. 7, 1881–Sept. 4, 1969); b. Phoenix, R.I. Persian art scholar, author. *Persian Art* (1925); *Persian Art and Culture* (1928); *An Introduction to Persian Art* (1930); *Masterpieces of Persian Art* (1960); etc. Editor: *A Survey of Persian Art,* 7v. (with Phyllis Driscoll, 1938–39). Chancellor, Asia Institute, 1947–53.

POPE, CLIFFORD HILLHOUSE (1899–); b. Washington, Ga. Herpetologist. *The Reptiles of China* (1935); *China's Animal Frontier* (1940); *Reptiles Round the World* (1957); *The Giant Snakes* (1961); etc.

POPE, EDITH (Mrs. Verle A. Pope) (July 23, 1905–Jan. 31, 1961); b. St. Augustine, Fla. Author, under maiden name Edith Everett Taylor: *The Black Lagoon* (poems, 1926); *Not Magnolias* (1928); *Old Lady* (1934); *Half Holiday* (1938); etc. Under married name: *The Colcorton* (1944); *The Biggety Chameleon* (1946); *River in the Wind* (1954).

POPENOE, PAUL [Bowman] (Oct. 16, 1888–); b. Topeka, Kan. Biologist, author. *Date Growing in the New and Old Worlds* (1913); *Modern Marriage* (1925); *Practical Applications of Heredity* (1930); *Marriage Is What You Make It* (1950); *Divorce—17 Ways to Avoid It* (1959); *Sex, Love, and Marriage* (with Evelyn Duvall and David Mace, 1963); *The Church Looks at Family Life* (1964); etc.

POPKIN, ZELDA (Mrs. Louis Popkin) (July 5, 1898–); b. Brooklyn, N.Y. Author. *The Journey Home* (1945); *Small Victory* (1947); *Walk Through the Valley* (1949); *Open Every Door* (autobiography, 1956). Author of many mystery novels.

"Poppy Juice." Long narrative poem by Genevieve Taggard (1926).

Popular Mechanics. New York. Monthly. Founded 1902. Published by Popular Mechanics Corp. Features material devoted to simple understanding of all areas of practical science and mechanics.

Popular Science Monthly. New York. Monthly. Founded 1872. Published by Popular Science Publishing Co. One of the earliest popular publications to stress the ordinary reader's relation to applied science and mechanics. Bought by Times Mirror Co. in 1967.

PORCHER, MARY F[anning] WICKHAM (June, 1898–); b. Philadelphia, Pa. Author. *The Tilted Cup* (poems, 1926); *Cherique* (1928); *Gloom Creek* (1929). Now writes as "Mary F. Wickham."

Porgy. Novel by Du Bose Heyward (1925). Story of Catfish Row in Charleston, S.C., where Porgy, a crippled Negro, becomes involved in a murder through a succession of sinister events. Dramatized (with his wife, Dorothy Heyward, prod. 1927), and made into an opera called *Porgy and Bess,* with music by George Gershwin (prod. 1935).

Port Folio. Philadelphia, Pa. Magazine. Founded Jan. 3, 1801, by Joseph Dennie. Editors: Joseph Dennie, 1801–11; Nicholas Biddle, 1812–14; Charles Caldwell, 1814–16; John Elihu Hall, 1816–27. It began as a weekly, but became a monthly in 1813. The pen name "Oliver Oldschool, Esq." was used by Dennie on the masthead, and was continued after his death. John Howard Payne, Philip Freneau, Charles Brockden Brown, Thomas G. Fessenden, William Dunlap, John Quincy Adams, James Hall, and Royal Tyler were among the distinguished contributors. *See* Albert H. Smyth's *Philadelphia Magazines and Their Contributors* (1892); Frank L. Mott's *A History of American Magazines,* v. I (1938).

PORTER, CHARLOTTE ENDYMION (1859–Jan. 16, 1942); b. Towanda, Pa. Poet, editor. *Lips of Music* (1910); etc. Editor (with Helen A. Clarke), of many editions of Robert Browning and Elizabeth Barrett Browning, *First Folio Shakespeare,* 40v.; co-founder (with Helen A. Clarke), *Poet-Lore,* 1888.

PORTER, COLE (June 9, 1893–Oct. 15, 1964); b. Peru, Ind. Composer, song writer. Has written the scores for many musical comedies, including: *Hitchy-Koo, 1919* (prod. 1919); *Greenwich Village Follies of 1924* (prod. 1924); *Fifty Million Frenchmen* (prod. 1929); *Gay Divorce* (prod. 1932); *Anything Goes* (prod. 1934); *Jubilee* (prod. 1935); *Leave It to Me* (prod. 1938); *Dubarry Was a Lady* (prod. 1939); *Let's Face It* (prod. 1941); *Something for the Boys* (prod. 1942); *Mexican Hayride* (prod. 1943); *Kiss Me, Kate* (prod. 1948); *Out of This World* (prod. 1950); *Silk Stockings* (prod. 1954); etc.

PORTER, DAVID (Feb. 1, 1780–Mar. 3, 1843); b. Boston, Mass. Naval officer, author. *Journal of a Cruise Made to the Pacific Ocean,* 2v. (1815); *Constantinople and its Environs,* 2v. (1835), comprising letters to James Kirke Paulding. See Archibald Douglas Turnbull's *Commodore David Porter, 1780–1843* (1929).

PORTER, DAVID DIXON (June 8, 1813–Feb. 13, 1891); b. Chester, Pa., son of David Porter. Naval officer, author. *Memoirs of Commodore David Porter* (1875); *Allan Dare and Robert le Diable* (in parts, 1884–85); *The Adventures of Harry Marline* (1885); *Incidents and Anecdotes of the Civil War* (1885); *History of the Navy During the War of the Rebellion* (1887).

PORTER, ELEANOR H[odgman] (Dec. 19, 1868–May 21, 1920); b. Littleton, N.H. Novelist. *Cross Currents* (1907); *Miss Billy* (1911); *The Story of Marco* (1911); *Pollyanna* (1913); *Miss Billy—Married* (1914); *Pollyanna Grows Up* (1915); *Just David* (1916); *Across the Years* (1919); *Dawn* (1919); *Mary Marie* (1920); etc.

PORTER, GENE STRATTON (Mrs. Charles Darwin Porter) (1868–1924); b. Wabash Co., Ind. Naturalist, novelist. *The Song of the Cardinal* (1902); *Freckles* (1904); *At the Foot of the Rainbow* (1908); *A Girl of the Limberlost* (1909); *Birds of the Bible* (1909); *Music of the Wild* (1910); *The Harvester* (1911); *Laddie* (1913); *Michael O'Halloran* (1915); *Friends in Feathers* (1922); *The Keeper of the Bees* (1925); etc. See Jeannette Porter Meehan's *The Lady of the Limberlost: The Life and Letters of Gene Stratton-Porter* (1928).

PORTER, HAROLD EVERETT (Sept. 19, 1867–June 20, 1936); b. Boston, Mass. Author. Pen name "Holworthy Hall." *Henry of Navarre, Ohio* (1914); *Pepper* (1915); *Paprika* (1915); *Help Wanted* (1916); *What He Least Expected* (1917); *The Man Nobody Knew* (1919); *The Six Best Cellars* (with Hugh M. Kahler, 1919); etc.

PORTER, HORACE (Apr. 15, 1837–May 29, 1921); b. Huntingdon, Pa. Soldier, diplomat, author. *West Point Life* (poems, 1866); *Campaigning with Grant* (1897); etc. U. S. Ambassador to France, 1897–1905. He succeeded in finding and identifying the body of John Paul Jones which he had transported and buried at Annapolis in 1905.

PORTER, KATHERINE ANNE (May 15, 1894–); b. Indian Creek, Tex. Author. *Flowering Judas* (1930); *Hacienda* (1934); *Noon Wine* (1937); *Pale Horse, Pale Rider* (1939); *The Itching Parrot* (trans. 1942); *The Leaning Tower* (1944); *The Days Before* (essays, 1952); *Ship of Fools* (1967); *Collected Short Stories of Katherine Anne Porter* (1965). See H. J. Mooney's *Fiction and Criticism of Katherine Anne Porter* (1957); William L. Nance's *Katherine Anne Porter and the Art of Rejection* (1964).

PORTER, LAURA SPENCER (Mrs. Francis Pope); b. Covington, Ky. Author. *The Greatest Books in the World* (1913); *Genevieve* (1914); *Story of the Little Angel* (1917); *Adventures in Indigence* (1918); *The Little Long Ago* (1927); etc.

PORTER, LINN BOYD (Dec. 20, 1851–June 29, 1916); b. Westfield, Mass. Author. Pen name, "Albert Ross." *Caring for No Man* (1875); *Her Husband's Friend* (1891); *His Private Character* (1889); *Speaking of Ellen* (1889); etc.

PORTER, NOAH (Dec. 14, 1811–Mar. 4, 1892); b. Farmington, Conn. Congregational clergyman, educator, editor, author. *The Human Intellect* (1868); *The Elements of Intellectual Science* (1871); *Science and Sentiment* (1882); *The Elements of a Moral Science* (1885); *Fifteen Years in the Chapel of Yale College* (1888); etc. He edited Noah Webster's dictionary in 1864. Prof. moral philosophy, Yale University, 1846–71, president, Yale University, 1871–86.

PORTER, REBECCA NEWMAN (1883–); b. Chicago, Ill. Novelist. *The Girl from Four Corners* (1920); *The Rest Hollow Mystery* (1921); *The Rhinestone Helmet* (1928); *I'd Love to Write* (1939); *Open House* (1955).

PORTER, ROBERT PERCIVAL (June 30, 1852–Feb. 28, 1917); b. Norwich, Eng. Editor, correspondent, author. *The West in 1880* (1882); *Life of William McKinley* (1896); *The Full Recognition of Japan* (1911), republished as *Japan, the New World-Power* (1915). Founder (with Frank Hatton), the *New York Press,* 1887, on staff, 1887–94.

PORTER, ROSE (1845–1906); b. New York. Author. *Summer Drift-Wood for the Winter Fire* (1870); *Uplands and Lowlands* (1872); *The Winter Fire* (1874); *In the Mist* (1879); *Honoria; or, The Gospel of a Life* (1885); *My Son's Wife* (1895); etc. Compiler: *About Women* (1894); *About Men* (1895); *About Children* (1896); etc.

PORTER, RUFUS (May 1, 1792–Aug. 13, 1884); b. Boxford, Mass. Inventor. Founder, the *Scientific American,* 1845.

PORTER, SYLVIA F[ield] (June 18, 1913–); b. Patchogue, N.Y. Journalist. *How To Make Money in Government Bonds* (1939); *Managing Your Money* (with J. K. Lasser, 1953); *How To Get More for Your Money* (1961); etc. With *New York Post,* since 1935; now financial columnist and editor.

PORTER, WILLIAM SYDNEY (Sept. 11, 1862–June 5, 1910); b. Greensboro, N.C. Short story writer. Pen name "O. Henry." *Cabbages and Kings* (1904); *The Four Million* (1906); *Heart of the West* (1907); *The Trimmed Lamp* (1907); *The Gentle Grafter* (1908); *The Voice of the City* (1908); *Options* (1909); *Roads of Destiny* (1909); *Whirligigs* (1910); *Let Me Feel Your Pulse* (1910); *Strictly Business* (1910); *The Two Women* (1910); *Sixes and Sevens* (1911); *The Gift of the Magi* (1911); *Rolling Stones* (1912); *Waifs and Strays* (1917); etc. See *Rolling Stone.* See also C. Alphonso Smith's *O. Henry Biography* (1916); Paul S. Clarkson's *A Bibliography of William Sydney Porter* (1938); E. Hudson Long's *O. Henry, the Man and His Work* (1949); Gerald Longford's *Alias O. Henry* (1957); Eugene Current-Garcia's *O. Henry* (1965).

PORTER, WILLIAM TROTTER (Dec. 24, 1809–July 19, 1858); b. Newbury, Vt. Editor, author, sportsman. Compiler: *The Big Bear of Arkansas, and Other Tales* (1835); *A Quarter Race in Kentucky* (1847); *Colonel Thorpe's Scenes in Arkansaw* (1858); etc. Founder, the sporting journal, *Spirit of the Times,* Dec. 10, 1831; editor, 1831–56; founder (with George Wilkes), *Porter's Spirit of the Times,* Sept., 1856. See Francis Brinley's *Life of William T. Porter* (1860).

PORTERFIELD, ALLEN WILSON (Aug. 30, 1877–May 10, 1952); b. Bedington, W. Va. Educator, author. *Karl Lebrecht Immermann* (1911); *Outline of German Romanticism* (1914). Editor: *Modern German Stories* (1927); etc. Prof. German, West Virginia University, 1924–40.

PORTERFIELD, AUSTIN LARIMORE (Oct. 16, 1896–); b. Salem, Ark. Sociologist. *Creative Factors in Scientific Research* (1941); *Youth in Trouble* (1946); *Wait the Withering Rain?* (1953); etc. Sociology dept., Texas Christian University, since 1937.

Portico, The. Baltimore, Md. Magazine. Founded Jan., 1816, by Tobias Watkins and Stephen Simpson. Its chief contributors were members of the Delphian Club. Expired June, 1818.

PORTIS, CHARLES. Author. *Norwood* (1966); *True Grit* (1968).

Portland Oregonian. Portland, Ore. Newspaper. The *Weekly Oregonian,* founded 1850; the *Morning Oregonian,* 1861. Robert C. Notson is publisher. Malcolm Bauer edits book reviews.

Portnoy's Complaint. Novel by Philip Roth (1968). Comic presentation of the Jewish male American caught between a domineering mother and the licentious freedom of American life.

"Portrait of a Lady." Poem by T. S. Eliot (1917).

Portraits and Prayers. By Gertrude Stein (1934). Includes some of her most characteristic vignette-like "poems" which engage a subject from a mixed perspective in which the lexical and linguistic overtones of words help form the intended meaning.

POSEY, ALEXANDER LAWRENCE (Aug. 3, 1873–May 27, 1908); b. near Eufaula, Indian Territory (now Okla). Creek Indian editor, poet. *The Poems,* ed. by his wife, Minnie H. Posey (1910). Editor, the *Indian Journal,* 1901–03. He wrote the satirical *Fus Fixico Letters* in the *Indian Journal,* and several poems under the pen name "Chinnubbie Harjo," the name of one of the central characters in Creek mythology.

POSIN, DANIEL Q. (Aug. 13, 1909–); b. in Turkestan. Educator, television lecturer, author. *Mendeleyev-The Story of a Great Scientist* (1948); *I Have Been to the Village* (1948); *Out of the This World* (1959); *What Is a Star?* (1961); *What Is a Chemical Change?* (1961); *What Is a Dinosaur?* (1961); *The Marvels of Physics* (1961); *Chemistry for the Space Age* (1961); *Experiments and Exercises in Chemistry* (1961); *What Is Matter?* (1962); *What is Electronic Communication?* (1962); *Dr. Posin's Giants* (1962); *Life Beyond Our Planet* (1962); *Man and the Sea* (1962); *Man and the Earth* (1962); *Man and the Jungle* (1962); *Man and the Desert* (1962); *Science in the Age of Space* (1965). Prof. physics, De Paul University, since 1956.

Possession. Novel by Louis Bromfield (1925). Ellen Tolliver, a relative of Lily Shane, portrayed in the author's earlier novel *The Green Bay Tree,* seeks to escape from the schemes her mother has made for her and from the Middle West which she hates. She goes to New York and Paris, and after tragic love entanglements is free to live her own life.

POSSONY, STEFAN THOMAS (Mar. 15, 1913–); b. Vienna. Educator, author. *Tomorrow's War* (1938); *Strategic Air Power* (1949); *International Relations* (with R. Strausz-Hupé, 1950); *A Century of Conflict* (1953); *Lenin, The Compulsive Revolutionary* (1964); *The Geography of Intellect* (with N. Weyl, 1963). Director, International Political Studies Program, Hoover Institution. Stanford University, since 1955.

POST, CHANDLER RATHFON (Dec. 14, 1881–Nov. 2, 1959); b. Detroit, Mich. Educator, author. *A History of European and American Sculpture* (1921); *A History of Spanish Painting,* 12 v. (1930–47); etc. Art and language depts., Harvard University, 1905–50.

POST, EMILY (Mrs. Price Post) (1873–Sept. 26, 1960); b. Baltimore, Md. Author. *The Flight of a Moth* (1904); *Purple & Fine Linen* (1905); *Woven in the Tapestry* (1908); *The Title Market* (1909); *The Eagle's Feather* (1910); *By Motor to the Golden Gate* (1916); *Etiquette* (1922); *Children Are People* (1940); *Emily Post Institute Cook Book* (with Edwin M. Post, Jr., 1949); *Motor Manners* (1950); *The Emily Post Cook Book* (1951); etc. Wrote daily newspaper column for the Bell Syndicate, 1932–60. Founder, Emily Post Institute, 1946.

Post, Maveric. Pen name of Victor Mapes.

POST, MELVILLE DAVISSON (Apr. 19, 1871–June 23, 1930); b. Romines Mills, W.Va. Novelist. *The Strange Schemes of Randolph Mason* (1896); *The Man of Last Resort* (1897); *Dwellers in the Hills* (1901); *The Corrector of Destinies* (1908); *The Gilded Chair* (1910); *Uncle Abner, Master of Mysteries* (1918); *The Mystery of the Blue Villa* (1919); *The Man Hunters* (1926); etc. *See* B. C. Williams's *Our Short Story Writers* (1920).

Postl, Karl. See Charles Sealsfield.

Postman Always Rings Twice The. Novel by James M. Cain (1934), dramatized in 1936.

POSTON, CHARLES DEBRILL (Apr. 20, 1825–June 24, 1902); b. in Hamlin, Co., Ky. Explorer, author. Called "The Father of Arizona." *Europe in the Summer-Time* (1868); *Apache Land* (poem, 1878); etc. *See* Raphael Pumpelly's *My Reminiscences,* 2v. (1918); F. C. Lockwood's *Arizona Characters* (1928).

POTEAT, EDWIN McNEILL (Feb. 6, 1861–June 26, 1937); b. in Caswell Co., N.C. Baptist clergyman, educator, author. *The Scandal of the Cross* (1928). Prof. ethics, Mercer University, Macon, Ga., 1931–34; Furman University, Greenville, S.C., 1934–37.

POTEAT, WILLIAM LOUIS (Oct. 20, 1856–Mar. 12, 1938); b. in Caswell Co., N.C. Educator, author. *The New Peace* (1915); *The Way of Victory* (1929); *Stop-Light* (1935); etc. President, Wake Forest College, N.C., 1905–27.

POTOK, CHAIM (Feb. 17, 1929–); b. New York. Editor, author. *The Chosen* (1967); *The Promise* (1970). Editor, Jewish Publication Society, since 1965.

Potowmac Guardian. Sheperdstown, W.Va. First newspaper in what is now West Virginia; founded 1790, by Nathaniel Willis. Moved to Martinsburg 1792. Expired 1800.

POTTER, ALFRED CLAGHORN (Apr. 4, 1867–Nov. 1, 1940); b. New Bedford, Mass. Librarian, author. *Librarians of Harvard College, 1667–1877* (1896); *Descriptive and Historical Notes on the Library of Harvard University* (1903); etc. On staff, Harvard College library, 1889–1940; asst. librarian, 1904–28; librarian, 1928–36.

POTTER, ALONZO (July 6, 1800–July 4, 1865); b. Beekman N.Y. Episcopal bishop, author. *Political Economy* (1840); *The School and the Schoolmaster* (with G. B. Emerson, 1842); *Religous Philosophy* (1872); etc.

POTTER, DAVID MORRIS (Dec. 6, 1910–); b. Augusta, Ga. Educator. *Lincoln and His Party in the Secession Crisis* (1942); *People of Plenty: Economic Abundance and the American Character* (1954); *The South and the Sectional Conflict* (1968); etc. Prof. history, Stanford University, since 1961.

POTTER, ELIPHALET NOTT (Sept. 20, 1836–Feb. 6, 1901); b. Schenectady, N.Y. Episcopal clergyman, educator, author. *Washington, a Model in His Library and Life* (1895); etc. President, Union college, 1871–84; president, Hobart College, 1884–97. *See* Frank H. Potter's *The Alonzo Potter Family* (1923).

POTTER, GEORGE W. (Sept. 20, 1899–Aug. 10, 1959); b. Fall River, Mass. Author. *An Irish Pilgrimage* (1950); *To the Golden Door* (1960).

POTTER, HENRY CODMAN (May 25, 1835–July 21, 1908); b. Schenectady, N.Y. Episcopal bishop, author. *Sisterhoods and Deaconesses* (1872); *The Scholar and the State, and Other Orations and Addresses* (1897); *The Modern Man and His Fellow Man* (1903); *Reminiscences of Bishops and Archbishops* (1906); etc.

POTTER, MARGARET HORTON (Mrs. J. D. Black) (1881–1911); b. Chicago, Ill. Novelist. *A Social Lion* (1899); *The House of De Mailly* (1901); *The Castle of Twilight* (1903); *The Genius* (1906); *The Princess* (1907); *The Golden Ladder* (1908); *Istar of Babylon* (1912).

POTTER, MARY KNIGHT (d. Oct. 5, 1915); b. Boston, Mass. Artist, author. *Love in Art* (1898); *Councils of Croesus* (1902); *Art of the Vatican* (1902); *How Richard Won Out* (1908).

POTTER, MIRIAM S. CLARK (May 2, 1886–); b. Minneapolis, Minn. Author and illustrator. *Rhymes of a Child's World* (1919); *The Pinafore Pocket Story Book* (1922); *Captain Sandman* (1926); *Mrs. Goose of Animal Town* (1939); *Hello, Mrs. Goose!* (1947); *Littlebits* (1951); *Our Friend Mrs. Goose* (1956); *No, No, Mrs. Goose!* (1962); etc.

POTTER, PAUL MEREDITH (June 3, 1853–Mar. 7, 1921); b. Brighton, Eng. Playwright. *The Ugly Duckling* (prod. 1890); *The American Minister* (prod. 1892); *Victoria Cross* (prod. 1894); *The Conquerors* (prod. 1898); etc. Potter dramatized Du Maurier's *Trilby*, and its first performance was in Boston, Mar. 11, 1895.

POTTER, ROBERT RUSSELL (Jan. 3, 1897–); b. Milton, Ia. Educator, author. *Modern French Art* (1927); *A Study of Shakespeare* (1928); *Little Red Ferry Boat* (1947).

Potter's American Monthly. See *American Historical Record.*

POTTLE, FREDERICK ALBERT (Aug. 3, 1897–); b. Lovell, Me. Educator, editor, author. *Shelley and Browning* (1923); *The Literary Career of James Boswell, Esq.* (1929); *Stretchers* (1929); *Boswell and the Girl from Botany Bay* (1937); *The Idiom of Poetry* (1941); *Boswell in Holland, 1763–1764* (1952); *Boswell on the Grand Tour, 1764* (1953); *Boswell in Search of a Wife, 1766–1769* (with Frank Brady, 1956); *Boswell for the Defence, 1769–1774* (with William K. Wimsatt, Jr., 1960); *Boswell, the Ominous Years, 1774–1776* (1963); *James Boswell, the Earlier Years, 1740–1769*; etc. Editor: *Boswell's Journal of a Tour of the Hebrides with Samuel Johnson* (with Charles E. Bennett, 1936); *Boswell's London Journal 1762–63* (1950). English dept., Yale University, since 1930; emeritus, 1966.

POTTLE, GILBERT EMERY BEMSLEY (1875–); Playwright, novelist. Writes under names, "Gilbert Emery," "Emery Pottle," and "Emery Bemsley Pottle." *The Late Mr. Rollins, and Other College Farces* (1899); *Handicapped* (1908); *Tarnish* (1924); *Riches* (1926); *Love-in-a-Mist* (with Amélie Rives, prod. 1926); etc.; also many scenarios.

Pottle, Mrs. Juliet Wilbur Tompkins. See Juliet Wilbur Tompkins.

POTTS, WILLIAM (May 5, 1838–1908); b. Philadelphia, Pa. Author. *Noblesse Oblige* (1880); *From a New England Hillside: Notes for Underledge* (1895); *More Notes from Underledge* (1904).

POULSON, ZACHARIAH (Sept. 5, 1761–July 31, 1844); b. Philadelphia, Pa. Publisher, philanthropist. Editor and publisher, *Poulson's American Daily Advertiser,* 1800–39. He printed Robert Proud's *The History of Pennsylvania,* 2v. (1797–98). *See* Henry Simpson's *The Lives of Eminent Philadelphians Now Deceased* (1859).

POULSSON, EMILIE (Sept. 8, 1853–Mar. 18, 1939); b. Cedar Grove, N.J. Author. *Through the Farmyard Gate* (1896); *Child Stories and Rhymes (1898); Holiday Songs* (1901); *The Runaway Donkey* (1905). Joint editor, *Kindergarten Review,* 1897–1904.

POUMMER, MARY WRIGHT (Mar. 8, 1856–Sept. 27, 1916); b. Richmond, Ind. Librarian, poet. *Hints to Small Libraries* (1894); *Verses* (1896); *Roy and Ray in Mexico* (1907); *Roy and Ray in Canada* (1908); *The Seven Joys of Reading* (1915); etc. Librarian, Pratt Institute, Brooklyn, 1894–1904; head, library school, 1896–1911.

POUND, ARTHUR (June 1, 1884–); b. Pontiac, Mich. Author. *Native Stock* (1931); *Mountain Morning, and Other Poems* (1932); *Once a Wilderness* (1934); *The Golden Earth*

(1935); *Detroit, Dynamic City* (1940); *Lake Ontario* (1945); etc. Editor, Atlantic Monthly Press, 1924–25; assoc. editor, *The Independent,* 1924–27.

POUND, EZRA [Loomis] (Oct. 30, 1885–   ); b. Hailey, Ida. Poet. *Personae* (1909); *Exultations* (1909); *Provença* (1910); *The Spirit of Romance* (1910); *Ripostes* (1912); *Lustra* (1917); *Indiscretions* (1923); *Cantos I–XVI* (1925); *Cantos XVII–XXVII* (1928); *A Draft of XXX Cantos* (1930); *A Draft of Cantos XXXI–XLI* (1934); *Jefferson and/or Mussolini* (1935); *The Fifth Decade of Cantos* (1937); *Cantos LII–LXXI* (1940); *The Pisan Cantos* (1948); *Letters, 1907–41* (1950); *Literary Essays* (1954); *Section: Rock Drill, 85–95 de los Cantares* (1956); *Brancusi* (1957); *Thrones: 96–109 de los Cantares* (1959); *Impact: Essays on Ignorance and the Decline of American Civilization* (1960); *Drafts and Fragments of Cantos CX–CXVII* (1968); etc. Translator: *The Sonnets and Ballate of Guido Cavalcanti* (1912); *Certain Noble Plays of Japan* (1916); Confucius' *The Unwobbling Pivot* and *The Great Digest* (1947); Sophocles's *The Women of Trachis* (1957); *Love Poems of Ancient Egypt* (1962); etc. Editor: *Confucius to Cummings* (with Marcella Spann, 1964). *See* Charles Norman's *The Case of Ezra Pound* (1949); Hugh Kenner's *The Poetry of Ezra Pound* (1950); H. H. Watts's *Ezra Pound and "The Cantos"* (1951); Donald Davie's *Ezra Pound: Poet as Sculptor* (1963); Noel Stock's *Poet in Exile: Ezra Pound* (1964); *Reading the Cantos* (1966) and *Life of Ezra Pound* (1970).

POUND, LOUISE (June 30, 1872–June 27, 1958); b. Lincoln, Neb. Educator, editor, author. *The Periods of English Literature* (1919); *Poetic Origins and the Ballad* (1921); *Selected Writings* (1949); etc. Editor: *American Ballads and Songs* (1922); Co-founder and editor, *American Speech,* 1925–33. Editor, *Southern Folklore Quarterly,* from 1937; *American Literature,* 1929–45; and other journals. English dept., University of Nebraska, 1894–1945.

POUND, ROSCOE (Oct. 27, 1870–July 1, 1964); b. Lincoln, Neb. Educator, author. *Readings on the Roman Law* (1906); *The Spirit of the Common Law* (1921); *Introduction to the Philosophy of Law* (1922); *Law and Morals* (1924); *Criminal Justice in America* (1930); *The Formative Era of American Law* (1938); *History and System of the Common Law* (1939); *Organization of Courts* (1940); *Administrative Law, Its Growth, Procedure, and Significance* (1942); *The Task of Law* (1944); *New Paths of the Law* (1950); *The Ideal Element in Law* (1958). Faculty, Harvard Law School, 1910–47.

POUNDS, NORMAN JOHN GREVILLE (Feb. 23, 1912–); b. Bath, Eng. Educator. *Historical and Political Geography of Europe* (1947); *The Ruhr* (1953); *The Geography of Iron and Steel* (1959); *Poland Between East and West* (1964); *An Atlas of Middle Eastern Affairs* (with R. C. Klingsbury, 1966); *World Geography: Economic, Political, Regional* (with J. W. Taylor, 1967); etc. Prof. history and geography, Indiana University, since 1968.

POWDERLY, TERENCE V[incent] (1849–1924); b. in Pennsylvania. *Thirty Years of Labor, 1859–89* (1889); *The Path I Trod* (1940). Leader of Knights of Labor, 1879–93.

POWDERMAKER, HORTENSE (1901–). Anthropologist. *Life in Lesu* (1933); *After Freedom* (1939); *Probing Our Prejudice* (1944); *Hollywood, the Dream Factory* (1950); *Stranger and Friend: The Way of an Anthropologist* (1967); etc. Prof. anthropology, Queens College, 1954–68; prof. emeritus, from 1968.

POWEL, HARFORD (Aug. 20, 1887–Aug. 17, 1956); b. Philadelphia, Pa. Editor, author. *Walter Camp* (1926); *The Virgin Queene* (1928); *Married Money* (1929); *The Invincible Jew* (1930); *Oh Glory!* (1931); *Widow's Might* (1935); etc. Editor, *Collier's,* 1919–22; *Youth's Companion,* 1925–28; etc.

POWELL, ADAM (1865–). Author. *Against the Tide* (autobiography, 1938); *Palestine and Saints in Caesar's Household* (1939); *Picketing Hell* (1942); *Riots and Ruins* (1945); etc.

POWELL, ADAM CLAYTON, Jr. (Nov. 29, 1908–d. Apr. 4, 1972); b. New Haven, Conn. Baptist clergyman, congressman, author. *Marching Blacks* (1945); *Adam Clayton Powell* (1960); *Keep the Faith, Baby!* (1967); etc.

POWELL, DAWN (Mrs. Joseph R. Gousha) (Nov. 28, 1897–Nov. 20, 1965); b. Mt. Gilead, O. Novelist, playwright. *She Walks in Beauty* (1928); *The Bride's House* (1929); *Big Night* (prod. 1933); *The Story of a Country Boy* (1934); *Jig Saw* (prod. 1934); *Turn, Magic Wheel* (1936); *Angels on Toast* (1940); *A Time to Be Born* (1942); *My Home Is Far Away* (1944); *The Locusts Have No King* (1948); *Sunday, Monday, and Always* (1952); *The Wicked Pavilion* (1954); *A Cage for Lovers* (1957); etc.

POWELL, E[dward] ALEXANDER (Aug. 16, 1879–Nov. 12, 1957); b. Syracuse, N.Y. Traveler, author. *The Last Frontier* (1912); *The Road to Glory* (1915); *Where the Strange Trails Go Down* (1921); *Asia at the Crossroads* (1922); *By Camel and Car to the Peacock Throne* (1923); *Beyond the Utmost Purple Rim* (1925); *In Barbary* (1926); *The Last Home of Mystery* (1929); *Yonder Lies Adventure* (1932); *Aerial Odyssey* (1936); *Free Lance* (1937); *Gone are the Days* (1938); *Adventure Road* (1954); etc.

POWELL, EDWARD PAYSON (May 9, 1833–May 14, 1915); b. Clinton, N.Y. Unitarian clergyman, editor, author. *Our Heredity from God* (1887); *Liberty and Life* (1889); *Nullification and Secession* (1897); and books on gardening and outdoor subjects. Co-editor *Unity,* a Unitarian weekly, 1894–96.

Powell, Frances. See Frances Powell Case.

POWELL, JOHN WESLEY (Mar. 24, 1834–Sept. 23, 1902); b. Mount Morris, N.Y. Geologist, author. *Explorations of the Colorado River of the West* (1875); *Canyons of the Colorado* (1895); *Truth and Error; or, The Science of Intellection* (1898).

POWELL, LAWRENCE CLARK (Sept. 3, 1906–); b. Washington, D.C. Librarian, author. *An Introduction to Robinson Jeffers* (1932); *Philosopher Pickett* (1942); *Islands of Books* (1951); *Heart of the Southwest* (1955); *Books in My Baggage* (1960); *The Little Package* (1963); *Fortune and Friendship* (1968); etc. Dean and prof. emeritus, University Library, University of California at Los Angeles, since 1966.

POWELL, LYMAN PIERSON (Sept. 21, 1866–Feb. 10, 1946); b. Farmington, Del. Educator, author. *The History of Education in Delaware* (1893); *Heavenly Heretics* (1910); *Lafayette* (1918); *The Human Touch* (1925); *Mary Baker Eddy* (1930); *The Better Part* (1933); *The House by the Side of the Road* (1933); *The Second Seventy* (with wife, 1936); etc. Editor, *American Historic Towns,* 4v. (1898–1902); etc. President, Hobart College and William Smith College, 1913–18.

POWELL, RALPH LORIN (Jan. 31, 1917–); b. Salt Lake City, Utah. Educator, author. *The Rise of Chinese Military Power, 1895–1912* (1955); *Politico-Military Relationships in Communist China* (1963). Prof. Far Eastern Studies, American University, since 1960.

POWELL, RICHARD PITTS, (Nov. 28, 1908–); b. Philadelphia, Pa. Author. *Don't Catch Me* (1942); *Shoot If You Must* (1946); *A Shot in the Dark* (1952); *False Colors* (1955); *The Philadelphian* (1957); *Pioneer, Go Home* (1959); *The Soldier* (1960); *Don Quixote U.S.A.* (1966); *Tickets to the Devil* (1968); etc.

Powell, Richard Stillman. Pen name of Ralph Henry Barbour.

POWELL, SUMNER CHILTON (Oct. 2, 1924–); b. Northampton, Mass. Educator, author. *From Mythical to Mediaeval Man* (1957); *Venture to Windward* (1958); *Puritan Village* (Pulitzer Prize in history, 1964). Prof. history and political science, Iona College, since 1967.

POWELL, TALCOTT WILLIAMS (Apr. 27, 1900–Apr. 4, 1937); b. Lansdowne, Pa. Journalist, explorer, author. *Tattered Banners* (1933). Editor, *Indianapolis Times,* 1933–35. With New York *Sun,* New York *World,* New York *Tribune,* etc.

POWELL, THOMAS (Sept. 3, 1809–Jan. 14, 1887); b. in England. Editor, playwright, poet. *The Wife's Revenge* (1842); *The Blind Wife* (1842); *Poems* (1844); *Dramatic Poems* (1845); *Marguerite* (1846); *Love's Rescue* (1848); *The Living Authors of England* (1849); *The Living Authors of America* (1850); *Chit Chat by Pierce Pungent* (1857); etc. First editor of *Frank Leslie's Illustrated Newspaper,* 1855. On staff, *The Lantern; Figaro; Young Sam;* the *New York Reveille;* etc.

POWELL, WILLIAM BRAMWELL (Dec. 22, 1836–Feb. 4, 1904); b. Castile, N.Y. Educational reformer, author. *How to See* (1880); *How to Talk* (1880); *How to Write* (1880); etc. Supt., Washington, D.C., public schools, 1885–1900.

Power Elite, The. By C. Wright Mills (1956). An intricate analysis of the control over social and economic life exercised by a small number of interest groups.

Power of Positive Thinking, The. By Norman Vincent Peale (1952). How to avoid worry and attain peace of mind through forceful optimism.

Power of Sympathy; or, The Triumph of Nature, The. The first novel written in America by an American (Boston, 1789). Long attributed to Sarah Wentworth Morton, it is now believed to have been written by her neighbor, William Hill Brown. It was printed by Isaiah Thomas. *See* Milton Ellis's *Philenia: The Life and Works of Sarah Wentworth Morton* (1931), and his *The Author of the First American Novel,* in *American Literature,* Jan., 1933.

POWERS, ANNE (May 7, 1913–); b. Cloquet, Minn. Author. *The Gallant Years* (1946); *No Wall So High* (1949); *The Only Sin* (1953); *Ride with Danger* (1958); *No King But Caesar* (1960); etc.

POWERS, ELLA MARIE (b. 1865–); b. Hamburg, N.Y. Lecturer, folklorist, author. *Stories the Iroquois Tell Their Children* (1917); *Around an Iroquois Story Fire* (1923); *The Portage Trail on Jahdahgwah* (1924). Compiler (with Hanson Hart Webster): *Famous Seamen of America* (1928). Adopted by the Iroquois and named "Yehsennohwehs."

POWERS, HORATIO NELSON (Apr. 30, 1826–1890); b. Amenia, N.Y. Episcopal clergyman, poet. *Poems, Early and Late* (1876); *Ten years of Song* (1887); *Lyrics of the Hudson* (1891).

POWERS, JAMES FARL (July 8, 1917–); b. Jacksonville, Ill. Short story writer. *Prince of Darkness and Other Stories* (1947); *The Presence of Grace* (1956); *Morte d'Urban* (1962).

POWERS, STEPHEN. Author. *Muskingum Legends* (1871); *Afoot and Alone* (1872); *Tribes of California* (1877); etc.

POYDRAS, JULIEN DE LALANDE (Apr. 3, 1746–June 23, 1824); b. Nantes, Fr. Poet. *La Prise du Morne du Bâton Rouge* (1779); the first epic poem written in Louisiana. *See* E. L. Tinker's *Les Écrits de Langue Française en Louisiane au XIXᵉ Siècle* (1932).

Praeger, Frederick A., Inc. New York. Publishers. Founded 1950, by Frederick A. Praeger, president and chief editor. Publishes books on international affairs, history, military science, art, etc., college texts and paperbacks. A subsidiary of Encyclopedia Britannica, Inc.

PRAEGER, FREDERICK AMOS (Sept. 16, 1915–); b. Vienna. Publisher. Pres., Frederick A. Praeger.

Prairie Schooner. Lincoln, Nebraska. Quarterly. Founded 1927, at the University of Nebraska, for the purpose of publishing mostly local writers. Later contributors included Anaïs Nin, Randall Jarrell, and Malcolm Lowry. Edited at one time by Karl Shapiro and later by Bernice Slote.

PRATT, AGNES EDWARDS ROTHERY (Mrs. Harry Rogers Pratt) (Jan. 31, 1888–Aug. 11, 1954); b. Brookline, Mass. Author. Wrote under name "Agnes Rothery." *The Romantic Store* (1915); *Cape Cod, Old and New* (under pen name "Agnes Edwards," 1918); *Central America and the Spanish Main* (1929); *South America, West Coast and East* (1930); *Sweden, the Land and the People* (1934); *Finland, the New Nation* (1936); *Denmark, Kingdom of Reason* (1937); *Virginia, the New Dominion* (1940); *Family Album* (1942); *Iceland Round-about (1948); Houses Virginians Have Loved* (1954); etc.

PRATT, CHARLES STUART (b. Feb. 10, 1854); b. Weymouth, Mass. Editor, author. Husband of Ella Farman. *Bye-O-Baby Ballads* (1886); *Mother Songs* (1888); *Buz-Buz* (1898); *Riddle-Rhymes* (1905); etc. Editor (with wife), *Wide Awake,* 1897–1907; *Little Folks,* 1907–09.

Pratt, Cornelia Atwood. See Cornelia A. P. Comer

PRATT, ELIZA ANNA FARMAN (Nov. 1, 1837–May 22, 1907); b. Augusta, N.Y. Editor, author. Pen name "Ella Farman." *Sugar Plums: Poems* (1877); *Mrs. White's Party, and Other Stories* (1879); *The Little Cave-Dwellers* (1901); etc. Editor, *Wide Awake,* 1875–93; *Babyland,* 1877–1900.

PRATT, FLETCHER (Apr. 25, 1897–June 10, 1956); b. Buffalo, N.Y. Author. *The Heroic Years: Fourteen Years of the Republic, 1801–1815* (1934); *Hail, Caesar* (1936); *The Lost Battalion* (with Thomas N. Johnson, 1938); *Secret and Urgent* (1939); *Road to Empire* (1939); *Short History of the Army and Navy* (1944); *Undying Fire* (1953); *All About Famous Inventors and Their Inventions* (1955); etc. Military analyst, the *New York Post.*

PRATT, HARRY NOYES (July 14, 1879–May 19, 1944); b. River Falls, Wis. Author. *Mother of Mine and Other Verse* (1918); *Hill Trails & Open Sky* (1919); etc. Editor, *Overland Monthly,* 1924–25.

PRATT, JAMES BISSETT (June 22, 1875–Jan. 15, 1944); b. Elmira, N.Y. Educator, author. *What is Pragmatism?* (1909); *Matter and Spirit* (1922); *Adventures in Philosophy and Religion* (1931); *Naturalism* (1939); etc. Philosophy dept., Williams College, from 1905.

PRATT, JOSEPH GAITHER (Aug. 31, 1910–); b. Winston-Salem, N.C. Psychologist, author. *Parapsychology: Frontier Science of the Mind* (with J. B. Rhine, 1957); *Parapsychology: An Insider's View of ESP* (1964); etc. Prof. psychiatry, University of Virginia Medical School, since 1966.

PRATT, LUCY (July 29, 1874–); b. Deerfield, Mass. Author. *Ezekiel* (1909); *Ezekiel Expands* (1914); *Felix Tells It* (1915).

PRATT, THEODORE (Apr. 26, 1901–Dec. 15, 1969); b. Minneapolis, Minn. Author. *Spring from Downward* (1934); *Big Blow* (1936); *Mr. Winkle Goes to War* (1943); *Miss Dilly Says No* (1945); *Big Bubble* (1951); *Florida Roundabout* (1959); etc. Also mystery novels under pen name "Timothy Brace."

PRATT, WALDO SELDEN (Nov. 10, 1857–July 29, 1939); b. Philadelphia, Pa. Musician, educator, author. *History of Music* (1907); *American Music and Musicians* (1920); *Music of the Pilgrims* (1921); etc. Editor: *St. Nicholas Songs* (1885); *American Supplement to Grove's Dictionary of Music and Musicians* (1920); *New Encyclopedia of Music and Musicians* (1924). Musical editor, *Century Dictionary,* etc. Prof. music and hymnology, Hartford Theological Seminary, 1882–1925.

PRATT, WALTER MERRIAM (July 13, 1880–); b. Chelsea, Mass. Author. *The Burning of Chelsea* (1908); *Seven Generations* (1930); *Adventure in Vermont* (1943); etc.

PRAY, ISAAC CLARK (May 15, 1813–Nov. 28, 1869); b. Boston, Mass. Actor, editor, author. *Prose and Verse* (1836); *Giuletta Gordoni, the Miser's Daughter* (1839); *Book of the Drama* (1851); *Memoirs of James Gordon Bennett and His Times* (1855); *The Hermit of Malta* (1856); etc. Editor *Pearl,* 1834; *Boston Daily Herald,* 1835–37; *Dramatic Guardian; Ladies' Companion; Philadelphia Inquirier;* etc.

PREBLE, GEORGE HENRY (Feb. 25, 1816–Mar. 1, 1885); b. Portland, Me. Naval officer, author. *Our Flag* (1872), republished as *History of the Flag* (1880); *A Chronological History of the Origin and Development of Steam Navigation, 1543–1882* (1883); etc.

PREECE, WARREN EVERSLEIGH (Apr. 17, 1921–); b. Norwalk, Conn. Editor, author. Co-author: *The Technological Order* (1962). Editor: *The Encyclopedia Britannica College Preparatory Series* (1964). Editor-in-chief, *Encylcopaedia Britannica,* since 1965.

Preface to a Life. Novel by Zona Gale (1926). Bernard Mead goes to Chicago to escape being tied to the family lumber business in Wisconsin, but does not reckon with a determined father.

Preface to Morals, A. By Walter Lippmann (1929). Essays on the intellectual and moral responsibilities of the modern world.

Prejudices. By H. L. Mencken, 6 series (1919–27). Sweeping denunciation of the ideas and personalities which seemed to the author to be stupid, dangerous, pompous, or intolerant.

Prentice-Hall, Inc. formerly New York, now Englewood Cliffs, N.J. Publishers. Founded 1913, by Charles William Gerstenberg, who was president until 1938; and Richard Prentice Ettinger, who is chairman of the board. The corporation was named after the maiden names of the mothers of the founders. The firm publishes mainly in four categories: business books, textbooks, secondary books, and trade books, the last since 1937. The first book of fiction appeared in 1945. Its divisions publish college books, business and financial planning materials, loose-leaf information services, correspondence courses, audio-visual aids, etc. Hawthorne Books, a subsidiary, was sold to Fred Kerner/Publishing Projects in 1965.

PRENTISS, ELIZABETH PAYSON (Mrs. George Lewis Prentiss) (Oct. 26, 1818–Aug. 13, 1878); b. Portland, Me. Author. *The Flower of the Family* (1854); *Stepping Heavenward* (1860); *Golden Hours* (poems, 1873); *Avis Benson* (1879); the *Little Susy* series; etc. See George L. Prentiss's *The Life and Letters of Elizabeth Prentiss* (1882).

PRENTISS, GEORGE LEWIS (May 12, 1816–Mar. 18, 1903); b. West Gorham, Me. Congregational clergyman, educator, author. *A Memoir of S. S. Prentiss,* 2v. (1855); *The Life and Letters of Elizabeth Prentiss* (1882); *The Union Theological Seminary in the City of New York,* 2v. (1889–99); *The Bright Side of Life: A Family Story,* 2v. (1901); etc. Prof. pastoral theology, Union Theological Seminary, 1873–97.

PRESBREY, EUGENE WILEY (Mar. 13, 1853–Sept. 9, 1931); b. Williamsburg, Mass. Stage manager, playwright. *Squirrel Inn* (with Frank R. Stockton, prod. 1893); *The Courtship of Miles Standish* (prod. 1894); *A Virginia Courtship* (prod. 1898); *The Garden of Eden* (prod. 1906); etc; also stage adaptations of many well-known stories.

Presbyterian Life. Philadelphia, Pa. Semimonthly. Founded 1948. A journal of Protestant interests.

PRESCOTT, FREDERICK CLARKE (Sept. 29, 1871–July 26, 1957); b. Salina, Kan. Educator, author. *Poetry and Dreams* (1912); *The Poetic Mind* (1922); *Poetry and Myth* (1927); *Hamilton and Jefferson* (1934); etc. Editor: *Critical Writings of Edgar Allan Poe* (1909); *Prose and Poetry of the Revolution* (with John H. Nelson; (1925); *An Introduction to*

American Poetry (with Gerald D. Sanders, 1932); etc. English dept., Cornell University, 1897–1940.

PRESCOTT, ORVILLE (Sept. 8, 1906–); b. Cleveland, O. Journalist, author. *In My Opinion: An Inquiry into the Contemporary Novel* (1952); *The Five-Dollar Gold Piece: The Development of a Point of View* (1956); *Princes of the Renaissance* (1969); etc. Editor: *The Undying Past* (1961); etc. Literary editor, *Cue,* 1936–47; daily book reviewer, *New York Times,* 1942—1966.

PRESCOTT, WILLIAM HICKLING (May 14, 1796–Jan. 28, 1859); b. Salem, Mass. Historian. *History of the Reign of Ferdinand and Isabella, the Catholic,* 3v. (1838); *History of the Conquest of Mexico,* 3v. (1843); *Biographical and Critical Miscellanies* (1845); *History of the Conquest of Peru,* 2v. (1847); *History of the Reign of Philip the Second,* 3v. (1855-58); etc. *Works,* 22v. (1904); *See* George Ticknor's *Life of William Hickling Prescott* (1864); C. Harvey Gardiner's *The Literary Memoranda of William Hickling Prescott,* 2v. (1961); C. Harvey Gardiner's *William Hickling Prescott: A Biography* (1969). Prescott's manuscripts are owned by the Massachusetts Historical Society.

"Present Crisis, The." Poem by James Russell Lowell (1845).

President Makers, The. By Matthew Josephson (1940). American politics from McKinley to Wilson.

Presidential Bibliographical Series, The. Comp. by John W. Cronin and W. Harvey Wise, Jr. (1935). Nos. 2–7 have so far been issued. No. 2 includes John Adams and John Quincy Adams; No. 3, Jefferson; No. 4, Madison and Monroe; No. 5, Jackson and Van Buren; No. 6, Harrison, Tyler, and Polk; No. 7, Taylor, Fillmore, Pierce, and Buchanan.

PRESTON, HARRIET WATERS (Aug. 6, 1836–May 14, 1911); b. Danvers, Mass. Editor, translator, author. *Aspindale* (1871); *Sea and Shore: A Collection of Poems* (with Martha Le Baron Goddard, 1874); *Is That All?* (1876); *A Year in Eden* (1887); *The Private Life of the Romans* (with Louise Dodge, 1893); etc. Translator of the works of Sainte-Beuve, Mistral, etc.

PRESTON, MARGARET JUNKIN (May 19, 1820–Mar. 28, 1897); b. Milton, Pa. Sister-in-law of "Stonewall" Jackson. Author. *Silverwood: A Book of Memories* (1856); *Beechenbrook: A Rhyme of the War* (1865); *Old Song and New* (1870); *Cartoons* (1875); *For Love's Sake: Poems of Faith and Comfort* (1886); *Aunt Dorothy* (1890); etc. *See* Elizabeth P. Allan's *The Life and Letters of Margaret Junkin Preston* (1903).

Pretty Story: Written in the Year of Our Lord 2774, A. Novel by "Peter Grievous" (Francis Hopkinson) (1774), reprinted in his *The Miscellaneous Essays* (1792). It also ran serially in the *Columbian Magazine.*

PRICE, CARL F[owler] (May 16, 1881–Apr. 12, 1948); b. New Brunswick, N.J. Hymnologist, author. *Who's Who in American Methodism,* v. I (1916); *One Hundred and One Hymn Stories* (1923); *More Hymn Stories* (1929); *Yankee Township* (1941); etc. Editor, *The Wesleyan Song Book* (with Karl P. Harrington, 1901); *Wesleyan Verse* (1914); *Intercollegiate Song Book* (1931); *Sing, Brothers Sing* (1940); etc.

PRICE, DON K[rasher], JR. (Jan. 23, 1910–); b. Middlesboro, Ky. Educator. *City Manager Government in the United States* (with others, 1940); *Government and Science* (1954); *The Scientific Estate* (1965); etc. Dean, Kennedy School of Government, Harvard University, since 1958.

PRICE, EDITH BALLINGER (Apr. 26, 1897–); b. New Brunswick, N.J. Artist, author. *Blue Magic* (1919); *Us and the Bottle Man* (1920); *Silver Shoal Light* (1920); *Garth, Able Seaman* (1923); *Gervaise of the Garden* (1927); *The Four Winds* (1927); *Ship of Dreams* (1927); *The Luck of Glenlorn* (1929); *The Fork in the Road* (1930); *Lubber's Luck* (1935); etc.

PRICE, [Edward] REYNOLDS (Feb. 1, 1933–); b. Macon, N.C. Author. *A Long and Happy Life* (1962); *The Names and Faces of Heroes* (1963); *A Generous Man* (1966); *Love and Work* (1968); *Late Warning: Four Poems* (1968); *Permanent Errors* (1970). Faculty, Duke University, since 1958.

PRICE, EUGENIA (June 22, 1916–   ); b. Charleston, W.Va. Author. *Discoveries* (1953); *The Burden Is Light* (1954); *Early Will I Seek Thee* (1956); *Woman to Woman* (1958); *The Wider Place* (1966); *Make Love Your Aim* (1967); etc.

PRICE, FRANK J. (Mar. 8, 1860–Oct. 6, 1939); b. Neosho, Mo. Journalist, author. *The Major's Daughter* (1891); *Ruth* (1892). Wrote over 200 short stories, many under the pen name "Faulkner Conway." Editorial writer and columnist for several newspapers, including the *New York Morning Telegraph,* 1914–24.

PRICE, GEORGE (June 9, 1901–); b. Coytesville, N.J. Cartoonist. Author, illustrator: *Good Humor Man* (1940); *Who's in Charge Here?* (1943); *Ice Cold War* (1951); *We Buy Old Gold* (1951); *My Dear 500 Friends* (1963); etc.

PRICE, GEORGE McCREADY (Aug. 26, 1870–); b. Havelock, N.B., Can. Educator, author. *Outlines of Modern Science* (1902); *The Fundamentals of Geology* (1913); *Poisoning Democracy* (1921); *Evolutionary Geology and the New Catastrophism* (1926); *A History of Some Scientific Blunders* (1930); *Genesis Vindicated* (1941); *The Greatest of the Prophets: A New Commentary on the Book of Daniel* (1955); etc. Prof. geology and philosophy, Walla Walla College, 1933–38.

PRICE, LAWRENCE MARSDEN (Feb. 14, 1881–); b. Titusville, Pa. Educator, author. *The Reception of English Literature in Germany* (1932); *The Publication of English Literature in Germany in the Eighteenth Century* (with Minnie Bell Price, 1934); *Vogue of Marmontel on the German Stage* (1944); *English Literature in Germany* (1953); etc. Editor: *Inkle and Yarico Album* (1937). German language dept., University of California, since 1915.

PRICE, LUCIEN (Jan. 6, 1883–Mar. 30, 1964); b. Kent, O. Author. *The Pillar of Fire* (1916); *Immortal Youth* (1919); *Winged Sandals* (1928); *We Northmen* (1936); *Dialogues of Alfred North Whitehead* (1954); *Another Athens* (1956). Editorial writer, *Boston Globe,* since 1914.

PRICE, MARGARET EVANS (Mar. 20, 1888–); b. Chicago, Ill. Artist, author. *A Child's Book of Myths* (1924); *Legends of the Seven Seas* (1929); *The Windy Shore* (1930); *Monkey-Do* (1934); *Mota and the Monkey Tree* (1935); *Night Must End* (1938); *Animals Marooned* (1943); *Mirage* (1955).

PRICE, WARWICK JAMES (Nov. 25, 1870–Apr. 6, 1934); b. Cleveland, Ohio. Author. *The Right Side* (poems, 1905); *Nearest Things* (poems, 1919); *The One Book* (1927).

PRICE, WILLARD [DeMille] (July 18, 1887–); b. Peterboro, Ont. Author. *Pacific Adventure* (1936); *Rip Tide in the South Seas* (1936); *Children of the Rising Sun* (1938); *Japan's Islands of Mystery* (1944); *Roving South* (1948); *Amazon Adventure* (1949); *I Cannot Rest from Travel* (1951); *Amazing Amazon* (1952); *South Sea Adventure* (1952); *Adventures in Paradise* (1955); *Whale Adventure* (1960); *Incredible Africa* (1962); *Lion Adventure* (1967); etc.

PRICE, WILLIAM THOMPSON (Dec. 17, 1845–May 3, 1920); b. in Jefferson Co., Ky. Drama critic. *The Technique of the Drama* (1892); *A Life of Charlotte Cushman* (1894); *The Analysis of Play Construction* (1908); etc. Editor, the *American Playwright,* 1912–15. Drama critic, the *Louisville Courier-Journal,* 1875–80; the *New York Star,* 1885–86. Play reader for A. M. Palmer and Harrison Grey Fiske.

Priceman, James. Pen name of Winifred Margaretta Kirkland.

PRICHARD, HAROLD ADYE (Dec. 14, 1882–May 7, 1944); b. Bristol, Eng. Episcopal clergyman, author. *Three Essays in Restatement* (1921); *Christian Stewardship* (1922); *The Sower* (1923); *A Country Parson Looks at Religion* (1931); *If They Don't Come Back* (1943); etc.

PRICHARD, SARAH JOHNSON (Jan. 11, 1830–1909); b. Waterbury, Conn. Author. *Martha's Hooks and Eyes* (1858); *Kate Morgan and Her Soldiers* (1862); *The Old Stone Chimney* (1865); *Rose Marbury* (1870); *Aunt Sadie's Cow* (1872); *The Only Woman in the Town, and Other Tales of the American Revolution* (1898); *The Wonderful Christmas in Pumpkin Delight Lane* (1908); etc.

PRIDGEN, TIM (1899–); Author. *Courage* (1938); *Tory Oath* (1941); *West Goes the Road* (1944).

PRIEST, GEORGE MADISON (Jan. 25, 1873–Feb. 17, 1947); b. Henderson, Ky. Educator, author. *A Brief History of German Literature* (1909); *Germany Since 1740* (1915); etc. Editor: *Anthology of German Literature in the Eighteenth Century* (1934); etc. Princeton University from 1895, prof. Germanic languages, 1912–41.

PRIEST, JOSIAH (1790–1850); b. New York. Author. *Wonders of Nature* (1826); *Stories of the Revolution* (1836); *The Robbers; or, The Narrative of Pye and the Highwayman* (1836); *Stories of Early Settlers in the Wildnerness* (1837); *A History of the Early Adventures of Washington* (1841); etc.

PRIESTLEY, HERBERT INGRAM (Jan. 2, 1875–Feb. 9, 1944); b. Fairfield, Mich. Historian, author. *The Mexican Nation, A History* (1923); *The Coming of the White Man* (1929); *Tristán de Luna, Conquistador* (1936); *France Overseas: A Study in Modern Imperialism* (1938); etc. Prof. Mexican history, University of California, from 1923; librarian, Bancroft Library, from 1920.

PRIESTLEY, JOSEPH (Mar. 13, 1733–Feb. 6, 1804); b. in England, came to the United States in 1794. Scientist, educator, author. *The Theological Works of Joseph Priestley*, ed. by J. T. Rutt, 26v. (1817–32). See E. F. Smith's *Priestley in America* (1920); Alice Holt's *A Life of Joseph Priestley* (1931).

PRIME, BENJAMIN YOUNGS (Dec. 9, 1733–Oct. 31, 1791); b. Huntington, L.I., N.Y. Physician, balladist. *The Patriot Muse; or, Poems on Some of the Principal Events of the Late War* (anon., 1764); *Columbia's Glory; or, British Pride Humbled* (1791); *Muscipula; sive, Cambromyomachia: The Mousetrap* (1840), containing a translation of Edward Holdsworth's poem.

PRIME, SAMUEL IRENAEUS (Nov. 4, 1812–July 18, 1885); b. Ballston, N.Y. Presbyterian clergyman, editor, author. *The Old White Meeting House* (1845); *Travels in Europe and the East*, 2v. (1885); *The Power of Prayer* (1859); *Letters from Switzerland* (1860); *The Alhambra and the Kremlin* (1873); *Autobiography and Memorials* (1888); etc. Editor, *The Observer*, 1840–85; conducted the "Editor's Drawer" in *Harper's Magazine*, 1853–85.

PRIME, WILLIAM COWPER (Oct. 31, 1825–Feb. 13, 1905); b. Cambridge, N.Y. Journalist, educator, author. *The Owl Creek Letters and Other Correspondence* (anon., 1848); *The Old House by the River* (1853); *Later Years* (1855); *Coins, Medals, and Seals* (1861); *Boat Life in Egypt and Nubia* (1868); *I Go A-Fishing* (1873); *Pottery and Porcelain* (1878); *Among the Northern Hills* (1895); etc. Editor, the *New York Journal of Commerce*, 1861–69. Prof. art, Princeton University, beginning in 1884.

Primitivism and Decadence. Work of literary criticism, by Yvor Winters (1937). Develops the author's theory of "expressive form" as a Romantic error in modern literature. See *In Defense of Reason* (1947).

PRINCE, HELEN CHOATE (Nov. 26, 1857–); b. Dorchester, Mass. Novelist. *The Story of Christian Rochefort* (1895); *At the Sign of the Silver Crescent* (1898); *The Strongest Master* (1903); etc.

PRINCE, L[e Baron] BRADFORD (July 3, 1840–Dec. 8, 1922); b. Flushing, L.I., N.Y. Jurist, governor, author. *Historical Sketches of New Mexico* (1883); *The Stone Lions of Cochiti* (1903); etc. Governor of New Mexico Territory, 1889–93.

PRINCE, MORTON (Dec. 21, 1854–Aug. 31, 1929); b. Boston, Mass. Neurologist, editor, author. *The Nature of Mind and Human Automatism* (1885); *The Dissociation of a Personality* (1906); *The Unconscious* (1913); etc. Founder and editor, *Journal of Abnormal Psychology*, 1906–29. Harvard Medical School, and Tufts College Medical School.

PRINCE, THOMAS (May 15, 1687–Oct. 22, 1758); b. Sandwich, Mass. Bibliophile, author. *A Chronological History of New England in the Form of Annals* (1736); *Annals of New England* (1755), being an unfinished continuation of the preceding. Wrote many sermons, memorials, etc. Many of his books are now preserved in the Boston Public Library. See W. H. Whitmore's *The Prince Library. A Catalogue* (1870); H. A. Hill's *History of Old South Church*, 2v. (1890).

Prince and the Pauper, The. By Mark Twain (1881). A satire on class distinctions. Tom Canty, a poor street urchin and Prince Edward, later Edward VI of England, exchange clothes and see life from the other's point of view, which is highly instructive to both, and leads to exciting adventures.

Prince of India, The. Novel by Lew Wallace (1893). Based on the legend of "The Wandering Jew."

Prince of Parthia, The. Play by Thomas Godfrey (prod. Philadelphia, Apr. 24, 1767).

Prince of the House of David, The. Popular biblical romance by Joseph Holt Ingraham (1855). It describes the advent of Christ.

Princess Casamassima, The. Novel by Henry James (1886). The current socialistic questions serve as a background.

Princeton Triangle Club. Theatrical organization at Princeton University. Founded 1888, as the Princeton Dramatic Association.

Princeton University Library Chronicle. Princeton, N.J. Quarterly. Founded 1940, with Lawrence Thompson as editor. Julian P. Boyd, Elmer Adler, Lawrence Heyl, Gilbert Chinard, and Willard Thorp have been associate editors.

Princeton University Press. Princeton, N.J. Founded 1905. Whitney Darrow, one of the founders, was manager, 1905–17; Paul Greene Tomlinson was manager, 1917–38; Frank D. Halsey was editor, 1922–41; Datus Smith became editor in 1941. Joseph A. Brandt was director 1938–41. The greatest benefactor of the Princeton University Press has been Charles Scribner (1854–1930), the New York publisher, who was instrumental in its founding, donated the land and building for the press, and served for many years as its president. His son, Charles Scribner, succeeded him as president. Herbert S. Bailey, Jr., is now president.

PRINDLE, FRANCES WESTON CARRUTH (July 12, 1867–); b. Newton, Mass. Author. *Those Dale Girls* (1899); *The Way of Belinda* (1901); *Fictional Rambles in and about Boston* (1902); *Vibrations* (poems, 1927).

PRINGLE, HENRY FOWLES (Aug. 23, 1897–Apr. 7, 1958); b. New York. Author. *Alfred E. Smith* (1927); *Big Frogs* (1928); *Theodore Roosevelt* (1931, Pulitzer Prize for biography, 1932); *The Life and Times of William Howard Taft*, 2v. (1939). Prof. journalism, Columbia University, 1936–43.

Printers' Ink. See *Marketing/Communications.*

Printz Hall. Novel by Lemuel Sawyer (1839). Story of the early Swedish settlement on the Delaware, and the conflict between the Swedes and Peter Stuyvesant.

PRIOR, MOODY E. (Sept. 29, 1901–); b. Fatsa, Turk. Educator, *The Language of Tragedy* (1947). Prof. English, Northwestern University, since 1930.

Prisoners of Hope. Novel by Mary Johnston (1898).

PRITCHETT, JOHN PERRY (June 3, 1902–); b. Brooks, Cal. Educator. *Canada and the Red River* (1938); *Calhoun, His Defence of the South* (1937); *The Red River Valley* (1942); *Black Robe and Buskin* (1960); Distinguished Prof. Mercer County Community College, Trenton, N.J. since 1967.

Private Life of Helen of Troy, The. Novel by John Erskine (1925). Modernization of an ancient story, recorded in conversations held with Eteoneus the gate-keeper by Helen, Menelaus, Hermione and others, who discuss the current events which formed the basis of the tragedies of Aeschylus.

Problems of Men. By John Dewey (1946). Essays written during a fifty-year period and, for the most part, published previously in periodicals.

Processional. Play by John Howard Lawson (prod. 1925). Sordid story of a strike in a West Virginia coal mining town, and the seduction of the jazz-crazy Sadie Cohen by Dynamite Jim.

PROCTER, ARTHUR (Jan. 4, 1889–Nov. 29, 1961); b. Omaha, Neb. Lawyer, author. *Principles of Public Personnel Administration* (1922); *Financing of Social Work* (with A. A. Schuck, 1926); *Murder in Manhattan* (1930). Co-author: *Savages Under the Skin* (play, 1927). Editor: *The Covered Wagon Centennial and Ox-Team Days* (1931).

PROCTOR, EDNA DEAN (Sept. 18, 1829–Dec. 18, 1923); b. Henniker, N.H. Poet. *Poems* (1866); *A Russian Journey* (1872); *The Song of the Ancient People* (1892); *The Mountain Maid, and Other Poems* (1900); *Songs of America, and Other Poems* (1905); *The Complete Poetical Works* (1925).

Prodigal Judge, The. Novel by Vaughan Kester (1911). Picture of a frontier settlement in Western Tennessee.

Professor at the Breakfast Table, The. By Oliver Wendell Holmes (1860). Genial, rambling discourse on a variety of subjects in the manner of *The Autocrat of the Breakfast Table,* but with more emphasis on theological subjects.

Professor's House, The. Novel by Willa Cather (1925). Professor St. Peter rebels against his wife's worldly desires, the pettiness of his daughters, and the vulgarization of the ideals he cherishes.

Professorships of Books and Reading. A significant report, in two parts, the first by F. B. Perkins, the second by William Mathews, which appeared in *Public Libraries in the United States of America* (1876); published by the U.S. Bureau of Education. These articles reported a lack of interest in American literature in schools and libraries, as compared to the attention given to English literature, and proposed ways of developing the study of our own literature.

PROFFITT, JOSEPHINE MOORE (Oct. 22, 1914–); b. Little Rock, Ark. Author. Writes under pen name "Sylvia Dee." *And Never Been Kissed* (1949); *Dear Guest and Ghost* (1950); *There Was a Little Girl* (1951). With Sidney Lippman, wrote the songs "Chickery Chick," "It Couldn't Be True," "Laroo Laroo Lilli Bolero," etc., and lyrics for *Barefoot Boy with Cheek* (prod. 1947).

Profiles in Courage. By John F. Kennedy (1956). A Collection of biographies of notable American legislators who rose above the demands of compromise and conciliation in politics to stand up for their most fervent political ideals.

Progress and Poverty. By Henry George (1858). Treatise on the single tax which became an international best seller. The author advocated that all unused land become public property, and that only land be taxed.

Progress of Dullness, The. Long poem by John Trumbull, 3 parts (1772–73). A satire on college instruction and its abuses.

Progressive, The. Madison, Wis. Monthly. Founded 1929, by the Progressive movement under the La Follettes, superseding *La Follette's Magazine.*

PROKOSCH, FREDERIC (May 17, 1909–); b. Madison, Wis. Novelist, poet. *The Asiatics* (1935); *The Assassins* (poems, 1936); *The Seven Who Fled* (1937); *The Carnival* (poems, 1938); *Night of the Poor* (1939); *The Skies of Europe* (1941); *The Conspirators* (1943); *Age of Thunder* (1945); *The Idols of the Cave* (1946); *Chosen Poems* (1947); *Storm and Echo* (1948); *Nine Days to Mukalla* (1953); *A Tale for Midnight* (1955); *A Ballad of Love* (1960).

Proletarian Literature in the United States. By Granville Hicks (1935). A survey of the new literary trend toward labor subjects, including some of the left-wing writings.

Promised Land, The. By Mary Antin (1912). The autobiography of an immigrant, setting forth the joys and hopes of the Russian Jews in America.

Prophet of the Great Smoky Mountains, The. Novel by "Charles Egbert Craddock" (Mary Noailles Murfree) (1885). Realistic portrayal of the lawless life led by a certain backwoods class in the mountains of Tennessee.

Prose. New York. Founded 1970. Twice yearly. Literary magazine. W.H. Auden, Edward Dahlberg, Parker Tyler, and Richard Howard have been among its contributors.

PROUD, ROBERT (May 10, 1728–July 5, 1813); b. in Yorkshire, Eng. came to America in 1759. Historian. *The History of Pennsylvania, in North America,* 2v. (1797–98).

PROUDFIT, DAVID LAW (Oct. 27, 1842–1897); b. Newburgh, N.Y. Author. Pen name, "Peleg Arkwright." *Love Among the Gamins, and Other Poems* (1877); *Mask and Domino* (1888).

PROUTY, CHARLES TYLER (May 30, 1909–); b. Washington, D.C. Educator. *George Gascoigne* (1942); *The Contention and Shakespeare's 2 Henry VI: A Comparative Study* (1954); etc. Editor: *Yale Facsimile Edition of Shakespeare's First Folio* (with H. Kökeritz, 1954); *Studies in the Elizabethan Theatre* (1961); etc. Prof. English, Yale University, since 1948.

PROUTY, OLIVE HIGGINS (Jan. 7, 1882–); b. Worcester, Mass. Author. *Bobbie, General Manager* (1913); *The Fifth Wheel* (1916); *The Star in the Window* (1918); *Stella Dallas* (1922); *Conflict* (1927); *White Fawn* (1931); *Lisa Vale* (1938); *Now, Voyager* (1941); *Home Port* (1947); *Fabia* (1951); etc.

Providence Bulletin. See *Providence Journal.*

Providence Journal. Providence, R.I. Newspaper. Founded Jan. 3, 1820, as the *Manufacturers' and Farmers' Journal and Providence and Pawtucket Advertiser.* William Ebenezer Richmond was its first editor, succeeded by Benjamin F. Hallett in 1821. Thomas Rivers was editor when the daily edition was established, July 21, 1829. The weekly continued until 1907, still under its original name. Other editors were Lewis Gaylord Clark, later editor of the *Knickerbocker Magazine,* George Paine, John B. Snow, Thomas H. Webb, Henry B. Anthony, James S. Ham, James B. Angell, George W. Danielson, Alfred M. Williams, Richard S. Howland, David S. Barry, Frederick Roy Martin, and John R. Rathom. When the Providence Journal Co. was incorporated William A. Hoppin was made president, followed by Lucian Sharpe, and Stephen O. Metcalf. Metcalf was president, 1904–41, being succeeded by his son, G. Pierce Metcalf. William Butler Yeats, Douglas Hyde, and Rudyard Kipling wrote for the *Providence Journal* before their fame became generally known. The *Providence Journal* was almost the only paper to proclaim the immediate greatness of Lincoln's *Gettysburg Address*. Noted contributors have been Thomas A. Jenckes, Augustus Hoppin, Emma Shaw Colcleugh, Alexis Caswell, Arthur W. "Jeff" Davis, and Ashmun Brown. It conducts a notable literary page. The *Evening Bulletin,* also published by the Providence Journal Co., was established in 1863. Now called the *Bulletin,* it is published evenings, except Sunday; the *Journal* appears mornings. The present executive editor is Michael J. Ogden. Maurice Dolbier edits book reviews.

Provincetown Players. Provincetown, Mass. Experimental group of actors, playwrights, and artists, organized in 1915 by George Cram Cook and others. The group had a wharf theatre in Provincetown, in 1916, and many of Eugene O'Neill's plays were first produced there. The same year the group moved to Macdougall Street, in Greenwich Village, New York, establishing first the Playwright's Theatre and two years later the Provincetown Playhouse, on the same street. The group disbanded in 1929. *See* Helen Deutsch and Stella Hanau's *The Provincetown* (1931).

Prue and I. Novel by George William Curtis (1856). A philosophical observer of life portrays that happiness which does not depend on wealth or material comfort.

PRUETTE, LORINE LIVINGSTON (1896–); b. Millersburg, Tenn. Author. *G. Stanley Hall: A Biography of a Mind* (1926); *Saint in Ivory* (1927); *School for Love* (1936); *Working with Words* (1940); *The Problem of Grandparents* (1951); etc.

Prufrock, and other Observations. Collection of poems by T. S. Eliot (1917). This first volume brought Eliot into prominence. *See* "The Love Song of J. Alfred Prufrock."

PRY, POLLY. Pen name of Leonel Campbell O'Bryan.

PRYCE-JONES, ALAN PAYAN (Nov. 18, 1908–); b. London, England. Critic, author. *Spring Journey* (1931); *People in the South* (1932); *Beethoven* (1933); *27 Poems* (1935); *Private Opinion* (1936); *Pink Danube* (opera, with L. Berkeley, 1939); *Nelson* (1954); *Vanity Fair* (musical, with R. Miller and J. Slade, 1962). Book critic, *New York Herald Tribune,* 1963–66.

PRYOR, SARA AGNES [Rice] (Mrs. Roger Atkinson Pryor) (Feb. 19, 1830–1912); b. in Halifax Co., Va. Author. *The Mother of Washington and Her Times* (1903); *Reminiscences of Peace and War* (1904); *The Birth of the Nation: Jamestown, 1607* (1907); *My Day: Reminiscences of a Long Life* (1909); etc.

"Psalm of Life, A." Poem by Henry Wadsworth Longfellow (1838).

Psychoanalytic Review. New York. Quarterly. Founded 1913. Published by the National Psychological Association for Psychoanalysis, Inc. Discontinued 1957 and combined with *Psychoanalysis* as *Psychoanalysis and the Psychoanalytic Review.*

Psychology Today. Del Mar, Cal. Monthly. Founded 1967. Concerned with psychology, society, and human behavior from a non-technical, literate point of view. Makes extensive use of the latest techniques in prints and graphics, emphasizing the modernity of its approach to information. Absorbed *Careers Today* in 1969.

Public Advertiser. Boston, Mass. Weekly magazine. Founded 1748, by Samuel Adams and a group of young friends.

Public Duty of Educated Men, The. Famous oration by George William Curtis (1877).

Public Interest, The. New York. Quarterly. Founded 1965. Published by Basic Books, Inc. Edited by Irving Kristol and Daniel Bell. Critical discussions of matters of public concern in all areas of culture.

Public Libraries in the United States of America: Their History, Condition, and Management: Special Report, Department of the Interior, Bureau of Education (1876). A monumental report on the American libraries, stimulated by the International Exhibition at Philadelphia, the organization of the American Library Association and the founding of *The Library Journal.*

Public Philosophy, Essays in the. By Walter Lippmann (1955). A consideration of the way in which democracy functions in the United States, stressing the philosophical basis of American political traditions.

Publick Occurrence. Boston, Mass. Founded Sept. 25, 1690, by Benjamin Harris. This, the first newspaper attempted in America, was suppressed after the first issue. *See* the *Boston News-Letter.*

Publicola. Political essays by John Quincy Adams, which were published in the *Columbian & Centinel* of Boston, June 8 to July 27, 1791. A reply to Paine's *The Rights of Man.*

Publishers' Trade List Annual. New York City. Founded 1873. Consolidated catalogue of the leading book publishers of America. Each publisher sends in a separate catalogue and these are bound in one volume. The nickname for this volume is the "Green Pig," since it is a fat volume bound in green.

Publishers' Weekly. New York. Book trade weekly. Founded Jan. 18, 1872, by Frederick Leypoldt. It grew out of the *Literary Bulletin,* founded 1868, and the *Monthly Book Trade Circular,* 1869. In Jan., 1872, Leypoldt issued the first number of the *Publishers' and Stationers' Weekly Trade Circular,* which changed its name to the *Publishers' Weekly* in 1873. Editors: Frederick Leypoldt, 1872–84; Richard R. Bowker, 1884–1933. Frederic G. Melcher, Alice P. Hackett, and Eugene Armfield were later editors. In 1872 the *American Literary Gazette and Publishers' Circular* was merged with it. This latter publication was an offspring of *Norton's Literary Advertiser,* founded by Charles B. Norton, in Philadelphia, 1851, and changed in 1852 to *Norton's Literary Gazette and Publishers' Circular.* In 1855 it was purchased by George W. Childs and superseded by the *American Publishers' Circular and Literary Gazette.* In 1856 the *Criterion* was merged with it. When Leypoldt bought it its name had changed to *American Literary Gazette and Publishers' Circular.* Leypoldt's *Monthly Book Trade Circular,* abandoned in 1872, was resumed in 1875 as the *Literary News,* which began a new series in 1880 and expired in 1904. The *Publishers' Weekly,* particularly since 1876, when booksellers and librarians systematized their records as a result of the exposition at Philadelphia, has attempted to list every book published in America. *See* Frank L. Mott's *History of American Magazines,* v.3 (1938).

Publishing House of the Methodist Episcopal Church South. Nashville, Tenn. Founded c. 1850. Incorporated 1855. The Cokesbury Press was established as a trade department; and The Parthenon Press for outside printing. Smith & Lamar were the agents 1903–22. Merged with the Methodist Book Concern in 1939.

Publius. Signature in *The Federalist* attached to the articles of Madison, Hamilton, and Jay, Oct. 27, 1787–Apr. 2, 1788.

Puck. New York. Comic magazine. Founded Mar., 1877, by Joseph Keppler and A. Schwarzmann, as an English edition of their German language *Puck,* founded 1876. Editors: Sydney Rosenfeld, 1877–78; Henry Cuyler Bunner, 1878–96; Harry Leon Wilson, 1896–1902; John Kendrick Bangs, 1904–05; Arthur Hamilton Folwell, 1905–16; Karl Schmidt, 1916. Among those who contributed to *Puck's* literary or artistic make-up were H. C. Bunner, whose *Short Sixes* appeared in its columns; Dana Burnet; James Huneker; "Hy" Mayer; Richard K. Munkittrick; F. Opper; and B. B. Valentine. Expired Sept., 1918. *See* Frank L. Mott's *A History of American Magazines*, v.3 (1938).

Puddin'head Wilson. By Mark Twain (1894). Frank Mayo, the actor, dramatized the story in 1895, and played the title rôle at Proctor's Opera House, Hartford, Conn., Apr. 8, 1895.

PUGH, ELLIS (June 1656–Oct. 3, 1718); b. Dolgelly, North Wales. Quaker preacher, author. *Annerch ir Cymru* (1721), the first book in Welsh printed in America. A translation by Rowland Ellis was published in Philadelphia under the title *A Salutation to the Britains* (1727).

PULITZER, JOSEPH (Apr. 10, 1847–Oct. 29, 1911); b. Budapest. Publisher. Owner and publisher of the *St. Louis Post-Dispatch*, 1878–1911; *New York World*, 1883–1911. Founder, School of Journalism, Columbia University. By the terms of his will he established the Pulitzer Prizes in 1915. *See* Donn C. Seitz's *Joseph Pulitzer* (1924); Alleyne Ireland's *An Adventure with a Genius* (1937); James Wyman Barrett's *Joseph Pulitzer and His World* (1941); William Swanberg's *Pulitzer* (1967).

PULITZER, JOSEPH (Mar. 21, 1885–Mar. 31, 1955); b. New York, son of Joseph Pulitzer. Editor and publisher. President, Pulitzer Publishing Co., publishers of the *St. Louis Post-Dispatch*, from 1912.

PULITZER, MRS. RALPH. *See* Margaret Kernochan Leech.

PULITZER, RALPH (June 11, 1879–June 14, 1939); b. St. Louis, Mo. Publisher, poet. *New York Society on Parade* (1910).

PULITZER, WALTER (Apr. 4, 1878–Sept. 5, 1926); b. New York. Author. *That Duel at the Château Marsanac* (1899); *A Cynic's Meditations* (1904).

Pulitzer Prizes. Established by bequest of Joseph Pulitzer (q.v.) to the Columbia University School of Journalism. Beginning in 1917, annual awards have been made by the Pulitzer Prize Committee for outstanding achievements in the fields of American biography, American history, drama, the novel, and poetry. The winners of the awards have been:

Fiction: For 1917, no award; 1918, *His Family*, by Ernest Poole; 1919, *The Magnificent Ambersons*, by Booth Tarkington; 1920, no award; 1921, *The Age of Innocence*, by Edith Wharton; 1922, *Alice Adams*, by Booth Tarkington; 1923, *One of Ours*, by Willa Cather; 1924, *The Able McLaughlins*, by Margaret Wilson; 1925, *So Big*, by Edna Ferber; 1926, *Arrowsmith*, by Sinclair Lewis (declined); 1927, *Early Autumn*, by Louis Bromfield; 1928, *The Bridge of San Luis Rey*, by Thornton Wilder; 1929, *Scarlet Sister Mary*, by Julia Peterkin; 1930, *Laughing Boy*, by Oliver La Farge; 1931, *Years of Grace*, by Margaret Ayer Barnes; 1932, *The Good Earth*, by Pearl Buck; 1933, *The Store*, by Thomas S. Stribling; 1934, *Lamb in His Bosom*, by Caroline Miller; 1935, *Now in November*, by Josephine Winslow Johnson; 1936, *Honey in the Horn*, by Harold L. Davis, 1937, *Gone with the Wind*, by Margaret Mitchell; 1938, *The Late George Apley*, by John Phillips Marquand; 1939, *The Yearling*, by Marjorie Kinnan Rawlings; 1940, *The Grapes of Wrath*, by John Steinbeck; 1941, no award; 1942, *In This Our Life*, by Ellen Glasgow; 1943, *Dragon's Teeth*, by Upton Sinclair; 1944, *Journey in the Dark*, by Martin Flavin; 1945, *A Bell for Adano*, by John Hersey; 1946, no award; 1947, *All the King's Men*, by Robert Penn Warren; 1948. *Tales of the South Pacific*, by James A. Michener; 1949, *Guard of Honor*, by James Gould Cozzens; 1950, *The Way West*, by A. B. Guthrie, Jr.; 1951, *The Town*, by Conrad Richter; 1952, *The Caine Mutiny*, by Herman Wouk; 1953, *The Old Man and the Sea*, by Ernest Hemingway; 1954, no award; 1955, *A Fable*, by William Faulkner; 1956, *Andersonville*, by MacKinlay Kantor; 1957, no award; 1958, *A Death in the Family*, by James Agee; 1959, *The*

Travels of Jaimie McPheeters, by Robert Lewis Taylor; 1960, *Advise and Consent*, by Allen Drury; 1961, *To Kill a Mockingbird*, by Harper Lee; 1962, *The Edge of Sadness*, by Edwin O'Connor; 1963, *The Reivers*, by William Faulkner; 1964, no award; 1965, *The Keepers of the House*, by Shirley Anne Grau; 1966, *Collected Short Stories*, by Katherine Anne Porter; 1967, *The Fixer*, by Bernard Malamud; 1968, *The Confessions of Nat Turner*, by William Styron; 1969, *House Made of Dawn*, by N. Scott Momaday; 1970, *Collected Stories*, by Jean Stafford; 1971, no award.

For American Biography: 1917, *Julia Ward Howe*, by Laura E. Richards, Maude H. Elliott, and Florence H. Hall; 1918, *Benjamin Franklin, Self-Revealed*, by William Cabell Bruce; 1919, *The Education of Henry Adams*, by Henry Adams; 1920, *The Life of John Marshall*, by Albert J. Beveridge; 1921, *The Americanization of Edward Bok*, by Edward Bok; 1922, *A Daughter of the Middle Border*, by Hamlin Garland; 1923, *The Life and Letters of Walter H. Page*, by Burton J. Hendrick; 1924, *From Immigrant to Inventor*, by Michael Pupin; 1925, *Barrett Wendell and His Letters*, by M. A. DeWolfe Howe; 1926, *The Life of Sir William Osler*, by Harvey Cushing; 1927, *Whitman* by Emory Holloway; 1928, *The American Orchestra and Theodore Thomas*, by Charles Edward Russell; 1929, *The Training of an American: The Earlier Life and Letters of Walter H. Page*, by Burton J. Hendrick; 1930, *The Raven: A Biography of Sam Houston*, by Marquis James; 1931, *Charles W. Eliot*, by Henry James; 1932, *Theodore Roosevelt*, by Henry F. Pringle; 1933, *Grover Cleveland*, by Allan Nevins; 1934, *John Hay*, by Tyler Dennett; 1935, *R. E. Lee*, by Douglas Southall Freeman; 1936, *The Thought and Character of William James*, by Ralph Barton Perry; 1937, *Hamilton Fish: The Inner History of the Great Administration*, by Allan Nevins; 1938, divided between *Pedlar's Progress: The Life of Bronson Alcott*, by Odell Shepard, and *Andrew Jackson*, by Marquis James; 1939, *Benjamin Franklin*, by Carl Van Doren; 1940, *Woodrow Wilson: Life and Letters*, vols. VII and VIII, by Ray Stannard Baker; 1941, *Jonathan Edwards*, by Ola Elizabeth Winslow; 1942, *Crusader in Crinoline*, by Forrest Wilson; 1943, *Admiral of the Ocean Sea*, by Samuel Eliot Morison; 1944, *The American Leonardo: The Life of Samuel F. B. Morse*, by Carleton Mabee; 1945, *George Bancroft: Brahmin Rebel*, by Russell Blaine Nye; 1946, *Son of the Wilderness*, by Linnie Marsh Wolfe; 1947, *The Autobiography of William Allen White*, by William Allen White; 1948, *Forgotten First Citizen: John Bigelow*, by Margaret Clapp; 1949 *Roosevelt and Hopkins*, by Robert E. Sherwood; 1950, *John Quincy Adams and the Foundations of American Foreign Policy*, by Samuel Flagg Bemis; 1951, *John C. Calhoun: American Portrait*, by Margaret Louise Coit; 1952, *Charles Evans Hughes*, by Merlo J. Pusey; 1953, *Edmund Pendleton, 1721–1803*, by David J. Mays; 1954, *The Spirit of St. Louis*, by Charles A. Lindbergh; 1955, *The Taft Story*, by William S. White; 1956, *Benjamin Henry Latrobe*, by Talbot F. Hamlin; 1957, *Profiles in Courage*, by John F. Kennedy; 1958, *George Washington*, 7v., by Douglas Southall Freeman, completed by John Alexander Carroll and Mary Wells Ashworth; 1959, *Woodrow Wilson, American Prophet*, by Arthur Walworth; 1960, *John Paul Jones*, by Samuel Eliot Morison; 1961, *Charles Sumner and the Coming of the Civil War*, by David Donald; 1962, no award; 1963, *Henry James: The Conquest of London, 1870–81*, vol. 2, and *Henry James: The Middle Years, 1881–95*, vol. 3, by Leon Edel; 1964, *John Keats*, by Walter Jackson Bate; 1965, *Henry Adams*, by Ernest Samuels; 1966, *A Thousand Days*, by Arthur M. Schlesinger, Jr.; 1967, *Mr. Clemens and Mark Twain*, by Justin Kaplan; 1968, *Memoirs, 1925–1950*, by George F. Kennan; 1969, *The Man from New York: John Quinn and His Friends*, by B. L. Reid; 1970, *Huey Long*, by T. Harry Williams; 1971, *Robert Frost: The Years of Triumph, 1915–1938*, by Lawrence R. Thompson.

For American History: 1917, *With Americans of Past and Present Days*, by J. J. Jusserand; 1918, *A History of the Civil War*, by James Ford Rhodes; 1919, no award; 1920, *The War with Mexico*, by Justin H. Smith; 1921, *The Victory at Sea*, by William S. Sims and Burton J. Hendrick; 1922, *The Founding of New England*, by James Truslow Adams; 1923, *The Supreme Court in United States History*, by Charles Warren; 1924, *The American Revolution*, by Charles H. McIlwain; 1925, *A History of the American Frontier*, by Frederick L. Paxson; 1926, *The History of the United States*, by Edward Channing; 1927, *Pinckney's Treaty*, by Samuel Flagg Bemis; 1928, *Main Currents in American Thought*, by Vernon L. Parrington; 1929, *The Organization and Administration of the Union Army*, by Fred Albert Shannon; 1930, *The War of Independence*, by Claude H. Van Tyne; 1931, *The Coming of the War: 1914*, by Bernadotte E. Schmitt; 1932, *My Experiences in the World War*, by John J. Pershing; 1933, *The Significance of Sections in American History*, by Frederick J. Turner; 1934, *The People's Choice*, by Herbert Agar; 1935, *The Colonial Period of American History*, by Charles McLean Andrews; 1936, *A Constitutional History of the United States*, by Andrew C. McLaughlin; 1937, *The Flowering of New England*, by Van Wyck Brooks; 1938, *The Road to Reunion: 1865-1900*, by Paul H. Buck; 1939, *A History of American Magazines*, by Frank Luther Mott; 1940, *Abraham Lincoln: The War Years*, by Carl Sandburg; 1941, *The Atlantic Migration*, by Marcus Lee Hansen; 1942, *Reveille in Washington*, by Margaret Leech; 1943, *Paul Revere and the World He Lived In*, by Esther Forbes; 1944, *The Growth of American Thought*, by Merle Curti; 1945, *Unfinished Business*, by Stephen Bonsal; 1946, *The Age of Jackson*, by Arthur M. Schlesinger, Jr.; 1947, *Scientists Against Time*, by Dr. James Phinney Baxter, III; 1948, *Across the Wide Missouri*, by Bernard De Voto; 1949, *The Disruption of American Democracy*, by Roy F. Nichols; 1950, *Art and Life in America*, by O. W. Larkin; 1951, *The Old Northwest, Pioneer Period 1815-1940*, by R. Caryle Buley; 1952, *The Uprooted*, by Oscar Handlin; 1953, *The Era of Good Feelings*, by George Dangerfield; 1954, *A Stillness at Appomattox*, by Bruce Catton; 1955, *Great River: The Rio Grande in North American History*, by Paul Horgan; 1956, *The Age of Reform*, by Richard Hofstadter; 1957, *Russia Leaves the War*, by George F. Kennan; 1958, *Banks and Politics in America: From the Revolution to the Civil War*, by Bray Hammond; 1959, *The Republican Era: 1869-1901*, by Leonard D. White and Jean Schneider; 1960, *In the Days of McKinley*, by Margaret Leech; 1961, *Between War and Peace: The Potsdam Conference*, by Herbert Feis; 1962, *The Triumphant Empire, Thunder-Clouds Gather in the West* by Lawrence H. Gipson; 1963, *Washington, Village and Capital: 1800-1878*, by Constance McLaughlin; 1964, *Puritan Village, The Formation of a New England Town*, by Sumner Chilton Powell; 1965, *The Greenback Era*, by Irwin Unger; 1966, *Life of the Mind in America*, by Perry Miller; 1967, *Exploration and Empire: The Explorer and Scientist in the Winning of the American West*, by William H. Goetzmann; 1968, *The Ideological Origins of the American Revolution*, by Bernard Bailyn; 1969, *Origins of the Fifth Amendment*, by Leonard W. Levy; 1970, *Present at the Creation*, by Dean Acheson; 1971, *Roosevelt: The Soldier of Freedom*, by James McGregor, Burns.

For Drama: 1917, no award; 1918, *Why Marry?* by Jesse Lynch Williams; 1919, no award; 1920, *Beyond the Horizon*, by Eugene O'Neill; 1921, *Miss Lulu Bett*, by Zona Gale; 1922, *Anna Christie*, by Eugene O'Neill; 1923, *Icebound*, by Owen Davis; 1924, *Hell-Bent for Heaven*, by Hatcher Hughes; 1925, *They Knew What They Wanted*, by Sidney Howard; 1926, *Craig's Wife*, by George Kelly; 1927, *In Abraham's Bosom*, by Paul Green; 1928, *Strange Interlude*, by Eugene O'Neill; 1929, *Street Scene*, by Elmer Rice; 1930, *The Green Pastures*, by Marc Connelly; 1931, *Alison's House*, by Susan Glaspell; 1932, *Of Thee I Sing*, by George S. Kaufman, Morris Ryskind, and Ira Gershwin; 1933, *Both Your Houses*, by Maxwell Anderson; 1934, *Men in White*, by Sidney Kingsley; 1935, *The Old Maid*, by Zöe Akins; 1936, *Idiot's Delight*, by Robert E. Sherwood; 1937, *You Can't Take It With You*, by George S. Kaufman and Moss Hart; 1938, *Our Town*, by Thorton Wilder; 1939, *Abe Lincoln in Illinois*, by Robert E. Sherwood; 1940, *The Time of Your Life*, by William Saroyan; 1941, *There Shall Be No Night*, by Robert E. Sherwood; 1942, no

award; 1943, *The Skin of Our Teeth*, by Thornton Wilder; 1944, no award; 1945, *Harvey*, by Mary Chase; 1946, *State of the Union*, by Russell Crouse and Howard Lindsay; 1947, no award; 1948, *A Streetcar Named Desire*, by Tennessee Williams; 1949, *Death of a Salesman*, by Arthur Miller; 1950, *South Pacific*, by Richard Rodgers, Oscar Hammerstein, II, and Joshua Logan; 1951, no award; 1952, *The Shrike*, by Joseph Kramm; 1953, *Picnic*, by William Inge; 1954, *Teahouse of the August Moon*, by John Patrick; 1955, *Cat on a Hot Tin Roof*, by Tennessee Williams; 1956, *The Diary of Anne Frank*, by Frances Goodrich and Albert Hackett; 1957, *A Long Day's Journey Into Night*, by Eugene O'Neill; 1958, *Look Homeward, Angel*, by Ketti Frings; 1959, *J.B.*, by Archibald MacLeish; 1960, *Fiorello*, by George Abbott, Jerome Weidman, Sheldon Harnick, and Jerry Bock; 1961, *All the Way Home*, by Tad Mosel; 1962, *How to Succeed in Business Without Really Trying*, by Frank Loesser and Abe Burrows; 1963, no award; 1964, no award; 1965, *The Subject Was Roses*, by Frank D. Gilroy; 1966, no award; 1967, *A Delicate Balance*, by Edward Albee; 1968, no award; 1969, *The Great White Hope*, by Howard Sackler; 1970, *No Place to Be Somebody*, by Charles Gordone; 1971, *The Effect of Gamma Rays on Man-in-the-Moon Marigolds*, by Paul Zindel.

For General Non-fiction: 1962, *The Making of the President, 1960*, by Theodore H. White; 1963, *The Guns of August*, by Barbara Tuchman; 1964, *Anti-Intellectualism in American Life*, by Richard Hofstadter; 1965, *O Strange New World*, by Howard Mumford Jones; 1966, *Wandering through the Winter*, by Edwin Way Teale; 1967, *The Problem of Slavery in Western Culture*, by David Brion Davis; 1968, *The Story of Civilization*, v. 10, by Will and Ariel Durant; 1969, *The Armies of the Night*, by Norman Mailer, and *So Human an Animal: How We Are Shaped by Surroundings and Events*, by Rene Jules Dubos; 1970, *Gandhi's Truth*, by Erik H. Erikson; 1971, *The Rising Sun*, by John Toland.

For Poetry: 1922, *Collected Poems*, by Edwin Arlington Robinson; 1923, *The Harp-Weaver (and Other Poems)*, by Edna St. Vincent Millay; 1924, *New Hampshire*, by Robert Frost; 1925, *The Man Who Died Twice*, by Edwin Arlington Robinson; 1926, *What's O'clock*, by Amy Lowell; 1927, *Fiddler's Farewell*, by Leonora Speyer; 1928, *Tristram*, by Edwin Arlington Robinson; 1929, *John Brown's Body*, by Stephen Vincent Benét; 1930, *Selected Poems*, by Conrad Aiken; 1931, *Collected Poems*, by Robert Frost; 1932, *The Flowering Stone*, by George Dillon; 1933, *Conquistador*, by Archibald MacLeish; 1934, *Collected Verse*, by Robert Hillyer; 1935, *Bright Ambush*, by Audrey Wurdemann; 1936, *Strange Holiness*, by Robert P. Tristram Coffin; 1937, *A Further Range*, by Robert Frost; 1938, *Cold Morning Sky*, by Marya Zaturenska; 1939, *Selected Poems*, by John Gould Fletcher; 1940, *Collected Poems*, by Mark Van Doren; 1941, *Sunderland Capture*, by Leonard Bacon; 1942, *The Dust Which Is God*, by William Rose Benét; 1943, *A Witness Tree*, by Robert Frost; 1944, *Western Star*, by Stephen Vincent Benét; 1945, *V-Letter and Other Poems*, by Karl Shapiro; 1946, no award; 1947, *Lord Weary's Castle*, by Robert Lowell; 1948, *The Age of Anxiety*, by W. H. Auden; 1949, *Terror and Decorum*, by Peter Viereck; 1950, *Annie Allen*, by Gwendolyn Brooks; 1951, *Complete Poems*, by Carl Sandburg; 1952, *Collected Poems*, by Marianne Moore; 1953, *Collected Poems*, by Archibald MacLeish; 1954, *The Waking*, by Theodore Roethke; 1955, *Collected Poems*, by Wallace Stevens; 1956, *North and South*, by Elizabeth Bishop; 1957, *Things of This World*, by Richard Wilbur; 1958, *Promises: Poems 1954-1956* by Robert Penn Warren; 1959, *Selected Poems 1928-1958*, by Stanley Kunitz; 1960, *Heart's Needle*, by W. D. Snodgrass; 1961, *Times Three: Selected Verse from Three Decades*, by Phillis McGinley; 1962, *Poems*, by Alan Dugan; 1963, *Pictures from Brueghel*, by William Carlos Williams; 1964, *At the End of the Open Road*, by Louis Simpson; 1965, *77 Dream Songs*, by John Berryman; 1966, *Selected Poems*, by Richard Eberhardt; 1967, *Live or Die*, by Anne Sexton; 1968, *The Hard Hours*, by Anthony Hecht; 1969, *On Being Numerous*, by George Oppen; 1970, *Untitled Subjects*, by

Richard Howard; 1971, *The Carrier of Letters,* by William S. Mervin.

PULSIFER, HAROLD TROWBRIDGE (Nov. 18, 1886–Apr. 8, 1948); b. Manchester, Conn. Editor, author. *Mothers and Men* (1916); *Harvest of Time* (1932); *First Symphony* (1935); *Elegy for a House* (1935); *Rowen* (1937); etc. President, The Outlook Co., and managing editor, *The Outlook,* 1923–28.

PUMPELLY, RAPHAEL (Sept. 8, 1837–Aug. 10, 1923); b. Owego, N.Y. Explorer, geologist, author. *Across America and Asis* (1869); *Geology of the Green Mountains* (1894); *Explorations in Central Asia* (1905); *Prehistoric Civilization of Anan* (1908); *My Reminiscences,* 2v. (1918); etc.

Punchinello. New York. Comic magazine. Founded Apr. 2, 1870. William A. Stephens and Charles Dawson Shanly were editors. Expired Dec. 24, 1870.

PUPIN, MICHAEL IDVORSKY (Oct. 4, 1858–Mar. 12, 1935); b. Idvor, Hung. Educator, physicist, inventor, author. *From Immigrant to Inventor* (autobiography, 1923); *The New Reformation* (1927); *Romance of the Machine* (1930); etc. Physics dept., Columbia University, 1889–1931. *See* A. E. S. Beard's *Our Foreign-Born Citizens* (1940).

Puppet Master, The. By Robert Nathan (1923). A graceful fantasy.

PURCELL, RICHARD J[oseph] (Dec. 19, 1887–Jan. 30, 1950); b. Minneapolis, Minn. Educator, author. *Connecticut in Transition* (1918); *The American Nation* (1929); etc. History dept., Catholic University of America, 1920–42.

PURDY, JAMES (1923–); Author. *The Color of Darkness* (1957); *Malcolm* (1959); *The Nephew* (1960); *Eustrace Chisholm and The Works* (1967); *An Oyster Is a Wealthy Beast* (1967); *Mr. Evening* (1968); etc.

Puritan and His Daughter, The. Novel by James Kirke Paulding (1849). Shows the conflict between Old World ideas and the new conditions faced by the Puritans in New England. In the preface Paulding satirizes the "blood-pudding fiction" of English writers who piled violent death upon violent death.

Puritan in Babylon, A. By William Allen White (1938). A biography of Calvin Coolidge.

Purloined Letter, The. Tale by Edgar Allan Poe (1845).

"Purple Cow." Celebrated quatrain by Gelett Burgess, in *The Lark,* 1895, beginning with the line "I never saw a purple cow."

Purslane. Novel by Bernice Kelly Harris (1940). The setting is in North Carolina. *Portulaca* (1941), by the same author, has a similar setting.

PURYEAR, VERNON JOHN (Mar. 31, 1901–); b. Sulphur Springs, Okla. *International Economics and Diplomacy in the Near East* (1935); *France and the Levant* (1941); *Napoleon and the Dardanelles* (1951). Dept. of history, University of California, since 1937.

PUSEY, CALEB (c. 1650–Feb. 25, 1727); b. in Berkshire, Eng. Quaker controversialist, pamphleteer. He founded Chester Mills, Pa., in 1683. His pamphlets, most of them printed in Philadelphia by Reiner Jansen, are now collected in the library of the Historical Society of Pennsylvania.

PUSEY, MERLO JOHN (Feb. 3, 1902–); b. Woodruff, Utah. Author. *The Supreme Court Crisis* (1937); *Charles Evans Hughes,* 2v. (1951); Pulitzer Prize for biography, 1952; *Eisenhower the President* (1956); *The Way We Go To War* (1969); etc.

PUSHKAREV, BORIS S. (Oct. 22, 1929–   ); b. Prague. Urban planner, author. *Man-Made America, Chaos or Control?* (with C. Tunnard, National Book Award, 1964).

Pussy Tip-Toes' Family. By Mrs. D. P. Sanford (1875). One of the better known children's books of the period.

PUTNAM, CARLETON (Dec. 19, 1901–); b. New York. Author. *High Journey: A Decade in the Pilgrimage of an Airline Pioneer* (1945); *Theodore Roosevelt: The Formative Years* (1958); *Race and Reason: A Yankee View* (1961); *Race and Reality: A Search for Solutions* (1967); etc.

PUTNAM, EBEN (Oct. 10, 1868–Jan. 22, 1933); b. Salem, Mass. Publisher, genealogist, historian. *A History of the Putnam Family in England and America,* 2v. (1891–1908); etc.

PUTNAM, ELEANOR. Pen name of Harrie Bates.

PUTNAM, EMILY JAMES (Apr. 15, 1865–Sept. 7, 1944); b. Canandaigua, N.Y. Educator, author. *The Lady* (1913); *Candaule's Wife, and Other Stories* (1926); etc. Barnard College, Columbia University, 1894–1929; dean, 1894–1900.

PUTNAM, FREDERICK WARD (Apr. 16, 1839–Aug. 14, 1915); b. Salem, Mass. Anthropologist. Co-founder, *The American Naturalist,* 1868. Associated with Essex Institute, Salem, Mass., 1856–73; curator, Peabody Museum, Harvard University, 1874–1909; prof. archaeology, Harvard University, 1886–1909.

PUTNAM, GEORGE HAVEN (Apr. 2, 1844–Feb. 27, 1930); b. London. Soldier, publisher, author. *Authors and Their Public in Ancient Times* (1894); *Books and Their Makers during the Middle Ages,* 2v. (1896–97); *The Censorship of the Church of Rome,* 2v. (1906–07); *Abraham Lincoln* (1909); *The Little Gingerbread Man* (1910); *George Palmer Putnam* (1912); *Memories of My Youth* (1914); *Memories of a Publisher* (1915); *Some Memories of the Civil War* (1924); etc. In 1886 he organized anew the American Publishers Copyright League, originally organized by George Palmer Putnam in 1851. He became the head of G. P. Putnam's Sons, publishers.

PUTNAM, GEORGE ISRAEL (1860–May 4, 1937). Journalist, novelist. *In Blue Uniform* (1893); *On the Offensive* (1894). On staff, the *New York Times;* the *Claremont* (N.H.) *Advocate and Daily Eagle.*

PUTNAM, GEORGE PALMER (Feb. 7, 1814–Dec. 20, 1872); b. Brunswick, Me. Publisher. He began his bookselling career with G. W. Bleecker in New York, and with Daniel and Jonathan Leavit, 1828–38. In 1851 he organized the American Publishers' Copyright League. In 1866 he founded the publishing firm of G. P. Putnam & Son. He was a lifelong friend and publisher of Washington Irving. *See* George Haven Putnam's *A Memoir of George Palmer Putnam,* 2v. (1903); Eben Putnam's *The Putnam Lineage* (1907).

PUTNAM, GEORGE PALMER (Sept. 7, 1887–Jan. 4, 1950); b. Rye, N.Y. Publisher, author. *The Southland of North America* (1913); *In The Oregon Country* (1915); *The Smiting of the Rock* (under pen name "Palmer Bend," 1918); *Andree: The Record of a Tragic Adventure* (1930); *Soaring Wings* (1939); etc. President, Knickerbocker Press, and treasurer, G. P. Putnam's Sons, 1919–30.

PUTNAM, HERBERT (Sept. 20, 1861–Aug. 14, 1955); b. New York. Librarian. Minneapolis Public Library, 1887–91; Boston Public Library, 1895–99; Librarian of Congress, 1899–1939.

PUTNAM, [Howard] PHELPS (July 9, 1894–1948); b. Boston, Mass. Poet. Author. *Trine* (1927); *The Five Seasons* (1931).

PUTNAM, J. Wesley. Pen name of Harry Sinclair Drago.

PUTNAM, JOHN BISHOP (July 17, 1847–Oct. 7, 1915); b. Staten Island, N.Y. Publisher, author. *Authors and Publishers* (1890); *A Norwegian Ramble* (1902); etc. Joined staff of G. P. Putnam's Sons, in 1868. President, Knickerbocker Press.

PUTNAM, MARY TRAIL SPENCE LOWELL (Dec. 3, 1810–1898); b. Boston, Mass. Author. *Records of an Obscure Man* (1861); *Tragedy of Errors* (poem, 1862); *Tragedy of Success* (poem, 1862); *Memoir of William Lowell Putnam* (1862); *Fifteen Days* (1966); etc.

PUTNAM, NINA WILCOX (Mrs. Christian Eliot) (Nov. 28, 1888–Mar. 8, 1962); b. New Haven, Conn. Author. *In Search of Arcady* (1912); *The Impossible Boy* (1913); *Esmerelda* (1918); *West Broadway* (1921); *Easy* (1924); *The Making of an American Humorist* (1929); *Laughing Through* (1930); *Paris Love* (1931); *The Inner Voice* (1941); *Lynn, Cover Girl* (1950); etc.

PUTNAM, PATER BROCK (June 11, 1920–); b. in Georgia. Author. *Keep Your Head Up, Mr. Putnam* (1952); *Seven Britons in Imperial Russia* (1952); *Cast Off the Darkness* (1957); *Triumph of Seeing* (1962).

PUTNAM, RUTH (July 18, 1856–Feb. 12, 1931); b. Yonkers, N.Y. Author. *William, Prince of Orange: The Moderate Man of the Sixteenth Century*, 2v. (1895); *William the Silent, Prince of Orange and the Revolt of the Netherlands* (1911); *Alsace and Lorraine from Caesar to Kaiser* (1915); *Life and Letters of Mary Putnam Jacobi* (1925); etc. Co-editor: *Historic New York* (1897–99).

PUTNAM, SALLIE A. BROCK. Author. *Richmond during the War* (1867); *Kenneth, My King* (1873); etc. Editor: *The Southern Amaranth* (1869).

PUTNAM, SAMUEL (1892–Jan. 17, 1950); b. Rossville, Ill. Translator, author. *François Rabelais: Man of the Renaissance* (1928); *The World of Jean Bosschère* (1932); *Marguerite of Navarre* (1935); *Paris Was Our Mistress* (1947); etc. Translator: *The Extant Works of Rabelais* (1929); *Don Quixote de la Mancha* by Cervantes (1949); and works by Aretino, Mauriac, Cocteau, Pirandello, etc.

Putnam's Monthly Magazine. New York. Founded Jan., 1853, by G. P. Putnam & Co. Editors: Charles F. Briggs (with George William Curtis and Parke Godwin, associates) 1853–57; Edmund Clarence Stedman, 1869–70; Parke Godwin, 1870; Jeanette Gilder and Joseph B. Gilder, 1906–10. The essays of George William Curtis which appeared in the magazine formed the basis of his *Potiphar Papers* and *Prue and I.* Longfellow, Thoreau, Melville, Lowell, Cooper, Charles Eliot Norton, Henry James, Bayard Taylor, and Charles Dudley Warner were among the contributors. Merged with *Emerson's United States Magazine* in 1857, and with *Scribner's Monthly* in 1870. It was revived in 1906 and took the title *Putnam's Monthly and the Critic.* In 1910 it was absorbed by the *Atlantic Monthly.*

Putnam's Sons, G.P. New York City. Publishers. In 1807 Charles Wiley opened a bookshop in New York and his son John branched out into publishing, taking George Long as publisher. In 1833 George Palmer Putnam entered the firm, and in 1840 the firm of Wiley & Putnam was formed. The partnership was dissolved in 1848. George Haven Putnam entered his father's business in 1866 to form G. P. Putnam & Son. Bishop Putnam followed in 1871, and Irving Putnam in 1872, the year of George Palmer Putnam's death. Edmund W. Putnam (1882–1940) was a later member of the firm. In 1872 the name was changed to G. P. Putnam's Sons. Walter J. Minton is now president. In 1853 George Palmer Putnam had founded *Putnam's Magazine.* In 1874 the firm established the Knickerbocker Press, which moved its plant to New Rochelle, N.Y., in 1891. A bookstore has always been an important adjunct to the firm. Washington Irving, a friend of the Putnams, was one of their successful authors. Two popular series, *The Stories of the Nation*, and *The Heroes of the Nation*, bore the Putnam imprint. Berkeley Publishing Corp., founded in 1954, is an affiliate. See *An American Reader*, ed. by Burton Rascoe (1938).

Put's Original California Songster. (1854). Popular songs of the gold-rush era.

PUZO, MARIO (1920–); Novelist. *The Fortunate Pilgrim* (1964); *The Runaway Summer of Davie Shaw* (1966); *The Godfather* (1969).

PYE, LUCIAN WILMOT (Oct. 21, 1921–); b. Shansi, China. Educator, author. *Guerrilla Communism in Malaya* (1956); *Politics, Personality and Nation Building* (1961); etc. Co-author: *The Politics of the Developing Areas* (1960); *The Emerging Nations* (1961). Editor: *Communications and Political Development* (1963). Prof. political science, Massachusetts Institute of Technology, since 1960.

PYLE, ERNIE (Ernest Taylor) (Aug. 3, 1900–Apr. 18, 1945); b. Dana, Ind. Journalist, author. *Ernie Pyle in England* (1941); *Here is Your War* (1943); *Brave Men* (1944); *Last Chapter* (1946). Syndicated columnist from 1935; war correspondent for Scripps-Howard newspapers from 1942 (Pulitzer Prize for correspondence, 1944). See G. Miller's *The Story of Ernie Pyle* (1950).

PYLE, HOWARD (Mar. 5, 1853–Nov. 9, 1911); b. Wilmington, Del. Artist, illustrator, author. *The Merry Adventures of Robin Hood* (1883); *Within the Capes* (1885); *Pepper and Salt* (1886); *The Wonder Clock* (1888); *Otto of the Silver Hand* (1888); *The Rose of Paradise* (1888); *Men of Iron* (1892); *Twilight Land* (1895); *The Story of Jack Ballister's Fortunes* (1895); *The Garden Behind The Moon* (1895); *The Ghost of Captain Brand* (1896); *Rejected of Men* (1903); *Stolen Treasure* (1907); *The Ruby of Kishmoor* (1908); *Howard Pyle's Book of Pirates* (1921); etc. See W. S. Morse and Gertrude Brinckle's *Howard Pyle* (1921); C. D. Abbott's *Howard Pyle* (1925).

PYLE, KATHARINE (d. Feb. 19, 1938); b. Wilmington, Del. Illustrator, author. *The Rabbit Witch* (1897); *The Counterpane Fairy* (1898); *Stories in Prose and Verse* (1899); *The Christmas Angel* (1900); *In the Green Forest* (1902); *Nancy Rutledge* (1906); *Tales from Many Lands* (1911); *Tales of Wonder and Magic* (1920); *History of Delaware* (1924); etc.

PYNCHON, THOMAS (May 8, 1937–). Novelist. *V* (1963); *The Crying of Lot 49* (1966).

Pynson Printers. New York. Founded 1923. Directed by Elmer Adler, 1923–40.

PYRNELLE, LOUISE CLARKE (b. 1852); b. "Ittabena," near Uniontown, Ala. Author. *Diddie, Dumps, and Tot; or, Plantation Child-Life* (1882); *The Marriage of Aunt Flora* (1895); *Miss Li'l' Tweetty* (1907).

Q

Quabbin: The Story of a Small Town. By Francis H. Underwood (1893). Intimate and homely biography of a New England town, based on Enfield, Mass., the author's birthplace.

"Quabi, or the Virtues of Nature, an Indian Tale." Poem by Sarah Wentworth Apthorp Morton (1790).

Quad, M. Pen name of Charles Bertrand Lewis.

Quadrangle Books. New York. Publishers. Founded 1959. Publishes nonfiction, college texts, and paperbacks. A subsidiary of *The New York Times.*

QUAIFE, MILO MILTON (Oct. 6, 1880–Sept. 1, 1959); b. Nashua, Ia. Author. *Chicago and the Old Northwest* (1913); *The Development of Chicago, 1674–1914* (1916); *Wisconsin: Its History and Its People, 1634–1924*, 4v. (1924); *The Kingdom of Saint James: A Narrative of the Mormons* (1930); *Checagou: From Indian Wigwam to Modern City, 1673–1835* (1933); *Lake Michigan* (1944); *The Life of John Wendell*

Anderson (1950); etc. Editor of many early American travels, narratives; etc. Editor, annual volumes of the *Lakeside Classics,* from 1916. Supt., Wisconsin State Historical Society, 1914–20, editor, 1920–22. Secretary and editor, Burton Historical Collection, Detroit Public Library.

Quaker City; or, The Monks of Monk Hall, The. Story by George Lippard (1844). An exposé of vice in Philadelphia.

"Quaker Graveyard in Nantucket, The." Poem by Robert Lowell, from *Lord Weary's Castle* (1944).

QUANTRILL, WILLIAM CLARKE (July 31, 1837–June 6, 1865); b. Canal Dover, O. Guerrilla chieftain who raided Kansas and Missouri. *See* William E. Connelley's *Quantrill and the Border Wars* (1910); J. N. Edwards's *Noted Guerrillas* (1877); John McCorkle's *Three Years with Quantrill* (1914); Kit Dalton's *Under the Black Flag* (1914); Wiley Britton's *The Civil War on the Border,* 2v. (1890–99).

Quare Women, The. Novel by Lucy Furman (1923). Social workers in the mountains of Kentucky encounter situations of tragedy and humor.

QUARLES, BENJAMIN ARTHUR (Jan. 23, 1904–); b. Boston, Mass. Educator, author. *Frederick Douglass* (1948); *The Negro in the Civil War* (1953); *The Negro in the American Revolution* (1961); *Lincoln and the Negro* (1962); *The Negro in the Making of America* (1964); *The Negro American: A Documentary Story* (with Leslie H. Fishel, Jr., 1967). Editor: *Narrative of the Life of Frederick Douglass* (1960). Prof. history, Morgan State College, Baltimore, since 1953.

"Quarry, The." Poem by William Vaughn Moody (1899). An expression of pride in America at her refusal to permit the dismemberment of China in 1899.

Quarter, a Magazine of the Arts. Utica, N.Y. Quarterly. Founded 1962. Occasionally publishes translations from Romance, Germanic, and Russian languages.

Quarter Race in Kentucky, A. By William Trotter Porter (1846). Written in the backwoods type of humor found in Longstreet's *Georgia Scenes.*

Quarterly Review of Literature. Chapel Hill, N.C.; New Haven, Conn., Annandale-on-Hudson, N.Y. Founded 1944. Edited by Warren Carrier and T. Weiss until 1946, and by T. Weiss after 1946.

QUAYLE, WILLIAM ALFRED (June 25, 1860–Mar. 9, 1925); b. Parkville, Mo. Methodist bishop, educator, author. *The Poet's Poet, and Other Essays* (1897); *A Hero and Some Other Folk* (1899); *Books and Life* (1901); *The Prairie and the Sea* (1905); *Lowell and the Christian Faith* (1906); *The Pastor-Preacher* (autobiography, 1910); *With Earth and Sky* (1922); etc. Classics dept., Baker University, 1883–91; president, 1890–94.

Queechy. Novel by Susan Warner (1852). The scene is Queechy, Vt. It is the story of an orphan, Fleda Ringgan, who survives hardships and marries Carleton Rossiter. It was a best seller of the day.

Queed. Novel by Henry Sydnor Harrison (1911). A bizarre novel about the eccentric and scholarly Mr. Queed, who wants to be an athlete and who takes lessons from Klinker, the pugilist. His love affairs are both comic and serious.

Queen, Ellery. Pen name of Manfred B. Lee and Frederic Dannay.

Queer Books. By Edmund Lester Pearson (1928). A study of curious oddities in literature.

Quentin, Patrick. Pen name of Hugh Callingham Wheeler.

Question of Our Speech, The. By Henry James (1905). An address before the graduating class of Bryn Mawr College, June 8, 1905, which was first published in the *Booklovers Magazine,* Aug., 1905.

QUICK, DOROTHY (1900–Mar. 15, 1962); Author. *Spears into Life* (1938); *To What Strange Altar* (1940); *Variations on a Theme* (1947); *One Night in Holyrood* (play, 1949); *Interludes* (1953); *Cry in the Night* (1957); *The Doctor Looks at Murder* (1959); *Enchantment* (1961); etc.

QUICK, HERBERT (Oct. 23, 1861–May 10, 1925); b. Grundy Co. Ia. Author. *In the Fairyland of America* (1901); *Aladdin & Co.* (1904); *Virginia of the Air Lanes* (1909); *Vandemark's Folly* (1921); *The Hawkeye* (1923); *The Invisible Woman* (1924); *One Man's Life* (autobiography, 1925); *Mississippi Steamboatin'* (1926). Editor, *La Follette's Magazine,* 1908–09; *Farm and Fireside,* 1909–16.

Quick or the Dead, The. Novel by Amelie Rives (1889), first published serially in *Lippincott's Magazine,* 1888. Barbara Pomfret's emotional struggle, when faced with the necessity of choosing between loyalty to her dead husband and a growing love for a man who strongly resembles him, is the psychological problem.

Quid Mirror, The. Anonymous book (1806). Sarcastic sketches of George Logan, Thomas M'Kean, William T. Donaldson and other prominent Philadelphians.

Quiet Cities. By Joseph Hergesheimer (1928). Stories of Pittsburgh, Natchez, New Orleans, Lexington, Albany, and Boston.

QUIGG, HORACE DASHER (Nov. 22, 1911–); b. Dennison, Minn. Journalist, author. *Gemini—America's Historic Walk in Space* (1965). Co-author: *Four Days* (1964).

QUIGLEY, CARROLL (Nov. 9, 1910–); Historian. *Evolution of Civilizations* (1961); *Tragedy and Hope: The World in Our Time* (1965). Prof. history, Georgetown University.

Quilibet, Philip. Pen name of George Edward Pond.

Quill, The. Chicago, Ill. Monthly. Founded 1912. Published by Sigma Delta Chi, professional journalistic fraternity. Features material for writers, editors, and publishers of press, radio, and television.

QUILLEN, ROBERT (Mar. 25, 1887–Dec. 19, 1948); b. Syracuse, Kan. Editor, author. *One Man's Religion* (1923); *The Path Wharton Found* (1924). Editorial writer, *Saturday Evening Post, Baltimore Sun,* etc. Creator of comic features "Aunt Het" and "Willie Willis."

Quin, Dan. Pen name of Alfred Henry Lewis.

QUINCY, EDMUND (Feb. 1, 1808–May 17, 1877); b. Boston, Mass. Reformer, editor of anti-slavery journals, author. *Wensley: A Story without a Moral* (1854); *The Haunted Adjutant, and Other Stories* (1885); *Life of Josiah Quincy* (with Eliza Susan Quincy, 1867).

QUINCY, JOSIAH (Feb. 4, 1772–July 1, 1864); b. Braintree, Mass. Reformer, educator, author. *The History of Harvard University,* 2v. (1840); *The History of the Boston Athenaeum* (1851); *Municipal History of Boston* (1852); *Memoir of John Quincy Adams* (1858); etc. President, Harvard University, 1829–45.

QUINCY, JOSIAH PHILLIPS (Nov. 28, 1829–Oct. 31, 1910); b. Boston, Mass. Poet, historian, author. *Lyteria* (poem, 1854); *Charicles* (poem, 1856); *Figures of the Past* (1883); *The Peckster Professorship* (1888). He was the "Little Josiah" of Bronson Alcott's *Conversations with Children on the Gospels,* and of Elizabeth Peabody's *Record of a School.*

Quincy Adams Sawyer. Novel by Charles Felton Pidgin (1900). Story of the son of a Boston millionaire who goes to Mason's Corner to regain his health. He joins in the simple life of the place and marries Alice Pettengill, local poet. Obadiah Stout, singing-master, is a leading character.

QUINE, WILLARD VAN ORMAN (June 25, 1908–); b. Akron, O. Philosopher, educator, author. *A System of Logistic* (1934); *Mathematical Logic* (1940); *Elementary Logic* (1941); *Methods of Logic* (1950); *From a Logical Point of View* (1953); *Word and Object* (1960); *Set Theory and Its Logic* (1963); *The Ways of Paradox* (1966); etc. Prof. philosophy, Harvard University, since 1941.

QUINN, ARTHUR HOBSON (Feb. 9, 1875–Oct. 16, 1960); b. Philadelphia, Pa. Educator, author. *Pennsylvania Stories* (1899); *A History of the American Drama from the Beginning to the Civil War* (1923); *A History of the American Drama from the Civil War to the Present Day,* 2v. (1927); *The Soul of America* (1932); *American Fiction: An Historical and Critical Survey* (1936); *Edgar Allan Poe* (1941); *The Establishment of National Literature* (1951); etc. Editor: *Representative American Plays* (1917); *Emerson's Essays* (1920); *Contemporary American Plays* (1923); *The Literature of America,* 2v. (with A. C. Baugh and W. D. Howe, 1929); *Edgar Allan Poe Letters and Documents in the Enoch Pratt Free Library* (with Richard H. Hart, 1941); *A Treasury of Edith Wharton* (1950); etc.

QUINN, [Elizabeth] VERNON (Jan. 5, 1881–Mar. 21, 1962); b. Waldorf, Md. Author. *Beautiful America* (1923); *Beautiful Mexico* (1924); *Beautiful Canada* (1925); *Roots: Their Place in Life and Legend* (1938); *Picture Map Geography of Canada and Alaska* (1944); *Pageant of the Seven Seas* (1948); *Picture Map Geography of Africa* (1952); etc.

Quinnebasset series. Books for girls, by "Sophie May" (Rebecca S. Clarke), 6v. (1871–81.

QUINT, WILDER DWIGHT (Nov. 15, 1863–Jan. 4, 1936); b. Salem, Mass. Journalist, author. *The Story of Dartmouth* (1914). Co-author with George Tilton Richardson, using the joint pen name "Dwight Tilton": *Miss Petticoats* (1902); *On Satan's Mount* (1903); *My Lady Laughter* (1904); *The Golden Greyhound* (1906); etc.; also, using the joint pen name "Charles Eustace Merriman": *Letters from a Son to His Self-Made Father* (1903); *A Self-Made Man's Wife: Her Letters to Her Son* (1905). On staff, the *Boston Adventurer;* the *Boston Traveler;* the *Boston Post;* and *Boston News;* etc.

QUINTANILLA, LUIS (June 13, 1895–); b. Santander, Sp. Artist, illustrator. Author: *Latin America Speaks* (1943); *Franco's Black Spain* (1946); *Pan Americanism and Democracy* (1952); etc.

QUIRK, LESLIE W. (May 12, 1882–); b. Alta, Ia. Editor, author. *The Fourth Down* (1912); *Freshmen Friends* (1913); *The Boy Scouts on Crusade* (1919); *Into Thin Air* (with Horatio Winslow, 1929); *Jimmy Goes to War* (1931); etc. Editor, *Editor Magazine,* 1903–08.

QUISENBERRY, ANDERSON CHENAULT (Oct. 26, 1850–Dec. 4, 1921); b. near Winchester, Ky. Editor, author. *Life and Times of Humphrey Marshall, the Elder* (1891); *Revolutionary Soldiers in Kentucky* (1896); *Zachary Taylor and the Mexican War* (1911). Editor, *Winchester Democrat,* 1870–73; *Lexington Transcript,* 1881–83; *Lexington Press,* 1883–85; founder, *Winchester Sun,* 1878.

Quodlibet. Story by John P. Kennedy (1840). A satire on Jacksonian democracy.

R

R. E. Lee. By Douglas Southall Freeman, 4v. (1934). Biography of General Robert E. Lee. Pulitzer Prize for American biography, 1935.

RABINOWITCH, EUGENE (Apr. 27, 1901–); b. St. Petersburg, Rus. Physical chemist, author. *Minutes to Midnight* (1950); *Dawn of a New Age* (1964); etc.

RABINOWITZ, SOLOMON J. (Feb. 18, 1859–May 13, 1916); b. Pereyaslev, Rus. Author, under pen name "Sholom Aleichem," of works in Yiddish. *Stempenyu* (1913); *Jewish Children* (1920); *The Old Country* (1946); *Inside Kasrilevke* (1948); *Tevye's Daughters* (1949); *Wandering Star* (1952); *The Adventures of Mottel, the Cantor's Son* (1953); *The Great Fair* (1955); etc., all English translations.

Rachel Dyer. Novel by John Neal (1828). The background is the witchcraft delusion in New England.

RADIN, EDWARD D. (d. Mar. 28, 1966). Author. *Twelve Against the Law* (1946); *Headline Crimes of the Year* (1952); *Lizzie Borden: The Untold Story* (1961); etc.

Radio Book Programs. Since World War II, and especially since the advent of Frequency Modulation (FM) broadcasting, there have been many programs devoted to books and authors. Some are conducted by a critic who reviews current books or interviews authors; others consist of talks by critics or authors, or readings by authors. Among the best-known programs have been: "Backgrounds of Literature" on WCBS, New York, moderated by John Dando; the Kenneth Banghart program on WCBS, covering books in conjunction with *Inside Books Newsletter* and including interviews of authors; "Books" on KPFA-FM, Berkeley, Calif., with Kenneth Rexroth reviewing books; "The Readers' Almanac" on WNYC, New York, conducted by Warren Bower; "Caspar Citron" on WNTA, Newark, N.J.; "Radio's Adventures in Bookland" transcribed over many stations, coast to coast, and edited by Scott Anderson, featuring book news; "Spoken Words" on WNYC, New York, directed by Martin Bush, which programs recordings of books and authors; "Book Briefs," conducted on KFUO, St. Louis, Mo.; "The Book Shelf," conducted on WSUI, Iowa City, Ia.; "The Barry Farber Show," featured on WOR, New York City; Jack D. Summerfield's program of reviews, interviews, and discussions held on WRVR-FM, New York City; and WFBM "News" which includes reviews on WFBM-AM and -FM, Indianapolis, Ind. The Pacifica group of listener-supported radio stations (KPFA-FM, Berkeley, Cal., KPFK-FM, North Hollywood, Cal., KPFT-FM, Houston, Tex., and WBAI-FM, New York City) have developed various kinds of book programs, including author interviews, dramatizations of books, readings from classics, recently published, and unpublished writings, etc. In the 1970's WBAI-FM experimented with audience reviews of books, consisting of taped materials sent in by listeners.

RAE, JOHN (July 4, 1882–Oct. 18, 1963); b. Jersey City, N.J. Artist, author. *The Big Family* (1916); *New Adventures of "Alice"* (1918); *Lucy Locket* (1927); etc.

RAFFERTY, MAX (May 7, 1917–   ); b. New Orleans, La. Educationist, author. *Practices and Trends in School Administration* (1961); *Suffer, Little Children* (1962); *What They Are Doing to Your Children* (1964).

RAFINESQUE, CONSTANTINE SAMUEL (Oct. 22, 1783–Sept. 18, 1840); b. Constantinople, Turk. Naturalist, author. *A History of Kentucky* (1824); *A Life of Travels and Researches in North America and South Europe* (1836); etc. See R. E. Call's *The Life and Writings of Rafinesque* (1895).

RAGAN, SAMUEL TALMADGE (Dec. 13, 1915–); b. Berea, N.C. Newspaper editor, author. *The Tree in the Far Pasture* (poems, 1964); *The Democratic Party: Its Aims and Purposes* (1964); *Free Press and Fair Trial* (1967); etc. Editor, *Raleigh News and Observer.*

RAGATZ, LOWELL JOSEPH (July 21, 1897–); b. Prarie du Sac, Wis. Educator, historian. *The Old Plantation System in the British Caribbean* (1925); *The Fall of the Planter Class in the British Caribbean* (1928); *March of Empire* (1948); *The Spud Papers* (1952); *Early Philatelic Forgeries* (1953); *Old*

Plantation System in the British West Indies (1955); *The New United States* (1962). Compiler: *Colonial Studies in the United States During the Twentieth Century* (1932); *A List of Books and Articles on Colonial Overseas Expansion Published in the United States, 1900–1935* (1938); *A Bibliography for the Study of European History 1815–1939,* 4v. (1957–60); etc. History dept., Ohio State University, since 1949.

RAGO, HENRY ANTHONY (Oct. 5, 1915–); b. Chicago, Ill. Educator, author. *The Philosophy of Esthetic Individualism* (1941); *The Travelers* (1949); *A Sky of Late Summer* (1963); *Praise of Comedy, A Discourse* (1963). Editor: *Poems in Folio,* with S. Kunitz and R. Wilbur, 1956–57. Prof., theology and literature, University of Chicago, since 1967. Editor, *Poetry,* since 1955.

RAGSDALE, LULAH [Tallulah] (deceased); b. in Lawrence Co., Miss. Poet, novelist. *Miss Dulcie from Dixie* (1917); *The Thorn* (1926); *If I See Green* (poems, 1929); etc.

RAHV, PHILIP (Mar. 10, 1908–); b. Kupin, Rus. Editor, critic. *Image and Idea* (1949). Editor: *The Short Novels of Tolstoy* (1946); *The Partisan Reader: Ten Years of the Partisan Review, 1934–44* (with William Phillips, 1946); *The Discovery of Europe: The Story of American Experience in the Old World* (1947); *Great Russian Short Novels* (1951); *Modern Occasions* (1966); *Literature and the Sixth Sense* (1969); etc. Co-founder (1933) and co-editor, *Partisan Review.*

Railroad Magazine. New York. Founded Oct., 1906. Merged Jan., 1919, with *Argosy All-Story Weekly.* Revived Dec., 1929. Name changed to *Railroad Stories,* Mar., 1932; and to *Railroad Magazine,* Sept., 1937. James W. Earp has written many stories for it.

Raimond, C. E. Pen name of Elizabeth Robins.

RAINE, NORMAN REILLY (June 23, 1895–); b. Wilkes-Barre, Pa. Author. *Hangman's Whip* (prod. 1933); "Tugboat Annie," "Mr. Gallup and the Dandy Man," and other series published in the *Saturday Evening Post;* etc. Also screenplays. Academy Award for screenplay *The Life of Emile Zola.*

RAINE, WILLIAM McLEOD (June 22, 1871–July 25, 1954); b. London. Novelist. *The Daughter of Raasay* (1902); *Wyoming* (1908); *Bucky O'Connor* (1910); *A Texas Ranger* (1911); *A Daughter of the Dons* (1914); *The Yukon Trail* (1917); *Iron Heart* (1923); *Colorado* (1928); *Famous Sheriffs & Western Outlaws* (1929); *Cattle* (with Will C. Barnes, 1930); *Border Breed* (1935); *Riders of the Rim Rocks* (1940); *Clattering Hoofs* (1946); *Saddletramp* (1950); *Dry Bones in the Valley* (1953); etc.

RAINER, DACHINE (1921–   ). Author. *Outside Time* (1948); *Room at the Inn* (1956); *Uncomfortable Inn* (1960); etc. Editor: *Prison Etiquette* (with Holley Cantine, 1950).

Raintree County. Novel by Ross Lockridge (1948). Epic novel depicting the events of a single day, July 4, 1892, in the life of Johnny Shawnessy of Indiana, and his recollections of the past.

Raleigh News and Observer. Raleigh, N.C. Newspaper. The *Daily Carolinian,* founded 1871, was followed in 1872 by the *Daily News.* The *Observer* was founded in 1876, by Laurence Saunders and Peter M. Hale. Saunders was editor until 1879. The *News* and the *Observer* merged in 1880. Jonathan Daniels is editor; Guy Munger edits book reviews. *See* the *Raleigh Times.*

Raleigh Times. Raleigh, N.C. Newspaper. Founded 1879, as the *Evening Visitor.* Became the *Raleigh Times-Visitor* in 1897, and the *Raleigh Times* in 1901. Merged with the *Raleigh News and Observer;* the *News and Observer* appears mornings and Sunday; the *Times,* evenings except Sunday. Herbert E. O'Keef is editor.

Raley, Rowena. Pen name of Johnston McCulley.

RALL, HARRIS FRANKLIN (Feb. 23, 1870–Oct. 13, 1964); b. Council Bluffs, Ia. Methodist clergyman, educator, author. *The Life of Jesus* (1917); *The Meaning of God* (1925); *Contemporary American Theology* (1933); *Christianity* (1940); *According to Paul* (1944); *Religion as Salvation* (1953). Prof. Garett Biblical Institute, since 1915.

RALPH, JAMES (c. 1695–Jan. 24, 1762); b. in New Jersey. Poet, playwright. *The Tempest* (poems, 1727); *Miscellaneous Poems* (1729), including *Night, Zeuma, Clarinda,* and *The Muses' Address to the King; The Fashionable Lady* (prod. 1730); *The Use and Abuse of Parliaments* (1744); *The Case of Authors by Profession or Trade* (1758); etc. Editor: *Miscellaneous Poems, by Several Hands* (1729). His plays were all produced in London. *See* Benjamin Franklin's *Autobiography* (1868).

RALPH, JULIAN (May 27, 1853–Jan. 20, 1903); b. New York. Journalist, author. *The Sun's German Barber* (1883); *On Canada's Frontier* (1892); *Our Great West* (1893); *Dixie; or, Southern Scenes and Sketches* (1895); *People We Pass* (1896); *A Prince of Georgia, and Other Tales* (1899); *The Millionaires* (1902); *War's Brightest Side: The Story of "The Friend" Newspaper* (1901); *The Making of a Journalist* (1903); etc. On staff, *New York Sun,* 1875–96.

RAMA RAU, SANTHA (Jan. 24, 1923–   ); b. Madras, India. Author. *Home to India* (1945); *East of Home* (1950); *This Is India* (1953); *View to the Southeast* (1955); *Remember the House* (1957); *My Russian Journey* (1959); *Gifts of Passage* (1961); *A Passage to India* (play, 1960); *The Adventuress* (1970).

Ramona. Novel by Helen Jackson (1885). Published serially in *The Outlook,* 1884. Popular story of California in the days of the Spanish ranchers. Ramona, daughter of Señora Moreno, marries Alessandro, an Indian, against her mother's wishes. The encroaching American settlers drive the couple from place to place, and the story ends in tragedy.

Ramparts. San Francisco, Cal. Monthly. Founded 1962. Edited by Robert Scheer. Introduced as a periodical expressing Catholic social conscience, it soon divested itself of all religious connections and espoused an aggressively radical political and social viewpoint. Noted for exposés of established government and business groups. *Ramparts* is also noted for its modernist graphic layout.

RAMSAY, DAVID (Apr. 2, 1749–May 8, 1815); b. Lancaster, Pa. Physician, author. *The History of the American Revolution,* 2v. (1789); *The Life of George Washington* (1807); *The History of South Carolina,* 2v. (1809); *History of the United States,* 3v. (1816–17); *Universal History Americanized,* 9v. (1819).

RAMSAY, ROBERT LEE (Dec. 14, 1880–1953); b. Sumter, S.C. Educator, author. *Introduction to a Survey of Missouri Place-Names* (1934). Editor: *Short Stories of America* (1921); *Poems by Missouri Students* (1935); *Mark Twain Lexicon* (with F. G. Emberson, 1938); etc. English dept., University of Missouri, from 1907.

RAMSAYE, TERRY (Nov. 2, 1885–Aug. 19, 1954); b. Tonganoxie, Kan. Editor, author. *A Million and One Nights: A History of the Motion Picture,* 2v. (1926). Editor: *Fame: Annual Audit of the Personalities of Screen, Radio and Television* (1950). Editor, the *Motion Picture Herald.*

RAMSEY, R[obert] PAUL (Dec. 10, 1913–   ); b. Mendenhall, Miss. Educator, author. *Basic Christian Ethics* (1950); *War and the Christian Conscience* (1961); *Christian Ethics and the Sit-In* (1961); *Nine Modern Moralists* (1962); *Who Speaks for the Church?* (1967); *War and Political Ethics* (1968); etc. Prof. religion, Princeton University, since 1954.

RANCK, EDWIN CARTY (July 18, 1879–); b. Lexington, Ky. Author. *History of Covington, Kentucky* (1903); *Poems for Pale People* (1906); *The Night Riders* (prod. 1912); *We the People* (prod. 1913); *The Mountain* (prod. 1913); *The Doughboy's Book* (1925); etc.

RAND, AYN (1908–); b. Petrograd, Rus. Author. *The Night of January 16th* (prod., 1935); *We, the Living* (1936); *Anthem* (1938); *The Fountainhead* (1943); *Atlas Shrugged* (1957); *For the New Intellectual* (1961); *The Virtue of Selfishness* (1965); *Capitalism: The Unknown Ideal* (1966); *Introduction to Objectivist Epistemology* (1967); etc. Editor, *The Objectivist,* since 1962.

RAND, BENJAMIN (July 17, 1856–Nov. 9, 1934); b. Canning, N.S. Librarian, author. *Rev. Aaron Cleveland* (1888). Editor: *The Life, Unpublished Letters and Philosophical Regimen of Anthony, Earl of Shaftesbury* (1900); *Berkeley and Percival* (1904); *The Correspondence of John Locke and Edward Clarke* (1927). Compiler: *Modern Classical Philosophers* (1907); *The Classical Moralists* (1909); *The Classical Psychologists* (1912); etc. Librarian, philosophy dept., Harvard University.

RAND, CHRISTOPHER (Feb. 14, 1912–   ); b. New York. Author. *Hong Kong* (1952); *A Nostalgia for Camels* (1957); *The Puerto Ricans* (1958); *Grecian Calendar* (1962); *Christmas in Bethlehem* (1963); *Cambridge, U.S.A.* (1964); *Mountains and Water* (1965); *Los Angeles* (1967). Writer, *New Yorker* magazine.

RAND, EDWARD AUGUSTUS (1837–Oct. 5, 1903); b. Portsmouth, N.H. Author. *Christmas Jack* (1878); *The Tent in the Notch* (1881); *Little Brown Top* (1883); *Sailor Boy Bob* (1888); etc.

RAND, EDWARD KENNARD (Dec. 20, 1871–Oct. 28, 1945); b. Boston, Mass. Educator, editor, author. *Ovid and His Influence* (1925); *Founders of the Middle Ages* (1928); *A Survey of the Manuscripts of Tours,* 2v. (1929); *In Quest of Virgil's Birthplace* (1930); *The Magical Art of Virgil* (1931); *A Toast to Horace* (1937); *Building of External Rome* (1943); etc. Editor, *Speculum,* 1926–28. Latin dept., Harvard University, from 1909–42.

RAND, FRANK PRENTICE (Nov. 8, 1889–); b. Worcester, Mass. Author. *Tiamat* (1917); *John Epps* (1921); *Phi Sigma Kappa: A History* (1922); *Phi Beta Kappa: A History, 1873–1923* (1923); *Yesterdays at Massachusetts State College, 1863–1933* (1933); *Heart o' Town* (poems, 1945); *Wordsworth's Mariner Brother* (1966); etc. English dept., Massachusetts State College, since 1914.

Rand, McNally and Company. Chicago, Ill. Publishers. Founded 1864, by Andrew McNally and William H. Rand. Noted for its publication of atlases and geographies, and, more recently, children's books. Andrew McNally III is president.

RANDALL, HENRY STEPHENS (May 3, 1811–Aug. 14, 1876); b. Brookfield, N.Y. Agriculturist, author. *The Life of Thomas Jefferson,* 3v. (1858).

RANDALL, J[ames] G[arfield] (June 24, 1881–Feb. 20, 1953); b. Indianapolis, Ind. Educator, author. *Constitutional Problems Under Lincoln* (1926); *The Civil War and Reconstruction* (1937); *Lincoln the President: Springfield to Gettysburg,* 2v. (1945); *Lincoln and the South* (1946); *Lincoln the Liberal Statesman* (1947); etc. Author of many articles on Abraham Lincoln and his period. History dept., University of Illinois, from 1920; prof., from 1930.

RANDALL, JAMES RYDER (Jan. 1, 1839–Jan. 14, 1908); b. Baltimore, Md. Poet, journalist. *Maryland, My Maryland, and Other Poems* (1908); *The Poems of James Ryder Randall* (1910), ed. by Matthew Page Andrews. His best-known poem was "Maryland, My Maryland."

RANDALL, JOHN HERMAN, JR. (Feb. 14, 1899–); b. Grand Rapids, Mich. Educator, author. *The Problem of Group Responsibility* (1922); *The Making of the Modern Mind* (1926); *Our Changing Civilization* (1929); *Philosophy: An Introduction* (with Justus Buchler, 1942); *Readings in Philosophy* (with others, 1946); *Nature and Historical Experience* (1957); *The Role of Knowledge in Western Religion* (1958); *Aristotle* (1960); *The Career of Philosophy: From the Middle Ages to Enlightenment* (1962); Vol. II, *From the German Enlightenment to the Age of Darwin* (1965); *Plato, Dramatist of the Life of Reason* (1969). Joint editor, *Journal of Philosophy.* Philosophy dept., Columbia University, since 1925.

RANDALL, JOHN WITT (1813–1892). Author. *Consolations of Solitude* (1856); *Poems of Nature and Life* (1899).

RANDALL, RUTH [Painter] (Mrs. J. G. Randall) (Nov. 1, 1892–); b. Salem, Va. Author. *Mary Lincoln: Biography of a Marriage* (1953); *Lincoln's Sons* (1956); *The Courtship of Mr. Lincoln* (1957); *I, Mary* (1959); *Colonel Elmer Ellsworth* (1960); *I, Varina* (1962); *I, Jessie* (1963); *I, Elizabeth* (1966); *I, Ruth: Autobiography of a Marriage* (1968); etc.

RANDALL, SAMUEL (Feb. 10, 1778–Mar. 5, 1864); b. Sharon, Miss. Jurist, playwright. *The Miser* (1812); *The Sophomore* (1812). See *Dictionary of American Biography,* v. 15 (1935).

RANDOLPH, DAVID (Dec. 21, 1914–   ); b. New York. Musician, conductor, author. *This Is Music* (1964). Editor: *David Randolph Choral Series.*

RANDOLPH, SARAH NICHOLAS (Oct. 12, 1839–Apr. 25, 1892); b. in Albemarle Co., Va. Educator, author. *The Domestic Life of Thomas Jefferson* (1871); *The Life of Gen. T. J. Jackson* (1876).

RANDOLPH, VANCE (Feb. 23, 1892–); b. Pittsburg, Kan. Author. *The Ozarks* (1931); *Ozark Mountain Folks* (1932); *From an Ozark Holler* (1933); *Ozark Outdoors* (1934); *The Camp on Wildcat Creek* (1934); *Hedwig* (1935); *Ozark Superstitions* (1947); *We Always Lie to Strangers* (1951); *Who Blowed Up the Church House?* (1952); *The Devil's Pretty Daughter* (1955); etc.

Random House. New York. Publishers. Founded 1927, by Bennett A. Cerf, Elmer Adler, and Donald Klopfer. Its first venture was Voltaire's *Candide,* illustrated by Rockwell Kent, and printed by Elmer Adler, at the Pynson Printers. Bennett Cerf bought *The Modern Library* from Boni and Liveright in 1925; it was later added to the Random House list and expanded to include *Modern Library Giants.* Adler organized the *Colophon* in 1930. Random House absorbed Smith & Haas, the successors to Jonathan Cape & Harrison Smith, founded in 1929. In 1960 the house bought an interest in Alfred A. Knopf, Inc., and absorbed L. W. Singer Co., of Syracuse, N.Y., publishers since 1924. In 1961 the firm bought Pantheon Books. Acquired by Radio Corporation of America in 1966.

Random House Dictionary of the English Language, The. Unabridged dictionary, first published in 1966. Jess Stein is editor-in-chief. A product of lexicographic research at the Reference Department of Random House.

RANKIN, CARROLL WATSON (May 11, 1870–Aug. 13, 1945); b. Marquette, Mich. Author. *Dandelion Cottage* (1904); *The Castaways of Pete's Patch* (1911); *Gipsy Man* (1926); *Wolf Rock* (1933); *Stump Village* (1935); etc.

RANKIN, HUGH FRANKLIN (June 17, 1913–); b. Arlington, Va. Educator, author. *North Carolina in the American Revolution* (1959); *Pirates of Colonial North Carolina* (1961); *Upheaval in Albemarle: The Story of Culpeper's Rebellion, 1675–1689* (1962); and other books on Colonial Southern history. Prof. history, Tulane University, since 1964.

RANKIN, JEREMIAH EAMES (Jan. 2, 1828–Nov. 28, 1904); b. Thornton, N.H. Congregational clergyman, educator, poet. *The Auld Scotch Mither, and Other Poems* (1873); *Ingleside Rhaims* (1887); etc. Author of the famous hymn, "God be with you till we meet again." President of Howard University, 1889–1903.

RANNEY, [Joseph] AUSTIN (Sept. 23, 1920–); b. Cortland, N.Y. Educator, author. *The Doctrine of Responsible Party Government* (1954); *Democracy and the American Party System* (with W. Kendall, 1956); *The Governing of Men* (1958); *Illinois Politics* (1960); *Pathways to Parliament* (1965); etc. Prof. political science, University of Wisconsin, since 1963.

RANOUS, DORA KNOWLTON (1859–Jan. 19, 1916); b. Ashfield, Mass. Editor, translator, author. *Diary of a Daly Débutante* (1910); *Good English in Good Form* (1916); etc. Editor: *The Literature of Italy*, 16v. (with Rossiter Johnson, 1907); *Authors Digest*, 20v. (with Rossiter Johnson, 1908); etc. Translator of the works of Guy de Maupassant, Gustave Flaubert, etc. See Rossiter Johnson's *Dora Knowlton Ranous* (1916).

RANSOM, JOHN CROWE (Apr. 30, 1888–); b. Pulaski, Tenn. Educator, editor, critic, poet. *Poems about God* (1919); *Chills and Fever* (1924); *Grace after Meat* (1924); *Two Gentlemen in Bonds* (poems, 1926); *God without Thunder* (1930); *The World's Body* (1938); *The New Criticism* (1941); *Selected Poems* (1945); *Lectures in Criticism* (1949); *Collected Poems* (1963); etc. Editor: *The Kenyon Critics* (1951); *Selected Poems of Thomas Hardy* (1961). Co-founder, *The Fugitive*, 1922, co-editor, 1922–25; editor, the *Kenyon Review*, since 1937. Prof. English, Vanderbilt University, 1927–37; prof. poetry, Kenyon College, since 1937. See Fred B. Millett's *Contemporary American Authors* (1940); Yvor Winter's *The Anatomy of Nonsense* (1943). See Karl F. Knight's *The Poetry of John Crowe Ransom* (1964).

RANSOM, WILL (Sept. 30, 1878–); b. St. Louis, Mich. Book designer, printer, bibliophile, author. *Private Presses and Their Books* (1929); etc. Compiler: *A Selective List of Press Books* (1946). With Harbor Press, J. J. Little & Ives, etc. With University of Oklahoma Press since 1941.

Ransome, Stephen. Pen name of Frederick Clyde Davis.

Ranson's Folly. Story by Richard Harding Davis (1902).

RAPER, ARTHUR FRANKLIN (Nov. 8, 1899–); b. in Davidson Co., N.C. Social scientist, author. *The Tragedy of Lynching* (1933). *Preface to Peasantry* (1936); *Tenants of the Almighty* (1943); *Rural Taiwan* (1953); etc.

RAPHAELSON, SAMSON (Mar. 30, 1896–); b. New York. Playwright. *The Jazz Singer* (prod. 1925); *The Store* (1926); *Young Love* (1928); *The Magnificent Heel* (1930); *The Wooden Slipper* (1933); *Accent on Youth* (prod. 1934); *Skylark* (prod. 1939); *Jason* (prod. 1942); *The Perfect Marriage* (1944); *The Human Nature of Playwriting* (1949); *Hilda Crane* (prod. 1950); *The Peanut Bag* (1967); etc. Also many screen plays.

RAPHALL, MORRIS JACOB (Oct. 3, 1798–June 23, 1868); b. Stockholm, Swe. Rabbi, author. *Post-Biblical History of the Jews*, 2v. (1855); *The Path to Immortality* (1859); etc. See Israel Goldstein's *A Century of Judaism in New York* (1930).

RAPP, WILLIAM JOURDAN (June 17, 1895–Aug. 12, 1942); b. New York. Editor, playwright, novelist. *Osman Pasha* (1925); *Whirlpool* (with Walter Marquiss, prod. 1929); *Harlem* (with Wallace Thurman, prod. 1929); *Holmes of Baker Street* (1936); *Poolroom* (1938); etc. Editor, *True Story Magazine*, from 1926.

Rappaccini's Daughter. Short story by Nathaniel Hawthorne (1844), which first appeared in the *Democratic Review* (1844). A scientist feeds his daughter poison so that her breath will be fatal to her lover.

RASCOE, BURTON (Oct. 22, 1892–Mar. 19, 1957); b. Fulton, Ky. Editor, author. *Theodore Dreiser* (1925); *A Bookman's Daybook* (1929); *Titans of Literature* (1932); *Prometheans, Ancient and Modern* (1933); *Before I Forget* (1936); *The Joys of Reading* (1937); *The Ten-Year Binge* (1938); *Rascoe Round-Up*, ed. by Lloyd Eshelman (1940); *Belle Starr* (1941); *We Were Interrupted* (1947); etc. Editor: *An American Reader* (1938). Editor, *The Bookman*, 1927–28; literary critic, *Esquire*, 1932–38, *American Mercury*, 1939–41; drama critic and editorial writer, *New York World-Telegram*, 1942–46; etc. Wrote syndicated column "The Daybook of a New Yorker," 1924–28.

Rat: Subterranean News. New York. Weekly. Founded 1968. Underground newspaper. Edited by Jeffrey Shero.

RATCLIFF, JOHN DRURY (May 4, 1903–); b. Huntington, W.Va. Author. *Modern Miracle Men* (1939); *Yellow Magic: The Story of Penicillin* (1945); *Birth* (1951); etc.

RATHBONE, HENRY BAILEY (July 3, 1871–June 13, 1945); b. Merrick, L.I., N.Y. Educator, journalist. On staff, the *New York Evening Sun*, and other newspapers in New York, San Francisco, and Chicago, 1895–1924. Prof. journalism, New York University, 1924–41.

RATHBONE, JOSEPHINE ADAMS (Sept. 10, 1864–May 17, 1941); b. Jamestown, N.Y. Author, librarian, *Viewpoints in Travel* (1919). With Pratt Institute Library, Brooklyn, N.Y., 1893–1938; instructor in library school, 1895–1911, vice director of library school, 1911–38. President, American Library Association, 1931–32. See *Bulletin*, American Library Association, June, 1941.

RATHBORNE, ST. GEORGE HENRY (Dec. 26, 1854–Dec. 16, 1928); b. Covington, Ky. Novelist, dime novelist, author of boys' books. Pen names "Aleck Forbes," "Duke Duncan," "Harrison Adams," "Harry St. George," "Marline Manly," and many others. *Old Solitaire* (1877); *The Marked Moccasin* (1878); *Old Hickory* (1878); *Hickory Harry* (1880); *Pittsburgh Landing* (1883); *Roaring Ralph Rockwood, the Reckless Ranger* (1884); *The Boy Cruisers* (1893); *A Goddess of Africa* (1897); *Miss Fairfax of Virginia* (1899); *The Pioneer Boys of the Ohio* (1912); *A Texan Thoroughbred* (1912); *Lend-a-Hand Boys' Team-Work* (1931); etc. The dates are not necessarily those of first editions.

RATIGAN, WILLIAM O. (Nov. 7, 1910–); b. Detroit, Mich. Author. *NBC War Poems* (1945); *Soo Canal!* (1954); *Young Mr. Big* (1955); *The Adventures of Captain McCargo* (1956); *Adventures of Paul Bunyan and Babe* (1958); *Highways over Broad Waters* (1959); *Straits of Mackinac* (1957); *The Blue Snow* (1958); *Tiny Tim Pine* (1958); *The Long Crossing* (1959); *Great Lakes Shipwrecks and Survivals* (1960); *School Counseling: View from Within* (1967).

RAUCH, BASIL (Sept. 6, 1908–); b. Dubuque, Ia. Historian. *The History of the New Deal, 1933–38* (1944); *American Interest in Cuba: 1848–1855* (1948); *Roosevelt from Munich to Pearl Harbor: A Study in the Creation of a Foreign Policy* (1950); *The Genesis and Growth of the United States of America* (with Dumas Malone, 2v. 1960, 6v. 1965). Dept. of history, Barnard College, since 1941.

RAUSCHENBUSCH, WALTER (Oct. 4, 1861–July 25, 1918); b. Rochester, N.Y. Baptist clergyman, educator, author. *Christianity and the Social Crisis* (1907); *Prayers of the Social Awakening* (1910); *Christianizing the Social Order* (1912); etc. Prof. church history, Rochester Theological Seminary, 1902–18.

RAUSHENBUSH, [Hilmar] STEPHEN (May 12, 1896–); b. New York. Author. *The Power Fight* (1932); *The March of Fascism* (1939); *Our Conservation Job* (1949); etc. Editor: *The Future of Our Natural Resources* (1952); etc.

"Raven, The." Poem by Edgar Allan Poe, which appeared in *The American Review*, Feb., 1845. By permission the poem

was printed in the New York *Evening Mirror,* Jan. 29, 1845, actually its first public appearance, but the poem had been purchased by the *American Review* and was in type for the forthcoming February issue of the magazine. *See* Henry E. Legler's *The Genesis of Poe's Raven* (1907).

Raven, The. By Marquis James (1929). A biography of Sam Houston.

RAVENEL, HARRIOTT HORRY RUTLEDGE (Aug. 12, 1832–July 2, 1912); b. Charleston, S.C. Author. *Eliza Pinckney* (1896); *Life and Times of William Lowndes of South Carolina, 1782–1822* (1901); *Charleston: The Place and the People* (1906); etc. *See* H. E. Ravenel's *Ravenel Records* (1898).

RAWLEY, JAMES ALBERT (Nov. 9, 1916–); b. Terre Haute, Ind. Educator, author. *Edwin D. Morgan: Merchant in Politics 1811–1833* (1955); *Turning Points of the Civil War* (1966); etc. Professor of history, University of Nebraska, since 1964.

RAWLINGS, MARJORIE KINNAN (Aug. 8, 1896–Dec. 14, 1953); b. Washington, D.C. Author. *South Moon Under* (1933); *Golden Apples* (1935); *The Yearling* (1938, Pulitzer Prize novel, 1939); *When the Whippoorwill* (1940); *Cross Creek* (1942); *The Sojourner* (1953).

RAWSON, [Edna] **MARION NICHOLL** (June 24, 1878–); b. Scotch Plains, N.J. Author. *Candle Days* (1927); *Country Auction* (1929); *Little Old Mills* (1935); *Of the Earth Earthy* (1937); *Forever the Farm* (1939); etc.

RAY, ANNA CHAPIN (Jan. 3, 1865–Dec. 13, 1945); b. Westfield, Mass. Author. *In Blue Creek Cañon* (1892); the *Teddy* books, 6v. (1898–1904); the *Sidney* books, 6v. (1905–10); *Sheba* (1903); *By the Good Sainte Anne* (1904); *Over the Quicksands* (1910); *Buddie* (1911); etc.

RAY, GORDON N[orton] (Sept. 8, 1915–); b. New York City. Educator. Author: *The Buried Life* (1952); *Thackeray (Vol. I): The Uses of Adversity* (1955), *(Vol. II): The Age of Wisdom* (1958). Editor: *Letters and Private Papers of William Makepeace Thackeray,* 4v. (1945–46); *Henry James and H. G. Wells* (with Leon Edel, 1958); etc. Prof. English, University of Illinois, since 1946.

RAY, LOUISE CRENSHAW (Mrs. Benjamin Franklin Ray), (d. Oct. 23, 1956); b. near Greenville, Ala. Poet. *Color of Steel* (1932); *Secret Shoes* (1939); *Strangers on the Stairs* (1944); *Autumn Token* (1957).

Ray Palmer Club. Newark, N.J. Women's literary club. Founded 1892. Amanda Minnie Douglas, novelist, was a leading member.

RAYFORD, JULIAN LEE (Apr. 7, 1908–); b. Mobile, Ala. Novelist. *Cotton-mouth* (1941). *Child of the Snapping Turtle* (1951); *Whistlin' Woman and Crowin' Hen* (1956).

RAYMOND, EVELYN [Hunt] (Nov. 6, 1843–Apr. 18, 1910); b. Watertown, N.Y. Author. *Mixed Pickles* (1892); *Monica* (1892); *A Cape May Diamond* (1896); *Little Red Schoolhouse* (1897); *Among the Lindens* (1898); *A Daughter of the West* (1899); *My Lady Barefoot* (1899); *Reels and Spindles* (1900); *The Mislaid Uncle* (1903); *Polly the Gringo* (1905); *The Brass Bound Box* (1905); *Dorothy Chester* (1907); *Dorothy's Schooling* (1908); etc.

RAYMOND, GEORGE LANSING (Sept. 3, 1839–July 11, 1929); b. Chicago, Ill. Presbyterian clergyman, educator, poet. *Poetry as a Representative Art* (1886); *Art in Theory* (1894); *Pictures in Verse* (1894); *The Aztec God, and Other Dramas* (1900); *Ballads, and Other Poems* (1901); *The Essentials of Aesthetics* (1906); *Comparative Aesthetics,* 8v. (1909); *Dante, and Collected Verse* (1909); *A Poet's Cabinet* (1914); *An Art Philosopher's Cabinet* (1915); etc. Compiler: *Colony Ballads* (1876); *Ballads of the Revolution* (1887). Prof. oratory and aesthetics, Princeton University, 1880–1905; prof. aesthetics, George Washington University, 1905–12.

RAYMOND, HENRY JARVIS (Jan. 24, 1826–June 18, 1869); b. Lima, N.Y. Editor, author. *History of the Administration of President Lincoln* (1864); *Disunion and Slavery* (1860); etc. On staff, the *New York Tribune,* 1841–43, the *Morning Courier and New-York Enquirer,* 1843–49; managing editor, *Harper's Monthly Magazine,* 1850–56. Founder, the *New York Times,* 1851, editor, 1851–69. *See* Augustus Maverick's *Henry J. Raymond and the New York Times* (1870); Elmer Davis's *History of the New York Times* (1921).

RAYMOND, ROSSITER WORTHINGTON (Apr. 27, 1840–Dec. 31, 1918); b. Cincinnati, O. Mining engineer, editor, author. *Camp and Cabin* (1880); *Peter Cooper* (1901); etc.

RAYMOND, WILLIAM LEE (Sept. 24, 1877–Mar. 19, 1942); b. Cambridge, Mass. Author. *An Occasional Diary by "X"* (1924); *Poems of Love and Life* (1928); *Later Poems* (1937); also books on politics and finance.

RAYNER, EMMA (d. Nov. 20, 1926); b. Cambridge, Eng. Author. *Free to Serve* (1897); *In Castle and Colony* (1899); *Visiting the Sin* (1900); *Doris Kingsley, Child and Colonist* (1901); etc. On staff *Youth's Companion,* 1896–1902.

RAYNOLDS, ROBERT (Apr. 29, 1902–Oct. 24, 1965); b. Santa Fe, N.M. Author. *Brothers in the West* (1931); *Saunders Oak* (1933); *The Scene of Fortune* (1935); *The Ugly Runts* (verse play, 1935); *Summer Song* (verse play, 1937); *Boadicea* (verse play, 1940); *May Bretton* (1944); *The Obscure Enemy* (1945); *Paquita* (1947); *The Sinner of Saint Ambrose* (1952); *The Quality of Quiros* (1955); *Far Flight of Love* (1957); *Choice to Love* (essays, 1959); *In Praise of Gratitude* (1961).

REA, GARDNER (Aug. 12, 1892–Dec. 28, 1966); b. Ironton, O. Cartoonist. *The Gentleman Says It's Pixies* (1944); *Gardner Rea's Sideshow* (1945).

Reactionary Essays on Poetry and Ideas. Collection of critical essays by Allen Tate (1936).

READ, ALLEN WALKER (June 2, 1906); b. Winnebago, Minn. Editor, author. *Lexical Evidence from Folk Epigraphy in Western North America* (1935). Asst. editor, *Dictionary of American English on Historical Principles,* editing words in A, B, C, and E (1934–38). Has written extensively on philological subjects in *American Speech, Dialect Notes, English Studies,* etc.

READ, CONYERS (Apr. 25, 1881–Dec. 23, 1959); b. Philadelphia, Pa. Educator, author. *The Tudors* (1936); *Social and Political Forces in the English Reformation* (1953); *Lord Burghley and Queen Elizabeth* (1960); *Mr. Secretary Walsingham and The Policy of Queen Elizabeth, 3v.* (1967). Editor: *The Bardon Papers* (1909); *Bibliography of British History 1485–1603* (1933); Clapham's *Elizabeth* (with E.P. Read, 1951); etc. Prof. English history, University of Pennsylvania, 1934–51.

READ, DANIEL (Nov. 16, 1757–Dec. 4, 1836); b. Rehoboth (now Attleboro), Mass. Musician. Compiler: *The American Singing Book* (1785); *The Columbian Harmonist* (1793); *The New Haven Collection of Sacred Music* (1818); etc. Founder, the *American Musical Magazine,* c. 1786.

READ, DAVID HAXTON CARSWELL (Jan. 2, 1910–); b. Cupar, Scot. Presbyterian clergyman. *The Spirit of Life* (1939); *Prisoners' Quest* (1944); *The Christian Faith* (1956); *God's Mobile Family: sermons, 1965–1966; Whose God is Dead?* (1966); *The Presence of Christ* (1968); etc.

READ, OPIE (Dec. 22, 1852–Nov. 2, 1939); b. Nashville, Tenn. Novelist, editor, humorist. *Len Gansett* (1888); *A Kentucky Colonel* (1890); *The Jucklins* (1895); *An Arkansas Planter* (1896); *Bolanyo* (1897); *Judge Elbridge* (1899); *The Carpet Bagger* (with Frank Pixley, 1899); *In the Alamo* (1900); *"Turk"* (1904); *Son of the Swordmaker* (1905); *"By* *the Eternal"* (1906); *Mr. Howerson* (1914); *Gold Gauze Veil* (1927); *I Remember* (autobiography, 1930); *The Autobiography of the Devil* (1939); *Mark Twain and I* (1940); etc. Founder, the *Arkansas Traveler,* Little Rock, Ark. *See* Maurice Eifer's *Opie Read* (1940).

READ, THOMAS BUCHANAN (Mar. 12, 1822–May 11, 1872); b. Guthriesville, Pa. Painter, poet. *Paul Redding: A Tale of the Brandywine* (1845); *Poems* (1847); *Lays and Ballads* (1849); *The Female Poets of America* (1849); *Rural Poems* (1857); *The Wagoner of the Alleghanies* (1862); *A Summer Story; Sheridan's Ride; and Other Poems* (1865); *The Poetical Works,* 3v. (1866); etc. His best-known poem is "Sheridan's Ride."

Reader's Adviser, The. See *Bookman's Manual.*

Readers Club. New York. Founded 1941 to publish at popular prices good books of the past which for some reason or another did not receive the attention due them. The first book published was E. H. Young's *William.*

Reader's Digest. Pleasantville, N.Y. Monthly digest. Founded 1921, by DeWitt Wallace, who edited it with Lila Acheson Wallace until 1965. Succeeded by Hobart D. Lewis in 1965. The magazine reprints digests of articles taken from other periodicals, but also originates many articles which are first printed in other magazines and then reprinted in *Reader's Digest.* It has a larger circulation than any other magazine in the world and publishes numerous foreign editions, a Braille edition, and a regular phonograph recording. Digests are also made from books, and a staff of roving editors contributes regular articles. Acquired Funk and Wagnall's in 1968.

Reader's Encyclopedia, The. By William Rose Benét (1948). Thousands of articles covering world literature, writers, literary movements, characters, and plots, etc. A second edition appeared in 1965.

Reader's Guide to Periodical Literature. New York. Founded 1900. Cumulative index to articles in magazines. It grew out of the *Cumulative Index,* 1896–1903. Published semimonthly, September-June; monthly, July-August; including some cumulative issues. There are bound annual and two-year volumes.

Reader's Scope. Monthly. Founded 1944, by Leverett Gleason. Partially a reprint digest, with several biographical articles each issue. Suspended 1950.

REALF, RICHARD (June 14, 1834–Oct. 28, 1878); b. Framfield, Sus., England. Poet. *Guesses at the Beautiful* (poem, 1852); *Poems by Richard Realf* (1898); etc. Hayden Douglas in Mary E. Jackson's novel, *The Spy of Osawotamie* (1881) is said to have been based on Realf.

Realist, The. New York. Irregular. Founded 1958. Published and edited by Paul Krassner. Magazine of free thought and satire, precursor of the "underground" weeklies in its willingness to challenge standards of obscenity and to express unpopular opinion even in criticism of radical thinking.

Realms of Being, The. Series of philosophical works by George Santayana. The series includes *Scepticism and Animal Faith* (1923); *The Realm of Essence* (1927); *The Realm of Matter* (1930); *The Realm of Truth* (1938); and *The Realm of Spirit* (1940).

"Reaper and the Flowers, The." Poem by Henry W. Longfellow (1838).

REASONER, HARRY (Apr. 17, 1923–); b. Dakota City, Ia. News reporter, author. *Tell Me About Women* (1964); *The Reasoner Report* (1966). Correspondent, CBS News, since 1956.

Rebecca of Sunnybrook Farm. Novel by Kate Douglas Wiggin (1903). Depicts the bright optimism of a little girl surrounded by poverty, whose winning ways obtain for her in due time an education, comfortable means, and romance.

Rebellion Record, The. Comp. by Frank Moore, 12v. (1861–65). A selection from *The War of the Rebellion: Official Records of the Union and Confederate Armies,* 228v. (1881–1900). Moore made his compilation from the unpublished records.

RECHT, CHARLES (Apr. 30, 1887–July 16, 1965); b. Varvazov, Czech. Author. *Rue with a Difference* (1924); *Manhattan Made* (poems, 1930); *Babylon-on-Hudson* (poems, 1932).

RECHY, JOHN FRANKLIN (March 10, 1934–); b. El Paso, Texas. Author. *City of Night* (1963); *Numbers* (1967); *This Day's Death* (1970).

Reconstruction in Philosophy. By John Dewey (1920). Lectures in which the author presents the modern American modes of thought, a thinking directed toward the pragmatic solution of immediate social problems rather than toward the search for absolute truth, long considered the true province of philosophical investigation.

Recordings. Since World War II there has been a notable increase in the number of recordings of spoken material, including readings and dramatizations of entire plays and books. Caedmon Records, Inc., is outstanding for its records of poetry and prose read by the authors or distinguished readers and performers. Among other such record companies are Folkways Records & Service Corp., National Council of Teachers of English, Riverside Records, The Spoken Word, Living Literature, and Living Shakespeare. Recording for the Blind, Inc., has recorded about 10,000 educational books for college students. A recent example of a new kind of venture in the recorded use of spoken words is Poetry Out Loud, a continuing edition of recordings based on taped rather than manuscript or printed verse.

Rector of St. Bardolph's, The. By Frederick William Shelton (1853). Tales of simple life in a country parish, written by an Episcopal clergyman.

Red Badge of Courage, The. By Stephen Crane (1895). A classic story of man's emotions in the stress of battle. Henry Fleming, young and inexperienced, is thrust suddenly into the thick of the Civil War. This book lifted Stephen Crane from obscurity to lasting literary fame.

Red Book, The. Baltimore, Md. Magazine. Founded 1818. It was an imitation of Irving's *Salmagundi.* Peter Hoffman Cruse contributed most of the poetry and John Pendleton Kennedy most of the prose. Expired 1819.

Red City, The. Novel by S. Weir Mitchell (1907). Story of Philadelphia during the second term of George Washington.

Red Decade, The. Study of communism in America, by Eugene Lyons (1942).

Red Pony, The. Short story by John Steinbeck (1937).

Red Republic, The. Novel by Robert W. Chambers (1894). First of a trilogy, including *Lorraine* (1898) and *Ashes of Empire* (1898).

Red Rock. Novel by Thomas Nelson Page (1899). Story of the struggles of Jacqueline Gray to face the problems of postbellum life in the South. The "carpet-baggers" and the Ku Klux Klan are prominently featured.

Red Rover, The. Novel by James Fenimore Cooper (1827). Sea tale about the pirate Red Rover and Henry Ark, of His Majesty's ship *Dart.* Ark, disguised, joins the Red Rover's crew on the *Dolphin.* A fight between the two ships is the climax.

Redbook Magazine. New York. Monthly. Founded 1903, at Chicago, Ill. Published by the McCall Corp. Moved to New York 1929. Devoted chiefly to fiction and general feature articles.

Redburn. Novel by Herman Melville (1849). Realistic portrayal of life on a merchantman and a man-of-war.

REDDICK, LAWRENCE DUNBAR (Mar. 3, 1910–); b. Jacksonville, Fla. Educator, author. *Emancipation Symphony* (1953); *Crusader Without Violence: A Biography of Martin Luther King, Jr.* (1959).

REDDING, JAY SAUNDERS (Oct. 13, 1906–); b. Wilmington, Del. Educator, author. *To Make a Poet Black* (1939); *No Day of Triumph* (autobiography, 1942); *Stranger and Alone* (1950); *On Being a Negro in America* (1952); *An American in India* (1954); *The Lonesome Road* (1958); *They Came in Chains* (1969); etc. Prof. English, Hampton Institute, since 1943.

Redeemed Captive, The. By John Williams (1707). A vivid story of Indian atrocities by a man who was carried to Canada by the savages after the massacre at Deerfield, Mass.

REDFIELD, JUSTUS STARR (Jan. 2, 1810–Mar. 24, 1888); b. Wallingford, Conn. Publisher. Took over the *Family Magazine*, in New York, in 1834, founded in 1833 by Origen Bacheler. Redfield hired the artist Benson J. Lossing as editor, 1839–41. From 1841 to 1860 Redfield ran a printing and publishing business. He was succeeded by W. J. Widdleton. J. S. Redfield published some of the works of William Gilmore Simms, Robert Montgomery Bird, Fitz-Greene Halleck, Edgar Allan Poe, Alice Cary, and others. See J. C. Derby's *Fifty Years among Authors, Books, and Publishers* (1884).

REDMAN, BEN RAY (Feb. 21, 1896–Aug. 2, 1961); b. Brooklyn, N.Y. Editor, author. *Masquerade* (poems, 1923); *Edwin Arlington Robinson* (1925); *Marriage for Three* (1929); *Down in Flames* (1930); *Reading at Random* (1933); *The Bannerman Case* (under pen name, "Jeremy Lord," 1935); *Sixty-Nine Diamonds* (1940); *The Meeker Case* (under pen name "Jeremy Lord," 1940); etc. Editor: *The Pleasures of Peacock* (1947); *The Portable Voltaire* (1949); etc. Editor, "Old Wine in New Bottles," in *New York Herald Tribune Books,* 1926–37. Translator of many French and Italian works.

REDPATH, JAMES (Aug. 24, 1833–Feb. 10, 1891); b. Berwick-upon-Tweed, Eng. Editor, lecture-promoter, author. *The Roving Editor; or, Talks With Slaves in the Southern States* (1859); *Guide to Haiti* (1860); *The Public Life of Capt. John Brown* (1860); *The John Brown Invasion* (1860); *John Brown, the Hero* (1862); *Talks About Ireland* (1881); etc. In 1868 he founded the Boston Lyceum Bureau, and among the lecturers he managed were Emerson, Thoreau, Sumner, Beecher, Bayard Taylor, Wendell Phillips, and Julia Ward Howe. James Burton Pond was associated with him. See Charles E. Horner's *The Life of James Redpath and the Development of the Modern Lyceum* (1926).

Redwood. Novel by Catherine Maria Sedgwick (1824). Tale of New England in the early days.

REED, EARL HOWELL (July 5, 1863–July 9, 1931); b. Geneva, Ill. Etcher, author. *The Voices of the Dunes* (1912); *The Dune Country* (1916); *Tales of a Vanishing River* (1920); *The Ghost in the Tower* (1921); *The Silver Arrow* (1926); etc.

REED, EDWARD BLISS (Aug. 19, 1872–Feb. 15, 1940); b. Lansingburgh, N.Y. Educator, editor, author. *English Lyrical Poetry* (1912); *Lyra Yalensis* (1913); *Sea Moods, and Other Poems* (1917); *Lyra Levis* (1922). Editor: *Christmas Carols Printed in the Sixteenth Century* (1932); Co-editor (with David Stanley Smith): *The Publications of the Carol Society,* New Haven, v. 1–15 (1924–35). Asst. editor, the *Yale Review,* 1911–28. English dept., Yale University, 1897–1927.

REED, ELIZABETH ARMSTRONG (May 16, 1842–June 16, 1915); b. Winthrop, Me. Orientalist, author. *Hindu Literature* (1891); *Persian Literature* (1893); *Primitive Buddhism* (1896); *Daniel Webster* (1899); etc. She was the mother of Earl Howell Reed, the etcher, and Myrtle Reed, the novelist.

REED, HELEN LEAH, b. St. John, N.B. Author. *Miss Theodora* (1898); the *Brenda* series, 5v. (1900–06); *Amy in Acadia* (1905); *Irma in Italy* (1908); *Serbia: A Sketch* (1916); *Memorial Day, and Other Verse* (1917); etc.

REED, HENRY HOPE (July 11, 1808–Sept. 27, 1854); b. Philadelphia, Pa. Editor, author. *Lectures on English Literature from Chaucer to Tennyson* (1855); *Lectures on the British Poets,* 2v. (1857); etc. Editor: *Wordsworth's Complete Works* (1851). He was the first to popularize Wordsworth in America.

REED, ISHMAEL (Feb. 22, 1938–   ); b. Chattanooga, Tenn. Author. *The Free-Lance Pallbearers* (1967); *Yellow Back Radio Broke-Down* (1969).

REED, JOHN (Oct. 22, 1887–Oct. 19, 1920); b. Portland, Ore. Journalist, poet. *The Day in Bohemia* (1913); *Sangar* (1913); *Insurgent Mexico* (1914); *Tamburlaine, and Other Poems* (1916); *Ten Days that Shook the World* (1919); *Daughter of the Revolution,* ed. by F. Dell (1927); etc. With the *American Magazine,* 1912, *The Masses,* 1913–18. His best known poem is "Sangar," in *Poetry,* Dec. 1912.

REED, KIT [Lillian Craig] (June 7, 1932–   ); b. San Diego, Calif. Author. *Mother Isn't Dead, She's Only Sleeping* (1961); *At War with Children* (1964); *The Better Part* (1967).

REED, MARY (1880?–Nov. 29, 1960). Editor. Adviser for Simon and Schuster's Golden Book series, from 1942.

REED, MYRTLE (Mrs. James Sidney McCullough) (Sept. 27, 1874–Aug. 17, 1911); b. Norwood Park, Ill. Author. *Love Letters of a Musician* (1899); *Lavender and Old Lace* (1902); *The Shadow of Victory* (1903); *Picaback Songs* (1903); *A Spinner in the Sun* (under pen name "Olive Green," 1906); *Love Affairs of Literary Men* (1907); *Flower in the Dusk* (1908); *Old Rose and Silver* (1909); *Sonnets of a Lover* (1910); *A Weaver of Dreams* (1911); *The Myrtle Reed Year Book* (1911); etc.

Reeder, George. Pen name of Arthur David Cloud.

REEDY, WILLIAM MARION (Dec. 11, 1862–July 2, 1920); b. St. Louis, Mo. Editor, essayist. *The Imitator* (1901); *The Law of Love* (1905); *A Golden Book and the Literature of Childhood* (1910); etc. In 1893 James Campbell, owner of the *St. Louis Sunday Mirror,* appointed Reedy editor, and in 1896 made him a present of the paper. It was re-named *Reedy's Mirror* and ran to thirty volumes before it expired. Reedy assisted many young writers including Edgar Lee Masters, Sara Teasdale, Fannie Hurst, John Hall Wheelock, Orrick Johns, Julia Peterkin, John Gould Fletcher, Zoë Akins, and Babette Deutsche. See Memorial number of *Reedy's Mirror,* Aug. 5, 1920.

REESE, CHARLOTTE PAUL (May 22, 1916–); b. Seattle, Wash. Author. *Hear My Heart Speak* (1950); *Gold Mountain* (1953); *Minding Our Own Business* (1955); *The Cup of Strength* (1958); *And Four to Grow* (1961).

REESE, LIZETTE WOODWORTH (Jan. 9, 1856–Dec. 17, 1935); b. Waverly, Md. Educator, poet. *A Branch of May* (1887); *A Handful of Lavender* (1891); *A Quiet Road* (1896); *A Wayside Lute* (1909); *Spicewood* (1920); *Wild Cherry* (1923); *The Selected Poems* (1926); *Little Henrietta* (1927); *A Victorian Village* (reminiscences, 1929); *White April, and Other Poems* (1930); *The York Road* (autobiography, 1931); *Pasture, and Other Poems* (1933); *The Old House in the Country* (1936). With the Baltimore, Md., Public Schools, 1873–1921. See Fred B. Millett's *Contemporary American Authors* (1940).

REEVE, ARTHUR BENJAMIN (Oct. 15, 1880–Aug. 9, 1936); b. Patchogue, L.I., N.Y. Author. *The Silent Bullet* (1912); *The Black Hand* (1912); *The Exploits of Elaine* (1915); *Constance Dunlap* (1915); *The Social Gangster*

(1916); *The Panama Plot* (1918); *The Master Mystery* (1919); etc. He created the detective "Craig Kennedy" in the *Adventures of Craig Kennedy,* in *Cosmopolitan,* 1910–18.

REEVE, FRANKLIN DOLIER (Sept. 18, 1928–); b. Philadelphia, Pa. Educator, author. *Aleksandr Blok: Between Image and Idea* (1962); *Robert Frost in Russia* (1964); *The Stone Island* (1964); *Six Poems* (1964); *On Some Scientific Concepts in Russian Poetry* (1966); *The Russian Novel* (1966). Editor and translator of several collections of Russian literature. Former prof. humanities, Wesleyan University.

REEVES, MARIAN C[alhoun] L[egaré] (c. 1854–); b. Charleston, S.C. Author. Pen name, "Fadette." *Ingemisco* (1867); *Randolph Honor* (1868); *Sea Drift* (1869); *Wearithorne* (1872); *Old Martin Boscawen's Jest* (with Emily Read, 1878); *Pilot Fortune* (with same, 1885); *A Little Maid of Acadia* (1888); etc.

REGNERY, HENRY (Jan. 5, 1912–); b. Hinsdale, Ill. Publisher. Pres., Henry Regnery Co., 1947–66; chairman of the board, since 1967.

Regnery, Henry, Co. Chicago, Ill. Founded 1947, by Henry Regnery. Bought The Reilly & Lee Co. in 1959. Publishes the Gateway Editions and Logos Books.

REICE, SYLVIE SCHUMAN; b. New York. Editor, author. *Should You be a Free-lance Writer?* (1955); *For Girls Only* (1956); *Season of Love* (1962). Youth editor, *McCall's* magazine, since 1967.

REICH, CHARLES ALAN (May 20, 1928–   ); b. New York. Educator, author. *The Greening of America* (1970). Prof. law, Yale University, since 1960.

REICH, WILHELM (Mar. 24, 1897–1957); b. in Austria. Psychotherapist. *The Function of the Orgasm* (1942); *The Sexual Revolution* (1945); *The Cancer Biopathy* (1948); *Listen, Little Man!* (1948); *Ether, God and Devil* (1951); *Cosmic Superimposition* (1951); *Selected Writings* (1960); etc.

REID, ALBERT CLAYTON (July 26, 1894–); b. High Rock, N.C. Educator. *Christ and the Present Crisis* (1936); *Elements of Psychology* (1938); *Invitation to Worship* (1942); *Man and Christ* (1954); *Christ and Human Values* (1961); *Tales from Cabin Creek* (1967); etc. Depts. of philosophy and psychology, Wake Forest College, since 1917.

REID, BENJAMIN LAWRENCE (May 3, 1918–); b. Louisville, Ky. Educator, author. *Art by Subtraction: A Dissenting Opinion of Gertrude Stein* (1958); *William Butler Yeats: The Lyric of Tragedy* (1961); etc. Professor of English, Mount Holyoke College, since 1957.

Reid, Christian. Pen name of Frances Christine Fisher Tiernan.

REID, MAYNE (Apr. 4, 1818–Oct. 22, 1883); b. Ballyroney, Ire. Soldier, novelist, playwright. *Love's Martyr* (prod. 1848); *The Rifle Rangers* (1850); *The Boy Hunters* (1852); *The Forest Exiles* (1854); *The Quadroon* (prod. 1856); *The White Chief* (1859); *Lost Lenore* (1864); *The Child Wife* (1868); *The Death Shot* (1874); *The Free Lance* (1881); *No Quarter!* (1888); etc. *See* Elizabeth Reid's *Mayne Reid* (1890).

REID, OGDEN MILLS (May 16, 1882–Jan. 3, 1947); b. New York. Son of Whitelaw Reid. Editor. With *New York Tribune* (later *New York Herald Tribune),* from 1908; editor-in-chief, from 1913.

REID, SAMUEL CHESTER (Aug. 25, 1783–Jan. 28, 1861); b. Norwich, Conn. Sea captain, author. *The Scouting Expeditions of McCulloch's Texas Rangers* (1847). Reid was the designer, in 1818, of the present form of the American flag, on which the number of stripes remains thirteen, while the stars represent the contemporary number of states.

REID, WHITELAW (Oct. 27, 1837–Dec. 15, 1912); b. Xenia, O. Editor, diplomat, author. *After the War* (1866); *Our New Duties* (1899); *American and English Studies* (1913); etc. Editor: the *New York Tribune,* 1869–1905. U.S. minister to France, 1889–92; ambassador to England, 1905–12. *See* Royal Cortissoz's *The Life of Whitelaw Reid,* 2v. (1921).

REIK, THEODOR (May 12, 1888–Dec. 31, 1969); b. Vienna. Psychologist, author. *Ritual* (1931); *The Unknown Murderer* (1936); *Surprise and the Psychoanalyst* (1937); *From Thirty Years With Freud* (1940); *Masochism in Modern Man* (1941); *A Psychologist Looks at Love* (1944); *Psychology of Sex Relations* (1945); *Listening with the Third Ear* (1948); *Fragment of a Great Confession* (1949); *Dogma and Compulsion* (1951); *The Secret Self* (1952); *The Haunting Melody* (1953); *The Search Within* (1956); *Myth and Guilt* (1957); *Of Love and Lust* (1957); *A Mystery on the Mountain: The Drama of the Sinai Revelation* (1959); *The Compulsion to Confess* (1959); *The Creation of Woman* (1960); *Sex in Man and Woman: Its Emotional Variations* (1960); *The Temptation* (1961); *Fragment of a Great Confession* (1965); *The Many Faces of Sex* (1966).

REILLY, HELEN (1890–Jan. 12, 1962), Author. *The Line-Up* (1934); *Dead for a Ducat* (1939); *Mourned on a Sunday* (1941); *Name Your Poison* (1942); *The Silver Leopard* (1947); *The Double Man* (1952); *Compartment K* (1955); *Ding Dong Bell* (1958); *Follow Me* (1960); *Certain Sleep* (1962); etc.

REILLY, JOSEPH JOHN (Jan. 16, 1881–Jan. 25, 1951); b. Springfield, Mass. Educator, librarian, author. *James Russell Lowell as a Critic* (1915); *Newman as a Man of Letters* (1925); *Dear Prue's Husband and Other People* (1932); *Of Books and Men* (1942). Prof. English, Hunter College, New York, from 1927; librarian 1928–48.

REILLY, WILLIAM JOHN (Mar. 6, 1899–Jan. 15, 1958); b. Pittsburgh, Pa. Business consultant, author. *Marketing Investigations* (1929); *Straight Thinking* (1935); *How to Avoid Work* (1949); *How to Get What You Want Out of Life* (1957); *In Search of a Working Philosophy of Life* (1959); *Opening Closed Minds* (1964); etc.

Reilly & Lee Company, The. Chicago, Ill. Book publishers. Founded 1900 by Frank K. Reilly and Sumner C. Britton, as the Madison Book Co. In 1902 the company was incorporated as the Reilly & Britton Co. Britton was president until 1913, and Reilly was president 1913–32. In 1919 the company became the Reilly & Lee Co. S. H. Darst was with the company 1911–36, and Leigh Reilly, 1919–29. Among the noted editors were Howard Vincent O'Brien and Clarke Venable. In 1916 the firm published Edgar A. Guest's *Heap O' Livin'* and this was the first of many popular books by Guest which Reilly & Lee Co., have published. In 1904 the company published Frank Baum's *Land of Oz,* and this with subsequent "Oz" books have been perennial favorites. Lulu Hunt Peters' *Diet and Health* in 1918 has been popular over the years. In 1930 the firm published *Tony's Scrap Book* by Tony Wons, the first of a successful series. Harold Bell Wright's books were sold through this firm for the J. N. Reynold's Company. Reilly & Lee was bought by Henry Regnery in 1959.

REINHARDT, GUENTHER (Dec. 13, 1904–Dec. 3, 1968); b. Mannheim, Ger. Author. *The Jews in Nazi Germany* (1933); *Crime Without Punishment* (1952); etc.

REINHARDT, JAMES MELVIN (Oct. 5, 1894–); b. near Dalton, Ga. Sociologist. *Current Social Problems* (with John M. Gillette, 1933); *Social Psychology* (1938); *Sex Perversions and Sex Crimes* (1957); etc. Dept. of sociology, University of Nebraska, since 1931.

REINHARDT, KURT FRANK (Nov. 2, 1896–); b. Munich, Ger. Educator, author. *Realistic Philosophy: The Perennial Principles of Thought and Action in a Changing World* (1944); *Germany: 2000 Years* (1950); *The Existentialist Revolt* (1952); *The Theological Novel of Modern Europe: An*

Analysis of Masterpieces by Eight Authors (1969); etc. Editor and translator: *St. John of the Cross, The Dark Night of the Soul* (1957); *Miguel de Unamuno, The Agony of Christianity* (1960); etc. Prof. Germanic languages, Stanford University, since 1930.

REINSCH, PAUL SAMUEL (June 10, 1869–Jan. 24, 1923); b. Milwaukee, Wis. Educator, diplomat, author. *World Politics at the End of the Nineteenth Century* (1900); *Colonial Government* (1902); *Colonial Administration* (1905); *Intellectual and Political Currents in the Far East* (1911); etc. Prof. political science, University of Wisconsin, 1901–13. Minister to China, 1913–19.

REISCHAUER, EDWIN OLDFATHER (Oct. 15, 1910–); b. Tokyo. Diplomat, historian. *Japan, Past and Present* (1946); *The United States and Japan* (1950); *Translations from Early Japanese Literature* (with Joseph Yamagiwa, 1951); *Wanted: An Asian Policy* (1955); *Ennin's Travels in T'ang Chine* (1955); *East Asia: The Great Tradition* (1960); *East Asia: The Modern Transformation* (with others, 1965); *Beyond Vietnam: The United States and Asia* (1967). Director, Harvard-Yenching Institute, from 1956. University professor, since 1966. Ambassador to Japan, 1961–66.

REISER, OLIVER LESLIE (Nov. 15, 1895–); b. Columbus, O. Educator. *Alchemy of Light and Color* (1928); *A New Earth and a New Humanity* (1942); *Nature, Man, and God* (1951); *The Integration of Human Knowledge* (1958); *Man's New Image of Man* (1961); *Cosmic Humanism* (1966); etc. Dept. of philosophy, University of Pittsburgh, since 1926.

Reizenstein, Elmer L. See Elmer Rice.

Remarkable Providences. Title usually used in referring to *An Essay for the Recording of Illustrious Providences* by Increase Mather (1684). Noted as a work on witchcraft.

REMARQUE, ERICH MARIA (June 22, 1898–Sept. 25, 1970); b. Osnabrück, Westphalia, Ger. Novelist. *All Quiet on the Western Front* (1929); *The Road Back* (1931); *Three Comrades* (1937); *Flotsam* (1941); *Arch of Triumph* (1946); *Spark of Life* (1952); *A Time to Love and a Time to Die* (1954); *Black Obelisk* (1957); *Heaven Has No Favorites* (1961); *The Night In Lisbon* (1964); etc. All translations from German.

Remembrance Rock. Novel by Carl Sandburg (1948). Panoramic view of the development of America conveyed through a flashback from the end of World War II in Europe. The reader follows the story forward from 17th-century England.

REMICK, GRACE MAY, b. Chelsea, Mass. Author. The *Glenlock Girls* series, 4v. (1909–12); the *Jane Stuart* series, 4v. (1913–16); the *Sheldon Six* series, etc.

REMINGTON, FREDERIC (Oct. 4, 1861–Dec. 26, 1909); b. Canton, N.Y. Painter, illustrator, author. *Pony Tracks* (1895); *Sundown Leflare* (1899); *Crooked Trails* (1898); *Men With the Bark On* (1900); *John Ermine of the Yellowstone* (1902); *The Way of an Indian* (1906); etc. Best known for his rugged paintings and drawings of cowboys, soldiers, Indians, and horses in scenes of swift action on the Western frontier. Many of his drawings are now in the New York Public Library, and the Remington Art Memorial, Ogdensburg, N.Y.

REMSEN, IRA (Feb. 10, 1846–Mar. 4, 1927); b. New York. Educator, chemist, author. *An Introduction to the Study of Chemistry* (1886); *Inorganic Chemistry* (1889); etc. Founder, the *American Chemical Journal,* 1879. President, Johns Hopkins University, 1901–13.

Renascence, and Other Poems. By Edna St. Vincent Millay (1917).

Renascence: A Critical Journal of Letters. Milwaukee, Wis. Quarterly. Founded 1948. Edited by John Pick. Devoted to criticism and book reviews.

Report from Iron Mountain (1967). About the possibilities of achieving international peace in the post-atomic-bomb world. The book is supposedly a secret U.S. government report leaked to Leonard Lewin. The report presumably was made by fifteen experts in various fields who convened at "Iron Mountain" to consider the feasibility of permanent peace. They come to the conclusion that war is necessary in human affairs, for it expresses an irrepressible need that would take violent form in any case.

Report of the President's Commission on the Assassination of President John F. Kennedy (1964). Sometimes known as the "Warren Report" because the Commission was headed by then Supreme Court Chief Justice Earl Warren. The Report occasioned the publication of numerous private studies of the assassination designed to argue against its conclusions.

Reporter, The. New York. Biweekly. Founded 1949, by Max Ascoli, who was also editor. Gouverneur Paulding was book review editor. Political and social opinion and reportage. Ceased publication 1968.

REPPLIER, AGNES (Apr. 1, 1855–Dec. 15, 1950); b. Philadelphia, Pa. Author. *Books and Men* (1888); *Points of View* (1891); *Essays in Miniature* (1892); *Essays in Idleness* (1893); *Varia* (1897); *Philadelphia* (1898); *The Fireside Sphinx* (1901); *Compromises* (1904); *In Our Convent Days* (1905); *The Cat* (1912); *Counter-Currents* (1915); *Père Marquette* (1929); *Mère Marie of the Ursulines* (1931); *Junípero Serra* (1933); *Agnes Irwin: A Biography* (1934); *In Pursuit of Laughter* (1936); *Eight Decades* (1937); *The Fireside Sphinx* (1939); etc. See Fred B. Millett's *Contemporary American Authors* (1940); George Stewart Stokes's *Agnes Repplier, Lady of Letters* (1949).

Requiem for a Nun. Novel by William Faulkner (1951). Written in a mixed, dramatic-narrative form as a sequel to *Sanctuary* (q.v.).

REQUIER, AUGUSTUS JULIAN (May 27, 1825–Mar. 19, 1887); b. Charleston, S.C. Author. *The Spanish Exile* (1842); *The Old Sanctuary: A Romance of the Ashley* (1846); *Poems* (1860); *Ode to Shakespeare* (1862); *The Legend of Tremaine* (1864); etc. His best known lyric is "Ashes of Glory."

Resistance to Civil Government. Essay by Henry David Thoreau. It first appeared in *Aesthetic Papers* (1849), ed. by Elizabeth Preston Peabody (1849). It was reprinted in several of Thoreau's collections of essays under the title "Civil Disobedience." This essay influenced Gandhi's non-resistance policy in India.

RESTON, JAMES BARRETT (Nov. 3, 1909–); b. Clydebank, Scot. Journalist, editor, author. *Sketches in the Sand* (1967); *The Artillery of the Press: Its Influence on American Foreign Policy* (1967). Staff, *New York Times,* since 1939; vice-president since 1969.

Return of Peter Grimm, The. Play by David Belasco (prod. 1911). A play of the supernatural; the ghost of Peter Grimm returns to earth to influence the lives of those left behind.

Reunion in Vienna. A play by Robert E. Sherwood (prod. 1931). A banished Hapsburg returns to Vienna and secretly visits his ex-mistress, Elena, now happily married. She succumbs to his attentions during his brief stay in Vienna.

REUTHER, WALTER PHILIP (Sept. 1, 1907–May 10, 1970); b. Wheeling, W. Va. Labor leader. *The Challenge of Automation* (with others, 1955); *Selected Papers,* ed. by Henry M. Christman (1961).

Reveille in Washington. Historical account of events in the U.S. capital during the Civil War, by Margaret Leech (1941).

REVELL, FLEMING H[ewitt] (Dec. 11, 1849–Oct. 11, 1931); b. Chicago, Ill. Publisher. Founder of Fleming H. Revell Company, Chicago, publishers of religious books. After the Chicago fire in 1871 Revell reestablished his business and in 1887 opened a branch in New York, which in 1906 became the main office of the firm, and is now one of the largest publishers of religious books. Revell's first success was the publication of the sermons of his brother-in-law Dwight L. Moody.

Reverberator, The. Novel by Henry James (1888).

REVERE, JOSEPH WARREN (May 17, 1812–Apr. 20, 1880); b. Boston, Mass. Military and naval officer, adventurer, author. *A Tour of Duty in California* (1849); *Keel and Saddle* (1872); etc.

Reveries of a Bachelor. By "Ik Marvel" (Donald Grant Mitchell) (1850). These popular sketches first appeared in the *Southern Literary Messenger* in 1849, and were reprinted in *Harper's New Monthly Magazine* in 1850. They include *A Bachelor's Reverie*, privately printed earlier in 1850.

Review of Reviews. New York. Monthly. Founded 1890, as the American edition of the *Review of Reviews*, London. In 1894 it became an independent magazine, under the editorship of Albert Shaw. It was a digest of international reviews. Shaw continued to edit it until 1937, when it was merged with the *Literary Digest* to form *The Digest*.

Reviewer, The. Richmond, Va. Monthly literary magazine. Founded 1921. Julia Peterkin, Frances Newman, Paul Green, and Du Bose Heyward were among the contributors. James Branch Cabell edited three issues. In 1925 it was moved to Chapel Hill, N.C., and in 1926 was absorbed by the *Southwest Review. See* Emily Clark.

Revolt of Mother, The. Short story by Mary E. Wilkins Freeman (1890).

Revolution for the Hell of It. By Abbie Hoffman (1968). Ideas about political and cultural revolution by the most notorious of the Youth International Party (Yippie) leaders.

REWALD, JOHN (May 12, 1912–); b. Berlin. Art historian. *Gauguin* (1938); *Maillol* (1939); *History of Impressionism* (1946); *Paul Cezanne* (1948); *Post-Impressionism: From Van Gogh to Gauguin* (1956); *Gauguin Drawings* (with others, 1958); etc. Editor: *Camille Pissarro, Letters to His Son Lucien* (1943); etc.

REXFORD, EBEN E[ugene] (July 16, 1848–Oct. 18, 1916); b. Johnsburg, N.Y. Poet. *Brother and Lover* (1886); *Grandmother's Garden* (1890); *Pansies and Rosemary* (poems, 1911); and many books on gardening. He was the author of the popular song "Silver Threads Among the Gold." *See* Mary L. P. Smith's *Eben E. Rexford: A Biographical Sketch* (1930).

REXROTH, KENNETH (Dec. 22, 1905–); b. South Bend, Ind. Painter, literary critic, poet. *In What Hour* (poems, 1940); *The Phoenix and the Tortoise* (poems, 1944); *The Signature of All Things* (1949); *The Art of Worldly Wisdom* (1949); *The Dragon and the Unicorn* (1952); *100 Poems from the Japanese* (1955); *100 Poems from the Chinese* (1956); *In Defense of the Earth* (poems, 1956); *The Bird in the Bush* (1959); *Assays* (1962); *The Homestead Called Damascus* (1962); *Natural Numbers* (1965); *An Autobiographical Novel* (1966); *Complete Collected Shorter Poems* (1966); *Beyond the Mountains* (plays, 1966); *Classics Revisited* (1968); *Collected Longer Poems* (1968); *Chinese Poems of Love and the Turning Year* (1969). San Francisco correspondent, *Nation,* after 1953. Co-founder, San Francisco Poetry Center.

Reynal & Hitchcock. New York. Publishers. Founded 1933, by Eugene Reynal and Curtice Hitchcock. Absorbed by Harcourt, Brace & Jovonovich in 1948.

REYNOLDS, CUYLER (Aug. 14, 1866–May 24, 1934); b. Albany, N.Y. Historian. *Janet* (1889); *Albany Chronicles* (1906). Editor: *Albany Authors* (1902); *The Banquet Book* (1902), republished as *Classified Quotations* (1905).

REYNOLDS, JOHN N. Author. *Mocha Dick: or, The White Whale of the Pacific* (1932).

REYNOLDS, MYRA (1853–Aug. 19, 1936); b. Troupsburg, N.Y. Educator, author. *The Treatment of Nature in English Poetry between Pope and Wordsworth* (1896); *The Learned Lady in England, 1650–1760* (1920). Compiler: *Selections from the Poetry of Alfred Tennyson* (1904); *Selections from the Poetry of Robert Browning* (1909); etc. English dept., University of Chicago, 1894–1936, prof. 1911–36.

REYNOLDS, PAUL REVERE (July 13, 1864–Aug. 19, 1944); b. Boston, Mass. Literary agent. Founded literary agency in New York in 1893. His son, Paul R. Reynolds, is a member of the firm, which is known as Paul R. Reynolds & Son.

REYNOLDS, QUENTIN [James] (Apr. 11, 1902–Mar. 17, 1965); b. New York. Editor, author. *The Wounded Don't Cry* (1941); *London Diary* (1941); *Dress Rehearsal* (1943); *The Curtain Rises* (1944); *Leave It to the People* (1949); *Courtroom* (1950); *I, Willie Sutton* (1953); *The Battle of Britain* (1953); *The F.B.I.* (1954); *The Life of St. Patrick* (1955); *The Fiction Factory* (1956); *They Fought for the Sky* (1957); *Known But to God* (1960); etc. Associate editor, *Collier's,* 1933–45.

REYNOLDS, TIM [othy Robin] (July 18, 1936–); b. Vicksburg, Miss. Poet. *Ryoanji: Poems* (1964); *Slocum: Poems* (1967).

REZNIKOFF, CHARLES (1894–). Poet. *Inscriptions: 1944–1956* (poems, 1959); *By the Waters of Manhattan* (poems, 1962); *Testimony: The United States 1885–1890; Recitative Poetry* (1965).

Rhapsodist, The. Essays by Charles Brockden Brown in the *Columbian Magazine,* Philadelphia, Aug.–Nov., 1789.

RHEES, WILLIAM JONES (Mar. 13, 1830–Mar. 18, 1907); b. Philadelphia, Pa. Bibliographer, author. *Manual of Public Libraries* (1859); *James Smithson and His Bequest* (1880); *The Smithsonian Institution,* 2v. (1901); etc.

RHINE, JOSEPH BANKS (Sept. 29, 1895–); b. Waterloo, Pa. Educator, psychologist, author. *Extra-Sensory Perception* (1934); *New Frontiers of the Mind* (1937); *The Reach of the Mind* (1947); *New World of the Mind* (1953); *Parapsychology, Frontier Science of the Mind* (1957); *Parapsychology* (1965); etc. Co-editor: *Parapsychology Today* (with Robert Brier, 1968). Psychology dept., Duke University, since 1928.

RHOADES, CORNELIA HARSEN (dec. 1, 1863–Nov. 28, 1940); b. New York. Author of children's books. Wrote under pen name, "Nina Rhoades." *The Little Girl Next Door* (1902); *Winifred's Neighbors* (1903); *How Barbara Kept Her Promise* (1905); *Little Miss Rosamond* (1906); *A Real Cinderella* (1915); etc.

Rhoades, Nina. See Cornelia Harsen Rhoades.

Rhode Island Gazette. Newport, R.I. Founded 1732, by James Franklin, brother of Benjamin Franklin. First newspaper in Rhode Island. Expired 1733.

RHODES, EUGENE MANLOVE (Jan. 19, 1869–June 26, 1934); b. Tecumseh, Neb. Author. *Good Men and True* (1911); *Bransford in Arcadia* (1913); *West Is West* (1917); *The Desire of the Moth,* and *The Come On* (1920); *Stepsons of Light* (1921); *Say Now Shibboleth* (1921); *Copper Streak Trail* (1922); *The Trusty Knaves* (1933); *Proud Sheriff* (1935); etc. *See* May Davison Rhodes's *The Hired Man on Horseback: My Story of Eugene Manlove Rhodes* (1938). *See* the introduction to Frank V. Dearing's *The Best Novels and Stories of Eugene Manlove Rhodes* (1949).

RHODES, HARRISON (Garfield) (June 2, 1871–Sept. 20, 1929); b. Cleveland, O. Author. *The Lady and the Ladder* (1906); *The Adventures of Charles Edward* (1907); *The Flight to Eden* (1907); *American Towns and People* (1920); etc.

RHODES, JAMES FORD (May 1, 1848–Jan. 22, 1927); b. Cleveland, O. Historian. *History of the United States,* 9v. (1893–1922); *Historical Essays* (1909); *A History of the Civil War* (1917, Pulitzer Prize for American history, 1918); etc. *See* M. A. De Wolfe Howe's *James Ford Rhodes* (1929).

"Rhodora, The." Poem by Ralph Waldo Emerson (1839).

Rhymes by Two Friends. Poems by William Allen White and Albert Bigelow Paine (1893).

Rhymes of Childhood Days. Poems by James Whitcomb Riley (1891).

RICE, ALICE HEGAN (Mrs. Cale Young Rice) (Jan. 11, 1870–Feb. 10, 1942); b. Shelbyville, Ky. Novelist. *Mrs. Wiggs of the Cabbage Patch* (1901); *Lovey Mary* (1903); *Sandy* (1905); *Captain June* (1907); *Mr. Opp* (1909); *A Romance of Billy Goat Hill* (1912); *Miss Mink's Soldier, and Other Stories* (1918); *Quinn* (1921); *Turn About Tales* (with husband, 1921); *The Buffer* (1929); *Mr. Pete & Co.* (1933); *The Lark Legacy* (1935); *Passionate Follies* (with husband, 1936); *Our Ernie* (1939); *The Inky Way* (autobiography, 1940); *Happiness Road* (1942); etc.

RICE, CALE YOUNG (Dec. 7, 1872–Jan. 23, 1943); b. Dixon, Ky. Poet, dramatist *From Dusk to Dusk* (1898); *Song-Surf* (1900); *David* (1904); *A Night in Avignon* (1907); *Many Gods* (1910); *Far Quests* (1912); *Collected Plays and Poems,* 2v. (1915); *Wraiths and Realities* (1918); *Songs to A. H. R.* (1918); *Turn About Tales* (with Alice Hegan Rice, 1920); *Sea Poems* (1921); *A Pilgrim's Scrip* (1924); *Bitter Brew* (1925); *Selected Plays and Poems* (1926); *High Perils* (1933); *Passionate Follies* (with Alice Hegan Rice, 1936); *Bridging the Years* (autobiography, 1939); etc.

RICE, CHARLES ALLEN THORNDIKE (June 18, 1851–May 16, 1889); b. Boston, Mass. Editor: *Reminiscences of Abraham Lincoln* (1886). In 1876, he bought the *North American Review,* then a quarterly, and moved it from Boston to New York, making it a successful monthly. *See* D. Charney's *The Ancient Cities of the New World* (1887).

RICE, EDWIN WILBUR (July 24, 1831–Dec. 3, 1929); b. Kingsborough, N.Y. Congregational clergyman, editor, author. *The Sunday-School Movement, 1780–1917, and the American Sunday School Union, 1817–1917* (1917); etc. With the American Sunday School Union, 1870–1929; editor of its publications, 1879–1915.

RICE, ELMER L. (Sept. 28, 1892–May 8, 1967); b. (Reizenstein) New York. Playwright, novelist, stage director. *On Trial* (prod. 1914); *The Iron Cross* (prod. 1917); *The Adding Machine* (prod. 1923); *Cock Robin* (with Philip Barry, prod. 1928); *The Subway* (prod. 1929); *Street Scene* (prod. 1929, Pulitzer Prize play, 1929); *See Naples and Die* (prod. 1929); *A Voyage to Purilia* (novel, 1930); *Counsellor at Law* (prod. 1931); *The Left Bank* (prod. 1931); *Black Sheep* (prod. 1932); *We, the People* (prod. 1933); *Judgment Day* (prod. 1934); *Between Two Worlds* (prod. 1934); *Imperial City* (novel, 1937); *Two on an Island* (prod. 1940); *Flight to the West* (prod. 1941); *A New Life* (prod. 1943); *Dream Girl* (prod. 1945); *The Show Must Go On* (1949); *Not for Children* (prod. 1951); *The Grand Tour* (prod. 1951); *The Winner* (1954); *Cue for Passion* (prod. 1958); *The Living Theatre* (1959); etc. *See* Joseph Wood Krutch's *The American Drama Since 1918: An Informal History* (1939); Fred B. Millett's *Contemporary American Authors* (1940).

RICE, GEORGE EDWARD (July 10, 1822–Aug. 10, 1861); b. Boston, Mass. Poet, playwright. *Ephemera* (poems, with John Howard Wainwright, 1852); *Blondel* (1854); *Nugamenta* (poems, 1859); etc.

RICE, GRANTLAND (Nov. 1, 1880–July 13, 1954); b. Murfreesboro, Tenn. Journalist, author. *Songs of the Stalwart* (1917); *Sportlights of 1923* (1924); *Songs of the Open* (1924); *Only the Brave* (poems, 1941); *The Tumult and the Shouting* (1954); Staff, *New York Tribune,* 1914–30. Wrote syndicated column, "The Sportlight," from 1930.

RICE, HARVEY (June 11, 1800–Jan. 18, 1891); b. Conway, Mass. Lawyer, editor, poet. *Mount Vernon, and Other Poems* (1858); *Nature and Culture* (1875); *Select Poems* (1878); *Pioneers of the Western Reserve* (1882); *Sketches of Western Life* (1887); etc.

RICE, JENNINGS (Oct. 8, 1900–   ); b. in Virginia. Author. *The Man Who Insulted Somerville* (1938); *Windmill Circle* (1943); etc.

RICE, PAUL NORTH (Feb. 9, 1888–Apr. 16, 1967); b. Lowell, Mass. Librarian. With the New York Public Library, 1914–27; librarian, Dayton Public Library, 1927–36; director of libraries, New York University, 1936–38; chief of reference dept., the New York Public Library, 1937–53.

RICE, REBECCA (Oct. 20, 1899–); b. Newtonville, Mass. Author. *The Brown Castle* (1926); *Carolina's Toy Shop* (1928); *Giles of the Star* (1928); *Creative Activities* (1947); *The Earth Is Full of His Riches* (1953); etc.

RICE, RICHARD ASHLEY (Jan. 29, 1878–Aug. 6, 1955); b. Burlington, Vt. Educator, author. *Robert Louis Stevenson: How to Know Him* (1916); *A Book of Narratives* (1917); *Studies in Wordsworth and Byron* (1924); *Rousseau and the Poetry of Nature* (1925); etc. Prof. English, Smith College, 1916–46.

RICE, ROSELLA (b. Aug. 11, 1827); b. Perrysville, O. Author. *Mabel; or, Heart Histories* (1858). She also wrote, under pen name "Pipsissiway Potts," *Other People's Windows,* in *Arthur's Home Magazine,* 1871–72; also, under pen name "Chatty Brooks," *My Girl and I,* and other serials; also, under own name, *Fifty Years Ago; or, The Cabins of the West,* and other serials.

RICE, THOMAS DARTMOUTH (May 20, 1808–Sept. 19, 1860); b. New York. Called the "Father of American Minstrelsy." He wrote the famous "Jim Crow" song in 1828, a hit in America and England, besides many Negro minstrel extravaganzas, sometimes called "Ethiopian Opera." *See* Ed. Leroy Rice's *Monarchs of Minstrelsy* (1911); D. Paskman and Sigmund Spaeth's *Gentlemen, Be Seated* (1928); Carl Wittke's *Tambo and Bones* (1930).

RICE, WALLACE (de Groot Cecil) (Nov. 10, 1859–Dec. 15, 1939); b. Hamilton, Ont. Lecturer, author. *A Chicago Boy in the 60's* (1928); *Palmer House, Old and New* (1929); etc. Wrote many historical pageants.

RICH, ALAN (June 17, 1924–   ); b. Boston, Mass. Music critic, author. *Careers and Opportunities in Music* (1964); etc. Contributor to newspapers and magazines on musical subjects.

RICH, DANIEL CATTON (Apr. 16, 1904–); b. South Bend, Ind. Museum director. *Seurat and the Evolution of "La Grande Jatte"* (1935); *Henri Rousseau* (1942); *Degas* (1951).

RICH, LOUISE DICKINSON (June 14, 1903–); b. Huntington, Mass. Author. *We Took to the Woods* (with Ralph Eugene Rich, 1942); *Happy the Land* (1946); *My Neck of the Woods* (1950); *Innocence Under the Elms* (1955); *The Coast of Maine* (1956); *The Peninsula* (1958); *Mindy* (1959); *The Natural World of Louise Dickinson Rich* (1962); *State O'-Maine* (1964); *First Book of the Fur Trade* (1965); *Star Island Boy* (1968); etc.

RICH, OBADIAH (1783–Jan. 20, 1850); b. Truro, Mass. Bibliographer, collector of Americana. Compiler: *A Catalogue of Books, Relating Principally to America* (1832); *Bibliotheca Americana Nova; or, A Catalogue of Books in Various Languages Relating to America, Printed Since the Year 1700,* 2v. (1835–46).

RICHARD, JAMES WILLIAM (Feb. 14, 1843–Mar. 7, 1909); b. near Winchester, Va. Lutheran clergyman, author. *Christian Worship: Its Principles and Forms* (with F. V. N. Painter, 1892); *Philip Melanchthon* (1898); *The Confessional History of the Lutheran Church* (1909); etc.

Richard Carvel. Novel by Winston Churchill (1900). Richard is rescued from pirates by John Paul Jones. Later, during the American Revolution, Richard forsakes London, rejoins Jones, and fights in the naval battle between the *Bon Homme Richard* and the *Serapis.*

"Richard Cory." Poem by Edwin Arlington Robinson (1897).

RICHARDS, ELIZABETH DAVIS (Apr. 1884–); b. Morgantown, W.Va. Composer, poet, author. *Leaves of Laurel* (1925); *The Peddler of Dreams, and Other Poems* (1928); etc. Editor: *Thistle Down* (a West Virginia anthology, 1929).

RICHARDS, HAROLD MARSHALL SYLVESTER (Aug. 28, 1894–); b. Davis City, Ia. Adventist clergyman. *Revival Sermons* (1947); *Promises of God* (1956); *What Jesus Said* (1957); *Look to the Stars* (1964); etc.

Richards, Harvey D. Pen name of Noel Everingham Sainsbury.

RICHARDS, I[vor] A[rmstrong] (Feb. 26, 1893–); b. in Cheshire, Eng. Educator, author. *The Meaning of Meaning* (with C. K. Ogden, 1923); *The Principles of Literary Criticism* (1926); *Coleridge on Imagination* (1934); *A Philosophy of Rhetoric* (1936); *Interpretation in Teaching* (1938); *How to Read a Page* (1942); *Nations and Peace* (1947); *Practical Criticism* (1950); *Speculative Instruments* (1955); *Goodbye Earth, and Other Poems* (1958); *The Screens, and Other Poems* (1960); *Tomorrow Morning, Faustus!* (play, 1962); *Why So, Socrates?* (play, 1964); *Plato's Republic* (1965); *So Much Nearer* (1968); *Design for Escape: World Education Through Modern Media* (1968). Lecturer on literary criticism, Harvard University, since 1939; university professor, since 1966. *See* J. P. Schiller's *I.A. Richard's Theory of Literature* (1969).

RICHARDS, LAURA ELIZABETH (Feb. 27, 1850–Jan. 14, 1943); b. Boston, Mass., daughter of Samuel Gridley Howe and Julia Ward Howe. Author. *Five Mice* (1881); *Captain January* (1890); *Rita* (1900); *Snow White* (1900); *Geoffrey Strong* (1901); *Grandmother* (1907); *Florence Nightingale* (1909); *Miss Jimmy* (1913); *Julia Ward Howe* (with Maude Howe Elliott and Florence Howe Hall, 1915, Pulitzer Prize for biography, 1917); *Life of Elizabeth Fry* (1916); *Pippin* (1917); *Abigail Adams and Her Times* (1917); *Joan of Arc* (1919); *Honor Bright* (1920); *Star Bright* (1927); *Laura Bridgman* (1928); *Stepping Westward* (autobiography, 1931); *Tirra-Lirra* (1932); *Samuel Gridley Howe* (1935); etc. Editor: *The Letters and Journals of Samuel Gridley Howe*, 2v. (1906–09).

RICHARDS, LELA HORN (Apr. 15, 1870–); b. Junction City, Kan. Author. The *Blue Bonnet* series, 5v. (1916–29); the *Caroline* series, 3v. (1921–23); *Poplars Across the Moon* (under pen name "Lee Neville," 1937); etc.

RICHARDS, THOMAS ADDISON (Dec. 3, 1820–June 28, 1900); b. London, Eng. Painter, illustrator, author. *The American Artist* (1838); *Georgia Illustrated* (1842); *Tallulah and Jocassee* (1852); *Summer Stories of the South* (1853); *American Scenery, Illustrated* (1854); *Appleton's Illustrated Hand-Book of American Travel* (1857); etc.

RICHARDSON, ABBY SAGE (Mrs. Albert Deane Richardson) (Oct. 14, 1837–Dec. 5, 1900); b. in Massachusetts. Author. *Stories from Old English Poetry* (1871); *The History of Our Country* (1875); *Familiar Talks on English Literature* (1881).

RICHARDSON, ALBERT D[eane] (Oct. 6, 1833–Dec. 2, 1869); b. Franklin, Mass. Journalist, author. *The Secret Service, the Field, the Dungeon, and the Escape* (1865); *Beyond the Mississippi* (1867); *Garnered Sheaves* (1871); etc. *See* A. R. Cazauran's *The Trial of Daniel McFarland* (1870).

RICHARDSON, CHARLES FRANCIS (May 29, 1851–Oct. 8, 1913); b. Hallowell, Me. Educator, author. *The Cross* (poems, 1879); *The Choice of Books* (1881); *American Literature, 1607–1885*, 2v. (1887–88); *The End of the Beginning* (anon., 1896); etc. Editor: *The International Cyclopedia*, 15v. (1893). Prof. Anglo-Saxon, Dartmouth College, 1882–1911. *See* J. A. Vinton's *The Richardson Memorial* (1876).

RICHARDSON, CYRIL C[harles] (June 13, 1909–); b. London. Episcopal clergyman, educator, author. *The Christianity of Ignatius of Antioch* (1935); *The Church through the Centuries* (1938); *The Sacrament of Reunion* (1940); *The Doctrine of the Trinity* (1958); *Living Thankfully* (1961); *Christianity on the March* (1963); *Ecumenical Dialogue at Harvard* (1964); etc. Dept. church history, Union Theological Seminary, since 1934.

RICHARDSON, DOROTHY (May 20, 1875–Mar. 27, 1955); b. Prospect, Pa. Journalist, author. *The Long Day* (1905); *The Book of Blanche* (1924). With the *New York Herald*, 1899–1909.

RICHARDSON, DOROTHY (Mrs. Robert C. Kissling) (Feb. 14, 1904–); b. Brownsville, Tex. Novelist. *Wait for Mrs. Willard* (1944); *Dark Medallion* (1945); *Mr. Bremble's Buttons* (1947); *The Hoogles and Alexander* (1948); etc.

RICHARDSON, ERNEST CUSHING (Feb. 9, 1860–June 3, 1939); b. Woburn, Mass. Librarian, author. *The Beginnings of Libraries* (1914); *Biblical Libraries* (1914); *Materials for a Life of Jacopo da Varagine* (1935); etc. Compiler: *Writings on American History* (1902); *A Union World Catalogue of Manuscript Books*, 6 parts (1933–37); etc. Librarian, Princeton University, 1890–1925.

RICHARDSON, EUDORA RAMSAY (Fitzhugh Briggs Richardson), b. Versailles, Ky. Author. *Little Aleck: A Life of Alexander H. Stephens* (1932); *The Influence of Men Incurable* (1936); etc.

RICHARDSON, FRANK HOWARD (July 1, 1882–May 26, 1970); b. Brooklyn, N.Y. Physician, author. *The Nursing Mother* (1953); *How to Get Along with Children* (1954); *For Teen-Agers Only* (1957); *For Young Adults Only* (1961); *For Parents Only: The Doctor Discusses Dicipline* (1962); *The Christian Doctor Talks with Young Parents* (1963); *Grandparents and Their Families* (1964); etc.

RICHARDSON, GEORGE TILTON (July 2, 1863–Sept. 11, 1938); b. Boston, Mass. Journalist, author. Co-author with Wilder Dwight Quint, using the joint pen name "Dwight Tilton": *Miss Petticoats* (1902); *On Satan's Mount* (1903); *My Lady Laughter* (1904); *The Golden Greyhound* (1906); etc.; also, using the joint pen name "Charles Eustace Merriman": *Letters from a Son to His Self-Made Father* (1903); *A Self-Made Man's Wife: Her Letters to Her Son* (1905). With several Boston newspapers; editor, the *Worcester Evening Post*, 1914–37.

RICHARDSON, HOWARD (Dec. 2, 1917–); b. Spartanburg, S.C. Playwright. *Dark of the Moon* (1945); *Design for a Stained Glass Window* (1949); *Protective Custody* (1956); etc.

RICHARDSON, JACK (Feb. 18, 1935–); b. New York. Author. *The Prodigal* (1960); *Gallows Humor* (1961); *Prison Life of Harris Filmore* (1963).

RICHARDSON, LEANDER [Pease] (Feb. 28, 1856–Feb. 2, 1918); b. Cincinnati, O. Editor, critic, novelist, playwright. *The Dark City* (1886); *The Prairie Detective* (1889); *Lord Dunmarsey* (1889); *The Millionarie* (prod. 1891); *Under the City Lamps* (prod. 1893); etc. Editor, the *Dramatic News*, 1891–96; on staff, the *New York Morning Telegraph*, 1896–1900; editor, the *New York Inquirer*.

RICHARDSON, LEON JOSIAH (Feb. 22, 1868–Nov., 1966); b. Keene, N.H. Educator, author. *Cronies: A Poetical Miscellany* (1934); *Arrows and Driftwood: Essays in Lifelong Learning* (1935); *Quintus Horatius Flaccus* (1935); *Old Cronies* (poems, 1951); etc. Latin dept., University of California, 1891–1938, professor, 1919–38.

RICHARDSON, LYON N[orman] (July 20, 1898–); b. Andover, O. Educator, author. *A History of Early American Magazines, 1741–1789* (1931). Editor: *Henry James* (1941). Co-editor: *The Heritage of American Literature,* 2v. (1951). English dept., Western Reserve University, since 1923.

RICHARDSON, NORVAL (Oct. 8, 1877–1940); b. Vicksburg, Miss. Author. *The Heart of Hope* (1905); *The Lead of Honour* (1910); *George Thorne* (1911); *Pagan Fire* (1920); *The Cave Woman* (1922); *My Diplomatic Education* (1923); *Mother of Kings* (1928); *Forgotten Lady* (1937); *Living Abroad* (1938).

RICHARDSON, RUFUS BYAM (Apr. 18, 1845–Mar. 10, 1914); b. Westford, Mass. Educator, Greek scholar, archaeologist, author. *Vacation Days in Greece* (1903); *History of Greek Sculpture* (1911). Director, American School of Classical Studies, Athens, Greece 1893–1903. See J. A. Vinton's *The Richardson Memorial* (1876).

RICHARDSON, RUPERT NORVAL (Apr. 28, 1891–); b. near Caddo, Tex. Educator, historian. *The Comanche Barrier to South Plains Settlements* (1933); *The Greater Southwest* (with C. C. Rister, 1934); *Texas: the Lone Star State* (1943); *Adventuring with a Purpose* (1952); *The Frontier of Northwest Texas* (1963); *Colonel Edward M. House* (1964); *Famous are the Halls* (1964); *Caddo, Texas: The Biography of a Community* (1966); etc. Prof. history Hardin-Simmons University, Abilene, Tex., since 1917.

RICHBERG, DONALD RANDALL (July 10, 1881–Nov. 27, 1960); b. Knoxville, Tenn. Lawyer, author. *The Shadow Men* (1911); *Who Wins in November?* (1916); *A Man of Purpose* (1922); *Tents of the Mighty* (1930); *The Rainbow* (1936); *Guilty!* (1936); *G. Hovah Explains* (1940); *Government and Business Tomorrow* (1943); *Old Faith and Fancies New* (1949); *My Hero* (autobiography, 1954); *Labor Union Monopoly* (1957). Co-author: *Only the Brave Are Free* (1958).

RICHMAN, ARTHUR (Apr. 16, 1886–Sept. 10, 1944); b. New York. Playwright. *Not So Long Ago* (prod. 1920); *Ambush* (prod. 1921); *The Serpent's Tooth* (prod. 1922); *The Far Cry* (prod. 1924); *All Dressed Up* (prod. 1925); *Heavy Traffic* (prod. 1928); *The Season Changes* (prod. 1935).

RICHMOND, EUPHEMIA JOHNSON (b. 1825); b. near Mt. Upton, N.Y. Novelist. Wrote early books as "Effie Johnson," later ones as "Mrs. E. J. Richmond." *The McAllisters* (1871); *The Jeweled Serpent* (1872); *The Fatal Dower* (1874); *Alice Grant* (1876); *Rose Clifton* (1881); *Woman, First and Last,* 2v. (1887), repub. as *The World's Woman* (1891); *Anna Maynard* (1888); *Aunt Chloe and Her Young Friends* (1891); *Fact & Fable* (1901); etc.

RICHMOND, GRACE [Louise] S[mith] (1866–Nov. 26, 1959); b. Pawtucket, R.I. Novelist. *The Second Violin* (1906); *Around the Corner in Gay Street* (1908); *A Court of Inquiry* (1909); *Red Pepper Burns* (1910); *Strawberry Acres* (1911); *The Twenty-Fourth of June, Midsummer's Day* (1914); *Red and Black* (1919); *Red of the Redfields* (1925); *The Listening Post* (1929); *Red Pepper Returns* (1931); etc.

RICHMOND, MARY ELLEN (Aug. 5, 1861–Sept. 12, 1928); b. Belleville, Ill. Social worker, author. *Friendly Visiting among the Poor* (1899); *The Good Neighbor in the Modern City* (1907); *Social Diagnosis* (1917); etc.

Richmond Enquirer. Richmond, Va. Newspaper. Founded 1804, by Spencer Roane. A second *Enquirer* was founded 1847, by John M. Daniel; they merged in 1867 to form the *Enquirer and Examiner,* shortened to *Enquirer* in 1870. Expired 1877.

Richmond News Leader. Richmond, Va. Newspaper. The *Richmond Leader* was founded 1888, by Joseph Bryan. The *Richmond News* was founded 1899, by John L. Williams. Merged 1903. Douglas Southall Freeman was editor from 1915 to 1949. Since 1940, the paper has been under the same management as the *Richmond Times-Dispatch.* D. T. Bryan is publisher; Virginius Dabney is editor. Ann Merriman is book editor.

Richmond Times-Dispatch. Richmond, Va. Newspaper. The *Richmond Dispatch* was founded Oct. 19, 1850, by James A. Cowardin and W. H. Davis. The *Richmond Times* was founded Oct. 22, 1886, as the *Daily Times,* by Lewis Ginter. Joseph Bryan, who had bought the *Times* in 1889, merged the two papers in 1903. He had on his staff such noted writers as William L. Royall, Philip Alexander Bruce, and Jacques Futrelle. Bryan was editor, 1904–08; Henry Sydnor Harrison, 1908–10; James Calvin Hemphill, 1910–12; John Stewart Bryan, 1912–14; Douglas Gordon, 1923–28. Douglas Southall Freeman, J. Rion McKissick, Louis I. Jaffe, William B. Smith, J. Fred Essary, were on the staff in later years. Virginius Dabney is the present editor. Since 1940, under the same management as the *Richmond News Leader.*

RICHTER, CONRAD MICHAEL (Oct. 13, 1890–Oct. 30, 1968); b. Pine Grove, Pa. Author. *Brothers of No Kin, and Other Stories* (1924); *Early Americana, and Other Stories* (1936); *The Sea of Grass* (1937); *The Trees* (1940); *Tacey Cromwell* (1942); *The Free Man* (1943); *The Fields* (1946); *Always Young and Fair* (1947); *The Town* (1950; Pulitzer Prize for fiction, 1951); *The Light in the Forest* (1953); *The Mountain on the Desert* (1955); *The Lady* (1957); *The Water of Kronos* (1960); *Simple Honourable Man* (1962); *Grandfathers* (1964); *Country of Strangers* (1966); *Awakening Land* (1966); *Over the Blue Mountain* (1967); *Aristocrat* (1968).

RICKENBACKER, EDWARD VERNON [Eddie] (Oct. 8, 1890–); b. Columbus, O. Aviator. *Fighting the Flying Circus* (1919); *Seven Came Through* (1943); *Rickenbacker: An Autobiography* (1967); etc.

RICKERT, EDITH (July 11, 1871–May 23, 1938); b. Dover, O. Educator, author. *Out of the Cypress Swamp* (1902); *The Reaper* (1904); *Folly* (1906); *The Golden Hawk* (1907); *The Beggar in the Heart* (1909); *The Bojabi Tree* (1923); *New Methods for the Study of Literature* (1927); *The Greedy Goroo* (1929); *Severn Woods* (1929). Editor: *American Lyrics* (with Jessie Paton, 1912); *The Writing of English* (with J. M. Manly, 1919); *Contemporary British Literature* (with same, 1921); *Contemporary American Literature* (with same, 1922); also many old English texts; etc. English dept., University of Chicago, 1924–38.

RICKETSON, DANIEL (July 30, 1813–July 16, 1898); b. New Bedford, Mass. Historian, poet. *The History of New Bedford* (1858); *The Autumn Sheaf* (1869); *The Factory Bell, and Other Poems* (1873); *New Bedford of the Past,* ed. by his daughter and son, Anna and Walton Ricketson (1903). At his county seat "Brooklawn" he often entertained Emerson, Thoreau, Bronson, Alcott, and George William Curtis, and carried on a voluminous correspondence with them, particularly with Thoreau. See *Daniel Ricketson and His Friends,* ed. by his daughter and son, Anna and Walton Ricketson (1902); and *Daniel Ricketson: Autobiographic and Miscellaneous,* ed. by same (1910).

Ricketts, Cid. See Cid Ricketts Sumner.

RICKOVER, HYMAN GEORGE (1900–); Naval officer. *Education and Freedom* (1959); *Swiss Schools and Ours* (1962); *American Education–A National Failure* (1963).

RICKS, PEIRSON (Aug. 21, 1908–   ); b. Mayodan, N.C. Novelist. *Bye-Bye Breeches* (1936); *The Hunter's Horn* (1947); etc.

Riddell, John Pen name of Corey Ford.

RIDDLE, ALBERT GALLATIN (May 28, 1816–May 16, 1902); b. Monson, Mass. Lawyer, biographer, novelist. *Bart Ridgeley* (1873); *The Portrait* (1874); *Alice Brand* (1875); *The Life of Benjamin F. Wade* (1886); *The House of Ross* (1887); *The Tory's Daughter* (1888); *Recollections of War Times* (1895).

"Ride of Paul Venarez, The." Ballad of Eben E. Rexford, which first appeared in *The Youth's Companion.* It was popular as a recitation and was later made over into a ballad called "The Ride of Billy Venero."

RIDEING, WILLIAM HENRY (Feb. 17, 1853–Aug. 22, 1918); b. Liverpool, Eng. Editor, author. *A-Saddle in the Wild West* (1879); *The Alpenstock* (1880); *Boys in the Mountains* (1882); *A Little Upstart* (1885); *The Boyhood of Living Authors* (1887); *In the Land of Lorna Doone* (1895); *At Hawarden with Mr. Gladstone* (1896); *Many Celebrities and a Few Others* (1912). Assoc. Editor, *Youth's Companion,* 1881–1918; managing editor, *North American Review,* 1888–99. On staff, the *New York Times* and other newspapers.

RIDEOUT, HENRY MILNER (Apr. 25, 1877–Sept. 17, 1927); b. Calais, Me. Critic, editor, author. *Beached Keels* (1906); *The Siamese Cat* (1907); *Admiral's Light* (1907); *Dragon's Blood* (1909); *The Twisted Foot* (1910); *William Jones* (1912); *White Tiger* (1915); *Fern Seed* (1921); *Barbry* (1923); *Man Eater* (1924); Tao Tales (1927).

RIDER, [Arthur] FREMONT (May 25, 1885–Oct. 26, 1962); b. Trenton, N.J. Librarian, author. *Between Seven and Eight* (1910); *The Bringing In of the Almeria* (1920); etc. Editor: *Rider's New York City* (1916); *Rider's Bermuda* (1922); *Rider's Washington* (1923); *Rider's California* (1925); *A Study of Library Policy* (1943); *The Scholar and the Future of the Research Library* (1944); *And Master of None* (1955); etc. Compiler: *Songs of Syracuse* (1905). Managing editor, Library Journal, 1914–17; *Publisher's Weekly,* 1910–17; editor, *American Library Annual,* 1912–17; *Monthly Book Review,* 1909–17; etc. President, Rider Press, 1914–33; librarian, Wesleyan University, Middletown, Conn., from 1933. Founder Godfrey Memorial Library, 1951.

RIDER, GEORGE T. Anthologist. *Lyra Americana; or, Verses of Praise and Faith, from American Poets* (1851); *Lyra Anglicana; or, A Hymnal of Sacred Poetry, Selected from the Best English Writers* (1865); etc.

Riders of the Purple Sage. Western Novel by Zane Grey (1912).

RIDGE, JOHN ROLLIN (Mar. 19, 1827–Oct. 5, 1867); b. near Rome, Ga. Cherokee Indian editor, poet. Pen name, "Yellow Bird," a translation of his Indian name, "Chees-quat-a-law-ny." *The Life and Adventures of Joaquin Murieta* (1854); *Poems* (1868). Editor, the *Sacramento Bee,* 1857; the *California Express,* 1857–58; the *San Francisco Herald,* 1861–63; etc. See *Chronicles of Oklahoma,* Dec. 1926, and Sept. 1936; and the *Southwest Review,* Autumn 1931.

RIDGE, LOLA (1884–May 19, 1941); b. Dublin. Poet. *The Ghetto, and Other Poems* (1918); *Sun-Up, and Other Poems* (1920); *Red Flag* (1927); *Firehead* (1929); *Dance of Fire* (1935). Her longest and best-known poem was "Firehead," which recorded the drama of the Crucifixion. See Fred B. Millett's *Contemporary American Authors* (1940).

RIDGEWAY, JAMES [Fowler] (Nov. 1, 1936–); b. Auburn, N.Y. Journalist, author. *The Closed Corporation* (1968). Contributing editor, *New Republic,* since 1968; editor, *Hard Times,* since 1968.

RIDGWAY, ERMAN JESSE (Aug. 6, 1867–June 16, 1943); b. near Otsego, O. Publisher. Vice-pres., The Frank A. Munsey Co., 1894–1903; president, The Ridgway Co., 1903–17. Director, The Butterick Co., 1910–17. Associated with Frank A. Munsey's publications, 1917–24.

RIDING, LAURA (Mrs. Schuyler Jackson) (Jan. 16, 1901–); b. New York. Poet, novelist, essayist. *The Close Chaplet* (1926); *Voltaire* (1927); *A Survey of Modernist Poetry* (with Robert Graves, 1927); *Contemporaries and Snobs* (1928); *Poems* (1930); *Laura and Francisca* (1931); *Poet: A Lying Word* (1933); *Americans* (1934); *Progress of Stories* (1935); *Trojan Ending* (1937); *Collected Poems* (1938); *The World and Ourselves* (1938); etc.

RIDPATH, JOHN CLARK (Apr. 26, 1840–July 31, 1900); b. in Putnam Co., Ind. Educator, historian. *A Popular History of the United States of America* (1876). Editor: *Cyclopaedia of Universal History,* in parts (1880–85); *Great Races of Mankind,* in parts (1884–94); *The Ridpath Library of Universal Literature,* 25v. (1898). Prof. English literature, Indiana Asbury (now De Pauw) University, 1869–71; prof. belles-lettres and history, 1871–82; prof. history and political philosophy, 1882–85; vice-president, 1879–85.

RIEFF, PHILIP (Dec. 15, 1922–   ); b. Chicago, Ill. Sociologist, author. *Freud: The Mind of the Moralist* (1959); *The Triumph of the Therapeutic: Uses of Faith After Freud* (1966). Editor: *The Collected Papers of Sigmund Freud* (10 v., 1961). Prof. sociology, University of Pennsylvania, since 1961.

RIEGEL, ROBERT EDGAR (Dec. 4, 1897–); b. Reading, Pa. Educator, author. *The Story of the Western Railroads* (1926); *American Moves West* (1930); *The American Story,* 2v. (with David F. Long, 1955); *American Feminists* (1963); etc. Prof. history, Dartmouth College, since 1922.

RIESENBERG, FELIX (Apr. 9, 1879–Nov. 19, 1939); b. Milwaukee, Wis. Engineer, master mariner, author. *Under Sail* (1915); *Vignettes of the Sea* (1926); *Endless River* (1931); *Clipper Ships* (1932); *Log of the Sea* (1933); *Cape Horn* (1939); *Living Again: An Autobiography* (1937); *The Pacific Ocean* (1940); etc. His son, Felix Riesenberg, Jr., is author of *Golden Gate: The Story of San Francisco Harbor* (1940).

RIESMAN, DAVID (Sept. 22, 1909–); b. Philadelphia, Pa. Social scientist, author. *The Lonely Crowd* (with others, 1950); *Faces in the Crowd* (1952); *Thorstein Veblen* (1953); *Individualism Reconsidered, and Other Essays* (1954); *Constraint and Variety in American Education* (1956); *Abundance for What? and Other Essays* (1963); *Conversations in Japan* (with Christopher Jencks, 1967); *The Academic Revolution* (1968); etc. Prof. social science, Harvard University, since 1958.

RIGG, EDGAR TAYLOR (Jan. 10, 1900–); b. Baltimore, Md. Publisher. Pres., Henry Holt and Co., from 1949; Chairman of board, Holt, Rinehart & Winston, Inc, 1960–67.

RIGGS, ARTHUR STANLEY (Apr. 8, 1879–Nov. 8, 1952); b. Cranford, N.J. Editor, author. *Vistas in Sicily* (1911); *France from Sea to Sea* (1913); *With Three Armies* (1918); *Spain: A Pageant* (1927); *The Romance of Human Progress* (1938); *Titian the Magnificent and the Venice of His Day* (1946); *Velázquez, Painter of Truth and Prisoner of a King* (1947); etc. Editor of Manila newspapers, etc.

RIGGS, LYNN (1899–June 30, 1954); b. near Claremore, Indian Terr. (now Oklahoma). Playwright, poet. *Big Lake* (prod. 1927); *Sump'n Like Wings, and A Lantern to See By* (plays, 1928); *The Iron Dish* (poems, 1930); *Roadside* (prod. 1930); *Green Grow the Lilacs* (prod. 1930; musical version, *Oklahoma!* by Rodgers and Hammerstein, prod. 1943); *The Russet Mantle,* and *The Cherokee Night* (plays, 1936); *World Elsewhere* (plays, 1940); *Four Plays* (1947); *Hang on to Love* (1948); *Toward the Western Sky* (1951); etc.

RIGGS, STEPHEN R[eturn] (Mar. 23, 1812–Aug. 24, 1883); b. Steubenville, O. Missionary, author. *Mary and I: Forty Years with the Sioux* (1880); also grammars, dictionaries, etc., of the Dakota language. Translator and compiler (with John P. Williamson): *Dakota Odowan* (hymns, 1853); etc.

Right Cross. Pen name of Paul Armstrong.

Rights of Man, The. By Tom Paine (1791). A revolutionary tract that urged men to free themselves from government tyranny. The author claimed that every age and generation must be free to act for itself and that it must not allow the State to set up artificial barriers to the free exercise of man's natural rights.

Rights of the Inhabitants of Maryland to the Benefits of the English Laws. By Daniel Dulany (1728). A pamphlet of importance in the colonial controversy in Maryland.

RIHANI, AMEEN [Fares] (Nov. 24, 1876–Sept. 14, 1940); b. Freiké, Mt. Lebanon, Syria. Poet, translator. *Makers of Modern Arabia* (1928); *Around the Coast of Arabia* (1929); etc. Interpreter of Arabic literature by his translations: *The Quatrains of Abu'l-Ala* (1903); *The Book of Khalid* (1911); *Ar-Rihaniyat,* 4v. (1910–24); etc.

RIIS, JACOB AUGUST (May 3, 1849–May 26, 1914); b. Ribe, Den. Journalist, reformer, author. *How the Other Half Lives* (1890); *Out of Mulberry Street* (1898); *The Making of an American* (1901); *The Battle with the Slum* (1902); *Children of the Tenements* (1903); *Is There a Santa Claus* (1904); etc. With the *New York Tribune* 1877–88; the *New York Sun* (1888–99). *See* Joseph Husband's *Americans by Adoption* (1920); Louise Ware's *Jacob A. Riis* (1938).

RIKER, THAD WEED (Nov. 2, 1880–Feb. 17, 1952); b. Stamford, Conn. Educator, historian. *Henry Fox, First Lord Holland,* 2v. (1911); *A Short Story of Modern Europe* (1935); *A History of Modern Europe* (1949); etc. History dept., University of Texas, from 1909.

RILEY, ALICE C. D. (Mar. 1867–1955); b. Morrison, Ill. Playwright, poet. *Elements of English Verse* (1906); *Lilts and Lyrics* (1912); *Taxi* (1927); *Skimming Spain in Five Weeks by Motor* (1931); *Aesop in Modern Dress* (1953); and many one-act plays and pageants, many for children.

RILEY, BENJAMIN FRANKLIN (July 16, 1849–Dec. 14, 1925); b. near Pineville, Ala. Baptist clergyman, educator, author. *Makers and Romance of Alabama History* (1914); *The Life and Times of Booker T. Washington* (1916); *The Baptists in the Building of the Nation* (1922). President, Howard College, Birmingham, Ala., 1888–93; prof. English, University of Georgia, 1893–1900.

RILEY, H[enry] H[iram] (Sept. 1, 1813–Feb. 8, 1888); b. Great Barrington, Mass. Lawyer, editor, author. *Puddleford, and Its People* (1854); *The Puddleford Papers* (1857).

RILEY, JAMES (b. Aug. 15, 1848–); b. in Co. Longford, Ireland. Author. *Poems* (1886); *Songs of Two Peoples* (1898); *Christy of Rathglin* (1906).

RILEY, JAMES WHITCOMB (Oct. 7, 1849–July 22, 1916); b. Greenfield, Ind. Poet. *"The Old Swimmin'-Hole," and 'Leven More Poems* (under pen name of "Benj. F. Johnson of Boone," 1883); *The Boss Girl* (1886), with cover design by Booth Tarkington; *Afterwhiles* (1887); *Pipes o' Pan at Zekesbury* (1888); *Old Fashioned Roses* (1888); *Rhymes of Childhood* (1891); *Green Field and Running Brooks* (1892); *Poems Here at Home* (1893); *Riley Child-Rhymes* (1899); *The Book of Joyous Children* (1902); *Old Schoolboy Romances* (1909); *Knee-Deep in June* (1912); *The Complete Works of James Whitcomb Riley,* 6v. (1913); *Old Times* (1915); *Letters of James Whitcomb Riley,* ed. by W. L. Phelps, 1930. Among the popular characters he created were The Raggedy Man, Doc Sifers, Old Aunt Mary, Squire Hawkins, Tradin' Joe, and Uncle Sidney. His small town, "Griggsby's Station" was the scene of many of his poems. Among his most popular poems were "When the Frost Is on the Punkin" and "Little Orphant Annie." He was know as the "Hoosier Poet." With *Indianapolis Journal,* 1877–85, and used the pen name, "Benj. F. Johnson of Boone" in this paper. *See* Meredith Nicholson's *The Hoosiers* (1900); Marcus Dickey's *The Youth of James Whit-*

comb Riley (1919), and his *The Maturity of James Whitcomb Riley* (1922); Peter Revell's *James Whitcomb Riley* (1970).

RILEY, WOODBRIDGE (May 20, 1869–Sept. 2, 1933); b. New York. Educator, author. *The Founder of Mormonism* (1902); *American Philosophy: The Early Schools* (1907); *American Thought from Puritanism to Pragmatism* (1915); *From Myth to Reason* (1926); *Men and Morals* (1929); *The Meaning of Mysticism* (1930). Prof. philosophy, Vassar College, 1908–33.

Rill from the Town Pump, A. Story by Nathaniel Hawthorne. (1836).

RIMANOCZY, RICHARD STANTON (Mar. 28, 1902–); b. Cincinnati, O. Editor, author. Co-author, with F. G. Clark: *Money* (1947); *How to Think About Economics* (1952); *Layman's Guide to Educational Theory* (with C.W. Coulter, 1955); *Where the Money Comes From* (1961); Editorial director, American Economic Foundation, since 1938.

RIMINGTON, CRITCHELL (Feb. 16, 1907–); b. Philadelphia, Pa. Editor. *Bon Voyage Book* (1934); *This Is the Navy* (1945); etc. Editor: *The Sea Chest: A Yachtman's Reader* (1947). Pres. and publisher, *Yachting* magazine, since 1955.

RINEHART, MARY ROBERTS (1876–Sept. 22, 1958); b. Pittsburgh, Pa. Novelist, playwright. *The Circular Staircase* (1908); *When a Man Marries* (1909); *The Man in Lower Ten* (1909); *The Case of Jennie Brice* (1913); *"K"* (1915); *Tish* (1916); *Bab, a Sub-Deb* (1917); *The Bat* (with Avery Hopwood, prod. 1920); *A Poor Wise Man* (1921); *Affinities* (1922); *The Breaking Point* (1922); *The Out Trail* (1923); *The Red Lamp* (1925); *Lost Ecstasy* (1927); *Two Flights Up* (1928); *The Romantics* (1929); *The Door* (1930); *My Story* (1931); *Miss Pinkerton* (1932); *Crime Book* (1933); *The Doctor* (1936); *Tish Marches On* (1937); *Married People* (1937); *The Wall* (1938); *The Great Mistake* (1940); *A Light in the Window* (1948); *The Mary Roberts Rinehart Crime Book* (1957); etc. Her son, Stanley M. Rinehart, Jr., was co-founder of Farrar and Rinehart; later of Rinehart and Co.

Rinehart & Co. See Farrar & Rinehart.

RIPLEY, CLEMENTS (Aug. 26, 1892–July 22, 1954); b. Tacoma, Wash. Author. *Dust and Sun* (1929); *Devil Drums* (1931); *Black Moon* (1933); *Gold Is Where You Find It* (1936); *Clear For Action* (1940); *Mississippi Belle* (1942); etc.

RIPLEY, GEORGE (Oct. 3, 1802–July 4, 1880); b. Greenfield, Mass. Reformer, editor, critic. *Discourses on the Philosophy of Religion* (1836); *Letters on the Latest Forms of Infidelity* (1840); *A Handbook of Literature and the Fine Arts* (with Bayard Taylor, 1852); *The American Cyclopaedia,* 16v. (1858–63); etc. Co-founder, *The Dial,* 1840; co-editor, 1840–41; editor, *The Harbinger,* 1845–46; co-editor, 1846–49; lit. critic, the *New York Tribune,* 1849–80. Co-founder of Brook Farm. *See* Octavius B. Frothingham's *George Ripley* (1882).

RIPLEY, KATHARINE BALL (Mrs. Clements Ripley) (March 20, 1899–July 24, 1955); b. Charleston, S.C. Author. *Sand in My Shoes* (1931); *Sand Dollars* (1933); etc.

RIPLEY, ROBERT LeROY (Dec. 25, 1893–May 27, 1949); Cartoonist, author. *Believe It or Not,* 2v. (1929–31); *Ripley's Big Book* (1935); etc. Creator of syndicated cartoon "Believe It or Not" in 1918.

RIPLEY, SHERMAN (Oct., 1889–); b. Hartford, Conn. Boy Scout executive, author. *Moon Shadows* (poems, 1918); *Games for Boys* (1922); *Beyond* (1930); *Introduction to Magic* (1946); *The Book of Games* (1952); etc.

RIPPERGER, HENRIETTA [Sperry] (1889–). Author. *112 Elm Street* (1943); *The Bretons of Elm Street* (1947); etc.

RIPPY, JAMES FRED (Oct. 27, 1892–); b. in Sumner Co., Tenn. Educator, author. Author or co-author: *The United States and Mexico* (1926); *Latin America in World Politics*

(1928); *Joel R. Poinsett* (1935); *Crusades of the Jungle* (1935); *Historical Evolution of Hispanic America* (1945); *Latin America and the Industrial Age* (1947); *Globe and Hemisphere* (1958); etc. Editor, Duke University Press, 1929–36. Prof. history, Duke University, 1926–36; University of Chicago, 1936–58.

Rise and Fall of the Third Reich, The. By William L. Shirer (1961). History of Nazi Germany. The author, a political correspondent during the period of the Third Reich, also wrote *Berlin Diary* (1941).

Rise of American Civilization, The. By Charles A. and Mary R. Beard, 2v. (1927). A history arranged by periods, from the English Colonization to the World War, with particular emphasis on the economic and social forces at work, and the conflict between agrarian and industrial groups and sections. *America in Midpassage,* Vol. III, appeared in 1939; and *A Study of the Idea of Civilization in the United States,* Vol. IV, in 1942.

Rise of David Levinsky, The. By Abraham Cohen (1917). Story of a Russian Jewish immigrant in America.

Rise of Silas Lapham, The. By William Dean Howells (1885). The story of a self-made Vermonter and his family transplanted to the Boston of the late nineteenth century.

Rise of the Common Man, The. By Carl Russell Fish (1927). Treats historically of the period in American life dominated by the new generation which came into power in 1830.

Rise of the Dutch Republic, The. By John Lothrop Motley, 3v. (1856). This scholarly work on the Netherlands and its history established Motley's fame, and was an immediate success. Not sure of its reception, the author had published the work at his own expense.

RISTER, CARL COKE (d. Apr. 16, 1955); b. Hayrich, Tex. Educator, author. *The Southwestern Frontier* (1928); *The Greater Southwest* (with Rupert Norval Richardson, 1934); *Southern Plainsmen* (1938); *Border Captives* (1940); *Border Command* (1944); *Oil! Titan of the Southwest* (1949); etc. History dept., University of Oklahoma, 1929–45.

RISTINE, FRANK HUMPHREY (Apr. 11, 1884–July 28, 1958); b. Crawfordsville, Ind. Educator, author. *English Tragicomedy* (1910). Editor: *Byron's Don Juan* (1927); etc. Prof. English, Hamilton College, 1912–52, dean, 1932–52.

***Ritchie, Anna Cora Ogden Mowatt. See* Anna Cora Mowatt.**

RITCHIE, LILY MUNSEL (Feb. 13, 1867–); b. Bloomington, Ill. Author. The *Chicken Little Jane* series, 4v. (1918–26); *The Man, the Woman and the University* (1923); *Pathological Realism* (1926); etc.

RITCHIE, ROBERT WELLES (June 17, 1879–Aug. 2, 1942); b. Quincy, Ill. Journalist, author. *Inside the Lines* (with Earl Derr Biggers, 1915); *Dust of the Desert* (1922); *Stairway of the Sun* (1924); *Deep Furrows* (1927); *The Hell-Roarin' Forty-Niners* (1928); *Wheat* (1935); etc. With *New York Sun,* 1906–13, *New York World,* 1913–18, *Country Gentleman,* 1919–27, etc.

RITTENHOUSE, JESSIE BELLE (Mrs. Clinton Scollard) (1869–Sept. 28, 1948); b. Mt. Morris, N.Y. Poet, editor. *The Door of Dreams* (1918); *The Lifted Cup* (1921); *The Secret Bird* (1930); *Patrician Rhymes* (with husband, 1930); *The House of Life* (autobiography, 1934); *The Moving Tide* (1939); etc. Editor: *The Younger American Poets* (1904); *The Little Book of American Poets, 1787–1900* (1915); *The Second Book of Modern Verse* (1919); *The Little Book of Modern British Verse* (1924); *The Third Book of Modern Verse* (1927); *The Bird-Lovers' Anthology* (with husband, 1930); etc.

RITTER, FREDERIC LOUIS (June 22, 1834–July 6, 1891); b. Strasbourg, Alsace. Composer, musicologist. *History of*

Music, 2v. (1870–74); *Music in America* (1883); etc. His wife, Frances Ritter (1840–1890), was the author of *Some Famous Songs* (1878); and *Songs and Ballads* (1887).

Rivers, Pearl. Pen name of Eliza Jane Poitevant Holbrook Nicholson.

RIVERS, WILLIAM JAMES (July 17, 1822–June 22, 1909); b. Charleston, S.C. Educator, historian. *A Sketch of the History of South Carolina* (1856), and supplement, *A Chapter in the Early History of South Carolina* (1874); *Addresses and Other Occasional Pieces* (1893). Prof. ancient languages, University of South Carolina, 1865–73; president, Washington College, Chestertown, Md., 1873–87.

Rivers of America Series. Separate volumes, each devoted to a notable American river, originally under the editorship of Constance Lindsay Skinner, and published by Farrar & Rinehart. It is now published by Holt, Rinehart & Winston, and by 1970 included over 85 volumes.

Riverside Magazine for Young People. Boston, Mass. Founded 1867. Published by Hurd and Houghton. Horace Scudder was editor. Many of Hans Christian Andersen's fairy tales appeared in it even before they were published in Denmark. It was merged with *Scribner's Monthly* in 1870.

Riverside Press. Cambridge, Mass. Founded by Henry O. Houghton in 1852. It has printed many books for Harvard University, and such notable series as the *American Commonwealth Series,* the *Riverside Literature Series,* etc. It is affiliated with Houghton, Mifflin Co. *See* Horace Scudder's *Henry Oscar Houghton* (1897).

Riverside Textbooks in Education. Ed. by E. P. Cubberley, 30v. (1914–31). Well known series of books on education written by leading educators in the United States.

RIVES, AMÉLIE (Princess Troubetzkoy) (Aug. 23, 1863–); b. Richmond, Va. Novelist, playwright. *The Quick or the Dead* (1889); *Seléné* (1905); *Augustine, the Man* (1906); *The Golden Rose* (1908); *Pan's Mountain* (1910); *Hidden House* (1911); *World's End* (1913); *Shadows of Flames* (1915); *The Fear Market* (prod. 1916); *Allegiance* (prod. 1918); *As the Wind Blew* (poems, 1922); *Firedamp* (1930); etc.

RIVES, GEORGE LOCKHART (May 1, 1849–Aug. 18, 1917); b. New York. Lawyer, author. *The United States and Mexico, 1821–1848,* 2v. (1913). A trustee, The New York Public Library, 1895–1917.

RIVES, HALLIE ERMINIE (Mrs. Post Wheeler) (May 2, 1878–1956); b. in Christian Co., Ky. Author. *Smoking Flax* (1896); *As the Hart Panteth* (1898); *Hearts Courageous* (1902); *The Castaway* (1904); *Satan Sanderson* (1907); *The Kingdom of Slender Swords* (1909); *The Valiants of Virginia* (1912); *The Golden Barrier* (1934); *The John Book* (with G. E. Forbush, 1947); *Dome of Many-Coloured Glass* (joint autobiography with husband, 1955); etc.

RIVES, JOHN COOK (May 24, 1795–Apr. 10, 1864); b. Franklin Co., Va. Journalist. Congressional reporter, the *Washington Daily Globe,* 1833–64.

"Road Not Taken, The." Poem by Robert Frost.

"Road to Avignon." Poem by Amy Lowell (1912).

Road to Rome, The. Play by Robert Sherwood (prod. 1926). Based on Hannibal's march through the Alps and his defeat at the very gates of Rome when victory seemed to be within his grasp.

Road to Serfdom, The. By F. A. von Hayek (1944). A conservative argument in favor of free enterprise.

Road to Xanadu, The. Analysis of Coleridge's poetic imagination, by John Livingston Lowes (1927).

ROARK, GARLAND (July 26, 1904–   ); b. Groesbeck, Tex. Novelist. *Wake of the Red Witch* (1946); *Fair Wind to Java* (1948); *Rainbow in the Royals* (1950); *Star in the Rigging* (1954); *Outlawed Banner* (1956); *The Lady and the Deep Blue Sea* (1958); *Should the Wind Be Fair* (1960); *Angels in Exile* (1967); etc. Also writes under pen name "George Garland."

Rob of the Bowl. Novel by John Pendleton Kennedy (1838). Historical tale which gives a faithful picture of life in St. Mary's, the old capital of colonial Maryland.

ROBACK, ABRAHAM AARON (1890–). Author. *A Bibliography of Character and Personality* (1927); *The Psychology of Common Sense* (1939); *A Dictionary of the International Slurs* (1944); *Personality in Theory and Practice* (1949); *A History of American Psychiatry* (1952); *Freudiana* (1957); *History of Psychology and Psychiatry* (1961).

ROBB, DAVID METHENY (Sept. 19, 1903–); b. Tak Hing Chau, South China. Educator, author. *Art in the Western World* (with J. J. Garrison, 1942); *The Harper History of Painting* (1951). Prof. art history, University of Pennsylvania, since 1939.

ROBB, JOHN S. Humorist. Pen name, "Solitaire." *Streaks of Squatter Life and Far-West Scenes* (1847), republished as *Western Scenes; or, Life on the Prairie* (1858); *Kaam; or, Daylight* (1847). See *Louisiana Swamp Doctor.*

Robbins, Harold. Pen name of Harold Rubin.

ROBBINS, HOWARD CHANDLER (Dec. 11, 1876–Mar. 20, 1952); b. Philadelphia, Pa. Episcopal clergyman, author. *Sursum Corda* (1927); *Cathedral Sermons* (1927); *Vita Nova* (1929); *Charles Lewis Slattery* (1931); *Paul Revere Frothingham* (1935); *Preaching the Gospel* (1939); etc. Prof. theology, General Theological Seminary, New York, 1929–49.

ROBBINS, MARY CAROLINE (1841–Nov. 5, 1912); b. Calais, Me. Author. *The Rescue of an Old Place* (1892). Translator of Eugene Fromentin's *Old Masters of Belgium and Holland* (1882); and other French books. Co-editor (with "Gail Hamilton," i.e., Mary Abigail Dodge), *Wood's Household Magazine,* 1871–72.

ROBBINS, REGINALD CHAUNCEY (Nov. 10, 1871–Nov. 19, 1955); b. Boston, Mass. Poet. *Love Poems,* 4v. (1903–12); *Poems of Personality,* 3v. (1904–19); *Earlier Poems* (1913); *Poems Domestic* (1919); etc. Founder, Robbins Library of Philosophy and Psychology, Harvard University, 1905.

Robe, The. Novel by Lloyd Douglas (1942). A Roman soldier wins Christ's robe in a dice game and eventually becomes converted. The rise of Christianity is the background.

"Robert of Lincoln." Poem by William Cullen Bryant, which first appeared in *Putnam's Magazine,* June, 1855.

ROBERTS, ANNA S[mith Rickey] (Mrs. Solomon White Roberts) (Dec. 23, 1827–Aug. 10. 1858); b. Philadelphia, Pa. Poet. *Forest Flowers of the West* (1851), all originally contributed to the *Columbian and Great West,* 1850–51.

ROBERTS, BRIGHAM HENRY (Mar. 13, 1857–Sept. 27, 1933); b. Warrington, Lancs., Eng. Mormon leader, author. *New Witnesses for God,* 3v. (1895); *The Rise and Fall of Nauvoo* (1900); *Missouri Persecutions* (1900); *The Seventy's Course in Theology,* 5v. (1907–12); *A Comprehensive History of the Church of Jesus Christ of Latter Day Saints, Century I,* 6v. (1930); etc. Editor, *Salt Lake Tribune,* 1890–96.

ROBERTS, CHALMERS MCGEAGH (Nov. 18, 1910–); b. Pittsburgh, Pa. Journalist. *Washington, Past and Present* (1950). Editor: *Can We Meet the Russians Halfway?* (1958). Staff, *Washington Post and Times-Herald,* since 1949.

ROBERTS, DOROTHY JAMES (Sept. 5, 1903–); b. Elizabeth, W.Va. Author. *More Than You Promise, A Business at Work in Society* (with Kathleen Anne Smallzried, 1942); *A Man of Malice Landing* (1943); *A Durable Fire* (1945); *The Mountain Journey* (1947); *Marshwood* (1949); *Enchanted Cup* (1953); *Lancelot, My Brother* (1954); *Missy* (1957); *With Night We Banish Sorrow* (1960); *Fire in The Ice* (1961).

Roberts, Edith. Pen name of Elizabeth Kneipple.

ROBERTS, ELIZABETH MADOX (1886–Mar. 13, 1941); b. near Springfield, Ky. Novelist, poet. *Under the Tree* (poems, 1922); *The Time of Man* (1926); *My Heart and My Flesh* (1927); *Jingling in the Wind* (1928); *The Great Meadow* (1930); *A Buried Treasure* (1931); *The Haunted Mirror* (1932); *He Sent Forth a Raven* (1935); *Black Is My Truelove's Hair* (1938); *Song In the Meadow* (poems, 1940); *Not by Strange Gods* (1941). See Fred B. Millett's *Contemporary American Authors* (1940); Harry M. Campbell's and Ruel E. Foster's *Elizabeth Madox Roberts: American Novelist* (1956).

ROBERTS, [GRANVILLE] ORAL (Jan. 24, 1918–); b. near Ada, Okla. Clergyman, author. *If You Need Healing, Do These Things* (1947); *The Fourth Man and Other Sermons* (1951); *Oral Roberts' Best Sermons and Stories* (1956); *God's Formula for Success and Prosperity* (1956); *Drama of End Time* (1963); *How to Be A Successful Soul Winner* (1964); etc. Founder and president, Oral Roberts Evangelistic Association, Inc.

ROBERTS, KENNETH [Lewis] (Dec. 8, 1885–July 21, 1957); b. Kennebunk, Me. Novelist, essayist. *Black Magic* (1924); *Florida* (1926); *Arundel* (1930); *The Lively Lady* (1931); *Rabble in Arms* (1933); *Captain Caution* (1934); *For Authors Only, and Other Gloomy Essays* (1935); *Northwest Passage* (1937); *Trending into Maine* (1938); *Oliver Wiswell* (1940); *Lydia Bailey* (1947); *Henry Gross and His Dowsing Rod* (1951); *Water Unlimited* (1957); etc.

ROBERTS, MARTIN ARNOLD (Oct. 28, 1875–June 15, 1940); b. Etna, Pa. Librarian. With Library of Congress, 1903–40; supt. of reading rooms, 1927–37; chief asst. librarian, 1937–40.

ROBERTS, OCTAVIA (Mrs. Barton Corneau), b. Springfield, Ill. Novelist. *Lady Valentine* (1914); *Lincoln in Illinois* (1917); *With Lafayette in America* (1919); *The Perilous Isle* (1926).

ROBERTS, WALTER ADOLPHE (Oct. 15, 1886–Sept. 15, 1962); b. Kingston, Jamaica. Editor, author. *Pierrot Wounded, and Other Poems* (1919); *Pan and Peacocks* (poems, 1928); *The Mind Reader* (1929); *The Moralist* (1931); *Sir Henry Morgan, Buccaneer and Governor* (1933); *Semmes of the Alabama* (1938); *The Pomegranate* (1941); *Royal Street* (1944); *Creole Dusk* (1948); *The Single Star* (1949); *Medallions* (1950); *Six Great Jamaicans* (1952); *Havana: The Portrait of a City* (1953); *Jamaica: The Portrait of an Island* (1955). Editor: *The American Parade,* 4v. (1925–26). Editor, *Ainslee's Magazine,* 1918–21; *Brief Stories,* 1928–30; Pioneer Press, Kingston, Jamaica, from 1956.

ROBERTSON, ARCHIBALD THOMAS (Nov. 6, 1863–Sept. 29, 1934); b. near Chatham, Va. Baptist clergyman, educator, author. *Life and Letters of John Albert Broadus* (1901); *Epochs in the Life of Jesus* (1908); *The Glory of the Ministry* (1911); *New Testament History* (1924); etc. Prof. New Testament interpretation, Southern Baptist Theological Seminary, Louisville, 1892–1934.

ROBERTSON, CONSTANCE NOYES (Sept. 27, 1897–); b. Niagara Falls, Ont. Author. *Enchanted Avenue* (1931); *Five Fatal Letters (under pen name "Dana Scott," 1937); Seek-No-Further* (1938); *Salute to the Hero* (1942); *Fire Bell in the Night* (1944); *The Unterrified* (1946); *Golden Circle* (1951); *Six Weeks in March* (1953); etc.

ROBERTSON, DAVID ALLAN (Oct. 17, 1880–July 15, 1961); b. Chicago, Ill. Educator, author. *The University of Chicago* (1916); *American Universities and Colleges* (1928); etc. Editor, *University Record,* 1915–20. English dept., University of Chicago, 1904–23.

ROBERTSON, FRANK CHESTER (Jan. 12, 1890–); b. Moscow, Ida. Author. *Foreman of the Forty-Bar* (1925); *Fall of Buffalo Horn* (1928); *The Silver Cow* (1929); *The Hidden Cabin* (1929); *Riders of the Sunset Trail* (1930); *The Mormon Trail* (1931); *Red Rustlers* (1932); *Song of the Leather* (1933); *Forbidden Trails* (1935); *The Rocky Road to Jericho* (under pen name "Frank Chester Field," 1935); *Branded Men* (1936); *The Pride of Pine Creek* (1938); *Fighting Jack Warbonnet* (1939); *Firebrand from Burnt Creek* (1940); *Longhorns of Hate* (1949); *A Ram in the Thicket* (autobiography, 1950); *Where Desert Blizzards Blow* (1952); *Sagebrush Sorrel* (1953); *Lawman's Pay* (1957); *Disaster Valley* (1957); *Rawhide* (1961); *Caribo* (1962); *Hoofbeats of Destiny, A History of the Pony Express* (1959); *A Man Called Paladin* (1964); *Valley of Frightened Men* (1967); *The Day the Colonel Wept* (1968); etc.

ROBERTSON, HARRISON (Jan. 16, 1856–Nov. 11, 1939); b. Murfreesboro, Tenn. Editor, author. *How the Derby Was Won* (1889); "*If I Were a Man*" (1899); *Red Blood and Blue* (1900); *The Inlander* (1901); *The Opponents* (1902); *The Pink Typhoon* (1906); etc. Editor, the *Louisville Courier-Journal,* 1929–39.

ROBERTSON, JAMES (b. 1740); b. Edinburgh. Royalist, printer, journalist. With Mein & Fleming, printers. Founder, with brother, Alexander Robertson (1742–84), the *New-York Chronicle,* May 8, 1769; also founder, the *Albany Gazette,* Nov. 25, 1771; the *Royal American Gazette,* New York, Jan. 16, 1777; the *Royal Pennsylvania Gazette, Philadelphia,* Mar. 3, 1778; and, with Donald Macdonald and Alexander Cameron, the *Royal South Carolina Gazette,* Charleston, 1780. *See* John C. Oswald's *Printing in the Americas* (1937).

ROBERTSON, JAMES ALEXANDER (Aug. 19, 1873–Mar. 20, 1939); b. Corry, Pa. Editor, archivist, author. *The Pacific Ocean in History* (with others, 1917); etc. Editor: *The Philippine Islands, 1493–1898,* 55v. (with Emma Helen Blair, 1902–09); *List of Documents in Spanish Archives Relating to the History of the United States* (1910); *Louisiana Under the Rule of Spain, France, and the United States, 1785–1807,* 2v. (1911); etc. His collection of Filipiniana numbered more than 20,000 pieces.

ROBERTSON, JOHN (Apr. 13, 1787–July 5, 1873); b. Petersburg, Va. Jurist, author. *Virginia; or, the Fatal Patent* (1825); *Riego; or, The Spanish Martyr* (1850); *Opuscula* (1870); etc.

ROBERTSON, MORGAN [Andrew] (Sept. 30, 1861–Mar. 24, 1915); b. Oswego, N.Y. Poet, novelist. *A Tale of a Halo* (poems, 1894); *Spun-Yarn Sea Stories* (1898); *Futility* (1898); "*Where Angels Fear to Tread,*" *and Other Tales* (1899); *Shipmates* (1901); *Masters of Men: A Romance of the New Navy* (1901); *Sinful Peck* (1903); *Down to the Sea* (1905); *Land Ho!* (1905); etc.

ROBINS, EDWARD (Mar. 2, 1862–May 21, 1943); b. Pau, Fr. Author. *Echoes of the Playhouse* (1895); *The Palmy Days of Nance Oldfield* (1898); *Benjamin Franklin* (1898); *Twelve Great Actors* (1900): *Twelve Great Actresses* (1900); *Romances of Early America* (1902); *William T. Sherman* (1905); etc. On staff the *Philadelphia Public Ledger,* 1884–97.

ROBINS, ELIZABETH (Mrs. George Richmond Parks) (1862–May 8, 1952); b. Louisville, Ky. Actress, author. Pen name "C. E. Raimond." *George Mandeville's Husband* (1894); *The Magnetic North* (1904); *A Dark Lantern* (1905); *The Convert* (1907); *Votes for Women* (prod. 1907); *Come and Find Me* (1908); *Way Stations* (1913); *Camilla* (1918); *Time Is Whispering* (1923); *Ibsen and the Actress* (memoirs, 1928); *Raymond and I* (1956); etc. Editor: *Theatre and Friendship* (letters from Henry James, 1932).

ROBINSON, ALFRED (1806–1895). Author. *Life in California* (1846). Robinson's marriage is described by Richard Henry Dana in his *Two Years Before the Mast* (1840).

ROBINSON, ANNIE DOUGLAS GREEN (Jan. 12, 1842–1913); b. Plymouth, N.H. Author. Pen name, "Marian Douglas." *Picture Poems for Young Folks* (1872); *Peter and Polly; or, Home Life in New England a Hundred Years Ago* (1876); *In the Poverty Year* (1901); *Days We Remember* (poems, 1903).

ROBINSON, ANTHONY [Christopher] (Mar. 10, 1931–); b. Hindenburg, Ger. Novelist. *A Departure from the Rules* (1960); *The Easy Way* (1963); *Home Again, Home Again* (1969).

ROBINSON, BOARDMAN (Sept. 6, 1876–Sept. 5, 1952); b. Somerset, Nova Scotia. Artist, cartoonist. *Cartoons of the War* (1916). Illustrated Dostoievsky's *The Idiot,* and *The Brothers Karamazov; King Lear;* etc. On staff, *The Liberator, Harper's Weekly,* etc. He accompanied John Reed to the Balkans to do the drawings for his *The War in Eastern Europe.*

ROBINSON, CHALFANT (Mar. 14, 1871–Dec. 31, 1946); b. Cincinnati, O. Educator, author. *Continental Europe, 1270–1598* (1916); *The Case of King Louis XI of France and Other Essays in Medieval History* (1929); etc. Curator, medieval manuscripts, Princeton, from 1920.

ROBINSON, C[harles] A[lexander], JR. (Mar. 30, 1900–); b. Princeton, N.J. Historian. Author: *Hellenic History* (with G. W. Botsford, 1939); *Ancient History* (1951); *History of Alexander the Great* (1953); *Athens in the Age of Pericles* (1959); *First Book of Ancient Egypt* (1961); etc. Editor: *The Ephemerides of Alexander's Expedition* (1932); *An Anthology of Greek Drama* (Vol. I, 1949; Vol. II, 1954); *Spring of Civilization* (1954); *Selections from Greek and Roman Historians* (1957). Classics dept., Brown University, since 1928.

ROBINSON, CHARLES MULFORD (Apr. 30, 1869–Dec. 30, 1917); b. Ramapo, N.Y. City planner, essayist, poet. *The Call of the City* (1908); *The City Sleeps* (1920); both collections of essays and poems.

ROBINSON, CHARLES SEYMOUR (Mar. 31, 1829–Feb. 1, 1899); b. Bennington, Vt. Presbyterian clergyman, hymnologist, author. *Annotations upon Popular Hymns* (1893). Compiler: *Hymns of the Church* (1862); *Songs for the Sanctuary* (1865); *Psalms and Hymns* (1875); *Laudes Domini* (1884).

ROBINSON, DANIEL SOMMER (Oct. 19, 1888–); b. N. Salem, Ind. Educator, author. *The Principles of Reasoning* (1924); *Illustrations of the Methods of Reasoning* (1927); *An Introduction to Living Philosophy* (1932); *Political Ethics* (1935); *Principles of Conduct* (1948); *Crucial Issues in Philosophy* (1955); etc. Editor: *An Anthology of Recent Philosophy* (1929); *An Anthology of Modern Philosophy* (1931); *The Story of Scottish Philosophy* (1961); etc. President, Butler University, since 1939.

ROBINSON, DAVID M[oore] (Sept. 21, 1880–Jan. 2, 1958); b. Auburn, N.Y. Educator, classicist, author. *Sappho and Her Influence* (1924); *Pindar: A Poet of Eternal Ideas* (1936); *A Short History of Greece* (1936); *America in Greece* (1948); *The Greek View of Life* (1953); etc. Co-editor: *Our Debt to Greece and Rome,* 45v. (1931–38); etc. Assoc. editor, the *Classical Weekly,* 1913–36; *Art and Archaeology,* 1918–34. Prof. archaeology, Johns Hopkins University, 1912–47.

ROBINSON, DOANE (Oct. 19, 1856–Nov. 27, 1946); b. (Jonah Leroy Robinson) Sparta, Wis. Author. *Coteaus of Dakota* (poems, 1899); *History of the Sioux Indians* (1904); *History of South Dakota,* 2v. (1904); *The Green Butte* (poems, 1920); *Life of Gen. Henry Leavenworth* (1931); etc. Founder, the *Monthly South Dakotan,* 1898. Supt. Dept. of History, State of South Dakota, 1901–26.

ROBINSON, EDGAR EUGENE (Apr. 5, 1887–); b. Oconomowoc, Wis. Historian. *Evolution of American Political Parties* (1924); *American Democracy in Time of Crisis* (1934); *The New United States* (1946); *Scholarship and Cataclysm* (1947); *The Roosevelt Leadership* (1955); *Powers of the President in Foreign Affairs, 1945–1965* (with others, 1966); etc. History dept., Carleton College, since 1910.

ROBINSON, EDITH (b. Feb. 17, 1858); b. Boston, Mass. Author. *A Loyal Little Maid* (1897); *A Little Puritan Rebel* (1898); *A Little Daughter of Liberty* (1899); *There Once Was a Queen* (1910); *The Story of Tea* (1918); etc.

ROBINSON, EDWARD (Apr. 20, 1794–Jan. 27, 1863); b. Southington, Conn. Philologist, Biblical scholar, editor, author. *Biblical Researches in Palestine, Mount Sinai and Arabia Petraea*, 3v. (1841); *Later Biblical Researches* (1856); etc. Founder, *American Biblical Repository*, 1831; *Bibliotheca Sacra*, 1843. Prof. Biblical literature, Union Theological Seminary, New York, 1837–63.

ROBINSON, EDWIN ARLINGTON (Dec. 22, 1869–Apr. 6, 1935); b. Head Tide, Me. Poet. *The Torrent and the Night Before* (1896); *The Children of the Night* (1897); *Captain Craig* (1902), augmented (1915); *The Town Down the River* (1910); *Van Zorn: A Comedy* (1914); *The Porcupine: A Drama* (1915); *The Man against the Sky* (1916); *Merlin* (1917); *Lancelot* (1920); *The Three Taverns* (1920); *Avon's Harvest* (1921); *Collected Poems* (1921, Pulitzer Prize for poetry, 1922); *Roman Bartholow* (1923); *The Man Who Died Twice* (1924, Pulitzer Prize for poetry, 1925); *Dionysus in Doubt* (1925); *Tristram* (1927, Pulitzer Prize for poetry, 1928); *Collected Poems*, 5v. (1927), also in 1v. (1927); *Fortunatus* (1928); *Sonnets, 1889–1927* (1928); *Three Poems* (1928); *Cavender's House* (1929); *Modred* (1929); *The Prodigal Son* (1929); *The Glory of the Nightingales* (1930); *The Valley of the Shadow* (1930); *Matthias at the Door* (1931); *Nicodemus* (1932); *Talifer* (1933); *Amaranth* (1934); *King Jasper* (1935); *Hannibal Brown* (1936); *Collected Poems* (1937); etc. See Ben R. Redman's *Edwin Arlington Robinson* (1926); Mark Van Doren's *Edwin Arlington Robinson* (1927); Charles Cestre's *An Introduction to Edwin Arlington Robinson* (1930); Charles Beecher Hogan's *A Bibliography of Edwin Arlington Robinson* (1936); Hermann Hagedorn's *Edwin Arlington Robinson* (1938); Yvor Winters' *Edwin Arlington Robinson* (1946); Ellsworth Barnard's *Edwin Arlington Robinson* (1952); Louis Untermeyer's *Edwin Arlington Robinson: A Reappraisal* (1963); Chard P. Smith's *Where the Light Falls: A Portrait of Edwin Arlington Robinson* (1965); W. R. Robinson's *Edwin Arlington Robinson: A Poetry of the Act* (1967); Louis O. Coxe's *Edwin Arlington Robinson: The Life of Poetry* (1969).

ROBINSON, EDWIN MEADE (Nov. 1, 1878–Sept. 20, 1946); b. Lima (now Howe), Ind. Critic, author. *The First Born* (1899); *Mere Melodies* (poems, 1918); *Piping and Panning* (poems, 1920); *Enter Jerry; etc.* Lit. editor, the *Cleveland Plain D* 1922.

ROBINSON, GEORGE LIVINGSTONE (Aug. 19, 1864–Dec. 17, 1958); b. W. Hebron, N.Y. Educator, author. *Leaders of Israel* (1906); *The Twelve Minor Prophets* (1926); *The Bearing of Archaeology on the Old Testament* (1941); *Live out Your Years* (1951); *Autobiography* (1957); etc. Prof. theology, McCormick Theological Seminary, from 1898.

ROBINSON, GEORGE WASHINGTON (Dec. 8, 1872–); b. Meredith, N.H. Educator, author. *Latin Literature from Paulus to Claudian* (1902); *Outlines of Historical Study* (1927); *Bibliography of Edward Channing* (1932); *Cinnus* (1938); etc. Secretary, Harvard Graduate School of Arts and Sciences, 1904–28.

ROBINSON, HARRIET JANE HANSON (Feb. 8, 1825–Dec. 22, 1911); b. Boston, Mass. Suffragist, author. *Captain Mary Miller* (1887); *The New Pandora* (1889); *Loom and Spindle; or, Life Among the Early Mill Girls: With a Sketch of "The Lowell Offering" and Some of Its Contributors* (1898); etc. Editor: *"Warrington" Pen Portraits* (1877). See E. C. Stanton, S. B. Anthony, and M. J. Gage's *History of Woman Suffrage*, 4v. (1881–1902).

ROBINSON, HENRY MORTON (Sept. 7, 1898–Jan. 13, 1961); b. Boston, Mass. Author. *Children of Morningside* (poems, 1924); *John Erskine: A Modern Acteon* (1928); *Buck Fever* (1929); *Stout Cortez* (1931); *Science vs. Crime* (1935); *Second Wisdom* (1936); *Private Virtue, Public Good* (1938); *A Skeleton Key to Finnegan's Wake* (with Joseph Campbell, 1944); *The Perfect Round* (1945); *The Great Snow* (1947); *The Cardinal* (1950); *The Enchanted Grindstone* (poems, 1952); *Water of Life* (1960). Assoc. editor, *Reader's Digest*, 1935–42; senior editor, 1942–45.

ROBINSON, JAMES HARVEY (June 29, 1863–Feb. 16, 1936); b. Bloomington, Ill. Educator, author. *An Introduction to the History of Western Europe* (1902); *The Development of Modern Europe*, 2v. (with Charles A. Beard, 1907); *The New History* (1911); *Medieval and Modern Times* (1915); *The Mind in the Making* (1921); *The Humanizing of Knowledge* (1923); *Our World Today and Yesterday* (1924); *The Ordeal of Civilization* (1926); etc. Editor: *Petrarch* (with Henry Winchester Rolfe, 1899); *Readings in European History*, 2v. (1904–05); *Readings in Modern European History*, 2v. (with Charles A. Beard, 1908–09). History dept., Columbia University, 1892–1919.

ROBINSON, JOHN HOVEY (b. 1825). Dime novelist. *Marietta; or, The Two Students* (1846); *The Boston Conspiracy* (1847); *Father Ildefonso* (1847); *The Lady's Dream* (1848); *Kosato, the Blackfoot Renegate* (1850); *The White Rover* (1852); *The Lone Star* (1852); republished as *The Texan Bravo* (1892); *Marion's Brigade* (1852); *Nightshade* (1878); *Ben Brion* (1881); etc. The dates are not necessarily those of first editions. Mrs. John Hovey Robinson was the author of *Evelyn, the Child of the Revolution* (1850).

ROBINSON, MABEL LOUISE (d. Feb. 21, 1962); b. Waltham, Mass. Educator, author. *Dr. Tam O'Shanter* (1921); the *Little Lucia* series, 4v. (1922–26); *Juvenile Story Writing* (1922); *Creative Writing* (1932); *Bright Island* (1937); *Runner of the Mountain Tops: The Life of Louis Agassiz* (1939); *Evacuation Christmas* (1940); *Island Noon* (1942); *Bitter Forfeit* (1947); *The Deepening Year* (1950); *Strong Wings* (1951); *Riley Goes to Obedience School* (1956); etc. English dept., Columbia University, 1910–58.

ROBINSON, ROWLAND EVANS (May 14, 1833–Oct. 15, 1900); b. Ferrisburg, Vt. Essayist, novelist. *Forest and Stream Fables* (1886); *Uncle Lisha's Shop* (1887); *Sam Lovel's Camps* (1889); *Danvis Folks* (1894); *In New England Fields and Woods* (1896); *Sam Lovel's Boy* (1901); *A Danvis Pioneer* (1901); *Out of Bondage, and Other Stories* (1905); etc.

ROBINSON, SOLON (Oct. 21, 1803–Nov. 3, 1880); b. Tolland, Conn. Pioneer, agriculturist, author. *The Will: A Tale of the Lake of the Red Cedars and Shabbona* (1841); *Hot Corn: Life Scenes in New York* (1854); etc. See *Solon Robinson, Pioneer and Agriculturist: Selected Writings*, ed. by Herbert A. Kellar, 2v. (1936).

ROBINSON, THÉRÈSE ALBERTINE LOUISE VON JAKOB (Mrs. Edward Robinson) (Jan. 26, 1797–Apr. 13, 1870); b. Halle, Ger. Novelist, translator, philologist. Pen name, "Talvj." *Historical View of the Slavic Language* (1834); *Heloise; or, The Unrevealed Secret* (1850); *Life's Discipline* (1851); *History of the Colonization of America*, 2v. (1851); *The Exiles* (1853); *Fifteen Years* (1870); etc. Her New York home was a literary salon in the 1840's. See Irma Elizabeth Voigt's *The Life and Works of Mrs. Thérèse Robinson* (Talvj) (1914).

ROBINSON, TRACY (Dec. 22, 1833–1915); b. Clarendon, N.Y. Author. *Song of the Palm, and Other Poems* (1889); *Panama: A Personal Record of Forty-Six Years, 1861–1907* (1907); *Fifty Years at Panama, 1861–1911* (1911).

ROBINSON, WILLIAM HENRY (Sept. 24, 1867–Apr. 5, 1938); b. Lexington, Ill. Author. *Her Navajo Lover* (1903); *The Golden Palace of Neverland* (1907); *The Story of Arizona* (1919); *The Witchery of Rita* (1919); *Yarns of the Southwest* (1921); *Under Turquoise Skies* (1928); *When the Red Gods Made Men* (1935); etc.

ROBINSON, WILLIAM STEVENS (Dec. 7, 1818–Mar. 11, 1876); b. Concord, Mass. Editor, letter-writer. He wrote letters to the *Springfield Republican* under the pen name "Warrington," and to the *New York Tribune* under the pen name "Gilbert." Editor, the *Yeoman's Gazette,* Concord, Mass., 1839–42; asst. editor, the *Lowell Courier and Journal,* 1842–48; editor, the *Boston Daily Whig,* 1848; editor, the *Lowell American,* 1848–54; etc.

ROBSJOHN-GIBBINGS, TERENCE HAROLD (1905–); b. London. Interior designer, author. *Good-Bye, Mr. Chippendale* (1944); *Mona Lisa's Mustache* (1947); *Homes of the Brave* (1954); *Furniture of Classical Greece* (1963).

ROCHE, ARTHUR SOMERS (Apr. 27, 1883–Feb. 17, 1935); b. Somerville, Mass. Author. *Loot* (1916); *Plunder* (1917); *The Sport of Kings* (1917); *Ransom* (1918); *Uneasy Street* (1920); *The Day of Faith* (1921); *Find the Woman* (1921); *The Eyes of the Blind* (1922); *A More Honorable Man* (1922); *What I Know About You* (1927); etc.

ROCHE, JAMES JEFFREY (May 31, 1847–Apr. 3, 1908); b. Mountmellick, Ire. Poet, journalist, novelist. *Songs and Satires* (1886); *The Story of the Filibusters* (1891); reissued as *By-Ways of War: The Story of the Filibusters* (1901); *Life of John Boyle O'Reilly* (1891); *Ballads of Blue Water, and Other Poems* (1895); *The V-a-s-e, & Other Bric-a-Brac* (poems, 1900); *The Sorrow of Sap'ed* (1904); etc. Asst. editor, *The Pilot,* Boston, 1883–90.

ROCHE, JOHN P[earson] (May 7, 1923–   ); b. Brooklyn, N.Y. Educator, author. *The Dynamics of Democratic Government* (with M. S. Stedman, Jr., 1954); *Courts and Rights* (1961); *The Quest for the Dream: Civil Liberties in Modern America* (1963); *Shadow and Substance: Studies in the Theory and Structure of Politics* (1964); *Origins of American Political Thought* (1966); *American Political Thought: Jefferson and the Progressives* (1967); *John Marshall* (1967). Prof. politics, Brandeis University, since 1956.

Rochester Democrat and Chronicle. Rochester, N.Y. Newspaper. Founded 1833, as the *Morning Advertiser;* became the *Daily Democrat,* 1834. The *Daily American* was founded in 1844, backed by Leonard Jerome, grandfather of Sir Winston Churchill. The *Democrat* and *American* merged in 1857; the *Daily Chronicle,* founded 1868, merged with them in 1870 as the *Democrat and Chronicle.* Ronald D. Martin is editor. Campbell Geeslin is book critic.

Rochester Times-Union. Rochester, N.Y. Newspaper. Founded 1826, as the *Rochester Daily Advertiser.* The *Rochester Daily Union,* founded 1855, merged with it within a year. The *Rochester Evening Times* was founded 1877; Frank Gannett bought it in 1918 and combined it with the *Union and Advertiser,* as the *Times-Union.* Gannett used it as his primary editorial organ, preferring it to his other papers. Paul Miller is editor. Jose Echaniz is book-review editor.

"Rock Me to Sleep." Poem by Elizabeth Chase Akers. It first appeared in the *Saturday Evening Post,* 1860.

"Rock Me to Sleep, Mother." Ballad by John Hill Hewitt.

"Rock-a-Bye, Baby." The familiar setting to the old lullaby was composed by Effie I. Canning Carlton in 1886, when she was a young girl. It was first sung in Denman Thompson's *The Old Homestead* and first published in Boston by C. D. Blake.

"Rocked in the Cradle of the Deep." Hymn by Emma Willard, written at sea, on the ship *Sully,* July 14, 1831, and set to music by John Philip Knight, English composer.

ROCKEY, HOWARD (June 3, 1886–May 27, 1934); b. Philadelphia, Pa. Novelist. *This Woman* (1924); *All That I Was* (under pen name, "Ronald Bryce," 1925); *Paradox* (1926); *The Varnoff Tradition* (under pen name, "Oliver Panbourne," 1926); *Through the Mill* (1927); *Masked Longing* (1931); *The Other Woman's Way* (1932); etc.

ROCKHILL, WILLIAM WOODVILLE (Apr. 1854–Dec. 8, 1914); b. Philadelphia, Pa. Diplomat, author. *The Life of the Buddha* (1884); *The Land of the Lamas* (1891); *Diary of a Journey in Mongolia and Tibet in 1891 and 1892* (1894); etc. Minister to China 1905–09; ambassador to Russia, 1909–11; to Turkey, 1911–13, etc. *See* Tyler Dennett's *Americans in Eastern Asia* (1922).

Rocky Mountain News. Denver, Colo. Newspaper. Founded 1859, at Cherry Creek (now Denver). First newspaper in Colorado. Became a daily in 1860. Jack Foster is editor and book review editor.

Rocky Mountain Review. Cedar City, Utah. Quarterly review of literature. Founded 1937, as *Inter-Mountain Review;* name changed in 1938.

RODALE, JEROME IRVING (Aug. 16, 1898–June 9, 1971); b. New York. Editor, publisher. *The King's English on Horseback* (1938); *Pay Dirt* (1945); *The Healthy Hunzas* (1948); *Organic Gardening* (1955); *The Organic Way to Plant Protection* (1966); *The Prostate* (1967); *Smoke and Die, Quit and Live* (1967); etc. Editor: *Encyclopedia of Organic Gardening* (1959); etc. Pres., Rodale Press, from 1932.

RODDIS, LOUIS HARRY (Feb. 16, 1886–); b. Cherokee, Ia. Naval medical historian. *Life of Edward Jenner* (1930); *A Short History of Nautical Medicine* (1942); *The Indian Wars of Minnesota* (1956); *The First European Medical Men in the New World* (1964); etc. Editor: Naval Medical History of World War II.

RODELL, FRED (Mar. 1, 1907–); b. Philadelphia, Pa. Educator, author. *Fifty-five Men: The Story of the Constitution* (1936); *Woe Unto You, Lawyers* (1939); *Nine Men: A Political History of the Supreme Court from 1790 to 1955* (1955); *Her Infinite Variety* (1966); etc. Faculty, School of Law, Yale University, since 1933.

RODEN, HENRY WISDOM (July 17, 1895–May 10, 1963); b. Dallas, Tex. Business executive, author. *You Only Hang Once* (1944); *Too Busy to Die* (1944); *One Angel Less* (1945); *Wake for a Lady* (1946).

Roderick Hudson. Novel by Henry James (1876). The story of a young sculptor who finds Northampton, Mass., unsuited to his genius and who goes to Rome for an atmosphere more inspiring.

RODICK, BURLEIGH CUSHING (June 12, 1889–); b. Freeport, Me. Educator, author. *The Doctrine of Necessity in International Law* (1928); *My Own New England: Tales of Vanishing Types* (1929); *American Constitutional Custom* (1953); *Appomattox: The Last Campaign* (1965). Political science dept., Brooklyn College, since 1938.

RODITI, EDOUARD (1910–). Author. *Prison Within Prison* (poems, 1941); *Oscar Wilde* (1947); *Poems, 1928–1948* (1949); *Dialogues on Art* (1960); etc.

RODMAN, SELDEN (Feb. 19, 1909–); b. New York City. Author. *Lawrence: The Last Crusade* (1937); *The Airmen* (poem, 1941); *The Amazing Year: A Diary in Verse* (1947); *Portrait of the Artist as an American: Ben Shahn* (1951); *Haiti: The Black Republic* (1954); *The Eye of Man* (1955); *Conversations with Artists* (1957); *The Insiders* (1960); *The Heart of Beethoven* (1961); *Quisqueya: A History of the Dominican Republic* (1964); *The Road to Panama* (1966); *The Guatemala Traveler* (1967); *The Caribbean* (1968); *The Mexican Traveler* (1969); etc. Editor: *A New Anthology of Modern Poetry* (1946).

ROE, AZEL STEVENS (Aug. 16, 1798–Jan. 1, 1886); b. New York. Novelist. *James Mountjoy* (1850); *Time and Tide; or, Strive and Win* (1852); *Looking Around* (1865); *True Love Rewarded* (1877); etc.

ROE, E[dward] P[ayson] (May 7, 1838–July 19, 1888); b. New Windsor, N.Y. Presbyterian clergyman, novelist. *Barriers Burned Away* (1872); *Opening a Chestnut Burr* (1874); *From Jest to Earnest* (1875); *Near to Nature's Heart* (1876); *A Knight of the Nineteenth Century* (1877); *A Face Illuminated* (1878); *Without a Home* (1881); *He Fell in Love with His Wife* (1886); *The Earth Trembled* (1887); etc. *See* Mary A. Roe's *E. P. Roe: Reminiscences of His Life* (1889).

ROE, MARY A[bigail] (c. 1840); b. New Windsor, N.Y., sister of E. P. Roe. Author. *Free, Yet Forging Their Own Chains* (under pen name, "C. M. Cornwall," (1876); *A Long Search* (1885); *E. P. Roe: Reminiscences of His Life* (1899).

ROE, VINGIE EVE (Mrs. Raymond C. Lawton) (Dec. 7, 1879–Aug. 13, 1958); b. Oxford, Kan. Author. *The Maid of the Whispering Hills* (1912); *A Divine Egotist* (1916); *Val of Paradise* (1921); *Nameless River* (1923); *Bitter Laurel* (1928); *Flame of the Border* (1933); *Black Belle Rides the Uplands* (1935); *Glory in the Gum Woods* (1937); *Guns of the Round Stone Valley* (1938); *Wild Harvest* (1941); *The Great Trace* (1948); etc.

ROERICH, NICHOLAS K[onstantin] (Sept. 27, 1874–Dec. 12, 1947); b. St. Petersburg, Rus. Artist, author. *Himalaya* (1926); *Joys of Sikkim* (1928); *Altai-Himalaya: A Travel Diary* (1929); *Flame in Chalice* (1930); *Heart of Asia* (1930); *Fiery Stronghold* (1933); *Gates into the Future* (1936). Founder, Roerich Museum, New York.

ROETHKE, THEODORE (May 25, 1908–Aug. 1, 1963); b. Saginaw, Mich. Educator, poet. *Open House* (1941); *The Lost Son and Other Poems* (1948); *Praise to the End!* (1951); *The Waking: Poems, 1933–53* (1953); *Words for the Wind* (collected poems, 1958); etc. English dept., University of Washington, from 1947. *See* Ralph J. Mills' *Theodore Roethke* (1963); Arnold Stein's *Theodore Roethke: Essays on the Poetry* (1965); William J. Martz's *The Achievement of Theodore Roethke* (1966).

ROGERS, AGNES (Mrs. Frederick Lewis Allen) (Sept. 16, 1893–); b. Hagerstown, Md. Author. *Flight* (1935); *From Man to Machine* (1941); *Women Are Here to Stay* (1949); etc. Co-author (with F. L. Allen): *The American Procession* (1933); *I Remember Distinctly* (1947); etc.

ROGERS, ARTHUR KENYON (Dec. 27, 1868–Nov. 1, 1936); b. Dunellen, N.J. Educator, author. *A Brief Introduction to Modern Philosophy* (1899); *Theory of Ethics* (1922); *English and American Philosophy Since 1800* (1922); *Morals in Review* (1927); *Ethics and Moral Tolerance* (1934); etc. Prof. philosophy, Yale University, 1914–20.

ROGERS, CAMERON (Dec. 20, 1900–); b. Santa Barbara, Cal. Author. *The Magnificent Idler: The Story of Walt Whitman* (1926); *Manila Galleon* (1936); *Flight Surgeon* (with H. E. Halland, 1940); *Trodden Glory* (1949); etc. Editor: *A County Judge in Arcady* (1954).

ROGERS, CLEVELAND (Mar. 3, 1885–); b. Greenville, S.C. Editor, playwright, biographer. *The Legend of the Hills* (1911); *Ransomed* (with Theodore B. Sayre, prod. 1912); *Walt Whitman's Life and Work* (1920); etc. With the *Brooklyn Eagle,* 1906–37.

ROGERS, DALE EVANS (Oct. 31, 1912); b. Uvalde, Tex. Actress, singer. *Angel Unaware* (1953); *My Spiritual Diary* (1955); *To My Son: Faith at Our House* (1957); *Christmas Is Always* (1958); *No Two Ways About It* (1963); *Dearest Debbie* (1965); *Time Out, Ladies* (1966); etc.

ROGERS, HENRY MUNROE (Feb. 27, 1839–Mar. 29, 1937); b. Boston, Mass. Lawyer, author. *Memories of Ninety Years* (autobiography, 1928); *Adam and Eve, and Other People* (poems, 1935).

ROGERS, JAMES GRAFTON (Jan. 13, 1883–); b. Denver, Colo. Lawyer, educator. *The Fire of Romance* (1919); *The Third Day* (1922); *American Bar Leaders* (1932); *World Policing and the Constitution* (1945); etc. Prof. law, Yale University, 1935–42.

ROGERS, JOHN RANKIN (Sept. 4, 1838–Dec. 26, 1901); b. Brunswick, Me. Merchant, governor, author. *The Irrepressible Conflict; or, An American System of Money* (1892); *The Grafton's; or, Looking Forward* (1893), republished as *Looking Forward* (1898). Founder, *The Kansas Commoner,* 1887. Governor of Washington, 1897–1901.

ROGERS, JULIA ELLEN (Jan. 21, 1866–); b. in La Salle Co., Ill. Naturalist, author. *Among Green Trees* (1902); *The Tree Book* (1905); *The Shell Book* (1907); *Earth and Sky* (1910).

ROGERS, LINDSAY (May 23, 1891–); b. Baltimore, Md. Educator, author. *The Problem of Government* (with W. W. Willoughby, 1921); *The American Senate* (1926); *Crisis Government* (1934); *Pollsters* (1949); etc. Law dept., Columbia University, since 1920.

ROGERS, MEYRIC REYNOLD (Jan. 8, 1893–); b. Birmingham, Eng. Museum curator. *Carl Milles: An Interpretation of His Work* (1940); *American Interior Design* (1947).

Rogers, Phillips. Pen name of Albert E. Idell.

ROGERS, ROBERT (Nov. 7, 1731–May 18, 1795); b. Methuen, Mass. Colonial ranger, frontiersman, author. *Journals* (1765); *A Concise Account of North America* (1765); *Ponteach; or, The Savages of America* (anon., 1766).

ROGERS, ROBERT CAMERON (Jan. 7, 1862–Apr. 20, 1912); b. Buffalo, N.Y. Author. *Old Dorset* (1897); *The Rosary, and Other Poems* (1906); *The Wind in the Clearing, and Other Poems* (1895); *For the King, and Other Poems* (1899).

ROGERS, ROBERT WILLIAM (Feb. 14, 1864–Dec. 12, 1930); b. Philadelphia, Pa. Educator, orientalist, author. *A History of Babylonia and Assyria,* 2v. (1900); *The Recovery of the Ancient Orient* (1912); *The History and Literature of the Hebrew People,* 2v. (1917); *A History of Ancient Persia* (1929); etc. Prof. Hebrew and Old Testament exegesis, Drew Theological Seminary, 1893–1930.

ROGERS, SAMUEL GREEN ARNOLD (Sept. 5, 1894–); b. Newport, R.I. Educator, author. *The Sombre Flame* (1928); *Dusk at the Grave* (1934); *Lucifer in Pine Lake* (1937); *Flora Shawn* (1942); *Don't Look Behind You* (1944); *You'll Be Sorry* (1945); *You Leave Me Cold* (1946); *Balzac and the Novel* (1953); etc. French and English depts., University of Wisconsin, since 1919.

ROGERS, WARREN JOSEPH, JR. (May 6, 1922–); b. New Orleans, La. Journalist, author. *The Floating Revolution* (1962); *Outpost of Freedom* (1965). Washington editor, *Look* magazine, from 1966.

ROGERS, WILL (Nov. 4, 1879–Aug. 15, 1935); b. Oologah, Indian Terr. (now Okla.). Humorist, actor, author. *Rogerisms,* 3 series (1919–20); *The Illiterate Digest* (1924); *There's Not a Bathing Suit in Russia* (1927); etc. Wrote daily syndicated humorous article for newspapers for many years. With Ziegfeld Follies; played in many motion pictures. *See* Patrick J. O'Brien's *Will Rogers* (1935); Jack Lait's *Our Will Rogers* (1936); Paula McSpadden Love's *The Will Rogers Book* (1961).

ROGERS, WILLIAM ALLEN (May 23, 1854–Oct. 20, 1931); b. Springfield, O. Cartoonist, illustrator, author. *A World Worth While* (1922); *Danny's Partner* (1923); *The Lost Caravan* (1927). Illustrated for *Harper's Weekly, Life,* etc. Illustrated James Otis Kaler's *Toby Tyler,* etc.

ROGERS, WILLIAM GARLAND (Feb. 29, 1896–); b. Chicopee Falls, Mass. Author. *Life Goes On* (1929); *When This You See Remember Me: Gertrude Stein In Person* (1948); *Ladies Bountiful* (1968); etc. Arts editor, Associated Press, since 1944.

ROGGE, O[etje] JOHN (Oct. 12, 1903–); b. in Cass Co., Ill. Lawyer. *Why Men Confess* (1959); *The First and the Fifth* (1960); *The Official German Report* (1961); *Obscenity Litigation in Ten American Jurisprudence Trials* (1965); etc. Editor, Harvard Law Review.

Rohde, Ruth Bryan Owen. See Ruth Bryan Owen.

ROLFE, EDWIN (1909–1954). Poet. *To My Contemporaries* (poems, 1939); *Lincoln Battalion: The Story of the Americans Who Fought in Spain* (1939); *Glass Room* (with Lester Fuller, 1946); *First Love* (poems, 1951).

ROLFE, JOHN CAREW (Oct. 15, 1859–Mar. 26, 1943); b. Lawrence, Mass. Educator, author. *Cicero and His Influence* (1923). Editor and translator of many classical texts, etc. Prof. Latin, University of Pennsylvania, 1902–32.

ROLFE, WILLIAM J[ames] (Dec. 10, 1827–July 7, 1910); b. Newburyport, Mass. Educator, editor, author. *Shakespeare the Boy* (1896); *A Life of William Shakespeare* (1904); etc. Editor: *Works of Shakespeare*, 40v. (1871–84); *Complete Works of Alfred Lord Tennyson*, 12v. (1895–98). Edited poetical works of Goldsmith, Gray, Scott, Browning, Milton, and Wordsworth, etc.

Rolling Stone. Austin, Tex. Magazine. Founded Apr. 28, 1894, by William Sydney Porter ("O. Henry"), as *The Iconoclast.* Name changed after two issues. Expired Aug. 28, 1894.

Rolling Stone. San Francisco, Cal. Semimonthly. Magazine. Founded 1967. Edited by Jann Wenner. Concerned with the new "longhair" youth culture, especially rock music.

ROLLINS, ALICE [Marland] WELLINGTON (June 12, 1847–Dec. 5, 1897); b. Boston, Mass. Poet, novelist. *My Welcome Beyond, and Other Poems* (1877); *The Ring of Amethyst* (poems, 1878); *The Story of a Ranch* (1885); *All Sorts of Children* (1886); *The Three Tetons* (1887); *Uncle Tom's Tenement* (1888); *From Snow to Sunshine* (poem, 1889); *From Palm to Glacier* (1892); *The Story of Azron* (poem, 1895); *Little Page Fern, and Other Verses* (1895); *The Finding of the Gentian* (1895); etc.

ROLLINS, HYDER EDWARD (Nov. 8, 1889–July 25, 1958); b. Abilene, Tex. Educator. *The Renaissance in England* (with H. Baker, 1954); etc. Editor: *Old English Ballads, 1553–1625* (1920); *Tottel's Miscellany*, 2v. (1928–29); *The Pepys Ballads*, 8v. (1929–32); *England's Helicon*, 2v. (1935); *The Passionate Pilgrim, by William Shakespeare* (1940); *Shakespeare's Sonnets*, 2v. (1944); *The Keats Circle*, 2v. (1948); *The Letters of John Keats*, 2v. (1958); etc. General editor, Harvard Studies in English, from 1933. English dept., Harvard University, from 1921.

ROLLINS, PHILIP ASHTON (Jan. 20, 1869–); b. Somersworth, N.H. Author. *The Cowboy: His Characteristics* (1922); *Jinglebob* (1927); *The Cowboy: An Unconventional History* (1936); *Gone Haywire* (1939); etc. Editor: *The Discovery of the Oregon Trail: Robert Stuart's Narratives* (1935). The Rollins Collection of Western Americana has been given to Princeton University.

Rollo Books. A series of books for boys by Jacob Abbott.

ROLSTON, HOLMES (Sept. 6, 1900–); b. Staunton, Va. Presbyterian clergyman. *A Conservative Looks to Barth and Brunner* (1932); *The Social Message of the Apostle Paul* (1942); *Personalities Around Paul* (1954); *Faces About the Christ* (1959); *The Bible in Christian Teaching* (1962); *The Layman's Bible Commentary* (1963); *The "We Knows" of the Apostle Paul* (1966); *Personalities Around David* (1968); etc.

ROLT-WHEELER, FRANCES WILLIAM (Dec. 16, 1876–Aug. 21, 1960); b. Forest Hill, London. Editor, author. *The Boy with the United States Survey* (1909); *The Boy with the United States Indians* (1913); *The Boy with the United States Explorers* (1914); *The Polar Hunters* (1917); *The Boy with the United States Naturalists* (1918); *The Aztec-Hunters* (1918); *The Boy with the United States Trappers* (1919); *The Book of Cowboys* (1921); *In the Days before Columbus* (1921); *Heroes of the Ruins* (1923); *The Gem Hunters* (1924); *Colonial Ways and Wars* (1925); *The Tamer of Herds* (1928); *The Tools of Magic* (1934); *Le Tarot Medieval* (1940); etc.

ROLVAAG, O[le] E[dvart] (Apr. 22, 1876–Nov. 5, 1931); b. in Helgeland, Nor.; came to the United States in 1896. Educator, novelist. His Norwegian novels have been translated as follows: *Pure Gold* (1930); *The Boat of Longing* (1933); *Giants in the Earth* (1927); *Peder Victorious* (1929); *Their Fathers' God* (1931). See Theodore Jorgenson's *Ole Edvart Rölvaag* (with Nora O. Solum, 1939); Fred B. Millett's *Contemporary American Authors* (1940).

Romance. Play by Edward Sheldon (prod. 1913). This most popular of Sheldon's plays deals with an Italian opera singer who gives up the clergyman she loves for fear a dark incident in her past life may wreck his career.

ROMANS, BERNARD (c. 1720–c. 1784); b. in the Netherlands. Naturalist, cartographer, author. *A Concise Natural History of East and West-Florida* (1775); *Annals of the Troubles in the Netherlands*, 2v. (1778–1782).

Romantic Revolution in America, The. By Vernon L. Parrington (1927). The second volume of his *Main Currents in American Thought* (q.v.).

ROMIG, EDNA DAVIS (Jan. 16, 1889–); b. Rarden, O. Educator, author. *Lincoln Remembers* (1930); *Marse Lee* (1930); *The Torch Undimmed* (1931); *An Amherst Garden* (1938); *These Are the Fields* (poems, 1955); etc. English dept., University of Colorado, since 1919.

ROMULO, CARLOS P[ena] (Jan. 14, 1901–); b. Manila. Diplomat, author. *Daughters for Sale and Other Plays* (1924); *Better English* (1924); *Rizal, a Chronicle Play* (1926); *Changing Tides in the Far East* (1928); *I Saw the Fall of the Philippines* (1942); *My Brother Americans* (1945); *The United* (1951); *Crusade in Asia* (1955); *I Walked with Heroes* (1961); *Identity and Change: Towards a National Definition* (1967); etc. Philippine ambassador to the United States, 1954–64.

ROOD, HENRY EDWARD (June 26, 1867–Jan. 3, 1954); b. Philadelphia, Pa. Editor, author. *The Company Doctor* (1895); *Hardwicke* (1902); *In Camp at Bear Pond* (1904); etc. Asst. editor, *Harper's Magazine,* 1900–1908.

ROOF, KATHARINE METCALF, b. Clifton Springs, N.Y. Author. *The Stranger at the Hearth* (1916); *The Life and Art of William Merritt Chase* (1917); *The Great Demonstration* (1920); *Colonel William Smith and Lady* (1929); *Murder on the Salem Road* (1931); etc.

ROOSEVELT, [Anna] ELEANOR (Mrs. Franklin Delano Roosevelt) (Oct. 11, 1884–Nov. 7, 1962); b. New York. Columnist, author. *It's Up to the Women* (1933); *This Is My Story* (1937); *My Days* (1938); *This Troubled World* (1938); *The Moral Basis of Democracy* (1940); *If You Ask Me* (1946); *This I Remember* (1949); *India and the Awakening East* (1953); *On My Own* (1958); *You Learn by Living* (1960); *Autobiography* (1961); etc. Editor: *Hunting Big Game in the Eighties: The Letters of Elliot Roosevelt, Sportsman* (1932). Wrote syndicated newspaper column, "My Day."

ROOSEVELT, ELLIOTT (Sept. 23, 1910–); b. New York. Author. *As He Saw It* (1946). Editor, with others: *F. D. R.: His Personal Letters,* 4v. (1947–50).

ROOSEVELT, FRANKLIN D[elano] (Jan. 30, 1882–Apr. 12, 1945); b. Hyde Park, N.Y. Thirty-second president of the

United States, author. *Whither Bound* (1926); *The Happy Warrior: Alfred E. Smith* (1928); *Government: Not Politics* (1932); *Looking Forward* (1933); *On Our Way* (1934); *The Public Papers and Addresses,* 5v. (1938); *Roosevelt's Foreign Policy, 1933–41: Unedited Speeches and Messages* (1942); *Nothing To Fear: Selected Addresses, 1932–45* (1946); *F. D. R.: His Personal Letters,* 3v. (1947–50); etc. Governor of New York, 1929–33; President of the U.S., 1933–45. See Frances Perkins' *The Roosevelt I Knew* (1946); Robert E. Sherwood's *Roosevelt and Hopkins* (1948); John Gunther's *Roosevelt in Retrospect* (1950); J. M. Burns's *Roosevelt: The Lion and the Fox* (1956); Arthur M. Schlesinger, Jr.'s *The Age of Roosevelt,* 3v. (1957–60); James Roosevelt's and Sidney Shalett's *Affectionately, F. D. R.* (1959); W. E. Leuchtenberg's *Franklin D. Roosevelt: A Profile* (1967); James MacGregor Burns's *Roosevelt: The Soldier of Freedom* (1970). His papers are in the Franklin D. Roosevelt Library at Hyde Park, N.Y.

ROOSEVELT, KERMIT (Oct. 10, 1889–June 4, 1943); b. Oyster Bay, N.Y., son of Theodore Roosevelt. Traveler, author. *War in the Garden of Eden* (1919); *The Happy Hunting Grounds* (1920); *Quentin Roosevelt* (1921); *East of the Sun and West of the Moon* (with Theodore Roosevelt, Jr. 1926); *Cleared for Strange Ports* (1927); *American Backlogs* (1928); *Trailing the Giant Panda* (with Theodore Roosevelt, 1929).

ROOSEVELT, NICHOLAS (June 12, 1893–); b. New York. Diplomat, publicist, author. *The Philippines: A Treasure and a Problem* (1926); *The Restless Pacific* (1928); *America and England?* (1930); *A New Birth of Freedom* (1938); *A Front Row Seat* (1953); *Creative Cook* (1956); *Good Cooking* (1959); *Theodore Roosevelt: The Man As I Knew Him* (1967). On editorial staff, the *New York Herald Tribune,* 1933–42.

ROOSEVELT, ROBERT BARNWELL (Aug. 7, 1829–June 14, 1906); b. New York. Reformer, pioneer in conservation, author. *Five Acres Too Much* (1869); *Progressive Petticoats* (1874); *Love and Luck* (1886); and books on game and conservation. Editor: *The Poetical Works of Charles G. Halpine* (1869). Congressman, 1871–73.

ROOSEVELT, THEODORE (Oct. 27, 1858–Jan. 6, 1919); b. New York. Twenty-sixth president of the United States, soldier, big game hunter, author. *The Naval War of 1812* (1882); *Hunting Trip of a Ranchman* (1885); *Thomas Hart Benton* (1886); *The Winning of the West,* 4v. (1889–96); *American Ideals, and Other Essays* (1897); *The Rough Riders* (1899); *The Strenuous Life* (1900); *Oliver Cromwell* (1900); *Outdoor Pastimes of an American Hunter* (1905); *The New Nationalism* (1910); *African Game Trails,* 2v. (1910); *History as Literature, and Other Essays* (1913); *Theodore Roosevelt: An Autobiography* (1913); *Life Histories of African Game Trails* (with Edmund Heller, 1914); *Through the Brazilian Wilderness* (1914); *America and the World War* (1915); *A Book-Lover's Holidays in the Open* (1916); *The Great Adventure* (1918); *Who Should Go West?* ed. by R. W. G. Vail (1927); *Theodore Roosevelt's Diaries of Boyhood and Youth* (1928); *The Works of Theodore Roosevelt,* Sagamore Edition, 15v. (1900); Elkhorn Edition, 28v. (1906–20); Memorial Edition, 24v. (1923–26); National Edition, 20v. (1926). Governor of New York, 1898–1900; Vice-President of the United States, 1900–01; president of the United States, 1901–08. Formed Progressive "Bull Moose" Party in 1912. See William Lewis Draper's *Theodore Roosevelt* (1919); Henry Cabot Lodge's *Theodore Roosevelt* (1919); William R. Thayer's *Theodore Roosevelt* (1919); J. B. Bishop's *Theodore Roosevelt and His Time Shown in His Own Letters,* 2v. (1920); John Hall Wheelock's *A Bibliography of Theodore Roosevelt* (1920); Herman Hagedorn's *Roosevelt in the Badlands* (1921); Earle Looker's *The White House Gang* (1929); Owen Wister's *Roosevelt: The Story of a Friendship* (1930); *Theodore Roosevelt Cyclopedia,* ed. by Albert Bushnell Hart and Herbert R. Ferleger (1941); H. F. Pringle's *Theodore Roosevelt;* George Edwin Mowry's *Theodore Roosevelt and the Progressive Movement* (1947); Nicholas Roosevelt's *Theodore Roosevelt* (1967). The Roosevelt Memorial in New York City contains a large collection of

Rooseveltiana, and many of his manuscripts are in the Library of Congress.

ROOSEVELT, THEODORE, JR. (Sept. 13, 1887–July 12, 1944); b. Oyster Bay, N.Y., son of Theodore Roosevelt. Governor general, army officer, explorer, author. *Average Americans* (1919); *East of the Sun and West of the Moon* (with Kermit Roosevelt, 1926); *All in the Family* (1929); *Taps* (with Grantland Rice, 1932); *Colonial Policies of the United States* (1937). Compiler: *The Desk Drawer Anthology* (with Alice Roosevelt Longworth, 1937); etc. Governor of Puerto Rico, 1929–32; governor general, Philippine Islands, 1932–33. Vice-president, Doubleday, Doran & Co.

Roosevelt and Hopkins. By Robert E. Sherwood (1948). Study of the relationship between Franklin D. Roosevelt and Harry Hopkins and its effect on United States political affairs.

ROOT, ELIHU (Feb. 15, 1845–Feb. 7, 1937); b. Clinton, N.Y. Lawyer, statesman, author. *The Citizen's Part in Government* (1907); *Addresses on International Subjects* (1916); *Addresses on Government and Citizenship* (1916); *Russia and the United States* (1917); *Miscellaneous Addresses* (1917); *Men and Policies* (1924). Secretary of War, 1899–1904; Secretary of State, 1905–09; U.S. Senator from New York, 1909–15; president, Carnegie Endowment for International Peace, 1910–25; member, Permanent Court of Arbitration at the Hague, 1910–37; etc. See Philip C. Jessup's *Elihu Root,* 2v. (1938); Richard W. Jessup's *Elihu Root and the Conservative Tradition* (1954).

ROOT, FRANK ALBERT (July 3, 1837–June 20, 1926); b. Binghamton, N.Y. Publisher, author. *The Overland Stage to California* (1901). Associated with *Telegraph, Courier, Express, Times, Mail,* all of Kansas, and the *Review Express* of Colorado.

ROOT, GEORGE FREDERICK (Aug. 30, 1820–Aug. 6, 1895); b. Sheffield, Mass. Musical educator, composer, author. *The Story of a Musical Life* (autobiography, 1891). Compiler of numerous hymnals. Among his popular songs are: "The First Gun is Fired," "The Battle Cry of Freedom," "Tramp, Tramp, Tramp, the Boys are Marching," "Just Before the Battle, Mother," "Hazel Dell," "Rosalie, the Prairie Flower," "The Shining Shore." See John T. Howard's *Our American Music* (1931).

ROOT, ROBERT KILBURN (Apr. 7, 1877–Nov. 20, 1950); b. Brooklyn, N.Y. Educator, editor, author. *Classical Mythology in Shakespeare* (1903); *The Poetry of Chaucer* (1906); *The Poetical Career of Alexander Pope* (1938); etc. Editor: *British Poetry and Prose,* 2v. (with P. R. Lieder and R. M. Lovett, 1928); *British Drama* (with same, 1929); etc. English dept., Princeton University, 1905–46; dean of faculty, from 1933.

ROOT, WAVERLEY LEWIS (Apr. 15, 1903–); b. Providence, R.I. Journalist, author. *The Truth About Wagner* (1929); *Secret History of the War* (1945); *Casablanca to Katyn* (1946); *The Food of France* (1958); *Contemporary French Cooking* (with R.D. Rochemont, 1962).

Rootabaga Stories. By Carl Sandburg (1922). Stories for children.

Roots of American Culture. By Constance Rourke (1942). An historical analysis.

ROPER, ELMO BURNS, JR. (July 31, 1900–); b. Hebron, Neb. Marketing consultant. *You and Your Leaders* (1958). Editor-at-large, *Saturday Review.*

ROPER, JOHN CASWELL (Nov. 4, 1873–Oct. 18, 1958); b. in Marlboro Co., S.C. Methodist clergyman. *Religious Aspects of Education* (1926); *The Supreme Law* (1932); *The Reality of the Invisible* (1949).

ROPES, JOHN CODMAN (Apr. 28, 1836–Oct. 28, 1899); b. St. Petersburg, Rus. Military historian, author. *The Army*

under Pope (1881); *The First Napoleon* (1886); *The Campaign of Waterloo* (1892); *The Story of the Civil War,* 2v. (1894–98); etc.

ROREM, NED (Oct. 23, 1923–); b. Richmond, Ind. Composer, author. *The Paris Diary of Ned Rorem* (1966); *Music from Inside Out* (1967); *The New York Diary of Ned Rorem* (1967).

RORIMER, JAMES JOSEPH (Sept. 7, 1905–May 11, 1966); b. Cleveland, O. Museum director. *The Cloisters* (1938); *The Unicorn Tapestries at the Cloisters* (1938); *Survival: The Salvage and Protection of Art in War* (with Gilbert Rakin, 1950); etc.

RORTY, JAMES (Mar. 30, 1890–May 11, 1966); b. Middletown, N.Y. Author. *Children of the Sun* (1926); *Where Life Is Better* (1936); *American Medicine Mobilizes* (1939); *Tomorrow's Food* (with N. P. Norman, 1947); *McCarthy and the Communists* (1954); etc.

ROSAIRE, FORREST (1902–). Author. *East of Midnight* (1945); *The Uneasy Years* (1950); *White Night* (1956).

"Rosary, The." Poem by Robert Cameron Rogers (1894). Set to music by Ethelbert Nevin in 1898.

ROSE, ADA CAMPBELL (Nov. 3, 1901–); b. Cincinnati, O. Editor. Compiler: *Jack and Jill Story Book* (1948); *Jack and Jill Mystery Book* (1959); etc. Editor, *Jack and Jill,* 1938–59.

ROSE, AQUILA (c. 1695–Aug. 22, 1723); b. in England. Poet. *Poems on Several Occasions* (1740). *See* Samuel Keimer's *Elegy on the Much Lamented Death of the Ingenious and Well-Beloved Aquila Rose* (1723); Elias Bockett's *A Poem to the Memory of Aquila Rose* (1723–24).

ROSE, ARNOLD M[arshall] (July 2, 1918–Jan. 2, 1968); b. Chicago, Ill. Sociologist. *Union Solidarity* (1952); *Sociology* (1956); *The Power Structure: Political Process in American Society* (1967); etc. Co-author: *An American Dilemma* (1944); *America Divided* (1948). Editor: *Race Prejudice and Discrimination* (1951); *Institutions of Advanced Societies* (1958); etc. Sociology dept., University of Minnesota, from 1949.

ROSE, DONALD FRANK [Don Rose] (June 29, 1890–Feb. 7, 1964); b. Street, Eng. Journalist. *Stuff and Nonsense: A Manual of Unimportances for Middlebrows* (1927); *Mother Nature Knows Best* (1940); *My Own Four Walls* (1941); *Mr. Wicker's War* (1943); *Full House* (1951); etc. Columnist, Philadelphia *Evening Bulletin,* from 1941.

ROSE, EDWARD EVERLEY (Feb. 11, 1862–Apr. 2, 1939); b. Stanstead, P.Q. Playwright. *The Great Train Robbery* (prod. 1897); *Rosa Machree* (prod. 1922); *Rose of the Ghetto* (1927); *Irish Eyes* (1933); and other plays. Adapter of many popular plays, including *David Harum, Janice Meredith, Richard Carvel, Alice of Old Vincennes, Eben Holden, Mr. Dooley, Gentleman from Indiana,* etc.

ROSE, HÉLOISE DURANT (Mrs. C. H. M. Rose), b. Brooklyn, N.Y. Poet, playwright. *Pine Needles* (poems, 1884); *A Ducal Skeleton* (1899); etc.

Rose of Dutcher's Coolly. Novel by Hamlin Garland (1895). The revolt of an idealist against the monotony and the intellectual starvation of Middle Western farm life.

ROSEBAULT, CHARLES J[erome] (Aug. 16, 1864–Mar. 18, 1944); b. Hartford, Conn. Journalist, author. *Saladin: Prince of Chivalry* (1930); *When Dana Was the Sun* (1931). With New York *Sun,* 1884–1907.

ROSEBORO', VIOLA, b. Pulaski, Tenn. Novelist. *Old Ways and New* (1892); *The Joyous Heart* (1903); *Players and Vagabonds* (1904).

ROSELIEP, RAYMOND (Aug. 11, 1917–); b. Farley, Ia. Clergyman, author. *Some Letters of Lionel Johnson* (1954); *Poems: The Linen Bands* (1961); *The Small Rain* (1963); *Love Makes the Air Light* (1965).

ROSEN, GEORGE (June 23, 1910–); b. New York. Physician. *The Specialization of Medicine* (1944); *A History of Public Health* (1958); etc. Editor (with B. C. Rosen): *Four Hundred Years of a Doctor's Life* (1947). Editor, *American Journal of Public Health,* since 1957.

ROSENBACH, A[braham] S[imon] W[olf] (July 22, 1876–July 1, 1952); b. Philadelphia, Pa. Rare book dealer, bibliophile, author. *The Unpublishable Memoirs* (1917); *An American Jewish Bibliography* (1926); *Books and Bidders: The Adventures of a Bibliophile* (1927); *Early American Children's Books* (1932). Has paid record auction prices for some of the world's greatest literary rarities. *See* Carl L. Cannon's *American Book Collectors* (1941).

ROSENBERG, HAROLD (Feb. 2, 1906–). Poet, art critic. *Trance Above the Streets* (poems, 1943); *The Tradition of the New* (1959); *Arshile Gorky* (1962); *The Anxious Object: Art Today and Its Audience* (1966); *Artworks and Packages* (1969); etc.

ROSENBERG, JAKOB (Sept. 5, 1893–); b. Berlin. Educator. *Rembrandt,* 2v. (1948); *Great Draughtsmen from Pisanello to Picasso* (1959); *Dutch Art and Architecture: 1600–1800* (1966); *Unfinished Business* (1967); etc. Prof. fine arts, Harvard University, since 1948.

ROSENBERG, NANCY SHERMAN (June 21, 1931–); b. New York. Author. *The Boy Who Ate Flowers* (1960); *Gwendolyn, the Miracle Hen* (1961); *Gwendolyn and the Weathercock* (1963); *The Story of Modern Medicine* (with Dr. L. Rosenberg, 1966).

ROSENFELD, LOUIS ZARA (Aug. 2, 1910–); b. New York. Author. Pen name, "Louis Zara." *Blessed Is the Man* (1935); *Give Us This Day* (1936); *Some for the Glory* (1937); *This Land Is Ours* (1940); *Against This Rock* (1943); *Ruth Middleton* (1946); *In the House of the King* (1952); *Rebel Run* (1951); *Blessed Is the Land* (1954); *Dark Rider* (1959); *Locks and Keys* (1969); etc.

ROSENFELD, MORRIS [Jacob] (Dec. 28, 1862–June 22, 1923); b. Bokscha, Pol. Poet. *Songs from the Ghetto* (1898); *The Works of Morris Rosenfeld,* ed. by Alex. Harkavy, 3v. (1908). Among his best known poems are "Songs of Labor," "My Boy," "Despair," and the "Candle Seller." *See* Leo Weiner's *The History of Yiddish Literature in the Nineteenth Century* (1899).

ROSENFELD, PAUL (May 4, 1890–July 22, 1946); b. New York. Music critic, essayist, novelist. *Port of New York* (1924); *Men Seen* (1925); *By Way of Art* (1928); *The Boy in the Sun* (1928); *Discoveries of a Music Critic* (1936). Music critic, the *Dial,* 1920–27.

ROSENHAUPT, HANS (Feb. 24, 1911–); b. Frankfurt-on-Main, Ger. Educator, author. *Isolation in Modern German Literature* (1939); *How To Wage Peace* (1949); *The True Deceivers* (1954); *Graduate Students' Experience of Columbia, 1940–56* (1958). With Woodrow Wilson National Fellowship Fund since 1958.

ROSENHEIM, EDWARD WEIL, JR. (May 15, 1918–); b. Chicago. Educator, author. *What Happens in Literature* (1960); *Swift and the Satirist's Art* (1963). Editor: *Selected Prose and Poetry of Jonathan Swift* (1958). Prof. English, University of Chicago, since 1962.

ROSENSTOCK-HUESSY, EUGEN (July 6, 1888–); b. Berlin. Educator, author. *Out of Revolution: Autobiography of Western Man* (1938); *The Christian Future* (1946); *The Driving Power of Western Civilization* (1950); *Judaism Despite Christianity* (1968); etc. Prof. social philosophy, Dartmouth College, since 1935.

ROSENTHAL, ABRAHAM MICHAEL (May 2, 1922–); b. Sault St. Marie, Ont., Can. Editor, author. *Thirty-Eight Witnesses* (1964); *One More Victim* (with others, 1967). Co-editor: *The Night the Lights Went Out* (1965); *The Pope's Journey* (1965). Assistant managing editor, *New York Times*, since 1967.

ROSEWATER, VICTOR (Feb. 13, 1871–July 13, 1940); b. Omaha, Neb., son of Edward Rosewater. Journalist, author. *History of the Liberty Bell* (1926); *History of Co-operative News-Gathering in the United States* (1930); *Back Stage in 1912* (1932); etc. Joined staff *Omaha Bee*, 1893; editor, 1906–20; publisher, 1917–23.

ROSMOND, BABETTE (Nov. 4, 1918–   ); b. New York. Novelist. *The Dewy, Dewy Eyes* (1946); *A Party for Grownups* (1948); *Lucy; or the Delaware Dialogues* (1952); *Children: A Comedy for Grownups* (1956); *Lawyers* (1962). Editor: *Seventeen's Stories* (1958).

ROSS, ALEXANDER (May 9, 1783–Oct. 23, 1856); b. Nairnshire, Scot. Fur-trader, explorer, Oregion pioneer, author. *Adventures of the First Settlers on the Oregon or Columbia River* (1849); *The Fur Hunters of the Far West*, 2v. (1855); *The Red River Settlement* (1856). See Harvey W. Scott's *History of the Oregon Country* (1924).

ROSS, ALEXANDER COFFMAN (May 31, 1812–Feb. 26, 1883); b. Zanesville, O. Jeweler, song writer. Author of the famous campaign song "Tippecanoe and Tyler, Too."

Ross, Barnaby. Pen name used jointly by Frederic Dannay and Manfred Bennington Lee.

ROSS, CHARLES GRIFFITH (Nov. 9, 1885–Dec. 5, 1950); b. Independence, Mo. Educator, author. *The Writing of News* (1911). Correspondent, the *St. Louis Post-Dispatch*, 1918–34; editor of editorial page, 1934–39. School of Journalism, University of Missouri, 1908–18.

ROSS, CLINTON (July 31, 1861–1920); b. Binghamton, N.Y. Author. *The Adventures of Three Worthies* (1891); *The Countess Bettina* (1895); *The Scarlet Coat* (1896); *The Puppet* (1896); *The Meddling Hussy* (1897); etc.

ROSS, EDWARD ALSWORTH (Dec. 12, 1866–1951); b. Virden, Ill. Educator, sociologist, author. *Sin and Society* (1907); *Changing America* (1912); *South of Panama* (1915); *Russia in Upheaval* (1918); *The Principles of Sociology* (1920); *Civic Sociology* (1925); *Seventy Years of It* (1936); *New Age Sociology* (1940); etc. Prof. sociology, University of Wisconsin, 1906–37.

ROSS, FLOYD HIATT (Jan. 19, 1910–); b. Indianapolis, Ind. Unitarian clergyman, author. *Personalism and the Problem of Evil* (1940); *Ethics and the Modern World* (with Frederick Mayer, 1952); *Questions That Matter Most* (with T. W. Hills, 1954); *Man Myth and Maturity* (1959); *Shinto—The Way of Japan* (1965); etc.

ROSS, HAROLD WALLACE (Nov. 6, 1892–Dec. 6, 1951); b. Aspen, Colo. Editor. Co-editor, *Stars and Stripes*, 1917–19; editor, the *American Legion Weekly*, 1919–24; *Judge*, 1925, the *New Yorker*, 1925–51.

ROSS, ISHBEL (Mrs. Bruce Rae) (1897–); b. in Sutherland-shire, Scot. Editor, author. *Through the Lich-Gate* (1931); *Promenade Deck* (1932); *Marriage in Gotham* (1933); *Highland Twilight* (1934); *Fifty Years a Woman* (1938); *Isle of Escape* (1942); *Child of Destiny* (1949); *Proud Kate* (1953); *Angel of the Battlefield* (1956); *First Lady of the South* (1958); *The General's Wife* (1959); *Grace Coolidge and Her Era* (1962); *American Family: The Tafts, 1678–1964* (1964); *Charmers and Cranks* (1965); etc. Editorial staff, *New York Herald Tribune*, 1919–33.

ROSS, JOHN DAWSON (Oct. 23, 1853–Oct. 29, 1939); b. Edinburgh, Scot. Author. *Scottish Poets in America* (1889); *Burnsiana* (1892); *All About Burns* (1896); *Burns' Clarinda* (1897); *All About Tam O'Shanter* (1900); *A Little Book of Burns Lore* (1926); *Who's Who in Burns* (1927); *The Poems of Clarinda* (1929); *The Burns Handbook* (1930); *The Story of the Kilmarnock Burns* (1933); etc.

ROSS, JOHN ELLIOT (Mar. 14, 1884–Sept. 18, 1946); b. Baltimore, Md. Roman Catholic clergyman, author. *Christian Ethics* (1918); *Five Minute Sermons*, 4 series (1925–37); *John Henry Newman* (1933); *Ethics from the Standpoint of Scholastic Philosophy* (1938); *Religions of Democracy* (with others, 1941); etc.

Ross, Leonard Q. Pen name of Leo Calvin Rosten.

ROSS, LILLIAN (June 8, 1926–   ); b. Syracuse, N.Y. Author. *Picture* (1952); *Portrait of Hemingway* (1961); *The Player* (with Helen Ross, 1962); *Vertical and Horizontal* (1963); *Reporting* (1964); *Adlai Stevenson* (1966); *Talk Stories* (1966).

ROSS, MALCOLM HARRISON (June 1, 1895–May 23, 1965); b. Newark, N.J. Author. *Deep Enough* (1926); *Penny Dreadful* (1929); *Hymn to the Sun* (1931); *Death of a Yale Man* (1939); *All Manner of Men* (1948); *The Man Who Lived Backward* (1950); etc.

ROSS, NANCY WILSON (Mrs. Stanley P. Young) b. Olympia, Wash. Author. *Friday to Monday* (1932); *Take the Lightning* (1940); *Farthest Reach: Oregon and Washington* (1941); *The Waves* (1943); *Westward the Women* (1944); *The Left Hand Is the Dreamer* (1947); *I, My Ancestor* (1950); *Time's Corner* (1952); *The Return of Lady Brace* (1957); etc.

ROSS, SAM (Mar. 10, 1912–Sept. 20, 1960); b. Kiev, Rus. Novelist. *He Ran All the Way* (1947); *Someday Boy* (1948); *The Sidewalks Are Free* (1950); *Port Unknown* (1951); *Tight Corner* (1956).

ROSSI, PETER HENRY (Dec. 27, 1921–   ); b. New York. Educator, author. *Why Families Move* (1956); *The Politics of Urban Renewal* (1962); *The Education of Catholic Americans* (1966); *New Media and Education* (1967). Dept. of social relations, Johns Hopkins University, since 1967.

ROSSITER, CLINTON [Lawrence], III (Sept. 18, 1917–July 11, 1970); b. Philadelphia, Pa. Educator. *Constitutional Dictatorship* (1948); *Seedtime of the Republic* (1953); *Conservatism in America* (1955); *The American Presidency* (1956); *Marxism: The View from America* (1960); *The Political Thought of the American Revolution* (1963); *Six Characters in Search of a Republic* (1964); *1787: The Grand Convention* (1966); etc. Editor: *The Essential Lippmann* (1963). Government dept., Cornell University, from 1946.

ROSSITER, WILLIAM SIDNEY (Sept. 9, 1861–Jan. 23, 1929); b. Westfield, Mass. Statistician, publisher. *A Century of Population Growth from the First Census of the United States to the Twelfth, 1790–1900* (1909). Editor: *Days and Ways in Old Boston* (1914). He joined the Census Bureau in 1900 and was connected with it until his death. He was with the Rumford Press, Concord, N.H., 1909–29, and its president for many years.

ROSTEN, LEO C[alvin] (Apr. 11, 1908–); b. Lodz, Poland. Author. Pen names, "Leonard Ross" and "Leonard Q. Ross." *The Washington Correspondents* (1937); *The Education of H-y-m-a-n K-a-p-l-a-n* (1937); *Dateline: Europe* (1939); *The Strangest Places* (1939); *Adventure in Washington* (1940); *Hollywood: The Movie Colony* (1941); *The Return of Hyman Kaplan* (1959); *Captain Newman, M.D.* (1961); *The Many Worlds of Leo Rosten* (1964); *A Most Private Intrigue* (1967); *The Joys of Yiddish* (1968); etc. Editor: *Guide to the Religions of America* (1955).

ROSTEN, NORMAN (Jan. 1, 1914–); Poet, playwright. *Return Again Traveler* (1940); *The Fourth Decade* (1943); *The Big Road* (1946); *Songs for Patricia* (1951); *The Plane and the Shadow* (1953); etc. Also radio verse plays.

ROSTOVTZEFF, MICHAEL I[vanovich] (Oct. 28, 1870–Oct. 20, 1952); b. Kiev, Rus. Educator, historian. *The Roman Empire* (1926); *A History of the Ancient World,* 2v. (1926–27); *Mystic Italy* (1927); *Out of the Past of Greece and Rome* (1932); *Caravan Cities* (1932); *Social and Economic History of the Hellenistic World,* 3v. (1941); etc. Prof. ancient history, Yale University, 1925–44.

ROSTOW, WALT WHITMAN (Oct. 7, 1916–); b. New York. Educator. *The American Diplomatic Revolution* (1947); *The Process of Economic Growth* (1952); *View From the Seventh Floor* (1966); etc. Co-author: *The Prospects for Communist China* (with M.F. Millikan, 1957); *The Dynamics of Soviet Society: The Krushchev Era and Beyond* (1967).

ROSZAK, THEODORE (1933–   ). Educator, editor, author. *The Making of a Counter Culture* (1969). Editor: *The Dissenting Academy* (1968); *Masculine/Feminine: Readings in Sexual Mythology and the Liberation of Women* (with Betty Roszak, 1970). Prof. history, California State College at Hayward.

ROTH, HENRY (Feb. 8, 1906–   ); b. Tysmenica, Aust.-Hung. Novelist. *Call It Sleep* (1934).

ROTH, PHILIP (Mar. 19, 1933–); Newark, N.J. Author. *Goodbye, Columbus, and Five Short Stories* (1959); *Letting Go* (1962). *Portnoy's Complaint* (1969); *Four by Philip Roth* (1970).

ROTHBERG, ABRAHAM (Jan. 14, 1922–   ); b. New York. Editor, author. *Eyewitness History of World War II* (1962); *The Thousand Doors* (1965); *The Other Man's Shoes* (1968); *The Boy and the Dolphin* (1969); etc. Editor: *U.S. Stories* (1949, 1952); *Flashes in the Night* (1958); *Anatomy of a Moral* (1959); *The Heresy of Cain* (1966); etc.

Rothery, Agnes. *See* Agnes Edwards Rothery Pratt.

ROUECHÉ, BERTON (1911–); Author. *Black Weather* (1945); *Greener Grass, and Some People Who Found It* (1948); *Eleven Blue Men* (1954); *Last Enemy* (1956); *Incurable Wound* (1958); *Delectable Mountains* (1959); *Neutral Spirit: A Portrait of Alcohol* (1960); *Annals of Epidemiology* (1967); *Reports on a Diminishing America* (1969); etc.

Rough Hewn. By Dorothy Canfield (1922). Story of athletic Neal Crittenden; brought up in New Jersey, educated in New York, he makes a quick success in business. In Rome, he meets Marise Allen, recovering from the shock of a family scandal. Sympathy leads to love and marriage.

Roughing It. By Mark Twain (1872). Based on the trip from St. Louis to San Francisco made by the author and his brother, Orion, in 1861.

ROULSTON, MARJORIE HILLIS (May 25, 1890–d. 1971); b. Peoria, Ill. Author. *Live Alone and Like It* (1936); *Orchids on Your Budget* (1937); *Work Ends at Nightfall* (1938); *New York, Fair or No Fair* (1939); *You Can Start All Over* (1951); *Keep Going and Like It* (1967).

ROUND, WILLIAM MARSHALL FITTS (Mar. 26, 1845–Jan. 2, 1906); b. Pawtucket, R.I. Journalist, prison reformer, novelist. Pen name, "Rev. Peter Pennot." *Achsah: A New England Life Study* (1876); *Torn and Mended: A Christmas Story* (1877); *Child Marian Abroad* (1878); *Hal: The Story of a Clodhopper* (1880); *Rosecroft: A Story of Common Places and Common People* (1881). With the *Boston Daily News;* the *New York Independent;* etc.

Round Table. New York. Weekly review. Founded 1863, and edited by Henry Edward Sweetser and Charles Humphreys Sweetser. Dorsey Gardner and Henry Sedley later joined the staff; many leading literary men were contributors. In 1869 it was sold to Robert B. Roosevelt, who merged it with his *The Citizen,* to form the *New York Citizen* and *Round Table.*

Round Table. New York. Informal literary club formed by the habitués of the Algonquin Hotel. It was started in 1919. Franklin P. Adams, Heywood Broun, Alexander Woollcott, Robert Benchley, Dorothy Parker, and Marc Connelly were prominent members. *See* Frank Case's *Tales of a Wayward Inn* (1938).

Round Table Dining Club. New York. One of the oldest dining clubs. Founded in winter of 1867–68. Its membership included prominent literary men. *See* Brander Matthews's preface in *The Roster of the Round Table Dining Club* (1926); Nicholas Murray Butler's *Across the Busy Years,* v. 2 (1940).

Round Up. By Ring Lardner (1929). Collection of short stories.

Roundup, The. Tucson, Ariz. Monthly. Founded 1953. Published by Western Writers of America, Inc. Edited by Betty Baker. Carries book reviews.

ROUNTREE, MAUDE McIVER (Oct. 22, 1875–); b. Wichita, Kan. Editor, author. *The Cross of Military Service* (1927); *Poems* (1929). Editor, the *Dixie Home Magazine,* 1898–1916.

ROUQUETTE, ADRIEN EMMANUEL (Feb. 13, 1813–July 15, 1887); b. New Orleans, La. Roman Catholic clergyman, poet. *Les Saranes* (1841); *Wild Flowers: Sacred Poetry* (1848); *L'Antoniade* (1860); *Patriotic Poems* (1860); *La Nouvelle Atala* (1879).

ROUQUETTE, FRANÇOIS DOMINIQUE (Jan. 2, 1810–May 1890); b. Bayou Lacombe, La. Poet. *Meschacébéennes* (1839); *Fleurs d'Amerique* (1856).

ROURKE, CONSTANCE [Mayfield] (Nov. 14, 1885–Mar. 23, 1941); b. Cleveland, O. Biographer. *Trumpets of Jubilee* (1927); *Troupers of the Gold Coast; or, The Rise of Lotta Crabtree* (1928); *American Humor: A Study of the National Character* (1931); *Davy Crockett* (1934); *Audubon* (1936); *Charles Sheeler* (1938); *The Roots of American Culture* (1942). *See* Fred B. Millett's *Contemporary American Authors* (1940).

ROURKE, FRANCIS EDWARD (Sept. 11, 1922–); b. New Haven, Conn. Educator, author. *Intergovernmental Relations in Employment Security* (1952); *The Campus and the State* (with M. Moos, 1959); *Secrecy and Publicity: Dilemmas of Democracy* (1961); *Bureaucratic Power in National Politics* (1965); *The Managerial Revolution in Higher Education* (with G. Brooks, 1966). Prof. political science, Johns Hopkins University, since 1961.

ROUSE, ADELAIDE LOUISE (d. 1912); b. Athens, N.Y. Editor, author. *Frontier and City* (1889); *Stephen Vance's Trust* (1890); *The Deane Girls* (1895); *Under My Own Roof* (1902); *The Letters of Theodora* (1905).

Rousseau and Romanticism. Critique of the Romantic idea, by Irving Babbitt (1919).

ROUTH, JAMES EDWARD (Jan. 1, 1879–); b. Petersburg, Va. Educator, editor, author. *The Fall of Tollan* (1905); *The Rise of Classical English Criticism* (1915); *The Theory of Verse* (1948); etc. Editor, *Bozart-Westminster* magazine; prof. English, Oglethorpe University, 1918–35; University of Georgia, since 1935.

Rover Boys Series. Books for boys written by Edward Stratemeyer. Begun in 1899, the thirtieth volume appeared in 1926. They were first published under the pen name of "Allen Winfield."

ROVERE, RICHARD H[alworth] (May 5, 1915–); b. Jersey City, N.J. Author. *Howe and Hummel: Their True and Scandalous History* (1947); *The General and the President* (with A. M. Schlesinger, Jr., 1951); *Affairs of State: The Eisenhower Years* (1956); *Senator Joe McCarthy* (1959); *The American Establishment and Other Conceits, Enthusiasms, and Hostilities* (1962); *The Goldwater Caper* (1965); *Waist Deep in the*

Big Muddy (1968); etc. *Staff writer, New Yorker.* Chairman of the board, *Washington Monthly,* since 1969.

ROWAN, ANDREW SUMMERS (Apr. 23, 1857–Jan. 10, 1943); b. Gap Mills, Va. Army officer, author. *The Island of Cuba* (1896); *How I Carried the Message to Garcia* (1923). This deed, accomplished in 1898, was the inspiration for Elbert Hubbard's *A Message to Garcia* (1908).

ROWAN, CARL T[homas] (1925–); Government official, journalist, author. *The Pitiful and the Proud* (1956); *Go South to Sorrow* (1957); *Wait Till Next Year* (with Jackie Robinson, 1960); etc.

ROWAN, RICHARD WILMER (Mar. 28, 1894–Aug. 12, 1964); b. Philadelphia, Pa. Author. *Spy and Counter-Spy* (1928); *The Baffle Book,* 3v. (with J. R. Colter, 1928–30); *The Pinkertons* (1931); *The Story of Secret Service* (1937); *Secret Agents against America* (1939); *Terror in Our Time* (1940); *The Sinister Front* (with Ruth J. Gerrard, 1940); *Japanese Secret Service and the Hundred Years War* (1943); *The Life Story of a Japanese Spy* (1944); *The Mountain Comes to Mohamet* (with Ruth G. Rowan, 1947); *The Devron Findings* (1948); *The United Nations Versus American Security* (1949); *Stalin's Secret Service* (1952); *A Family of Outlaws* (1955); etc.

Rowans, Virginia. Pen name of Edward Everett Tanner III.

ROWE, FYNETTE (Apr. 20, 1910–   ); b. Chatham, N.Y. Novelist. *The Chapin Sisters* (1945); *The Burning Spring* (1947).

ROWE, HENRIETTA GOULD (1835–1910); b. East Corinth, Me. Author. *Retold Tales of the Hills and Shores of Maine* (1892); *Queenshithe* (1895); *A Maid of Bar Harbor* (1902).

ROWE, HENRY KALLOCH (Nov. 30, 1869–1941); b. Boston, Mass. Educator, author. *Landmarks of Christian History* (1912); *The History of Religion in the United States* (1924); *Tercentenary History of Newton* (1930); *History of Andover Theological Seminary* (1933); *A Centennial History, 1837–1937; Colby Academy, Colby Junior College* (1937); etc. History dept., Andover-Newton Theological Seminary, from 1906; prof., from 1917.

ROWELL, GEORGE PRESBURY (July 4, 1838–Aug. 28, 1908); b. Concord, Vt. Publisher, author. *Forty Years an Advertising Agent* (1906). Founded firm of Geo. P. Rowell and Co., which published the *American Newspaper Directory* from 1869 to 1908, when it was absorbed by N. W. Ayer & Son's *American Newspaper Annual.* Founder, *Advertiser's Gazette,* Boston, 1866; *Printer's Ink,* July 15, 1888.

Rowfant Club. Cleveland, O. Club for bibliophiles. Founded 1892, in honor of Frederick Locker-Lampson. Incorporated 1895. See Arthur H. Clarke's *Bibliography of the Publications of the Rowfant Club* (1925).

ROWLAND, DUNBAR (Aug. 25, 1864–Nov. 1, 1937); b. Oakland, Miss. Archivist, editor, author. *History of Mississippi,* 4v. (1925); *Courts, Judges, and Lawyers of Mississippi, 1798–1935* (1935); etc. Editor: *The Mississippi Territorial Archives* (1905); *Mississippi,* 3v. (1907); *Mississippi Provincial Archives . . . English Dominion,* v. I (1911); *Official Letter Books of W. C. C. Claiborne, 1801–1816,* 7v. (1917); *Jefferson Davis, Constitutionalist: His Letters, Papers, and Speeches,* 10 v. (1923); *Mississippi Provincial Archives . . . French Dominion,* v. 1-3 (with Albert G. Sanders, 1927–32); etc. Founder and director, Mississippi State Department of Archives and History, 1902; editor, *Publications,* Mississippi Historical Society.

ROWLAND, ERON O[pha Moore] (Mrs. Dunbar Rowland,) b. near Okolona, Miss. Author. *Andrew Jackson's Campaign against the British* (1926); *Varina Howell, Wife of Jefferson Davis,* 2v. (1927–31); etc.

ROWLAND, HELEN, b. Washington D. C. Author. *The Digressions of Polly* (1905); *Reflections of a Bachelor Girl* (1909); *The Sayings of Mrs. Solomon* (1913); *A Guide to Men* (1922); *This Married Life* (1927).

ROWLAND, HENRY. Playwright. *Simple Simon Simple* (1936); *Aunt Abbey Answers an Ad* (1936); *Aunt Minnie from Minnesota* (1937); *Aunt Bessie Beats the Band* (1938); *Three Little Maids* (1938); *Uncle Josh Perkins* (1939); *Hi and Sis in New York* (1945); etc.

ROWLAND, HENRY C[ottrell] (May 12, 1874–June 6, 1933); b. New York. Physician, traveler, author. *Sea Scamps* (1903); *To Windward* (1904); *The Apple of Discord* (1913); *Duds* (1920); etc.

ROWLAND, J[oseph] M[edley] (Jan. 9, 1880–Aug. 17, 1938); b. Rowland, N.C. Methodist clergyman, editor, author. *Blue Ridge Breezes* (1914); *A Pilgrimage to Palestine* (1915); *The Hill Billies* (1921); *Travels in the Old World* (1923); *Bright Angel Trail* (1924); etc.

ROWLAND, KATE MASON (d. June 28, 1916). Author. *The Life of George Mason,* 2v. (1892); *The Life of Charles Carroll of Carrollton,* 2v. (1898). Editor: *Poems of Frank Q. Ticknor* (1879). Editor (with Mrs. Morris L. Croxall): *The Journal of Julia Le Grand, New Orleans, 1862–1863* (1911).

ROWLANDSON, MARY WHITE (c. 1635–c. 1678); b. in England. Indian captive, author. *The Sovereignty & Goodness of God Together, with the Faithfulness of His Promises Displayed; Being a Narrative of the Captivity and Restauration of Mrs. Mary Rowlandson* (1682), republished many times as, *The Narrative of the Captivity and Restoration of Mrs. Mary Rowlandson.*

ROWLEY, THOMAS (Mar. 24, 1721–Aug. 1796); b. Hebron, Vt. Vermont's first poet. *Selections and Miscellaneous Works* (1802). His verses appeared mostly in the *Vermont Gazette* and the *Rural Magazine.* See *The Vermonter,* v. 34, 1929.

ROWSOME, FRANK H[oward] JR. (Mar. 12, 1914–); b. Dedham, Mass. Editor, author. *Trolley-Car Treasury* (1956); *They Laughed When I Sat Down* (1959); *The Verse By the Side of the Road* (1965).

ROWSON, SUSANNA HASWELL (C. 1762–Mar. 2, 1824); b. Portsmouth, Eng. Novelist, playwright. *Victoria* (1786); *Charlotte: A Tale of Truth* (1791), republished as, *Charlotte Temple: A Tale of Truth,* and as, *The History of Charlotte Temple,* 145 editions in all; *Mentoria; or, The Young Lady's Friend* (1791); *The Fille de Chambre* (1793), republished as, *Rebecca; or, The Fille de Chambre; The Inquisitor; or, Invisible Rambler* (1794); *Slaves in Algiers* (prod. 1794); *Trials of the Human Heart* (1795); *Americans in England* (prod. 1797); *Reuben and Rachel* (1798); *Miscellaneous Poems* (1804); *Sarah, the Exemplary Wife* (1813); *Charlotte's Daughter; or, The Three Orphans* (1828), republished as, *Lucy Temple, One of the Three Orphans.* See Robert W. G. Vail's *Susannah Haswell Rowson, The Author of Charlotte Temple* (1933); *Charlotte Temple, a Tale of Truth,* ed. by Clara M. and Rudolf Kirk (1965).

Roxy. Novel by Edward Eggleston (1878). Depicts life in Indiana in the author's early days.

Royal American Magazine; or, Universal Repository of Instruction and Amusement. Boston, Mass. Founded Jan., 1774. Published and edited by Isaiah Thomas and Joseph Greenleaf. Illustrated with copper plates, some by Paul Revere. Expired Mar., 1775.

Royal Road to Romance, The By Richard Halliburton (1925). A wealthy American youth, offered a deluxe trip around the world by his family as a graduation present, decides to go the hard way and ships as a seaman on a freighter. The success of the book launched the author on a career of adventure which ended in his death at sea.

ROYALL, ANNE NEWPORT (June 11, 1769–Oct. 1, 1854); b. in Maryland. Author. *Sketches of History, Life and Manners in the United States* (anon., 1826); *The Tennessean: A Novel* (1827); *The Black Book; or, A Continuation of Travels in the United States*, 3v. (1828–29); *Pennsylvania; or, Travels Continued in the United States*, 2v. (1829); *Letters from Alabama on Various Subjects* (1830); *Southern Tour; or, Second Series of the Black Book*, 2v. (1830–31). Founder, *Paul Pry*, Washington D.C., Dec. 2, 1836. *See* George S. Jackson's *Uncommon Scold: The Story of Anne Royall* (1937); Richardson L. Wright's *Forgotten Ladies* (1928); Marquis James's *Andrew Jackson* (1938).

ROYCE, JOSIAH (Nov. 20, 1855–Sept. 14, 1916); b. Grass Valley, California. Educator, philosopher, author. *The Religious Aspect of Philosophy* (1885); *California* (1886); *The Spirit of Modern Philosophy* (1892); *Studies of Good and Evil* (1898); *The World and the Individual*, 2 series (1900, 1901); *Outlines of Psychology* (1903); *William James, and Other Essays on the Philosophy of Life* (1911); *The Sources of Religious Insight* (1912); *The Hope of the Great Community* (1916); *Lectures on Modern Idealism* (1919). Philosophy dept., Harvard University, 1882–1916; prof., 1892–1916. *See* John Edwin Smith's *Royce's Social Infinite* (1950); Vincent Buranelli's *Josiah Royce* (1963); Peter L. Fuss's *Moral Philosophy of Josiah Royce* (1965); Thomas Powell's *Josiah Royce* (1967).

ROYLE, EDWIN MILTON (Mar. 2, 1862–Feb. 16, 1942); b. Lexington, Mo. Actor, playwright. *The Squaw Man* (prod. 1905); *The Struggle Everlasting* (prod. 1907); *The Silent Call* (1910); *The Unwritten Law* (prod. 1913); *Peace and Quiet* (1916); *The Conqueror* (1923); *Edwin Booth as I Knew Him* (1933); etc.

ROYSTER, VERMONT CONNECTICUT (Apr. 30, 1914–); b. Raleigh, N.C. Editor, author. *Main Street and Beyond* (with others, 1959); *Journey Through the Soviet Union* (1962); *A Pride of Prejudices* (1967). Editor, *The Wall Street Journal*.

RUARK, ROBERT CHESTER (Dec. 29, 1915–July 1, 1965); b. Wilmington, N.C. Columnist, author. *Grenadine Etching* (1947); *I Didn't Know It Was Loaded* (1948); *One for the Road* (1950); *Grenadine's Spawn* (1952); *Horn of the Hunter* (1953); *Something of Value* (1955); *The Old Man and the Boy* (1957); *Poor No More* (1959); *The Old Man's Boy Grows Older* (1961); *Uhuru* (1962). Columnist, Washington *Daily News*, 1937–42; Scripps-Howard Newspapers and United Features, from 1946.

RUBIN, HAROLD (May 21, 1912–   ); b. New York. Novelist. Writes under pen name "Harold Robbins." *Never Love a Stranger* (1948); *The Dream Merchants* (1949); *A Stone for Danny Fisher* (1952); *79 Park Avenue* (1955); *The Carpetbaggers* (1961); *Where Love Has Gone* (1962); *The Inheritors* (1969); etc.

RUBIN, JERRY Political activist, author. *Do It!* (1970).

RUBIN, THEODORE ISAAC (Apr. 11, 1923–); b. Brooklyn, N.Y. Psychiatrist, author. *Jordi* (1960); *Lisa and David* (1961); *In the Life* (1961); *Sweet Daddy* (1963); *Platzo and the Mexican Pony Rider* (1965); *The Thin Book by a Formerly Fat Psychiatrist* (1966); *The 29th Summer* (1966); *Cat* (1966); *Coming Out* (1967); *The Winner's Note Book* (1967).

RUBIO, DAVID (Dec. 29, 1884–Dec. 28, 1962); b. Leon, Spain. Educator, author. *Symbolism and Classicism in Modern Literature* (1924); *Classical Scholarship in Spain* (1934); etc. Compiler: *Spanish Anthology* (1928); *Spanish Fables* (1930); *Spanish Wit and Humor* (1932); *The Mystic Soul of Spain* (1946). Prof. Romance languages, Catholic University of America, from 1916.

RUDD, HUGHES DAY (Sept. 14, 1921–   ); b. Wichita, Kan. Journalist, author. *My Escape from the CIA and Other Improbable Events* (1966). Staff member, CBS news, since 1959.

Rudder Grange. By Frank R. Stockton (1879). Humorous story of young married couple who select a canal-boat as an inexpensive summer home, and start housekeeping with the aid of a most unusual servant named Pomona, whose passion for thrilling love-stories gives a romantic tinge to all her actions.

RUDGE, WILLIAM EDWIN (Nov. 23, 1876–June 12, 1931); b. Brooklyn, N.Y. Printer of fine books, publisher. His printing house, first located in New York City, and then at Mt. Vernon, N.Y., 1921, produced many beautiful editions. He was assisted by such book designers as Frederic W. Goudy, Bruce Rogers, Frederic Warde, and W. A. Dwiggins. One of the best-known works he published was Mary Vaux Walcott's *North American Wild Flowers*, 5v. (1925).

RUDHYAR, DANE (May 23, 1895–); b. Paris. Composer, author. *Rebirth of Hindu Music* (1928); *Toward Man* (poems, 1929); *Astrology of Personality* (1936); *White Thunder* (poems, 1938); *The Pulse of Life* (1943); *Modern Man's Conflicts* (1948); *Gifts of the Spirit* (1956); *Fire Out of the Stone* (1959); *The Rhythm of Human Fulfillment* (1966); *A Study of Psychological Complexes* (1966); *The Lunation Cycle* (1967); *The Practice of Astrology* (1968); *Triptych* (1968); *Birth Patterns* (1969); etc.

RUDWIN, MAXIMILIAN [Joseph] (Jan. 22, 1885–); b. in Poland. Educator, author. *The Origin of the Carnival Comedy* (1920); *Historical and Bibliographical Survey of the Religious Drama* (1924); *The Devil in Legend and Literature* (1931); etc. Editor: *Devil Stories: Anthology* (1921). Prof. modern languages, Swarthmore College, University of Pittsburgh; etc.

RUDYARD, CHARLOTTE (Mrs. Robert Hallowell), b. New York. Critic, author. Lit. editor, Harper & Brothers, 1907–10; asst. editor, *Harper's Magazine*, 1910–13; assoc. editor, the *New Republic*, 1914–16.

RUFF, G. ELSON (Feb. 9, 1904–); b. Dunkirk, N.Y. Lutheran clergyman, editor. Author: *The Dilemma of Church and State* (1954). Editor-in-chief, United Lutheran Publishing House, since 1946; editor, *The Lutheran*, since 1945.

RUFFIN, EDMUND (Jan. 5, 1794–June 18, 1865); b. in Prince George Co., Va. Planter, agriculturist, author. *Essays and Notes on Agriculture* (1855); *Anticipations of the Future* (1860); etc. Editor and publisher, the *Farmer's Register*, 1833–43. He fired the first shot at Fort Sumter on Apr. 14, 1861. His manuscript diary in 14v., from 1856 to 1865, is in the Library of Congress. *See* Avery O. Craven's *Edmund Ruffin, Southerner* (1932).

RUFFIN, M[argaret] E[llen] HENRY (b. 1857); b. Daphne, Ark. Author. *John Gilbert* (poem, 1901); *The North Star* (1904); etc.

RUGG, HAROLD (Jan. 17, 1886–May 17, 1960); b. Fitchburg, Mass. Educator, author. *Introduction to American Civilization* (1929); *Changing Civilizations in a Modern World* (1929); *Culture and Education in America* (1931); *A History of American Civilization* (1931); *The Great Technology* (1933); *That Men May Understand* (1941); *Now Is the Moment* (1943); *The Teacher in School and Society* (1950); etc. Founder, New World Education series (1950); editor, from 1950. Editor, *Frontiers of Democracy*, 1939–43. Prof. education, Teachers College, Columbia University, 1920–51.

RUGGLES, ELEANOR (June 24, 1916–); b. Boston, Mass. Author. *Gerard Manley Hopkins: A Life* (1944); *Journey Into Faith: The Anglican Life of John Henry Newman* (1948); *Prince of Players: Edwin Booth* (1953); *The West-Going Heart: A Life of Vachel Lindsay* (1959).

Ruggles of Red Gap. Novel by Harry Leon Wilson (1915). The adventures of a rough-and-ready American from the West Coast who visits Paris and brings home a docile English butler and makes a man of him by exposing him to democracy.

RUHL, ARTHUR BROWN (Oct. 1, 1876–June 7, 1935); b. Rockford, Ill. Correspondent, drama critic, author. *The Other Americans* (1912); *Second Nights* (1914); *New Masters of the Baltic* (1921); *White Nights* (1921); *The Central Americas* (1928); etc. With the *New York Evening Sun,* 1899–1904; *Collier's Weekly,* 1904–13; drama critic, the *New York Tribune,* 1913–14; war correspondent, *Collier's Weekly,* 1914–19; foreign correspondent, the *New York Evening Post,* 1920; the *New York Herald Tribune,* 1925–26.

RUITENBECK, Hendrik M. (Feb. 26, 1928–); b. Leyden, Holl. Psychoanalyst, author. *The Individual and the Crowd: A Study of Identity in America* (1965); *Freud and America* (1966); *The Male Myth* (1967). Editor: *The Creative Imagination* (1965); *The Psychotherapy of Perversions* (1967); etc.

RUKEYSER, MURIEL (Dec. 15, 1913–); b. New York. Poet, biographer. *Theory of Flight* (1935); *U. S. 1* (1938); *Mediterranean* (1938); *A Turning Wind* (1939); *The Soul and Body of John Brown* (1941); *Wake Island* (1942); *Willard Gibbs* (biography, 1942); *Beast in View* (1944); *The Green Wave* (1948); *Elegies* (1949); *Orpheus* (1949); *The Life of Poetry* (1949); *Selected Poems* (1951); *Come Back, Paul* (1955); *One Life* (1957); *Houdini* (1957); *The Body of Waking* (1958); *I Go Out* (1958); *Collected Poems* (1960); *The Speaking Tree* (1960); *The Orgy* (1965); *The Speed of Darkness* (1968); *The Traces of Thomas Hariot* (1969); etc.

RUMAKER, MICHAEL (Mar. 5, 1932–   ); b. Philadelphia. Author. *Exit 3* (1959); *The Butterfly* (1962); *The Bar* (1964); *Gringos and Other Stories* (1967).

Rumor and Reflection. By Bernard Berenson (1952). Diaries of the years 1941–1945, when the author was hiding from the Nazis.

RUNBECK, MARGARET LEE (1910–1956); b. Des Moines, Ia. Author. *People Will Talk* (1929); *For Today Only* (1938); *Our Miss Boo* (1942); *Time for Each Other* (1944); *Your Kids and Mine* (with Joe E. Brown, 1944); *Hope of the Earth* (1947); *Pink Magic* (1949); *Hungry Man Dreams* (1952); *Year of Love* (1956); etc.

RUNCIE, CONSTANCE FAUNT LE ROY (Jan. 15, 1836–1911); b. Indianapolis, Ind. Musician, poet, author. *Poems, Dramatic and Lyric* (1888); *Divinely Led* (autobiography, 1895). Founder, Minerva Club, New Harmony, Ind., 1859, the first woman's club in the United States; the Bronte Club, Madison, Ind., 1867; the Runcie Club, St. Joseph, Mo., 1894.

RUNES, DAGOBERT DAVID (1902–); Publisher, author. *Letters to My Son* (1949); *Of God, the Devil and the Jews* (1952); *Letters to My Daughter* (1954); *Book of Contemplation* (1957); *Letters to My Teacher* (1961); *The War Against the Jews* (1968); *The Bible for the Liberal* (1946); etc. *Wisdom of the Torah* (1956); *Treasury of Thought: Observations Over Half A Century* (1967). Pres. and editor, Philosophical Library.

RUNKLE, BERTHA (Mrs. Louis H. Bash), b. Berkeley Heights, N.J. Author. *The Helmet of Navarre* (1901); *The Truth About Tolna* (1906); *The Scarlet Rider* (1913); *Straight Down the Crooked Lane* (1915); *The Island* (1921).

RUNYON, DAMON (Oct. 4, 1884–Dec. 10, 1946); b. Manhattan, Kan. Sports writer, short story writer, journalist. *Tents of Trouble* (poems, 1911); *Rhymes of the Firing Line* (1912); *Guys and Dolls* (1932); *Blue Plate Special* (1934); *Money from Home* (1935); *A Slight Case of Murder* (with Howard Lindsay, 1935); *The Best of Runyon* (1938); *Furthermore* (1938); *My Old Man* (1939); *My Wife Ethel* (1939); *Take It Easy* (1939); *Runyon à la Carte* (1944); *In Our Town* (1946); *Short Takes* (1946); *Poems for Men* (1947); *Trials and Other Tribulations* (1948). With *Denver Post, San Francisco Post, New York American,* and other Newspapers. Writer of syndicated column, from 1918.

RUPP, ISRAEL DANIEL (July 10, 1803–May 31, 1878); b. in Cumberland Co., Pa. Editor, historian, translator. *History of Lancaster County* (1844); *Early History of Western Pennsylvania* (1846); etc. Compiler: *A Collection of Thirty Thousand Names of German Immigrants in Pennsylvania, 1727–1776* (1856). Editor, the *Carlise Herald,* 1833; the *Practical Farmer,* 1837.

Rural Poems. By John Hayes (1807). About American birds and flowers.

RUSH, BENJAMIN (Dec. 24, 1745–Apr. 19, 1813); b. Byberry, Pa. Patriot, humanitarian, medical pioneer, author. *Sermons to Gentlemen upon Temperance and Exercise* (1772); *Essays, Literary, Moral, and Philosophical* (1798); etc. See Nathan G. Goodman's *Benjamin Rush* (1934); Carl Van Doren's *Benjamin Franklin* (1938); Richard M. Gummere's *Seven Wise Men of Colonial America* (1967).

RUSH, EMMY MATT (Mrs. Edward Frederick Rush); b. St. Louis, Mo. Lecturer, author. *Sweet Mother o' Mine* (poems, 1920); *My Garden of Roses* (poems, 1925); *Arts and Crafts of the American Indian* (1929).

RUSK, RALPH LESLIE (July 11, 1888–June 30, 1962); b. Rantoul, Ill. Educator, editor, author. *The Literature of the Middle Western Frontier,* 2v. (1925); *The Life of Ralph Waldo Emerson* (1949). Editor: *Emerson-Clough Letters* (with Howard F. Lowry, 1934); *The Letters of Ralph Waldo Emerson,* 6v. (1939); *Letters to Emma Lazarus* (1939). Co-editor, *American Literature,* 1929–38. English dept., Indiana University, 1915–25; Columbia University, since 1925.

RUSS, CAROLYN [Ernestine] HALE (Mrs. Willis R. Russ) (1865–Feb. 12, 1944); b. Newburyport, Mass. Author. *America's Pilgrims* (1921); *Kuhio, Last Scion of Hawaii's Royal House* (1921); *Ebb of the Tide* (1922); *Last Inhabitant of Uncle Tom's Cabin* (1923); *Adventure Island* (1927). Editor: *The Log of a Forty-Niner: Journal . . . Kept by Richard L. Hale* (1923).

RUSSEL, FLORENCE KIMBALL (Mrs. Edgar Russel); b. Ft. Riley, Kan. Author. *Born to the Blue* (1906); *A Woman's Journey through the Philippines* (1907); *In West Point Gray* (1908); *From Chevrons to Shoulder Straps* (1914).

RUSSELL, ADDISON PEALE (Sept. 8, 1826–1912); b. Wilmington, O. Author. *Half Tints* (1867); *Thomas Corwin* (1882); *Characteristics* (1884); *In a Club Corner* (1890); *Sub-Coelum* (1893).

RUSSELL, ARTHUR JOSEPH (b. Mar. 14, 1861–); b. Hallowell, Me. Columnist, author. *Stony Lonesome* (1903); *Illumination of Walt Whitman* (1901); *Fourth Street* (1917); *The Other Side of a Street* (1931); etc. Writes "The Long Bow" column in the *Minneapolis Times-Tribune.*

RUSSELL, BENJAMIN (Sept. 13, 1761–Jan. 4, 1845); b. Boston, Mass. Journalist. Founder, the *Massachusetts Centinel* (later the *Columbian Centinel*), Boston , Mass., Mar. 24, 1784; editor, 1784–1828.

RUSSELL, CHARLES EDWARD (Sept. 25, 1860–Apr. 23, 1941); b. Davenport, Iowa. Editor, author. *Such Stuff as Dreams* (1902); *The Uprising of the Many* (1907); *Thomas Chatterton: The Marvelous Boy* (1908); *Why I Am a Socialist* (1910); *Stories of the Great Railroads* (1912); *The Story of Wendell Phillips* (1915); *Bolshevism and the United States* (1919); *Julia Marlowe: Her Life and Art* (1926); *The American Orchestra and Theodore Thomas* (1927; Pulitzer Prize for biography, 1928); *From Sandy Hook to 62°* (1929); *Blaine of Maine* (1931); *Bare Hands and Stone Walls* (1933); etc. City editor, *New York World,* 1894–97; managing editor, *New York American,* 1897–99; publisher, *Chicago American,* 1900–02.

RUSSELL, CHARLES MARION (Mar. 19, 1864–Oct. 24, 1926); b. St. Louis, Mo. Painter, illustrator, author. *Rawhide Rollins* (1921).

RUSSELL, CHARLES TAZE (Feb. 16, 1852–Oct. 31, 1916); b. Pittsburgh, Pa. Religious leader. *The Object and Manner of Our Lord's Return* (1872); *Food for Thinking Christians* (1881). Founder, *The Watch Tower and Herald of Christ's Presence,* 1879.

RUSSELL, CHARLES WELLS (1818–1867). Lawyer, author. *Roebuck: A Novel* (anon., 1868); *The Fall of Damascus* (1878).

RUSSELL, CHARLES WELLS (Mar. 16, 1856–Apr. 5, 1927); b. Wheeling, W.Va. Lawyer, diplomat, poet. *The Secret Place, and Other Poems* (1911); *Iranian Rest, and Other Lyrics* (1912); *Poems* (1921). Editor: *The Memoirs of Colonel John S. Mosby* (1917).

RUSSELL, FRANCES THERESA (May, 1873–Feb. 15, 1936); b. Anamosa, Ia. Educator, author. *Satire in the Victorian Novel* (1920); *One Word More on Broadway* (1927); *Touring Utopia* (1932); *Two Poets, a Dog, and a Boy* (1933). Prof. English, Stanford University.

RUSSELL, FRANKLIN ALEXANDER (Oct. 9, 1926–); b. Christchurch, New Zealand. Author. *Watchers at the Pond* (1961); *Argen the Gull* (1964); *The Secret Islands* (1966).

RUSSELL, HENRY B[enajah] (Mar. 9, 1859–June 30, 1941); b. Russell, Mass. Editor, author. *The Lives of William McKinley and Garret A. Hobart* (1896); *The Story of Two Wars* (1899); *Man Proposes* (1939); etc. With the *Springfield Union,* 1917–41, editor, 1926–41.

RUSSELL, IRWIN (June 3, 1853–Dec. 23, 1879); b. Port Gibson, Miss. Poet. *Poems by Irwin Russell* (1888), augmented as *Christmas Night in the Quarters, and Other Poems* (1917). He was a pioneer in the use of Negro dialect.

RUSSELL, JOHN (Apr. 22, 1885–Mar. 6, 1956); b. Davenport, Ia., son of Charles Edward Russell. Explorer, author. *The Society Wolf* (under pen name, "Luke Thrice," 1910); *The Red Mark, and Other Stories* (1919); *In Dark Places* (1923); *Where the Pavement Ends* (1928); *Color of the East* (1929); *Cops 'n Robbers* (1930); *The Lost God and other Adventure Stories* (1947); etc.

RUSSELL, NELSON VANCE (Apr. 15, 1895–Oct. 12, 1951); b. Birmingham, Mich. Educator, historian. *The British Regime in Michigan and the Old Northwest, 1760–1796* (1939). Prof. American History, Coe College, 1929–35; Carleton College, 1938–46. Pres. Carroll College, Waukesha, Wis., from 1946. Organized the Division of Reference, National Archives, 1935; chief, 1935–38.

RUSSELL, OSBORNE (June 12, 1814–c. 1865); b. Hallowell, Me. Trapper, Oregon and California pioneer, author. *Journal of a Trapper; or, Nine Years in the Rocky Mountains, 1834–1843* (1914).

RUSSELL, PHILLIPS (Aug. 5, 1884–); b. Rockingham, N.C. Author. *Benjamin Franklin, the First Civilized American* (1926); *John Paul Jones, Man of Action* (1927); *Emerson, The Wisest American* (1929); *Red Tiger* (1929); *Harvesters* (1932); *William the Conqueror* (1933); *The Glittering Century* (1936); *The Woman Who Rang the Bell* (1949); *Jefferson, Champion of the Free Mind* (1956).

RUSSELL, THOMAS HERBERT (b. Mar. 12, 1862–); b. Plymouth, Eng. Editor, author. *Life and Work of Theodore Roosevelt* (1919); *The Illustrious Life and Work of Warren G. Harding* (1923). Editor: *The Railway Library,* 17v. (1924–25); etc.

RUSSELL, WALTER [Bowman] (May 19, 1871–May 19, 1963); b. Boston, Mass. Painter, sculptor, author. *The Sea Children* (1901); *The Bending of the Twig* (1903); *The Age of Innocence* (1904); *Salutation to the Day* (9127); *The Secret of Light* (1946); *Book of Early Whisperings* (1949); *Atomic Suicide* (with Lao Russell, 1958); *The One World Purpose* (with same, 1960); etc.

RUSSELL, WILLIAM FLETCHER (May 18, 1890–Mar. 26, 1956); b. Delhi, N.Y. Educator, author. *The Early Teaching of History in New York and Massachusetts* (1915); *Schools in Siberia* (1919); *New Common Sense* (1941); *How to Judge a School* (1954); etc. Teachers College, Columbia University, from 1923; dean, 1927–49; pres. 1949–54.

Russell's Magazine. Charleston, S.C. Founded Apr., 1857, by John Russell, a book-seller, whose shop was the literary rendezvous of Charleston. Paul Hamilton Hayne was editor. Russell was often called "Lord John." Hayne, Henry Timrod, William Gilmore Simms, were contributors. Expired Mar., 1860.

Russian Hill. A section of San Francisco inhabited by artists and writers, a sort of "Greenwich Village." The Montgomery Block, on Montgomery Street, called the "Monkey Block," is the heart of the city's Bohemia.

Russian Review, The. Hanover, N.H.; Stanford, Cal. Quarterly. Founded 1941. Edited by Dimitri von Mohrenschildt. Devoted to Russian history and current affairs.

Rusticus. Pen name of MacGregor Jenkins.

RUTHERFORD, MILDRED LEWIS (July 16, 1851–Aug. 15, 1928); b. Athens, Ga. Educator, historian. *English Authors: A Hand Book* (1906); *The South in History and Literature* (1907); *Georgia: The Thirteenth Colony* (1926); etc. Founder and editor, *Miss Rutherford's Scrap Book,* 1923–27. Prof. Southern history and literature, Lucy Cobb Institute, Athens, Ga., 1917–26; president, 1917–22.

RUTLEDGE, ARCHIBALD HAMILTON (Oct. 23, 1883–); b. McClellanville, S.C. Author. *Under the Pines* (poems, 1907); *The Banners of the Coast* (poems, 1908); *Old Plantation Days* (1911); *New Poems* (1917); *Songs from a Valley* (1919); *South of Richmond* (poems, 1922); *Days Off in Dixie* (1923); *Collected Poems* (1925); *Tales of Dogs* (1929); *Veiled Eros* (poems, 1933); *Wild Life of the South* (1935); *Brimming Chalice* (1936); *My Colonel and His Lady* (1937); *Home by the River* (1941); *The Everlasting Light and Other Poems* (1949); *The Brimming Tide* (1954); *The World Around Hampton* (1960); etc.

Rutledge, Marice. Pen name of Marie Louise Gibson Hale.

RUTSALA, VERN (Feb. 5, 1934–   ); b. McCall, Idaho. Poet. *The Window* (1964). Poetry editor, *December,* 1959–62. Faculty, Lewis and Clark College, since 1961.

RUUD, MARTIN BROWN (Aug. 2, 1885–); b. Fergus Falls, Minn. Author. *A History of Shakespeare in Norway* (1917); *A History of Shakespeare in Denmark* (1920); *Thomas Chaucer* (1926). Editor: *Norwegian Emigrant Songs and Ballads* (with Theodore C. Blegen, 1936). English dept., University of Minnesota, since 1915.

RYAN, ABRAM JOSEPH (Feb. 5, 1838–Apr. 22, 1886); b. Hagerstown, Md. Roman Catholic clergyman, poet. Recognized Poet of the Confederacy. *Father Ryan's Poems* (1879); *Poems: Patriotic, Religious, Miscellaneous* (1880); etc. Among his poems are "The Conquered Banner," "The Lost Cause," "The Sword of Robert E. Lee," "The March of the Deathless Dead," "Reunited."

RYAN, JAMES HUGH (Dec. 15, 1886–Nov. 23, 1948); b. Indianapolis, Ind. Roman Catholic bishop, educator, author. *An Introduction to Philosophy* (1924); *The Encyclicals of Pius XI* (1927); *The Peace Points of Pope Pius XII* (1942); etc. Philosophy dept., Catholic University of America, 1922–29.

RYAN, JOHN A[ugustine] (May 25, 1869–Sept. 16, 1945); b. Vermillion, Dakota County, Minn. Roman Catholic clergyman, educator, social worker, author. *Francisco Ferrer* (1910); *Distributive Justice* (1916); *Social Reconstruction* (1920); *The Church and Labor* (1920); *Questions of the Day* (1931); *Social Doctrine in Action* (autobiography, 1941); etc.

Prof. theology and industrial ethics, Catholic University, 1915-39.

RYAN, MARAH ELLIS (Feb. 27, 1866-July 11, 1934); b. in Butler Co., Pa. Author. *Squaw Eloise* (1892); *Told in the Hills* (1892); *A Flower of France* (1894); *Comrades* (1896); *The Bondwoman* (1899); *That Girl Montana* (1901); *My Quaker Maid* (1906); *Indian Love Letters* (1907); *Pagan Prayers* (1913); *The House of the Dawn* (1914); *The Druid Path* (1917); *Treasure Trail* (1919); etc.

RYDELL, FORBES. Novelist. *Annalisa* (1959); *If She Should Die* (1961); *They're Not Home Yet* (1962).

RYDER, ARTHUR WILLIAM (Mar. 8, 1877-Mar. 21, 1938); b. Oberlin, O. Educator, author. *Original Poems: Together with Translations from the Sanskrit* (1939), and several collections of verse translated from the Sanskrit. Sanskrit dept., University of California, 1906-38.

RYERSON, FLORENCE (Mrs. Colin Clements); b. Glendale, Calif. Playwright. *A Cup of Tea* (1927); *Seven Suspects* (1930); *This Awful Age* (with husband, 1930); *Diana Laughs* (1932); *Mild Oats* (1933); *Blind-Man's-Buff* (1933); *The Borgia Blade* (1937); *Glamour Preferred* (with husband, 1941); *Spring Green* (with same, 1944); *Strange Bedfellows* (with same, 1948); etc. Many one-act plays, screen plays, etc.

RYLAND, CALLY [Thomas], b. Richmond, Va. Journalist, author. *Daphne and Her Lad* (with Mary Julia Lagen, 1904); *Aunt Jemimy's Maxims* (1907). Editor of woman's page, the *Richmond News-Leader.*

RYLE, WALTER HARRINGTON (June 1, 1896-); b. Yates, Mo. Educator, author. *Missouri: Union or Secession* (1931); *The Story of Missouri* (with C. E. Garner, 1938). President, Northeast Missouri State Teachers College, Kirksville, Mo. since 1937.

RYLEE, ROBERT (Sept. 17, 1908-); b. Memphis, Tenn. Novelist. *Deep Dark River* (1935); *St. George of Weldon* (1937); *The Ring and the Cross* (1947).

RYSKIND, MORRIE (1895-); b. New York. Playwright. *Unaccustomed As I Am* (poems, 1921); *Of Thee I Sing* (with George S. Kaufman and Ira Gershwin, prod. 1931, Pulitzer Prize play, 1932); *The Diary of an Ex-President, by John P. Wintergreen* (1932); *Let 'Em Eat Cake* (with George S. Kaufman and Ira Gershwin, prod. 1933); etc.

S

SAALFIELD, ADA LOUISE [Sutton], b. Brooklyn, N.Y. Author. *Mr. Bunny: His Book* (1902); *Sweeter Still Than This* (1905); *Teddy Bears* (1906); the *Peter Rabbit* series; etc.

SAARINEN, ALINE LOUCHHEIM (Mar. 25, 1914-); b. New York. Art critic. *The Proud Possessors* (1958). Editor: *Eero Saarinen on His Work* (1968). Assoc. art editor and critic, *New York Times,* 1948-53; assoc. art critic, since 1954.

SABIN, EDWIN L[egrand] (Dec. 23, 1870-); b. Rockford, Ill. Novelist. *The Making of Iowa* (1900); *Circle K* (1911); *Old Four Toes* (1912); *On the Plains with Custer* (1913); *Buffalo Bill and the Overland Trail* (1914); *Kit Carson Days* (1914); *Sam Houston in Texas* (1916); *On the Overland Stage* (1918); *Building the Pacific Railway* (1919); *Boys' Book of Frontier Fighters* (1919); *The Rose of Santa Fé* (1923); *Old Jim Bridger on the Moccasin Trail* (1928); *Gold!* (1929); *Wild Men of the Wild West* (1929); *Adventures with Carson and Fremont* (1938); etc.

SABIN, JOSEPH (Dec. 9, 1821-June 5, 1881); b. Braunston, Northants., Eng. Bibliographer, bookseller. Compiler: *Bibliotheca Americana: A Dictionary of Books Relating to America, from its Discovery to the Present Time,* 29v. (1868-1936), of which he edited vols. 1-14. Vols. 15-20 were edited by Wilberforce Eames, and the remaining vols. were completed by Robert W. G. Vail and assistants. Both Eames and Vail were with The New York Public Library at the time, that library being the repository of the Sabin catalogues and manuscripts. Editor, *American Bibliopolist,* 1869-; etc. His book business, opened in New York in 1856, was continued by his son Joseph Sabin (b. 1845-d. 1926). In 1861 H. A. Jennings joined with Sabin to open a book auction business.

SABINE, LORENZO (July 28, 1803-Apr. 14, 1877); b. Lisbon, N.H. Author. *The American Loyalists* (1847), augmented as *Sketches of Loyalists,* 2v. (1864); *Notes on Duels and Duelling* (1855); etc.

SACHS, CURT (June 29, 1881-Feb. 5, 1959); b. Berlin. Music historian, educator, author. *World History of the Dance* (1937); *The History of Musical Instruments* (1940); *The Rise of Music in the Ancient World, East and West* (1943); *The Commonwealth of Art* (1946); *Our Musical Heritage* (1948); *Rhythm and Tempo: A Study in Music History* (1953); etc. Faculty, New York University, 1937-57; Columbia University, from 1953. Consultant to New York Public Library, 1937-52.

Sachs, Emanie. See Emanie Arling.

Sacramento Bee. Sacramento, Calif. Newspaper. Founded 1857, by James McClatchy. Still owned by the McClatchy family. John Rollin Ridge was its first editor. Walter P. Jones is the present editor. Philip C. Freshwater edits book reviews.

Sacred Fount, The. Novelette by Henry James (1901).

Sacred Harp, The. Compiled by B. F. White and E. J. King (1844). A hymnal which had a great influence on the singing habits of the South.

Sacred Wood, The. Critical essays by T. S. Eliot (1920). Influential work in modern American and British literary criticism. A re-evaluation of the literary tradition and of the function of poetry.

SADLIER, DENIS (1817-Feb. 4, 1885); b. in Co. Tipperary, Ire. Roman Catholic book publisher. Founder, with his brother James, of D. & J. Sadlier & Co., bookbinders, in New York, 1836. They became publishers in 1837. Published the annual *Sadlier's Catholic Directory* (1864-96). Founder, the *New York Tablet,* 1857, which he conducted until 1881. The firm published a *Household Library* of 164 titles, besides Bibles, text books, etc.

SADLIER, MARY ANNE MADDEN (Mrs. James Sadlier) (Dec. 31, 1820-Apr. 5, 1903); b. Cootehill, Ire. Novelist, short-story writer, translator. *The Red Hand of Ulster* (1850); *Alice Rorodan* (1851); *The Blakes and the Flanagans* (1855); *The Confederate Chieftains* (1860); *The Fate of Father Sheehy* (1863); *Con O'Regan* (1864); *Aunt Honor's Keepsake* (1866); *Maureen Dhu* (1870); and over fifty other novels. See *A Round Table of Representative American Catholic Novelists* (1897).

SAERCHINGER, CÉSAR [Victor Charles] (Oct. 23, 1884-); b. Aix-la-Chapelle, Fr. Lecturer, broadcaster, author. *A Narrative History of Music* (with Leonard Hall, 1915); *Hello, America!* (1938); *The Way Out of War* (1939); *Artur Schnabel: A Biography* (1956). Editor: *International Who's Who in Music* (1918).

SAGE, AGNES CAROLYN (Agnes Carr Sage) (b. Mar. 17, 1854); b. Brooklyn, N.Y. Author. *Christmas Elves* (1887); *The Jolly Ten and Their Year of Stories* (1888); *A Little Colonial Dame* (1898); *A Little Daughter of the Revolution* (1899); etc.

SAGE, KAY (June 25, 1898–Jan. 8, 1963); b. Albany, N.Y. Artist, author. *The More I Wonder* (poems, 1957); etc.

SAGE, RUFUS B. (b. 1817). Author. *Scenes in the Rocky Mountains* (1846), republished as, *Wild Scenes in Kansas and Nebraska, the Rocky Mountains* (1855), and augmented and republished as, *Rocky Mountain Life* (1857).

SAGE, WILLIAM (b. May 8, 1864); b. Manchester, N.H. Author. *Robert Tournay* (1900); *The Clayborness* (1902); *Frenchy: The Story of a Gentleman* (1904); *The District Attorney* (1906); etc.

SAGENDORPH, ROBB HANSELL (Nov. 20, 1900–July 4, 1970); b. Newton Center, Mass. Publisher. Compiler: *The Old Farmer's Almanac*. Editor: *That New England* (with J. D. Hale, 1966). Founder, *Yankee Magazine*, 1935.

SAINSBURY, NOEL [Everingham] (June 11, 1884–); b. New York. Author. The *Great Ace* series, 7v.; the *Bill Bolton Aviation* series, 6v.; the *Dorothy Dix Air Mystery* series, 6v. (under pen name "Dorothy Wayne"); the *Malay Jungle* series (under pen name "Harvey D. Richards"); the *Champion Sports* series, 5v.; and many other books on aviation for younger readers.

St. Botolph Club. Boston, Mass. Founded Jan. 10, 1880. An organization meeting was held Jan. 3, 1880. Francis Parkman was its first president. The Club's original headquarters were at 87 Boylston Street. In 1887 it moved to 4 Newbury Street. It was modeled after the Century Club of New York. *See* Joseph Henry Curtis's *The St. Botolph Club: Its Birth and Early History* (n.d.).

St. Denis le Cadet. Pen name of Paul Allen.

St. Elmo. Novel by Augusta Jane Evans (1866). Popular story of Edna Earl and her laconic and pessimistic lover whose waywardness she reforms through patience and wisdom.

SAINT-GAUDENS, AUGUSTUS (Mar. 1, 1848–Aug. 3, 1907); b. Dublin, Ireland. Sculptor, author. *The Reminiscences of Augustus Saint-Gaudens*, 2v. (1913). His best-known pieces of sculpture are "Hiawatha," "Admiral Farragut," "Lincoln," "Bastien-Lepage," "Silence," "Amor Caritas," "Diana," "Sherman." He was one of the founders of the Cornish group at Cornish, N.H., and his Cornish home, "Aspet," is now the Augustus Saint-Gaudens Memorial. *See* Royal Cortissoz's *Augustus Saint-Gaudens* (1907).

ST. JOHN, ADELA ROGERS (May 20, 1894–); b. Los Angeles, Calif. Author. *A Free Soul* (1924); *Single Standard* (1925); *Affirmative Prayer in Action* (1955); *Final Verdict* (1962); *Tell No Man* (1965); etc. Author of numerous short stories and serials in magazines.

St. John, J. Hector. Pen name of Michel-Guillaume St. Jean de Crèvecoeur.

ST. JOHN, ROBERT (Mar. 9, 1902–); b. Chicago, Ill. Foreign correspondent, lecturer, author. *From the Land of Silent People* (1942); *It's Always Tomorrow* (1944); *The Silent People Speak* (1948); *Shalom Means Peace* (1949); *Tongue of the Prophets* (1952); *This Was My World* (1953); *Through Malan's Africa* (1954); *Foreign Correspondent* (1957); *Ben-Gurion: The Biography of an Extraordinary Man* (1959); *The Boss: The Story of Gamal Abdel Nasser* (1960); etc. Correspondent, Associated Press, 1939–41; commentator, National Broadcasting Company, 1942–46.

St. Louis Globe-Democrat. St. Louis, Mo., Newspaper. Founded Aug. 1852, by William McKee and William Hill as the *Missouri Democrat*. The *Globe* was founded in 1872 by William McKee and Daniel M. Houser. Merged May, 1875, as the *Globe-Democrat*. John Hay and John G. Nicolay were on the staff of the *Democrat*, together with Joseph Burbage McCullagh, Henry M. Stanley, the explorer, and James Redpath, lyceum bureau founder. McCullagh was editor, 1875–96, followed by Henry King, 1897–1915. In 1918 E. Lansing Ray became editor and president, succeeding Charles H. McKee. Casper S. Yost, on the staff, 1889–1941, was editor of the editorial page for many years. Joseph J. McAuliffe joined the staff in 1913, becoming managing editor in 1915. G. A. Killenberg is the present editor. C. K. Boeschenstein is book review editor. In 1919 the *Globe-Democrat* absorbed the *St. Louis Republic*, a descendant of the *Missouri Gazette*, Missouri's oldest newspaper. See *Historical Sketch of the St. Louis Globe-Democrat* (1935).

St. Louis Post-Dispatch. St. Louis, Mo. Newspaper. The *Missouri Argus* was founded 1835, and followed in 1841 by the *Missouri Reporter*. The *Daily Missourian* was founded 1844. Merged 1846, as the *St. Louis Daily Union*. The *St. Louis Dispatch* was founded 1864, and c. 1867 absorbed the *Daily Union*. The *St. Louis Evening Post* was founded 1878. Joseph Pulitzer bought the two papers in 1878 and merged them as the *St. Louis Post-Dispatch*. Joseph Pulitzer, Jr., has been editor and publisher since 1912. Charles H. Jones was editor, 1895–97. John A. Cockrill was the elder Pulitzer's chief editorial assistant. John G. Neihardt was literary editor, 1922–38. Bart B. Howard was chief editorial writer, 1919–41. George Sibley Johns (Dec. 27, 1857–July 16, 1941), on staff, 1883–1941, was editor of editorial page, 1898–1939. Charles Griffith Ross, on staff, 1906–07 and since 1918, was editor of editorial page, 1934–39. *See* Orrick Johns's *Time of Our Lives* (1937).

St. Martin's Press, Inc. New York. Founded 1952. Affiliated with The Macmillan Company of Canada and Macmillan & Company, London. Publishes fiction, biography, history, and scholarly books. Frank A. Upjohn is Chairman of the Board.

St. Paul Dispatch. See *St. Paul Pioneer Press.*

St. Paul Pioneer Press. St. Paul, Minn. Newspaper. Founded 1849, as the *Minnesota Pioneer*, the first newspaper in the state. The *St. Paul Press* was founded 1861, and merged with the *Pioneer* in 1675. The *St. Paul Dispatch*, founded 1868, combined later with the *Pioneer Press*; the former appears evenings, except Sunday; the latter, mornings. Charles M. Flandrau, Joseph C. Pyle, Lawrence C. Hodgson, and Joseph A. Wheelock have been connected with the papers. William Sumner is editor. Kathryn Boardman is book review editor.

St. Petersburg Times. St. Petersburg, Fla. Newspaper. Founded 1884. Nelson Poynter is editor. William Smith is book review editor.

Saints and Sinners. Group of literary men and bibliophiles in Chicago described by Eugene Field in his *The Love Affairs of a Bibliomaniac*. They gathered at the "Saints and Sinners Corner" in McClurg's bookstore.

SALE, "CHIC" (Charles Partlow) (1885–Nov. 7, 1935); b. Huron, S.D. Actor, humorist, author. *The Specialist* (1929); *I'll Tell You Why* (1930); *The Champion Cornhusker Crashes the Movies* (1933); etc. *See* William T. Sullivan's *Comments and Commentaries on The Specialist and Other Things* (1932).

SALE, WILLIAM M[erritt], JR. (Feb. 16, 1899–); b. Louisville, Ky. Educator. *Samuel Richardson, a Bibliographical Record* (1936); *The Use of Language* (with H. F. Pommer, 1947); *Samuel Richardson, Master Printer* (1950). Editor: *Henry James' Hawthorne* (1956); *Prose Readings* (1958). Prof. English, Cornell University, since 1948.

SALINGER, HERMAN (Dec. 23, 1903–); b. St. Louis, Mo. Educator. *A Sigh Is the Sword* (1963). Editor: *An Index to the Poems of Rainer Maria Rilke* (1942); *Twentieth Century German Verse: A Selection* (1952); etc. Prof. German, Duke University, since 1955.

SALINGER, J[erome] D[avid] (1919–); b. New York. Author. *The Catcher in the Rye* (1951); *Nine Stories* (1953); *Franny and Zooey* (1961); *Raise High the Roof Beam, Carpenters, and Seymour—an Introduction* (1962).

SALISBURY, HARRISON EVANS (Nov. 14, 1908–); b. Minneapolis, Minn. Journalist, author. *Russia on the Way* (1946); *An American in Russia* (1955); *The Shook-Up Generation* (1958); *To Moscow—And Beyond* (1960); *Moscow Journal* (1961); *Orbit of China* (1967); etc. With United Press, 1930–48; *New York Times*, since 1949.

Salmagundi Club. New York. Founded 1871, as the Sketch Class; name changed 1877 to the Salmagundi Sketch Club. *See* William Henry Shelton's *The Salmagundi Club* (1918), and his *The History of the Salmagundi Club* (1927).

Salmagundi; or, The Whim-Whams and Opinions of Launcelot Langstaff, Esq., and Others. New York. Comic periodical written by Washington Irving, William Irving, and James Kirke Paulding. Founded 1807. A series of humorous papers designed to instruct the young and reform the old, and to polish the manners of New York society. The papers ceased in 1808.

SALMON, LUCY MAYNARD (July 27, 1853–Feb. 14, 1927); b. Fulton, N.Y. Educator, historian. *The Newspaper and the Historian* (1923); *The Newspaper and Authority* (1923); *Historical Material* (1933); etc. History dept., Vassar College, 1887–1927; prof., 1889–1927.

SALOUTOS, THEODORE (Aug. 3, 1910–   ); b. Milwaukee, Wis. Educator, author. *Agricultural Discontent in the Middle West, 1900–1939* (1951); *They Remember America* (1956); *Farmer Movements in the South, 1865–1933* (1960); *The Greeks in the United States* (1964); *Twentieth Century Populism* (1964); *The Greeks in America* (1967). Prof. history, University of California at Los Angeles, since 1956.

Salt-Box House, The. By Jane de Forest Shelton (1900). The biography of an actual house of that kind built by Daniel Shelton near Stratford, Conn., in 1758.

Salt Lake City Tribune. Salt Lake City, Utah. Newspaper. Founded 1870, as an anti-Mormon paper. The *Salt Lake Telegram*, founded 1902, is its evening edition. New combined with the *Desert News and Telegram.*

SALTER, JOHN THOMAS (Jan. 17, 1898–); b. Three Oaks, Mich. Educator. *Boss Rule—Portraits in City Politics* (1935); *The Pattern of Politics* (1940). Editor: *The American Politician* (1938); *Public Men: In and Out of Office* (1946). Political science dept., University of Wisconsin, since 1930.

SALTER, WILLIAM (Nov. 17, 1821–Aug. 15, 1910); b. Brooklyn, N.Y. Congregational clergyman, historian, biographer. *The Life of James R. Grimes* (1876); *Augustus C. Dodge* (1887); *James Clarke* (1888); *Iowa: The First Free State in the Louisiana Purchase* (1905); *Sixty Years, and Other Discourses* (1907); etc.

SALTER, WILLIAM MACKINTIRE (Jan. 30, 1853–July 18, 1931); b. Burlington, Ia. Ethical Culture leader, philósopher, author. *Ethical Religion* (1889); *First Steps in Philosophy* (1892); *Walt Whitman* (1899); *Nietzsche, the Thinker* (1917); etc.

Saltillo Boys. By William O. Stoddard (1882). Boys' book filled with adventure of many sorts. Saltillo was the name of a small town where the action begins.

SALTUS, EDGAR [Evertson] (Oct. 8, 1855–July 31, 1921); b. New York. Author. *Balzac* (1885); *The Anatomy of Negation* (1886); *Mr. Incoul's Misadventure* (1887); *The Truth about Tristrem Varick* (1888); *Eden* (1888); *The Transient Guest* (1889); *Love and Lore* (1890); *Mary Magdalen* (1891); *Imperial Purple* (1892); *Enthralled* (1894); *Historia Amoris* (1906); *The Monster* (1913); *The Paliser Case* (1919); *The Imperial Orgy* (1920); etc.

Salvation Nell. Play by Edward Brewster Sheldon (prod. 1908). Nell's lover goes to prison, and on his release reverts to a life of crime in the New York City slums. Nell regenerates him and he finally joins a religious organization.

Sam Patch. Play by E. H. Thompson (1836). Based on Sam Patch's celebrated leap into the waters of Niagara.

Sampo, The. By James Baldwin (1912). Story based on the Finnish saga of the *Kalevala.*

SAMPSON, EMMA SPEED (Dec. 1, 1868–May 7, 1947); b. Louisville, Ky. Pen name "Nell Speed." Author. *Billy and the Major* (1917); *Mammy's White Folks* (1919); *Miss Minerva's Baby* (1920); and other Miss Minerva stories, a continuation of Frances Boyd Calhoun's *Miss Minerva and William Green Hill* (1909); *The Spite Fence* (1929); the *Tucker Twins* series, *Carter Girls* series, etc.

Sams and Co., Howard W., Inc., Publishers. Indianapolis, Ind. Publishers. Founded 1946. Howard W. Sams is chairman of the board. The Bobbs-Merrill Company is a subsidiary. Acquired by International Telephone and Telegraph in 1966.

SAMUEL, MAURICE (Feb. 8, 1895–); b. Macin, Rum. Author. *The Outsider* (1921); *You Gentiles* (1924); *King Mob* (1931); *Beyond Woman* (1934); *The Great Hatred* (1940); *The World of Sholom Aleichem* (1943); *Harvest in the Desert* (1944); *Prince of the Ghetto* (1948); *The Gentleman and the Jew* (1950); *The Devil That Failed* (1952); *Certain People of the Book* (1955); *The Professor and the Fossil* (1956); *The Second Crucifixion* (1960); *Little Did I Know* (1963); *Blood Accusation* (1967); *Light on Israel* (1968); etc.

SAMUELS, ADELAIDE FLORENCE (Mrs. Orville Bassett) (b. Sept. 24, 1845); b. Boston, Mass. Author. *Saved from the Street* (1871); *Adrift in the World* (1872); *Little Cricket* (1873); *Daisy Travers; or, The Girls of Hive Hall* (1876); *Father Gander's Melodies for Mother Goose's Grandchildren* (1894); etc.

SAMUELS, ERNEST (May 19, 1903–); b. Chicago, Ill. Educator. *Business English Projects* (1936); *The Young Henry Adams* (1948); *Henry Adams: The Middle Years* (1958); *Henry Adams: The Major Phase.* (1964, Pulitzer Prize, 1965). Prof. English, Northwestern University.

SAMUELS, MAURICE VICTOR (Oct. 3, 1873–Apr. 1, 1945); b. San Francisco, Calif. Author. *The Florentines* (1904); *Pageant of the Strong* (1923); etc.

SAMUELS, S[amuel] (Mar. 14, 1823–1908). Seaman, author. *From the Forecastle to the Cabin* (1887).

SAMUELSON, PAUL ANTHONY (May 15, 1915–); b. Gary, Ind. Economist. *Foundations of Economic Analysis* (1947); *Economics, an Introductory Analysis* (1948); *Linear Programming and Economic Analysis* (1958); *Collected Scientific Papers*, 2v. (1966). Editor: *Readings in Economics* (with others, 1955).

San Antonio Express and News. San Antonio, Tex. Newspaper. The *Express* was founded 1865. Its evening edition, *News* was founded 1918. Charles Kilpatrick is editor. Gerald R. Ashford is book review editor.

San Antonio Light. San Antonio, Tex. Newspaper. Founded 1881, by Tom and Benjamin Franklin. Possibly stemmed from the *Alamo Express*, founded 1860, by James P. Newcomb. William Randolph Hearst bought control of it in 1924. Frank A. Bennack, Jr., is publisher.

San Antonio News. See *San Antonio Express and News.*

San Diego Tribune. See *San Diego Union.*

San Diego Union. San Diego, Calif. Newspaper. Founded 1868. Its evening paper, the *Tribune* (founded 1895), had already merged with the *Sun* (founded 1881) at the time it was acquired. Herbert G. Klein is editor. George Jones is book review editor.

San Francisco Chronicle. San Francisco, Calif. Newspaper. Founded 1865, as the *Dramatic Chronicle.* Mark Twain and

Bret Harte were early contributors. In 1868 the word "Dramatic" was omitted from the title. George Hamlin Fitch was literary editor, 1880–1915. Joseph Henry Jackson became literary editor in 1930. Combined with *San Francisco Examiner* (q.v.) as evening paper. Sunday edition is the *Examiner and Chronicle.* Charles Thieriot edits the *Chronicle;* Ed Dooley edits the *Examiner.* William Hogan is book review editor.

San Francisco Examiner. San Francisco, Calif. Newspaper. Founded 1865, as the *Evening Examiner.* Bought by George Hearst in 1880 and changed to a morning paper. William Randolph Hearst became owner in 1887. Associated with it have been Ambrose Bierce, Mark Twain, Jack London, Joaquin Miller, Gertrude Atherton, Kathleen Norris, Arthur McEwen. Edwin Markham's "The Man with the Hoe" and E. L. Thayer's "Casey at the Bat" originally appeared in the *Examiner.* Combined with *San Francisco Chronicle* (q.v.).

San Francisco News. San Francisco, Calif. Newspaper. Founded 1903. Merged with the *Call-Bulletin* in 1959, as the *News-Call Bulletin.*

San Francisco News-Call Bulletin. San Francisco, Calif. Newspaper. The *Bulletin* was founded 1855 by James King, who was killed in 1856 for opposing lawless government. His death gave rise to the Vigilantes. The *Call,* founded 1856, was merged with the *Bulletin* in 1929. Fremont Older edited the *Bulletin* after 1895 and continued editing both papers after the merger until his death in 1933. Among those associated with the *Call* have been Mark Twain, John Medbury, Evelyn Wells, T. A. Dorgan, Russ Westover, Rube Goldberg, and Jimmy Murphy. *Bulletin* writers have included Rose Wilder Lane, Maxwell Anderson, Kathleen Norris, Sinclair Lewis, and Sophie Treadwell. In 1959 the *San Francisco News,* owned by Scripps-Howard, and the *Call-Bulletin,* owned by the Hearst Corporation, merged as the *News-Call Bulletin.* Now merged with *San Francisco Examiner* (q.v.).

San Francisco News Letter. San Francisco, Calif. Weekly. Founded 1856, by Frederick Marriott. Merged with *The Wasp* in 1928.

San Francisco Oracle. San Francisco, Cal. Newspaper. Founded 1967. Ceased publication 1969. Underground newspaper in tabloid format.

San Francisco Review. San Francisco, Calif. Quarterly. Founded 1959. Edited by R. H. Miller and others. Literary magazine.

SANBORN, ALVAN FRANCIS (July 8, 1866–Oct. 25, 1966); b. Marlboro, Mass. Correspondent, author. *Moody's Lodging House, and Other Tenement Sketches* (1895); *Meg McIntyre's Raffle, and Other Stories* (1896); *Paris and the Social Revolution* (1903); etc. Paris correspondent, *Boston Transcript,* 1907–36, etc.

SANBORN, FRANKLIN BENJAMIN (Dec. 15, 1831–Feb. 24, 1917); b. Hampton Falls, N.H. Editor, author. *Henry D. Thoreau* (1882); *The Life and Letters of John Brown* (1885); *Dr. S. G. Howe, the Philanthropist* (1891); *A. Bronson Alcott's Life and Philosophy,* 2v. (1893); *Ralph Waldo Emerson* (1901); *A History of New Hampshire* (1903); *Hawthorne and His Friends* (1908); *Fruitlands, New England, 1842–1844* (1908); *Recollections of Seventy Years,* 2v. (1909); *Sixty Years in Concord* (1916); etc. Editor, the *Boston Commonwealth,* 1863–67; the *Springfield Republican,* 1868–72; contributing editor, 1873–1914.

SANBORN, FREDERIC ROCKWELL (Feb. 14, 1899–Aug. 29, 1968); b. Glens Falls, N.Y. Jurist, author. *Origins of the Early English Maritime and Commercial Law* (1930); *Design for War* (1951).

SANBORN, HERBERT CHARLES (Feb. 18, 1873–July 6, 1967); b. Winchester, Mass. Educator, philosopher, author. *Sudermann* (1905); *Eckstein* (1906); *Schiller* (1906); *A Personal View of Art* (1922); *Aesthetics and Civilization* (1923);

The Function of Philosophy in Liberal Education (1926); etc. Prof. philosophy, Vanderbilt University, 1911–1942.

SANBORN, J[ohn] PITTS (1879–Mar. 7, 1941); b. Port Huron, Mich. Music critic, author. *Vie de Bordeaux* (poems, 1917); *Prima Donna: A Novel of the Opera* (1928); *Greek Night* (1933); *Metropolitan Book of the Opera* (1937); etc. Music editor, *New York Globe,* 1905–23; *New York Evening Mail; New York World-Telegram,* 1931–41.

SANBORN, KATE (Katharine Abbott) (July 11, 1839–July 9, 1917); b. Hanover, N.H. Educator, lecturer, author. *Home Pictures of English Poets* (1869); *Adopting an Abandoned Farm* (1891); *Abandoning an Adopted Farm* (1894); *Memories and Anecdotes* (1915); etc. Prof. literature, Smith College. See Edwin W. Sanborn's *Kate Sanborn* (1918).

SANBORN, MARY FARLEY (May 8, 1853–Nov. 25, 1941); b. Manchester, N.H. Novelist, poet. *Sweet-and-Twenty* (1890); *Paula Ferris* (1892); *The Revelation of Herself* (1904); *The Canvas Door* (1909); *The First Valley* (1920); *Behind the Counter* (poems, 1935); etc.

SANCHEZ, NELLIE VAN DE GRIFT (b. Nov., 1854); b. Indianapolis, Ind. Historian. *The Life of Mrs. Robert Louis Stevenson* (1920); *Spanish Arcadia* (1929); *A Short History of California* (1929); *Stories of the States* (1931); etc. Translator of Spanish documents for Bancroft Library, University of California.

SANCHEZ [y Sanchez], GEORGE ISIDORE (Oct. 4, 1906–); b. Albuquerque, N.M. Educator. *Mexico—A Revolution by Education* (1936); *Forgotten People* (1940); *The Development of Higher Education in Mexico* (1944); *Arithmetic in Maya* (1961); *The Development of Education in Venezuela* (1963); *Mexico* (1965). Prof. Latin American education, University of Texas, since 1940.

Sanctuary. Novel by William Faulkner (1931). A horror story involving rape, sexual perversion, and murder. Temple Drake, a college girl, and Popeye, a moronic criminal, are the most important characters.

SANDBURG, CARL (Jan. 6, 1878–July 28, 1967); b. Galesburg, Ill. Poet, biographer. *Chicago Poems* (1916); *Cornhuskers* (poems, 1918); *Smoke and Steel* (poems, 1920); *Slabs of the Sunburnt West* (poems, 1922); *Rootabaga Stories* (1922); *Rootabaga Pigeons* (1923); *Abraham Lincoln: The Prairie Years,* 2v. (1926); *Good Morning America* (poems, 1928); *Steichen, the Photographer* (1929); *Potato Face* (1930); *Early Moon* (poems, 1930); *Mary Lincoln, Wife and Widow,* 2v. (with Paul McClelland Angle, 1932); *The People, Yes* (poems, 1936); *Abraham Lincoln: The War Years,* 4v. (1939, Pulitzer Prize for American history, 1940); *Storm Over the Land* (1942); *Home Front Memo* (1943); *Remembrance Rock* (1948); *Lincoln Collector* (1949); *Complete Poems* (1950); *Always the Young Strangers* (autobiography, 1952); *Prairie Town Boy* (1955); *The Sandburg Range* (1957); *Wind Song* (1960); etc. Editor: *The American Songbag* (1927); etc. See Karl W. Detzer's *Carl Sandburg: A Study in Personality and Background* (1941); Richard Crowder's *Carl Sandburg* (1963).

SANDERS, ED (Aug. 17, 1939–); b. Kansas City, Mo. Poet, editor, singer. *Poems from Jail* (1963); *King Lord-Queen Freak* (1964); *The Toe-Queen Poems* (1965); *Peace Eye* (1965); *The Complete Sex Poems of Ed Sanders* (1965); *Banana: An Anthology* (1965); etc. Composer, lyricist, singer, rock group The Fugs.

SANDERS, FRANK KNIGHT (June 5, 1861–Feb. 20, 1933); b. Batticotta, Ceylon. Congregational clergyman, educator, historian. *History of the Hebrews* (1914); *Old Testament History* (1922); etc. Semitic languages dept., Yale University, 1891–1905; president, Washburn College, Topeka, Kan., 1908–14.

SANDERS, HENRY ARTHUR (Oct. 22, 1865–Nov. 16, 1956); b. Livermore, Me. Educator, philologist. Editor: *Roman Historical Sources and Institutions* (1904); *Roman History and Mythology* (1910); *The Old Testament Manuscripts in the Freer Collection,* 2 parts (1910–17); *The New Testament Manuscripts in the Freer Collection,* 2 parts (1912–17); *Latin Papyri in the University of Michigan Collection* (1947); etc. Latin dept., University of Michigan, 1899–1939; prof., 1909–39.

SANDERS, IRWIN TAYLOR (Jan. 17, 1909–); b. Millersburg, Ky. Educator. Author or co-author: *Balkan Village* (1949); *The Community* (1958); *The Rainbow in the Rock* (1962); *The Professional School and World Affairs* (1968); etc. Sociology dept., University of Kentucky, 1940–58; lecturer in sociology, Harvard University.

SANDERS, JAMES ALVIN (Nov. 28, 1927–); b. Memphis, Tenn. Clergyman, educator, author. *Suffering as Divine Discipline in the Old Testament and Post-Biblical Judaism* (1955); *The Old Testament in the Cross* (1961); *The Psalms Scrolls of Qumram Cave II* (1967); *The Dead Sea Psalms Scrolls* (1967); Prof. Old Testament, Union Theological Seminary, since 1965.

SANDERS, THOMAS JEFFERSON (Jan. 18, 1855–Dec. 26, 1946); b. Burbank, O. Educator, author. *Philosophy of the Christian Religion* (1888); *The Nature and End of Education* (1896); *The Place of Music in a Liberal Education* (1930); etc. Prof. philosophy, Otterbein College, 1901–31.

SANDERSON, IVAN TERRANCE (Jan., 1911–); b. Edinburgh. Biologist, author. *Animal Treasure* (1937); *Caribbean Treasure* (1939); *Living Treasure* (1941); *How to Know the American Mammals* (1951); *The Silver Mink* (1952); *Follow the Whale* (1956); *The Abominable Snowmen* (1961); *The Continent We Live On* (1961); *Invisible Residents: A Disquisition Upon Certain Matters Maritime and the Possibility of Intelligent Life under Waters of this Earth* (1970); etc.

SANDERSON, JOHN (1783–Apr. 5, 1844); b. Carlisle, Pa. Editor, author. *Sketches of Paris,* 2v. (1838), published in London as *The American in Paris,* 2v. (1838); etc. Editor: *Biography of the Signers of the Declaration of Independence,* v. 1-2 (with Joseph M. Sanderson, 1820), completed by Richard Waln, Jr., v. 3-9 (1823–27).

SANDMEL, SAMUEL (Sept. 23, 1911–   ); b. Dayton, Ohio. Educator, author. *A Jewish Understanding of the New Testament* (1956); *Philo's Place in Judaism* (1956); *The Genius of Paul* (1958); *The Hebrew Scriptures* (1963); *We Jews and Jesus* (1965); *Herod: Profile of a Tyrant* (1967). Prof. Bible and Hellenistic Literature, Jewish Institute of Religion.

SANDOZ, MARI [Susette] (1901–Mar. 10, 1966); b. in Sheridan Co., Neb. Author. *Old Jules* (1935); *Slogum House* (1937); *Capital City* (1939); *Crazy Horse* (1942); *The Tom-Walker* (1947); *Cheyenne Autumn* (1953); *The Buffalo Hunters* (1954); *Miss Morissa* (1955); *The Horsecatcher* (1957); *Hostiles and Friendlies* (1959); *The Christmas of the Phonograph Records: A Recollection* (1966).

SANDS, BILL. Author. *My Shadow Ran Fast* (1964); *The Seventh Step* (1967).

SANDS, ROBERT CHARLES (May 11, 1799–Dec. 16, 1832); b. New York. Editor, author. *The Writings of Robert C. Sands, in Prose and Verse,* ed. by Guilian C. Verplanck, 2v. (1834). Editor, the *Atlantic Magazine,* 1824–25; asst. editor, the *New York Commercial Advertiser,* 1827–32; editor (with William C. Bryant and G. C. Verplanck), *The Talisman,* 1828–30; etc. His best-known poem was "Yamoden," based on the Indian chief, Philip, and his best short story was *Boyuca.*

Sandy. Novel by Alice Hegan Rice (1905). Story of an Irish boy, Sandy Kilday, an orphan who crosses the sea when he is sixteen to try his luck in a new land of promise.

SANDYS, GEORGE (Mar. 2, 1577/78–Mar. 4, 1643/44); b. Bishopsthorpe, Yorks, Eng. Colonist, poet, translator. *A Relation of a Journey Begun An: Dom: 1610* (1615); *Ovid's Metamorphosis Englished* (1626); *A Paraphrase Upon the Divine Poems* (1637); *The Poetical Works,* ed. by Richard Hooper, 2v. (1872); etc. See R. B. Davis's *George Sandys, Poet-Adventurer* (1955).

SANFORD, HUGH WHEELER (Apr. 22, 1879–Nov. 15, 1961); b. Knoxville, Tenn. Author. *The Business of Life* (1924); *Science and Faith* (1930); *Concerning Knowledge* (1935); *Major Premise of Albert Einstein* (1950); etc.

SANFORD, ROBERT NEVITT (May 31, 1909–); b. Chatham, Va. Psychologist. *Physique, Personality, and Scholarship* (with others, 1943); *The Authoritarian Personality* (with others, 1950). Prof. psychology, University of California, since 1949.

SANGER, MARGARET (Sept. 14, 1883–Sept. 6, 1966); b. Corning, N.Y. Leader of birth control movement, author. *What Every Girl Should Know* (1916); *The Case for Birth Control* (1917); *Happiness in Marriage* (1927); *My Fight for Birth Control* (1931); *Margaret Sanger: An Autobiography* (1938); etc. Editor, *Birth Control Review,* 1917–28.

SANGER, WILLIAM CARY (Feb. 9, 1893–deceased); b. Brooklyn, N.Y. Poet. *When Hearts Are Young, and Other Stories* (1921); *The City of Toil and Dreams* (1924); *Springtime and the Harbor, and Other Poems* (1924); *In the Land of the Harvest* (1924); *Tides of Commerce* (1924); *Songs of the Hill and Sea* (1927); etc.

SANGSTER, MARGARET E[lizabeth] (Mrs. Gerrit Van Deth) (Feb. 22, 1838–June 4, 1912); b. New Rochelle, N.Y. Editor, author. *Little Janey* (1855); *Poems of the Household* (1882); *On the Road Home* (poems, 1893); *Little Knights and Ladies* (1895); *Easter Bells* (poems, 1897); *Lyrics of Love, of Hearth and Home & Field and Garden* (1901); *Janet Ward, a Daughter of the Manse* (1902); *Eleanor Lee* (1903); *The Joyful Life* (1907); *An Autobiography: From My Youth Up: Personal Reminiscences* (1909); *A Little Book of Homespun Verse* (1911); *Eastover Parish* (1912); etc. Editor, *Harper's Bazar,* 1889–99. See Francis E. Willard and Mary A. Livermore's *A Woman of the Century* (1893).

SANGSTER, MARGARET E[lizabeth] (1894–); b. Brooklyn, N.Y. Poet, novelist. *Friends o' Mine: A Book of Poems and Stories* (1914); *Real People and Dreams: A New Book of Stories and Poems* (1915); *Cross Roads* (poems, 1919); *The Island of Faith* (1921); *The Rugged Road* (1930); *The Littlest Orphan, and Other Christmas Stories* (1935); *The Stars Come Close* (1936); *Singing on the Road* (1936); *All Through the Day* (1939); *Reluctant Star* (1940); *Bible Quiz Book* (1944); etc.

SANKEY, IRA DAVID (Aug. 28, 1840–Aug. 13, 1908); b. Edinburgh, Pa. Associated with Dwight L. Moody, as Moody and Sankey, evangelists. Author: *My Life and the Story of the Gospel Hymns* (1906). Compiler: *Sacred Songs and Solos* (1873); *Gospel Hymns* (1875); and other hymnals. See W. R. Moody's *D. L. Moody* (1930).

SANN, PAUL (Mar. 17, 1914–); b. Brooklyn, N.Y. Journalist, author. *A Century of Journalism* (1943); *More Post Biographies* (1947); *Pictorial History of the Wild West* (with J.D. Horan, 1954); *The Lawless Decade* (1957); *Fads, Follies and Delusions of the American People* (1967); *Red Auerbach: Winning the Hard Way* (with Red Auerbach, 1967). With *New York Post,* since 1931.

SANTAYANA, GEORGE (Dec. 16, 1863–Sept. 26, 1952); b. Madrid, Spain. Educator, poet, essayist. *Sonnets, and Other Verses* (1894); *The Sense of Beauty* (1896); *Interpretation of Poetry and Religion* (1900); *A Hermit of Carmel, and Other Poems* (1901); *The Life of Reason,* 5v. (1905–06); *Winds of Doctrine* (1913); *Egotism in German Philosophy* (1916); *Poems* (1922); *Soliloquies in England, and Later Soliloquies*

(1922); *Skepticism and Animal Faith* (1923); *The Realm of Essence* (1927); *The Realm of Matter* (1930); *The Last Puritan* (1935); *Obiter Scripta* (1936); *The Works*, 14v. (1936–37); *The Realm of Truth* (1937); *The Realm of Spirit* (1940); *Dominations and Powers* (1951); *Persons and Places*, 3v. (autobiography, 1944–53). Philosophy dept., Harvard University, 1889–1912. See George W. Howgate's *George Santayana* (1938); Fred B. Millett's *Contemporary American Authors* (1940); *The Letters of George Santayana*, ed. by Daniel Cory (1955); and *Santayana: The Later Years*, ed. by Daniel Cory (1963).

SANTEE, ROSS (Aug. 16, 1889–June 30, 1965); b. Thornburg, Ia. Illustrator, author. *Men and Horses* (1926); *Cowboy* (1928); *Pooch* (1931); *Sleepy Black: The Story of a Horse* (1933); *Spike, the Story of a Cowpuncher's Dog* (1934); *Apache Land* (1947); *Bubbling Spring* (1949); *Hardrock and Silver Sage* (1951); *Dog Days* (autobiography, 1955); etc.

SANTMYER, HELEN HOOVEN (Nov. 25, 1895–); b. Cincinnati, O. Author. *Herbs and Apples* (1925); *The Fierce Dispute* (1929); etc. Prof. English, Cedarville College, since 1936.

Saplings. See *Scholastic Magazines.*

Sapphira and the Slave Girl. Novel by Willa Cather (1940).

Saracinesca. Novel by F. Marion Crawford (1887). First of a group of four novels laid in Italy after the unification, and dealing with the fortunes of the Saracinesca family, especially Giovanni and his son, Don Orsino. The others are: *Sant' Ilario* (1889); *Don Orsino* (1892); and *Corleone* (1897).

SARASON, SEYMOUR BERNARD (Jan. 12, 1919–); b. Brooklyn, N.Y. Psychologist, educator. *Psychological Problems in Mental Deficiency* (1949); *The Clinical Interaction* (1954); *Psychological and Cultural Problems in Mental Subnormality* (with Thomas Gladwin, 1958). Co-author: *Anxiety in Elementary School Children* (1960); *The Preparation of Teachers, An Unstudied Problem in Education* (1962); *Psychology in Community Settings* (1966). Prof. psychology, Yale University, since 1955.

Saratoga Trunk. Novel by Edna Ferber (1941). Love affair of aristocratic Clio, brought up in France, and Clint, a former cowboy, after they meet in New Orleans. Clint abandons horses and becomes successful as a railroad magnate.

SARETT, LEW (May 16, 1888–Aug. 17, 1954); b. Chicago, Ill. Educator, poet, lecturer, bibliophile. *Many, Many Moons* (1920); *The Box of God* (1922); *Slow Smoke* (1925); *Wings against the Moon* (1931); *Collected Poems* (1941); etc. Advisory editor, *Poetry*, from 1921. Prof. speech, Northwestern University, 1921–53.

SARG, TONY (Anthony Frederick) (Apr. 24, 1880–Mar. 7, 1942); b. in Guatemala. Artist, author. *Tony Sarg's Book for Children* (1924); *Tony Sarg's Animal Book* (1925); *A Book of Marionette Plays* (with Anne Stoddard, 1927); *Tony Sarg's Wonder Zoo* (1927); *Tony Sarg's New York* (1927); etc.

SARGENT, DWIGHT EMERSON (Apr. 3, 1917–); b. Pembroke, Mass. Editor. With *Portland Press Herald* and *Sunday Telegram*, 1949–59; editor, editorial page, *New York Herald Tribune*, 1959–64.

SARGENT, EPES (Sept. 27, 1813–Dec. 30, 1880); b. Gloucester, Mass. Editor, poet, playwright. *The Bride of Genoa* (1837); *Velasco* (1839); *American Adventure by Land and Sea* (1841); *Fleetwood* (1845); *Songs of the Sea and Other Poems* (1847); *Arctic Adventures by Sea and Land* (1857); *Peculiar: A Tale of the Great Transition* (1864); *The Woman Who Dared* (poems, 1870); etc. Editor: *Harper's Cyclopedia of British and American Poetry* (1881); etc. Editor, the *Boston Transcript*, 1847–53; *Sargent's New Monthly Magazine*, 1843, etc. His best-known poem was "A Life on the Ocean Wave." See Emma W. Sargent and C. S. Sargent's *Epes Sargent of Gloucester and His Descendants* (1923).

SARGENT, GEORGE HENRY (May 5, 1867–Jan. 14, 1931); b. Warner, N.H. Bibliographer, journalist. *The French Revolution and Napoleon in Literature and Caricature* (1906); *Romances of Books* (1913); *Lauriats: A Sketch of Early Boston Booksellers* (1922); *Amy Lowell: A Mosaic* (1926); *The Writings of A. Edward Newton: A Bibliography* (1927); *A Busted Bibliophile and His Books* (1928); etc. With the *Boston Evening Transcript*, 1895–1931, conducting a column called "The Bibliographer." His library was sold at auction, Dec. 19, 1931.

SARGENT, LUCIUS MANLIUS (June 25, 1786–June 2, 1867); b. Boston, Mass. Antiquary, temperance reformer, author. *The Culex of Virgil: with a Translation into English Verse* (1807); *Hubert and Ellen, and Other Poems* (1812); *James Talbot* (1821); *The Stage Coach* (1838); *The Temperance Tales* (1848); *Dealings with the Dead* (1856); etc. See J. H. Sheppard's *Reminiscences of Lucius Manlius Sargent* (1871).

SARGENT, NATHAN (May 5, 1794–Feb. 2, 1875); b. Putney, Vt. Jurist, editor, correspondent, author. *Brief Outline of the Life of Henry Clay* (1844); *Public Men and Events*, 2v. (1875). Founder, *Commercial Herald*, Philadelphia, 1830. Wrote the "Oliver Oldschool" letters for the *United States Gazette*, beginning Jan. 3, 1842.

SARGENT, PORTER E[dward] (June 6, 1872–Mar. 27, 1951); b. Brooklyn, N.Y. Editor, publisher, author. *Spoils: Poems from a Crowded Life* (1935); *Education in Wartime* (1942); *Dangerous Trends* (1948); etc. Editor and publisher of *Sargent's Handbook of Private Schools*, many editions; *Sargent's Handbook of Summer Camps*, many editions; and other popular handbooks.

SARGENT, RALPH MILLARD (May 10, 1904–); b. Austin, Minn. Educator. *At the Court of Queen Elizabeth* (1935); etc. Prof. English, Haverford College, Pennsylvania, 1941–62.

SARGENT, WINTHROP (Sept. 23, 1825–May 18, 1870); b. Philadelphia, Pa. Author. *History of an Expedition against Fort Duquesne in 1755 under Major-General Edward Braddock* (1855); *The Loyalist Poetry of the Revolution* (1857); *The Life and Career of Major John André* (1861). Editor: *The Loyal Verses of Joseph Stansbury and Doctor Jonathan Odell, Relating to the American Revolution* (1860); etc.

SAROYAN, ARAM (Sept. 25, 1943–   ); Poet. *Poems* (with Jenni Caldwell and Richard Kolmar, 1963); *In* (1965); *Works* (1966); *Poems* (1967); *Lines Press series* (six magazines, four books completed in 1966); *Aram Saroyan* (1968); *Random* (1969); *Words and Photographs* (1970).

SAROYAN, WILLIAM (Aug. 31, 1908–); b. Fresno, Calif. Author. *The Daring Young Man on the Flying Trapeze, and Other Stories* (1934); *Inhale & Exhale* (1936); *Three Times Three* (1936); *The Gay and Melancholy Flute* (1937); *Little Children* (1937); *Love, Here Is My Hat* (1938); *A Native American* (1938); *The Trouble with Tigers* (1938); *Peace, It's Wonderful* (1939); *My Heart's in the Highlands* (prod. 1939); *The Time of Your Life* (prod. 1939, Pulitzer Prize play, 1940); *Love's Old Sweet Song* (prod. 1940); *My Name Is Aram* (1940); *The Beautiful People* (prod. 1941); *The Human Comedy* (1943); *Dear Baby* (1944); *The Adventures of Wesley Jackson* (1946); *Jim Dandy* (play, 1947); *Rock Wagram* (1951); *Mama, I Love You* (1956); *Papa, You're Crazy* (1957); *The Cave Dwellers* (play, 1958); *Here Comes, There Goes You Know Who* (1962); *Not Dying* (1963); *One Day in the Afternoon of the World* (1964); *After Thirty Years: The Daring Young Man on the Flying Trapeze* (1964); etc. See James Gray's *On Second Thought* (1946).

SARRIS, ANDREW (Oct. 31, 1928–   ); b. Brooklyn, N.Y. Film critic, author. *The Films of Josef von Sternberg* (1966); *The American Cinema: Directors and Directions* (1968); *Confessions of a Cultist: On the Cinema, 1955–1969* (1970). Editor: *Interviews with Film Directors* (1967); *The Film* (1968). Film Critic, *Village Voice*, since 1960. Faculty, New York University, since 1967.

SARTAIN, JOHN (Oct. 24, 1808–Oct. 25, 1897); b. London. Engraver, editor, author. *The Reminiscences of a Very Old Man, 1808–1897* (1899); etc. He came to America in 1830 and executed plates for *Godey's Lady's Magazine, The Casket,* etc. In 1841 he joined *Graham's Magazine,* and in 1848 purchased, with William Sloanaker, the *Union Magazine,* issuing it as *Sartain's Union Magazine of Literature and Art* in 1849. See *Annals of the Sartain Tribe* (privately printed, 1886).

SARTON, GEORGE ALFRED LEON (Aug. 31, 1884–Mar. 22, 1956); b. Ghent, Belg. Editor, author. *Introduction to the History of Science,* 2v. (1927–31); *The History of Science and the New Humanism* (1931); *The Study of the History of Science* (1936); *Science and Learning in the Fourteenth Century,* 2v. (1947); *Six Wings: Men of Science in the Renaissance* (1957); etc. Founder and editor, *Isis,* 1912, *Osiris,* 1936. Lecturer on history of science, Harvard University, from 1920; professor, 1940–51.

SARTON, MAY (May 3, 1912–); b. Wondelgem, Belg. Poet, novelist. *Encounter in April* (1937); *The Single Hound* (1938); *Inner Landscape* (poems, 1939); *The Bridge of Years* (1946); *The Lion and the Rose* (poems, 1948); *Shadow of a Man* (1950); *A Shower of Summer Days* (1952); *The Land of Silence* (poems, 1953); *Faithful Are the Wounds* (1954); *The Birth of a Grandfather* (1957); *In Time Like Air* (poems, 1957); *I Knew a Phoenix* (autobiography, 1959); *Cloud, Stone, Sun, Vine* (poems, 1961); *The Small Room* (1961); *Joanna and Ulysses* (1963); *Mrs. Stevens Hears the Mermaids Singing* (1965); *A Private Mythology* (1966); *Miss Pickthorn and Mr. Hare* (1966); etc.

SASS, GEORGE HERBERT (Dec. 24, 1845–Feb. 19, 1908); b. Charleston, S.C. Lawyer, author. Pen name "Barton Gray." *The Heart's Quest* (1904).

SASS, HERBERT RAVENEL (Nov. 2, 1884–Feb. 18, 1958); b. Charleston, S.C., son of George Herbert Sass. Author. *The Way of the Wild* (1925); *Adventures in Green Places* (1926); *Gray Eagle* (1927); *On the Wings of a Bird* (1929); *Look Back to Glory* (1933); *Hear Me, My Chiefs!* (1940); *Emperor Brims* (1941); *The Story of the South Carolina Low Country* (1956); etc.

Satanstoe. Novel by J. Fenimore Cooper (1845). First of a trilogy, including also *The Chainbearer* (1845), and *The Redskins* (1845), which records the history of three generations of a New York family.

Saturday Evening Gazette. Boston, Mass. Founded 1814, by William Burdick, and edited and published by William Warland Clapp, and William Warland Clapp, Jr. Noted for its theatrical news. The younger Clapp's *Records of the Boston Stage* appeared in it. Expired 1906.

Saturday Evening Post. Philadelphia, Pa. Weekly magazine. Founded Aug. 4, 1821, by Charles Alexander and Samuel C. Atkinson. It claims descent from the *Pennsylvania Gazette.* T. Cottrell Clarke was editor until 1826. John Du Solle, who had bought an interest in the paper, sold it in 1840 to Charles Jacobs Peterson, who in 1843 sold it to Samuel D. Patterson. He in turn sold it in 1848 to Edmund Deacon and Henry Peterson, who published it under the firm name Deacon & Peterson. Peterson was editor, 1846–74. In 1873, Peterson sold his interest to the Post Publishing Co. The *Post* had been a newspaper, but gradually changed into a weekly magazine, the change being clearly indicated in 1871 by the omission of legal notices. The *Post* entered upon its modern and successful period in 1897, when it was bought by Cyrus H. K. Curtis. Upon his death in 1933, he was succeeded by George Horace Lorimer, who in turn was succeeded in 1937 by Walter D. Fuller. The *Post* had begun to feature fiction during the editorship of Henry Peterson, and since 1897 had specialized in this field, proving a stimulus to short-story writings in the United States. It became equally known for its feature articles on topical material. Ceased publication 1969. *See* Otto Friedrich's *Decline and Fall* (1970).

Saturday Night. Philadelphia, Pa. Family journal. Founded 1865, by James Elverson. Expired 1902.

Saturday Press. New York. Weekly. Founded 1858, by Henry Clapp, Edward H. Clapp, and Edward Howland. Walt Whitman and William Winter were contributors in 1865, when it was revived after a five year suspension. Mark Twain's *The Celebrated Jumping Frog of Calaveras County* appeared in it, Nov. 18, 1865. "Josh Billings" made his debut in the same issue. Clapp was known as the "Prince of the Bohemians." Expired 1866.

Saturday Review. New York. Weekly literary review. Founded as the *Saturday Review of Literature,* in 1924, by Christopher Morley and William Rose Benét. The name was changed in 1952 after new departments were added. Henry Seidel Canby was editor in chief for many years, assisted by Amy Loveman, Harrison Smith, Bernard De Voto, George Stevens and others. Bought by McCall Corp., 1961.

Saturday Visiter. Baltimore, Md. Weekly magazine. Founded 1832, by Charles F. Cloud, as the *Saturday Morning Visiter.* Lambert A. Wilmer was editor in 1832, and was followed by John H. Hewitt. In 1833 it offered a prize of one hundred dollars, which was won by Edgar Allan Poe's *MS. Found in a Bottle.* Merged with the *National Era,* c. 1847.

SAUL, GEORGE BRANDON (Nov. 1, 1901–); b. Shoemakersville, Pa. Educator, author. *The Cup of Sand* (poems, 1923); *Bronze Woman* (1930); *Unimagined Rose* (1937); *Selected Lyrics* (1947); *Elusive Stallion* (1948); *Shadow of the Three Queens* (1953); *Prolegomena to the Study of Yeats's Poems* (1957); *Prolegomena to the Study of Yeats's Plays* (1958); *Luminous Wind* (1966); *Quintet: Essays on Five American Women Poets* (1967). Editor: *The Age of Yeats* (1964); *Owl's Watch* (1965). Prof. English, University of Connecticut, since 1942.

SAUL, LEON JOSEPH (Apr. 26, 1901–); b. New York. Psychiatrist. *Emotional Maturity—The Development and Dynamics of Personality* (1947); *The Bases of Human Behavior* (1951); *The Hostile Mind* (1956); *Technique and Practice of Psychoanalysis* (1958); *Fidelity and Infidelity: What Makes or Breaks a Marriage* (1967). Prof. clinical psychiatry, University of Pennsylvania, since 1948.

SAULNIER, RAYMOND J. (Sept. 20, 1908–); b. Hamilton, Mass. Educator, economist. *Contemporary Monetary Theory* (1938); *Costs and Returns on Farm Mortgage Lending* (1949); *Urban Mortgage Lending by Life Insurance Companies* (1950); *Federal Lending and Loan Insurance* (with others, 1958); *Strategy of Economic Policy* (1962). Prof. economics, Columbia University, since 1949.

SAUNDERS, CHARLES FRANCIS (b. July 12, 1859); b. in Bucks Co., Pa. Author. *In a Poppy Garden* (1903); *A Window in Arcady* (1911); *With the Flowers and Trees in California* (1914); *The California Padres and Their Missions* (1915); *Finding the Worth While in California* (1916); *Finding the Worth While in the Southwest* (1918); *The Southern Sierras of California* (1923); *A Little Book of California Missions* (1925); *Capistrano Nights* (with St. John O'Sullivan, 1930); etc.

SAUNDERS, CHARLES HENRY (Sept. 25, 1818–July 15, 1857); b. Boston, Mass. Playwright. *The Gambler* (prod. 1844); *The Paint King* (prod. 1845); *The Pirate's Legacy; or, The Wrecker's Fate* (prod. 1848); *The North End Caulker* (prod. 1851).

SAUNDERS, DERO AMES (Sept. 27, 1913–); b. Starkville, Miss. Public relations executive. Contributor to *Why Do People Buy?* (1953); *The Changing American Market* (1954). Editor: *The Portable Gibbon* (1952). Co-editor: *The History of Rome* (1958). Executive Editor, *Forbes* magazine, since 1966.

SAUNDERS, FREDERIC (Aug. 14, 1807–Dec. 12, 1902); b. London. Librarian, compiler, author. *Memories of the Great Metropolis* (1852); *Salad for the Solitary* (anon., 1853); *Salad for the Social* (anon., 1856); *Mosaics* (anon., 1859); *New-York in a Nutshell* (anon., 1859); *Festival of Song: A Series of Evenings with the Poets* (anon., 1866); *Evenings with the Sacred Poets* (anon., 1869); *About Women, Love, and Marriage* (1874); *Pastime Papers* (1885); *The Story of Some Famous Books* (1887); *Stray Leaves of Literature* (1888); *Character Studies, with Some Personal Recollections* (1894); etc. Editor: *Homes of American Authors* (with Henry T. Tuckerman, 1853). Asst. librarian, Astor Library, New York, 1859–76, librarian, 1876–96.

SAUNDERS, JOHN BERTRAND DECUSANCE MORANT (July 2, 1903–); b. Grahamstown, South Africa. Educator, author. *Illustrations from the Works of Andreas Vesalius* (with C. D. O'Malley, 1950); *Leonardo Da Vinci on the Human Body* (ed., trans., 1952); *Ancient Egyptian and Cnidian Medicine* (with R. O. Steuer, 1958). Prof. anatomy, University of California, San Francisco, since 1938.

SAUNDERS, JOHN MONK (Nov. 22, 1897–Mar. 11, 1940); b. Hinckley, Minn. Author. *Single Lady* (1931). Wrote many aviation scenarios for the motion pictures. Associate editor, *American Magazine*, 1924.

SAUNDERS, LOUISE (Mrs. Maxwell Evarts Perkins) (May 8, 1893–); b. New York. Author. *Magic Lanterns: A Book of Plays* (1923); *The Knave of Hearts* (1925).

Saunders, Richard. Name under which Benjamin Franklin wrote his *Poor Richard's Almanac.*

SAUNDERS, WILLIAM LAURENCE (July 30, 1835–Apr. 2, 1891); b. Raleigh, N.C. Editor, historian. Editor: *The Colonial Records of North Carolina.* Founder (with Peter M. Hale), the *Raleigh Observer*, 1876; editor, 1876–79.

Saur, Christopher. See Christopher Sower.

SAVAGE, [Charles] COURTENAY (July 29, 1890–Aug. 23, 1946); b. New York. Playwright, author. *The Buzzard* (with Wallace Peck, prod. 1928); *The Queen of Kingdom Corners* (1929); *The Queen at Home* (prod. 1930); *The Flying Vagabond* (1931); *Nellie was a Lady* (prod. 1933); *Loose Moments* (with Bertram Hobbs, prod. 1935); *Forever and Forever* (1937); *Home Is the Hero* (1945); etc.

SAVAGE, ELIZABETH FITZGERALD (1918–); b. Hingham, Mass. Author. *Summer Pride* (1960); *But Not for Love* (1970).

SAVAGE, HOWARD JAMES (May 10, 1886–); b. Meriden, Conn. Author. *Games and Sports in British Schools and Universities* (1927); *American College Athletics* (1929); *Current Developments in American College Sport* (1931); *Fruit of an Impulse: Forty-five Years of The Carnegie Foundation* (1953).

SAVAGE, JAMES (July 13, 1784–Mar. 8, 1873); b. Boston, Mass. Antiquarian. Editor: *The History of New England from 1630 to 1649; by John Winthrop, Esq.*, 2v. (1825–26); *A Genealogical Dictionary of the First Settlers of New England*, 4v. (1860–62).

SAVAGE, JOHN (Dec. 13, 1828–Oct. 9, 1888); b. Dublin. Journalist, author. *'98 and '48: The Modern Revolutionary History and Literature of Ireland* (1856); *Sybil* (prod. 1858); *Faith and Fancy* (poems, 1864); *Poems* (1870); etc. His best-known poem was "The Starry Flag."

SAVAGE, MINOT JUDSON (June 10, 1841–May 22, 1918); b. Norridgewock, Me. Congregational clergyman, lecturer, author. *Bluffton* (1878); *Belief in God* (1881); *Poems* (1882); *The Religious Life* (1886); *To My Creed* (1887); *Life* (1890); *America to England, and Other Poems* (1905); etc.

SAVAGE, PHILIP HENRY (Feb. 11, 1868–June 4, 1899); b. North Brookfield, Mass. Poet. *First Poems and Fragments* (1895); *The Poems* (1898); both reprinted in the *Poems of Philip Henry Savage*, ed. by Daniel Gregory Mason (1901).

SAVAGE, RICHARD HENRY (June 12, 1846–1903). Author. *My Official Wife* (1891); *For Life and Love* (1893); *Miss Devereux of the Mariquita* (1895); *After Many Years* (poems, 1895); *An Exile from London* (1896); *A Modern Corsair* (1897); *Brought to Bay* (1900); etc.

SAVAGE, SARAH (1785–1837). Author. *The Factory Girl* (anon., 1814); *James Talbot* (anon., 1821); *Life of Philip, the Indian Chief* (anon., 1827); *Trial and Self-Discipline* (anon., 1835).

SAVAGE, THOMAS. Author. *Bargain with God* (1953); *Trust in Chariots* (1962); *The Power of the Dog* (1967); *The Liar* (1969); *Daddy's Girl* (1970).

SAVELLE, MAX (Jan. 8, 1896–); b. Mobile, Ala. Educator. *George Morgan, Colony Builder* (1932); *The Diplomatic History of the Canadian Boundary, 1749–63* (1940); *Foundations of American Civilization* (1942); *Seeds of Liberty* (1948); *A Short History of American Civilization* (with T. McDowell, 1957); *Is Liberalism Dead? and Other Essays* (1967); etc. General editor: *A History of World Civilization*, 2v. (1957). Prof. history, Stanford University, 1932–47; University of Washington, since 1947.

SAVERY, WILLIAM (Sept. 14, 1750–June 19, 1804); b. Philadelphia, Pa. Quaker preacher, author. *A Journal of the Life, Travels, and Religious Labors of William Savery* (1837). *See* Francis R. Taylor's *Life of William Savery* (1925).

Saw-Mill; or, A Yankee Trick, The. Comic opera by Micah Hawkins (prod. 1824).

SAWYER, CAROLINE M[ehitabel Fisher] (Mrs. Thomas Jefferson Sawyer) (Dec. 8, 1812–May 19, 1894); b. Newton, Mass. Editor, author. *The Merchant's Widow, and Other Tales* (1841); *The Juvenile Library*, 4v. (1845); *The Rose of Sharon*, 8v. (1850–58). Editor, the *Ladies' Repository*, 1861–64, etc. *See* Richard Eddy's The *Life of Thomas J. Sawyer ... and of Caroline M. Sawyer* (1900).

SAWYER, EUGENE T[aylor] (1846–Oct. 29, 1924). Author, dime novelist. *The Life and Career of Tiburcio Vasquez* (1875); *Millions at Stake; or, The Gambler Detective* (1884); *The Maltese Cross* (1888); *The Los Huecos Mystery* (1900); *Old Quartz* (1900); etc.; including dime novels of the "Old Cap Collier" and the "Nicholas Carter" libraries.

SAWYER, LEMUEL (1777–Jan. 9, 1852); b. Camden Co., S.C. Author. *Blackbeard: A Comedy* (1824); *The Wreck of Honor: A Tragedy* (1826); *Printz Hall* (1839); *A Biography of John Randolph of Roanoke* (1844); *Autobiography of Lemuel Sawyer* (1844).

SAWYER, RUTH (Mrs. Albert C. Durand) (Aug. 5, 1880–); b. Boston, Mass. Author. *The Primrose Ring* (1915); *Seven Miles to Arden* (1916); *The Silver Sixpence* (1921); *Gladiola Murphy* (1923); *Folkhouse: The Autobiography of a Home* (1932); *Gallant: The Story of Storm Veblen* (1936); *Roller Skates* (1936); *The Least One* (1941); *The Little Red Horse* (1950); *Maggie Rose* (1952); *A Cottage for Betsy* (1954); *The Enchanted Schoolhouse* (1956); *The Way of the Storyteller* (1966); etc.

SAXE, JOHN G[odfrey] (June 2, 1816–Mar. 31, 1887); b. Highgate, Vt. Poet. *Progress: A Satirical Poem* (1846); *Humorous and Satirical Poems* (1850); *Poems* (1850); *The Money-King, and Other Poems* (1860); *Clever Stories of Many Nations Rendered in Rhyme* (1865); *The Masquerade, and Other Poems* (1866); *Leisure-Day Rhymes* (1875); *Selections from the Poems* (1905); etc. Editor, the *Burlington Sentinel*, 1850–56. *See* W. H. Crockett's *Vermonters* (1931).

SAXON, CHARLES DAVID (Nov. 13, 1920–); b. Brooklyn, N.Y. Artist, author. *Oh, Happy, Happy, Happy!* (1960); *Cold Comfort Farm* (1964). Cartoonist: *The New Yorker* magazine.

SAXON, LYLE (Sept. 4, 1891–Apr. 9, 1946); b. Baton Rouge, La. Author. *Father Mississippi* (1927); *Fabulous New Orleans* (1928); *Old Louisiana* (1929); *LaFitte, the Pirate* (1930); *Children of Strangers* (1937); etc. Editor, *New Orleans City Guide* (1938); *Friends of Joe Gilmore* (1948).

SAXTON, ALEXANDER [Plaisted]; b. Great Barrington, Mass. Novelist. *Grand Crossing* (1943); *The Great Midland* (1948); *Bright Web in the Darkness* (1958).

SAXTON, MARK (Nov., 1914–); b. New York. Editor, author, publisher. *Danger Road* (1939); *Broken Circle* (1941); *Year of August* (1943); *Prepare for Rage* (1947); *Paper Chase* (1964). Director and editor-in-chief Gambit, Inc. since 1968.

SAY, THOMAS (June 29, 1787–Oct. 10, 1834); b. Philadelphia, Pa. Naturalist, author. Called the "Father of Descriptive Entomology in America." *American Entomology*, 3v. (1824–28); *Complete Writings on the Conchology of the United States*, ed. by W. G. Binney (1858); *The Complete Writings ... on the Entomology of North America*, ed. by J. L. Le Conte, 2v. (1859); etc. Prof. natural history, University of Pennsylvania, 1822–28.

SAYLER, HARRY LINCOLN (Feb. 13, 1863–1913); b. Little York, O. Author of boys' books. Pen names, "Ashton Lamar," "Elliott Whitney," "Gordon Stuart." *Johnny Hep* (1908); *The Air Ship Boys* (1909); *The Airship Boys Due North* (1910); *Battling the Bighorn* (1911); *White Tiger of Nepal* (1912); *Giant Moose* (1912); *The Blind Lion of the Congo* (1912); *Black Fox of Yukon* (1917); *Boss of the Big Horns* (1930).

SAYLOR, HENRY HODGMAN (May 5, 1880–Aug. 22, 1967); b. Baltimore, Md. Architect, editor, author. *Bungalows* (1910); *Making a Rose Garden* (1912); *The Book of Annuals* (1913); *Tinkering with Tools* (1924); *Dictionary of Architecture* (1952). Editor: *Architectural Styles for Country Houses* (1912); *Collecting Antiques for the Home* (1938). Editor, *Architecture*, 1926–36; *Journal of the American Institute of Architects*, 1944–57.

SAYLOR, [John] GALEN (Dec. 12, 1902–); b. Carleton, Neb. Educator. *Secondary Education: Basic Principles and Practices* (with William Alexander, 1950); *Curriculum Planning For Better Teachers* (with same, 1954); *Modern Secondary Education* (1959); *Curriculum Planning for Modern Schools* (1966); etc. Prof. secondary education, University of Nebraska, since 1940.

SAYLOR, OLIVER M[artin] (Oct. 23, 1887–); b. Huntington, Ind. Drama critic, author. *Russia, White or Red* (1919); *The Russian Theatre under the Revolution* (1920); *Our American Theatre* (1923); *Max Reinhardt and His Theatre* (1924); *Revolt in the Arts* (1930); etc. On staff, the *Indianapolis News*, 1909–20, etc.

Sayonara. Novel by James Michener (1954). Love affair of an American air force major and a Japanese girl.

Sayre, Gordon. Pen name of Josiah Pitts Woolfolk.

SAYRE, JOEL (Dec. 13, 1900–); b. Marion, Ind. Author. *Rackety Rax* (1932); *Persion Gulf Command* (1945); *The House Without a Roof* (1948); etc. For many years staff writer and correspondent, *The New Yorker.*

SAYRE, PAUL (July 26, 1894–Aug. 10, 1959); b. Hinsdale, Ill. Educator, author. *Life of Roscoe Pound* (1948); *Philosophy of Law* (1954); etc. Editor: *Interpretations of Modern Legal Philosophies* (1947); *Essays on Family Law* (1950). Prof. law, State University of Iowa, from 1930.

SAYRE, THEODORE BURT (Dec. 18, 1874–Nov. 1954); b. New York. Playwright, author. *Charles O'Malley* (1897); *Two Summer Girls and I* (1898); *The Son of Carley Croft* (1900); *A Classical Cowboy* (1900); *Tom Moore: An Unhistorical Romance* (1902); *Edmund Burke* (1905); *O'Neill of Derry* (1907); *The Wearing of the Green* (1910); *The Irish Dragoon* (1915); etc.

SAYRE, WALLACE STANLEY (June 24, 1905–); b. near Point Pleasant, W.Va. Political scientist. *Your Government* (1932); *Outline of American Government* (1933); *Training for Specialized Mission Personnel* (with Clarence Thurber, 1952); *Governing New York City* (with Herbert Kaufman, 1960).

SCAIFE, ROGER LIVINGSTON (Aug. 14, 1875–Oct. 19, 1951); b. Boston, Mass. Publisher, author. *Confessions of a Debutante* (anon., 1913); *Cape Coddities* (1920); *The Reflections of a T.B.M.* (anon., 1922); etc. With Houghton, Mifflin Co., for many years; vice-president, Little, Brown & Co., Boston, from 1934.

Scanlan's Monthly. New York. Magazine. Founded 1970 by Warren Hinckle III and Sydney Zion. Radical appraisal of matters of public interest. Expired 1971.

SCARBOROUGH, DOROTHY (d. Nov. 7, 1935); b. Mt. Carmel, Tex. Author. *Fugitive Verse* (1912); *The Supernatural in Modern English Fiction* (1917); *From a Southern Porch* (1919); *In the Land of Cotton* (1923); *On the Trail of Negro Folk-Songs* (with Ola Lee Gulledge, 1925); *The Wind* (anon., 1925); *A Song Catcher in the Southern Mountains* (1937); etc. Editor: *Famous Modern Ghost Stories* (1921); etc.

SCARBOROUGH, GEORGE MOORE (June 3, 1875–); b. Mt. Carmel, Tex. Playwright. *The Girl* (Prod. 1913), rewritten as *Oklahoma* (prod. 1916), again rewritten as *The Heart of Wetona* (with David Belasco, prod. 1916); *The Son-Daughter* (with David Belasco, prod. 1919); *Bluebonnet* (prod. 1920); *The Mad Dog* (prod. 1921).

Scarecrow, The. Play by Percy MacKaye (prod. 1911). Based on Nathaniel Hawthorne.

Scarlet Letter. Famous letter by William L. Yancey (1858). It predicted the forthcoming secession of the Southern states.

Scarlet Letter, The. Novel by Nathaniel Hawthorne (1850). Puritan Boston two hundred years ago, with the leading character, Hester Prynne, involved in a love triangle with her lover, Arthur Dimmesdale, and her husband, Roger Chillingworth. As a mark of her sin, she was forced to wear a scarlet "A," indicating adultery.

Scarlet Sister Mary. Novel by Julia Peterkin (1928). A chronicle of a Negro woman's life in South Carolina.

Scarlett, Rebecca. Pen name of Katherine Newlin Burt.

Scenes, Incidents, and Adventures in the Pacific Ocean. By T. Jacobs (1844).

SCHAAP, RICHARD JAY (Sept 27, 1934–   ); b. Brooklyn, N.Y. Columnist, author. *Mickey Mantle* (1961); *Paul Hornung* (1962); *Illustrated History of the Olympics* (1963); *Turned On* (1967); *The Masters* (1970); etc.

SCHACHNER, NATHAN (Jan. 16, 1895–Oct. 2, 1955); b. New York. Author. *Aaron Burr* (1937); *The Mediaeval Universities* (1938); *By the Dim Lamps* (1941); *The King's Passenger* (1942); *The Sun Shines West* (1943); *The Wanderer* (1944); *Alexander Hamilton* (1946); *Thomas Jefferson* (1951); *Space Lawyer* (1953); *The Founding Fathers* (1954); etc.

SCHACHTEL, IRVING I. (Mar. 2, 1909–); b. London. Lawyer, author. *Patent Pools and the Federal Anti-Trust Laws* (1932); *Conservation of Children's Hearing* (1948); etc.

SCHAEFER, JACK WARNER (Nov. 19, 1907–); b. Cleveland, O. Novelist, editor. *Shane* (1949); *First Blood* (1953); *The Big Range* (stories, 1953); *The Canyon* (1953); *The Pioneers* (stories, 1954); *Company of Cowards* (1957); *The Kean Land and Other Stories* (1959); *Old Ramon* (1960); *The Plainsman* (1963); *Monte Walsh* (1963); *Stubby Pringle's Christmas* (1964); *Heroes Without Glory* (1965); *Collected Stories* (1966); *Mavericks* (1967); *New Mexico* (1967); *Collected Short Novels* (1967); etc. Editor and publisher, *Theatre News*, 1935–40; *The Movies*, 1939–41.

SCHAFER, JOSEPH (Dec. 29, 1867–1941); b. Muscoda, Wis. Editor, author. *The Pacific Slope and Alaska* (1905); *History of the Pacific Northwest* (1905); *Francis Parkman* (1923); *Carl Schurz, Militant Liberal* (1930); etc. Editor: *Intimate Letters of Carl Schurz* (1929); *California Letters of Lucius Fairchild* (1931); *Memoirs of Jeremiah Curtin* (1940). Editor, *Wisconsin Magazine of History*. History dept., University of Oregon, 1900–20; superintendent, State Historical Society of Wisconsin, from 1920.

SCHAFF, DAVID SCHLEY (Oct. 17, 1852–Mar. 2, 1941); b. Mercersburg, Pa., son of Philip Schaff. Presbyterian clergyman, educator, author. *Commentary on Acts* (1882); *Life of Philip Schaff* (1897); *History of the Christian Church*, 2v. (1907–10); *John Huss* (1915). Co-editor: *Schaff-Herzog Encyclopedia*, 4v. (1883). Prof. ecclesiastical history, Western Theological Seminary, 1903–25.

SCHAFF, PHILIP (Jan. 1, 1819–Oct. 20, 1893); b. Chur, Switz. Educator, editor, church historian. *The Principle of Protestantism* (1845); *History of the Christian Church* (1853); *A Companion to the Greek Testament and the English Version* (1883); etc. Editor: *A Commentary on the Holy Scriptures*, 25v. (1865–80); *The Religious Encyclopedia*, 3v. (1882–84); etc. Founder, *Deutsche Kirchenfreund*, 1846, the first theological journal in the German language in the United States. President, Mercersburg Theological Seminary, 1844–65; prof. theology, Union Theological Seminary, New York, 1870–93. See David S. Schaff's *The Life of Philip Schaff* (1897).

SCHAFFER, AARON (May 18, 1894–Feb. 24, 1957); b. Baltimore, Md. Educator, author. *Selected Poems* (1916); *George Rudolf Weckherlin* (1918); *Parnassus in France: Currents and Cross-Currents in Nineteenth Century French Lyric Poetry* (1929); *Genres of Parnassian Poetry* (1944); etc. Prof. French, University of Texas, from 1928.

SCHAPIRO, J[acob] SALWYN (Dec. 19, 1879–); b. Hudson, N.Y. Educator, author. *Social Reform and the Reformation* (1909); *Modern and Contemporary European History* (1918); *Modern Times in Europe* (1927); *Condorcet and the Rise of Liberalism* (1934); *Liberalism and the Challenge of Fascism* (1949); *World in Crisis* (1950); *Anticlericalism: Conflict Between Church and State in France, Italy, and Spain* (1967); etc. History dept., College of the City of New York, since 1907, prof., since 1922.

SCHAPIRO, MEYER (Sept. 23, 1904–); b. Shavly, Lith. Educator, art critic. *Vincent Van Gogh* (1950); *Paul Cézanne* (1952). Prof. fine arts, Columbia University, since 1952.

SCHARF, JOHN THOMAS (May 1, 1843–Feb. 28, 1898); b. Baltimore, Md. Lawyer, historian. *The Chronicles of Baltimore* (1874); *History of Maryland*, 3v. (1879); *History of Philadelphia* (1884); *History of the Confederate States Navy* (1887); *History of the State of Delaware* (1888); etc. His collection of Americana is now in the library of the Johns Hopkins University.

SCHARPER, PHILIP JENKINS (Sept. 15, 1919–); b. Baltimore, Md. Editor. *American Catholics: A Protestant-Jewish View* (1959); *Torah and Gospel* (1966). Editor-in-chief, Sheed and Ward.

SCHARY, DORE (Aug. 31, 1905–); b. Newark, N.J. Motion-picture producer, playwright. *Sunrise at Campobello* (prod. 1958).

SCHAUB, EDWARD LEROY (Aug. 13, 1881–May 24, 1953); b. Decorah, Ia. Educator, editor. Editor: *Immanuel Kant* (1925); *Philosophy Today* (1928); *Spinoza* (1933); *William Torrey Harris* (1936). Editor, *The Monist*, 1926–37. Prof. philosophy, Northwestern University, 1913–46.

SCHAUFFLER, ROBERT HAVEN (Apr. 8, 1879–Nov. 24, 1964); b. Brünn, Austria, of American parentage. Author, compiler. *Through Italy with the Poets* (1908); *Romantic*

America (1913); *Fiddler's Luck* (1920); *The White Comrade and Other Poems* (1923); *Peter Pantheism* (1925); *Plays for Our American Holidays*, 4v. (1928); *Hobnails in Eden* (1929); *Beethoven, the Man Who Freed Music*, 2v. (1929); *A Manthology* (1931); *The Unknown Brahms* (1933); *The Days We Celebrate*, 4v. (1940); *Florestan: The Life and Works of Robert Schumann* (1945); *Franz Schubert, the Ariel of Music* (1949); etc. Has compiled and edited books on Christmas, Washington's Birthday, Lincoln's Birthday, Easter, Arbor Day, Thanksgiving, Flag Day, Mother's Day, Halloween, Graduation Day, Columbus Day, Lincoln's Birthday, Memorial Day, Independence Day, etc.

SCHECTER, SOLOMON (Dec. 7, 1850–Nov. 15, 1915); b. Fokshaa, Rum. Rabbi, educator, Hebraist, author. *Studies in Judaism*, 3 series (1896, 1908, 1924); *Seminary Addresses, and Other Papers* (1915); etc. One of the editors of the *Jewish Encyclopedia*, 12v. (1901–06). President, Jewish Theological Seminary, New York, 1902–15.

SCHEER, JULIAN WEISEL (Feb. 20, 1926–); b. Richmond, Va. Government official, author. *Tweetsie: The Blue Ridge Stemwinder* (1958); *Choo-Choo: The Charlie Justice Story* (1958); *First Into Outer Space* (1959); *Rain Makes Applesauce* (1964). With NASA since 1962.

SCHEER, ROBERT (Apr. 4, 1936–   ); b. New York. Editor, author. *Cuba: Tragedy on Our Hemisphere* (with M. Zeitlin, 1961; retitled *Cuba: An American Tragedy*, 1962); *How the United States Got Involved in Vietnam* (1965). Editor, *The Diary of Che Guevara, Bolivia: November 7, 1966–October 7, 1967* (1968). Editor, *Ramparts* magazine, since 1965.

SCHEFFAUER, HERMAN GEORGE (Feb. 3, 1878–1927); b. San Francisco, Calif. Poet, playwright. *Of Both Worlds* (poems, 1903); *Sons of Baldur* (prod. 1908); *Looms of Life* (1908); *The Masque of the Elements* (1911); *Drake in California: Ballads and Poems* (1912); etc. He wrote plays for the Bohemian Grove productions, and was a member of the literary colony at Carmel, California.

SCHEFFLER, ISRAEL (Nov. 25, 1923–   ); b. New York. Educator, author. *The Language of Education* (1960); *The Anatomy of Education* (1963); *Conditions of Knowledge* (1965). Editor: *Science and Subjectivity* (1967); etc. Prof. education and philosophy, Harvard University, since 1961.

SCHELE DE VERE, MAXIMILIAN (Nov. 1, 1820–May 12, 1898); b. Wexio, Swe. Educator, philologist, author. *Outlines of Comparative Philology* (1853); *Stray Leaves from the Book of Nature* (1855); *Studies in English: or, Glimpses of the Inner Life of Our Language* (1867); *The Great Empress: A Portrait* (1870); *Wonders of the Deep* (1871); *Americanisms: The English of the New World* (1872); *Modern Magic* (1873); etc. Professor, modern languages, University of Virginia, 1844–95. See Philip A. Bruce's *History of the University of Virginia*, v. 3, (1921).

SCHELLING, FELIX EMANUEL (Sept. 3, 1858–Dec. 15, 1945); b. New Albany, Ind. Educator, author. *The Queen's Progress* (1904); *Elizabethan Drama*, 2v. (1908); *The English Lyric* (1913); *English Drama* (1914); *Appraisements and Asperities as to Some Contemporary Writers* (1922); *Elizabethan Playwrights* (1925); *Shakespeare Biography* (1927); etc. Editor: *A Book of Elizabethan Lyrics* (1895); *A Book of Seventeenth Century Lyrics* (1899); etc. Prof. English literature, University of Pennsylvania, from 1893.

SCHELLING, THOMAS CROMBLE (Apr. 14, 1921–); b. Oakland, Cal. Economist. *National Income Behavior* (1951); *International Economics* (1958); *The Strategy of Conflict* (1960); *Arms and Influence* (1966).

SCHEM, ALEXANDER JACOB (Mar. 16, 1826–May 21, 1881); b. Wiedenbruck, Westphalia, Ger. Encyclopedist, editor, author. *The War in the East* (1878). Editor: *Deutsch-*

Amerikanisches Conversations-Lexikon, 11v. (1869–74); *The Cyclopedia of Education* (with Henry Kiddle, 1877); etc.

SCHERER, JAMES AUGUSTIN BROWN (May 22, 1870–Feb. 15, 1944); b. Salisbury, N.C. Educator, author. *Four Princes* (1902); *The Holy Grail* (1906); *The First Forty-Niner* (1925); *The Romance of Japan* (1926); *Japan: Whither?* (1932); *"The Lion of the Vigilantes": William T. Coleman and the Life of Old San Francisco* (1939); and many books on modern Japan. President, California Institute of Technology, Pasadena, 1908–20; director, Southwest Museum, Los Angeles, 1926–31, etc.

SCHERER, PAUL EHRMAN (June 22, 1892–Mar. 26, 1969); b. Mt. Holly Springs, Pa. Lutheran clergyman, author. *When God Hides* (1934); *Facts that Undergird Life* (1938); *The Place Where Thou Standest* (1942); *For We Have This Treasure* (1944); *Event in Eternity* (1945). Prof. homiletics, Union Theological Seminary, 1946–60.

SCHERF, MARGARET (Apr. 1, 1908–Mar. 26, 1969); b. Fairmont, W.Va. Author. *The Corpse Grew a Beard* (1940); *The Case of the Kippered Corpse* (1941); *They Came to Kill* (1942); *The Owl in the Cellar* (1945); *Always Murder a Friend* (1948); *The Gun in Daniel Webster's Bust* (1949); *The Curious Custard Pie* (1950); *The Green Plaid Pants* (1951); *The Elk and the Evidence* (1952); *Dead: Senate Office Building* (1953); *Glass on the Stairs* (1954); *The Cautious Overshoes* (1956); *Judicial Body* (1957); *Never Turn Your Back* (1958).

SCHERMAN, HARRY (Feb. 1, 1887–Nov. 12, 1969); b. Montreal, Can. Book club executive, author. *The Promises Men Live By* (1938); *The Real Danger in Our Gold* (1940); *Will We Have Inflation?* (1941); *The Last Best Hope of Earth* (1942). Founder (with Robert K. Haas and Max B. Sackheim), the Book-of-the-Month Club, New York, 1926; pres. 1931–50; chairman of the board, since 1950.

SCHERMERHORN, JAMES (Mar. 13, 1865–Dec. 2, 1941); b. Hudson, Mich. Editor, author. *Testing the Beatitudes* (1915); *Schermerhorn's Stories* (1928); *Schermerhorn's Speeches* (1930). Founder, the *Detroit Times,* 1900, president, 1900–21.

SCHERR, MARIE, b. New York. Author. Pen name "Marie Cher." *Life in Still Life* (1926); *Up at the Villa* (1929); *Charlotte Corday and Certain Men of the Revolutionary Torment* (1929); *Poison at Court* (1931); etc.

SCHEVILL, FERDINAND (Nov. 12, 1868–Dec. 10, 1954); b. Cincinnati, O. Educator, author. *Political History of Modern Europe* (1899); *The Making of Modern Germany* (1916); *Karl Bitter* (1917); *The History of the Balkan Peninsula* (1922); *A History of Europe* (1925); *History of Florence* (1936); *The Medici* (1950); etc. History dept., University of Chicago, 1892–1937.

SCHIFF, DOROTHY (Mar. 11, 1903–); b. New York. Publisher. Director, *New York Post,* 1939–42; pres. and publisher, 1942; owner and publisher, since 1943.

SCHILLER, A. ARTHUR (Sept. 7, 1902–); b. San Francisco, Cal. Educator. Author or co-author: *Cases in the Law of Agency* (1948); *The Formation of Federal Indonesia, 1945–1949* (1955); etc. Prof. law, Columbia University, since 1949.

SCHILLER, FERDINAND CANNING SCOTT (1864–Aug. 6, 1937); b. in Germany. Educator, author. *Riddles of the Sphinx* (1894); *Humanism* (1903); *Formal Logic* (1912); *Problem of Belief* (1924); *Tantalus; or, The Future of Man* (1924); *Cassandra; or, The Future of the British Empire* (1926); *Must Philosophers Disagree?* (1934); etc. Prof. philosophy, University of Southern California.

SCHILPP, PAUL ARTHUR (Feb. 6, 1897–); b. Dillenberg, Hesse-Nassau, Ger. Methodist clergyman, educator, author. *Commemorative Essays* (1930); *The Quest for Religious Realism* (1938); *Kant's Pre-Critical Ethics* (1938). Editor: *Philos-*

ophy of Alfred North Whitehead (1941); *Philosophy of Bertrand Russell* (1944); *Albert Einstein, Philosopher-Scientist* (1949); *Human Nature and Progress* (1954); *Philosophy of Karl Jaspers* (1958); *The Philosophy of Martin Buber* (with M. S. Friedman, 1967). Philosophy dept., Northwestern University, since 1936.

SCHINZ, ALBERT (Mar. 9, 1870–Dec. 19, 1943); b. Neuchâtel, Switz. Educator, author. *J. J. Rousseau, a Forerunner of Pragmatism* (1909); *Anti-Pragmatism* (1909); etc. Wrote much in English and French on J. J. Rousseau and his period. Prof. French, Smith College, 1913–28, University of Pennsylvania, 1928–41.

SCHISGAL, MURRAY (Nov. 25, 1926–   ); b. New York. Playwright. *The Typist and The Tiger* (1963); *Knit One, Purl Two* (1963); *Luv* (1964); *Fragments, Windows and Other Plays* (1965).

SCHLAMM, WILLIAM S. (June 10, 1904–); b. Przemysl, Aust.-Hung. Editor, author. *Dictatorship of the Lie* (1936); *This Second War of Independence* (1940); *Germany and the East-West Crisis* (1959); *Who Is A Jew?* (1964); etc. Editor, *Freeman,* 1950–53; *National Review,* 1955–57.

SCHLESINGER, ARTHUR M[eier] (Feb. 27, 1888–Oct. 30, 1965); b. Xenia, O. Educator, author. *The Colonial Merchants and the American Revolution* (1917); *Salmon Portland Chase* (1919); *New Viewpoints in American History* (1922); *The Rise of the City* (1933); *Political and Social History of the United States, 1829–1925* (1925); *The New Deal in Action* (1938); *Learning How to Behave: A Historical Study of American Etiquette Books* (1946); *Paths to the Present* (1949); *The American as Reformer* (1950); *Prelude to Independence: The Newspaper War on Britain, 1764–76* (1957); etc. Prof. history, Harvard University, 1925–54.

SCHLESINGER, ARTHUR M[eier], JR. (Oct. 15, 1917–); b. Columbus, O. Educator, author. *Orestes A. Brownson: A Pilgrim's Progress* (1939); *The Age of Jackson* (1945, Pulitzer Prize for history, 1946); *The Vital Center* (1949); *The General and the President* (with Richard H. Rovere, 1951); *The Age of Roosevelt,* 3v.: *The Crisis of the Old Order* (1957); *The Coming of the New Deal* (1958); *The Politics of Upheaval* (1960); *The Bitter Heritage: Vietnam and American Democracy 1941–1966* (1967); etc. Co-editor: *Harvard Guide to American History* (1954); *Guide to Politics—1954* (1954); *A Thousand Days* (1965, Pulitzer Prize, 1966). Prof. history, City College of the City University of New York.

SCHLINK, FREDERICK JOHN (Oct. 26, 1891–); b. Peoria, Ill. Mechanical engineer, physicist, author. *Eat, Drink, and Be Wary* (1935). Co-author: *Your Money's Worth* (1927); *One Hundred Million Guinea Pigs* (1933); *Meat Three Times a Day* (1946); *Don't You Believe It!* (1966).

SCHMECKEBIER, LAURENCE E[li] (Mar. 1, 1906–); b. Chicago Heights, Ill. Educator, author. *Handbook of Italian Painting* (1938); *Modern Mexican Art* (1939); *John Steuart Curry's Pageant of America* (1943); *Art in Red Wing* (1946); *Ivan Mestrovic—Sculptor and Patriot* (1959). Editor, *College Art Journal,* 1949–53. Prof. and dir., school of arts, Syracuse University, since 1954.

SCHMECKEBIER, LAURENCE FREDERICK (Jan. 24, 1877–1959); b. Baltimore, Md. Political scientist, author. *The Customs Service* (1924); *The Government Printing Office* (1925); *The Office of Indian Affairs* (1927); *The Bureau of Engraving and Printing* (1929); *Government Publications and Their Use* (1936); *Congressional Apportionment* (1941); etc. Chief, division of publications, Dept. of Interior, 1907–17; on staff, Institute for Government Research, Brookings Institution, from 1921.

SCHMIDT, DANA ADAMS (Sept. 6, 1915–); b. Bay Village, Ohio. Journalist, author. *Anatomy of a Satellite* (1952); *Journey Among Brave Men* (1964). Correspondent, *New York Times,* since 1943.

SCHMIDT, ERICH FRIEDRICH (Sept. 13, 1897–); b. Baden-Baden, Ger. Archeologist. *Flights Over Ancient Cities of Iran* (1940); *Persepolis,* vol. I: *Structures—Reliefs—Inscriptions* (1953); Vol. II: *Contents of the Treasury* (1957).

SCHMIEDELER, EDGAR (Dec. 15, 1892–); b. Kansas City, Kan. Roman Catholic clergyman, educator, author. *Introductory Study of the Family* (1930); *Readings on the Family* (1932); *A Better Rural Life* (1938); *The Sacred Bond* (1940); *Co-operation* (1941); *25 Years of Uncontrol* (1943); *Marriage and the Family* (1946); etc. Sociology department, Catholic University of America, 1932–33, 1937–45.

SCHMITT, BERNADOTTE EVERLY (May 19, 1886–Mar. 22, 1969); b. Strasburg, Va. Educator, author. *England and Germany, 1740–1914* (1916); *The Coming of the War, 1914,* 2v. (1930, Pulitzer Prize for history, 1931); *Triple Alliance and Triple Entente* (1934); *The Annexation of Bosnia, 1908–1909* (1937); *From Versailles to Munich, 1918–1938* (1939); *The Origin of the First World War* (1958); etc. Editor in chief: *Documents on German Foreign Policy, 1918–45,* series D, vols. III, IV, V (1950–53); *The First World War, 1914–1919* (1957). Editor, the *Journal of Modern History,* from 1929. History dept., University of Chicago, 1925–46.

SCHMITT, GLADYS (Mrs. Simon Goldfield) (May 31, 1909–); b. Pittsburgh, Pa. Author. *The Gates of Aulis* (1942); *David, the King* (1946); *Alexandra* (1947); *Confessors of the Name* (1952); *The Persistent Image* (1955); *A Small Fire* (1957); *Rembrandt* (1961); *Electra* (1965); etc. With *Scholastic,* since 1933.

SCHMUCKER, SAMUEL CHRISTIAN (Dec. 18, 1860–Dec. 27, 1943); b. Allentown, Pa. Educator, author. *The Study of Nature* (1907); *Under the Open Sky* (1910); *The Meaning of Evolution* (1913); *Man's Life on Earth* (1920); etc. Prof. biology, State Teachers College, West Chester, Pa., 1895–1923.

Schmucker, Samuel Mosheim. See Samuel Mosheim Smucker.

SCHMUTZ, CHARLES AUSTIN (June 15, 1900–); b. Richmond Hill, N.Y. Publisher. Successively managing editor, editor-in-chief, Standard & Poor's Corp., 1941–57; vice chairman, since 1958.

SCHNEIDER, ELISABETH WINTERSTEEN (Sept. 7, 1897–); b. Salt Lake City, Utah. Educator, author. *The Aesthetics of William Hazlitt* (1933); *Aesthetic Motive* (1939); *Poems and Poetry* (1964). Editor: *Samuel Taylor Coleridge, Selected Prose and Poetry,* (1951); etc. *Coleridge, Opium, and Kubla Khan* (1953); etc. Prof. English, Temple University, since 1945.

SCHNEIDER, HERBERT WALLACE (Mar. 16, 1892–); b. Berea, O. Educator, author. *Making Fascists* (1929); *The Puritan Mind* (1930); *Meditations in Season* (1939); *A History of American Philosophy* (1946); *Religion in Twentieth Century America* (1952); *Three Dimensions of Public Morality* (1956); *Morals for Mankind* (1960); *Ways of Being* (1962); etc. Compiler: *Bibliography of John Dewey* (1930). Philosophy dept., Columbia University, since 1918; prof. religion, since 1929.

SCHNEIDER, ISIDOR (Aug. 25, 1896–); b. Horodenko, Pol. Poet, novelist. *Doctor Transit* (under initials, "I.S." 1925); *The Temptation of Anthony: A Novel in Verse; and Other Poems* (1928); *Comrade: Mister* (poems, 1934); *From the Kingdom of Necessity* (1935); *The Judas Time* (1947); *World of Love,* 2v. (1964). Editor: *Enlightenment* (1965). Translator: Gorki's *Autobiography* (1949). *See* Fred B. Millet's *Contemporary American Authors* (1940).

SCHNEIDERS, ALEXANDER A[loysius] (Feb. 2, 1909–); b. Sioux City, Ia. Educator. *Introductory Psychology* (1948); *Psychology of Adolescence* (1951); *Personal Adjustment and Mental Health* (1955). Prof. psychology, Fordham University, since 1953.

SCHNELLBACHER, EMIL ST. ELMO (Dec. 18, 1901–); b. Quincy, Ill. Government official, author. *Credit and Payment Terms* (1931); *Sources of Foreign Credit Information* (1931); *Export and Import Practice* (with F. R. Eldridge, 1938); *Government and Foreign Trade* (1954).

SCHNITTKIND, HENRY THOMAS (Aug. 18, 1888–); b. in Lithuania. Pen name, "Henry Thomas." Author. *Giuseppe* (1914); *Shambles* (1915); *Weavers of Words* (1933); *The Story of the Human Race* (1935); *The Wonder Book of History* (1937); *Stories of the Great Dramas and Their Authors* (1939); *George Washington Carver* (1958); *The Wright Brothers* (1960); etc. Co-author with D. A. Schnittkind as "Henry and Dana Lee Thomas": *Living Biographies of Famous Women* (1942); *Forty Famous Composers* (1948); *Living Adventures in Philosophy* (1954). Editor, the *Stratford Magazine,* 1916–32.

Schocken Books, Inc. New York. Publishers. Founded 1945. Theodore Schocken is president; and Nahum N. Glatzer is chief editor. Publishes religious, historical, philosophical books, especially those dealing with Hebrew literature and Jewish studies.

SCHOENBRUN, DAVID FRANZ (Mar. 15, 1915–); b. New York. Foreign Correspondent. *As France Goes* (1955); *The Three Lives of Charles De Gaulle* (1965). With Columbia Broadcasting Co., since 1945.

SCHOFIELD, WILLIAM HENRY (Apr. 6, 1870–June 24, 1920); b. Brockville, Ont. Educator, translator, author. *English Literature from the Norman Conquest to Chaucer* (1905); *Chivalry in English Literature* (1912); *Mythical Bards and the Life of William Wallace* (1920); and many books on Scandinavian subjects, etc. English dept., Harvard University, 1897–1920.

Scholarly Books in America. New York. Quarterly. Founded 1959. Bibliography published by the Association of American University Presses.

Scholastic Magazines. New York. *The Scholastic* was founded in 1920 as the *Western Pennsylvania Scholastic.* Named changed in 1922 to *Scholastic.* It developed into a notable periodical for school children, distinguished for its literary contributions from students. The anthology of student writings, *Saplings,* first appeared in 1926. Maurice Richard Robinson was the first editor and publisher of *Scholastic.* Discontinued in 1936 and later resumed in various editions. *World Week* appeared in 1942; *Junior Scholastic,* in 1943; *Practical English,* in 1946; *Literary Cavalcade,* in 1948; *Newstime,* in 1952; *Scholastic Teacher,* in 1953; *Co-ed,* in 1956.

SCHOLES, FRANCE V[inton] (Jan. 26, 1897–); b. Bradford, Ill. Educator, author. *Church and State in New Mexico* (1937); *Troublous Times in New Mexico, 1659–1670* (1942); *The Maya Chontal Indians of Acalan-Tixchel* (with others, 1948). Prof. history, University of New Mexico, since 1946.

SCHOLL, JOHN WILLIAM (Aug. 17, 1869–Sept. 2, 1952); b. near Springfield, O. Educator, poet. *The Light-Bearer of Liberty* (1899); *Social Tragedies, and Other Poems* (1900); *Hesper-Phosphor, and Other Poems* (1910); *Children of the Sun* (1916); *Edith: A Sonnet Sequence* (1930); *The Nymph and the Rose* (1931); *The Rose Jar* (1936); *Strenae* (1943); *The Unknown Soldier and Other Poems* (1950); etc. German dept., University of Michigan, 1902–39.

SCHOMBURG, ARTHUR A[lfonso] (Jan. 24, 1874–June 10, 1938); b. San Juan, P.R. Antiquarian, bibliophile. Compiler: *A Bibliographical Checklist of American Negro Poetry* (1916); etc. His collection of Negro Americana is in the 135th Street Branch of The New York Public Library.

SCHOMER, HOWARD (June 9, 1915–); b. Chicago, Ill. Congregationalist clergyman, educator. Translator: *The Prayer of the Church Universal* by Marc Boegner (1954).

Editor-at-large, *Christian Century,* since 1959. President, Chicago Theological Seminary, since 1959.

SCHONBERG, HAROLD C. (Nov. 29, 1915–); b. New York. Music critic. *The Guide to Long-Playing Records* (1955); *The Collector's Chopin and Schumann* (1959); *The Great Pianists* (1963); *The Great Conductors* (1967); *The Lives of the Great Composers* (1970). Assoc. editor, *American Music Lover,* 1939–41; music critic, *New York Sun,* 1946–50; music and record critic, *New York Times,* since 1950.

School, College, and Character. By Le Baron R. Briggs (1902). Informal summary of American educational ideals by one of Harvard's best-loved professors, who was also the head of Radcliffe College.

"School Days." Popular song by Gus Edwards, from a revue of the same name (1916).

SCHOOLCRAFT, HENRY ROWE (Mar. 28, 1793–Dec. 10, 1864); b. in Albany Co., N.Y. Explorer, ethnologist, author. *A View of the Lead Mines of Missouri* (1819); *Narrative Journal of Travels through the Northwestern Regions* (1821); *Narrative of an Expedition through the Upper Mississippi to Itasca Lake* (1934); *Algic Researches,* 2v. (1839); *Alhalla; or, The Lord of Talladega* (under pen name "Henry Rowe Colcraft," 1843); *Notes on the Iroquois* (1846); *The Red Race of America* (1847); *Personal Memoirs of a Residence of Thirty Years with the Indian Tribes on the American Frontiers* (1851); *Historical and Statistical Information Respecting the History, Condition and Prospects of the Indian Tribes of the United States,* 6v. (1851–57); etc.

Schoolmaster of Yesterday. By Millard Fillmore Kennedy and Alvin F. Harlow (1940). Account of the Kentucky Kennedys and Kentucky schools of the past.

SCHOONMAKER, FRANK MUSSELMAN (Aug. 20, 1905–); b. Spearfish, S.D. Author. *Through Europe on $2 a Day* (1927); *Come with Me through France* (1928); *Come with Me through Belgium and Holland* (1928); *Come with Me through Italy* (1929); *Come with Me through Germany* (1930); *Spain—The Traveler's Guidebook* (with Lowell Thomas, 1932); *The Complete Wine Book* (with Tom Marvel, 1934); *American Wines* (with same, 1941); *A Dictionary of Wines* (1951); *The Wines of Germany* (1957); *Encyclopedia of Wine* (1965); etc.

SCHOONOVER, LAWRENCE L[ovell] (Mar. 6, 1906–); b. Anamosa, Ia. Author. *The Burnished Blade* (1949); *The Gentle Infidel* (1951); *The Golden Exile* (1952); *The Quick Brown Fox* (1954); *The Spider King* (1955); *The Queen's Cross* (1956); *The Revolutionary* (1958); *The Prisoner of Tordesillas* (1959); *The Chancellor* (1961).

SCHORER, MARK (May 17, 1908–); b. Sauk City, Wis. Educator, author. *A House Too Old* (1935); *The Hermit Place* (1941); *William Blake: The Politics of Vision* (1946); *The Story* (1950); *The Wars of Love* (1954); *Sinclair Lewis* (1961); *The World We Imagine: Selected Essays* (1968); etc. Prof. English, University of California, since 1946.

SCHOULER, JAMES (Mar. 20, 1839–Apr. 16, 1920); b. Arlington, Mass. Educator, author. *History of the United States of America, under the Constitution,* 7v. (1880–1913); *Thomas Jefferson* (1893); *Alexander Hamilton* (1901); *Americans of 1776* (1906); *Ideals of the Republic* (1908); and many law books. Prof. law, Boston University, 1882–1902.

SCHOULER, WILLIAM (Dec. 31, 1814–Oct. 24, 1872) b. Kilbarchan, near Glasgow, Scot. Editor, historian. *A History of Massachusetts in the Civil War,* 2v. (1868–71). Editor, *Boston Daily Atlas, Cincinnati Gazette, Ohio State Journal, Lowell Courier.*

SCHOYER, PRESTON (June 13, 1911–   ); b. Pittsburgh, Pa. Novelist. *The Foreigners* (1942); *The Indefi-*

nite River (1947); *The Ringing Glass* (1950); *The Typhoon's Eye* (1959).

SCHRADER, FREDERICK FRANKLIN (Oct. 27, 1857–Mar. 7, 1943); b. Hamburg, Ger. Editor, playwright. *José* (1890); *At the French Ball* (prod. 1896); *The Germans in the Making of America* (1923); etc. Editor, the *New York Dramatic Mirror,* 1912–16.

SCHRAGG, OTTO (Oct. 11, 1902–   ); b. Karlsruhe, Ger. Novelist. *The Locusts* (1943); *Sons of the Morning* (1945); *Bedrock* (1947); etc.

SCHREIBER, GEORGES (Apr. 25, 1904–); b. Brussels, Bel. Painter, illustrator, author. Author and illustrator: *Bambino the Clown* (1947); *Bambino Goes Home* (1959); etc. Coauthor and illustrator, *Professor Bull's Umbrella* (1956). Illustrator: *Ride on the Wind* (1956). Editor: *Portraits and Self-Portraits* (1936).

SCHRIFTGIESSER, KARL (Nov. 12, 1903–); b. Boston, Mass. Journalist, author. *Families* (1940); *The Amazing Roosevelt Family, 1613–1942* (1942); *Oscar of the Waldorf* (1943); *The Gentleman from Massachusetts: Henry Cabot Lodge* (1944); *This Was Normalcy* (1948); *The Lobbyists* (1951); *The Farmer from Merna* (1955); *Business Comes of Age* (1960); etc.

SCHROTH, FRANK (Oct. 18, 1884–); b. Trenton, N.J. Editor, publisher. Editor and publisher, *Brooklyn Daily Eagle,* 1938–55.

SCHUELER, HERBERT (Feb. 9, 1914–); b. New York. Educator. *Hebbel and the Dream* (1941); *Practical American English* (with H. Lenz, 1956); *Teacher Education and the New Media* (1967). Prof. education, Hunter College, since 1956.

SCHULBERG, BUDD (Mar. 27, 1914–);b. New York. Author. *What Makes Sammy Run?* (1941); *The Harder They Fall* (1947); *The Disenchanted* (1950); *Some Faces in the Crowd* (stories, 1953); *Waterfront* (1955); *From the Ashes—Voices of Watts* (1967); *Sanctuary V* (1969); and motion picture scenarios.

SCHULER, LORING ASHLEY (Aug. 24, 1886–June 4, 1968); b. New Bedford, Mass. Editor. On staff *Country Gentleman,* 1913–20, 1924–27; editor, 1924–27; editor, *Ladies' Home Journal,* 1927–35.

SCHULTZ, JAMES WILLARD (Aug. 26, 1869–June 11, 1947); b. Boonville, N.Y. Adopted by the Blackfeet Indians of Montana, as "Ap-i-juni." Author. *My Life as an Indian* (1907); *With the Indians in the Rockies* (1910); *Simopah, the Indian Boy* (1911); *Apauk, Caller of Buffalo* (1913); *On the War Path* (1915); *Blackfeet Tales of Glacier National Park* (1917); *Bird Woman* (1918); *In the Great Apache Forest* (1920); *Sun Woman* (1926) *Signposts of Adventure* (1926); *Red Crow's Brother* (1927); *William Jackson, Indian Scout* (1927); *The Sun God's Children: The Blackfeet Indian Tribes* (with Jessie L. Donaldson, 1929); *The White Beaver* (1930); *Stained Gold* (1937); etc.

SCHULTZ, THEODORE WILLIAM (Apr. 30, 1902–); b. Arlington, S.D. Economist. *Redirecting Farm Policy* (1943); *Food for the World* (1945); *Production and Welfare of Agriculture* (1950); *The Economic Organization of Agriculture* (1953); *The Economic Test in Latin America* (1956); *The Economic Value of Education* (1963); *Transforming Traditional Agriculture* (1964); *Economic Crisis in World Agriculture* (1965); *Economic Growth and Agriculture* (1968); etc.

SCHULTZE, CARL EMIL (May 25, 1866–Jan. 18, 1939); b. Lexington, Ky. Cartoonist. Pen name "Bunny." Creator of "Foxy Grandpa" cartoon, Jan. 7, 1900. These drawings first appeared in the *New York Herald.*

SCHULZ, CHARLES M[onroe] (Nov. 26, 1922–); b. Minneapolis, Minn. Cartoonist. *Peanuts* (1952); *More Peanuts*

(1954); *Good Grief, More Peanuts* (1956); *Collected Cartoons* (1963); *Happiness is a Warm Puppy* (1962); *Love is Walking Hand in Hand* (1965); *A Charlie Brown Christmas* (1965); *You Need Help, Charlie Brown* (1966); *Charlie Brown's All-Stars* (1966); etc.

SCHUMAN, FREDERICK LEWIS (Feb. 22, 1904–); b. Chicago, Ill. Educator, author. *Soviet Politics at Home and Abroad* (1946); *The Commonwealth of Man* (1952); *Russians Since 1917* (1957); *Russia since 1917* (1957); *Government in the Soviet Union* (1961); *The Cold War: Retrospect and Prospect* (1962). Prof. political science, Williams College, since 1936.

SCHURMAN, JACOB GOULD (May 22, 1854–Aug. 12, 1942); b. Freetown, P.E.I. Educator, author. *Kantian Ethics and the Ethics of Evolution* (1881); *Agnosticism and Religion* (1886); *The Ethical Import of Darwinism* (1888); *Philippine Affairs* (1902); etc. President Cornell University, 1892–1920.

SCHURZ, CARL (Nov. 2, 1829–May 14, 1906) b. Cologne, Ger., came to the United States in 1852. Soldier, statesman, diplomat, editor, author. *Life of Henry Clay*, 2v. (1887); *The Reminiscences of Carl Schurz*, 3v. (1907–08); *Speeches, Correspondence and Political Papers*, 6v. (1918); *Intimate Letters*, ed. by Joseph Schafer (1928); etc. Editor, the *Detroit Post*, 1866–67; co-editor, the *St. Louis Westliche Post*, 1867–69; editor, the *New York Evening Post*, 1881–83; editorial writer, *Harper's Weekly*, 1892–98. Minister to Spain, 1861–62; U.S. Senator, 1869–75; Secretary of the Interior, 1877–81. His papers are in the Library of Congress and in the Wisconsin Historical Society. *See* Joseph Schafer's *Carl Schurz, Militant Leader* (1930); Claude M. Fuess's *Carl Schurz* (1932).

SCHURZ, WILLIAM LYTLE (Nov. 25, 1886–July 26, 1962); b. South Lebanon, O. Educator, author. *Paraguay, a Commercial Handbook* (1920); *Bolivia, an Industrial Handbook* (1921); *Rubber Production in the Amazon Valley* (with O. D. Hargis, 1924); *The Manila Galleon* (1939); *Latin America: A Descriptive Survey* (1941); *This New World: A Study of Latin-American Civilization* (1953). Prof. area studies in international relations, American Institute for Foreign Trade, Phoenix, Ariz., since 1951.

SCHUSTER, MAX LINCOLN (Mar. 2, 1897–Dec. 20, 1970); b. Kalusz, Austria. Publisher, editor. Editor: *A Treasury of the World's Great Letters* (1940). Founder, with Richard L. Simon, Simon & Schuster, publishing firm, New York, 1924.

SCHUTZ, ANTON [Friedrich Joseph] (Apr. 19, 1894–); b. Berndorf, Ger. Artist, publisher. *New York in Etchings* (1939); *Blue Book Color Reproductions* (1951); *Fine Art Reproductions: Old and Modern Masters* (1961–1965); *Reproductions of American Paintings* (1961); etc. Founder and pres., New York Graphic Society, since 1925; Publisher and co-editor of the UNESCO World Art Series.

SCHUTZE, MARTIN (1866–July 19, 1950); b. Germany. Educator, author. *Crux Aetatis, and Other Poems* (1904); *Hero and Leander* (1908); *Judith* (1910); *Poems and Songs* (1914); *Towards a Modern Humanism* (1934); *An Approach to an Understanding of Art* (1938); *Johann Gottfried Herder* (1944); etc. Prof. German, University of Chicago.

SCHUYLER, EUGENE (Feb. 26, 1840–July 16, 1890); b. Ithaca, N.Y. Diplomat, scholar, author. *Turkistan: Notes of a Journey in Russian Turkistan, Buckhara, and Kuldja*, 2v. (1876); *Peter the Great*, 2v. (1884); *Selected Essays* (1901). Minister to Greece, Serbia, and Rumania, 1882–84.

SCHUYLER, GEORGE SAMUEL (Feb. 25, 1895–); b. Providence, R.I. Editor, author. *Black No More* (1931); *Slaves Today* (1931); *Black and Conservative* (1966); etc. Business manager, *The Crisis*, 1937–44.

SCHUYLER, GEORGE WASHINGTON (Feb. 2, 1810–Feb. 1, 1888); b. Stillwater, N.Y. Author. *Colonial New York: Philip Schuyler and His Family*, 2v. (1885).

SCHUYLER, JAMES. Author. *Salute* (1960); *May 24th or So* (1966); *Freely Espousing* (1969). Co-author, with John Ashbery: *A Nest of Ninnies* (1969).

SCHUYLER, MONTGOMERY (Aug. 19, 1843–July 16, 1914); b. Ithaca, N.Y. Historian of architecture. *Studies in American Architecture* (1892); *Westward the Course of Empire* (1906); etc. With the *New York World*, 1865–83; the *New York Times*, 1883–1907.

SCHUYLER, MONTGOMERY (Sept. 2, 1877–Nov. 1, 1955); b. Stamford, Conn., son of Montgomery Schuyler. Consul, Orientalist. Compiler: *Index Verborum of the Fragments of the Avesta* (1901); *Bibliography of the Sanscrit Drama* (1906); etc. In consular service in Russia, Japan, Siam, Servia, Ecuador, Mexico, Salvador, etc., 1902–25.

SCHUYLER, ROBERT LIVINGSTON (Feb. 26, 1883–); b. New York. Educator, author. *The Constitution of the United States* (1923); *Parliament and the British Empire* (1929); *Josiah Tucker* (1931); *The Fall of the Old Colonial System* (1945); etc. Editor: *The Making of English History* (with Herman Ausubel, 1952); *Frederic William Maitland, Historian* (1960); etc. History dept., Columbia University, since 1910, prof., since 1924.

SCHWAB, JOHN CHRISTOPHER (Apr. 1, 1865–Jan. 12, 1916); b. New York. Educator, economist, librarian, author. *The Confederate States of America, 1861–1865* (1901); etc. Dept. political science, Yale University, 1890–1916; prof., 1898–1916; librarian, 1905–16.

SCHWARTZ, DELMORE (Dec. 8, 1913–July 11, 1966); b. Brooklyn, N.Y. Poet, critic. *In Dreams Begin Responsibilities* (1938); *Shenandoah* (verse play, 1941); *Genesis, Book I* (1943); *The World Is a Wedding* (stories, 1948); *Vaudeville for a Princess and Other Poems* (1950); *Summer Knowledge* (1959); *Successful Love, and Other Stories* (1961). Translator: Rimbaud's *A Season in Hell* (1939).

SCHWARTZ, JULIA AUGUSTA (Feb. 3, 1873–); b. Albany, N.Y. Author. *Vassar Studies* (1899); *Five Little Strangers and How They Came to Live in America* (1904); *Little Star Gazers* (1917); *From Then Till Now* (1929); etc.

SCHWATKA, FREDERICK (Sept. 29, 1849–Nov. 2, 1892); b. Galena, Ill. Arctic explorer, author. *Along Alaska's Great River* (1885); *Nimrod in the North* (1885); *The Children of the Cold* (1886); *Among the Apaches* (1887); *In the Land of Cave and Cliff Dweller* (1893); etc.

SCHWEIKERT, H[arry] **C**[hristian] (Feb. 24, 1877–June 5, 1937); b. Bernville, Pa. Editor, compiler. Editor: *French Short Stories* (1918); *Russian Short Stories* (1919); *Short Stories* (1925); *Early English Plays* (1928); etc.

SCIDMORE, ELIZA RUHAMAH (Oct. 14, 1856–Nov. 3, 1928); b. Madison, Wis. Traveler, author. *Guide to Alaska and the Northwest Coast* (1890); *Jinrikisha Days in Japan* (1891); *Java, the Garden of the East* (1897); *China, the Long-Lived Empire* (1900); *Winter India* (1903); *As the Hague Ordains* (1907); etc.

Science and Health. By Mary Baker Eddy (1875). The principles evolved in this famous work became the foundations of Christian Science. It held that matter was negative and that mind was supreme. All disease could be cured through mental therapy. Many editions have been printed. Only a thousand copies of the original edition were printed. John Wilson was the printer.

Science and Survival. By Barry Commoner (1966). An influential book written about the ecological concerns that became one of the dominant issues in public life in the late 1960's.

Science Fiction. Treatment in fiction of scientific subjects, especially as projected into the future. Notable modern American writers of science fiction include Ray Bradbury, Robert Heinlein, and Frederick Pohl. Science fiction began appearing in magazines with Hugo Gernsback's "Ralph 124C 41t," which was published in 1911 in his periodical *Modern Electrics*. *Amazing Stories, Astounding Stories, Fantasy & Science Fiction, International Science Fiction, World of If,* and *Galaxy Science Fiction* have been the leading science fiction magazines. See Howard Bruce Franklin's *Future Perfect: American Science Fiction of the 19th Century* (1966); Samuel Moskowitz's *Science Fiction by Gaslight: A History and Anthology of Science Fiction in the Popular Magazines, 1891–1911* (1968); E. L. Ferman's and R. P. Mills' *Twenty Years of the Magazine of Fantasy and Science Fiction* (1970).

Scientific American. New York. Monthly. Founded 1845, by Rufus Porter, as a weekly of science news. Became a monthly in 1921. In 1947 it was bought by Gerard Piel, now publisher, and Dennis Flanagan, now editor, who changed it into a forum for all scientists. The magazine features profuse illustrative material.

SCOGGINS, C[harles] E[lbert] (Mar. 17, 1888–Dec. 6, 1955); b. Mazatlan, Sinaloa, Mex. Author. *The Proud Old Name* (1925); *The Red Gods Call* (1926); *White Fox* (1928); *John Quixote* (1929); *The House of Darkness* (1931); *Flame* (1931); *Tycoon* (1932); *Pampa Joe* (1935); *Lost Road* (1941); etc.

SCOLLARD, CLINTON (Sept. 28, 1860–Nov. 19, 1932); b. Clinton, N.Y. Poet. *Pictures in Song* (1884); *With Reed and Lyre* (1886); *Giovio and Julia* (1891); *Songs of Sunrise Lands* (1892); *The Hills of Song* (1895); *Lawton* (1900); *Lyrics of the Dawn* (1902); *The Lyric Bough* (1904); *Odes and Elegies* (1905); *A Southern Flight* (1905); *Easter Song* (1907); *Voices and Visions* (1908); *From the Lips of the Sea* (1911); *Arms, and Other Poems* (1915); *War Voices and Memories* (1919); *The Singing Heart: Selected Lyrics and Other Poems,* with a memoir by his wife, Jessie B. Rittenhouse (1934). Editor, *Ballads of American Bravery* (1900); etc.

SCOTFORD, JOHN RYLAND (Sept. 7, 1888–); b. Chicago, Ill. Congregational clergyman, author. *Mating Ministers and Churches* (1930); *The Church Beautiful* (1945); *Church Union, Why Not?* (1948); *Within These Borders* (1953); *When You Build Your Church* (1955).

SCOTT, ANNA MILLER (Mrs. Walter Dill Scott) (Jan. 22, 1871–); b. Lockport, Ill. Author. *A Year with the Fairies* (1914); *Flower Babies* (1915); etc.

SCOTT, CARRIE EMMA (Aug. 22, 1874–July 27, 1943); b. Mooresville, Ind. Librarian, author. *Manual for Institution Libraries* (1916). Compiler: *Popular Books for Boys and Girls* (1911). Editor: *Anthology of Children's Literature* (with Edna Johnson, 1935). Supervisor, children's work, Indianapolis Public Library, from 1917.

Scott, Dana. Pen name of Constance Noyes Robertson.

SCOTT, ELLEN C. (Mrs. Julius E. Scott) (July 27, 1862–June 18, 1936); b. Kensington, Conn. Author. *Elizabeth Bess* (1917); *The Loyalty of Elizabeth Bess* (1918); etc.

SCOTT, EMMETT JAY (Feb. 13, 1873–Dec. 12, 1957); b. Houston, Tex. Author. *Tuskegee and Its People* (with Booker T. Washington, 1910); *Booker T. Washington, Builder of a Civilization* (with Lyman Beecher Stowe, 1916); *The American Negro in the World War* (1919); etc. Secretary, Howard University, 1919–38, etc.

SCOTT, ERNEST FINDLAY (Mar. 18, 1868–July 21, 1954); b. Durham, Eng. Educator, author. *The Fourth Gospel* (1906); *The Beginning of the Church* (1914); *The Ethical Teachings of Jesus* (1924); *The First Age of Christianity* (1925); *The Nature of the Early Church* (1941); *Man and Society in the New Testament* (1946); etc. Prof. New Testament, Union Theological Seminary, New York, 1919–38.

SCOTT, EVELYN [D.] (Mrs. John Metcalfe) (Jan. 17, 1893–); b. Elsie Dunn, at Clarksville, Tenn. Novelist, poet.

Precipitations (poems, 1920); *The Narrow House* (1921); *Narcissus* (1922); *Escapade* (autobiography, 1923); *The Golden Door* (1925); *Ideals* (1927); *Migrations* (1927); *The Wave* (1929); *Witch Perkins* (1929); *The Winter Alone* (1930); *A Calendar of Sin: American Melodramas,* 2v. (1931); *Eva Gay* (1933); *Breathe Upon These Slain* (1934); *Bread and a Sword* (1937); *Background in Tennessee* (autobiography, 1937); *Shadow of the Hawk* (1941); etc. See Fred B. Millett's *Contemporary American Authors* (1940).

SCOTT, FRANKLIN DANIEL (July 4, 1901–); b. Cambridge, Mass. Educator, author. *Bernadotte and the Fall of Napoleon* (1935); *Guide to American Historical Review, 1895–1945* (1945); *The Twentieth Century World* (1948); *The U.S. and Scandinavia* (1950); *Scandinavia Today* (1951); *American Experience of Swedish Students* (1956); etc. Editor: *Pictorial History of Northwestern University* (1951). Prof. history, Northwestern University, since 1943.

SCOTT, FRANKLIN WILLIAM (Nov. 12, 1877–Jan. 10, 1950); b. Centralia, Ill. Editor, educator, author. *Composition for College Students* (with others, 1923); *New Handbook of Composition* (with E. C. Woolley, 1927); etc. Compiler: *Newspapers and Periodicals of Illinois* (1910). Editor, *Alumni Quarterly of the University of Illinois,* 1906–18. English dept., University of Illinois, 1901–1925. Editor-in-chief, D. C. Heath & Co., 1925–46.

SCOTT, FRED NEWTON (Aug. 20, 1860–May 29, 1931); b. Terre Haute, Ind. Educator, translator, author. *Aesthetics in Problems and Literature* (1890); *Principles of Style* (1890); *An Introduction to the Methods and Materials of Literary Criticism* (with C. M. Gayley, 1899); *The Standard of American Speech and Other Papers* (1926); etc. English dept., University of Michigan, 1889–1927. See *The Fred Newton Scott Anniversary Papers,* ed. by C. D. Thorpe and C. E. Whitmore (1929).

SCOTT, HARVEY WHITEFIELD (Feb. 1, 1838–Aug. 7, 1910); b. near Groveland, Tazewell Co., Ill. Editor, author. *Religion, Theology and Morals,* 2v. (1917); *History of the Oregon Country,* 6v. (1924); etc. Editor, the *Portland Oregonian,* 1877–1910.

SCOTT, JAMES BROWN (June 3, 1866–June 25, 1943); b. in Bruce Co., Ont. Lawyer, author. *The Hague Peace Conferences of 1899 and 1907,* 2v. (1909); *The United States of America* (1920); *Robert Bacon* (1923); *Law, the State, and the International Community,* 2v. (1939); etc. Editor, *American Journal of International Law* 1907–24. Secretary, Carnegie Endowment for International Peace, 1910–40.

SCOTT, JAMES WILMOT (June 29, 1849–Apr. 14, 1895); b. in Walsworth Co., Wis. Editor, publisher. Founder, the *Chicago Herald,* 1881. In 1895, he purchased the *Chicago Times,* to consolidate it with the *Herald,* but did not live to see the merger accomplished.

SCOTT, JOHN (Mar. 26, 1912–); b. Philadelphia, Pa. Author. *Behind the Urals* (1942); *Duel for Europe* (1942); *Europe in Revolution* (1945); *Political Warfare* (1955); *Democracy is Not Enough* (1960).

SCOTT, JOHN IRVING ELIAS, b. in Jamaica, B.W.I. Educator, author. *Living with Others* (1939); *Students and Their Colleges* (1949); etc. Editor-in-chief, *The Negro Educational Review.* Director, Negro education, Jacksonville and Duval Co., Florida, since 1953.

SCOTT, JOHN REED (Sept. 8, 1869–); b. Gettysburg, Pa. Author. *The Colonel of the Red Huzzars* (1906); *Beatrix of Clare* (1907); *The Last Try* (1912); *The Red Emerald* (1914); *The Duke of Oblivion* (1915); *The Cab of the Sleeping Horse* (1916); *The Man in Evening Clothes* (1917); etc.

SCOTT, JONATHAN FRENCH (Dec. 10, 1882–May 30, 1942); b. Newark, N.J. Author. *Patriots in the Making* (1916); *Five Weeks* (1927); *Twilight of the Kings* (1938); etc. History dept., University of Rochester, 1918–24.

Scott, Kerry. Pen name of Harold Norling Swanson.

SCOTT, LEROY (May 11, 1875–July 21, 1929); b. Fairmount, Ind. Author. *The Walking Delegate* (1905); *To Him that Hath* (1907); *The Shears of Destiny* (1910); *Counsel for the Defense* (1912); *Partners of the Night* (1916); *Mary Regan* (1918); *Cordelia the Magnificent* (1923); etc.

SCOTT, MARTIN J. (Oct. 16, 1865–Nov. 29, 1954). Roman Catholic clergyman, lecturer, author. *God and Myself* (1917); *Convent Life* (1919); *The Boy Knight* (1921); *Father Scott's Radio Talks* (1928); *The Church and the World* (1934); *Introduction to Catholicism* (1939); *All You Who Are Burdened* (1946); etc.

SCOTT, NATALIE ANDERSON (1906–); b. Ekaterinoslav, Russia. Author. *So Brief the Years* (1935); *The Sisters Livingston* (1946); *The Story of Mrs. Murphy* (1947); *The Husband* (1949); *Romance* (1951); *The Little Stockade* (1954); *Salvation Johnny* (1958); *The Golden Trollop* (1961).

SCOTT, R[eginald] M[aitland] (Aug. 14, 1882–); b. Woodstock, Ont. Author. *The Black Magician* (1925); *Aurelius Smith: Detective* (1927); *The Mad Monk* (1931); *Murder Stalks the Mayor* (1936); *Agony Column Murders* (1946); etc.

SCOTT, ROBERT BLAGARNIE YOUNG (July 16, 1899–); b. Toronto, Can. Educator, author. *Relevance of the Prophets* (1944); *Treasures from Judean Caves* (1955); *The Psalms as Christian Praise* (1958). Prof. religion, Princeton University, since 1955.

SCOTT, ROBERT LEE, JR. (Apr. 12, 1908–); b. Macon, Ga. Author. *God Is My Co-Pilot* (1943); *Damned to Glory* (1944); *Runway to the Sun* (1945); *Between the Elephant's Eyes* (1954); *Samburu the Elephant* (1957); *The Flying Tiger* (1959); *Boring a Hole in the Sky* (1961); etc.

SCOTT, S. SPENCER (June 21, 1892–Jan. 1, 1971); b. Elizabeth, N.J. Publisher. With Henry Holt and Co., 1914–20; with Harcourt, Brace and Co., 1920–55; pres., 1948–55.

SCOTT, SAMUEL PARSONS (July 8, 1846–May 30, 1929); b. Hillsboro, O. Hispanic scholar, author. *Through Spain* (1886); *History of the Moorish Empire in Europe,* 3v. (1904). Translator of Spanish laws, etc.

SCOTT, VIRGIL [Joseph] (Aug. 1, 1914–   ); b. Vancouver, Wash. Author. *The Dead Tree Gives No Shelter* (1947); *The Hickory Stick* (1948); *I, John Mordaunt* (1964); etc. Editor: *Studies in the Short Story* (with Adrian Jaffe, 1949).

SCOTT, WINFIELD (June 13, 1786–May 29, 1866); b. near Petersburg, Va. Army officer, author. *Memoirs,* 2v. (1864); etc. See M. J. Wright's *General Scott* (1894); J. H. Smith's *The War with Mexico,* 2v. (1919).

SCOTT, WINFIELD LIONEL. Editor, poet. *St. Blasien's Maid* (1904); *Azure and Silver* (1911). Editor, *Smoke* magazine, since 1931.

SCOTT, WINFIELD TOWNLEY (Apr. 30, 1910–Apr. 28, 1968); b. Haverhill, Mass. Author, editor. *Elegy for Robinson* (1936); *Biography for Traman* (1937); *Wind the Clock* (poems, 1941); *The Sword on the Table* (1942); *To marry Strangers* (poems, 1945); *Mr. Whittier and Other Poems* (1948); *The Dark Sister* (poems, 1958); *Exiles and Fabrications* (1961). With *The Providence Journal,* 1931–51; literary editor, 1941–51.

Scott's Monthly. Atlanta, Ga. Magazine. Founded Dec., 1865, by W. J. Scott. It contained some of the early work of Sidney Lanier, Paul Hamilton Hayne, and Maurice Thompson. Expired Dec., 1869.

Scourge of the Ocean: A Story of the Atlantic, The. Novel by Robert Burts, published anonymously (1837). A story of the American Revolution.

SCOVILLE, JOSEPH ALFRED (Jan. 30, 1815–June 25, 1864); b. Woodbury, Conn. Journalist, novelist. *Marion,* 3v. (under pen name "Manhattan," 1864), republished in England as *Vigor* (under pen name "Walter Barrett," 1864); *The Old Merchants of New York City,* 4v. (1863–66); etc. Founder, *Pick,* 1852; editor, *The Spectator,* Washington, D.C., 1843; the *New York Picayune,* 1850–52; etc.

SCOVILLE, SAMUEL, JR. (June 9, 1872–Dec. 4, 1950); b. Norwich, N.Y. Naturalist, author. *Brave Deeds of Union Soldiers* (1915); *Abraham Lincoln: His Story* (1918); *Boy Scouts in the Wilderness* (1919); *Every Day Adventures* (1920); *Wild Folk* (1922); *More Wild Folk* (1924); *Man and Beast* (1926); *Lords of the Wild* (1928); *The Snakeblood Ruby* (1932); *Alice in Blunderland* (1934); etc.

SCRIBNER, ARTHUR HAWLEY (Mar. 15, 1859–July 3, 1932); b. New York, brother of Charles Scribner (1854–1930). President, Charles Scribner's Sons.

SCRIBNER, BENJAMIN F. Soldier, author. *Camp Life of a Volunteer* (anon., 1847); *A Campaign in Mexico* (anon., 1850); *How Soldiers Were Made* (1887); etc.

SCRIBNER, CHARLES (Feb. 21, 1821–Aug. 26, 1871); b. New York. Publisher. Founder, publishing and bookselling firm, Baker & Scribner, New York, 1846, which became Charles Scribner, 1850, Scribner, Armstrong & Co., 1871, and Charles Scribner's Sons, 1878.

SCRIBNER, CHARLES (Oct. 18, 1854–Apr. 19, 1930); b. New York, son of Charles Scribner (1821–1871). Publisher. President, Charles Scribner's Sons, 1879–1930. Founder, *Scribner's Magazine.* One of the founders of the Princeton University Press, to which he donated land and buildings, etc.

SCRIBNER, CHARLES (Jan. 26, 1890–Feb. 11, 1952); b. New York, son of Charles Scribner (1854–1930). Publisher. With Charles Scribner's Sons, New York, from 1913; secretary, 1918–26; vice president, 1926–32; president, from 1932. President, Princeton University Press.

SCRIBNER, CHARLES, JR. (July 13, 1921–); b. Quogue, N.Y. Publisher. With Charles Scribner's Sons, since 1946; pres., since 1952; pres. Princeton University Press, since 1957.

SCRIBNER, FRANK KIMBALL (Feb. 22, 1867–Nov. 10, 1935); b. New York. Author. *The Honor of the Princess* (1897); *The Fifth of November* (1898); *The Love of the Princess Alice* (1898); *In the Land of the Loon* (with Earl W. Mayo, 1899); *A Maid of the Colonies* (1900); etc.

Scribner's, Charles, Sons. New York. Publishers and booksellers. Founded 1846, by Charles Scribner and Isaac D. Baker under the name Baker and Scribner. It began by purchasing the religious book stock of John S. Taylor. Baker died in 1850, and in 1857 Charles Scribner took as partner, Charles Welford, formerly of the book importing firm of Bartlett and Welford (John Russell Bartlett retiring from this business in 1849). Two firm names were adopted, Scribner and Welford, which imported foreign books, and Charles Scribner, which carried on the American trade. In 1864 Andrew Armstrong was admitted as a partner, and in 1869 Edward Seymour was admitted into partnership. On the death of Scribner in 1871, the business was headed by his son, John Blair Scribner, the name of the American firm becoming Scribner, Armstrong and Company, and the importing firm, Scribner, Welford & Armstrong. The year following the death of Edward Seymour in 1877, John Blair Scribner and his brother Charles (1854–1930) bought out the Armstrong interest and the entire business reverted to the family of the founder and became known as Charles Scribner's Sons, the name it still bears. John Blair Scribner died in 1879, and his brother, Arthur H. Scribner (1859–1932), joined the firm in 1884. Charles Scribner, grandson of the founder, entered the business in 1913, became president of the company in 1932. Charles Scribner, Jr., is now president. The first great success of Scribner's was J. T. Headley's *Napoleon and His Marshalls.* A large venture was the

American edition of *The Encyclopaedia Britannica*. Among the Scribner authors were Joel Chandler Harris, Thomas Nelson Page, Frank R. Stockton, Robert Louis Stevenson, J. M. Barrie, Francis Hodgson Burnett, Richard Harding Davis, John Galsworthy, G. A. Henty, James G. Huneker, Edith Wharton, Henry van Dyke, Theodore Roosevelt, Harold Frederic, Ernest Thompson Seton, Arthur Train, Will James, James Truslow Adams, Thomas Wolfe, Ernest Hemingway, Stark Young, Robert Sherwood, and Marjorie Kinnan Rawlings. Major works have been *Lange's Commentary, The Ante Nicene, The Nicene and Post Nicene Fathers, International Critical Commentary, The Dictionary of American Biography, The Dictionary of American History* and the *Modern Student's Library*. In the juvenile field is the *Scribner Illustrated Classics*. Among the editors of Scribner's have been Maxwell Perkins, John Hall Wheelock, Wallace Myers, and Will D. Howe. In the magazine field Scribner's has published *Scribner's Monthly, Hours at Home, St. Nicholas, Scribner's Magazine*, and the *Book Buyer. See* Roger Burlingame's *Of Making Many Books* (1946).

Scribner's Magazine. New York. Founded Jan., 1887. Published by Charles Scribner's Sons. Not to be confused with *Scribner's Monthly.* Editors: Edward L. Burlingame, 1887–1914, Robert Bridges, 1914–30; Alfred Dashiell, 1930–36, Harlan Logan, 1936–39. Stanford White designed the original cover. August F. Jaccaci and Joseph H. Chapin were art directors. The leading writers of Europe and America were contributors, many literary classics appearing originally as serials in this well-illustrated magazine. For many years *Scribner's* vied with *Harper's* and the *Century* for leadership in the literary magazine field. In 1939 it was sold by Charles Scribner's Sons, and was merged with the *Commentator*. See *Scribner's Magazine. Fiftieth Anniversary Number*, Jan., 1937.

Scribner's Monthly. New York. Founded 1870 by Scribner & Company. In 1881 it was acquired by the Century Company, and its name changed to *The Century Illustrated Monthly Magazine.* Editors: Josiah Gilbert Holland, 1870–81; Richard Watson Gilder, 1881–1901; Robert Underwood Johnson, 1909–13; Robert Sterling Yard, 1913–14; Douglas Zabriskie Doty, 1915–18; Thomas R. Smith, 1919; W. Morgan Shuster, 1920–21; Glenn Frank, 1921–25; Hewitt H. Howland, 1925–30. It grew out of the literary magazine, *Hours at Home.* It absorbed *Putnam's* in 1870, the *Riverside Magazine*, 1870, and *Old and New* in 1875. Josiah Holland, H. H. Boyesen, Bret Harte, Edward Everett Hale, Helen Hunt Jackson, Charles Dudley Warner, W. C. Brownell, John Muir, John Burroughs, Joel Chandler Harris, John Fox, Jr., George W. Cable, Frank Stockton, Frances Hodgson Burnett, Thomas Nelson Page, James Lane Allen, F. Marion Crawford, William Dean Howells, S. Weir Mitchell, and Henry James were only a few of its distinguished contributors. Alexander W. Drake was art director, 1870–1916, and its illustrations during that period were unexcelled. It was printed by Theodore Low Devinne. Stanford White and Augustus Saint-Gaudens designed a new cover for it in 1881. It took its name from the Century Club. Noted articles on the Civil War appeared in its early issues, alongside Nicolay and Hay's *Lincoln.* Timothy Cole, Frederic Remington, John La Farge, Joseph Pennell, Howard Pyle, Charles Dana Gibson, Maxfield Parrish, A. B. Frost, E. W. Kemble, Jay Hambridge, and N. C. Wyeth were among its illustrators.

SCRIPPS, CHARLES EDWARD (Jan. 27, 1920–); b. San Diego, Cal. Publisher. Director, E. W. Scripps Co., since 1946.

SCRIPPS, EDWARD WYLLIS (June 18, 1854–Mar. 12, 1926); b. Rushville, Ind., half-brother of James Edmund Scripps. Publisher, philanthropist. Founder, *Cleveland Penny Press*, Nov. 2, 1878, later called the *Cleveland Press*. He acquired interests in the *St. Louis Evening Chronicle*, the *Cincinnati Post*, and in 1895, with Milton Alexander McRae, formed the Scripps-McRae League of Newspapers. Founded Scripps-McRae Press Association in 1897, and in 1907 merged it with the Publishers Press to form the United Press. Founded Newspaper Enterprise Association in 1902, known as NEA.

He later gained control of a chain of newspapers on the West Coast. The organization, now known as Scripps-Howard, controls many newspapers including the *New York World-Telegram, Cleveland Press, Cincinnati Post, Columbus Citizen, Toledo News-Bee, Pittsburgh Press, Indianapolis Times, Buffalo Times, San Francisco Daily News, San Diego Sun, Rocky Mountain News, Birmingham Post, Memphis Press-Scimitar, Knoxville News-Sentinel, Oklahoma City News, Kentucky Post, Fort Worth Press, Houston Press, Washington Daily News, Evansville Press, Youngstown Telegram, Akron Times-Press, El Paso Herald, New Mexico State Tribune*, etc. George B. Parker has been editor in chief of twenty-one of these newspapers, since 1927. Roy W. Howard is president. Edward Wyllis Scripps, with his half-sister Ellen Browning Scripps, endowed the Scripps Institution for Biological Research at La Jolla, Calif., which was formerly the Marine Biological Association of San Diego. In 1925 it became the Scripps Institution of Oceanography, and is affiliated with the University of California. *See* N. D. Cochran's *E. W. Scripps* (1933); Gilson Gardner's *Lusty Scripps* (1932).

SCRIPPS, EDWARD WYLLIS (May 21, 1909–); b. San Diego, Cal. Publisher. Chairman of the board, Scripps League of Newspapers, later Scripps-Howard Newspapers, since 1931.

SCRIPPS, ELLEN [Browning] (Oct. 18, 1836–Aug. 3, 1932); b. London, sister of James Edmund Scripps, and half-sister of Edward Wyllis Scripps. Newspaperwoman, philanthropist. Associated with *Detroit Advertiser and Tribune* and *Detroit Evening News.* She edited a special feature section of miscellany in the latter, which developed into the Newspaper Enterprise Association in 1902, known as NEA. Founder, Scripps College, Claremont, Calif.

SCRIPPS, JAMES EDMUND (Mar. 19, 1835–May 29, 1906); b. London, half-brother of Edward Wyllis Scripps. Editor, publisher, author. *Five Months Abroad* (1882); *Memorials of the Scripps Family* (1891); etc. Joined staff of *Detroit Daily Advertiser* in 1859, became part owner in 1861, and in 1862, when it was merged with the *Detroit Tribune*, he became editor. Founder, *Detroit Evening News*, Aug. 23, 1873, which became the *Detroit News. See* L. A. White's *The Detroit News: 1873–1917* (1918).

SCRIPPS, JOHN P. (Oct. 5, 1912–); b. Cleveland, O. Publisher. Chairman of the board, John P. Scripps Newspapers.

SCRIPPS, ROBERT PAINE (Oct. 27, 1895–Mar. 3, 1938); b. San Diego, Calif., son of Edward Wyllis Scripps. Journalist. Editorial director Scripps-Howard and Scripps-McRae Newspapers, 1917–38.

SCRIPPS, WILLIAM EDMUND (May 6, 1882–June 12, 1952); b. Detroit, Mich., son of James Edmund Scripps. Industrialist, publisher. Publisher *Detroit News;* president, Evening News Association.

Script. Hollywood, Calif. Biweekly. Founded 1929, by Rob Wagner. Became monthly in 1947 after it was bought by Robert L. Smith and others. Suspended 1949.

Scuba Duba. Play by Bruce Jay Friedman (prod. 1967).

SCUDDER, ANTOINETTE QUINBY (1898–Jan. 27, 1958); b. Newark, N.J., daughter of Wallace McIlvane Scudder. Poet, playwright. *Provincetown Sonnets, and Other Poems* (1925); *The Soul of Ilaria* (poem, 1926); *Huckleberries* (poems, 1929); *Maples Bride, and Other One Act Plays* (1930); *Out of Peony and Blade* (poems, 1931); *The Henchman and the Moon* (poems, 1934); *Grey Studio* (1934); *East End, West End* (poems, 1935); *The Cherry Tart, and Other Plays* (1938); *Italics for Life* (poems, 1947); *The World in a Match Box* (plays, 1949); etc.

SCUDDER, ELIZA (Nov. 14, 1821–1896); b. Boston, Mass. Author. *Hymns and Sonnets* (1880).

SCUDDER, HORACE ELISHA (Oct. 16, 1838–Jan. 11, 1902); b. Boston, Mass. Editor, author. *Seven Little People and Their Friends* (1862); *Dream Children* (1864); *Life and Letters of David Coit Scudder* (1864); the *Bodley* books, 8v. (1876–84); *Stories and Romance* (1880); *Noah Webster* (1882); *Men and Letters* (1887); *George Washington* (1889); *Childhood in Literature and Art* (1894); *Henry Oscar Houghton* (1897); *James Russell Lowell*, 2v. (1901); etc. Editor: *Life and Letters of Bayard Taylor*, 2v. (1884). Founder and editor, the *Riverside Magazine for Young Folks*, 1867–70; editor, the *Atlantic Monthly*, 1890–98. With Hurd & Houghton, and later, Houghton, Mifflin Co., 1864–1902.

SCUDDER, JANET (Oct. 27, 1873–June 9, 1940); b. Terre Haute, Ind. Sculptor, painter, author. *Modeling My Life* (autobiography, 1925).

SCUDDER, VIDA DUTTON (Dec. 15, 1861–Oct. 9, 1954); b. Madura, India. Educator, author. *The Life of the Spirit in the Modern English Poets* (1894); *Introduction to the Study of English Literature* (1901); *A Listener in Babel* (1903); *The Disciple of a Saint* (1907); *Brother John* (1927); *The Franciscan Adventure* (1931); *On Journey* (autobiography, 1937); *The Privilege of Age* (1939); etc. English dept., Wellesley College, 1892–1927.

SCUDDER, WALLACE McILVANE (Dec. 26, 1853–Feb. 24, 1931); b. Trenton, N.J. Father of Antoinette Quinby Scudder. Editor, publisher. Founder, the *Newark Evening News*, 1883; editor and publisher, 1883–1931.

SCULL, JOHN (1765–Feb. 8, 1828); b. Reading, Pa. Newspaper editor, publisher. Founder (with Joseph Hall), the *Pittsburgh Gazette*, July 29, 1786, the first newspaper west of the Allegheny Mountains. He published v. 3 of Hugh Henry Brackenridge's *Modern Chivalry*, in 1792. He relinquished the *Gazette* in 1816.

SCULLY, FRANK (Francis Joseph Xavier) (1892–June 23, 1964); b. Steinway, L.I., N.Y. Author. *My Reminiscences as a Cowboy* (with Frank Harris, 1929); *Fun in Bed* (1932); *Sir Basil Zaharoff* (with John Hanscom, 1933); *Rogues' Gallery* (1943); *Behind the Flying Saucers* (1950); *Blessed Mother Goose* (1951); *Cross My Heart* (1955); etc.

SCULLY, VINCENT JOSEPH, Jr. (Aug. 21, 1920–); b. New Haven, Conn. Art historian, author. *Frank Lloyd Wright* (1960); *Modern Architecture* (1961); *The Earth, the Temple and the Gods: Greek Sacred Architecture* (1962); *Louis I. Kahn* (1962). Prof., Yale University, since 1961.

Sea Around Us, The. Discussion of the sea as a subject in itself, by Rachel Carson (1951).

"Sea Bird's Song, The." Poem by John G. C. Brainerd.

Sea Island Lady. Novel by Francis Griswold (1929). Story of Emily Fenwick, a New England girl who goes to the South as the wife of a carpetbagger, whom she despises. She later becomes free to marry the man she loves and settles down in the Sea Islands of South Carolina and overcomes all prejudice against her by her courageous character.

Sea of Grass, The. By Conrad Richter (1937). Novelette of the Southwest. The delicate woman in the story leaves her husband's ranch and flees to the city. Her son becomes a desperado, and she finally returns to the ranch. It is similar in many respects to Willa Cather's *A Lost Lady.*

Sea Serpent; or, Gloucester Hoax, The. By William Crafts (1819).

Sea Wolf, The. Novel by Jack London (1904). "Wolf Larson," captain of the sealing schooner *Ghost*, is one of the toughest characters in American fiction, and his cruelty is matched by his courage.

SEABROOK, WILLIAM BUEHLER (Feb. 22, 1886–Sept. 20, 1945); b. Westminster, Md. Author. *Adventures in Arabia* (1927); *The Magic Island* (1929); *The White Monk of Timbuctoo* (1934); *Asylum* (1935); *An Analysis of Magic and Witchcraft* (1940); *No Hiding Place: An Autobiography* (1942); etc.

SEABURY, DAVID (Sept. 11, 1885–Apr. 1, 1960); b. Boston, Mass. Psychologist, lecturer. *Unmasking Our Minds* (1924); *Growing into Life* (1928); *Keep Your Wits* (1935); *Why We Love and Hate* (1939); *High Hopes for Low Spirits* (1955); *The Art of Living Without Tension* (1958); etc.

SEABURY, PAUL (May 6, 1923–   ); b. Hempstead, N.Y. Educator, author. *Wilhelmstrasse: A Study of German Diplomacy Under the Nazi Regime* (1954); *Power, Freedom and Diplomacy* (1963); *The Balance of Power* (1965); *The Rise and Decline of the Cold War* (1967). Prof. government, University of California at Berkeley, since 1967.

SEABURY, SAMUEL (Nov. 30, 1729–Feb. 25, 1796); b. Groton, Conn. Episcopal bishop, loyalist, author. *Discourses on Several Subjects*, 2v. (1793); *Discourses on Several Important Subjects* (1798); etc. His grandson, Samuel Seabury (1801–72), became editor of *The Churchman* in 1833, and was the author of several religious books.

SEAGER, ALLAN (Feb. 5, 1906–May 10, 1968); b. Adrian, Mich. Author. *Equinox* (1943); *The Inheritance* (1948); *The Old Man of the Mountain* (stories, 1950); *Hilda Manning* (1956); *Death of Anger* (1960).

SEAGLE, WILLIAM (Jan. 14, 1898–); b. New York. Lawyer, author. *To the Pure . . . A Study of Obscenity and the Censor* (with Morris L. Ernst, 1928); *Cato; or, The Future of Censorship* (1930); *There Ought to Be a Law* (1933); *The Quest for Law* (1941); *Men of Law: From Hammurabi to Holmes* (1947); *Law: The Science of Inefficiency* (1952); *Acquitted of Murder* (1958).

Seal in the Bedroom and Other Predicaments, The. Collection of humorous sketches by James Thurber (1932).

SEALOCK, RICHARD BURL (June 15, 1907–); b. Lexington, Ill. Librarian. *Long Island Bibliography* (with Pauline A. Seely, 1940); *Bibliography of Place Name Literature: U.S., Canada, Alaska, Newfoundland* (with same, 1948).

SEALSFIELD, CHARLES (Mar. 3, 1793–May 26, 1864); b. (Karl Anton Postl) Poppitz, Moravia. Novelist. Translations of his books in German have been published as: *Tokeah; or, The White Rose*, 2v. (1828); *The United States as They Are* (1828); *The Cabin Book* (1844); *Life in the New World* (1844); *North and South* (1844); etc. He wrote anonymously until 1845. His collected works, published in German in 15v., 1845–47, bore the name Charles Sealsfield. He created the ethnological novel. *See* Otto Heller and Thomas Leon's *Charles Sealsfield Bibliography and Handbook* (1939).

SEAMAN, AUGUSTA HUIELL (Mrs. Francis P. Freeman) (Apr. 3, 1879–June 4, 1950); b. New York. Author. *The Sapphire Signet* (1916); *The Girl Next Door* (1917); *The Crimson Patch* (1920); *The Secret of Tate's Beach* (1926); *The Disappearance of Anne Shaw* (1928); *The Stars of Sabra* (1932); *The Figurehead of the Folly* (1935); *The Vanderlyn Silhouette* (1938); *The Mystery of Linden Hall* (1939); *The Half-Penny Adventure* (1945); etc.

SEAMAN, ELIZABETH COCHRANE (May 5, 1867–Jan. 27, 1922); b. Cochran Mills, Pa. Journalist, traveler, author. Pen name, "Nellie Bly." *Ten Days in a Mad-House* (1887), written on a newspaper assignment; *Six Months in Mexico* (1888); *Nelly Bly's Book: Around the World in Seventy-Two Days* (1890). The *New York World* sent her around the world in 1889–90, in an effort to lower the record set by Jules Verne's "Phineas Fogg"; she completed the trip in 72 days. With the *Pittsburgh Gazette*, 1881–88; the *New York World*, 1888–95; the *New York Journal*, c. 1920–22.

Searching Wind, The. Play by Lillian Hellman (1944). Deals with the family of a former American ambassador in the period before and during World War II.

SEARING, LAURA CATHERINE REDDEN (Feb. 9, 1840–Aug. 10, 1923); b. in Somerset Co., Md. Pen name "Howard Glyndon." Journalist, author. *Idyls of Battle* (1864); *Sounds from Secret Chambers* (1873); *Of El Dorado* (1897); *Echoes of Other Days* (1921); etc. Wrote for the *St. Louis Republican* under her pen name. With the *New York Mail*, 1868–76.

SEARLE, ROBERT WYCKOFF (May 25, 1894–June 16, 1967); b. New Brunswick, N.J. Protestant clergyman, author. *Contemporary Religious Thinking* (1933); *City Shadows* (1938); *Author of Liberty* (1941); *Tell It to the Padre* (1943).

SEARS, CLARA ENDICOTT (Dec. 16, 1863–Mar. 25, 1960); b. Boston, Mass. Author. *Bronson Alcott's Fruitlands* (1915); *The Bell-Ringer* (1918); *The Romance of Fidler's Green* (1922); *Days of Delusion* (1924); *Whispering Pines* (1930); *The Great Powwow* (1934); *Wind from the Hills, and Other Poems* (1936); *Some American Primitives* (1941); *Highlights Among the Hudson River Artists* (1947); *Snapshots from Old Registers* (1955); etc. Compiler: *Gleanings from Old Shaker Journals* (1916).

SEARS, EDMUND HAMILTON (Apr. 6, 1810–Jan. 16, 1876); b. Sandisfield, Mass. Unitarian clergyman, hymn writer. His best known hymns are "Calm on the listening ear of night," and "It came upon the midnight clear."

SEARS, EDWARD I. (1819–Dec. 7, 1876); b. in Co. Mayo, Ireland. Educator, editor, author. *Legends of the Sea* (under pen name "H. W. Chevalier," 1863); etc. Editor and owner, the *National Quarterly,* 1860–76. Prof. languages, Manhattan College.

SEARS, JOSEPH HAMBLEN (Apr. 10, 1865–Feb. 15, 1946); b. Boston, Mass. Publisher, author. *Fur and Feather Tales* (1897); *None but the Brave* (1902); *A Box of Matches* (1904); *The Career of Leonard Wood* (1916); etc. With Harper & Brothers; president, D. Appleton Co., 1904–18; founder and president J. H. Sears and Company, 1922–34.

SEARS, LORENZO (Apr. 18, 1838–Mar. 1, 1916); b. Searsville, Mass. Educator, author. *The History of Oratory* (1896); *Principles and Methods of Literary Criticism* (1898); *American Literature in the Colonial and National Periods* (1902); *The Makers of American Literature* (1904); *Wendell Phillips* (1909); *John Hancock* (1912); *John Hay* (1914); etc. English dept., Brown University, 1890–1906.

SEARS, LOUIS MARTIN (June 4, 1885–); b. Chicago, Ill. Educator, author. *John Slidell* (1925); *Purdue University* (1925); *Jefferson and the Embargo* (1927); *A History of American Foreign Relations* (1927); *George Washington* (1932); *George Washington and the French Revolution* (1958); etc. History dept., Purdue University, 1920–55.

SEARS, MINNIE EARL (Nov. 17, 1873–Nov. 28, 1933); b. Lafayette, Ind. Librarian, editor. Compiler: *A Thackeray Dictionary* (with Isidore G. Mudge, 1910); *A George Eliot Dictionary* (with same, 1924); *Children's Catalog* (1925); *Song Index* (with Phyllis Crawford, 1926); *Standard Catalog: Biography Section* (1927); *Standard Catalog for Public Libraries: Fine Arts Section* (1928); etc.

SEARS, PAUL BIGELOW (Dec. 17, 1891–); b. Bucyrus, O. Educator, author. *Deserts on the March* (1935); *This Is Our World* (1937); *Who Are These Americans?* (1939); *Life and Environment* (1939); *This Useful World* (1941); *Charles Darwin* (1950); *The Living Landscape* (1960). Prof. botany, Oberlin College, 1938–50; chairman, conservation program, Yale University, since 1950.

SEARS, ROBERT (June 28, 1810–Feb. 17, 1892); b. St. John, N.B. Publisher. Compiler: *Two Hundred Pictorial Illustra-*

tions of the Holy Bible, 3v. (1840–41); *The Wonders of the World,* 2v. (1843); *The Pictorial History of the American Revolution* (1845); *The Pictorial Bible* (1858); and similar works. Editor and publisher, the *New Pictorial Family Magazine,* 1844–49.

SEARS, ROBERT RICHARDSON (Aug. 31, 1908–); b. Palo Alto, Cal. Educator. *Objective Studies of Psychoanalytic Concepts* (1943); *Patterns of Child Rearing* (with others, 1957). Prof. psychology, Harvard University, 1949–53; Stanford University, since 1953.

SEARSON, JOHN. Poet. *Poems on Various Subjects* (1797); *Art of Contentment; With Several Pieces of Poetry* (1798); *Mount Vernon* (1799); etc.

SEASHORE, CARL EMIL (Jan. 28, 1866–Oct. 16, 1949); b. Mörlunda, Swe. Educator, psychologist, author. *Psychology in Daily Life* (1913); *The Psychology of Musical Talent* (1919); *Introduction to Psychology* (1922); *Psychology of Music* (1938); *The People's College* (1940); *In Search of Beauty in Music* (1947); etc. Prof. psychology, State University of Iowa, 1902–36.

Seasoned Timber. Novel by Dorothy Canfield Fisher (1939). The story of the school teacher, Timothy Hulme, and his courageous life in a small New England town where private lives are kept under close scrutiny.

SEATON, WILLIAM WINSTON (Jan. 11, 1785–June 16, 1866); b. "Chelsea," King William Co., Va. Editor. Assoc. editor, the *National Intelligencer,* Washington, D.C., 1812–60. *See* Josephine Seaton's *William Winston of the "National Intelligencer"* (1871).

Seattle Post-Intelligencer. Seattle, Wash. Newspaper. The *Seattle Gazette* was founded 1863; after various changes of name and mergers, it combined in 1881 with the *Seattle Daily Post,* founded 1878. The historian Edward S. Meany was connected with the paper. William Randolph Hearst purchased it in 1921. D. L. Starr is the present publisher. Louis R. Guzzo is managing editor. Nard Jones is book review editor.

Seattle Times. Seattle, Wash. Newspaper. Founded 1886. Merged with the *Seattle Press* in 1891, as the *Press-Times.* Original name restored 1896. Henry MacLeod is managing editor. Larry Rumley is book review editor.

SEAVER, EDWIN (Jan. 18, 1900–); b. Washington, D.C. Author. *The Company* (1920); *All in the Racket* (with W. E. Weeks, 1930); *Between the Hammer and the Anvil* (1937). Editor: *Cross Section: A Collection of New American Writing* (1944, 1945, 1947, 1948); *Pageant of American Humor* (1948); etc.

"Seaward." Elegy written by Richard Hovey in 1893 on the death of Thomas William Parsons, the Dante scholar.

SEAWELL, MOLLY ELLIOT (Oct. 23, 1860–Nov. 15, 1916); b. in Gloucester Co., Va. Novelist. *Little Jarvis* (1890); *Throckmorton* (1890); *A Virginia Cavalier* (1896); *Twelve Naval Captains* (1897); *The History of the Lady Betty Stair* (1897); *The Lively Adventures of Gavin Hamilton* (1899); *The House of Egremont* (1900); *Papa Bouchard* (1901); *Francezka* (1902); *The Fortunes of Fifi* (1903); *The Secret of Toni* (1907); *Betty's Virginia Christmas* (1914); etc.

Secession. Literary magazine. Founded 1922. It was edited by Gorham Munson, Kenneth Burke, and Matthew Josephson. Discontinued in 1924.

SECHRIST, ELIZABETH HOUGH (Aug. 31, 1903–); b. Media, Pa. Editor, author. *Christmas Everywhere* (1931); *A Little Book of Hallowe'en* (1934); etc. Editor: *Thirteen Ghostly Yarns* (1932); *Red-Letter Days* (1940); *Once in the First Time* (1949); *It's Time to Give a Play* (with Janette Woolsey, 1955); *It's Time for Thanksgiving* (with same, 1957). Children's library, Carnegie Library, Pittsburgh, 1937–39.

Second Coming Magazine, The. New York. Bi-monthly. Founded 1961, by Samuel Pitts Edwards and Jack Rennert, while students at Columbia University. Devoted to literature, cultural and social opinion, and the arts.

SECONDARI, JOHN HERMES (Nov. 1, 1919–); b. Rome. News broadcaster, author. *Coins in the Fountain* (1952); *Temptation for a King* (1954); *Spinner of the Dream* (1955). Chief, Washington news bureau, American Broadcasting Company, 1956–68. Founder, John H. Secondari Productions, Ltd., 1968.

Secondsight, Solomon. Pen name of James McHenry.

Secondthoughts, Solomon. Pen name of John Pendleton Kennedy.

SECORD, ARTHUR WELLESLEY (Nov. 7, 1891–May 16, 1957); b. Emporia, Kan. Educator, author. *Studies in the Narrative Method of Defoe* (1924); *Robert Drury's Journal and Other Studies* (1961); etc. Editor, *Defoe's Review,* 22v. (1938); and other works by Defoe. Prof. English, University of Illinois.

Secret History of the American Revolution. By Carl Van Doren (1941).

Secret Life of Walter Mitty, The. Story by James Thurber.

Secret Service. Play by William Gillette (prod. 1896).

Secular City, The. By Harvey Cox (1965). A theological interpretation of modern life, arguing that God will be found outside the churches.

SEDGWICK, ANNE DOUGLAS (Mrs. Basil de Selincourt) (Mar. 28, 1873–July 21, 1935); b. Englewood, N.J. Novelist. *The Dull Miss Archinard* (1898); *The Rescue* (1902); *Paths of Judgment* (1904); *Annabel Channice* (1908); *Tante* (1911); *The Encounter* (1914); *Adrienne Toner* (1921); *The Little French Girl* (1924); *Dark Hester* (1929); etc. *See* Basil de Selincourt's *Anne Douglas Sedgwick* (1936).

SEDGWICK, ARTHUR GEORGE (Oct. 6, 1844–July 14, 1915); b. New York. Lawyer, editor, lecturer, author. *The Democratic Mistake* (1912); etc. Asst. editor, *The Nation,* 1872–84; asst. editor, the *New York Evening Post,* 1881–85.

SEDGWICK, CATHARINE MARIA (Dec. 28, 1789–July 31, 1867); b. Stockbridge, Mass. Author. *A New England Tale* (1822); *Redwood* (1824); *The Travellers* (1825); *Hope Leslie* (1827); *Clarence* (1830); *The Linwoods* (1835); *Home* (1835); all anonymous; *Tales and Sketches,* 2 series (1835, 1844); *Wilton Harvey* (1845); *The Works,* 3v. (1849); *Married or Single?* (1857); *Life and Letters* (1871); etc.

SEDGWICK, ELLERY (Feb. 27, 1872–Apr. 21, 1960); b. New York. Editor, author. *Thomas Paine* (1899); *The Happy Profession* (1946). Assistant editor, *The Youth's Companion,* 1896–1900; editor, *Leslie's Monthly Magazine,* 1900–05; *American Magazine,* 1906–07; *Atlantic Monthly,* 1909–38.

SEDGWICK, HENRY DWIGHT (Sept. 24, 1861–Jan. 5, 1957); b. Stockbridge, Mass. Author. *Life of Father Hecker* (1897); *Life of Samuel Champlain* (1901); *Essays on Great Writers* (1902); *Life of Francis Parkman* (1904); *Italy in the Thirteenth Century* (1912); *Dante* (1919); *Marcus Aurelius* (1921); *Pro Vita Monastica* (1923); *Life of Ignatius Loyola* (1923); *Life of Lafayette* (1927); *Henry of Navarre* (1930); *Alfred de Musset* (1931); *The Black Prince* (1932); *Dan Chaucer* (1934); *The House of Guise* (1937); *Vienna* (1939); *Madame Récamier* (1940); *Horace* (1947); etc.

SEDGWICK, SUSAN ANN LIVINGSTON [Ridley] (Mrs. Theodore Sedgwick) (c. 1789–Jan. 20, 1867). Author. *The Morals of Pleasure* (1829); *The Young Emigrants* (1830); *Allen Prescott* (1834); *Alida; or, Town and Country* (1844); *Walter Thornley* (1859); all published anonymously.

SEDGWICK, THEODORE (Dec. 1780–Nov. 7, 1839); b. Sheffield, Mass. Lawyer, author. *Hints to My Countrymen* (1826); *Public and Private Economy,* 3v. (1836–39); etc.

SEDGWICK, THEODORE (Jan. 27, 1811–Dec. 8, 1859); b. Albany, N.Y., son of Susan Ann Livingston Sedgwick. Lawyer, author. *A Memoir of the Life of William Livingston* (1833); *Constitutional Reform* (1843); *Thoughts on the Proposed Annexation of Texas* (1844); *A Treatise on the Measurement of Damages* (1847); etc. Editor: *A Collection of the Political Writings of William Leggett,* 2v. (1840); etc.

SEDLEY, HENRY (b. Apr. 4, 1831); b. Boston, Mass. Journalist, author. *Dangerfield's Rest; or, Before the Storm* (1864); *Marion Rooke; or, The Quest for Fortune* (1865); etc.

SEEGER, ALAN (June 22, 1888–July 4, 1916); b. New York. Soldier, poet. *Poems* (1916); *Letters and Diary* (1917); both edited by his father, Charles Louis Seeger. His best-known poem is "I Have a Rendezvous with Death."

SEEGER, CHARLES LOUIS (Jan. 13, 1860–Nov. 6, 1943); b. Springfield, Mass. Father of Alan Seeger. Merchant, editor, author. *Americans in Foreign Lands* (1914). Editor: *Poems of Alan Seeger* (1916); *Letters and Diary of Alan Seeger* (1917).

SEELE, KEITH C[edric] (Feb. 13, 1898–); b. Warsaw, Ind. Egyptologist, educator. *Medinet Habu II: Later Historical Records of Ramses III* (with others, 1932); *Medinet Habu III: The Calendar, the Slaughterhouse, and Minor Records of Ramses III* (with others, 1934); *The Mastaba of Mereruka* (with others, 1938); *When Egypt Ruled the East* (with G. Steindorff, 1941); *Medinet Habu V: The Temple Proper, Part I* (with others, 1957); *The Tomb of Tjanefr* (1959); and other reports of archeological investigations in Egypt. Editor, *Journal of Near Eastern Studies,* since 1948. Prof. Egyptology, University of Chicago, since 1950.

SEELEY, MABEL (Mar. 25, 1903–); b. Herman, Minn. Author. *The Listening House* (1938); *The Crying Sisters* (1939); *The Whispering Cup* (1940); *The Chuckling Fingers* (1941); *Eleven Came Back* (1942); *Woman of Property* (1947); *The Beckoning Door* (1950); *The Stranger Beside Me* (1951); *The Whistling Shadow* (1954).

SEELYE, ELIZABETH EGGLESTON (Dec. 15, 1858–Nov. 11, 1923); b. St. Paul, Minn., daughter of Edward Eggleston. Author. *Lake George in History* (1896); *Saratoga and Lake Champlain in History* (1898); *Montezuma and the Conquest of Mexico* (with Edward Eggleston, 1908); etc.

SEELYE, JULIUS HAWLEY (Sept. 24, 1824–May 12, 1895); b. Bethel, Conn. Educator, author. *The Way, the Truth and the Life* (1873); *Christian Missions* (1875); *Duty* (1891); *Citizenship* (1894); etc. President, Amherst College, 1876–90.

SEELYE, L[aurenus] CLARK (Sept. 20, 1837–Oct. 12, 1924); b. Bethel, Conn. Congregational clergyman, educator, author. *The Early History of Smith College* (1923); *Prayers of a College Year* (1925); etc. President, Smith College, 1873–1910.

SEEMÜLLER, A[nne] M[oncure] C[rane] (Mrs. Augustus Seemüller) (1838–1872). Author. *Emily Chester* (anon., 1864); *Reginald Archer* (1871); etc.

SEGAL, ERICH W. (June 16, 1937–   ); b. Brooklyn, N.Y. Educator, author. *Euripides: A Collection of Critical Essays* (1968); *Roman Laughter: The Comedy of Plautus* (1968); *Love Story* (novel, 1970). Dept. of classics, Yale University.

SEGAL, LORE GROSZMANN (Mar. 1928–); b. Vienna. Author. *Other People's Houses* (1964); *Tell Me a Mitzi* (1970).

SEIBEL, GEORGE (Sept. 13, 1872–July 24, 1958); b. Pittsburgh, Pa. Editor, librarian, author. *The Fall* (1918); *Bacon versus Shakespeare* (1919); *The Mormon Saints* (1919); *The*

Concert (sonnets, 1934); *The Stories He Told* (1939); *Book and Heart* (poems, 1951); etc. Editor, the *Pittsburgh Gazette-Times*, 1896–1911; *Volksblatt Freiheits-Freund*, 1912–25; drama editor, the *Pittsburgh Sun-Telegraph*, 1927–36; director, Allegheny Carnegie Library, 1939–54.

SEID, RUTH (July 1, 1913–); b. Brooklyn, N.Y. Author. Pen name "Jo Sinclair." *Wasteland* (1946); *Sing at My Wake* (1951); *The Long Moment* (play, 1951); *The Changelings* (1955); *Anna Teller* (1960).

SEIDEL, FREDERICK LEWIS (Feb. 19, 1936–); b. St. Louis, Mo. Poet. *Final Solutions* (1963).

SEIFERT, SHIRLEY (1889–September 1, 1971); b. St. Peters, Mo. Novelist. *Land of Tomorrow* (1937); *The Wayfarer* (1938); *River out of Eden* (1940); *Waters of the Wilderness* (1941); *Those Who Go Against the Current* (1943); *Captain Grant* (1946); *The Proud Way* (1948); *The Turquoise Trail* (1950); *The Three Lives of Elizabeth* (1952); *Let My Name Stand Fair* (1956); *Destiny in Dallas* (1958); *Look to the Rose* (1960); *The Senator's Lady* (1967).

SEIFFERT, MARJORIE ALLEN, b. Moline, Ill. Poet. *A Woman of Thirty* (1919); *Ballads of the Singing Bow!* (1927); *The King with Three Faces, and Other Poems* (1929); *The Name of Life* (1938); etc.

SEISS, JOSEPH AUGUSTUS (Mar. 18, 1823–June 20, 1904); b. in Frederick Co., Md. Lutheran clergyman, editor, author. *Lectures on the Gospels,* 2v. (1868–72); *Luther and the Reformation* (1884); *Lectures on the Epistles,* 2v. (1885); etc. Editor, *The Lutheran,* 1867–79.

SEITZ, DON CARLOS (Oct. 24, 1862–Dec. 4, 1935); b. Portage, O. Editor, author. *The Last Piracy of the Spanish Main* (1903); *Elba and Elsewhere* (1910); *The Buccaneers* (1912); *Whistler Stories* (1913); *Paul Jones* (1917); *Artemus Ward* (1919); *Braxton Bragg* (1923); *Joseph Pulitzer* (1924); *Uncommon Americans* (1925); *The Dreadful Decade* (1926); *Horace Greeley* (1926); *A Chapter on Autobiography* (1926); *The James Gordon Bennetts* (1928); *The Also Rans* (1928); *Famous American Duels* (1929); etc. With the *New York World,* 1895–1923, manager, the *Evening World,* 1923–26; assoc. editor, *The Outlook,* 1926–27; *The Churchman,* 1929–32.

SELBY, HUBERT JR. (July 23, 1928–   ); b. Brooklyn, N.Y. Author. *Last Exit to Brooklyn* (1964).

SELBY, JOHN [Allen] (Feb. 7, 1897–); b. Gallatin, Mo. Editor, author. *Sam* (1939); *Island in the Corn* (1941); *Starbuck* (1943); *Elegant Journey* (1944); *The Man Who Never Changed* (1954); *Time Was* (1956); *The Days Dividing* (1958); *A Few Short Blocks Between* (1959); *Madame* (1961); *Beyond Civil Rights* (1966); etc. Editor-in-chief, Rinehart & Co., 1945–53.

SELDES, GEORGE [Henry] (Nov. 16, 1890–); b. Alliance, N.J. Author. *You Can't Print That!* (1929); *Can These Things Be?* (1931); *The Vatican* (1934); *Freedom of the Press* (1935); *Sawdust Caesar* (1935); *Lords of the Press* (1938); *The Catholic Crisis* (1939); *Facts and Fascism* (1943); *1000 Americans* (1947); *The People Don't Know* (1949); *Tell the Truth and Run* (1953); *The World's Great Quotations* (1959); *Never Tire of Protesting* (1968). Editor, *In Fact,* 1940–50.

SELDES, GILBERT [Vivian] (Jan. 3, 1893–Oct. 5, 1970); b. Alliance, N.J. Critic, editor, playwright. *The Seven Lively Arts* (1924); *The Wise-Crackers* (prod. 1925); *The Stammering Century* (1928); *The Square Emerald* (1928); *The Future of Drinking* (1930); *Against Revolution* (1932); *The Years of the Locust* (1932); *Mainland* (1936); *The Movies Come from America* (1937); *The Great Audience* (1950); *The Public Arts* (1956); etc. Also under pen name "Foster Johns": *The Victory Murders* (1927), and other mystery novels. Columnist, the *New York Journal,* 1931–37; director of television programs, Columbia Broadcasting System, 1937–45; prof. and director,

The Annenberg School of Communications, University of Pennsylvania, from 1959.

SELEKMAN, BENJAMIN MORRIS (Mar. 26, 1893–Apr. 7, 1962); b. Bethlehem, Pa. Educator. *Labor Relations and Human Relations* (1947); *Power and Morality in a Business Society* (with Sylvia K. Selekman, 1956); *A Moral Philosophy for Management* (1959); etc. Prof. labor relations, Harvard University, from 1935.

Self. Play by Sidney F. Bateman (prod. 1856). Comedy of manners.

SELF, MARGARET CABELL (Feb. 12, 1902–); b. Cincinnati, O. Author. *Teaching the Young to Ride* (1935); *Horses, Their Selection, Care and Handling* (1943); *Those Smith Kids* (1945); *The Horseman's Encyclopedia* (1945); *Riding Simplified* (1948); *Horseman's Companion* (1949); *Horsemastership* (1953); *The American Horse Show* (1958); *Riding and Hunting Simplified* (1959); *At the Horse Show with Margaret Cabell Self* (1966); *In Ireland with Margaret Cabell Self* (1967); *The Morgan Horse in Pictures* (1967); *Come Away* (1968); *The Quarter Horse in Pictures* (1969); *The Young Rider and His First Pony* (1969); etc.

Self-Culture. Essay by William Ellery Channing (1838). It had a profound influence on Emerson, Curtis, and Higginson and other writers imbued with humanitarian impulses.

SELIGMAN, BEN B[aruch] (Nov. 20, 1912–); b. Newark, N.J. Economist, author. *Main Currents in Modern Economics: Economic Thought Since 1870* (1962); *Most Notorious Victory: Man in an Age of Automation* (1966). Editor: *Poverty as a Public Issue* (1965).

Selkirk, Jane. Pen name of John Stanton Higham Chapman and Mary Hamilton Illsley Chapman.

SELL, HENRY BLACKMAN (Nov. 14, 1889–); b. Whitewater, Wis. Editor. *Buffalo Bill and the Wild West* (with Victor Weybright, 1955). Editor, *Harper's Bazaar,* 1920–26; *Town and Country,* since 1949.

SELLARS, ROY WOOD (July 9, 1880–); b. Egmondville, Ont. Educator, author. *Critical Realism* (1916); *The Essentials of Logic* (1917); *The Essentials of Philosophy* (1917); *Principles and Problems of Philosophy* (1926); *Religion Coming of Age* (1928); *Lending a Hand to Hylas* (1968); *Reflections on American Philosophy from Within* (1969); etc. Editor: *Philosophy for the Future* (with others, 1949). Philosophy dept., University of Michigan, since 1905.

SELLERS, ISAIAH (c. 1802–Mar. 6, 1864); b. in Iredell Co., N.C. Mississippi River pilot, author. He wrote articles for the *New Orleans Daily Picayune* under the pen name "Mark Twain," which was later adopted by Samuel L. Clemens. *See* "Mark Twain's" *Life on the Mississippi* (1883); E. W. Gould's *Fifty Years on the Mississippi* (1889).

SELLERS, [James] CLARK (Oct. 16, 1891–); b. Heber, Utah. Handwriting expert. *Handwriting Identification and Expert Testimony* (1930); *Spurious Typewritten Documents* (1934); *Scientific Identification vs. Guesswork* (1938).

SELLERY, GEORGE CLARKE (Jan. 21, 1872–Jan. 21, 1962); b. Kincardine, Ont. Educator, author. *Lincoln's Suspension of Habeas Corpus as Viewed by Congress* (1907); *The Renaissance, Its Nature and Origins* (1950); *E. A. Birge: a Memoir* (1956); *Some Ferments at Wisconsin, 1901–1947* (1960); etc. Co-author: *Medieval Foundations of Western Civilization* (1929); etc. History dept., University of Wisconsin, 1901–42.

SELLIN, [Johan] THORSTEN (Oct. 26, 1896–); b. Örnsköldsvik, Swe. Educator. *Marriage and Divorce Legislation in Sweden* (with J. P. Shalloo, 1922); *A Bibliographical Manual for the Student of Criminology* (1935); *Research Memorandum on Crime in the Depression* (1937); *Culture, Conflict, and Crime* (1938); *The Criminality of Youth* (1940); *Pioneer-*

ing in Penology (1944); *The Death Penalty* (with M. E. Wolfgang, 1959); *The Measurement of Delinquency* (1964).

Selling of Joseph, The. By Samuel Sewall (1700). One of the first anti-slavery documents in America. It also touched on the then novel subject of woman's rights.

Selling of the President, The. Inside story of the advertising campaign used to "sell" Richard M. Nixon's image to American television viewers, by Joe McGinniss (1968).

SELTZER, CHARLES ALDEN (Aug. 15, 1875–1942); b. Janesville, Wis. Novelist. *The Range Riders* (1911); *The Two-Gun Man* (1911); *The Range Boss* (1916); *The Trail Horde* (1920); *Beau Rand* (1921); *The Way of the Buffalo* (1924); *Channing Comes Through* (1925); *The Mesa* (1928); *Gone North* (1930); *A Son of Arizona* (1931); *Silverspurs* (1935); *Coming of the Law* (1938); *Treasure Ranch* (1940); etc.

SELTZER, LEON EUGENE (Aug. 14, 1918–); b. Auburn, Me. Editor, publisher. Editor: *Columbia Lippincott Gazeteer of the World* (1946–52). With Columbia University Press, 1939–56; director, Stanford University Press, since 1956.

SELTZER, LOUIS BENSON (Sept. 19, 1897–); b. Cleveland, O. Editor. *The Years Were Good* (1956). With *Cleveland Press,* since 1917; editor, since 1928; editor-in-chief, Scripps-Howard newspapers of Ohio, since 1937.

SELWYN, EDGAR (Oct. 20, 1875–Feb. 13, 1944); b. Cincinnati, O. Playwright. *The Arab* (prod. 1910); *The Country Boy* (prod. 1910); *Nearly Married* (prod. 1913); *Rolling Stones* (prod. 1914); *The Mirage* (prod. 1920); *Anything Might Happen* (prod. 1923); *Dear Sir* (prod. 1924); *Possession* (prod. 1928); etc.

SELZ, PETER HOWARD (Mar. 27, 1919–); b. Munich, Germany. Art historian, author. *German Expressionist Painting* (1957); *New Images of Man* (1959); *Art Nouveau* (1960); *Directions in Kinetic Sculpture* (1966); *Funk* (1967); etc. Prof. art, University of California at Berkeley, since 1965.

SEMMES, RAPHAEL (Sept. 27, 1809–Aug. 30, 1877); b. in Charles Co., Md. Naval officer, author. *Service Afloat and Ashore during the Mexican War* (1851); *The Campaign of General Scott, in the Valley of Mexico* (1852). *Memoirs of Service, Afloat, during the War between the States* (1869); etc.

SENARENS, LUIS PHILIP (1863–Dec. 26, 1939); b. Brooklyn, N.Y. Dime novelist. Author of over 1500 books. Creator of the mechanically minded Frank Reade, hero of the *Frank Reade* books. He also wrote the *Frank Reade Weekly,* beginning in 1902. He wrote under twenty-seven pen names, including "Noname," "Police Captain Howard," "W. J. Earle," "Ned Sparling," and "Kit Clyde." He was connected for many years with the Frank Tousey Co., publishers of dime novels. The usual *Frank Reade* book consisted of 16 pages, three columns to a page, containing about 50,000 words, with a black and white cover illustration showing some mechanical marvel.

SENDAK, MAURICE BERNARD (June 10, 1928–); b. Brooklyn, N.Y. Author, illustrator. *Kenny's Window* (1956); *Very Far Away* (1957); *The Sign on Rosie's Door* (1960); *The Nutshell Library* (1963); *Where the Wild Things Are* (1963); *In the Night Kitchen* (1970); etc. Illustrator of numerous other children's books.

SENDER, RAMON JOSÉ (1902–); b. Alcolea de Cinca, Sp. Educator, author. Works translated into English include: *Pro Patria* (1934); *Counterattack in Spain* (1938); *Dark Wedding* (1943); *The Sphere* (1949); *Affable Hangman* (1954); *Before Noon* (1957); *Requiem for a Spanish Peasant* (1960); *Exemplary Novels of Cibola* (1963); etc. Prof. Spanish, successively Amherst College, University of Denver, University of New Mexico.

SENIOR, CLARENCE (June 9, 1903–); b. Clinton, Mo. Educator, author. *Puerto Rican Emigration* (1947); *The Puerto Rican in New York City* (1948); *Strangers and Neighbors* (1952); *The Puerto Ricans* (1965); etc. Prof. sociology, Brooklyn College, since 1961.

SENN, ALFRED H. (Mar. 19, 1899–); b. Blotzheim, Haut-Rhin, Fr. Educator, linguist. *Cortina's Russian Conversaphone* (with A. A. Rozhdestvensky, 1951); *Prehistory of the Russian Language* (1954); Editor, *Swiss Record,* since 1948. Prof. philology, University of Wisconsin, 1931–38; University of Pennsylvania, since 1938.

SENNETT, RICHARD. Author. *Families against the City: Middle Class Homes of Industrial Chicago, 1872–1890* (1970); *The Uses of Disorder: Personal Identity and City Life* (1970).

SENSABAUGH, GEORGE FRANK (July 15, 1906–); b. Dublin, Tex. Educator, author. *The Tragic Muse of John Ford* (1944); *Purposeful Prose* (with V. K. Whitaker, 1951); *That Grand Whig, Milton* (1952); *The Study of English in California Schools* (1953); *Milton in Early America* (1963). Prof. English, Stanford University, since 1947.

Sense of the Past, The. By Henry James (1917), published posthumously. A contemporary Englishman engrossed in the diary of an ancestor steps back to those vanished days to relive the events mentioned in the diary.

Sentimental Novel in America, 1789–1860, The. By Herbert Ross Brown (1940).

Separate Peace, A. By John Knowles (1963). Novel about a boys' preparatory school.

"September 1, 1939." Poem by W. H. Auden.

Sequoyah. Indian name of George Guess (or Gist) (c. 1770–1843). Guess created the Cherokee alphabet, and founded the *Cherokee Phoenix* (q.v.), Feb. 22, 1828. The giant Sequoia trees in California were named in his honor. *See* Grant Foreman's *Sequoyah* (1938); *The Colophon,* part 9, 1932, part 13, 1933.

SERL, EMMA, b. Clinton, Wis. Author. *In Fableland* (1911); *The Story of Kansas City* (1924); *Every Day Doings in Heathville* (1927); *In Rabbitville* (1929); *What They Say in Rabbitville* (1936); etc.

SERLING, ROD (Dec. 25, 1924–); b. Syracuse, N.Y. Playwright. *Patterns* (prod. 1957); *More Stories from the Twilight Zone* (1961); *The Season to Be Wary* (1968); etc.

SERT, JOSÉ LUIS (July 1, 1902–); b. Barcelona, Sp. Architect, city planner, author. *Can Our Cities Survive?* (1947); *The Heart of the City* (with others, 1952); *The Shape of Our Cities* (with Jacqueline Tyrwhitt, 1957); *Antoni Gaudi* (with James Johnson Sweeney, 1960).

Servant in the House, The. Play by Charles Rann Kennedy (prod. 1908). The action takes place in an English vicarage, and the series of events which ensues brings out the Christian brotherhood of all the characters, some of high degree, some of lower rank.

SESSIONS, ROGER HUNTINGTON (Dec. 28, 1896–); b. Brooklyn, N.Y. Composer, educator. *The Musical Experience of Composer, Performer, and Listener* (1950); *Harmonic Practice* (1951). Prof. music, University of California, 1945–65. Faculty, Julliard School of Music, since 1965.

Seth Jones; or, The Captive of the Frontier. Dime novel by Edward S. Ellis (1860). Story of the Revolutionary hero, Ethan Allan. A sensational best seller.

Seth's Brother's Wife. Novel by Harold Frederic (1887). Bitter tale of drab farm life in New York State.

SETON, ANYA, b. New York. Author. *My Theodosia* (1941); *Dragonwyck* (1944); *The Turquoise* (1946); *The Hearth and the Eagle* (1948); *Foxfire* (1950); *Katherine* (1954); *The Mistletoe and the Sword* (1955); *The Winthrop Woman* (1958); *Devil Water* (1962); *Avalon* (1965); etc.

SETON, ELIZABETH ANN BAYLEY (Aug. 28, 1774–Jan. 4, 1821); b. New York. Founder of the Sisters of Charity; known as Mother Seton. Author: *Memoir, Letters and Journal,* 2v. (1869). *See* Joseph B. Code's *Mother Seton and Her Sisters of Mercy* (1930), and his numerous other books on Mother Seton.

SETON, ERNEST THOMPSON (Aug. 14, 1860–Oct. 23, 1946); b. South Shields, Eng. Name changed from Ernest Seton-Thompson. Naturalist, artist, author. *Wild Animals I Have Known* (1898); *The Trail of the Sandhill Stag* (1899); *The Biography of a Grizzly* (1900); *Lobo, Rag and Vixen* (1900); *Lives of the Hunted* (1901); *Krag and Johnny Bear* (1902); *American Woodcraft for Boys* (1902); *Two Little Savages* (1903); *Monarch, the Big Bear of Tallac* (1904); *Animal Heroes* (1905); *The Arctic Prairies* (1911); *Rolf in the Woods* (1911); *Wild Animals at Home* (1913); *Bannertail* (1922); *Famous Animal Stories* (1932); *Great Historic Animals* (1937); *Trail of an Artist Naturalist* (autobiography, 1940); *Santana, Hero Dog of France* (1945); etc.

SETON, GRACE THOMPSON (Mrs. Gallatin Thompson Seton) (1872–Mar. 19, 1959); b. Sacramento, Calif. Author. *A Woman Tenderfoot in the Rockies* (1900); *Nimrod's Wife* (1907); *A Woman Tenderfoot in Egypt* (1923); *Chinese Lanterns* (1924); *Log of the "Look-See"* (1932), also published as *Magic Waters* (1933); *Poison Arrows* (1940); *The Singing Traveller* (1947); *Singing Heart* (1957); etc.

SETON, WILLIAM (Jan. 28, 1835–Mar. 15, 1905); b. New York. Novelist, poet. *Nat Gregory* (1867); *Romance of the Charter Oak* (1871); *The Pride of Lexington* (1873); *The Pioneer* (poem, 1874); etc.

SETTLE, RAYMOND W. (Mar. 11, 1888–); b. Pleasant Gap, Mo. Baptist clergyman, author. *Empire on Wheels* (with Mary L. Settle, 1949); *Story of Wentworth* (1949); *Saddles and Spurs: The Saga of the Pony Express* (with Mary L. Settle, 1955). Editor: *March of the Mounted Riflemen* (1940).

SETTON, KENNETH M. (June 17, 1914–); b. New Bedford, Mass. Historian. *The Christian Attitude toward the Emperor in the Fourth Century* (1941); *Catalan Domination of Athens, 1311–1388* (1948); *Great Problems in European Civilization* (with Henry R. Winkler, 1954). Editor-in-chief, *History of the Crusades,* 5v. (1956). Prof. history, University of Pennsylvania, since 1953.

Seuss, Dr. Pen name of Theodor Seuss Geisel.

SEVAREID, [Arnold] ERIC (Nov. 26, 1912–); b. Velva, N.D. News analyst, author. *Canoeing with the Cree* (1935); *Not So Wild a Dream* (1946); *In One Ear* (1952); *Small Sounds in the Night* (1956); *This Is Eric Sevareid* (1964); etc.

Seven Arts. New York. Monthly magazine. Founded Nov., 1916. Expired Oct., 1917.

Seven Days in May. Novel by Fletcher Knebel (1962). Imaginary takeover of the U.S. government in the Atomic Age.

Seven Keys to Baldpate. Novel by Earl Derr Biggers (1913), dramatized by George M. Cohan (prod. 1913). An author makes a bet that he can write a play during a weekend. He goes to a house on Baldpate Mountain, a hangout for thieves. He becomes mixed up in their affairs, but manages to win his bet.

Seven Little Sisters. By Jane Andrews (1861). Stories of foreign lands for girls.

Seven Lively Arts, The. Discussion of the popular arts of the motion picture, comic strip, jazz, etc., by Gilbert Seldes (1924). Influential as one of the first thorough treatments of popular culture.

Seven Storey Mountain, The. By Thomas Merton (1949). Autobiography of a poet who became converted to Catholicism and entered a Trappist monastery.

Seventeen. By Booth Tarkington (1916). Humorous account of the ups and downs of William Sylvanus Baxter, aged seventeen, called "Willie" by his family and "Silly Bill" by his schoolmates.

Seventeen. New York. Monthly. Founded 1944. Magazine covering all interests of teen-age girls.

Seventh Heaven. Play by Austin Strong (1922). Moving story of heroic sacrifice on the part of a soldier who lost his sight in World War I, and on the part of the girl who waited for him in a dingy attic.

Seventies, The. Madison, Minn. Irregular. Founded 1958, as *The Fifties;* name changed to *The Sixties* in 1960. Edited by Robert Bly and others. Devoted to poetry and cultural comment.

77 Dream Songs. Poem sequence by John Berryman (1964).

Seventy Years of Best Sellers, 1895–1965. Edited by Alice Payne Hackett. Brings up to date *Sixty Years of Best Sellers.*

SEVERANCE, FRANK HAYWARD (Nov. 28, 1856–Jan. 26, 1931); b. Manchester, Mass. Editor, author. *Old Trails on the Niagara Frontier* (1899); *The Story of Joncaire* (1906); *Studies of the Niagara Frontier* (1911); *An Old Frontier of France,* 2v. (1917); and many books on Niagara and Western New York history. Managing editor, the *Illustrated Buffalo Express,* 1886–1902.

SEVERSKY, ALEXANDER P. de (June 7, 1894–); b. Tiflis, Rus. Aeronautical engineer, airplane designer, author. *Victory through Air Power* (1942); *Air Power—Key to Survival* (1950); *America: Too Young to Die* (1961).

Sevier, Clara Driscoll. See Clara Driscoll.

SEVIER, JOHN (Sept. 23, 1745–Sept. 24, 1815); b. near New Market, Va. Pioneer, governor, diarist. *The Diary of John Sevier,* in the *Tennessee Historical Magazine,* Oct. 1919–Apr. 1920. Governor of Tennessee, 1796–1801, 1803–09. *See* James R. Gilmore's *John Sevier, Commonwealth-Builder* (1887); Francis M. Turner's *Life of Gen. John Sevier* (1910); Carl S. Driver's *John Sevier* (1932).

Sewall, Alice Archer. See Alice Archer Sewall James.

SEWALL, JONATHAN (Aug. 17, 1728–Sept. 26, 1796); b. Salem, Mass. Lawyer, loyalist, author. *A Cure for the Spleen; or, Amusement for a Winter's Evening* (under pen name "Sir Roger de Coverley," 1775), reprinted as *The American's Counsel, in a Cure for the Spleen* (1775); etc. *See* J. H. Stark's *The Loyalists of Massachusetts* (1910).

SEWALL, JONATHAN MITCHELL (1748–Mar. 29, 1808); b. Salem, Mass. Poet. *Eulogy on the Late General Washington* (1800); *Miscellaneous Poems* (1801); etc. He wrote the ballad, "War and Washington," which was sung by the soldiers.

SEWALL, SAMUEL (Mar. 28, 1652–Jan. 1, 1730); b. Bishopstoke, Eng. Merchant, printer, magistrate, diarist. *The Selling of Joseph* (1700); *Diary of Samuel Sewall,* 3v. (1878–82); *Samuel Sewall's Diary,* abridged edition, ed. by Mark Van Doren (1927). *See* Ola E. Winslow's *Samuel Sewall of Boston* (1964).

Sewanee Review. Sewanee, Tenn. Literary quarterly. Founded 1892, at the University of the South. Its first editor was William Peterfield Trent, 1892–1900. Other editors have included John Bell Henneman, William S. Knickerbocker, Andrew Lytle, Allen Tate, J. E. Palmer, and Monroe Spears. Mark Van Doren, Delmore Schwartz, R. P. Blackmur, Richard Ellman, Howard Nemerov, and other notable poets and critics have been among its contributors in recent years.

SEWARD, WILLIAM HENRY (May 16, 1801–Oct. 10, 1872); b. Florida, N.Y. Statesman, author. *The Works of William H. Seward,* 5v. (1884); *Autobiography of William H. Seward,* ed. by F. W. Seward (1877). See *William H. Seward's Travels around the World,* ed. by Olive R. Seward (1873); F. W. Seward's *Seward at Washington,* 2v. (1891); Frederic Bancroft's *Life of William H. Seward,* 2v. (1900). Governor of New York, 1839–42; U.S. Senator, 1848–61; Secretary of State, 1861–69.

SEWELL, HELEN MOORE (June 27, 1896–1957); b. Mare Island, Calif. Illustrator, author. *Blue Barns* (1933); *Cinderella* (1934); *Ming and Mehitable* (1936); *Peggy and the Pony* (1937); *Jimmy and Jemima* (1940); *Belinda the Mouse* (1944). Illustrated many books by other authors.

Sex and the Single Girl. By Helen Gurley Brown (1962). The unmarried American female working in white-collar jobs in her search for amusement, romance, and husbands.

SEXTON, ANNE HARVEY (Nov. 9, 1928–); b. Newton, Mass. Author. Poet. *To Bedlam and Part Way Back* (1960); *All My Pretty Ones* (1962); *Eggs of Things* (with M. W. Kumin, 1963); *More Eggs of Things* (with M. W. Kumin, 1964); *Live or Die* (1966; Pulitzer Prize, 1967).

SEXTON, PATRICIA CAYO. Sociologist, author. *Spanish Harlem: An Anatomy of Poverty* (1965); *The American School* (1967).

Sexual Behavior in the Human Male. By Alfred C. Kinsey, Wardell B. Pomeroy, and Clyde E. Martin (1948). Based on surveys made by faculty members of Indiana University and supported by the National Research Council's Committee for Research on Problems of Sex. Financed by the Medical Division of the Rockefeller Foundation. This work, and its successor *Sexual Behavior in the Human Female* (1953), aroused considerable controversy because of its revelation of what supposedly were the sexual habits of average people. Published primarily for scholars and social scientists, it soon unexpectedly became a best-seller. *See* Donald Geddes' *An Analysis of the Kinsey Reports on Sexual Behavior in the Human Male and Female* (1954); Seward Hiltner's *Sex Ethics and the Kinsey Reports* (1953).

Sexual Politics. By Kate Millet (1970). Study of the "power-structured relationships" by which men govern women in modern society. The author argues that the basic idea of power in Western society derives from the wielding of sexual control by men over women.

SEYBOLT, ROBERT FRANCIS (Feb. 25, 1888–Feb. 5, 1951); b. Kearny, N.J. Educator, author. *The Colonial Citizen of New York City* (1918); *Source Studies in American Colonial Education* (1925); *The Public Schools of Colonial Boston* (1935); *The Private Schools of Colonial Boston* (1935); *The Public Schoolmasters of Colonial Boston* (1939); *The Town Officials of Colonial Boston* (1939); etc. History dept., University of Illinois, from 1920.

SEYMOUR, CHARLES (Jan. 1, 1885–Aug. 11, 1963); b. New Haven, Conn. Educator, author. *The Diplomatic Background of the War, 1870–1914* (1916); *Woodrow Wilson and the World War* (1921); *American Diplomacy during the World War* (1934); *American Neutrality, 1914–1917* (1935); etc. Editor: *The Intimate Papers of Colonel House,* 4v. (1926–28). President, Yale University, 1937–50.

SEYMOUR, CHARLES, JR. (Feb. 26, 1912–); b. New Haven, Conn. Educator. *Notre Dame of Noyon in the Twelfth Century* (1939); *Masterpieces of Sculpture in the National Gallery of Art* (1949); *Tradition and Experiment in Modern Sculpture* (1949); *Art Treasures for America* (1961); *Italian Sculpture 1400–1500* (1966); *Michelangelo's David, A Search for Identity* (1967). Prof. and curator, Renaissance art, Yale University, 1954–1966.

SEYMOUR, FLORA WARREN (Mrs. George Steele Seymour) (1888–Dec. 9, 1948); b. Cleveland, O. Lawyer, author. *William De Morgan* (1922); *The Boys' Life of Frémont* (1928); *The Boys' Life of Kit Carson* (1929); *Lords of the Valley* (1930); *Women of Trail and Wigwam* (1931); *Daniel Boone, Pioneer* (1931); *Meriwether Lewis, Trail-Blazer* (1937); *La Salle* (1939); *We Called Them Indians* (1940); *Handbook of Indian Wardship* (1943); *Pocahontas, Brave Girl* (1946); etc. Editor, *The Step Ladder,* from 1919.

SEYMOUR, GEORGE STEELE (Jan. 20, 1878–Sept. 7, 1945); b. Jersey City, N.J. Author. *Adventures with Books and Autographs* (1921); *Chronicles of Bagdad* (1923); *Cargoes of Ivory* (1937); *Hilltop in Michigan* (1940); etc.

SEYMOUR, THOMAS DAY (Apr. 1, 1848–Dec. 31, 1907); b. Hudson, O. Educator, classicist, editor, author. *Life in the Homeric Age* (1907); *Introduction to the Language and Verse of Homer* (1885); etc. Editor, Ginn & Co., publishers. Prof. Greek, Yale University, 1880.

SHAABER, MATTHIAS ADAM (Dec. 13, 1897–); b. Reading, Pa. Educator. *Some Forerunners of the Newspaper in England, 1476–1622* (1929); *The Art of Writing Business Letters* (1930); *Shakespeare's Seventeenth Century Editors* (with Matthew W. Black, 1937). Editor: *Seventeenth Century English Prose* (1957). Prof. English, University of Pennsylvania, since 1942.

SHACKFORD, MARTHA HALE (Aug. 25, 1875–); b. Dover, N.H. Educator, author. *A First Book of Poetics* (1906); *Plutarch in Renaissance England* (1929); *E. B. Browning; R. H. Horne: Two Studies* (1935); *Talks on Ten Poets, Wordsworth to Moody* (1958); etc. Editor: *Wellesley Verse, 1875–1925* (1925); *Letters from Elizabeth Barrett to B. R. Haydon* (1939); etc. English literature dept., Wellesley College, 1901–43.

SHACKLETON, ROBERT (Dec. 26, 1860–Mar. 1923); b. in Wisconsin. Editor, author. *Toomey and Others* (1900); *Many Waters* (1902); *The Great Adventure* (1904); *Touring Great Britain* (1914); *The Book of Boston* (1916); *The History of Harper's Magazine* (1916); *The Book of New York* (1917); *The Book of Philadelphia* (1919); *The Book of Chicago* (1920); *The Book of Washington* (1921); etc. Editor, the *Saturday Evening Post,* 1900–02.

SHADEGG, STEPHEN (Dec. 8, 1909–   ); b. Minneapolis, Minn. Author. *Barry Goldwater: Freedom Is His Flight Plan* (1962); *How to Win an Election* (1964); *What Happened to Goldwater* (1965).

Shadows on the Rock. Novel by Willa Cather (1931). The events of a single year as they appear to a child of Quebec in the last days of Frontenac, embellished with descriptions of the city and contemporary events.

SHAFER, BOYD CARLISLE (May 8, 1907–); b. Crestline, O. Editor, author. *Life, Liberty, and the Pursuit of Bread* (with Carol Shafer, 1940); *Nationalism, Myth, and Reality* (1955); *Nationalism, Interpreters and Interpretations; History of the United States* (1966); *Historical Study in the West* (in collaboration, 1968). Editor, *American Historical Review,* since 1953.

SHAFER, ROBERT (Dec. 24, 1889–Jan. 6, 1956); b. Hagerstown, Md. Editor, critic, author. *The English Ode to 1600* (1918); *Progress and Science* (1922); *Christianity and Naturalism* (1926); *Humanism and America* (1930); etc. Editor: *From Beowulf to Thomas Hardy* (1924); *American Literature* (1926); *Seventeenth Century Studies,* 2 series (1933, 1937); etc. Dept. of literature, University of Cincinnati, 1923–55.

SHAFFER, LAURANCE FREDERIC (Aug. 12, 1903–); b. Johnstown, N.Y. Psychologist. Author or co-author: *Children's Interpretations of Cartoons* (1930); *The Psychology of Adjustment* (1936); *Child Psychology* (1937); *Fields of Psychology* (1940); *Foundations of Psychology* (1948); etc.

SHALER, NATHANIEL SOUTHGATE (Feb. 20, 1841–Apr. 10, 1906); b. Newport, Ky. Educator, geologist, author. *Aspects of the Earth* (1889); *The Interpretation of Nature* (1893); *The Individual: A Study of Life and Death* (1900); *Elizabeth of England: A Dramatic Romance*, 5v. (1903); *Man and Earth* (1905); *Autobiography* (1909); etc. Prof. paleontology, Harvard, 1869–88; prof. geology, 1888–1906; dean, Lawrence Scientific School, Harvard, 1891–1906.

SHAMBAUGH, BERTHA M. H. (Mrs. Benjamin Franklin Shambaugh) (Feb. 12, 1871–); b. Cedar Rapids, Ia. Author. *Amana: The Community of True Inspiration* (1908); *Amana That Was and Amana That Is* (1932); etc.

Shandygaff. By Christopher Morley (1918). Collection of bookish essays on life and letters.

SHANE, PEGGY [Woodward] (Mrs. Ted Shane) (Nov. 24, 1898–); b. Washington, Ind. Novelist. *The Love Legend* (1922); *Lazy Laughter* (1923); *The Unpaid Piper* (1927); *Tangled Wives* (1932); *Change Partners* (1934).

SHANKLIN, JOHN F[erguson] (Feb. 9, 1903–); b. Fishers Island, N.Y. Forester. *Fifty Years of Forestry in the U.S.A.* (with others, 1950).

SHANKS, WILLIAM F[ranklin] G[ore] (Apr. 20, 1837–1905); b. Shelbyville, Ky. Editor, author. *Recollections of Distinguished Generals* (1865); *A Noble Treason* (1876); etc. On staff, the *New York Herald*, the *New York Times*, the *New York Tribune*, *Harper's Monthly*, etc.

SHANLY, CHARLES DAWSON (Mar. 9, 1811–Aug. 15, 1875); b. Dublin, Ire. Journalist, humorist, poet. *A Jolly Bear and His Friends* (1866); *The Monkey of Porto Bello* (1866); *The Truant Chicken* (1866); etc. His best known poem was "The Brier Wood Pipe." He wrote the "Mrs. Grundy Papers" and the "Mrs. Mehitable Ross" sketches, the latter for *Vanity Fair*, which he edited, 1862–63.

SHANNON, DAVID ALLEN (Nov. 30, 1920–); b. Terre Haute, Ind. Educator, author. *The Socialist Party in America: A History* (1955); *The Decline of American Communism* (1959); *Twentieth Century America* (1963); *Between the Wars* (1965). Editor: *The Great Depression* (1960); *Beatrice Webb's American Diary, 1898* (1963); *Progressivism and Postwar Reaction* (1966). Prof. history, University of Maryland, since 1965.

SHANNON, FRED ALBERT (Feb. 12, 1893–Feb. 4, 1963); b. Sedalia, Mo. Educator, author. *The Organization and Administration of the Union Army, 1861–65* (1928, Pulitzer Prize for American history, 1929); *Economic History of the People of the United States* (1934); *America's Economic Growth* (1940); *The Farmer's Last Frontier* (1945); *The Nation's Centennial Years: 1877–1890* (1959). History dept., Kansas State College of Agriculture and Applied Science, 1926–39; University of Illinois, from 1939.

SHANNON, JASPER BERRY (June 15, 1903–); b. Carlisle, Ky. Educator, author. *Towards a New Politics in the South* (1950); *Money and Politics* (1959). Editor: *The Study of Comparative Government* (1949). Prof. political science, University of Nebraska, since 1957.

SHANNON, MONICA, b. Belleville, Ont. Author. *California Fairy Tales* (1926); *Eyes for the Dark* (1928); *Tawnymore* (1931); *Dobry* (1934); etc. With Los Angeles Public Library, 1916–25.

SHANNON, WILLIAM VINCENT (Aug. 24, 1927–); b. Worcester, Mass. Journalist, author. *The Truman Merry-Go-Round* (with R. S. Allen, 1950); *The American Irish* (1964); *The Heir Apparent* (1968). With *New York Times*, since 1964.

SHAPIRO, DAVID (Jan. 2, 1947–   ); b. Newark N.J. Poet. *January* (1965). Editor: *An Anthology of New York Poets* (with Ron Padgett, 1970).

SHAPIRO, HARRY L[ionel] (Mar. 19, 1902–); b. Boston, Mass. Anthropologist, author. *Heritage of the Bounty* (1936); *Migration and Environment* (1939); *Aspects of Culture* (1956); *The Jewish People* (1960). Editor: *Man, Culture, and Society* (1956).

SHAPIRO, HARVEY (Jan. 27, 1924–   ); b. Chicago, Ill. Poet. *The Eye* (1953); *The Book and Other Poems* (1955); *Mountain, Fire, Thornbush* (1961); *Battle Report* (1966). Staff, *New York Times*, since 1957.

SHAPIRO, KARL [Jay] (Nov. 10, 1913–); b. Baltimore, Md. Poet, critic. *Poems* (1935); *Person, Place, and Thing* (1942); *V-Letter and Other Poems* (1944); *Essay on Rime* (1945); *Trial of a Poet and Other Poems* (1947); *Poems 1940–1953* (1953); *Beyond Criticism* (1953); *Poems of a Jew* (1958); *In Defense of Ignorance* (1960); *Prose Keys to Modern Poetry* (1962); *The Bourgeois Poet* (with Robert Beum, 1964); *White–Haired Lover* (1968); etc. Editor, *Poetry: A Magazine of Verse*, 1950–56; *Prairie Schooner*, since 1956. Prof. English, University of California at Davis.

SHAPLEN, ROBERT MODELL (Mar. 22, 1917–); b. Philadelphia, Pa. Author. *A Corner of the World* (1949); *Free Love and Heavenly Sinners* (1954); *A Forest of Tigers* (1956); *Kreuger: Genius and Swindler* (1960); *Toward the Welfare of Mankind—The Story of the Rockefeller Foundation* (1963); *The Lost Revolution* (1965); *Time Out of Hand: Revolution and Reaction in Southeast Asia* (1970); *The Road from War* (1970). Staff writer, *New Yorker* magazine, since 1952.

SHAPLEY, FERN RUSK (Sept. 20, 1890–); b. Mahomet, Ill. Museum curator, author. *George Caleb Bingham, The Missouri Artist* (1917); *European Paintings from the Gulbenkian Collection* (1950); *Paintings from the Samuel H. Kress Collection: Italian Schools*, Vol. I (1966); Vol. II (1968). Co-author: *Comparisons in Art* (1957).

SHAPLEY, HARLOW (Nov. 2, 1885–); b. Nashville, Mo. Astronomer. *Starlight* (1926); *Flights from Chaos* (1930); *Galaxies* (1943); *The Inner Metagalaxy* (1957); *Of Stars and Men* (1958); *The View from a Distant Star* (1964); *Beyond the Observatory* (1967); etc. Astronomer, Mt. Wilson Observatory, 1914–21; Harvard Observatory, 1921–52; Prof. astronomy, Harvard, 1952–56.

SHARP, DALLAS LORE (Dec. 13, 1870–Nov. 29, 1929); b. Haleyville, N.Y. Educator, naturalist, author. *Wild Life Near Home* (1901); *A Watcher in the Woods* (1903); *The Face of the Fields* (1911); *Beyond the Pasture Bars* (1914); *Where Rolls the Oregon* (1914); *The Seer of Slabsides* (1921); *The Better Country* (1928); etc. English dept., Boston University, 1902–22.

SHARP, FRANK CHAPMAN (July 30, 1866–May 4, 1943); b. Union City, N.J. Educator, author. *Shakespeare's Portrayal of the Moral Life* (1902); *The Influence of Custom on the Moral Judgment* (1908); *Ethics* (1928); etc. Philosophy dept., University of Wisconsin, 1893–1936; prof. 1905–36.

SHARP, PAUL FREDERICK (Jan. 19, 1918–); b. Kirksville, Mo. Educator, author. *Agrarian Revolt in Western Canada* (1948); *Old Orchard Farm: Story of an Iowa Boyhood* (ed., 1952); *Whoop-Up Country: Canadian-American West* (1955). Pres., Drake University, Des Moines, since 1966.

Sharp, Sidney. Pen name of Victor Mapes.

SHARPLESS, ISAAC (Dec. 16, 1848–Jan. 16, 1920); b. in Chester Co., Pa. Quaker leader, educator, author. *A Quaker Experiment in Government* (1898); *The Quaker in the Revolution* (1899); the two forming *A History of Quaker Government in Pennsylvania; Quakerism and Politics* (1905); *A Quaker Boy on the Farm and at School* (1908); *The Story of a Small College* (1918); etc. President, Haverford College, 1887–1917.

"Sharps and Flats." Column of wit and satire in verse and prose written by Eugene Field in the *Chicago Daily News,* 1883–95.

SHARROCK, MARIAN EDNA [Dormitzer] (May 12, 1897–); b. New York. Author. Pen name, "M. A. Dormie." *Snobs* (1913); *Expatriates* (1932); *Middle Age Madness* (1934); etc.

SHARTS, JOSEPH [William] (Sept. 14, 1875–); b. Hamilton, Ohio. Lawyer, author. *Ezra Caine* (1901); *The Romance of a Rogue* (1902); *The Hills of Freedom* (1904); *The Black Sheep* (1909); *The King Who Came* (1913); *Biography of Dayton* (1922); etc.

SHASTID, THOMAS HALL (July 19, 1866–Feb. 15, 1947); b. Pittsfield, Ill. Poet, novelist. *Newspaper Ballads* (1880); *Poems* (1881); *A Country Doctor* (1898); *Simon of Cyrene* (1923); *The Duke of Duluth* (1926); *Tramping to Failure* (autobiography, 1937); *My Second Life* (autobiography, 1944); etc.

SHATTUCK, ROGER WHITNEY (Aug. 20, 1923–); b. New York. Educator, author. *The Banquet Years* (1958); *Proust's Binoculars* (1963); *Half Tame* (poems 1964); etc. Prof. romance languages, University of Texas, since 1960.

Shaughraun, The. Play by Dion Boucicault (prod. 1874). Based on the experiences of Irish political prisoners who were being held in English jails.

SHAW, ADÉLE MARIE, b. Concord, N.H. Author. *The Coast of Freedom* (1902); *The Lady of the Dynamos* (1909); etc.

SHAW, ALBERT (July 23, 1857–June 25, 1947); b. Shandon, O. Editor, author. *Icaria: A Chapter in the History of Communism* (1884); *Political Problems of American Development* (1907); *Abraham Lincoln,* 2v. (1929); *International Bearings of American Policy* (1943); etc. Editor, the *Minneapolis Tribune,* 1883–90; founder, the *American Review of Reviews,* 1891; editor, 1891–1937.

SHAW, ANNA HOWARD (Feb. 14, 1847–July 2, 1919); b. Newcastle-upon-Tyne, Eng. Methodist minister, reformer, physician, author. *The Story of a Pioneer* (autobiography, 1915); etc. President, National American Woman Suffrage Association, 1904–15.

SHAW, CHARLES BUNSEN (June 5, 1894–Jan. 28, 1962); b. Toledo, O. Librarian. Compiler: *Reading List of Biographies* (1922); *Arm Chair Travels* (1924); *American Painters* (1927); *A List of Books for College Libraries,* 2v. (1931–40). Librarian, Woman's College of the University of North Carolina, 1920–27; librarian, Swarthmore College, from 1927.

SHAW, CHARLES GRAY (June 23, 1871–July 28, 1949); b. Elizabeth, N.J. Educator, author. *Christianity and Modern Culture* (1906); *The Ego and Its Place in the World* (1913); *Outline of Philosophy* (1930); *The Road to Culture* (1931); *The Road to Happiness* (1937); etc. Philosophy dept., New York University, 1899–1941.

SHAW, CHARLES G[reen] (1892–); Author. *The Low-Down* (1928); *Nightlife* (1931); *Lady by Chance* (1932); *New York—Oddly Enough* (1938); *The Giant of Central Park* (1940); *Into the Light* (1959); *Image of Life* (1962); *Time Has No Edge* (1966); etc.

SHAW, EDGAR DWIGHT (1871–Apr. 13, 1931); b. Leominster, Mass. Editor, publisher. Managing editor, the *Boston Journal,* 1903–04, 1914–17; the *Washington Times,* 1904–12; the *Boston Herald,* 1912–13; the *Boston Traveler,* 1913–14. Founder, the *Rochester Journal,* 1922; and other newspapers. Publisher, the *Washington Times;* the *Boston American;* the *Boston Advertiser.*

SHAW, HENRY WHEELER (Apr. 21, 1818–Oct. 14, 1885); b. Lanesboro, Mass. Pen name "Josh Billings." Humorist. *Josh Billings: His Book of Sayings* (1858); *Josh Billings on Ice, and Other Things* (1868); *Josh Billings' Farmer's Allminax* (annual vols. 1870–80); *Everybody's Friend* (1874); *Josh Billings: His Works Complete* (1880); *Josh Billings' Spice Box* (1881); etc. See J. R. Tandy's *Crackerbox Philosophers in American Humor and Satire* (1925).

SHAW, IRWIN (Feb. 27, 1913–); b. New York. Author. *Bury the Dead* (prod. 1936); *The Gentle People* (prod. 1939); *Sailor of the Bremen, and Other Stories* (1939); *Sons and Soldiers* (prod. 1943); *The Assassin* (prod. 1945); *Act of Faith* (stories, 1946); *The Young Lions* (1948); *Mixed Company* (stories, 1950); *The Troubled Air* (1951); *Lucy Crown* (1956); *Two Weeks in Another Town* (1959); *Selected Short Stories* (1962); *In the Company of Dolphins* (1964); *Voices of a Summer Day* (1965); *Love on a Dark Street* (1965); *Rich Man, Poor Man* (1970).

SHAW, JOHN (May 4, 1778–Jan. 10, 1809); b. Annapolis, Md. Naval surgeon, poet. *Poems by the Late Doctor John Shaw* (1810); etc.

SHAW, WARREN CHOATE (Nov. 16, 1887–); Lowell, Mass. Educator, author. *The Art of Debate* (1927); *History of American Oratory* (1928); etc. Prof. history, Blackburn College, Carlinville, Ill., since 1939.

SHAW, WILFRED BYRON (Jan. 10, 1881–); b. Adrian, Mich. Editor, author. *The University of Michigan* (1920). Editor: *From Vermont to Michigan: Correspondence of James Burrill Angell, 1860–1871* (1936); *The University of Michigan: An Encyclopedic Survey,* 4v. (with Walter A. Donnelly, 1942–58). Editor, the *Michican Alumnus,* 1904–29, the *Quarterly Review,* since 1934.

SHAW, WILLIAM SMITH (Aug. 12, 1778–Apr. 25, 1826); b. Haverhill, Mass. Librarian, Boston Athenaeum, 1807–22. Co-founder, the Anthology Society, 1805. He was known as "Athenaeum Shaw."

SHAWKEY, MORRIS PURDY (Feb. 17, 1868–1941); b. Sigel, Pa. Educator, author. *West Virginia in History, Life, Literature, and Industry,* 5v. (1928); etc. Pres., Marshall College, 1921–35.

SHAWN, TED [Edwin M.] (Oct. 21, 1891–1972); b. Kansas City, Mo. Dancer, author. *Ruth St. Denis, Pioneer and Prophet,* 2v. (1920); *The American Ballet* (1926); *Gods Who Dance* (1929); *Fundamentals of a Dance Education* (1937); *Dance We Must* (1940); *How Beautiful Upon the Mountains* (1943); *Every Little Movement: A Treatise on François Delsarte* (1954); *Sixteen Dances in Sixteen Rythms* (1956); *Thirty-Three Years of American Dance* (1959); *One Thousand and One Night Stands* (1960); etc.

SHAWN, WILLIAM (Aug. 31, 1907–); b. Chicago, Ill. Editor. With *The New Yorker,* since 1933; editor, since 1952.

Shawnee Sun. First periodical in Kansas. Founded 1835, by the Baptist missionary Jotham Meeker, at a mission on the outskirts of what is now Kansas City. Printed in Shawnee under the title, *Siwinowe Kesibwi.* Expired about 1844.

SHAY, FRANK (Apr. 8, 1888–Jan. 14, 1954); b. East Orange, N.J. Author. *Iron Men and Wooden Ships* (1924); *Here's Audacity!* (1930); *Incredible Pizarro* (1932); *Judge Lynch: His First Hundred Years* (1938); *Democracy in Action* (1940); etc. Editor: *My Pious Friends and Drunken Companions* (1927); and other song collections, etc.

SHEA, JOHN AUGUSTUS (1802–Aug. 15, 1845); b. Cork, Ire., came to the U.S. in 1827. Journalist, poet. *Rudekki* (1826); *Adolph, and Other Poems* (1831); *Parnassian Wild Flowers* (1836); *Clontarf . . . and Other Poems* (1841); *Poems,* ed. by his son, George Augustus Shea (1846); etc.

SHEA, JOHN [Dawson] GILMARY (July 22, 1824–Feb. 22, 1892); b. New York. Roman Catholic historian, editor. *Discovery and Exploration of the Mississippi Valley* (1852); *His-*

tory of the Catholic Missions among the Indian Tribes of the United States (1854); History of the Catholic Church in the United States, 4v. (1886–92); etc. Editor: The Library of American Linguistics, v. (1860–74); The Fallen Brave (1861); etc. He reprinted the original French text of the Jesuit Relations in 26v. (1857–87). With the Historical Magazine, 1855–67; the Catholic News, 1889–92. Founder, the United States Catholic Historical Society. See Peter Guilday's John Gilmary Shea (1926).

SHEAHAN, HENRY BESTON. See Henry Beston.

SHEARER, AUGUSTUS HUNT (Feb. 21, 1878–May 31, 1941); b. Philadelphia, Pa. Librarian, educator, historian. Co-author: History of the State of New York, ed. by Alexander C. Flick, 10v. (1933–37). Co-editor (with George Matthews Dutcher): A Guide to Historical Literature (1931).

SHEATS, PAUL HENRY (Dec. 5, 1907–); b. Tiffin, O. Educator. Citizenship Education Through the Social Studies (with R. W. Frederick, 1936); Education and the Quest for a Middle Way (1938); Adult Education (with others, 1953). Prof. education, University of California at Los Angeles, since 1949.

SHECUT, J[ohn] L[innaeus] E[ward] W[hitridge] (Dec. 4, 1770–June 1, 1836); b. Beaufort, S.C. Physician, botanist, novelist. Medical and Philosophical Essays (1819); Ish-Noo-Ju-Lut-Sche; or, The Eagle of the Mohawks (anon., 1841); The Scout; or, The Fast of Saint Nicholas (1844); etc.

SHEDD, CLARENCE PROUTY (June 24, 1887–); b. Worcester, Mass. Educator. Two Centuries of Student Christian Movements (1934); The Church Follows Its Students (1938); History of World's Alliance of YMCA's (with others, 1955); Religion in State Universities. (1959). Prof. religion, Yale Divinity School, since 1939.

SHEDD, GEORGE CLIFFORD (Nov. 19, 1877–Jan. 8, 1937); b. Ashland, Neb. Author. Miniatures (1900); Princess of Forge (1910); The Isle of Strife (1919); In the Shadow of the Hills (1919); Cryder (1922); The Silver Skull (1927); Up Purgatory Trail (1939); Rustlers of the Basin (1940); etc.

SHEDD, MARGARET [Cochran] (Mrs. Oliver Michael Kisich). (1900–); b. Urumia, Pers. Novelist. Hurricane Caye (1942); Inherit the Earth (1944); Return to the Beach (1950); Run (1956); Hosannah Tree (1967); etc.

SHEDD, WILLIAM G[reenbough] T[aylor] (June 21, 1820–Nov. 17, 1894); b. Acton, Mass. Educator, author. Discourses and Essays (1856); Lectures upon the Philosophy of History (1856); Literary Essays (1878); Dogmatic Theology, 3v. (1888–94); etc. Editor: Complete Works of Samuel Taylor Coleridge, 7v. (1853); etc. Prof. sacred rhetoric and systematic theology, Union Theological Seminary, New York, 1862–93.

SHEEAN, [James] VINCENT (Dec. 5, 1899–); b. in Christian Co., Ill. Correspondent, novelist. An American among the Riffi (1926); The Anatomy of Virtue (1927); The New Persia (1927); Gog and Magog (1930); The Tide (1933); Personal History (autobiography, 1935); Sanfelice (1936); The Pieces of a Fan (1937); A Day of Battle (1938); Not Peace but a Sword (1939); Bird of the Wilderness (1941); Between the Thunder and the Sun (1943); A Certain Rich Man (1947); Lead, Kindly Light (1949); Indigo Bunting (1951); Rage of the Soul (1952); Lily (1954); Mahatma Gandhi (1955); Nehru, Ten Years of Power (1959); Dorothy and Red (1963); etc.

SHEED, WILFRED JOHN JOSEPH (Dec. 27, 1930–); b. London. Author. A Middle Class Education (1961); The Hack (1963); Square's Progress (1965); Office Politics (1966); The Blacking Factory (1969); Max Jamison (1970). Editor: G. K. Chesterton's Essays and Poems (1957). Book editor, Commonweal magazine, since 1964.

Sheed & Ward. Publishers. New York City. The American branch of this London firm was established in New York in 1933 and specializes in Christian theology, philosophy, history, etc.

SHEEHAN, PERLEY POORE (June 11, 1875–1943); b. Cincinnati, O. Author. The Seer (1912); Those Who Walk in Darkness (1915); The Passport Invisible (1916); The House with a Bad Name (1920); etc.

SHEEHY, MAURICE S[tephen] (Apr. 26, 1898–); b. Irwin, Ill. Roman Catholic clergyman, author. Christ and the Catholic College (1926); Problems of Student Guidance (1929); College Men (1936); Head Over Heels (1951); Six O'Clock Mass (1952); The Priestly Heart (1956); Communist War on God (1956); Father Nick of Hickory Creek (1966).

SHEEN, FULTON JOHN (May 8, 1895–); b. El Paso, Ill. Roman Catholic clergyman, educator, author. God and Intelligence (1925); The Life of All Living (1929); Old Errors and New Labels (1931); Moods and Truths (1932); The Eternal Galilean (1934); Domestic Prelate (1935); The Moral Universe (1936); Communism and Religion (1937); The Rainbow of Sorrow (1938); Liberty, Equality and Fraternity (1938); Victory Over Vice (1939); For God and Country (1941); Peace (1942); Seven Words to the Cross (1944); Preface to Religion (1946); Peace of Soul (1949); Three to Get Married (1951); The Way to Happiness (1954); Life of Christ (1958); This is the Mass (1958); This is Rome (1960); The Power of Love (1964); Guide to Contentment (1966); Footprints in a Darkened Forest (1967); Easter Inspirations (1967); The Quotable Fulton J. Sheen (1967); That Tremendous Love (1967); etc. Catholic University of America, 1926–60; director, Society for the Propagation of the Faith, 1950–67.

Shelburne Essays. By Paul Elmer More, 11 v. (1904–27). These essays on a variety of subjects, chiefly literary, religious, and philosophical, take their name from Shelburne, N.H., where the author lived for a short time.

SHELBY, GERTRUDE [Singleton] MATHEWS (Mrs. John L. Mathews; Mrs. Edmund P. Shelby) (Apr. 13, 1881–Nov. 1, 1936); b. Momence, Ill. Author. Treasure (1917); Galusha A. Grow (with James T. Du Bois, 1917); Deporté (1927); Black Genesis (with Samuel G. Stoney, 1930); Po. Buckra (with same, 1930).

SHELDON, ADDISON ERWIN (Apr. 15, 1861–Nov. 24, 1943); b. Sheldon, Minn. Editor, author. History and Stories of Nebraska (1913); Nebraska: The Land and the People, 3v. (1930). Nebraska Old and New (1937); and many other books on Nebraska. Editor, Nebraska History, 1918–39; supt. Nebraska State Historical Society, from 1917.

SHELDON, CHARLES MONROE (Feb. 26, 1857–Feb. 24, 1946); b. Wellsville, N.Y. Congregational clergyman, author. Richard Bruce (1891); In His Steps (1896); Malcolm Kirk (1897); The Redemption of Freetown (1898); The Narrow Gate (1902); Howard Chase (1917); Heart Stories (1920); Charles M. Sheldon: His Life and Story (1925); Two Old Friends (1925); Scrap Book (1942); etc. Editor, Christian Herald, New York, 1920–25.

SHELDON, EDWARD BREWSTER (Feb. 4, 1886–Apr. 1, 1946); b. Chicago, Ill. Playwright. Salvation Nell (prod. 1908); The Nigger (prod. 1909); The Boss (prod. 1911); Romance (prod. 1913); The Garden of Paradise (prod. 1914); Lulu Belle (with Charles MacArthur, prod. 1926); etc. See Fred B. Millett's Contemporary American Authors (1940); Eric Wollencott Barnes's Edward Sheldon: The Man Who Lived Twice (1952).

SHELDON, EDWARD STEVENS (Nov. 21, 1851–Oct. 16, 1925); b. Waterville, Me. Philologist. Revised the etymologies in Webster's International Dictionary, for 1890 and later issues. Philology dept., Harvard University, 1877–1921; prof., 1894–1921.

Sheldon, Mrs. Georgie. Pen name of Sarah Elizabeth Downs.

SHELDON, WALTER L[orenzo] (Sept. 5, 1858–June 5, 1907); b. West Rutland, Vt. Ethical Culture leader, author. *Ethics and the Belief in God* (1892); *An Ethical Movement* (1896); *Thoughts from the Writings and Addresses,* ed. by Cecilia Boette (1919); etc.

SHELDON, WILLIAM HERBERT (Nov. 19, 1899–); b. Warwick, R.I. Medical and psychological researcher, author. *Psychology and the Promethean Will* (1936); *The Varieties of Human Physique* (with S. S. Stevens, 1940); *The Varieties of Temperament* (with same, and W. B. Tucker, 1942); *Varieties of Delinquent* (1949); *Atlas of Men* (with others, 1954); *Penny Whimsy* (1958); *Prometheus Revisited* (1969); etc.

SHELLABARGER, SAMUEL (May 18, 1888–Mar. 20, 1954); b. Washington, D.C. Educator, author. Pen names, "John Esteven," "Peter Loring." Under own name: *The Chevalier Bayard* (1928); *The Black Gale* (1929); *Lord Chesterfield* (1935); *Captain from Castile* (1945); *Prince of Foxes* (1947); *The King's Cavalier* (1950); *Lord Vanity* (1953); *Tolbecken* (1955); also under pen name "John Esteven": *The Door of Death* (1928); *Voodoo* (1930); *Graveyard Watch* (1938); and under pen name "Peter Loring": *Grief before Night* (1938); *Miss Rolling Stone* (1939). English dept., Princeton University, 1914–23.

Sheltered Life, The. Novel by Ellen Glasgow (1932). Study of General Archbold, gentleman of the old school, who is surrounded by women whom he cherishes.

Sheltering Sky, The. Novel by Paul Bowles (1949). Three well-to-do Americans, a man and wife and their male friend, seek personal fulfillment in North Africa but come to disaster.

SHELTON, DON ODELL (May 5, 1867–Jan. 29, 1941); b. Odessa, N.Y. Educator, editor, author. *Higher Ideals of Christian Stewardship* (1897); *Heroes of the Cross in America* (1904); *My Mother* (1916); *The Bible and Modern Civilization* (1921); etc. Founder and editor, the *Young Men's Journal,* Elmira, N.Y., 1886; *The Bible To-Day,* 1907; etc. President, National Bible Institute, New York, 1906–41.

SHELTON, FREDERICK WILLIAM (May 20, 1815–June 20, 1881); b. Jamaica, N.Y. Episcopal clergyman, humorist, essayist. *The Trolliopiad; or, Travelling Gentlemen in America* (under pen name "Nil Admirari, Esq.," 1837); *Salander and the Dragon* (1850); *The Rector of St. Bardolph's* (1853); *Up the River* (1853); *Crystalline; or, The Heiress of Fall Down Castle* (1854); *Peeps from a Belfry; or, The Parish Sketch Book* (1855); etc.

SHELTON, WILLIAM HENRY (Sept. 4, 1840–Oct. 4, 1932); b. in Ontario, Co., N.Y. Author. *A Man without a Memory* (1895); *The Last Three Soldiers* (1897); *The Three Prisoners* (1904); *The Jumel Mansion* (1910); *The Salmagundi Club* (1918); etc.

Shenandoah. Civil War play by Bronson Howard (prod. 1888). The play begins in Charleston the morning after the fall of Fort Sumter, and ends in Washington after Lee's surrender.

Shenandoah. Lexington, Va. Quarterly. Founded 1950. Published at Washington and Lee University. Literary magazine.

SHENTON, EDWARD (Nov. 29, 1895–); b. Pottstown, Pa. Illustrator, author. *The Gray Beginning* (1924); *Lean Twilight* (1928); *Riders of the Wind* (1929); *On Wings for Freedom* (1942); *The Rib and Adam* (1959); *This Mortal Moment* (poems, 1961); *Exploring the Ocean Depths* (1968); etc. Editor, Macrae Smith Co., since 1926. Illustrated Marjorie Kinnan Rawlings's *The Yearling,* etc.

SHENTON, JAMES PATRICK (Mar. 17, 1925–); b. Passaic, N.J. Educator, author. *Robert John Walker, a Politician from Jackson to Lincoln* (1960); *Reconstruction: the South after the War* (1963); *An Historian's History of the United States* (1966). Prof. history, Columbia University, since 1967.

SHEPARD, ISAAC FITZGERALD (July 7, 1816–Aug. 25, 1889); b. Natick, Mass. Editor, author. *Pebbles from Castalia* (poems, 1840); *Poetry of Feeling* (poems, 1844); *Scenes and Songs of Social Life* (1846); *Household Tales* (1861); etc. Editor, the *Boston Daily Bee,* 1846–48; the *Missouri Democrat,* 1868–69; the *Missouri State Atlas,* 1871–72.

Shepard, Jesse. See Francis Grierson.

SHEPARD, MORGAN VAN ROERBACH (Apr. 8, 1877–); b. Brooklyn, N.Y. Editor, author. Pen name, "John Martin." *Standard Upheld* (poems, 1900); *Letters to Children,* 2v. (1909–10); the *Read Out Loud Books,* 5v. (1911); *The Children's Munchausen* (1921); *Aesop's Fables in Rhyme* (1924); *God's Dark, and Other Bedtime Verses and Songs* (1927); *Stories for Children* (1936); etc. Founder, *John Martin's Book* magazine, 1913; editor, 1913–32.

SHEPARD, ODELL (July 22, 1884–July 19, 1967); b. Sterling, Ill. Educator, author. *A Lonely Flute* (poems, 1917); *Bliss Carman* (1923); *The Harvest of a Quiet Eye* (1927); *The Joys of Forgetting* (1928); *The Lore of the Unicorn* (1929); *Pedlar's Progress: The Life of Bronson Alcott* (1937, Pulitzer Prize for biography, 1938); *Connecticut, Past and Present* (1939); *Holdfast Gaines* (with Willard O. Shepard, 1946); *Jenkins' Ear* (with same, 1951). Prof. English, Trinity College, Hartford, Conn., 1917–46.

SHEPARD, THOMAS (Nov. 5, 1605–Aug. 25, 1649); b. Towcester, Eng. Congregational clergyman, author. *The Sincere Convert* (1641); *Theses Sabbaticae* (1649); *The Parable of the Ten Virgins* (1660); *Three Valuable Pieces* (1647); *The Autobiography of Thomas Shepard,* ed. by Nehemiah Adams (1832); etc.

SHEPERD, MASSEY HAMILTON (Mar. 14, 1913–); b. Wilmington, N.C. Episcopal clergyman, author. *The Living Liturgy* (1946); *The Oxford American Prayer Book Commentary* (1950); *The Worship of the Church* (1952); *The Liturgy and the Christian Faith* (1957); *The Eucharist and Liturgical Reward* (1960); *Worship in Scripture and Tradition* (1963); etc. Prof. liturgics, School of the Pacific, California, since 1954.

SHEPHERD, JEAN. Radio monologist, author. *In God We Trust: All Others Pay Cash* (1966). Editor: *The America of George Ade* (1962); *The Night People's Guide to New York* (1965). Regular program, WOR-AM.

SHEPPARD, NATHAN (Nov. 9, 1834–Jan. 24, 1888); b. Baltimore, Md. Correspondent, lecturer, author. *Shut Up in Paris* (1871); *Before an Audience* (1886); etc. Editor: *Saratoga Chips and Carlsbad Wafers* (1887); etc. Founder, Saratoga Athenaeum, 1884; president, 1884–88. Civil War correspondent for the *New York World.*

SHEPPARD, W[illiam H.] CRISPIN (Jan. 1, 1871–); b. Philadelphia, Pa. Artist, author. The *Rambler Club* series, 15v. (1909–1916); the *Don Hale* series, 4v. (1917–1920); etc.

Sheppard Lee. Novel by Robert Montgomery Bird (1836). Traces the transmigration of the soul in contemporary times.

SHERA, JESSE H[auk] (Dec. 8, 1903–); b. Oxford, O. Educator. Co-Editor: *Documentation in Action* (1956); *Information Systems in Documentation* (1957); *Information Resources: A Challenge to American Science and Industry* (1958); *Documentation and the Organization of Knowledge* (1966); etc. Dean, school of library science, Western Reserve University, since 1952.

SHERBURN, GEORGE WILEY (Nov. 1884–Nov. 28, 1962); b. Northfield, Vt. Author. *The Early Popularity of Milton's Minor Poems* (1920); *The Early Career of Alexander Pope* (1934); *Roehenstart, a Late Stuart Pretender* (1961); etc. Editor: Pope's *Correspondence,* 5v. (1956). English dept., University of Chicago, 1913–36; prof. English, Harvard University, since 1939.

SHERBURNE, JOHN HENRY (1794–c. 1850); b. Portsmouth, N.H. Poet, naval historian. *Life and Character of the Chevalier John Paul Jones* (1825); *Naval Sketches* (1845); etc.

SHERIDAN, PHILIP HENRY (Mar. 6, 1831–Aug. 5, 1888); b. Albany, N.Y. Army officer, author. *Personal Memoirs*, 2v. (1888). See John McElroy's *Gen. Philip Henry Sheridan* (1896); William H. Van Orden's *Gen. Philip H. Sheridan* (1896); Joseph Hergesheimer's *Sheridan* (1931).

"Sheridan's Ride." Poem by Thomas Buchanan Read (1864).

SHERMAN, CHARLES PHINEAS (June 8, 1874–); b. West Springfield, Mass. Educator, author. *First Year of Roman Law* (1906); *Roman Law in the Modern World*, 3v. (1917); *Epitome of Roman Law* (1937); *Roman Law in the Modern World* (1942); *Academic Adventures* (1944); etc. Professor, Boston University Law School, since 1939.

SHERMAN, CLIFTON LUCIEN (Sept. 1, 1866–Feb. 6, 1946); b. East Dover, Vt. Editor. Managing editor, the *Hartford Courant*, 1904–19; the *Hartford Times*, 1919–21, editor 1921–29.

SHERMAN, EDITH BISHOP (Dec. 25, 1889–); b. Des Moines, Ia. Author. *Milady at Arms* (1927); *Upstairs, Downstairs* (1930); *Mistress Madcap* (1935); *The Hay Chariot* (1936); *Mystery at High Hedges* (1937); *Flying Banners* (1942); *Bright College Year* (1950); etc.

SHERMAN, ELLEN BURNS (May 4, 1867–Jan. 15, 1956); b. Montgomery Center, Vt. Author. *Taper Lights* (1907); *Words to the Wise—and Others* (1907); *Poems* (1936); *Balm for Men's Souls* (1953); etc.

SHERMAN, FRANK DEMPSTER (May 6, 1860–Sept. 19, 1916); b. Peekskill, N.Y. Author. *Madrigals and Catches* (1887); *New Waggings of Old Tales* (with John Kendrick Bangs, 1887); *Lyrics for a Lute* (1890); *Little-Folk Lyrics* (1892); *Lyrics of Joy* (1904); *A Southern Flight* (with Clinton Scollard, 1905); *The Poems* (1917); etc.

SHERMAN, FREDERICK FAIRCHILD (c. 1874–Oct. 23, 1940); b. Peekskill, N.Y. Art critic, collector, editor, author. *Day Dreams & Even Song* (poems, 1904); *American Painters of Yesterday and Today* (1919); *Early American Painting* (1932); *Sonnets & Lyrics* (1937); etc. Editor and publisher, *Art in America*, a quarterly, 1913–40.

Sherman, Joan. Pen name of Peggy [Gaddis] Dern.

SHERMAN, LUCIUS ADELNO (Aug. 28, 1847–Feb. 13, 1933); b. Douglas, Mass. Educator, author. *Analytics of Literature* (1893); etc. Editor: Shakespeare's *Macbeth* (1899); Shakespeare's *Hamlet* (1903); etc. English dept., University of Nebraska, 1882–1933.

SHERMAN, RICHARD (1905–Jan. 8, 1962); b. Bancroft, Ia. Novelist. *To Mary with Love* (1936); *The Unready Heart* (1944); *The Bright Promise* (1947); *The Kindred Spirit* (1951).

SHERMAN, STUART P[ratt] (Oct. 1, 1881–Aug. 21, 1926); b. Anita, Ia. Educator, editor, critic. *On Contemporary Literature* (1917); *The Genius of America* (1923); *Points of View* (1924); *The Main Stream* (1927); *Shaping Men and Women* (1928); etc. Editor: *The Cambridge History of American Literature*, 4v. (with William P. Trent and others, 1917–21); etc. Editor, *New York Herald-Tribune Books*, 1924–26. See Jacob Zeitlin and Homer Woodbridge's *Life and Letters of Stuart P. Sherman*, 2v. (1929); Fred B. Millett's *Contemporary American Authors* (1940).

SHERMAN, WILLIAM TECUMSEH (Feb. 8, 1820–Feb. 14, 1891); b. Lancaster, O. Army officer, author. *Memoirs*, 2v. (1875); etc. See J. D. Cox's *The March to the Sea* (1905); *Home Letters of General Sherman*, ed. by M. A. DeWolfe Howe (1909); Lloyd Lewis's *Sherman, Fighting Prophet* (1932); A. H. Burne's *Lee, Grant and Sherman* (1939); etc.

SHERRILL, CHARLES HITCHCOCK (Apr. 13, 1867–June 25, 1936); b. Washington, D.C. Lawyer, author. The *Stained Glass Tours* series, 5v. (1908–1927); *French Memories of Eighteenth Century America* (1915); *Bismarck & Mussolini* (1931); *My Story Book* (autobiography, 1937); etc.

SHERROD, ROBERT LEE (Feb. 8, 1909–); b. in Thomas Co., Ga. Editor, author. *Tarawa: The Story of a Battle* (1944); *History of Marine Corps Aviation in World War II* (1952); *On to Westward* (1955). With *Saturday Evening Post*, 1952–66.

SHERWOOD, ADIEL (Oct. 3, 1791–Aug. 18, 1879); b. Fort Edward, N.Y. Baptist clergyman, educator, author. *Notes on the New Testament*, 2v. (1856); etc. Compiler: *A Gazetteer of the State of Georgia* (1827). President, Shurtleff College, Alton, Ill., 1841–46; Masonic College, Lexington Mo., 1848–49; Marshall College, Griffin, Ga., 1857–61.

SHERWOOD, GRACE BUCHANAN (d. Sept. 16, 1969); Poet. *Winter Bird Song* (1936); *Water Meadows* (1937); *What If the Spring—* (1938); *No Final Breath* (1940).

SHERWOOD, HENRY NOBLE (Dec. 8, 1882–); b. Mitchell, Ind. Educator, author. *Life of Paul Cuffee* (1923); *Makers of America* (1929); *Citizenship* (1934); etc. President Georgetown College, Georgetown, Ky., since 1934.

SHERWOOD, ISAAC RUTH (Aug. 13, 1835–Oct. 15, 1925); b. Stanford, N.Y. Editor, soldier, congressman, author. *Memories of the War* (1923). His best known poem is "The Army Graybook." Editor, the *Williams County Gazette*, Bryan, O.; with the *Toledo Commercial;* with the *Cleveland Leader;* editor and owner, the *Toledo Journal*, 1874–84; editor, the *Canton News-Democrat*, 1888–98. Congressman, 1873–75, 1907–21; 1923–25.

SHERWOOD, KATE [Katherine Margaret Brownlee] (Mrs. Isaac Ruth Sherwood) (Sept. 24, 1841–Feb. 15, 1914); b. Poland, O. Editor, reformer, poet. *Camp-Fire; Memorial-Day; and Other Poems* (1885); *Dream of the Ages: A Poem of Columbia* (1893). Best known poem is "The Flag That Makes Men Free." With the *Toledo Journal*, 1875–83; editor, woman's department, the *National Tribune*, 1883–98.

SHERWOOD, MARGARET [Pollock] (Nov. 1, 1864–Sept. 24, 1955); b. Ballston, N.Y. Educator, author. Pen name "Elizabeth Hastings." *An Experiment in Altruism* (1895); *A Puritan Bohemia* (1896); *Daphne* (1903); *The Coming of the Tide* (1905); *The Princess Pourquoi* (1907); *Familiar Ways* (1917); *The Upper Slopes* (poems, 1924); *Undercurrents of Influence in English Romantic Poetry* (1934); *Pilgrim Feet* (1949); etc. English dept., Wellesley College, 1889–1931.

SHERWOOD, M[ary] E[lizabeth] W[ilson] (Mrs. John Sherwood) (Oct. 27, 1826–Sept. 12, 1903); b. Keene, N.H. Poet, novelist, short-story writer. Wrote under the initials "M.E.W.S." *The Sarcasm of Destiny* (1878); *Home Amusements* (1881); *Etiquette* (1884); *Sweet-Brier* (1889); *Poems* (1892); *An Epistle to Posterity* (recollections, 1897); *Here and There and Everywhere: Reminiscences* (1898).

SHERWOOD, ROBERT EMMET (Apr. 4, 1896–Nov. 14, 1955); b. New Rochelle, N.Y. Playwright. *The Road to Rome* (prod. 1926); *The Queen's Husband* (prod. 1928); *Waterloo Bridge* (prod. 1930); *Reunion in Vienna* (prod. 1931); *The Petrified Forest* (prod. 1935); *Idiot's Delight* (1936, Pulitzer Prize play, 1936); *Abe Lincoln in Illinois* (prod. 1938, Pulitzer Prize play, 1939); *There Shall Be No Night* (prod. 1940, Pulitzer Prize play, 1941); *Roosevelt and Hopkins: An Intimate History* (1948, Pulitzer Prize for biography, 1949); *Miss Liberty* (1949); etc. Dramatic editor, *Vanity Fair*, 1919–20; assoc. editor, *Life*, 1920–24, editor, 1924–28; etc.

SHIDLE, NORMAN GLASS, b. Pittsburgh, Pa. Editor, author. *Finding Your Job* (1921); *Motor Vehicles and Their Engines* (with T. A. Bissell, 1941); *Clear Writing for Easy Reading* (1951).

Shield of Achilles, The. Collection of poems by W. H. Auden (1955).

SHIELDS, CHARLES WOODRUFF (Apr. 4, 1825–Aug. 26, 1904); b. New Albany, Ind. Presbyterian clergyman, educator, author. *Philosophia Ultima* (1861); *The Final Philosophy* (1877); etc. Prof. philosophy and religion, Princeton, 1865–1903.

SHIELDS, GEORGE OLIVER (Aug. 26, 1846–Nov. 1925); b. Batavia, O. Editor, author. *Rustlings in the Rockies* (1883); *The Battle of the Big Hole* (1889); *Cruisings in the Cascades* (1889); *The Big Game of North America* (1890); *American Game Fishes* (1892); *The Blanket Indian of the Northwest* (1921); etc. Founder and editor, *Recreation,* 1894; organized Camp Fire Club, 1897; editor, *Shields Magazine,* 1905–25. He sometimes signed his articles with the pen name "Coquina."

SHILLABER, BENJAMIN PENHALLOW (July 12, 1814–Nov. 25, 1890); b. Portsmouth, N.H. Editor, humorist, poet. Pen name, "Mrs. Partington." *Rhymes, With Reason and Without* (1853); *Life and Sayings of Mrs. Partington* (1854); *Partingtonian Patchwork* (1873); *Lines in Pleasant Places* (1874); the *Ike Partington* stories, 3v. (1879–81); etc. On staff, the *Boston Post,* 1840–50; editor, the *Carpet Bag,* 1851–53; on staff, the *Saturday Evening Gazette,* 1856–66.

Shiloh. Novel by "W.M.L. Jay" (J. L. M. Woodruff) (1870). This book was the first best seller published by E. P. Dutton & Co.

SHIMKIN, LEON (Apr. 7, 1907–); b. Brooklyn, N.Y. Publisher. With Simon and Schuster, Inc., since 1924; now president. Co-founder, Pocket Books, Inc., 1939; pres., since 1950.

SHINDLER, MARY STANLEY BUNCE PALMER DANA (Mrs. Charles E. Dana; Mrs. Robert D. Shindler) (Feb. 15, 1810–1883); b. Beaufort, S.C. Author. *The Southern Harp* (1840); *The Northern Harp* (1841); *The Temperance Lyre* (1842); *The Parted Family, and Other Poems* (1842); *Charles Morton* (1843); *The Young Sailor* (1846); *Forecastle Tom* (1846).

"Shine, Perishing Republic." Poem by Robinson Jeffers (1924).

SHINN, ASA (May 3, 1781–Feb. 11, 1853); b. in New Jersey. Methodist clergyman, author. *An Essay on the Plan of Salvation* (1812); *On the Benevolence and Rectitude of the Supreme Being* (1840); and many pamphlets.

Ship of Fools. Novel by Katherine Anne Porter (1962). A number of characters of different nationalities sail from Veracruz to Bremerhaven in 1931. Presents the characters as resonant types in their relations to each other as they seek love and self-justification. The book was known for many years, while being written, under the tentative title *No Safe Harbor.*

SHIPLEY, JOSEPH T[wadell] (Aug. 19, 1893–); b. Brooklyn, N.Y. Drama critic, author. *King John* (1924); *The Art of Eugene O'Neill* (1928); *The Quest for Literature* (1931); *Trends in Literature* (1949); *Dictionary of World Literature* (1953); *Guide to Great Plays* (1956); *Playing with Words* (1960); *Mentally Disturbed Teacher* (1961); *Word Games for Play and Power* (1962); *Five Plays by Ibsen* (1965); *Vocabulary* (1968); etc. Drama editor, *The New Leader,* since 1922. English dept., College of the City of New York, 1928–38; Yeshiva College, 1928–44.

SHIPMAN, LOUIS EVAN (Aug. 2, 1869–Aug. 2, 1933); b. Brooklyn, N.Y. Playwright, novelist. *D'Arcy of the Guards* (1899); *Predicaments* (1899); *The Curious Courtship of Kate Poins* (1901); *On Parole* (prod. 1906); *The Admiral* (prod. 1909); *The True Adventures of a Play* (1914); *The Fountain of Youth* (prod. 1918); *Fools Errant* (prod. 1922); *Three Comedies* (1923); *Ben Franklin: A Comedy* (1933); etc.

SHIPMAN, SAMUEL (Dec. 25, 1883–Feb. 9, 1937); b. New York. Playwright. *The Crooked Square* (prod. 1923);

Friendly Enemies (with Aaron Hoffman, 1923); *Children of To-Day* (1926); *Cheaper to Marry* (prod. 1926); etc.

SHIPP, CAMERON (Nov. 10, 1903–Aug. 20, 1961); b. Dallas, Tex. Author. *With a Feather on My Nose* (with Billy Burke, 1949); *We Barrymores* (with Lionel Barrymore, 1951); *King of Comedy* (with Mack Sennett, 1954).

SHIPPEE, LESTER BURRELL (Jan. 28, 1879–Feb. 9, 1944); b. East Greenwich, R.I. Educator, author. *Recent American History* (1924); *Canadian - American Relations, 1849–1874* (1939); etc. History dept., University of Minnesota, from 1917, prof. from 1925.

SHIPPEY, LEE (Feb. 26, 1884–Dec. 30, 1969); b. Memphis, Tenn. Journalist, author. *The Testing Crowd* (1926); *Personal Glimpses* (1929); *Where Nothing Ever Happens* (1935); *The Girl Who Wanted Experience* (1937); *The Great American Family* (1938); *It's an Old California Custom* (1948); *The Los Angeles Book* (1950); *The Luckiest Man Alive* (autobiography, 1959); etc. Editor of column "Lee Side o' Los Angeles" in *Los Angeles Times,* from 1927.

SHIRER, WILLIAM L[awrence] (Feb. 23, 1904–); b. Chicago, Ill. Journalist, author. *Berlin Diary* (1941); *End of a Berlin Diary* (1947); *The Traitor* (1950); *Midcentury Journey* (1952); *Stranger Come Home* (1954); *The Challenge of Scandinavia* (1955); *The Consul's Wife* (1956); *The Rise and Fall of the Third Reich* (1961); *The Rise and Fall of Adolf Hitler* (1961); *The Sinking of the Bismarck* (1962); *The Collapse of the Third Republic* (1969). With *Chicago Tribune,* 1925–33; Universal News Service, 1935–37; Columbia Broadcasting System, 1937–47; Mutual Network, 1947–49.

Shirley, Dame. Pen name of Louise A. K. Clappe.

SHIVELL, PAUL (Sept. 25, 1874–); b. Indianapolis, Ind. Poet. *Ashes of Roses* (1898); *Stillwater Valley Pastorals* (1908); *Stillwater Pastorals and Other Poems* (1915); *The Spring-Brook in the Dell* (1940); *Selections from Published Poems* (1944); etc.

Shock of Recognition, The. Anthology of criticism of American literature, by Edmund Wilson (1943).

SHOEMAKER, DON[ald Cleavenger] (Dec. 6, 1912–); b. Montreal, Can. Editor: *Henry George: Citizen of the World* (1950); *With All Deliberate Speed* (1957). Editor, *Asheville* (N.C) *Citizen,* 1947–55; *Miami Herald,* since 1958.

SHOEMAKER, HENRY WHARTON (Feb. 24, 1882–July 14, 1958); b. New York. Journalist, author. *General William Sprague* (1916); *Chief John Logan* (1917); *Gifford Pinchot* (1922); *John Brown* (1931). President, the *Altoona Times-Tribune,* 1912–50. Director, State Museum, Harrisburg, Pa., 1939–40.

SHOEMAKER, VAUGHN RICHARD (Aug. 11, 1902–); b. Chicago, Ill. Cartoonist. Author of annual cartoon collections, 1939–46; *The Best of Shoemaker Cartoons* (1966). Art dept., the *Chicago Daily News,* since 1922; chief cartoonist, 1925–52.

Shoes of the Fisherman, The. Novel by Morris West (1963).

SHOLL, ANNA McCLURE. b. Philadelphia, Pa. Author. *The Law of Life* (1903); *The Port of Storms* (1905); *Blue Blood and Red* (under pen name "Geoffrey Corson," (1915); *Carmichael* (1915); *The Ancient Journey* (1917); etc.

Shore Acres. By James A. Herne (1892). Down east melodrama featuring homely scenes in the Shore Acres subdivision, with Uncle Nat a central character. A turkey dinner, a shipwreck and a snowstorm add realism to the play. *Shore Acres* is similar in setting to the author's *Sag Harbor* (1899) and *Hearts of Oak* (1879).

SHORES, LOUIS (Sept. 14, 1904–); b. Buffalo, N.Y. Librarian, author. *Origins of the American College Library,*

1638–1800 (1935); *Bibliographies and Summaries in Education* (1936); *Basic Reference Books* (1937); *Highways in the Sun* (1947); *Challenges to Librarianship* (1953); *Basic Reference Sources* (1954); *Instructional Materials* (1960); *Tex-Tec* (1968); etc. Conducts review column in the *Wilson Bulletin.* Dean emeritus, Library School, Florida State University since 1967. Editor-in-chief, Collier's Encyclopedia, since 1960.

SHORES, ROBERT JAMES (Mar. 14, 1881–Jan. 5, 1950); b. Minneapolis, Minn. Editor, poet. *At Molokai, and Other Verse* (1910); *New Brooms* (1913); etc. Founder and editor, *The Idler,* 1910–12.

Shores of Light, The. By Edmund Wilson (1952). Essays in criticism of American writing of the 1920's and 1930's.

SHOREY, PAUL (Aug. 3, 1857–Apr. 24, 1934); b. Davenport, Ia. Educator, author. *The Idea of God in Plato's Republic* (1895); *The Unity of Plato's Thought* (1903); *The Assault on Humanism* (1917); *What Plato Said* (1933); *Platonism, Ancient and Modern* (1938); etc. Editor, *Classical Philology,* 1908–34. Prof. Greek, University of Chicago, 1892–1934.

SHORT, JOSEPHINE HELENA, b. Urbana, Ill. Author. *Oberammergau* (1910); *Chosen Days in Scotland* (1911); *Reading Journey through Scotland* (1913); etc.

"SHORTFELLOW, TOM." Real name unknown. Novelist. *Eva Labree* (1845); *Evelyn of Alleyne Cliff* (1845); *Mary Kale* (1845); *Annie, the Orphan Girl of St. Mary* (1846); etc.

SHORTRIDGE, WILSON PORTER (July 28, 1880–); b. Medora, Ill. Educator, author. *The Transition of a Typical Frontier* (1922); *The Development of the United States* (1929). Prof. history, West Virginia University, since 1922.

SHOTWELL, JAMES THOMPSON (Aug. 6, 1874–July 15, 1965); b. Strathroy, Ont. Educator, author. *The Religious Revolution of Today* (1913); *An Introduction to the History of History* (1921); *War as an Instrument of National Policy* (1929); *The Heritage of Freedom* (1934); *On the Rim of the Abyss* (1936); *At the Paris Peace Conference* (1937); *The Great Decision* (1944); *Balkan Mission* (1949); *Poems* (1954); *The United States in History* (1956); *Autobiography* (1961); etc. Editor: *Records of Civilization, Sources and Studies,* 5v. (1915–21); etc. Co-editor: *Lessons on Security and Disarmament from the History of the League of Nations* (1949). History dept., Columbia University, 1902–42.

SHOUP, CARL SUMNER (Oct. 26, 1902–); b. San Jose, Cal. Educator. Author or co-author: *The Sales Tax in France* (1930); *A Report on the Revenue System of Cuba* (1932); *The Sales Tax in the American States* (1934); *Facing the Tax Problem* (1937); *The Fiscal System of Cuba* (1939); *Federal Finances in the Coming Decade* (1941); *Taxing to Prevent Inflation* (1943); *Principles of National Income Analysis* (1947); *Ricardo on Taxation* (1958); *Federal Estate and Gift Taxes* (1966); *Public Finance* (1969). Prof. economics, Columbia University, since 1945.

Show: The Magazine of the Performing Arts. New York. Monthly. Founded 1961 by Huntington Hartford. Edited by Robert M. Wool. Expired 1965. Republished as *Show* in 1970. Noted for its thorough and sophisticated coverage of both the live and recorded performing arts.

Show Boat, The. Novel by Edna Ferber (1926). Captain Andy Hawks, river pilot, buys a show boat on the Mississippi, and the troupe of actors live on the boat to the delight of Andy and to the annoyance of his wife Parthenia. Magnolia, a daughter, who shares her father's love for the river, becomes the leading lady.

Show-Off, The. Comedy by George Kelly (prod. 1924). Story of the braggart Aubrey Piper, who earns $32.50 per week and talks like a millionaire. He tries to prove to his family that he is a business genius, and in the end one of his crack-pot ideas brings sudden wealth.

SHOWERMAN, GRANT (Jan. 9, 1870–Nov. 13, 1935); b. Brookfield, Wis. Educator, author. *With the Professor* (1910); *The Indian Stream Republic and Luther Parker* (1915); *A Country Chronicle* (1916); *A Country Child* (1917); *Horace and His Influence* (1922); *Eternal Rome,* 2v. (1924); etc. Prof. classics, University of Wisconsin, 1900–35.

SHREVE, THOMAS HOPKINS (Dec. 17, 1808–Dec. 22, 1853); b. Alexandria, Va. Editor, publisher, poet. *Drayton: A Story of American Life* (1851). Publisher (with William Davis Gallagher), the *Cincinnati Mirror,* 1833–35; editor, 1833–36; with the *Louisville Daily Journal,* 1842–53.

SHRIVER, PHILIP RAYMOND (Aug. 16, 1922–); b. Cleveland, O. Educator, author. *The Years of Youth* (1960); *George A. Bowman: The Biography of an Educator* (1963); *Ohio's Military Prisons of the Civil War* (with D. J. Breen), 1964). President, Miami University, since 1965.

SHROYER, FREDERICK BENJAMIN (Oct. 28, 1916–); b. Decatur, Ind. Novelist, newspaper columnist. *Wall Against the Night* (1957); *It Happened in Wayland* (1963); *There None Embrace* (1966). Editor of several anthologies.

SHRYOCK, [Edwin] HAROLD (Apr. 14, 1906–); b. Seattle, Wash. Anatomist, author. *Happiness for Husbands and Wives* (1949); *Happiness and Health* (1950); *On Becoming a Man* (1951); *On Becoming a Woman* (1951); *Highways to Health* (1953); *Mind If I Smoke?* (1959); *On Being Sweethearts* (1966); etc.

SHRYOCK, RICHARD HARRISON (Mar. 29, 1893–); b. Philadelphia, Pa. Educator, author. *Georgia and the Union in 1850* (1926); *The Development of Modern Medicine* (1936); *American Medical Research: Past and Present* (1947); *Unique Influence of the Johns Hopkins University on American Medicine* (1953); *The University of Pennsylvania Faculty: A Study in American Higher Education* (1959); *Medicine and Society in America, 1660–1860* (1960); *Medical Licensing In America 1650–1965* (1967); etc. Prof. history, University of Pennsylvania, since 1938.

SHUGG, ROGER W[allace] (May 22, 1905–); b. Needham, Mass. Publisher, author. *Origins of Class Struggle in Louisiana* (1939); *World War II: A Concise History* (with Harvey DeWeerd, 1946). Director, University of New Mexico Press, since 1967.

SHULMAN, CHARLES E. (July 25, 1900–June 2, 1968); b. in the Ukraine. Rabbi, author. *Problems of Jews in the Contemporary World* (1934); *Europe's Conscience in Decline* (1939); *A People That Did Not Die* (1956); *What It Means to Be a Jew* (1960); etc.

SHULMAN, IRVING (May 21, 1913–); b. Brooklyn, N.Y. Motion picture scenarist, novelist. *The Amboy Dukes* (1947); *Cry Tough* (1949); *The Big Brokers* (1951); *The Square Trap* (1953); *Children of the Dark* (1956); *The Velvet Knife* (1959); *The Roots of Fury* (1961); *Harlow* (1964); *Valentino* (1967); etc.

SHULMAN, MAX (Mar. 14, 1919–); b. St. Paul, Minn. Author. *Barefoot Boy with Cheek* (1943); *The Feather Merchants* (1944); *The Zebra Derby* (1946); *Sleep Till Noon* (1949); *The Tender Trap* (prod. 1954); *Rally Round the Flag Boys* (1957); *I Was A Teen-Age Dwarf* (1959); *Anyone Got a Match?* (1964); etc.

SHUMAN, EDWIN LLEWELLYN (Dec. 13, 1863–Dec. 13, 1941); b. Lancaster Co., Pa. Editor, author. *Practical Journalism* (1903); *How to Judge a Book* (1910). Lit. editor, the *Chicago Tribune,* 1895–1901, the *Chicago Record-Herald,* 1901–13, managing editor, *Current History Magazine,* 1916–22; assoc. editor, *International Book Review,* 1922–26; on editorial staff *Literary Digest,* 1926–33. Book editor, Funk and Wagnalls Co.

SHUMWAY, HARRY IRVING (Oct. 26, 1883–); b. Naugatuck, Conn. Author. *The Wonderful Voyages of Cap'n Pen* (1929); *I Go South* (1930); *The Story of Paper* (1932); *Lawrence, the Arabian Knight* (1935); *Good Man Gone Wrong?* (1940); *Bernard M. Baruch* (1946); etc.

SHURTER, EDWIN DuBOIS (Oct. 24, 1863–Oct. 13, 1946); b. Samsonville, N.Y. Educator, author. *Science and Art of Debate* (1908); *The Rhetoric of Oratory* (1909); etc. Editor: *The Modern American Speaker* (1901); *Oratory of the South* (1908); *Speeches of Henry W. Grady* (1908); *American Oratory of Today* (1911); *Masterpieces of Modern Verse* (1926); *Winning Declamations* (1929); etc. Prof. public speaking, University of Texas, 1899–1923.

SHURTLEFF, NATHANIEL BRADSTREET (June 29, 1810–Oct. 17, 1874); b. Boston, Mass. Antiquarian, author. *A Decimal System for the Arrangement and Administration of Libraries* (1856); *A Topographical and Historical Description of Boston* (1871); etc. Editor: *Records of the Governor and Company of the Massachusetts Bay in New England,* 5v. (1853–54); *Records of the Colony of New Plymouth in New England,* 8v. (1855–57); etc. Mayor of Boston, 1868–70. His extensive library was sold at auction, Nov. 30, 1875.

SHUSTER, GEORGE NAUMAN (Aug. 27, 1894–); b. Lancaster, Wis. Educator, author. *The Catholic Spirit in Modern English Literature* (1922); *Newman: Prose and Poetry* (1925); *English Literature* (1926); *The Catholic Church and Current Literature* (1929); *The Germans* (1932); *Brother Flo* (1938); *Look Away* (1939); *Religion Behind the Iron Curtain* (1954); *In Silence I Speak* (1956); *The Ground I Walked On* (1961); *UNESCO* (1963); *Catholic Education in a Changing World* (1967); etc. Managing editor, *The Commonweal,* 1929–37. President, Hunter College, 1940–59.

SHUTE, HENRY AUGUSTUS (Nov. 17, 1856–Jan. 25, 1943); b. Exeter, N.H. Author. *The Real Diary of a Real Boy* (1902); *Letters to Beany and Love Letters of Plupy Shute* (1905); *Real Boys* (1905); *A Few Neighbors* (1906); *A Profane and Somewhat Unreliable History of Exeter* (1907); *Plupy* (1910); *A Country Lawyer* (1911); *Misadventures of Three Good Boys* (1914); *The Lad with the Downy Chin* (1917); *Brite and Fair* (1918); *Plupy, the Wirst Yet* (1929); etc. "Plupy" Shute, the hero of most of the stories, is his own boyhood phase.

Shuttle, The. Novel by Frances Hogdson Burnett (1907). Rosalie Vanderpool, American girl, sells herself for a foreign title and lives to regret it.

SIBLEY, EDWARD CARROLL (Jan. 18, 1906–1949); b. Toledo, O. Lecturer, author. *Barrie and His Contemporaries: Cameo Portraits of Ten Living Authors* (1936); *Nor Time Nor Tide* (1937); *Uncle Dan* [Beard] (1938); etc.

SIBLEY, JOHN LANGDON (Dec. 29, 1804–Dec. 9, 1885); b. Union, Me. Librarian, author. *Biographical Sketches of Graduates of Harvard University,* 3v. (1873–85); etc. Editor, *American Magazine of Useful and Entertaining Knowledge,* 1833–36. Assistant librarian, Harvard College Library, 1841–56; librarian, 1856–77. The Massachusetts Historical Society continued his unfinished biographical sketches of Harvard graduates.

"Sidewalks of New York, The." Song, words by James W. Blake (Sept. 23, 1862–May 24, 1935), music by Charles Lawler, published 1894. Its first line is "Down in front of Casey's"; but it is best known by the opening line of the refrain: "East Side, West Side."

Sidney, Margaret. Pen name of Harriet Mulford Stone Lothrop.

SIEBERT, WILBUR HENRY (Aug. 30, 1866–); b. Columbus, O. Educator, author. *The Underground Railroad* (1899); *The Loyalists in Pennsylvania* (1920); *The Loyalists in East Florida,* 2v. (1929); *Ohio State University in the Great War*

(1935–39); *The Mysteries of Ohio's Underground Railroads* (1951); etc. History dept., Ohio State University, from 1898; prof. 1902–25; research prof. since 1925.

SIEGAL, JACK [Jacob] (Feb. 14, 1913–); b. New York. Author. *Squeegee* (1965); *Dawn at Kahlenberg* (1966).

Siege of London, The. Collection of short stores by Henry James (1883).

SIEGEL, ELI (Aug. 16, 1902–); b. Dvinsk, Latvia. Author. *The Scientific Criticism* (1923); *Hot Afternoons Have Been in Montana* (poems, 1925); *The Aesthetic Method in Self-Conflict* (1946); *Psychiatry, Economics, Aesthetics* (1946); *Is Beauty the Making One of Opposites?* (1955); *William Carlos Williams' Poetry Talked About and William Carlos Williams Present and Talking* (1964); *A Rosary of Evil* (1964); *Damned Welcome: Aesthetic Realism Maxims* (1964); *What's There—Lou Bernstein's Photographs* (1965); *James and the Children* (1967); *Hail American Development* (1968); *Goodbye Profit System* (1970).

SIEGMEISTER, ELIE (Jan. 15, 1909–); b. New York. Composer. *Invitation to Music* (1961); etc. Compiler: *Treasury of American Song* (with Olin Downes, 1940); *Harmony and Melody,* 2v. (1965); *The New Music Lover's Handbook* (1968); etc.

SIEGRIST, MARY (d. Mar., 1953); b. Jonestown, Pa. Author. *You That Come After* (1927); *Sentinel* (1928); *Flame Rises on the Mountain* (poems, 1942); etc. Compiler: *The New Humanity* (1928).

Sierra Club Bulletin. San Francisco, Cal. Monthly. Founded 1893. Devoted to the conservation of natural resources.

SIGAL, CLANCY (Sept. 6, 1926–); b. Chicago, Ill. Author. *Weekend in Dinlock* (1961); *Going Away* (1962).

SIGMUND, JAY G. (Dec. 11, 1885–Oct. 29, 1937); b. Waubeek, Ia. Author. *Frescoes* (poems, 1922); *Land o' Maize Folk* (poems, 1924); *Wapsipinicon Tales* (1927); *Ridge Road* (1930); *Altar Panels* (poems, 1931); *The Least of These* (1935); *Burr Oak and Sumac* (poem, 1935); etc.

SIGOURNEY, L[ydia] H[oward Huntley] (Sept. 1, 1791–June 10, 1865); b. Norwich, Conn. Editor, author. Called "The American Hemans." *Moral Pieces, in Prose and Verse* (1815); *Poems* (1827); *How to Be Happy* (1833); *Letters to Young Ladies* (1833); *Sketches* (1834); *Pocahontas, and Other Poems* (1841); *Poems, Religious and Elegiac* (1841); *Pleasant Memories of Pleasant Lands* (1842); *The Faded Hope* (1853); *Letters of Life* (autobiography, 1866); etc. Co-editor, *Godey's Lady's Book,* 1839–42. See Gordon S. Haight's *Mrs. Sigourney, the Sweet Singer of Hartford* (1930).

SIKES, ENOCH WALTER 19, 29, 1868–Jan. 8, 1940); b. in Union Co., N.C. Educator, historian. *From Colony to Commonwealth* (1897); *The Confederate Congress* (1904); *Joseph Hewes* (1904); *Sketches in Biographical History of North Carolina* (1909); *The First Constitution of North Carolina* (1909); etc. Prof. History, Wake Forest College, 1897–1916; president, Coker College, 1916–25; Clemson College, 1925–40.

Sikes, Mrs. Wirt. See Olive Logan.

SIKES, WIRT (Nov. 23, 1836–Aug. 18, 1883); b. Watertown, N.Y. Journalist, author. *A Book for the Winter-Evening Fireside* (1858); *British Goblins: Welsh Folk-Lore, Fairy Mythology, Legends, and Traditions* (1880); *Rambles and Studies in Old South Wales* (1881).

SIKORSKY, IGOR I[van] (May 25, 1889–); b. Kiev, Rus. Aeronautical engineer, author. *The Story of the Winged-S* (1941); *The Invisible Encounter* (1947).

SILBERMAN, CHARLES ELIOT (Jan. 31, 1925–); b. Des Moines, Iowa. Editor, author. *Crisis in Black and White*

(1964); *The Myths of Automation* (1966); *Crisis in the Classroom: The Remaking of American Education* (1970). Editor, *Fortune* magazine, since 1953.

SILBERMAN, JAMES HENRY (Mar. 21, 1927–); b. Boston, Mass. Editor. With Dial Press, since 1953; editor-in-chief, 1959–1963; editor, *The Dial*, 1959. With Random House, since 1963. Vice-president and editor-in-chief, since 1970.

Silent Language, The. By Edward T. Hall (1959). Non-verbal communication systems on which modern Western culture depends.

Silent Partner, The. Novel by Elizabeth Stuart Phelps (1871). A plea for justice for the New England mill hands.

Silent Snow, Secret Snow. Story by Conrad Aiken.

Silent Spring. By Rachel Carson, 1962.

Silent Storms. Novel by Ernest Poole (1927). Barry McClurg, wealthy American, marries Madeleine de Granier, a young French intellectual. They fail to reconcile their conflicting ideas and ideals, and the disparity in their ages adds to their unhappiness.

SILL, EDWARD ROWLAND (Apr. 29, 1841–Feb. 27, 1887); b. Windsor, Conn. Educator, poet. *The Hermitage, and Other Poems* (1868); *Venus of Milo, and Other Poems* (1883); *The Prose of Edward Rowland Sill* (1900); *The Poems of Edward Rowland Sill* (1902); etc. "The Fool's Prayer" and "Opportunity" are among his best known poems. Prof. English, University of California, 1874–82.

SILLS, KENNETH CHARLES MORTON (Dec. 5, 1879–Nov. 15, 1954); b. Halifax, N.S. Educator, author. *The First American, and Other Poems* (1911); etc. President, Bowdoin College, 1918–52.

SILVER, ABBA HILLEL (Jan. 28, 1893–Nov. 28, 1963); b. Neinstadt, Lith. Rabbi, author. *Messianic Speculations in Israel* (1927); *Democratic Impulse in Jewish History* (1928); *Religion in a Changing World* (1930); *World Crisis and Jewish Survival* (1941); *Vision and Victory* (1949); *Where Judaism Differed* (1956); *Moses and the Original Torah* (1961); etc.

SILVER, JAMES W[esley] (June 28, 1907–); b. Rochester, N.Y. Educator. *Edmond Pendleton Gaines: Frontier General* (1949); *Confederate Morale and Church Propaganda* (1956); *A Life for the Confederacy* (ed., 1959); *The Closed Society* (1964); etc. Prof. history, University of Notre Dame, since 1965.

Silver Burdett Company. Morristown, N.J. Textbook publishers. Founded 1885 in Boston by Edgar O. Silver and later moved to New York. Silver's first publishing venture was *Normal Music Course,* planned by Hosea Edson Holt and arranged by John Wheeler Tufts. In 1886 M. Thatcher Rogers was admitted to partnership and the firm became Silver, Rogers & Co. Elmer Silver, a brother, and Henry C. Deane were admitted to partnership at this time. The firm then began the publication of textbooks with *Normal Course in Reading,* based on new educational methods worked out by William B. Powell and Emma J. Todd. M. Thatcher Rogers sold his interest to Frank W. Burdett in 1888, and the name was changed to Silver, Burdett & Company, and incorporated in 1892. Meanwhile a New York branch had been opened, and in 1890 a Chicago branch was opened, and in later years branches were established at Dallas and San Francisco. In 1891 the popular *Ward Readers* by Edward Ward were begun. Edgar Silver died in 1909 and was succeeded as president by Arthur Lord. In 1914 Haviland Stevenson succeeded Lord as president, and on his death in 1927 was succeeded by George L. Buck, who had been with the firm since 1903. In 1935 the corporate name was shortened to Silver Burdett Company. Now a division of The General Learning Corp.

Silver Cord, The. Play by Sidney Howard (prod. 1926). Mrs. Phelps tries to control the lives of her two sons, but is thwarted by David's wife, Christina, and by the attempted suicide of her younger son Robert's intended bride.

"Silver Threads Among the Gold." Song, words by Eben H. Rexford, music by Hart Pease Danks (1873).

SILVERBERG, ROBERT; b. New York. Author. Fiction: *Lost Race of Mars* (1960); *Collision Course* (1961); *The Seed of Earth* (1962); *Next Stop the Stars* (1962); *Recalled to Life* (1962); *Conquerors from the Darkness* (1965); *Thorns* (1967); *The Masks of Time* (1968); *Nightwings* (1969); etc. Non-fiction: *Treasures Beneath the Sea* (1960); *First American Into Space* (1961); *Lost Cities and Vanished Civilizations* (1962); *The Fabulous Rockefellers* (1963); *Sunken History: The Story of Underwater Archaeology* (1963); *15 Battles That Changed the World* (1963).

SILVERCRUYS, SUZANNE (Mrs. Edward Ford Stevenson), b. Maeseyck, Belg. Sculptor, painter, author. *Suzanne of Belgium (autobiography, 1932); There Is No Death* (play, 1933); *A Primer of Sculpture* (1941).

SILVERMAN, MORRIS (Nov. 19, 1894–); b. Newburgh, N.Y. Rabbi. Editor: *Junior Prayer Book,* 2v. (1933, 1937); *Sabbath and Festival Service* (1936); and other prayer books; *Hartford Jews, 1959–1969* (1969).

SILVERMAN, SIME (May 18, 1873–Sept. 22, 1933); b. Cortland, N.Y. Editor, publisher. Founder, *Variety,* New York, 1905. Publisher, the *New York Clipper,* 1922–24. See *Dictionary of American Biography,* v. 17; *Variety,* Sept. 26, 1933; Dayton Stoddard's *Lord Broadway: Variety's Sime* (1941).

SILVERS, EARL REED (Feb. 22, 1891–Mar. 26, 1948); b. Jersey City, N.J. Author. *Dick Arnold of Raritan College* (1920); and other "Dick Arnold" stories; *Ned Beals, Freshman* (1922), and other "Ned Beals" stories; *The Hillsdale High Champions* (1924); *The Spirit of Menlo* (1926); *Sons of Tomorrow* (1947); etc. Editor, *Rutgers Alumni Monthly.* Director, Rutgers University Press, 1938–44. English dept., Rutgers, 1929–44.

SILVERS, ROBERT B. (Dec. 31, 1929–); b. Mineola, New York. Editor. *Writing in America* (1960). Translator: *La Gangrene* (1961). Co-editor: *New York Review of Books,* since 1963.

SILZ, WALTER (Sept. 27, 1894–); b. Cleveland, O. Educator. *Heinrich von Kleist's Conception of the Tragic* (1923); *Early German Romanticism* (1929); *German Romantic Lyrics* (1934); *Realism and Reality* (1954); *H. V. Kleist* (1961). Prof. German, Columbia University, since 1954.

SIMMONS, ERNEST J[oseph] (Dec. 8, 1903–); b. Lawrence, Mass. Educator, author. *Pushkin* (1937); *Dostoevsky: The Making of a Novelist* (1940); *Tolstoy* (1946); *Russian Fiction and Soviet Ideology* (1958); etc. Editor: *U.S.S.R.: A Concise Handbook* (1947); *Through the Glass of Soviet Literature* (1953); *Continuity and Change in Russian and Soviet Thought* (1955); *Introduction to Russian Realism* (1965); *Introduction to Tolstoy's Writings* (1968).

SIMMONS, LEO WILLIAM (Oct. 31, 1897–); b. Kinston, N.C. Sociologist. *Sun Chief* (ed., 1942); *Role of the Aged in Primitive Society* (1945); *Social Science in Medicine* (with H. G. Wolff, 1954); *Nursing Research* (with V. Henderson, 1964); *The Aged Ill* (with Dorothea Jaeger, 1969). Visiting prof. sociology, Case Western Reserve University, since 1967.

SIMMS, HENRY HARRISON (1896–). *The Rise of the Whigs in Virginia* (1929); *Life of John Taylor* (1932); *Life of Robert M. T. Hunter* (1935); *Decade of Sectional Controversy, 1851–1861* (1942); etc.

SIMMS, JEPTHA ROOT (Dec. 31, 1807–May 31, 1883); b. Canterbury, Conn. Author. *The American Spy; or, Freedom's Early Sacrifice* (1846); *Trappers of New York* (1850); *The Frontiersmen of New York,* 2v. (1882–83).

SIMMS, WILLIAM GILMORE (Apr. 17, 1806–June 11, 1870); b. Charleston, S.C. Editor, novelist, poet. *Atalantis* (1832); *Martin Faber* (anon., 1833); *Guy Rivers* (anon., 1834); *The Yemassee* (anon., 1835); *The Partisan* (anon., 1835); *Mellichampe* (anon., 1836); *Richard Hurdis* (anon., 1838); *Carl Werner* (anon., 1838); *Pelayo* (anon., 1838); *Border Beagles* (anon., 1840); *Confession* (anon., 1841); *The Kinsmen* (anon., 1841); *Beauchampe* (anon., 1842); *Castle Dismal* (anon., 1844); *The Prima Donna* (1844); *Helen Halsey* (1845; *Count Julian* (anon., 1845); *The Wigwam and Cabin*, 2 series (anon., 1845); *Areytos; or, Songs of the South* (1846); *The Lily and the Totem* (anon., 1850); *Flirtation at the Moultrie House* (anon., 1851); *Katharine Walton* (1851); *Poems, Descriptive, Dramatic, Legendary, and Contemplative* (1853); *Vasconselos* (1853); *The Sword and Distaff* (1853), published as *Woodcraft* (1854); *The Forayers* (1855); *Eutaw* (1856); *Charlemont* (1856); *The Cassique of Kiawah* (1859); etc. Many of his novels were republished as *Border Romances*, 17v. (1859). Editor: *War Poetry of the South* (1867). Editor, the *Charleston City Gazette*, 1828–33. *See* William P. Trent's *William Gilmore Simms* (1892); Clement Eaton's *The Mind of the Old South* (1964); *Cavalier of Old South Carolina: William Gilmore Simms's Captain Porgy*, ed. by H. W. Hetherington (1966).

SIMON, [Anthony] TONY (Apr. 7, 1921–); b. New York. Editor, author. *Ripsnorters and Ribticklers* (1958); *North Pole, Life of Robert E. Peary* (1960); *The Search for Planet X* (1962); etc. Editor: *The Hit Parade of Horse Stories* (1963); *The Heart Explorers* (1966). With *Scholastic* magazines, since 1948.

Simon, Charlie May. Pen name of Mrs. John Gould Fletcher.

SIMON, HENRY WILLIAM (Oct. 9, 1901–Oct. 1, 1970); b. New York. Editor, author. *The Teaching of Poetry Appreciation* (1932); *The Reading of Shakespeare* (1933); *Preface to Teaching* (1938); *A Treasury of Grand Opera* (1946); *Festival of Operas* (1957); *What Is a Music Teacher?* (1964); *Victor Book of the Opera* (1967); *An Audio-Visual History of Music* (1968); etc. Editor: *Five Great Tragedies by Shakespeare* (1939); and other Shakespeare collections.

SIMON, [Marvin] NEIL (July 4, 1927–); b. New York. Playwright. Co-author: *Come Blow Your Horn* (1961). Author: *Little Me* (musical, 1962); *Barefoot in the Park* (1963); *Sweet Charity* (1966); *The Odd Couple* (1965); *Star-Spangled Girl* (1967); *Plaza Suite* (1967); *Promises, Promises* (1969); *Last of the Red Hot Lovers* (1970). Screenplays for *Come Blow Your Horn* (1963); *After the Fox* (1966); *Barefoot in the Park* (1967); *The Odd Couple* (1968); *The Out of Towners* (1969).

SIMON, RICHARD LEO (Mar. 6, 1899–July 29, 1960); b. New York. Publisher. Founder, with Max Lincoln Schuster, Simon & Schuster, 1924.

SIMON, YVES R[ené Marie] (Mar. 14, 1903–May 11, 1961); b. Cherbourg, Fr. Philosopher. *Philosophy of Democratic Government* (1951). Translator: *The Material Logic of John of St. Thomas, Basic Treatises* (with others, 1955).

Simon and Schuster. New York. Publishers. Founded Jan. 2, 1924, by Richard L. Simon and M. Lincoln Schuster. The firm started with a crossword puzzle book, which was one of its perennial best-sellers. Other books which enjoyed wide success were Abbé Dimnet's *The Art of Thinking*, Will Durant's *The Story of Philosophy*, Dale Carnegie's *How to Win Friends and Influence People*, *The Bible Designed to be Read as Living Literature*, edited by Ernest Sutherland Bates, Hendrik Willem Van Loon's *The Arts*, M. Lincoln Schuster's *A Treasury of the World's Great Letters* and Wendell Willkie's *One World*, issued in an inexpensive edition. In 1942 the firm introduced its juvenile line, *Golden Books* (q.v.). In 1944 Marshall Field bought a major interest in the company. Leon Shimkin is president. Its divisions or subsidiaries include Pocket Books, Trident Press, Washington Square Press, Julian Messner, Monarch Press.

SIMONDS, FRANK H[erbert] (Apr. 5, 1878–Jan. 23, 1936); b. Concord, Mass. Editor, author. *They Shall Not Pass* (1916); *History of the World War*, 5v. (1927); *Can Europe Keep the Peace* (1931); etc. With the *New York Sun*, 1908–14; editor, the *Evening Sun*, 1913–14; assoc. editor, the *New York Tribune*, 1915–18; contrib. editor, *Review of Reviews*, 1914–33.

SIMONDS, WILLIAM (Oct. 30, 1822–July 7, 1859); b. Charlestown, Mass. Editor, author. *The Pleasant Way* (1841); the *Aimwell Stories*, 7v. (under pen name "Walter Aimwell," 1853–70); etc. Editor, the *Boston Saturday Rambler*, 1846–50; the *New England Farmer*, 1850–59.

SIMONDS, WILLIAM ADAMS (Sept. 19, 1887–Oct. 19, 1963); b. Central City, Neb. Author. *Henry Ford, Motor Genius* (1929); *From the Ground Up* (with Fred L. Black, 1930); *A Boy with Edison* (1931); *Edison: His Life, His Work, His Genius* (1934); *Henry Ford and Greenfield Village* (1938); *Henry Ford, His Life, His Work, His Genius* (1943); *Kamaaina, A Century in Hawaii* (1949); *The Hawaiian Telephone Story* (1958); etc.

SIMONDS, WILLIAM EDWARD (Sept. 10, 1860–June 24, 1947); b. Peabody, Mass. Educator, author. *Sir Thomas Wyatt and His Poems* (1889); *An Introduction to the Study of English Fiction* (1894); *A Student's History of English Literature* (1902); *A Student's History of American Literature* (1909); etc. Professor English Literature, Knox College, 1889–1930; dean, 1912–30.

SIMONSON, LEE (June 26, 1888–Jan. 23, 1967); b. New York. Scenic designer, author. *Minor Prophecies* (1927); *The Stage Is Set* (1932); *Settings and Costumes of the Modern Stage* (1933); *Theatre Art* (1934); *Part of a Lifetime—Drawings and Designs, 1919–1940* (1943); *The Art of Scenic Design* (1949); etc.

SIMONT, MARC (Nov. 23, 1915–); b. Paris, France. Artist, author. *Opera Soufflé* (1950); *Polly's Oats* (1951); *The Lovely Summer* (1952); *How To Get To First Base* (with Red Smith, 1952); *Mimi* (1955); *The Plumber Out of the Sea* (1955); *The Contest at Paca* (1959); *How Come Elephants?* (1965); *Afternoon in Spain* (1965).

Simple Cobler of Aggawam in America, The. By Nathaniel Ward (1647). Sprightly New England satire of its time, and a commentary on the sad plight of England. *See* edition edited by Lawrence C. Wroth (1937); V. L. Parrington's *Colonial Mind* (1927).

SIMPSON, CHARLES TORREY (June 3, 1846–Dec. 17, 1932); b. Tiskilwa, Ill. Naturalist, author. *In Lower Florida Wilds* (1920); *Out of Doors in Florida* (1923); *Florida Wild Life* (1932); etc.

SIMPSON, GEORGE GAYLORD (June 16, 1902–); b. Chicago, Ill. Vertebrate paleontologist, author. *Attending Marvels, a Patagonian Journal* (1933); *The Meaning of Evolution* (1949); *Horses* (1951); *Life of the Past* (1953); *The Major Features of Evolution* (1953); *Life* (with others, 1957); *The Principles of Animal Taxonomy* (1961); *This View of Life: The World of an Evolutionist* (1964); *The Geography of Evolution* (1965); *Biology and Man* (1969); etc. Prof. geology University of Arizona, since 1967.

SIMPSON, JOHN ERNEST (Jan. 17, 1889–); b. Washington, Ia. Presbyterian clergyman, author. *This Grace Also* (1933); *He That Giveth* (1936); *This World's Goods* (1939); *Faithful Also in Much* (1941); *Stewardship and the World Mission* (1944); *Great Stewards of the Bible* (1947); etc.

SIMPSON, ROBERT (Oct. 12, 1886–Jan. 7, 1934); b. Strathy, Scot. Author. *The Bite of Benin* (1919); *Swamp Breath* (1921); *The Gray Charteris* (1923); *Eight Panes of Glass* (1924); *Calvert of Allobar* (1925); etc. Managing editor, *Argosy*, 1917–20; editor, *Mystery Magazine*, 1925–27.

SIMPSON, STEPHEN (July 24, 1789–Aug. 17, 1854); b. Philadelphia, Pa. Editor, economist, author. *The Author's Jewel* (1823); *The Working Man's Manual* (1831); *Biography of Stephen Girard* (1832); *The Lives of George Washington and Thomas Jefferson: With a Parallel* (1833); etc. Co-editor, *The Portico, Baltimore*, 1816–17; the *Columbian Observer*, Philadelphia, 1822.

SIMS, DOROTHY RICE (Mrs. P. Hal Sims) (d. Mar. 24, 1960). Author. *Curiouser and Curiouser* (1940); *How to Live on a Hunch* (1944); etc.

SIMS, EDWARD HOWELL (May 29, 1923–); b. Orangeburg, S.C. Editor, author. *American Aces–Great Fighter Battles of World War II* (1958); *Greatest Fighter Missions* (1962); *The Fighter Pilots* (1967). Editor, *Orangeburg Times and Democrat*.

SIMS, HENRY UPSON (June 27, 1873–Oct. 31, 1961); b. Columbus, Miss. Lawyer, author. *Covenants Which Run with Land other than Covenants with Title* (1901); *Chancery Pleading and Practice in Alabama* (1909); *Origin and Development of the Civilization of the Gulf States* (1952). Editor: *150 Great Hymns in the English Language* (1949).

SIMS, MARIAN [McCamy] (Oct. 16, 1899–July 9, 1961); b. Dalton, Ga. Author. *Morning Star* (1934); *The World with a Fence* (1936); *Call It Freedom* (1937); *Memo to Timothy Sheldon* (1938); *The City on the Hill* (1940); *Beyond Surrender* (1942); *Storm Before Daybreak* (1946); etc.

SINAI, ISAAC ROBERT (Oct. 10, 1924–   ); b. in Lithuania. Educator, author. *The Challenge of Modernization* (1964); *The Dynamics of Modern History* (1967); *In Search of the Modern World* (1967). Prof. political science, L.I.U., since 1966.

Sinbad, Smith & Co. By Albert Stearns (1896). An American boy's adventures in the land described in the *Arabian Nights*.

SINCLAIR, HAROLD AUGUSTUS (May 8, 1907–May 24, 1966); b. Chicago, Ill. Novelist. *Journey Home* (1936); *American Years* (1938); *The Years of Growth* (1940); *Westward the Tide* (1940); *Years of Illusion* (1941); *The Port of New Orleans* (1942); *Music Out of Dixie* (1952); *The Horse Soldiers* (1956); *The Cavalryman* (1958); etc.

Sinclair, Jo. Pen name of Ruth Seid.

SINCLAIR, UPTON [Beall] (Sept. 20, 1878–Nov. 25, 1968); b. Baltimore, Md. Author. *Springtime and Harvest* (1901), also published as *King Midas* (1901); *The Jungle* (1906); *The Metropolis* (1908); *King Coal* (1917); *The Brass Check* (1919); *The Goose-Step* (1923); *Oil!* (1927); *Boston* (1928); *Mountain City* (1930); *Roman Holiday* (1931); *American Outpost* (reminiscences, 1932); *Our Lady* (1938); *Marie Antoinette: A Play* (1939); *World's End* (1940); *Between Two Worlds* (1941); *Dragon's Teeth* (1942); *Wide Is the Gate* (1943); *Presidential Agent* (1944); *Dragon Harvest* (1945); *A World to Win* (1946); *Presidential Mission* (1947); *One Clear Call* (1948); *O Shepherd, Speak!* (1949); *The Return of Lanny Budd* (1953); *The Cup of Fury* (1956); *It Happened to Didymus* (1958); *My Lifetime in Letters* (1960); *Affectionately, Eve* (1961); *The Autobiography of Upton Sinclair* (1963); *The Cry for Justice* (1915); etc. Also numerous books for boys under pen names "Ensign Clarke Fitch, U.S.N.," "Clark Fitch," and "Lieut. Frederick Garrison." *See* Floyd Dell's *Upton Sinclair* (1927); James L. Harte's *This Is Upton Sinclair* (1938); David Mar Chalmers' *The Social and Political Ideas of the Muckrakers* (1965); *Political Literature of the Progressive Era*, ed. by G. L. Groman (1967).

Sinclair-Cowan, Bertha Muzzy. See B. M. Bower.

SINGER, CAROLINE (Mrs. C. Le Roy Baldridge) (Apr. 6, 1888–); b. Colfax, Wash. Author. *White Africans and Black* (1929); *Boomba Lives in Africa* (1935); *Half the World Is Isfahan* (1936); *Santa Claus Comes to America* (1942); etc.

SINGER, EDGAR ARTHUR, Jr. (Nov. 13, 1873–Apr. 4, 1954); b. Philadelphia, Pa. Educator, author. *Modern Thinkers and Present Problems* (1923); *Mind as Behavior and Studies in Empirical Idealism* (1924); *Fool's Advice* (1925); *On the Contented Life* (1936); *In Search of a Way of Life* (1948); etc. Prof. Philosophy, University of Pennsylvania, from 1909.

SINGER, ISAAC BASHEVIS (July 14, 1904–); b. Radzymin, Pol. Author of books written in Yiddish. *Satan in Goray* (1935); *The Family Moskat* (1950); *Gimpel the Fool* (1957); *The Magician of Lublin* (1960); *The Spinoza of Market Street* (1961); *The Slave* (1962); *Short Friday* (1964); *In My Father's Court* (1966); *Zlateh the Goat and other Stories* (1966); *Selected Short Stories* (1966); *The Manor* (1967); *A Friend of Kafka* (1970); *Joseph and Koza* (1970); *Elijah the Slave* (1970); etc.

SINGER, ISIDORE (Nov. 10, 1859–Feb. 20, 1939); b. Weisskirchen, Austria. Editor, publisher, author. *Social Justice* (1923); *Theology at the Crossroads* (1928); *One God, One Mankind* (1935); etc. Wrote many books in German. Managing editor and founder, *Jewish Encyclopedia*, 12v. (1901–05).

SINGER, ISRAEL JOSHUA (Nov. 30, 1893–Feb. 10, 1944); b. Bilgoraj, Pol. Author of novels and stories in Yiddish. *The Brothers Ashkenazi* (1936); *The River Breaks Up* (1938); *East of Eden* (1939); etc.

SINGER, KURT D[eutsch] (Aug. 10, 1911–   ); b. Vienna, Aus. Editor, commentator, author. *The Coming War* (1934); *Spies and Saboteurs in Argentina* (1943); *Spies and Traitors of World War II* (1945); *Who Are the Communists of America?* (1948); *3000 Years of Espionage* (1951); *Hemingway—Life and Death of a Giant* (1961); *Dr. Albert Schweitzer, Medical Missionary* (1962); *Kurt Singer's Ghost Omnibus* (1965); *I Can't Sleep At Night* (1966); and numerous other books on spies, politics, and ghosts.

SINGERLY, WILLIAM MISKEY (Dec. 27, 1832–Feb. 27, 1898); b. Philadelphia, Pa. Editor, publisher. He bought the *Public Record*, Philadelphia, in 1877, and changed its name in 1879 to the *Philadelphia Record*.

Singing Sibyl. Pen name of Metta Victoria Victor.

Singleton, Anne. Pen name of Ruth Benedict.

SINGLETON, CHARLES SOUTHWARD (Apr. 21, 1909–); b. McLoud, Okla. Educator. *An Essay on the Vita Nuova* (1949); *Il Decameron* (1955); *Journey to Beatrice* (1958). Editor: *Art, Science and History in the Renaissance* (1967); *Interpretation, Theory and Practice* (1969); etc. Prof. Italian, Johns Hopkins University, since 1937.

SINGLETON, ESTHER (Nov. 4, 1865–July 2, 1930); b. Baltimore, Md. Editor, author. *Turrets, Towers and Temples: The Great Buildings of the World* (1898); *A Guide to the Opera* (1899); *The Furniture of Our Fore-fathers*, 8 parts (1900–01); *Social New York under the Georges* (1902); *The White House* (1907); *Landmarks of American History* (1907); *Famous Cathedrals* (1909); *Dutch New York* (1909); *A Daughter of the Revolution* (1915); *Shakespearian Fantasias* (1930); etc. Editor, *The Antiquarian*, 1923–30.

SINGMASTER, ELSIE (Mrs. Harold Lewars) (Aug. 29, 1879–Sept. 30, 1958); b. Schuylkill Haven, Pa. Author. *When Sarah Saved the Day* (1909); *When Sarah Went to School* (1910); *Gettysburg: Stories of the Red Harvest and the Aftermath* (1913); *Katy Gaumer* (1914); *The Long Journey* (1917); *Ellen Levis* (1921); *The Hidden Road* (1923); *A Boy at Gettysburg* (1924); *The Book of the Colonies* (1927); *What Everybody Wanted* (1928); *Virginia's Bandit* (1929); *The Young Ravenels* (1932); *The Loving Heart* (1937); *Stories of Pennsylvania*, 4v. (1937–40); *A High Wind Rising* (1942); *I Speak for Thaddeus Stevens* (1947); *I Heard of a River* (1948); etc.

Singular Life, A. Novel by Elizabeth Stuart Phelps (1896). Story of Emanuel Bayard, brought up in luxurious surroundings, who gives up a life of ease to devote himself to the cause of Christ.

Sinners in the Hands of an Angry God. By Jonathan Edwards (1742). Famous sermon preached at Enfield, Mass., July 8, 1741.

SINNOTT, EDMUND WARE (Feb. 5, 1888–Jan. 7, 1968); b. Cambridge, Mass. Botanist, author. *Two Roads to Truth* (1953); *The Biology of the Spirit* (1955); *Matter, Mind, and Man* (1957); *Cell and Psyche* (1961); etc. Prof. botany, Yale University, 1940–56.

Siogvolk, Paul, Pen name of Albert Mathews.

SIPLE, PAUL ALLMAN (Dec. 18, 1908–Nov. 25, 1968); b. Montpelier, O. Explorer, author. *A Boy Scout with Byrd* (1931); *Exploring at Home* (1932); *Scout to Explorer* (1936); *Adaptation of the Explorer to the Climate of Antarctica* (1939); *90° South: The Story of The American South Pole Conquest* (1959); etc.

SIRINGO, CHARLES A. (Feb. 7, 1855–Oct. 19, 1928); b. Matagorda, Tex. Cowboy, author. *A Texas Cowboy; or, Fifteen Years on the Hurricane Deck of a Spanish Pony* (1885); *A Cowboy Detective* (1912); *A Lone Star Cowboy* (1919); *History of "Billy the Kid"* (1920); *Riata and Spurs* (autobiography, 1927); etc.

SISSON, EDWARD OCTAVIUS (May 24, 1869–Jan. 24, 1949); b. Gateshead, Eng. Educator, author. *The Essentials of Character* (1910); *Educating for Freedom* (1935); etc. President, State University of Montana, 1917–21; prof. philosophy, Reed College, 1921–39.

Sister Carrie. Novel by Theodore Dreiser (1900). Story of Carrie Meeber who goes from a small town to Chicago to become an actress. She becomes the mistress of two men, and one, Hurstwood, is ruined by her.

SITTERLY, CHARLES FREMONT (June 4, 1861–Nov. 8, 1945); b. Liverpool, N.Y. Methodist clergyman, author. *Praxis in Manuscripts of the Greek New Testament* (1898); *History of the English Bible* (with S. G. Ayres, 1899); *Henry Anson Buttz,* 2v. (1922); *The Building of Drew University* (1937); etc. Prof. Biblical literature, Drew University, 1895–1935.

Sixties, The. See *Seventies, The.*

Sixty Years of Best Sellers. By Alice Hackett (1956). Covers the period from 1895 to 1955.

SIZOO, JOSEPH RICHARD (May 15, 1884–Aug. 28, 1966); b. in the Netherlands. Dutch Reformed clergyman, author. *Abraham Lincoln* (1924); *William Jennings Bryan* (1925); *Make Life Worth Living* (1937); *Not Alone* (1940); *Preaching Unashamed* (1949); *On Guard* (1954); etc.

SKARIATINA, IRINA (Mrs. Victor Franklin Blakeslee) (d. Nov. 17, 1962); b. St. Petersburg, Rus. Author. *A World Can End* (1931); *A World Begins* (1932); *First to Go Back* (1933); *Tamara* (1941); *Skyroad to Moscow* (1944); etc.

"Skeleton in Armor, The." Poem by Henry Wadsworth Longfellow (1841).

"Sketch." Poem by Carl Sandburg, in his *Chicago Poems* (1916). Evocative silhouette of shadowy ships slipping quietly into their lake harbor.

Sketch Book, The. By Washington Irving (1819). The author's earliest and most popular work. It contains two of Irving's best known tales, *The Legend of Sleepy Hollow* and *Rip Van Winkle.*

Sketch Book Magazine. New York. Monthly. Founded 1923. Art and literary magazine edited and published by DeWitt H. Fessenden. Discontinued 1943.

Sketch for a Self-Portrait. By Bernard Berenson (1949). Autobiography of an art critic, connoisseur, and man of letters.

Skiddoo. Humorous sketch by George Vere Hobart (1906). "Skiddoo" was a popular slang expression at that time.

SKIDMORE, HOBERT DOUGLAS (Apr. 11, 1909–); b. Webster Springs, W.Va. Novelist. *Valley of the Sky* (1944); *More Lives than One* (1945); *Disturb Not Our Dreams* (1947); *O Careless Love* (1949); *The Years Are Even* (1952); etc.

SKIDMORE, HUBERT STANDISH (Apr. 11, 1909–Feb. 2, 1946); b. Webster Springs, W.Va. Author. *I Will Lift Up Mine Eyes* (1936); *Heaven Came So Near* (1938); *River Rising* (1939); *Hawk's Nest* (1941).

Skin of Our Teeth, The. Play by Thornton Wilder (prod. 1942). Allegorical comedy of a New Jersey family who represent the first created men and women, in Biblical analogy, and overcome cataclysmic disasters to continue the advance in culture of the human race.

SKINNER, ADA M[aria] (1878–); b. Worcester, Eng. Co-author (with sister, Eleanor Louise Skinner): *The Emerald Story Book* (1915); *Merry Tales* (1915); *The Turquoise Story Book* (1918); *Children's Plays* (1919); *Happy Tales for the Story Hour* (1920); etc. Compiler (with same): *A Child's Book of Country Stories* (1951).

SKINNER, B[urrhus] F[rederic] (Mar. 20, 1904–); b. Susquehanna, Pa. Educator, author. *Behavior of Organisms* (1938); *Walden Two* (1948); *Science and Human Behavior* (1953); *Verbal Behavior* (1957); *Cumulative Record* (1959); *Analysis of Behavior* (1961); *The Technology of Teaching* (1968); etc. Prof. psychology, Harvard University, since 1948.

SKINNER, CHARLES M[ontgomery] (Mar. 15, 1852–1907); b. Victor, N.Y. Editor, author. *Do-Nothing Days* (1899); *Myths and Legends Beyond Our Border* (1899); *Flowers in the Pane* (1900); *American Myths & Legends,* 2v. (1903); etc. On editorial staff, the *Brooklyn Eagle.*

SKINNER, CLARENCE RUSSELL (Mar. 23, 1881–Aug. 27, 1949); b. Brooklyn, N.Y. Universalist clergyman, educator, author. *Liberalism Faces the Future* (1937); *Human Nature and the Nature of Evil* (1939); *Religion for Greatness* (1945); etc. Prof. applied Christianity, Tufts College, from 1914; dean, from 1933.

SKINNER, CONSTANCE LINDSAY (d. Mar. 27, 1939); b. in British Columbia. Author. *Pioneers of the Old Southwest* (1919); *Silent Scott, Frontier Scout* (1925); *Becky Landers, Frontier Warrior* (1926); *Andy Breaks Trail* (1928); *Red Willows* (1929); *Songs of the Coast-Dwellers* (1930); *Beaver, Kings and Cabins* (1933); etc. Editor, *Rivers of America* series.

SKINNER, CORNELIA OTIS (May 30, 1901–); b. Chicago, Ill., daughter of Otis Skinner. Actress, author. *Excuse It, Please!* (1936); *Dithers and Jitters* (1938); *Our Hearts Were Young and Gay* (with Emily Kimbrough, 1942); *Family Circle* (1948); *Nuts in May* (1950); *Bottoms Up!* (1955); *The Ape in Me* (1959); *Elegant Wits and Grand Horizontals* (1962); *Madame Sarah* (1967); etc.

SKINNER, ELEANOR LOUISE (1872–Oct. 20, 1951); b. Worcester, Eng. Author (with sister, Ada M. Skinner): *The Emerald Story Book* (1915); *Merry Tales* (1915); *The Turquoise Story Book* (1918); *Children's Plays* (1919); *Happy Tales for the Story Hour* (1920); *Fun in Our Busy World* (1940); *A Child's Book of Country Stories* (1951); etc.

SKINNER, G[eorge] WILLIAM (Feb. 14, 1925–); b. Oakland, Cal. Anthropologist, author. *Chinese Society in Thailand* (1958); *Marketing and Social Structure in Rural China* (1967). Editor: *The Social Sciences and Thailand* (1956); *Local, Ethnic and National Loyalties in Village Indonesia* (1959). Prof. anthropology, Stanford University, since 1966.

SKINNER, HARLEY CLAY (May 3, 1895–); b. Croton, O. Educator. *Psychology for the Average Man* (1927); *Educational Biology* (with others, 1937); etc. Prof. psychology, Arizona State College, since 1938.

SKINNER, HUBERT MARSHALL (Jan. 15, 1855–June 4, 1916); b. Valparaiso, Ind. Lecturer, author. *Readings in Folk-Lore* (1893); *The Schoolmaster in Literature* (1893); *The Schoolmaster in Comedy and Satire* (1895); etc.

SKINNER, JOHN STUART (Feb. 22, 1788–Mar. 21, 1851); b. in Calvert Co., Md. Editor. Editor, *American Farmer*, 1819–30; the *American Turf Register and Sporting Magazine*, 1829–35; the *Farmer's Library and Monthly Journal of Agriculture*, 1845–48; *The Plough, the Loom, and the Anvil*, 1848–51.

SKINNER, KATE RUMSEY (Apr. 25, 1929–); b. St. Louis, Mo. Poet. *Stranger With a Watch* (1965); *A Close Sky Over Killaspuglonane* (1967).

SKINNER, OTIS (June 28, 1858–Jan. 4, 1942); b. Cambridge, Mass. Actor, author. *Footlights and Spotlights* (1924); *Mad Folk of the Theatre* (1928); *One Man in His Time* (with Maud Skinner, 1938); *The Last Tragedian: Booth Tells His Own Story* (1939); etc.

SKINNER, OTIS AINSWORTH (July 3, 1807–Sept. 18, 1861); b. Royalton, Vt. Universalist clergyman, educator, editor, reformer. *Universalism Illustrated and Defended* (1839); *Miller's Theory Exploded* (1940); *The Death of Daniel Webster* (1852); etc. Editor, the *Universalist Miscellany*, Boston, 1844–49. President, Lombard College, Galesburg, Ill., 1857–58.

"Skipper Ireson's Ride." Poem by John Greenleaf Whittier (1857).

SKLAR, GEORGE (June 1, 1908–); b. Meriden, Conn. Author. *Merry-Go-Round* (with Albert Maltz, prod. 1931); *Peace on Earth* (with same, prod. 1933); *Stevedore* (with Paul Peters, prod. 1934); *Parade* (with same, prod. 1935); *Life and Death of An American* (prod. 1939); *The Two Worlds of Johnny Truro* (1947); *Laura* (with Vera Caspary, prod. 1946); *The Promising Young Men* (1951); *The Housewarming* (1953); *The Identity of Dr. Frazier* (1961); *And People All Around* (1966); etc.

SKLAR, ROBERT ANTHONY (Dec. 3, 1936–); b. New Brunswick, N.J. Author. *F. Scott Fitzgerald, the Last Laocoön* (1967). Faculty, University of Michigan, since 1965.

SLADE, CAROLINE [Beach] (Mrs. John A. Slade) (Oct. 7, 1886–); b. Minneapolis, Minn. Novelist. *Sterile Sun* (1936); *The Triumph of Willie Pond* (1940); *Job's House* (1941); *Lilly Crackell* (1943); *Margaret* (1946); *Susie* (1947); *Mrs. Party's House* (1948); etc.

SLADE, WILLIAM ADAMS (Sept. 27, 1874–May 16, 1950); b. Fall River, Mass. Librarian. With Library of Congress, 1898–1930; chief reference librarian, 1934–40. Director, Folger Shakespeare Library, 1930–34.

SLAFTER, EDMUND FARWELL (May 30, 1816–Sept. 22, 1906); b. Norwich, Vt. Episcopal clergyman, genealogist. Editor: *Sir William Alexander and American Colonization* (1873); *Voyages of the Northmen to America* (1877); *Voyages of Samuel de Champlain*, 3v. (1878–82); *John Checkley*, 2v. (1897); etc. Associated with New England Historic-Genealogical Society, 1861–1906. President, Prince Society, 1880–1906.

SLAUGHTER, FRANK G[ill] (Feb. 25, 1908–); b. Washington. Physician, author. *That None Should Die* (1941); *Battle Surgeon* (1944); *Sangaree* (1948); *Fort Everglades* (1951); *The Galileans* (1953); *Flight from Natchez* (1955); *The Warrior* (1956); *Daybreak* (1958); *Life of Christ* (1959); *The Land and the Promise* (1960); *David: Warrior and King* (1962); *Tomorrow's Miracle* (1962); *Devil's Harvest* (1963); *Upon This Rock* (1963); *A Savage Place* (1964); *The Purple Quest* (1965); *Constantine: The Miracle of the Flaming Cross* (1965); *Surgeon U.S.A.* (1966); *God's Warrior* (1967); *Doctor's Wives* (1967); *The Sins of Herod* (1968); *Surgeon's Choice* (1969); etc.

SLAUGHTER, GERTRUDE [Elizabeth Taylor] (Mrs. Moses Stephen Slaughter) (Nov. 29, 1870–); b. Cambridge, O. Author. *Two Children in Old Paris* (1918); *Shakespeare and the Heart of a Child* (1922); *Heirs of Old Venice* (1927); *The Amazing Frederick* (1927); *Calabria, the First Italy* (1939); *Saladin: A Biography* (1955); etc.

SLAUGHTER, PHILIP (Oct. 26, 1808–June 12, 1890); b. "Springfield," Culpeper Co., Va. Episcopal clergyman, historian. *A History of Bristol Parish* (1846); *The Virginian History of African Colonization* (1855); *A Sketch of the Life of Randolph Fairfax* (1864); *A History of St. Mark's Parish* (1877); *The History of Truro Parish*, ed. by Edward L. Goodwin (1908); etc.

Slave; or, Memoir of Archy Moore, The. Novel by Richard Hildreth (1836). Fictional autobiography of a slave, probably the first anti-slavery novel in America.

Slave Songs of the United States. Ed. by William Francis Allen, Charles Pickard Ware, and Lucy McKim Garrison (1867).

Slavery in the Southern States. By Edward Pringle (1852). Important statement of the moderate Southern position.

SLAVSON, SAMUEL RICHARD (Dec. 25, 1891–); b. in Russia. Psychotherapy consultant, author. *Science in the New Education* (with Robert K. Speer, 1934); *Creative Group Education* (1937); *Character Education in a Democracy* (1939); *Introduction to Group Therapy* (1943); *Recreation and the Total Personality* (1946); *Analytic Group Psychotherapy* (1950); *Re-educating the Delinquent* (1954); *The Fields of Group Psychotherapy* (1956); *Child-Centered Group Guidance of Parents* (1958); *A Textbook in Analytic Group Psychotherapy* (1964); *Reclaiming the Delinquent Through Para-Analytic Group Psychotherapy and the Inversion Technique* (1965); *Because I Live Here, Vita-Erg Therapy with Regressed Psychotic Women* (1969); etc. Editor: *Child Psychotherapy* (1952); *The Practice of Group Therapy* (1947).

SLEDD, BENJAMIN (Aug. 27, 1864–Jan. 4, 1940); b. in Bedford Co., Va. Educator, poet. *From Cliff and Scar* (1897); *The Watchers of the Hearth* (1901); *When Freedom Came* (1910); *A Virginian in Surrey* (1914); *To England* (1919); *The Dead Grammarian* (1924); *The Modernist and the Megatherium* (1927); etc. Prof. English, Wake Forest College, 1888–1940.

SLEEPER, HAROLD REEVE (Mar. 18, 1893–Nov. 10, 1960); b. Pueblo, Col. Architect. *Architectural Graphic Standards* (with others, 1932); *Architectural Specifications* (1940); *Realistic Approach to Private Investment in Urban Redevelopment* (1946); *The House for You—To Build, Buy, or Rent* (with wife, 1948); *Building, Planning and Design Standards* (1955).

SLEEPER, JOHN SHERBURNE (Sept. 21, 1794–Nov. 14, 1878); b. Tyngsboro, Mass. Mariner, journalist, author. Pen name, "Hawser Martingale." *Tales of the Ocean* (1841); *Salt-Water Bubbles* (1854); *Ocean Adventures* (1857); *Jack in the Forecastle* (1860); *Mark Rowland* (1867); etc.

"Sleeping Sentinel, The." Civil War poem by Francis de Haes Janvier (1863).

SLEIGHT, MARY BRECK, b. New York, daughter of Henry C. Sleight. Author. *The House at Craque* (1886); *The Flag on the Mill* (1887); etc.

SLESINGER, TESS (July 16, 1905–); b. New York. Novelist. *The Unpossessed* (1934); *Time: The Present* (1935). *See* Fred B. Millett's *Contemporary American Authors* (1940).

SLICHTER, SUMNER H[uber] (Jan. 8, 1892–Sept. 27, 1959); b. Madison, Wis. Economist. *Modern Economic Society* (1931); *Towards Stability* (1934); *Trade Union Policy and Industrial Management* (1941); *The Challenge of Industrial Relations* (1947); *The American Economy* (1948); *What's Ahead for American Business* (1951); *The Impact of Collective Bargaining on Management* (with others, 1960); etc. Prof. economics, Harvard University, 1930–40; Lamont University from 1940.

Slim. Novel by William Wister Haines (1934). Story of the awkward American soldier adventurer. The character was later put into several motion pictures.

SLOAN, HAROLD STEPHENSON (Nov. 23, 1887–); b. Brooklyn, N.Y. Economist, author. *Today's Economics* (1936); *Farming in America* (1947). Co-author: *Classrooms in the Factories* (1958); *Classrooms in the Stores* (1962); *Classrooms in the Military* (1964); *Classrooms on Main Street* (1966); etc.

SLOANE, ERIC (Feb. 27, 1910–   ); b. New York. Meteorologist, artist, author. *Clouds, Air and Wind* (1941); *Skies and the Artist* (1951); *Eric Sloane's Weather Book* (1952); *Our Vanishing Landscape* (1955); *American Yesterday* (1957); *Eric Sloane's Americana* (1957); *Return to Taos* (1960); *ABCs of Early Americana* (1963); *Folklore of American Weather* (1963); *Museum of Early American Tools* (1964); *Reverence for Wood* (1965); *Mr. Daniels and the Grange* (1967); etc.

SLOANE, WILLIAM (Mar. 13, 1910–); b. Glasgow, Scot. Educator, author. *The British Isles* (1946); *Children's Books in England and America in the Seventeenth Century* (1955). Prof. English, Dickinson College, since 1952.

SLOANE, WILLIAM MILLIGAN (Nov. 12, 1850–Sept. 11, 1928); b. Richmond, O. Educator, author. *Life of Napoleon Bonaparte,* 4v. (1896); *The Life of James McCosh* (1896); *The Balkans* (1914); *The Powers and Aims of Western Democracy* (1919); *Greater France in Morocco* (1924); etc. Prof. history, Princeton University, 1876–96, Columbia University, 1896–1928.

SLOANE, WILLIAM [Milligan, III] (Aug. 15, 1906–); b. Plymouth, Mass. Publisher, editor, author. *To Walk the Night* (1937); *The Edge of Running Water* (1939). Editor: *Space, Space, Space* (1953); *Stories for Tomorrow* (1954). Founder, William Sloane Associates, 1946; president, 1946–52. Editorial director, Funk & Wagnall's Co., 1952–55; Rutgers University Press, since 1955.

SLOBODKIN, LOUIS (Feb. 19, 1903–); b. Albany, N.Y. Sculptor, illustrator, author. *Sculpture—Principles and Practice* (1949); *Mr. Mushroom* (1950); *Our Friendly Friends* (1951); *The Space Ship Under the Apple Tree* (1952); *Circus April 1st* (1953); *The Horse with the High-Heeled Shoes* (1954); *The Amiable Giant* (1955); *Millions and Millions* (1955); *The Little Mermaid Who Could Not Sing* (1956); *The Space Ship Returns* (1958); *The First Book of Drawing* (1958); *Trick or Treat* (1959); *Excuse Me, Lovely Animals* (1960); *A Good Place to Hide* (1961); *Picco* (1961); *The Three-Seated Spaceship* (1962); *The Late Cuckoo* (1962); *Luigi and the Long-Nosed Soldier* (1963); *Moon Blossom and the Golden Penny* (1963); *The Polka Goat* (1964); *Yasu and the Strangers* (1965); *Colette and the Princess* (1965); *Read About the Policeman* (1966); *Read About the Postman* (1966); *Read about the Fireman* (1967); *Read About the Busman* (1967); *Read About the Garbageman* (1967); *Round Trip Spaceship* (1968); etc.

SLOCUM, JOSHUA (Feb. 20, 1844–1909); b. in Wilmot Township, N.S. Author. *Voyage of the Liberdade* (1890); *Sailing Alone Around the World* (1900); etc. *See* C. E. Slocum's *A Short History of the Slocums,* 2v. (1882–1908); W. M. Teller's *The Search for Captain Slocum* (1956). He last sailed on Nov. 14, 1909, was never heard from again, and was declared legally dead as of that date.

Slogum House. By Mari Sandoz (1937). Novel of pioneer life in Nebraska.

SLONIM, MARC [L'vovich]. Author. *Epic of Russian Literature from Its Origins through Tolstoy* (1950); *Modern Russian Literature: From Chekhov to the Present* (1953); *The Three Loves of Dostoevsky* (1955); *Outline of Russian Literature* (1958); *Russian Theater: From the Empire to the Soviets* (1961); *Soviet Russian Literature* (1964).

SLONIMSKY, NICOLAS (Apr. 27, 1894–); b. St. Petersburg, Rus. Conductor, composer, author. *Music Since 1900* (1937); *Music of Latin America* (1945); *Lexicon of Musical Invective* (1953); etc. Editor: *International Cyclopedia of Music and Musicians,* 4th–7th ed. (1946–56); Theodore Baker's *Biographical Dictionary of Musicians,* 5th ed. (1958); etc.

SLOSSON, ANNIE TRUMBULL (May 18, 1838–Oct. 4, 1926); b. Stonington, Conn. Author. *China Hunters Club* (1878); *Fishin' Jimmy* (1889); *Seven Dreamers* (1891); *Dumb Foxglove, and Other Stories* (1898); *Aunt Abby's Neighbors* (1902); *A Local Colorist* (1912); *Other Folks* (1918); etc.

SLOSSON, EDWIN EMERY (June 7, 1865–Oct. 15, 1929); b. Albany, Kansas. Chemist, editor, author. *Major Prophets of To-Day* (1914); *Creative Chemistry* (1919); *Plots and Personalities* (1922); *Chats on Science* (1924); *A Number of Things* (1930); etc. lit. Editor, *The Independent,* 1903–21.

SLOSSON, PRESTON WILLIAM (Sept. 2, 1892–); b. Lafayette, Wyo. Educator, author. *The Decline of the Chartist Movement* (1916); *The Twentieth Century Europe* (1927); *The Great Crusade and After, 1914–1928* (1930); *Europe Since 1870* (1935); *After the War: What?* (1943); *Europe Since 1815* (1954); *The History of Our World* (with others, 1959); etc. History dept., University of Michigan, since 1921.

SMALL, ALBION WOODBURY (May 11, 1854–Mar. 24, 1926); b. Buckfield, Me. Sociologist, educator, author. *General Sociology* (1905); *The Meaning of Social Science* (1910); *Origins of Sociology* (1924); etc. Founder, the *American Journal of Sociology;* editor, 1895–1926. President, Colby College, 1889–92; prof. sociology, University of Chicago, 1892–1926.

SMALL, ELDEN (July 22, 1876–Aug. 29, 1934); b. Marshall, Mich. Critic, author. *At the Court of Bohemia* (1903); *Songs in Twilight* (1919); *The Singing Woman* (1925); etc. Drama critic, the *Detroit News,* 1904–07; drama and music critic, the *Detroit Evening Journal,* 1920–23; feature writer, the *Detroit Free Press,* 1923–25.

Small, Maynard & Co. Boston, Mass. Publishers. Founded 1897. Its editorial work was under the direction of Laurens Small. Absorbed by Dodd, Mead & Company in 1926.

SMALL, SIDNEY HERSCHEL (Feb. 17, 1893–); b. San Francisco, Cal. Author. *The Lord of Thundergate* (1923); *Fourscore* (1924); *Snow and Candle* (1927); *The Splendid Californians* (1928); *Dangerous Duty* (1954); etc.

Small Boy and Others, A. Autobiographical work by Henry James (1913).

Small Publishers Company. New York. Distributes books and other publications of a number of small publishers specializing in modernist, experimental books and graphics, such as Croton Press, Jargon Society, Frontier Press, Caterpillar Press, Something Else Press, and Stony Brook Press.

Small Town in American Literature, The. By Ima Honaker Herron (1939).

SMALLEY, EUGENE VIRGIL (July 18, 1841–Dec. 30, 1899); b. Randolph, O. Journalist, author. *American Journalism* (1884); *The Great Northwest: A Guide Book and Itinerary* (1889); etc. Founder and editor, the *Northwest Illustrated Monthly Magazine.*

SMALLEY, GEORGE WASHBURN (June 2, 1833–Apr. 4, 1916); b. Franklin, Mass. Journalist, author. *London Letters, and Some Others,* 2v. (1891); *Studies of Men* (1895); *Anglo-American Memories,* 2v. (1911–12). Foreign correspondent for the *New York Tribune* during the Civil War, Austro-Prussian War, Franco-Prussian War, etc. *See* F. L. Bullard's *Famous War Correspondents* (1914).

SMART, CHARLES ALLEN (Nov. 30, 1904–Mar. 11, 1967); b. Cleveland, O. Author. *New England Holiday* (1931); *The Brass Cannon* (1933); *R. F. D.* (autobiography, 1938); *Rosscommon* (1940); *Wild Geese and How to Chase Them* (1941); *Sassafras Hill* (1947); *Green Adventure* (play, 1954); *At Home in Mexico* (1957); etc.

SMEDES, SUSAN DABNEY (Aug. 10, 1840–1913); b. Raymond, Miss. Author. *Memorials of a Southern Planter* (1887).

SMEDLEY, AGNES (1894–May 6, 1950); Author. *Daughter of Earth* (1929); *Chinese Destinies* (1933); *China's Red Army Marches* (1934); *China Fights Back* (1939); *Battle Hymn of China* (1943); etc.

SMELSER, MARSHALL (Feb. 4, 1912–); b. Joliet, Ill. Historian. *American Colonial and Revolutionary History* (1950); *Conceived in Liberty* (with Harry Kirwin, 1955); *Congress Founds the Navy, 1787–1798* (1959); *The Democratic Republic 1801–1815* (1968).

SMET, PIERRE-JEAN DE (Jan. 30, 1801–May 23, 1873); b. Termonde, Belg. Roman Catholic clergyman, missionary to the Indians, author. Came to America in 1821. *Letters and Sketches* (1843); *Oregon Missions and Travels over the Rocky Mountains* (1847); *New Indian Sketches* (1863); etc. See *Life, Letters and Travels of Pierre-Jean De Smet,* ed. by H. M. Chittenden and Alfred T. Richardson (1905); E. Laveille's *Life of Father De Smet* (1915); Helene Magaret's *Father De Smet* (1940).

Smiley, Jim. Pen name of Raymond S. Spears.

Smith, Adam. Pen name of George J. W. Goodman.

SMITH, ALFRED E[manuel] (Dec. 30, 1873–Oct. 4, 1944); b. New York. Governor, editor, author. *Progressive Democracy* (1928); *Up to Now* (autobiography, 1929); *Citizen and His Government* (1935); etc. Editor, *New Outlook,* 1932–34. Governor of New York, 1919–20, 1923–28. *See* Franklin D. Roosevelt's *Happy Warrior* (1928); Norman Hapgood and Henry Moskowitz's *Up from the City Streets* (1928).

SMITH, ARABELLA EUGENIA (1844–July 24, 1916); b. Litchfield, O. Poet. Author of "If I Should Die Tonight."

SMITH, ARTHUR COSSLETT (Jan. 19, 1852–May 22, 1926); b. Lyons, N.Y. Lawyer, novelist. *The Monk and the Dancer* (1900); *The Turquoise Cup and the Desert* (1903); etc.

SMITH, ARTHUR DOUGLAS HOWDEN (Dec. 29, 1887–); b. New York. Author. *The Audacious Adventures of Miles McConaughy* (1918); *Porto Bello Gold* (1924); *Commodore Vanderbilt* (1927); *John Jacob Astor* (1929); *Conqueror: The Story of Cortes and Montezuma* (1933); *Alan Breck Again* (1934); *Men Who Run America* (1936); *Old Fuss and Feathers* (1937); *Mr. House of Texas* (1940); etc.

SMITH, ARTHUR HENDERSON (July 18, 1845–Aug. 31, 1932); b. Vernon, Conn. Congregational clergyman, author. *Chinese Characteristics* (1890); *Village Life in China* (1899); *The Uplift of China* (1907); etc.

SMITH, BENJAMIN ELI (Feb. 7, 1857–Feb. 24, 1913); b. Beirut, Syria. Editor. Succeeded William Dwight Whitney as editor-in-chief of the *Century Dictionary* in 1894. Editor, *Century Cyclopedia of Names* (1894); revised edition of the *Century Dictionary,* 12v. (1911).

SMITH, BERNARD (Sept. 20, 1906–); b. New York. Editor, author. *Forces in American Criticism* (1939). Editor: *Books that Changed Our Minds* (with Malcolm Cowley, 1939); *The Democratic Spirit: A Collection of American Writings from the Earliest Times to the Present Day* (1941); *The Holiday Reader* (with P. V. Stern, 1947).

SMITH, BETTY [Wehner] (Dec. 15, 1904–Jan. 17, 1972); b. Brooklyn, N.Y. Author. *A Tree Grows in Brooklyn* (1943); *The Boy Abe* (one-act play, 1944); *Tomorrow Will Be Better* (1948); *Maggie-Now* (1958); *Joy in the Morning* (1963).

SMITH, BRADFORD (May 13, 1909–July 14, 1964); b. North Adams, Mass. Author. *To the Mountain* (1936); *This Solid Flesh* (1937); *American Quest* (1938); *The Arms Are Fair* (1943); *Americans from Japan* (1948); *Bradford of Plymouth* (1951); *Captain John Smith: His Life and Legend* (1953); *Dan Webster—Union Boy* (1954); *Yankees in Paradise* (1956); *Our Debt to the Pilgrims* (1957); *Why We Behave like Americans* (1957); *The Islands of Hawaii* (1957); *Portrait of India* (1962); *Indian American Adventure* (1962); *Meditation: The Inward Art* (1963); *Men of Peace* (1964); *The Seasoned Mind* (1965).

SMITH, BUCKINGHAM (Oct. 31, 1810–Jan. 5, 1871); b. on Cumberland Island, Ga. Lawyer, antiquarian. Translator: *The Narrative of Alvar Nuñez Cabeça de Vaca* (1851); *Narratives of the Career of Hernando de Soto* (1866); etc. His papers and library are now in the New-York Historical Society.

Smith, Carmichael. Pen name of Paul Myron Anthony Linebarger.

SMITH, CHARD POWERS (Nov. 1, 1894–); b. Watertown, N.Y. Poet. *Along the Wind* (1925); *Lost Address* (1928); *Hamilton: A Poetic Drama* (1930); *The Quest of Pan* (1930); *Pattern and Variety in Poetry* (1932); *Annals of the Poets* (1935); *Prelude to Man* (1936); *Artillery of Time* (1939); *Ladies' Day* (1941); *Turn of the Dial* (1943); *The Housatonic* (1946); *Yankees and God* (1956); *Where the Light Falls, A Portrait of Edwin Arlington Robinson* (1965); etc.

SMITH, CHARLES ALPHONSO (May 28, 1864–June 13, 1924); b. Greensboro, N.C. Educator, author. *What Can Literature Do for Me?* (1913); *O. Henry* (1916); *Edgar Allan Poe: How to Know Him* (1921); *Southern Literary Studies* (1927). Literary editor, *Library of Southern Literature,* 17v. (1907–23). Founder, Virginia Folk-Lore Society, 1913. Prof. English, University of Virginia, 1909–17; U.S. Naval Academy, 1917–24.

SMITH, CHARLES EMORY (Feb. 18, 1842–Jan. 19, 1908); b. Mansfield, Conn. Editor, diplomat, cabinet officer. Editor, the *Philadelphia Press,* 1880–1908. Minister to Russia, 1890–92; Postmaster-General, 1898–1901.

SMITH, CHARLES FORSTER (June 30, 1852–Aug. 3, 1931); b. in Abbeville Co., S.C. Educator, classicist, author. *Reminiscences and Sketches* (1908); *Charles Kendall Adams* (1924); etc. Assoc. editor, *Classical Philology,* 1906–31. Prof. Greek and classical philology, University of Wisconsin, 1894–1917. See *Classical Studies in Honor of Charles Forster Smith* (1919).

SMITH, CHARLES HENRY (June 15, 1826–Aug. 24, 1903); b. Lawrenceville, Ga. Journalist, humorist. Pen name "Bill Arp." *Bill Arp, So Called* (1866); *Bill Arp's Peace Papers* (1873); *Bill Arp's Scrap Book* (1884); *The Farm and the Fireside* (1891); *Bill Arp: From the Uncivil War to Date* (1903); etc. Wrote weekly letters to the *Atlanta Constitution* for over twenty-five years.

SMITH, CHARLES SPRAGUE (Apr. 27, 1853–Mar. 30, 1910); b. Andover, Mass. Educator, author. *Barbizon Days* (1902); *Poems* (1908); etc. Prof. German, Columbia University, 1880–91.

SMITH, CHARLES WESLEY (June 20, 1877–); b. Elizabeth City, N.C. Librarian. Compiler: *Bibliography of Marcus Whitman* (1909); *Checklist of Books and Pamphlets Relating to the Pacific Northwest* (1909); *Pacific Northwest Americana* (1921); *Union List of Manuscripts in the Libraries of the Pacific Northwest* (1931); etc. With University of Washington Library, from 1905; librarian, from 1929.

SMITH, CHARLES WILLIAM (June 22, 1893–); b. Lofton, Va. Artist. Collections of his woodcuts have been published as: *Old Virginia in Block Prints* (1929); *Old Charleston* (1933); *The University of Virginia* (1937); *Abstractions* (1939); etc.

SMITH, DAVID EUGENE (Jan. 21, 1860–July 29, 1944); b. Cortland, N.Y. Librarian, educator, mathematician, book collector, editor, author. *Rara Arithmetica* (1907); *Number Stories of Long Ago* (1919); *History of Mathematics*, 2v. (1924); *Rubaiyat of Omar Khayyam* (1933); *Poetry of mathematics and Other Essays* (1934); etc. Editor, *American Mathematical Monthly*, from 1916; *Scripta Mathematica*, from 1932. Prof. mathematics, Teachers College, Columbia University, 1901–26; librarian, 1902–20. Owned extensive collection of early writing materials and books on the history of bookmaking in all countries.

SMITH, DONNAL VORE (Jan. 3, 1901–); b. in Van Wert Co., O. Educator, author. *Chase and Civil War Politics* (1931); *Our Own Age* (with C. A. Beard, 1937); *Social Learning* (1937); *Community Living* (1941); etc. Pres., New York State Teachers College, Cortland, 1943–59.

SMITH, DOROTHY WHITEHILL (Feb. 10, 1893–); b. New York. Author. The *Polly* series, 7v. (1915–25); the *Somewhere* series, 6v. (under pen name, "Martha Trent," 1916); the *Twin* series, 7v. (1918–1925); *Mary Cinderella Brown* (1924).

SMITH, EDGAR F[ahs] (May 23, 1854–May 3, 1928); b. York, Pa. Educator, chemist, author. *The Life of Robert Hare* (1917); *James Woodhouse* (1918); *Chemistry in Old Philadelphia* (1919); *James Cutbush* (1919); *Priestley in America* (1920); etc. Prof. chemistry, University of Pennsylvania, 1888–1920; vice-provost, 1898–1911; provost, 1911–20.

SMITH, EDGAR McPHAIL (Dec. 9, 1857–Mar. 8, 1938); b. Brooklyn, N.Y. Playwright. *The Blue Paradise* (with Herbert Reynolds and Edmund Eysler, prod. 1915); and over 150 other plays and adaptations.

SMITH, EDGAR WADSWORTH (Apr. 1, 1894–Sept. 17, 1960); b. Bethel, Conn. Author. *Foreign Trade and Domestic Welfare* (1935); *Price Equilibrium* (1937); *Appointment in Baker Street* (1938); *Baker Street Inventory* (1945); *A Survey of the Middle East* (1952); *Baker Street and Beyond* (1957); etc.

SMITH, ELIHU HUBBARD (Sept. 4, 1771–Sept. 19, 1798); b. Litchfield, Conn. Poet, playwright, editor. *Edwin and Angelina; or, The Bandit* (prod. 1794), produced as a ballad opera (1796). Editor: *American Poems, Selected and Original* (1793); etc. He was one of the first American poets to use the sonnet form. Member of "Hartford Wits."

SMITH, ELIZABETH OAKES [Prince] (Mrs. Seba Smith) (Aug. 12, 1806–Nov. 15, 1893); b. North Yarmouth. Me. Lecturer, reformer, poet. Pen name "Ernest Helfenstein." *Riches without Wings* (1838); *The Western Captive* (1842); *The Sinless Child, and Other Poems* (1843); *The Poetical Writings* (1845); *The Salamander* (1848); *Old New York* (1853); *The Newsboy* (1854); *Black Hollow* (1864); *Bald Eagle* (1867); *The Sagamore of Saco* (1868); *Selections from the Autobiography of Elizabeth Oakes Smith*, ed. by Alice Wyman, (1924); etc. See Mary Alice Wyman's *Two American Pioneers: Seba Smith and Elizabeth Oakes Smith* (1927).

SMITH, E[lmer] BOYD (May 31, 1860–1943); b. St. John, N.B., Can. Artist, illustrator, author. *My Village* (1896); *The Story of Pocahontas and Captain John Smith* (1906); *The Seashore Book* (1912); *The Country Book* (1924); *So Long Ago* (1944); etc.

SMITH, ELSDON C[oles] (Jan. 25, 1903–); b. Virginia, Ill. Lawyer, author. *Naming Your Baby* (1943); *Story of Our Names* (1950); *The Dictionary of American Family Names* (1956); *Treasury of Name Lore* (1967); *American Surnames* (1969); etc. Editor: *Bibliography of Personal Names* (1950).

SMITH, F. BERKELEY (Aug. 24, 1868–); b. Astoria, L.I., N.Y., son of F. Hopkinson Smith. Author. *The Real Latin Quarter* (1901); *Budapest* (1903); *In London Town* (1905); *The Street of Two Friends* (1912); *A Village of Vagabonds* (1912); *Babette* (1916); *Enoch Crane* (with F. Hopkinson Smith, 1916).

Smith, Ford. Pen name of Oscar Jerome Friend.

Smith, Frances Burge. *See* Frances Irene Burge Smith Griswold.

SMITH, FRANCIS H[enry] (Oct. 14, 1829–July 5, 1928); b. Leesburg, Va. Educator, author. *Thoughts on the Discord and Harmony of Science and the Bible* (1888); *Outlines of Physics* (1894); *Christ and Science* (1906); etc. Prof. natural philosophy, University of Virginia, 1853–1907. See Mary Stuart Smith.

SMITH, FRANCIS S[hubael] (b. Dec. 29, 1819). Publisher, author. *Poems for the Million* (1871). Co-founder of the publishing firm of Street and Smith.

SMITH, F[rancis] HOPKINSON (Oct. 23, 1838–Apr. 7, 1915); b. Baltimore, Md. Artist, author. *Well-Worn Roads* (1886); *A White Umbrella in Mexico* (1889); *Colonel Carter of Cartersville* (1891); *A Day at Laguerre's and Other Days* (1892); *Tom Grogan* (1896); *Gondola Days* (1897); *The Veiled Lady* (1897); *Caleb West, Master Diver* (1898); *The Other Fellow* (1899); *The Fortunes of Oliver Horn* (1902); *The Tides of Barnegat* (1906); *Kennedy Square* (1911); *The Armchair at the Inn* (1912); etc.

SMITH, FREDERICK MILLER (June 16, 1870–); b. Richmond, Ind. Educator, author. *The Stolen Signet* (1909); *Eight Essays* (1927); *Some Friends of Doctor Johnson* (1931); etc. Editor: *Essays and Studies* (1922). English dept., Cornell University, 1910–37.

SMITH, GEORGE HENRY (Oct. 20, 1873–Jan. 9, 1931); b. Knoxville, Tenn. Editor, author. *Daddy's Goodnight Stories* (1910); *Oh, Look Who's Here* (1911); *The Dollie Stories* (1912); etc. His syndicated stories were written under the pen names "Farmer Smith" and "Uncle Henry." He was editor of the children's page of the *New York Globe*, the *Philadelphia Public Ledger*, the *Newark Ledger*, etc.

SMITH, GEORGE JAY (Oct. 7, 1866–Jan. 2, 1937); b. Lebanon, O. Educator, author. *A Synopsis of English and American Literature* (1890); *Longman's English Lessons* (1905); *Forbidden Fruit* (prod. 1915); etc. With Public School System, New York, 1898–1937.

SMITH, GERALD BIRNEY (May 3, 1868–Apr. 3, 1929); b. Middlefield, Mass. Editor, educator, author. *Social Idealism and the Changing Theology* (1913). Editor: *Religious Thought in the Last Quarter-Century* (1927); etc. Compiler: *A Dictionary of Religion and Ethics* (with Shailer Matthews, 1921). Editor, *Journal of Religion*, 1921–29.

SMITH, GERTRUDE (1860–1917); b. in California. Author. *The Rousing of Mrs. Potter, and Other Stories* (1894); *Dedora Heywood* (1896).

SMITH, GORDON ARTHUR (Nov. 18, 1886–May 7, 1944); b. Rochester, N.Y. Author. *Mascarose* (1913); *The Crown of Life* (1915); *The Pagan* (1920); *There Goes the Groom* (1922); etc.

SMITH, HALLETT [Darius] (Aug. 15, 1907–); b. Chattanooga, Tenn. Educator, author. *The Golden Hind* (1942); *The Critical Reader* (1949); *Elizabethan Poetry* (1952); etc. Editor: *Renaissance England* (with Roy Lamson, 1956); Prof. English, California Institute of Technology, since 1949.

SMITH, HARRIET LUMMIS (Mrs. William M. Smith) (d. May 9, 1947); b. Auburndale, Mass. Author. The *Peggy Raymond* series, 3v. (1913–22); *Pollyanna* series, 4v. (1924–29); *Other People's Business* (1916); etc. Continued "Pollyanna" books begun by Eleanor Porter (q.v.).

SMITH, HARRISON (Aug. 4, 1888–Jan. 8, 1971); b. Hartford, Conn. Publisher. Editor: *From Main Street To Stockholm: Letters of Sinclair Lewis* (1952). With Harcourt, Brace & Co., 1918–28. Co-founder of publishing firm, Jonathan Cape and Harrison Smith, New York, 1931, dissolved in 1932. Later founded Harrison-Hilton Books, Inc., which changed to Smith and Durrell in 1940. President, Harrison Smith & Robert Haas, 1931–36; president, *Saturday Review of Literature.*

SMITH, H[arry] ALLEN (Dec. 19, 1907–); b. McLeansboro, Ill. Author. *Robert Gair: A Study* (1939); *Low Man on a Totem Pole* (1941); *Life in a Putty-Knife Factory* (1943); *Lost in the Horse Latitudes* (1944); *We Went Thataway* (1949); *People Named Smith* (1950); *The Rebel Yell* (1954); *Don't Get Perconel With a Chicken* (1959); *How to Write Without Knowing Nothing* (1961); *Son of Rhubarb* (1967); etc.

SMITH, HARRY B[ache] (1860–Jan. 1, 1936); b. Buffalo, N.Y. Librettist, book collector, author. *Robin Hood* (1890); *The Fencing Master* (1894); *The Wizard of the Nile* (1895); *The Mandarin* (1896); *The Fortune Teller* (1898); *Babette* (1899); *The Siren* (1911); *The Girl From Utah* (1912); *Sybil* (1912); *Angel Face* (1919); *Carolina* (1922); *First Nights and First Editions* (1931); etc. He wrote the book or lyrics for over three hundred stage productions, many with Reginald DeKoven. *See* Margaret G. Mayorga's *A Short History of the American Drama* (1934).

SMITH, HARRY JAMES (May 24, 1880–Mar. 16, 1918); b. New Britain, Conn. Playwright, novelist. *Amedee's Son* (1908); *Enchanted Ground* (1910); *Mrs. Bumpstead-Leigh* (prod. 1911); *A Tailor-Made Man* (1917); *The Little Teacher* (1918); *Letters* (1919); *Cape Breton Tales* (1920).

SMITH, HARRY WORCESTER (Nov. 5, 1865–Apr. 5, 1945); b. Worcester, Mass. Book collector, sportsman, author. *Life and Sport in Aiken and Those Who Made It* (1935); *A Sporting Family of the Old South* (1937); etc. Edited the works of "Frank Forester" (William Henry Herbert) and helped erect a memorial to Herbert at Warwick, Orange Co., N.Y. His collection of books by and about Herbert were sold in New York in 1931.

SMITH, HELEN AINSLIE. Author. *The Great Cities of the Ancient World* (under pen name "Hazel Shepard," 1885); *The Great Cities of the Modern World* (1885); *One Hundred Famous Americans* (1886); *Stories of Persons and Places in America* (1888); *The Thirteen Colonies,* 2v. (1901); etc.

SMITH, HELEN EVERTSON (b. Aug. 22, 1839); b. Sharon, Conn. Author. *Colonial Days and Ways* (1900).

SMITH, HENRY AUGUSTINE (Oct. 17, 1874–Mar. 16, 1952); b. Naperville, Ill. Educator, author. *Lyric Religion: The Romance of Immortal Hymns* (1931); etc. Compiler: *The Century Hymnal* (1921); *The Army and Navy Hymnal* (1922); *The New Church Hymnal* (1937); etc. Prof. hymnology, Boston University, from 1917.

SMITH, HENRY BOYNTON (Nov. 21, 1815–Feb. 7, 1877); b. Portland, Me. Presbyterian clergyman, educator, author. *Textbook of Church History,* 5v. (1855–79); *Apologetics* (1882); etc. Editor, *American Theological Review,* 1859–74. Prof. Church history and theology, Union Theological Seminary, New York, 1850–74. *See* E. L. Smith's *Henry Boynton Smith: His Life and Work* (1881).

SMITH, HENRY ERSKINE (c. 1842–Mar. 8, 1932); b. New York. Author. *On and Off the Saddle* (1894); *Love's Diplomacy* (1899); and a number of plays.

SMITH, HENRY JUSTIN (June 19, 1875–Feb. 9, 1936); b. Chicago, Ill. Journalist, author. *Deadlines* (1922); *Chicago: A Portrait* (1931); *The Master of the Mayflower* (1936); etc. With the *Chicago Daily News,* 1901–1936; managing editor, 1926–36. He helped develop such writers as Carl Sandburg, Ben Hecht, Harry Hansen, Keith Preston, and Howard Vincent O'Brien.

SMITH, HENRY PRESERVED (Oct. 23, 1847–Feb. 26, 1927); b. Troy, O. Presbyterian clergyman, Biblical scholar, author. *A Critical and Exegetical Commentary on the Books of Samuel* (1899); *The Religion of Israel* (1914); *The Heretic's Defense* (autobiography, 1926); etc.

SMITH, HENRY NASH (Sept. 29, 1906–   ); b. Dallas, Tex. Educator, author. *Virgin Land: The American West as Symbol and Myth* (1950); *Mark Twain: The Development of a Writer* (1962); *Mark Twain's Fable of Progress* (1964). Editor: *Popular Culture and Industrialism, 1865–1890* (1965) and several volumes relating to the writings of Mark Twain and other American authors. Prof. English, University of California at Berkeley, since 1953.

SMITH, HOMER WILLIAM (Jan. 2, 1895–); b. Denver Colo. Educator, author. *Kamongo* (1932); *The End of Illusion* (1935); *Man and His Gods* (1952); *From Fish to Philosopher* (1953). Prof. physiology, New York University, since 1928.

SMITH, HORATIO ELWIN (May 8, 1886–Sept. 9, 1946); b. Cambridge, Mass. Educator, author. *The Literary Criticism of Pierre Bayle* (1912); *Masters of French Culture* (1937); etc. Editor: *Columbia Dictionary of Modern European Literature* (1947). Editor, *Romantic Review,* from 1937. Prof. French, Amherst College, 1919–25; prof. Romance languages, Brown University, 1925–36; prof. French, Columbia University, from 1936.

SMITH, HOWARD KINGSBURY (May 12, 1914–); b. Ferriday, La. News commentator, author. *Last Train from Berlin* (1942); *The State of Europe* (1949); *Washington, D.C.* (1967); etc. Correspondent, Washington bureau, Columbia Broadcasting System, since 1959.

SMITH, HUNTINGTON (Dec. 4, 1857–July 23, 1926); b. Hudson, N.Y. Editor. Lit. editor, the *Boston Daily Evening Traveler,* 1879–85; assoc. editor, the *Literary World,* 1882–88; the *Boston Beacon,* 1889–98; owner and editor, 1898–1903.

SMITH, JAMES ROBINSON (Dec. 27, 1876–); b. Hartford, Conn. Author. *The Soul-at-Arms, and Other Poems* (1900); *Life of Cervantes* (1914); *The Solution of the Homeric Question* (1923); etc. Compiler: *English Quotations* (1906); *The Flower of English Poetry* (1912).

SMITH, JEDEDIAH STRONG (June 24, 1798–May 27, 1831); b. Bainbridge, N.Y. Western explorer. See *The Ashley-Smith Explorations,* ed. by H. C. Dale (1918); *The Travels of Jedediah Smith,* ed. by M. S. Sullivan (1934).

SMITH, JEROME van CROWNINSHIELD (July 20, 1800–Aug. 21, 1879); b. Conway, N.H. Physician, educator, author. *Memoirs of Andrew Jackson* (1828); *A Pilgrimage to Palestine* (1851); *Pilgrimage to Egypt* (1852); *Turkey and the Turks* (1854); etc. Founder, *Boston Medical Intelligencer, 1823.* Editor, *Boston Medical and Surgical Journal,* 1828–56. Mayor of Boston, 1854. Prof. anatomy, New York Medical College.

SMITH, JOHN (1580–June 21, 1631); b. Willoughby, Eng. Explorer, colonizer, author. *A True Relation of Such Occurrences and Accidents of Noate as Hath Hapnd in Virginia since the First Planting of That Collony* (at first anon., then under pen name "Th. Watson," 1608); *New Englands Trials*

(1620); *The Generall Historie of Virginia, New-England and the Summer Isles* (1624). *See* Wilberforce Eames's *A Bibliography of Captain John Smith* (1927); J. G. Fletcher's *John Smith: Also Pocahontas* (1928); *The True Travels... of Captain John Smith,* ed. by J. G. Fletcher and L. C. Wroth (1930); John M. Gwathmey's *The Love Affairs of Captain John Smith* (1935); Philip L. Barbour's *The Three Worlds of Captain John Smith* (1964); Paul Lewis's *The Great Rogue* (1966).

SMITH, JOHN COTTON (Aug. 4, 1826–Jan. 9, 1882); b. Andover, Mass. Episcopal clergyman, editor, author. *Miscellanies, Old and New* (1876); *Briar Hill Lectures* (1881); etc. Editor, *Church and State* until it was absorbed by *The Churchman.*

SMITH, JOHN JAY (June 16, 1798–Sept. 23, 1881); b. Green Hill, N.J. Editor, librarian, author. *A Summer's Jaunt Across the Water,* 2v. (1846); *Recollections of John Jay Smith* (1892); etc. Editor: *American Historical and Literary Curiosities,* 2 series (with John F. Watson, 1847, 1860). Founder, with John Taylor, the *Pennsylvania Gazette,* Philadelphia, 1827; founder, with Adam Waldie, of a weekly reprint of foreign literature known as *Waldie's Select Circulating Library,* Oct. 1, 1832. Librarian, Library Company of Philadelphia, 1829–51.

SMITH, JOHN MERLIN POWIS (Dec. 28, 1866–Sept. 26, 1932); b. London, England. Educator, Orientalist, author. *The Moral Life of the Hebrews* (1923); *The Prophets and Their Times* (1925); *The Origin and History of Hebrew Law* (1931); etc. Semitics dept., University of Chicago, 1899–32.

SMITH, JOSEPH (Dec. 23, 1805–June 27, 1844); b. Sharon, Vt. Mormon prophet, author. *A Book of Commandments* (1833); etc. *See* W. A. Linn's *The Story of the Mormons* (1902); Woodbridge Riley's *The Founder of Mormonism* (1902); J. H. Evans's *Joseph Smith* (1933).

SMITH, JOSEPH FIELDING (July 19, 1876–Aug. 29, 1964); b. Salt Lake City, Utah. Mormon leader, author. *Essentials in Church History* (1922); *The Way to Perfection* (1931); *The Progress of Man* (1936); *Life of Joseph F. Smith* (1938); *Restoration of All Things* (1945); *Man: His Origin and Destiny* (1954); *Doctrines of Salvation,* 3v. (1954–56); etc.

SMITH, J[oseph] RUSSELL (Feb. 3, 1874–Feb. 25, 1966); b. near Lincoln, Va. Geographer, author. *The Organization of Ocean Commerce* (1905); *The Story of Iron and Steel* (1908); *Commerce and Industry* (1915); *The World's Food Resources* (1919); *Peoples and Countries* (1921); *World Folks* (1931); *Foreign Lands and Peoples* (1933); *Men and Resources* (1937); *The Devil of the Machine Age* (1941); *Neighbors at Home* (1947); etc.

SMITH, JULIE P. Author. *Chris and Otho* (1870); *The Married Belle* (1872); *Ten Old Maids* (1874); *Widow Goldsmith's Daughter* (1875); *Courting and Farming* (1876); *Kiss and Be Friends* (1879); *Lucy* (1880); *Blossom-Bud and Her Genteel Friends* (1883); etc.

SMITH, JUSTIN HARVEY (Jan. 13, 1857–Mar. 21, 1930); b. Boscawen, N.H. Author. *The Troubadours at Home,* 2v. (1899); *Arnold's March from Cambridge to Quebec* (1903); *A Tale of Two Worlds and Five Centuries* (1903); *Our Struggle for the Fourteenth Colony: Canada and the American Revolution,* 2v. (1907); *The Annexation of Texas* (1911); *The War with Mexico,* 2v. (1919, Pulitzer Prize for American history, 1920); etc. Editor: *The Letters of Santa Anna* (1919). With Ginn & Co., 1890–98. Prof. history, Dartmouth College, 1899–1908.

SMITH, LACEY BALDWIN (Oct. 3, 1922–); b. Princeton, N.J. Educator, author. *Tudor Prelates and Politics* (1953); *A Tudor Tragedy: the Life and Times of Catherine Howard* (1961); *This Realm of England, 1399–1689* (1966); *The Elizabethan Epic* (1966). Prof. history, Northwestern University, since 1955.

SMITH, LAURA ROUNTREE (July 30, 1876–Feb. 22, 1924); b. Chicago, Ill. Author. *The Tale of Bunny Cotton-Tail* (1904), and sequels; *Little Bear* (1908), and sequels; *The Roly-Poly Book* (1910); *Little Eskimo* (1911); *The Circus Book* (1913); *The Pixie in the House* (1915), and sequels; etc., some under pen name, "Caroline Silver June."

SMITH, LEONARD KINGSLEY (Apr. 7, 1876–); b. Boston, Mass. Episcopal clergyman, author. *Songs East and West* (poems, 1909); *Moods and Memories* (1923); *Corley of the Wilderness Trail* (1937); *Forty Days to Santa Fé* (1938); *Lyrics and Meditations* (1952); etc.

SMITH, LEWIS WORTHINGTON (Nov. 22, 1866–Dec. 27, 1947); b. Malta, Ill. Educator, author. *God's Sunlight* (1901); *In the Furrow* (poems, 1906); *The English Tongue, and Other Poems* (1915); *Ships in Port* (poems, 1916); *The Mechanics of English Style* (1916); etc. Prof. English, Drake University, 1902–1940.

SMITH, LILLIAN [Eugenia] (Dec. 12, 1897–Sept. 28, 1966); b. Jasper, Fla. Author. *Strange Fruit* (1944); *Killers of the Dream* (1949); *The Journey* (1954); *Now Is the Time* (1955); *One Hour* (1959).

SMITH, LLOYD PEARSALL (Feb. 6, 1822–July 2, 1886); b. Philadelphia, Pa. Editor, librarian. *On the Classification of Books* (1892). Editor, *Lippincott's Magazine,* 1868–69. Librarian, Library Company of Philadelphia, 1851–86, succeeding his father, John Jay Smith (q.v.). Founder, *Smith's Weekly Volume,* in 1845, a successor to *Waldie's Select Circulating Library.*

SMITH, LOGAN PEARSALL (Oct. 18, 1865–Mar. 2, 1946); b. Millville, N.J. Author. *The Youth of Parnassus, and Other Stories* (1895); *Trivia* (1902); *More Trivia* (1921); *Afterthoughts* (1931) [including the three preceding, together with *Last Words*] (1933); *Reperusals and Re-collections* (1936); *Unforgotten Years* (autobiography, 1938); *Milton and His Modern Critics* (1941); etc. Editor: *A Treasury of English Prose* (1919); *A Treasury of English Aphorisms* (1928); etc. *See* Robert Granthorne-Hardy's *Recollections of Logan Pearsall Smith* (1950).

SMITH, LUCY [Henderson] HUMPHREY (Mrs. Preserved Smith) (d. Nov. 18, 1939); b. New York. Author. *Memories and Poems,* ed. by her husband (1940); etc. Compiler: *The Poetic Old-World* (1908); *The Poetic New-World* (1910).

SMITH, MABELL SHIPPIE CLARKE (Nov. 14, 1864–May 23, 1942); b. Boston, Mass. Author. *A Tar-Heel Baron* (1903); *The Spirit of French Letters* (1912); *Twenty Centuries of Paris* (1913); *The Ethel Morton* books, 6v. (1915); *The Story of Napoleon* (1928); *Cousins* (1931); etc.

SMITH, MARGARET BAYARD (Mrs. Samuel Harrison Smith) (Feb. 20, 1778–June 7, 1844). Society leader, editor, author. *A Winter in Washington; or, Memoirs of the Seymour Family,* 2v. (anon., 1824); *What Is Gentility?* (anon., 1828); *The First Forty Years of Washington Society* (1906); etc. She wrote extensively for the *Southern Literary Messenger* and *Godey's Lady's Book.* Her papers in 28 vols. are now in the Library of Congress.

SMITH, MA[r]Y [Louise] RILEY (May 27, 1842–Jan. 14, 1927); b. Rochester, N.Y. Poet. *A Gift of Gentians, and Other Verses* (1882); *The Inn of Rest* (1888); *Cradle and Armchair* (1893); *Sometime, and Other Poems* (1893); etc.

SMITH, MARY PRUDENCE WELLS (July 23, 1840–Dec. 17, 1930); b. Attica, N.Y. Author. The *Jolly Good* series, 8v. (1875–95); the *Young Puritans* series, 4v. (1897–1900); the *Old Deerfield* series; the *Summer Vacation* series; etc.

SMITH, MARY STUART [Harrison] (Mrs. Francis H. Smith) (b. Feb. 10, 1834); b. University, Va. Author. *The Heirs of the Kingdom* (1872); *Lang Syne; or, the Wards of Mount Vernon* (1889). Translated many German novels.

SMITH, MATTHEW JOHN WILFRED (June 9, 1891–June 15, 1960); b. Altoona, Pa. Roman Catholic clergyman, editor. *Letters to an Infidel* (1925); *Great Controversies* (1928); *The Church upon the Rock* (1941); *The Unspotted Mirror of God* (1943); etc. Editor, *Denver Catholic Register*, from 1913.

SMITH, MAXWELL A[ustin] (Nov. 3, 1894–); b. Madison, Wis. Educator, author. *Short History of French Literature* (1924); *Jean Giono* (1966); etc. Editor: *Short Stories by French Romanticists* (1929); *Knight of the Air: Life and Works of Antoine de Saint-Exupéry* (1956); etc. Prof. French, University of Chattanooga, since 1922.

SMITH, MERRIMAN (Feb. 10, 1913–Apr. 13, 1970); b. Savannah, Ga. Journalist, author. *Thank You, Mr. President* (1946); *A President Is Many Men* (1948); *Meet Mister Eisenhower* (1955); *A President's Odyssey* (1961); *The Good New Days* (1962); etc. Staff correspondent, United Press, from 1936.

SMITH, MICHAEL TOWNSEND (Oct. 5, 1935–); b. Kansas City, Mo. Author. *Getting Across* (1962); *Near the End* (1965). Plays: *I Like It* (1961); *The Next Thing* (1963); *A Dog's Love* (1965). Theater critic, *The Village Voice*, since 1959.

SMITH, MILTON MYERS (Oct. 28, 1890–); b. Springfield, Mass. Educator, author. *Magic in the Making* (with John Mulholland, 1925); *The Book of Play Production* (1926); *A Guide to Play Selection* (1934); etc. English dept., Teachers College, Columbia University, since 1921.

Smith, Mr. Pen name of Ralph Ingersoll Lockwood.

Smith, Mrs. Seba. *See* Elizabeth Oakes Smith.

SMITH, MUNROE (Dec. 8, 1854–Apr. 13, 1926); b. Brooklyn, N.Y. Educator, editor, author. *Bismarck and German Unity* (1898); *Militarism and Statecraft* (1918); etc. Law dept., Columbia University, 1880–1926.

SMITH, NICHOLAS (Oct. 31, 1836–1911); b. Blackburn, Eng. Soldier, editor, author. *Stories of Great National Songs* (1899); *Grant, the Man of Mystery* (1909); *Fifty-Two Years at the Labrador Fishery* (1936). Editor: *Hymns Historically Famous* (1901). Editor, the *Janesville* (Wis.) *Daily Gazette*, 1874–91.

SMITH, NORA ARCHIBALD (d. Feb. 1, 1934); b. Philadelphia, Pa., sister of Kate Douglas Wiggin. Author. *The Children of the Future* (1898); *Under the Cactus Flag* (1899); *The Menage of Froebel* (1900); *The Adventures of a Doll* (1907); *Boys and Girls of Bookland* (1923); *Kate Douglas Wiggin As Her Sister Knew Her* (1925); etc. Author of several books with her sister and engaged with her in kindergarten work.

SMITH, ORMOND GERALD (Apr. 30, 1860–Apr. 17, 1933); b. New York. Publisher. President, Street and Smith, New York. Founder, *Ainslee's*, *Top Notch*, *Smith's*, and other fiction magazines.

SMITH, PAGE (Sept. 6, 1917–); b. Baltimore, Md. Author. *Historian and History* (1964); *As A City Upon a Hill* (1966); *Daughters of the Promised Land* (1970).

SMITH, PRESERVED (July 22, 1880–May 15, 1941); b. Cincinnati, O. Educator, author. *Life and Letters of Martin Luther* (1911); *The Age of the Reformation* (1920); *Erasmus* (1923); *A History of Modern Culture*, 2v. (1930–34); etc. Prof. history, Cornell University, 1922–41.

SMITH, RALPH LEE (Nov. 6, 1927–); b. Philadelphia, Pa. Author. *The Health Hucksters* (1960); *The Bargain Hucksters* (1962); *The Grim Truth About Mutual Funds* (1963); *The New Nations of Africa* (1963); *Getting to Know the World Health Organization* (1963); *The Tarnished Badge* (1965).

SMITH, RAY (May 1, 1915–); b. Minneapolis, Minn. Poet. *No Eclipse* (1945); *The Greening Tree* (1965).

SMITH, REED (Jan. 16, 1881–July 24, 1943); b. Washington, D.C. Educator, author. *South Carolina Ballads* (1928); *The Teaching of Literature* (1935). Compiler: *American Anthology of Old-World Ballads* (1937); etc. Prof. English, University of South Carolina, from 1910.

SMITH, RICHARD AUSTIN (Dec. 3, 1911–); b. Clarksburg, W.Va. Editor, author. *The Sun Dial* (1942); *Why Do People Buy?* (1953); *The Art of Success* (1956); *The Space Industry* (1962); etc. Member board of editors, *Fortune*, since 1958.

SMITH, RICHARD PENN (Mar. 13, 1799–Aug. 12, 1854); b. Philadelphia, Pa. Lawyer, editor, playwright. *William Penn* (prod. 1829); *The Deformed* (prod. 1830); *The Triumph at Plattsburg* (prod. 1830); *Caius Marius* (prod. 1831); *The Forsaken* (anon., 1831); *The Actress of Padua, and Other Tales*, 2v. (anon., 1836); *The Miscellaneous Works*, ed. by his son, Horace W. Smith (1856); etc. *Col. Crockett's Exploits and Adventures in Texas* (1836) has been attributed to him. He also translated and adapted many plays from the French. Editor, *The Aurora*, 1822–27. *See* Bruce W. McCullough's *The Life and Writings of Richard Penn Smith* (1917).

SMITH, ROBERT AURA (Jan. 12, 1899–Nov. 11, 1959); b. Denver, Col. Journalist, author. *Our Future in Asia* (1940); *Your Foreign Policy* (1941); *Divided India* (1947); *Philippine Freedom* (1958). Editorial writer, *New York Times*, from 1949.

SMITH, ROBERT METCALF (Mar. 29, 1886–Jan. 15, 1952); b. Worcester, Mass. Educator, editor, author. *Froissart and the English Chronicle Play* (1915); *The Shelley Legend* (with M. M. Schlegel, 1945). Editor: *Types of World Literature* (1930); *A Book of Biography* (1930); etc. Prof. English, Lehigh University, from 1925.

SMITH, ROBERT PAUL (Apr. 16, 1915–); b. New York. Author. *So It Doesn't Whistle* (1941); *The Journey* (1943); *Because of My Love* (1946); *The Time and the Place* (1952); *Where Did You Go? Out. What Did You Do? Nothing.* (1957); *Where He Went* (1958); *How To Do Nothing with Nobody All Alone By Yourself* (1958); *Translations from the English* (1958); *And Another Thing* (poems, 1959); *Jack Mack* (1960); *How to Grow Up in One Piece* (1963); etc. Co-author: *The Tender Trap* (with Max Shulman, prod. 1954).

SMITH, ROSWELL (Mar. 30, 1829–Apr. 19, 1892); b. Lebanon, Conn. Lawyer, publisher. Co-founder, *Scribner's Monthly*, 1870. *St. Nicholas*, 1873; the *Century Magazine*, 1881; the *Century Dictionary and Cyclopedia*, 1882.

SMITH, RUEL PERLEY (Dec. 16, 1869–July 30, 1937); b. Bangor, Me. Author. The *Rival Campers* series, 3v. (1905–07); *Prisoner of Fortune* (1907); *Jack Harvey's Adventures* (1908).

SMITH, SAMUEL FRANCIS (Oct. 21, 1808–Nov. 16, 1895); b. Boston, Mass. Baptist clergyman, poet, editor. *Lyric Gems* (1843); *Missionary Sketches* (1879); *History of Newton, Massachusetts* (1880); *Rambles in Mission-Fields* (1883); *Poems of Home and Country* (1895); etc. Editor: *The Psalmist* (with Baron Stow, 1843). Editor, the *Christian Review*, Boston, 1842–48. Best known for his poems "America," "The Morning Light Is Breaking," and "The Lone Star." Oliver Wendell Holmes mentioned him in his poem "The Boys." *See America: Our National Hymn*, by G. H. W. Whittemore (1884); H. S. Burrage's *Baptist Hymn Writers and Their Hymns* (1888).

SMITH, S[amuel] STEPHENSON (Apr. 3, 1897–Oct. 3, 1961); b. Albia, Ia. Editor, author. *The Craft of the Critic* (1931); *The Command of Words* (1947); *The Style Rule* (1947). Editor, *Funk and Wagnalls Standard Dictionaries*, 1955–58; John H. Winston Co., from 1959.

SMITH, SARAH LOUISA HICKMAN (June 30, 1811–Feb. 12, 1832); b. Detroit, Mich. Poet. *Poems* (1829).

SMITH, SEBA (Sept. 14, 1792–July 28, 1868); b. Buckfield, Me. Political satirist, author. Pen name "Major Jack Downing." *The Life and Writings of Major Jack Downing of Downingville* (1833); *Letters Written During the President's Tour "Down East," by Myself, Major Jack Downing* (1833); *The Select Letters of Major Jack Downing* (1834); *John Smith's Letters, with "Picters" to Match* (1839); *May-Day in New York; or, House-Hunting and Moving* (1845); *Dew-Drops of the Nineteenth Century* (1846); *'Way Down East* (1854); *My Thirty Years's Out of the Senate* (1859); etc. Founder, the *Portland Courier*, 1829; co-editor, *The Rover*, 1843–44. *See* Mary A. Wyman's *Two American Pioneers: Seba Smith and Elizabeth Oakes Smith* (1927).

SMITH, SEYMOUR ALFRED (Oct. 30, 1916–); b. Jamestown, N.Y. Educator, author. *American College Chaplaincy* (1954); *Religious Co-operation in State Universities* (1957). Pres. Stephens College, Missouri, since 1958.

SMITH, SIDNEY (Feb. 13, 1877–Oct. 20, 1935); b. Bloomington, Ill. Cartoonist. With the *Chicago Tribune*, 1911–35. Creator of comic strips "The Gumps," and "Old Doc Yak."

SMITH, SOPHIA (Aug. 27, 1796–June 12, 1870); b. Hatfield, Mass. Left endowment for the founding of Smith College. Her papers are in the Smith College Library. *See* Elizabeth D. Hanscom and Helen F. Greene's *Sophia Smith and the Beginnings of Smith College* (1925).

SMITH, THOMAS R. (Dec. 13, 1880–Apr. 11, 1942); b. Phillipsburg, N.J. Editor. Editor: *Swinburne's Poems* (1917); *Baudelaire's Poems* (1918); Managing editor, the *Century Magazine*, 1914–20. Director, Boni and Liveright, 1921–28; Horace Liveright, Inc., from 1928.

SMITH, THORNE (1892–June 21, 1934); b. Annapolis, Md. Humorist, author. *Biltmore Oswald* (1918); *Topper* (1926); *The Stray Lamb* (1929); *The Night Life of the Gods* (1931); *Turnabout* (1931); *Topper Takes a Trip* (1932); *The Bishop's Jaegers* (1932); etc.

SMITH, WILLIAM (Sept. 7, 1727–May 14, 1803); b. Aberdeen, Scot. Anglican clergyman, educator, author. *A General Idea of the College of Mirania* (1753); *A Poem on Visiting the Academy of Philadelphia* (1753); *A Sermon on the Present Situation of American Affairs* (1773). Editor, the *American Magazine and Monthly Chronicle for the British Colonies*, 1757–58. Provost, College of Philadelphia, 1755–79, 1789–91; president, Washington College, Chestertown, Md., 1782–89.

SMITH, WILLIAM (June 25, 1728–Nov. 3, 1793); b. New York. Jurist, Loyalist, historian. *The History of the Province of New-York, from the First Discovery to the Year M.DCC.XXXII* (1732), reprinted, with his continuations, by the New-York Historical Society, as *The History of the Late Province of New York*, 2v. (1829). His unpublished diary and other papers are in the New York Public Library.

SMITH, WILLIAM BENJAMIN (Oct. 26, 1850–Aug. 6, 1934); b. Stanford, Ky. Educator, author. *The Color Line* (1905); *Ecce Deus* (1912); *Mors Mortis* (1915); and books on mathematics. Prof. mathematics and philosophy, Tulane University, 1893–1915.

SMITH, WILLIAM HENRY (Dec. 4, 1806–Jan. 17, 1872); b. in Mont., Wales. Actor, playwright. *Aaron Burr, Emperor of Mexico* (prod. 1837); *The Drunkard; or, The Fallen Saved!* (prod. 1844).

SMITH, WILLIAM HENRY (Dec. 1, 1883–July 27, 1896); b. Austerlitz, N.Y. Journalist, author. *A Political History of Slavery*, 2v. (1903); *Life of Rutherford Birchard Hayes*, 2v. (1914, completed by Charles R. Williams); etc. Editor: *The St. Clair Papers*, 2v. (1882). In 1870 he took charge of the West-

ern Associated Press. In 1882 he combined this organization with the New York Associated Press, and became its head. He helped organize the Mergenthaler Linotype Co., with White-law Reid. He was one of the editors of the *Cincinnati Evening Chronicle*.

SMITH, WILLIAM RUSSELL (Mar. 27, 1815–Feb. 26, 1896); b. Russellville, Ky. Lawyer, congressman, author. *College Musings; or, Twigs from Parnassus* (1833); *The Uses of Solitude* (poem, 1860); *Reminiscences of a Long Life* (1889); etc. *See* Anne Easby-Smith's *William Russell Smith of Alabama* (1931).

SMITH, WILLIAM STEVENSON (Feb. 7, 1907–Jan. 13, 1969); b. Indianapolis, Ind. Archaeologist. *Ancient Egypt as Represented in the Museum of Fine Arts* (1942); *A History of Egyptian Sculpture and Painting in the Old Kingdom* (1946); *The Art and Architecture of Ancient Egypt* (1958); etc.

SMITH, WINCHELL (Apr. 5, 1871–June 10, 1933); b. Hartford, Conn. Playwright. *Polly of the Circus* (with Margaret Mayo, prod. 1907); *The Fortune Hunter* (prod. 1909); *The Only Son* (prod. 1911); *The Boomerang* (with Victor Mapes, prod. 1915); *Turn to the Right* (with John E. Hazzard, prod. 1916); *Lightnin'* (with Frank Bacon, prod. 1918); *The Wheel* (prod. 1921); *A Holy Terror* (with George Abbott, prod. 1925); etc.

Smith & Lamar. *See* Publishing House of the Methodist Episcopal Church South.

SMITHERS, WILLIAM WEST (May 5, 1864–Mar. 19, 1947); b. Philadelphia, Pa. Lawyer, author. *Relation of Attorney and Client* (1887); *A Coaching Trip through Delaware* (1892); *The Life of John Lofland, "the Milford Bard"* (1894); etc.

Smoke and Steel. Poems by Carl Sandburg (1920).

Smoke Bellew. Novel by Jack London (1912). Wild adventures in the Klondike, with Christopher "Smoke" Bellew as hero.

Smoky. By Will James (1926). Classic juvenile relating the early experiences of a colt on the western range and his exciting adventures with Clint the cowboy and with the horses that roamed the open range.

SMUCKER, SAMUEL MOSHEIM (Jan. 12, 1823–May 12, 1863); b. (Schmucker) at New Market, Va. Lawyer, author. *The Life and Times of Alexander Hamilton* (1857); *Arctic Explorations and Discoveries During the Nineteenth Century* (1857); *A History of the Four Georges* (1860); etc.

SMYTH, ALBERT H[enry] (June 18, 1863–May 4, 1907); b. Philadelphia, Pa. Educator, author. *American Literature* (1889); *The Philadelphia Magazines and Their Contributors, 1741–1850* (1892); *Bayard Taylor* (1896); etc. Editor: *The Writings of Benjamin Franklin*, 10v. (1905–07).

SMYTH, HERBERT WEIR (Aug. 8, 1857–July 16, 1937); b. Wilmington, Del. Educator, author. *Greek Dialects* (1894); *Greek Melic Poetry* (1900); *Aeschylean Tragedy* (1924); etc. Editor, *Transactions and Proceedings of the American Philological Association*, 1889–1904. Prof. Greek, Harvard University, 1902–25.

SMYTH, JOSEPH HILTON (Dec. 4, 1901–); b. Plymouth, Mass. Editor, publisher, author. *Tropical Fragments* (poems, 1927); *The World Over* (1938); *The Autobiography of a Puritan* (1940); *That French Girl* (pen name "Joseph Hilton," 1960). Editor and publisher, *The Living Age*, since 1938; *North American Review*, since 1938; co-publisher, *Saturday Review of Literature*, since 1939. Co-founder, with Harrison Smith, of Harrison-Hilton Books, Inc., 1939.

SMYTH, NEWMAN (June 25, 1843–Jan. 6, 1925); b. Brunswick, Me. Congregational clergyman, author. *Christian Ethics*

(1892); *A Story of Church Unity* (1923); *Recollections and Reflections* (1926); etc.

SMYTH, WILLIAM HENRY (b. May 16, 1855–); b. Birkenhead, Cheshire, Eng. Inventor, author. *Technocracy* (1917); *Federation of Nations* (1922); *Women in Industry* (1934); *Problem of Crime* (1938); etc.

Snake Pit, The. Novel by Mary Jane Ward (1946). About a young woman committed to an insane asylum.

SNEDDON, ROBERT W[illiam] (1880–); b. in Scotland. Author. Pen name, "Robert Guillaume." *Galleon's Gold* (1925); *Monsieur X* (1928).

SNEDEKER, CAROLINE DALE [Parke] (Mrs. Charles H. Snedeker) (Mar. 23, 1871–Jan. 22, 1956); b. New Harmony, Ind., granddaughter of Robert Dale Owen. Author of books for young people. *The Spartan* (1912); *Seth Way: A Romance of the New Harmony Community* (under name, "Caroline Dale Owen," 1917); *The Perilous Seat* (1923); *Theras and His Town* (1924); *Downright Dencey* (1927); *The Beckoning Road* (1929); *The Black Arrowhead* (1929); *The Town of the Fearless* (1931); *The Forgotten Daughter* (1933); *Uncharted Ways* (1935); *White Isle* (1940); *Luke's Quest* (1947); *A Triumph for Flavius* (1954).

SNELL, GEORGE (Apr. 4, 1909–   ); b. Caldwell, Ida. Radio producer, author, editor. *The Great Adam* (1934). *Root, Hog and Die* (1936); *And If Man Triumph* (1938); *Shapers of American Fiction* (1947); etc. Co-editor, *Western Review*. Producer, National Broadcasting Co., San Francisco, since 1945.

SNELL, ROY JUDSON (Nov. 12, 1878–); b. Laddonia, Mo. Author. *Little White Fox and His Arctic Friends* (1916); *An Eskimo Robinson Crusoe* (1917); *Skimmer and His Thrilling Adventures* (1919); *Soolook, Wild Boy* (1920); *The Black Schooner* (1923); *Told Beneath the Northern Lights* (1925); *Johnny Longbow* (1928); *The Rope of Gold* (1929); *Hour of Enchantment* (1933); *Red Dynamite* (1936); *The Shadow Passes* (1938); *Sign of the Green Arrow* (1939); *Wings for Victory* (1942); *The Jet Plane Mystery* (1945); etc.

SNELLING, WILLIAM JOSEPH (Dec. 26, 1804–Dec. 24, 1848); b. Boston, Mass. Fur trapper, miner, journalist, poet. *Tales of the Northwest; or, Sketches of Indian Life and Character* (anon., 1830); *Truth: A New Year's Gift for Scribblers* (1831); *The Rat Trap; or Cogitations of a Convict in the House of Correction* (1839); etc. Editor, *Boston Herald,* 1847.

SNIDER, DENTON J[aques] (Jan. 9, 1841–Nov. 25, 1925); b. Mt. Gilead, O. Educator, author. *Delphic Days* (poems, 1880); *A Walk in Hellas,* 2v. (1881–82); *Psychology and the Psychosis* (1890); *Homer in Chios* (poem, 1891); *Johnny Appleseed's Rhymes* (1895); *Ancient European Philosophy* (1903); *Modern European Philosophy* (1904); *A Tour in Europe* (1907); *Music and the Fine Arts* (1913); *The St. Louis Movement in Philosophy ... With Chapters of Autobiography* (1920); *The Collected Writings,* 8v. (1921–23); etc. A founder of the St. Louis School of Philosophy, 1866.

SNIDER, FELIX EUGENE (Jan. 14, 1908–); b. Fremont, Mo. Librarian. Author or editor: *Great Cities and How They Grow* (with V. C. Myers, 1944); *Missouri, Midland State, A History* (with E. A. Collins, 1955); *Cape Girardeau, Biography of a City* (with same, 1956); *Workbook in Missouri History* (with Paul Hines, 1969); etc. Librarian, Southeast Missouri State Teachers College, since 1943.

SNOW, EDGAR PARKS (July 19, 1905–Feb. 14, 1972); b. Kansas City, Mo. Correspondent, author. *Far Eastern Front* (1934); *Red Star over China* (1937); *The Battle for Asia* (1941); *People on Our Side* (1944); *Pattern of Soviet Power* (1945); *Journey to the Beginning* (1958); *Red China* (1962); *One Fourth of Humanity—The China Story* (documentary film 1968); *Four Hour Interview with Mao-Tse-tung* (1965); *Washington–Tokyo–Peking* (1969). Editor: *Living China* (1936). With *Saturday Evening Post,* 1942–53.

SNOW, ELIZA R[oxey] (Jan. 21, 1804–Dec. 5, 1887); b. Becket, Mass. Sister of Lorenzo Snow. Mormon poet. *Poems, Religious, Historical, and Political,* 2v. (1856–77); *Biography and Family Record of Lorenzo Snow* (1884). She was the author of several Mormon hymns.

SNOW, LORENZO (Apr. 3, 1814–Oct. 10, 1901); b. Mantua, O. Mormon leader, follower of Brigham Young. *See* Eliza R. Snow Smith's *Biography and Family Record of Lorenzo Snow* (1884).

SNOW, ROYALL H[enderson] (Jan. 1899–); b. Chicago, Ill. Educator, poet. *Igdrasil* (1921); *Thomas Lovell Beddoes, Eccentric & Poet* (1928); *This Experimental Life* (1930). Prof. English, Ohio State University.

SNOW, WILBERT (Apr. 6, 1884–); b. White Head Island, St. George, Me. Educator, poet. *Maine Coast* (1923); *The Inner Harbor* (1926); *Down East* (1932); *The Selected Poems* (1936); *Before the Wind* (1938); *Maine Tides* (1940); *Sonnets to Steve* (1957); *Spruce Head* (1959); etc. English dept., Wesleyan University, since 1921.

"Snow-Bound: A Winter Idyll." Poem by John Greenleaf Whittier (1866). The theme is family tradition and solidarity against a Quaker background.

SNOWDEN, RICHARD (fl. 1794). Author. *The American Revolution,* 2v. (1793–94); *The Columbiad* (poem, 1795); *The History of North and South America* (1805).

Snows of Kilimanjaro, The. Story by Ernest Hemingway (1938).

SNYDER, CHARLES McCOY (b. Apr. 17, 1859); b. Bellefonte, Pa. Author. *Comic History Of Greece* (1897); *Comic History of Spain* (1898); *Runaway Robinson* (1901); etc. On staff, *Texas Siftings,* 1885. Wrote "With the Wits" column for *Lippincott's Magazine,* etc.

SNYDER, DONALD B[ertram] (Jan. 15, 1897–); b. Wabash, Ind. Publisher, *Atlantic Monthly,* since 1933.

SNYDER, FRANKLYN BLISS (July 26, 1884–May 11, 1958); b. Middletown, Conn. Educator, author. *The Life of Robert Burns* (1932); *Robert Burns: His Personality, His Reputation and His Art* (1936). Editor: *A Book of English Literature* (with Robert Grant Martin, 1916); *A Book of American Literature* (with Edward D. Snyder, 1927). English dept., Northwestern University, 1909–39; president, 1939–49.

SNYDER, GARY SHERMAN (May 8, 1930–); b. San Francisco, Cal. Poet. *Riprap* (1959); *Myths and Texts* (1960); *Six Sections from Mountains and Rivers without End* (1965); *A Range of Poems* (1966); *The Back Country* (1968).

SNYDER, JOHN FRANCIS (Mar. 22, 1830–Apr. 30, 1921); b. Prairie du Pont, Ill. Physician, archaeologist, author. *The Field for Archaeological Research in Illinois* (1900); *Captain John Baptiste Saucier at Fort Chartres in the Illinois* (1901); *Adam W. Snyder* (1903). A founder of the Illinois State Historical Society, 1899.

So Big. Novel by Edna Ferber (1924). Popular story of a gambler and his daughter Selina who takes her philosophy of life from his pronounced views in support of an active and adventurous life.

So Red the Rose. Novel by Stark Young (1934). Southern family life in Mississippi during the Civil War and the years prior to the conflict.

SOARES, THEODORE GERALD (Oct. 1, 1869–); b. Abridge, Eng. Baptist clergyman, author. *The Supreme Miracle* (1904); *Heroes of Israel* (1909); *Religious Education* (1928); *The Story of Paul* (1930); *Origins of the Bible* (1941). Theology dept., University of Chicago, 1899–1930.

SOBEL, BERNARD (d. Mar. 13, 1964); b. Attica, Ind. Author. *Burleycue: An Underground History of Burlesque Days* (1931); *The Indiscreet Girl* (1933); *The Theatre Handbook and Digest of Plays* (1940); *Broadway Heartbeat* (1953); *A Pictorial History of Vaudeville* (1961); etc. Co-author, *A Book of One Act Plays* (n.d.); etc.

SOBEL, LESTER A[lbert] (Oct. 3, 1919–   ); b. New York. Editor, author. *National Issues* (1956); *Space: From Sputnik to Gemini* (1965); *South Vietnam: U.S.-Communist Confrontation in Southeast Asia* (1966); *Civil Rights* (1967). With *Facts on File* since 1946.

SOBOL, LOUIS (Aug. 10, 1896–); b. New Haven, Conn. Columnist, author. *Six Lost Women* (1936); *Some Days Were Happy* (1947); *Along the Broadway Beat* (1950). Columnist, the *New York Journal-American*, since 1931.

SOBY, JAMES THRALL (Dec. 14, 1906–); b. Hartford, Conn. Art critic, editor, author. *After Picasso* (1935); *The Early Chirico* (1941); *Tchelitchew* (1942); *Georges Rouault* (1945); *Ben Shahn* (1947); *Contemporary Painters* (1948); *Balthus* (1956); *Modern Art and the New Past* (1957); *Juan Gris* (1958); *Joan Miro* (1959); *Ben Shahn* (1963); *Rene Magritte* (1965); etc. Art columnist, *Saturday Review*, since 1946.

Social Sciences and Humanities Index. See *International Index to Periodicals.*

Social Silhouettes. By Edgar Fawcett (1885). A series of ironic sketches of New York society.

Society of Midland Authors. Chicago, Ill. Founded 1915.

SOCKMAN, RALPH WASHINGTON (Oct. 1, 1889–Aug. 29, 1970); b. Mt. Vernon, O. Methodist clergyman, author. *Men of the Mysteries* (1927); *Morals of Tomorrow* (1931); *The Paradoxes of Jesus* (1936); *Recoveries in Religion* (1938); *The Higher Happiness* (1950); *A Life for Living* (1956); *Man's First Love* (1958); etc.

SOGLOW, OTTO (Dec. 23, 1900–); b. New York. Cartoonist, author. *Pretty Pictures* (1931); *The Little King* (1933); *Wasn't the Depression Terrible?* (with David G. Plotkin, 1934); *A Confidential History of Modern England* (1939); etc.

SOHN, JOSEPH (Mar. 22, 1867–Mar. 16, 1935); b. New York. Musician, music critic, author. *Robert Schumann: A Lyrical Poet* (1896); *Music in America and Abroad* (1904); *Joseph Joachim* (1904); *Opera in New York* (1907); *The Music of Richard Wagner* (1910). Music critic, *New York American and Journal, The Forum,* etc.

SOKOLSKY, GEORGE [Ephraim] (Sept. 5, 1893–Dec. 13, 1962); b. Utica, N.Y. Columnist, author. *Outlines of Universal History* (1928); *The Tinder Box of Asia* (1932); *Labor's Fight for Power* (1934); *We Jews* (1935); *The American Way of Life* (1939). Syndicated columnist, *New York Sun*, 1940–50; editorial writer, *New York Mirror*, from 1946.

SOLBERG, THORVALD (Apr. 22, 1852–July 15, 1949); b. Manitowoc, Wis. Copyright authority, author. *Bibliography of Literary Property* (1886); *Foreign Copyright Laws* (1904); *Copyright Enactments 1783–1906* (1906); *Revision of Copyright Laws* (1936); *Copyright Miscellany* (1939); etc. On staff Library of Congress, 1876–1889; manager, Library Dept., Boston Book Co., 1889–97; Register of Copyrights, Washington, D.C., 1897–1930.

Soldiers of Fortune. Novel by Richard Harding Davis (1897). Olancho, capital of a South American republic, is on the eve of a revolution, and many soldier adventurers become involved in the affairs of the city.

Soldiers' Pay. First novel of William Faulkner (1926).

SOLEY, JAMES RUSSELL (Oct. 1, 1850–Sept. 11, 1911); b. Roxbury, Mass. Lawyer, educator, naval author. *Historical Sketch of the United States Naval Academy* (1876); *The Blockade and the Cruisers* (1883); *The Boys of 1812 and Other Naval Heroes* (1887); *The Sailor Boys of 61* (1888); *Admiral Porter* (1903); etc. Prof. English, U.S. Naval Academy, 1871–82.

SOLMSEN, FRIEDRICH (Feb. 4, 1904–); b. Bonn, Ger. Educator. *Aristotle's Logic* (1929); *Antiphon the Orator* (1931); *Plato's Theology* (1942); *Hesiod and Aeschylus* (1949); *Aristotle's System of the Physical World* (1960); *Aisthesis in Aristotelian and Epicurean Thought* (1961); *Cleanthes or Posidonius?* (1962); *Electra and Orestes* (1967); *Kleine Schriften* (1968); etc. Prof. philosophy, Cornell University, since 1947.

Solomon. Short story by Constance Fenimore Woolson (1874).

Solon Shingle; or, The People's Lawyer. Play by Joseph Stevens Jones (prod. 1839). Hugh Winslow, an unscrupulous character, is convicted of forgery by Robert Howard, a young lawyer, aided by Solon Shingle, a clever Yankee.

SOLOW, HERBERT (Nov. 20, 1903–Nov. 26, 1964); b. New York. Editor. With *Time*, 1943–45; editor, *Fortune*, since 1945.

Some Adventures of Captain Simon Suggs, Late of the Tallapoosa Volunteers. By Johnson Jones Hooper (1846). Chronicle of the backwoods sharper Simon Suggs.

Some Came Running. Novel by James Jones (1958).

Some Considerations on the Keeping of Negroes. By John Woolman (1753). An early anti-slavery tract.

"Somebody's Darling." Poem attributed to Marie LaCoste, or Maria La Conte (c. 1863).

"Somebody's Mother." Poem by Mary D. Brine, in her *Madge, the Violet Girl, and Other Poems* (1881).

SOMERBY, FREDERICK THOMAS (1814–1871). Author. Pen name, "Cymon." *Hits and Dashes* (1852).

Something Else Press, Inc. New York. Publishers. Founded 1965. Publishes avant-garde books and bound graphics; devoted to rethinking the idea of literature in the medium of print. Dick Higgins is president. Emmett Williams is editor-in-chief.

"Song and Story." Weekly page in the *Nashville Banner*, conducted by Will Allen Dromgoole.

"Song for the Public Celebration of the National Peace." Ode by Sarah Wentworth Morton (1815). Set to the music of "Rule, Britannia."

Song of Hugh Glass, The. By John G. Neihardt (1915). The first of a cycle of epic poems on the West. The others are *The Song of Three Friends* (1919); *The Song of the Indian Wars* (1925).

"Song of Marion's Men, The." Poem by William Cullen Bryant (1832).

"Song of Myself." Poem by Walt Whitman (1855).

"Song of the Chattahoochee." Poem by Sidney Lanier (1877).

Song of the Lark. Novel by Willa Cather (1915). Story of Thea Kronberg, a poor girl who becomes an opera star after years of struggle.

SONNECK, OSCAR GEORGE THEODORE (Oct. 6, 1873–Oct. 30, 1928); b. Jersey City, N.J. Musician, editor, author. *Seufzer* (German poems, 1895); *Report on "The Star Spangled Banner," "Hail Columbia," "America," "Yankee Doo-*

dle" (1909); etc. Compiler: *Bibliography of Early Secular American Music* (1905); etc. Editor, *Musical Quarterly,* 1915–28. Chief of music division, Library of Congress, 1902–17; with G. Schirmer Co., New York, 1917–28.

SONNICHSEN, ALBERT (May 5, 1878–Aug. 15, 1931); b. San Francisco, Calif. War correspondent, author. *Deep Sea Vagabonds* (1903); *Ten Months a Captive among Filipinos* (1901); *Confessions of a Macedonian Bandit* (1909); etc. On staff, the *New York Tribune,* 1901–02; Balkan correspondent, the *New York Evening Post,* 1904–06.

SONTAG, FREDERICK EARL (Oct. 8, 1924–); b. Long Beach, Cal. Educator, author. *Divine Perfection: Possible Ideas of God* (1962); *The Existentialist Prolegomena* (1964). Editor: Kierkegaard's *Authority and Revelation* (1966). Prof. philosophy, Pomona College, since 1962.

SONTAG, RAYMOND JAMES (Oct. 2, 1897–); b. Chicago, Ill. Educator, author. *The Middle Ages* (with Dana C. Munro, 1928); *European Diplomatic History, 1871–1932* (1933); *Germany and England* (1938). Editor: *Documents on German Foreign Policy, 1918–45* (1949). History dept., 1939–41; University of California, since 1941.

SONTAG, SUSAN (Jan. 28, 1933–   ); Author. *The Benefactor* (1963); *Against Interpretation and Other Essays* (1966); *Death Kit* (1967); *Styles of Radical Will* (1969).

Sooth. Short story by Wilbur Daniel Steele (1927).

SOPER, ALEXANDER COBURN (Feb. 18, 1904–); b. Chicago, Ill. Educator, author. *Evolution of Buddhist Architecture in Japan* (1942); *Literary Evidence for Early Buddhist Art in China* (1959); *Chinese, Korean, Japanese Bronzes* (1966); *Textual Evidence for the Secular Arts of China in the Period from Liu Sung through Sui* (1967); etc. Prof. art history, Bryn Mawr College, since 1948. Translator: *Kue-Kuo Jo-hsu's Experiences in Painting* (1951).

SORENSEN, THEODORE CHAIKIN (May 8, 1928–); b. Lincoln, Neb. Politician, author. *Decision Making in the White House* (1963); *Kennedy* (1965).

SORENSEN, VIRGINIA [Eggertsen] (Feb. 17, 1912–); b. Provo, Utah. Author. *A Little Lower than the Angels* (1942); *On This Star* (1946); *The Neighbors* (1947); *The Evening and the Morning* (1949); *The Proper Gods* (1951); *Many Heavens* (1954); *The House Next Door* (1954); *Plain Girl* (1955); *Miracles on Maple Hill* (1956); *Kingdom Come* (1960); *Where Nothing is Long Ago* (1963); *Lotte's Locket* (1964); etc.

SORIN, EDWARD FREDERICK (Feb. 6, 1814–Oct. 31, 1893); b. near Laval, France. Roman Catholic clergyman, educator, editor. Founder, University of Notre Dame, South Bend, Ind., Jan. 15, 1844. Founder, *Ave Maria,* 1865.

SOROKIN, PITRIM ALEXANDROVITCH (Jan. 21, 1889–Feb. 10, 1968); b. Touria, Vologda, Russia. Educator, sociologist, author. *Leaves from a Russian Diary* (1924); *Contemporary Sociological Theories* (1929); *A Source Book in Rural Sociology,* 3v. (1930–31); *Social and Cultural Dynamics,* 4v. (1937–41); *The Crisis of Our Age* (1941); *Society, Culture and Personality* (1947); *Altruistic Love* (1950); *S.O.S.: The Meaning of Our Crisis* (1951); *The Ways and Powers of Love* (1954); *Forms and Techniques of Altruistic and Spiritual Growth* (1954); *The American Sex Revolution* (1956); etc. Also many books in Russian. Professor sociology, Harvard University, from 1930.

SORRELLS, JOHN HARVEY (Mar. 31, 1896–Feb. 25, 1948); b. Pine Bluff, Ark. Publisher, author. *The Working Press* (1930). Editor, the *Fort Worth Press,* 1927–30; president and publisher, the *Memphis Commercial Appeal,* from 1936.

SOSKIN, WILLIAM (May 1, 1899–Mar. 24, 1952); b. New York. Critic, publisher. Lit. editor, the *New York Evening Post,* 1928–33; the *New York American,* 1934–40. Cofounder, Howell, Soskin & Co., publishers, New York, 1940.

Sot-Weed Factor; or, A Voyage to Maryland, The. Satire by Ebenezer Cook (1708). Account of an early journey by the "factor" or agent of a British merchant. "Sot-weed" is tobacco, "the weed that makes one besotted."

SOTHERN, EDWARD HUGH (Dec. 6, 1859–Oct. 28, 1933); b. New Orleans, La. Actor, author. *The Melancholy Tale of "Me"* (1916). His best known acting role was in *The Prisoner of Zenda.*

Soul on Ice. Autobiography of Eldridge Cleaver (1968). Regeneration of a so-called Negro criminal as he develops political consciousness about the plight of blacks in a racist society.

SOULE, GEORGE HENRY, JR. (June 11, 1887–Apr. 14, 1970); b. Stamford, Conn. Statistician, editor, author. *A Planned Society* (1932); *The Coming American Revolution* (1934); *The Future of Liberty* (1936); *Sidney Hillman, Labor Statesman* (1939); *Introduction to Economic Science* (1948); *Economic Forces in American History* (1952); *Time for Living* (1955); *Longer Life* (1958); *Economics, Measurements, Theories, Case Studies* (1961); *Economics for Living* (1961); *The New Science of Economics* (1964); *Planning U.S.A.* (1967). With the *New Republic,* since 1914; editor, 1924–47.

Souls of Black Folks, The. By W. E. Burghardt DuBois (1903).

Sound and the Fury, The. Novel by William Faulkner (1929). Concerns the decline of the Compson family, once one of the grand types of the Southern aristocracy. The story is told in stream-of-consciousness narrative by different members of the family.

Sources of Culture in the Middle West. Ed. by Dixon Ryan Fox (1934). A symposium.

SOUSA, JOHN PHILIP (Nov. 6, 1854–Mar. 6, 1932); b. Washington, D.C. Bandmaster, composer, author. Known as "The March King." *The Fifth String* (1902); *Pipetown Sandy* (1905); *Transit of Venus* (1920); etc. He composed "The Washington Post March," "Semper Fidelis," "The Stars and Stripes Forever," "El Capitán," "The High School Cadets," etc.

South Atlantic Quarterly. Durham, N.C. Quarterly review of history, economics, and literature. Founded 1902, by J. S. Bassett. Concentrates, in particular, on Southern affairs.

South Bend Tribune. South Bend, Ind. Newspaper. Founded 1872. Franklin D. Schurz is editor and publisher. Walton R. Collins is book-review editor.

South-Carolina Gazette. Charleston, S.C. Newspaper. Founded 1732, by Thomas Whitmarsh, a printer sent to Charleston by Benjamin Franklin. First newspaper in the state. Suspended 1775; revived 1777, as the *Gazette of the State of South Carolina;* in 1794, the *South-Carolina State Gazette.* Expired 1802.

"South Carolina to the States of the North." Poem by Paul Hamilton Hayne, written in protest against the horrors of the Reconstruction period.

South Moon Under. Novel by Marjorie Kinnan Rawlings (1933). The setting is in the "Big Scrub" of Florida and deals with its slow, brave, and peaceful people.

South Sea Idyls. By Charles Warren Stoddard (1873). A classic work on the romantic South Seas based on the author's travels.

SOUTHALL, JAMES COCKE (Apr. 2, 1828–Sept. 13, 1897); b. Charlottesville, Va. Editor, author. *The Recent Origin of Man* (1875); *Man's Age in the World* (1878); etc. Founder (with Green Peyton), the *Charlottesville Review,*

1861; editor and owner, the *Charlottesville Daily Chronicle,* 1865–68; editor, the *Richmond Enquirer,* 1868–74.

SOUTHERN, TERRY (May 1, 1928–   ); b. Alvarado, Tex. Author. *Flash and Filigree* (1958); *The Magic Christian* (1959); *Candy* (with M. Hoffenberg, 1958); *Red Dirt Marihuana and Other Tastes* (1967); *Blue Movie* (1970). Screenplays for *Dr. Strangelove* (with Stanley Kubrick, 1963); *The Loved One* (with Christopher Isherwood, 1964); *The Cincinnati Kid* (with Ring Lardner, Jr., 1965); *Barbarella; Easy Rider.* Co-author: *Writers in Revolt* (with Alex Trocchi, 1960).

SOUTHERN, WILLIAM NEIL, JR. (Nov. 4, 1864–Feb. 11, 1956); b. Morristown, Tenn. Newspaper editor and publisher. Founder, *Independence Examiner,* Independence, Mo., 1905, editor and publisher from 1905. Wrote daily column "In Missouri Language."

Southern Address. By Howell Cobb (1849). It called for the united action of all Southerners and anticipated the later struggles between the States.

Southern Amaranth, The. Ed. by Sallie A. Brock (1869). Anthology of Confederate poetry.

Southern and Western Monthly Magazine and Review. Charleston, S.C. Founded Jan., 1845, and edited by William Gilmore Simms. Merged with the *Southern Literary Messenger,* 1845.

Southern Bivouac. Louisville, Ky. Monthly magazine. Founded Sept., 1882, by the Southern Historical Association. Chiefly devoted to the publication of Civil War papers, but in later years became more literary in tone, with Lafcadio Hearn, Paul Hamilton Hayne, John Esten Cook among its contributors. Merged with *The Century,* 1887.

"Southern Cross, The." Poem by St. George Tucker (1861).

Southern Illinois University Press. Carbondale, Ill. Founded 1953. Publishes scholarly nonfiction and reprints of fiction.

Southern Literary Journal. Charleston, S.D. Monthly. Founded Sept., 1835, by Daniel K. Whitaker. William Gilmore Simms was the chief contributor. Expired Dec., 1838.

Southern Literary Messenger. Richmond, Va. Magazine. Founded Aug., 1834, by Thomas Willys White. Editors: James F. Heath, 1834–35; Edward V. Sparhawk, 1835; Thomas W. White, 1835, 1837–39; Edgar Allan Poe, 1835–37; Matthew F. Maury, 1840–43; Benjamin B. Minor, 1843–47; John R. Thompson, 1847–60; George W. Bagby, 1860–64; Frank H. Alfriend, 1864. Poe, Simms, Beverly Tucker, Matthew F. Maury, Philip Pendleton Cooke, Robert Montgomery Bird, Paul Hamilton Hayne, John R. Thompson, Henry Timrod, and Donald G. Mitchell were among the distinguished contributors. The magazine expired in 1864. It was revived in 1939 by the Dietz Press. *See* Benjamin B. Minor's *The Southern Literary Messenger* (1905); David K. Jackson's *The Contributors and Contributions to the Southern Literary Messenger, 1834–1864* (1936). Frank Luther Mott's *History of American Magazines,* v. 1 (1938).

Southern Magazine. Baltimore, Md. See *Land We Love.*

Southern Monthly. Memphis, Tenn. Founded Sept., 1861. It contained Quincy Quackenboss's *Idlewild: A Tale of West Tennessee.* Expired May, 1862.

Southern Quarterly Review. New Orleans, La. Literary magazine. Founded Jan., 1842, by Daniel K. Whitaker in New Orleans, but moved to Charleston, S.C., after the first year. William Gilmore Simms edited it from 1849 to 1855. The magazine expired in Columbia, S.C., Feb., 1857.

Southern Review. Charleston, S.C. Quarterly. Founded Feb., 1828, by Stephen Elliott, who edited it at first. Hugh Swinton Legaré was a later editor and contributor. Expired Feb., 1832.

Southern Review. Baltimore, Md. A literary quarterly. Founded Jan., 1867, and edited by Albert Taylor Bledsoe and William Hand Browne. Later edited by A. T. Bledsoe and Sophia Bledsoe Herrick. Devoted to the literature of the South, and faithful throughout to The Lost Cause. Paul Hamilton Hayne was its chief literary critic. Expired Oct., 1879.

Southern Review. Baton Rouge, La. Quarterly. Founded July, 1935. Published at Louisiana State University. Edited by Charles W. Pipkin, 1935–41; Cleanth Brooks and Robert Penn Warren, 1941–42. Contributors included John Peale Bishop, Kenneth Burke, Allen Tate, J. C. Ransom, Lionel Trilling, Arthur Mizener. Discontinued 1942. Revived under editors Lewis P. Simpson and Donald E. Stanford in 1965.

Southwest Magazine. Fort Worth, Tex. Monthly. Founded 1905. Magazine section distributed to numerous Texas and Oklahoma newspapers.

Southwest Review, The. Dallas, Tex. Quarterly. Founded 1912 as *The Texas Review* and edited by Stark Young, 1912–17; and Robert Adger Law, 1917–24. Reorganized as *The Southwest Review* in 1924 at Southern Methodist University. Editors have included Jay B. Hubbell, George Bond, and Alan Maxwell. Devoted to essays on Southwestern culture and American literature, as well as to fiction and poetry.

Southwest Writer's Guild. Founded 1935, by Royal Dixon and others.

Southwester, The. Dallas, Tex. Literary magazine. Founded 1935. Editors: Florence E. Barns, 1935–36; W. T. Tardy, 1937–38. Expired 1938.

SOUTHWICK, ALBERT PLYMPTON (b. May 11, 1855); b. Charleston, Mass. Author. *Quizzism, and its Key* (1884); *Bijou* (1889); *Wisps of Wit and Wisdom* (1892); *The Catherwood Mystery* (1893); *A Fact in Fiction* (1893); *Brown the Lawyer* (1893); etc.

SOUTHWICK, SOLOMON (Dec. 25, 1773–Nov. 18, 1839); b. Newport, R.I. Editor, poet. *The Pleasures of Poverty* (1823). Editor, *Albany Register,* 1808–17. Founded and edited, *The Ploughboy,* 1819–23, and wrote for it under pen name of "Henry Homespun."

SOUTHWORTH, E[mma] D[orothy] E[liza] N[evitte] (Dec. 26, 1819–June 30, 1899); b. Washington, D.C. Novelist. *Retribution* (1849); *The Curse of Clifton* (1852); *The Discarded Daughter* (1852); *Broken Pledges* (1855); *The Missing Bride* (1855); *The Hidden Hand* (1859); *The Haunted Homestead* (1860); *Ishmael* (1863); *The Fatal Marriage* (1863); *The Bride of Llewellyn* (1868); *Changed Brides* (1867); *Fair Play* (1868); *How He Won Her* (1869); *Tried for Her Life* (1969); *The Maiden Widow* (1870); *David Lindsay* (1877); *A Leap in the Dark* (1881); *The Gypsy's Prophecy* (1886); *Her Love or Her Life* (1905); etc. *See* Regis Louise Boyle's *Mrs. E. D. E. N. Southworth, Novelist* (1939).

SOUTHWORTH, GEORGE CHAMPLIN SHEPARD (Dec. 13, 1842–Feb. 19, 1918); b. West Springfield, Mass. Educator, author. *Six Lectures Introductory to the Study of English Literature* (1887); etc. Prof. English, Kenyon College, 1881–88.

SOUTHWORTH, JAMES G[ranville] (Oct. 18, 1896–); b. Monroe, Mich. Educator, author. *Sowing the Spring: Studies in British Poets from Hopkins to MacNeice* (1940); *Vauxhall Gardens* (1941); *The Poetry of Thomas Hardy* (1947); *Some Modern American Poets* (1950); *Verses of Cadence* (1954); etc. Prof. English, University of Toledo, since 1934.

SOUVAINE, MABEL HILL, b. Elizabeth, N.J. Editor. staff, *Woman's Day,* 1937–43; editor-in-chief, 1943–57.

Soveraignty & Goodness of God Together, With the Faithfulness of His Promises Displayed; Being a Narrative of the Captivity and Restauration of Mrs. Mary Rowlandson, The. By Mary Rowlandson (1682). The Indians sacked the town of

Lancaster, Mass., Feb. 10, 1675, and killed most of the inhabitants. Mary Rowlandson was taken as a prisoner, along with her small daughter, Sarah. After a harrowing experience she was ransomed.

SOWER, CHRISTOPHER (1693–Sept. 25, 1758); b. Laasphe, Ger. Printer, publisher. His name is sometimes spelled Saur or Sauer. Came to Philadelphia in 1724 and set up a press at Germantown in 1738. Built paper mill in 1774. Most famous of his undertakings was the translations of Bible into German (1743), the first American edition, except for the Indian version by John Eliot. See John Clyde Oswald's *Printing in the Americas* (1937).

SOWER, CHRISTOPHER (Jan. 27, 1754–July 3, 1799); b. Germantown, Pa., grandson of Christopher Sower, Pennsylvania publisher and loyalist. He published, besides Pennsylvania papers in the German language, the *Royal Gazette and Weekly Advertiser*, at New Brunswick, N.J. Continued father's business. See S. W. Pennypacker's *Pennsylvania in American History* (1910).

SPAETH, JOHN WILLIAM, JR. (July 2, 1895–); b. Philadelphia, Pa. Educator. *A Study of the Causes of Rome's Wars from 343 to 265 B.C.* (1926); *Vergiliana: A Selected List of Books for Library Exhibits* (1930); *Index Verborum Ciceronis Poeticorum Fragmentorum* (1955). Prof. Wesleyan University, Connecticut, since 1932.

SPAETH, SIGMUND [Gottfried] (Apr. 10, 1885–Nov. 11, 1965); b. Philadelphia, Pa. Musician, lecturer, author. *The Common Sense of Music* (1926); *Read 'Em and Weep* (1926); *American Mountain Songs* (1927); *Gentlemen Be Seated* (1928); *The Art of Enjoying Music* (1933); *Stories Behind the World's Great Music* (1937); *Fun with Music* (1941); *Great Symphonies* (1950); and guide books to operas, songs, etc. Music editor, *McCall's Magazine*, 1931–33, *Esquire*, 1934, the *Literary Digest*, 1937–38; editor, *Music Journal*, from 1955.

SPALDING, JOHN LANCASTER (June 2, 1840–Aug. 25, 1916); b. Lebanon, Ky., nephew of Martin John Spalding. Roman Catholic bishop, poet, essayist. *Essays and Reviews* (1876); *Lectures and Discourses* (1882); *America, and Other Poems* (1885); *The Poet's Praise* (1887); *Education and the Higher Life* (1890); *Things of the Mind* (1894); *Opportunity, and Other Essays* (1898); *Aphorisms and Reflections* (1901); *Religion, Art, and Other Essays* (1905); *A Kentucky Pioneer* (poem, 1932); etc.

SPALDING, MARTIN JOHN (May 23, 1810–Feb. 7, 1872); b. Rolling Fork, Ky. Roman Catholic archbishop, author. *Sketches of the Early Catholic Missions in Kentucky* (1844); *General Evidences of Catholicity* (with John McGill, 1847); *Miscellanea* (1855); etc. Founder of the *Louisville Guardian*, 1858, an outgrowth of the *Catholic Advocate*, founded 1835. See John Lancaster Spalding's *Life of the Most Rev. M. J. Spalding* (1873).

SPARGO, JOHN (Jan. 31, 1876–); b. Stithians, Cornw., Eng. Author. *The Bitter Cry of the Children* (1906); *Not Guilty* (1907); *The Common Sense of Socialism* (1908); *The Socialism of William Morris* (1908); *Karl Marx* (1909); *Americanism and Social Democracy* (1918); *Anthony Haswell, Printer, Patriot, Balladist* (1925); *Ethan Allen at Ticonderoga* (1926); *The Consecrated Century* (1934); *Notes on the Ancestry of Ethan and Ira Allen and Their Immediate Descendants* (1948); *Covered Wooden Bridges of Bennington and Vicinity* (1953); etc.

SPARGO, JOHN WEBSTER (Mar. 6, 1896–Sept. 6, 1956); b. St. Louis, Mo. Educator, author. *Virgil, the Necromancer* (1934); *Some Reference Books of the 16th and 17th Centuries* (1937); *Bibliographical Manual for Students of Language and Literature of England and the United States* (1939); *Imaginary Books and Libraries* (1952); etc. Editor: *Charles Neely: Tales and Songs of Illinois* (1938); etc. English dept., Northwestern University, from 1927; prof. from 1935.

SPARHAWK, FRANCES CAMPBELL (b. July 28, 1847); b. Amesbury, Mass. Author. *A Lazy Man's Work* (1881); the *Dorothy Brooke* series, 5v. (1909–13); *Whittier at Close Range* (1925); etc.

SPARKES, BOYDEN (Jan. 6, 1890–May 18, 1954); b. Cincinnati, O. Author. *Crime in Ink* (with Claire Carvalho, 1929); *Hetty Green* (with S. T. Moore, 1930); *Father Struck It Rich* (with Evalyn Walsh McLean, 1936); *Life of an American Workman* (with Walter P. Chrysler, 1937); *Judge Mellon's Sons* (with M. L. Mellon, 1948); etc.

SPARKS, EDWIN ERLE (July 16, 1860–June 15, 1924); b. Newark, O. Educator, author. *The Man Who Made the Nation* (1900); *The Expansion of the American People* (1900); *The United States of America*, 2v. (1904); *The Lincoln-Douglas Debates of 1858* (1908). President, Pennsylvania State College, 1908–20.

SPARKS, JARED (May 10, 1789–Mar. 14, 1866); b. Willington, Conn. Educator, historian, biographer, editor. *The Life of George Washington* (1839); etc. Editor: *The Writings of George Washington*, 12v. (1833–39); *The Works of Benjamin Franklin*, 10v. (1836–40); *The Library of American Biography*, 25v. (1834–48); *Correspondence of the American Revolution*, 4v. (1853); etc. Editor, *North American Review*, 1824–31; founder and editor, *American Almanac and Repository of Useful Knowledge*, 1830–61. Prof. history, Harvard College, 1839–49; president, Harvard College, 1849–53. See H. B. Adams's *The Life and Writings of Jared Sparks*, 2v. (1893); *Correspondence of George Bancroft and Jared Sparks, 1823–1832* (1917, 1969) ed. by J. S. Bassett.

Sparling, Ned. Pen name of Luis Philip Senarens.

SPARROW, LOUISE [Winslow] **KIDDER** (Mrs. Herbert George Sparrow) (Jan. 1, 1884–Aug. 17, 1966); b. Malden, Mass. Sculptor, poet. *Lyrics and Translations* (1904); *The Last Cruise* (1926).

Sparrow Magazine. West Lafayette, Ind. Twice yearly. Published and edited by Felix and Selma Stefanile. Literary magazine.

Spartacus to the Gladiators. Declamation written by Elijah Kellogg. It appeared originally in the *School Reader*, by Epes Sargent (1846). Kellogg also wrote *Regulus to the Carthaginians*, *Hannibal at the Altar*, and *Pericles to the People*.

SPAULDING, EDWARD GLEASON (Aug. 6, 1873–Jan. 31, 1940); b. Burlington, Vt. Educator, philosopher, author. *The New Rationalism* (1918); *What Am I?* (1928); *A World of Chance* (1936). Philosophy dept., Princeton University, 1905–40.

SPAULDING, FRANK ELLSWORTH (Nov. 30, 1866–June 6, 1960); b. Dublin, N.H. Educator, author. *The Individual Child and His Education* (1904); etc. Compiler: *Living Thoughts for All Ages*, 3v. (with Catherine T. Bryce, 1903); *The Aldine Readers*, 8v. (1907); *One School Administrator's Philosophy: Its Development* (1952); *School Superintendent in Action* (1955); etc. Prof. education, Yale University, 1920–35.

SPAULDING, SOLOMON (1761–Oct. 20, 1816); b. Ashford, Conn. Soldier, preacher, novelist. *The Manuscript Found* (1812). This novel describing a pre-Columbian civilization in America, purported to have been found in an ancient mound. It was charged later that Joseph Smith derived *The Book of Mormon* from it. Spaulding's original manuscript was republished by the Mormons in 1885. See *Tract 77* of the Western Reserve Historical Society, 1892.

Speakers of the House of Representatives of the United States. By W. H. Smith (1928). Biographical and historical study.

Speaking Frankly. By James F. Byrnes (1947). Political autobiography of a U.S. Secretary of State and observer at the

Yalta Conference, covering the period February, 1945, to October, 1946.

SPEARE, DOROTHY (Dec. 13, 1898–Feb. 3, 1951); b. Newton Centre, Mass. Novelist. *Dancers in the Dark* (1922); *The Gay Year* (1923); *A Virgin of Yesterday* (1925); *The Road to Needles* (1937); *Spring on Fifty-Second Street* (1947); etc.

SPEARE, ELIZABETH GEORGE (Nov. 21, 1908–); b. Melrose, Mass. Author. *Calico Captive* (1957); *The Witch of Blackbird Pond* (1958); *The Bronze Bow* (1961); *Life in Colonial America* (1963); *The Prospering* (1967); etc.

SPEARE, MORRIS EDMUND (1884–); b. Boston, Mass. Editor, author. *The Political Novel* (1924); *The Essay* (1927); *Geography and Travel* (1933); etc. General editor, *The Chelsea Classics,* 46v. (1932–33). With Oxford University Press, Alfred A. Knopf, Robert M. McBride Co., Stanford University Press. Prof. English, St. John's University, New York, 1933–40.

SPEARMAN, FRANK H[amilton] (Sept. 6, 1859–Dec. 29, 1937); b. Buffalo, N.Y. Author. *The Nerve of Foley* (1900); *Held for Orders* (1901); *Doctor Bryson* (1902); *The Daughter of a Magnate* (1904); *Whispering Smith* (1906); *Laramie Holds the Range* (1921); *Selwood of Sleepy Cat* (1925); *Flambeau Jim* (1927); and many movie scenarios.

SPEARS, JOHN RANDOLPH (1850–Jan. 25, 1935); b. in Van Wert Co., O. Author. *The Fugitive* (1899); *The History of Our Navy,* 5v. (1897–99); *The American Slave-Trade* (1900); *David G. Farragut* (1905); *The Story of the New England Whalers* (1908); *The Story of the American Merchant Marine* (1910).

SPEARS, RAYMOND S[miley] (Aug. 2, 1876–Jan., 1950); b. Bellevue, O. Author. Pen name, "Jim Smiley." *A Trip on the Great Lakes* (1913); *Camping on the Great Lakes* (1913); *Diamond Tolls* (1920); *The River Prophet* (1920); *Driftwood* (1921); *Camping, Woodcraft and Wildcraft* (1924); etc.

Specialist, The. By Charles "Chic" Sale (1925). Story about the outdoor privy as an American institution.

Specimens of American Poetry. By Samuel Kettell, 3v. (1829). First comprehensive anthology of native verse, selections from 189 writers from Cotton Mather to John Greenleaf Whittier.

SPECK, FRANK GOULDSMITH (Nov. 8, 1881–Feb. 6, 1950); b. Brooklyn, N.Y. Educator, anthropologist, author. *Ceremonial Songs of the Creek and Yuchi Indians* (1911); *Penobscot Shamanism* (1920); *The Rappahannock Indians of Virginia* (1925); *Native Tribes and Dialects of Connecticut* (1926); *Penobscot Tales and Religious Beliefs* (1935); *Penobscot Man* (1940); *The Iroquois* (1946); and many more books on the American Indian. Anthropology dept., University of Pennsylvania, from 1909; prof. from 1925.

SPECKING, INEZ (Apr. 8, 1895–); b. Washington, Mo. Author. The *Martha Jane* series, 4v. (1925–33); *Boy* (1925); *So That's That* (1930); *I Get Married* (1933); *Shakespeare for Children* (1956); and other books for children. Editor: *Simon Bolivar* (1947). English dept., Harris' Teachers College, Toledo, O., since 1925.

SPECTORSKY, A[uguste] C[omte] (Aug. 13, 1910–Jan. 17, 1972); b. Paris. Editor, author. *Invitation to Skiing* (1947); *Man into Beast* (1948); *The Book of the Sea* (1954); *The Exurbanites* (1955); *The College Years* (1958); *The New Invitation to Skiing* (1958); *The New Invitation to Modern Skiing* (with Fred Iselin, 1965). With *The New Yorker,* 1938–41; The *Chicago Sun,* 1941–46; *Park East,* 1951–54; *Playboy,* from 1956.

Spectra. Literary hoax by Witter Bynner and Arthur Davison Ficke, under the pen names of "Ann Knish" and "Emmanuel Morgan" (1917). *See* William Jay Smith's *The Spectra Hoax* (1961).

Spectre Bridegroom, The. Story by Washington Irving in *The Sketch Book.*

Speculum. Cambridge, Mass. Quarterly. Founded 1925. Published by the Mediaeval Academy of America. Journal of medieval studies.

Speech at Plymouth. By Daniel Webster (1820). One of his famous orations, delivered at the Plymouth bicentenary, Dec. 22, 1820.

SPEED, JOHN GILMER (Sept. 21, 1853–1909); b. in Kentucky. Journalist, author. *The Horse in America* (1905); etc. Editor, the *American Magazine,* 1888–89; on editorial staff, the *New York World,* 1877–83, *Leslie's Weekly,* etc.

Speed, Nell. Pen name of Emma Speed Sampson.

SPEER, ROBERT ELLIOTT (Sept. 10, 1867–Nov. 23, 1947); b. Huntington, Pa. Missionary, executive, author. *Missions and Politics in Asia* (1898); *Missions and Modern History* (1904); *The Light of the World* (1911); *Race and Race Relations* (1924); *Sir James Ewing* (1928); *Owen Crimmins* (1931); *Memoir of John Bowen* (1938); *Memoir of John J. Eagan* (1939); *Five Minutes a Day* (1943); *Jesus and Our Human Problems* (1946); etc.

SPELLMAN, FRANCIS JOSEPH (May 4, 1889–Dec. 2, 1967); b. Whitman, Mass. Roman Catholic cardinal, author. *No Greater Love* (1945); *Prayers and Poems* (1946); *The Foundling* (1951); *What America Means to Me, and Other Poems and Prayers* (1953). Translator of papal broadcasts and encyclicals. Editorial writer for Boston *Pilot,* 1918–22.

SPENCE, HARTZELL (Feb. 15, 1908–); b. Clarion, Ia. Author. *One Foot in Heaven* (1940); *Radio City* (1941); *Get Thee Behind Me* (1943); *Vain Shadow* (1947); *No Place Like Home* (1948); *Happily Ever After* (1949); *Bride of the Conqueror* (1954); *The Story of America's Religions* (1960); *A Foot in the Door* (with A. C. Fuller, (1960); *The Clergy and What They Do* (1961); *Portrait in Oil* (1962); *For Every Tear a Victory* (1964); *A Great Name in Oil* (1966); *The New York Life 1845–1968* (1969); *Marcos of the Philippines* (1969); etc.

SPENCER, BENJAMIN TOWNLEY (Apr. 23, 1904–); b. Winchester, Ky. Educator, author. *The Quest for Nationality* (1957); Co-author: *Seventeenth Century Studies* (1933). Editor: *The Bondman* (1932). Prof. English, Ohio Wesleyan University, since 1937; director of library, 1938–40.

SPENCER, CLAIRE (Mrs. J. G. Evans) (Apr. 20, 1899–); b. Glasgow, Scot. Author. *Gallows' Orchard* (1930); *The Quick and the Dead* (1932); *The Island* (1935).

Spencer, Cornelia. Pen name of Grace Sydenstricker Yaukey.

SPENCER, CORNELIA PHILLIPS (Mar. 20, 1825–Mar. 11, 1908); b. Harlem, N.Y. Historian of North Carolina. *The Last Ninety Days of the War in North Carolina* (1866); *First Steps in North Carolina History* (1889); etc. *See* Hope S. Chamberlain's *Old Days in Chapel Hill: Being the Life and Letters of Cornelia Phillips Spencer* (1926).

SPENCER, ELIZABETH (July 19, 1921–); b. Carrollton, Miss. Novelist. *Fire in the Morning* (1948); *This Crooked Way* (1952); *Voice at the Back Door* (1956); *The Light in the Piazza* (1960); *Knights and Dragons* (1965); *No Place for an Angel* (1967); *Ship Island and Other Stories* (1968).

SPENCER, FLOYD ALBERT (Oct. 23, 1899–); b. Bedford, Ia. Educator, author. *Trends of Civilization and Culture* (with others, 1932); *Beyond Damascus: A Biography of Paul the Tarsian* (1934); *Agent Extraordinary* (1942); *War and Postwar Greece* (1952). Classics dept., New York University, 1930–38.

SPENCER, HAZELTON (July 7, 1893–July 28, 1944); b. Methuen, Mass. Educator, author. *Shakespeare Improved* (1927); *The Art and Life of William Shakespeare* (1940); etc.

Editor: *Elizabethan Plays* (1933); etc. English dept., Johns Hopkins University, from 1928; prof., from 1937.

SPENCER, JESSE AMES (June 17, 1816–Sept. 2, 1898); b. Hyde Park, N.Y. Episcopal clergyman, educator, author. *History of the Reformation in England* (1846); *The East: Sketches of Travel in Egypt and the Holy Land* (1850); *History of the United States*, 3v. (1858); *Memorabilia of Sixty-five Years* (1890); etc. Founder, *Young Churchman's Miscellany*, 1845. Prof. Greek, College of the City of New York, 1869–79.

SPENCER, ROBIN EDGERTON (Dec. 23, 1896–); b. Ogden, Utah. Novelist. *The Lady Who Came to Stay* (1931); *The Incompetents* (1933); *Felicita* (1937); *The Death of Mark* (1938).

SPENCER, SAMUEL REID, JR. (1919–); b. Rock Hill, S.C. Educator. *Decision for War* (1953); *Booker T. Washington and the Negro's Place in American Life* (1955). Prof. history, Davidson College, 1955–57; pres., Mary Baldwin College, since 1957.

Spencer, Warren. Pen name of William Charles Lengel.

Spencerian handwriting. A form of handwriting perfected by Platt Rogers Spencer (Nov. 7, 1800–May 16, 1864), an Ohio schoolmaster. His first textbooks appeared in 1848, and his five sons continued to publish these popular manuals long after his death.

Spenser, Avis S. See Emma Carra.

SPERRY, WILLARD LEAROYD (Apr. 5, 1882–May 15, 1954); b. Peabody, Mass. Educator, author. *The Disciplines of Liberty* (1921); *Reality in Worship* (1925); *The Paradox of Religion* (1927); *Signs of These Times* (1929); *Strangers and Pilgrims* (1939); *Rebuilding Our World* (1943); *Religion in America* (1946); etc. Dean of divinity school, and prof. practical theology, Harvard University, from 1922.

SPEWACK, BELLA COHEN (Mrs. Samuel Spewack) (Mar. 1899–); b. in Hungary. Playwright. Co-author (with husband): *Poppa* (prod. 1928); *Clear All Wires* (prod. 1932), rewritten as *Leave It to Me* (prod. 1938); *Spring Song* (prod. 1934); *Boy Meets Girl* (prod. 1935); *The Solitaire Man* (prod. 1936); *Miss Swan Expects* (prod. 1939); *Woman Bites Dog* (prod. 1946); *My Three Angels* (prod. 1953); etc. Co-author (with Cole Porter): *Kiss Me Kate* (prod. 1949). Motion picture scenarist, with husband.

SPEWACK, SAMUEL (Sept. 16, 1898–); b. in Russia. Playwright, author. *The Busy Busy People* (1948); *Two Blind Mice* (prod. 1949); *Under the Sycamore Tree* (1952). Author (under pen name "A. A. Abbott"): *Mon Paul* (1928); *The Skyscraper Murder* (1928); *The Murder in the Gilded Cage* (1929). Co-author of plays with wife, Bella Spewack (q.v.); *Boy Meets Girl* (prod. 1935); *The Solitaire Man* (prod. 1936); *Miss Swan Expects* (prod. 1939); *Woman Bites Dog* (prod. 1946); *My Three Angels* (prod. 1953); and motion picture scenarios.

SPEYER, LEONORA (Nov. 7, 1872–Feb. 10, 1956); b. Washington, D.C. Poet. *A Canopie Jar* (1921); *Fiddler's Farwell* (1926, Pulitzer Prize for poetry, 1927); *Naked Heel* (1931); *Slow Wall: New and Selected Poems* (1939); *The Slow Wall: Poems, together with Nor Without Music* (1946).

SPICER, ANNE HIGGINSON (Mrs. Vibe K. Spicer) (1874–Sept. 9, 1935); b. Burlington, Ia. Poet. *Songs of the Skokie, and Other Verse* (1917); *The Last Crusade* (1918); *A Cookshire Lad* (1922); etc.

SPICER, JACK (1925–   ); b. Hollywood, Cal. Poet. *After Lorca* (1957); *Billy the Kid* (1959); *The Heads of the Town Up to the Aether* (1962); *Language* (1965); *Book of Magazine Verse* (1966); *Homage to Creeley*; etc.

Spider, Spider. Short story by Conrad Aiken (1928).

"Spider and the Fly, The." Song, words by Jesse Hutchinson, music adapted by S. O. Dyer (1847).

SPIEGEL, CLARA GATZERT; b. Chicago, Ill. Author with Jane Mayer under pen name "Clare Jaynes": *Instruct My Sorrows* (1942); *These Are the Times* (1944); *This Eager Heart* (1947); *The Early Frost* (1952).

SPILLANE, MICKEY [Frank Morrison] (1918–). Author. *I, the Jury* (1947); *Big Kill* (1951); *Kiss Me, Deadly* (1952); *The Deep* (1961); etc.

SPILLER, ROBERT E[rnest] (Nov. 13, 1896–); b. Philadelphia, Pa. Educator, author. *The Americans in England During the First Half Century of Independence* (1926); *Fenimore Cooper, Critic of His Times* (1931); *A Descriptive Bibliography of James Fenimore Cooper* (with P. C. Blackburn, 1934); *The Cycle of American Literature* (1955); *Eight American Authors* (with others, 1956); *The Early Lectures of Ralph Waldo Emerson* (1959); *A Time of Harvest* (1961); etc. Editor: *The Roots of National Culture: American Literature to 1830* (1933). Co-editor: *Literary History of the United States* (1948). *American Perspectives* (1961); *Social Control in a Free Society* (1960). Advisory editor, *American Literature*, 1928–31; editor 1932–39, and since 1940. English dept., Swarthmore College, since 1921.

SPINGARN, J[oel] E[lias] (May 17, 1875–July 26, 1939); b. New York. Publicist, educator, editor, author. *A History of Literary Criticism in the Renaissance* (1899); *The New Hesperides, and Other Poems* (1911); *Creative Criticism* (1917); *Poems* (1924); *Poetry and Religion* (1924); etc. Editor: *Critical Essays of the Seventeenth Century*, 3v. (1908–09); *European Library*, 25v. (1920–25); *Criticism in America* (1924). Owner, the *Amenia* (N.Y.) *Times*, 1911–26. A founder and literary advisor, Harcourt, Brace and Co. Comparative literature dept., Columbia University, 1899–1911.

Spinners' Club. San Francisco, Calif. Literary club. An informal group which had no established headquarters. Gertrude Atherton and Mrs. Ednah Aiken were among its active leaders. It published *The Spinners' Book of Fiction* (1907), in honor of Ina Coolbrith. Among the contributors to this volume were George Sterling, Jack London, Gertrude Atherton, Charles Warren Stoddard, Frank Norris, Mary Halleck Foote.

Spirit. New York. A bi-monthly magazine of poetry. Founded 1934. John Gilland Brunini and David Roth were among its editors. Published by the Catholic Poetry Society.

Spirit of the Times. New York. Sporting journal. Founded Dec. 10, 1831, by William T. Porter. In 1856 the journal was sold to George Wilkes, founder of the *National Police Gazette*. Wilkes changed the name to *Porter's Spirit of the Times*, which expired in June, 1861. Wilkes started the *Spirit of the Times and Sportsman*, Sept. 10, 1859, which was usually known as *Wilkes' Spirit of the Times* to distinguish it from *Porter's Spirit of the Times*. Wilkes' journal ran until Dec. 13, 1902, when it was merged with the *Horseman*. These sporting journals contained many literary articles by Porter, "Frank Forester," Thomas B. Thorpe, Albert Pike and others.

Spiritual Aspects of the New Poetry. By Amos Niven Wilder (1940). A critical survey of twentieth-century poetry as it affects the thought of America.

SPITZ, ARMAND N[eustadter] (July 7, 1904–); b. Philadelphia, Pa. Inventor, author. *The Pinpoint Planetarium* (1940); *A Start in Meteorology* (1941); *Dictionary of Astronomy and Astronautics* (1958).

SPIVAK, JOHN L[ouis] (June 13, 1897–); b. New Haven, Conn. Author. *The Devil's Brigade* (1930); *Georgia Nigger* (1932); *America Faces the Barricades* (1935); *Europe Under the Terror* (1936); *Secret Armies* (1939); *Honorable Spy* (1939); *Shrine of the Silver Dollar* (1940); *A Pattern for American Fascism* (1947); *A Man in His Time* (1967).

SPOCK, BENJAMIN [McLane] (May 2, 1903–); b. New Haven, Conn. Physician, educator. *Common Sense Book of Baby and Child Care* (1946); *A Baby's First Year* (with others, 1954); *Feeding Your Baby and Child* (with M. Lowenberg, 1955); *Dr. Spock Talks with Mothers* (1961); *Problems of Parents* (1962); *Caring for Your Disabled Child* (with M. Lerrigo, 1965); *Dr. Spock on Vietnam* (with Mitchell Zimmerman, 1968); etc. Prof. psychiatry, Mayo Foundation, 1947–51; prof. child development. University of Pittsburgh, 1951–55; Western Reserve University, since 1955.

SPOFFORD, AINSWORTH RAND (Sept. 12, 1825–Aug. 11, 1908); b. Gilmanton, N.H. Librarian, editor, author. *A Book for All Readers* (1900). Editor: *The Library of Choice Literature,* 10v. (1881–88); *The Library of Wit and Humor,* 5v. (1884); *The Library of Historic Characters and Famous Events,* 10v. (1894–95); etc. Librarian of Congress, 1864–97. See Appleton P. C. Griffin's *Ainsworth R. Spofford* (1909); *The Independent,* Nov. 19, 1908.

SPOFFORD, HARRIET ELIZABETH PRESCOTT (Apr. 3, 1835–Aug. 14, 1921); b. Calais, Me. Poet, novelist. *Sir Rohan's Ghost* (1860); *The Amber Gods, and Other Stories* (1863); *Azarian: An Episode* (1864); *New England Legends* (1871); *Poems* (1882); *Ballads About Authors* (1887); *A Scarlet Poppy, and Other Stories* (1894); *In Titania's Garden, and Other Poems* (1897); *Old Madame, & Other Tragedies* (1900); etc. Her best known story was *The Madonna of the Tubs. See* Elizabeth K. Halbeisen's *Harriet Prescott Spofford, a Romantic Survival* (1935).

Spoilers, The. Novel by Rex Beach (1905). Story of the gold rush in the Klondike. Roy Glenister, the central character, thirsted for power and believed that everything could be accomplished by brute force. The basis of the story was the McKenzie-Noyes conspiracy trial at Nome, Alaska.

Spoils of Poynton, The. Novel by Henry James (1897). Squabble between a widow and her son over the possession of a house and objects of art which she had collected during a lifetime.

Spokane Chronicle. See *Spokane Spokesman Review.*

Spokane Spokesman-Review. Spokane, Wash. Newspaper. The *Spokane Falls Review,* founded 1883; the *Spokane Spokesman,* founded 1890; merged 1893, by William Hutchinson Cowles. George Washington Fuller was editorial writer. Stoddard King (1889–1933) wrote the column "Facetious Fragments". Combined with the *Spokane Chronicle,* founded 1881; the *Chronicle* appears evenings and Thursdays; the *Spokesman-Review,* mornings and Sundays.

Spoon River Anthology, The. Poems by Edgar Lee Masters (1915). Made up of imaginary epitaphs of various men and women of a drab village of the Middle West, couched in satire and irony. One of the most widely quoted of the epitaphs is the one on Anne Rutledge, Abraham Lincoln's sweetheart.

SPOONER, ALDEN JEREMIAH (Feb. 2, 1810–Aug. 2, 1881); b. Sag Harbor, L.I., N.Y. Antiquarian, editor. Editor: *Notes Geographical and Historical Relating to the Town of Brooklyn . . . by Gabriel Furman* (1865); *A Sketch of the First Settlement of the Several Towns on Long Island . . . by Silas Wood* (1865). Editor, *Long Island City Star,* founded by his father, Alden Spooner. Founder, Long Island Historical Society, 1863.

SPOONER, SHEARJASHUB (Dec. 3, 1809–Mar. 14, 1859); b. Orwell, Vt. Dentist, editor. Compiler: *Anecdotes of Painters, Engravers, Sculptors and Architects; and Curiosities of Art,* 3v. (1850); *A Biographical and Critical Dictionary of Painters, Engravers, Sculptors and Architects* (1853); etc. He bought the copper plates for John Boydell's illustrations for Shakespeare while on a tour of Europe, and published an American edition of *Boydell's Shakespeare* in 2v. (1852). Also wrote books on dentistry.

Sports Illustrated. New York. Weekly. Founded 1954. Concerned with all aspects of sports in relation to the general culture rather than limited to technical discussion only.

Spotted Horses. Short story by William Faulkner (1931).

SPRAGUE, ACHSA W. (c. 1828–July 6, 1862); b. Plymouth Notch, Vt. Poet, spiritualist. *I Still Live: Poem for the Times* (1862); *The Poet, and Other Poems* (1865).

SPRAGUE, CHARLES (Oct. 26, 1791–Jan. 22, 1875); b. Boston, Mass. Banker, poet. *Writings of Charles Sprague, Now First Collected* (1841). Best known for his "Ode to Shakespeare." See C. J. Sprague's *The Poetical and Prose Writings of Charles Sprague* (1876).

SPRAGUE, HOMER BAXTER (Oct. 19, 1829–Mar. 23, 1918); b. Sutton, Mass. Educator, lecturer, author. *The True Macbeth* (1909); *Caesar and Brutus* (1912); *Studies in Shakespeare* (1916); etc. Founder, The Martha's Vineyard Summer Institute, 1879, the first summer school in the United States. President of Mills College, and of the University of North Dakota.

SPRAGUE, JESSE RAINSFORD (Mar. 23, 1872–Sept. 4, 1946); b. Le Roy, N.Y. Author. *The Middleman* (1929); *On the Road* (1930); *James Read* (1930); *King Cotton Carries On* (1932); *The Lumberman* (1933); *The Romance of Credit* (1943); etc.

SPRAGUE, WILLIAM BUELL (Oct. 16, 1795–May 7, 1876); b. Andover, Conn. Congregational clergyman, autograph collector, author. *Visits to European Celebrities* (1856); *The Life of Jedidiah Morse* (1874). Compiler: *Annals of the American Pulpit,* 9v. (1857–69). He collected over 40,000 autographs. *See* A. H. Joline's *The Autograph Hunter, and Other Papers* (1907).

SPRENGLING, MARTIN (Oct. 9, 1877–Sept. 5, 1959); b. Centre, Wis. Educator, Orientalist, author. *Descriptive Catalogue of Manuscripts in the Library of the University of Chicago* (with E. J. Goodspeed, 1912); *The Alphabet; Its Rise and Development from the Sinai Inscriptions* (1931); *From Persian to Arabic* (1939); *Kartir, Founder of Sassanian Zoroasterism* (1940); etc. Editor, *Journal of Semitic Languages and Literatures,* from 1932. Oriental languages dept., University of Chicago, from 1915.

"Spring." Poem by Richard Hovey, set to music by Frederic Field Bullard. Once a popular favorite with American college youth. The poem was first read at a college fraternity convention in 1896.

SPRING, LEVERETT WILSON (Jan. 5, 1840–Dec. 23, 1917); b. Grafton, Vt. Congregational clergyman, educator. *Kansas: The Prelude to the War for the Union* (1885); *Mark Hopkins* (1888); *A History of Williams College* (1917). Prof. English, Williams College, 1886–1909.

SPRING, SAMUEL. Author. *Giafar al Barmeki: A Tale of the Court of Haroun al Raschid* (1836), republished as, *The Rose of Persia; or, Giafar al Barmeki* (1847); *The Monk's Revenge; or, The Secret Enemy* (1847).

SPRINGER, REBECCA RUTER (Mrs. Rebecca William McKendree Springer) (Nov. 8, 1832–1904); b. Indianapolis, Ind. Poet, novelist. *Beechwood* (1873); *Self* (1881); *Songs by the Sea* (1889); *Intra Muros* (1898); *Marcus and Miriam* (1908).

SPRINGER, THOMAS GRANT (Dec. 26, 1873–); b. Sacramento, Calif. Author. *The Red Cord* (1925); *Coffee and Conspiracy* (1926); *Wild Game* (with Fleta C. Springer and Joseph Noel, 1932); *The Sagebrush Buckaroo* (1932); *Rodeo* (1935); *The Californian* (1936).

"Springfield Mountain." Ballad of New England, written late in the eighteenth century.

Springfield News. See *Springfield Republican.*

Springfield Republican. Springfield, Mass. Newspaper. Founded 1824, as a weekly, by Samuel Bowles. Became a daily in 1844. Editors have been Samuel Bowles, his son and grandson of the same name, Richard Hooker, and Waldo Linden Cook. Present editor is Walter R. Graham. Solomon Buckley Griffin (1852–1925) wrote the department "State and Local Topics." Other notable staff members have included Charles Goodrich Whiting, Franklin Benjamin Sanborn, Josiah Gilbert Holland, and Edward Smith King. Now combined with the *Springfield News,* founded 1880, published evenings, except Sunday; the *Springfield Union,* founded 1878, published mornings, except Sunday. The *Republican* appears only on Sunday. H. B. Hill is book review editor.

Springfield Union. See *Springfield Republican.*

SPRINGS, ELLIOTT WHITE (July 31, 1896–Oct. 16, 1959); b. Lancaster, S.C. Author. *Nocturne Militaire* (1927); *Leave Me with a Smile* (1928); *Contact* (1930); *In the Cool of the Evening* (1930); *Pent-Up in a Penthouse* (1931); *Clothes Make the Man* (1948). Editor: *War Birds* (1926).

SPRUNT, JAMES (June 9, 1846–July 9, 1924); b. Glasgow, Scot. Author. *Tales and Traditions of the Lower Cape Fear, 1661–1896* (1896); *Chronicles of the Cape Fear River* (1914); *Derelicts* (1920).

Spy, The. Novel by James Fenimore Cooper (1821). A tale of the American Revolution, with the spy Harvey Birch in a series of adventures behind the British lines, gathering information for General Washington, called William Harper in the book.

Squibob, John P. Pen name of George Horatio Derby.

Squibob Papers. By George Horatio Derby (1859). Humorous articles by the California editor.

SQUIER, EMMA-LINDSAY (Dec. 1, 1892–); b. Marion, Ind. Author. *The Wild Heart* (1922); *On the Human Trails* (1923); *The Bride of the Sacred Well, and Other Tales* (1928); *The Golden Trail* (1931); *Pirate Plunder* (1933); *Gringa: An American Woman in Mexico* (1934); etc.

SQUIER, E[phraim] G[eorge] (June 17, 1821–Apr. 17, 1888); b. Bethlehem, N.Y. Archaeologist, editor, diplomat. *Aboriginal Monuments of the State of New York* (1849); *Antiquities of the State of New York* (1851); *Serpent Symbols* (1852); *Nicaragua* (1852); *Notes on Central America* (1855); *Peru: Incidents and Explorations in the Land of the Incas* (1877); etc. Founder, *Poet's Magazine,* Albany, N.Y., 1842. Publisher, *Scioto Gazette,* Scioto, O. He was chief editor for the publishing house of Frank Leslie. Chargé d'affaires in Central America, 1849–50; Commissioner to Peru, 1863–65.

SQUIRES, JAMES DUANE (Nov. 9, 1904–); b. Grand Forks, N.D. Jurist, educator, author. *Mirror to America* (1952); *The Granite State: A History of New Hampshire, 1623–1955* (1956); *The Story of New Hampshire 1923–1955* (1956); *The Story of New Hampshire* (1964); *New Hampshire: A Student's Guide to Localized History* (1966); etc. Prof. history, Colby Junior College, since 1933.

SQUIRES, WILLIAM HENRY TAPPEY (Apr. 14, 1875–Apr. 20, 1948); b. Petersburg, Va. Presbyterian clergyman, author. *William Maxwell* (1918); *Peregrine Papers* (1923); *The Days of Yester-Year* (1928); *Through Centuries Three* (1929); *The Land of Decision* (1931); *Through the Years in Norfolk* (1937); etc.

Squirrel Cage, The. Problem novel by Dorothy Canfield Fisher (1912). Protest against the demands of social life, offering handicraft as a substitute.

St. For names and titles beginning with this abbreviation, *see* Saint.

STACE, WALTER TERENCE (Nov. 17, 1886–Aug. 2, 1967); b. London. Educator, author. *A Critical History of Greek Philosophy* (1920); *The Philosophy of Hegel* (1924); *The Meaning of Beauty* (1929); *The Concept of Morals* (1937); *The Nature of the World* (1940); *The Destiny of Western Man* (1942); *Gate of Silence* (1952); *Time and Eternity* (1952); *Mysticism and Philosophy* (1960); etc. Prof. philosophy, Princeton University, since 1932.

STACKPOLE, EDWARD JAMES (Jan. 18, 1861–Jan. 2, 1936); b. McVeytown, Pa. Editor, author. *Tales of My Boyhood* (1922); etc. With the *Harrisburg Telegraph,* since 1883; editor, since 1901.

STACKPOLE, EDWARD J[ames] (June 21, 1894–Oct. 1, 1967); b. Harrisburg, Pa. Publisher, author. *They Met at Gettysburg* (1956); *Drama on the Rappahannock: The Fredericksburg Campaign* (1957); *Chancellorsville, Lee's Greatest Battle* (1958). Pres. and director, Salesmen Telegraph Press, Harrisburg, Pa., from 1936; Military Service Publishing Co., from 1932.

STACTON, DAVID [Derek] (Apr. 25, 1925–); b. near Minden, Nev. *A Ride on a Tiger* (1954); *Dolores* (1954); *A Fox Inside* (1955); *The Self Enchanted* (1956); *Remember Me* (1957); *On a Balcony* (1958); *Segaki* (1959); *A Dancer in Darkness* (1962); *A Signal Victory* (1960); *Tom Fool* (1962); *Sir William* (1963); *The Judges of the Secret Court* (1964); *Old Acquaintance* (1964); *Kaliyuga: A Quarrel with the Gods* (1965); *People of the Book* (1965); *The Bonapartes* (1966); etc.

STAFFELBACH, ELMER HUBERT (July 29, 1893–); b. Pocahontas, Ill. Educator, author. *Stanford Speller* (with J. C. Almack, 1931); *Toward Oregon* (1946); *For Texas and Freedom* (1948); *Long Rifle Vanguard* (1953); etc. Prof. education, San José State College, 1926–58.

STAFFORD, JEAN (July 1, 1915–); b. Covina, Cal. Author. *Boston Adventure* (1944); *The Mountain Lion* (1947); *The Catherine Wheel* (1952); *Children Are Bored on Sunday* (1953); *A Mother in History* (1966); *Collected Stories* (1969); etc.

STAFFORD, MARIE AHNIGHITO [Peary] (Mrs. Edward Stafford) (Sept. 12, 1893–); b. in Greenland, daughter of Robert Edwin and Josephine Diebitsch Peary. Known as "the Snow Baby." Author. *Little Tooktoo* (1930); *The Red Caboose* (1932); *The Snowbaby's Own Story* (1934); *Ootah and His Puppies* (1942); *Discoverer of the North Pole* (1959); etc.

STAFFORD, RUSSELL HENRY (Apr. 4, 1890–); b. Wauwatosa, Wis. Congregational clergyman, author. *Finding God* (1923); *Christian Humanism* (1928); *Religion Meets the Modern Mind* (1934); *A Religion for Democracy* (1938); *We Would See Jesus* (1947); etc.

STAFFORD, THOMAS ALBERT (Apr. 23, 1885–); b. Enniskillen, N. Ire. Methodist church official, author. *The Pension Regulations of the Methodist Episcopal Church* (1934); *The Practice of His Presence* (1940); *Christian Symbolism in the Evangelical Churches* (1942); etc.

STAFFORD, WENDELL PHILLIPS (b. May 1, 1861); b. Barre, Vt. Jurist, poet. *North Flowers* (poems, 1902); *Dorian Days* (1909); *Speeches* (1913); *The Land We Love* (poems, 1916); *War Poems* (1917).

STAFFORD, WILLIAM EDGAR (June 17, 1914–); b. Hutchinson, Kan. Educator, author. *Down in My Heart* (1947); *West of Your City* (poems, 1960); *Traveling Through the Dark* (1962, National Book Award, 1963); *The Rescued Year* (poems, 1966); *Allegiances* (1970). Prof. English, Lewis and Clark College, since 1960.

Stagge, Jonathan. Pen name of Hugh Callingham Wheeler and R. Wilson Webb.

STAHL, JOHN M[eloy] (Aug. 24, 1860–Oct. 17, 1944); b. Mendon, Ill. Author. *Just Stories* (1916); *The Battle of Plattsburg* (1918); *"The Invasion of the City of Washington"* (1918); *Battle of New Orleans* (1930); *Growing with the West* (autobiography, 1930); etc.

STALLINGS, LAURENCE (Nov. 25, 1894–Feb. 28, 1968); b. Macon, Ga. Playwright. *Plumes* (1924); *What Price Glory?* (with Maxwell Anderson, prod. 1924); *The Buccaneer* (with same, prod. 1925); *First Flight* (with same, prod. 1925); *Deep River* (opera, music by Frank Harling, prod. 1926); *Rainbow* (music by Oscar Hammerstein II, prod. 1928); etc. Also screen plays. Editor: *The World War in Photographs Uncensored* (1934). See Fred B. Millett's *Contemporary American Authors* (1940).

STALLMAN, ROBERT WOOSTER (Sept. 27, 1911–); b. Milwaukee, Wis. Educator, author. *The House That James Built and Other Literary Studies* (1961). Editor: *Critiques and Essays in Criticism, 1920–48* (1949); *The Critic's Notebook* (1950); *Stephen Crane: An Omnibus* (1952); *Stephen Crane: Stories and Tales* (1955); *Seventeen American Poets* (1958); *The Art of Joseph Conrad* (1960); etc. Prof. English, University of Connecticut, since 1953.

STAMPP, KENNETH M[ilton] (July 12, 1912–); b. Milwaukee, Wis. Educator, author. *Indiana Politics During the Civil War* (1949); *And the War Came: The North and the Secession Crisis* (1950); *The Peculiar Institution* (1956); *The Era of Reconstruction 1865–1877* (1965). Editor: *The Causes of the Civil War* (1959). Prof. American history, University of California, since 1951.

STANARD, MARY [Mann Page] NEWTON (Mrs. William Glover Stanard) (Aug. 15, 1865–June 5, 1929); b. Westmoreland Co., Va. Virginia historian, author. *The Story of Bacon's Rebellion* (1907); *The Dreamer: A Romantic Rendering of the Life-Story of Edgar Allan Poe* (1909); *Colonial Virginia: Its People and Customs* (1917); *Richmond: Its People and Its Story* (1923); *The Story of Virginia's First Century* (1928); and biographies of several Virginians.

STANARD, WILLIAM GLOVER (Oct. 2, 1858–May 6, 1933); b. Richmond, Va. Antiquarian, editor, author. *Some Emigrants to Virginia* (1911); etc. Editor: *The Colonial Virginia Register* (1902). Corresponding secretary, Virginia Historical Society, and editor, the *Virginia Magazine of History and Biography,* 1898–1933.

"Stand Up, Stand Up for Jesus." Hymn by George Duffield (1858).

Standard Dictionary. Published by Funk and Wagnalls, New York (1893). Constantly revised and enlarged. F. H. Vizetelly, I. K. Funk, and Calvin Thomas were prominent editors of this American dictionary.

STANDING BEAR, LUTHER (Dec. 1868–); b. in So. Dakota. Sioux Indian chief, lecturer, author. *My People, the Sioux* (1928); *My Indian Boyhood* (1931); *Land of the Spotted Eagle* (1933); *Twenty True Stories* (1934).

Standish, Burt L. Pen name of Gilbert Patten.

STANFORD, ALFRED BOLLER (Mar. 12, 1900–); b. East Orange, N.J. Author. *The Ground Swell* (1923); *A City Out of the Sea* (1924); *Navigator: The Story of Nathaniel Bowditch of Salem* (1927); *Invitation to Danger* (1929); *Men, Fish and Boats* (1934); *Pleasures of Sailing* (1942); *Force Mulberry* (1951); *Mission in Sparrow Bush Lane* (1966); etc.

Stanford University Press. Stanford, Cal. Founded 1917. Publishes scholarly works.

Stanley, Chuck. Pen name of Charles Stanley Strong.

STANLEY, HIRAM ALONZO (b. Feb. 12, 1859); b. Vestal, N.Y. Author. *Rex Wayland's Fortune* (1898); *The Backwoodsman* (1902); *The Smugglers of Twin-Cove Rock* (1906); etc. Founder, the *Binghamton* (N.Y.) *Herald,* 1889.

STANLEY, SIR HENRY MORTON (1841–May 10, 1904); b. Denbigh, Wales. Explorer, author. *How I Found Livingstone* (1872); *Coomassia and Magdala* (1874); *Through the Dark Continent,* 2v. (1878); *The Congo and the Founding of Its Free State,* 2v. (1885); *In Darkest Africa,* 2v. (1890); *The Autobiography* (1909); etc.

STANOYEVICH, MILIVOY STOYAN (Feb. 14, 1882–); b. Koprivnitsa on Timok, Yugo. Educator, author. *Early Yugoslav Literature* (1922); *Modern Yugoslav Literature* (1923); *Slavonic Nations of Yesterday and Today* (1925); etc. Wrote many books in Slavonic languages and editor of many Yugoslav newspapers in the U.S.

STANTON, ELIZABETH CADY (Nov. 12, 1815–Oct. 26, 1902); b. Johnstown, N.Y. Reformer, author. *Eighty Years and More, 1815–1897* (1897). Compiler: *History of Woman Suffrage,* 6v. (with Susan B. Anthony and Matilda Joslyn Gage, 1881–1922). See Alma Lutz's *Created Equal: A Biography of Elizabeth Cady Stanton, 1815–1902* (1940).

STANTON, FRANK LEBBY (Feb. 22, 1857–Jan. 7, 1927); b. Charleston, S.C. Poet, editor. Called "The Riley of the South." *Songs of a Day and Songs of the Soil* (1892); *Comes One with a Song* (1898); *Songs from Dixie Land* (1900); *Up from Georgia* (1902); *Little Folks Down South* (1904); etc. On staff, *Atlanta Constitution,* conducting for many years a column entitled "Just from Georgia." His best known poems were "Mighty Lak a Rose," "Georgia Land," and "Just a Wearyin' for You." See Frank L. Stanton's *"Just from Georgia": Compiled by His Daughter* (1927).

STANTON, HENRY THROOP (June 30, 1834–May 7, 1899); b. Alexandria, Va. Lawyer, poet. *The Moneyless Man, and Other Poems* (1871); *Jacob Brown, and Other Poems* (1875); the two combined and augmented as *Poems of the Confederacy* (1900), and republished as *The Poetical Works* (1901).

STANTON, STEPHEN BERRIEN (b. Mar. 12, 1864); b. Detroit, Mich. Author. *The Essential Life* (1908); *Soul and Circumstance* (1910); *Foam Flowers* (poems, 1913); *Collected Poems* (1930); etc.

STANWOOD, EDWARD (Sept. 16, 1841–Oct. 11, 1923); b. Augusta, Me. Editor, author. *Boston Illustrated* (1872); *A History of Presidential Elections* (1884), augmented as, *A History of the Presidency* (1898). Editor, the *Boston Daily Advertiser,* 1867–83; *Youth's Companion,* 1887–1911.

STAPLES, WILLIAM READ (Oct. 10, 1798–Oct. 19, 1868); b. Providence, R.I. Librarian, historian. *Rhode Island in the Continental Congress* (1870); etc. Librarian, Rhode Island Historical Society, 1822–68.

STAPP, WILLIAM PRESTON, b. in Kentucky. Author. *The Prisoners of Perote* (1845).

Star Journal. New York. Dime novel magazine. Founded 1870, and published by Beadle & Adams. It was followed by *Beadle's Weekly* (1882–97). From 1886 this latter magazine bore the name *The Banner Weekly. See* Dime Novels.

"Star Spangled Banner, The." American national anthem. Written by Francis Scott Key, and first printed in the *Baltimore American,* Sept. 21, 1814. Key had boarded the British frigate *Surprise,* under a flag of truce, and was detained overnight during the bombardment of Fort McHenry. When he saw the United States flag still flying the next morning, he wrote the song as an expression of his feelings.

STARBUCK, GEORGE EDWIN (June 15, 1931–); b. Columbus, O. Poet. *Bone Thoughts* (1960); *White Paper* (1966). Prof., University of Iowa, since 1964.

STARBUCK, ROGER. Dime novelist. *The Golden Harpoon* (1865); *Cast Away* (1866); *Foul-Weather Jack* (1867); *The Blue Anchor* (1868); *The Rival Rovers* (1873); *The Slaver Captain* (1874); *The Boy Sea-Thugs* (1877); *The Black*

Schooner (1879); *Old Tar Knuckle and His Boy Chums* (1882); *The Phantom Light-House* (1884); *Dead-Shot Ike* (1890); *Frisky Frank in Idaho* (1890); etc. The dates are not necessarily those of first editions.

STARCH, DANIEL (Mar. 8, 1883–); b. La Crosse, Wis. Psychologist, author. *Experiments in Educational Psychology* (1911); *Advertising* (1914); *Educational Psychology* (1919); *Principles of Advertising* (1923); *Faith, Fear, and Fortunes* (1934); *How To Develop Your Executive Ability* (1943); *Measuring Advertising Readership and Results* (1966); etc. Lecturer on business psychology, Harvard University, 1919–26; etc.

STARK, PAUL CLARENCE (July 20, 1891–); b. Louisiana, Mo. Nurseryman, author. *Stark Orchard Book* (1913); *Stark Orchard and Spray Book* (1914); *Simplified Landscaping* (1916); etc.

Stark, Richard. Pen name of Donald E. Westlake.

STARR, BELLE (Feb. 5, 1848–Feb. 3, 1889); b. near Carthage, Mo. Notorious woman bandit of the southwest. *See* Richard K. Fox's *Belle Starr, the Bandit Queen; or, The Female Jesse James* (anon., 1889); S. W. Harmon's *Hell on the Border* (1898); Burton Rascoe's *Belle Starr, "The Bandit Queen"* (1941).

STARR, ELIZA ALLEN (Aug. 29, 1824–Sept. 7, 1901); b. Deerfield, Mass. Art critic, author. *Pilgrims and Shrines,* 2v. (1885); *Patron Saints,* 2 series (1871, 1881); *Songs of a Life Time* (1888); etc.

STARR, FREDERICK (Sept. 2, 1858–Aug. 14, 1933); b. Auburn, N.Y. Anthropologist, author. *Some First Steps in Human Progress* (1895); *American Indians* (1898); *Truths about the Congo* (1907); *In Indian Mexico* (1908); *Philippine Studies* (1909); *Filipino Riddles* (1909); *Liberia* (1913); *Fujiyama* (1924); etc. Compiler: *Readings from Modern Mexican Authors* (1904). Anthropology dept., University of Chicago, 1892–1923.

STARR, MARK (Apr. 27, 1894–); b. Shoscombe, England. Educator, author. *A Worker Looks at History* (1917); *A Worker Looks at Economics* (1925); *Lies and Hate in Education* (1928); *Labor in America* (with H. U. Faulkner, 1944); *Labor Looks at Education* (1946); *Labor Politics in the U.S.* (1949); etc.

STARRETT, VINCENT [Charles Vincent Emerson] (Oct. 26, 1886–); b. Toronto, Ont. Critic, editor, bibliophile, novelist. *Arthur Machen* (1918); *Estrays* (with others, 1918); *Ambrose Bierce* (1920); *The Unique Hamlet* (1920); *Ebony Flame* (1922); *Buried Caesars* (1923); *Persons from Porlock* (1923); *Murder on "B" Deck* (1929); *Penny Wise and Book Foolish* (1929); *The Blue Door* (1930); *The Private Life of Sherlock Holmes* (1933); *Exits and Entrances* (1933); *Oriental Encounters* (1938); *Books Alive* (1940); *Brillig* (1949); *Poems* (1951); *Best Loved Books of the Twentieth Century* (1956); *Book Column* (1958); *Born in a Bookshop* (1965); etc. Book columnist, *Sunday Chicago Tribune,* from 1942.

Stars and Stripes. Newspaper originally published by the American Expeditionary Force in France. Founded Feb. 1918. Guy T. Viskniskki, Harold Wallace Ross, Linton Lincoln Davies, John T. Winterich, Alexander Woollcott, Charles Phelps Cushing, Grantland Rice, and others were on the staff. Expired 1919. Revived in Washington, D.C., 1919–26, and again, 1942, in London, first as a weekly, then as a daily. During the course of World War II other editions appeared in various cities abroad. A beachhead edition was set up in Normandy less than two weeks after the invasion of Europe on June 6, 1944, but the plant was destroyed by bombs shortly afterward. Bill Mauldin's "Up Front" appeared in it, as well as George Baker's "Sad Sack."

"Stars and Stripes, The." Poem by Theodosia Garrison (1917).

Stars Fell on Alabama. By Carl Carmer (1934). A firsthand description of contemporary life in Alabama, with emphasis on the folk ways of the poor whites and Negroes, interspersed with songs, ballads, dialects, proverbs, superstitions, etc.

STASSEN, HAROLD EDWARD (Apr. 13, 1907–); b. West St. Paul, Minn. Lawyer, government official. *Where I Stand* (1947). Governor of Minnesota, 1939–45. Pres., University of Pennsylvania, 1948–53. Special assistant to the President for disarmament, 1955–58. With Stassen, Kephart, Sarkis and Scullin.

State Fair. Novel by Phil Stong (1932). Story of an Iowa farm family who enter a hog in the state fair exhibit and win a prize —with domestic issues hinging on the contest.

State of the Union. Play by Howard Lindsay and Russell Crouse (prod. 1945).

Status. New York. Founded 1965 by Igor Cassini. Absorbed in 1967 by *Diplomat* and published as *Status and Diplomat.* Name later reverted to *Status.* Bought by Curtis Publishing Co. in 1968. Concerned with all aspects of good living and social elegance.

STAUFFER, DAVID McNEELY (Mar. 24, 1845–Feb. 5, 1913); b. Richland, Pa. Civil engineer, collector, book-plate designer, author. *American Engravers Upon Copper and Steel,* 2v. (1907).

STEAD, WILLIAM HENRY (Jan. 22, 1899–June 12, 1959); b. Galesburg, Ill. Economist, author. *Democracy Against Unemployment* (1942); *The Tasks of Non-military Defense* (1955); *Fomento–The Economic Development of Puerto Rico* (1958).

Steamer. Pen name of Leonard Hastings Nason.

STEARNS, FRANK PRESTON (Jan. 4, 1846–Jan. 1917); b. Medford, Mass. Author. *The Real and the Ideal in Literature* (1892); *Life of Tintoretto* (1894); *The Midsummer of Italian Art* (1895); *Concord Sketches* (1895); *Modern English Prose Writers* (1897); *Life in Bismarck* (1899); *Napoleon and Machiavelli* (1903); *Cambridge Sketches* (1905); *The Life and Genius of Nathaniel Hawthorne* (1906); etc.

STEARNS, HAROLD EDMUND (May 7, 1891–Aug. 13, 1943); b. Barre, Mass. Author. *Liberalism in America* (1919); *America and the Young Intellectual* (1921); *Rediscovering America* (1934); *The Street I Know* (autobiography, 1935); *America: A Re-Appraisal* (1937). Editor: *America Now* (a symposium, 1939).

STEARNS, JOHN NEWTON (May 24, 1829–Apr. 21, 1895); b. New Ipswich, N.H. Temperance advocate, editor. Compiler: *Temperance Hymn-Book* (1869); *The Prohibition Songster* (1884); *Foot-Prints of Temperance Pioneers* (1885); etc. Editor, *National Temperance Advocate; National Temperance Almanac and Teetotaler's Year Book;* etc.

STEARNS, RAYMOND PHINEAS (Jan. 11, 1904–); b. Canton, Ill. Educator, author. *Introduction to World History, Man's Great Adventure* (with E. Pahlow, 1949); *The Strenuous Puritan: Hugh Peter, 1598–1660* (1954); *A History of the World,* 2v. (with others, 1960); etc. Editor: *The Pageant of Europe* (1947). Prof. history, University of Illinois, since 1948.

STEARNS, WILLIAM AUGUSTUS (Mar. 17, 1805–June 8, 1876); b. Bedford, Mass. Congregational clergyman, educator, author. *Life of Rev. Samuel H. Stearns* (1846); *Adjutant Stearns* (1862); etc. President, Amherst College, 1854–76. *See* W. S. Tyler's *A History of Amherst College* (1895).

STEBBINS, GEORGE LEDYARD, Jr. (Jan. 6, 1906–); b. Lawrence, N.Y. Educator. *Variation and Evolution in Plants* (1950); *The Human Organism and the World of Life* (with C. W. Young, 1951); *Processes of Organic Evolution* (1966); etc. Prof. genetics, University of California, since 1947.

STEDMAN, EDMUND CLARENCE (Oct. 8, 1833–Jan. 18, 1908); b. Hartford, Conn. Poet, editor. *Poems Lyrical and Idyllic* (1860); *Alice of Monmouth: An Idyl of the Great War; with Other Poems* (1864); *The Blameless Prince, and Other Poems* (1869); *Poems, Now First Collected* (1897); Editor: *Victorian Poets* (1875); *Poets of America*, 2v. (1885); *A Library of American Literature*, 11v. (1889–90); *The Works of Edgar Allan Poe*, 10v. (with George E. Woodberry, 1894–95); *A Victorian Anthology* (1837–1895); *An American Anthology, 1787–1899* (1900). See Laura Stedman and G. M. Gould's *Life and Letters of Edmund Clarence Stedman*, 2v. (1910).

STEDMAN, LAURA (Mrs. George Milbry Gould) (Feb. 18, 1881–); b. New York, granddaughter of Edmund Clarence Stedman. Editor: *The Poems of Edmund Clarence Stedman* (1908), *Life and Letters of Edmund Clarence Stedman*, 2v. (with husband, 1910); *Stedman's Genius and Other Essays* (with husband, 1911); etc.

STEEGER, HENRY (May 26, 1903–); b. New York. Publisher, editor. *You Can Remake America* (1969). Publisher and pres., Popular Publications, since 1930; pres. Fictioneers, Inc., 1939–58; All-Fiction Field, 1942–58; editor, *Argosy*, since 1946.

STEEGMULLER, FRANCIS (July 3, 1906–); b. New Haven, Conn. Author under own name and pen names "Byron Steel" and "David Keith": *O Rare Ben Jonson* (1928); *Java-Java* (1928); *Sir Francis Bacon* (1930); *The Musicale* (1930); *Flaubert and Madame Bovary* (1939); *A Matter of Iodine* (1940); *A Matter of Accent* (1943); *States of Grace* (1946); *French Follies and other Follies* (1946); *The Blue Harpsichord* (1949); *Maupassant: A Lion in the Path* (1949); *The Two Lives of James Jackson Jarves* (1951); *The Grand Mademoiselle* (1956); *The Christening Party* (1960); *Cocteau* (1970); etc. Editor: *The Selected Letters of Gustave Flaubert* (1954). Editor and Translator: *Flaubert's Intimate Notebook 1840-41.*

Steel, Byron. Pen name of Francis Steegmuller.

Steel, Kurt. Pen name of Rudolf Kagey.

STEELE, FREDERIC DORR (Aug. 6, 1873–July 6, 1944); b. Marquette, Mich. Illustrator. Worked under Edward Penfield. Illustrated for *Life, Century, Scribner's, Harper's, Collier's*, etc., and made illustrations for books by Frank S. Stockton, Richard Harding Davis, Mark Twain, Conan Doyle, Rudyard Kipling, Joseph Conrad, etc. See *The Colophon,* 1938.

STEELE, JAMES. Author. *Sons of the Border* (1873); *Old Californian Days* (1892); etc. Wrote for the *Kansas Magazine* under pen name "Deane Monahan."

STEELE, JAMES KING (June 30, 1875–Dec. 25, 1937); b. Keokuk, Ia. Author. *Wandering Feet* (1919); *Strange Beds* (1921); *Bits of Jade* (1923).

STEELE, JOHN LAWRENCE (June 9, 1917–); b. Chicago, Ill. Journalist. Editor: *The Private Papers of Senator Vandenberg* (with A. H. Vandenberg, Jr., and Joe A. Morris, 1952). Chief Washington bureau, *Time-Life*, since 1958.

STEELE, MAX. Author. *Debby* (1950); *The Cat and the Coffee Drinkers* (1969).

STEELE, RUFUS [Milas] (Mar. 3, 1877–Dec. 25, 1935); b. Hope, Ark. Author. *The City That Is* (1909); *The Fall of Ug* (Bohemian Grove play, pub. 1913); *Rule G* (1915); *Aces for Industry* (1919); *Scar Neck* (1930); etc.

STEELE, THOMAS SEDGWICK (June 11, 1845–1903); b. Hartford, Conn. Artist, author. *Canoe and Camera* (1880); *Paddle and Portage* (1882); *A Voyage to Viking-Land* (1896); etc.

STEELE, WILBUR DANIEL (Mar. 17, 1886–May 26, 1970); b. Greensboro, N.C. Author. *Storm* (1914); *Land's End, and Other Stories* (1918); *The Shame Dance, and Other Stories* (1923); *Taboo* (1925); *Meat* (1928); *Urkey Island* (1926); *The Man Who Saw Through Heaven, and Other Stories* (1927); *Tower of Sand, and Other Stories* (1929); *Diamond Wedding* (1931); *Post Road* (with Norma Mitchell, prod. 1934); *Sound of Rowlocks* (1938); *Their Town* (1952); *The Way to the Gold* (1955); etc. See Fred B. Millett's *Contemporary American Authors* (1940).

STEELE, WILLIAM OWEN (Dec. 22, 1917–); b. Franklin, Tenn. Author. *The Golden Root* (1951); *The Buffalo Knife* (1952); *Wilderness Journey* (1953); *Winter Danger* (1954); *Francis Marion* (1954); *Tomahawks and Trouble* (1955); *Davy Crockett's Earthquake* (1956); *De Soto, Child of the Sun* (1956); *The Lone Hunt* (1956); *Flaming Arrows* (1957); *The Perilous Road* (1958); *Andy Jackson's Waterwell* (1959); *The Far Frontier* (1959); *The Spooky Thing* (1960); *Westward Adventure: The True Stories of Six Pioneers* (1962); *The Year of the Bloody Sevens* (1963); *Wayah of the Real People* (1964); *The No Name Man of the Mountains* (1964); *Trail Through Danger* (1965); *Tomahawk Border* (1966); *The Old Wilderness Road: An American Journey* (1968); etc.

STEELL, WILLIS (1866–Jan. 31, 1941); b. Detroit, Mich. Author. *Isidra* (1888); *Benjamin Franklin of Paris* (1928); *In a Little Garden* (poems, 1935); etc.

STEENDAM, JACOB (1616–1672); b. in the Netherlands. First poet of New Netherlands. *Den Distelvink*, 3v. (poems, 1649–50); etc.

Steeplejack. By James G. Huneker, 2v. (1919). A frank autobiography of a critic who knew most of the celebrities in the art world of America and Europe.

STEEVES, HARRISON ROSS (Apr. 8, 1881); b. New York. Educator, author. *Learned Societies and English Scholarship* (1913); *Literary Aims and Art* (1927); *Good Night, Sheriff* (1941); *Before Jane Austen: The Shaping of the English Novel in the 18th Century* (1965). Co-author: *A College Program in Action* (1946). Editor: *Representative Essays in Modern Thought* (with F. H. Ristine, 1913); etc. English dept., Columbia University, from 1905; prof., 1926–49.

STEFÁNSSON, VILHJALMUR (Nov. 3, 1879–Aug. 26, 1962); b. Arnes, Manitoba, Can. Explorer, lecturer, author. *My Life with the Eskimo* (1913); *The Friendly Arctic* (1921); *Hunters of the Great North* (1922); *The Adventure of Wrangel Island* (1925); *Adventures in Error* (1936); *Unsolved Mysteries of the Arctic* (1938); *Iceland, the First American Republic* (1939); *Ultima Thule* (1940); *Greenland* (1942); *Arctic Manual* (1944); *Northwest to Fortune* (1958); *Cancer: Disease of Civilization?* (1960); etc. Editor: *Great Adventures and Explorations* (1947).

STEFFENS, LINCOLN (Apr. 6, 1866–Aug. 9, 1936); b. San Francisco, Calif. Editor, author. *The Shame of the Cities* (1904); *Upbuilders* (1909); *The Least of These* (1910); *Autobiography*, 2v. (1931); *Boy on Horseback* (1935); *The Letters of Lincoln Steffens*, 2v. (1938); etc. City editor, *New York Commercial Advertiser*, 1898–1902; managing editor, *McClure's Magazine*, 1902–06; assoc. editor, *American Magazine*, 1906–11, etc. He was one of the "Muckrakers."

STEGNER, PAGE (Jan. 31, 1937–   ); b. Salt Lake City, Utah. Educator, author. *Escape Into Aesthetics: The Art of Vladimir Nabokov* (1966); *The Edge* (1968). Faculty, University of California at Santa Cruz, since 1968.

STEGNER, WALLACE EARLE (Feb. 18, 1909–); b. near Lake Mills, Ia. Educator, author. *Remembering Laughter* (1937); *The Potter's House* (1938); *On a Darkling Plain* (1940); *The Big Rock Candy Mountain* (1943); *Second Growth* (1947); *The Women on the Wall* (1950); *Beyond the Hundredth Meridian* (1954); *The City of the Living* (1956); *A Shooting Star* (1961); *Wolf Willow* (1963); *The Gathering* of Zion (1964); *All the Little Live Things* (1967); *The Sound of Mountain Water* (1969); etc. English dept., Harvard University, 1939–45; prof., Stanford University, since 1945.

STEIG, WILLIAM (Nov. 14, 1907–); b. New York. Artist, wood sculptor, cartoonist, author. *About People* (1939); *The Lonely Ones* (1942); *All Embarrassed* (1944); *Small Fry* (1944); *Persistent Faces* (1945); *The Rejected Lovers* (1951); *Dreams of Glory* (1953); *Roland, the Minstrel Pig* (1968); *CDB* (1968); *Sylvester and the Magic Pebble* (1969); etc. His humorous drawings have appeared in *Life, New Yorker, Vanity Fair, Collier's, Judge,* etc.

STEIN, EVALEEN (Oct. 12, 1863–Dec. 11, 1923); b. Lafayette, Ind. Artist, poet, author of children's books. *One Way to the Woods* (poems, 1897); *Among the Trees Again* (1902); *Child Songs of Cheer* (1918); *A Little Shepherd of Provence* (1910); *The Little Count of Normandy* (1911); *Pepin: A Tale of Twelfth Night* (1914); *The Christmas Porringer* (1914); *Rosechen and the Wicked Magpie* (1917); *When Fairies Were Friendly* (1922); *The Circus Dwarf Stories* (1927); etc.

STEIN, GERTRUDE (Feb. 3, 1874–July 27, 1946); b. Allegheny, Pa. Author. *Three Lives* (1909); *Tender Buttons* (1914); *The Making of Americans* (1925); *Useful Knowledge* (1928); *Lucy Church Amiably* (1930); *Operas and Plays* (1932); *Matisse, Picasso, and Gertrude Stein* (1933); *The Autobiography of Alice B. Toklas* (1933); *Four Saints in Three Acts* (1934); *Lectures in America* (1935); *Narration* (1936); *Everybody's Autobiography* (1937); *Picasso* (1938); *The World . . . Is Round* (1939); *Paris France* (1940); *Wars I Have Seen* (1945); *Brewsie and Willie* (1946); *Four in America* (1947); *Blood on the Dining Room Floor* (1948); *Last Operas and Plays* (1949); etc. See W. G. Roger's *When This You See Remember Me* (1948); Elizabeth Sprigge's *Gertrude Stein, Her Life and Work* (1957); John Malcolm Brinnin's *The Third Rose: Gertrude Stein and Her World* (1959); Allegra Stewart's *Gertrude Stein and the Present* (1967); Norman Weinstein's *Gertrude Stein and the Literature of the Modern Consciousness* (1970).

STEIN, HAROLD (Oct. 21, 1902–May 8, 1966); b. New York. Political scientist, author. *Studies in Spenser's Complaints* (1933). Editor: *Public Administration and Policy Development* (1952); etc.

STEIN, HERBERT (Aug. 27, 1916–); b. Detroit, Mich. Economist. *U.S. Government Price Policy During the World War* (1938); *Jobs and Markets* (with others, 1946); *The Fiscal Revolution in America* (1969); etc. Editor: *Policies to Combat Depression* (1956).

STEIN, JACK MADISON (Apr. 25, 1914–); b. Newark, N.J. Educator, author. *Schnitzler-Kafka-Mann* (with Henry Hatfield, 1953); *Richard Wagner and the Synthesis of the Arts* (1960); *The German Scientific Heritage* (1962); etc. Prof. German, Harvard University, since 1958.

STEIN, ROBERT (Mar. 4, 1924–); b. New York. Assoc. editor, *Redbook,* 1953–58; editor-in-chief, 1958-65; editor-in-chief, McCall's Magazine, 1965–67; Director McCall's Book Division, since 1969.

Stein and Day Publishers. New York. Founded 1962. Publishes belles lettres, drama, science, and practical books. Sol Stein is president and editor-in-chief.

STEINBECK, JOHN [Ernst] (Feb. 27, 1902–Dec. 20, 1968); b. Salinas, Calif. Novelist. *Cup of Gold* (1929); *The Pastures of Heaven* (1932); *To a God Unknown* (1933); *Tortilla Flat* (1935); *In Dubious Battle* (1936); *Of Mice and Men* (1937); *The Red Pony* (1937); *The Long Valley* (1938); *The Grapes of Wrath* (1939, Pulitzer Prize novel, 1940); *The Moon Is Down* (1942); *Cannery Row* (1945); *The Wayward Bus* (1947); *A Russian Journal* (1948); *The Log from the Sea of Cortez* (1951); *East of Eden* (1952); *Sweet Thursday* (1954); *Pipe Dream* (prod. 1955); *The Short Reign of Pippin IV* (1957); *Once There Was a War* (1958); *The Winter of Our*

Discontent (1961); *Travels with Charley in Search of America* (1962); etc. See Harry Thornton Moore's *The Novels of John Steinbeck: A First Critical Study* (1939); Peter Lisca's *The Wide World of John Steinbeck* (1958).

STEINBERG, SAUL (June 15, 1914–); b. Ramnic-Sarat, Rum. Artist, illustrator. Author of books of drawings: *All in Line* (1945); *The Art of Living* (1949); *Passport* (1954); *The Labyrinth* (1960); *New World* (1965); etc.

STEINCROHN, PETER JOSEPH (Nov. 28, 1899–); b. Hartford, Conn. Physician, author. *More Years for the Asking* (1940); *How to Keep Fit Without Exercise* (1942); *Heart Disease Is Curable* (1943); *How to Stop Killing Yourself* (1950); *How to Master Your Fears* (1952); *A Doctor Looks at Life* (1953); *Live Longer and Enjoy It* (1956); *You Can Increase Your Heart Power* (1958); *Your Life to Enjoy* (1963); *Common Sense Coronary Care and Prevention* (1963); *You Live As You Breathe* (1967); *How To Get A Good Night's Sleep* (1968); *How to Be Lazy, Healthy and Fit* (1969); *Your Heart is Stronger Than You Think* (1970); etc.

STEINEM, GLORIA (Mar. 25, 1936–   ); b. Toledo, Ohio. Author. *The Thousand Indias* (1957); *The Beach Book* (1963). Writer for various publications, TV panelist, etc.

STEINER, BERNARD CHRISTIAN (Aug. 13, 1867–Jan. 12, 1926); b. Guilford, Conn. Librarian, author. *Life of Roger Brooke Taney* (1922); etc. Editor, *Maryland Archives,* vols. 18, 36–45. Librarian, Enoch Pratt Free Library, Baltimore, 1892–1926.

STEINER, H. ARTHUR (Feb. 22, 1905–); b. St. Louis, Mo. Political scientist, author. *Government in Fascist Italy* (1938); *Principles and Problems of International Relations* (1940); *Communist China in the World Community* (1961); etc. Editor: *Maoism: A Source Book* (1952). Prof. political science, University of California at Los Angeles, since 1947.

STEINER, JESSE FREDERICK (Feb. 25, 1880–); b. St. Paris, O. Educator, author. *The North Carolina Chain Gang* (1927); *Americans at Play* (1933); *Recreation in the Depression* (1937); *Behind the Japanese Mask* (1943). Prof. sociology, University of Washington, since 1931.

STEINER, LEE R[abinowitz] (Nov. 18, 1901–); b. New York. Author. *Where Do People Take Their Troubles?* (1945); *A Practical Guide for Troubled People* (1952); *Make the Most of Yourself* (1954); *Understanding Juvenile Delinquency* (1960); *Romantic Marriage: The Twentieth Century Illusion* (1964); etc.

STEINER, STANLEY. Author. *The New Indians* (1968); *La Raza: The Mexican Americans* (1970).

STEINER, WILLIAM HOWARD (Dec. 30, 1894–June 2, 1966); b. New York. Economist, author. *Some Aspects of Banking Theory* (1920); *The Mechanism of Commercial Credit* (1922); *Investment Trusts: American Experience* (1929); *Money and Banking* (1933); *Credits and Collections* (with H. S. Kane, 1950).

STEINHAEUSER, WALTER PHILIP (Aug. 10, 1878–); b. Coshocton, N.Y. Educator, author. Pen name, "S. P. Retlaw." *Selected Love Sonnets* (1933); etc. Editor, *Camp News,* 1898–1922; with *Baldwin's Monthly, Overland Magazine,* etc. President, Le Master Institute, since 1926.

STEINMAN, DAVID BARNARD (June 11, 1886–Aug. 22, 1960); b. New York. Bridge engineer, author. *Famous Bridges of the World* (1953); *Miracle Bridge at Mackinac* (with J. T. Nevill, 1957).

Stella. Pen name of Estelle Anna Lewis.

Stelligeri. By Barrett Wendell (1893). Contains a sketch of James Russell Lowell as a teacher of Dante at Harvard University, and other literary reminiscences. Name means those bearing stars, i.e., the dead.

STELZLE, CHARLES (June 4, 1869–Feb. 27, 1941); b. New York. Presbyterian clergyman, sociologist, author. *Boys of the Street* (1904); *Letters from a Working Man* (1908); *Church and Labor* (1910); *A Son of the Bowery* (autobiography, 1926); etc.

STEPANCHEV, STEPHEN (1915–   ); b. in Yugoslavia. Educator, critic, poet. *American Poetry Since 1945* (1965); *Spring in the Harbor* (poems, 1967); *A Man Running in the Rain* (1969). English dept., Queens College, New York.

STEPHENS, ALEXANDER HAMILTON (Feb 11, 1812–Mar. 4, 1883); b. in Wilkes (now Taliaferro) Co., Ga. Statesman, author. *A Constitutional View of the Late War between the States,* 2v. (1868–70); etc. Congressman, 1843–59, 1873–82; Vice-President, Confederate States of America, 1861–65. *See* Eudora R. Richardson's *Little Aleck* (1932).

STEPHENS, ANN S[ophia] Winterbotham (1813–Aug. 20, 1886); b. Derby, Conn. Editor, novelist. *High Life in New York* (under pen name "Jonathan Slick," 1843); *Alice Copley* (1844); *David Hunt, and Malina Gray* (1845); *The Tradesman's Boast* (1846); *The Diamond Necklace, and Other Tales* (1846); *Fashion and Famine* (1854); *The Old Homestead* (1855); *Malaeska* (1860), first of the Beadle *Dime Novels; The Rejected Wife* (1863); *Ahmo's Plot* (1863); *The Indian Queen* (1864); etc. Founder, *Portland Magazine,* 1834; *Mrs. Stephens' Illustrated New Monthly,* 1856. On editorial staff, *Peterson's Magazine; Brother Jonathan; Lady's Wreath,* etc.

STEPHENS, CHARLES ASBURY (Oct. 21, 1844–Sept. 22, 1931); b. Norway Lake, Me. Author. *Lynx Hunting* (1872); *Left on Labrador* (1872); *On the Amazons* (1872); *The Knockabout Club Alongshore* (1882); *Living Matter* (1888); *Pluri-cellular Man* (1892); *When Life Was Young* (1912); *Stories of My Home Folks* (1926); *Katahdin Camps* (1928); etc. He wrote over 3,000 short stories and over 100 serials. On staff, *Youth's Companion,* 1870–1929.

STEPHENS, EDWIN WILLIAM (Jan. 21, 1849–May 22, 1931); b. Columbia, Mo. Publisher, author. *Around the World* (1909). Editor and publisher, the *Columbia Herald,* Columbia, Mo., 1870–1905. Founder, the publishing house of E. W. Stephens Co., Jefferson City, Mo.

STEPHENS, HENRY MORSE (Oct. 3, 1857–Apr. 16, 1919); b. Edinburgh. Educator, author. *A History of the French Revolution,* 2v. (1886–91); *The Story of Portugal* (1891); *Revolutionary Europe, 1789–1815* (1893); etc. A founder of the *American Historical Review,* 1895. Prof. history, University of California, 1902–19.

STEPHENS, JOHN LLOYD (Nov. 28, 1805–Oct. 12, 1852); b. Shrewsbury, N.J. Traveler, author. *Incidents of Travel in Egypt, Arabia Petraea, and the Holy Land,* 2v. (1837); *Incidents of Travel in Greece, Turkey, Russia, and Poland,* 2v. (1838); *Incidents of Travel in Central America, Chiapas, and Yucatan,* 2v. (1841), to which were added as supplementary volumes, *Incidents of Travel in Yucatan,* 2v. (1843).

STEPHENS, KATE (Feb. 27, 1853–May 10, 1938); b. Moravia, N.Y. Author. *American Thumb-Prints* (1905); *A Woman's Heart* (1906); *Delphic Kansas* (1911); *The Greek Spirit* (1914); *Life at Laurel Town: In Anglo-Saxon Kansas* (1920); *A Curious History in Book-Editing* (1927); *Lies and Libels of Frank Harris* (1929); etc. Editor, *The Love Life of Bryon Caldwell Smith* (1930); *Stories From Old Chronicles* (1909); etc. Greek dept., University of Kansas, 1878–85.

STEPHENS, ROBERT NEILSON (July 22, 1867–1906); b. New Bloomfield, N.J. Novelist, playwright. *An Enemy to the King* (prod. 1896); *The Ragged Regiment* (prod. 1898); *The Continental Dragoon* (1898); *Philip Winwood* (1900); *Captain Ravenshaw* (1901).

STEPHENSON, GENEVA; b. Portsmouth, Ohio. Novelist. *Spring Journey* (1939); *Melody in Darkness* (1943).

STEPHENSON, GEORGE MALCOLM (Dec. 30, 1883–Oct. 11, 1958); b. Olds, Ia. Educator, author. *Political History of the Public Lands* (1917); *History of American Immigration* (1926); *John Lind of Minnesota* (1935); *American History Since 1865* (1939); *American History to 1865* (1940); *Puritan Heritage* (1952); *Pilgrim and Stranger* (1953); *America's Major Prophetess: Harriet Beecher Stowe* (1953); etc. History dept., University of Minnesota, 1914–52.

STEPHENSON, HENRY THEW (Apr. 22, 1870–); b. Cincinnati, O. Educator, author. *The Fickle Wheel* (1901); *Shakespeare's London* (1905); *The Elizabethan People* (1910); *The Study of Shakespeare* (1915); *The Ettrick Shepherd* (1922); etc. English dept., Indiana University, from 1895.

STEPHENSON, HOWARD (Sept. 2, 1903–); b. Indianapolis, Ind. Author. *Glass* (1934); *They Sold Themselves* (with Joseph C. Keeley, 1937); *The Art of Being a Boss* (1946); *Publicity for Prestige and Profit* (with Wesley F. Pratzner, 1954). Editor-in-chief: *Public Relations Handbook* (1959).

STEPHENSON, NATHANIEL WRIGHT (July 10, 1867–Jan. 17, 1935); b. Cincinnati, O. Educator, author. *The Beautiful Mrs. Moulton* (1902); *Abraham Lincoln and the Union* (1918); *Texas and the Mexican War* (1921); *Lincoln* (1922); *Nelson W. Aldrich* (1930); *A History of the American People* (1934); etc. Prof. history, College of Charleston, 1902–23; Scripps College, 1927–35.

STEPHENSON, WENDELL HOLMES (Mar. 13, 1899–); b. Cartersburg, Ind. Educator, editor, author. *The Political Career of General James H. Lane* (1930); *Alexander Porter, Whig Planter of Old Louisiana* (1934); *Isaac Franklin, Slave Trader and Planter of the Old South* (1938); *Southern Lives in History* (1955); *A Basic History of the Old South* (1959); *Southern History in the Making* (1964). Editor: C. W. Ramsdell's *Behind the Lines in the Southern Confederacy* (1944). Editor, *Journal of Southern History,* 1935–41. History dept., Louisiana State University, 1927–45; Tulane University, 1946–53; University of Oregon, since 1953.

STERLING, ADA (1870–Sept. 1, 1939); b. near Holyoke, Mass. Author. *A Lucky Man* (1912); *Mary Queen of Scots* (poems, 1921); *Lions and Lambs* (1921); *Nica* (1924); *The Jew and Civilization* (1924); etc. Editor: *A Belle of the Fifties* (1904).

STERLING, CHARLES F. Novelist. *Buff and Blue; or, The Privateers of the Revolution* (1847); *The Red Coats; or, The Sack of Unquowa* (1848).

STERLING, GEORGE (Dec. 1, 1869–Nov. 17, 1926); b. Sag Harbor, N.Y. Poet. *The House of Orchid, and Other Poems* (1911); *The Caged Eagle* (1916); *Rosamund* (1920); *Lilith* (1920); *Sails and Mirrors, and Other Poems* (1921); *Selected Poems* (1923); *Robinson Jeffers, the Man and the Artist* (1926); *Sonnets to Craig* (1928); *Poems to Vera* (1938); etc. Editor: *Continent's End* (1925). Among his best known poems are "Autumn in Carmel," "Spring in Carmel," "Willy Pitcher," "The Last Days," and "Beyond the Breakers."

STERLING, JAMES (c. 1701–Nov. 10, 1763); b. Dowrass, Kings Co., Ire. Anglican clergyman, poet, playwright. *The Rival Generals* (prod. 1722); *The Parricide* (prod. 1736); *An Epistle to the Hon. Arthur Dobbs* (poem, 1752); etc. Wrote poems for the *American Magazine* and the *Maryland Gazette,* etc.

STERLING, SARA HAWKS, b. Philadelphia, Pa. Author. *Shakespeare's Sweetheart* (1905); *A Lady of King Arthur's Court* (1907); *Robin Hood and His Merry Men* (1920); etc.

STERN, DAVID, III (Sept. 2, 1909–); b. Philadelphia, Pa. Journalist, publisher, author. *Francis* (1946); *Stop Press Murder* (1947); *Francis Goes to Washington* (1948); and screenplays. Publisher, *Camden Courier Post,* 1939–47; *New Orleans Item,* 1949–58; *Philadelphia Daily News,* 1957–58.

STERN, EDITH MENDEL (June 24, 1901–); b. New York. Author. *Mental Illness: A Guide for the Family* (1942; rev. ed. 1968); *The Housemother's Guide* (1947); *The Handicapped Child: A Guide for Parents* (1950); *You and Your Aging Parents* (1952); *Notes for After Fifty* (1955); *A Full Life After 65* (1963); etc.

STERN, ELIZABETH (Eleanor Morton) (1890–Jan. 9, 1954); b. in Poland. Novelist. Pen name "Leah Morton." Under own name: *My Mother and I* (1917); *A Friend at Court* (with Leon Stern, 1923); *This Ecstasy* (1927); *A Marriage Was Made* (1928); *Josiah White, Prince of Pioneers* (1947); *Women Behind Gandhi* (1954); also, under pen name: *I Am a Woman and a Jew* (1926); *When Love Comes to Woman* (1929); etc.

STERN, FRITZ (Feb. 2, 1926–   ); b. Breslau, Ger. Educator, author. *The Politics of Cultural Despair: A Study of the Germanic Ideology* (1961). Editor: *The Varieties of History from Voltaire to the Present* (1956). Prof. history, Columbia University, since 1953.

STERN, GLADYS BERTHA (June 17, 1890–); b. London. Author. *The Reasonable Shores* (1946); *The Donkey Shoe* (1953); *For All We Know* (1956); *And Did He Stop and Speak to You?* (1958); *Travels with a Donkey* (1959); *Unless I Marry* (1959); *One is Only Human, Bernadette* (1960); etc.

STERN, JULIUS DAVID (Apr. 1, 1886–); b. Philadelphia, Pa. Editor, publisher. *Eidolon* (1952); *Memoirs of a Maverick Publisher* (1962). Until 1947, publisher of *New Brunswick Times, Springfield News, Springfield Record, Camden Evening Courier, Camden Morning Post, Philadelphia Record, New York Post.*

STERN, PHILIP MAURICE (May 24, 1926–); b. New York. Author. *The Great Treasury Raid* (with H. Stern, 1964); *The Shame of a Nation* (1965); *Oh, Say Can You See: A Bifocal Tour of Washington* (with H. Stern and G. de Vincent, 1968); *The Oppenheimer Case: Security on Trial* (with H. P. Green, 1969).

STERN, PHILIP VAN DOREN (Sept. 10, 1900–); b. Wyalusing, Pa. Publisher, designer, author. *An Introduction to Typography* (1932); *The Breathless Moment* (with Herbert Asbury, 1935); *The Thing in the Brook* (under pen name, "Peter Storme," 1936); *The Man Who Killed Lincoln* (1939); *The Midnight Reader* (ed., 1942); *The Greatest Gift* (1944); *Travelers in Time* (ed., 1947); *Our Constitution* (1953); *Tin Lizzie, the Story of the Fabulous Model-T Ford* (1955); *An End to Valor: The Last Days of the Civil War* (1958); *Secret Missions of the Civil War* (1959); *They Were There: The Civil War in Action as Seen by Its Combat Artists* (1959); *Prologue to Sumter* (1961); *The Confederate Navy: A Pictorial History* (1962); *Robert E. Lee, The Man and The Soldier* (1963); *The Annotated Uncle Tom's Cabin* (1964); *When the Guns Roared: World Aspects of the American Civil War* (1965); *Beyond Paris: A Touring Guide to the French Provinces* (with Lillian D. Stern, 1967); *Prehistoric Europe From Stone Age Man to Early Greeks* (1969); etc.

STERN, RENÉE B[ernd] (c. 1875–May 19, 1940); b. Philadelphia, Pa. Editor, librarian, author. *Neighborhood Entertainments* (1910); *The Standard Letter Writer* (1925); *Clubs, Making and Management* (1927); etc. Editor, *Woman's Weekly;* asst. editor, *Mother's Magazine;* woman's editor, *Philadelphia Record,* 1932–39.

STERN, RICHARD GUSTAVE (Feb. 25, 1928–); b. New York. Educator, author. *Golk* (1960); *Europe or Up and Down with Baggish and Schreiber* (1961); *In Any Case* (1961); *Teeth, Dying and Other Matters* (1964); *Stitch* (1965). Editor: *Honey and Wax* (1966). Prof. English, University of Chicago, since 1965.

STERN, RICHARD MARTIN (Mar. 17, 1915–); b. Fresno, Cal. Author. *The Bright Road to Fear* (1958); *Suspense* (1959); *The Search for Tabitha Carr* (1960); *Those Unlucky*

Deeds (1961); *High Hazard* (1962); *Cry Havoc* (1963); *Right Hand, Opposite* (1964); *I Hide, We Seek* (1965); *The Kessler Legacy* (1967); *Manuscript for Murder* (1970).

STERNBERG, HARRY (July 19, 1904–); b. New York. Artist, author. *Silk Screen Color Printing* (1942); *Modern Methods and Materials of Etching* (1949); *Compositions* (1957); *Modern Drawing* (1958); *Woodcut* (1962).

STERNE, ELAINE (1894–); b. New York. Author. *Sunny Jim* (1916); *The Road of Ambition* (1917). Editor: *Over the Seas for Uncle Sam* (1918).

STERNE, EMMA GELDERS (Mrs. Roy M. Sterne) (May 13, 1894–); b. Birmingham, Ala. Author. *White Swallow* (1927); *Loud Sing Cuckoo* (1930); *The Calico Ball* (1934); *Drums of Monmouth* (1935); *Miranda Is a Princess* (1937); *Some Plant Olive Trees* (1937); *European Summer* (1938); *The Pirate of Chatham Square* (1939); *We Live to Be Free* (1941); *Printer's Devil* (1952); *Let the Moon Go By* (1955); *The Sea* (1959); *Benito Juarez: Master Builder of a Nation* (1967); *They Took Their Stand* (1968); etc.

Sterne, Stuart. Pen name of Gertrude Bloede.

STERRETT, FRANCES ROBERTA (1869–Nov. 11, 1947); b. Red Wing, Minn. Author. *Up the Road with Sallie* (1915); *Mary Rose of Mifflin* (1916); *Rebecca's Promise* (1919); *The Amazing Inheritance* (1922); *Sophie* (1927); *Rusty of Tall Pines* (1929); *Rusty of the Meadow Lands* (1931); *Years of Achievement* (1932); etc.

STERRETT, JOHN ROBERT SITLINGTON (Mar. 4, 1851–June 15, 1914); b. Rockbridge Baths, Va. Archaeologist, educator. *An Epigraphical Journey in Asia Minor* (1888); *The Wolfe Expedition to Asia Minor* (1888); *Leaflets from the Notebooks of an Archaelogical Traveler* (1889); *The Torch-Race at Athens* (1902); etc. Prof. Greek, Amherst College, 1892–1901; Cornell University, 1901–14.

STETSON, HARLAN TRUE (June 28, 1885–Sept. 16, 1964); b. Haverhill, Mass. Astronomer, geophysicist, author. *Man and the Stars* (1930); *Earth, Radio and the Stars* (1934); *Sunspots and Their Effects* (1937); *Sunspots in Action* (1947); etc. Prof. astronomy, Ohio Wesleyan University, 1929–34; research associate, Massachusetts Institute of Technology, 1936–49.

Stetson, Mrs. Charlotte Perkins. See Charlotte Perkins Gilman.

Stetson, Mrs. Charles Walter. See Grace Ellery Channing.

STEVENS, ABEL (Jan. 17, 1815–Sept. 11, 1897); b. Philadelphia, Pa. Methodist clergyman, editor, author. *Sketches & Incidents,* 2v. (1844–45); *Tales from the Parsonage* (1846); *Life and Times of Nathan Bangs,* 2v. (1863); *History of the Methodist Episcopal Church in the United States,* 2v. (1864, augmented to 4v. 1866–67); *Madame de Staël,* 2v. (1881); etc. Editor, *Zion's Herald,* 1840–52, the *National Magazine,* 1852–56, etc.

STEVENS, ALDEN (July 1, 1907–Apr. 28, 1968); b. Chicago, Ill. Author. *Dove Creek Rodeo* (1936); *Arms and the People* (1942); *Victory Without Peace* (with Roger Burlingame, 1944); *Mobil Travel Guides* (with Marion Alden, revised annually).

STEVENS, ASHTON (Aug. 11, 1872–July 11, 1951); b. San Francisco, Calif. Dramatic critic, author. *Mary's Way Out* (with Charles Michelson, prod. 1918); *Actorviews: Intimate Portraits* (1923); *The Colonel's Lady* (with Gene Markey, 1948); etc. Drama critic, the *Chicago Herald and Examiner,* 1910–32; the *Chicago Herald-American,* from 1932.

STEVENS, BARBARA BAGG (Dec. 5, 1901–); b. West Springfield, Mass. Author. *Walk Humbly* (1935); *The Strongest Son* (1938).

STEVENS, BENJAMIN FRANKLIN (Feb. 19, 1833–Mar. 5, 1902); b. Barnet, Vt., brother of Henry Stevens. Bookseller, bibliographer. *Introduction to the Catalogue Index of Manuscripts in the Archives of England, France, Holland, and Spain Relating to America, 1763 to 1783* (1902), an index in 180 manuscript volumes now deposited in the Library of Congress; *Report on American Manuscripts in the Royal Institution of Great Britain,* ed. by H. J. Brown, 4v. (1904–09); etc. He also printed facsimiles of many valuable manuscripts relating to America in 25 vols. (1889–98). He was a London bookseller and agent for American libraries, 1860–1902.

STEVENS, DAVID HARRISON (Dec. 20, 1884–); b. Berlin, Wis. Educator, author. *Types of English Drama* (1923); *College Composition* (1927); *A Reference Guide to Milton from 1800 to the Present Day* (1929; rev. ed. 1967); *The Changing Humanities: An Appraisal of Old Values and New Uses* (1953); etc. Editor: *Ten Talents in the American Theatre* (1957). *Party Politics & English Journalism 1702–1742* (1967); English dept., University of Chicago, 1914–30. With Rockefeller Foundation, 1932–50.

STEVENS, DAVID [Kilburn] (Aug. 12, 1860–June 29, 1946); b. Fitchburg, Mass. Editor, author. *Lays of a Lazy Dog by Teddy* (poems, 1909); *The Lyrics of Eliza* (poems, 1911); *Azora, the Daughter of Montezuma* (1917); also librettos. With C. C. Birchard & Co., Publishers, from 1914.

STEVENS, EDMUND WILLIAM (July 22, 1910–); b. Denver, Col. Journalist, author. *Russia Is No Riddle* (1945); *This Is Russia Uncensored* (1950); *North Africa Powder Keg* (1955). With *Christian Science Monitor,* from 1939; chief, Moscow bureau, *Time and Life,* since 1958.

STEVENS, GEORGE (Feb. 20, 1904–); b. Atlanta, Ga. Publisher. *Lincoln's Doctor's Dog* (1939). Vice-president, W. W. Norton & Co., 1929–33; managing editor, *Saturday Review of Literature,* 1933–38; editor, 1938–40; director, J. B. Lippincott Co., since 1940.

STEVENS, GEORGE WASHINGTON (Jan. 16, 1866–Oct. 29, 1926); b. Utica, N.Y. Museum director, poet. *The King and the Harper, together with Other Poems* (1900); *Things* (1902). Director, Toledo Museum of Art, 1903–26.

STEVENS, HALSEY (Dec. 3, 1908–); b. Scott, N.Y. Composer, educator. *The Life and Music of Bela Bartok* (1953). Prof. music, University of Southern California, since 1951.

STEVENS, HENRY (Aug. 24, 1819–Feb. 28, 1886); b. Barnet, Vt. Bookman, author. *Historical Nuggets* (1862); *Bibliotheca Historica* (1870); *Recollections of Mr. James Lenox of New York and the Formation of His Library* (1886); etc. He collected books for John Carter Brown, James Lenox, the Library of Congress, etc. His brother, Benjamin Franklin Stevens (1833–1902), was also a book collector of note, and published many facsimiles of documents relating to America in foreign archives. *See* F. P. Wells's *History of Barnet, Vt.* (1923).

STEVENS, HENRY BAILEY (July 13, 1891–); b. Hooksett, N.H. Playwright, editor, author. *A Cry Out of the Dark* (1919); *Tolstoy* (1928); *Johnny Appleseed and Paul Bunyan* (1930); *Rediscovery of Culture* (1951).

STEVENS, JAMES [Floyd] (Nov. 15, 1892–); b. Albia, Ia. Author. *Paul Bunyan* (1925); *Brawnyman* (1926); *Mattock* (1927); *Homer in the Sagebrush* (1928); *The Saginaw Paul Bunyan* (1932); *Timber!* (1942); *Paul Bunyan's Bears* (1947); *Big Jim Turner* (1948); *Tree Treasure* (1950); *Green Power* (1958); etc.

STEVENS, JOHN AUSTIN (Jan. 21, 1827–June 16, 1910); b. New York. Financier, author. *The Valley of the Rio Grande* (1864); *Progress of New York in a Century, 1776–1876* (1876); *The Burgoyne Campaign* (1877); *Albert Gallatin* (1884); etc. Founder, the *Magazine of American History,* 1877; editor, 1877–81. He contributed several chapters to the

Memorial History of the City of New York, ed. by James Grant Wilson, 4v. (1892–93).

STEVENS, LOUIS (Jan. 6, 1899–   ); b. in South Ukraine. Novelist. *All the King's Horses* (1928); *Here Comes Pancho Villa* (1932); *Days of Promise* (1948); etc.

STEVENS, ROBERT SPROULE (May 29, 1888–Nov. 17, 1968); b. Attica, N.Y. Educator, author. *Stevens on Corporations* (1936); *Cases and Materials on the Law of Corporations* (with A. Larson, 1947); etc. Prof. law, Cornell University, 1921–54.

STEVENS, S[tanley] SMITH (Nov. 4, 1906–); b. Ogden, Utah. Psychologist. *Hearing: Its Psychology and Physiology* (with Hallowell Davis, 1938); *The Varieties of Human Physique* (with others, 1940); *The Varieties of Temperament* (with W. H. Sheldon, 1942); *Sound and Hearing* (with F. Warshofsky, 1965). Editor: *Handbook of Experimental Psychology* (1951).

STEVENS, SYLVESTER K[irby] (July 10, 1904–); b. Harrison Valley, Pa. Historian, author. *American Expansion in Hawaii, 1842–1898* (1945); *Pennsylvania—Titan of Industry* (1948); *Exploring Pennsylvania* (with others, 1953); etc. Editor: *Pennsylvania, Keystone of Democracy,* 2v. (1956).

STEVENS, THOMAS (Dec. 24, 1855–); b. Great Berkhamstead, Herts., Eng. Bicyclist, correspondent, author. *Around the World on a Bicycle,* 2v. (1887–88); *Scouting for Stanley in East Africa* (1890); *Through Russia on a Mustang* (1891); etc. He was a representative of the *New York World* during the search for Livingstone in Africa, and was the Richard Halliburton of his day.

STEVENS, THOMAS WOOD (Jan. 26, 1880–Jan. 29, 1942); b. Daysville, Ogle Co., Ill. Author. *The Morning Road* (poems, 1902); *Masques of East and West* (with Kenneth Sawyer Goodman, 1914); *The Theatre from Athens to Broadway* (1932); *Westward Under Vega* (poem, 1938); and numerous pageants.

STEVENS, WALLACE (1879–Aug. 2, 1955); b. Reading, Pa. Poet. *Harmonium* (1923); *Ideas of Order* (1935); *Owl's Clover* (1936); *The Man with the Blue Guitar, and Other Poems* (1937); *Parts of a World* (1942); *Notes Toward a Supreme Fiction* (1942); *Esthétique du Mal* (1944); *Transport to Summer* (1947); *Three Academic Pieces* (1947); *A Primitive Like an Orb* (1948); *Auroras of Autumn* (1950); *The Necessary Angel* (1951); *Collected Poems* (1954); *Opus Posthumous* (1957). *See* William Van O'Connor's *The Shaping Spirit: A Study of Wallace Stevens* (1950); Daniel Fuchs's *The Comic Spirit of Wallace Stevens* (1963); Joseph Riddle's *The Clairvoyant Eye: The Poetry and Poetics of Wallace Stevens* (1965); R. H. Pearce's and J. H. Miller's *The Act of the Mind: Essays on the Poetry of Wallace Stevens* (1966); Samuel French Morse's *Wallace Stevens: Life As Poetry* (1970).

STEVENS, WALTER BARLOW (July 25, 1848–Aug. 28, 1939); b. Meriden, Conn. Author. *Through Texas* (1892); *The Ozark Uplift* (1900); *A Trip to Panama* (1907); *Missouri the Center State, 1821–1915,* 4v. (1915); *St. Louis, the Fourth City, 1764–1911,* 2v. (1911); *Lincoln and Missouri* (1916); *Centennial History of Missouri,* 4v. (1921), etc.

STEVENS, WILLIAM (1925–   ). Author. *Peddler* (1966); *The Gunner* (1968); *The Cannibal Isle* (1970).

STEVENS, WILLIAM BACON (July 13, 1815–June 11, 1887); b. Bath, Me. Episcopal bishop, author. *A History of Georgia,* 2v. (1847–59); *Early History of the Church in Georgia* (1873); *Sermons* (1879); etc.

STEVENS, WILLIAM OLIVER (Oct. 7, 1878–Jan. 15, 1955); b. Rangoon, Burma. Educator, author. *"Pewee" Clinton, Plebe* (1912); *Messmates* (1913); *Boy's Book of Famous Warships* (1915); *A History of Sea Power* (with Allan Westcott, 1920); *Nantucket* (1936); *Annapolis* (1937); *Old Wil-*

liamsburg and Her Neighbors (1938); *Charleston* (1939); *Discovering Long Island* (1939); *The Patriotic Thing* (1940); *Pistols at Ten Paces* (1940); *The Shenandoah and Its By-Ways* (1941); *Drummer Boy of Burma* (1943); *The Quiet Hour* (1947); *Famous Men of Science* (1952); *Famous Humanitarians* (1952); etc.

STEVENSON, ADLAI E[wing] (Feb. 5, 1900–July 14, 1965); b. Los Angeles, Calif. Government official, lawyer, author. *Call to Greatness* (1954); *What I Think* (1956); *The New America* (1957); *Friends and Enemies* (1959); *Putting First Things First: A Democratic View* (1960). Governor of Illinois, 1949–53; U.S. ambassador to the U.N., from 1961. See Stuart G. Brown's *Conscience in Politics* (1961); *Looking Outward: Years of Crisis at the United Nations* (ed. by R. L. and S. Schiffler, 1963); Lillian Ross' *Adlai Stevenson* (1966).

STEVENSON, ALEC BROCK (Dec. 29, 1895–); b. Toronto, Ont. Investment banker, author. *Shares in Mutual Investment Funds* (1946); *Investment Company Shares* (1947). Member of group editing and publishing *The Fugitive,* 1922–25.

STEVENSON, BURTON EGBERT (Nov. 9, 1872–May 13, 1962); b. Chillicothe, O. Author. *A Soldier of Virginia* (1901); *The Heritage* (1902); *The Young Apprentice* (1912); *The Charm of Ireland* (1914); *Famous Single Poems, and the Controversies Which Have Raged around Them* (1923); *The House Next Door* (1932); *Villa Aurelia* (1932); *The Red Carnation* (1939); etc. Compiler: *Days and Deeds* (verse, 1906); *Days and Deeds* (prose, 1907); *The Home Book of Verse* (1912); *Home Book of Modern Verse* (1925); *Home Book of Quotations* (1934); *Home Book of Shakespeare Quotations* (1937); *Home Book of Bible Quotations* (1949); etc. Founder and librarian, American Library in Paris, 1918–20, 1925–30; librarian, Chillicothe Public Library, 1899–1957.

STEVENSON, CHARLES LESLIE (June 27, 1908–); b. Cincinnati, O. Educator. *Ethics and Language* (1945); *Facts and Values* (1963). Prof. philosophy, University of Michigan, since 1949.

STEVENSON, DONALD MACLAREN (Sept. 13, 1902–); b. Bridgeport, Conn. Publisher. With William Morrow & Co., since 1928; pres. 1958–64.

STEVENSON, EDWARD IRENAEUS [Prime] (1868–July 23, 1942); b. in the United States. Editor, author. *White Cockades* (1887); *Janus* (1889); *Her Enemy* (1913); *Long-Haired Iopas* (1927); etc. Co-editor, *Library of the World's Best Literature.* On staff *Harper's Weekly, The Independent,* etc.

STEVENSON, E[lias] ROBERT (Aug. 29, 1882–); b. New Haven, Conn. Editor, author. *The Damnation of Sandy MacGregor* (1911); *Connecticut History Makers,* 3v. (1929). With *Springfield Republican,* 1909–17; editor, *Waterbury Republican,* 1917–22; editor, *Waterbury American,* 1922–27; editor, both newspapers, 1927–49.

STEVENSON, ELISABETH (June 13, 1919–); b. Ancon, Canal Zone. Author. *The Crooked Corridor: A Study of Henry James* (1949); *Henry Adams, A Biography* (1955); *Lafcadio Hearn* (1961); *Babbits and Bohemians: The American 1920's* (1967); etc. Editor: *A Henry Adams Reader* (1958).

STEVENSON, ELMO NALL (Feb. 25, 1904–); b. in California. Educator, author. *Nature Rambles in the Wallowas* (1937); *Nature Games Book* (1941); *Key to the Nests of the Pacific Coast Birds* (1942); *Pets: Wild and Western* (1953); etc. Pres., South Oregon College, since 1946.

STEVENSON, LIONEL (July 16, 1902–); b. Edinburgh. Educator, author. *Appraisals of Canadian Literature* (1926); *Darwin Among the Poets* (1932); *The Wild Irish Girl: The Life of Sydney Owenson, Lady Morgan* (1936); *Dr. Quicksilver: The Life of Charles Lever* (1939); *The Showman of Vanity Fair* (1947); *The Ordeal of George Meredith* (1953); *The English Novel* (vol. I, 1961; vol. II, 1967). English dept.,

University of Southern California, 1937–55; prof., Duke University, since 1955.

STEVENSON, MATILDA COXE (Mrs. James Stevenson) (1850–June 24, 1915); b. San Augustine, Tex. Ethnologist, author. *Zuñi and Zuñians* (1881); *The Zuñi Indians* (1905); and other books on the Indians of the Southwest. On staff, Bureau of American Ethnology, Smithsonian Institution, 1889–1915.

STEVERS, MARTIN DELAWAY (June 28, 1892–); b. Chicago, Ill. Editor, author. *Steel Trails* (1933); *Sea Lanes* (with Jonas Pendlebury, 1935); *Mind Through the Ages* (1940); Managing editor, *Compton's Pictured Encyclopedia,* since 1946.

STEWARD, ANN (Aug. 29, 1898–   ); b. Cincinnati, O. Novelist. *Let the Earth Speak* (1940); *Take Nothing for Your Journey* (1943); etc.

STEWARD, JULIAN H. (Jan. 31, 1902–); b. Washington, D.C. Anthropologist. *Theory of Culture Change* (1955). Co-author: *People of Puerto Rico* (1956); *Native People of South America* (1959). Editor: *Handbook of South American Indians,* 6v. (1946–49); *Contemporary Change in Traditional Societies,* 3v. (1967).

STEWART, ANNA BIRD, b. Cincinnati, O. Educator, author. *The Gentlest Giant* (1915); *Little Brother Goose* (1928); *Three White Cats of Avignon* (1929); *Bibi, the Baker's Horse* (1942); *Two Young Corsicans* (1944); *Young Miss Burney* (1947); *Enter David Garrick* (1951); etc. English dept., St. Mary's College, Notre Dame, Ind., since 1936.

STEWART, CHARLES D[avid] (Mar. 18, 1868–); b. Zanesville, O. Author. *The Fugitive Blacksmith* (1905); *Partners of Providence* (1907); *Essays on the Spot* (1910); *Finerty of the Sand-House* (1913); *Some Textual Difficulties in Shakespeare* (1914); *Buck* (1919); *Valley Waters* (1922); *Fellow Creatures* (1935); etc.

STEWART, CHARLES DAVID (Feb. 17, 1910–); b. Detroit, Mich. Government official, author. *Economic Reconstruction* (1945); *Principles of Economic Development* (1955); etc. U.S. Dept. of Labor, since 1967.

STEWART, DONALD OGDEN (Nov. 30, 1894–); b. Columbus, O. Humorist, actor, screenwriter, author. *A Parody Outline of History* (1921); *Perfect Behavior* (1922); *Aunt Polly's Story of Mankind* (1923); *Mr. and Mrs. Haddock Abroad* (1924); *The Crazy Fool* (1925); *Father William* (1929); *Rebound* (prod. 1930); *Fine and Dandy* (prod. 1930); *The Kidders* (prod. 1957); etc. Editor: *Fighting Words* (1940). Also numerous screenplays.

STEWART, GEORGE (Feb. 11, 1892–); b. Webb City, Mo. Presbyterian clergyman, educator, author. *Life of Henry B. Wright* (1925); *The White Armies of Russia* (1933); *Reluctant Soil* (1936); *The Church* (1938); *God in Our Street* (1939); *A Face to the Sky* (1940); *I Met Them Once* (1940); *These Men My Friends* (1954). Lecturer, Yale Divinity School, 1930–36.

STEWART, GEORGE R[ippey] (May, 1895–); b. Sewickley, Pa. Educator, author. *The Technique of English Verse* (1930); *Bret Harte, Argonaut and Exile* (1931); *Ordeal by Hunger: The Story of the Donner Party* (1936); *John Phoenix, Esq., the Veritable Squibob: A Life of Captain George H. Derby, U. S. A.* (1937); *East of the Giants* (1938); *Storm* (1941); *Man: An Autobiography* (1946); *Fire* (1948); *Sheep Rock* (1951); *U.S. 40* (1953); *The Years of the City* (1955); *N.A.1* (1957); *Pickett's Charge* (1959); *The California Trail* (1962); *Committee of Vigilance 1851* (1964); *Good Lives* (1967); *Not So Rich As You Think* (1968). English dept., University of California, since 1923.

STEWART, GRACE BLISS (Apr. 18, 1885–Apr. 24, 1969); b. Atchison, Kan. Artist, author. *In and Out of the Jungle*

(1922); *Jumping into the Jungle* (1923); *The Good Fairy* (1930); etc.

STEWART, IRVIN (Oct. 27, 1899–); b. Fort Worth, Tex. Educator. *Consular Privileges and Immunities* (1926); *Organizing Scientific Research for War* (1948). Editor: *Radio* (1929). Pres. West Virginia University, 1946–58; prof. government, 1958–67. Consultant, National Academy of Public Administration, since 1967.

STEWART, JUDD (May 14, 1867–c. 1920); b. near Lawrence, Kan. Author. *Some Lincoln Correspondence with Southern Leaders Before the Outbreak of the Civil War* (1909); and other pamphlets on Lincoln. His collection of Lincolniana was one of the largest ever assembled.

STEWART, KENNETH NORMAN (June 6, 1901–); b. Leadville, Col. Educator, author. *News Is What We Make It: A Running Story of the Working Press* (1943); *Makers of Modern Journalism* (with John Tebbel, 1952). Prof. journalism, University of Michigan, since 1952.

STEWART, RANDALL (July 25, 1896–June 17, 1964); b. Fayetteville, Tenn. Educator, author. *Nathaniel Hawthorne: A Biography* (1948); *American Literature and Christian Doctrine* (1958). Editor: *The Literature of the South* (with others, 1952). Prof. English, Vanderbilt University, since 1955.

STEWART, ROBERT ARMISTEAD (1877–1950); b. Norfolk, Va. Educator, poet. *Knights of the Golden Horseshoe, and Other Lays* (1909); *Golden Stairs* (poems, 1923); *The History of Virginia's Navy of the Revolution* (1933); etc. Author, under pen name "Gordon Stuart," of many Boy Scout books. Editor: *Letters of Patrick Henry* (1926); *Letters of Thomas Jefferson* (1928).

Stewart, Will. Pen name of John Stewart Williamson.

Stewart and Bowen. Indianapolis, Ind. Publishers and booksellers. Founded in 1854. In 1860 the firm was called Bowen, Stewart and Company. In 1885 it was merged with Merrill, Meigs and Co., now known as Bobbs-Merrill. During its first year it published Harriet Beecher Stowe's *Memories in Foreign Lands.*

STICKNEY, JULIA NOYES (b. July 5, 1830); b. West Newbury, Mass. Poet. *Poems on Lake Winnepesaukee* (1884); *One Hundred Sonnets* (1895); *In the Valley of the Merrimack* (1901); etc.

Sticks and Stones: A Study of American Architecture and Civilization. By Lewis Mumford (1924). A study of the parallel development of American culture and American architecture.

STIDGER, WILLIAM LEROY (Mar. 16, 1885–Aug. 7, 1949); b. Moundsville, W.Va. Methodist clergyman, author. *Giant Hours with Poet Preachers* (1918); *Soldier Silhouettes* (1919); *Henry Ford* (1923); *The Epic of Earth* (1923); *Finding God in Books* (1924); *Edwin Markham* (1932); *How to Get the Most Out of Life* (1939); *Sermon Nuggets in Stories* (1945); etc.

STIEGLITZ, ALFRED (Jan. 1, 1864–July 13, 1946); b. Hoboken, N.J. Photographer. Founder, *Camera Notes,* 1897; editor, 1897–1903; editor and publisher, *Camera Work,* from Jan. 1, 1903.

STIFF, EDWARD. Author. *The Texas Emigrant* (1840), augmented as *A New History of Texas* (1849).

STIGLER, GEORGE JOSEPH (Jan. 17, 1911–); b. Renton, Wash. Educator, economist, author. *Production and Distribution Theories* (1941); *The Theory of Price* (1946); *Five Lectures on Economic Problems* (1949); *Trends in Employment in the Service Industries* (1956); *Demand and Supply for Scientific Personnel* (with D. Blank, 1957); *The Intellectual and The Market Place* (1964); *Essays in the History of Economics* (1965); *The Organization of Industry* (1968). Prof. economics,

Columbia University, 1947–58; University of Chicago, since 1958.

STILES, EZRA (Nov. 29, 1727–May 12, 1795); b. North Haven, Conn. Congregational clergyman, educator, author. *The Literary Diary of Ezra Stiles,* ed. by F. B. Dexter, 3v. (1901); *Letters and Papers of Ezra Stiles,* ed. by Isabel M. Calder (1933). Librarian, Redwood Library, Newport, R.I., 1756–75. President, Yale University, 1778–95. His manuscripts are at Yale. *See* Abiel Holmes's *Life of Ezra Stiles* (1798); Edmund S. Morgan's *Gentle Puritan* (1962).

STILES, HENRY REED (Mar. 10, 1832–Jan. 7, 1909); b. New York. Genealogist, editor, author. *The History of Ancient Windsor, Connecticut* (1859), revised as *The History and Genealogies of Ancient Windsor, Connecticut,* 2v. (1891); *A History of the City of Brooklyn,* 3v. (1867–70); *Bundling* (1869); *The Stiles Family in America* (1895); *The History of Ancient Wethersfield, Connecticut,* 2v. (1904); etc. Editor, the *New York Genealogical and Biographical Record,* 1900–02; etc.

STILES, HINSON (June 28, 1893–); b. Albert, N.B., Can. Journalist, author. *Room with the Black Door* (1927); *Song o' the Sea* (1928). With the *New York Daily Mirror,* from 1933; managing editor, from 1935.

STILES, LINDLEY JOSEPH (July 1, 1913–); b. Tatum, N.M. Educator, author. *Supervision as Guidance* (with Inga Olla Helseth, 1946); *Democratic Teaching in Secondary Schools* (with Mattie F. Dorsey, 1950); *Mood and Moments* (poems, 1955); etc. Dean, School of Education, University of Wisconsin, 1955–56; prof. education, Northwestern University, since 1966.

STILL, JAMES (July 16, 1906–); b. Double Creek, Ala. Author. *Hounds on the Mountain* (poems, 1937); *River of Earth* (1940); *On Troublesome Creek* (1941); etc.

STILL, LOUISE MORGAN, b. Honolulu. Poet, translator. *In Sun or Shade* (1906); *The Hell-God, and Other Poems* (1928). With Harper & Brothers, 1899–1905; on staff *Harper's Magazine,* 1905–10.

"Still, Still with Thee, When Purple Morning Breaketh." Hymn by Harriet Beecher Stowe (1855).

STILL, WILLIAM (Oct. 7, 1821–July 14, 1902); b. Shamong, N.J. Reformer, author. *The Underground Railroad* (1872); etc.

STILLÉ, CHARLES JANEWAY (Sept. 23, 1819–Aug. 11, 1899); b. Philadelphia, Pa. Educator, author. *The Social Spirit* (1839); *Studies in Medieval History* (1882); *The Life and Times of John Dickinson* (1891); *Reminiscences of a Provost, 1866–1880* (n.d.). Provost, University of Pennsylvania, 1868–80. Benefactor of "Gloria Dei" (Old Swedes') Church, Philadelphia.

STILLMAN, HENRY (Apr. 10, 1884–); b. Brooklyn, N.Y. Director, playwright. *Nightshade* (prod. 1920); *Lally* (prod. 1927); etc. Associated with David Belasco, Daniel Frohman, Harrison Grey Fiske, and the Theatre Guild.

STILLMAN, WILLIAM JAMES (June 1, 1828–July 6, 1901); b. Schenectady, N.Y. Artist, correspondent, author. *Poetic Localities of Cambridge* (1876); *On the Track of Ulysses* (1887); *Billy and Hans* (1897); *Little Bertha* (1898); *The Old Rome and the New and Other Studies* (1898); *Francesco Crispi* (1899); *The Autobiography of a Journalist,* 2v. (1901). Founder, *The Crayon,* Jan. 1855. Correspondent, *London Times,* 1877–98; U.S. Consul, Rome, 1861–65; Crete, 1865–68.

Stillness at Appomatox, A. By Bruce Catton (1953). Dramatic account of the final events of the Civil War.

STILLWELL, MARGARET BINGHAM (1887–); b. Providence, R.I. Librarian, bibliographer, author. *The Influence of*

William Morris and the Kelmscott Press (1912); *Incunabula and Americana* (1931); *Gutenberg and the Catholicon* (1936); *Noah's Ark in Early Woodcuts and Modern Rhyme* (1942); *While Benefit Street Was Young* (1943); *The Pageant of Benefit Street Down Through the Years* (1945); etc. Curator and librarian, The Annmary Brown Memorial Library, Providence, R.I., 1917–54.

STILWELL, HART (1902–   ); b. in Texas. Author. *Border City* (1945); *Hunting and Fishing in Mexico* (1946); *Uncovered Wagon* (1947); *Fishing in Mexico* (1948); *Campus Town* (1950); etc.

STIMSON, A[lexander] L[ovett] (Dec. 14, 1816–Jan. 2, 1906); b. Boston, Mass. Author. *Poor Caroline, the Indiaman's Daughter* (anon., 1845); *Easy Nat; or, The Three Apprentices* (1854), reprinted as *New England Boys* (1856); *History of the Express Companies* (1858); *Waifwood* (1864).

STIMSON, FREDERIC JESUP (July 20, 1855–Nov. 19, 1943); b. Dedham, Mass. Lawyer, author. Pen name, "J. S. of Dale." Under pen name: *Guerndale* (1882); *The Crime of Henry Vane* (1884); *The Sentimental Calendar* (1886); under own name: *First Harvests* (1888); *Mrs. Knollys, and Other Stories* (1894); *Pirate Gold* (1896); *King Noanett* (1896); *In Cure of Her Soul* (1906); *The Light of Provence* (poem, 1917); *My Story* (pretended autobiography of Benedict Arnold, 1917); *The Western Way* (1929); *My United States* (autobiography, 1931); etc.

STIRLING, YATES, JR. (Apr. 30, 1872–Jan. 27, 1948); b. Vallejo, Calif. Naval officer, author. The *U. S. Midshipman* series, 5v. (1908–12); *Sea Duty* (memoirs, 1939); etc.

STITH, WILLIAM (1707–Sept. 19, 1755); b. in Virginia. Educator, author. *The History of the First Discovery and Settlement of Virginia* (1747); *The Sinfulness and Pernicious Spirit of Gaming* (1752). President, College of William and Mary, 1752–55.

STOCKBRIDGE, FRANK PARKER (June 11, 1870–Dec. 7, 1940); b. Gardiner, Me. Journalist, author. *Yankee Ingenuity in the War* (1919); *The New Capitalism* (1926); *So This Is Florida* (1938); etc. Editorial writer, the *Buffalo Express,* 1894–1901; founder and editor, the *American Home Magazine,* 1901–02; editor, *Popular Mechanics,* 1913–15; president, the *New York Evening Mail,* 1915–17; etc.

STOCKING, CHARLES FRANCIS (Sept. 4, 1873–); b. Freeport, Ill. Author. *The Diary of Jean Evarts* (1912); *The Mayor of Filbert* (1916); *Carmen Ariza* (1916); *The Identity of Douglas Bain* (1928); *Modern Parables* (1931); *Doorstep Ann* (1936); *Out of the Dust* (1939); etc.

STOCKTON, FRANK R. [Francis Richard] (Apr. 5, 1834–Apr. 20, 1902); b. Philadelphia, Pa. Author. *Ting-a-Ling* (1870); *What Might Have Been Expected* (1874); *Tales Out of School* (1875); *Rudder Grange* (1879); *The Floating Prince, and Other Fairy Tales* (1881); *The Lady or the Tiger* (1884); *The Casting Away of Mrs. Lecks and Mrs. Aleshine* (1886); *The Bee Man of Orn, and Other Fanciful Tales* (1887); *The Merry Chanter* (1890); *The Clocks of Rondaine and Other Stories* (1892); *Pomona's Travels* (1894); *The Adventures of Captain Horn* (1895); *The Great Stone of Sardis* (1898); *The Novels and Stories,* 23v. (1899–1904); *The Captain's Toll Gate,* ed. by his wife, Marian Edwards Stockton (1903); etc. Asst. editor, *St. Nicholas Magazine,* 1873–81. *See* W. W. Ellsworth's *A Golden Age of Authors* (1919); L. F. Tooker's *The Joys and Tribulations of an Editor* (1924); M. I. J. Griffin's *Frank R. Stockton* (1939).

STOCKTON, LOUISE (1838–1914); b. Philadelphia, Pa., sister of Frank R. Stockton. Author. *Dorothea* (1882); *A Sylvan City* (1883); republished as, *Quaint Corners* (1900); etc.

Stoddard, Charles. Pen name of Charles Stanley Strong.

STODDARD, CHARLES AUGUSTUS (May 28, 1833–June 5, 1920); b. Boston, Mass. Presbyterian clergyman, author. *Across Russia from the Baltic to the Danube* (1891); *Spanish Cities* (1892); *Beyond the Rockies* (1894); *A Spring Journey in California* (1895); *Cruising among the Caribbees* (1895). Editor, the *New York Observer,* 1885–1902.

STODDARD, CHARLES WARREN (Aug. 7, 1843–Apr. 23, 1909); b. Rochester, N.Y. Author, poet. *Poems* (1867); *South-Sea Idylls* (1873); *The Lepers of Molokai* (1885); *Hawaiian Life* (1894); *In the Footprints of the Padres* (1902); *For the Pleasure of His Company* (1903); *Exits and Entrances* (1903); *Poems of Charles Warren Stoddard* (1917). Wrote poems for the *Golden Era,* 1862–63, under pen name "Pip Pepperpod." *See* F. Walker's *San Francisco's Literary Frontier* (1939).

STODDARD, ELIZABETH DREW BARSTOW (Mrs. Richard Henry Stoddard) (May 6, 1823–Aug. 1, 1902); b. Mattapoisett, Mass. Novelist, poet. *The Morgesons* (1862); *Two Men* (1865); *Temple House* (1867); *Lolly Dinks's Doings* (1874); *Poems* (1895).

STODDARD, FRANCES HOVEY (Apr. 25, 1847–Feb. 6, 1936); b. Middlebury, Vt. Educator, author. *The Modern Novel* (1883); *Psycho-Biography* (1885); *Literary Spirit in the Colleges* (1893); *The Evolution of the English Novel* (1900); *The Life and Letters of Charles Butler* (1903). Prof. English language and literature, New York University, 1888–1936.

STODDARD, GEORGE DINSMORE (Oct. 8, 1897–); b. Carbondale, Pa. Educator, author. *Iowa Placement Examinations* (1920); *Getting Ideas from the Movies* (with P. W. Holaday, 1933); *The Meaning of Intelligence* (1943); *Frontiers in Education* (1945); *On the Education of Women* (1950); *The Dual Progress Plan* (1961). Prof. psychology, University of Iowa, 1929–42; pres., University of Illinois, 1946–53; dean, School of Education, New York University, 1956–60; Acting Chancellor for Academic Affairs, L. I. U., since 1968.

STODDARD, JOHN LAWSON (Apr. 24, 1850–June 5, 1931); b. Brookline, Mass. Lecturer, hymn writer, author. *Red-Letter Days Abroad* (1884); *Glimpses of the World* (1892); *John L. Stoddard's Lectures,* 10v. (1897–98); *Poems* (1913); *The Evening of Life* (1929); etc. Compiler: *The Stoddard Library: A Thousand Hours of Entertainment with the World's Greatest Writers,* 12v. (1910); etc. *See* D. Crane Taylor's *John L. Stoddard* (1935).

STODDARD, RICHARD HENRY (July 2, 1825–May 12, 1903); b. Hingham, Mass. Poet, critic, editor, author. *Foot-Prints* (1849); *Poems* (1852); *Songs of Summer* (1857); *The King's Bell* (1863); *Abraham Lincoln: A Horation Ode* (1865); *The Book of the East, and Other Poems* (1871); *The Lion's Cub, with Other Verse* (1890); *Recollections, Personal and Literary* (1903); etc. Editor, *The Late English Poets* (1865); editor, *The Aldine,* 1871–75. He also edited two popular series of books, *The Bric-a-Brac* and the *Sans-Souci.* Lit. reviewer, *New York World,* 1860–70, *Mail and Express,* 1880–1903.

STODDARD, S[eneca] R[oy]. Publisher, author. *Ticonderoga, Past and Present* (1873); *Lake George* (1873); *The Adirondacks* (1874); *Saratoga Springs* (1881); *"In Mediterranean Lands"* (1896); etc.

STODDARD, [Theodore] **LOTHROP** (June 29, 1883–May 1, 1950); b. Brookline, Mass. Author. *Present-Day Europe* (1917); *The Rising Tide of Color Against White World-Supremacy* (1920); *The New World of Islam* (1921); *The Revolt Against Civilization* (1922); *Scientific Humanism* (1926); *Luck—Your Silent Partner* (1929); *Lonely America* (1932); *Into the Darkness* (1940).

STODDARD, WILLIAM OSBORN (Sept. 24, 1835–Aug. 29, 1925); b. Homer, N.Y. Inventor, assistant private secretary to Abraham Lincoln, author. *The Crawling Snake* (under pen name "Col. Cris Forrest," 1868); *Verses of Many Days* (1875); *Dismissed* (1878); *Dab Kinzer* (1881); *Saltillo Boys* (1883); *Abraham Lincoln* (1884); *The Lives of the Presidents*, 10v. (1886–89); *Chuck Purdy* (1887); *The Red Mustang* (1890); *Inside the White House in War Times* (1890); *Gid Granger* (1890); *Battle of New York* (1892); *Guert Ten Eyck* (1893); *On the Old Frontier* (1893); *The First Cruise Out* (1898); *Running the Cuban Blockade* (1899); *Lincoln at Work* (1899); *Jack Morgan* (1901); *The Spy of Yorktown* (1903); etc.

STODDARD, WILLIAM OSBORN, Jr. (Mar. 5, 1873–); b. New York. Author. *Longshore Boys* (1909); *Captain of the Cat's-Paw* (1914); *The Farm That Jack Built* (1916); etc. Editor: *Lincoln's Third Secretary: Memoirs of William Osborn Stoddard* (1955).

STODDART, JOSEPH MARSHALL (Aug. 10, 1845–Feb. 25, 1921); b. Philadelphia, Pa. Editor and publisher. Opened a publishing business in Philadelphia, 1874, and his first book was Charles Heber Clark's *Out of the Hurly Burly*. From 1875 to 1884 he published American editions of the *Encyclopedia Britannica*. He also published Stoddart's *Encyclopedia Americana*, 4v. (1883–89). Publisher, *Stoddart's Review*, 1880–82. He published the Gilbert and Sullivan light operas in America, and was manager of *Lippincott's Magazine*. Editor, *Collier's Weekly*, *The Literary Era*, etc.

STOKE, HAROLD WALTER (May 11, 1903–); b. Bosworth, Mo. Educator. *The Foreign Relations of the Federal State* (1931); *The Background of European Governments* (with Norman L. Hill, 1935); *The American College President* (1959). Pres., Queens College, New York, since 1958.

STOKES, ANSON PHELPS (Apr. 13, 1874–Aug. 13, 1958); b. New Brighton, S.I., N.Y. Episcopal clergyman, author. *Memorials of Eminent Yale Men*, 2v. (1914); etc.

STOKES, FREDERICK ABBOT (Nov. 4, 1857–Nov. 15, 1939); b. Brooklyn, N.Y. Publisher. Author: *College Tramps* (1880); *A Publisher's Random Notes, 1880–1935* (1935). Founder publishing house of Frederick A. Stokes Company in New York in 1881. Among the early associates of Stokes were Maynard Dominick and William Morrow. Among later associates were his sons, Horace W. and Frederick Brett Stokes, assisted by Thomas Mahony, George Shively, Helen Dean Fish, and Munro Leaf. The publishing firm was first called White and Stokes. In 1883 it changed to White, Stokes & Allen, in 1887 it became Frederick A. Stokes & Brother. In 1890 it became Frederick A. Stokes Company. In 1941 it was consolidated with J. B. Lippincott & Co. (q.v.). Among the authors published by Stokes have been Sir Anthony Hope, W. W. Jacobs, Stephen Crane, Robert E. Peary, James Branch Cabell, Susan Glaspell, Robert Barr, Louis Bromfield, Clinton Scollard, Robert Chambers, Helen Bannerman and Hugh Lofting. From 1898 to 1901 Stokes published and edited *The Pocket Magazine*. He delivered the first R. R. Bowker Memorial Lecture at The New York Public Library in 1935. See *The House of Stokes, 1881–1926* (1926).

STOKLEY, JAMES (May 19, 1900–); b. Philadelphia, Pa. Educator, author. *Stars and Telescopes* (1936); *Science Remakes Our World* (1942); *Electrons in Action* (1946); *The New World of the Atom* (1957). Editor: *Science Marches On* (1951). Assoc. prof. journalism, Michigan State College, 1956–69; prof. emeritus, journalism and astronomy, since 1969.

Stolen Story, The, and Other Newspaper Stories. By Jesse Lynch Williams (1899). The title story is regarded as one of the classics of journalism.

STOLL, ELMER EDGAR (Feb. 11, 1874–); b. Orrville, O. Educator, author. *John Webster* (1905); *Othello* (1915); *Hamlet* (1919); *Shakespeare Studies* (1927); *Poets and Playwrights* (1929); *Shakespeare's Young Lovers* (1937); *Shakespeare and Other Masters* (1940); *From Shakespeare to Joyce* (1944); *Art and Artifice in Shakespeare* (1951); etc. Prof. English, University of Minnesota, 1915–42.

STOLZ, LOIS MEEK (Oct. 19, 1894–); b. Washington, D.C. Psychologist, educator. *A Study of Learning and Retention of Young Children* (1925); *Personal-Social Development of Young Boys and Girls* (1940); *Father Relations of War-Born Children* (with others, 1954); *Influences on Parent Behavior* (1967). Prof. psychology, Stanford University, 1947–57.

STOLZ, MARY SLATTERY (Mar. 24, 1920–); b. Boston, Mass. Author. *The Seagulls Woke Me* (1951); *In a Mirror* (1953); *Pray Love, Remember* (1954); *Hospital Zone* (1956); *Second Nature* (1958); *Great Rebellion* (1961); *Pigeon Flight* (1962); *Bully of Barkham Street* (1963); *The Noonday Friends* (1965); *A Wonderful Terrible Time* (1967); *Say Something* (1968); etc.

STONE, ALBERT EDWARD, Jr. (Jan. 1, 1924–); b. New London, Conn. Educator, author. *The Innocent Eye: Childhood in Mark Twain's Imagination* (1961). Editor: *Letters from an American Farmer*. Prof. English, Emory University, since 1962.

STONE, DAVID MARVIN (Dec. 23, 1817–Apr. 2, 1895); b. Oxford, Conn. Editor, publisher, novelist. *Frank Forrest* (1850). With the *New York Journal of Commerce*, 1849–93; editor, 1866–1893; owner, 1884–93.

STONE, EZRA CHAIM (Dec. 2, 1917–   ); b. New Bedford, Mass. Actor, producer, author. *Coming Major* (1945); *Puccini Opera* (with Deems Taylor, 1951). Director or producer of numerous motion pictures, plays and television programs; best known as "Henry Aldrich" in the radio serial "The Aldrich Family."

STONE, GRACE ZARING (Jan. 9, 1896–); b. New York. Novelist. *Letters to a Djinn* (1922); *The Heaven and Earth of Doña Elena* (1929); *The Bitter Tea of General Yen* (1930); *The Almond Tree* (1931); *The Cold Journey* (1934); *Escape* (under pen name "Ethel Vance," 1939); *Reprisal* (1942); *Winter Meeting* (1946); *The Secret Thread* (1948); *The Grotto* (1951).

STONE, IRVING (July 14, 1903–); b. San Francisco, Calif. Author. *Pageant of Youth* (1933); *Lust for Life* (1934); *Sailor on Horseback* (1938); *False Witness* (1940); *They Also Ran* (1943); *Immortal Wife* (1944); *Adversary in the House* (1947); *Earl Warren* (1948); *We Speak for Ourselves* (1950); *Love Is Eternal* (1954); *Men to Match My Mountains* (1956); *The Agony and the Ecstasy* (1961); *A Contemporary Portrait* (1962); *The Story of Michelangelo's Pieta* (1963); *Those Who Love* (1965); *The Passions of the Mind* (1971).

STONE, I[sidor] F[einstein] (Dec. 24, 1907–   ); b. Philadelphia. Journalist, author. *The Court Disposes* (1937); *Business as Usual* (1941); *Underground to Palestine* (1946); *This Is Israel* (1948); *The Hidden History of the Korean War* (1952); *The Truman Era* (1953); *The Haunted Fifties* (1964); *In a Time of Torment* (1967). Publisher of *I. F. Stone's Weekly* from 1953 to 1971.

Stone, Jane Dransfield. See Jane Dransfield.

STONE, JOHN AUGUSTUS (Dec. 15, 1800–May 29, 1834); b. Concord, Mass. Actor, playwright. *Restoration of the Diamond Cross* (prod. 1824); *Tancred; or, The Siege of Antioch* (1827); *Metamora; or, The Last of the Wampanoags* (prod. 1828); *The Ancient Briton* (prod. 1833); *The Knight of the Golden Fleece; or, The Yankee in Spain* (prod. 1834); etc.

STONE, LUCY (Aug. 13, 1818–Oct. 18, 1893); b. West Brookfield, Mass. Reformer, editor. Founder, *Woman's Journal*, 1870; editor, 1872–93. See Alice Stone Blackwell's *Lucy Stone* (1930).

STONE, MELVILLE ELIJAH (Aug. 22, 1848–Feb. 15, 1929); b. Hudson, Ill. Publisher, author. *Fifty Years a Journalist* (1929). Founder (with Victor F. Lawson), the *Chicago Daily News*, 1876. General Manager, Associated Press, 1893–1921. Herbert Stuart Stone, of Stone and Kimball, publishers, was a son. *See* Oliver Gramling's *AP: The Story of News* (1940).

STONE, PETER H. (Feb. 27, 1930–); b. Los Angeles, Cal. Playwright. *Kean* (1961); *Skyscraper* (1965); *Charade* (novel, 1963). Author of motion picture scenarios, television scripts.

STONE, ROBERT. Author. *A Hall of Mirrors* (1966).

STONE, WILLIAM LEETE (Apr. 20, 1792–Aug. 15, 1844); b. New Paltz, N.Y. Editor, author. *Matthias and His Impostures* (1833); *Tales and Sketches,* 2v. (1834); *The Mysterious Bridal, and Other Tales,* 3v. (1835); *Maria Monk and the Nunnery of Hôtel Dieu* (1836); *Life of Joseph Brant, Thayendanegea,* 2v. (1838); *Life and Times of Red Jacket, or Sa-go-ye-wat-ha* (1841); *The Poetry and History of Wyoming* [Valley] (1841); *The Atlantic Club-Book,* 2v. (1834); *Uncas and Miantonomoh* (1842); *Ups and Downs in the Life of a Distressed Gentleman* (anon., 1836); *The Witches* (anon., 1837); *Border Wars of the American Revolution,* 2v. (1843); etc. Editor, the *New York Commercial Advertiser,* 1820–44.

STONE, WILLIAM LEETE (Apr. 4, 1835–June 11, 1908); b. New York, son of William Leete Stone. Printer, editor, author. *The Life and Times of Sir William Johnson, Bart.,* 2v. (1865), a work left unfinished by his father; *Saratoga Springs* (1866); *History of New York City* (1868); *Reminiscences of Saratoga and Ballston* (1875); *Ballads and Poems Relating to the Burgoyne Campaign* (1893); etc. Editor, the *College Review,* 1870–74.

STONE, WITMER (Sept. 22, 1866–May 24, 1939); b. Philadelphia, Pa. Naturalist, editor, author. *Mammals of New Jersey* (1908); *Birds of New Jersey* (1909); *The Plants of Southern New Jersey* (1911); etc. Editor, *The Auk,* 1912–39. Curator, Academy of Natural Sciences, Philadelphia, 1908–24; director of museum, 1925–28.

Stone and Kimball. Chicago, Ill. Publishers. Founded 1893, by Herbert Stuart Stone and Ingalls Kimball, at Cambridge, Mass. In 1894 the firm moved to Chicago. Noted for its fine printing. In 1896 Kimball purchased his partner's share in the business and moved to New York. The firm was dissolved in 1897. Stone and Kimball published the *Chap-Book.* Stone, son of Melville Stone, publisher of the *Chicago Record,* lost his life on the *Lusitania. See* Sidney Kramer's *History and Bibliography of Stone and Kimball and Herbert S. Stone* (1940).

STONEHOUSE, NED BERNARD (Mar. 19, 1902–); b. Grand Rapids, Mich. Theologian, author. *The Witness of Matthew and Mark to Christ* (1944); *The Witness of Luke to Christ* (1951); *J. Gresham Machen: A Biographical Memoir* (1954); *Paul Before the Areopagus and Other New Testament Studies* (1957).

STONER, WINIFRED [d'Estcourte] SACKVILLE (1883–1931). Educational reformer, author. *Castles in Spain, and Other Sketches in Rhyme* (1901); *Natural Education* (1914); *Songs of the Allies* (1917); etc. Founder, Natural Educational System, 1902; head, Mother Stoner, Inc., publishing firm.

STONER, WINIFRED SACKVILLE (Countess Charles P. de Bruche) (Aug. 19, 1902–); b. Norfolk, Va., daughter of Winifred Sackville Stoner. Author. *Jingles* (1909); *Freakish Animals* (1916); *Giants of Old* (1919); etc. Founder, *Pocket-Book Magazine,* 1923.

"Stonewall Jackson's Way." Civil War poem by John W. Palmer. Written during the battle of Antietam, Sept. 17, 1862.

STONG, PHIL[ip Duffield] (Jan. 27, 1899–Apr. 26, 1957); b. Keosauqua, Ia. Novelist. *State Fair* (1932); *Stranger's Return* (1933); *Farm Boy* (1934); *The Farmer in the Dell* (1935); *Week-End* (1935); *Honk the Moose* (1935); *Career* (1935); *The Hound* (1936); *Buckskin Breeches* (1937); *The Hired Man's Elephant* (1939); *Ivanhoe Keeler* (1939); *Horses and*

Americans (1939); *Hawkeyes: A Biography of the State of Iowa* (1940); *The Iron Mountain* (1942); *One Destiny* (1942); *Marta of Muscovy* (1945); *Jessamy John* (1947); *Return in August* (1953); *Blizzard* (1955); etc.

"Stopping by Woods on a Snowy Evening." Poem by Robert Frost (1923).

Store, The. Novel by Thomas S. Stribling (1932). It depicts the moral and cultural decadence of a small Alabama town. The central figure is Miltiades Vaiden. It is a part of a trilogy, the first book being *The Forge* (1931), and the third book being *Unfinished Cathedral* (1933). Overweening love for money brings about the ruin of the leading family in the trilogy.

STORER, JAMES WILSON (Dec. 1, 1884–); b. Burlington, Kans. Baptist clergyman, author. *Truth Enters Lowly Doors* (1937); *By Ways to High Ways* (1938); *Major Messages of the Minor Prophets* (1940); *These Historical Scriptures* (1952); *The Preacher: His Belief and Behavior* (1953).

STOREY, MOORFIELD (Mar. 19, 1845–Oct. 24, 1929); b. Roxbury, Mass. Lawyer, author. *Charles Sumner* (1900); *Ebenezer Rockwood Hoar* (with Edward Waldo Emerson, 1911); *The Negro Question* (1918); *Problems of Today* (1920); etc. *See* M. A. De Wolfe Howe's *Portrait of an Independent: Moorfield Storey, 1845–1929* (1932).

STOREY, VIOLET ALLEYN (Nov. 24, 1900–); b. New York. Poet. *Green of the Year* (1927); *Tea in an Old House* (1933); *A Poet Prays* (1959).

Stories by American Authors, 10v. (1884–96). Contains stories by H. C. Bunner, J. W. De Forest, Harold Frederic, Frank R. Stockton, etc.

Stories of a Western Town. By Octave Thanet (1883). Western life as illustrated by scenes and characters drawn from Davenport, Iowa.

STORK, CHARLES WHARTON (Feb. 12, 1881–); b. Philadelphia, Pa. Poet, educator, editor, translator. *Day Dreams of Greece* (1908); *The Queen of Orplede* (1910); *Sea and Bay* (1916); *Sunset Harbor* (1933); *On Board Old Ironsides, 1812–1815* (1948); *Navpac* (poem, 1952); etc. Editor: *Contemporary Verse Anthology* (1920); *Second Contemporary Verse Anthology* (1923); *Modern Swedish Masterpieces* (1923); *Anthology of Swedish Stories* (1928); *Anthology of Norwegian Lyrics* (1942); etc. Editor, *Contemporary Verse,* 1917–26. Translator and editor of many Swedish works. English dept., University of Pennsylvania, 1903–16.

STORRS, RICHARD SALTER (Feb. 6, 1787–Aug. 11, 1873); b. Longmeadow, Mass. Congregational clergyman, editor, author. *A Dialogue Exhibiting Some of the Principles and Practical Consequences of Modern Infidelity* (1806); *Memoir of the Rev. Samuel Green* (1836); *American Slavery and the Means of Its Removal* (1844); etc. Editor, *The Congregationalist,* 1850–56.

STORRS, RICHARD SALTER (Aug. 21, 1821–June 5, 1900); b. Braintree, Mass., son of Richard Salter Storrs. Congregational clergyman, orator, author. *The Constitution of the Human Soul* (1857); *Bernard of Clairvaux* (1892); *Orations and Addresses* (1901); etc. Co-editor, *The Independent,* 1848–61. *See* Charles Storrs' *The Storrs Family* (1886).

Story. New York. Magazine devoted to short stories. Founded 1931, in Vienna, Austria, by Whit Burnett and Martha Foley (Mrs. Whit Burnett). *Story* was transferred to New York in 1933. Discontinued 1953, but resumed publication 1960. Sponsored by the University of Missouri and published by Story Magazine, Inc., five times yearly. Edited by Mrs. Hallie Burnett, William Peden, Whit Burnett, and Richard Wathen. Ceased publication 1963.

STORY, ISAAC (Aug. 7, 1774–July 19, 1803); b. Marblehead, Mass. Essayist, poet. His essays, written "from the Desk of Beri Headin," appeared in the *Newburyport Political Gazette.* Another series of essays, "by the Traveler," appeared in the *Columbian Centinel.* His poems by "Peter Quince" were written for the *Newburyport Political Gazette* and the *Farmer's Museum.* These last were collected and published as *A Parnassian Shop, Opened in the Pindaric Stile* (1801).

STORY, JOSEPH (Sept. 18, 1779–Sept. 10, 1845); b. Marblehead, Mass. Jurist, constitutional lawyer, author. *On the Constitution,* 3v. (1833); *The Conflict of Laws* (1834); *The Miscellaneous Writings of Joseph Story,* ed. by W. W. Story (1852); etc. See *Life and Letters of Joseph Story,* ed. by W. W. Story, 2v. (1851).

Story, Sydney A. Pen name of Mary Hayden Green Pike.

STORY, WALTER SCOTT (June 23, 1879–June 23, 1955); b. Springfield, Mass. Author. *Skinny Harrison, Adventurer* (1922); *The Uncharted Island* (1926); *Boy Heroes of the Seas* (1928); etc.

STORY, WILLIAM WETMORE (Feb. 12, 1819–Oct. 7, 1895); b. Salem, Mass. Sculptor, essayist, poet. *Poems* (1847); *Roba di Roma,* 2v. (1862–64); *Graffiti d'Italia* (poems, 1868); *Vallombrosa* (1881); *He and She; or, A Poet's Portfolio* (1883); *Fiametta: A Summer Idyl* (1886); *Conversations in a Studio,* 2v. (1890); *Excursions in Art and Letters* (1891). Editor: *Life and Letters of Joseph Story,* 2v. (1851). His apartment in the Palazzo Barberini in Rome was frequented by the Brownings, Hawthorne, Thackeray, Walter Savage Landor, etc. *See* Henry James's *William Wetmore Story and His Friends,* 2v. (1903); Mary E. Phillips's *Reminiscences of William Wetmore Story* (1897).

Story of a Bad Boy, The. By Thomas Bailey Aldrich (1870). Based on the author's own boyhood in Portsmouth, N.H., and its environs, reflecting the New England manners and customs of the period, and the irresponsible instincts of boys of every period, everywhere.

Story of a Country Town, The. By E. W. Howe (1883). Chronicle of the dreary life of Twin Mounds, a small town in the Middle West, as seen by a boy. Based on the author's early life in Missouri.

Story of America, The. By Hendrik Van Loon (1927). Popular history of America, concentrating on the United States. Written in a personal, chatty style but shrewdly stressing some of the most significant forces and events recognized by scholarly historians.

Story of Civilization, The. Multi-volume work, by Will Durant, comprising *Our Oriental Heritage* (1935); *The Life of Greece* (1939); *Caesar and Christ* (1944); *The Age of Faith* (1944); *The Renaissance* (1953); *The Reformation* (1957); *The Age of Reason Begins* (1961); *The Age of Louis XIV* (with Ariel Durant, 1963); *The Age of Voltaire* (1965); and *Rousseau and Revolution* (1967).

Story of Don Miff, The. Novel by Virginius Dabney (1886). Don Miff is a lisping version of the name John Smith. A supposed record of Virginia, 1860–1865.

Story of Kennett, The. Novel by Bayard Taylor (1866). Real characters of about 1796 in his own neighborhood of Kennett Square, Philadelphia.

Story of Mankind, The. By Hendrik Van Loon (1921). Popular history illustrated by the author, dramatizing world events from a storyteller's standpoint rather than in the more formal historical manner.

Story of Margaret Kent, The. Novel by "Henry Hayes" (Ellen Warner Olney Kirk) (1886). Portrays the efforts of Margaret Kent, deserted by her husband, to make a living for herself and her little daughter Gladys, by writing. The situation is complicated by suitors who think she is a widow.

Story of My Boyhood and Youth, The. Autobiography by John Muir (1913).

Story of the Other Wise Man, The. By Henry van Dyke (1896). A story of Christmas, first read as a sermon at the Brick Presbyterian church in New York City, as was also the author's *The First Christmas Tree* (1897).

Story of Thyrza, The. Novel by Alice Brown (1909). Presents the woman who suffers martyrdom from her first encounter with passions.

Story Teller's Story, A. By Sherwood Anderson (1924). Autobiography relating the adventures of an imaginative mind as it sought to adjust itself to a world of tragic realities.

STOUT, GEORGE LESLIE (Oct. 5, 1897–); b. Winterset, Ia. Museum director, author. *Painting Materials: A Short Encyclopedia* (with Rutherford J. Gettens, 1942); *The Care of Pictures* (1948).

STOUT, REX [Todhunter] (Dec. 1, 1886–); b. Noblesville, Ind. Author. *How Like a God* (1929); *Golden Remedy* (1931); *Forest Fire* (1933); *The President Vanishes* (1934); *Fer-de-Lance* (1934); *O Careless Love!* (1935); *The Rubber Band* (1936); *The Red Box* (1936); *The Hand in the Glove* (1937); *Mr. Cinderella* (1938); *Some Buried Caesar* (1939); *Mountain Cat* (1939); *The Broken Vase* (1941); *Black Orchids* (1942); *The Silent Speaker* (1946); *The Second Confession* (1949); *Curtains for Three* (1951); *The Golden Spiders* (1953); *Before Midnight* (1955); *Three for the Chair* (1957); *And Four to Go On* (1958); *Plot It Yourself* (1959); *The Final Deduction* (1961); *Gambit* (1962); *The Mother Hunt* (1963); *Trio for Blunt Instruments* (1964); *The Doorbell Rang* (1965); *Death of a Dude* (1969); etc.

Stout Gentleman, The. Short story by Washington Irving, in *Bracebridge Hall* (1822). A romance of the stage coach.

STOUTENBURG, ADRIEN (Dec. 1, 1916–   ); b. Darfur, Minn. Author. *Wild Animals of the Far West* (1958); *Good-by Cinderella* (1958); *Beloved Botanist* (with L. N. Baker, 1961); *Little Smoke* (1961); *Secret Lions* (1962); *Window on the Sea* (1962); *Dear, Dear Livy: Story of Mrs. Mark Twain* (with L. N. Baker, 1963); *Walk into the Wind* (1964); *The Things that Are* (poems, 1964); *Heroes Advise Us* (poems, 1964); *Rain Boat* (1965); *Explorer of the Unconscious: Sigmund Freud* (with L. N. Baker, 1965); *The Crocodile's Mouth* (1966); *A Vanishing Thunder* (1967); *Short History of the Fur Trade* (1968); etc. Also writes under the name "Lace Kendall."

STOVALL, FLOYD (July 7, 1896–); b. Temple, Tex. Educator, author. *Desire and Restraint in Shelley* (1931); *American Idealism* (1943). Co-author: *The Development of American Literary Criticism* (1955). Prof. English, University of Virginia, since 1955.

Stover at Yale. By Owen Johnson (1911). One of the popular college stories.

STOWE, CALVIN ELLIS (Apr. 26, 1802–Aug. 22, 1886); b. Natick, Mass. Congregational clergyman, educator, author. Husband of Harriet Beecher Stowe. *Introduction to the Criticism and Interpretation of the Bible* (1835); *Origin and History of the Books of the Bible* (1867); etc.

STOWE, CHARLES EDWARD (b. July 8, 1850); b. Brunswick, Me., son of Mrs. Harriet Beecher Stowe. Lecturer, author. *Life of Harriet Beecher Stowe* (1889); *Lives of Distinguished Americans* (1889); *Harriet Beecher Stowe: The Story of Her Life* (with son, Lyman Beecher Stowe, 1911); *Rhymes from the Santa Barbara Hills* (1920).

STOWE, HARRIET [Elizabeth] BEECHER (June 14, 1811–July 1, 1896); b. Litchfield, Conn. Author. *A New England Sketch* (1834); *The Mayflower* (1843); *Uncle Tom's Cabin; or, Life Among the Lowly* (1851); *Memories in Foreign Lands* (1854); *Dred, A Tale of the Great Dismal Swamp* (1856); *The

Minister's Wooing (1859); *The Pearl of Orr's Island* (1862); *Religious Poems* (1867); *Old Town Folks* (1869); *Sam Lawson's Oldtown Fireside Stories* (1872); *Poganuc People* (1878); *The Writings*, 16v. (1896); etc. See C. E. Stowe's *Life of Harriet Beecher Stowe* (1889); A. A. Fields's *Life and Letters of Harriet Beecher Stowe* (1897); Forrest Wilson's *Crusader in Crinoline* (1941); Edward Wagenknecht's *Harriet Beecher Stowe: The Known and the Unknown* (1965); *Essays on American Literature in Honor of Jay B. Hubbell,* ed. by C. Gohdes (1967).

STOWE, LELAND (Nov. 10, 1899–); b. Southbury, Conn. Journalist, lecturer, author. *Nazi Means War* (1933); *No Other Road to Freedom* (1941); *They Shall Not Sleep* (1944); *While Time Remains* (1946); *Target: You* (1949); *Conquest by Terror: The Story of Satellite Europe* (1952); *Crusoe of Lonesome Lake* (1957). With *New York Herald Tribune,* 1926–39; foreign staff *Chicago Daily News,* from 1939. Prof. journalism, University of Michigan, since 1956.

STOWE, LYMAN BEECHER (Dec. 22, 1880–Sept. 25, 1963); b. Saco, Me., grandson of Harriet Beecher Stowe. Lecturer, author. *Harriet Beecher Stowe: The Story of Her Life* (with Charles Edward Stowe, 1912); *Booker T. Washington* (with Emmet J. Scott, 1916); *Saints, Sinners and Beechers* (1934); etc. Editorial staff, Doubleday, Page & Co., later Doubleday, Doran & Co., New York, 1918–30.

STOWELL, WILLIAM AVERILL (Mar. 29, 1882–May 29, 1950); b. Appleton, Wis. Educator, author. *The Wake of the Setting Sun* (1923); *The Mystery of the Singing Walls* (1925); *The Marston Murder Case* (1930). Prof. Romance languages, Amherst College, 1909–20.

STRABEL, THELMA (1900–May 28, 1959); b. Crown Point, Ind. Novelist. *Smart Woman* (1933); *Streamline Marriage* (1947); *Reap the Wild Wind* (1941); *Storm to the South* (1944); *Caribee* (1957).

STRACHEY, WILLIAM (fl. 1610). Historian, first secretary of the Virginia colony. *A True Reportory of the Wracke, and Redemption of Sir Thomas Gates* (1625); *The Historie of Travaile into Virginia Britannia* ed. by Richard H. Major (1849).

STRAHAN, KAY CLEAVER (Mrs. William Nicholas Strahan) (Jan. 4, 1888–); b. La Grande, Ore. Novelist. *Peggy-Mary* (1915); *Something That Begins with "T"* (1918); *Desert Moon* (1928); *Footprints* (1928); *October House* (1931); *Meriwether Mystery* (1933); *The Desert Lake Mystery* (1936); etc.

STRAIGHT, MICHAEL WHITNEY (Sept. 1, 1916–); b. Southampton, New York. Editor. *Make This the Last War* (1943); *Trial by Television* (1954); *Carrington* (1960); *A Very Small Remnant* (1963); etc. Editorial staff, *The New Republic,* 1941–43; now contributing editor.

STRAIGHT, WILLARD DICKERMAN (Jan. 31, 1880–Dec. 1, 1918); b. Oswego, N.Y. Consul, publicist. Founder, the *New Republic,* 1914; *Journal of the American Asiatic Association,* 1915, later called *Asia.* See Herbert Croly's *Willard Straight* (1924); Louis Graves's *Willard Straight in the Orient* (1922). U.S. consular service in Far East.

STRAIN, FRANCES BRUCE, b. Milwaukee, Wis. Author. *But You Don't Understand* (1950); *Framework for Family Life Education* (with C. L. Egger, 1955); etc.

STRAND, MARK (Apr. 11, 1934–   ); b. Summerside, Prince Edward Island, Can. Poet. *Sleeping With One Eye Open* (1964); *Reasons for Moving* (1968).

STRANG, JAMES JESSE (Mar. 21, 1813–July 9, 1856). Religious fanatic, author. *The Diamond* (1848); *Ancient and Modern (Michilimackinac)* (1854); *The Prophetic Controversy* (1854); *The Book of the Law of the Lord* (1856); etc. Founder of a religious cult at Voree, Wis. Founder, Order of the Iluminati. Established his new Zion at St. James on Big

Beaver Island, Wis., in 1849, and was crowned king in 1850. See Milo M. Quaife's *The Kingdom of Saint James* (1930).

STRANG, LEWIS CLINTON (Dec. 4, 1869–Jan. 14, 1935); b. Westfield, Mass. Author. *Famous Actresses of the Day* (1899); *Famous Actors of the Day* (1900); *Celebrated Comedians of Light Opera and Musical Comedy in America* (1901); *Players and Plays of the Last Quarter Century,* 2v. (1902); etc. With the *Boston Journal,* the *Washington Times,* etc.

STRANGE, MICHAEL (Mrs. Harrison Tweed) (1890–Nov. 5, 1950); b. (Blanche Marie Louise Oelrichs), Newport, R.I. Actress, poet. *Poems* (1919); *Resurrecting Life* (1921); *Selected Poems* (1928); *Who Tells Me True* (autobiography, 1940); etc.

Strange Fruit. Novel by Lillian Smith (1944). Treats race relations in the South.

Strange Interlude. Play by Eugene O'Neill (prod. 1928). A psychological drama illustrating the duality of character. What each character says and what each character thinks is revealed by the device of the stage "aside," giving the audience an insight not vouchsafed to the players themselves.

STRATEMEYER, EDWARD L. (Oct. 4, 1862–May 10, 1930); b. Elizabeth, N.J. Author. Pen names "Allen Winfield," "Arthur M. Winfield," "Captain Ralph Bonehill," etc. *Richard Dare's Venture; or, Striking Out for Himself* (1894); *Under Dewey at Manila* (1898); etc., including the *Bound to Win* series, *Old Glory* series, *Rover Boys* series, *Flag of Freedom* series, *Frontier* series, *Boy Hunters* series, *Mexican War* series, *Tom Swift* series, *Motor Boys* series, *Bobbsey Twins* series, *American Boys Biographical* Series. Founder, Stratemeyer Literary Syndicate, New York, 1906. After Stratemeyer's death, the Syndicate was directed by his daughter Harriet S. Adams, later joined by Andrew E. Svenson.

STRATTON, CLARENCE (Sept. 17, 1880–Sept. 13, 1950); b. Philadelphia, Pa. Educator, author. *Producing in Little Theatres* (1921); *Literature and Life* (1922); *Theatron* (1928); *Theatres: An Illustrated Record* (1928); *Harbor Pirates* (1929); *Robert the Roundhead* (1930); *In Singapore* (1932); *Mastering Your Language* (1947); etc. Editor: *Great American Speeches* (1920); etc. Lecturer, Western Reserve University, 1933–37, 1939–40.

STRATTON, SAMUEL SOMMERVILLE (Feb. 23, 1898–Mar. 1, 1969); b. Lynn, Mass. Educator. Co-author: *Problems in Corporation Finance* (1936); *Economics of the Iron and Steel Industry* (1937); *Financial Instruments and Institutions* (1938); etc. Pres., Middlebury College, since 1943.

STRAUS, NATHAN (May 27, 1889–); b. New York. Business executive. *Seven Myths of Housing* (1944); *Two Thirds of a Nation—A Housing Program* (1952).

STRAUS, OSCAR SOLOMON (Dec. 23, 1850–May 3, 1926); b. Otterberg, Bav. Jurist, diplomat, author. *The Origin of the Republican Form of Government in the United States* (1885); *Roger Williams, the Pioneer of Religious Liberty* (1894); *The American Spirit* (1913); *Under Four Administrations: From Cleveland to Taft* (autobiography, 1922). U.S. minister to Turkey, 1887–89, 1898–1900; secretary of commerce and labor, 1906–09; ambassador to Turkey, 1909–11.

STRAUSS, HAROLD (June 18, 1907–); b. New York. Editor. Editor-in-chief, Covici, Friede, 1934–38; with Alfred A. Knopf since 1939, editor-in-chief since 1942.

STRAUSS, LEO (Sept. 20, 1899–); b. Kirchhain, Ger. Educator, author. *The Political Philosophy of Hobbes* (1936); *On Tyranny* (1948); *Persecution and the Art of Writing* (1952); *Natural Right and History* (1953); *Thoughts on Machiavelli* (1958). Prof. political philosophy, University of Chicago, 1949–68; scholar in residence, St. John's College, since 1969.

STRAUSZ-HUPÉ, ROBERT (Mar. 25, 1903–); b. Vienna, Aus. Educator, author. *Axis-America* (1941); *Geopolitics* (1942); *The Balance of Tomorrow* (1945); *International Relations* (with S. T. Possony, 1950); *The Zone of Indifference* (1952); *Power and Community* (1956); etc. Prof. political science, University of Pennsylvania, since 1952. U.S. Ambassador to Morocco since 1969.

STRAVINSKY, IGOR FEDOROVICH (June 5, 1882–April 6, 1971); b. near St. Petersburg, Rus. Composer. *Poetics of Music* (1947); *Conversations with Igor Stravinsky* (with Robert Craft, 1959); *Memories and Commentaries* (with same, 1960); *Expositions and Developments* (with same, 1962).

STRECKER, EDWARD ADAM (Oct. 16, 1886–Jan. 2, 1959); b. Philadelphia, Pa. Educator, author. *Clinical Psychiatry* (1925); *Discovering Ourselves* (1931); *Alcohol: One Man's Meat* (with F. T. Chambers, 1938); *Their Mothers' Sons* (1946); *Their Mothers' Daughters* (with V. T. Lathbury, 1956), Prof. psychiatry, University of Pennsylvania, 1931–53.

STREET, ALFRED BILLINGS (Dec. 18, 1811–June 2, 1881); b. Poughkeepsie, N.Y. Lawyer, poet, librarian. *The Burning of Schenectady, and Other Poems* (1842); *Drawings and Tintings* (1844); *The Poems of Alfred B. Street* (1845); *Frontenac* (1849). His best known poems are "The Gray Forest Eagle," "Lost Hunter," "The Settler." Editor, *Northern Light,* Albany, N.Y., 1843–44. Librarian, New York State Library, 1848–62.

STREET, JAMES [Howell] (Oct. 15, 1903–Sept. 28, 1954); b. Lumberton, Miss. Journalist, author. *Look Away! A Dixie Notebook* (1936); *Oh, Promised Land* (1940); *In My Father's House* (1941); *Tap Roots* (1942); *By Valour and Arms* (1944); *The Gauntlet* (1945); *Short Stories* (1945); *Tomorrow We Reap* (with James Childers, 1949); *Mingo Dabney* (1950); *The High Calling* (1951); *Velvet Doublet* (1953); *Captain Little Ax* (1956); etc.

STREET, JULIAN [Leonard] (Apr. 12, 1879–Feb. 19, 1947); b. Chicago, Ill. Novelist, *The Need of Change* (1909); *The Goldfish* (1912); *Abroad at Home* (1914); *American Adventures* (1917); *After Thirty* (1919); *Rita Coventry* (1922); *Cross-Sections* (1923); *Mr. Bisbee's Princess* (1925); *Wines* (1933); *Men, Machines and Morals* (1942); etc.

Street and Smith. Publishers. New York. Founded 1855, by Francis S. Smith and Francis S. Street. The presidents of the firm have been Ormond G. Smith, George C. Smith, Jr., Artemas Holmes, and Allen L. Grammer. The firm published popular fiction in a cheap format, including "dime novels" and numerous "pulp" magazines featuring Western fiction, detective stories, adventure stories, etc. Many well-known writers got their start with Street and Smith. No longer active in book publishing, it now owns many magazines, including *Mademoiselle.*

Street Scene. Play by Elmer Rice (prod. 1929). Various scenes from a tenement section in New York City, showing the comedy and tragedy of the daily life of a crowded cosmopolitan neighborhood. Pulitzer Prize play, 1929.

Streetcar Named Desire, A. Play by Tennessee Williams (prod. 1947). The setting is a New Orleans slum and the theme concerns a woman who is obsessed by her own dreams, and her brother-in-law, who is a selfish, sensual man of strong animal attraction to her.

STREETER, CARROLL PERRY (Nov. 12, 1898–); b. Groton, S.D. Editor, *Farm Journal,* since 1955.

STREETER, EDWARD (Aug. 1, 1891–); b. New York. Humorist, author. *Dere Mable* (1918); *That's Me All Over, Mable* (1919); *Same Old Bill, Eh, Mable?* (1919); *Daily Except Sundays* (1938); *Father of the Bride* (1949); *Skoal Scandinavia* (1952); *Merry Christmas, Mr. Baxter* (1956); *Mr. Robbins Rides Again* (1957); *Window on America* (1959); *Chairman of the Bored* (1961); *Along the Ridge* (1964); *Ham Martin, Class of '17* (1969); etc.

STREIT, CLARENCE KIRSHMAN (Jan. 21, 1896–); b. California, Mo. Journalist, author. *Union Now* (1940); *Union Now with Britain* (1941); *Freedom Against Itself* (1954); *Freedom's Frontier; Atlantic Union Now* (1961); etc. On staff, the *New York Times,* since 1925; editor, *Freedom and Union,* since 1946.

Strenuous Life, The. By Theodore Roosevelt (1900). Thirteen essays and addresses reflecting the philosophy of a man of action.

STRIBLING, T[homas] S[igismund] (Mar. 4, 1881–July 8, 1965); b. Clifton, Tenn. Novelist. *The Cruise of the Dry Dock* (1917); *Birthright* (1922); *Fombombo* (1923); *Red Sand* (1924); *Teeftallow* (1926); *Bright Metal* (1928); *East Is East* (1928); *Strange Moon* (1929); *Clues of the Caribbees* (1929); *Backwater* (1930); *The Forge* (1931); *The Store* (1932, Pulitzer Prize novel, 1933); *Unfinished Cathedral* (1933); *The Sound Wagon* (1935); *These Bars of Flesh* (1938). See Fred B. Millett's *Contemporary American Authors* (1940).

Strictures on a Pamphlet Entitled "A Friendly Address to All Reasonable Americans." By Charles Lee (1775). Reply to Thomas Bradbury Chandler's conciliatory pamphlet.

STRINGER, ARTHUR [John Arbuthnott] (Feb. 26, 1874–Sept. 15, 1950); b. Chatham, Ont. Novelist. *Watchers of Twilight* (1894); *Pauline, and Other Poems* (1895); *The Loom of Destiny* (1898); *The Silver Poppy* (1899); *Lonely O'Malley* (1901); *Irish Poems* (1911); *Open Water* (1912); *Gun Runner* (1912); *The Prairie Wife* (1915); *City of Peril* (1923); *White Hands* (1927); *The Wolf Woman* (1928); *A Woman at Dusk, and Other Poems* (1928); *The Mud Lark* (1931); *Man Lost* (1934); *Heather of the High Hand* (1937); *Intruders in Eden* (1942); *Red Wine of Youth: A Biography of Rupert Brooke* (1948); etc.

Stringtown on the Pike. Novel by John Uri Lloyd (1909). A story of drab life as lived in the region between the Ohio and Kentucky rivers. The folks of Stringtown are not without virtue, but they have little to do with strangers and cling to old prejudices.

STROBEL, MARION (Mrs. James Herbert Mitchell) (Aug. 26, 1895–); b. Chicago, Ill. Poet, novelist. *Once in a Blue Moon* (poems, 1925); *Lost City* (poems, 1928); *Saturday Afternoon* (1930); *A Woman of Fashion* (1931); *Fellow Mortals* (1935); *Ice Before Killing* (1943); *Kiss and Kill* (1946); etc.

STRODE, HUDSON (Oct. 31, 1892–); b. Cairo, Ill. Educator, author. *The Story of Bermuda* (1932); *The Pageant of Cuba* (1934); *South by Thunderbird* (1937). Editor: *Immortal Lyrics* (1938); *Sweden: Model for a World* (1949); *Denmark Is a Lovely Land* (1951); *Jefferson Davis: American Patriot* (1955); *Jefferson Davis: Confederate President* (1959). English dept., University of Alabama, since 1916.

STROHM, JOHN LOUIS (June 22, 1912–); b. near West Union, Ill. Editor, radio commentator, author. *I Lived with Latin Americans* (1943); *Just Tell the Truth* (1947). Assoc. editor, *Country Gentleman,* 1947–55. Editor: *Ford Almanac.*

STRONG, ANNA LOUISE (Nov. 24, 1885–); b. Friend, Neb. Author. *Songs of the City* (1906); *Ragged Verse by Anise* (1918); *China's Millions* (1928); *Red Star in Samarkand* (1929); *The Road to the Grey Pamir* (1931); *I Change Worlds* (autobiography, 1935); *This Soviet World* (1936); *Spain in Arms* (1937); *My Native Land* (1940); *Peoples of the U.S.S.R.* (1944); *Tomorrow's China* (1948); *The Chinese Conquer China* (1949); *The Stalin Era* (1956); etc.

STRONG, AUGUSTUS HOPKINS (Aug. 3, 1836–Nov. 29, 1921); b. Rochester, N.Y. Baptist clergyman, educator, author. *Systematic Theology* (1886); *Philosophy and Religion* (1888); *The Great Poets and Their Theology* (1897); *Miscellanies,* 2v. (1912); *American Poets and Their Theology* (1916); etc. President, Rochester Baptist Theological Seminary, 1872–1912. He influenced John D. Rockefeller to found the University of Chicago. Founder, Rochester Historical Society. *See* Allan Nevins's *John D. Rockefeller*, 2v. (1940).

STRONG, AUSTIN (Apr. 18, 1881–Sept. 17, 1952); b. San Francisco, Calif. Playwright. *The Exile* (with Lloyd Osbourne, prod. 1903); *The Little Father of the Wilderness* (with same, prod. 1905); *The Drums of Oude* (prod. 1906); *The Toymaker of Nüremburg (prod. 1907); Rip Van Winkle* (prod. 1911); *Three Wise Fools* (prod. 1918); *Seventh Heaven* (prod. 1922); *A Play without a Name* (prod. 1928).

STRONG, CHARLES AUGUSTUS (Nov. 28, 1862–Jan. 23, 1940); b. Haverhill, Mass. Educator, author. *The Origin of Consciousness* (1918); *The Wisdom of the Beasts* (1921); *A Theory of Knowledge* (1923); *A Creed for Skeptics* (1936). Psychology dept., Columbia University, 1895–1910.

STRONG, CHARLES STANLEY (Nov. 29, 1906–Oct. 10, 1962); b. Brooklyn, N.Y. Author. *The Spectre of Masuria* (1932); *Betrayed* (1935); *Cruise Hosters* (1936); *Professional Model* (1938); *Flying Lovers* (1939); *Confessional* (1939). Under pen name "Carl Sturdy": *Society Doctor* (1936); *Registered Nurse* (1937); *Resort Doctor* (1938); etc.; under pen name "Kelvin McKay": *Murder at Barclay House* (1937); under pen name "Nancy Bartlett": *Embassy Ball* (1938); under pen name "William McClellan": *Waterfront Waitress* (1937); *Penthouse Pagan* (1938); etc. Under pen name "Chuck Stanley": *Boss of Golden River* (1952); *Indian Fighter* (1955); *Professor Colt* (1958); *King of Cimarron Crossing* (1959). Also books under pen names "Myron Keats," "Charles Stoddard."

Strong, Harrington. Pen name of Johnston McCulley.

STRONG, JAMES (Aug. 14, 1822–Aug. 7, 1894); b. New York. Educator, editor. Compiler: *Cyclopoedia of Biblical, Theological, and Ecclesiastical Literature*, 10v. (with John M'Clintock, 1867–81); with *Supplement*, 2v. (1885–86); *The Exhaustive Concordance of the Bible* (1894); etc. Prof. Biblical literature, Troy (N.Y.) University, 1858–63; prof. exegetical theology, Drew Theological Seminary, 1867–93.

STRONG, JOSIAH (Jan. 19, 1847–Apr. 28, 1916); b. Naperville, Ill. Congregational clergyman, reformer, author. *Our Country* (1885); *The New Era* (1893); *The Next Great Awakening* (1902); *The Challenge of the City* (1907); *My Religion in Every-Day Life* (1910); etc. He originated the "Safety First" movement.

STRONG, LATHAM CORNELL (June 12, 1845–Dec. 17, 1879); b. Troy, N.Y. Author. *Castle Windows* (1876); *Poke o' Moonshine* (1878); *Midsummer Dream* (1879); etc.

STRONG, WALTER ANSEL (Aug. 13, 1883–May 10, 1931); b. Chicago, Ill. Editor, publisher. With the *Chicago Daily News*, 1905–31; owner and president, 1925–31.

Strongheart. Play by William C. De Mille (prod. 1905). Story of an educated Indian chief who feels compelled to forego his love for a white girl to return to his tribe and work for their improvement.

STROTHER, DAVID HUNTER (Sept. 26, 1816–Mar. 8, 1888); b. Martinsburg, Va. (now W.Va.). Soldier, illustrator, author. Pen name, "Porte Crayon." *Virginia Illustrated* (1857); *The Adventures of Porte Crayon and His Cousins* (1857). His first "Porte Crayon" article, illustrated by himself, *The Virginia Canaan*, was published in *Harper's Weekly*, 1853. Other series of iustrated articles which he contributed to *Harper's Weekly* were: *North Carolina Illustrated*, 1857; *A Winter in the South*, 1857–58; *A Summer in New England*, 1860–61; *Personal Recollections of the War*, 1866–68; *The Mountains*, 1872–75. He illustrated John P. Kennedy's *Swallow Barn;* Pendleton Kennedy's *The Blackwater Chronicle;* etc.

STROUP, HERBERT HEWITT (May 1, 1916–); b. Philadelphia, Pa. Educator, author. *Jehovah's Witnesses* (1945); So-

cial Work: *An Introduction to the Field* (1948); *Community Welfare Organization* (1952); *Toward A Philosophy of Student Activities* (1965); *Church and State in Confrontation* (1967); etc. Prof. sociology and anthropology, Brooklyn College, since 1954.

STROUT, RICHARD LEE (Mar. 14, 1898–); b. Cohoes, N.Y. Journalist. *Farewell to the Model T* (with E. B. White, 1936); etc. Editor: *Maud* (1939). With *Christian Science Monitor*, since 1921.

STRUIK, DIRK JAN (Sept. 30, 1894–); b. Rotterdam, Neth. Educator, author. *Linear Connections* (1934); *Yankee Science in the Making* (1948); *Concise History of Mathematics*, 2v. (1948). Prof. mathematics, Massachusetts Institute of Technology, since 1940.

STRUNK, [William] OLIVER (Mar. 22, 1901–); b. Ithaca, N.Y. Educator, author. *State and Resources of Musicology in the United States* (1932); *Source Readings in Music History* (1950). Editor: *Music from the Days of George Washington* (with Carl Engel, 1931). Prof. music, Princeton University, 1950–66; Prof. Emeritus since 1966.

STRUNSKY, SIMEON (July 23, 1879–Feb. 5, 1948); b. Vitebsk, Rus. Journalist, essayist. *The Patient Observer and His Friends* (1911); *Post-Impressions* (1914); *Belshazzar Court* (1914); *Professor Latimer's Progress* (1918); *Sinbad and His Friends* (1921); *The Rediscovery of Jones* (1931); *The Living Tradition* (1939); *No Mean City* (1944); *Two Came to Town* (1947). Editorial staff, *New York Evening Post*, 1906–20; *New York Times*, from 1924.

STRYKER, LLOYD PAUL (Jan. 5, 1885–June 21, 1955); b. Chicago, Ill. Lawyer, author. *Andrew Johnson: A Study in Courage* (1929); *Courts and Doctors* (1932); *For the Defense: A Biography of Thomas Erskine* (1947); *The Art of Advocacy* (1954).

STRYKER, MELANCTHON WOOLSEY (Jan. 7, 1857–Dec. 6, 1929); b. Vernon, N.Y. Presbyterian clergyman, educator, hymn writer, poet. *The Song of Miriam, and Other Hymns & Verses* (1888); *Hamilton, Lincoln & Other Addresses* (1896); *Vesper Bells* (poems, 1919); *Embers: Hymns and Other Verse* (1926); etc. President, Hamilton College, 1892–1917.

STRYKER, PERRIN (Mar. 6, 1908–); b. Passaic, N.J. Journalist, editor. *Arms and the Aftermath* (1942); *The Men From the Boys* (1960); *The Character of the Executive* (1961); *The Hidden Areas of the President's Decision Making* (1966); *The Incomparable Salesman* (1967); etc. Co-author: *A Guide to Modern Management Methods* (1954); *The Executive Life* (1956). With *Fortune*, since 1946.

Stuart, Arabella W. *See* Arabella M. Willson.

Stuart, Eleanor. *See* Eleanor Stuart Childs.

Stuart, Gordon. See Robert Armistead Stewart.

STUART, GRAHAM HENRY (Jan. 27, 1887–); b. Cleveland, O. Educator, author. *Latin America and the United States* (1922); *The Tacna-Arica Dispute* (1927); *American Diplomatic and Consular Practice* (1936); *Department of State* (1949); *The International City of Tangier* (with others, 1955); etc. Prof. political science, Stanford University, since 1924.

STUART, GRANVILLE (Aug. 27, 1834–Oct. 2, 1918); b. Clarksburg, Va. (now W.Va.). Montana pioneer, author. *Montana as It Is* (1865); *Forty Years on the Frontier*, ed. by P. C. Phillips, 2v. (1925).

STUART, ISAAC WILLIAM (June 13, 1809–Oct. 2, 1861); b. New Haven, Conn. Historian, orator, author. *Hartford in the Olden Time* (1853); *Life of Captain Nathan Hale* (1856); *Life of Jonathan Trumbull, Sen., Governor of Connecticut* (1859); etc.

STUART, J[ames] E[well] B[rown] (Feb. 6, 1833–May 12, 1864); b. in Patrick Co., Va. Confederate cavalry officer. *See* J. E. Cooke's *The Wearing of the Gray* (1867); George C. Eggleston's *A Rebel's Recollections* (1875); H. B. McClellan's *The Life and Campaigns of Major-General J. E. B. Stuart* (1885); G. W. Beale's *A Lieutenant of Cavalry in Lee's Army* (1918); John W. Thomason's *Jeb Stuart* (1930); Douglas S. Freeman's *R. E. Lee*, 4v. (1934–35). Best remembered for his romantic and dashing exploits at the battles of Fredericksburg and Gettysburg.

STUART, JESSE [Hilton] (Aug. 8, 1907–); b. near Riverton, Ky. Poet, novelist. *Man with a Bull-Tongue Plow* (poems, 1934); *Head o' W-Hollow* (1936); *Beyond Dark Hills* (autobiography, 1938); *Trees of Heaven* (1940); *Mongrel Mettle* (1944); *Foretaste of Glory* (1946); *The Thread That Runs So True* (1949); *Hie to the Hunters* (1950); *Kentucky Is My Land* (poems, 1952); *Red Mule* (1954); *The Year of My Rebirth* (1956); *Plowshare in Heaven* (1958); *The Rightful Owner* (1960); *Andy Finds A Way* (1961); *Hold April* (1962); *Save Every Lamb* (1964); *Daughter of the Legend* (1965); *My Land Has a Voice* (1966); *Mr. Gallion's Novel* (1967); *To Teach to Love* (1969); etc.

STUART, RUTH McENERY (May 21, 1849–May 6, 1917); b. Marksville, La. Author. *A Golden Wedding, and Other Tales* (1893); *Carlotta's Intended, and Other Tales* (1894); *In Simpkinsville: Character Tales* (1897); *Sonny, a Christmas Guest* (1897); *Napoleon Jackson, the Gentlemen of the Plush Rocker* (1902); *Aunt Amity's Silver Wedding, and Other Stories* (1909); *Daddy Do-Funny's Wisdom Jingles* (1913); *Plantation Songs* (1916).

Stuart Little. By E. B. White (1945). Children's Story about an ingenious and adventurous little mouse.

STUBBS, HARRY C[lement] (May 30, 1922–); b. Somerville, Mass. Teacher, science-fiction writer. Pen name "Hal Clement." *Needle* (1950); *Ice World* (1952); *Mission of Gravity* (1954); *The Ranger Boys in Space* (1956); *Cycle of Fire* (1957); *Close to Critical* (1958); *Natives of Space* (stories, 1965).

STUCK, HUDSON (Nov. 11, 1863–Oct. 10, 1920); b. London. Episcopal clergyman, missionary, author. *Ten Thousand Miles with a Dog Sled* (1914); *Voyages on the Yukon and Its Tributaries* (1917); *A Winter Circuit of Our Arctic Coast* (1920); etc.

STUDEBAKER, JOHN WARD (June 10, 1887–); b. McGregor, Ia. Publisher. Vice-president and chairman of board, *Scholastic*, since 1948. Author of numerous textbooks.

Student in Economics, A. Short story by George Milburn (1933).

Studs Lonigan. Novel by James T. Farrell (1936). A trilogy embracing *Young Lonigan* (1932), *The Young Manhood of Studs Lonigan* (1934), and *Judgment Day* (1935). Studs is a young Chicago hoodlum, victim of his environment. His daily life with its spiritual frustration is the theme of this realistic chronicle.

STUMPF, SAMUEL ENOCH (Feb. 3, 1918–); b. Cleveland, O. Educator. *A Democratic Manifesto* (1954). Prof. philosophy, Vanderbilt University, 1952–67; Pres., Cornell College, Ia., since 1967.

Sturdy, Carl. Pen name of Charles Stanley Strong.

Sturgeon, Theodore. Pen name of Edward Hamilton Waldo.

STURGIS, RUSSELL (Oct. 16, 1836–Feb. 11, 1909); b. Baltimore, Md. Architect, critic, editor, author. *A History of Architecture*, 4v. (1906–15); etc. Compiler: *Catalogue of Ancient and Modern Engravings, Woodcuts, and Illustrated Books, Parts of the Collection of C. E. Norton and R. Sturgis* (with Charles Eliot Norton, 1879). Editor: *A Dictionary of Architecture and Building*, 3v. (1901–02); *Outlines of the History*

of Art, 2v. (1904). Editor, "The Field of Art" dept., in *Scribner's Magazine*, 1897–1909. Founder, *The New Path*, 1863.

STURM, JUSTIN (Apr. 21, 1899–Aug. 1967); b. Nehawka, Neb. Sculptor, author. *The Bad Samaritan* (1926); *I Know What I Like* (prod. 1939); *The Clover Ring* (play, 1945); *Index to Sybil* (1951); *One Eye Closed* (play, 1954).

STUTLER, BOYD BLYNN (July 10, 1889–); b. Coxs Mills, W.Va. Journalist, editor, author. *Captain John Brown and Harper's Ferry* (1926); *West Virginia Yesterday and Today* (with Phil Conley 1952). Managing editor, the *American Legion Magazine*, 1936–54.

STYRON, WILLIAM (1925–). Author. *Lie Down in Darkness* (1957); *Set This House on Fire* (1960); *Confessions of Nat Turner* (1967, Pulitzer Prize, 1968); *Long March* (1968).

Subject Guide to Books in Print. Published by R. R. Bowker Co., since 1957. A one-volume bibliography listing U. S. books now in print. The list covers subject headings and cross-references.

Subject Index to Poetry. Ed. by Herbert Bruncken (1940).

SUBLETTE, CLIFFORD MacCLELLAN (Aug. 16, 1887–1939); b. Charleston, Ill. Author. *The Scarlet Cockerel* (1925); *The Bright Face of Danger* (1926); *The Golden Chimney* (1931); *Greenhorn's Hunt* (1934).

Subtreasury of American Humor. Edited by E. B. and K. S. White (1941). Standard collection of humorous writings.

"Success." Poem by Emily Dickinson, first published in *A Masque of Poets*, an anthology, in 1878. Helen Hunt Jackson was responsible for sending the poem to the editor.

SUCKOW, RUTH (Aug. 6, 1892–Jan. 23, 1960); b. Hawarden, Ia. Novelist. *Country People* (1924); *The Odyssey of a Nice Girl* (1925); *Iowa Interiors* (1926); *The Bonney Family* (1928); *Cora* (1929); *The Kramer Girls* (1930); *Children and Older People* (1931); *The Folks* (1934); *Carry-Over* (1936); *New Hope* (1942); *Some Others and Myself: A Memoir* (1952); *The John Wood Case* (1959).

Sudden Guest, The. Novel by Christopher La Farge (1946).

Sugartail. Pen name of George Washington Harris.

SULLIVAN, EDWARD DEAN (Nov. 24, 1888–Apr. 4, 1938); b. New Haven, Conn. Journalist, author. *Rattling the Cup* (1928); *Look at Chicago* (1930); *Benedict Arnold, Military Racketeer* (1932); *The Fabulous Wilson Mizner* (1935); *This Labor Union Racket* (1936); etc. With *New York Herald, Chicago Herald Examiner, New York Herald Tribune,* etc.

SULLIVAN, FRANCIS WILLIAM (Feb. 16, 1887–); b. Evanston, Ill. Author. *Children of Banishment* (1914); *Alloy of Gold* (1915); *Star of the North* (1916); etc.

SULLIVAN, FRANK [Francis John] (Sept. 22, 1892–); b. Saratoga Springs, N.Y. Humorist. *The Life and Times of Martha Hepplethwaite* (1926); *The Adventures of an Oaf* (1927); *Broccoli and Old Lace* (1931); *In One Ear* (1933); *A Pearl in Every Oyster* (1938); *Sullivan at Bay* (1938); *A Rock in Every Snowball* (1946); *The Night the Old Nostalgia Burned Down* (1953); *Sullivan Bites News* (with Sam Berman, 1954); *A Moose in the Hoose* (1959).

SULLIVAN, JOHN PATRICK (July 13, 1930–); b. Liverpool, Eng. Educator, author. *Ezra Pound and Sextus Propertius: A Study in Creative Translation* (1964); *The Satyricon of Petronius: A Literary Study* (1967). Editor: *Critical Essays on Roman Literature*, vol. 1 (1962), vol. 2 (1963). Prof. classics, University of Texas, since 1963.

SULLIVAN, KEVIN (Oct. 22, 1920–   ); b. New York. Educator, author. *Joyce Among the Jesuits* (1958); *Oscar Wilde* (1967). Associate dean of graduate faculties, Columbia University, since 1964.

SULLIVAN, LAWRENCE (Aug. 5, 1898–Mar. 7, 1968); b. San Francisco, Cal. Journalist, author. *All About Washington* (1932); *Prelude to Panic* (1936); *The Dead Hand of Bureaucracy* (1940); *Bureaucracy Runs Amuck* (1944); etc. Founder, *National Business News,* 1934.

SULLIVAN, LOUIS HENRI (Sept. 3, 1856–Apr. 14, 1924); b. Boston, Mass. Architect, author. *The Autobiography of an Idea* (1924); *Kindergarten Chats on Architecture, Education, and Democracy* (1934). He was responsible for the skyscraper, America's distinct contribution to architecture. *See* Frank Lloyd Wright's *Genius and Mobocracy: The Life and Drawings of Louis Sullivan* (1949); Sherman Paul's *Louis Sullivan* (1962).

SULLIVAN, MARK (Sept. 10, 1874–Aug. 13, 1952); b. Avondale, Pa. Journalist, author. *Our Times: The United States, 1900–1925,* 6v. (1926–35); *The Education of an American* (autobiography, 1938). Political columnist, *New York Herald Tribune,* and other papers.

SULLIVAN, RICHARD (Nov. 29, 1908–   ); b. Kenosha, Wis. Novelist. *Summer after Summer* (1942); *The Dark Continent* (1943); *The World of Idella May* (1946); *First Citizen* (1948); *The Fresh and Open Sky* (stories, 1950); *Notre Dame* (1951); *311 Congress Court* (1953); *Three Kings* (1956); etc.

SULLIVAN, THOMAS RUSSELL (Nov. 21, 1849–June 28, 1916); b. Boston, Mass. Novelist. *Day and Night Stories,* 2 series (1890–93); *Ars et Vita, and Other Stories* (1898); *The Courage of Conviction* (1902); *The Heart of Us* (1912); *Boston, New and Old* (1912); *The Hand of Petrarch* (1913); *Passages from the Journal* (1917); etc.

SULLIVAN, WALTER SEAGAR (Jan. 12, 1918–); b. New York. Editor, author. *Quest for a Continent* (1957); *White Land of Adventure* (1957); *Assault on the Unknown* (1961); *We Are Not Alone* (1964). Editor: *America's Race for the Moon* (1962). Science Editor, *New York Times,* since 1964.

SULLIVAN, WILLIAM (Nov. 1774–Sept. 3, 1839); b. Biddeford, Me. Lawyer, author. *The Moral Class Book* (1831); *Sea Life* (1837); *Familiar Letters on Public Characters and Public Events from the Peace of 1783 to the Peace of 1815* (1834), republished, as *The Public Men of the Revolution,* ed. by his son, J. T. S. Sullivan (1847).

SULZBERGER, ARTHUR HAYS (Sept. 12, 1891–Dec. 11, 1968); b. New York. Publisher. Director, Times Printing Co., Chattanooga, Tenn.; owner and publisher, the *New York Times,* succeeding his father-in-law, Adolph S. Ochs.

Summerfield, Charles. Pen name of Alfred W. Arrington.

SUMMERS, FESTUS PAUL (Mar. 2, 1895–); b. near Summersville, W.Va. Educator. *Johnson Newlon Camden: A Study in Individualism* (1937); *The Baltimore and Ohio in the Civil War* (1939); *William L. Wilson and Tariff Reform* (1953); *West Virginia: The Mountain State* (1958). Editor: *The Cabinet Diary of William L. Wilson, 1896–97* (1957). Prof. history, University of West Virginia, since 1946; prof. emeritus since 1965.

SUMMERS, HOLLIS (June 21, 1916–   ); b. Eminence, Ky. Educator, author. *City Limit* (1948); *Brighten the Corner* (1952); *The Weather of February* (1957); *Teach You a Lesson* (with J. Rourke, 1955); *The Walks Near Athens* (poems, 1959); *Someone Else* (1962); *Seven Occasions* (1965); *The Peddler and Other Domestic Matters* (1967); etc. Faculty, Ohio University, since 1959.

SUMNER, CHARLES (Jan. 6, 1811–Mar. 11, 1874); b. Boston, Mass. Orator, statesman, abolitionist, author. *The Works of Charles Sumner,* 15v. (1870–83); *The Complete Works,* 20v. (1900). His best known oration was *The Crime of Kansas,* delivered in the U.S. Senate, Mar. 20, 1856. The Sumner collection at Harvard University contains over 40,000 letters re-

ceived by him. Famous orations on Sumner were delivered by George W. Curtis, Carl Schurz, and Lucius Q. C. Lamar. U.S. Senator, 1851–74. *See* E. L. Pierce's *Memoir and Letters of Charles Sumner,* 4v. (1877–93); Moorfield Storey's *Charles Sumner* (1900); George H. Haynes's *Charles Sumner* (1909).

SUMNER, CID RICKETTS (Sept. 27, 1890–Oct. 15, 1970); b. Brookhaven, Miss. Novelist. *Ann Singleton* (1938); *Quality* (1946); *Tammy out of Time* (1948); *But the Morning Will Come* (1949); *Sudden Glory* (1951); *The Hornbeam Tree* (1953); *Traveler in the Wilderness* (1957); *Tammy, Tell Me True* (1959); *Christmas Gift* (1961); etc.

SUMNER, WILLIAM GRAHAM (Oct. 30, 1840–Apr. 12, 1910); b. Paterson, N.J. Educator, biographer, essayist. *Andrew Jackson* (1883); *Alexander Hamilton* (1890); *Robert Morris* (1892); *Folkways* (1907); *The Forgotten Man, and Other Essays,* ed. by Albert G. Keller (1919); *Selected Essays,* ed. by same and Maurice R. Davis (1924); *The Science of Society,* 4v. (with Albert G. Keller and Maurice R. Davis, 1927); *Essays,* ed. by Albert G. Keller and Maurice R. Davis, 2v. (1934); etc. Prof. political and social science, Yale University, 1872–1909. *See* Harris E. Starr's *William Graham Sumner* (1925); Albert G. Keller's *Reminiscences of William Graham Sumner* (1933).

Sun Also Rises, The. Novel by Ernest Hemingway (1926). A chronicle of frustration and dissipation as recorded in the café conversation of a group of disillusioned expatriates, stranded in Europe after World War I, with Paris and a Spanish fiesta in Pamplona as the background.

Sun Do Move, The. Famous sermon by the Negro preacher, John Jasper (1882).

Sun-Up. Play by Lulu Vollmer (prod. 1923). The Widow Cagle's conflict with the law in the mountain country of North Carolina.

Sunday Mercury. New York. Magazine. Founded 1838. Distinguished for its fiction, for its humor, and for its illustrations, many of which were drawn by F. O. C. Darley. Expired 1896.

"Sunday Morning." Poem by Wallace Stevens.

Sunderland Capture. Collection of poems by Leonard Bacon (1940).

Sunny South. Atlanta, Ga. Magazine. Founded 1875. Expired 1907. Succeeded by *Uncle Remus Magazine.*

Sunset Magazine. San Francisco, Cal.; Menlo Park, Cal. Monthly. Founded 1898. Now Known as *Sunset, The Magazine of Western Living.* Published by Lane Magazine and Book Co.

SUPER, DONALD E[dwin] (July 10, 1910–); b. Honolulu. Psychologist. *Avocational Interest Patterns* (1940); *The Psychology of Careers* (1957); *Vocational Development* (with others, 1957); *The Professional Preparation of Counseling Psychologists* (1964); etc. Prof. psychology, Teachers College, Columbia University, since 1949.

Superstition. Play by James Nelson Barker (prod. 1824). Based on New England witchcraft and its terrors.

Survey Graphic. New York. Magazine. Founded 1897, as *Charities.* Name changed to *Survey* 1909, and later to *Survey Graphic.* It was known for its political liberalism and interest in social welfare.

Susan and God. Play by Rachel Crothers (prod. 1937). A mild satire on a new religious movement, presumably the so-called "Oxford Group." Susan tries to convince her friends that she is a changed woman, but her dilettantism shows through.

Susan Lenox: Her Fall and Rise. Novel by David Graham Phillips (1917). A bitter indictment of society, with a woman of easy virtue as the central character.

SUSANN, JACQUELINE. Author. *Every Night, Josephine* (1963); *Valley of the Dolls* (1966); *The Love Machine* (1968).

SUTHERLAND, EVELYN GREENLEAF (1855–1908); b. Cambridge, Mass. Journalist, playwright. *Po' White Trash, and Other One-Act Dramas* (1900); *A Rose o' Plymouth-Town* (with Beulah Marie Dix, prod. 1902); *The Road to Yesterday* (with same, prod. 1906); *Matt of Merrymount* (with same, prod. 1907); etc. Drama critic, the *Boston Commonwealth;* the *Boston Transcript,* 1888–96; the *Boston Journal,* 1897–98.

SUTHERLAND, HOWARD VIGNE (Aug. 3, 1868–); b. Cape Town, S. Africa. Author. *Jacinta: A California Idyll; and Other Verses* (1900); *Bigg's Bar, and Other Klondyke Ballads* (1901); *Songs of a City* (1904); *Idylls of Greece,* 3 series (1908–1914); *Isis and Marpessa* (1912); *Out of the North* (1913). Translator: *Préma-gîtâ* (1940).

SUTLIFF, MILO JOSEPH (Oct. 8, 1899–Sept. 22, 1964); b. Washington, D.C. Publisher. Director and executive vice-president, Doubleday & Co., 1936–48; pres. Literary Guild, 1942–48; managing director, Dollar Book Club, 1937–48. Director, Greystone Press, from 1948.

SUTPHEN, WILLIAM GILBERT VAN TASSEL (May 11, 1861–Sept. 20, 1945); b. Philadelphia, Pa. Novelist. *The Golf-cide, and Other Tales of the Fair Green* (1898); continued as *The Nineteenth Hole: Being Tales of the Fair Green . . . 2d Series* (1901); *The Gates of Chance* (1904); *In Jeopardy* (1922); *King's Champion* (1927); *The Glorious Company* (1940); *I, Nathaniel, Knew Jesus* (1941); etc.

SUTRO, ADOLPH HEINRICH JOSEPH (Apr. 29, 1830–Aug. 8, 1898); b. Aachen, Prussia. Engineer, bibliophile, author. *The Mineral Resources of the United States* (1868). His scientific library of over 200,000 volumes, partly destroyed by fire in 1906, is now owned by the San Francisco Public Library. It includes incunabula. Mayor of San Francisco, 1895–96.

SUTTER, JOHN AUGUSTUS (Feb. 1803–June 18, 1880); b. Kandern, Baden. Adventurer, colonist, diarist. *The Diary of Johann August Sutter* (1932), which appeared originally in the *San Francisco Argonaut,* Jan 26–Feb. 16, 1878; etc. *See* T. J. Schoonover's *The Life and Times of Gen. John A. Sutter* (1895); and Julian Dana's *Sutter of California* (1934).

Sutton, Ada Louise. *See* Ada Louise Saalfield.

SUTTON, ALBERT ALTON (Aug. 14, 1906–); b. Minneapolis, Kans. Educator, author. *Education for Journalism in the United States from Its Beginning to 1940* (1945); *Design and Makeup of Newspapers* (1948). Chairman, Advanced Studies, Northwestern University, since 1960.

SUTTON, GEORGE MIKSCH (May 16, 1898–); ornithologist, artist, author. *Introduction to Birds of Pennsylvania* (1928); *Eskimo Year* (1934); *Birds in the Wilderness* (1936); *Mexican Birds* (1951); *Aloha, Hawaii* (1967); etc.

SUTTON, HENRY. Author. *The Exhibitionist* (1967); *Vector* (1970).

SUZZALLO, HENRY (Aug. 22, 1875–Sept. 25, 1933); b. San Jose, Cal. Educator, author. *Our Faith in Education* (1924); etc. Editor, Collier's *The National Encyclopedia,* 10v. (1932); *Riverside Educational Monographs,* beginning in 1900; The *Houghton Mifflin Educational Classics,* etc. Pres. University of Washington, 1915–26.

SWADOS, HARVEY. Author. *Out Went the Candle* (1955); *On the Line* (1957); *False Coin* (1959); *Nights in the Gardens of Brooklyn* (stories, 1960); *A Radical's America* (1962); *The Will* (1963); *A Story for Teddy and Others* (1965); *The American Writer and the Great Depression* (1966); etc.

SWAIN, ANNA SPENCER CANADA (Mrs. Leslie Swain) (Mar. 18, 1889–); b. Versailles, O. Author. *My Book of Mis-*sionary Heroines (1930); *Pioneer Missionary Heroines in America* (1932); *Youth Unafraid* (1935); *Christ and the World Community* (1939).

SWAIN, JOSEPH WARD (Dec. 16, 1891–); b. Yankton, S.D. Educator, author. *The Ancient World,* 2v. (1950); *The Harper History of Civilization,* 2v. (1958); *The People of the Ancient World* (with W. H. Armstrong, 1959); *Edward Gibbon: The Historian* (1966); etc. Prof. history, University of Illinois, since 1937.

Swallow Barn; or, A Sojourn in the Old Dominion. Novel by John Pendleton Kennedy, 2v. (anon., 1832). Idyllic story of a southern plantation, one of the first American novels to catch the romance of plantation life in the South, a theme fully exploited by the novelists who came after Kennedy.

SWAN, EMMA (1914–). Poet. *The Lion and the Lady, and Other Poems* (1949); *Poems* (1958).

SWANN, WILLIAM FRANCIS GRAY (Aug. 29, 1884–); b. Ironbridge, Eng. Physicist, author. *Architecture of the Universe* (1934); *Physics* (1941); Co-author: *The Story of Human Error* (1936). Prof. physics, Yale University, 1924–27; director, Bartol Research Foundation of Franklin Institute, since 1927.

SWANSON, HAROLD NORLING (Aug. 28, 1899–); b. Centerville, Ia. Editor, literary agent, author. *Corn: Moods from Mid-America* (1922); *Big Business Girl* (with others, anon. 1930); *They Fell in Love* (under pen name "Kerry Scott," 1932). Editor, *College Humor,* 1923–33; now pres. H. N. Swanson, Inc., literary agency.

SWANSON, NEIL H[armon] (June 30, 1896–); b. Minneapolis, Minn. Editor, novelist. *The Judas Tree* (1933); *The First Rebel* (1937); *The Forbidden Ground* (1938); *The Silent Drum* (1940); *The Unconquered* (1947); *The Star Spangled Banner* (1958). With *Baltimore Evening Sun,* 1931–54.

SWEARINGEN, TILFORD TIPPETT (May 9, 1902–); b. Glasgow, Mo. Educator, author. *Planning for Young People in the Local Church* (1933); *Must a Man Live?* (1941); *The Community and Christian Education* (1950). Pres. William Woods College, Missouri, since 1951.

SWEENEY, JAMES JOHNSON (May 30, 1900–); b. Brooklyn, N.Y. Art curator. Author or co-author: *Henry Moore* (1947); *Modern Art and Tradition* (1950); *African Folk Tales and Sculpture* (with Paul Radin, 1952); *Atmosphere Miro* (1959); *Vision and Image* (1968); *Alexander Calder* (1969); etc.

SWEENEY, TOM [Thomas Bell] (Jan. 19, 1874–Feb. 2, 1957); b. Wheeling, W.Va. Poet. *Horizon Frames* (1931); *Sunward* (1933); *Legend of Leonardo* (1936); *Flight to Erin* (1945); *Makers of War* (1950); etc.

"Sweeney Among the Nightingales." Poem by T. S. Eliot (1917).

SWEET, FRANK HERBERT (Aug. 1, 1856–Feb. 3, 1930); b. West Greenwich, R.I. Author. *A Mountain Hero* (1902); *Rufe and Ruth* (1902); *Judy, Pioneer Girl* (1907); *Blue and Gray* (1907); *Grandfather Tales* (1907); *Grandmother Tales* (1907); *Buzzard's Den* (1916); *In the Midst of the Deep Woods* (1925); etc.

SWEET, LOUIS MATTHEWS (Oct. 10, 1869–Oct. 3, 1950); b. Southold, N.Y. Presbyterian clergyman, educator, author. *The Self-Portrayal of Shakespeare* (1906); *Roman Emperor Worship* (1919); *The Makin' o' Joe* (1919); *To Christ through Evolution* (1925); *The Head of the Corner* (1931); etc. With Presbyterian Theological Seminary, from 1929; prof., 1931–39.

SWEET, WILLIAM WARREN (Feb. 15, 1881–Jan. 3, 1959); b. Baldwin, Kan. Educator, author. *Circuit Rider Days in Indiana* (1916); *A History of Latin America* (1919); *The*

Rise of Methodism in the West (1920); The Story of Religions in America (1930); Religion on the American Frontier (v. 1. Baptists, 1931, v. 2. Presbyterians, 1936, v. 3, Congregationalists, 1939); Methodism in American History (1933); Men of Zeal (1935); Makers of Christianity (1937); The American Church (1947); Religion in the Development of American Culture (1952); A Short History of Methodism (1956); etc. Prof. history of American Christianity, University of Chicago, 1927–46.

"Sweet Adeline." Popular song, words by Richard H. Gerard, music by Harry Armstrong (1903). Gerard had written the song in 1902, as "Sweet Rosalie," but it met with no success until Armstrong persuaded him to change the wording.

"Sweet By and By, The." Hymn, words by Sanford Fillmore Bennett, music by J. P. Webster (1868).

"Sweet Genevieve." Song by George Cooper, music by Henry Tucker (1869).

"Sweet Marie." Popular song by Cy Warman (1893).

"Sweet Rosy O'Grady." Song by Maude Nugent.

"Sweet Spring." Poem by E. E. Cummings.

Sweet Thursday. Novel by John Steinbeck (1954).

Sweet William. By Marguerite Bouvet (1890). A popular book for children, with Mont St. Michel as the scene, and William the Conqueror as a central character.

"Sweetest Flower That Blows, The." Poem by Frederick Peterson, set to music by James H. Rogers (1886). The song is entitled "At Parting."

"Sweetest Story Ever Told, The." Song by R. M. Stults (1892).

SWEETSER, KATE DICKINSON (d. Mar. 22, 1939); b. New York. Author. Ten Boys from Dickens (1901); Ten Girls from Dickens (1902); Boys and Girls from George Eliot (1906); Ten Girls from History (1912); Book of Indian Braves (1913); Ten Great Adventures (1915); Famous Girls of the White House (1930); etc.

SWEEZY, PAUL MARLOR (1910–). Economist. Monopoly and Competition in the English Coal Trade, 1550–1850 (1938); Theory of Capitalist Development (1942); The Present as History (1962); etc.

SWEM, EARL GREGG (Dec. 29, 1870–Apr. 14, 1965); b. Belle Plains, Ia. Librarian, editor, compiler. Bibliography of Virginia (1916); Virginia Historical Index, 2v. (1934); and many bibliographical works for the Virginia State Library; 23 Jamestown Historical Booklets (1957). Editor, William and Mary Historical Magazine, since 1921. Asst. librarian, Virginia State Library, 1907–19; librarian, College of William and Mary, 1920–44.

SWENSON, MAY (May 28, 1919–   ); b. Logan, Utah. Poet. Another Animal (1954); A Cage of Spines (1958); To Mix with Time (1963); Poems to Solve (1966); Half Sun Half Sleep (1967).

SWETT, SOPHIE [Miriam] (1858–Nov. 12, 1912); b. Brewer, Me. Author. Stories of Maine (1899); The Young Ship Builder (1902).

SWIFT, ERNEST FREMONT (Sept. 15, 1897–July 24, 1968); b. Tracy, Minn. Conservation administrator, author. Wildlife as a Forest Crop in the Lake States (1948); Education, the Sharpest Tool for Conservation of Resources (1953); Business of Conservation (1953).

SWIFT, FLETCHER HARPER (May 20, 1876–May 28, 1947); b. New York. Educator, author. The Most Beautiful Thing in the World (1905); Education in Ancient Israel (1919); Studies in Public School Finance, 4v. (1922–25); Emma Marwedel, 1818–1893 (1931); etc. Prof. education, University of California, from 1925.

SWIFT, IVAN (June 24, 1873–Oct. 5, 1945); b. in Wayne Co., Mich. Artist, author. The Blue Crane, and Shore Songs (1918); Fagots of Cedar (1926); Nine Lives in Letters (1930).

SWIFT, JOHN FRANKLIN (Feb. 28, 1829–Mar. 10, 1891); b. Bowling Green, Mo. Orator, diplomat, author. Going to Jericho (1868); Robert Greathouse (1870). Minister to Japan, 1889–91.

SWIFT, J[osiah] OTIS (Mar. 1, 1871–May 14, 1948); b. Farmington, Me. Naturalist, journalist. With New York World and World-Telegram from 1900, conducting a nature column entitled "News Outside the Door." Founder, "Yosian Brotherhood," a hiking organization.

SWING, RAYMOND Gram (Mar. 25, 1887–Dec. 22, 1968); b. Cortland, N.Y. News commentator, author. Forerunners of American Fascism (1935); How War Came (1939); Preview of History (1943); In the Name of Sanity (1946). Editor: This I Believe (1954).

SWINTON, JOHN (Dec. 12, 1829–Dec. 15, 1901); b. near Edinburgh, brother of William Swinton. Editor, social reformer. Chief of editorial staff, The New York Times, 1860–70; the New York Sun, 1875–83; founder, John Swinton's Paper, 1883; editor, 1883–87; with the New York Sun, 1888–97.

SWINTON, WILLIAM (Apr. 23, 1833–Oct. 24, 1892); b. near Edinburgh, brother of John Swinton. Correspondent, educator, author. The "Times" Review of McClellan (1864), also published as McClellan's Military Career Reviewed and Exposed (1864); Campaigns of the Army of the Potomac (1866); The Twelve Decisive Battles of the War (1867); etc. Wrote many popular textbooks in various fields. On staff, the New York Times, 1858–64; Civil War correspondent, 1861–64. Prof. English, University of California, 1869–74.

SWISSHELM, JANE GREY CANNON (Dec. 6, 1815–July 22, 1884); b. Pittsburgh, Pa. Abolitionist, editor, advocate of woman's rights, author. Letters to Country Girls (1853); Half a Century (autobiography, 1880). Editor: Behind the Scenes: By Elizabeth Keckley (1868). Founder, the Pittsburgh Saturday Visiter, 1847; editor, 1847–57; founder, The St. Cloud (Minn.) Visiter 1858; The St. Cloud Democrat, 1858; editor, 1858–63. See Crusader and Feminist: Letters of Jane Grey Swisshelm, 1858–1865, ed. by A. J. Larsen (1934); Mississippi Valley Historical Review, Dec. 1920; Collections of the Minnesota Historical Society, v. 12, 1908.

SWITZLER, WILLIAM FRANKLIN (Mar. 16, 1819–May 24, 1906); b. in Fayette Co., Ky. Editor, historian. Early History of Missouri (1872); etc. Editor, the Columbian Patriot, 1841, which he bought in 1842 and renamed the Missouri Statesman; editor, 1842–85; editor, the Missouri Democrat, Boonville, 1893–98.

Sword Blades and Poppy Seeds. Poems by Amy Lowell (1914). The poet adopted the patterns of free verse in many of the poems in this volume and set a vogue for free verse among the younger American poets.

"Sword in the Sea, The." Poem by Francis Orray Ticknor, after the surrender of Captain Semmes of the "Alabama" following its fight with the "Kearsarge" (1864).

"Sword of Robert E. Lee, The." Poem by Abram J. Ryan.

Sybil. Play by John Savage (prod. 1858). Romantic treatment of the American scene, as contrasted with other plays of the period which took classical or European subjects as their theme.

SYDNOR, CHARLES S[ackett] (July 21, 1898–Mar. 2, 1954); b. Augusta, Ga. Educator, historian. Mississippi History (1930); Slavery in Mississippi (1933); A Gentleman of the

Old Natchez Region, Benjamin L. C. Wailes (1938); *Gentleman Freeholders: Political Practices in Washington's Virginia* (1952); etc. Prof. history, University of Mississippi, 1925–36; Duke University, from 1936.

SYKES, CHARLES HENRY (Nov. 12, 1882–Dec. 19, 1942); b. Athens, Ala. Cartoonist. Cartoonist for Philadelphia *Evening Public Ledger,* from 1914. Political cartoonist, *Life,* New York, 1922–28.

SYKES, GERALD. Author. *The Children of Light* (1955); *The Hidden Remnant* (1962); *The Cool Millennium* (1967); *The Nice American; The Center of the Stage;* etc. Editor: *Alienation: The Cultural Climate of Our Time* (1964). Faculty, New School for Social Research.

Sylvester, Arthur. Pen name of Arthur Lewis Tubbs.

SYLVESTER, FREDERICK OAKES (Oct. 8, 1869–Mar. 2, 1915); b. Brockton, Mass. Artist, poet. *Verses* (1903); *The Great River: Poems and Pictures* (1911).

SYLVESTER, HARRY (Jan. 19, 1908–); b. Brooklyn, N.Y. Novelist. *Dearly Beloved* (1942); *Dayspring* (1945); *Moon Gaffney* (1947); *All Your Idols* (1948); *A Golden Girl* (1950); etc.

SYLVESTER, HERBERT MILTON (b. Feb. 20, 1840); b. Lowell, Mass. Author. *Prose Pastorals* (poems, 1887); *Maine Pioneer Settlements,* 5v. (1909); *Indian Wars of New England,* 3v. (1910); *Early Voyages to New England* (1910); etc.

SYLVESTER, ROBERT (Feb. 7, 1907–); b. Newark, N.J. Journalist, novelist. *Dream Street* (1946); *Rough Sketch* (1947); *The Second Oldest Profession* (1950); *Indian Summer* (1952); *The Big Boodle* (1954); *No Cover Charge* (1956); *Tropical Paradise* (1960); *Memoirs of An Unidentified Man* (1961); *We Were Younger* (1968); etc. Also television and film scripts. Drama and amusement writer, *New York Daily News,* since 1936.

SYNON, MARY; b. Chicago, Ill. Author. *The Fleet Goes By* (1914); *McAdoo: The Man and His Times* (1924); *The Good Red Bricks* (1929); *Copper Country* (1931); *Washington Night* (1935); etc.

Syntopicon. See *Great Books of the Western World.*

SYPHER, WYLIE (Dec. 12, 1905–); b. Mt. Kisco, N.Y. Educator, author. *Guinea's Captive Kings* (1942); *Enlightened England* (1947); *Four Stages of Renaissance Style* (1955); *Rococo to Cubism in Art and Literature* (1960); *Loss of the Self* (1962); *Art History* (1963); *Literature and Technology* (1968). Chairman of English, Simmons College, since 1966.

Syracuse Herald-Journal and Sunday Herald-American. Syracuse, N.Y. Newspaper. The *Western State Journal,* founded 1839; later became the *Syracuse Weekly Journal,* which founded the *Syracuse Daily Journal* in 1844. The *Syracuse Herald* was founded 1877. Merged 1939. The Sunday edition is known as the *Syracuse Herald-American.* Acquired the *Syracuse Post-Standard* (q.v.), as a morning paper; the *Herald-Journal* appears evenings. J. L. Gorman is editor. William D. Cotter is book-review editor.

Syracuse Post-Standard. Syracuse, N.Y. Newspaper. The *Onondaga Journal,* founded 1821. The *Syracuse Advertiser,* founded 1826. Merged 1829, as the *Onondaga Standard,* at Syracuse. Became the *Syracuse Standard* in 1874. The *Syracuse Post,* founded 1894. Merged c. 1898. Paul Mayo Paine conducted weekly column "Books and Folks." See *Syracuse Herald-Journal and Sunday Herald-American.*

Syracuse University Press. Syracuse, N.Y. Founded 1945. Publishes non-technical, technical, and scholarly books in English, Spanish, and French.

SYRETT, HAROLD C[offin] (Oct. 13, 1913–); b. New York. Educator, editor, author. *The City of Brooklyn, 1865–1898* (1944); *A History of the American People* (with Harry J. Carman, 1952); *Andrew Jackson* (1953); Editor: *The Gentleman and the Tiger* (1956); *American Historical Documents* (1960); etc. Co-editor: *Papers of Alexander Hamilton,* 4v. (1961–62); etc. Prof. history, City University of N.Y., since 1969.

SZASZ, THOMAS STEPHEN (Apr. 15, 1920–); b. Budapest, Hung. Psychiatrist, author. *Pain and Pleasure* (1957); *The Myth of Mental Illness* (1961); *Law, Liberty and Psychiatry* (1963); *Psychiatric Justice* (1965); The *Ethics of Psychoanalysis* (1965).

SZULC, TAD (July 25, 1926–); b. Warsaw. Journalist, author. *Twilight of the Tyrants* (1959); *The Cuban Invasion* (with K. E. Meyer, 1962); *The Winds of Revolution* (1963); *Dominican Diary* (1965); *Latin America* (1966); *Bombs of Palomares* (1967). Staff, *New York Times,* since 1953.

T

"Ta-ra-ra-boom-de-ay!" Song by Henry J. Sayers (1891).

TABAK, ISRAEL (Dec. 7, 1904–); b. Bucovina, Rum. Rabbi, author. *Maimonides, Master Builder of Jewish Law* (1935); *Judaic Lore in Heine: The Heritage of a Poet* (1948); *Treasury of Holiday Thoughts* (1958); *Essay On Life and Work of Abraham Rise, First Ordained Rabbi in the U.S.* (1963).

TABB, JOHN BANISTER (Mar. 22, 1845–Nov. 19, 1909); b. Amelia Co., Va. Roman Catholic clergyman, poet. *An Octave to Mary* (1893); *Poems* (1894); *Lyrics* (1897); *Child Verse* (1899); *Poems Grave and Gay* (1899); *Later Lyrics* (1902); *The Rosary in Rhyme* (1904); *Quips and Quiddits* (1907); *Later Poems* (1910); *The Poetry of Father Tabb* (1928); etc. See Jennie M. Tabb's *Father Tabb* (1922); F. A. Litz's *Father Tabb* (1923); *American Book Collector,* v. 6, 1935.

TABER, GLADYS [Bagg] (Apr. 12, 1899–); b. Colorado Springs, Colo. Author. *A Star To Steer By* (1938); *Harvest at Stillmeadow* (1940); *Nurse in Blue* (1943); *The Heart Has April Too* (1944); *The Family on Maple Street* (1946); *Daisy and Dobbin* (1948); *Especially Father* (1949); *Stillmeadow Seasons* (1950); *When Dogs Meet People* (short stories, 1952); *Spring Harvest* (1959); *Stillmeadow Calendar, A Countrywoman's Journal* (1967); *Especially Dogs, Especially at Stillmeadow* (1968); *Flower Arranging, A Book to Begin On* (1969); etc. Columnist, *Ladies Home Journal,* 1937–58.

TABER, RALPH GRAHAM (May 2, 1866–); b. Red Wing, Minn. Traveler, author. *Northern Lights and Shadows* (1900); *Chained Lightning: An Adventurous Travelogue of Mexico* (1915); *Stray Gold* (1915).

Tablet, The. New York. Roman Catholic weekly. Founded 1852 as the *American Celt,* by Thomas D'Arcy McGee. Name changed 1857.

TABOR, H[orace] A[ustin] W[arner] (1830–1899); b. Holland, Vt. Colorado pioneer, gold miner, philanthropist. He built the opera house in Leadville, Col., in 1879, and the Tabor Grand Opera House in Denver, 1881. *See* David Karsner's *Silver Dollar* (1932); Lewis C. Gandy's *The Tabors* (1934).

Tad. Pen name of Thomas Aloysius Dorgan.

TAFT, CHARLES PHELPS (Sept. 20, 1897–); b. Cincinnati, O. Public official. Author. *City Management: The Cincinnati Experiment* (1933); *Why I Am for the Church* (1947); *Democracy in Politics and Economics* (1950); *Trade Barriers and the National Interest* (1955); etc.

TAFT, WILLIAM HOWARD (Sept. 15, 1867–Mar. 8, 1930); b. Cincinnati, O. Twenty-seventh president of the United States, jurist, author. *Popular Government* (1913); *Our Chief Magistrate and His Powers* (1916); etc. Chief Justice of the Supreme Court of the United States, 1921–30. Kent prof. of constitutional law, Yale University, 1913–21. See Mrs. William Howard Taft's *Recollections of Full Years* (1914); H. S. Duffy's *William Howard Taft* (1930). His papers are in the Library of Congress.

TAGGARD, GENEVIEVE (Nov. 28, 1894–Nov. 8, 1948); b. Waitsburg, Wash. Poet. *For Eager Lovers* (1922); *Hawaiian Hilltop* (1923); *Words for the Chisel* (1926); *Travelling Standing Still* (1928); *The Life and Mind of Emily Dickinson* (1930); *Remembering Vaughan in New England* (1933); *Not Mine to Finish* (1934); *Calling Western Union* (1936); *Collected Poems, 1918–1938* (1938); *Long View* (1942); *Falcon* (1942); *A Part of Vermont* (1945); *Slow Music* (1946); *Origin Hawaii* (1947).

TAGGART, MARION AMES (Miss) (1866–Jan. 19, 1945); b. Haverhill, Mass. Author. *The Blissylvania Post Office* (1897); *Miss Lochinvar* (1902); *The Wyndham Girls* (1902); *At Aunt Anna's* (1903); *The Doctor's Little Girl* (1907); *Six Girls and Betty* (1911); *Captain Sylvia* (1918); *Pilgrim Maid* (1920); *The Cable* (1923); etc.

TAGLIABUE, JOHN (July 1, 1923–); b. Cantu, Italy. *Poems 1941–57* (1959); *A Japanese Journal* (1966); *The Buddhist Uproar* (1967). Prof. English, Bates College, since 1953.

Taine, John. Pen name of E. T. Bell.

TALBOT, CHARLES REMINGTON (1851–1891). Episcopal clergyman, author of children's books. Pen names "John Brownjohn" and "Magnus Merriweather." *Miltiades Peterkin Paul* (1877); *The Story of Honor Bright* (1881); *A Double Masquerade* (1885); *A Midshipman at Large* (1887); *Romulus and Remus: A Dog Story* (1888); etc.

TALBOT, CHARLES S. Playwright. *Paddy's Trip to America; or, The Husband with Three Wives* (prod. 1822); *Captain Morgan; or, The Conspiracy Unveiled* (prod. 1827); *Squire Hartley* (prod. 1825).

TALBOT, FRANCIS XAVIER (Jan. 25, 1889–Dec. 3, 1953); b. Philadelphia, Pa. Roman Catholic clergyman, editor, author. *Jesuit Education in Philadelphia* (1927); *Shining in Darkness* (1932); *Saint Among Savages* (1935); *Saint Among the Hurons* (1949); etc. Editor: *The America Book of Verse* (1927). Lit. editor, *America*, 1922–36; editor-in-chief, 1936–44; editor, *Thought*, 1936–40.

Tales for the Marines. By Henry Augustus Wise (1855). Humorous and exaggerated naval exploits.

Tales of a Wayside Inn. By Henry Wadsworth Longfellow (1863). Narrative poems related by a group of friends gathered at an old inn in Sudbury, Mass., including such favorite poems as "The Midnight Ride of Paul Revere," and the "Saga of King Olaf."

Tales of the South Pacific. Sketches by James Michener (1947). Adapted by Rodgers and Hammerstein into a musical comedy, *South Pacific* (prod. 1949).

TALESE, GAY (Feb. 7, 1922–); b. Ocean City, N.J. Author. *New York—A Serendipiter's Journey* (1961); *The Bridge* (1964); *The Overreachers* (1965); *The Kingdom and the Power* (1969); *Fame and Obscurity* (1970). Staff, *New York Times*, 1953–65.

TALIAFERRO, HARDEN E. (c. 1818–1875). Author. *Fisher's River (North Carolina) Scenes and Characters* (Under pen name, "Skitt," 1859); *Carolina Humor: Sketches* (1938), first published in the *Southern Literary Messenger*, 1860–63.

Talisman. San Jose, Calif. Semiannual literary magazine. Founded 1952. Discontinued 1958.

Talks to Teachers on Psychology; and to Students on Some of Life's Ideals. By William James (1899).

Tall Tale. Type of anecdote or story told during frontier days, marked by caricature and exaggeration, either understated or overstated. The folk legends that gave rise to this form concerned such heroes as Paul Bunyan, Davy Crockett, John Henry, Pecos Bill, Daniel Boone. See Percy Mackay's *Tall Tales of the Kentucky Mountains* (1926); Lowell Thomas's *Tall Stories* (1931); *God Bless the Devil*, by the Tennessee Writers' Project (1940); J. Frank Dobie's *Tales of Old-Time Texas* (1955); *Life Treasury of American Folklore* (1961).

TALLANT, ROBERT (Apr. 20, 1909–1957); b. New Orleans, La. Author. *Gumbo Ya-Ya, A Collection of Louisiana Folklore* (1945); *Voodoo in New Orleans* (1946); *Mrs. Candy and Saturday Night* (1947); *Mardi Gras* (1948); *Angel in the Wardrobe* (1948); *Mr. Preen's Salon* (1949); *A State in Mimosa* (1950); *The Romantic New Orleanians* (1950); *Louisiana Purchase* (1952); *Ready to Hang* (1952); *Mrs. Candy Strikes It Rich* (1954); *Voodoo Queen* (1956); *Evangeline and the Acadians* (1957).

TALMAGE, T[HOMAS] DE WITT (Jan. 7, 1832–Apr. 12, 1902); b. Bound Brook, N.J. Presbyterian clergyman, lecturer, editor, author. *Old Wells Dug Out* (1874); *Every-Day Religion* (1875); *The Night Sides of City Life* (1878); *The Earth Girdled* (1895); *T. De Witt Talmage As I Knew Him* (autobiography, 1912); *Fifty Short Sermons* (1923); etc. Editor, *Frank Leslie's Sunday Magazine*, 1880–90; the *Christian Herald*, 1890–1902.

"Tamar." Long poem by Robinson Jeffers (1925).

Tampa Tribune. Tampa, Fla. Newspaper. Founded 1875, as the *Sunland Tribune*. Name changed 1882. Daily established 1894. Edwin Dart Lambright, on staff since 1898, was editor, 1912–17, and after 1923. James A. Clendinen is now editor. Holmes Alexander is book-review editor. Now combined with *Tampa Times*.

Tanglewood Tales. By Nathaniel Hawthorne (1853). A juvenile classic.

TANNENBAUM, FRANK (Mar. 4, 1893–June 1, 1968); b. in Austria. Educator, author. *Wall Shadows* (1922); *Osborne of Sing Sing* (1933); *Whither Latin America?* (1934); *Crime and the Community* (1938); *Slave and Citizen* (1947); *Mexico* (1950); *A Philosophy of Labor* (1951); *American Tradition in Foreign Policy* (1955); etc. History dept., Columbia University, since 1935.

TANNENBAUM, SAMUEL AARON (May 1, 1874–Oct. 31, 1948); b. in Hungary. Physician, Shakespeare scholar, author. *Problems in Shakespeare's Penmanship* (1927); *The Assassination of Christopher Marlowe* (1928); *Shakespeare Forgeries in the Revels Account* (1928); *The Handwriting of the Renaissance* (1930); *Shakespearean Scraps, and Other Elizabethan Fragments* (1933); *The Patient's Dilemma* (1935); *John Ford and Thomas Nashe* (1941); etc. Compiler: *Christopher Marlowe: a Concise Bibliography* (1937).

TANNER, EDWARD EVERETT, III (May 18, 1921–); b. Chicago, Ill. Author. Under pen name "Virginia Rowans": *Oh What a Wonderful Wedding* (1953); *House Party* (1954); *The Loving Couple* (1956); *Love and Mrs. Sargent* (1961); etc. Under pen name "Patrick Dennis": *Auntie Mame* (1955); *Around the World with Auntie Mame* (1958); *Little Me* (1961); *Genius* (1962); *The Joyous Season* (1965); *Tony* (1966); *How Firm a Foundation* (1968); etc. Drama critic, *New Republic*, since 1957.

TANNER, HENRY SCHENCK (1786–1858); b. New York. Cartographer, statistical geographer, author. *Memoir on the Recent Surveys* (1829), to accompany his *A New American*

Atlas, in parts (1818–22); *The American Traveller* (1834); *A Description of the Canals and Railroads of the United States* (1840); etc.

TANNER, JOHN (c. 1780–1847); b. in Kentucky. Indian captive, scout. See *Narrative of the Captivity and Adventures of John Tanner During Thirty Years' Residence Among the Indians,* ed. by Edwin James (1830).

TANSILL, CHARLES CALLAN (Dec. 9, 1890–Nov. 12, 1964); b. Fredericksburg, Tex. Educator. Author: *The Canadian Reciprocity Treaty of 1854* (1922); *America Goes to War* (1938); *The Foreign Policy of Thomas F. Bayard* (1941); *Back Door to War* (1952); *America and the Fight for Irish Freedom* (1957); *The Purchase of the Danish West Indies* (1966); *The United States and Santo Domingo 1798–1873* (1967); etc. Prof. American history, Georgetown University, since 1944.

Tante. Novel by Anne Douglas Sedgwick (1911). Study in the psychology of genius.

TAPPAN, ARTHUR (May 22, 1786–July 23, 1865); b. Northampton, Mass., brother of Lewis Tappan. Abolitionist, editor. Founder, the *New York Journal of Commerce,* 1827, which he sold to his brother in 1828. Founder, the *American and Foreign Anti-Slavery Reporter,* 1840. Helped to found the *National Era, The Unionist,* etc. See Lewis Tappan's *Arthur Tappan* (1870); C. W. Bowen's *Arthur and Lewis Tappan* (1883).

TAPPAN, ELI TODD (Apr. 30, 1824–Oct. 23, 1888); b. Steubenville, O. Educator, editor. Founder the *Ohio Press,* Columbus, O., 1846. President, Kenyon College, 1869–75.

TAPPAN, EVA MARCH (Dec. 26, 1854–Jan. 29, 1930); b. Blackstone, Mass. Educator, author. *Charles Lamb* (1896); *In the Days of Alfred the Great* (1900); *Our Country's Story* (1902); *In the Days of Queen Elizabeth* (1902); *In the Days of Queen Victoria* (1903); *A Short History of America's Literature* (1906); *American Hero Stories* (1906); *A Friend in the Library,* 12v. (1910); *Ella, a Little Schoolgirl of the Sixties* (1923); etc.

TAPPAN, LEWIS (May, 23, 1788–June 21, 1873); b. Northampton, Mass., brother of Arthur Tappan. Journalist, merchant, abolitionist. *The Life of Arthur Tappan* (1870). Became owner of the *New York Journal of Commerce,* 1828, and sold it to David Hale and Gerard Hallock in 1831. See C. W. Bowen's *Arthur and Lewis Tappan* (1883); J. A. Scoville's *The Old Merchants of New York,* v. 1 (1863).

TAPPAN, WILLIAM BINGHAM (Oct. 29, 1794–June 18, 1849); b. Beverly, Mass. Poet. *New England, and Other Poems* (1819); *Songs of Judah, and Other Melodies* (1820); *Lyrics* (1822); *Poems* (1822); *Poems* (1834); *The Poems ... Not Contained in a Former Volume* (1836); *Poems and Lyricks* (1842); *Poetry of the Heart* (1845); *Sacred and Miscellaneous Poems* (1846); *Poetry of Life* (1847); *The Sunday-School, and Other Poems* (1849); *Late and Early Poems* (1849); etc.

Tar Baby Story, and Other Rhymes by Uncle Remus. Joel Chandler Harris (1904).

Tar-Heel Baron, A. Novel by Mabell Shippie Clarke Smith (1903). Story of Western North Carolina.

TARBELL, IDA M[INERVA] (Nov. 5, 1857–Jan. 6, 1944); b. Erie Co., Pa. Author. *A Short Life of Napoleon Bonaparte* (1895); *The Life of Abraham Lincoln,* 2v. (1900); *The History of the Standard Oil Company,* 2v. (1904); *The Ways of Women* (1915); *Boy Scout's Life of Lincoln* (1921); *In the Footsteps of Lincoln* (1924); *Owen D. Young* (1932); *All in the Day's Work* (autobiography, 1939); etc. Assoc. editor, the *American Magazine,* 1906–15. See Muckrakers.

TARBOX, INCREASE NILES (Feb. 11, 1915–May 3, 1888); b. East Windsor, Conn. Congregational clergyman, author. *Life of Israel Putnam* (1876); *Rambles in Old Pathways,* 2v. (1868); *Songs and Hymns for Common Life* (1885); etc. Edi-

tor: *Dairy of Thomas Robbins, 1796–1854,* 2v. (1886–87). One of the founders and editors of the *Congregationalist,* 1849.

TARDY, MARY T., b. in Alabama. Author. Pen name, "Ida Raymond." *Southland Writers,* 2v. (1870), republished as, *The Living Female Writers of the South* (1872).

TARG, WILLIAM (Mar. 7, 1907–   ); b. Chicago, Ill. Editor, author. *Rare American Books* (1941); *The American West* (1946); *Bibliophile in the Nursery* (1957). Editor-in-chief, G. P. Putnam's Sons, since 1965.

TARKINGTON, BOOTH [Newton] (July 29, 1869–May 19, 1946); b. Indianapolis, Ind. Novelist, playwright, illustrator. *The Gentleman from Indiana* (1899); *Monsieur Beaucaire* (1900); *Cherry* (1903); *The Conquest of Canaan* (1905); *The Guardian* (with Harry Leon Wilson, prod. 1907); *The Man from Home* (with same, prod. 1907); *Penrod* (1914); *Penrod and Sam* (1916); *Seventeen* (1916); *The Country Cousin* (with Julian Street, prod. 1917); *The Magnificent Ambersons* (1918, Pulitzer Prize novel, 1919); *Clarence* (prod. 1919); *The Gibson Upright* (with Harry Leon Wilson, prod. 1919); *Alice Adams* (1921, Pulitzer Prize novel, 1922); *The Wren* (prod. 1921); *Gentle Julia* (1922); *The Collector's Whatnot* (with others, 1923); *The Midlander* (1923); *Looking Forward and Others* (1926); *The Plutocrat* (1927); *The World Does Move* (reminiscences, 1928); *Claire Ambler* (1928); *Mirthful Heaven* (1930); *Mary's Neck* (1932); *Little Orvie* (1934); *The Lorenzo Bunch* (1936); *Some Old Portraits* (1939); *The Works of Booth Tarkington,* 27v. (1922–32); *The Heritage of Hatcher Ide* (1941); *Kate Fennigate* (1943); *The Image of Josephine* (1945); etc. Illustrated James Whitcomb Riley's *The Boss Girl* (1886); Kenneth Roberts's *Antiquamania* (1928); etc. See Barton Currie's *Booth Tarkington; A Bibliography* (1932); Fred B. Millett's *Contemporary American Authors* (1940); James Woodress' *Booth Tarkington: Gentleman from Indiana* (1955).

TARLETON, FISWOODE (1890–Apr. 2, 1931). Author. *Bloody Ground: A Cycle of the Southern Hills* (1929); *Some Trust in Chariots* (1930). Co-editor, the *Modern Review.*

TARSKI, ALFRED (Jan. 14, 1902–); b. Warsaw. Mathematician. *Introduction to Logic* (1941); *Cardinal Algebras* (1949); *Ordinal Algebras* (1956); *Logic, Semantics, Metamathematics: Papers from 1923 to 1938* (1956); *The Completeness of Elementary Algebra and Geometry* (1967); etc. Prof. mathematics, University of California, since 1946.

TATE, ALLEN [John Orley] (Nov. 19, 1899–); b. in Clarke Co., Ky. Critic, poet. *Mr. Pope, and Other Poems* (1928); *Stonewall Jackson* (1928); *Jefferson Davis: His Rise and Fall* (1929); *Three Poems* (1930); *Poems, 1928–1931* (1932); *Robert E. Lee* (poem, 1932); *The Mediterranean, and Other Poems* (1936); *Reactionary Essays* (1936); *Selected Poems* (1937); *The Fathers* (1938); *Invitation to Learning* (with Huntington Cairns and Mark Van Doren, 1941); *Reason in Madness* (1941); *On the Limits of Poetry* (1948); *The Hovering Fly* (1949); *The Forlorn Demon: Didactic and Critical Essays* (1953); *The Man of Letters in the Modern World* (1955); *Collected Essays* (1959); *Poems* (1960); *Essays of Four Decades* (1969). Co-founder, *The Fugitive,* 1922; co-editor, 1922–25; editor, *Sewanee Review,* 1944–46; Henry Holt and Co., 1946–48. Prof. English, University of Minnesota, since 1951.

TATE, JAMES (Dec. 8, 1943–   ); b. Kansas City, Mo. Author. *The Lost Pilot* (1967); *The Notes of Woe* (1967). Yale Series of Younger Poets award, 1967. Poetry editor, *Dickinson Review.*

TATLOCK, JOHN S[trong] P[erry] (Feb. 24, 1876–June 24, 1948); b. Stamford, Conn. Educator, editor, author. *The Development and Chronology of Chaucer's Works* (1907); etc. Editor: *The Modern Reader's Chaucer: The Complete Works ... Now Put into Modern English* (with Percy MacKaye, 1912); *Representative English Plays* (with Robert G. Martin,

1916); *A Concordance to the Complete Works of Geoffrey Chaucer* (with Arthur G. Kennedy, 1927); etc. Prof. English, Harvard University, 1925–29; University of California, 1929–46.

TAUBMAN, [Hyman] HOWARD (July 4, 1907–); b. New York. Music and drama critic, author. *Opera Front and Back* (1938); *Music as a Profession* (1939); *Music on My Beat* (1943); *The Maestro: The Life of Arturo Toscanini* (1951); *How to Build a Record Library* (1954); *How to Bring Up Your Child to Enjoy Music* (1958); *The Making of the American Theatre* (1967). Editor: Guilio Gatti-Casazza's *Memories of Opera* (1941); Frances Perkins' *The Roosevelt I Knew* (1946). Music critic, *New York Times*, to 1960; drama critic, 1960–66; critic at large, since 1966.

TAUSSIG, CHARLES WILLIAM (Aug. 9, 1896–May 9, 1948); b. New York. Author. *The Book of Hobbies* (with Theodore Arthur Meyer, 1924); *Rum, Romance and Rebellion* (1928); *Philip Kappel* (1929); etc.

TAUSSIG, FRANK WILLIAM (Dec. 28, 1859–1940); b. St. Louis, Mo. Educator, author. *Tariff History of the United States* (1888); *Wages and Capital* (1896); *Principles of Economics* (1911); *Social Origins of American Business Leaders* (1932); etc. Editor, the *Quarterly Journal of Economics*, 1896–1937. Political economy dept., Harvard University, 1882–1935.

TAVEL, RONALD (1940–   ); b. New York. Author. *Street of Stairs* (novel, 1968); *Boy on the Straight-Back Chair* (prod. 1968); *Arenas of Lutetia* (prod. 1968). Wrote numerous film scenarios, produced by Andy Warhol Films, Inc., since 1964.

TAX, SOL (Oct. 30, 1907–); b. Chicago, Ill. Anthropologist. Author: *Heritage of Conquest: The Ethnology of Middle America* (1952); etc. Editor: *Selected Papers of the 29th International Congress of Americanists*, 3v. (1951–52); *Evolution after Darwin*, 3v. (1960); etc. Dept. of anthropology, University of Chicago, since 1940.

TAYLEURE, CLIFTON W. (1832–Apr. 10, 1891); b. Charleston, S.C. Actor, manager, playwright. *The Boy Martyrs of September 12, 1814* (prod. 1859); etc. Dramatized John P. Kennedy's *Horse-Shoe Robinson* (prod. 1858); etc. Editor, the *Long Branch News*, 1883–91.

TAYLOR, BAYARD (Jan. 11, 1825–Dec. 19, 1878); b. Kennett Square, Pa. Traveler, diplomat, translator, author. *Ximena; or, The Battle of the Sierra Morena, and Other Poems* (1844); *Views A-Foot* (1846); *Eldorado* (1850); *A Journey to Central Africa* (1854); *Poems of the Orient* (1855); *Northern Travel* (1858); *At Home and Abroad* (1860); *The Poet's Journal* (1862); *Hannah Thurston* (1863); *The Poems* (1865); *The Story of Kennett* (1866); *Lars: A Pastoral of Norway* (1873); *The Echo Club and Other Literary Diversions* (1876); etc. Translator Goethe's *Faust*, 2v. (1870–71); etc. Taylor was the traveler in Whittier's poem, "The Tent on the Beach." Minister to Germany, 1878. *See* Marie Hansen Taylor and H. E. Scudder's *The Life and Letters of Bayard Taylor*, 2v. (1884); A. H. Smyth's *Bayard Taylor* (1896).

TAYLOR, BENJAMIN FRANKLIN (July 19, 1819–Feb. 24, 1887); b. Lowville, N.Y. Editor, traveler, author. *Mission Ridge and Lookout Mountain* (1872); *Old Time Pictures and Sheaves of Rhyme* (1874); *The World on Wheels* (1874); *Songs of Yesterday* (1875); *Between the Gates* (1878); *Summer-Savory* (1879); *Dulce Domum* (poems, 1884); *Complete Poetical Works* (1886); *Theophilus Trent* (1887); etc. Lit. editor, the *Chicago Daily Journal*, 1845–65; Civil War correspondent, same.

TAYLOR, BERT LESTON (Nov. 13, 1866–Mar. 19, 1921); b. Goshen, Mass. Poet, columnist. Wrote under initials "B. L. T." *The Bilioustine* (1901); *The Book Booster* (1901); *Line-o'-Type Lyrics* (1902); *The Well in the Wood* (1904); *The Charlatans* (1906); *A Line-o'-Verse or Two* (1911); *The Pipesmoke Carry* (1912); *Motley Measures* (1913); *A Line o' Gowf or Two* (1923); *The East Window, and the Car Window* (1924); etc. Editor of the column, "A Line-o'-Type or Two" in the *Chicago Daily Tribune*, 1902–20. *See* Richard Henry Little.

TAYLOR, CHARLES JAY (Aug. 11, 1855–Jan. 18, 1929); b. New York. Illustrator, author. *In the "400" and Out* (1897); *England* (1899); etc. Illustrated H. C. Bunner's *Short Sixes*, works of Williston Fish, C. D. Stewart, etc. His drawings appeared in *Puck, Life, Judge, Punch*, etc.

Taylor, Edith Everett. See Edith Pope.

TAYLOR, EDWARD (1642–June 29, 1729); b. in England, came to Massachusetts in 1668. Congregational clergyman, poet. *The Poetical Works* (1939). Donald E. Stanford's *The Poems of Edward Taylor* (1960) is the complete annotated edition. *See* Norman S. Grabo's *Edward Taylor* (1962) and *Edward Taylor's "Christographia"* (1962); *A Transcript of Edward Taylor's Metrical History of Christianity*, ed. by D. E. Stanford (1962); Peter Nicolaisen's *Die Bildichkeit in der Dichtung Edward Taylors* (1966).

TAYLOR, ELKANAH EAST (July 26, 1888–); b. Norfolk, Va. Editor, poet, critic. *Whispering and Other Poems* (1919); *Dust and Flame* (1923); *Candles on the Sill* (1927); etc. Founder and editor, *Will-o'-the-Wisp*, a magazine of verse, 1925.

TAYLOR, EMERSON GIFFORD (June 9, 1874–); b. Pittsfield, Mass. Author. *The Upper Hand* (1906); *The Day after Dark* (1922); *Paul Revere* (1930); *Governeur Kemble Warren: The Life and Letters of an American Soldier, 1830–1882* (1932); etc.

TAYLOR, FITCH WATERMAN (1803–1865); b. Middle Haddam, Conn. Author. *The Flag Ship; or, A Voyage Around the World, in the U. S. Frigate Columbia*, 2v. (1840); *The Broad Pennant; or, A Cruise in the United States Flag Ship of the Gulf Squadron* (1848); etc.

TAYLOR, FRANK J[ohn] (Oct. 8, 1894–); b. Wessington, S.D. Author. *Land of Homes* (1929); *Democracy's Air Arsenal* (1947); *Black Bonanza* (1950); *High Horizons* (1951); *Southern Pacific* (1952); and co-author of several Western guide-books, *Grand Canyon Country* (1929); *The Rainbow Canyons* (1931); etc.

TAYLOR, GEORGE E. (Dec. 13, 1905–); b. Coventry, Eng. Historian. Author: *The Struggle for North China* (1940); *America in the New Pacific* (1942); *The Philippines and the United States: Problems of Partnership* (1964); etc. Co-author: *The Phoenix and the Dwarfs* (play, 1944); *The Far East in the Modern World* (with Franz Michael, 1956). Director, Far Eastern Institute, University of Washington, since 1956.

TAYLOR, GEORGE ROGERS (June 15, 1895–); b. Beaver Dam, Wis. Economist. Author: *The Transportation Revolution, 1815–60* (1951); etc. Co-author: *The United States, A Graphic History* (1937); *The American Railroad Network, 1861–90* (1956); etc. Editor, *Journal of Economic History*, since 1955. Prof. economics, Amherst College, since 1951.

TAYLOR, HAROLD (Sept. 28, 1914–   ); b. Toronto, Can. Educator, author. *On Education and Freedom* (1954); *Art and the Intellect* (1960); *The University and Social Change* (1962); *Students Without Teachers: The Crisis in the University* (1969). Editor, co-author: *Essays in Teaching* (1950). Past president, Sarah Lawrence College.

TAYLOR, HENRY JUNIOR (Sept. 2, 1902–); b. Chicago, Ill. Journalist, author. *Why Hitler's Economy Fooled the World* (1941); *Time Runs Out* (1942); *Men and Power* (1946); *An American Speaks His Mind* (1957); *The Big Man* (1964); *Men and Moments* (1966). Foreign correspondent for Scripps-Howard Newspaper Syndicate, since 1949. Ambassador to Switzerland, 1957–60.

TAYLOR, HENRY OSBORN (Dec. 5, 1856–Apr. 13, 1941); b. New York. Lawyer, author. *Ancient Ideals* (1896); *The Classical Heritage of the Middle Ages* (1901); *The Medieval Mind*, 2v. (1911); *Deliverance: The Freeing of the Spirit in the Ancient World* (1915); *Freedom of Mind in History* (1922); *Human Values and Verities* (1928); *Fact: The Romance of Mind* (1932); *A Layman's View of History* (1935); *A Historian's Creed* (1939).

TAYLOR, HORACE (June 30, 1894–); b. Chireno, Tex. Educator. Author. *Making Goods and Making Money* (1928). Co-author: *The American Economy in Operation* (1949); etc. Dept. economics, Columbia University, 1924–59; prof. emeritus, since 1959.

TAYLOR, JAMES MONROE (Aug. 5, 1848–Dec. 19, 1916); b. Brooklyn, N.Y. Baptist clergyman, educator, author. *Elements of Psychology* (1892); *Practical or Ideal* (1901); *Before Vassar Opened* (1914); *Vassar* (with Elizabeth Hazelton Haight, 1915). President, Vassar College, 1886–1914.

TAYLOR, JOHN (Dec. 19, 1753–Aug. 21, 1824); b. in Virginia. Agriculturist, political author. *Arator* (1814); *An Inquiry into the Principles and Policy of the Government of the United States* (1814); *Construction Construed and Constitutions Vindicated* (1820); *Tyranny Unmasked* (1822); etc.

TAYLOR, JOHN F[rank] A[dams] (Oct. 8, 1915–); b. Dallas, Tex. Educator, author. *Design and Expression in the Visual Arts* (1964); *The Masks of Society* (1966). Prof. philosophy, Michigan State University, since 1952.

TAYLOR, [Joseph] DEEMS (Dec. 22, 1885–July 3, 1966); b. New York. Composer, music critic. *Of Men and Music* (1937); *The Well-Tempered Listener* (1940); *Pictorial History of the Movies* (with others, 1943); *Music to My Ears* (1949); *Moments Mousical* (1949); *Some Enchanted Evenings* (1953); etc. Compiler of music handbooks, etc. Composed music for *The King's Henchman*, by Edna St. Vincent Millay, etc. Music critic, the *New York World*, 1921–25; editor, *Musical America*, 1927–29; etc. Radio commentator.

TAYLOR, JOSEPH RICHARD (Jan. 11, 1858–Aug. 12, 1955); b. New York. Educator, author. *The Story of the Drama* (1930); *European and Asiatic Plays* (1936); etc. Editor, *Bostonia*, 1904–31. Classics dept., Boston University, 1891–1938.

TAYLOR, KATHARINE HAVILAND (d. 1941); b. Mankato, Minn. Author. *Cecilia of the Pink Roses* (1917); *Barbara of Baltimore* (1919); *Yellow Soap* (1920); *Natalie Page* (1921); *Cross Currents* (1922); *Stanley John's Wife* (1926); *Pablito* (1929); *The Nine Hundred Block* (1932); *Night Club Daughter* (1933); *The Sea Gull's Daughter, and Other Poems* (1937); *Back Roads* (1939); also many plays.

TAYLOR, MARIE HANSEN (Mrs. Bayard Taylor) (June 2, 1829–1925); b. Gotha, Ger. Author. *Letters to a Young Housekeeper* (1892); *On Two Continents: Memories of Half a Century* (1905); etc. Editor: *Bayard Taylor's Poetical Works* (1880); *Bayard Taylor's Dramatic Works* (1880); *Life and Letters of Bayard Taylor* 2v. (with Horace E. Scudder, 1884); etc. Translated her husband's works into German.

TAYLOR, MARION SAYLE (Aug. 16, 1889–1942); b. Louisville, Ky. Radio lecturer and author under name "The Voice of Experience." *The Voice of Experience* (1933); *Stranger than Fiction* (1934); *Making Molehills out of Mountains* (1936); *Best Collected Writings* (1936).

TAYLOR, MARY IMLAY (1878–Aug. 28, 1938); b. Washington, D.C. Author. *On the Red Staircase* (1896); *The Home of the Wizard* (1899); *Anne Scarlett* (1901); *The Rebellion of the Princess* (1903); *The Impersonator* (1906); *Caleb Trench* (1910); *The Long Way* (1913); *A Candle in the Wind* (1919); *The Wild Fawn* (1920).

TAYLOR, NORMAN (May 18, 1883–Nov. 5, 1967); b. Hereford, Eng. Botanist. *Botany: Science of Plant Life* (1924); *The Garden Dictionary* (1936); *Encyclopedia of Gardening* (1948); *Flight from Reality* (1949); *Wild Flower Gardening* (1955); *Taylor's Garden Guide* (1957); etc.

TAYLOR, PETER H[ILLSMAN] (Jan. 8, 1917–); b. in Tennessee. Author. *A Long Fourth, and Other Stories* (1948); *A Woman of Means* (1950); *The Widows of Thornton* (1954); *Tennessee Day in St. Louis* (play, 1957); *Happy Families Are All Alike* (1959); *When Last Seen* (1964); *The Collected Stories of Peter Taylor* (1969).

TAYLOR, ROBERT LEWIS (Sept. 24, 1912–); b. Carbondale, Ill. Author. *Adrift in a Boneyard* (1947); *Doctor, Lawyer, Merchant, Chief* (1948); *W. C. Fields, His Follies and Fortunes* (1949); *The Running Pianist* (1950); *Professor Fodorski* (1950); *Winston Churchill, An Informal Study of Greatness* (1952); *The Bright Sands* (1954); *Center Ring, The People of the Circus* (1956); *The Travels of Jaimie McPheeters* (1958); *A Journey to Matecumbe* (1961); *Two Roads to Guadalupe* (1964); *Vessel of Wrath: The Life and Times of Carry Nation* (1966); etc.

TAYLOR, ROBERT LOVE [Bob] (July 31, 1850–Mar. 31, 1912); b. Happy Valley, Carter Co., Tenn. Governor, editor, author. *Gov. Bob Taylor's Tales* (1896); *Lectures and Best Literary Productions* (1912). Founder, *Bob Taylor's Magazine* (1905). See *Taylor-Trotwood Magazine. See also* Paul D. Augsburg's *Bob and Alf Taylor* (1925), and DeLong Rice's *"Old Limber"; or, The Tale of the Taylors* (1921).

TAYLOR, ROSEMARY [Drachmann] (Mrs. John Winchcombe-Taylor) (May 8, 1899–); b. Phoenix, Ariz. Novelist. *Chicken Every Sunday* (1943); *Ridin' the Rainbow* (1944); *Bar Nothing Ranch* (1947); *Come Clean, My Love* (1949); *Harem Scare'm* (1951); *Ghost Town Bonanza* (1954); *Broadway in a Barn* (with Charlotte Harmon, 1957); etc.

TAYLOR, ROSS McLAURY (Dec. 29, 1909–); b. Snyder, Okla. Educator, author. *Brazos* (1938); *The Saddle and the Plow* (1942); *We Were There Along the Chisholm Trail* (1957); *On the Santa Fe Trail* (1960); etc. Dept. English, University of Wichita, since 1939.

TAYLOR, SAMUEL ALBERT (June 13, 1912–); b. Chicago, Ill. Playwright. *The Happy Time* (1950); *Sabrina Fair* (1953); *The Pleasure of His Company* (with C. O. Skinner, 1958); *First Love* (1961); *No Strings* (with R. Rodgers, 1962); *Beekman Place* (1964).

TAYLOR, TELFORD (Feb. 24, 1908–); b. Schenectady, N.Y. Lawyer, author. *The Nuremberg Trials: War Crimes and International Law* (1949); *Sword and Swastika: Generals and Nazis in the Third Reich* (1952); *Grand Inquest: The Story of Congressional Investigations* (1955); *The March of Conquest* (1958); *The Breaking Wave* (1967); *Two Studies in Constitutional Interpretation* (1969); etc.

TAYLOR, WALTER FULLER (1900–). Author. *A History of American Letters* (1936); *The Economic Novel in America* (1942).

TAYLOR, WILLIAM (May 2, 1821–May 18, 1902); b. in Rockbridge Co., Va. Methodist bishop, author. *Seven Years' Street Preaching in San Francisco* (1857); *California Life Illustrated* (1858); *Story of My Life* (1895); etc.

TAYLOR, WILLIAM LADD (Dec. 10, 1854–Dec. 26, 1926); b. Grafton, Mass. Illustrator, author. *Our Home and Country* (1908). His illustrations appeared in the *Ladies Home Journal* for many years. He accompanied Lucius L. Hubbard on his trips and illustrated his *Woods and Lakes of Maine* (1884); etc.

TAYLOR, WILLIAM MACKERGO (Oct. 23, 1829–Feb. 8, 1895); b. Kilmarnock, Scot. Congregational clergyman, author. *Moses, the Lawgiver* (1879); *John Knox* (1885); *At the*

End of Twenty Years (1892); *Contrary Winds, and Other Sermons* (1899); etc.

TAYLOR, ZACHARY (Nov. 24, 1784–July 9, 1850); b. Montebello, Orange Co., Va. Twelfth president of the United States, soldier. *See* C. Frank Powell's *Life of Major General Zachary Taylor* (1846); J. Reese Fry and Robert T. Conrad's *A Life of General Zachary Taylor* (1847); John Frost's *Life of Major General Zachary Taylor* (1847); Oliver O. Howard's *General Taylor* (1892).

Taylor-Trotwood Magazine. Nashville. Monthly. Founded 1905, by John Trotwood Moore, as *Trotwood's Monthly*. In 1907, it was merged with *Bob Taylor's Magazine* (founded 1905, by Robert Love Taylor), as the *Taylor-Trotwood Magazine*. Absorbed 1911, by *Watson's Jeffersonian Magazine*, which later became *Watson's Magazine*.

TEAD, ORDWAY (Sept. 10, 1891–); b. Somerville, Mass. Editor, author. *The Art of Leadership* (1935); *The Case for Democracy* (1937); *Democratic Administration* (1945); *Equalizing Opportunities Beyond the Secondary School* (1947); *The Climate of Learning* (1958); etc. Co-author: *Modern Education and Human Values* (1947); *Trustees, Teachers, Students* (1951); *Character Building and Higher Education* (1953); *The Climate of Learning* (1958); *Administration: Its Purpose and Performance* (1959). Chairman, Board of Higher Education of New York City, 1938–53; with Harper and Bros., since 1925.

TEAGUE, WALTER DORWIN (Dec. 18, 1883–Dec. 5, 1960); b. Decatur, Ill. Industrial designer, author. *Design This Day* (1940); *You Can't Ignore Murder* (with Ruth Teague, 1942); *Land of Plenty, A Summary of Possibilities* (1947); *Flour for Man's Bread, A History of Milling* (with John Storck, 1952); etc.

TEAL, VAL[entine] (Mrs. Clarence W. Teal); b. Bottineau, N.D. Author. *The Little Woman Wanted Noise* (1943); *Angel Child* (1946); *It Was Not What I Expected* (1948); *With Sirens Blowing* (prod. 1949); etc.

TEALE, EDWIN WAY (June 2, 1899–); b. Joliet, Ill, Naturalist, author. *Grassroot Jungles* (1937); *The Golden Throng* (1940); *Near Horizons* (1942); *Dune Boy: The Early Years of a Naturalist* (1943); *The Lost Woods* (1945); *Days Without Time* (1948); *North with the Spring* (1951); *Circle of the Seasons* (1953); *Insect Friends* (1955); *Autumn Across America* (1956); *Journey into Summer* (1960); *The Lost Dog* (1961); *The Strange Lives of Familiar Insects* (1962); etc.

TEALL, EDWARD NELSON (Mar. 23, 1880–Feb. 17, 1947); b. Brooklyn, N.Y. Author. *Vagrom Verses* (1915); *Books and Folks* (1921); *Meet Mr. Hyphen* (1937); *Putting Words to Work* (1940); Wrote "Watch Tower" department in *St. Nicholas*, 1917–27; on staff, *Inland Printer*, from 1923.

TEALL, GARDNER [Callahan] (Mar. 6, 1878–July 22, 1956); b. Eau Claire, Wis. Illustrator, author. *The Garden Primer* (1910); *The Contessa's Sister* (1911); *The Pleasures of Collecting* (1920); *Book Plates by Sidney L. Smith* (1921); *The Art of Sidney Lawton Smith* (1931); *The Color Prints of Treeva Wheete* (1935).

"Tears." Best known poem of Lizette Woodworth Reese (1889).

Tears and Smiles. First play by James N. Barker (prod. 1807). A satire on American manners. Fluttermore, an American fop, goes abroad to polish his etiquette.

TEASDALE, SARA (Aug. 8, 1884–Jan. 29, 1933); b. St. Louis, Mo. Poet. *Sonnets to Duse, and Other Poems* (1907); *Helen of Troy, and Other Poems* (1911); *Rivers to the Sea* (1915); *Love Songs* (1917); *Flame and Shadow* (1920); *Dark of the Moon* (1926); *Stars To-Night* (1930); *Strange Victory* (1933); *The Collected Poems* (1937). *See* Fred B. Millett's *Contemporary American Authors* (1940).

TEBBEL, JOHN [William] (Nov. 16, 1912–); b. Boyne City, Mich. Author. *An American Dynasty* (1947); *George Horace Lorimer and the Saturday Evening Post* (1948); *The Conqueror* (1951); *The Life and Good Times of William Randolph Hearst* (1952); *George Washington's America* (1954); *The Magic of Balanced Living* (1956); *The American Indian Wars* (with K. W. Jennison, 1960); *The Inheritors* (1962); *The Epicure's Companion* (1962); *David Sarnoff* (1963); *Compact History of the American Newspaper* (1964). Dept. of journalism, New York University; director, Graduate Institute of Book Publishing, since 1958.

TEILHET, DARWIN [Le Ora] (May 20, 1904–); b. Wyanette, Ill. Author. *Bright Destination* (1935); *Journey to the West* (1938); *Trouble Is My Master* (1941); *Fear Makers* (1944); *My True Love* (1945); *The Avion My Uncle Flew* (under pen name "Cyrus Fisher," 1946); *Something Wonderful to Happen* (1947); *Ab Carmody's Treasure* (under pen name "Cyrus Fisher," 1948); *The Happy Island* (1950); *Steamboat on the River* (1952); *Road to Glory* (1956); etc.

Television Book Programs. Since the late 1940's a number of television programs have incidentally, occasionally, or regularly been concerned with books and authors. Among the best-known offerings devoted to literature have been "Books and Authors" on KQED, San Francisco, Calif., consisting of book discussions and author interviews; "Dave Garroway" on NBC-TV, featuring reviews; "Today Show," featuring interviews and reviews on NBC-TV; "I've Been Reading," on WGBH-TV, Cambridge, Mass., moderated by Albert P. Duhamel, featuring book critiques; "Landmarks in the Evolution of the Novel" on WCBS-TV, in which Floyd Zulli has conducted a college-credit course; "Face the Nation" and "Eye on New York," both on WCBS-TV; "My Favorite Reading" on KETC, St. Louis Mo., with Julie Hershey conducting conversations and interviews; "Carnival of New Books" on WMAQ, Chicago, Ill., in which Ruth Harshaw has conducted interviews of authors of juveniles and group discussions; "David Susskind Show," in which literary and cultural topics have been dealt with through panel discussions with authors; "The Opinionated Man," moderated by Roysce Smith on WNHC-TV, New Haven, Conn.; "Focus on Books" on WNYC-TV, New York City; Robert Cromie on "Book Beat," WTTW-TV, Chicago, Ill.; "Caspar Citron Interviews," on WNYC-TV, New York City.

Television Quarterly. New York City. Founded 1962. Edited by David Manning White. Published by National Academy of Television Arts and Sciences.

TELLER, EDWARD (Jan. 15, 1908–); b. Budapest. Physicist. Author: *Basic Concepts of Physics* (1960). Co-author: *The Structure of Matter* (1949); *Our Nuclear Future* (1958); *The Legacy of Hiroshima* (1962); *The Reluctant Revolutionary* (1964); *The Constructive Uses of Nuclear Explosives* (with G. W. Johnson, W. K. Talley, and G. H. Higgins, 1965). Prof. physics, University of California, since 1952.

"Telling the Bees." Poem by John Greenleaf Whittier (1858).

Tempest and Sunshine; or, Life in Kentucky. First novel by Mary Jane Holmes (1854). Most popular of her books.

Ten Boys Who Lived on the Road from Long Ago to Now. By Jane Andrews (1885). Hero tales from many lands.

TEN BROEK, JACOBUS (July 6, 1911–Mar. 27, 1968); b. in Alberta, Can. Educator. *The Antislavery Origins of the 14th Amendment* (1951); *Prejudice, War, and the Constitution* (with others, 1954); *Hope Deferred* (with F.W. Matson, 1959); etc. Chairman, speech dept., University of California, from 1955.

Ten Days That Shook the World. Eyewitness account of the Russian Revolution, by John Reed (1919).

TEN HOOR, MARTEN (Apr. 21, 1890–); b. Franeker, Neth. Educator. *The Problems of Thinking and Knowing* (1933);

Freedom Limited (1954); *Education for Privacy* (1960); etc. Prof. philosophy, University of Alabama, since 1944.

Ten Nights in a Barroom and What I Saw There. By Timothy Shay Arthur (1854). Sensationally popular temperance novel showing the decay of a once happy village. Joe Morgan, the drunkard, is shown in the tavern "Sickle and Sheaf" while his noble wife Fanny attempts to save him from disgrace. Dramatized by William W. Pratt (prod. 1858), it became a popular melodrama.

Ten North Frederick. Novel by John O'Hara (1955).

Tender Buttons. Experimental poems by Gertrude Stein (1914).

Tender Is the Night. Novel by F. Scott Fitzgerald (1934).

Tennessee's Partner. By Bret Harte (1870). One of the early local color stories. It portrays an extraordinary friendship between two men.

TENNEY, EDWARD PAYSON (Sept. 29, 1835–July 24, 1916); b. Concord, N.H. Congregational clergyman, author. *The Silent House* (1876); *Agamenticus* (1878); *Constance of Acadia* (1886); *Agatha and the Shadow* (1887); *The Dream of My Youth* (1901); *Contrasts in Social Progress* (1907); *Looking Forward into the Past* (1910).

TENNEY, MERRILL CHAPIN (Apr. 16, 1904–); b. Chelsea, Mass. Baptist clergyman, educator. *John: The Gospel of Belief* (1948); *The New Testament: A Survey* (1953); *Interpreting Revelation* (1957); *Proclaiming the New Testament: The Reality of Resurrection* (1963); *New Testament Times* (1965); etc. Prof. Bible and theology, Wheaton College (Illinois), since 1945.

TENNEY, SARAH BROWNSON (June 7, 1839–Oct. 30, 1876); b. Chelsea, Mass., daughter of Orestes A. Brownson. Novelist. *Marion Elwood* (1859); *At Anchor* (1865); *Life of Demetrius Augustine Gallitzin, Prince and Priest* (1873); etc.

TENNEY, TABITHA GILMAN (Apr. 7, 1762–May 2, 1837); b. Exeter, N.H. Novelist. *The Pleasing Instructor* (1799), of which no copy is known to exist, but which was announced in the *Newburyport Herald*, May 7, 1799; *Female Quixotism* (anon., 1801).

Tensas, Madison. See *Louisiana Swamp Doctor.*

Tent on the Beach, The. By John Greenleaf Whittier (1867). A series of narrative poems.

"Tenting on the Old Camp Ground." Popular Civil War song, words and music by Walter Kittredge, written in 1862 and first published in 1864.

Terence. Play by Florence Hower Morgan (Mrs. Edmund Nash Morgan) (prod. 1904). This play, based on a novel by Mrs. B. M. Croker, ran for two years on Broadway.

TERHUNE, ALBERT PAYSON (Dec. 21, 1872–Feb. 18, 1942); b. Newark, N.J., son of Mary Virginia Terhune ("Marion Harland"). Author. *Syria from the Saddle* (1896); *Columbia Stories* (1897); *Dr. Dale: A Story without a Moral* (with mother, 1900); *The Fighter* (1909); *Lad, A Dog* (1919); *Bruce* (1920); *Buff: a Collie* (1921); *Black Gold* (1921); *Wolf* (1924); *Treve* (1924); *Now That I'm Fifty* (1925); *Treasure* (1926); *Gray Dawn* (1927); *The Luck of the Laird* (1927); *To the Best of My Memory* (autobiography, 1930); *The Way of a Dog* (1934); *The Book of Sunnybank* (1935); *A Book of Famous Dogs* (1937); *Grudge Mountain* (1939); etc. On staff, the *New York World*, 1894–1916.

TERHUNE, ANICE [Morris Stockton] (Mrs. Albert Payson Terhune); b. Hampden, Mass. Composer, author. *Ballade of Dead Ladies* (1917); *Sins of the Fathers* (1918); *Grey Dawn* (1919); *The Story of Canada* (1919); *The Eyes of the Village* (1921); *The Boarder up at Em's* (1925); *The White Mouse* (1929); *Sunnybank Songs* (1929); *The White Mouse* (1929); *A Flier in Paris* (1930); *The Bert Terhune I Knew* (1943); *Across the Line* (1945).

TERHUNE, MARY VIRGINIA [Hawes] (Dec. 21, 1830–June 3, 1922); b. Dennisville, Va. Mother of Albert Payson Terhune. Novelist. Pen name "Marion Harland." *Alone* (1846); *The Hidden Path* (1859); *Nemesis* (1860); *True as Steel* (1872); *Loiterings in Pleasant Paths* (1880); *Judith* (1883); *A Gallant Fight* (1888); *His Great Self* (1892); *William Cowper* (1899); *Charlotte Bronte at Home* (1899); *Hannah More* (1900); *Dr. Dale: A Story without a Moral* (with Albert Payson Terhune, 1900); *Marion Harland's Autobiography* (1910); *Looking Westward* (1914); *The Long Lane* (1915); *The Carringtons of High Hill* (1919); etc.

TERKEL, STUDS [Louis] (May 16, 1912–); b. New York. Author. *Giants of Jazz* (1956); *Amazing Grace* (1959); *The Republican Establishment* (with Stephen Hess, 1967); *Division Street: America* (1967); *Hard Times: An Oral History of the Great Depression* (1970).

"Terminus." Poem by Ralph Waldo Emerson (1872).

TERRELL, JOHN UPTON (Dec. 9, 1900–); b. Chicago, Ill. Author. *Jean Blue* (1929); *Adam Cargo* (1934); *The Little Dark Man* (1934); *Sunday Is the Day You Rest* (1939); *Plume Rouge* (1942); *Pueblo of the Hearts* (1966); *The United States Department of Commerce* (1966); *The United States Department of Defense* (1967); etc.

TERRES, JOHN K[enneth] (Dec. 17, 1905–); b. Philadelphia, Pa. Naturalist, editor, author. *Songbirds in Your Garden* (1953); *The Wonders I See* (1960); *An Encyclopedia of American Birds* (1965); etc. Editor of numerous volumes relating to wildlife.

Territorial Enterprise and Virginia City News. Virginia City, Nev. Newspaper. Founded 1858, as *Territorial Enterprise*, at Genoa, Nev., by W. L. Jernegan and Alfred James. Moved to Carson City and later to Virginia City, in 1860. Mark Twain was city editor in its early years. Nevada's first newspaper. Expired 1916. Revived in early 1950's by Lucius Beebe. Janice Franks is editor. *See* Beebe's *Comstock Commotion: The Story of the Territorial Enterprise* (1954).

Territorial Imperative, The. By Robert Ardrey (1966). A personal study of the animal origins of property and national groups. The author argues that man's territorial sense is not the result of custom and that his ideas about property are biologically determined.

Terror and Decorum. Collection of poems, by Peter Viereck (1948).

TERRY, HOWARD LESLIE (Jan. 4, 1877–); b. St. Louis, Mo. Poet, novelist. *The Cave Diggers* (1891); *Poems* (1894); *Waters from an Ozark Spring* (poems, 1909); *California, and Other Poems* (1912); *A Voice from the Silence* (1914); *Sung in Silence: Selected Poems* (1929).

TERRY, RODERICK (Apr. 1, 1849–Dec. 28, 1933); b. Brooklyn, N.Y. Presbyterian clergyman, book collector. Author of a number of pamphlets on Rhode Island history. See *The Library of the Late Rev. Dr. Roderick Terry*, a catalogue, 3v. (1934–35).

TERRY, T[homas] (June 6, 1864–deceased); b. Georgetown, Ky. Traveler, lecturer, author. *Terry's Guide to Mexico* (1909); *Terry's Japanese Empire* (1914); *Terry's Guide to Cuba* (1926); *Terry's Guide to the Japanese Empire and Manchoukuo* (1940); etc.

TERRY, WALTER (May 14, 1913–); b. Brooklyn, N.Y. Dance critic. *Invitation to Dance* (1942); *Star Performance: The Story of the World's Great Ballerinas* (1954); *Ballet in Action* (with Paul Himmel, 1954); *The Dance in America* (1956); *Ballet: A New Guide to the Liveliest Art* (1959); *On Pointe* (1962); *Isadora Duncan* (1964); *The Ballet Company*

(1968). Dance critic, *New York Herald Tribune*, 1939–42, from 1945 to 1967.

Tess of the Storm Country. Novel by Grace Miller White (1909). Popular rural romance of a brave girl.

TESTUT, CHARLES (c. 1818–July 1, 1892); b. in France. Physician, journalist, author. *Les Échos* (poems, 1849); *Portraits Littéraires* (1850); *Fleurs d'Été* (poems, 1851); *Les Mystères de la Nouvelle-Orléans*, 2v. (1852–53); *Le Vieux Salomon* (1872); etc. Editor: *Les Veillées Louisianaises*, 2v. (1849). Founder, *La Semaine de la Nouvelle Orléans*, 1852; *L'Equité*, 1871; *La Semaine Littéraire*, 1876; *Le Journal des Famille*, c. 1888.

Texas Quarterly, The: A Review of the Arts and Sciences. Austin, Tex. Founded at the University of Texas, 1958.

Texas Republican. Nacogdoches, Tex. Founded 1819, by Horatio Bigelow. Editor, Eli Harris. First newspaper published in English in Texas. A Spanish paper, *Gaceta de Texas*, preceded it by a few years.

Texas Siftings. Austin, Tex. Comic magazine. Founded 1881, by Alex E. Sweet and J. Amory Knox, co-authors of *On a Mexican Mustang* (1883). In 1885 the magazine was transferred to New York. Expired 1897.

Texas Steer; or, "Money Makes the Mare Go," A. Comedy by Charles H. Hoyt (prod. 1890). Travesty on a Texas congressman. Cf. Frank H. Murdock's *Davy Crockett.*

THACHER, JAMES (Feb. 14, 1754–May 23, 1844); b. Barnstable, Mass. Army surgeon, historian. *A Military Journal during the American Revolutionary War* (1823); *American Medical Biography* (1828); *An Essay on Demonology, Ghosts, and Apparitions* (1831); etc.

THACHER, JOHN BOYD (Sept. 11, 1847–Feb. 25, 1909); b. Ballston, N.Y. Bibliophile, author. *The Continent of America* (1896); *Charlecote; or, The Trial of William Shakespeare* (1896); *The Cabotian Discovery* (1897); *Christopher Columbus*, 3v. (1903–04); etc. His collection of books and autographs is now in the Library of Congress. See Frederick W. Ashley's *Catalogue of the John Boyd Thacher Collection of Incunabula* (1915).

THACKER, MAY DIXON (May 4, 1875–); b. Shelby, N.C. Author. *The Strength of the Weak* (1910); *The Outcast* (1927); *Young Sinners* (1928); *Cell No. 33* (1929); etc.

THADDEUS, VICTOR (Jan. 24, 1896–); b. London. Author. *Julius Caesar & the Grandeur That Was Rome* (1927); *Voltaire, Genius of Mockery* (1928); *Frederick the Great: Philosopher King* (1930); *Benvenuto Cellini and His Florentine Dagger* (1933); etc.

Thalatta: A Book for the Seaside. Ed. by Samuel Longfellow and T. W. Higginson (1853). An anthology of poems by Lowell, Longfellow, Whittier, Holmes, etc.

THALER, ALWIN (Jan. 10, 1891–); b. Hamburg, Ger. Educator, author. *Shakespeare to Sheridan* (1922); *Shakespeare's Silences* (1929); *Shakespeare and Democracy* (1941); *Shakespeare and Sir Philip Sidney* (1947); *Shakespeare and Our World* (1966); etc. Editor: *Tennessee Studies in Literature*, 3v. (with R. B. David, 1956–58). Prof. English, University of Tennessee, since 1923; prof. emeritus since 1961.

"Thanatopsis." Poem by William Cullen Bryant, which appeared anonymously in the *North American Review*, Sept., 1817.

THANE, ELSWYTH (Mrs. William Beebe) (1900–); b. Burlington, Ia. Author. *Riders of the Wind* (1925); *The Tudor Wench* (prod. 1934); *Young Mr. Disraeli* (prod. 1935); *The Queen's Folly* (1937); *From this Day Forward* (1942); *Ever After* (1945); *Letter to a Stranger* (1954); *Homing* (1957); *Washington's Lady* (1960); *Potomac Squire* (1963); *Mt. Ver-*

non is Ours (1966); *Mt. Vernon, the Legacy* (1967); *Mt. Vernon Family* (1968); *The Virginia Colony* (1969); etc.

Thanet, Octave. Pen name of Alice French.

THARP, LOUISE [Marshall Hall] (June 19, 1898–); b. Oneonta, N.Y. Author. *Tory Hole* (1940); *Down to the Sea: A Life of Nathaniel Bowditch* (1942); *Champlain Northwest Voyager* (1944); *The Peabody Sisters of Salem* (1950); *Three Saints and a Sinner* (1956); *Adventurous Alliance: The Agassiz Family of Boston* (1959); *Louis Agassiz* (1961); *The Baroness and the General* (1962); *Mrs. Jack: A Biography of Isabella Stewart Gardner* (1965); etc.

That Mainwaring Affair. By Anna Maynard Barbour (1900). One of the most popular mystery novels of its day.

THATCHER, BENJAMIN BUSSEY (Oct. 8, 1809–July 14, 1840); b. Warren, Me. Lawyer, editor, author. *Indian Biography*, 2v. (1832); *Indian Traits*, 2v. (1833); *Memoir of Phillis Wheatley* (1834); etc. Compiler: *The Boston Book* (1837), an anthology.

THAXTER, CELIA [Laighton] (June 29, 1835–Aug. 26, 1894); Portsmouth, N.H. Poet. *Poems* (1872); *Among the Isles of Shoals* (1873); *Drift Weed* (1879); *Poems for Children* (1884); *Idyls and Pastorals* (1886); *The Cruise of the Mystery* (1886); *An Island Garden* (1894); *Letters* (1895); *Poems* (1896); *The Heavenly Guest, with Other Unpublished Writings* (1935); etc. See Annie Fields's *Authors and Friends* (1896); Oscar Laighton's *Ninety Years at the Isles of Shoals* (1930).

THAYER, EMMA REDINGTON LEE (Apr. 5, 1874–); b. Troy, Pa. Author. Writes as "Lee Thayer." *The Mystery of the 13th Floor* (1919); *That Affair at the Cedars* (1921); *Q. E. D.* (1922); *The Key* (1924); *Alias Dr. Ely* (1927); *Hell-Gate Tides* (1933); *Sudden Death* (1935); *Dead Storage* (1935); *Last Trump* (1937); *That Strange Sylvester Affair* (1939); *Accessory After the Fact* (1943); *Jaws of Death* (1946); *Pig in a Poke* (1948); *Blood on the Knight* (1952); *Still No Answer* (1958); *And One Cried Murder* (1961).

THAYER, JOHN ADAMS (Feb. 20, 1861–Feb. 21, 1936); b. Boston, Mass. Publisher, author. *Astir: A Publisher's Life-Story* (1910), published in England as *Getting On: The Confessions of a Publisher* (1911), republished as *Out of the Rut: A Business Life Story* (1912). Co-founder, Ridgeway-Thayer Co., 1903, publishers of *Everybody's Magazine*. Publisher and owner, *Smart Set*, 1911–14.

THAYER, JOSEPH HENRY (Nov. 7, 1828–Nov. 26, 1901); b. Boston, Mass. Congregational clergyman, educator, author. *The Change of Attitude Towards the Bible* (1891); *Books and Their Use* (1893); etc. Prof. sacred literature, Andover Theological Seminary, 1864–82; Bussey Prof. of New Testament criticism and interpretation, Harvard University, 1884–1901.

THAYER, MARY DIXON (Dec. 16, 1896–); b. Philadelphia, Pa. Poet. *The Intellectuals* (1921); *Songs of Youth* (1922); *New York, and Other Poems* (1925); *The Child on His Knees* (1926); *Foam* (1926); *Ends of Things* (1927); *Songs before the Blessed Sacrament* (1932); *Sonnets* (1933).

THAYER, MRS. J. Author. *The Drunkard's Daughter* (1842); *The Widow's Son* (1843); *Passion, and Other Tales* (1846).

THAYER, STEPHEN HENRY (Dec. 16, 1839–Dec. 16, 1919); b. New Ipswich, N.H. Banker, poet, novelist. *Songs of Sleepy Hollow, and Other Poems* (1886); *Daughters of the Revolution* (1900); *Songs from Edgewood* (1902).

THAYER, TIFFANY ELLSWORTH (Mar. 1, 1902–Aug. 23, 1959); b. Freeport, Ill. Novelist. *Thirteen Men* (1930); *Illustrious Corpse* (1930); *Call Her Savage* (1931); *The Greek* (1931); *Thirteen Women* (1932); *An American Girl* (1933); *Doctor Arnoldi* (1934); *Old Goat* (1937); *Little Dog Lost* (1938); *Rabelais for Boys and Girls* (1939); *Three Musketeers*

(1939); *One Woman* (1943); *Mona Lisa: I, The Prince of Taranto,* 3v. (1956); etc.

THAYER, WILLIAM M[akepeace] (Feb. 23, 1820–Apr. 7, 1898); b. Franklin, Mass. Congregational clergyman, editor, author. *The Gem and the Casket* (1953); *The Poor Girl and the True Woman: The Life of Mary Lyon* (1857); *The Bobbin Boy* (1860); *The Pioneer Boy and How He Became President* (1863); *A Youth's History of the Rebellion,* 4v. (1864–65); *Charles Jewett: Life and Recollections* (1880); *Marvels of the New West* (1887); *From Boyhood to Manhood: The Life of Benjamin Franklin* (1889); *Men Who Win* (1896); *Women Who Win* (1896); etc. Editor, the *Home Monthly,* 1858–62; *The Nation,* 1864–68; *Mother's Assistant,* 1868–72.

THAYER, WILLIAM ROSCOE (Jan. 16, 1859–Sept. 7, 1923); b. Boston, Mass. Editor, author. *The Dawn of Italian Independence,* 2v. (1893); *Poems, New and Old* (1894); *Throne-Makers* (1899); *A Short History of Venice* (1905); *The Life and Times of Cavour,* 2v. (1911); *The Life and Letters of John Hay,* 2v. (1915); *Theodore Roosevelt: An Intimate Biography* (1919); *The Art of Biography* (1920); *The Letters,* ed. by C. D. Hazen (1926); etc. Editor, *Harvard Graduates' Magazine,* 1892–1915.

Theatre Arts. New York. Monthly. Founded 1916, as the quarterly *Theatre Arts Magazine.* Name changed in 1924 to the *Theatre Arts Monthly.* Name *Theatre Arts* adopted in 1939. Sheldon Cheney, Edith J. R. Isaacs, Charles MacArthur, Bruce Bohle have been editors. Expired 1964.

Theatre Guild. New York. Founded 1919. Grew out of the Washington Square Players. The Guild Theatre, New York (now the Anta), was opened April 13, 1925. Before the Guild built its own theatre it used the Garrick Theatre. It is now solely a producing organization. *See* Walter Prichard Eaton's *The Theatre Guild, The First Ten Years* (1929). *See also* Lawrence Langner.

THEBAUD, AUGUSTUS J. (Nov. 20, 1807–Dec. 17, 1885); b. Nantes, Fr. Roman Catholic clergyman, educator, author. *The Church and the Moral World* (1881); *Louisa Kirkbride* (1879); *Forty Years in the United States of America* (1904); *Three-Quarters of a Century,* 2v. (1912–13). Prof. Fordham University, 1860–63, 1874–75; etc.

Their Wedding Journey. Novel by William Dean Howells (1871). Description of a wedding journey from Boston to Ohio, based on Howells's own wedding journey from Ohio to Boston.

THEISS, LEWIS EDWIN (Sept. 29, 1878–May 22, 1963); b. Birmingham (now Derby) Conn. Editor, educator, author. *In Camp at Fort Brady* (1914); *Lumberjack Bob* (1916); the *Young Wireless Operator* series, 5v. (1920–24); *The Flume in the Mountains* (1925); *Piloting the U. S. Air Mail* (1927); *Wings of the Coast Guard* (1932); *The Flying Explorer* (1935); *Guardians of the Sea* (1935); *Wings Over the Pacific* (1938); *Wings Over the Andes* (1939); *Aboard a U. S. Submarine* (1940); *Flying with the Coastal Patrol* (1943); *Flying with the Air-Sea Rescue Service* (1946); *Lives of Danger and Daring* (1955); etc. Prof. journalism, Bucknell University, since 1924.

Theory of Literature. By Austin Warren and René Wellek (1949). A comprehensive analysis of the critical approach to literature.

Theory of the Leisure Class, The. By Thorstein Veblen (1899). The author's thesis is that people of wealth buy their leisure at the expense of laborers whom they enslave, that this leisure is an economic waste and tends to widen the breach between the upper and lower classes.

There Are Smiles. Short story by Ring Lardner (1929).

"There Is a Tavern in the Town." Song by William H. Hills (1883).

There She Blows! or, The Log of the Arethusa. Novel by William Hussey Macy (1877). A whaling classic by a whaling captain.

"There was a little girl who had a little curl." From a poem by Henry Wadsworth Longfellow. A version of this bit of verse appeared in *Balloon Post,* April 11, 1871. Its first appearance in a book was in *The Home Life of Henry W. Longfellow,* by Blanche Roosevelt Tucker-Macchetta (1882).

"There'll Be a Hot Time in the Old Town Tonight." See "Hot Time in the Old Town."

These United States. Ed. by Ernest Henry Gruening, 2v. (1923). Collection of essays on each state in the United States, written by several authors.

Thespian Mirror. New York. Theatrical journal. Founded 1805. John Howard Payne was editor. Expired 1806.

Thespian Oracle. Philadelphia, Pa. Theatrical review. Founded 1798, by J. B. Freeman. It had a short life, but was probably the first of its kind in America.

They Knew What They Wanted. Play by Sidney Howard (prod. 1925). Tony, a California fruit grower, wants a wife and child. Amy, who answers Tony's advertisement for a wife, wants a home. Joe, Tony's hired hand, wants love. Amy provides Tony with a child, but Joe is its father. Pulitzer Prize play, 1926.

They Went On Together. Novel by Robert Nathan (1941). About a group of people dispossessed by World War II.

They Were Expendable. By W. L. White (1942). The adventures of men in a patrol boat squadron during World War II.

THIELEN, BENEDICT (Apr. 29, 1902–); b. Newark, N.J. *Deep Streets* (1932); *Women in the Sun* (1933); *Dinosaur Tracks and Other Stories* (1937); *Stevie* (1941); *The Lost Men* (1946); *Friday at Noon* (1947); etc.

THIERRY, CAMILLE (Oct. 1814–Apr. 1875); b. New Orleans, La. Poet. *Les Vagabondes* (1874); etc. *See* E. L. Tinker's *Les Écrits de Langue Française en Louisiane* (1932).

THILLY, FRANK (Aug. 18, 1865–Dec. 28, 1934); b. Cincinnati, O. Educator, author. *An Introduction to Ethics* (1900); *A History of Philosophy* (1914); etc. Editor and translator, Paulsen's *A System of Ethics* (1898); Weber's *History of Philosophy* (1896); etc. Editor, *University of Missouri Studies,* 1901–04. Prof. philosophy, Cornell University, 1906–34.

Third Press. New York. Publishers. Founded 1969, by Joe Okpaku. Concerned with black interests, social change, and modern literature.

"Thirteen Ways of Looking at a Blackbird." Poem by Wallace Stevens (1923).

Thirty Years' View; or, History of the Working of the American Government from 1820 to 1850. Autobiography by Thomas Hart Benton, 2v. (1854–56). Chronicle of frontier life in the West and of a long residence in Washington as United States Senator from Missouri. This was parodied by "Major Jack Downing" (Seba Smith) in his *My Thirty Years Out of the Senate* (1859).

This Body the Earth. Novel by Paul Green (1935). Portrayal of the struggle of the poor share-croppers of the South against the agricultural system which has long prevailed there.

This I Believe. Edited by Edward P. Morgan, with an introduction by Edward R. Murrow (1953). Statements of personal faith by one hundred contributors, developed from Murrow's radio program "This I Believe." Followed by *This I Believe, 2,* edited by Raymond Swing (1954).

This Is the Army. Musical show by Irving Berlin (prod. 1942).

This Side of Paradise. Novel by F. Scott Fitzgerald (1920). Jazz-age story of gay but philosophical college youth in revolt against the conservatism of their elders.

This Week Magazine. New York. Sunday newspaper magazine section, published by United Newspapers Magazine Corp. Founded 1935. Distributed with newspapers throughout the United States. Contains topical feature articles. Suspended 1969.

THOBURN, JAMES MILLS (Mar. 7, 1836–Nov. 28, 1922); b. St. Clairsville, O. Methodist bishop, missionary, author. *My Missionary Apprenticeship* (1887); *India and Malaysia* (1892); *Life of Isabella Thoburn* (1903); etc. His autobiography appeared in the *Western Christian Advocate,* Jan.–Dec. 1911.

THOBURN, JOSEPH BRADFIELD (Aug. 8, 1868–); b. Bellaire, O. Archeologist, historian. *History of Oklahoma* (1916); *Oklahoma: A History of the State and Its People* (with Muriel H. Wright, 1929). Co-editor: Washington Irving's *Tour on the Prairies* (1955). With Oklahoma Historical Society, from 1903; curator, 1926–31, 1938.

THOMAS, ABEL C[harles] (June 11, 1807–Sept. 28, 1880); b. Exeter, Pa. Universalist clergyman, author. *Allegories and Divers Day-Dreams* (1841); *Autobiography* (1852). Co-author: *The Lowell Tracts* (with Thomas B. Thayer, 1840–42). Founder (with Thomas B. Thayer), the *Lowell Offering,* 1840.

THOMAS, A[lbert] E[llsworth] (Sept. 16, 1872–June 18, 1947); b. Chester, Mass. Playwright, novelist, journalist. *Cynthia's Rebellion* (1903); *Thirty Days* (with Clayton Hamilton, prod. 1910); *Her Husband's Wife* (prod. 1910); *The Rainbow* (prod. 1912); *The Big Idea* (with Clayton Hamilton, prod. 1914); *The Better Understanding* (with same, prod. 1917); *The Matinee Hero* (prod. 1918); *Just Suppose* (prod. 1920); *The Champion* (with Thomas Loudon, prod. 1921); *Our Nell* (with Brian Hooker, prod. 1922); *White Magic* (prod. 1926); *The Big Pond* (with George Middleton, prod. 1928); *Her Friend the King* (with Harrison Rhodes, prod. 1929); *Vermont* (prod. 1929); *No More Ladies* (prod. 1934); etc. On staff successively, the *New York Tribune,* the *New York Evening Post,* the *New York Times,* the *New York Sun,* 1895–1909.

THOMAS, AUGUSTUS (Jan. 8, 1857–Aug. 12, 1934); b. St. Louis, Mo. Playwright. *Alone* (prod. 1875); *A Proper Impropriety* (1888); *Alabama* (prod. 1890); *In Mizzoura* (prod. 1893); *The Capitol* (prod. 1894); *The Man Upstairs* (prod. 1895); *The Hoosier Doctor* (prod. 1897); *Oliver Goldsmith* (prod. 1899); *Arizona* (prod. 1899); *Colorado* (prod. 1901); *The Other Girl* (prod. 1902); *The Earl of Pawtucket* (prod. 1903); *Mrs. Leffingwell's Boots* (prod. 1905); *Delancey* (prod. 1904); *The Witching Hour* (prod. 1907); *The Harvest Moon* (prod. 1909); *As a Man Thinks* (1911); *Rio Grande* (prod. 1916); *The Copperhead* (prod. 1918); *The Print of My Remembrance* (autobiography, 1922); *Still Waters* (prod. 1925); etc.

THOMAS, CALVIN (Oct. 28, 1854–Nov. 4, 1919); b. Lapeer, Mich. Educator, author. *The Life and Works of Friedrich Schiller* (1901); *A History of German Literature* (1909); *Goethe* (1917); *Scholarship, and Other Essays* (1924). Editor: *Goethe's Faust,* 2v. (1892–97). Compiler: *An Anthology of German Literature* (1907). Prof. Germanic languages, Columbia University, 1896–1919.

THOMAS, CHARLES SWAIN (Dec. 29, 1868–Jan. 26, 1943); b. Pendleton, Ind. Educator, editor, author. *How to Teach English Classics* (1909). Editor: *Tom Brown's Schooldays* (1909); Cooper's *The Spy* (1911). Compiler: *Milton's Minor Poems;* Bret Harte's *Stories and Poems* (1912); *Selected Lyrics,* 2v. (1913); *Atlantic Narratives,* 2v. (1918); *Modern Atlantic Stories* (1932). Wrote, "The Saunterer Col-

umn" in the *Harvard Educational Review,* from 1936. Editorial staff, Atlantic Monthly Press, 1920–25. English dept., Harvard University, 1920–36.

THOMAS, CHAUNCEY (July 15, 1872–deceased); b. Denver, Colo. Editor, author. *The Crystal Button* (1891). Assoc. editor *Smart Set,* 1903; with Munsey publications, 1910–13; assoc. editor, *Outdoor Life,* 1913–25.

THOMAS, CYRUS (July 27, 1825–June 26, 1910); b. Kingsport, Tenn. Ethnologist, author. *The Indians of North America in Historic Times* (1903); *Prehistoric North America* (with W. J. McGee, 1905). He published many monographs on Maya culture.

THOMAS, DAVID YANCEY (Jan. 19, 1872–Apr. 18, 1943); b. in Fulton Co., Ky. Educator, author. *History of the University of Arkansas* (1910); *One Hundred Years of the Monroe Doctrine* (1923); *Arkansas in War and Reconstruction* (1926); etc. Editor, *Arkansas and Its People,* 4v. (1930). History dept., University of Arkansas, from 1907.

THOMAS, DOROTHY (1898–); b. in Kansas. Novelist. *Ma Jeeter's Girls* (1933); *The Home Place* (1936); *Hi-Po the Hippo* (1942); *The Elephant's Dilemma* (1946).

THOMAS, EBENEZER SMITH (June 1780–Aug. 1844); b. Lancaster, Mass. Editor, author. *Reminiscences of the Last Sixty-Five Years,* 2v. (1840); *Reminiscences of South Carolina,* 2v. (1840). Editor, the *Charleston City Gazette,* 1810–16; the *Cincinnati Daily Advertiser,* 1829–35; the *Cincinnati Evening Post,* 1835–39.

THOMAS, EDITH M[atilda] (Aug. 12, 1854–Sept. 13, 1925); b. Chatham, O. Poet. *A New Year's Masque, and Other Poems* (1885); *Lyrics and Sonnets* (1887); *The Inverted Torch* (1890); *In Sunshine Land* (1895); *The Dancers, and Other Legends and Lyrics* (1903); *The Flower from the Ashes* (1915); *Selected Poems* (1926); etc. Reader for *Harper's Magazine,* 1908–25.

THOMAS, EUGENE (Feb. 21, 1893–); b. Seneca, S.C. Author. Pen name "Donald Grey." *Black Echo* (1932); *Intimate Stranger* (1932); *Death Rides the Dragon* (1932); *Shadow of Chu-Sheng* (1933); *The Morning After* (1934); *Yellow Magic* (1934); *The Lady from Hell* (1935); *Exiled to Heaven* (1937); *The Brotherhood of Mount Shasta* (1946); etc.

THOMAS, FREDERICK WILLIAM (Oct. 25, 1806–Aug. 27, 1866); b. Providence, R.I. Editor, novelist. *The Emigrant* (poem, 1833); *Clinton Bradshaw,* 2v. (anon. 1836); *East and West* (anon., 1836); *Sketches of Claymore, and Tales Founded on Fact* (1840); *Howard Pinckney* (anon., 1840); *The Beechen Tree: A Tale Told in Rhyme* (1844); *An Autobiography of William Russell* (anon., 1852); *John Randolph of Roanoke, and Other Sketches* (1853); etc. See Ebenezer S. Thomas's *Reminiscences of the Last Sixty-Five Years,* 2v. (1840). Lit. editor, the *Richmond Enquirer,* 1860.

THOMAS, G[eorge] ERNEST (Feb. 16, 1907–); b. Bolton, Eng. Methodist clergyman, author. *Old Covered Wagon Show Days* (with Bob Barton, 1939); *What Jesus Was Like* (1946); *Spiritual Life in the New Testament* (1955); *Steps to the Christian Life* (1956); *Meditations on the Seven Last Words* (1959); *Personal Power Through the Spiritual Disciplines* (1960); *Jesus and Discipleship* (1961); *Disciplines of the Spiritual Life* (1963); *The Meaning of the Resurrection* (1964); *Holy Habits and You* (1966); etc.

THOMAS, GEORGE FINGER (July 31, 1899–); b. Ladonia, Tex. Educator. *Spirit and Its Freedom* (1939); *Poetry, Religion and the Spiritual Life* (1951); *Christian Ethics and Moral Philosophy* (1955); *Religious Philosophies of the West* (1965). Editor: *The Vitality of the Christian Tradition* (1944). Prof. religious thought, Princeton University, since 1940.

THOMAS, ISAIAH (Jan. 19, 1749–Apr. 4, 1831); b. Boston, Mass. Printer, publisher, author. *The History of Printing in*

America, 2v. (1810); The Diary, 2v. (1909). Publisher, the Royal American Magazine, 1774–75; the Worcester Magazine, 1786–88; the Massachusetts Magazine, 1789–96; Thomas's New England Almanac; co-founder, the Massachusetts Spy, 1770. Founder, American Antiquarian Society, 1812. He became the largest publisher of juvenile books in America. See Charles Lemuel Nichols's Isaiah Thomas, Printer, Writer & Collector (1912); Annie Russell Marble's From 'Prentice to Patron: The Life Story of Isaiah Thomas (1935).

THOMAS, JAMES AUGUSTUS (b. Mar. 6, 1862–); b. Lawsonville, N.C. Merchant, traveler, author. A Pioneer Tobacco Merchant in the Orient (1928); Trailing Trade a Million Miles (1931).

THOMAS, JEAN[nette Bell] (1881–); b. Ashland, Ky. Folklorist. Known to the mountain people as "The Traipsin' Woman." Devil's Ditties (1931); The Traipsin' Woman (1933); The Singin' Fiddler of Lost Hope Hollow (1938); Ballad Makin' in the Mountains of Kentucky (1939); Big Sandy (1940).

THOMAS, JOHN MARTIN (Dec. 27, 1869–Feb. 26, 1952); b. Covington, N.Y. Presbyterian clergyman, educator, author. The Christian Faith and the Old Testament (1908). President, Middlebury College, 1908–21; Pennsylvania State College, 1921–25; Rutgers University, 1925–30, Norwich University, 1939–44.

THOMAS, JOHN R. (b. 1812); b. Newport, Wales. Songwriter. Wrote "The Cottage by the Sea" (1856); wrote music for such popular songs as "Bonnie Eloise" (1858); " 'Tis But a Little Faded Flower" (1860); George Pope Morris's "Annie of the Vale" (1861), and "Down by the River Side I Stray" (1861); "Croquet" (1867); etc.

THOMAS, JOSEPH (Sept. 23, 1811–Dec. 24, 1891); b. Ledyard, N.Y. Lexicographer, author. Travels in Egypt and Palestine (1853); etc. Editor: Lippincott's Pronouncing Gazetteer (1855); Universal Pronouncing Dictionary of Biography and Mythology, 2v. (1870). With J. B. Lippincott & Co., Philadelphia, 1854–71.

THOMAS, JOSEPH MORRIS (Nov. 15, 1876–); b. Saugatuck, Mich. Educator. Editor: Great English Prose Writers (with others, 1934); Great English Writers, 2v. (with others, 1938). English dept., University of Michigan, 1901–09; Senior College, since 1909; prof., since 1921.

THOMAS, LEWIS FOULKE (1815–May 26, 1868); b. Baltimore, Md., son of Ebenezer Smith Thomas. Poet, playwright. India and Other Poems (1842); Osceola (prod. 1838); Cortez the Conqueror (prod. 1857); etc.

Thomas, Lida Larrimore. See Lida Larrimore Turner.

THOMAS, LOWELL [Jackson] (Apr. 6, 1892–); b. Woodington, O. Traveler, lecturer, radio commentator, author. With Lawrence in Arabia (1924); Beyond the Khyber Pass (1925); The Boy's Life of Colonel Lawrence (1927); Woodfill of the Regulars (1929); Tall Stories (1931); The Untold Story of Exploration (1935); A Life of Rudyard Kipling (1936); Seeing India with Lowell Thomas (1936); Pageant of Adventure (1940); Back to Mandalay (1951); The Seven Wonders of the World (1956); The Vital Spark (1959); One Hundred and One Outstanding Lives (1959); Sir Hubert Wilkins: His World of Adventure (1961); More Great True Adventures (1963); Book of the High Mountains (1964); etc.

THOMAS, LOWELL JR. (Oct. 6, 1923–   ); b. London. Lecturer, author. Out of This World, A Flight to Tibet (1950); Our Flight to Adventure (with Mrs. L. Thomas, Jr., 1956); The Silent War in Tibet (1959); The Dalai Lama (1961); The Trail of Ninety-Eight (1962). Producer, travel and documentary motion pictures, and television series.

THOMAS, M[artha] CAREY (Jan. 2, 1857–Dec. 2, 1935); b. Baltimore, Md. Educator, author. The Higher Education of Women (1900); Should the Higher Education of Women Differ from that of Men? (1901). Organizer of Bryn Mawr College in 1884; dean and prof. English, 1885–94; President, 1894–1922.

THOMAS, MILTON HALSEY (Feb. 3, 1903–); b. Troy, N.Y. Librarian. Editor: The Diary of George Templeton Strong, 4v. (with Allan Nevins, 1952); Elias Boudinot's Journey to Boston in 1809 (1955); etc. University archivist, Princeton University, since 1959.

THOMAS, NORMAN (Nov. 20, 1884–Dec. 19, 1968); b. Marion, O. Socialist, author. The Conscientious Objector in America (1923); As I See It (1932); What Is Our Destiny? (1944); A Socialist's Faith (1951); The Test of Freedom (1954); Great Dissenters (1962); etc. See Murray B. Seidler's Norman Thomas: Respectable Rebel (1962).

THOMAS, PIRI (1928–   ). Author. Down These Mean Streets (1967).

THOMAS, RICHARD HENRY (Jan. 26, 1854–Oct. 3, 1904); b. Baltimore, Md. Physician, author. Echoes and Pictures (poems, 1895); Penelve (1898); Present Day Papers, 5v. (1898–1902); The History of the Society of Friends in America (with Allen C. Thomas, 1894).

THOMAS, ROBERT BAILEY (Apr. 24, 1766–May 19, 1846); b. Grafton, Mass. Editor, publisher. Founder, The Farmer's Almanack, 1792. It was later called The Farmer's Almanack, and The Old Farmer's Almanack. It has had a continuous existence. See George Lyman Kittredge's The Old Farmer and His Almanac (1905).

THOMAS, ROBERT JOSEPH (Jan. 26, 1922–); b. San Diego, Cal. Journalist, author. The Art of Animation (1958); Flesh Merchants (1959); The Massie Case (1966); King Cohn (1967); Walt Disney: Magician of the Movies (1967).

THOMAS, STANLEY POWERS ROWLAND (June 22, 1879–); b. Castine, Me. Author. Writes as Rowland Thomas. The Little Gods (1909); Fatima (1913); Felicidad (1914).

THOMASON, JOHN WILLIAM, JR. (Feb. 28, 1893–Mar. 12, 1944); b. Huntsville, Texas. Marine Corps officer, illustrator, author. Fix Bayonets (1926); Red Pants (1927); Marines and Others (1929); Jeb Stuart (1930); Salt Winds and Gobi Dust (1934); Gone to Texas (1937); Lone Star Preacher (1941). Editor and illustrator: Adventures of General Marbot, by Himself (1935).

THOMES, WILLIAM HENRY (May 5, 1824–Mar. 6, 1895); b. Portland, Me. Publisher, novelist. A Gold Hunter's Adventures; or, Life in Australia (1864), and sequel The Bushrangers (1866); The Whaleman's Adventures (1872); A Slaver's Adventures on Land and Sea (1872); Running the Blockade (1875); On Land and Sea (1883); Lewey and I (1884); The Ocean Rovers (1896); etc. Member of the publishing firm of Elliott & Thomes, Boston, known later as Elliott, Thomes, and Talbot.

THOMPSON, ADELE E[ugenia], b. Middlefield, O. Author of books for girls. Beck's Fortune (1899); Betty Seldon, Patriot (1901); Brave Heart Elizabeth (1902); Polly of the Pines (1906); American Patty (1909); Nobody's Rose (1911).

THOMPSON, AUGUSTUS CHARLES (Apr. 30, 1812–1901); b. Goshen, Conn. Congregational clergyman, author. Morning Hours in Patmos (1860); Moravian Mission (1882); etc. Compiler: Songs in the Night (1854); Lyra Coelestis (1863); etc.

THOMPSON, BENJAMIN, COUNT RUMFORD (Mar. 26, 1753–Aug. 21, 1814); b. Woburn, Mass. Physician, physicist, Loyalist, expatriate, philanthropist, author. Proposals for Forming . . . a Public Institution (1799), which led to the founding of the Royal Institution, London; Philosophical Pa-

pers, v. 1 (1802), no more published; *On the Excellent Qualities of Coffee* (1812); etc. See James Alden Thompson's *Count Rumford of Massachusetts* (1935).

THOMPSON, CHARLES MINER (Mar. 24, 1864–Dec. 19, 1941); b. Montpelier, Vt. Author. *The Nimble Dollar* (1896); *The Calico Cat* (1908); *An Army Mule* (1910); etc. Lit. editor, the *Boston Advertiser,* 1887–90; editor, *Youth's Companion,* 1911–25.

THOMPSON, CHARLES WILLIS (Mar. 15, 1871–Sept. 8, 1946); b. Kalamazoo, Mich. Author. *Presidents I've Known* (1929); *The Fiery Epoch* (1931); etc. With the *New York Times,* 1897–1921.

THOMPSON, DANIEL PIERCE (Oct. 1, 1795–June 6, 1868); b. Charlestown, Mass. Lawyer, author. *May Martin* (1835); *The Green Mountain Boys* (1839); *Locke Amsden* (1847); *Lucy Hosmer* (1848); *The Rangers* (1851); *Gaut Gurley* (1857); *The Doomed Chief* (1860); *Centeola, and Other Tales* (1864), all written anonymously. Editor, *The Green Mountain Freeman,* 1849–56. See John Ehret Flitcroft's *The Novelist of Vermont: A Biographical and Critical Study of Daniel Pierce Thompson* (1929).

THOMPSON, DENMAN (Oct. 15, 1833–Apr. 14, 1911); b. Girard, Pa. Actor, playwright. *Joshua Whitcomb* (prod. 1877), later rewritten as *The Old Homestead* (with George W. Ryer, prod. 1887); *The Sunshine of Paradise Alley* (with same, 1896); etc. See J. J. Brady's *The Life of Denman Thompson* (1888).

THOMPSON, DOROTHY (July 8, 1894–Jan. 30, 1961); b. Lancaster, N.Y. Journalist, author. *The Depths of Prosperity* (with Phyllis Bottome, 1925); *The New Russia* (1928); *I Saw Hitler!* (1932); *Refugees* (1938); *Political Guide* (1938); *Let the Record Speak* (1939); *Listen, Hans* (1942); *The Courage to Be Happy* (1957); etc. Political columnist, *New York Herald Tribune,* 1936–40; *New York Post,* from 1941; *The Ladies' Home Journal.*

THOMPSON, DUNSTAN (1918–). Poet. *Poems* (1943); *Lament for the Sleepwalker* (poems, 1947).

THOMPSON, EDWARD HERBERT (Sept. 28, 1860–May 11, 1935); b. Worcester Co., Mass. Consul, archaeologist, author. *Children of the Cave* (1929); *People of the Serpent* (1932); etc. Wrote many monographs on Mayan civilization. Discovered the "Hidden City" in Yucatan, and explored Chichen Itza, etc. U.S. consul, Yucatan, 1885–1909.

THOMPSON, ELBERT NEVIUS SEBRING (Dec. 15, 1877–Sept. 13, 1948); b. Orange, N.J. Educator, author. *Controversy between the Puritans and the Stage* (1903); *Essays on Milton* (1914); *Literary Bypaths of the Renaissance* (1924); etc. English dept., State University of Iowa, from 1909; prof., from 1921.

THOMPSON, ERA BELL; b. Des Moines, Ia. Editor, author. *American Daughter* (1946); *Africa, Land of My Fathers* (1954). Editor: *White on Black* (1963). With *Ebony* magazine since 1951.

Thompson, Ernest Seton. See Ernest Thompson Seton.

THOMPSON, GEORGE. Author. Pen name "Greenhorn." *Venus in Boston* (1840); *The House Breaker* (1848); *City Crimes* (1849); *The G'hals of Boston* (1850); *Black Bess; or, The Knight of the Road* (1866); *Blueskin!* (1866); etc. See "Pisanus Fraxi's" (i.e., Henry Spencer Ashbee) *Catena Librorum Tacendorum* (1885).

THOMPSON, HAROLD WILLIAM (June 5, 1891–); b. Buffalo, N.Y. Educator, author. *Anthems of Today* (1927); *Church Organ Music* (1927); *Anecdotes and Egotisms of Henry Mackenzie* (1927); *Cornplanter's Legends of the Longhouse* (1938); etc. English dept., Cornell University, 1940–59.

THOMPSON, HOLLAND (July 30, 1873–Oct. 21, 1940); b. Randolph Co., N.C. Author. *History of Our Land* (1911); *The United States* (1915); *The New South* (1919); etc. Co-editor-in-chief; *The Book of Knowledge,* 20v. (1910–11); editor; *Lands and Peoples,* 7v. (1929–30).

THOMPSON, HUGH MILLER (June 5, 1830–Nov. 18, 1902); b. Londonderry, Ireland. Episcopal bishop, author. *"Copy": Essays from an Editor's Drawer* (1897); *More "Copy": A Second Series of Essays from an Editor's Drawer* (1897); etc. Editor, the *American Churchman,* 1860–71; etc.

THOMPSON, JAMES WESTFALL (June 3, 1869–1941); b. Pella, Ia. Educator, author. *The Last Pagan* (1916); *The Lost Oracles* (1921); *Feudal Germany* (1929); *Economic and Social History of the Middle Ages* (1929); *Economic and Social History of the Later Middle Ages* (1931); *The Living Past* (1931); *The Middle Ages,* 2v. (1931); *Byways in Bookland* (1935); *European Civilization* (1939); *Ancient Libraries* (1940); etc. History dept., University of Chicago, 1895–1932; prof. history, University of California, 1932–39.

THOMPSON, JEAN[ette] M[ay] (Sept. 20, 1867–Mar. 4, 1944); b. Guilford, Conn. Author. *Three Bears of Porcupine Ridge* (1913); *Wild Kindred of Fur, Feather, and Fin* (1914); *Over Indian and Animal Trails* (1918); *Animal Adventures in the Deep Forest* (1920); etc. Known as the "Jack Frost Lady."

THOMPSON, JOHN R[euben] (Oct. 23, 1823–Apr. 30, 1873); b. Richmond, Va. Editor, poet. *Across the Atlantic* (1856); *Poems* (1920); *The Genius and Character of Edgar Allan Poe,* ed. by James H. Whitty and James H. Rindfleisch (1929); etc. Editor, the *Southern Literary Messenger,* 1847–60; owner, 1847–53. His best known poems are "The Burial of Latane," "Lee to the Rear," "Music in Camp," and "The Window-Panes at Brandon."

THOMPSON, JOSEPH PARRISH (Aug. 7, 1819–Sept. 20, 1879); b. Philadelphia, Pa. Congregational clergyman, editor, author. *Memoir of Timothy Dwight* (1844); *Memoir of David Hall* (1850); *Egypt, Past and Present* (1856); *Church and State in the United States* (1873); *The United States as a Nation* (1877); *American Comments on European Questions* (1884); etc. On editorial staff, *The Independent,* 1848–62.

THOMPSON, KAY (1912–); b. St. Louis, Mo. Entertainer, author. *Eloise* (1955); *Eloise in Paris* (1957); *Eloise at Christmastime* (1958); *Eloise in Moscow* (1959); *Eloise in Bawth* (1964); etc.

THOMPSON, LAWRANCE ROGER (Apr. 3, 1906–); b. Franklin, N.H. Educator, author. *Young Longfellow* (1938); *Fire and Ice: The Art and Thought of Robert Frost* (1942); *Melville's Quarrel with God* (1952); *Robert Frost* (1959); etc. Editor: *Selected Letters of Robert Frost* (with Edward Connery Latham, 1964); *New Hampshire's Child: The Derry Journals of Lesley Frost* (with Arnold Grade, 1969). Dept. of English, Princeton University, since 1947.

THOMPSON, LAWRENCE SIDNEY (Dec. 21, 1916–); b. Raleigh, N.C. Librarian. Author: *The Kentucky Novel* (with A.D. Thompson, 1953); *The Kentucky Tradition* (1956); *Bibliogia Comica* (1968); *A Bibliography of French Plays on Microcards* (1967); *A Bibliography of Spanish Plays on Microcards* (1968); etc. Director libraries, University of Kentucky.

THOMPSON, LEWIS; b. Jersey City, N.J. Author of mystery stories. *The Girl in the Stateroom* (with C. Boswell, 1951); *The Girl in Lover's Lane* (1953); *The Girl with the Scarlet Brand* (1954); *The Girls in Nightmare House* (1955); *Surrender to Love* (1955). Co-editor: *Curriculum of Murder* (1962); *Business of Murder* (1963); etc.

THOMPSON, MARAVENE KENNEDY (Mrs. C. Bertrand Thompson), b. Decatur, O. Author. *No Middle Ground* (1902); *Under Twenty* (1905); *The Yellow Flower* (1909); *The Woman's Law* (1914); *Persuasive Peggy* (1916); *The Net* (prod. 1919); *The Secret Love House* (1926).

THOMPSON, MARY WOLFE (Mrs. Charles D. Thompson) (Dec. 7, 1886–); b. Winsted, Conn. Author. *Farmtown Tales* (1923); *My Grandpa's Farm* (1929); *The Circle of the Braves* (1931); *Cherry Farm* (1932); *Highway Past Her Door* (1938); *Blueberry Muffin* (1942); *Crossroads for Penelope* (1943); *Hillhaven* (1949); *Green Threshold* (1954); *Snow Slopes* (1957); *Two in the Wilderness: Before Vermont Had a Name* (1967).

THOMPSON, MAURICE (Sept. 9, 1844–Feb. 15, 1901); b. Fairfield, Ind., brother of Will Henry Thompson. Poet, novelist, archer. *Hoosier Mosaics* (1875); *The Witchery of Archery* (1878); *A Tallahassee Girl* (1881); *His Second Campaign* (1883); *Songs of Fair Weather* (1883); *By-Ways and Bird Notes* (1885); *At Love's Extremes* (1885); *A Banker of Bankersville* (1886); *Sylvan Secrets, in Bird-Songs and Books* (1887); *Poems* (1892); *The King of Honey Island* (1892); *The Ethics of Literary Art* (1893); *Alice of Old Vincennes* (1900); *My Winter Garden* (1900); etc. See *The Independent*, Feb. 21, 1901.

THOMPSON, MORTIMER NEAL (Sept. 2, 1831–June 25, 1875); b. Riga, N.Y. Pen name "Q. K. Philander Doesticks, P. B." Humorist, author. *Doesticks: What He Says* (1855); *Plu-ri-bus-tah, a Song That's-by-No-Author* (1856), a parody on Longfellow's "Hiawatha"; *The History and Records of the Elephant Club* (1856); *Nothing to Say* (1857), a parody on William Allen Butler's *Nothing to Wear; The Lady of the Lake* (1860), a parody on Scott's poem; etc. Editor, the *New York Picayune*, 1858; *Frank Leslie's Illustrated Weekly*, 1873–75.

THOMPSON, MORTON (1908?–1953); Author. *Joe, the Wounded Tennis Player* (1945); *How to Be a Civilian* (1946); *Not as a Stranger* (1954).

THOMPSON, OSCAR (Oct. 10, 1887–July 2, 1945); b. Crawfordsville, Ind. Editor, music critic, author. *Practical Musical Criticism* (1934); *How to Understand Music* (1935); *The American Singer* (1937); *Debussy, Man and Artist* (1937); etc. Editor: *The International Cyclopedia of Music and Musicians* (1938); etc. Compiler: *A Tabulated Biographical History of Music* (1936); etc. Editor, *Musical America;* on staff, the *New York Sun.*

THOMPSON, RALPH (Nov. 11, 1904–); b. West Orange, N.J. Critic, author. *American Literary Annuals & Gift Books, 1825–1865* (1936). Translator: Uhde's *Five Primitive Masters* (1948). On staff, *Current History* until 1936. Book columnist, *New York Times Book Review*, 1948–49. Editor, Book-of-the-Month Club, 1951–56, Secretary, since 1956.

THOMPSON, RICHARD WIGGINTON (June 9, 1809–Feb. 9, 1900); b. in Culpeper Co., Va. Lawyer, author. *The Papacy and the Civil Power* (1876); *Recollections of Sixteen Presidents* (1894); etc.

THOMPSON, ROBERT ELLIS (Apr. 5, 1844–Oct. 19, 1924); b. County Down, Ireland. Educator, author. *Social Science and National Economy* (1875), revised as *Elements of Political Economy* (1881). Editor, *Penn Monthly*, 1870–81; *American*, 1880–91; on staff, *Sunday School Times*, 1892–1924. President, Central High School, Philadelphia, 1894–1920. See Richard Montgomery's *Robert Ellis Thompson* (1934).

THOMPSON, RUTH PLUMLY (July 27, 1895–); b. Philadelphia, Pa. Author. *The Princess of Cozytown* (1922); *The Cowardly Lion of Oz* (1923); *The Lost King of Oz* (1925); *Pirates in Oz* (1931); *Captain Salt in Oz* (1936); *King Kojo* (1939); and many other books about the fabulous country of Oz.

THOMPSON, SAMUEL HUNTER (Apr. 19, 1876–Oct. 27, 1952); b. Chuckey, Tenn. Author. *The Highlanders of the South* (1910); *Southern Hero Tales* (1914); *Namjika, an Indian Princess* (1915); etc. Supt. public instruction, Tennessee, for many years, beginning in 1913.

THOMPSON, SLASON (Jan. 5, 1849–Dec. 22, 1935); b. Fredericton, N.B. Journalist, author. *Eugene Field*, 2v. (1901); *A Short History of American Railways* (1925); *Life of Eugene Field* (1927); *Way Back When* (autobiography, 1930); etc. Compiler: *The Humbler Poets* (1886); etc. Co-founder, the *Chicago Herald*, 1881. With Railway News Bureau, 1903–35, and on staff of several Chicago newspapers.

THOMPSON, STITH (Mar. 7, 1885–); b. Bloomfield, Ky. Educator, author. *British Poets of the Nineteenth Century* (with Curtis Hidden Page, 1929); *Motif-Index of Folk Literature*, 6v. (1932–37); *The Folktale* (1946); etc. Editor: *Tales of the North American Indians* (1929; rev. ed. 1966); *Our Heritage of World Literature* (1938); etc. Editor, *Publications of the Folk-Lore Society of Texas*, 1916. English dept., Indiana University, since 1921.

THOMPSON, VANCE (Apr. 17, 1863–June 5, 1925). Author. *The Life and Letters of Ethelbert Nevin* (1913); *The Night Watchman and Other Poems* (1914); *Verse* (1915); *Take It From Me* (1916); *Woman* (1917); *Louisa* (1924); etc.

THOMPSON, WADDY (Sept. 8, 1798–Nov. 23, 1868); b. Pickensville, S.C. Diplomat, author. *Recollections of Mexico* (1846). Minister to Mexico, 1842–44.

THOMPSON, WADDY (Aug. 13, 1867–Mar. 19, 1939); b. Columbia, S.C., grandnephew of Waddy Thompson. Author. *A History of the United States* (1904); *A History of the People of the United States* (1919); *History of American Progress* (with Fremont P. Wirth, 1933); etc.

THOMPSON, WADE C[layton] (Sept. 28, 1923–); b. Sand Point, Idaho. Educator, author. *The Egghead's Guide to America* (1962). English dept., State University of New York at New Paltz, since 1965.

THOMPSON, WILL HENRY (Mar. 10, 1848–1918); b. Calhoun, Ga. Brother of James Maurice Thompson. Lawyer, archer, author. *How to Train in Archery* (with Maurice Thompson, 1879); *The High Tide at Gettysburg* (1888); *Bond of Blood* (1899); etc.

THOMPSON, WILL LAMARTINE (Nov. 7, 1847–Sept. 20, 1909); b. Beaver Co., Pa. Song writer. His best known songs are "Come Where the Lilies Bloom," "Jesus Is All the World to Me," "There's a Great Day Coming," "Drifting With the Tide," "Gathering Shells from the Seashore," "Softly and Tenderly Jesus Is Calling," and "My Home on the Ohio." Founder, Will L. Thompson & Co., music publishers, 1875.

THOMPSON, WILLIAM TAPPAN (Aug. 31, 1812–Mar. 24, 1882); b. Ravenna, O. Editor, humorist. Pen name "Major Jones." *Major Jones's Courtship* (1843); *Major Jones's Scenes in Georgia* (1843); *Major Jones's Sketches of Travel* (1848); *John's Alive* (1883); etc. Founder, *The Mirror*, Augusta, Ga., 1838; founder, the *Savannah Morning News*, 1850; editor, 1850–82.

THOMPSON, ZADOCK (May 23, 1796–Jan. 19, 1856); b. Bridgewater, Vt. Naturalist, historian. *History of the State of Vermont* (1833); *Appendix to the History of Vermont* (1853).

THOMSON, CHARLES GOFF (Feb. 9, 1883–Mar. 23, 1937); b. Little Falls, N.Y. Author. *Terry: A Tale of the Hill People* (1921); *Time Is a Gentleman* (1929).

THOMSON, CHARLES WEST (1798–Apr. 17, 1879); b. Philadelphia, Pa. Poet. *The Limner* (1822); *The Phantom Barge, and Other Poems* (1822); *Ellinor, and Other Poems* (1826); *The Sylph, and Other Poems* (1828); *The Love of Home, and Other Poems* (1845).

THOMSON, EDWARD WILLIAM (Feb. 12, 1849–Mar. 5, 1924); b. Toronto, Ont. Editor, author. *Old Man Savarin* (1895); *Walter Gibbs, the Young Boss* (1896); *Between Earth and Sky* (1897); *Smoky Days* (1901); *When Lincoln Died, and Other Poems* (1909); etc. Editorial writer, the *Toronto Globe*, 1879–91; editor, *Youth's Companion*, 1891–1901.

THOMSON, JOHN STUART (June 6, 1869–); b. Montreal, P.Q. Author. *Estabelle, and Other Verse* (1897); *A Day's Song* (poems, 1900); *Bud and Bamboo* (1912); *China Revolutionized* (1913); *The Animal Kingdom* (1923).

Thomson, Mortimer. See Mortimer Thompson.

THOMSON, O[smund] R[hoads] HOWARD (Dec. 5, 1873–Dec. 23, 1943); b. London. Poet, librarian. *History of the Bucktails* (with W. H. Rauch, 1906); *Resurgam: Poems and Lyrics* (1915); *The Modern Comedy, and Other Poems* (1918). Librarian, J. V. Brown Library, Williamsport, Pa., from 1906.

THOMSON, VIRGIL (Nov. 25, 1896–); b. Kansas City, Mo. Composer, music critic. *State of Music* (1939); *The Musical Scene* (1945); *The Art of Judging Music* (1948); *Music Right and Left* (1951); *Virgil Thomson: Music Reviewed, 1950–54* (1967). Music critic, *New York Herald Tribune,* 1940–54.

THORBURN, GRANT (Feb. 18, 1773–Jan. 21, 1863); b. near Dalkeith, Scotland. Merchant, author. Pen name "Laurie Todd." *Forty Years Residence in America* (1834); *Men and Manners in Britain* (1834); *Fifty Years' Reminiscences of New-York* (1845); *Lawrie Todd's Notes on Virginia* (1848); *Life and Writings of Grant Thorburn* (1852); John Galt's novel *Lawrie Todd* (1830) was based on Thorburn's life. Thorburn's seed catalogue, *The Gentleman and Gardener's Kalendar* (1812), was the first printed in America.

THOREAU, HENRY DAVID (July 12, 1817–May 6, 1862); b. Concord, Mass. Naturalist, poet, essayist, philosopher. *A Week on the Concord and Merrimack Rivers* (1849); *Walden* (1854); *Excursions* (1863); *The Maine Woods* (1864); *Cape Cod* (1865); *A Yankee in Canada* (1866); *Early Spring in Massachusetts* (1881); *Summer* (1884); *Winter* (1888); *Autumn* (1892); *Poems of Nature* (1895); *Journal* (1906); *The Writings,* 20v. (Walden Edition, 1906); *Consciousness in Concord: Thoreau's Lost Journal, 1840–41* (1958). W. H. Harding is editing a definitive collection of the *Works. See* Francis H. Allen's *A Bibliography of Henry David Thoreau* (1908); William Ellery Channing's *Thoreau the Poet-Naturalist* (1873); F. B. Sanborn's *The Life of Henry David Thoreau* (1917); Henry S. Canby's *Thoreau* (1939); Carl Bode's *Collected Poems* (1943); Joseph Wood Krutch's *Henry David Thoreau* (1948); Carl Bode's *Correspondence of Henry David Thoreau* (1958); August Derleth's *Concord Rebel: A Life of Henry David Thoreau* (1962); W. Harding's *The Days of Henry Thoreau* (1965); Philip Van Doren Stern's *The Annotated Walden* (1971);

THORNDIKE, ASHLEY HORACE (Dec. 26, 1871–Apr. 17, 1933); b. Houlton, Me. Educator, author. *The Elements of Rhetoric and Composition* (1905); *Tragedy* (1908); *Everyday English,* 2v. (with F. T. Baker, 1912–13); *Shakespeare's Theatre* (1916); *Literature in a Changing Age* (1920); *English Comedy* (1929); *The Outlook for Literature* (1931); etc. Editor: *The Minor Elizabethan Drama,* 2v. (1910); *The Tudor Shakespeare,* 39v. (with William A. Neilson, 1913–15); *The Warner Library,* 30v. (rev. edition, with John W. Cunliffe, 1917); *A History of English Literature* (with William A. Neilson, 1920); etc. Prof. English, Columbia University, 1906–33.

THORNDIKE, CHARLES JESSE [Chuck] (Jan. 20, 1897–); b. Seattle, Wash. Cartoonist. *Are You a Doodler?* (1940); *Arts and Crafts for Children* (1945); *Susie and Sam in Silver Springs* (1949); *Susie and Sam in Rock City* (1950); *How to Enjoy Good Health* (1966); etc.

THORNDIKE, EDWARD LEE (Aug. 31, 1874–Aug. 9, 1949); b. Williamstown, Mass. Educator, psychologist, author. *Educational Psychology* (1903); *Elements of Psychology* (1905); *Animal Intelligence* (1911); *The Psychology of Learning* (1914); *The Measurement of Intelligence* (1926); *Your City* (1939); *Human Nature and the Social Order* (1940); *Man and His Works* (1943); etc. Psychology dept., Teachers College, Columbia University, from 1899; prof., 1904–40.

THORNDIKE, LYNN (July 24, 1882–Dec. 28, 1965); b. Lynn, Mass. Educator, author. *The Place of Magic in the Intellectual History of Europe* (1905); *The History of Medieval Europe* (1917); republished as *Medieval Europe* (1920); *A History of Magic and Experimental Science,* 6v. (1923–41); *A Short History of Civilization* (1926); *Science and Thought in the Fifteenth Century* (1929); *University Records and Life in the Middle Ages* (1944); etc. History dept., Western Reserve University, 1909–24; Columbia University, from 1924.

THORNE, DIANA (Oct. 7, 1895–); b. Winnipeg, Canada. Illustrator, author. *Dog-Basket* (1930); *Your Dogs and Mine* (1932); *Polo* (1936); *Tails Up!* (1936); *Peter the Goat* (1940); *Dogs: An Album* (1944); *How to Draw the Dog* (1950); etc. Illustrated E. G. Beandry's *Puppy Stories* (1934); R. Orton's *Pepito the Colt* (1933); A. P. Terhune's *The Dog Book* (1932); etc.

Thorne, Victor. Pen name of Frederick Jackson.

THORNTON, JOHN WINGATE (Aug. 12, 1818–June 6, 1878); b. Saco, Me. Author. *The Landing at Cape Anne* (1854); *Ancient Pemaquid* (1857); *The Pulpit of the American Revolution* (1860); *The Historical Relation of New England to the English Commonwealth* (1874); etc. One of the founders of the New England Historic-Genealogical Society, 1844, and the Prince Society, 1858. His journal, etc., is in the Boston Athenaeum, and his correspondence in the New England Historic-Genealogical Society library.

THORNTON, RICHARD H[opwood] (1845–Mar. 1925). Philologist, author. *An American Glossary,* 2v. (1912). This unfinished dictionary in revised form was completed in *Dialect Notes* after the compiler's death.

THORP, WILLARD (Apr. 20, 1899–); b. Sidney, N.Y. Educator. *The Triumph of Realism in Elizabethan Drama* (1928); *Trollope's America* (1950); *American Writing in the 20th Century* (1960). Co-editor: *American Issues* (1941); *Literary History of the United States* (1948); etc. Dept. of English, Princeton University, since 1926.

THORPE, FRANCIS NEWTON (Apr. 16, 1857–May 8, 1926); b. Swampscott, Mass. Lawyer, educator, author. *Franklin and the University of Pennsylvania* (1893); *A Constitutional History of the American People, 1776–1850,* 2v. (1898); *The Constitutional History of the United States, 1765–1895,* 3v. (1901); *The Spoils of Empire* (1903); *The Divining Rod: A Story of the Oil Regions* (1905); etc. Prof. political science and constitutional law, University of Pittsburgh, 1910–26.

Thorpe, Kamba. Pen name of Elizabeth Whitfield Croom Bellamy.

THORPE, MERLE (Nov. 1, 1879–Oct. 31, 1955); b. Brimfield, Ill. Editor, educator, author. *The Coming Newspaper* (1915); etc. Editor and publisher, *The Nation's Business,* Washington, D.C., 1916–44. Prof. journalism, University of Kansas, 1911–16.

THORPE, ROSE HARTWICK (July 18, 1850–July 19, 1939); b. Mishawaka, Ind. Poet, novelist. *Fred's Dark Days* (1881); *The Yule Log* (1881); *Curfew Must Not Ring To-Night* (1882); *The Fenton Family* (1884); *Nina Bruce* (1886); *The Chester Girls* (1887); *Ringing Ballads* (1887); *White Lady of La Jolla* (1904); *Poetical Works* (1912); *From California* (1914); etc.

THORPE, THOMAS BANGS (Mar. 1, 1815–Sept. 20, 1878); b. Westfield, Mass. Artist, humorist, chronicler of backwoods life. *The Big Bear of Arkansas* (1845); *Our Army on the Rio Grande* (1846); *The Mysteries of the Backwoods* (1846); *Our Army at Monterey* (1847); *The Taylor Anecdote Book* (1848); *Lynde Weiss: An Autobiography* (1852); *The Hive of the Bee Hunter* (1854); *The Master's House* (1854); *Colonel Thorpe's Scenes in Arkansaw* (1858); etc. Co-editor, the *Spirit of the Times,* 1860. He was known as "Tom Owen, the Bee Hunter."

Thought. New York. Quarterly magazine. Founded 1926, at Spencer, Mass.; transferred to Fordham University, 1940. Concerned with culture and ideas. J. E. O'Neill is editor.

Thousand, Days, A. By Arthur Schlesinger, Jr. (1965). A historian's presentation of the Kennedy Administration, based largely on the testimony of the author, who participated as a Presidential adviser.

Three Lives. Stories by Gertrude Stein (1909). One of the earliest examples of experimental writing using expressive form to reveal inner feelings and consciousness. The stories are *The Good Anna, The Gentle Lena,* and *Melanctha.*

Three Soldiers. Novel by John Dos Passos (1921). One of the first unvarnished accounts of the realism and disillusionment of World War I.

Three Who Made a Revolution. By Bertram D. Wolfe (1948). History of the Russian Revolution seen through biographical studies of Lenin, Trotsky, and Stalin.

Three Wise Fools. Play by Austin Strong (prod. 1918). A judge, a doctor, and a financier live in a bachelor's heaven until it is invaded and conquered by the daughter of a woman whom all three had loved in earlier years.

"Threnody." Poem by Richard Henry Stoddard, which first appeared in *Putnam's Magazine,* Oct., 1906.

"Threnody." Poem by Ralph Waldo Emerson (1841). An elegy on his son Waldo, who died at the age of five.

Through Hell and High Water. By members of the Explorers Club (1941). Personal adventure narratives of members of the Explorers Club of New York City.

Through the Dark Continent. By Henry Morton Stanley (1878). An account of the remarkable experiences of the author in crossing the African continent from East to West, partly through unexplored country.

Through the Gates of Old Romance. Novel by W. Jay Mills (1903). Based on the love story of Nathaniel Fish Moore, president of Columbia College, New York, and Ellen Conover, the "belle of Chambers Street."

Through the Wheat. Novel by Thomas Boyd (1923). One of the best known of the novels written about the American soldiers in France during World War I.

"Throw Out the Life-Line." Hymn by Edward Smith Ufford (1884).

THRUELSEN, RICHARD DELMAR (Jan. 19, 1908–); b. Hackensack. N.J. Editor, author. *Men at Work* (1950); *Transocean: Story of an Unusual Airline* (1953); etc. Editor: *Adventures of the Mind* (with John Kobler, 1959). Editor, *Saturday Evening Post,* since 1958.

THRUSTON, LUCY M[eacham] (b. Mar. 29, 1862); b. in King and Queen Co., Va. Novelist. *Mistress Brent* (1901); *A Girl of Virginia* (1902); *Where the Tide Comes In* (1904); *Jenifer* (1907); *The Heavens of the Unexpected* (1910); etc.

Thunder on the Left. Novel by Christopher Morley (1925). Martin, the child, wonders if adults have a good time in life. He never grows up, and becomes a symbol of youthful simplicity. The author shows that men and women are only superficially mature and serious-minded. The story is told through Martin, still in his child personality, projected into adult life twenty years later.

THURBER, JAMES [Grover] (Dec. 8, 1894–Nov. 2, 1961); b. Columbus, O. Artist, author. *Is Sex Necessary?* (with E. B. White, 1929); *The Owl in the Attic, and Other Perplexities* (1931); *The Seal in the Bedroom, and Other Predicaments* (1932); *My Life and Hard Times* (1933); *The Middle-Aged Man on the Flying Trapeze* (1935); *Let Your Mind Alone* (1937); *The Last Flower* (1939); *The Male Animal* (with Elli-

ott Nugent, prod. 1940); *My World—And Welcome to It!* (1942); *Men, Women and Dogs* (1943); *Many Moons* (1943); *The Great Quillow* (1944); *The Thurber Carnival* (1945); *The White Deer* (1945); *The Beast in Me and Other Animals* (1948); *The Thirteen Clocks* (1950); *Further Fables for Our Time* (1956); *The Wonderful O* (1957); *Alarms and Diversions* (1957); *The Years With Ross* (1959); *Lanterns and Lances* (1961). With Columbus (Ohio) *Dispatch,* 1921–24; contributor to *The New Yorker,* 1926–61.

Thurman, A. R. Pen name of Arthur William Mann.

THURMAN, WALLACE (1902–1934). Co-author: *Harlem* (prod. 1929); *The Interne* (1932). Author: *The Blacker the Berry* (1929); *Infants of the Spring* (1932).

THURSTON, ERNEST LAWTON (Feb. 13, 1873–July 10, 1958); b. Fall River, Mass. Editor, author. *The Iroquois Geography* series (with G. R. Bodley and A. W. Abrams, 1929–44); *The Black Shadow* (1934); *Tongues of Flame* (1934); *The Young Boss of Camp Eighteen* (1935); *Living with Science* (1948); *Homelands Beyond the Seas* (1955); etc. With George Washington University. Editor, Iroquois Publishing Co., Syracuse, N.Y., 1926–32, 1935–40.

THURSTON, IDA T[readwell] (1848–June 3, 1918); b. Author. Pen name "Marion Thorne." *A Bachelor Maid and Her Brother* (1898); *The Captain of the Cadets* (1899); *Citizen Dan of the Junior Republic* (1901); *The Torch Bearer* (1913); *The Big Brother of Sabin Street* (1919); etc.

THURSTON, LORRIN ANDREWS (July 31, 1858–May 11, 1931); b. Honolulu, Hawaii. Lawyer, author. *Memoirs of the Hawaiian Revolution* (1936). *Writings* (1936). Held many offices in the Kingdom and the Republic of Hawaii.

THWAITES, REUBEN GOLD (May 15, 1853–Oct. 22, 1913); b. Dorchester, Mass. Librarian, editor, author. *Historic Waterways* (1888); *The Story of Wisconsin* (1890); *The Colonies* (1891); *Afloat on the Ohio* (1897); *Stories of the Badger State* (1900); *Daniel Boone* (1902); *Father Marquette* (1902); etc. Editor: *The Jesuit Relations and Allied Documents,* 73 v. (1896–1901); *Original Journals of the Lewis and Clark Expedition,* 8v. (1904–05); *Early Western Travels,* 32v. (1904–07); etc. Librarian, State Historical Society of Wisconsin, 1887–1913.

THWING, CHARLES FRANKLIN (Nov. 9, 1853–Aug. 29, 1937); b. New Sharon, Me. Congregational clergyman, educator, author. *American Colleges* (1878); *The Reading of Books* (1883); *The Family* (with wife, Carrie F. Butler Thwing, 1886); *A Liberal Education and a Liberal Faith* (1903); *A History of Higher Education in America* (1906); *A History of Education in the United States Since the Civil War* (1910); *Universities of the World* (1911); *The American College* (1914); *Education and Religion* (1929); *Guides, Philosophers and Friends,* 2 series (1927, 1933); etc. President, Western Reserve University and Adelbert College, 1890–1921.

THWING, EUGENE (Jan. 17, 1866–May 29, 1936); b. Quincy, Mass. Author. *The Red-Keggers* (1903); *The Man from Red-Keg* (1905); *The Life and Meaning of Theodore Roosevelt* (1919); etc. Compiler: *The World's Best 100 Detective Stories,* 10v. (1929). With Funk and Wagnalls Co., 1882–1908. With the *Literary Digest,* 1918–36.

TICKNOR, CAROLINE (1866–May 11, 1937); b. Boston, Mass. Author. *Hawthorne and His Publisher* (1913); *Poe's Helen* (1916); *Glimpses of Authors* (1922); *May Alcott* (1928).

TICKNOR, FRANCIS ORRAY (Nov. 13, 1822–Dec. 18, 1874); b. Fortville, Ga. Physician, poet. *The Poems,* ed. by Paul Hamilton Hayne (1879), reëd. by Michelle C. Ticknor (1911). His best known poem was "Little Giffin," based on an incident in a Confederate hospital during the Civil War.

TICKNOR, GEORGE (Aug. 1, 1791–Jan. 26, 1871); b. Boston, Mass. Educator, author. *History of Spanish Literature* (1849), augmented (1872); *Life of William Hickling Prescott* (1864); *Remarks on the Life and Writings of Daniel Webster* (1831); *Life, Letters, and Journals of George Ticknor,* 2v. (1876); *Travels in Spain,* ed. by G. T. Northup (1913). His library of Spanish literature was presented to the Boston Public Library, which he had helped found in 1852. It was catalogued by J. L. Whitney in 1879. Prof. French and Spanish and belles-lettres, Harvard University, 1819–35. *See* Charles Henry Hart's *Memoirs of George Ticknor* (1871); Orie W. Long's *Literary Pioneers* (1935); David B. Tyack's *George Ticknor and the Boston Brahmins* (1967).

TICKNOR, WILLIAM DAVIS (Aug. 6, 1810–Apr. 10, 1864); b. Lebanon, N.H. Publisher. Founder, publishing firm of Allen and Ticknor, Boston, 1832. In 1833 it was called William D. Ticknor and Company, in 1849 Ticknor, Reed, and Fields; and in 1854, Ticknor and Fields (q.v.).

Ticknor & Fields. Boston, Mass. Publishers. William Davis Ticknor founded the publishing firm of Allen and Ticknor in 1832. In 1833 it was called William D. Ticknor and Company, in 1849, Ticknor, Reed, and Fields, and in 1854, Ticknor & Fields. The firm published the *Atlantic Monthly,* and *Our Young Folks,* and owned and operated the "Old Corner Bookstore." During the latter half of the nineteenth century it published the most outstanding list of authors in America, a list which included Hawthorne, Emerson, Lowell, Holmes, Longfellow, Whittier, Thoreau, and such English writers as Tennyson, Browning, Leigh Hunt, and De Quincey. James T. Fields, and his wife, Annie Adams Fields, were also writers of note. In 1868, four years after the death of Ticknor, a new firm was formed called Fields, Osgood & Co. In 1871 Fields retired and Benjamin H. Ticknor, son of William Davis Ticknor, formed the firm of James R. Osgood & Co. In 1878 this firm was merged with H. O. Houghton's publishing business to form Houghton, Osgood & Co., now known as Houghton Mifflin Company. *See* Caroline Ticknor's *Hawthorne and His Publisher* (1913); Annie Adams Fields's *Memoirs of James T. Fields* (1881).

Tid-Bits. New York. Comic journal. Founded 1884. Merged with *Munsey's Weekly,* 1890.

Tides of Barnegat, The. By F. Hopkinson Smith (1906). Story of a fishing community on the coast of New Jersey.

TIEDE, TOM ROBERT (Feb. 24, 1937–   ); b. Huron, S.D. Journalist, author. *Your Men at War* (1965); *Coward* (1968). War correspondent, Newspaper Enterprise Association, since 1964.

TIEDJENS, VICTOR ALPHONS (June 13, 1895–); b. Brillion, Wis. Horticulturist. *Vegetable Encyclopedia and Gardener's Guide* (1943); *The Handbook of Gardening* (with Albert E. Wilkinson, 1950); *More Food From Soil Science* (1966); *Olena Farm U.S.A.* (1969); etc.

Tiempo, El. New York. Newspaper. Founded 1964. Concerned with news of the Latin-American community in New York, other than Puerto Ricans. Stanley Ross is editor.

TIERNAN, FRANCES CHRISTINE FISHER (July 5, 1846–Mar. 24, 1920); b. Salisbury, N.C. Novelist. Pen name "Christian Reid." *Valerie Aylmer* (1870); *Morton House* (1871); *A Daughter of Bohemia* (1874); *A Question of Honor* (1875); *The Land of the Sky* (1876); *Bonny Kate* (1878); *Armine* (1884); *Carmela* (1891); *The Land of the Sun* (1894); *Weighed in the Balance* (1896); *Fairy Gold* (1897); *The Man of the Family* (1898); *The Chase of an Heiress* (1898); *Under the Southern Cross* (1900); *A Daughter of Bohemia* (1902); *A Daughter of the Sierra* (1903); *Princess Nadine* (1908); *The Light of the Vision* (1912); *The Daughter of a Star* (1913); *The Wargrave Trust* (1913); *A Far-Away Princess* (1914); *The Secret Bequest* (1920); etc.

TIETJENS, EUNICE (Mrs. Cloyd Head) (July 29, 1884–Sept. 6, 1944); b. Chicago, Ill. Poet, novelist. *Profiles from China* (1917); *Body and Raiment* (1919); *Jake* (1921); *Profiles from Home* (1925); *Leaves in Windy Weather* (1929); *The Romance of Antar* (1929); *Boy of the South Seas* (1931); *The World at My Shoulder* (autobiography, 1938); etc. On staff, *Poetry,* Chicago, from 1913.

TIFFANY, NINA MOORE (d. Sept. 29, 1958); b. Cincinnati, O. Author. *Pilgrims and Puritans* (1888); *From Colony to Commonwealth* (1891); etc.

TIFFANY, OSMOND (July 16, 1823–Nov. 18, 1895); b. Baltimore, Md. Author. *The Canton Chinese* (1849); *Brandon* (1858).

Tiger Lilies. By Sidney Lanier (1867). Prose romance, semi-autobiographical. The theme is music, poetry, and nature, with the Tennessee mountains as a background.

Tiger Lily. Pen name of Lillie Devereux Blake.

Tikhonov, Valentin. Pen name of Robert Payne.

'Tilda Jane. By Margaret Marshall Saunders (1901). Popular children's book relating the story of an amusing and plucky orphan.

TILDEN, FREEMAN (Aug. 22, 1883–); b. Malden, Mass. Author. *That Night, and Other Satires* (1915); *Second Wind* (1917); *Khaki* (1918); *Mr. Podd* (1923); *The Spanish Prisoner* (1928); *A World in Debt* (1936); *Better See George* (1941); *National Parks* (1951); *Interpreting Our Heritage* (1957); etc.

TILDEN, SAMUEL JONES (Feb. 9, 1814–Aug. 4, 1886); b. New Lebanon, N.Y. Lawyer, governor, presidential nominee, author. *The Writings and Speeches of Samuel J. Tilden,* 2v. (1885); *Letters and Literary Memorials of Samuel J. Tilden,* 2v. (1908); etc. Governor of New York, 1874–76. He established the Tilden Trust for the building of a free public library in New York City, and this became, with the merger of the Astor and Lenox libraries, The New York Public Library. *See* John Bigelow's *The Life of Samuel J. Tilden,* 2v. (1895).

TILESTON, MARY WILDER (Aug. 20, 1843–July 3, 1934); b. Salem, Mass. Author. *Caleb and Mary Wilder Foote* (1918). Compiler: *Quiet Hours,* 2 series (poems, 1874, 1880); *Sursum Corda* (1877); *Selections from Epictetus* (1877); *The Blessed Life: Favorite Hymns* (1878); *Heroic Ballads* (1883); *Sugar and Spice* (1885); *The Child's Harvest of Verse* (1910); etc.

TILLETT, WILBUR FISK (Aug. 25, 1854–June 4, 1936); b. Henderson, N.C. Methodist clergyman, author. *Our Hymns and Their Authors* (1889); *The Doctrines of Methodism* (1903); *Hymns and Hymn Writers of the Church* (1911). Theology dept., Vanderbilt University, 1882–1919; dean and vice-chancellor, 1886–1919.

TILLICH, PAUL [Johannes] (Aug. 20, 1886–Oct. 22, 1965); b. Starzeddel, Kreis Guben, Prus. Theologian, author. *The Interpretation of History* (with others, 1936); *The Protestant Era* (1948); *The Shaking of the Foundations* (1948); *Systematic Theology,* 2v. (1950–57); *The Courage to Be* (1952); *Love, Power and Justice* (1954); *The New Being* (1955); *Biblical Religion and the Search for Ultimate Reality* (1955); *Dynamics of Faith* (1957); *Theology of Culture* (1959); *Christianity and the Encounter of the World Religions* (1963); *Morality and Beyond* (1963); *The Eternal Beyond* (1963). etc. Prof. philosophy and theology, Union Theological Seminary, New York, 1933–55; Harvard University, after 1955. *See* Walter Leibrecht's *Religion and Culture: Essays in Honor of Paul Tillich* (1959) and G. H. Tavard's *Paul Tillich and the Christian Message* (1962).

Tilton, Dwight. Pen name used jointly by Wilder Dwight Quint and George Tilton Richardson.

TILTON, THEODORE (Oct. 2, 1835–May 25, 1907); b. New York. Poet, journalist, editor. *The Sexton's Tale, and Other Poems* (1867); *Tempest-Tossed* (1873); *Thou and I: A Lyric of Human Life* (1880); *Swabian Stories* (1882); *The Chameleon's Dish* (1893); *Heart's Ease* (1894); *Sonnets to the Memory of Frederick Douglass* (1895); *The Complete Works* (1897); *The Fading of the Mayflower* (1906); etc. Editor, *The Independent,* 1863–70; founder, the *Golden Age,* 1871. See *Theodore Tilton vs. Henry Ward Beecher* (1874).

Time. New York. Weekly news magazine. Founded 1923 by Henry R. Luce and Briton Hadden. Pioneer in combining research, reportage, and comprehensiveness of coverage within an interpretive news framework. "Time style" has come to mean a deft, incisive condensation of information in language that appears factual but expresses attitudes. Among those who have worked as editors or writers for *Time* have been Louis Kronenberger, James Agee, Whittaker Chambers, and T. S. Matthews.

Time for Decision, The By Sumner Welles (1944). Discussion of American foreign policy and peace plans after the end of World War II.

Time of Man, The. Novel by Elizabeth Madox Roberts (1926). Best known of the author's works. It is an idyl of the Kentucky hill country, with Ellen Dresser the heroine. A "poor white" family travels from place to place in a wagon to find work among the more prosperous farmers.

Time of Your Life, The. Play by William Saroyan (prod. 1939).

Time-Life Books. New York. Publishers. Founded 1961. A division of Time Inc. Rhett Austell is publisher. Publishes nonfiction, art books, books devoted to business and current events, as well as other kinds. New York Graphic Society, Ltd., is a division of Time-Life Books.

Time-Piece, and Literary Companion. New York. Newspaper. Founded, 1797, by Philip Freneau. Expired 1798.

Times, The. Political satire in verse by Benjamin Church (1765). In defense of the colonists.

Times and Patowmack Packet. Georgetown, D.C. Newspaper. Founded Feb. 12, 1789, by Charles Fierer, who soon took Thomas U. Fosdick into partnership. First newspaper published in the District of Columbia. Expired 1791.

Times Mirror Co., The. Los Angeles, Calif. Publishers. Martin P. Levin is president. Subsidiaries include Harry N. Abrams, Inc., religious and encyclopedic books; The New American Library, Inc. (q.v.); The World Publishing Co. (q.v.); and other concerns.

TIMROD, HENRY (Dec. 8, 1828–Oct. 6, 1867); b. Charleston, S.C. Poet. Called the "Poet Laureate of the Confederacy." *Poems* (1860); *The Poems of Henry Timrod* (1873), republished by the Timrod Memorial Association (1899). Cofounder, *Russell's Magazine,* 1857. His best known poems are "The Cotton-Boll," "Carmen Triumphale," "Charleston," "Spring," "Magnolia Cemetery Ode," "A Cry to Arms," "Carolina," and "Katie." *See* H.T. Thompson's *Henry Timrod, Laureate of the Confederacy* (1928); G. A. Wauchope's *Henry Timrod, Man and Poet* (1915); Virginia Pettigrew Clare's *Harp of the South* (1936); *The Collected Poems of Henry Timrod: A Variorum Edition,* ed. by Edd Winfield Parks and Aileen Wells Parks (1965).

TINCKER, MARY AGNES (July 18, 1831–Nov. 27, 1907); b. Ellsworth, Me. Essayist, poet, novelist. *Signor Monaldini's Niece* (1879); *By the Tiber* (1881); *Aurora* (1886); *Two Coronets* (1889); *San Salvador* (1892); *Autumn Leaves* (1899); etc.

TINDALL, WILLIAM YORK (Mar. 7, 1903–); b. Williamstown, Vt. Educator. *D. H. Lawrence and Susan His Cow* (1939); *Forces in Modern British Literature* (1947); *James Joyce, His Way of Interpreting the Modern World* (1950);

The Literary Symbol (1955); *A Reader's Guide to James Joyce* (1959). Editor: *The Later D. H. Lawrence* (1952). Dept. of English, Columbia University, since 1931.

TING, WALASSE (Oct. 13, 1929–); b. Shanghai, China. Artist, poet. *One Cent Life* (1964); *Chinese Moonlight* (1967); *Hot and Sour Soup* (1967).

Ting-a-Ling. By Frank R. Stockton (1870). Children's book dealing with an Eastern king, a prince, and a princess, with dwarfs, giants, and magicians supplying mystery and romance.

TINKER, CHAUNCEY BREWSTER (Oct. 22, 1876–Mar. 16, 1963); b. Auburn, Me. Educator, author. *Dr. Johnson and Fanny Burney* (1911); *The Salon and English Letters* (1915); *Young Boswell* (1922); *Nature's Simple Plan* (1922); *The Good Estate of Poetry* (1929); *Painter and Poet* (1938); *The Poetry of Matthew Arnold* (with H. F. Lowry, 1940); *The Age of Johnson* (1949); etc. Editor: *Letters of James Boswell,* 2v. (1924). English dept., Yale University, 1903–45.

TINKER, EDWARD LAROCQUE (Sept. 12, 1881–Jan. 6, 1968); b. New York. Author. *Lafcadio Hearn's American Days* (1924); *Toucoutou* (1928); *Les Cenelles* (1930); *Old New Orleans,* 4v. (1930); *Les Écrits de Langue Française en Louisiane au XIXe Siècle* (1932); *Bibliography of French Newspapers and Periodicals of Louisiana* (1933); *Gombo, the Creole Dialect of Louisiana* (1936); *The Cult of the Gaucho and the Birth of a Literature* (1948); *The Horseman of the Americas and the Literatures They Inspired* (1953); *Creole City* (1953); etc. He wrote the department, "New Editions Fine and Otherwise" for the *New York Times Book Review,* 1937–42.

TINKLE, [Julien] LON (Mar. 20, 1906–); b. Dallas, Tex. Educator, author. *13 Days to Glory: The Alamo* (1958); *The Story of Oklahoma* (1962); *The Valiant Few* (1964); *The Key to Dallas* (1965); *Miracle in Mexico* (1965). Co-editor: *The Cowboy Reader* (1959). Faculty, Southern Methodist University, since 1932.

Tinnecum Papers. By Frederick William Shelton. A series of humorous sketches written for the *Knickerbocker Magazine* over a long period of years, beginning in 1838.

Tiny Alice. Play by Edward Albee (prod. 1969).

"Tippecanoe and Tyler Too." Song by Alexander Coffman Ross (1840). Written for the presidential campaign of 1840 in support of William Henry Harrison, called "Old Tippecanoe," and John Tyler, his running mate. Written to the tune "Little Pigs."

TIPPLE, BERTRAND MARTIN (Dec. 1, 1868–); b. Camden, N.Y. Author. *Italy of the Italians* (1911); *Europe's God* (1914); *The People of the Great Sea* (1918); *The Eighth Hill* (1922); *Alien Rome* (1924); etc.

" 'Tis Said That Absence Conquers Love." Song by Frederick William Thomas (1833).

TITCHENER, EDWARD BRADFORD (Jan. 11, 1867–Aug. 3, 1927); b. Chichester, England. Educator, psychologist, author. *An Outline of Psychology* (1896); *Experimental Psychology,* 2v. (1901–05). Editor, *American Journal of Psychology,* 1921–25; American editor, *Mind,* 1894–1920. Psychology dept., Cornell University, 1892–1927; Sage professor, 1895–1927.

Titcomb, Timothy. Pen name of Josiah Gilbert Holland.

TITTERINGTON, SOPHIE BRONSON (b. Mar. 13, 1846); b. Assam, India. Author. *Mabel Livingstone* (1871); *Rachel Hastings' Girls* (1873); the *Tropic Land* series (1893); the *Little Pilgrim* series (1897); *Hill-Top Farm* (1899); etc.

TITUS, HAROLD (Feb. 20, 1888–); b. Traverse City, Mich. Novelist. *I Conquered* (1916); *Bruce of the Circle A* (1918);

The Last Straw (1920); *Timber* (1922); *The Beloved Pawn* (1923); *Spindrift* (1924); *Code of the North* (1933); *Flame in the Forest* (1933); *The Man from Yonder* (1934); *Black Feather* (1936); etc.

"To a Caty-Did." Poem by Philip Freneau (1815).

"To a Mocking Bird." Poem by Albert Pike (1834).

"To a Waterfowl." Poem by William Cullen Bryant (1818).

To an Early Grave. Novel by Wallace Markfield (1964). Jewish intellectuals in New York going to a funeral of one of their friends.

"To Brooklyn Bridge." Poem by Hart Crane.

To Have and Have Not. Novel by Ernest Hemingway (1937). An American living in Florida becomes involved in smuggling and other illegal activities in order to provide for his family during the Depression. He is killed by bank robbers whom he has helped escape. The novel expresses the desperation of a lonely man in his attempt to survive as one of the "have-nots" of the world.

To Have and To Hold. Novel by Mary Johnston (1900). Best selling novel dealing with the romantic life in Virginia in the early part of the seventeenth century.

"To Helen." Poem by Edgar Allan Poe, in *Graham's Magazine*, Sept., 1841.

To Kill a Mockingbird. Novel by Harper Lee (1960). Narrated by the girl Scout Finch whose lawyer father is defending a Negro on trial for raping a white woman in an Alabama town during the 1930's.

To the Finland Station. Political and social analyses by Edmund Wilson (1940).

"To the Fringed Gentian." Poem by William Cullen Bryant (1832).

Tobacco Road. Novel by Erskine Caldwell (1932). A chronicle of the sordid life of the Lester family in the backwoods country of Georgia. It was dramatized in 1933 by Caldwell and Jack Kirkland, and enjoyed the longest run of any American play up to that time, having been performed continuously for over seven years. It closed May 31, 1941, after a run of 3,180 consecutive performances.

TOBENKIN, ELIAS (Feb. 10, 1882–Oct. 19, 1963); b. in Russia. Author. *Witte Arrives* (1916); *The House of Conrad* (1918); *The Road* (1922); *God of Might* (1925); *Stalin's Ladder* (1933); *The People Want Peace* (1938); etc.

TOBIN, RICHARD LARDNER (Aug. 9, 1910–); b. Chicago, Ill. Journalist, author. *Invasion Journal* (1944); *Golden Opinions* (1948); *The Center of the World* (1951); *Decisions of Destiny* (1961).

Toby Tyler. By James Otis Kaler (1880). Most popular children's book on circus life. Illustrated by William Allen Rogers.

Today. See *Newsweek*.

TODD, ARTHUR JAMES (May 6, 1878–Nov. 28, 1948); b. Petaluma, Cal. Educator, author. *Theories of Social Progress* (1918); *The Scientific Spirit and Social Work* (1919); *Three Wise Men of the East* (1927); *Industry and Society* (1933); etc. Prof. sociology, Northwestern University, 1921–43.

TODD, CHARLES BURR (b. Jan. 9, 1849); b. Redding, Conn. Author. *The History of Redding, Connecticut* (1880); *Life and Letters of Joel Barlow* (1886); *The Story of the City of New York* (1888); *Story of Washington, the National Capital* (1897); *The True Aaron Burr* (1902); *The Real Benedict Arnold* (1903); *The Confessions of a Railroad Man* (1904); *In Olde Connecticut* (1906); *In Olde Massachusetts* (1907); *In Olde New York* (1907); etc.

TODD, DAVID P[eck] (Mar. 19, 1855–June 1, 1939); b. Lake Ridge, N.Y. Educator, author. *Stars and Telescopes* (1899); *Astronomy To-Day* (1924); etc. Editor: *Columbian Knowledge Series*, 3v. (1893–95). Prof. astronomy, Amherst College, 1881–1920.

TODD, HELEN (Aug. 23, 1912–Aug. 16, 1953); b. St. Louis, Mo. Author. *So Free We Seem* (1936); *A Man Named Grant* (1939); *The Roots of the Tree* (1944); *High Places* (1947); etc.

TODD, HENRY ALFRED (Mar. 13, 1854–Jan. 3, 1925); b. Woodstock, Ill. Philologist, educator, editor. Founder, with A. M. Elliott, *Modern Language Notes*, 1886; the *Romantic Review*, with others, 1909, of which he was co-editor until his death. Prof. Romance langs., Columbia University, 1893–1925. See *Todd Memorial Volumes*, 2v. (1930).

TODD, JOHN (Oct. 9, 1800–Aug. 24, 1873); b. Rutland, Vt. Congregational clergyman, author. *Lectures to Children* (1834); *The Student's Manual* (1835); *Truth Made Simple* (1839); *Woman's Rights* (1869); etc.

Todd, Lawrie. Pen name of Grant Thorburn.

TODD, MABEL (Loomis) (Nov. 10, 1856–Oct. 14, 1932); b. Cambridge, Mass. Lecturer, editor, author. *Footprints* (1883); *A Cycle of Sonnets* (1896); *Corona and Coronet* (1898); *Tripoli, the Mysterious* (1912); etc. Editor: *Poems by Emily Dickinson*, 3v. (v. 1 and 2 with Thomas W. Higginson, 1890–96); *Letters of Emily Dickinson*, 2v. (1894), augmented (1931).

TODD, MARION (b. Mar. 1841); b. Plymouth, N.Y. Lawyer, author. *Professor Goldwin Smith and His Satellites in Congress* (1880); *Pizarro and John Sherman* (1891); *Railways of Europe and America* (1893); *Claudia* (1902); etc.

Todd, Millicent. See Millicent Todd Bingham.

TODRIN, BORIS (May 1, 1915–   ); b. Brooklyn. N.Y. Editor, author. *First Furrow* (poems, 1932); *The Room by the River* (poems, 1936); *Five Days* (poems, 1936); *Seven Men* (1938); *At the Gates* (poems, 1944); *Out of These Roots* (1944); *Paradise Walk* (1946); *The Plundered Heart* (1948); etc. Departmental editor, *PM*.

TOFFLER, ALVIN (Oct. 28, 1928–   ); b. New York. Author. *The Culture Consumers* (1964); *Future Shock* (1970). Associate editor, *Fortune*, 1959–61.

Together. Novel by Robert Herrick (1906). Based on the marriage and divorce problem, and revealing the shallow lives of mismated couples.

Toinette's Philip. By Cecilia Viets Dakin Jamison (1894). A tale for children, laid in the French quarter in old New Orleans.

Token, The. Boston, Mass. Literary annual. Founded 1828. Published by S. C. Goodrich. It was the leading literary annual during the gift-book age. Expired 1842.

TOKLAS, ALICE B[abette]. (d. Mar. 7, 1967). *The Alice B. Toklas Cook Book* (1957); *Aromas and Flavors of Past and Present* (1958). See Gertrude Stein.

TOLAND, JOHN WILLARD (June 29, 1912–); b. La Crosse, Wis. Author. *Ships in the Sky* (1957); *Battle: The Story of the Bulge* (1959); *But Not in Shame* (1961); *The Dillinger Days* (1963); *The Flying Tigers* (1963); *The Last 100 Days* (1966); *The Battle of the Bulge* (1966); *The Rising Sun* (1970).

TOLBERT, FRANK [Francis Xavier] (July 27, 1912–); b. Amarillo Tex. Author. *Nieman-Marcus, Texas* (1953); *Bigamy Jones* (1954); *The Staked Plain* (1958); *The Day of San Jacinto* (1960); *Sabine Pass* (1961); *Dick Dowling at Sabine Pass* (1962).

TOLEDANO, RALPH DE (Aug. 17, 1916–   ); b. Tangier, Mor. Columnist, author. *Seeds of Treason* (1950);

Spies, Dupes and Diplomats (1952); *Day of Reckoning* (1955); *Nixon* (1956); *Lament for a Generation* (1960); *The Greatest Plot in History* (1963); *The Winning Side* (1963); *The Goldwater Story* (1964). Co-editor: *The Conservative Papers* (1964).

Toledo Blade. Toledo, O. Newspaper. Founded 1836. In 1846, changed from a weekly to a tri-weekly; in 1847, became a daily. David R. Locke ("Petroleum V. Nasby") joined it in 1865, and edited it until 1887. Succeeded by his son, Robinson Locke, who was president of the company, 1888–1920. Nathaniel Curwin Wright was editor until 1923. Paul Block was owner 1926–41; Paul Block, Jr., and William Block are present publishers. Albert Cross is editor; Herbert Knowlton, book critic. Now combined with the *Toledo Times*: the *Times* appears mornings, except Saturday and Sunday; the *Blade* appears evenings.

Toledo Times. Toledo, O. Newspaper. Founded 1849, as the *Toledo Commercial Republican.* Present name adopted 1899. Under same ownership as the *Toled. Blade* (q.v.). Joseph V. Knack is executive editor.

TOLLES, FREDERICK BARNES (Apr. 18, 1915–); b. Nashua, N.H. Educator, author. *The Meeting House and Counting House: The Quaker Merchants of Colonial Philadelphia* (1948); *George Logan of Philadelphia* (1953); *James Logan and the Culture of Provincial America* (1957); *Quakers and the Atlantic Culture* (1960); etc. Dept. of history, Swarthmore College, since 1941.

TOLLEY, WILLIAM PEARSON (Sept. 13, 1900–); b. Honesdale, Pa. Methodist clergyman, educator, author. *The Idea of God in the Philosophy of St. Augustine* (1930); etc. Editor: *Alumni Record of Drew Theological Seminary, 1867–1925* (1926); *Preface to Philosophy* (1945). President Allegheny College, 1931–42; chancellor, Syracuse University, 1942–69, Chancellor emeritus since 1969.

TOLMAN, ALBERT WALTER (Nov. 29, 1866–Mar. 7, 1965); b. Rockport, Me. Educator, author. The *Jim Spurling* series, 4v. (1918–1927); etc. English dept., Bowdoin College, 1889–94.

TOLMAN, HERBERT CUSHING (Nov. 4, 1865–Nov. 24, 1923); b. South Scituate, Mass. Episcopal clergyman, educator, Orientalist, author. *Herodotus and the Empires of the East* (1899); *The Art of Translating* (1901); *Urbs Beata* (1902); *Mycenaean Troy* (with G. C. Scoggin, 1904); *"Via Crucis"* (1907); *Christi Imago* (1915); and numerous Greek and Latin text books. Professor, Greek, Vanderbilt University, 1894–1923.

Tom Grogan. By F. Hopkinson Smith (1895). A study of laboring life in Staten Island, N.Y.

Tom Owen, the Bee-Hunter. By Thomas Bangs Thorpe, which first appeared in his *The Mysteries of the Backwoods; or, Sketches of the Southwest* (1846). Tom Owen is also described in Thorpe's *The Hive of "The Bee-Hunter": A Repository of Sketches* (1854). Both books were illustrated by F. O. C. Darley. This is one of the classic American sketches on bee lore.

TOME, PHILIP (Mar. 22, 1782–Apr. 30, 1855); b. in Dauphin Co., Pa. Hunter, author. *Pioneer Life; or, Twenty Years a Hunter* (1854), republished (1928).

TOMES, ROBERT (Mar. 27, 1817–Aug. 24, 1882); b. New York. Physician, author. *Panama in 1855* (1855); *Battles of America by Sea and Land* (1861); *The Great Civil War*, 3v. (1862), also published as *The War with the South; The Champagne Country* (1867); *My College Days* (1880); etc.

TOMLINSON, EVERETT TITSWORTH (May 23, 1859–Oct. 30, 1931); b. Shiloh, N.J. Educator, author of boys' books. *Three Colonial Boys* (1895); *Camping Out on the St. Lawrence* (1899); *The Winner* (1903); *The Fort in the Forest*

(1904); *The Young Rangers* (1906); *Four Boys in the Yellowstone* (1906); *Four Boys in the Land of Cotton* (1907); *The Book of Pioneers* (1926); etc.

TOMLINSON, PAUL GREENE (Feb. 8, 1888–); b. New Brunswick, N.J. Author. *To the Law of the Caribou* (1914); *In Camp on Bass Island* (1915); *The Trail of Black Hawk* (1915); *The Trail of Tecumseh* (1916); *The Strange Gray Canoe* (1916); *A Princeton Boy in the Revolution* (1922); etc.

Tomorrow. New York. Founded 1952. Edited by Eileen J. Garrett. Devoted to speculative science and extrasensory perception, clairvoyance, telepathy, etc.

TOMPKINS, ELIZABETH KNIGHT (b. Oct. 17, 1865); b. Oakland, Calif. Author. *Her Majesty* (1895); *An Unlessoned Girl* (1895); *The Broken Ring* (1896); *Talks with Barbara* (1900).

TOMPKINS, JULIET WILBOR (Mrs. Juliet Wilbor Tompkins Pottle) (May 13, 1871–Jan. 29, 1956); b. Oakland, Calif. Author. *Dr. Ellen* (1908); *Diantha* (1915); *Pleasures and Palaces* (1917); *At the Sign of the Oldest House* (1917); *The Startling* (1919); *The Millionaire* (1930); etc.

TOMPSON, BENJAMIN (July 14, 1642–Apr. 10, 1714); b. Quincy, Mass. Educator, author. *New Englands Crisis* (1676); *New Englands Tears for Her Present Miseries* (1676); *Benjamin Tompson ... His Poems*, ed. by Howard Judson Hall (1924).

Tomson, Graham Rosamund. Pen name of Rosamund Marriott Watson.

TONER, JOSEPH MEREDITH (Apr. 30, 1825–July 30, 1896); b. Pittsburgh, Pa. Physician, book collector, editor, author. *Maternal Instinct* (1864); *The Medical Men of the Revolution* (1876); etc. Editor: *Washington's Rules of Civility and Decent Behavior* (1888); Washington's *Journal of My Journey over the Mountains ... in 1747–8* (1892); *The Daily Journal of Major George Washington, in 1751–2* (1892); *Journal of Colonel George Washington ... in 1754* (1893); etc.

Too Late. Short story by Rose Terry Cooke (1875). A study in grim New England realism.

TOOHEY, JOHN PETER (1880–Nov. 7, 1946); b. Binghamton, N.Y. Author. *Fresh Every Hour* (1922); *Growing Pains* (1929); also several plays.

TOOKER, LEWIS FRANK (Dec. 18, 1854–Sept. 17, 1925); b. Port Jefferson, L.I., N.Y. Editor, poet. *The Call of the Sea, and Other Poems* (1902); *Under Rocking Skies* (1905); *John Paul Jones* (1916); *The Middle Passage* (1920); *The Joys and Tribulations of an Editor* (1924); etc. His best known poem is "The Sea Fight." On editorial staff, the *Century Magazine,* 1885–1925.

TOOMER, JEAN (Dec. 26, 1894–); b. Washington, D.C. Lecturer, author. *Cane* (1923); *Essentials* (1931); *Portage Potential* (1932).

Top-Notch. New York. Fiction monthly. Founded 1910. Expired 1937.

TOPKINS, KATHARINE (July 22, 1927–   ); b. Seattle, Wash. Author. *All the Tea in China* (1962); *Kotch* (1965).

TOPLIFF, SAMUEL (Apr. 25, 1789–Dec. 11, 1864); b. Boston, Mass. News-dealer, author. *Topliff's Travels* (1906). He wrote the story of Pitcairn's Island and the mutiny of the *Bounty* in the *New England Galaxy,* Jan. 12, 1821. He sold foreign news to papers in Boston, New York, and Philadelphia.

Topper. Novel by Thorne Smith (1926). Later books about the character Topper, a ghost, appeared until Smith's death in 1934. All were written in a vein of fantasy mixed with sexual suggestiveness.

TORRANCE, ARTHUR FREDERICK (July 26, 1887–Dec. 12, 1944); b. Blackpool, Eng. Physician, anthropologist, author. *The Moros in the Philippines* (1916); *Tracking Down the Enemies of Man* (1928); *Jungle Mania* (1933); etc.

TORRENCE, [Frederic] RIDGELY (Nov. 27, 1875–Dec. 1950); b. Xenia, O. Poet, playwright. *The House of a Hundred Lights* (poems, 1900); *El Dorado: A Tragedy* (1903); *Abelard and Heloise* (poetic drama, 1907); *Hesperides* (poems, 1925); *The Undefended Line* (1938); *Poems* (1941); *The Story of John Hope* (1947); etc. Editor, *The Critic,* 1903; assoc. editor, *Cosmopolitan,* 1905–07; *The New Republic,* 1920–24; etc.

TORRES RIOSECO, ARTURO (Oct. 17, 1897–); b. Talca, Chile. Educator. Author: *Walt Whitman* (1922); *The Epic of Latin American Literature* (1942); *New World Literature* (1949); etc. Prof. Latin-American literature, University of California, since 1928.

TORREY, BRADFORD (Oct. 9, 1843–Oct. 7, 1912); b. Weymouth, Mass. Ornithologist, editor, essayist. *Birds in the Bush* (1885); *A Rambler's Lease* (1889); *The Foot-Path Way* (1892); *Spring Notes from Tennessee* (1896); *A World of Green Hills* (1898); *Footing it in Franconia* (1901); *The Clerk of the Woods* (1903); *Friends on the Shelf* (1906); *Field Days in California* (1913); etc. Editor: *The Journal of Thoreau,* 14v. (1906).

TORREY, CHARLES CUTLER (Dec. 20, 1863–1956) b. Hardwick, Vt. Educator, translator, author. *Ezra Studies* (1910); *The Composition and Date of Acts* (1916); *The Second Isaiah* (1928); *Pseudo-Ezekiel and the Original Prophecy* (1930); *The Jewish Foundation of Islam* (1933); *Documents of the Primitive Church* (1941); *Apocryphal Literature* (1945); *Chronicler's History of Israel: Chronicles-Ezra-Nehemiah Restored to Its Original Form* (1954); etc. Editor and translator of Arabic and Semitic texts. Prof. Semitic languages, Yale University, 1900–32.

TORREY, JOHN (Aug. 15, 1796–Mar. 10, 1873); b. New York. Physician, botantist, chemist, author. *A Flora of North America* (1838); etc. Sabin attributes to him *America: A Dramatic Poem* (1863). Prof. chemistry, U. S. Military Academy, 1824–27; New York College of Physicians and Surgeons, 1827–55; Princeton, 1830–55. The Torrey Botanical Club, founded 1867, is named in his honor.

Tortesa the Usurer. Play by Nathaniel Parker Willis (prod. 1839). A romantic comedy representing the character of the money-lender.

Tortilla Flat. By John Steinbeck (1935). Story of Monterey, California, panhandlers of mixed Indian and Spanish blood.

Tory Lover, The. Novel by Sarah Orne Jewett (1901). The scene is laid in Berwick, Maine, on the Piscataqua River, and the American Revolution serves as a background.

TOTHEROH, DAN [W]. (1895–); b. San Francisco, Calif. Playwright, novelist. *Wild Birds* (prod. 1922); *David Hotfoot* (1926); *Wild Orchard* (1927); *The Last Dragon* (1927); *Men Call Me Fool* (1929); *One-Act Plays for Everyone* (1931); *Distant Drums* (prod. 1932); *Moon Born* (1934); *Deep Valley* (1942); etc. See Fred B. Millett's *Contemporary American Authors* (1940).

TOTTEN, JOE BYRON (June 1, 1875–Apr. 1946); b. Brooklyn, N.Y. Director, playwright. *The Cowboy and the Squaw* (prod. 1907); *Alibi Bill* (prod. 1912); *So That's That* (prod. 1925); etc.

Touch of the Poet, A. Play by Eugene O'Neill (prod. 1957).

TOURGEE, ALBION WINEGAR (May 2, 1838–May 21, 1905); b. Williamsfield, O. Novelist. *Toinette* (under pen name "Henry Churton," 1874), republished as *A Royal Gentleman* (1881); *A Fool's Errand* (anon., 1879); *Figs and Thistles* (1879); *Bricks Without Straw* (1880); *John Eax and Mamelon* (1882); *Hot Ploughshares* (1883); *The Veteran and His Pipe*

(1886); *Black Ice* (1888); *Pactolus Prime* (1890); etc. See Roy Floyd Dibble's *Albion W. Tourgée* (1921).

TOURSCHER, FRANCIS EDWARD (May 10, 1870–Jan. 30, 1939); b. Dushore, Pa. Educator, translator, author. *The Hogan Schism of 1820–29* (1930); etc. Editor: *The Diary of Rt. Rev. Francis Patrick Kenrick* (1916); *Old St. Augustine's in Philadelphia* (1937); etc. Translator of numerous works by St. Augustine. Professor Latin and church history, Villanova College, 1898–1939, librarian, 1925–39.

TOUSEY, FRANK. Publisher. Editor and publisher, *Our Boys,* 1876–78; *Young Men of America,* 1877–88; the *Boys' Weekly,* 1877–78; the *Boys of New York,* 1878–94; the *Wide Awake Library,* 1878–91; etc.

TOUSEY, SINCLAIR (July 18, 1815–June 16, 1887); b. New Haven, Conn. Journalist, book and magazine distributor, author. *Life in the Union Army* (1864); *Papers from Over the Water* (1869); *Indices of Public Opinion* (1871). One of the founders of the American News Company, New York.

"Tower Beyond Tragedy." Dramatic poem by Robinson Jeffers (1924).

TOWLE, GEORGE MAKEPEACE (Aug. 27, 1841–Aug. 9, 1893); b. Washington, D.C. Journalist, author. *Glimpses of History* (1866); *American Society,* 2v. (1870); *Pizarro* (1878); *Marco Polo* (1880); *Certain Men of Mark* (1880); *Raleigh* (1881); *Drake* (1883); *England in Egypt* (1885); *The Literature of the English Language* (1892); etc. Foreign editor, the *Boston Post,* 1871–76, and author of "American Notes" for the *London Graphic,* 1871–76.

Town and Country. See *Home Journal.*

Town and Country Mouse, The. Short story by Rose Terry Cooke. Considered one of the best of her stories.

"Town Down the River, The." Poem by Edwin Arlington Robinson (1910).

Town Journal. See *Pathfinder.*

"Town Meeting, The." Long poem by Joseph Stansbury. Loyalist satire on the Revolution.

TOWNE, BENJAMIN (d. July 8, 1793); b. Lincolnshire, England. Printer, journalist. Founder, the *Pennsylvania Evening Post,* Jan. 24, 1775.

TOWNE, CHARLES HANSON (Feb. 2, 1877–Feb. 28, 1949); b. Louisville, Ky. Editor, author. *A World of Windows* (1919); *The Bad Man* (1921); *Loafing Down Long Island* (1922); *Ambling Through Acadia* (1923); *The Gay Ones* (1924); *Tinsel* (1925); *Adventures in Editing* (1926); *This New Year of Mine* (1931); *Good Old Yesterday* (1935); *An April Song, New Poems* (1937); *Jogging Around New England* (1939); *The Shop of Dreams* (1939); *So Far, So Good* (autobiography, 1945); etc. Editor, *Harper's Bazaar,* 1926–31; with *McClure's, Smart Set, The Designer,* etc. Wrote column in the *New York American,* 1931–37.

TOWNE, CHARLES WAYLAND (Nov. 14, 1875–); b. Dover, N.H. Author. *The Foolish Dictionary* (1904); etc. Also books under pen name "Gideon Wurdz." Co-author (with Edward N. Wentworth): *Shepherd's Empire* (1945); *Pigs: From Cave to Corn Belt* (1950); *Cattle and Men* (1955).

TOWNE, ELIZABETH (May 11, 1865–June 1, 1961); b. Portland, Ore. Editor, New Thought leader, author. *Joy Philosophy* (1903); *The Life Power* (1906); *Lessons in Living* (1910); etc. Founder, *Nautilus,* Porland, Ore., 1898.

TOWNSEND, CHARLES WENDELL (Nov. 10, 1859–Apr. 3, 1934); b. Boston, Mass. Physician, naturalist, author. *Along the Labrador Coast* (1907); *A Labrador Spring* (1910); *Sand Dunes and Salt Marshes* (1913); *In Audubon's Labrador* (1918); *Beach Grass* (1923); *From Panama to Patagonia* (1931); etc.

TOWNSEND, EDWARD WATERMAN (Feb. 10, 1855–Mar. 16, 1942); b. Cleveland, O. Congressman, author. *"Chimmie Fadden," Major Max, and Other Stories* (1895); *Chimmie Fadden Explains* (1895); *A Daughter of the Tenements* (1895); *Days Like These* (1901); *Lees and Leaven* (1903); *Reuben Larkmead* (1905); *Beaver Creek Farm* (1907); etc. His "Chimmie Fadden" stories of the Bowery first appeared in the *New York Sun.* Congressman, 1911–15.

TOWNSEND, GEORGE ALFRED (Jan. 30, 1841–Apr. 15, 1914); b. Georgetown, Del. Journalist, novelist. *The Bohemians* (1861); *Poems* (1870); *Washington, Outside and Inside* (1873); *Bohemian Days* (1880); *Tales of the Chesapeake* (1880); *Poetical Addresses* (1881); *The Entailed Hat* (1884); *Katy of Catoctin* (1886); *Mrs. Reynolds and Hamilton* (1890); *Poems of Men and Events* (1899); etc. Wrote for the *Chicago Tribune* and the *Cincinnati Daily Enquirer,* and other papers under the pen name "Garth." See *North American Review,* v. 170, 1900.

TOWNSEND, HARVEY GATES (Jan. 27, 1885–Dec. 19, 1948); b. David City, Neb. Educator, author. *Philosophical Ideas in the United States* (1934); *On the History of Philosophy* (1946); etc. Philosophy dept., Smith College, 1914–26; prof. philosophy, University of Oregon, from 1926.

TOWNSEND, JAMES BLISS (Sept. 30, 1855–Mar. 10, 1921); b. New York. Editor, author. *Random Fancies, Sonnets and Translations* (1901); Editor, *Art Interchange,* 1879; art editor, *New York World,* 1881–87; art critic, *New York Times,* 1894–1900; with *New York Herald,* 1902–07; founder, *American Art News* (later *Art News),* 1904, editor, 1904–21.

TOWNSEND, JOHN WILSON (Nov. 2, 1885–deceased); b. near Lexington, Ky. Author. *Richard Hickman Menefee* (1907); *Kentuckians in History and Literature* (1907); *Lore of the Meadowland* (1911); *Kentucky in American Letters, 1784–1912,* 2v. (1913); *James Lane Allen* (1928); *Irvin S. Cobb* (1933); *Three Kentucky Gentlemen of the Old Order* (1946); etc.

TOWNSEND, MARY ASHLEY (Sept. 24, 1832–June 27, 1901); b. Lyons, N.Y. Poet. *The Brother Clerks* (1857); *Xariffa's Poems* (1870); *The Captain's Story, and Other Verse* (under pen name "Xariffa," 1874); *Down the Bayou, and Other Poems* (1882); *Distaff and Spindle* (1895); etc.

TOWNSEND, REGINALD T[ownsend] (Aug. 3, 1890–); b. Newport, R.I. Business executive, editor, author. *This, That and the Other Thing* (1929); *A Twenty-Five Year Record* (1937); *The Comical Chronicle of the Circus Saints and Sinners* (1956); etc. Editor, *Country Life,* 1920–35.

TOWNSEND, VIRGINIA FRANCES (1836–Aug. 11, 1920); b. New Haven, Conn. Editor, author. *Living and Loving* (1857); *Amy Deane* (1862); *Janet Strong* (1865); *Only Girls* (1872); *That Queer Girl* (1874); *Lenox Dare* (1881); *A Boston Girl's Ambition* (1887); *Life of Washington* (1887); *Our Presidents* (1889); etc., including the *Maidenhood* series, the *Breakwater* series. Assoc. editor, *Lady's Home Magazine,* 1856–72.

TOWNSEND, WILLIAM H[enry] (May 31, 1890–July 25, 1964); b. Glensboro, Ky. Lawyer, author. *Abraham Lincoln, Defendant* (1923); *Lincoln, the Litigant* (1925); *Lincoln's Rebel Niece* (1945); *Lincoln and the Bluegrass: Slavery and Civil War in Kentucky* (1955); etc.

TOY, CRAWFORD HOWELL (Mar. 23, 1836–May 12, 1919); b. Norfolk, Va. Educator, author. *The Religion of Israel* (1882); *Commentary on Proverbs* (1899); *Judaism and Christianity* (1890); *Introduction to the History of Religions* (1913). Hancock prof. Hebrew and other Oriental languages, Harvard University, 1880–1909.

TOZIER, JOSEPHINE (b. Aug. 12, 1861); b. Boston, Mass. Author. *Among English Inns* (1904); *A Spring Fortnight in France* (1907); *Susan in Sicily* (1910); etc.

Trace. Hollywood, Calif., and London, Eng. Quarterly. Founded 1952. International quarterly of literary events, poetry, fiction, articles. Edited by James Boyer May. Has published Lawrence Spingarn, Harry Hooton, Curtis Zahn, Gil Orlovitz. Features a running supplement of information about little magazines.

TRACHSEL, MYRTLE JAMISON. b. Gower, Mo. Author. Pen name, "Jane Jamison." *The Garden of the Little Lame Princess* (1927); *Mistress Jennifer and Master Jeremiah* (1937); *Linda and Dick of Colonial Williamsburg* (1938); *Sally Sue Visits Old Natchez* (1939); *Elizabeth of the Mayflower* (1950); etc.

Track of the Cat, The. Novel by Walter Van Tilburg Clark (1949). A panther hunt in the Northwest, with symbolic overtones.

"Tract." Poem by William Carlos Williams.

TRACY, DON[ald Fiske] (Aug. 20, 1905–   ). Author. *Round Trip* (1935); *Criss Cross* (1936); *How Sleeps the Beast* (1938); *Last Year's Snow* (1939); *Chesapeake Cavalier* (1949); *Streets of Askelon* (1951); *Second Try* (1954); *Bride of Possession* (with James Street, 1960); *No Trespassing* (1961); *The Hated One* (1963); *The Big Brass Ring* (1963); *Bazzaris* (1965). Under pen name "Roger Fuller": *Sign of the Pagan* (1954); *Carolina Corsair* (1955); *Cherokee* (1957); *On the Midnight Tide* (1957); *Big Blackout* (1959).

TRACY, HENRY CHESTER (Aug. 26, 1876–Dec. 19, 1958); b. Athens, Pa. Author. *Toward the Open: A Preface to Scientific Humanism* (1927); *English As Experience* (1928); *American Naturists* (1930); *Morning Land* (1938); etc.

Tradition of the New, The. By Harold Rosenberg (1959). Essays on social forces, literature, and painting.

Tragic Ground. Novel by Erskine Caldwell (1944). Racy story of a Georgia boom town during World War II in which a jobless backwoodsman figures as hero.

Tragic Muse, The. Novel by Henry James (1890). The conflict between art and material comfort exemplified by a member of parliament who resigns to become a painter, and a woman who turns down marriage with a diplomat in order to become an actress.

Trail, The. Denver, Colo. Magazine. Founded 1906, as *Sons of Colorado.* Name changed 1908. Expired 1928.

Trail of the Lonesome Pine, The. Novel of the Kentucky mountains by John Fox, Jr. (1908). Romance of John Hale, an engineer working in the Kentucky mountains, and June Tolliver, a beautiful and intelligent but uneducated mountain girl.

TRAIN, ARTHUR (Sept. 6, 1875–Dec. 22, 1945); b. Boston, Mass. Lawyer, author. *McAllister and His Double* (1905); *The Prisoner at the Bar* (1906); *Confessions of Artemus Quibble* (1909); *The Goldfish* (1914); *The World and Thomas Kelly* (1917); *Tutt and Mr. Tutt* (1920); *His Children's Children* (1923); *On the Trail of the Bad Men* (1925); *Page Mr. Tutt* (1926); *When Tutt Meets Tutt* (1927); *The Horns of Ramadan* (1928); *Illusion* (1929); *The Adventures of Ephraim Tutt* (1930); *Puritan's Progress* (1931); *Jacob's Ladder* (1935); *Tutt's Case Book* (1937); *From the District Attorney's Office* (1939); *My Day in Court* (autobiography, 1939); *Tassels on Her Boots* (1940); *Mr. Tutt Comes Home* (1941); etc.

TRAIN, ELIZABETH PHIPPS (b. Sept. 1, 1856); b. Dorchester, Mass. Novelist. *Doctor Lamar* (1891); *A Social Highwayman* (1896); *The Autobiography of a Professional Beauty* (1896); etc.

TRAIN, ETHEL KISSAM (Mrs. Arthur Train) (Dec. 29, 1875–May 15, 1923); b. New York. Author. *Son* (1911); *Bringing Out Barbara* (1917); etc.

TRAIN, GEORGE FRANCIS (Mar. 24, 1829–Jan. 19, 1904); b. Boston, Mass. Merchant, traveler, author. *An Ancient Merchant in Europe, Asia, and Australia* (1857); *My Life in Many States and in Foreign Lands* (1902).

Tramp Printer, The. By Ben Hur Lampman (1934). Story of a vanishing type of itinerant printer.

"Tramp! Tramp! Tramp!" Civil War song by George Frederick Root (1864). Known as "The Prisoner's Hope."

Trans-Action. New Brunswick, N.J. Monthly. Founded 1963 by A.W. Gouldner. Edited by Irving Louis Horowitz. Devoted to furthering the understanding and use of the social sciences.

Transatlantic Review, The. New York and Rome. Quarterly. Founded 1959. Devoted to fiction, articles, poetry. Known for its sophisticated cartoons and drawings. Edited by Joseph F. McCrindle.

Transcendentalists. New England school of thinkers headed by Ralph Waldo Emerson. It represented the flowering of Puritan idealism, a spiritual renascence which implied the communion of the human spirit with a directing "oversoul" which shaped men's destinies. Brook Farm (q.v.) was associated with the movement, and *The Dial* (q.v.) was the organ of transcendentalism. The Transcendental Club held its first meeting at the home of George Ripley, Sept. 19, 1836. *See* Emerson, Ripley, A. B. Alcott, Margaret Fuller, Elizabeth Peabody, F. H. Hedge, Orestes A. Brownson, James F. Clarke, Theodore Parker, Minot Pratt, Charles A. Dana. See also *The Harbinger;* Sylvester Judd's *Margaret,* 2v. (1845); Nathaniel Hawthorne's *The Blithedale Romance* (1852); O. B. Frothingham's *Transcendentalism in New England* (1876); Harold Clarke Goddard's *Studies in New England Transcendentalism* (1908); Henry David Gray's *Emerson: A Statement of New England Transcendentalism* (1931); C. L. F. Gohdes' *The Periodicals of American Transcendentalism* (1931); *The Transcendentalists: An Anthology,* ed. by Perry Miller (1950); Myron Simon's and T. H. Parson's *Transcendentalism and its Legacy* (1966); W. L. Leighton's *French Philosophers and New England Transcendentalism* (1968); G. F. Whicher's and G. Kennedy's *Transcendentalist Revolt* (1968).

Transients, The. Novel by Mark Van Doren (1934). The adventures of two Olympian visitors to New England.

Transition. Paris; The Hague; New York. Monthly, and later quarterly, literary magazine. Founded 1927. It was edited by Eugene Jolas and Elliot Paul. Devoted to experiments in the free use of language, especially as influenced by dreams, hallucinations, and free association. Published work by Gertrude Stein, Ernest Hemingway, Richard Eberhardt, and Kay Boyle. Discontinued in 1938.

TRAPP, MARIA AUGUSTA (Jan. 26, 1905–); b. Vienna. Musician, author. *The Story of the Trapp Family Singers* (1949); *Yesterday, Today, and Forever* (1952); *A Family on Wheels* (with R. T. Murdoch, 1959); *The Trapp Family Singers* (1966); etc.

Traprock, Walter E. Pen name of George Shepard Chappell.

TRASK, KATE NICHOLS (1853–Jan. 8, 1922); b. Brooklyn, N.Y. Poet, novelist. Wrote as "Katrina Trask." *Under King Constantine* (poems, 1892); *Sonnets and Lyrics* (1894); *John Leighton, Jr.* (1898); *Christalan* (poems, 1903); *Free, Not Bound* (1903); *Mors et Victoria* (1906); *Night and Morning* (1906); *King Alfred's Jewel* (1908); *In the Vanguard* (1913); etc.

TRATTNER, ERNEST ROBERT (Nov. 4, 1898–May 28, 1963); b. Denver, Colo. Rabbi, author. *Unravelling the Book of Books* (1929); *As a Jew Sees Jesus* (1931); *Architect of Ideas* (1938); *Biography of Omar Khayyam* (1940); *The Story of the World's Great Thinkers* (1943); *Understanding the Talmud* (1955); etc.

TRAUBEL, HORACE (Dec. 19, 1858–Sept. 8, 1919); b. Camden, N.J. Editor, author. *Chants Communal* (1904); *With Walt Whitman in Camden,* 3v. (1906–14); *Optimos* (1910); *Collects* (1915); etc. Founder, *The Conservator, Philadelphia,* 1890. *See* W. E. Walling's *Whitman and Traubel* (1916); David Karsner's *Horace Traubel* (1919); Walt Whitman.

Travel. New York. Monthly. Founded 1902. Editor and book-review editor, Malcolm Davis. Merged in 1931 with the American Automobile Association's *Holiday,* founded 1930.

Travel Is So Broadening. Short story by Sinclair Lewis (1928).

Traveler from Altruria, A. Novel by William Dean Howells (1894). Utopian romance.

TRAVEN, B. (May 3, 1882 or Mar. 5, 1890 or 1894–Mar. 27, 1969); b. probably in Germany. Wrote novels and stories in German, some of which he translated into English. These were either re-translated or edited by different hands, some published first in England, others in the United States. Other books were translated directly. Reputed to have lived in Mexico during most of his writing life. Real name unknown. No record of authenticated meetings with him by editors or publishers. Works include *The Death Ship* (1934); *The Treasure of the Sierra Madre* (1935); *Bridge in the Jungle* (1938); *The Rebellion of the Hanged* (1952); *The Cotton Pickers* (1956); *Stories by the Man Nobody Knows* (1963); *March to the Monteria* (1963); *The Night Visitor and Other Stories* (1967); *The Creation of the Sun and the Moon* (1968).

Traver, Robert. Pen name of John Donaldson Voelker.

TREADWELL, DANIEL (Oct. 10, 1791–Feb. 27, 1872); b. Ipswich, Mass. Educator, inventor, author. Wrote numerous pamphlets on physics and on his inventions. Co-editor, *Boston Journal of Philosophy and the Arts,* 1823–26. Rumford prof. application of science to the arts, Harvard, 1824–45.

TREADWELL, WILLIAM FRANK [Bill] (Jan. 3, 1914–); b. New York. Public relations executive. Author: *Give It to Me Easy* (1944); *Fifty Years of American Comedy* (1951); *Head, Heart and Heal* (1958); *The Penetration of Propaganda* (1959); etc. Editor: *Big Book of Swing* (1946).

Treasury of American Folklore. Edited by B. A. Botkin (1944). Stories, tall tales, and legends that comprise the folklore of America.

Treasury of the World's Great Letters. Edited by M. L. Schuster (1940). Letters of famous figures of various periods and places.

TREAT, MARY (Adelia Davis) (b. Sept. 7, 1830); b. Tompkins Co., N.Y. Naturalist, author. *Chapters on Ants* (1879); *Home Studies in Nature* (1885).

Tree Grows in Brooklyn, A. Novel by Betty Smith (1943). A charming story of family life in the Williamsburg section of Brooklyn, as it appeared to a sensitive young girl.

Trees, and Other Poems. By Joyce Kilmer (1914).

TREGASKIS, RICHARD WILLIAM (Nov. 28, 1916–); b. Elizabeth, N.J. Journalist, author. *Guadalcanal Diary* (1943); *Stronger Than Fear* (1945); *Seven Leagues to Paradise* (1951); *Last Plane to Shanghai* (1961); *John F. Kennedy and PT-109* (1962); *Vietnam Diary* (1963); *China Bomb* (1967); etc.

TREMAINE, FREDERICK ORLIN (Jan. 7, 1889–Oct. 22, 1956); b. Harrisville, N.Y. Editor, publisher, author. *One Burning Minute* (1926); *The First Person Story* (1927); *Aviation Conquests* (1931); etc. Editor: *Smart Set,* 1924–26; *Everybody's Magazine,* 1931; Street and Smith magazines, 1933–38. President and editor, Orlin Tremaine Co., publishers, 1939–42.

Tremont House. Boston, Mass. Built in 1829. Famous as the popular stopping place for literary visitors to Boston and Cambridge. At one time managed by Paran Stevens, called the father of the American hotel system.

TRENT, LUCIA (Mrs. Ralph Cheyney) (Dec. 1897–); b. Richmond, Va. Poet. *Dawn Stars* (1926); *Children of Fire and Shadow* (1929); *Dreamers' House* (with Ralph Cheyney, 1931); *More Power to Poets!* (with same, 1934); *Sierra Dreamers' House* (with same, 1935); *Thank You, America* (with same, 1937); etc.

Trent, Martha. Pen name of Dorothy Whitehill Smith.

TRENT, WILLIAM PETERFIELD (Nov. 10, 1862–Dec. 6, 1939); b. Richmond, Va. Educator, editor, author. *English Authors in Virginia* (1889); *William Gilmore Simms* (1892); *Southern Statesmen of the Old Regime* (1897); *Verses* (1899); *John Milton* (1899); *The Authority of Criticism, and Other Essays* (1899); *Robert E. Lee* (1899); *A History of American Literature, 1607–1865* (1903); *Greatness in Literature, and Other Papers* (1905); *Longfellow, and Other Essays* (1910); *Great American Writers* (with J. Erskine, 1912); *Daniel Defoe: How to Know Him* (1916); *Verse Jottings* (1924); etc. Editor: *Southern Writers* (1905); etc. Prof. English, University of the South, 1888–1900; Columbia University, 1900–29.

TRESCOT, WILLIAM HENRY (Nov. 10, 1822–May 4, 1898); b. Charleston, S.C. Diplomat, historian. *The Position and Course of the South* (1850); *Diplomacy of the Revolution: An Historical Study* (1852); *The Diplomatic History of the Administrations of Washington and Adams* (1857); etc. Asst. Secretary of State, June–Dec. 1860; special commissioner to China, 1880; to Chile, 1881; to Mexico, 1882; etc.

Tri-Quarterly. Evanston, Ill. Founded 1958. Published by Northwestern University. Successively edited by Edward Hungerford and Charles Newman. Has devoted special sections to Soviet literature, new African writing, work of Eastern European writers. Contributors include Richard Ellmann, Kenneth Rexroth, and Sylvia Plath.

Trial of Mary Dugan, The. Play by Bayard Veiller (prod. 1927).

Trials of the Human Heart: A Novel in Four Volumes. By Susanna Haswell Rowson (1795). In the form of letters from Meriel Howard to Celia Shelburne.

Tribune Novels. Extra sheets of the *New York Tribune,* containing popular novels. These extras were started in 1873, and continued until 1883.

TRILLING, LIONEL (July 4, 1905–); b. New York. Educator, author. *Matthew Arnold* (1939); *E. M. Forster* (1943); *The Middle of the Journey* (1947); *The Liberal Imagination* (1950); *The Opposing Self* (1955); *A Gathering of Fugitives* (1956). Editor: Keats, *Selected Letters* (1950); *The Experience of Literature: A Reader with Commentaries* (1967); etc. English dept., Columbia University, since 1931.

TRINE, RALPH WALDO (Sept. 9, 1866–1958); b. Mt. Morris, Ill. Author. *In Tune with the Infinite* (1897); *On the Open Road* (1908); *My Philosophy and My Religion* (1921); *The Best of Ralph Waldo Trine* (1957); etc.

Trip to Chinatown, A. Popular play by Charles H. Hoyt (prod. 1891).

Triple Thinkers, The. By Edmund Wilson (1938). Twelve essays on literature.

Tristram. Narrative poem by Edward Arlington Robinson (1927). Based on the Arthurian legend. Tristram and Isolt of the White Hands, and King Mark are the leading characters.

Triumph of Willie Pond, The. Novel by Caroline Slade (1940). The story of a man hired by the Works Progress Administration, who later becomes a public ward in a tuberculosis sanitarium.

TROEGER, JOHN W[inthrop] (Aug. 20, 1849–Dec. 17, 1936); b. Oswego, Ill. Educator, author. The *Harold* series of books for boys, 5v. (1897–1902).

Trollopiad; or, Travelling Gentlemen in America, The. By Frederick William Shelton (under pen name "Nil Admirari, Esq.," 1837). Satire on the books written by English travelers in America who sent back unfavorable reports of American manners and customs, particularly the account written by Mrs. Trollope.

TROMBLY, ALBERT EDMUND (Aug. 21, 1888–); b. Chazy, N.Y. Educator, author. *The Springtime of Love, and Other Poems* (1914); *Love's Creed, and Other Poems* (1915); *Songs of Daddyhood, and Other Poems* (1916); *Rosetti the Poet* (1920); *Vachel Lindsay* (1929); *North of the Rio Grande* (poems, 1936); *Acorns and Apples from Old Missouri and New* (poems, 1942); *Grain of Sand* (poems, 1944); *Little Dixie* (poems, 1955); etc. Professor Romance languages, University of Missouri, since 1922.

Tropic of Cancer. Narrative of experiences as a penniless American writer in Paris, by Henry Miller (1934). Published in France. Because of its use of obscene expressions and its description of sexual encounters, it was not published in the United States until 1961, when Grove Press put out an edition. Numerous seizures of the book by police in various states occurred throughout 1962 and the publisher was involved in litigation. The book was an immediate best-seller after American publication.

Trotty Book, The. Stories by Elizabeth Stuart Phelps Ward (1870). It was followed by *Trotty's Wedding Tour and Story Book* (1873).

Trotwood. Pen name of John Trotwood Moore.

Troubetzkoy, Amélie Rives, Princess. See Amélie Rives.

TROW, JOHN FOWLER (Jan. 30, 1810–Aug. 8, 1886); b. Andover, Mass. Printer and publisher. He began his printing business in New York in 1834, forming a partnership known as West & Trow. From 1837 to 1844 he was in business under his own name. In 1844 he joined with Jonathan Leavitt, a partnership that lasted until 1849. In 1852 he published *Trow's New York City Directory,* a directory issued by the firm until 1925.

TROWBRIDGE, JOHN TOWNSEND (Sept. 18, 1827–Feb. 12, 1916); b. Monroe Co., N.Y. Poet, editor, author of books for boys. Pen name "Paul Creyton." *Father Brighthopes* (1853); *The Vagabonds* (1863); *Cudjo's Cave* (1864); *The South: A Tour of Its Battlefields and Ruined Cities* (1866); *Lucy Arlyn* (1866); *The Poetical Works of John Townsend Trowbridge* (1903); *My Own Story* (1903); etc. Contributing editor *Our Young Folks,* 1865–70; managing editor, 1870–73. Author of the *Jack Hazard, Tidemill* and *Toby Trafford* series for boys. His best known poems are "Darius Green and His Flying Machine," and "Pewee."

TROYER, HOWARD WILLIAM (Sept. 4, 1901–); b. in LaGrange Co., Ind. Educator, author. *Ned Ward of Grubstreet* (1946); *The Salt and the Savor* (1950); *The Four Wheel Drive Story* (1954). Dean, Cornell College (Mt. Vernon, Ia.), since 1957.

TRUDEAU, EDWARD LIVINGSTON (Oct. 5, 1848–Nov. 15, 1915); b. New York. Physician, student of tuberculosis. *An Autobiography* (1915), title page, (1916). Founder, the Adirondack Cottage Sanitarium (now the Trudeau Sanatorium), 1884, the first tuberculosis sanitarium in the United States.

True: For Today's Man. New York. Monthly. Founded 1937. Robert Ruark, C. S. Forester, Budd Schulberg, and Richard Tregaskis have been associated with it. Once known as *True: The Man's Magazine.*

TRUE, CHARLES KITTREDGE (Aug. 14, 1809–June 20, 1878); b. Portland, Me. Educator, author. *The Elements of Logic* (1840); *Shawmut; or, The Settlement of Boston by the Puritans* (anon., 1845), also published as *Tri-Mountain; or, The Early History of Boston* (anon., 1845); *John Winthrop* (1875); *The Life and Times of Sir Walter Raleigh* (1877); *The Life and Times of John Knox* (1878); etc. Prof. philosophy, Wesleyan University, 1849–60.

TRUE, JOHN PRESTON (Feb. 13, 1859–Jan. 4, 1933); b. Bethel, Me. Editor, author. *Their Club and Ours* (1883); *Shoulder Arms* (1889); *Morgan's Men* (1901); *The Iron Star* (1902); *Scouting for Light Horse Harry* (1911); etc. Editorial dept., Houghton, Mifflin & Co., 1879–1919.

True Believer. By Eric Hoffer (1951). An informal analysis of the individual's relation to the masses in modern society.

True Flag. Boston, Mass. Story magazine. Founded 1851. John W. Nichols was a prominent editor. Expired 1908.

True Grandeur of Nations, The. Oration by Charles Sumner, at Tremont Temple, Boston, July 4, 1845. This marked the beginning of his political career.

TRUEBLOOD, D[avid] ELTON (Dec. 12, 1900–); b. Pleasantville, Ia. Editor, educator, author. *The Essence of Spiritual Religion* (1936); *The Knowledge of God* (1939); *The Life We Prize* (1951); *Your Other Vocation* (1952); *The Yoke of Christ* (1958); *The People Called Quakers* (1966); *The Incendiary Fellowship* (1967); *The Lord's Prayer* (1967); *The Predicament of Modern Man* (1967). Editor, *The Friend*, 1935–47. Prof. philosophy of religion, Stanford University, 1936–45; prof. philosophy, Earlham College since 1946; Prof.-at-large, since 1966.

TRUEBLOOD, THOMAS CLARKSON (Aug. 6, 1856–June 4, 1951); b. Salem, Ind. Educator, author. *Essentials of Public Speaking* (1909); *British and American Eloquence* (1912). Compiler: *Patriotic Eloquence Relating to the Spanish-American War* (with Robert Fulton, 1900); etc. Prof. public speaking, University of Michigan, 1889–1926.

TRUMAN, BEN[jamin] C[ummings] (Oct. 25, 1835–July 18, 1916); b. Providence, R.I. Journalist, author. *Life, Adventures, and Capture of Tiburcio Vasquez, the Great California Bandit and Murderer* (1874); *Occidental Sketches* (1881); *The Field of Honor* (1883); etc. Editor, the *Los Angeles Evening Express*, 1872. Correspondent, the *New York Times.*

TRUMAN, HARRY S (May 8, 1884–); b. Lamar, Mo. Thirty-third President of the U.S. *The Truman Program* (1949); *Memoirs*, 2v. (I, *Years of Decisions*, 1955; II, *Years of Trial and Hope*, 1956); *Mr. Citizen* (autobiography, 1960); *Truman Speaks* (1960); etc. U.S. senator from Missouri, 1934–44; vice-president of the U.S., 1944–45. See William Hillman's *Mr. President: Personal Papers of Harry S Truman* (1952). *See also* R. Alton Lee's *Truman and the Taft-Hartley* (1966); Barton J. Bernstein's and A. J. Matusow's *Truman Administration: A Documentary History* (1966).

TRUMBO, DALTON (Dec. 9, 1905–); b. Montrose, Colo. Novelist, playwright. *Eclipse* (1935); *Washington Jitters* (1936); *Johnny Got His Gun* (1939); *The Remarkable Andrew* (1941); *Biggest Thief in Town* (play, 1949); etc. Also screenplays. See *Additional Dialogue: Letters of Dalton Trumbo, 1942–1962*, edited by Helen Manfull (1970).

TRUMBULL, ANNIE ELIOT (1857–Dec. 23, 1949); b. Hartford, Conn. Author. *An Hour's Promise* (1889); *White Birches* (1893); *A Christmas Accident* (1897); *Rod's Salvation* (1898); *A Cape Cod Week* (1898); *Mistress Content Craddock* (1899); *Life's Common Way* (1903); etc.

TRUMBULL, CHARLES GALLAUDET (Feb. 20, 1872–Jan. 13, 1941); b. Hartford, Conn. Editor, author. *A Pilgrimage to Jerusalem* (1904); *Taking Men Alive* (1907); *Men Who Dared* (1907); *Anthony Comstock* (1913); *Life Story of C. I.*

Scofield (1920); *Prophecy's Light on Today* (1937); etc. Editor, the *Sunday School Times*, Philadelphia, 1893–1941.

TRUMBULL, HENRY. Author. Pen name, "Rev. James Steward." *History of the Discovery of America* (1810), also published anonymously; frequently republished under various titles, especially *History of the Indian Wars.*

TRUMBULL, HENRY CLAY (June 8, 1830–Dec. 8, 1903); b. Stonington, Conn. Sunday School missionary, author. *The Knightly Soldier* (1865); *Kadesh-Burnea* (1884); *Teaching and Teachers* (1888); *A Lie Never Justifiable* (1893); *The Memories of an Army Chaplain* (1898); etc. See Philip R. Howard's *The Life Story of Henry Clay Trumbull* (1905).

TRUMBULL, JAMES HAMMOND (Dec. 20, 1821–Aug. 5, 1897); b. Stonington, Conn. Philologist, historian, bibliographer. *The Rev. Samuel Peters* (1876); etc. Editor: *The Public Records of the Colony of Connecticut*, 3v. (1850–59); *The Memorial History of Hartford County* (1886); etc. Compiler: *Catalogue of the American Library of the Late Mr. George Brinley, of Hartford, Conn.*, 5v. (1878–97); *List of Books Printed in Connecticut, 1709–1800* (1904); etc. Librarian, Watkinson Library, Hartford, Conn., 1866–90.

TRUMBULL, JOHN (Apr. 13, 1750–May 11, 1831); b. Westbury, Conn. Jurist, poet. *An Essay on the Uses and Advantages of the Fine Arts* (1770); *The Progress of Dulness*, 2 parts (in verse, 1772–73); *An Elegy on the Times* (1774); *M'Fingal* (poem, 1776, first complete edition, 1782); *The Poetical Works* (1820). One of the Hartford Wits. See *The Anarchiad. see Also* Alexander Cowie's *John Trumbull: Connecticut Wit* (1936).

TRUMBULL, JOHN (June 6, 1756–Nov. 10, 1843); b. Lebanon, Conn. Painter of the Revolution, author. *Autobiography, Letters and Reminiscences of John Trumbull* (1841). Among his best known paintings are the "Battle of Bunker Hill," "The Surrender of Cornwallis," and the "Signing of the Declaration of Independence." *See* John Durand's *John Trumbull* (1881); P. Boswell's *Modern American Painting* (1939).

TRUMBULL, ROBERT (May 26, 1912–   ); b. Chicago, Ill. Journalist, author. *The Raft* (1942); *Silversides* (1945); *India Since Independence* (1954); *As I See India* (1956); *Nine Who Survived Hiroshima and Nagasaki* (1957); *Paradise in Trust* (1959); *The Scrutable East* (1964); Correspondent to *New York Times.*

Truth: A New Year's Gift for Scribblers. By William Joseph Snelling (1931). Satire on contemporary poets in Boston.

"Truth, crushed to earth, shall rise again." Line from William Cullen Bryant's poem, "The Battlefield."

Truth, The. Play by Clyde Fitch (prod. 1907). Study of a woman who finds it difficult to tell the truth, with complications which place her in embarrassing predicaments.

TRYON, LILLIAN WAINWRIGHT HART (Mrs. Winthrop Pitt Tryon) (June 3, 1870–); b. New Britain, Conn. Author. *Speaking of Home: Being Essays of a Contented Woman* (1916); *The Story of New Britain* (1925); *Life of William H. Hart* (1929); etc.

TSANOFF, RADOSLAV ANDREA (Jan. 3, 1887–); b. Sofia. Educator. Author: *Pawns of Liberty* (with Corrinne S. Tsanoff, 1914); *The Nature of Evil* (1931); *Ethics* (1947); *The Ways of Genius* (1949); *The Great Philosophers* (1953); etc. Philosophy dept., Rice Institute, 1914–56.

TUBBS, ARTHUR LEWIS (July 2, 1867–Jan. 27, 1946); b. Glens Falls, N.Y. Drama and music critic, playwright. Pen name "Arthur Sylvester." *The Heart of a Home* (1898); *Followed by Fate* (1903); *The Finger of Scorn* (1911); *The Village Lawyer* (1916); etc. Drama and music critic, the *Philadelphia Evening Bulletin,* 1897–1936.

TUCCI, NICCOLO (1908–   ). Author. *Tico-Tico* (with Ylla, 1950); *Before My Time* (1962); *Unfinished Funeral* (1964).

TUCHMAN, BARBARA [Wertheim] (Jan. 30, 1912–). Author. *Bible and Sword: England and Palestine from the Bronze Age to Balfour* (1956); *The Zimmermann Telegram* (1958); *The Guns of August* (1962); *The Proud Tower* (1966).

TUCKER, AUGUSTA (1904–   ); b. Saint Francisville, La. Novelist. *Miss Susie Slagle's* (1939); *The Man Miss Susie Loved* (1942); *It Happened at Hopkins: A Teaching Hospital* (1960); etc.

TUCKER, BEVERLEY RANDOLPH (Apr. 26, 1874–June 19, 1945); b. Richmond, Va. Neurologist, author. *S. Weir Mitchell* (1914); *Verses of Virginia* (1923); *The Lost Lenore* (1929); *The Gift of Genius* (1930); *Narna Darrell* (1936); *Tales of the Tuckers* (1942); also technical books. Prof. nervous diseases, Medical college of Virginia, Richmond, 1912–38.

TUCKER, GEORGE (Aug. 20, 1775–Apr. 10, 1861); b. in Bermuda. Political economist, author. *Essays on Various Subjects* (1822); *The Valley of Shenandoah,* 2v. (anon., 1824); *A Voyage to the Moon* (under pen name, "Joseph Atterley," 1827); *The Life of Thomas Jefferson,* 2v. (1837); *The History of the United States,* 4v. (1856–57); *Political Economy for the People* (1859); etc. Contrib. editor, the *Virginia Literary Museum,* 1929. Congressman, 1819–25. Prof. moral philosophy, University of Virginia, 1825–45.

TUCKER, GEORGE FOX (Jan. 19, 1852–Feb. 14, 1929); b. New Bedford, Mass. Lawyer, novelist. *The Monroe Doctrine* (1885); *A Quaker Home* (1891); *Uncle Calup's Christmas Dinner* (1892); *Mildred Marvel* (1899).

TUCKER, GILBERT M[illigan] (Aug. 26, 1847–Jan. 13, 1932); b. Albany, N.Y. Editor, author. *Our Common Speech* (1895); *A Layman's Apology* (1913); *American English* (1921). Editor, *Country Gentleman,* 1897–1911.

TUCKER, GLENN [Irving] (Nov. 30, 1892–); b. Tampico, Ind. Author. *Poltroons and Patriots* (1954): *Tecumseh* (1956); *High Tide at Gettysburg* (1958); *Hancock the Superb* (1960); *Chickamauga* (1961); *Front Rank* (1962); *Dawn Like Thunder, The Barbary Wars and the Birth of the U.S. Navy* (1963); *Zeb Vance, Champion of Personal Freedom* (1966); *Lee and Longstreet at Gettysburg* (1968).

TUCKER, LUTHER (May 7, 1802–Jan. 26, 1873); b. Brandon, Vt. Editor. Founder, the *Rochester Daily Advertiser,* Oct. 1826; the *Genesee Farmer,* Jan. 1, 1831; the *Horticulturist,* July 1846; and the *Country Gentleman,* 1853.

TUCKER, NATHANIEL BEVERLEY (Sept. 6, 1784–Aug. 26, 1851); b. Chesterfield Co., Va. Educator, novelist. *George Balcombe* (anon., 1836); *The Partisan Leader* (under pen name "Edward William Sidney," and intentionally dated 1856, 1836); *Gertrude* (1844–45); etc. Prof. law, College of William and Mary, 1834–51. *See* Maude H. Woodfin's *Nathaniel Beverley Tucker, in Richmond College Historical Papers,* v. 2, (1917); Vernon L. Parrington's *Main Currents in American Literature,* v. 2 (1927).

TUCKER, ST. GEORGE (June 29, 1752–Nov. 10, 1827); b. Poet Royal, Bermuda. Poet. *Liberty: A Poem on the Independence of America* (1788); *The Probationary Odes of Jonathan Pindar* (1796). His best known poem is "Day of My Youth, Ye Have Glided Away." *See* May Haldane Coleman's *St. George Tucker* (1938).

TUCKER, SAMUEL MARION (Nov. 25, 1876–Feb. 19, 1962); b. Sanford, Fla. Educator, author. *Verse Satire in England Before the Renaissance* (1908); *Public Speaking for Technical Men* (1939). Editor of several collections of modern plays. Prof. English, Brooklyn Polytechnic Institute, 1911–45.

TUCKER, SOPHIE [Sophie Abuza] (1884–Feb. 9, 1966); b. in Russia. Entertainer. *Some of These Days* (autobiography, 1945).

TUCKERMAN, ARTHUR (Jan. 6, 1896–Oct. 5, 1955); b. New York. Author. *Breath of Life* (1922); *Galloping Dawns* (1924); *Possible Husbands* (1926); *High Walls* (1929); *Old School Tie* (1954).

TUCKERMAN, BAYARD (July 2, 1855–Oct. 20, 1923); b. New York. Editor, author. *A History of English Prose Fiction* (1882); *Life of General Lafayette,* 2v. (1889); *Peter Stuyvesant* (1893); *Life of General Philip Schuyler, 1733–1804* (1903). Editor: *The Diary of Philip Hone, 1828–1851,* 2v. (1889).

TUCKERMAN, FREDERICK GODDARD (Feb. 4, 1821–May 9, 1873); b. Boston, Mass. Poet. *Poems* (1860, 1864, 1869); *The Sonnets* (1931), with introduction by Witter Bynner.

TUCKERMAN, HENRY THEODORE (Apr. 20, 1813–Dec. 17, 1871); b. Boston, Mass. Essayist, poet, critic. *Isabel; or, Sicily* (1830); *The Italian Sketch Book* (1835); *Rambles and Reveries* (1841); *Thoughts on the Poets* (1843); *Characteristics of Literature,* 2v. (1849–51); *The Optimist* (1850); *Poems* (1851); *Leaves from the Diary of a Dreamer* (anon., 1853); *Essays, Biographical and Critical* (1857); *America and Her Commentators: With a Critical Sketch of Travel in the United States* (1864); *The Criterion* (1866); *Book of the Artists* (1867); *The Life of John Pendleton Kennedy* (1871); etc. *See* Evart A. Duyckinck's *A Memorial of Henry T. Tuckerman* (1872).

TUDOR, TASHA (Mrs. Thomas L. McCready, Jr.) (Aug. 28, 1915–); b. Boston, Mass. Author, illustrator: *Pumpkin Moonshine* (1938); *Alexander the Gander* (1939); *The Dolls' Christmas* (1950); *Edgar Allan Crow* (1953); *One Is One* (1956); *Around the Year* (1957); *Take Joy! The Tasha Tudor Christmas Book* (1966); *First Poems of Childhood* (1967); etc. Editor: *The Tasha Tudor Book of Fairy Stories* (1961). Illustrator; *The Real Diary of a Real Boy,* by H. A. Shute (1967); etc.

TUDOR, WILLIAM (Jan. 28, 1779–Mar. 9, 1830); b. Boston, Mass. Editor, author. *Letters on the Eastern States* (anon., 1820); *Miscellanies* (anon., 1821); *The Life of James Otis* (1823); *Gebel Teir* (anon., 1829); etc. Founder, the *North American Review,* 1815; editor, 1815–17. Co-founder, the Anthology Society, 1805, and the Boston Athenaeum, 1805.

TUEL, JOHN E. Author. Wrote also under initials, "J. E. T." and under pen name, "Jet." *The Age of Times: A Satire* (in verse, anon., 1843); *St. Clair; or, the Protégé* (1846); *The Prisoner of Perote* (1848); *Putnam Portraits* (1852); etc.

Tuesday Club. Philadelphia, Pa. Literary club. Charles Brockden Brown, Joseph Dennie, and the other members wrote articles for the *Port Folio,* edited by Joseph Dennie. In 1809 Nicholas Biddle joined the club.

Tuesday Club. Annapolis, Md. Professional society which flourished in the middle of the eighteenth century. Jonas Green, publisher of the *Maryland Gazette,* was secretary and was dubbed "P.P.P.P.P." meaning "poet, printer, punster, purveyor and punchmaker."

Tuesday Evening Club. Boston, Mass. Literary society whose brilliant members supplied many of the articles in the early volumes of the *North American Review.*

TUFTS, JAMES HAYDEN (July 9, 1862–Aug. 5, 1942); b. Monson, Mass. Educator, author. *Ethics* (with John Dewey, 1908); *Our Democracy* (1917); *The Real Business of Living* (1918); *America's Social Morality* (1934); etc. Editor, the *International Journal of Ethics,* 1914–30. Psychology dept., University of Chicago, 1892–1930, prof. 1900–30.

TUGWELL, REXFORD GUY (July 10, 1891–); b. Sinclairville, N.Y. Economist, governor, author. *The Economic Basis of Public Interest* (1922); *American Economic Life* (with others, 1925); *Industry's Coming of Age* (1927); *The Industrial Discipline* (1933); *The Battle for Democracy* (1935); *The*

Fourth Power (1939); *The Stricken Land* (1946); *A Chronicle of Jeopardy* (1955); *The Democratic Roosevelt* (1957); *The Art of Politics* (1958); *The Light of Other Days* (autobiography, 1962); *How They Became President: Thirty-Five Ways to the White House* (1965); *F.D.R.: Architect of an Era* (1967); *Grover Cleveland: A Biography* (1968); *The Brain Trust* (1968); etc. Economics dept., Columbia University, 1920–37; political science dept., University of Chicago, 1946–57. Governor of Puerto Rico, 1941–46.

Tulane Drama Review. See *Drama Review, The.*

Tulips and Chimneys. First collection of poems by E. E. Cummings (1923).

TULLY, ANDREW FREDERICK, JR (Oct. 24, 1914–); b. Southbridge, Mass. Journalist, author. *Era of Elegance* (1947); *Treasury Agent* (1958); *A Race of Rebels* (1960); *CIA: The Inside Story* (1962); *Supreme Court* (1963); *The Time of the Hawk* (1967); *White Tie and Dagger* (1967); etc.

TULLY, JIM (June 3, 1891–June 22, 1947); b. near St. Marys, O. Author. *Emmett Lawler* (1922); *Beggars of Life* (1924); *Jarnegan* (1925); *Circus Parade* (1927); *Shanty Irish* (1928); *Shadows of Men* (1929); *Blood on the Moon* (1931); *Laughter in Hell* (1932); *Men in the Rough* (1933); *A Hollywood Decameron* (1937); *Men I Remember* (1940); *Rave Lafferty* (1943); etc.

TULLY, RICHARD WALTON (May 7, 1877–Jan. 31, 1945); b. Nevada City, Cal. Playwright, producer. *Rose of the Rancho* (with David Belasco, prod. 1906); *Omar, the Tent Maker* (prod. 1914); *His Blossom Bride* (prod. 1927); etc.

Tulsa Tribune. Tulsa, Okla. Newspaper. Founded 1904, as the *Tulsa-Democrat;* in 1919, became first the *Tulsa-Tribune-Democrat,* then the *Tulsa Tribune.* J. L. Jones is publisher and editor. Combined with the *Tulsa World* (q.v.), a morning paper. The *Tribune* appears evenings, except Sunday.

Tulsa World. Tulsa, Okla. Newspaper. Founded 1905. Byron V. Boone is publisher; Sid Steen is editor. See *Tulsa Tribune.*

TUNISON, JOSEPH S[alathiel] (Nov. 9, 1849–1916); b. Bucyrus, O. Journalist, author. *Master Virgil* (1890); *Dramatic Traditions of the Dark Ages* (1907); etc. On staff, the *Cincinnati Gazette,* 1874–83; the *New York Tribune,* 1884–96; etc.

TUNLEY, ROUL (May 12, 1912–); b. Chicago, Ill. Editor, author. *Kids, Crime and Chaos* (1962); *The American Health Scandal* (1966).

TUNNARD, CHRISTOPHER (July 7, 1910–); b. Victoria, B. C., Canada. City planner, author. *Gardens in the Modern Landscape* (1938); *The City of Man* (1953); *American Skyline* (with H. H. Reed, Jr., 1955); *Man-Made America: Chaos or Control* (with B. Pusharev, 1963); etc. Director, City Planning Studies, Yale University, since 1950.

Tunnel of Love, The. Novel by Peter De Vries (1954). One couple wants to adopt a baby and another vouches for their character as foster parents. Satirizes middle-class suburban life and behavior.

TUNNEY, GENE [James Joseph] (May 25, 1897–); b. New York. Executive, athlete. *A Man Must Fight* (1932); *Arms For Living* (autobiography, 1941).

TUPPER, EDITH SESSIONS. Novelist. *By a Hair's Breadth* (1889); *By Whose Hand?* (1889); *Hearts Triumphant* (1906); *The Stuff of Dreams* (1908).

TUPPER, FREDERICK (Dec. 17, 1871–Feb. 11, 1950); b. Charleston, S.C. Educator, editor. Editor: *Representative English Dramas from Dryden to Sheridan* (with James W. Tupper, 1914); *Walter Map's Courtiers' Trifles* (with M. B. Ogle, 1923); *Grandmother Tyler's Book* (1925); *Types of Society in Medieval Literature* (1926); etc. Prof. English, University of Vermont, from 1894.

TUPPER, JAMES WADDELL (Mar. 31, 1870–June 2, 1953); b. Sheet Harbor, N.S. Educator, editor. Editor: *Representative English Dramas from Dryden to Sheridan* (with Frederick Tupper, 1914); *Narrative and Lyric Poems* (1927); *English Poems from Dryden to Blake* (1933); etc. English dept., Lafayette College, from 1906.

TUPPER, SAMUEL; b. in Atlanta, Ga. Novelist. *Some Go Up* (1931); *Old Lady's Shoes* (1934).

TUPPER, TRISTRAM (Sept. 11, 1886–Dec. 30, 1954); b. in Caroline Co., Va. Author. *The House of Five Swords* (1922); *Adventuring* (1923); *Jorgensen* (1926); *The River* (1927); *A Storm at the Cross-Roads* (1930); *Ambrose* (1951).

TURBYFILL, MARK (1896–); b. Wynnewood, Okla. Poet. *The Living Frieze* (1921); *Evaporation* (1923); *A Marriage with Space* (1927); etc.

TURELL, JANE (Feb. 25, 1708–Mar. 26, 1745); b. Boston, Mass. Poet. See Benjamin Colman's *Reliquiae Turellae, et Lachrymae Paternae* (1735). This book contains two sermons on her death by her father, Benjamin Colman, and a memoir of her by her husband, Ebenezer Turell, which includes her poems.

Turmoil. Novel by Booth Tarkington (1915). Big Business, personified in old Sheridan of the Sheridan Trust Company, dominates the life of a middlewestern city and converts its earlier charm into noise and smoke and industry.

Turn of the Screw, The. By Henry James (1898). Terrifying ghost story about two children who are haunted by the evil spirits of a pair of vengeful servants who seek to gain possession of the children's souls. Regarded as a classic of its kind.

TURNBULL, AGNES SLIGH (Mrs. James Lyall Turnbull); (Oct. 14, 1888–); b. New Alexandria, Pa. Author. *Far Above Rubies* (1926); *The Wife of Pontius Pilate* (1928); *In the Garden* (1929); *The Four Marys* (1932); *Old Home Town* (1933); *This Spring of Love* (1934); *The Rolling Years* (1936); *Remember the End* (1938); *Elijah the Fish-bite* (1940); *Dear Me, a Diary* (1941); *The Day Must Dawn* (1942); *The Bishop's Mantle* (1947); *The Gown of Glory* (1952); *The Golden Journey* (1955); *Out of My Heart* (1958); *The Nightingale* (1960); *The King's Orchard* (1963); *Little Christmas* (1964); *George* (1965); *The Wedding Bargain* (1966); *Many a Green Isle* (1968); *The White Lark* (1968); etc.

TURNBULL, MARGARET (d. June 12, 1942); b. Glasgow, Scot. Author. *Classmates* (with William C. De Mille, prod. 1907); *W.A.G.'s Tale* (1913); *Looking After Sandy* (1914); *Alabaster Lamps* (1925); *Rogues' March* (1928); *In The Bride's Mirror* (1934); etc.

TURNER, EDWARD RAYMOND (May 28, 1881–Dec. 31, 1929); b. Baltimore, Md. Educator, historian. *Ireland and England* (1919); *Europe, 1789–1920* (1920); *Europe Since 1870* (1921); *Europe, 1450–1789* (1923); *Europe Since 1789* (1924); *The Privy Council of England in the Seventeenth and Eighteenth Centuries,* 2v. (1927–28); etc. Prof. European history, University of Michigan, 1911–24; Yale University, 1924–25; John Hopkins University, 1925–29.

TURNER, FREDERICK JACKSON (Nov. 14, 1861–Mar. 14, 1932); b. Portage, Wis. Educator, historian of the Frontier. *The Significance of the Frontier in American History* (1893); *Rise of the New West, 1819–1829* (1906); *The Frontier in American History* (1920); *The Significance of Sections in American History* (1932, Pulitzer Prize for American history, 1933); *The United States, 1830–1850* (1935); *The Early Writings* (1938); etc. History dept., University of Michigan, 1885–1910; prof. history, Harvard University, 1910–24. *See* W. R. Jacobs' *Frederick Jackson Turner's Legacy* (1965).

TURNER, GEORGE KIBBE (Mar. 23, 1869–Feb. 15, 1952); b. Quincy, Ill. Author. *The Taskmasters* (1902); *Memories of a Doctor* (1913); *Red Friday* (1919); *Hagar's Hoard* (1920);

White Shoulders (1921); etc. Editorial staff, *McClure's Magazine*, 1906–17.

TURNER, LIDA LARRIMORE (Mrs. Charles Edwin Thomas) (June 27, 1897–); b. Girdletree, Md. Writes under name "Lida Larrimore." Author. *The Blossoming of Patricia-the-Less* (1924); *Tarpaner Palace* (1928); *Mulberry Square* (1930); *Robin Hill* (1932); *No Lovelier Spring* (1935); *Stars Still Shine* (1940); *Jonathan's Daughter* (1943); *The Silver Flute* (1945); *Each Shining Hour* (1948); *The Lovely Duckling* (1951); etc.

TURNER, NANCY BYRD (July 29, 1880–); b. Boydton, Va. Author. *A Riband on My Rein* (poems, 1929); *The Mother of Washington* (with Sidney Gunn, 1930); *In the Days of Young Washington* (1931); *Star in a Well* (poems, 1935); *Hopskips* (with Gertrude Nichols, 1940); *When It Rained Cats and Dogs* (1946); etc. Editor of children's page, *Youth's Companion*, 1918–22. On editorial staff, Houghton, Mifflin Co., etc.

TURPIN, EDNA HENRY LEE (July 26, 1869–June 7, 1952); b. Mecklenburg Co., Va. Author. *Happy Acres* (1913); *Whistling Jimps* (1922); *Cotton* (1924); *The Old Mine's Secret* (1925); *Honey-Sweet* (1927); *Echo Hill* (1933); *Lost Covers* (1937); *Zickle's Luck* (1938); *Story of Virginia* (1949); etc.

TURRELL, CHARLES ALFRED (Oct. 15, 1875–Dec. 23, 1961); b. Fishkill, N.Y. Educator, editor. Editor: *Spanish-American Short Stories* (1921); etc. Prof. modern languages, University of Arizona, 1904–24; prof. romance languages, Oregon Institute of Technology, 1934–37.

TUSIANI, JOSEPH (Jan. 14, 1924–   ); b. Foggia, It. Educator, author. *Two Critical Essays on Emily Dickinson* (1952); *The Complete Poems of Michelangelo* (1960); *Rind and All* (poems, 1962); *Lust and Liberty: The Poems of Machiavelli* (1963); *The Fifth Season* (1963); *Dante's Inferno Introduced to Young People* (1964); *Envoy from Heaven* (1965); and other volumes in Italian.

TUTTLE, EMMA ROOD (Mrs. Hudson Tuttle) (b. July 21, 1838); b. Braceville, O. Poet. *Blossoms of Our Spring* (with husband, 1864); *From Soul to Soul* (1890).

TUTTLE, JULIUS HERBERT (Mar. 7, 1857–Feb. 10, 1945); b. Littleton, Mass. Librarian, author. *The Libraries of the Mathers* (1910); etc. With Massachusetts Historical Society, 1878–1934, librarian, 1919–34; Asst. editor, its *Proceedings*, 1909–34.

TUTTLE, MARGARETTA [Muhlenberg] (1880–); b. Cincinnati, O. Author. *His Worldly Goods* (1912); *Feet of Clay* (1923); *The Cobweb* (1925); *Kingdoms of the World* (1927); etc.

TUVE, ROSEMOND (Nov. 27, 1903–Dec. 20, 1964); b. Canton S.D. Educator. *Seasons and Months* (1933); *Elizabethan and Metaphysical Imagery* (1947); *A Reading of George Herbert* (1952); *Allegorical Imagery: Some Medieval Books and Their Posterity* (1966); *Essays on Spenser, Herbert and Milton* (1969); etc. Prof. English, Connecticut College, from 1947.

TV Guide. Radnor, Pa. Weekly. Founded 1953. Printed in seventy-nine separate editions. Edited by Merritt Panitt. Consists essentially of a weekly listing of television programs, with short articles on current, popular television topics and personalities. Acquired by *Philadelphia Inquirer* in 1969.

Twain, Mark. Pen name of Samuel Langhorne Clemens. He first used the name in the *Territorial Enterprise* in 1862. It had been used earlier by Isaiah Sellers in the *New Orleans Picayune*. It was an expression used by the leadsmen on Mississippi steamboats to designate a certain depth of water, specifically, two fathoms, or twelve feet.

Tweed, Mrs. Harrison. See Michael Strange.

Twentieth Century Literature. Denver, Colo., Los Angeles, Cal. Quarterly. Founded 1955. Published articles on modern literature. Alan Swallow was the first editor.

Twentieth Century Short Stories. Ed. by Sylvia Chatfield Bates (1933). A selection of stories with biographical notes on their authors.

Twenty Years at Hull House. By Jane Addams (1910). Autobiographical account of social settlement work in Chicago told by a pioneer in the field.

Twice a Year. New York. Semi-annual literary magazine of literature, the arts, and civil liberties. Founded 1938. Noted for its translations of European authors. Contributors included Henry Miller, William Saroyan, and Kenneth Patchen. Discontinued 1948.

Twice-Told Tales. By Nathaniel Hawthorne, 2 series (1837, 1847). Old New England tales and legends, embellished and refined through the literary genius of an author who sensed their dramatic value.

TWICHELL, JOSEPH HOPKINS (May 27, 1838–Dec. 20, 1918); b. Southington, Conn. Congregational clergyman, author. *John Winthrop* (1891). Editor: *Some Old Puritan Love-Letters: John and Margaret Winthrop: 1618–1638* (1893). During his fifty years as minister in Hartford, Conn., he became a member of the literary group which included Mark Twain, Harriet Beecher Stowe, Charles Dudley Warner, and others; he accompanied Mark Twain on his travels, and is the "Harris" of *A Tramp Abroad.*

Two Little Confederates. Boy's book by Thomas Nelson Page (1888). Frank and Willy, Southern boys, have many adventures during the Civil War, and play a part in trapping a group of marauding Union soldiers.

Two Lives. Autobiographical sonnet sequence by William Ellery Leonard (1925).

"Two Mysteries, The." Poem by Mary Mapes Dodge, in *Scribner's Monthly,* Oct., 1876. It was inspired by the death of a child. Wrongly attributed to Walt Whitman.

Two-Way Passage. By Louis Adamic (1941). Suggests an experiment involving Americans of European background who would teach Europeans about the American way of life.

Two Worlds. New York. Literary quarterly. Founded, 1925. Expired, 1927.

Two Years Before the Mast. By Richard H. Dana (1840). Classic record of a sailor's life in the days of the sailing ship. Dana graduated from Harvard in 1837 and sailed on the brig *Pilgrim* around Cape Horn to California and back.

TYBOUT, ELLA MIDDLETON MAXWELL, b. near New Castle, Del. Author. *Poketown People* (1904); *The Wife of the Secretary of State* (1905); *The Smuggler* (1907).

TYLER, JOHN (Mar. 20, 1790–Jan. 18, 1862); b. "Greenway," Charles City Co., Va. Tenth president of the United States. Congressman, 1816–21; Governor of Virginia, 1825–27; U. S. Senator, 1827–36; Confederate Congressman, 1861. *See* Hiram Cumming's *Secret History of the Tyler Dynasty* (anon., 1845); Lyon G. Tyler's *The Letters and Times of the Tylers*, 3v. (1884–96); Oliver P. Chitwood's *John Tyler* (1939).

TYLER, LYON GARDINER (Aug. 1853–Feb. 12, 1935); b. in Charles City, Va., son of President John Tyler. Educator, author. *The Letters and Times of the Tylers*, 3v. (1884–96); *The Cradle of the Republic* (1900); *England in America. 1580–1652* (1904); *Williamsburg, the Colonial Capital* (1907); *Ripples of Rhyme* (1933); etc. Editor: *Narratives of Early Virginia, 1606–1625* (1907); *Encyclopedia of Virginia Biography*, 5v. (1915). Pres., College of William and Mary, 1888–1919.

TYLER, MOSES COIT (Aug. 2, 1835–Dec. 28, 1900); b. Griswold, Conn. Educator, author. *The Brawnville Papers* (1869); *A History of American Literature during the Colonial Time 1607–1765,* 2v. (1878); *Patrick Henry* (1887); *Three Men of Letters* (1895); *The Literary History of the American Revolution 1763–1783,* 2v. (1897); *Glimpses of England* (1898). Prof. English literature, University of Michigan, 1867–81; prof. American history, Cornell University, 1881–1900. *See* H. M. Jones's *The Life of Moses Coit Tyler* (1933).

TYLER, PARKER (1907–); b. New Orleans, La. Poet, critic. *The Young and Evil* (with C. H. Ford, 1933); *The Metaphor in the Jungle* (poems, 1940); *The Hollywood Hallucination* (1944); *The Granite Butterfly* (poems, 1945); *Yesterday's Children* (poems, 1947); *Magic and Myth of the Movies* (1947); *Chaplin: Last of the Clowns* (1948); *The Three Faces of the Film* (1960; rev. ed. 1967); *The Divine Comedy of Pavel Tchelitchew: A Biography* (1967); *Classics of the Foreign Film: A Pictorial Treasury* (1967); etc.

TYLER, ROBERT (Sept. 9, 1816–Dec. 3, 1877); b. in Charles City Co., Va., son of President John Tyler. Lawyer, editor, poet. *Ahasuerus* (poem, 1842); *Death; or, Medorus's Dream* (poem, 1843); etc. Editor, the *Montgomery Mail and Advertiser.*

TYLER, ROYALL (July 18, 1757–Aug. 26, 1826); b. Boston, Mass. Jurist, poet, novelist, playwright. *The Contrast* (prod. 1787); *May Day in Town; or, New York in an Uproar* (1787); *The Algerine Captive,* 2v. (1797); *The Georgia Spec; or, Land in the Moon* (1797); *The Yankey in London,* v. I (anon., 1809), of which no further vols. were published; *The Chestnut Tree* (poem, 1931), written in 1824; *The Farm House; or, The Female Duellists* (n.d.); etc. He was "Spondee" in the "Colon and Spondee" column of the *Farmers' Weekly Museum* and other magazines, Joseph Dennie being "Colon." *See* Milton Ellis's *Joseph Dennie and His Circle* (1915); *Grandmother Tyler's Book* (1925), ed. by Frederick Tupper.

TYNG, STEPHEN HIGGINSON (Mar. 1, 1800–Sept. 3, 1885); b. Newburyport, Mass. Episcopal clergyman, author. *Recollections of England* (1847); *The Rich Kinsman* (1855); *Forty Years' Experience in Sunday Schools* (1860); etc.

Typee. Novel by Herman Melville (1854). Record of the author's sojourn in the Marquesas Islands in the South Seas, embellished with a romantic story of adventure among cannibals. Melville was in these islands in 1842.

Typographic Miscellany. By Joel Munsell (1850). Essays on numerous subjects connected with the graphic arts. Contains material on the publishers and printers of the time.

Tyranny of Words, The. By Stuart Chase (1938). Discussion of the confusions that arise from misinterpreting and misunderstanding the meanings of words. Popularized the study of semantics.

U

U. S. A. Trilogy of novels, by John Dos Passos (1938). The separate parts are *The 42nd Parallel* (1930), *1919* (1932), and *The Big Money* (1936). These works treat the social forces of the twentieth century as an underlying theme to which the characters themselves are subordinated. By means of various literary devices adapted from techniques of the mass media, Dos Passos narrates dramatically the changes in American life influenced by commercialism and loss of national purpose.

U.S. 40. Description, in words and photographs, of the transcontinental highway, by George R. Stewart (1953).

UDALL, STEWART LEE (Jan. 31, 1920–); b. St. Johns, Ariz. Government official, author. *The Quiet Crisis* (1963); *The Conservation Challenge of the Sixties* (1963); *The National Parks of America* (1966). U.S. Secretary of the Interior, 1961–69.

Ugly Club. New York. Literary club founded by a group of New York writers. Fitz-Green Halleck was a leading member. The club met in "Ugly Hall," near Broadway and Wall Street.

UHLAN, EDWARD (Oct. 12, 1912–); b. New York. Publisher, author. *The Rogue of Publishers' Row* (1955); *Dynamo Jim Stiles* (1959); *What Every Writer Should Know About Publishing* (1962); etc. Pres., Exposition Press, since 1950.

UKERS, WILLIAM HARRISON (July 30, 1873–Jan. 19, 1954); b. Philadelphia, Pa. Author. *All about Coffee* (1922); *A Trip to Brazil* (1924); *A Trip to China* (1926); *All About Tea,* 2v. (1935); *The Romance of Tea* (1936); etc.

"Ulalume." Poem by Edgar Allan Poe (1847).

ULANOV, BARRY (Apr. 10, 1918–); b. New York. Educator, author. *The Recorded Music of Mozart* (1941); *Duke Ellington* (1946); *A Handbook of Jazz* (1957); *Sources and Resources* (1960); *The Making of a Modern Saint: A Biographical Study of Thérèse of Lisieux* (1966); etc. Co-translator: *Bernanos' Last Essays* (1955); *Mother Marie des Douleurs' Joy Out of Sorrow* (1958). Editor, *Metronome Magazine,* 1943–55. English dept., Barnard College, since 1951.

ULLMAN, JAMES RAMSEY (Nov. 24, 1907–June 20, 1971); b. New York. Author. *Mad Shelley* (1930); *High Conquest* (1941); *The White Tower* (1945); *River of the Sun* (1951); *Windom's Way* (1952); *The Sands of Karakorum* (1953); *The Age of Mountaineering* (1954); *The Day on Fire* (1958); *Fia Fia* (1962); *Where the Bong Tree Grows* (1963); *Americans on Everest* (1964); *Straight Up* (1967); *None but Ourselves* (1970).

ULMANN, ALBERT (July 2, 1861–Oct. 8, 1948); b. New York. Author. *Frederick Struthers' Romance* (1889); *Chaperoned* (1894); *A Landmark History of New York* (1901, revised 1939); *Tales of Old New York* (with Grace C. Strachan, 1914).

ULRICH, CHARLES KENMORE (1861–July 5, 1941); b. Cincinnati, O. Journalist, novelist, playwright. *The Dawn of Liberty* (1906); *In Plum Valley* (1915); *Fires of Faith* (1919); *The Wolf of Purple Canyon* (1921); etc. Joined staff of *Cincinnati Enquirer* in 1877. He was also with newspapers in New York, Chicago, San Francisco and Denver, until his retirement in 1931.

ULRICH, HOMER (Mar. 27, 1906–); b. Chicago, Ill. Music historian. *Chamber Music* (1948); *The Education of a Concert-Goer* (1949); *Symphonic Music* (1952); *Music: A Design for Listening* (1957); *History of Music and Musical Style* (1963); etc. Music dept., University of Maryland, since 1953.

ULVESTAD, MARTIN (b. Dec. 24, 1865–); b. in Norway. Author. *English-Norwegian Dictionary* (1895); *History and Record of the Norwegians in America,* 2v. (1907–13).

Uncle Ray. Pen name of Ramon Coffman.

Uncle Remus. By Joel Chandler Harris (1880). Fables told by an elderly Negro to a little boy, a melange of folklore and pleasant memories of slavery. Written in a distinctively sensitive representation of dialect speech.

Uncle Remus Magazine. Atlanta, Ga. Monthly. Founded 1907, superseding *Sunny South.* Absorbed the *Home Magazine,* 1908. Absorbed by *Pulitzer's Magazine,* c. 1913.

Uncle Tom's Cabin. Novel by Harriet Beecher Stowe, 2v. (1852). It first appeared serially in the *National Era,* Washington, D.C., from June 5, 1851 to Apr. 1, 1852. Published in book form in two volumes, Mar. 20, 1852, by Jewett & Co., Boston. This American classic, which fanned the controversy between the North and the South on the subject of Negro slavery, relates the story of little Eva, Topsy, Uncle Tom, and the brutal slave driver, Simon Legree. The climax of the story is the flight of the slave girl Eliza, with her baby, across broken ice, pursued by the villain. The book broke all sales records of the time. Dramatized by George L. Aiken (1852). At least fourteen pro-slavery novels followed *Uncle Tom's Cabin*, among which were L. B. Chase's *English Serfdom and American Slavery* (1854); J. W. Page's *Uncle Robin in His Cabin in Virginia and Tom without One in Boston* (1855); and S. H. Elliott's *New England Chatells* (1858). *Pro-Slavery Argument* (1852) was a collection of material from the novels and essays which followed the publication of *Uncle Tom's Cabin*.

Uncle Tom's Tenement. By Alice Marland Wellington Rollins (1888). Based on tenement life in New York City. A reform book.

Uncle Wiggily. Series of books for children by Howard R. Garis.

Undefeated, The. Short story by Ernest Hemingway (1927).

Under the Gaslight. Melodrama by Augustin Daly (prod. 1867). Laura Courtlandt, reared by a family of wealth, discovers that she is the daughter of a criminal. Her lover deserts her, and she descends to dire poverty. The climax of the play is her rescue from an oncoming locomotive by a one-armed soldier.

"Under the spreading chestnut tree." Familiar opening line of "The Village Blacksmith," poem by Henry Wadsworth Longfellow.

Underground press. Periodicals, usually weeklies, ranging from dissident to radical and revolutionary in social and political outlook. Their concerns include anarchism, pacifism, sexual freedom, women's liberation, rights of minority groups, drugs, ecology, and rock music, among others identified with the so-called youth culture, or counter culture, of the 1960's. Among such periodicals have been *The Realist, New Left Notes, The Los Angeles Free Press, The Berkeley Barb, The East Village Other, Rat, Rolling Stone, Zap Comics*. The Underground Press Syndicate, founded in 1966, was organized by the *East Village Other* of New York, the *Los Angeles Free Press*, the *Berkeley Barb*, East Lansing's *The Paper*, and Detroit's *The Fifth Estate* to share material, advertising, and profits. *Los Angeles Free Press* was the first (1964). By 1971 there were 700 such publications with a circulation of 20 million.

Underground Press Digest. New York. Founded 1971. Published and edited by Robert W. Farrell. Condenses articles from the underground press.

UNDERHILL, John Garrett (Jan. 10, 1876–May 15, 1946); b. Brooklyn, N.Y. Editor, author. *Spanish Literature in the England of the Tudors* (1899); etc. Translator: *Plays by Jacinto Benavente*, 4 series (1917–24); *Plays of G. Martinez Sierra*, 2v. (1923); *Four Plays by Lope de Vega* (1936); etc. Editor, *Poet Lore*, 1918.

UNDERHILL, RUTH MURRAY (Aug. 22, 1884–); b. Ossining, N.Y. Ethnologist, author. *First Penthouse Dwellers of America* (1938); *Social Organization of the Papago Indians* (1939); *Hawk Over Whirlpools* (1940); *Papago Indian Religion* (1946); *Red Man's America* (1953); *The Navajos* (1956); *First Came The Family* (1958); *Beaverbird* (1959); Editor: *Autobiography of a Papago Woman* [Chona] (1936). Prof. anthropology, Denver University, 1949–52.

UNDERHILL, ZOE DANA (Mrs. Walter Mitchell Underhill) (Mar. 4, 1847–Dec. 5, 1934); b. Brook Farm, West Roxbury, Mass., daughter of Charles A. Dana. Compiler and translator: *The Dwarfs' Tailor, and Other Fairy Tales* (1896).

Understanding Media. By Marshall McLuhan (1964). An explanation of modern social reality in terms of the psychological and esthetic influence of technology, especially the mass media. "McLuhanism" has come to mean a belief in the effectiveness of forms of information regardless of content.

Understanding Poetry. Textbook of poetic appreciation by Robert Penn Warren and Cleanth Brooks (1939). The most thorough application of the principles of the New Criticism in textbook form.

UNDERWOOD, CHARLOTTE (Mar. 5, 1914–); b. Cincinnati, O. Author, translator. Writes under pen name "Joan Charles." *The Dark Glass* (1944); *Son and Stranger* (1945); *And the Hunter Home* (1946); etc. Translator of works by André Maurois, Honoré de Balzac, and Gustave Flaubert.

UNDERWOOD, EDNA WORTHLEY (1873–); b. Phillips, Me. Poet, novelist. *A Book of Dear Dead Women* (1911); *Garden of Desire* (poems, 1913); *Songs from the Plains* (1917); *Attic Twilights* (1918); *Egyptian Twilights* (1918); *The Whirlwind* (1919); *Maine Summers* (poems, 1940); etc. Compiler and translator: *The Slav Anthology* (1931); *Anthology of Mexican Poets* (1932); *The Poets of Haiti, 1782–1934* (1934).

UNDERWOOD, FRANCIS HENRY (Jan. 12, 1825–Aug. 7, 1894); b. Enfield, Mass. Lawyer, diplomat, author. *A Hand-Book of English Literature ... British Authors* (1871); *A Hand-Book of English Literature ... American Authors* (1872); *Cloud-Pictures* (1872); *Lord of Himself* (1874); *Henry Wadsworth Longfellow* (1882); *John Greenleaf Whittier* (1884); *Man Proposes* (1885); *Quabbin: the Story of a Small Town* (1893); *James Russell Lowell* (1895); *Doctor Gray's Quest* (1895); etc. While on the staff of the publishing house of Phillips, Sampson & Co., Boston, he proposed the founding of the *Atlantic Monthly*.

UNDERWOOD, JOHN CURTIS (July 26, 1874–); b. Rockford, Ill. Poet. *The Iron Muse* (1910); *Americans* (1912); *Literature and Insurgency* (1914); *Processionals* (1915); *War Flames* (1917); *Trail's End* (1921); *Pioneers* (1923); *Interpreters* (1939).

Underwood, Sophie Kerr. See Sophie Kerr.

Undiscovered Country, The. Novel by W. D. Howells (1880). A country doctor becomes interested in spiritualistic manifestations and believes that his delicate and nervous daughter is a medium. Branded as a faker, he seeks refuge in a Shaker community with his daughter.

UNGER, GLADYS BUCHANAN (d. May 25, 1940); b. San Francisco, Cal. Playwright. *Edmund Kean* (prod. 1903); *The Knave of Hearts* (prod. 1907); *The Son and Heir* (prod. 1913); *Toto* (prod. 1916); *Our Mr. Hepplewhite* (prod. 1919); *Two Girls Wanted* (prod. 1926); *Ladies of Creation* (prod. 1931); etc.

UNGERER, JEAN TOMI (Nov. 28, 1931–); b. Strasbourg, Fr. Illustrator, author. *The Mellops Go Flying* (1957); *Adelaide* (1959); *Moon Man* (1966); *The Hat* (1969); *The Fornicon* (1969); *Compromises* (1969); etc.

Unified Encyclopedia. See *Grolier Encyclopedia*.

Union Catalog of the Library of Congress. A cooperative check list of the books in various American libraries, designed to assist scholars in locating copies of any given book.

"Union Forever, The." Civil War song written and composed by William Shakespeare Hays (1861).

Union List of Serials. Published in New York (1927). Ed. by Winifred Gregory, with an advisory committee consisting of H. M. Lydenburg, C. W. Andrews, Nathan Van Patten, Willard Austen, A. E. Bostwick, and J. T. Gerould. It is kept up to date with *Supplements*. A comprehensive cooperative list of periodicals showing where files of each may be found in the

United States and Canada. The third edition was edited in five volumes by E. B. Titus (1965).

Union Magazine of Literature and Art. New York. Founded July, 1847, by Israel Post. Caroline W. Kirkland was its first editor. Poe's "To Helen" appeared in the Nov., 1848 number. John Sartain, noted engraver, bought the magazine in 1848, renaming it *Sartain's Union Magazine of Literature and Art,* and moving it to Philadelphia. It was distinguished by fine engravings, and articles by the leading writers of the period, particularly women.

Union Now. By Clarence K. Streit (1939). Controversial book advocating the federal union of the United States and Great Britain and the other democracies for the purpose of guaranteeing world peace.

Union Square. Novel by Albert Halper (1933). Deals with the famous square in New York, and the struggles of the poor.

United Fraternity. Literary society at Dartmouth College. Founded 1786. Disbanded 1904. Its library is now a part of the college library.

United Nations World. See *Free World.*

United Service. Philadelphia and New York. Military and naval magazine. Founded Jan. 1879, by Lewis R. Hamersly. Editors: Lewis R. Hamersly and George A. Woodward, 1879–84; T. H. S. Hamersly, 1885–86; L. R. Hamersly, 1889–1904; Lewis R. Hamersly, Jr., 1904–05; W. D. Walker, 1906–08; T. N. Horn, 1908–09; W. D. Walker, 1909. In 1906 it became *Army and Navy Life and United Service;* in 1908, *Army and Navy Life;* and in 1909, *Uncle Sam's Magazine.* Besides military and naval intelligence it featured fiction of a high order, chiefly sea tales and military adventures. Expired 1909. See Frank L. Mott's *History of American Magazines,* v. 3 (1938).

United States Book Company. New York. Founded 1890. Not to be confused with the American Book Company, founded the same year. The United States Book Company was a large distributor of cheap reprints.

United States Catalogue. New York. Published by H. W. Wilson Co. An index to books in print. First edition, 1900, second edition, 1903, third edition, 1912, all ed. by Marion E. Potter; fourth edition, 1928, ed. by Mary Burnham and Carol Hurd, who have edited subsequent cumulations. Continued as *Cumulative Book Index,* 1932, the first permanent supplement to the fourth edition. Another permanent supplement was published in 1938. Annual supplements keep the work up to date. Gives author, title, date, publisher and price of books in print.

United States Literary Gazette. Boston, Mass. Founded Apr., 1824. James G. Carter and Theophilus Parsons were editors. In 1826 it became the *United States Review and Literary Gazette.* Longfellow and Bryant were among the contributors. Expired Sept., 1826. See *Miscellaneous Poems Selected from the United States Literary Gazette* (1826).

United States Magazine. New York. Monthly. Founded May 15, 1854, by Alexander Jones. Seba Smith was editor. In 1857 its name was changed to *Emerson's United States Magazine,* and later in the same year it absorbed *Putnam's Monthly* and became *Emerson's Magazine and Putnam's Monthly.* Expired Nov., 1858.

United States News & World Report. Washington, D.C. Weekly. Founded 1946 by David Lawrence as *World Report* and merged with his *United States News* (founded 1933) in the same year.

United States Service Magazine. New York. Founded Jan., 1864. Its chief editor was Henry Coppee. Noted for its Civil War literature. Expired June, 1866.

Unity of God. Celebrated sermon by Samuel Cooper Thacher (1817). A defense of Unitarianism.

Universalist, The. Boston, Mass. Monthly family magazine. Founded 1832. In 1839 the title was changed to the *Universalist and Ladies' Repository;* and in 1843, to the *Ladies Repository; A Universalist Monthly Magazine for the Home Circle.* Expired 1873.

University Club. New York. Founded Apr., 28, 1865. Its purpose is to promote literature and the arts, and it maintains an art gallery and library. The club building is noted for its architectural details and its furnishings.

University of California Press. Berkeley, California. Founded 1893. Noted for scholarly and scientific nonfiction, translations, and professional journals.

University of Chicago Press. Chicago. Founded 1891. Publishes scholarly books and journals. *Phoenix Books* is its paperbound imprint. Its notable journals include *The American Journal of Sociology, Comparative Politics, The Journal of Modern History, The Library Quarterly, Technology and Culture.*

University of Illinois Press. Urbana, Ill. Founded 1918.

University of Michigan Press. Ann Arbor, Michigan. Founded 1930.

University of Minnesota Press. Minneapolis, Minn. Founded 1925. Publishes scholarly books. Directed by John Ervin, Jr.

University of Nebraska Press. Lincoln, Neb. Founded 1941. Specializes in general scholarly fiction, regional history, and poetry.

University of New Mexico Press. Albuquerque, N.M. Founded 1930. Publishes scholarly books, especially those dealing with the Southwest. Also publishes *New Mexico Quarterly.*

University of North Carolina Press. Chapel Hill, N.C. Founded 1922.

University of Oklahoma Press. Norman, Okla. Founded 1928. Joseph A. Brandt was director, 1928–38. Specializes in Indian and pioneer periods.

University of Pennsylvania Press. Philadelphia, Pa. Founded 1927.

University of Pittsburgh Press. Pittsburgh, Pa. Founded 1937. Publishes scholarly books in all fields. Director and editor is Frederick A. Hetzel.

University of Wisconsin Press. Madison, Wis. Founded 1937.

Unleavened Bread. Novel by Robert Grant (1900). Story of Selma White's unscrupulous attempt to climb the social ladder regardless of the cost, including the honor of her husband.

"Unmanifest Destiny." Poem by Richard Hovey (1898).

Unquiet. Autobiographical novel by Joseph Gollomb (1935). A story of youth in the dirty, crowded streets of New York.

UNTERECKER, JOHN (Dec. 14, 1922–   ); b. Buffalo, N.Y. Author. *A Reader's Guide to W. B. Yeats* (1959); *Lawrence Durrell* (1964); *The Dreaming Zoo* (1965); *Voyager: The Life of Hart Crane* (1969).

UNTERMEYER, JEAN STARR (May 13, 1886–June 27, 1970); b. Zanesville, O. Poet. *Growing Pains* (1918); *Dreams out of Darkness* (1921); *Steep Ascent* (1927); *Winged Child* (1936); *Love and Need: Collected Poems* (1940); *Private Collection, A Memoir* (1965); *Job's Daughter* (1967); *Re-Creation* (1970).

UNTERMEYER, LOUIS (Oct. 1, 1885–); b. New York. Poet, editor, anthologist. *The Younger Quire* (1910); *First Love* (1911); *Challenge* (1914); *These Times* (1917); *The New Adam* (1920); *American Poetry Since 1900* (1923); *Roast*

Leviathan (1923); *Collected Parodies* (1926); *Burning Bush* (1928); *Moses* (1928); *The Donkey of God* (1932); *Chip* (1933); *The Last Pirate* (1934); *Selected Poems and Parodies* (1935); *Heinrich Heine* (1937); *Doorways to Poetry* (1937); *Play in Poetry* (1938); *From Another World* (autobiography, 1939); *Makers of the Modern World* (1955); *Lives of the Poets* (1959); *Long Feud* (poems, 1962); *Bygones: An Autobiography* (1965); etc. Editor: *Modern American Poetry* (1919, rev. ed. 1936); *Modern British Poetry* (1920, rev. ed. 1936); *This Singing World* (1923); *Yesterday and Today* (1927); *American Poetry from the Beginning to Whitman* (1931); *The Book of Living Verse* (1932); *A Treasury of Great Poems* (1955); *A Treasury of Ribaldry* (1956); *Lots of Limericks* (1961); *The Letters of Robert Frost to Louis Untermeyer* (1963); *Songs of Joy from the Book of Psalms* (1967); *Merry Christmas* (1967).

UNWIN, NORA SPICER (Feb. 22, 1907–); b. Surbiton, Eng. Artist, author. Author, illustrator: *Round the Year* (1940); *Doughnuts for Lin* (1950); *Poquito* (1959); *Too, Too Many* (1962); *The Way of the Shepherd* (1963); *Joyful the Morning* (1963); *The Midsummer Witch* (1966); etc.

Up from Slavery. Autobiography of Booker T. Washington (1901). Born in Virginia, a slave until freed by the Emancipation Proclamation, the author rose to the leadership of his race. Education for the Negro was his major objective.

Up Front. Collection of cartoons by Bill Mauldin (1945). The most famous cartoons about American soldiers in Europe during World War II.

"Up in a Balloon." Song by H. B. Farnie (1869).

Up Stream. Autobiography of Ludwig Lewisohn (1922).

Up the Down Staircase. By Bel Kaufman (1966). Fictional account of the author's experiences as a teacher in the New York City public school system.

UPDEGRAFF, ALLAN [Eugene] (Feb. 14, 1883–Dec., 1965); b. Grinnell, Ia. Editor, novelist, *Second Youth* (1915); *Strayed Revellers* (1918); *Dancers in the Wind* (1925); *Native Soil* (1929); *The Hills Look Down* (1941); *Poems and Impressions* (1953); *Grantham's Moor* (poems, 1960); etc. Editorial staff, the *Literary Digest*, 1918–25.

UPDEGRAFF, ROBERT R[awls] (Apr. 17, 1889–); b. Salt Lake City, Utah. Author. *Captains in Conflict* (1927); *Survey of the Music Industry* (1930); *Yours to Venture* (1937); *All the Time You Need* (1958); etc.

UPDIKE, JOHN (March 18, 1932–); b. Shillington, Pa. Author. *The Carpentered Hen, and Other Tame Creatures* (poems, 1958); *The Same Door* (stories, 1959); *The Poorhouse Fair* (1959); *Rabbit, Run* (1960); *Pigeon Feathers, and Other Stories* (1962); *The Centaur* (1963); *Couples* (1968); *Midpoint* (1969); *Bech: A Book* (1970); etc.

UPHAM, CHARLES WENTWORTH (May 4, 1802–June 15, 1875); b. St. John, N.B. Unitarian clergyman, author. *The Life of General Washington*, 2v. (1851); *Life, Explorations, and Public Services of John Charles Fremont* (1856); *Salem Witchcraft*, 2v. (1867); etc. He was the brother-in-law of Oliver Wendell Holmes, and is said to have been the model for Judge Pyncheon in Hawthorne's *The House of the Seven Gables.*

UPHAM, GRACE LeBARON (b. June 22, 1845–); b. Lowell, Mass. Author. *Little Miss Faith* (1894); *Queer Janet* (1897); *Told under the Cherry Trees* (1899); *The Children of Bedford Court* (1905); etc.

Uprooted. Short story by Ruth Suckow (1926).

UPSON, ARTHUR [Wheelock] (Jan. 10, 1877–1908); b. Camden, N.Y. Poet. *At the Sign of the Harp* (1900); *Westwind Songs* (1902); *Poems* (1902); *The City: A Poem-Drama; and Other Poems* (1905); *The Tides of Spring, and Other Poems* (1907); *The Collected Poems* (1909); *Sonnets and Songs* (1911); etc.

UPSON, WILLIAM HAZLETT (Sept. 26, 1891–); b. Glen Ridge, N.J. Author. *The Piano Movers* (1927); *Me and Henry and the Artillery* (1928); *Alexander Botts: Earthworm Tractors* (1929), and its sequels; *How to be Rich Like Me* (1947); *Hello, Mr. Henderson* (1949); etc.

UPTON, CHARLES ELMER. Author. *Pioneers of El Dorado* (1906); *Down Wild Goose Canyon* (1910).

UPTON, GEORGE PUTNAM (Oct. 25, 1834–May 19, 1919); b. Boston, Mass. Pen name "Peregrine Pickle." Journalist, music critic, author. *Letters of Peregrine Pickle* (1869); *Woman in Music* (1880); *Standard Symphonies* (1889); *Musical Pastels* (1902); *Musical Memories* (1908); *Standard Musical Biographies* (1910); etc. With the *Chicago Tribune*, 1862–1919; music critic, 1863–81, assoc. editor, 1872–1905.

UPTON, WILLIAM TREAT (Dec. 17, 1870–); b. Tallmadge, O. Musicologist, educator, author. *Art-Song in America* (1930); *Anthony Philip Heinrich: A Nineteenth Century Composer in America* (1939); *William Henry Fry* (1954); etc. Music critic, *Oberlin Review*, 1918–36. Piano dept., Oberlin Conservatory of Music, 1898–1936.

URBAN, WILBUR MARSHALL (Mar. 27, 1873–); b. Mt. Joy, Pa. Educator, author. *Valuation* (1909); *The Intelligible World* (1929); *Fundamentals of Ethics* (1930); *Language and Reality* (1939); *Humanity and Deity* (1951). Prof. philosophy, Dartmouth College, 1920–30; Yale University, since 1931.

UREY, HAROLD C[layton] (Apr. 29, 1893–); b. Walkerton, Ind. Chemist. Author: *Atoms, Molecules, and Quanta* (with A. E. Ruark, 1930); *The Planets* (1952). Prof. chemistry, University of California, since 1958.

URIS, LEON (Aug. 3, 1924–); b. Baltimore, Md. Author. *Battle Cry* (1953); *Exodus* (1958); *Mila 18* (1961); *Armageddon* (1964); *Topaz* (1967); etc.

URNER, MABEL HERBERT (Mrs. Lathrop Colgate Harper) (June 28, 1881–Mar., 1957); b. Cincinnati, O. Author. *Journal of a Neglected Wife* (1909); *The Woman Alone* (1914); *The Married Life of Helen and Warren* (1925); etc. Her "Helen and Warren" stories were syndicated in newspapers for over twenty-five years.

US. New York. Quarterly. Founded 1969. Published as a paperback magazine by Bantam Books. Edited by Richard Goldstein. Has published Ed Sanders, Steve Katz, R. Crumb, Richard Kostelanetz, Jim Morrison, and other representatives of Pop Culture writing and graphics.

USHER, ROLAND G[reene] (May 3, 1880–); b. Lynn, Mass. Educator, author. *The Reconstruction of the English Church*, 2v. (1910); *Pan-Germanism* (1913); *The Rise of the American People* (1914); *Pan-Americanism* (1915); *The Pilgrims and Their History* (1918); *The Story of the Great War* (1919); etc. History dept., Washington University, St. Louis, from 1907.

"Usury" canto. Canto XLV of the *Cantos*, by Ezra Pound.

UTLEY, FREDA (Jan. 23, 1898–); b. London. Author. *China at War* (1939); *The Dream We Lost: Soviet Russia Then and Now* (1940); *The High Cost of Vengeance* (1949); *The China Story* (1951); *Will the Middle East Go West?* (1957); etc.

UTLEY, GEORGE BURWELL (Dec. 3, 1876–Oct. 4, 1946); b. Hartford, Conn. Librarian, author. *The Life and Times of Thomas Claggett* (1913); *Fifty Years of the American Library Association* (1926); etc. Secretary, American Library Association, 1911–20. Librarian, Newberry Library, Chicago, 1920–42.

UTTER, REBECCA PALFREY (May, 1844–1905); b. Barnstable, Mass. Poet. *The King's Daughter, and Other Poems* (1888).

UTTER, ROBERT PALFREY (Nov. 23, 1875–Feb. 17, 1936); b. Olympia, Wash. Educator, author. *A Guide to Good*

English (1914); *Every-day Words and Their Uses* (1916); *Pearls and Pepper* (1924); *Pamela's Daughter* (with Gwendolyn Bridges Needham, 1936); etc. English dept., Amherst College, 1906–19; University of California, 1920–36.

UZZELL, THOMAS H. (Oct. 25, 1884–); b. Denver, Colo. Editor, author. *Narrative Technique* (1923); *Writing as a Career* (1938); *Technique of the Novel* (1947); etc. Editor and publisher, *Blue Pencil,* since 1934.

V

V. Novel by Thomas Pyncheon (1963).

V. V.'s Eyes. Novel by Henry Sydnor Harrison (1913). Deals with labor reform.

"V-Letter." Long poem by Karl Shapiro (1944). Thoughts of a soldier in the South Pacific during World War II. Published in *V-Letter, and Other Poems* (1944).

"Vagabondia." Opening poem of *Songs from Vagabondia* by Bliss Carman and Richard Hovey (1894).

VAIL, HENRY HOBART (May 27, 1839–Sept. 2, 1925); b. Pomfret, Vt. Editor, publisher, author. *A History of the McGuffey Readers* (1910); *Pomfret, Vermont,* 2v. (1930). In 1886 he entered the publishing firm of Sargeant, Wilson, Hinkle & Co., Cincinnati, and became a partner in Wilson, Hinkle & Co., in 1874. He remained a partner in the firm of its successor, Van Antwerp, Bragg & Co., which merged with the American Book Co., 1890–1907. Directed and edited *McGuffey's Revised Readers,* beginning in 1878.

VAIL, ROBERT WILLIAM GLENROIE (Mar. 26, 1890–June 21, 1966); b. Victor, N.Y. Librarian, bibliographer, author. *A Message to Garcia* (1930); *The Ulster County Gazette and Its Illegitimate Offspring* (1931); *Susanna Haswell Rowson* (1933); *James Johns, Vermont Pen Printer* (1933); *Random Notes on the History of the Early American Circus* (1934); *Literature of Book Collecting* (1936); *A Guide to the Resources of the American Antiquarian Society* (1937); *The Voice of the Old Frontier* (1949); *Knickerbocker Birthday* (1954); etc. Editor: Sabin's *Bibliotheca Americana: A Dictionary of Books Relating to America,* v. 22–29 (1931–36); etc. With New-York Public Library, 1914–20, 1928–29; librarian, American Antiquarian Society, Worcester, Mass., 1930–39; librarian, New York State Library, Albany, after 1940; director, New York Historical Society, from 1944.

Vain Oblations. Short story by Katharine Fullerton Gerould (1914).

VAJNA, GEORGE (Apr. 18, 1889–May 13, 1968); b. Budapest. Publisher. Founder (1939), pres., Transatlantic Arts.

VAKA, DEMETRA (Mrs. Kenneth Brown) (1877–1947); b. Island of Prinkipo in the Sea of Marmora. Author. *The First Secretary* (with husband, 1907); *Haremlik* (1909); *The Duke's Price* (with husband, 1910); *Finella in Fairyland* (1910); *In the Shadow of Islam* (1911); *A Child of the Orient* (1914); *The Grasp of the Sultan* (1916); *In the Heart of the Balkans* (1917); *The Unveiled Ladies of Stamboul* (1923); *Delarah* (1943); *Bribed to Be Born* (1951); etc.

VALE, GILBERT (1788–Aug. 17, 1866); b. London, Eng. Editor, author. *Fanaticism: Its Source and Influence* (1835); *The Life of Thomas Paine* (1841). Editor, *The Citizen of the World; The Beacon; etc.*

VALENCY, MAURICE [Jacques] (Mar. 22, 1903–); b. New York. Educator, playwright. *The Thracian Horses* (play, 1940); *In Praise of Love* (1958). Translator, adapter: Girau-

doux's *The Madwoman of Chaillot* (prod. 1948), *The Enchanted* (prod. 1950), *Ondine* (prod. 1954), *The Apollo of Bellac* (1957); Duerrenmatt's *The Visit* (prod. 1958); etc. Editor: *The Palace of Pleasure* (1960). Advisory editor, *The Encylopedia of Americana.* Comparative literature dept., Columbia University, since 1946.

VALENTINE, ALAN (Feb. 23, 1901–); b. Glen Cove, N.Y. Educator, author. *The English Novel* (1927); *Biography* (1927); *Dusty Answer* (1941); *The Age of Conformity* (1954); *Vigilante Justice* (1956); *Trial Balance* (1956); *Education of an American* (1958); *Lord George Germain* (1962); *1913: Year of Transition* (1962); *Fathers to Sons* (1963); *Lord North,* 2v. (1967); *The Establishment, 1760–84,* 2v. (1968); *Lord Stirling* (1968); etc. Editor: *Oxford of Today* (1928). Editor, the *American Oxonian,* 1930–35. President, University of Rochester, 1935–50.

VALENTINE, DAVID THOMAS (Sept. 15, 1801–Feb. 25, 1869); b. East Chester, N.Y. Editor, author. *History of the City of New York* (one vol. only of a projected set, 1853); etc. Compiler of the *Manual of the Corporation of the City of New York,* which he issued annually from 1841 to 1867. This compilation is popularly known as *Valentine's Manual.*

VALENTINE, EDWARD [Abram] UFFINGTON (Jan. 29, 1870–); b. Bellefonte, Pa. Author. *The Ship of Silence, and Other Poems* (1901); *Hecla Sandwith* (1905); etc.

VALLENTINE, BENJAMIN BENNATON (Sept. 7, 1843–Nov. 30, 1926); b. London, Eng. Journalist, playwright. *Fadette* (comic opera, prod. 1892); *A Southern Romance* (prod. 1897); *In Paradise* (prod. 1899); etc. He wrote for *Puck* under the pen name "Fitznoodle." He was one of the founders of *Puck,* managing editor, 1877–84.

Valley of Decision, The. Novel by Marcia Davenport (1942). The Scott family, owners of an iron works, followed from the years 1873 through 1941.

Valley of the Dolls. Novel by Jacqueline Susann (1966). Best-selling novel about sexual adventures of various women and their reliance on pills and prescription drugs to keep their lives in order.

Values for Survival. By Lewis Mumford (1946). Essays, addresses, and letters on politics and education, written between 1938 and 1946.

VAN AMBURGH, F[red] D[e Witt] (Apr. 5, 1866–Oct. 23, 1934); b. Newburgh, N.Y. Publisher, author. *By the Side of the Road* (1916); *The Buck Up Book* (1918); *A Book of Sentiment* (1925); etc.

VAN ANDA, CARR V. (Dec. 2, 1864–Jan. 29, 1945); b. Georgetown, O. Editor. With the *New York Sun,* 1888–1904; managing editor, the *New York Times,* 1904–32. *See* Barnett Fine's *A Giant of the Press* (1933).

Van Bibber and Others. Short stories by Richard Harding Davis (1892). The adventures of a New York man-about-town.

Van Buren, Abigail. Pen name of Pauline Friedman Phillips.

VAN BUREN, MARTIN (Dec. 5, 1782–July 24, 1862); b. Kinderhook, N.Y. Eighth president of the United States, author. *The Autobiography of Martin Van Buren,* ed. by J. C. Fitzpatrick, in the *Annual Report of the American Historical Association for the Year 1918,* v. 2 (1920). *See* Edward M. Shepard's *Martin Van Buren* (1900); Holmes M. Alexander's *The American Talleyrand* (1935); Robert V. Remini's *Martin Van Buren and the Making of the Democratic Party* (1959).

VAN BUREN, MAUD (Dec. 9, 1869–Jan. 2, 1959); b. Montfort, Wis. Librarian, anthologist. Compiler (with Katharine I. Bemis): *Christmas in Modern Story* (1927); *Mother in Modern Story* (1928); *Thanksgiving in Modern Story* (1928); *Easter in Modern Story* (1929); *Father in Modern Story*

(1929); etc. Editor: *Quotations for Special Occasions* (1938). Librarian, Owatonna Public Library, Owatonna, Minn., 1920–36.

VAN CAMPEN, HELEN (1882–). Novelist. *The Actor's Boarding House, and Other Stories* (1906); *The Maison de Shine: Other Stories of the Actor's Boarding House* (1908).

VAN DE WATER, FREDERIC F[ranklyn] (Sept. 30, 1890– July 16, 1968); b. Pompton, N.J. Author. *Grey Riders* (1921); *The Eye of Lucifer* (1927); *Alibi* (1930); *The Real McCoy* (1931); *Glory Hunter: A Life of General Custer* (1934); *Death in the Dark* (1937); *Fathers Are Funny* (1939); *Fool's Errand* (1945); *Catch a Falling Star* (1949); *The Captain Called It Mutiny* (1954); *This Day's Madness* (1957); etc.

VAN DE WATER, VIRGINIA TERHUNE (d. Oct. 17, 1945); b. Newark, N.J., daughter of Mary Virginia Terhune. Author. *The Shears of Delilah* (1914); *The Heart of a Child* (reminiscences, 1927); etc.

VAN DEN HAAG, ERNEST (Sept. 15, 1914–); b. Den Haag, Neth. Psychoanalyst, author. *The Fabric of Society* (1957); *Passion and Social Restraint* (1963); *The Jewish Mystique* (1969).

Van Deusen, Elizabeth Kneipple. See Elizabeth Kneipple.

VAN DEUSEN, GLYNDON GARLOCK (Sept. 22, 1897–); b. Clifton Springs, N.Y. Educator, author. *Sieyes; His Life and His Nationalism* (1932); *The Life of Henry Clay* (1937); *Thurlow Weed: Wizard of the Lobby* (1947); *Horace Greeley: Nineteenth Century Crusader* (1952); *The Jacksonian Era, 1828–1848* (1959); *The United States of America: A History* (1962); *The American Democracy: Its Rise to Power* (1964); *William Henry Seward* (1967); *The Rise and Decline of Jacksonian Democracy* (1970). History dept., University of Rochester, since 1930.

Van Dine, S.S. Pen name of Willard Huntington Wright.

VAN DOREN, CARL [Clinton] (Sept. 10, 1885–July 18, 1950); b. Hope, Ill. Educator, editor, critic, author. *The American Novel* (1921); *Contemporary American Novelists, 1900–1920* (1922); *The Roving Critic* (1923); *Many Minds* (1924); *Other Provinces* (1925); *American and British Literature Since 1890* (with Mark Van Doren, 1925); *The Ninth Wave* (1926); *Swift* (1930); *Sinclair Lewis* (1933); *American Literature: An Introduction* (1933); *Three Worlds* (autobiography, 1936); *Benjamin Franklin* (1938, Pulitzer Prize for American biography, 1939); *An Illinois Boyhood* (1939); *Secret History of the American Revolution* (1941); *Mutiny in January* (1943); *American Scriptures* (with Carl Carmer, 1946); *The Great Rehearsal* (1948); *Jane Mecom, the Favorite Sister of Benjamin Franklin* (1950). Editor: *The Cambridge History of American Literature*, 4v. (with William P. Trent and others, 1917–21); *An Anthology of World Prose* (1935); etc. Editor, The Literary Guild, 1926–34; etc. English dept., Columbia University, 1911–30.

VAN DOREN, DOROTHY GRAFFE (Mrs. Mark Van Doren) (May 2, 1896–); b. San Francisco, Cal. Author. *Strangers* (1926); *Flowering Quince* (1927); *Brother and Brother* (1928); *Those First Affections* (1938); *Dacey Hamilton* (1942); *The Country Wife* (1950); *The Professor and I* (1959). Editor: *The Lost Art: Letters of Seven Women* (1929).

VAN DOREN, IRITA (Mrs. Carl Van Doren) (Mar. 16, 1891–Dec. 19, 1966); b. Birmingham, Ala. Editor. Editorial staff, *The Nation*, 1919–22, editor, 1923-24; assoc. editor, the *New York Herald Tribune Books*, 1924–26, lit. editor, from 1926.

VAN DOREN, MARK (June 13, 1894–); b. Hope, Ill. Poet, editor, compiler. *Henry David Thoreau* (1916); *Spring Thunder, and Other Poems* (1924); *American and British Literature since 1890* (with Carl Van Doren, 1925); *7 P.M. and Other Poems* (1926); *Edwin Arlington Robinson* (1927); *Now*

the Sky, and Other Poems* (1928); *Jonathan Gentry* (poems, 1931); *Dick and Tom* (1931); *A Winter Diary, and Other Poems* (1935); *The Transients* (1935); *The Last Look, and Other Poems* (1937); *Collected Poems, 1922–1938* (1939, Pulitzer prize for poetry, 1940); *Shakespeare* (1939); *Windless Cabins* (1940); *The Transparent Tree* (1940); *Nathaniel Hawthorne* (1949); *Short Stories* (1950); *Selected Poems* (1954); *Benjamin Franklin* (1956); *Home with Hazel, and Other Stories* (1957); *Autobiography* (1958); *The Last Days of Lincoln* (1959); *The Happy Critic* (1961); *Somebody Came* (1966); *That Shining Place* (1969); etc. Editor: *An American Bookshelf,* 5v. (1927–28). Compiler: An Anthology of World Poetry (1928); *The Oxford Book of American Prose* (1932); *American Poets, 1630–1930* (1932); *An Anthology of English and American Poetry* (1936); *Introduction to Poetry* (1951); etc. See Warren Bush's *The Dialogues of Archibald MacLeish and Mark Van Doren* (1964).

VAN DUSEN, HENRY PITNEY (Dec. 11, 1897–); b. Philadelphia, Pa. Educator, author. *In Quest of Life's Meaning* (1926); *God in These Times* (1935); *For the Healing of the Nations* (1940); etc. Editor: *The Church Through Half a Century* (1936); *Church and State in the Modern World* (1937); *They Found the Church There* (1945); *God in Education* (1951); *Spirit, Son and Father* (1958); *One Great Ground of Hope* (1961); *The Vindication of Liberal Theology* (1963); *Dag Hammarskjold: The Statesman and His Faith* (1967); etc. With Union Theological Seminary, New York, since 1926; pres. since 1945.

VAN DUYN, MONA (May 9, 1921–); b. Waterloo, Ia. Poet. *Valentines to the Wide World* (1959); *A Time of Bees* (1964); *To See, To Take* (1970). Lecturer in English, Washington University, since 1950. Editor, *Perspective*, since 1947.

VAN DYKE, HENRY (Nov. 10, 1852–Apr. 10, 1933); b. Germantown, Pa., brother of Paul van Dyke. Presbyterian clergyman, poet, educator. *The Poetry of Tennyson* (1889); *Little Rivers* (1895); *The Story of the Other Wise Man* (1896); *Ships and Havens* (1897); *The Builders, and Other Poems* (1897); *The First Christmas Tree* (1897); *Fisherman's Luck* (1899); *The Friendly Year* (1900); *The Ruling Passion* (1901); *The Blue Flower* (1902); *The Open Door* (1903); *The School of Life* (1905); etc. Prof. English Literature, Princeton University, 1900–23. See Edwin Mims's *The Van Dyke Book* (1905); Tertius Van Dyke's *Henry van Dyke* (1935).

VAN DYKE, JOHN CHARLES (Apr. 21, 1856–Dec. 5, 1932); b. New Brunswick, N.J. Librarian, educator, critic. *Books and How to Use Them* (1883); *Principles of Art* (1887); *History of Painting* (1894); *Old Dutch and Flemish Masters* (1895); *Modern French Masters* (1896); *The Desert* (1901); *The Opal Sea* (1906); *New Guides to Old Masters* (1914); *The Mountain* (1916); *The Raritan* (1916); *The Grand Canyon of the Colorado* (1920); *The Open Spaces* (1922); *Rembrandt and His School* (1923); *The Meadows* (1926); etc. Librarian, Sage Library, New Brunswick, 1878–1932. Prof. history of art, Rutgers University, 1889–1932.

VAN DYKE, PAUL (Mar. 25, 1859–Aug. 30, 1933); b. Brooklyn, N.Y., brother of Henry van Dyke. Presbyterian clergyman, educator, author. *The Age of the Renascence* (1897); *Renascence Portraits* (1905); *Catherine de Medicis,* 2v. (1923–27); *Ignatius Loyola* (1926); *The Story of France* (1928); *George Washington, the Son of His Country* (1931); etc. Prof. modern European history, Princeton University, 1898–1928.

VAN DYKE, TERTIUS (Jan. 18, 1886–Feb. 28, 1958); b. New York, son of Henry van Dyke. Presbyterian clergyman, educator, author. *Songs of Seeking and Finding* (1920); *Light My Candle* (with Henry van Dyke, 1926); *Henry van Dyke* (1935). Headmaster, Gunnery School, Washington, Conn., 1936–42. Dean, Hartford Theological Seminary, 1943–54.

Van Dyne, Edith. Pen name of L. Frank Baum.

VAN ETTEN, WINIFRED [Florence Mayne] (Jan. 23, 1902–); b. Emmetsburg, Ia. Author. *I Am the Fox* (1936).

VAN EVERY, DALE (July 23, 1896–); b. Levering, Mich. Author. *A.E.F. in Battle* (1928); *Westward the River* (1945); *The Shining Mountains* (1948); *Bridal Journey* (1950); *The Captive Witch* (1951); *The Trembling Earth* (1953); *The Scarlet Feather* (1958); *Forth to the Wilderness* (1961); *A Company of Heroes* (1962); *Ark of Empire* (1963); *The Final Challenge* (1964); *The Disinherited* (1966); etc.

VAN GELDER, ROBERT (Oct. 19, 1904–Apr. 3, 1952); b. Baltimore, Md. Critic, author. *Marjory Fleming* (1940); *Writers and Writing* (1946); *Important People* (1948); etc. With *New York Times* from 1928; editor, *New York Times Book Review,* 1943–46.

VAN HOESEN, HENRY BARTLETT (Dec. 25, 1885–Jan. 6, 1965); b. Truxton, N.Y. Librarian, author. *Roman Cursive Writing* (1915); *Bibliography, Practical, Enumerative and Historical* (1928); *The Brown University Library* (1940); *Greek Horoscopes* (with Otto Neugebauer, 1959). With Princeton University library, 1915–29; librarian, Brown University, since 1930; John Hay prof. bibliography, from 1930.

VAN HOOK, LA RUE (Jan. 20, 1877–1951); b. Illiopolis, Ill. Educator, author. *Greek Life and Thought* (1924). Greek and Latin dept., Barnard College, New York, 1910–30; prof. 1920–30. Jay prof. Greek, Columbia University, 1931–42.

VAN KEUREN, FLOYD (1880–Oct. 21, 1968); b. Sioux City, Ia. Episcopal clergyman. Author: *The Open Door* (1942); *Christian Marriage* (1947); *The Game of Living* (1953); etc.

VAN LOON, HENDRIK WILLEM (Jan. 14, 1882–Mar. 11, 1944); b. Rotterdam, Neth. Journalist, historian. *The Fall of the Dutch Republic* (1913); *The Rise of the Dutch Kingdom* (1915); *Ancient Man* (1920); *The Story of Mankind* (1921); *The Story of the Bible* (1923); *Tolerance* (1925); *America* (1927); *Life and Times of Peter Stuyvesant* (1928); *R. v. R.* (1931); *Geography* (1932); *Ships & How They Sailed the Seven Seas* (1935); *The Arts* (1937); *Our Battle* (1939); *The Story of the Pacific* (1940); *Simón Bolívar* (1943); etc. Editor: *The Songs We Sing* (with Grace Castagnetta, 1936); *Folk Songs of Many Lands* (with same, 1938); *The Songs America Sings* (with same, 1939); etc.

VAN NOSTRAND, DAVID (Dec. 5, 1811–June 14, 1886); b. New York. Publisher. He worked for John P. Haven, New York bookseller, until 1834, when he went into the publishing business with William Dwight. In 1848 he established D. Van Nostrand Company. From 1864 to 1868 he published vols. 7–11 of the *Rebellion Record,* ed. by Frank Moore. Later he published many technical books and magazines, chiefly in the field of military science and engineering. The company continues to publish extensively in the technical field.

Van Nostrand Co., Inc. Princeton, N.J. Publishers. Founded 1848. Publishes technical and scientific works, reference books, and general nonfiction. Acquired by Litton Industries in 1968.

VAN PAASSEN, PIERRE [Pieter Antonie Laurusse van Paassen] (Feb. 7, 1895–Jan. 6, 1968); b. Gorcum, Neth. Unitarian clergyman, author. *Days of Our Years* (autobiography, 1939); *The Time Is Now* (1941); *That Day Alone* (1941); *The Forgotten Ally* (1943); *Earth Could Be Fair* (1946); *Why Jesus Died* (1949); *Jerusalem Calling!* (1950); *Visions Rise and Change* (1955); *A Pilgrim's Vow* (autobiography, 1956); *A Crown of Fire* (1960). Editor: *Nazism: An Assault on Civilization* (with James Waterman Wise, 1934).

VAN PATTEN, NATHAN (Mar. 24, 1887–Mar. 17, 1956); b. Niskayuna, N.Y. Librarian, bibliographer, author. *Printing in Greenland* (1939); etc. Compiler, *An Index to Biographies and Bibliographical Contributions Relating to the Work of American and British Authors, 1923–1932* (1933). Director, University libraries, Stanford University, 1927–47; prof. bibliography, 1947–52.

VAN RENSSELAER, MARIANA GRISWOLD (Mrs. Schuyler Van Rensselaer) (Feb. 25, 1851–Jan. 20, 1934); b. New York. Poet, critic. *American Etchers* (1886); *Book of American Figure Painters* (1886); *Henry Hobson Richardson and His Works* (1888); *English Cathedrals* (1892); *History of the City of New York in the Seventeenth Century,* 2v. (1909); *Poems* (1910); *Many Children* (poems, 1921).

VAN RENSSELAER, MAY KING (Mrs. John King Van Rensselaer) (May 25, 1848–May 11, 1925); b. New York. Author. *The Goede Vrouw of Mana-ha-ta* (1898); *New Yorkers of the 19th Century* (1897); *Newport, Our Social Capital* (1905); *The Social Ladder* (with Frederic Van de Water, 1924); etc.

Van Saanen, Marie Louise. See Marie Louise Gibson Hale.

VAN SAHER, LILLA (d. July 15, 1968); b. Budapest. Novelist. *The Echo* (1947); *Macamba* (1949).

VAN SCHAACK, HENRY CRUGER (Apr. 2, 1802–Dec. 16, 1887); b. Kinderhook, N.Y. Antiquarian, editor of manuscripts dealing with the Loyalists in America, author. *The Life of Peter Van Schaack* (1842); *Memoirs of the Life of Henry Van Schaack* (1892); etc. His collection of autograph letters and manuscripts was one of the largest in America.

VAN SCHAICK, JOHN, JR. (Nov. 18, 1873–1949); b. Cobleskill, N.Y. Universalist clergyman, editor, author. *The Little Corner Never Conquered* (1921); *Cruising Around a Changing World* (1923); *Cruising Across Country* (1926); *The Little Hill Farm* (1930); *Memories of the World War* (1933); *The Characters in the Tales of a Wayside Inn* (1939); etc. Editor, the *Christian Leader,* Boston, from 1922.

VAN TYNE, CLAUDE HALSTEAD (Oct. 16, 1869–Mar. 21, 1930); b. Tecumseh, Mich. Educator, author. *The Loyalists in the American Revolution* (1902); *The American Revolution* (1905); *The Causes of the War of Independence* (1922); *India in Ferment* (1923); *England and America, Rivals in the American Revolution* (1927); *The War of Independence: American Phase* (1929, Pulitzer Prize for American history, 1930); etc. Editor: *The Letters of Daniel Webster* (1902); etc. History dept., University of Michigan, 1903–30; head of dept., 1911–30.

VAN URK, JOHN BLAN (Apr. 15, 1902–); b. in Michigan. Public relations counsel. *The Story of American Foxhunting,* 2v. (1940, 1941); *The Story of Rolling Rock* (1950); etc.

VAN VECHTEN, CARL (June 17, 1880–Dec. 21, 1964); b. Cedar Rapids, Ia. Critic, author. *Music and Bad Manners* (1916); *Interpreters and Interpretations* (1916); *The Merry-Go-Round* (1918); *In the Garret* (1920); *Interpreters* (1920); *The Tiger in the House* (1920); *Lords of the Housetops* (1921); *Peter Whiffle* (1922); *The Blind Bow-Boy* (1923); *The Tattooed Countess* (1924); *Firecrackers* (1925); *Nigger Heaven* (1926); *Excavations* (1926); *Spider Boy* (1928); *Parties* (1930); *Feathers* (1930); *Sacred and Profane Memories* (1932); etc. Editor: *Selected Works of Gertrude Stein* (1946); *Last Operas and Plays of Gertrude Stein* (1949). *See* Edward Lueder's *Carl Van Vechten and the Twenties* (1955).

VAN VOGT, A[lfred] E[lton] (Apr. 26, 1912–); b. Manitoba, Can. Novelist. *Slan* (1946); *The Weapon Makers* (1947); *The Book of Ptath* (1947); *The World of A* (1948); *Out of the Unknown* (stories, 1948); *The Voyage of the Space Beagle* (1950); *The House That Stood Still* (1950); *Away and Beyond* (stories, 1950); *Destination: Universe!* (1952); *Empire of the Atom* (1957); *The War Against the Rull* (1959); *The Winged Man* (1967); etc.

VAN VORST, BESSIE (Mrs. John Van Vorst) (1873–deceased); b. New York, sister of Marie Van Vorst. Author. *Bagsby's Daughter* (with sister, 1901); *Letters to Women in Love* (1906); etc.

VAN VORST, MARIE (Mrs. Gaetano Cagiati) (Nov. 23, 1867–Dec. 16, 1936); b. New York, sister of Bessie Van Vorst. Author. *Bagsby's Daughter* (with sister, 1901); *Philip Longstreth* (1902); *Poems* (1902); *Amanda of the Mill* (1905); *The Tiber* (1907); *The Nile* (1908); etc.

Van Winkle, Rip. See Rip Van Winkle.

VAN WYCK, WILLIAM (Mar. 10, 1863–Dec. 11, 1956); b. Terre Haute, Ind. Editor, author. *Jessica's Book* (1922); *Florentines* (1923); *Savonarola* (1926); *Some Gentlemen of the Renaissance* (1928); *On the Terrasse* (1931); *Robinson Jeffers* (1928); *How to Enjoy Poetry* (1956); etc. Editor: *Berner's Fishing with a Hook* (1933); Chaucer's *The Miller's Tale* (1939); *Aucassin and Nicolette* (1939); etc.

VAN ZILE, EDWARD SIMS (May 2, 1863–May 29, 1931); b. Troy, N.Y. Author. *Don Miguel* (1891); *The Manhattaners* (1895); *The Dreamers, and Other Poems* (1897); *With Sword and Crucifix* (1900); *A Duke and His Double* (1903); *Perkins, the Fakeer* (1903); etc.

Vanardy, Varick. Pen name of Frederic Van Rensselaer Dey.

VANCE, ARTHUR TURNER (Oct. 10, 1872–Sept. 8, 1930); b. Scranton, Pa. Editor, author. *The Real David Harum* (1900); etc. Associate editor, *New England Magazine;* editor, *Woman's Home Companion,* 1900–07; editor, *Pictorial Review,* 1908–30.

Vance, Clara. Pen name of Mary Andrews Denison.

Vance, Ethel. Pen name of Grace Zaring Stone.

Vance, Jack. Pen name of Henry Kuttner.

VANCE, LOUIS JOSEPH (Sept. 19, 1879–Dec. 16, 1933); b. Washington, D.C. Novelist. *Terence O'Rourke, Gentleman Adventurer* (1905); *The Brass Bowl* (1907); *The Black Bag* (1908); *The Bronze Bell* (1909); *The Fortune Hunter* (1910); *The Bandbox* (1912); *The Lone Wolf* (1914); *Beau Revel* (1919); *Baroque* (1923); etc.

VANCE, MARGUERITE (Nov. 27, 1889–May 22, 1965). Author. *Marta* (1937); *Capitals of the World* (1938); *While Shepherds Watched* (1946); *Martha, Daughter of Virginia* (1947); *Patsy Jefferson of Monticello* (1948); *Marie Antoinette: Daughter of an Empress* (1950); *Lady Jane Grey, Reluctant Queen* (1952); *The Jacksons of Tennessee* (1953); *On Wings of Fire* (1955); *Flight of the Wildling: Elisabeth of Austria* (1957); *Ashes of Empire: Carlota and Maximilian of Mexico* (1959); *Jephtha and the New People* (1960); *Dark Eminence* (1961); etc.

VANCE, RUPERT BAYLESS (Mar. 15, 1899–); b. Plumerville, Ark. Sociologist. Author: *Human Geography of the South* (1935); *Farmers Without Land* (1937); etc. Co-author: *Exploring the South* (1949). Co-editor: *Urban South* (1954); etc. Prof. sociology, University of North Carolina, since 1945.

Vandegrift, Margaret. Pen name of Margaret Thomson Janvier.

Vandemark's Folly. Novel by Herbert Quick (1922). Story of pioneer life in Iowa before and after the Civil War. The first novel in a trilogy, the other titles being *The Hawkeye* (1923) and *The Invisible Woman* (1924).

VANDENBERG, ARTHUR HENDRICK (Mar. 22, 1884–Apr. 18, 1951); b. Grand Rapids, Mich. United States senator, author. *Alexander Hamilton, the Greatest American* (1921); *If Alexander Hamilton Were Here Today* (1923); *The Trail of Tradition* (1925); *The Private Papers of Senator Vandenberg* (1952), edited by Arthur J. Vandenberg, Jr., and Joe Alex Morris, etc.

VANDERBILT, AMY (July 22, 1908–); b. Staten Island, N.Y. Journalist, author. *Amy Vanderbilt's Complete Book of Etiquette* (1952); *Amy Vanderbilt's Everyday Etiquette* (1956); *Amy Vanderbilt's Complete Cookbook* (1961). Author syndicated column "Amy Vanderbilt's Etiquette," since 1954.

VANDERBILT, CORNELIUS, Jʀ. (Apr. 30, 1898–); b. New York. Journalist, author. *Personal Experiences of a Cub Reporter* (1922); *The Far West* (1923); *Reno* (1929); *Park Avenue* (1930); *Farewell to Fifth Avenue* (1935); *Personal European Travel Directory* (1954); *The Living Past of America* (1955); *Queen of the Golden Age* (1956); *Man of the World: My Life on Five Continents* (1959); *Ranches and Ranch Life in America* (1968); etc. See Wayne Andrews's *The Vanderbilt Legend* (1941).

VANDERCOOK, JOHN W. (Apr. 22, 1902–Jan. 5, 1963); b. London, Eng. Author, radio commentator. *"Tom-Tom"* (1926); *Black Majesty* (1928); *Forty Stay In* (1931); *Murder in Trinidad* (1933); *Murder in Fiji* (1936); *Dark Islands* (1937); *Caribbee Cruise* (1938); *King Cane* (1939); *Discover Puerto Rico* (1939); *Empress of the Dusk: A Life of Theodora of Byzantium* (1940); *One Day More* (1950); *Great Sailor* (1956); *Murder in Haiti* (1956); *Murder in New Guinea* (1959). Staff commentator, American Broadcasting Company, from 1953.

VANDERCOOK, MARGARET [O'Bannon Womack] (Jan. 12, 1876–); b. Louisville, Ky. *The Loves of Ambrose* (1913); *The Lady of Desire, and Other Imaginary Portraits* (1930); the *Ranch Girl* series; the *Camp Fire Girls* series; the *Girl Scout* series; etc.

VANDERPOEL, EMILY [C] NOYES (d. Feb. 20, 1939); b. New York. Painter, author. *Chronicles of a Pioneer School* (1903); *More Chronicles of a Pioneer School* (1927); and books on art.

VANDIVER, FRANK E[verson] (Dec. 9, 1925–); b. Austin, Tex. Educator, author. *Ploughshares into Swords: Josiah Gorgas and Confederate Ordnance* (1952); *Rebel Brass: The Confederate Command System* (1956); *Mighty Stonewall* (1957); *Fields of Glory* (with W. H. Nelson, 1960); *Jubal's Raid* (1960); *Basic History of the Confederacy* (1962); *Jefferson Davis and the Confederate State* (1964); *Their Tattered Flags: The Epic of the Confederacy* (1970). Editor of several volumes of documents relating to Southern history. Prof. history, Rice University, since 1955.

Vanguard Press. New York. Publishers. Founded 1926. Evelyn Shrifte is president. It grew out of the American Fund for Public Service established by Charles Garland.

Vanity Fair. New York. Comic weekly. Founded Dec. 31, 1859. Published by Louis Henry Stephens, with his brothers, William Allan Stephens as editor, and Henry Louis Stephens as art editor. Charles Farrar Browne contributed humorous articles under the pen name "Artemus Ward," and was managing editor, 1861–62. Charles Godfrey Leland was managing editor, 1860–61. Expired July 4, 1863.

Vanity Fair. New York. Monthly. Founded 1889, as *Illustrated Sport, Music and Drama.* After various changes of title, it became *Vanity Fair* in 1912. Absorbed *Dress* (founded 1906) in 1913. Frank Crowninshield was editor 1914–35. Absorbed by *Vogue,* 1935. See *Vanity Fair: A Cavalcade of the 1920's and 1930's,* edited by Cleveland Amory and Frederic Bradlee (1970).

VANN, WILLIAM HARVEY (Feb., 1887–); b. Wake Forest, N.C. Educator, editor. *The Other End of the Log* (1959). Editor: *Texas Poems* (1936). Editor, *The Torch Bearer,* a magazine of verse. Head, English dept., Baylor College, Belton, Tex.

VARBLE, RACHEL McBRAYER (Mrs. Pinckney Varble III). b. in Anderson Co., Ky. Author. *The Red Cape* (1928); *A Girl from London* (1929); *Marie of the Gypsies* (1931); *Julia Ann Tevis* (1939); *Romance for Rosa* (1946); *Pepys' Boy* (1955); etc.

Varieties of Religious Experience, The. Analysis of religion as a universal experience having psychological validity, by William James (1902).

Variety. New York. Weekly journal of the amusement world. Founded 1905, by Sime Silverman, who directed it until his death in 1933. Jack Conway was an editor. It is noted for its slang and theatre jargon, some of its articles being unintelligible to persons not familiar with the slangy speech of Broadway. The headline "Stix Nix Hix Pix," for example, means that the rural sections do not care for pictures depicting farm life.

Varmint, The. By Owen Johnson (1910). Story of a boy's exciting experiences at a preparatory school in New Jersey. The hero has a penchant for becoming involved in escapades which threaten disastrous consequences.

VEBLEN, THORSTEIN [Bunde] (July 30, 1857–Aug. 3, 1929); b. in Manitowoc Co., Wis. Educator, author. *The Theory of the Leisure Class* (1899); *The Instinct of Workmanship* (1914); *The Higher Learning in America* (1918); *Vested Interests* (1919); *The Place of Science in Modern Civilization* (1920); etc. Economics dept., University of Chicago, 1893–1906; University of Missouri, 1911–18; New School for Social Research, New York, 1918–27. *See* Joseph Dorfman's *Thorstein Veblen and His America* (1934); John Hobson's *Veblen* (1936); Carlton C. Qualey's *Thorstein Veblen* (1968). *See also* Warner Berthoff's *The Ferment of Realism* (1965); Thomas R. West's *Flesh of Steel and the Machine in American Culture* (1967).

VEDDER, ELIHU (Feb. 26, 1836–Jan. 29, 1923); b. New York. Painter, illustrator, author. *The Digressions of V* (1910); *Miscellaneous Moods in Verse* (1914); *Doubt and Other Things* (poems, 1922); etc. Illustrated *Rubaiyat of Omar Khayyam* (1884); etc.

VEDDER, HENRY CLAY (Feb. 26, 1853–Oct. 13, 1935); b. DeRuyter, N.Y. Educator, author. *A History of the Baptists of the Middle States* (1898); *American Writers of To-Day* (1894); *The Baptists* (1903); *The Reformation in Germany* (1913); *The Fundamentals of Christianity* (1921). Prof. church history, Crozer Theological Seminary, 1894–1935.

VEILLER, BAYARD (Jan. 2, 1869–1943); b. Brooklyn, N.Y. Playwright. *The Primrose Path* (prod. 1907); *Gordon's Wife* (prod. 1911); *Within the Law* (1912); *The Fight* (prod. 1913); *The Thirteenth Chair* (prod. 1916); *The Chatterbox* (prod. 1917); *Danger* (prod. 1919); *Mary Dugan* (prod. 1927); *The Fun I've Had* (autobiography, 1941).

VELIKOVSKY, IMMANUEL (June 10, 1895–); b. Vitebsk, Rus. Scientist, author. *Thirty Days and Nights of Diego Pires on the Bridge of St. Angelo* (1935); *Worlds in Collision* (1950); *Age in Chaos* (1952); *Earth in Upheaval* (1955); *Oedipus and Akhaton: Myth and History* (1960).

VENABLE, CLARKE (Apr. 1, 1892–); b. Liberty, Mo. Author. Pen name "Covington Clarke." *Fleetfin: An Idyll of a Little River* (1925); *"Aw Hell"* (1927); *All the Brave Rifles* (1929); *Mosby's Night Hawk* (1931); etc.

VENABLE, EDWARD CARRINGTON (July 4, 1884–May 17, 1936); b. Petersburg, Va. Author. *Pierre Vinton* (1914); *Short Stories* (1915); *Lasca* (1916); *At Isham's* (1918); etc.

VENABLE, EMERSON (Dec. 22, 1875–); b. Cincinnati, O., son of William Henry Venable. Educator, author. *A Speculation Regarding Shakespeare* (1905); *Poets of Ohio* (1909); *The Hamlet Problem and Its Solution* (1912); *Joan of Arc* (drama, 1956). Editor: *The Poems of William Henry Venable* (1925). He presented the D. C. Venable collection of manuscripts to the Ohio Archaeological and Historical Society in 1931. With public school system, Cincinnati, 1900–34.

VENABLE, WILLIAM HENRY (Apr. 29, 1836–July 6, 1920); b. Waynesville, O. Poet, educator. *June on the Miami,*

and Other Poems (1871); *Melodies of the Heart, and Other Poems* (1884); *Historical Sketch of Western Periodical Literature* (1888); *Beginnings of Literary Culture in the Ohio Valley* (1891); *Tom Tad* (1902); *Saga of the Oak, and Other Poems* (1904); *Ohio Literary Men and Women* (1904); *A Buckeye Boyhood* (1911); *The Poems of William Henry Venable* (ed. by his son, Emerson Venable 1925); etc.

Venetian Glass Nephew, The. By Elinor Wylie (1925). A flesh and blood woman, Rosalba, marries a hero made of glass, Virginio. Rosalba is turned into porcelain in order to harmonize this impossible marriage.

VERBECK, BLANCHE A VICESTILL HARRIMAN (Aug. 7, 1890–); b. Oshkosh, Wis. Writes under maiden name. Author. *Home Made Philosophy* (1916); *Short Stories* (1917); *The Avatar* (1917); *Moods* (verse, 1926); etc.

VERBECK, WILLIAM FRANCIS (June 1, 1858–July 13, 1933); b. Mansfield, O. Illustrator, author. *The Dumpies and the Arkansas Bear* (with A. B. Paine, 1896); *The Three Bears* (1899); *Beasts and Birds* (1900); *Book of Bears* (1906); *The Little Lost Bear* (1916); *The Little Cat Who Journeyed to St. Ives* (1921); etc.

Vermilye, Mrs. Frederick M. See Kate Jordan.

Vermont Gazette and Green Mountain Post-Boy. Westminster, Vt. Founded 1780, by Judah Padeck Spooner and Timothy Green IV. First newspaper in Vermont. Anthony Haswell was editor. Expired c. 1781.

VERNADSKY, GEORGE (Aug. 20, 1887–); b. St. Petersburg, Rus. Historian. *Lenin, Red Dictator* (1931); *Political and Diplomatic History of Russia* (1936); *Ancient Russia* (1943); *The Origins of Russia* (1959); *Tsardom of Moscow* (1969); etc. Prof. Russian history, Yale University, 1946–56.

VERNER, ELIZABETH O'NEILL. b. Charleston, S.C. Etcher, author. *Prints and Impressions of Charleston* (1939); *Mellowed By Time* (1941); *Other Places* (1946). Illustrated the Charleston edition of Dubose Heyward's *Porgy,* etc.

VERNON, AMBROSE WHITE (Oct. 13, 1870–1951); b. New York. Congregational clergyman, educator, author. *The Religious Value of the Old Testament* (1907); *Turning Points in Church History* (1917); *Ten Pivotal Figures of History* (1925); *Nobler Risk, and Other Sermons* (1955). Prof. biography, Dartmouth College, 1924–31.

Vernon, Max. Pen name of Vernon Lyman Kellogg.

VERPLANCK, GULIAN CROMMELIN (Aug. 6, 1786–Mar. 18, 1870); b. New York. Editor, author. *The Bucktail Bards* (1819); *The State Triumvirate: A Political Tale* (1819); *Discourses and Addresses on Subjects of American History, Arts and Literature* (1833); etc. Editor: *Shakespeare's Plays,* 3v. (1847). Founder (with Charles King), the *New York American.* Co-editor, *The Talisman,* 1828–30. His best known oration was "The Advantages and the Dangers of the American Scholar," delivered at Union College, 1836. He was one of the early Shakespearean scholars in America. See *American Literature,* v. 8, 1936.

VERRILL, ALPHEUS HYATT (July 1871–Nov. 14, 1954); b. New Haven, Conn. Explorer, author. *In Morgan's Wake* (1915); *Book of the West Indies* (1917); *Panama Past and Present* (1921); *Rivers and Their Mysteries* (1922); *Boys' Book of Buccaneers* (1927); *Under Peruvian Skies* (1930); *Barton's Mills* (1932); *Romantic and Historic Maine* (1933); *Romantic and Historic Virginia* (1935); *Romantic and Historic Florida* (1935); *Our Indians* (1935); *Heart of Old New England* (1936); *They Found Gold* (1936); *Along New England Shores* (1936); *My Jungle Trails* (1937); *The Real Americans* (1954); etc.

VERY, JONES (Aug. 28, 1813–May 8, 1880); b. Salem, Mass. Poet, transcendentalist. *Essays and Poems* (1839); *Poems* (1883); *Poems and Essays* (1886). *See* Edwin Gittleman's *Jones Very: The Effective Years, 1833–1840* (1967).

VERY, LYDIA L[ouisa] A[nn] (Nov. 2, 1823–Sept. 10, 1901); b. Salem, Mass. Author. *Poems* (1856); *Poems and Prose Writings* (1890); *The Better Path; or, Sylph, the Organ-Grinder's Daughter* (1898); *A Strange Disclosure* (1898); *A Strange Recluse* (1899); *An Old-Fashioned Garden* (1900); etc.

Vestal, Stanley. Pen name of Walter Stanley Campbell.

Via Crucis. Novel by F. Marion Crawford (1898). Romance of the Crusaders of the twelfth century, beginning in England, shifting to the French court and then to Syria.

VICTOR, FRANCES [Aurette] FULLER (Mrs. Jackson Barritt; Mrs. Henry Clay Victor) (May 23, 1826–Nov. 14, 1902); b. in Oneida Co., N.Y., sister of Metta Victoria [Fuller] Victor. Author. She and her sister were known as "The Sisters of the West." *Anizetta, the Guajira* (1848); *Poems of Imagination and Sentiment* (with sister, 1851); *The Land Claim* (1862); *The River of the West* (1870); rewritten as *Eleven Years in the Rocky Mountains,* 2v. (1877); *All over Oregon and Washington* (1872); *The New Penelope, and Other Poems and Stories* (1877); *The Early Indian Wars of Oregon* (1894); *Poems* (1900); the following parts of Bancroft's *History of the Pacific States: History of Oregon,* 2v. (1886–88); *History of Washington, Idaho, and Montana* (1890); *History of Nevada, Colorado, and Wyoming* (1890); etc. She wrote the *Florence Fane Sketches* in the *San Francisco Bulletin,* 1863–65.

VICTOR, METTA VICTORIA [Fuller] (Mrs. Orville James Victor) (Mar. 2, 1831–June 26, 1886); b. near Erie, Pa., sister of Frances Aurette Fuller Victor. Editor, author, dime novelist. She and her sister were known as "The Sisters of the West." Pen names, "Singing Sibyl," "Mrs. Mark Peabody," "Rose Kennedy," "Seeley Regester," etc. *Last Days of Tul* (1847); *Poems of Imagination and Sentiment* (with sister, 1851); *The Senator's Son* (1853); *Mormon Wives* (1856); *Miss Slimmens' Window, and Other Papers* (1859); *Alice Wilde* (1860); *The Backwoods Bride* (1860); *Maum Guinea* (1861); *Myrtle, the Child of the Prairie* (1863); *The Dead Letter* (1867); *Too True: A Story of Today* (anon., 1868); *Passing the Portal* (1876); *Blunders of a Bashful Man* (anon., 1881); etc. Many of her books were reprinted under other titles. Asst. editor, the *United States Journal,* 1857–60; editor, *Beadle's Home Monthly,* 1859–60; the *Cosmopolitan Art Journal,* 1860–61.

VICTOR, ORVILLE JAMES (Oct. 23, 1827–Mar. 14, 1910); b. Sandusky, O. Author, publisher. *The History, Civil, Political, and Military, of the Southern Rebellion,* 4v. (1861–68); *Incidents and Anecdotes of the War* (1862); etc. Editor: *Beadle's Dime Biographical Library; Beadle's Magazine of Today;* the *New York Saturday Journal,* 1872–80; etc. It is claimed that he started the fad for dime novels in 1860.

Victory. Bimonthly published by the Office of War Information during World War II in six languages for overseas distribution.

Vida, La. By Oscar Lewis (1966). Study of Puerto Ricans in poverty. The work is the first in a series concerned with one hundred Puerto Ricans belonging to the same extended family in San Juan and New York City.

VIDAL, GORE (Oct. 23, 1925–); b. West Point, N.Y. Novelist, dramatist. *Williwaw* (1946); *In a Yellow Wood* (1947); *The City and the Pillar* (1948); *The Season of Comfort* (1949); *A Search for the King* (1950); *Dark Green, Bright Red* (1950); *The Judgment of Paris* (1952); *Messiah* (1954); *A Thirsty Evil* (short stories, 1956); *Visit to a Small Planet* (prod. 1957); *The Best Man* (prod. 1960); *Washington, D.C.* (1967); *Myra Breckenridge* (1968); *Two Sisters* (1970); etc.

VIELÉ, EGBERT LUDOVICUS (May 26, 1863–Nov. 12, 1937); b. Norfolk, Va. Pen name, "Francis Vielé-Griffin." Poet. *Oeuvres,* 4v. (1924–30); etc.

VIELÉ, HERMAN KNICKERBOCKER (Jan. 31, 1856–1908); b. New York. Author. *The Inn of the Silver Moon* (1900); *The Last of the Knickerbockers* (1901); *Myra of the Pines* (1902); *Random Verse* (1903); *The House of Silence* (prod. 1906); *Heartbreak Hill* (1908).

VIERECK, GEORGE SYLVESTER (Dec. 31, 1884–Mar. 18, 1962); b. Munich, Ger. Author. *Nineveh, and Other Poems* (1907); *Confessions of a Barbarian* (1910); *The Candle and the Flame* (1912); *My First Two Thousand Years: The Autobiography of the Wandering Jew* (with Paul Eldridge, 1928); *Glimpses of the Great* (1931); *The Temptation of Jonathan* (1938); *Nude in the Mirror* (1953); etc. Editor: *America: A Litany of Nations* (1906); etc.

VIERECK, PETER (Aug. 5, 1916–); b. New York, son of George Sylvester Viereck. Educator, poet. *Metapolitics–From the Romantics to Hitler* (1941); *Terror and Decorum* (poems, 1948); *Who Killed the Universe?* (1948); *Conservatism Revisited–The Revolt Against Revolt—1815–1949* (1949); *Strike Through the Mask: New Lyrical Poems* (1950); *The First Morning: New Poems* (1952); *Shame and Glory of the Intellectuals* (1953); *The Unadjusted Man: A New Hero for Americans* (1956); *Conservatism: From John Adams to Churchill* (1956); *The Persimmon Tree* (poems, 1956); *Education in a Free Society* (1958); *The Tree Witch* (poems, 1960); *Soviet Policy Making* (1967); *New and Selected Poems 1932–1967* (1967); etc. Prof. history, Mount Holyoke College, since 1955.

VIERTEL, PETER (Nov. 16, 1920–); b. Dresden, Ger. Author. *The Survivors* (with Irwin Shaw, play, 1948); *The Canyon* (1940); *Line of Departure* (1947); *White Hunter, Black Heart* (1953); etc.

View. New York. Founded 1940. Edited by Charles Henri Ford. Published irregularly as a quarterly. Devoted to the avant-garde in art. Discontinued 1947.

Views Afoot. By Bayard Taylor (1860). Account of the author's travels in Europe.

Vignettes of Manhattan. By Brander Matthews (1894). Stories of New York life.

Viking Press. New York. Publishers. Founded 1925. Absorbed the firm of B. W. Huebsch, founded 1905. Thomas Guinzburg is president. Viking Press initiated the Viking Portable Library in 1943, which included the selected works of Steinbeck, Hemingway, and Dorothy Parker in one-volume editions. Many others were later added. Acquired Grossman Publishers and Orion Press (qq.v.).

VILAS, FAITH VAN VALKENBURGH (d. May 25, 1955); b. Milwaukee, Wis. Poet. *The Drummer of Fyvie, and Other Verse* (1926); *Aromancy, and Other Poems* (1929); *Roads of Earth* (1934); *Certificate of Flight* (1939); etc.

VILES, JONAS (May 3, 1875–Feb. 6, 1948); b. Waltham, Mass. Educator, author. *Archives of Missouri* (1910); *History of Missouri* (1912); *The University of Missouri 1839–1939* (1939); etc. History dept., University of Missouri, 1902–45.

VILLA, JOSÉ GARCIA (Aug. 5, 1914–); b. Manila. Poet. *Footnote to Youth* (stories, 1933); *Poems, by Doveglion* (under pen name "Doveglion," 1941); *Have Come, Am Here* (1942); *Volume Two* (1949); *Selected Poems* (1958); etc. Editor: *Celebration for Edith Sitwell* (1948); etc.

"Village, The." Poem by Enoch Lincoln (1816).

"Village Blacksmith, The." Poem of Henry W. Longfellow, which first appeared in *Ladies' Magazine of Literature, Fashion and the Fine Arts,* Aug., 1844.

Village Press. Private press founded 1903, by Frederic W. Goudy and Bertha M. Goudy, at Park Ridge, Ill. It was moved in 1904 to Hingham, Mass., and in 1906, to New York. There it was destroyed by fire in 1908. It was re-established in 1911 at Brooklyn, and later moved to Garden City, N.Y. In 1923 it was moved to Deepdene, Marlborough-on-Hudson, N.Y. It was again destroyed by fire in 1939. *See* Melbert B. Cary's *A Bibliography of the Village Press* (1938).

Village Voice, The. New York. Newspaper. Founded 1955 as a weekly. Edited by Daniel Wolf and, later, Edwin Fancher. In 1962 a monthly four-page book section was added. By the mid-1960's *The Village Voice* had become one of the most important organs of advanced opinion in the east, noted for its enterprising, unconventional, and candid views. It has served as a forum for a large body of iconoclastic and reformist ideas ranging from liberal to radical, but often giving space to those unrepresented in any part of the political press. Distinguished for personal journalism written in highly colloquial language. In art and culture more oriented toward popular and avant-garde forms, especially in the plastic arts, interpretive arts, movies, off-off Broadway theatre, etc.

VILLARD, HENRY (Apr. 10, 1835–Nov. 12, 1900); b. (Ferdinand Heinrich Gustav Hilgard) Speyer, Bavaria; came to the United States in 1853. Publisher, financier, author. *The Past and Present of the Pike's Peak Gold Regions* (1860); *Memoirs,* 2v. (1904). Civil War correspondent, the *New York Herald,* the *New York Tribune;* etc. Became owner of the *New York Evening Post,* 1881. *See* J. B. Hedges's *Henry Villard and the Railways of the Northwest* (1930).

VILLARD, HENRY S[errano] (Mar. 30, 1900–); b. New York. Diplomat, author. *Libya, the New Arab Kingdom of North Africa* (1956); *Affairs of State* (1965). Director of programs, Washington Institute of Foreign Affairs.

VILLARD, OSWALD GARRISON (Mar. 13, 1872–Oct. 1, 1949); b. Wiesbaden, Ger. Editor, author. *John Brown* (1910); *Germany Embattled* (1915); *Some Newspapers and Newspaper Men* (1923); *Prophets True and False* (1928); *The German Phoenix* (1933); *Fighting Years: Memoirs of a Liberal Editor* (1939); *Within Germany* (1940); *Disappearing Daily* (1944); *Free Trade—Free World* (1947); etc. Editorial writer and president, the *New York Evening Post,* 1897–1918; editor and owner, *The Nation,* 1918–32.

VINAL, HAROLD (Oct. 17, 1891–Mar. 9, 1965); b. Vinal Haven, Me. Poet, editor, essayist, publisher. *White April* (poems, 1922); *Voyage* (poem, 1923); *Nor Youth Nor Age* (poems, 1924); *A Stranger in Heaven* (poems, 1927); *Hymn to Chaos* (1931); *Attic for the Nightingale* (1934); *Hurricane: A Marine Coast Chronicle* (poem, 1936); *The Compass Eye* (1944); *Selected Poems* (1948); etc. Founder and editor, *Voices,* Vinal Haven, Me., 1921.

VINCENT, FRANCIS (Mar. 17, 1822–June 23, 1882); b. Bristol, Eng. Editor, author. *Essay Recommending the Union of Great Britain and Her Colonies and the United States, and the Final Union of the World into One Great Nation* (1868); *A History of the State of Delaware* (1870). Founder, *The Blue Hen's Chickens,* Wilmington, Del., Aug. 22, 1845.

VINCENT, FRANK (Apr. 2, 1848–June 19, 1916); b. Brooklyn, N.Y. Traveler, author. *The Land of the White Elephant* (1874); *Through and through the Tropics* (1876); *Wonderful Ruins of Cambodia* (1878); *Norsk, Lapp, and Finn* (1881); *Around and About South America* (1890); *In and Out of Central America* (1891); *Actual Africa* (1895); etc.

VINCENT, HOWARD P[aton] (Oct. 9, 1904–); b. Galesburg, Ill. Educator. *The Trying-Out of Moby Dick* (1949); *Melville and Hawthorne in the Berkshires* (1968); *Daumier and His World* (1969); etc. Editor: *Collected Poems of Herman Melville* (1946); etc. English dept., Illinois Institute of Technology, since 1942.

VINCENT, LEON HENRY (b. Jan. 1, 1859), b. Chicago, Ill. Author. *A Few Words on Robert Browning* (1891); *The Bibliotaph and Other People* (1898); *Corneille* (1901); *Moliere* (1902); *American Literary Masters* (1906); *Dandies and Men of Letters* (1913); *A Memoir of John Heyl Vincent* (1925); etc.

VINCENT, MARVIN RICHARDSON (Sept. 11, 1834–Aug. 18, 1922); b. Poughkeepsie, N.Y. Methodist clergyman, educator, author. *The Two Prodigals* (1876); *Faith and Character* (1880); *Word Studies in the New Testament* (1877); *In the Shadow of the Pyrenees* (1883); *That Monster the Higher Critic* (1894); *The Age of Hildebrand* (1896); etc. Prof. New Testament exegesis and criticism, Union Theological Seminary, New York, 1888–1922.

Vinegar Tree, The. Play by Paul Osborn (prod. 1930). Laura Merrick believes she has found an old lover she had not seen for twenty years. He turns out to be a total stranger.

VINGUT, GERTRUDE F[airfield] (Mrs. Francisco Javier Vingut) (b. 1830); b. Philadelphia, Pa., daughter of Sumner L. Fairfield. Author. *Irene; or, The Autobiography of an Artist's Daughter* (1853); *Naomi Torrente* (1864); etc.

VINING, ELIZABETH [Janet] GRAY (1902–). Author. *Meggy MacIntosh* (1930); *Young Walter Scott* (1935); *Adam of the Road* (1943); *Windows for the Crown Prince* (1952); *The Virginia Exiles* (1955); *Friend of Life* (1958); *Return to Japan* (1960); *Take Heed of Loving Me* (1964); *Flora: A Biography* (1966); *I, Roberta* (1968); *William Penn: Mystic* (1969); *Quiet Pilgrimage* (1970); etc.

VINTON, FREDERIC (Oct. 9, 1817–Jan. 1, 1890); b. Boston, Mass. Librarian. Compiler: *Index to the Catalogue of Books in the Bates Hall* (1861); *Alphabetical Catalogue of the Library of Congress: Index of Subjects* (1869); *Subject-Catalogue of the Library of the College of New Jersey at Princeton* (1884); etc. Librarian, Princeton University, 1873–90.

"Virginal, A." Poem by Ezra Pound.

Virginia. Play by John Parke (1784). Written in the form of a pastoral poem on Washington's birthday.

Virginia. Novel by Ellen Glasgow (1913). Intellectual and emotional conflict of a Southern woman who tries unsuccessfully to adapt herself to new ideas alien to her temperament and background. Her playwright husband deserts her, her daughters are independent, and only her brilliant young son stands by her.

Virginia Comedians, The. Novel by John Esten Cooke (1854). Intimate picture of the artificial life of the Virginia cavaliers before the Revolution.

Virginia Gazette. Williamsburg, Va. Five weekly newspapers of this name were founded at Williamsburg before the Revolution, and others afterward. These were: Parks's *Virginia Gazette* (1736–50); Hunter's *Virginia Gazette* (1751–78); Rind's *Virginia Gazette* (1766–76); Purdie's *Virginia Gazette* (1775–80); and Dixon and Nicholson's *Virginia Gazette* (1779–80). Parks's newspaper was the first in Virginia.

Virginia Quarterly Review. Charlottesville, Va. Founded Apr., 1925, by James Southall Wilson, who became its first editor. Other editors have been Stringfellow Barr, Lambert Davis, Lawrence Lee, Archibald Shepperson, and Charlotte Kohler. Contributors have included Conrad Aiken, Charles Beard, J. B. Cabell, T. S. Eliot, Waldo Frank, Allen Tate, Stark Young.

Virginian, The. Novel by Owen Wister (1902). A Virginian goes to the wilds of Montana and falls in love with a Vermont school teacher, Molly Wood. The difference in their cultural background is a barrier which love finally overcomes.

Virginian-Pilot and Norfolk Landmark. See *Norfolk Virginian-Pilot and Sunday Star.*

Vision of Sir Launfal, The. Poem by James Russell Lowell (1848). A version of the Holy Grail legend. It reveals Sir Launfal as a young knight, and finally as an old man, poor and broken, who ponders upon his fruitless search for the unattainable.

"Visit from St. Nicholas, A." See "The Night Before Christmas."

VISSCHER, WILLIAM LIGHTFOOT (Nov. 25, 1842–Feb. 10, 1924); b. Owingsville, Ky. Actor, poet, novelist. *Black Mammy: A Song of the South; and Other Poems* (1886); *Chicago: An Epic* (1897); *Blue Grass Ballads, and Other Verses* (1900); *A Thrilling and Truthful History of the Pony Express* (1908); *Ten Wise Men and Some More* (autobiography, 1909); *Poems of the South, and Other Verse* (1911). Editor: *Buffalo Bill's Own Story* (1917).

VIVAS, ELISEO (July 13, 1901–); b. Pamplona, Colombia. Educator. *The Moral Life and The Ethical Life* (1950); *Creation and Discovery* (1955); *D. H. Lawrence: The Failure and the Triumph of Art* (1960); *D. H. Lawrence* (1960); *The Artistic Transaction* (1963). Co-editor: *The Problems of Aesthetics* (1953). Philosophy dept., Northwestern University, 1951–69; emeritus since 1969.

VIZETELLY, FRANK (Francis) H[orace] (Apr. 2, 1864–Dec. 21, 1938); b. London, England. Lexicographer, editor. Author or editor: *The Preparation of Manuscripts for the Press* (1905); *Desk-Book of Errors in English* (1906); *Essentials of English Speech and Literature* (1915); *Desk Book of 25,000 Words Frequently Mispronounced* (1917); *Idioms and Idiomatic Phrases* (1921); etc. Editor: A *Practical Standard Dictionary* (1922); A *Desk Standard Dictionary* (1920); *Funk & Wagnalls New Standard Encyclopedia of Universal Knowledge,* 25v. (1931); *The New International Year Book,* 1932–38; *The New Comprehensive Standard Dictionary* (1937); etc. On editorial staff, Funk & Wagnalls, 1891–1938. Wrote "Lexicographer's Easy Chair" dept. for the *Literary Digest* for many years.

VOELKER, JOHN D[onaldson] (June 29, 1903–); b. Ishpeming, Mich. Lawyer, author. *Troubleshooter* (1943); *Danny and the Boys* (1951); *Small Town D.A.* (1954); *Anatomy of a Murder* (1957; film, 1959); *Trout Madness* (1960); *Hornstein's Boy* (1962); *The Laughing Whitefish* (1965); *Anatomy of a Fisherman* (1964); *The Jealous Mistress* (1968); etc.

VOGEL, JOSEPH (Nov. 21, 1904–); b. New York. Author. *At Madame Bonnard's* (1935); *Man's Courage* (1938); *The Straw Hat* (1940); etc. Editor of *Blues; Morada; Front; Dynamo;* all "little magazines."

Vogue. New York. Twenty issues yearly. Founded 1892, by Arthur Turnure and Harry McVickar; bought by Condé Nast in 1909. Absorbed *Vanity Fair* in 1935. Magazine of fashion, women's interests, and topical culture.

Voice of the People, The. Novel by Ellen Glasgow (1900). The spiritual triumph of a character heavily handicapped in youth.

Voices. Vinal Haven, Me. Poetry quarterly. Founded 1921, by Harold Vinal, who was editor from that date.

VOLCK, ADALBERT JOHN (Apr. 14, 1828–Mar. 26, 1912); b. Augsburg, Bavaria. Caricaturist. *Confederate War Etchings* (n.d.). He illustrated Emily V. Mason's *A Popular Life of Robert E. Lee* and James Fairfax McLaughlin's *Bombastes Furiosa Buncombe,* etc.

VOLLMER, LULA (d. May 2, 1955); b. Keyser, N.C. Playwright. *Sun-Up* (prod. 1923); *The Shame Woman* (prod. 1923); *The Dunce Boy* (prod. 1925); *Trigger* (prod. 1927); *Sentinels* (prod. 1931); *The Hill Between* (prod. 1938); etc.

VOLWILER, ALBERT TANGEMAN (Aug. 25, 1888–June 25, 1957); b. Cincinnati, O. Educator, author. *George Croghan and the Westward Movement* (1926). Editor: *Correspondence Between Benjamin Harrison and James G. Blaine* (1940). History dept., Wittenberg College, 1923–33; Ohio University, 1933–55.

VON BRAUN, WERNHER (Mar. 23, 1912–); b. Wirsitz, Ger. Engineer. *The Mars Project* (1953). Co-author: *Conquest of the Moon* (1953); *The Exploration of Mars* (1956); *Project Satellite* (1958); *First Men to the Moon* (1960); *A Journey Through Space and the Atom* (1962); *History of Rocketry and Space Travel* (with Frederick I. Ordway, 1967); etc.

VON GOTTSCHALCK, OSCAR HUNT (b. Oct. 1, 1865); b. Providence R.I. Humorist, author. *Yankee Doodle Gander* (1901); *Gnome Man's Land* (1902); *Lives of the Haunted* (1902); etc.

VON HAGEN, VICTOR WOLFGANG (Feb. 29, 1908–); b. St. Louis, Mo. Explorer, author. *Off with Their Heads* (1937); *Ecuador the Unknown* (1940); *Riches of South America* (1941); *The Four Seasons of Manuela* (with C. B. Von Hagen, 1952); *Highway of the Sun (1955); The Sun Kingdom of the Aztecs* (1958); *Maya: Land of the Turkey and the Deer* (1960); *The Ancient Sun Kingdoms of America* (1961); *People's War, People's Army* (1962); *The Mochicas and the Chimus* (1963); *Desert Kingdoms of Peru* (1965); *Aztec: Man and Tribe* (1965); *Roman Roads* (1966); etc. Editor: Cieza de León's *Incas* (1959).

VON HAYEK, FRIEDRICH AUGUST (May 8, 1899–); b. Vienna. Educator, author. *Price and Production* (1931); *Collective Economic Planning* (1935); *The Pure Theory of Capital* (1941); *John Stuart Mill and Harriet Taylor* (1951); *The Counter-Revolution of Science* (1952); *The Sensory Order* (1952); *The Road to Serfdom* (1956); *The Constitution of Liberty* (1960); *Studies in Philosophy, Politics and Economics* (1967); *Freiburger Studies* (1969); etc. Prof. social and moral science, University of Chicago, since 1950.

VON HOFFMAN, NICHOLAS (Oct. 16, 1929–); b. New York. Journalist, author. *Mississippi Notebook* (1964); *Multiuniversity* (1966); *We Are the People Our Parents Warned Us Against* (1968).

Von Holst, Hermann Eduard. See Holst, Hermann Eduard.

VON HUTTEN ZUM STOLZENBERG, BETSEY RIDDLE, FREIFRAU (Feb. 14, 1874–Jan. 26, 1957); b. Erie, Pa. Wrote under name, "Bettina von Hutten." Author. *Miss Carmichael's Conscience* (1898); *Violett* (1903); *Pam* (1905); *What Became of Pam* (1906); *The Halo* (1907); etc.

VON MISES, LUDWIG [Edler] (Sept. 29, 1881–July 26, 1946); b. Lemberg, Aust. Economist. *The Theory of Money and Credit* (1912); *Omnipotent Government: The Rise of the Total State and Total War* (1944); *Human Action: A Treatise on Economics* (1949); *Planning for Freedom* (1952); *Theory and History* (1957); etc. Economics dept., New York University, from 1946.

VON REDLICH, MARCELLUS DONALD ALEXANDER (Aug., 1893–July 26, 1946); b. Austria-Hungary. Lawyer, author. *Persian Language and Literature* (1928); *The Queen of the Azure Coast* (1935); *The Unconquered Albania* (1935); *Albania Yesterday and Today* (1936–37); etc.

VON TEMPSKI, ARMINE (Mrs. Alfred L. Ball) (Apr. 1, 1899–Dec. 2, 1943); b. Maui, Ter. Hawaii. Novelist. *Hula* (1927); *Dust* (1928); *Fire* (1929); *Lava* (1930); *Ripe Breadfruit* (1935); *Born in Paradise* (1940); *Aloha* (1945); etc.

Von Teuffel, Blanche Willis Howard. See Blanche Willis Howard.

VONNEGUT, KURT, JR. (Nov. 11, 1922–); b. Indianapolis, Ind. Novelist. *Player Piano* (1951); *Sirens of Titan* (1959); *Mother Night* (1961); *Cat's Cradle* (1963); *God Bless You, Mr. Rosewater* (1964); *Welcome to the Monkey House* (1968); *Slaughterhouse-Five* (1969); *Happy Birthday, Wanda June* (prod. 1970).

VOORHIES, FRANK COREY (June 1, 1877–); b. Woodbury, N.J. Author. *Story of Lizzie McGuire* (1902); *Reflections of Bridget McNulty* (1902); *Mrs. McPiggs of the Very Old Scratch* (1903); *Twisted History* (1904); etc.

VOORHIES, JOHN STEVENS (May 9, 1809–Nov. 19, 1865); b. New York. Publisher. Partner of Oliver Halsted, lawbook publisher. The firm of Baker, Voorhies and Co. continued the publishing business after his death.

VORSE, ALBERT WHITE (Aug. 18, 1866–1910); b. Littleton, Mass. Editor, explorer, author. *Laughter of the Sphinx* (1900); etc. Lit. editor, the *Boston Commonwealth*, 1894–96; editor, *Criterion*, 1900–1901.

VORSE, MARY [Marvin] HEATON (Mrs. Joseph O'Brien) (d. June 14, 1966); b. New York. Author. *The Breaking in of a Yachtsman's Wife* (1908); *Autobiography of an Elderly Woman* (anon., 1911); *The Very Little Person* (1911); *The Heart's Country* (1913); *The Prestons* (1918); *Growing Up* (1920); *Men and Steel* (1921); *Passaic* (1926); *A Footnote to Folly* (reminiscences, 1935); *Time and the Town* (1942); *Here Are the People* (1943); etc.

VOSE, EDWARD NEVILLE (Aug. 1, 1870–Aug. 31, 1949); b. Albany, N.Y. Editor, author. *The Spell of Flanders* (1915); *The World's Market* (1916); etc. Editor, *Dun's International Review,* 1903–25.

VOSS, CARL HERMANN (Dec. 8, 1910–); b. Pittsburgh, Pa. Congregational clergyman, author. *The Palestine Problem Today* (1953); *This is Israel* (with Theodore Huebner, 1956); *Rabbi and Minister* (1964); *Living Religions of the World* (1968). Editor: *The Universal God* (1953); *Stephen S. Wise: Servant of the People* (1969).

VOSS, ELIZABETH. b. Cincinnati, O. Poet. *The Soul's Voice* (1920); *Poems* (1926); *Archway of Dreams* (1932); *Shelter of Song* (1933); etc.

Voyage of the Hoppergrass, The. By Edmund L. Pearson (1913). Children's book about pirates and a treasure hunt.

Voyage of the Rattletrap, The. By Hayden Carruth (1897). Classic tale for boys depicting exciting adventures and episodes of travel across the prairie country from Dakota Territory to the West Coast.

Voyage to the Moon, A. Satirical tale by George Tucker (1827).

VOYNICH, ETHEL LILLIAN [Boole] (1864–Jul. 27, 1960). Author. *The Gadfly* (1897); *An Interrupted Friendship (1928); Put Off Thy Shoes* (1945); etc.

VREELAND, WILLIAMSON UPDIKE (Aug. 30, 1870–Nov. 6, 1942); b. Rocky Hill, N.J. Educator, author. *French Syntax and Composition* (with William Koren, 1907). Compiler: *Anthology of French Prose and Poetry* (with Regis Michaud, 1910); *Anthology of Seventeenth Century Literature* (with others, 1927); etc. Romance languages dept., Princeton University, 1894–1938.

Vulgarisms and Other Errors of Speech. By Richard Meade Bache (1868). A plea for the purity of language.

W

W.P.A. See Federal Theatre Project; Federal Writers Project.

WACK, HENRY WELLINGTON (1869–Dec. 13, 1954); b. Baltimore, Md. Author. *In the Snow of the Alps* (1901); *The Story of the Congo Free State* (1905); *The Camping Ideal* (1905); *The Romance of Victor Hugo and Julienne Drouet* (1905); *In Thanesland* (1906); *Hive Farm Ballads* (1918); *You and I and Life* (1925); *Songs of the Trail* (1926); *Explorations in Friendship* (1930); *Early History of Field and Stream* (1949); etc.

WADE, BOB (1920–). Co-author of mystery novels with Billy Miller (q.v.), under pen name "Wade Miller." *Uneasy Street* (1966); *Play Like You're Dead* (under pen name "Whit Masterson," 1967); *The Stroke of Seven* (under pen name "Bob Wade," 1965).

WADE, DECIUS SPEAR (Jan. 23, 1835–Aug. 3, 1905); b. in Ashtabula Co., O. Jurist, author. *Clair Lincoln* (1876), said to be the first novel written in Montana.

WADE, IRA OWEN (Oct. 4, 1896–); b. Richmond, Va. Educator. *Voltaire and Madame Du Châtelet* (1941); *Voltaire's Micromégas: A Study in the Fusion of Science, Myth, and Art* (1950); *The Search for a New Voltaire* (1958); *Voltaire and Candide* (1959); etc. Prof. French, Princeton University, since 1940.

WADE, JOHN DONALD (Sept. 28, 1892–Oct. 9, 1963); b. Marshallville, Ga. Educator, foundation executive, author. *Augustus Baldwin Longstreet: A Study of the Development of Culture in the South* (1924); *John Wesley* (1930); *Culture in the South* (1934); Co-editor: *Masterworks of World Literature* (1947). Founder, *Georgia Quarterly Review,* (1946); editor, 1946–50. Prof. English, University of Georgia, 1934–46; founder, Marshallville Foundation, 1944; pres., from 1944.

WADE, MARY HAZELTON (Mar. 23, 1860–Mar. 5, 1936); b. Charlestown, Mass. Author. *Little Japanese Cousin* (1901), and other "Little Cousin" books, including ones on the *Indian* (1901); *Russian* (1901); *Eskimo* (1902); *African* (1902); *Philippine* (1902); *Hawaiian* (1902); *Cuban* (1902); *Porto Rican* (1902); *Italian* (1903); *Swiss* (1903); *Siamese* (1903); *Norwegian* (1903); *German* (1904); *Turkish* (1904); *Jewish* (1904); *Irish* (1904); *Armenian* (1905); *Ten Little Indians* (1904); *The Coming of the White Men* (1905); *Ten Big Indians* (1905); *Indian Fairy Tales* (1906); *Abraham Lincoln* (1914); *Pilgrims of To-Day* (1916); *Twin Travelers in South America* (1918); and other "Twin Traveler" books; *Adventurers All* (1921); etc.

WAGENKNECHT, EDWARD (March 28, 1900–); b. Chicago, Ill. Educator, author. *Values in Literature* (1928); *Geraldine Farrar* (1929); *A Guide to Bernard Shaw* (1929); *The Man Charles Dickens* (1929); *Jenny Lind* (1931); *Mark Twain: The Man and His Work* (1935); *Cavalcade of the English Novel* (1943); *Cavalcade of the American Novel* (1952); *A Preface to Literature* (1953); *Longfellow: A Full Length Portrait* (1955); *The Seven Worlds of Theodore Roosevelt* (1958); *Movies in the Age of Innocence* (1962); *John Greenleaf Whittier* (1967); *Marilyn Monroe: A Composite View* (1969); *William Dean Howells: The Friendly Eye* (1969); etc. Prof. English, Boston University, since 1945.

WAGER, WALTER H. (Sept. 4, 1924–); b. New York. Author. *Death Hits the Jackpot* (1954); *Operation Intrigue* (1956); *Camp Century* (1962); *History of the O.S.S.* (1962); *I Spy* (1965); *Masterstroke* (1966); *Wipeout* (1967); *Death Twist* (1968); *The Girl Who Split* (1969); *Sledgehammer* (1970); etc.

WAGGAMAN, MARY T[eresa McKee] (Sept. 21, 1846–July 30, 1931); b. Baltimore, Md. Poet. *Little Comrades* (1894); *Tom's Luck-Pot* (1897); *Little Missy* (1900); *Corrine's Vow* (1902); *Carroll Dare* (1903); *The Secret of Pocomoke* (1914); *The Finding of Tony* (1919); etc.

WAGLEY, CHARLES [Walter] (Nov. 9, 1913–); b. Clarksville, Tex. Anthropologist. *Social and Religious Life of a Guatemala Village* (1949); *Amazon Town: A Study of Man in the Tropics* (1953); *Minority Groups in the New World* (with M. Harris, 1958); *Book Introduction to Brazil* (with others, 1963); etc. Anthropology dept., Columbia University, since 1946.

WAGNALLS, ADAM WILLIS (Sept. 24, 1843–Sept. 3, 1924); b. Lithopolis, O. Publisher. Joined Isaac Kaufman Funk in 1878 to form the publishing firm of Funk & Wagnalls, dictionary publishers. Their *New Standard Dictionary* appeared in 1912.

WAGNALLS, MABEL, b. Kansas City, Mo. Musician, author. *Miserere* (1892); *Stars of the Opera* (1898); augmented as *Opera and Its Stars* (1924); *Selma the Soprano* (1898); *Letters to Lithopolis* (1921); *The Light in the Valley* (1925); *The Mad Song* (1926); *The Immortal Sinner* (1933); etc.

WAGNER, CHARLES ABRAHAM (May 30, 1901–); b. New York. Journalist, poet. *Poems of the Soil and Sea* (1923); *Nearer the Bone* (1929); *Harvard: Four Centuries and Freedoms* (1950). Literary editor, *New York Daily Mirror* and *Sunday Mirror*, from 1932.

WAGNER, HARR (Mar. 20, 1857–June 20, 1936); b. Pennsylvania. Editor, author. *The Street and the Flower* (1883); *California History* (with Mark Keppel, 1922); *A Man Unafraid: The Story of John Charles Frémont* (with Herbert Bashford, 1927); *Joaquin Miller and His Other Self* (1929); etc. Editor, the *Golden Era*, San Francisco, 1881. Founder, Harr Wagner Publishing Co., San Francisco.

WAGNER, HENRY R[aup] (Sept. 27, 1862–Mar. 28, 1957); b. Philadelphia, Pa. Bibliographer, collector, author. *The Plains and the Rockies: A Bibliography of Original Narratives of Travel and Adventure, 1800–1865* (1921); *The Spanish Southwest, 1542–1794: An Annotated Bibliography* (1924); *Sir Francis Drake's Voyage around the World* (1926); *Peter Pond, Fur Trader and Explorer* (1955); etc. His extensive collection of Western Americana was acquired by Henry E. Huntington, Apr., 1922.

WAGONER, DAVID. Author. *Poems* (1959); *The Nesting Ground* (1963); *The Escape Artist* (1965); *Staying Alive* (1966); *Where is My Wandering Boy Tonight?* (1970).

"Wagoner of the Alleghanies, The." Poem by Thomas Buchanan Read (1862).

WAGSTAFF, BLANCHE SHOEMAKER (Mrs. Donald Carr) (July 10, 1888–); b. New York. Editor, poet. *Song of Youth* (1905); *Atys: A Grecian Drama; and Other Poems* (1909); *Alcestis* (1911); *Eris* (1912); *Narcissus, and Other Poems* (1918); *Quiet Waters* (1921); *Mortality, and Other Poems* (1930); *Beloved Son* (1944); *After the Flesh* (1953); etc. Editor: *Rhythmus; Poetry Journal*, Boston.

WAGSTAFF, HENRY McGILBERT (Jan. 27, 1876–1945); b. Roxboro, N.C. Educator, historian. Editor: *The Harrington Letters* (1914); *The Harris Letters* (1916); *The Papers of John Steele*, 2v. (1924); *Impressions of Men and Movements at the University of North Carolina* (1950); etc. History dept., University of North Carolina, from 1907; prof., from 1909.

WAID, EVA CLARK (Jan. 10, 1869–June 11, 1929); b. Ottawa, Kan. Poet. *Personal Letters and an Outline of Her Life*, ed. by Theodora Fields (1931); *Poems* (1932). Compiler: *From Plaza, Patio, and Palm* (1916).

WAINWRIGHT, JONATHAN MAYHEW (Feb. 24, 1792–Sept. 21, 1854); b. Liverpool, England. Episcopal bishop, author. *The Pathways and Abiding-Places of Our Lord* (1851); *The Land of Bondage . . . Being a Journal of a Tour in Egypt* (1852). One of the founders of New York University.

WAINWRIGHT, VIRGINIA (Mar. 14, 1891–); b. Chestnut Hill, Mass. Poet. *Poems* (1899); *Cleaning* (1920); *Youth, Love and Laughter* (poems, 1931); etc. Called the "Daisy Ashford of America."

"Wait Till the Clouds Roll By." Song by J. T. Wood, with music by H. J. Fulmer (1881).

"Waiting." Poem by John Burroughs, which first appeared in the *Knickerbocker Magazine*, March, 1863.

Waiting for Lefty. One-act play by Clifford Odets (prod. 1935).

"Waiting for News." Poem by Lucy Larcom.

Waiting for the End. Essays by Leslie A. Fiedler (1964).

Wake-Robin. By John Burroughs (1871). A sympathetic study of familiar birds.

Wakefield. By Nathaniel Hawthorne (1836). Story of the man who disappeared from his place in life, though he remained in the neighborhood unknown.

WAKEFIELD, DAN (May 21, 1932–); b. Indianapolis, Ind. Author. *Island in the City: The World of Spanish Harlem* (1959); *Revolt in the South* (1961); *The Addict, an Anthology* (1963); *Between the Lines* (1966); *Supernation at Peace and War* (1968); *Going All The Way* (1970).

WAKEMAN, FREDERIC (Dec. 26, 1909–); b. Scranton, Kan. Author. *Shore Leave* (1944); *The Hucksters* (1946); *Saxon Charm* (1947); *Mandrake Root* (1953); *Deluxe Tour* (1956); *Virginia Q* (1959); *Fault of the Apple* (1960); *A Free Agent* (1962); *The Flute Across the Pond* (1966); etc.

Waking, The. Collection of poems by Theodore Roethke (1953).

WAKOWSKI, DIANE (Aug. 3, 1937–); b. Whittier, Cal. Poet. *Coins and Coffins* (1962); *Discrepancies and Apparitions* (1966); *The George Washington Poems* (1967); *Greed, Parts I and II* (1968); *Inside the Blood Factory* (1968); *Motorcycle Betrayal Poems* (1971).

Walam Olum. Called the Red Score of the Lenni Lenape. An Indian record on birch bark strips, the earliest American Indian literature extant. It was discovered by Constantine S. Rafinesque, of Transylvania University, and he printed a translation in 1836. It contained a creation myth. *See* Daniel G. Boonton's *The Lenâpé and Their Legends* (1885).

WALCOT, CHARLES MILTON (c. 1816–May 15, 1868); b. London. Actor, playwright. *Don Giovanni in Gotham* (prod. 1844); *The Imp of the Elements; or, The Lake of the Dismal Swamp* (prod. 1844); *Hiawatha; or, Ardent Spirits and Laughing Water* (prod. 1856); *One Coat for Two Suits* (prod. 1857); etc.

WALCOTT, GREGORY DEXTER (Aug. 29, 1869–Mar. 20, 1959); b. Lincoln, R.I. Educator. *An Elementary Logic* (1931); *Logic and Scientific Method* (1952); etc. Philosophy dept., Long Island University, 1928–54.

WALD, LILLIAN D. (Mar. 10, 1867–Sept. 1, 1940); b. in Cincinnati, O. Social worker, author. *The House on Henry Street* (1915); *Windows on Henry Street* (1934); etc. Founder, Henry Street Settlement, New York, 1893. *See* Robert L. Duffus's *Lillian Wald, Neighbor and Crusader* (1938).

WALDEN, WALTER (June 1, 1870–); b. Milan, Ill. Author. *Boy Scouts Afloat* (1918); *The Hidden Islands* (1920); *The Voodoo Gold Trail* (1922).

Walden; or, Life in the Woods. By Henry David Thoreau (1854). A classic exposition of the simple life, giving an account of Thoreau's social and economic experiment at "Walden" and setting forth his philosophy of life.

Walden Two. Utopian novel by B. F. Skinner (1948). Describes a community formed on rational principles of Skinner's "operant conditioning."

Waldie's Select Circulating Library. Begun Oct. 1, 1832, by Adam Waldie and John Jay Smith in Philadelphia. A republication of important foreign books in the form of a weekly, a venture made possible by the lack of an international copyright. In 1845, it was succeeded by *Smith's Weekly Volume*, founded by Lloyd Pearsall Smith, son of John Jay Smith.

Waldimar. Play by John J. Bailey (prod. 1831).

WALDMAN, MILTON (Oct. 4, 1895–); b. Cleveland, O. Editor, author. *Americana: The Literature of American History* (1925); *Sir Walter Raleigh* (1928); *The Disinherited*

(1929); *England's Elizabeth* (1933); *Joan of Arc* (1935); *Biography of a Family: Catherine de Medici and Her Children* (1936); *Elizabeth and Leicester* (1945); *Queen Elizabeth* (1952); etc.

WALDO, EDWARD HAMILTON (1918–); Author. Pen name "Theodore Sturgeon." *The Dreaming Jewels* (1950, later known as *The Synthetic Man); Thunder and Roses* (stories, 1957); *The Cosmic Rape* (1958); *Venus Plus X* (1960); *The Joyous Invasions* (1965); *Starshine* (1968); *Caviar* (stories, 1968).

WALDO, FULLERTON LEONARD (Apr. 5, 1877–Oct. 24, 1933); b. Cambridge, Mass. Correspondent, music critic, author. *America at the Front* (1918); *Down the Mackenzie* (1923); *Grenfell* (1924); *The Saga of a Supercargo* (1926); *German and Russian Opera* (1926); *Early Italian & French Opera* (1927); *Modern French and Italian Opera* (1927); etc. With the *Philadelphia Public Ledger,* 1908–33; war correspondent, 1917–18; music critic, 1920–33.

WALDO, S[amuel] PUTNAM (Mar. 12, 1779–Feb. 23, 1826); b. Pomfret, Conn. Editor, author. *Memoirs of Andrew Jackson* (1818); *Life and Character of Stephen Decatur* (1821); *Biographical Sketches of Distinguished American Naval Heroes in the War of the Revolution* (1823); and many other naval and military biographies.

Waldron, Mrs. Webb. See Marion Patton.

WALDRON, WEBB (Sept. 8, 1882–Aug. 5, 1945); b. Vergennes, Mich. Editor, author. *The Road to the World* (1922); *We Explore the Great Lakes* (1923); *Shanklin* (1925); *Blue Glamor* (1929); *Uncharted* (1936); *The Americans* (1941); etc. On editorial staff, *Collier's Weekly,* 1917–20.

Walk in the Sun, A. Novel by Harry Brown (1944). An American platoon lands on an Italian beach and proceeds to its assigned objective.

WALKER, ABBIE PHILLIPS (Mrs. Fred Allan Walker) (June 6, 1867–Jan. 10, 1943); b. Exeter, R.I. Author. *The Sandman* series, 12v. (1916–23); and other children's books; also more than 2,000 children's stories in newspapers.

WALKER, ALBERT PERRY (June 9, 1862–1911); b. Alton Bay, N.H. Educator, author. *Essentials in English History* (1905). Editor of several English textbooks.

WALKER, ALEXANDER (Oct. 13, 1818–Jan. 24, 1893); b. Fredericksburg, Va. Journalist, author. *Jackson and New Orleans* (1856); augmented as *The Life of Andrew Jackson* (1859). On staff, *New Orleans Daily Delta, Daily Picayune, New Orleans Times,* etc.

WALKER, ALICE JOHNSTONE (Aug. 13, 1871–); b. New Haven, Conn. Author. *Little Plays from American History for Young Folks* (1914); *Dolly Peckham's Clothesline* (1928); etc.

WALKER, AMASA (May 4, 1799–Oct. 29, 1875); b. Woodstock, Conn. Reformer, economist, author. *The Nature and Uses of Money and Mixed Currency* (1857); *The Science of Wealth* (1866); etc.

WALKER, CHARLES RUMFORD (July 31, 1893–); b. Concord, N.H. Author. *Steel: The Diary of a Furnace Worker* (1922); *Bread and Fire* (1927); *Our Gods Are Not Born* (1931); *American City* (1937); *American Productivity* (1946); *Steeltown: An Industrial Case History* (1950); *The Man on the Assembly* (with Robert H. Guest, 1952); *Toward the Automatic Factory* (1957); *Modern Technology and Civilization* (1962); *Technology, Industry and Man: The Age of Acceleration* (1968). Editorial staff, the *Atlantic Monthly; The Independent; The Bookman.*

WALKER, DANTON MACINTYRE (July 26, 1899–Aug. 8, 1960); b. Marietta, Ga. Author. *Danton's Inferno* (autobiography, 1955); *Spooks Deluxe: Some Excursions into the Supernatural* (1956); etc.

WALKER, FRANCIS AMASA (July 2, 1840–Jan. 5, 1897); b. Boston, Mass., son of Amasa Walker. Educator, economist, statistician, author. *The Indian Question* (1874); *Money* (1878); *Political Economy* (1883); *The Making of the Nation* (1895); etc. President, Massachusetts Institute of Technology, 1881–97.

WALKER, FRANKLIN DICKERSON (Nov. 13, 1900–); b. Republic, Mich. Educator, author. *Frank Norris* (1932); *San Francisco's Literary Frontier* (1939); *Ambrose Bierce* (1941); *A Literary History of Southern California* (1950); *Seacoast of Bohemia* (1966); *Jack London and the Klondike* (1966); etc. Prof. American literature, Mills College, since 1946.

WALKER, FRED ALLAN (Mar. 27, 1867–Mar. 25, 1947); b. Berwick, Me. Editor, publisher. Managing editor, the *Boston Journal,* 1896–1909; publisher, the *Washington Times,* 1911–19; the *New York Evening Telegram,* 1920–25; with the *New York Sun,* 1925–34.

Walker, Helen. See Helen Walker Homan.

WALKER, JAMES (Aug. 16, 1794–Dec. 23, 1874); b. Woburn, Mass. Unitarian clergyman, educator, author. *Sermons Preached in the Chapel of Harvard College* (1861); *Reason, Faith, and Duty* (1876). President, Harvard University, 1853–60.

WALKER, JAMES BARR (July 29, 1805–Mar. 6, 1887); b. Philadelphia, Pa. Congregational clergyman, educator, author. *The Philosophy of the Plan of Salvation* (1839); *Experiences of Pioneer Life in the Early Settlements and Cities of the West* (1881). Founder, *The Watchman of the Valley,* Cincinnati, 1840; and the *Herald of the Prairies,* Chicago, 1846. Prof. intellectual and moral philosophy and belles-lettres, Wheaton College, Wheaton, Ill., 1870–84.

WALKER, JAMES PERKINS (1829–May 10, 1868); b. Portsmouth, N.H. Publisher, author. *Faith and Patience* (1860); *Sunny-Eyed Tim* (1861); etc. Co-founder, publishing firm, Walker, Wise, and Co., Boston, c. 1860.

WALKER, JESSE (1810–1852). Novelist, poet. *Fort Niagara* (anon., 1845); *Queenston* (anon., 1845); *Poems* (1854).

WALKER, JOHN BRISBEN (Sept. 10, 1847–July 7, 1931); b. near Pittsburgh, Pa. Editor, publisher. Managing editor, the *Washington Chronicle,* 1876–77; owner and publisher, *Cosmopolitan,* 1889–94; editor, 1886–1905.

WALKER, MILDRED (Mrs. Mildred Merrifield Walker Schemm) (May 2, 1905–); b. Philadelphia, Pa. Author. *Fireweed* (1934); *Light from Arcturus* (1935); *Winter Wheat* (1944); *The Quarry* (1947); *The Southwest Corner* (1951); *The Curlew's Cry* (1955); *The Body of a Young Man* (1960); etc.

WALKER, ROBERT SPARKS (Feb. 4, 1878–); b. Chickamauga, Tenn. Editor, naturalist, author. *Anchor Poems* (1925); *My Father's Farm* (poems, 1927); *Chattanooga, Its History and Growth* (1929); *Torchlights to the Cherokees* (1931); *Eating Thunder, and Other Stories* (1933); *Weedland and Woodland Walks* (1933); *When God Failed* (poems, 1938); *Lookout: The Story of a Mountain* (1941); *As the Indians Left It* (1955).

WALKER, STANLEY (Oct. 21, 1898–Nov. 25, 1962); b. Lampasas, Texas. Editor, author. *The Night Club Era* (1933); *City Editor* (1934); *Mrs. Astor's Horse* (1935); *Dewey: An American of This Century* (1944); *Journey Toward the Sunlight* (1947); *Home to Texas* (1956). With the *New York Herald Tribune,* the *Philadelphia Evening Public Ledger,* etc.

WALKER, STUART (Mar. 4, 1888–Mar. 13, 1941); b. Augusta, Ky. Playwright. *Portmanteau Plays* (1917); *More Portmanteau Plays* (1919); *Five Flights Up* (prod. 1922); etc.

WALKER, WILLIAM (May 8, 1824–Sept. 12, 1860); b. Nashville, Tenn. Adventurer, leader of expedition against Nicaragua, author. *The War in Nicaragua* (1860); etc. See W. V. Wells's *Walker's Expedition to Nicaragua* (1860); Richard Harding Davis's *Real Soldiers of Fortune* (1906).

WALKER, WILLISTON (July 1, 1860–Mar. 9, 1922); b. Portland, Me. Congregational clergyman, author. *A History of the Congregational Churches in the United States* (1894); *Ten New England Leaders* (1901).

Walking-Stick Papers. Essays by Robert Cortes Holliday (1918).

WALL, ALEXANDER JAMES (Oct. 25, 1884–Apr. 15, 1944); b. New York. Librarian. Compiler: *List of New York Almanacs 1694–1850* (1921); *Books on Architecture Printed in America, 1775–1830* (1925); *A Sketch of the Life of Horatio Seymour* (1929); *American Genealogical Research* (1942); etc. Librarian, New-York Historical Society, 1921–37; director, from 1937,

WALL, E[vander] BERRY (Jan. 14, 1861–May 4, 1940); b. New York. Author. *Neither Pest nor Puritan* (autobiography, 1940).

Wall, The. Novel by John Hersey (1950). About the uprising of the Jews of Warsaw against the Nazis in World War II.

Wall Street Journal. New York. Newspaper. Founded 1882. Financial paper which also contains both literary and historical material. It is edited by Vermont Royster and publishes book reviews.

Wall Street Stories. By Edwin Le Fevre (1901).

WALLACE, CHARLES WILLIAM (Feb. 6, 1865–Aug. 7, 1932); b. Hopkins, Mo. Educator, author. *Lyrics for Leisure Moments* (1892); *Spider-Webs in Verse* (1892); *The Children of the Chapel at Blackfriars, 1597–1603* (1908); *The Evolution of the English Drama up to Shakespeare* (1912); *The First London Theatre* (1913). English dept., University of Nebraska, 1901–32.

WALLACE, DAVID DUNCAN (May 23, 1874–Apr. 29, 1951); b. Columbia, S.C. Educator, historian. *Constitutional History of South Carolina, 1725–1775* (1899); *Life of Henry Laurens* (1915); *The History of South Carolina*, 3v. (1934); etc. Prof. history, Wofford College, from 1899.

WALLACE, DE WITT (Nov. 12, 1889–); b. St. Paul, Minn. Editor. Founder, *Reader's Digest*, 1921; editor, since 1921.

WALLACE, DILLON (June 24, 1863–Sept. 28, 1939); b. Craigsville, N.Y. Author. *The Lure of the Labrador Wild* (1905); *Ungava Bob* (1907); *The Wilderness Castaways* (1913); *Story of Grenfell of the Labrador* (1922); *The Lost Mine* (1930); and many other books of adventure, chiefly in the Labrador.

WALLACE, HENRY (Mar. 19, 1836–Feb. 22, 1916); b. West Newton, Pa. Editor, author. *Uncle Henry's Letters to the Farm Boy* (1897); *Uncle Henry's Own Story of His Life*, 3v. (1917–19). Editor, *Wallace's Farmer*, 1895–1916. He was succeeded by his son, Henry Cantwell Wallace (1866–1924), father of Henry A. Wallace, vice-president of the United States.

WALLACE, HENRY A[gard] (Oct. 7, 1888–Nov. 18, 1965); b. in Adair Co., Ia., grandson of Henry Wallace. Government official, editor, author. *America Must Choose* (1934); *New Frontiers* (1934); *Statesmanship and Religion* (1934); *Paths to Plenty* (1938); *The American Choice* (1940); *The Century of the Common Man* (1943); *Democracy Reborn* (1944); *Sixty Million Jobs* (1945); *Toward World Peace* (1948); *Corn and the Midwestern Farmer* (with W. L. Brown, 1956); *The Long Look Ahead* (1960); etc. Assoc. editor, *Wallace's Farmer*, 1910–24; editor, 1924–29; editor, *Iowa Homestead and Wallace's Farmer*, 1929–33; editor, *New Republic*, 1946–48. Secretary of agriculture, 1933–40; vice-president of the United States 1941–45; secretary of commerce, 1945–46.

WALLACE, HORACE BINNEY (Feb. 26, 1817–Dec. 16, 1852); b. Philadelphia, Pa. Critic, legal writer. *Stanley; or, The Recollections of a Man of the World* (anon., 1838); *Art, Scenery and Philosophy in Europe* (1855); *Literary Criticism, and Other Papers* (1856).

WALLACE, IRVING (Mar. 19, 1916–). Author. *Fabulous Originals* (1955); *Square Pegs* (1957); *Fabulous Showman: The Life and Times of P.T. Barnum* (1959); *The Chapman Report* (1960); *The Twenty-Seventh Wife* (1961); *The Prize* (1962); *The Three Sirens* (1963); *The Man* (1964); *The Plot* (1967); *The Seven Minutes* (1969); *Nymphos and Other Maniacs* (1971);etc.

WALLACE, LEW[is] (Apr. 10, 1827–Feb. 15, 1905); b. Brookville, Ind. Soldier, lawyer, diplomat, novelist. *The Fair God* (1873); *Ben Hur: A Tale of the Christ* (1880); *The Boyhood of Christ* (1888); *The Prince of India* (1893); *The Wooing of Malkatoon* (poem, 1898); *Lew Wallace: An Autobiography* (1906); etc. See Irving McKee's *Ben-Hur Wallace* (1947).

WALLACE, LILA ACHESON, b. Virden, Manitoba, Can. Co-founder, co-editor and co-owner with her husband, De-Witt Wallace, of *Reader's Digest*.

WALLACE, ROBERT (Jan. 10, 1932–); b. Springfield, Mo. Poet. *This Various World, and Other Poems* (1957); *Views from a Ferris Wheel* (1965). Editor: *Poems on Poetry* (1965). Faculty, Western Reserve University, since 1965.

WALLACE, S[amuel] MAYNER (Dec. 25, 1886–); b. New York. Educator. *Our Governmental Machine* (1925); *The New Deal in Action* (1934); etc. Government dept., Columbia University, since 1920.

WALLACE, SUSAN [Arnold] E[lston] (Mrs. Lew Wallace) (Dec. 25, 1830–Oct. 1, 1907); b. Crawfordsville, Ind. Author. *The Storied Sea* (1883); *Ginevra; or, The Old Oak Chest* (1887); *The Land of the Pueblos* (1888); *The Repose in Egypt* (1888); *Along the Bosphorus, and Other Sketches* (1898). Her best known poem is "The Patter of Little Feet."

WALLACE, WILLARD MOSHER (Oct. 11, 1911–); b. South Portland, Me. Educator, author. *Appeal to Arms* (1951); *Traitorous Hero* (1954); *Friend William* (1958); *Sir Walter Raleigh* (1959); *Interview in Weehawken* (with H. C. Syrett and J. G. Cooke, 1960); *Soul of the Lion* (1960); *East to Bagaduce* (1963); *Jonathan Dearborn* (1967). Prof. history, Wesleyan University, since 1955.

WALLACE, WILLIAM KAY (Nov. 10, 1886–); b. New York. Author. *Greater Italy* (1917); *The Trend of History* (1922); *Thirty Years of Modern History* (1926); etc.

WALLACE, WILLIAM ROSS (1819–May 5, 1881); b. Lexington, or Paris, Ky. Poet. *The Battle of Tippecanoe* (1837); *Alban the Pirate* (poem, 1848); *Meditations in America, and Other Poems* (1851). Author of the familiar lines, "And the hand that rocks the cradle is the hand that rules the world."

WALLACH, IRA JAN (Jan. 22, 1913–); b. New York. Author. *The Horn and the Roses* (1947); *Hopalong-Freud* (1951); *Gutenberg's Folly* (1954); *Drink To Me Only* (play, 1958); *Muscle Beach* (1959); *Smiling, the Boy Fell Dead* (play, 1961); *Absence of a Cello* (play, 1964); etc.

WALLACK, LESTER (Jan. 1, 1820–Sept. 6, 1888); b. New York. Actor, manager, playwright. *Two to One* (prod. 1854); *First Impressions* (1856); *The Veteran* (prod. 1859); *Central Park* (prod. 1861); *Rosedale* (prod. 1863); *Memories of Fifty Years* (autobiography, 1889); etc. Succeeded his father, James William Wallack, as manager of Wallack's Theatre, New York, 1864. See Montrose J. Moses's *Famous Actor-Families in America* (1906).

WALLANT, EDWARD LEWIS (1926–1962). Author. *The Human Season* (1960); *The Pawnbroker* (1961); *Tenants of Moonbloom* (1963); *The Children at the Gate* (1964).

WALLBANK, THOMAS WALTER (July 27, 1901–); b. Swadlincote, Eng. Educator. *India in the New Era* (1951); *Contemporary Africa: Continent in Transition* (1956); *Living World History* (with Arnold Fletcher, 1957); *Man's Story: World History in Its Geographic Setting* (1961); *The Clash of Ideas* (1969); etc. Prof. history, University of Southern California, since 1944.

WALLER, LESLIE (Apr. 1, 1923–); b. Chicago, Ill. Novelist. *Three Day Pass* (1945); *Show Me the Way* (1947); *The Bed She Made* (1951); *Witching Night* (under pen name "C. S. Cody," 1952); *Phoenix Island* (1958); *Explorers* (1961); etc. Book review staff, *Chicago Sun-Times.*

WALLER, MARY ELLA (1855–June 14, 1938). Author. *The Wood-Carver of 'Lympus* (1904); *Through the Gates of the Netherlands* (1907); *A Cry in the Wilderness* (1912); *A Daughter of the Rich* (1925); *The Windmill on the Dune* (1931).

Wallet of Time, The. By William Winter, 2v. (1913). Reminiscences, chiefly of the theatre world, with sidelights on the author's contemporaries.

WALLIS, WILSON D. (Mar. 7, 1886–); b. Forest Hill, Md. Educator, anthropologist, author. *Messiahs* (1918); *Introduction to Anthropology* (1926); *Culture and Progress* (1930); *Religion in Primitive Society* (1939); *Messiahs, Their Role in Civilization* (1943); *Canadian Dakota* (1947); *The Micmac Indians of Eastern Canada* (1955); *Welfare Programs: An Economic Appraisal* (1968); etc. Anthropology dept., University of Minnesota, since 1923.

WALLOP, [John] DOUGLASS, III (Mar. 8, 1920–); b. Washington, D.C. Author. *The Year the Yankees Lost the Pennant* (1954); *So This Is What Happened to Charlie Moe* (1965).

WALMSLEY, JAMES ELLIOTT (June 24, 1872–); b. Mingo, Va. Educator, historian. *The Making of South Carolina* (1921); *The Peaks of Otter* (1922); *The Shadow of the Peaks* (1923). Professor history, Winthrop College, Rock Hill, S.C., 1912–25; State Teachers College, Farmville, Va., since 1925.

WALN, NORA (June 4, 1895–Feb. 27, 1964); b. Grampian Hills, Pa. Author. *The Street of Precious Pearls* (1921); *The House of Exile* (1933); *Reaching for the Stars* (1939).

WALN, ROBERT (Oct. 20, 1794–July 4, 1825); b. Philadelphia, Pa. *The Hermit in America on a Visit to Philadelphia* (under pen name "Peter Atall," 1819); *American Bards* (1820); *Sisyphi Opus* (poems, 1820); *The Hermit in Philadelphia: Second Series* (under pen name "Peter Atall," 1821); *Life of the Marquis de La Fayette* (1825). Editor: *Biography of the Signers of the Declaration of Independence,* v. 3–6 (1823–24).

WALSH, CHAD (May 10, 1914–   ); b. South Boston, Va. Educator, author. *Stop Looking and Listen* (1947); *C. S. Lewis: Apostle to the Skeptics* (1949); *The Factual Dark* (1949); *The Early Christians of the 21st Century* (1950); *Knock and Enter* (1953); *Campus Gods on Trial* (1953); *Faith and Behavior* (with E. Montizambert, 1954); *Eden Two-Way* (1954); *Behold the Glory* (1956); *Nelly and Her Flying Crocodile* (1956); *The Rough Years* (1960); *Why Go to Church?* (with E. Walsh, 1962); *Doors into Poetry* (1962); *From Utopia to Nightmare* (1962); *The Psalm of Christ* (1964); *The Unknowing Dance* (1964); *Today's Poets* (1964); *Garlands for Christmas* (1965). Prof. English, Beloit College, since 1952.

WALSH, CHARLES CLINTON (May 20, 1867–Dec. 20, 1943); b. Kirkwood, Ill. Author. *Early Days on the Western Range* (1917); *The Nester and the Tenderfoot* (1918); *The Old Quartette* (1923); *Passing of the Years* (1928); *Memories of '93* (1928).

WALSH, EDMUND [Aloysius] (Oct. 10, 1885–Oct. 31, 1956); b. Boston, Mass. Roman Catholic clergyman, educator, author. *The Fall of the Russian Empire* (1928); *Woodcarver of Tyrol* (1935); *Total Power* (1948); *Total Empire* (1951); etc. Regent, School of Foreign Affairs, Georgetown University, from 1919.

WALSH, GEORGE ETHELBERT (Mar. 12, 1865–Feb. 4, 1941); b. Brooklyn, N.Y. Author. *The Mysterious Burglar* (1901); *Polly Comes to Woodbine* (1915); *Twilight Animal Stories,* 10v. (1917); *White Tail the Deer* (1917); etc.

WALSH, HENRY COLLINS (Nov. 23, 1863–Apr. 29, 1927); b. Florence, It. Explorer, editor, author. *By the Potomac, and Other Verses* (1889); *The Last Cruise of the Miranda* (1896); *The White World* (with others, 1902); etc. Founder, *American Notes and Queries,* 1888; co-editor, *The Smart Set,* 1902–06; *Travel Magazine,* 1907–10. One of the founders of the Arctic Club and the Explorers' Club.

WALSH, JAMES JOSEPH (Apr. 12, 1865–Feb. 28, 1942); b. Archbald, Pa. Physician, author. *Makers of Modern Medicine* (1904); *The Thirteenth, Greatest of Centuries* (1907); *The Century of Columbus* (1914); *History of Medicine in New York,* 5v. (1919); *What Civilization Owes to Italy* (1923); *A Catholic Looks at Life* (1928); *A Golden Treasury of Mediaeval Literature* (1930); *Mother Alphonsa, Rose Hawthorne Lathrop* (1930); *American Jesuits* (1934); etc.

Walsh, Mrs. Richard John. See Pearl S. Buck.

WALSH, RICHARD JOHN (Nov. 20, 1886–May 28, 1960); b. Lyons, Kans. Publisher, editor, author. *Kidd* (poems, 1922); *The Making of Buffalo Bill* (with Milton S. Salsbury, 1928). Editor: *The Adventures of Marco Polo* (1928); *Collier's Weekly,* 1922–24; assoc. editor, *Judge,* 1927–33; editor, *Asia,* 1933–46; editorial board, *United Nations World,* 1947–49. Pres., John Day Co., 1926–59; chairman of board, 1959–60.

WALSH, ROBERT (Aug. 30, 1784–Feb. 7, 1859); b. Baltimore, Md. Editor, consul, author. *Genius and Disposition of the French Government* (1810); *Didactics, Social, Literary, and Political,* 2v. (1836); etc. Editor: *The Works of the British Poets,* v. 25-50 (1822). Editor, *American Register,* 1809–10; *Museum of Foreign Literature and Science,* 1822–23; founder, *American Review of History and Politics,* 1811; co-founder (with William Fry), *American Quarterly Review,* 1827. U.S. consul at Paris, 1845–51. See Joseph C. Walsh's *Robert Walsh* (1927).

WALSH, THOMAS (Oct. 14, 1871–Oct. 29, 1928); b. Brooklyn, N.Y. Poet, critic, editor, compiler. *The Prison Ships, and Other Poems* (1909); *The Pilgrim Kings* (1915); *Gardens Overseas, and Other Poems* (1918); *Don Foluet, and Other Poems* (1920); *Selected Poems* (1930); etc. Compiler: *The Catholic Anthology* (1927); etc. Asst. editor, *The Commonweal,* 1924–28.

WALSH, WARREN BARTLETT (Dec. 21, 1909–); b. Brookfield, Mass. Educator. *Russia: A Handbook* (with R. A. Price, 1947); *Russia and the Soviet Union* (1958); *Perspective and Patterns, Discourses on History* (1962); *International Conflict and Cooperation* (1964); *Science and International Public Affairs* (1967); etc. History dept., Syracuse University, since 1935. Assoc. editor, *Russian Review,* since 1948.

WALSH, WILLIAM SHEPARD (Feb. 1, 1854–Dec. 8, 1919); b. Paris, France, grandson of Robert Walsh. Editor, critic, author. Wrote also as "William Shepard." *Authors and Authorship* (1882); *Handy-Book of Literary Curiosities* (1893); *Abraham Lincoln and the London Punch* (1909); *Handy Book of Curious Information* (1913); *Heroes and Heroines in Fiction,* 2 series (1914–15); etc. Editor: *Enchiridion of Criticism* (1885). Editor, *Lippincott's Magazine,* 1885–89; lit. editor, the *New York Herald.*

WALSH, WILLIAM THOMAS (Sept. 11, 1891–Feb. 22, 1949); b. Waterbury, Conn. Educator, author. *Isabella of Spain* (1930); *Out of the Whirlwind* (1935); *Shekels* (1937); *Philip II* (1937); *Poems* (1939); *St. Teresa of Avila* (1943); *St. Peter the Apostle* (1948); etc. Prof. of English, Manhattanville College of the Sacred Heart, New York, 1933–47.

WALTER, ELLERY (June 16, 1906–Apr. 2, 1935); b. Petersburg, Fla. Author. *The World on One Leg* (1928); *High Hats and Low Bows* (1931); *Manchurian Empire* (1934).

WALTER, EUGENE (Nov. 27, 1874–1941); b. Cleveland, O. Playwright. *The Undertow* (prod. 1906); *Paid in Full* (prod. 1907); *The Wolf* (prod. 1907); *The Easiest Way* (prod. 1908); *The Real Issue* (prod. 1908); *Fine Feathers* (prod. 1911); *The Onlooker* (prod. 1922); *Jennie, the Watercress Girl* (1947); etc.

WALTER, FRANK KELLER (July 23, 1874–Oct. 28, 1945); b. Point Pleasant, Pa. Librarian, author. Co-author: *Modern Drama and Opera*, 2v. (1911–15). Compiler: *Abbreviations and Technical Terms* (1912); *Bibliography, Practical, Enumerative, Historical* (with H. V. Van Hoesen, 1928); etc. Librarian, University of Minnesota, 1921–43.

WALTER, PAUL ALFRED FRANCIS (Sept. 29, 1873–); b. Berlin. Editor, author. *The Cities That Died of Fear* (1916); *Yesterdays in the Spanish Southwest* (1929); *Social Sciences, a Problem Approach* (1949); *Race and Culture Relations* (1952). Editor, *El Palacio*, and *The New Mexico Historical Review.*

WALTER, THOMAS (Dec. 13, 1696–Jan. 10, 1725); b. Roxbury, Mass. Congregational clergyman, author. *A Choice Dialogue Between John Faustus, a Conjurer, and Jack Tory His Friend* (1720); *The Grounds and Rules of Musick Explained* (1721); *The Sweet Psalmist of Israel* (1722).

WALTERS, RAYMOND (Aug. 25, 1885–Oct., 1970); b. Bethlehem, Pa. Educator, author. *The Bethlehem Bach Choir* (1918); *Educational Jottings* (1924); *Stephen Foster: Youth's Golden Gleam* (1936); *Historical Sketch of the University of Cincinnati* (1941); *Gifts and Bequests to Higher Education* (1959). President, University of Cincinnati, 1932–55.

WALTERS, RAYMOND, Jr. (Aug. 23, 1912–); b. Bethlehem, Pa. Editor, Author. *Alexander James Dallas* (1943); *Albert Gallatin: Jeffersonian Financier and Diplomat* (1957); *The Virginia Dynasty* (1965); etc. Staff, *New York Times Book Review*, since 1958.

WALTON, EDA LOU (Jan. 19, 1896–); b. Deming, N.M. Educator, author. *Dawn Boy: Blackfoot and Navajo Songs* (1926); *Jane Matthew, and Other Poems* (1931); *Turquoise Boy and White Shell Girl* (1933); *So Many Daughters* (poems, 1952); etc. Editor: *The City Day* (1929); *This Generation* (with G.K. Anderson, 1940). With New York University.

WALTZ, ELIZABETH CHERRY (Dec. 10, 1866–1903); b. Columbus, O. Journalist, novelist. *Pa Gladden* (1903); *The Ancient Landmark* (1905). With the *Louisville Courier-Journal*, 1899–1903.

Waltz, The. Short story by Dorothy Parker (1930).

WALVOORD, JOHN FLIPSE (May 1, 1910–); b. Sheboygan, Wis. Educator. *The Doctrine of the Holy Spirit* (1943); *The Return of the Lord* (1955); *To Live is Christ* (1960); *Israel in Prophecy* (1962); *The Church in Prophecy* (1964); *The Revelation of Jesus Christ* (1966); *The Nations in Prophecy* (1967); etc. Pres., Dallas Theological Seminary, since 1952.

WALWORTH, ARTHUR [Clarence] (July 9, 1903–); b. Newton, Mass. Author: *Black Ships Off Japan* (1946); *Cape Breton* (1948); *Woodrow Wilson*, 2v. (1958; Pulitzer Prize for biography, 1958); etc.

WALWORTH, CLARENCE AUGUSTUS (May 30, 1820–Sept. 19, 1900); b. Plattsburg, N.Y., brother of Mansfield Tracy Walworth. Roman Catholic clergyman, author. *The Gentle Skeptic* (1863); *Andiatorocté ... and Other Poems* (1888); *Reminiscences of Edgar P. Wadhams* (1893); *The Oxford Movement in America* (1895); etc.

WALWORTH, DOROTHY (Mrs. Merle Crowell) (Mar. 15, 1900–Nov. 5, 1953); b. Cornwall, N.Y. Author. *Faith of Our Fathers* (1925); *The Pride of the Town* (1926); *Chickens Come Home to Roost* (1927); *The Glory and the Parlour* (1929); *They Thought They Could Buy It* (1930); *Reno Fever* (1932); *Rainbow at Noon* (1935); *Feast of Reason* (1941); *Nicodemus* (1946).

WALWORTH, ELLEN HARDIN (Mrs. Mansfield Tracy Walworth) (Oct. 20, 1832–June 23, 1915); b. Jacksonville, Ill. Author. *Saratoga* (1877); *Battles of Saratoga* (1891). See *Americana*, v. 29, 1935.

WALWORTH, ELLEN HARDIN (Oct. 2, 1858–Sept. 20, 1932); b. Saratoga Springs, N.Y., daughter of Mansfield Tracy Walworth and Ellen Hardin Walworth. Author. *An Old World as Seen through Young Eyes* (1877); *The Life and Times of Kateri Tekakwitha, the Lily of the Mohawks, 1656–1680* (1891); *Life Sketches of Father Walworth* (1907).

WALWORTH, JEANNETTE RITCHIE HADERMANN (Mrs. Douglas Walworth) (Feb. 22, 1837–Feb. 4, 1918); b. Philadelphia, Pa. Author. Early books under maiden name. *Forgiven at Last* (1870); *Dead Men's Shoes* (1872); *Against the World* (1873); *Heavy Yokes* (1876); *Nobody's Business* (1878); *The Bar Sinister* (anon. 1885), republished as *His Celestial Marriage* (1899) and *His Three Wives* (1900); *Southern Silhouettes* (1887); *The New Man at Rossmere* (1886); *A Little Radical* (1889); *Uncle Scipio* (1896); etc. See C. A. Walworth's *The Walworths of America* (1897).

WALWORTH, MANSFIELD TRACY (Dec. 3, 1830–June 3, 1873); b. Albany, N.Y., brother of Clarence Augustus Walworth. Novelist. *Mission of Death* (1853); *Lulu: A Tale of the National Hotel Poisoning* (1863); *Hotspur* (1864); *Stormcliff* (1865); *Warwick; or, The Lost Nationalities of America* (1869); *Delaplaine* (1871); *Beverly* (1872); *Married in Mask* (1880); *Tahara* (1888); etc.

WALZ, JAY (Oct. 26, 1907–   ); b. South Bend, Ind. Journalist, author. *The Middle East* (1965); *The Bizarre Sisters* (with A. Walz, 1950); *The Undiscovered Country* (1958). Staff, *New York Times*, since 1943.

WANGNER, ELLEN [J.] D[iffin] (Oct. 1872–); b. Fenwick, Ont. Editor, author. *Bobby Lynx* (1919); *Mother Fox* (1921). Editor, *The American Home.*

WANN, LOUIS (Aug. 30, 1885–Apr. 21, 1956); b. Claypool, Ind. Educator, author. *Century Readings in the English Essay* (1926); *Effective English: A Handbook of Composition* (1932); etc. Editor, *The Rise of Realism*, v. 3 of *American Literature: A Period Anthology* (1933). Editor, *The Parchment*, 1926–30; associate editor, *The Personalist*, from 1941. Prof. English, University of Southern California, 1919–51.

"Wanted—A Man." Poem by Edmund Clarence Stedman (1862). Voicing the public discontent over the failure of the Union troops to capture Richmond.

WAPLES, DOUGLAS (Mar. 3, 1893–); b. Philadelphia, Pa. Educator, author. *What People Want to Read About* (with R. W. Tyler, 1931); *National Libraries and Foreign Scholarship* (1936); *People and Print* (1937); *Research Methods and Teachers' Problems* (1930); *What Reading Does to People* (with others, 1940). Education dept., University of Chicago, since 1925.

Wapshot Chronicle. Novel by John Cheever (1957).

War Cry. New York. Weekly paper published by the Salvation Army. Founded 1881.

War Is Kind. Collection of poems by Stephen Crane (1899). A notable early example of poems written in free verse.

WARBURG, JAMES PAUL (Aug. 18, 1896–); b. Hamburg, Ger. Author. Writes under pen name "Paul James." *Wool and Wool Manufacture* (1920); *Shoes, Ships and Sealing Wax* (poems, 1932); *The Money Muddle* (1934); *Our War and Our Peace* (1941); *Last Call for Common Sense* (1949); *The United States in a Changing World* (1954); *The West in Crisis* (1959); *Reveille for Rebels* (1960); etc.

WARD, ANNA LYDIA (1850–Feb. 2, 1933); b. Bloomfield, N.J. Editor, author. *Surf and Wave* (1883); *Waterbury Illustrated* (1889). Co-editor: *Town and City of Waterbury, Connecticut,* 3v. (1896). Compiler: *Dictionary of Quotations from the Poets* (1883); *Dictionary of Quotations in Prose* (1889).

Ward, Artemus. Pen name of Charles Farrar Browne.

WARD, CATHARINE WEED [Barnes] (Mrs. H. Snowden Ward) (Jan. 10, 1851–July 31, 1913); b. Albany, N.Y. Artist, author. *Shakespeare's Town and Times* (with husband, 1896); *Shakespeare and Stratford-on-Avon* (with same, 1897); etc.

WARD, CHRISTOPHER LONGSTRETH (Oct. 6, 1868–Feb. 20, 1943); b. Wilmington, Del. Lawyer, author. *The Triumph of the Nut, and Other Parodies* (1923); *Gentleman into Goose* (1924); *Twisted Tales* (1924); *Foolish Fiction* (1925); *The Dutch & Swedes on the Delaware* (1930); *A Yankee Rover* (1932); *Strange Adventures of Jonathan Drew* (1932); *Sir Galahad, and Other Rimes* (1936); *New Sweden on the Delaware* (1938); *Delaware Continentals* (1941); etc.

WARD, ELIZABETH STUART PHELPS (Mrs. Herbert Dickinson Ward) (Aug. 31, 1844–Jan. 28, 1911); b. Boston, Mass., daughter of Austin Phelps and Elizabeth Stuart Phelps. Author. *The Gates Ajar* (1868, but dated 1869); *The Trotty Book* (1870); *The Silent Partner* (1871); *Trotty's Wedding Tour and Story Book* (1873); *Poetic Studies* (1875); *The Story of Avis* (1877); *An Old Maid's Paradise* (1879); *Doctor Zay* (1882); *Beyond the Gates* (1883); *Songs of the Silent Word, and Other Poems* (1885); *The Madonna of the Tubs* (1887); *The Gates Between* (1887); *Jack the Fisherman* (1887); *A Lost Hero* (with husband, 1891); *Austin Phelps* (1891); *A Singular Life* (1895); *Chapters from a Life* (1896); *Within the Gates* (1901); *Walled In* (1907); *Comrades* (1911); etc. *See* Mary A. Bennett's *Elizabeth Stuart Phelps* (1939).

WARD, FLORENCE [Jeannette Baier] (Aug. 21, 1886–Mar. 27, 1959); b. Minneapolis, Minn. Author. *Phyllis Anne* (1921); *Spread Circles* (1927); *Second Eden* (1929); *Wild Wine* (1932); *Dalesacres* (1939).

WARD, HERBERT DICKINSON (June 30, 1861–June 18, 1932); b. Waltham, Mass. Publicist, editor, author. *The Master of the Magicians* (with wife, Elizabeth Stuart Phelps Ward, 1890); *A Lost Hero* (with same, 1891); *Come Forth* (with same, 1891); *The White Crown* (1894); *The Light of the World* (1901); etc.

WARD, JAMES WARNER (June 5, 1816–June 28, 1897); b. Newark, N.J. Librarian, author. *Home Made Verses and Stories in Rhyme* (1857); *Higher Water* (1858); a parody on Longfellow's *Hiawatha.* Librarian, Grosvenor Library, Buffalo, N.Y., 1874–95.

WARD, LYDIA [Arms] AVERY COONLEY (Jan. 31, 1845–Feb. 26, 1924); b. Lynchburg, Va. Poet. *Under the Pines, and Other Verses* (1895); *Singing Verses for Children* (1897); *Love Songs* (1898); etc.

WARD, LYND KENDALL (June 26, 1905–); b. Chicago, Ill. Artist, author of novels in woodcuts. *God's Man* (1929); *Madman's Drum* (1930); *Wild Pilgrimage* (1932); *Prelude to a Million Years* (1933); *Song Without Words* (1936); *Vertigo* (1937); *The Biggest Bear* (1952); *Nic of the Woods* (1965); etc.

WARD, MARY JANE (Aug. 27, 1905–); b. Fairmount, Ind. Author. *The Tree Has Roots* (1937); *The Wax Apple* (1938); *The Snake Pit* (1946); *The Professor's Umbrella* (1948); *A Little Night Music* (1951); *It's Different for a Woman* (1952); *The Other Caroline* (1970); etc.

WARD, MAY ALDEN (Mar. 1, 1853–Jan. 15, 1918); b. in Ohio. Author. *Dante* (1887); *Petrarch* (1891); *Old Colony Days* (1896); *Prophets of the Nineteenth Century* (1900).

WARD, MAY WILLIAMS, b. Holden, Mo. Poet, author. *In Double Rhythm* (1929); *Seesaw Poems* (1929); *From Christmas Time to April* (1938); *Approach to Social Studies Through Choral Speaking* (with Dorothy Harvel, 1945). Editor, *The Harp* (1926–32).

WARD, NATHANIEL (c. 1578–Oct., 1652); b. Haverhill, Eng. Congregational clergyman, author. Pen name, "Theodore de la Guard." *The Simple Cobler of Aggawam in America* (1647), and the edition edited by Lawrence C. Wroth (1937); *Mercurius Anti-Mechanicus* (1648); etc.

WARD, PAUL WILLIAM (June 27, 1893–); b. Indianapolis, Ind. Educator. *Intelligence in Politics* (1931); *A Short History of Political Thinking* (1939); etc. Philosophy dept., Syracuse University, from 1922.

WARD, SAMUEL (Jan. 25, 1814–May 19, 1884); b. New York. Financier, author. *Lyrical Recreations* (1865). He was the uncle of F. Marion Crawford, and Julia Ward Howe was his sister. The character Horace Bellingham in Crawford's *Dr. Claudius* is based on Ward. *See* Maude Howe Elliott's *Three Generations* (1923).

WARD, SAMUEL A. (1847–1903); b. Newark, N.J. Composer. "America the Beautiful," patriotic song (q.v.) is set to his tune "Materna," long familiar in connection with the hymn "O Mother Dear, Jerusalem."

WARD, THOMAS (June 8, 1807–Apr. 13, 1873); b. Newark, N.J. Poet, musician, playwright. *A Month of Freedom: An American Poem* (anon., 1837); *Passaic: A Group of Poems Touching that River, with Other Poems* (under pen name "Flaccus," 1842); *Flora; or, The Gipsy's Frolic* (1858); *War Lyrics* (1865); *The Fair Truant* (1867); etc.

WARD, WILLIAM G. (Nov. 5, 1848–Nov. 3, 1923); b. Sandusky, O. Educator, author. *The Poetry of Robert Browning* (1898); *Studies in Literature* (1901); etc. English dept., Emerson College of Oratory, Boston, 1898–1923.

WARD, WILLIAM HAYES (June 25, 1835–Aug. 28, 1916); b. Abington, Mass. Congregational clergyman, editor, author. *Report of the Wolfe Expedition to Babylonia, 1884–85* (1885); *The Seal Cylinders of Western Asia* (1910); *What I Believe and Why* (1915). On staff, *The Independent,* 1868–1913; editor, 1896–1913.

WARDE, FREDERIC (July 29, 1894–July 31, 1939); b. (Arthur Frederick Ward) Wells, Minn. Book designer, editor, author. *Bruce Rogers* (1925). Editor, *The Dolphin,* 1933. Director of printing, Princeton University Press, 1922–24; co-founder (with Crosby Gaige), the Watch Hill Press, 1925; with William Edwin Rudge, 1927–32; with Limited Editions Club, 1929–37; with Oxford University Press, New York, 1937–39. See *Print,* May–June, 1941.

Warde, Margaret. Pen name of Edith Kellogg Dunton.

WARDEN, DAVID BAILLIE (1772–Oct. 9, 1845); b. Ballycastle, Co. Down, Ireland. Consul, book-collector. Compiler: *Bibliotheca Americana-Septentrionalis* (anon., 1820); *Bibliotheca Americana* (anon., 1831); etc. U.S. Consul at Paris, 1810–14.

WARDNER, HENRY STEELE (1867–Mar. 5, 1935); b. Windsor, Vt. Author. *The Birthplace of Vermont: A History of Windsor to 1781* (1927).

WARE, EUGENE FITCH (May 29, 1841–July 1, 1911); b. Hartford, Conn. Author. Pen name, "Ironquill." *Rhymes of Ironquill* (1885); *Some Rhymes of Ironquill* (1892); *The Indian War of 1864* (1892); etc. See the *Collections* of the Kansas State Historical Society, v. 13, 1915.

WARE, HENRY (Apr. 1, 1764–July 12, 1845); b. Sherborn, Mass. Congregational clergyman, educator, author. *Letters Addressed to Trinitarians and Calvinists* (1820); *An Inquiry into the Foundation, Evidences, and Truths of Religion* (1842); etc. Hollis prof. divinity, Harvard College, 1805–16; prof. systematic theology, Harvard Divinity School, 1816–40.

WARE, HENRY (Apr. 21, 1794–Sept. 22, 1843); b. Hingham, Mass., son of Henry Ware. Unitarian clergyman, editor, author. *The Recollections of Jotham Anderson* (anon., 1824); *David Ellington* (1846); *The Works*, ed. by Chandler Robbins, 4v. (1846–47); etc. Editor, the *Christian Disciple*, 1819–23.

WARE, KATHARINE AUGUSTA [Rhodes] (1797–1843); b. Quincy, Mass. Editor, poet. *Power of the Passions, and Other Poems* (1842). Editor, the *Bower of Taste*, Boston, 1828–30.

WARE, WILLIAM (Aug. 3, 1797–Feb. 19, 1852); b. Hingham, Mass. Unitarian clergyman, novelist, biographer. *Letters of Lucius M. Piso from Palmyra, to His Friend Marcus Curtius, at Rome* (1837), republished as *Zenobia; or, The Fall of Palmyra* (1838); *Palmyra* (1839); *Letters from Palmyra* (1851); and *The Last Days and Fall of Palmyra* (1890); *Probus; or, Rome in the Third Century* (1838), republished as *The Last Days of Aurelian; or, The Nazarenes of Rome* (London, 1838); *Aurelian; or, Rome in the Third Century* (1849); and *Rome and the Early Christians* (1851); *Julian; or, Scenes in Judea* (1841); etc. Editor: *American Unitarian Biography*, 2v. (1850–51).

WARFEL, HARRY R[edcay] (Mar. 21, 1899–); b. Reading, Pa. Educator, author. *Charles Brockden Brown* (1949); *American Novelists of Today* (1951); *American English in Its Cultural Setting* (with D. J. Lloyd, 1956); *Language: A Science of Human Behavior* (1962); *Noah Webster, Schoolmaster to America* (1967); etc. Editor: *Uncollected Letters of James Gates Percival* (1959); etc. Prof. English, University of Florida, since 1948.

WARFIELD, CATHARINE ANN WARE (June 6, 1816–May 21, 1877); b. Natchez, Miss. Poet, novelist. *The Wife of Leon, and Other Poems* (with Eleanor Percy Lee, 1844); *The Indian Chamber, and Other Poems* (with same, 1846); *The Household of Bouverie* (1860); *The Romance of the Green Seal* (1866); *Miriam Comfort* (1873); *Lady Ernestine* (1876); *The Cardinal's Daughter* (1877); *Ferne Fleming* (1877); etc.

WARHOL, ANDY (Aug. 8, 1931–); b. Cleveland, O. Artist, film-maker. *A, a Novel* (1968). Since 1963 has made such "underground" films as *Eat, Kiss, Harlot, Chelsea Girls, Loves of Ondine, Trash, Blue Movie,* and numerous others.

WARING, GEORGE E[dwin] (July 4, 1833–Oct. 29, 1898); b. Poundridge, N.Y. Agriculturist, sanitary engineer, author. *Whip and Spur* (1875); *A Farmer's Vacation* (1876); *The Bride of the Rhine* (1878); *Tyrol and the Skirt of the Alps* (1880); *Horse Stories* (1882); etc.

WARMAN, CY (June 22, 1855–Apr. 7, 1914); b. Greenup, Ill. Journalist. *Tales of an Engineer* (1895); *The Express Messenger, and Other Stories of the Rail* (1897); *Frontier Stories* (1898); *The Story of the Railroad* (1898); *The White Mail* (1899); *Snow on the Headlight* (1899); *Short Rails* (1900); *The Last Spike, and Other Railroad Stories* (1906); *Songs of Cy Warman* (1911). His song "Sweet Marie" was very popular.

Warmed-Overland. Name given by Ambrose Bierce to the *Second Series* of the *Overland Monthly*. Given in jest, it had an unfortunate effect on the magazine's popularity.

Warne, Frederick, & Co., Inc. New York. Publishers. Founded 1865 in London by Frederick Warne, formerly a partner in the firm of Routledge, Warne & Routledge. Charles Scribner and Company were the American representatives until 1881, when the American branch was established in New York by P. C. Leadbeater. Leadbeater was the head of the firm until 1921. Richard Billington is president. The firm now publishes juveniles and general nonfiction.

WARNER, ANNA B[artlett] (Aug. 31, 1827–Jan. 22, 1915); b. New York. Sister of Susan Warner. Novelist, author of children's books. Pen name "Amy Lothrop." *Dollars and Cents* (1852); *Say and Seal* (with sister, 1860); *Stories of Vinegar Hill*, 6v. (1872); etc. See Olivia E. P. Stokes's *Letters and Memories of Susan and Anna Bartlett Warner* (1925).

WARNER, ANNE [Richmond] (Mrs. Charles Ellis French) (Oct. 14, 1869–Feb. 1, 1913); b. St. Paul, Minn. Novelist. *A Woman's Will* (1904); *Susan Clegg and Her Friend Mrs. Lathrop* (1904); *The Rejuvenation of Aunt Mary* (1905); *Susan Clegg and Her Neighbor's Affairs* (1906); *Susan Clegg and a Man in the Home* (1907); *Your Child and Mine* (1909); *Woman Proposes* (1911); etc.

WARNER, CHARLES DUDLEY (Sept. 12, 1829–Oct. 20, 1900); b. Plainfield, Mass. Editor, essayist, novelist. *My Summer in a Garden* (1871); *Backlog Studies* (1873); *Baddeck* (1874); *My Winter on the Nile* (1876); *In the Levant* (1877); *Being a Boy* (1878); *In the Wilderness* (1878); *Washington Irving* (1881); *A Roundabout Journey* (1883); *Their Pilgrimage* (1887); *On Horseback* (1888); *Studies in the South and West* (1889); *A Little Journey in the World* (1889); *As We Were Saying* (1891); *Our Italy* (1891); *As We Go* (1893); *The Golden House* (1895); *The Relation of Literature to Life* (1896); *The People for Whom Shakespeare Wrote* (1897); *That Fortune* (1899); *Fashions in Literature* (1902); *The Complete Writings*, ed. by Thomas R. Lounsbury, 15v. (1904); etc. Editor (with his brother, George H. Warner): *Library of the World's Best Literature*, 31v. (1896–97) (q.v.). Editor, the *Hartford Evening Press*, 1861–67; co-editor, the *Hartford Courant*, 1867–1900; contrib. editor, *Harper's New Monthly Magazine*, 1884–98. See Annie A. Field's *Charles Dudley Warner* (1904); Albert B. Paine's *Mark Twain*, 3v. (1912); *Mark Twain's Autobiography*, 2v. (1924).

WARNER, FRANCES LESTER (Mrs. Mayo Dyer Hersey) (July 19, 1888–); b. Putnam, Conn., sister of Gertrude Chandler Warner. Author. *Endicott and I* (1919); *Life's Minor Collisions* (with sister, 1921); *Pilgrim Trails* (1921); *Steel and Holly* (1925); *Pleasures and Palaces* (with sister, 1933); *On a New England Campus* (1937); *Amateur's Holiday* (1939); *Inner Springs* (1942); etc.

WARNER, GERTRUDE CHANDLER (Apr. 16, 1890–); b. Putnam, Conn., sister of Frances Lester Warner. Author. *House of Delight* (1916); *Life's Minor Collisions* (with sister, 1921); *The Box Car Children* (1924); *The World in a Barn* (1927); *Pleasures and Palaces* (with sister, 1933); *Surprise Island* (1949); *The Yellow House Mystery* (1953); *Mystery Ranch* (1958); *Blue Bay Mystery* (1961).

Warner, Hannah. Pen name of John Howard Jewett.

WARNER, HENRY EDWARD (Jan. 17, 1876–Apr. 11, 1941); b. Elyria, O. Journalist, humorist, poet, song writer. *That House I Bought* (1912); *Songs of the Craft* (1929); *Uncle Ed and His Dream Children* (1929); etc. On staff, the *Baltimore Sun*, 1910–41. His best known song was his popular doll song, "I've Got a Pain in My Sawdust" (1911).

WARNER, SUSAN BOGERT (July 11, 1819–Mar. 17, 1885); b. New York, sister of Anna B. Warner. Author. Pen name "Elizabeth Wetherell." *The Wide, Wide World* (1850); *Queechy* (1852); *Mrs. Rutherford's Children*, 2v. (with sister, 1853–55); *The Old Helmet* (1863); *Melbourne House* (1864); *Daisy* (1868); *Wych Hazel* (with sister, 1876); *Diana* (1877); *My Desire* (1879); *Nobody* (1882); *Stephen, M.D.* (1883); etc. Her best known hymn is "Jesus Loves Me" (q.v.). See Anna

B. Warner's *Susan Warner* (1909); Olivia E. P. Stokes's *Letters and Memories of Susan and Anna Bartlett Warner* (1925).

Warner Library. See *Library of the World's Best Literature.*

WARREN, ARTHUR (May 18, 1860–Apr. 16, 1924); b. Dorchester, Mass. Editor, critic, author. *The Charles Whittinghams, Printers* (1896). With the *Boston Herald,* 1888–1909; editor, 1907–09; drama critic, the *New York Tribune,* 1909–12.

WARREN, AUSTIN (July 4, 1899–); b. Waltham, Mass. Educator, author. *Alexander Pope as Critic and Humanist* (1929); *The Elder Henry James* (1934); *Richard Crashaw* (1938); *Rage for Order* (1947); *New England Saints* (1956). Co-author: *Literary Scholarship* (1941); *Theory of Literature* (1948). Assoc. editor, the *New England Quarterly,* 1937–40, 1942–46; *American Literature,* 1940–42, *Comparative Literature,* 1948–50. English dept., University of Michigan, since 1948.

WARREN, CHARLES (Mar. 9, 1868–Aug. 16, 1954); b. Boston, Mass. Lawyer, educator, author. *The Girl and the Governor* (1900); *History of the American Bar, Colonial and Federal, to 1860* (1911); *The Supreme Court in United States History,* 3v. (1922, Pulitzer Prize for American history, 1923); *Congress, the Constitution, and the Supreme Court* (1925); *The Making of the Constitution* (1928); *Bankruptcy in United States History* (1935); *Odd Byways in American History* (1942); etc.

WARREN, FREDERICK MORRIS (June 9, 1859–Dec. 7, 1931); b. Durham, Me. Educator, author. *A Primer of French Literature* (1889); *A History of the Novel Previous to the Seventeenth Century* (1895); etc. Prof. modern languages, Yale University, 1900–20.

WARREN, HOWARD CROSBY (June 12, 1867–Jan. 4, 1934); b. Montclair, N.J. Educator, psychologist, author. *History of the Association Psychology* (1921); *Elements of Human Psychology* (1922); etc. Editor: *Dictionary of Psychology* (1934). Editor, *Psychological Review,* 1916–34; co-editor, *Psychological Bulletin,* 1904–34. Psychology dept., Princeton University, 1893–1934; prof., 1903–34; Stuart prof., 1914–34.

WARREN, INA RUSSELLE; b. Inverness, Scot. Editor, compiler. Editor: *The Doctor's Window* (1898); *The Lawyer's Alcove* (1900); *In Cupid's Court* (1900); *Under the Holly Bough* (1907); *The Girdle of Friendship* (1910); *Mother Love* (1911). Editor, the *Magazine of Poetry,* 1893–96.

WARREN, ISRAEL P[erkins] (Apr. 8, 1814–Oct. 9, 1892); b. Woodbridge (now Bethany), Conn. Congregational clergyman, editor, author. *The Sisters; A Memoir* (1859); *The Three Judges* (1873); *Chauncey Judd* (1874); etc. Editor, the *Christian Mirror,* 1875–92.

WARREN, LELLA (Mar. 22, 1899–); b. Clayton, Ala. Author. *A Touch of Earth* (1926); *Foundation Stone* (1940); *Whetstone Walls* (1952).

WARREN, LOUIS AUSTIN (Apr. 23, 1885–); b. Holden, Mass. Disciples clergyman, author. *Lincoln's Parentage and Childhood* (1926); *Abraham Lincoln's Birthplace* (1927); *Little Known Lincoln Episodes* (1934); *Abraham Lincoln* (1934); *Lincoln's Youth* (1959); *Lincoln's Gettysburg Declaration* (1964); and other books on Lincoln and the Lincoln country.

WARREN, MAUDE [Lavinia] RADFORD (1875–July 6, 1934); b. Wolfe Island, Ont. Author. *The Land of the Living* (1908); *The Main Road* (1913); *Robin Hood* (1915); *Little Pioneers* (1916); *The White Flame of France* (1918); *The House of Youth* (1923); *Never Give All* (1927); etc. War and Far Eastern correspondent, the *Saturday Evening Post,* 1916–20.

WARREN, MERCY OTIS (Sept. 14, 1728–Oct. 19, 1814); b. Barnstable, Mass. Poet, playwright. *The Adulateur* (1773);

The Group (1775); *Poems, Dramatic and Miscellaneous* (1790); *History of the Rise, Progress, and Termination of the American Revolution,* 3v. (1805); etc. *See* Alice Brown's *Mercy Warren* (1898); Katherine Anthony's *First Lady of the Revolution* (1958).

WARREN, ROBERT PENN (Apr. 24, 1905–); b. Guthrie, Ky. Author. *John Brown: The Making of a Martyr* (1929); *Thirty-Six Poems* (1935); *An Approach to Literature* (with John T. Purser and Cleanth Brooks, 1936); *Night Rider* (1939); *Eleven Poems on the Same Theme* (1942); *At Heaven's Gate* (1943); *All The King's Men* (1946; Pulitzer Prize for fiction, 1947); *A Modern Rhetoric* (with Cleanth Brooks, 1949); *World Enough and Time* (1950); *Brother to Dragons* (1953); *Band of Angels* (1955); *Segregation* (1956); *Promises: Poems* (1957; Pulitzer Prize for poetry, 1958); *The Cave* (1960); *Wilderness* (1961); *Flood* (1964); *Who Speaks for the Negro?* (1965); *Selected Poems, New and Old, 1923–1966* (1966); *Incarnations* (1968); *Audubon: A Vision* (1969); etc. Co-founder and editor, the *Southern Review.* Member Fugitive group of poets, 1923–25. Prof. English, University of Minnesota, 1942–50; Yale University, 1950–56. *See* Leonard Casper's *Robert Penn Warren: The Dark and Bloody Ground* (1960).

Warren Report. See *Report of the President's Commission on the Assassination of President John F. Kennedy.*

"Warren's Address to the American Soldiers." Poem by John Pierpont, written in honor of the laying of the cornerstone of the Bunker Hill Monument, June 17, 1825. It was published in his *Airs of Palestine, and Other Poems* (1840). This poem was a favorite declamation of generations of school boys. *See* John T. Winterich's *Savonarola of Hollis Street,* in *The Colophon,* pt. 20, 1935.

Wars I Have Seen. Reminiscences of the two world wars, by Gertrude Stein (1945).

Wars of New England with the Eastern Indians. By Samuel Penhallow (1726).

WASHBURN, CHARLES AMES (Mar. 16, 1822–Jan. 26, 1889); b. Livermore, Me. Editor, historian, novelist. *Philip Thaxter* (1861); *Gomery of Montgomery* (1865); *History of Paraguay,* 2v. (1871).

WASHBURN, EDWARD ABIEL (Apr. 16, 1819–Feb. 2, 1881); b. Boston, Mass. Episcopal clergyman, essayist, poet. *Epochs in Church History, and Other Essays* (1883); *Voices from a Busy Life* (poems, 1883); etc.

WASHBURN, ROBERT [Morris] (Jan. 4, 1868–Feb. 26, 1946); b. Worcester, Mass. Author. *Footprints* (1923); *Calvin Coolidge* (1923); *Smith's Barn* (1923); *My Pen* (1940); *The Nine Intimates* (1942).

WASHBURN, STANLEY (Feb. 7, 1878–Dec. 14, 1950); b. Minneapolis, Minn. War correspondent, author. *Trails, Trappers and Tenderfeet* (1912); *The Spirit of the Wilds* (1913); *Two in the Wilderness* (1914); *Field Notes from the Russian Front* (1915); *The Russian Campaign, April to August, 1915* (1915); *The Russian Advance* (1917); etc.

WASHBURNE, CARLETON WOLSEY (Dec. 2, 1889–Nov. 27, 1968); b. Chicago, Ill. Educator, author. *Remakers of Mankind* (1932); *A Living Philosophy of Education* (1940); and many textbooks in education. Supt. of schools, Winnetka, Ill., 1919–45; department of education, Brooklyn College, from 1949.

WASHBURNE, ELIHU BENJAMIN (Sept. 23, 1816–Oct. 23, 1887); b. Livermore, Me. Statesman, diplomat, author. *Recollections of a Minister to France, 1869–1877* (1887); etc. Editor: *The Edwards Papers* (1884); etc; Congressman, 1853–69; secretary of state, 1869; U.S. minister to France, 1869–77.

WASHBURNE, HELUIZ CHANDLER (Mrs. Carleton W. Washburne) (Jan. 25, 1892–); b. Cincinnati, O. Lecturer, author of children's books. *The Story of the Earth* (with husband, 1916); *Letters to Channy* (1933); the *Little Elephant* series, 3v. (1937–39); *Tomas Goes Trading* (1959); etc. Coauthor: *Children of the Blizzard* (1952).

WASHINGTON, BOOKER T[aliaferro] (Apr. 5, 1856–Nov. 14, 1915); b. Franklin Co., Va. Educator, orator, author. *The Future of the American Negro* (1899); *Sowing and Reaping* (1901); *Up from Slavery* (autobiography, 1901); *Character Building* (1902); *Working with the Hands* (1904); *Frederick Douglass* (1907); *The Story of the Negro* (1909); *My Larger Education* (1911); *Selected Speeches* (1932); etc. *See* Emmett Jay Scott and Lyman Beecher Stowe's *Booker T. Washington* (1916); Basil Joseph Mathew's *Booker T. Washington, Educator and Interracial Interpreter* (1948); August Meier's *Negro Thought in America, 1880–1915* (1963); E. Thornbrough's *Booker T. Washington* (1969).

WASHINGTON, GEORGE (Feb. 11, 1731, O.S., or Feb. 22, 1732, N.S.–Dec. 14, 1799); b. in Westmoreland Co., Va. Commander-in-chief of the Continental Armies during the American Revolution, first President of the United States, author. Called the "Father of His Country." *Farewell Address to the People of the United States* (1796), published under many titles in that year and later; *The Writings*, ed. by Jared Sparks, 12v. (1834–39); *The Diaries . . . 1748–1799*, ed. by John C. Fitzpatrick, 4v. (1925). The Washington MSS. in the Library of Congress are bound in over 400 volumes. *See* John Marshall's *The Life of George Washington*, 5v. (1804–07); Mason L. Weems's *The Life of Washington the Great* (1806); Jared Sparks's *The Life of George Washington* (1839); Washington Irving's *Life of George Washington*, 5v. (1855–59); Henry C. Lodge's *George Washington*, 2v. (1889); William M. Thayer's *From Farm House to the White House* (1890); Paul L. Ford's *The True George Washington* (1896); Worthington C. Ford's *George Washington*, 2v. (1900); Norman Hapgood's *George Washington* (1901); Paul L. Haworth's *George Washington, Country Gentleman* (1925); Rupert Hughes's *George Washington*, 3v. (1926–30); John C. Fitzpatrick's *George Washington Himself* (1933); James Thomas Flexner's *George Washington* (1965) and *George Washington in the American Revolution, 1775–1783* (1968); Clark Kinnaird's *George Washington* (1966); Douglas S. Freeman's *George Washington*, 7v., ed. by John A. Carroll and Mary W. Ashworth (1969).

Washington Daily Globe. Washington, D.C. Founded 1838, by Francis Preston Blair and John Cook Rives. Followed in 1843 by the *Daily Union*, edited by Thomas Ritchie. This became the *Washington Union* in 1857. Followed in 1859 by the *Constitution*, which expired 1861. Noted for its reports on debates in Congress. Amos Kendall was on the staff.

Washington Monthly, The. Washington, D.C. Founded 1969. Edited by Charles Peters; advisory board includes Richard Rovere, Murray Kempton, Russell Baker. An independent public opinion monthly devoted to the expression of informed views based on professional experience, usually in the field of journalism. The articles range over all areas of American political, social, and cultural life, with an emphasis on the insider's view of politics.

"Washington Monument." Poem by Carl Sandburg (1922).

Washington News. Washington, D.C. Newspaper. Founded 1921, by E. W. Scripps. Associated with it have been Ernie Pyle, Len Hall, and Charter Heslep. Richard Hollander is editor. Tom Donnelly is book-review editor.

Washington Post. Washington, D.C. Newspaper. Founded Dec. 6, 1877, by Stilson Hutchins. Sold in 1889 to Frank Hatton and Beriah Wilkins. The Wilkins estate sold it to John B. McLean who, on his death in 1916, was succeeded by his son Edward B. McLean (d. 1941). In 1933 it was sold to Eugene Meyer. Prominent early editors were Beriah Wilkins,

Henry Litchfield West and George Harvey. Arthur Charles Johnson, on the staff, 1901–23, was editor, 1912–23. Felix Morley was editor, 1933–40. Benjamin Bradlee is editor; Geoffrey Wolff edits book reviews. Ralph West Robey, Elliott Thurston, Raymond Clapper, and Franklyn Waltman, Jr., have been columnists. The *Post* bought the *Times-Herald* in 1954. See *Washington Post–Times-Herald*.

Washington Post–Times-Herald. Washington, D.C. Newspaper. The *Times*, founded 1894, as a morning paper; discontinued 1902. The *Evening Times*, founded 1895. The *Herald*, founded 1906. W. R. Hearst bought both in 1922 and made the *Herald* into the morning edition of the *Times*. Published by Eleanor Patterson, 1930–48. The *Times* and *Herald* were merged as the *Times-Herald* in 1939. Bought by the *Washington Post* (q.v.) in 1954.

Washington Square. Novel by Henry James (1881).

Washington Star. Washington, D.C. Newspaper. Founded 1852. On the staff have been Victor Kauffman, Frank B. Noyes, Theodore W. Noyes, Newbold Noyes, John H. Cline, Rex Collier, Mary Carter Roberts, and Philander Chase Johnson. Newbold Noyes is editor; Day Thorpe and Charles Cooke review books. Hudson Grunewald edits the book page; Barbara Nolen reviews juveniles. Mary McGrory writes the column "Reading and Writing."

WASON, ROBERT ALEXANDER (Apr. 6, 1874–May 11, 1955); b. Toledo, Ohio. Novelist. *Happy Hawkins* (1909); *The Steering Wheel* (1910); *The Dog and the Child and the Ancient Sailor Man* (1911); *Friar Tuck* (1912); etc.

Wasp, The. San Francisco, Cal. Weekly illustrated magazine. Founded 1856. Ambrose Bierce was one of its editors. Mark Twain and Bret Harte wrote for it. Later called the *Wasp News-Letter*.

WASSERMAN, DALE (Nov. 2, 1917–   ); b. Rhinelander, Wis. Playwright. *Livin' The Life* (with B. Geller, 1957); *The Pencil of God* (1961); *998* (1962); *Man of La Mancha* (1966).

WASSERMAN, EARL REEVES (Nov. 11, 1913–); b. Washington, D.C. Educator. *Elizabethan Poetry in the Eighteenth Century* (1947); *The Subtler Language: Critical Reading of Neoclassic and Romantic Poems* (1959); *Pope's Epistle to Bathurst* (1960); *Prometheus Unbound: A Critical Reading* (1965); etc. Faculty, Johns Hopkins University, since 1948.

WASSON, DAVID ATWOOD (May 14, 1823–Jan. 21, 1887); b. West Brooksville, Me. Transcendentalist, author. *Poems* (1888); *Essays* (1889).

WASSON, GEORGE SAVARY (Aug. 27, 1855–Apr. 28, 1931); b. Groveland, Mass., son of David Atwood Wasson. Artist, author. *Cap'n Simeon's Store* (1903); *The Green Shay* (1905); *Home from Sea* (1908); *Sailing Days on the Penobscot* (1932).

WASSON, MILDRED COES (Apr. 2, 1890–); b. Woburn, Mass. Author. *The Big House* (1926); *Churchill Street* (1928); *The Everlasting Harpers* (1929); *Nancy: A Story of the Younger Set* (1932); *Bill and Nancy* (1940).

WASSON, ROBERT GORDON (Sept. 22, 1898–); b. Great Falls, Mont. Banker, author. *The Hall Carbine Affair; A Study in Contemporary Folklore* (1941). Co-author: *Mushrooms, Russia and History* (1957).

Waste Land, The. Long poem by T. S. Eliot (1922). The landmark of post-World-War-I poetry. It dramatized the breakup of the old cultural order in Europe and the despair of twentieth-century man faced with the loss of accepted standards of value.

Watanna, Onoto. Pen name of Winnifred Babcock.

Watch on the Rhine. Play by Lillian Hellman (prod. 1941).

Water Witch, The. Novel by J. Fenimore Cooper (1830). An attempt to localize a legend in New York harbor. The author regarded this as his most imaginative book.

WATERLOO, STANLEY (May 21, 1846–Oct. 11, 1913); b. in St. Clair, Mich. Author. *A Man and a Woman* (1892); *An Odd Situation* (1893); *The Story of Ab* (1897); *Armageddon* (1898); *The Wolf's Long Howl* (1899); *The Seekers* (1900); *The Cassowary* (1906); *A Son of the Ages* (1914).

WATERMAN, NIXON (Nov. 12, 1859–Sept. 1, 1944); b. Newark, Ill. Poet. *A Book of Verses* (1900); *In Merry Mood* (1902); *Sonnets of a Budding Bard* (1907); *For You and Me* (1913); *A Rose to the Living, and Other Poems* (1930).

WATERS, CLARA ERSKINE CLEMENT (Aug. 28, 1834–Feb. 20, 1916). Author. Wrote under maiden name. *Charlotte Cushman* (1882); *A Handbook of Christian Symbols and Stories of the Saints* (1886); *Eleanor Maitland* (1890); *Venice* (1893); *Constantinople* (1895); *Angels in Art* (1898); and many other books on art.

WATERS, FRANK (July 25, 1902–); b. Colorado Springs, Colo. Author. *Fener Pitch* (1930); *The Wild Earth's Nobility* (1935); *Below Grass Roots* (1937); *Midas of the Rockies* (1937); *People of the Valley* (1941); *The Man Who Killed the Deer* (1942); *The Yogi of Cockroach Court* (1948). *Masked Gods* (1951); Co-author: *River Lady* (1942); *Diamond Head* (1949).

WATERS, ROBERT (May 9, 1835–Nov. 28, 1910); b. Thurso, Scotland. Educator, author. *William Shakespeare Portrayed by Himself* (1888); *John Selden and His Table-Talk* (1899); *Culture by Conversation* (1907); etc. Supt., West Hoboken Public Schools, 1883–1908.

WATIE, STAND (Dec. 12, 1806–Sept. 9, 1871); b. near Rome, Ga. Cherokee Indian chief, Confederate general. See Mabel W. Anderson's *Life of General Stand Watie* (1915); *Cherokee Cavaliers*, ed. by Edward Everett Dale and Gaston Litton (1939).

WATKINS, FRANCES ELLEN (Mrs. Frances Ellen Watkins Harper) (1825–1911); b. Baltimore, Md. Poet, novelist. *Poems on Miscellaneous Subjects* (1857); *Iola Leroy* (1892); *Idylls of the Bible* (poems, 1901); *The Sparrow's Fall, and Other Poems* (n.d.).

WATKINS, JOHN ELFRETH (Feb. 12, 1875–Feb. 13, 1946); b. Vincentown, N.J. Editor, short story writer. *Famous Mysteries* (1919); and over 100 detective and mystery stories. Wrote the "Watson Letter" on Washington events for a number of newspapers, 1894–1914. Founder, Watkins Syndicate, Inc., 1935.

WATKINS, SHIRLEY. Author of books for girls. *The Island of Green Myrtles* (1897); *Nancy of Paradise Cottage* (1921); *Georgina Finds Herself* (1922); *Jane Lends a Hand* (1923); *This Poor Player* (1929); etc.

WATKINS, TOBIAS (1780–Nov. 14, 1855); b. in Maryland. Physician, editor, author. *A History of the American Revolution,* 2v. (with John Neal, 1819), projected by Paul Allen, but written by Neal and Watkins; *Tales of the Tripod; or, A Delphian Evening* (under pen name "Pertinax Particular," 1821); etc. Founder, the *Portico,* Baltimore, 1816; co-editor, 1816–20. Co-founder and first president, the Delphian Club.

WATSON, EDWARD WILLARD (Jan. 2, 1843–Nov. 20, 1925); b. Newport, R.I. Physician, poet. *Today and Yesterday* (1895); *Songs of Flying Hours* (1897); *Old Lamps and New, and Other Verse* (1905); *If Love Were King, and Other Poems* (1915).

WATSON, E[rnest] BRADLEE (Apr. 19, 1879–); b. Boston, Mass. Author, editor, educator. *Sheridan to Robertson* (1926). Co-editor (with Benfield Pressey): *Contemporary Drama: European Plays,* 4v. (1931–34); *Contemporary Drama: English and Irish Plays,* 2v. (1931); *Contemporary Drama: American Plays,* 2v. (1931–38); the eight volumes republished in one as *Contemporary Drama* (1941). Prof. English, Dartmouth College, from 1924.

WATSON, ERNEST W[illiam] (Jan. 14, 1884–Jan. 23, 1969); b. Conway, Mass. Artist, editor. *Linoleum Printing* (1925); *Twenty Painters and How They Work* (1950); *Gallery of Pencil Techniques* (1958); etc. Editor-in-chief, *American Artist,* 1937–55.

WATSON, GOODWIN BARBOUR (July 9, 1899–); b. Whitewater, Wis. Educator, author. *Orient and Occident* (1927); *Tests of Personality and Character* (1932); *Human Resources* (1936); *Youth After Conflict* (1947); etc. Psychology dept., Teachers College, Columbia University, since 1925; prof. education, since 1935.

WATSON, HELEN ORR (Mrs. James T. Watson, Jr.); b. Pipestone, Minn. Author. *Chanco, A U.S. Army Homing Pigeon* (1938); *High Stepper* (1946); *Black Horse of Culver* (1950); *Beano, Circus Dog* (1953); etc.

WATSON, HENRY CLAY (1831–June 24, 1869); b. Baltimore, Md. Editor, author. *Camp-Fires of the Revolution; or, The War of Independence* (1850); *The Old Bell of Independence; or, Philadelphia in 1776* (1851); *The Yankee Tea-Party; or, Boston in 1773* (1852); *Nights in a Block-House; or, Sketches of Border Life* (1852); *Thrilling Adventures of Hunters* (1853); *The Camp-Fires of Napoleon* (1854). Editor, the *Sacramento Daily Union,* 1861–67.

WATSON, HENRY GOOD (Nov. 4, 1818–Dec. 2, 1875); b. London, came to the United States in 1841. Editor, music critic, author. *A Familiar Chat about Musical Instruments* (1852). Founder, the *Musical Chronicle,* 1843; co-editor, the *Broadway Journal,* 1845; managing editor, *Frank Leslie's Illustrated Newspaper,* 1855–61; music critic, the *New York Tribune,* 1863–67; founder, *Watson's Art Journal,* 1864; editor, 1864–75. Co-founder, the New York Philharmonic Society, 1852.

WATSON, JAMES D. (Apr. 6, 1928–   ); b. Chicago, Ill. Biochemist. *Molecular Biology of the Gene* (1965); *The Double Helix: A Personal Account of the Discovery of the Structure of DNA* (1970). Prof. biology, Harvard University, since 1955.

WATSON, JOHN B[roadus] (Jan. 9, 1878–Sept. 25, 1958); b. Greenville, S.C. Educator, psychologist, editor, author. *Behavior* (1914); *Psychology from the Standpoint of the Behaviorist* (1919); *Behaviorism* (1925); *Ways of Behaviorism* (1928); etc. Editor, *Psychological Review,* 1908–15; *Journal of Experimental Psychology,* 1915–27. Psychology dept., Johns Hopkins University, 1908–20.

WATSON, JOHN FANNING (June 13, 1779–Dec. 23, 1860); b. in Burlington Co., N.J. Historian, editor. *Annals of Philadelphia* (1830); *Historic Tales of Olden Times Concerning New York City and State* (1932); *Historic Tales of Olden Times Concerning Philadelphia and Pennsylvania* (1933); *Annals and Occurrences of New York City and State* (1846); etc. Founder, the *Select Reviews of Literature and Spirit of the Foreign Magazines* (later the *Analectic Magazine*), 1809; editor, 1809–12.

WATSON, JOHN WHITAKER (Oct. 14, 1824–July 18, 1890); b. New York. Poet. *Beautiful Snow, and Other Poems* (1869). His best known poem is "Beautiful Snow."

Watson, Mary Devereaux. See Mary Devereaux.

WATSON, PAUL BARRON (Mar. 25, 1861–Mar. 19, 1948); b. Morristown, N.J. Author. *Marcus Aurelius Antoninus* (1884); *The Swedish Revolution under Gustavus Vasa* (1889); *Tales of Normandie* (1930); *Some Women of France* (1936); *Commodore James Barron* (1942); *Our Constitution* (1946); etc.

WATSON, THOMAS EDWARD (Sept. 5, 1856–Sept. 26, 1922); b. Thomson, Ga. Editor, author. *The Story of France*, 2v. (1896); *Napoleon* (1902); *The Life and Times of Thomas Jefferson* (1903); *Bethany: A Story of the Old South* (1905); *Life and Speeches of Thos. E. Watson* (1908); etc. Founder, *Tom Watson's Magazine*, New York, 1905. The "Thomas E. Watson Song," a ballad, is still sung in backwoods Georgia.

Watson's Magazine. Atlanta, Ga. Monthly magazine. Thomas Edward Watson founded and edited two magazines bearing his name. *Tom Watson's Magazine* was founded in 1905 in New York, and expired in 1906. In 1907, he began *Watson's Jeffersonian Magazine* in Atlanta, not assuming the volume numbering of the earlier magazine. This absorbed the *Taylor-Trotwood Magazine* in 1911 and was moved to Thomson, Ga., in the same year. In 1912, it became *Watson's Magazine*. Expired 1917.

WATT, HOMER ANDREW (Sept. 11, 1884–Oct. 4, 1948); b. Wilkes-Barre, Pa. Educator, author. *Ideas and Forms in English and American Literature* (1925); *The Literature of England* (with others, 1936, 1941, 1947); *Dictionary of English Literature* (with W. W. Watt, 1945). English dept., New York University from 1916; head of dept., from 1938.

WATTERSON, HENRY (Feb. 16, 1840–Dec. 22, 1921); b. Washington, D.C. Editor, author. *Oddities in Southern Life and Character* (1882); *The Compromises of Life, and Other Lectures* (1903); *Old London Town* (1910); *"Marse Henry": An Autobiography*, 2v. (1919); *The Editorials of Henry Watterson* (1923); etc. On staff *Harper's Weekly;* the *New York Times;* the *New York Tribune;* the *Nashville Banner;* etc.; editor, the *Louisville Courier-Journal*, 1868–1918. See *Louisville Courier-Journal*.

WATTERSTON, GEORGE (Oct. 23, 1783–Feb. 4, 1854); b. on board ship, New York harbor. Librarian, novelist. *The Lawyer; or, Man as He Ought Not to Be* (anon., 1808); *The Child of Feeling* (1809); *Glencarn; or, The Disappointment of Youth* (1810); *The Wanderer in Jamaica* (poem, 1810); *The Scenes of Youth* (poem, 1813); *Letters from Washington* (1818); *The L . . . Family at Washington* (anon., 1812); *The Wanderer in Washington* (anon., 1827); *Gallery of American Portraits* (1830); *A Picture of Washington* (1840); etc. Editor, the *Washington City Gazette*, 1813. Librarian of Congress, 1815–29. See Julia E. Kennedy's *George Watterston, Novelist* (1933).

WATTLES, WILLARD AUSTIN (June 8, 1898–Sept. 25, 1950); b. Bayneville, Kan. Educator, poet. *Lanterns in Gethsemane* (1918); *The Funston Double-Track, and Other Poems* (1919); *A Compass for Sailors* (1928). Compiler: *Sunflowers: A Book of Kansas Poems* (1914). Prof. English, Rollins College, Winter Park, Fla., from 1927.

WATTS, ALAN WILSON (Jan. 6, 1915–); b. Chislehurst, Eng. Author. *Legacy of Asia and Western Man* (1938); *Behold the Spirit* (1947); *The Way of Zen* (1957); *Nature, Man, and Woman* (1958); *This Is It* (1960); *The Joyous Cosmology* (1962); *The Two Hands of God* (1963); *Beyond Theology* (1964); *The Book on the Taboo Against Knowing Who You Are* (1966); etc.

WATTS, MARY S[tanbery] (Nov. 4, 1868–May 21, 1958); b. in Delaware Co., O. Novelist. *The Tenants* (1908); *Nathan Burke* (1910); *The Legacy* (1911); *The Rise of Jennie Cushing* (1914); *The Boardman Family* (1918); *The House of Rimmon* (1922); *Luther Nichols* (1923); etc.

WATTS, RICHARD, JR. (Jan. 12, 1898–); b. Parkersburg, W. Va. Journalist. Motion picture critic, *New York Herald Tribune*, 1924–36; drama critic, 1936–42; drama critic, *New York Post*.

Wau Bun. By Juliette A. Kinzie (1856). Early novel of Chicago, the Black Hawk War, and Northwest Territory. Reprinted and edited by Louise Phelps Kellogg in 1932.

WAUCHOPE, GEORGE ARMSTRONG (May 26, 1862–June 6, 1943); b. Natural Bridge, Va. Educator, author. *From Generation to Generation* (1905); *The Writers of South Carolina* (1910); *Henry Timrod: Man and Poet* (1915); *Contemporary English Drama* (1921); *Literary South Carolina* (1923); etc. Editor of textbook editions of Lamb's *Essays*, Eliot's *Silas Marner*, etc. Prof. English, University of South Carolina, since 1898.

Wave, The Novel by Evelyn Scott (1929). Panorama of the Civil War period.

Wave, The. San Francisco, Calif. Literary weekly. Founded 1887, by Ben Truman, at Del Monte, Calif., but later moved to San Francisco. John O'Hara Cosgrave was editor, 1889–1900. Will Irwin was assistant editor, 1899, and editor, 1900. Hugh Hume was at one time editor. Frank Norris was on the staff, 1896–98. William Jonathan Neidig was book editor, 1899–1900. Perry Newberry bought *The Wave* in 1901, but it lived only a short while thereafter. See Oscar Lewis's *Frank Norris and the Wave* (1931).

Wave of the Future, The. By Anne Morrow Lindbergh (1940). Political philosophy expressed in terms of suggested reforms in American life.

Waverly Magazine. Boston, Mass. Founded 1850, by Moses A. Dow. A great favorite with young amateur writers. Expired 1908.

WAXMAN, PERCY (Sept. 25, 1880–Jan. 12, 1948); b. in Australia. Editor, author. *Versiflage* (poems, 1922); *The Black Napoleon* (1931); *What Price Mallorca?* (1933); *Napoleon's Madcap Sister* (1940); etc. Assoc. editor *Cosmopolitan*, from 1935.

"Way down upon the Suwanee River." First line of "The Old Folks at Home," song by Stephen Foster.

"Way to Arcady, The." Poem by Henry Cuyler Bunner (1884).

WAYLAND, FRANCIS (Mar. 11, 1796–Sept. 30, 1865); b. New York. Baptist clergyman, educator, author. *The Elements of Moral Science* (1835); *Domestic Slavery Considered as a Scriptural Institution* (1845); *University Sermons* (1849); *The Elements of Intellectual Philosophy* (1854); etc. President, Brown University, 1827–55.

WAYLAND, JOHN WALTER (Dec. 8, 1872–); b. Mt. Jackson, Va. Educator, historian. *The Twelve Apostles* (1905); *The Political Opinions of Thomas Jefferson* (1907); *Sidney Lanier at Rockingham Springs* (1912); *Guide to the Shenandoah Valley* (1923); *Historic Landmarks of the Shenandoah* (1924); *Rambles in Europe* (1927); *Whispers of the Hills* (poems, 1928); *Virginia Valley Records* (1930); *The Pathfinder of the Seas: The Life of Matthew Fontaine Maury* (1930); *Historic Homes of Northern Virginia* (1937); *The Washingtons and Their Home* (1944); *Historic Harrisonburg* (1949); *The Lincolns in Virginia* (1953); *Twenty-five Chapters on the Shenandoah Valley* (1957); *John Kagi and John Brown* (1961); etc. Prof. history, State Teachers College, Harrisonburg, Va., from 1909.

WAYMAN, DOROTHY G. (Jan. 7, 1893–); b. San Bernardino Co., Cal. Author or co-author. Pen name, "Theodate Geoffrey." *An Immigrant in Japan* (1926); *Powdered Ashes* (1926); *Edward Sylvester Morse* (1942); *Bite the Bullet* (1948); *David I. Walsh: Citizen Patriot* (1952); *Cardinal O'-Connell of Boston* (1955); *Dumaine of New England* (1958); *Quaker Pioneers in Quaker History* (1962); *Friends on the Frontier in Quaker History* (1965); etc.

WAYNE, CHARLES STOKES (b. Mar. 18, 1858); b. Philadelphia, Pa. Author. Pen name, "Horace Hazeltine." *Mrs. Lord's Moonstone, and Other Stories* (1888); *The Lady and Her Tree* (1895); *A Prince to Order* (1905); *The City of Enchantments* (1908); *The Sable Lorcha* (1912); *The Snap-*

dragon (1913); *Susan Clegg and Her Love Affairs* (1916); *The King Pin* (1923); etc.

Wayne, Dorothy. Pen name of Noel Everingham Sainsbury, Jr.

Wayward Bus, The. Novel by John Steinbeck (1947).

"We." By Charles A. Lindbergh (1927). An account of his epochal transatlantic flight from New York to Paris, May 20–21, 1927, in the "Spirit of St. Louis."

"We are coming, Father Abraham, three hundred thousand strong." Civil War song by James Sloan Gibbons, first published anonymously in the New York *Evening Post*, July 16, 1862. Attributed to William Cullen Bryant, it has now been established as the work of James Sloan Gibbons (1810–92), an abolitionist.

"We must love one another and die." Line from the poem "September 1, 1939," by W. H. Auden.

WEALES, GERALD [Clifford] (June 12, 1925–); b. Connersville, Ind. Author. *Miss Grimsbee Is a Witch* (1957); *Tale for a Bluebird* (1960); *Religion in Modern English Drama* (1961); *American Drama Since World War II* (1962); *Miss Grimsbee Takes a Vacation* (1965). Editor: *Five Edwardian Plays* (1962); *The Play and Its Parts* (1964); etc.

"Wearing of the Grey." A Confederate song, written by "Georgins," with music adapted by A. E. Blackmar. It was first published in 1865.

WEATHERFORD, WILLIS DUKE (Dec. 1, 1875–); b. Weatherford, Tex. Author. *Negro Life in the South* (1910); *Personal Elements in Religious Life* (1910); *The Negro from Africa to America* (1924); *Life Sketch of James Brownson Dunwoody De Blow* (1935); *The American Churches and the Negro* (1946); *Pioneers of Destiny* (1955).

WEAVER, ANDREW THOMAS (July 28, 1890–May 19, 1965); b. Waukesha, Wis. Editor, author. Author or coauthor: *The Elements of Speech* (1933); *Basic Speech and Voice Science* (1933); *Speech* (1946); *The Teaching of Speech* (1952); *Fundamentals and Forms of Speech* (1957). Editor, *Quarterly Journal of Speech,* 1930–33. Speech dept., University of Wisconsin, from 1918; prof. from 1925.

WEAVER, BENNETT (Aug. 11, 1892–); b. Sussex, Wis. Educator, author. *The Garden of Seven Trees* (poems, 1921); *Toward the Understanding of Shelley* (1932); *Shelley: Values and Imagination* (1934); *Wordsworth: the Poetic Function of Memory* (1937); *The Interpreter of Literature* (1938); *Wordsworth: Forms and Images* (1938); *The English Romantic Poets* (with others, 1950); *Prometheus Unbound* (1957); *Wordsworth, Poet of the Unconquerable Mind* (1965). Editor: *The Major English Romantic Poets* (with others, 1957). Prof. English, University of Michigan.

Weaver, Charley. Pen name of Cliff Arquette.

WEAVER, GUSTINE [Nancy] **COURSON** (Mrs. Clifford Selden Weaver) (Dec., 1873–); b. Abingdon, Ill. Author. *The Minister's Wife* (1927); *Hop-Run, and Six Other Pageants* (1927); *Our Guest* (1928); *Canticles of a Minister's Wife* (1930). Creator of the "Cotton Dolls," and known as the "Texas Doll Lady."

WEAVER, HARRIET SHAW (1876–Oct. 14, 1961). Publisher, Egoist Press, Paris, under whose imprint the early work of James Joyce, T. S. Eliot, and other then "modernist" writers appeared.

WEAVER, JOHN D[OWNING] (Feb. 4, 1912–); b. Washington, D.C. Author. *Wind Before Rain* (1942); *Another Such Victory* (1948); *As I Live and Breathe* (1959); *Warren: The Man, the Court, the Era* (1967); etc.

WEAVER, JOHN V[an] **A**[lstyn] (July 17, 1893–June 14, 1938); b. Charlotte, N.C. Poet, novelist. *In American: Poems* (1921); *Finders: More Poems in American* (1923); *More "In American" Poems* (1926); *To Youth* (1928); *Her Knight Comes Riding* (1928); *Turning Point* (poems, 1930); *Trial Balance* (poems, 1931); *Joy-Girl* (1932). Lit. editor, the *Brooklyn Daily Eagle,* 1920–24.

WEAVER, WARREN JR. (Feb. 7, 1923–   ); b. Madison, Wis. Journalist, author. *Making Our Government Work* (1964). Co-author: *The Kennedy Years* (1964); *The New York Times Election Handbook* (1964); *The Road to the White House* (1965). Staff, *New York Times,* since 1948.

Web and the Rock, The. Novel by Thomas Wolfe (1939). George Weber comes east to New York but leaves for Germany after a stormy love affair. He decides to forge a new life for himself to escape the influences of his previous experiences and the conditioning of his ancestry. See *You Can't Go Home Again.*

WEBB, CHARLES HENRY (Jan. 24, 1834–May 24, 1905); b. Rouse's Point, N.Y. Editor, parodist, poet. Pen name, "John Paul." *Liffith Lank; or, Lunacy* (1866); *John Paul's Book* (1874); *Parodies: Prose and Verse* (1876); *Sea-Weed and What We Seed* (1876); *Vagrom Verses* (1868); *With Lead and Line along Varying Shores* (1901); etc. Founder, the *Californian,* 1864; editor, 1864–68.

WEBB, JAMES WATSON (Feb. 8, 1802–June 7, 1884); b. Claverack, N.Y. Soldier, diplomat, editor, author. *Altowan; or, Incidents of Life and Adventures in the Rocky Mountains,* 2v. (1846); *Slavery and Its Tendencies* (1856); *Reminiscences* (1882); etc. Editor, the *New York Courier,* 1827; the *New York Morning Courier and New York Enquirer,* 1829–61. One of the founders of the Associated Press. U.S. Minister to Brazil, 1861–69. *See* James Parton's *Men of Progress* (1870).

WEBB, WALTER PRESCOTT (Apr. 3, 1888–Mar. 8, 1963); b. in Panola Co., Tex. Educator, author. *The Growth of a Nation* (with E. C. Barker and W. E. Dodd, 1928); *The Story of Our Nation* (with same, 1929); *The Great Plains* (1931); *The Texas Rangers* (1935); *Divided We Stand* (1937); *The Great Frontier* (1952); *More Water for Texas* (1954); *An Honest Preface* (1959). Editor: *The Handbook of Texas* (1952). Editor, *Southwestern Historical Quarterly.* History dept., University of Texas, from 1918; prof. from 1933.

WEBBER, CHARLES W[ilkins] (May 29, 1819–Apr., 1856); b. Russellville, Ky. Explorer, journalist, naturalist, author. *Old Hicks, the Guide* (1848); *Adventures in the Camanche* [sic] *Country* (1848); *The Hunter-Naturalist* (1851); *The Wild Girl of Nebraska* (1852); *The Texan Virago . . . and Other Tales* (1852); *The Prairie Scout* (1852); *Tales of the Southern Border* (1852); *Yieger's Cabinet* (1853); *The Romance of Forest and Prairie Life* (1853); *"Sam"; or, The History of Mystery* (1855); etc. His best-known story was *The Shot in the Eye,* which appeared originally in the *Whig Review,* Feb., 1845, and simultaneously in the *Democratic Review.* It was published in book form in 1846 under the title *Jack Long; or, Shot in the Eye,* and as *The Shot in the Eye* (1847). He wrote many of his adventures in the *Whig Review* under the pen name "Charles Winterfield." Webber introduced camel transport on the plains of the west.

WEBBER, GORDON (Oct. 25, 1912–); b. Lindon, Mich. Advertising executive, author. *Years of Eden* (1951); *The Far Shore* (1954); *What End But Love* (1959); etc. Vice-president, Benton & Bowles, since 1948.

WEBER, BROM (May 14, 1917–   ); b. New York. Educator, author. *Hart Crane: A Biographical and Critical Study* (1948); *Sherwood Anderson* (1964). Editor: *The Letters of Hart Crane, 1916–1932* (1952); *Sut Lovingood* (1954); *An Anthology of American Humor* (1962); *The Story of a Country Town* (1964); *Sense and Sensibility in Twentieth Century Writing* (1970). Prof. English, University of California at Davis, since 1963.

WEBER, CARL JEFFERSON (Jan. 20, 1894–Dec. 18, 1966); b. Baltimore, Md. Educator. Author or editor: *Biography of Edward Lucas White* (1923); *Four Centuries of Literature* (with others, 1925); *The Best of Browning* (1930); *Hardy of Wessex* (1940); Hardy's *Revenge is Sweet* (1940); *1001 Fore-Edge Paintings* (1949); *Hardy and the Lady from Madison Square* (1952); *Letters of Thomas Hardy* (1954); *The Rise and Fall of James Ripley Osgood* (1959). English dept., Colby College, from 1922; Roberts prof., from 1928.

WEBER, EUGEN (Apr. 24, 1925–); b. Bucharest, Rom. Educator, author. *The Nationalist Revival in France* (1959); *The Western Tradition* (1959); *Paths to the Present* (1960); *Action Française* (1962); *Satan Franc-Maccon* (1964); *Varieties of Fascism* (1964); *The European Right* (with H. Rogger, 1965). Prof. history, University of California at Los Angeles, since 1956.

WEBER, LENORA MATTINGLY (Oct. 1, 1895–Jan. 29, 1971); b. Dawn, Mo. Author. *Wind on the Prairie* (1929); *The Gypsy Bridle* (1930); *Rocking Chair Ranch* (1936); *Happy Landing* (1941); *Meet the Malones* (1943); *Riding High* (1946); *Beany Malone* (1948); *Beany and the Beckoning Road* (1952); *Make a Wish for Me* (1956); *The More the Merrier* (1958); *Pick a New Dream* (1961); etc.

WEBER, MAX (Apr. 18, 1881–Oct. 4, 1961); b. Byelostok, Rus. Artist, author. *Cubist Poems* (1914); *Essays on Art* (1916); *Primitives* (1927); *Woodcuts* (1957).

WEBSTER, ALBERT FALVEY (1848–Dec. 27, 1876); b. Boston, Mass. Short story writer. Wrote many short stories for *Scribner's, Appleton's,* and the *Atlantic Monthly,* including *Our Friend Sullivan; Little Majesty; An Operation in Money; My Daughter's Watch;* and *Miss Eunice's Glove.* His stories have not been collected in book form.

WEBSTER, BARBARA (Mrs. Edward Shenton) (Apr. 5, 1900–); b. St. Louis, Mo. Artist, author. *Nick, Nac, Nob and Nibble* (1930); *Shadows on the Valley* (1940); *The Magic Water* (1942); *Mrs. Heriot's House* (1945); *The Color of the Country* (1947); *A Horse of Her Own* (1951); *Green Year* (1956); etc. Editor: *Country Matters* (1959).

WEBSTER, DANIEL (Jan. 18, 1782–Oct. 24, 1852); b. Salisbury, N.H. Statesman, author. *The Writings and Speeches of Daniel Webster,* ed. by Edward Everett (1903). Congressman, 1813–17, 1823–27; U.S. senator, 1827–41, 1845–50; secretary of state, 1841–43, 1850–52. See George T. Curtis's *Life of Daniel Webster,* 2v. (1870); Henry C. Lodge's *Daniel Webster* (1883); Frederic A. Ogg's *Daniel Webster* (1916); Claude M. Fuess's *Daniel Webster* (1930); Richard H. Current's *Daniel Webster and the Rise of National Conservatism* (1955); Norman D. Brown's *Daniel Webster and the Politics of Availability* (1968).

WEBSTER, HAROLD TUCKER (Sept. 21, 1885–Sept. 22, 1952); b. Parkersburg, W.Va. Cartoonist. *Our Boyhood Thrills, and Other Cartoons* (1915); *Boys and Folks* (1917); etc. Creator of cartoons "Life's Darkest Moment," "The Thrill That Comes Once in a Life Time," "The Boy Who Made Good," "How to Torture Your Wife," "Poker Portraits," "They Don't Speak Our Language," "The Timid Soul." With *New York Herald Tribune,* from 1931.

WEBSTER, HENRY KITCHELL (Sept. 7, 1875–Dec. 8, 1932); b. Evanston, Ill. Novelist. *The Short Line War* (with Samuel Merwin, 1899); *Calumet "K"* (with Samuel Merwin, 1901); *Traitor and Loyalist* (1904); *A King in Khaki* (1909); *The Sky Man* (1910); *June Madness* (prod. 1912); *The Butterfly* (1914); *The Thoroughbred* (1917); *An American Family* (1918); *Mary Wollaston* (1920); *Real Life* (1921); *The Alleged Great-Aunt* (1935); etc.

WEBSTER, HUTTON (Mar. 24, 1875–May 20, 1955); b. Malone, N.Y. Educator, author. *Primitive Secret Societies* (1908); *Rest Days* (1916); *World History* (1923); *History of Civilization* (1940); *Taboo* (1942); *Magic* (1947); also a number of textbooks on ancient, medieval, and modern history. Sociology dept., Stanford University, 1933–40.

WEBSTER, JEAN [Alice Jean Chandler] (July 24, 1876–June 11, 1916); b. Fredonia, N.Y. Author. *When Patty Went to College* (1903); *The Wheat Princess* (1905); *Jerry Junior* (1907); *Much Ado About Peter* (1909); *Just Patty* (1911); *Daddy-Long-Legs* (1912); *Dear Enemy* (1915); etc.

WEBSTER, MARGARET (May 15, 1905–); b. New York. Actress, director. *Shakespeare Without Tears* (1942).

WEBSTER, NOAH (Oct. 16, 1758–May 28, 1843); b. West Hartford, Conn. Lexicographer. Called the "Schoolmaster to America." Compiler: *A Grammatical Institute of the English Language,* 3 parts (1783, 1784, 1785), part 1 was republished as *The American Spelling Book* (1793), beginning the long line of the "Blue-Back Spellers," part 2 was a grammar, and part 3 was a reader; *A Compendious Dictionary of the English Language* (1806), which, though frequently revised, did not formally achieve a *Second Edition* until 1936; etc. See Horace E. Scudder's *Noah Webster* (1881); Emily E. F. Ford's *Notes on the Life of Noah Webster,* ed. by Emily E. F. Skeel, 2v. (1912); Harry R. Warfel's *Noah Webster: Schoolmaster to America* (1936); Ervin C. Shoemaker's *Noah Webster: Pioneer of Learning* (1936); Mark Sullivan's *Our Times,* v. 2 (1932); Homer D. Babbidge, Jr.'s *Noah Webster* (1967). See also G. & C. Merriam Company.

Webster's Biographical Dictionary. Published by G. & C. Merriam Co. (1943). Contains tens of thousands of proper-name entries from all historical periods covering all countries of the world. Periodically revised.

Webster's New International Dictionary. See G. & C. Merriam Company.

Webster's Reply to Hayne. Famous oration given on the floor of the U. S. Senate, Jan. 26, 1830, by Daniel Webster, containing the line, "Liberty and union, now and forever, one and inseparable."

WECHSBERG, JOSEPH (Aug. 29, 1907–); b. Moravska Ostrava, Czech. Author. *Looking for a Bluebird* (1945); *Homecoming* (1946); *Sweet and Sour* (1948); *The Continental Touch* (1948); *Blue Trout and Black Truffles* (1953); *The Self-Betrayed* (1955); *Avalanche!* (1958); *Red Plush and Black Velvet* (1961); *Dining at the Pavilion* (1962); *The Best Things in Life* (1964); *Journey Through the Land of Eloquent Silence* (1964); *The Merchant Bankers* (1966); *Vienna, My Vienna* (1968); *The Voices* (1969); etc. Staff, *New Yorker,* since 1948.

WECHSLER, JAMES A. (Oct. 31, 1915–); b. New York. Editor, author. *Revolt on the Campus* (1935); *Labor Baron: A Portrait of John L. Lewis* (1944); *The Age of Suspicion* (1953); *Reflections of an Angry Middle-Aged Editor* (1960). Editor, *New York Post,* since 1949.

WECTER, DIXON (Jan. 12, 1906–June 24, 1950); b. Houston, Texas. Educator, author. *The Saga of American Society: A Record of Social Aspiration, 1607–1937* (1937); *Edmund Burke and Kinsmen* (1939); *The Hero in America* (1941); *When Johnny Comes Marching Home* (1944); *The Age of the Great Depression* (1948); etc. Associate editor: *Literary History of the United States* (1948). Literary editor of Mark Twain estate, from 1946. English dept., University of Colorado, 1933–39; prof. English, University of California at Los Angeles, from 1939.

WEDDELL, ALEXANDER W[ilbourne] (Apr. 6, 1876–Jan. 1, 1948); b. Richmond, Va. Diplomat, editor, author. *Introduction to Argentina* (1939); etc. Editor: *A Memorial Volume of Virginia Historical Portraiture* (1930); *Portraiture in the Society* (1945); etc. Ambassador to Argentina, 1933–39; Ambassador to Spain, 1939–42.

WEDEL, THEODORE OTTO (Feb. 19, 1892–); b. Halstead, Kan. Episcopal clergyman. Author: *The Medieval Attitude toward Astrology* (1920); *The Coming Great Church* (1945); *The Pulpit Rediscovers Theology* (1956); etc.

WEED, CLARENCE MOORES (Oct. 5, 1864–July 20, 1947); b. Toledo, O. Educator, naturalist, author. *Stories of Insect Life* (1897); *Our Trees* (1908); *Over and Over Stories* (with Margaret Weed, 1929); *Insect Ways* (1930); etc. With State Teachers College, Lowell, Mass., 1904–35; president, 1932–35.

WEED, THURLOW (Nov. 15, 1797–Nov. 22, 1882); b. Cairo, N.Y. Editor, author. *Letters from Europe and the West Indies* (1866); *Selections from the Newspaper Articles* (1877); *Life of Thurlow Weed Including His Autobiography,* ed. by Harriet A. Weed and Thurlow Weed Barnes, 2v. (1883–84). Editor, the *Rochester Telegraph,* 1824–26; founder, the *Anti-Masonic Enquirer,* 1826; editor, 1826–30; owner and editor, the *Albany Evening Journal,* 1830–62; editor, the *New York Commercial Advertiser,* 1867–68.

WEEDEN, (Miss) HOWARD (July 6, 1847–Apr. 11, 1905); b. Huntsville, Ala. Artist, poet. *Shadows on the Wall* (1898); *Bandanna Ballads* (1899); *Songs of the Old South* (1900); *Old Voices* (1904).

WEEDEN, WILLIAM BABCOCK (Sept. 1, 1834–Mar. 28, 1911); b. Bristol, R.I. Manufacturer, historian. *The Social Law of Labor* (1882); *Indian Money as a Factor in New England Civilization* (1884); *Economic and Social History of New England,* 2v. (1890); *Early Rhode Island* (1910); etc.

Weekly Trade Circular. New York. Founded Jan. 18, 1872. It soon changed its title to the *Publishers' Weekly.*

WEEKS, ARLAND D[eyett] (Dec. 13, 1871–Nov. 13, 1936); b. McLean, N.Y. Educator, author. *The Education of To-Morrow* (1913); *Playdays on Plum Blossom Creek* (1916); *Squaw Point* (1919); *Children of the Pines* (1926); *The Silver Fox* (1929); etc. Education dept., North Dakota State Agricultural College, 1907–36; dean, 1917–36.

WEEKS, EDWARD [Augustus] (Feb. 19, 1898–); b. Elizabeth, N.J. Editor, author. *This Trade of Writing* (1935); *The Open Heart* (1955); *In Friendly Candor* (1959). Editor: *Jubilee: 100 Years of the Atlantic* (with E. Flint, 1957). Assoc. editor, the *Atlantic Monthly,* 1924–28; editor, 1938–66; senior consultant from 1966. Editor, Atlantic Monthly Press, 1928–37.

WEEKS, EDWIN LORD (1849–Nov. 17, 1903); b. Boston, Mass. Artist, traveler, author. *From the Black Sea through Persia and India* (1896); *Some Episodes of Mountaineering* (1897).

WEEKS, RAMONA [Maher] (Oct. 25, 1934–); b. Phoenix, Ariz. Editor, author. *Their Shining Hour* (1960); *The Abracadabra Mystery* (1960); *A Dime for Romance* (1962); *Secret of the Dark Stranger* (under pen name "Agatha Mayer," 1964); *Secret of the Sundial* (1966); *Shifting Sands* (1968); *The Blind Boy, and Other Eskimo Myths* (1969).

WEEKS, RAYMOND (Jan. 2, 1863–Feb. 16, 1954); b. Tabor, Ia. Educator, poet, novelist. *Ode to France* (1917); *The Hound-Tuner of Callaway* (1927). Prof. Romance languages, Columbia University, 1909–29.

WEEKS, ROBERT KELLEY (Sept. 21, 1840–Apr. 13, 1876); b. New York. Poet. *Poems* (1866); *Episodes and Lyric Pieces* (1870); *Twenty Poems* (1876); *Poems* (selections, 1881).

WEEKS, STEPHEN BEAUREGARD (Feb. 2, 1865–May 3, 1918); b. in Pasquotank Co., N.C. Bibliographer, historian. *The Press of North Carolina in the Eighteenth Century* (1891); *Southern Quakers and Slavery* (1896); etc. Compiler: *A Bibliography of the Historical Literature of North Carolina* (1895). Co-founder, the *Southern Historical Association,* Washington, D.C., 1896.

WEEMS, MASON LOCKE (Oct. 11, 1759–May 23, 1825); b. in Anne Arundel Co., Md. Episcopal clergyman, book agent, biographer. Known as "Parson Weems." *A History of the Life and Death, Virtues and Exploits, of General George Washington* (1800), augmented as *The Life of Washington the Great* (1806), and further augmented as *The Life of George Washington* (1808); *The Life of General Francis Marion* (1809); *God's Revenge against Drunkenness* (1812), republished as *The Drunkard's Looking Glass* (1813); *The Life of Doctor Benjamin Franklin* (1815); *The Life of William Penn* (1822); etc. The familiar story of the cherry tree first appears in the 1806 edition of the Washington biography. *See* Lawrence C. Wroth's *Parson Weems* (1911); Paul L. Ford and Emily E. F. Skeel's *Mason Locke Weems: His Works and Ways,* 3v. (1929); Dixon Wecter's *The Hero in America* (1941).

"Weeping Sad and Lonely; or, When This Cruel War Is Over." Song, words by Charles Carroll Sawyer, music by Henry Tucker (1863).

WEGELIN, OSCAR (1876–). Compiler: *Early American Plays, 1714–1830* (1900); *Early American Fiction, 1774–1830* (1902); *Early American Poetry* [1650–1820], 2v. (1903–07); etc.

WEIDMAN, JEROME (Apr. 4, 1913–); b. New York. Author. *I Can Get It for You Wholesale* (1937); *What's In It for Me?* (1938); *The Horse That Could Whistle "Dixie"* (1939); *Letter of Credit* (1940); *I'll Never Go There Any More* (1941); *The Lights Around the Shore* (1943); *Too Early to Tell* (1946); *The Captain's Tiger* (1947); *The Price Is Right* (1949); *The Hand of the Hunter* (1951); *The Third Angel* (1953); *Traveler's Cheque* (1954); *Your Daughter Iris* (1955); *A Dime a Throw* (1957); *The Enemy Camp* (1958); *Before You Go* (1960); *The Sound of Bow Bells* (1962); *Word of Mouth* (1964); *The Death of Dickie Draper* (1965); *Other People's Money* (1967); *Center of the Action* (1969); *Fourth St. East* (1971); *Last Respects* (1971); etc.

WEIGAND, HERMANN JOHN (Nov. 17, 1892–); b. Philadelphia, Pa. Educator. Author: *The Modern Ibsen* (1925); *Three Chapters on Courtly Love in Arthurian France and Germany* (1956); *The Modern Ibsen: A Reconsideration* (1960). Editor, translator: *Goethe: Wisdom and Experience* (1949). Prof. German, Yale University, 1929–61.

WEIGLE, LUTHER ALLAN (Sept. 11, 1880–); b. Littlestown, Pa. Educator, author. *The Pupil and the Teacher* (1911); *American Idealism* (v. 10 in the *Pageant of America,* 1928); *We Are Able* (1937); *The Living Word* (1956); *A Bible Word Book* (with Ronald Bridges, 1959); *The Genesis Octapla* (1965); etc. Yale Divinity School, 1916–49; dean, 1928–49.

WEIK, JESSE WILLIAM (Aug. 23, 1857–Aug. 19, 1930); b. Greencastle, Ind. Author. *Herndon's Lincoln: The True Story of a Great Life,* 3v. (with William Henry Herndon, 1889); *The Real Lincoln* (1922). Owner of a large collection of Lincoln letters and MSS., now the Jesse W. Weik Collection, Library of Congress.

WEIKEL, ANNE HAMLIN, b. in Clinton Co., Pa. Author. The *Betty Baird* Series, 3v. (1906–09) for girls.

WEIMAN, RITA (1889–June 23, 1954); b. Philadelphia, Pa. Novelist, playwright. *Playing the Game* (1910); *The Stage Door* (1920); *The Acquittal* (prod. 1920); *Footlights* (1923); *Moon Magic* (1925); *What Manner of Love* (1935); *Headline News* (1939); *Paths of Judgment* (1945); *Mist* (1949); etc.

WEINBERG, BERNARD (Aug. 23, 1909–); b. Chicago, Ill. Educator. Author: *French Realism: The Critical Reaction* (1937); *A History of Literary Criticism in the Italian Renaissance,* 2v. (1961). Editor: *Critical Prefaces of the French Renaissance* (1950); *French Poetry of the Renaissance* (1954); *The Limits of Symbolism* (1966); etc. Prof. Romance languages, University of Chicago, since 1955.

WEINSTEIN, NORMAN C. (Jan. 26, 1948–); b. Philadelphia, Pa. Poet, critic. *Gertrude Stein and Literature of Modern Consciousness* (1970). Editor, *Upuver,* 1964–68; editor, *Lampeter Muse.*

WEINSTOCK, HERBERT (Nov. 16, 1905–   ); b. Milwaukee, Wis. Music critic, author. *The Opera* (1941); *Tschaikovsky* (1943); *Handel* (1946); *Chopin, the Man and His Music* (1949); *Music as an Art* (1953); *Through an Opera Glass* (with Irene Cass, 1958); *Donizetti* (1963); *Rossini, a Biography* (1968).

WEIR, HUGH C. (May 18, 1884–Mar. 16, 1934); b. Virginia, Ill. Editor, author. *The Conquest of the Isthmus* (1909); *With the Flag at Panama* (1911); *The Young Skipper of the Great Lakes* (1912); *"Cinders"* (1914); *Miss Madelyn Mack, Detective* (1914); etc. Founder (with Catherine McNelis), the Tower Magazines, Inc.

WEIR, JAMES (June 16, 1821–1906); b. in Kentucky. Lawyer, banker, novelist. *Lonz Powers; or, The Regulators* (1850); *Simon Kenton; or, The Scout's Revenge* (1852), republished as *Sharp-Eye; or, The Scout's Revenge* (1855); *The Winter Lodge* (1854).

WEISS, JOHN (June 28, 1818–Mar. 9, 1879); b. Boston, Mass. Unitarian clergyman, author. *Life and Correspondence of Theodore Parker,* 2v. (1864); *American Religion* (1871); *Wit, Humor, and Shakespeare* (1876); etc.

WEISS, PAUL (May 19, 1901–); b. New York. Philosopher, author. Author: *Reality* (1938); *Nature and Man* (1947); *Man's Freedom* (1950); *Modes of Being* (1958); *Our Public Life* (1959); *The World of Art* (1961). Co-editor: *Collected Papers of Charles S. Peirce,* 6v. (1931–35). Founder, editor, *Review of Metaphysics,* since 1947. Prof. philosophy, Yale University, since 1946.

WEISS, THEODORE [Russell] (Dec. 16, 1916–); b. Reading, Pa. Poet. *Catch* (poems, 1950); *Outlanders* (1960); *Gunsight* (1962); *The Medium* (1965); *The Last Day and the First* (1968). Editor, *Quarterly Review of Literature.*

WEITENKAMPF, FRANK (Aug. 13, 1866–Aug. 23, 1962); b. New York. Librarian, author. Pen name, prior to 1893, "Frank Linstow White." *How to Appreciate Prints* (1908); *American Graphic Art* (1912); *The Etching of Contemporary Life* (1916); *The Quest of the Print* (1932); *The Illustrated Book* (1938); *A Century of Political Cartoons* (1944); *Manhattan Kaleidoscope* (1947); *Political Caricature in the United States* (1953); etc. With the Astor Library, 1881–95; with The New York Public Library, from 1895; chief, Art Division, 1910–20; chief, Prints Division, from 1921.

WEITZENKORN, LOUIS (May 28, 1893–); b. Wilkes-Barre, Pa. Editor, playwright. *First Mortgage* (prod. 1929); *Five Star Final* (prod. 1931); *Two Bones and a Dog* (1934); *And the Sun Goes Down* (1935); etc. Editor-in-chief, the *New York Evening Graphic.*

WELBY, AMELIA BALL COPPUCK (Feb. 3, 1819–May 3, 1852); b. St. Michaels, Md. Author. Pen name "Amelia." *Poems* (1845). *See* Edgar Allan Poe's *The Literati* (1850).

WELCH, CLAUDE (1922–). *In This Name: The Doctrine of the Trinity in Contemporary Theology* (1952); *The Reality of the Church* (1958); etc.

WELCH, GALBRAITH (Mrs. James Francis Dwyer); b. Plankinton, S.D. Author. *The Unveiling of Timbuctoo* (1939); *North African Prelude: The First 7,000 Years* (1949); *The Jet Lighthouse* (1960); *Africa Before They Came* (1965); *The World and the Earth* (1969); etc.

WELCH, PHILIP H[enry] (Mar. 1, 1849–Feb. 24, 1889); b. Angelica, N.Y. Humorist, author. *The Tailor Made Girl* (1888); *Said in Fun* (1889). Wrote humorous dialogue for *Life, Puck, Judge, San Francisco Argonaut, New York Sun,* etc.

WELCH, WILLIAM HENRY (Apr. 8, 1850–Apr. 30, 1934); b. Norfolk, Conn. Physician, educator, author. *Papers and Addresses,* ed. by Walter C. Butler, 3v. (1920), and many medical books. Baxley prof. pathology, Johns Hopkins University, 1884–1926; prof., history of medicine, 1926–30. See *William Henry Welch at Eighty,* ed. by Victor O. Freeburg (1930); Simon Flexner and James Thomas Flexner's *William Henry Welch and the Heroic Age of American Medicine* (1941).

WELD, HORATIO HASTINGS (Feb. 4, 1811–Aug. 27, 1888); b. Baltimore, Md. Episcopal clergyman, author. *Corrected Proofs* (1836); *Jonce Smiley* (under pen name, "Ezekiel Jones," 1845); etc.

WELD, J. H. Author. *Fourth Experiment of Living: Living without Means* (anon., 1837).

Well Wrought Urn, The. By Cleanth Brooks (1947). Essays on the structure of poetry. One of the best-known books of critical analysis according to the modes of the New Criticism.

WELLEK, RENÉ (Aug. 22, 1903–); b. Vienna. Educator. Author: *Kant in England* (1931); *The Rise of English Literary History* (1941); *Theory of Literature* (with Austin Warren, 1949); *A History of Modern Criticism,* 2v. (1955); *Dostoevsky* (1962); *Concepts of Criticism* (1963); *Essays on Czech Literature* (1963); *Confrontations* (1965); *Discriminations* (1969); etc. Prof. Slavic and comparative literature, Yale University, since 1946.

WELLER, GEORGE ANTHONY (July 13, 1907–); b. Boston, Mass. Journalist, author. *Not to Eat, Not for Love* (1933); *The Crack in the Column* (1949); *The Story of the Paratroops* (1958); *Story of Submarines* (1962); etc. Foreign correspondent, *Chicago Daily News,* since 1940.

WELLES, GIDEON (July 1, 1802–Feb. 11, 1878); b. Glastonbury, Conn. Statesman, editor, author. *Lincoln and Seward* (1874); *Diary,* ed. by Edgar T. Welles, 3v. (1911). Editor, the *Hartford Times,* 1826–36; co-founder, the *Hartford Evening Press,* 1856. Secretary of the navy, 1861–69.

WELLES, ORSON [George] (May 6, 1915–); b. Kenosha, Wis. Actor, producer, editor. *Mr. Arkadin* (1957). Editor: *Everybody's Shakespeare* (with Roger Hill, 1934); *The Mercury Shakespeare* (with same, 1939).

WELLES, SUMNER (Oct. 14, 1892–Sept. 24, 1961); b. New York. Former government official, author. *Naboth's Vineyard* (1928); *The World of the Four Freedoms* (1943); *The Time for Decision* (1944); *Where Are We Heading?* (1946); *We Need Not Fail* (1948); *Seven Decisions That Shaped History* (1951); etc. In government service from 1915; undersecretary of state, 1937–43.

WELLES, WINIFRED (Jan. 26, 1893–1939); b. Norwichtown, Conn. Poet. *The Hesitant Heart* (1919); *This Delicate Love* (1929); *Skipping along Alone* (1931); *Blossoming Antlers* (1933); *A Spectacle for Scholars* (1935); *The Park That Spring Forgot* (1940).

WELLMAN, HILLER CROWELL (Mar. 2, 1871–Feb. 3, 1956); b. Boston, Mass. Librarian. City Library Association, Springfield, Mass., 1902–49.

WELLMAN, PAUL I[selin] (Oct. 14, 1898–Sept. 17, 1966); b. Enid, Okla. Historian, novelist. Author: *Death on the Prairie* (1934); *Broncho Apache* (1936); *Jubal Troop* (1939); *The Walls of Jericho* (1947); *The Chain* (1949); *The Iron Mistress* (1951); *Glory, God, and Gold* (1954); *Ride the Red Earth* (1958); *Indian Wars and Warriors,* 2v. (1959); *Portage Bay* (1959); etc.

WELLMAN, RITA (Mrs. Edgar F. Leo) (Dec. 2, 1890–); b. Washington, D.C. Author. *The Gentle Wife* (1919); *The Wings of Desire* (1919); *The House of Hate* (1924); *Victoria Royal* (1939); *Eugenie* (1941).

WELLS, AMOS RUSSELL (Dec. 23, 1862–Mar. 6, 1933); b. Glens Falls, N.Y. Editor, author. *Sunday-School Problems* (1905); *That They All May Be One* (1905); *Sunday-School Essentials* (1911); etc.; and many books and pamphlets for young people, written chiefly for the *Christian Endeavor World,* of which he was managing editor, 1891–1933.

WELLS, ANNA MARY (Oct. 22, 1906–); b. Newark, N.J. Educator, author. *A Talent for Murder* (1942); *Murderer's Choice* (1943); *Sin of Angels* (1948); *Fear of Death* (1951); *The Night of May Third* (1956); *Dear Preceptor: The Life and Times of Thomas Wentworth Higginson* (1963). Prof. English, Rutgers University, since 1963.

WELLS, BENJAMIN WILLIS (Jan. 31, 1856–Dec. 19, 1923); b. Walpole, N.H. Educator, editor, author. *Modern German Literature* (1895); *Modern French Literature* (1896); *A Century of French Fiction* (1898); etc. Co-editor: *Colonial Prose and Poetry* (1902). On staff, *The Churchman,* New York, 1899–1912. Prof. modern languages, University of the South, 1891-99.

WELLS, CAROLYN (d. Mar. 26, 1942); b. Rahway, N.J. Poet, parodist, novelist. Author or compiler: *At the Sign of the Sphinx* (1896); *The Jingle Book* (1899); *Folly in Fairyland* (1901); *Abeneki Caldwell* (1902); *A Nonsense Anthology* (1902); *A Parody Anthology* (1904); *A Satire Anthology* (1905); *A Whimsey Anthology* (1906); *Emily Emmins Papers* (1907); *Fluffy Ruffles* (1907); *Baubles* (1917); *Mark of Cain* (1917); *The Book of Humorous Verse* (1920); *All at Sea* (1921); *More Lives Than One* (1923); *Book of Limericks* (1925); *Book of Charades* (1927); *Horror House* (1931); *The Cat in Verse* (1935); *The Wooden Indian* (1935); *For Goodness' Sake* (1935); *Murder in a Bookshop* (1936); *Money Musk* (1936); *The Rest of My Life* (autobiography, 1937); *The Importance of Being Murdered* (1939); *Murder on Parade* (1940); *Who Killed Caldwell?* (1942); also many juveniles; etc.

WELLS, CATHERINE BOOTH GARNETT (1838–1911); b. in England. Essayist, novelist. Wrote as "Kate Garnett Wells." *About People* (1885); *Miss Curtis* (1888); *Two Modern Women* (1890); etc.

WELLS, DAVID AMES (June 17, 1828–Nov. 5, 1898); b. Springfield, Mass. Editor, political economist, author. *Our Burden and Our Strength* (1864); *The Silver Question* (1877); *Our Merchant Marine* (1882); *Practical Economics* (1889); etc. Assoc. editor, the *Springfield Republican,* 1847–48; co-editor, the *Annual of Scientific Discovery,* 1849–66; with G. P. Putnam & Co., 1857–58.

WELLS, DAVID DWIGHT (Apr. 22, 1868–June 15, 1900); b. Norwalk, Conn. Author. *Her Ladyship's Elephant* (1898); *His Lordship's Leopard* (1900); *Parlous Times* (1900); *The Tie That Binds* (with Charles Emerson Cook, 1909); etc.

WELLS, EDMUND [Williams] (b. Feb. 14, 1846); b. Lancaster, O. Author. *Argonaut Tales* (1927).

WELLS, [Grant] CARVETH (Jan. 21, 1887–Feb., 1957); b. Barnes, Surrey, Eng. Explorer, lecturer, author. *Six Years in the Malay Jungle* (1925); *In Coldest Africa* (1929); *Let's Do the Mediterranean* (1929); *Adventure* (1931); *Kapoot* (1933); *Exploring the World* (1934); *Bermuda in Three Colors* (1935); *Panamexico* (1937); *North of Singapore* (1940); *Introducing Africa* (1943); *Raffles, The Bird Who Thinks He's a Person* (1945); etc.

WELLS, HENRY WILLIS (1895–). Author. *Poetic Imagery* (1924); *The Judgment of Literature: An Outline of Aesthetics* (1928); *New Poets from Old: A Study in Literary Genetics* (1940); *The American Way of Poetry* (1943); *Introduction to Emily Dickinson* (1947); *Poet and Psychiatrist: Merrill Moore, M.D.* (1955); etc.

WELLS, JOEL FREEMAN (Mar. 17, 1930–); b. Evansville, Ind. Editor, author. *Grim Fairy Tales for Adults: Parodies of*

the Literary Lions (1967). Co-editor: *Bodies and Souls* (1961); *Blithe Spirits* (1962); *Bodies and Spirits* (1964); *Through Other Eyes* (1965); *Moments of Truth* (1966).

WELLS, JOHN EDWIN (Feb. 12, 1875–June 23, 1943); b. Philadelphia, Pa. Educator, author. *A Manual of the Writings in Middle English, 1050-1400* (1916, with eight supplements, 1919–1941); *The Story of Wordsworth's Cintra* (1921). Head English dept., Connecticut College for Women, New London, from 1917.

Wells, Kate Garnett. See Catherine Booth Garnett Wells.

WELLS, LINTON (Apr. 1, 1893–); b. Louisville, Ky. Traveler, aviator, radio broadcaster, author. *Around the World in Twenty-Eight Days* (1926); *Jumping Meridians* (1926); *Blood on the Moon* (autobiography, 1937); *Salute to Valor* (1942).

WELLS, RHEA (Sept. 24, 1891–); b. Jonesboro, Tenn. Illustrator, author. *Costuming a Play* (with Elizabeth B. Grimball, 1925); *Peppi, the Duck* (1927); *An American Farm* (1928); *Coco the Goat* (1929); *Beppo the Donkey* (1930); *Ali the Camel* (1931); *Zeke the Raccoon* (1933); *Judy and Grits and Honey* (1938); etc.

WELSH, CHARLES (Dec. 22, 1850–Sept. 12, 1914); b. Ramsgate, Kent, Eng., came to the United States in 1895. Editor, author. *A Bookseller of the Last Century* (1885); *Publishing a Book* (1900); etc. Editor: *Chauffeur Chaff; or, Automobilia* (1905); *The Fragrant Weed* (1907); *The Golden Treasury of Irish Songs and Lyrics,* 2v. (1907); etc.

WELTY, EUDORA (Apr. 13, 1909–); b. Jackson, Miss. Novelist and short-story writer. *A Curtain of Green* (stories, 1941); *The Robber Bridegroom* (1942); *The Wide Net* (stories, 1943); *Delta Wedding* (1946); *Music from Spain* (stories, 1948); *The Golden Apples* (stories, 1949); *The Ponder Heart* (1954); *The Bride of the Innesfallen* (stories, 1955); *The Shoe Bird* (1964); *Losing Battles* (1970).

WEMYSS, FRANCIS COURTNEY (May 13, 1797–Jan. 5, 1859); b. London, came to the United States in 1822. Actor, manager, author. *Twenty-Six Years of the Life of an Actor and Manager,* 2v. (1847); republished as *Theatrical Biography* (1848); *Chronology of the American Stage, from 1752 to 1852* (1852); etc.

WENDELL, BARRETT (Aug. 23, 1855–Feb. 8, 1921); b. Boston, Mass. Educator, author. *The Duchess Emilia* (1885); *Runkell's Remains* (1887); *Cotton Mather* (1891); *English Composition* (1891); *Stelligeri, and Other Essays* (1893); *William Shakespeare* (1894); *A Literary History of America* (1900); *Raleigh in Guiana, Rosamond, and a Christian Masque* (1902); *A History of Literature in America* (with Chester N. Greenough, 1904); *The Temper of the Seventeenth Century in English Literature* (1904); *Liberty, Union and Democracy* (1906); *The Privileged Classes* (1908); *The Mystery of Education* (1909); *The Traditions of European Literature* (1920); etc. English dept., Harvard, 1880–1917; prof., 1898–1917. *See* M. A. De Wolfe Howe's *Barrett Wendell and His Letters* (1924).

WENDT, GERALD [Louis] (Mar. 3, 1891–); b. Davenport, Ia. Chemist. Author: *Matter and Energy* (1930); *Science for the World of Tomorrow* (1939); *You and the Atom* (1955); *Prospects of Nuclear Power and Technology* (1957); *Atoms for Industry* (1960). Editor, *The Humanist,* since 1959.

WENGER, JOHN CHRISTIAN (Dec. 25, 1910–); b. Honey Brook, Pa. Mennonite clergyman. *Christ the Redeemer and Judge* (1942); *Separated Unto God* (1951); *The Mennonites in Indiana and Michigan* (1961); *The Church Nurtures Faith* (1963); *God's Written Word* (1966); *The Mennonite Church in America* (1967); etc.

WENLEY, ROBERT MARK (July 19, 1861–Mar. 29, 1929); b. Edinburgh, Scot. Educator, author. *Socrates and Christ* (1889); *Aspects of Pessimism* (1894); *Kant and His Philo-*

sophical Revolution (1910); *The Anarchist Ideal, and Other Essays* (1913); *Stoicism and Its Influence* (1924). Head philosophy dept., University of Michigan, 1896–1929.

WENTWORTH, FRANKLIN HARCOURT (Mar. 27, 1866–Oct. 4, 1954); b. Chicago, Ill. Journalist, author. *The Pride of Intellect* (1901); *Wendell Phillips* (1908); *The Woman's Portion* (1910); *Decreasing the Fire Hazard* (1930); etc. Washington correspondent for socialist press, 1904–05; editor, National Fire Protection Association, 1909–39.

WENTWORTH, GEORGE ALBERT (July 31, 1835–May 24, 1906); b. Wakefield, N.H. Mathematician, educator, author. *Elements of Geometry* (1878); *Elements of Algebra* (1881); *Practical Arithmetick* (with Thomas Hill, 1881); *College Algebra* (1888); etc. His textbooks helped establish the reputation of his publishers, Ginn & Co., in the field of education. They ran into many editions.

WERKMEISTER, WILLIAM HENRY (Aug. 10, 1901–); b. Asendorf, Ger. Educator. Author: *A Philosophy of Science* (1940); *A History of Philosophical Ideas in America* (1949); *Theories of Ethics* (1961); *Man and His Values* (1967); etc. Prof. philosophy, University of Southern California, since 1953.

WERNER, HEINZ (Feb. 11, 1890–May 14, 1964); b. Vienna. Educator. *Origins of Metaphor* (1919); *Origins of Lyrics* (1924); *Dynamics in Binocular Depth* (1937); *Acquisition of Word Meanings* (1952); *On Expressive Language* (1955); *Perceptual Development* (with Seymour Wapner, 1957); etc. Chairman, psychology dept., Clark University, from 1947.

WERNER, M[orris] R[obert] (Mar. 6, 1897–); b. New York. Author. *Barnum* (1923); *Brigham Young* (1925); *Tammany Hall* (1928); *Bryan* (1929); *"Orderly!"* (1930); *Privileged Characters* (1935); *Julius Rosenwald* (1939); *A House near Paris* (with Dorothy Tartière, 1946); *It Happened in New York* (1957); *Teapot Dome* (with John Starr, 1959); etc.

WERTENBAKER, CHARLES [Christian] (Feb. 11, 1901–Jan. 8, 1955); b. Lexington, Va. Author. *Boojum!* (1928); *Peter the Drunk* (1929); *To My Father* (1936); *Invasion* (1944); *Write Sorrow on the Earth* (1947); *The Barons* (1950); etc.

WERTENBAKER, THOMAS JEFFERSON (Feb. 6, 1879–Apr. 22, 1966); b. Charlottesville, Va. Educator, author. *Patrician and Plebeian in Virginia* (1910); *Virginia under the Stuarts* (1914); *The American People* (1926); *The First Americans, 1607–1690* (1927); *The United States of America* (with Donald E. Smith, 1931); *Norfolk: Historic Southern Port* (1931); *The Founding of American Civilization* (1938); *The Old South—the Founding of American Civilization* (1942); *Princeton, 1746–1896* (1946); *The Puritan Oligarchy—the Founding of American Civilization* (1947); *Bacon's Rebellion* (1957); *The Government of Virginia in the Seventeenth Century* (1957); *The Shaping of Colonial Virginia* (1958); *Give Me Liberty: The Struggle for Self-Government in Virginia* (1958). History dept., Princeton University, from 1910.

WERTHAM, FREDRIC (1895–); b. in Germany. Psychiatrist, author. *The Brain as an Organ* (1935); *Dark Legend: A Study in Murder* (1941); *The Show of Violence* (1949); *Seduction of the Innocent* (1954); *The Circle of Guilt* (1956); *A Sign for Cain: An Exploration of Human Violence* (1966); etc.

WESCOTT, GLENWAY (Apr. 11, 1901–); b. Kewaskum, Wis. Novelist, poet. *The Bittern* (poems, 1920); *The Apple of the Eye* (1924); *Natives of Rock: XX Poems, 1921–1922* (1925); *Like a Lover* (1926); *The Grandmothers: A Family Portrait* (1927); *Good-Bye, Wisconsin* (1928); *Fear and Trembling* (1932); *A Calendar of Saints for Unbelievers* (1932); *The Deadly Friend* (1933); *The Pilgrim Hawk* (1940); *Apartment in Athens* (1945); *Images of Truth* (1962); etc. See Fred B. Millett's *Contemporary American Authors* (1940).

WESEEN, MAURICE HARLEY (Dec. 15, 1890–Apr. 14, 1941); b. Oakland, Neb. Educator, author. *Everyday Uses of English* (1922); *Words Confused and Misused* (1932). Compiler: *A Dictionary of American Slang* (1934). English dept., University of Nebraska, 1918–41.

WESLEY, EDGAR BRUCE (Dec. 5, 1891–); b. Bethelridge, Ky. Educator, author. *Social Problems of Today* (with G. S. Dow, 1925); *Guarding the Frontier* (1935); *America's Road to Now* (1939); *American History in Schools and Colleges* (1944); *Our United States: Its History in Maps* (1956); etc. Education dept., University of Minnesota, from 1931; prof. from 1937.

Wesleyan University Press. Middletown, Conn. Publishers. Founded 1956. Devoted to scholarly nonfiction, works of regional interest, and poetry.

WESSELHOEFT, LILY [Elizabeth] F[oster Pope] (Oct. 20, 1840–Jan. 31, 1919); b. Dorchester, Mass. Author. *Jerry the Blunderer* (1896); *Madam Mary of the Zoo* (1899); *Torpeanuts the Tomboy* (1905); *Sparrow the Tramp* (1919); etc.

WEST, ANDREW FLEMING (May 17, 1853–Dec. 27, 1943); b. Allegheny, Pa. Educator, classicist, author. *Alcuin and the Rise of the Christian Schools* (1893); *Short Papers on American Liberal Education* (1907); *Presentations for Honorary Degrees at Princeton University, 1905–1925* (1929); *Stray Verse* (1931); etc. Prof. Latin, Princeton University, 1883–1928; dean, Graduate School, 1901–28.

WEST, ANTHONY [Panther] (Aug. 4, 1914–); b. Hunstanton, Norf., Eng. Author. *The Vintage* (1949); *D. H. Lawrence* (1951); *Another Kind* (1951); *Heritage* (1955); *Principles and Persuasions* (1957); *The Trend Is Up* (1960). Staff, *New Yorker,* since 1950.

WEST, BENJAMIN (Mar. 1730–Aug. 26, 1813); b. Rehoboth, Mass. Almanac-maker. *An Almanack, for the Year of Our Lord Christ, 1763* (1762). This was printed at Providence, R.I., by William Goddard. It was soon changed to the *New-England Almanack; or, Lady's and Gentleman's Diary.* West also issued *Bickerstaff's Boston Almanac,* etc.

WEST, ELIZABETH HOWARD (Mar. 27, 1873–Jan. 3, 1948); b. Pontotoc, Miss. Librarian, bibliographer. *Texas Historical Notebook* (1905). Editor: *Calendar of the Papers of Martin Van Buren* (1910); *Calendar of the Papers of Mirabeau Buonaparte Lamar* (1912). State librarian, Texas, 1918–25; librarian, Texas Technological College, Lubbock, Tex. 1925–42.

WEST, JAMES E[dward] (May 16, 1876–May 15, 1948); b. Washington, D.C. Author. *The Lone Scout of the Sky* (1928); *He-Who-Sees-in-the-Dark: The Boys' Story of Frederick Burnham, the American Scout* (with Peter O. Lamb, 1932); *Making the Most of Yourself* (1941); etc. Editor, *Boys' Life,* 1922–43.

West, Kenyon. Pen name of Frances Louise Morse Howland.

WEST, LEVON (Feb. 3, 1900–Apr. 25, 1968); b. Centerville, S.D. Etcher, photographer, author. Pen name, "Ivan Dmitri." *A Catalogue of the Etchings of Levon West* (1929); *Making an Etching* (1932); *Color in Photography* (1939); *Kodachrome and How to Use It* (1940); *Flight to Everywhere* (1944).

WEST, LILLIE (Mrs. Henry Brown; Mrs. Frank Howard Buck) (Oct. 11, 1860–July 3, 1939); b. West Burlington, Ia. Actress, drama critic, author. Pen names, "Amy Leslie" and "Marie Stanley." *Amy Leslie at the Fair* (1893); *Some Players* (1899); *Gulf Stream* (1930); etc. Drama critic, the *Chicago Daily News,* 1890–1930.

WEST, MAE (Apr. 17, 1893–   ); b. Brooklyn, N.Y. Actress, author. *Sex* (1926); *The Drag* (1926); *The Wicked Age* (1927); *Pleasure Man* (1928); *Diamond Lil* (1928); *The Constant Sinner* (1930); *Catherine Was Great*

(1944); *Goodness Had Nothing to Do with It* (1959); *The Wit and Wisdom of Mae West* (1967).

WEST, NATHANAEL [Nathan Wallenstein Weinstein] (Oct. 17, 1902–Dec. 21, 1940); b. New York. Novelist. *The Dream Life of Balso Snell* (1931); *Miss Lonelyhearts* (1933); *A Cool Million* (1934); *The Day of the Locust* (1939); *See* Randall C. Reid's *The Fiction of Nathanael West* (1967); Jay Martin's *Nathanael West: The Art of His Life* (1970).

WEST, PAUL (Feb. 23, 1930–   ); b. Eckington, Eng. Author. *The Fantasy Poets: Number Seven* (1952); *The Growth of the Novel* (1959); *The Spellbound Horses* (poems, 1960); *Byron and the Spoiler's Art* (1960); *A Quality of Mercy* (1961); *I Said the Sparrow* (1963); *Robert Penn Warren* (1964); *The Snow Leopard* (poems, 1964); *Tenement of Clay* (1965); *The Wine of Absurdity* (1966); *Alley Jaggers* (1966); *Words for a Deaf Daughter* (1969); *I'm Expecting to Live Quite Soon* (1970).

WEST, PAUL [Clarendon] (Jan. 26, 1871–Oct. 30, 1918); b. Boston, Mass. Journalist, author. *The Pearl and the Pumpkin* (with William W. Denslow, 1904); *Innocent Murderers* (with William A. Johnston, 1910); *Just Boy* (1912); etc.

WEST, RAY [Benedict], Jʀ. (1908–). Author. *Writing in the Rocky Mountains* (1947); *Essays in Modern Literary Criticism* (1952); *Kingdom of the Saints* (1957); etc. Editor: *The Art of Modern Fiction* (with R. W. Stallman, 1949); *American Short Stories* (1960); etc.

West, Ward. Pen name of Hal Borland.

West Virginia Review. Charleston, W. Va. Monthly. Founded 1923. Discontinued 1943.

Westchester Farmer, Letters of a. Written by Samuel Seabury just before the Revolution. He opposed those who advocated armed resistance to England.

WESTCOTT, ALLAN FERGUSON (Nov. 22, 1882–May 2, 1953); b. Alexandria Bay, N.Y. Educator, editor, author. *A History of Sea Power* (with W. O. Stevens, 1920); *The United States Navy, A History* (with C. S. Alden, 1943); etc. Editor: *New Poems of James I of England* (1910). *Four Centuries of Literature* (with others, 1925). Editor and co-author: *American Sea Power since 1775* (1947). English dept., U.S. Naval Academy, 1911–48.

WESTCOTT, EDWARD NOYES (Sept. 27, 1846–Mar. 31, 1898); b. Syracuse, N.Y. Banker, author. *David Harum: A Story of American Life* (1898); *The Teller* (1901).

WESTCOTT, JAN (1912–); b. Philadelphia, Pa. Novelist. *The Border Lord* (1946); *Captain for Elizabeth* (1949); *The Hepburn* (1950); *Captain Barney* (1951); *The Walsingham Woman* (1953); *The Queen's Grace* (1959); etc.

WESTCOTT, THOMPSON (June 5, 1820–May 8, 1888); b. Philadelphia, Pa. Editor, author. *Life of John Fitch* (1857); *The Historic Mansions and Buildings of Philadelphia* (1877); *History of Philadelphia*, 3v. (with John Thomas Scharf, 1884); etc. Editor, the *Philadelphia Sunday Dispatch*, 1848–84.

WESTERMAN, HARRY JAMES (Aug. 8, 1876–June 27, 1945); b. Parkersburg, W. Va. Cartoonist. *A Book of Cartoons* (1902). Illustrated Robert O. Ryder's *The Young Lady across the Way* (1913); etc. Cartoonist, the *Ohio State Journal*, from 1901.

WESTERMANN, WILLIAM LINN (Sept. 15, 1873–Oct. 4, 1954); b. Belleville, Ill. Educator, historian. *The Story of the Ancient Nations* (1912); *Slave Systems of Greek and Roman Antiquity* (1955). Editor: *Upon Slavery in Ptolemaic Egypt* (1929); etc. Prof. history, Columbia University, 1923–48.

Western. A genre of popular fiction originated in the United States. It derives from the settlement of the West, the pushing back of the frontier, and the transformation of the frontiers-

man and Indian scout into the cowboy. The source of the Western American male hero who lives by his wits and physical prowess closer to nature than to society is the historical romances of Fenimore Cooper. The first Western to attain critical notice was Owen Wister's *The Virginian* (1902). Notable writers of Westerns have included Frederick Faust, Zane Grey, Ernest Haycox, Edward Zane Carroll Judson, Walter Van Tilburg Clark. See *Great Tales of the American West*, ed. by Harry E. Maule (1945); Irwin R. Blacker's *The Old West in Fiction* (1961); Leslie A. Fiedler's *The Return of the Vanishing American* (1968).

Western, The. St. Louis, Mo. Magazine. Founded 1866, as the *Western Educational Review*. Name and scope changed 1872. Editor, H. H. Morgan. Distinguished for its literary content and scholarly editing. Expired 1881.

Western Clearings. Stories by Carolina Matilda Stansbury Kirkland (1845). Graphic sketches of pioneer life in the Northwest Territory.

Western Humanities Review, The. University of Utah, Salt Lake City, Utah. Quarterly. Founded 1941. Devoted to academic work in poetry, essays, fiction. Contributors have included William Arrowsmith, John Ciardi, Allan Swallow, and Sheridan Baker.

Western Messenger. Cincinnati, O. Unitarian monthly. Founded June, 1835. Ralph Waldo Emerson's poems, "Goodbye, Proud World," "Each and All," "Rhodora," and "The Humble-Bee" appeared in this magazine. Its literary content was outstanding. Expired Apr., 1841.

Western Monthly Review. Cincinnati, O. Founded May, 1827. E. Hubbard Flint was publisher, and Timothy Flint was editor. Expired June, 1830.

Western Publishing Co., Inc. Racine, Wis. Acquired Golden Press in 1964. Also owns Odyssey Press and Pegasus.

Western Review, The. Murray, Utah. Quarterly. Founded 1937 as *The Intermountain Review* by Ray B. West, Jr. In 1938 became *The Rocky Mountain Review*, published at Ogden, Utah, and edited by Ray B. West, Jr. Moved to Lawrence, Kans., in 1946, and title changed to *The Western Review*. In 1949 moved to State University of Iowa, Iowa City, Ray B. West, Jr., continuing as editor. Known for its fiction, poetry, and literary criticism. Suspended 1960 and incorporated with *Contact*.

Western Star. Long poem by Stephen Vincent Benét (1943). Part of a planned epic poem about America. Describes the part played by the Jamestown and Plymouth settlements.

Western Story Magazine. New York. Weekly fiction magazine, published by Street & Smith. Founded 1917.

Western Writers of America. Organization of writers of fiction about the U.S. West. Publishes a professional magazine, *The Roundup*. Established the Western Writers of America Awards in 1953 for craftsmanship in the field.

WESTHEIMER, DAVID (1917–   ); b. Houston, Tex. Novelist. *Summer on the Water* (1948); *The Magic Fallacy* (1950); *Watching out for Dulie* (1960).

WESTLAKE, DONALD E[dwin] (July 12, 1933–); b. New York. *The Mercenaries* (1960); *Killing Time* (1961); *Killy* (1963); *Pity Him Afterwards* (1964); *The Fugitive Pigeon* (1965); *The Busy Body* (1966); *The Spy in the Ointment* (1966); *God Save the Mark* (1967); *The Hot Rock* (1970). Under pen name "Richard Stark": *The Hunter* (1963); *The Man with the Getaway Face* (1963); *The Outfit* (1963); *The Mourner* (1963); *The Score* (1964); *The Jugger* (1965); *The Seventh* (1966); *The Handle* (1966); *The Rare Coin Score* (1967).

WESTLEY, GEORGE HEMBERT (Jan. 28, 1865–Sept. 25, 1936); b. (George Hippisley) in Newfoundland. Columnist, author. *The Maid and the Miscreant* (1906); *Clementina's Highwayman* (with Robert N. Stephens, 1907); etc. Editor: *For Love's Sweet Sake* (1905). Wrote column, "Fads and Fancies," for the *Boston Evening Transcript*, 1906–29.

Westminster Historical Atlas to the Bible. Edited by George E. Wright and Floyd V. Filson (1945). Atlas and geography based on modern researches, with a topographical concordance.

Westminster Magazine. Oglethorpe University, Ga. Quarterly review. Founded 1911. Absorbed *Bozart,* 1935, to form the *Bozart-Westminster.* Has published D. C. DeJong, Marianne Moore, Parker Tyler, Louis Zukofsky.

Westminster Press, The. Philadelphia, Pa. Publishers. Founded 1838, by the General Assembly of the Presbyterian Church in the United States of America. Its first publication was *Psalms and Hymns* (1840). In 1923, the Board of Christian Education of the Presbyterian Church in the United States of America established a separate publication department, which now conducts the Westminster Press. Westminster Press was not used as a publishing trade name until 1870. The press publishes Sunday School books and tracts, hymnals, and periodicals. One of its most popular books over a period of almost a hundred years is *Calvin's Institutes of the Christian Religion.* As early as 1735 the General Assembly of the Presbyterian Church in the United States exercised jurisdiction over printed matter designed for its members, and in 1809 organized a Tract Society for the distribution of Presbyterian literature.

WESTON, CHRISTINE [Goutiere] (1904–); b. in India, came to the United States in 1923. Author. *Be Thou the Bride* (1940); *The Devil's Foot* (1942); *Indigo* (1944); *Bhimsa, the Dancing Bear* (1945); *The Dark Wood* (1946); *There and Then* (stories, 1947); *The World Is a Bridge* (1950); *Wise Children* (1957); *Ceylon* (1960).

WESTON, GEORGE (June 28, 1880–); b. New York. Novelist. *The Apple Tree Girl* (1918); *The Horseshoe Nails* (1927); *Wings of Destiny* (1929); *The American Marquis* (1930); *His First Million Women* (1934); etc.

Westward Ho! Novel by James Kirke Paulding (1832). Romance of early days of adventure in Kentucky.

"Westward Ho!" Poem by Joaquin Miller.

Wetherell, Elizabeth. Pen name of Susan Bogert Warner.

WETHERELL, JUNE (Mrs. Daniel Frame) (June 8, 1909–); b. Bellingham, Wash. Novelist. *Every Ecstasy* (1941); *Run with the Pack* (1942); *But That Was Yesterday* (1943); *The Glorious Three* (1951); etc.

WETJEN, ALBERT RICHARD (Aug. 20, 1900–Mar. 8, 1948); b. London. Author. *Captains All* (1924); *Way For a Sailor!* (1928); *Fiddlers' Green* (1931); *Beyond Justice* (1936); *Shark Gotch of the Islands* (1936); *In the Wake of the Shark* (1939); *Outland Tales* (1940); etc. Co-founder and editor, *The Outlander,* 1933.

WETMORE, CLAUDE HAZELTINE (b. 1863); b. Cuyahoga Falls, O. Traveler, author. *Sweepers of the Sea* (1900); *Under the Southern Cross* (1901); *Incaland* (1902); *In a Brazilian Jungle* (1903); *Out of a Fleur-de-Lis* (1903); etc.

WEXLEY, JOHN (Sept. 14, 1907–); b. New York. Playwright. *The Last Mile* (prod. 1930); *Steel* (prod. 1931); *They Shall Not Die* (prod. 1935); *The Judgment of Julius and Ethel Rosenberg* (1955); etc.

WEYBRIGHT, VICTOR (Mar. 16, 1903–); b. Keymar, Md. Publisher. Author: *Spangled Banner* (1935); *Buffalo Bill and the Wild West* (with Henry B. Sell, 1955); *Making of a Publisher* (1967); etc. Editor-in-chief, New American Library, 1945–1966.

Weybright and Talley, Inc. New York. Publishers. Founded 1966. Victor Weybright, formerly with New American Library (q.v.), is chairman of the board. Publishes works of biography, history, politics, and poetry.

WEYGANDT, CORNELIUS (Dec. 13, 1871–Aug., 1957); b. Germantown, Pa. Educator, author. *Irish Plays and Playwrights* (1913); *A Century of the English Novel* (1925); *Tuesdays at Ten* (1928); *The Red Hills* (1929); *The Wissahickon Hills* (1930); *A Passing America* (1932); *The White Hills* (1934); *The Time of Tennyson* (1936); *The Blue Hills* (1936); *New Hampshire Neighbors* (1937); *The Time of Yeats* (1937); *Philadelphia Folks* (1938); *The Dutch Country* (1939); *Down Jersey* (1940); *November Rowen* (1941); *The Plenty of Pennsylvania* (1942); *On the Edge of Evening* (autobiography, 1945); etc. English dept., University of Pennsylvania, 1897–1942.

WHALEN, PHILIP (Oct. 20, 1923–); b. Portland, Ore. Author. *Like I Say* (1960); *Memoirs of an Interglacial Age* (1960); *Monday in the Evening* (1963); *Everyday* (1965); *Highgrade: Doodles, Poems* (1966); etc.

WHALEN, RICHARD JAMES (Sept. 23, 1935–); b. New York. Journalist, author. *The Founding Father: The Story of Joseph P. Kennedy* (1964); *A City Destroying Itself* (1965).

WHALEN, WILLIAM WILFRID (May 7, 1886–); b. near Mt. Carmel, Pa. Priest, playwright, novelist. *The Golden Squaw* (1926); *Strike* (1927); *The Irish Sparrow* (1927); *Give Me a Chance!* (1929); *The Priest Who Vanished* (1942); etc.

WHARTON, ANNE HOLLINGSWORTH (Dec. 15, 1845–July 29, 1928); b. Southampton Furnace, Pa. Author. *Through Colonial Doorways* (1893); *Martha Washington* (1897); *Social Life in the Early Republic* (1902); *Italian Days and Ways* (1906); *An English Honeymoon* (1908); *In Château Land* (1911); *A Rose of Old Quebec* (1913); *In Old Pennsylvania Towns* (1920).

WHARTON, EDITH [Newbold Jones] (Jan. 24, 1862–Aug. 11, 1937); b. New York. Novelist. *The Greater Inclination* (1899); *The Touchstone* (1900); *Crucial Instances* (1901); *The Valley of Decision* (1902); *Sanctuary* (1903); *The House of Mirth* (1905); *Madame de Treymes* (1907); *The Fruit of the Tree* (1907); *Ethan Frome* (1911); *The Custom of the Country* (1913); *The Age of Innocence* (1920, Pulitzer Prize novel, 1921); *The Glimpses of the Moon* (1922); *Old New York,* 4v. (1924); *Twilight Sleep* (1927); *The Children* (1928); *Hudson River Bracketed* (1929); *Certain People* (1930); *The Gods Arrive* (1932); *Human Nature* (1933); *A Backward Glance* (1934); *Ghosts* (1937); *The Buccaneers* (1938); etc. Among her non-fiction books are: *The Decoration of Houses* (with Ogden Codman, 1897); *Italian Backgrounds* (1905); *The Writing of Fiction* (1925). See Robert M. Lovett's *Edith Wharton* (1925); Lavinia Davis's *A Bibliography of the Writings of Edith Wharton* (1933); Fred B. Millett's *Contemporary American Authors* (1940); Blake Nevius's *Edith Wharton, a Study of Her Fiction* (1953); D.E.S. Maxwell's *American Fiction: The Intellectual Background* (1963); Michael Millgate's *American Social Fiction: James to Cozzens* (1964); Millicent Bell's *Henry James and Edith Wharton* (1965).

WHARTON, HENRY MARVIN (Sept. 11, 1848–June 23, 1928); b. in Culpeper Co., Va. Baptist clergyman, lecturer, author. *Pulpit, Pew, and Platform* (1890); *Stories, Short and Sweet* (1910); *Messages of Mercy* (1927); etc. Editor: *War Songs and Poems of the Southern Confederacy* (1904).

WHARTON, THOMAS [Isaac] (Aug. 1, 1859–Apr. 6, 1896); b. Philadelphia, Pa. Journalist, novelist. *A Latter-Day Saint* (anon. 1884); *Hannibal of New York* (1886).

"What hath God wrought!" The message which Samuel F. B. Morse ticked off on the telegraph from Washington to Alfred Vail in Baltimore, May 24, 1844. It was not the first message, for others had been sent earlier in May.

"What is so rare as a day in June?" Line from the poem "The Vision of Sir Launfal" by James Russell Lowell.

What Maisie Knew. Novel by Henry James (1897). The inner development of a young girl whose divorced parents shunt her between governesses.

What Makes Sammy Run? Novel by Budd Schulberg (1941). Sammy Glick, an energetic go-getter, becomes a Hollywood big shot by unscrupulous maneuvering.

What Price Glory? Play by Maxwell Anderson and Laurence Stallings (prod. 1924). Robust story of the A.E.F. in France during World War I. Captain Flagg, and Sergeant Quirt and Charmaine, daughter of the innkeeper, are the leading characters.

What Was It? Short story by Fitz James O'Brien (1859). Scene laid in a New York boarding house.

WHATMOUGH, JOSHUA (June 30, 1897–Apr. 25, 1964); b. Rochdale, Lancs. Eng. Philologist. *Language* (1956); *Poetic, Scientific, and Other Forms of Discourse* (1956); etc. Linguistics dept., Harvard University, from 1951.

"What's O'Clock?" Poem by Amy Lowell (1926).

"What's the Matter with Kansas?" Famous editorial by William Allen White in the *Emporia Gazette,* Aug. 15, 1896.

WHEAT, CARL IRVING (Dec. 5, 1892–June 23, 1966); b. Holliston, Mass. Lawyer, author. *Trailing the Forty-Niners through Death Valley* (1939); *Mapping the American Transmississippi West, 1540–1804,* vl. 1 (1957), vl. 2 (1958). Editor: Lewis Hector Garrand's *Wah-to-Yah & the Taos Trail* (1935); and other historical journals. Editor, the *Quarterly* of the Historical Society of Southern California, 1933–36.

WHEATLEY, PHILLIS (Mrs. Phillis Peters) (c. 1753–Dec. 5, 1784); b. in Africa. Poet. *An Elegiac Poem, on the Death of that Celebrated Divine George Whitefield* (1770); *Poems on Various Subjects, Religious and Moral* (1773); *Memoir and Poems of Phillis Wheatley* (1834); *Letters of Phillis Wheatley, the Negro Slave Poet of Boston,* ed. by C. Deane (1864); *Poems and Letters: First Collected Edition,* ed. by Charles Fred Heartmann (1915); etc. *See* Benjamin B. Thatcher's *Memoir of Phillis Wheatley* (1834).

WHEATON, HENRY (Nov. 27, 1785–Mar. 11, 1848); b. Providence, R.I. Jurist, historian. *History of the Northmen* (1831); *Elements of International Law* (1836); *History of the Law of Nations in Europe and America* (1845).

Wheel of Life, The. Novel by Ellen Glasgow (1906). The scene is New York City and the theme, marital difficulties.

WHEELER, ANDREW CARPENTER (June 4, 1835–Mar. 10, 1903); b. New York. Journalist, critic, author. Pen names "J. P. Mowbray," "J. P. M.," "Trinculo," "Nym Crinkle." *The Chronicles of Milwaukee* (1861); *The Iron Trail* (1876); *The Toltec Cup* (1890); *The Primrose Path of Dalliance* (1892); *A Journey to Nature* (1901); *The Making of a Country Home* (1901); *Tangled up in Beulah Land* (1902); *The Conquering of Kate* (1903). See *World's Work,* v. 6, 1903.

WHEELER, BENJAMIN IDE (July 15, 1854–May 2, 1927); b. Randolph, Mass. Educator, author. *Alexander the Great* (1900); *The Abundant Life* (1926). President, University of California, 1899–1919.

WHEELER, DANIEL EDWIN (Mar. 1, 1880–); b. New York. Editor, author. *Abraham Lincoln* (1916); *Autobiography* (1917). Editor: *Life and Writings of T. Paine,* 10v. (1908). Editor, *McClure's Magazine,* 1928–29; *Smart Set,* 1929–30; fiction editor, *Liberty,* 1931–33; on editorial staff, from 1935.

WHEELER, EDWARD L. Dime novelist. *Bob Wood* (1878); *Nobby Nick of Nevada* (1880); *Sierra Sam* (1882); *Apollo Bill* (1882); *Yreka Jim's Joker* (1884); *The Phantom Miner* (1884); *Corduroy Charlie* (1885); *Deadwood Dick on Deck; or, Calamity Jane, the Heroine of Whoop-Up* (1885); *Deadwood Dick, Jr., in Denver* (1888); *Colorado Charlie's Detective Dash* (1890); etc. The dates are not necessarily those of first editions.

WHEELER, HOWARD DURYEE (Nov. 3, 1880–Feb. 25, 1958); b. Montclair, N.J. Editor. Editor, the *San Francisco Daily News* 1906–08; *Everybody's Magazine,* 1915–1919; chief editorial writer, the *New York Daily Mirror,* 1932–36; etc.

WHEELER, HUGH CALLINGHAM (Mar. 19, 1913–); b. London. Author. *The Crippled Muse* (1952); *Big Fish, Little Fish* (1961); *Look: We've Come Through* (1963); *We Have Always Lived in the Castle* (prod. 1967); etc. Under pen name "Patrick Quentin": seventeen novels; latest, *Family Skeleton* (1965). Under pen name "Q. Patrick," with R. Wilson Webb: five novels; latest, *Return to the Scene* (1952). Under pen name "Jonathan Stagge," with R. Wilson Webb: eight novels; latest, *The Three Fears* (1953).

WHEELER, JOSEPH LEWIS (Mar. 16, 1884–); b. Dorchester, Mass. Librarian, author. *The Library and the Community* (1924); *The American Public Library Building* (with Alfred Morton Githens, 1941); *The 1776 Hubbardton Military Road* (1956); *Location of Public Library Buildings* (1956). Librarian, Youngstown Public Library, 1915–26; Enoch Pratt Free Library, Baltimore, 1926–45.

WHEELER, MONROE (Feb. 13, 1900–); b. Evanston, Ill. Museum director. Author: *Bookbindings of I. Wiemeler* (1935); *Modern Painters and Sculptors as Illustrators* (1936); *Soutine* (1950); *The Last Works of Henri Matisse* (1961); *Bonnard and His Environment* (1964); etc. Editor: *Textiles and Ornaments of India* (1956); etc.

WHEELER, POST (Aug. 6, 1869–Dec. 23, 1956); b. Owego, N.Y. Diplomat, author. *The Writer* (1893); *Reflections of a Bachelor* (1897); *Love-in-a-Mist* (poems, 1901); *Poems* (1902); *Russian Wonder Tales* (1910); *Albanian Wonder Tales* (1936); *The Golden Legend of Ethiopia* (1936); *Ho-Dan-Zo,* 10v. (1938); *India Against the Storm* (1944); *Dragon in the Dust* (1946); etc. Editor, the *New York Press,* 1896–1900. U.S. Minister to Paraguay, 1929–33; to Albania, 1933–34.

WHEELER, RAYMOND HOLDER (Mar. 9, 1892–Aug. 24, 1961); b. Berlin, Mass. Educator, psychologist, author. *The Science of Psychology* (1929); *The Laws of Human Nature* (1931). Assoc. editor, the *Journal of General Psychology.* Founder, *Journal of Human Ecology,* 1951; editor, from 1951. Prof. psychology, University of Kansas, 1925–47; Erskine College, 1947–48; faculty of Babson Institute of Business Administration, from 1948.

WHEELER, WILLIAM ADOLPHUS (Nov. 14, 1833–Oct. 28, 1874); b. Leicester, Mass. Librarian, philologist, author. *An Explanatory and Pronouncing Dictionary of the Noted Names of Fiction; Including Also Familiar Pseudonyms* (1865); *Familiar Allusions* (completed by Charles G. Wheeler, 1882). Editor: *Mother Goose Melodies* (1869); *Who Wrote It?* (1881). With Boston Public Library, 1866–74.

WHEELIS, ALLEN B. (Oct. 23, 1915–); b. Marion, La. Psychoanalyst, author. *The Quest for Identity* (1958); *The Seeker* (1960); *The Illusionless Man* (1966); *The Desert* (1970).

WHEELOCK, JOHN HALL (Sept. 9, 1886–); b. Far Rockaway, L.I., N.Y. Poet. *Verses by Two Undergraduates* (with Van Wyck Brooks, 1905); *The Human Fantasy* (1911); *The Beloved Adventure* (1912); *Love and Liberation; The Songs of Adsched of Meru, and Other Poems* (1913); *Dust and Light* (1919); *The Black Panther* (1922); *The Bright Doom* (1927); *Poems, 1911–1936* (1936); *Poems Old and New* (1956); *The Gardener* (1961). Editor: *The Letters of Maxwell Perkins* (1950); *Poets of Today Annual,* since 1954. Editor, Charles Scribner's Sons, since 1926; director and secretary, since 1932.

See Fred B. Millett's *Contemporary American Authors* (1940).

WHEELOCK, JOSEPH A[lbert] (Feb. 8, 1831–May 9, 1906); b. Bridgetown, N.S. Editor, author. *Minnesota: Its Place among the States* (1860); *Minnesota: Its Progress and Capabilities* (1862). Editor, *St. Paul Daily Press,* 1861–75; *St. Paul Pioneer-Press,* 1875–1906.

WHEELWRIGHT, JERE HUNGERFORD, JR. (1905?–Jan. 21, 1961). Author. *Gentleman, Hush* (1948); *Wolfshead* (1949); *Gray Captain* (1955); *Kentucky Stand* (1951); *Draw Near to Battle* (1953); etc.

WHEELWRIGHT, JOHN (c. 1592–Nov. 15, 1679); b. Saleby, Lincolnshire, Eng. Congregational clergyman, author. *Mercurius Americanus* (1645); *John Wheelwright: His Writings,* in the *Publications* of the Prince Society, v.9 (1876). *See* John Heard, Jr.'s *John Wheelwright, 1592–1679* (1930).

WHEELWRIGHT, JOHN [Brooks] (c. 1897–Sept. 15, 1940); b. Milton, Mass. Poet. *Northwest Passage* (1917); *Rock and Shell* (1933); *Mirrors of Venus* (1938); *Political Self-Portrait* (1940).

WHEELWRIGHT, JOHN TYLER (Feb. 26, 1856–Dec. 23, 1925); b. Roxbury, Mass. Lawyer, author. *Rollo's Journey to Cambridge* (with Frederic Jesup Stimson, anon., 1880); *A Child of the Century* (1887); *Uncle Micajah's Treat at Slanbasket Beach* (1888); *A Bad Penny* (1896); *War Children* (1908); etc.

WHEELWRIGHT, PHILIP ELLIS (July 6, 1901–); b. Elizabeth, N.J. Educator. Author. *The Way of Philosophy* (1954); *The Burning Fountain: A Study in the Language of Symbolism* (1954); *Heraclitus* (1959); *Valid Thinking,* (1962)*'; Metaphor and Reality* (1962); *The Presocratics* (1966); etc. Prof. philosophy, University of California at Riverside, since 1954.

WHEILDON, WILLIAM W[illder] (Oct. 17, 1805–1892); b. Boston, Mass. Editor, author. *Contributions to Thought* (1874); *Curiosities of History* (1880); etc. Founder, the *Bunker Hill Aurora,* Charlestown, Mass.; editor and publisher, 1827–70.

WHELEN, TOWNSEND (Mar. 6, 1877–Dec. 23, 1961); b. Philadelphia, Pa. Army officer, author. *The American Rifle* (1918); *Wilderness Hunting and Wildcraft* (1927); *The Hunting Rifle* (1940); *On Your Own in the Wilderness* (with B. Angier, 1958); etc.

"When I Saw Sweet Nellie Home." Song, words by Frances Kyle, music by J. Fletcher (1856). Also known as "The Quilting Party" and as "Seeing Nellie Home."

"When Johnny Comes Marching Home Again." Popular Civil War song by Patrick Sarsfield Gilmore, written under the pen name of "Louis Lambert" (1863).

When Knighthood was in Flower. Novel by "Edwin Caskoden" (Charles Major) (1898). Historical romance of sixteenth century England, describing the courtship and marriage of Mary Tudor and Charles Brandon.

"When Lilacs Last in the Dooryard Bloom'd." Poem by Walt Whitman (1865). Tribute to Abraham Lincoln.

"When the Frost Is on the Punkin." Poem by James Whitcomb Riley (1882).

"When the Great Gray Ships Come In." Poem by Guy Wetmore Carryl, written in New York Harbor, Aug. 20, 1898.

"When the Robins Nest Again." Song by Frank Howard (1883).

"When the Roll Is Called up Yonder." Popular hymn by James M. Black.

"When Will My Darling Boy Return?" Popular Civil War song.

"When You and I Were Young, Maggie." Song, words by George W. Johnson, music by J. A. Butterfield (1866).

"When You Were Sweet Sixteen." Song by James Thornton (1898).

Where the Blue Begins. Fantasy by Christopher Morley (1922). Story of Gissing and a group of stray dogs. The dogs become personified and enter the business and social life of New York City.

WHICHER, GEORGE FRISBIE (Nov. 5, 1889–Mar. 7, 1954); b. Lawrenceville, N.J., son of George Meason Whicher. Educator, author. *On the Tibur Road* (with George M. Whicher, poems, 1911); *The Life and Romances of Mrs. Eliza Haywood* (1915); *This Was a Poet: A Critical Biography of Emily Dickinson* (1938); *Walden Revisited* (1945); *Mornings at 8:50* (1951); etc. Editor, *Amherst Graduates' Quarterly,* 1919–32. English dept., Amherst College, from 1915.

WHICHER, GEORGE MEASON (July 29, 1860–Nov. 2, 1937); b. Muscatine, Ia. Author. *On the Tibur Road* (with George Frisbie Whicher, 1911); *Roman Pearls, and Other Verses* (1926); *Vergiliana* (1931); *Amity Street* (poems, 1935). Prof. Greek and Latin, Hunter College, 1899–1924.

WHIGHAM, HENRY JAMES (Dec. 24, 1869–Mar. 16, 1954); b. Ayrshire, Scot. Editor, author. *The Persian Problem* (1903); *Manchuria and Korea* (1904). Editor, *Town and Country,* 1909–35; editor and publisher, *Metropolitan Magazine,* 1912–22; editor, *International Studio,* 1928–31; etc.

Whilomville Stories. By Stephen Crane (1900). A record of New Jersey village life. Crane was born at No. 14 Mulberry Street, in Newark, N.J., and is buried at Elizabeth, New Jersey.

WHIPPLE, EDWIN PERCY (Mar. 8, 1819–June 16, 1886); b. Gloucester, Mass. Critic, lecturer, author. *Essays and Reviews,* 2v. (1848–49); *Lectures in Subjects Connected with Literature and Life* (1850); *Character and Characteristic Men* (1866); *Literature of the Age of Elizabeth* (1869); *Success and Its Conditions* (1871); *Recollections of Eminent Men* (1887); *American Literature and Other Papers* (1887); *Outlooks on Society, Literature and Politics* (1888); etc. Compiler: *Family Library of British Poetry* (with James T. Fields, 1878).

WHIPPLE, GUY MONTROSE (June 12, 1876–Aug. 1, 1941); b. Danvers, Mass. Psychologist, educator, author. *How to Study Effectively* (1916); *Problems in Educational Psychology* (1922); etc. Psychology dept., Cornell University, 1898–1914; University of Illinois, 1914–18; prof. experimental education, University of Michigan, 1919–25.

WHIPPLE, THOMAS KING (1890–1939). Author. *Spokesmen: Modern Writers and American Life* (1928); *Study Out the Land* (1943); etc.

WHIPPLE, WAYNE (Nov. 17, 1856–Oct. 22, 1942); b. near Meadville, Pa. Author of American biographies for young people. *The Story-Life of Lincoln* (1908); *The Heart of Washington* (1911); *The Heart of Lee* (1918); *Hero Tales from History* (1922); etc. With D. Lothrop Co., Boston, publishers, 1882–1905.

Whirligigs. By O. Henry (1910). Short stories of adventure, each with an ironic ending, the characters being overcome by quirks of fate.

WHISTLER, JAMES [Abbott] **McNeill** (July 10, 1834–July 17, 1903); b. Lowell, Mass. Painter, author. *Ten O'Clock* (1888); *The Gentle Art of Making Enemies* (1890). *See* Elizabeth R. and Joseph Pennell's *The Life of James McNeill Whistler,* 2v. (1908).

Whistling Dick's Christmas Stocking. First story by O. Henry (1899).

WHITAKER, ALMA (Mrs. Jerome Reynolds) (1881–Nov. 23, 1956); b. London. Naturalized, 1915. Author. *Trousers and Skirts* (1924); *The Governor's Wife Pays a Call* (prod. 1932); *Bacchus Behave!* (1933). With McClure's Syndicate 1924–40.

WHITAKER, ARTHUR PRESTON (June 6, 1895–); b. Tuscaloosa, Ala. Educator, historian. *The Spanish-American Frontier* (1927); *The Mississippi Question, 1795–1803* (1934). Compiler: *Documents Relating to Spanish Commercial Policy in the Floridas and Louisiana, 1778–1808* (1931); *The Western Hemisphere Idea: Its Rise and Decline* (1954); *The United States and Argentina* (1955); *Argentine Upheaval* (1956); *Nationalism in Contemporary Latin America* (1966); etc. Prof. American history, Cornell University, 1930–36; prof. Latin-American history, University of Pennsylvania, from 1936.

WHITAKER, CHARLES HARRIS (May 19, 1872–Aug. 12, 1938); b. in Rhode Island. Editor, author. *The Joke about Housing* (1920); *Rameses to Rockefeller: The Story of Architecture* (1934); etc. Editor, the *Journal* of the American Institute of Architects, 1913–27.

WHITAKER, DANIEL KIMBALL (Apr. 13, 1801–Mar. 24, 1881); b. Sharon, Mass. Editor. Founder and editor, the *New Orleans Monthly Review,* 1874–76; editor, the *Southern Literary Journal and Magazine of Arts,* Charleston, S.C., 1835; the *Southern Quarterly Review,* New Orleans, 1842–47.

WHITAKER, VIRGIL KEEBLE (Dec. 31, 1908–); b. Spokane, Wash. Educator, author. *The Religious Basis of Spenser's Thought* (1950); *Shakespeare's Use of Learning* (1953); etc. English dept., Stanford University, since 1934.

WHITAKER, WALTER CLAIBORNE (Jan. 28, 1867–Sept. 2, 1938); b. Lenoir, N.C. Episcopal clergyman, author. *Dives and Lazarus: Six Studies* (1898); *Richard Hooker Wilmer* (1907); *The Southern Highlands and Highlanders* (1915); etc.

WHITCHER, FRANCES M[iriam Berry] (Nov. 1, 1814–Jan. 4, 1852); b. Whitesboro, N.Y. Humorist. *The Widow Bedott Papers* (1856); *Widow Spriggins, Mary Elmer, and Other Sketches* (1867).

WHITCOMB, CATHARINE (Mrs. Daniel A. Davis) (Dec. 13, 1911–); b. Philadelphia, Pa. Novelist. *I'll Mourn You Later* (1936); *In the Fine Summer Weather* (1938); *The Malfreys* (1944); *The Hill of Glass* (1950); etc.

WHITCOMB, SELDEN L[incoln] (July 19, 1866–Apr. 22, 1930); b. Grinnell, Ia. Educator, author. *Chronological Outlines of American Literature* (1894); *Lyrical Verse* (1898); *The Study of a Novel* (1905); *Poems* (1912); *Random Rhymes, and the Three Queens* (1913); *Via Crucis* (1915). English dept., University of Kansas, 1905–1930.

WHITE, ALBERT BEEBE (Sept. 11, 1871–May 10, 1952); b. E. Randolph (now Holbrook), Mass. Educator, historian. *The Making of the English Constitution* (1898); *Self-Government at the King's Command* (1933); etc. History dept., University of Minnesota, 1899–1940.

WHITE, ALMA (June 16, 1862–June 26, 1946); b. Lewis Co., Ky. Educator, author. *The Story of My Life,* 6v. (1919–31); *Hymns and Poems* (1931); *Everlasting Life* (1944); etc. Founder of Pillar of Fire Church, and bishop of same.

WHITE, ANDREW DICKSON (Nov. 7, 1832–Nov. 4, 1918); b. Homer, N.Y. Diplomat, educator, author. *History of the Warfare of Science with Theology in Christendom* (1896); *Autobiography,* 2v. (1905); *The Work of Benjamin Hale* (1911); etc. President, Cornell University, 1868–85. U.S. minister to Germany, 1879–81, to Russia, 1892–94; ambassador to Germany, 1897–1902.

WHITE, CAROLINE EARLE (Sept. 28, 1833–Sept. 7, 1916); b. Philadelphia, Pa. Novelist. *Love in the Tropics* (1890); *A Modern Agrippa* (1893); *Patience Barker* (1893); *A Holiday in Spain* (1896); *An Ocean Mystery* (1903).

White, Charles Erskine. Pen name of Laughton Osborn.

WHITE, CHARLES LINCOLN (Jan. 22, 1863–Apr. 20, 1941); b. Nashua, N.H. Baptist clergyman, educator, author. *The Churches at Work* (1915); *Children of the Lighthouse* (1916). President, Colby College, 1901–08.

WHITE, CHARLES WILLIAM (1906–). Author. *Anna Becker* (1937); *Tiger, Tiger* (1940); *How I Feed My Friends* (1947); *The Man Who Carved Women from Wood* (1949); etc.

White, David, Co., New York. Publishers. Founded 1963. David W. White is president and editor. Specializes in general adult nonfiction and juveniles.

WHITE, DAVID MANNING (June 28, 1917–); b. Milwaukee, Wis. Educator, author. *Elementary Statistics for Journalists* (1954); *Mass Culture: The Popular Arts in America* (1957); *From Dogpatch to Slobbovia* (with A. Capp, 1964). Co-editor: *Introduction to Mass Communications Research* (1958); *Publishing for the New Reading Audience* (1959); *Identity and Anxiety: Survival of the Individual in Mass Society* (1960); *The Funnies, An American Idiom* (1963); *People, Society and Mass Communications* (1964). Prof. journalism, Boston University, since 1947.

WHITE, EDWARD LUCAS (May 18, 1866–Mar. 30, 1934); b. Bergen, N.J. Novelist. *Narrative Lyrics* (1908); *El Supremo* (1916); *The Unwilling Vestal* (1918); *The Song of the Sirens, and Other Stories* (1919); *Andivius Hedulio* (1921); *Helen: The Story of the Romance of Helen of Troy* (1925); *Lukundoo, and Other Stories* (1927); *Matrimony* (autobiography, 1932).

WHITE, ELIZA ORNE (Aug. 2, 1856–Jan. 23, 1947); b. Keene, N.H. Author. *Miss Brooks* (1890); *Winterborough* (1892); *When Molly Was Six* (1894); *A Lover of Truth* (1898); *Lesley Chilton* (1903); *An Only Child* (1905); *The First Step* (1914); *William Orne White: A Record of Ninety Years* (1917); *The Blue Aunt* (1918); *Nancy Alden* (1936); *Patty Makes a Visit* (1939); *When Esther Was a Little Girl* (1944); etc.

WHITE, E[lwyn] B[rooks] (July 11, 1899–); b. Mount Vernon, N.Y. Editor, humorist, author of children's books. *The Lady Is Cold* (poems, 1929); *Is Sex Necessary?* (with James Thurber, 1929); *Every Day Is Saturday* (1934); *The Fox of Peapack* (1938); *Quo Vadimus* (1939); *One Man's Meat* (1942); *Stuart Little* (1945); *The Wild Flag* (1946); *Here Is New York* (1949); *Charlotte's Web* (1952); *The Second Tree from the Corner* (1954); *The Points of My Compass* (1962). Editor: *Ho Hum* (1931); *Another Ho Hum* (1932); *A Subtreasury of American Humor* (with wife, Katherine S. White, 1941); Strunk's *The Elements of Style* (1959). With *New Yorker* since 1925.

WHITE, FRANCES HODGES (June 18, 1866–); b. Washington, Me. Author. *Sea Tales* (1898); *Helena's Wonderworld* (1900); *Aunt Nabby's Children* (1902); *Captain Jinks: The Autobiography of a Shetland Pony* (1909); etc.

WHITE, GRACE MILLER (Mrs. Friend H. Miller) (d. Dec. 21, 1965); b. New York. Author. *Tess of the Storm Country* (1909); *From the Valley of the Missing* (1911); *Judy of Rogues' Harbor* (1918); *The Shadow of the Sheltering Pines* (1919); *Ghost of Glen Gorge* (1925); *Susan of the Storm* (1927).

WHITE, HELEN C[onstance] (Nov. 28, 1896–June 7, 1967); b. New Haven, Conn. Educator, author. *The Mysticism of William Blake* (1927); *English Devotional Literature, 1600–1640* (1931); *A Watch in the Night* (1933); *Not Built with

Hands (1935); *The Metaphysical Poets* (1936); *To the End of the World* (1939); *Dust on the King's Highway* (1947); *Tudor Books of Private Devotion* (1951); *The Four Rivers of Paradise* (1955); *Bird of Fire* (1958); *Prayer and Poetry* (1960); etc. English dept., University of Wisconsin, from 1919; prof., since 1936.

WHITE, HENRY ADELBERT (Apr. 1880–Nov. 25, 1951); b. near Syracuse, N.Y. Educator, author. *English Study and English Writing* (1922); *Sir Walter Scott's Novels on the Stage* (1927). Prof. English, University of Nebraska, 1926–50.

WHITE, HENRY ALEXANDER (Apr. 15, 1861–Oct. 8, 1926); b. in Virginia. Presbyterian clergyman, educator, author. *Robert E. Lee and the Southern Confederacy* (1897); *The Making of South Carolina* (1906); *Stonewall Jackson* (1909). Prof. Greek, Columbia (S.C.) Theological Seminary, 1902–26.

WHITE, HERVEY (Nov. 26, 1866–1944); b. New London, Ia. Poet, novelist. *Differences* (1899); *Quicksand* (1900); *New Songs for Old* (1908); *In an Old Man's Garden* (1910); *A Ship of Souls* (poems, 1910); *Karon* (1914); *Man Overboard* (1922); *Snake Gold* (1926); *Childhood Fancies* (1927); *Tinker Town* (1930); *Border Freaks* (play, 1935); etc.

WHITE, JOHN BLAKE (Sept. 2, 1781–Aug. 24, 1858); b. Eutaw Springs, S.C. Lawyer, poet, artist. *Foscari* (1806); *The Mysteries of the Castle* (1807); *Modern Honor* (1812); *The Triumph of Liberty* (1819); *Intemperance* (1839); *The Forgers* (poem, 1899); etc. He painted portraits of the celebrated southerners of his time.

WHITE, JOHN WILLIAMS (Mar. 5, 1849–May 9, 1917); b. Cincinnati, O. Educator, Hellenist, author. *The Verse of Greek Comedy* (1912); *The Scholia on the Aves of Aristophanes* (1914); etc. Co-founder (with J. B. Greenough), the *Harvard Studies in Classical Philology.* Greek dept., Harvard University, 1874–1909; professor, 1884–1909.

WHITE, LEE A. (Nov. 23, 1886–); b. Flint, Mich. Author. *The Detroit News, 1873–1917* (1918); *Cranbrook Institute of Science* (with others, 1959). Editor: *Poems of Harold Brian Steele* (1908); Editor, *The Quill,* 1915–20; editorial staff, the *Detroit News,* 1917–52.

WHITE, LIONEL (July 9, 1905–). Author. *Flight into Terror* (1955); *Invitation to Violence* (1958); *The Time of Terror* (1960); *A Grave Undertaking* (1961); *Obsession* (1962); *The Money Trap* (1963); *The Night of the Rape* (1967); *The Crimshaw Memorandum* (1967); etc.

WHITE, LYNN TOWNSEND, Jr. (Apr. 29, 1907–); b. San Francisco, Cal. Educator, author. *Latin Monasticism in Norman Sicily* (1938); *Educating Our Daughters: A Challenge to Colleges* (1950); *Frontiers of Knowledge in the Study of Man* (1956); *Medieval Technology and Social Change* (1962); *The Transformation of the Roman World* (1966). Prof. history, University of California at Los Angeles, since 1958. Past pres., Mills College.

WHITE, MATTHEW (Sept. 21, 1857–Sept. 17, 1940); b. New York. Dramatic critic, author. *Eric Dane* (1889); *One of the Profession* (1893); *The Affair at Islington* (1897); *A Born Aristocrat* (1898); *Two Boys and a Fortune* (1907); and other boy's books. Editor, *Argosy,* beginning in 1889; drama editor for *Munsey's Magazine* for twenty-eight years.

WHITE, MORTON GABRIEL (Apr. 29, 1917–); b. New York. Philosopher. Author: *Social Thought in America* (1949); *Toward Reunion in Philosophy* (1956); *Religion, Politics, and Higher Learning* (1959); *The Intellectual versus the City* (1962); etc. Editor: *The Age of Analysis* (1955). Philosophy dept., Harvard University, since 1948.

WHITE, NANCY (Mrs. Ralph Delahaye Payne, Jr.) (July 25, 1916–); b. Brooklyn, N.Y. Editor. Editor-in-chief, *Harper's Bazaar,* 1958–1971.

WHITE, NELIA GARDNER (Nov. 1, 1894–June 12, 1957); b. Andrews Settlement, Pa. Novelist. *Mary* (1925); *Marge* (1926); *And Michael* (1927); *Kristin* (1929); *Hathaway House* (1931); *Family Affairs* (1934); *Daughter of Time* (1942); *Brook Willow* (1944); *No Trumpet Before Him* (1948); *The Pink House* (1950); *The Spare Room* (1954); *The Gift and the Giver* (1957); etc.

WHITE, NEWMAN IVEY (Feb. 3, 1892–Dec. 6, 1948); b. Statesville, N.C. Educator, author. *American Negro Folk-Songs* (1928); *The Unextinguished Hearth: Shelley and His Contemporary Critics* (1938); *Shelley,* 2v. (1940); *Portrait of Shelley* (1945). Editor: *An Anthology of Verse by American Negroes* (with Walter Clinton Jackson, 1924). Prof. English, Duke University, from 1919.

WHITE, OLIVE BERNARDINE (May 28, 1899–); b. New Haven, Conn. Educator, author. *The King's Good Servant* (1936); *Late Harvest* (1940); etc. Prof. English, Bradley University, since 1940.

WHITE, RICHARD GRANT (May 23, 1821–Apr. 8, 1885); b. New York. Editor, philologist, author. *A Tale of the Hospital* (1840); *Handbook of Christian Art* (1853); *Shakespeare's Scholar* (1854); *The New Gospel of Peace,* 4v. (anon., 1863–66); *The Adventures of Sir Lyon Bouse, Bart., in America during the Civil War* (1867); *Words and Their Uses* (1870); *The Chronicles of Gotham,* 2v. (anon., 1871–72); *Every-Day English* (1880); *The Fate of Mansfield Humphreys* (1884); etc. Editor, *The Works of William Shakespeare,* 12v. (1857–66); founder and editor, *Yankee Doodle,* 1846.

WHITE, ROBB (June 20, 1909–); b. Baquio, Luzon, P.I. Author. *The Nub* (1935); *Three Against the Sea* (1940); *Candy* (1949); *Deep Danger* (1952); *Up Periscope* (1956); *Flight Deck* (1961); *Torpedo Run* (1962); *The Survivor* (1964); *Surrender* (1966); *Silent Ship, Silent Sea* (1967); etc.

WHITE, ROBIN (1928–). Author. *House of Many Rooms* (1958); *Elephant Hill* (1959); *Foreign Soil* (1962); *His Own Kind* (1967); etc.

WHITE, STEWART EDWARD (Mar. 12, 1873–Sept. 18, 1946); b. Grand Rapids, Mich. Novelist. *The Claim Jumpers* (1901); *The Westerners* (1901); *The Blazed Trail* (1902); *The Forest* (1903); *The Mountains* (1904); *The Silent Places* (1904); *Arizona Nights* (1907); *Camp and Trail* (1907); *The Riverman* (1908); *The Cabin* (1910); *Footprints* (1912); *Gold* (1913); *The Grey Dawn* (1915); *The Leopard Woman* (1916); *Simba* (1918); *The Forty-Niners* (1918); *Daniel Boone* (1922); *The Glory Hole* (1924); *Credo* (1925); *Back of Beyond* (1927); *The Long Rifle* (1932); *Ranchero* (1933); *Folded Hills* (1934); *Wild Geese Calling* (1940); *The Unobstructed Universe* (1941); *Speaking for Myself* (1943); *The Stars Are Still There* (1946); etc. See Fred B. Millett's *Contemporary American Authors* (1940).

WHITE, THEODORE H[arold] (May 6, 1915–); b. Boston, Mass. Journalist, author. *Thunder out of China* (with Annalee Jacoby, 1946); *Fire in the Ashes* (1953); *The Mountain Road* (1958); *The View from the Fortieth Floor* (1960); *The Making of the President, 1960* (1961); *The Making of the President, 1964* (1965); *Caesar at the Rubicon* (1968); *The Making of the President, 1968* (1969); etc. Editor: J. W. Stillwell's *Papers* (1948).

WHITE, THOMAS WILLIS (Mar. 28, 1788–Jan. 19, 1843); b. Williamsburg, Va. Printer. Founder, the *Southern Literary Messenger,* Aug. 1834. He printed the books of his friends, including James E. Heath and James Ware. One of his editors was Edgar Allan Poe.

WHITE, TRUMBULL (Aug. 12, 1868–Dec. 13, 1941); b. Winterset, Ia. Editor, author. *The Wizard of Wall Street* (1893); *Our War with Spain* (1898); *Pacific Tours and around the World* (1900); *Martinique and the World's Great Disasters* (1902); *San Francisco Earthquake* (with R. Linthicum, 1906); *Puerto Rico and Its People* (1938). Editor, *Red Book,*

1903–06; *Appleton's Magazine,* 1906–09; *Adventure,* 1910–11; *Everybody's,* 1911–15.

WHITE, WALTER [Francis] (July 1, 1893–Mar. 21, 1955); b. Atlanta, Ga. Author. *The Fire in the Flint* (1924); *Flight* (1926); *Rope & Faggot: A Biography of Judge Lynch* (1929); *A Man Called White* (autobiography, 1948); *How Far the Promised Land* (1955); etc.

WHITE, WILLIAM (Sept. 4, 1910–); b. Paterson, N.J. Educator, editor, author. *John Donne Since 1900* (1942); *This Is Detroit* (with M. M. Quaife, 1951); *Sir William Osler, Historian and Literary Essayist* (1951). Bibliographer, works of Thoreau, D. H. Lawrence, John Ciardi, W. D. Snodgrass, Karl Shapiro, Wilfred Owen. Co-editor, Modern Humanities Research Association *Annual Bibliography of English Literature* (with others,) since 1949; *The Collected Writings of Walt Whitman,* since 1961; *Serif Series in Bibliography,* since 1966. Prof. journalism, Wayne State University, since 1960.

WHITE, WILLIAM ALLEN (Feb. 10, 1868–Jan. 29, 1944); b. Emporia, Kan. Editor, author. *The Real Issues, and Other Stories* (1896); *The Court of Boyville* (1899); *Stratagems and Spoils* (1901); *In Our Town* (1906); *A Certain Rich Man* (1909); *The Old Order Changeth* (1910); *God's Puppets* (1916); *In the Heart of a Fool* (1916); *The Martial Adventures of Henry and Me* (1918); *Woodrow Wilson* (1924); *The Editor and His People* (1924); *Calvin Coolidge* (1925); *Masques in a Pageant* (1928); *Forty Years on Main Street* (1937); *A Puritan in Babylon* (1938); *The Changing West* (1939); etc. Owner and editor, the *Emporia Gazette,* from 1895. *See* Everett Rich's *William Allen White* (1941).

WHITE, WILLIAM ANTHONY PARKER (Aug. 21, 1911–Apr. 30, 1968); b. Oakland, Cal. Editor and author. Under pen name "Anthony Boucher": *The Case of the Seven of Calvary* (1937); *The Case of the Crumpled Knave* (1939); *The Case of the Baker Street Irregulars* (1940); *The Case of the Solid Key* (1941); *Far and Away* (1955). Under pen name "H. H. Holmes": *Nine Times Nine* (1940); *Rocket to the Morgue* (1942). Editor: *The Pocket Book of True Crime Stories* (1943); *Great American Detective Stories* (1945); *The Best from Fantasy and Science Fiction* (annual, 1952–58). Mystery reviewer, *New York Times Book Review,* from 1949; sci-fantasy reviewer, *New York Herald Tribune Book Review,* from 1951; editor, *The Magazine of Fantasy and Science Fiction,* 1949–58.

WHITE, WILLIAM CHARLES (1777–May, 1818); b. Boston, Mass. Playwright. *Orlando; or, Parental Persecution* (prod. 1797); and two adaptations: *The Clergyman's Daughter* (prod. 1809); and *The Poor Lodger* (prod. 1811).

WHITE, WILLIAM L[indsay] (June 17, 1900–); b. Emporia Kan., son of William Allen White. Publisher, author. *What People Said* (1938); *Journey for Margaret* (1941); *They Were Expendable* (1942); *Queens Die Proudly* (1943); *Report on the Russians* (1945); *Report on the Germans* (1947); *Lost Boundaries* (1948); *Land of Milk and Honey* (1949); *Bernard Baruch* (1950); *Back Down the Ridge* (1953); *The Captives of Korea* (1957); *The Little Toy Dog* (1962); *Report on the Asians* (1969); etc. Co-publisher of the *Emporia* (Kan.) *Gazette.*

WHITE, WILLIAM PATTERSON (Jan. 22, 1884–); b. St. Paul, Minn. Novelist. *The Owner of the Lazy D* (1919); *Lynch Lawyers* (1920); *Hidden Trails* (1920); *The Heart of the Range* (1921); *The Wagon Wheel* (1923); *Buster* (1926); *Sweetwater Range* (1927); *Adobe Walls* (1933); *Willow Canyon* (1933).

WHITE, WILLIAM S[mith] (May 20, 1907–); b. DeLeon, Tex. Journalist, author. *The Taft Story* (1954, Pulitzer Prize for biography, 1955; *Citadel: The Story of the U.S. Senate* (1957); *Majesty and Mischief: A Mixed Tribute to FDR* (1961); *The Professional: Lyndon B. Johnson* (1965); *Home Place: The Story of the U.S. House of Representatives* (1965); etc. Washington staff, *New York Times,* since 1945.

White Fang. Novel by Jack London (1905). Story of a wolf in the northern wilds that joins a pack of dogs, reversing the theme of the *Call of the Wild.*

White Heron, A. By Sarah Orne Jewett (1886). Story of the Maine sea coast.

White Jacket. Novel by Herman Melville (1850). Describes the rough life on a United States frigate on a homeward voyage from Japan. It was influential in ending flogging in the navy.

White Mule. Novel by William Carlos Williams (1937). Scandinavian immigrants adjust to life in America. Written in a matter-of-fact impressionistic style describing the minor incidents of life so that what they suggest gives the story its resonance. *In the Money* (1940) is a sequel to it.

White Negro, The. Essay by Norman Mailer (1959).

WHITEFIELD, GEORGE (Dec. 16, 1714–Sept. 30, 1770); b. Gloucester, Eng. Evangelist, author. *A Journal of a Voyage from London to Savannah in Georgia* (1738); *The Two First Parts of His Life, with His Journals, Revised* (1756); *Works,* 6v. (1771–72), ed. by John Gillies. *See* Luke Tyerman's *The Life of the Rev. George Whitefield,* 2v. (1876–77). Whitefield is buried at Newburyport, Mass.

WHITEFORD, ROBERT NAYLOR (June 28, 1870–Jan. 6, 1959); b. Crawfordsville, Ind. Educator, editor, author. *Motives in English Fiction* (1918). Editor: *Anthology of English Poetry: Beowulf to Kipling* (1903); works of Oliver Goldsmith, etc. Prof. English, Toledo University, 1910–38.

WHITEHALL, HAROLD (May 14, 1905–); b. Ramsbottom, Lancs., Eng. Educator. *Structural Essentials of English* (1956); etc. English dept., Indiana University, since 1941.

WHITEHEAD, ALFRED NORTH (Feb. 15, 1861–Dec. 30, 1947); b. Ramsgate, Eng. Educator, philosopher, author. *Principia Mathematica* (with Bertrand Russell, 1910); *The Organization of Thought* (1916); *The Principles of Natural Knowledge* (1919); *The Concept of Nature* (1920); *Science and the Modern World* (1925); *Religion in the Making* (1926); *The Aims of Education* (1928); *Process and Reality* (1929); *The Function of Reason* (1929); *Adventures of Ideas* (1933); *Nature and Life* (1934); *Modes of Thought* (1938); *Essays in Science and Philosophy* (1947); etc. Prof. philosophy, Harvard University, 1924–36.

WHITEHEAD, DON (Apr. 8, 1908–); b. Inman, Va. Journalist, author. *The FBI Story* (1960); *Border Guard* (1963); *Attack on Terror: The FBI Against The Ku Klux Klan in Mississippi* (1970).

WHITEHEAD, WILLIAM ADEE (Feb. 19, 1810–Aug. 8, 1884); b. Newark, N.J. Historian. *East Jersey under the Proprietary Governments* (1846); etc. Editor: *The Papers of Lewis Morris, Governor of the Province of New Jersey* (1852); *Documents Relating to the Colonial History of the State of New Jersey,* 8v. (1880–85); etc.

WHITELOCK, LOUISE CLARKSON (1865–); b. Baltimore, Md. Author. *The Gathering of the Lilies* (1877); *The Rag Fair, and Other Reveries* (1879); *Heartsease and Happy Days* (1883); *Violet among the Lilies* (1885); *A Mad Madonna, and Other Stories* (1895); *How Hindsight Met Provincialatis* (1898).

WHITELOCK, WILLIAM WALLACE (Apr. 1, 1869–Jan. 29, 1940); b. Mt. Washington, Md. Editor, critic, playwright, poet. *When the Heart Is Young* (1902); *The Literary Guillotine* (anon., 1903); *The Man Who Told the Truth* (prod. 1906); *Just Love Songs* (1906); *When Kings Go Forth to Battle* (1907); *Foregone Verses* (1907); etc. Assoc. editor, *The Criterion;* European correspondent, the *New York Times;* contributor to *Life,* 1915–30. His poem "Nude Descending a Staircase" was often reprinted.

WHITEMAN, MAXWELL (1914–); b. Philadelphia, Pa. Author. *A Century of Fiction by American Negroes, 1853–1952* (1955); *History of the Jews of Philadelphia from Colonial Times to the Age of Jackson* (with Edwin Wolf, 1957); *Mankind and Medicine: A History of Albert Einstein Medical Center* (1966); *Copper for America* (1971); etc.

WHITING, CHARLES GOODRICH (Jan. 30, 1842–June 20, 1922); b. St. Albans, Vt. Editor, critic, poet. *The Saunterer* (1886); *Walks in New England* (1903); etc. With the *Springfield Republican*, 1868–1919; lit. editor, 1874–1910.

WHITING, EDWARD ELWELL (Feb. 18, 1875–Dec. 24, 1956); b. Springfield, Mass. Author. *President Coolidge: A Contemporary Estimate* (1923); *Changing New England* (1929); etc. Writer of "Whiting's Column" in the *Boston Herald;* the "Boston Letter" in the *Springfield Republican;* and "Beacon Hill" in the *Worcester Telegram,* etc.

WHITING, HENRY (1790–Sept. 16, 1851); b. Lancaster, Mass. Soldier, poet. *Otway: A Poem* (1822); *Sannilac: A Poem* (1831); etc. Editor: *Washington's Revolutionary Orders* (1844); etc.

WHITING, LILIAN (Oct. 3, 1859–Apr. 30, 1942); b. Niagara Falls, N.Y. Author. *The World Beautiful,* 3 series (1896–98); *Boston Days* (1902); *Paris the Beautiful* (1908); *Louise Chandler Moulton* (1909); *The Brownings* (1911); *Athens* (1913); *Lure of London* (1914); *Canada the Spellbinder* (1917); etc.

WHITLOCK, BRAND (Mar. 4, 1869–May 24, 1934); b. Urbana, O. Diplomat, novelist. *The 13th District* (1902); *The Turn of the Balance* (1907); *Abraham Lincoln* (1909); *The Gold Brick* (1910); *Forty Years of It* (autobiography, 1914); *Belgium: A Personal Record,* 2v. (1919); *J. Hardin & Son* (1923); *Uprooted* (1926); *Big Matt* (1928); *Lafayette,* 2v. (1929); *Narcissus* (1931); *The Stranger on the Island* (1933); *The Letters and Journals,* 2v. (1936); U.S. Minister to Belgium, 1913–19; Ambassador to Belgium, 1919–22.

WHITLOCK, HERBERT PERCY (1868–Feb. 22, 1948); b. New York. Curator, mineralogist, author. *The Story of the Minerals* (1925); *The Story of the Gems* (1936); *The Story of Minerals* (1946); etc. With the New York State Museum, 1901–18; state mineralogist, 1916–18; curator of mineralogy, American Museum of Natural History, New York, 1918–41.

WHITMAN, ALBERY A[llson] (May 30, 1851–June 29, 1901); b. Hart Co., Va. Methodist clergyman, poet. *Not a Man and Yet a Man* (1877); *Lelah Misled* (1873); *The Rape of Florida* (1884), republished as *Twasinta's Seminoles* (1885); *An Idyl of the South* (1877); etc.

WHITMAN, MARCUS (Sept. 4, 1802–Nov. 29, 1847); b. Rushville, N.Y. Physician, missionary, pioneer. *See* W. A. Mowry's *Marcus Whitman and the Early Days of Oregon* (1901); C. W. Smith's *A Contribution Toward a Bibliography of Marcus Whitman* (1908); Myron Eells's *Marcus Whitman* (1909); Archer B. Hulbert's *Marcus Whitman,* 2 pts. (with Dorothy Hulbert, 1936–38).

WHITMAN, SARAH HELEN POWER (Jan. 19, 1803–June 27, 1878); b. Providence, R.I. Poet. *Hours of Life, and Other Poems* (1853); *Edgar Poe and His Critics* (1860); *Poems* (1879); *Letters* (1907); etc. Friend of Edgar Allan Poe. *See* Caroline Ticknor's *Poe's Helen* (1916).

WHITMAN, STEPHEN F[rench] (Jan. 10, 1880–); b. Philadelphia, Pa. Novelist. *Predestined* (1910); *Sacrifice* (1922).

WHITMAN, WALT (May 31, 1819–Mar. 26, 1892); b. West Hills, L.I., N.Y. Poet, editor, journalist. *Franklin Evans; or, The Inebriate* (1842); *Leaves of Grass* (1855); *Drum Taps* (1865); *Democratic Vistas* (1871); *Memoranda During the War* (1875); *Two Rivulets* (1876); *Specimen Days & Collect* (1882); *November Boughs* (1888); *Goodbye, My Fancy* (1891); *Complete Prose Works* (1892); *Autobiography*

(1892); *The Complete Writings of Walt Whitman,* 10v. (1902); *The Uncollected Poetry and Prose of Walt Whitman,* ed. by Emory Holloway, 2v. (1921); etc. On staff, the *Brooklyn Eagle;* the *Brooklyn Times; Brother Jonathan;* the *Democratic Review;* the *Long Islander; the American Review;* etc. The *Collected Writings of Walt Whitman* are being issued in fifteen volumes under the general editorship of G. W. Allen and Sculley Bradley, including Edwin Haviland Miller's *The Correspondence of Walt Whitman,* 2v. (1961) and H. W. Blodgett's and Sculley Bradley's *Leaves of Grass: Comprehensive Reader's Edition* (1965). Notable collections of Whitmaniana are at Brown University and the Library of Congress. The Whitman Library assembled by Adrian Van Sinderen has been given to Yale University. *See* Bliss Perry's *Walt Whitman* (1906); Carolyn Wells and Alfred F. Goldsmith's *A Concise Bibliography of the Works of Walt Whitman* (1922); Emory Holloway's *Whitman* (1926); Gay Wilson Allen's *A Walt Whitman Handbook* (1946); *The Solitary Singer: A Critical Biography of Walt Whitman* (1955); and *Walt Whitman As Man, Poet, and Legend* (1961); Richard Chase's *Walt Whitman* (1961); Roger Asselineau's *The Evolution of Walt Whitman,* 2v. (trans., 1960, 1962); Howard J. Waskow's *Exploration in Form* (1966); Jean Didier's *Homage to Walt Whitman* (1969); William White's *Walt Whitman's Journalism: A Bibliography* (1969).

WHITMORE, WILLIAM HENRY (Sept. 6, 1836–June 14, 1900); b. Dorchester, Mass. Antiquarian, editor, author. *A Handbook of American Genealogy* (1862); *Abel Brown, Engraver* (1884); etc. Editor: *The Andros Tracts,* 3v. (1868–74); co-editor, *Sewall's Diary* (1878–82); etc. Founder, the *Historical Magazine,* 1857; the *Heraldic Journal,* 1863; Prince Society, 1858; Boston Antiquarian Society, 1879. Editor, *New England Historical and Genealogical Register.*

WHITNEY, ADELINE DUTTON TRAIN (Sept. 15, 1824–Mar. 20, 1906); b. Boston, Mass. Author. *Boys at Chequasset* (1862); *Faith Gartney's Girlhood* (1863); *The Gayworthys* (1865); *A Summer in Leslie Goldthwaite's Life* (1866); *We Girls* (1870); *Real Folks* (1871); *Pansies* (1872); *The Other Girls* (1873); *Bonnyborough* (1886); *White Memories* (1893); *Friendly Letters to Girl Friends* (1896).

WHITNEY, CASPAR (Sept. 21, 1862–Jan. 18, 1929); b. Boston, Mass. Editor, explorer, author. *A Sporting Pilgrimage* (1895); *Hawaiian America* (1899); *Jungle Trails and Jungle People* (1905); *Charles Adelbert Canfield* (1930). Editor, *Outing Magazine,* 1900–09.

WHITNEY, ELINOR. Author. *Tyke-y: His Book and His Mark* (1925); *Tod of the Fens* (1928); *Timothy of the Blue Cart* (1930); *Try All Ports* (1931); *The Mystery Club* (1933). Compiler: *Contemporary Illustrators of Children's Books* (with Bertha E. Mahony, 1930); *Realms of Gold in Children's Books* (with same, 1935); *Five Years of Children's Books* (with same, 1936); etc.

WHITNEY, GERTRUDE CAPEN (Mrs. George Erastus Whitney) (May 13, 1861–May 22, 1941); b. Canton, Mass. Novelist. *I Choose* (1910); *Above the Shame of Circumstance* (1913); *The House of Landell* (1917); *Where the Sun Shines* (1920); *On the Other Side of the Bridge* (1922); *The Interpreter* (1925); *In the Fulness of Time* (1936); etc.

WHITNEY, HELEN HAY. b. New York. Author. *Some Verses* (1898); *The Rose of Dawn* (1901); *Sonnets and Songs* (1905); *Gypsy Verses* (1907); *Herbs and Apples* (1910); etc.

WHITNEY, JAMES AMAZIAH (June 30, 1839–c. 1910); b. Rochester, N.Y. Lawyer, author. *Shobab: A Tale of Bethesda* (poem, 1884); *Sonnets and Lyrics* (1884); *The Tale of the Children of Lamech* (poem, 1885); *The Poetical Works,* 3v. (1886).

WHITNEY, JANET PAYNE (Mrs. George Gillett Whitney) (1894–). Author. *Elizabeth Fry, Quaker Heroine* (1936); *Jennifer* (1941); *Judith* (1943); *Abigail Adams* (1947); *Intrigue in Baltimore* (1951); *Ilex Avenue* (1956).

WHITNEY, LEON FRADLEY (Mar. 29, 1894–); b. Brooklyn, N.Y. Biologist. *The Basis of Breeding* (1928); *The Partners* series (boys' books, 1932); *How to Breed Dogs* (1937); *The Complete Book of Home Pet Care* (1950); *The Coon Hunter's Handbook* (with A. B. Underwood, 1952); *The Truth about Dogs* (1959); *Keep Your Pigeons Flying* (1960); *Feed Your Dog* (1960); *The Natural Method of Dog Training* (1965); *People and Pets* (1967); *Training You to Train Your Cat* (1968); *The Basis of Breeding Racing Pigeons* (1968); etc.

WHITNEY, PHYLLIS AYAME (Sept. 9, 1903–); b. Yokohama, Jap. Author. *A Place for Ann* (1941); *Writing Juvenile Fiction* (1947); *Step to the Music* (1953); *The Fire and the Gold* (1956); *The Trembling Hills* (1956); *Secret of the Samurai Sword* (1958); *Moonflower* (1958); *Blue Fire* (1961); *Mystery of the Haunted Pool* (1961); *Mystery of the Angry Idol* (1965); *Secret of the Spotted Shell* (1967); *Secret of Goblin Glen* (1968); *Winter People* (1969); etc.

WHITNEY, WILLIAM DWIGHT (Feb. 9, 1827–June 7, 1894); b. Northampton, Mass. Philologist, editor, author. *Language and the Study of Language* (1867); *Oriental and Linguistic Studies,* 2v. (1873–74); *Life and Growth of Language* (1875); *Essentials of English Grammar* (1877); *Sanskrit Grammar* (1879); *Max Müller and the Science of Language* (1892). Editor-in-chief, *The Century Dictionary,* 6v. (1889–91). See *The Whitney Memorial Meeting* (1897) for full bibliography.

WHITRIDGE, ARNOLD (June 29, 1891–); b. New Rochelle, N.Y. Educator, author. *Critical Ventures in Modern French Literature* (1924); *Dr. Arnold of Rugby* (1928); *Men in Crisis* (1949); *Simon Bolivar* (1954); *No Compromise* (1960); *Rochambeau* (1965); etc. English dept., Yale University, 1932–42.

WHITSON, JOHN HARVEY (Dec. 28, 1854–May 2, 1936); b. Seymour, Ind. Novelist, dime novelist. Pen name for dime novels, "Lieut. A. K. Sims." *Captain Cactus* (1888); *Huckleberry, the Foot Hills Detective* (1888); *Signal Sam* (1890); *The Rival Rustlers* (1891); *The Doctor Detective in Texas* (1893); *The King-Pin of the Leadville Lions* (1894); *Barbara, a Woman of the West* (1903); *With Frémont the Pathfinder* (1903); *The Rainbow Chasers* (1904); *The Castle of Doubt* (1907); etc. The dates are not necessarily those of first editions. See the *Saturday Evening Post,* Feb. 28, 1931.

WHITTAKER, FREDERIC (b. Dec. 12, 1838); b. London. Dime novelist *The Mustang-Hunters* (1862); *The Grizzly-Hunters* (1872); *Boone, the Hunter* (1872); *A Complete Life of General George A. Custer* (1876); *Silver Sam* (1878); *The Cadet Button* (1878); *Old Double Sword* (1883); *The Saucy Jane, Privateer* (1884); *Woods and Waters* (1884); *The Great Kenton Feud* (1891); *The Black Tiger* (1892); *Transgressing the Law* (1893); *The Column of Death* (1917). Editor: *Handbook of Summer Sports* (1880). He wrote *A Defense of Dime Novels, by a Writer of Them,* in the *New York Tribune,* in March, 1884. The dates are not necessarily those of first editions.

WHITTELSEY, ABIGAIL GOODRICH (Nov. 29, 1788–July 16, 1858); b. Ridgefield, Conn. Editor. Founder, the *Mother's Magazine,* 1833; editor, 1833–44; co-editor, 1844–49; founder, *Mrs. Whittelsey's Magazine for Mothers,* 1850; editor, 1850–52.

WHITTEMORE, [Edward] REED II (Sept. 11, 1919–). Educator, author. *Heroes and Heroines* (poems, 1946); *An American Takes a Walk* (poems, 1956); *Self-Made Man, and Other Poems* (1959); *The Boy from Iowa* (poems and essays, 1962); *The Fascination of the Abomination* (1963); *Poems: New and Selected* (1967); *From Zero to the Absolute* (1967); etc.

WHITTEMORE, THOMAS (Jan. 1, 1800–Mar. 21, 1861); b. Boston, Mass. Universalist clergyman, author. *Life of Rev. Hosea Ballou,* 4v. (1854–55); *The Modern History of Universalism* (1830); *The Early Days of Thomas Whittemore: An*

Autobiography (1859); etc. Compiler: *Songs of Zion* (1937); etc. Editor, the *Trumpet and Universalist Magazine,* 1828–57.

WHITTIER, JOHN GREENLEAF (Dec. 17, 1807–Sept. 7, 1892); b. Haverhill, Mass. Poet, abolitionist. *Legends of New England* (1831); *Lays of My Home, and Other Poems* (1843); *Voices of Freedom* (1846); *Old Portraits and Modern Sketches* (1850); *Literary Recreations and Miscellanies* (1854); *Songs of Labor, and Other Poems* (1850); *The Chapel of the Hermits, and Other Poems* (1853); *The Panorama, and Other Poems* (1856); *Home Ballads and Poems* (1860); *In War Times, and Other Poems* (1864); *Snow-Bound* (1866); *The Tent on the Beach, and Other Poems* (1867); *Among the Hills, and Other Poems* (1869); *Miriam, and Other Poems* (1871); *Hazel-Blossoms* (1875); *The Vision of Echard, and Other Poems* (1878); *Saint Gregory's Guest, and Recent Poems* (1886); *At Sundown* (1890); *The Writings of John Greenleaf Whittier,* 7 vls. (rev., 1894). See Mary B. Claflin's *Personal Recollections of John Greenleaf Whittier* (1893); Samuel T. Pickard's *Life and Letters of John Greenleaf Whittier* (1894); T. W. Higginson's *John Greenleaf Whittier* (1902); Bliss Perry's *Whittier* (1907); A. Mordell's *Quaker Militant* (1933); Thomas Franklin Currier's *A Bibliography of John Greenleaf Whittier* (1937); and his *Elizabeth Lloyd and the Whittiers* (1939); Fredericka Shumway Smith's *John Greenleaf Whittier, a Narrative Biography* (1948); Lewis Leary's *John Greenleaf Whittier* (1962); Edward Wagenknecht's *John Greenleaf Whittier, A Portrait in Paradox* (1967).

WHITTY, JAMES HOWARD (Feb. 8, 1859–June 2, 1937); b. Baltimore, Md. Editor: compiler. Editor; *Complete Poems of Edgar Allan Poe* (1911). Compiler: *A Record of Virginia Copyright Entries, 1790–1844* (1911). Claimed to have owned largest general collection of Poeana in the world.

Whiz Bang. See *Captain Billy's Whiz Bang.*

Who Owns America? Symposium edited by Herbert Agar and Allen Tate (1936).

Whole Case for Toleration, The. Written by William Penn while he was in prison, about 1680.

Whole Earth Catalogue, The. Published periodically by the Portola Institute, Inc., since 1969, with supplements. It contains articles about and illustrations of items useful as tools, as well as suggestions about enterprises, ideas, and practices of imaginative types. The catalogue subjects are relevant to independent education as distinguished from formal education; the various items are of high quality or low cost and available through the mails. The catalogue has become the "Sears-Roebuck" of the so-called youth movement or counterculture.

Who'll Turn Grindstone. By Charles Miner in the *Luzerne Federalist* (Sept 7, 1810). Contains *The Ballad of James Bird,* in which first occurs the phrase "to have an axe to grind."

Who's Afraid of Virginia Woolf? Play by Edward Albee (prod 1961). Mordant view of marital strife among the educated middle classes.

Who's Who in America. Published by the A. N. Marquis Co. Biennially, since 1899. Biographies of notable Americans; also includes some famous world figures. Material gathered from the persons themselves. Notable deceased persons are listed in *Who Was Who in America,* Vol. I (1897–1942); Vol. II (1943–1950); Vol. III (1951–1960); Vol. IV (1961–1968).

Why Johnny Can't Read. By Rudolf Flesch (1955). Criticism of the Look and Say whole-word method of teaching reading. Argues in favor of a return to the alphabetical-phonetic method.

Why Marry? Play by Jesse Lynch William (prod. 1917). A comedy dealing with the conflict between careers and marriage, particularly as it concerns Helen and Dr. Ernest Hamilton, both scientists. Pulitzer Prize play, 1918.

WHYTE, WILLIAM FOOTE (June 27, 1914–); b. Springfield, Mass. Educator. *Street Corner Society* (1943); *Pattern for Industrial Peace* (1951); *Money and Motivation* (with others, 1955); *Man and Organization* (1959); *Men at Work* (1961); *Action Research for Management* (1965); *Organizational Behavior* (1969). Prof., School of Industrial and Labor Relations, Cornell University, since 1948.

WHYTE, WILLIAM HOLLINGSWORTH, JR. (Oct. 1, 1917–); b. West Chester, Pa. Editor, author. *Is Anybody Listening?* (1952); *The Organization Man* (1956); *Open Space Action* (1962); *Cluster Development* (1964); *The Lost Landscape* (1968); etc. Staff, *Fortune* magazine, since 1946.

Wichita Eagle and Beacon. Wichita, Kans. Newspaper. Founded 1872. Daily established 1884. Marcellus M. Murdock is publisher. John H. Colburn is editor. Howard Sparks edits book reviews and a book supplement.

WICKENDEN, DAN [Leonard Daniel] (Mar. 24, 1913–); b. Tyrone, Pa. Novelist. *The Running of the Deer* (1937); *Walk Like a Mortal* (1940); *The Wayfarers* (1945); *Tobias Brandywine* (1948); *The Dry Season* (1950); *The Red Carpet* (1952).

WICKER, THOMAS GREY (June 18, 1926–); b. Hamlet, N.C. Journalist, author. *The Kingpin* (1953); *The Devil Must* (1957); *The Judgment* (1961); *Kennedy Without Tears* (1964); *JFK and LBJ: The Influence of Personality upon Politics* (1968). Under pen name "Paul Connolly": *Get Out of Town* (1951); *Tears Are for Angels* (1952); *So Fair, So Evil* (1955). Staff member, *New York Times*, since 1960.

WICKERSHAM, GEORGE WOODWARD (Sept. 19, 1858–Jan. 25, 1936); b. Pittsburgh, Pa. Lawyer, author. *The Changing Order* (1914); *Spring in Morocco and Algiers* (1923).

WICKERSHAM, JAMES (Aug. 24, 1857–Oct. 24, 1939); b. Patoka, Ill. Jurist, bibliophile, historian. *A Bibliography of Alaskan Literature, 1724–1924* (1927); *Old Yukon* (1938); etc. He presided at the McKenzie-Noyes conspiracy trial at Nome, Alaska, which provided material for *The Spoilers* by Rex Beach.

WICKHAM, HARVEY (May 30, 1872–Nov., 1930); b. Middletown, N.Y. Critic, novelist. *Jungle Terror* (1920); *The Clue of the Primrose Petal* (1921); *The Scarlet X* (1922); *The Boncoeur Affair* (1923); *The Misbehaviorists* (1928); *The Impuritans* (1929); *The Unrealists* (1930), the last three forming a trilogy.

Wickham, Mary F. See Mary F. Wickham Porcher.

WICKS, KATHARINE GIBSON (Mrs. Frank Scott Wicks) (Sept. 13, 1893–); b. Indianapolis, Ind. Author. Writes under maiden name. *The Golden Bird* (1927); *The Goldsmith of Florence* (1929); *The Oak Tree House* (1936); *Cinders* (1939); *Jock's Castle* (1940); *Nathaniel's Witch* (1941); *Tell It Again* (1942); *Bow Bells* (1943); *Arrow Fly Home* (1945); *Fairy Tales* (1950); *To See the Queen* (1954); *The Tall Book of Bible Stories* (1957).

WIDDEMER, MARGARET (Mrs. Robert Haven Schauffler) (1880–); b. Doylestown, Pa. Poet and novelist. *The Factories, with Other Lyrics* (1915); *The Rose-Garden Husband* (1915); *The Board Walk* (1919); *Cross Currents* (poems, 1921); *Tree with a Bird in It* (parodies, 1922); *Graven Image* (1923); *Ballads and Lyrics* (1925); *Gallant Lady* (1926); *The Singing Word* (1926); *Collected Poems* (1928); *All the King's Horses* (1931); *Golden Rain* (1933); *Years of Love* (1933); *Hill Garden* (poems, 1936); *Hand on Her Shoulder* (1938); *Some Day I'll Find You* (1940); *Constancia Herself* (1945); *Lani* (1948); *Red Cloak Flying* (1950); *Prince in Buckskin* (1952); *The Golden Wildcat* (1954); *Dark Cavalier: Collected Poems* (1958); and other books, including the *Winona* series for girls.

Wide, Wide World, The. Novel by Susan Warner (1850). One of the most popular romances of the nineteenth century, featuring the life of Ellen Montgomery from early childhood to womanhood. Placed under the care of a carping aunt she lived in unpleasant surroundings, brightened only by the friendship of Alice Humphreys.

Wide Awake: An Illustrated Magazine for Boys and Girls. Boston, Mass. Founded July, 1875, by Daniel Lothrop, Boston publisher of children's books. Editors: Ella Farman Pratt, 1875–91; Ella F. Pratt and Charles Stuart Pratt, 1891–93. Among its writers were Sarah Orne Jewett, Edward Everett Hale, James Whitcomb Riley, Imogen Guiney, Charles Egbert Craddock, Louise Chandler Moulton, Edgar Fawcett, Mary H. Catherwood, Kirk Munroe, John T. Trowbridge, and Margaret Sidney, who began in *Wide Awake* in 1880 her popular *Five Little Peppers and How They Grew*. Absorbed by *St. Nicholas*, 1893.

WIDGERY, ALBAN GREGORY (May 9, 1887–); b. Bloxwich, Eng., came to the United States in 1928. Educator, author. *The Comparative Study of Religions* (1923); *Contemporary Thought of Great Britain* (1927); *Christian Ethics in History and Modern Life* (1940); *What Is Religion?* (1953); etc. Prof. philosophy, Duke University, from 1930.

Widow Bedott Papers, The. By Frances Miriam Whitcher (1856). Humorous sketches in the "Samantha" and "Major Jack Downing" vein, purporting to be the wise and witty sayings of a sprightly widow.

WIEAND, ALBERT CASSEL (Jan. 17, 1871–July 24, 1954); b. Wadsworth, O. Educator, author. *The Child's Life of Christ* (1918); *Studies in the Gospel According to Matthew* (1929); *Studies in the Gospel of Mark* (1939); *The Gospel of Prayer* (1953); etc. Founder, Bethany biblical Seminary, Chicago, 1905; president, 1905–32; prof. Biblical literature, 1932–46.

Wieland; or, The Transformation. Novel by Charles Brockden Brown (1798). A man murders his wife and children because of a muddled state of mind induced by the power of ventriloquism.

WIEMAN, HENRY NELSON (Aug. 19, 1884–); b. Richhill, Mo. Educator, author. *The Wrestle of Religion with Truth* (1927); *The Issues of Life* (1931); *The Growth of Religion* (with Walter Horton, 1938); *The Source of Human Good* (1947); *Man's Ultimate Commitment* (1958); *The Intellectual Foundation of Faith* (1961); etc. Prof. religion, University of Chicago Divinity School, from 1927.

WIENER, LEO (July 26, 1862–Dec. 12, 1939); b. Bialystok, Pol. Philologist, educator, compiler. *The History of Yiddish Literature in the Nineteenth Century* (1899); *Africa and the Discovery of America*, 3v. (1919); *Mayan and Mexican Origins* (1926); etc. Compiler: *Anthology of Russian Literature*, 2v. (1902–03). Translator of *Complete Works of Tolstoy*, 24v. (1904–05); etc. Slavic languages dept., Harvard University, 1896–1930, prof. 1911–30.

WIENER, NORBERT (Nov. 26, 1894–Mar. 18, 1964); b. Columbia, Mo. Mathematician. *Cybernetics* (1948); *The Human Use of Human Beings* (1950); *Ex-Prodigy* (autobiography, 1953); *I Am a Mathematician* (autobiography, 1956); *Nonlinear Problems in Random Theory* (1958); *The Tempter* (1959); etc.

WIENERS, JOHN (Jan. 6, 1934–); b. Boston, Mass. Poet. *The Hotel Wentley Poems* (1958); *Ace of Pentacles* (1964); *Chinoiserie* (1965); *Record* (1967); *Six Poems* (1967); *Pressed Wafer* (1967); *Selected Poems* (1967). Plays: *Still-Life* (1961); *Asphodel, In Hell's Despite* (1963); *Jive Shoelaces and Anklesox* (1967).

WIESE, KURT (1887–); b. Minden, Ger. Painter, illustrator, author. *Karoo, the Kangaroo* (1929); *The Chinese Ink Stick* (1929); *Liang & Lo* (1930); *Wallie the Walrus* (1930); *Ella, the Elephant* (1931); *Buddy, the Bear* (1936); *The Rabbit's*

Revenge (1940); *You Can Write Chinese* (1945); *The Fish in the Air* (1948); *The Dog, the Fox and the Fleas* (1953); *The Groundhog and His Shadow* (1959); etc. Illustrator of Salten's *Bambi*, Mukerji's *Hindu Fables*, Weber's *Wind on the Prairie*, Bonsel's *Adventures of Mario*, Lin Yutang's *With Love and Irony*, Gatti's *Saranga the Pygmy*, North's *Greased Lightning*, etc.

WIESEL, ELIE (Sept. 30, 1928–); b. Sighet, Rom. Journalist, author. *Night* (1960); *Dawn* (1961); *The Accident* (1962); *The Town Beyond the Wall* (1964); *The Gates of the Forest* (1966); *The Jews of Silence* (1966); *A Beggar in Jerusalem* (1970); *One Generation After* (1970).

WIESNER, JEROME B[ert] (May 30, 1915–); b. Detroit, Mich. Communications engineer, author. *Where Science and Politics Meet* (1964). Faculty, Massachusetts Institute of Technology, since 1950. Special assistant to the President on science and technology, 1961–64.

WIGGAM, ALBERT EDWARD (1871–Apr., 1957); b. Austin, Ind. Lecturer, author. *The New Decalogue of Science* (1923); *The Fruit of the Family Tree* (1924); *The Next Age of Man* (1927); *Exploring Your Mind* (1927); *The Marks of an Educated Man* (1930); *New Techniques of Happiness* (1948); etc.

WIGGIN, KATE DOUGLAS (Mrs. Samuel Bradley Wiggin; Mrs. George Christopher Riggs) (Sept. 28, 1856–Aug. 24, 1923); b. Philadelphia, Pa. Editor, novelist. *The Story of Patsy* (1883); *The Birds' Christmas Carol* (1887); *Timothy's Quest* (1890); *The Story Hour* (with Nora A. Smith, 1890), and fourteen other books with same; *Polly Oliver's Problem* (1893); *A Cathedral Courtship* (1893); *Penelope's Progress* (1898); *Penelope's Irish Experiences* (1901); *Rebecca of Sunnybrook Farm* (1903); *The Story of Waitstill Baxter* (1913); *Ladies in Waiting* (1918); *My Garden of Memories: An Autobiography* (1923); etc. See Nora A. Smith's *Kate Douglas Wiggin as Her Sister Knew Her* (1925).

WIGGLESWORTH, MICHAEL (Oct. 18, 1631–May 27, 1705); b. in England. Anglican clergyman, poet. *The Day of Doom* (1662), and many later editions; *Meat out of the Eater* (1669); etc. See John Ward Dean's *Memoir of Rev. Michael Wigglesworth* (1871); Kenneth B. Murdock's edition of *The Day of Doom* (1929).

WIGHT, ORLANDO WILLIAMS (Feb. 19, 1824–Oct. 19, 1888); b. Centreville, N.Y. Author, *The Romance of Abelard and Heloise* (1853); *Life of Peter the Great*, 2v. (1859); *People and Countries Visited in a Winding Journey around the World* (1888); etc. Editor: *Standard French Classics*, 14v. (1858–60); *The Household Library*, 18v. (1859); etc. Translator of Balzac, Victor Cousin, Henry Martin, Pascal, etc.

WIKOFF, HENRY (c. 1813–May 2, 1884); b. Philadelphia, Pa. Adventurer, author. *My Courtship and Its Consequences* (1855); *The Adventures of a Roving Diplomatist* (1857); *The Four Civilizations of the World* (1875); *The Reminiscences of an Idler* (1880); etc.

Wilbur, Anne Tappan. See Anne Tappan Turner Wood.

WILBUR, RAY LYMAN (Apr. 13, 1875–June 26, 1949); b. Boonesboro, Ia. Educator, cabinet officer, author. *Conservation* (with W. A. Du Puy, 1931); *Stanford Horizons* (1936); *The Hoover Policies* (with A. M. Hyde, 1937); *The March of Medicine* (1938); *Human Hopes* (1940); etc. Secretary of the interior, 1929–33. President, Stanford University, 1916–43.

WILBUR, RICHARD [Purdy] (Mar. 1, 1921–); b. New York. Educator, poet. *The Beautiful Changes* (1947); *Ceremony* (1950); *Things of This World* (1956; Pulitzer Prize for poetry, 1957); *Candide* (comic opera, with Lillian Hellman, 1957); *Poems, 1943–56* (1957); *Advice to a Prophet* (1961); *Walking to Sleep* (1969); etc. Translator: Molière's *Misanthrope* (1955); Molière's *Tartuffe* (1963). Editor: *A Bestiary* (1955). Prof. English, Wesleyan University, since 1957.

WILCOX, ELLA WHEELER (Nov. 5, 1850–Oct. 30, 1919); b. Johnstown Center, Wis. Poet. *Drops of Water* (1872); *Shells* (1873); *Maurine* (1876); *Poems of Passion* (1883); *The Story of a Literary Career* (1905); etc. Her best known poem is "Solitude," with the line "Laugh and the world laughs with you," which first appeared in *Poems of Passion; Perdita, and Other Stories* (1886).

WILCOX, MARRION (Apr. 3, 1858–Dec. 26, 1926); b. Augusta, Ga. Author. *Real People* (1886); *Señora Villena and Gray* (1887); *Vengeance of the Female* (1899); etc.

WILCOX, WALTER DWIGHT (Sept. 24, 1869–); b. Chicago, Ill. Author. *Camping in the Canadian Rockies* (1896); *Picturesque Landscapes in the Canadian Rockies* (1898); *The Rockies of Canada* (1900); *Caoba, the Mahogany Tree* (1924); etc.

WILD, JOHN D[aniel] (Apr. 10, 1902–); b. Chicago, Ill. Educator, author. *Open Court* (1929); *George Berkeley* (1936); *Plato's Theory of Man* (1946); *Plato's Modern Enemies and the Theory of Natural Law* (1953); *Challenge of Existentialism* (1957); etc. Editor: *Spinoza: Selections* (1930). Prof. philosophy, Harvard University, since 1946.

WILD, PAYSON SIBLEY (May 25, 1869–Feb. 6, 1951); b. Craftsbury, Vt. Author. *The Links of Ancient Rome* (with Bert Leston Taylor, 1912); *The Valley and Villa of Horace* (1915); *Idylls of the Skillet Fork* (1918); *How Old Is Horace?* (1937); etc.

Wild Animal Round-Up, A. By William T. Hornaday (1908). Stories of exciting hunts for wild animals in many parts of the world by the curator of the New York Zoological Park, with special chapters on the American buffalo and grizzly bear.

Wild Animals I Have Known. By Ernest Thompson Seton (1898).

Wild Geese. Novel by Martha Ostenso (1925). The setting is the American prairie country.

"Wild Honey Suckle, The." Poem by Philip Freneau (1786).

Wild Men of the Wild West. By Edwin Legrand Sabin (1929).

Wild Palms, The. Novel by William Faulkner (1939). Two separate stories are interwoven in this work, *The Old Man* and *The Wild Palms.*

WILDE, IRENE. b. Wadesboro, N.C. Librarian, poet. *Driftwood Fires* (1928); *Fire Against the Sky* (1938); *Red Turban* (1943).

WILDE, PERCIVAL (Mar. 1, 1887–Sept. 19, 1953); b. New York. Playwright, author. *Dawn and Other One-Act Plays of Life Today* (1915); *The Aftermath* (prod. 1921); *Catesby* (1925); *The Devil's Booth* (novel, 1930); *There Is a Tide* (novel, 1932); *The One-Act Plays of Percival Wilde*, 2 series (1933, 1934); *Over the Teacups* (1937); *Inquest* (novel, 1939); *Mr. F* (1941); *P. Moran, Operative* (short stories, 1947); *The One-Act Plays of Percival Wilde*, new series (1953); etc.

WILDE, RICHARD HENRY (Sept. 24, 1789–Sept. 10, 1847); b. Dublin, Ire. Poet, translator. *Conjectures and Researches Concerning the Love, Madness, and Imprisonment of Torquato Tasso*, 2v. (1842); *Hesperia: A Poem* (1867); etc. His best known poem was "My Life Is Like the Summer Rose," originally called "The Lament of the Captive," which first appeared in the *Analectic Magazine*, Apr., 1819. His unfinished life of Dante and his unfinished work on the Italian lyric poets are in the Library of Congress. See Charles C. Jones's *Life, Labors, and Neglected Grave of Richard Henry Wilde* (1887); *American Book Collector*, v. 4–5 (1933).

WILDER, AMOS NIVEN (Sept. 18, 1895–); b. Madison, Wis. Congregational clergyman, educator, poet. *Battle-Retrospect, and Other Poems* (1923); *Arachne: Poems* (1928); *The Spiritual Aspects of the New Poetry* (1940); *The Healing* of the Waters (poems, 1943); *Modern Poetry and the Christian Tradition* (1952); *Other Worldliness and the New Testament* (1954); *Theology and Modern Literature* (1958); *The Language of the Gospel* (1964); etc. With Andover-Newton Theological School, 1933–43; prof., New Testament, Chicago Theological Seminary, 1943–54; Harvard Divinity School, since 1954.

WILDER, DANIEL WEBSTER (July 15, 1832–1911); b. Blackstone, Mass. Editor, publisher, author. *The Annals of Kansas* (1875); etc. President, State Historical Society of Kansas.

WILDER, ROBERT [Ingersoll] (Jan. 25, 1901–); b. Richmond, Va. Author. *Sweet Chariot* (prod. 1928); *Stardust* (prod. 1937); *God Has a Long Face* (1940); *Flamingo Road* (1942); *And Ride a Tiger* (1951); *Autumn Thunder* (1952); *The Wine of Youth* (1955); *Walk with Evil* (1958); *The Sun Is My Shadow* (1960); *Plow the Sea* (1961); *Wind from the Carolinas* (1963); *Fruit of the Poppy* (1965); *The Sea and the Stars* (1967); *An Affair of Honor* (1969); etc.

Wilder, Rose. See Rose Wilder Lane.

WILDER, THORNTON [Niven] (Apr. 17, 1897–); b. Madison, Wis. Novelist, playwright. *The Cabala* (1926); *The Trumpet Shall Sound* (1926); *The Bridge of San Luis Rey* (1927, Pulitzer Prize novel, 1928); *The Angel that Troubled the Waters* (1928); *The Woman of Andros* (1930); *The Long Christmas Dinner* (1931); *Heaven's My Destination* (1934); *Our Town* (prod. 1938, Pulitzer Prize play, 1938); *The Merchant of Yonkers* (1938); revised as *The Matchmaker* (prod. 1955); *The Skin of Our Teeth* (prod. 1942, Pulitzer Prize for drama, 1943); *The Ides of March* (1948); *Plays for Bleecker Street* (prod. 1962); *The Eighth Day* (1967); etc. *See* Edmund Wilson's *Classics and Commercials* (1950).

Wilderness and the Warpath, The. Frontier novel by James Hall (1846).

WILDES, HARRY EMERSON (Apr. 3, 1890–); b. Middletown, Del. Journalist, author. *Social Currents in Japan* (1927); *Alien in the East* (1937); *Valley Forge* (1938); *The Delaware* (1940); *Anthony Wayne* (1941); *Twin Rivers* (1943); *Lonely Midas* (1943); *Typhoon in Tokyo* (1952); *Voice of the Lord* (1964); etc. Lit. editor, the *Philadelphia Forum Magazine,* 1933–45. Writes daily column "Of Making Many Books."

WILDMAN, MARIAN WARNER (Mrs. Jesse A. Fenner) (Oct. 14, 1876–); b. Norwalk, O. Author. *A Hill Prayer, and Other Poems* (1904); *Loyalty Island* (1904); *Theodore and Theodora* (1905); *What Robin Did Then* (1907); etc.

Wildwood, Will. Pen name of Frederick Eugene Pond.

WILE, FREDERIC WILLIAM (Nov. 30, 1873–Apr. 7, 1941); b. La Porte, Ind. Journalist, author. *Our German Cousins* (1909); *Men around the Kaiser* (1913); *Explaining the Britishers* (1918); *News Is Where You Find It* (autobiography, 1939); etc. Correspondent for *Chicago Daily News, New York Times,* etc. Radio news commentator, 1923–38.

WILEY, BELL IRVIN (Jan. 5, 1906–); b. Hall, Tenn. Educator, author. *Southern Negroes, 1861–65* (1938); *The Life of Johnny Reb* (1943); *The Life of Billy Yank* (1952); *The Road to Appomattox* (1956); *Embattled Confederates: An Illustrated History of Southerners at War* (1964); etc. Editor: G. M. Sorrel's *Recollections of a Confederate Staff Officer* (1958); etc. Prof. history, Emery University, since 1948.

WILEY, CALVIN HENDERSON (Feb. 3, 1819–Jan. 11, 1887); b. in Guilford Co., N.C. Presbyterian clergyman, publisher, editor, author. *Alamance; or, The Great and Final Experiment* (anon., 1847); *Adventures of Old Dan Tucker, and His Son Walter* (1851); *Life in the South: A Companion to Uncle Tom's Cabin* (1852); *Roanoke; or, Where Is Utopia?* (1886); etc. Editor: *The North-Carolina Reader,* 3 parts (1851–59). Co-founder (with William D. Cooke), the *Southern Weekly Post,* Raleigh, N.C.

WILEY, FRANKLIN BALDWIN (Sept. 28, 1861–Aug. 1930); b. New York. Editor, poet. *Roadside Rhymes* (1885); *The Harvard Guide Book* (1895); *Flowers That Never Fade* (1897); *Voices and Visions* (1904); etc. Lit. editor, the *Ladies' Home Journal,* 1899–1930.

WILEY, HUGH (Feb. 26, 1884–); b. Zanesville, O. Author. *The Wildcat* (1920); *Jade, and Other Stories* (1921); *Lady Luck* (1922); *Lily* (1923); *The Prowler* (1924); *Fo' Meals a Day* (1927); *Manchu Blood* (1927); *Copper Mask* (1930).

WILEY, JOHN (Apr., 1899–); b. New York. Novelist. *The Education of Peter* (1924); *Triumph* (1926); *Queer Street* (1928); *Mushroom Heaven* (1935).

Wiley, John, and Sons. New York. Publishers. John Wiley established his publishing business in 1828, and in 1832 took George Long into the firm. George Palmer Putnam entered the firm in 1833, to form Wiley & Putnam. This partnership was dissolved in 1848. In 1865 Charles Wiley, son of the founder, entered the business, and William Halsted Wiley, another son, joined the firm in 1876, to form John Wiley & Sons. Charles Wiley, father of the founder, had a bookstore in New York as early as 1807, and soon began to publish books. His shop was a celebrated literary rendezvous. The firm published Cooper's *The Spy* (1821); Poe's *The Raven, and Other Poems* (1845); Hawthorne's *Mosses from an Old Manse* (1846); and Melville's *Typee* (1846). In 1961 it merged with Interscience Publishers, and W. Bradford Wiley became president.

WILEY, WILLIAM BRADFORD (Nov. 17, 1910–); b. Orange, N.J. Publisher. Pres., John Wiley & Sons, since 1956.

WILEY, WILLIAM HALSTED (July 10, 1842–May 21, 1925); b. New York. Congressman, publisher, author. *The Yosemite, Alaska, and the Yellowstone* (1893). With John Wiley & Sons, publishers, after 1876, a firm founded by his father, John Wiley. Congressman, 1903–07, 1909–11.

WILGUS, A[lva] CURTIS (Apr. 2, 1897–); b. Platteville, Wis. Educator, author. *A History of Hispanic America* (1931); *Histories and Historians of Hispanic America* (1936); *A Caravan Tour to Argentina and Brazil* (1936); *The Other Americas* (with G. L. Swiggett, 1937); *The Caribbean: Contemporary Trends* (1953); *The Caribbean: Natural Resources* (1959); *The Caribbean: Contemporary Education* (1960); *The Caribbean: Contemporary Colombia* (1962); *The Caribbean: Venezuelan Development* (1963); *The Caribbean: Mexico Today* (1964); *The Caribbean: Its Health Problems* (1965); *The Caribbean: United States Relations* (1966); *The Caribbean: Its Role in the Hemisphere* (1967); *Historical Atlas of Latin America* (1967); etc. History dept., University of Southern California, 1924–30, George Washington University, 1930–51.

WILHELM, DONALD [George] (Jan. 23, 1887–Feb. 25, 1945); b. Defiance, O. Lecturer, author. *Theodore Roosevelt as an Undergraduate* (1910); *The Story of Steel* (1915); *The Book of Metals* (1931); *The Story of Iron and Steel* (1934); *Writing for Profit* (1941); etc.

WILHELM, GALE (Apr. 26, 1908–); b. Eugene, Ore. Novelist. *We Too Are Drifting* (1935); *No Letters for the Dead* (1936); *Torchlight to Valhalla* (1938); *Bring Home the Bride* (1940); *The Time Between* (1942); *Never Let Me Go* (1945).

WILHELM, STEPHEN ROGER (June 22, 1905–Aug. 28, 1967); b. East Jordan, Mich. Advertising executive. *Texas, Yesterday and Tomorrow* (1947); *Cavalcade of Hooves and Horns* (1958); etc.

WILKES, CHARLES (Apr. 3, 1798–Feb. 8, 1877); b. New York. Naval officer, explorer, author. *Narrative of the United States Exploring Expedition,* 5v. (1844); *Western America* (1849); etc. His manuscript autobiography is in the Library of Congress. Wilkes Land in Antarctica is named for him. *See* J. C. Palmer's *Thulia* (poem, 1843); T. L. Harris's *The Trent Affair* (1896).

WILKES, GEORGE (1817–Sept. 23, 1885); b. New York. Journalist. *The Mystery of the Tombs* (1844); *History of Oregon* (1845); *Europe in a Hurry* (1853); *Shakespeare from an American Point of View* (1877). Co-founder (with Enoch E. Camp), the *National Police Gazette,* 1845; co-founder (with William T. Porter), *Porter's Spirit of the Times,* 1856; founder, *Wilkes' Spirit of the Times,* 1859. *See* James O'Meara's *Broderick and Gwin* (1881).

Wilkes' Spirit of the Times. See *Spirit of the Times.*

WILKIE, FRANC B[angs] (July 2, 1832–Apr. 12, 1892); b. West Charlton, N.Y. Editor, author. Pen name "Poliuto." *Walks about Chicago* (1869); *Sketches beyond the Sea* (1879); *Pen and Powder* (1888); *The Gambler* (1888); *Personal Reminiscences of Thirty-Five Years of Journalism* (1891); *A Life of Christopher Columbus* (1892); etc. Editor, the *Dubuque Daily Herald;* war correspondent, the *New York Times;* on editorial staff, the *Chicago Times,* 1863–88.

WILKINS, ERNEST HATCH (Sept. 14, 1880–Jan. 2, 1966); b. Newton Centre, Mass. Educator, author. *Dante: Poet and Apostle* (1921); *Above Pompeii* (1930); *The College and Society* (1932); *Living in Crisis* (1937); *Toward Unity* (1946); *A History of Italian Literature* (1954); *Petrarch's Later Years* (1959); etc. Pres., Oberlin College, 1927–46.

Wilkins, Mary E. See Mary E. Wilkins Freeman.

WILKINSON, ELIZABETH HAYS (Feb. 29, 1880–); b. Pittsburgh, Pa. Author. *The Lane to Sleepy Town, and Other Verses* (1910); *Peter and Polly* (1912); *Little Billy 'Coon* (1914); etc.

Wilkinson, Florence. See Florence Wilkinson Evans.

WILKINSON, JAMES (1757–Dec. 28, 1825); b. in Calvert Co., Md. Soldier, author. *Memoirs . . . Volume II* (1811), no more published; *Memoirs of My Own Times,* 3v. (1816). *See* James Wilkinson's *Wilkinson* (1933); R. O. Shreve's *The Finished Scoundrel* (1933); Thomas R. Hay's *The Admirable Trumpeter* (with M. R. Werner, 1941).

WILKINSON, [John] BURKE (Aug. 24, 1913–); b. New York. Novelist. *Proceed at Will* (1948); *Run, Mongoose* (1950); *Last Clear Chance* (1954); *Night of the Short Knives* (1964); *By Sea and by Stealth* (1965); *The Helmet of Navarre* (1965); *Cardinal in Armor* (1966); etc.

WILKINSON, SYLVIA (Apr. 3, 1940–); b. Durham, N.C. Novelist. *Moss on the North Side* (1964); *A Killing Frost* (1967); *Cale* (1970).

WILKINSON, WILLIAM CLEAVER (Oct. 19, 1833–Apr. 25, 1920); b. Westford, Vt. Baptist clergyman, educator, author. *A Free Lance in the Field of Life and Letters* (1874); *Poems* (1883); *Poetical Works,* 5v. (1905); *Some New Literary Valuations* (1909); *The Good of Life, and Other Little Essays* (1910); etc. Also many college texts. Prof. poetry and criticism, University of Chicago, 1892–1920.

WILL, ALLEN SINCLAIR (July 28, 1868–Mar. 10, 1934); b. Antioch, Va. Journalist, educator, author. *Life of James Cardinal Gibbons* (1911); *Education for Newspaper Life* (1931); etc. With the *Baltimore Sun,* 1889–1912; with the *New York Times,* 1917–34.

WILLARD, ASHTON ROLLINS (Apr. 14, 1858–Oct. 3, 1918); b. Montpelier, Vt. Art critic. *A Sketch of the Life and Work of the Painter Domenico Morelli* (1895); *History of Modern Italian Art* (1898); *The Land of the Latins* (1902).

WILLARD, EMMA [Hart] (Feb. 23, 1787–Apr. 15, 1870); b. Berlin, Conn. Educator, author. *Advancement of Female Education* (1833); *Journal and Letters from France and Great-Britain* (1833); *Late American History* (1856); etc. She wrote many textbooks and was the author of the poem "Rocked in the Cradle of the Deep." She was the founder of Troy Female Seminary. *See* John Lord's *The Life of Emma Willard* (1873); Alma Lutz's *Emma Willard, Daughter of Democracy* (1929).

WILLARD, FRANCES ELIZABETH CAROLINE (Sept. 28, 1839–Feb. 18, 1898); b. Churchville, N.Y. Reformer, editor, author. *Nineteen Beautiful Years* (1864); *Glimpses of Fifty Years* (autobiography, 1889); *A Classic Town: The Story of Evanston* (1892); etc. Editor: *A Woman of the Century* (with Mary A. Livermore, 1893), augmented as *American Women,* 2v. (1897). *See* Lydia Jones Trowbridge's *Frances Willard of Evanston* (1938).

WILLARD, JOSIAH FLINT (Jan. 23, 1869–1907); b. Appleton, Wis. Author. Wrote under name "Josiah Flynt." *Tramping with Tramps* (1899); *Notes of an Itinerant Policeman* (1900); *The World of Graft* (1901); *The Little Brothers* (1902); *My Life* (1908).

WILLARD, NANCY (June 26, 1936–); Author. *An Experiment in Objectivity* (1963); *In His Country* (1966); *Skin of Grace* (1967).

WILLARD, SIDNEY (Sept. 19, 1780–Dec. 6, 1856); b. Beverly, Mass. Educator, writer. *A Hebrew Grammar* (1817); *Memories of Youth and Manhood,* 2v. (1855). Co-founder, the *Literary Miscellany,* 1805; founder, the *American Monthly Review,* 1832; editor, 1832–33. Co-founder, the Anthology Society, 1805.

WILLCOX, LOUISE COLLIER (Apr. 24, 1865–Sept. 13, 1929); b. Chicago, Ill. Critic, translator, essayist, editor. *Answers of the Ages* (1900); *The Human Way* (1909); *The Road to Joy* (1911); *The House in Order* (1917); etc. Compiler: *The Torch,* an anthology of children's verse (1924). Reader, Macmillan Co., 1903–09; E. P. Dutton & Co., 1910–17.

WILLETS, GILSON (Aug. 10, 1869–); b. Hempstead, L.I., N.Y. Editor, traveler, author. *His Neighbor's Wife* (1897); *Anita, the Cuban Spy* (1898); *Travels in India* (1901); *The Double Cross* (1910); etc.

WILLETT, HERBERT LOCKWOOD (May 5, 1864–Mar. 27, 1944); b. Ionia, Mich. Educator, author. *Life and Teachings of Jesus* (1898); *Prophets of Israel* (1899); *Our Bible* (1917); *The Bible through the Centuries* (1929); *The Jew through the Centuries* (1931). Dept. Oriental languages, University of Chicago, 1896–1929; prof., 1915–29.

WILLEY, MALCOLM MACDONALD (Nov. 13, 1897–); b. Portland, Me. Educator, author. *The Country Newspaper* (1926); *An Introduction to Sociology* (with others, 1927); *Depression, Recovery, and Higher Education* (1937); etc. Sociology dept., University of Minnesota, 1924–34; dean, 1934–43; vice-pres. academic administration, since 1943.

William Henry Letters, The. By Abby Morton Diaz (1870). These letters from a schoolboy to his relatives first appeared in *Our Young Folks.* A sequel, *William Henry and His Friends,* was published in 1871.

William Wilson. Short story by Edgar Allan Poe (1839). An allegory of man's double nature.

William-Frederick Press, The. New York. Founded 1941. Subsidy publisher, noted for its poets series. Directed by Alvin Levin.

WILLIAMS, ALBERT RHYS (Sept. 28, 1883–Feb. 27, 1962); b. Greenwich, O. Author. *The Russian Land* (1927); *The Soviets* (1937); *Russians: The Land, the People and Why They Fight* (1943); and numerous other books about the Soviet Union.

WILLIAMS, ALFRED MASON (Oct. 23, 1840–Mar. 9, 1896); b. Taunton, Mass. Journalist, poet. *Sam Houston and the War of Independence in Texas* (1893); *Studies in Folk-Song and Popular Poetry* (1894); *Under the Trade Winds* (1898); etc. Editor: *The Poets and Poetry of Ireland* (1881).

WILLIAMS, ANNA BOLLES (b. 1840); b. New London, Conn. Author. Pen name "J. A. K." The *Birchwood* series, 8v. (1885–89); etc.

WILLIAMS, BEN AMES (Mar. 7, 1889–Feb. 4, 1953); b. Macon, Miss. Short story writer, novelist. *All the Brothers Were Valiant* (1919); *The Sea Bride* (1919); *Audacity* (1924); *Splendor* (1927); *Immortal Laughter* (1927); *Great Oaks* (1930); *Touchstone* (1930); *Pirate's Purchase* (1931); *Money Musk* (1932); *Mischief* (1933); *Hostile Valley* (1934); *Small Town Girl* (1935); *Crucible* (1937); *Thread of Scarlet* (1939); *Come Spring* (1940); *The Strange Woman* (1941); *Time of Peace* (1942); *Leave Her to Heaven* (1944); *House Divided* (1947); *Owen Glen* (1950); *The Unconquered* (1953); etc.

WILLIAMS, BENJAMIN HARRISON (Mar. 23, 1889–); b. Eugene, Ore. Author. *Economic Foreign Policy of the United States* (1929); *American Diplomacy: Policies and Practice* (1936). Editor: *The Search for National Security* (1951).

WILLIAMS, "BERT" [Egbert Austin] (1875–Mar. 4, 1922); b. on Island of New Providence, Bahamas. Comedian, song writer. See Mabel Rowland's *Bert Williams, Son of Laughter* (1923).

WILLIAMS, B[ertye] Y[oung] (Mrs. Karl H. Williams) (d. Feb., 1951); b. Hamersville, O. Editor, poet. *House of Happiness* (1928); *Apples of Gold* (1932); *For Each a Star: Zodiac Sonnets* (1942); *What Else Matters?* (1949); etc. Founder and editor (with Annette Patten Cornell), *Talaria* magazine of verse, 1936.

WILLIAMS, BLANCHE COLTON (Feb. 10, 1879–Aug. 9, 1944); b. in Attala Co., Miss. Educator, editor, author. *A Handbook on Story Writing* (1917); *Our Short Story Writers* (1920); *Studying the Short Story* (1926); *George Eliot—A Biography* (1936); etc. Editor: *O. Henry Memorial Prize Stories*, 14v. (1919–32); *Thrice Told Tales* (1924); *A Book of Essays* (1931); *The Mystery and the Detective* (1938); etc. English dept., Hunter College, 1910–39.

WILLIAMS, CATHARINE READ ARNOLD (Dec. 31, 1787–Oct. 11, 1872); b. Providence, R.I. Poet, novelist. *Original Poems, on Various Subjects* (1828); *Religion at Home* (1829); *Aristocracy; or, The Holbey Family* (1832); *Tales, National and Revolutionary*, 2v. (1830–35); *The Neutral French; or, The Exiles of Nova Scotia* (1841); *Annals of the Aristocracy*, 2 nos. (1845), no more published; etc. See Sidney Smith Rider's *Biographical Memoirs of Three Rhode Island Authors* (1880).

WILLIAMS, CHANCELLOR. Author. *The Raven* (1943); *Have You Been to the River?* (1952); *The Rebirth of American Civilization* (1961).

WILLIAMS, CHARLES RICHARD (Apr. 16, 1853–May 6, 1927); b. Plattsburg, N.Y. Editor, author. *In Many Moods* (1910); *The Life of Rutherford Birchard Hayes*, 2v. (1914); *Hours in Arcady* (poems, 1926); *The Return of the Prodigal, and Other Religious Poems* (1927); etc. Editor: *Diary and Letters of Rutherford Birchard Hayes*, 5v. (1922–26). Editor, the *Indianapolis News*, 1892–1911.

WILLIAMS, CLARA ANDREWS (Dec. 6, 1882–); b. Newark, N.J. Author. The *Blue Book* series, 16v. (1905–1910); *The Magic Book* (1912); *The Indian Wigwam* (1915); etc.

WILLIAMS, DANIEL DAY (Sept. 12, 1910–); b. Denver, O. Congregational clergyman, educator, author. *The Andover Liberals* (1941); *God's Grace and Man's Hope* (1949); *What Present-Day Theologians Are Thinking* (1952); *Alfred North Whitehead: Essays on His Philosophy* (1963); *The Spirit and the Forms of Love* (1968). Co-author: *The Advancement of Theological Education* (1957); *The Shaping of American Religion* (1961). Prof. theology, Union Theological Seminary, since 1954.

WILLIAMS, DAVID (Dec. 23, 1841–Oct. 28, 1927); b. Waterford, Ireland. Publisher. Publisher of *Iron Age*, founded by his father in 1855. Founder, Williams Printing Co., 1884; founder, David Williams Co., publishers, 1897; president, 1897–1909.

WILLIAMS, EDWARD HUNTINGTON (Nov. 1, 1868–June 24, 1941); b. Durand, Ill. Physician, author. *Every-Day Science*, 11v. (with Henry Smith Williams, 1909–10); *The Wonders of Science in Modern Life*, 10v. (with same, 1912); *The Forest Pilot* (1915); *Red Plume* (1925); *Larry of the North* (1926); *Red Plume Returns* (1927); *Red Plume of the Northwest Mounted* (1928); *The Doctor in Court* (1929); *Animal Autobiographies* (1930); etc.

WILLIAMS, EDWARD THOMAS (Oct. 17, 1854–Jan. 27, 1944); b. Columbus, O. Disciples clergyman, educator, author. *The State Religion of China under the Manchus* (1913); *China Yesterday and To-Day* (1923); *A Short History of China* (1928); *Tibet and Her Neighbors* (1937); etc. Missionary and legation secretary, etc., in China, 1878–1913; chief, Far Eastern Affairs Div., Dept. of State, 1914–18. Prof. Oriental languages, University of California, 1918–27.

WILLIAMS, EDWIN (Sept. 25, 1797–Oct. 21, 1854); b. Norwich, Conn. Editor, author. *Narrative of the Recent Voyage of Captain Ross to the Arctic Regions* (1835); *The Presidents of the United States* (1849); *The Twelve Stars of Our Republic* (1850); *The Napoleon Dynasty* (anon., with Charles Edwards Lester, 1852); etc. Compiler, *The New York Annual Register*, 1830–45; *The Statesman's Manual*, 1846–58; etc.

WILLIAMS, EDWIN BUCHER (Sept. 20, 1891–); b. Columbia, Pa. Educator, editor, author. *Life and Dramatic Works of Gertrudis Gomez de Avellaneda* (1924); *From Latin to Portuguese* (1938); etc. Editor: *French Short Stories of the 19th Century* (1933); *Spanish-English Dictionary* (1955); *The New College Spanish and English Dictionary* (1968); etc. Romance languages dept., University of Pennsylvania; prof. emeritus since 1961.

WILLIAMS, ELEAZAR (c. 1789–Aug. 28, 1858); b. Caughnawaga, P.Q. Indian scout, missionary. Known erroneously as the "Lost Dauphin." Translated the *Book of Common Prayer*, etc., into Mohawk. J. H. Hanson's *Have We a Bourbon among Us?* in *Putnam's Magazine*, Feb., 1853, started the controversy as to Williams's real identity. See Hanson's *The Lost Prince* (1854); Meade Minnigerode's *The Son of Marie Antoinette* (1934).

WILLIAMS, ESPY [William Hendricks] (Jan. 30, 1852–1908); b. New Orleans, La. Playwright, poet. *Dream of Art* (poems, 1892); *Parrhasius* (prod. 1892); *The Husband* (prod. 1895); *The Man in Black* (prod. 1897); *A Royal Joke* (comic opera, prod. 1901); etc.

WILLIAMS, FRANCIS CHURCHILL (Apr. 23, 1869–Apr. 11, 1945); b. Philadelphia, Pa. Editor, author. *J. Devlin, Boss* (1901); co-author, *Stories of the College* (1902); *The Captain* (1903); etc. Assoc. editor, *Saturday Evening Post*, 1907–27.

WILLIAMS, FRANCIS HOWARD (Sept. 2, 1844–June 18, 1922); b. Philadelphia, Pa. Poet, playwright. *The Princess Elizabeth: a Lyric Drama* (1880); *Master and Man* (1884); *Atman: The Documents in a Strange Case* (1891); *The Flute-Player, and Other Poems* (1894); etc.

WILLIAMS, GARTH MONTGOMERY (Apr. 16, 1912–); b. New York. Illustrator, author. *Baby Animals* (1952); *Tall Tale of Make Believe* (1950); *Rabbit's Wedding* (1958); etc. Illustrator of many children's books.

WILLIAMS, GEORGE FORRESTER (1837–Dec. 30, 1920); b. Gibraltar. Journalist, adventurer, author. *Bullet and Shell* (1883); *Lucy's Rebel; Unfair in Love and War; Half a Century of New York Newspaper Life*, etc. Civil War correspondent, the *New York Times*, 1861–65; managing editor, the *New York Times*, 1871–73; the *New York Herald*, 1874.

WILLIAMS, GEORGE WASHINGTON (Oct. 16, 1849–Aug. 4, 1891); b. Bedford Springs, Pa. Baptist clergyman, soldier, author. *History of the Negro Race in America*, 2v. (1883); *A History of the Negro Troops in the War of the Rebellion* (1888); etc.

WILLIAMS, GLUYAS (July 23, 1888–); b. San Francisco, Calif. Illustrator, author. *The Gluyas Williams Book* (1929); *Fellow Citizens* (1940); *The Gluyas Williams Gallery* (1957). Has illustrated all the books by Robert Benchley, and made numerous comic drawings for magazines.

WILLIAMS, HENRY SMITH (Mar. 4, 1863–July 4, 1943); b. Durand, Ill. Physician, author. *The Story of Nineteenth-Century Science* (1900); *The History of the Art of Writing,* 4v. (1902); *Every-Day Science,* 11v. (with Edward Huntington Williams, 1909–10); *The Wonders of Science in Modern Life,* 10v. (with same, 1912); *The Dope Ring* (1937); *The Private Lives of Birds* (1929); etc. Editor: *The Historians' History of the World,* 25v. (1904); *Luther Burbank,* 12v. (1915); etc.

WILLIAMS, HERSCHEL (1874–Sept. 15, 1935); b. North Manchester, England. Author. *Fairy Tales from Folk Lore* (1908); *Young People's Story of Massachusetts* (1916); the *Merrymakers* series, 2v. (1919–20); *The Jolly Old Whistle, and Other Tales* (1927); *Children of the Clouds* (1929).

WILLIAMS, IRVING (Aug. 4, 1873–Sept., 1957); b. Watertown, Wis. Author. *Mistah Robinson's Remembery Book* (1913); *Big Wallace* (1914); *Joe Manning* (1915); *Bruce Wright* (1916).

WILLIAMS, JAMES (July 1, 1796–Apr. 10, 1869); b. Grainger County, Tenn. Editor, author. *Letters on Slavery from the Old World* (1861); *The Rise and Fall of the Model Republic* (1863). Founder, the *Knoxville Post,* 1841.

WILLIAMS, JESSE LYNCH (Aug. 17, 1871–Sept. 14, 1929); b. Sterling, Ill. Editor, playwright, short-story writer. *Princeton Stories* (1895); *The Stolen Story, and Other Newspaper Stories* (1899); *New York Sketches* (1902); *My Lost Duchess* (1908); *And So They Were Married* (prod. 1914), revised as *Why Marry?* (prod. 1917, Pulitzer Prize play, 1918); *Not Wanted* (1923); *Lovely Lady* (prod. 1925); *They Still Fall in Love* (1929); etc.

WILLIAMS, JOHN (Dec. 10, 1664–June 12, 1729). Congregational clergyman, Indian captive, author. *The Redeemed Captive, Returning to Zion* (1707).

WILLIAMS, JOHN (Apr. 28, 1761–Oct. 12, 1818); b. London, Eng. Satirist, critic, poet. Pen name "Anthony Pasquin." *Poems* (1789); *The Children of Thespis* (1792); *The Pin-Basket to the Children of Thespis* (1797); *The Hamiltoniad* (1804); etc.

WILLIAMS, JOHN A. (1925–); b. Jackson, Miss. Novelist. *The Angry Ones* (1960); *Night Song* (1961); *Cissie* (1963); *The Man Who Cried I Am* (1967); *Sons of Darkness, Sons of Light* (1969).

WILLIAMS, JOHN H[arvey] (b. Jan. 1, 1864); b. Canandaigua, N.Y. Author. *The Mountain That Was "God"* (1910); *The Guardians of the Columbia* (1912); *Yosemite and Its High Sierra* (1914).

WILLIAMS, JONATHAN [Chamberlain] (Mar. 8, 1929–); b. Asheville, N.C. Poet. *Red/Gray* (1951); *Four Stoppages* (1953); *The Empire Finals at Verona* (1959); *amen/huzza/-selah* (1960); *In England's Green* (1962); *Emblems for the Little Dolls and Nooks and Corners of Paradise* (1962); *Lullabies, Twisters, Gibbers, Drags* (1963); *Elegies and Celebrations* (1963); *Lines About Hills Above Lakes* (1964); *Jammin' the Greek Scene* (1964). Publisher, Jargon Books, since 1951.

WILLIAMS, JOSEPH JOHN (Dec. 1, 1875–Oct. 28, 1940); b. Boston, Mass. Roman Catholic clergyman, anthropologist, author. *Whisperings of the Caribbean* (1925); *Voodoos and Obeahs* (1932); *Africa's God* (1937); *The Maroons of Jamaica* (1938); etc. Prof. anthropology, Boston College, 1934–40.

WILLIAMS, MARTHA McCULLOCH, b. in Montgomery Co., Tenn. Author. *Field-Farings* (1892); *Two of a Trade* (1894); *Milre* (1894); *Next to the Ground* (1902); *Dishes & Beverages of the Old South* (1913).

WILLIAMS, MARY WILHELMINE (May 14, 1878–Mar. 10, 1944); b. Stanislaus Co., Cal. Educator, author. *Anglo-American Isthmian Diplomacy, 1815–1915* (1914); *Social Scandinavia in the Viking Age* (1920); *The People and Politics of Latin America* (1930); etc. History dept., Goucher College, 1915–40.

WILLIAMS, MICHAEL (Feb. 5, 1877–Oct. 12, 1950); b. Halifax, N.S. Editor, author. *The Book of the High Romance* (1918); *Little Brother Francis of Assisi* (1926); *Catholicism and the Modern Mind* (1928); *The Shadow of the Pope* (1932); *The Catholic Church in Action* (1935); etc. Founder, *The Commonweal,* 1924; editor, 1924–37; contrib. editor, from 1937.

WILLIAMS, OSCAR (Dec., 1900–Oct. 10, 1964). Poet, editor. *The Golden Darkness* (1921); *In Gossamer Grey* (1921); *The Man Coming Toward You* (1940); *That's All That Matters* (1945); *Selected Poems* (1947); etc. Editor: *New Poems: 1940, 1942, 1943, 1944,* 4v. (1941–44); *Little Treasury of Modern Poetry* (1946); *Little Treasury of British Poetry* (1951); *New Pocket Anthology of American Verse* (1955); etc.

WILLIAMS, RALPH OLMSTEAD (May 12, 1838–1908); b. Palmyra, N.Y. Author. *Our Dictionaries and Other English Language Topics* (1890); *Some Questions of Good English* (1897).

WILLIAMS, REBECCA YANCEY (Mrs. John Bell Williams); b. Lynchburg, Va. Author. *The Vanishing Virginian* (1940); *Carry Me Back* (1942).

WILLIAMS, ROGER (c. 1603–1682/83); b. London. Baptist clergyman, author. *The Bloudy Tenent, of Persecution* (1644); *The Bloudy Tenent Yet More Bloudy* (1652), a reply to John Cotton's *The Bloudy Tenent, Washed, and Made White* (1647); etc. Founder, Providence Plantation, 1636. President, Rhode Island and Providence Plantations, 1654–57. See *Narragansett Club Publications,* 6v. (1866–74); Emily Easton's *Roger Williams, Prophet and Pioneer* (1930); James E. Ernst's *Roger Williams* (1932); Charles S. Longacre's *Roger Williams* (1939); Samuel H. Brockunier's *The Irrepressible Democrat, Roger Williams* (1940); Edmund Morgan's *Roger Williams: The Church and the State* (1967).

WILLIAMS, SAMUEL COLE (Jan. 15, 1864–Dec. 14, 1947); b. Gibson Co., Tenn. Educator, author. *History of the Lost State of Franklin* (1924); *Beginnings of West Tennessee* (1930); etc. Editor: *Lieut. Henry Timberlake's Memoirs, 1756–1765* (1927); *Early Travels in the Tennessee Country* (1928); *Adair's History of the American Indians* (1930); *The Lincolns and Tennessee* (1942); *William Tatham, Wautagan* (1947); etc. Dean, Lamar School of Law, Emory University, 1920–25.

WILLIAMS, SAMUEL WELLS (Sept. 22, 1812–Feb. 16, 1884); b. Utica, N.Y. Editor, educator, author. *The Topography of China* (1844); *The Middle Kingdom,* 2v. (1848); etc. Editor, the *Chinese Repository,* 1836–51. He set up a printing press at Cantoñ, China, and was interpreter of Japanese to Commodore Perry in 1833. Prof. Chinese, Yale University, 1877–84.

WILLIAMS, SIDNEY CLARK (Mar. 2, 1878–May 24, 1949); b. Wells, Me. Editor, critic, author. *A Reluctant Adam* (1915); *The Eastern Window* (1918); *An Unconscious Crusader* (1920); *Mystery in Red* (1925); *The Drury Club Case* (1927); *The Aconite Murders* (1936); etc. Drama critic, the *Boston Daily Advertiser,* 1902–14; lit. editor, the *Boston Herald,* 1914–19; the *Philadelphia North American,* 1920–25; the *Philadelphia Inquirer,* 1925–39.

WILLIAMS, STANLEY THOMAS (Oct. 25, 1888–Feb. 4, 1956); b. Meriden, Conn. Educator, editor, author. *Life and Dramatic Works of Richard Cumberland* (1917); *Studies in Victorian Literature* (1923); *The American Spirit in Letters* (1926); *American Literature* (1933); *The Life of Washington Irving* (1935); *The Beginnings of American Poetry, 1620–*

1855 (1951); *Two in a Topolino* (1956); etc. Editor: *Irving's Letters from Sunnyside and Spain* (1928); *Journal of Washington Irving, 1823–24* (1931); *Journal of Washington Irving, 1803* (1934); *Journal of Washington Irving, 1828* (1937); *The Journal of Emily Foster* (with Leonard B. Beach, 1938); etc. Co-editor: *Around the Horn* (1944); etc. English dept., Yale University, from 1915.

WILLIAMS, TALCOTT (July 20, 1849–Jan. 24, 1928); b. Abeih, Turkey, of American parentage. Editor, educator, author. *Turkey: A World Problem of To-Day* (1921); *The Newspaperman* (1922); etc. Co-editor: *International Encyclopedia;* etc. Wrote for *Book News* 1889–1909. First director, Columbia University School of Journalism, 1912–19. With the *Philadelphia Press,* 1881–1912. *See* Elizabeth Dunbar's *Talcott Williams, Gentleman of the Fourth Estate* (1936).

WILLIAMS, TENNESSEE [Thomas Lanier] (Mar. 26, 1914–); b. Columbus, Miss. Playwright, novelist. *American Blues* (play, 1939); *Battle of Angels* (prod. 1940); *The Glass Menagerie* (prod. 1944); *Twenty-seven Wagons Full of Cotton* (1946); *You Touched Me* (prod. 1946); *A Streetcar Named Desire* (prod. 1947; Pulitzer Prize for drama, 1948); *Summer and Smoke* (prod. 1948); *One Arm, and Other Stories* (1948); *The Rose Tattoo* (prod. 1950); *The Roman Spring of Mrs. Stone* (1950); *Camino Real* (1953); *Hard Candy: A Book of Stories* (1954); *Cat on a Hot Tin Roof* (prod. 1954; Pulitzer Prize for drama, 1955); *In the Winter* (poems, 1956); *Orpheus Descending* (prod. 1957); *Garden District* (prod. 1958); *Sweet Bird of Youth* (prod. 1959); *The Night of the Iguana* (prod. 1962); *The Milk Train Doesn't Stop Here Anymore* (prod. 1963); *Slapstick Tragedy* (prod. 1966); *In a Bar of a Tokyo Hotel* (1969), etc.

WILLIAMS, THOMAS HARRY (May 19, 1909–); b. Vinegar Hill, Ill. Historian. *Lincoln and the Radicals* (1941); *Lincoln and His Generals* (1952); *P.G.T. Beauregard* (1955); *Romance and Realism in Southern Politics* (1961); *The Civil War Volunteer Officer* (1965); etc. Editor: *Abraham Lincoln, Selected Speeches, Messages, and Letters* (1957). Boyd prof. of history, Louisiana State University, since 1953.

WILLIAMS, WALTER (July 2, 1864–July 29, 1935); b. Boonville, Mo. Educator, journalist, author. *The Practice of Journalism* (1911); *The World's Journalism* (1915); *A History of Missouri since the Civil War* (1927); *Missouri, Mother of the West,* 5v. (with Floyd C. Shoemaker, 1930). Editor, the *Columbia* (Mo.) *Herald,* 1890–1908. Founder, School of Journalism, University of Missouri, and dean of same, 1908–31; president, University of Missouri, 1931–35. President, Press Congress of the World, 1915–25.

WILLIAMS, WAYLAND WELLS (Aug. 16, 1888–May 6, 1945); b. New Haven, Conn. Artist, poet, novelist. *The Whirligig of Time* (1916); *Goshen Street* (1920); *The Seafarers, and Other Poems* (1924). Edited: *Castle in Spain* (poems by W. B. D. Henderson, 1942).

WILLIAMS, WILLIAM APPLEMAN (June 12, 1921–); b. Atlantic, Ia. Educator, author. *American-Russian Relations 1784–1947* (1950); *The Shaping of American Diplomacy 1763–1955* (1956); *The Tragedy of American Diplomacy* (1962); *The Contours of American History* (1961); *The United States, Cuba and Castro* (1962); *The Great Evasion* (1964). Prof. history, Oregon State University.

WILLIAMS, WILLIAM CARLOS (Sept. 17, 1883–Mar. 4, 1963); b. Rutherford, N.J. Physician, poet, novelist, essayist. *Poems* (1909); *The Tempers* (poems, 1913); *A Book of Poems, Al Que Quiere!* (1917); *Kora in Hell* (poems, 1920); *Sour Grapes* (poems, 1921); *Spring and All* (1922); *The Great American Novel* (1923); *In the American Grain* (1925); *A Voyage to Pagany* (1928); *The Knife of the Times, and Other Stories* (1932); *A Novelette, and Other Prose, 1921–1927* (1932); *Collected Poems, 1921–1931* (1934); *An Early Martyr, and Other Poems* (1935); *Adam & Eve & The Coty* (poems, 1936); *White Mule* (1937); *The Complete Collected Poems, 1906–1938* (1938); *Life along the Passaic River* (1938); *In the Money* (1940); *The Wedge* (1944); *Paterson,* Books I-IV (poem, 1946–51); *Selected Poems* (1949); *Make Light of It* (stories, 1950); *Autobiography* (1951); *The Build-Up* (1952); *The Desert Music, and Other Poems* (1954); *Selected Essays* (1954); *Journey to Love* (1956); *Selected Letters of William Carlos Williams* (1957); *Yes, Mrs. Williams* (1959); *Many Loves and Other Plays* (1961); *Pictures from Breughel, and Other Poems* (1962); etc. *See* Lloyd Frankenberg's *Pleasure Dome* (1949); Vivienne Koch's *William Carlos Williams* (1950) and *The Poems of William Carlos Williams: A Critical Study* (1964); *Imaginations,* ed. by Webster Schott (1970).

WILLIAMS, WIRT (1921–). Educator, author. *The Enemy* (1951); *Love in a Windy Space* (1957); *Ada Dallas* (1959). Prof. English, Los Angeles State College.

WILLIAMS, WYTHE (Sept. 18, 1881–July 13, 1956); b. Meadville, Pa. Correspondent, editor, author. *Passed by the Censor* (1916); *This Flesh* (1931); *Dusk of Empire* (1937); *Washington Broadcast* (1944); *The Tiger of France* (1949); etc. European correspondent for several newspapers, 1910–31; editor and publisher of the *Greenwich Time,* Greenwich, Conn., 1937–40, and radio news analyst.

Williams & Wilkins Company, The. Baltimore, Md. Publishers. Founded by John H. Williams, a commercial printer, who took Harry Wilkins as a partner a few years later. The modern development of the firm as a leader in the field of scientific books and periodicals dates from 1900 when Edward B. Passano became manager. Passano became sole proprietor around 1907, and in 1909 the firm published its first periodical. In 1920 the firm began to publish books as well as scientific periodicals, and was incorporated in 1925 as a separate publishing concern, distinct from the printing corporation which was named the Waverly Press. In 1932 the company absorbed the William Wood & Co., of New York, founded in 1804. In 1933 Passano helped organize Reynal and Hitchcock. William M. Passano is president.

WILLIAMSON, GEORGE (Feb. 20, 1898–Sept. 8, 1968); b. Galesburg, Ill. Educator. Author: *The Talent of T. S. Eliot* (1929); *The Donne Tradition* (1930); *The Senecan Amble* (1951); *A Reader's Guide to T. S. Eliot* (1953); *Seventeenth Century Contexts* (1961); *Milton and Others* (1965); *Alfred North Whitehead: Essays on His Philosophy* (1963); *The Spirit and the Forms of Love* (1968); etc. Prof. English, University of Chicago, 1940–59.

Williamson, Jack. Pen name of John Stewart Williamson.

WILLIAMSON, JOHN STEWART (Apr. 29, 1908–); b. Brisbee, Ariz. Teacher, science-fiction writer. Pen names "Jack Williamson" and "Will Stewart." *Legion of Space* (1947); *Darker Than You Think* (1948); *The Humanoids* (1949); *The Green Girl* (1950); *The Cometeers* (1950); *One Against the Legion* (1950); *The Not-Men* (1951, originally *Dragon's Island*); *The Legion of Time* (1952); *After World's End* (1952); *Dome Around America* (1955); *The Trial of Terra* (1962); *Golden Blood* (1964); *The Reign of Wizardry* (1965); *Bright New Universe* (1967). Under pen name "Will Stewart": *Setee Shock* (1950); *Setee Ship* (1951); etc. Co-author with Frederick Pohl: *Undersea Quest* (1954); *Undersea Fleet* (1956); *Undersea City* (1958); *The Reefs of Space* (1964); *Starchild* (1965). Co-author with James E. Gunn: *Star Bridge* (1955).

WILLIAMSON, JULIA MAY (Mar. 13, 1859–1909); b. New Sharon, Me. Poet. Pen name "Lura Bell." *The Choir of the Year* (1875); *Echoes of Time and Tide* (1879); *Star of Hope, and Other Songs* (1892).

WILLIAMSON, THAMES [Ross] (Feb. 7, 1894–); b. on Indian reservation near Genesee, Idaho. Novelist. *Run, Sheep, Run* (1925); *Gypsy down the Lane* (1926); *The Man Who Cannot Die* (1926); *Stride of Man* (1928); *Hunky* (1929); *Opening Davy Jones's Locker* (1930); *Sad Indian* (1932);

Against the Jungle (1933); *The Woods Colt* (1933); *North after Seals* (1934); *The Lobster War* (1935); *Beginning at Dusk* (1935); *Under the Linden Tree* (1935); *The Falcon Mystery* (1936); *Saltar the Mongol* (1938); *A Tamer of Beasts* (1938); *Christine Roux* (1945); *The Gladiator* (1948); etc. Also writes under pen names of "S. S. Smith," "Waldo Fleming," "Edward Dragonet," "Gregory Trent," and "De Wolfe Morgan," used for his boy's books and mystery novels. *See* Fred B. Millett's *Contemporary American Authors* (1940).

WILLIS, NATHANIEL (June 6, 1780–May 26, 1870); b. Boston, Mass. Editor. Father of Nathaniel Parker Willis and Sara Payson (Willis) Parton ("Fanny Fern"). Founder and editor, the *Eastern Argus,* Portland, Me., 1803; founder, *The Recorder,* Boston, Mass., Jan. 3, 1816.

WILLIS, NATHANIEL PARKER (Jan. 20, 1806–Jan. 20, 1867); b. Portland, Me., son of Nathaniel Willis. Poet, editor, journalist, playwright. *Fugitive Poetry* (1829); *Melanie, and Other Poems* (1835); *Inklings of Adventure,* 2v. (anon., 1836); *Pencillings by the Way* (1836); *Tortesa the Usurer* (prod. 1839); *Bianca Visconti* (1839); *A l'Abri; or, The Tent Pitch'd* (1839); *Romance of Travel* (anon., 1840); *Loiterings of Travel,* 3v. (1840); *Lady Jane, and Other Poems* (1844); *Dashes at Life with a Free Pencil* (1845); *Complete Works* (1846); *The Miscellaneous Works* (1847); *Prose Works* (1849); *Rural Letters* (1849); *People I Have Met* (1850); *Life, Here and There* (1850); *Fun-Jottings* (1853); *Famous Persons and Places* (1854); etc. Founder, the *American Monthly Magazine,* 1829, the *New York Mirror,* 1842. With George Pope Morris, bought the *National Press* in 1846, which became the *Home Journal* (q.v.). *See* H. W. Beers's *Nathaniel Parker Willis* (1885).

WILLIS, WILLIAM (Aug. 31, 1794–Feb. 17, 1870); b. Haverhill, Mass. Lawyer, historian of Maine. *The History of Portland,* 2v. (1831–33); *A History of the Law, the Courts, and the Lawyers of Maine* (1863).

WILLISON, GEORGE F[indlay] (July 24, 1896–); b. Denver, Colo. Author. *Here They Dug the Gold* (1931); *Why Wars Are Declared* (1935); *Saints and Strangers* (1945); *Behold Virginia* (1951); *Patrick Henry and His World* (1969); etc. Editor: *Let's Make a Play* (1940).

WILLKIE, WENDELL L[ewis] (Feb. 18, 1892–Oct. 8, 1944); b. Elwood, Ind. Lawyer, executive, author. *Speeches and Statements* (1940); *This Is Wendell Willkie* (1940); *One World* (1943). Republican candidate for President of the United States, 1940.

WILLOUGHBY, [Florence] BARRETT (Mrs. Robert H. Prosser) (d. Aug., 1959), b. in Alaska. Author. *Where the Sun Swings North* (1922); *Rocking Moon* (1925); *Gentlemen Unafraid* (1928); *Sitka, Portal to Romance* (1930); *Alaskans All* (1933); *Sondra O'Moore* (1939); *Alaska Holiday* (1940); *The Golden Totem* (1945); etc.

WILLOUGHBY, HAROLD RIDEOUT (Mar. 3, 1890–Feb. 2, 1962); b. North Haverhill, N.H. Educator, author. *Religious Thought in the Last Quarter Century* (with others, 1927); *Pagan Regeneration: A Study of Mystery Initiations in the Graeco-Roman World* (1929); *The Miniatures* (1932); *Codex 2400 and Its Miniatures* (1933); *A Greek Corpus of Revelation Iconography* (1939); *The First Authorized English Bible and the Cranmer Preface* (1942); *Soldiers' Bibles Through Three Centuries* (1944); *Munera Studiosa* (with others, 1946); *Religious Import of the Tushingham Placque* (1958); etc. Editor of literary remains of Ernest Dewitt Burton. Dept. New Testament literature, University of Chicago, 1924–55.

WILLOUGHBY, WESTEL WOODBURY (July 20, 1867–Mar. 26, 1945); b. Alexandria, Va. Educator, author. *The Supreme Court of the United States* (1890); *Government and Administration of the United States* (1891); *The Nature of the State* (1896); *Social Justice* (1900); *The Political Theme of the Ancient World* (1903); *Constitutional Law of the United*

States, 3v. (1929); *The Ethical Basis of Political Authority* (1930); etc. Managing editor, the *American Political Science Review,* 1907–17. Prof. political science, Johns Hopkins University, 1897–1933.

WILLS, GARRY. Author. *Nixon Agonistes: The Crisis of the Self-Made Man* (1970).

WILLS, HELEN NEWINGTON (Oct. 6, 1906–); b. Centerville, Cal. Tennis player, author. *Tennis* (1928); *Fifteen-Thirty* (1937); *Death Serves an Ace* (1939).

Willsie, Honoré. See Honoré Willsie Morrow.

WILLSON, ARABELLA M. (Arabella W. Stuart). Author. *The Lives of Mrs. Ann H. Judson and Mrs. Sarah B. Judson* (1851), augmented as *The Lives of the Three Mrs. Judsons* (1872); *Disaster, Struggle, Triumph* (1870).

WILLSON, FORCEYTHE (Apr. 10, 1837–Feb. 2, 1867); b. Little Genesee, N.Y. *The Old Sergeant* (1866), augmented as *The Old Sergeant, and Other Poems* (1867). His best known poems are "In State," "Boy Brittan" and his masterpiece "The Old Sergeant."

WILLSON, MEREDITH (May 18, 1902–); b. Mason City, Ia. Composer, musical director, author. *What Every Musician Should Know* (1948); *And There I Stood With My Piccolo* (1948); *Who Did What to Fedalia?* (1952); *Eggs I Have Laid* (1955); *But He Doesn't Know the Territory* (1959). Author book, music and lyrics, *The Music Man* (1958).

WILMER, LAMBERT A. (c. 1805–Dec. 21, 1863). Journalist, author. *The Quacks of Helicon* (poems, 1851); *Life, Travels and Adventures of Hernando de Soto* (1858); *Our Press Gang* (1859); etc. With the *Baltimore Saturday Visitor, The Pennsylvanian,* etc. He was a close friend of Edgar Allan Poe, who wrote about him in his *The Literati* (1850).

WILMSHURST, ZAVARR (Nov. 25, 1824–Jan. 27, 1887); b. (William Bennet) Tunbridge Wells, England. Poet, playwright. *The Viking* (1849); *The Winter of the Heart, and Other Poems* (1874); *The Siren* (poem, 1876); *Liberty's Centennial* (1876); *Ralph and Rose; or, Faith's Defense* (poem, 1879); etc.

WILSON, ALBERT FREDERICK (Aug. 26, 1883–June 25, 1940); b. Greenfield Hills, Conn. Educator, editor, author. *The Township Line* (1919); *Pok O'Moonshine* (1927); *Higher Than the Wind Can Blow* (1934). Managing editor, *Leslie's Weekly,* 1912–14. Prof. journalism, New York University, 1914–40.

WILSON, ALEXANDER (July 6, 1766–Aug. 23, 1813); b. Paisley, Scotland. Ornithologist, poet. *Watty and Meg* (poem, 1782); *Poems, Humorous, Satirical, and Serious* (1789); *The Foresters* (1805); *American Ornithology,* 9v. (1808–14); *Poems* (1816); etc. *See* Alexander B. Grosart's *Memoir and Remains of Alexander Wilson,* 2v. (1876); biographical sketch by George Ord in v. 9 of Wilson's *American Ornithology;* James S. Wilson's *Alexander Wilson, Poet-Naturalist* (1906).

WILSON, AUGUSTA [Jane] EVANS (Augusta J. Evans) (May 8, 1835–May 9, 1909); b. Columbus, Ga. Novelist. *Inez* (1855); *Beulah* (1859); *Macaria; or, Altars of Sacrifice* (1864); *St. Elmo* (1867); *Vashti* (1869); *Infelice* (1876); *At the Mercy of Tiberius* (1887); etc.

WILSON, CALVIN DILL (July 1857–Apr. 28, 1946); b. Baltimore, Md. Presbyterian clergyman, author. *The Child's Don Quixote* (1901); *Making the Most of Ourselves* (1909); *Black Masters* (1915); *Caesar* (poems, 1937); *Exiled Savants* (poems, 1938); *Turannoi* (poems, 1939); *One Octogenarian to Another* (poem, 1943); etc.

WILSON, CHARLES MORROW (June 16, 1905–); b. Fayetteville, Ark. Author. *Acres of Sky* (1930); *Backwoods America* (1934); *Meriwether Lewis of Lewis and Clark* (1934); *Aroostook: Our Last Frontier* (1937); *Country Living*

(1938); *Ginger Blue* (1939); *Challenge and Opportunity: Central America* (1941); *Man's Reach* (1944); *Liberia* (1947); *Butterscotch and the Happy Barnyard* (1953); *Bodacious Ozarks* (1959); *Grass and People* (1961); *Mountain Toy Makers* (1965); *The Fights Against Hunger* (1969); *William Jennings Bryan* (1970); etc.

WILSON, CHERRY [Rose] (July 12, 1894–); b. Mystic, Pa. Novelist. *Thunder Brakes* (1929); *Empty Saddles* (1929); *Stormy* (1930); *Black Wing's Rider* (1934); *Stirrup Brother* (1935).

WILSON, DAVID (Sept. 17, 1818–June 9, 1887); b. West Hebron, N.Y. Author. *Life in Whitehall* (anon., 1849); *The Life of James McCrea* (1853); *Henrietta Robinson* (1855); *A Narrative of Nelson Lea* (1859); etc.

WILSON, DOROTHY CLARKE (May 9, 1904–); b. Gardiner, Me. Author. *Twelve Months of Drama for the Average Church* (plays, 1934); *The Brother* (1944); *Prince of Egypt* (1949); *House of Earth* (1952); *Jezebel* (1955); *The Gifts* (1957); *The Journey* (1965); *Handicap Race, the Story of Roger Arnett* (1967); *Lone Woman, a Biography of Dr. Elizabeth Blackwell* (1970); etc.

WILSON, EARL (May 3, 1907–); b. Rockford, O. Columnist. *Jungle Performers* (with Clyde Beatty, 1941); *I Am Gazing Into My Eight-Ball* (1945); *Let 'Em Eat Cheesecake* (1949); *Look Who's Abroad Now* (1953); *Earl Wilson's New York* (1964); etc. Columnist, "It Happened Last Night," New York *Post*, since 1942.

WILSON, EDMUND (May 8, 1895–); b. Red Bank, N.J. Critic, author. *The Undertaker's Garland* (with John Peale Bishop, 1922); *Discordant Encounters* (1926); *I Thought of Daisy* (1929); *Poets, Farewell!* (poems, 1929); *Axel's Castle: A Study in the Imaginative Literature of 1870–1930* (1931); *The American Jitters* (1932); *Travels in Two Democracies* (1936); *The Triple Thinkers* (1938); *To the Finland Station* (1940); *The Boys in the Back Room* (1941); *The Wound and the Bow* (1941); *Note-Books of Night* (1942); *Memoirs of Hecate County* (1946); *Europe Without a Baedeker* (1947); *The Little Blue Light* (play, 1950); *Classics and Commercials* (1950); *The Shores of Light* (1952); *Five Plays* (1954); *The Scrolls from the Dead Sea* (1955); *Red, Black, Blond and Olive* (1956); *A Piece of My Mind* (1956); *The American Earthquake* (1958); *Apologies to the Iroquois* (1960); *Night Thoughts* (1961); *Patriotic Gore* (1962); *The Cold War and the Income Tax* (1963); *Bit Between My Teeth* (1965); *O Canada* (1965); *A Prelude* (1967); *The Dead Sea Scrolls: 1955–69* (1969); *Upstate* (1971). Editor: *The Shock of Recognition* (1943). *See* Sherman Paul's *Edmund Wilson* (1965).

WILSON, ERNEST HENRY (Feb. 15, 1876–Oct. 15, 1930); b. Chipping Campden, Eng. Plant collector, botanist, author. *Aristocrats of the Garden* (1917); *Plant Hunting*, 2v. (1927); *China: Mother of Gardens* (1929). With Arnold Arboretum, Boston, 1907–30.

WILSON, FORREST (Jan. 20, 1883–1942); b. Warren, O. Author. *The Living Pageant of the Nile* (1924); *Paris on Parade* (1925); *Rich Brat* (1929); *Crusader in Crinoline: The Life of Harriet Beecher Stowe* (1941); etc.

WILSON, FRANCIS (Feb. 7, 1854–Oct. 7, 1935); b. Philadelphia, Pa. Author. *Recollections of a Player* (1897); *The Eugene Field I Knew* (1898); *Joseph Jefferson* (1906); *Francis Wilson's Life of Himself* (1924); *John Wilkes Booth* (1929); etc.

WILSON, FRANCIS GRAHAM (Nov. 26, 1901–); b. Junction, Tex. Educator. *Labor in the League System* (1934); *The American Political Mind* (1949); *The Case for Conservatism* (1951); *Political Thought in National Spain* (1967); etc. Member of the staff at C. W. Post College, since 1967.

WILSON, GROVE (Dec. 6, 1863–Oct. 11, 1954); b. Greenville, Ohio. Author. *Man of Strife* (1925); *The Human Side of*

Science (1929); *Temperamental Jane: The Strange Story of Carlyle's Wife* (1931); *Sneckles of Mowbrey Street* (1933); *The Defiant Corpse* (1946); etc. Assoc. editor, *Smart Set*, 1921–28; assoc. editor, *Popular Science Monthly*, 1930–34.

Wilson, H. W. Co. New York. Publishers. Founded by Halsey William Wilson in Minneapolis in 1898. Incorporated 1903. In 1913 the firm moved to White Plains, N.Y., and in 1917 to New York City. It specializes in library reference works. Among its outstanding publications are: *The United States Catalogue* and *Cumulative Supplements;* the *Standard Catalogue Series;* the *Book Review Digest;* the *Essay and General Literature Index;* the *Art Index;* the *Education Index;* the *Reader's Guide to Periodical Literature;* the *International Index to Periodicals;* the *Union List of Serials; American Authors, 1600–1900; Living Authors; Junior Book of Authors; Authors Today and Yesterday; Twentieth Century Authors;* etc. Howard Haycraft is chairman of the board.

WILSON, HALSEY WILLIAM (May 12, 1868–Mar. 1, 1954); b. Wilmington, Vt. Publisher. Founder of H. W. Wilson Co. in 1898.

WILSON, HARRY LEON (May 1, 1867–June 28, 1939); b. Oregon, Ill. Novelist. *Mavericks* (1892); *Zig Zag Tales* (1896); *The Spenders* (1902); *The Lions of the Lord* (1903); *The Seeker* (1904); *The Boss of Little Arcady* (1905); *The Man from Home* (with Booth Tarkington, 1908); *Bunker Bean* (1913); *Ruggles of Red Gap* (1915); *Somewhere in Red Gap* (1916); *Merton of the Movies* (1922); *Lone Tree* (1929); *Two Black Sheep* (1931); *Exit* (1931); *When in the Course* (1940); etc. Editor, *Puck*, 1896–1902.

WILSON, HENRY (Feb. 16, 1812–Nov. 22, 1875); b. (Jeremiah Jones Colbath) Farmington, N.H. Statesman, editor, author. Known as "The Natick Cobbler." *History of the Rise and Fall of the Slave Power in America*, 3v. (1872–75). Editor and owner, the *Boston Republican*, 1848–51. Vice-president of the United States, 1872–75.

WILSON, JAMES (Sept. 14, 1742–Aug. 21, 1798); b. near St. Andrews, Scot. Jurist, congressman, educator, author. *The Works*, ed. by Bird Wilson, 3v. (1804); reëd. by James De W. Andrews, 2v. (1896). Member Continental Congress, 1775–77; associate justice, U.S. Supreme Court, 1789–94. Prof. law, College of Philadelphia, 1790. The Wilson MSS. in 10 volumes are in the Historical Society of Pennsylvania.

WILSON, JAMES GRANT (Apr. 28, 1832–Feb. 1, 1914); b. Edinburgh, Scot. Soldier, editor, author. *The Life and Letters of Fitz-Greene Halleck* (1869); *The Poets and Poetry of Scotland*, 2v. (1876); *Bryant and His Friends* (1886); *Life of General Grant* (1897); *Memoirs of an American Lady* (1901); *Thackeray in the United States*, 2v. (1904); etc. Editor: *Appleton's Cyclopedia of American Biography*, 6v. (1886–89); *The Memorial History of the City of New York*, 4v. (1892–93); etc. Founder, *The Record*, Chicago, 1857.

WILSON, JAMES HARRISON (Sept. 2, 1837–Feb. 23, 1925); b. Shawneetown, Ill. Engineer, soldier, author. The *Life of Ulysses S. Grant* (with Charles A. Dana, 1887); *The Life of Charles A. Dana* (1907); *Under the Old Flag*, 2v. (autobiography, 1912).

WILSON, JAMES SOUTHALL (Nov. 12, 1880–Nov. 25, 1958); b. in Surry Co., Va. Educator, editor, author. *Alexander Wilson, Poet-Naturalist* (1906); etc. Editor: *Facts about Poe* (1926); *Tales of Edgar Allan Poe* (1927); etc. Editor, the *Virginia Quarterly Review*, 1925–30.

WILSON, JOHN (c. 1591–Aug. 7, 1667); b. Windsor, Eng. Congregational clergyman, poet. *A Song or Story for the Lasting Remembrance of Divers Famous Works* (1626), long poem for children.

WILSON, JOHN FLEMING (Feb. 22, 1877–Mar. 5, 1922); b. Erie, Pa. Author. *Across the Latitudes* (1911); *The Land Claimers* (1911); *They Who Came Back* (1912); *Tad Shelton,*

Boy Scout (1913); *Tad Shelton's Fourth of July* (1913); *The Master Key* (1915); *Scouts of the Desert* (1920); *Somewhere at Sea, and Other Tales* (1923).

WILSON, JOHN LAIRD (1832–1896); b. Croftshead, Bridge of Weir, Renfrewshire, Scot., came to the United States in 1866. Presbyterian clergyman, author. *The Battles of the Civil War*, 2v. (1878); *John Wycliffe* (1884). On staff, the *New York Herald*, 1866–74.

WILSON, KEITH (Dec. 26, 1927–); b. Clovis, N.M. Poet, educator. *Sketches for a New Mexico Hill Town* (1966); *The Old Car and Other Black Poems* (1968); *Lion's Gate* (1968); *The Shadow of Our Bones* (1968). Faculty, New Mexico State University, since 1965.

WILSON, LOUIS R[ound] (Dec. 27, 1876–); b. Lenoir, N.C. Librarian, editor, author. *The Geography of Reading* (1938); *Library Planning* (1944); *The University Library* (with M. F. Tauber, 1956); *The University of North Carolina, 1900–1930* (1957). Editor: *Library Trends* (1936). Librarian, University of North Carolina library, 1901–32; dean, graduate library school, University of Chicago, from 1932. Director, University of North Carolina Press, 1922–32. On editorial board, *Library Quarterly*, from 1932.

WILSON, MARGARET (Mrs. G. D. Turner) (Jan. 16, 1882–); b. Traer, Ia. Novelist. *The Able McLaughlins* (1923, Pulitzer Prize novel, 1924); *The Kenworthys* (1925); *Daughters of India* (1928); *Trousers of Taffeta* (1929); *One Came Out* (1932); *The Valiant Wife* (1933); *The Law and the McLaughlins* (1936); *The Devon Treasure Mystery* (1939); etc.

WILSON, MITCHELL A. (July 17, 1913–); b. New York. Author. *Footsteps Behind Her* (1941); *Stalk the Hunter* (1943); *None So Blind* (1945); *The Panic-Stricken* (1946); *The Kimballs* (1947); *Live with Lightning* (1949); *My Brother, My Enemy* (1952); *American Science and Invention* (1954); *The Lovers* (1954); *The Human Body* (1959); *Meeting at a Far Meridian* (1961); *Energy* (1963); *The Huntress* (1968); etc.

WILSON, PHILIP WHITWELL (May 21, 1875–June, 1956); b. Kendal, Westmoreland, Eng. Journalist, author. *The Christ We Forget* (1917); *An Explorer of Changing Horizons: William Edgar Geil* (1927); *General Evangeline Booth* (1938); *Bride's Castle* (1944); *Old Mill* (1946); etc. Editor: *The Greville Diary*, 2v. (1927); *William Pitt, the Younger* (1930); etc. With the *London Daily News*, the *New York Times*, etc.

WILSON, ROBERT BURNS (Oct. 30, 1850–Mar. 31, 1916); b. Washington, Pa. Painter, poet, novelist, *Life and Love* (1887); *Chant of a Woodland Spirit* (1894); *The Shadows of the Trees* (1898); *Until the Day Break* (1900). Best known poems are "Remember the Maine," "When Evening Cometh On," and "Such Is the Death the Soldier Dies."

Wilson, Rose Cecil O'Neill. See Rose Cecil O'Neill.

WILSON, RUFUS ROCKWELL (Mar. 15, 1865–Dec. 14, 1949); b. Troy, Pa. Publisher, author. *Rambles in Colonial Byways*, 2v. (1901); *New York, Old & New*, 2v. (1902); *Historic Long Island* (1902); *New England in Letters* (1904); *Out of the West* (1933); *Intimate Memories of Lincoln* (1945); *New York in Literature* (1947); etc. President, Primavera Press, Inc., Wilson Book Co.

WILSON, RUTH DANENHOWER (Mrs. Albert Frederick Wilson) (Feb. 10, 1887–); b. Annapolis, Md. Author. *Giving Your Child the Best Chance* (1924); *Here Is Haiti* (1957); etc.

WILSON, SAMUEL GRAHAM (Feb. 11, 1858–July 2, 1916); b. Indiana, Pa. Presbyterian clergyman, missionary, author. *Persian Life and Customs* (1895); *Mariam: A Romance of Persia* (1906); *Modern Movements among Moslems* (1916).

WILSON, SAMUEL MACKAY (Oct. 15, 1871–Oct. 10, 1946); b. Louisville, Ky. Lawyer, author. *George Robertson* (1908); *Isaac Shelby and the Genêt Mission* (1920); *Kentucky Blue Grass* (1924); *The Ohio Company of Virginia, 1748–1798* (1926); *History of Kentucky* (1928); etc.

WILSON, SLOAN (May 8, 1920–); b. Norwalk, Conn. Novelist. *Voyage to Somewhere* (1946); *The Man in the Gray Flannel Suit* (1955); *The Summer Place* (1958); *A Sense of Values* (1960); *Janius Island* (1966); *Away from It All* (1969); etc.

WILSON, STANLEY [Kidder] (Apr. 16, 1879–Nov. 15, 1944); b. Madison, N.J. Author. *John Leech* (1914); *The Scream of the Doll* (1931); *Guess Who?* (under pen name, "Pliny the Youngest," 1934); *Blind Dawn* (poem, 1942); etc.

WILSON, THOMAS JAMES (Oct. 25, 1902–June 27, 1969); b. Chapel Hill, N.C. Publisher. Translator: *The Correspondence of Romain Rolland and Malwida von Meysenburg* (1934).

WILSON, [Thomas] WOODROW (Dec. 28, 1856–Feb. 3, 1924); b. Staunton, Va. Twenty-eighth President of the United States, educator, historian. *Congressional Government* (1885); *Division and Reunion, 1829–1889* (1893); *George Washington* (1897); *A History of the American People*, 5v. (1902); *Public Papers*, ed. by Ray Stannard Baker and William E. Dodd, 3v. (1927); etc. Prof. jurisprudence, Princeton University, 1890–1910; president, Princeton University, 1902–10. *See* William E. Dodd's *Woodrow Wilson and His Work* (1920); Joseph P. Tumulty's *Woodrow Wilson As I Know Him* (1921); David Lawrence's *The True Story of Woodrow Wilson* (1924); Ray Stannard Baker's *Life and Letters of Woodrow Wilson*, 2v. (1927); Arthur Stanley Link's *Wilson: The Road to the White House* (1947); E. M. Hugh-Jones's *Woodrow Wilson and American Liberalism* (1948), Gene Smith's *When the Cheering Stopped* (1964).

WILSON, WILLIAM (Dec. 25, 1801–Aug. 25, 1860); b. Crieff, Scot. Publisher, bookseller, poet. *Poems* (1869). In 1834 he became a member of the bookstore staff of Paraclete Potter at Poughkeepsie, N.Y., and in 1841 took over the business. He published a number of books.

WILSON, WILLIAM E[dward] (Feb. 12, 1906–); b. Evansville, Ind. Educator, author. *The Wabash* (1940); *Abe Lincoln of Pigeon Creek* (1949); *The Strangers* (1952); *The Raiders* (1955); *On the Sunny Side of a One Way Street* (autobiography, 1959); *The Angel and the Serpent* (1964); *Indiana: A History* (1966); etc. James A. Work Prof. of English, Indiana University, since 1967.

WILSTACH, FRANK JENNERS (Oct. 20, 1865–Nov. 28, 1933); b. Lafayette, Ind. Theatre manager, author. *Wild Bill Hickok* (1926). Compiler: *A Dictionary of Similes* (1916), etc.

WILSTACH, JOHN AUGUSTINE (July 14, 1824–1897); b. Washington, D.C. Poet. *The Battle Forest* (1890); *The Angel and the King, and Other Poems* (1893). Translator: *The Divine Comedy of Dante*, 2v. (1888).

WILSTACH, PAUL (July 1, 1870–Feb. 10, 1952); b. Lafayette, Ind. Author. *Richard Mansfield* (1908); *Mount Vernon* (1916); *Potomac Landings* (1921); *Along the Pyrenees* (1925); *Jefferson and Monticello* (1925); *Islands of the Mediterranean* (1926); *Patriots off Their Pedestals* (1927); *An Italian Holiday* (1928); *Tidewater Virginia* (1929); *Tidewater Maryland* (1931); *Hudson River Landings* (1933); etc.

WILTSE, SARA ELIZA (b. 1849); b. Burns, Mich. Educator, author. *Stories for Kindergartens* (1885); *The Place of the Story in Early Education* (1892); *A Brave Baby, and Other Stories* (1894); *Myths and Mother Plays* (1895); etc.

WIMBERLY, CHARLES FRANKLIN (Nov. 19, 1866–July 10, 1946); b. in Jefferson Co., Ill. Methodist clergyman, author. *New Clothes for the Old Man* (1907); *The Vulture's*

Claw (1910); *The Winepress* (1913); *Modern Apostles of Faith* (1931); etc.

WIMBERLY, LOWRY CHARLES (Dec. 25, 1890–July 8, 1959); b. Plaquemine, La. Educator, author. *Death and Burial Lore in the English and Scottish Popular Ballads* (1927); *Folklore in English and Scottish Ballads* (1928); etc. Compiler: *Famous Cats of Fairyland* (1938). Editor: *Mid Country: Writings From the Heart of America* (1945); *Selected Writings of Louise Pound* (1949). Editor, *Prairie Schooner,* until 1956. Engliah dept., University of Nebraska, from 1917; prof., 1928–56.

WIMSATT, WILLIAM KURTZ, Jr. (Nov. 17, 1907–); b. Washington, D.C. Educator, author. *The Prose Style of Samuel Johnson* (1941); *The Verbal Icon* (1954); *Literary Criticism: A Short History* (with Cleanth Brooks, 1957); *Hateful Contraries* (1965); *The Portraits of Alexander Pope* (1965); etc. Editor: *The Idea of Comedy: Essays in Prose and Verse: Ben Johnson to George Meredith* (1969). Prof. English, Yale University, since 1955.

WINCHELL, ALEXANDER (Dec. 31, 1824–Feb. 19, 1891); b. in Dutchess Co., N.Y. Educator, geologist, author. *The Doctrine of Evolution* (1874); *World-Life* (1883); *Walks and Talks in the Geological Field* (1886); etc. Prof. geology, University of Michigan, 1855–73, 1879–91; chancellor, Syracuse University, 1873–74.

WINCHELL, CONSTANCE M[abel] (Nov. 2, 1896–); b. Northampton, Mass. Librarian. *Locating Books for Interlibrary Loan* (1930); *Guide to Reference Books* (7th ed., 1951); etc. Reference librarian, Columbia University Libraries, since 1941.

WINCHELL, WALTER (Apr. 7, 1897–1972); b. New York. Journalist. Columnist, the *New York Evening Graphic,* 1924–29; the *New York Mirror,* from 1929. *See* St. Clair McKelway's *Gossip: The Life and Times of Walter Winchell* (1940).

WINCHESTER, ALICE (July 26, 1907–); b. Chicago, Ill. Editor, author. *How to Know American Antiques* (1951). Editor: *The Antiques Treasury of Furniture and Other Decorative Arts at Winterthur* (1959); *Collectors and Collections* (1961); *Living with Antiques* (1963); etc. Co-editor: *Primitive Painters in America, 1750–1950* (1950).

WINCHESTER, CALEB THOMAS (Jan. 18, 1847–Mar. 24, 1920); b. Montville, Conn. Editor, author. *Some Principles of Literary Criticism* (1899); *The Life of John Wesley* (1906); *William Wordsworth: How to Know Him* (1916); *An Old Castle, and Other Essays* (1922).

WINCHESTER, JAMES HUGH (June 1917–); b. Midlothian, Tex. Author. *Wonders of Water* (1964); *Wonders of Storms* (1966). Columnist, "World Today," King Features-Central Press.

WINCHEVSKY, MORRIS (Aug. 9, 1856–Mar. 18, 1932); b. (Leopold Benedict) Yanovo, Lith. Poet. Known as the "Ghetto Poet." *Gesamlte Werk,* 10v. (1927–28). Some of his poems were translated into English.

WIND, G[erhard] L[ewis] (Dec. 8, 1896–); b. Cheyenne, Wyo. *Natalie* (1925); *The Land of Sunny Days* (1926); *The Pride of Graystone* (1927); *Rex Amoris* (1928); *Dreams Come True* (1937); *The Soldier's Daughter* (1946); *Chuck Dressler* (1947); *Patriot Blood* (1956); etc.

Wind Without Rain. Novel by Herbert Arthur Krause (1939). Rural life in Minnesota.

WINDHAM, DON (July 2, 1920–). Playwright, author. *You Touched Me!* (with Tennessee Williams, 1947); *The Dog Star* (1950); *The Hero Continues* (1960); *The Warm Country* (1962); *Emblems of Conduct* (1963); *Two People* (1965); etc.

WINDLE, MARY JANE (b. 1825). Author. *Truth and Fancy* (1850), augmented as *A Legend of the Waldenses, and Other Tales* (1852); *Life at the White Sulphur Springs* (1857); *Life in Washington, and Life Here and There* (1859).

WINDOLPH, F[rancis] LYMAN (June 10, 1889–); b. in Lancaster Co., Pa. Lawyer. *The Country Lawyer: Essays in Democracy* (1938); *Leviathan and Natural Law* (1951); *Reflections of the Law in Literature* (1956).

Winds of Morning, The. Novel by H. L. Davis (1952).

Windsor, Anne. Pen name of Annette Barrett Dewey.

Windy McPherson's Son. Novel by Sherwood Anderson (1916).

Wine Press, The. A cellar at No. 74 Warren Street, New York, which was a favorite gathering place of the New York literati in the 1850's. Its founder was Frederick S. Cozzens, wine merchant and humorist. Irving and Halleck were frequent visitors.

WINES, ENOCH COBB (Feb. 17, 1806–Dec. 10, 1879); b. Hanover, N.J. Congregational clergyman, prison reformer, author. *Two Years and a Half in the Navy,* 2v. (1832); *A Trip to Boston* (1838); *The State of Prisons and of Child-Saving Institutions in the Civilized World* (1880).

Winesburg, Ohio. By Sherwood Anderson (1919). A book of twenty-three short sketches of middlewestern life, told with stark realism.

WING, FRANK [Francis Marvin] (July 24, 1873–); b. Elmwood, Ill. Cartoonist, author. *Yesterdays* (1910); *Old Forty Dollars* (1916). Cartoonist, the *Minneapolis Journal,* 1900–14.

WINGATE, CHARLES E[dgar] L[ewis] (Feb. 14, 1861–May 15, 1944); b. Exeter, N.H. Editor, author. *Shakespeare's Heroines on the Stage* (1895); *Life and Letters of Paul Wingate,* 2v. (1930); etc. Editor: *Famous American Actors of To-day* (with Frederick Edward McKay, 1896); etc. General manager, the *Boston Journal,* 1898–1913; editor, the *Boston Sunday Post,* 1913–41.

WINGER, OTHO (Oct. 23, 1877–Aug. 13, 1946); b. Marion, Ind. Educator, author. *History and Doctrines of the Church of the Brethren* (1919); *Letters from Foreign Lands* (1928); *The Last of the Miamis* (1933); *The Lost Sister among the Miamis* (1936); *The Potawatomi Indians* (1939); *The Frances Slocum Trail* (1943); etc. Pres., Manchester College, Manchester, Ind., 1911–41.

WINGFIELD, MARSHALL (Feb. 19, 1893–Apr. 5, 1964); b. in Franklin Co., Va. Disciples clergyman, author. *History of Caroline County, Va.* (1924); *Notes of a Pilgrim* (1935); *Nostalgia, and Other Poems* (1937); *A Piedmont Chronicle* (1937); *Hills of Home* (1938); *Strangers First* (1958).

Wings. Mill Valley, Cal. Quarterly of verse. Founded 1933, by Stanton A. Coblentz. Discontinued 1960.

Wings of the Dove, The. Novel by Henry James (1902). Kate Croy struggles against the domination of a father and a complaining widowed sister who paint a gloomy picture of poverty and its attendant evils and who place the wrong value on wealth.

WINLOW, CLARA VOSTROVSKY (Mrs. Albert E. Winlow) (Oct. 27, 1871–); b. West Point, Neb. Author. *Our Little Cousin* series, 9v. (1911–1925); etc.

WINNER, PERCY (Oct. 16, 1899–); b. New York. Author. *Dario* (1947); *Scene in the Ice-Blue Eyes* (1947).

WINNER, SEPTIMUS (1827–1902); b. Philadelphia, Pa. Song writer. Pen name, "Alice Hawthorne." Best known songs are "Listen to the Mocking Bird," "How Sweet Are the Roses," "Whispering Hope," and "What is Home without a Mother?"

Winner Take Nothing. Collection of stories by Ernest Hemingway (1933).

Winning of Barbara Worth, The. Novel by Harold Bell Wright (1911). Frontier life in Rubio City on the banks of the Colorado River.

Winning of the West, The. By Theodore Roosevelt, 4v. (1889–96). Study of the land movements developed through a century of expansion.

WINSHIP, ALBERT EDWARD (Feb. 24, 1845–Feb. 17, 1933); b. West Bridgewater, Mass. Editor, author. *The Shop* (1889); *Horace Mann, the Educator* (1896); *Great American Educators* (1900); *Jukes-Edwards* (1900); *The Louisiana Purchase* (with R. W. Wallace, 1903); etc. Editor, the *Journal of Education,* 1886–1933.

WINSHIP, GEORGE PARKER (1871–June 22, 1952); b. Bridgewater, Mass. Editor, bibliographer, librarian, author. *The Coronado Expedition* (1896); *Geoffrey Chaucer* (1900); *Cabot Bibliography* (1900); *Early Mexican Printers* (1909); *William Caxton* (1909); *Gutenberg to Plantin* (1926); *The Merrymount Press* (1929); *The First Cambridge Press* (1938); *The Cambridge Press, 1638–1692* (1945); *Guide to Sources of English History, 1603–60* (with E. S. Upton, 1952); etc. Editor: *Wafer's Darien* (1903); *Sailor's Narratives* (1905); *Census of XVth Century Books Owned in America* (1919); *Madame Knight's Journal* (1920); etc.

WINSLOW, ANNE GOODWIN (Mrs. Eveleth Winslow); b. Memphis, Tenn. Author. *The Long Gallery* (poems, 1925); *The Dwelling Place* (poems, 1943); *A Winter in Geneva* (stories, 1945); *Cloudy Trophies* (1946); *A Quiet Neighborhood* (1947); *It Was Like This* (1949); etc.

WINSLOW, EDWARD (Oct. 18, 1595–May 8, 1655); b. Droitwich, Eng. Governor, author. *Good News from New-England* (1624); *Hypocrisie Unmasked* (1646); etc. Governor of Plymouth Colony, 1633–34, 1636–37, 1644–45. *See* Roland G. Usher's *The Pilgrims and Their History* (1918).

WINSLOW, HELEN MARIA (1851–Mar. 27, 1938); b. Westfield, Vt. Author. *The Shawsheen Mills* (1882); *Concerning Cats* (1900); *Literary Boston of To-Day* (1903); *Spinster Farm* (1908); *The Road to a Loving Heart* (1926); etc.

WINSLOW, HORATIO GATES (May 5, 1882–); b. Racine, Wis. Editor, author. *Rhymes and Meters* (1906); *Some Wander Songs, and Other Verse* (1908); *Spring's Banjo* (1927); *Into Thin Air* (with Leslie Quirk, 1929); etc. Editor, *The Masses,* 1910–11.

WINSLOW, HUBBARD (Oct. 30, 1799–Aug. 13, 1864); b. Williston, Vt. Congregational clergyman, author. *The Young Man's Aid to Knowledge, Virtue and Happiness* (1837); *Are You a Christian?* (1839); *The Christian Doctrines* (1844); *Elements of Intellectual Philosophy* (1850); *Moral Philosophy* (1864); etc.

WINSLOW, ROSE GUGGENHEIM (1881–). Author. Pen name, "Jane Burr." *City Dust* (poems, 1916); *The Glorious Hope* (1918); *I Build My House* (poems, 1918); *The Passionate Spectator* (1921); *Married Men* (1925); *Marble and Mud* (1935); *The Queen Is Dead* (1938); *Fourteen Radio Plays* (1945); etc.

WINSLOW, THYRA SAMTER (Mar. 15, 1903–Dec. 2, 1961); b. Ft. Smith, Ark. Author. *A Cycle of Manhattan* (with Arthur Richman, 1923); *Picture Frames* (1923); *Show Business* (1926); *People Round the Corner* (1927); *Blueberry Pie* (1932); *My Own, My Native Land* (1935); *Think Yourself Thin* (1951); *The Winslow Weight Watcher* (1953); *The Sex Without Sentiment* (1954); *Be Slim, Stay Slim* (1955); etc. Theatre and book reviewer, *Gotham Guide;* contributor to many periodicals. Also television and screenplays.

WINSLOW, WILLIAM COPLEY (Jan. 13, 1840–Feb. 2, 1925); b. Boston, Mass. Episcopal clergyman, Egyptologist,

author. *Israel in Egypt* (1883); *The Store City of Pithom* (1885); *A Greek City in Egypt* (1887); *The Pilgrim Fathers in Holland* (1891); etc.

WINSOR, JUSTIN (Jan. 2, 1831–Oct. 22, 1897); b. Boston, Mass. Librarian, editor, author. *Christopher Columbus* (1891); *Cartier to Frontenac* (1894); *The Mississippi Basin* (1895); *The Westward Movement* (1897); etc. Editor: *The Memorial History of Boston,* 4v. (1880–81); *Narrative and Critical History of America,* 8v. (1884–89); etc. One of the founders of the American Library Association, and of the *Library Journal* in 1876. Librarian, Boston Public Library, 1868–77; Harvard Library, 1877–97.

WINSOR, KATHLEEN; b. Olivia, Minn. Author. *Forever Amber* (1944); *The Lovers* (1952); *America, with Love* (1957); *Wanderers Eastward, Wanderers West* (1965); etc.

WINSTON, JOHN C. (Nov. 22, 1856–May 6, 1920); b. Darlington, Ind. Publisher. Founded publishing firm of John C. Winston Co., in Philadelphia, Pa., in 1884.

WINSTON, ROBERT WATSON (Sept. 12, 1860–Oct. 14, 1944); b. Windsor, N.C. Jurist, author. *Andrew Johnson, Plebeian and Patriot* (1928); *High Stakes and Hair Trigger: The Life of Jefferson Davis* (1930); *Robert E. Lee: A Biography* (1934); *It's a Far Cry* (autobiography, 1937); *Winston's Journal and Scrapbook, 1932–44,* 4v. (1944); etc.

Winston, The John C., Co. Philadelphia, Pa. Publishers. Founded 1884 by John C. Winston. It specializes in dictionaries, Bibles, children's books, and educational books. Merged with Henry Holt & Co. and Rinehart & Co., as Holt, Rinehart & Winston, Inc. (q.v.), in 1959.

Winston Simplified Dictionary, The. First published by the John C. Winston Co. in 1919. An *Advanced Edition* was published in 1926, and the original was then called the *Intermediate Edition.* In 1936 the *Winston Dictionary for Schools* was issued. In 1939 the word "simplified" was dropped and the three editions were designated the *Primary,* the *Intermediate,* and the *Advanced.* William Dodge Lewis and Edgar A. Singer edited the original edition. William Dodge Lewis, Henry Seidel Canby, and Thomas Kite Brown edited the *Advanced Edition.* The last printing was in 1961.

WINTER, ALICE AMES (Nov. 25, 1865–Apr. 5, 1944); b. Albany, N.Y. Author. *The Prize to the Hardy* (1905); *Jewel-Weed* (1907); *The Heritage of Woman* (1927); etc.

WINTER, CHARLES EDWIN (Sept. 13, 1870–Apr. 22, 1948); b. Muscatine, Ia. Author. *Grandon of Sierra* (1907); *Ben Warman* (1917); *Gold of Freedom* (1948); etc.

WINTER, EDWARD HENRY (Aug. 21, 1923–); b. Poughkeepsie, N.Y. Anthropologist, author. *Bwamba Economy* (1955); *Bwamba* (1956); *Beyond the Mountains of the Moon* (1959); *Witchcraft and Sorcery* (with J. Middleton, 1963). Prof. anthropology, University of Virginia, since 1959.

WINTER, ELIZABETH C[ampbell] (Mrs. William Winter) (Dec. 19, 1841–Apr. 7, 1922); b. Ederline, Scot. Novelist. Pen name, "Isabella Castelar." *The Spanish Treasure* (1893); *A Girl's First Love* (1905); etc.

WINTER, JOHN GARRETT (Feb. 14, 1881–Mar. 23, 1956); b. Holland, Mich. *The Myth of Hercules at Rome* (1910); *Life and Letters in the Papyri* (1933); etc. General editor: University of Michigan Studies (Humanistic Series), 1928–50. Classics dept., University of Michigan, from 1906; prof., 1906–51.

WINTER, NEVIN OTTO (June 14, 1869–Sept. 1, 1936); b. Benton, O. Author. *Texas the Marvellous* (1916); *A History of Northwest Ohio,* 3v. (1917); *Florida, the Land of Enchantment* (1918); etc.

WINTER, WILLIAM (July 15, 1836–June 30, 1917); b. Gloucester, Mass. Drama critic, historian, essayist, poet. *The Convent* (poems, 1854); *My Witness* (poems, 1871); *Thistle-*

down (poems, 1878); *The Poems* (1881); *The Jeffersons* (1881); *Henry Irving* (1885); *The Wanderers* (poems, 1888); *Gray Days and Gold* (1891); *Shadows of the Stage,* 3 series (1892–95); *Old Shrines and Ivy* (1892); *Life and Art of Edwin Booth* (1893); *Other Days* (1908); *Old Friends* (1909); *The Wallet of Time,* 2v. (1913); *Vagrant Memories* (1915); etc. Drama critic, the *New York Album,* 1861–66; the *New York Tribune,* 1866–1909.

Winter Circuit of Our Arctic Coast, A. By Hudson Stuck (1920). A classic account of a journey around Alaska.

Winterfield, Charles. Pen name of Charles W. Webber.

WINTERICH, JOHN T[racy] (May 25, 1891–Aug. 15, 1970); b. Middletown, Conn. Editor, book collector, author. *A Primer of Book Collecting* (1927); *Collector's Choice* (1928); *Books and the Man* (1929); *An American Friend of Dickens* (1933); *Early American Books and Printing* (1935); *Twenty-three Books* (1938); *Another Day, Another Dollar* (1947); *Three Lantern Slides* (1949); *The Grolier Club, 1884–1950: An Informal History* (1950); *Writers in America, 1842–1967* (1967); etc. Editor, the *American Legion Weekly,* 1924–26, and its successor, the *American Legion Monthly,* 1926–38, editorial staff, *The Colophon,* 1930–39; *The New Colophon,* from 1947; contributing editor, *The Saturday Review,* from 1946.

WINTERS, YVOR (Oct. 17, 1900–Jan. 25, 1968); b. Chicago, Ill. Educator, poet, critic. *The Immobile Wind* (poems, 1921); *The Magpie's Shadow* (poems, 1922); *The Bare Hills* (poems, 1927); *The Proof* (poems, 1930); *The Journey, and Other Poems* (1931); *Before Disaster* (poems, 1934); *Primitivism and Decadence* (1937); *Maule's Curse* (1938); *Poems* (1940); *Giant Weapon* (poems, 1943); *The Anatomy of Nonsense* (1943); *Edward Arlington Robinson* (1946); *In Defense of Reason* (1947); *Collected Poems* (1952); *The Function of Criticism* (1957); *On Modern Poets* (1959); *The Poetry of W. B. Yeats* (1960); *The Poetry of J. V. Cunningham* (1961); *Forms of Discovery* (1967). Editor: *Twelve Poets of the Pacific* (1937); *Poets of the Pacific,* 2d series (1947). Prof. English, Stanford University, 1949–68.

Winterset. Play by Maxwell Anderson (prod. 1935). The effort of Mio to avenge the unjust execution of his father. Finding the gang which was responsible, he is killed by them, together with his sweetheart Miriamne.

WINTHER, OSCAR OSBURN (Dec. 22, 1903–); b. Weeping Water, Neb. Historian. Author: *Via Western Express and Stagecoach* (1945); *The Great Northwest* (1947); *Diary of a Dying Empire* (1955); *The Transportation Frontier: Trans-Mississippi West 1865–1890* (1964); *The Old Oregon Country: A History of Frontier Trade, Transportation and Travel* (1969); *The Story of Our Heritage* (with W. H. Cartwright, 1966); etc. Editor: *With Sherman to the Sea* by T. F. Upson (1943); etc. University prof. history, Indiana University, since 1965.

WINTHER, SOPHUS KEITH (June 24, 1895–); b. Aarhus, Denmark. Author. *Eugene O'Neill: A Critical Study* (1934); *Take All to Nebraska* (1936); *Mortgage Your Heart* (1937); *This Passion Never Dies* (1938); *Beyond the Garden Gate* (1946). English dept., University of Washington, since 1927.

WINTHROP, JOHN (Jan. 12, 1587/8–Mar. 26, 1649); b. Edwardston, Suffolk, Eng. Governor, author. *A Journal of the Transactions and Occurrences in the Settlement of Massachusetts and the Other New-England Colonies, from the Year 1630 to 1644* (1790), revised from the original MS. as *The History of New England,* 2v. (1825–26), and again revised in *Winthrop Papers,* published by the Massachusetts Historical Society, 2v. (1929–31). Governor of Massachusetts Bay Colony, 1629–34, 1637–40, 1642–44, 1646–49. *See* Robert C. Winthrop's *Life and Letters of John Winthrop,* 2v. (1864–67); Robert G. Raymer's *John Winthrop* (1963); Loren Baritz's *City on a Hill: A History of Ideas and Myths in America* (1965).

WINTHROP, LAURA (Mrs. W. Templeton Johnson) (Sept. 13, 1825–1889); b. New Haven, Conn., sister of Theodore Winthrop. Poet. Pen name, "Emily Hare." *Little Blossom's Reward* (1854); *Poems of Twenty Years* (1874); *The Life and Poems of Theodore Winthrop* (1884); etc.

WINTHROP, ROBERT CHARLES (May 12, 1809–Nov. 16, 1894); b. Boston, Mass. Senator, orator, author. *Life and Letters of John Winthrop,* 2v. (1864–67); *Memoir of Henry Clay* (1880); *Reminiscences of Foreign Travel: A Fragment of Autobiography* (1894); etc. Gave chief address at laying of cornerstone of the Washington Monument, Washington, D.C., 1848, and again at its dedication, 1885. Congressman, 1840–50; Speaker of the House, 1847–49; U.S. senator, 1850.

WINTHROP, THEODORE (Sept. 28, 1828–June 10, 1861); b. New Haven, Conn. Author. *Cecil Dreeme* (1861); *John Brent* (1862); *Edwin Brothertoft* (1862); *The Canoe and the Saddle* (1862); *Life in the Open Air, and Other Papers* (1863); *The Life and Poems* (1884); *Mr. Waddy's Return* (1904). He was the subject of Thomas William Parson's "Dirge for One Who Fell in Battle." *See* Laura Winthrop Johnson's *The Life and Poems of Theodore Winthrop* (1884).

WINWAR, FRANCES (May 3, 1900–); b. Francesca Vinciguerra, at Taormina, It. Author. *The Ardent Flame* (1927); *The Golden Round* (1928); *Pagan Interval* (1929); *Poor Splendid Wings* (1933); *The Romantic Rebels* (1935); *Gallows Hill* (1937); *Puritan City* (1938); *Farewell the Banner* (1938); *Oscar Wilde and the Yellow Nineties* (1940); *The Sentimentalist* (1943); *Life of the Heart: George Sand and Her Time* (1946); *Saint and the Devil: Joan of Arc and Gilles de Rais* (1948); *The Immortal Lovers* (1950); *The Eagle and the Rock* (1953); *Wingless Victory* (1956); *The Haunted Palace* (1959); *Jean-Jacques Rousseau: Conscience of an Era* (1961); *All about Napoleon* (1967); etc.

WIRRIES, MARY MABEL (Jan. 14, 1894–); b. South Bend, Ind. Author. *The Mary Rose* series, 7v. (1924–1932); *Praying Pines* (1932); *Wayside Idyls* (1934); *The Road Is Long* (1938); *Juan of San Bruno* (1948); etc.

WIRT, MILDRED [Augustine] (1905–). Author. Writes under own name and under pen names "Frank Bell," "Joan Clark," "Don Palmer," "Dorothy West." *Carolina Castle* (1936); *The Clock Strikes Thirteen* (1942); *Swamp Island* (1947); *Dan Carter and the Great Carved Face* (1952); *Dangerous Deadline* (1957); *The Quarry Ghost* (1959); etc.

WIRT, WILLIAM (Nov. 8, 1772–Feb. 18, 1834); b. Bladensburg, Md. Statesman, author. *The Letters of the British Spy* (1803); *The Old Bachelor* (1814); *Sketches of the Life and Character of Patrick Henry* (1817); etc. Attorney general of the United States, 1817–29. *See* John P. Kennedy's *Memoirs of the Life of William Wirt,* 2v. (1849).

WISE, CLAUDE MERTON (Dec. 21, 1887–Jan. 4, 1966); b. Memphis, Mo. Educator, author. *Dramatics for School and Community* (1923); *A Book of Dramatic Costume* (1930); *A Friend at Court* (1931); and other works on dramatics. Head, dept. speech, Louisiana State University, 1928–58.

WISE, DANIEL (Jan. 10, 1813–Dec. 19, 1898); b. Portsmouth, N.H. Methodist clergyman, editor, author. Pen names, "Francis Forester," "Lawrence Lancewood." *The Path of Life* (1847); *Dick Duncan* (1860); *Janie Carlton* (1861); the *Glen Morris* series; the *Lindendale* series; the *Winwood Cliff* series; etc.

WISE, DAVID (May 10, 1930–); b. New York. Journalist, author. *The U-2 Affair* (with T.B. Ross, 1962); *The Invisible Government* (1964). Contributing author: *The Kennedy Circle* (1961).

WISE, HENRY AUGUSTUS (May 12, 1819–Apr. 2, 1869); b. Brooklyn, N.Y. Naval officer, author. Pen name, "Harry Gringo." *Los Gringos; or, An Inside View of Mexico and California* (1849); *Tales for the Marines* (1855); *Scamperings from Gibel Tarek to Stamboul* (1857); *Captain Brand, of the "Centipede"* (1864); etc.

WISE, ISAAC MAYER (Mar. 29, 1819–Mar. 26, 1900); b. Steingrub, Bohemia. Rabbi, educator, author. *History of the Israelitish Nation* (1854); *Selected Writings* (1900); *Reminiscences* (1901); etc. Founder, Hebrew Union College, 1875; president, 1875–1900.

WISE, JAMES WATERMAN (Dec. 7, 1901–); b. Portland, Ore., son of Stephen Samuel Wise. Lecturer, author. *Synagogue Songs* (1924); *Jews Are Like That* (under pen name, "Analyticus," 1928); *Mr. Smith, Meet Mr. Cohen* (1940); *A Jew Revisits Germany* (1950); *From Bigotry to Brotherhood* (1952); Co-editor: *The Intimate Letters of Stephen Wise* (1955). Founder: *Opinion: A Journal of Jewish Life and Letters,* 1931; editor, 1931–36.

WISE, JENNINGS CROPPER (Sept. 10, 1881–); b. Richmond, Va. Lawyer, soldier, author. *Ye Kingdome of Accawmacke* (1911); *The Long Arm of Lee,* 2v. (1915); *Colonel John Wise of England and Virginia: His Ancestors and Descendants* (1917); *The Turn of the Tide* (1920); *The Red Man in the New World Drama* (1931); *On the Way to Perpignan* (1937); *Woodrow Wilson, Disciple of Revolution* (1938); *America: The Background of Columbus* (1946); *The Mystery of Columbus* (1947); *Philosophic History of Civilization* (1955); and many books on military science.

WISE, JOHN (Aug. 1652–Apr. 8, 1725); b. Roxbury, Mass. Congregational clergyman, author. *The Churches Quarrel Espoused* (1710); *A Vindication of the Government of the New-England Churches* (1717); etc. Supposed author of *A Word of Comfort to a Melancholy Country* (under pen name, "Amicus Patriae," 1721).

WISE, JOHN SERGEANT (Dec. 27, 1846–May 12, 1913); b. Rio de Janeiro, Brazil, of American parentage. Lawyer, author. *Diomed: The Life, Travels and Observations of a Dog* (1897); *The End of an Era* (1899); *The Lion's Skin* (1905); *Recollections of Thirteen Presidents* (1906).

WISE, STEPHEN SAMUEL (Mar. 17, 1874–Apr. 19, 1949); b. Budapest, Hung. Rabbi, editor, author. *The Ethics of Solomon Ibn Gabirol* (1901); *The Great Betrayal* (1930); *Challenging Years* (autobiography, 1949); etc. Editor, *Opinion: A Journal of Jewish Life and Letters,* from 1936.

WISH, HARVEY (Sept. 4, 1909–); b. Chicago, Ill. Educator, author. *George Fitzhugh, Propagandist of the Old South* (1943); *Contemporary America* (rev. ed., 1966); *Thought and Society in America* (2v., 1950, 1952); *The American Historian* (1960). Prof. history, Western Reserve University, since 1945.

WISHART, CHARLES FREDERICK (Sept. 3, 1870–Apr. 11, 1960); b. Ontario, O. Presbyterian clergyman, author. *The Unwelcome Angel* (1919); *The God of the Unexpected* (1923); *Coverdale Speaks* (1935); etc. Pres., College of Wooster, Ohio, 1919–44.

WISSLER, CLARK (Sept. 18, 1870–Aug. 25, 1947); b. Wayne Co., Ind. Anthropologist, educator, author. *North American Indians of the Plains* (1912); *The American Indian* (1917); *Man and Culture* (1923); *Adventures in the Wilderness* (with Constance Lindsay Skinner and William Wood, 1925); *Indian Cavalcade* (1938); *Indians of the United States* (1940); etc. Prof. anthropology, Yale University, 1924–40; curator, American Museum of Natural History, 1906–41.

Wistar Parties. Social and literary gatherings at the home of Dr. Caspar Wistar in Philadelphia, at Fourth and Prune streets, from 1799 to 1818. After his death the Wistar Association continued the parties. The members of the American Philosophical Society formed the nucleus of this Wistar group. *See* H. L. Carson's *The Centenary of the Wistar Party* (1918).

WISTER, OWEN (July 14, 1860–July 21, 1938); b. Philadelphia, Pa. Novelist. *The New Swiss Family Robinson* (1882); *The Dragon of Wantley* (1892); *Red Men and White* (1896); *Lin McLean* (1898); *Ulysses S. Grant* (1900); *Done in the Open* (poems, 1902); *The Virginian* (1902); *Philosophy 4* (1903); *Lady Baltimore* (1906); *The Seven Ages of Washington* (1907); *Neighbors Henceforth* (1922); *The Writings,* 11v. (1928); *When West Was West* (1928); *Roosevelt: The Story of a Friendship, 1880–1919* (1930); etc. *See* Fred B. Millett's *Contemporary American Authors* (1940).

WISTER, SARAH (July 20, 1761–Apr. 21, 1804); b. Philadelphia, Pa. Diarist. *Sally Wister's Journal, A True Narrative, Being a Quaker Maiden's Account of Her Experiences with Officers of the Continental Army, 1777–1778,* ed. by Albert Cook Myers (1902).

"Witch of Coös, The." Poem by Robert Frost.

Witching Hour, The. Play by Augustus Thomas (prod. 1908). A murder mystery involving the use of telepathy.

WITCOVER, JULES. Journalist, author. *85 Days ... The Last Campaign of Robert Kennedy* (1969); *The Resurrection of Richard Nixon* (1970). Washington correspondent, *Los Angeles Times.*

Witherspoon, Halliday. Pen name used by William H. Nutter in the *Boston Traveler* for many years. Nutter (1875–1941), created the *Liverpool Jarge* adventure stories.

WITHERSPOON, JOHN (Feb. 5, 1723–Nov. 15, 1794); b. Edinburgh, Scot. Presbyterian clergyman, educator, author. *The Works,* 4v. (1800–01). President, College of New Jersey (now Princeton University), 1768–94. Member, Continental Congress, 1776–79, 1780–82. *See* V. Lansing Collins's *President Witherspoon,* 2v. (1925).

Within the Law. Play by Bayard Veiller (prod. 1912). Story of Mary Turner, imprisoned for stealing from a department store, a crime she did not commit. To gain revenge she marries the son of the store's owner.

WITHINGTON, ROBERT (June 7, 1884–Aug. 31, 1957); b. Roxbury, Mass. Educator, editor, author. *Arma Virumque* (poems, 1917); *English Pageantry,* 2v. (1918–20); *Excursions in English Drama* (1937); *Smith College Studies in Honor of President W. A. Neilson* (1939); Editor: *Essays and Characters,* 2v. (1933); *Eminent British Writers of the Nineteenth Century: Prose* (with Cortlandt Van Winkle, 1934). English dept., Smith College, from 1917.

Witness. By Whittaker Chambers (1952). Account of the author's Communist past and the Hiss-Chambers trial, by the accuser of Alger Hiss.

WITTENBERG, PHILIP (Apr. 4, 1895–); b. Brooklyn, N.Y. Lawyer. Author: *Protection and Marketing of Literary Property* (1937); *Dangerous Words: A Guide to the Law of Libel* (1947); *The Law of Literary Property* (1957); *The Protection of Literary Property* (1968); etc. Editor: *The Lamont Case: History of a Congressional Investigation* (1957).

WITTENBERG, RUDOLPH M. (Mar. 24, 1906–); b. Berlin. Psychoanalyst. *So You Want to Help People* (1947); *The Art of Group Discipline* (1951); *Adolescence and Discipline* (1959); *The Troubled Generation* (1967); *Postadolescence: Theoretical and Clinical Aspects of Psychotherapy* (1968); etc.

Wittenborn, George, Inc. New York. Publishers. Founded 1938 by George Wittenborn. Specializes in contemporary fine arts, art, architecture, typography, industrial design.

WITTKE, CARL FREDERICK (Nov. 13, 1892–May 24, 1971); b. Columbus, O. Educator. *A History of Canada* (1928); *Tambo and Bones: A History of the American Minstrel Stage* (1930); *We Who Built America: The Saga of the Immigrant* (1939); *Refugees of Revolution* (1952); *The Ger-*

man-Language Press in America (1957); etc. Prof. history, Western Reserve University, from 1948.

WITTKOWER, RUDOLF (June 22, 1901–); b. Berlin. Educator. *Architectural Principles in the Age of Humanism* (1950); *Gian Lorenzo Bernini* (1955); *Art and Architecture in Italy, 1600–1750* (1958); *Born Under Saturn* (1963); etc. Prof. fine arts and archaeology, Columbia University, since 1956.

WITWER, H[arry] C[harles] (Mar. 11, 1890–Aug. 9, 1929); b. Athens, Pa. Humorist, author. *From Baseball to Boches* (1918); *There's No Base Like Home* (1920); *Fighting Blood* (1923); *Bill Grimm's Progress* (1926); etc.

WODEHOUSE, P[elham] G[renville] (Oct. 15, 1881–); b. Guildford, Surrey, Eng. Author of numerous works especially of fiction since 1909, such as *Mike and Smith* (1909); *Fish Preferred* (1929); *The Code of the Woosters* (1938); *Uncle Fred in the Springtime* (1939); *Nothing Serious* (1951); *Angel Cake* (1952); *America, I Like You* (1956); *Jeeves in the Offing* (1960); *Author!, Author!* (1961); *Stiff Upper Lip, Jeeves* (1962); *Do Butlers Burgle Banks?* (1968). Columnist, "By the Way," *London Globe*, 1903–09; came to the U.S., 1909. Created the characters "Jeeves" and "Bertie Wooster."

WOJCIECHOWSKA, MAIA TERESA (Aug. 7, 1927–); b. Warsaw, Pol. Author. *Market Day for Ti Andre* (1952); *Shadow of a Bull* (1965); *Odyssey of a Courage* (1965); *A Kingdom in a Horse* (1965); *The Hollywood Kid* (1966); *Hey, What's Wrong with This One?* (1967); *"Don't Play Dead Before You Have To"* (1970).

WOLCOTT, ROGER (Jan. 4, 1679–May 17, 1767); b. Windsor, Conn. Soldier, poet. *Poetical Meditations* (1725); etc.

WOLCOTT, ROGER (July 25, 1877–deceased); b. Milton, Mass. Lawyer, author. *Family Jottings* (1939); etc. Editor, *The Correspondence of William Hickling Prescott, 1833–1847* (1925).

WOLF, EMMA (b. June 15, 1865); b. San Francisco, Cal. Author. *Other Things Being Equal* (1892); *A Prodigal In Love* (1894); *The Joy of Life* (1897); *Heirs of Yesterday* (1900); *Fulfillment* (1916); etc.

WOLF, LUTHER BENAIAH (Nov. 29, 1857–Nov. 25, 1939); b. Abbottstown, Pa. Lutheran clergyman, missionary, educator, author. *After Fifty Years* (1895); *Missionary Heroes of the Lutheran Church* (1911); etc. Principal, American Evangelical Lutheran Mission College, Guntur, India, 1883–1907.

WOLF, WILLIAM JOHN (Jan. 17, 1918–); b. Hartford, Conn. Protestant Episcopal clergyman. *Man's Knowledge of God* (1955); *Almost Chosen People: The Religion of Abraham Lincoln* (1959); *A Plan of Church Union* (1965); *A United and Uniting Church* (1968); etc.

WOLFE, BERTRAM DAVID (Jan. 19, 1896–); b. Brooklyn, N.Y. Author. *Portrait of America* (1934); *Portrait of Mexico* (1937); *Civil War in Spain* (1937); *Diego Rivera* (1939); *Deathless Days* (1940); *Three Who Made a Revolution* (1948); *Six Keys to the Soviet System* (1956); *Khrushchev and Stalin's Ghost* (1957); *Communist Totalitarianism* (1961); *Rosa Luxemburg and the Russian Revolution* (1961); *The Fabulous Life of Diego Rivera* (1963); *Marxism: 100 Years in the Life of a Doctrine* (1965); *Strange Communists I Have Known* (1965); *The Bridge and the Abyss: The Troubled Friendship of Maxim Gorky and V.I. Lenin* (1967); *Lenin, The Architect of 20th Century Totalitarianism* (1967); *The Ideology of the Barracks and the Street* (1968); *Marx and the Russian Revolution* (1968); *An Ideology in Power: Reflections on the Russian Revolution* (1969); etc.

WOLFE, HENRY CUTLER (Jan. 11, 1898–); b. Newcomerstown, O. Lecturer, journalist, author. *The German Octopus* (1938); *Human Dynamite* (1939); *The Imperial Soviets* (1940). Writer of column, "The European Scene," *Columbus Sunday Dispatch*, until 1937.

WOLFE, LINNIE MARSH (Jan. 8, 1881–); b. Big Rapids, Mich. Author. *John Muir, Friend and Interpreter of Nature, 1838–1914* (1937); *Son of the Wilderness: The Life of John Muir* (1945). Editor: *John of the Mountains: The Unpublished Journals of John Muir* (1938).

WOLFE, THOMAS [Clayton] (Oct. 3, 1900–Sept. 15, 1938); b. Asheville, N.C. Novelist, playwright. *The Return of Buck Gavin* (prod. 1919); *The Third Night* (prod. 1919); *Look Homeward, Angel* (1929); *Of Time and the River* (1935); *From Death to Morning* (1935); *The Story of a Novel* (1936); *The Web and the Rock* (1939); *You Can't Go Home Again* (1940); *The Hills Beyond* (1941); *Gentlemen of the Press* (1942); *Mannerhouse* (play, 1948); *A Western Journal* (1951). Poetical passages from his books were published as *The Face of a Nation* (1939). See *Thomas Wolfe's Letters to His Mother*, ed. by J. S. Terry (1943); *The Letters of Thomas Wolfe*, ed. by Elizabeth Nowell (1956); *Herbert J. Muller's Thomas Wolfe* (1947); Pamela H. Johnson's *Hungry Gulliver* (1947); *Richard Walser's The Enigma of Thomas Wolfe* (1953); Louis D. Rubin's *Thomas Wolfe, The Weather of His Youth* (1955); Elizabeth Nowell's *Thomas Wolfe* (1960); *Richard Walsen's Thomas Wolfe* (1962); *Richard S. Kennedy's The Window of Memory: The Literary Career of Thomas Wolfe* (1962); Andrew Turnbull's *Thomas Wolfe* (1967); *The Notebooks of Thomas Wolfe*, 2v., ed. by Richard S. Kennedy and Paschal Reeves (1970).

WOLFE, THOMAS KENNERLY, JR. (Mar. 2, 1931–); b. Richmond, Va. Journalist, author. *The Kandy-Kolored Tangerine-Flake Streamline Baby* (1965); *The Electric Kool-Aid Acid Test* (1968); *The Pump House Gang* (1968); *Radical Chic and Mau-Mauing the Flak Catchers* (1970). Staff, *New York Herald Tribune*, 1962–66; *New York World Journal Tribune*, 1966–67; *New York* magazine, since 1962.

WOLFERT, IRA (Nov. 1, 1908–); b. New York. Author. *Tucker's People* (1943); *American Guerrilla in the Philippines* (1945); *Act of Love* (1948); *Married Men* (1953); *An Epidemic of Genius* (1960); etc.

Wolff, Mary Evaline. See Sister M. Madeleva.

WOLFF, PERRY (June 12, 1921–   ); b. Chicago, Ill. Author. *The Friend* (1950); *A Tour of the White House with Mrs. John F. Kennedy* (1962); *The Italians* (1967).

WOLFF, ROBERT PAUL (Dec. 27, 1933–   ); b. New York. Educator, author. *Kant's Theory of Mental Activity* (1963); *A Critique of Pure Tolerance* (1965); *Political Man and Social Man* (1966); *Kant: A Collection of Critical Essays* (1967). Assoc. prof. philosophy, Columbia University, since 1964.

WOLFSON, HARRY AUSTRYN (Nov. 2, 1887–); b. Austryn, Wilna, Rus. Educator, author. *Crescas' Critique of Aristotle* (1929); *The Philosophy of Spinoza*, 2v. (1929); *The Internal Senses* (1935); *Philo* (1947); *The Philosophy of the Church Fathers*, Vol. I (1956). Prof. Hebrew literature and philosophy, Harvard University.

Wolfville. See Alfred Henry Lewis.

WOLLE, MURIEL SIBELL (1898–); b. Brooklyn, N.Y. Artist, educator, author. *Ghost Cities of Colorado* (1933); *Cloud Cities of Colorado* (1933); *Stampede to Timberline* (1949); *The Bonanza Trail* (1953); *Montana Pay Dirt* (1963); etc. Prof. fine arts, University of Colorado, since 1936.

WOLMAN, LEO (Feb. 24, 1890–Oct. 2, 1961); b. Baltimore, Md. Economist, author. *The Boycott in American Trade Unions* (1916); *Planning and Control of Public Works* (1930); *Ebb and Flow in American Trade Unions* (1936); etc. Prof. economics, Columbia University, 1931–58.

Woman in The Nineteenth Century. By Margaret Fuller (1845).

Woman of Andros, The. Novel by Thornton Wilder (1930). A modern application of the theme set forth in Terence's *Andria.*

Woman Within, The. Autobiography of Ellen Glasgow (1954).

Woman's Day. New York. Monthly. Founded 1937. Distributed only by stores of the Great Atlantic and Pacific Tea Company as a women's service magazine.

Woman's Home Companion. New York. Fashion and story magazine. Founded 1873, at Cleveland, O., as the *Home Companion,* a juvenile monthly. Bought by the publishers of *Farm and Fireside* and transferred to Springfield, O., in 1884. Serial fiction was a feature in recent years. Gertrude Battles Lane was editor, 1911–40. Expired 1956.

Woman's Journal. Boston, Mass. Founded 1870, by Lucy Stone and others. Devoted to woman suffrage. Editors: Mary A. Livermore, 1870–73; Lucy Stone and Henry B. Blackwell, 1873–1909; Alice Stone Blackwell, 1909–17. Expired 1931.

Women at Point Sur, The. Poems by Robinson Jeffers (1927).

Women: In All Ages and In All Countries. 10v. (1907–08). A popular series giving sketches of great women who have figured in history. Vol. 10 is entitled *Women of America,* by John Rouse Larus.

Wonder-Book, The. By Nathaniel Hawthorne (1852). A book for children which has been popular among several generations of readers.

Wonder-Working Providence of Sion's Saviour in New England. Running title of *A History of New England,* by Edward Johnson (publ. 1653, dated 1654). Long poem, in which the colonists are pictured as under the direct leadership of God, chosen to fight His foes, both seen and unseen.

"Wonderful One-Hoss Shay." See "Deacon's Masterpiece."

"Wonderful Sack, The." Poem by J. T. Trowbridge in *Our Young Folks,* May, 1865.

Wonderful Wizard of Oz, The. By Frank Baum (1900). Fairy tale of perennial popularity. In 1902 it was made into a musical extravaganza and in 1939, into a motion picture in color. The imaginary land of Oz has been used as a background for numerous children's books. For other titles see L. Frank Baum.

Wonders of the Invisible World, The. By Cotton Mather (1693).

Wondersmith, The. Famous short story by Fitz-James O'Brien, depicting life in the New York slums.

WOOD, ANNE TAPPAN WILBUR (Mrs. Joseph Wood) (June 20, 1817–Sept. 14, 1864); b. Wendell, Mass. Editor, translator. Translator of a number of novels from the French and other languages. Editor, the *Ladies' Casket,* Lowell, Mass., 1848.

WOOD, ASA BUTLER (Aug. 26, 1865–May 7, 1945); b. Wapello Co., Ia. Printer, journalist, author. *Pioneer Stories of the Nebraska Panhandle* (1938); *Fifty Years of Yesterdays* (1944). Founder, the *Gering* (Neb.) *Courier,* 1887, and editor and publisher. Established newspapers at Torrington, Wyo., 1907; Scottsbluff, Neb., 1912.

WOOD, CHARLES ERSKINE SCOTT (Feb. 20, 1852–Jan. 22, 1944); b. Erie, Pa. Poet. *A Book of Tales* (1901); *The Poet in the Desert* (1915); *Maia: A Sonnet Sequence* (1918); *Heavenly Discourse* (1927); *Poems from the Rangere* (1929); *Earthly Discourse* (1937); *Collected Poems* (1949); etc.

WOOD, CHARLOTTE DUNNING (b. 1858). Novelist. Wrote as "Charlotte Dunning." *Upon a Cast* (1885); *A Step Aside* (1886); *Cabin and Gondola* (1886).

WOOD, CLEMENT (Sept. 1, 1888–Oct. 26, 1950); b. Tuscaloosa, Ala. Poet, editor, compiler. *Glad of Earth* (poems, 1917); *The Earth Turns South* (poems, 1919); *Folly* (1925); *The Eagle Flies: Sonnets* (1925); *Poets of America* (1925); *Amy Lowell* (1926); *The Greenwich Village Blues* (poems, 1926); *Flesh, and Other Stories* (1929); *The Craft of Poetry* (1929); *Bernarr McFadden* (1929); *Honeymoon* (1931); *The Man Who Killed Kitchener* (1932); *The Glory Road* (autobiography, 1934); *A History of the World,* 5v. (1937); *Tom Sawyer Grows Up* (1939); *The Complete Handbook for Poets* (1940); *Eagle Sonnets* (1942); *Death in Ankara* (1944); *The Eagle Returns* (poems, 1947); *Desire, and Other Stories* (1950); *Strange Fires* (1951); etc. Compiler: *A Slang Dictionary* (with Gloria Goddard, 1926); etc.

WOOD, EDITH ELMER (Sept. 24, 1871–Apr. 29, 1945); b. Portsmouth, N.H. Author. *The Spirit of the Service* (1903); *An Oberland Chalet* (1910); and books on housing.

WOOD, ERIC FISHER (Jan 4, 1889–Oct. 4, 1962); b. New York. Architect, army officer, author. *The Note Book of an Attaché* (1915); *The Writing on the Wall* (1916); *The Note Book of an Intelligence Officer* (1917); *Conservator of Americanism* (1920); *Basic Manual Field Artillery* (1934); *Troop Leading and Staff Procedure* (1941).

WOOD, FRANCES GILCHRIST (Mrs. Lansing P. Wood) (Nov. 25, 1859–Dec. 21, 1944); b. Hillsgrove, Ill. Author. *Gospel Four Corners* (1930); *Turkey Red* (1932); etc.

WOOD, GEORGE (1799–Aug. 24, 1870); b. Newburyport, Mass. Author. *Peter Schlemihl in America* (1848); *Modern Pilgrims,* 2v. (1855); *Marrying Too Late* (1857); *Future Life; or, Scenes in Another World* (1858), republished as *The Gates Wide Open; or, Scenes in Another World* (1869); etc.

WOOD, HENRY ALEXANDER WISE (Mar. 1, 1866–Apr. 9, 1939); b. New York. Inventor, author. *Fancies* (poems, 1903); *The Book of Symbols* (1904); *Money Hunger* (1908).

WOOD, [James] PLAYSTED (Dec. 11, 1905–); b. New York. Author. *The Presence of Everett March* (1937); *Magazines in the United States: Their Social and Economic Influence* (1949); *The Beckoning Hill* (1954); *Elephant in the Family* (1957); *Advertising and the Soul's Belly: Repetition and Memory in Advertising* (1960); *The Queen's Most Honorable Pirate* (1961); *A Hound, A Bay Horse, and a Turtle Dove* (1963); *Trust Thyself* (1964); *The Lantern Bearer* (1965); *Very Wild Animal Stories* (1965); *Elephant on Ice* (1965); *The Snark Was a Boojum* (1966); *What's the Market?* (1966); *When I Was Jersey* (1967); *Alaska, the Great Land* (1967); *Spunkwater, Spunkwater* (1968); *Mr. Jonathan Edwards* (1968); *This Is Advertising* (1968); *I Told You So* (1969); *The Mammoth Parade* (1969); etc.

WOOD, JOHN (c. 1775–May 15, 1822); b. in Scotland. Political pamphleteer. *The History of the Administration of John Adams* (1802); etc. See James Cheetham's *A Narrative of the Suppression by Col. Burr, of The History of the Administration of John Adams...by John Wood* (1802).

WOOD, JOHN SEYMOUR (b. Oct. 1, 1853); b. Utica, N.Y. Lawyer, author. *Gramercy Park: A Story of New York* (1892); *An Old Beau, and Other Stories* (1892); *A Coign of Vantage* (1893); *College Days* (1894); *Yale Yarns* (1895); etc.

WOOD, JUNIUS B[oyd] (May 27, 1877–Apr. 2, 1957); b. Coatesville, Pa. Correspondent, author. *The Negro in Chicago* (1917); *The Race to Sedan* (1918); *Incredible Siberia* (1927); *Flying the World's Longest Airmail Route* (1930); *Illinois: Crossroads of the Nation* (1931); etc. Correspondent, the *Chicago Daily News,* 1907–34.

Wood, Madam. See Sarah Sayward Barrell.

WOOD, ODELLA PHELPS. Author. *Recaptured Echoes* (1944); *High Ground* (1946).

WOOD, ROBERT COLDWELL (Sept. 16, 1923–); b. St. Louis, Mo. Government official, author. *Suburbia, Its People and Their Politics* (1958); *Metropolis Against Itself* (1959); *1400 Governments, The Political Economy of the New York Region* (1960); *Schoolmen and Politics* (with others, 1962); *Government and Politics of the U. S.* (with others, 1965). Prof. political science, Massachusetts Institute of Technology, 1962–66; undersecretary, Department, of Housing and Urban Development, since 1966.

WOOD, SAMUEL (July 17, 1760–May 5, 1844); b. Oyster Bay, L.I., N.Y. Publisher. In 1804 he opened a book store in New York, and soon began to print children's books. In 1815 he took into partnership his sons, Samuel S. and John, to form the company of Samuel Wood and Sons. In 1817, a third son, William (1797–1877) was admitted to the firm. The firm later became William Wood & Co., which specialized in scientific publications. In 1932 it was merged with the Williams & Wilkins Co., Baltimore.

Wood, Sarah Sayward Barrell Keating. See Sarah Sayward Barrell.

WOOD, WILLIAM (fl. 1629–35); b. in England. Colonist, author. *New Englands Prospect* (1634); first printed account of Masaachusetts Bay Colony.

Wood, William, & Co. See Samuel Wood.

WOODBERRY, GEORGE EDWARD (May 12, 1855–Jan. 2, 1930); b. Beverly, Mass. Poet, critic, educator. *Edgar Allan Poe* (1885); *The North Shore Watch, and Other Poems* (1890); *Studies in Letters and Life* (1890); *Wild Eden* (poems, 1899); *Nathaniel Hawthorne* (1902); *Poems* (1903); *The Torch* (1905); *The Appreciation of Literature* (1907); *Ralph Waldo Emerson* (1907); *The Inspiration of Poetry* (1911); *The Flight, and Other Poems* (1914); *Literary Essays* (1920); *The Roamer, and Other Poems* (1920); *Literary Memoirs of the Nineteenth Century* (1921); *Selected Letters* (1933); *Selected Poems* (1933); etc. Prof. comparative literature, Columbia University, 1891–1904.

WOODBRIDGE, FREDERICK JAMES EUGENE (Mar. 26, 1867–June 1, 1940); b. Windsor, Ont. Educator, author. *Philosophy of Hobbes* (1903); *The Purpose of History* (1916); *The Realm of Mind* (1926); *The Son of Apollo* (1929); *Nature and Mind* (1937); *An Essay on Nature* (1940); etc. Prof. philosophy, Columbia University, 1902–39.

WOODBRIDGE, HOMER EDWARDS (Sept. 28, 1882–Jan. 21, 1958); b. Williamstown, Mass. Educator, author. *Essentials of English Composition* (1920); *Life and Letters of Stuart P. Sherman*, 2v. (with Jacob Zeitlin, 1929); *Sir William Temple, the Man and His Work* (1940). Prof. English, Wesleyan University, from 1920.

WOODBURN, JAMES ALBERT (Nov. 30, 1856–Dec. 12, 1943); b. Bloomington, Ind. Educator, historian. *The American Republic and its Government* (1903); *Political Parties and Party Problems in the United States* (1903); *American Politics* (1903); *The Life of Thaddeus Stevens* (1913); *History of Indiana University* (1940); and many other books on American history. President, Indiana Historical Society, 1928–31. Prof. American history, Indiana University, 1890–1924.

Woodford, Jack. Pen name of Josiah Pitts Woolfolk.

WOODHULL, VICTORIA CLAFLIN (Mrs. Canning Woodhull; Mrs. James H. Blood; Mrs. John Biddulph Martin) (Sept. 23, 1838–June 20, 1927); b. Homer, O. Lecturer, editor, author. *The Origin, Tendencies and Principles of Government* (1871); *The Human Body the Temple of God* (with sister, Tennessee C. Claflin, 1890). Editor, *Woodhull and Claflin's Weekly*, New York, 1879. See Erminie Arling's *The Terrible Siren: Victoria Woodhull* (1929).

"Woodman, Spare That Tree." Poem by George Pope Morris (1830).

"Woodnotes." Poem by Ralph Waldo Emerson (1840).

WOODROW, JAMES (May 30, 1828–Jan. 17, 1907); b. Carlisle, England. Presbyterian clergyman, educator, author. *Evolution* (1884). Editor, the *Southern Presbyterian Review,* 1861–85; publisher, the *Southern Presbyterian,* 1865–93. President, University of South Carolina, 1891–97.

WOODROW, Mrs. Wilson (Nancy Mann Waddel Woodrow) (c. 1870–Sept. 7, 1935); b. Chillicothe, O. Novelist. *The Bird of Time* (1907); *The Silver Butterfly* (1908); *The Beauty* (1910); *Sally Salt* (1912); *The Hornet's Nest* (1917); *Burned Evidence* (1925); etc.

WOODRUFF, ANNE HELENA (b. Dec. 28, 1850); b. St. David's Ont. Author. *Betty and Bob* (1903); *The Pond in the Marshy Meadow* (1906); *Three Boys and a Girl* (1906); etc.

WOODRUFF, JULIA LOUISA MATILDA (Apr. 29, 1833–1909); b. Newtown, Conn. Author. Pen name, "W. M. L. Jay." *Shiloh; or, Without and Within* (1870); *My Winter in Cuba* (1871); *Holden with the Cords* (1874); *The Daisy Seekers* (1885); *Bellerue* (1891); etc.

WOODS, BERTHA GERNEAUX [Davis] (1873–Feb. 14, 1952); b. Penn Yan, N.Y. Poet. *Verses* (1903); *The Guest, and Other Verse* (1926); *Patient Scientists, and Other Verse* (1928); *The Little Gate* (1935); *World Communion, and Other Verse* (1943).

WOODS, GEORGE BENJAMIN (Nov. 14, 1878–Nov. 8, 1958); b. Morris, Ill. Educator, editor, author. *A College Handbook of Writing* (1922); *Problems in English,* 3 series (1926–27–28); *A Guide to Good English* (1934). Editor: *English Poetry and Prose of the Romantic Movement* (1916); *Prose of the Victorian Period* (1930); *The Literature of England,* 2v. (with H. A. Watt and George Anderson, 1936); *Versification in English Poetry* (1958); etc. Prof. English, Carleton College, 1913–25; American University, Washington, D.C., 1925–44.

WOODS, KATE TANNATT (1838–1910); b. Peekskill, N.Y. Author. *All Around a Rocking Chair* (1879); *Six Little Rebels* (1879); *Doctor Dick* (1881); *That Dreadful Boy* (1886); *A Fair Maid of Marblehead* (1889); *Across the Continent* (1897); etc.

WOODS, KATHARINE PEARSON (Jan. 28, 1853–Feb. 19, 1923); b. Wheeling, W. Va. Author. *Metzerott, Shoemaker* (1889); *The Mark of the Beast* (1890); *The True Story of Captain John Smith* (1901); etc.

WOODS, KATHERINE IRVIN (Mar. 29, 1886–Feb. 5, 1968); b. Philadelphia, Pa. Author. *The Other Château Country* (1931); *Murder in a Walled Town* (1934). Translator of works by M. Haedrich, J. Kessel, L. Massé, Saint Exupéry, R. Vercel, Zola; etc. With the *New York Times Book Review,* 1912–19, 1928–31, and from 1935.

WOODS, THOMAS FRANCIS (Jan. 17, 1882–Dec. 17, 1949); b. Albany, N.Y. Lawyer, poet. *New York, and Other Poems* (1931); *Three Waters* (1933).

WOODS, WILLIAM HOWARD (b. June 25, 1916–); b. Port Chester, N.Y. Novelist. *The Edge of Darkness* (1942); *The Street of the Seven Monks* (1948); *Riot at Gravesend* (1952); *Manuela* (1957); *The Mask* (1960); *Poland: Eagle of the East* (1968); *Mermaid in Nikoli* (1967); etc.

WOODS, WILLIAM SEAVER (Aug. 13, 1872–Dec. 3, 1962); b. Bath, N.Y. Editor, author. *Colossal Blunders of the War* (1930). On staff, the *Literary Digest,* 1897–1933; editor-in-chief, 1905–33.

"Woods are full of them, The." Line from the preface of Alexander Wilson's *American Ornithology* (1825).

WOODSON, CARTER GODWIN (Dec. 19, 1875–Apr. 3, 1950); b. New Canton, Va. Author. *The Education of the*

Negro Prior to 1861 (1915); *History of the Negro Church* (1921); *The Negro in Our History* (1922); *Negro Orators and Their Orations* (1925); *African Myths* (1928); *Negro Makers of History* (1928); *African Heroes and Heroines* (1939); etc. President Associated Publishers, Inc. Founder and editor, *Journal of Negro History,* 1916; *Negro History Bulletin,* 1937.

Woodville; or, The Anchoret Reclaimed. Novel by Charles W. Todd (1932). One of the first novels written by a native of Tennessee. The locale of the novel is Montvale Springs, Tenn.

WOODWARD, C[omer] VANN (Nov. 13, 1908–); b. Vanndale, Ark. Educator, author. *Tom Watson: Agrarian Rebel* (1938); *The Battle for Leyte Gulf* (1947); *Origins of the New South, 1877–1913* (1951); *Reunion and Reaction* (1951); *The Strange Career of Jim Crow* (1955); *The Burden of Southern History* (1960). History dept., Johns Hopkins University, since 1946.

WOODWARD, HELEN (Mrs. William E. Woodward) (Mar. 19, 1882–); b. New York. Author. *Through Many Windows* (1926); *Way of the Lancer* (with Richard Boleslavski, 1932); *Lances Down* (with same, 1932); *Three Flights Up* (autobiography, 1935); *It's an Art* (1938); *Money to Burn* (1945); etc. Editor: *William E. Woodward's Years of Madness* (1951).

WOODWARD, WALTER CARLETON (Nov. 28, 1878–Apr. 14, 1942); b. Mooresville, Ind. Editor, author. *The Rise and Early History of Political Parties in Oregon, 1843–1868* (1913); *Friendly Tales of Foreign Travel* (1923); *Timothy Nicholson, Master Quaker* (1927); etc. Editor, the *American Friend,* from 1917.

WOODWARD, WILLIAM E. (Oct. 2, 1874–Sept. 27, 1950); b. Ridge Spring, S.C. Author. *Bunk* (1923); *Lottery* (1924); *Bread and Circuses* (1925); *George Washington, the Image and the Man* (1926); *Meet General Grant* (1928); *Evelyn Prentice* (1933); *A New American History* (1936); *Lafayette* (1938); *The Way Our People Lived* (1944); *The Gift of Life* (autobiography, 1947); *Years of Madness* (1951); etc.

WOODWORTH, FRANCIS C[hanning] (1812–June 5, 1859); b. Colchester, Conn. Naturalist, editor, author. *Uncle Frank's Fables for Children,* 6v. (1851); *Stories about Birds* (1851); *Wonders of the Insect World* (1854); etc. Editor: *American Miscellany of Entertaining Knowledge,* 12v. (1853).

WOODWORTH, HERBERT G[rafton] (b. Feb. 27, 1860); b. Boston, Mass. Author. *In the Shadow of Lantern Street* (1920); *Where the Twain Met* (1935); etc.

WOODWORTH, ROBERT SESSIONS (Oct. 17, 1869–July 4, 1962); b. Belchertown, Mass. Educator, psychologist, author. *The Care of the Body* (1912); *Dynamic Psychology* (1917); *Psychology* (1929); *Heredity and Environment* (1941); *Dynamics of Behavior* (1958). Editor, *Archives of Psychology,* 1906–45. Prof. psychology, Columbia University, 1909–42.

WOODWORTH, SAMUEL (Jan. 13, 1784–Dec. 9, 1842); b. Scituate, Mass. Editor, poet, playwright. Pen name, "Selim." *New-Haven* (1809); *Beasts at Law* (1811); *Quarter-Day* (1912); *The Poems, Odes, Songs, and Other Metrical Effusions* (1818); *The Deed of Gift* (prod. 1822); *La Fayette* (prod. 1824); *The Forest Rose* (prod. 1825); *The Widow's Son* (prod. 1825; *King's Bridge Cottage* (prod. 1833); *The Poetical Works,* ed. by his son, F. A. Woodworth (1861); etc. Wrote "The Hunters of Kentucky" and "The Bucket" ("The Old Oaken Bucket"). Editor, the *New York Mirror,* 1823.

WOODY, CLIFFORD (June 2, 1884–Nov. 19, 1948); b. Thorntown, Ind. Educator, author. *Measurements of Some Achievements in Arithmetic* (1916); *Problems of Elementary School Instruction* (1923); *Guidance Implications from Measurements of Achievements, Aptitudes and Interest* (1944); etc. Prof. education, University of Michigan, from 1921.

WOODY, WALTER THOMAS (Nov. 3, 1891–Sept. 11, 1960); b. Thorntown, Ind. Educator, author. *Early Quaker Education in Pennsylvania* (1920); *Educational Views of Benjamin Franklin* (1931); *Liberal Education for Free Men* (1951). Prof. history of education, University of Pennsylvania, from 1924.

WOOLEY, EDWARD MOTT (Feb. 25, 1867–May 31, 1947); b. Milwaukee, Wis. Author. Pen names "Robert Bracefield" and "Richard Bracefield." *Roland of Altenburg* (1904); *Miss Huntington* (1908); *Free-Lancing for Forty Magazines* (autobiography, 1927); *The Curve* (1928); *100 Paths to a Living* (1931); etc. Compiler: *The Real America in Romance,* 3v. (1909–10).

WOOLF, DOUGLAS (Mar. 23, 1922–   ); b. New York. Author. *The Hypocritic Days* (1955); *Fade Out* (1959); *Wall to Wall* (1962); *Signs of a Migrant Worrier* (1965).

WOOLF, SAMUEL JOHNSON (Feb. 12, 1880–Dec. 3, 1948); b. New York. Artist, author. *A Short History of Art* (1909); *Drawn from Life* (1931); *Here Am I* (autobiography, 1941); etc. His personality sketches appeared in the magazine section of the *New York Times.*

WOOLFOLK, JOSIAH PITTS (Mar. 25, 1894–); b. Chicago. Author. Under own name: *Trial and Error* (1933). Under pen name "Jack Woodford": *The Evangelical Cockroach* (1929); *Sin and Such* (1930); *White Meat* (1931); *Unmoral* (1932); *Delinquent* (1934); *Gentlemen from Parnassus* (1936); *How To...* (1950); *Loud Literary Lamas of New York* (1950); *Writer's Cramp* (1955); *The Motive Key* (1956); etc. Under pen name "Gordon Sayre":*Assistant Wife* (1933); *Male and Female* (1934); *Possessed* (1935); *Three Gorgeous Hussies* (1936). Under pen name "Sappho Henderson Britt": *Love in Virginia* (1935). Under pen name "Howard Kennedy": *Lady Killer* (1935); *Lady Mislaid* (1937).

WOOLLCOTT, ALEXANDER (Jan. 19, 1887–Jan. 23, 1943); b. Phalanx, N.J. Critic, actor, author. *Mrs. Fiske—Her Views on Acting* (1917); *Shouts and Murmurs* (1922); *Enchanted Aisles* (1924); *Going to Pieces* (1928); *While Rome Burns* (1934); *The Good Companions* (1936); etc. Editor: *The Woollcott Reader* (1935); *Woollcott's Second Reader* (1937); etc. Drama critic, the *New York Times,* 1914–22; the *New York Herald,* 1922; the *New York World,* 1925–28. The chief character in the play, *The Man Who Came to Dinner,* by George Kaufman and Moss Hart (1939), is based on Woollcott. See Fred B. Millett's *Contemporary American Authors* (1940).

WOOLLEY, CELIA PARKER (June 14, 1848–Mar. 9, 1918); b. Toledo, O. Novelist. *Love and Theology* (1887); *A Girl Graduate* (1889); *Roger Hunt* (1892); *The Western Slope* (1903); etc.

WOOLLEY, LAZELLE THAYER (June 17, 1872–); b. Port Allegany, Pa. Author. The *Faith Palmer* series, 4v. (1912–15); *The Just Alike Twins* (1912); etc.

WOOLLEY, MARY EMMA (July 13, 1863–Sept. 5, 1947); b. Norwalk, Conn. Educator, author. *The Early History of the Colonial Post Office* (1894); etc. Pres. Mt. Holyoke College, 1900–37.

WOOLMAN, JOHN (Oct. 19, 1720–Oct. 7, 1772); b. Ancocas, province of West Jersey. Quaker leader, abolitionist, author. *Some Considerations on the Keeping of Negroes* (1754); *A Plea for the Poor* (1763); *A Journal of the Life, Gospel, Labours and Christian Experiences of John Woolman* (1774). See Janet Whitney's *John Woolman, American Quaker* (1942); Edwin H. Cady's *John Woolman* (1965).

WOOLRICH, CORNELL (Dec. 4, 1903–Sept. 25, 1968); b. New York. Author. Pen name "William Irish." *The Bride Wore Black* (1940); *Black Alibi* (1942); *Deadline at Dawn* (1944); *The Dancing Detective* (1946); *I Married a Dead Man* (1948); *Rendezvous in Black* (1948); *Dead Man Blues* (1948);

The Blue Ribbon (1949); *Fright* (1950); *Somebody on the Phone* (1950); *Stranger's Serenade* (1951); *Eyes That Watch You* (1952); *Nightmare* (1956); *Hotel Room* (1958); etc.

WOOLSEY, SARAH CHAUNCEY (Jan. 29, 1835–Apr. 9, 1905); b. Cleveland, O. Author. Pen name, "Susan Coolidge." The *Katy Did* series, 5v. (1873); *Verses* (1880); *A Few More Verses* (1889); *Last Verses* (1906); etc.

WOOLSEY, THEODORE DWIGHT (Oct. 31, 1801–July 1, 1889); b. New York. Educator, author. *Political Science*, 2v. (1877); *Communism and Socialism* (1880); etc. Editor of texts of many Greek plays. President, Yale University, 1846–71.

WOOLSON, ABBA [Louisa] GOOLD (Apr. 30, 1838–Feb. 6, 1921); b. Windham, Me. Educator, lecturer, author. *Women in American Society* (1873); *Browsing among Books, and Other Essays* (1881); *George Eliot and Her Heroines* (1886); *With Garlands Green* (poems, 1915); etc.

WOOLSON, CONSTANCE FENIMORE (Mar. 1840–Jan. 24, 1894); b. Claremont, N.H., grandniece of James Fenimore Cooper. Novelist. Pen name "Anne March." *The Old Stone House* (1873); *Castle Nowhere: Lake-Country Sketches* (1875); *Two Women: 1862* (poem, 1877); *Rodman the Keeper: Southern Sketches* (1880); *Anne* (1882); *For the Major* (1883); *East Angels* (1886); *Jupiter Lights* (1889); *Horace Chase* (1894); *The Front Yard, and Other Italian Stories* (1895); *Dorothy* (1896); etc. *See* John Dwight Kern's *Constance Fenimore Woolson* (1934).

WOON, BASIL [Dillon] (1893–). Author. *The Real Sarah Bernhardt* (1925); *The Paris That's Not in the Guide Books* (1926); *The Frantic Atlantic* (1927); *Incredible Land* (1933); *San Francisco and the Golden Empire* (1935); *Atlantic Front: The Merchant Navy in the War* (1941); etc. Compiler: *The Current Publishing Scene* (1952).

WORCESTER, DONALD EMMET (Apr. 29, 1915–); b. Tempe, Ariz. Educator, author. *The Interior Provinces of New Spain, 1786* (1951); *The Growth and Culture of Latin America* (with Wendell G. Schaeffer, 1956); *Sea Power and Chilean Independence* (1962); *The Three Worlds of Latin America* (1963); *American Civilization* (with Maurice Boyd, 1964); *Man and Civilization* (with others, 1965); *Makers of Latin America* (1966). Prof. history, Texas Christian University, since 1963.

WORCESTER, JOSEPH EMERSON (Aug. 24, 1784–Oct. 27, 1865); b. Bedford, N.H. Lexicographer, geographer, historian. *A Comprehensive Pronouncing and Explanatory Dictionary of the English Language* (1830); *A Universal and Critical Dictionary of the English Language* (1846); *A Dictionary of the English Language* (1860); etc.

Worcester Gazette. Worcester, Mass. Newspaper. The *Worcester Transcript*, founded 1801; the *Worcester Daily Transcript*, established 1845. Richard C. Steele, publisher, also publishes the *Worcester Telegram*, founded 1884, as a morning paper. The *Gazette* appears evenings, except Sunday. Forrest W. Seymour is editor. Sunday book-review editor is Ivan Sandrof.

Worcester Telegram. See *Worcester Gazette.*

WORDEN, HELEN (Mrs. W. H. H. Cranmer); (July 12, 1896–); b. Denver, Colo. Journalist, author. *The Real New York* (1932); *Round Manhattan's Rim* (1934); *Society Circus* (1937); *Here is New York* (1939); *Discover New York* (1943); *Out of This World* (1953). With the *New York World* and the *World-Telegram*, 1931–44.

WORDEN, [J.] PERRY (May 25, 1866–Mar. 20, 1945); b. Hastings-on-Hudson, N.Y. Lecturer, author. *Delft and Delft Ware* (1900); *Stories and Legends of the Rhine and the Neckar* (1910); *California of Yesterday* (1916); etc.

WORK, HENRY CLAY (Oct. 1, 1832–June 8, 1884); b. Middletown, Conn. Song-writer, author. *The Upshot Family* (1868). His best-known songs are "Marching through Georgia" (1865); "Kingdom Coming" (1861); also known as "De Year ob Jubilo";"Babylon Is Fallen!" (1863); "Wake, Nicodemus!" (1864); "Grandfather's Clock"; "The Ship That Never Return'd"; "Come Home, Father!" (1864).

Workers, The. By Walter A. Wychoff, 2v. (1897–98). These remarkable personal reminiscences describe the experiences of a young college graduate who, in order to solve for himself some of the social problems of the day, goes out into the world as a day laborer.

Working with Hands. By Booker T. Washington (1904). Sequel to his *Up from Slavery.*

WORKMAN, FANNY BULLOCK (Mrs. W. Hunter Workman) (Jan. 8, 1859–Jan. 22, 1925); b. Worcester, Mass. Explorer, author. *In the Ice World of Himalaya* (with husband, 1900); *Peaks and Glaciers of Nun-Kun* (with same, 1909); and other books of travel and exploration.

WORKMAN, W[illiam] HUNTER (Feb. 16, 1847–Oct. 7, 1937); b. Worcester, Mass. Explorer, author. *In the Ice World of Himalaya* (with wife, Fanny Bullock Workman, 1900); *Peaks and Glaciers of Nun-Kun* (with same, 1909); and other books of travel and exploration.

World Almanac & Book of Facts. New York. Founded by the *New York World*, 1868. Published annually since that date. Standard yearbook of statistics, world events, personalities, and miscellaneous information.

World Book Encyclopedia, The. Ed. by Michael Vincent O'Shea and others, 19v. (1933). First published as *The World Book*, 8v. (1917); revised in 10v. (1919); and in 13v. (1929–30). A standard juvenile encyclopedia, illustrated. *The World Book Encyclopedia Annual* has been published since 1931.

World Enough and Time. Novel by R. P. Warren (1950). About a famous crime, the Beauchamp case, also known as the Kentucky Tragedy.

World I Never Made, A. Novel by James T. Farrell (1936).

World Publishing Company, The. Cleveland, New York. Founded 1905, by Alfred Cahen, as the Commercial Book Bindery. Produced millions of books for premium distribution by newspapers and mail-order concerns. Tower Books, reprints, were launched in 1940; later Rainbow Classics and Living Library were brought out. Has operated Meridian Books, Inc., founded 1955, as a wholly owned subsidiary since 1960. Acquired by the Times-Mirror Co. (q.v.) in 1963.

World's Best Literature. See *Library of the World's Best Literature.*

World's Work. New York. Monthly record of current events. Founded 1901 by Walter Hines Page. Absorbed 1932 by the *Review of Reviews.*

WORMELEY, KATHARINE PRESCOTT (Jan. 14, 1830–Aug. 4, 1908); b. Ipswich, Eng. *The United States Sanitary Commission* (1863); *The Other Side of War* (1889); *A Memoir of Honoré de Balzac* (1892); *The Cruel Side of War* (1898).

Wormeley, Mary Elizabeth. See Mary Elizabeth Wormeley Latimer.

Wormwood Review. Storrs, Conn.; Stockton, Cal. Quarterly. Founded 1959. Literary magazine, devoted to experimental writing.

Worth, Nicholas. Pen name of Walter Hines Page.

WORTHINGTON, MARJORIE b. New York. Author. *The House on the Park* (1946); *The Enchanted Heart* (1949); *Miss Alcott of Concord* (1958); *Abelard and Heloise* (1960); *The Strange World of Willie Seabrook* (1966); etc.

WORTS, GEORGE FRANK (Mar. 16, 1892–); b. Toledo, O. Author. Pen name, "Loring Brent." *Peter the Brazen* (1919); *The Return of George Washington* (1932); *Greenfield Mystery* (1934); *The Phantom President* (1934); *The Blue Lacquer Box* (1939); *Dangerous Young Man* (1940); *Laughing Girl* (1941); *Overboard* (1943); *Five Who Vanished* (1945).

WOTHERSPOON, MARION FOSTER (Aug. 31, 1863–May 15, 1944); b. Northampton, Mass. Author. *Every Day Essays* (1904); *Study of Child Life* (1907); *The House on the North Shore* (1909); *Old Fashioned Fairy Tales* (1909); *A Search for a Happy Country* (1940); etc.

WOUK, HERMAN (May 27, 1915–); b. New York. Author. *Aurora Dawn* (1947); *The City Boy* (1948); *The Traitor* (play, 1949); *The Caine Mutiny* (1951; Pulitzer Prize for fiction, 1952); *The Caine Mutiny Court-Martial* (prod. 1953); *Marjorie Morningstar* (1955); *Nature's Way* (Play, 1958); *This Is My God* (1959); *Youngblood Hawke* (1962); *Don't Stop the Carnival* (1965); *The Winds of War* (1971).

Wound and the Bow, The. Collection of critical essays by Edmund Wilson (1941).

Wound Dresser, The. Letters and memoranda of Walt Whitman published by R. M. Bucke.

"Wreck of the Hesperus, The." Poem by Henry W. Longfellow (1841).

"Wreck of the Old 97." Ballad claimed to have been written by David Graves George (1903).

WREDEN, NICHOLAS (Nov. 30, 1901–Aug. 6, 1955); b. St. Petersburg, Rus. Editor, translator, author. *The Unmaking of a Russian* (1935). Translator: *The Fifth Seal* (1943), and other novels by Mark Aldanov; also other books by Russian writers. Head, Scribner Bookstore, New York, 1939–44; director, Charles Scribner's Sons, 1941–44. Editor-in-chief, E. P. Dutton and Co., 1944–54; Little, Brown and Co., from 1954.

WRIGHT, CARROLL DAVIDSON (July 25, 1840–Feb. 20, 1909); b. Dunbarton, N.H. Statistician, social economist, author. *The Industrial Evolution of the United States* (1895); *Outline of Practical Sociology* (1899).

WRIGHT, CATHARINE [Morris] (Mrs. Sidney Longstreth Wright) (Jan. 20, 1899–); b. Philadelphia, Pa. Artist, author. *The Simple Nun* (poems, 1929); *Seaweed Their Pasture* (poem, 1946); *The Color of Life* (autobiography, 1957); etc.

WRIGHT, C[harles] **H**[enry] **C**[onrad] (Nov. 16, 1869–May 16, 1957); b. Chicago, Ill. Editor, educator, author. *A History of the Third French Republic* (1916); *French Classicism* (1920); *A History of French Literature* (1925); *The Background of Modern French Literature* (1926). Editor of many college texts in French. French dept., Harvard University, 1895–1936, prof., 1913–36.

WRIGHT, CHARLES [Stevenson] (June 4, 1932–); b. New Franklin, Mo. Author. *The Messenger* (1963); *The Wig* (1966).

WRIGHT, ERNEST HUNTER (Mar. 20, 1882–Dec. 20, 1968); b. Lynchburg, Va. Educator, author. *The Authorship of Timon of Athens* (1910); *The Meaning of Rousseau* (1929). Editor-in-chief: *The Richards Cyclopedia* (1933). English dept., Columbia University, from 1910.

WRIGHT, FRANCES (Sept. 6, 1795–Dec. 13, 1852); b. Dundee, Scot. Reformer, editor, author. *Altorf* (prod. 1819); *Views of Society and Manners in America* (1821); *Course of Popular Lectures,* 2 series (1829, 1836). Co-editor, *New Harmony Gazette,* 1828.

WRIGHT, FRANK LLOYD (June 8, 1869–Apr. 9, 1959); b. Richland Center, Wis. Architect, author. *Modern Architecture* (1931); *The Disappearing City* (1932); *An Autobiography* (1932); *Architecture and Modern Life* (1937); *Organic*

Architecture: Frank Lloyd Wright on Architecture, ed. by Frederick Gutheim (1941); *Genius and the Mobocracy* (1949); *The Natural House* (1954); *American Architecture* (1955); *The Future of Architecture* (1955); *The Story of the Tower* (1956); *Testament* (1957); *Living City* (1958); *Drawings for a Living Architecture* (1959); etc.

WRIGHT, GEORGE FREDERICK (Jan. 22, 1838–Apr. 20, 1921); b. Whitehall, N.Y. Congregational clergyman, geologist, author. *The Ice Age in North America* (1889); *Story of My Life and Work* (1916); etc.

WRIGHT, GRANT (Sept. 1, 1865–Oct. 20, 1935); b. Decatur, Mich. Illustrator. *Art of Caricature* (1904); etc.

WRIGHT, HAROLD BELL (May 4, 1872–May 24, 1944); b. Rome, N.Y. Novelist. *That Printer of Udell's* (1903); *The Shepherd of the Hills* (1907); *The Calling of Dan Mathews* (1909); *The Uncrowned King* (1910); *The Winning of Barbara Worth* (1911); *Their Yesterdays* (1912); *The Eyes of the World* (1914); *When a Man's a Man* (1916); *The Re-Creation of Brian Kent* (1919); *Helen of the Old House* (1921); *The Mine with the Iron Door* (1923); *A Son of His Father* (1925); *Exit* (1930); *To My Sons* (1934); *The Man Who Went Away* (1942); etc.

WRIGHT, HELEN (Dec. 20, 1914–); b. Washington, D.C. Astronomer, author. *Sweeper in the Sky: The First Woman Astronomer in America* (1949); *Palomar, the World's Largest Telescope* (1952); *A New Treasury of Science* (1965); *Explorer of the Universe: A Biography of George Ellery Hale* (1966). Editor of numerous popular works on science.

WRIGHT, HELEN S[aunders Smith] (Feb. 9, 1874–); b. Washington, D.C. Author. *The Great White North* (1910); *Valley of Lebanon* (1916); *The Seventh Continent* (1917); *Voices of the Wind* (poems, 1930).

WRIGHT, HENRIETTA CHRISTIAN (d. 1899). Author. *Children's Stories in English Literature* (1889); *Children's Stories in American Literature* (1899); *Children's Stories of American Progress* (1906); *Children's Stories of the Great Scientists* (1906); etc.

WRIGHT, HERBERT F[rancis] (Mar. 28, 1892–Apr. 12, 1945); b. Washington, D.C. Lawyer, author. *Biography of Philander Chase Knox* (1929); *Catholic Founders of International Law* (1934); etc. Editor: *The Constitutions of the States at War* (1919); etc.

WRIGHT, IRENE ALOHA (Dec. 19, 1879–); b. Lake City, Colo. Author. *Cuba* (1910); *Isle of Pines* (1910); *Santiago de Cuba and Its District* (1918); *History of Havana in the 16th Century* (1927); *History of Havana in the 17th Century* (1930); *English Voyages to the Spanish Main, 1569–1580* (1932). Editor and translator: *Further English Voyages to Spanish America, 1583–1594* (1951).

WRIGHT, JAMES [Arlington] (1927–); b. Martin's Ferry, O. Poet. *The Green Wall* (Yale Series of Younger Poets, 1957); *Saint Judas* (1959); *The Lion's Tail and Eyes* (1962); *The Branch Will Not Break* (1963); *Shall We Gather at the River?* (1968). Faculty, Hunter College.

WRIGHT, JOHN HENRY (Feb. 4, 1852–Nov. 25, 1908); b. in Persia. Educator, editor. Editor: *A History of All Nations,* 24v. (1902). Editor, the *American Journal of Archaeology,* 1897–1906; assoc. editor, the *Classical Review,* 1888–1906; the *Classical Quarterly,* 1907–08. Prof. Greek, Dartmouth College, 1878–86; with American School of Classical Studies, Athens, 1906–07; Harvard University, 1908. He was the husband of Mary Tappan Wright.

WRIGHT, JOHN KIRTLAND (Nov. 30, 1891–Mar. 24, 1969); b. Cambridge, Mass. Geographer, author. *Aids to Geographical Research* (1923); *The Geographical Lore of the Time of the Crusaders* (1925); *New England's Prospect* (with others, 1933); *Geography in the Making* (1952). Librarian,

American Geographical Society, 1920–37; director, from 1938.

WRIGHT, JULIA McNAIR (May 1, 1840–Sept. 2, 1903); b. Oswego, N.Y. Author. *The Best Fellow in the World* (1871); *Saints and Sinners* (1873); *Bricks from Babel* (1876); *A Wife Hard Won* (1882); etc. See Edmund Pearson's *Queer Books* (1928).

WRIGHT, LOUIS BOOKER (Mar. 1, 1899–); b. in Greenwood Co., S.C. Educator, author. *Middle-Class Culture in Elizabethan England* (1935); *Puritans in the South Seas* (with Mary Isabel Fry, 1936); *The First Gentleman of Virginia* (1940); *Religion and Empire* (1943); *The First Americans in North Africa* (with Julia MacLeod, 1945); *The Atlantic Frontier* (1947); *Culture on the Moving Frontier* (1955); *The Cultural Life of the American Colonies* (1957); *Shakespeare for Everyman* (1964); *Dream of Prosperity in Colonial America* (1965). Editor: *Royster Memorial Studies* (1931); *The American Tradition* (with H. T. Swedenborg, 1941); *The Historie of Travell into Virginia Britania* (with Virginia Freund, 1953). Editor, *Huntington Library Quarterly*, 1945–48. Director, Folger Shakespeare Library, Washington, D.C., since 1948.

WRIGHT, MABEL OSGOOD (Jan. 26, 1859–July 21, 1934); b. New York. Author. Pen name, "Barbara." *The Friendship of Nature* (1894); *Tommy-Anne and the Three Hearts* (1896); *The Dream Fox Story Book* (1900); *Dogtown* (1902); *At the Sign of the Fox* (1905); *The Garden, You, and I* (1906); *My New York* (1926); *Eudora's Men* (1931); etc.

WRIGHT, MARCUS JOSEPH (June 5, 1831–Dec. 27, 1922); b. Purdy, Tenn. Soldier, editor, author. *Reminiscences of the Early Settlement and Early Settlers of McNairy County, Tennessee* (1882); *General Scott* (1894); *Tennessee in the War, 1861–1865* (1908); etc. Editor: *Battles and Commanders of the Civil War* (1908).

WRIGHT, MARIE ROBINSON (1866–Feb. 1, 1914); b. Newnan, Ga. Traveler, author. *Picturesque Mexico* (1897); *The New Brazil* (1901); *The Republic of Chile* (1904); and many other books on Latin America.

WRIGHT, MARY TAPPAN (Mrs. John Henry Wright) (Dec. 1851–1917); b. Steubenville, O., daughter of Eli Todd Tappan. Author. *A Truce, and Other Stories* (1895); *The Test* (1900); *Aliens* (1902); *The Tower* (1906); *Charioteers* (1912); etc.

WRIGHT, PHILIP GREEN (Oct. 3, 1861–Sept. 4, 1934); b. Boston, Mass. Economist, poet. *The Dial of the Heart* (1904); *The Dreamer* (1906); *Elizur Wright, the Father of Life Insurance* (with Elizabeth Q. Wright, 1937); also books on the tariff question.

WRIGHT, QUINCY (Dec. 28, 1890–); b. Medford, Mass. Educator. *Control of American Foreign Relations* (1922); *Mandates Under the League of Nations* (1930); *A Study of War* (1942); *The Study of International Relations* (1955); *International Law and the United Nations* (1960); *Role of International Law in the Elimination of War* (1962); *Preventing World War III: Some Proposals* (with others, 1962); *Study of War* (1964); etc. prof. international law, University of Virginia, since 1958.

WRIGHT, RICHARD (Sept. 4, 1908–Nov. 28, 1960); b. near Natchez, Miss. Author. *Uncle Tom's Children* (1938); *Native Son* (1940); *Twelve Million Black Voices* (1941); *Black Boy* (1945); *The Outsider* (1953); *Black Power* (1954); *The Color Curtain* (1956); *Pagan Spain* (1957); *White Man, Listen* (1957); *The Long Dream* (1958); *Eight Men* (1961); *Lawd Today* (1963); etc. See James Baldwin's *Nobody Knows My Name* (1961); Constance Webb's *Richard Wright* (1968).

WRIGHT, RICHARD ROBERT, Jr. (Apr. 16, 1878–Dec. 12, 1967); b. Cuthbert, Ga. Methodist bishop, editor, author. *The Teachings of Jesus* (1903); *The Negro in Pennsylvania* (1911); *Social Service* (1922); *My Church* (1944). Editor: *Po-*

ems of Phillis Wheatley (1909); *The Mission Study Course* (1943). Editor, the *Christian Recorder*, Philadelphia, 1909–36.

WRIGHT, RICHARDSON LITTLE (June 18, 1886–Aug. 6, 1961); b. Philadelphia, Pa. Editor, author. *Through Siberia* (1913); *The Open Door* (1914); *Feodor Vladmir Larrovitch* (with W. G. Jordan, 1918); *Hawkers and Walkers in Early America* (1927); *Forgotten Ladies* (1928); *The Bed-Book of Travel* (1931); *The Story of Gardening* (1934); *Revels in Jamaica* (1937); *Grandfather Was Queer* (1939); *The Bed-Book of Eating and Drinking* (1943); *Anatomy of Saints* (1946); *Gardener's Tribute* (1949); *Book of Days for Christmas* (1951); *Greedy Gardeners* (1955); and many books on houses and gardens. Editor, *House and Garden*, from 1914.

WRIGHT, ROBERT WILLIAM (Feb. 22, 1816–Jan. 9, 1885); b. Ludlow, Vt. Editor, author. *The Poetry and Poets of Connecticut* (1872); *Life: Its True Genesis* (1880); also several political satires. Editor, between 1856 and 1877, of the *Waterbury Journal*, the *Hartford Daily Post*, the *New Haven Daily News*, the *New York Daily News*, the *New Haven Daily Lever*, the *Richmond* (Va.) *Daily State Journal*, and the *New Haven Daily Register*.

WRIGHT, WILLARD HUNTINGTON (1888–Apr. 11, 1939); b. Charlottesville, Va. Editor, author. Pen name "S. S. Van Dine." Under own name: *Songs of Youth* (1913); *Modern Painting: Its Tendency and Meaning* (1915); *The Man of Promise* (1916); *The Creative Will* (1916); *The Future of Painting* (1923); *Modern Literature* (1926); etc. Under pen name: *The Benson Murder Case* (1926); *The Canary Murder Case* (1927); *The Greene Murder Case* (1928); *The Bishop Murder Case* (1929); *The Scarlet Murder Case* (1930); *The Kennel Murder Case* (1932); *The Dragon Murder Case* (1933); *The Casino Murder Case* (1934); *The Garden Murder Case* (1935); *The Kidnap Murder Case* (1936); *Philo Vance Murder Cases* (1936); *The Gracie Allen Murder Case* (1938); etc. Lit. critic, *Town Topics*, 1910–14; editor, *Smart Set*, 1912–14; art critic, *Hearst's International Magazine*, 1922–23.

WRIGHT, WILLIAM KELLEY (Apr. 18, 1877–Mar. 29, 1956); b. Canton, Ill. Educator, philosopher, author. *Ethical Significance of Feeling, Pleasure, and Happiness* (1907); *A Student's Philosophy of Religion* (1922); *General Introduction to Ethics* (1929); *A History of Modern Philosophy* (1941); etc. Philosophy dept., Dartmouth College, 1916–47.

WRISTON, HENRY MERRITT (July 4, 1889–); b. Laramie, Wyo. Educator, author. *The Nature of a Liberal College* (1937); *Challenge to Freedom* (1943); *Strategy of Peace* (1944); *Wriston Speaking* (1957); *Academic Procession: Reflections of a College President* (1959); *Perspectives on Policy* (1963); etc. Pres., Brown University, 1937–55.

Writer, The. Boston, Mass. Monthly. Founded 1887, by Robert Luce and William Hills. Magazine for professional writers. A. S. Burack has been editor since 1935. Publishes *The Writer's Handbook*. See the April, 1962, Diamond Anniversary number, featuring articles by Anya Seton, Richard Armour, Faith Baldwin, Sloan Wilson, John Holmes, William E. Barrett, and others.

Writer's Digest. Cincinnati, Ohio. Monthly. Founded 1920. Magazine for writers. Publishes *The Writer's Market* and *The Writer's Year Book* annually.

Writer's Monthly. Springfield, Mass. Founded 1912. Editor, J. B. Esenwein. Discontinued 1951.

Writings on American History. Washington, D.C. Founded 1906. An annual bibliography and index to all books and articles on American and Canadian history. Compiled by Grace Gardner Griffin.

WRONG, DENNIS HUME (Nov. 22, 1923–); b. Toronto, Ca. Sociologist, author. *American and Canadian Viewpoints*

(1955); *Population and Society* (1961). Graduate faculty, New School for Social Research, 1961–63; prof. sociology, New York University, since 1966.

WROTH, LAWRENCE C[ounselman] (Jan. 14, 1884–Dec. 25, 1970); b. Baltimore, Md. Librarian, bibliographer, author. *Parson Weems* (1911); *A History of Printing in Colonial Maryland* (1922); *Abel Buell of Connecticut* (1926); *William Parks* (1926); *The Colonial Printer* (1931); *An American Bookshelf, 1755* (1934); *Roger Williams* (1937); *The Way of a Ship* (1937); *The Book in America* (with H. Lehmann-Haupt and Ruth S. Granniss, 1939); *Early Cartography of the Pacific* (1944); *Typographic Heritage* (1949); *Abel Buell of Connecticut: Silversmith, Type Founder and Engraver* (1958); *Colonial Printer* (1964); etc. Editor: *A History of the Printed Book* (1938). Asst. librarian, Enoch Pratt Free Library, Baltimore, 1912–23; librarian, John Carter Brown Library, Providence, R.I., since 1923, and editor of v. 3 of its catalogue. Writer of "Notes for Bibliophiles" for the *New York Herald Tribune Books,* succeeding Leonard Mackall in 1937.

WURDEMANN, AUDREY (Mrs. Joseph Auslander) (Jan. 1, 1911–May 19, 1960); b. Seattle, Wash. Poet. *The House of Silk* (1927); *Bright Ambush* (1934, Pulitzer Prize for poetry, 1935); *The Seven Sins* (1935); *Splendour in the Grass* (1936); *Testament of Love: A Sonnet Sequence* (1938); *My Uncle Jan* (with husband, 1948); *Islanders* (with husband, 1951).

Wurdz, Gideon. Pen name of Charles Wayland Towne.

WYATT, EDITH FRANKLIN (Sept. 14, 1873–Oct., 1958); b. Tomah, Wis. Author. *Every One His Own Way* (1901); *True Love* (1903); *Great Companions* (1917); *The Wind in the Corn, and Other Poems* (1917); *The Satyr's Children* (1939); etc.

Wycliffe, John. Pen name of H. Bedford-Jones.

WYDEN, PETER H. (Oct. 2, 1923–); b. Berlin, Ger. Editor, author. *Suburbia's Coddled Kids* (1961); *The Hired Killers* (1962); *The Overweight Society* (1965). Executive editor, *Ladies Home Journal,* since 1965.

WYER, JAMES INGERSOLL (May 14, 1869–Nov. 1, 1955); b. Red Wing, Minn. Librarian, author. *The College and University Library* (1921); *Reference Work* (1930); etc. Compiler: *The Bibliography of the Study and Teaching of History* (1900); *Annual Bibliography of Education,* 1899–1907. Librarian, University of Nebraska, 1898–1905. Director, New York State Library School, 1908–26; director, New York State Library, 1908–38.

WYETH, N[ewell] C[onvers] (Oct. 22, 1882–Oct. 19, 1945); b. Needham, Mass. Artist, illustrator, editor. Editor: *Marauders of the Sea* (1935); *Great Stories of the Sea & Ships* (1940). Besides his well-known murals, Wyeth is known for his illustrations, notably for the volumes of *Scribner's Juvenile Classics.* Illustrator: Rawlings' *The Yearling;* Baldwin's *Sampo;* Boyd's *Drums;* Creswide's *Robin Hood;* Cooper's *Deerslayer;* Bulfinch's *Legends of Charlemagne;* Defoe's *Robinson Crusoe;* Homer's *Odyssey;* Irving's *Rip Van Winkle;* Kingsley's *Westward Ho!* Malory's *Boys' King Arthur;* Stevenson's *Treasure Island;* Verne's *Michael Strogoff;* etc.

WYLIE, ANDREW (Apr. 12, 1789–Nov. 11, 1851); b. Washington, Pa. Episcopal clergyman, educator, author. *The Uses of History* (1831); *An Eulogy of General Lafayette* (1835); etc. President, Indiana University, 1812–28.

WYLIE, ELINOR [Hoyt] (Mrs. William Rose Benét) (Sept. 7, 1885–Dec. 16, 1928); b. Somerville, N.J. Poet, novelist. *Incidental Numbers* (poems, anon., 1912); *Nets to Catch the Wind* (poems, 1921); *Black Armour* (poems, 1923); *Jennifer Lorn* (1923); *The Venetian Glass Nephew* (1925); *The Orphan Angel* (1926); *Trivial Breath* (1928); *Mr. Hodge & Mr. Hazard* (1928); *Angels and Earthly Creatures* (poems, 1929); *Collected Poems* (1932); *Collected Prose* (1933); *The Novels* (1934). *See* Nancy Hoyt's *Elinor Wylie* (1935); Fred B. Millett's *Contemporary American Authors* (1940).

WYLIE, MAX (May 12, 1904–); b. Beverly, Mass. Author. *Hindu Heaven* (1933); *Radio Writing* (1939); *Go Home and Tell Your Mother* (1950); *Clear Channels* (1955); *Trouble in the Flesh* (1959); *Never the Twain* (1961); *Juvenile Crime and Open Hearings* (1966); *Delinquency Can Be Stopped* (1967); etc.

WYLIE, PHILIP GORDON (May 12, 1902–1971); b. Beverly, Mass. Author. *Heavy Laden* (1928); *Babes and Sucklings* (1929); *Footprint of Cinderella* (1931); *Finnley Wren* (1934); *The Golden Hoard* (1934); *The Shield of Silence* (1936); *An April Afternoon* (1938); *The Big Ones Get Away* (1940); *Salt Water Daffy* (1941); *The Other Horseman* (1942); *A Generation of Vipers* (1942); *Night Unto Night* (1944); *An Essay on Morals* (1947); *The Best of Crunch and Des* (1955); *The Answer* (1956); *The Innocent Ambassadors* (1957); *Triumph* (1963); *They Both Were Naked* (1965); *The Magic Animal* (1968); etc.

WYMAN, LEVI PARKER (July 12, 1873–Apr. 16, 1950); b. Skowhegan, Me. Educator, chemist, author. The *Golden Boys* series, 9v. (1920); the *Lakewood Boys* series, 5v. (1924); the *Hunniwell Boys* series, 7v. (1929–30); *Donald Price's Victory* (1930); *The Mystery of Eagle Lake* (1931); *After Many Years* (1941); etc. Prof. chemistry, Pennsylvania Military College, Chester, Pa., from 1905; dean, 1920–43.

WYMAN, LILLIE BUFFUM CHACE (Mrs. John C. Wyman) (Dec. 10, 1847–Jan. 10, 1929); b. Valley Falls, R.I. Author. *American Chivalry* (1913); *Gertrude of Denmark* (1924); *Syringa at the Gate* (poems, 1926).

WYMAN, SETH (Mar. 4, 1784–Apr. 2, 1843); b. Goffstown, N.H. Burglar, author. *The Life and Adventures of Seth Wyman: Embodying the Principal Events of a Life Spent in Robbery, Theft, Gambling* (1843).

WYN, AARON ARTHUR (May 22, 1898–); b. New York. Publisher. Pres., A. A. Wyn.

"Wynken, Blynken and Nod." Poem by Eugene Field (1889).

WYSE, LOIS HELENE (Oct. 30, 1926–); b. Cleveland, O. Advertising executive, author. *The I Don't Want to Go to Bed Book for Boys* (1963); *The I Don't Want to Go to Bed Book for Girls* (1963); *The Absolute Truth About Marriage* (1964); *What Kind of Girl Are You, Anyway?* (1965); *P.S. Happy Anniversary* (1966); *The Compleat Child* (1966); *Help! I am the Mother of a Teen-aged Girl* (1967); *Grandfathers Are to Love* (1967); *Love Poems for the Very Married* (1967); *Are You Sure You Love Me?* (1969); *I Love You Better Now* (1970).

X

X Bar X Boys. Popular juvenile series for boys by James Cody Ferris.

Xariffa. Pen name of Mary Ashley Townsend.

Xerox Corp. New York. The Xerox Educational Division, the publishing branch of the corporation, now owns R. R. Bowker Co., Jacques Cattell Press, Ginn & Co., and other concerns. Acquired Wesleyan University Press and University Microfilms in 1965.

Ximena. First volume of verse by Bayard Taylor (1844).

Xingu. Short story by Edith Wharton, which first appeared in *Scribner's Magazine,* Dec., 1911. Satire on a pseudointellectual woman's club.

Y

"Yachts, The." Poem by William Carlos Williams.

Yaddo. Colony for artists at the Trask estate, Saratoga, N.Y.

YALE, ELIHU (Apr. 5, 1649–July 8, 1721); b. Boston, Mass. Official of East India Company. Yale College was named in his honor in 1718. *See* Hiram Bingham's *Elihu Yale, the American Nabob of Queen Square* (1999, i.e., 1939).

Yale Review. New Haven, Conn. Quarterly. Founded 1911. Editors: Wilbur L. Cross, 1911–39; William C. DeVane, Edgar S. Furniss, Arnold Wolfers, J. E. Palmer, and others since 1940.

Yale University Press. New Haven, Conn. Founded 1908, by George Parmly Day. *See* Clarence Day's *The Story of the Yale University Press Told by a Friend* (anon., 1920).

Yamoyden: A Tale of the Wars of King Philip. Poem by Charles Robert Sands (1820). Based on the life of King Philip, the Indian chief. It was begun in joint authorship with James Eastburn, who died before the poem was completed.

Yank. Weekly newspaper published by the United States Army during World War II. Founded 1942. Edited largely in New York. Noted for the literary quality of its contributions. Its managing editor, Joe McCarthy, was primarily responsible for its distinctiveness. Expired 1945.

Yankee Blade. Waterville, Me. Magazine. Founded 1841, by William Matthews as *The Watervillonian.* It was later moved to Gardiner, Me., and then to Boston. Merged with the *Port Folio* in 1856. Revived in 1862 as *Harry Hazel's Yankee Blade,* it expired in 1894.

"Yankee Doodle." A skit sung by the British soldiers in America prior to the American Revolution, which poked fun at the provincial militia. Its catchy tune made it popular and new stanzas were added to it and its development followed the usual pattern of folk balladry. Our native humor began with this song. Yankee Doodle became the prototype of many humorous characters. *See* O. G. T. Sonneck's *Report on the Star-Spangled Banner, Hail Columbia, America, Yankee Doodle* (1909), and John Tasker Howard's *Our American Music* (1939).

Yankee Notions. New York. Comic magazine. Founded 1852 by a comic-valentine printer, T. W. Strong. Some of the leading humorists wrote for it. Expired 1875.

Yankey in England, The. Play by David Humphreys (1815). In order to make this play intelligible to English audiences Humphreys added a glossary of Americanisms. See *Dialect Notes,* v. 5, 1926.

YARD, ROBERT STERLING (Feb. 1, 1861–May, 1945); b. Haverstraw, N.Y. Editor, publisher, author. *The Publisher* (1915); *Glimpses of Our National Parks* (1916); *The Top of the Continent* (1917); *The Book of the National Parks* (1919); *Our Federal Lands* (1928); etc. Founder (with William David Moffat), Moffat, Yard & Co., publishers, 1905; editor-in-chief, 1905–11. Editor, *The Lamp,* 1903–05, a magazine published by Charles Scribner's Sons. Organizer and general secretary, National Parks Association, 1919–34.

YARDLEY, HERBERT O[sborn] (Apr. 13, 1889–1958); b. Worthington, Ind. Author. *The American Black Chamber* (1931); *The Blonde Countess* (1934); *Red Sun of Nippon* (1934); *Crows Are Black Everywhere* (with C. H. Grabo, 1945); *The Education of a Poker Player* (1957).

YARMOLINSKY, AVRAHM (Jan. 1, 1890–); b. in Russia. Librarian, author. *Turgenev: The Man, His Art, and His Age* (1926); *Russian Literature* (1931); *Dostoevsky: A Life* (1934); *Russian Americana* (1943); *Road to Revolution* (1957); *More*

Tales of Faraway Folk (1963); *The Russian Literary Imagination* (1969); etc. Editor and translator: *Modern Russian Poetry* (with wife, Babette Deutsch, 1921); *Contemporary German Poetry* (with same, 1923). Editor: *The Works of Alexander Pushkin* (1936); *Early Polish Americana* (1937); *Eugene Onegin* (1943); *The Idiot* (1956); etc. Chief of Slavonic division, New York Public Library, 1918–55.

Yarmolinsky, Mrs. Avrahm. *See* Babette Deutsch.

YATES, ELIZABETH (Mrs. William McGreal) (Dec. 6, 1905–); b. Buffalo, N.Y. Author. *High Holiday* (1938); *Quest in the Northland* (1940); *Patterns on the Wall* (1943); *Wind of Spring* (1945); *Once in the Year* (1947); *Guardian Heart* (1950); *Hue and Cry* (1953); *Rainbow Round the World* (1954); *Pebble in a Pool: The Widening Circles of Dorothy Canfield Fisher's Life* (1958); *The Lighted Heart* (autobiography, 1960); *Sir Gibbie* (1962); *With Pipe, Paddle and Song* (1968); *On That Night* (1969); etc.

YATES, KATHERINE MERRITTE (b. 1865); b. Drumbo, Ont. Author of children's books. *What the Pine Tree Heard* (1903); *Through the Woods* (1906); *"Chat"* (1909); *Tales from the Rainbow Land* (1914); *On the Hill-Top* (1919); *In the Valley* (1922); etc.

YATES, RICHARD (Feb. 3, 1926–). Author. *Revolutionary Road* (1961); *Eleven Kinds of Loneliness* (stories, 1962). Editor: *Stories for the Sixties* (1963).

YAUKEY, GRACE SYDENSTRICKER (May 12, 1899–); b. Chinkiang, China, sister of Pearl Buck. Author. Writers under pen name "Cornelia Spencer." *Three Sisters: The Story of the Soong Family of China* (1939); *China Trader* (1940); *Made in China* (1943); *Made in India* (1946); *The Missionary* (1947); *Understanding the Japanese* (1949); *Romulo, Voice of Freedom* (1953); *More Hands for Man* (1960); *Claim to Freedom: The Rise of the Afro-Asian Peoples* (1961); etc.

YEAGER, DORR G[raves] (June 23, 1902–); b. Gilman, Ia. Naturalist, author. *Our Wilderness Neighbors* (1931); *Bob Flame: Ranger* (1933); *Bob Flame in Death Valley* (1937); *Chita* (1939); *Grey Dawn, the Wolf Dog* (1942); *Bob Flame Among the Navajo* (1946); *National Parks in California* (1959; rev. ed., 1969).

Year of Decision: 1846, The. By Bernard De Voto (1943).

Yearling, The. Novel by Marjorie Kinnan Rawlings (1938). Story of the boy Jody, son of Penny Baxter, a poor Florida backwoods farmer. Jody's pet fawn plays an important part in the story, adding poignancy to this rural classic which was awarded the Pulitzer Prize in 1939. (Pulitzer Prize, 1931.)

Years of Grace. Novel by Margaret Ayer Barnes (1930). A story with a Chicago background (Pulitzer Prize, 1931).

Yechton, Barbara. Pen name of Lyda Farrington Krause.

Yehoash. Pen name of Solomon Bloomgarden.

Yekl: A Tale of the New York Ghetto. By Abraham Cahan (1896). A novel of Jewish life in the New York Ghetto. Yekl worked in a sweatshop in Pitt Street. Israel Zangwill called Yekl the first real Jew in American fiction.

Yellow Jack. Play by Sidney Howard and Paul De Kruif (prod. 1934). Based on a chapter in De Kruif's *Microbe Hunters.* It gives a dramatic picture of medicine's fight to isolate the typhoid germ. The locale is Cuba.

Yellow Jacket, The. Play by George C. Hazelton and J. G. Benrimo (prod. 1912).

"Yellow Kid." Comic character created by the cartoonist, R. F. Outcault, in the *New York World* (1896). The comic strip was first called "Hogan's Alley." Outcault left the *World* for the *New York Journal* and continued the cartoon. George B. Luks drew a "Yellow Kid" for the *World* in competition, and "Yellow Kid" posters were used everywhere for advertising purposes, leading to the coinage of the opprobrious terms "Yellow Press" and "Yellow Journalism."

Yemassee, The. Novel by William Gilmore Simms (1835). Romance of South Carolina as revealed in the history of the Yemassee tribe of Indians.

YENDES, LUCY A. (b. Jan. 31, 1851); b. Champion, N.Y. Author. *Preston Papers* (1882); *Miss Preston's Leaven* (1895); *What Shall I Do?* (with J. S. Stoddard, 1899); etc.

YENNI, JULIA TRUIT (Mrs. Charles R. Hikes); (Feb. 21, 1913–); b. Birmingham, Ala. Novelist. *Never Say Goodbye* (1937); *This Is Me, Kathie* (1938); *House for the Sparrows* (1942); *The Spellbound Village* (1951).

YERBY, FRANK [GARVIN] (Sept. 5, 1916–); b. Augusta, Ga. Novelist. *The Foxes of Harrow* (1946); *The Vixens* (1947); *The Golden Hawk* (1948); *Pride's Castle* (1949); *Floodtide* (1950); *A Woman Called Fancy* (1951); *The Saracen Blade* (1952); *The Devil's Laughter* (1953); *Benton's Row* (1954); *Captain Rebel* (1956); *Fair Oaks* (1957); *Jarrett's Jade* (1959); *The Garfield Honor* (1962); *Griffin's Way* (1962); *The Old Gods Laugh* (1964); *An Odor of Sanctity* (1965); *Goat Song* (1967); *Judas, My Brother* (1968); *Speak Now* (1969); etc.

Yesterdays with Authors. By James T. Fields. These studies appeared in the *Atlantic Monthly* in 1871, in a series of papers called "Our Whispering Gallery."

YEZIERSKA, ANZIA (1885–); b. in Russia. Sociologist, author. *Hungry Hearts* (1920); *Salome of the Tenements* (1922); *Children of Loneliness* (1923); *Bread Givers* (1925); *Arrogant Beggar* (1927); *All I Could Never Be* (1932); *Red Ribbon on a White Horse* (autobiography, 1950).

"Yield Not to Temptation." Popular Hymn by Horatio Richmond Palmer, which first appeared in *The Song King* (1872), under the title "Looking to Jesus."

YINGER, J[ohn] MILTON (July 25, 1916–); b. Quincy, Mich. Educator, author. *Religion in the Struggle for Power* (1946); *Racial and Cultural Minorities* (with George E. Simpson, 1953); *Religion, Society, and the Individual* (1957); *Sociology Looks at Religion* (1963); *Toward a Field Theory of Behavior* (1965); *A Minority Group in American Society* (1965). Prof. sociology, Oberlin College, since 1952.

YOAKUM, H[enderson] (Sept. 6, 1810–Nov. 30, 1856); b. Powell's Valley, Tenn. Author. *History of Texas from Its First Settlement in 1685 to Its Annexation to the United States in 1846*, 2v. (1855).

YORE, CLEM[ent] (May 6, 1875–Oct. 24, 1936); b. St. Louis, Mo. Novelist, poet. *Songs of the Underworld* (1914); *Raw Gold* (1924); *Trigger Justice* (1928); *Ranger Bill* (1931); *Sudden Slim* (1934); etc.

YOSELOFF, MARTIN (July 26, 1919–); b. Sioux City, Ia. Novelist. *No Greener Meadows* (1946); *The Family Members* (1948); *The Girl in the Spike-Heeled Shoes* (1949); *Magic Margin* (1954); *Lily and the Sergeant* (1957); *A Time to Be Young* (1967); etc.

YOSELOFF, THOMAS (Sept. 8, 1913–); b. Sioux City, Ia. Publisher. Author. *A Fellow of Infinite Jest* (1945). Editor: *Comic Almanac* (1963). Editor, translator: *Merry Adventures of Till Eulenspiegel* (with Lillian Stuckey, 1944); etc. Also books under pen name "Thomas Young." Pres., Beechhurst Press, since 1946; American History Publishing Society, since 1951; Fine Editions Club, since 1956; A. S. Barnes & Co., since 1958; Sagamore Press, since 1958.

YOST, CASPER SALATHIEL (July 1, 1864–May 30, 1941); b. Sedalia, Mo. Editor, author. *Patience Worth* (1916); etc. Joined staff of *St. Louis Globe Democrat* in 1889; Sunday editor, 1890–1915; editor of the editorial page, 1915–1941.

"You, Andrew Marvell." Poem by Archibald MacLeish (1930).

You Can't Go Home Again. Novel by Thomas Wolfe (1940), sequel to *The Web and the Rock* (1939). George Weber returns to New York from Germany and becomes a novelist. Reflects the personal upheaval of one whose home town attachments are shaken and of the cultural horror of the Third Reich in a Germany the hero had once found exhilarating.

You Know Me, Al. By Ring Lardner (1916). Humorous stories of a braggart baseball player.

Youma. Novel by Lafcadio Hearn (1890). Deals with slaves in Martinique, culminating in a remarkable picture of a slave insurrection.

YOUMANS, EDWARD LIVINGSTON (June 3, 1821–Jan. 18, 1887); b. Coeymans, N.Y., brother of William Jay Youmans. Editor, lecturer. Editor: *The Culture Demanded by Modern Life* (1867); etc. Founder, the *International Scientific Series* of books, 1871; founder, *Popular Science Monthly* (now the *Scientific Monthly*), 1872; editor, 1872–86.

YOUMANS, ELEANOR. b. St. Louis, Mo. Author. The *Skitter Cat* series, 4v. (1925–28); *Cinder* (1933); *Little Dog Mack* (1936); *The Forest Road* (1939); *Timmy, the Dog That Was Different* (1941); *Mount Delightful* (1944); etc.

YOUMANS, WILLIAM JAY (Oct. 14, 1838–Apr. 10, 1901); b. Milton, N.Y. Editor, author. *Pioneers of Science in America* (with others, 1896); etc. Editor, *Popular Science Monthly* (now the *Scientific Monthly*), 1887–1900.

Young, Agatha. Pen name of Agnes Brooks Young.

YOUNG, AGNES BROOKS (Mrs. George Benham Young) (Nov. 18, 1898–); b. Cleveland, O. Author. *Stage Costuming* (1927); *Recurring Cycles of Fashion* (1937). Under pen name "Agatha Young": *Light in the Sky* (1948); *Blaze of Glory* (1950); *Clown of the Gods* (1954); *Scalpel* (1956); *Women and the Crisis: Women of the North in the Civil War* (1959); *Men Who Made Surgery* (1961); *Manual of Statistics* (1964); *The Town and Dr. Moore* (1966); *I Swear by Apollo* (1968); etc.

YOUNG, ALEXANDER (Sept. 22, 1800–Mar. 16, 1854); b. Boston, Mass. Unitarian clergyman, historian. Editor: *Chronicles of the Pilgrim Fathers of the Colony of Plymouth, from 1602 to 1625* (1841); *Chronicles of the First Planters of the Colony of Massachusetts Bay, from 1623 to 1636* (1846); etc.

YOUNG, ALFRED (Jan. 21, 1831–Apr. 4, 1900); b. Bristol, Eng. Roman Catholic clergyman, hymn writer, leader in the movement to restore Gregorian music in America. Compiler: *The Catholic Hymnal* (1884); *Carols for a Merry Christmas and a Joyous Easter*, 2v. (1885–86); and other collections.

YOUNG, ART[hur Henry] (Jan. 14, 1866–Dec. 29, 1943); b. Orangeville, Ill. Cartoonist, author. *Trees at Night* (1927); *On My Way* (1928); *The Best of Art Young* (1936); *Art Young: His Life and Times* (1939); etc. Co-editor, *The Masses*, 1911–19; on staff, *Metropolitan Magazine*, 1912–17. Made drawings for *Life, Judge, Saturday Evening Post, Collier's*, etc.

YOUNG, BRIGHAM (June 1, 1801–Aug. 29, 1877); b. Whitingham, Vt. Mormon leader, author. *Discourses* (1925). See Frank J. Cannon and George L. Knapp's *Brigham Young and His Mormon Empire* (1913); Morris R. Werner's *Brigham Young* (1925); Susa Young Gates and Leah D. Widtsoe's *The Life Story of Brigham Young* (1930); Preston Nibley's *Brigham Young: The Man and His Work* (1936).

YOUNG, DAVID (Jan. 27, 1781–Feb. 13, 1852); b. Pine Brook, N.Y. Astronomer, almanac-maker, poet. *The Contrast* (poem, 1804); *The Perusal; or, The Book of Nature Unfolded* (1818); *The Wonderful History of the Morristown Ghost* (1826); etc. From 1814 to 1852, he was editor of various almanacs, one coming almost annually from his pen: *The*

Citizens' & Farmers' Almanac (1814); his first; *The Family Almanac; Harper's United States Almanac; Knickerbocker's Almanac; The Methodist Almanac; New York Almanac; Paul Pry's Almanac;* etc.

YOUNG, EDWARD JOSEPH (Nov. 29, 1907–); b. San Francisco. Presbyterian clergyman. Author: *The Prophecy of Daniel* (1949); *Studies in Isaiah* (1954); *The Study of Old Testament Theology Today* (1959); *Book of Isaiah,* Vol. I *(New International Commentary on the Old Testament)* (1964); etc. Prof. Old Testament, Westminster Theological Seminary, Philadelphia, since 1936.

YOUNG, FRANK CRISSEY (1844–1919); b. New York. Author. *Echoes from Arcadia* (1903); *Across the Plains in '65* (1905).

YOUNG, GORDON (Sept. 27, 1886–Feb. 10, 1948); b. in Ray Co., Mo. Author. *Savages* (1921); *Wild Blood* (1922); *Hurricane Williams* (1923); *Seibert of the Island* (1925); *Days of '49* (1925); *Treasure* (1928); *The Devil's Passport* (1933); *Red Clark of the Arrowhead* (1935); *Huroc the Avenger* (1937); *Poems in Prose* (1938); *Mr. Beamish* (1940); *Quarter Horse* (1947); etc.

YOUNG, HOWARD IRVING (Apr. 24, 1893–); b. Jersey City, N.J. Producer, playwright. *March On!* (prod. 1924); *Not Herbert* (prod. 1926); *Hawk Island* (prod. 1931); *The Drums Begin* (prod. 1933); etc.

YOUNG, JAMES CAPERS (1892–Oct. 27, 1945). Author. *Marse Robert, Knight of the Confederacy* (1929); *Liberia Rediscovered* (1934); *Roosevelt Revealed* (1936).

YOUNG, JOHN RUSSELL (Nov. 20, 1840–Jan. 17, 1899); b. in Co. Tyrone, Ireland. Journalist, diplomat, librarian, author. *Around the World with General Grant,* 2v. (1879); *Men and Memories,* 2v. (1901). With the *New York Tribune,* 1866–70; the *New York Herald,* 1872–77, 1885–90. U.S. Minister to China, 1882–85; Librarian of Congress, 1987–99.

YOUNG, JULIA EVELYN (b. Dec. 4, 1857); b. Buffalo, N.Y. Author. *Adrift: A Story of Niagara* (1889); *Black Evan* (poem, 1901); *Barham Beach* (poem, 1908); etc.

YOUNG, KARL (Nov. 2, 1879–Nov. 27, 1943); b. Clinton, Ia. Educator, author. *The Drama of the Medieval Church,* 2v. (1933); etc. English dept., University of Wisconsin, 1908–23; prof. English, Yale University, from 1923.

YOUNG, KIMBALL (Oct. 26, 1893–); b. Provo, Utah. Educator, author. *Bibliography on Censorship and Propaganda* (with R. D. Lawrence, 1928); *Social Psychology* (1930); *An Introductory Sociology* (1934); *Isn't One Wife Enough?* (1954); *Principles of Sociology* (with Raymond Mark, 1968); and other works in the fields of sociology and social psychology. Prof. sociology, Northwestern University, since 1947.

YOUNG, MARGUERITE VIVIAN; b. Indianapolis, Ind. Author. *Prismatic Ground* (poems, 1937); *Moderate Fable* (1945); *Miss MacIntosh, My Darling* (1965); *Angel in the Forest* (1966).

YOUNG, MARTHA (b. 1868); b. near Greensboro, Ala. Author. *Plantation Bird Legends* (1902); *Somebody's Little Girl* (1910); *Minute Dramas* (poems, 1921); etc.

Young, Robert. Pen name of Robert Payne.

YOUNG, ROSE E[mmett] (1869–July 6, 1941); b. Lexington, Mo. Editor, suffragist, novelist. *Sally of Missouri* (1903); *Henderson* (1904); *Murder at Manson's* (1927); *A Complete Record* (1929); etc. With University Publishing Co., New York, 1903–07; the *New York Evening Post,* 1912–13; editor, the *Woman Citizen,* 1917–21.

YOUNG, SAMUEL (b. Dec. 29, 1821); b. near Pittsburgh, Pa. Editor, novelist. *The Orphan and Other Tales* (1844); *The*

Smoky City: A Tale of Crime (1845); *Tom Hanson, the Avenger* (1847); *The History of My Life* (1890). Editor, the *Clarion* (Pa.) *Banner,* c. 1853–68; the *Conoquenessing Valley News.*

YOUNG, SAMUEL HALL (Sept. 12, 1847–Sept. 2, 1927); b. Butler, Pa. Presbyterian clergyman, missionary to Alaska, author. *Alaska Days with John Muir* (1915); *The Klondike Clan* (1916); *Adventures in Alaska* (1919); *Hall Young of Alaska* (autobiography, 1927).

YOUNG, STANLEY [Preston] (Feb. 3, 1906–); b. Greencastle, Ind. Author. *Robin Landing* (verse play, 1938); *Ship Forever Sailing* (1938); *Sons Without Anger* (1939); *Brothers in the Dark* (1940); *Ask My Friend Sandy* (prod. 1943); *Mayflower Boy* (1944); *A Bunyan Yarn* (in *Best One-act Plays,* 1945); *Mr. Pickwick* (1952); *The Sound of Apples* (verse play, 1957); *Laurette* (1965); etc. Critic, the *New York Times Book Review,* since 1936.

YOUNG, STARK (Oct. 11, 1881–Jan. 6, 1963); b. Como, Miss. Editor, critic, novelist, playwright. *The Blind Man at the Window, and Other Poems* (1906); *Guenevere* (1906); *The Three Fountains* (1924); *Glamour* (1925); *Encaustics* (1926); *Theatre Practice* (1926); *Heaven Trees* (1926); *Theatre* (1927); *The Torches Flare* (1928); *The Street of the Islands* (1930); *River House* (1929); *So Red the Rose* (1934); *Feliciana* (1935); *Immortal Shadows* (1948); *The Pavilion* (1951); etc. Editor: *A Southern Treasury of Life and Literature* (1937); *Best Plays of Chekhov* (1956); etc. Translator: Chekhov's *The Sea Gull* (1939). With *New Republic,* 1921–47; editor, *Theatre Arts Monthly,* 1921–40. See Fred B. Millett's *Contemporary American Authors* (1940).

Young, Thomas. Pen name of Thomas Yoseloff.

YOUNG, THOMAS DANIEL (Oct. 22, 1919–); b. Louisville, Miss. Educator, author. *Jack London and the Era of Social Protest* (1950); *The Literature of the South* (1952); *Donald Davidson, an Essay and a Bibliography* (1965); *American Literature, a Critic's Survey* (1967). Prof. English, Mississippi Southern College, since 1964.

YOUNG, WILLIAM (WALLACE) (1847–1920); b. in Illinois. Playwright, poet. *The Rajah* (prod. 1883); *Wishmakers' Town* (poems, 1898); *Ah, What Riddles These Women Be* (1900); etc. He dramatized Lew Wallace's *Ben Hur* (prod. 1899).

Young Alaskans, The. By Emerson Hough (1908). A classic narrative for children, depicting adventure in the Far North.

"Young Charlotte." American ballad. It was composed at Bensontown, Vt., prior to 1835, and spread westward during the settlement of the western states. It recounts the death of Charlotte who froze to death in her lover's sleigh on the way to a ball.

Young Kate; or, The Rescue: A Tale of the Great Kanawha. Anonymous novel (1844). Attributed to John Lewis. Story of Henry Bellenger and his sister Matilda, and their adventures in the backwoods of the Upper Ohio. Republished as *New Hope; or, The Rescue: A Tale of the Great Kanawha* (anon., 1855), and as *The Allens: A Tale of the Great Kanawha Valley.*

Young Lions, The. Novel by Irwin Shaw. (1948). World War II novel about two American soldiers, a Jew and a Gentile.

Young Marooners, The. By F. R. Goulding (1852). Adventure story for boys, one of the popular juveniles immediately before the era of dime novels.

Young New Yorkers. New York. Ten issues yearly. Founded 1957. Title changed 1958 to *Young Americans.* Discontinued 1960.

YOUNGDAHL, LUTHER W. (May 29, 1896–); b. Minneapolis, Minn. Lawyer, jurist. *The Ramparts We Watch* (1961). Governor of Minnesota, 1947–51.

Youngstown Vindicator. Youngstown, Ohio. Newspaper. Founded 1868. William F. Maag, Jr., is editor.

Youth and Life. By Randolph Bourne (1913). In this book the author sounded the trumpet call to youth, asserting that youth was the creative ferment of life, the hope and the salvation of a world forever decaying from within.

Youth of Washington, The. Imaginary autobiography written by S. Weir Mitchell (1904).

Youth's Companion, The. Boston, Mass. Juvenile magazine. Founded Apr. 16, 1827, by Nathaniel Willis and Asa Rand. In 1857 it was sold to Daniel Sharp Ford and J. W. Olmstead. Ford increased its circulation from 7,000 to half a million subscribers. Editors: Nathaniel Willis, 1827–56; Daniel Sharp Ford and Nathaniel Willis, 1857–62; Daniel Sharp Ford, 1863–70; Daniel Sharp Ford and Hezekiah Butterworth, 1870–86; Daniel Sharp Ford, Butterworth, and Edward Stanwood, 1887–94; Ford and Stanwood, 1894–99; Stanwood, 1900–11; Charles Miner Thompson, 1911–25; Harford H. W. Powel, Jr., 1925–29. Contributing editors included James Parton, William E. Barton, John Clair Minot, Theron Brown, Joseph Edgar Chamberlin, Thomas Hart Clay, George William Douglas, Roswell Martin Field, Charles Macomb Flandrau, Arthur Stanwood Pier, Paul F. Foster, M. A. De Wolfe Howe, William H. Rideing, Charles Asbury Stephens, Edward William Thompson, Jefferson L. Harbour, Heloise E. Hersey, Ira Rich Kent, Dallas Lore Sharp, Will N. Harben, Walter Leon Sawyer, John Macy, Ellery Sedgwick, John L. Mathews, etc. It absorbed *Merry's Museum* in 1872. In Sept., 1929, it was merged with the *American Boy,* and ceased its independent existence. See Frank L. Mott's *A History of American Magazines,* v. 3 (1938); C. A. Stephens's *Story of My Homefolks* (1926); *Youth's Companion,* v. 75, 1901 and v. 100, 1926.

YOUTZ, PHILIP NEWELL (Apr. 27, 1895–); b. Quincy, Mass. Author. *Sounding Stones of Architecture* (1929); *American Life in Architecture* (1932). Editor, *Outline of Aesthetics,* 5v. (1928); *The New Arts,* 5v. (1927). Director, Brooklyn Museum, 1934–36; dean, College of Architecture and Design, University of Michigan, since 1957.

Yugen. New York. Quarterly of literature. Founded 1958. Edited by Le Roi Jones. Expired 1962.

YURICK, SOL (Jan. 18, 1925–); b. New York. Author. *The Warriors* (1965); *Fertig* (1966); *The Bag* (1968).

YUST, WALTER (May 16, 1894–Feb. 29, 1960); b. Philadelphia, Pa. Editor. Lit. editor of the *Philadelphia Public Ledger,* 1926–30. Assoc. editor, the *Encyclopaedia Britannica,* 1932–38; editor, 1938–60.

YUST, WILLIAM FREDERICK (Nov. 10, 1869–Nov. 16, 1947); b. Canton, Mo. Librarian, author. *Fred Yust, Kansas Pioneer* (1937). Librarian, Louisville Free Public Library, 1905–12); Rochester Public Library, 1912–32; Rollins College, 1931–42.

Z

ZABEL, MORTON DAUWEN (Aug. 10, 1901–Apr. 28, 1964); b. Minnesota Lake, Minn. Editor, author. *The Romantic Idealism of Art in England, 1800–1848* (1933); *The Critical and Popular Background of Art in England 1800–1848* (1937); *Two Years of Poetry, 1937–39* (1939); *The Situation in American Criticism* (1939); *Craft and Character in Modern Fiction* (1957); *The Art of Ruth Draper* (1959); etc. Coauthor: *A Book of English Literature* (1943); *The Question of Henry James* (1945); *Forms of Modern Fiction* (1949); *Critiques and Essays on Modern Fiction* (1952); *The Make of Man: Craft and Character in Modern Poetry* (1958). Editor: *Literary Opinion in America* (1937); *The Portable Joseph Conrad* (1947); Henry James's *The Art of Travel* (1958). Assoc. editor, *Poetry: A Magazine of Verse, 1928–36;* editor-in-chief, 1936–37. Prof. English, Loyola University, Chicago, Ill., 1929–46; University of Chicago, from 1947.

Zaca Venture. By William Beebe (1938).

ZACHARIAS, ELLIS M. (Jan. 1, 1890–June 28, 1961); b. Jacksonville, Fla. Naval officer. *Secret Missions* (1946); *Behind Closed Doors: The Secret History of the Cold War* (with Ladislas Farago, 1950).

Zadoc Pine, and Other Stories. By Henry C. Bunner (1891).

"Zagonyi." Poem on Missouri, written by George Henry Boker.

ZAHM, JOHN AUGUSTINE (Sept. 14, 1851–Nov. 10, 1921); b. New Lexington, O. Roman Catholic clergyman, author. Pen name (for travel books), "H. J. Mozans." *Sounds and Music* (1892); *Science and the Church* (1896); *Up the Orinoco and Down the Magdalena* (1910); *Along the Andes and Down the Amazon* (1911); *Through South America's Southland* (1916); *The Quest of El Dorado* (1917); *From Berlin to Bagdad to Babylon* (1922); etc.

ZAHN, CURTIS (Nov. 12, 1912–); b. Detroit, Mich. Painter, editor, author. *American Contemporary* (1963); *One Extraordinary AM, some poems* (1964). Associate editor, *Trace* magazine.

ZAIDENBERG, ARTHUR (Aug. 15, 1903–); b. Brooklyn, N.Y. Artist, author. *The Emotional Self* (1930); *Anyone Can Paint* (1942); *The Art Student's Encyclopedia* (1948); *The Joy of Painting* (1955); *Drawing the Human Figure in Action* (1960); *How to Draw Heads and Faces* (1966); *The Painting of Pictures* (1966); *Drawing All Animals* (1967); *How to Draw Shakespeare's People* (1967); *Creative Way to Draw Women* (1968); *Creative Way to Draw Heads and Portraits* (1969); *How to Draw a Circus* (1969); etc. Editor: *The Art of the Artist* (1951).

ZARA, LOUIS (Aug. 2, 1910–); b. Louis Zara Rosenfeld, New York. Author. *Blessed Is the Man* (1935); *This Land Is Ours* (1940); *Against This Rock* (1943); *Ruth Middleton* (1946); *Rebel Run* (1951); *Blessed Is the Land* (1954); *Dark Rider* (1961); *Jade* (1969); *Locks and Keys* (1969); etc.

ZEIGEN, FREDERIC (Apr. 18, 1874–May 26, 1942); b. Saginaw, Mich. Author. *Breezes from Pines* (1898); *Collected Poems* (1900); *Lava* (1926); *Black Christ* (1929); etc.

ZEITLIN, JACOB (Jan. 6, 1883–Dec. 8, 1937); b. Gorky, Mogilev, Rus. Author. *Life and Letters of Stuart P. Sherman,* 2v. (with Homer Woodbridge, 1929). Compiler: *Types of Poetry* (with Clarissa Rinaker, 1927).

ZELIE, JOHN SHERIDAN (May 3, 1866–Nov. 9, 1942); b. Princeton, Mass. Congregational clergyman, author. *Bill Pratt, the Sawbuck Philosopher* (with Carroll Perry, 1895); *Joseph Conrad, the Man* (with E. L. Adams, 1925); etc.

ZEMACH, HARVE [Harvey Fischtrom] (Dec. 5, 1933–); b. Newark, N.J. Author. *Small Boy Is Listening* (1958); *A Hat with a Rose* (1960); *Nail Soup* (1964); *The Tricks of Master Dabble* (1965); *The Speckled Hen* (1966); etc.

ZENGER, JOHN PETER (1697–July 28, 1746); b. in Germany. Printer, journalist, public printer for Colonial New York and New Jersey. Author: *A Brief Narrative of the Case and Tryal of John Peter Zenger* (1736). Founder, the *New-York Weekly Journal,* 1733; editor, 1733–1746. His acquittal on a charge of criminal libel, 1735, established freedom of the press in America. See Livingston Rutherfurd's *John Peter Zenger* (1904).

Zenobia; or, The Fall of Palmyra. Novel by William Ware (1838). Originally published as *Letters of Lucius M. Piso from Palmyra, to his Friend Marcus Curtius, at Rome* (1837).

ZENOS, ANDREW C. (b. Aug. 13, 1855); b. Constantinople, Turkey. Educator, author. *Elements of Higher Criticism* (1895); *The Son of Man* (1914); *Presbyterianism in America* (1937); etc. Prof. theology, Presbyterian Theological Seminary, Chicago, from 1891.

Zeph. Unfinished story by Helen Hunt Jackson (1885). Scene is Colorado.

ZERBE, JAMES SLOUGH (b. Sept. 18, 1849); b. Womelsdorf, Pa. Author. *Castaways* (1912); *The Mysterious Caverns* (1912); *From New York to the Golden Gate* (1915); *From San Francisco to Japan* (1915); *From Tokyo to Bombay* (1915); etc.

ZEYDEL, EDWIN HERMANN (Dec. 31, 1893–); b. Brooklyn, N.Y. Educator, author. Author or editor: *The German Theatre in New York City* (1915); *The Holy Roman Empire in German Literature* (1918); *Ludwig Tieck and England* (1931); *Ludwig Tieck, the German Romanticist* (1935); *Sebastian Brant's Ship of Fools* (1944); *Poems of Walther von der Vogelweide* (1952); *Goethe the Lyrist* (1955); *Escape of A Certain Captive* (1964); *Sebastian Brant* (1967); etc. Prof. German, University of Cincinnati, from 1926.

ZIEGLER, EDWARD (Mar. 25, 1870–Oct. 25, 1947); b. Baltimore, Md. Music critic, author. *Critique on Tristan and Isolde* (1909). Music critic, *New York World*, 1903–08; *New York Herald*, 1908–16; asst. general manager, Metropolitan Opera House, New York, from 1920.

ZIFF, WILLIAM BERNARD (Aug. 1, 1898–Dec. 20, 1953); b. Chicago, Ill. Publisher, author. *The Rape of Palestine* (1938); *The Gentlemen Talk of Peace* (1944); *Two Worlds* (1948); etc. Chairman, Ziff-Davis Publishing Co., Chicago, from 1946. Publisher of *Amazing Stories; Photography; Radio and Television News;* and other magazines.

ZIFF, WILLIAM BERNARD (June 24, 1930–); b. Chicago, Ill. Publisher. Pres., Ziff-Davis Publishing Co.

Zig Zag Tales. By Harry Leon Wilson (1896).

Zig-Zag Journeys. Popular travel sketches written for children by Hezekiah Butterworth, 17v. (1880–95). They appeared originally in *The Youth's Companion.*

ZIGROSSER, CARL (Sept. 28, 1891–); b. Indianapolis, Ind. Museum curator. Author: *Six Centuries of Fine Prints* (1937); *The Artist in America* (1942); *Kaethe Kollwitz* (1946); *The Expressionists: A Survey of Their Graphic Art* (1957); *Mauricio Lasansky* (1960); *Misch Kohn* (1961); *A Guide to the Collecting and Care of Original Prints* (with Christa M. Gaehde, 1965); *The Complete Etchings of John Marin* (1969); *Prints and Drawings of Kaethe Kollwitz* (1969); *Medicine and the Artist* (1969); etc.

Zigzagging the South Seas. By Isabel Anderson (1936).

ZILBOORG, GREGORY (Dec. 25, 1890–Sept. 17, 1959); b. Kiev, Rus. Psychiatrist. *History of Medical Psychology* (with G. W. Henry, 1941); *Mind, Medicine, and Man* (1943); *Sigmund Freud: His Exploration of the Mind of Man* (1951); *The Psychology of the Criminal Act and Punishment* (1954); *Psychoanalysis and Religion* (1962); etc.

ZIM, HERBERT SPENCER (July 12, 1909–); b. New York. Editor, author. *The Universe* (1961); *Gamebirds* (1961); *Butterflies and Moths* (1964); *Non-Flowering Plants* (1967); etc. Editor-in-chief, *Our Wonderful World Encyclopedia,* 1952–63; *Golden Encyclopedia of Natural Science,* since 1960; editor, *Golden Guide Series,* since 1947; *Junior Golden Guides,* since 1964.

ZIMMERMAN, EUGENE (May 25, 1862–Mar. 26, 1935); b. Basle, Switz. Caricaturist, author. *This and That about Caricature* (1905). Illustrated the works of "Bill Nye" and James Whitcomb Riley and others; also made drawings for *Puck, Judge,* etc.

ZIMMERMAN, LEANDER M. (b. Aug. 29, 1860–); b. Manchester, Md. Lutheran clergyman, author. *A Wedding Token* (1898); *Yvonne* (1900); *"Dot": A Novel of Today* (1909); *Sparks* (1912); *Reminiscences* (1919); *My Philosophy and Life* (1929).

ZIMMERMAN, ROBERT (May 24, 1941–); b. Duluth, Minn. Folk singer, composer-lyricist, under name "Bob Dylan." Author of words and music to "Blowin' in the Wind" (1962), "The Times They Are A-Changin," (1964), "Masters of War" (1964), "Like a Rolling Stone" (1965), "Mr. Tambourine Man" (1965), "Desolation Row" (1965), and dozens of other songs issued on records and record albums since the first one, "Bob Dylan," appeared in 1962.

ZINN, HOWARD (Aug. 24, 1922–); b. New York. Historian, author. *La Guardia in Congress* (1959); *SNCC: The New Abolitionists* (1964); *New Deal Thought* (1966); *Vietnam: The Logic of Withdrawal* (1967). Prof. government, Boston University, since 1966.

ZINSSER, HANS (Nov. 17, 1878–Sept. 4, 1940); b. New York. Bacteriologist, author. *Rats, Lice and History* (1935); *As I Remember Him: The Biography of R. S.* (autobiography, 1940); and books on bacteriology. Prof. bacteriology, Harvard Medical School, 1923–1940.

ZINSSER, WILLIAM KNOWLTON (Oct. 7, 1922–); b. New York. Author. *Any Old Place with You* (1957); *Seen Any Good Movies Lately?* (1958); *Search and Research* (1961); *The City Dwellers* (1962); *Weekend Guests* (1963); *The Haircurl Papers* (1964); *Pop Goes America* (1966); *The Paradise Bit* (1967).

ZIOLKOWSKI, THEODOR JOSEPH (Sept. 30, 1932–); b. Birmingham, Ala. Educator. author. *Hermann Broch* (1964); *The Novels of Hermann Hesse* (1965); *Hermann Hesse* (1966). Prof. German, Princeton University, since 1964.

ZITKALA-SA, (Gertrude Simmons Bonnin) (1878–Jan. 26, 1938); b. Yankton Indian Reservation, S. D. granddaughter of Sitting Bull. Sioux Indian author. *Old Indian Legends* (1901); *American Indian Stories* (1921).

Zoe; or, The Quadroon's Triumph. Novel by Elizabeth D. Livermore, 2v. (1855).

ZOGBAUM, BAIRD LEONARD (Mrs. Harry St. Clair) (c. 1889–Jan. 23, 1941). Critic, poet. Wrote under maiden name. *Simple Confession* (1930). Editor: *Cora Scovil's Lady's Book* (1940). Columnist, the *New York Morning Telegraph.*

ZOGBAUM, RUFUS FAIRCHILD (Aug. 28, 1849–Oct. 22, 1925). Illustrator and author. *Horse, Foot, and Dragoons* (1888); *The Junior Officer of the Watch* (1908). Illustrated for many magazines.

ZOLOTOW, MAURICE (Nov. 23, 1913–); b. New York. Author. *Never Whistle in a Dressing Room* (1944); *The Great Balsamo* (1946); *No People Like Show People* (1951); *It Takes All Kinds* (1952); *Oh Careless Love* (1959); *Marilyn Monroe* (1960); *Stagestruck: The Romance of Alfred Lunt and Lynn Fontanne* (1965).

Zone of Quiet. Short story by Ring Lardner (1926).

ZOOK, GEORGE FREDERICK (Apr. 22, 1885–Aug. 17, 1951); b. Ft. Scott, Kan. Educator, author. *The Royal Adventurers Trading into Africa* (1919); *The Role of the Federal Government in Education* (1945); etc. History dept., Pennsylvania State College, 1912–20. President, American Council of Education, 1934–50.

Zophiel; or, The Bride of Seven. Long narrative poem by Marie Gowen Brooks (1833).

ZUCKER, PAUL (Aug. 14, 1890–Feb. 14, 1971); b. Berlin. Educator, author. *Stage Setting at the Time of the Baroque* (1925); *Theatres and Moving Picture Houses* (1926); *The Development of the City* (1929); *American Bridges and Dams* (1941); *Styles in Painting* (1950); *Town and Square* (1959); *Fascination of Decay: Ruins, Relic, Symbol, Ornament* (1968); etc. Faculty, Cooper Union Art School, from 1938.

ZUGSMITH, LEANE (Jan. 18, 1903–Oct. 13, 1969); b. Louisville, Ky. Novelist. *All Victorians Are Alike* (1929); *Goodbye and Tomorrow* (1931); *Never Enough* (1932); *The Reckoning* (1934); *A Time to Remember* (1936); *Home Is Where You Hang Your Childhood* (1937); *The Summer Soldier* (1938); *The Visitor* (with husband, Carl Randau, 1944). *See* Fred B. Millett's *Contemporary American Authors* (1940).

ZUKOFSKY, LOUIS (Jan. 23, 1904–   ); b. New York. Poet. *A Test of Poetry* (1952); *Some Time* (1956); *"A" 1–12* (1959); *Bottom: On Shakespeare* (1963); *After I's* (1964); *All the Collected Short Poems, 1923–1958* (1965); *Prepositions* (1967); *Ferdinand* (1968); *Zukovsky's Catullus* (1969); *"A" 13–21* (1969); *Autobiography* (1970); *Little* (1970). Prof. English, Polytechnic Institute of Brooklyn, since 1947.

ZURCHER, ARNOLD JOHN (Oct. 20, 1902–); b. S. Amherst, O. Educator. *Experiment with Democracy in Central Europe* (1933); *Dictionary of Economics* (with H. S. Sloan, 1949); *The Struggle to Unite Europe, 1940–58* (1958); etc. Dept. of political science, New York University, from 1928.

Zury: The Meanest Man in Spring County. Novel by Joseph Kirkland (1887). A study of the development of character in the hard life of the pioneers in the covered-wagon days just prior to the Civil War.

ZWEMER, SAMUEL MARINUS (Apr. 12, 1867–Apr. 2, 1952); b. Vriesland, Mich. Missionary, author. *Across the World of Islam* (1920); *The Golden Milestone* (reminiscences, with James Cantine, 1938); *Into All the World* (1943); *The Glory of the Empty Tomb* (1947); *Sons of Adam* (1951); etc.